# LLOYD'S

# INTRODUCTION

## TO

# JURISPRUDENCE

EIGHTH EDITION

by

## M.D.A. FREEMAN, LL.M.

*Professor of English Law*
*University College London*

SWEET & MAXWELL  THOMSON REUTERS

| | | | |
|---|---|---|---|
| First Edition | - | - | *1959* |
| Second Edition | - | - | *1965* |
| Third Edition | - | - | *1972* |
| Fourth Edition | - | - | *1979* |
| Fifth Edition | - | - | *1985* |
| Sixth Edition | - | - | *1994* |
| Second Impression | - | - | *1996* |
| Third Impression | - | - | *1997* |
| Fourth Impression | - | - | *1999* |
| Fifth Impression | - | - | *2000* |
| Seventh Edition | - | - | *2001* |
| Second Impression | - | - | *2002* |
| Third Impression | - | - | *2005* |
| Fourth Impression | - | - | *2006* |
| Eighth Edition | - | - | *2008* |

Published in 2008 by Thomson Reuters (Legal) Limited
(Registered in England & Wales, Company No 1679046.
Registered Office and address for service:
100 Avenue Road, London, NW3 3PF) trading as Sweet & Maxwell
For further information on our products and services, visit
www.sweetandmaxwell.co.uk
Computerset by YHT Ltd, London
Printed and bound in Great Britain by TJ International, Padstow, Cornwall

*No natural forests were destroyed to make this product; only farmed timber
was used and replanted.*

A CIP catalogue record for this book is available from the British Library

ISBN 978–0–421–90790–4

# Preface to the Eighth Edition

*Lloyd on Jurisprudence* now enters its fiftieth year. It has grown from edition to edition as the subject has expanded. Previous editions have all incorporated new schools of jurisprudential thought—Critical Race Theory was included for the first time in the last edition. There are no new schools explored this time.

This edition does however include, for the first time, a separate chapter on Ronald Dworkin's interpretivism. The thoughts and insights of Dworkin feature elsewhere in the book as well, notably in the chapter on "Theories of Justice". Dworkin is now established as the most significant jurist of our times. Whole courses could, I am sure, focus on his jurisprudence.

Since the last edition of *Lloyd* was published Dworkin has published prolifically. Most significant is his *Justice In Robes*: this new edition contains a substantial extract from this. There is now considerable critical exegesis of Dworkin's work: some of this (Hershovitz, Postema, Waldron) is extracted too.

There is new work on natural law (from Mark Murphy) to comment upon and extract too. Murphy's work is the most significant since Finnis published *Natural Law and Natural Rights* in 1980. A new extract from Kent Greenawalt "How Persuasive Is Natural Law Theory?" is also included. Until now most students have picked up Radbruch's thinking from the Hart-Fuller debate (or Alexy which is also in the book). But we now have a key text from Radbruch in English, and this is included in this edition for the first time.

*Lloyd* has always introduced the subject through the dual approaches of texts and commentary. There are several new commentaries this time. On *Jackson's* case and its implications for sovereignty, on the theory of human rights (a subject upon which a separate chapter will be warranted next time), on Nussbaum's "capabilities" approach to justice, on global justice. These are issues which are likely to feature more prominently in Jurisprudence courses: I hope appetites are whetted by their introduction here. It would be nice to think that students explored the "frontiers" of justice beyond Rawls's well-trodden terrain, and Martha Nussbaum's work offers the scope for debate.

Interest in law and social theory is expanding. There have been reassessments of Durkheim, Ehrlich and Luhmann recently, as of legal feminism (by Ann Scales) and Pashukanis (by Michael Head). This book discusses Bourdieu for the first time and includes an extract by Villegas on his legal thought. Roger Cotterrell's chapter "Law and Social Theory" from his "Law, Culture and Society" is included in the extracts.

Much else of significance is acknowledged in the book, if no more fully than in references in notes. The past few years have been a productive period for legal thinking, stimulated no doubt by outside events such as 9/11 and the ensuing "War on Terror" (I include Fitzpatrick and Joyce on the "normality of the exception" as an example of this). But jurisprudential scholarship does not need such stimuli. Thus, there has also been important work by Duxbury (on precedent), Galligan, Weinreb, Tamanaha and MacCormick. There is Rumble's sympathetic re-assessment of Austin (the 150th anniversary of whose death falls in 2009) and Griffin's new book on human rights. The positivism—natural law debates continue apace (see for example Coleman). There is more discussion of "obligation": hence the extracts in this book from Perry and Edmundson. There is, of course, also Nicola Lacey's thoroughly readable biography of H.L.A. Hart, which can be recommended to any student of jurisprudence. The list is endless: thus I have found Nigel Simmonds's *Law As a Moral Idea* thought-provoking, but (unfortunately) there was not space to include it. Ginsburg and Moustafa's new book on the role of the judge in authoritarian systems (*Law As Rule*, 2008) has made me wish there was a section on this important subject. It is certainly one I hope to include next time. Legal anthropology is expanding too, as I discovered at UCL's "Law and Anthropology" colloquium held in July 2008: this too is likely to be reflected in future editions.

Lord Lloyd stated the aims of this book as "to provide the student of jurisprudence with a textbook which will enable him [or her] to become acquainted with the theories, attitudes, and insights of leading jurists from selected texts culled from their own writings", and "to afford him [or her] a coherent picture of the subject, by means of a full commentary setting out the background and inter-connections between the differing approaches, and a critical appraisal of the viewpoints illustrated in the selected texts". This remains the aim of this book 50 years on.

It remains to acknowledge the assistance I have received from many colleagues—UCL remains a vibrant nest of jurisprudential thinking and also to thank Linda Thomas for her secretarial skills. Without her producing this new edition would have been much more difficult.

M.D.A. Freeman
July 2008

# ACKNOWLEDGMENTS

GRATEFUL acknowledgment is made for permission to reproduce from the undermentioned works:

ALEXANDER, LARRY and KRESS, KEN, "Against Legal Principles" from Andrei Marmor (Ed.), *Law and Interpretation* (1995), (Clarendon Press).

AQUINAS, *Summa Theologica*, trans. J.G. Dawson, ed. d'Entrèves (Basil Blackwell).

ARISTOTLE, *Ethics*, trans. Sir D. Ross (Oxford Univ. Press).

AUSTIN, J., "The Uses of the Study of Jurisprudence", from *The Province of Jurisprudence Determined*, ed. H.L.A. Hart (published in 1954 by George Weidenfeld & Nicolson Ltd. and reprinted by kind permission of the Editor).

AXLEY, R., "A Defence of Radbruch's Formula" from David Dyzenhaus (ed.), *Recrafting the Rule of Law: The Limits of Legal Order* (1999), (Hart Publishing).

BALKIN, J.M. "Understanding Legal Understanding: The Legal Subject and the Problem of Legal Coherence" (1993) 103 Yale L.J. 105.

BALL, MILNER S., "The Legal Academy and Minority Scholars" (1990) 103 Harvard Law Review 1855 (The Harvard Law Review Association).

BARNES, R.D., "Race Consciousness: The Thematic Content of Racial Distinctiveness in Critical Race Scholarship" (1990) 103 Harvard Law Review 1864 (The Harvard Law Review Association).

BARTLETT, K., "Feminist Legal Methods" (1990) 103 Harvard Law Review 829. (Copyright © 1990 by the Harvard Law Review Association).

BENTHAM, J., *An Introduction to the Principles of Morals and Legislation* (ed. J.H. Burns and H.L.A. Hart, 1970) (The Athlone Press, Univ. of London).

BENTHAM, J., *Of Laws in General*, ed. H.L.A. Hart (The Athlone Press, Univ. of London, 1970 and also by kind permission of the editor).

BOHANNAN, PAUL, Selections from "The Differing Realms of the Law" which appears in *Law and Warfare* by Paul Bohannan. (Copyright © 1967 by Paul Bohannan. The American Anthropological Association from American Anthropologist 67 (6. Pt. II): 34–37, 1965. Not for further reproduction).

CAIN, P.A., "Feminism and the Limits of Equality". (This article was originally published at 24 Ga.L.Rev. 803 (1990) and is reprinted with permission).

CARDOZO, B., *Nature of the Judicial Process* (Yale Univ. Press. Reprinted by permission).

CICERO, *De Republica*, trans. C.W. Keyes. Reprinted by permission of the publishers and the Trustees of the Loeb Classical Library from CICERO: VOLUME XVI, Loeb Classical Library ® Volume 213, translated by Clinton W. Keyes, Cambridge, Mass.: Harvard University Press, Copyright © 1928 by the President and Fellows of Harvard College. The Loeb Classical Library ® is a registered trademark of the President and Fellows of Harvard College.

COHEN, G.A., *Karl Marx's Theory of History*, (Reprinted by kind permission of A.D. Peters & Co.).

COLEMAN, J., "Beyond the Separability Thesis" (2007) 27 Oxford Journal of Legal Studies 581–608.

COLEMAN, J., "Inclusive Legal Positivism" from *The Practice of Principle* (2001), (Oxford University Press).

COTTERRELL, R., *Law's Community* (1995), (By permission of Oxford University Press).

COTTERRELL, R., "Law and Social Theory" in *Law, Culture and Society* (2006) (Ashgate).

COTTERRELL, R., "Why Must Legal Ideas be Interpreted Sociologically?" (1998) Journal of Law and Society vol. 25, 171 (Blackwell Publishers).

CRENSHAW, K., "Race, Reform and Retrenchment: Transformation and Legitimation in AntiDiscrimination Law" (1988) 101 Harvard Law Review 1331. (Copyright © 1988 by the Harvard Law Review Association).

DE SOUZA SANTOS, B., "The Postmodern Tradition: Law and Politics" in *The Fate of Law*, Austin Sarat and Thomas Kearns, editors (Ann Arbour: The University of Michigan Press).

DELGADO, RICHARD and STEFANCIC, JEAN, "Critical Race Theory: An Annotated Bibliography" (1993) 79 Virginia Law Review 461 (The Virginia Law Review Association).

DALTON, C., "An Essay in the Deconstruction of Contract Doctrine" (1985) 94 Yale L.J. 1095–1114. (Reprinted by kind permission of The Yale Law Journal Company and Fred B. Rothman from *The Yale Law Journal*, Vol. 94, pp. 9971114).

DEWEY, J., "Logical Method and Law" from (1924) 10 *Cornell Law Quarterly* 17 (Cornell Law Review and Fred B. Rothman & Co. © Copyright 1924, by Cornell University).

DIAMOND, S., "The Rule of Law versus the order of custom", *Social Research*, Vol. 38, No. 1, Spring 1971, pp. 42–72. (Copyright © 1971 *Social Research*. By permission of the Graduate Faculty, New School for Social Research, New York).

DOUZINAS, C., and Warrington, R., "A wellfounded fear of Justice: Law and Ethics in Postmodernism" Law and Critique Vol. 2(2), 115 pp. 115–131. (This article has been republished in a different version in Costas Douzinas & Ronnie Warrington "Justice Miscarried: Ethics, Aesthetics and the Law" (Harvester 1994)).

DURKHEIM, E., *The Division of Labour in Society*, translated by W.D. Halls. (Reprinted by permission of Macmillan, London & Basingstoke).

DWORKIN, R., "What is Equality? Part 2: Equality of Resources" (1981) 10 Philosophy and Public Affairs 283 (Wiley-Blackwell).

DWORKIN, R., *Laws Empire* (1986), (First published by Fontana Press and reprinted by Hart Publishing, 1998).

DWORKIN, R., *Justice in Robes* (Harvard University Press (Copyright © 2006 by the President and Fellowes of Harvard College)).

DWORKIN, R., *Taking Rights Seriously*. (Reprinted by kind permission of the author and Gerald Duckworth & Co.).

DWORKIN, R., "Law as Interpretation" (Published originally in 60 Texas L.Rev. 527 (1982). Copyright © 1982 by the *Texas Law Review*. Reprinted by permission).

DWORKIN, R., "A Trump Over Utility" (1981) 1 O.J.L.S. 177.

EHRLICH, E., Reprinted by permission of the publisher from "The Structure of the Legal Proposition," in FUNDAMENTAL PRINCIPLES OF THE SOCIOLOGY OF LAW, by Eugen Ehrlich, translated by Walter Lewis Moll, pp. 198-203, 501-503, Cambridge, Mass.: Harvard University Press, Copyright © 1936 by the President and Fellows of Harvard College.

ENGELS, F., "AntiDühring" from M. Oakeshott, *Social and Political Doctrines of Contemporary Europe* (Cambridge Univ. Press).

ENGELS, F., Letter to J. Bloch, September 21, 1890 from *Selected Correspondence*. (Reprinted by kind permission of Lawrence and Wishart Ltd).

ENGELS, F., Letter to Conrad Schmidt, October 27, 1890 from *Selected Correspondence*. (Reprinted by kind permission of Lawrence and Wishart Ltd).

ENGELS, F., "Ludwig Feuerbach and the End of Classical German Philosophy" from Marx and Engels, *Collected Works*, Vol. III. (Reprinted by kind permission of Lawrence and Wishart Ltd).

ENGELS, F., "The Housing Question" from Marx and Engels, *Selected Works*, Vol. III. (Reprinted by kind permission of Lawrence and Wishart London 1975).

ESPERANZA, B., Hernández – Truyol, "Borders (En)Gendered: Normativities, Latinas and Latcrit Paradigm" (1997) 72 New York Univ. L. Rev. 882.

EDMUNDSON, W.A., *The Duty to obey the Law*, Legal Theory 10, pp. 228–238 (2000), © Cambridge University Press, reproduced with permission.

FINLEY, L., "Breaking Women's Silence in Law: The Dilemma of the Gendered Nature of Legal Reasoning", Notre Dame Lawyer, page 885–910 (1989) reprinted with permission © by *Notre Dame Law Review*, University of Notre Dame.

FINNIS, J., *Natural Law and Natural Rights* (1980), (Clarendon Press)

FINNIS, J. et al, *Nuclear Deterrence, Morality and Realism* (1987), (Clarendon Press).

FITZPATRICK, P., and Joyce, R., "The Normality of the Exception in Democracy's Empire (2007) 34 Journal of Law and Society 65–76.

FOUCAULT, M., "Two Lectures" from *Power/Knowledge: Selected Interviews and other Writings 1972–1977*, by Michael Foucault, edited by Colin Gordon. Copyright © 1977 by Michael Foucault. (Reprinted by permission of Harvester Press and Pantheon Books, a division of Random House Inc.).

FRANK, J., *Law and the Modern Mind*. (Copyright © 1930, 1933, 1949 by

Coward McCann Inc., Copyright © 1930 by Brentano's Inc., from Anchor Books edition 1963. Copyright renewed in 1958 by Florence K. Frank. Reprinted by arrangement with estate of Barbara Frank Kristein).

FULLER, L.L., "Human Interaction and the Law" from (1969) 14 Amer. J. of Jurisprudence 1 (American Journal of Jurisprudence).

FULLER, L.L., "Positivism and Fidelity to Law—A Reply to Professor Hart" (1958) 71 Harv.L.Rev. 630. (Copyright © 1958 by the Harvard Law Review Association).

FULLER, L.L., *The Morality of Law* (Yale Univ. Press, Copyright © 1964, by Yale University).

FULLER, L.L., "The Case of the Speluncean Explorers" 62 Harvard Law Review 616 (1949). (Copyright © 1949 by the Harvard Law Review Association).

GABEL, P., "Reification in Legal Reasoning" from "Research in Law and Sociology" Vol. 3 (1980) 25–46 *Critical Legal Studies*.

GLUCKMAN, M., *Judicial Process Among the Barotse* (Published on behalf of the Institute for Social Research, Univ. of Zambia, by Manchester Univ. Press. First published 1955; 2nd edition with corrections and two additional chapters 1967).

GORDON, R.W., "Law and Theology" from Tikkun (1988) Vol. 13(1), 14–18, 83–86.

GORDON, R.W., "New Developments in Legal Theory" from *The Politics of Law: A Progressive Critique*, edited by David Kairys. Compilation copyright © 1982 by David Kairys. Reprinted by permission of Pantheon Books, a division of Random House Inc.

GREENWALT, K., "How Persuasive is Natural Law Theory?" (2000) 75 Notre Dame Law Review 1647.

HABERMAS, J., "Between Facts and Norms: An Author's Reflections, (1999) 76 Denver University Law Review 937.

HAGERSTRÖM, AXEL, *Inquiries into the Nature of Law and Morals*, trans. C.D. Broad (Almqvist and Wiksell).

HARRIS, A.P., "The Jusrisprudence of Reconstruction" © 1994 by the California Law Review, Inc. Reprinted from California Law Review, Vol. 82, No. 4, pp. 759–766 by permission of the California Law Review, Inc.

HART, H.L.A., "Positivism and the Separation of Law and Morals" (1958) 71 Harv.L.Rev. 593. (Copyright © 1958 by the Harvard Law Review Association).

HART, H.L.A., "Problems of Philosophy of Law; Substantive Law". (Reprinted with permission of the Publisher from the *Encyclopedia of Philosophy*, Paul Edwards, Editor in Chief, Vol. 6, pp. 264–276. Reprinted with permission of Macmillan Publishing Company. Copyright © 1967 by Macmillan Publishing Company).

HART, H.L.A., "Definition and Theory in Jurisprudence" (1954) 70 L.Q.R. 37. (Reprinted by kind permission of the author, and the Editor of *Law Quarterly Review*, Stevens & Sons Ltd).

HEGEL, F., *Philosophy of Right*, trans. T.M. Knox (by permission of Oxford Univ. Press).

HERSHOVITZ, S. "Integrity and Stare Decisis" in (ed) Scott Hershovitz *Exploring Law's Empire*, (2006) (Oxford University Press).

HERNÀNDEZTRUYOL, BERTA ESPERANZA, "Borders (En)Gendered: Normativities, Latinas and a LatCrit Paradigm" (1997) New York University Law Review 882 (New York University Law Review).

HOEBEL, E.A., "The Functions of Law," reprinted by permission of the publisher from THE LAW OF PRIMITIVE MAN: A STUDY IN COMPARATIVE LEGAL DYNAMICS by E. Adamson Hoebel, pp. 275–288, Cambridge, Mass.: Harvard University Press, Copyright © 1954 by the President and Fellows of Harvard College © renewed 1982 by Edward Adamson Hoebel.

HOHFELD, W.N., *Fundamental Legal Conceptions as Applied in Judicial Reasoning* (Yale Univ. Press).

HOLMES, O.W., "The Path of Law" (1897) 10 Harv.L.Rev. 457–478. (Copyright © 1897 by the Harvard Law Review Association).

HUNT, A., "Dichotomy and Contradictions in the Sociology of Law" (1981) 8 *British Journal of Law and Society* 47. (Reprinted by kind permission of Basil Blackwell Ltd).

JHERING, R. VON, *Law as Means to an End*, trans. I. Husik. (Reprinted by permission of Augustus M. Kelley, Publishers).

JOHNSON, K.R., "Celebrating LatCrit Theory: What Do We Do When the Music Stops?" This work, copyright 2000 by Kevin R. Johnson, was originally published in the *UC Davis Law Review*, vol. 33, pp. 753–786, copyright 2000 by The Regents of the University of California. All rights reserved. Reprinted with permission.

JUSTINIAN, *Institutes*, trans. R.W. Lee (Sweet & Maxwell Ltd).

KELMAN, M., "Interpretive Construction in the Substantive Criminal Law" 33 Stan.L.Rev. 591–605, 611–616, 669–673. (Reproduced by kind permission of The Stanford Law Review).

KELSEN, H., *General Theory of Law and State* (Harvard Univ. Press. Copyright 1946 by the President and Fellows of Harvard College).

KELSEN, H., "Professor Stone and the Pure Theory of Law" originally from *Stanford Law Review*, Vol. 17, p. 1128. (Copyright 1965, by the Board of Trustees of the Leland Stanford Junior University).

KELSEN, H., "The Pure Theory of Law", trans. Max Knight. (Originally published by the University of California Press; reprinted by permission of the Regents of the Univ. of California).

KELSEN, H., *What is Justice?* (Originally published by the Univ. of California Press; reprinted by permission of the Regents of the Univ. of California).

KELSEN, H., *The Function of a Constitution*, trans. Dr. I. Stewart. (Reprinted by kind permission of the translator).

KENNEDY, D., "The Ideological Content of Legal Education" from *The Politics of Law: A Progressive Critique*, edited by David Kairys. Compilation copyright © 1982 by David Kairys. Reprinted by permission of Pantheon Books, a division of Random House Inc.

KRAMER, M., "How Moral Principles Can Enter Into the Law" (2000) 6 Legal Theory 83 © Cambridge University Press, reproduced with permission.

KUHN, T.S., *The Structure of Scientific Revolutions*. (Reprinted by permission of the University of Chicago Press. Copyright © 1962, 1970 by the University of Chicago. All rights reserved).

LACEY, N., *Unspeakable Subjects* (1998), (Hart Publishing).

LENIN, V.I., "State and Revolution" from M. Oakshott, *Social and Political Doctrines of Contemporary Europe* (Cambridge Univ. Press).

LEVI, E.H., *An Introduction to Legal Reasoning*. (Reprinted by permission of the University of Chicago Press. Copyright © 1949 by The University of Chicago. All rights reserved).

LITTLETON, C., "Reconstructing Sexual Equality" © 1987 by the *California Law Review, Inc.* Reprinted from *California Law Review* Vol. 75, pp. 1279–1337 by permission of the California Law Review, Inc.

LLEWELLYN, K.N., *The Common Law Tradition: Deciding Appeals* (1960), pp. 35–45, 178–180 (Wolters Kluwer). Reprinted with permission of the publisher.

LLEWELLYN, K.N., "On Reading and Using the Newer Jurisprudence" This article originally appeared at (1940) 40 Col.L.R. 581.

LLEWELLYN, K.N., "Some Realism about Realism—Responding to Dean Pound" (1931) 44 Harv. L.Rev. 1222–1256. (Copyright © 1931 by the Harvard Law Review Association).

LLEWELLYN, K.N., *My Philosophy of Law* (Boston Law Co.).

LLEWELLYN, K.N., "The Normative, the Legal and the Law Jobs: The Problem of Juristic Method" (1940) 49 Yale L.J. 1373. (Reprinted by permission of the Yale Law Journal Company and Fred B. Rothman & Company from *The Yale Law Journal* Vol. 49, pp. 1373–1395).

LUHMAN, N., "Operational Closure and Structural Coupling: The Differentiation of the Legal System" (1992) 13 Cardozo L.Rev. 1419.

LUKES, S., "Can the Base be Distinguished from the Superstructure?" from D. Miller (ed.), *The Nature of Political Theory*. (Oxford University Press).

LYOTARD, J., "Answering the Question: What is Postmodernism" (1984) in *The Postmodernist Condition: A Report on Knowledge*. (Manchester University Press).

MACCORMICK, N., "A Very British Revolution?" from *Questioning Sovereignty* (1999), (Oxford University Press).

MACCORMICK, N., "Contemporary Legal Philosophy: The Rediscovery of Practical Reason" (1983) 10 *Journal of Law and Society* 1. (Reprinted by kind permission of Basil Blackwell Ltd).

MACCORMICK, N., "Formal Justice and the Form of Legal Arguments" from *Etudes de Logique Juridique* (1976), Vol. 6, ed. Perelman (Establissements Emile Bruylant).

MACDONALD, M., "Natural Rights" (1947/8), Proc.A.S. (Reprinted by courtesy of the Editor of the Aristotelian Society. Copyright © 1948 The Aristotelian Society).

MACKINNAN, C, "Difference and Dominance: On Sex Discrimination" from *Feminism Unmodified: Discourses on Life and Law*. (Harvard University Press. Copyright © 1987 by the President and Fellows of Harvard College).

MAINE, SIR HENRY, *Ancient Law*, ed. Sir. F. Pollock (by permission of Oxford Univ. Press).

MARITAIN, J., *Man and the State*. (Reprinted by permission of the University of Chicago Press. Copyright © 1951 The University of Chicago. All rights reserved).

MARX, K., "Critique of Hegel's Philosophy of Right" from McLennan (ed.),

*Early Texts*. (Reprinted by kind permission of Basil Blackwell Ltd).

MARX, K., "Preface to Contribution to Critique of Political Economy" trans. T.B. Bottomore, from Bottomore and Rubel, *Selected Writings in Sociology and Social Philosophy*. (Reprinted by permission of Pitman Publishing Ltd).

MARX, K., "The German Ideology" from Marx and Engels, *Selected Works*, Vol. V. (Reprinted by kind permission of Lawrence and Wishart London 1970).

MARX, K., "Critique of the Gotha Programme" from McLennan, *The Thought of Marx* (1973) (reproduced with permission of Palgrave Macmillan).

MARX, K., "Preface to the Critique of Political Economy" from McLennan, *The Thought of Marx* (Macmillan, London and Basingstoke).

MARX, K., "The Civil War in France" from McLennan, *The Thought of Marx* (1973) (reproduced with permission of Palgrave Macmillan).

MARX, K., "The German Ideology" from McLennan, *The Thought of Marx* (Macmillan, London and Basingstoke).

MEAD, M., "Some Anthropological Consideration Concerning Natural Law" 6 *Natural Law* Forum 51. (Reprinted by kind permission of the *American Journal of Jurisprudence*).

MOLLER OKIN, S., *Justice, Gender and the Family* (1989), Reprinted by permission of BASIC BOOKS, a member of Perseus Books Group.

MOLLER OKIN, S., *Is Multiculturalism Bad for Women?* (1999), (Eds. Joshua Cohen, Matthew Howard and Martha C. Nussbaum), (Princeton University Press).

MURPHY, M.C., "Natural Law Jurisprudence", *Legal Theory*, 9, pp. 243–264, 2003 © Cambridge University Press, reproduced with permission.

MURPHY, M.C., "Natural Law Jurisprudence Defended," pp. 25–47 in *Natural Law Jurisprudence and Politics* (2006) © Mark C. Murphy 2006, reproduced with permission of the publisher and author.

NELKEN, D., "Blinding Insights? The Limits of a Reflexive Sociology of Law" (1998) Journal of Law and Society vol. 25, 407 (Blackwell Publishers).

NOZICK, R., *Anarchy, State and Utopia* Reprinted by permission of BASIC BOOKS, a member of Perseus Books Group.

OAKESHOTT, M., *Social and Political Doctrines of Contemporary Europe*, (1950) Cambridge University Press.

OLIVECRONA, K., *Law as Fact* (Ejnar Monksgaard).

PASHUKANIS, E., *Law and Marxism*, edited and introduced by Chris Arthur and translated from the German by Barbara Einhorn. (Published by Inks Links Ltd. in 1978).

PERRY, S., "Law and Obligation" (2005) 50 American Journal of Jurisprudence.

PERRY, S., "Hart's Methodological Positivism" (1998) 4 Legal Theory 427 © (Cambridge University Press reproduced with permission).

POPPER, K., *The Poverty of Historicism* (Routledge & Kegan Paul).

POSNER, R., "The Ethical and Political Basis of Wealth Maximization", reprinted by permission of the publisher from THE ECONOMICS OF JUSTICE by Richard A. Posner, pp 88–107, Cambridge, Mass: Harvard University Press, Copyright © 1981, 1983 by the President and

Fellows of Harvard College. Based on articles in volume 8 of the *Hofstra Law Review* and volume 9 of the *Journal of Legal Studies*, 1980.

POSTEMA, G., "Integrity: Justice in Work Clothes" in (ed) Justine Burley, *Dworkin and his Critics* (Wiley-Blackwell) (2004).

POUND, R., *Contemporary Juristic Theory* (Friends of the Claremont Colleges).

POUND, R., *Outlines of Jurisprudence* (1954), Harvard University Press.

POUND, R., *Philosophy of Law* (Yale Univ. Press. Reprinted by permission).

POUND, R., *Social Control Through Law* (Yale Univ. Press. Reprinted by permission).

RADBRUCH, G., Statutory Lawlessness and Supra–Statutory Law" (2006) Oxford Journal of Legal Studies 1–11.

RAWLS, J., *A Theory of Justice*, Oxford University Press (1972).

RAWLS, J., "The Laws of Peoples" (1993) from *On Human Rights*, Shute & Hurley (eds.) (Basic Books Inc.).

RAZ, J., *Ethics in the Public Domain* (1994), (by permission of Oxford University Press).

RAZ, J., *Practical Reason and Norms*. (Reprinted by kind permission of the author).

RAZ, J., "The Problem About the Nature of Law" from *Contemporary Philosophy*, (1982) Vol. 3. © Springer Science and Business Media published with kind permission.

RAZ, J., "The Purity of the Pure Theory" (1983) *Revue International de Philosophie* 442–459. (Copyright © J. Raz. Reprinted by permission of the author).

RENNER, K., *The Institutions of Private Law* (Routledge & Kegan Paul).

ROSS, A., *Directives and Norms* (Routledge & Kegan Paul).

ROSS, A., *On Law and Justice* (Stevens & Sons Ltd).

ROSS, A., "Tûtû" (1957) 70 Harv.L.Rev.812. (Copyright © 1957 by the Harvard Law Review Association).

SARTORIUS, R., "Social Policy and Judicial Legislation", 8 *American Philosophical Quarterly* 151.

SCALES, A.C., "The Emergence of Feminist Jurisprudence: An Essay" (1986) Yale L.J., Vol. 95, 1373. Reprinted by kind permission of the Yale Law Journal Company and Fred B. Rothman & Company from *The Yale Law Journal*, Vol. 95, pp. 1373–1986.

SCHLAG, P., "Normativity and the Politics of Form" 139 U.Pa.L.Rev.834 (1991). (Reproduced by kind permission of *The University of Pennsylvania Law Review* and Fred B. Rothman & Company).

SELZNICK, P., "The Sociology of Law" from *Sociology Today: Problems and Prospects*, ed. Robert K. Merton, Leonard Broom and Leonard S. Cottrell, Jr. (Copyright © 1959 Reprinted by permission of BASIC BOOKS, a member of Perseus Books Group).

SHKLAR, J., "Law and Ideology," reprinted by permission of the publisher from LEGALISM: LAW, MORALS, AND POLITICAL TRIALS by Judith N. Shklar, pp. 8–13, Cambridge, Mass.: Harvard University Press, Copyright © 1964, 1986 by the President and Fellows of Harvard College. Copyright © renewed 1992 by Judith N. Shklar.

SIBLEY, S. & SARAT, A., "Critical Traditions in Law and Society Research" (1987) *Law and Society Review*, Vol. 21:1. (Reproduced by permission of the Law and Society Association).

SOPER, P., "Choosing a Legal Theory on Moral Grounds" *Social Philosophy and Policy*, 4(1): 32–42, 1986 © Social Philosophy and Policy Foundation, published by Cambridge University Press, reproduced with permission.

STONE, J., *Law and the Social Sciences*, The Second HalfCentury (Univ. of Minnesota Press, Mpls. Copyright © 1966 by Univ. of Minnesota).

THOMPSON, E.P., *Whigs and Hunters: The Origin of the Black Act.* (Copyright © 1975 by E.P. Thompson. Reprinted by permission of D. Thompson.

TRUBEK, D.M. "Back to the Future: The Short Happy Life of the Law and Sociology Movement" (1990) © Florida State University Law Review 1.

TWINING, W., *Karl Llewellyn and the Realist Movement.* (Reprinted by kind permission of George Weidenfeld & Nicolson Ltd. and the author).

TWINING, W., "Some Jobs for Jurisprudence" (1974) *British Journal of Law and Society* 157–161 (Basil Blackwell Ltd).

UNGER, R., *What Should Legal Analysis Become?* (1996), (Verso).

VILLEGÁS, M.G., "On Pierre Bourdieu's Legal Thought" (2004) Droit et Société.

WALDRON, J., "The Rule of Law as a Theatre of Debate" in (ed) Justine Barley and his critics, (2006 Wiley-Blackwell).

WEBER, M., "Economy and Society" from Rheinstein (ed.), *Max Weber on Law in Economy and Society* (Harvard University press. Copyright © 1954 by the President and Fellows of Harvard College).

WEST, R., "Jurisprudence and Gender" (1988) *University of Chicago Law Review*, Vol. 55:1. (Reprinted by permission of the University of Chicago Press. Copyright © 1988 by the University of Chicago. All rights reserved).

WICKE, J., *Postmodern Identity and the Legal Subject* 62 U. Colo. L. Rev. 455 (1991). Reprinted with permission of the University of Colorado Law Review and the author.

WILLIAMS, G.L., "International Law and the Controversy Surrounding the Word 'Law'" from 22 B.Y.I.L. 146 (Fred B. Rothman & Co.).

WILLIAMS, G.L., "Language and the Law" (1945) 61 L.Q.R. 71, 179, 293, 384. (Reprinted by kind permission of the author and the Editor of the *Law Quarterly Review*).

WILLIAMS, R., *Marxism and Literature.* (Oxford University Press).

WISDOM, J., "Gods" (from 1944 Proc.A-S.). (Reprinted by courtesy of the Editor of the Aristotelian Society. Copyright © 1944 The Aristotelian Society).

WOLLHEIM, R., "The Nature of Law" from *Political Studies* (1954), Vol. 2.

YOUNG Irs, M., *JUSTICE AND THE POLITICS OF DIFFERENCE* © 1990 Princeton University Press Reprinted by permission of Wiley-Blackwell.

# CONTENTS

## EXTRACTS

## EXTRACTS

## EXTRACTS

## EXTRACTS

## EXTRACTS

## EXTRACTS

## EXTRACTS

## EXTRACTS

## EXTRACTS

## EXTRACTS

# EXTRACTS

# EXTRACTS

# EXTRACTS

# TABLE OF CASES

# TABLE OF STATUTES

1

# NATURE OF JURISPRUDENCE

## What is Jurisprudence?

To ask this question is to be reminded of the old adage, *quot homines, tot sententiae*.[1] For not only does every jurist have his own notion of the subject-matter and proper limits of jurisprudence, but his approach is governed by his allegiances, or those of his society, by his "ideology".[2] No doubt such ideological factors are frequently implicit rather than openly avowed; thus Holmes's description of them as "inarticulate major premises".[3] It has been said that "traditional theories in jurisprudence reflect the old "ideologies",[4] as we may readily see in such theories as those of natural law[5] or of utilitarianism.[6] It may be, however, that lawyers, whatever their philosophical leaning, have through their training and environment more in common than divides them.[7]

Nor is law unique in this tendency to reflect the ideologies of its place and time, for similar characteristics will be encountered in many other fields, in history, ethics, psychology and in all social sciences. Nor have the natural sciences escaped.[8] However, the close relation of law to the social structure[9] inevitably brings into prominence the ideological context of legal theory.[10]

---

[1] Terence, *Phormio*, II, 14. The word "jurisprudence" is not generally used in other languages in the English sense. Thus in French it refers to something like our "case-law", *théorie générale du droit* being used to cover our meaning of jurisprudence.

[2] See *post*, 1141 for the Marxist view.

[3] *Collected Legal Papers*, 203, 209. "To be sure, there are lawyers, judges and even law professors who tell us they have no legal philosophy. In Law, as in other things, we shall find that the only difference between a person 'without a philosophy' and someone with a philosophy is that the latter knows what his philosophy is, and is, therefore, more able to make clear and justify the premises that are implicit in his statement of the facts of his experience and his judgment about those facts" (F.C.S. Northrop, *The Complexity of Legal and Ethical Experience* (1959), p. 6).

[4] Northrop (1949) *Journal of Legal Education* 791.

[5] See *post*, Chap. 3.

[6] See *post*, 248.

[7] *Cf.* Shklar, *post*, 20.

[8] *Cf.* Kuhn, *post*, 27.

[9] *Cf.* Schwartz and Miller (1964) 70 Am. J. Sociology 159.

[10] *Cf. post*, 6.

THE RELEVANCE OF JURISPRUDENCE[11]

The hard-headed and pragmatic attitude of common lawyers to the law and the absence of any philosophical tradition informing legal education or the practice of law in common law countries have tended to provoke scepticism towards theory among judges, legal practitioners and even academic lawyers; a scepticism which may be shared by law students. This has been considerably reinforced by the fact that it is only in comparatively recent times that legal education has established itself as an acknowledged discipline in English universities. Law was previously taught under an apprenticeship system whereby knowledge of the law was picked up in the course of legal practice without any systematic instruction. The lawyer was expected to apply himself to the problem of his clients without pausing, either as student, practitioner or even judge, to explore or speculate upon what the law was about; what was or should be the role of the law and the lawyer in society; whether it was capable of responding to contemporary needs.

Very different has been the tradition of civil law countries where universities were founded for the purpose of educating for the professions, especially that of the law.[12] The academic approach to legal education, with its more philosophic and rationalistic orientation, thus became an essential feature of the civil law. An academic tradition, as against training by apprenticeship, is more likely to inspire more philosophical attitudes and less impatience with "mere theory".[13]

It has been pointed out with great force by Kahn-Freund that any serious academic discipline must entail instilling in the student a capacity for critical thought.[14] He believed the deep concern of English law with the concept of "authority" has encouraged pragmatism and diminished critical faculties of students and that this, in turn, has cast doubt on the legitimacy of law studies in English universities.[15] However, education which consists in the instilling of dogma, authoritative though it may be, is hardly worthy of its name. It was Kahn-Freund's view, which we endorse, that legal education needs to teach both law and its context, social, political, historical and theoretical.

When the first edition of this book appeared in 1959 jurisprudence was still something of a "dirty word". Since then, it may be said to have come of age. Instead of regarding rules of law as simply something to be accepted as part of the natural order of society, every aspect of the legal system, the legislative and judicial process, the working of the legal profession, the nature and functioning of law are now recognised as

---

[11] *Cf.* W. Twining, *post,* 17.
[12] See A. Hunt, *The Sociological Movements in Law* (1978), p. 111, on Weber's view of the influence of legal education on the rationalisation of law.
[13] *Cf.* H.J. Laski in 1924 (*Holmes-Laski Letters*, vol. 1, p. 694) "There has not been a reading judge in England since Lord Bowen".
[14] "Reflections on Legal Education" (1966) 29 M.L.R. 121, 123.
[15] *Cf.* R.H.S. Tur, "Jurisprudence and Practice" (1976) 14 J.S.P.T.L. 38, 41–42.

legitimate and indeed pressing fields of study. The urge to understand and appraise the relevance of the subject-matter must lead directly from the apparatus of the rules and principles of the law to jurisprudential exploration of their meaning and their effects in society.

Again, the view, rather hesitatingly adumbrated in the preface to the first edition, that there were links between jurisprudence and other fields of study, such as sociology, psychology and anthropology, which could contribute substantially to our understanding of law,[16] has now been overtaken by a situation where such interdisciplinary study and research have been greatly developed and expanded.[17]

Jurisprudence involves the study of general theoretical questions about the nature of laws and legal systems, about the relationship of law to justice and morality and about the social nature of law. A proper discussion of questions such as these involves understanding and use of philosophical and sociological theories and findings in their application to law. A study of jurisprudence should encourage the student to question assumptions and to develop a wider understanding of the nature and working of law. Questions of theory constantly spring up in legal practice, though they may not be given very sophisticated answers.

Consider the question that was posed by the case of *Oppenheimer v. Cattermole*.[18] A German Jewish refugee was deprived of his German nationality by a Nazi decree. The question (over 30 years later) was whether an English court should regard him as effectively deprived of his German nationality. If so, he would be unable to claim dual nationality entitling him to exemption from United Kingdom tax on a pension paid by the Federal Republic of Germany. The Federal Constitutional Court had decided in 1968 that the law was so obviously inconsistent with fundamental principles of justice as not to be regarded as valid law, but that a person was not to be treated as a German unless he applied for renaturalisation. The House of Lords accordingly felt itself bound to hold that Oppenheimer had lost his German citizenship in 1949 (the date of the German Basic Law[19]) since he never applied for renaturalisation. *Obiter* views were expressed as to whether, apart from the renaturalisation provision, an English court would have upheld the deprivation of nationality under the Nazi decree. A majority favoured rejecting it, reliance being placed on public policy. But Lord Cross also said that to his mind "a law of this sort constitutes so grave an infringement of

---

[16] *Cf.* P. Brett, *Essay on a Contemporary Jurisprudence* (1975); Law Commission, 11th Annual Report (1977), ss. 6–7. But note the danger, referred to by J. Hall, *Law, Social Science and Criminal Theory* (1982), p. 299, "that legal concepts, rules and values should not be permitted to dissolve in the concepts of a non-legal discipline".

[17] For a useful review of present developments, see D.R. Harris, "Socio-legal Studies in the United Kingdom" 3 *Legal Studies* 315. For examples in one area see B.A. Hepple and W.A. Brown, "Tasks for Labour Law Research" (1981) 1 *Legal Studies* 56. UCL has since 1997 had an inter-disciplinary colloquium in which the relationship between law and another discipline, for example literature, geography, psychology and anthropology, has been explored.

[18] [1976] A.C. 249; see also F. Mann (1973) 89 L.Q.R. 194.

[19] The relevant Article is 116.

human rights that the courts of this country ought to refuse to recognise it as a law at all".[20] But what are "human rights", indeed what are "rights" and what is a sufficiently "grave" infringement and who is to decide[21] and what are the effects of so deciding? Is such a law not a law at all? And if it is not, are citizens released from their obligation to obey?[22] Indeed, do citizens have a obligation to obey law[23] and if so what is the nature of this obligation and is it absolute or qualified and, if qualified, qualified in which ways?[24] Jurisprudence does not provide answers to these questions but it does offer pointers, clues, insights: it teaches students the rudiments of moral arguments.[25]

A second example centres on the so-called *Grundnorm* cases, notably *Madzimbamuto v. Lardner-Burke*,[26] litigation pursued in the aftermath of the Rhodesian unilateral declaration of independence. The immediate question concerned the validity of a detention effected by those in charge of a colonial state which purported to throw off its shackles of dependence. But the case raised fundamental questions. What is a legal system?[27] What is meant by "revolution"?[28] It is juridically different from a coup d'état? What is the role of a judge in such a situation? What is the relationship between validity and effectiveness?[29] These questions lead on to others. What is the relationship of laws to each other? Are all rules equally authoritative? What gives rules their authority? Is there an all-or-nothing concept of law? Is law affected by selective enforcement? What is the effect on a legal system of attenuation of consent? Is the force of authority of a law diminished by poor reasoning? The questions could be multiplied. Judges in a number of countries believed the pure science of law, as developed by Kelsen,[30] could assist them to resolve the more immediate of these issues. We will see in Chapter 5 some of the problems this view causes and some answers that have been posited to some of these questions. None of them is a question which any thinking lawyer can ignore.

A third question relates to justification.[31] It is well accepted that judges must give reasoned decisions. But what constitutes good reasons? In the run-of-the-mill cases there is a straightforward answer: there is statutory authority or the case clearly falls within an existing precedent which

---

[20] [1976] A.C. 249, 278.
[21] The people, other officials, jurists? (*cf.* Fuller, *post*, 121).
[22] This problem was perceived as early as Aquinas, *post*, 101.
[23] *Cf.* M.B.E. Smith (1983) 82 Yale L.J. 950. And *post*, 405 and Edmundson, *post*, 574.
[24] See P. Singer, *Democracy and Disobedience* (1973).
[25] See J. Glover, *Causing Deaths and Saving Lives* (1977), Chap. 2.
[26] (1968) 2 S.A. 284 and, on appeal to the Privy Council, [1969] 1 A.C. 645. *Cf. post*, 311.
[27] See J. Raz, *The Concept of A Legal System* (1970).
[28] See J. Eekelaar, "Principles of Revolutionary Legality" in Simpson (ed.) *Oxford Essays in Jurisprudence* (1973), p. 22 and J.M. Finnis, "Revolution and Continuity of Law", *op. cit.*, p. 44.
[29] See F.M. Brookfield (1969) 19 Univ. of Toronto L.J. 326; J. Harris (1971) C.L.J. 103.
[30] See Chap. 5.
[31] A question brought into prominence in the writings of Ronald Dworkin; see, *post*, Chap. 8. See also S. Guest, *Ronald Dworkin* (2nd ed., 1997).

cannot be rationally distinguished from it. But what of the "hard case", what happens when the law appears to have gaps? Can the judge turn to nonlegal sources? Are there legal sources to which he can go when he appears to run out of rules? If so, what is it that makes these non-rules into law? Are they validated in the same way as rules? What light does this throw on a legal system's "pedigree test"?[32] To what sort of standards, other than rules, may judges appeal? Is it legitimate for them to invoke teleological considerations, goals or policies? Or should they confine themselves to the deontological, to rights and principles? Is there a right answer and is that answer to be found embedded in the law? What is meant by "the law"? How far does it extend? These questions only occasionally surface in litigation (see for example, the case of *McLoughlin v. O'Brian*[33]) but they are pervasive if implicit and inarticulate.

The recent case of *Jackson and Others v. Attorney General*[34] is a further example of the importance of jurisprudential thinking to the resolution of legal problems. The House of Lords had to decide whether the Hunting Act 2004 was a valid Act of Parliament. The Act had been forced though under the Parliament Acts of 1911 and 1949. The Lords held that the 1949 Act had been validly enacted under the procedure established by the 1911 Act, and that the Hunting Act had been validly enacted under the amended procedure. Most of what they said on wider issues is strictly obiter but is interesting to the jurist because it raised questions about the foundations of the legal order and about sovereignty.

Can Parliament (as we learn from Dicey, who derived his views from Austin and beyond) pass any law or are there fundamental values such as human rights, democracy and the rule of law embedded within the constitution? Are there limits on what Parliament can do? Could it abolish elections? Can it extend the period for which there can be detention without trial, and, if so, to what? In *Jackson*, the proposition was entertained, for the first time judicially,[35] that courts might be able to strike down an Act of Parliament as incompatible with fundamental values. This conflict between orthodoxy[36] and revisionism is mirrored by the different views of Hart and Dworkin, considered at various places in this book.[37] If, as Dworkin argues, there are principles underlying the law, such as justice and fairness, if "propositions of law are true if they figure in and follow from the principles of justice, fairness, and procedural due process that provide the best constructive interpretation of the political structure and legal doctrine of the community[38]", then perhaps we should accept that the sovereignty of Parliament is not absolute. Are the judges being influenced by Dworkinian jurisprudence as earlier

[32] The phrase is Dworkin's. See *Taking Rights Seriously* (1977).
[33] [1983] 1 A.C. 410 and see *post*, 810.
[34] [2006] 1 A.C. 262. *Jackson's* case is further considered at 260, n. 73.
[35] It had been extra-judicially, by Sir John Laws (1995) Public Law 72, 87 and by Lord Woolf of Barnes (1995) Public Law 57, 67–69.
[36] Well-illustrated today by J. Goldsworthy, *The Sovereignty of Parliament* (1999).
[37] See 386, 717.
[38] *Law's Empire*, p. 225.

generations were by Dicey's (and Austin's)? Austin's mentor (Bentham), we shall see, saw that there could be limits on sovereignty (he sketched the rudiments of a doctrine of judicial review).[39] English constitutional law might have looked different if Dicey had been able to read Bentham.[40]

ACQUIRING SOCIAL KNOWLEDGE

One of the "jobs" of jurisprudence is to supply an epistemology of law, a theory as to the possibility of genuine knowledge in the legal sphere. But how is such knowledge to be acquired? What are its sources? Can its methodology be compared with that of the natural sciences or of, what have come to be called, the social sciences? Is objective knowledge possible or must it be distorted by our values and biases?

In the nineteenth century, there were fairly clear answers to these questions.[41] The noteworthy development of the natural sciences had earned for them overwhelming prestige and this had marked effects on other fields of study, which sought to share in this prestige by claiming also scientific status and thus the ability to produce empirical knowledge by similar procedures to those accepted as the conventional methods of the natural sciences. The apotheosis of this view is John Stuart Mill's defence of a "naturalistic" social science in *A System of Logic* (1843).[42]

Mill believed that there were scientific laws of society: that causal laws governed man in society as well as the physical world of science. He was not alone in holding this view: Auguste Comte's *Cours de Philosophie Positive* (1830–1842) developed laws of social evolution holding not dissimilar views.[43] And there were many others. The belief spread even beyond the nascent social sciences to art[44] and literature. Consider, for example, impressionist art and naturalism in literature.

There are different conceptions of natural science explanation. There is the empiricist account which holds that only those statements which can be empirically verified can be considered to be true knowledge. The

---

[39] See 252.
[40] Bentham's seminal text on this, *Of Laws In General*, was not published until 1970.
[41] For the development of this view see R. Brown, *The Nature of Social Laws* (1984).
[42] Discussed *ibid.*, Chap. 9 and *post*, 7–8.
[43] *Post*, 836.
[44] The realism of Courbet was influenced by the positivism of Comte. Courbet regarded reality as only what is observed and can be expressed scientifically. Again, the impressionist painters were concerned with the scientific theory of vision and Seurat sought to establish a scientific method of rendering light (see B. Taylor, *The Impressionists and their World*, pp. 6–15). In 1836, John Constable wrote, "Painting is a science, and should be pursued as an enquiry into the laws of nature" (Leslie, *Life of Constable*, p. 323). Ruskin, too, was persuaded that there was such a close connection between art and science that he believed his aesthetic observations were as conclusive as those of a scientist (see Quentin Bell, *Ruskin* (1963), pp. 16–17).

empiricist relies on induction[45]: the observation of empirical facts, the propounding of a hypothesis to explain those facts followed by inference and testing leading to an explanatory theory. He rejects judgements of value. At one stage such a process was believed to result in scientific laws of complete generality and uniformity. This view of the natural sciences, rigid and deterministic, has now been rejected.

First, it has been shown that natural science is not mechanistic. Induction does not lead to the inference of absolutely rigid causal laws, rather to "statistical regularities" which we assume will apply until we find they do not. Secondly, there are good scientific reasons for believing that in any event there remains an element of indeterminacy or "chance" such that the physical world cannot be explained solely in terms of pre-dictable deterministic laws.[46] The myth of determinism has been destroyed by modern physics. Thirdly, verification is not, or not always, possible. For this reason the influential philosopher Karl Popper prefers the method of "falsification".[47] All scientific theories (or laws) are in this view tentative and provisional and liable to possible refutation. Clearly, the more tests a hypothesis survives, the greater its explanatory power. Fourthly, the natural sciences are not value-free. What Kuhn[48] has called "normal science" has a moral or value base: as a system it classifies those facts which are considered worthy of study; it has its own technology and material apparatus and carries the commitment of the community of scientists. It may have the organised support and direction of government or industrial enterprise. Change from such an existing "world view" is slow and tortuous. Theories long refuted ("falsified") may nonetheless be clung to. New "world views" or "paradigms" evolve as increasing anomalies in an existing pattern break down the resistance of the old paradigms' adherents.

Our conception of the natural sciences is not what it was when Mill and Comte tried to construct social laws. Nevertheless, can social sciences be fitted into the modified empiricist account of the natural sciences, just depicted, and, if so, how far? The mere fact that social sciences involve a more complex subject-matter does not necessarily entail that there can be no unity of method between them, since the complexity of phenomena is only a matter of degree, and even in physical experiments certain ideal conditions are often postulated.[49] Mill was aware of this problem.

---

[45] Even then Hume's tormenting argument that there was no possibility of finding a logical justification for induction raised nagging doubts, at least for philosophers (*A Treatise of Human Nature*, Bk. 1, s. 6). See also L. Kolakowski, *Positivist Philosophy* (1972), p. 52.

[46] A brief clarification of this point and its philosophic significance will be found in Pass-more, *A Hundred Years of Philosophy* (1957), p. 332. Consider also the part played by intuition in scientific method. See Sir Peter Medawar's *Pluto's Republic* (1982), p. 73.

[47] *Post*, 24. *Cf*. T. Kuhn, *post* 27. See also A. Giddens, *New Rules of Sociological Method* (1976), pp. 135–144.

[48] In *The Structure of Scientific Revolutions* (revised ed., 1970) and see *post*, 30. This thesis may do something to explain resistance to legal change as well. But here there is the additional factor of pressure groups.

[49] K. Popper, *Poverty of Historicism*, pp. 139–140.

"Effects," he noted, "are commonly determined by a *concurrence* of causes".[50] How, he asked, "can we obtain a crucial experiment on the effect of a restrictive commercial policy upon national wealth? We must find two nations alike in every other respect ... but differing in this only, that one of them adopts a system of commercial restrictions, and the other adopts free trade. This would be a decisive experiment, similar to those which we can almost always obtain in experimental physics."[51] Mill concedes that the likelihood of being able to make such an experiment is infinitesimally small. In some fields, psychology for example, there may be more scope for controlled experiments than in others. Nevertheless, it remains undeniable that the social sciences cannot hope to obtain the sort of theories or laws found in the natural sciences. The social scientist confronts in particular two problems.

First, the phenomena with which he concerns himself are not the same in kind. The objects of enquiry are different: the natural sciences being concerned with matter; the social sciences with man. Matter reacts to a stimulus (subject to what has been said already). It does not understand its own behaviour. It has no subjective intentions. It is meaningless until the scientist imposes his frame of reference upon it. To understand the logic of the behaviour of matter, one observes the behaviour itself. But the action of men is meaningful to them. Men define their situation and act in certain ways to achieve their ends. In doing so, they construct a social world. Social life has an internal logic which must be understood by the social scientist. By contrast, the natural scientist can impose an external logic on his data. An understanding of man's subjective intentions requires interpretive understanding by theorists who share these subjective meanings. This is to deny the existence of objective social knowledge and to reject the positivist attempt to separate theories, facts and values. The interpretive approach is often labelled hermeneutical.[52] Understanding is thought to result from a complex process linking experiences to perceptions, meanings and values, all of which in their turn are rooted in a particular culture.

This leads to another problem. The social scientist cannot experience the experience of another person. Indeed, his own experience may make him perceive what is going on in a way which distorts its meanings to the actors involved. The ethnocentricity of early anthropologists, including those who were concerned with "primitive" law, is partly attributable to this barrier.

With these phenomenological problems confronting him, how is the social scientist to acquire knowledge of the social world, the jurist of the legal world? How is understanding possible? One suggestion is to observe

---

[50] *Essays on Some Unsettled Questions of Political Economy* (1844), p. 160.
[51] *ibid.*, p. 148.
[52] On hermeneutics see R. Palmer, *Hermeneutics* (1969); P. Rabinow and W. Sullivan (eds.), *Interpretive Social Science* (1979); J. Bleicher *Contemporary Hermeneutics* (1980). Perhaps the most important interpreter of hermeneutical theory is Hans-Georg Gadamer: see his *Truth and Method* (1975). See also R. Bernstein, *op. cit.*

behaviour, the argument being that this is concrete, quantifiable and susceptible to scientific analysis. This is an approach adopted by the school of judicial behaviouralists with a view to predicting judicial behaviour (decisions).[53] But aside from the problems already referred to and others, such as the ignoring of the normative, this approach has severe limitations. To make sense of an act, an observer must place it within a category which he can comprehend, and it may mean something totally different to the actor himself. The danger is of missing the significance of the act to the participants themselves. Rather than focusing on behaviour, it is commonly suggested that the theorist should be concerned with action.[54] Action arises from meanings which define social reality.[55] People assign meanings to situations and to the actions of others, and react in terms of the interpretation suggested by these meanings. Action is the result of expectations arising out of past experience. Meaning is found within social life and history. The meaning of our social world is given to us by the past history and present structure of our society. Thus, when the social scientist observes the social world, what he sees is structured. In Alfred Schutz's words:

> "It has a particular meaning and relevance structure for the human beings living, thinking and acting therein. They have preselected and pre-interpreted this world by a series of common-sense constructs of the reality of daily life, and it is these thought-objects which determine their behaviour, define the goal of their action, and the means available for obtaining them."[56]

When we enter the social world it is already organised and coherent, and we rarely question what we regard as part of the natural order of things. We experience the world as an unquestioned reality. We know this social world through a shared stock of knowledge and the correctness of this knowledge is continually reinforced by the actions of others. It follows from this that explanations of human actions must take account of the meanings which those concerned assign to their acts. But, as already indicated, the outside world is complex. The result is we are likely to be selective, to oversimplify and to lose information in the process. Further, our ability to test information diminishes as objects recede into the distance. It becomes very easy for us to reduce the strange, the problematic to inconsequentiality, even triviality.

This is the subject-matter the social scientist confronts.[57] He does not find the social world structureless but faces what society has preselected and pre-interpreted by means of common-sense constructs of reality of

---

[53] See the work of Schubert, *Judicial Behavior* (1964). See also the writings of Donald Black, for example, *The Behavior of Law* (1976). And *post*, 861–862.

[54] See A. Giddens, *Central Problems in Social Theory* (1979).

[55] See P. Berger and T. Luckmann, *The Social Construction of Reality* (1967).

[56] *The Phenomenology of the Social World* (1972), p. 121.

[57] The differences between natural and social sciences can be over-emphasised. See M. Hesse, *Revolutions and Reconstructions in the Philosophy of Science* (1980), pp. 61–110.

daily life. He uses constructs of the second degree: what Schutz calls "constructs of constructs made by actors on the social scene".[58]

The task of the social scientist is thus to transcend the common-sense world to discern its working and patterns and relationships between actors. He must make sense of it. Further, he must elicit meanings for they are often not clear. They may be implicit, disguised or even confused. In addition, far from ignoring what society has chosen to trivialise, he must concentrate on it. The anomalous,[59] the problematic is often that which provides test-beds for his theory. The theory which cannot explain, or only explain inadequately,[60] the anomalous cases may not stand up to critical examination. It is important that the theorist distances himself, in so far as this is possible. None of this is intended to suggest that rational explanation is impossible. Indeed, rational explanation is more likely to be attained by the theorist who is aware of, and can take steps to neutralise, his pre-scientific understandings, concepts and values.

Debates have raged over the question as to whether particular disciplines, psychotherapy[61] and medicine[62] for example, are sciences and similarly on the limits and scope of the social sciences. There are historians like Spengler[63] and Toynbee[64] who claim to construct laws of history.

It is difficult to characterise jurisprudence; there are many rooms in its mansion. But, broadly, we shall see it is concerned with rule-governed action, with the activities of officials such as judges and with the relationship between them and the population of a given society. Hart, indeed, categorised his elucidation of the concept of law as an "essay in descriptive sociology."[65] But whether jurisprudence is a social science or not, the debates about methodology in the social sciences between positivists or empiricists and practitioners of hermeneutics are echoed in juristic literature. Much classical jurisprudence (the writings of Austin and Bentham for example) is positivist in its approach to social knowledge and indeed we call their legal theories positivist. There is much, however, in contemporary juristic writing, that of Hart[66] and Dworkin[67] to take just two outstanding examples, which uses the insight of hermeneutics. Contemporary jurisprudence reflects philosophical debates about

---

[58] *Op. cit.*, n. 60, p. 137.

[59] In the context of jurisprudence the place of international law or constitutional law is a good example. See in relation to Austin, *post*, 256. H.L.A. Hart (*The Concept of Law* (1994), Chap. 1) does not think our difficulties of definition in relation to law are the result of anomalous cases.

[60] For example, the difficulties encountered by positivistic jurisprudence with the common law. See A.W.B. Simpson (ed.), *Oxford Essays in Jurisprudence* (1973), p. 77.

[61] *Cf.* P. Alexander, in *Proceedings of Arist. Soc.*, Supp., vol. 29, pp. 27–42.

[62] See the discussion in Nowell-Smith, *Ethics*, p. 64.

[63] *Cf. post*, 1080.

[64] See in particular Arnold J. Toynbee, *Study of History*, vol. 9, pp. 395–405; and vol. 12, pp. 239–242, 650–677. See A.J.P. Taylor's comment in Ashley Montagu (ed.), *Toynbee and History* (1956), p. 115; "This is not history".

[65] *The Concept of Law* (1994), Preface.

[66] On Hart and hermeneutics see N. MacCormick, *H.L.A. Hart* (1981), pp. 37–40.

[67] *A Matter of Principle* (1985) and *Law's Empire* (1987).

the meaning of social knowledge: if for no other reason students should be aware of the issues discussed in this section.

## NORMATIVE CHARACTER OF LAW

The emphasis on law as a science can lead to a neglect or even a denial of a critical aspect of the concept of law. This is particularly so where jurisprudence is seen, as the Realists see it, as a study of factual patterns of behaviour. But human laws are not in themselves statements of fact[68]; they are rules or norms, which prescribe a course of conduct, and indicate what should happen in default.[69] The sanction, however, is not usually connected in an empirical sense with the rule or its breach, but is merely indicative of what the rule itself prescribes, as the consequence of non-compliance.[70] This is, therefore, a particular form or use of language different from that part of language concerned with propositions of fact, but it is no less legitimate usage than factual statements, and, is indeed, related to a whole group of similar "normative" usages, such as commands, exhortations, and moral, ethical, or religious codes or rules of conduct.[71] Hence normative rules must be carefully distinguished from physical laws, which state causal connections. The latter are subject to verification,[72] that is, they can be true or false; but the notion of truth or falsity is inapplicable to normative rules. Such rules simply state what should or "ought to" happen. This is the distinction made by Kant between *sein* (being) and *sollen* (ought) which is so emphatically brought out by Kelsen,[73] and which tended to be obscured or even rejected in the earlier writings of the Realists.[74] Of course, it must be borne in mind that the use of the word "ought" does not necessarily imply *moral* obligation, for in relation to a purely positive rule, such as a legal duty of care, the "ought" merely relates to the duty of compliance with the rule on pain of suffering the prescribed penalty.[75]

---

[68] Whether the norm *itself* is a correct statement within a particular system is another matter; this will depend not on factual verification but on whatever tests are accorded by that system.

[69] Austin endeavoured to stress this by his imperative theory of law as a command, but his actual analysis was not *free* from objection; see *post*, 256.

[70] The clearest statement of this view is found in Kelsen. See *post*, 328–329. See in particular Olivecrona's caustic response on 329, n. 34.

[71] On the difference between norms and value judgements see C. Fried, *Right and Wrong* (1978), pp. 11–12. Fried defines a norm as "a judgement addressed to an agent, directing choice" (p. 11).

[72] *Cf.* Popper, *post*, 24.

[73] *Post*, 305.

[74] *Post*, Chaps 10 and 11.

[75] This is not to say that the *legal* "ought" may not in some instances, correspond with the *moral* "ought"; *cf. post*, 41.

## "Ought" And "Is"

The tendency to derive normative rules from physical or natural laws, or to analyse or define them in terms of physical qualities or phenomena, is a pervasive one. Thus many of the attempts to base positive law on an immutably established natural law governing the universe have involved an attempt to link normative rules directly with what are really con-jectural hypotheses of factual character (*i.e.* in the nature of physical laws). However, in 1740, Hume pointed out the fallacy of trying, as he put it, to derive "ought" from "is", and argued that a normative state-ment could not be inferred from a purely factual one.[76] So, too, the efforts to define moral norms in terms of something else, which can be ascer-tained or verified as a fact, such as pleasure or utility, involve a similar confusion which has been stigmatised by G.E. Moore as "the naturalistic fallacy".[77] There is, in other words, an unbridgeable gap between "ought" and "is", or norm and fact, but this does not mean, as has sometimes been thought, that "ought" statements occupy a special world of exis-tence of their own, distinct from physical reality. In the last century, the work of the philosopher Wittgenstein on the uses of language as a solvent of many of the puzzles and paradoxes that have perplexed philosophers[78] also helped to bring out more clearly the distinction between normative and factual usages of language. In this connection close consideration has been given by moral philosophers and, more recently, jurists like Hart, the Scandinavians and Raz, to the logical structure of the imperative and normative forms of language, and although finality of opinion is not by any means attained or perhaps attainable, much of this sort of analysis is illuminating not only in regard to ethics but also in relation to the nature and logic of legal rules.[79] Thus the notion that a statement that something ought to be done is not to give a factual description but to prescribe a course of conduct based on the implication that reasons exist for so acting, and also on the existence of standards and criteria of appraisal, by

---

[76] But J.M. Finnis denies that the true classical doctrine of natural law, which he identifies in Aristotle and Aquinas, did this. He claims that classical natural law derives its nor-mative conclusions not from an observation of human nature or physical law but a reflective grasp of what is self-evidently good for men (*Natural Law and Natural Rights* (1980), pp. 33–36 and *Fundamentals of Ethics* (1983), pp. 10–17).

[77] *Post*, 1044. Hume's "law" has been challenged. A useful collection of essays on this theme is W.D. Hudson (ed.), *The Is/Ought Question* (1969); the editor's lucid introduc-tion is particularly recommended. See also L. Kolakowski, *Positivist Philosophy* (1972), pp. 42–59. An excellent analysis of Hume's views is J. Harrison, *Hume's Moral Episte-mology* (1976), pp. 110–25. For the view that Hume himself offends against the principle see J.M. Finnis, *op. cit.*, pp. 37–38. P. Milton argues that the dichotomy anyway owes more to Kant than Hume (1982) *Legal Studies* 14.

[78] *Cf. post*, 33.

[79] Recent juristic writings adopting a linguistic approach include Ross, *Directives and Norms* (1968), *post*, 1068, Olivecrona, *Law As Fact* (2nd ed., 1971), particularly Chaps 9 and 10, *post*, 858; the writings of H.L.A. Hart, see, for example, *post*, 59, 444 and Raz, *The Concept of a Legal System* and *Practical Reason and Norms* (1975).

which those reasons may be judged. A rule of law, however, differs[80] from this in that, though it does not state a fact but only prescribes a course of conduct, it does not necessarily imply that reasons for compliance could be sought and perhaps given, but rather that it is derived from a valid authority.[81] Such an authority can, as both Hume and Kelsen have pointed out, consist in another norm.[82]

## FORM (OR STRUCTURE) AND CONTENT

Those jurists who have stressed the form or logical structure of legal and other normative propositions have been disposed to adopt a "conceptual" kind of jurisprudence, laying emphasis on the fundamental form of legal concepts without regard to their content. This was no doubt in the mind of Austin when he sought to lay down a universal definition of law, and to adumbrate the distinction between what he called general and particular jurisprudence. Austin, indeed, fell a good deal short of applying this notion with logical rigidity, since he sought to derive his ultimate source of law, *viz.*, sovereignty, from a basis of fact,[83] but his idea of general jurisprudence as concerned with the principles common to various systems of law, and which those systems inevitably involve, appears to recognise a structural identity which does not arise merely *de facto*, but is *logically* inherent. This distinction is applied a good deal more deliberately and consistently in the writings of Hans Kelsen.[84]

## PHILOSOPHY OF LAW?

The choice between a philosophy or a science of law is no doubt to a large extent a matter of terminology. Philosophy was once the fashionable word, when physics was known as "natural philosophy".[85] But since that day science has become all the rage, and as we have seen, many studies beyond the physical sciences have sought shelter under the comforting umbrella of science. Science, however, is concerned with empirically observable facts and events, whereas philosophy is concerned with certain ultimate questions of structure. Bertrand Russell once put it rather neatly by saying that science is what we know, philosophy what we don't

---

[80] But on the rediscovery within the last decade of the relationship between law and practical reason see MacCormick, *post*, 449.

[81] *Cf.* Nowell-Smith, *op. cit.*, Chap. 13. Many rules of law also, however, like moral rules, contain, so to speak, a built-in standard of appraisal, *e.g.* a legal duty of care implies that reasons exist for taking such care, and criteria exist for appraising these reasons. Such criteria, however, need not necessarily coincide with those of morals in a comparable case. *Cf. post*, 40.

[82] *Post*, 24, 329, but *cf.* 325.

[83] *Post*, 299.

[84] *Post*, Chap. 5.

[85] *Cf.* Ryle, in *British Philosophy in Mid-Century* (Mace, ed.), pp. 257–258.

jurisprudence, so is the exposition of such principles its exclusive or appropriate object. With the goodness or badness of laws, as tried by the test of utility (or by any of the various test which divide the opinions of mankind), it has no immediate concern. If, in regard to some of the principles which form its appropriate subject, it adverts to considerations of utility, it adverts to such considerations for the purpose of explaining such principles, and not for the purpose of determining their worth. And this distinguishes the science in question from the science of legislation: which affects to determine the test or standard (together with the principles subordinate or consonant to such test) by which positive law ought to be made, or to which positive law ought to be adjusted.

If the possibility of such a science appear doubtful, it arises from this; that in each particular system, the principles and distinctions which it has in common with others, are complicated with its individual peculiarities, and are expressed in a technical language peculiar to itself.

It is not meant to be affirmed that these principles and distinctions are conceived with equal exactness and adequacy in every particular system. In this respect different systems differ. But, in all, they are to be found more or less nearly conceived; from the rude conceptions of barbarism, to the exact conceptions of the Roman lawyers or of enlightened modern jurists.

I mean, then, by General Jurisprudence, the science concerned with the exposition of the principles, notions, and distinctions which are common to systems of law: understanding by systems of law, the ampler and maturer systems,[92] which, by reason of their amplitude and maturity, are pre-eminently pregnant with instruction.

Of the principles, notions, and distinctions which are the subjects of general jurisprudence, some may be esteemed necessary. For we cannot imagine coherently a system of law (or system of law as evolved in a refined community), without conceiving them as constituent parts of it.[93]                [pp. 365–367]

The word Jurisprudence itself is not free from ambiguity; it has been used to denote—

The knowledge of Law as a science, combined with the art of practical habit or skill of applying it; or, secondly,

Legislation,—the science of what *ought to be done* towards making good laws, combined with the art of doing it.

Inasmuch as the knowledge of what ought to be, supposes a knowledge of what

---

[92] [Note that Austin *expressly* excludes from his conception and jurisprudence immature systems, such as primitive customary and feudal laws. *Cf. post,* 40. M. Barberis (1996) 9 Ratio Juris. 1 throws some contemporary light on Austin's project, using insights from debates on conceptual relativism. W. Twining, *Globalisation and Legal Theory* (2000), Chap. 2 offers valuable context to Austin's thinking.]

[93] [Austin proceeds to give as examples of such necessary principles, notions and distinctions, the following notions of duty, right, liberty, punishment, redress; with their various relations to one another, and to law, sovereignty and independent political society; the distinction between written and unwritten law; the distinction between rights availing against the world at large and variously restricted rights; the division of obligations into those arising from contract and from injuries, and from other sources; and the distinction between civil injuries and crimes (see W.L. Morison, *John Austin* (1982), pp. 118–121).

Stone, *Legal System and Lawyers' Reasonings* (1964), pp. 82–85, sees here "Austin's tendency to straddle the particularist and universalist view". He believes that Austin makes unwarranted inferences from English and Roman law, the only two systems with which he was familiar.

Austin goes on to refer to other principles, notions and distinctions which are not "necessary" in the above sense, but which on grounds of utility occur very generally in mature systems of law, and, therefore, may be ranked with the general principles which are the subjects of general jurisprudence. He gives as an example, the distinction between the law of persons and the law of things, as a basis for a scientific arrangement of a body of law. *Cf.* Margaret Mead, *post,* 225.]

is, legislation supposes jurisprudence, but jurisprudence does not suppose legislation. What laws have been and are, may be known without a knowledge of what they ought to be. Inasmuch as a knowledge of what ought to be, is bottomed on a knowledge of antecedents *cognato genere*, legislation supposes jurisprudence.

With us, Jurisprudence is the science of what is essential to law, combined with the science of what it ought to be. It is particular or universal. Particular Jurisprudence is the science of any actual system of law, or of any portion of it. The only practical jurisprudence is particular.

The proper subject of General or Universal Jurisprudence (as distinguished from Universal Legislation) is a description of such subjects and ends of Law as are common to all systems; and of those resemblances between different systems which are bottomed in the common nature of man, or correspond to the resembling points in their several positions.

And these resemblances will be found to be very close, and to cover a large part of the field. They are necessarily confined to the resemblances between the systems of a few nations; since it is only a few systems with which it is possible to become acquainted, even imperfectly. From these, however, the rest may be presumed. And it is only the system of two or three nations which deserve attention:—the writings of the Roman Jurists; the decisions of English Judges in modern times; the provisions of French and Prussian Codes as to arrangement.   [pp. 372–373]

## W.L. TWINING
### Some Jobs for Jurisprudence
(1974)[94]

[T]he most widely held view of jurisprudence as a subject, that which was expressed by Julius Stone as "the lawyer's extraversion" ...

> It is lawyer's examination of the precepts, ideals and techniques of the law in the light derived from present knowledge in disciplines other than the law. It is an attempt, which always remains imperfect, to fulfil for the law the object strikingly posed by the late Mr Justice Holmes of showing "the rational connection between your fact and the frame of the Universe. To be master of any branch of knowledge you must muster those which lie next to it."[95]

In this view, the main function of the jurist is as a conduit. He ventures forth from the law to garner what one or more neighbouring disciplines have to offer respecting questions of a general nature that have been thrown up in legal contexts. His role is to bring back the ideas, techniques, and insights of that other discipline and to integrate or assimilate them into the intellectual milieu of the law. The achievements of many leading jurists can be interpreted in this way; for instance, perhaps the main contribution of Roscoe Pound was to import into Anglo-American law some of the ideas of nineteenth century German jurists and social thinkers, such as Ihering, Post and Kohler. Similarly one of the main achievements of H.L.A. Hart has been to introduce, or at least to reintroduce, to us the techniques and modes of thought of English analytical philosophy. More recently Albert Ehrenzweig has tried to do something similar with psychoanalysis.[96]

The role of conduit is not necessarily an easy nor an exclusive one: often in performing this function the jurist has done something more and has typically produced some additional element which can be justly claimed as an original

[94] [From (1974) 1 *British J. of Law and Society* 149.]
[95] J. Stone, *Legal Systems and Lawyers' Reasoning* (1964), p. 16.
[96] A. Ehrenzweig, *Psychoanalytic Jurisprudence* (1971).

contribution. But the essential nature of the process is for someone to venture forth from the intellectual milieu of the law and to come back with spoils from elsewhere and to present them in assimilable form.[97]

Of course the role of jurist as conduit is by no means the only function of juristic activity. Fundamental issues, what might be termed "high theory", have a central place in jurisprudence. Very general questions about the nature and functions of law, the concept of a legal system, the relationship between law and morality, the differences between law and other types of social control, perennial questions about justice, and ultimate questions about the epistemological and other fundamental assumptions of legal discourse, stand at the core of legal theory. Most of these questions are in a sense philosophical; but even at this rarified level the approach of jurists is often influenced, more or less directly, by the centripetal, participant-orientation of law. However, few, if any, of these questions are exclusively of jurist concern. For at this level the boundaries between disciplines recede to vanishing point. I do not want to pursue here the question whether it is even meaningful to talk of an "autonomous discipline", but it is scarcely open to question that many, if not all, of the more general and fundamental questions of jurisprudence are not only shared with philosophers, political theorists, and social theorists, but also require for their resolution concepts and techniques which have been largely developed by people other than jurists.

It is important to emphasize that concern with "high theory" represents only *one* part of jurisprudence, as I have used this term. There is a wide range of questions of a lower order which are also a proper focus of juristic attention; and it is a dis-service to dismiss concern with such questions as being unphilosophical or untheoretical or in some way not worthy of the attention of serious jurists. It is difficult to make this point without appearing to be siding with the philistines or involving oneself in a particular sterile kind of controversy. But while it is perfectly proper that some jurists should be concentrating primarily on "high theory", there are dangers that if this is accompanied by mandarin over-refinement or by certain kinds of unnecessary intellectual snobbery, jurisprudence and juristic activity may get out of touch with the general intellectual milieu of the law; as a result a nation's jurisprudence may fail to make some of its most important, but more modest, contributions to its legal culture. There are some who would maintain that this has happened to some extent in recent years with analytical jurisprudence in England; and that as a result, certain important kinds of juristic concern have to a large extent been neglected. In particular three such concerns are germane to the theme of this paper.

(*a*)  the study, criticism and improvement of the working theories and operative ideas of participants in legal activities;

(*b*)  the formulation of theories of the middle order (in the Mertonian sense) and of fertile hypotheses to guide research and enquiry in various areas, especially in new and neglected fields of study; and

(*c*)  the synthesizing function: to chart and, where appropriate, to re-draw the general map of the intellectual milieu of the law.

All that is a bit of a mouthful and needs some clarification. First, working theories. All participants in legal activities, from solicitors to judges, from law reformers to writers of textbooks, have working theories, in the sense that they have conceptions of the nature of their tasks, how best to go about them and what is the relationship of their activity to some broader picture. Such conceptions may be more or less articulate, more of less coherent or more or less suited to the actual potential tasks involved. One function of jurisprudence is to identify, to articulate   and   to   examine   critically,   these   working   theories.   In   short,

---

[97]  On the pitfalls of eclecticism see Campbell (1974) 1 *British J. of Law and Society* 24–26.

jurisprudence is not only the lawyer's extraversion; for some purposes it is also the lawyer's introspection. One such purpose is to suggest changes or improvements.

One service demanded of the academic lawyer and the jurist by their clients to provide guidance, especially general guidance, on how to set about performing their tasks. Some of this guidance is quite specific, *e.g.* detailed proposals for law reform, or specialized advice on abstruse points of law, but in a broader sense what is wanted is general guidelines on how to set about performing their tasks. Juristic literature abounds with attempts to provide such theories: Bentham's Science of Legislation. Karl Llewellyn's theory of the Grand Style of appellate judging and advocacy, and, in a less pure form, the articulated more general assumptions of the Ormrod Committee on Legal Education are examples.[98] I would include under this head a recommended set of general intellectual procedures for planning a contextual course or book. On the whole the response of jurists to such demands have been patchy and unsystematic, perhaps because of the strongly pragmatic tendencies of the common law. One of the main failures of jurisprudence in England in the 20th century has been its failure systematically to examine and bring into the open the working assumptions and operative ideas of various kinds of participant in legal processes and to examine these critically in the light of some more general conceptions about the nature of our legal culture and the actual and potential role of law and lawyers in society. This failure of jurisprudence is clearly illustrated in the field of so-called "law reform" and more generally of law making in this country. The public debate on the Eleventh Report of the Criminal Law Revision Committee on Evidence, published in 1972, provides a particularly striking example.[99] For neither the authors of the report nor the majority of their critics seem to have had very clear conceptions about the nature of the exercise—there was lacking not only a coherent theory of the nature of the law of evidence and its place in criminal process and in social control of crime, but also, more generally, a coherent theory of law reform analogous to Bentham's Science of Legislation.[1]

A similar kind of guidance is needed in the academic sphere in respect of developing new fields, re-thinking old ones and guiding research. The pragmatism of the common law approach to legal problems in the world of practice is matched to quite remarkable degree by a similar distrust not only of very general, but even of middle order, theorizing in respect of research and other intellectual activities.[2] This is a large and controversial subject, but suffice to say here that the continued vitality of the rather wild and largely discredited generalizations of Sir Henry Maine is perhaps less a tribute to his perspicuity, than an indication of a dearth of comparable middle order hypotheses even today.

Next, the synthesizing function: to chart and, where appropriate, to redesign the general map of the intellectual milieu of the law. In other words, to explore and articulate general frames of reference for law as an academic discipline. What I have in mind is very close to Karl Llewellyn's idea of a working whole view of law[3] and Blackstone's conception of the lawyer's map of his world.[4] Such maps can be evaluated partly in terms of the criteria of relevance they adopt and the criteria of significance they incorporate. But ultimately they rest on a more general ideology, whether or not that ideology is fully articulated. It would be

---

[98] J. Bentham, *Works, passim* (Bowring ed.) [and see *post*, 248]; K.N. Llewellyn, *The Common Law Tradition: Deciding Appeals* (1960) [and see *post*, 1021]; *Report of the Committee on Legal Education* (1971); Cmnd. 4595.

[99] (1972) Cmnd. 4991. [This debate continues. Some of its proposals were implemented in the Police and Criminal Evidence Act 1984.]

[1] See Twining, "The Way of the Baffled Medic" (1973) 12 *J. Society of Public Teachers of Law (N.S.)* 348. [On evidence and legal theory see Twining (1984) 47 M.L.R. 261.]

[2] See generally, R.K. Merton, *Social Theory and Social Structure* (revised ed., 1957).

[3] See *Karl Llewellyn and the Realist Movement, op. cit.*, Chap. 9 and Appendix C.

[4] 1 *Commentaries* 35 (on the study of law).

crying for the moon to expect a general consensus at this level in Britain at the present time. My complaint is not that we do not have one map, but that we do not have any which are both modern and accessible, whereas we should have several competing alternative ones. That is to say British academic lawyers do not at present seem to have any clearly usable general theories to their short term and middle term needs, to give some coherence to their approach to their subject. The incoherence of many of our present efforts are in part attributable to different aims and concerns, but they are also in part attributable to lack of coherent frames of reference for those who have similar concerns and aims.

I have so far concentrated on five functions of legal theorizing: the conduit function, high theory, the development of working theories and of theories of the middle order, and the synthesizing function. In selecting these five jobs of jurisprudence I do not wish to imply that they are the only ones. For instance, nothing has been said here of the educational functions of jurisprudence courses, the therapeutic functions of certain kinds of juristic analysis, nor the allegations of radical jurists that the main function or orthodox, bourgeois jurisprudence has been to obfuscate and to legitimate the existing legal order.[5] Nor is there time to digress on jurisprudence as part of the history of ideas. More important, I do not think that an adequate account of jurisprudence can be given solely in functional terms. But to talk in these terms helps to emphasize the participant-orientation of much of juristic as well as legal discourse and to set the stage for consideration of the part played by jurisprudence in the expository tradition of academic law and of the reaction against it.　　　　　　　　　　　　　　　　　　[pp. 157–161]

## J. SHKLAR
### Legalism
#### (1964)

#### *Law and Ideology*

What is legalism? It is the ethical attitude that holds moral conduct to be a matter of rule following, and moral relationship to consist of duties and rights determined by rules. Like all moral attitudes that are both strongly felt and widely shared it expresses itself not only in personal behaviour but also in philosophical thought, in political ideologies, and in social institutions. As an historical phenomenon, it is, moreover, not something that can be understood simply by defining it. Such a morality must be seen in its various concrete manifestations, in its diverse applications, and in the many degrees of intensity with which men in different places and conditions have abided by it. It is in short, a complex of human qualities, not a quantity to be measured and labelled.

Legalism, so understood, is thus often an inarticulate, but nonetheless consistently followed, individual code of conduct. It is also a very common social ethos, though by no means the only one, in Western countries. To a great extent it has provided the standards of organization and the operative ideals for a vast number of social groups, from governmental institutions to private clubs. Its most nearly complete expression is in the great legal system of the European world. Lastly, it has also served as the political ideology of those who cherish these systems of law and, above all, those who are directly involved in their maintenance—the legal profession, both bench and bar. The court of law and the trial according to law are the social paradigms, the perfection, the very epitome, of legalistic morality. They are, however, far from being its only expressions. Indeed, they are inconceivable without the convictions, mores, and ideology that must permeate any society which wished to maintain them. Yet the spirit of legalism is

---

[5] See Campbell, *op. cit.*, p. 54.

not now, and never has been, the only morality among men even in generally legalistic societies. The full implication of this moral and political diversity, though its existence is commonly acknowledged and often regretted, has rarely been thoroughly investigated. This is by no means surprising, since almost all those who have devoted themselves to the study of legalistic morality and institutions have been their zealous partisans and promoters, anxious to secure their moral empire.

Even though it is no sign of disaffection for legalism to treat it as but one morality among others, such a view has not been congenial to any of the traditional theories of law. These have been devised almost exclusively by lawyers and philosophers who agree in nothing but in taking the prevalence of legalism and of law for granted, as something to be simply defined and analysed. The consequences for legal theory have not been altogether fortunate. The urge to draw a clear line between law and non-law has led to the constructing of ever more refined and rigid systems of formal definition. This procedure has served to isolate law completely from the social context within which it exists. Law is endowed with its own discrete, integral history, its own "science," and its own values, which are all treated as a single "block" sealed off from general social history, from general social theory, from politics, and from morality. The habits of mind appropriate, within narrow limits, to the procedures of law courts in the most stable legal systems have been expanded to provide legal theory and ideology with an entire system of thought and values. This procedure has served its own ends very well: it aims at preserving law from irrelevant considerations, but it has ended by fencing legal thinking off from all contact with the rest of historical thought and experience.

As an alternative to this unsatisfactory situation, it is suggested here that one ought not to think of law as a discrete entity that is "there," but rather to regard it as part of a social continuum. At one end of the scale of legalistic values and institutions stand its most highly articulate and refined expressions, the courts of law and the rules they follow; at the other end is the personal morality of all those men and women who think of goodness as obedience to the rules that properly define their duties and rights. Within this scale there is a vast area of social beliefs and institutions, both more and less rigid and explicit, which in varying degrees depend upon the legalistic ethos. This would provide an approach suitable to law as an historical phenomenon, and would replace the sterile game of defining law, morals, and politics in order to separate them as concepts both "pure" and empty, divorced from each other and from their common historical past and contemporary setting... [pp. 1–3]

Lastly, there is legalism itself. To say that it is an ideology is to criticise only those of its traditional adherents who, in their determination to preserve law from politics, fail to recognise that they too have made a choice among political values. In itself this would hardly be a new accusation, nor a very important one. What does matter is again the intellectual consequences of this denial, and the attendant belief that law is not only separate from political life but that it is a mode of social action superior to mere politics. This is what will later be discussed as "the policy of justice," for legalism as an ideology does express itself in policies, in institutional structures, and in intellectual attitudes. As a social ethos which gives rise to the political climate in which judicial and other legal institutions flourish, legalism is beyond reproach. It is the rigidity of legalistic categories of thought, especially in appraising the relationship of law to the political environment within which it functions, that is so deleterious. This is the source of the artificiality of almost all legal theories and is what prevents its exponents from recognising both the strength and weaknesses of law and legal procedures in a complex social world.

Legalism as an ideology is the common element in all the various and conflicting modes of legal thinking ... It is what gives legal thinking its distinctive flavour on a vast variety of social occasions, in all kinds of discourse, and among

men who may differ in every oth\ss" of law as a cover in orc            l habits of
operative outlook of the legal p is rarely so rational or so            he formal
legal history, whether it be analy\er natural law nor positivis\        [pp. 8–13]
on categories of thought deriv\d to protect the judiciary or
tendency to think of law as "the\way, to the professional expe.
morals and politics, has its deep\ help to maintain their identit\
functions, and forms the very \wever, both natural law theorie\
procedures.                     \ve that there always is a rule
... The dislike of vague gener\pf society or of its wise men, a
of all social issues, the structurin\t (however twisted in meaning),         \rhaps,
claims and counter-claims under\ns to which a judge must resort            \therto
"there"—these combine to ma\galistic conscience and his office            in the
becomes self-conscious, when it \(                                        \bser-
Since lawyers are engaged in th\ecognize that the courts do leg-          \ that
some kind, they are bound to ru\ true and even less accepted in           \h no
their own. As law serves ideally\reover, the public at large and          \ge is
tions, so legalism with its concei\r functions thus. The courts are       \ught
conservative. It is not, however,\ofessional ideology and public          \ be
nomic interest. Not only do la\e judiciary and its perception of          for
conservative social groups, bus\sus that can serve in place of a          ion
for anything. It is an openly, int\and it affects his choices in ways      \nly
because law is itself a conserv\nts. To avoid the appearance of           \am
judicial ethos, it becomes clear t\ trouble is that the possibility of     of
on what appears already to h\ur alone, but also on the public            \ed
stitutional and social changes h\ of Parliamentary sovereignty,
adapts itself to the new order. T\nsive as that in America. Here
involved the whole federal benc\ourts and the greater scope of
For the judiciary to remain un\co the very midst of the great
Adjustment is therefore its natu\iaries, moreover, are bound to
The limits to such adaptatio\ish judiciary is spared.
society itself, when no consensu\ade by court or legislation, can
When a consensus does emerge\geneous society. Without con-
with which the English judiciar\very offended party character-
lation, but even bent backwards\ges of "legislating." It is not the
in statute law as "there" can h\ judge, who is at fault, and an
adapt itself to political *force ma*\g party begins its case by pre-
Parliament that it was impossi\hat, as denunciations of "law-/
standing of the nature of social\d and the likelihood of judge/       \ned with
to Marxism, Harold Laski as\g as substantial interests ar/         \otheses is
could save the English judicia\, there can be no realization          \ universal
barristers have not as a group b\ exists to satisfy legally arg        \se are not
It is not likely that the judiciary\e judge, not the law, has /
Far from it. However, men liv\rt, under such circumstan/          \uman, Coons
imposes upon them and to the d\n. For American judges             \e telling illus-
that supported the reforming \\alytical legal theory, it           \nner-take-all".
judiciary demonstrated its neu\hat is already a built-i\           \only two solu-
supported the old.[7]           \e incomprehensible \               \eorists describe
Aloofness from politics and                                        \8 Northwestern
with other, more powerful poli                                     \p. 10–15 is also
exposed as such only when the\
them, decisions seem to be not c                                   "ought", *i.e.* pro-
                                                                   s on the other. The
                                                                   \lt that we cannot
                                                                   \ast without a good
                                                                   For a detailed study
                                                                   \ght", see A. Brecht,
                                                                   Hume and attributes
                                                                   \istory of positivism is
                                                                   \ 2.]

[6] Laski, *Studies In Law and Politi\*
[7] [But see O'Higgins and Partingt\
    *Judiciary* (1997) and J. Hackne\
    Problems 113.]                      . 51–56.

considered as problematic—for example, some initial conditions—we deduce some prognosis. We then confront this prognosis, whenever possible, with the results of experiment or other observations. Agreement with them is taken as corroboration of the hypothesis, though not as final proof; clear disagreement is considered as refutation or falsification.

The result of tests is the *selection* of hypotheses which have stood up to tests, or the *elimination* of those hypotheses which have not stood up to them and which are therefore rejected. It is important to realize the consequences of this view. They are these: all tests can be interpreted as attempts to weed out false theories— to find the weak points of a theory in order to reject it if it is falsified by the test. This view is sometimes considered paradoxical; our aim, it is said, is to establish theories, not to eliminate false ones. But just because it is our aim to establish theories as well as we can, we must test them as severely as we can; that is, we must try to find fault with them, we must try to falsify them. Only if we cannot falsify them in spite of our best efforts can we say that they have stood up to severe tests.[11] This is the reason why the discovery of instances which confirm a theory means very little if we have not tried, and failed, to discover refutations. For if we are uncritical we shall always find what we want; we shall look for, and find, confirmations, and we shall look away from, and not see, whatever might be dangerous to our pet theories. In this way it is only too easy to obtain what appears to be overwhelming evidence in favour of a theory which, if approached critically, would have been refuted. In order to make the method of selection by elimination work, and to ensure that only the fittest methods survive, their struggle for life must be made severe.

This, in outline, is the method of all sciences which are backed by experience. But what about the method by which we *obtain* our theories or hypotheses? What about *inductive generalizations*, and the way in which we proceed from observation to theory? To this question ... I shall give two answers.[12] (*a*) I do not believe that we ever make inductive generalizations in the sense that we start with observations and try to derive our theories from them. I believe that the prejudice that we proceed in this way is a kind of optical illusion, and that at no stage of scientific development do we begin without something in the nature of theory, such as a hypothesis, or a prejudice, or a problem—often a technological one— which in some way *guides* our observations, and helps us to select from the innumerable objects of observation those which may be of interest.[13] But if this is so, then the method of elimination—which is nothing but that of trial and error ...—can always be applied. However, I do not think that it is necessary for our present discussion to insist upon this point. For we can say (*b*) that it is irrelevant from the point of view of science whether we have obtained our theories by jumping to unwarranted conclusions or merely by stumbling over them (that is, by "intuition")[14] or by some inductive procedure. The question, "How did you first *find* your theory?" relates, as it were, to an entirely private matter, as opposed to the question "How did you *test* your theory?" which alone is scientifically

---

[11] [But many theories which nobody accepts today have never been falsified. Medawar, *Induction and Intuition in Scientific Thought* (1969), has commented: "Theories are repaired more often than they are refuted ... Sometimes theories meekly fade away ... More often they are merely assimilated into wider theories in which they rank as special cases. [Some theories] ... have been trivialised" (p. 30).]

[12] [*Cf.* Medawar, *ibid.*, pp. 40–44 for a catalogue of the deficiencies of inductivism.]

[13] [It is interesting to note that so creative a scientific theorist as Darwin seem gradually to have changed his view from the idea that science consists in collecting facts from which general laws may be deduced, to the notion that observation of facts needs to be guided by theory: see N. Barlow (ed.) *Autobiography of Charles Darwin*, (1958), especially pp. 70, 98, 119 and 157–164. See also J.O. Wisdom, *Foundations of Inference in Natural Science*.]

[14] [*Cf.* Medawar, *ibid.*, pp. 56 *et seq.* on the role of "luck" in scientific discovery.]

relevant. And the method of testing described here is fertile; it leads to new observations, and to a mutual give and take between theory and observation.

Now all this, I believe, is not only true for the natural but also for the social sciences. And in the social sciences it is even more obvious than in the natural sciences that we cannot see and observe our objects before we have thought about them. For most of the objects of social sciences if not all of them, are abstract objects; they are *theoretical* constructions.[15] (Even "the war" or "the army" are abstract concepts, strange as this may sound to some. What is concrete is the many who are killed; or the men and women in uniform, etc.) These objects, these theoretical constructions used to interpret our experience, are the result of constructing certain *models*[16] (especially of institutions), in order to explain certain experiences[17]—a familiar theoretical method in the natural sciences (where we construct our models of atoms, molecules, solids, liquids, etc.) It is part of a method of explanation by way of reduction, or deduction from hypotheses. Very often we are unaware of the fact that we are operating with hypotheses or theories, and we therefore mistake our theoretical models for concrete things. This is a kind of mistake which is only too common.[18]                    [pp. 132–136]

A very brief remark may be added here on the problem of complexity. There is no doubt that the analysis of any concrete social situation is made extremely difficult by its complexity. But the same holds for any concrete physical situation.[19] The widely held prejudice that social situations are more complex than physical ones seems to arise from two sources. One of them is that we are liable to compare what should not be compared; I mean on the one hand concrete social situations and on the other hand artificially insulated experimental physical situation. (The latter might be compared, rather, with an artificially insulated social situation—such as a prison, or an experimental community.) The other source is the old belief that the description of a social situation should involve the mental and perhaps even physical states of everybody concerned (or perhaps that it should even be reducible to them). But this belief is not justified; it is much less justified even than the impossible demand that the description of a concrete chemical reaction should involve that of the atomic and sub-atomic states of all the elementary particles involved (although chemistry may indeed be reducible to physics). The belief also shows traces of the popular view that social entities such

---

[15] [This applies with particular force to law; hence the oddity of the view of some of the Scandinavian Realists who seek to eliminate legal concepts as mere flights of fancy and therefore superfluous. *Cf. post*, Chap. 12.]

[16] [Such as Hart's construction of a legal system in *The Concept of Law, post*, 335 or Dworkin's of positivism, *post*, ???. See also McBride, *The Essential Role of Models and Analogies in the Philosophy of Law*, 43 N.Y.U.L. Rev. 53.]

[17] [*Sed quaere*, do not these ideas exist in the minds of people long before the social scientist arrives with his explanations? *Cf.* P. Winch, *The Idea of a Social Science* (1958), p. 127.]

[18] ["When we verify a model by testing how far it does or does not correspond to the phenomena, this is, of course, not an end in itself but only a means to an end. Our ulterior purpose is not to learn whether the model is or is not valid; it is to get a new insight into the structure and nature of Reality by applying a model that is valid and is therefore an effective tool." A. J. Toynbee, *A Study of History*, vol. 12, p. 160. *Cf.* p. 224: "Definitions ... are frozen models ... If definition are to be used at all in the study of human affairs they will be less hampering, if, instead of making them, *more mathematico*, at the beginning of our enquiry, we work them out retrospectively, as a check on the results we have obtained by the application of ill-defined and therefore flexible 'models' ". *Cf. post*, 59.]

[19] [But for an argument that the complexity involved in introducing the human element results in a difference in kind both in the concepts used and the nature of the problems from those of natural science, see P. Winch, *op. cit.*, Chap. 3.]

to suspect the "legal caste" of using the "thereness" of law as a cover in order to exercise political power irresponsibly.[8] Ideology is rarely so rational or so purposefully designed a Machiavellian scheme. Neither natural law nor positivism is "there" to hide anything. They are not contrived to protect the judiciary or the bar. They are ideas that correspond, each in its way, to the professional experiences and necessities of bench and bar, and that help to maintain their identity, their social place, and their sense of purpose. However, both natural law theories and analytical positivism allow judges to believe that there always is a rule somewhere for them to follow. The consensus of society or of its wise men, a statute (however broadly interpreted), a precedent (however twisted in meaning), all are somehow present to serve as rationalizations to which a judge must resort if his decisions are to meet the demands that a legalistic conscience and his office make upon him.

If many lawyers, in American especially, do recognize that the courts do legislate and make basic social choices, this is less true and even less accepted in other countries. Even in the United States, moreover, the public at large and important sections of the bar do not perceive their functions thus. The courts are expected to interpret the law, not to alter it. Professional ideology and public expectations, in fact, do mould the conduct of the judiciary and its perception of its role. To seek rules, or at least a public consensus that can serve in place of a rule, must be the judge's constant preoccupation, and it affects his choices in ways that are unknown to less constrained political agents. To avoid the appearance of arbitrariness is a deep inner necessity for him. The trouble is that the possibility of aloofness does not depend on the judge's behaviour alone, but also on the public responses to it. In England, given the acceptance of Parliamentary sovereignty, the judiciary is not exposed to controversy as extensive as that in America. Here both the nature of the issues placed before the courts and the greater scope of choice available put the judiciary inevitably into the very midst of the great political battles of the nation. Elective state judiciaries, moreover, are bound to remain subject to public scrutiny, which the English judiciary is spared.

In any case, no basic social decision, whether made by court or legislation, can ever meet with unanimous approval in a heterogeneous society. Without consensus the appearance of neutrality evaporates. Every offended party characteristically responds to a decision by accusing the judges of "legislating." It is not the law, which is clearly far from self-evident, but the judge, who is at fault, and an erring judge is a legislating judge, since the losing party begins its case by presenting its version of the true law. The result is that, as denunciations of "lawmaking" multiply, the legalistic ethos is reinforced and the likelihood of judges satisfying it becomes increasingly rare. As long as substantial interests and expectations are disappointed by judicial decisions, there can be no realization of legalistic hopes for a neutral judicial process. Law exists to satisfy legally argued expectations, and the loser is sure to feel that the judge, not the law, has arbitrarily deprived him of "his own." The easiest resort, under such circumstances, is for judges to escape into formalism when they can. For American judges this is frequently not possible. In England it is. As for analytical legal theory, it is more than anything an effort to enhance the formalism that is already a built-in feature of legal discourse. Modern legal theory would be incomprehensible if it were

[8] Watkins, *The State As A Political Concept* (1934), pp. 51–56.

forgotten that its creators are themselves lawyers and that professional habits of mind exercise a real influence upon them as they strive to extract the formal essence of law from the confusion of its historical reality.[9]          [pp. 8–13]

## D. HUME
### A Treatise of Human Nature
### (ed. 1777)

*"Is" and "Ought"*

I cannot forbear adding to these reasonings an observation, which may, perhaps, be found of some importance. In every system of morality, which I have hitherto met with, I have always remark'd, that the author proceeds for some time in the ordinary way of reasoning, and establishes the being of God, or makes observations concerning human affairs; when of a sudden I am surpriz'd to find that instead of the usual copulations of propositions, *is* and is not, I meet with no proposition that is not connected with an *ought*, or an *ought not*. This change is imperceptible; but is, however, of the last consequence. For as this *ought*, or *ought not*, expresses some new relation or affirmation, 'tis necessary that it shou'd be observ'd and explain'd; and at the same time that a reason should be given, for what seems altogether inconceivable, how this new relation can be a deduction from others, which are entirely different from it. But as authors do not commonly use this precaution, I shall presume to recommend it to the readers; and am persuaded, that this small attention wou'd subvert all the vulgar systems of morality, and let us see, that the distinction of vice and virtue is not founded merely on the relations of objects, nor is perceiv'd by reason.[10]

## K. POPPER
### The Poverty of Historicism
### (1957)

*Method of science*

What is important is to realize that in science we are always concerned with explanations, predictions, and tests, and that the method of testing hypotheses is always the same. From the hypothesis to be tested—for example, a universal law—together with some other statements which for this purpose are not

---

[9] [Shklar's book formed the focus of a symposium to which Shklar herself, Shuman, Coons and Jones contributed. See (1966) 19 *J. of Legal Education* 49 *et seq*. One telling illustration of legalism is described by Coons, *ibid.*, p. 67, as the "cult of winner-take-all". "For any given dispute submitted to adjudication" he rightly remarks, "only two solutions exist: for plaintiff or defendant: it makes litigation what the game theorists describe as a zero-sum game." On this theme see Coons, further, in (1964) 58 Northwestern University L. Rev. 50. Arnold, *The Symbols of Government* (1935), pp. 10–15 is also critical.]

[10] [This passage makes a point of great significance between "is" and "ought", *i.e.* propositions which state facts on the one hand, and which prescribe norms on the other. The "logic" of these two types of statements is different, with the result that we cannot properly infer norms from facts, or translate one into the other, at least without a good deal of qualification. See further on this, *ante*, 11, and *post*, 257, 864. For a detailed study of the historical origins of the distinction between "is" and "ought", see A. Brecht, *Political Theory* (1959), Chap. 5. Brecht minimises the influence of Hume and attributes much greater importance to later German philosophy. The early history of positivism is also traced by L. Kolakowski, *Positivist Philosophy* (1972), Chap. 2.]

considered as problematic—for example, some initial conditions—we deduce some prognosis. We then confront this prognosis, whenever possible, with the results of experiment or other observations. Agreement with them is taken as corroboration of the hypothesis, though not as final proof; clear disagreement is considered as refutation or falsification.

The result of tests is the *selection* of hypotheses which have stood up to tests, or the *elimination* of those hypotheses which have not stood up to them and which are therefore rejected. It is important to realize the consequences of this view. They are these: all tests can be interpreted as attempts to weed out false theories—to find the weak points of a theory in order to reject it if it is falsified by the test. This view is sometimes considered paradoxical; our aim, it is said, is to establish theories, not to eliminate false ones. But just because it is our aim to establish theories as well as we can, we must test them as severely as we can; that is, we must try to find fault with them, we must try to falsify them. Only if we cannot falsify them in spite of our best efforts can we say that they have stood up to severe tests.[11] This is the reason why the discovery of instances which confirm a theory means very little if we have not tried, and failed, to discover refutations. For if we are uncritical we shall always find what we want; we shall look for, and find, confirmations, and we shall look away from, and not see, whatever might be dangerous to our pet theories. In this way it is only too easy to obtain what appears to be overwhelming evidence in favour of a theory which, if approached critically, would have been refuted. In order to make the method of selection by elimination work, and to ensure that only the fittest methods survive, their struggle for life must be made severe.

This, in outline, is the method of all sciences which are backed by experience. But what about the method by which we *obtain* our theories or hypotheses? What about *inductive generalizations*, and the way in which we proceed from observation to theory? To this question ... I shall give two answers.[12] (*a*) I do not believe that we ever make inductive generalizations in the sense that we start with observations and try to derive our theories from them. I believe that the prejudice that we proceed in this way is a kind of optical illusion, and that at no stage of scientific development do we begin without something in the nature of theory, such as a hypothesis, or a prejudice, or a problem—often a technological one—which in some way *guides* our observations, and helps us to select from the innumerable objects of observation those which may be of interest.[13] But if this is so, then the method of elimination—which is nothing but that of trial and error ...—can always be applied. However, I do not think that it is necessary for our present discussion to insist upon this point. For we can say (*b*) that it is irrelevant from the point of view of science whether we have obtained our theories by jumping to unwarranted conclusions or merely by stumbling over them (that is, by "intuition")[14] or by some inductive procedure. The question, "How did you first *find* your theory?" relates, as it were, to an entirely private matter, as opposed to the question "How did you *test* your theory?" which alone is scientifically

---

[11] [But many theories which nobody accepts today have never been falsified. Medawar, *Induction and Intuition in Scientific Thought* (1969), has commented: "Theories are repaired more often than they are refuted ... Sometimes theories meekly fade away ... More often they are merely assimilated into wider theories in which they rank as special cases. [Some theories] ... have been trivialised" (p. 30).]

[12] [*Cf.* Medawar, *ibid.*, pp. 40–44 for a catalogue of the deficiencies of inductivism.]

[13] [It is interesting to note that so creative a scientific theorist as Darwin seem gradually to have changed his view from the idea that science consists in collecting facts from which general laws may be deduced, to the notion that observation of facts needs to be guided by theory: see N. Barlow (ed.) *Autobiography of Charles Darwin*, (1958), especially pp. 70, 98, 119 and 157–164. See also J.O. Wisdom, *Foundations of Inference in Natural Science*.]

[14] [*Cf.* Medawar, *ibid.*, pp. 56 *et seq.* on the role of "luck" in scientific discovery.]

relevant. And the method of testing described here is fertile; it leads to new observations, and to a mutual give and take between theory and observation.

Now all this, I believe, is not only true for the natural but also for the social sciences. And in the social sciences it is even more obvious than in the natural sciences that we cannot see and observe our objects before we have thought about them. For most of the objects of social sciences if not all of them, are abstract objects; they are *theoretical* constructions.[15] (Even "the war" or "the army" are abstract concepts, strange as this may sound to some. What is concrete is the many who are killed; or the men and women in uniform, etc.) These objects, these theoretical constructions used to interpret our experience, are the result of constructing certain *models*[16] (especially of institutions), in order to explain certain experiences[17]—a familiar theoretical method in the natural sciences (where we construct our models of atoms, molecules, solids, liquids, etc.) It is part of a method of explanation by way of reduction, or deduction from hypotheses. Very often we are unaware of the fact that we are operating with hypotheses or theories, and we therefore mistake our theoretical models for concrete things. This is a kind of mistake which is only too common.[18]                    [pp. 132–136]

A very brief remark may be added here on the problem of complexity. There is no doubt that the analysis of any concrete social situation is made extremely difficult by its complexity. But the same holds for any concrete physical situation.[19] The widely held prejudice that social situations are more complex than physical ones seems to arise from two sources. One of them is that we are liable to compare what should not be compared; I mean on the one hand concrete social situations and on the other hand artificially insulated experimental physical situation. (The latter might be compared, rather, with an artificially insulated social situation—such as a prison, or an experimental community.) The other source is the old belief that the description of a social situation should involve the mental and perhaps even physical states of everybody concerned (or perhaps that it should even be reducible to them). But this belief is not justified; it is much less justified even than the impossible demand that the description of a concrete chemical reaction should involve that of the atomic and sub-atomic states of all the elementary particles involved (although chemistry may indeed be reducible to physics). The belief also shows traces of the popular view that social entities such

---

[15]  [This applies with particular force to law; hence the oddity of the view of some of the Scandinavian Realists who seek to eliminate legal concepts as mere flights of fancy and therefore superfluous. *Cf. post*, Chap. 12.]

[16]  [Such as Hart's construction of a legal system in *The Concept of Law, post*, 335 or Dworkin's of positivism, *post*, ???. See also McBride, *The Essential Role of Models and Analogies in the Philosophy of Law*, 43 N.Y.U.L. Rev. 53.]

[17]  [*Sed quaere*, do not these ideas exist in the minds of people long before the social scientist arrives with his explanations? *Cf.* P. Winch, *The Idea of a Social Science* (1958), p. 127.]

[18]  ["When we verify a model by testing how far it does or does not correspond to the phenomena, this is, of course, not an end in itself but only a means to an end. Our ulterior purpose is not to learn whether the model is or is not valid; it is to get a new insight into the structure and nature of Reality by applying a model that is valid and is therefore an effective tool." A. J. Toynbee, *A Study of History*, vol. 12, p. 160. *Cf.* p. 224: "Definitions ... are frozen models ... If definition are to be used at all in the study of human affairs they will be less hampering, if, instead of making them, *more mathematico*, at the beginning of our enquiry, we work them out retrospectively, as a check on the results we have obtained by the application of ill-defined and therefore flexible 'models'". *Cf. post*, 59.]

[19]  [But for an argument that the complexity involved in introducing the human element results in a difference in kind both in the concepts used and the nature of the problems from those of natural science, see P. Winch, *op. cit.*, Chap. 3.]

as institutions or associations are concrete natural entities such as crowds of men, rather than abstract models constructed to interpret certain selected relations between individuals.[20]                                                                    [pp. 139–140]

## T.S. KUHN
### The Structure of Scientific Revolution
### (1970)

History, if viewed as a repository for more than anecdotes or chronology, could produce a decisive transformation in the image of science by which we are now possessed. That image has previously been drawn, even by scientists themselves, mainly from the study of finished scientific achievements as these recorded in the classics, and, more recently, in the textbooks from which each new scientific generation learns to practise its trade. Inevitably, however, the aim of such books is persuasive and pedagogic; a concept of science drawn from them is no more likely to fit the enterprise that produced them than an image of a national culture drawn from a tourist brochure of a language text ... we have been misled by them in fundamental ways. There follows a sketch of the quite different concept of science that can emerge from the historical record of the research activity itself.

Even from history, however, that new concept will not be forthcoming if historical data continue to be sought and scrutinised mainly to answer questions posed by the unhistorical stereotype drawn from science texts. Those texts have, for example, often seemed to imply that the content of science is uniquely exemplified by the observations, laws and theories described in their pages ... The result has been a concept of science with profound implications about its nature and development.

In recent years, however, a few historians of science have been finding it more and more difficult to fulfil the functions that the concept of development-byaccumulation assigns to them. As chroniclers of an incremental process, they discover that additional research makes it harder not easier, to answer questions like: When was oxygen discovered? Who first conceived of energy conservation? Increasingly, a few of them suspect that these are simply the wrong sorts of question to ask. Perhaps science does not develop by the accumulation of individual discoveries and inventions. Simultaneously, these same historians confront growing difficulties in distinguishing the "scientific" component of past observation and belief from what their predecessors had readily labelled "error" and "superstition." The more carefully they study, say, Aristotelian dynamics, phlogistic chemistry, or caloric thermodynamics, the more certain they feel that those once current views of nature were, as a whole, neither less scientific nor more than the product of human idiosyncrasy than those current today. If these out-of-date beliefs are to be called myths, then myths can be produced by the same sorts of methods and held for the same sorts of reasons that now lead to scientific knowledge. If, on the other hand, they are to be called science, then science has included bodies of belief quite incompatible with the ones we hold today. Given these alternatives, the historian must choose the latter...

The result of all these doubts and difficulties is a historiographic revolution in the study of science, though one that is still in its early stages. Gradually, and often entirely without realising they are doing so, historians of science have begun to ask new sorts of questions and to trace different, and often less than cumulative developmental lines for the sciences. Rather than seeking the permanent contributions of an older science to our present vantage, they attempt to display the

---

[20] [Consider here, *e.g.* the Scandinavian Realist criticism of the common theory of law, which regards that theory as untenable in a modern state since it is impossible to attribute any command to particular determinate individuals. *Cf. post*, 1060].

historical integrity of that science in its own time. They ask, for example, not about the relation of Galileo's views to those of modern science, but rather about the relationship between his views and those of his group, *i.e.* his teachers, contemporaries, and immediate successors in the sciences. Furthermore, they insist upon studying the opinions of that group and other similar ones from the viewpoint—usually very different from that of modern science—that gives those opinions the maximum internal coherence and the closest possible fit to nature...

The early developmental stages of most sciences have been characterised by continual competition between a number of distinct views of nature, each partially derived from, and all roughly compatible with, the dictates of scientific observation and method. What differentiated these various schools was not one or another failure of method—they were all "scientific"—but what we shall come to call their incommensurable way of seeing the world and practising science in it. Observation and experience can and must drastically restrict the range of admissible scientific belief, else there would be no science. But they cannot alone determine a particular body of such belief. An apparently arbitrary element, compounded of personal and historical accident, is always a formative ingredient of the beliefs espoused by a given scientific community at a given time.

The element of arbitrariness does not, however, indicate that any scientific group could practise its trade without some set of received beliefs. Nor does it make less consequential the particular constellation to which the group, at a given time, is in fact committed. Effective research scarcely begins before a scientific community thinks it has acquired firm answers to questions like the following: What are the fundamental entities of which the universe is composed? How do these interact with each other and with the senses? What questions may legitimately be asked about such entities and what techniques employed in seeking solutions? At least in the mature sciences, answers (or full substitutes for answers) to questions like these are firmly embedded in the educational initiation that prepares and licenses the student for professional practice. Because that education is both rigorous and rigid, these answers come to exert a deep hold on the scientific mind. That they can do so does much to account both for the peculiar efficiency of the normal research activity and for the direction in which it proceeds at any given time...

Yet that element of arbitrariness is present and it too has an important effect on scientific development ... Normal science, the activity in which most scientists inevitably spend almost all their time, is predicted on the assumption that the scientific community knows what the world is like. Much of the success of the enterprise derives from the community's willingness to defend the assumption, if necessary at considerable cost. Normal science, for example, often suppresses fundamental novelties because they are necessarily subversive of its basic commitments. Nevertheless, so long as those commitments retain an element of the arbitrary, the very nature of normal research ensures that novelty shall not be suppressed for very long. Sometimes a normal problem, one that ought to be solvable by known rules and procedures, resists the reiterated onslaught of the ablest members of the group within whose competence it falls. On other occasions a piece of equipment designed and constructed for the purpose of normal research fails to perform in the anticipated manner, revealing an anomaly that cannot, despite repeated effort, be aligned with professional expectation. In these and other ways besides, normal science repeatedly goes astray. And when it does— when, that is, the profession can no longer evade anomalies that subvert the existing tradition of scientific practice—then begin the extraordinary investigations that lead the profession at last to a new set of commitments, a new basis for the practice of science. The extraordinary episodes in which that shift of professional commitments occurs are the ones known in this essay as scientific revolutions. They are the tradition-shattering complements to the tradition-bound activity of normal science.

The most obvious examples of scientific revolutions are those famous episodes in scientific development that have often been labeled revolutions before ... the major turning points in scientific development associated with the names of Copernicus, Newton, Lavoisier, and Einstein. More clearly than most other episodes in the history of at least the physical sciences, these display what all scientific revolutions are about. Each of them necessitated the community's rejection of one time honoured scientific theory in favour of another incompatible with it. Each produced a consequent shift in the problems available for scientific scrutiny and in the standards by which the profession determined what should count as an admissible problem or as a legitimate problem-solution. And each transformed all the scientific imagination in ways that we shall ultimately need to describe as a transformation of the world within which scientific work was done. Such changes, together with the controversies that almost always accompany them, are the defining characteristics of scientific revolutions. ...

A new theory, however special its range of application, is seldom or never just an increment to what is already known. Its assimilation requires the reconstruction of prior theory and the re-evaluation of prior fact, an intrinsically revolutionary process that is seldom completed by a single man and never overnight. No wonder historians have had difficulty in dating precisely this extended process that their vocabulary impels them to view as an isolated event.

Nor are new inventions of theory the only scientific events that have revolutionary impact upon the specialists in whose domain they occur. The commitments that govern normal science specify not only what sorts of entities the universe does contain, but also, by implication, those that is does not. It follows ... that a discovery like that of oxygen or X-rays does not simply add one more item to the population of the scientist's world. Ultimately it has that effect, but not until the professional community has re-evaluated traditional experimental procedures, altered its conception of entities with which it has long been familiar, and, in the process, shifted the network of theory through which it deals with the world. Scientific fact and theory are not categorically separable, except perhaps within a single tradition of normal-scientific practice. That is why the unexpected discovery is not simply factual in its import and why the scientist's world is qualitatively transformed as well as quantitatively enriched by fundamental novelties of either fact or theory. ...

A theory of scientific inquiry, replace[s] the confirmation or falsification procedures made familiar by our usual image of science. Competition between segments of the scientific community is the only historical process that ever actually results in the rejection of one previously accepted theory or in the adoption of another. ...

"Normal science" means research firmly based upon one of more past scientific achievements, achievements that some particular scientific community acknowledges for a time as supplying the foundation for its further practice. ...

Their achievement was sufficiently unprecedented to attract an enduring group of adherents away from competing modes of scientific activity. Simultaneously, it was sufficiently open-ended to leave all sorts of problems for the redefined group of practitioners to resolve.

Achievements that share these two characteristics I shall henceforth refer to as "paradigms", a term that relates closely to "normal science". By choosing it, I mean to suggest that some accepted examples of actual scientific practice—examples which include law, theory, application, and instrumentation together—provide models from which spring particular coherent traditions of scientific research. ...

The study of paradigms, including many that are far more specialised than those named illustratively above, is what mainly prepares the student for membership in the particular scientific community with which he will later practice. Because he there joins men who learned the bases of their field from the same concrete models, his subsequent practice will seldom evoke overt disagreement over fundamentals. Men whose research is based on shared paradigms are committed to the same rules and standards for scientific practice. That commitment and the apparent consensus it produces are prerequisites for normal science, *i.e.* for the genesis and continuation of a particular research tradition. . . .

[pp. 1–11]

Discovery commences with the awareness of anomaly, *i.e.* with the recognition that nature has somehow violated the paradigm-induced expectations that govern normal science. It then continues with a more or less extended exploration of the area of anomaly. And it closes only when the paradigm theory has been adjusted so that the anomalous has become the expected. Assimilating a new sort of fact demands a more than additive adjustment of theory, and until that adjustment is completed—until the scientist has learned to see nature in a different way—the new fact is not quite scientific fact at all. . . .                 [pp. 52–53]

Once it has achieved the status of paradigm, a scientific theory is declared invalid only if an alternative candidate is available to take its place. No process yet disclosed by the historical study of scientific development at all resembles the methodological stereotype of falsification by direct comparison with nature. That remark does not mean that scientists do not reject scientific theories, or that experience and experiment are not essential to the process in which they do so. But it does mean—what will ultimately be a central point—that the act of judgment that leads scientists to reject a previously accepted theory is always based upon more than a comparison of that theory with the world. The decision to reject one paradigm is always simultaneously the decision to accept another, and the judgment leading to that decision involves the comparison of both paradigms with nature *and* with each other. . . .                 [p. 77]

If an anomaly is to evoke crisis, it must usually be more than just an anomaly. There are always difficulties somewhere in the paradigm-nature fit; most of them are set right sooner or later, often by processes that could not have been foreseen. The scientist who pauses to examine every anomaly he notes will seldom get significant work done. We therefore have to ask what it is that makes an anomaly seem worth concerted scrutiny, and to that question there is probably no fully general answer. The cases we have already examined are characteristic but scarcely prescriptive. Sometimes an anomaly will clearly call into question explicit and fundamental generalisations of the paradigms, as the problem of ether drag did for those who accepted Maxwell's theory. Or, as in the Copernican revolution, an anomaly without apparent fundamental import may evoke crisis if the applications that it inhibits have a particular practical importance, in this case for calendar design and astrology. . . .

When, for these reasons or others like them, an anomaly comes to seem more than just another puzzle of normal science, the transition to crisis and to extraordinary science has begun. The anomaly itself now comes to be more generally recognised as such by the profession. More and more attention is devoted to it by more and more of the field's most eminent men. If it still continues to resist, as it usually does not, many of them may come to view its resolution as *the* subject matter of their discipline. For them the field will no longer look quite the same as it had earlier. Part of its different appearance results simply from the new fixation point of scientific scrutiny. An even more important source of change is the divergent nature of the numerous partial solutions that concerted attention to the problem has made available. The early attacks upon the resistant problem will have followed the paradigm rules quite closely. But with continuing resistance, more and more of the attacks upon it will have involved some minor or not so minor articulation of the paradigm, no two of them quite alike, each partially successful, but not sufficiently so to be accepted as paradigm by the group. Through this proliferation of divergent articulations (more and more frequently they will come to be described as ad hoc adjustments), the rules of normal science becomes increasingly blurred. Though there is still a paradigm, few practitioners prove to be entirely agreed about what it is. Even formerly standard solutions of solved problems are called in question. . . .

All crises begin with the blurring of a paradigm and the consequent loosening of the rules for normal research. In this respect research during crisis very much resembles research during the pre-paradigm period, except that in the former the locus of difference is both smaller and more clearly defined. And all crises close in one of three ways. Sometimes normal science ultimately proves able to handle the crisis-provoking problem despite the despair of those who have seen it as the end of an existing paradigm. On other occasions the problem resists even apparently radical new approaches. Then scientists may conclude that no solution will be forthcoming in the present state of their field. The problem is labeled and set aside for future generation with more developed tools. Or finally, . . . a crisis may end with the emergence of a new candidate for paradigm and with the ensuing battle over its acceptance. . . .

The transition from a paradigm in crisis to a new one from which a new tradition of normal science can emerge is far from a cumulative process, one achieved by an articulation or extension of the old paradigm. Rather it is a reconstruction of the field from new fundamentals, a reconstruction that changes some of the field's most elementary theoretical generalisations as well as many of its paradigm methods and applications. During the transition period there will be a large but never complete overlap between the problems that can be solved by the old and by the new paradigm. But there will also be a decisive difference in the modes of solution. When the transition is complete, the profession will have changed its view of the field, its methods, and its goals. . . .

Just because the emergence of a new theory breaks with one tradition of scientific practice and introduces a new one conducted under different rules and within a different universe of discourse, it is likely to occur only when the first tradition is felt to have gone badly astray. That remark is, however, no more than a prelude to the investigation of the crisis-state, and, unfortunately, the questions to which it leads demand the competence of the psychologist even more than that of the historian. What is extraordinary research like? How is anomaly made lawlike? How do scientists proceed when aware only that something has gone fundamentally wrong at a level with which their training has not equipped them to deal? Those questions need far more investigation, and it ought not all be historical. . . .                                                    [pp. 82–86]

Almost always the men who achieve these fundamental inventions of a new paradigm have been either very young or very new to the field whose paradigm they change. And perhaps that point need not have been made explicit, for obviously these are the men who, being little committed by prior practice to the traditional rules of normal science, are particularly likely to see that those rules no longer define a playable game and to conceive another set that can replace them. The resulting transition to a new paradigm is scientific revolution . . .   [p. 90]

If any and every failure to fit were ground for theory rejection, all theories ought to be rejected at all times. On the other hand, if only severe failure to fit justifies theory rejection, then the Popperians will require some criterion of "improbability" or of "degree" of falsification." . . .

Falsification, though it surely occurs, does not happen with, or simply because of, the emergence of an anomaly or falsifying instance. Instead, it is a subsequent and separate process that might equally well be called verification since it consists in the triumph of a new paradigm over the old one. Furthermore, it is in that joint verification-falsification process that the probabilist's comparison of theories plays a central role. Such a two-stage formulation has, I think the virtue of great verisimilitude, and it may also enable us to begin explicating the role of agreement (or disagreement) between fact and theory in the verification process. To the historian, at least, it makes little sense to suggest that verification is establishing the agreement of fact with theory. All historically significant theories have agreed with the facts, but only more or less. There is no more precise answer to the question whether or how well an individual theory fits the facts. But questions much like that can be asked when theories are taken collectively or even in pairs. It makes a great deal of sense to ask which of two actual competing theories fits the facts *better....*                                                        [pp. 146–147]

The man who embraces a new paradigm at an early stage must often do so in defiance of the evidence provided by problem-solving. He must, that is, have faith that the new paradigm will succeed with the many large problems that confront it, knowing only that the older paradigm has failed with a few. A decision of that kind can only be made on faith....

At the start a new candidate for paradigm may have few supporters, and on occasion the supporters' motives may be suspect. Nevertheless, if they are competent, they will improve it, explore its possibilities, and show what it would be to to belong to the community guided by it. And as that goes on, if the paradigm is one destined to win its fight, the number and strength of the persuasive arguments in its favour will increase.[21]                                           [pp. 158–159]

---

[21]  [Kuhn's model has been used to illustrate the reversal in juvenile justice policy in California in the 1960s. See Lemert, *Social Action and Legal Change* (1970). For other uses see Freeman, *Current Legal Problems* (1982), pp. 84, 99–105 (on matrimonial property).]

# 2

# MEANING OF LAW

## The Nature of Definitions

Since much juristic ink has flowed in an endeavour to provide a universally acceptable definition of law,[1] but with little sign of attaining that objective, some comment on the general nature of definitions is pertinent. Two confusions need here to be dispelled.

### *"Naming a Thing"*

One approach with a long history has been to regard the act of giving the meaning of or defining a word as equivalent to naming or "denoting" the thing for which it stands. This leads to somewhat odd results in many cases, for instance, those of *classes* of things, non-existent things, or fictitious creations. These difficulties have caused many philosophers, especially those associated with the so-called "linguistic" philosophy initiated by Wittgenstein,[2] to reject this theory of meaning, save in relation to proper names, and to treat the meaning or definition of a word as given not so much by denoting what it stands for, but by showing the ways in which a word is used in the context of a particular language.[3] Such usage may indeed vary even within the same language, and it may therefore be necessary to distinguish between the "logical grammar" of a word as it may be used in different contexts.[4] A useful analogy here, and one much favoured by Wittgenstein himself, is that of various games, so that, for instance, it is said that the "meaning" of a knight is given by the part it plays in the game of chess. Wittgenstein commonly employed the phrase "language games" to describe how we develop a conventional

---

[1] "The concept of law fulfils as central a role in jurisprudence as Kant claimed for the moral obligation in ethics. No simple definition will satisfy us in the absence of a clear grasp of the ramifications of the concept throughout its domain and an acceptable criterion of adequacy." (P. M. S. Hacker in *Law, Morality, and Society* (eds. Hacker and Raz) (1977), p. 5.)

[2] *Cf. ante*, 12, and *post*, 36.

[3] "For a large class of statements—though not all—in which we employ the word 'meaning' it can be defined thus: the meaning of a word is its use in the language" (L. Wittgenstein, *Philosophical Investigations* (1953), p. 43).

[4] See D. Pole, *The Later Philosophy of Wittgenstein* (1958), p. 31.

usage of words within the four corners of a particular type of activity,[5] and it may readily be seen how this approach affords an insight into the manner in which lawyers give words a special and conventional use as "counters," so to speak, in the "game" of operating a legal system.

One great benefit of this new attitude is that it acts as a kind of "Ockham's razor",[6] eliminating the need to postulate fictitious or non-existent *entities* to correspond with the meaning of particular conceptual words.[7] Thus, the fact that we have and frequently use words such as the state, the law, sovereignty and so on, does not necessarily imply the existence of a mysterious "entity" denoted by such words.[8]

### *"Essentialism"*[9]

Essentialism, by no means unconnected with the previous confusion, has a history stretching back to Plato's notion of ideal universals, namely, the notion that every class or group of things has an essential or fundamental nature, common to every member of the class, and that the process of defining consists in isolating and identifying this common nature or intrinsic property. In this way, to define a class expression, such as "law", is to state an inherent fact about the world as it is. This attitude may be detected in such legal writers as Austin, who seeks to define law "properly so called", or Kelsen, who aims at identifying the essential logical structure of a legal system. Some of those who follow the linguistic approach have perhaps been rather too eager in rejecting this confusion, and have not limited themselves to demonstrating that this doctrine of "essentialism" is another futile search for a metaphysical entity, the "essence" of a thing. One of the strongest critics of this approach, Hart, has, it has been suggested, succumbed to it himself.[10] What is also suggested by way of *riposte* is that definition is only a matter of choice of criteria, and that this choice cannot be right or wrong, for it is simply *arbitrary* and, therefore, a mere matter of words; another way of putting it is to say that a definition is a "linguistic recommendation" to be accepted or rejected, but which, being put forward as an axiom, cannot be proved or disproved.[11] This assertion really proves too much, for while it may be correct to say that truth or falsity is inapplicable to definitions,

---

[5]　See, especially, his *Philosophical Investigations* (1953), *op. cit.* His influence is reflected in Hart, *Essays in Jurisprudence and Philosophy* (1983), Chap. 1.

[6]　See B. Russell, *A History of Western Philosophy*, pp. 494–495.

[7]　See the discussion of this by H. L. A. Hart, in "Definition and Theory in Jurisprudence" (1954) 70 L.Q.R. 37 (*Essays in Jurisprudence and Philosophy* (1983), Chap. 2).

[8]　*Pace* the Scandinavian Realists, as to which, see *post*, Chap. 11.

[9]　So called by Popper, in *Poverty of Historicism* (1957), pp. 26–34.

[10]　*Cf.* Stone, *Legal System and Lawyers' Reasonings* (1964), p. 166.

[11]　See Glanville Williams, *post*, 58.

what it overlooks is that these may be good or bad in the very real sense that they may or may not be appropriately correlated to the nature of the facts or phenomena which are being described.[12]

Thus, suppose we desire to frame a definition of "law", we are surely obliged to study the legal activities to which this word is usually appropriated. In addition there may be borderline or peripheral matters which are for some purposes differentiated, but which possess some features in common with or bear a close analogy to the matter generally accepted without question as being legal. Examples are customs in a tribal society or informal controls in a small, well-integrated community such as the *kibbutz* described by Schwartz,[13] or the practice in this country whereby collective industrial bargains are not legally enforceable.[14] Here, certainly, our definition may be said to be arbitrary in the sense that we may, for instance, like Austin, choose so to frame it as to exclude primitive law, and no one can say that we are *wrong*. Yet even here the matter is not one *purely* of words, since we may legitimately inquire into the factual background in order to compare the character and function of law in stateless societies with that of developed law, and reach our choice as to whether the concept of law may be suitably extended to comprise both types on a reasoned consideration of the facts to be described. It may even be that our understanding of law in the more developed complex systems will be furthered if we focus our attention upon simpler societies and systems.[15] To describe such a proceeding as necessarily arbitrary is thus highly misleading. The requirements of a "good" definition of law should therefore (a) include what is generally accepted as properly within this sphere; (b) exclude which is universally regarded as not being "law" (*e.g.* the rules of a robber band); and (c) include or exclude borderline cases in the light of a reasoned comparison of the phenomena in question. As has been pointed out, a good definition is, therefore, one framed with a close eye on the nature of things; for even statements true by definition may be said "to feel the pressure of facts".

---

[12] *Cf.* J. Wisdom, *post*, 1473 *et seq.*; it should be noted in considering the passages referred to that Wisdom was himself one of Wittgenstein's closest followers. As Weldon points out (*Vocabulary of Politics*, pp. 156, 170) a definition of something like "law" is a kind of appraisal; it is not merely arbitrary or based on mere prejudice, but resembles rational judgment, one which can be supported by good reasons.

[13] See (1954) 63 Yale L.J. 471. The Kibbutz is a collective community in Israel in which informal controls operate with sufficient effectiveness to obviate the necessity for the development of distinctively legal institutions.

[14] Collective agreements are not legally binding, unless the parties expressly stipulate to the contrary (see Trade Union and Labour Relations Act 1974, s. 18).

[15] See, for example, the approach of Barkun, *Law Without Sanctions* (1968), where the thesis is presented that the "essence" of law (custom, conflict and mediation) can be seen clearly in societies based upon kingship (segmentary lineage societies), and international systems. But note the author's starting point, itself an *a priori* definition of law. See also Bohannan, *The Differing Realms of Law* in *Law and Warfare* (ed. Bohannan) (1967), pp. 43–56 and see *post*, 1121 and Fuller, *post*, 1111. See also S. Roberts, *Order and Dispute* (1980).

### ANALYSIS OF WORDS OR FACTS

The limits of defining should also be considered from a further viewpoint. To define is strictly to substitute a word or words for another set of words, and these further words may and generally will stand in need of additional explanation. It must, therefore, be borne in mind that when what is to be discussed is a highly complex concept such as "law" the vital and illuminating feature is not so much the form of words chosen as a definition, but the accompanying elucidation of the manner in which those words are to function in all the diverse contexts in which they may be used. Thus, in Hart's *Concept of Law* no definition of law is posited. Instead we are treated to a description of a working model of a standard legal system. His concern is with the conditions which are necessary and sufficient for the existence of a legal system. Quoting J. L. Austin, he claims that he is "using a sharpened awareness of words to sharpen our perception of phenomena," and on this basis, perhaps somewhat dubiously, puts forward *The Concept of Law* as "an essay in descriptive sociology".[16]

### ARE DEFINITIONS UNNECESSARY?

Does this imply, as some have contended, that to define our concepts is really a waste of time?[17] Sometimes this view is put forward as a form of hard-headed practicality. Or again, definitions may be rejected as a misleading substitute for concrete examples in sentences showing the actual function or use of the word in question.[18] The former view can really only be met by a demonstration that even in practical life clarity is often attained, and futile dispute avoided, by a careful defining of our terms. Such precision may not always be attainable, but an attempt at an approximation is not necessarily futile. As to the latter view, we may concede that we can only adequately understand our concepts by seeing how they function in a particular linguistic or logical framework, but this does not necessarily condemn general definitions as worthless, for though in complex matters they cannot afford complete explanations in themselves, they may help, in the light of the functional exposition, to provide an overall picture and to emphasise certain key criteria.[19] They may thus

---

[16] *Cf.* A. J. Ayer, *The Problem of Knowledge* (1956), particularly at pp. 2–3, 26: "Inquiry into the use of words can equally be regarded as inquiring into the nature of the facts which they described." And see *post*, 376.

[17] Stone is of the opinion that quite the reverse may be the case, that those who seek for definitions are seeking mnemonics, "short cut(s) or even substitute(s) for exposition. . . . It is this [he argues] which is the gravest sense in which *omnis definitio periculosa est.*" *Legal Systems and Lawyers' Reasonings* (1964), p. 185.

[18] *Cf.* Hart, *op. cit., post*, 65, n. 59.

[19] *Cf.* the discussion between Hart and Cohen, in *Proc. of Arist. Soc.*, Suppl., vol. 29, pp. 213 *et seq.* Cohen not only argues in favour of the need for criteria to distinguish "legal" from "non-legal" but also that juristic definitions should take account of the politico-moral factors which are entailed in the construction of legal rules. As to these, *cf. post*, 39.

serve to illuminate our understanding, provided we avoid the confusions to which reference has been made, and provided also they are treated as more in the nature of a summing-up of the discussion than as a series of axioms from which all subsequent conclusions may logically be inferred. This, indeed, is the cardinal weakness of such an approach as Austin's, which begins by postulating the "nature" of law and then goes on to deduce conclusions from such postulates, instead of first discussing and analysing the relevant phenomena and then providing a definition not as a logically deduced conclusion, but as a rational generalisation[20] in relation to the subject-matter so analysed.

## IDEOLOGICAL FACTORS

Apart from the foregoing considerations, it must also be remembered that choices will be influenced by the ideology of the chooser; whether, for instance, his general outlook is idealist or positivist. Thus linguistic recommendations may be activated, consciously or subconsciously, by such underlying premises.[21] It must always be borne in mind that beneath even the most apparently technical of rules there may lurk deeply held social or political philosophies. Thus, the doctrine of *"caveat emptor"*[22]— the rule that it is for the purchaser to take the risk whether he has made a good or bad bargain—is certainly no mere legalistic technicality but involves the whole philosophy of laissez-faire, which has played such an influential part in the classical theory both of the common and of the civil law of property and contract. Moreover, words themselves contain many emotional overtones and the choice of language may act as what have been termed "persuasive definitions",[23] inducing practical and psychological consequences or effects on the part of those to whom they are offered. Accordingly, although a state may be an "organism unknown to biology" it may make a considerable difference whether we define it in a legalistic way as a contract between the citizens or as a type of "moral person", and much of the conflict between political theorists may be traceable to this source.[24] So again, we may recall that some of the most bitter attacks on Austin's jurisprudence were by those who rejected his classification of international law as not being law; nor is this a merely

---

[20] *Cf.* W. L. Morison, 68 Yale L.J. 212, and in *John Austin* (1982), p. 99 who argues that Austin's jurisprudence was an empirical science, though Stone (*op. cit.*, p. 66) sums up his empiricism as no more than that of "any thinker [who] approaches his problems on the basis of his own experience and knowledge".

[21] *Cf. ante*, 1, 20, 27. See further Friedmann, *Legal Theory* (5th ed.), Chap. 6.

[22] An excellent historical analysis of the economic significance of this is M. J. Horwitz, *The Transformation of American Law 1780–1860* (1977) (see particularly pp. 58–62). See also P. Gabel and J. M. Feinman, "Contract Law As Ideology" in D. Kairys (ed.), *The Politics of Law* (1998), p. 497.

[23] See C. L. Stevenson, in (1937) *Mind*, p. 47, and Glanville Williams, *Philosophy, Politics and Society* (ed. Laslett) (1956), 1st series, p. 134.

[24] See M. Macdonald, in *Logic and Language* (1955), 1st series, pp. 167 *et seq.* On Marxist analyses of the state see *post*, Chap. 13.

verbal question, even from this point of view, since much might turn, so far as the influence of international law itself is concerned, on people generally linking it with the emotional associations normally induced by the very word "law", as something which must be unquestionably obeyed, in contrast with morality, compliance with which may depend on the individual conscience.

### CRITERION OF VALIDITY

Wollheim has pointed out that much of the confusion in defining law has been due to the different type of purpose sought to be achieved, and in particular that jurists have not clearly distinguished between three types of question, *viz.* (1) a definition, in the sense of an elucidation of meaning; (2) a criterion for the validity of law; and (3) a general scheme for the criterion of validity of *any* legal system whatever. As to the second, this must be relative to a particular legal system and is therefore a question more appropriately of constitutional law; the third, on the other hand, involves a search for a general criterion of a formal kind which therefore relates to *any legal* system.[25] It is this that Bentham and Austin in the nineteenth century and Kelsen and Hart in the twentieth have tried to attain, with varying degrees of success.[26] A serious limitation of this method is that there is no guarantee that the criteria selected can be shown to be applicable to the actual content of particular legal systems, since these have empirical characteristics not necessarily capable of being confined within the particular strait-jacket it is desired to impose upon them.[27] But it is no coincidence that the problem of content is one which has little exercised those jurists who have sought to construct a model of a legal system.[28] Content, the problem of whether systems must satisfy any minimal requirements,[29] is no further explicated in two of the most recent forays into the "grand theory"[30] of legal systems. For Fuller's "internal moral structure", whilst an exemplary code of legality, shows no awareness of any relationship between this and laws so processed,[31] and Raz's searching analysis of the writings of these earlier jurists merely

[25]  R. Wollheim, "Nature of Law", in (1954) 2 *Political Studies,* 128; see *post,* 61.
[26]  See *post,* Chaps 4, 5 and 6 and the account in Joseph Raz, *The Concept of a Legal System* (2nd ed., 1980).
[27]  A difficulty encountered by Austin and Kelsen, *post,* 257, and 325. Both wrote against the backgrounds of particular systems and hoped to structure a logically self-contained formal skeleton with general, if not universal, validity upon knowledge culled from such sources.
[28]  With the notable exception of Hart. *Cf. post,* 123.
[29]  *Cf.* Raz, *op. cit.,* p. 2.
[30]  The phrase is C. Wright Mills, *The Sociological Imagination* (1959), Chap. 2.
[31]  *Cf. post,* 121.

em.[32] And the three other criteria which
gal system must adequately tackle, *viz.*
iish between existing systems and those
ments of the imagination?[33]); *identity* and
to which system a given law belongs?) and
ystem or are certain patterns of relations
ind in the writings of leading analytical
ith such precision or emphasis.[35]

validity a number of approaches have been
*oural* approach, associated with the Rea-
stion of effectiveness. But, as Kelsen points
be a necessary pre-condition of validity, it is
al system valid.[37] In other words, is effec-
tion of validity?[38] Secondly, a *socio-psycho-*
lopted. Those adopting this view will relate
officials[40] and citizens obey the laws of a
in Hart's analysis, will be on critical and
iws, in this view, are those that are used as
are regarded as normative. A third view, the
the hypothesis that what is crucial is for laws
s of the society. According to this view it is
s necessary that laws should guide. Of course,
ition as to when laws are binding. Olivercrona,
is particularly scathing on the variegated
'bindingness" of law.[41] The traditional positivist
is to say that laws are binding when they are
[42] Natural lawyers have tended to respond that
they satisfy certain ethical standards. Social
y of whom would identify with natural law
some recognition by members of the society that
ding on them, a conclusion not far removed from
l position already adumbrated. Others, in
'hy laws are binding, would adopt a behaviourist

're lack of interest in the problem of content, but also his failure
oral and cultural factors that act upon a legal systems, a con-
is "momentary legal systems" (pp. 34, 189), and his rule-centred
oversimplified model of the legal process.
'8–479.
conclusions are expressed in a number of theses (pp. 155, 156,

edly in the so-called "Grundnorm" or revolution cases. See *post*,

ach. See *ante*, 8. On Hart's rejection of behaviourism see Mac-
rt (1981), p. 148. See also *post*, 379.
fficient if officials have this critical reflective attitude.

e, according to a "pedigree test".

stance: laws are binding when they are enforced. This view, wh
close to a "might is right" position, ignores the lesson that Hur
instill more than 200 years ago that "ought" cannot be ded
"is".[43] But many jurists, including those who would accep
"guillotine" come close at times to identifying "right" with "n

## LAW AND REGULARITY

Law requires a certain minimum degree of regularity and cert
without this it would be impossible to assert that what was oper
given territory amounted to a legal *system*. Clearly, however,
criterion can be applied for determining what degree of regu
certainty is necessary to achieve this aim, and states may va
arbitrary tyrannies, where all are subject to the momentary capr
tyrant, to the elaborate and orderly governed states associated
eral democracies. Pollock urged that the exercise of a merely ca
power, according to the whim of the moment, is not law, and c
Austin on the ground that, on this theory, the capricious orders of
despot would still be law until revoked.[45] It is not an answer to th
that the tyrant's whims would, to satisfy Austin's theory, at least
be expressed in general terms, for this is by no means inconceiv
beyond the experience of actual tyrannies.

It may be, however, that a system pivoted on the caprice of a
could not long function effectively. But this goes no way towar
stantiating the very different thesis of some naturalists that con
issuing from such a source could not be described as law, any mo
their source would merit the description as a "legal system."[46] Lon
for example, has posited eight *sine qua non* of a legal system: th
issued from such a source must be promulgated, intelligible, prosp
non-contradictory, general, avoid impossible demands and fr
change, and official actions must be congruent with promulgated r
But, as Friedmann[48] has pointed out, the laws of the Nazi régime f
were consonant with these requirements. Furthermore, in spite of

---

[43] *Ante*, 24.

[44] Thus Austin in grounding sovereignty on a habit of obedience derived the autho
make law from power; see *post*, 261. Even more extreme is Kelsen's conceptualisa
the Grundnorm in terms of an obligation to comply with an effective constitut
terms of international law to the effect that "states ought to behave as they ha
tomarily behaved" (see *post*, 321) and note Hart's scathing criticism in *The Con
Law* (1994), p. 236.

[45] *Jurisprudence and Legal Essays* (ed. A. L. Goodhart), pp. 18, 162–163: Others,
contrary, have seen this as a positive merit of Austinian or Kelsenian jurispruden
its ability to embrace all institutional set-ups. See, for example, McBride, 43 N.Y
Rev. 52, 62.

[46] See *post*, Chap. 3.

[47] See *The Morality of Law* (1969), Chap. 2 and *post*, 118, 154.

[48] *Legal Theory* (5th ed.), p. 19 with, he admits, the exception to some extent of
mulgation. *Cf.* Grunberger, *A Social History of the Third Reich* (1971), Chap. 8.

subject to the whims of Hitler, the legal system of the Third Reich did not operate in a total vacuum. A large structure of laws and customs continued to operate with some measure of regularity. The question in all such cases will be whether the degree of capricious intervention is so far-reaching as to deprive the citizenry of any expectation of the orderly and regular application of even that (possibly large) segment of rules which is outside the probable sphere of the tyrant's particular interest. It is one thing to deny that such a system is a legal system: quite another to prophesy that its inefficacy will lead to its eventual downfall.

## LAW AND MORALS

We have already seen how the normative structure of the language of the law resembles that of ethics, a point that is brought out by their common use of "ought", "obligation" and "duty".[49] Even linguistically, however, this may be no coincidence, for it has been argued that logically you lay yourself open to a request for reasons for asserting a moral duty, whereas legal obligation is more in the nature of a command, depending not on reason but on authority.[50] In this respect law resembles religion more closely than ethics, for religion also appeals to authority in the shape of what is decreed by God.[51] Some ethical approaches, however, such as that of certain natural law thinkers, have reduced morals to a series of imperatives comparable to rules of law,[52] but these have often involved a close interconnection between religion and moral obligation.

Apart from differences in the language of law and morals, attempts have long been made to detect distinctions of substance between these two closely related spheres.[53] Thus, even the natural lawyers have recognised that the two do not altogether coincide, and that there is a field of positive law not deducible from any pre-existing or presupposed system of natural law and, therefore, morally neutral.[54] Certainly one of the firmest tenets of the positivist jurists from Bentham and Austin onwards has been that positive law is quite distinct from and its validity in no way dependent upon morals. This is not put forward as a purely logical or formal contrast, but as asserting a distinction *de facto* between two normative systems to be found side by side in human society. As a

---

[49] *Ante*, 12–13.
[50] See Nowell-Smith, *Ethics*, pp. 190–198. But it is now regarded as of the essence of a *judicial* decision that reasons should be given. *Cf. post*, 1550.
[51] *Cf.* Kantorowicz, *Definition of Law* (1958), p. 34.
[52] *Post*, 83.
[53] Thus Hart has pointed out that the main differences between moral and legal responsibility is due to substantive differences between the content of legal and moral rules and principles, rather than in semantic distinctions, *e.g.* there may be important differences in the criteria applied, as, for instance, where the law may rely upon concepts of strict or even absolute liability, which are hard, if not impossible, to reconcile with our present concept of morality. See 83 L.Q.R. 346, 358–359, also in *Punishment and Responsibility* (1968), pp. 224–225. See also *The Concept of Law* (1994), pp. 167–180.
[54] *Post*, Chap. 340.

matter of social fact there may be many reasons why these two systems should fail to correspond in particular instances, even though a broad measure of coincidence between them may be essential to the working of human society. Moral sentiments on some matters may be insufficiently developed or mobilised to be translated into law,[55] as witness the comparatively recent legal prohibition of cruelty to children in England, or, more recently still, the abolition of capital punishment or the prohibition of racial discrimination. The law may be too cumbersome an instrument to justify legal intervention in some spheres, and might thus do more harm than good, as in the case of some sexual irregularities,[56] or it may be felt that certain moral duties are best left to the individual conscience, as, for instance, the duty to rescue a drowning man.[57] Again, many legal questions are morally indifferent, for instance, the rule of the road, and others are afforded no certain guide by appeal to moral considerations, for example where a choice is to be made whether a loss is to fall on one or other of two innocent persons.[58]

Is it then possible to point to any distinction of substance which can enable us to differentiate legal from moral norms? The more philosophical approach has generally been to follow or adapt the thought of Kant by regarding laws as prescribing external conduct whereas morals

[55] The question whether the passing of legislation in such a case actually effects morality has come in for a lot of recent discussion and socio-legal research. The views of the Scandinavians, notably Olivecrona, are considered *post*, 1048, 1063. But particularly interesting are the findings of Berkowitz and Walker. "There appears to be a comparatively small but nevertheless significant tendency for some people to alter their views of the morality of some actions in accord with laws specifying that these actions are legal or illegal. Knowledge of the existence of these laws, however, does not have as much effect in changing the moral judgments as knowledge of the consensus of opinions among one's peers" ((1967) 30 *Sociometry* 410, 418). These conclusions were based on the testing and retesting of some 87 English university students, hardly, therefore, a representative sample. Furthermore, as the authors of the survey admit, the dichotomy between the impact of the law and the attitudes of one's peers whilst distinguishable in a laboratory setting, does not exist in the "real world". See also Colombotos's article showing the change in doctors' attitudes to *Medicare* before the passage of legislation, after this but before its operation, and after six months of operation. Whilst 38 per cent were in favour of compulsory health insurance through social security to cover hospitalisation of the over-sixty-fives before the law, the figures were 70 per cent and 81 per cent at the later times. See (1969) 34 Amer.Soc.Rev. 318.

[56] The success rate for the legislation of morality depends upon a number of variables. The chances of success are greatest where violation of the new law involves a *victim* who can act as a "plaintiff" and where the arena for the occurrence of the offence is *visible*. "Laws which affect both the public arena and concern victimisation will be most effective in changing the existing moral order. Thus civil rights legislation is placed in a new light. . . . It is at the exact opposite pole of discussions about moral legislation on prostitution and drug addiction." *Per* Troy Duster, *The Legislation of Morality* (1970), p. 26.

[57] Not a legal duty by the common law, though some systems, *e.g.* French law, take a different view. On which see Radcliffe, *The Good Samaritan and the Law* (1966) and Linden (1971) 34 M.L.R. 241. A survey conducted by Kaufman found that where the law required aid, failure to intervene was considered significantly less moral than where the law did not require one to intervene. See "Legality and Harmfulness of a Bystander's Failure to Intervene as Determinant of Moral Judgment" in *Altruism and Helping* (ed. Macaulay and Berkowitz) (1969), p. 77.

[58] See, *e.g.* an innocent purchaser, as against the lawful owner of stolen goods. And see Hughes, "The Existence of a Legal System" in 35 N.Y.U.L. Rev. 1001.

prescribe internal conduct, that is, morals alone are concerned with subjective factors, such as motive.[59] Thus it is said that law, even when purporting to deal with motive, is really only concerned with its external manifestations,[60] on the well-known principle that "the thought of man is not triable, for the devil himself knoweth not the thought of man".[61] Yet for the lawyer this is really a matter of difficulty of proof, and it is hardly possible to draw a precise line at the point where law can be said to ignore subjective considerations. Lawyers have, therefore, tended to put their faith rather in the element of sanctions as the characteristic feature differentiating law from morals. Yet even morals are not without a sanctioning element, if only in the form of incurring peer disapprobation, which may indeed be the most powerful of all pressures in human society.[62] This difficulty it is sought to overcome by asserting that law calls for a regularised, if not a specific, sanction. More will be said of this in later sections of this book, but it should be pointed out here that the sanctionists do not rely upon this as a merely formal characteristic of legal rules, but appeal to the history of human society as bearing out the indispensability of regular sanctions as part of any recognised legal system.[63]

## MORALS AS PART OF LAW

The controversies do not, however, end here, for there are some who assert that even if law and morals are distinguishable it remains true that morality is in some way an integral part of law or of legal development, that morality is "secreted in the interstices" of the legal system, and to that extent is inseparable from it. There are various ways in which this viewpoint has been put forward. Thus it has been said that law in action is not a mere system of rules, but involves the use of certain principles, such as that of the equitable and the good (*aequum et bonum*). By the skilled application of these principles to legal rules the judicial process distills a moral content out of the legal order, though it is admitted that this does not permit the rules themselves to be rejected on the general ground of their immorality.

Another approach would go much further and confer upon the legal process an inherent power to reject immoral rules as essentially non-legal; this seems to resemble the classical natural law mode of thought, but, it is

---

[59] See H. Kantorowicz, *op. cit.*, pp. 41–51, *Cf.* pp. xxi–xxiii.
[60] *Cf.* Holmes J. in *Collected Legal Papers* (1920), p. 177. The much-criticised decision in *DPP v. Smith* [1961] A.C. 290 was based on this philosophy.
[61] *Per* Brian C.J. in Y.B. 17 Edw. IV, 1.
[62] For Hacker (in *Oxford Essays in Jurisprudence* (ed. Simpson, 1973), p. 131) the essential element in moral duty is the existence of reasons justifying the duty, rather than any possible sanction.
[63] So Kelsen, at least; see *post*, 311. Equally, if all peoples were found to obey the rules laid down by constituted authority without sanction, no one would suggest sanctions as the criterion of law.

urged, the difference is that according to the present doctrine it is a matter of the internal structure of the legal system, which treats immoral rules as inadmissible rather than as being annulled by an external law of nature.[64] At any rate, it should not be overlooked that even the positivist does not deny that many factors, including morality, may and do concur in the development of a legal rule, and that where there is a possible choice in adjudication, moral or other extra-legal considerations may induce the coming to one decision rather than another.[65] What the positivist insists is, that once the rule is laid down or determined, it does not cease to be law because it may be shown to be in conflict with morality.

### LAW AND VALUE JUDGEMENTS[66]

Some positivists, such as Kelsen, have desired to banish any element of value judgements from the juristic study of law, on the ground that these are purely subjective and, therefore, cannot be admitted into the scientific study of law as an objective phenomenon.[67] Yet, if value judgements, such as moral factors, form an inevitable feature of the climate of legal development, as is generally admitted, it is difficult to see the justification for this exclusive attitude. For not only, even in the realm of pure science, are valuations almost inescapable,[68] but also the value judgements which enter into law, such as consideration of what would be a just rule or decision, even though not "objective" in the sense of being based on absolute truth, may, nevertheless, be relatively true, in the sense of corresponding to the existing moral standards of the community. Certain standards of conduct, for instance, if not patterns laid up in heaven, may be at least part of what have been called the "operative ideals" of a particular society,[69] a part of its accepted system of values, and whether this is so or not is a matter of objective social fact. And if lawyers and legislators do in fact have regard to such values in the working of the legal system, this is just as much a part of the legal system in action as rules contained in a statute, and can no more be ignored by the jurist than by the legal practitioner advising his client, or the judge determining a case. So that whether it is convenient or not to define law without reference to subjective factors,[70] when we come to observe the phenomena with which law is concerned and to analyse the meaning and use of legal

---

[64] See L. L. Fuller, referred to *ante*, 40, and see extracts *post*, 154.

[65] *Cf.* Lloyd, *Public Policy* (1953), Chaps 1 and 7. How this process works is subject to considerable controversy today, largely stimulated by the writings of Ronald Dworkin, as to which see *post*, 720.

[66] *Cf. post*, 263.

[67] *Post*, 307.

[68] *Cf.* Kuhn, *ante*, 27.

[69] *Cf.* R. Pound, *post*.

[70] For an argument as to the desirability of importing subjective factors into the definition of law, see H. Kantorowicz, *op. cit.*, pp. 72–73.

rules in relation to such phenomena, it will be found impossible to disregard the role of value judgements in legal activity, and we cannot exorcise this functional role by stigmatising such judgments as merely subjective or unscientific.[71]

---

## L.L. FULLER
### The Case of the Speluncean Explorers
(1949)

*In the Supreme Court of Newgarth, 4300*

The defendants, having been indicted for the crime of murder, were convicted and sentenced to be hanged by the Court of General Instances of the County of Stowfield. They bring a petition of error before this Court. The facts sufficiently appear in the opinion of the Chief Justice.

TRUEPENNY, C. J. The four defendants are members of the Speluncean Society, an organization of amateurs interested in the exploration of caves. Early in May of 4299, they, in the company of Roger Whetmore, then also a member of the Society, penetrated into the interior of a limestone cavern. ... While they were in a position remote from the entrance to the cave, a landslide occurred. Heavy boulders fell in such a manner as to block completely the only known opening to the cave. When the men discovered their predicament they settled themselves near the obstructed entrance to wait ... a rescue party. When the imprisoned men were finally released it was learned that on the twenty-third day after their entrance into the cave, Whetmore had been killed and eaten by his companions.[72]

From the testimony of the defendants, which was accepted by the jury, it appears that it was Whetmore who first proposed that they might find the nutriment without which survival was impossible in the flesh of one of their own number. It was also Whetmore who first proposed the use of some method of casting lots, calling the attention of the defendants to a pair of dice he happened to have with him. ...

Before the dice were cast, however, Whetmore declared that he withdrew from the arrangement, as he had decided on reflection to wait for another week before embracing an expedient so frightful and odious. The others charged him with a breach of faith and proceeded to cast the dice. When it came Whetmore's turn, the dice were cast for him by one of the defendants, and he was asked to declare any objections. The throw went against him, and he was then put to death and eaten by his companions.

After the rescue of the defendants ... they were indicted for the murder of Roger Whetmore. ... [T]he trial judge then sentenced them to be hanged, the law of our Commonwealth permitting him no discretion with respect to the penalty to be imposed. After the release of the jury, its members joined in a communication to the Chief Executive asking that the sentence be commuted to an imprisonment of six months. The trial judge addressed a similar communication to the Chief Executive. ...

It seems to me that in dealing with this extraordinary case the jury and the trial judge followed a course that was not only fair and wise, but the only course that was open to them under the law. The language of our statute is well known: "Whoever shall willfully take the life of another shall be punished by death."

---

[71] *Cf. post*, 305.
[72] [The model for this is *R. v. Dudley and Stephens* as to which see A. W. B. Simpson, *Cannibalism and the Common Law* (1984).]

N.C.S.A.(n.s.) § 12–A. This statute permits of no exception applicable to this case, however our sympathies may incline us to make allowance for the tragic situation in which these men found themselves.

In a case like this the principle of executive clemency seems admirably suited to mitigate the rigors of the law, and I propose to my colleagues that we follow the example of the jury and the trial judge by joining in the communications they had addressed to the Chief Executive. There is every reason to believe that these requests for clemency will be heeded, coming as they do from those who have studied the case and had an opportunity to become thoroughly acquainted with all its circumstances. It is highly improbable that the Chief Executive would deny these requests unless he were himself to hold hearings at least as extensive as those involved in the trial below, which lasted for three months. The holding of such hearings (which would virtually amount to a retrial of the case) would scarcely be compatible with the function of the Executive as it is usually conceived. I think we may therefore assume that some form of clemency will be extended to these defendants. If this is done, then justice will be accomplished without impairing either the letter or spirit of our statutes and without offering any encouragement for the disregard of law.

Foster, J. I am shocked that the Chief Justice, in an effort to escape the embarrassments of this tragic case, should have adopted, and should have proposed to his colleagues, an expedient at once so sordid and so obvious. I believe something more is on trial in this case than the fate of these unfortunate explorers; that is the law of our Commonwealth. If this Court declares that under our law these men have committed a crime, then our law is itself convicted in the tribunal of common sense, no matter what happens to the individuals involved in this petition of error. For us to assert that the law we uphold and expound compels us to a conclusion we are ashamed of, and from which we can only escape by appealing to a dispensation resting within the personal whim of the Executive, seems to me to amount to an admission that the law of this Commonwealth no longer pretends to incorporate justice.

For myself, I do not believe that our law compels the monstrous conclusion that these men are murderers. I believe, on the contrary, that it declares them to be innocent of any crime. I rest this conclusion on two independent grounds, either of which is of itself sufficient to justify the acquittal of these defendants.

The first of these grounds rests on a premise that may arouse opposition until it has been examined candidly. I take the view that the enacted or positive law of this Commonwealth, including all of its statutes and precedents, is inapplicable to this case, and that the case is governed instead by what ancient writers in Europe and America called "the law of nature."

This conclusion rests on the proposition that our positive law is predicated on the possibility of men's coexistence in society. When a situation arises in which the coexistence of men becomes impossible, then a condition that underlies all of our precedents and statutes has ceased to exist. When that condition disappears, then it is my opinion that the force of our positive law disappears with it. We are not accustomed to applying the maxim *cessante ratione legis, cessat et ipsa lex* to the whole of our enacted law, but I believe that this is a case where the maxim should be so applied.

The proposition that all positive law is based on the possibility of men's coexistence has a strange sound, not because the truth it contains is strange, but simply because it is a truth so obvious and pervasive that we seldom have occasion to give words to it. Like the air we breathe, it so pervades our environment that we forget that it exists until we are suddenly deprived of it. Whatever particular objects may be sought by the various branches of our law, it is apparent on reflection that all of them are directed toward facilitating and improving men's coexistence and regulating with fairness and equity the relations of their life in common. When the assumption that men may live together loses its truth, as it obviously did in this extraordinary situation where life only became possible by the taking of life, then the basic premises underlying our whole legal order have lost their meaning and force.

Had the tragic events of this case taken place a mile beyond the territorial limits of our Commonwealth, no one would pretend that our law was applicable to them. We recognize that jurisdiction rests on a territorial basis. The grounds of this principle are by no means obvious and are seldom examined. I take it that this principle is supported by an assumption that it is feasible to impose a single legal order upon a group of men only if they live together within the confines of a given area of the earth's surface. The premise that men shall coexist in a group underlies, then, the territorial principle, as it does all of law. Now I contend that a case may be removed morally from the force of a legal order, as well as geographically. If we look to the purposes of law and government, and to the premises underlying our positive law, these men when they made their fateful decision were as remote from our legal order as if they had been a thousand miles beyond our boundaries. Even in a physical sense, their underground prison was separated from our courts and writ-servers by a solid curtain of rock that could be removed only after the most extraordinary expenditures of time and effort.

I conclude, therefore, that at the time Roger Whetmore's life was ended by these defendants, they were to use the quaint language of nineteenth-century writers, not in a "state of civil society" but in a "state of nature." This has the consequence that the law applicable to them is not the enacted and established law of this Commonwealth, but the law derived from those principles that were appropriate to their condition. I have no hesitancy in saying that under those principles they were guiltless of any crime.

What these men did was done in pursuance of an agreement accepted by all of them and first proposed by Whetmore himself. Since it was apparent that their extraordinary predicament made inapplicable the usual principles that regulate men's relations with one another, it was necessary for them to draw, as it were, a new charter of government appropriate to the situation in which they found themselves.

It has from antiquity been recognized that the most basic principle of law or government is to be found in the notion of contract or agreement. Ancient thinkers, especially during the period from 1600 to 1900, used to base government itself on a supposed original social compact.[73] Skeptics pointed out that this theory contradicted the known facts of history, and that there was no scientific evidence to support the notion that any government was ever founded in the manner supposed by the theory. Moralists replied that, if the compact was a fiction from a historical point of view, the notion of a compact or agreement furnished the only ethical justification on which the powers of government, which include that of taking life, could be rested. The powers of government can only be justified morally on the ground that these are powers that reasonable men would agree upon and accept if they were faced with the necessity of constructing anew some order to make their life in common possible.

Fortunately, our Commonwealth is not bothered by the perplexities that beset the ancients. We know as a matter of historical truth that our government was founded upon a contract or free accord of men. The archeological proof is conclusive that in the first period following the Great Spiral the survivors of that holocaust voluntarily came together and drew up a charter of government. Sophistical writers have raised questions as to the power of those remote contractors to bind future generations, but the fact remains that our government traces itself back in an unbroken line to that original charter.

If, therefore, our hangmen have the power to end men's lives, if our sheriffs have the power to put delinquent tenants in the street, if our police have the

---

[73] [Also modern thinkers such as Rawls: see *post*, 583.]

power to incarcerate the inebriated reveler, these powers find their moral justification in that original compact of our forefathers. If we can find no higher source
for our legal order, what higher source should we expect these starving unfor-
tunates to find for the order they adopted for themselves? I believe that the line of
argument I have just expounded permits of no rational answer. I realize that it
will probably be received with a certain discomfort by many who read this opinion, who will be inclined to suspect that some hidden sophistry must underlie a
demonstration that leads to so many unfamiliar conclusions. The source of this
discomfort is, however, easy to identify. The usual conditions of human existence
incline us to think of human life as an absolute value, not to be sacrificed under
any circumstances. . . .

Every highway, every tunnel, every building we project involves a risk to
human life. Taking these projects in the aggregate, we can calculate with some
precision how many deaths the construction of them will require; statisticians can
tell you the average cost in human lives of a thousand miles of a four-lane
concrete highway. Yet we deliberately and knowingly incur and pay this cost on
the assumption that the values obtained for those who survive outweigh the loss.
If these things can be said of a society functioning above ground in a normal and
ordinary manner, what shall we say of the supposed absolute value of a human
life in the desperate situation in which these defendants and their companion
Whetmore found themselves?

This concludes the exposition of the first ground of my decision. My second
ground proceeds by rejecting hypothetically all the premises on which I have so
far proceeded. I concede for purposes of argument that I am wrong in saying that
the situation of these men removed them from the effect of our positive law, and I
assume that the Consolidated Statutes have the power to penetrate five hundred
feet of rock and to impose themselves upon these starving men huddled in their
underground prison.

Now it is, of course, perfectly clear that these men did an act that violates the
literal wording of the statute which declares that he who "shall willfully take the
life of another" is a murderer. But one of the most ancient bits of legal wisdom is
the saying that a man may break the letter of the law without breaking the law
itself. Every proposition of positive law, whether contained in a statute or a
judicial precedent, is to be interpreted reasonably, in the light of its evident
purpose. This is a truth so elementary that it is hardly necessary to expatiate on it.
Illustrations of its application are numberless and are to be found in every branch
of the law. In *Commonwealth v. Staymore* the defendant was convicted under a
statute making it a crime to leave one's car parked in certain areas for a period
longer than two hours. The defendant had attempted to remove his car, but was
prevented from doing so because the streets were obstructed by a political
demonstration in which he took no part and which he had no reason to anticipate. His conviction was set aside by this Court, although his case fell squarely
within the wording of the statute. . . .

The statute before us for interpretation has never been applied literally. Centuries ago it was established that a killing in self-defense is excused. There is
nothing in the wording of the statute that suggests this exception. Various
attempts have been made to reconcile the legal treatment of self-defense with the
words of the statute, but in my opinion these are all merely ingenious sophis-
tries.[74] The truth is that the exception in favor of self-defense cannot be reconciled
with the *words* of the statute, but only with its *purpose*.

The true reconciliation of the excuse of self-defence with the statute making it a
crime to kill another is to be found in the following line of reasoning. One of the
principal objects underlying any criminal legislation is that of deterring men from

---

[74] [Self-defence has also puzzled philosophers. An excellent exploration is J. J. Thomson
(1991) 20 *Phil. and Public Affairs* 283.]

crime. Now it is apparent that if it were declared to be the law that a killing in self-defense is murder such a rule could not operate in a deterrent manner. A man whose life is threatened will repel his aggressor, whatever the law may say. Looking therefore to the broad purposes of criminal legislation, we may safely declare that this statute was not intended to apply to case of self-defense.

When the rationale of the excuse of self-defence is thus explained, it becomes apparent that precisely the same reasoning is applicable to the case at bar. If in the future any group of men ever find themselves in the tragic predicament of these defendants, we may be sure that their decision whether to live or die will not be controlled by the contents of our criminal code. Accordingly, if we read this statute intelligently it is apparent that it does not apply to this case. The withdrawal of this situation from the effect of the statute is justified by precisely the same considerations that were applied by our predecessors in office centuries ago to the case of self-defense.

I accept without reservation the proposition that this Court is bound by the statutes of our Commonwealth. ... The line of reasoning I have applied above raises no question of fidelity to enacted law, though it may possible raise a question of the distinction between intelligent and unintelligent fidelity. ... The correction of obvious legislative errors or oversights is not to supplant the legislative will, but to make that will effective.

I therefore conclude that on any aspect under which this case may be viewed these defendants are innocent of the crime of murdering Roger Whetmore, and that the conviction should be set aside.

TATTING, J. ... As I analyze the opinion just rendered by my brother Foster, I find that it is shot through with contradictions and fallacies. Let us begin with his first proposition: these men were not subject to our law because they were not in a "state of civil society" but in a "state of nature." I am not clear why this is so, whether it is because of the thickness of the rock that imprisoned them, or because they were hungry, or because they had set up a "new charter of government" by which the usual rules of law were to be supplanted by a throw of the dice. Other difficulties intrude themselves. If these men passed from the jurisdiction of our law to that of "the law of nature," at what moment did this occur? Was it when the entrance to the cave was blocked, or when the threat of starvation reached a certain undefined degree of intensity, or when the agreement for the throwing of the dice was made? These uncertainties in the doctrine proposed by my brother are capable of producing real difficulties. Suppose, for example, one of these men had had his twenty-first birthday while he was imprisoned within the mountain. On what date would we have to consider that he had attained his majority—when he reached the age of twenty-one, at which time he was, by hypothesis, removed from the effects of our law, or only when he was released from the cave and became again subject to what my brother calls our "positive law"? These difficulties may seem fanciful, yet they only serve to reveal the fanciful nature of the doctrine that is capable of giving rise to them.

But it is not necessary to explore these niceties further to demonstrate the absurdity of my brother's position. Mr Justice Foster and I are the appointed judges of a court of the Commonwealth of Newgarth, sworn and empowered to administer the laws of that Commonwealth. By what authority do we resolve ourselves into a Court of Nature? If these men were indeed under the law of nature, whence comes our authority to expound and apply that law? Certainly *we* are not in a state of nature.

Let us look at the contents of this code of nature that my brother proposes we adopt as our own and apply to this case. What a topsy-turvey and odious code it is! It is a code in which the law of contracts is more fundamental than the law of murder. It is a code under which a man may make a valid agreement empowering his fellows to eat his own body. Under the provision of this code, furthermore, such an agreement once made is irrevocable, and if one of the parties attempts to withdraw, the others may take the law into their own hands and enforce the contract by violence—for though my brother passes over in convenient silence the effect of Whetmore's withdrawal, this is the necessary implication of his argument.

The principles my brother expounds contain other implications that cannot be tolerated. He argues that when the defendants set upon Whetmore and killed him ... they were only exercising the rights conferred upon them by their bargain. Suppose, however, that Whetmore had had concealed upon his person a revolver, and that when he saw the defendants about to slaughter him he had shot them to death in order to save his own life. My brother's reasoning applied to these facts would make Whetmore out to be a murderer, since the excuse of self-defense would have to be denied to him. If his assailants were acting rightfully in seeking to bring about his death, then of course he could no more plead the excuse that he was defending his own life than could a condemned prisoner who struck down the executioner lawfully attempting to place the noose about his neck.

All of these considerations make it impossible for me to accept the first part of my brother's argument. I can neither accept his notion that these men were under a code of nature which this Court was bound to apply to them, nor can I accept the odious and perverted rules that he would read into that code. I come now to the second part of my brother's opinion, in which he seeks to show that the defendants did not violate the provisions of N.C.S.A. (N.S.) § 12–A. Here the way, instead of being clear, becomes for me misty and ambiguous, though my brother seems unaware of the difficulties that inhere in his demonstrations.

The gist of my brother's argument may be stated in the following terms: No statute, whatever its language, should be applied in a way that contradicts its purpose. One of the purposes of any criminal statute is to deter. The application of the statute making it a crime to kill another to the peculiar facts of this case would contradict this purpose, for it is impossible to believe that the contents of the criminal code could operate in a deterrent manner on men faced with the alternative of life or death. The reasoning by which this exception is read into the statute is, my brother observes, the same as that which is applied in order to provide the excuse of self-defense. . . .

Now let me outline briefly, however, the perplexities that assail me when I examine my brother's demonstration more closely. It is true that a statute should be applied in the light of its purpose, and that *one* of the purposes of criminal legislation is recognized to be deterrence. The difficulty is that other purposes are also ascribed to the law of crimes. It has been said that one of its objects is to provide an orderly outlet for the instinctive human demand for retribution. . . . It has also been said that its object is the rehabilitation of the wrongdoer. . . . Other theories have been propounded. Assuming that we must interpret a statute in the light of its purpose, what are we to do when it has many purposes or when its purposes are disputed?

A similar difficulty is presented by the fact that although there is authority for my brother's interpretation of the excuse of self-defense, there is other authority which assigns to that excuse a different rationale. . . . The taught doctrine of our law schools, . . . runs in the following terms: The statute concerning murder requires a "willful" act. The man who acts to repel an aggressive threat to his own life does not act "willfully," but in response to an impulse deeply ingrained in human nature. I suspect that there is hardly a lawyer in this Commonwealth who is not familiar with this line of reasoning. . . .

Now the familiar explanation for the excuse of self-defense just expounded obviously cannot be applied by analogy to the facts of this case. These men acted not only "willfully" but with great deliberation and after hours of discussing what they should do. Again we encounter a forked path, with one line of reasoning leading us in one direction and another in a direction that is exactly the opposite. This perplexity is in this case compounded, as it were, for we have to set off one explanation, incorporated in a virtually unknown precedent of this Court, against another explanation, which forms a part of the taught legal tradition of our law schools, but which, so far as I know, has never been adopted in any judicial decision....

...I have difficulty in saying that no deterrent effect whatever could be attributed to a decision that these men were guilty of murder. The stigma of the word "murderer" is such that it is quite likely, I believe, that if these men had known that their act was deemed by the law to be murder they would have waited for a few days at least before carrying out their plan. During that time some unexpected relief might have come. I realize that this observation only reduces the distinction to a matter of degree, and does not destroy it altogether. It is certainly true that the element of deterrence would be less in this case than is normally involved in the application of the criminal law.

There is still a further difficulty in my brother Foster's proposal to read an exception into the statute to favor this case, though again a difficulty not even intimated in his opinion. What shall be the scope of this exception? Here the men cast lots and the victim was himself originally a party to the agreement. What would we have to decide if Whetmore had refused from the beginning to participate in the plan? Would a majority be permitted to overrule him? Or, suppose that no plan were adopted at all and the others simply conspired to bring about Whetmore's death, justifying their act by saying that he was in the weakest condition. Or again, that a plan of selection was followed but one based on a different justification than the one adopted here, as if the others were atheists and insisted that Whetmore should die because he was the only one who believed in an afterlife. These illustrations could be multiplied, but enough have been suggested to reveal what a quagmire of hidden difficulties my brother's reasoning contains.

Of course I realise on reflection that I may be concerning myself with a problem that will never arise, since it is unlikely that any group of men will ever again be brought to commit the dread act that was involved here. Yet, on still further reflection, even if we are certain that no similar case will arise again, do not the illustrations I have given show the lack of any coherent and rational principle in the rule my brother proposes? Should not the soundness of a principle be tested by the conclusions it entails, without reference to the accidents of later litigational history? Still, if this is so, why is it that we of this Court so often discuss the question whether we are likely to have later occasion to apply a principle urged for the solution of the case before us? Is this a situation where a line of reasoning not originally proper has become sanctioned by precedent, so that we are permitted to apply it and may even be under an obligation to do so?

The more I examine this case and think about it, the more deeply I become involved. My mind becomes entangled in the meshes of the very nets I throw out for my own rescue. I find that almost every consideration that bears on the decision of the case is counterbalanced by an opposing consideration leading in the opposite direction. My brother Foster has not furnished to me, nor can I discover for myself, any formula capable of resolving the equivocations that beset me on all sides.

I have given this case the best thought of which I am capable. I have scarcely slept since it was argued before us. When I feel myself inclined to accept the view of my brother Foster, I am repelled by a feeling that his arguments are intellectually unsound and approach mere rationalization. On the other hand, when I incline toward upholding the conviction, I am struck by the absurdity of directing that these men be put to death when their lives have been saved at the cost of the lives of ten heroic workmen. It is to me a matter of regret that the Prosecutor saw fit to ask for an indictment for murder. If we had a provision in our statutes making it a crime to eat human flesh, that would have been a more appropriate charge. If no other charge suited to the facts of this case could be brought against the defendants, if would have been wiser, I think, not to have indicted them at all.

Unfortunately, however, the men have been indicted and tried, and we have therefore been drawn into this unfortunate affair.

Since I have been wholly unable to resolve the doubts that beset me about the law of this case, I am with regret announcing a step that is, I believe, unprecedented in the history of this tribunal. I declare my withdrawal from the decision of this case.[75]

KEEN, J. I should like to begin by setting to one side two questions which are not before this Court.

The first of these is whether executive clemency should be extended to these defendants if the conviction is affirmed. Under our system of government, that is a question for the Chief Executive, not for us. I therefore disapprove of that passage in the opinion of the Chief Justice in which he in effect gives instructions to the Chief Executive as to what he should do in this case and suggests that some impropriety will attach if these instructions are not heeded. This is a confusion of governmental functions—a confusion of which the judiciary should be the last to be guilty. I wish to state that if I were the Chief Executive I would go farther in the direction of clemency than the pleas addressed to him propose. I would pardon these men altogether, since I believe that they have already suffered enough to pay for any offense they may have committed. I want it to be understood that this remark is made in my capacity as a private citizen who by the accident of his office happens to have acquired an intimate acquaintance with the facts of this case. In the discharge of my duties as judge, it is neither my function to address directions to the Chief Executive, nor to take into account what he may or may not do, in reaching my own decision, which must be controlled entirely by the law of this Commonwealth.

The second question that I wish to put to one side is that of deciding whether what these men did was "right" or "wrong", "wicked" or "good". That is also a question that is irrelevant to the discharge of my office as a judge sworn to apply, not my conceptions of morality, but the law of the land. In putting this question to one side I think I can also safely dismiss without comment the first and more poetic portion of my brother Foster's opinion. The element of fantasy contained in the arguments developed there has been sufficiently revealed in my brother Tatting's somewhat solemn attempt to take those arguments seriously. . . .

Whence arise all the difficulties of the case, then, and the necessity for so many pages of discussion about what ought to be so obvious? The difficulties, in whatever tortured form they may present themselves, all trace back to a single source, and that is a failure to distinguish the legal from the moral aspects of this case. To put it bluntly, my brothers do not like the fact that the written law requires the conviction of these defendants. Neither do I, but unlike my brothers I respect the obligations of an office that requires me to put my personal predilections out of my mind when I come to interpret and apply the law of this Commonwealth.

Now, of course, my brother Foster does not admit that he is actuated by a personal dislike of the written law. Instead he develops a familiar line of argument according to which the court may disregard the express language of a statute when something not contained in the statute itself, called its "purpose", can be employed to justify the result the court considers proper. Because this is an old issue between myself and my colleague, I should like, before discussing his particular application of the argument to the facts of this case, to say something

---

[75] [The dilemma of the judge in the unjust legal system was the subject of debate between South African scholars under apartheid. See R. Wacks 101 *South African Law J.* 266 (1984) and J. Dugard 101 S.A. L.J. 286 with Wacks's rejoinder at p. 295. See also R. Dworkin, *Law's Empire* (1986), pp. 104–108, R. Abel in D. Dyzenhaus, *Recrafting The Rule of Law* (1999), p. 66, D. Dyzenhaus, *Hard Cases In Wicked Legal Systems* (1991) and R. Teitel, *Transitional Justice* (2000) and *post*, 92.]

about the historical background of this issue and its implications for law and government generally....

We now have a clear-cut principle, which is the supremacy of the legislative branch of our government. From that principle flows the obligation of the judiciary to enforce faithfully the written law, and to interpret that law in accordance with its plain meaning without reference to our personal desires or our individual conceptions of justice. I am not concerned with the question whether the principle that forbids the judicial revision of statutes is right or wrong, desirable or undesirable: I observe merely that this principle has become a tacit premise underlying the whole of the legal and governmental order I am sworn to administer.

Yet though the principle of the supremacy of the legislature has been accepted in theory for centuries, such is the tenacity of professional tradition and the force of fixed habits of thought that many of the judiciary have still not accommodated themselves to the restricted role which the new order imposes on them. My brother Foster is one of that group: his way of dealing with statutes is exactly that of a judge living in the 3900's.

We are all familiar with the process by which the judicial reform of disfavored legislative enactments is accomplished....

The process of judicial reform requires three steps. The first of these is to divine some single "purpose" which the statute serves. This is done although not one statute in a hundred has any such single purpose, and although the objectives of nearly every statute are differently interpreted by the different classes of its sponsors. The second step is to discover that a mythical being called "the legislator," in the pursuit of this imagined "purpose," overlooked something or left some gap or imperfection in his work. Then comes the final and most refreshing part of the task, which is, of course, to fill in the blank thus created. *Quod erat faciendum....*

One could not wish for a better case to illustrate the specious nature of this gap-filling process than the one before us. My brother thinks he knows exactly what was sought when men made murder a crime, and that was something he calls "deterrence." My brother Tatting has already shown how much is passed over in that interpretation. But I think the trouble goes deeper, I doubt very much whether our statute making murder a crime really has a "purpose" in any ordinary sense of the term. Primarily, such a statute reflects a deeply felt human conviction that murder is wrong and that something should be done to the man who commits it. If we were forced to be more articulate about the matter, we would probably take refuge in the more sophisticated theories of the criminologists, which, of course, were certainly not in the minds of those who drafted our statute. We might also observe that men will do their own work more effectively and live happier lives if they are protected against the threat of violent assault....

If we do not know the purpose of § 12–A, how can we possibly say there is a "gap" in it? How can we know what its draftsmen thought about the question of killing men in order to eat them? ... [I]t remains abundantly clear that neither I nor my brother Foster knows what the "purpose" of § 12–A is.

Considerations similar to those I have just outlined are also applicable to the exception in favor of self-defense, which plays so large a role in the reasoning of my brothers Foster and Tatting. As in dealing with the statute, so in dealing with the exception, the question is not the conjectural *purpose* of the rule, but its *scope*. Now the scope of the exception in favor of self-defence as it has been applied by this Court is plain: it applies to cases of resisting an aggressive threat to the party's own life. It is therefore too clear for argument that this case does not fall within the scope of the exception, since it is plain that Whetmore made no threat against the lives of these defendants.

The essential shabbiness of my brother Foster's attempts to cloak his remaking of the written law with an air of legitimacy comes tragically to the surface in my brother Tatting's opinion. Justice Tatting struggles manfully to combine his colleague's loose moralisms with his own sense of fidelity to the written law. The issue of this struggle could only be that which occurred, a complete default in the discharge of the judicial function. You simply cannot apply a statute as it is written and remake it to meet your own wishes at the same time.

Now I know that the line of reasoning I have developed in this opinion will not be acceptable to those who look only to the immediate effects of a decision and ignore the long-run implications of an assumption by the judiciary of a power of dispensation. A hard decision is never a popular decision. Judges have been celebrated in literature for their sly prowess in devising some quibble by which a litigant could be deprived of his rights where the public thought it was wrong for him to assert those rights. But I believe that judicial dispensation does more harm in the long run than hard decisions. Hard cases may even have a certain moral value by bringing home to the people their own responsibilities toward the law that is ultimately their creation, and by reminding them that there is no principle of personal grace that can relieve the mistakes of their representatives.

Indeed, I will go farther and say that not only are the principles I have been expounding those which are soundest for our present conditions, but that we would have inherited a better legal system from our forefathers if those principles had been observed from the beginning. For example, with respect to the excuse of self-defense, if our courts had stood steadfast on the language of the statute the result would undoubtedly have been a legislative revision of it. Such a revision would have drawn on the assistance of natural philosophers and psychologists, and the esulting regulation of the matter would have had an understandable and rational basis, instead of the hodge-podge of verbalisms and metaphysical distinctions that have emerged from the judicial and professional treatment.

These concluding remarks are, of course, beyond any duties that I have to discharge with relation to this case, but I include them here because I feel deeply that my colleagues are insufficiently aware of the dangers implicit in the conceptions of the judicial office advocated by my brother Foster.

I conclude that the conviction should be affirmed.

HANDY, J. I have listened with amazement to the tortured ratiocinations to which this simple case has given rise. I never cease to wonder at my colleagues' ability to throw an obscuring curtain of legalisms about every issue presented to them for decision. We have heard this afternoon learned disquisitions on the distinction between positive law and the law of nature, the language of the statute and the purpose of the statute, judicial functions and executive functions, judicial legislation and legislative legislation. . . .

What have all these things to do with the case? The problem before us is what we, as officers of the government, ought to do with these defendants. That is a question of practical wisdom, to be exercised in a context, not of abstract theory, but of human realities. When the case is approached in this light, it becomes, I think, one of the easiest to decide that has ever been argued before this Court.

Before stating my own conclusions about the merits of the case, I should like to discuss briefly some of the more fundamental issues involved—issues on which my colleagues and I have been divided ever since I have been on the bench.

I have never been able to make my brothers see that government is a human affair, and that men are ruled, not by words on paper or by abstract theories, but by other men. They are ruled well when their rulers understand the feelings and conceptions of the masses. They are ruled badly when that understanding is lacking.

Of all branches of the government, the judiciary is the most likely to lose its contact with the common man. The reasons for this are, of course, fairly obvious. Where the masses react to a situation in terms of a few salient features, we pick into little pieces every situation presented to us. Lawyers are hired by both sides to analyze and dissect. Judges and attorneys vie with one another to see who can discover the greatest number of difficulties and distinctions in a single set of facts. Each side tries to find cases, real or imagined, that will embarrass the demonstrations of the other side. To escape this embarrassment, still further distinctions are invented and imported into the situation. When a set of facts has been subjected to this kind of treatment for a sufficient time, all the life and juice have gone out of it and we have left a handful of dust.

Now I realize that wherever you have rules and abstract principles lawyers are going to be able to make distinctions. To some extent the sort of thing I have been describing is a necessary evil attaching to any formal regulation of human affairs. But I think that the area which really stands in need of such regulation is greatly overestimated. There are, of course, a few fundamental rules of the game that must be accepted if the game is to go on at all. I would include among these the rules relating to the conduct of elections, the appointment of public officials, and the term during which an office is held. Here are some restraint on discretion and dispensation, some adherence to form, some scruple for what does and what does not fall within the rule, is, I concede, essential. Perhaps the area of basic principle should be expanded to include certain other rules, such as those designed to preserve the free civilmoign system.

But outside of these fields I believe that all government officials, including judges, will do their jobs best if they treat forms and abstract concepts as instruments. We should take as our model, I think, the good administrator, who accommodates procedures and principles to the case at hand, selecting from among the available forms those most suited to reach the proper result.

The most obvious advantage of this method of government is that it permits us to go about our daily tasks with efficiency and common sense. My adherence to this philosophy has, however, deeper roots. I believe that it is only with the insight this philosophy gives that we can preserve the flexibility essential if we are to keep our actions in reasonable accord with the sentiments of those subject to our rule. More governments have been wrecked, and more human misery caused, by the lack of this accord between ruler and ruled than by any other factor that can be discerned in history. Once drive a sufficient wedge between the mass of people and those who direct their legal, political, and economic life, and our society is ruined. Then neither Foster's law of nature nor Keen's fidelity to written law will avail us anything.

Now when these conceptions are applied to the case before us, its decision becomes, as I have said, perfectly easy. In order to demonstrate this I shall have to introduce certain realities that my brothers in their coy decorum have been seen fit to pass over in silence, although they are just as acutely aware of them as I am.

The first of these is that this case has aroused an enormous public interest, both here and abroad. Almost every newspaper and magazine has carried articles about it; columnists have shared with their readers confidential information as to the next governmental move; hundreds of letters-to-the-editor have been printed. One of the great newspaper chains made a poll of public opinion on the question, "What do you think the Supreme Court should do with the Speluncean explorers?" About ninety per cent expressed a belief that the defendants should be pardoned or let off with a kind of token punishment. It is perfectly clear, then, how the public feels about the case. We could have known this without the poll, of course, on the basis of common sense, or even by observing that on this Court there are apparently four-and-a-half men, or ninety per cent, who share the common opinion.

This makes it obvious, not only what we should do, but what we must do if we are to preserve between ourselves and public opinion a reasonable and decent accord. Declaring these men innocent need not involve us in any undignified quibble or trick. No principle of statutory construction is required that is not consistent with the past practices of this Court. Certainly no layman would think that in letting these men off we had stretched the statute any more than our ancestors did when they created the excuse of self-defense. If a more detailed demonstration of the method of reconciling our decision with the statute is required, I should be content to rest on the arguments developed in the second and less visionary part of my brother Foster's opinion.

Now I know that my brothers will be horrified by my suggestion that this Court should take account of public opinion. They will tell you that public opinion is emotional and capricious, that it is based on half-truths and listens to witnesses who are not subject to cross-examination. They will tell you that the law surrounds the trial of a case like this with elaborate safeguards, designed to insure that the truth will be known and that every rational consideration bearing on the issues of the case has been taken into account. They will warn you that all of these safeguards go for naught if a mass opinion formed outside this framework is allowed to have any influence on our decision.

But let us look candidly at some of the realities of the administration of our criminal law. When a man is accused of crime, there are, speaking generally, four ways in which he may escape punishment. One of these is a determination by a judge that under the applicable law he has committed no crime. This is, of course, a determination that takes place in a rather formal and abstract atmosphere. But look at the other three ways in which he may escape punishment. These are: (1) a decision by the Prosecutor not to ask for an indictment; (2) an acquittal by the jury; (3) a pardon or commutation of sentence by the executive. Can anyone pretend that these decisions are held within a rigid and formal framework of rules that prevents factual error, excludes emotional and personal factors, and guarantees that all the forms of the law will be observed?

In the case of the jury we do, to be sure, attempt to cabin their deliberations within the area of the legally relevant, but there is no need to deceive ourselves into believing that this attempt is really successful. In the normal course of events the case now before us would have gone on all of its issues directly to the jury. Had this occurred we can be confident that there would have been an acquittal or at least a division that would have prevented a conviction. If the jury had been instructed that the men's hunger and their agreement were no defense to the charge of murder, their verdict would in all likelihood have ignored this instruction and would have involved a good deal more twisting of the letter of the law than any that is likely to tempt us. Of course the only reason that didn't occur in this case was the fortuitous circumstances that the foreman of the jury happened to be a lawyer. His learning enabled him to devise a form of words that would allow the jury to dodge its usual responsibilities.

My brother Tatting expresses annoyance that the Prosecutor did not, in effect, decide the case for him by not asking for an indictment. Strict as he is himself in complying with the demands of legal theory, he is quite content to have the fate of these men decided out of court by the Prosecutor on the basis of common sense. The Chief Justice, on the other hand, wants the application of common sense postponed to the very end, though like Tatting, he wants no personal part in it.

This brings me to the concluding portion of my remarks, which has to do with executive clemency. Before discussing that topic directly, I want to make a related observation about the poll of public opinion. As I have said, ninety per cent of the people wanted the Supreme Court to let the men off entirely or with a more or less nominal punishment. The ten per cent constituted a very oddly assorted group, with the most curious and divergent opinions. ... [A]lthough almost every conceivable variety and shade of opinion was represented in this group, there was, so far as I know, not one of them, nor a single member of the majority of ninety per cent, who said, "I think it would be a fine thing to have the courts sentence these men to be hanged, and then to have another branch of the government come along and pardon them." Yet this is a solution that has more or less dominated our discussions and which our Chief Justice proposes as a way by which we can avoid doing an injustice and at the same time preserve respect for law. He can be assured that if he is preserving anybody's morale, it is his own, and not the public's, which knows nothing of his distinctions. I mention this matter because I wish to emphasize once more the danger that we may get lost in the patterns of our own thought and forget that these patterns often cast not the slightest shadow on the outside world.

I come now to the most crucial fact in this case, a fact known to all of us on this Court, though one that my brothers have seen fit to keep under the cover of their judicial robes. This is the frightening likelihood that if the issue is left to him, the Chief Executive will refuse to pardon these men or commute their sentences. As we all know, our Chief Executive is a man now well advanced in years, of very stiff notions. Public clamor usually operates on him with the reverse of the effect intended. . . .

Their scruple about acquiring accurate information directly does not prevent them from being very perturbed about what they have learned indirectly. Their acquaintance with the facts I have just related explains why the Chief Justice, ordinarily a model of decorum, saw fit in his opinion to flap his judicial robes in the face of the Executive and threaten him with excommunication if he failed to commute the sentence. It explains, I suspect, my brother Foster's feat of levitation by which a whole library of law books was lifted from the shoulders of these defendants. It explains also why even my legalistic brother Keen emulated Pooh-Bah in the ancient comedy by stepping to the other side of the stage to address a few remarks to the Executive "in my capacity as a private citizen." . . .

I must confess that as I grow older I become more and more perplexed at men's refusal to apply their common sense to problems of law and government, and this truly tragic case has deepended my sense of discouragement and dismay. I only wish that I could convince my brothers of the wisdom of the principles I have applied to the judicial office since I first assumed it. . . .

. . . I conclude that the defendants are innocent of the crime charged, and that the conviction and sentence should be set aside.

TATTING, J. I have been asked by the Chief Justice whether, after listening to the two opinions just rendered, I desire to re-examine the position previously taken by me. I wish to state that after hearing those opinions I am greatly strengthened in my conviction that I ought not to participate in the decision of this case.

The Supreme Court being evenly divided the conviction and sentence of the Court of General Instances is *affirmed*. It is ordered that the execution of the sentence shall occur at 6 A.M., Friday, April 2, 4300, at which the Public Executioner is directed to proceed with all convenient dispatch to hang each of the defendants by the neck until he is dead.

### Postscript

Now that the court has spoken its judgment, the reader puzzled by the choice of date may wish to be reminded that the centuries which separate us from the year 4300 are roughly equal to those that have passed since the Age of Pericles. There is probably no need to observe that the *Speluncean Case* itself is intended neither as a work of satire nor as a prediction in any ordinary sense of the term. As for the judges who make up Chief Justice Truepenny's court, they are, of course, as mythical as the facts and precedents with which they deal. The reader who refuses to accept this view, and who seeks to trace out contemporary resemblances where none is intended or contemplated, should be warned that he is engaged in a frolic of his own, which may possibly lead him to miss whatever modest truths are contained in the opinions delivered by the Supreme Court of Newgarth. The case was constructed for the sole purpose of bringing into a common focus certain divergent philosophies of law and government. These philosophies presented men with live questions of choice in the days of Plato and Aristotle. Perhaps they will continue to do so when our era has had its say about them. If there is any element of prediction in the case, it does not go beyond a suggestion that the questions involved are among the permanent problem of the human race. [pp. 616–645.][76]

## G. WILLIAMS
### International Law and the Controversy Concerning the Word "Law"
(Revised version, 1956)[77]

It will be seen ... that the error as to the "proper" meaning of words and as to "true definitions" is still widespread....
    ...Arising out of the proper-meaning fallacy is the idea that words have not only a proper meaning but a single proper meaning. This involves a denial of the fact that words change their meanings from one context to another. To illustrate the difficulties into which this idea lands one: we commonly speak of "early customary law", yet a municipal lawyer refuses to say that all social customs at the present day are law. Conventions of the constitution, for instance, are not usually called "law" by the modern lawyer. Now it is a fact that it is practically impossible to frame a definition of "law" in short and simple terms that will *both* include early customary law *and* exclude modern conventions of the constitution. If it includes the one it will include the other, and if it excludes the one it will exclude the other. This leads the single-proper-meaning theorists to argue among themselves whether conventions are to be put in or early custom to be left out. The misconception again comes from supposing that there is an entity suspended somewhere in the universe called "law", which cannot truthfully be described as both including custom and excluding custom. When we get rid of the entity idea and realize that we are defining words, we see also that there is no absolute need to use words consistently. The word "law" has one meaning in relation to early customary law and a different meaning in relation to municipal law....
    Closely connected with the last misconception is the idea that there are natural differences of "kind" quite independent of human classification. Thus, Leslie Stephen, in a discussion of Austin, asks whether the fact that Austin's "laws improperly so called" do not conform to his definition of law "corresponds to a vital difference in their real nature. Is he simply saying, 'I do not call them laws', or really pointing out an essential and relevant difference of 'kind'?" And again: "The question then arises whether the distinction between laws and customs is essential or superficial—a real distinction of kinds or only important in classification."[78] This language is misleading because it overlooks the fact that the concept of kind results from the process of classification, and that all classification is a man-made affair. An inquiry into whether a given difference is one of kind or of degree is a verbal, not a scientific, inquiry.
    This error as to the existence of natural kinds is again closely connected with, if not simply an aspect of, the error as to the existence of natural essences. The latter error consists in the idea that the search for "essences" or "fundamental features" is in some way a factual investigation, and not merely an inquiry into the meaning of words.                                                                    [pp. 148–153]
    Must these dusty disputes last for ever? They will unless we bring ourselves to realize that definitions have no importance in themselves, no importance apart from the expression and ascertainment of meaning. The only intelligent way to deal with the definition of a word of multiple meaning like "law" is to recognize

---

[76] [For nine new opinions see P. Suber, *The Case of The Speluncean Explorers* (1998).]
[77] [From (1945) 22 B.Y.B.I.L. 146, and reprinted in a revised version in *Philosophy, Politics and Society* (ed. Laslett, 1956), p. 134, to which present page references are given.]
[78] *The English Utilitarians* (1900), iii, pp. 322, 324.

that the definition, if intended to be of the ordinary meaning, must itself be
multiple.                                                                    [p. 155]

When jurisprudence comes to disembarrass itself of verbal controversies ...
there will still be some questions that may usefully be saved for discussion on their
own account. Thus a comparison of international law with *municipal law* would
be a factual, not a verbal, discussion.                                     [p. 156]


## H.L.A. HART
### Definition and Theory in Jurisprudence[79]
(1954)


In law as elsewhere, we can know and yet not understand. Shadows often obscure
our knowledge which not only vary in intensity but are cast by different obstacles
to light. These cannot all be removed by the same methods and till the precise
character of our perplexity is determined we cannot tell what tools we shall need.

The perplexities I propose to discuss are voiced in those questions of analytical
law? What is a State? What is a right? What is possession? I choose this topic
because it seems to me that the common mode of definition is ill-adapted to the
law and has complicated its exposition; its use has, I think, led at certain points to
a divorce between jurisprudence and the study of the law at work, and has helped
to create the impression that there are certain fundamental concepts that the
lawyer cannot hope to elucidate without entering a forbidding jungle of philosophical argument. I wish to suggest that this is not so; that legal notions however
fundamental can be elucidated by methods properly adapted to their special
character. Such methods were glimpsed by our predecessors but have only been
fully understood and developed in our own day.

Questions such as those I have mentioned "What is a State?" "What is law?"
"What is a right?" have great ambiguity. The same form of words may be used to
demand a definition or the cause or the purpose or the justification or the origin
of a legal or political institution. But if, in the effort to free them from this risk of
confusion with other questions, we rephrase these requests for definitions as
"What is the meaning of the word 'State'?" "What is the meaning of the word
'right'?", those who ask are apt to feel uneasy as if this had trivialised their
question. For what they want cannot be got out of a dictionary and this transformation of their question suggests it can. This uneasiness is the expression of an
instinct which deserves respect: it emphasises the fact that those who ask these
questions are not asking to be taught how to use these words in the correct way.
This they know and yet are still puzzled. Hence it is no answer to this type of
question merely to tender examples of what are correctly called rights, laws, or
corporate bodies, and to tell the questioner if he is still puzzled that he is free to
abandon the public convention and use words as he pleases. For the puzzle arises
from the fact that though the common use of these words is known it is not
understood; and it is not understood because compared with most ordinary words
these legal words are in different ways anomalous. Sometimes, as with the word
"law" itself, one anomaly is that the range of cases to which it is applied has a
diversity which baffles the initial attempt to extract any principle behind the
application, yet we have the conviction that even here there is some principle and
not an arbitrary convention underlying the surface differences; so that whereas it
would be patently absurd to ask for elucidation of the principle in accordance
with which different men are called Tom, it is not felt absurd to ask why, within
municipal law the immense variety of different types of rules are called law, nor

---

[79] [Essay 1 of *Essays in Jurisprudence and Philosophy* (1983), originally in (1954) 70 L.Q.R.
37.]

why municipal law and international law, in spite of striking differences, are so called.

But in this and other cases, we are puzzled by a different and more troubling anomaly. The first efforts to define words like "corporation," "right" or "duty" reveal that these do not have the straightforward connection with counterparts in the world of fact which most ordinary words have and to which we appeal in our definition of ordinary words. There is nothing which simply "corresponds" to these legal words and when we try to define them we find that the expressions we tender in our definition specifying kinds of persons, things, qualities, events, and processes, material or psychological, are never precisely the equivalent of these legal words though often connected with them in some way. This is most obvious in the case of expressions for corporate bodies and is commonly put by saying that a corporation is not a series of aggregate of persons. But it is true of other legal words. Though one who has a right usually has some expectation or power the expression "a right" is not synonymous with words like "expectation" or "power" even if we add "based on law" or "guaranteed by law." And so, too, though we speak of men having duties to do or abstain from certain actions the word "duty" does not stand for or describe anything as ordinary words do. It has an altogether different function which makes the stock form of definition, "a duty is a ..." seem quite inappropriate.

These are genuine difficulties and in part account for something remarkable: that out of these innocent requests for definitions of fundamental legal notions there should have arisen vast and irreconcilable theories so that not merely whole books but whole schools of juristic thought may be characterised by the type of answer they give to questions like "What is a right?" or "What is a corporate body?" This alone, I think, suggests that something is wrong with the approach to definition: can we really not elucidate the meaning of words which every developed legal system handles smoothly and alike without assuming this incubus of theory? And the suspicion that something is amiss is confirmed by certain characteristics that many such theories have. In the first place they fall disquietingly often into a familiar triad. Thus the American Realists striving to give us an answer in terms of plain fact tell us that a right is a term by which we described the prophecies we make of the probable behaviour of courts or officials; the Scandinavian jurists after dealing the Realist theory blows that might well be thought fatal (if these matters were strictly judged) say that a right is nothing real at all but an ideal or fictitious or imaginary power, and then join with their opponents to denigrate the older type of theory that a right is an "objective reality"—an invisible entity existing apart from the behaviour of men. These theories are in form similar to the three great theories of corporate personality, each of which has dealt deadly blows to the other. There, too, we have been told by turn that the name of a corporate body like a limited company or an organisation like the State is really just a collective name or abbreviation for some complex but still plain facts about ordinary persons, or alternatively that it is the name of a fictitious person, or that on the contrary it is the name of a real person existing with a real will and life, but not a body of its own. And this same triad of theories has haunted the jurist even when concerned with relatively minor notions. Look, for example, at Austin's discussion of status[80] and you will find that the choice lies for him between saying that it is a mere collective name for a set of special rights and duties, or that it is an "ideal" or "fictitious" basis for these rights and duties, or that it is an "occult quality" in the person who has the status, distinguishable both from the rights and duties and from the facts engendering them.

Secondly, though these theories spring from the effort to define notions actually involved in the practice of a legal system they rarely throw light on the precise

---

[80] *Jurisprudence* (5th ed.), pp. 609–700.

work they do there. They seem to the lawyer to stand apart with their head at least in the clouds; and hence it is that very often the use of such terms in a legal system is neutral between competing theories. For that use "can be reconciled with any theory, but is authority for none."[81]

Thirdly, in many of these theories there is often an amalgam of issues that should be distinguished. It is, of course, clear that the assertion that corporate bodies are real persons and the counter-assertion that they are fictions of the law were often not the battle cries of analytical jurists. They were ways of asserting or denying the claims of organised groups to recognition by the State. But such claims have always been confused with the baffling analytical question "What is a corporate body?" so that the classification of such theories as Fiction or Realist or Concessionist is a criss-cross between logical and political criteria. So, too, the American Realist theories have much to tell us of value about the judicial process and how small a part deduction from predetermined premises may play in it, but the lesson is blurred when it is presented as a matter of definition of "law" or "a right"; not only analytical jurisprudence but every sort of jurisprudence suffers by this confusion of aim.

Hence though theory is to be welcomed, the growth of theory on the back of definition is not. Theories so grown indeed represent valuable efforts to account for many puzzling things in law: and among these is the great anomaly of legal language—our inability to define its crucial words in terms of ordinary factual counterparts. But here, I think, they largely fail because their method of attack commits them all, in spite of their mutual hostility, to a form of answer that can only distort the distinctive characteristic of legal language.[82]     [pp. 21–26]

## R. WOLLHEIM
### The Nature of Law
### (1954)[83]

The question: What is the nature, or essence, of law? has long perplexed legal and political philosophers. .... Perhaps the failure to produce a conclusive answer in this matter is to be ascribed not so much to the difficulty of the question as to the ambiguity of it. And perhaps many of the traditional answers are to be seen not as incompatible answers to the same question but as compatible answers to different questions: and the various "schools of jurisprudence" not as the champions of conflicting views but as the reflections of divergent yet complementary lines of research. And this supposition is further confirmed by the way the question is phrased: What is the nature, or essence, of law? For questions of the form. What is the nature of *X*? or What is the essence of *X*? are notoriously equivocal. Indeed the unsatisfactory condition of political philosophy can largely be attributed to the dominating position occupied within it by questions posed in this form.

1. The first and the simplest interpretation that can be put on the formula What is the nature, or essence, of law? is to see it as raising the question, *What is the definition of "law"?* That is to say, the question might be a linguistic question: not a question about the phenomenon of law at all but a question about the word "law"—this distinction between questions about the phenomena and questions about words being well brought out by the use of inverted commas in the for-mulation of the latter. Such linguistic questions can be answered in one or more of three possible ways. In the first place they can be answered by giving an *explicit* or *equipollent definition, i.e.,* by giving a word or set of words that can in any sentence be substituted for any occurrence of the word to be defined so as to yield

---

[81]   P. W. Duff, *Personality in Roman Private Law*, p. 215.
[82]   [See further, *post*, 444.]
[83]   [From (1954) 2 *Political Studies* 128.]

a new sentence equivalent in meaning to the old. Or they can be answered by giving a *definition in use, i.e.*, by giving a series of equivalences each consisting of one sentence in which the word to be defined occurs and one sentence in which the word to be defined does not occur and that also differs from the first sentence in some further respect. From such a series we gather the use of the original word. Or finally such linguistic questions can be answered by giving an *elucidation* of the word, by giving a general characterization of what we mean by it. Such elucidations can, however, be very misleading, for the fact that they are generally couched in the material mode of speech may make us forget or overlook their essentially verbal character. We say "Law is ..." rather than "The word 'law' means ..." and in saying the first may well forget that we are saying nothing that we could not say if we said the second.

But once we have recognized the purely linguistic character of these elucidations, we may easily come to question their value or importance. For how, we might ask, can a question that is merely verbal be anything but trivial? Certainly the extreme claims put forward by philosophers, either for the process of elucidation in general or for their own particular elucidation, cannot be admitted. But setting aside these exaggerated claims, can we not establish a more moderate case for the utility of these elucidations? Some philosophers will no doubt want to deny even this on the grounds that we know perfectly well how to use the words in question and that any further effort to instruct us in this matter can only result in barren scholasticism. Such an attitude is certainly congenial in its impatience with futile word-chopping. And there seems to me to be at least this much truth in it: that the value of such elucidations lies not so much in revealing to us senses of words hitherto unsuspected but in separating the real meaning of a word from accretions due to association and custom. But this in itself is no mean or otiose task.                                                                      [pp. 128–130]

2. A second question that the formula. What is the nature of essence of law? can be used to raise is the question that we could express more precisely by asking *What is the criterion of validity of law?* Now though Analytical Jurisprudence has done much to dispel many of the confusions that perplex legal philosophers, it has made little or no attempt to differentiate clearly between a definition and a criterion of validity. I think that the best way of exhibiting the distinction I have in mind is this: when we define the word "law," we aim at producing or eliciting a rule for the use of the word that applies equally well whether we are talking about English, French, Swiss, or Bantu social life. But a criterion of validity is necessarily relative to the particular legal system. It may, of course, be the case that two legal systems employ the same criterion of validity, but this would only be coincidental. Before we can justifiably declare that a certain law is valid we must know, first, of which system it purports to be an element, and secondly what is the operative criterion for that system. A definition is relative to a language, a criterion of validity is relative to a legal system.

Now to talk of a criterion of validity in respect of legal systems may well sound artificial. And of course it is, and intentionally so. Lawyers, judges, use the law, present cases, produce decisions, and their activity seems at first sight chaotic and without principle. However, we find that there is a permanent effort made to distinguish between statements that are statements of law and statements that are not statements of law. A task that confronts the jurist is to elicit the general principles on which this is done. We may profitably compare this activity to that of the logician who, confronted by the apparently irregular and "natural" linguistic behaviour of people, makes a "rational reconstruction" of a language: and, having done so, can talk about the criterion of significance of that language. Such a "rational reconstruction" of a language does not imply that people consciously use statements prohibited by this criterion. Linguistic discrimination of this sort is intuitive and unconscious. The logician's task is to draw up the principles that logically justify such an activity—not those that psychologically prompt it. Even in such a rigorous language-system as a logical calculus, we may well have little difficulty in determining, in an intuitive fashion, whether certain formulae are or are not theorems of that calculus: and only later attempt to formalize what we have been doing by laying down the decision-procedure for that calculus.

3. However, there also exists an important and interesting line of inquiry which has been almost universally misunderstood—and certainly no less by its practitioners than by its critics. Let us look at this. As we have seen, a criterion of legal validity is necessarily relative to a legal system; each system has its own criterion, and to ask for a criterion without specifying the system is analogous to asking for the method of scoring without specifying the game. But, it has been felt, perhaps what we can give is, not a general criterion of validity for all systems, but *a general schema for the criterion of validity of any system*; a skeleton, as it were, that any criterion satisfy if it is to fulfil its proper task—just as we might hope to give, not a general method of scoring, but a scheme that any method must satisfy.[84]

## J. RAZ
## The Problem About the Nature of Law
## (1982)[85]

The theory of knowledge attempts to clarify the nature of knowledge, the philosophy of logic examines the definition of logic, moral philosophy reflects on the nature and boundaries of morality and so on. Since the identity of such disciplines depends on the identity of their subject matter, preoccupation with their own self-identity is typical of many philosophical inquiries. Philosophy of law is no exception. It too is partly engaged in an investigation of the nature of law and of the boundary of the legal and thus it is perennially reflecting upon its own nature. . . .[86]

In this article I shall describe and comment upon three current approaches to the question of the nature of law. To explain them and justify my comments I shall have to venture some remarks towards a theory concerning the nature of law but these will be, in the context of the present article, both incomplete and incidental to the main task of clarifying the problem about the nature of law.

### 1. The Linguistic Approach

Both among the classical exponents of legal philosophy[87] and among its modern practitioners[88] one finds philosophers who took the enquiry concerning the nature of law to be an attempt to define the meaning of the word "law". The linguistic approach was boosted by the anti-essentialist spirit of much of modern analytical philosophy and in particular by its tendency in its early years to regard all philosophical questions as linguistic questions.

Recently philosophers have grown dissatisfied with the linguistic approach, and

---

[84] [This, in Wollheim's view, was what Austin's theory of sovereignty aimed at achieving (see *op. cit.*, pp. 133–137). But it should be borne in mind that Austin was expressly limiting his criterion to developed systems: see *ante*, 15.]

[85] [From *Contemporary Philosophy*, vol. 3.]

[86] H. L. A. Hart has repeatedly commented on this feature of legal philosophy. *Cf. Definition and Theory in Jurisprudence* (1953), and *The Concept of Law* (1994), Chap. 1.

[87] *Cf.* for example, John Austin's treatment of the question in *The Province of Jurisprudence Determined* (1832).

[88] For reasonably sophisticated discussions of the linguistic approach *cf.* G. Williams "The Controversy Concerning the Word 'Law'", in *Philosophy, Politics and Society*, 1st series (ed. P. Laslett, 1967), and R. Wollheim, "The Nature of Law", *Political Studies* (1954), p. 128. [See also *ante*, 58 and 61.]

I introduce it first only to dismiss it by surveying some of the flaws and defects associated with it. The first and most common response to the linguistic approach is that philosophers are not lexicographers. This, though true, is obviously incomplete. What then are philosophers of law after? The answer will be found in our examination of the other two approaches to be discussed below. Yet even while allowing that the final verdict on the linguistic approach must await the emergence of a viable alternative we can examine the internal weakness of the linguistic approach itself.

Traditionally those who adopted the linguistic approach concentrated on the word "law". They encountered the overwhelming problem that that word is used in a multiplicity of non-legal contexts. We have laws of nature and scientific laws, laws of God and of thought, of logic and of language, etc. Clearly the explanation of "law" has to account for its use in all these contexts and equally clearly any explanation which is so wide and general can be of very little use to legal philosophers.

Only on one assumption can the explanation of "law" hope to provide the answer to the legal philosopher's inquiry into the nature of law. That assumption is that the use of "law" in all its contexts but one is analogical or metaphorical or in some other way parasitical on its core meaning as displayed in its use in one type of context and that that core meaning is the one the legal philosopher has at the centre of his enquiry. Unfortunately, the assumption is mistaken, Its implausibility is best seen by examining the most thorough and systemic attempt to provide an analysis of "law" based on this assumption, that proposed by John Austin in *The Province of Jurisprudence Determined*. For the failure of Austin's analysis does not depend on his espousal of a general command model of law. Quite independently of the shortcomings of the command theory Austin was doubly wrong. First, there is no reason to regard discourse about purely theoretical laws, like laws of nature, as parasitical extensions of discourse about purely practical laws, such as legal rules. Secondly, when considering purely practical laws there seems no reason to give legal rules and their special features preferred status compared with that of, *e.g.* moral laws.

The fate of the linguistic approach is not yet sealed. The explanation of the meaning of the word "law" has little to do with legal philosophy,[89] but it is possible that the meaning of some other terms is closely associated with the concerns of legal philosophers. The most promising candidates are "legal" and "legally". They are not used in theoretical contexts and in practical contexts seem to be excluded from moral and all other usages apart from those which directly concern legal philosophy.

"Legally" is, *inter alia*, a sentence-forming operator on sentences. The claim that its semantics explains the nature of law amounts to saying that "legally p" is the general form of all legal statements. To examine the claim one should consider the five types of sentences standardly used to make legal statements.

---

[89] Lon Fuller (see especially his *The Morality of Law* (1964, revised edition 1969)) represents an interesting line. He is totally uninterested in the special features of legal systems. His theory is best seen as an inquiry into some putative features of practical laws generally, whether legal or not. In following this line he may have been influenced, consciously or unconsciously, by the linguistic approach focusing on "law." If the philosophy of law is the study of "law" then why bother with any finer demarcations. It should instead study all kinds of practical laws.

First, some other legal operators such as "It is the law that ..." and "According to law ..." are roughly synonymous with "Legally. ..."[90] The main other legal operator "There is a law that ..." though not synonomous with "legally ..." can be explained by its use. "There is a law that p" is logically equivalent to "Legally, there is a rule that p."

Second, "legal" can be defined in terms of "legally." "x has a legal duty" (or "a legal right" or "legal authority," etc.), is logically equivalent to "Legally, x has a duty" (or "a right" or "authority," etc.). Similarly "This is a legal transaction" is logically equivalent to "Legally this is a transaction," and so on.

Third, purely legal predicates are predicates such as "a mortgage," "a share," "a copyright," "fee simple" which, we intuitively judge, are used only to make legal statements. Any sentence containing a purely legal predicate should, therefore, count as a legal sentence even though it does not display the form "Legally p." However any sentence "p" containing a purely legal predicate is logically equivalent to "legally p." For example, "he has the copyright" is logically equivalent to "legally he has the copyright."

Fourth, semi-legal predicates are predicates which are normally used to make legal statements but which can also be used in other contexts. "Ownership," "marriage," "contract" are semi-legal. "They make a contract," "They are married," "He owns the house," "The house is his" are normally used to make what we intuitively judge to be legal statements. But my son is right in saying that his books are his, even if in law they are mine, and Marian Evans could quite sensibly regard herself as G. H. Lewes' wife, not merely consider that she deserves to be. In contrast, if it is not the case that according to law one has the copyright then it is not true that one has the copyright, however much one deserves to have it. Given these facts about semi-legal predicates it is clear that the condition specified above respecting legal predicates does not apply to them. Sentences containing semi-legal predicates are *not* logically equivalent to the sentences resulting from them by prefixing "legally" to them.

At the same time it is true that any legal statement made by the use of a sentence "p" containing a semi-legal predicate is logically equivalent to the statement standardly made by the use of "Legally p."

Fifth, legal statements are often made by the use of ordinary deontic sentences where the content of the sentence and the context of its utterance indicate that it is used to make a legal statement (*e.g.* "It is prohibited to park here"). Here again all one can say is that when such a deontic sentence "p" is used to make a legal statement the statement thus made is logically equivalent to the one standardly made by "Legally p."

Consideration of the first three points may suggest that all sentences standardly used to make legal statements are, or are logically equivalent to, sentences of the form "Legally p." The fourth and fifth points, however, disprove any such suggestion. It is true that all the foregoing observations strongly suggest that all legal statements can be expressed by sentences having the form "legally p", yet this judgment is based on an intuitive notion of "legal statement" which is not itself explained by reference to "legally." One may therefore conclude that any theory of the nature of law must observe the Linguistic Condition.

*LC:* All legal statements are statable by the use of sentences of the form "Legally p."

---

[90] Note that "The rule is legally valid" is logically equivalent to "Legally, the rule is valid." In equating "legally ...", "According to law ..." and "It is the law that ..." I do not mean to deny that there are stylistic and conversational differences between them which make one or the other of them more appropriate than the others in different contexts. Being here concerned merely with their semantic properties I shall disregard such differences and use "legally" even in contexts where one of the others will be conversationally more apposite.

But one must at the same time reject the claim that the theory of the nature of law is simply an investigation of the meaning of "legally."

This claim is also defeated by an independent argument. The argument above shows that not all the sentences frequently used to make what we intuitively judge to be legal statements can be analysed in terms of "legally." It can also be shown that not all the statements standardly made by the used of sentences of the form "Legally p" are intuitively judged to be legal statements in the sense relevant to legal philosophy. "Legally p"-sentences can be used to make statements of religious law or of international law or indeed of the law of some other kinds of powerful social associations but the credentials of such statements as legal statements in the relevant sense (whatever that may be) is not a question which philosophers will allow to be settled by the appropriateness of the use of "legally" in such cases. To say this is essentially no more than to reassert that philosophy is not lexicography.

## 2. The Lawyers' Perspective

The upshot of the discussion so far is that linguistic considerations impose a constraint on the acceptability of legal theories but that the inquiry into the nature of law is not a study of the meaning of any term or family of terms. What then is the object of such an inquiry? Many legal philosophers start from an unstated basic intuition:

*BI:*    The law has to do with those considerations which it is appropriate for courts to rely upon in justifying their decisions.

I have left the formulation vague because it is meant to capture a common basic intuition. Many legal philosophers accepting the basic intuition as an unconscious starting point regard their task as refining it to yield a philosophical theory of the nature of law which is in fact an elaboration of the basic intuition.

It may be thought, and the thought may have influenced various philosophers, that the basic intuition is justified by the linguistic approach (or perhaps even by LC). It may be thought, in other words, that "legal rules" and "legal facts" mean the same as "the considerations that it is appropriate for courts to rely upon." But this cannot be accepted on the strength of linguistic usage. The case of constitutional conventions in English Law provides a good counter-example.[91] In England constitutional conventions constitute a major part of the English constitution regulating as they do the relations between the organs of government. An example is the convention that the monarch is not entitled to refuse royal assent to a bill properly passed by Parliament. According to most standard theories of English constitutional law one defining feature of conventions is that they are not considerations on which courts can base decisions. If this is so then according to the basic intuition they are not legal rules. This indeed was Dicey's view and it is shared by many other legal theorists. But this conclusion cannot be supported by linguistic usage, since many native English speakers would not hesitate to dub various conventions "legal rules." Having rejected the linguistic approach above, it will be clear that I am not presenting the case of constitutional convention as a refutation of the basic intuition, but merely as a refutation of the suggestion that it is necessitated by the linguistic approach. In fact it is at odds with facts about linguistic usage and although it is compatible with LC it is by no means justified or required by it.

I shall assume, and will say a little below to justify the assumption, that BI is

---

[91]  The classical discussion of constitutional conventions is in A. V. Dicey, *Introduction to the Study of the Law of the Constitution* (1885). For an interesting recent discussion see G. Marshall and G. C. Moodie, *Some Problems of the Constitution* (4th ed., 1967), esp. Chap. 2.

true. This still leaves unexplained the question why it should have been taken by so many as an unexamined assumption which serves, most unconsciously, to define their own subject and thus gives shape to their theories. If I am right in suggesting that many tended to regard BI as justified by linguistic usage this provides a partial explanation for the willingness to adopt BI without further questioning. But since this belief is so evidently ill-founded there must be additional reasons, if only to explain why legal philosophers were so myopic in their perception of linguistic usage. The explanation is simple. Most theorists tend to be by education and profession lawyers and their audience often consists primarily of law students. Quite naturally and imperceptibly they adopted the lawyers' perspective on the law. Lawyers' activities are dominated by litigation in court, actual or potential. They not only conduct litigation in the courts. They draft documents, conclude legal transactions, advise clients, etc., always with an eye to the likely outcome of possible litigation in which the validity of the document or transaction or the legality of the client's action may be called into question. From the lawyer's point of view the law does indeed consist of nothing but considerations appropriate for courts to rely upon.[92]

The lawyer's perspective consists of the unquestioning acceptance of BI as the starting point for legal philosophy and as determining its subject matter. But perhaps BI need not be accepted unquestioningly. Perhaps it can be justified by more fundamental assumptions. Therefore, accepting BI does not commit one to accepting the lawyer's perspective.

Kelsen can be taken as an instructive example of a philosopher who adopts the lawyer's perspective without being aware of this. That if he did so he was unaware of this would probably be generally conceded. Indeed most of Kelsen's interpreters either did not notice or underplayed the point. This is quite natural. Kelsen himself says he is following a combination of the linguistic approach and the institutional approach: "Any attempt to define a concept must take for its starting point the common usage of the word denoting the concept in question. In defining the concept of law we must begin by examining the following questions: Do the social phenomena generally called law present a common characteristic distinguishing them from other social phenomena of a similar kind? And is this characteristic of such importance ... that it may be made the basis of a concept serviceable for the cognition of social life?"[93] But in fact Kelsen is merely paying lip-service to what he regards as a proper methodological procedure. He never seriously examined any linguistic evidence and he assumed dogmatically and in the face of all the glaring evidence to the contrary, that law is the only social institution using sanctions (other than divine sanctions).[94]

The clue to the methodological approach he was in fact pursuing is in his insistence that legal theory must be a pure theory. He regarded it as doubly pure. It is pure of all moral argument and it is pure of all sociological facts. We shall return to the purity from morality below. For the time being let us concentrate on purity from social facts. By this Kelsen indicates his belief that the analysis of legal concepts and the determination of the content of any legal system depends in no way at all on the effects the law has on the society or the economy, nor does it involve examination of people's motivation in obeying the law or in breaking it. The picture of law dictated by the methodology of the Pure Theory is of law in the

---

[92] My "Sociological" generalisations should be regarded as crude approximations to the truth, *e.g.* there are specialist constitutional lawyers who advise on the application of constitutional conventions. But such exceptions to the general rule do not affect the thrust of the argument.

[93] *General Theory of Law and State* (1945), p. 4 and see further pp. 5, 14 *et seq.*

[94] It is not my claim that law does not resort to sanctions, merely that sanctions play a major role in informal social norms and in non-legal organisations as well. See further my *Practical Reason and Norms* (1975), pp. 154–162; H. Oberdiek, "The Role of Sanctions and Coercion in Understanding Law and Legal Systems", in (1977) Am. J. of Juris.

books, of an analysis of law using as the raw material only law reports and statute books. Now the only possible justification for legal studies to ignore the social realities behind the law is a conception of law and legal studies which concentrates on the lawyers' perspective.

On the assumption that Kelsen embraces the lawyers' perspective it is easier to understand why Kelsen was tempted by two of his best known doctrines. If the law consists of considerations appropriate for courts to rely upon then it is tempting to regard all laws as addressed to courts. Furthermore, if one thinks of every law as determining the result of a (class of) potential disputes then it is tempting to regard every law as stipulating a remedy (Kelsen says that every law stipulates a sanction but his notion of a sanction is wide enough to cover all remedies excepting declaratory judgments). After all every litigation is about the applicability or non-applicability of certain remedies. I am not suggesting that these doctrines are plausible nor that they are necessitated by the lawyers' perspective, merely that they are made comprehensible on the assumption that Kelsen endorsed this perspective.

The basic intuition says that law has to do with reasons for courts' decisions. It does not say that *all* the considerations that courts may rely upon are legal considerations. Nor does it reject such a view. Kelsen himself however rejected it. He regarded law as consisting of enacted law, case law and customary law and he acknowledged that there are other considerations on which courts may rely. These are extra-legal considerations. So far as the law is concerned the courts are left with discretion when the law runs out and other considerations come into play. Kelsen's reasons for such a position have nothing to do with BI. They derive from the other aspect of the purity of legal theory: its purity from moral considerations.

For Kelsen it is self-evident that legal theory is free of all moral considerations. Given his essentially emotivist theory of ethics this is a prerequisite for legal theory to be "scientific." But this argument, quite apart from its dependence on a particular view of the nature of morality, is clearly misconceived. The task of legal theory is clearly to study law. If law is such that it cannot be studied scientifically then surely the conclusion must be that legal theory is not "a science." One can even accept the conclusion that if the law does involve moral considerations and therefore cannot be studied scientifically, then legal theory will study only those aspects of the law which can be studied scientifically. What one cannot conclude is that since only morally neutral considerations can be studied scientifically therefore the law is such that its study does not involve moral considerations.

Since Kelsen has no good reason to insist that legal theory should be free from moral considerations, he has no good reason to delimit the law in the way he does. He is aware that courts do rely on moral considerations. He regards enacted law, case law and customary law as exhausting the content of the law even though he is aware that courts quite appropriately rely on moral considerations not incorporated in legislation, custom or precedent. I remarked above that BI does not require that such considerations shall be taken as law. But since BI postulates that at least some of the considerations appropriate for courts are legal, it imposes a burden on anyone who claims that some such considerations are not legal to explain what difference between them and legal considerations makes them non-legal and why. Kelsen has no such explanation. The logic of his own doctrines can be used against him: if enacted and case law can be represented as instructions for courts to apply sanctions in certain circumstances so can those moral considerations which it is appropriate for courts to rely upon. If all the considerations which guide courts in applying sanctions are legal considerations, why are not moral considerations which do so part of the law even if they are not incorporated in legislation, precedent or custom?

Legal theory in America has always been dominated by the thought that law is just what the courts do. American theorists not only embraced the lawyers' perspective but jumped to the conclusion that all the considerations which courts may use are legal. The most sophisticated and accomplished representative of this tradition is R. M. Dworkin who in a series of articles during the last 15 years developed a theory of law out of a theory of adjudication.[95] In fact he developed a theory of adjudication and regards it willy nilly and without further argument as a theory of law. Dworkin points out that judges must use moral considerations in addition to enacted and case law. He argues that the moral considerations which they should use are those which belong to a moral theory justifying the enacted and case law binding on them i.e. that moral theory which constitutes the ideology of the law.[96] One may agree or disagree with this theory of adjudication. Either way one has to ask a separate question, namely, which of all these considerations constitute the law? Dworkin, however, does not pause to ask this question. He unquestionably assumes, without even stating the assumption or providing any reason for it, that all the considerations which courts legitimately use are legal considerations.

Dworkin's identification of a theory of adjudication with a theory of law looks, however, very natural from the lawyer's perspective. Lawyers' activities, as we saw, revolve, directly or indirectly, round litigation in the courts. From the lawyer's perspective all the considerations pertaining to judicial reasoning are equally relevant. A lawyer has to concern himself not only with legislation and precedent but also with other considerations relevant to judicial reasoning. A lawyer, therefore, fortified in virtue of BI with the knowledge that the law has to do with judicial reasoning finds no reason from the perspective of his own professional preoccupations to stop short of identifying the theory of law with a theory of adjudication.

### 3. *The Institutional Approach*

I have suggested that from the lawyer's perspective in the disagreement between Kelsen and Dworkin the latter must be declared winner. But we have also seen that neither the basic intuition BI nor the linguistic constraint LC contributes to this verdict. They are compatible with both Kelsen's and Dworkin's theories of law.[97] It is the lawyer's perspective which delivers the verdict. Yet there is something inherently implausible in adopting the lawyer's perspective as one's fundamental methodological stance. There is no doubting the importance of the legal profession and of the judicial system in society. It is entirely appropriate to make them the object of a separate study and to regard legal theory as that study. It is, however, unreasonable to study such institutions exclusively from the lawyers' perspective. Their importance in society results from their interaction with other social institutions and their centrality in the wider context of society. The law is of interest to students of society generally, and legal philosophy, especially when it inquires into the nature of law, must stand back from the lawyer's perspective, not in order to disregard it, but in order to examine lawyers and courts in their location in the wider perspective of social organization and political institutions generally.

The institutional approach has had many representatives in the history of legal

---

[95] Most of Dworkin's articles are collected in his *Taking Rights Seriously* (1978). See also his "No Right Answer" in P. M. S. Hacker and J. Raz (eds.), *Law, Morality and Society* (1977) [and his *A Matter of Principle* (1985) and *Law's Empire* (1986)].

[96] *Cf.* "Hard Cases" in *Taking Rights Seriously*. See also my explanation and criticism in "Prof. Dworkin's Theory of Rights", *Political Studies* (1978).

[97] It is arguable that further linguistic evidence may provide support for one or the other theory. I believe, however, that the linguistic evidence in itself without the backing of theoretical considerations is likely to remain indecisive. *Cf. The Authority of Law* (1979), Chap. 3.

necessary to enable people to plan ahead, to determine themselves to act in advance of the occasion for the action. For large organizations a distinction between deliberative and executive stages is essential to secure planned and efficient institutional action. In institutions such division often includes a division of responsibility between different persons. Some will be responsible for deliberating and deciding, others for executing those decisions. In general, social co-operation either negative (people refraining from hurting each other) or positive can be viewed as a form of social action decided upon by some social institutions and carried out by individuals. Some societies allow individuals a share in deciding on their schemes of co-operative action and other plans. But even they have to distinguish between the deliberative stage where individuals contribute to the decision-making process and the executive stage, where perhaps those very same individuals are bound to observe those decisions.

In the deliberative stage the question what is to be done is open to argument based on all sorts of considerations. Reasons of a moral character will often dominate. Once the matter has been decided to the satisfaction of the social institution involved, its appropriate organ will formulate "the social intention," i.e. it issues an authoritative instruction. Since this instruction represents the conclusion of the deliberative stage and belongs itself to the executive stage it will be identifiable without resort to further moral argument. Those belong by definition to the deliberative stage. Only positivist considerations can belong to the executive stage. Furthermore executive considerations are authoritatively binding. Those subject to them are not, normally, allowed, by the social institution concerned, to challenge or query their validity or conclusiveness. To do so is to reopen the deliberative process and unless there are limitations on the freedom with which this can be done the considerations cannot be regarded as executive. So long as argument is free the executive stage has not been reached.

Executive considerations are therefore authoritative positivist considerations. This brings us back to the definition of courts of law. It included the fact that they are guided in part by authoritative positivist considerations and that they issue authoritative rulings (which being issued by the action of members of the court are themselves authoritative positivist rulings). This suggests that the law consists of the authoritative positivist considerations binding on the courts and belongs essentially to the executive stage of the political institution (the state, the church, etc.), of which it is a part. The resulting picture has the courts applying both legal (i.e. authoritative positivist) and non-legal considerations. They rely both on executive and deliberative reasons, yet the law belongs to the first kind only.

The two stage picture presented above may make one surprised with a doctrine by which the courts are guided by considerations belonging to both stages. But the surprise is due merely to the oversimplification in the representation of the two stages above. Consider again the case of the individual. A person may stagger the process of decision-making, moving towards the "pure" executive stage in several separate steps. First, for example, he decides to act on the balance of economic considerations and to discount considerations of prestige. Then he decides that one of the half dozen alternatives open to him is to be rejected since at least one of the others is better supported by economic considerations, etc. The law often proceeds in a similar way. On many issues statutes represent but the first step towards a "pure" executive stage. They may have to be supplemented by delegated legislation and perhaps even by further administrative action. Sometimes litigation reaches the courts in matters which have not reached a "pure" executive stage in the matter at issue and the courts have to resort to non-legal, *i.e.* non-executive considerations to resolve the dispute. Even this picture is oversimplified. It suggests, *e.g.* that the survival of a deliberative stage down to the adjudicative level is always to be regretted. This is far from the truth. It is often advantageous for a person while forming a general intention in advance (I'll stay the night in Nottingham) to leave the precise details to the last moment (I'll choose an hotel when there). The same kind of reasons suggests that often, especially when dealing with very broad categories, it is better not to fix too inflexibly the precise details in advance. It is better to settle for executive reasons, *i.e.* laws, which fix the framework only and leave the courts room to apply deliberative reasons within that framework.

Be that as it may, our concern here is not to comment on various law-making policies but on the nature of law. Our analysis yielded only one element: the law consists of authoritative positivist considerations enforceable by courts. Clearly not all the considerations which meet this condition are part of the law. Other conditions have to be added. However, the fact that law consists of considerations enforceable by courts (as required by BI) which are authoritative and positivist is suggested by the definition of a legal court and is supported by the common distinction between the two functions of the courts as law-makers and law-appliers which roughly coincides with the distinction between cases where the law is unsettled and those where it is not. It is further supported by the fact that any analysis of law based in part on this feature focuses on a distinction of paramount importance to social organization, *i.e.* the distinction between the deliberative and the executive stages.

### 4. Is legal philosophy value free?

The analysis outlined above is intended to show how at the level of highest philosophical abstraction the doctrine of the nature of law can and should be concerned with explaining law within a wider context of social and political institutions. It shows how the lawyers' perspective is an arbitrary starting point for legal philosophy, disregarding the wider political context in which the law is moored. It also shows how from this point of view the inclination to identify the theory of law with a theory of adjudication and legal considerations with all those appropriate for courts is based on a short sighted doctrine overlooking the connection of law with the distinction between executive and deliberative considerations.

It may be thought that the arguments of the last section support legal positivism against natural law. But this is not so. It is true that positivists do generally regard legal considerations as authoritative and positivist.[3] But they are not the only ones. The theories of several prominent natural lawyers conform with all the features contributing to a doctrine of the nature of law mentioned above.[4] There still remains the general question about the moral character of the doctrine of the nature of law. Is it a moral doctrine based on moral considerations or not?

Clearly a theory of adjudication is a moral theory. It concerns all the considerations affecting reasoning in the courts, both legal and non-legal. In pronouncing which extra-legal considerations have force and how much weight is due to them it is engaged in moral argument. When the doctrine of the nature of law is identified with a theory of adjudication it becomes itself a moral theory. The question what is the law of England is identified with the question which considerations should courts rely upon. This is clearly a question of political morality, at least inasmuch as it concerns the content of one or the other of the extra-legal considerations. For example, the question whether an English court today is entitled to declare a ministerial regulation null and void on the ground that it violates human rights is clearly a moral and political question. It is a question one

---

[3] Though see for doubts as to whether Hart conforms with this condition: P. Soper "Legal Theory and the Obligation of a Judge: The Hart/Dworkin Dispute", Mich. L. Rev. (1977), p. 473, and D. Lyons "Principles, Positivism and Legal Theory—Dworkin, *Taking Rights Seriously*" (1977), p. 415.

[4] See, *e.g.* L. L. Fuller, *The Morality of Law* and J. M. Finnis, *Natural Law and Natural Rights* (1980).

however conscientious, will be stigmatized by the legal officials as a moral wrongdoer and a moral danger."[9]

The fact that law comes "morally loaded" regardless of one's legal theory makes it difficult to see how one might vary the Gandhi/Eichmann example to sustain MacCormick's claim. Here are two possibilities. First, it might be suggested that my example is flawed because it assumes citizens who are already conscientious or not and thus no longer subject to reform through the choice of legal theory. MacCormick's claim might be an educational one: the way to bring up citizens so that they become Gandhis and not Eichmanns is to teach the positivist view from the beginning, instilling in yet-unformed citizens the understanding that no moral tests are part of the criteria for law and urging such citizens to develop for themselves the capacity of sifting formal law through moral filters. But this suggestion highlights the difficulty. It is indeed the case that what we want to do, given my assumption about the correctness of the moral half of MacCormick's argument, is train citizens to be conscientious. (We ought also to put Eichmann back in school and retrain him.) The question is how one's view about the conceptual distinction between law and morality can have any bearing on this educational goal. If we succeed in making citizens conscientious, it will not be because of the legal theory. It will be because of the arguments about why individual autonomy and moral reflection are inescapable and the judgments of others always potentially fallible. Those arguments are not arguments of legal theory, because they are arguments that both positivists and natural law theorists can and do accept. A good positivist knows there is no necessary connection between law and morality. But nothing in that knowledge explains whether he knows what morality is or, more importantly, whether he cares about finding out. Graduates of schools of positivism or of natural law, it seems, must both make their way to some other school to find their moral consciences.

The above response, however, shows only that legal theory, whether natural law or positivist, cannot ensure conscientiousness. It does not yet show us whether one or the other theory might actually interfere with the development of individual moral sovereignty. This claim, that natural law results in the diminution of individual, moral, and political responsibility, has been made by others.[10] The basis for the indictment, as MacCormick's argument makes clear, is the assumption that there is some additional power of officials to secure obedience and deter individual moral evaluation of "law," if they can present law as already consistent with morality. Thus, a society that adopts the natural law position will present citizens with the claim that law is not only valid by reference to the required formal tests, but that these laws have already been inspected for moral adequacy because otherwise they could not be claimed to be "laws." Of course, a conscientious citizen should not take this moral endorsement at face value, and citizen Gandhi presumably will not. But ordinary people lie somewhere between the extremes of Gandhi and Eichmann, and many of them will find that the official moral endorsement is just the excuse or reason they need to defer their own judgment and obey the law. To put the argument in constitutional terms, imagine two Supreme Court decisions rejecting, say, a challenge to the draft laws. One decision sustains the state's action on the basis of the Court's interpretation

[9] MacCormick, *H. L. A. Hart*, p. 161. MacCormick makes this point, apparently not to qualify the moral argument for positivism which he accepts, *ibid.*, at p. 162, but as a criticism of Hart's failure to recognize that law itself is "in the sense of 'positive morality' a moral order." *ibid.*, p. 160.

[10] See S. I. Shuman, *Legal Positivism* (1963), pp. 204–209. For criticism of the claim, see J. Stone, *Human Law and Human Justice* (1965), pp. 253–254. Professor Stone's discussion of this issue has been valuable to my own thinking and may explain why I share his similarly skeptical conclusions about the attempt to resolve this debate on moral grounds.

of existing statutes, but the Court explicitly disavows any opinion about the justice or morality of the draft law itself. The other decision reaches the same conclusion about the statute but also explicitly indicates—because of the due process clause in the Constitution—that the statute passes minimum requirements of fairness and, thus, is not too immoral to be enforced. Is not the latter decision more likely to deter citizens from making their own evaluation? If citizen conscientiousness is our goal, would we not sooner achieve that goal by removing any moral filters—even as a contingent matter in connection with our own Constitution— as tests for deciding what is "law"?

This argument, I believe, has some force, but it does not raise a question about the desirability of the natural law position so much as about the desirability of establishing particular, official institutions to pass on the moral merits of official directives. With or without a due process clause, the officials who enact and support the draft law will presumably claim that it is morally justified. Thus, the legislators will purport to have made and will continue to endorse the judgment about the moral validity of the law which the Supreme Court, in the first imagined case, refused to make. It may be true that fewer citizens would defer to the legislature's moral judgment than would defer to the moral judgment of the Court for reasons familiar to those who explain why judicial review is lodged in the Court in the first place. But none of this seems to me to be a consequence of adopting a natural law view about the connection between law and morality. It is a consequence of deciding to filter official directives through institutions which, for whatever reason, enjoy sufficient respect and prestige to give their moral judgments extra weight. If one accepts the empirical premise—that these institutions enjoy more prestige as moral judges—then a positivist society could also happily use the same institution to reenforce its claims about the morality of its laws. (The monarch who also has the Church behind him has more chance of persuading citizens to defer their moral judgments to the official moral judgment.) Of course, doing so involves risks—the risk that the more prestigious judiciary (or other institution) will disagree about the moral merits of legislation; but weighing that risk against the possibility of reducing citizen disobedience can occur independently of the underlying legal theory.

### The moral case for natural law

In the Hart/Fuller exchange, it was positivism that found itself on the defensive against the charge that it was responsible for the abdication of individual moral responsibility in Nazi Germany. It should be clear from what has been said that this charge seems no more capable of being sustained as an indictment of positivism than of natural law. Indeed, Hart's response to the charge was similar in many respects to the response given above: the fact that law and morality were seen as separate does not explain why individuals in Germany would defer to law rather than to their own assessment of the morality of action.[11] It is easy to imagine ways in which such deference *might* be explained. It might, for example, have something to do with the acceptance of an erroneous political theory about the absolute moral authority of the state, however unjust its laws. Or the explanation might lie in social-psychological theories about the "tendency of most people to submit to actual power, and even to the 'normative tendency of the factual.'"[12] But the suggestion that the legal theory itself had a causal influence is difficult to defend.

Fuller, however, levels another charge against positivism. This charge focuses not on the connection between legal theory and individual moral responsibility, but on the connection between legal theory and the ability of those bent on doing

[11] See Hart 71 Harv. L.R. 593, 617–618. [And see *post*, 444].
[12] See Stone, *Human Law*, p. 255.

dilemma these judges faced as proof that legal theory was partly to blame for judicial failure to move the country more rapidly toward the abolition of slavery.[17] Dworkin's interpretation, however, is not one that will help us in deciding whether there are moral implications in the debate between natural law and positivism as I am using those terms. Dworkin's claim is that if judges had correctly interpreted the available institutional materials, they would have seen that the law supported the antislavery result the judge wanted to reach. Thus, there need not have been a dilemma between the judge's role and the morally correct decision. Whether or not Dworkin is correct about what the institutional materials indicated at the time[18] makes no difference, because the "rights thesis" which underlies Dworkin's claim about how judges were supposed to decide cases is independent of the natural law/positivism distinction. A positivist regime, if it thought it made sense to tell judges to seek the best answer even in hard cases, could so instruct judges with the result that the failure here, if it was one, must again be charged not to legal theory but to the particular theory of adjudication judges were using.

The argument that must be made in the case of the antislavery judge goes something like this. Judges in a natural law regime who are morally ahead of the rest of society will be free to express their moral judgments and base their opinions on them without fear of criticism for stepping outside the limits of their role. In doing so, they are more likely to move society ahead in line with their, presumably correct, moral views. This is not possible in a positivist regime which insists on separating "the law" that the judge must enforce from judgments about its morality.

One difficulty with this argument, of course, is that it assumes that the individual judges who are being "freed" to advance society in accordance with their own views do indeed have the correct views. If natural law has the posited freeing effect for those who do not like the accepted rules, it will free in both directions: the proslavery judge after the Civil War, who wants to return, as well as the antislavery judge who wants to "move forward." But there are other problems. Individual judges acting on their own moral lights are not likely to have much chance of reversing the contrary moral judgment of the rest of society. Indeed, if such judges are continually reversed by other judges or replaced by society, at some point the invitation to keep moral tests in view in reaching legal decisions is going to be so obviously futile that a good judge would do better to resign or look for other ways to change opinion. Even in a natural law society, some Court at some point must have the final say about whether the moral tests for law have been met; individual judges who continue to flout that highest court's decisions are not likely to find that they are any more "free" to do so than their positivist analogues.

Yet the argument might still have purchase. Even though individual judges are not likely to immediately effect a change in the rest of society, the fact that they are encouraged to engage in moral evaluation in reaching their decisions might initiate a dialogue that could lead to reevaluation of existing doctrine as other courts and society attempt to respond to the moral arguments of the enlightened judges. If judges continue to be reversed, then presumably at some point the prevailing moral judgment should be seen as preventing further argument within the role of judge. But the constant possibility of being allowed to test existing doctrine and force a definitive moral response could well result at least sometimes in greater forward progress.

This argument will be seen to have considerable affinity with Fuller's argument

---

[17] See Dworkin, "The Law of the Slave-Catchers", *The Times Literary Supplement* (December 5, 1975), p. 1437.
[18] Serious doubts about this part of Dworkin's claim are raised in Greenawalt, "Policy, Rights, and Judicial Decision" in (1977) 11 Ga. L. Rev. 993, 1050–1051.

about evil judges. Indeed, it rests on similar assumptions about the relationship between moral dialogue and the direction of moral progress. Where Fuller focused on preventing evil by requiring justification, we are now focusing on undoing evil through the same means: requiring the system to respond to the demand to justify. Because the arguments are so similar, it should not surprise that the same response is available here that we gave above. There is no necessary connection between the society's prevailing legal theory and whether or not it has designed courts to permit this continued possibility of built-in challenge and response. A natural law society, if it preferred not to allow judges to demand justification for settled doctrine, could restrict their role to determining only whether directives passed the required formal tests. In that case, legislators could still claim to have made the judgment that the necessary moral tests had been passed and citizens would have to treat the judicial decision as "law," unless, being conscientious citizens who disagreed with the legislative claim, they decided it was too immoral. Conversely, a positivist society that valued the chance to constantly reevaluate doctrine by responding to moral challenge could empower courts to check doctrine for moral adequacy—though the power could be withdrawn at any time, consistent with the positivist claim that the connection is only contingent. [pp. 32–42]

## J. FINNIS
### Evaluation and the Description of Law
### (1980)[19]

The evaluations of the theorist himself are an indispensable and decisive component in the selection or formation of any concepts for use in description of such aspects of human affairs as law or legal order. For the theorist cannot identify the central case of that practical viewpoint which he uses to identify the central case of his subject-matter, unless he decides what the requirements of practical reasonableness really are, in relation to this whole aspect of human affairs and concerns. In relation to law, the most important things for the theorist to know and describe are the things which, in the judgment of the theorist, make it important from a *practical* viewpoint to have law—the things which it is, therefore, important in practice to "see to" when ordering human affairs. And when these "important things" are (in some or even in many societies) in fact missing, or debased, or exploited or otherwise deficient, then the most important things for the theorist to describe are those aspects of the situation that manifest this absence, debasement, exploitation, or deficiency.

Does this mean that descriptive jurisprudence (and social science as a whole) is inevitably subject to every theorist's conceptions and prejudices about what is good and practically reasonable? Yes and no. "Yes", in so far as there is no escaping the theoretical requirement that a judgment of *significance* and *importance* must be made if theory is to be more than a vast rubbish heap of miscellaneous facts described in a multitude of incommensurable terminologies. "No", in so far as the disciplined acquisition of accurate knowledge about human affairs—and thus about what other men have considered practically important, and about the actual results of their concern—is an important help to the reflective and critical theorist in his effort to convert his own (and his culture's) practical "prejudices" into truly reasonable judgments about what is good and practically reasonable. Descriptive knowledge thus can occasion a modification of the judgments of importance and significance with which the theorist first approached his data, and can suggest a reconceptualization. But the knowledge will not have been attained without a preliminary conceptualization and thus a

---

[19] [From J. Finnis, *Natural Law and Natural Rights* (1980).]

preliminary set of principles of selection and relevance drawn from some practical viewpoint.

There is thus a movement to and fro between, on the one hand, assessments of human good and of its practical requirements, and on the other hand, explanatory descriptions (using all appropriate historical, experimental, and statistical techniques to trace all relevant causal interrelationships) of the human context in which human well-being is variously realized and variously ruined. Just as there is no question of deriving one's basic judgments about human values and the requirements of practical reasonableness by some inference from the facts of the human situation, so there is no question of reducing descriptive social science to an apologia for one's ethical or political judgments, or to a project for apportioning praise or blame among the actors on the human scene: in this sense, descriptive social science is "value-free". But when all due emphasis has been given to the differences of objective and method between practical philosophy and descriptive social science, the methodological problems of concept-formation as we have traced it in this chapter compel us to recognize that the point of reflective equilibrium in descriptive social science is attainable only by one in whom wide knowledge of the data, and penetrating understanding of other men's practical viewpoints and concerns, are allied to a sound judgment about all aspects of genuine human flourishing and authentic practical reasonableness.    [pp. 16–18]

### J. RAZ
### Ethics in the Public Domain
(1994)

The concept of law is part of our culture and of our cultural traditions. It plays a role in the way in which ordinary people as well as the legal profession understand their own and other people's actions. It is part of the way they "conceptualize" social reality. But the culture and tradition of which the concept is a part provide it with neither sharply defined contours nor a clearly identifiable focus. Various, sometimes conflicting, ideas are displayed in them. It falls to legal theory to pick on those which are central and significant to the way the concept plays its role in people's understanding of society, to elaborate and explain them.

Legal theory contributes in this respect to an improved understanding of society. But it would be wrong to conclude, as Lyons has done,[20] that one judges the success of an analysis of the concept of law by its theoretical sociological fruitfulness. To do so is to miss the point that, unlike concepts like "mass" or "electron", "the law" is a concept used by people to understand themselves. We are not free to pick on any fruitful concepts. It is a major task of legal theory to advance our understanding of society by helping us understand how people understand themselves.

To do so it does engage in evaluative judgment, for such judgment is inescapable in trying to sort out what is central and significant in the common understanding of the concept of law. It was my claim in this chapter that one such feature is the law's claim to authority and the mediating role it carries with it. The significance of this feature is both in its distinctive character as a method of social organization and in its distinctive moral aspect, which brings special considerations to bear on the determination of a correct moral attitude to authoritative institutions. This is a point missed both by those who regard the law as a gunman situation writ large and by those who, in pointing to the close connection between law and morality, assume a linkage inconsistent with it.[21]          [p. 237]

---

[20] *Ethics and The Rule of Law* (1983), pp. 57–59.
[21] [An excellent monograph which debates these issues is Julie Dickson, *Evaluation and Legal Theory* (2001). See also Dickson (2004) 10 Legal Theory 117]

# 3

# NATURAL LAW

Natural law thinking has occupied a pervasive role in the realms of ethics, politics, and law from the time of Greek civilisation. At some periods its appeal may have been essentially religious or supernatural: in modern times it has formed an important weapon in political and legal ideology. Essentially it has afforded a moral justification for existing social and economic systems and their legal systems. By arguing that what "is" the law is based on a higher law dictated by reason and so is also what the law "ought" to be, positive law is thought to acquire a sanctity that puts it beyond question.[1] The idea of natural rights similarly had its origin in conservative forces anxious to sanctify property (symbol of the existing order) as the fundamental human right overriding even the right to life itself.[2] Yet there lurked behind this notion an equally revolutionary factor in its emphasis on human equality, which was already in evidence in the American Declaration of Rights and became fully manifest with the outbreak of the French Revolution. The reaction which this provoked,[3] coupled with other factors which will be mentioned later, resulted in a diminished respect for natural law during the nineteenth century. But natural law thinking revived[4] in the twentieth century, particularly since the Second World War. Indeed, in the last thirty years or so, there has been a revival of interest in natural law theory within mainstream legal, political and moral theory.[5]

---

[1] *Cf.* Kelsen, *What is Justice?*, pp. 137 *et seq.*; see also V. Gordon Childe, *What Happened in History*, pp. 211–217; and Ross, *On Law and Justice* (1958), pp. 258–262.

[2] See R. Tuck, *Natural Rights Theories* (1979), Chap. 1. For a particularly trenchant attack on this aspect of naturalism, see A. Ross, *On Law and Justice* (1958), Chaps 10 and 11.

[3] See particularly Bentham's *Anarchical Fallacies*.

[4] Finnis however argues that talk of revival, decline, etc., is misconceived. To him natural law has no history, though there is a history of doctrines which assert that there are principles of natural law (*Natural Law and Natural Rights* (1980), p. 24).

[5] This may be gauged from an excellent collection of essays edited by R. George, *Natural Law Theory: Contemporary Essays* (1992). See also his *Natural Law, Liberalism and Morality* (1996) and *In Defense of Natural Law* (1999). See also P. Soper (1988) 22 Creighton L. Rev. 67 and P. Johnson (1987) 75 California L. Rev. 217. Recently symposia to reflect the revived interest are in (1992) 90 Michigan L. Rev. 2203–2533, (1992) 61 U. Cinn. L. Rev. 1–222 and (1993) 26 U.C. Davis L. Rev. 503–789.

## WHAT IS NATURAL LAW?

With 2,500 years of history it is not surprising that the question "what is natural law?" provokes so many different answers. The expression "natural law" has continuity but this does not mean that the concept has remained static. It has had very different meanings and has served entirely different purposes. As D'Entrèves points out, "many of the ambiguities of the concept of natural law must be ascribed to the ambiguity of the concept of nature that underlies it".[6] There have been different doctrines of natural law. The Romans lacked a concept of natural rights.[7] They did not subordinate positive law to natural law in the way in which later ages have.[8] Medieval and modern notions of natural law have little in common.[9] Despite these different doctrines, what has remained constant is an assertion that there are principles of natural law. Views as to the content of these principles have sometimes diverged but the essence of natural law may be said to lie in the constant assertion that there are objective moral principles which depend upon the nature of the universe and which can be discovered by reason. These principles constitute the natural law. This is valid of necessity because the rules governing correct human conduct are logically connected with immanent truths concerning human nature. Natural law is believed to be a rational foundation for moral judgement. Natural lawyers accept that natural law principles do not always have the effect that they would like them to have but they argue that the principles remain true even if they are ignored, misunderstood, abused in practice,[10] or defied in practical thinking. An appropriate analogy are mathematical axioms which hold good even when misunderstood or undiscovered.

One of the principal obstacles which natural law must surmount centres about the problem whether moral propositions can be derived from propositions of fact, whether an "ought" can be deduced from an "is". Finnis, denies that natural law attempts to "make this illicit transition".[11] Indeed, he accepts, though he re-interprets, Hume's dualism.[12] We will see later in this chapter how Finnis deals with this question.[13] Bridging the gap between "is" and "ought" remains a critical problem. Of course, it is understandable why natural lawyers should wish to derive normative propositions from factual statements. Factual statements (water boils at 100° centigrade, for example) are verifiable; moral judgments (capital

---

6. *Natural Law* (rev. ed., 1970), p. 16.
7. The Greeks did not even have a concept of rights.
8. See D'Entrèves, *op. cit.*, p. 34.
9. Though forms of Thomism re-appear. See Maritain *post*, 150 and Finnis *post*, 168.
10. The comment of Leo Strauss (*Natural Rights and History* (1953), p. 9) should not be overlooked: "By proving that there is no principle of justice that has not been denied somewhere or at some time, one has not yet proved that any given denial was justified or reasonable."
11. *Op. cit.*, n. 4, p. 34.
12. *ibid.*, pp. 36–42.
13. *Post*, 88.

punishment is the right punishment for murder, for example) cannot be proved. We may differ over the latter[14] but not over the former. So, if moral propositions could be deduced from factual statements, we would be able to set up moral truths which would demand general consensus. Much attention has been focused by natural lawyers on the question of how to get from "is" to "ought" without making an unacceptable logical inference.

One way in which natural law seeks to do this is by arguing that if it is a natural law for men to act in a particular way (this it is argued can be discovered by observation of his behaviour patterns), then he ought morally to act in this way. For example, it is a natural law for mankind to reproduce itself: therefore, mankind ought to do so and it would be contrary to this natural law for human beings not to produce children. It is easy to see how, using this type of reasoning, conclusions on the moral impropriety of contraception and abortion[15] as well as the unacceptability of gay unions[16] can be reached. The positivist response to this reasoning is to argue that it confuses scientific laws (which *describe* what does occur) with moral and legal ones (which *prescribe* what should occur).[17] It does not follow from the undoubted fact that mankind generally does reproduce itself that particular human beings are under a moral or legal duty to comply with this practice.

Some natural lawyers might respond to this by arguing that scientific laws (for example, the law of gravity) describe the manner it is laid down that things should behave. Such a view presupposes a creator who has subjected all things to laws. The falsification[18] of a scientific law would, in these terms, prove no more than that scientists had not as yet accurately discovered what had been ordained. This defence does not necessarily involve a confusion of scientific and moral law. But it rests on a pre-supposition that many would not accept and it may be said to involve the proof of the existence of a deity, itself a problem not easily resoluble.

Another way to justify the view that there are immanent norms and values in the nature of things is to consider nature teleologically. To Aristotle and his followers natural processes tended towards pre-determined ends: acorns grew into oaks, etc.[19] In doing this they fulfilled their natural function. Man, too, according to this view had his own proper function which could be discovered by reason and thought. This gives us an idea of "the good". The good for a species is the "end" it will reach if its progress is not impeded. Similarly, a part of something can be understood only by reference to its contribution to the whole to which it belongs. In these terms man can be understood only as part of a properly

---

[14] As Finnis and Grisez, for example, do. For Finnis, capital punishment instantiates an intrinsic good (justice); for Grisez, it is the use of an evil means to a good end.

[15] As in *Humanae Vitae* (1968), for example. See P. Harris, *On Human Life* (1968).

[16] See Finnis (1997) 42 Amer. J. Jurisprudence 97 (see also A. Koppelman at p. 51).

[17] See *ante*, 24.

[18] See K. Popper's views, *ante*, 24.

[19] "What each thing is when fully developed we call its nature, whether we are speaking of a man, a horse or a family" (*Politics* i, 2 (in Jowett's translation), p. 28).

functioning social whole. This view was developed by Aquinas in the thirteenth century within a Christian world-view: the goods disclosed by nature belonged within the *lex aeterna*, God's plan for the universe into which rational man could gain insight through revelation (the *lex divina*) and conscious participation (the *lex naturalis*).[20] The tradition is continued in Finnis's work.[21] There are, he asserts, certain basic goods for human beings, objective values, in the sense that every reasonable human being must assent to their value as objects of human striving. These goods must be seen in the light of a community of human beings for only in communal life are there the conditions for the pursuit of basic goods. The teleological view thus sees man as having ends which can be ascertained by reflecting on his nature and his needs. One way of looking at this is to ask who gives man his purposes. This can lead us back to a deity and to a problem already referred to. Even if the existence of God could be satisfactorily established, a theory which relied on his existence might disappoint. After all, one of the attractions of natural law is that we can reach moral truths through pure reason. Another possible defence of the teleological account of natural law is to introduce the notion of rational beings having free will. For rational beings with free will the law says what ought to be done but it does not necessarily describe what happens in practice. But the introduction into the debate of free will causes manifold problems. If someone has free will, how can he be obligated to do anything? This requires us to posit some act of will, either of the person himself (subjecting himself through the institution of promising[22]) or of some superior will, such as that of a sovereign. If we take the latter case, the binding force of natural law would be seen to derive from the command of a superior. This might lead to the conclusion, as in Pufendorf,[23] that natural law is binding because it is willed by God.

However, to define morality in terms of God's will is objectionable. Suppose we were created by an evil deity for a malevolent purpose. The riposte, that we were created by a morally perfect God, brings out the circularity in attempting to define morality in terms of God's will.[24] It is because the Judaic-Christian God is defined partially in terms of moral perfection that a denial of God's goodness is itself a rejection of the Judaic-Christian God. To say that God deserves our obedience because he is morally perfect can only make sense if we understand the notion of moral perfection before we relate it to God. We are using a logically independent standard in morally judging the appropriateness of respecting the God in whom we were taught to believe. We are not

[20] *Post*, 100.
[21] Discussed *post*, 126 *et seq.*
[22] As to which see P. Atiyah, *Promises, Morals and Laws* (1981).
[23] On whom, see Stone, *Human Law and Human Justice* (1965), pp. 65–73. See also C. L. Carr and M. J. Seidler (1996) 17 *History of Political Thought* 354 and J. B. Schneewind (1987) 72 *Synthese* 123.
[24] This is the argument of an early Platonic dialogue (the *Euthyphro*). In it Socrates attempts to make Euthyphro distinguish between the claim that an "act is right because God wills it" and "God wills an act because it is right."

abandoning independent moral appraisal. It is not God's fiat that makes an act right, but the reasons that a God in whom we believe, or define to be good, would give for his actions. Natural lawyers like Suárez[25] and Grotius,[26] in the seventeenth century, saw this. To them natural law was willed by God, but was willed by him because it is that which is rationally good. It is not good merely because he happens to have willed it. Hence Grotius could conclude that natural law would hold good even if there were no God.[27]

The superior will could equally be that of a human sovereign. The existence of, indeed the need for, positive law is not denied by natural law.[28] In the view of natural lawyers much positive law should embody natural law. But this will not always be so. On many matters natural law is indifferent (the precise rules of conveyancing, for example). This does not mean that natural law is indifferent to whether there are such rules at all. Of course, human rulers with free will can and may make unjust laws. How natural lawyers have dealt with this question must be reserved until later in this section.[29]

For we must return to the thorny problem of how moral norms and values can be established. Another argument is that propositions of natural law are self-evident. This is, it must be admitted, a retreat from the claim that they can be proved. Even so, doubt may be cast on the argument. Statements such as "slavery is wrong" or "it is wrong to kill" may be self-evident to us but the Greeks and Americans in the antebellum South, for example, had no problem in accepting slavery as a morally justifiable institution.[30] There are definitional problems as well. Neither the concept of slavery[31] nor homicide is clear. All societies,[32] it seems, have prohibited some killing but there is far from complete agreement on what killing should be outlawed, or justified.

One twentieth century attempt to rescue natural law from this problem is the theory, largely associated with Stammler, of natural law with a variable content.[33] This view holds that while the ideal of justice is absolute, its application must vary with time, place and circumstance. But we must not overlook the fact that one of the reasons for variability in application, arguably the most significant one, are differences in moral attitude. The Greeks did not think slavery was wrong: we do. In which case to concede that the content of natural law may vary with social

---

[25] *Post*, 102.

[26] *Post*, 102.

[27] *Post*, 102.

[28] See the views of Aquinas, *post*, 142, Locke, *post*, 145 and Finnis, *post*, 174. See also George, *In Defense of Natural Law*, Chap. 5.

[29] *Post*, 90–94.

[30] See, for example, Aristotle, *Politics*.

[31] The Marxist would include all employees of capitalism as wage-slaves. Natural lawyers today, Finnis for example, would say that proslavery arguments were wrong and those who accepted them were wrong so to do.

[32] *Cf*. M. Mead, *post*, 225.

[33] A full account of Stammler is J. Stone, *Human Law and Human Justice* (1965), Chap. 6.

differences is to give up any attempt to construct objective norms and values.

Another attempt to rescue natural law is found in the writings of a leading contemporary positivist, Hart. His "minimum content of natural law"[34] is premised on biology and psychology. He starts with certain truisms about human nature: human vulnerability, limited altruism, approximate equality. He assumes we have a commitment to survive (we are not a "suicide club"). We can accordingly work out a set of principles to satisfy our needs and enhance our chances of survival. Two problems with this may be noted here.[35] First, calling the premises platitudes and clothing them in scientific and social-scientific language does not avoid the recognition that what Hart is doing is deducing moral principles and legal norms from facts.[36] Secondly, it may be said that the "minimum content" provides us with very little guidance: it tells us we need some prohibitions on violence, some recognition of private property (in itself contentious[37]), but not which. This does not take us very far.

An important contemporary restatement of natural law is Finnis's *Natural Law and Natural Rights*.[38] He denies that true classical natural law ever purported to derive "ought" from "is". He concedes that the Stoics,[39] renaissance jurists[40] and even many catholic writers,[41] including contemporary ones, have claimed to draw normative inferences from nature and so to confuse fact with value. He argues, however, that this was not true of Aristotle[42] or Aquinas. He maintains the latter's views have been misunderstood by later writers. Finnis's own exposition of natural law is a reinterpretation of Aquinas. He argues that the normative conclusions of natural law are not based on the observation of human or any other nature but rather on a reflective grasp of what is self-evidently good for human beings. He reasons thus:

> "When discerning what is good ... intelligence is operating in a different way, yielding a different logic, from when it is discerning what is the case (historically, scientifically, or metaphysically); but there is no good reason for asserting that the latter operations of intelligence are more rational than the former ...
> The basic forms of good grasped by practical understanding are what is good for human beings with the nature they have."[43]

Finnis claims that Aquinas considered that practical reasoning began "not by understanding this nature from the outside ... by way of

---

[34] This is discussed *post*, 123–126.
[35] See *post*, 124–125.
[36] And thus transgressing Hume's "law". See *ante*, 24, and *post*, 124, n. 42.
[37] As to which see L.C. Becker, *Property Rights* (1977) and discussion of Locke, *post*, 115.
[38] Published in 1980.
[39] *ibid.*, p. 35. On Stoics see *post*, 98 and extract from Cicero, *post*, 137.
[40] Vazquez and Suàrez, for example. See Finnis's discussion at pp. 43–48.
[41] Finnis does not cite Dabin or Maritain (see *post*, 150) but they are clearly "guilty" of this.
[42] Aristotle clearly distinguished "speculative reason" (reasoning about what is the case) and "practical reason" (reasoning about ought to be done).
[43] *Op. cit.*, n. 4, p. 34.

psychological, anthropological, or metaphysical observations and judgments defining human nature, but by experiencing one's nature ... from the inside, in the form of one's inclinations".[44] He denies that this involves a process of inference.

"One does not judge that I have [or everybody has] an inclination to find out about things and then infer that therefore 'knowledge is a good to be pursued'. Rather, by a simple act of non-inferential understanding one grasps that the object of the inclination which one experiences is an instance of a general form of good, for oneself (and others like one)."[45]

Finnis himself argues that objective knowledge of what is right is made possible first by the existence of "basic forms of human flourishing"[46] which we all use (even if in practice we come to wrong conclusions). Secondly, by a set of "basic methodological requirements"[47] of practical reasonableness (for example, "a coherent plan of life", "no arbitrary preferences amongst values" or amongst "persons", "detachment and commitment", "the [limited] relevance of consequences", "the requirements of the common good" and "following one's conscience"[48] which, taken together enable us to determine the morally right ways of acting. The "basic goods" and the "basic methodological requirements" together constitute the universal and unchanging principles of natural law. But can the drawing of inferences from inside our nature, as opposed to understanding nature from the outside, offer a more credible foundation for the normative propositions of natural law?

Finnis stresses that the basic forms of human flourishing are "obvious to anyone acquainted ... with the range of human opportunities" and the general requirements of reasonableness are likewise "as obvious as the norms of rationality, principles of logic, and canons of explanation that are presupposed in *any* explanation, whether in our practical context or in natural science or analytical philosophy".[49] He reasons:

"The fact that human beings have a certain range of urges, drives, or inclinations; and the fact that these have a certain correspondence ... with the states of affairs that anyone intelligent would consider human flourishing; and the fact that without reasonable direction the inclinations will bring about individual and communal ruin ...; and the fact that certain psychological, biological, climatic, physical, mechanical, and other like principles, laws, state of affairs, or conditions affect the realisation of human well-being in discoverable ways—all these are facts in an order, external to our own understanding, which our understanding can only discover. This order is often called the order of nature."[50]

[44] *ibid.*
[45] *ibid.*
[46] *ibid.*, p. 23 and see *post*, 170.
[47] Set out in Chap. V.
[48] On the association between these requirements and the Roman Catholic Church, see Finnis, *op. cit.*, p. 124.
[49] *Natural Law and Natural Rights*, p. 371.
[50] *ibid.*, p. 380.

He concedes, however, there is also disorder in nature. This leads him to conclude that "*direct* speculative questions about the significance, implications, or source of the orderliness of things yield, by *themselves*, no clear or certain answers".[51] For Finnis further explanation can only lie in theology: "As well as the orderliness of the order(s) of things, there is their sheer existence ...".[52] He reasons that concern for the "basic value of truth" is essential if our "reasoning is to lead from questions about states of affairs which we experience to knowledge of the existence of a state of affairs which we do not as such experience. For principles of theoretical rationality, although they do not describe anything ... are objective, not conventional or relative to individual purposes or commitments."[53] One cannot but be impressed with the force and sincerity of Finnis's arguments. Yet what is this reality we must experience and believe in to be satisfied that there are objective goods or values which exist independently of anyone's valuation of them? Finnis seems to be saying that what one has to believe in is itself one of the basic goods (religion). Is this not a boot-strap argument? We would agree with MacCormick[54] that, to say the least, Finnis's claim is "not proven".

## THE ATTRACTIONS OF NATURAL LAW

It was Pascal who seized on the irony that, as he put it, "there are people in the world who, having renounced all the laws of God and nature, have themselves made law which they rigorously obey".[55] Yet throughout civilisation human beings have striven for something better than they found in their own laws and institutions. So long as these are not perfect, so long as there is perceived to be injustice, the search for an ideal system will continue. From the tirades of Old Testament prophets through Antigone's impassioned plea in Sophocles' play[56] to the prosecutors' arguments at the Nuremberg War Trials[57] the plea has been similar: there

---

[51] *ibid.*, p. 382.
[52] *ibid.*
[53] *ibid.*, p. 387.
[54] "Natural Law Reconsidered" (1981) 1 O.J.L.S. 99, 107. And see also in George (ed.) *op. cit.*, n. 5, p. 128. On Finnis and religion see J. Finnis (2006) 51 Am. J. Jurisprudence 107.
[55] This is quoted by D'Entrèves at the beginning of his *Natural Law, op. cit.*, n. 6.
[56]     "Not of today or yesterday they are,
        But live eternal (none can date their birth)
        Nor would I fear the wrath of any man
        (And brave's God's vengeance) for defying these."
    Polyneikes had broken Creon's law but burial of the dead was a sacred duty to be upheld even when positive law had been broken. W. Jaeger in (ed.) Sayre, *Modern Legal Philosophies*, p. 352, is useful in locating *Antigone* within its context. See also J. Butler, *Antigone's Claim* (2000), and T. Staehler in M. Freeman and R. Harrison (eds.), *Law and Philosophy* (2007), p. 137.
[57] See A. Tusa and J. Tusa, *The Nuremberg Trial* (1983). Scepticism about the existence of objective human goods is found in the C.L.S. movement (*post*, 1209) and on this see J. Finnis (1985) 30 Am. J. of Jurisp. 21, 40–42.

are more important obligations, higher ideals, than obedience to the positive laws of the state. This raises three questions.

First, there is the problem of defining injustice. For Aquinas "the force of a law depends on the extent of its justice ... according to the rule of reason. But the first rule of reason is the law of nature ... Consequently, every human law has just so much of the nature of law as it is derived from the law of nature. But if in any point it departs from the law of nature, it is no longer a law but a perversion of law."[58] Aquinas was not in doubt as to when human laws were just. They were when they served the common good, distributed burdens fairly, promoted religion and were within the bounds of the law-maker's authority. All these concepts are, of course, value-laden and require interpretation. Opinions differ not only on what constitutes the common good,[59] but on whether it exists. It should be added that injustice may be done not just by following the law but by applying it unfairly[60] or arbitrarily favouring the interests of some citizens over others.[61]

Secondly, there is the question of who decides whether a "law" is so flagrant a breach of principles of justice as not to merit the appellation of law? Is this a decision that can be left to everyone's conscience or can it only be taken by professionals, judges or jurists, applying criteria which they consider principled and morally coherent? If the basis for valuation is reason, it is difficult to deny this decision to anyone. The consequences of so doing have disturbed many natural lawyers, including Aquinas.[62] Fuller, on the other hand, comes close to reserving the decision to professional opinion.[63]

Thirdly, what are the consequences of deciding that a "law" should not be regarded as law? Aquinas was in no doubt that such perversions of law did not bind the moral conscience of man and could be ignored but this was subject to one highly significant caveat. The "law" should be obeyed when to break it would lead to scandal or civic disturbance. Aquinas, in other words, weighed up the consequences of disobedience to unjust laws against the possibly deleterious consequences of permitting it, including the example that disobedience sets to others who may, as a result, choose to flout other laws which may not be morally defective.[64] Finnis's conclusion on this is close to Aquinas's. "The good citizen", he argues, "may be morally required to conform to [an unjust] stipulation to the extent

---

[58] Q.95, art. 2. See also *post*, 101; 142–143.

[59] But *cf.* Finnis *ante*, 89 and *post*, 173 *et seq.*

[60] See Hart, *The Concept of Law* (1994).

[61] But what if the interests of those being discriminated against are base? See George, *In Defense of Natural Law*, p. 131 on the interests of those who want access to pornography. And *cf.* Dworkin, *A Matter of Principle* (1985), Chap. 17 and R. Langton (1993) 22 Phil. and Public Affairs 293. See also D Scoccia (1996) 106 Ethics 776.

[62] See *post*, 101. See also how Finnis tackles this problem, *post*, 92, 181.

[63] *Cf.* discussion of Fuller, *post*, 121.

[64] This "domino effect" argument is sometimes used today to counter advocates of civil disobedience. But the evidence does not suggest that law-breaking is particularly rife at times when civil disobedience is commonly practised.

necessary to avoid weakening 'the law,' the legal system ... as a whole".[65] However, since the ruler should repeal such a law rather than enforce it, he has no right to expect conformity to it. Presumably, though Finnis does not address the issue, he may, however, punish those who disobey it.[66]

Finnis also passes over the dilemma that such "laws" present to officials such as judges. Are judges supposed to enforce unjust laws? There is an argument, found in Hart's *Concept of Law*,[67] that not to enforce such a law would infringe a principle of justice (though this does not commit Hart to the view that unjust laws should always be enforced for the value of implementing a law, fidelity to law, may be outweighed by the worse injustice which enforcing the law might perpetrate).[68] What is the judge to do?[69] Much must depend on the political context. What independence does he have? Is there a rule of law in his society? Is he merely a puppet of the régime? If he has merely been "planted" by an authoritarian régime to give it a veneer of respectability by lending his good name to its adjudicative processes, it is difficult to see what moral dilemma this presents. Failure to implement an unjust law in such circumstances might well lead to unpleasant consequences for him but he would not be violating a moral principle. His assumed obligation of fidelity to law is overridden by the circumstances of his appointment.

Even within a democratic system there are circumstances where a judge, or other official, may be said not to be in violation of his duties to uphold the law when he refuses to implement an unjust law. Just as a soldier's duty to obey commands does not extend to orders to shoot unarmed civilians,[70] so a judge's obligation to implement the law has moral limits. What these are will depend on the content of the law, the social and political context and the consequences of applying it and not applying it.

The dilemma of the moral judge provoked a lot of interest and controversy in South Africa when the system of apartheid still existed?[71] An

---

[65] Finnis, *op. cit.*, n. 37, pp. 361–362.

[66] But according to MacCormick, positivism "yields the same conclusion"—if the duties imposed by "a valid law" validate the demands of justice (he used the "Poll Tax" as an example), if will follow that the moral issue whether or not to comply is "prima facie an open one" (see in George (ed.), *op. cit.*, n. 5, p. 109).

[67] Hart, *op. cit.*, n. 60, pp. 156–157. See also D. Lyons, *Ethics and the Rule of Law* (1984), p. 82.

[68] *Cf.* R. M. Hare, *Moral Thinking* (1981).

[69] An excellent study of the judicial conscience under stress is R. Cover, *Justice Accused: Anti-Slavery and The Judicial Process* (1975). On the moral-philosophical problems involved see B. Williams, *Problems of The Self* (1975), p. 166.

[70] *Cf.* the *Calley* case in the U.S. (see T. Taylor, *Nuremberg and Vietnam*).

[71] See R. Wacks (1984) 101 *South African Law Journal* 266 and *cf.* J. Dugard (1984) 101 *South African Law J.* 286. See also Wacks' reply at p. 295 and Dugard's subsequent admission that Wacks' views had force (1987) 3 *South African Journal on Human Rights* 295. See also further Wacks (1988) 12 *Bulletin of the Australian Society of Legal Philosophy* 221.

official has a general obligation of fidelity to law, but, it may be argued, there are moral bounds to this. As Lyons[72] puts it:

"A misguided or naive official under the Third Reich, who initially believes that the law he shall be called upon to administer will not be outrageously immoral, may find that it requires him to verify the eligibility of persons for extermination in the gas chambers because they are Jews. He may in good conscience have undertaken to apply the law as he finds it, but I see no reason to suppose that this resulting obligation of fidelity to law extends this far. Such an obligation has moral limits."

Should the judge who finds the law he has to apply radically immoral "give up his job as judge and join the revolution"?[73]

The judge might think that there are reasons for staying in his post. He may think most of the law is just (what percentage of the law in Nazi Germany or apartheid South Africa was racially polluted?) so that most of his judging takes place on morally neutral terrain. Secondly, he may believe that there are the opportunities for him to interpret the law humanely, even giving him the capacity to frustrate the immoral intentions of the legislature. And thirdly, there is the understandable intuition that, should he resign, he is likely to be replaced by a less moral judge.

The second response may well be that of the positivist. Hart,[74] for example, held that open-textured rules—and many discriminatory laws by virtue of their very vagueness[75] would come into this category—gave judges scope to make law and to draw upon moral principles to reach a decision.[76] This version of the judicial enterprise gives the judge "slightly thicker ice on which to skate". It produces an area of strong discretion[77] by which he might do good.[78] Certainly, in South Africa liberals sought to show how, "within the interstices of unjust law, humane interpretations [were] possible".[79]

It is also the response of Dworkin, though, as we shall see, it is not as easy for him to sustain it in his adjudicative theory. Dworkin's judge must ask "which interpretation of his country's legal practices would put them in what we believe would be their least bad light".[80] The judge has to think of himself not as giving voice to his own personal moral convictions, but "as an author in the chain of the common law".[81] In Dworkin's view, the dilemma is best solved by the judge lying because "he cannot be of any help unless he is understood as saying, in his official

---

[72] *Ethics and the Rule of Law* (1984), p. 85.
[73] *Per* R. M. Hare, *Moral Thinking* (1981), p. 163.
[74] *The Concept of Law, post*, 1546.
[75] See Fuller, *post*, 165.
[76] *Per* R. Wacks in W. Sadurski (ed.), *Ethical Dimension of Legal Theory* (1990).
[77] Dworkin's expression: see *post*, 721.
[78] R. Wacks, *op. cit.*, n. 71.
[79] *ibid.*
[80] *Law's Empire* (1986), p. 107.
[81] *ibid.*, p. 239.

role, that the legal rights are different from what he believes they are". [82]
He says that resigning is of "little help",[83] but, given the legitimacy that
the role of the judge gives the system, this is a somewhat pessimistic
analysis: public resignation might be thought to provoke debate at the
very least about the moral propriety of the laws in question. Perhaps it is
not surprising that Dworkin should encounter this dilemma. His theory
of adjudication is based on the concept of "constructive interpretation"[84]
which is to be understood as an explanation for the process of "law as
integrity". But this process does not operate independently of the
"dimension of fit". The quest is for the "right answer". And an answer is
"right" not only in the sense that it is morally the best justification of the
law, but also in that it "fits" in with "institutional history". The judge is
now an oracle for the values immanent in the legal system. Where these
values are not just, then in hard cases involving unjust laws, in Dworkin's
view, the judge must lie.[85] This is, of course, to place fidelity to justice
above fidelity to law. But to "be of any help" the judge would have to
institutionalize lying. Would a judge who did this survive? And, if he did,
would his competence, his integrity, not be called into question? Further,
even a lying judge may lend the system he deplores much-needed legitimacy. Resignation for all its problems may thus be the most justifiably
moral decision. But, it may be asked, why only judges? Should lawyers
too refuse to participate in a system they regard as morally unacceptable
or can a distinction be drawn between their roles? Like Wacks,[86] I think it
can. Lawyers are not state officials: they may have duties to the state but
their primary obligation is to their clients. Nor do they only work within
a court system. Those oppressed under an unjust system need the independent advice and protection that moral lawyers—and sometimes only
such lawyers—can offer.[87]

Those who espouse naturalism also see other attractions in natural law.
It is, D'Entrèves noted, part of the "unrelenting quest of man to rise
above the letter of the law to the realm of the spirit".[88] It is a useful
corrective to counteract the tendency to exaggerate the historical, fortuitous growth of law. It can explain why positive laws have obligatory
force, even when those laws cannot be deduced from natural law principles. It can give us insight into why laws are made, for, like other social

---

[82] *Taking Rights Seriously* (1977), p. 326.
[83] Note the appeal to consequentialism.
[84] This is discussed more fully, *post*, 721 *et seq.*
[85] And see also Wacks, *op. cit.*, n. 71, p. 275 (liberal judgments by liberal judges best
understood as lies.) *cf.* Dugard, *op. cit.*, n. 71, adopting a positivist account, who sees
such judges as calling upon the liberal principles of the common law rather than apply
unjust legislation. See also Mureinik in Corder (ed.), *Essays on Law and Social Practice in
South Africa* (1988), p. 210 who sees it rather as an example of constructive
interpretation.
[86] *Op. cit.*, n. 71.
[87] Brooks (1989) 6 J. Applied Phil. 31 argues that those who live in an unjust society have a
duty to mitigate the injustice so as to avoid being held responsible for it, and, if they are
being unjustly enriched, to compensate those deprived.
[88] D'Entrèves, *op. cit.*, n. 6, p. 127.

institutions, laws are only fully intelligible by reference to the values they ought to realise, such as justice and the public good.

Perhaps, though, the most compelling attraction of natural law for the student of jurisprudence is that, in exposing deficiencies in positivist thinking, it broadens the whole scope of the discipline. We must agree with Finnis that "a theorist cannot give a theoretical description and analysis of social facts, unless he also participates in the work of evaluation, of understanding what is really good for human persons, and what is really required by practical reasonableness".[89] Positivist jurisprudence, as we shall see, gives us both description and analysis of law as a social institution but it has tended, as Shklar notes,[90] to be legalistic, to assume a "discrete entity".[91] As she notes, and Finnis re-emphasises, "the subject-matter of the theorist's description does not come neatly, demarcated from other features of social life and practice".[92] The jurist's subject-matter is "law" but how does he decide what is to count as law for the purposes of his theory?

Neither Austin nor Bentham[93] shows much awareness of this problem. Each starts with a definition of law which is then taken as an unproblematic given.[94] Neither advances any justification for the definitions postulated, nor for their conceptions of jurisprudence, built, as so often is the case, on the backs of the definitions.[95] Kelsen is at least aware that function is intrinsic to the subject matter of law (he defines law as a specific "social technique"[96]) but he too gives no critical attention to the problem of justifying his definition of law. Thus, he asks what it is that unites disparate social orders and finds an answer in "law": "the word refers", he tells us, "to that specific social technique which ... is ... essentially the same ...".[97] By looking for the lowest common denominator, Kelsen is forced to employ an explanatory term to a series of situations even though participants in those disparate environments would not use the concepts or use them in the same way. To say, as he does, that a stateless society under a despotic chieftain and the Swiss republic both use the "social technique" of law is to assume a level of sophistication in the notional "primitive society" such that it is able to distinguish law from morality or custom or religion or might even be interested in so doing.

Both Hart and Raz have consciously abandoned this spurious quest for unity. They concentrate on central cases and build up a concept of law by appealing to the practical components of the concept. For Hart law is

---

[89] *Op. cit.*, n. 49, p. 14.
[90] *Ante*, 20.
[91] *ibid.*, p. 21.
[92] *Op. cit.*, n. 49, p. 4.
[93] *Post*, 273 and 291 respectively.
[94] Bentham's is on 273; Austin's on 291.
[95] *Cf.* Hart, *Essays in Jurisprudence and Philosophy* (1983), p. 21 and *post*, 375.
[96] *General Theory of Law and State*, p. 19. The law is an ordering "for the promotion of peace" (*ibid.*, p. 21).
[97] See discussion of this *post*, 332–333.

described in terms of rules *for* the guidance of officials and citizens[98]: for Raz it is a system of norms providing a method of settling disputes authoritatively.[99] But what is a central case? How are importance and significance to be assessed? Hart and Raz insist that a descriptive theorist in "deciding to attribute a central role"[1] to some feature must "reproduce"[2] a particular practical viewpoint, Hart gives explanatory priority to the concerns and evaluations of those with an "internal point of view".[3] Raz has shifted from the "ordinary man's point of view"[4] to "the legal point of view" (the view of those like judges who believe in the validity of norms and follow them).[5] There are central and peripheral cases of "the internal view" and "the legal point of law," but Hart and Raz seem unwilling to acknowledge this. They refuse "to attribute significance to differences that any actor in the field ... would count as practically significant".[6] It is not clear which viewpoints bring law, as opposed to some other form of social order, into existence. To Finnis the conclusion is clear.

> "If there is a point of view in which legal obligation is treated as at least presumptively a moral obligation, ... a viewpoint in which the establishment and maintenance of legal as distinct from discretionary or statistically customary order is regarded as a moral ideal if not a compelling demand of justice, then such a viewpoint will constitute the central case of the legal viewpoint. For only in such a viewpoint is it a matter of overriding importance that law as distinct from other forms of social order should come into being, and thus become an object of the theorists' description."[7]

To Finnis, the key is "practical reasonableness".[8] He argues that a theorist cannot identify "the central case of that practical viewpoint which he uses to identify the central case of his subject-matter, unless he decides what the requirements of practical reasonableness really are ... In relation to law, the most important things for the theorist to ... describe" are the things which in his judgement (for his values inevitably influence his selection of concepts to use in describing law) "make it important from a *practical* viewpoint to have law".[9] It follows that when these important things are missing or debased the theorist must explain what it is in the situations of such societies that causes absence or debasement. Finnis concludes that a theory of natural law distinguishes "the

---

[98] *The Concept of Law* (1994).
[99] *Practical Reason and Norms* (1975). See *post*, 391.
[1] *Per* J. Raz, *The Concept of a Legal System*, p. 200, n. 2.
[2] *Per* Hart, *The Concept of Law*, p. 88.
[3] *Post*, 379.
[4] *Per* J. Raz, *op. cit.*, n. 99.
[5] *Practical Reason and Norms*, p. 177.
[6] *Per* Finnis, *op. cit.*, n. 49, p. 13. *cf.* Kelsen's remark (*Pure Theory of Law*, p. 218) that even an anarchist, if he were a professor of law, could describe positive law as a system of valid norms.
[7] *Op. cit.*, n. 49, pp. 14–15.
[8] *ibid.*, p. 88 and Chap. V.
[9] *ibid.*, p. 16.

practically unreasonable from the practically reasonable",[10] It claims "to be able to identify conditions and principles of practical right-mindedness, of good and proper order among men and in individual conduct".[11] Whether it succeeds is considered later.[12]

## GREEK ORIGINS

If there are traces to be discerned of a conception of natural law among almost all peoples,[13] it is nevertheless to the Greeks that we must first look.[14] Whether the law of nature was first conceived as governing the cosmos and only later applied to man or society, or whether (as Kelsen contends) the idea of universal law was a projection of the law of the state into the physical universe, may well be disputed. Certainly the notion of divine retribution operating in human affairs tended to create confusion between natural law as a norm prescribing conduct and physical law compelling it, and Kelsen even suggests that it was not until Hume that the idea of causality as a norm directed at nature by the divine will was substantially abandoned.[15]

The Greeks themselves, though comparatively uninterested in the technical development of law, were much concerned in exploring its philosophical foundations, and in doing so evolved many fundamental concepts, of which natural law was one of the most important. In the classical period, however, little attention was paid to the idea of universal law, though it was current doctrine that there was in each city-state a body of law, fundamental and unchangeable and often unwritten, and which it was a usurpation to override, though the assembly might pass decrees changing the law in matters of less moment.[16] Plato, by his idealist philosophy, laid the foundations for much of subsequent speculation on natural law, but he had nothing to say on natural law as such. Indeed his *Republic* was based on the substitution for law of the philosopher-king, who could attain absolute justice by consulting the mystery locked in his own heart, which partook of the divine wisdom but remained

---

[10] *ibid.*, p. 18.

[11] *ibid.*

[12] *Post*, 126.

[13] See, *e.g.* as to China, J. Needham, *Science and Civilisation in China* (1956), vol. 2, Chap. 18, pp. 518 *et seq.*; and for Hebraic civilisation see H. Silving (1953) 28 N.Y.U.L. Rev. 1129, and Lloyd, *The Idea of Law* (1985), pp. 48–51. For the influence of Hebrew sources—particularly the Noahite Code—on Selden, see M. Crowe (1977) 12 *Natural Law Forum* 184.

[14] On the Greek contribution see L. Weinreb, *Natural Law and Justice* (1987), Chap. 1.

[15] Kelsen, *op. cit.*, pp. 314 *et seq.*

[16] See Aristotle, *Politics* (ed. E. Barker), pp. 127–128. The odium attached to legislative innovation is dramatically illustrated by the fact that the existing law had to be arranged in a prosecution and that among the Locrians, the "prosecutor" had to arraigned in a prosecution and that among the Locrians, the "prosecutor" had to appear with a halter round his neck, which was drawn tight if his proposal was rejected. *cf.* Ehrenberg, *The Greek State* (2nd ed., 1969), pp. 56–58.

uncommunicable to lesser mortals.[17] And even Aristotle, for whom nature played a cardinal role in the unfolding of man's social development, was so little interested in natural law in the form of normative rules that he contented himself with a passing reference to the distinction between natural and conventional justice, while immediately qualifying this by pointing out that, among men, even natural justice is not necessarily unchanging.[18]

It is with the decline of the city-state and the rise of large empires and kingdoms in the Greek world, associated with the conquests of Alexander, that natural law as a universal system comes to the fore, and for this the Stoic philosophers were particularly responsible. Until the Stoics "nature"[19] had meant "the order of things": with them it came to be identified with man's reason. When man lived according to "reason" he was living "naturally". To the Stoics precepts of reason had universal force. They stressed the ideas of individual worth, moral duty and universal brotherhood, and though in the early days theirs was a philosophy of withdrawal enjoining conformity to the universal law upon the select few of wise men alone, in its later development, stress was placed on its universal aspects as laying down a law not only for the wise, but for all men.

## Jus Gentium

It was in this form, especially through the Greek-loving Scipionic circle, that Stoicism passed over to and influenced Roman thought. The best representative of this thinking is the Roman orator, Cicero.[20] His definition of natural (true) law as "right reason in agreement with nature" has been enormously influential. Cicero was the first natural lawyer to contend for the striking down of positive laws which contravened natural law. A legislature, he said, which said that theft or forgery of wills or adultery was lawful would no more be making law than what a band of robbers might pass in their assembly. It is not clear whether the standards were natural because they derived from human nature, because our natural human reason could lead us to them, or because they were to be found in the physical world about us (or a combination of the three)—a recurrent ambiguity. But the more pragmatic mind of the Roman jurist was little interested in "higher law" and regarded it as more suitable for oratorical rhetoric. The opening sentence of Gaius's *Institutes* (A.D. 160)

---

[17] On which see C. Bobonich (2007) 24(2) *Social Philosophy and Policy* 153.
[18] See *Ethics*, 1134b. On nature in Aristotle see R. Kraut (2007) 24(2) *Social Philosophy and Policy* 199.
[19] For the different meanings of this for the Stoics, see Finnis, *op. cit.*, pp. 374–377.
[20] See *post*, 137 and see Weinreb, *op. cit.*, n. 12, p. 39–41, and H. Arkes in (ed.) R. George, *Natural Law Theory* (1992), Chap. 9.

may be regarded in this light,[21] as can Ulpian's "what nature has taught all animals",[22] though the latter was taken at face-value by Aquinas, and vestiges plague even contemporary polemics.[23]

But conquest and commerce necessitated the development of law which could be applied to foreigners, *peregrini*. *Jus Gentium*, the *jus civile* stripped of formalities and with cosmopolitan trimmings, was the result.[24] Against the intellectual background of stoicism, the Roman jurists can be forgiven the fact that they confused the law they applied universally with the law of nature which stoicism had taught was of universal validity. In truth, this was but an early example of the "naturalistic fallacy",[25] a confusion of "is" and "ought", of what Jolowicz called "practical" and "theoretical" *jus gentium*.[26]

## MEDIEVAL PERIOD

Throughout the Middle Ages, the theology of the Catholic Church set the tone and pattern of all speculative thought. As Gierke has pointed out, two vital principles animated medieval thought: *unity*, derived from God, and involving one faith, one Church, and one empire, and the *supremacy of law*, not merely man-made, but conceived as part of the unity of the universe.[27] Yet, until Aquinas in the thirteenth century, Christian thought[28] was also bedevilled by the notion of law and human dominion being rooted in sin. It was not the least of Aquinas's contributions that, in his synthesis of Aristotelian philosophy and Catholic faith in a universal divine law, he rejected the idea that civil government was necessarily tainted with original sin and argued for the existence of a hierarchy of law

---

[21] *Viz.* "That law which a people establishes for itself is peculiar to it, and is called *jus civile* (civil law) as being the special law of that *civitas* (state), while the law that natural reason establishes among all mankind is followed by all peoples alike, and is called *jus gentium* (law of nations, or law of the world) as being the law observed by all mankind", as translated by De Zulueta, *The Institutes of Gaius*, Pt 1. For the relationship between natural law and Roman law see J. Kroger (2004) Wisconsin L.R. 905.

[22] See Justinian's *Institutes*, 1, 2. This definition is thought to have been Ulpian's until its incorporation in the *Digest* (see Weinreb, p. 45). On the history of Ulpian's remarks see M. Crowe, *The Changing Profile of Natural Law* (1977), pp. 43–51, 142–55.

[23] See, for example, the Papal Encyclical, *Humanae Vitae* in Harris *et al.*, *On Human Life* (1968).

[24] But this is not the sole origin. According to F.S.C. Northrop, *The Complexity of Ethical and Legal Experience* (1959): "it finds its basis ... in a novel scientific way of thinking about ... practical transactions and disputes" (p. 219).

[25] *Ante*, 12–13.

[26] *Historical Introduction to Roman Law* (3rd ed., 1972), pp. 102–107. A good example of this is Gaius's definition in n. 19. The institution of slavery demonstrated the confusion but it was a sensing that slavery was contrary to the *jus naturale* that went some way towards mitigating the lot of the Roman slave, D'Entrèves, *Natural Law*, provides a glowing account of natural law in Roman writings and a panegyric of its heritage. See Chap. 1. The distinction and confusion dogged later thinking, for example that of Vitoria (1485–1546) and Suàrez (1548–1617) (see Q. Skinner, *The Foundations of Modern Political Thought*, (1978), vol. 2, Chap. 5, particularly pp. 151–154).

[27] *Political Theories of the Middle Ages* (ed. Maitland), pp. 9 *et seq.* and 73 *et seq.*

[28] See, for example, Chap. 5 of St Augustine's *Civitas Dei*.

derived ultimately from God, and in which human or positive law had a rightful though lowly place and was worthy for its own sake.[29]

Aquinas (1224–1274)[30] is in many senses the "paradigm 'natural law theorist' and dominates the period from the church fathers to Kant".[31] He divides law into four categories, though the concept as a whole is unified. The *lex aeterna* is divine reason, known only to God and "the blessed who see God in his essence". It is God's plan for the universe, a deliberate act of God and everything, not only man, is subject to it. The *lex aeterna* is necessary since man is ordained to a particular end (eternal happiness) and cannot attain this through his own powers alone but needs guidance and direction. The *lex divina* is the law of God revealed in the Scriptures. The *lex naturalis* consists of participation of the eternal law in rational creatures.[32] It is thus the eternal law in so far as this is intuitively and innately known and knowable. Natural law is the same for all men since all are rational and "it is proper for man to be inclined to act according to reason". This only applies to the general or primary principles of natural law. As far as the detailed working out of the principles is concerned, it is the same only for the majority of cases. Aquinas conceded that the will to do right and awareness of what is right may be distorted by habit, custom or temperament.

Aquinas believed that natural law could be added to, though, as far as first principles were concerned, not subtracted from. Secondary precepts, however, could be changed in rare cases. This does raise considerable problems. First, it is not clear which precepts are primary and which secondary. Nor is it clear how the secondary principles are derived from the primary ones. There may be only one primary precept: "good is to be done and evil to be avoided". But what is "good" and what "evil"? According to neo-scholastic interpreters, "good" refers to those actions that conform to properly human ends, and "evil" to those actions that fail so to conform. This view has, however, been challenged by Grisez. "Good", as he understands Aquinas, refers not only to what is morally good, but to whatever within human power can be understood as "intelligibly worthwhile", and "evil" to "any privation of intelligible goods". How can change in secondary precepts be explained? It cannot be that human nature changes so that obligations change also. Aquinas admits that human law, which derives its validity from natural law, changes with human circumstances and human reason. Attitudes to usury are an example. Aquinas proscribed this as contrary to natural law but Cardinal Cajetan, a sixteenth-century commentator on Aquinas, had no difficulty in abandoning this doctrine.[33] The growth of commerce and

---

[29] See T. Gilby, *Principality and Polity*, pp. 146 *et seq.*

[30] A useful introduction to Aquinas is A-H. Chroust (1974) 19 Am. J. Jurisp. 1. See also G. Grisez (1965) 10 *Natural Law Forum* 168, and A. Lisska, *Aquinas's Theory of Natural Law* (1996).

[31] *Per* Finnis, *op. cit.*, p. 28. For a somewhat controversial view of Aquinas (seen in Darwinian terms) see L. Arnhart (2001) 18(1) *Social Philosophy and Policy* 1.

[32] This is explained and expanded upon by Finnis, *op. cit.*, pp. 398–403.

[33] See O'Connor, *Aquinas and Natural Law* (1967), p. 78.

industry and the need for investment justified the change. But may not other natural law doctrines by similarly interpreted? Can the "bellum justum" doctrine, as formulated in St. Augustine and expounded by Aquinas, survive the growth of nuclear weapons?[34] (It was under attack already in the early sixteenth century from humanists such as Erasmus and More).[35] Can the ban on contraception, explicitly restated in the Papal Encyclical *Humanae Vitae* in 1968, be defended in a world plagued by over-population and challenged by the changed status of women?[36]

There is finally the *lex humana* or positive law. This derives its validity from secondary natural law but "it is not a mere emanation from or copy of natural law".[37] It is necessary for two reasons. First, natural law does not provide all or even most of the solutions to everyday life in society. Secondly, there is "need for compulsion, to force selfish people to act reasonably".[38] Human laws are either just or unjust. To be just a positive law must be virtuous, necessary, useful, clear and for the common good. Slavery is thus justified.[39] Unjust laws are a perversion of law and do not bind man's moral conscience. If contrary to divine will, for example laws commanding idolatry, man is released from obedience ("We ought to obey God rather than men"). With other unjust laws obedience is recommended to avoid scandal. Man is to "yield his right of rebellion," though such a law clearly does not bind his conscience. It is difficult to distinguish these classes of unjust law. One defence of Aquinas would argue that "perversion of law" does not mean that the law is not law, but rather not law in its fullest sense.[40] Aquinas also distinguishes between the positive laws of particular societies and the *jus gentium*. He implied that where a law was common to all societies this fact itself supplied its moral underpinning. The *jus gentium* was thus analogous to the natural law, though separate from it. It was also more fundamental than ordinary positive laws. One of the consequences of this was that Aquinas was able to endow certain common institutions like private property with a special sanctity.

The difference between practice and theory was never more manifest

---

[34] On the idea of the just war see J.T. Johnson (2006) 23 *Social Philosophy and Policy* 167 and A. Buchanan (2006) 34 *Phil and Public Affairs* 2.

[35] See R.P. Adams, *The Better Part of Valor: More, Erasmus, Colet and Vives on Humanism, War and Peace 1496–1535* (1962). For the view that natural law, as a result of this and other developments, requires the development of a world government see George, *In Defense of Natural Law* (1999).

[36] See P. Harris, *On Human Life* (1968). The new natural law of Grisez, Finnis, Boyle and George has no difficulty in defending the outlawing of contraception. It puts con-tracepted sex on a moral plane with sodomitical acts.

[37] *Per* Finnis, *op. cit.*, p. 28.

[38] *ibid.*, p. 29.

[39] As it was by Aristotle. So is private property: on this see McLaren, *Private Property and the Natural Law* (1948) (Aquinas Papers No. 8). On later developments see Q. Skinner, *op. cit.*, vol. 2, pp. 152–154.

[40] This is Finnis's argument and see also B. Bix, "Natural Law Theory" in D. Patterson, *A Companion to Philosophy of Law and Legal Theory* (1996), pp. 223, 226. In Murphy's view, Aquinas sees unjust laws as "defective" (2003) 9 *Legal Theory* 241, 243–254. On unjust laws see also N. Kretzmann (1988) 33 Am J. Jurisprudence 99.

than in the medieval period, with its high-sounding moral doctrine combined with barbarous usages and strong-arm justice.

## RENAISSANCE, REFORMATION AND COUNTER-REFORMATION

The Renaissance[41] led to an emphasis on the individual and free will and human liberty and a rejection of the universal collective society of medieval Europe in favour of independent national states, and, where the Reformation followed, separate national Churches.[42] Thought begins to take a secular cast, as exemplified by Machiavelli,[43] who examined human institutions without regard for divine prescriptions, and in the light of naked expediency.

The sixteenth century also saw the revival of Thomism, a revival of crucial importance for the development of the modern natural law theory of the state. The central figures in this were Vitoria[44] and Suàrez. They reacted against what they saw as the heresies of Lutheranism.[45] As Suàrez put it, the error which above all needed to be extirpated was "the blasphemous suggestion of Luther" that it is impossible even for a just man to follow the law of God.[46]

They took their thinking about law and society from Aquinas though there are significant developments. Our knowledge of the principles of natural justice was said to be wholly independent of any knowledge of revelation. It was not possible to neglect the law of nature since "all men from the beginning of creation have in fact been subject to it.[47] The Jesuit Bellarmine (1542–1611) even anticipates Grotius's formulation when he states that "even if *per impossibile* man were not God's creation", he would still be able to interpret natural law, since "he would still be a rational creature",[48] Aquinas's distinction between natural law, the *jus gentium* and positive law,[49] though initially accepted by sixteenth-century Thomists such as Vitoria, was subsequently rejected. Thus Suàrez believed that the *ius gentium* differed in an "absolute" sense from natural

---

[41] For a valuable discussion of political thought in the Renaissance see Q. Skinner, *The Foundations of Modern Political Thought* (1978), vol. 1. He emphasises the remarkable extent to which the vocabulary of Renaissance moral and political thought was derived from Roman Stoic sources.

[42] The Lutheran vision of man's relationship with God undermined any attempt to base political thinking on the foundations of natural law.

[43] An excellent introduction to whose thought, placed in its historical context, is Q. Skinner, *Machiavelli* (1981). *The Prince* is discussed in Chap. 2, where the essential break with other humanist thought is succinctly explained.

[44] On whom see J.A. Fernandez-Santamaria, *The State, War and Peace: Spanish Political Thought in the Renaissance 1516–1559* (1977).

[45] See Q. Skinner, *op. cit.,* vol. 2, Chap. 1.

[46] Quoted *ibid.,* p. 139.

[47] Quoted *ibid.,* p. 151.

[48] Quoted *ibid.*

[49] *Ante,* 100.

law and was "straightforwardly a case of human positive law".[50] It followed that private property, justified as part of the law of nature in Thomist theory,[51] had no further basis than the laws men had made for themselves—an awkward conclusion. Locke was later to escape from this dilemma by arguing that the right to hold property was a right of nature,[52] not a mere privilege from positive law. Suàrez purported to do so by reverting to a distinction in Aquinas between "positive" and "negative" injunctions of the law of nature. This enabled him to suggest that whilst communal property-holding is an injunction of the law of nature, it is only a negative injunction reminding us that "all property would be held in common by the force of this law if it had not happened that men decided to introduce a different system".[53] He was thus able to argue that natural law could be used to sanction either the continuation or abolition of communal ownership and to adopt the view that the division of property was one left for men to decide for themselves. This was a conclusion to which Grotius also came.

There is another link with Grotius for, once it was accepted that the *jus gentium* was an aspect of positive law, it was but a short step to the suggestion that it ought to be formulated into a code of law to govern relationships between nations.[54] The concept of international law is at least implicit in the writing of Vitoria,[55] though it is to Grotius (1583–1645) that the development of this is usually attributed.[56]

The social contract ideologies that we associate with Hobbes, Locke and Rousseau[57] can also be traced to sixteenth-century Thomist thought.[58] The concept of consent[59] was invoked to explain how it is possible for a free individual to become the subject of a legitimate state. Suàrez was the first to give attention to the problem of how the idea of political authority could be brought into existence by a general act of consent performed by men in a state of nature. His answer was that people were able to conceive of themselves as a *universitas* and so participate univocally in corporate legal acts. This answer may be thought to rest on the same fictions as the idea of social contract itself. It is, however, significant that the problem was being perceived: neither Hobbes nor Locke really grasps the nettle at all.[60]

Another question to which Counter-Reformation Thomist thinkers devoted their attention was that as to whether the commands of a human sovereign were always binding. The Lutherans had insisted that the

---

[50] Quoted by Skinner, *op. cit.*, p. 153.
[51] See further Finnis, *op. cit.*, pp. 169–173.
[52] See *post*, 148.
[53] Quoted by Skinner, *op. cit.*, pp. 153–154.
[54] C. Barcia Trelles, "Suàrez" in (1933) *43 Receuil des Cours*, pp. 458–462.
[55] See J.B. Scott, *The Spanish Origin of International Law* (1934) who hails Vitoria as the "creator" of international law (p. 98).
[56] *Post*, 105.
[57] *Post*, 111.
[58] See R. Tuck, *Natural Rights Theories* (1979).
[59] On consent see J. Dunn (1967) 10 *Historical Journal* 153.
[60] See further, O. von Gierke, *Political Theories of The Middle Ages* (1900), pp. 67–73.

commands of an ungodly ruler could never be binding in a court of conscience. The Thomists' response was that it was not possible for anything to be a precept of the civil law "which is not a precept of the law of nature".[61] In their terms this meant that someone who claimed the right to disobey the commands of a legitimate ruler was also claiming to be able to set aside natural law, and this was not merely a dictate of right reason but also an expression of the will of God; this meant, as Bellarmine explained, that "anyone who sets aside either the natural, the positive, the divine or the human law must in every case be sinning against the eternal law of God."[62]

If this shows natural law as a defender of the *status quo*, it should be pointed out that these same thinkers were upholding the rights of Indians of the New World against the depredations of the Conquistadores. Champions of the Spanish conquests such as Sepulveda (1490–1573) argued that since Indians possessed no knowledge of Christianity they could not be said to be living a life of genuine "political liberty and human dignity".[63] Their status was the Aristotelian category of "slaves by nature", and it was accordingly proper to see Spanish conquests as a just war against infidels. Vitoria's response, derived from Aquinas, is that there is an equal capacity in all men, Christians or not, to establish their own political societies. This the Indians had done. He is led to the conclusion that "even if the Christian faith has been announced to the barbarians with complete and sufficient arguments, and they have still refused to receive it, this does not supply a reason for making war on them and despoiling them of their goods".[64] Even in the sixteenth century men were prepared to stand up against powerful régimes using natural law thinking as their main weapon.[65] At the same time it was used, together with the more popular though not in itself novel[66] theory of the social contract, either to bolster up,[67] or in some cases to restrain,[68] the new-found weapon in the lawyers' and politicians' armoury of legal sovereignty.

---

[61] *Per* Suàrez, quoted in Skinner, *op. cit.*, pp. 167–168.

[62] Quoted *ibid.*, p. 168.

[63] *Per* L. Hanke, *The Spanish Struggle For Justice In The Conquest of America* (1949), p. 132.

[64] Quoted by Skinner, *op. cit.*, pp. 169–170.

[65] *Cf.* A. D'Entrèves, *Natural Law* (1970).

[66] This idea can be traced at least as far back as the Greek Sophists; see *per* Glaucon in Plato's *Republic*, Bk. II. Silving, *op. cit.* sees the seeds of social contract in God's covenant with man as reported in the Old Testament. On social contract theories, generally, see Gough, *The Social Contract* (1957) and Barker's Introduction to the World Classics edition of *The Social Contract* (1947). For a contemporary example, see J. Rawls, *A Theory of Justice, post*, 524.

[67] As in Hobbes.

[68] As in Locke, whose doctrine of natural rights were later embodied in the United States Declaration of Independence and Constitution.

GROTIUS AND INTERNATIONAL LAW

The secularisation of natural law is usually held to begin with Grotius. He is said to have inaugurated a new, modern era in natural law thinking by his assertion that natural law would subsist even if God did not exist (*etiamsi daremus non esse Deum*).[69] But, as we have seen, this was anticipated by Bellarmine in the previous century and possibly by others even earlier.[70] Finnis believes that the "standard reading" of Grotius is misconceived. He argues that what Grotius is claiming is that what is right and wrong depends on the nature of things, and not on a decree of God, but the normative significance of moral rightness depends fundamentally upon there being a decree expressing God's will that the right be done. Grotius is not expelling God from his doctrine of natural law. He is saying that "due and undue acts are therefore understood to be necessarily enjoined or forbidden by God", though they would remain due or undue, even if there were no such divine decrees.[71] The significance of Grotius's thought is in a shift of emphasis towards the natural reason of man.

Grotius's main concern was to establish a system of international law to regulate the affairs and warfare of the rising nation states.[72] A precondition of such a system is stable, orderly government within nations. He saw government as resting on social contract, the people surrendering their freedom for security. Having done this, Grotius advocates that they should lack the right of repudiating the sovereign, however unjust the laws he makes. It is not easy to reconcile this prescription for stability with the precepts of natural law he advocates. It is further complicated by Grotius's argument that sovereigns are bound by natural law. It is as if Grotius's own reasoning has to give in to utilitarian demands of expediency. Though the progenitor of his political theory, natural law ends up with a subsidiary role as its details are worked out.

NATURAL LAW AND THE SOCIAL CONTRACT

The "social contract" is a wholly formal and analytic construct that can be used as a means of presenting conflicting political ideals.[73] In Hobbes (or Bodin or Grotius) it is used in defence of absolutism: in Locke in support of limited constitutionalism. Though explicitly rejected by Hume

---

[69] *De Jure Belli ac Pacis*, Prolegomena, para. 11.

[70] See also Finnis, *op. cit.*, p. 43. The origins are traced by M. B. Crowe (1976) 38 *Tijdschrift Joor Filoscofie* 379.

[71] *Op. cit.*, pp. 43–44. Further Grotius makes the point that natural law cannot be altered even by God. "He cannot cause that which is intrinsically evil be not evil."

[72] K. Haakonssen, *Grotius, Pufendorf and Modern Natural Law* (1999) is an excellent compendium of materials.

[73] See J. Plamenatz, *Man and Society* (1963), vol. 1, pp. 163–164.

and Bentham, many liberal theorists[74] continue to emphasise it either in terms of consent theory or, as in Rawls's theory of justice,[75] as something close to traditional notions of social contract. At root the political theory is that "no man can be subjected to the political power of another without his own consent",[76] Obedience to authority is thus legitimated by voluntary submission to those who exercise authority. But what individuals have consented to differs radically according to the particular values of the contract theorist.

To Thomas Hobbes (1588–1679) the state of nature in which man lived before the social contract was "a war of every Man against every Man",[77] a condition of internecine strife in which the life of man was "solitary, poor, nasty, brutish and short".[78] Self-preservation is the great lesson of natural law. Law and government thus become necessary as a means of promoting order and personal security. For each citizen to preserve his own life, he must give absolute and unconditional obedience to the law. The social contract is thus used by Hobbes, as it was by Grotius, to justify authoritarian government. Hobbes's own goal was to rule out the legitimacy of civil rebellion and thus to eliminate the possibility of civil war, which he regarded as the greatest of evils. Hobbes informs us that we should infer the characteristics of political obligation from "the *intention* of him that submitteth himself to his power, which is to be understood by the *end* for which he so submitteth".[79] His theory of political obligation is thus derived from a consideration of "the end of the institution of sovereignty, namely, the peace of the subjects within themselves, and their defence against a common enemy."[80] Natural law does not loom large in Hobbes's commonwealth.[81] Its importance lies in the fact that he expressed the main precept of natural law in terms of man's right to self-preservation. Earlier[82] natural law thinkers had seen the natural law in terms of duties imposed on man, a pattern to which he had to conform. In Hobbes's there is the germ of a concept of natural rights, the idea that man may make certain legitimate demands on his fellow men.

The use of a social contract to construct a natural rights doctrine is

---

[74] For example, J. Plamenatz, *Consent, Freedom and Political Organisation* (2nd ed., 1968); M. Walzer, *Obligations* (1970).

[75] *Post*, 583.

[76] *Per* Locke, *Two Treatises of Government*, vol. 2, s. 95.

[77] *Leviathan*, Pt 1, Chap. 13. For a similar notion today, see M. Foucault, *Power/Knowledge* (1980), pp. 97–98.

[78] But less frightening and less anarchic than that described by contemporaries such as Digges, Taylor or Chief Justice Vaughan. See Tuck, *op. cit.*, p. 125.

[79] *Leviathan*, Pt 2, Chap. 21.

[80] *ibid.*

[81] Hobbes' views changed in the course of his writings. There is a good account of these changes and Hobbes's relationship to contemporary writers in Tuck, *op. cit.*, Chap. 6 and see M. Murphy (1995) 105 Ethics 846.

[82] That is those of the Renaissance and Reformation period. There were natural rights theories in the fourteenth century (see Tuck, *op. cit.*, Chap. 1). It was humanism with its contempt for untutored nature that made it impossible for humanist lawyers to talk of natural rights. Nor were Calvinists interested in natural rights: their theories of resistance were not linked to natural law (see further Tuck, Chap. 2).

articulated most fully in the writings of John Locke (1632–1704).[83] To Locke the state of nature that preceded the social contract was not, as conceived by Hobbes, one of brutal horror, but rather a golden age, an Eden before the Fall. One thing was lacking in this near-paradise: property was insecure. According to Locke, it was to remedy this that man renounced his otherwise idyllic natural condition and by contract gave up part of his liberty to a sovereign. The purpose of government was the protection of human entitlements. In his later writings[84] he developed a theory of political authority which countenanced resistance to unjust authority.

In his early writings Locke distinguished the ruler and the ruled. The ruled were beasts who needed taming.[85] But in *Two Treatises of Government* this gulf has disappeared. The ruler is just as likely as his subjects, to enter upon "force, the way of Beasts".[86] The opposite of force is reason. It is this that distinguishes man from beast and it is the way of reason that God wills men to follow. It is through exercising reason that men can and should know what God wills them to do. Reason further supplies the answers where God's will is not clear. All humans (though not children[87] or the mentally ill) have reason and are equal. As such they confront each other in a state of nature. God's requirement for all men in a state of nature is that they live according to the law of nature. Reason enables every man to grasp the content of this law. But how were men to acquire this knowledge? How could they distinguish the law of nature from the conventions, the prejudices, of their own societies? As will be apparent Locke did not find the secular natural law of Hobbes attractive. His answers were accordingly couched, as in natural law thinking of earlier centuries, in terms of a Deity. Knowledge of natural law was accordingly compulsive, "writ in the hearts of all mankind".[88] Man was fully instructed by God on how he ought to live. This goes some way towards explaining the seemingly different opinions in Hobbes and Locke on what the state of nature is. Hobbes told us how he thought men would behave in a state of nature: Locke what rights and duties men have as creatures of God in a pre-civil society.[89]

In the state of nature man's duties under natural law are matched by

[83] An excellent introduction to the thought of whom is J. Dunn, *Locke* (1984). See also K. M. McClure, *Judging Rights* (1996).

[84] *Two Treatises of Government*, completed by 1683. In his earlier writings (*Two Tracts on Government* (1660) and *Essay on Toleration* (1667)) he had argued that the subject should obey the unjust commands of the sovereign passively to recognise the authority from which they had come, though not to endorse their justice. See also J. Dunn, *The Political Thought of John Locke* (1969), p. 49: "the law of God forbids disturbance or dissolution of governments" (written in 1676).

[85] *Two Tracts on Government* (ed. P. Abrams, 1967), p. 158.

[86] *Two Treatises on Government* (ed. P. Laslett, 1967), II, p. 181.

[87] There are, however, muted hints of children's rights in Locke. See M. D. A. Freeman, *The Rights and Wrongs of Children* (1983), pp. 53–54.

[88] Quoted by J. Dunn, *op. cit.*, n. 83, p. 30. See also J. Dunn, *op. cit.*, n. 84, pp. 95–97, 187–202. Many of Locke's ideas reiterate the central assumptions of 16th-century Thomist thought.

[89] As explained *ibid.*, pp. 46–47.

his rights under that same law. The most important of these is the right to hold other men responsible for breaches of this law. Any man could do this but, by joining civil society, he abandoned these powers to the sovereign.[90] It was the massive increase in coercive power and the dangers of abuse of this power that particularly concerned Locke. But he had to explain first the "contract" by which men gave others political authority over them. This raised two problems. First, could it be shown that such contracts were historically-based (both generally and in the specific English context)? Although there were "states" of nature in Locke's time[91] and the foundation of political societies could be observed, Locke evaded this problem. This remains a stumbling-block to contractarian theories still.[92]

Secondly, how could it be shown that every adult member of a legitimate political society could reasonably be supposed to have consented to its political sovereign? Locke distinguished two kinds of consent, express consent and "tacit and scarce avoidable consent".[93] The latter involves "no Expressions of it at all"[94] but which nevertheless is as morally binding as express acts of consent.[95] Locke claims that individuals tacitly consent to obey the law by their mere presence within the territorial confines of a society, since to be within a society means taking advantage of the benefits derived from the actions of a political sovereign. Express consent made a man a full member of his society: tacit consent made him subject to the laws of the country but did not give him either full membership of the society or the rights, above all rights of political choice, which followed from such membership. Express consent would explain why a sovereign had political authority but it overlooked the fact that few, if any, Englishmen in Locke's day (or any other) had made an express undertaking at adulthood. Tacit consent is a useful construct for demanding obedience to the law by those present in a society but the line between express and tacit consent is not easy to draw so that Locke leaves us with a hazy notion as to who has full rights of membership in a society.

Locke wrote *Two Treatises* to proclaim a right of revolution but he was not an enemy of political authority. He saw it as a human good. Rulers had the right to rule, to use their political power for the public good. But

---

[90] On Locke and the right to punish, see Simmons (1991) 20 Phil. and Public Affairs 311.
[91] Most obviously in America.
[92] As with Rawls's original position, *post*, 637.
[93] *Op. cit.*, n. 86, II, p. 360.
[94] *ibid.*, II, p. 392.
[95] On "tacit consent" see J. Dunn, "Consent In the Political Theory of John Locke" in (1967) 10 *Historical Journal* 153; M. Seliger, *The Liberal Politics of John Locke* (1969), pp. 267–293 and D-H. Ruben, (1972) 83 *Ethics* 71. Bentham thought Locke's theory of "tacit consent" was nothing other than a doctrine of "virtual consent" and since Locke accepted a restircted and undemocratic suffrage (as to which see J. Steinberg, *Locke, Rousseau and the Idea of Consent* (1978)) became a doctrine of "virtual representation" (A. Gewirth, "Political Justice" in R. B. Brandt, *Social Justice* (1962)).

all men had the right to resist the ruler, even of a legitimate political society, where he manifestly abuses his power. Central to Locke's conception of government was the idea of trust.[96] There is a conceptual shift involved here from contract to fiduciary relationship. Whereas the concept of contract emphasises the conduct of individual citizens, that of trust stresses the conduct of the rulers.[97] Men put their trust in the sovereign. A ruler who betrays this trust may be overthrown. He puts himself into a state of war with his subjects and each of these has the same right to resist him as any other unjust aggressor. As Dunn notes: "In the England of Locke's day this was a very extreme doctrine."[98] Locke, not surprisingly, therefore, played down its practical implications. Only "a long train of Actings",[99] a clear threat to the estates, liberties and lives of the majority will justify resistance.[1] And Locke was in no doubt who was responsible for resistance. To disturb government was, for Locke, a breach of the law of nature: to rebel without just cause was thus in itself unjust. "But when the oppressed people resist tyranny it is not they who disturb government or bring back the state of war. Rebellion is an 'Opposition, not to Persons, but Authority'. A tyrant has no authority. It is tyrants who are the true rebels."[2] Tyrants were like "Beasts", "noxious brutes",[3] and the right to destroy such vermin was the right of every human being.[4] However, revolution, for Locke, is not to be seen as an "act of revenge": rather an "act of restoration, of the recreation of a violated political order".[5]

We have seen that man gave up his liberty to secure his property. Property thus for Locke ante-dated civil society and was not a creation of it.[6] Locke's theory of property is at once his most influential and controversial contribution to jurisprudence.[7] Some[8] have seen in it an explanation of the moral legitimacy of capitalist production, though the fact that Locke believed in rights more basic than property, such as the

---

[96] As to which see J. W. Gough, *John Locke's Political Philosophy: Eight Studies* (1950), p. 136 and P. Laslett's Introduction to *op. cit.*, n. 82, pp. 126–130. Men, Locke said, *"live upon trusts". The Correspondence of John Locke* (ed. E. S. de Beer, 1976), vol. 1, p. 123.

[97] Locke was not the first to use the trust concept. An earlier example is found in the *Observations* of Henry Parker in 1642. See the discussion of this in Tuck, *op. cit.*, n. 66, p. 146.

[98] *Per* J. Dunn, *op. cit.*, n. 88, p. 55.

[99] *Op. cit.*, n. 86, II, p. 220.

[1] *ibid.*, II, p. 209.

[2] *Per* J. Dunn, *op. cit.*, n. 83, p. 55, quoting *Two Treatises of Government*, II, p. 226.

[3] Laslett, *op. cit.*, n. 86, II, p. 172.

[4] An early example of justification of tyrannicide for breach of social compact is the thought of the Humanist jurist, Mario Salamonio writing in 1530 (see Tuck, *op. cit.*, n. 58, p. 35 and Skinner, *op. cit.*, vol. 1, pp. 148–152.

[5] *Per* J. Dunn, *op. cit.*, n. 83, pp. 55–56.

[6] *Cf.* Pashukanis's idea (*post*, 1158–1159), that property existed prior to law.

[7] It is also apparently that part of his work which Locke esteemed most (*Two Treatises of Government*, I, p. 15). On Locke and property see P. Rahe (2005) 22 *Social Philosophy and Policy* 1

[8] Notably C.B. Macpherson, *The Political Theory of Possessive Individualism* (1962).

right to physical subsistence, has caused others[9] to doubt this. The subtlety of Locke's explanation of property lies in its synthesis of notions of
common property and private rights. He accepts it as a truth both of
human reason and revelation that the earth belongs to God, who has
given it to human beings in common for them to enjoy it.[10] He dismisses
the idea that there could be any right of private property (God has given
the whole earth to "Adam and his Heirs in Succession") but justifies
private right to common heritage through the concept of labour. Labour
belongs to the labourer, and, by mixing his labour with material objects,
he acquires the right to what he has worked on. The "Condition of
Human Life, which requires Labour and Materials to work on, necessarily introduces private *Possessions*".[11] In Locke's terms it was important that it was God, and not a sovereign, who had given men a title to
the fruits of their labour. Locke's ruler thus was under a duty to use his
powers to protect rights which God himself had bestowed on mankind.
Locke was thus able to refute claims, such as those that Charles I had
made,[12] that rulers could dispose of their subjects' property without their
consent for the public good. The implications of this thesis are indeed
profound. Locke himself defended the notion of "no taxation without
representation" which figured so prominently in the American colonists'
complaints nearly a century later.[13] The American constitution went on to
embody Lockean ideas about the protection of life, liberty and
property.[14]

Locke's ideas about property are, however, more complex and
sophisticated than this brief summary indicates. At the initial stage of
human history property right was uncontentious. As Locke noted, there
"could then be no reason of quarrelling about Title, nor any doubt about
the largeness of Possession it gave. Right and conveniency went together;
for as a Man had a right to all he could employ his Labour upon, so he
had no temptation to labour for more than he could make use of."[15] But
the invention of money changed all that. It increased the inequality of
possessions made possible by the "different degrees of Industry"[16] which
men display. In Locke's view, it made it possible for a man to "possess

---

[9] In particular J. Dunn, *op. cit.*, n. 95, and J. Tully, *A Discourse on Property* (1980).
[10] Laslett, *op. cit.*, n. 86, II, pp. 6, 25, 31.
[11] *ibid.*, II, p. 35.
[12] And Filmer for one defended. The jumping-off point for Locke is an attack on Filmer's
ultra-royalist tract, *Patriarcha*.
[13] But Locke is not proposing a democratic legislature. He favours only limited representation as a means of limiting the legitimate exercise of royal authority. For the view
that "Locke's use of consent theory is little more than a demand for the restoration of the
medieval practice of the shared exercise of political power and authority" see J. Steinberg, *op. cit.*, n. 95. Unsurprisingly, Locke defended the franchise resting on ownership of
property.
[14] See W. Hamilton (1932) 41 Yale L.J. 864; J. Grant (1931) 31 Col. L.R. 56. P. Maier,
*American Scripture* (1997) 123–143, 160–170.
[15] Laslett, *op. cit.*, n. 86, II, p. 51. More pithily: "In the beginning all the World was
America" (II, p. 49) see further A. John Simmons (1994) 11 (2) *Social Philosophy and
Policy* 63.
[16] *ibid.*, II, p. 48.

more than he can use the product of".[17] He saw labour as an uncontentious good: it increased the value of a thing.[18] But as Dunn points out, "the role of money was altogether more ambiguous".[19] Money meant that "right and conveniency no longer went together. The entire social and economic order of seventeenth-century England rested upon a human institution about whose moral status Locke felt deeply ambivalent."[20] Taking away the produce of a man's labour was not justifiable but Locke had less qualms about taking away profits of speculation or property which had reached its present owner through royal favouritism to a distant ancestor though, as Dunn thinks, "there is no reason to believe that he would have *felt* any less disapproval in their case than in the former".[21] Not surprisingly, there is ambiguity here.

However, to see Locke as an apologist for commercial capitalism does not altogether fit with his espousal of, what we today might call, welfare rights. Like Aquinas he defended the right to physical subsistence even where it undermined property rights. He argued that if a man insisted on the market price for a man dying of hunger and caused his death by so doing, he was guilty of murder.[22] He believed that those who laboured had the right in their old age to a decent standard of living. He even argued that charity gave every man a title "to so much out of another's Plenty, as will keep him from extream want" for "God requires him to afford to the wants of his Brother".[23] These rights hinged upon God's gift of the world to men in common. The idea, Dunn notes, that "subsequent human conventions (like monetary exchange) might be entitled to entrench on them is fundamentally at odds with Locke's conception of property".[24]

The social contract approach to natural law culminated in the writing of Rousseau (1712–1778). As Barker has noted: "Rousseau is a Januslike figure in the history of natural law. He turns to it and belongs to it, he turns away from it and belongs elsewhere."[25] Rousseau's conception of a state of nature is closer to Locke's than Hobbes's, though without Locke's emphasis on the sanctity of property. To Rousseau the social contract is a mystical construct by which the individual merges into the community and becomes part of the "general will". Ideally the people should govern themselves. But, as he acknowledged, "it is unimaginable that the people should remain continually assembled to devote their time

---

[17] *ibid.*, II, p. 50.
[18] *ibid.*, II, p. 40.
[19] Dunn, *op. cit.*, n. 83, p. 40. See also McClure, *op. cit.*, n. 79, Chap. 4.
[20] *ibid.*
[21] *ibid.*, p. 42.
[22] *Venditio* in J. Dunn, "Justice and the Interpretation of Locke's Political Theory" (1968) XVII *Political Studies*, p. 84.
[23] *Two Treatises of Government*, I, p. 42.
[24] Dunn, *op. cit.*, n. 83, p. 43.
[25] Introduction to *Social Contract*. In the first draft of the *Social Contract* Rousseau dismissed natural law as "nonsense". On Rousseau and natural law see R. Wokler (1994) 15 *History of Political Thought* 373.

to public affairs".[26] Accordingly there is need for some specialisation: Rousseau favoured "elective aristocracy".[27] As J. S. Mill put it: "There is a radical distinction between controlling the business of government and actually doing it."[28]

Law is "the register of the general will". Government can only be tolerated so long as it accurately reflects the general will. On the other hand, in language reminiscent of twentieth-century totalitarianism, Rousseau insists that whoever refuses to obey the general will shall be compelled to do so by the whole body: "he will be forced to be free".[29] This appears "self-contradictory" but on a true understanding of Rousseau is not.[30] What Rousseau is saying is that disobedience is morally illegitimate because it constitutes a failure to discharge a moral obligation a citizen incurred when acting as a citizen. Rousseau is, however, refusing to draw a distinction between law and morality: the general will is the "moral will" of each citizen.

Rousseau was, of course, critical of the theories of legislative representation accepted by Hobbes and Locke and of actual English political experience. "The people of England regards itself as free; but it is grossly mistaken; it is free only during the election of members of parliament. As soon as they are elected, slavery overtakes it and it is nothing."[31] He argued that "Every law the people has not ratified in person is null and void—is, in fact, not a law."[32] Direct citizen participation is thus a necessary condition of establishing the moral basis of obedience to law.

Rousseau's political theory has only tenuous links with natural law. The General Will has come almost to replace the higher law standard that natural law has typically represented. Rousseau is a paradox: "the supreme prophet and theorist of modern democracy"[33] and yet the beginning of the road to totalitarianism. D'Entrèves is surely right when he remarks that Rousseau's definition of democracy "thus appears as a landmark as well as a warning. It provides the strongest argument in favour of democracy, indicating that ... the cleavage between legal and moral obligation can be overcome, in as much as that principle will ensure that the laws express a prevailing moral conviction. But it also indicates the dangers that lie at hand ... Rousseau's 'general will', which is always right, is the prototype of the modern tyrant."[34]

---

[26] *Social Contract* (trans. G. D. H. Cole), Bk. III, Chap. 4, p. 217.
[27] *ibid.*, p. 219.
[28] *Representative Government* (in *Utilitarianism, Liberty and Representative Government*) (Everyman ed.), pp. 229–230.
[29] *Social Contract*, Bk. I, Chap. 7, p. 18.
[30] See J. Steinberg, *op. cit.*, pp. 87–90.
[31] *Op. cit.*, n. 22, Bk. III, Chap. 15, p. 240.
[32] *ibid.* On Rousseau and representation see Wokler, *op. cit.*, n. 21, pp. 393.
[33] Per D'Entrèves, *Natural Law* (1970), p. 142. See further, A. Ryan, "Mill and Rousseau: Utility and Rights" in G. Duncan, *Democratic Theory and Practice* (1983), p. 39.
[34] Per D'Entrèves, *op. cit.*, n. 33, p. 143.

KANT AND HUMAN FREEDOM

The complexities and, what at first seem like contradictions in the thinking of the German philosopher, Immanuel Kant (1724–1804) make his contributions to our understanding of the individual and the State elusive. He is very much a bridge thinker with his ideas looking back to the Greeks, Aquinas, as well as the social contract writers, and forward to much contemporary critical thought.[35]

For Kant morality "arises and can only arise from freedom".[36] Not only does freedom make morality possible, but it determines it too. In this way, Kant believes he is able to answer both of the central questions of natural law together *viz.* how is freedom possible?[37] And, how exercising freedom, ought I to act? Kant accepted that human beings do not always act as morality requires—they lack, what he calls, "holy will".[38] But, since morality and freedom are one and the same, provided the law is in conformity with morality, one can be forced to obey without forfeiting freedom. This conclusion, so similar to Rousseau's,[39] is thus reached without the necessity of a fictionalized "general will". In addition, since the positive law is the only possible public manifestation of the moral law,[40] to oppose it is "to oppose the possibility of a community governed by the moral law".[41] A conclusion drawn is that resistance to established legal authority must be wrong because it undermines the rule of law and frustrates the achievement of a community in conformity with the moral law.[42] This imperative is mitigated somewhat by Kant's vision of a human community as a "kingdom of ends", with the freedom of each person honoured consistently with the freedom of every other person. Kant tells us that the "history of the human race ... can be regarded as the realization of a hidden plan of nature to bring about an internally— and for this purpose also externally—perfect political constitution as the only possible state with which all natural capacities of mankind can be developed completely".[43] A noble ideal no doubt—but, in the 200 years since Kant, have we taken steps towards this goal or regressed from it?

More fundamentally, it is not clear why freedom should inevitably lead to the moral law any more than, to use an analogue in Aquinas's thinking, participation in the *lex aeterna* should produce the *lex naturalis*.[44] Nor is it clear whether Kant's basis of civil authority amounts to

---

[35] On Kant and natural law ethics see J. B. Schneewind (1993) 104 *Ethics* 53.

[36] *Per* Weinreb, *Natural Law and Justice*, p. 90.

[37] *Critique of Pure Reason* (trans. N. Kemp Smith, 1929), p. 409.

[38] *Groundwork of the Metaphysics of Morals* (trans. as *The Moral Law* by H. Paton, 1956), pp. 80–81.

[39] See *ante*, 112.

[40] And see Aquinas, *ante*, 101.

[41] Weinreb, *op. cit.*, n. 36, p. 93.

[42] "It is the people's duty to endure even the most intolerable abuse of supreme authority." (*The Metaphysical Elements of Justice*, trans. J. Ladd, 1965), p. 86.

[43] "Idea for a Universal History with a Cosmopolitan Purpose" in *Kant's Political Writings* (trans. H.B. Nisbet, 1970), p. 50.

[44] See *ante*, 100.

anything more than practical necessity—essentially the argument adduced by Hobbes.[45] Where Kant struck out in a new direction was his insistence that freedom meant autonomy—that subjection to any determination from a source other than oneself is heteronomy. Earlier natural law theories had concluded that, since human activity is constrained by natural law, freedom amounted to nothing more than striving to accord with this law. For Kant, subjection even to the will of God is heteronomy, not freedom. To understand freedom is to understand the moral law and to act only according to it. "No other law counts, because in the realm of freedom there is no other law."[46] And this is the direction which natural law was to take, with every form of heteronomy rejected.[47]

## THE ENLIGHTENMENT

The eighteenth century has been called the age of reason.[48] With its secularism and rationalism natural law came under attack. The idea of a universal natural law common to all mankind was vigorously refuted by Vico (1668–1774), Herder (1744–1803)[49] and Montesquieu (1689–1755).[50] Vico's starting point was the affirmation of humanism. He had no doubt that "the world of civil society has certainly been made by men".[51] For Montesquieu mankind was influenced by a variety of factors: climate, religion, laws, maxims of government, morals and customs. The structure of a society thus hinged on the workings of many factors. He saw the individual as merely the instrument of historical change, "a passive element within a system conceived as the ceaseless interaction of moral and physical forces".[52]

The eighteenth century was also the period of the Scottish Enlightenment.[53] Hume (1711–76), Adam Smith (1723–90).[54] Ferguson (1723–1816),[55] Millar (1735–1801)[56] were a group of intellectuals dedicated to

---

[45]  See *ante*, 106.

[46]  Weinreb, *op cit.*, n. 36, p. 95.

[47]  And see further Weinreb, *op. cit.*, particularly Chaps 4 *et seq*. But see N. MacCormick's comment: "None of us starts off other than as totally heteronomous. ... If autonomy is supposed to involve the experience of inventing a moral universe from scratch it is non-existent...." (*Legal Reasoning and Legal Theory* (1978), p. 273).

[48]  Thus whole systems of natural law were expounded as derivable from pure reason, though they strongly bore the influence of Roman law, which was believed to embody the *ratio juris*. Cf. Schulz, *Principles of Roman Law*, pp. 38–39, 100.

[49]  See I. Berlin, *Vico and Herder* (1976), pp. 34–35, 175. See also W. Cahnmann in B. Rhea (ed.) *The Future of the Sociological Classics* (1981).

[50]  See *The Spirit of the Laws* (1748). See also F. Neumann, *The Democratic and Authoritarian State* (1957), Chap. 4. On Montesquieu and natural law see M. Zuckert (2001) 18 Soc. Phil. & Pol. 227.

[51]  *The New Science* (ed.) Bergin and Frisch) (1948) (originally published 1725), s. 331.

[52]  Per A. Swingewood, *A Short History of Sociological Thought* (1984), p. 17.

[53]  On the Enlightenment generally see P. Gay, *The Enlightenment: An Interpretation* (1967, 1970). On Scotland see A. Chitnis, *The Scottish Enlightenment* (1977).

[54]  On the contribution to jurisprudence of whom see D. D. Raphael, *Adam Smith* (1985).

[55]  *An Essay On The History of Civil Society* (1767) (an edition was published in 1966).

[56]  See J. Lehmann (ed.) *John Millar of Glasgow* (1960).

studying society scientifically. They rejected social contractarian explanations of society. Hume argued that it was government which made promises possible. He wrote:

> "'Tis reasonable for those philosophers, who assert justice to be a natural virtue, and antecedent to human conventions, to resolve all civil allegiance into the obligation of a promise, and assert that 'tis our consent alone, which binds us to any submission to magistracy. For as all government is plainly an invention of men, and the origin of most governments is known in history, 'tis necessary to mount higher, in order to find the source of our political duties, if we wou'd assert them to have any *natural* obligation of morality."[57]

But Hume was not deceived in this way:

> "Having found that *natural* as well as *civil* justice derives from human conventions, we shall quickly perceive, how fruitless it is to resolve the one into the other, and seek, in the laws of nature, a stronger foundation for our political duties than interest, and human conventions; while the laws themselves are built on the very same foundation."[58]

Hume, however, did not totally reject natural law. He developed, what has been called, "a modern theory of natural law",[59] an exclusively empirical version of the fundamental principles of natural law. His secularism led him to attempt to found a science of morality and law in a science of man which had no need of a religious hypothesis. This meant "pruning the idea of justice of its universal or superior meaning".[60] Hume found no immediate relationship between justice and any natural inclination. He argued that for an act to be moral, there had to be a motive considered good independently of the sense of the virtue of the action. His difficulty was to find one in the case of justice because there is no natural inclination to be just. Analysis of justice showed that the "passion" involved was contrary to just action and socially destructive in itself. So justice and human society were possible because the socially destructive passion was redirected by the understanding with reason acting obliquely on the passion. Justice was thus "an invention of a naturally inventive species, and from that point of view 'natural': the spontaneous product of life in society, and like that, as old as the species".[61] Hume called the rules of justice "natural laws" since "they are as old and universal as society and the human species, but prior to government and positive law".[62] Observation of the rules of justice is "palpable and evident, even to the most rude and uncultivated of the

---

[57] *Treatise On Human Nature*, Bk., III, Pt II, s. VIII, pp. 542–543.
[58] *ibid.*
[59] By D. Forbes, *Hume's Philosophical Politics* (1975), Chap. 2.
[60] *ibid.*, p. 68.
[61] *ibid.*, p. 70.
[62] *ibid.*

human race; and 'tis almost impossible for anyone, who has experience of society, to be mistaken in this particular".[63]

The contribution of Burke (1729–97) to political thought remains controversial even today. Celebrated as moderate Whig, arch-conservative, forerunner of nineteenth-century liberalism, as utilitarian, as revolutionary and as counter-revolutionary, the question for us is whether he was a natural lawyer.[64] Stanlis certainly thinks so and there is cogent evidence for this. He writes, "The true nature of Burke's cardinal political principles cannot be understood apart from its connection with the Natural Law."[65] His political philosophy is said to supply the answer to those who still rely on the utilitarian, positivist or materialist traditions. Stanlis asserts: "In every important political problem he ever faced ... Burke *always* appealed to the Natural Law. What is more, by Natural Law Burke always meant essentially the same thing, and he applied it as the ultimate test of justice and liberty in all human affairs."[66] He gives as an example Burke's speech in Parliament in 1787 protesting against those who wished to obstruct the impeachment of Warren Hastings. The greatest obstruction came from lawyers, a body of men whom he venerated.[67] Of them he said, as they put up an endless series of legal impediments, they drive us "from law to law" and would "in the end leave us no law at all". He by contrast supported "the eternal principles of truth and justice".[68] Burke was here using natural law to attack rule by arbitrary power.

But he also used natural law to shore up capitalist institutions and practices. He identified the laws of commerce as laws of nature "and consequently the laws of God".[69] He saw a competitive, self-regulating market economy as a necessary part of the natural order of the universe. He attacked the Speenhamland system.[70] "Whenever it happens that a man can claim nothing according to the rules of commerce, and the principles of justice, he passes out of that department, and comes within the jurisdiction of mercy. In that province the magistrate has nothing at all to do: his interference is a violation of the property which it is his office to protect."[71] It was "pernicious to disturb the natural course of

---

[63] Hume, *op. cit.*, n. 57, p. 534.
[64] C.B. Macpherson, *Burke* (1980) argues that he was all these things and that there is no fundamental inconsistency between such apparently opposite positions. He shows the key to lie in Burke's political economy, a constant factor in his political reasoning.
[65] *Edmund Burke and The Natural Law* (1958), p. 34.
[66] *ibid.*, p. 83.
[67] Stanlis, *op. cit.*, n. 65, for evidence of this.
[68] Stanlis, *op. cit.*, n. 65, pp. 60–61. See also Macpherson, *op. cit.*, n. 64, pp. 30–32. Burke's case rested on general principles of right. His major premise (like Locke, *ante*, 108) was that political power is a trust. The trust had been abused: so the property right (the charter) should go. Natural rights older than chartered rights had been broken, rights going back to Magna Carta.
[69] *Thoughts and Details on Scarcity*, para. 7.404.
[70] Justices at Speenhamland paid labourers a sum supplementary to wages on a scale related to the size of the labourer's family and the cost of bread.
[71] Burke, *op. cit.*, n. 69, paras 7.390–7.391.

things".[72] The wage relation was part of a natural "chain of subordination".[73] It is right that the people should accept this subordination because it fits "the final proportions of eternal justice".[74] Burke opposed the egalitarian propaganda of the French revolutionists[75] because, if accepted, it would undermine this whole natural, and therefore just, social order. To say, as Burke did, that the capitalist order was part of the divine and natural order is patently absurd. Although the dating of the emergence of capitalism is contentious,[76] it is not in doubt that it has not always existed. Indeed, the Christian Natural Law, to which Burke turned, had on the whole been sharply critical of market morality. So, as Macpherson explains, Burke had to change the content of this natural law. To Burke capitalist order was traditional because it *"had in fact been* the traditional order in England for a whole century".[77]

Burke has much in common with Blackstone who appealed to natural law to sanctify the English common law.[78] Blackstone's justification of the common law has not recovered from the assault on it by Bentham.[79] Burke's views remain influential within conservative political thought today.[80] He thus looks forward to the contemporary political scene as well as back with his somewhat anachronistic revival of Christian Natural Law.

## THE NINETEENTH AND TWENTIETH CENTURIES

The nineteenth century, the century of materialism and sovereignty, belonged to positivism.[81] Those who sought an understanding of the relationship between self and reality, the individual and society, discovered laws of social order which had the same inevitability as the laws of nature, but they did not seek these laws in natural law.[82]

In the twentieth century, there was a revival of interest in natural law.[83] A "school" of neo-scholastics, following and refining the doctrines of

---

[72] *Reflections on the Revolution in France* (1969), p. 271.
[73] Burke, *op. cit.*, n. 69, paras 7.383–7.384. In this chain workers were superior to cattle and cattle to carts, ploughs and spades.
[74] Burke, *op. cit.*, n. 72, p. 372.
[75] And their English supporters.
[76] See *post*, 1161–1162.
[77] Macpherson, *op. cit.*, n. 64, p. 63.
[78] See D. Kennedy, (1979) 28 Buffalo Law Rev. 205.
[79] But Bentham was in agreement with Burke in attacking "natural rights" doctrines emanating from the French Revolution. For Bentham's attack on the fictitious character of natural law ("a mere work of the fancy"), see K. Olivecrona, "Bentham's Veil of Mystery" in (1978) *Current Legal Problems*, p. 227.
[80] For example, R. Scruton, *The Meaning of Conservatism* (2nd ed., 1985).
[81] *Post*, Chap. 4.
[82] See, *e.g.* the laws of historical materialism in Marx (Chap. 12) or of Social Darwinism in Herbert Spencer (*post*, 837).
[83] Reasons may be sought in a multiplicity of factors, ranging from doubts about the epistemology of the empirical sciences to the growth of nuclear weapons, policies of genocide, recognition of human rights abuses like *apartheid*, to a decline in economic and social stability and other "certainties".

Aquinas emerged.[84] A formal idealist school, associated with Stammler in Germany and Del Vecchio in Italy, sought to set up a formal structure of just law and to strive to give it material content. There were also a group of empirical and sociological lawyers, most notable Gény and Duguit,[85] who, while rejecting metaphysical natural law, sought to re-establish overriding principles in the name of social solidarity. In England, until well after the Second World War, natural law was dormant. In the United States, there was greater interest: the existence of fundamental rights in the Constitution giving greater scope for the natural lawyer.[86]

But all this has changed and natural law has regained its place in legal and political theory. The rediscovery of the concept of practical reason[87] as at the heart of both law and morality shows their connectedness and argues that the gulf between positivism and natural law may not be as great as stereotypical pictures of the "schools" suggest. The discovery by Hart of a core of good sense in natural law—which he expresses as a minimum content of natural law[88]—by MacCormick of, what he calls "ethical legalism"[89] and by Campbell of "ethical positivism"[90] brings leading contemporary positivist thinkers closer to natural law than has been the case before. Whether this can also be said of Dworkin depends on how (or whether) you categorise him. Is "law as integrity",[91] natural law theory? Dworkin himself seems less than sure.[92] However, in a theory in which moral evaluation is so central it would be difficult to avoid categorising Dworkin as totally outwith the modern natural law tradition.[93]

## FULLER AND THE MORALITY OF LAW

One of the most significant contributions to contemporary natural law thinking is the writing of Lon Fuller (1902–1978).[94] He parted company

---

[84] See Maritain, *post*, 150. Also the writings of Jean Dabin. And see also Finnis, *post*, 126.
[85] (1917) 31 Harvard L. Rev. 1.
[86] Bodenheimer, *Jurisprudence* (1962) gives a useful resumé of immediate post-war natural law writing in the U.S.
[87] See respectively, the very different writings of Finnis and Raz, *Practical Reason and Norms* (1975).
[88] *Post*, 123.
[89] See his article in 2 *Ratio Juris* 184.
[90] *The Legal Theory of Ethical Positivism* (1996).
[91] See (1989) 2 *Ratio Juris* 184.
[92] See *Law's Empire* (1986), pp. 35–36, 263, 397 and (1982) 34 Univ. of Florida L. Rev. 165. George, *In Defense of Natural Law* (1999) does not see Dworkin's theories are compatible with natural law: indeed, it is Robert Bork's (see *The Tempting of America* (1990)) which (in George's view) is so compatible (pp. 110–111).
[93] *Post*, 717 and *post*, 724.
[94] See *The Law in Quest of Itself* (1940) (1958) 71 Harv.L.Rev. 630, *post*, 396. *The Morality of Law* (rev. ed.) (1969), *Anatomy of the Law* (1968) and (1969) 14 *American J. of Jurisprudence* 1. See also "The Case of the Speluncean Explorers" *ante*, 45 and *The Principles of Social Order* (1981). There is a full study of Fuller's thought by R. Summers (*Lon L. Fuller*) (1984)).

with much of the earlier natural law tradition,[95] rejecting Christian doctrines of natural law and seventeenth and eighteenth century rationalist doctrines of natural rights. He did not subscribe to a system of absolute values. His principal affinity was, he tells us, with Aristotle. He found a "family resemblance" in the various natural law theories: the search for principles of social order.[96] "I discern, and share, one central aim common to all the schools of natural law, that of discovering those principles of social order which will enable men to attain a satisfactory life in common."[97] He believed that in all theories of natural law it was assumed that "the process of moral discovery is a social one, and that there is something akin to a 'collaborative articulation of shared purposes' by which men come to understand better their own ends and to discern more clearly the means for achieving them".[98] To Fuller, the most fundamental tenet of natural law is an affirmation of the role of reason in legal ordering.[99]

Summers believes that Fuller did not go "much further" in the general direction of natural law than this.[1] But he did, however, also stress the universal importance of two broadly procedural dictates: "Keep man's purpose-forming processes healthy" and "keep the channel of communication between men open".[2] The latter he described as the "one central indisputable principle of ... substantive natural law".[3] In addition he believed in the objective determination of "right orderings" of human relations, within limits. Reasoning on some issues could be objectively grounded in human nature as such. He did not, however, develop in any detail what he meant by human nature. Certainly, the illustrations he gives of such decision-making (for example, five men in a motor boat in the Pacific, strangers with different skills and no hierarchic ranking carrying on a joint task with no principle of organisation other than recognised human need[4]) seem to reduce human nature to little more than "necessities of the situation".[5] He talked of "mastering a segment of reality",[6] as if his real concern was with means and not, as is more normal in natural law theorising, about ends. Fuller himself denied this: indeed, he argued for a closer, more integrated relationship of means and ends

---

[95] See R. Moffat, "Lon Fuller: Natural Lawyer After All!" 26 Amer. J. of Jurisp. 190 (1981). *Cf.* A. D'Amato "Lon Fuller and Substantive Natural Law" 26 Amer. J. of Jurisp. 202 (1981).

[96] See, particularly, *The Principles of Social Order* (ed. K. Winston, 1981).

[97] *Per* Fuller (1958) 3 Natural L. Forum 83, 84.

[98] *ibid.* But he said the term "natural law" had about it "a rich deep odor of the witches' cauldron" and mere mention of it sufficed "to unloose a torrent of emotions and tears" ((1946) 59 Harv. L. Rev. 376, 379).

[99] *Anatomy of The Law* (1968), p. 163.

[1] *Lon L. Fuller* (1984), p. 66.

[2] *The Law in Quest of Itself* (1940), p. 110. See further, D. Sturm, "Fuller's Multi-Dimensional Natural Law Theory" (1966) 18 Stan. L. Rev. 612–616.

[3] *The Morality of Law* (rev. ed. 1969), p. 186.

[4] *The Problems of Jurisprudence* (temp. ed., 1949), pp. 694–695 (this and other examples are in Summers, *op. cit.*, n. 94, pp. 68–69).

[5] *ibid.*, p. 695.

[6] (1946) 59 Harv.L.Rev. 376.

than is common. Thus, he stated that "means and ends no longer arrange themselves in tandem fashion, but move in circles of interaction"[7]: ends cannot be judged without also considering means. For Fuller ends or purposes require particular rules as means. To the criticism that this is to derive an "ought" from an "is", Fuller would respond impatiently (according to Summers[8]). He interpreted it "as a sweeping doctrine to the effect that facts cannot tell lawyers, legislators, and judges what they ought to do"[9] and this he could not accept.[10]

For Fuller the connection between law and morality is a necessary one.[11] This had implications for substantive law, as we have seen. Perhaps, though, Fuller's lasting contribution to jurisprudence lies in his extension of this analysis to encompass "processual" arrangements, legislation, adjudication,[12] customary practice,[13] contract,[14] and electoral methods. He believed these processes were "governed by objectively determinable "laws" and that these laws were "natural" in the sense that "they represent compulsions necessarily contained in certain ways of *organising* men's relations with each other".[15] D'Entrèves classified this as "technological" natural law.[16]

Let us look at the implications of this for understanding the legal system. Fuller's initial premise was that a legal system is the purposive human "enterprise of subjecting human conduct to the governance of rules".[17] According to Fuller a legal system had other purposes as well. Whatever its substantive purposes, certain procedural purposes had to be acknowledged as goals if the system were to qualify as a system of law, rather than a set of institutions using arbitrary force. As far as statutes (and other "made law"[18]) were concerned this required that they be sufficiently general (there must be rules); publicly promulgated; sufficiently prospective; clear and intelligible; free of contradictions; sufficiently constant through time so that people can order their relations accordingly; not require the impossible; and be administered in a way sufficiently congruent with their wording so that people can abide by

---

[7] (1958) 3 Nat.L.For.83. Fuller was considering "Means and Ends" as the first chapter in his *The Principles of Social Order.*

[8] Summers, *op. cit.*, n. 94, p. 70.

[9] *Per* Summers, *ibid.*

[10] Savarese (1964) 53 Geo. L.J. 250 criticises Fuller for not going far enough to formulate a substantive natural law. But Fuller's concerns were directed more to process and procedure.

[11] For a telling criticism of Fuller's attempt to establish this, see Raz (1977) 93 L.Q.R. 195.

[12] See *The Principles of Social Order* (1981), pp. 86–124; (1978) 92 Harv. L. Rev. 353; *The Anatomy of the Law* (1968), pp. 121–158, and Summers, *op. cit.*, Chap. 7.

[13] *The Principles of Social Order* (1981), pp. 212–224; *The Anatomy of the Law* (1968), pp. 64–75, 101–120.

[14] (1936–37) Yale L.J. 52, 373 and Summers, *op. cit.*, Chap. 10.

[15] "American Legal Philosophy at Mid-Century" (1954) 6 *J. of Legal Education* 457, 476.

[16] *Natural Law* (1970).

[17] *The Morality of Law* (revised ed., 1969), p. 106.

[18] Fuller distinguished "made law" and "implicit law" (*e.g.* customary law) (see *The Anatomy of The Law*, pp. 63–119).

them.[19] These principles he described as an "internal morality" of law. They are "internal" because they are implicit in the concept of law. They can be described as "morality" because they set up standards for evaluating official conduct.

But what of a system which failed to meet any one of these conditions, or failed substantially in regard to several? Fuller is ambivalent. At one point, he says that "a total failure in any one of these eight directions does not simply result in a bad system of law; it results in something that is not properly called a legal system at all ..."[20] A few pages later conditions have been downgraded to "kinds of legal excellence toward which a system of rules may strive".[21] There is an aspiration of a utopia, but this is "not actually a useful target for guiding the impulse toward legality".[22] Instead, it suggests "distinct standards by which excellence in legality may be tested".[23] It is also not clear whether any of the conditions (if that is what they are) are more important than any others. What Fuller is setting out are principles of legality, a restatement of the rule of law. He seems to be saying that the closer a government comes to meeting the criteria, the more fully legal such a system would be. Implicit in this analysis is a rejection of a finite definition of law: for Fuller, the existence of a legal system is thus a matter of degree.[24] But how useful is a theory which cannot tell us when something is law or not, or whether a particular society has a legal system or not? Who is to make the decisions: officials (if so, are they to be the same ones who have made the rules in the first place?) or ordinary people or is this an elitist theory which leaves critical decisions to jurists? And, further, on what level (if at all) does the theory make sense? Is it the case that retrospective legislation is not law? If so, does this apply also to Finance Acts? And if not, in what way are they conceptually different from laws made by Hitler or Stalin? A response—certainly the positivist response—is that they may be unjust law but law nevertheless.

Fuller deals only cursorily with the relationship between the form in which legal rules are expressed and their content. Is the internal morality of law (procedural natural law) a means or an end in itself? He said, as we noted above, that the relation of ends and means was an interactive conception. He wrote that "order itself will do us no good unless it is good for something"[25] and "justice itself is impossible without order."[26] Summers notes[27] that part of the significance attached to the legal system being purposive in the sense set out in the eight ideals "is that this

---

[19] These "ideals" are set out in *The Morality of The Law*, Chap. 2.
[20] *The Morality of Law* (1964), p. 39.
[21] *ibid.*, p. 41.
[22] *ibid.*
[23] *ibid.*, p. 42.
[24] And see Dworkin (1965) 10 Villanova L. R. 677–678.
[25] (1958) 71 Harv.L.Rev. 630, and *post*, 417.
[26] *ibid.*
[27] *Lon L. Fuller* (1984), p. 28. See also Pappe's remark ((1960) 23 M.L.R. 260, 271) that "a dictatorship would of necessity be driven to perverting procedure rather than law".

constrains the kinds of specific purpose that at least officials can pursue through law. For example, once officials adopt a general rule and promulgate it, this will constrain what they themselves can thereafter do." This is all very well in theory but in practice does this happen, in particular does it happen outside systems which do not need the constraints of procedural natural law? As was indicated in an earlier chapter, the Nazi legal system[28] was faithful, with one possible exception, to Fuller's standards, yet it was able to promulgate laws contrary to the most fundamental principles of humanitarian morality.[29] Fuller's response is far from convincing. We *ought* to say, he intimates, that a system which purports to be one of law has these procedural purposes. This device, it is said, would keep law-makers conscious of the demands of legality.[30]

But what bearing does this have on the content of the law? Can we claim, as critics have,[31] that the principles of procedural legality are nothing more than the tools of an efficient craftsman?[32] Is Fuller confusing efficacy and morality? He denies this. He suggests that a régime might actually find it effective to violate the principles of legality. He refers to the Soviet statutes of 1961 making economic crimes capital offences and legal practice which applied the statutes retroactively. Soviet lawyers apparently did not like this, but, from the perspective of the law-maker, the laws may well have been effective in stamping out a particular form of deviance.[33] One argument that Fuller puts for a link between the principle of legality and moral value draws on the German sociologist, Simmel.[34] He contends that a legal system rests on a tacit reciprocity between lawgiver and subject. Fuller's uses of this are critically examined by Kramer,[35] who shows that he draws upon reciprocity in different ways. Thus, at one point Fuller sees reciprocity as offering the individual fair opportunity to plan in the "confident awareness that governmental

---

[28] Fuller was present in Germany during 1933–34 and seems to have flirted with Nazism. See N. E. H. Hull, *Roscoe Pound and Karl Llewellyn* (1997), pp. 244–245.

[29] *Cf.* Radbruch's remarks quoted *post*, 415, 421 and 426.

[30] See as to this Summers, *op. cit.*, n. 27, p. 29.

[31] See particularly the symposium in (1965) 10 Villanova L.Rev. 631–678 and see Hart (1965) 78 Harv.L.Rev. 1281 alleging Fuller confuses "the notions of purposive activity and morality" (p. 1285). See also Weinreb, *op. cit.*, n. 31, p. 103 and see MacCormick's defence of Fuller in (ed.) George, *op. cit.*, n. 5, pp. 122–123: the rule of law has real value even when the substance of what is done falls short of any relevant ideal of substantive justice. See also George, *In Defense of Natural Law* (1999), Chap. 6. *Cf.* the view of Raz (1977) 93 L.Q.R. 208.

[32] See also D. Lyons, *Ethics and The Rule of Law* (1984), p. 77. Cohen (1965) 10 Villanova L. Rev. 640, 651) asks: "Is there a lapse in morality when an assassin forgets to load his gun?"

[33] *The Morality of Law*, pp. 202–203. He quotes Berman on Soviet jurists' unhappiness with the 1961 laws.

[34] *ibid.*, pp. 216–217. Reciprocity in Fuller's work is explored fully by M. Kramer, *In Defense of Legal Positivism* (1999) (more briefly in (1998) 18 Ox. J.L.S. 235). See also J. Boyle (1993) 78 Cornell L.R. 371, 392–397 and J. Waldron (1994) 13 *Law and Philosophy* 259, 277–282. For the view that Fuller sees natural law as "professional ethics", see D. Luban (2001) 18(1) *Social Philosophy and Policy* 176.

[35] (1998) 18 Ox. J.L.S. 235 and, more fully, in *In Defense of Legal Positivism: Law Without Trimmings* (1999), Chap. 3. See also T. Allan (1996) 55 Cambridge L.J. 89.

officials will not arbitrarily clamp down on her undertakings".[36] A second way in which Fuller draws a connection between law's reciprocity and the dignity of the individual is the contention that governance by law "entails an acknowledgment of each citizen's capacity for autonomous decision-making".[37] The subject is to be given fair opportunity.[38] He knows the rules he has to follow and he is told which rules will be applied to his conduct. The lawgiver who violates principles of legality destroys this understanding and forfeits some governmental legitimacy. Legitimacy is, of course, a moral value. Extensive violation could remove all legitimacy and destroy the moral basis of government totally. But what Fuller has done here is to jump from the "inner morality of law" to questions of moral obligation and judgment of authority by moral standards. The ruler who infringes the principles of legality, by making unclear laws or requiring the impossible, presumably is frustrated in his objectives but this is not to say that he has acted immorally or unjustly. Fuller may believe the connection between law and morality is a necessary one, but he has not established this.[39]

## HART ON NATURAL LAW

Positivists today are less positivistic than they were a very few years ago, and Hart has attempted to restate a natural law position from a semi-sociological point of view.[40] Hart points out that there are certain substantive rules which are essential if human beings are to live together in close proximity. "These simple facts constitute a core of indisputable truth in the doctrines of natural law."[41] Hart places primary emphasis on an assumption of survival as a principal human goal. We are concerned with social arrangements for continued existence, and not with those of a suicide club. There are, therefore, certain rules which any social organisation must contain, and it is these facts of human nature which afford a reason for postulating a "minimum content" of natural law.

Hart does not state the actual minimum universal rules, but rather certain facts of the "human condition" which must lead to the existence of some such rules (but not necessarily rules with any specific content). These facts of the human condition Hart describes as consisting of human vulnerability; approximate equality; limited altruism; limited resources; and limited understanding and strength of will which leads some to favour their short-term interests at the expense of their long-term ones. What he argues is that, in the light of these inevitable features of the

---

[36] *Per* Kramer, *In Defense of Legal Positivism* (1999), p. 54.
[37] *Per* Kramer, *ibid.*, p. 58.
[38] See also H. L. A. Hart, *Punishment and Responsibility* (1968) on, what he calls, the "doctrine of fair opportunity".
[39] There are valuable insights into Fuller in Nigel Simmonds, *Law as a Moral Idea* (2007).
[40] *The Concept of Law*, pp. 193–200 and *Essays in Jurisprudence and Philosophy* (1983), pp. 111–116.
[41] *ibid.*, p. 181.

human condition, there follows[42] a "natural necessity" for certain minimum forms of protection for persons, property and promises. "It is in this form that we should reply to the positivist thesis 'law may have *any* content'."[43] Hart is not, however, claiming that law is derived from moral principles or that there is some necessary conceptual link between the legal and moral.[44]

However, Hart does not seek to suggest that, even if this analysis of human society is accepted,[45] this must inevitably lead to a system of even minimal justice within a given community. On the contrary, he accepts the fact, as indeed is hardly to be denied, that human societies at all periods of history have displayed a melancholy record of oppression and discrimination in the name of security and legal order, as, for instance, in the case of systems based on slavery, or systems based on positive religious or racial discrimination, all too familiar in the modern world.[46]

A number of comments may be made. First it must be clear that this approach should not be confused with an attempt to establish some kind of "higher law" in the sense of overriding or eternally just moral or legal principles, but is merely an attempt to establish a kind of sociological foundation for a minimum content for natural law. The justification for the use of the term natural law here is that regard is paid to what is suggested to be the fundamental nature of man as indicated in Hart's five facts of the human condition. It must be pointed out, however, that these "facts", apart from being extremely vague and uncertain in most respects, do not depend upon sociological investigation, but are really an intuitive appraisal of the character of the human condition.[47]

Further, as MacCormick points out, it contains striking omissions, of which the most obvious is sex "which in almost all of us is at times an urge whose promptings far transcend the limits of our strength of will

---

[42] Is Hart attempting to derive a value from a fact, thus transgressing Hume's law (*ante*, 27)? See Sir Isaiah Berlin for a suggestion that Hart is doing this, in *Does Political Theory still Exist? in Philosophy, Politics and Society* (2nd series, ed. Laslett and Runciman, 1962), p. 27.

[43] *The Concept of Law*, p. 199.

[44] See N. MacCormick, *H. L. A. Hart* (1981), pp. 23–24, and Chap. 8 for a penetrating analysis of Hart's "minimum content". His verdict is that it is "very far from being a guarantee of a just or good society" (p. 97). For the view that the minimum content of natural law is "not so minimal after all" see R. Epstein (2005) 25 Ox J.L.S. But contrast J. Allan (2007) 20 Ratio Juris 213.

[45] But can it be? For example, is there really "approximate equality"? Do women have equality with men, children with adults? Is Hart not ignoring every form of stratification (social, economic, sexual) in society? And when we talk of "limited resources" are we referring to deficiencies in the environment or in human beings? Where is the line to be drawn between limited resources and limited altruism?

[46] See Kramer, *In Defense of Legal Positivism* (1999), pp. 263–265 who points out that some people, for example slaves, might be better off in a situation of lawlessness.

[47] For a discussion of this point and a comparison with the method of Hobbes, see D'Entrèves, *Natural Law* (1970), p. 194.

guided even by a supremely rational understanding of long term, or even immediate, self-interest".[48]

Moreover, it is difficult to see how any real minimum content whatever can be based upon such principles as those formulated. For example, the factor of human vulnerability seems necessarily to restrict the use of violence. But the need for human survival has not prevented the acceptance in many societies of the exposure of infants or the killing of slaves or children by those exerting power over them. Moreover, a society may actually base its survival upon the need for human slaughter. Thus the ancient Mexican civilisation possessed a religious and state system which required the perpetual propitiation of the gods by continuous human sacrifice on a massive scale. In relation to such a society, which attained in other respects a high measure of civilisation, it seems difficult to talk in terms of individual human vulnerability as it might be conceived in a developed modern state, which acknowledges as a fundamental principle the value of individual life and security.[49]

Again, although Hart refers to the implications of what he calls the approximate equality between human beings, he himself recognises that no universal system of natural law or justice can be based upon the principle of impartiality, or that of treating like cases alike. For the essential question here is by what criteria we are to determine which cases are to be treated as alike, and no such feature of the physical or psychosomatic condition of human beings as embodied in the idea of approximate equality can indicate how a society may decide which cases are alike for this purpose. Hindu society may justify distinguishing between categories of persons on the footing of the caste system, and other societies may regard as essentially unlike, slaves and freemen, male and female, or black and white. The rule of equality, therefore, cannot be derived from any formal principle of impartiality, any more than it can be derived from the physical or psychic nature of human beings or from the character of human practice and experience in this or other ages. The idea of equality or non-discrimination is essentially a value-judgment which cannot be derived from any assertions or speculations regarding the nature of man. No insistence, therefore, on the idea of impartiality, or the rules of natural justice, or the "inner morality" of the law can afford a basis for arriving at such a principle as that of non-discrimination. This is

---

[48] *Per* MacCormick, *op. cit.*, p. 98. He points out that Hume, with whom he shows Hart has great affinity on the question of a minimum content (p. 93), devotes considerable attention to a consideration of sexual restrictions (p. 99). He suspects that Hart is reluctant to include rules about sexual conduct which he regards (*Law, Liberty and Morality*, p. 83) as a hangover from the "prehistory of morality". Hart himself was ambivalent as regards his own sexuality: see N. Lacey, *A Life of H.L.A. Hart* (2004), particularly 73–79, 203–205.

[49] Though developed modern states accept killing in war, execute criminals, abort foetuses. No modern society has abolished the motor car. Minimum content based on human vulnerability will always be culturally-biased, or a general principle with stated exceptions. *Cf.* Mead, *post*, 225.

fully recognised by Hart himself, when he remarks that the idea of impartiality is "unfortunately compatible with very great iniquity".[50]

D'Entrèves,[51] a sympathetic critic of Hart's minimum content, has pointed to yet another gap in his treatment of natural law. For, whilst Hart unequivocally accepts that the validity of a legal norm "does not depend in any way on its equity or iniquity",[52] he tells us that natural law contains "the elementary principles which men must respect as long as men are what they are and propose to set up a viable society".[53] "Are we", D'Entrèves asks, "to conclude that natural law is a central and privileged sphere of morality distinguished by its sacred and inviolable character?"[54] Does this mean that outside the area of the minimum content laws of any iniquity may stand? And, even within it, what is the status of laws which flagrantly violate that minimum protection for which Hart's natural law stands? Are such laws laws and, if so, what, if any, is the right of resistance? To what extent can "evil laws" permeate a system before that set-up becomes no more than a suicide club? D'Entrèves is clearly right to ask for clarification.[55]

## FINNIS AND THE RESTATEMENT OF NATURAL LAW

The most authoritative modern statement of natural law is that of John Finnis.[56] Leading positivists see in Finnis's account "very great merit"[57]: it requires us to "abandon our caricature version of what a natural law theory is".[58] On the other hand Finnis has been accused of offering us "natural law without nature", so that he is forced to rely on claims that certain propositions in normative ethics and political theory are self-evidently true.[59]

Finnis rejects much in the natural law tradition. His is an attempt to rescue from its accretions and misconceptions "pure" naturalism, which he associates with Aristotle and Aquinas. He denies that what others, including us in this chapter, regard as central tenets of natural law are essential to it at all. In particular, he claims that natural law does not necessitate a belief in morality as comprising observance of rationally demonstrable principles of behaviour, and he denies that natural law requires laws which infringe such principles be impugned as invalid. He

---

[50] *The Concept of Law*, p. 207. *Cf.* Barry, *Political Argument*, pp. 124–126.
[51] See *Natural Law*, App. C.
[52] *ibid.*, p. 199.
[53] *ibid.*
[54] *ibid.*
[55] D'Entrèves makes a number of other pertinent comments on Hart's approach. See pp. 198–203.
[56] *Natural Law and Natural Rights* (1980).
[57] *Per* H. L. A. Hart, *Essays in Jurisprudence and Philosophy* (1983), p. 11.
[58] *Per* Neil MacCormick "Natural Law Reconsidered" (1981) 1 O.J.L.S. 99, 109.
[59] See L. Weinreb, *Natural Law and Justice* (1987), Chap. 4. See also R. Hittinger, *A Critique of the New Natural Law Theory* (1987) and J. Goldsworthy (1996) 41 Amer. J. of Jurisp. 21.

accordingly argues that the positivist who refutes these claims does not effectively deny the true doctrine of natural law.

For Finnis, "natural law" is "the set of principles of practical reasonableness in ordering human life and human community".[60] Drawing on Aristotle and Aquinas. Finnis sets up the proposition that there are certain basic goods for human beings. The basic principles of natural law are pre-moral.[61] These basic goods are objective values in the sense that every reasonable person must assent to their value as objects of human striving.[62] Finnis lists seven. There are, he believes, "countless objectives and forms of good" but those not listed are "ways or combinations of ways" of pursuing one of the seven.[63] These are:

(1) *Life*: "the first basic value, corresponding to the drive for self-preservation, is the value of life. The term 'life' . . . signifies every aspect of vitality . . . which puts a human being in good shape for self-determination."[64]

(2) *Knowledge*: a preference for true over false belief.[65] It corresponds to that basic drive we call curiosity, a drive which leads us to reject any celebration of self-proclaimed ignorance or superstition. It is "knowledge . . . for its own sake, not merely instrumentally"[66] that Finnis has in mind. It can range from the speculations of a great philosopher or scientist to knowledge of how often Middlesex have been county cricket champions.

(3) *Play*: "each one of us can see the point of engaging in performances which have no point beyond the performance itself."[67]

(4) *Aesthetic experience*: the appreciation of beauty.[68]

(5) *Sociability or friendship*: "acting for the sake of one's friend's purposes, one's friend's well-being."[69]

(6) *Practical reasonableness*: "the basic good of being able to bring one's own intelligence to bear effectively . . . on the problems of choosing one's actions and life-style and shaping one's own character."[70]

---

[60] *Natural Law and Natural Rights*, p. 280.

[61] See J. Finnis and G. Grisez, "The Basic Principles of Natural Law" (1981) 26 Amer.J. of Jurisp. 21, 28, where Finnis distinguishes "proportionalism". He describes the basic human goods as "aspects of the full-being of human persons, aspects essentially immeasurable and incommensurable. For the proportionalist, the right choice is one which realises as much premoral good and as little premoral evil as possible". *Cf.* Bentham, *post*, 248 and Pound, *post*, 849.

[62] See Finnis, *post*, 169. There is no objective hierarchy: *ibid.*, pp. 92–95; *post*, 173–174.

[63] Finnis, *op. cit.*, n. 60, p. 90; *post*, 173–174.

[64] *ibid.*, p. 86; *post*, 170.

[65] *ibid.*, Chap. III.

[66] *ibid.*, p. 59 and *post*, 170.

[67] *ibid.*, p. 87; *post*, 170.

[68] *Post*, 171.

[69] *ibid.*, p. 88; *post*, 171.

[70] *ibid.*, *post*, 171.

(7) *Religion*: "questions of the origins of cosmic order and of human freedom and reason."[71] Expressed thus, this view is a good that even an atheist can value.

How do we know that these basic goods are good? According to Finnis, they are self-evident. Take knowledge, for example. Although the proposition that knowledge is a basic human good is not susceptible to proof, it cannot be denied. Finnis explains why: one who denies it is "implicitly committed to the proposition that he believes his assertion is worth making, and worth making *qua* true; he thus is committed to the proposition that he believes the truth is a good worth pursuing or knowing. But the sense of his original assertion was precisely that truth is not a good worth pursuing or knowing."[72] Anyone who denies that knowledge is a good cuts the ground from under his own feet. As MacCormick puts it: "why should ... anyone ... care to *know* that knowledge is not worth having unless, after all, at least that knowledge *is* worth having?"[73] Of course, not all that we do is aimed at knowledge for its own sake but, Finnis argues, it must be aimed at something for its own sake, some form of completeness which needs no ulterior justification. It may be there is a psychological explanation linking certain urges or drives with our acceptance of certain basic goods. Psychology may *explain* this but it does not, according to Finnis, *justify* the value of the basic goods. Psychology may also be able to explain less positive urges (towards greed or cruelty, for example). These, it must be conceded, do not support any basic value. They need an explanation whereas, according to Finnis, inclinations like curiosity, friendliness do not.

In more recent writing, Finnis (with Grisez and Boyle) has identified additionally "the first moral principle".[74] This principle commands persons to "choose and otherwise will those and only those possibilities whose willing is compatible with integral human fulfilment".[75] As George concedes,[76] this concept is "easily misunderstood". But its relationship with the basic human goods is reasonably clear. It is neither above nor apart from the basic goods. It reflects the fact that there are many ways of serving and sharing in the basic goods, and that human beings "can only do so much",[77] so that choices must be made. And no choice can bring about overall fulfilment. Thus, the principle of integral human fulfilment is an ideal,[78] a standard to guide choices. What Finnis (and Grisez) have called "modes of responsibility"[79] are derived from the first principle of morality. These identify the incentives to choose incompatibly with a will

---

[71] *ibid.*, p. 89; *post*, 172.
[72] *ibid.*, pp. 74–75.
[73] Per MacCormick, *op. cit.*, n. 58, p. 103. See also his *Legal Reasoning and Legal Theory* (1978).
[74] *Nuclear Deterrence, Morality and Realism* (1987), and *post*, 188.
[75] *ibid.*, p. 193.
[76] *In Defense of Natural Law*, p. 51.
[77] *ibid.*, p. 53.
[78] But not in the Platonic form of the good existing in a realm transcending this world.
[79] *Op. cit.*, n. 62a, p. 194.

to integral human fulfilment, and direct the chooser not to act on these incentives. Identification of the modes is necessary because the first principle of morality is too general to enable the specification of moral norms. Without more, the injunction to choose with a will toward integral human fulfilment would not assist in the formulation of norms about (say) capital punishment or abortion or whether to separate conjoined twins where one will necessarily die as a consequence.[80] The modes are intermediate moral principles and, unlike the first principle of morality, are not self-evident. But does this mean they derive from no more than personal conviction? It is difficult to see from where else they come, and Finnis himself has not offered any other answer.[81]

The question may be asked as to where law fits into all this. Finnis's answer is that human goods must be seen in the light of a community of human beings. Only in communal life are there the conditions for the pursuit of basic goods. The common good requires a legal system. Finnis acknowledges that legal systems can work against the common good. What is man to do then? Finnis refuses to believe that such complex questions can be reduced to a simple formula such as *lex iniusta non est lex*. Unjust laws are, in his view, a subordinate concern of natural law theory.[82] He argues that the "stipulations of those in authority have presumptive obligatory force",[83] that a ruler has authority to act for the common good, so that if he uses this authority to make stipulations "against the common good, or against any of the basic principles of practical reasonableness, those stipulations altogether lack the authority they would otherwise have *by virtue of being his*".[84]

What Finnis is doing here is distinguishing the focal or central meaning of our concept of law from its penumbral meaning.[85] The focal meaning is of an authoritative common ordering of a community, aimed at facilitating the realisation of the common good.[86] In these terms, much unjust law will not be law in its focal sense. It will be at best "an imperfect or fringe instance of law in its focal meaning"; at worst "a mere corruption of law in that focal sense".[87] It is, as MacCormick puts it, "the focal meaning which has to be grasped". It is there we find "a direct link with the moral order".[88]

The link between practicable reasonableness and law is brought out in Finnis's discussion of justice and rights. For Finnis the object of distributive justice is the common good. There are, he concedes, "no very

---

[80] See *Re A* [2000] 4 All E.R. 961.
[81] George attempts one (*op. cit.*, n. 76, pp. 52–54).
[82] But *cf. ante*, 91.
[83] *Op. cit.*, p. 359.
[84] *ibid.*, pp. 359–360. The principles of practical reasonableness are set out in Chap. 5. The product of these principles is morality.
[85] See the discussion of this in relation to positivist thinking, *ante*, 101–102.
[86] See a somewhat lengthier definition in *op. cit.*, n. 56, pp. 276–277.
[87] *Per* MacCormick, *op. cit.*, n. 58, p. 106.
[88] *ibid.*

precise yardsticks" for assessing this.[89] He maintains that there is no
single criterion universally applicable for resolving questions of distribution, though in relation to basic human goods "up to a certain
threshold level" the primary criterion is "need".[90] A second criterion is
"function", that is "need relative ... to roles and responsibilities in the
community"; a third is "capacity, relative not only to roles in communal
enterprise but also to opportunities for individual advancement".[91] He
also cites deserts and contributions and the fact that some have "created
or at least foreseen and accepted avoidable risks" while others have not.
Finnis gives two reasons for maintaining a régime of private property.
First, "the good of personal autonomy in community" suggests private
ownership as a requirement of justice,[92] Secondly, a "rule of human
experience indicates that resources are more productively exploited by
private enterprise". He does, however, see that in a more ideal world,
where people were more "other-directed", common ownership and
enterprise would be more productive of benefits for all.[93]

Finnis has pertinent comments to make on commutative justice also.
The term is Aquinas's: Aristotle used the term "corrective" justice and
this remains the more usual terminology. As Finnis rightly remarks, the
distinction between the two types of justice is "no more than an analytical
convenience".[94] In some fields of law it is difficult to say whether the rules
are intended to secure distributive or commutative justice. He cites as an
example the shift in the law of torts from the "classical" period (1850–
1950) to contemporary times: a shift from rules conceived to be an
instrument of commutative justice to one where the proper function of
the law has come to be seen, in some places more so than others, as
essentially distributive. Where once the question was "what are the
standards of conduct which one person must live up to in relation to his
"neighbours?", now increasingly it is phrased in terms of the appor-
tionment of the risks of common life.[95] Finnis does not account for these
changes[96] nor, surprisingly, does he believe that there is any necessity to
express an opinion on their propriety. To him the fundamental issue is
"How reasonable is it to regard the persons whose activities are in
question as engaged in a common enterprise?"[97] And rightly perceiving

---

[89]  Finnis, *op. cit.*, n. 56, p. 174.
[90]  *ibid.* He brings this out very clearly in his excellent discussion of bankruptcy law (pp.
      188–193).
[91]  *ibid.*, p. 175.
[92]  *ibid.*, p. 169.
[93]  This may explain why Finnis can accept redistributive taxation: "the State need be doing
      no more than crystallise and enforce duties that the property-holder *already* had" (p.
      187). Finnis makes some critical and highly pertinent comments on Nozick (on whom see
      *post*, 595).
[94]  Finnis, *op. cit.*, p. 179. See also *post*, 583, 629.
[95]  See his discussion of these issues and also questions relating to contract, particularly the
      doctrine of frustration, at pp. 180–183.
[96]  See for this P. Atiyah, *Accidents, Compensation and the Law* (6th ed., 1999) and R.
      Pound, *Introduction to the Philosophy of Law*.
[97]  *Per* Finnis, *op. cit.*, n. 56.

the origins of the development to lie in schemes to compensate industrial accidents, he does not think that the rationale for this (participation in a common enterprise) should be extended to encompass the whole of society.

Finnis's analysis of rights (which shows him to be fully within the analytical tradition) cannot be pursued here.[98] But the significance of a number of his comments on rights must be noted. The maintenance of human rights (Finnis uses the modern idiom rather than "natural rights"[99]) is a "fundamental component of the common good".[1] They are not subject to the common good, as utilitarians might claim.[2] But Finnis argues most human rights are "subject to or limited by each other and by other *aspects* of the common good".[3] These aspects, he acknowledges, can probably be subsumed under "a very broad conception of human rights but ... are fittingly indicated ... by expressions such as 'public morality', 'public health', 'public order'"[4] The difference between this and the utilitarian position is not easy to distinguish. But, unlike utilitarians, Finnis does believe in some absolute human rights: "the right not to have one's life taken directly as a means to any further end; ... the right not to be positively lied to in any situation ... in which factual communication ... is reasonably expected; and the related right not to be condemned on knowingly false charges; and the right not to be deprived, or required to deprive oneself, of one's pro-creative capacity"[5] and the right to be taken into respectful consideration in any assessment of what the common good requires.[6] It is no answer to say that such absolute rights are not recognised generally for Finnis responds that natural law theorists have never claimed or expected that "what I have called requirements of practical reasonableness ... are clearly recognised by all or even most people—on the contrary".[7] This is a highly significant statement and not the usual claim that we have come to expect from proponents of natural law. Of course, if a substantial consensus of opinion does not support a particular right, how can we be sure of its existence? This doubt does not concern Finnis for reasons given and discussed earlier in this chapter.[8]

There is much of value and interest in Finnis's discussion of many other matters (authority,[9] obligation and others). Space prevents any further elaboration. One point, however, cannot be ignored: the place of God in Finnis's scheme. As a rational reconstruction of Aquinas, it might

[98] See Finnis, *op. cit.*, n. 56, Chap. VIII and (1972) 4 Adel. L. Rev. 377 on Hohfeld (*cf. post*, 396).
[99] *Per* Finnis, *op. cit.*, n. 56, p. 198.
[1] *ibid.*, p. 218.
[2] See *post*, 248.
[3] *Per* Finnis, *op. cit.*, n. 56, p. 218.
[4] *ibid.*
[5] *ibid.*
[6] *ibid.*
[7] *ibid.*
[8] *Ante*, 88.
[9] *Per* Finnis, *op. cit.*, n. 56, pp. 231–239.

be expected that God would loom large in Finnis's theory. He does not. Finnis is a committed Christian but God is Finnis's conclusion, not his premise. Like Grotius[10] he believes a theory of natural law does not have to stipulate God. It stands without need of religious doctrine. Finnis, however, thinks that if you accept the arguments of his book you will have a strong reason to believe in an Uncaused Cause of the Universe.[11] What the non-believer or doubter might find attractive in this is that it allows a suspension of belief and does not require belief in a deity as a necessary preliminary to initial investigation.

We conclude this discussion of Finnis with a few critical comments. Finnis's thesis has many virtues. It integrates natural law within analytical jurisprudence. At the same time it emphasises the misleading effects of studying law in isolation from natural law. By studying it in the context of natural law Finnis shows the meaning and significance of law as part of a strategy of structuring human life in accordance with the requirements of practical reasonableness.

Some questions remain. We have already queried Finnis's concept of self-evidence. His argument for the basic good of knowledge, the retorsive argument already considered, is logically convincing. It is, however, notable that Finnis offers us no real parallel arguments for the other basic goods. It is believed that he would have difficulty in so doing.

Unlike positivists (we would include within this all empiricist jurisprudence including realism) Finnis does not purport to describe social reality. What he tries to do is construct a régime that it would be desirable to have in human communities. There is much of value in an evaluable conception of law but we cannot readily do without a criterion for law that would enable us to identify law unambiguously. There are many important purposes for which we need a non-moral criterion for identifying law. Finnis at places within his book seems to agree. But does his theory enable us to do this?

The relationship between law and the basic goods he lists is also not beyond doubt. Law is an aspect of the basic goods (practical reasonableness). It is also an instrument which stands outside of, and is thus logically prior to, human flourishing. Finnis is a social theorist who wants to use law to improve society. His arguments for law thus, not surprisingly, centre on its instrumental value. The focal meaning of law concentrates on what it achieves, not on what it is. As a result of this orientation we are left with the suspicion that Finnis gives us no substantial reason why social ordering through law is the most appropriate way of organising political life, that it has, in other words, the greatest moral value.

---

[10] *Ante*, 105.
[11] *Per* Finnis, *op. cit.*, n. 46, Chap. XIII. It was apparently Hart's advice to place the chapter on "God" as an appendix. Hart was worried that a theological conclusion might undermine the book as a work of philosophy. See Lacey, above n. 48. p. 347. On Finnis and religion see J. Finnis (2006) 51 Am. J. Jurisprudence 107. See also M. Murphy (2007) 13 *Legal Theory* 187, and Finnis's response at (2007) 13 *Legal Theory* 315, 339–344.

Besides this problem other questions pall into insignificance. But other nagging doubts remain. How, for example, did Finnis choose his list of basic goods? If they are the chief objects to which human beings incline, there is a suspicion that he has paid too much attention to good, too little to evil. Linked to this is the distinct feeling that reason may not always point us in Finnis's directions. It is not altogether clear what Finnis would suppose we ought to do then. Further, as with much natural law theorising, we are left at the end not with a blueprint for legal and political action, for his conclusions are too vague for any real value choices, but with hints, no more, of how to better ourselves and the communities within which we live.

The critical comments of Weinreb should also be noted. If, he says, Finnis's claim to provide the basic principles of law is to be supported, "his principles of practical reasonableness must indicate in a not inconsiderable number of cases what the law ought to be, with certainty".[12] Finnis argues that they do: the central principle of the law of murder, of theft, of marriage, of contract may be "straightforward applications of universally valid requirements of reasonableness", although their full integration into a legal system requires "countless elaborations" that are not all obvious or determinate.[13] Finnis writes as if there are "central principles" of law and that these are "ascertainable with certainty by his method"[14] with other less basic obligations indeterminate matters of detail. But, does the law contain central principles of that kind? It may contain very general abstract ones—the sanctity of life, for example—but these leave even the most basic legal obligations to be further determined. To take one of Finnis's examples: the law of murder is a "directive not to intentionally kill (or attempt to kill) any human being, unless in self-defence".[15] This corresponds to the "requirement of practical reason ... that one is not to deliberately kill the innocent".[16] But this leaves any number of questions unanswered. Does practical reason prohibit abortion?[17] (is a foetus a human being?) And is it innocent if it threatens the life or health of the mother? Is killing in war prohibited? Does practical reason rule out the July Plot to kill Hitler? What does practical reason have to say about capital punishment?[18] Similar questions dog Finnis's references to the central principle of the law of theft, marriage and contract. Take marriage, for example. It might be easy to formulate a central principle such as fidelity, but does practical reason dictate whether there should be a law of divorce and, if so, on what grounds, whether marriage should be monogamous, whether same sex marriages should be

---

[12] *Natural Law and Justice* (1987), p. 113.
[13] *Op. cit.*, n. 56, p. 289.
[14] *Per* Weinreb, *op. cit.*, n. 59, p. 113.
[15] *Op. cit.*, n. 56, p. 281.
[16] *ibid.*
[17] Finnis's view on this is clear: see in R. Dworkin (ed.), *The Philosophy of Law*.
[18] And what of the execution of children who kill, a practice which still operates in several Third World countries and did in the U.S. until recently? See (1993) 33 Santa Clara L. Rev. 283.

permitted?[19] The questions are legion: but the answers despite Finnis's urgings, are not there.


## Murphy and Natural Law

Finnis's book was published in 1980. The most significant book on natural law since is Mark Murphy's *Natural Law in Jurisprudence and Politics*.[20] It is central to natural law jurisprudence, according to Murphy, that "law is backed by decisive reasons for compliance". Natural law political philosophy claims, in contrast, that "law has this reason-giving force through the common good of the political community".[21] The connection between law and reasons for action thus has to be explained.

There are different possible explanations. There is a strong reading which emphasizes legal validity: a law not supported by decisive reasons for compliance is not a law at all. This is the classical natural law position (though, of course, Finnis contests this[22]). There is also a weak reading that a law not supported by decisive reasons is defective, both morally and legally. There is also a moral reading of natural law: on this understanding a law not backed by decisive reasons for action cannot be regarded as morally binding.

Murphy favours the weak reading. There are, he argues, three possible arguments for this. One is Finnis's: law which lacks moral force is not law in the "focal" sense of the term.[23] Murphy does not accept this reasoning. He raises instead two other possible arguments: one emanates from law's function—it is the characteristic activity of law to provide dictates which are backed by decisive reasons for action. A law which does not do this fails as law. Secondly, he argues that it is proper to understand the law as a speaker and to see its norms as demands to those to whom it applies. He then argues that a demand to do x is defective (as an illocutionary act) unless there are decisive reasons for those to whom it is directed to x. A law not backed by decisive reasons for action is defective as law. Murphy employs both of these routes to support the weak reading.

But how is this different from Raz's thesis—discussed in a later chapter[24]—that law claims authority? "The authority's directives become our reasons", Raz emphasizes.[25] The difference is that Raz invokes the concept of "authority" and Murphy the support of "decisive reasons". It can be argued that the law would not be authoritative unless one reason why obedience is expected is that it is the law. Murphy puts distance

---

[19]  Finnis's view on this is clear! (1997) 42 Amer. J. Jurisprudence 97.
[20]  (2006). See also below, 208. This account of Murphy relies heavily on J. Crowe (2007) 27 OX. J. *Legal Studies* 775.
[21]  *Natural Law in Jurisprudence and Politics* (2006), pp.1–2.
[22]  See above, 126.
[23]  See above, 129. Note the influence of Hart on "core" and "penumbra".
[24]  Below, p. 391.
[25]  *Practical Reason and Norms* (1990), p. 193.

between himself and Raz, but their positions may not be as far apart as Murphy believes.

Having concluded that law which is not supported by decisive reasons for compliance is defective as law, Murphy turns to natural law political theory and asks how law can come to be backed by decisive reasons for action. His answer is in terms of the "common good". But in what does this consist? There are, Murphy argues, three different conceptions of the common good. The instrumentalist view sees it as consisting of those conditions either necessary or helpful for members of the community to pursue the ends they consider valuable. The distinctive good view focuses on what is good for the community as a whole irrespective of what is good for members of the community. The aggregative view—Murphy's favoured conception—sees the common goods belonging to particular citizens.[26]

This produces the "common good principle" viz., every person has an obligation to do his/her share for the common good. The common good is an ideal, the total realisation of which is unlikely to happen. It is also open-ended: there are many ways in which it can be brought about. To tackle these characteristics of the common good, Murphy introduces the concept of a "determination". As explained by Crowe:

> "[A] determination of some objective O is a secondary objective that stands to O either as an approximation of an unattainable ideal or as a more precise rendering of an open-ended goal".[27]

In Murphy's view, law gains its normative force "as a partial determination of the common good principle".[28] But why law? Why should law play this role? Granted that we all have to do our share for the common good it must be asked "why should one adhere to the law's determination of the principle, rather than following one's own determination or that offered by some other person or body".[29]

Finnis's answer emphasizes the status of law as a "salient co-ordinator" of action with regard to the common good.[30] But does the law hold authority because it offers a salient solution to the co-ordination problem, as Finnis believes? That there is value in the law doing so does not mean that law actually is authoritative. As Crowe points out, "at the most, it means that members of the community have reason to make law authoritative".[31] Without authority, there is no obligation to follow the law's determination. Murphy rejects Finnis' explanation, and finds one instead in consent. Not, it should be added, in consent constituted by a speech act or in an attitude of approval, but rather in the "acceptance"

[26] *Per* J. Crowe, n. 20, above, p. 779.
[27] *ibid.*
[28] *ibid.*
[29] *ibid.*
[30] See *Natural Law and Natural Rights* (1980), and (1984) 1 Notre Dame Journal of Law, Policy and Ethics 114.
[31] Above, n. 20, p. 780.

sense, "where one adopts open-ended determination to be filled—by the dictates of other parties".[32] Consent is not irrevocable: "even if a person accepts a determination of the common good principle that includes acting as the law requires ... he or she may free himself or herself from obligation simply by rejecting that determination".[33] Crowe observes that Murphy's account "fails to establish that all citizens are bound by the laws of their community; at most, it shows that all *practically reasonable* citizens of a *generally just* legal system will choose to accept its authority".[34]

## CONCLUSION

In what lies the value of natural law thinking? Natural law deflects our attention from the historically fortuitous in human laws and institutions to the universal, or near-universal,[35] principles which underlie them. It shows us the need to study law in the context of other disciplines: in particular, it makes us aware of the way in which moral goals enter the law and play a part in its administration and in the adjudication of cases. Of course, these lessons, important though they are, can be learnt elsewhere. The social context of law can be appreciated by studying social theory and law (American realism, the sociology of law, Marxism) and within positivism explanations are to be found of ways in which moral aims enter the law and its adjudication.[36] But natural law does make us think about why we have law, what law can achieve and what we should do when we think it is failing. Some may find the link depicted by natural lawyers between law and human good[37] exaggerated, even naive. After all, it may be said, look at the oppression, the injustices perpetrated in the name of law. Positivists will continue to criticise the refusal of natural lawyers to answer the question *quid juris*,[38] their refusal to tell us categorically whether something is or is not law. Finnis's distinction between "focal meaning" of law and laws which are "less legal"[39] only seems to perpetuate old confusions between what is law and what are appropriate standards of criticism of law.

In the next chapters we must see whether positivists overcome these problems. Are they able satisfactorily to distinguish valid law from non-valid "law", law from morality? And if they are, do they sacrifice anything in the process?

---

[32] *ibid*, p. 781.
[33] Above, n. 20, p. 125.
[34] Above, n. 20, p. 781.
[35] *cf*. Mead, *post*, 225.
[36] In Hart, *The Concept of Law* and D. N. MacCormick, *Legal Reasoning and Legal Theory* (1978).
[37] Most obviously in Aquinas and Finnis, but more generally as well.
[38] D'Entrèves, *Natural Law*, p. 176 concedes positivism "contains an answer to the question *quid juris*". But *cf*. Finnis, *ante*, 95 *et seq*.
[39] *Ante*, 129.

### ARISTOTLE
#### Nicomachean Ethics[40]
Natural and Legal Justice

Of political justice part is natural,[41] part legal—natural, that which everywhere has the same force and does not exist by people's thinking this or that; legal, that which is originally indifferent, but when it has been laid down is not indifferent, e.g. that a prisoner's ransom shall be a mina, or that a goat and not two sheep shall be sacrificed, and again all the laws that are passed for particular cases, e.g. that sacrifice shall be made in honour of Brasidas, and the provisions of decrees. Now some think that all justice is of this sort, because that which is by nature is unchangeable and has everywhere the same force (as fire burns both here and in Persia), while they see change in the things recognised as just. This, however, is not true in this unqualified way, but is true in a sense; or rather, with the gods it is perhaps not true at all, while with us there is something that is just even by nature, yet all of it is changeable; but still some is by nature, some not by nature. It is evident which sort of thing, among things capable of being otherwise, is by nature; and which is not but is legal and conventional, assuming that both are equally changeable. And in all other things the same distinction will apply; by nature the right hand is stronger, yet it is possible that all men should come to be ambidextrous. The things which are just by virtue of convention and expediency are like measures; for wine and corn measures are not everywhere equal, but larger in wholesale and smaller in retail markets. Similarly, the things which are just not by nature but by human enactment are not everywhere the same, since constitutions also are not the same, though there is but one which is everywhere by nature the best.[42]                                          [pp. 124; 1134 b; 18–1135 a. 5]

### CICERO
#### De Re Publica

True law is right reason in agreement with nature; it is of universal application, unchanging and everlasting; it summons to duty by its commands, and averts from wrongdoing by its prohibitions. And it does not lay its commands or prohibitions upon good men in vain, though neither have any effect on the wicked. It is a sin to try to alter this law, nor is it allowable to attempt to repeal any part of it, and it is impossible to abolish it entirely. We cannot be freed from its obligations by senate or people, and we need not look outside ourselves for an expounder or interpreter of it. And there will not be different laws at Rome and at Athens, or different laws now and in the future, but one eternal and unchangeable law will be valid for all nations and all times, and there will be one master and ruler, that is, God, over us all, for he is the author of this law, its promulgator, and its enforcing judge. Whoever is disobedient is fleeing from himself and

---

[40] [Translated, Sir David Ross.]
[41] [*Cf.* the discussion on the nature of justice in Plato, *Republic*, 367 (Cornford's translation, pp. 51–52).]
[42] [The doctrine of natural justice is an attempt to justify philosophically the Greek belief in a fundamental law but it played little part in Aristotle's ethics, *e.g.* he does not say that positive law which conflicts with natural justice is invalid. *Cf.* Kelsen, *What is Justice?*, p. 384. For a modern attempt to re-interpret the distinction between nature and convention, see Stuart Hampshire, in *Utilitarianism and Beyond* (eds. A. Sen and B. Williams, 1983), Chap. 7. He argues that there are two kinds of moral claim, one referable to universal human needs, and the other operating within a desired way of life and thought essential within that way of life and equally valid within that context.]

denying his human nature, and by reason of this very fact he will suffer the worst penalties, even if he escapes what is commonly considered punishment.

[p. 21; III, 22]

## JUSTINIAN
### Institutes[43]
### Of the Law of Nature, Universal Law and the Civil Law

The law of nature is the law which nature has taught all animals. This law is not peculiar to the human race, but belongs to all living creatures, birds, beasts and fishes. This is the source of the union of male and female, which we called matrimony, as well as of the procreation and rearing of children; which things are characteristic of the whole animal creation.

The civil law is distinguished from universal law as follows. Every people which is governed by laws and customs uses partly a law peculiar to itself, partly a law common to all mankind. For the law which each people makes for itself is peculiar to itself, and is called the civil law, as being the law peculiar to the community in question. But the law which natural reason has prescribed for all mankind is held in equal observance amongst all peoples and is called universal law, as being the law which all peoples use. Thus the Roman People uses a law partly peculiar to itself, partly common to all mankind.

The civil law takes its name from the country to which it belongs. ... But universal law is common to the whole human race. For under the pressure of use and necessity the peoples of mankind have created for themselves certain rules. Thus, wars arose and captivity and slavery, which is contrary to natural law, for almost all contracts are derived, such as sale, hire, partnership, deposit, loan and countless others.

The laws of nature which are observed amongst all people alike, being established by a divine providence, remain ever fixed and immutable, but the laws which each State makes for itself are frequently changed either by tacit consent of the people, or by a later statute.                                   [pp. 41–43; 1.2.]

## AQUINAS
### Summa Theologica[44]
### Law in General

*(Qu. 90)*

*The Nature of Law* (Art. 1, concl.)

Law is a rule or measure of action in virtue of which one is led to perform certain actions and restrained from the performance of others. The term "law" derives [etymologically] from "binding," because by it one is bound to a certain course of action. But the rule and measure of human action is reason, which is the first principle of human action: this is clear from what we have said elsewhere. It is reason which directs action to its appropriate end; and this, according to the Philosopher,[45] is the first principle of all activity.

---

[43]  [Translated, R. W. Lee.]
[44]  [Translated, J. G. Dawson.]
[45]  [*i.e.* Aristotle.]

*Reason and Will in Law* (*ibid.* ad 3um.)

Reason has power to move to action from the will, as we have shown already: for reason enjoins all that is necessary to some end, in virtue of the fact that that end is desired. But will, if it is to have the authority of law, must be regulated by reason when it commands. It is in this sense that we should understand the saying that the will of the prince has the power of law. [46] In any other sense the will of the prince becomes an evil rather than law.

*The Object of the Law is the Common Good* (*ibid.* Art. 2, concl.)

Since every part bears the same relation to its whole as the imperfect to the perfect, and since one man is a part of that perfect whole which is the community, it follows that the law must have as its proper object the well-being of the whole community. So the Philosopher, in his definition of what pertains to law, makes mention both of happiness and of political union. He says (*Ethics* V. chap. 1): "We call that legal and just which makes for and preserves the well-being of the community through common political action": and the perfect community is the city, as is shown in the first book of the *Politics* (chap. 1).

*Who has the right to promulgate Law* (*ibid.* Art. 3, concl.)

Law, strictly understood, has as its first and principal object the ordering of the common good. But to order affairs to the common good is the task either of the whole community or of some one person who represents it. Thus the promulgation of law is the business either of the whole community or of that political person whose duty is the care of the common good. Here as in every other case it is the one who decrees the end who also decrees the means thereto.

*(ibid.* ad 2um.)

A private person has no authority to compel right living. He may only advise; but if his advice is not accepted he has no power of compulsion. But law, to be effective in promoting right living, must have such compelling force; as the Philosopher says (*X Ethics*, chap. 9). But the power of compulsion belongs either to the community as a whole, or to its official representative whose duty it is to inflict penalties, as we shall see later. He alone, therefore, has the right to make laws.

*(ibid.* ad 3um.)

Just as one man is a member of a family, so a household forms part of a city: but a city is a perfect community, as is shown in the first book of the *Politics*. Similarly, as the well-being of one man is not a final end, but is subordinate to the common good, so also the well-being of any household must be subordinate to the interests of the city, which is a perfect community. So the head of a family may make certain rules and regulations, but not such as have, properly speaking, the force of law.

*Definition of Law* (*ibid.* Art. 4, concl.)

From the foregoing we may gather the correct definition of law. It is nothing else than a rational ordering of things which concern the common good; promulgated by whoever is charged with the care of the community.

---

[46] [The reference is to the text in the Roman law: "*Quod principi placuit legis habet vigorem.*" (*Dig.*, I, iv, 1, Ulpianus.)]

*The various types of law*

(Qu. 91)

### The Eternal Law

As we have said, law is nothing else but a certain dictate of the practical reason "in the prince" who rules a perfect community. It is clear, however, supposing the world to be governed by divine providence ... that the whole community of the Universe is governed by the divine reason. Thus the rational guidance of created things on the part of God, as the Prince of the universe, has the quality of law. ... This we can call the eternal law.[47]

### The Natural Law (Art. 2, concl.)

Since all things which are subject to divine providence are measured and regulated by the eternal law—as we have already shown—it is clear that all things participate to some degree in the eternal law; in so far as they derive from it certain inclinations to those actions and aims which are proper to them. But, of all others, rational creatures are subject to divine providence in a very special way; being themselves made participators in providence itself, in that they control their own actions and the actions of others. So they have a certain share in the divine reason itself, deriving therefrom a natural inclination to such actions and ends as are fitting. This participation in the eternal law by rational creatures is called the natural law.

### Human Law (Art. 3, concl.)

Just as in speculative reason we proceed from indemonstrable principles, naturally known, to the conclusions of the various sciences, such conclusions not being innate but arrived at by the use of reason; so also the human reason has to proceed from the precepts of the natural law, as though from certain common and indemonstrable principles, to other more particular dispositions. And such particular dispositions, arrived at by an effort of reason, are called human laws: provided that the other conditions necessary to all law, which we have already noted, are observed.

*The natural law[48]*

(Qu. 94)

### Precepts of the Natural Law (Art. 2, concl.)

The order of the precepts of the natural law corresponds to the order of our natural inclinations. For there is in man a natural and initial inclination to good which he has in common with all substances; in so far as every substance seeks its own preservation according to its own nature. Corresponding to this inclination, the natural law contains all that makes for the preservation of human life, and all that is opposed to it dissolution. Secondly, there is to be found in man a further

[47] [The Scholastic approach to natural law was in a sense a form of rationalism in that from its own premises it claimed to reason with rigorous logic, but it must not be overlooked that these premises themselves were derived from certain theological dogmas and traditions which it was forbidden to deny or even doubt. These, therefore, form fundamental presuppositions of the system which were not open to rational refutation.]

[48] [See, generally, O'Connor, *Aquinas and Natural Law* (1967), particularly Chap. VII.]

inclination to certain more specific ends, according to the nature which man shares with other animals. In virtue of this inclination there pertains to the natural law all those instincts "which nature has taught all animals,"[49] such as sexual relationship, the rearing of offspring, and the like. Thirdly, there is in man a certain inclination to good, corresponding to his rational nature: and this inclination is proper to man alone. So man has a natural inclination to know the truth about God and to live in society. In this respect there come under the natural law, all actions connected with such inclinations: namely, that a man should avoid ignorance, that he must not give offence to others with whom he must associate and all actions of like nature.

### The Universality of the Natural Law (Art. 4, concl.)

As we have just said, all those actions pertain to the natural law to which man has a natural inclination: and among such it is proper to man to seek to act according to reason. Reason, however, proceeds from general principles to matters of detail ... The practical and the speculative reason, however, go about this process in different ways. For the speculative reason is principally employed about necessary truths, which cannot be otherwise than they are; so that truth is to be found as surely in its particular conclusions as in general principles themselves. But practical reason is employed about contingent matters, into which human actions enter: thus, though there is a certain necessity in its general principles, the further one departs from generality the more is the conclusion open to exception.

So it is clear that as far as the general principles of reason are concerned, whether speculative or practical, there is one standard of truth or rightness for everybody, and that this is equally known by every one. With regard to the particular conclusions of speculative reason, again there is one standard of truth for all; but in this case it is not equally known by every one. With regard to the particular conclusions of speculative reason, again there is one standard of truth for all; but in this case it is not equally known to all; it is universally true, for instance, that the three interior angles of a triangle equal two right angles; but this conclusion is not known by everybody. When we come to the particular conclusions of the practical reason, however, there is neither the same standard of truth or rightness for everyone, nor are these conclusions equally known to all. All people, indeed, realize that it is right and true to act according to reason. And from this principle we may deduce as an immediate conclusion that debts must be repaid. This conclusion holds in the majority of cases. But it could happen in some particular case that it would be injurious, and therefore irrational, to repay a debt; if, for instance, the money repaid were used to make war against one's own country. Such exceptions are all the more likely to occur the more we get down to particular cases: take, for instance, the question of repaying a debt together with a certain security, or in some specific way. The more specialised the conditions applied, the greater is the possibility of an exception arising which will make it right to make restitution or not.

So we must conclude that the law of nature, as far as general first principles are concerned, is the same for all as a norm of right conduct and is equally well known to all. But as to more particular cases which are conclusions from such general principles it remains the same for all only in the majority of cases, both as a norm and as to the extent to which it is known. Thus in particular instances it can admit of exceptions: both with regard to rightness, because of certain impediments (just as in nature the generation and change of bodies is subject to accidents caused by some impediment), and with regard to its knowability. This can happen because reason is, in some persons, depraved by passion or by some evil habit of nature; as Caesar relates in *De Bello Gallico* (VI, 23), of the Germans,

[49] [*Cf. ante*, 99.]

that at one time they did not consider robbery to be wrong; though it is obviously against natural law.

### The Immutability of Natural Law (Art. 5.)

There are two ways in which natural law may be understood to change. One, in that certain additions are made to it. And in this sense there is no reason why it should not change. Both the divine law and human laws do, in fact, add much to the natural law which is useful to human activity.

Or again the natural law would be understood to change by having something subtracted from it. If, for instance, something ceased to pertain to the natural law which was formerly part of it. In this respect, and as far as first principles are concerned, it is wholly unchangeable. As to secondary precepts, which, as we have said, follow as immediate conclusions from first principles, the natural law again does not change; in the sense that it remains a general rule for the majority of cases that what the natural law prescribes is correct. It may, however, be said to change in some particular case, or in a limited number of examples; because of some special causes which make it observation impossible, as we have already pointed out.

*Human law*

(Qu. 95)

### The Necessity for Human Laws (Art. 1, concl.)

From the foregoing it is clear that there is in man a natural aptitude to virtuous action. But men can achieve the perfection of such virtue only by the practice of a "certain discipline."—And men who are capable of such discipline without the aid of others are rare indeed.—So we must help one another to achieve that discipline which leads to a virtuous life. There are, indeed, some young men, readily inclined to a life of virtue through a good natural disposition or upbringing, or particularly because of divine help; and for such, paternal guidance and advice are sufficient. But there are others, of evil disposition and prone to vice, who are not easily moved by words. These it is necessary to restrain from wrongdoing by force and by fear. When they are thus prevented from doing evil, a quiet life is assured to the rest of the community; and they are themselves drawn eventually, by force of habit, to do voluntarily what once they did only out of fear, and so to practise virtue. Such discipline which compels under fear of penalty is the discipline of law. Thus, the enactment of laws was necessary to the peaceful and virtuous life of men. And the Philosopher says (I *Politics*, 2): "Man, when he reaches the perfection of virtue is the best of all animals: but if he goes his way without law and justice he becomes the worst of all brutes." For man, unlike other animals, has the weapon of reason with which to exploit his base desires and cruelty.

### The Subordination of Human Laws to the Natural Law (Art. 2, concl.)

Saint Augustine says (I *De Lib. Arbitrio*, 5): "There is no law unless it be just." So the validity of law depends upon its justice. But in human affairs a thing is said to be just when it accords aright with the rule of reason: and, as we have already seen, the first rule of reason is the natural law. Thus all humanly enacted laws are in accord with reason to the extent that they derive from the natural law. And if a human law is at variance in any particular with the natural law, it is no longer legal, but rather a corruption of law.

But it should be noted that there are two ways in which anything may derive from natural law. First, as a conclusion from more general principles. Secondly, as a determination of certain general features. The former is similar to the method of the sciences in which demonstrative conclusions are drawn from first principles. The second way is like to that of the arts in which some common form is determined to a particular instance: as, for example, when an architect, starting from the general idea of a house, then goes on to design the particular plan of this or that house. So, therefore, some derivations are made from the natural law by way of formal conclusion: as the conclusion, "Do no murder," derives from the precept, "Do harm to no man." Other conclusions are arrived at as determinations of particular cases. So the natural law establishes that whoever transgresses shall be punished. But that a man should be punished by a specific penalty is a particular determination of the natural law.

Both types of derivation are to be found in human law. But those which are arrived at in the first way as sanctioned not only by human law, but by the natural law also; while those arrived at by the second method have the validity of human law alone.

## T. HOBBES
### Leviathan
(1651)

Whatsoever therefore is consequent to a time of Warre, where every man is Enemy to every man; the same is consequent to the time, wherein men live without other security, than what their own strength, and their own invention shall furnish them withall. In such condition, there is no place for Industry; because the fruit thereof is uncertain: and consequently no Culture of the Earth; no Navigation, nor use of the commodities that may be imported by Sea; no commodious Building; no Instruments of moving, and removing such things as require much force; no Knowledge of the face of the Earth; no account of Time; no Arts; no Letters; no Society; and which is worst of all, continuall feare, and danger of violent death; And the life of man, solitary, poore, nasty, brutish, and short...

To this warre of every man against every man, this also is consequent; that nothing can be Unjust. The notions of Right and Wrong, Justice and Injustice have there no place. Where there is no common Power, there is no Law: where no Law, no Injustice. Force, and Fraud, are in warre the two Cardinall vertues. Justice, and Injustice are none of the Faculties neither of the Body, nor Mind. If they were, they might be in a man that were alone in the world, as well as his Senses, and Passions. They are Qualities, that relate to men in Society, not in Solitude. It is consequent also to the same condition, that there be no Propriety, no Dominion, no *Mine and Thine* distinct; but onely that to be every mans that he can get; and for so long, as he can keep it. And thus much for the ill condition, which man by meer Nature is actually placed in; though with a possibility to come out of it, consisting partly in the Passions, partly in his Reason...

And because the condition of Man, (as hath been declared in the precedent Chapter) is a condition of Warre of every one against every one; in which case every one is governed by his own Reason; and there is nothing he can make use of, that may not be a help unto him, in preserving his life against his enemyes; It followeth, that in such a condition, every man has a Right to every thing; even to one anothers body. And therefore, as long as this naturall Right of every man to every thing endureth, there can be no security to any man, (how strong or wise soever he be), of living out the time, which Nature ordinarily alloweth men to live. And consequently it is a precept, or generall rule of Reason, *That every man, ought to endeavour Peace, as farre as he has hope of obtaining it; and when he cannot obtain it, that he may seek, and use, all helps, and advantages of Warre.* The first branch of which Rule, containeth the first, and Fundamentall Law of Nature; which is, *to seek Peace, and follow it.* The Second, the summe of the Right of Nature; which is, *By all means we can, to defend our selves.*

From this Fundamental Law of Nature, by which men are commanded to endeavour Peace, is derived this second Law; *That a man be willing, when others are so too, as farre-forth, as for Peace, and defence of himselfe he shall think it necessary, to lay down this right to all things; and be contented with so much liberty against other men, as he would allow other men against himselfe.* For as long as every man holdeth this Right, of doing any thing he liketh; so long as all men in the condition of Warre. But if other men will not lay down their Right, as well as expose himself to Prey, (which no man is bound to) rather than to dispose himselfe to Peace. This is that Law of the Gospell; *Whatsoever you require that others should do to you, that do ye to them.* And that Law of all men, *Quod tibi fieri non vis, alteri ne feceris.* [pp. 186–190]

THE finall Cause, End, or Designe of men, (who naturally love Liberty, and Dominion over others), in the introduction of that restraint upon themselves, (in which wee see them live in Common-wealths,) is the foresight of their own pre-servation, and of a more contented life thereby; that is to say, of getting them-selves out from that miserable condition of Warre, which is necessarily consequent (as hath been shewn) to the naturall Passions of men, when there is no visible Power to keep them in awe, and tye them by feare of punishment to the performance of their Covenants, and observation of those Lawes of Nature ...

[T]he agreement of these creatures is Naturall; that of men, is by Covenant only, which is Artificiall: and therefore it is no wonder if there be somewhat else required (besides Covenant) to make their Agreement constant and lasting; which is a Common Power, to keep them in awe, and to direct their actions to the Common Benefit.

The only way to erect such a Common Power, as may be able to defend them from the invasion of Forraigners, and the injuries of one another, and thereby to secure them in such sort, as that by their owne industrie, and by the fruites of the Earth, they may nourish themselves and live contentedly; is, to conferre all their power and strength upon one Man, or upon one Assembly of men, that may reduce all their Wills, by plurality of voices, unto one Will: which is as much as to say, to appoint one man, or Assembly of men, to beare their Person; and every one to owne, and acknowledge himselfe to be Author of whatsoever he that so beareth their Person, shall Act, or cause to be Acted, in those things which concerne the Common Peace and Safetie; and therein to submit their Wills, every one to his Will, and their Judgments, to his Judgment. This is more than Consent, or Concord; it is a reall Unitie of them all, in one and the same Person, made by Covenant of every man with every man, in such manner, as if every man should say to every man, *I Authorise and give up my Right of Governing my selfe, to this Man, or to this Assembly of men, on this condition, that thou give up thy Right to him, and Authorise all his Actions in like manner.* This done, the Multitude so united in one Person, is called a COMMON-WEALTH, in latine CIVITAS. This is the Generation of that great LEVIATHAN, or rather (to speake more reverently) of that *Mortall God*, to which wee owe under the *Immortall God*, our peace and defence. For by this Authoritie, given him by every particular man in the Common-Wealth, he hath the use of so much Power and Strength conferred on him, that by terror thereof, he is inabled to forme the wills of them all consisteth the Essence of the Common-wealth; which (to define it), is *One Person, of whose Acts a great Multitude, by mutuall Covenants one with another, have made themselves every one the Author, to the end he may use the strength and means of them all, as he shall think expedient, for their Peace and Common Defence.*

And he that carryeth this Person, is called SOVERAIGNE, and said to have *Soveraigne Power*; and everyone besides, his SUBJECT.

The attaining to this Soveraigne Power, is by two wayes. One, by Naturall force; as when a man maketh his children, to submit themselves, and their children to his government, as being able to destroy them if they refuse; or by Warre subdueth his enemies to his will, giving them their lives on that condition. The other, is when men agree amongst themselves, to submit to some Man, or Assembly of men, voluntarily, on confidence to be protected by him against all others. This later, may be called a Political Common-wealth or Common-wealth by *Institution*; and the former, a Common-wealth by *Acquisition*. [pp. 223–228]

## LOCKE
### Two Treatises of Government
Civil Government

But though this be a state of liberty,[50] yet it is not a state of licence; though man in that state have an uncontrollable liberty to dispose of his person or possessions, yet he has not liberty to destroy himself, or so much as any creature in his possession, but where some nobler use than its bare preservation calls for it. The state of Nature has a law of Nature to govern it, which obliges everyone, and reason, which is that law, teaches all mankind who will but consult it, that being all equal and independent, no one ought to harm another in his life, health, liberty or possessions; for men being all the workmanship of one omnipotent and infinitely wise Maker; all the servants of one sovereign Master, sent into the world by His order and about His business; they are His property, whose workmanship they are made to last during His, not one another's pleasure. And, being furnished with like faculties, sharing all in one community of Nature, there cannot be supposed any such subordination among us that may authorise us to destroy one another, as if we were made for one another's uses, as the inferior ranks of creatures are for ours. Everyone as he is bound to preserve himself, and not to quit his station wilfully, so by the like reason, when his own preservation comes not in competition, ought he as much as he can to preserve the rest of mankind, and not unless it be to do justice on an offender, take away or impair the life, or what tends to the preservation of the life, the liberty, health, limb, or goods of another.

And that all men may be restrained from invading others' rights, and from doing hurt to one another, and the law of Nature be observed, which willeth the peace and preservation of all mankind, the execution of the law of Nature is in that state put into every man's hands, whereby every one has a right to punish the transgressors of that law to such a degree as may hinder its violation. For the law of Nature would, as all other laws that concern men in this world, be in vain if there were nobody that in the state of Nature had a power to execute that law, and thereby preserve the innocent and restrain offenders; and if any one in the state of Nature may punish another for any evil he has done, every one may do so. For in that state of perfect equality, where naturally there is no superiority or jurisdiction of one over another, what any may do in prosecution of that law, every one must needs have a right to do.

And thus, in the state of Nature, one man comes by a power over another, but yet no absolute or arbitrary power to use a criminal, when he has got him in his hands, according to the passionate heats or boundless extravagancy of his own will, but only to retribute to him so far as calm reason and conscience dictate, what is proportionate to his transgression, which is so much as may serve for reparation and restraint. For these two are the only reasons why one man may lawfully do harm to another, which is that we call punishment. In transgressing the law of Nature, the offender declares himself to live by another rule than that of reason and common equity, which is that measure God has set to the actions of

[50]  [*i.e.* the state of nature, as described by Locke.]

men for their mutual security, and so he becomes dangerous to mankind: the tie which is to secure them from injury and violence being slighted and broken by him, which being a trespass against the whole species, and the peace and safety of it, provided for by the law of Nature, every man upon this score, by the right he hath to preserve mankind in general, may restrain, or where it is necessary, destroy things noxious to them, and so may bring such evil on any one who hath transgressed that law, as may make him repent the doing of it, and thereby deter him, and, by his example, other from doing the like mischief. And in this case, and upon this ground, every man hath a right to punish the offender, and be executioner of the law of nature. [Bk. II, cap. 2]

Man being born, as has been proved, with a title to perfect freedom and an uncontrolled enjoyment of all the rights and privileges of the law of Nature, equally with any other man, or number of men in the world, hath by nature a power not only to preserve his property[51]—that is, his life, liberty, and estate, against the injuries and attempts of other men, but to judge of and punish the breaches of that law in others, as he is persuaded the offence deserves, even with death itself, in crimes where the heinousness of the fact, in his opinion, requires it. But because no political society can be, nor subsist, without having in itself the power to preserve the property, and in order thereunto punish the offences of all those of that society, there, and there only, is political society where every one of the members hath quitted this natural power, resigned it up into the hands of the community in all cases that exclude him not from appealing for protection to the law established by it.[52] And thus all private judgment of every particular member being excluded, the community comes to be umpire, and by understanding indifferent rules and men authorised by the community for their execution, decides all the differences that may happen between any members of that society concerning any matter of right, and punishes those offences which any member hath committed against the society with such penalties as the law has established; whereby it is easy to discern who are, and are not, in political society together. Those who are united into one body, and have a common established law and judicature to appeal to, with authority to decide controversies between them and punish offenders, are in civil society one with another; but those who have no such common appeal, I mean on earth, are still in the state of Nature, each being where there is no other, judge for himself and executioner; which is, as I have before showed it, the perfect state of Nature. [Bk. II, cap. 7]

Though the legislative, whether placed in one or more, whether it be always in being or only by intervals, though it be the supreme power in every commonwealth, yet, first, it is not, nor can possibly be, absolutely arbitrary over the lives and fortunes of the people. For it being but the joint power of every member of the society given up to that person or assembly which is legislator, it can be no more than those persons had in a state of Nature before they entered into society, and gave it up to the community. For nobody can transfer to another more power than he has in himself, and nobody has an absolute arbitrary power over himself, or over any other, to destroy his own life, or take away the life or property of another. A man, as has been proved, cannot subject himself to the arbitrary power of another; and having, in the state of Nature, no arbitrary power over the life, liberty, or possession of another, but only so much as the law of Nature gave him for the preservation of himself and the rest of mankind, this is all he doth, or can give up to the commonwealth, and by it to the legislative power, so that the legislative can have no more than this. Their power in the utmost bounds of it is limited to the public good of the society. It is a power that hath no other end but

---

[51] [The so-called Whig theory of government was primarily aimed at the preservation of private property, even against the ruler himself. Life and liberty are characteristically treated as mere aspects of the fundamental property right, see *ante*, 109.]

[52] [This is Locke's version of the social contract.]

preservation, and therefore can never have a right to destroy, enslave, or designedly to impoverish the subjects; the obligations of the law of Nature cease not in society, but only in many cases are drawn closer, and have, by human laws, known penalties annexed to them to enforce their observation. Thus the law of Nature stands as an eternal rule to all men, legislators as well as others. The rules that they make for other men's actions must, as well as their own and other men's actions, be conformable to the law of Nature—*i.e.*, to the will of God, of which that is a declaration, and the fundamental law of Nature being the preservation of mankind, no human sanction can be good or valid against it.   [Bk. II, cap. 11]

## J.J. ROUSSEAU
### The Social Contract
That We Must Always Go Back to an Original Compact

. . . Not matter how many isolated individuals may submit to the enforced control of a single conqueror, the resulting relationship will ever be that of Master and Slave, never of People and Ruler. The body of men so controlled may be an agglomeration; it is not an association. It implies neither public welfare nor a body politic. An individual may conquer half the world, but he is still only an individual. His interests, wholly different from those of his subjects, are private to himself. When he dies his empire is left scattered and disintegrated. He is like an oak which crumbles and collapses in ashes so soon as the fire consumes it.

"A People," says Grotius, "may give themselves to a king." His argument implies that the said People were already a People before this act of surrender. The very act of gift was that of a political group and presupposed public deliberation. Before, therefore, we consider the act by which a People is constituted as their king, it were well if we considered the act by which a People chooses such. For it necessarily precedes the other, and is the true foundation on which all Societies rest.

Had there been no original compact, why, unless the choice were unanimous, should the minority ever have agreed to accept the decision of the majority? What right have the hundred who desire a master to vote for the ten who do not? The institution of the franchise is, in itself, a form of compact, and assumes that, at least once in its operation, complete unanimity existed.

### *Of the social fact*

I assume, for the sake of argument, that a point was reached in the history of mankind when the obstacles to continuing in a state of Nature were stronger than the forces which each individual could employ to the end of continuing in it. The original state of Nature, therefore, could no longer endure, and the human race would have perished had it not changed its manner of existence.

Now, since men can by no means engender new powers, but can only unite and control those of which they are already possessed, there is no way in which they can maintain themselves save by coming together and pooling their strength in a way that will enable them to withstand any resistance exerted upon them from without. They must develop some sort of central direction and learn to act in concert.

Such a concentration of powers can be brought about only as the consequence of an agreement reached between individuals. But the self-preservation of each single man derives primarily from his own strength and from his own freedom. How, then, can he limit these without, at the same time, doing himself an injury and neglecting that care which it is his duty to devote to his own concerns? This difficulty, in so far as it is relevant to my subject, can be expressed as follows:

"Some form of association must be found as a result of which the whole strength of the community will be enlisted for the protection of the person and property of each constituent member, in such a way that each, when united to his fellows, renders obedience to his own will, and remains as free as he was before." That is the basic problem of which the Social Contract provides the solution.

The clauses of this Contract are determined by the Act of Association in such a way that the least modification must render them null and void. Even though they may never have been formally enunciated, they must be everywhere the same, and everywhere tacitly admitted and recognised. So completely must this be the case that, should the social compact be violated, each associated individual would at once resume all the rights which once were his, and regain his natural liberty, by the mere fact of losing the agreed liberty for which he renounced it.

It must be clearly understood that the clauses in question can be reduced, in the last analysis, to one only, to wit, the complete alienation by each associate member to the community of *all his rights*. For, in the first place, since each has made surrender of himself without reservation, the resultant conditions are the same for all: and, because they are the same for all, it is in the interest of none to make them onerous to his fellows.

Furthermore, this alienation having been made unreservedly, the union of individuals is as perfect as it well can be, none of the associated members having any claim against the community. For should there be any rights left to individuals, and no common authority be empowered to pronounce as between them and the public, then each, being in some things his own judge, would soon claim to be so in all. Were that so, a state of Nature would still remain in being, the conditions of association becoming either despotic or ineffective.

In short, who so gives himself to all gives himself to none. And, since there is no member of the social group over whom we do not acquire precisely the same rights as those over ourselves which we have surrendered to him, it follows that we gain the exact equivalent of what we lose, as well as an added power to conserve what we already have.

If, then, we take from the social pact all that is not essential to it, we shall find it to be reduced to the following terms: "each of us contributes to the group his person and the powers which he wields as a person under the supreme direction of the general will and we receive into the body politic each individual as forming an indivisible part of the whole."

As soon as the act of association becomes a reality, it substitutes for the person of each of the contracting parties a moral and collective body made up of as many members of the constituting assembly has votes, which body receives from this very act of constitution its unity, its dispersed *self*, and its will. The public person thus formed by the union of individuals was known in the old days as a *City*, but now as the *Republic* or *Body Politic*. This, when it fulfills a passive role, is known by its members as *The State*, when an active one, as *The Sovereign People*, and, in contrast to other similar bodies, as a *Power*. In respect of the constituent associates, it enjoys the collective name of *The People*, the individuals who compose it being known as *Citizens* in so far as they share in the sovereign authority, as *Subjects* in so far as they owe obedience to the laws of the State. But these different terms frequently overlap, and are used indiscriminately one for the other. It is enough that we should realise the difference between them when they are employed in a precise sense.

### Of the sovereign

It is clear from the above formula that the act of association implies a mutual undertaking between the body politic and its constituent members. Each individual comprising the former contracts, so to speak, with himself and has a twofold function. As a member of the sovereign people he owes a duty to each of his neighbours, and, as a Citizen, to the sovereign people as a whole. But we cannot here apply that maxim of Civil Law according to which no man can be held to an undertaking entered into with himself, because there is a great difference between a man's duty to himself and to a whole of which he forms a part.

Here it should be pointed out that a public decision which can enjoin obedience on all subjects to their Sovereign, by reason of the double aspect under which each is seen, cannot, on the contrary, bind the sovereign in his dealings with himself. Consequently, it is against the nature of the body politic that the sovereign should impose upon himself a law which he cannot infringe. For, since he can regard himself under one aspect only, he is in the position of an individual entering into a contract with himself. Whence it follows that there is not, nor can be, any fundamental law which is obligatory for the whole body of the People, not even the social contract itself. This does not mean that the body politic is unable to enter into engagements with some other Power, provided always that such engagements do not derogate from the nature of the Contract; for the relation of the body politic to a foreign Power is that of a simple individual.

But the body politic, or Sovereign, in that it derives its being simply and solely from the sanctity of the said Contract, can never bind itself, even in its relations with a foreign Power, by any decision which might derogate from the validity of the original act. It may not, for instance, alienate any portion of itself, nor make submission to any other sovereign. To violate the act by reason of which it exists would be tantamount to destroying itself, and that which is nothing can produce nothing.

As soon as a mob has become united into a body politic, any attack upon one of its members is an attack upon itself. Still more important is the fact that, should any offence be committed against the body politic as a whole, the effect must be felt by each of its members. Both duty and interest, therefore, oblige the two contracting parties to render one another mutual assistance. The same individuals should seek to unite under this double aspect all the advantages which flow from it.

Now, the Sovereign People, having no existence outside that of the individuals who compose it, has, and can have, no interest at variance with theirs. Consequently, the sovereign power need give no guarantee to its subjects, since it is impossible that the body should wish to injure all its members, nor, as we shall see later, can it injure any single individual. The Sovereign, by merely existing, is always what it should be. But the same does not hold true of the relation of subject to sovereign. In spite of common interest, there can be no guarantee that the subject will observe his duty to the sovereign unless means are found to ensure his loyalty.

Each individual, indeed, may, as a man, exercise a will at variance with, or different from, that general will to which, as citizen, he contributes. His personal interest may dictate a line of action quite other than that demanded by the interest of all. The fact that his own existence as an individual has an absolute value, and that he is, by nature, an independent being, may lead him to conclude that what he owes to the common cause is something that he renders of his own free will; and he may decide that by leaving the debt unpaid he does less harm to his fellows than he would to himself should he make the necessary surrender. Regarding the moral entity constituting the State as a rational abstraction because it is not a man, he might enjoy his rights as a citizen without, at the same time, fulfilling his duties as a subject, and the resultant injustice might grow until it brought ruin upon the whole body politic.

In order, then, that the social compact may not be but a vain formula, it must contain, though unexpressed, the single undertaking which can alone give force to the whole, namely, that whoever shall refuse to obey the general will must be constrained by the whole body of his fellow citizens to do so: which is no more than to say that it may be necessary to compel a man to be free—freedom being that condition which, by giving each citizen to his country, guarantees him from all personal dependence and is the foundation upon which the whole political machine rests, and supplies the power which works it. Only the recognition by the individual of the rights of the community can give legal force to undertakings entered into between citizens, which, otherwise, would become absurd, tyrannical, and exposed to vast abuses.

### Of the civil state

The passage from the state of nature to the civil state produces a truly remarkable change in the individual. It substitutes justice for instinct in his behaviour, and gives to his actions a moral basis which formerly was lacking. Only when the voice of duty replaces physical impulse and when right replaces the cravings of appetite does the man who, till then, was concerned solely with himself, realise that he is under compulsion to obey quite different principles, and that he must now consult his reason and not merely respond to the promptings of desire. Although he may find himself deprived of many advantages which were his in a state of nature, he will recognise that he has gained others which are of far greater value. By dint of being exercised, his faculties will develop, his ideas taken on a wider scope, his sentiments become ennobled, and his whole soul be so elevated, that, but for the fact that misuse of the new conditions still, at times, degrades him to a point below that from which he has emerged, he would unceasingly bless the day which freed him for ever from his ancient state, and turned him from a limited and stupid animal into an intelligent being and a Man.

Let us reduce all this to terms which can be easily compared. What a man loses as a result of the Social Contract is his natural liberty and his unqualified right to lay hands on all that tempts him, provided only that he can compass its possession. What he gains is civil liberty and the ownership of what belongs to him. That we may labour under no illusion concerning these compensations, it is well that we distinguish between natural liberty which the individual enjoys so long as he is strong enough to maintain it, and civil liberty which is curtailed by the general will. Between possessions which derive from physical strength and the right of the first-comer, and ownership which can be based only on a positive title.

To the benefits conferred by the status of citizenship might be added that of Moral Freedom, which alone makes a man his own master. For to be subject to appetite is to be a slave, while to obey the laws laid down by society is to be free.                                                   [Chaps V–VIII, pp. 253–263]

### J. MARITAIN
### Man and the State
#### (1951)

Since I have not time here to discuss nonsense (we can always find very intelligent philosophers, not to name Mr. Bertrand Russell, who defend it most brilliantly) I take it for granted that we admit that there is a human nature, and that this human nature is the same in all men.[53] I take it for granted that we also admit that man is a being who is gifted with intelligence, and who, as such, acts with an understanding of what he is doing, and therefore with the power to determine for himself the ends which he pursues. On the other hand, possessed of a nature, of an ontological structure which is a locus of intelligible necessities, man possesses ends which necessarily correspond to his essential constitution and which are the same for all—as all pianos, for instance, whatever their particular type and in whatever place they may be, have as their end the production of certain attuned sounds. If

---

[53] [But see, on this facile generalisation, M. Macdonald, *post*, 152.]

they do not produce these sounds they must be tuned, or discarded as worthless. But since man is endowed with intelligence and determines his own ends, it is for him to attune himself to the ends that are necessarily demanded by his nature. This means that there is, by force and virtue of human nature itself, an order or disposition which human reason can discover and according to which the human will must act in order to attune itself to the essential and necessary ends of the human being. The unwritten law, or natural law, is nothing more than that.... [p. 78]

Natural law is not a written law. Men know it with greater or less difficulty, and in different degrees, here as elsewhere being subject to error. The only practical knowledge all men have naturally and infallibly in common as a self-evident principle, intellectually perceived by virtue of the concepts involved, is that we must do good and avoid evil. This is the preamble and the principle of natural law; it is not the law itself. Natural law is the ensemble of things to do and not to do which follow therefrom in *necessary* fashion. That every sort of error and deviation is possible in the determination of these things merely proves that our sight is weak, our nature coarse, and that innumerable accidents can corrupt our judgment. Montaigne *maliciously* remarked that, among certain peoples, incest and theft were considered virtuous acts. Pascal was scandalized by it. All this proves nothing against natural law, any more than a mistake in addition proves anything against arithmetic, or the mistakes of certain primitive peoples, for whom the stars were holes in the tent which covered the world, prove anything against astronomy.

Natural law is an unwritten law. Man's knowledge of it has increased little by little as man's moral conscience has developed. The latter was at first in a twilight state. Anthropologists have taught us within what structures of tribal life and in the midst of what half-conscious magic it was first formed. This proves merely that the knowledge men have had of the unwritten law has passed through more diverse forms and stages than certain philosophers or *theologians* have believed. The knowledge that our own moral conscience has of this law is doubtless still imperfect, and very likely it will continue to develop and to become more refined as long as mankind exists. Only when the Gospel has penetrated to the very depths of our human substance will natural law appear in its full flower and its perfection.

So the law and the knowledge of the law are to different things. Yet the law has force of law only when it is promulgated. It is only insofar as it is known and expressed in affirmations of practical reason that natural law has the force of law.

At this point let us stress that human reason does not discover the regulations of natural law in an abstract and theoretical manner, as a series of geometrical theorems. Nay more, it does not discover them through the conceptual exercise of the intellect, or by way of rational knowledge. I think that Thomas Aquinas' teaching, here, needs to be understood in a much deeper and more precise fashion than is common. When he says that human reason discovers the regulations of natural law through the guidance of the *inclinations* of human nature, he means that the very mode or manner in which human reason knows natural law is not rational knowledge, but knowledge *through inclination*. That kind of knowledge is not clear knowledge through concepts and conceptual judgments; it is obscure, unsystematic, vital knowledge by connaturality or affinity, in which the intellect, in order to form its judgment, consults and listens to the inner melody that the vibrating strings of abiding tendencies awaken in us. [pp. 81–83]

... *Positive Law*, or the body of laws (either customary law or statute law) in force in a given social group, deals with the rights and duties which are connected with the first principle, but in a *contingent* manner, by virtue of the determinate ways of conduct prescribed by the reason and the will of man when they institute the laws or mould the customs of a particular society, thus stating of themselves that in the particular group in question certain things will be good and permissible, certain other things bad and not permissible.

But it is by virtue of natural law that the law of Nations and positive law take on the force of law, and impose themselves upon the conscience. They are a prolongation or an extension of natural law, passing into objective zones which are less and less able to be adequately determined by the essential inclinations of human nature. For it is *natural law itself which requires that whatever it leaves undetermined shall subsequently be determined*, either as a right or a duty existing for all men, and of which they are made aware, not by knowledge through inclination but by conceptual reason—that is the *jus gentium*,—or—and this is positive law—as a right or a duty existing for certain men by reason of the human and contingent regulations proper to the social group of which they are a part. Thus there are imperceptible transitions (at least from the point of view of historical experience) between Natural Law, the Law of Nations, and Positive Law. There is a dynamism which impels the unwritten law to show forth in human law, and to render the latter ever more perfect and just in the very field of its contingent determinations. It is in accordance with this dynamism that the rights of human persons take political and social form in the community.

Man's right to existence, to personal freedom, and to the pursuit of perfection in his moral life, belongs, strictly speaking, to natural law.

The right to the private ownership of material goods pertains to natural law, in so far as mankind is naturally entitled to possess for its own common use the material goods of nature; it pertains to the law of Nations, or *jus gentium*, in so far as reason necessarily concludes in the light of the conditions naturally required for their management and for human work that for the sake of the common good those material goods must be privately owned. And the particular modalities of the right to private ownership, which vary according to the form of a society and the state of the development of its economy, are determined by positive law.[54]

[pp. 90–91]

## M. MACDONALD
### Natural Rights
(1948)

[After citing Maritain's view on the common nature of man (*ante*, 153) Miss Macdonald comments as follows.]

And men's rights depend upon this common nature and end by which they are subject to the natural or "unwritten" law. But this seems to me a complete mistake. Human beings are not like exactly similar bottles of whisky each marked "for export only" or some device indicating a common destination or end. Men do not share a fixed nature, nor, therefore, are there any ends which they must necessarily pursue in fulfilment of such nature. There is no definition of "man." There is a more or less vague set of properties which characterise in varying degrees and proportions those creatures which are called "human." These determine for each individual human being what he *can* do but not what he *must* do. If he has an I.Q. of 85 his intellectual activities will be limited; if he is physically weak he cannot become a heavyweight boxer. If a woman has neither good looks nor acting ability she is unlikely to succeed as a film star. But what people may do with their capacities is extremely varied, and there is no one thing which they must do in order to be human.... There is no end set for the human race by an abstraction called "human nature." There are only ends which individuals choose, or are forced by circumstances to accept. There are none which

---

[54] [One may pertinently ask how the natural law character of private ownership is vouchsafed to us; also does this merely refer to the abstract concept, since the particular modalities rest with positive law? See L. Becker, *Property Rights* (1977).]

they *must* accept. Men are not created for a purpose as a piano is built to produce certain sounds. Or if they are we have no idea of the purpose.

It is the emphasis on the individual sufferer from bad social conditions which constitutes the appeal of the social contract theory and the "natural" origin of human rights. But it does not follow that the theory is true as a statement of verifiable fact about the actual constitution of the world. The statements of the Law of Nature are not statements of the laws of nature, not even of the laws of an "ideal" nature. For nature provides no standards or ideals. All that exists, exists at the same level, or is of the same logical type. There are not, by nature, prize roses, works of art, oppressed or unoppressed citizens. Standards are determined by human choice, not set by nature independently of men. Natural events cannot tell us what we ought to do until we have made certain decisions, when knowledge of natural fact will enable the most efficient means to be chosen to carry out those decisions. Natural events themselves have no value, and human beings as natural existents have no value either, whether on account of possessing intelligence or having two feet.

One of the major criticisms of the doctrine of natural rights is that the list of natural rights varies with each exponent. For Hobbes, man's only natural right is self-preservation. More "liberal" theorists add to life and security; liberty, the pursuit of happiness and sometimes property. Modern socialists would probably include the right to "work or adequate maintenance." M. Maritain enumerates a list of nine natural rights which include besides the rights to life, liberty, and property of the older formulations, the right to pursue a religious vocation, the right to marry and raise a family, and, finally, the right of every human being to be treated as a person and not as a thing. It is evident that these "rights" are of very different types which would need to be distinguished in a complete discussion of the problem . . .

. . . When the lawyers said that a slave had a right in natural law to be free, they thought of a legal right not provided for by any existing statute, enactment or custom and to whose universal infringement no penalties attached. But this, surely, is the vanishing point of law and of legal right? It indicates that there just wasn't a law or legal right by which a slave might demand his freedom. But perhaps there was a moral right and a moral obligation. The slave ought to be free and maybe it was the duty of every slave-holder to free his slaves and of legislators to enact laws forbidding slavery. But until this happened there was no law which forbade a man to keep slaves. Consequently, there is no point in saying there was "really" a natural law which forbade this. For the natural law was impotent. Statements about natural law were neither statements of natural fact nor legal practice.

So, does it follow that a "natural" right is just a "moral" right? Kant said, in effect, that to treat another human being as a person, of intrinsic worth, an end in himself, is just to treat him in accordance with the moral law applicable to all rational beings on account of their having reason. But this is not quite the sense in which the term "natural rights" has been historically used. Declarations of the Rights of Man did not include his right to be told the truth, to have promises kept which had been made to him, to receive gratitude from those he had benefited, etc. The common thread among the variety of natural right is their *political* character. Despite their rugged individualism, no exponent of the Rights of Man desired to enjoy them, in solitude, on a desert island. They were among the articles of the original Social Contract; clauses in Constitutions, the inspiration of social and governmental reforms. But "Keep promises"; "Tell the truth"; "Be grateful" are not inscribed on banners carried by aggrieved demonstrators or circulated among the members of an oppressed party. Whether or not morality can exist without society, it is certain that politics cannot. Why then were "natural rights" conceived to exist independently of organised society and hence of political controversies? I suggest that they were so considered in order to emphasises their basic or fundamental character. For words like freedom, equality, security, represented for the defenders of natural rights what they considered to be the fundamental moral and social values which should be or should continue to be realised in any society fit for intelligent and responsible citizens.[55]    [pp. 44–47]

### L.L. FULLER
### The Morality of Law
### (1969)

*The morality that makes law possible*

This chapter will begin with a fairly lengthy allegory. It concerns the unhappy reign of a monarch.

*Eight ways to fail to make law*

Rex came to the throne filled with the zeal of a reformer. He considered that the greatest failure of his predecessors had been in the field of law. For generations the legal system had known nothing like a basic reform. Procedures of trial were cumbersome, the rules of law spoke in the archaic tongue of another age, justice was expensive, the judges were slovenly and sometimes corrupt. Rex was resolved to remedy all this and to make his name in history as a great lawgiver. It was his unhappy fate to fail in this ambition. Indeed, he failed spectacularly, since not only did he not succeed in introducing the needed reforms, but he never even succeeded in creating any law at all, good or bad.

His first official act was, however, dramatic and propitious. Since he needed a clean slate on which to write, he announced to his subjects the immediate repeal of all existing law, of whatever kind. He then set about drafting a new code. Unfortunately, trained as a lonely prince, his education had been very defective. In particular he found himself incapable of making even the simplest generalisations. Though not lacking in confidence when it came to deciding specific controversies, the effort to give articulate reasons for any conclusion strained his capacities to the breaking point.

Becoming aware of his limitations. Rex gave up the project of a code and announced to his subjects that henceforth he would act as a judge in any disputes that might arise among them. In this way under the stimulus of a variety of cases he hoped that his latent powers of generalisation might develop, proceeding case by case, he would gradually work out a system of rules that could be incorporated in a code. Unfortunately the defects in his education were more deep-seated than he had supposed. The venture failed completely. After he had handed down literally hundreds of decisions neither he nor his subjects could detect in those decisions any pattern whatsoever. Such tentatives toward generalisation as were to be found in his opinions only compounded the confusion, for they gave false leads to his subjects and threw his own meager powers of judgment off balance in the decision of later cases.

After this fiasco Rex realised it was necessary to take a fresh start. His first move was to subscribe to a course of lessons in generalisation. With his intellectual powers thus fortified, he resumed the project of a code and, after many hours of solitary labor, succeeded in preparing a fairly lengthy document. He was still not confident, however, that he had fully overcome his previous defects.

[55] [For a discussion of some of the values underlying the legal systems of Western democracy, see Dennis Lloyd, *The Idea of Law* (1985), Chap. 7, Stein and Shand, *Legal Values in a Western Society* (1974).]

Accordingly, he announced to his subjects that he had written out a code and would henceforth be governed by it in deciding cases, but that for an indefinite future the contents of the code would remain an official state secret, known only to him and his scrivener. To Rex's surprise this sensible plan was deeply resented by his subjects. They declared it was very unpleasant to have one's case decided by rules when there was no way of knowing what those rules were.

Stunned by this rejection Rex undertook an earnest inventory of his personal strengths and weaknesses. He decided that life had taught him one clear lesson, namely, that it is easier to decide things with the aid of hindsight than it is to attempt to foresee and control the future. Not only did hindsight make it easier to decide cases, but—and this was of supreme importance to Rex—it made it easier to give reasons. Deciding to capitalise on this insight. Rex hit on the following plan. At the beginning of each calendar year he would decide all the controversies that had arisen among his subjects during the preceding year. He would accompany his decisions with a full statement of reasons. Naturally, the reasons thus given would be understood as not controlling decisions in future years, for that would be to defeat the whole purpose of the new arrangement, which was to gain the advantages of hindsight. Rex confidently announced the new plan to his subjects, observing that he was going to publish the full text of his judgments with the rules applied by him, thus meeting the chief objection to the old plan. Rex's subjects received this announcement in silence, then quietly explained through their leaders that when they said they needed to know the rules, they meant they needed to know them *in advance* so they could act on them. Rex muttered something to the effect that they might have made that point a little clearer, but said he would see what could be done.

Rex now realised that there was no escape from a published code declaring the rules to be applied in future disputes. Continuing his lessons on generalisation, Rex worked diligently on a revised code, and finally announced that it would shortly be published. This announcement was received with universal gratification. The dismay of Rex's subjects was all the more intense, therefore, when his code became available and it was discovered that it was truly a masterpiece of obscurity. Legal experts who studied it declared that there was not a single sentence in it that could be understood either by an ordinary citizen or by a trained lawyer. Indignation became general and soon a picket appeared before the royal palace carrying a sign that read, "How can anybody follow a rule that nobody can understand?"

The code was quickly withdrawn. Recognising for the first time that he needed assistance, Rex put a staff of experts to work on a revision. He instructed them to leave the substance untouched, but to clarify the expression throughout. The resulting code was a model of clarity, but as it was studied it became apparent that its new clarity had merely brought to light that it was honeycombed with contradictions. It was reliably reported that there was not a single provision in the code that was not nullified by another provision inconsistent with it. A picket again appeared before the royal residence carrying a sign that read, "This time the king made himself clear—in both directions."

Once again the code was withdrawn for revision. By now, however, Rex had lost his patience with his subjects and the negative attitude they seemed to adopt toward everything he tried to do for them. He decided to teach them a lesson and put an end to their carping. He instructed his experts to purge the code of contradictions, but at the same time to stiffen drastically every requirement contained in it and to add a long list of new crimes. Thus, where before the citizen summoned to the throne was given ten days in which to report, in the revision the time was cut to ten seconds. It was made a crime, punishable by ten years' imprisonment, to cough, sneeze, hiccough, faint or fall down in the presence of the king. It was made treason not to understand, believe in, and correctly profess the doctrine of evolutionary, democratic redemption.

When the new code was published a near revolution resulted. Leading citizens declared their intention to flout its provisions. Someone discovered in an ancient author a passage that seemed apt: "To command what cannot be done is not to make law; it is to unmake law, for a command that cannot be obeyed serves no end but confusion, fear and chaos." Soon this passage was being quoted in a hundred petitions to the king.

The code was again withdrawn and a staff or experts charged with the task of revision. Rex's instructions to the experts were that whenever they encountered a rule requiring an impossibility, it should be revised to make compliance possible. It turned out that to accomplish this result every provisions in the code had to be substantially rewritten. The final result was, however, a triumph of draftsmanship. It was clear, consistent with itself, and demanded nothing of the subject that did not lie easily within his powers. It was printed and distributed free of charge on every street corner.

However, before the effective date for the new code had arrived, it was discovered that so much time had been spent in successive revisions of Rex's original draft, that the substance of the code had been seriously overtaken by events. Ever since Rex assumed the throne there had been a suspension of ordinary legal process and this had brought about important economic and institutional changes within the country. Accommodation to these altered conditions required many changes of substance in the law. Accordingly as soon as the new code became legally effective, it was subjected to a daily stream of amendments. Again popular discontent mounted; an anonymous pamphlet appeared on the streets carrying scurrilous cartoons of the king and a leading article with the little: "A law that changes every day is worse than no law at all."

Within a short time this source of discontent began to cure itself as the pace of amendment gradually slackened. Before this had occurred to any noticeable degree, however, Rex announced an important decision. Reflecting on the misadventures of his reign, he concluded that much of the trouble lay in bad advice he had received from experts. He accordingly declared he was reassuming the judicial power in his own person. In this way he could directly control the application of the new code and insure his country against another crisis. He began to spend practically all of his time hearing and deciding cases arising under the new code.

As the king proceeded with this task, it seemed to bring to a belated blossoming his long dormant powers of generalisation. His opinions began, indeed, to reveal a confident and almost exuberant virtuosity as he deftly distinguished his own previous decisions, exposed the principles on which he acted, and laid down guidelines for the disposition of future controversies. For Rex's subjects a new day seemed about to dawn when they could finally conform their conduct to a coherent body of rules.

This hope was, however, soon shattered. As the bound volumes of Rex's judgments became available and were subjected to closer study, his subjects were appalled to discover that there existed no discernible relation between those judgments and the code they purported to apply. Insofar as it found expression in the actual disposition of controversies, the new code might just as well not have existed at all. Yet in virtually every one of his decisions Rex declared and redeclared the code to be the basic law of his kingdom.

Leading citizens began to hold private meetings to discuss what measurers, short of open revolt, could be taken to get the king away from the bench and back on the throne. While these discussions were going on Rex suddenly died, old before his time and deeply disillusioned with his subjects.

The first act of his successor, Rex II, was to announce that he was taking the powers of government away from the lawyers and placing them in the hands of psychiatrists and experts in public relations. This way, he explained, people could be made happy without rules.

*The consequences of failure*

Rex's bungling career as legislator and judge illustrates that the attempt to create and maintain a system of legal rules may miscarry in at least eight ways: there are in this enterprise, if you will, eight distinct routes to disaster. The first and most obvious lies in a failure to achieve rules at all, so that every issue must be decided on an ad hoc basis. The other routes are: (2) a failure to publicise, or at least to make available to the affected party, the rules he is expected to observe; (3) the abuse of retroactive legislation, which not only cannot itself guide action, but undercuts the integrity of rules prospective in effect, since it puts them under the threat of retrospective change; (4) a failure to make rules understandable; (5) the enactment of contradictory rules or (6) rules that require conduct beyond the powers of the affected party; (7) introducing such frequent changes in the rules that the subject cannot orient his action by them; and, finally, (8) a failure of congruence between the rules as announced and their actual administration.

A total failure in any one of these eight directions does not simply result in a bad system of law; it results in something that is not properly called a legal system at all, except perhaps in the Pickwickian sense in which a void contract can still be said to be one kind of contract. Certainly there can be no rational ground for asserting that a man can have a moral obligation to obey a legal rule that does not exist, or is kept secret from him, or that came into existence only after he had acted, or was unintelligible, or was contradicted by another rule of the same system, or commanded the impossible, or changed every minute. It may not be impossible for a man to obey a rule that is disregarded by those charged with its administration, but at some point obedience becomes futile—as futile, in fact, as casting a vote that will never be counted. As the sociologist Simmel has observed, there is a kind of reciprocity between government and the citizen with respect to the observance of rules.[56] Government says to the citizen in effect, "These are the rules we expect you to follow. If you follow them, you have our assurance that they are the rules that will be applied to your conduct." When this bond of reciprocity is finally and completely ruptured by government, nothing is left on which to ground the citizen's duty to observe the rules.

The citizen's predicament becomes more difficult when, though there is no total failure in any direction, there is a general and drastic deterioration in legality, such as occurred in Germany under Hitler. A situation begins to develop, for example, in which though some laws are published, others, including the most important, are not. Though most laws are prospective in effect, so free a use is made of retrospective legislation, that no law is immune to change ex post facto if it suits the convenience of those in power. For the trial of criminal cases concerned with loyalty to the regime, special military tribunals are established and these tribunals disregard, whenever it suits their convenience, the rules that are supposed to control their decisions. Increasingly the principal object of government seems to be, not that of giving the citizen rules by which to shape his conduct, but to frighten him into impotence. As such a situation develops, the problem faced by the citizen is not so simple as that of a voter who knows with certainty that his ballot will not be counted. It is more like that of the voter who knows that the odds are against his ballot being counted at all, and that if it is counted, there is a good chance that it will be counted for the side against which he actually voted. A citizen in this predicament has to decide for himself whether to stay with the system and cast his ballot as a kind of symbolic act expressing the hope of a better day. So it was with the German citizen under Hitler faced with

---

[56] *The Sociology of Georg Simmel* (1950), trans. Wolff, § 4, "Interaction in the Idea of 'Law'", pp. 186–189; see also Chapter 4, "Subordination under a Principle," pp. 250–67. Simmel's discussion is worthy of study by those concerned with defining the conditions under which the ideal of "the rule of law" can be realised.

deciding whether he had an obligation to obey such portions of the laws as the Nazi terror had left intact.

In situations like these there can be no simple principle by which to test the citizen's obligations of fidelity to law, any more than there can be such a principle for testing his right to engage in a general revolution. One thing is, however, clear. A mere respect for constituted authority must not be confused with fidelity to law. Rex's subjects, for example, remained faithful to him as king throughout his long and inept reign. They were not faithful to his law, for he never made any.

### The aspiration towards perfection in legality

So far we have been concerned to trace out eight routes to failure in the enterprise of creating law. Corresponding to these are eight kinds of legal excellence toward which a system of rules may strive. What appear at the lowest level as indispensable conditions for the existence of law at all, become, as we ascend the scale of achievement, increasingly demanding challenges to human capacity. At the height of the ascent we are tempted to imagine a utopia of legality in which all rules are perfectly clear, consistent with one another, known to every citizen, and never retroactive. In this utopia the rules remain constant through time, demand only what is possible, and are scrupulously observed by courts, police, and everyone else charged with their administration ... [T]his utopia, in which all eight of the principles of legality are realised to perfection, is not actually a useful target for guiding the impulse toward legality; the goal of perfection is much more complex. Nevertheless it does suggest eight distinct standards by which excellence in legality may be tested.

In expounding in my first chapter the distinction between the morality of duty and that of aspiration, I spoke of an imaginary scale that starts at the bottom with the most obvious and essential moral duties and ascends upward to the highest achievements open to man. I also spoke of an invisible pointer as marking the dividing line where the pressure of duty leaves off and the challenge of excellence begins. The inner morality of law, it should now be clear, presents all of these aspects. It too embraces a morality of duty and a morality of aspiration. It too confronts us with the problem of knowing where to draw the boundary below which men will be condemned for failure, but can expect no praise for success and at worst pitied for the lack of it.

In applying the analysis of the first chapter to our present subject, it becomes essential to consider certain distinctive qualities of the inner morality of law. In what may be called the basic morality of social life, duties than run toward other persons generally (as contrasted with those running toward specific individuals) normally require only forbearances, or as we say, are negative in nature: Do not kill, do not injure, do not deceive, do not defame, and the like. Such duties lend themselves with a minimum of difficulty to formalised definition. That is to say, whether we are concerned with legal or moral duties, we are able to develop standards which designate with some precision—though it is never complete—the kind of conduct that is to be avoided.

The demands of the inner morality of the law, however, though they concern a relationship with person generally, demand more than forbearances; they are, as we loosely say, affirmative in nature: make the law known, make it coherent and clear, see that your decisions as an official are guided by it, etc. To meet these demands human energies must be directed toward specific kinds of achievement and not merely warned away from harmful acts.

Because of the affirmative and creative quality of its demands, the inner morality of law lends itself badly to realisation through duties, whether they be moral or legal. No matter how desirable a direction of human effort may appear to be, if we assert there is a duty to pursue it, we shall confront the responsibility of defining at what point that duty has been violated. It is easy to assert that the legislator has a moral duty to make his laws clear and understandable. But this remains at best an exhortation unless we are prepared to define the degree of clarity he must attain in order to discharge his duty. The notion of subjecting clarity to quantitative measure presents obvious difficulties. We may content ourselves, of course, by saying that the legislator has at least a moral duty to try to be clear. But this only postpones the difficulty, for in some situations nothing can be more baffling than to attempt to measure how vigorously a man intended to do that which he has failed to do. In the morality of law, in any event, good intentions are of little avail, as King Rex amply demonstrated. All of this adds up to the conclusion that the inner morality of law is condemned to remain largely a morality of aspiration and not of duty. Its primary appeal must be to a sense of trusteeship and to the pride of the craftsman.

To these observations there is one important exception. This relates to the desideratum of making the laws known, or at least making them available to those affected by them. Here we have a demand that lends itself with unusual readiness to formalisation. A written constitution may prescribe that no statute shall become law until it has been given a specified form of publication. If the courts have power to effectuate this provision, we may speak of a legal requirement for the making of law. But a moral duty with respect to publication is also readily imaginable. A custom, for example, might define what kind of promulgation of laws is expected, at the same time leaving unclear what consequences attend a departure from the accepted mode of publication. A formalisation of the desideratum of publicity has obvious advantages over uncanalised efforts, even when they are intelligently and conscientiously pursued. A formalised standard of promulgation not only tells the lawmaker where to publish his laws; it also lets the subject—or a lawyer representing his interests— know where to go to learn what the law is.

One might suppose that the principle condemning retroactive laws could also be very readily formalised in a simple rule that no such law should ever be passed, or should be valid if enacted. Such a rule would, however, disserve the cause of legality. Curiously, one of the most obvious seeming demands of legality—that a rule passed today should govern what happens tomorrow, not what happened yesterday—turns out to present some of the most difficult problems of the whole internal morality of law.

With respect to the demands of legality other than promulgation, then, the most we can expect of constitutions and courts is that they save us from the abyss; they cannot be expected to lay out very many compulsory steps toward truly significant accomplishment. [pp. 33–44]

### The concept of law

#### Legal Morality and Natural Law

[T]he first task is to relate what I have called the internal morality of the law to the ages-old tradition of natural law. Do the[se] principles represent some variety of natural law? The answer is an emphatic, though qualified, yes.

What I have tried to do is to discern and articulate the natural law of a particular kind of human undertaking, which I have described as "the enterprise of subjecting human conduct to the governance of rules." These natural laws have nothing to do with any "brooding omnipresence in the skies."[57] Nor have they the slightest affinity with any such proposition as that the practice of contraception is

---

[57] [This phrase is Holmes's.]

a violation of God's law.[58] They remain entirely terrestrial in origin and application. They are not "higher" laws; if any metaphor of elevation is appropriate they should be called "lower" laws. They are like the natural laws of carpentry, or at least those laws respected by a carpenter who wants the house he builds to remain standing and serve the purpose of those who live in it.

Though these natural laws touch one of the most vital of human activities they obviously do not exhaust the whole of man's moral life. They have nothing to say on such topics as polygamy, the study of Marx, the worship of God, the progressive income tax, or the subjugation of women. If the question be raised whether any of these subjects, or others like them, should be taken as objects of legislation, that question relates to what I have called the external morality of law.

As a convenient (though not wholly satisfactory) way of describing the distinction being taken we may speak of a procedural, as distinguished from a substantive natural law. What I have called the internal morality of law is in this sense a procedural version of natural law, though to avoid misunderstanding the word "procedural" should be assigned a special and expanded sense so that it would include, for example, a substantive accord between official action and enacted law. The term "procedural" is, however, broadly appropriate as indicating that we are concerned, not with the substantive aims of legal rules, but with the ways in which a system of rules for governing human conduct must be constructed and administered if it is to be efficacious and at the same time remain what it purports to be.

In the actual history of legal and political thinking what association do we find between the principles I have expounded [. . .] and the doctrine of natural law? Do those principles form an integral part of the natural law tradition? Are they invariably rejected by the positivist thinkers who oppose that tradition? No simple answer to these questions is possible.

With the positivists certainly no clear pattern emerges. Austin defined law as the command of a political superior. Yet he insisted that "laws properly so called" were general rules and that "occasional or particular commands" were not law.[59] Bentham, who exploited his colorful vocabulary in castigating the law of nature, was at all times concerned with certain aspects of what I have called the internal morality of law. Indeed, he seemed almost obsessed with the need to make the law accessible to those subject to them. On the other hand, in more recent times Gray has treated the question whether law ought to take the form of general rules as a matter of "little importance practically," though admitting that specific and isolated exercises of legal power do not make a fit subject for jurisprudence. . . ."[60]

With respect to thinkers associated with the natural law tradition it is safe to say that none of them would display the casualness of . . . Gray . . . toward the demands of legal morality. On the other hand, their chief concern is with what I have called substantive natural law, with the proper ends to be sought through legal rules. When they treat of the demands of legal morality it is, I believe, usually in an incidental way, though occasionally one aspect of the subject will receive considerable elaboration. Aquinas is probably typical in this respect. Concerning the need for general rules (as contrasted with a case-by-case decision of controversies) he develops a surprisingly elaborate demonstration, including an argument that wise men being always in short supply it is a matter of economic prudence to spread their talents by putting them to work to draft general rules which lesser men can then apply.[61] On the other hand, in explaining why Isidore

---

[58]  [*Cf.* the Papal Encyclical *Humanae Vitae* (1968), referred to *ante*, 85.]
[59]  [See *post*, 246–247.]
[60]  [See *post*, 803.]
[61]  *Summa Theologica*, Pt I–II, ques. 95, Art. 1.

required laws to be "clearly expressed" he contents himself with saying that this is desirable to prevent "any harm ensuing from the law itself."[62]

With writers of all philosophic persuasions it is, I believe, true to say that when they deal with problems of legal morality it is generally in a casual and incidental way. The reason for this is not far to seek. Men do not generally see any need to explain or to justify the obvious. It is likely that nearly every legal philosopher of any consequence in the history of ideas has had occasion to declare that laws ought to be published so that those subject to them can know what they are. Few have felt called upon to expand the argument for this proposition or to bring it within the cover of any more inclusive theory.

From one point of view it is unfortunate that the demands of legal morality should generally seem so obvious. This appearance has obscured subtleties and has misled men into the belief that no painstaking analysis of the subject is necessary or even possible. When it is asserted, for example, that the law ought not to contradict itself, there seems nothing more to say. Yet ... in some situations the principle against contradiction can become one of the most difficult to apply to those which make up the internal morality of the law.    [pp. 96–99]

### *Law as a Purposeful Enterprise and Law as a Manifested Fact of Social Power*

... I have insisted that law be viewed as a purposeful enterprise, dependent for its success on the energy, insight, intelligence, and conscientiousness of those who conduct it, and fated, because of this dependence, to fall always somewhat short of a full attainment of its goals. In opposition to this view it is insisted that law must be treated as a manifested fact of social authority or power, to be studied for what it is and does, and not for what it is trying to do or become.

In dealing with this fundamental opposition let me begin with a statement of the considerations that seem to me to have led to the view which I oppose. Since I have no authority to speak for the opposition, this statement will have to be hypothetical in form. I shall, however, try to phrase it as persuasively as I can.

Such a statement would begin with a concession that purpose has a property role to play in the interpretation of individual legal enactments. A statute is obviously a purposive thing, serving some end or congeries of related ends. What is objected to is not the assignment of purposes to particular laws, but to law as a whole.

Any view that ascribes some purpose or end to a whole institutional complex has, it may be said, very unattractive antecedents in the history of philosophy. It calls to mind the excesses of German and British idealism. It suggests that if we start talking about the purpose of law we may end by talking about the Purpose of the State. Even if we dismiss an unreal danger that the spirit of Hegel[63] may ride again, the view under consideration has other affinities that are far from reassuring ... A naïve teleology, it may be said, has shown itself to be the worst enemy that the scientific pursuit of objective truth can have.

Even if its historic affinities were less disturbing, there is an intrinsic improbability about any theory that attempts to write purpose in a large hand over a whole institution. Institutions are constituted of a multitude of individual human actions. Many of these follow grooves of habit and can hardly be said to be purposive at all. Of those that are purposive, the objectives sought by the actors are of the most diverse nature. Even those who participate in the creation of institutions may have very different views of the purpose or function of the institutions they bring into being.

In answering these criticisms I shall begin by recalling that the purpose I have attributed to the institution of law is a modest and sober one, that of subjecting

---

[62] *ibid.*, Art. 3.
[63] [On Hegel see *post*, 1130, 1166.]

human conduct to the guidance and control of general rules. Such a purpose scarcely lends itself to Hegelian excesses. The ascription of it to law would, indeed, seem a harmless truism if its implications were not, as I believe I have shown [. . .], far from being either self-evident or unimportant.

Before denying ourselves the modest indulgence in teleology I have proposed, we should consider carefully the cost entailed in this denial. The most significant element of that cost lies in the fact that we lose wholly any standard for defining legality. If law is simply a manifested fact of authority or social power, then, though we can still talk about the substantive justice or injustice of particular enactments, we can no longer talk about the degree to which a legal system as a whole achieves the ideal of legality; if we are consistent with our premises we cannot, for example, assert that the legal system of Country $X$ achieves a greater measure of legality than that of Country $Y$. We can talk about contradictions in the law, but we have no standard for defining what a contradiction is. We may bemoan some kinds of retroactive laws, but we cannot even explain what would be wrong with a system of laws that were wholly retroactive. If we observe that the power of law normally expresses itself in the application of general rules, we can think of no better explanation for this than to say that the supreme legal power can hardly afford to post a subordinate at every street corner to tell people what to do. In short, we can neither formulate nor answer the problems to which my second chapter was devoted.

It may be said that if in truth these problems cannot be formulated in a manner that enables us to answer them then we ought to face that fact courageously and not deceive ourselves with fictions. It is at this point that issue is most sharply joined. The question becomes, not which view is most comforting and reassuring, but which view is right, which view corresponds most faithfully to the reality with which we must deal. In the remainder of this chapter I shall seek to show that the view which pretends to abstract from the purpose of law and to treat law simply as a manifested fact of social power cannot be supported except through a falsification of the reality on which it purports to build.

The view I am criticising sees the reality of law in the fact of an established lawmaking authority. What this authority determines to be law *is* law. There is in this determination no question of degree; one cannot apply to it the adjectives "successful" or "unsuccessful." This, it seems to me, is the gist of the theory which opposes that underlying these chapters.

Now this theory can seem tenable, I submit, only if we systematically strike from view two elements in the reality it purports to describe. The first of these lies in the fact that the established authority which tells us what is law is itself the product of law.[64] In modern society law is typically created by corporate action. Corporate action—by a parliament, for example—is possible only by adopting and following rules of procedure that will enable a body of men to speak legally with one voice. These rules of procedure may meet shipwreck in all of the eight ways open to any system of law. So when we assert that in the United Kingdom Parliament has the final say as to what law is, we are tacitly assuming some measure of success in at least one legal enterprise, that directed toward giving Parliament the corporate power to "say" things. This assumption of success is normally quite justified in countries with a long parliamentary tradition. But if we are faithful to the reality we purport to describe, we shall recognise that a parliament's ability to enact law is itself an achievement of purposive effort, and not simply a datum of nature.

The second falsification of reality consists in ignoring the fact that a formal structure of authority is itself usually dependent on human effort that is not required by any law or command. Weber points out that all formal social

---

[64] [Fuller discusses this in connection with Parliamentary supremacy (*The Morality of Law*, p. 115).]

structures—whether embodied in a tradition or a written constitution—are likely to have gaps that do not appear as such because they are filled by appropriate actions taken, often, without any awareness that an alternative is open.[65] Men do not, in other words, generally do absurd things that would defeat the whole undertaking in which they are engaged, even though the formal directions under which they operate permit these absurdities.

A good example of a gap in formal structure is to be found in the Constitution of the United States. That laws should be promulgated is probably the most obvious demand of legality. It is also the demand that is most readily reduced to a formal constitutional requirement. Yet the Constitution says nothing about the publication of laws. Despite this lack I doubt if it has ever entered the mind of any Congressman that he might curry favour with the taxpayers through a promise to save them money by seeing to it that the laws were left unpublished. One can, of course, argue that a constitutional requirement of publication can be reached by interpretation, since otherwise the provisions against certain retrospective laws would make little sense. But the point is that no such interpretation was in fact engaged in by those who from the first assumed as a matter of course that laws ought to be published.

The scholar may refuse to see law as an enterprise and treat it simply as an emanation of social power. Those whose actions constitute that power, however, see themselves as engaged in an enterprise and they generally do the things essential for its success. To the extent that their actions must be guided by insight rather than by formal rule, degrees in the attainment of success are inevitable.

Hart's problem of "the persistence of law"[66]—how can the law made by Rex IV still be law when Rex V comes to the throne?—is another example of a gap in postulated formal structure that does not appear as such in practice. The need for continuity in law despite changes in government is so obvious that everyone normally assumes this continuity as a matter of course. It becomes a problem only when one attempts to define law as an emanation of formal authority and excludes from its operations the possible influence of human judgment and insight.

The heavy emphasis theory tends to place on an exact definition of the highest legal power expresses, no doubt, a concern that obscurity on this point may cause the legal system as a whole to disintegrate. Again, it is forgotten that no set of directions emanating from above can ever dispense with the need for intelligent action guided by a sense of purpose. Even the lowly justice of the peace, who cannot make head or tail of the language by which his jurisdiction is limited, will usually have the insight to see that his powers derive from an office forming part of a larger system. He will at least have the judgment to proceed cautiously. Coordination among the elements of a legal system is not something that can simply be imposed; it must be achieved. Fortunately, a proper sense of role, reinforced by a modicum of intelligence, will usually suffice to cure any defaults of the formal system.

There is, I think, a curious irony about any view that refuses to attribute to law as a whole any purpose, however modest or restricted. No school of thought has ever ventured to assert that it could understand reality without discerning in it structure, relatedness, or pattern. If we were surrounded by a formless rain of discrete and unrelated happenings, there would be nothing we could understand or talk about. When we treat law as a "fact," we must assume that it is a special kind of fact, possessing definable qualities that distinguish it from other facts.

---

[65] Weber, *Law in Economy and Society*, pp. 31–33. Weber writes, "It is a fact that the most 'fundamental' questions often are left unregulated by law even in legal orders which are otherwise thoroughly rationalised." He goes on to say that generally men act so that "the absurd' though legally possible situation" does not arise in practice.

[66] [*Post*, 382.]

Indeed, all legal theorists are at great pains to tell us just what kind of fact it is—it is not "the gunman situation writ large," it normally involves the application of general rules to human behavior, etc., etc.

This effort to discover and describe the characteristics that identify law usually meets with a measure of success. Why should this be? The reason is not at all mysterious. It lies in the fact that in nearly all societies men perceive the need for subjecting certain kinds of human conduct to the explicit control of rules. When they embark on the enterprise contains a certain inner logic of its own, that it imposes demands that must be met (sometimes with considerable inconvenience) if its objectives are to be attained. It is because men generally in some measure perceive these demands and respect them, that legal systems display a certain likeness in societies otherwise quite diverse.

It is, then, precisely because law is a purposeful enterprise that it displays structural constancies which the legal theorist can discover and treat as uniformities in the factually given. If he realised on what he built his theory, he might be less inclined to conceive of himself as being like the scientist who discovers a uniformity of inanimate nature. But perhaps in the course of rethinking his subject he might gain a new respect for his own species and come to see that it, too, and not merely the electron, can leave behind a discernible pattern.

[pp. 145–151]

### The substantive aims of law

The two principal distinctions ... are ... the distinction between the moralities of duty and of aspiration and the distinction between the internal and external moralities of law.

#### The Neutrality of the Law's Internal Morality toward Substantive Aims

In presenting my analysis of the law's internal morality I have insisted that it is, over a wide range of issues, indifferent toward the substantive aims of law and is ready to serve a variety of such aims with equal efficacy. One moral issue in lively debate today is that of contraception. Now it is quite clear that the principles of legality are themselves incapable of resolving this issue. It is also clear that a legal system might maintain its internal integrity whether its rules were designed to prohibit or to encourage contraception.

But a recognition that the internal morality of law may support and give efficacy to a wide variety of substantive aims should not mislead us into believing that *any* substantive aim may be adopted without compromise of legality. Even the adoption of an objective like the legal suppression of contraception may, under some circumstances, impair legal morality. If, as sometimes seems to be the case, laws prohibiting the sale of contraceptives are kept on the books as a kind of symbolic act, with the knowledge that they will not and cannot be enforced, legal morality is seriously affected. There is no way to quarantine this contagion against a spread to other parts of the legal system. It is unfortunately a familiar political technique to placate one interest by passing a statute, and to appease an opposing interest by leaving the statute largely unenforced.

One of the tasks of the present chapter is to analyse in general terms the manner in which the internal and external moralities of law interact.      [p. 153]

#### Legality as a Condition of Efficacy

...[T]he internal morality of the law is not something added to, or imposed on, the power of law, but is an essential condition of that power itself. If this conclusion is accepted, then the first observation that needs to be made is that law is a precondition of good law. A conscientious carpenter, who has learned his trade well and keeps his tools sharp, might, we may suppose, as well devote himself to building a hangout for thieves as to building an orphans' asylum. But it still remains true that it takes a carpenter, or the help of a carpenter, to build an orphans' asylum, and that it will be a better asylum if he is a skillful craftsman equipped with tools that have been used with care and kept in proper condition.

If we had no carpenters at all it would be plain that our first need would be, not to draft blueprints for hospitals and asylums or to argue about the principles of good design, but to recruit and train carpenters. It is in this sense that much of the world today needs law more than it does good law. [pp. 155–156]

*Legal Morality and Laws Aiming at Alleged Evils That Cannot Be Defined*

The simple demand that rules of law be expressed in intelligible terms seems on its face ethically neutral toward the substantive aims law may serve. If any principle of legal morality is, in Hart's words, "compatible with very great iniquity," this would seem to be it. Yet if a legislator is attempting to remove some evil and cannot plainly identify the target at which his statute is directed, it is obvious he will have difficulty in making his laws clear. I have already tried to illustrate this point by a reference to statutes designed to prevent "a return of the old saloon."[67] In that case, however, we have to do with legislative foolishness, rather than with anything touching on iniquity.

It is quite otherwise with laws attempting to make legal rights depend on race. It is common today to think of the government of South Africa as combining a strict observance of legality with the enactment of a body of law that is brutal and inhuman. This view could only arise because of the now inveterate confusion between deference for constituted authority and fidelity to law. An examination of the legislation by which racial discrimination is maintained in South Africa reveals a gross departure from the demands of the internal morality of law.

The following extracts are taken from a careful and objective study of the racial laws enacted by the Union of South Africa:

> The Legislation abounds with anomalies and the same person may, in the result, fall into different racial categories under different statutes ... the Minister of the Interior on the 22nd March 1957, stated that approximately 100,000 race classification cases were then pending before the Director of Census and Statistics which were regarded as "borderline cases." ... As the present study has revealed, the absence of uniformity of definition flows primarily from the absence of any uniform or scientific basis of race classification. ... In the final analysis the legislature is attempting to define the indefinable.[68]

Even the South African judge who in his private life shares the prejudices that have shaped the law he is bound to interpret and apply, must, if he respects the ethos of his calling, feel a deep distaste for the arbitrary manipulations this legislation demands of him.[69]

It should not be supposed it is only in South Africa that statutes attaching legal consequences to differences in race have given rise to serious difficulties of interpretation. In 1948 in *Perez v. Sharp*[70] the Supreme Court of California authorising the marriage of a white person with a Negro, mulatto, Mongolian or member of the Malay race." The holding that the statute was invalid was rested in part on the ground that it did not meet the constitutional requirement "that a law

---

[67] [Prohibition Laws: these are discussed by A. Sinclair, *Prohibition: An Era of Excess* (1962). Fuller discusses them at pp. 89–91.]

[68] Suzman, "Race Classification and Definition in the Legislation of the Union of South Africa, 1910–1960" in *Acta Juridica* (1960), pp. 339–367; the extracts quoted in the text are taken from pp. 339, 355 and 367.

[69] [But *cf.* our discussion of this issue, *ante*, 92.]

[70] 32 Cal. 2d 711.

be definite and its meaning ascertainable by those whose rights and duties are governed thereby."                                                    [pp. 159–161]

### The View of Man Implicit in Legal Morality

I come now to the most important respect in which an observance of the demands of legal morality can serve the broader aims of human life generally. This lies in the view of man implicit in the internal morality of law. I have repeatedly observed that legal morality can be said to be neutral over a wide range of ethical issues. It cannot be neutral in its view of man himself. To embark on the enterprise of subjecting human conduct to the governance of rules involves of necessity a commitment to the view that man is, or can become, a responsible agent, capable of understanding and following rules, and answerable for his defaults.

Every departure from the principles of the law's inner morality is an affront to man's dignity as a responsible agent. To judge his actions by unpublished or retrospective laws, or to order him to do an act that is impossible, is to convey to him your indifference to his powers of self-determination. Conversely, when the view is accepted that man is incapable of responsible action, legal morality loses its reason for being. To judge his actions by unpublished or retrospective laws is no longer an affront, for there is nothing left to affront—indeed, even the verb "to judge" becomes itself incongruous in this context: we no longer judge a man, we act upon him.                                                    [pp. 162–163]

### The Minimum Content of a Substantive Natural Law

In seeking to know whether it is possible to derive from the morality of aspiration anything more imperative than mere counsel and encouragement, I have then so far concluded that, since the morality of aspiration is necessarily a morality of human aspiration, it cannot deny the human quality to those who possess it without forfeiting its integrity. Can we derive more than this?

The problem may be stated in another form. In my third chapter I treated what I have called the internal morality of law as itself presenting a variety of natural law. It is, however, a procedural or institutional kind of natural law, though, as I have been at pains in this chapter to show, it affects and limits the substantive aims that can be achieved through law. But can we derive from the morality of aspiration itself any proposition of natural law that is substantive, rather than procedural, in quality?

In his *Concept of Law* H. L. A. Hart presents what he calls "the minimum content of natural law" (pp. 193–200).[71] Starting with the single objective of human survival, conceived as operating within certain externally imposed conditions, Hart derives, by a process I would describe as purposive implication, a fairly comprehensive set of rules that may be called those of natural law. What is expounded in his interesting discussion is a kind of minimum morality of duty.

Like every morality of duty this minimum natural law says nothing about the question, Who shall be included in the community which accepts and seeks to realise cooperatively the shared objective of survival? In short, who shall survive? No attempt is made to answer this question. Hart simply observes that "our concern is with social arrangements for continued existence, not with those of a suicide club."

In justifying his starting point of survival Hart advances two kinds of reasons. One amounts to saying that survival is a necessary condition for every other human achievement and satisfaction. With his proposition there can be no quarrel.

But in addition to treating survival as a precondition for every other human

[71] [*Ante*, 123.]

good, Hart advances a second set of reasons for his starting point—reasons of a very different order. He asserts that men have properly seen that in "the modest aim of survival" lies "the central indisputable element which gives empirical good sense to the terminology of Natural Law." He asserts further that in the teleological elements that run through all moral and legal thinking there is "the tacit assumption that the proper end of human activity is survival." He observes that "an overwhelming majority of men do wish to live, even at the cost of hideous misery."

In making these assertions Hart is, I submit, treading more dubious ground. For he is no longer claiming for survival that it is a necessary condition for the achievement of other ends, but seems to be saying that it furnishes the core and central element of all human striving. This, I think, cannot be accepted. As Thomas Aquinas remarked long ago, if the highest aim of a captain were to preserve his ship, he would keep it in port forever.[72] As for the proposition that the overwhelming majority of men wish to survive even at the cost of hideous misery, this seems to me of doubtful truth. If it were true, I question whether it would have any particular relevance to moral theory.

Hart's search for a "central indisputable element" in human striving raises the question whether in fact this search can be successful. I believe that if we were forced to select the principle that supports and infuses all human aspiration we would find it in the objective of maintaining communication with our fellows.

In the first place—staying within the limits of Hart's own argument—man has been able to survive up to now be?ause of his capacity for communication. In competition with other creatures, often more powerful than he and sometimes gifted with keener senses, man has so far been the victor. His victory has come about because he can acquire and transmit knowledge and because he can consciously and deliberately effect a co-ordination of effort with other human beings. If in the future man succeeds in surviving his own powers of self-destruction, it will be because he can communicate and reach understanding with his fellows. Finally, I doubt if most of us would regard as desirable survival into a kind of vegetable existence in which we could make no meaningful contact with other human beings.

Communication is something more than a means of staying alive. It is a way of being alive. It is through communication that we inherit the achievements of past human effort. The possibility of communication can reconcile us to the thought of death by assuring us that what we achieve will enrich the lives of those to come. How and when we accomplish communication with one another can expand or contract the boundaries of life itself. In the words of Wittgenstein, "The limits of my language are the limits of my world."

If I were asked, then, to discern one central indisputable principle of what may be called substantive natural law—Natural Law with capital letters—I would find it in the injunction: Open up, maintain, and preserve the integrity of the channels of communication by which men convey to one another what they perceive, feel, and desire. In this matter the morality of aspiration offers more than good counsel and the challenge of excellence. It here speaks with the imperious voice we are accustomed to hear from the morality of duty. And if men will listen, that voice, unlike that of the morality of duty, can be heard across the boundaries and through the barriers that now separate men from one another.     [pp. 184–186]

---

[72] *Summa Theologica*, Pt I–II, Q. 2, Art. 5. "Hence a captain does not intend as a last end, the preservation of the ship entrusted to him, since a ship is ordained to something else as its end. *viz.*, to navigation."

**J. M. FINNIS**
**Natural Law and Natural Rights**
(1980)

*Theoretical Studies of "Universal" Values*

Knowledge is not the only basic aspect of human well-being. . . . So we may now widen our reflections on our interests and commitments, and ask whether there are other basic values besides knowledge, other indemonstrable but self-evident principles shaping our practical reasoning.

Such a course of reflection is, in a way, an attempt to understand one's own character, or nature. The attempt thus parallels attempts made, in quite another way, by those anthropologists and psychologists who ask (in effect) whether there is a human nature and what are its characteristics. The anthropological and psychological studies ought to be regarded as an aid in answering our own present question—not, indeed, by way of any "inference" from universality or "human nature" to values (an inference that would be merely fallacious), but by way of an assemblage of reminders of the range of possibly worthwhile activities and orientations open to one.

To anyone who surveys the literature, whether on ethics (or other practical modes of thinking about values) or on anthropology(or other "theoretical" modes of investigating what humans value) it is obvious that investigation of the basic aspects of human well-being (real or supposed) is not easy. The difficulty manifests itself (*a*) in arbitrary and implausible reductions of the many basic values to one (or two, or three) values, or of the many basic inclinations or interests to one (or two, or three) basic inclinations or interests: (*b*) in lists of basic tendencies (or values, or features of human nature) which as lists are incoherent because drawn up on shifting criteria; and (*c*) in short-winded analyses which mention a few tendencies, values, or features, and then tail off into "etc." or "and other basic values" . . . etc. (not for convenience, as in this sentence, but for want of sustained attention to the problem).

Reductionism, cross-categorisation, and the daunting variety of the lists offered by investigators, can be overcome by steady attention to distinctions drawn and emphasised in the preceding chapter. Recall, first of all, the distinction between the brute fact of an urge (or drive or inclination or tendency) and the forms of good which one who has such urges can think it worthwhile to pursue and realise, on the ground not that he has the urges but that he can see the good of such pursuit and realisation. Secondly, and *a fortiori*, recall the distinction between the material conditions for, or affecting, the pursuit of value and the value itself. A sound brain and intelligence are necessary conditions for the understanding, pursuit, and realisation of truth, but neither brainpower nor intelligence should appear in a list of basic values: knowledge is the relevant value. Or again, H. L. A. Hart's "natural facts and aims,"[73] or "truisms" about human beings, concern the material and psychological conditions ("the setting") under which persons seek their various ends (and his list of universally recognised or "indisputable" ends contains only one entry: survival). Thirdly, in listing the basic values in which human beings may participate, recall the distinctions between general value and particular goal, and between ends and the means for attaining, realising, or participating in those ends. Amongst these means are to be included the many intermediate and subordinate ends involved in such wide-ranging, long-lasting and fecund means as languages, institutions like laws or property, or an economy. Thus, for example, John Rawls's "primary goods" (liberty, opportunity, wealth, and self-respect) are primary, in his view, not because they are the

---

[73] *Concept of Law*, pp. 193, 195. [See *ante*, 123 and also Fuller's comments *ante*, 166–167.]

basic *ends* of human life but because "it is rational to want these goods whatever else is wanted, *since* they are in general *necessary for* the framing and the execution of a rational plan of life."[74]

Students of ethics and of human cultures very commonly assume that cultures manifest preferences, motivations, and evaluations so wide and chaotic in their variety that no values or practical principles can be said to be self-evident to human beings, since no value or practical principle is recognised in all times and all places.... But those philosophers who have recently sought to test this assumption, by surveying the anthropological literature (including the similar general surveys made by professional anthropologists), have found with striking unanimity that this assumption is unwarranted.[75]

These surveys entitle us, indeed, to make some rather confident assertions. All human societies show a concern for the value of human life; in all, self-pre-servation is generally accepted as a proper motive for action, and in none is the killing of other human beings permitted without some fairly definite justification. All human societies regard the procreation of a new human life as in itself a good thing unless there are special circumstances. No human society fails to restrict sexual activity; in all societies there is some prohibition of incest, some opposition to boundless promiscuity and to rape, some favour for stability and permanence in sexual relations. All human societies display a concern for truth, through education of the young in matters not only practically (*e.g.* avoidance of dangers) but also speculative or theoretical (*e.g.* religion). Human beings, who can survive infancy only by nurture, live in or on the margins of some society which invari-ably extends beyond the nuclear family, and all societies display a favour for the values of co-operation, of common over individual good, of obligation between individuals, and of justice within groups. All know friendship. All have some conception of *meum* and *tuum*, title or property and of reciprocity. All value play, serious and formalised, or relaxed and recreational. All treat the bodies of dead members of the group in some traditional and ritual fashion different from their procedures for rubbish disposal. All display a concern for powers or principles which are to be respected as suprahuman; in one form or another, religion is universal.                                                  [pp. 81–84]

### *The Basic Forms of Human Good: A Practical Reflection*

It is now time to revert, from the descriptive or "speculative" findings of anthropology and psychology, to the critical and essentially practical discipline in which each reader must ask himself: What *are* the basic aspects of my well-being? Here each one of us, however extensive his knowledge of the interests of other people and other cultures, is alone with his own intelligent grasp of the inde-monstrable (because self-evident) first principles of his own practical reasoning. From one's capacity to grasp intelligently the basic forms of good as "to-bepursued" one gets one's ability, in the descriptive disciplines of history and anthropology, to sympathetically (though not uncritically) see the point of actions, life-styles, characters, and cultures that one would not choose for oneself. And one's speculative knowledge of other people's interests and achievements does not leave unaffected one's practical understanding of the forms of good that lie open to one's choice. But there is no inference from fact to value. At this point in our discourse (or private meditation), inference and proof are left behind (or left until later), and the proper form of discourse is: "... is a good, in itself, don't you think?"

Remember: by "good," "basic good," "value," "well-being." etc. I *do not* yet mean "moral good," etc.

---

[74] *Theory of Justice*, p. 433 (emphasis added). [And *post*, 583.]
[75] [See, *e.g.* M. Mead, *post*, 225.]

What, then, are the basic forms of good for us?

## A. Life

A life basic value, corresponding to the drive for self-preservation, is the value of life. The term "life" here signifies every aspect of the vitality (*vita*, life) which puts a human being in good shape for self-determination. Hence, life here includes bodily (including cerebral) health, and freedom from the pain that betokens organic malfunctioning or injury. And the recognition, pursuit, and realisation of this basic human purpose (or internally related group of purposes) are as various as the crafty struggle and prayer of a man overboard seeking to stay afloat until his ship turns back for him; the teamwork of surgeons and the whole network of supporting staff, ancillary services, medical schools, etc.; road safety laws and programmes; famine relief expeditions; farming and rearing and fishing; food marketing; the resuscitation of suicides; watching out as one steps off the kerb ...

Perhaps we should include in this category the transmission of life by pro-creation of children. Certainly it is tempting to treat procreation as a distinct, irreducibly basic value, corresponding to the inclination to mate/reproduce/rear. But while there are good reasons for distinguishing the urge to copulate from both the urge to self-preservation and the maternal or paternal instincts, the analytical situation is different when we shift from the level of urges/instincts/ drives to the level of intelligently grasped forms of good. There may be said to be one drive (say, to copulate) and one physical release for that drive (or a range of such physical forms); but as a human action, pursuit and realisation of value, sexual intercourse may be play, and/or expression of love or friendship, and/or an effort to procreate. So, likewise, we need not be analytically content with an anthropological convention which treats sexuality, mating, and family life as a single category or unit of investigation; nor with an ethical judgment that treats the family, and the procreation and education of children, as an indistinguishable cluster of moral responsibilities. We can distinguish the desire and decision to have a child, simply for the sake of bearing a child, from the desire and decision to cherish and to educate the child. The former desire and decision is a pursuit of the good of life, in this case life-in-its transmission; the latter desires and decisions are aspects of the pursuit of the distinct basic values of sociability (or friendship) and truth (truth-in-its-communication), running alongside the continued pursuit of the value of life that is involved in simply keeping the child alive and well until it can fend for itself.

## B. Knowledge

The second basic value I have already discussed: it is knowledge, considered as desirable for its own sake, not merely instrumentally.

## C. Play

The third basic aspect of human well-being is play. A certain sort of moralist analysing human goods may overlook this basic value, but an anthropologist will not fail to observe this large and irreducible element in human culture. More importantly, each one of us can see the point of engaging in performances which have no point beyond the performance itself, enjoyed for its own sake. The performance may be solitary or social, intellectual or physical, strenuous or relaxed, highly structured or relatively informal, conventional or ad hoc in its pattern ... An element of play can enter into any human activity, even the drafting of enactments, but is always analytically distinguishable from its "serious" context; and some activities, enterprises, and institutions are entirely or primarily pure play. Play, then, has and is its own value.

## D. Aesthetic experience

The fourth basic component in our flourishing is aesthetic experience. Many forms of play, such as dance or song or football, are the matrix or occasion of aesthetic experience. But beauty is not an indispensable element of play. Moreover, beautiful form can be found and enjoyed in nature. Aesthetic experience, unlike play, need not involve an action of one's own; what is sought after and valued for its own sake may simply be the beautiful form "outside" one, and the "inner" experience of appreciation of its beauty. But often enough the valued experience is found in the creation and/or active appreciation of some *work* of significant and satisfying form.

## E. Sociability (friendship)

Fifthly, there is the value of that sociability which in its weakest form is realised by a minimum of peace and harmony amongst men, and which ranges through the forms of human community to its strongest form in the flowering of full friendship. Some of the collaboration between one person and another is no more than instrument to the realisation by each of his own individual purposes. But friendship involves acting for the sake of one's friends' purposes, one's friend's well-being. To be in a relationship of friendship with at least one other person is a fundamental form of good, is it not? . . .

## F. Practical reasonableness

Sixthly, there is the basic good of being able to bring one's own intelligence to bear effectively (in practical reasoning that issues in action) on the problems of choosing one's actions and lifestyle and shaping one's own character. Negatively, this involves that one has a measure of effective freedom; positively, it involves that one seeks to bring an intelligent and reasonable order into one's own actions and habits and practical attitudes. This order in turn has (i) an internal aspect, as when one strives to bring one's emotions and dispositions into the harmony of an inner peace of mind that is not merely the product of drugs or indoctrination nor merely passive in its orientation; and (ii) an external aspect, as when one strives to make one's actions (which are external in that they change states of affairs in the world and often enough affect the relations between persons) authentic, that is to say, genuine realisations of one's own freely ordered evaluations, preferences, hopes, and self-determination. This value is thus complex, involving freedom and reason, integrity and authenticity. But it has a sufficient unity to be treated as one; and for a label I choose "practical reasonableness" . . .

## G. Religion

Seventhly, and finally in this list, there is the value of what, since Cicero, we summarily and lamely call "religion." For, as there is the order of means to ends, and the pursuit of life, truth, play, and aesthetic experience in some individually selected order of priorities and pattern of specialisation, and the order that can be brought into human relations through collaboration, community, and friendship, and the order that is to be brought into one's character and activity through inner integrity and outer authenticity, so, finally there arise such questions as: (*a*) How are all these orders, which have their immediate origin in human initiative and pass away in death, related to the lasting order of the whole cosmos and to the origin, if any, of that order? (*b*) Is it not perhaps the case that human freedom, in which one rises above the determinism of instinct and impulse to an intelligent grasp of worthwhile forms of good, and through which one shapes and masters one's environment but also one's own character, is itself somehow subordinate to something which makes that human freedom, human intelligence, and human mastery possible (not just "originally" but from moment to moment) and which is free, intelligent and sovereign in a way (and over a range) no human being can be?

Misgivings may be aroused by the notion that one of the basic human values is the establishment and maintenance of proper relationships between oneself (and the orders one can create and maintain) and the divine. For there are, always, those who doubt or deny that the universal order-of-things has any origin beyond the "origins" known to the natural sciences, and who answer question (*b*) negatively. But is it reasonable to deny that it is, at any rate, peculiarly important to have thought reasonably and (where possible) correctly about these questions of the origins of cosmic order and of human freedom and reason—whatever the answer to those questions turns out to be, and even if the answers have to be agnostic or negative? And does not that importance in large part consist in this: that if there is a transcendent origin of the universal order-of-things and of human freedom and reason, then one's life and actions are in fundamental disorder if they are not brought, as best one can, into some sort of harmony with whatever can be known or surmised about that transcendent other and its lasting order? More important for us than the ubiquity of expressions of religious concerns, in all human cultures, is the question: Does not one's own sense of "responsibility," in choosing what one is to be and do, amount to a concern that is not reducible to the concern to live, play, procreate, relate to others, and be intelligent? Does not even a Sartre, taking as his *point de départ* that God does not exist (and that therefore "everything is permitted"), none the less appreciate that he is "responsible"—obliged to act with freedom and authenticity, and to will the liberty of other persons equally with his own—in choosing what he is to be; and all this, because, *prior to* any choice of his, "man" is and is-to-be free?[76] And is this not a recognition (however residual) of, and concern about, an order of things "beyond" each and every man? And so, without wishing to beg any question, may we not for convenience call that concern, which is concern for a good consisting in an irreducibly distinct form of order, "religious"? . . .

### An Exhaustive List?

Now besides life, knowledge, play, aesthetic experience, friendship, practical reasonableness, and religion, there are countless objectives and forms of good. But I suggest that these other objectives and forms of good will be found, on analysis, to be ways or combinations of ways of pursuing (not always sensibly) and realising (not always successfully) one of the seven basic forms of good, or some combination of them.

Moreover, there are countless aspects of human self-determination and self-realisation besides the seven basic aspects which I have listed. But these other aspects, such as courage, generosity, moderation, gentleness, and so on, are not themselves basic values; rather, they are ways (not means, but modes) of pursuing the basic values, and fit (or are deemed by some individual, or group, or culture, to fit) a man for their pursuit.

In this way we can analytically unravel even very "peculiar" conventions, norms, institutions, and orders of preference, such as the aristocratic code of honour that demanded direct attacks on life in duelling.

Again, though the pursuit of the basic values is made psychologically possible by the corresponding inclinations and urges of one's nature, still there are many inclinations and urges that do not correspond to or support any basic value: for example, the inclination to take more than one's share, or the urge to gratuitous cruelty. There is no need to consider whether these urges are more, or less, "natural" (in terms of frequency, universality, intensity, etc.) than those urges

---

[76]  J.-P. Sartre, *L'Existentialisme est un Humanisme* (1946), pp. 36, 83–84.

which correspond to the basic values. For I am not trying to justify our recognition and pursuit of basic values by deducing from, or even by pointing to, any set of inclinations. The point, rather, is that selfishness, cruelty, and the like, simply do not stand to something self-evidently good as the urge to self-preservation stands to the self-evident good of human life. Selfishness, cruelty, etc., stand in need of some explanation, in a way that curiosity, friendliness, etc., do not . . .

But are there just seven basic values, no more and no less? And what is meant by calling them basic? . . .

### All Equally Fundamental

. . . First, each is equally self-evidently a form of good. Secondly, none can be analytically reduced to being merely an aspect of any of the others, or to being merely instrumental in the pursuit of any of the others. Thirdly, each one, when we focus on it, can reasonably be regarded as the most important. Hence there is no objective hierarchy amongst them. Let me amplify this third point, which includes the other two.

If one focuses on the value of speculative truth, it can reasonably be regarded as more important than anything; knowledge can be regarded as the most important thing to acquire; life can be regarded as merely a pre-condition, of lesser or no intrinsic value; play can be regarded as frivolous; one's concern about "religious" questions can seem just an aspect of the struggle against error, superstition, and ignorance; friendship can seem worth forgoing, or be found exclusively in sharing and enhancing knowledge; and so on. But one can shift one's focus. If one is drowning, or, again, if one is thinking about one's child who died soon after birth, one is inclined to shift one's focus to the value of life simply as such. The life will not be regarded as a mere pre-condition of anything else; rather, play and knowledge and religion will seem secondary, even rather optional extras. But one can shift one's focus, in this way, one-by-one right round the circle of basic values that constitute the horizon of our opportunities. We can focus on play, and reflect that we spend most of our time working simply in order to afford leisure; play is performances enjoyed for their own sake as performances and thus can seem to be the point of everything; knowledge and religion and friendship can seem pointless unless they issue in the playful mastery of wisdom, or participation in the play of the divine puppetmaster (as Plato said),[77] or in the playful intercourse of mind or body that friends can most enjoy . . .

Of course, each one of us can reasonably *choose* to treat one or some of the values as of more importance in *his* life. A scholar chooses to dedicate himself to the pursuit of knowledge, and thus gives its demands priority, to a greater or lesser degree (and perhaps for a whole lifetime), over the friendships, the worship, the games, the art and beauty that he might otherwise enjoy. He might have been out saving lives through medicine or famine relief, but he chooses not to. But he may change his priorities; he may risk his life to save a drowning man, or give up his career to nurse a sick wife or to fight for his community. The change is not in the relation between the basic values as that relation might reasonably have seemed to him before he chose his life-plan (and as it should always seem to him when he is considering human opportunity and flourishing in general); rather, the change is in his chosen life-plan. That chosen plan *made* truth more important and fundamental for him. His new choice changes the status of that value *for him*; the change is in him. Each of us has a subjective order of priority amongst the basic values; this ranking is no doubt partly shifting and partly stable, but is in any case essential if we are to act at all to some purpose. But one's reasons for

[77] *Laws*, VII: 685, 803–804; see XIII, 5, below.

choosing the particular ranking that one does choose are reasons that properly relate to one's temperament, upbringing, capacities, and opportunities, not to differences of rank of intrinsic value between the basic values.

Thomas Aquinas, in his formal discussion of the basic forms of good and self-evident primary principles of practical reasoning—which he calls the first principles and most general precepts of natural law[78]—sets a questionable example. For he arranges the precepts in a threefold order: (i) human life is a good to be sustained, and what threatens it is to be prevented; (ii) the coupling of man and woman, and the education of their young, etc., is to be favoured, and what opposes it is to be avoided; (iii) knowledge (especially of the truth about God), sociable life, and practical reasonableness are goods, and ignorance, offence to others, and practical unreasonableness are to be avoided. And his rationale for this threefold ordering (which all too easily is interpreted as a ranking) is that the self-preservative inclinations corresponding to the first category are common not just to all men but to all things which have a definite nature; that the sexual-reproductive inclinations corresponding to the second category of goods are shared by human beings with all other animate life; and that the inclinations corresponding to the third category are peculiar to mankind. Now all this is no doubt true, and quite pertinent in a metaphysical mediation on the continuity of human order with the universal order-of-things (of which human nature is a microcosmos, incorporating all levels of being; inorganic, organic, ... mental...). But is it relevant to a mediation on the *value* of the various basic aspects of human well-being? Are not speculative considerations intruding into a reconstruction of principles that are practical and that, being primary, indemonstrable, and self-evident, are not derivable (nor sought by Aquinas to be derived) from any speculative considerations?...                                    [pp. 81–94]

### A Definition of Law

Throughout this chapter, the term "law" has been used with a focal meaning so as to refer primarily to rules made, in accordance with regulative legal rules, by a determinate and effective authority (itself identified and standardly, constituted as an institution by legal rules) for a "complete" community, and buttressed by sanctions in accordance with the rule-guided stipulations of adjudicative institutions, this ensemble of rules and institutions being directed to reasonably resolving any of the community's co-ordination problems (and to ratifying, tolerating, regulating, or overriding co-ordination solutions from any other institutions or sources of norms) for the common good of that community, according to a manner and form itself adapted to that common good by features of specificity, minimisation of arbitrariness, and maintenance of a quality of reciprocity between the subjects of the law both amongst themselves and in their relations with the lawful authorities.

This multi-faceted conception of law has been reflectively constructed by tracing the implications of certain requirements of practical reason, given certain basic values and certain empirical features of persons and their communities. The intention has not been lexicographical; but the construction lies well within the boundaries of common use of "law" and its equivalents in other languages. The intention has not been to describe existing social orders; but the construction corresponds closely to many existing social phenomena that typically are regarded as central cases of law, legal system, Rule of Law, etc. Above all, the meaning has been constructed as a *focal* meaning, not as an appropriation of the term "law" in a univocal sense that would exclude from the reference of the term anything that failed to have all the characteristics (and to their full extent) of the

---

[78] *S.T.* I–II, q. 94, a. 2c. [And *ante*, 140.]

central case. And, equally important, it has been fully recognised that each of the terms used to express the elements in the conception (e.g. "making," "determinate," "effective," "a community," "sanctioned," "rule-guided," "reasonable," "non-discriminatory," "reciprocal," etc.) has itself a focal meaning and a primary reference, and therefore extends to analogous and secondary instances which lack something of the central instance. For example, custom is not *made* in the full sense of "made"—for making is something that someone can set himself to do, but no one sets himself (themselves) to make a custom. Yet customs are "made," in a sense that requirements of practical reason are not made but discovered. The way in which each of the other crucial terms is *more or less* instantiated is quite obvious ... Law, in the focal sense of the term, is *fully* instantiated only when each of these component terms is fully instantiated.

If one wishes to stress the empirical/historical importance, or the practical/rational desirability of sanctions, one may say, dramatically, that an unsanctioned set of laws is "not really law." If one wishes to stress the empirical/historical importance, or the practical/rational desirability of determinate legislative and/or adjudicative institutions one may say, dramatically, that a community without such institutions "lacks a real legal system" or "cannot really be said to have 'a legal system.'" If one wishes to stress the empirical/historical importance, or the practical/rational desirability, of rules authorising or regulating private or public change in the rules or their incidence, one may say, dramatically, that a set of rules which includes no such rules "is not a legal system." All these things have often been said, and can reasonably be said provided that one is seeking to draw attention to a feature of the central case of law and not to banish the other non-central cases to some other discipline.

I have by now sufficiently stressed that one would be simply misunderstanding my conception of the nature and purpose of explanatory definitions of theoretical concepts if one supposed that my definition "ruled out as non-laws"[79] laws which failed to meet, or meet fully, one or other of the elements of the definition. But I should add that it would also be a misunderstanding to condemn the definition because "it fails to explain correctly our ordinary concept of law which does allow for the possibility of laws of [an] objectionable kind."[80] For not only does my definition "allow for the possibility"; it also is not advanced with the intention of "explaining correctly our [sc. the ordinary man's] ordinary concept of law." For the truth is that the "ordinary concept of law" (granting, but not admitting, that there is *one* such concept) is quite unfocused. It is a concept which allows "us" to understand lawyers when they talk about sophisticated legal systems, and anthropologists when they talk about elementary legal systems, and tyrants and bandits when they talk about the orders and the customs of their Syndicate, and theologians and moralists ... There is no point in trying to explain a common-sense concept which takes its meanings from its very varied contexts and is well understood by everyone in those contexts. My purpose has not been to explain an unfocused "ordinary concept" but to develop a concept for use in a theoretical explanation of a set of human actions, dispositions, interrelationships, and conceptions which (i) hang together as a set by virtue of their adaptation to a specifiable set of human needs considered in the light of empirical features of the human condition, and (ii) are accordingly found in very varying forms and with varying degrees of suitability for, and deliberate or unconscious divergence from, those needs as the fully reasonable person would assess them. To repeat: the intention has been not to explain a concept, but to develop a concept which would explain the various phenomena referred to (in an unfocused way) by "ordinary" talk about law—and explain them by showing how they answer (fully or partially)

---

[79] See Raz, *Practical Reason and Norms* (1975), p. 164.
[80] *ibid.*

to the standing requirements of practical reasonableness relevant to this broad area of human concern and interaction.

The lawyer is likely to become impatient when he hears that social arrangements can be *more or less* legal, that legal systems and the rule of law exist as a matter of degree ... and so on. For the lawyer systematically strives to use language in such a way that from its use he can read off a definite solution to definite problems—in the final analysis, judgment for one party rather than the other in a litigable dispute. If cars are to be taxed at such and such a rate, one must be able, as a lawyer, to say (i.e. to rule) of every object that it simply is or is not a car: qualifications, "in this respect ... but in that respect," *secundum quids*, and the like are permissible in argument (and a good lawyer is well aware how open-textured and analogous in structure most terms and concepts are); but just as they do not appear in statutory formulae, so they cannot appear in the final pronouncement of law. And the lawyer, for the same good practical reasons, intrinsic to the enterprise of legal order as I have described it in this chapter, extends his technical use of language to the terms "law," "rule," "legal," "legal system" themselves. To make his point prepositionally he will say that a purported law or rule is either valid or invalid. There are no intermediate categories (though there are intermediate states of affairs, e.g. voidable laws, which now are valid, or are treated as valid, or are deemed to be valid, but are liable to be rendered or treated as or deemed invalid). Equipped with this concept of validity, the lawyer aspires to be able to say of every rule that, being valid, it is a legal rule, or, being invalid, is not. The validity of a rule is identified with membership of the legal system (conceived as a set of valid rules), which thus can be considered legally as the set of all valid rules, including those rules which authorised the valid rule-originating acts of enactment and/or adjudication which are (in this conception) the necessary and sufficient conditions for the validity of the valid rules.

There is no need to question here the sufficiency of this set of concepts and postulates for the practical purposes of the lawyer—though questions could certainly be raised about the role of principles (which have no determinate origin and cannot without awkwardness be called valid) in legal argumentation. Rather it must be stressed that the set is a technical device for use within the framework of legal process, and in legal thought directed to arriving at solutions within that process. The device cannot be assumed to be applicable to the quite different problems of describing and explaining the role of legal process within the ordering of human life in society, and the place of legal thought in practical reason's effort to understand and effect real human good. It is a philosophical mistake to declare, in discourse of the latter kinds, that a social order or set of concepts must either be law or not be law, be legal or not legal.                    [pp. 276–280]

### Derivation of "Positive" From "Natural" Law

"In every law positive well made is somewhat of the law of reason ...; and to discern ... the law of reason from the law positive is very hard. And though it be hard, yet it is much necessary in every moral doctrine, and in all laws made for the commonwealth."[81] These words of the sixteenth-century English lawyer Christopher St. German express the fundamental concern of any sound "natural law theory" of law; to understand the relationship(s) between the particular laws of particular societies and the permanently relevant principles of practical reasonableness.

Consider the law of murder. From the layman's point of view this can be

---

[81] *Doctor and Student*, I, c. 4. As St German remarks, *ibid.*, I, c. 5, English lawyers are not used to reasoning in terms of what is and is not a matter of "the law of nature"; instead they frame their reasoning "in that behalf" in terms of what is and is not "against reason" (*i.e.* unreasonable).

regarded as a directive not to intentionally kill (or attempt to kill) any human being, unless in self-defence ... The legal rule, conceived from this viewpoint, corresponds rather closely to the requirement of practical reason, which would be such a requirement whether or not repeated or supported by the law of the land: that one is not to deliberately kill the innocent (in the relevant sense of "innocent"). Now this requirement is derived from the basic principle that human life is a good, in combination with the seventh of the nine basic requirements of practical reason. Hence Aquinas says that this sort of law is derived from natural law by a process analogous to deduction of demonstrative conclusions from general principles; and that such laws are not positive law only, but also have part of their "force" from the natural law (*i.e.* from the basic principles of practical reasonableness ...[82]) Aquinas's general idea here is fundamentally correct, but vaguely stated and seriously under-developed.

True, some parts of a legal system commonly do, and certainly should, consist of rules and principles closely corresponding to requirements of practical reason which themselves are conclusions directly from the combination of a particular basic value (e.g. life) with one or more of those nine basic "methodological" requirements of practical reasonableness. Discussion in courts and amongst lawyers and legislators will commonly, and reasonably, follow much the same course as a straightforward moral debate such as philosophers or theologians, knowing nothing of that time and place, might carry on. Moreover, the threat of sanctions is ... an "expedient" supplementation for the legislator to annex to the moral rule, with an eye to the recalcitrant and wayward in his own society.

But the process of receiving even such straightforward moral precepts into the legal system deserve closer attention. Notice, for example, that legislative draftsmen do *not* ordinarily draft laws in the form imagined by Aquinas: "There is not to be killing"[83]—nor even "Do not kill," or "Killing is forbidden," or "A person shall not [may not] kill." Rather they will say "It shall be [or:is] an offence to ..." or "Any person who kills ... shall be guilty of an offence." Indeed, it is quite possible to draft an entire legal system without using normative vocabulary at all. Now why does the professional draftsman prefer this indicative propositional form? At the deepest level it is because he has in his mind's eye the pattern of a future social order, or of some aspect of such an order, and is attempting to reproduce that order (on the assumption, which need not be stated or indicated grammatically because it is contextually self-evident, that the participants are to, shall, must, may, etc., act conformably to the pattern). More particularly, a lawyer sees the desired future social order from a professionally structured viewpoint, as a stylised and manageable drama. In this drama, many characters, situations, and actions known to common sense, sociology, and ethics are missing, while many other characters, relationships, and transactions known only or originally only to the lawyer are introduced. In the legally constructed version of social order there are not merely the "reasonable" and "unreasonable" acts which dominate the stage in an individual's practical reasoning; rather, an unreasonable act, for example of killing, may be a crime (and one of several procedurally significant classes of offence), and/or a tort, and/or an act which effects automatic vacation or suspension of office or forfeiture of property, and/or an act which insurers and/or public officials may properly take into account in avoiding a contract or suspending a licence ... etc. So it is the business of the draftsman to specify, precisely, into which of these costumes and relationships an act of killing-under-such-and-such-circumstances fits. That is why "*No one may kill ...*" is legally so defective a formulation.

Nor is all this of relevance only to professional lawyers. The existence of the legal rendering of social order makes a new train of practical reasoning possible,

---

[82] *S.T.* I–II, q. 95, a. 2c.
[83] *S.T.* I–II, q. 95, a. 2c.

and necessary, for the law-abiding private citizen … For example, the pro-fessionally drafted legislative provision, "It is an offence to kill," contextually implies a normative direction to citizens. For there is a legal norm, so intrinsic to any legal ordering of community that it need never be enacted: criminal offences are not to be committed. Behind this norm the citizen need not go. Knowing the law of murder (at least in outline), he need not consider the value of life or the requirement of practical reason that basic values be respected in every action…. As part of the law of the land concerning offences, it adds … (i) a precise elaboration of any other legal (and therefore social) consequences of the act and (ii) a distinct new motive for the law-abiding citizen, who acts on the principle of avoiding legal offences as such, to abstain from the stipulated class of action.

Thus, in a well-developed legal system, the integration of even an un-controversial requirement of practical reasonableness into the law will not be a simple matter. The terms of the requirement *qua* requirement (e.g., in the case we were considering, the term "intentionally") will have to be specified in language coherent with the language of other parts of the law. And then the part which the relevant acts are to play in the legal drama will have to be scripted—their role as, or in relation to, torts, contracts, testamentary dispositions, inheritances, tenures, benefits, matrimonial offences, proofs, immunities, licences, entitlements and forfeitures, offices and disqualifications, etc., etc.

Now very many of these legal implications and definitions will carry the legislator or judge beyond the point where he could regard himself as simply *applying* the intrinsic rule of reason, or even as deducing conclusions from it. Hence the legal project of *applying* a permanent requirement of practical reason will itself carry the legislator into the second of the two categories of human or positive law discerned by Aquinas…

For, in Aquinas's view, the law consists in part of rules which are "derived from natural law like conclusions deduced from general principles," and for the rest of rules which are "derived from natural laws like implementations [*determinationes*] of general directives."[84] This notion of *determinatio* he explains on the analogy of architecture (or any other practical art), in which a general idea or "form" (say, "house," "door," "door-knob") has to be made determinate as this particular house, door, door-knob, with specifications which are certainly derived from and shaped by the general idea but which could have been more or less different in many (even in every!) particular dimension and aspect, and which therefore require of the artificer a multitude of choices. The (making of the) artefact is controlled but not fully determined by the basic idea (say, the client's order), and until it is fully determinate the artefact is non-existent or incomplete. To count as a door in a human habitation, an object must be more than half a metre high and need not be more than 2.5 metres, but no door will be built at all if the artificer cannot *make up his mind* on a particular height. Stressing, as it were, the artificer's virtually complete freedom in reason to choose say 2.2 rather than 2.1 or 2.3 metres, Aquinas says that laws of this second sort have their force "*wholly* from human law"…

These last formulae, so strongly emphasising the legislator's rational freedom of choice in such cases, can be misleading unless one bears in mind that they enunciate only a subordinate theorem within a general theory. The general theory is that, in Aquinas's words, "*every* law laid down by men has the character of law just in so far as it is derived from the natural law,"[85] or in St. German's words, already quoted, "in *every* law positive well made is somewhat of the law of

---

[84] *S.T.* I–II, q. 95, a. 2c. There seems to be no happy English equivalent of "*determinatio*": perhaps Kelsen's "concretization"—would do; "implementation" is more elegant. [On Kelsen see *post*, Chap. 5.]

[85] I–II, q. 95, a. 2c.

reason." The compatibility between this theory and the subordinate theorem can be best understood by reference to [an example]...

If material goods are to be used efficiently for human well-being ... there must normally be a regime of private property ... This regime will be constituted by rules assigning property rights in such goods, or many of them, to individuals or small groups. But precisely what rules should be laid down in order to constitute such a regime is not settled ("determined") by this general requirement of justice. Reasonable choice of such rules is to some extent guided by the circumstances of a particular society, and to some extent "arbitrary." The rules adopted will thus for the most part be *determinationes* of the general requirement—derived from it but not entailed by it even in conjunction with a description of those particular circumstances...

Moreover, in the vast area where the legislator is constructing *determinationes* rather than applying or ratifying determinate principles or rules of reason, there are relatively few points at which his choice can reasonably be regarded as "unfettered" or "arbitrary" (in the sense that it reasonably can be when one confronts two or more feasible alternatives which are in *all* respects equally satisfactory, or equally unsatisfactory, or incommensurably satisfactory/unsatisfactory). The basic legal norms of a law-abiding citizen are "Do not commit offences," "abstain from torts," "perform contracts," "pay debts," "discharge liabilities," "fulfil obligations," etc.; and, taking these norms for granted without stating them, the lawmaker defines offences (from murder to road-traffic offences), torts, the formation, incidents, and discharge of contracts, etc., etc. But this task of definition (and re-definition in the changing conditions of society) has its own principles, which are not the citizen's. The reasonable legislator's principles include the desiderata of the Rule of Law ... But they also include a multitude of other substantive principles related, some very closely, others more remotely, some invariably and others contingently, to the basic principles and methodological requirements of practical reason.

What are these basic norms for the legislator? Normally they are not the subject of direct and systematic enquiry by lawyers. But it should be recalled that "legislator" here, for convenience (and at the expense of some significant differentiations), includes any judiciary that, like the judge at common law, enjoys a creative role. Now the principles that should guide the judge in his interpretation and application of both statutory and common or customary law to particular issues are the subject of scientific discussion by lawyers. *These* principles are almost all "second-order," in that they concern the interpretation and application of other rules or principles whose existence, they presuppose. They therefore are not directly the concern of legislators who have authority not merely to interpret and supplement but also to change and to introduce novel rules. Nevertheless, the second-order principles are themselves mostly crystallisations or versions (adapted to their second-order role) of "first-order" principles which ought to guide even a "sovereign legislature" in its acts of enactment. Moreover, a legislator who ignores a relevant first-order principle in his legislation is likely to find that his enactment are controlled, in their application by citizens, courts, and officials, by that principle in its second-order form, so that in the upshot the law on the particular subject will tend to turn out to be a *determinatio* of that principle (amongst others).

Many of the second-order principles or maxims employed by lawyers express the desirability of stability and predictability in the relations between one person and another, and between persons and things. Such maxims are obviously connected very closely not only with the formal features of law and the desiderata of the Rule of Law, but also with the willingness of lawyers and indeed of men in society in every age to attribute authoritative force to usage, principles to which any legislator ought to give considerable weight—that those human goods which are the fragile and cumulative achievements of past effort, investment, discipline, etc. are not to be treated lightly in the pursuit of future goods...

Starting with these second-order maxims favouring continuity in human affairs—i.e. favouring the good of diachronic order, as distinct from the good of a future end-state—we can trace a series of related second-order principles which include the principle of stability but more and more go beyond it to incorporate new principles or values. In each case these are available in first-order form to guide a legislator. Prose-form requires a linear exposition here which over-simplifies and disguises their interrelations: (i) compulsory acquisition of property rights to be compensated, in respect of *damnum emergens* (actual losses) if not of *lucrum cessans* (loss of expected profits), (ii) no liability for unintentional injury, without fault; (iii) no criminal liability without *mens rea*; (iv) estoppel (*nemo contra factum proprium venire potest*); (v) no judicial aid to one who pleads his own wrong (he who seeks equity must do equity); (vi) no aid to abuse of rights; (vii) fraud unravels everything; (viii) profits received without justification and at the expense of another must be restored; (ix) *pacta sunt servanda* (contracts are to be performed); (x) relative freedom to change existing patterns of legal relationships by agreement; (xi) in assessments of the legal effects of purported acts-in-the-law, the weak to be protected against their weaknesses; (xii) disputes not to be resolved without giving both sides an opportunity to be heard; (xiii) no one to be allowed to judge his own cause.

These "general principles of law" are indeed principles. That is to say, they justify, rather than require, particular rules and determinations, and are qualified in their application to particular circumstances by other like principles. Moreover, any of them may on occasion be outweighed and overridden (which is not the same as violated, amended, or repealed) by other important components of the common good, other principles of justice. Nor is it to be forgotten that there are norms of justice that may never be overridden or outweighed, corresponding to the absolute rights of man. Still, the general principles of law which have been recited here do operate, over vast ranges of legislative *determinationes*, to modify the pursuit of particular social goods. And this modification need not be simply a matter of abstaining from certain courses of conduct: the principles which require compensation, or ascertainment of *mens rea*, or "natural justice" ... can be adequately met only by the positive creation of complex administrative and judicial structures.

In sum: the derivation of law from the basic principles of practical reasoning has indeed the two principal modes identified and named by Aquinas; but these are not two streams flowing in separate channels. The central principle of the law of murder, of theft, of marriage, of contract ... may be a straightforward application of universally valid requirements of reasonableness, but the effort to integrate these subject-matters into the Rule of Law will require of judge and legislator countless elaborations which in most instances partake of the second mode of derivation. This second mode, the sheer *determinatio* by more or less free authoritative choice, is itself not only linked with the basic principles by intelligible relationship to goals (such as traffic safety ...) which are directly related to basic human goods, but also is controlled by wide-ranging formal and other structuring principles (in both first- and second-order form) which themselves are derived from the basic principles by the first mode of derivation.

In the preceding chapter I said that a principal source of the need for authority is the luxuriant variety of appropriate but competing choices of "means" to "end." Now we can see how this range of choices is both increased *and* controlled by the complex of interacting "principles of law." True, the reasoning of those in authority frequently ends without identifying any uniquely reasonable decision; so the rulers must choose, and their choice (*determinatio*) determines what thereafter is uniquely just for those subject to their authority. But, having stressed that it is thus authority, not simply reasoning, that settles most practical questions in the life of a community, I know must stress the necessary rider. To be, itself, authoritative in the eyes of a reasonable man, a *determinatio* must be consistent with the basic requirements of practical reasonableness, though it need not necessarily or even usually be the *determinatio* he would himself have made had he had the opportunity; it need not even be one he would regard as "sensible." Our jurisprudence therefore needs to be completed by a closer analysis of this authoritativeness or "binding force" of positive law, and by some consideration of the significance of wrongful exercises of authority.

It may, however, be helpful to conclude the present discussion by reverting to the textbook categories, "[positive] law," "sources of law," "morality." The tradition of "natural law" theorising is not characterised by any particular answer to the questions: "Is every 'settled' legal rule and legal solution settled by appeal exclusively to 'positive' sources such as statute, precedent, and custom? Or is the 'correctness' of some judicial decisions determinable only by appeal to some 'moral' ('extra-legal') norm? And are the boundaries between the settled and the unsettled law, or between the correct, the eligible, and the incorrect judicial decision determinable by reference only to positive sources or legal rules?" The tradition of natural law theorising is not concerned to minimise the range and determinacy of positive law or the general sufficiency of positive sources as solvents of legal problems.

Rather, the concern of the tradition ... has been to show that the act of "positing" law (whether judicially or legislatively or otherwise) is an act which can and should be guided by "moral" principles and rules; that those moral norms are a matter of objective reasonableness, not of whim, convention, or mere "decision"; and that those same moral norms justify (*a*) the very institution of positive law, (*b*) the man institutions, techniques, and modalities within that tradition (e.g. separation of powers), and (*c*) the main institutions regulated and sustained by law (e.g. government, contract, property, marriage, and criminal liability). What truly characterises the tradition is that it is not content merely to observe the historical or sociological fact that "morality" thus affects " 'law,' " but instead seeks to determine what the requirements of practical reasonableness really are, so as to afford a rational basis for the activities of legislators, judges, and citizens. [pp. 281–290]

*Unjust Laws*

*A Subordinate Concern of Natural Law Theory*

The long haul through the preceding chapters will perhaps have convinced the reader that a theory of natural law need not have as its principal concern, either theoretical or pedagogical, the affirmation that "unjust laws are not law." Indeed, I know of no theory of natural law in which that affirmation, or anything like it, is more than a subordinate theorem. The principal concern of a theory of natural law is to explore the requirements of practical reasonableness in relation to the good of human beings who, because they live in community with one another, are confronted with problems of justice and rights, of authority, law, and obligation. And the principal jurisprudential concern of a theory of natural law is thus to identify the principles and limits of the Rule of Law and to trace the ways in which sound laws, in all their positivity and mutability, are to be derived (not, usually deduced) from unchanging principles—principles that have their force from their reasonableness, not from any originating acts or circumstances....

The ultimate basis of a ruler's authority is the fact that he has the opportunity, and thus the responsibility, of furthering the common good by stipulating solutions to a community's co-ordination problems. Normally, though not necessarily, the immediate source of this opportunity and responsibility is the fact that he is designated by or under some authoritative rule as bearer of authority in respect of certain aspects of those problems. In any event, authority is useless for the common good unless the stipulations of those in authority (or which emerge through the formation of authoritative customary rules) are treated as exclusionary reasons, i.e. as sufficient reason for acting notwithstanding that the subject would not himself have made the same stipulation and indeed considers the actual stipulation to be in some respect(s) unreasonable, not fully appropriate for the common good.... The principles set out in the preceding three sentences control our understanding both of the types of injustice in the making and administration of law, and of the consequences of such injustice.

### Types of Injustice in Law

First, since authority is derived solely from the needs of the common good, a ruler's use of authority is radically defective if he exploits his opportunities by making stipulations intended by him not for the common good but for his own or his friends' or party's or faction's advantage, or out of malice against some person or group. In making this judgment, we should not be deflected by the fact that most legal systems do not permit the exercise of "constitutional" powers to be challenged on the ground that that exercise was improperly motivated. These restrictions on judicial review are justified, if at all, either by pragmatic considerations or by a principle of separation of powers. In either case, they have no application to the reasonable man assessing the claims of authority upon him. On the other hand, it is quite possible that an improperly motivated law may happen to be in its contents compatible with justice and even promote the common good.

Secondly, since the location of authority is normally determined by authoritative rules dividing up authority and jurisdiction amongst separate office-holders, an office-holder may wittingly or unwittingly exploit his opportunity to affect people's conduct, by making stipulations which stray beyond his authority. Except in "emergency" situations in which the law (even the constitution) should be bypassed and in which the source of authority reverts to its ultimate basis, an *ultra vires* act is an abuse of power and an injustice to those treated as subject to it. (The injustice is "distributive" inasmuch as the official improperly seeks to subject others to his own decisions.) Lawyers sometimes are surprised to hear the *ultra vires* actions of an official categorised as abuse of power, since they are accustomed to thinking of such actions as "void and of no effect" in law. But such surprise is misplaced; legal rules about void and voidable acts are "deeming" rules, directing judges to treat actions, which are empirically more or less effective, *as if* they had not occurred (at least, as juridical acts), or *as if* from a certain date they had been overridden by an *intra vires* act of repeal or annulment. Quite reasonably, purported juridical acts of official are commonly presumed to be lawful, and are treated as such by both fellow officials and laymen, unless and until judicially held otherwise. Hence, *ultra vires* official acts, even those which are not immune-for-procedural-or-pragmatic-reasons from successful challenge, will usually subject persons to effects which cannot afterwards be undone; and the bringing about of (the likelihood of) such effects is an abuse of power and an unjust imposition.

Thirdly, the exercise of authority in conformity with the Rule of Law normally is greatly to the common good (even when it restricts the efficient pursuit of other objectives); it is an important aspect of the commutative justice of treating people as entitled to the dignity of self-direction and of the distributive justice of affording all an equal opportunity of understanding and complying with the law. Thus the exercise of legal authority otherwise than in accordance with due requirements of manner and form is an abuse and an injustice, unless those involved consent, or ought to consent, to an accelerated procedure in order to cut out "red tape" which in the circumstances would prejudice substantial justice.

Fourthly, what is stipulated may suffer from none of these defects of intention, author, and form, and yet be substantively unjust. It may be distributively unjust, by appropriating some aspect of the common stock, or some benefit of common life or enterprise, to a class not reasonably entitled to it on any of the criteria of distributive justice, while denying it to other persons; or by imposing on some a burden from which others are, on no just criterion, exempt. It may be commutatively unjust, by denying to one, some, or everyone an absolute human right, or a human right the exercise of which is in the circumstances possible, consistent with the reasonable requirements of public order, public health, etc., and compatible with the due exercise both of other human rights and of the same human rights by other persons.

### Effects of Injustice on Obligation

How does injustice, of any of the foregoing sorts, affect the obligation to obey the law?

It is essential to specify the exact sense of this question. Any sound jurisprudence will recognise that someone uttering the question might conceivably mean by "obligation to obey the law" either (i) empirical liability to be subjected to sanction in event of non-compliance; or (ii) legal obligation in the intra-systemic sense ("legal obligation in the legal sense") in which the practical premiss that conformity to law is socially necessary is a framework principle insulated from the rest of practical reasoning; or (iii) legal obligation in the moral sense (i.e. the moral obligation that presumptively is entailed by legal obligation in the intra-systemic or legal sense); or (iv) moral obligation deriving not from the legality of the stipulation-of-obligation but from some "collateral" source (to be explained shortly). None of these interpretations is absurd, and a sound jurisprudence will show to what extent the answers to each will differ and to what extent they are interrelated.

An unsound jurisprudential method will seek to banish the question, in some of its senses, to "another discipline,"[86] or even declare those senses to be nonsense...

The first of the four conceivable senses of the question listed above is the least likely, in practice, to be intended by anyone raising the question. (Nevertheless, it is the only sense which Austin explicitly recognises). Someone who asks how injustice affects his obligation to conform to law is not likely to be asking for information on the practically important but theoretically banal point of fact, "Am I or am I not likely to be hanged for non-compliance with this law?"

The second of the four listed senses of the question of obligation might seem, at first glance, to be empty. For what is the point of asking whether there is a legal obligation in the legal sense to conform to a stipulation which is in the legal sense obligatory? This objection is, however, too hasty. In my discussion of the formal features of legal order, of the Rule of Law, and of legal obligation. I emphasised the way in which the enterprise of exercising authority through law proceeds by positing a system of rules which derive their authority not from the intrinsic appropriateness of their content but from the fact of stipulation in accordance with rules of stipulation. I emphasised the degree to which the resulting system is conceived of, in legal thought, as internally complete ("gapless") and coherent, and thus as sealed off (so to speak) from the unrestricted flow of practical reasoning about what is just and for the common good. I treated these "model" features of legal system and legal thought not as mere items in some "legal logic" (which as a matter of logic could certainly differ widely from that mode!), but as practically reasonable responses to the need for security and predictability, a need which is indeed a matter of justice and human right. But all this should not disguise the extent to which legal thought in fact (and reasonably) does allow the system of rules to be permeated by principles of practical reasonableness which derive their authority from their appropriateness (in justice and for the common good) and not, or not merely, from their origin in some past act of stipulation or

---

[86]  *Cf.* Hart, *Concept of Law*. [See also Austin's opinion, *post*, 262.]

some settled usage. The legal system, even when conceived strictly as a set of normative meaning-contents (in abstraction from institutions, processes, personnel, and attitudes), is more open that the model suggests—open, that is to say, to the unrestricted flow of practical reasoning, in which a stipulation, valid according to the system's formal criteria of validity ("rules of recognition")[87] may be judged to be, or to have become, unjust and, therefore, after all, wholly or partially inapplicable.

In some legal systems this openness to unvarnished claims about the injustice of an existing or purported law is particularly evident, as in the United States of America. In others, as in English law, it is less obvious but still is familiar to lawyers, for example from the "golden rule" that statutes are to be interpreted so as to avoid "absurdity" or injustice and from debates, quite frequent in the highest courts, about the propriety of amending or abandoning even well-established rules or "doctrines" of common law. Those who doubt or minimise the presence of open-ended principles of justice in professional legal thought will usually be found, on close examination, to be making a constitutional claim, *viz.* that the judiciary ought to leave change and development of law to the legislature. Conversely, those who stress the pervasiveness of such principles and minimise the coverage of practical problems by black-and-white rules will usually be found to be advancing the contradictory constitutional claim. In other words, what is presented[88] as a dispute about the "legal system" *qua* set of normative meaning contents is in substance, typically, a dispute about the "legal system" *qua* constitutional order of institutions.

In short, even in well-developed legal orders served by a professional caste of lawyers, there are (and reasonably) quite a few opportunities of raising "intra-systemically," for example before a court of law, the question whether what would otherwise be an indubitable legal obligation is in truth not (*legally*) obligatory because it is unjust. On the other hand, since there is little point in mediating about the legal-obligation-imposing force of normative meaning contents which are not treated as having legal effect in the principal legal institutions of a community (*viz.* the courts), it is idle to go on asking the question in this sense (the second of the four listed) after the highest court has ruled that in its judgment the disputed law is not unjust or, if unjust, is none the less law, legally obligatory, and judicially enforceable. It is not conducive to clear thought, or to any good practical purpose, to smudge the positivity of law by denying the legal obligatoriness *in the legal or intra-systemic sense* of a rule recently affirmed as legally valid and obligatory by the highest institution of the "legal system." ...

The question in its *third* sense therefore arises in clear-cut form when one is confident that the legal institutions of one's community will not accept that the law in question is affected by the injustice one discerns in it. The question can be stated thus: Given that legal obligation presumptively entails a moral obligation, and that the legal system is by and large just, does a particular unjust law impose upon me any moral obligation to conform to it?

Notoriously, many people (let us call them "positivists") propose that this question should not be tackled in "jurisprudence" but should be left to "another discipline," no doubt "political philosophy" or "ethics." Now it is not a purpose of this book to conduct a polemic against anybody's conception of the limits of jurisprudence. Suffice it to mention some disadvantages of this proposal. First the proposed division is artificial to the extent that the arguments and counter-arguments which it is proposed to expel from jurisprudence are in fact (as we observed in the preceding paragraphs) to be found on the lips of lawyers in court and of judges giving judgment. Of course, the arguments about justice and obligation that find favour in the courts of a given community at a given time may

---

[87] [*Cf.* Hart, *post*, 382.]
[88] As in Dworkin, *Taking Rights Seriously* (London, 1977), Chaps 2–4. [See *post*, 386.]

be arguments that would be rejected by a sound and critical ethics or political philosophy. But they are part of the same realm of discourse. One will not understand either the "logic" or the "sociology" of one's own or anyone else's legal system unless one is aware (not merely in the abstract but in detail) how both the arguments in the courts, and the formulation of norms by "theoretical" jurists, are affected, indeed permeated, by the vocabulary, the syntax, and the principles of the "ethics" and "political philosophy" of that community, or of its élite or professional caste. In turn, one will not well understand the ethics or political philosophy of that community or caste unless one has reflected on the intrinsic problems of "ethics" and "political philosophy," i.e. on the basic aspects of human well-being and the methodological requirements of practical reasonableness. Finally, one will not well understand these *intrinsic* problems and principles unless one is aware of the extent to which the language in which one formulates them for oneself, and the concepts which one "makes one's own," are themselves the symbols and concepts of a particular human civilisation, a civilisation which has worked itself out, as much as anywhere, in its lawcourts and law schools. This set of considerations affords the first reason why I would not myself accept the proposal to banish to some "other discipline" the question of the moral obligation of an unjust law.

The second reason, not unconnected with the first, is ... that a jurisprudence which aspires to be more than the lexicography of a particular culture cannot solve its theoretical problems of definition or concept-formation unless it draws upon at least some of the considerations of values and principles of practical reasonableness which are the subject-matter of "ethics" (or "political philosophy"). Since there can be no sharp distinction between the "two disciplines" at that basic level, it is not clear why the distinction, if such there be, should be thought so very important at other levels.

The third reason is that (not surprisingly, in view of what I have just said) the programme of separating off from jurisprudence all questions or assumptions about the moral significance of law is not consistently carried through by those who propose it. Their works are replete with more or less undiscussed assumptions such as that the formal features of legal order contribute to the practical reasonableness of making, maintaining, and obeying law; that these formal features have some connection with the concept of justice as principles of *legality*[89] and that the fact that a stipulation is *legally* valid gives some reason, albeit not conclusive, for treating it as *morally* obligatory or *morally* permissible to act in accordance with it.[90] But none of these assumptions can be shown to be warranted, or could even be discussed, without transgressing the proposed boundary between jurisprudence and moral or political philosophy—in the way that I have systematically "transgressed" it in the preceding five chapters. Thus the state of the scholarly literature testifies, so to speak, to what a sound philosophy of practical reason establishes abstractly: the principles of practical reasonableness and their requirements form one unit of inquiry which can be subdivided into "moral," "political," and "jurisprudential" only for a pedagogical or expository convenience which risks falsifying the understanding of all three.

What, then, are we to say in reply to the question whether an unjust law creates a moral obligation *in the way* that just law *of itself* does? The right response begins by recalling that the stipulations of those in authority have presumptive obligatory force (in the eyes of the reasonable person thinking unrestrictedly about what to do) only because of what is needed if the common good is to be secured and realised.

All my analyses of authority and obligation can be summed up in the following theorem: the ruler has, very strictly speaking, no right to be obeyed; but he has the

[89] See Hart, *Concept of Law*, pp. 160–161, 206.
[90] *ibid.*

authority to give directions and make laws that are morally obligatory and that he has the responsibility of enforcing. He has this authority for the sake of the common good (the needs of which can also, however, make authoritative the opinions—as in custom—or stipulations of men who have no authority). Therefore, if he uses his authority to make stipulations against the common good, or against any of the basic principles of practical reasonableness, those stipulations altogether lack the authority they would otherwise have *by virtue of being his*. More precisely, stipulations made for partisan advantage, or (without emergency justification) in excess of legally defined authority, or imposing inequitable burdens on their subjects, or directing the doing of things that should never be done, simply fail, of themselves, to create any moral obligation whatever.

This conclusion should be read with precision. First, it should not be concluded that an enactment which itself is for the common good and compatible with justice is deprived of its moral authority by the fact that the act of enacting it was rendered unjust by the partisan motives of its author. Just as we should not be deflected from adjudging the act of enactment unjust by the fact that improper motivation is not, in a given system, ground for judicial review, so we should not use the availability of judicial review for that ground, in certain other systems of law, as a sufficient basis for concluding that a private citizen (to whom is not entrusted the duty of disciplining wayward officials or institutions) is entitled to treat the improper motives of the authors of a just law as exempting him from his moral duty of compliance. Secondly, it should not be concluded that the distributive injustice of a law exempts from its moral obligation those who are *not* unjustly burdened by it.

Understood with those precision, my response to the question in its third sense corresponds to the classical position: *viz.* that for the purpose of assessing one's legal obligations in the moral sense, one is entitled to discount laws that are "unjust" in any of the ways mentioned. Such laws lack the moral authority that in other cases comes simply from their origin, "pedigree," or formal source. In this way, then, *lex injusta non est lex and virtutem obligandi non habet* whether or not it is "legally valid" and "legally obligatory" in the restricted sense that if (i) emanates from a legally authorised source, (ii) will in fact be enforced by courts and/or other officials, and/or (iii) is commonly spoken of as a law like other laws.

But at the same time I must add that the last-mentioned facts, on which the lawyer *qua* lawyer (normally but, as I have noted, not exclusively) may reasonably concentrate, are not irrelevant to the moralist, the reasonable man with his unrestricted perspective.

At this point there emerges our question in the *fourth* of the sense I listed at the beginning of this section. It maybe the case, for example, that if I am *seen* by fellow citizens to be disobeying or disregarding this "law," the effectiveness of other laws, and/or the general respect of citizens for the authority of a generally desirable ruler or constitution, will probably be weakened, with probable bad consequences for the common good. Does not this collateral fact create a moral obligation? The obligation is to comply with the law, but it should not be treated as an instance of what I have called "legal obligation in the moral sense." For it is not based on the good of *being* law-abiding, but only on the desirability of not rendering ineffective the just parts of the legal system. Hence it will not require compliance with unjust laws according to their tenor or "legislative intent," but only such degree of compliance as is necessary to avoid bringing "the law" (as a whole) "into contempt." This degree of compliance will vary according to time, place, and circumstance; in some limiting cases (e.g. of judges or other officials administering the law) the morally required degree of compliance may amount to full or virtually full compliance, just *as if* the law in question had been a just enactment.

So, if an unjust stipulation is, in fact, homogeneous with other laws in its formal source, in its reception by courts and officials, and in its common acceptance, the good citizen may (not always) be morally required to conform to that stipulation to the extent necessary to avoid weakening "the law," the legal system (of rules, institutions, and dispositions) as a whole. The ruler still has the responsibility of repealing rather than enforcing his unjust law, and in this sense has no right that it should be conformed to. But the citizen, or official, may meanwhile have the diminished, collateral, and in an important sense extra-legal, obligation to obey it. [pp. 351–362]

## Lex Injusta Non Est Lex

...Aquinas carefully avoids saying flatly that "an unjust law is not a law: *lex injusta non est lex*." But in the end it would have mattered little had he said just that. For the statement either is pure nonsense, flatly self-contradictory, or else is a dramatisation on the point more literally made by Aquinas when he says that an unjust law is not law in the focal sense of the term "law" [i.e. *simpliciter*] notwithstanding that it is law in a secondary sense of that term [i.e. *secundum quid*].

Perhaps we can dwell on this a little. The central tradition of natural law theorising in which the "lex injusta ..." doctrine is embedded has not chosen to use the slogans attributed to it by modern critics, for example that "*what is utterly immoral* cannot be law,"[91] or that "*certain rules* cannot be law because of their moral iniquity,"[92] or that "*these evil things* are not law,"[93] or that "*nothing iniquitous* can *anywhere* have the status of law,"[94] or that "*morally iniquitous demands* [are] *in no sense* law,[95] or that "*there cannot be* an unjust law.'"[96] On the contrary, the tradition, even in its most blunt formulations,[97] has affirmed that unjust LAWS are not law. Does not this formula itself make clear, beyond reasonable question, that the tradition is not indulging in "a refusal, made *once and for all*, to recognise evil laws as valid *for any purpose*?"[98] Far from "denying legal validity to iniquitous rules,"[99] the tradition explicitly (by speaking of "unjust *laws*")[1] accords to iniquitous rules legal validity, whether on the ground and in the sense that these rules are accepted in the courts as guides to judicial decision, or on the ground and in the sense that, in the judgment of the speaker, they satisfy the criteria of validity laid down by constitutional or other legal rules, or on both these grounds and in both these senses. The tradition goes so far as to say that there may be an obligation to conform to some such unjust laws in order to uphold respect for the legal system as a whole (what I call a "collateral obligation"[2])...

[Normative] statements may, in one and the same grammatical form, intend to assert (S:1) what is justified or required by practical reasonableness *simpliciter*, or (S:2) what is treated as justified or required in the belief or practice of some group, or (S:3) what is justified or required *if* certain principles or rules are justified (but

---

[91] Hart, "The Separation of Law and Morals" (1958) 71 *Harvard L. Rev.* 593, reprinted in Dworkin (ed.), *The Philosophy of Law* (1977), p. 33 (emphasis added). [And in *Essays In Jurisprudence and Philosophy*.]

[92] *ibid.* (emphasis added).

[93] *ibid.*, p. 34 (emphasis added).

[94] Hart, *Concept of Law*, p. 211 (emphasis added).

[95] *ibid.*, p. 211 (emphasis added).

[96] Arthur C. Danto, "Human Nature and Natural Law" in S. Hook (ed.), *Law and Philosophy* (1964), p. 187 (emphasis added), ascribing this "dictum" to "the Thomistic defenders of natural law".

[97] See, *e.g.* Blackstone, I *Comm.* 41.

[98] Hart, *Concept of Law*, p. 211 (emphasis added); and see p. 156, ascribing that view to the "Thomist tradition."

[99] *ibid.*, p. 211.

[1] And such references are not merely in the context of "non est lex" formulations: see, *e.g.* S.T. I–II, q. 94, a. 6 ad 3.

[2] *S.T.* I–II, q. 96, a. 4c and ad 3.

without taking any position on the question whether those principles or rules *are* so justified)...

[it is] natural and frequent to shift from the expository (S:3) or sociological/ historical (S:2) viewpoint to the fully critical (S:1) viewpoint within the space of a single sentence. *Lex injusta non est lex* is such a sentence: it implies (i) that some normative meaning-content has for some community the status (S:2/S:3) of law, (ii) that that law is unjust (a critical judgment of practical reasonableness, whether correct or incorrect), and (iii) that compliance with that law is (S:1) *not* justified or required by the derivative and defeasible principle of practical reasonableness that laws impose moral obligations.

Plato, Aristotle, Augustine, and Aquinas did not draw attention to the distinction between the intra-systemic expository viewpoint, the historical/sociological viewpoint, and the viewpoint of unrestricted practical reasonableness. They took it for granted, and shifted easily from one to another while treating the last-mentioned viewpoint as their primary concern: "we hold that, in all such matters [pertaining to human passions and actions], whatever appears to the mature man of practical wisdom [the *spoudaios* to be the case really is the case."[3] [pp. 364–366]

J. FINNIS, J. BOYLE, G. GRISEZ
**The First Moral Principle**
(1987)[4]

To understand right and wrong, one must bear two things in mind. First, the possibilities of fulfilment are always unfolding, for there are several basic human goods, and endless ways of serving and sharing in them. Second, human beings, even when they work together, can only do so much. No one can undertake every project, or serve in every possible way. Nor can any community. Choices must be made.

Irresistibly compulsive behaviour, bad luck, ineptitude, and the unwelcome results of honest human error are not wrongs. Only by choosing badly can individuals and groups go wrong morally. On any ethical theory, moral norms are standards for choosing well.

But how can there be bad choosing, if human goods are as we have said? Without reasons for choosing grounded in basic human goods, there could be no options; yet, we have also said, the choice of an option is never rationally necessary—otherwise there would not be two or more real options. Every choice is grounded in some intelligible good, and to that extent is rational, yet no choice has a monopoly on rationality. Moreover, virtually every choice has some negative impact on some good or other; no possibility can be chosen without setting aside at least some reason against choosing it.

Partly in response to this complexity, the consequentialist tries to distinguish good from bad choices by their effectiveness in maximizing good or minimizing evil. But consequentialism cannot serve as a coherent method of moral judgment. For, although one may in various ways and for various purposes commensurate the measurable value and disvalue promised by different instantiations of goods, one cannot commensurate the goods and bads which make diverse possibilities choiceworthy opportunities: such goods and bads go beyond what is definite at any moment of choice.

But if consequentialism is unworkable, how can basic human goods mark the moral distinction between choosing well and choosing badly?

The basic principle of the distinction between right and wrong is not easy to

---

[3]  Aristotle, *Nic Eth*. X, 5: 1176a 16–17.
[4]  [From *Nuclear Deterrence, Morality and Realism*.]

discern reflectively and articulate. Before attempting to formulate it, we shall sketch, but only sketch, the outline of morality's foundation, as we see it.

All moral theorists, including consequentialists, recognize that the foundation of morality is broader and deeper than the prospective results of the options between which one must choose. Common morality suggested an ultimate foundation in "the blessings of the covenant", "the Kingdom", "beatitude", "the order of charity", and so forth. Secular moral theories pointed towards realities such as "the kingdom of ends", "the realm of freedom", "the greatest good of the greatest number", and so forth.

Like consequentialists, we think it clear that morality's foundation is to be located in the goods of human persons, as individuals and in community. Unlike consequentialists, we believe that an adequate description of morality's foundation will take into account aspects of these goods irreducible to even the widest and most long-run prospective consequences of eligible options. Among the important aspects of human goods are possibilities still unknown, for example the answers to questions no one today is in a position to ask, and forms of human community to which present aspirations for a better world do not even reach out. Other aspects of human goods, of the first importance for morality, come to be in the personalities and communities of those who cherish and serve them, and so act rightly in respect of their instantiations. For example, authenticity, neighbourliness, and just social order come to be in good persons and communities, in and through their morally right choices, yet are not among the pre-moral values and disvalues upon which the consequentialist tries to ground moral judgment.

Plainly, the basic human goods, conceived so inclusively, cannot ground morality by differentiating possible choices with respect to the potential effectiveness of those choices in realizing instances of the goods. Rather, the moral foundation determines the rightness and wrongness of choices by differentiating attitudes toward basic goods. Underlying the willingness to make one choice or another, there can be entirely different dispositions of the moral agent toward the basic human goods.

Right choices are those which can be made by moral agents whose attitude towards the moral foundation is one for which there is no single adequate word. Certainly, it involves respect for all of the basic human goods in all their aspects, yet "respect" has too passive a connotation. The right attitude is one of concern and interest, but all connotations of partiality must be excluded from these words. The right attitude is perhaps best called "appreciation", provided that this word is used with its connotation of readiness to serve and to cherish what one appreciates. Morally right choices are those choices which can be made by one whose will is disposed toward the entire moral foundation with this attitude of appreciation.

Having completed a sketch of the outline of morality's foundation, we shall now articulate as best we can the moral truths which are at and very near the beginning of the process of moral judgment. First, we propose a formulation of the first principle of morality, and then, in the next section, we unfold some of its most immediate specifications. The very abstract language in which the first principle has to be articulated renders it, we realize, quite opaque; but the somewhat less abstract language in which its specifications will be discussed will help make the first principle itself more understandable.

The first principle of morality can, perhaps, best be formulated: In voluntarily acting for human goods and avoiding what is opposed to them, *one ought to choose and otherwise will those and only those possibilities whose willing is compatible with integral human fulfilment.*

This formulation can be misunderstood. "Integral human fulfilment" does not refer to individualistic self-fulfilment, but to the good of all persons and communities. All the goods in which any person can share can also fulfil others, and individuals can share in goods such as friendship only with others.

Nor is integral human fulfilment some gigantic synthesis of all the instantiations of goods in a vast state of affairs, such as might be projected as the goal of a world-wide billion-year plan. Ethics cannot be an architectonic art in that way; there can be no plan to bring about integral human fulfilment. It is a guiding ideal rather than a realizable idea, for the basic goods are open ended.

And integral human fulfilment is not a supreme human good, beyond basic human goods such as truth and friendship. It does not provide reasons for acting as the basic goods do. It only moderates the interplay of such reasons, so that deliberation will be thoroughly reasonable.

Common morality's fundamental principles were formulated in theistic terms, while the ideal of integral human fulfilment is not. The primary principles of biblical morality were: Love God above all things; Love your neighbour as yourself. The first principle of morality as we formulate it captures much, if not all, the moral content of those love commands. For Jews and Christians, God is the supreme good and source of all goods; loving him therefore requires the cherishing of all goods. Among these are the basic human goods, which the ideal of integral human fulfilment, too, requires be cherished. And loving one's neighbour as oneself at least excludes egoism and means accepting the fulfilment of others as part of one's own responsibility; the same demand is made by the first principle of morality as we formulate it.

### Specifications of the first moral principle

But this principle may at first seem too abstruse to be of service. How can any specific moral norms be derived from it?

No specific moral norm can be derived *immediately* from the first principle. But it does imply intermediate principles from which specific norms can be deduced. Among these intermediate principles is the Golden Rule, or the related principle of universalizability—for a will marked by egoism or partiality cannot be open to integral human fulfilment. And this intermediate principle in turn leads to some specific moral judgments—*e.g.* Jane who wants her husband Jack to be faithful plainly violates it by sleeping with Sam.

Thus there is a route from the first moral principle to specific moral norms. By reflection on the case we have just identified, we try in the next four paragraphs to clarify the intuitively obvious relationship between the first principle and the Golden Rule, and between the Golden Rule and specific norms of fairness.

Human choices are limited in many ways; some limits are inevitable but others are not. Among inevitable limits are those on people's insight into the basic goods, ideas of how to serve them, and available resources. In so far as such limits are outside one's control, morality cannot demand that they be transcended.

Some limits on choice, however, are avoidable. For one can voluntarily narrow the range of people and goods one cares about. Sometimes this voluntary narrowing has an intelligible basis, as when a person of many gifts chooses a profession and allows other talents to lie fallow. But sometimes avoidable limitations are voluntarily set or accepted without any such reason.

Sources of limitations of this last kind thus meet two conditions: (i) they are effective only by one's own choices; and (ii) they are non-rational motives, not grounded in intelligible requirements of the basic goods. Normally, the acting person either can allow these non-rational limiting factors to operate, or can transcend them. For they are one's own feelings and emotions, in so far as these are not integrated with the rational appeal of the basic goods and of communal fulfilment in those goods. Such non-integrated feelings offer motives for behaviour, yet are *not* in themselves reasons for action. (However, one who gives in to them, whether through malice or weakness of will, always can find some reason for choosing in line with them.)

The first and master principle of morality rationally prescribes that non-integrated feelings be transcended. The Golden Rule requires one not to narrow one's interests and concerns by a certain set of such feelings—one's preference for oneself and those who are near and dear. It does not forbid one to treat different persons differently, when that is required by inevitable limits, or by intelligible requirements of shared goods themselves.

The first principle has other specifications, besides the Golden Rule, because non-rational preferences among persons are not the only feelings which incline one to prefer limited to integral human fulfilment. Hostile feelings such as anger and hatred towards oneself or others lead intelligent, sane, adult persons to actions which are often called "stupid", "irrational", and "childish". Self-destructive and spiteful actions destroy, damage, or block some instantiations of basic human goods; willing such actions is plainly not in line with a will to integral human fulfilment. Yet behaviour motivated by hostility need not violate the Golden Rule. People sometimes act self-destructively without being unfair to others. Moreover, revenge can be fair: an eye for an eye. But fairness does not eliminate the unreasonableness of acting on hostile feelings in ways that intelligibly benefit no one. Thus the Golden Rule is not the only intermediate principle which specifies the first principle of morality and generates specific moral norms.

So an ethics of Kantian type is mistaken if it claims that universalizability is the only principle of morality. Respect for persons—treating them always as ends in themselves, and never as mere means—must mean more than treating others fairly. The dignity of persons, as bearers of and sharers in human goods, sets at least one other moral demand: Do not answer injury with injury, even when one can do so fairly.

Not only feelings of hostility, but positive feelings can motivate one to do evil—i.e. to destroy, damage, or impede an instantiation of some basic human good. One can choose to bring about evil as a means. One does evil to avoid some other evil, or to attain some ulterior good.

In such cases, the choice can seem entirely rational, and consequentialists might commend it. But, as we have said, the appearance of rationality is based on a false assumption: that human goods do not matter except in so far as they are instantiated and can be commensurated. As we have argued (IX.5–6), this way of trying to deal with human goods cannot be rational; the preceding sections of the present chapter indicate part of the reason why. What is morally important includes possible instantiations of goods diverse in kind from one another, and also includes not only those instantiations one now considers but the field of possibility opened up by the basic human goods. The indeterminacy of this aspect of the good utterly defies measurement.

Thus, it is unreasonable to choose to destroy, damage, or impede some instance of a basic good for the sake of an ulterior end. In doing this, one does not have the reason of maximizing good or minimizing evil—there is no such *reason*, for the goods at stake in choosable options are not rationally commensurable. Rather one is motivated by different feelings towards different instances of good involved. In this sort of case, one willy-nilly plays favourites among instantiations of goods, just as in violating the Golden Rule one plays favourites among persons.

And so, in addition to the Golden Rule and the principle which excludes acting on hostile feelings, there is another intermediate principle: Do not do evil that good may come.

Because this principle generates moral absolutes, it is often considered a threat to people's vital concrete interests. But while it may be a threat to some interests, the moral absolutes it generates also protect real human goods which are parts of the fulfilment of actual persons, and it is reasonable to sacrifice important concrete interests to the integral fulfilment of persons.

Why? Because otherwise one plays favourites among the goods. Why not play favourites? Because doing so is incompatible with a will towards integral human fulfilment. Why worry about integral human fulfilment? That is like asking why man is man. Integral human fulfilment is not something alien to the moral agent, but is what the moral agent as a person is, and is together with others, and is most abundantly, and is still to be. And is, not only as moral in *distinction from* other human concerns, but as moral *including* most perfectly and harmoniously every truly human concern.

The Golden Rule and the other two principles enunciated in this section shape the rational prescription of the first principle of morality into definite responsibilities. Hence, we here call such intermediate principles "modes of responsibility". Besides the three modes we have discussed, there are others which moral reflection in the great cultures has uncovered: detachment, creative fidelity, purity of heart, and so on. Although we will not treat them here, the theory of moral principles we propose has a place for such fruits of previous moral reflection. [pp. 281–287]

**MARK C. MURPHY**

**Natural Law Jurisprudence**[4a]

(2003)

*Formulating the Natural Law Thesis*

The dominant contemporary understanding of natural law theory is, strangely enough, not drawn from any reading of natural law theorists themselves, but from Hart. Natural-law theory is the view that Hart rejects in his 1957 Holmes Lecture on "Positivism and the Separation of Law and Morals."[5] Positivism believes in the separation, or at least the separability, of law and morals; natural law theory must be the denial of that claim. To be a natural law theorist is, then, to reject the view that law and morality are separable.

This way of putting the natural law thesis is unsatisfactory in a number of ways. It is first of all unclear as to whether the natural law view should be framed in terms of *morality*. The notion of morality is arguably a peculiarly modern notion,[6] and it would be courting anachronism to refer to the views of Aquinas, the paradigmatic natural law theorist, in such terms. Better to adopt Finnis's suggestion and simply appeal to "practical reasonableness," a semitechnical term that is meant to cover the entire range of good reasons for action rather than suggesting a subset of them.[7] Nor is *inseparability* a sufficiently precise concept to

---

[4a] (From *Legal Theory*, Vol. 9.)

[5] H.L.A. Hart, *Positivism and the Separation of Law and Morals*, 71 Harv. L. Rev. 593–629 (1958); cited to the reprint in Hart, Essays in Jurisprudence and Philosophy 49–87, 55 (1983).

[6] *See, e.g.*, Alasdair MacIntyre, After Virtue 1–5 (2nd ed., 1984); and Bernard Williams, Ethics and the Limits of Philosophy 6 (1985).

[7] "The term 'moral' is of somewhat uncertain connotation. So it is preferable to frame our conclusion in terms of practical reasonableness. If there is a viewpoint in which the institution of the Rule of Law, and compliance with rules and principles of law according to their tenor, are regarded as at least presumptive requirements of practical reasonableness itself, such a viewpoint is the viewpoint which should be used as the standard of reference by the theorist describing the features of the legal order"; Finnis, *Natural Law and Natural Rights*, at 15. Michael Moore essentially follows this line as well; though formulating the natural law thesis in terms of a necessary constraint on law by moral reasons, he explicitly counts *all* normative reasons as moral reasons. *See* Moore, *Law as a Functional Kind, in* Natural Law Theory 188–242, 189, 196–197 (Robert P. George, ed., 1992).

get at what the natural law theorist has in mind:[8] The natural law theorist is concerned with a necessary continuity between law and the requirements of practical reasonableness. Positively put, the natural law thesis is that, necessarily, law is a rational standard for conduct. It is of the nature of law to provide a set of standards that rational agents should take as a guide to their conduct.

This first cut at the natural law thesis is rough, but it has the benefits of closely following Aquinas' formulation of the position[9] and would be affirmed by contemporary writers self-consciously working in this tradition. What has separated writers in this tradition is how the natural law thesis ought to be understood and developed. The central difficulty has been to provide a clearer understanding of the natural law thesis that is both interesting—that is, an understanding that is or would be denied by some otherwise sensible legal theorists—and not obviously false.

One way to understand the basic natural law thesis is what I will call the *strong* reading of the natural law thesis. According to the strong reading, the fact that it is of the nature of law to provide a set of standards that rational agents should take as a guide to their conduct entails that any standard that rational agents could not take as a guide to their conduct is not law but is simply invalid. *Lex iniusta*—or, better *lex sine rationem*—*non est lex*. While there have been some doubts expressed as to whether anyone actually held this view,[10] it does seem to have been pretty clearly affirmed by Blackstone, and Michael Moore's recent sketch of the core natural law position includes the strong reading as the target at which the natural law theorist is aiming.[11]

Law that cannot serve as an adequate guide to conduct for a rational being is no law at all. Critics—even those otherwise sympathetic to some reading of the natural law thesis—have been very exuberant in their zeal to show that this sort of view is on its face paradoxical or otherwise deeply implausible. Finnis, George, and Soper have charged that the *lex iniusta non est lex* slogan expresses an absurd view—literally, "unjust law is not law"—that carries its self-contradiction out in the open and hence should not be considered an accurate statement of the natural law position. Finnis has argued that the natural law motto that unjust law is not law is, construed literally, "pure nonsense, flatly self-contradictory",[12] Soper has written that "the very obviousness of this contradiction" shows that no one could ever have meant to affirm the strong natural law thesis;[13] and George has remarked that the fact that Aquinas was perfectly willing to talk about unjust

---

[8] Leslie Green, *Legal Positivism, in* THE STANFORD ENCYCLOPEDIA OF PHILOSOPHY (Edward N. Zalta, ed., Spring 2003) available at http://plato.stanford.edu/archives/spr2003/entries/legal-positivism/.

[9] SUMMA THEOLOGIAE IaIIae Q. 90. A. 4; IaIIae Q. 91, A. 3.

[10] Norman Kretzmann notes that no occurrence of the sentence *lex iniusta non est lex* appears either in Aquinas or in Augustine, whom Aquinas cites in introducing the idea into his discussion of law; Kretzmann, *Lex Iniusta Non Est Lex: Laws on Trial in Aquinas' Court of Conscience*, AM. J. JURIS. 99–122, 100–101 (1988). Of course, this does not at all settle the question of whether anyone in that tradition affirmed the rather stark proposition about the connection between law and practical reasonableness that the slogan suggests. Finnis expresses doubts about whether anyone in the natural law tradition affirmed it, and Finnis, George, and Soper are particularly confident that Aquinas did not mean to assert so stark a claim. Their main reasons for doubting that Aquinas held this view was that they find the view incoherent; on this alleged incoherence, *see* below in this paper.

[11] Moore, *supra* note 7, at 194–195; *see also* Moore, *Law as Justice*, 18 SOC. PHIL. & POL'Y 115–145, 115–117 (2001).

[12] Finnis, *supra*, note 7, at 364.

[13] Philip Soper, *Legal Theory and the Problem of Definition*, 50 U. CHI. L. REV 1170–1200, 1181 (1983).

laws shows that the paradigmatic natural law position does not affirm the *lex iniusta* thesis.[14] But none of this is at all persuasive. For, first of all, the core of the strong view can remain without the paradoxical formulation. This is obvious. All that one needs to do is to restate the position as the claim that no norm or social rule (etc.) that is unreasonable can be law. This lacks even the appearance of paradox to which the critics object.

But for all that there may be good reasons to stick with the formulation and to reject the view that it is at all paradoxical. Norman Kretzmann has made one case for this view in his exposition of Aquinas' position.[15] Kretzmann has defended the *lex iniusta* slogan by noting that it is a common phenomenon for one term to have two sets of conditions of application, one of which is nonevaluative, the other of which is evaluative. So one might claim that this doctor is no doctor at all; or that one's son is no son at all. In each of these cases, the correct application of the former term depends entirely on nonevaluative conditions (having the socially recognized credentials of physicians for the former, and perhaps being one's male biological offspring or being legally recognized as a male dependent of a certain sort), while the correct application of the latter term depends at least in part on evaluative conditions (having a proper care and competence with respect to furthering health or showing the proper sort of care for and deference to one's parents). The crucial point to be made here is that this is not merely a matter of equivocation: the former and latter conditions of application are nonarbitrarily related to one another. Kretzmann does not elaborate sufficiently on the nature of this nonarbitrary relationship, leaving his view open to the charge that the sense in which the *lex iniusta* claim is true may be a sense that everyone, including the most hard-boiled positivists, can accept.[16]

There is another way to respond to the charge. A claim of the form "a————X is not an X" is not self-contradictory—even assuming it to have existential import—if the blank is filled by an *alienans*, a certain sort of attributive adjective. "Fake" is always an *alienans*, and so "fake diamonds are not diamonds" is not self-contradictory: "fake diamonds are not diamonds" is not properly analyzed as "nothing that is both fake and a diamond is a diamond." But there are adjectives that count as instances of the *alienans* only in certain contexts, that is, as applied to certain nouns. "Glass" is not generally an *alienans* (a glass slipper is a slipper), but it can be (a glass diamond is not a diamond). A natural law theorist who takes the strong view could hold that "inadequately serving as a rational standard for conduct" is, when applied to law, an *alienans*, and thus escape the charge that the strong version of natural law jurisprudence is flatly self-contradictory.

Even if the strong reading of the natural law thesis can be defended from the charge that its central thesis is paradoxical, it is nonetheless subject to the accusation that it is open to other obvious, devastating objections. Here, for example, is Brian Bix:

> The basic point is that the concept of "legal validity" is closely tied to what is recognized as binding in a given society and what the state enforces, and it seems fairly clear that there are plenty of societies where immoral laws are recognized as binding and enforced. Someone might answer that these immoral laws are not *really* legally valid, and the officials are making a mistake when they treat the rules as if they were legally valid. However, this is just to play games with words, and confusing games at that. "Legal validity" is the term we use to refer to *whatever* is conventionally recognized as binding;

---

[14] Robert P. George, *Kelsen and Aquinas on "the Natural Law Doctrine,"* 75 NOTRE DAME L. REV. 1625–1646, 1641 (2000).

[15] Kretzmann, *supra* note 10, at 102–107.

[16] J.S. Russell, *Trial by Slogan: Natural Law and Lex Iniusta Non Est Lex*, 19 LAW & PHIL. 433–449 (2000).

to say that all the officials could be wrong about what is legally valid is close to nonsense.[17]

The Fugitive Slave Act of 1850, to take one example, required citizens not to hinder and even to aid federal marshals who sought to return runaway slaves to bondage. This act was passed in order to enforce a constitutional provision and was enacted in due form by the federal legislature. It was socially acknowledged and judicially enforced. It seems that as a matter of social practice, the Fugitive Slave Act *was* law—regardless of the fact that those under it did not have anything like decisive reason to comply with it. It hence serves nothing but obfuscation to deny—as the defender of the strong reading must deny—that the Fugitive Slave Act was law.

It still seems to me an inconclusive objection. We should grant, of course, that if it were a criterion for success in any account of law that it designate as "law" all those things that are designated "law" by citizens or perhaps by officials, then this understanding of the natural law view would be doomed, for it undoubtedly does deny the designation "law" to some of those items. But the question to be raised is whether this general agreement is to be treated as infallible. Consider, as an instructive analogy, van Inwagen's story of the "bligers":

> When the first settlers arrived in the hitherto unpopulated land of Pluralia, they observed (always from a fair distance) what appeared to be black tigers, and they coined the name "bliger" for them. ... A few centuries after the settlement of Pluralia, however, a foreign zoological expedition discovered that, in a way, there were no bligers. "A bliger (*Quasi-Tigris Multiplex Pluralianus*)," their report read, "is really six animals. Its 'legs' are four monkey-like creatures, its 'trunk' a sort of sloth, and its 'head' a species of owl. Any six animals of the proper species can combine temporarily to form a bliger. (Combinations lasting for several hours have been observed telescopically.) The illusion is amazing. Even a trained zoologist observing a bliger from a distance of ten meters would swear he was observing a single, unified animal. While the purpose of this combination is doubtless to protect its members from predators by producing the illusion of the presence of a large, dangerous carnivore, we can only guess as the evolutionary history of this marvelous symbiosis.[18]

Now, it is not perfectly clear what moral to draw from this story. Van Inwagen draws the moral that Pluralians nonetheless spoke truly when they said "there is a bliger in the back field!" and the like; in saying "there is a bliger in the back field!" the Pluralians did not express a view on whether the various objects arranged bligerwise composed an additional object, a bliger. It I understand Trenton Merricks correcuy, he would hold that the Pluralians spoke falsely when they said "there is a bliger in the back field!": Though what they said is nearly as good as true and good enough for normal practical purposes, what they said is nevertheless simply false.[19] Whichever way one goes in reading this fable, it seems to me that there is room for one to make the sensible claim—as van Inwagen does—that really there are no bligers. By van Inwagen's lights, what needs to be done to give his assertion sense and to distinguish it from the Pluralian folk's way of speaking is to provide a gloss on his claim. By Merrick's lights, the assertion really—if we were uncorrupted—requires no gloss; what requires explanation is why the Pluralians are less confused in saying "there is a bliger in the back field" than in saying "there is a unicorn in the back field." On either view, one can make sense, in the context of van Inwagen's story, of eliminativism about bligers.

[17] Brian Bix, *Natural Law Theory: the Modern Tradition, in* OXFORD HANDBOOK OF JURISPRUDENCE AND PHILOSOPHY OF LAW 72–73 (Jules Coleman & Scott Shapiro, eds., 2002).
[18] Peter van Inwagen, MATERIAL BEINGS 104 (1990).
[19] Trenton Merricks, OBJECTS AND PERSONS 162–185 (2001).

What the strong natural law theorist should claim is that laws unsuitable to serve as rational guides to conduct occupy the role that bligers occupy in van Inwagen's story. Such rules have been recognized as law by citizens and officials and have been treated as binding as a matter of social practice. But that fact does not make citizens and officials infallible with respect to the philosophical problem of whether these rules insufficiently grounded in reasons are really laws. As with the case of the bligers, the strong natural law theorist can go one of two ways here. He or she can claim that while folks are perfectly right when they say that some unjust laws are laws, there is an important sense in which they are not laws. The central task for the strong natural law theorist taking this route is that of explaining what that sense is and showing that this sense is sufficiently interesting. On the other hand, the natural law theorist can claim that in the ordinary sense of law, law that it is not reasonable to comply with is no law at all. The task here is, I take it, that of showing that there are presuppositions of the designation of social rules as laws which could be brought to light by closer analysis and which could nevertheless turn out to be false. Closer inspection yielded the result that a bliger is not one animal but six; and given the centrality to the practice of bliger-talk that a bliger is one animal, a straightforward inference to draw is that there are not really any bligers. Closer inspection may yield the result that laws unbacked by decisive reasons for action lack some feature whose assumed presence is central to any practice that we would count as the practice of law. And if it turned out that this were the case, a straightforward inference to draw would be that there are not really any laws unbacked by decisive reasons for action.

Now, one might respond: Even if it is not incoherent for the strong natural law theorist to claim that laws unbacked by decisive reasons for compliance are no laws at all, there is a key disanalogy between the case of the bligers and the case of laws unbacked by insufficient reasons. We see the situation with the bligers and we recognize that something is amiss, recognize that there is at least potential tension between Pluralians' bliger-talk and what is the case with bligers. But we see the strong natural law theorist's purported claim about law—that it is necessarily a rational standard for conduct—and we are yet unmoved. Officials go on applying unjust laws (or recognizing that they are laws yet refusing to apply them), citizens go on obeying or reforming them, and there is no tension felt. Does this not show that even if there is conceptual room for the sort of claim that a natural law theorist might want to make, there must be in fact no basis for the view that law must be backed by such reasons?

No. For, first of all, the claim that the natural law theorist wants to make does not immediately imply that folks—ordinary folk or legal officials—cannot go on using the term "law" very much as they did before. This much is clear from (at least seemingly) revisionary metaphysical theories that do not of themselves include recommendations for changes in ordinary linguistic practice. Second, the fact that folks have remained unmoved by the claims of strong natural law theory does not show that the claims of strong natural law theory are false. Ordinary users of the langauge do not enjoy a final authority on the correctness of analyses of the terms they employ nor on the presuppositions of the practices that they are engaged in.

Again, think of the bligers. Suppose that a Pluralian is shown the facts about bligers yet continues to think that there are bligers. A philosopher might note that there are features of bliger-talk that show pretty clearly that it was essential to the designation of that mass in the back field (and others like it) as bligers that they be individual enduring objects rather than temporary animal collectives. Yet the Pluralians just might not see it. While how they use the term "bliger" fixes its reference, they do not enjoy some sort of infallibility, either individually or collectively, on how their use fixes its reference and whether on any given occasion they are applying that term correctly. The same holds of law. The starting point for marking out a set of phenomena as law is the practices of human agents, but that does not make those agents infallible about whether they are correct in thinking that any particular instance is a case of law.

For example, even if there were complete agreement among competent users of the language of law that certain instances were cases of laws and all other instances were not, this would not be sufficient to show that all of those instances are in fact laws. For there might be some platitude about law that is accepted, either explicitly or implicitly, by all of those users and that is absolutely central to the practice of law-talk but that, nevertheless, some of those instances fail to satisfy. Suppose it were true, for example, that all competent users of the language of law believe that A, B, and C are laws and that nothing else is, but all such competent users of the language of law also accept as a deep and crucial platitude about law that compliance with laws is morally obligatory. (This corresponds to the platitude about bligers that they are individual enduring objects, not temporary animal collectives.) If we are able to show that compliance with A is not morally obligatory, this would give us a basis to say that A really is not a law.

I acknowledge, of course, that Bix's point places a weighty burden on the strong natural law theorist. But this burden is no greater than that which falls on any philosopher when his or her view runs contrary to common opinion. The strong natural law theorist bears the burden of showing that it is central to law that it be backed by decisive reasons, and this burden is made weighty by the fact that this view commits him or her to the thesis that a number of socially sanctioned rules called by consensus "laws" are not really laws at all. But we knew this already. It is no criticism of a controversial philosophical position that the defender of that position needs a good argument for it.

Here is another way to respond to Bix's claim of incoherence. If Bix were right, then it would be a condition of the eligibility of a jurisprudential theory that, necessarily, if all of the legal officials in some society hold that X is law in that society, then the theory implies that X is law in that society. But neither unsophisticated Austinian nor sophisticated Hartian positivism satisfies this constraint. So Bix's argument fails through proving too much.

Re Austin's view: in Austin's general jurisprudence, every law is a command issued by a sovereign and backed by a sanction.[20] A sanction is a credible threat of harm to a subject attendant on a violation of the order.[21] It follows from Austin's view that there is no law that is not backed by a sanction. But, possibly, all of the legal officials in some society might hold that some particular norm, a norm unbacked by a sanction, is law. If Austin's view is true, law without sanction is no law at all. Hence Austinian positivism violates Bix's constraint.

Re Hart's view: in Hart's view, whether something is law in a given society depends on whether it is recognized as such by the rule of recognition, the usually tremendously complex rule that guides legal officials in making, identifying, and applying law.[22] It follows from Hart's view that there is no law that is not acknowledged as such by the rule of recognition. But, possibly, all of the legal officials in some society might hold that some particular norm, a norm not acknowledged by the rule of recognition, is law. The rule of recognition might hold that if norm N was part of the originally adopted constitution, then it is law; but they might all hold a false view about whether some particular norm n was part of the originally adopted constitution. If Hart's view is true, law unacknowledged by the rule of recognition is no law at all. Hence Hartian positivism violates Bix's constraint.

It might be objected that while all of the legal officials could be confused about what is acknowledged as law by the rule of recognition, they could not all be

---

[20] John Austin, The Province of Jurisprudence Determined 21 (Wilfrid E. Rumble, ed., 1995) (1832), Lecture 1.

[21] Austin, *supra* note 20, at 22.

[22] H.L.A. Hart, The Concept of Law 94–95 (1994) (1961).

confused about what the rule of recognition is. I think that this is false. We may grant that the practice of legal officials makes the rule of recognition what it is. But because the rule of recognition is not something that legal officials need to be able to make explicit—the rule of recognition is typically shown rather than said[23]—it is possible for all legal officials to be deeply confused in their explicit judgments of what the rule of recognition is. All that is really justified in the end by the doctrine of the rule of recognition is that there is *something* about the actual practice of legal officials that fixes the content of the rule of recognition. But it is consistent with this position to hold that there is a necessary truth about whatever activities that we would be willing to call the "actual practices of legal officials" that would commit us to affirming the view that the rule of recognition cannot confer legal validity on any rule that is insufficiently backed by reasons for action. It may be *false* that there is any such necessary truth, but it is by no means *incoherent* to hold this.

We will return to this strong formulation of the natural law thesis below; I will suggest that we ought to reject it, but not on account of its incoherence or its obvious falsity. We ought to reject it just because the key argumentative strategies employed by natural law theorists fail to establish that thesis. These lines of defense of this strong understanding of the natural law thesis notwithstanding, it is obvious that contemporary advocates and friendly critics of natural law theory have, by and large, treated the strong natural law thesis as hopeless and perhaps even as a thesis that no natural law theorist has ever really been concerned to affirm. Soper writes that it is confusion to think of the classic natural law theorists as concerned with the tasks of analytical jurisprudence; they were instead concerned to provide a theory of political obligation and of the subject's moral relationship to law generally.[24] Bix, in a number of accounts of natural law theories classic and contemporary, has affirmed much the same position.[25] This reading of the history of natural law jurisprudence is open to doubt,[26] but even if it were acknowledged as true, it would leave behind the task of providing a clearer understanding of what it is that the natural law theorist wants to assert.

Robert George has proposed that "What is being asserted by natural law theorists [is] . . . that the moral obligatoriness which may attach to positive law is *conditional* in nature."[27] All that the natural law theorist wants to do in affirming a connection between law and reasons is to issue a reminder that adherence to some laws would constitute such a departure from reasonableness that there could not be adequate reason to obey them; the only law that merits our obedience is law that meets a certain minimum standard of reasonableness. We can call this the *moral* reading of the natural law thesis, and Bix and Soper have agreed with George in holding that this is the point that classical natural law views meant to emphasize. The main problem with this reading is, as Bix notes, that it makes the natural law thesis excruciatingly uninteresting.[28] It is not merely

---

[23]  Hart, *supra* note 22, at 101.

[24]  Soper, *supra* note 13, at 1181.

[25]  *See, e.g.,* Bix, *supra* note 17, at 63.

[26]  Again, the reason to doubt that this is a correct interpretation of the natural law tradition as a whole is that it is false of Aquinas' view, and Aquinas is the paradigm natural law theorist. Aquinas' conclusion about the status of *lex iniusta* is the result of not a primarily *practical* investigation but a primarily *speculative* one—it is a straightforward inference from the fact that human law is a kind of law, and law in general (including the eternal law, which is for the most part unknowable and as such of little practical interest to us) is a rational standard.

[27]  Robert P. George, *Preface, in* THE AUTONOMY OF LAW viii (Robert P. George, ed., 1996).

[28]  *See* Bix, *Patrolling the Boundaries: Inclusive Legal Positivism and the Nature of Jurisprudential Debate,* 12 CAN. J. L. & JURIS. 17–33, 30 (1999); *see also* Bix, *On the Dividing Line Between Natural Law Theory and Legal Positivism,* 75 NOTRE DAME L. REV. 1613–1624, 1620, n. 34 (2000).

that the natural law theorists would have no basis to disagree with the legal positivists, for whom it has been a central point to emphasize that the rightness of compliance with law depends on an evaluation of the law's merits.[29] If the moral reading were all there is to the natural law thesis, the natural law theorist would have almost no one to disagree with in the entire history of philosophy.

Given the reluctance of contemporary natural law theorists to affirm a strong reading of the basic natural law thesis, and given the trivial dullness of the moral reading of the natural law thesis, it is of course worthwhile to ask whether there is a third formulation—one that grants that the Fugitive Slave Act really was law without saying merely that it was a law that ought not to be obeyed. There seems to be. Recall again the basic natural law thesis: *necessarily, law is a rational standard for conduct*. The defender of the strong reading understands this thesis as of the same sort as *necessarily, triangles have three sides*. From *necessarily, triangles have three sides* we can deduce that *if X does not have three sides, then X is not a triangle;* and from *necessarily, law is a rational standard for conduct* we can deduce that *if X is not a rational standard for conduct, then X is not law.* The defender of the *weak* reading of the natural law thesis, by contrast, does not hold that *necessarily, law is a rational standard for conduct* is a proposition of the same sort as *necessarily, triangles have three sides:* rather, it is of the same sort as *necessarily, the duck is a skillful swimmer.* From *necessarily, the duck is a skillful swimmer* we cannot deduce that *if X is not a skillful swimmer, then X is not a duck;* we can deduce no more than *if X is not a skillful swimmer, then X is not a duck or is a defective duck.* The necessity attaches not to individual ducks but to the kind *duck;* and while it is possible for a duck-instance to lack the feature of being a skillful swimmer, the absence of that feature marks it as defective.[30]

Finnis suggests this sort of move in *Natural Law and Natural Rights*: His preferred way of putting the point is that some law is law in the focal sense, whereas some law is law in a secondary, peripheral sense.[31] Hence Finnis writes that attention to the principles of practical reasonableness that govern human conduct "justifies regarding certain positive laws as radically defective, *precisely as laws*, for want of conformity to those principles.[32] It also seems to be in the spirit of Kretzmann's reading of the natural law thesis. Kretzmann, in order to make the *lex iniusta non est lex* claim interesting, must hold that "*lex*" is not used merely equivocally here. One way to pull this off is by making the claim, following Finnis, that the latter sense is somehow primary, whereas the former sense is derivative, truncated, or incomplete. Some of Kretzmann's examples tend to distract one from this point: "a badly disobedient son is no son at all" seems to lean far more toward metaphor than does "an entirely incompetent doctor is no doctor at all."[33] This gives support to Russell's charge against Kretzmann that his interpretation of the *lex iniusta* slogan is not just available for natural law theorists but open to adoption by anybody who wants to trade on positive connotations of "law" to use the slogan to criticize unjust legal systems or unjust individual legal norms.[34] But while it does seem right that Kretzmann's official statement of his position does provide some ammunition for Russell's criticisms, the overall thrust of his view seems to be toward the weak reading of the natural law thesis, though he does not himself go very far in showing why the weak reading should be taken as correct.

---

[29] *See* Jeremy Bentham, A FRAGMENT ON GOVERNMENT ch. iv, §§18–22 (Ross Harrison, ed., 1988); *see also* Hart, *supra* note 22, at 50–56.

[30] *Cf.* Michael Thompson, *The Representation of Life, in* VIRTUES AND REASONS 247–296 (Rosalind Hursthouse, Gavin Lawrence & Warren Quinn, eds., 1995); and Philippa Foot, NATURAL GOODNESS 20 (2001).

[31] Finnis, *supra*, note 7, at 364.

[32] Finnis, *supra*, note 7, at 24, emphasis in original.

[33] Kretzmann, *supra*, note 10, at 102–104.

[34] Russell, *supra*, note 16, at 446.

The weak reading of the natural law thesis is clearly distinct from the strong reading, allowing that there can be laws with which it is unreasonable to comply. But one might wonder whether it is really distinct from the uninteresting moral reading. Hence Bix, who puzzles a bit over why anyone would think that the moral reading of the natural law thesis is anything but "banal," immediately identifies the moral reading with the view that immoral law is a perversion of law or defective as law.[35] But this identification is illegitimate. The weak reading of the natural law thesis does *not* say simply that some laws might fail to be adequate rational standards and that this is *in some way* objectionable; it takes the further step of saying that this way of being objectionable counts as a *defect* in law. The standards for counting something a defect are far more stringent than those for counting something objectionable. To count the absence of a feature as a defect in something, one must show that it is intrinsic to the kind to which that thing fundamentally belongs to possess that feature. We might object to a particular coloring pattern in a duck's feathers on aesthetic grounds, but that objection would not suffice to show that the pattern counts as a defect in the duck. We might find the duck's propensity to leave its droppings around ponds objectionable, but that would hardly count as making ducks that leave their droppings around defective ducks. On the other hand, a duck that cannot fly or swim is defective, regardless of whether a duck's inability to fly or swim suits our own purposes.

To affirm that the moral reading is the proper understanding of the natural law thesis would be the end of natural law theory as an interesting jurisprudential view. The strong reading, while often quickly dismissed, even by those sympathetic to natural law theory, possesses adequate resources to fend off the most straightforward objections and is hence worthy of further scrutiny. And the weak reading, since it is entailed by the strong reading and distinct from the moral reading, must be worthy of further scrutiny as well. We may hence turn to the task of seeing what sort of arguments have been put forward for the fundamental natural law thesis, seeing what success those arguments have had, and seeing whether any such success militates only in favor of the weak reading or also in favor of the strong reading as well.

## Defending the Natural Law Thesis

There are three interesting and initially plausible[36] lines of argument toward the central natural law thesis: Finnis's "internal point of view" argument, Moore's

---

[35]  Bix, *Patrolling the Boundaries, supra*, note 28, at 1620, n. 34; *see also* Bix, *On the Dividing Line, supra*, note 28, at 30.

[36]  I put to the side the defense of natural law theory, popular in the mid-twentieth century, of arguing on behalf of natural law theory and against positivism that only natural law theory can serve as a bulwark against abuse of law. *Cf.* Gustav Radbruch, *Fünf Minuten Rechtsphilosophie* (1945) and *Gesetzliches Unrecht und übergesetzliches Recht* (1946), both reprinted in Rechtsphilosophie 327–329, 339–350 (8th ed., Erik Wolf & Hans-Peter Schneider, eds., 1973); *cf. also* Lon Fuller, *Positivism and Fidelity to Law: A Reply to Professor Hart*, 71 Harv. L. Rev. 630–672 (1958). The proper criticism and reform of statutes can intelligibly take place regardless of whether one is a positivist or a natural law theorist; whether one is better able to do so if one is a natural law theorist or a positivist is of merely psychological interest. For criticism of this approach to defending theories of the nature of law, *see* Philip Soper, *Choosing a Legal Theory on Moral Grounds*, 4 Soc. Phil. & Pol'y 31–48 (1987) (and *ante*, p. 74).

functional-kind argument, and Raz's self-image-of-law argument.[37] I want to make clear the structure of each of these arguments and offer a brief assessment of the prospects of each. While Finnis's argument is ultimately unsuccessful, it does bring out a point that can be exploited for natural law purposes by the sorts of arguments that Moore and Raz employ. The Moorean and Razian arguments, however, do not provide support for the strong natural law thesis, though they suggest bases for affirming the weak thesis.

### Finnis's Internal-Point-of-View Argument

Finnis's argument for the natural law thesis is that the natural law thesis drops out of Hart's and Raz's jurisprudential method, a method that has shown itself to be fundamentally sound. Finnis writes in praise of Hartian and Razian jurisprudence that Hart's and Raz's views were able to advance so far beyond earlier positivist views by their more or less self-conscious employment of three methodological features: attention to the practical point of legal systems, use of a focal-meaning approach to definition, and adoption of the viewpoint of those who take an insider's point of view.[38] Hart had argued against earlier positivist views that such views had failed to take into account the point of view of the person who takes the internal point of view with respect to a legal system, treating it as a standard by which he or she guides his or her conduct. So Hart's view privileges the internal point of view, and it is the point of view of one who treats the law as a standard for conduct. Hart is insistent that no further differentiation of the internal point of view is called for. People who treat the law as a basis for their conduct out of a calculation of long-term advantage, on a whim, out of altruistic concerns, out of the demands of morality, to please one's parents, to conform to time-honored tradition, and so on are all taking the internal point of view, and Hart is not interested in taking their different motives as shaping his theory of law.[39]

Finnis's argument for the natural law thesis is to take Hart's starting point—that analytical jurisprudence must adequately take into account this insider's point of view—and to try to show that its characterization of the internal point of view is too undifferentiated, that it fails to take into account that some of these insiders' points of view are more paradigmatically insiders' points of view than others. By Finnis's lights, there is a clearly *most central* internal point of view with respect to the law:

> If there is a point of view in which legal obligation is treated as at least presumptively a moral obligation ..., a viewpoint in which the establishment and maintenance of a legal as distinct from discretionary or statically customary order is regarded as a moral ideal if not a compelling demand of justice, then such a viewpoint will constitute the central case of the legal viewpoint.[40]

But even within this central legal viewpoint we should recognize that

---

[37] It is undoubtedly *prima facie* bizarre to think that Raz, who is a hard positivist, offers a defense of natural law jurisprudence. But Raz's hard positivism is a hard positivism only about legal validity—that is, for law's existence conditions—and, as is clear already and will be discussed further below, the weak natural law thesis is compatible with at least the canonical formulations of the hardest such positivisms out there.

[38] Finnis, *supra*, note 7, at 6–18. Finnis develops the importance of each of these separately, noting with respect to each that he is simply following themes explicit in Hart and Raz. Hence Finnis takes himself to be answering the same questions that Hart and Raz are trying to answer, and using a basically similar methodology. The difference is that on Finnis's view, Hart and Raz arbitrarily stop short of fully embracing that methodology's relevant set of implications.

[39] Hart, *supra* note; 22, at 203.

[40] Finnis, *supra* note 7, at 14–15.

Among those who, from a practical viewpoint, treat law as an aspect of practical reasonableness, there will be some whose views about what practical reasonableness actually requires in this domain are, in detail, more reasonable than others. Thus the central case viewpoint itself is the viewpoint of those who not only appeal to practical reasonableness but also are practically reasonable.[41]

Law that fails to be morally obligatory will be viewed, from this central legal viewpoint, as defective, deficient, falling short. And since the central legal viewpoint is the proper vantage point from which to do analytical jurisprudence, we have a basis for holding that law that fails to serve as a mandatory requirement of practical reasonableness is defective precisely as law. So the weak natural law thesis is true.[42]

If we take for granted the fundamental soundness of Hart's approach, the key questions are first, whether Finnis has taken up what is in fact Hart's method, and second, whether Hart's method thus understood admits of arbitrariness if it stops short of the natural law thesis. The answer to the first, it seems to me, is that he has gone much further than Hart, who holds merely that analytical jurisprudence must characterize law in such a way that exhibits how it is possible for persons to take the internal point of view with respect to it. Finnis seems to want to make the further claim that the internal point of view is the privileged point of view with respect to the description of law. But it seems that this massive privileging of the internal perspective carries Finnis beyond the descriptive jurisprudence that he takes himself, along with Hart and Raz, to be practicing and into a more straightforwardly normative jurisprudence.[43]

Second, it seems that Finnis's argument here for the centrality of the point of view of the party who treats the law as presumptively obligatory is, to say the least, not self-sufficient. Hart repeatedly compares legal rules to rules of games, and the comparison is useful here as well. In understanding the rules of cricket, one needs to understand them not just from a third-person perspective but from the perspective of a participant in the game; one needs to understand how the rules of cricket function in the decision-making of players and officials in a cricket match. But it is not relevant why the cricketer takes the rules of cricket as a guide to his conduct. All the descriptive theorist need do is to provide an account of those rules that shows how it is possible for one to take such a stance with respect to the rules.

Now, law is not cricket, and so it might be that there is reason to privilege the view of one who treats the law as morally obligatory while there is no reason to privilege the view of one who treats the rules of cricket as governing his conduct for some particular reasons. But the explanation will have to be driven by something other than remarks about point of view; it will instead have to be driven by some features of law that distinguish its rules from the rules of cricket. Perhaps these will be further facts about the function of law in contrast to the

---

[41] Finnis, *supra* note 7, at 15.

[42] Finnis emphatically rejects the strong natural law thesis; *see* Finnis, *supra* note 7, at 363–365.

[43] One might wonder whether Finnis did take himself to be doing descriptive jurisprudence. The answer that he did could not be clearer. As I note above, Finnis takes his views to be rival answers to the same questions posed by Hart and Raz, who are undoubtedly doing descriptive jurisprudence. It is also worth looking closely at sections 1.4 and 1.5 of Finnis, *supra* note 7, along with the accompanying notes. There Finnis holds his natural law jurisprudence to be, just as Hart described his own view (*supra* note 34, at vi), part of descriptive social science (Finnis, *supra* note 7, at 21); he distinguishes the fundamentally descriptive jurisprudence of Hart and Raz from the normative jurisprudence of Dworkin and aligns his own jurisprudential project with the former rather than with the latter. For Finnis, the fact that the descriptive theorist "needs the assistance of a general normative theory" (Finnis, *supra* note 7, at 21) does not render the resulting theory simply an exercise in normative jurisprudence.

function of cricket; or perhaps these will be further facts about the claims made by legal officials—those in a privileged position to speak on behalf of the law—that contrast with claims made by cricket officials. And both of these do seem to be fruitful points of departure for defenses of the natural law thesis.

## Moore's Functional-Kind Argument

Michael Moore has suggested that the most promising route to the natural law jurisprudential thesis is through an argument concerning the function of law.[44] When characterizing the nature of law, writers have often thought that law is to be defined in terms of some set of distinctive structures. But Moore wants to say that it is far more likely that law is to be defined in terms of its *function*, by its serving some end. In order for this to be the case, Moore claims, we would have to find some *distinctive* goal that law serves—otherwise we would not be able to define law in terms of the function of serving that goal. If it turns out that there is such an end, then if it can be shown that law must be moral-obligation-imposing in order to promote this goal, we have a basis to say that there is a necessary dependence of law on moral obligation; law must be morally obligatory, and any norm that cannot be morally obligatory cannot be law. Indeed, Moore thinks that if the premises of this argument can be established, the conclusion would be the strong natural law thesis.

As Moore notes, there are all sorts of difficulties involved in making a plausible argument that fits this schema. His constraint on definition by functional-kind-membership generates, on his view, a dilemma for the natural law theorist: Either the attempt to define law in terms of its serving some end will fail or the attempt to show that the law must be moral-obligation-imposing in order for it to serve this end will fail. The problem is this: In order for law to be defined by its serving some end, that end must be distinctive—it must be an end that is served only through or by law. So the goal that law serves cannot simply be "everything that is worth pursuing and promoting." But, Moore wonders, how can anything short of "everything that is worth pursuing and promoting" be the source of the moral obligation that is, on the natural law theorist's view, essential to human law?[45]

As the argument is laid out, the second horn of Moore's dilemma strikes me as unproblematic. Given the way that Moore has set out the law-as-functional-kind argument for the natural law thesis, it is not necessary that the source of the moral obligation to obey the law be identical with the goal that law serves. So one might hold that while there is some distinctive goal G that law serves, it is not the law's serving G that is alone sufficient to make law morally obligatory. It might be, however, that for G to be served, or to be served properly, folks must be under a moral obligation to obey the law; and this moral obligation might arise from various sources—consent, fairness with respect to the promotion of G, gratitude to the law for helping us to promote G, and so forth. If there is a genuine difficulty to which Moore's formulation of the second horn of the dilemma points, it is that of finding some end of law that can be promoted *only through* obligatory norms, regardless of the source of that obligation. Suppose, for example, that serving the Finnisian common good were the function of law. It is obvious that this can be served other than through means that impose obligations. Moore mentions that a regime of sanctions might do the trick.[46] Or a set of

---

[44] *See* Moore, *supra* note 17; Moore, *supra* note 11.

[45] Moore suggests a tentative response to this dilemma: that the end that law serves, while not identical to "all the values there are," is so connected to their realization that moral obligation must result. Moore takes Finnis's understanding of the common good, which is the sum total of those conditions that individuals can draw upon in order to realize their own choice-worthy conceptions of the good (Finnis, *supra* note 7, at 154), to be potentially such an end (Moore, *supra* note 7, at 223).

[46] Moore, *supra* note 7, at 225.

common standards that did not impose obligations might be sufficient in a community where citizens were extremely public-minded and extremely conformist. Their public-spiritedness and conformism could be sufficient to lead them to act on a common standard.

More troubling is the difficulty that it just seems obvious that there is no good "distinctively served by law" in Moore's sense. There is no good that is served *only* by institutions that could by any stretch of the imagination be thought of as legal systems. The Finnisian common good, Dworkinian integrity, whatever—all of these can be served by institutions that are obviously pretheoretically extra-legal. Moore sees the problem and thinks that if this is true, then the upshot is that law cannot be a purely functional kind.[47]

While I agree there is a real worry in the vicinity, part of the fault must lie with Moore's overly strict understanding of what makes something a functional kind. There is, so far as I can see, no reason to think that for something to be a functional kind it must be adequately marked off simply in terms of its serving some goal. Functional kinds are typically marked off by serving some goal *through some characteristic activity*. Hence functional ascriptions involve both ends and means; to say that X is a member of functional kind F is to say, in part, that its characteristic activity tends toward the realization of some particular end. Not every X whose characteristic activity tends toward the realization of the same end E belongs to the same functional kind, for their characteristic activities may be of such different sorts that they could not be placed in the same kind. Moore is obviously right that *heart* is a functional kind, that there could be hearts of various structures and made of various materials. But while the end of the heart is to circulate the blood, it is pretty clear that only objects whose characteristic activity is that of *pumping* can be classified as hearts.

What causes unnecessary trouble for Moore's argument is his spartan understanding of functional kinds in which such kinds are individuated entirely by the ends they serve. Given an understanding of functional kinds in which such kinds are individuated also by the characteristic activities of the members of that kind, it could be that it is law's characteristic activity for the sake of its end that provides the needed support for the natural law thesis. So one might say that while legal systems might promote various ends, all of these involve the imposition of order; but one might say that it is the characteristic activity of law to realize this end through the provision of rules with which agents have decisive reason to comply. This would give us reason to say that the or a function of law is to impose order by laying down rules with which agents have decisive reasons to comply. And hence the natural law thesis would take its warrant not from the end that law serves (as in Moore's view) but from the characteristic activity of law in serving this end.

How would one show that this is law's characteristic activity? As Moore suggests: Look at the various particular ways that systems pretheoretically designated as "legal" operate and see whether their activities tend to be explicable in terms of and regulated by the giving of dictates backed by decisive reasons for the sake of imposing order. Look at the features of legal systems to which Raz has drawn our attention, that is, that they claim to be authoritative[48] and that, characteristically, their dictates go with the flow of normative reasons rather than against them.[49] Look at the way in which law characteristically ties sanctions to certain activities in order to give agents further reason to abstain from them. Look at Fuller's eight ways to fail to make law; each of them indicates some way

---

[47]  Moore, *supra* note 7, at 223.
[48]  *See* Raz, THE AUTHORITY OF LAW 30 (1979).
[49]  This is Raz's "service" conception of authority: *see* Raz, THE MORALITY OF FREEDOM 56 (1986).

in which law can fail to serve as a reason for action for those living under it.[50] On the basis of such considerations, one might well come to the conclusion that it is part of law's characteristic activity to lay down norms with which agents will have sufficient reason to comply.

Moore sets up the functional-kind argument as an argument for the strong natural law thesis (though he does not consider the weak natural law thesis as an alternative). But it seems false to suppose that, whether on Moore's functional-kind argument or on the emendation I suggested, the strong natural law thesis would be the result. The law cannot carry out its function if it is not backed by decisive reasons for compliance, on this view, but why would we think that there is no law unbacked by decisive reasons for compliance rather than merely that all such law is defective? There is, after all, nothing more ordinary than things that have the function of $\phi$-ing but which at the moment are not $\phi$-ing and in their present condition cannot $\phi$: witness broken alarm clocks, broken arms, and so on. A broken alarm clock is an alarm clock; it is just a defective alarm clock. To have one's arm broken in a skiing accident is not to lose (or even just temporarily misplace) an arm in a skiing accident. The functional-kind argument should aspire to no more than the weak natural law thesis.

## Raz's Self-Image Argument

Raz is a positivist, but it seems to me that his work can be conscripted for natural law causes. (I am not alone in this suspicion; Goldsworthy[51] and Kramer[52] have made similar suggestions.) The way that Razian jurisprudence can be co-opted for natural law theory is by appeal to the cornerstone of Raz's legal theory, that is, that the law's self-image is that it is authoritative. On Raz's view, law necessarily claims to be a practical authority. For law to be authoritative would be, in part, for law's dictates that those in class C $\phi$ to provide protected reasons[53] for those in class C to $\phi$. Now, it seems to me that this view provides evidence for the weak natural law thesis, that is, the thesis that law that fails to serve as a standard of conduct for those rational agents under it is defective. For a thing to be defective is for it to fail to satisfy a standard that is internal to the kind to which it belongs. But that law essentially makes a claim to authority suffices to indicate that *providing a particularly important sort of reason for action* is a standard that is internal to the kind *law*. And so Raz's view that law necessarily claims authority entails that law that is not authoritative is defective and hence that something like the weak natural law thesis is true.

Why think that the fact that law necessarily claims authority would show that *being authoritative* is a standard internal to legality? Well, *if* the fact that law necessarily claims authority shows that *being authoritative* is an appropriate standard by which legal norms are measured, that standard is surely internal to the kind *law* rather than imposed on it from without, for after all, it is law's *self*-image that it is authoritative. That it is making this claim for itself suffices to meet the condition that the standard be relevantly *internal*, the sort of standard of which the failure to attain it would count as a defect. But why think that being authoritative is shown to be a standard for law at all? Because law's claim to authority is not just an interesting fact that it is reporting about itself, just as I might claim to be able to slam-dunk (which is false) or might claim to be from Texas (which is true). Rather, law's claim to authority is made in the context of justifying its other activities, its activities of laying burdens on citizens and

---

[50] *See* Fuller, *The Morality of Law*, at 39 (and *ante*, 154–156).

[51] Jeffrey D. Goldsworthy, *The Self-Destruction of Legal Positivism*, 10 OXFORD J. LEGAL STUD. 449–486 (1990).

[52] Matthew Kramer, IN DEFFENSE OF LEGAL POSITIVISM: LAW WITHOUT TRIMMINGS (1999).

[53] A reason to $\phi$ is a protected reason if it is a reason to $\phi$ and a reason to disregard reasons not to $\phi$. *See* Raz, *supra* note 49, at 18.

punishing those that fail to comply, of rendering decisions on allocations of goods and putting to the side rival ways to allocate those goods. Hence its being authoritative is not just a feature it has self-reported but a standard to which it has held itself accountable. Because it holds itself to this standard, it can rightly be treated as a *defect* in law if it fails to be authoritative. Raz's views about law's essential claim to authority, which underwrite Raz's hard positivism about legal validity,[54] can therefore also be used to underwrite a weak formulation of the natural law view.

I will not here enter into the debate on whether Raz is right that law necessarily makes this claim to authority.[55] I will, however, note that it is not at all clear that one need go as far as Raz in order to show that laws that are not decisively backed by reasons for compliance are defective as laws. Suppose that we allow that Kramer is right that law does not necessarily claim for itself practical authority, for there is, Kramer writes, a possible legal system in which all mandatory norms are stark imperatives, simply the demands of law.[56] Even in such a case we might think that demands of law that are not backed by decisive reasons for compliance are defective. Here is why: It is standard in speech-act theory to distinguish between success conditions, the conditions under which a speech-act is performed, and nondefectiveness conditions, the conditions under which all the presuppositions of a speech-act are satisfied.[57] Now, it is plausibly a presupposition of the illocutionary act *demanding that A ϕ* that, upon receiving the demand, A has decisive reasons to ϕ. The most straightforward way of arguing for this claim is the paradox test: It seems to be pragmatically inconsistent for one to demand that A ϕ while allowing that A might perfectly reasonably refrain from ϕ-ing.[58] So even if mandatory legal norms were mere demands, we would have some basis to think that a mandatory legal norm insufficiently backed by reasons for compliance is defective precisely as law.

It is pretty clear that neither the Razian argument nor the illocutionary-act variation on it would provide any basis to affirm the strong natural law thesis. So none of the plausible routes to natural law theory leads to the strong natural law thesis; they lead to but not beyond the weak thesis. While the initial objections to strong natural law theory can be avoided, the view fails simply for lack of evidence in its favor. But the weak natural law view is distinctive and defensible. The kind *law* may well be necessarily connected to reasons for action even if individual legal systems and individual laws can be unreasonable in the extreme.

### Is there Substantial Disagreement with the Positivists?

It is obvious that the strong reading of the natural law thesis is incompatible with legal positivism; it is the strong thesis that the positivists were concerned to deny. It is obvious that the moral reading of the natural law thesis is compatible with

[54]  *See* Raz, *Authority, Law, and Morality*, 68 Monist 295–324, 315 (1984).

[55]  *See, e.g.*, Kramer, *supra* note 26, at 83–89; *see also* Philip Soper, *Law's Normative Claims, in* The Autonomy of Law: Essays on Legal Positivism 215–248, 229–240 (Robert P. George, ed., 1996).

[56]  Kramer, *supra* note 52, at 83–89; *see also* Hart, *Introduction, in* Essays in Jurisprudence and Philosophy 1–18, 10 (1983): "It seems to me unrealistic to suppose that judges in making statements of legal obligation *must* always either believe or pretend to believe in the false theory that there is always a moral obligation to obey the law. It seems to me that such statements may be better construed as stating what may be properly *demanded* of their subjects by way of action according to the law which the judges accept as setting the correct standard of legal adjudication and law enforcement" (emphases in original).

[57]  *See* John Searle and Daniel Vanderveken, Foundations of Illocutionary Logic 12–13 (1985).

[58]  I make this argument at greater length and for a different purpose in An Essay on Divine Authority 24–29 (2002).

legal positivism; the positivists have taken as a central part of their program the emphasis on the need to scrutinize the merits of laws to determine whether they are worthy of obedience. What, then, about the weak reading? Is it contrary to the letter or spirit of positivism to affirm that law that is insufficiently backed by reasons for compliance is defective precisely as law?

It is not contrary to the letter of positivism. For if there is any canonical understanding of positivism, it is a thesis about legal validity; but the weak reading does not call into question the claim that whether law is valid is a matter of social fact. It claims that just as there are straightforward truths about when a duck or a heart is defective, there are straightforward truths about when laws are defective; and it claims that just as it is straightforwardly true that an adult duck that cannot fly is defective and that a heart that is fibrillating is defective, it is straightforwardly true that law that is not backed by adequate reasons for compliance is defective as well. Neil MacCormick, a positivist, describes and endorses this combination of positions in discussing Finnis's view:

> Of course there may be legislation properly enacted by competent authorities which falls far short of or cuts against the demands of justice. The validity of the relevant statutory norms as members of the given system of law is not as such put into doubt by their injustice. The legal duties they impose, or the legal rights they grant, do not stop being genuinely legal duties or legal rights in virtue of the moral wrongfulness of their impo-sition or conferment. *They are, however, defective or substandard or corrupt instances of what they genuinely are—laws, legal duties, legal rights.*[59]

The weak natural law thesis may, however, be contrary to the spirit of posi-tivism. For if the weak natural law thesis is true, it follows that one cannot have a complete descriptive theory of law without having a complete understanding of the requirements of practical reasonableness. For one cannot have a complete descriptive theory of law without an exhaustive account of the ways that law can be defective; and one cannot have an exhaustive account of the ways that law can be defective without having a complete understanding of the requirements of practical reasonableness.

That one cannot have an exhaustive account of the ways that law can be defective without having a complete understanding of the requirements of prac-tical reasonableness is a pretty straightforward inference from the weak natural law thesis. But what is the warrant for claiming that there cannot be a complete descriptive theory of law without an exhaustive account of the ways that law can be defective? In any of those cases that are not at issue here, we would find very peculiar a theory of Xs that claimed to be a complete descriptive theory of Xs but did not offer an exhaustive account of the ways that Xs can be defective.

Suppose, for example, that I claimed to have an exhaustive descriptive theory of automobiles but freely acknowledged that I did not have an exhaustive account of when automobiles are defective and when they are not. Or suppose that I claimed to have an exhaustive theory of the kidney but freely acknowledged that I did not have an exhaustive account of when kidneys are defective and when they are not. It seems perfectly obvious in these cases that a complete descriptive theory of the automobile or kidney would include a correspondingly complete theory of automobile or kidney defect. The burden of proof, then, seems to be on one who would hold that one can have a complete descriptive theory of law without a complete account of when and how law can be defective. But I have not the slightest idea how one would meet this burden.

Insofar, then, as positivism has presupposed a methodology that allows one to proceed further in jurisprudence without commitment to a particular conception

---

[59] Neil MacCormick, *Natural Law and the Separation of Law and Morals, in* NATURAL LAW THEORY 105–133, 108 (Robert P. George, ed., 1992), emphasis added.

of how agents ought individually and collectively to act, defenders of the weak natural law thesis must reject positivist methodology. As I noted at the beginning of this article, the natural law thesis in analytical jurisprudence can be formulated and initially defended without appeal to the particulars of a moral or political theory. But the weak natural law thesis, once defended, implies that a rich jurisprudence—even one that aims to be just descriptively adequate—cannot forego moral and political theory.[60]

## MARK C. MURPHY
### Natural Law in Jurisprudence and Politics
(2006)

*Natural Law Jurisprudence Defended*

*2.1 Three Routes to the Weak Natural Law Thesis*

The strong natural law thesis holds that law unbacked by decisive reasons for compliance is no law at all. The weak natural law thesis holds that law unbacked by decisive reasons for compliance is defective precisely as law. I have two central aims in this chapter—first, to defend the truth of the weak natural law thesis; second, to show that the success of this defense of the weak natural law thesis is not merely a way station to the defense of the strong natural law thesis but provides the premises to call the strong natural law thesis into question. So while the standard criticisms of natural law jurisprudence fall short of providing serious reasons to reject the strong natural law thesis, reasons to reject the strong thesis emerge in prosecuting the task of defending the natural law view.

I will consider three initially plausible routes to the weak natural law thesis. What makes each of these an initially plausible route to that thesis is that each exhibits on its face a technique for distinguishing between law's existence conditions and its non-defectiveness conditions, and provides some clue to identifying what law's non-defectiveness conditions are. One route, the "legal point of view" route endorsed by Finnis, appeals to the notion that there is a distinctively legal point of view, and it is law as characterized from this point of view that is paradigmatically law (2.2). Another route, the "law as functional kind" argument described, but not quite endorsed, by Moore, appeals to the notion that law has a function, and fails to perform that function if not backed by decisive reasons for compliance (2.3). A third route, the "law as illocutionary act" argument, likens or identifies law with speech-acts of a certain sort, and notes that the non-defectiveness conditions of these speech-acts obtain only if law is backed by decisive reasons for compliance (2.4).[61] I will not endorse the first of these arguments: it seems to me that the legal point of view argument generates theses of normative rather than descriptive jurisprudence. But the second and third of these argumentative strategies succeed; and that they both succeed is not merely a (suspicious) coincidence.

---

[60]  *Cf.* Finnis, *supra* note 7, at 15–19.
[61]  One might be surprised that I fail to consider Dworkin's views here, since Dworkin expresses at least a limited willingness to describe himself as an advocate of natural law theory. But it is hard to square the notion of Dworkin as natural law theorist with Dworkin's limited theoretical ambitions—that is, to provide an account simply of *our* practice of law: "General theories of law, for us, are general interpretations of our own legal practice" (Dworkin 1986, p. 410). A parochial natural law theory is no natural law theory at all.

## 2.2 The Legal Point of View and the Weak Natural Law Thesis

Finnis writes that we should not hope to provide an account of the necessary and sufficient conditions for law, such that some legal systems and individual norms and decisions in cases will count as law through exemplifying these conditions, whereas the remainder will not. Rather, we should hope for an account that provides us with the central, paradigmatic instances of law and legality. With this account, we will be able to classify some social systems and social norms as clearly law, some as entirely extralegal, and some as simply falling short of or distinct from the central case in one or another specific way (Finnis 1980, pp. 9–11).

Finnis's argument for the natural law thesis is that the natural law thesis thus drops out of Hart's and Raz's jurisprudential method, a method that in Finnis's view has shown itself to be fundamentally sound. Finnis writes in praise of Hartian and Razian jurisprudence that Hart's and Raz's views were able to advance so far beyond earlier positivist views by their more-or-less self-conscious employment of three methodological features: attention to the practical point of legal systems, use of a focal meaning approach to definition, and adoption of the viewpoint of those who take an insider's point of view. It is the third of these that serves as the basis for Finnis's argument for the natural law thesis. Hart had argued against earlier positivist views that such views had failed to take into account the point of view of the person who takes the internal point of view with respect to a legal system, treating it as a standard by which he or she guides his or her conduct. So Hart's view privileges the internal point of view, and it is the point of view of one who treats the law as a standard for conduct. Hart is insistent that no further differentiation of the internal point of view is called for. People who treat the law as a basis for their conduct out of a calculation of long-term advantage, on a whim, out of altruistic concerns, out of the demands of morality, to please their parents, to conform to time-honored tradition, and so on are all taking the internal point of view, and Hart is not interested in taking their different motives as shaping his theory of law (Hart 1994 [1961], p. 203).

Finnis's argument for the natural law thesis is to take Hart's starting point—that analytical jurisprudence must adequately take into account this insider's point of view—and to try to show that its characterization of the internal point of view is too undifferentiated, that it fails to take into account that some of these insiders' points of view are more paradigmatically insiders' points of view than others. By Finnis's lights, there is a clearly *most central* internal point of view with respect to the law:

> If there is a point of view in which legal obligation is treated as at least presumptively a moral obligation . . ., a viewpoint in which the establishment and maintenance of a legal as distinct from discretionary or statically customary order is regarded as a moral ideal if not a compelling demand of justice, then such a viewpoint will constitute the central case of the legal viewpoint.
> (Finnis 1980, pp. 14–15)

But even within this central legal viewpoint, we should note the following distinction:

> Among those who, from a practical viewpoint, treat law as an aspect of practical reasonableness, there will be some whose views about what practical reasonableness actually requires in this domain are, in detail, more reasonable than others. Thus the central case viewpoint itself is the viewpoint of those who not only appeal to practical reasonableness but also are practically reasonable.
> (Finnis 1980, p. 15)

Law that fails to be morally obligatory will be seen, from this central legal viewpoint, as defective, deficient, falling short. And since the central legal viewpoint is the proper vantage point from which to do analytical jurisprudence, we have a basis for holding that law that fails to serve as a mandatory requirement of practical reasonableness is defective precisely as law.

This strategy is meant only to establish the weak natural law thesis, and it is obvious that it can establish no more than that: its appeal to the central, paradigmatic notion of law is not meant to preclude the presence of a limited, technical sense of legal validity. But it is hard to see why we would follow Finnis in his extension of Hart's methodology on the basis of this argument. Hart has good reason for taking the burden of proof to be on those who wish to make some particular version of the internal point of view more privileged: while his arguments against the legal realists show that legal theory must account for the datum that people can take the internal point of view with respect to a system of legal norms (Hart 1994 [1961], pp. 88–91), this datum just is that people treat the existence of legal rules as reasons or constituent parts of reasons for action; it does not naturally extend further to the *basis* on which they so treat those norms. Far from the internal point of view's just being an "amalgam" of different viewpoints, Hart's undifferentiated take has a clear rationale, and so is not unstable; it is up to Finnis to destabilize it. But nothing he says in the crucial stretch of argument discussed above succeeds in destabilizing it. The law tends not to care for the motivations that one has for complying with it; and while Finnis appeals to the greater efficacy of some points of view in generating a legal system, one might rightly retort not only that the tasks of explaining how a legal system comes into being and explaining what it is for a legal system to be in place are, while interestingly related, different questions, but also that there are some points of view that may have greater efficacy in generating and sustaining a legal system than that of the person of full practical reasonableness—for example, that of the person who holds a false tribal or nationalistic morality.

By so closely identifying the task of characterizing law with the task of saying what a fully practical reasonable person should be interested in when dealing with the law, Finnis's view seems to become simply applied ethics—he is asking what features of the law the fully reasonable citizen, or the fully reasonable judge, should be interested in responding to, and in particular what features of the law are such that, when present, the fully reasonable citizen or judge may treat the law as authoritative. But this seems to make Finnis's view too much like the uninteresting moral reading, leaving his critics to wonder what all the fuss was about natural law theory (1.1). This massive privileging of the internal perspective carries Finnis beyond the descriptive jurisprudence that he takes himself, along with Hart and Raz, to be practicing, and into a more straightforwardly normative jurisprudence. (One might wonder whether Finnis did take himself to be doing descriptive jurisprudence. That he did seems to me very clear—see Finnis 1980, p. 21—though for a contrary view, see Leiter 2003, pp. 33–37.)

It seems, then, that Finnis's argument here for the centrality of the point of view of the party who treats the law as presumptively obligatory is, to say the least, not self-sufficient. Hart repeatedly compares legal rules to rules of games, and it is useful here as well. In understanding the rules of cricket, one needs to understand them not just from a third-person perspective, but from the perspective of a participant in the game: one needs to understand how the rules of cricket function in the decision-making of players and officials in a cricket match. But it is not relevant *why* the cricketer takes the rules of cricket as a guide to his conduct. All the descriptive theorist need do is provide an account of those rules that shows how it is possible for one to take such a stance with respect to its rules. Now, law is not cricket, and so it might be that there is reason to privilege the view of one who treats the law as morally obligatory, while there is not reason to privilege the view of one who treats the rules of cricket as governing his conduct for some particular reasons. But the explanation will have to be driven by something other than remarks about point of view; it will instead have to be driven by some features of law that distinguish its rules from the rules of cricket. Perhaps these will be further facts about the *function* of law, in contrast to the function of cricket; or perhaps these will be further facts about the *claims* made by legal officials, those in a privileged position to speak on behalf of the law, that contrast with claims made by cricket officials. And both of these do seem to be fruitful points of departure for defenses of the natural law thesis.

### 2.3 Law's Function and the Weak Natural Law Thesis

A promising line of argument for the weak natural law thesis takes as its starting point the common notion of *function*. We can, according to this line of argument, see that some legal systems or individual legal norms have non-defectiveness conditions that include the presence of reasons for action by getting clear on the functions of those systems or of those norms. One might worry that this sort of argument for the natural law thesis is doomed to triviality: what could be easier, one might ask, than to assign a morally charged function to law and then, on the basis of such an ascription, hold that law that does not perform this function, or perform it satisfactorily, is either no law at all or law only defectively? It is obvious that no interesting argument for the natural law thesis that proceeds from the idea that the law has a function can follow this pattern. But the ascription of a function to an object is a much more constrained matter than such an argument would suggest. I cannot simply assign the function "keeping New Haven populated" to law professors, and then declare that law school faculty who do not reside in New Haven are no law professors at all, or are law professors only defectively. What *are* the conditions that must be met to ascribe a function to some object or institution, and how can these be brought to bear to show that one or another formulation of the natural law thesis is correct?

Roughly (and not at all originally, and not entirely uncontroversially), we can say that for an x to have the function of $\phi$-ing, the following conditions must be satisfied:

(*characteristic activity*) x is the kind of thing that $\phi$s
(*goal productivity*) x's $\phi$-ing tends to bring about some end-state S
(*teleology*) x $\phi$s because x's $\phi$-ing tends to bring about some end-state S
(*value*) S exhibits some relevant variety of goodness

There is reason to think that each of these conditions is individually necessary; and there is reason to think that they are jointly sufficient. The heart has a characteristic activity: it pumps. Its pumping tends to bring about the circulation of the blood, and indeed the heart pumps because its pumping contributes to the circulation of the blood. (This is so in two ways: in animals with hearts, there is a feedback loop such that the circulation of the blood is in part what causes the heart to be able to continue pumping; and the very structure and activity of the heart was selected because of efficiency in causing the circulation of the blood.) Some would take these first three conditions to be jointly sufficient, but it seems to me that it is also important that the circulation of the blood is beneficial for the animal. As Mark Bedau has noted, a stick pinned against a rock in a stream by the backwash that that very stick has created may exhibit the first three features: it is pinned against a rock, its being pinned against a rock causes the backwash, and it is pinned against the rock because its being pinned against the rock causes the backwash. But no one would be tempted by the view that it is the stick's function to be pinned against the rock (Bedau 1992a, p. 786). One way to accommodate such cases is to emphasize that functions are ascribed when there is, in some sense, a good realized through the activity: either an end sought out by the designer of the object, or the self-maintenance of the thing in question, or the like (see also Bedau 1992b and Murphy 2001a, pp. 26–28).

To show, then, that the natural law thesis is true in virtue of the law's function (or one of the law's functions), one needs to show that these various conditions are satisfied, and that a particular legal system or law fails to perform its function when it fails to serve as a rational standard for conduct. An instance of this strategy is the argument offered by Moore. Moore has suggested that the most promising route to the natural law jurisprudential thesis is through an argument concerning the function of law. When characterizing the nature of law, writers have often thought that law is to be defined in terms of some set of distinctive structures. But Moore wants to say that it is far more likely that law is to be defined in terms of its *function*, by its serving some end. In order for this to be the case, Moore claims, we would have to find some *distinctive* goal that law serves— otherwise, we would not be able to define law in terms of the function of serving that goal. If it turns out that there is such an end, then if it can be shown that law must be moral-obligation-imposing in order to promote this goal, then we have a basis to say that there is a necessary dependence of law on moral obligation: law must be morally obligatory, and any norm that cannot be morally obligatory cannot be law. Indeed, Moore thinks that if the premises of this argument can be established, the conclusion would be the strong natural law thesis (Moore 1992 and Moore 2001).

As Moore notes, there are all sorts of difficulties involved in making out a plausible argument that fits this schema. His constraint on definition by func-tional-kind-membership generates, on his view, a dilemma for the natural law theorist: either the attempt to define law in terms of its serving some end will fail, or the attempt to show that the law must be moral-obligation-imposing in order for it to serve this end will fail. The problem is this. In order for law to be defined by its serving some end, that end must be distinctive—it must be an end that is served *only* through or by law. So the goal that law serves cannot simply be "everything that is worth pursuing and promoting." But, Moore wonders, how can anything short of "everything that is worth pursuing and promoting" be the source of the moral obligation that is, on the natural law theorist's view, essential to human law?[62]

As the argument is laid out, the second horn of the dilemma strikes me as unproblematic. For as Moore sets out the argument, it is not necessary that the source of the moral obligation to obey the law be identical with the goal that law serves. So one might hold that while there is some distinctive goal S that law serves, it is not the law's serving S that is alone sufficient to make law morally obligatory. It might be, however, that for S to be served, or to be served properly, people must be under a moral obligation to obey the law, and this moral obli-gation might arise from various sources—consent, fairness with respect to the promotion of S, gratitude to the law for helping us to promote S, and so forth. If there is a genuine difficulty to which Moore's formulation of the second horn of the dilemma points, it is that of finding some end of law that can be promoted *only through* obligatory norms, regardless of the source of that obligation. Sup-pose, for example, that serving the Finnisian common good (3.3) were the function of law. It is obvious that this can be served other than through means that impose obligations. Moore mentions that a regime of sanctions might do the trick (Moore 1992, p. 225). Or a set of common standards that did not impose

---

[62] Moore suggests a tentative response to this dilemma: that the end that law serves, while not identical to "all the values there are," is so connected to their realization that moral obligation can result. Moore takes Finnis's understanding of the common good, which is the sum total of those conditions that individuals can draw upon in order to realize their own choiceworthy conceptions of the good (Finnis 1980, p. 154; for discussion, see 3.3), to be potentially such an end (Moore 1992, p. 223).

obligations might be sufficient in a community where citizens were extremely public-minded and extremely conformist. Their public-spiritedness and conformism could be sufficient to lead them to act on a common standard.

More troubling still is the difficulty that it just seems obvious that there is no good "distinctively served by law" in Moore's sense. There is no good that is served *only* by institutions that could by any stretch of the imagination be thought of as legal systems. The Finnisian common good, Dworkinian integrity (Dworkin 1986, pp. 95–96)—these can be served by institutions that are obviously pretheoretically extralegal. Moore sees the problem and thinks that, if this is true, then the upshot is that law cannot be a purely functional kind (Moore 1992, p. 223).

While I agree there is a real concern in the vicinity, part of the fault must lie with Moore's overly strict understanding of what makes something a functional kind. There is, so far as I can see, no reason to think that for something to be a functional kind it must be adequately marked off simply in terms of its serving some goal. As we have seen, functional kinds are typically marked off by the serving of some goal *through some characteristic activity*. Thus, functional ascriptions involve both ends and means: to say that x is a member of functional kind F is to say, in part, that its characteristic activity of $\phi$-ing tends toward the realization of some particular end-state S. Not every x whose characteristic activity tends toward the realization of the same end-state S belongs to the same functional kind, for their characteristic activities may be of such different sorts that they could not be placed in the same kind. Moore is obviously right that *heart* is a functional kind, that there could be hearts of various structures and made of various materials. But while the end of the heart is to circulate the blood, it is clear that only objects whose characteristic activity is that of *pumping* can be classified as hearts.

What causes unnecessary trouble for Moore's argument is his spartan understanding of functional kinds in which such kinds are individuated entirely by the ends they serve. Given an understanding of functional kinds in which such kinds are individuated also by the characteristic activities of the members of that kind, it could be that it is law's characteristic activity for the sake of its end that provides the needed support for the natural law thesis. So, one might say that while legal systems might promote various ends, all of these involve the imposition of order; but one might say that it is the characteristic activity of law to realize this end through the provision of rules with which agents have decisive reason to comply. This would give us reason to say that the (or a) function of law is to impose order by laying down rules with which agents have decisive reasons to comply. And thus the natural law thesis would take its warrant not from the end that law serves (as in Moore's view) but from the characteristic activity of law in serving this end.

It is clear that there is nothing incoherent about holding that it is some object's function to provide dictates backed by decisive reasons for action, and thus that that object would be defective if its dictates were to fail to be backed by such reasons. Suppose, for example, that I attempt to build a "reason-backed rule" machine. When a person pulls the handle of the machine, the machine is supposed to display on its screen a rule, in the handle-puller's language, with which the handle-puller has decisive reason to comply. It is an accurate description of the machine to say that its function is to exhibit rules with which its operators have decisive reason to comply. If one is going to provide a fuller account of when the machine is functioning as it is designed to function and when it is not, one would have to draw on one's views, theorized or not, about what agents have reason to do: if, for example, you were to pull the handle on the machine and it were to display "You should give one-third of your income to Oxfam," you would not be able to say whether the machine is functioning as designed unless you could say whether one in circumstances such as yours has reasons to make sacrifices of this sort. So normative conditions enter into the account of the machine's function, and normative argument would be needed to establish when the machine is defective and when it is not. But there is no doubt that the ascription of this function to the machine is a descriptive matter: we are describing what the machine's function is, not imposing such a function or recommending that we conceive of the machine as having that function.

Now, in the case of this reason-backed rule machine, it is easy to see why the giving of dictates backed by decisive reasons for action is its characteristic activity: we have an authoritative statement from the designer of the artifact that this activity is what the machine is meant to do. How, then, would one show that this is the law's characteristic activity? Since we lack an authoritative statement from the designer of the institution of law, we might be suspicious of the claim that we could come up with a defensible account of law's characteristic activity, or suspicious of the claim that any such account would include "provide rules backed by decisive reasons for action" among law's characteristic activities. But we need not be suspicious of the possibility of providing an account of the law's function; and once we see how this can be done, it turns out that the ascription of the function "provides rules backed by decisive reasons for action" is plausible after all.

Consider, first, how you would show that the reason-backed dictates machine has the function of providing dictates backed by decisive reasons for action in the absence of an authoritative statement from the machine's designer. All you have at your disposal is your observations of what people do to the machine, of the machine's outputs, the inner workings of the machine, and the environments in which the machine operates. Suppose that you have the following evidence. The machine's handle is often pulled by rational beings. Usually the machine's output is a dictate with which the handle-puller has decisive reason to comply. That the machine's output is a dictate with which the handle-puller has decisive reason to comply is explicable by appeal to the inner workings of the machine: its parts are, most of the time, structured so that the machine's output is a dictate backed by decisive reasons. When there appear several dictates that are not backed by decisive reasons for action, this is explainable by some change in the inner workings or environment of the machine, and people appear and begin to tinker with the inner workings of the machine or move the machine to a different environment or try to alter the present environment, and they do this until the machine again begins to produce a series of dictates backed by decisive reasons for action. This is the sort of evidence you would need to ascribe the function of providing dictates backed by decisive reasons for action to the machine: its activity is to provide such dictates, and it seems to be constructed and adjusted to enable it to continue to carry out that activity.

The way to show that it is law's function to provide dictates backed by decisive reasons for action is, then, as Moore suggests: look at the various ways that systems pre-theoretically designated as "legal" operate, and see whether their activities tend to be explicable in terms of, and regulated by, the giving of dictates backed by decisive reasons. One might note the features of legal systems to which Raz has drawn our attention—that they claim to be authoritative (see Raz 1979b, p. 30) and that, characteristically, their dictates go with the flow of normative reasons rather than against them (Raz 1985 and Raz 1986, pp. 53–69). One might note the way that law characteristically ties sanctions to certain activities, which sanctions give agents further reason to abstain from them. One might also take notice of Fuller's eight ways to fail to make law: on his view, putative legal rules can fail to achieve legality when they are *ad hoc*, inadequately promulgated, retroactive, incomprehensible, contradictory, requiring conduct adherence to which is beyond the powers of subjects, ephemeral, or insincere (see Fuller 1964, p. 39). For our purposes, what is relevant about Fuller's eight ways is that each of them indicates in some way in which law can fail to serve as a reason for action for those living under it. On the basis of such considerations, one might well come to the conclusion that it is part of law's characteristic activity to lay down norms with which agents will have decisive reason to comply. Even, then, if the end that law's characteristic activity serves is itself not an obviously obligatory end—if it is, to follow Hart and Fuller, something like that of realizing social order, or social control—the natural law thesis could be sustained if law's characteristic activity is to provide dictates that are rational standards for conduct and that it provides these dictates as a means to, and because they are a means to, realizing social order.

Now, one might retort: it can hardly be the case that it is law's characteristic activity to provide dictates that are rational standards for conduct, when it is clear that so many dictates of law are no such thing. To take the low road, we can appeal to cases as dramatic as the Fugitive Slave Law or as banal as parking ordinances. To take the high road, we can appeal to the growing literature in support of the claim that the law lacks authority, that its dictates do not in fact typically constitute decisive reasons for agents to comply with them.[63]

The initial response here is just that to say that $\phi$-ing is x's characteristic activity is not to say that all x's always $\phi$. It is to say that x's are *the kind of thing that* $\phi$, and this is compatible with there being instances—even perhaps in the majority of cases—where x's fail to $\phi$. But the retort does raise an important question: how do we know that these cases in which law fails to provide dictates that are backed by decisive reasons for action count not as counterexamples to the claim that this is law's characteristic activity but rather as cases in which law is failing to perform its characteristic activity?

With artifacts, often the answer is easy: our source of information about what kind an object belongs to, and what is the characteristic activity of that kind, is usually determined at least in large part by the maker's intentions. But with law, as with other large-scale social institutions, we have something that is not the product of some thinker's intentions. Here the more apt analogies are the systems of organisms. We know that a heart's characteristic activity is to pump blood, and that this is its function; and we can know this without appeal a designer's intentions. We can know this in spite of the fact that animals can have heart attacks. We say that the heart's characteristic activity is to pump blood not just because of statistical frequency—again, we can imagine states of affairs in which heart attacks were disastrously more frequent, and this would give us reason to say that hearts were malfunctioning all over the place, not that its characteristic activity had changed or that we were wrong about what its characteristic activity is. We persist in the judgment that the characteristic activity is pumping blood because judgments of characteristic activity are made against a background, a privileged background of normalcy. An object's departure from its characteristic activity is to be accounted for through appeal to a change in the normal background.

To sustain the claim that law's characteristic activity is to provide dictates with which agents have decisive reason to comply, even in the face of divergences from this activity, we have to say that in such cases, the privileged background for the description of institutions such as the law does not obtain, and that departures from the activity of providing dictates with which agents have decisive reason to comply is to be explained by reference to the departure from this background. Here is the crucial move: the background from which human institutions are to be assessed, so far as possible, is one in which humans are properly functioning. But human beings are rational animals, and when properly functioning act on what the relevant reasons require. And so law would not be able to realize the end of order by giving dictates in a world in which humans are properly functioning

---

[63] The literature is large and growing. Influential pieces include Simmons 1979, Raz 1979a, Smith 1973, and Green 1990. The literature has been surveyed in Edmundson 1999b, 1999c, and (most extensively) in Edmundson 2004 [and below, 574].

unless those dictates are backed by adequate reasons. Thus we should say that it is law's characteristic activity to provide dictates backed by compelling reasons for action, and that law that fails to do so is defective as law.

As I said earlier, the crucial move is to hold that the privileged background of normalcy for assessing human institutions like law is, so far as possible, that in which humans are properly functioning. This conception of the normal background is, I hope, intuitively appealing, but it can also be defended in terms of the constraints under which functions are ascribed to systems and their parts. When a system has a function, and its parts also have functions, it is important to have— again, as far as possible—an account of the system's and the parts' functions according to which those functions are not at odds with one another. For to have a function is, in part, to tend toward an equilibrium state; and so for the system's and the parts' ascribed functions to be at odds with each other is to call into question either the view that the putative parts genuinely are parts of that system or the view that the functions have been correctly ascribed to the system or to the parts. For if the system's and its parts' activities are at odds with each other, then either the system or its parts will fail to tend toward its ascribed equilibrium state, and thus we should either revise our specific functional attributions to the system and its parts or reassess our understanding of one or more items as parts of that system.

The ascription of functions to systems and their parts thus proceeds in a way that generates coordination between them, and in the abstract, there is no reason to think that our judgments of the function of the system should be more or less prone to revisions than our judgments of the function of the parts of that system. But there is a class of cases in which the function of the parts does have priority over the function of the system: it is that class of cases in which the parts have a function (logically) independent of and (logically) prior to their existence as parts of that system. This is true with respect to law. In understanding the function of legal systems and of laws within those systems, there is excellent reason to treat the function of the parts as fixed, as the background by which the function of law is understood: for humans are natural objects whose basic proper functioning is prior to the various institutions in which they find or make for themselves. And so the assessment of law in functional terms rightly presupposes as its privileged background properly functioning human beings.

There may of course remain some skepticism about the notion that law is to be understood in functional terms at all, so that dictates that do not live up to those standards are defective as law. Another way to reduce this skepticism is to note that there are non-legal phenomena that also seem to call for functional analyses, the particular functional analyses of which implicate reasons for action. Consider the ("first, rough") notion of a convention as characterized by Lewis:

> A regularity R in the behavior of members of a population P when they are in a recurrent situation S is a convention if and only if, in any instance of S among members of P,
> 1. everyone conforms to R;
> 2. everyone expects everyone else to conform to R;
> 3. everyone prefers to conform to R on condition that the others do, since S is a coordination problem and uniform conformity to R is a proper coordination equilibrium in S.
>
> (Lewis 1969, p. 42)

This definition is a functional definition: we cannot properly understand conventions except as ways of solving problems of certain sorts. And it would not be surprising to say that some regularities of behavior are conventions, but defective: a regularity of behavior that is not universally preferred among the members of P but which can survive and be preferred by the vast majority of P, even in awareness of the existence of defectors, can be plausibly described as a convention, though in some ways a defective one. Nor would it be surprising to say that even a convention that meets Lewis's first statement of the criteria is defective: if uniform conformity to $R_1$ is a coordination equilibrium in S yet there is an available Pareto-superior coordination equilibrium $R_2$ in S, then we might think of $R_1$ as in one important way defective: while it does what conventions are supposed to do, it does not do it as well as $R_2$ would have.

Functional analysis is inescapable in dealing with convention, and there is little reason to worry about the way that functional analysis of conventions implicates practical rationality. Neither then should we balk at functional analysis of law or at the notion that the proper functional analysis of law appeals to certain sorts of reasons for compliance.

### 2.4 Illocutionary Acts and the Weak Natural Law Thesis

The third plausible route to the weak natural law thesis appeals to the idea that laws are or are akin to illocutionary acts. I will argue, first, that it is legitimate to understand the law as a speaker, and that a mandatory legal norm just is the law's demand to those under its jurisdiction that they carry out a certain course of action. However, it is one of the non-defectiveness conditions on demands that there be decisive reasons for the party to whom the demand is issued to comply with the demand. It thus follows that mandatory legal norms are essentially defective if they are not backed by decisive reasons for compliance: and this is equivalent to the weak natural law thesis as applied to mandatory legal norms. I will conclude the illocutionary acts argument for the weak natural law thesis by extending the argument offered for mandatory legal norms to other sorts of laws.

#### The Law as Speaker

It is commonplace, both in ordinary talk and in philosophical writing, to attribute to the law the performance of speech-acts of various sorts. No one is or would be puzzled by the report that United States law demands that residents pay their taxes by April 15; or by the report that United States law once declared that blacks are not and could not be citizens, but that now it does not say this; or by the report that Virginia law tells us that a valid will must, *inter alia*, be signed by two witnesses. And philosophers, though with a bit more hesitation, have been willing to treat the law and its institutions as a speaker. A central thesis of Raz's jurisprudence is that the law claims to be a practical authority.[64] While there has been a great deal of disagreement concerning the content of what Raz holds the law to claim (see, for example, Soper 2002, pp. 51–88), those responding to Raz have been mostly content to allow the legitimacy of treating the law as itself a speaker.

Now, one might complain that this way of describing the law's activities seems to presuppose a very peculiar "animism" (Moore's term: see his 1987, p. 837), or more particularly, *anthropomorphism* vis-à-vis the law by ascribing to the law claims, assertions, demands. While there have been some sketches of defense of this way of treating the law, these sketches, while seeming to be on the right track, nevertheless require further filling out before we can be confident of the legitimacy of treating the law as a speaker. Leslie Green, for example, defends the propriety of speaking of the state's making claims to authority as follows.

> Is it not a dangerous metaphor to speak of the state "acting" and "making claims" on us …? Not all metaphors are dangerous, however, and this one has utility in avoiding cumbersome circumlocutions about the activities of the officials of the state, in particular its legislative and executive officials. Of course when we say the state claims our allegiance

[64] See the discussions in Raz 1979a, pp. 29–33, 146–159, and Raz 1984a, pp. 123–131.

we are only summarizing certain politically relevant actions of officials: that they have passed a law which purports to impose obligations on us, that the police and courts regard these obligations as binding and will enforce them, and so on. In principle, we could replace talk of the state as an agent with a more convoluted vocabulary of individuals, officials, and social rules, but there would be little profit in it.

(Green 1990, p. 66)

In fairness to Green, he is clearly here only gesturing at the form such an account would take, and such gestures are to be assessed by whether they illuminate promising ways that a full account of the notion of the state as a speaker might be developed; and it does seem that the appeal to the activities of officials—real, live, paradigmatic speakers—would be a helpful way to clarify the law's status as a speaker. But it also contains seeds of doubt. For when Green does spell out some of what is involved in the state's making claims, he relies on the notion that there is "a law which purports to impose obligations on us"; and surely the notion that the law *purports* to be doing something is not a bit less anthropomorphic on its face than the notion that the state *claims* to be doing something.

Raz and Green are right to follow common talk in allowing the propriety of ascribing speech-acts to the law, but it is worth examining why the ascription of speech-acts to the law is appropriate; the propriety of such ascriptions is central to my argument for the weak natural law thesis, and any suspicions that this way of thinking of the law really is mere metaphor and insusceptible of illuminating analysis will cast doubt on that argument. We can begin with the more general question. What conditions must be satisfied for *any* entity to be a speaker?

For an entity to be a speaker, it must be susceptible of a certain range of belief and desire-states; it must be susceptible of a certain range of normative standings; and it must be capable of producing a certain range of events. Normal adult human beings paradigmatically satisfy the constraints in question. They are able to form beliefs, desires and intentions; they are able to subject themselves to critical standards of appraisal; and they are capable of producing auditory and visual events that express beliefs, desires, and intentions, and thereby make themselves responsible in specific ways. For example: a paradigmatic asserter is able to form beliefs about the propositions that he or she asserts; can express those beliefs in virtue of his or her capacity to grasp and use certain words and phrases; can intentionally produce the requisite words and phrases; and can thereby make himself or herself responsible for the content and occasion of the utterance, subject to adverse criticism for any mistaken assertion.[65] Now, it is clear that the law will not be a paradigmatic speaker. *Believing that p* and *desiring that p* and *being responsible for p* are states of minded beings, and the law, unlike humans, angels, and God, does not have a mind and thus cannot possess beliefs and desires in the standard way and cannot be a responsible agent in the most straightforward sense. The question, though, is not whether the law is a paradigmatic speaker but whether it is legitimate to ascribe these features to law in any more than a metaphorical sense.

*The law as believer and desirer*: On the one hand, we have paradigmatic believers and desirers—that is, mature adult human beings. On the other hand, we have objects to which beliefs and desires are sometimes ascribed, but in what is a clearly metaphorical way. I sometimes say that my computer thinks that I am pushing the "a" key when I in fact am not, or that my car wants to engage its traction control system at the slightest hint of ice on the road. But while speaking

---

[65] Different views on the nature of illocutionary acts place these necessary features of speakerhood in different orders of explanatory importance: some views place the expression of belief and desire as crucial, still others place the intention to bring about a certain belief or desire state in the audience as crucial, still others place the imposition of a certain normative standing as being of first importance. I have no need to enter into these disputes here.

thus of my computer and my car is intelligible—everybody knows what I mean when I say these things—its intelligibility is through interpretation by metaphor. But the notion that the law believes or wants something is not metaphorical in this way. The believing and wanting of the law occupies an intermediate place between the paradigmatic believing and wanting of natural persons and the merely metaphorical believing and wanting of artifacts such as the computer and the car.

Begin with desire. What the literal desiring of the human and the metaphorical desiring of the car have in common is their teleological structure: to ascribe a desire is to hold that there is some end-state toward which the object tends, and that the object will (*ceteris paribus*) act until that end-state is realized (cf. Smith 1994, pp. 111–116). Now, in full-blooded desire, there is a typical phenomenology of desire, and the adjustment of action toward the realization of the end-state is accomplished through full-blooded belief. The car's "desire" to activate its traction control system is not accompanied by the characteristic phenomenology of desire, nor is its realization of the goal accomplished through full-blooded belief.

Now, with respect to desiring, law occupies a place intermediate between these two extremes. Legal systems are teleological systems—all legal systems tend to order through the imposition of standards of conduct—and different sorts of legal order are distinguished by the basic ends toward which they tend and subordinate ends that they employ or refrain from employing to realize them. Thus it is at least as appropriate to say that the law wants to achieve order as it is to say that my car wants to activate its traction control system. But with the law there is a further point—that its goal-achievement is realized through the motivational systems of real, live, paradigmatic desirers. As the passage earlier by Green notes, the law's activities are carried out first and foremost through what Tuomela calls its "operative" members—officials—and also through those citizens who take what Hart calls the internal point of view with respect to it. The law's adjustment of its activities in order to achieve certain end-states is the result of the desires of the operative agents of the law motivated *qua* operative agents (Tuomela 1995, pp. 232–234).[66]

It is also legitimate and not merely metaphorical to ascribe to the law beliefs. Again: what is common to paradigmatic believers and to my computer is that they possess some way of representing states of affairs, which representations can be used as the basis for further representations or for the adjustment of goal-promoting activity. The common fact of representation is what makes the metaphor of belief apt in the case of the computer's representation of my having pressed the "a" key. Now, while the law is of course not a paradigmatic believer, its having beliefs and forming judgments is not merely metaphorical, for its representations of states of affairs works through the cognitive equipment of paradigmatic believers: legal officials, whose judgments about the effectiveness of law's present activity in realizing the sought ends make possible the read-justment of the law's activities in light of those ends, as well as those persons who take the internal point of view with respect to the law.

The argument, then, is that it should be uncontroversial to ascribe to the law goals and representations, and that the particular way that these goals and representations are instantiated in law—through operative agents that are paradigmatic desirers and believers—legitimates our understanding the law's having

---

[66] Suppose that I were to inform you that my car is *very* special—the way that its traction control system gets activated is that there are homunculi occupying observation posts who want the traction control to be turned on when the road is slippery and who thus activate that system when they observe that the road is slippery. I take it that this would make my claim that the car wants to activate its traction system closer to literal truth and further from mere metaphor.

of goals as desiring and its having of representations as believing. Now, one might ask whether it is the case, then, that it is only possible to understand the law as a speaker where the legal system has developed to the point at which there is a distinct class of operatives—legislators, judges, and so forth—through whose motivational and cognitive capacities the law functions. Without such operatives—imagine the more primitive system of norms described by Hart, which possesses primary rules of obligation but lacks rules of change, adjudication, and recognition (Hart 1994 [1961], pp. 91–92)—it would seem that there would be no basis to ascribe to the law any judgments or aims.

I do not think that this precisely follows. What follows is that ascription to the law of desires and beliefs (and the illocutionary acts ascription of which presupposes the possibility of the ascription of desires and beliefs) will be more vague and uncertain than they would be in a situation in which there is a clear set of officials responsible for the law's operations. Compare the situations in primitive and developed legal systems with the cases of what Tuomela calls "joint" belief/desire and "group" belief/desire (Tuomela 1995, pp. 307–308). The conditions for group belief/desire require the presence of operative agents who can have such beliefs/desires *qua* operatives. By the presence of such agents, the conditions for ascription of a belief or desire to a group is fairly clearly defined. Joint belief/desire requires no such official capacities, but results in a less clearly defined set of conditions for joint belief or desire: if there is not unanimity among the members, it becomes unclear to what extent a joint belief or desire can be ascribed. The situation is similar in the case of the primitive and developed legal systems. In developed legal systems, a well-defined class of officials makes possible the identification of law even though there may be plenty of dissenters living under the legal system. But without a well-defined class of officials, the presence of dissenters makes it difficult to say whether there are in fact rules in place and what the goals or beliefs of the law are. (On this point, see also Gilbert 1999b, p. 144.)

*The law as possessing normative standing.* To speak, one must also possess the proper normative standing. To speak is to make oneself responsible in certain ways, where the sort of responsibility involved differs for different sorts of illocutionary acts. It is to render oneself subject to criticism and blame for falling short with respect to one's responsibilities.

Such responsibility is commonly ascribed to the law. The law is blamed for the content of its demands, or for what it fails to demand; it is blamed for making certain commitments, or for failing to live up to the commitments that it has made. Its general dictates and particular rulings are subject to criticism. It is not simply an unresponsive source from which dictates emerge, etched in stone and uncriticizable. Criticism can be launched and revision expected in light of the force of good arguments. Of course, it is because of the powers of the officials of a legal system, through whom the content and application of the law can be changed, that such criticism has a point. It is enough for the law to have the normative standing requisite for speaking that it can sensibly be called to account for what it says.

*The law as causally efficacious.* Finally, in order to speak, one must have the requisite causal powers, the power to produce the written or spoken words that are the vehicle by which the illocutionary act takes place. As the law is an institution, its capacity to intervene by producing the necessary linguistic items is through the officials occupying its institutional roles. The law has the causal power requisite for speaking because its officials have the causal power requisite for speaking.

### Mandatory Legal Norms and Demands

To call the law a speaker, then, is to use the notion of "speaker" in a way that is without a doubt extended but not simply metaphorical. It is legitimate and informative to treat the law as a speaker. As I will argue later, there are various sorts of legal propositions whose truth is interestingly connected to the performance of speech-acts by the law. But for the sake of simplicity, and for the sake of dealing first with the sort of legal rule that has historically been at the center of the dispute between natural law theorists and legal positivists, we can begin with duty-imposing laws—laws that make some conduct mandatory.

The claim that I want to make here is that duty-imposing rules essentially involve the demands of law: a duty-imposing legal rule that all members of class M $\phi$ is the law's demand on all members of class M that they $\phi$. Here is the most straightforward argument for this view. Whenever it is by consensus true that there is a law that imposes a mandatory norm on those under it, it is also by consensus true that the law demands the conduct mandated by the norm. We acknowledge that the U.S. legal system contains a mandatory norm requiring the payment of taxes by April 15; we also acknowledge that U.S. law demands the payment of taxes by April 15. We acknowledge that the U.S. legal system contains a mandatory norm forbidding the theft of the mails; we also acknowledge that U.S. law demands that we not steal the mails. And while we acknowledge that U.S. law does not demand that we make payments toward the support of an established religion, we correspondingly acknowledge that the U.S. legal system does not contain a mandatory norm requiring the making of payments toward the support of an established religion. All of this is exceedingly obvious, and there is no need to multiply examples.

We should allow that there is a mandatory legal norm requiring $\phi$-ing if and only if the law demands $\phi$-ing. But the status of this biconditional is obviously not merely contingent: it is absurd to think that the demands of law and the presence of mandatory norms just happen to correspond to each other. And this connection is also clearly not a mere mutual entailment between two *independent* states of affairs: it is rather far-fetched to think that whenever there is a mandatory norm to $\phi$ there is also some further, distinct state of affairs, that of *the law's demanding $\phi$-ing*; and whenever there is not such a mandatory norm, the law also must refrain from demanding that conduct. Given the non-contingency of the connection between the law's demands and the presence of mandatory norms, surely it is more plausible to suppose that there being a mandatory legal norm requiring $\phi$-ing *just is* the law's demanding $\phi$-ing.

Again: consider the sorts of analysis that have recently been offered for the existence of mandatory legal norms and compare them with those states of affairs to which I appealed in making the case for the claim that the law speaks. The law's speaking involves its having certain beliefs and desires, its making itself accountable in certain ways, and its intervening linguistically, and each of these is to be understood, at least in developed legal systems, in terms of the responses of officials acting as officials. But it seems that on any account of what the existence of a legal rule consists in, it will appeal to these very states of affairs (see, for example, Hart 1994 [1961], pp. 55–58). So a further reason to think that a mandatory legal norm requiring $\phi$-ing just is the law's demanding $\phi$-ing is that the very same states of affairs will appear in the analyses of both of these notions.

Again: consider the following *explanandum*. When a legal system contains a mandatory norm requiring $\phi$-ing of all members of class M, we thereby know that the law *has an interest* in the $\phi$-ing of the members of class M—the law *intends* for them to $\phi$, *aims* at their $\phi$-ing, *wants* them to $\phi$. But the mere presence of a rule in a system does not give of itself any indication why we would thereby think that anyone has as an *aim* or *purpose* or *goal* that persons perform the required act. But if we think of the law's mandatory norms as being the demands of law, we would thereby render unmysterious the fact that when there is a mandatory norm requiring $\phi$-ing, then we know that the law wants people to $\phi$. For when one makes a demand, it is normally the case that he or she wants those to whom the demand is addressed to act on it. (It is, to use the terminology of the theory of illocutionary acts (see later in this section), a sincerity condition of one's demanding that A $\phi$ that one intends that A $\phi$.) This gives us further reason to think that the law's mandatory norms are invariably to be identified with the demands of law.

Now, there may be some resistance to the idea that mandatory legal norms are to be understood as the law's demands. Is this not the sort of command conception of law that Hart decisively refuted in *The Concept of Law*?

It is not. It is essential to Hart's objections to the Austin-inspired command conception of law both (1) that command is taken to be the essence of law, present in every case in which there is genuine law, and (2) that the commands in question are those of a *sovereign*, some supreme, legally unlimited party to whom there is habitual obedience. And against such a view, Hart rightly notes that (1) there are types of law, most notably those that confer powers either on private individuals or on public officials, that cannot plausibly be understood in terms of the command conception, and (2) that selecting as law only those commands proceeding from such a sovereign precludes proper understanding of the way that law persists through changes in lawmaking authority (Hart 1994 [1961], pp. 26–49, 51–61). But it has been no part of the argument of this section that the mandatory legal norms, which I say are the demands of law, are the primitive normative element out of which all other legal norms are to be constructed; so Hart's criticism of the Austinian view's sole focus on command does not apply to the view that I have defended. Nor has it been any part of the argument of this section that we must identify, without reference to legal concepts, some party whose demands are the demands of law. The demands that I have identified with mandatory legal norms are not the demands of some Austinian sovereign but the demands of the law itself. So none of the criticisms that Hart levels against the way that Austinian theory appeals to the notion of sovereignty has application here.

## *Demands and Decisive Reasons for Action*

The law's mandatory norms are its demands. The relevance of this identification is that it is through understanding these norms as demands that we can see how there are, internal to law, standards of defectiveness and non-defectiveness that make essential reference to reasons for action. For demands are one species of illocutionary act; and illocutionary acts have standards of defectiveness and non-defectiveness internal to them; and some of the standards of defectiveness and non-defectiveness for the species of illocutionary act to which demands belong make essential reference to reasons for action.

In order to make this part of the case for the weak natural law thesis, I first need to say a few things, none of them original, about illocutionary acts. Illocutionary acts are, as Searle and Vanderveken write, "minimal units of human communication" (1985, p. 1). An illocutionary act is an attempt to do something with language, an attempt to realize some state of affairs by the performance of a speech-act. Every such act can be analyzed in terms of its illocutionary force and its propositional content. Illocutionary acts may have the same propositional content yet be distinct as a result of their differing illocutionary force: commanding you to be in class on time is distinct from predicting that you will be in class on time, begging you to be in class on time, cheering your being in class on time, and so on, even though the propositional content of all of these illocutionary acts—that you be in class on time—is the same. An illocutionary force is identified and distinguished from other illocutionary forces by the conditions under which the illocutionary act partly constituted by that force is successful and non-defective: the success conditions for an illocutionary act of a certain type are those conditions that must be realized for one to perform an illocutionary act of that type at all; the non-defectiveness conditions of an illocutionary act are those conditions that are presupposed in illocutionary act of that type and thus to whose obtaining the performer of that illocutionary act is committed by its performance.

Most fundamental to the distinguishing of illocutionary forces is the *illocutionary point*, which is the goal internal to being an illocutionary act of that type. For example, one of the fundamental illocutionary points is that of *assertion*, on which the point of presenting the proposition is to represent the world. While there are other components of illocutionary force, the illocutionary point is most basic, and defines what constitutes the success of the performance of the illocutionary act (Searle and Vanderveken 1985, pp. 51–59). No act of assertion is successful, really counts as an act of assertion at all, if it does not represent the world as being in fact a certain way.

There are, however, ways that illocutionary acts can go wrong other than through being entirely unsuccessful. One who attempts to make an assertion can fail to make any assertion through sheer linguistic incompetence, and can end up making no assertion at all. But assertions can be successful though defective: for there is a variety of ways that assertions can fall short without failing altogether to count as assertions. For aside from the illocutionary point, there are various components of an illocutionary force whose obtaining is presupposed by the speaker in the illocutionary act. Among these are the sincerity conditions—those speaker's mental states that are presupposed in an illocutionary act—and preparatory conditions—those states of the world that are presupposed in an illocutionary act. For example: in the case of assertion, it is among the sincerity conditions that the proposition asserted is believed by the speaker, and it is among the preparatory conditions that the proposition asserted has some positive epistemic status. One who asserts that p presupposes these conditions in making that assertion, and is committed to them; the clearest test of this is that it is invariably paradoxical to assert that p while denying that one believes that p, and it is inevitably paradoxical to assert that p while denying that p has any positive epistemic status for the speaker (Searle and Vanderveken 1985, pp. 17, 18–19; also Alston 1999, pp. 77–78). Nevertheless, these non-defectiveness conditions on assertion are not success conditions. To lie is to make an assertion contrary to one's mind (cf. *Summa Theologiae* IIaIIae 110, 1) and to bullshit is to make an assertion without regard to that assertion's positive epistemic status (cf. Frankfurt 1988b), and lying and bullshitting *are* possible. Nevertheless, lying and bullshitting are intrinsically flawed forms of asserting, defective in their kind. To make this assessment is not to make any moral pronouncements about lying and bullshitting. It is just to say that lying and bullshitting are of the genus of asserting and are intrinsically defective instances of that genus.

There are different success and nondefectiveness conditions corresponding to speech-acts with different illocutionary forces. My aim here is to argue that it is among the nondefectiveness conditions for demands that the party demanded have decisive reasons to comply with the demand. The argument is this.

1. Demanding is a species of *directive* illocutionary act: the point internal to the laying down of demands is to present an act as to-be-done.
2. When one directs another to $\phi$, then one necessarily implies that the other has some reason to $\phi$.
3. Though some directive acts give the addressed party the option of not acting on the directive, demanding does not give this option.
4. The features of demands noted in (2) and (3)—commitment to reasons for compliance and the non-optionality of such compliance—yield the result that when one demands that another $\phi$, then one necessarily implies that the other has *decisive* reasons to $\phi$.

**1.** Assume Searle's now-standard taxonomy of basic illocutionary points—assertive, directive, commissive, declarative, expressive. On this view, the point of *assertion* is to present a proposition as representing the world accurately, the point of *commission* is to present a proposition so as to commit the speaker to actualizing it, the point of *direction* is to present the proposition so as to have the addressee(s) carry out the action represented in the proposition, the point of *declaration* is to present a proposition so as to make it true by the performance of the act itself, and the point of *expression* is to present a proposition so as to express one's attitude toward the state of affairs represented by it. While, as we said, there are other components of illocutionary force—it is these other components that distinguish the various species of illocutionary acts—the illocutionary point is most basic, and defines what constitutes the success of the performance of the illocutionary act (Searle and Vanderveken 1985, pp. 51–59).

It is clear that, given this standard taxonomy of basic illocutionary forces, *demanding that p* belongs to the genus of directive illocutionary acts. But there is a problem with the way this illocutionary point has been formulated. For one can successfully make a demand even if the party demanded fails to be motivated by that demand. (We should be sure to keep clear the distinction between the success of the illocutionary act, the communication itself, and that of the perlocutionary act—what one means to accomplish by means of it.) It seems better to say that in issuing a directive, the point internal to that act is to present a proposition as to-be-done. For that is what counts as success in issuing a directive: the most basic achievement required for the issuing of a directive is that one manages to present it as to-be-done. And it is obvious that this is the illocutionary point exhibited by demands: a demand presents an action as to-be-done.

**2.** In performing a directive act, one invariably implies that the party addressed has a reason to perform the directed act. (Note well: to say that in performing a directive illocutionary act one implies that the directed party addressed has a reason to comply is not to say that whenever one directs another to $\phi$, the other has a reason to $\phi$; it is only to say that whenever one directs another to $\phi$, one puts himself or herself forward as *affirming that*—at least once the directive is issued— the other has reason to $\phi$.) One way to give evidence for this view is just to survey the various sorts of directive acts—pleas, demands, orders, and so on—and to note that in each case, it seems to be the case that one who performs that act puts himself or herself forward as holding that there is some reason, of some strength, to perform the directed act. But the more persuasive and more straightforward way to show that a proposition is a necessary implication of a type of speech-act is to employ the "paradox test": to show that it is invariably paradoxical to perform that speech-act while denying that proposition. If one considers any directive act chosen at random, it is clear that it is paradoxical to perform that act while denying that the person directed has any reason to go along. Suppose that I give you the following demand to bring me a book. "There is, in fact, nothing—not even the demand that I am about to make—that gives you the slightest reason to bring me a copy of Raz's *The Authority of Law*. But bring me that book!" The paradox is apparent. Even with milder directives, such as requests, it is paradoxical to deny the existence of any reason for compliance while making the request. Directives are issued by rational beings to rational beings, and thus they carry with them the implication that compliance with the directive is, in some respect, supported by reasons (Searle and Vanderveken 1985, pp. 17, 18–19; also Alston 1999, pp. 77–78).

**3.** In performing directive acts, and *a fortiori* in making demands, one implies that there are reasons for the addressed party to act as directed: one who directs an agent to $\phi$ implies that the agent has reasons to $\phi$. What I want to say now is that in the particular case of demands, the reasons whose existence is implied by the directive act are decisive ones. To show this we need to note a component of commanding acts that does not hold of all directive acts. Some directive acts allow the addressee the option of non-compliance; others do not allow such an option (Searle and Vanderveken 1985, pp. 198–199). A request, for example, allows the one to whom the request is addressed to opt out, while an order, by contrast, does not. In this broad division of directives, demands clearly fall on the side of the non-optional. One can, after all, non-paradoxically say "I request that you do this, though you may refrain if you choose"; one cannot non-paradoxically say "I demand that you do this, though you may refrain if you choose."

**4.** Together, the fact that (a) demands display a non-optionality feature, and (b) all directive acts, including those of making demands, imply the existence of reasons for action on the part of those addressed gives us grounds to believe that the reasons for action implied by demands are of a specific sort—that is, decisive ones. In making a demand, one implies that there is no option other than compliance. But how can rational beings be left with no option other than compliance unless the reasons that favor compliance are decisive ones? To confirm this result, we can again appeal directly to the paradox test: one can non-paradoxically say "I hereby request that you $\phi$, while recognizing that you can reasonably, all things considered, refrain from $\phi$-ing"; one cannot non-paradoxically say "I hereby demand that you $\phi$, while recognizing that you can reasonably, all things considered, refrain from $\phi$-ing." The reasons for action implied in all directive acts and the strength of the directive force partially constitutive of demands together entail that in demanding one implies the existence of decisive reasons for compliance.[67]

## MARGARET MEAD
### Some Anthropological Considerations Concerning Natural Law
### (1961)[68]

... In asking what conceptions of human rights are universal to all known cultures, it is, of course, necessary to recognise that we can only ask this question about the assemblage of societies that have been observed and recorded. Inevitably, our universe excludes all cultures that have vanished without leaving any record, and the steadily shrinking number of existing cultures that exist in the present but have not yet been studied. The culturally regulated relationship among persons within a given environment is characterised both by certain persistent regularities, due to the species-specific characteristics of human beings, and a wide variety of forms having historical uniqueness. It is only those areas of human life which are most closely based in our common biological heritage in which we may not expect still to find, among existing cultures, instances which alter existing generalisations.

Nevertheless, the systematic observations of constancies among all known cultures make it highly probable that the kinds of cultural behavior found in all of them have been an integral part of their survival system up to the present time. Among such constancies we may note the distinction between the sacredness of human life within and without the group, or the existence of a category of human life within and without the group, or the existence of a category of murder—a

---

[67] One might wonder whether this puts the point too strongly. Think of the variety of unreasonable demands made by small children on parents, for example—are we to suppose that these demands carry the implication that the parents have decisive reason to comply? Well, yes, we are. Whether an illocutionary act has certain implications is not a feature of the performance of an act of that type on any given occasion, so it is not as if the fact that the child knows not of decisive reasons is any strike against the claim that demands imply decisive reasons for compliance.

[68] [From 6 *Natural Law Forum* 51.]

type of killing that is different from all other killings, falling in specified ways within the circle of protected persons.[69] The distinctions vary from one group to another; a new born infant may be excluded, or an adulterer caught in *flagrante delicto*; expected revenge may even take the form of a man's obligation to kill the foster father, who once killed his father, married his mother, and reared him from childhood. But the categories of justified versus unjustified killing remain for all known societies. As human beings, to survive, must live in aggregations of more than one biological family, this distinction can be regarded as a vital one for the development of a viable society. The extension of the category of those whose killing constitutes murder, in contradistinction to legitimate vengeance, or conventional head hunting or warfare, has been a conspicuous marker of the evolution of civilisations in spite of its carrying with it the inescapable corollary of increasing the number of those who become at one stroke—as with a declaration of war—legitimate victims.

With the same universality we find incest rules governing the three primary incest relationships—mother-son, father-daughter, and brother-sister—occurring in all known societies. Although in special cases they may be occasionally waived, as in royal marriages between brother and sister, or in cases of small in marrying groups in which there are no possible mates, such exceptions are treated as exceptions, marking royalty off from commoners or signalling a desperate population emergency. The circumstance that the taboo is frequently broken—especially in the father-daughter form—under conditions of cultural breakdown, only serves to demonstrate that its maintenance is socio-cultural rather than instinctive. Clinical and anthropological evidence suggests that the attraction and repulsion of members of a biological family are such that social regulation has been necessary. The function of the incest taboo may be seen as preventing competition among members of the same sex within the family group during the long period when human young are not mature enough to fend for themselves, and as providing forms in which the search for mates outside the immediate family strengthens ties within families.[70]

It is in those instances where incest rules have been elaborated to include large numbers of persons, all members of one clan, all members of one village or district, etc., that the compensatory need for religio-legal devices for breaking a rule that has become too onerous is found, and the complementary right to find a mate is brought into relief. Again those instances in which marriage is denied require strong cultural elaborations or religious and ethical sanctions, in which individuals become completely dedicated to a religious life.

Finally, in spite of the widespread notions of primitive communism, there is no known culture without some institution of private property. The forms in which this is expressed may appear bizarre—the right to a name, or the right to certain forms of privacy such as the right to sleep without being awakened, or to eat without being spoken to—but the association of social identity with rights against the invasion of others is universal.[71] Practice such as the destruction or interment of an individual's personal possessions, weapons, tools, dress and adornment, etc., combined with ownership of camping sites and hunting territories by larger corporate groups, have misled some observers into thinking that no property was held by individuals. Experience with attempts to impose modern ideas of state

---

[69] Edward Westermarck, *The Origin and Development of the Moral Ideas*, 2 vols: vol. I, 1906; vol. II, 1908).

[70] Robert H. Lowie, *Primitive Society* (1920); George Peter Murdock, *Social Structure* (1949); Reo F. Fortune, *Incest*, in (1932) 7 *The Encyclopaedia of the Social Sciences* 620; Maurice J. Barry, Jr. & Adelaid M. Johnson, "The Incest Barrier" (1958) 27 *The Psychoanalytic Quarterly* 485; Margaret Mead, *Male and Female* (1949).

[71] Lawrence K. Frank, "The Concept of Inviolability in Culture" in *Society as the Patient* (1948), pp. 143–150.

capitalism or collective ideologies upon "communistic" primitive people very rapidly exposes the error of this assumption.

Effective use of case studies from primitive cultures requires a recognition that no matter how primitive the people under discussion are, rules concerning the sacredness of life (under some circumstances), rules concerning the prohibition of incest in the primary familial relationships in most circumstances, and rules governing an individual's rights over some differentiated physical or cultural items will be found. That such recognitions have been universal in the past does not, however, argue conclusively for their necessary continuance in the future. But they appear to have provided a minimal culturally transmitted ethical code without which human societies were not viable. The English geneticist C. H. Waddington has argued persuasively,[72] on purely naturalistic grounds, that the capacity to accept a division of behavior into that which is right and that which is wrong, is a distinctively human species-specific type of behavior which has played an essential part in the evolution of culture.

"Natural law" might thus be defined as those rules of behavior which had developed from a species-specific capacity to ethicalise as a feature of those examples of such ethicalising that appear in all known societies.[73]    [pp. 51–54]

We have seen that recognition of natural rights, to life, property, and reproduction, is found in all societies, although with profound variations in interpretation. However, when Western law and traditional law or primitive custom have confronted each other, it is rather the question of sanctions, authority, order which have constituted the aspects of the law which have become salient. It would be worthwhile to undertake a series of intensive explorations of societies on the verge of intensive modernization who are at the moment attempting to formulate their legal systems, relying variously upon British, American, Swiss, French. Soviet models and others. In each such case two sets of cultural envelopes are involved, the culturally embedded system of the donor or model country, and the culture of the receiver or model-seeking country. If such situations were analysed with a view to finding a minimal set of legal principles which might be regarded as stripped universals, the creation of new legal systems might be effectively streamlined—in contrast to the present attempt to tinker with models which are hoary with specific traditional accretions, many of which are inappropriate in the new situation. Is it possible to regard law as having such a set of universals, which can in any way be compared with scientific principles such as govern nutrition, or can we only arrive at a scientific study of the law by way of the study of comparative legal systems, each seen as part of a particular culture and one link in a long historical chain of legal inventions?[74]                  [p. 64]

[72] C.H. Waddington, *The Ethical Animal* (1960). See also Thomas H. & Julian Huxley, *Evolution and Ethics, 1893–1943* (1947). American edition, *Touchstone For Ethics, 1893–1943* (1947).

[73] To argue this position fully it is necessary to circumscribe the definition of a viable human society by including survival over a generation span, which excludes both the nonviable Nazi experiment in mass murder, which lacked ethical sanctions, and such bizarre experiments as religious cults like the Oneida Community or experimental cult communities in which all sex relations are forbidden...

[74] [Anthropoligical evidence is only part of the answer to what is natural, for even where an indisputable case is established, this says nothing about its moral rectitude. Slavery might exist everywhere but this would not prove it was a just ordering of society. Attempts to deny this look to a second meaning of nature, nature as an ideal standard. See further Lloyd, in *Essays to Castberg*, p. 111.]

KENT GREENAWALT
**How Persuasive is Natural Law Theory?**
(2000)[75]

*1. Some Basic Questions About Natural Law Theory*

1.  How far is a natural law approach a general inquiry about human ful-
    fillment and common good, and how far is it a distinctive tradition with
    long-standing and settled ways of approaching moral and political
    problems?
2.  Are forms of moral reasoning and, in particular, the categorical approa-
    ches of a traditional natural law view universally valid?
3.  How culturally relative are specific moral conclusions?
4.  How crucial are religious convictions for (1) belief in something like a
    natural law and (2) specific conclusions on moral and political issues?
5.  What judgments about the place of human law and the roles of actors
    within legal systems need to be made, if one is to recommend adoption of
    moral conclusions for official action and for citizens?

I raise these questions about a full, robust, natural law position—a view that
has roots in Aristotle and the Stoics and has found its most influential formulation in the writings of Saint Thomas Aquinas. There are, of course, very
important disagreements *among* natural lawyers, and I risk insensitivity to those.
Perhaps the most general disagreement is whether one should (and Aquinas did)
build a theory of good and of moral action from a teleological (purposive)
understanding of human beings or whether one should (and Aquinas did) begin
with self-evident human goods. Following Germain Grisez, Finnis has powerfully
defended the second position. I remark briefly on this difference in connection
with homosexual acts, but most of what I say has application to both positions.

*II. The Basic Natural Law Position*

According to my understanding, the standard natural law position rests on a
number of premises.

1.  Human life is integrally related to all of existence.
2.  Human nature is universal.
3.  The defining characterstic of human beings is their reason or rationality.
4.  Human beings have inherent purposes (the teleological approach) or self-
    evident goods (the approach Finnis defends).
5.  These purposes, or goods, are dicoverable by reason, reason being
    understood in a broad sense to include the light of experience.
6.  Morality is objective, universal, and discoverable by reason.
7.  People's moral obligations are consonant with their own true purposes, or
    their realization of self-evident goods, and with their true happiness.
8.  At the deepest levels, no conflict arises between individual good and the
    common good.
9.  Human laws appropriately reflect the natural law (though not every dictate
    of natural law should be subject to state coercion). Human laws appro-
    priately determine details left open by natural law, such as the precise
    punishments for various crimes, and they settle matters of indifference.
10. Human laws that are not in accord with natural law are not "really" law in
    some sense. A failure to accord with natural law may occur if a human law

---

[75] [From 75 *Notre Dame Law Review* 1647].

requires behavior that natural law forbids, or if a law forbids behavior that natural law values, or if the burdens and benefits of a law are highly unjust.

My first comment about this list concerns the idea that a human law that violates natural law is "really" not a law. Perhaps because the subject has seemed especially legal in some sense, theorists interested in law have expended a good deal of effort arguing over whether an unjust law is "really" a law and this has often appeared to be the major point of division between natural lawyers and positivists. Finnis rightly relegates this argument to a secondary position, carefully explaining the different senses in which a law might be said to have authority, acknowledging that in an important sense, an immoral law is law, but maintaining that such a law does not create the moral obligation to obey that is produced by other laws within a generally just system.[76] Even then Finnis does not claim that as far as moral duty is concerned an unjust law is like no law at all, but instead he develops a frequently overlooked passage in Aquinas to suggest that one's obligation not to undermine a just system may require one to obey an unjust law if disobedience would have destructive consequences.[77]

Since most political theorists who are not natural lawyers believe that moral reasons may justify disobedience of immoral laws, what distinguishes them from natural lawyers in this respect? Their conceptual apparatus and their exact approach to issues of obligation and obedience may differ subtly, but these differences do not mark some major disagreement. The query whether an unjust law is "really" a law has less significance than may have appeared before Finnis wrote.

My second comment ties closely to the first. Natural law theory is dominantly about human good and morality. Legal positivism, *by itself*, is a theory about what makes a human law a law; that legal theory can be joined with a wide range of theories about moral truth, about how judges should interpret, and about a citizen's obligation to obey the law. The true opponents of the most important claims of natural law are not legal positivists as such, but proponents of competing theories of morality (many of whom are also legal positivists).[78] If we assess how useful various conclusions about natural law may be for the development of human law, we must ask how well natural law theory serves as an account of moral understanding, *and* how much that account ties moral conclusions to judgments about human law. For the latter inquiry, we need to inquire how moral determinations should affect actors in legal systems. We *might* conclude, for example, that legislators should take account of the truths of natural law, but that judges interpreting statutes should be guided by standards of original meaning.

My third and fourth comments are about omissions from my list. I have not included any connection between natural law and God. Although in modern times, belief in natural law is strongly correlated to belief in God, *and* opponents of natural law views often have mistakenly supposed these views are simply religious, natural law theorists have consistently asserted that individuals can discover the natural law, independent of their particular religious beliefs. Finnis strongly claims, further, that one can establish the validity of natural law theory without invoking religious premises. These assertions raise central issues about the plausibility of a robust natural law theory.

My last comment concerns natural rights theory of the sort developed by John Locke that has been highly influential in our history. Claims about natural rights may or may not be based on a state of nature analysis of the kind found in Locke.

---

[76] *See* FINNIS, *Natural Law and Natural Rights*, at 245–342.

[77] *See id.* at 365.

[78] Bentham, Austin, and Kelsen are striking examples. Bentham and Austin were both utilitarians about moral theory (though Austin's rule-utilitarianism differed from Bentham's act-utilitarianism); in many respects utilitarianism is sharply opposed to natural law claims. Kelsen was a relativist about morality.

According to the dominant version of natural rights theory, what reason mainly teaches that is relevant for political society are the limits of justified interference with the freedom of individuals.[79] These limits constrain other individuals and the government. Typically, natural rights theory connects to a social contract explanation of the legitimacy of government. The government has authority because people have created it to protect them from wrongful interferences with liberty. If the government trespasses against protected liberty, it becomes illegitimate and may be overthrown. Much of what I say applies to typical natural rights theory as well as to traditional natural law theory. But I am mainly interested in the latter here and do not pause to work out implications for natural rights.

### III.  The Role of Natural Law in Developing Human Law

Let us assume for the moment that some natural law approach is the correct way to discern moral truth, that a government official recognizes this, and that the official has reached a confident conclusion about a moral truth that seems to bear on how a social problem should be resolved. The official is convinced, for example, that capital punishment is wrong, that an embryo has the value of a full human being from the moment of conception, or that every individual should have an opportunity to work. What obstacles might the official conceive to the appropriateness of converting one of these moral conclusions into positive human law?

The official recognizes, of course, that any decision about legal coercion involves judgment about the place of government and law as well as about moral truth. Many serious lies, for example, may violate natural law but not be subject to legal redress. The official recognizes, further, that decisions about enforcing natural law involve judgments about the proper responsibilities of particular officials in particular societies.

Constraints on implementing moral truths are most obvious for judges. When judges interpret legal materials, they usually do not (and should not) decide simply what they think are moral standards the state should enforce. They must consider their responsibilities vis-à-vis other political actors: the makers of constitutions, legislatures, administrators, higher courts, and earlier judges on their own court. Frequently, judges should do what statutes, executive orders, or precedents require rather than what they think would (otherwise) be morally best.

Even if a decision comes down to moral evaluation, a strong argument exists, at least for common law cases, that judges should be guided substantially by community sentiments, rather than their own assessments under the best moral theory, if the two diverge. I do not mean direct moral evaluation has *no* proper place for judges. Indeed, I think it has considerably more place in constitutional adjudication than strict originalist approaches allow. But any judge needs to devote substantial thought to the role of courts in various cases before concluding that he or she should implement some principle of morality. Answers will depend not only on general considerations about judicial authority in liberal democracies, but also on various. "local" aspects, such as whether traditions encourage flexible

---

[79]   Finnis accepts natural rights, understood in a certain way, but his foundations are at variance with common natural rights theory. He examines moral duties to determine what rights people have. He says, "[W]hen we come to explain the requirements of justice, ... we find that there is reason for treating the concept of duty, obligation, or requirement as having a more strategic explanatory role than the concept of rights." FINNIS, *supra* note 76, at 210.

interpretation of statutes, and whether the Constitution is grounded on natural law premises.[80]

When executive officials administer clear statutory directions and when lower executive officials carry out the orders of higher-ups, the constraints they face are similar to those on judges. Their job is mainly to do what they are told, not to decide what approach to a problem is best morally.

The appropriateness of relying on natural law conclusions about morality may seem simpler for legislators and for executive officials who are exercising broad discretion, since their task is to adopt good laws and regulations. Even here complexities face us. How far should government discourage actions that are immoral, but which most citizens do not regard as such? Former Governor Mario Cuomo has given us the most famous modern exploration of this problem by an official who believes in natural law. He defended support of a permissive law despite his conviction that abortion is deeply wrong from a moral point of view.[81] He might conclude that if a proposed restrictive law flies in the face of the morality of most citizens, it would be ineffective or too harsh. A legislator might believe that he has a responsibility to represent public attitudes, as well as to conform the law to correct moral judgment.

Even when an official has a clear domain of private discretion, questions about implementing moral judgments arise. What should a governor do if he believes capital punishment violates natural law, but the state authorizes capital punishment and many murderers are sentenced to death? Should the governor commute *every* death sentence, and thus achieve a morally correct outcome for each case, or would a uniform exercise of executive clemency that so directly rejects legislative judgment be improper?[82]

If natural law theory is sound and useful, natural law should figure significantly in the work of legislators and high executive officials, but concerns about role and about the functions of law preclude any easy assumption that what is called for is unblinking application of natural law to positive law.

### IV. Is There a Helpful Universal Natural Law?

We now reach much more difficult terrain. Is a natural law approach the correct, or best, way to resolve moral questions? Put differently, is the fundamental core of a traditional natural law theory persuasive, or even plausible? I am interested here in what I shall call a distinctive natural law approach and its ability to yield convincing or defensible answers to genuine moral problems. Against the claim that a distinctive natural law approach can yield such answers are arrayed challenges that its methodology is seriously flawed and that, at most, any answers it gives lack universal validity. For me, these two challenges are closely related. I use examples that test the soundness of natural law theorizing for problems that face our culture to develop concerns about universal validity.

### A. An Approach That Is Helpful and Distinctive?

From the time I first studied natural law in college, I was skeptical about the value of a genuine natural law approach to assist in the resolution of moral problems and the development of human laws. The nub of my difficulty was that some

---

[80] A plausible claim about the United States Constitution is that it largely reflects a natural rights philosophy.

[81] *See* Mario M. Cuomo. *Religious Belief and Public Morality: A Catholic Governor's Perspective*, 1 NOTRE DAME J.L. ETHICS & PUB. POL'Y 13 (1984); *see also* Terry Hall, *Legislation, in* NATURAL LAW, *supra* note 5, at 135.

[82] It might matter how recently the death penalty has been endorsed by the legislature and its degree of public support.

highly general moral premises seemed persuasive but not very useful, and that many principles and conclusions that would be useful, if persuasive, did not seem persuasive. Thus, for example, the idea that life is generally preferable to death is persuasive but not very helpful in resolving genuine moral problems; the idea that a distinction between intentional and knowing killing is *the* crucial principle for deciding whether to cause death in order to save life is unpersuasive, as is the notion that use of artificial contraception is morally wrong. (I do not mean to imply that all natural lawyers agree on all issues; many reject the conclusion about artificial contraception.[83]) Simply put, I have believed that the plausibility of natural law views has depended substantially on their level of generality and that, as plausibility has increased, usefulness for actual choice has decreased.

My view has shifted somewhat in the last few years, primarily through exposure to arguments that have started with relatively uncontroversial premises about human good and have worked through to significant ideas about public policy. George Wright, for example, has urged that if people have a right to realize their capacities, they must be able to exercise their reason, and this requires educational opportunities greater than those our society now provides to many of its children.[84] James Murphy has argued that if work is a crucial element of human fulfillment, we must do more to see that everyone has an opportunity to work.[85]

About such arguments, my concern is the distinctiveness of natural law theory. In an after-dinner talk, Judge John Noonan made a stirring defense of a commitment to natural law.[86] Building partly on an illustration of simple, voluntary cooperation between strangers to achieve the desired end of crossing a bridge with enough passengers to drive in the fast, no toll lane, he suggested that everyone does natural law as everyone speaks prose.[87] But, if this is so, we are left to ask what the distinctive natural law tradition offers for the resolution of social problems. Much of the arguments of Wright and Murphy could be cast in terms of widely accepted values, values that a utilitarian or a liberal perfectionist[88] would also endorse. Are the *distinctive* components of natural law theory crucial? I am not sure, but I believe it is important to distinguish between (1) reasoning broadly about public problems from the standpoint of human fulfillment and common good, and (2) using the vocabulary, concepts, and modes of analysis characteristic of the particular natural law tradition. My doubts about the potential usefulness of most general natural law precepts has partially transmuted into doubts whether practical conclusions based on some of these precepts *need* the precepts or could be equally well grounded in other approaches.

As the last paragraphs indicate, on one general moral issue natural lawyers line up with utilitarians and those who think society should promote human autonomy above all. Adherents of all these positions think that moral conclusions relevant for political and legal choice should start with ideas of human fulfillment and common good. They are opposed to the view that the morality relevant for government and law rests primarily on ideas of moral rights. I do not address whether those who begin with human fulfillment and common good have the better of the argument against those who start with moral rights, if one can put

---

[83]  *See, e.g.,* THE CATHOLIC CASE FOR CONTRACEPTION (Daniel Callahan ed., 1969).

[84]  *See* R. George Wright, *Welfare, in* NATURAL LAW, *supra* note 5, at 280.

[85]  *See* JAMES BERNARD MURPHY, THE MORAL ECONOMY OF LABOR: ARISTOTELIAN THEMES IN ECONOMIC THEORY 4 (1993); James Bernard Murphy, *A Natural Law of Human Labor*, 39 AM. J. JURIS. 71 (1994).

[86]  *See* John T. Noonan, Jr., *The Natural Law Banner, in* NATURAL LAW, *supra* note 5, at 380.

[87]  *See id.* at 380–81.

[88]  By a liberal perfectionist, I mean broadly a liberal whose moral philosophy is built on some idea of human fulfillment, not on ideas of "right" that are detached from specific conclusions about good. *See* JOHN STUART MILL, ON LIBERTY (1859); JOSEPH RAZ, THE MORALITY OF FREEDOM (1986).

the issue so crudely.[89] I am interested in whether the more distinctive approaches of the natural law tradition are persuasive.

On some issues, the distinctive natural law tradition adopts approaches and conclusions that are not generally shared. In contemporary public life, abortion, assisted suicide, and homosexual relations are sharply contested subjects. Natural lawyers often write as if the general tenor of modern permissiveness in law is a baleful commentary on the state of contemporary society, and that we are quickly moving toward a culture of narcissism and death that substitutes selfish satisfaction of preference for human good. It is with the reasoning and conclusions about such issues in mind that I want to examine the claims of universality that natural lawyers typically make.

### B. *The Challenge of Historicism and Cultural Relativism*

Three of the vital premises of natural law theory—that human nature is universal, that human purposes or goods are discoverable by reason, and that moral principles are objective and discoverable by reason—are sharply challenged by varieties of historicism and cultural relativism. We are the people we are, so the challenge goes, because we are members of a particular culture. Our concepts of understanding, and what we take as good reasons, as well as our more specific moral beliefs, are the products of that culture. There is no universal human nature, no transcultural reason, no objective moral perspective. The notion of a fundamental human reason that can discern moral principles is a delusion, one of the culturally bound premises of traditional Western society.

In its most radical form, the challenge asserts that many moral questions do not have correct answers. A less radical version does not attack the idea of correct answers but doubts both that these answers will reach across cultures and that they can be discovered by cross-cultural reason. I am primarily interested in the less radical version. That is, I do not mean to dispute the idea that moral questions do have correct answers.

Even in the less radical version, the challenge to universality attacks some of the basic premises of traditional natural law theory. I believe that the real issue about universality is not either/or, but more or less.

Is there a universal human nature? Anthropologists tell us how different mainstream modern Americans are from people who have lived in various parts of the globe across the ages of history; but all people want food, a sense of well being, and companionship. Some human characteristics are universal, but much is culture-dependent. The same is true about human reason; to a substantial degree our sense of what is reasonable depends on our culture *and* our particular place within it.

If some human goods are universal, the understandings of those goods and their orderings in context are different. Natural lawyers, of course, acknowledge that individuals order goods in various ways in developing the best life for themselves and that different cultures also have different orderings.[90] If these variations concerned *only* the lives individuals choose for themselves, they might pose little problem for natural law theory; but the variations also concern what people regard as appropriate interferences with others and as appropriate laws. To some extent, the moral principles in which people believe are relative to culture.

---

[89] Finnis challenges Rawls's reliance on a "thin theory of the good" to build political rights. FINNIS, *supra* note 76, at 105–06, 108–09.

[90] *See* FINNIS, *supra* note 76, at 117: *see also* JOHN FINNIS, FUNDAMENTALS OF ETHICS 91 (1983).

### C. Are Cultural Variations in Social Morality Consonant with Universal, Objective Moral Answers?

Where does this leave us? Cultural variations certainly do not rule out the possibility of objectively determinable, universally valid, moral judgments,[91] but they do raise a problem. To see just what the problem is, we need to distinguish between what I shall call fundamentals and non-fundamentals.

Natural lawyers can comfortably concede that, on some non-fundamentals, both social institutions and moral opinion may appropriately differ across cultures. Most obviously, matters that might require legal enforcement in some societies may be handled well enough by conscience and social morality in others. Exactly when to use the coercive apparatus of positive law is a question of prudence. More importantly, as James Stoner has pointed out, the genuine achievement of basic human goods can be accomplished by variant structures of rights and duties, and the best structures may depend partly on stages of economic growth.[92] For example, we should expect the rights and duties connected with the ownership of private property to vary at different stages of economic development.[93] Thus, a natural law approach is hardly rigid and static in its implications for legal orders. Since many people's moral sense about these matters will be influenced by legal provisions and by other aspects of the social environment, that moral sense will also vary among cultures. We should not expect members of a small tribe of Native Americans in 1650 to have had the same idea about *moral rights* to property as modern Americans. The theorist who stands back and reviews the rich variety of cultures may be able to see that no single moral attitude toward private property is universally correct, but few ordinary members of a culture will achieve that detached perspective. With an adequate degree of complexity, a natural law theorist may handle variations in moral attitude about non-fundamentals.

More serious difficulties arise with moral conclusions that natural lawyers assert are universally valid. For natural lawyers, these include a great many highly specific moral judgments, including, for example, the wrongness of abortion and suicide, even in extreme circumstances. Cultural variations, as we observe them, show that even on many significant and fundamental moral questions, people of ordinary goodwill in different cultures do not take the same view. No doubt, people everywhere believe that murder of other full members of the community is wrong, but that hardly helps settle difficult moral questions. On reflection, we can see that universal human reactions cannot directly settle difficult moral questions; because when reactions are uniform, questions are not regarded as difficult.

Modern natural lawyers are well aware that controversial issues divide people. Their arguments for their own views do not depend on these attracting anything like unanimous acceptance. In a passage responding to misconceptions of natural law theory, Finnis says that, although Aquinas thought any sane person could recognize basic goods of human existence, even the most elementary moral implications of first principles could be distorted for individuals and whole cultures by "prejudice, oversight, convention, [and] the sway of desire," and that

---

[91] Finnis has said, "A genuine requirement of practical reasonableness is not the less a part of natural law (to use the classical phrase) just because it is not universally recognized or is actively disputed." FINNIS, *supra* note 76, at 31.

[92] *See* James R. Stoner, Jr., *Property, the Common Law, and John Locke, in* NATURAL LAW, *supra* note 5, at 193, 193–218.

[93] Finnis says cautiously, "The good of personal autonomy in community ... suggests that the opportunity of exercising some form of private ownership, including of means of production, is in most times and places a requirement of justice." FINNIS, *supra* note 76, at 169.

"many moral questions . . . can only be rightly answered by someone who is wise, and who considers them searchingly."[94]

What difficulties, if any, do cultural variations pose for natural law theory? As *more* about social morality is seen as culturally dependent, a higher percentage of moral questions will be seen as troublesome, at least if one tries to think in cross-cultural terms. For example, someone confident that monogamy is best for human beings in general might hesitate upon learning about apparently healthy cultures with polygamy.[95] The presence of many troublesome moral problems is *a* difficulty, but by no means the greatest.

Cultural variations may cast doubt on the very processes by which natural lawyers move from premises to conclusions. Very roughly, we can think of arguments by natural law theorists as beginning from initial premises that have a very strong claim to acceptance, such as that life and friendship are inherent human goods. These premises are usually supported by broad, cross-cultural acceptance (though perhaps not in the conceptual formulation given them by natural law theory). From the premises, a careful process of reasoning yields conclusions that are much more controversial. This process of reasoning carefully from powerful premises may be defended as the basis for a belief in answers to moral questions that are universal, objective, and discoverable by reason. Thus, even when slavery remained widely accepted, one might have begun from a compelling and broadly shared view about human beings to show that it was morally wrong. How could people make the moral mistake of accepting slavery? They might somehow not recognize that certain groups of people are full human beings, a factual mistake about the fundamental characteristics of the people made slaves. Or they might mistakenly suppose that moral respect extends only to an "in group," whereas reason can somehow establish that we owe respect to all people. Or they might reach a conclusion about what victory in war entails that reason can show to be faulty. In any event, refined reason might build on basic judgments to reach conclusions that are not universally shared. A more modern example of a controversial judgment is a rejection of all forms of suicide and assisted suicide, built on premises that life is of great value, and that one should not act intentionally against such values.

Despite the rejection in some cultures of specific conclusions reached by natural lawyers, these conclusions, supported by reason from indisputable premises, could have universal force. But a serious problem remains with the claims of reason itself. May not the reasoning employed by natural lawyers rest on categories and methods of thought that themselves are culture-dependent? I put this question to the side for the moment, but I shall return to it after addressing three specific moral conclusions of natural law theorists.

### D. Is the Reasoning of Traditional Natural Law Too Abstract and Categorical?

In this Part, I shift from focus on cultural variations to a more direct critique of the process of reasoning in which natural lawyers commonly engage. This critique is more suggestive than systematic. It is not meant to resolve the three moral problems I address, much less make conclusive arguments in favor of some different way of proceeding across a broad range of moral issues. For two of the problems, I draw from personal experience, partly to exemplify a different way of reasoning about moral issues than one is likely to find in discussions by natural lawyers. Once my truncated critique from within a single society is complete. I connect my general conclusions to the broader theme of cultural variation.

---

[94] FINNIS, *supra* note 76, at 30 (footnote omitted).
[95] Of course, if one became persuaded that monogamy was "non-fundamental," one might accommodate it in the manner that one might accommodate various views about the range of property rights.

### 1. The Rule Against Intentionally Taking Innocent Life

According to virtually all of those who have adopted a traditional natural law position, one should not intentionally take innocent human life. As a basic moral principle, this has wide appeal, but what I want to examine is the absoluteness with which it is held. Suppose a unit of an invading army approaches a town that has surrendered and is offering no armed resistance. The captain, bearing a personal grudge against the mayor, plans to destroy the town's 5000 inhabitants, including the mayor. A lieutenant, Lief, is horrified and warns the captain he will be committing a terrible war crime if he goes ahead. The captain tells Lief, of whom he is fond, that if Lief kills the mayor and brings her body to him, he will spare the other residents. Lief, having seen the captain do similar things, has no doubt the captain will obliterate the town if he fails to act. The unit is cut off from radio contact with all higher military personnel. Lief is not in a position to kill the captain. What should he do?

The position of Finnis and most other natural lawyers is clear; Lief should not kill the mayor. It helps to place this position within Finnis's broader claims in *Natural Law and Natural Rights*. Forgoing reliance on speculative principles, facts, or a teleological conception of nature, Finnis asserts that the intrinsic goodness of certain things will be perceived as self-evident by humans with social experience.[96] He names knowledge, life, play, aesthetic experience, sociability (friendship), practical reasonableness, and "religion" (taken in a broad sense).[97] Among the standards of practical reasonableness, the standards by which participation in the other values is intelligently fulfilled, are a stricture against arbitrary preferences amongst persons, requirements of respect for basic values, and promotion of the common good.[98]

Beginning with the premise that his seven basic values are not reducible to each other, Finnis moves to the proposition that they are not commensurable.[99] The incommensurability of basic values shows the indefensibility, indeed the senselessness, of consequentialism. The implausibility of consequentialism helps us to see the self-evidence of the position that one should never act directly against a basic value. One formulation of this requirement of practical reasonableness is that "one should not choose to do any act which *of itself does nothing* but damage or impede a realization or participation of any one or more of the basic forms of human good."[1]

I confess to difficulties with the notion that attempting to engage in computations when basic values are in conflict is not only impossible but senseless.[2] Not only do individuals make such choices between values, something Finnis readily acknowledges, on some occasions a particular choice is morally required. If someone must choose between having a few people suffer a modest deprivation of aesthetic experience or having an innocent person lose his life, she should choose the deprivation of aesthetic experience. On a day a small museum is closed, ten foreign visitors who will fly back to Asia that evening are admitted. A man who has just been denied admission suffers museum deprivation rage, produces a gun, and says he will shoot the museum guard immediately unless the ten visitors are put out. The manager should deprive the visitors of aesthetic experience in order to save the guard's life.

We need not pause over problems including *different values*, because Lief's dilemma does not raise those problems. The only value at stake for him is life. He

---

[96] *See* FINNIS, *supra* note 76, at 85.
[97] *See id.* at 86–90.
[98] *See id.* at 106–07.
[99] *See id.* at 112.
[1] *Id.* at 118.
[2] *See* FINNIS, *Fundamentals of Ethics*, at 87–92.

can save 4999 lives by taking one, and that life, along with the 4999, will be lost if he does not act. Those who adopt the absolute position that taking an innocent life can never be morally justified do not doubt that a person saving lives in a rescue operation should save 4999 rather than one, if a choice is required. So the wrongness of taking innocent life is not commonly thought to rest on any radical skepticism about the relevance of numbers.[3] Rather, intentionally killing a person is barred by the principle that one can never act against a basic value. It is permitted to perform acts that will have the certain consequence of killing innocent people,[4] but one cannot act for that purpose, even if the accomplishment of the purpose is to serve a greater good. (In Lief's case he would aim to kill the mayor, in order to save other lives.)

Someone might defend the absolute principle that requires Lief to stay his hand in various ways. One might talk about the harmful long-term consequences of admitting any exceptions, or defend a religious conception under which we should comply with God's injunction against the intentional taking of innocent life, and rely on God's providence when we contemplate the awful consequences to follow. But Finnis does not make a consequentialist argument, and he asserts that natural law principles can be defended without reference to God. This leaves, as possible supports for the absolute position, the incommensurability of basic values and the idea that one should not choose against a basic good.[5] Whatever the incommensurability of values may plausibly entail, it does not provide support for the absolute position here.

The notion that one should not choose against a basic good is related to the idea that people should not be used as mere means.[6] Killing the mayor would be to use her as a means to the good end of saving others. Our museum example tests the proposition that people should *never* be used as mere means; is not the exclusion of the foreign visitors from the museum a mere means to save the life of the guard? Shifting to the idea that people should not be used as means from the idea that no one should choose against a basic value does not make the absolute principle more compelling.

The absoluteness of the principle seems particularly vulnerable when we focus on the borderlines of its coverage—borderlines of intentions, action, and innocence.[7] The principle relies on a critical distinction between intended and merely

---

[3] *See, e.g.*, Germain Grisez, *Against Consequentialism*, 23 Am. J. Juris 21, 51 (1978).

[4] According to the so-called principle of "double effect," an act that predictably causes the loss of innocent life may be warranted if the actor's intention is good, and there are proportionately grave reasons for allowing the evil to occur. Thus, an engineer may divert a flood to save a town although she knows that the inhabitants of a farm will be killed. Similarly, fliers may bomb military targets, if their aim is to attack those targets, though it is certain some civilians will die. (For these purposes, enemy *soldiers* do not count as innocents.)

[5] For some situations, there is an argument that one should not yield to extortion. That argument may bear on the museum hypothetical because the enraged gunman is extorting behavior from the manager, but it hardly bears on Lief's dilemma since the captain is quite content to destroy the entire town, and is only hesitating in order to do Lief a favor. Another argument is that, if one participates in wrong, one compromises one's identity and dirties one's hands, but this hardly seems decisive if many lives are at stake.

[6] *See* Germain Grisez, Abortion: The Myth, the Realities. and the Arguments 319 (1970). Finnis refers to the saying that "the end does not justify the means" and to Kant's principle to treat humanity "always as an end and never as a means only." Finnis, *supra* note 1, at 122 (quoting Immanuel Kant, Foundations of the Metaphysics of Morals., 1963.

[7] One might resist this conclusion in various ways, and Finnis acknowledges the complexities in how one decides what counts as a single act and how to describe the act. *See* Finnis, *supra* note 76, at 122–23; John Finnis, *Intention and Side-Effects, in* Liability and Responsibility 32, 56–61 (R.G. Frey & Christopher W. Morris eds., 1991).

foreseen results. Could we say that Lief does not "intend" the mayor's death if Lief would be delighted if somehow the mayor survived being shot through the heart and appearing dead to the captain?[8] If the principle condemns action, not a failure to act,[9] can it matter whether someone's choice is to flick a switch that will kill or refrain from flicking a switch that will save? As far as innocence is concerned, may someone kill (in self-defense) a small child unwittingly advancing with a bomb, when killing the child is the only way to prevent the bomb from killing oneself?

Let me be clear that I believe both that these concepts of intention, action, and non-innocence matter for moral appraisal of acts, and that we need to worry about how to define their borders. But the delicateness and contestability of these borders give us reason to doubt whether these distinctions can support absolute moral norms that condemn every instance of conduct that falls on the "wrong side" of the borders.

In summary, the absolutist approach of Finnis and most other natural law theorists seems unfaithful to the complexities of moral choice, and to be more abstract and categorical than the circumstances of life justify.

## 2. The Wrongness of Homosexual Acts

Finnis, and most other theorists in the natural law tradition, have claimed that sexual acts between persons of the same sex are morally defective. In discussing this problem, I am interested in that basic moral judgment, rather than whatever conclusions one might draw about criminal penalties or benefits for same-sex couples or same-sex marriage. In respect to the moral judgment, my special concern is the manner in which one reasons to the judgment, rather than the judgment itself. Others have discussed the subject extensively, and I do not undertake a thorough exploration of all the relevant arguments.

In his reasoning about sexual acts, Finnis does not follow most older writers in the natural law tradition.[10] They claimed that homosexual acts, as well as artificial contraception, frustrated the natural purposes, or teleology, of sexual acts and sexual organs.[11] According to Finnis,

> The union of the reproductive organs of husband and wife really unites them biologically (and their biological reality is part of, not merely an instrument of, their *personal* reality); reproduction is one function and so, in respect of that function, the spouses are indeed one reality, and their sexual union therefore can *actualize* and allow them to *experience* their *real common good—their marriage* with the two goods, parenthood and friendship.[12]

---

[8] See Finnis, *supra* note 2, at 54–61, for a discussion that bears on whether that claim about intent would be reasonable.

[9] Even if one cannot act to hasten the death of someone suffering a painful terminal illness, some people believe one can refuse extraordinary measures of care for a similar motive. Finnis rejects this position. *See* John Finnis. *A Philosophical Case Against Euthanasia, in* EUTHANASIA EXAMINED: ETHICAL, CLINICAL AND LEGAL PERSPECTIVES 23, 28 (J. Keown ed., 1995). The widely discussed variations on "the trolley problem" raise issues about action and inaction. *See* 2 FRANCES M. KAMM, MORALITY, MORTALITY: RIGHTS, DUTIES, AND STATUS 144–267 (1996): *see also* Judith Jarvis Thomson, *The Trolley Problem*, 94 YALE L.J. 1395 (1985).

[10] *See* Paul J. Weithman, *A Propos of Professor Perry: A Plea for Philosophy in Sexual Ethics*, 9 NOTRE DAME J.L. ETHICS & PUB. POL'Y 75, 78–79 (1995).

[11] Finnis says that he does not mean to "seek to infer normative conclusions or theses from non-normative (natural-fact) premises." John M. Finnis, *Law, Morality, and "Sexual Orientation*," 69 NOTRE DAME L. REV. 1049, 1068 (1990).

[12] *Id.* at 1066.

Friends who are incapable of marriage (this includes all couples of the same gender) cannot become a "biological unit" through their sexual acts, so these acts "cannot do what they may hope and imagine."[13] Because they cannot experience "the *marital* good" through their sexual acts, these acts "can do no more than provide each partner with an individual gratification."[14] They are treating their bodies as instruments for their own experience; "their choice to engage in such conduct thus dis-integrates each of them precisely as acting persons."[15] "The attempt to express affection by orgasmic non-marital sex [is] the pursuit of an illusion."[16]

Finnis's basic line is not between all heterosexual acts and all homosexual acts; it is not between all genital intercourse between men and women and all other sexual acts arousing orgasm; and it is not between sexual acts capable of reproduction and all sexual acts not capable of reproduction. On the "good" side of the line are standard sexual acts between committed married partners, even though they know that reproduction is impossible (because of various physical factors) or extremely unlikely. On the "bad" side of the line are orgasmic acts by married couples achieved by other than genital intercourse, genital intercourse with artificial contraceptives, and, apparently, all heterosexual intercourse outside of marriage, even by couples who are engaged and will shortly be married.

I have compressed an argument of Finnis's that is already compressed. In trying to reconstruct the argument, Paul Weithman breaks it down into forty-six separate explicit or implicit claims.[17] But it is fair to say that the argument can be taken as one about the inherent nature of acts or about the experience of those who participate in the acts, or both. Suppose a man says he can fly, and further claims that he has been flying when observers have seen him firmly rested on the ground. If he says he has had the experience *of flying*, we can conclude that he has not actually experienced flying, however close his experiences may be to those of beings actually capable of flight. Suppose, instead, in some distant time when we can communicate minimally with dolphins, a superior human swimmer says his experiences are like those of a dolphin. This claim is about the quality of lived experience, and one could evaluate the truth of the claim only by comparing the quality of the person's subjective experiences with those of dolphins.

If Finnis's argument is essentially about the inherent quality of various acts and does not depend on the qualities of lived experience, it is immune to evidence from that experience. In that event, the argument does not seem so different from more standard teleological arguments. Persons of the same gender, incapable of reproductive acts, cannot participate in a marital common good; they can participate in the good of friendship but that alone does not include sexual acts. So put, the argument seems highly abstract and categorical, and many will wonder why intercourse with artificial contraception is radically different from intercourse when one is certain that physical impairment renders procreation impossible.

Suppose we take Finnis as making a claim about lived experience that, at least in theory, can be confirmed or rebutted by reference to that experience. If his fundamental distinction was between heterosexual and homosexual acts, most people would have a fundamental difficulty in evaluating the claim; they would have to evaluate their own experience against the described experience of others with different sexual inclinations. A heterosexual who experienced the union possible in genital intercourse might doubt that those involved in homosexual acts could have quite that experience, even if they said that they did. But Finnis seems

[13] *Id.*
[14] *Id.*
[15] *Id.* at 1067.
[16] *Id.* at 1065.
[17] *See* Weithman, *supra* note 10, at 89–92.

to make things easier for the high proportion of his readership who have been married and have at one time or another engaged in intercourse in marriage with a substantial possibility of procreation, intercourse with artificial contraceptives, and intercourse in which physical factors will prevent procreation.

My own experience, which has to be *my* starting point, is that intercourse within marriage does have an extra element when one is aware that it may produce a (wanted) child, but that the lived experience of intercourse when procreation is precluded by physical impossibility does not vary (significantly) from that when contraceptives are used. The mix of selfish satisfaction and loving care is incredibly complex in almost all sexual experiences, but the supposition that a distinctive good is possible for marital intercourse without contraceptives and impossible altogether for all other forms of sexual intercourse, including marital intercourse with contraceptives, is belied by my experience. The notion that all else is relegated to pursuit of one's own satisfaction is strikingly implausible.

Developing a much fuller analysis along these lines, Michael Perry concludes that "[t]he reality apprehended by many married couples who practice contraception, and by many homosexual couples, is directly contrary to the reality postulated by John Finnis."[18] Responding to Finnis's claim that many people may suffer illusions about the quality of their sexual experiences, Perry wonders why Finnis himself is under the illusions that he is under.[19]

I am especially interested in a response by Paul Weithman to Perry's rebuttal of Finnis. Professor Weithman is a Roman Catholic, natural law philosopher who disagrees with Finnis's basic thesis, but who also suggests that Perry's challenge is not compelling.[20] Contending that Perry does not provide a sound argument that the experiences on which he relies are veridical, Weithman says that Finnis has a sophisticated sense of the ways in which fantasy and illusion can affect human sexuality.[21] Finnis, Weithman proposes, can accept what Perry claims descriptively and still maintain his fundamental thesis, though Weithman himself does not believe that deliberate contraceptive sex should be assimilated to homosexual activity.[22]

To some degree, Weithman's quarrel with Perry seems to be over the extent to which we can rely on experience to reach moral conclusions. No doubt, the vast majority of the population could be under, an illusion, and a plausible theory of why that might be so should make us more likely to think that most people suffer in this way than if no such theory were available. But it is also true that coherent theories that have seemed convincing at one time appear to be shot with error, even ridiculous, at a later time. As moral agents, we must choose between the weight to give to theory and the weight to give to experience when the two seem to conflict. Finnis does emphasize that ethical judgment depends on experience,[23] but Finnis, and Weithman, in accord with traditional natural law approaches, give a high place to theory. Perry, in this instance reflecting a more Protestant approach to moral judgment, emphasizes lived experience. In this division, I side with Perry.

Another point about experience is important here. Finnis, in calling homosexual acts "unacceptable,"[24] strongly implies that persons of dominant homosexual inclinations should remain celibate rather than engage in homosexual

[18] Michael J. Perry. *The Morality of Homosexual Conduct: A Response to John Finnis*, 9 NOTRE DAME J.L. ETHICS & PUB. POL'Y 41, 59 (1995).

[19] *See id.* at 59–61.

[20] *See* Weithman, *supra* note 10, at 75. Weithman considers Finnis's arguments more fully in his contribution to *Sex, Preference, and Family. See* Paul J. Weithman, *Natural Law, Morality and Sexual Complementarity, in* SEX, PREFERENCE AND FAMILY 227 (David M. Estlund & M. Nussbaum eds., 1997).

[21] *See* Weithman, *supra* note 10, at 80–82.

[22] *See id.* at 88.

[23] *See* FINNIS, *supra* note 76, at 101.

[24] Finnis, *supra* note 11, at 1064.

intercourse. Robert George, whose views about these acts substantially accord with those of Finnis, is more explicit.[25]

George talks of "the basic good of marriage itself as a two-in-one flesh communion of persons"[26] that is consummated and actualized by acts of the reproductive type. Only such sexual acts can be "truly unitive."[27] Other sexual acts fail to accomplish this basic good and are immoral. Acknowledging that two to five percent of the population may be strongly inclined from birth to desire homosexual unions.[28] George says that the moral course of action for them, as for non-married heterosexuals, is to remain celibate.[29]

In my own life, love in marriage has had a transforming power; it, and the children of marital union, have been the two greatest blessings of my life. My experience tells me that to consign to permanent celibacy many persons who are not called to such a life by devotion or inclination is to insist that they should deprive themselves of one of the richest sources of human affection and understanding. This substantive position, though not the intentions of those who defend it, strikes me as harsh, even cruel. Even if one could plausibly defend the proposition that, all in all, heterosexual relations with genital union can be more enriching than homosexual relations, it certainly would not follow that the latter are morally defective, to be avoided by responsible people with strong homosexual inclinations.

### 3. Suicide and Assisted Suicide

My third example is the problem of suicide and assisted suicide. I should perhaps start here by saying that I thought *Roe v. Wade*[30] was wrongly decided; that I have not expected a constitutional right to commit suicide, much less to be assisted in the effort, in my lifetime; that I do not favor a general legal right to commit suicide and would be troubled if I were a legislator considering a limited right of the terminally ill to have assistance in dying. Further, I am uncertain whether suicide and assistance toward that end are ever morally justified.

What I want to highlight is a certain form of categorical argument about this problem.[31] In a paper on the subject, David Novak hardly acknowledges the nearly unbearable pain that some persons suffer as they slowly die.[32] He remarks,

> Of course, now such a suicidal course of action is only advocated for those who are "terminal." But if death is our inevitable lot in the world into which we have been cast, then who is terminal and who is not can only be a matter of inherently imprecise degree, not one of essential kind.[33]

Novak, no doubt, has a valid philosophical point about "degree," but the sentence in which the point is made asks me to deny what life has taught me. The

---

[25] *See* Robert P. George, *Nature, Morality, and Homosexuality, in* NATURAL LAW, *supra* note 11, at 29, 38.

[26] *Id.* at 36.

[27] *Id.*

[28] *See id.* at 29.

[29] *See id* at 38.

[30] 410 U.S. 113 (1973).

[31] Finnis makes a categorical argument against suicide and assisted suicide, but that argument does not include the particular formulation on which I focus. *See* Finnis, *supra* note 76.

[32] *See* David Novak, *Privacy, in* NATURAL LAW, *supra* note 11, at 13, 24. I agree with Novak that fear of lack of control has much to do with the wish of many people to "die with dignity." *Id.* at 24. Indeed, I think that graceful acceptance of dependence is a lesson that many who are dying teach us all.

[33] *Id* at 24.

two months between the discovery that my late wife Sanja had incurable cancer and her death was a time of far greater stress and intensity than I had ever experienced. Although sadness about her approaching death was never absent from my feelings, our already strong love was deepened yet more as she embraced my support, and I was moved by her incredible spirit and courage. For Sanja, suicide was never an option; she expressed her powerful will to live until she lost consciousness for the last time. This period was unlike any other in my life, and I know that was true for Sanja. Novak's implication that terminal illness is just a matter of degree seems insensitive, if not actually insulting, and remote from the lives of people who themselves are terminally ill or who have loved ones in that condition. The suggestion that, since all is a matter of degree, no exceptions from moral constraints on suicide are warranted seems not to respect the special plight of those who suffer painful terminal illness.

### 4. Lessons from the Three Moral Problems: Possible Limits of Reason

In each example I have chosen, the recommended natural law approach relies on abstract, categorical modes of thought in preference to greater emphasis on qualities of lived experience and contextual distinctions drawn from that experience.[34] I have always had a distinct distrust for highly abstract ideas, whether they come from the political left or the political right. Reflection on lived experience seems to me a better guide to moral choice than abstract categorization. Of course, one makes sense of experience by abstracting and categorizing, but there is a difference between top-down and bottom-up thinking, and experience can be given more or less weight if it seems to conflict with abstract arguments. When Finnis writes, "[r]eality is known in judgment, not in emotion,"[35] he implicitly assigns emotional response a less significant place than I would give it.

What has this particular challenge to common forms of natural law reasoning to do with the problem of cultural variations? Most straightforwardly, I am objecting to a certain approach to moral reasoning and proposing a preferable alternative. This critique assumes that we have sounder and less sound ways to reason about moral matters, and that an approach in which experience receives greater weight is sounder than highly abstract, categorical analysis. Since I am located within the same broad culture as the natural lawyers with whom I disagree, my claims about the three moral issues I discuss are not directly about cultural variations.

Here are the crucial connections. Whether people are attracted more to abstract principles or to contextual evaluation of experience itself depends significantly on habits of mind and personal psychology. Perhaps it is my Protestant upbringing or some deep-seated intellectual skepticism that influences my resistance to abstract theory. In one sense, all each of us can do is to pay attention to a wide range of positions, to reason as best we can, and to adopt and defend the positions that seem to us most persuasive, with the humility that we may be mistaken. But we should be aware of the possibility that the reasoning of actual human beings, limited as we are, may not resolve which among certain plausible approaches to moral reasoning is the most sound. If such differences exist within single cultural traditions, we can expect yet greater differences if our reference point shifts to a broad range of human cultures. If the abstract, categorical

---

[34] In relation to the widely cited and widely attacked thesis that women, in general, and men, in general, adopt different approaches to moral problems, *see generally* CAROL GILLIGAN, IN A DIFFERENT VOICE: PSYCHOLOGICAL THEORY AND WOMEN'S DEVELOPMENT (1982), we can easily place traditional natural law theorizing far on the male side of the spectrum.

[35] Finnis, *supra* note 11, at 1067.

approaches of traditional natural lawyers seem closely connected to *one particular strand* of the wide culture of Western Europe, they will seem even less universal from a transcultural perspective.

I am not claiming that the positions taken by members of one culture are unintelligble to members of another culture who try to understand them. Some level of mutual intelligibility exists among those who disagree about what is morally right. My claim is that we may have no transcultural method of eva-luation of the strength of competing assessments.

In sum, my theoretical point is this—we do not have an evidently correct, universal form of moral reason that can build an imposing edifice of moral norms on the basis of simple, compelling, widely-shared judgments about human goods and moral obligations. Our processes of moral reasoning no more escape cultural dependence than do particular moral judgments that are outside some shared universal core.

How may natural lawyers respond to this pervasive concern about whether the answers to moral questions are objective, universal, and discoverable by reason?

## E. Natural Law Theory as the Best System Yet Developed?

Natural lawyers may acknowledge that, over some range, different cultures make different moral judgments and employ different forms of moral reason; but they may further claim that the system of reason and judgments represented by the natural law tradition is indeed the best, or the best yet developed by human understanding. A theorist might combine such a view with belief in a certain kind of moral progress—namely, that thoughtful people of goodwill can make more accurate moral appraisals as human civilization develops[36] The forms of reason employed by most natural lawyers may be both culture dependent to a degree *and* the best available.

Such an account can save the crucial claims of universality and objectivity, but it carries a certain cost. Natural lawyers could not reasonably suppose that all their moral norms should seem valid to thoughtful, reasonable people in all cultures. Suppose a moral conclusion rests significantly on a kind of moral rea-soning that is not characteristic in another culture. Members of that culture will think the norm is valid only if they can be persuaded to exchange their dominant forms of moral reasoning for the approach of natural lawyers. Since we are here supposing that a particular type of Western reasoning about morality—natural law reasoning—is actually superior to other forms of moral reasoning, perhaps that persuasion could be effective. However, people of another culture may have deeply ingrained forms of reasoning that will not be easy to displace, and many people of other cultural backgrounds may simply be unable to see the superiority of natural law reasoning.[37] that leads to specific moral norms at variance with those of their culture. In any event, many people of goodwill in other cultures will remain unpersuaded by natural law reasoning

Another difficulty, one I have already mentioned, is still more fundamental. If forms of moral reasoning differ in crucial ways, how can natural lawyers be confident their forms are best? They may believe their approaches are self-evi-dently right,[38] but if others on reflection do not find them to be so, there is an impasse. Natural lawyers might rely on critical standards of evaluation that transcend cultures. They might claim, for example, that natural law reasoning and

---

[36] This particular version of the idea of moral progress may be able to explain the increasing rejection of slavery without being refuted by horrors like the Holocaust.

[37] Scientific reasoning may be different from moral and social evaluation in this respect. Scientific successes may give some approaches a very strong appeal across cultures.

[38] I mean "self-evident" in the sense that Finnis uses about intrinsic good. *See* FINNIS, *supra* note 76, at 70. A truth is self-evident if it does not derive from some other proposition; it can be self-evident without being obvious or undisputed.

conclusions, if followed, yield lives that are recognized by all as more fulfilling than the lives lived according to the conclusions of other approaches. Unfortunately, it seems much more likely that forms of reasoning within cultures fit fairly well the ideas of human fulfillment within those cultures. Observance of moral norms asserted by natural lawyers will lead to lives that proponents of natural law find fulfilling; observance of the norms yielded by other approaches will lead to lives that are fulfilling judged by the standards of those cultures. Lack of agreement on what lives are fulfilling does not rule out the possibility that some ways of life are *really* the most fulfilling *and* that some disputed moral norms are *really* best; but establishing this by reason will be difficult, to the extent that reason itself is culture bound.

## F. Use for Intracultural Evaluation

A natural lawyer might make a significant retreat, believing in a kind of natural law for a particular culture, and claiming that if one begins with the premises of one's own culture, a single answer to any moral question will be correct. What counts as a single culture could be troublesome. For some issues of international commercial practice and human rights, the relevant culture might be the modern international community; for other issues "a culture" might be conceived much more narrowly. If natural lawyers lowered their sights to this degree, they would still have to face the worry that internal conflicts or contradictions in values within a culture might preclude uniquely correct moral answers. But the main problem with this idea of intracultural natural law is that it surrenders a central aspect of natural law theories, as well as natural rights theories: their claim to universality. One aspect of this surrender would be the loss of a basis to claim that the dominant values of a culture are misconceived.

## G. Religious Premises

Natural lawyers may invoke religious premises to support their claim to universality and to deflect the argument that practical reason is culture dependent. Even if practical reason seems to depend on culture, perhaps a Higher Spirit exists who loves us and to whom moral standards and ways of reasoning are connected.[39] Finnis has maintained that his claims about natural law are persuasive independent of claims about God,[40] but some natural lawyers think that religious conviction plays a more central role than it does in Finnis's exposition. One's attachment to valid religious belief may be thought to establish that objective moral standards do exist and to underlie one's confidence about specific standards.[41] A natural lawyer who relies significantly on religious premises can retain the claim to universal objective moral standards, but he cannot expect all reasonable people of goodwill to accept those standards, unless his religious beliefs include the idea that God gives everyone the reasoning power to ascertain the validity of true moral norms.

An approach that relies on religious conviction faces another obstacle. Why should we suppose that religious perception are any less culture dependent than moral understandings? Someone who began without any religious commitment would conclude that religious perspectives are at least as culture dependent as moral perspectives, to which they are intimately tied. Nevertheless, the believer

---

[39]  I put the point in this way to avoid the question of what exactly is the relation between God and moral standards. Two possibilities are that God establishes moral standards and that moral standards exist independent of God, but God perfectly perceives those standards and encourages human beings to live by them.

[40]  *See* FINNIS, *supra* note 76, at 48–49.

[41]  *See* Novak, *supra* note 32, at 21–22 (arguing forcefully that ideas of natural law are much more deeply rooted in religion than has commonly been recognized).

may suppose, based on faith or on overwhelming evidence of some kind, that the core of his convictions is reliably true. Once this is granted, he may think that moral understandings tied to the convictions in various ways are either true to a high degree of certainty or at least are more likely to be true than moral understandings developed in some other way.

A Christian believer in natural law may think that detailed moral norms that have been developed in the Christian natural law tradition (especially the Roman Catholic tradition) are reliable partly because they, and the forms of reasoning that lead to them, have the authority of the tradition. Religious persons who are skeptical about the unique validity of their own tradition may conclude that religious truth helps bolster belief in universal moral truths, but they will have less confidence about the soundness of their particular religious understandings and about whatever moral insights flow from those understandings.

## H. Norms That Vary by Culture

I want now to develop a bit more extensively a possibility I suggested earlier in the Article, exploring a rather different set of assumptions about basic premises and detailed conclusions than one commonly sees in natural law writing. One might think that certain, minimum, basic moral premises can be established, but that their proper application may vary widely among cultures. One might conclude, for example, that human beings should count equally and should care for each other's welfare. In some cultural settings, these basic premises might properly yield a "rights" focused morality; in other cultural settings, informal mutual care might predominate. One could then believe in a universal, objective standard for morality, but one whose best application varies significantly.[103] That is, even the best set of specific *moral norms* might vary significantly. One could acknowledge that many detailed moral conclusions might be valid only for some times and some places. To return to one of our examples, assisted suicide might be appropriate for some cultures, but not all.

As with the more detailed norms of traditional natural law theories, such a "flexible" system might be grounded on various underlying premises. One might base such a system on (1) compelling, widely-shared moral judgments about human good plus reasoned development, (2) the best reasoned understanding among culturally variant forms of reason, (3) religious convictions, or (4) some combinations of these.

A system in which desirable moral norms vary is more modest in its universal claims than the traditional natural law approach, which assigns universal validity to many specific moral norms. Belief in such a "flexible" system may seem easier to sustain. The problem of supporting basic premises remains, but the more limited these premises are, the more reasonably one can assert their transcultural validity. For example, the premise that people should care for each other is at the core of the moral understanding of many religions, and that premise is more *indisputably* enjoined by Christianity than are most highly specific norms—such as the principle of double effect or the inappropriateness of homosexual acts. A Christian may be able to move more confidently from a belief in religious truth to a belief in the validity of this basic premise than he can move to disputable, specific norms.

With what confidence could one move from some fundamental premise to more specific norms for particular cultures? We are generally better able to assess our own culture than other cultures. We are more familiar with the social conditions of our own culture, and its dominant forms of reasoning are more likely to reflect how broad principles can best be worked out in that culture than in other cultures.

This does not mean we are foreclosed from all assessments of other cultures or that we need accept all the basic premises of our own. We may see plainly that another culture does not treat people equally or even that some of its members are regarded as mere objects. We should not adopt without examination the dominant forms of reasoning in our own culture. Feminists and critical race theorists, for example, have argued that forms of reason in our culture tend to thwart genuine equality. Any assessment of how well fundamental moral premises are achieved in context needs to approach our own cultural reasoning, as well as our specific cultural norms, with a critical eye.

## Conclusion

My own views lie along the lines of belief in certain fundamental moral perspectives that are universally valid, with appropriately different manifestations in different cultures; and my belief in the truth of these views rests on a mix of ordinary reason and religious conviction.

I have focused on difficulties in the relation between natural law approaches and different approaches in other cultures. I claim that these difficulties are exhibited to a degree in disagreements between natural lawyers and proponents of competing approaches within our own culture. Offering a challenge from the inside to approaches that are too abstract and categorical and detached from human experience, I have turned to the problem of other cultures. The claim that disagreements can ultimately be resolved (at least in theory) on the basis of a common reason seems most vulnerable as to them.

I should emphasize that natural law reasoning and conclusions, not the least those of Finnis, have an important place in our society, even if skepticism is warranted about assertions of universality, reason, and unique correctness. We must all make moral judgments, and natural law approaches are one fruitful source of evaluation, with a rich tradition in our culture. The value of these approaches extends to legislators and judges as well as ordinary citizens. But natural lawyers want to claim much more than this; it is these more ambitious claims to which I have responded. . . .                                              [pp. 1644–1679]

# 4

# BENTHAM, AUSTIN AND CLASSICAL ENGLISH POSITIVISM

## Sovereignty and its Origins

The modern doctrine of sovereignty derived essentially from two lines of development which heralded the end of the medieval period.[1] On the one hand there was the rise of the new national states anxious to assert their total independence in a new age of economic expansion and to reject all feudal notions of overlordship or papal interference; on the other, a departure from the medieval idea of law as being fundamentally custom, and legislation as merely a form of declaring the existence of new customs.[2] On the contrary each national territory was now recognized as constituting both a self-sufficient unit and an independent legal entity, so that the notion naturally followed that, within each such nation-state, there must be located some supreme power, the decisive feature of which was its virtually unlimited capacity to make new law. This doctrine was more than a reassertion of the earlier theory that *rex est imperator in regno suo*.[3] For it emphasised in a way that to the earlier theorists would have been unacceptable the idea of unfettered legislative capacity. The new approach was secular and positivist, and though lip-service continued to be paid to a notional subjection to overriding natural law,[4] the supporters of legal sovereignty tended increasingly to whittle down

[1] In the Middle Ages, sovereignty in the sense of unfettered power of legislation was more easily associated with the Pope than with secular rulers. For the latter were regarded not only as bound by feudal law, but also as coming within the ecclesiastical jurisdiction, whereas the Pope was regarded as outside and even above the Church. (See W. Ullman, *Principles of Government and Politics in the Middle Ages* (1961), pp. 72, 139, 150; and *A History of Political Thought in the Middle Ages* (1965), pp. 103 *et seq.*) On the transmission and persistence of medieval thought to the modern world see B. Tierney, *Religion, Law and the Growth of Constitutional Thought 1150–1650* (1982).

[2] The declaratory theory of precedent is a survival of this thinking.

[3] The maxim employed by French lawyers in the fourteenth century to resist imperial pretensions: *cf.* McIlwain, *Growth of Political Thought in the West*, p. 268; and by Henry VIII in his dispute with the Pope regarding Royal supremacy over a national Church. See J.J. Scarisbrick, *Henry VIII* (1968), pp. 267–273 and see, in particular, the preamble to the Act in Restraint of Appeals 1533: "... this realm of England is an empire ..." (*ibid.*, pp. 309–310). The growth of these ideas and their significance is traced in Q. Skinner, *The Foundations of Modern Political Thought* (2 vols., 1978).

[4] *Cf.* Bodin, *Six Books of the Republic* (ed. Tooley), p. 35. On Bodin see J. H. Franklin, *Jean Bodin and the Sixteenth-Century Revolution in The Methodology of Law and History* (1963) and Skinner, *op. cit.*, vol. 2, pp. 284–301.

natural law from a system of norms either to a mere statement of human impulses explaining the need for a sovereign power in human society, as with Hobbes, or to a mere formal category to justify a belief in inalienable sovereignty, as in Rousseau's theory of the general will.[5] But as became apparent in the writings of Hume, true empiricism really involved the rejection of natural law as a system of norms since, as Hume argued, the validity of normative rules cannot logically be treated as an objective fact, but depends on the relative viewpoint of those who apply them.[6] On the other hand, *positive* law, in the sense of the law of the state, is something ascertainable and valid without regard to subjective considerations. Hence it must be regarded as separate from morals (which were equated with natural law, if this term was still used at all), although it might correspond in many respects to current moral standards and be subject to their influence.

## Bentham and the Utilitarians[7]

Did this entail that, for the positivist, mankind was thrown upon a sea of conflicting moralities with no compass by which he might legitimately choose to follow or reject these? If natural law was dethroned, could some scientific or rational standard be found? Hume himself asserted that only utility could supply the answer,[8] but it was left to Bentham to expound in detail the significance and working of the principle of utility. Bentham, though he gave credit to Priestley as "the first who taught my lips to pronounce this sacred truth",[9] gave currency to its formulation as the principle of the greatest happiness of the greatest number, and sought to make himself the Newton of the legal and moral world by establishing the principles of an experimental science governing that sphere, much as Newton had formulated the fundamental laws of the physical world. To this end Bentham began with a savage but well-directed attack upon the traditional *clichés* of natural law and the social contract as embodied in Blackstone's complacent and uncritical panegyric on the British

---

[5] On the importance of this concept in Rousseau see J. Steinberg, *Locke, Rousseau and the Idea of Consent* (1978), Chap. 4. On Hobbes and Rousseau, see *ante*, 146, 150,

[6] But *cf. ante*, 115.

[7] See in general R. Harrison, *Bentham* (1983).

[8] See *Enquiry concerning the Principles of Morals*, Chap. V.

[9] *Works*, vol. 10, p. 142. It may in fact derive originally from Beccaria: "La massima felicità divisa nel maggior numero", as Bentham himself admitted. See W. Harrison (ed.), *A Fragment on Government*. See H. L. A. Hart, *Essays on Bentham* (1982), Chap. 2 ("Bentham and Beccaria"). Letwin comments: "It had been suggested to him by everyone, or at any rate, he attributed his inspiration to different authors—Beccaria, Helvetius, Bacon, Hume. In fact, from each of them Bentham drew only what he was looking for. He borrowed phrases but the principle of utility as he came to understand and use it was entirely his own invention" (*The Pursuit of Certainty* (1965), p. 139).

Constitution.[10] This was followed by an attempt to analyse the springs of human actions in terms of pleasures and pains, and to reduce human needs to a "calculus of felicity" where different "lots" of happiness could be weighed by certain quantitative tests, in order to ascertain what utility decreed.[11]

The somewhat crude psychology of the Utilitarians, has long been jettisoned, though the notion of utility still plays an important role in the philosophical justification of ethics.[12] Bentham, despite his occasional naïvetés, was a profound thinker, an acute social critic, and an untiring campaigner for the reform of antiquated law, and he became, and has indeed remained, one of the cardinal influences on modern society. By rejecting both natural law and subjective values and replacing these by standards based on human advantages, pleasures and satisfactions, he provided what may be, as many think, an insufficient substitute for ethics or aesthetics, but was at least a valuable signpost by which men in society might direct the external welfare of that society. Bentham himself was a believer in *laisser-faire* once the antiquated legal system had been renovated, but ironically, his emphasis on reform and social welfare has made

*ADD TO BIBLIOGRAPHY*

[10] Contained in the introduction to Blackstone's *Commentaries*. Bentham described natural rights as nonsense—"nonsense upon stilts." See "Anarchical Fallacies", *Works*, vol. 2, p. 501. Bentham's approach to natural rights is well elucidated in R. Harrison, *Bentham* (1983), Chap 4. Bentham's objection was not just to their fictitious character, "the pestilential breath of fiction" as denounced by him in "The Fragment on Government," for he also recognised the utility of fiction in the use of legal concepts such as "legal rights", where these could be analysed into and verified in terms of real entities, such as a threat of sanctions. But this process could not be applied to *natural* rights which are incapable of being analysed in terms of what actually *is*, and are no more than as assertion of what *ought* to be the case. (See especially, *op. cit.*, pp. 100–101). Also Bentham opposed entrenched, unalterable rights as a block in the path of change in the law, and therefore of reform (p. 104).

[11] See *Principles of Morals and Legislation*, Chap. 4. Hazlitt's comment is not without justice. "He turns wooden utensils in a lathe for exercise, and fancies he can turn men in the same manner" (*Spirit of the Age* (World's Classics ed.), p. 18).

[12] A modern refinement is the growth of so-called "rule-utilitarianism" whereby a *practice*, rather than an isolated incident is tested by reference to utility. Instead of asking whether hanging *this* innocent man has good consequences it asks whether the practice of hanging *the* innocent is beneficial. See D. B. Lyons, *Forms and Limits of Utilitarianism* (1965). Bentham himself may have hinted as much. (See Hart, "Bentham", 48 Proc. of Br. Acad. 297, 302–303, and in Summers, *More Essays in Legal Philosophy* (1971), pp. 16, 23–24. R. Harrison (*Bentham*, Chap. 9) argues that Bentham's spirit is that of act-utilitarianism, while adopting many of the procedures of a rule-utilitarian. Thus in working out the application of the principle of utility generally desirable criteria should sometimes yield to individual judgment (see pp. 242–243). Austin, however, apparently favoured rule-utilitarianism: see W. E. Rumble (1979) 24 Am.J.Jurisprud. 149–150. For a recent survey of pro- and anti-utilitarian theories, see Sen and Williams (eds.), *Utilitarianism and Beyond* (1982). It should be noted that the whole study of welfare economics is largely founded on utilitarian ideas (*op. cit.*, Chap. 4). See, further *post*, 620.

him one of the creators of the welfare state.[13]

Bentham was mainly interested in law reform and he distinguished what he called censorial jurisprudence, or the science of legislation, from expository jurisprudence. The latter was concerned with law as it is, without regard to its moral or immoral character. The science of legislation, however, was for him really a branch of morals, being the principles upon which men's actions were to be directed to the greatest quantity of possible happiness[14] by rules of a permanent kind, as distinguished from private morals, which are directed only to oneself.[15]

Bentham's writings of expository jurisprudence became readily available less than 40 years ago. It became apparent that these are no mere appendage to the Bentham canon. Nor are they mere chips from which Austin was able to build. On the contrary, there is little of Austin, or, indeed, a century of later jurists, which is not foreseen in Bentham. It is apparent from Raz,[16] for example, that no subsequent writer developed a formal concept of a legal system with such ingenuity. No doubt lawyers will still read Austin as the fount of nineteenth century positivism. He appeals to lawyers because he was a lawyer and Austinian jurisprudence

[13] A contrasting picture of Bentham's vision of governmental activity is given in Manning, *The Mind of Jeremy Bentham* (1968), pp. 53, 86–97. Bentham believed in reducing law to a minimum; ("In France, where they have so much less liberty than we have, they have much more law") in economic matters he believed that the governmental watchword shold be "Be quiet". He, however, calibrated the degree of intervention with opulence, the greater the opulence, the less was the need of governmental interference. But "the problem in England was ... one of growing unemployment and visible poverty. And in this circumstance, Bentham did gradually commit himself, by degrees, to an increasing measure of state intervention in the life of the individual ... There is nothing in Bentham ... to suggest that he could not have been a supporter of Fabian Socialism had he lived a hundred years later" (pp. 91, 97). For a full discussion of the matter see Harrison's exposition in *Bentham* (1983), pp. 106 *et seq.*

[14] The greatest happiness of the greatest number may on Bentham's calculations, require the greatest misery of the few. This is well brought out in Bentham's scheme for prison reform by way of his celebrated "Panopticon". It is clear that Bentham's ideas for a modern prison involved the infliction of appallingly inhuman conditions, and making the conditions of gaol a terror for all prisoners actual and potential, in the interests of the greatest number, who presumably were never to experience the torments of the Panopticon.

[15] *Principles of Morals and Legislation*, Chap. 17, para. 1. Bentham did not offer a systematic theory of ethics based on exact calculation, but a series of prudential rules addressed to legislators and judges based on a new vocabulary and logic. He was not concerned to describe every conceivable species of human behaviour, but only those with social consequences, the public and observable kinds the judge might have to estimate in court. The Panopticon is used by Foucault as a symbol of repressive authoritarian control (*Discipline and Punish*) (1977), esp. Pt III, Chap. 3). But for a defence see J. Semple, *Bentham's Prison* (1993) and in (1992) 4 *Utilitas* 105. Private morals (or "deontology" as Bentham called it) consisted of persuading people that is in their interest to reach their own happiness. And in so far as their interest coincides with the general interest it serves as an auxiliary method of attaining the final end of general happiness and thus fills in the gaps in the legislative programme. Bentham's general happiness may have been for practical reasons confined to that of specific nations, but his ultimate aim was universalistic, appropriately enough as the inventor of the term "international law." (See R. Harrison, *Bentham*, Chap. 10.)

[16] *Ante*, 38–39, and 391.

is full of painstaking searching legal analysis. But there is no doubt who is the master, who the student.

## BENTHAM'S "OF LAWS IN GENERAL"

*Of Laws in General* is Bentham's main contribution to analytical jurisprudence. Yet, it was not until 1970 that we had an authoritative edition. Its editor has remarked, with justification, that "Had it been published in his lifetime, it, rather than John Austin's later and obviously derivative work, would have dominated English jurisprudence."[17] Nor must it be thought that it stands in isolation from Bentham's censorial jurisprudence. Bentham was a life-long law-reformer, but he believed (and Austin was his disciple in this as well) that no reform of the substantive law could be effectuated without a reform of its form and structure. A thoroughly scientific conceptual framework was thus but a prelude to reform.[18]

In the extracts which follow the reader may gain some insight into Bentham's contribution to analytical jurisprudence.[19] Like Austin's theory, Bentham's is an imperative theory of law, in which the key concepts are those of sovereignty and command. But, whilst their respective definitions of these concepts are closely related,[20] Bentham, to quote his editor again, "expounds those ideas with far greater subtlety and flexibility than Austin and illuminates aspects of law largely neglected by him".[21] A few illustrations of Bentham's originality are sketched in this section.

Austin's sovereign was postulated as an illimitable, indivisible entity: Bentham's is neither. There may be sound practical reasons for having one all-powerful sovereign, but Bentham saw the distinction, as Austin did not, between social desirability and logical necessity. From a conceptual standpoint there is no necessity for a sovereign to be undivided and unlimited. Indeed, in the complex societies that have developed since Bentham's day, particularly the modern collectivist states and federal systems, quite the reverse is true. Bentham thus accepts divided and partial sovereignty.[22] Furthermore, he discussed the legal restrictions that

---

[17] H. L. A. Hart, *Rechtstheorie* (1971), pp. 55, 57. Hart's article is now to be found in a revised version as Chap. 5 of his *Essays on Bentham* (1982); see p. 108 for previous cited references, and later page references will be to the last-mentioned work. The discussion of Bentham's *Of Laws in General* which follows is largely based on Hart's article, which provides an invaluable introduction to that work. See also M. H. James (ed.), *Bentham and Legal Theory* (1974) (also in (1973) 24 N.I.L.Q. No. 3), and M. D. A. Freeman, in *Gli Italiani e Bentham* (1982), vol. 1, pp. 36–44.

[18] *Cf.* Stone, *Legal Systems and Lawyer's Reasonings* (1964), pp. 64–69. Bentham himself brings out the relationship in Chap. XIX of *Of Laws in General*.

[19] See *post*, 269, 273.

[20] *Post*, 273, 291.

[21] Hart, *op. cit.*, pp. 108, 227–242.

[22] *Of Laws in General*, p. 18, n. 6. On the role of judges (and juries) see O. Ben-Dor (2007) *Legal Studies* 216.

may be imposed upon sovereign power. "The business of the ordinary sort of laws is to prescribe to the people what *they* shall do: the business of this transcendent class of laws is to prescribe to the sovereign what *he* shall do."[23] Bentham believes a sovereign may bind his successors, explaining that "if by accident a sovereign should in fact come to the throne with a determination not to adopt the covenants of his predecessors, he would be told that he had adopted them notwithstanding".[24] Without spelling it out Bentham comes close to conceptualising a doctrine of judicial review, for, though he thought that enforcement would be extra-legal (moral or religious), he did not rule out the use of legal sanctions.

Sanctions generally play a less prominent part in Bentham's theory than they do in Austin's. And Bentham, perhaps for this reason, is prepared to undertake a more detailed, less crude, taxonomy of motivating forces than Austin was. Thus, Bentham thought a sovereign's commands would be law even if supported only by religious or moral sanctions.[25] Further, Bentham's account admits "alluring motives", the concept of rewards. Bentham accepts that, what he calls, "praemiary or invitative laws"[26] are likely to be rare. "By reward alone", he contends, "it is most certain that no material part of that business [of government] could be carried on for half an hour."[27] It is on "punishments" that "everything turns".[28]

But "what chiefly differentiates Bentham from Austin and makes him so interesting a philosopher of law is that he was a conscious innovator of new forms of enquiry into the structure of law, and that he makes explicit his method and general logic of enquiry in a way in which no other writer on these topics does".[29] This contrast comes out when Austin's definition of law is compared with Bentham's. On the surface, they are strikingly similar: both are framed in terms of superiority and inferiority,[30] in terms of conduct to be adopted by those in a habit of obedience to a sovereign. But there the similarity ceases. Austin's "model", consciously or unconsciously, was the criminal statute. Bentham, anticipating a trend in modern analytical jurisprudence, has undertaken "rational reconstruction",[31] wider than Austin's "model" and current usage. With his ultimate goal the erection of a structure within which law reform could take place, Bentham was prepared to "fix the meaning of terms",[32] so as not to be restricted by contemporary patterns. Thus, in his definition of law as

[23] *ibid.*, p. 64 and *post*, 279.
[24] *ibid.*, p. 66 and *post*, 280.
[25] *Of Laws in General*, p. 70.
[26] *ibid.*, p. 136.
[27] *ibid.*, p. 135.
[28] *ibid.*, p. 136. For a discussion of Bentham's theory of sanctions and its reliance on the *probable* infliction of pain, see Hart, *op. cit.*, pp. 132–147.
[29] Hart, *op. cit.*, p. 109.
[30] On which see Raz's comments in *The Concept of a Legal System* (1970), pp. 13–14.
[31] On this trend see Summers, *Essays in Legal Philosophy* (1968), pp. 4–6. See also Wollheim, *ante*, 61.
[32] Raz, *op. cit.*, p. 10.

an expression of volition, he covers not only general laws made by legislatures (supreme and subordinate), but also judicial, administrative and
even domestic orders, such as those given by a parent to a child:
declaratory laws[33] are also within its ambit. One reason why Bentham
prefers this "model" of a law as a tool of analysis is clear, for a statute
with usually only contain part of a law and, indeed, will frequently
contain parts of different laws.

One of Bentham's "greatest insights" (according to Hart) into the
structure of a legal system is his distinctive doctrine that the power of
legislation (or "imperation") as Bentham calls it must be "broken into
shares." Thus the legislator himself is confined to enacting general laws
but these may confer mandates on individuals to legislate *de singulis*,
concerning individual persons or things, such as a power to appoint
judges or officials. And the same reasoning comprises particular legal
powers, such as the power of alienation of property or of making contracts. Bentham, however, seeks to bring this theory of imperation within
the scope of his general attribution of all laws to the command of the
sovereign, by explaining it in terms of adoption, that is, the sovereign's
grant of permission to issue what would otherwise be an illegal mandate.
As Hart points out, however, here Bentham falls into the error of confusing illegality with invalidity. For in a modern legal system it is the
validity of the exercise of a legal power, and not its legality, which is all
important. Hart therefore suggests that what is valuable in Bentham's
insight can still be preserved by relating such acts of subordinate
imperation to accepted rules and procedures rather than to sovereign
command.[34]

Another difference between Austin's concept of law and Bentham's is
that, for Bentham, a command is only one of four "aspects" which the
legislator's will may bear to the acts concerning which he is legislating.
Bentham believed that an understanding of the structure of law entails an
appreciation of the "necessary relations" of "opposition and con-
comitancy"[35] between these four aspects of the legislator's will. To
demonstrate these relationships, Bentham developed, what modern jurists and logicians call, "deontic" logic, the logic of imperatives.[36] Bentham can rightly claim to be the discoverer of this insight and to have
demonstrated how this can afford a coherent guide to the structure of any
law.

Without discussing this in detail,[37] it may be said to commit Bentham
to the view that there are no laws which are neither imperative nor
permissive. All laws command or prohibit or permit some form of

---

[33] *Cf. The Province of Jurisprudence Determined*, p. 27.
[34] See Hart, *Essays on Bentham* (1982), Chap. 8 and pp. 241–242.
[35] Raz, *op. cit.*, p. 97.
[36] See, for example, Ross, *Directives and Norms*; Raz, *The Concept of a Legal System*; Von
Wright, *Norm and Action*. See also D. Lyons, *In the Interests of the Governed* (1973),
Chap. 6.
[37] A fuller discussion will be found in Hart, *op. cit.*, pp. 111–122 and Chap. 8 and Raz, *op.
cit.*, pp. 54–59.

conduct. Bentham recognised, however, that the imperative character of law is often concealed, that law is expressed descriptively ("whoever steals shall be sentenced to five years of imprisonment"), or, further, that reference to any offence or sanction is often hidden "in the course of many sentences or even pages or even volumes."[38] An example of the latter approach is an area such as the law of property. Every developed legal system sets out the requirements of a valid title, explains what conditions must be fulfilled to make a person an owner or vest in him some lesser form of proprietary right, and explains what an owner must do to divest himself of his property. One of the most interesting sections of *Of Laws in General* is Bentham's reconciliation of such provisions, which are indisputably law, with his thesis that all laws other than merely permissive ones are *in part* imperative and penal. Title to property is nothing more than a rationalisation of a particular permission taken out of a general prohibition. The prohibition relates to the act of "meddling"[39] with, for example, a piece of land, but the owner is excepted from this prohibition. So the acts or events which confer proprietary title are merely exceptions limiting the scope of the basic prohibitory law. It follows from Bentham's analysis that those laws he regarded as civil laws (that is laws which do not impose obligations or duties or provide sanctions for them[40]) were not "complete laws", but only parts of laws. Convenience of exposition dictated that we detach such civil laws into separate codes, but there was nothing inherent in the laws themselves which made such division necessary.[41]

It must be understood also that though Bentham rejected any idea of "natural" rights,[42] his analysis still left scope for the values which he sought to incorporate, such as liberty, equality or property. Thus duties enforced by sanctions lead to security[43] and thereby to greater happiness. This is achieved by creating a wall of protection within which the individual can do what he chooses. Protection from murder, imprisonment or dispossession results not from abstract natural rights to life, liberty or property but because the security resulting from legally enforced duties leads to general happiness. "It enables people to choose for themselves within the limits laid down how they will attempt to maximise their own, separate, portions of happiness."[44]

---

[38]  *Of Laws in General*, p. 106.
[39]  See *post*, 287.
[40]  So "penal" in Bentham's terminology is much wider than the accepted use of "criminal" and includes such civil wrongs as torts, breaches of contract and breaches of trust. Much property legislation and constitutional law would be classified as "civil" and therefore "incomplete." It should be added that *Of Laws in General* is the outcome of Bentham's pursuit of the difference, if any, between "penal" and "civil" law. See, on this, *Principles of Morals and Legislation*, p. 299. Bentham's analysis fails to characterise legal techniques other than the penal and the civil, for example, the administrative regulatory technique. See, further, Summers (1971) 59 Calif.L.Rev. 733.
[41]  *Of Laws in General*, p. 192.
[42]  See *ante*, 249, n. 10.
[43]  *Cf. post*, 275, n. 34.
[44]  R. Harrison, *Bentham* (1983), pp. 244 *et seq.*, and 250.

Bentham's analysis, it will be noticed, steers clear of a number of the pitfalls into which Austin fell. We are not forced into postulating nullity as a sanction, or into rejecting laws in common usage as "law improperly so-called", or into setting up fictions like "tacit command". Bentham's *Of Laws in General* is undoubtedly the best defence of the imperative theory.[45] Where it fails and where modern jurisprudence picks up the strands is in a failure to develop the concept of a rule. Bentham, like Austin, is rooted to the concepts of sovereignty and the habit of obedience which as Hart and other leading contemporary jurists have demonstrated are deficient in aim and unsatisfactory in scope.

## AUSTIN[46]

Following Bentham's lead Austin attempted to work out what he believed to be the legal and logical implications of sovereignty as viewed by a legal positivist. There are few, at the present day, who regard him as either wholly successful in this undertaking or as being altogether clear-minded in his basic aims, but, nevertheless, Austin's thought still remains worthy of examination not only on account of his widespread influence, especially in common law countries, but also by reason of his penetrating powers of applying analysis to jurisprudence.[47]

As a positivist Austin sought to show what law really is, as opposed to moral or natural law notions of what it ought to be. It has been pointed out that there is no necessary logical connection between positivism and the command theory,[48] and it is certainly true that we are logically free to insist on the separation of law from morals, while rejecting the command theory. Yet to the Benthamites positivism seemed to require some simple empirical explanation of law devoid of metaphysics or mysticism. Bentham, ever critical of "judge-made" law, once compared this to the way of teaching conduct to one's dog,[49] by waiting until it has done something objectionable and then beating it. What was rationally needed was merely

---

[45] Twining attributes Bentham's displacement by Austin to the fact that Austin was more sympathetic to the common law, less critical of the legal profession and less "dangerously radical" than his master (1998) 51 C.L.P. 1, 14).

[46] Critical accounts of Austin and his thought are W. Morison, *John Austin* (1982); W. Rumble, *The Thought of John Austin* (1985). For a defence of Austin against the criticisms of Hart see R. Moles, *Definition and Rule in Legal Theory* (1987). See now the spirited defence by W. Rumble, *Doing Austin Justice* (2005). On his life, see L. and J. Hamburger, *Troubled Lives: John and Sarah Austin* (1985).

[47] It is said that once he was a religion, but today (in fact 1974) he is a disease (Buckland, *Some Reflections on Jurisprudence* (1974), p. 2). On his criminal law theories see K. Smith, *Lawyers, Legislators and Theorists: Developments in English Criminal Jurisprudence 1800–1957* (1998).

[48] See H. L. A. Hart, "Positivism and the Separation of Law and Morals" (1958) 71 Harv.L.Rev. 593; and in Edwards (ed.), *Encyclopaedia of Philosophy* (1967). Olivecrona (*Law as Fact* (2nd ed.), pp. 50–62) limits the expression "legal positivism" to its "original and traditional sense of the German *Rechtspositivismus*" (p. 61). This connotes that all law is positive in the sense of being an expression of the will of a supreme authority.

[49] See *Works*, V, p. 235.

some prior command, so that law was really no more than a series of orders given to human beings, with penalties or sanctions attached for disobedience. Whether this was an over-simplification, or in what sense the word "command" was here used, were questions not fully explored by those to whom this approach seemed so obvious an explanation of the essence of law; to Austin[50] the problem was merely to link this logically with the long-established doctrine of legal sovereignty.

Much of the criticism directed at Austin has been concerned with the deductions that he made from his fundamental positions, such as the illimitable and indivisible nature of sovereignty, or of international and constitutional law and custom as mere positive morality,[51] with the object thereby of casting doubt on the correctness of Austin's own definitions and assumptions. Of the validity and significance of a choice of a definition we have already written,[52] so that it is only necessary here to discuss some specific points of criticism.

## Law as a Command

To conceive of law as command invites the questions *who* issued it? And *when*? And with what authority? Law is clearly portrayed as an artificial creation of human society ... Law is not just descriptive of social order, but is its "cause".[53] A fundamental objection to the command theory is that the idea of a command presupposes the order of a determinate person, and that since law emanates from the ever-changing multitude which comprises the political machinery of the state, it cannot be treated as the command of one person. Curiously enough, Austin himself insisted on a determinate person or body as the source of a command, presumably on the footing that a command is an exercise of will of some particular person or persons. But the justification for calling law a command is really quite different,[54] namely, that it refers to the *logical* classification of legal propositions as "imperatives", that is, they are

---

[50] This does not, of course, mean that Austin's sovereignty and imperative theories cannot stand independently of each other. See Stone, *Legal Systems and Lawyers' Reasonings* (1964), pp. 75–76: "They are independent starting points both of which Austin adopts: one is not deduced from the other."

[51] As to Austin's view regarding international law and custom, see *post*, 298, 300–301. On custom see J. Waldron (1998) 51 C.L.P. 93.

[52] *Ante*, Chap. 2.

[53] G. Postema, *Bentham and the Common Law Tradition* (1986), p. 316. As Postema notes, this had important implications for Bentham: law was not sacred to impervious to change.

[54] *Cf.* Hart, *Essays on Bentham* (1982), Chap. X. Hart regards the concept of "command" as relevant to law, authority or legislation so far as it refers to a *normative* attitude and not a mere "habit of obedience." Such an attitude arises where the mere issue of the command functions as a peremptory reason for doing the act commanded, independently of the nature or character of the act to be done. But only with the development of effective law-applying and law-enforcing agencies will such a normative command situation lead to a legal system in force. (*Op. cit.*, pp. 256–258, and *cf. post*, 336.) The courts will then function by construing what is said or done by certain persons as constituting peremptory reasons for actions, and thus as law-making events (p. 260).

normative statements laying down rules to guide human conduct as distinguished from statements of fact.[55] Hence it is a mere matter of terminology whether the word "command" is appropriate to bring out this distinction, or whether it should be confined to such specific instances as the order of a sergeant-major rapped out on the barrack square or a police officer at a demonstration. Olivecrona, who raises this objection, in effect recognises that Austin is, nonetheless, justified in classifying legal rules as imperative statements, and suggests the term "independent imperatives".[56] Perhaps the word "command" is undesirable for its psychological associations, and it is frequently replaced nowadays by the more colourless designation of "imperatives" or "directives".

Others, such as Duguit, asserted that the notion of command is in any event inapplicable to modern social legislation, which binds the state itself rather than the individual. To the suggestion that there is here no command at all, Austin's reply is that there can be a command where some organ of the sovereign, as against the sovereign itself—(Austin avoids the word "state")—is commanded, and this would certainly cover most legislation of the type envisaged. But it must be admitted that the whole notion of the state or sovereign being unable to command itself is a wholly unrealistic one, in the ambit of the highly complex web of modern public law.[57] This unreality is underlined, for instance, by Austin's treatment of constitutional law as not being positive law, since either it is a mere question of fact as to who is habitually obeyed, or it consists of commands to the sovereign by itself. This is grotesque in relation to modern conditions, but the problem can be resolved if "command" is regarded merely as denoting the logically imperative form of legal rules, for there is nearly always legal machinery for enforcing public law rules against some person or body within the state. And to say that the state cannot bind itself is merely to assert that the sovereign may be able to change the law. Yet it can only do so by observing the procedure constitutionally laid down, and in the meantime existing imperatives remain law.[58]

### Sovereignty

Much of the keenest criticism is directed against Austin's rather rigid views as to the nature of sovereignty. Thus his notion that sovereignty is indivisible is falsified by federal constitutions, and certainly Austin's attempt to locate the sovereign in the United States was a singularly unhappy venture.[59] The mistake here was to assume that sovereignty has

[55] *Cf. ante*, 11.

[56] See *post*, 859. Similarly, Kelsen insists that the word "command" can only be used here in an impersonal and anonymous way, and divested of any psychological association, such as the "will" of the legislator. In this sense it has hardly anything in common with a command properly so called: H. Kelsen, *General Theory of Law and State*, pp. 33–36.

[57] See further, and more generally, N. MacCormick, *Questioning Sovereignty* (1999).

[58] *Cf.* Bentham, quoted *post*, 279.

[59] See Hart (ed.), *Province*, pp. 250–251.

an inherent "nature" (though whether as a matter of logic or physical fact is far from clear) which it cannot avoid. Thus any attempt by the sovereign to divide itself can, on Austin's view, owing to the nature of sovereignty itself, be countermanded and the original sovereign resume its former powers. The same argument applied to establish its illimitability. Here Austin was taking over, and seeking to justify logically, the notions of sovereignty propounded by his predecessors such as Bodin, Hobbes and Rousseau. The fallacy is that sovereignty is not a metaphysical entity with an ineradicable logical structure. On the contrary it is a practical device of law and politics whereby effect is given to the practical need in any political community for some final or ultimate legal authority. But there is no logical or any other compulsion to make this authority indivisible. Ultimate authority may be vested as to different matters in various bodies, though a need will then be felt to have a tribunal resolve conflicts. This does not mean, however, that the tribunal is thus constituted the Austinian sovereign, for in this setting there is no such animal. Sovereignty is divided and the constitutional court is itself subject to or controlled by the legal system. Nor need a sovereign's power be unlimited, and, indeed, many constitutions impose entrenched clauses, so that to that extent no change is possible without a change of constitution.[60] Unlimited sovereignty, therefore, can properly only refer to a body being without a superior in the structure of the state, but this implied nothing either logically or legally as to the degree of its freedom of action.

That these questions are by no means purely theoretical, but have a distinctly practical implication, is sufficiently indicated by the problems that arose in interpreting the effect of the Statute of Westminster of 1931 on Dominion constitutions. For instance, how far can the Westminster Parliament bind itself not to legislate in a certain way for the future?[61] And to what extent can a sovereign Parliament effectively define its own structure so as to constrain itself to comply with a particular procedure for legislative purposes, *e.g.* to sit in two separate bodies? Such questions have arisen in an acute form in the courts of South Africa, which have displayed a laudable unwillingness to be tied to any rigid formula.[62] Indeed, it is sometimes overlooked in this sort of discussion, that Austin himself based sovereignty on habitual obedience. There is no doubt whom the people of South Africa habitually then obeyed and thus no doubt on Austin's test where sovereignty lay. But, in a revolutionary

---

[60] The provision in the U.S. Constitution whereby no state can be deprived of its equal representation in the Senate without its consent is usually cited in this connection (Art. 5).

[61] See *British Coal Corporation v. R.* [1953] A.C. 500 at 520, and the comment thereon of Lord Denning quoted in *Blackburn v. Att.-Gen.* [1971] 2 All E.R. 1380.

[62] See *Harris v. Dönges* [1952] 1 T.L.R. 1245.

setting, a military takeover, a revolution, a secession,[63] Austin's test of habitual obedience is too open-textured to be useful as a criterion. One must keep in mind Austin's failure to distinguish *de jure* sovereignty (authority to make law) from *de facto* sovereignty (power to enforce obedience).[64]

The problems of sovereignty have once again come to the fore since the United Kingdom became a member of the European Economic Community, now Union. Under the terms of the Treaty of Rome certain parts of the Treaty as well as regulations made thereunder were made directly applicable in each member-state,[65] and all questions of legal interpretation subjected to the final decision of the European Court in Luxembourg.[66] Following the orthodox Austinian view that no external legislator can make laws for the United Kingdom without the sanction of Parliament, this novel situation was made the subject of an express provision of the European Communities Act 1972 whereby U.K. courts are to give effect to E.C. legislation passed or to be passed in the future in accordance with the provisions of the Act.[67] This, however, still leaves open the question as to the retention of parliamentary supremacy where there is a conflict between an E.U. regulation and a later statute. The European Court has come down firmly in favour of the view that where Community regulations and subsequent national legislation are in conflict Community law prevails.[68] This doctrine has also been generally accepted by the courts of the original member state[69] but it remains far from clear[70] whether it is reconcilable with the orthodox view of parliamentary supremacy, whereby a later statute can always repeal expressly or impliedly, the operation of previous legislation.[71] It has been suggested

---

[63] Examples such as Pakistan (see *State v. Dosso* (1958) 2 P.S.C.R. 180), Uganda (*Uganda v. Commissioner of Prisons* (1966) E.A.L.R. 514), Nigeria (*Lakanmi and K. Ola v. Att.-Gen. (Western State)*, discussed by Ojo in 20 I.C.L.Q. 117), Ghana (*Sallah v. Att.-Gen.*, discussed by Date-Bah in I.C.L.Q. 315) or, most notably, Southern Rhodesia (*Madzimbamuto v. Lardner-Burke* [1969] 1 A.C. 645).

[64] *Cf.* Bryce, *Studies in History and Jurisprudence*, II, pp. 51–62. See W. Rumble, *Doing Austin Justice* (2003), p. 235.

[65] See E.C. Treaty, Art. 249 and European Communities Act 1972, s. 2(1).

[66] *ibid.*, Art. 234.

[67] s. 2.

[68] *Costa v. E.N.E.L.* [1964] C.M.L.R. 425; *Internationale Handelsgesellschaft v. Einfuhr* [1972] C.M.L.R. 255; *Italian Tax Administration v. Simmenthal* [1978] 3 C.M.L.R. 263.

[69] See H. Kutcher in (1973) 89 L.Q.R. 487, 502–503, and M. Simon in (1976) 92 L.Q.R. 85, 357. The German Constitutional Court has expressed some reservation in the case of basic human rights guaranteed by the Constitution: see [1974] 2 C.M.L.R. 540.

[70] *Cf. Blackburn v. Att.-Gen.* [1971] 2 All E.R. 1380. And see J.-P. Warner (1977) 93 L.Q.R. 349.

[71] In *Macarthys Ltd v. Smith* [1979] 3 All E.R. 325 and [1981] 1 All. E.R. 120, the Court of Appeal decided that a provision of the Equal Pay Act 1970, as amended by the Sex Discrimination Act 1975, was (after a reference to the European Court: see [1981] All E.R. 111) in conflict with the EEC Treaty which therefore prevailed over U.K. law. The implication seems to be that a subsequent Act of Parliament which is inconsistent with a directly applicable rule of Community law will be read subject to s. 2(4) of the EEC Act 1972 whereby existing or future enactments are to be construed subject to giving legal effect in the U.K. of relevant Community law. (See also *Garland v. British Rail Engineering* [1982] 2 All E.R. 402.) The question remains open, however, as to the effect of

that it might well remain open to a U.K. court to sacrifice the full measure of rigid logic imposed by the Austinian theory of parliamentary sovereignty, by holding that there has been an effective partial transfer of sovereignty over matters within the ambit of EEC and E.U. legislation to the new legislature constituted by the Treaty, and that the United Kingdom Parliament has thereby effectively surrendered its powers over those legislative questions within the prerogative of the EEC (now E.U.). In support of this, appeal is made to the argument that this could be treated as not a substantive limitation on sovereignty so far as the content of legislation is concerned, but no more than a change in the manner and form of legislation[72] so that, for specific purposes, Parliament can be regarded as redefined by way of comprising the legislative organs of the Community or Union.[73] Whatever may be the merit of this particular argument it does seem clear that with the passage of time the unreality of repeating the formula of irreversible parliamentary sovereignty may become so manifest that English courts will eventually come to accept a change in the ultimate ground rules[74] of the constitution and that some part of its sovereign power has been irrevocably transferred by Parliament to other legislative organs. It may be said that there is nothing to stop this development save the force of tradition[75] and, if and when it does occur, the result may then appear disarmingly simple and even self-evident so long as the political climate of the time renders it acceptable. But the decision would certainly have political implications and would

subsequent inconsistent legislation which is intended, expressly or impliedly, to repeal that legislation, either generally, or so far as relates specifically thereto (see previous note and Lord Denning M.R. in *Macarthys Ltd v. Smith* [1979] 3 All E.R. 329). Nor is it yet clear how an English court will respond to the ruling in *Simmental, op. cit.*, n. 68, that a national court should give full effect to Community Law without awaiting repeal of inconsistent legislation. The question as to the effect of subsequent inconsistent legislation, intended to repeal European law, still remains unresolved, notwithstanding the decision of the House of Lords and of the Court of Justice in *Factortame Ltd v. Secretary of State for Transport* [1991] A.C. 603 (holding that a national court was required to set aside a rule of national law which was the sole obstacle preventing grant of interim relief). For the time being Lord Diplock's view in *Garland* (p. 415) that a subsequent statute is to be construed, if reasonably so capable, as not to be inconsistent with prior EEC (or E.U.) legislation, remains the prevailing doctrine. But see MacCormick, *post*, 497.

[72] See *ante*, 211.

[73] G. Winterton, "The British Grundnorm: Parliamentary Supremacy Re-examined" (1976) 92 L.Q.R. 591, especially pp. 597, 607, 613–617. It is also suggested that the Parliament Acts 1911 and 1949 may be regarded as providing an alternative legislature of Commons and Monarch for many purposes: *ibid.*, p. 607. The abolition or reconstruction of the House of Lords might be similarly so regarded. Interest has been rekindled by the case of *Jackson v. Attorney General* [2006] 1 A.C. 262. Judges spoke of limitations on sovereignty: community legislation, the European Convention on Human Rights, the Scotland Act 1998, the Acts of Union and even the common law and the rule of law. There is disagreement between the judges but agreement that the rule of law may constraint legislative competence. Thus Baroness Hale, for example, states:
"The courts will treat with particular suspicion (and might even reject) any attempt to subvert the rule of law by removing governmental action affecting the rights of the individual from all judicial scrutiny".
See, further, T. Mullen (2007) 27 *Legal Studies* 1.

[74] Cf. *post*, 267.

[75] See Dennis Lloyd, *The Idea of Law* (revised ed., 1985), pp. 192, 198.

therefore call for considerable sensitivity from the judiciary as to its timing and presentation.[76]

The attempt by Austin to base sovereignty on habitual obedience has been strongly criticised, as confusing the legal with the *de facto* or political sovereign. It has been suggested in answer, that Austin was looking for neither of these, but for the logically presupposed ultimate source of law in any state, viewed as an abstract concept. Thus his sovereign would be comparable to Rousseau's general will.[77] It seems likely, however, that this was not Austin's aim. Austin was a lawyer, and what he sought to provide was an unfailing test for locating legal sovereignty in the state.[78] He recognised, however, that law cannot itself be based on law but must be based on something outside law. He therefore, sought to base it upon fact,[79] *viz.*, the habitual obedience of the mass of the population. This was certainly not a confusion with a *de facto* sovereign. Indeed this latter concept is really meaningless, for the location of actual power in a modern state, whether attributed to a power élite,[80] a pressure group, a social class, or different categories of individuals, is a sociological inquiry entirely distinct from locating the legal sovereign. Austin, for instance, never imagined that the body of electors was in itself the *de facto* power of the state, or was not subject to all the force of pressure of those able to direct it. That something was wrong with Austin's invocation of fact in the form he used it is, however, sufficiently shown by his refusal to accept the King in Parliament as England's legal sovereign. But to avoid repetition, the further examination of this point will be reserved until Kelsen's theory has been reviewed.[81]

It should, however, be added that Austin has been defended by Morison from another viewpoint.[82] He describes Austin approvingly as a "naive empiricist" by which he apparently means one who treats propositions of or concerning either law or morals as simply true or false or as making no sense at all.[83] Morison argues that Austin (like Hart) defines law by reference to rules but regards that as a failure on Austin's part to recognise that a "true" account of law in terms of "sociological fact"

---

[76] *Cf. post*, 260. See further G. Marshall, *Constitutional Theory* (1971), pp. 43–53; and P. Fitzgerald (1972) *Irish Jurist* 28.

[77] C. W. Manning, in *Modern Theories of Law* (1933), pp. 180 *et seq.* See also J. Stone, *Legal Systems and Lawyers' Reasonings* (1964), who argues that Austin is merely putting forward a formal theory, to enable the legal order to be seen as a coherent system of norms. But Stone admits that he is not always consistent on this plane (see pp. 73–88). On Rousseau's "general will" see *ante*, 147.

[78] *Cf.* W. L. Morison, "Some Myths about Positivism" (1958) 68 Yale L.J. 212.

[79] Ignoring the difficulty raised by Hume, that a norm (or system of norms) cannot be derived from existential propositions alone. On this account Kelsen relies on an ultimate norm outside the legal system, *cf. post*, 309.

[80] As in C. Wright Mills, *Power Elite* (1956). See also R. Miliband, *The State in Capitalist Society* (1969), and R. Dahrendorf, *Class and Class Conflict in Industrial Society* (1963). See also the Marxist approach in Chap. 13.

[81] *Post*, Chap. 5.

[82] See W. L. Morison, *John Austin* (1982), and especially Chap. 6.

[83] Morison, *op. cit.*, p. 189.

needs to be given other than in terms of rules.[84] Thus, we must not indulge in a preconceived "legal centre of gravity" in any community, but rather recognise the wide variety of factors which determine the course of any authoritative decision-making.[85] Morison accordingly reaches the intriguing conclusion that Austin's real aims were similar to those of Lasswell and McDougal.[86] Law, we are told, is not to be regarded as a concept but as a "slice of observable reality".[87] But where Austin failed to carry his insight through was in trying to reconcile it with a crude and "untrue" theory of sovereignty, rather than in seeking to explain decision-making in such terms as the shared commitments of judges.[88] Such a thesis, it may be said, resembles generally that of Olivecrona's treatment of law as *fact*,[89] and is open to similar objections. At the same time it seems to blur the distinction between the normative character of law itself and a descriptive "science of law" which might be regarded as true or false in relation to any particular legal system. And while rightly stressing Austin's concern to show what law is really about, it attributes to him a consistency and clarity of purpose which are hardly confirmed by Austin's own writings.[90]

### Law and Morals

The positivist aspect of Austinianism is most in evidence in the rigid separation of law and morals.[91] Most of the critics of this approach may

---

[84]  *ibid.*, p. 183.

[85]  *ibid.*, pp. 183–184.

[86]  *ibid.*, pp. 179–188. For Lasswell and McDougal, see *post*, 856.

[87]  Morison, *op. cit.*, p. 190.

[88]  *ibid.*, p. 197.

[89]  *Post*, 856.

[90]  See also W. E. Rumble (1979) 24 Am.J. of Jurisprud. 168–173.

[91]  Hart usefully identifies five different meanings of "positivism":

(1) The contention that laws are commands of human beings.

(2) The contention that there is no necessary connection between law and morals or law as it is and ought to be.

(3) The contention that the analysis (or study of the meaning) of legal concepts is (a) worth pursuing and (b) to be distinguished from historical inquiries into the causes or origins of laws, from sociological inquiries into the relation of law and other social phenomena, and from the criticism or appraisal of law whether in terms or morals, social aims, "functions," or otherwise.

(4) The contention that a legal system is a "closed logical system" in which correct legal decisions can be deduced by logical means from predetermined legal rules without reference to social aims, policies, moral standards.

(5) The contention that moral judgments cannot be established or defended, as statements of facts can, by rational argument, evidence, or proof. (See (1958) 71 Harv. L. Rev. 601–602.)

For an extended list, see Summers (1966) 41 N.Y.U.L.Rev. 861, 889. (*Cf.* Morison, *John Austin* (1982), pp. 170–177.) There is a good deal of truth in Summers' remark that it would be best in legal philosophy to drop the term "positivist", for it is now radically ambiguous and dominantly pejorative" (in *Essays in Legal Philosophy*, p. 16). Olivecrona believes that much confusion over the meaning of "positivism" has been caused by failure to distinguish twin-origins of the concept: in the sense of law by position "*positum*", it designates a theory on the nature of law, and, as a philosophy, it stands for a particular approach to legal problems, the "separation of positive law from morals, mores, religion ..." (Hall, 33 U. Cinc.L.Rev. 29). See Olivecrona, *Law As Fact* (2nd ed.), pp. 50–62.

be classified in one way or another as supporters of an external natural law, which has already been discussed above.[92] Another approach, which appeals to some modern thinkers, is to claim that law is a kind of order which has an *internal* moral structure to which it must conform in order to be law.[93] Much of this sort of thinking is animated by the strong aversion to recognising some of the frenzied output of the Nazi legal system as "law." This is to set up some sort of an objective moral law as part of the universe and involves a rejection of Hume's distinction between objective existential propositions ("is") and valuations ("ought"), and implies that the truth of value judgments at least in morals is as ascertainable as the truth of the physical fact. Yet until some criteria are established comparable to those available in the realm of fact it seems to add little to the argument to conceive the moral order as part of the inner structure of the legal order, rather than as an external system.[94] The approach remains essentially an idealist search for absolute truth in the realm of values, curiously enough at a time when this search has virtually been abandoned in the field of scientific fact.[95]

## *Sanctions*[96]

Austin's insistence on sanctions as a mark of law has frequently been objected to as concealing or distorting the real character and functions of law in a community. Sanctions, it is said, do not explain why law is changed and place an undue emphasis on fear. The essence of a legal system is the inherent fact, based on various psychological factors, that law is accepted by the community as a whole as binding, and the element of sanction is not an essential, or perhaps even an important, element in the functioning of the system.[97] "It is because a rule is regarded as obligatory that a measure of coercion may be attached to it; it is not

---

[92] *Ante*, Chap. 3.

[93] See the writings of Lon Fuller, *ante*, 45 and 154 and *post*, 417.

[94] For an attempt to attain what some may regard as inherently unattainable, see F.S.C. Northrop, *The Complexity of Legal and Ethical Experience* (1959), Chap. 21. It may be said that the positivist looks at the actual *decision*, and says this is law, good or bad; the moralist looks at the process, and says morality has been taken into account. But a court is not *bound* to take account of moral factors, and even if it were, this would not establish a pre-existing objective ethical standard.

[95] *Cf. ante*, 5. Note that this position also resembles the Kantian view that the absolute is only attainable in the moral sphere (the category of "essence") and not in the sphere of human knowledge; *cf.* Mackinnon, *Ethical Theory* (1957), Chap. 3. An attempt to bridge this gap in the realm of phenomenology, see the lucid exposition in W. Friedmann, *Legal Theory* (5th ed.), pp. 197–208.

[96] For an account of the inconsistencies and ambiguities underlying Austin's discussion of sanctions, see C. Tapper [1965] C.L.J. 271. See also G. Lamond (2000) 20 Ox. J.L.S. 39, and (2001) 7 *Legal Theory* 35, A. Ripstein (2004) 32 *Phil and Public Affairs* 2 argues that the state's claim to authority is inseparable from the rationale for coercion.

[97] *Cf.* A. L. Goodhart, "An Apology for Jurisprudence" in *Interpretations of Modern Legal Philosophy* (ed. Sayre), p. 283. Goodhart restated his case in (1967) 41 Tulane L.Rev. 769. See also Hart, *The Concept of Law* (1994), for the view that sanctions play the secondary role of ensuring that "those who would voluntarily obey shall not be sacrificed to those who do not" (p. 198).

obligatory because there is coercion."[98] As has already been pointed out, law essentially depends on authority.[99] What does this mean? Authority implies that obedience is rendered by one person to another because the former recognises that the latter has a *right* to obedience. In other words, the person laying down the rule to be obeyed is claiming that he is legitimately entitled to do so and the subject in obeying is acknowledging that legitimacy. The position is therefore one of hierarchical subordination between subject and ruler, and is to be contrasted with a readiness to conform to a practice or rule which is accepted as appropriate to govern conduct as between equals or, in the language of sociology, as between members of "peer groups". The present argument is therefore that the threat or application of sanctions is only a peripheral feature of law, which at least theoretically could exist and function without a specific apparatus of law enforcement.

Support for this view is found in the well known experiments of Milgram, which demonstrated the enormous impact of authority, believed in as legitimate, in securing voluntary obedience to instructions lacking any sort of sanctions, and even involving actions going contrary to the moral beliefs of those concerned.[1] The explanation put forward for this rather startling outcome is that social indoctrination takes place at a very early age both in the family and at school, and that in this way social obedience is internalised in the structure of the mental attitudes of the individual and this conditions him to give voluntary obedience to anyone exerting what he accepts as legitimate authority. Thus, even without the Orwellian nightmare of Big Brother operating in a totalitarian society,[2] the internalised basis of obedience in any society, including even a liberal society dedicated to freedom of the individual, will result in the acceptance of authority, believed in as legitimate. Hence the legislature (or sovereign), being the supreme legitimate source of authority in the state, is able to secure a readier and more unquestioning obedience than any other source of social or moral rules. Accordingly, even if coercive sanctions are commonly associated with legal rules they are by no means the source of legal obligation.

Those who do stress the part which sanctions play, on the other hand, seek to deploy two arguments to oppose this. First, it is said that the question is not the precise psychological[3] explanation why people obey the law. This is a matter of social psychology, not law. What it is sought

---

[98] A. L. Goodhart, *English Law and the Moral Law*, p. 17.

[99] *Ante*, 44.

[1] See S. Milgram, *Obedience to Authority* (1974) as to which see M.D.A. Freeman (1979) 1 Liverpool L.R. 45. *Cf.* Olivecrona, *post*, 1062.

[2] See G. Orwell, *Animal Farm and Nineteen Eighty-Four*.

[3] A socio-legal study undertaken to determine why people (in this case taxpayers) obeyed the law found that "the threat of sanction can deter people from violating the law, perhaps in important part by inducing a moralistic attitude toward compliance". See Schwartz and Orleans (1967) 34 U. Chi.L.Rev. 274, 300. T. Tyler (*Why People Obey The Law* (1990)) has found that "normative concerns are an important determinant of law-abiding behaviour", in particular the person's assessment that following the law accords with his sense of right and wrong.

to attain by invoking sanctions is some characteristic *formal* feature of legal systems, which differentiate them from others. Moreover, the fact that no sanction may actually exist to enforce a particular rule is not necessarily vital if one has regard to the fact that the legal system *as a whole* does provide sanctions.[4] But it may be doubted whether Austin would have agreed with this defence. Certainly his reference to sanctions is expressed in admittedly crude psychological terms, and appears to suggest that he believed he was describing the way law actually operates. Moreover, he is not very explicit about the structure of a legal system. Is there any internal relationship between commands or are they, as in Cardozo's phrase, nothing more than "isolated dooms?"[5] Raz maintains that "the fact that every law is a command entails that every law can be an independent unit, the existence, meaning or application of which is not logically affected by other laws".[6] All the same it is difficult[7] to find any distinctive feature of all legal systems other than the existence of some kind of sanctioning procedure.[8] Admittedly sanctions may exist in non-legal systems, such as codes of morals or etiquette, but these are not usually specific or governed by specific procedures: if they are, as in canon law, we seem justified in calling such rules "law". Certainly the notion of general acceptance lacks any distinctive character enabling us to distinguish law from the rules of a club, or of a robber gang, as well as being, save in the sense of generally internalised obedience to authority as such, a fiction comparable to the old social contract theory.[9]

The second objection, on the other hand, seeks to meet the argument from social psychology on its own terms by insisting that, despite the admittedly strong impulse towards voluntary obedience to authority, there are aggressive and anti-social forces at work both in individuals and in society generally which militate decisively against the functioning of any legal system not ultimately backed by force.[10] On this view, although

---

[4] In this way can be avoided those highly pedantic discussions as to whether sanctions can be spelt out in certain individual cases such as enabling statutes, imperfect obligations, duties of judges and juries, etc. Austin's problem may be surmounted by looking, as Hart does, not for sanctions, but for "critical reactions", which may, or may not, include sanctions. See the useful discussion in Raz, *op. cit.*, pp. 152–154.

[5] *The Nature of the Judicial Process* (1921), p. 126.

[6] *The Concept of a Legal System* (1970), p. 26. Raz makes no reference to *The Lectures*, in which Tapper, *op. cit.*, pp. 284–287, finds oblique equivocal evidence that Austin accepted legal rules without sanctions, provided they were part of a chain of obligations with ultimate infliction of an evil. It is as if Austin has seen the problem but has been unable to grasp fully its implications or work out its logical ends.

[7] Thus even Kelsen, who relies primarily on a structural means of identifying law, still considers sanctions as an essential element of any legal system: *post*, 311.

[8] It has come to be thought by some that the impression conveyed in the text results from adopting municipal legal systems in Western democracies as the norm and that, if, for example, we were to widen our horizon and look at law in stateless societies, colonial law, international relations or, indeed, areas of our law where sanctions are very much in the background, such as industrial relations or the family, then we might find some other distinctive feature in social control than the existence of sanctions. (See, for example, P. Bohannan, *post*, 1121 or M. Barkun, *Law Without Sanctions* (1968).)

[9] As pointed out by F. Castberg, *Problems of Legal Philosophy* (2nd ed., 1957), p. 50.

[10] *Cf.* K. Olivecrona, *post*, 1062.

any particular individual may obey the law without thought of sanctions, it is practically certain that if the law ceased to apply sanctions *as a whole* society would disintegrate, for the recalcitrant minority would otherwise tyrannise over the majority. Indeed, the probable consequence would be simply a power movement within the state prior to a reaffirmation of a sanctioning legal system in favour of those who have seized control in defiance of previous law. It is, therefore, quite realistic to regard the policeman as the ultimate mark of the legal process, and the experience of Tolstoyan[11] or other seekers after a society containing justice without force, show these to be Utopian seekers of an ideal world.

A further attempt to justify a coercion theory of law has recently been put forward from a more fundamental philosophical viewpoint.[12] This rejects the need, as positivists generally felt, to link a theory of coercion with the identification of a set of rules constituting the law. If, it is suggested, we substitute for the question, what is law?, the question, what is "illegal behaviour?" the answer can be given in purely sanctionist terms as simply behaviour which the sovereign or governmental power is disposed to punish. This is not to deny that law does often involve an appeal to rules, as for instance when legal officials use legal reasoning to reach decisions as to what behaviour is illegal; this, however, is not the same as the question what makes certain behaviour illegal.

Theoretically it does appear possible to separate out these two issues, and also to treat what is illegal behaviour as in a sense the more fundamental. It is not altogether clear what advantages flow from this procedure. In the first place we are told that what makes behaviour illegal is more easily identified by seeing what conduct officials in a given country are disposed to punish rather than by identifying a fundamental rule and ascertaining what is to be deemed illegal by derivation from that rule. Secondly, it is argued that the coercion theory supplies a uniform account of illegal behaviour which cannot be provided by a rule-oriented theory. Certainly theories which seek to explain law exclusively in terms of rules do give rise to certain difficulties to which Dworkin and others have referred.[13] It may well be that these can be avoided or evaded by posing the seemingly simple question, what is illegal behaviour? What, however, may be doubted is whether the proposed answer, relying solely on the test of what the sovereign or officials on his behalf are disposed to punish, provides the straightforward criterion which is claimed. At the same time it does help to provide some insight into the way coercion is built into the framework of illegality and therefore of law itself. It is therefore one, if not the only, way in which the contention of the anti-sanctionist that coercion is not indispensable to law, may perhaps be refuted.

---

[11] See Aylmer Maude's *Life of Tolstoy*, II, Chap. 8.
[12] See R. Foley, "Illegal Behaviour" (1982) 1 *Law and Philosophy* 131.
[13] *Cf. post*, 386.

MacCormick[14] has agreed, on the other hand, that the fundamental objection to law being regarded as essentially coercive is logical rather than practical. Even if it is true that coercion has actually proved necessary in all known human societies this is only a contingent feature, and not a logically necessary feature of a legal order which determines rights and defines offences for the members of any society. As to civil remedies, even if the possibility of coercion lies in the background as an inducement to respect the legal rights of others this amounts to no more than a vague and diffuse awareness of available coercive processes for enforcing such remedies. Such an awareness is not to be compared with any form of coercion and even its existence is a matter of mere conjecture, worthy in itself of empirical investigation. As to criminal law, even in this case there is nothing logically absurd in supposing a noncoercive system of criminal law. In regarding penalties as intrinsically a variety of coercion by threats we are unnecessarily building into our theory of law the theory of general deterrence, which is itself both controversial and unproved. Furthermore, the extent to which law may be sanctioned by rewards rather than penalties, as suggested by Bentham,[15] remains an area which still lacks empirical exploration. For all this, however, it may be said that in so far as a theory of law is rooted in the practical necessities of human society it cannot be lightly brushed aside merely because its acceptance rests on contingent rather than formal logical necessity. Perhaps this is an instance where, in Holmes's words,[16] logic must yield to experience.

## Hart's "Concept of Law" and Austin[17]

By far the most searching criticism of the Austinian position has come from Hart,[18] who has linked this criticism with his own concept of law as a system of rules. Hart rejects any model of law based simply on coercive orders, on the ground that this is derived too exclusively from the criminal pattern of law and is inapplicable to that large section of a modern legal system which confers public and private legal *powers*, for instance, in the case of the law relating to wills, contracts, marriage, the jurisdiction of the courts, or the powers of the legislature. Moreover, Hart points out that to try and extend the notion of a sanction to cover

---

[14] See N. MacCormick, *Legal Rights and Social Democracy* (1982), Chap. 12. *Cf.* J. Raz in *Practical Reason and Norms* (1977).

[15] See *ante*, 252. These may take the form of coercive proposals as distinct from coercive threats ("an offer you cannot refuse"): see V. Haksar (1976) 4 *Political Theory* 65–79.

[16] See *post*, 986.

[17] On which see M. Bayles, *Hart's Legal Philosophy* (1992), Chap. 2.

[18] W. Rumble in *Doing Austin Justice* (2005) points to nineteenth century criticisms of Austin which anticipate Hart's critique (see pp. 225–227).

nullity of a transaction, as Austin did,[19] is really absurd, for in criminal law the purpose of a sanction is to *discourage* conduct, whereas the purpose of legal rules conferring power is to provide for the implementation of certain acts-in-the-law.[20]

In place, of Austin's monolithic model, Hart suggests a dual system consisting of two types of rules.[21] These he describes as "primary" and "secondary" rules. The primary rules are those which lay down standards of behaviour and are rules of obligation,[22] that is, rules that impose duties. The secondary rules, on the other hand, are ancillary to and concern the primary rules in various ways; for instance, they specify the ways in which the primary rules may be ascertained, introduced, eliminated or varied, and the mode in which their violation may be conclusively determined. These secondary rules are, therefore, mainly procedural and remedial and include, but go far beyond, the rules governing sanctions. For instance, they extend to the rules of judicial procedure and evidence,[23] as well as the rules governing the procedure by which new legislation may be introduced. For Hart, therefore, it is the union of primary and secondary rules which constitutes the core of a legal system.[24]

## CONCLUSION

Any attempt to evaluate Bentham and Austin's contribution to jurisprudence must stress both the strength and the weaknesses of the analytical approach. On the one hand, the determination to see things as they are, to resist metaphysical allurements, and to probe analytically and with rigour into the fundamental concepts of law on which so much confused thinking existed, has had a lastingly beneficial effect in persuading lawyers in common law countries that, as Holmes J. put it, "the common law is not a brooding omnipresence in the sky" but a

---

[19] See *Lectures on Jurisprudence* (5th ed., 1885), p. 505. Raz remarks that Austin did not need this doctrine: "It is introduced to explain private powers which can be completely accounted for by his doctrine of capacity" (*op. cit.*, p. 22). Austin also regarded inconvenience and a declaration of infamy as sanctions, but, unlike Bentham, was careful to exclude rewards from their ambit, which seems odd for a utilitarian.

[20] For the view that Hart's arguments are not as convincing as many have assumed see D. Lyons, *Ethics and The Rule of Law* (1984), pp. 43–48.

[21] H. L. A. Hart, *The Concept of Law* (1994), Chap. 5.

[22] Hart carefully distinguishes between being "obliged", which results from the "gun-man situation" (A orders B to hand over his money under threat of shooting him), from being "under an obligation", which entails the existence of social (including legal) rules: see *The Concept of Law*, pp. 82–88. *Cf. post*, 379.

[23] *Cf.* Austin's remark, *op. cit.*, p. 249: "All laws or rules determining the practice of the courts, or all laws or rules determining judicial procedure, are purely subsidiary to the due execution of others." Tapper comments with some justice: "This passage anticipates a whole body of later thought, and most strikingly the analysis of primary and secondary rules to be found in Hart's *The Concept of Law*", *op. cit.*, p. 285. It should be noted that it seems unlikely that Austin envisaged a court being liable to sanctions if it contravened procedural requirements, much less for exercising any judicial power wrongly.

[25] See *Holmes-Laski Letters*, II, p. 822.

phenomenon susceptible of scientific analysis and investigation. Austin's aims were to establish the autonomy of jurisprudence as a separate field of study, and to place it on a factual and scientific basis. The fundamental and general concepts of law that Austin explored were not regarded by him as *a priori* concepts, but were regarded as facts to be derived from experience. At the same time this approach did tend, especially among Austin's followers, to induce a rather coldly logical and analytical approach to law as a set of rules existing separately and in its own right, and containing within itself the seeds of its own development. Austin himself, as a Benthamite reformer, was certainly not unmindful of the need to relate law to the needs of society,[25] and he had a positive view on judicial legislation,[26] which has been overlooked subsequently by his followers and his critics. Even Austin, however, displayed some strong leanings in favour of conceptual thinking, especially in regard to sovereignty. But the suggestion that the positivist insistence on distinguishing law and morals has been instrumental in leading to dictatorship seems fanciful in the extreme,[27] for if Nazi Germany is cited in support of this contention, this not only ignores the role of German idealism and neo-Hegelianism, but also leaves totally unexplained why England, with its strong leaning to empiricism, and the United States, home of pragmatism, have not gone much further along this particular road.

---

### J. BENTHAM
### A Fragment on Government

When a number of persons (whom we may style *subjects*) are supposed to be in the *habit* of paying *obedience* to a person, or an assemblage of persons, of a known and certain description (whom we may call *governor* or *governors*) such persons altogether (*subjects* and *governors*) are said to be in a state of *political* SOCIETY ...

   ...As to the LAW *of Nature*, if (as I trust it will appear) it be nothing but a

---

[25] See *Holmes-Laski Letters*, II, p. 822.

[26] See *Holmes-Laski Letters*, II, p. 822.

[25] Serious doubt has been cast on Austin's sympathy for social reform in respect of the community as a whole (see E. Ruben, "John Austin's Political Pamphlets 1824–1859" in *Perspectives in Jurisprudence* (ed. Attwooll, 1977), p. 20). Even early on, as a follower of Bentham's radical utilitarianism, his main aim was to sustain the propertied middle classes. In his later writings he affirms that to give power to the mass of the working class would spell anarchy or (even worse) socialism. This led him to reject utility in favour of traditionalism and to oppose the extension of the franchise. For Austin unfettered so vereignty was not just a logical concept but an ideology of social discipline. And the habit of obedience was no mere rational basis of law but a necessary pre-requisite of a stable legal order. Like many positivists Austin found it hard to resist slipping into his notion of the law as it is, what he believed the law ought to be. But *cf.* Morison, *op. cit.*, pp. 122–132.

[26] Austin accepted that judicial legislation was inevitable. His view was that judicial legislation was qualitatively better than statutory law (*Lectures on Jurisprudence*, pp. 218–219).

[27] This view is urged by Fuller in (1958) 71 Harv.L.Rev. 657–661, and denied by Hart, *ibid.*, pp. 616 *et seq.*

phrase; if there be no other medium for proving a law of the *state* to be contrary to it, than the *inexpediency* of such law, unless the bare unfounded disapprobation of any one who thinks of it be called a proof; if a test for distinguishing such laws as would be *contrary* to the Law *of Nature* from such as, *without* being contrary to it, are simply *inexpedient*, be that which neither our Author[28] nor any man else so much as pretended ever to give; if, in a word, there be scarce any law whatever but what those who have not liked it have found, on some account or another, to be repugnant to some text of scripture; I see no remedy but that the natural tendency of such doctrine is to impel a man, by a force of conscience, to rise up in arms against any law whatever that he happens not like. What sort of government it is that can consist with such a disposition, I must leave to our Author to inform us.

It is the principle of *utility*, accurately apprehended and steadily applied, that affords the only clue to guide a man through these straits. It is for that, if any, and for that alone to furnish a decision which neither party shall dare in *theory* to disavow. It is something to reconcile men even in theory. They are at least, *something* nearer to an effectual union, than when at variance as well in respect of theory as of practice...

## J. BENTHAM
### An Introduction to the Principles of Morals and Legislation
(Edited by J.H. Burns and H.L.A. Hart, 1970)

*Of the Principle of Utility*

Nature has placed mankind under the governance of two sovereign masters, *pain* and *pleasure*. It is for them alone to point out what we ought to do, as well as to determine what we shall do. On the one hand the standard of right and wrong, on the other the chain of causes and effects, are fastened to their throne. They govern us in all we do, in all we say, in all we think: every effort we can make to throw off our subjection, will serve but to demonstrate and confirm it. In words a man may pretend to abjure their empire: but in reality he will remain subject to it all the while. The *principle of utility*[29] recognises this subjection, and assumes it for the

---

[28] [Blackstone in *Commentaries*, vol. 1, p. 42.]

[29] To this denomination has of late been added, or substituted, the *greatest happiness* or *greatest felicity* principle: this for shortness, instead of saying at length *that principle* which states the greater happiness of all those whose interest is in question, as being the right and proper, and only right and proper and universally desirable, end of human action: of human action in every situation, and in particular in that of a functionary or set of functionaries exercising the powers of Government. The word *utility* does not so clearly point to the ideas of *pleasure* and *pain* as the words *happiness* and *felicity* do: nor does it lead us to the consideration of the *number*, of the interests affected; to the *number*, as being the circumstance, which contributes, in the largest proportion, to the formation of the standard here in question; the *standard of right and wrong*, by which alone the propriety of human conduct, in every situation, can with propriety be tried. This want of a sufficiently manifest connexion between the ideas of *happiness* and *pleasure* on the one hand, and the idea of *utility* on the other, I have every now and then found operating, and with but too much efficiency, as a bar to the acceptance, that might otherwise have been given, to this principle.

[For recent explorations of the limits of utilitarianism as a system of moral and legal justification, see D. B. Lyons, *Forms and Limits of Utilitarianism* (1965), D. H. Hodgson, *Consequences of Utilitarianism* (1967), J. Rawls, *A Theory of Justice* (1972), R. Sartorious, *Individual Conduct and Social Norms* (1975), H. L. A. Hart "Utility and Rights" (1979) 79 Col. L. R. 823 and M.D.A. Freeman in *Gli Italiani e Bentham* (1982), vol. 1, pp. 28–32. Much modern criticism turns on the view that it is an illusion that moral issues can be determined by reference to a single consistent criterion or test: see Sen and Williams (eds.), *Utilitarianism and Beyond* (1983), Chap. 6 (C. Taylor), and Chap. 7 (Stuart

foundation of that system, the object of which is to rear the fabric of felicity by the hands of reason and of law. Systems which attempt to question it, deal in sounds instead of sense, in caprice instead of reason, in darkness instead of light.

But enough of metaphor and declamation: it is not by such means that moral science is to be improved.

The principle of utility is the foundation of the present work: it will be proper therefore at the outset to give an explicit and determinate account of what is meant by it. By the principle of utility is meant that principle which approves or disapproves of every action whatsoever, according to the tendency which it appears to have to augment or diminish the happiness of the party whose interest is in question: or, what is the same thing in other words, to promote or to oppose that happiness. I say of every action whatsoever; and therefore not only of every action of a private individual, but of every measure of government.

By utility is meant that property in any object, whereby it tends to produce benefit, advantage, pleasure, good or happiness, (all this in the present case comes to the same thing) or (what comes again to the same thing) to prevent the happening of mischief, pain, evil, or unhappiness to the party whose interest is considered: if that party be the community in general, then the happiness of the community: if a particular individual, then the happiness of that individual.

The interest of the community is one of the most general expressions that can occur in the phraseology of morals: no wonder that the meaning of it is often lost. When it has a meaning, it is this. The community is a fictitious *body*, composed of the individual persons who are considered as constituting as it were its *members*. The interest of the community then is, what?—the sum of the interests of the several members who compose it.

It is in vain to talk of the interest of the community, without understanding what is the interest of the individual.[30] A thing is said to promote the interest, or to be *for* the interest of an individual, when it tends to add to the sum total of his pleasures: or, what comes to the same thing, to diminish the sum total of his pains.[31]

An action then may be said to be conformable to the principle of utility, or, for shortness sake, to utility, (meaning with respect to the community at large) when the tendency it has to augment the happiness of the community is greater than any it has to diminish it.

A measure of government (which is but a particular kind of action, performed by a particular person or persons) may be said to be conformable to or dictated by the principle of utility, when in like manner the tendency which it has to augment the happiness of the community is greater than any which it has to diminish it.                                                      [pp. 11–13]

Hampshire). See also the Warnock Report of the Committee on Inquiry into *Human Fertilisation and Embryology* (1984) Cmnd. 9314: "A strict utilitarian would suppose that given certain procedures, it would be possible to calculate their benefits and their costs . . . However, even if such a calculation were possible, it could not provide a final or verifiable answer to the question whether it is *right* that such procedures should be carried out. There would still remain the possibility that they were unacceptable, whatever their long-term benefits were supposed to be." (p. 2). The Report adds: "We have necessarily been mindful of the truth that matters of ultimate values are not susceptible of proof" (*ibid.*.]

[30]  (Interest, etc.) Interest is one of those words, which not having any superior *gènus*, cannot in the ordinary way be defined.

[31]  [But to assess alternative measures by their probable effects on people's pleasures or pains is clearly fraught with difficulty. An alternative has been suggested in the so-called "economic analysis" of law. As to this, see *post*, 620.]

*Of the Four Sanctions or Sources of Pain and Pleasure*

**1.** It has been shown that the happiness of the individuals, of whom a community is composed, that is their pleasures and their security, is the end and the sole end which the legislator ought to have in view: the sole standard, in conformity to which each individual ought, as far as depends upon the legislator, to be *made* to fashion his behaviour. But whether the this or any thing else that is to be *done*, there is nothing by which can ultimately be *made* to do it, but either pain or pleasure. Having taken a general view of these two grand objects (*viz.* pleasure, and what comes to the same thing, immunity from pain) in the character of *final* causes; it will be necessary to take a view of pleasure and pain itself, in the character of *efficient* causes or means.

**2.** There are four distinguishable sources from which pleasure and pain are in use to flow: considered separately, they may be termed the *physical*, the *political*, the *moral*, and the *religious*: and inasmuch as the pleasures and pains belonging to each of them are capable of giving a binding force to any law or rule of conduct, they may all of them be termed *sanctions*.

**3.** If it be in the present life, and from the ordinary course of nature, not purposely modified by the interposition of the will of any human being, nor by any extraordinary interposition of any superior invisible being, that the pleasure or the pain takes place or is expected, it may be said to issue from or to belong to the *physical sanction*.

**4.** If at the hands of a *particular* person or set of persons in the community, who under names correspondent to that of *judge*, are chosen for the particular purpose of dispensing it, according to the will of the sovereign or supreme ruling power in the state, it may be said to issue from the *political sanction*.

**5.** If at the hands of such *chance* persons in the community, as the party in question may happen in the course of his life to have concerns with, according to each man's spontaneous disposition, and not according to any settled or concerted rule, it may be said to issue from the *moral* or *popular sanction*.

**6.** If from the immediate hand of a superior invisible being, either in the present life, or in a future, it may be said to issue from the *religious sanction*.

**7.** Pleasures or pains which may be expected to issue from the *physical, political* or *moral* sanctions, must all of them be expected to be experienced, if ever, in the *present* life: those which may be expected to issue from the *religious* sanction, may be expected to be experienced either in the *present* life or in a *future*.[32]

[pp. 34–35]

---

[32] [Bentham never claims that the principle of utility was a scientific law. It combined this opinion as to the proper end of government with the fact that men always seek to maximise pleasure and minimise pain. Therefore, the value of the Greatest Happiness Principle could not be measured by utility in prediction; it had a different logical status from scientific laws. Still, though his system began and ended with an ultimate value-judgment, in almost every other respect his new art-and-science conformed to the method of the natural sciences (see Mack, *op. cit.*, pp. 143–144). The principle of utility was Bentham's single initial axiom, the one extra-empirical assumption underlining the conditions or means of his new science, but everything in the system depended upon it. "If it be denied me, I must confess I shall be altogether at a loss to prove it ... nor shall I easily be brought to think it necessary" (Bentham quoted, *op. cit.*, pp. 204–205; and *cf.* M. D. A. Freeman, in *Gli Italiani e Bentham* (1982), vol. 1, pp. 28–30). It could also be partly justified as a procedure which leads to "an agreed public language of discussion": see R. Harrison, *Bentham* (1983), Chap. 7. Manning (*op. cit.*, p. 12) suggests Bentham's "blunder" followed from "belief that the truth is manifest in sense experience and available to all who will free their minds from the shackles of received opinion." Taken alone, the principle of utility is empty, or is too general to be applied to practice. Its value really depends on its middle level "laws" or subordinate principles. Thus to take his example in relation to sexual freedom, by his rule, evil was measured by the number of people affected. It was not utilitarian to punish sexual offences, for they usually took

## J. BENTHAM
## Of Laws in General
(ed. Hart (1970))

*A Law Defined and Distinguished*

A law may be defined as an assemblage of signs declarative of a volition conceived or adopted by the *sovereign* in a state, concerning the conduct to be observed in a certain *case* by a certain person or class of persons, who in the case in question are or are supposed to be subject to his power: such volition trusting for its accomplishment to the expectation of certain events which it is intended such declaration should upon occasion be a means of bringing to pass, and the prospect of which it is intended should act as a motive upon those whose conduct is in question.

According to this definition, a law may be considered in eight different respects.

(1)  In respect to its *source*: that is in respect to the person or persons of whose will it is the expression.

(2)  In respect to the quality of its *subjects*: by which I mean the persons and things to which it may apply.

(3)  In respect to its *objects*: by which I meant the *acts*, as characterized by the *circumstances*, to which it may apply.

(4)  In respect to its *extent*, the generality or the amplitude of its application: that is in respect of the determinateness of the persons whose conduct it may seek to regulate.

(5)  In respect to its *aspects*: that is in respect to the various manners in which the will whereof it is the expression may apply itself to the acts and circumstances which are its objects.

(6)  In respect to its *force*: that is, in respect to the *motives* it relies on for enabling it to produce the effect it aims at, and the laws or other means which it relies on for bringing those motives into play: such laws may be styled its *corroborative appendages*.

place in private and had no public consequences. As to the calculus, he offered this, not as a dogma of ethics, but as a useful rule of thumb. The legislator must become an impartial calculator, a moral mathematician for whom each man had a numerical value of one. To answer what he should do, the legislator was given evidence and forced to estimate its reliability and consequences, and to help him Bentham tried to establish a rudimentary calculus based on external observable phenomena that could be measured. Bentham regarded the science of legislation as a practical science. He gradually sought to replace the word "science" with the phrase "art-and-science". Science was concerned with theory; art with practice. Bentham wanted to substitute the word "discipline" to include both. He regarded law and morals as essentially a practical discipline with a particularly close analogy with chemistry and more particularly with medicine. "The art of legislation is but the art of healing practised upon a large scale" (p. 264). Experience, observation and experiment are the foundations of well-grounded medical practice as they are of legislative practice. Bentham had no illusions about the practical possibility of an effective science of legislation, before the science of social statistics had been developed. For this reason he concentrated mainly on penal law, where he considered that adequate material already existed upon which conclusions could be based. For Bentham's suggestion as to how the "value of a lot of pleasure or pain" might be measured, see *Principles and Morals and Legislation*, Chaps 4–6. At the present day, a stronger defence of Bentham's "moral arithmetic" might be adduced in the light of such developments as psychological and personality tests; the use of computers; opinion-polls and cost-benefit analysis and similar sociological and economic techniques.]

(7)  In respect of its *expression*: that it is in respect to the nature of the *signs* by which the will whereof it is the expression may be made known.

(8)  In respect to its *remedial appendages*, where it has any: by which I mean certain other laws which may occasionally come to be subjoined to the principal law in question; and of which the design is to obviate the mischief that stands connected with any individual act of the number of those which are made offences by it, in a more perfect manner than can be done by the sole efficacy of the subsidiary appendages to which it stands indebted for its force.

The latitude here given to the import of the word *law* is it must be confessed rather greater than what seems to be given to it in common[33]: the definition being such as is applicable to various objects which are not commonly characterized by that name. Taking this definition for the standard it matters not whether the expression of will in question, so as to have but the authority of the sovereign to back it, were his by immediate conception or only by adoption: whether it be of the most public or of the most private or even domestic nature: whether it be sovereign from whom it derives its force be an individual or a body: whether it be issued *propter quid* as the phrase may be, that is on account of some particular act or event which is understood to warrant it (as is the case with an order of the judicial kind made *litis causa* in the course of a cause); or *mero motu* without the assignment of any such special ground: or whether it be susceptible of an indefinite duration or whether it be *suā naturā* temporary and undurable: as is most commonly the case with such expressions of will the uttering of which is looked upon as a *measure of administration*: whether it be a command or a countermand: whether it be expressed in the way of statute, or of customary law. Under the term "law" then if this definition be admitted of, we must include a judicial order, a military or any other kind of executive order, or even the most trivial and momentary order of the domestic kind, so it be not illegal: that is, so as the issuing of it be not forbidden by some other law.

Judging however from analogy, it would naturally be expected that the signification given to the word *law* should be correspondent to that of its conjugates *legislation* and *legislative power*: for what, it will be said, is legislation but the act of making laws? or legislative power but the power of making them? that consequently the term *law* should be applied to every expression of will, the uttering of which was an act of legislation, an exertion of legislative power; and that on the other hand it should not be applied to any expression of will of which those two propositions could not be predicted. Accordingly in the former of these points it does indeed quadrate with these two expressions: but it can not be said to do so in the latter. It has all the amplitude which they have, but the import of it is not everywhere confined within the bounds which limit theirs. This will be seen in a variety of examples.

(1)  In the first place, according to the definition, the word *law* should be applicable to any the most trivial order supposing it to be not illegal, which a man may have occasion to give for any of the most inconsiderable purposes of life: to any order which a master may have occasion to give to his servant, a parent to his child, or (where the request of a husband assumes the harsh form of a command) of a husband to his wife. Yet it would seem a strange catachresis to speak of the issuing of any such order as an act of legislation, or as an exercise of legislative power. Not but that in cases like these the word *law* is frequently enough employed: but then it is in the way of figure. Even where there is no such legal superiority, a man may say to another out of compliment, "your commands are laws to me":

---

[33]  [On Bentham's attitude and approach, see *ante*, 252–254.]

but on occasions like these the impropriety of the expression is the very reason of its being chosen.

(2) With equal propriety (according to the definition) would the word *law* be applicable to a temporary order issued by any magistrate who is spoken of as exercising thereby a branch of *executive* power, or as exercising the functions belonging to any department of *administration*. But the executive power is continually mentioned as distinct from the legislative: and the business of administration is as constantly opposed to that of legislation. Let the Board of Treasury order a sum of money to be paid or issued to such or such a person, let the Commander in chief order such or such a body of troops to march to such a place, let the Navy Board order such or such a ship to be fitted out, let the Board of Ordnance order such or such a train of artillery to be dispatched to such a destination—Who would ever speak of any of these orders as acts of legislative power, as acts of legislation?

(3) With equal propriety again would the word law according to the definition be applicable to any *judicial* order, to any order which in the course of a cause of any kind a man might have occasion to issue in the capacity of a judge. Yet the business of judicature is constantly looked upon as essentially distinct from the business of legislation and as constantly opposed to it: and the case is the same between the judicial and the legislative power. Even suppose the order to have been ever so general, suppose the persons to whom it is addressed to be ever so numerous and indeterminate, and the duration of it ever so indefinite, still if issued in the course of a forensic contestation, the act of issuing it would not be looked upon in general as coming under the notion of an act of legislation, or as an exercise of legislative power. The fate of a province may be determined by a judicial decrees: but the pronouncing of the decree will not on that account be looked upon as being capable with any sort of propriety of being termed an act of legislation... [pp. 1–5]

Such then are the various sorts of expressions of will to which men would be apt for one reason or other to deny the appellation of *a* law: such therefore are the points in which the definition here given of that important word outstretches the idea which common usage has annexed to it. And these excluded objects have in every point except that of the manner of their appertaining to the sovereign, in every point in short except their immediate *source*, the same nature with those whose title to the appellation stands clearest of dispute. They are all referrable *ultimately* to one common source: they have all of them alike their subjects and their objects, their local extent and their duration: in point of logical extent as it may be called they must all of them be either general or particular, and they may in most instances be indifferently either the one or the other: they are all of them susceptible of the same diversities with respect to the *parties* whom they may affect, and the *aspects* which they have present to the acts which are their objects: they require all of them the same *force* to give them effect, and the same *signs* to give them utterance. [p. 9]

### Source of a Law

First then with respect to its *source*. Considered in this point of view, the will of which it is the expression must, as the definition intimates, be the will of the sovereign in *a* state.[34] Now by a sovereign I mean any person or assemblage of

---

[34] [For natural lawyers like Pufendorf legal phenomena such as rights and duties were moral entities which were inherent in human beings. Bentham rejected this as sophistry and fiction and instead asserted that all legal concepts derived their significance solely

persons to whose will a whole political community are (no matter on what account) supposed to be in a disposition to pay obedience: and that in preference to the will of any other person.[35] Suppose the will in question not to be the will of *a* sovereign, that is of some sovereign or other; in such case, if it come backed with motives of a coercive nature, it is not a law, but an illegal mandate: and the act of issuing it is an offence.

If the person of whose will it is the expression be a sovereign, but a sovereign to whose power in the case in question a person of the description in question happens not to be subject, it is a law, which as to that person indeed has no force, yet still it is a law. The law having no force, the not obeying it is either no offence or an offence which cannot be punished. Yet still it cannot here be said that the issuing it is an offence: because the person from whom it issues is one whose act, as such, cannot be invested with the character of an offence. Were the Lord High Treasurer of Great Britain to issue of his own authority an order for levying a tax on all the inhabitants of Great Britain the issuing of that order would indeed be an offence: since the Lord High Treasurer of Great Britain is no more a sovereign in Great Britain than he is anywhere else. But were the King of France to issue an order to the same effect addressed to the same persons, such law would indeed be of no force, but yet it would hardly be looked upon as coming under the name of an offence: why?—because the King of France, though not sovereign in Great Britain is sovereign elsewhere; to wit in France: on his part then it would be an act not of delinquency but of hostility.

Now a given will or mandate may be the will or mandate of a given person in either of two ways: in the way of *conception* as it may be called (that is of original conception) or 2, in the way of *adoption*. A will or mandate may be said to belong to a sovereign in the way of conception when it was he himself who issued it and who first issued it, in the words or other signs in which it stands expressed: it may be said to belong to him by adoption when the person from whom it immediately emanes is not the sovereign himself (meaning the sovereign for the time being) but some other person: insomuch that all the concern which he to whom it belongs by adoption has in the matter is the being known to entertain a will that in case such or such another person should have expressed or should come to have expressed a will concerning the act or sort of act in question, such will should be observed and looked upon as his.

Where a mandate appertains to the sovereign only by adoption, such adoption may be distinguished in several respects: 1. in respect of the *time* in which the mandate adopted appears with reference to that of the adopting mandate: 2. in respect of the persons whose mandates are thus adopted: 3. in respect of the *degree* in which the adoption is performed: fourthly in respect of the *form* of expression by which it may be performed.

(1) First then, with regard to *time*, the mandate which the sovereign in question is supposed to adopt may be either already issued, or not: in the former case it may be said to be his by *susception*; in the latter by *pre-adoption*. Where the sovereign holds himself thus in readiness to adopt the mandates of another person whensover they shall happen to have been issued, he may thereby be said to invest that person with a certain species of power, which may be termed a *power of imperation*.[36] Examples of this distinction we shall see immediately.

from the commands and prohibitions imposed by the will of the sovereign. He did not pause however to consider whether that "will" itself was not a fiction. (See K. Olivecrona, "Bentham's Veil of Mystery" in *Current Legal Problems* (1978), p. 227). And see generally on Bentham's view of legal concepts, such as rights and duties, as fictions and how they should be analysed, H. L. A. Hart, *Essays on Bentham* (1982), pp. 128–132.]

[35] [But note Bentham's omission of any negative condition such as is found in Austin's description of sovereignty. Austin commented: "Mr Bentham has forgotten to notice the necessity of a negative condition" (*Province*, p. 212). See, further, Raz, *op. cit.*, pp. 6–8.]

[36] [On powers of imperation see Hart, *Essays on Bentham* (1982), Chap. 8.]

(2) As to the *persons* whose mandates the sovereign may have occasion to adopt, it would be to little purpose here, and indeed it would be premature, to attempt reducing the enumeration of them to an analytic method. In the way of susception, the sovereign for the time being adopts as well the mandates of former sovereigns as those of subordinate *power-holders*: in the way of pre-adoption, he can adopt the last mentioned mandates only: for to pre-adopt the mandates of subsequent sovereigns would be nugatory, since whatever actual force there is in sovereignty rests in the sovereign for the time being: in the living, not in the dead. As the propensity to obedience may admit of every imaginable modification, it is just conceivable indeed that the people should in certain points obey the mandates of a deceased sovereign in preference to those of his living successor. Lycurgus, if the story be a true one, found means by a trick, thus to reign after his death: but it is a trick that would hardly succeed a second time: and the necessity he found himself under of having recourse to that expedient would be a sufficient proof, if there required any, how little need the sovereign who is recognized as such for the time being has to be beholden for his power to his departed predecessors.

As to the subordinate power-holders whose mandates the sovereign pre-adopts, these are of course as many and as various as the classes of persons to whom the law gives either powers of *imperation* or the contrary powers of *de-imperation*, if such is the name that may be given to the power of undoing what by imperation has been done. These powers it may give to the power-holder on his own account, in which case the power is beneficial, or on that of another; in which case it is fiduciary: and in this latter case, on account of an individual, or on account of the public at large; in which latter case again the power is of the public or constitutional kind. It is thus that every mandate that is issued within the limits of the sovereignty and that is not illegal, is in one sense or the other the mandate of the sovereign. Take any mandate whatsoever, either it is of the number of those which he allows or it is not: there is no medium: if it is, it is his; by adoption at least, if not by original conception: if not, it is illegal, and the issuing it an offence. Trivial or important makes no difference: if the former are not his, then neither are the latter. The mandates of the master, the father, the husband, the guardian, are all of them the mandates of the sovereign: if not, then neither are those of the general or of the judge. Not a cook is bid to dress a dinner, a nurse to feed a child, an usher to whip a school boy, an executioner to hang a thief, an officer to drive the enemy from a post, but it is by his orders. If anyone should find a difficulty in conceiving this, he has only to suppose the several mandates in question to meet with resistance; in one case as well as in another the business of enforcing them must rest ultimately with the sovereign. Nor is there anything of fiction in all this: if there were, this is the last place in which it should be found.

To continue the laws of preceding sovereigns, and the powers of the various classes of magistrates, domestic as well as civil, is (in every tolerably well settled commonwealth at least) a matter of course. To suffer either of those systems of institutions to perish, and not to establish anything in their stead, would be to suffer the whole machine of government to drop to pieces. The one course no sovereign was ever yet mad enough, the other none was ever yet industrious enough, to pursue. If the adoption be not declared in words, it is because the fact is so notorious, that any express form of words to signify it would be unnecessary. It is manifested by means not less significant than words, by every act of government, by which the enforcement of the mandates in question is provided for. If it be alleged that the trivial transactions that pass in the interior of a family are not specifically in the contemplation of the sovereign: (trivial as they may be termed when individually considered, though in their totality they are the stuff that human life is made of) the same may be said of the transactions of fleets and armies: of those which become the objects of the mandates issued by the general or the judge. The same may even be said of those laws which emane directly from the very presence of the sovereign. It is only by the general tenor of their effects and not by any direct specification that individual acts of any kind can be comprised under extensive and general descriptions.

It is in this very way that conveyances and covenants acquire all the validity they can possess, all the connection they have with the system of the laws: adopted by the sovereign, they are converted into mandated laws. If you give your coat to a man, and the gift is valid, and nobody else has a right to meddle[37] with your coat, it is because a mandate subsists on the part of the sovereign, commanding all persons whatever to refrain from meddling with it, he to whom you gave it alone excepted, upon the event of your declaring such to be your pleasure. If a man engages or covenants to mend your coat for you, and such an engagement is valid, it is because on the part of the sovereign a mandate hath been issued, commanding any person upon the event of his entering into any engagement, (exception excepted) and thereby that particular person in consequence of his having entered into that particular engagement, (if not being within the exceptions) to perform it: in other words to render you that particular service which is rendered to you by performance of the act which he has engaged for.

Thus then in all cases stands the distinction between the laws which belong to the legislator in the way of conception, and those which belong to him in the way of pre-adoption. The former are the work of the legislator solely: the latter that of the legislator and the subordinate power-holder conjunctively, the legislator sketching out a sort of imperfect mandate which he leaves it to the subordinate power-holder to fill up. In the first case there are no other mandates in the case than those which emane from the subordinate legislator *immediate*: in the latter case whatever mandates there are emane from the subordinate power-holder *immediate*, and whenever they happen to be issued can only be said to emane *potestative* from the legislator. In the former case there are mandates from the first that exist *in actu:* in the latter until issued by the subordinate power-holder, whatever mandates there may be conceived to be exist only *in potentia.* In the former case the law will more readily than in the other be perceived to be occupied in issuing or repeating commands: In the other case it will be apt to appear as if it were employed solely in giving descriptions: for example of the *persons* by whom powers shall be possessed: of the *things* over which, or persons over whom, such powers shall be possessed: of the *acts* to which such power shall extend; that is of which the performance shall be deemed an exercise of such power: of the *place* in which and the *time* during which such powers shall be exercised, and so on. Yet still such descriptions have so much in them of the nature of a command or what stands opposed to it, that whenever the power which they confer or limit comes to be exercised, the expression of will whereby it is exercised may, without any alteration made in the import of it, be translated into the form and language of a mandate: of a mandate issuing from the mouth of the lawgiver himself.

Next as to the degree in which the mandate of a subordinate power-holder may be adopted by the sovereign: or in other words the degree of force which such mandate acquires by the adoption. Take any single manifestation of the sovereign's will, and all the assistance that the mandate of a subordinate power-holder can receive from it consists in a bare permission: this is the first step that the sovereign takes towards the giving validity to subordinate mandates: the first and least degree of assistance or rather countenance that the inferior can receive from the superior: the not being made the subject of a law commanding him not to issue the subordinate mandate which is in question. The part thus far taken by the sovereign is, we see, merely a negative one. Nor would it be worthwhile, or indeed proper, to notice him as taking any part at all, since it is no more than what is taken by even the merest stranger, were it not for its lying so much in his way to take the contrary part; a part which he actually does take in relation to the greater

---

[37] [For Bentham's concept of "meddling" see *post,* 287–288.]

number of the other members of the community. If any further degree of countenance is shown it must be by another law or set of laws: a law permitting the
subordinate power-holder to punish with his own hand the party who is made
subject to the mandate in case of disobedience, by a law permitting others to assist
in the administering such punishment, by a law commanding others to assist; and
so on. Such ulterior corroborative laws however are not to be reckoned as
exclusively necessary to the particular business of adoption: for a set of subsidiary
laws like these are equally necessary, as will be seen hereafter, to the giving *force*
and efficacy to such laws as emane from the sovereign himself in the most
immediate manner. [pp. 18–28]

## *Parties affected by a law*

...There yet remain a class of laws which stand upon a very different footing
from any of those that have hitherto been brought to view. The laws of which we
have hitherto been speaking have for their passible subjects not the sovereign
himself, but those who are considered as being in subjection to his power. But
there are laws to which no other person in quality of passible subjects can be
assigned than the sovereign himself. The business of the ordinary sort of laws is to
prescribe to the people what *they* shall do: the business of this transcendent class
of laws is to prescribe to the sovereign what *he* shall do: what mandates *he* may or
may not address to *them*; and in general how he shall or may conduct himself
towards them. Laws of this latter description may be termed, in consideration of
the party who is their passible subject, laws *in principem*[38]: in contradistinction to
the ordinary mass of laws which in this view may be termed laws *in subditos* or *in
populum*.

These laws *in principem* may be of either of two sorts according to the party
from whom they emane and the party whose conduct they are designed to
influence. This latter party may be the individual sovereign himself from whom
they emane, or any future sovereign or sovereigns his successor or successors; in
the former case they are what are strictly and properly termed pacts or covenants:
and to distinguish them from the ordinary covenants entered into by subjects,
they may be styled *pacta regalia* or *royal covenants*: in the latter case, they have
not as yet acquired any separate denomination. In the common way of speaking
these indeed are likewise termed pacts or covenants, one man being considered as
having covenanted in virtue of a covenant actually entered into by his predecessor. But this way of speaking, familiar as it is, is improper: it is inaccurate,
inconsistent and productive of confusion: to obviate which, acts of this sort may
be styled *recommendatory mandates*. When a reigning sovereign then in the tenor
of his laws engages for himself and for his successors he does two distinguishable
things. By an expression of will which has his own conduct for its object, he enters
*himself* into a covenant; by an expression of will which has the conduct of his
successors for its object, he addresses to *them* a recommendatory mandate. This
mandate the successor whenever the sovereignty devolves to him will probably
adopt: and then and not till then it is his covenant.

The causes which originally produced the original covenant and the considerations of expediency which justified the engaging in it on the part of the
predecessor will in general subsist to produce and justify the adoption of it on the
part of the successor. In most instances therefore it will have happened that upon
any change taking place in the sovereignty such adoption shall have taken place:
it will have become customary for it so to do: the people, influenced partly by the
force of habit and partly by the consideration of the expediency of such adoption,
will be expecting it as a thing of course: and this expectation will add again to the

---

[38] [For Hart's discussion, see *Essays on Bentham* (1982), pp. 239–242.]

motives which tend to produce such effect in any given instance. So great in short is the influence of all these causes when taken together, that in any tolerably well settled government the successor is as much expected to abide by the covenants of his predecessor as by any covenants of his own: unless where any change of circumstances has made a manifest and indisputable change in the utility of such adherence. This expectation may even become so strong, as to equal the expectation which is entertained of the prevalence of that disposition to obedience on the part of the people by which the sovereignty *de facto* is constituted: in-somuch that the observance of the covenant on the one part shall be looked upon as a condition *sine qua non* to the obedience that is to be paid on the other. Things are most apt to be upon this footing in those governments in which the sovereignty is ascribed nominally to a single person, who in reality possesses only a part, though perhaps the most conspicuous part, in it. But in all governments where either the whole or a principal part of the sovereignty is in the hands of a single person, the exercise of the sovereignty and the observance of the covenants entered into by preceding sovereigns are looked upon as being in such a degree connected that upon taking upon him the former a man is universally understood to have taken upon him the latter: understood, not only by the people, but by the sovereign himself. This notion is so universal and deep-rooted that if by accident a sovereign should in fact come to the throne with a determination not to adopt the covenants of his predecessors, he would be told that he had adopted them notwithstanding: adopting them tacitly by taking upon him those powers to the exercise of which the obligation of adopting those covenants, stood annexed. Nor would this way of speaking, how untrue soever it may be by the very supposition, seem mis-applied: since it has become the habit among men of law to speak of the matter of right in the same terms in which they would speak of the matter of fact: that which, according to the general opinion, *ought* to be done being spoken as if it *were* done.

It appears then that there are two distinct sorts of laws, very different from each other in their nature and effect: both originating indeed from the sovereign, (from whom mediately or immediately all ordinances in order to be legal must issue) but addressed to parties of different descriptions: the one addressed to the sovereign, imposing an obligation on the sovereign: the other addressed to the people, imposing an obligation on the people. Those of the first sort may again be addressed either to the sovereign himself who issues them, (the sovereign for the time being) or to his successors, or (what is most common) to the one as well as to the other. It is evident then that in the distinction between these two classes of laws it is the quality of the parties who are respectively bound by them that is the essential and characteristic feature.

Here it may naturally enough be asked what sense there is in a man's addressing a law to himself? and how it is a man can impose an obligation upon himself? such an obligation to wit as can to any purpose be effectual. Admit indeed we must that for a man to address a law to himself, is what indeed there would be little sense in, were there no other *force* in the world but his: nor can a man by his own single unassisted force impose upon himself any effectual obli-gation: for granting him to have bound himself, what should hinder him on any occasion from setting himself free? On the other hand, take into account an exterior force, and by the help of such force it is as easy for a sovereign to bind himself as to bind another. It is thus, as was seen in a former chapter, that in transactions between subject and subject a man binds himself by the assistance of that force which is at the disposal of the sovereign. Nor is the assertion we make in speaking of a man's binding himself so wide from the literal truth as at first sight might appear. The force which binds, depends indeed upon the will of a third person: but that will itself waits to receive its determination from the person who is said to bind, from the person who is the promulgator of the law. Without the covenantor, there would be no law at all: without the *guarantee*, as he is called, none that can be effectual. The law then may in strictness be considered as the word of both: and therefore in part, of either: but the share which the covenantor takes in it is by much the more conspicuous. It is this at all events that is taken first: it is seen to be taken while the other perhaps is expected only: it is certain; while the other perhaps is but contingent. In short the part which the sovereign for the time being has in the establishment of a *pactum regium* whereby he binds himself and his successors may be as considerable, and as independent of the part which may come to be taken by those to whom belongs the enforcement of such covenant, as the part which is taken by the legislator in the case of a law of the ordinary stamp *in populum* is of the part which may come to be taken by the judge.

By what means then can a law *in principem* be enforced and rendered efficacious: what force is there in the nature of things that is applicable to his purpose? To answer this question, we have nothing to do but to resort to the enumeration, that has been already given on a former occasion, of the several sorts of forces by which the human will is liable to be influenced. The forces and the only forces by which the human will is influenced are *motives*: these, when considered in the mass, may be distinguished according to the sources from whence they issue: to these sources we set out with giving the name of *sanctions*. Of these sanctions that which we termed the *physical* is out of the question: for the force in the case in question is supposed to be directed *by design*. There remain the political, the religious and the moral. The force of the political sanction is inapplicable to this purpose by the supposition: within the dominion of the sovereign there is no one who while the sovereignty subsists can judge so as to coerce the sovereign: to maintain the affirmative would be to maintain a contradiction.[39] But the force of

---

[39] This proposition stands in need of explanation: the truth of it depends upon the idea annexed to the word *sovereign*. The case is, that supposing the powers in the state to be thus distributed, there is no one person or body of persons in whose hands the sovereignty is reposed. Suppose two bodies of men, or for shortness' sake two men, the one possessing every power of the state, except that the other in case of a public accusation, preferred in such or such forms, has the power of judging him; including such power as may be necessary to carry the judgment into execution. It is plain the sovereignty would not be exclusively in either: it would be conjunctively in both. Yet in common speech it is probable that the first man would be styled *the* sovereign, or at least *a* sovereign: because his power would be constantly in exercise: the other's only occasionally, or perhaps never. Now then if the narrow sense were to be given to the word *sovereign*, it is plain that the proposition above mentioned concerning the impossibility of the sovereign's being judged by anyone, would not be true. A logician of the ordinary stamp (for nothing is more common than to be versed in the forms of dialects without any clear notions of terminology) would find no difficulty in maintaining the contrary, and proving it by what to him might seem a demonstration. Taking advantage of the inexplicit notions annexed to the words *superior* and *inferior*, he would perhaps assume for his medium this proposition, that it is impossible for a man to be superior and inferior to another at the same time: or perhaps in different propositions he would use the same word *sovereign* in two different sense: at one time in its strict and proper sense; at another time in its popular and improper sense, according to the distinction above taken. Till men are sufficiently aware of the ambiguity of words, political discussions may be carried on continually, without profit and without end. It may occur, that the distribution of power above supposed is not an expedient one, or that it cannot be a lasting one. This may or may not be the case: but the expediency or the durability of such an arrangement are points with which we have nothing to do here. I consider here only what is possible: now it is possible: for every distribution as well as every limitation of power is possible that is conceivable. The power of the governor is constituted by the obedience of the governed: but the obedience of the governed is susceptible of every modification of which human conduct is susceptible: and the rules which mark it out, of every diversity which can be clearly described by words. Wheresoever one case can be distinguished from another, the same distinction may obtain in the disposition to obedience which may have established itself among the people. In the former case they may be disposed to pay it to one

the religious sanction is as applicable to this purpose as to any other; and this is one of the great and beneficial purposes to which the religious sanction, where it happens to have an influence, is wont to be applied. The same may be said of the force of the moral sanction. Now the force of the moral sanction as applied to the purpose in question may be distinguished into two great branches: that which may be exerted by the subjects of the state in question acting without, and perhaps even against, the sanction of political obligations, acting in short as in a state of nature; and that which may be exerted by foreign states. When a foreign state stands engaged by express covenant to take such a part in the enforcement of such a law as that in question, this is one of the cases in which such foreign state is said to stand with reference to such law in the capacity of a guarantee. Of a covenant of this sort many examples are to be met with in the history of international jurisprudence.

To all or any of these forces may a law *in principem* stand indebted for its efficacy. Of all these forces even when put together the efficacy it must be confessed is seldom so great as that of the political. How should it? when it is in the nature of the political sanction to draw with it in most instances a great part if not the whole of the force of the other two? But to deny them all efficacy would be to go too far on the other side. It would be as much as to say that no privileges were ever respected, no capitulation ever observed. It would be as much as to say, that there is no such system in Europe as the Germanic body: that the inhabitants of Austrian Flanders are upon no other footing than the inhabitants of Prussia: those of the *pays d'états* in France than those of the *pays d'élection*: that no regard was ever paid to the American charters by the British Parliament: and that the Act of Union has never been anything but a dead letter . . .        [pp. 64–71]

### Force of a law

. . . With respect to the *force* of the law: that is, with respect to the motives it relies upon for enabling it to produce the effects it aims at.[40] Motives of some sort or

magistrate, in the latter to another: or in the former case they may be disposed to obey one of those magistrates, and in the latter nobody. Many are the commonplace phrases in use which would seem to assert the contrary: that an *imperium in imperio* is a monster in politics: that no man can serve two masters: that a house divided against itself cannot stand: and these phrases are made to pass for arguments. There is indeed something specious in them at first sight: and without due examination a man may be easily mislead by them. Thus much is indeed true, that the same individual branch of power cannot be possessed, and that exclusively, by two persons at the same time. But any two branches of power may that are distinguishable: and any one branch of power may be shared amongst ever so many. What gives rise to the internal contests by which states are agitated or destroyed, is that two different men or bodies of men claim exclusively the same individual branch: which in governments that are not purely monarchical may ever be the case, and that on all sides with the best faith imaginable, while laws are wanting to decide the matter, or those which there are ambiguous or obscure. The minuteness and refinement of which the distribution of powers in a state is susceptible depends upon the proficiency that is made in the anatomy of language, and the use that is made of the proficiency in the body of laws. [In the text Bentham is describing by what sanctions a sovereign can be bound. In this note he develops the germ of a doctrine of judicial review, showing that where sovereignty is divided, one part of the sovereign could be bound by another. See also J. H. Burns, "Bentham on Sovereignty: An Exploration" in (ed.) M. H. James, *Bentham and Legal Theory*, pp. 133–150.]

[40]  [*Cf.* D. Lyons, *In the Interests of the Governed* (1973), pp. 130–137.]

other[41] to trust to it evidently must have: for without a cause, no such thing as an effect: without a motive, no such thing as action. What then are motives: We have seen that they are but the expectations of so many lots of pain and pleasure, as connected in a particular manner in the way of causality with the actions with reference to which they are termed *motives*. When it is in the shape of pleasure they apply, they may be termed *alluring* motives: when in the shape of pain, *coercive*. It is when those of the alluring kind are held up as being connected with an act, that a *reward* is said to be offered: it is when those of the coercive kind are thus held up, that a *punishment* is said to be denounced.[42]

The next question is from what source these motives may issue. Now it has already been observed, that of the four sources from whence pain and pleasure may be said to take their rise, there are three which are under the influence of intelligent and voluntary agents; *viz*: the political, the moral, and the religious sanctions. The legislator then may, in the view of giving efficacy to his laws take either of two courses: he may trust altogether to the auxiliary force of the two foreign sanctions, or he may have recourse to motives drawn from that fund which is of his own creation. The former of these courses is what has sometimes been taken with success: there seem even to be cases in which it is to be preferred to any other. These cases however are in comparison but rare. For the most part it is to some pleasure or some pain drawn from the political sanction itself, but more particularly, as we shall see presently, to pain that the legislator trusts for the effectuation of his will.

This punishment then, or this reward, whichever it be, in order to produce its effect must in some manner or other be announced: notice of it must in some way or other be given, in order to produce an expectation of it, on the part of the people whose conduct it is meant to influence. This notice may either be given by the legislator himself in the text of the law itself, or it may be left to be given, in the way of customary law by the judge; the legislator, commanding you for example to do an act; the judge in his own way and according to his own measure punishing you in case of your not doing it, or, what is much less frequent, rewarding you in case of your doing it . . .

But the most eligible and indeed the most common method of giving notice is by inserting a clause on purpose: by subjoining to that part of the law which is expressive of the legislator's will, another part, the office of which is to indicate the motive he furnishes you with for complying with such will.

In this case the law may plainly enough be distinguished into two parts: the one serving to make known to you what the inclination of the legislator is: the other serving to make known to you what motive the legislator has furnished you with for complying with that inclination: the one addressed more particularly to your understanding; the other, to your will. The former of these parts may be termed the *directive*: the other, the *sanctional* or *incitative*.

---

[41] [The four motives are described in detail in *The Rationale of Judicial Evidence* (Chaps IX and XI of Book 1) where Bentham's concern is with the problem of ensuring truthfulness in testimony in court. (See Bowring (ed.), *Collected Works*, vol. VI, pp. 247–275). For discussions of this aspect of Bentham, see Hacker in *Oxford Essays in Jurisprudence* (Simpson ed., 1973), pp. 135–148, Lyons, *In the Interest of the Governed* (1973), pp. 130–137, Knowles in *Perspectives in Jurisprudence* (Attwooll ed., 1977), pp. 1–19.]

[42] [But *cf.* R. S. Summers's remark on the "implementive mechanisms or devices" required by laws. "The naive instrumentalist has but one type . . . in his inventory: sanctions . . . But the reality is more varied and complex. Among other things, it includes educational effort, rewards and other incentives, symbolic deployment of legal forms, publicity (favourable or adverse), continuous supervision, public signs and signals, recognised statuses and entities, grants with strings attached, and on and on and on. Jurisprudence (sociological?) awaits an imaginative and systematic analysis of the wide-ranging varieties of implementive devices and mechanisms" (Hacker and Raz (eds.), *Law, Morality and Society* (1977), p. 126).]

As to the incitative this it is evident may be of two kinds: when the motive furnished is of the nature of punishment, it may be termed the *comminative* part, or *commination*: when it is of the nature or reward, the *invitative* part, or *invitation*.

Of the above two methods of influencing the will that in which punishment is employed is that with which we are chiefly concerned at present. It is that indeed of which we hear the most and of which the greatest use is made. So great indeed is the use that is made of it, and so little in comparison is that which is made of reward, that the only names which are in current use for expressing the different aspects of which a will is susceptible are such as suppose punishment the motive. Command, prohibition, and permission, all of them point at punishment: hence the impropriety we were obliged to set out with, for want of words to remedy it.

The case is that for ordinary use punishment is beyond comparison the most efficacious upon the whole. By punishment alone it seems not impossible but that the whole business of government might be carried on: though certainly not so well carried on as by a mixture of that and reward together. But by reward alone it is most certain that no material part of that business could ever be carried on for half an hour.[43]

---

[43] The reasons why the principal part of the business of government cannot be carried on any otherwise than by punishment are various: among which there are several which would each of them be abundantly sufficient of itself.

1. In the first place, any man can at any time be much surer of administering pain than pleasure.

2. The law (that is, the set of persons employed for this purpose by the legislator) has it still less in its power to make sure of administering pleasure than particular persons have: since the power of administering pleasure depends upon the particular and ever-changing circumstances of the individual to whom it is to be applied: of which circumstances the law is not in any way of being apprised. In short the law seems to have no means of administering pleasure to any man by its own immediate operation: all it can do is to put the instrument in his way, and leave him at liberty to apply it himself for that purpose if he thinks proper: this is accordingly what the law does when it is said to give a man a pecuniary reward.

3. The scale of pleasure supposing it actually applied is very short and limited: the scale of pain is in comparison unlimited.

4. The sources of pleasure are few and soon exhausted: the sources of pain are in numerable and inexhaustible. It has already been observed that the only means the law has of administering pleasure to a man is by placing the instruments of it within his reach. But the number and value of these instruments is extremely limited. Any object in nature may be converted into an instrument of pain: few in comparison and rare are those which are calculated to serve as instruments of pleasure.

5. The law has no means of producing pleasure without producing pain at the same time: which pleasure and which pain being considered by themselves apart from their effects, the pain is more than equivalent to the pleasure. For, an instrument of pleasure before it can be given to one man must have been taken from another: and since *ceteris paribus* it is more painful to lose a given sum than it is pleasurable to gain it, the pain produced by the *taking* is upon an average always more than equivalent to the pleasure produced by the *giving*.

6. The insufficiency of rewards is more particularly conspicuous when applied to acts of the negative kind. The acts of a positive kind of which it is necessary to enjoin the performance are always made refereable to some definite possible subject, and included within a definite portion of time: such as to pay money on a certain occasion to a certain person: to lend a hand to the repair of certain road for such a number of days; and so forth. But acts of a negative kind are commonly comprised under no such limitations. Take for instance the not stealing, and the not doing damage to the roads. Now by not stealing is meant the not stealing from any person any stealable articles at any time: but persons are numerous, stealable articles still more so, and time indefinitely divisible. If then Paul for example were to be rewarded for not stealing it must be in some way as this: for not stealing from Peter a farthing at 12 o'clock one shilling: for not stealing another farthing from the same Peter at the same time, another shilling, for not stealing another

The sense of mankind on this head is so strong and general, however confused and ill developed, that where the motives presented to the inclination of him whose conduct it is proposed to influence are of no other than the alluring kind, it might appear doubtful perhaps whether the expression of the will of which such conduct is the object could properly be styled a law. The motives which the law trusts to are in most cases of a coercive nature: hence the idea of coercion shall in their minds have become inseparably connected with that of a law. Being then an invitation, that is an expression of will trusting for its efficacy to motives not coercive, they will conclude that it can not with propriety be styled a law.

The conclusion however seems not to be a necessary one. For as these invitations are as much the expressions of the will of a lawgiver as commands themselves are, as they issue from the same source, tend to the same ends, are susceptible of the same aspects, applicable to the same objects, and recorded indiscriminately in the same volumes with those expressions of will which beyond dispute are entitled to the appellation of a law, it should seem that without any great incongruity, they might be established in the possession of the same name. To distinguish, however, a law of this particular kind from the other, it should never be mentioned but under some particular name, such as than of an *invitative* or *praemiary* law; or it might be styled a *legislative invitation*, or a *bounty*.

As a law may have sometimes a penal sanction to back it, sometimes a sanction of the praemiary kind, so may it, (as is obvious) be provided with two opposite sanctions, one of the one kind, the other of the other. A law thus provided may be styled *a law with an alternative sanction*. In this case the mode of conduct with which the one of these sanctions is connected is the opposite to that with which the other is connected. If the one sanction is connected with the positive act, the other sanction is connected with the correspondent negative act. Take the following example. Whosoever comes to know that a robbery has been committed, let him declare it to the judge: if he declares it accordingly, he shall receive such or such a reward: if he fails to declare it, he shall suffer such or such a punishment.

We are now arrived at the notion of an object which might in a certain sense admit of the appellation of a law. It may even be looked upon as constituting a law and something more: since there are to be found in it two distinguishable parts: the directive part, which must of itself be a complete expression of will, and an article of a different nature, *a prediction*. But nothing hath as yet been brought to view by which the efficacy of the directive part, or the verity of the predictive can have been established upon any solid footing. Let the law stop here, and let the influence of the two auxiliary sanctions be for a moment set aside, what has been done by the law as yet amounts to nothing: as an expression of will, it is impotent; as a prediction, it is false. The will of the legislator concerning the matter in question has indeed been declared: and punishment has been threatened in the case of non-compliance with such will: but as to the means of carrying such threats into execution, nothing of this sort hath as yet been made appear.

What course then can the legislator take? There is but one, which is to go on commanding as before: for as to taking upon himself the infliction of the punishment with his own hands, this, were it practicable in every case which it manifestly can not be, would be overstepping the bounds of his own function and exercising a different sort of power. All he can do then in his capacity of legislator is to issue a second law, requiring some person to verify the prediction that accompanied the first. This secondary law being issued in aid of the primary may with reference thereto be termed the *subsidiary* law: with reference to which the primary law may on the other hand be termed the *principal*.

To whom is it then that this subsidiary law should be addressed? It can never be

---

farthing from the same Peter at a moment after 12, another shilling: for not stealing another John a farthing at such a place at 12 o'clock, another shilling: the same sums to be given also to Peter and John for not stealing from Paul: and so on for everlasting.

to the same person to whom the principal law was addressed: for a man *can* not reward himself; nor *will* he punish himself. It must therefore be to some other person: a circumstance which of itself is sufficient to shew that the principal and subsidiary are two distinct laws, and not parts of one and the same law. It may be any other person indefinitely. Commonly however it is to some particular class of persons, who occupying some particular station or civil condition instituted for the purpose, such as that of judge, are presumed on the one hand to be properly qualified, on the other hand to be previously disposed, to execute or cause to be executed any such commands when issued by the legislature.

But neither can the hand nor the eye of the judge reach everywhere: to be in a condition to discharge his functions he must be provided with a variety of assistants: which assistants must for certain purposes be of various ranks, occupations and descriptions: witnesses, registers, court-keepers, jail-keepers, bailiffs, executioners, and so forth. Of these there are many who must begin to act in their respective characters even before the matter is submitted to his cognizance: consequently before they can be in a way to receive any commands from him. On this and other accounts they too must have their duties prescribed to them by the law itself: and hence the occasion for so many more subsidiary laws or sets of subsidiary laws, of which they are respectively the agible subjects, and their acts the objects.

It is evident that the number and nature of the subsidiary laws of this stamp will be determined by the number and nature of the different sorts of acts which on the part either of the same person or of different person it is thought proper should be performed or abstained from in the course of the *procedure*. Now by the procedure is meant on the present occasion the suite of steps which are required to be taken in the view of ascertaining whether a man has or has not done an act of the number of those which stand prohibited by some principal law: and thereby of ascertaining whether he is or is not of the number of those persons, on whom a punishment of the sort denounced by the principal law in question is required to be inflicted.

Amidst this various train of laws subsidiary, that which is addressed to the judge and contains the command to punish, may for distinction's sake be termed the punitive or *punitory* law: and with reference to the rest the *proximate* subsidiary law: the rest may indiscriminately be termed *remote*. Where the principal law is of the praemiary kind, the proximate subsidiary law may be termed *remunerative*.

Now it is evident that in like manner as a principal law must have its subsidiary laws, so also must each of those subsidiary laws have a train of subsidiary laws to itself, and that for the same reason. This is a circumstance that belongs alike to every law which takes its support from the political sanction. *A* commits an offence: it is thereupon rendered the duty of *B* to contribute in such or such a way to the bringing of him to punishment in the event of his proving guilty: and a particular process is appointed to be carried on for ascertaining whether he be or no. In the course of that process such and such steps are required to be taken by *C* in such and such contingencies: such and such others by *D* and *E* and *F*: and so on indefinitely. But what if *B* also prove refractory? a similar process must thereupon be carried on and a similar provision made by the law for the bringing of him also to punishment: and so on if any failure should arise on the part of *D* or *E* or *F*. In this way must commands follow upon commands: if the first person called does not obey, the second may: if the second should not, yet a third may: if even the third should fail, yet there may be hopes of a fourth.[44] If it is not expected that

---

[44]  [It was from arguments such as these that Petrazycki argued that a sanction of any kind cannot be essential to a rule of law, for the transgression of a rule with a sanction would bring another rule and sanction into play and so on *ad infinitum*. But, as Stone puts out (*Legal System, op. cit.*, pp. 77–78), though logically sound, in sociological terms the

anyone will obey, the law is plainly impotent and falls to the ground: but let obedience be but expected from any one of the persons addressed, at whatever distance he stands from him who was addressed first, this expectation may prove sufficient to keep all the intermediate persons to their duty. If an offence then be committed, until obedience takes place on the part of some one person or other of the persons thus connected, the law is as it were asleep, and the whole machine of government is at a stand: but let any one law in the whole penal train meet with obedience, let punishment take place in any quarter, the law awakens out of its trance, and the whole machine is set agoing again: the influence of that law which has met with obedience flows back as if it were through all the intermediate laws till it comes to the principal one to which they are all alike subsidiary...

[pp. 133–141]

### Idea of a complete law[45]

...The laws relative to property may be considered in various points of view. To apprehend the nature of them, the relation they bear to the rest of the system, and how they are reducible to the nature of a mandate or its opposite, we must call back to mind what was said of the offences relative to property in the preceding chapter.[46] Let us begin with that sort of property which is the most simple.... The most simple case is where the proprietary subject as we may call it is corporeal, determinate and single...

To understand the nature of the laws of property it will be requisite to recur to the enumeration we had occasion to make in the last chapter of the possible offences relative to property. It will also be necessary to recollect that an offence and the law whereby that offence is created are a sort of correlatives; so that for every offence there is a law: *viz*: a law of the mandative or imperative kind, and for every law of the imperative kind there is an offence: and that accordingly the offence being given the law is given also, or the law being given, the offence. Now in the list of the offences against property the radical one seems to be that which we have styled *wrongful occupation of property:* it is to that offence that the law, by which the most simple and elementary species of proprietary right is created, corresponds. This is the leading offence by reference to which the nature of those other offences may most commodiously be explained.

But without the idea of some particular sort of corporeal object before our eyes it will be difficult to reason clearly. Let the proprietary subject then be a certain piece of land, a field, the offence which consists in the wrongful occupation of this property will be any act in virtue of which the agent may be said to meddle with this field. But the name of the offence reflects the act which is the object of the law: now the offence is that of meddling with the field. But that object when represented by the name of the offence is represented just as natural objects are

support given by public opinion and power to the law renders the chance of violation of the first rule relatively small and the chance of violation of subsequent rules less and less likely.]

45 [For a detailed exposition of Bentham's analysis of "a law" see M. H. James (ed.), *Bentham and Legal Theory*, especially "Bentham on the Individuation of Laws" by M. H. James, at pp. 91–116 and "Bentham on the Aspects of a Law" by L. J. Lysaght, at pp. 117–132. Bentham's system was based on the assumption that the business of the legal system is to tell the population what acts they may expect to be followed by sanctions and what acts they may perform without fear of legal interference. Every complete law is thus a duty-imposing norm; for though permissive laws are possible each individual law should be constructed round a principal provision which is obligative in character (*op. cit.*, pp. 115 and 132). For criticism, see Raz, *Concept of a Legal System* (1970), pp. 170–175 and Dworkin, "Legal Principles and the Limits of Law" (1972) 81 Yale L. J. 823.]

46 [The reference intended is to Chap. XVI, para. 35 of *An Introduction to the Principles* (in *CW*, 226–232). *CW* refers to Collected Works 1968—: the edition by Hart and Burns.]

represented in certain mirrors, in an inverted position. The offence then being the act of meddling with the field, the act which is the object of the law, the act commanded is the negative act of not meddling with the field. Annexing then the expression of will to the act thus expressed, we have the whole substance of the law; which amounts to this, "Let no one, Rusticus excepted," (so we will call the proprietor) "and those whom he allows meddle with such or such a field." Here then we have an example of one form in which the substance of law of property creating property may be expressed.

But in this law we see there is an exceptive clause. Now every law in which there is an exceptive clause may be resolved into two provisions. These provisions where the law is, as it is here, of the negative or prohibitive kind are 1. a primordial mandate of the prohibitive kind, the more extensive of the two: 2. a superventitious mandate of the permissive kind which is the least extensive of the two, being revocative but revocative *pro tanto* only and not *pro toto* of the former. No man shall meddle with the garment (describing it): Praetextatus and such other persons as he allows may meddle with the garment.

Viewing the matter in this light it is not to be wondered if a man should be alarmed at first at the multitude of the laws to which the head of property may give occasion. To that multitude it must be acknowledged there are no bounds. In the first place we have a different law for every distinct proprietary subject: and matter is infinitely divisible. In the next place we have a new law every time the subject changes hands, and time also is infinitely divisible and that may happen fifty times a day. But we are as yet got but a very little way in the enumeration of the circumstances which may give occasion to different laws relative to the same individual subject. In the example above exhibited it is taken for granted that the subject belongs solely to one person, that it is his not only for a certainty but at present, and not only for the present but for ever, that when he chooses to make use of it, he may make what use of it he pleases, and that he may make use of one part of it as well as of another, and that to warrant him in making use of it he has no need to wait for any particular event or for the consent of any other person...

The laws then to which any one single proprietary subject may give occasion being infinite, how is it possible, it may be asked, to comprise the collection of the whole body of the laws relative to property within the limited compass of a code? Certainly to draw them out at length and conceived in the imperative form is not possible. But the modes of expressing imperation as there hath already been occasion to observe are indefinitely numerous. Of these many are indirect and have nothing of imperation upon the face of them; bearing the form not of imperative but of common assertive propositions: as if they were the words not of the lawgiver but of some one else who was giving an account of what the lawgiver had done. Now as in the imperative form the laws relative to this head would swell to an infinite degree of expansion: so in the narrative or assertive form they may be reduced to an almost infinite degree of compression. To describe and distinguish the several contrivances by which in different cases this concentration may be effected, would require a volume. All that can be done here is to give notice to the reader: inasmuch that being aware of the metamorphoses, he may be master of a thread which will conduct him at any time from the artificial and super-induced, to the native and primeval form of the several provisions of the law. To exhibit in this latter form all these provisions collectively is impossible, but it is no more than what a man must be able to do with regard to each of them taken separately, ere he can possess any accurate comprehension either of the nature and operation of such provision taken by itself, or of the relation it bears towards the other parts of the system. For a law of any kind or any part of the law of any kind to have any effect, a man must be punishable in case of his disobeying it: but to have an idea of a case in which a man is punishable for any act is to have the idea of an offence: and to have the idea of an offence, the signification of the will of him who makes it such being added, is to have the idea of a command.

It hath already been observed on a former occasion that private conveyances in as far as they are legal, that is adopted by the legislator, are so many laws or assemblages of laws. This being admitted, a body of the laws to be complete must be understood as including *inter alia* the whole body of conveyances: a complete body of the laws taken at any given period will therefore include a complete collection of the several conveyances which within the dominion of the state are in force at the instant of that period. Not that conveyances are on this account to be reckoned laws in any other sense than that in which any other commands issued in the exercise of powers are laws; those not excepted which are issued by parents, masters and other domestic power-holders for any the most trivial purposes of a private family. For the legislator then to take any separate notice of them is impossible. All that he can do, and all that it is requisite he should do is to describe in general terms such as he thinks proper to adopt, and thereupon explicitly or implicitly such others as he thinks proper not to adopt: in other words such as are deemed *good* or *valid*, and such as are to be deemed *void*. Now those are good or valid which are made in such *form* as it is thought proper to acknowledge for good form, by him who has a good title, or to speak shortly a title to convey, in favour of him who has good title to take or receive: those bad or void which are made in such form as it is thought proper to hold for bad, by one who has no good title, or as the phrase is no title to convey, or in favour of one who has no good title or not title to take or receive. But an event which is allowed to give a man a title to one sort of proprietary subject may not perhaps be allowed to give a man a title to a proprietary subject may not perhaps be allowed to give him a title to a proprietary subject of another sort: and an individual event: which gives a man a title to an individual proprietary subject does not thereby give him a title to another individual proprietary subject. Moreover an event which is allowed to give to a person of one sort a title to a proprietary subject of any given sort, may not be allowed to give a title to a proprietary subject of that sort to a man of another sort. Also as to events that depend upon the act of man, an event which if it resulted from the act of a person of one sort would be allowed to give to a person of a given sort a title as to a proprietary subject of a given sort, may not be allowed to produce that effect where it results from the act of a person of another sort, as in the case of minors, prodigals, trust-holders and the like. Hence the whole branch of the law relative to conveyances may be comprised in the exposition of a few such words as proprietary, proprietary subject, proprietary rights, proprietor or right-holder, title, formal conveyance, and the like: of which exposition every distinguishable clause by being applied to any particular conveyance that came into controversy might be translated into a command.

It is thus that by being applied to and combined in a manner with the expression of the wills of individual power-holders that branch of the law which concerns conveyances is transformable into and carries the effect of a command. But there is another branch of the law, still referable to the offence of wrongful occupation in which the matter of the command is furnished by the legislator solely and immediately without needing to be applied to the mandate of any private power-holder. This includes the cases where the title of him in whose favour the law is made is constituted either by an event which is altogether in his own power or by an event of any other kind in which, in as far at least as concerns the effect thus given to it, no other person's will has any participation: as is the case for instance with the title derived from occupancy, improvement, natural increment and succession *ab intestato*. In this latter sort of case the connection between the assertive matter of the law and the idea of a command emaning from the legislator will not be quite so remote as in the former. In the one case we may have a complete law, in the other case we can not without descending to that degree of minuteness and particularity as to take in the mandates of individuals. Thus it is that in one or other of these ways a great part of the matter of law is naturally and in a manner necessarily thrown into the assertive form constituting a kind of exposition of some such word as the word *title*.

This word then we see is a word that will be wanted to make part of the definition of the offence entitled wrongful occupation of property. But this same word of what is equivalent to it will be equally stood in need of for completing the several definitions of the several other acts which are ranked under the head of offences concerning property. Thus wrongful non-investment of property is the forbearing to render a man that sort of service which consists in the conveying to him or investing him with a title to a certain proprietary subject, he having a title to such service: wrongful investment of property, in the doing of any of those acts which are deemed by the law to divest a man of such a title, the wrongdoer having no title so to do: and so on in a manner that may be easily imagined.

We have shewn how it is that to the single offence of wrongful occupation, considering the matter in a certain point of view, there may belong an infinite multitude of laws. But such as the offence is such is the law: therefore if the offence is *one*, the law considered in a certain point of view, must be *one* also. Considered in this point of view the law when expressed in the imperative form will run in this wise, "Let no man perform" or "let no man commit wrongful occupation, that is an act of wrongful occupation understood of property." This law then as we have shewn already will in order to be explicit enough stand in need of ample, and those very ample, expositions: out of which expositions and the several distinguishable clauses in them may be constructed, by a proper method of translation, as many laws as there may be occasion for to match with the several individual offences that may come under this title.

In the formulary just exhibited the law may be considered as being couched in the conditional form; the epithet *wrongful* prefixed to the term occupation being expressive of a specificant circumstance: *viz*: the *wrongfulness* of the act of occupation. But a law in the conditional form may always be converted into an unconditional provision with exceptive clauses and with exceptions taken out of it. This accordingly is the case with the law in question. Omitting in the first instance the conditionalizing or limitative epithet *wrongful*, the law in the unconditional form will stand thus, "Let no man perform any act of occupation": or to express the same meaning with less stiffness: "Let no man occupy any proprietary subject." After that come the several exceptions which may be all included under some such single formulary as this: "except he have a title so to do": and then in order to accommodate the general proposition to the particular case of each proprietary right-holder, will come the exposition of the word title and of the other leading terms, such as proprietary subject, proprietary right, proprietary right-holder, proprietary right-giver, proprietary right-taker, form of conveyance, and so forth, as above.

Of the several forms above-mentioned perhaps this latter is the clearest, and that which places the station which the fundamental law of property occupies in the most satisfactory point of view. Upon this plan the leading provision is one simple mandate: a mandate which is the primordial work of the law itself without needing the co-operation of individuals, which contains what there is universal in the law of property and what must necessarily be applicable to every *corpus juris* whatsoever.

Thus much in the way of description: a word or two here may not be amiss in the way of caution. It is not enough that the law be really complete: to have the effect of a complete law it should be made to appear such in the eyes of those who are concerned in it: to the citizen who is to take it, that is to take the whole of it together, for the measure of his conduct; to the judge who is to take it for the measure of his decision: and to the legislator, who in order to know whether anything that is requisite remains to be done should be able to see at a moment's glance what it is he hath done. It ought accordingly to be consigned to paper, and that in such a form that anyone who opens a volume of the code may lay his finger upon it and say this is one law: and that is another: here the first of these begins, and there ends: here are all the parts, and these together are what make the whole of it.

This being the description of a complete law, where then it may naturally be asked is there a specimen of such a law to be met with? I answer—nowhere...

[pp. 176–183]

# J. AUSTIN
## The Province of Jurisprudence Determined
### (ed. Hart (1954))

*The definition of law*

The matter of jurisprudence is positive law: law, simply and strictly so called: or law set by political superiors to political inferiors. But positive law (or law, simply and strictly so called) is often confounded with objects to which it is related by resemblance, and with objects to which it is related in the way of analogy: with objects which are also signified, properly and improperly, by the large and vague expression law.

A law, in the most general and comprehensive acceptation in which the term, in its literal meaning, is employed, may be said to be a rule laid down for the guidance of an intelligent being by an intelligent being having power over him. In this the largest meaning which it has, without extension by metaphor or analogy, the term law embraces the following objects:—Laws set by God to his human creatures, and laws set by men to men.

The whole or a portion of the laws set by God to men is frequently styled the law of nature, or natural law: being, in truth, the only natural law of which it is possible to speak without a metaphor, or without a blending of objects which ought to be distinguished. But, rejecting the appellation Law of Nature as ambiguous and misleading, I name those laws or rules, as considered collectively or in a mass, the *Divine law*, or the *law of God*.

Laws set by men to men are of two leading or principal classes. Some are established by *political* superiors, sovereign and subject: by persons exercising supreme and subordinate government, in independent nations, or independent political societies. The aggregate of the rules thus established, or some aggregate forming a portion of that aggregate, is the appropriate matter of jurisprudence, general or particular. To the aggregate of the rules thus established, or to some aggregate forming a portion of that aggregate, the term law as used simply and strictly, is exclusively applied. But, as contradistinguished to natural law, or to the law of nature (meaning, by those expressions, the law of God), the aggregate of the rules, established by political superiors, is frequently styled positive law, or law existing *by position*. As contradistinguished to the rules which I style positive morality, and on which I shall touch immediately, the aggregate of the rules, established by political superiors, may also be marked commodiously with the name of positive law. For the sake, then, of getting a name brief and distinctive at once, and agreeably to frequent usage, I style that aggregate of rules, or any portion of that aggregate, positive law: though rules, which are not established by political superiors, are also positive, or exist by position, if they be rules or laws, in the proper signification of the term.

Though some of the laws or rules, which are set by men to men, are established by political superiors, others are not established by political superiors, or are not established by political superiors in that capacity or character.

Closely analogous to human laws of this second class, are a set of objects frequently but improperly termed laws, being rules set and enforced by *mere opinion*, that is, by the opinions or sentiments held or felt by an indeterminate body of men in regard to human conduct. Instances of such a use of the term *law* are the expressions—"The law of honour"; "The law set by fashion"; and rules of this species constitute much of what is usually termed "International law."

The aggregate of human laws properly so called belonging to the second of the classes above mentioned, with the aggregate of objects improperly but by close analogy termed laws, I place together in a common class, and denote them by the term *positive morality*. The name morality severs them from positive law, while the epithet positive disjoins them from the law of God. And to the end of obviating confusion, it is necessary or expedient that they should be disjoined from the latter by that distinguishing epithet. For the name morality (or morals), when standing unqualified or alone, denotes indifferently either of the following objects: namely, positive morality *as it is*, or without regard to its merits; and positive morality, *as it would be*, if it conformed to the law of God, and were, therefore, deserving of approbation.

Besides the various sorts of rules which are included in the literal acceptation of the term law, and those which are by a close and striking analogy, though, improperly, termed laws, there are numerous applications of the term law, which rest upon a slender analogy and are merely metaphorical or figurative. Such is the case when we talk of laws observed by the lower animals; of laws regulating the growth or decay of vegetables; of laws determining the movements of inanimate bodies or masses.[47] For where intelligence is not, or where it is too bounded to take the name of reason, and, therefore, is too bounded to conceive the purpose of a law, there is not the will which law can work on, or which duty can incite or restrain.[48]

Having suggested the purpose of my attempt to determine the province of jurisprudence; to distinguish positive law, the appropriate matter of jurisprudence, from the various objects to which it is related by resemblance, and to which it is related, nearly or remotely, by a strong or slender analogy: I shall now state the essentials of *a law* or *rule* (taken with the largest signification which can be given to the term *properly*).

Every *law* or *rule* (taken with the largest signification which can be given to the term *properly*) is a *command*. Or, rather, laws or rules, properly so called, are a species of commands.

Now, since the term command comprises the term law, the first is the simpler as well as the larger of the two. But, simple as it is, it admits of explanation. And, since it is the key to the sciences of jurisprudence and morals, its meaning should be analysed with precision.

Accordingly, I shall endeavour, in the first instance, to analyse the meaning of "command": an analysis which, I fear, will task the patience of my hearers, but which they will bear with cheerfulness, or, at least, with resignation, if they

---

[47] [This suggests that normative law is the basic idea and is extended to physical law by metaphor. For the view that the actual development was the other way.]

[48] The classification may be arranged in tabular form:

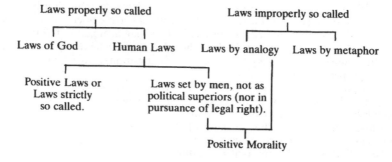

consider the difficulty of performing it. The elements of a science are precisely the parts of it which are explained least easily. Terms that arc the largest, and, therefore, the simplest of a series, are without equivalent expressions into which we can resolve them concisely. And when we endeavour to define them, or to translate them into terms which we suppose are better understood, we are forced upon tedious circumstances.

If you express or intimate a wish that I shall do or forbear from some act, and if you will visit me with an evil in case I comply not with your wish, the expression or intimation of your wish is a command.[49] A command is distinguished from other significations of desire, not by the style in which the desire is signified, but by the power and the purpose of the party commanding to inflict an evil or pain in case the desire be disregarded. If you cannot or will not harm me in case I comply not with your wish, the expression of your wish is not a command, although you utter your wish in imperative phrase. If you are able and willing to harm me in case I comply not with your wish, the expression of your wish amounts to a command, although you are prompted by a spirit of courtesy to utter it in the shape of a request. "Preces erant, sed quibus contradici non posset." Such is the language of Tacitus, when speaking of a petition by the soldiery to a son and lieutenant of Vespasian.

A command, then, is a signification of desire. But a command is distinguished from other significations of desire by this peculiarity: that the party to whom it is directed is liable to evil from the other, in case he comply not with the desire.

Being liable to evil from you if I comply not with a wish which you signify, I am *bound* or *obliged* by your command, or I lie under a *duty* to obey it.[50] If, in spite of that evil in prospect, I comply not with the wish which you signify, I am said to disobey your command, or to violate the duty which it imposes.

Command and duty are, therefore, correlative terms: the meaning denoted by each being implied or supposed by the other. Or (changing the expression) wherever a duty lies, a command has been signified; and whenever a command is signified, a duty is imposed.

The evil which will probably be incurred in case a command be disobeyed or (to use an equivalent expression) in case a duty be broken, is frequently called a *sanction*, or an *enforcement of obedience*. Or (varying the phrase) the command or the duty is said to be *sanctioned* or *enforced* by the chance of incurring the evil...                                                                    [pp. 9–15]

Accordingly, I distribute laws proper, with such improper laws as are closely analogous to the proper, under three capital classes.

The first comprises the laws (properly so called) which are set by God to his human creatures.

[49] [For Austin only a command which obliges *generally* to acts or forbearances of a *class* is a law or rule. He does not, like Blackstone, insist on generality as to *persons*. Hence *privilegia, i.e.* laws passed in regard to an individual, are laws so far as they enjoin or forbid generally acts of a class (Hart ed., p. 19). Thus a private divorce Act, though directed only to two persons, has general legal consequences which bring it within the category of a law. *Cf. Liyanage v. R.* [1967] 1 A.C. 259 and *Kariapper v. Wijesinha* [1968] A.C. 717. Tapper in [1965] C.L.J. 271 at 276, believes that Austin's motive was "to remove judgments in particular cases from the category of law". He remarks that if this was so Austin chose "a singularly blunt" instrument to achieve his objective. Why did he not limit his exclusion "to commands to do particular acts addressed to particular persons"? Tapper's suggestion is that Austin may have tried to achieve a pattern like Blackstone's: for "persons commanded" read "acts commanded". "The demands of an Augustan balance," he comments, "seem to have outweighed those of clarity and accuracy".]

[50] [For Austin, as for Kant, duty is therefore primary. Rights only arise when a person to whom a duty is owed has at his disposal the means of enforcement through state sanctions. On this analysis some duties are absolute (see Austin, *Lectures on Jurisprudence*, lectures 16 and 17), as not giving rise to a relative right.

The second comprises the laws (properly so called) which are set by men as political superiors, or by men, as private persons, in pursuance of legal rights.

The third comprises laws of the two following species: 1. The laws (properly so called) which are set by men to men but not by men as political superiors, nor by men, as private persons, in pursuance of legal rights: 2. The laws, which are closely analogous to laws proper, but are merely opinions or sentiments held or felt by men in regard to human conduct.—I put laws of these species into a common class, and I mark them with the common name of positive morality or positive moral rules.[51]

### Positive law and morality

My reasons for using the two expressions "*positive* law" and "*positive* morality," are the following:

There are two capital classes of human laws. The first comprises the laws (properly so called) which are set by men as political superiors, or by men, as private persons, in pursuance of legal rights. The second comprises the laws (proper and improper) which belong to the two species above mentioned.

As merely distinguished from the second, the first of those capital classes might be named simply *law*. As merely distinguished from the first, the second of those capital classes might be named simply *morality*. But both must be distinguished from the law of God: and, for the purposes of distinguishing both from the law of God, we must qualify the names *law* and *morality*. Accordingly, I style the first of those capital classes "positive law": and I style the second of those capital classes "positive morality." By the common epithet *positive*, I denote that both classes flow from human sources. By the distinctive names *law* and *morality*, I denote the difference between the human sources from which the two classes respectively emanate.

Strictly speaking, every law properly so called is a positive law. For it is put or set by its individual or collective author, or it exists by the position or institution of its individual or collective author.

But, as opposed to the law of nature (meaning the law of God), human law of the first of those capital classes is styled by writers on jurisprudence "positive law." This application of the expression "positive law" was manifestly made for the purpose of obviating confusion; confusion of human law of the first of those capital classes with the Divine law which is the measure or test of human.

And, in order to obviate similar confusion, I apply the expression "positive morality" to human law of the second capital class. For the name *morality*, when standing unqualified or alone, may signify the law set by God, or human law of that second capital class. If you say that an act or omission violates morality, you speak ambiguously. You may mean that it violates the law which I style "positive morality," or that it violates the Divine law which is the measure or test of the former...                                                              [pp. 122–125]

From the expression *positive law* and the expression *positive morality*, I pass to certain expressions with which they are closely connected.

The *science of jurisprudence* (or, simply and briefly, *jurisprudence*) is concerned with positive laws, or with laws strictly so called, as considered without regard to their goodness or badness.

Positive morality, as considered without regard to its goodness or badness, *might* be the subject of a science closely analogous to jurisprudence. I say "*might*

---

[51] [By treating "law" as an aggregate of nothing but rules, Austin fails to take into account, the extent to which it consists of principles or standards such as "good faith," "reasonableness", etc. These cannot be reduced to rules, and they represent one of the main points of contact between law and the "operative" values of society (*cf. ante*, 49), and see Dworkin's criticisms of Hart, discussed *post*, 347.]

be;" since it is only in one of its branches (namely, the law of nations or inter-national law) that positive morality, as considered without regard to its goodness or badness, has been treated by writers in a scientific or systematic manner.—For the science of positive morality, as considered without regard to its goodness or badness, current or established language will hardly afford us a name. The name *morals*, or *science of morals*, would denote it ambiguously: the name *morals*, or *science of morals*, being commonly applied (as I shall show immediately) to a department of ethics or deontology. But, since the science of jurisprudence is not unfrequently styled "the science of positive law," the science in question might be styled analogically "the science of positive morality." . . .          [pp. 126–127]

*The science of ethics* (or, in the language of Mr. Bentham, *the science of deontology*) may be defined in the following manner.—It affects to determine the test of positive law and morality. In other words, it affects to expound them as they should be: as they would be if they were good or worthy of praise; or as they would be if they conformed to an assumed measure.

The science of ethics (or, simply and briefly, ethics) consists of two depart-ments: one relating specially to positive law, the other relating specially to positive morality. The department which relates specially to positive law is commonly styled *the science of legislation*, or briefly, *legislation*. The department which relates specially to positive morality is commonly styled *the science of morals*, or briefly, *morals*.

The foregoing attempt to define the science of ethics naturally leads me to offer the following explanatory remark. When we say that a human law is good or bad, or is what it ought to be or what it ought not to be, we mean (unless we intimate our mere liking or aversion) that the law agrees with or differs from a something to which we tacitly refer it as to a measure or test. For example, to the adherent of the theory of utility, a human law is good if it be generally useful, and a human law is bad if it be generally pernicious. For, in *his* opinion, it is consonant or not with the law of God, inasmuch as it is consonant or not with the principle of general utility.[52] To the adherent of the hypothesis of a moral sense, a human law is good if he likes it he knows not why, and a human law is bad if he hates it he knows not wherefore. For, in *his* opinion, his inexplicable feeling of liking or aversion shows that the human law pleases or offends the Deity. . . .[pp. 127–128]

. . . Besides the human laws which I style positive law, there are human laws which I style positive morality, rules of positive morality, or positive moral rules. The generic character of laws of the class may be stated briefly in the following negative manner. No law belonging to the class is a direct or circuitous command of a monarch or sovereign number in the character of political superior. . . .

But of positive moral rules, some are laws proper, or laws properly so called: others are laws improper, or laws improperly so called.

The positive moral rules which are laws properly so called, are distinguished from other laws by the union of two marks.—1. They are imperative laws or rules set by men to men. 2. They are not set by men as political superiors, nor are they set by men as private persons, in pursuance of legal rights. Inasmuch as they bear the latter of these two marks, they are not commands of sovereigns in the

[52] [It has been argued that despite Austin's rigid demarcation between law and morals there was still a crucial relation between Austin's philosophy of law and his utilitarian ethics. Thus for Austin understanding of laws involves explaining their purposes, and these cannot be grasped without understanding of the principle of utility. Also the evaluation of or choice between various juristic concepts involves the need for utilitarian calcula-tions. It is further contended that Austin's basing of positive law on the commands of a sovereign whose powers are legally unlimited rested not only on logical consideration but also on Austin's perception of practical necessity, that is, on what would promote general happiness on utilitarian grounds. Like Hobbes, for Austin the alternative to a supreme authority would be anarchy and chaos. See W. E. Rumble, "Divine Law, Utilitarian Ethics, and Positive Jurisprudence" (1979) 24 Am.J. of Jurisprud. 139.]

character of political superiors. Consequently, they are not positive laws: they are not clothed with legal sanctions, nor do they oblige legally the persons to whom they are set. But being commands (and therefore being established by determinate individuals or bodies) they are always properly so called, they are armed with sanctions, and impose duties, in the proper acceptation of the terms.

Of positive moral rules which are laws properly so called, some are established by men who are not subjects, or are not in a state of subjection to a monarch or sovereign number. Of these some are established by men living in the negative state which is styled a state of nature or a state of anarchy: that is to say, by men who are *not* members, sovereign or subject, of any political society: others are established by sovereign individuals or bodies, but not in the character of political superiors.

Of laws properly so called which are set by subjects, some are set by subjects as subordinate political superiors; others are set by subjects as private persons: Meaning by "private persons," subjects not in the class of subordinate political superiors, or subordinate political superiors not considered as such.—Laws set by subjects as subordinate political superiors, are positive laws: they are clothed with legal sanctions, and impose legal duties. They are set by sovereigns or states in the character of political superiors, although they are set by sovereigns circuitously or remotely. Although they are made directly by subject or subordinate authors, they are made through legal rights granted by sovereigns or states, and held by those subject authors as mere trustees for the granters. Of laws set by subjects as private persons, some are not established by sovereign or supreme authority. And these are rules of positive morality: they are not clothed with legal sanctions, nor do they oblige legally the parties to whom they are set.—But of laws set by subjects as private persons, others are set or established in pursuance of legal rights residing in the subject authors. And these are positive laws or laws strictly so called. Although they are made directly by subject authors, they are made in pursuance of rights granted or conferred by sovereigns in the character of political superiors: they legally oblige the parties to whom they are set, or are clothed with legal sanctions. They are commands of sovereigns as political superiors, although they are set by sovereigns circuitously or remotely. . . .

A law set by a subject as a private person, but in pursuance of a legal right residing in the subject author, is either a positive law purely or simply, or it is a positive law as viewed from one aspect, and a rule of positive morality as viewed from another. The person who makes the law in pursuance of the legal right, is either legally bound to make the law, or he is not. In the first case, the law is a positive law purely or simply. In the second case, the law is compounded of a positive law and a positive moral rule.

For example, A guardian may have a right over his pupil or ward, which he is legally bound to exercise, for the benefit of the pupil or ward, in a given or specified manner. Now if, in pursuance of his right, and agreeably to his duty or trust, he sets a law or rule to the pupil or ward, the law is a positive law purely or simply. It is properly a law which the state sets to the ward through its minister or instrument the guardian. It is not made by the guardian of his own spontaneous movement, or is made in pursuance of a duty which the state has imposed upon him. The position of the guardian is closely analogous to the position of subordinate political superiors; who hold their delegated powers of direct or judicial legislation as mere trustees for the sovereign granters.

Again: the master has legal rights, over or against his slave, which are conferred by the state upon the master for his own benefit. And, since they are conferred upon him for his own benefit, he is not legally bound to exercise or use them. Now if, in pursuance of these rights, he sets a law to his slave, the law is compounded of a positive law and a positive moral rule. Being made by sovereign authority, and clothed by the sovereign with sanctions, the law made by the master is properly positive law. But, since it is made by the master of his own spontaneous movement, or is not made by the master in pursuance of a legal duty, it is properly a rule of positive morality, as well as a positive law. Though the law set by the master is set circuitously by the sovereign, it is set or established by the sovereign at the pleasure of the subject author. The master is not the instrument of the sovereign or state, but the sovereign or state is rather the instrument of the master....

Laws which are positive law as viewed from one aspect, but which are positive morality as viewed from another, I place simply or absolutely in the first of those capital classes. If, affecting exquisite precision, I placed them in each of those classes, I could hardly indicate the boundary by which those classes are severed without resorting to expressions of repulsive complexity and length....

It appears from the foregoing distinctions, that positive moral rules which are laws properly so called are of three kinds.—1. Those which are set by men living in a state of nature. 2. Those which are set by sovereigns, but not by sovereigns as political superiors. 3. Those which are set by subjects as private persons, and are not set by the subject authors in pursuance of legal rights.

To cite an example of rules of the first kind were superfluous labour. A man living in a state of nature may impose an imperative law: though, since the man *is* in a state of nature, he cannot impose the law in the character of sovereign, and cannot impose the law in pursuance of a legal right. And the law being *imperative* (and therefore proceeding from a *determinate* source) is a law properly so called: though, for want of a sovereign author proximate or remote, it is not a positive law but a rule of positive morality.

An imperative law set by a sovereign to a sovereign, or by one supreme government to another supreme government, is an example of rules of the second kind. Since no supreme government is in a state of subjection to another, an imperative law set by a sovereign to a sovereign is not set by its author in the character of political superior. Nor is it set by its author in pursuance of a legal right: for every legal right is conferred by a supreme government, and is conferred on a person or persons in a state of subjection to the granter. Consequently, an imperative law set by a sovereign to a sovereign is not a positive law or a law strictly so called. But being imperative (and therefore proceeding from a determinate source), it amounts to a law in the proper signfication of the term, although it is purely or simply a rule of positive morality.

If they be set by subjects as private persons, and not in pursuance of legal rights, the laws following are examples of rules of the third kind: namely, imperative laws set by parents to children; imperative laws set by masters to servants: imperative laws set by lenders to borrowers; imperative laws set by patrons to parasites. Being imperative (and therefore proceeding from determinate sources), the laws foregoing are laws properly so called: though, if they be set by subjects as private persons, and be not set by their authors in pursuance of legal rights, they are not positive laws but rules of positive morality.

Again: a club or society of men, signifying its collective pleasure by a vote of its assembled members, passes or makes a law to be kept by its members severally under pain of exclusion from its meetings. Now if it be made by subjects as private persons, and be not made by its authors in pursuance of a legal right, the law voted and passed by the assembled members of the club is a further example of rules of the third kind.

The positive moral rules which are laws improperly so called, are *laws set* or *imposed by general opinion:* that is to say, by the general opinion of any class or any society of persons. For example, some are set or imposed by the general opinion of persons who are members of a profession or calling: others, by that of persons who inhabit a town or province: others, by that of a nation or independent political society: others, by that of a larger society formed of various nations.

A few species of the laws which are set by general opinion have received appropriate names.—For example, There are laws or rules imposed upon gentlemen by opinions current amongst gentlemen. And these are usually styled *the rules of honour*, or *the laws or law of honour*.—There are laws or rules imposed upon people of fashion by opinions current in the fashionable world. And these are usually styled *the law set by fashion*.—There are laws which regard the conduct of independent political societies in their various relations to one another: Or, rather, there are laws which regard the conduct of sovereigns or supreme governments in their various relations to one another. And laws or rules of this species, which are imposed upon nations or sovereigns by opinions current amongst nations, are usually styled *international law*.[53]

Now a law set or imposed by general opinion is a law improperly so called. It is styled a *law* or *rule* by an analogical extension of the term. When we speak of a law set by general opinion, we denote, by that expression, the following fact.— Some intermediate body or uncertain aggregate of persons regards a kind of conduct with a sentiment of aversion or liking. In consequence of that sentiment or opinion, it is likely that they or some of them will be displeased with a party who shall pursue or not pursue conduct of that kind. And, in consequence of that displeasure, it is likely that *some* party (*what* party being undermined) will visit the party provoking it with some evil or another.

The body by whose opinion the law is said to be set, does not command, expressly or tacitly, that conduct of the given kind shall be forborne or pursued. For, since it is not a body precisely determined or certain, it cannot, *as a body* express or intimate a wish. As a body, it cannot signify a wish by oral or written words, or by positive or negative deportment. The so-called law or rule which its opinion is said to impose, is merely the sentiment which it feels, or the opinion which it holds, in regard to a kind of conduct.

A determinate member of the body, who opines or feels with the body, may doubtless be moved or impelled, by that very opinion or sentiment, to command that conduct of the kind shall be forborne or pursued. But the command expressed or intimated by that determinate party is not a law or rule imposed by general opinion. It is a law properly so called, set by a determinate author.—For example, The so-called law of nations consists of opinions or sentiments current among nations generally. It therefore is not law properly so called. But one supreme government may doubtless command another to forbear from a kind of conduct which the law of nations condemns. And, though it is fashioned on law which is law improperly so called, this command is a law in the proper signification of the term. Speaking precisely, the command is a rule of positive morality set by a determinate author. For, as no supreme government is in a state of subjection to another, the government commanding does not command in its character of political superior.[54] If the government receiving the command were in a state of subjection to the other, the command, though fashioned on the law of nations would amount to a positive law...                    [pp. 134–142]

...In consequence of the frequent coincidence of positive law and morality, and of positive law and the law of God, the true nature and fountain of positive law is often absurdly mistaken by writers upon jurisprudence. Where positive law has been fashioned on positive morality, or where positive law has been fashioned

---

[53]  [At the Nuremberg Trials reliance was placed on the defences of act of state, superior orders and *ex post facto* laws. All of them, to a greater or less extent, were related to the Austinian view that only state law could be positive law in the strict sense as derived from national sovereignty and that no obligations under international law could override the legal duties of a subject to his own sovereign. Such arguments were rejected both by the terms of the Nuremberg Charter and in the judgment of the Tribunal: see S. L. Paulson, "Classical Legal Positivism at Nuremberg" (1975) 4 *Phil. and Public Affairs* 132. For the upholding of the legal status of international law within a framework of positivism, *pace* Austin, see the views of Kelsen (*post*, 338) and Hart, (*post*, 386).]

[54]  [Habitual obedience cannot be founded on one law. *cf.* Raz, *op. cit.*, pp. 15–16.]

on the law of God, they forget that the copy is the creature of the sovereign, and impute it to the author of the model.

For example: Customary laws are positive laws fashioned by judicial legislation upon pre-existing customs. Now, till they become the grounds of judicial decisions upon cases, and are clothed with legal sanctions by the sovereign one or number, the customs are merely rules set by opinions of the governed, and sanctioned or enforced morally: Though, when they become the reasons of judicial decisions upon cases, and are clothed with legal sanctions by the sovereign one or number, the customs are rules of positive law as well as of positive morality. But, because the customs were observed by the governed before they were clothed with sanctions by the sovereign one or number, it is fancied that customary laws exist *as positive laws* by the institution of the private persons with whom the customs originated.[55]

Again: The portion of positive law which is parcel of the *law of nature* (or, in the language of the classical jurists, which is the parcel of the *jus gentium*) is often supposed to emanate, even as positive law, from a Divine or Natural source. But (admitting the distinction of positive law into law natural and law positive) it is manifest that law natural, considered as a portion of positive, is the creature of human sovereigns, and not of the Divine monarch. To say that it emanates, as positive law, from a Divine or Natural source, is to confound positive law with law whereon it is fashioned, or with law whereunto it conforms...[pp. 162–164]

The existence of law is one thing; its merit or demerit is another. Whether it be or be not is one inquiry; whether it be or be not conformable to an assumed standard, is a different inquiry. This truth, when formally announced as an abstract proposition, is so simple and glaring that it seems idle to insist upon it.[56] But simple and glaring as it is, when enunciated in abstract expression, the enumeration of the instances in which it has been forgotten would fill a volume.

[p. 184]

### The Definition of Sovereignty

The superiority which is styled sovereignty, and the independent political society which sovereignty implies, is distinguished from other superiority, and from other society, by the following marks or characters.—1. The *bulk* of the given society are in a *habit* of obedience or submission to a *determinate* and *common* superior: let that common superior be a certain individual person, or a certain body or aggregate of individual persons. 2. That certain individual, or that certain body of individuals, is *not* in a habit of obedience to a determinate human superior. Laws (improperly so called) which opinion sets or imposes, may permanently affect the

---

[55] [Austin here accepts a similar theory to Bentham's on delegated legislation *ante*, 276. But Austin himself has a very much more satisfactory explanation of delegated legislation in terms of what Raz calls "obedience laws" (pp. 21–22, 166–167), *i.e.* "laws imposing a duty to obey a certain person, if he commands". So, for example, where a local authority imposes traffic restrictions in exercise of a power conferred by the sovereign, then the sovereign wishes citizens to obey the local authority, and the local authority wishes citizens to, say, drive only one way up a particular street. As Raz remarks, "their wishes are not identical, though practically they amount to the same thing" (p. 21).]

[56] [After referring to a passage in Blackstone to the effect that no human law which conflicts with divine law is binding. Austin makes the following comment: "Now, to say [this] is to talk stark nonsense. The most pernicious laws, have been, and are continually enforced as laws by judicial tribunals. Suppose an act innocuous, or positively beneficial, be prohibited by the sovereign under the penalty of death; if I commit this act I shall be tried and condemned, and if I object to the sentence, on the ground that it is contrary to the law of God, ... the Court of Justice will demonstrate the inconclusiveness of my reasoning by hanging me up": J. Austin (Hart ed., p. 185). On conflict between the law of the land and a moral imperative see *Francombe* v. *Mirror Group Newspapers* [1984] 2 All E.R. 408.

conduct of that certain individual or body. To express or tacit commands of other determinate parties, that certain individual or body may yield occasional submission. But there is no determinate person, or determinate aggregate or persons, to whose commands, express or tacit, that certain individual or body renders habitual obedience.

Or the notions of sovereignty and independent political society may be expressed concisely thus.—If a determinate human superior, not in a habit of obedience to a like superior, receive habitual obedience from the bulk of a given society, that determinate superior is sovereign in that society, and the society (including the superior) is a society political and independent.[57]

To that determinate superior, the other members of the society are *subject*: or on that determinate superior, the other members of the society are *dependent*. The position of its other members towards that determinate superior, is a *state of subjection* or *a state of dependence*. The mutual relation which subsists between that superior and them, may be styled *the relation of sovereign and subject*, or *the relation of sovereignty and subjection*.[58]

In order that a given society may form a society political and independent, the two distinguishing marks which I have mentioned above must unite. The generality of the given society must be in the habit of obedience to a determinate and common superior: whilst that determinate person, or determinate body of persons must not be habitually obedient to a determinate person or body. It is the union of that positive, with the negative mark, which renders that certain superior sovereign or supreme, and which renders that given society (including that certain superior) a society political and independent. I proceed to illustrate these marks.

(1) In order that a given society may form a society political, the generality or bulk of its members must be in a *habit* of obedience to a determinate and common superior.

In case the generality of its members obey a determinate superior, but the obedience be rare or transient and not habitual or permanent, the relation of sovereignty and subjection is not created thereby between that certain superior and the members of that given society . . .　　　　　　　　　　　　[pp. 193–196]

. . . (2) In order that a given society may form a society political, habitual obedience must be rendered, by the *generality* or *bulk* of its members, to a determinate and *common* superior. In other words, habitual obedience must be rendered, by the generality or bulk of its members, to one and the same determinate person, or determinate body of persons. . . .

For example: In case a given society be torn by intestine war, and in case the conflicting parties be nearly balanced, the given society is in one of two positions. If the bulk of each of the parties be in a habit of obedience to its head, the given society is broken into two or more societies, which, perhaps, may be styled independent political societies.—If the bulk of each of the parties be not in that habit of obedience, the given society is simply or absolutely in a state of nature or anarchy. It is either resolved into its individual elements, or into numerous societies of an extremely limited size: of a size so extremely limited, that they could hardly be styled societies independent and political. For, as I shall show hereafter, a given independent society would hardly be styled political, in case it

---

[57]　[The basis of sovereignty is thus the *fact* of obedience. For a comment on this position, see *ante*, 261.]

[58]　[Austin assumes that such habitual submission must result in unlimited legal sovereignty. Study of the legal position of the Roman emperor under the principate could have shown him how a *de facto* sovereign might possess only a limited legislative power, which was gradually developed on a customary basis (see Jolowicz and Nicholas, *Historical Introduction to Roman Law*, pp. 363–364, 460). No doubt, arguing syllogistically from Austin's axioms, we will conclude that only moral restraints bound the early emperors, and some may say that this was actually the position. Equally, however, we may be led to question Austin's axioms.]

fell short of a number which cannot be fixed with precision, but which may be called considerable, or not extremely minute.

(3) In order that a given society may from a society political, the generality or bulk of its members must habitually obey a superior *determinate* as well as common.

On this position I shall not insist here. For I have shown sufficiently ... that no indeterminate party can command expressly or tacitly, or can receive obedience or submission: that no indeterminate body is capable of corporate conduct, or is capable, as a body, of positive or negative deportment.

(4) It appears from what has preceded, that, in order that a given society may form a society political, the bulk of its members must be in a habit of obedience to a certain and common superior. But, in order that the given society may form a society political and independent, that certain superior may *not* be habitually obedient to a determinate human superior. He may render occasional submission to commands of determinate parties. But the society is not independent, although it may be political, in case that certain superior habitually obey the commands of a certain person or body....

Let us suppose, for example, that a viceroy obeys habitually the author of his delegated powers. And, to render the example complete, let us suppose that the viceroy receive habitual obedience from the generality or bulk of the persons who inhabit his province. The viceroy is not sovereign within the limits of his province, nor are he and its inhabitants an independent political society. The viceroy, and (through the viceroy) the generality or bulk of its inhabitants, are habitually obedient or submissive to the sovereign of a larger society. He and the inhabitants of his province are therefore in a state of subjection to the sovereign of that larger society. He and the inhabitants of his province are a society political but subordinate....

A natural society, or a society in a state of nature, is composed of persons who are connected by mutual intercourse, but are not members, sovereign or subject, of any society political. None of the persons who compose it lives in the positive state which is styled a state of subjection: or all the persons who compose it live in the negative state which is styled a state of independence.

Considered as entire communities, and considered in respect of one another, independent political societies live, it is commonly said, in a state of nature. The expression, however, is not perfectly apposite. Since all the members of each of the related societies are members of a society political, none of the related societies is strictly in a state of nature: nor can the larger society formed by their mutual intercourse be styled strictly a natural society. Speaking strictly, the sovereign and subject members of each of the related societies form a society political: but the sovereign portion of each of the related societies lives in the negative condition which is styled a state of independence.

Society formed by the intercourse of independent political societies, is the province of international law, or of the law obtaining between nations. For (adopting a current expression) international law is conversant about the conduct of independent political societies considered as entire communities: *circa negotia et causas gentium integrarum.* Speaking with greater precision, international law, or the law obtaining between nations, regards the conduct of sovereigns considered as related to one another.

And hence it inevitably follows, that the law obtaining between nations is not positive law:[59] for every positive law is set by a given sovereign to a person or

---

[59] [*cf.* D. Bederman, *The Spirit of International Law* (2002): international law now exhibits "many features of 'mature' domestic legal systems": p. 22. But see O. Hathaway (2002) 111 Yale L.J. 1935 (discussing the persistence of non-compliance in human rights law). There is now more discussion as to why states comply with international law: see e.g. A. Guzman (2002) 90 California L.R. 1823, who argues they do so to protect their reputations and avoid the negative consequences of non-compliance.]

persons in a state of subjection to its author. As I have already intimated, the law obtaining between nations is law (improperly so called) set by general opinion. The duties which it imposes are enforced by moral sanctions: by fear on the part of nations, or by fear on the part of sovereigns, of provoking general hostility, and incurring its probable evils, in case they shall violate maxims generally received and respected... [pp. 198–201]

### The limits of sovereign power

... Every positive law, or every law simply and strictly so called, is set, directly or circuitously, by a sovereign person or body, to a member or members of the independent political society wherein that person or body is sovereign or supreme. It follows that the power of a monarch properly so called, or the power of a sovereign number in its collegiate and sovereign capacity, is incapable of *legal* limitation.[60] A monarch or sovereign number bound by a legal duty, were subject to a higher or superior sovereign: that is to say, a monarch or sovereign number bound by a legal duty, were sovereign and not sovereign. Supreme power limited by positive law is a flat contradiction in terms.

Nor would a political society escape from legal despotism, although the power of the sovereign were bounded by legal restraints. The power of the superior sovereign immediately imposing the restraints, or the power of some other sovereign superior to that superior, would still be absolutely free from the fetters of positive law. For unless the imagined restraints were ultimately imposed by a sovereign not in a state of subjection to a higher or superior sovereign, a series of sovereigns ascending to infinity would govern the imagined community which is impossible and absurd.[61] [pp. 253–254]

... In short, when we style an act of a sovereign an unconstitutional act (with that more general import which is sometimes given to the epithet), we mean, I believe, this: That the act is inconsistent with some given principle or maxim: that the given supreme government has expressly adopted the principle, or, at least, has habitually observed it: that the bulk of the given society, or the bulk of its influential members regard the principle with approbation: and that, since the supreme government has habitually observed the principle, and since the bulk of the society regard it with approbation, the act in question must thwart the expectations of the latter, and must shock their opinions and sentiments. Unless we mean this, we merely mean that we deem the act in question generally pernicious: or that, without a definite reason for the disapprobation which we feel, we regard the act with dislike.[62]

The epithet unconstitutional as applied to conduct of a sovereign, and as used with the meaning which is more special and definite, imports that the conduct in question conflicts with constitutional law. And by the expression *constitutional law*, I mean the positive morality, or the compound of positive morality and positive law, which fixes the constitution or structure of the given supreme government. I mean the positive morality, or the compound of positive morality and positive law, which determines the character of the person, or the respective

---

[60] [*Cf.* Bentham, *ante*, 279.]

[61] [*i.e.* absurd on Austin's assumption that law is a derivative of sovereignty, rather than that sovereignty is itself a product of law.]

[62] [Dicey, while accepting Austin's dichotomy between laws and conventions of the constitution, argued that the reason why the latter were obeyed was that a breach of a convention would ultimately lead to a breach of law, *e.g.* failure to assembly a parliament would result in the illegal collection of taxes. But breach of a convention would not necessarily have such an effect, *e.g.* collective ministerial responsibility. Munro in (1975) 91 L.Q.R. 218 is critical of any attempt to blur the distinction between law and convention.]

characters of the persons, in whom, for the time being, the sovereignty shall reside: and, supposing the government in question an aristocracy or government of a number, which determines moreover the mode wherein the sovereign powers shall be shared by the constituent members of the sovereign number or body.[63]                                              [pp. 258–259]

---

[63] [From Lecture VI.]

# 5

# THE PURE THEORY OF LAW

There is no single legal writer in the last century who made a more illuminating analysis of the legal process than Hans Kelsen (1881–1973).[1] And certainly, it cannot be denied that he has done as much as anyone, by his lucid analysis and tenacious defence, to stimulate thought and provoke further inquiry into the meaning, structure and validity of law. Yet some of the controversy that has resulted from his writings has partly been due to misunderstanding caused, for all his general clarity of thought, by the use of language which is apt to prove deceptive.[2] For, although Kelsen is the very antithesis of those whom, rightly or wrongly, English lawyers may regard as the typical continental legal philosopher dealing in wordy abstractions, it must be admitted that, especially in his earlier writing, fondness for Kantian terminology may have resulted in confusion which has, been to some extent cleared up in his later writings.[3]

Kelsen has undoubtedly shown a leaning towards the Kantian approach to the theory of knowledge, according to which the objective world is transmuted by certain formal categories applied to it by the mind of the onlooker.[4] This lies at the root of his search for the formal elements, as concepts of the human mind, which enable us to grasp the inherent structure of any legal system, and also to his acceptance of

---

[1] Ota Weinberger has described him as "the jurist of our century" (Hans Kelsen, *Essays in Legal and Moral Philosophy* (1973), p. ix). Scholarship centered on Kelsen has developed rapidly since his death: see in particular Tur and Twining, *Essays on Kelsen* (1986), S. Paulson's articles (in particular (1992) 12 O.J.L.S. 265, 311, I. Stewart (1990) 17 J.L.S. 273), and Lars Vinx's new book (2008).

[2] Also by a failure to appreciate the political and intellectual background, against which Kelsen developed his *Rechtswissenschaft*. The influence of Freud, the "Vienna Circle" of philosophy, and the remaking of central Europe after World War I are described by Stone, *Legal Systems and Lawyers' Reasonings* (1964), pp. 98–100. See also the philosophical controversies described by McBride (1968) 43 N.Y.U.L. Rev. 53, 66–70.

[3] That Kelsen's jurisprudence is rooted in the critical philosophy of Kant is beyond serious dispute. See Moore, *Legal Norms and Legal Science* (1978), p. 7. In Stanley Paulson's mind the neo-Kantian dimension of Kelsen's thought is clear (1992) 12 Oxford J. of Legal Studies 265). See also I. Stewart (1980) Jurid. Rev. 199, 200.

[4] For a concise account of Kant's epistemology or theory of knowledge, see R. Scruton, *Kant* (1982), Chaps 2 and 3. Relationship between Kant's thought and Hume is brought out at pp. 13–18, 34–36. For an illustration of Kelsen's use of Kant's epistemology, see *Pure Theory of Law*, p. 202.

monism, a single "world of law".[5] Also Kelsen follows Kant in distinguishing between the two categories of existence and of normative relations ("is" and "ought").

## NORMATIVISM

Kelsen is often described, and was described in earlier editions of this book, as a positivist.[6] And, if as Shiner suggests,[7] positivism and, what he calls, anti-positivism are exhaustive of the possibilities of speculation about the nature of law,[8] then Kelsen would have to be categorised as a positivist. But Kelsen's normativism is conceptually distinct from the empirical tradition of legal positivism, upheld in the post-war period by Hart.[9] Kelsen rejects legal positivism because it confuses the law with fact. He rejects natural law theory because it confuses the law with morality. Kelsen thus rules out both the appeal to morality and that to fact. For Kelsen the law consists of norms: a norm cannot be derived from facts, but only from other norms. The relationship between norms is one of "imputation", not causality.[10] Natural science is concerned with causal explanations of the physical world, whereas normative science, such as law or ethics, is concerned with conduct as it ought to take place, determined by norms. "Under certain conditions a certain consequence ought to take place. This is the grammatical form of the principle of imputation."[11] The old natural law is, therefore, rejected, as it was also by Hume,[12] on the ground that it is an illogical and impermissible attempt to establish the objective character of what is necessarily normative.[13]

Raz[14] has shown that Kelsen's normativism can be supported without reference to the neo-Kantianism associated with notions like normative imputation. According to Raz, Kelsen advances "a cognitivist interpretation of all normative discourse". For Kelsen, a normative proposition (whether legal or moral or other) expresses "a belief in the existence

---

[5] See also Harris's criticism of Kelsen's assumption that there is only one field of normative meaning to which scientific discourse can refer when it uses the concept of validity. The "unfortunate metaphysical gloss" to which Harris refers is yet another legacy of Kelsen's Kantian background ([1971] C.L.J. 103, 115–116).

[6] See 5th ed, p. 320 (a positivist of positivists).

[7] *Norm and Nature* (1992), pp. 2–5.

[8] But where does Realism fit? (see *post*, 985, 1035) It must be doubted whether jurisprudence can be dichotomised in this way.

[9] Note the appeal to social facts in grounding the rule of recognition.

[10] See *What is Justice?*, pp. 324 *et seq*. Kelsen's preference for "imputation" rather than "causality" has an ideological as well as philosophical basis. He believes in individual responsibility (the German Zurechnung, translated as "imputation" is associated with the concept of accountability in the sense of responsibility; causality, on the other hand, connotes determinism.) See, further, Ebenstein, 59 Calif. L. Rev. 617, 635–637 and *post*, 329.

[11] See *What is Justice?*, p. 349.

[12] See *ante* 24, but see also 120–121.

[13] On Kelsen's reason for rejecting natural law see J. Raz, *The Authority of Law* (1979), pp. 129–132.

[14] *Post*, 357.

of a valid norm, and a norm constitutes a value".[15] There is a difficulty with this: if the normative import of legal propositions is to be explained by the fact that they state the existence of a binding norm *qua* value, then legal propositions would appear to be moral statements, and, to quote Raz, "the law and its existence and content ... seem to be essentially moral facts".[16] How could this be squared with Kelsen's "purity" thesis?[17] There is a real dilemma here: if Kelsenian legal propositions have normative import they state moral facts, and this sullies the "purity" thesis. But, if they do not state moral facts, they have no normative import.[18] As Paulson points out: "the idea that legal propositions might lack normative import is an idea fraught with far-reaching consequences, among them the fact that legal science would lose this basis for claiming the special status of a normative science."[19] And Kelsen's theory would "collapse" in something approximating empirico-positivist theory.

Raz, as will be seen in the extract from him in this chapter,[20] offers a reconstruction and an escape hatch for Kelsen. He asks us to imagine an individual "whose moral beliefs are *identical* with the law".[21] Legal scientists study the law as a normative system but this does not commit them to its normativity. The legal propositions that legal scientists formulate are conditional: "if the legal man is right, then one ought to do thus-and-so."[22] Or, transposing this into language that Kelsen would have used: "if the basic norm is valid, then one ought to do thus-and-so." Raz claims by this means to have reconstructed a legal science which has purity and describes the law as a normative system.

## THE PURE SCIENCE OF LAW

Kelsen's goal is a pure science of law: it is not a theory of pure law.[23] He envisages no such chimera as a "pure norm".[24] Kelsen is not disinterested in justice or sociology or psychology.[25] The pure theory provides the basic forms under which meanings can be known scientifically as legal norms—which will have a content, although the particular content is empirically contingent, and which, once determined as having a particular content,

---

[15] *Post*, 362.
[16] *Post*, 363.
[17] *Post*, 326.
[18] In his posthumous *General Theory of Norms* (1979), published in an English translation in 1991, Kelsen appears to argue just this (see p. 216).
[19] (1993) 6 Ratio Juris. 227, 234–235.
[20] *Post*, 357.
[21] *Post*, 363.
[22] *Post*, 363.
[23] See I. Stewart in Tur and Twining (eds.) *op. cit.*, note 1, p. 123 at 127 and (1998) 51 C.L.P. 181, 183.
[24] *Cf.* J. Harris, *Law and Legal Science* (1979), pp. 34–35.
[25] How else could Kelsen have written widely on political philosophy (see, for example, the collection *What is Justice?* (1957) or critiqued the Bolshevik experience of law and legal theory (*The Communist Theory of Law*)?

can be morally evaluated.[26] Thus, "far from being an attempt to exclude consideration of experience,[27] content[28] and justice,[29] the pure theory is intended to make attention to them more rigorously possible."[30] Therefore, the theory's object of cognition—the norm—is seen without reference to its content or to such questions as why it is (or is not) obeyed. But Kelsen intends thereby to clarify the field for those who are primarily interested in these questions. That the study of law has been "adulterated" by other disciplines is, according to Kelsen, perfectly understandable. These disciplines deal with subject matters "closely connected" with law. But the pure theory of law, Kelsen insists, "undertakes to delimit the cognition of law against these disciplines ... because it wishes to avoid the uncritical mixture of methodologically different disciplines ... which obscures the essence of the science of law".[31]

### NORMS AND THE BASIC NORM

Norms are regulations setting forth how persons are to behave and positive law is thus a normative order regulating human conduct in a specific way. A norm is an "ought" proposition; it expresses not what is, or must be, but what ought to be, given certain conditions[32]; its existence can only mean its *validity*,[33] and this refers to its connection with a system

[26]  *Per* Stewart, *op. cit.*, note 1, p. 128.
[27]  As Laski maintained (see *post*, 326).
[28]  On which see Hart, *Essays in Jurisprudence and Philosophy* (1983), pp. 309, 313.
[29]  For example, the criticism of Michel Villey, *Philosophie du Droit* (1975), p. 198.
[30]  *Op. cit.*, note 1, p. 128.
[31]  *The Pure Theory of Law*, p.1.
[32]  "Ought" here does not refer to moral obligation but simply to the normative form of legal propositions. For Kelsen these are mainly differentiated by the fact that the reaction of law consists in a measure of coercion enacted by the legal order and socially organised. Morality works by direct motivation, *i.e.* it regulates the behaviour of one individual. Law is indirect as involving not only the person whose conduct is in question but also the one who is to apply the sanction. Religious norms are nearer to law than morals, as providing for supernatural sanctions. See H. Kelsen, *What is Justice?*, pp. 235–244. In his later writings, notably *The Pure Theory of Law* (English translation, 1967), Kelsen has indicated that "ought" covers such other modalities as "can" and "may" (see pp. 5, 16). So a norm "permits the use of force in self-defence" (p. 16); another allows the institution of court proceedings (pp. 134 *et seq.*) this goes some way towards countering the type of criticism that Hart makes of Austin's common concept as failing to explain the "variety of laws" (*The Concept of Law*, Chap. 3) and answers Bobbio's point (in Hughes, *Law, Reason and Justice* (1969), pp. 189 *et seq.*) that Kelsen's theory fits the nineteenth century negative liberal state but not the contemporary social welfare ideal.
[33]  A concept with various meanings and one not used with any consistency by Kelsen. Harris demonstrates that there are four, possibly five, senses in which validity is used to qualify a legal norm. It may suggest conformity to a higher norm ("is not *ultra vires*, is not void"); or that it "is a consistent part of a normative field of meaning"; or correspondence with social reality; or that it "has inherent claim to fulfilment." As Harris points out, Kelsen himself uses "valid" primarily in the second sense, but sometimes without recognising the distinction in the first. The third and fourth uses of the concept are alien to Kelsenian thought: the third equates validity and effectiveness and Kelsen specifically distinguishes them: the fourth suggests that a rule has political or moral values and is thus inconsistent with the pure theory of law. See *op. cit.*, pp. 112–116 and Christie (1964) 48 Minn. L. Rev. 1049.

of norms of which it forms a part. It cannot be proved to exist factually, but simply to be derivable from other norms, and is, therefore, valid in that sense.

But if a norm can only be derived from another norm, does this mean one can continue this derivation *ad infinitum?* Theoretically, yes, but, in practice, since norms are concerned with human conduct, there must be some ultimate norm postulated on which all the others rest. This is the Grundnorm (basic norm). So far as the legal system is concerned this basic norm must be extra-legal, since *ex hypothesi* it does not rest upon another legal norm. But Kelsen is at pains to point out that the choice of the basic norm[34] is not arbitrary. On the contrary it must be selected by the legal scientist on the principle of efficacy, that is to say that the legal order as a whole must rest on an assumption that is by and large efficacious, in the sense that in the main people do conduct themselves in conformity with it.[35] The basic norm is non-positive and so is not the concern of legal science, but it is really purely formal in giving unity to the legal system and marking the limits of those norms which are the subject of legal science.[36] The choice of the basic norm may also have important implications in determining the relation of national state law to international law. For if the basic norm is in conformity to the constitution of each state, there will be a pluralistic congeries of independent legal systems, while if that norm is taken in relation to international law, there will be a monistic world order, from which each national law will derive.[37] Kelsen does not, however, make very clear how far this choice is pre-determined by the principle of effectiveness,[38] though the fact that all states purport to regard themselves as bound by international law (subject to their own construction of what may be its particular rules), may perhaps bring the voice of a monistic system, unquestionably favoured by Kelsen himself, within this principle.

Kelsen spurns all metaphysical entities, such as the state[39] or rights and duties. Thus, the imputation of acts to the state is a figure of speech, which, in legal context merely refers to norms of the legal order. But the term "legal order" is wider than that of the state, since it is only a relatively centralised order which is termed a state, and this would exclude, for instance, primitive societies and the present international legal order.[40] Again, rights and duties are not entities existing in

---

[34] Kelsen's clearest formulation of this is his answer to Professor Stone's critique. See 17 Stan. L. Rev. 1128, 1140–1151 and *see post*, 339.

[35] *What is Justice?*, p. 268.

[36] *ibid.*, pp. 360–361.

[37] For a defence of the monistic interpretation of the relationship between international and domestic legal orders see Kelsen, "The Concept of the Legal Order" in (1982) 27 Am.J. of Jurisprud. 64 (written in 1958).

[38] *Cf.* Benn in *Political Philosophy* (ed. Quinton) (1967), pp. 75–77.

[39] On law and state in Kelsen see A. Somek (2006) 26 OX. J.L.S. 753.

[40] *What is Justice*, p. 293, *cf.* Barkun, *ante*, 35, n. 15. Kelsen refers to the animistic tendency to imagine a spirit behind phenomena, as Helios and the sun, and explains the idea of "the State" as an entity on the same basis.

themselves, but merely the expression of legal norms related to the concrete conduct of individuals.

<br>

## HIERARCHY OF NORMS AND LAW-MAKING PROCESS

Kelsen's description of the legal process as a hierarchy of norms, the validity of each norm (apart from the basic norm) resting upon a higher norm, and each level in the hierarchy representing a movement from complete generality to increasing individualisation, has sometimes been misunderstood as suggesting that the interpretation and application of general rules are of a purely mechanical character. This is far from being Kelsen's view. On the contrary, he points out that, though law has the peculiarity of regulating its own creation, a higher norm can determine the creation and content of another norm only to a certain extent. In so far as there is a discretion or a choice as to the applicable rule, the normcreating function takes on a political character. This is obvious in the case of the American Supreme Court interpreting the Constitution, but it is the same with the application of law by any legal authority. And the function does not cease to be legal on this account, for it still take place within the framework of norms.[41]

Kelsen does not negate the value of the sociology of law. This stands side by side with normative jurisprudence and neither can replace the other. The latter deals with validity and the former with efficacy, but the two are inter-connected, since the sociology of law presupposes the normative concept of law.[42] But Kelsen makes a curious distinction between the role of the legal scientist and of a law-making authority, such as a judge. The former can only describe and not prescribe, and, therefore, he cannot exercise any choice open to the latter. The legal scientist must, therefore, accept any decision as valid, since it is outside his competence to say whether it is within the framework of the general norm in question. And, though he can point out possible interpretations, he must leave the law-making authority to make the choice, for to try to influence this authority is to exercise a political and not a legal function.[43] This seems to involve an act of renunciation on the part of legal science in

---

[41] *What is Justice?*, pp. 372–373. The emphasis on the political elements in the work of the judge is most common in connection with constitutional interpretation. But not only here: see Dworkin's *Law Empire* (1986), *post*, 720.

[42] *What is Justice?*, pp. 267–271.

[43] *ibid.*, pp. 367–368. This is discussed more fully in *The Pure Theory of Law* (1967). The distinction in this later work is not so much between respective roles as between the products of the actors in each: law-making authorities issue *norms*; a jurist describes *normative statements*. See pp. 72–75, and Raz's discussion, *The Concept of a Legal System*, pp. 45–47. *cf.* Hart's contrast of an external observer who can observe signs and predict accordingly but does not know the reasons for a pattern of behaviour with the official who has a critical reflective attitude. (*The Concept of Law*, pp. 55–58.) Hart discussed Kelsen's distinction in *Essays in Jurisprudence and Philosophy* (1983), pp. 286, 287–289.

which it is hardly likely to acquiesce, and apparently treats the advocate arguing a case as a politician, rather than a lawyer.[44]

## SANCTIONS

For Kelsen, every system of norms rests on some type of sanction, though this may be of an undifferentiated kind, such as disapproval[45] by a group. The essence of law is an organisation of force, and law thus rests on a coercive order designed to bring about certain social conduct. Sanctions are the key characteristic of law not because of any supposed psychological effectiveness but because it stipulates that coercion ought to be applied by officials where delicts are committed. The law attaches certain conditions to the use of force, and those who apply it act as organs of the community. Kelsen bases this view on the historical facts (as he asserts) that there has never been a "large" community which was not based on a coercive order. This applies equally to primitive and international[46] society, which simply lack the elements of specific centralised organs for law-creating and law-applying. The notion of a social order requiring no sanctions either looks back to a Golden Age or forward (as with Marxism) to a Utopian society. It is in fact the "negation of society," based on the illusion of the natural goodness of man.[47]

Kelsen commits himself to the view that every norm to be "legal" must have a sanction, though this may be found, as for instance in

---

[44] In a number of cases judges have failed to appreciate Kelsen's dichotomy between the respective roles of jurist and judge. For example, Udoma C.J. in *Uganda* v. *Commissioner of Prisons, ex p. Matovu* (1966) E.A. 514 said: "Applying the Kelsenian principles ... our view is that the 1966 Constitution is a legally valid Constitution and the supreme law of Uganda ... the 1962 Constitution abolished as a result of victorious revolution does not longer exist." But Kelsenian dogma is not really helpful to him. He had a practical decision to take which he did by weighing up relevant considerations such as peace and stability. The pure science of law could not assist in this task. All it can do is to declare upon the new reality, one of the primary factors of which is judicial recognition. This interpretation is not supported by Harris (*op. cit.*, pp. 125–127) who, whilst admitting that this is no direct justification for his thesis in Kelsen's writings, has suggested that "judges in developed legal systems do act as legal scientists," so that, for example, they, as well as jurists, are capable of presupposing the grundnorm. His premise is that legal science "is a socially useful activity" (p. 119) and "can only continue to be socially useful so long as judges also indulge in it" (p. 126). It is difficult to see how the latter statements would have Kelsen's support, though its sentiments is one with which one would readily agree. *Cf. post*, 267.

[45] Woozley ((1968) 77 *Mind* 461, 475) points out that Kelsen fails to distinguish "disapproval" from "expressions of disapproval." The latter depends on "the supposed gravity of the infringement, the extent to which the society was a conformist society and the degree of tolerance which members of the society extended to each others' failings." Unlike legal sanctions, "they are the likely, not the necessary consequences of the infringement."

[46] The sanctions of international law are, for Kelsen, war and reprisals, comparable to self-help in primitive law: see *General Theory of Law and the State* (1964), pp. 328 *et seq.* This is cogently criticised by Herz, *Law, State and International Legal Order* (ed. Engel and Metall, 1968), p. 108.

[47] See especially, *What is Justice?*, pp. 231–256. *Cf.* Cowan's plea for Kelsen to substitute for force the notion of "control" (1971) 59 Calif. L. Rev. 683, 693–694.

constitutional law, by taking it together with other norms with which it is interconnected.[48]

Kelsen treats any breach of a legal norm as a "delict," whether this would normally be described in traditional terms as falling within the criminal or the civil law. For Kelsen, to be legally obligated to a certain behaviour means that the contrary behaviour is a delict and as such is the condition of a sanction stipulated by a legal norm.[49] Since Kelsen regards a sanction as an essential characteristic of law, no conduct can amount to a delict unless a sanction is provided for it. This view has been criticised,[50] with some warrant, on the ground that though the absence of a sanction may make law ineffective, this is not the same as its being invalid, nor does the absence of a sanction necessarily entail invalidity. Emphasis on sanctions also underplays the significance of duties. There are many examples of public authorities which have obligations imposed on them but where no sanctions as such follow from default. We would, nevertheless, rightly say of such defaults that the authorities were "flouting the law." If this is a correct characterisation, Kelsen's analysis does not fully explain it. It is true that Kelsen does recognise that a legislature could make laws without considering it necessary to attach sanctions for violations.[51] He still objects, however, that although, under such a system it would be possible to decide whether a norm was legal or not by determining whether it had emanated from the appropriate authority, we would even so not be able to provide thereby a criterion by which law could be distinguished from other social norms. But, as has been pointed out, even if sanctions were essential to law, it is the legality of legal sanctions, not their character as coercive acts, which would contribute to the essence of law, since other social norms may also have coercive acts attached to them as sanctions.[52]

A further feature of Kelsen's analysis of the sanctionist view of law is that legal norms are stated in the form that, if a person does not comply with a certain prohibition, then the consequence is that the courts ought to inflict a penalty, whether criminal or civil. It follows that for Kelsen the content of legal norms is not primarily to impose duties on the subject to conform, but rather to lay down what judges or officials are expected to do in the event of a delict. Accordingly, for Kelsen the norm which lays down the sanction, involving a direction to the judge, is the primary norm, though he recognised that there is a secondary norm which stipulates the behaviour which the legal order endeavours to bring about by announcing the sanction. This conflicts with the orthodox view that legal

---

[48] *General Theory of Law and State*, pp. 29, 143–44.
[49] *ibid.*, p. 59; *The Pure Theory of Law*, pp. 34, 115.
[50] By A.D. Woozley (1968) 77 *Mind 461*, 463–465 and Raz, *The Concept of a Legal System*, pp. 78 *et seq.*
[51] *General Theory of Law and State*, p. 122.
[52] *Cf.* Raz, *op. cit.*, p. 82 where lynching, vendetta (in "certain positive moral systems"), or the imposition of corporal punishment by parents and teachers are pointed to as examples of non-legal agencies of social control employing coercion to enforce non-legal norms.

duties set standards of conduct and accordingly impose obligations on society as a whole. Moreover, as Woozley points out,[53] although the official ought to impose the sanction on a deviant, they may not have a legal duty to do so. Whether they have will depend on further conditions. For if the judge has such a legal duty, it can be only because there is a higher norm prescribing a sanction against him for failing to apply the lower-order norm. And such a hierarchy can lead to a "vicious regress." "The stop is provided by having as a last norm one 'such that the sanction which it stipulates is not a legal duty in the sense defined,' *i.e.* the last norm is itself a sanctionless norm," of the permissive or power-conferring kind. Woozley justifiably comments: "This is a serious watering-down ... the proposition that an organ of the state ought to act in a certain way may mean nothing more than that, if it does not, its actions (legislative, judicial, or administrative) have no validity."[54]

A further criticism of the sanctionist view, whether, indeed, that of Kelsen or Austin, is that not only does it blur the distinction between criminal and civil law,[55] but also makes it difficult to distinguish between penal and administrative coercion. Thus, Kelsen seeks to exclude cases of administrative enforcement, such as the compulsory evacuation of buildings threatened by fire, or enforced isolation of a person suffering from a contagious disease, from the ambit of legal sanctions, on the ground that it is circumstances other than human which lead to the application of coercion whereas sanctions are always the consequent of human conduct.[56] This distinction seems somewhat unrealistic, since it fails to take account of the fact that many forms of administrative coercion, such as a compulsory purchase order on an owner unwilling to sell, or taxation, are the consequent of human conduct.[57] Perhaps the difficulty could be avoided by conceding that administrative coercion is just as much penal as any other coercion if it is buttressed in any particular case by one form of penalty or another.[58]

---

[53] *Op. cit.*, pp. 470–474.

[54] *ibid.*, p. 473; *cf.* the predictive view of Ross, *post*, 1068. See further Hart "Self-Referring Laws" in *Essays in Jurisprudence and Philosophy* (1983), pp. 170–173.

[55] *Cf.* Bentham, *Of Laws in General*, Chap. 16.

[56] *General Theory of Law and State*, pp. 278–279. *The Pure Theory of Law*, pp. 40–42. For a detailed taxonomy of coercion in terms of their dominant purpose or effect, see Packer, *The Limits of the Criminal Sanction* (1969), pp. 23–31, 251–257. His rough classification of coercion is into four categories; compensation, regulation, punishment and treatment. Both treatment and compensation are also the consequent of human conduct, and neither are explained by a sanctionist view of law. Packer's work draws particular attention to the neglect of the concept of sanction, which is strange bearing in mind its prominence in so many jurisprudential writings.

[57] Nor could Kelsen extricate himself by defining a sanction as a consequent of "socially undesired behaviour," for "this is precisely an element which Kelsen considers to be excluded from the juristic definition of delict," *per* Hart, *Essays in Jurisprudence and Philosophy* (1983) at pp. 295–301. Apart from which much administrative coercion may be directed against "socially undesired behaviour" (*e.g.* high rates of tax on luxury items and alcoholic beverages).

[58] Kelsen admits his theory implies that in the type of socialist society envisaged by Marx (see *post*, 1188) law would lose its legal character (*Pure Theory of The Law*, p. 54). And see T. Campbell, *The Left and Rights* (1983), pp. 65–76.

CRITIQUE

Kelsen's analysis of the formal structure of law as a hierarchical system of norms, and his emphasis on the dynamic character of this process, are certainly illuminating and avoid some, at any rate, of the perplexities of the Austinian system.[59] But is Kelsen nor unduly rigid in his desire to make precise lines of demarcation between the legal scientist and the legal sociologist, between the legal and political function? A legal system is not an abstract collection of bloodless categories but a living organism in a constant state of movement. Is it enough to recognise, for instance, the discretionary process of courts as a dynamic function and then to hand over to an entirely different inquirer in order to ascertain the scope and significance of this function? Kelsen himself recognises that to call a judge's function "political"[60] as he does, does not deprive it of its legal quality. Then what is the virtue of this highly misleading description?

There are certain more specific points that need to be answered.

*The Basic Norm*

This is a very troublesome feature of Kelsen's system. We are not clear what sort of norm this really is, nor what it does, nor, indeed, where we find it. Part of the problem lies in Kelsen's own obliqueness. In his last published article[61] he tells us that it is not "positive" (which means for Kelsen that it is *not* a norm of positive law, *i.e.* created by *a real* act of will of a legal organ, but is *presupposed in juristic thinking*).[62] Hence, he argues, it is "meta-legal"; but, it is "legal" if by this term we understand anything which has legally relevant functions." And, since it enables anyone to interpret a command, permission or authorisation as an

---

[59] Kelsen's own analysis of the differences may be found in *What is Justice?*, pp. 271 *et seq.*
[60] Alf Ross also speaks of "legal politics" though, unlike Kelsen, he contends that the doctrinal study of law cannot be detached from the sociology of law: see *On Law and Justice* (1958), pp. 19–24, and Chaps 14–16.
[61] In (1965) 17 Stan. L. Rev. 1130, 1140–1142, *and post*, 289. Later articles are published but these are translations from the German and appeared in the original earlier than 1965. *See post*, 302.
[62] *ibid.*, p. 1141. Kelsen reiterates in German terminology that the basic norm is not *gesetzt by a real will, but vorausgesetzt* in juristic thinking. Though Kelsen ultimately believed that the basic norm is *a fictitious* norm presupposing a *fictitious act of will* that lays down this norm. See 1 Israel L. Rev. 1, 6–7. In this way Kelsen seemingly aimed at encompassing both his view that a norm must ultimately be based on an act of will, and that a norm can only rest on another norm. But postulating a "fictive act of violition" he hoped to surmount his dilemma. That the attempt failed is brought out by A. Wilson, "The Imperative Fallacy in Kelsen's Theory" (1981) 44 M.L.R. 270, who justly remarks that a fictive act of volition does not bring us back "to human will and reality" (p. 280). Moreover, Kelsen, in his last writing, seemed to render the basis of his whole theory untenable, by recognising that not only does the basic norm as fiction contradict reality, but is also self-contradictory, since it is defined as the meaning of an act of will that is known *a priori* cannot exist. (See I. Stewart, "The Basic Norm as Fiction" (1980) Jurid. Rev. 199, 207–208, 221–222). Perhaps, however, Harris's idea of the sovereign will (in Bentham and Austin) as a "constructive metaphor" might also be relevant to Kelsen's notion of a fictive act of will. See also, I. Stewart, *op. cit.*, pp. 209–211. See, further, Stewart in Tur and Twining, *op. cit.*, note 1, pp. 123, 132.

objectively valid legal norm,[63] its legal functions are not in doubt. Nonetheless, we are told it is purely formal, is a juristic value judgment, and has a hypothetical character[64]; yet it forms the keystone of the whole legal arch (it is ... "at the top of the pyramid[65] of norms of each legal order"[66]). Goodhart was doubtful of the value of an analysis which did not explain the existence of a basic norm on which the whole legal system was founded.[67] However, it may be argued that we have reached the stage where it is pointless to look for further *legal* justification. And this is what Kelsen recognises. Accordingly, he refers us to the principle of effectiveness. Kelsen tells us that every jurist assumes this to be the basis of the legal order (which, of course, is unlikely to be true); and that it merely means that the legal order is as a whole effective (*i.e.* that people do in fact behave according to the norms of this order), and that it may be stated in the form that men ought to behave in conformity with the legal

---

[63] Though, according to Harris, *op. cit.*, pp. 112–113, "The citizen or lawyer who distinguishes [for example] the tax officer's demand from the gangster's demand as "valid" or "lawful" does not need to presuppose a basic norm, unless he is a legal scientist seeking to show that the contents of the tax officer's directive form part of a unified field of meaning constituted by it and all other valid legal norms." (*cf. General Theory of Law and the State*, p. 437). The citizen or the lawyer need only go as far as the *particular* act of Parliament: he need not question Parliament's authority: only a legal scientist need do that.

[64] *What is Justice?*, pp. 224–225, and see n. 60.

[65] In *Legal System and Lawyers' Reasonings* (1964), Stone asserts that "The commonplace figure of a pyramid for the norms of a legal order is acceptable, with perhaps the modification (in view of the fact that the highest norm—those of the constitution—may themselves be numerous and complex) that the top of the figure may be a plateau rather than a point ... Indeed, since after all the norms of the pyramid are constructs out of the actual words of the constitutional and other laws, no harm is done by representing the constitution as a single point in the model, and in words, as a basic (or rather apex) norm. All that the logical theory of the structure of a legal order tells us is that the apex norm of any legal order, *i.e.* its constitution, ought to be obeyed" (pp. 203–204). Stone here fuses, and thus confuses, the basic norm and ultimate constitutional norms. If there is only one basic norm, as is suggested in the text, then the figures will be a point, not a plateau, though Stone's term "apex-norm," if the idea of a pyramid is retained, would approximately describe this.

[66] See 1 Israel L.R. 1.

[67] *English Law and Moral Law* (1953), p. 16. But *cf.* p. 51. Kelsen distinguished carefully between validity and efficacy. The validity of the legal order as a whole, as well as of any particular norm within the legal order, depends on conformity with the basic norm. The efficacy of the legal order on the other hand is no more than the *condition* of validity, and not validity itself. The validity is conditioned by efficacy in the sense that a legal order as a whole, just as a single norm, *loses* its validity if it does not become by and large effective. "A legal order does not *lose* its validity by the fact that a single legal norm loses its efficacy, that is to say that this legal norm is not at all or in some particular case not applied. A legal order is considered to be valid if its norms are *by and large* effective, that is, actually obeyed and applied." See Kelsen's reaffirmation of his views in (1965) 17 Stan. L. Rev. 1139–1140. It should be noted, that effectiveness in only one "condition" of validity. So, for example a court which applies a statute immediately after enactment—before the statute had a chance to become effective—applies a valid legal norm. (*cf. Pure Theory of Law*, p. 11.) See also, pp. 211–214.

order only if it is as a whole effective.[68] This seems to invoke either a totally unnecessary fictitious hypothesis, on the one hand, or on the other, a statement of fact, dressed up in the shape of a general norm, but which is not unlike Austin's much-condemned reliance on habitual obedience.[69]

Moreover, the basic norm is propounded as the means of giving unity to the legal system, and enabling the legal scientist to interpret all valid legal norms as a non-contradictory field of meaning.[70] Presumably, therefore, there can be only one basic norm. But is this so? And, if so, how is it related, if at all, to the constitution of a given country? These questions are complicated by a lack of clarity in Kelsen's thought.

Kelsen latterly distinguished between what he calls the constitution in a legal-logical sense (what we have called the basic norm) and the constitution in a positive legal sense, which contains those rules governing the process of government which we call the constitution.[71] In the majority of countries this latter is usually contained in a document, but Kelsen admits that reduction to such a form is not necessary.[72] How are the basic norm and constitution in a positive legal sense related? Kelsen's answer is that we must trace back the existing constitution to a historically first constitution, which cannot be traced back to a positive norm created by a legal authority: "we arrive, instead, at a constitution that became valid in a revolutionary way, that is, either by breach of a former constitution, or for a territory that formerly was not the sphere of validity of a constitution and of a national legal order based on it."[73] The presupposition that this first constitution is valid is the basic norm. Furthermore, Kelsen has argued that this initial hypothesis is not a vague abstraction, but is based on objectively ascertainable facts, *viz.*, effectiveness.[74] We must, therefore, draw a distinction between the basic norm and the ultimate constitutional norms. There is necessarily only one basic norm, but the number of ultimate constitutional norms need not be so limited. Indeed,

---

[68]   *ibid.* Kelsen was influenced by the "coherence theory" of truth propounded by the Vienna Circle of logical positivists. According to this the criterion whether a statement is true is its *consistency* with other statements. Since incompatible systems might each be internally consistent, we are told that we should accept that system *actually accepted by* scientists of our cultural circle. For Kelsen's association with the Vienna Circle, see Jerome Hall, *Studies in Jurisprudence and Criminal Theory* (1958), p. 35.

[69]   Cf. Eckhoff and Sundby. "The Notion of Basic Norm(s) in Jurisprudence" in (1975) *Scandinavian Studies in Law* 123, 134–136, who attribute the search for a single basic norm to the tendency in Western thought to seek after a supreme source of authority, whether God, Reason or the will of a Sovereign.

[70]   Cf. *The Pure Theory of Law*, p. 72. See also Harris, *op. cit.*, pp. 106–108. But in his final writings Kelsen abandoned this doctrine of non-contradiction. See "Law and Logic" in *Essays in Legal and Moral Philosophy* (ed. O. Weinberger) (1973): there he says "*both* the conflicting norms are valid" (p. 233). The conflict cannot be resolved "by way of knowledge with the aid of legal science" (p. 235) (*i.e.* by interpretation, as he suggests in *Pure Theory of Law*, pp. 205–208). In *Law and Logic* he leaves resolution of the conflict to legislation or "customary non-observance."

[71]   (1965) 17 Stan.L.Rev. 1141, 1143.

[72]   See *The Pure Theory of Law*, p. 222 (the distinction between rules and a document).

[73]   *ibid.*, p. 200.

[74]   Cf. *What is Justice?*, pp. 262–263. See also (1965) 17 Stan.L.Rev. 1141.

one of the functions of the basic norm is to resolve any conflict or seeming contradiction between the different constitutional norms.[75]

The difficulty in relating this structure to a national legal order like that of the United Kingdom is that we have never had a constitution[76] and our ultimate constitutional norms have been established by custom. It is, nevertheless, possible, as Harris has demonstrated, to express our national legal order in Kelsenian terms. He suggests that the basic norm of the United Kingdom legal order is that "coercive acts ought to be applied only under conditions and in the ways customarily recognised as constitutional from time to time[77] by the population at large,"[78] and that there are two, possibly three,[79] ultimate constitutional norms. So, we should obey the courts, for example, because of an ultimate constitutional norm that "coercive acts ought to be applied in accordance with judge-making rules established in conformity to the doctrine of binding precedent."[80] Is this to suggest that one should conform to an unwritten customary rule of the constitution?[81] And, if so, is this additional hypothesis merely superfluous?

There is little doubt that in the majority of cases, certainly where stable democracies such as the United Kingdom are in issue, the basic norm is needless reduplication. But, if it can be shown that the basic norm is a useful guide in countries torn by revolution or other upheaval, it may prove a valuable construct. Certainly, in the aftermath of such cataclysmic change, lawyers have believed that Kelsen's theory of the change of the basic norm was the key to unlock the mystery of the validity of pre- and post-revolutionary laws.[82] If it can be shown that their faith in Kelsen

---

[75] *General Theory of Law and State*, pp. 401, 406; *The Pure Theory of Law*, pp. 74, 195. See also Raz, *op. cit.*, p. 96.

[76] In the sense of a single document. But *cf*. MacCormick, *Current Legal Problems* (1983), pp. 13, 21.

[77] Thus the recognition that the Convention, which acknowledged William and Mary as the new Sovereign, could be turned into a parliament with authority to pass valid legislation, can be explained as a new ultimate constitutional norm customarily adopted in accordance with this basic norm: *cf*. Macaulay, *History of England* (Everyman's ed.), vol. 2, p. 235 ("It was plain that the Convention was the fountainhead from which the authority of all future parliaments must be derived, and that on the validity of the votes of the Convention must depend the validity of every future statute. And how could the stream rise higher than the source?"). On the change effected by the European Communities Act 1972 see N. MacCormick, *Questioning Sovereignty* (1999), Chap. 6 and, *post*, 556.

[78] *Op. cit.*, p. 111.

[79] Is custom an independent source of law today? See Cross, *Precedent in English Law* (3rd ed.), pp. 159–165.

[80] *Op. cit.*, pp. 109, 111.

[81] For the difficulties in reconciling Kelsen's theory to constitutions based either wholly or partially on custom, see G. Maher, "Custom and Constitutions" (1981) O.J.L.S. 167.

[82] See *The State v. Dosso* (1985) 2 Pakistan S.C.R. 180 at 185–186, 195; *Uganda v. Commissioner of Prisons, ex p. Matovu* (1966) E.A. 514; *Madzimbamuto v. Lardner-Burke* (1986) 2 S.A. 284 at 315; *Lakanmi and Kikelomo Ola v. Att.-Gen. (Western State)* in 20 I.C.L.Q. 117 at 127–128; *Mitchell v D.P.P.* [1986] A.C. 73 *cf. Sallah v. Att.-Gen* [1970] C.C. 54 in 20 I.C.L.Q. 315 at 320–321 where Sowah J.A. declared: "It seems to me we will not derive much assistance from the foreign theories." (Plato and Marx were also quoted!) And *Asma Jilani v. Govt. of Punjab* (discussed in Iyer (1973) 21 Am.J.Comp. Law 759) in which the Supreme Court of Pakistan rejected Kelsen's theory. See also Eekelaar in (1969) 32 M.L.R. 19 at 22–23.

is well-placed, then there may be some justification for Kelsen's setting up of an additional extra-legal hypothesis. But, in deciding whether their expectations are legitimate ones, we must again return to Kelsen's curious distinction between the role of the legal scientist and the law-making authority.[83] For, it may be argued that Kelsen's theory, being descriptive of legal science, can only indicate the role of the jurist and can in no way assist the judge.[84] This would suggest that those judges who relied upon Kelsen's theory to solve post-revolution legal problems were labouring under self-deception that Kelsen could assist them. But, this would in no way detract from any assistance that a legal scientist might seek in Kelsenian analysis.

Harris, however, goes further and, implying from Kelsen that a judge is a legal scientist, takes the view that the judges in Pakistan, Uganda and Southern Rhodesia were acting properly. "It is true," he argues, "that Kelsen's theory does not directly authorise a judge to make any particular decision. But indirectly it suggests that, when legal science gives a clear solution to a case, the judge ought to accept that solution, and this is true when, soon after the occurrence of a revolution, the question arises: has the grundnorm changed? The reason why it has this suggestive force for a judge is that the theory assumes that legal science is a socially useful activity, which it could not be if it were not an essential part of the role of a judge to act as a legal scientist and to apply the conclusions of legal science.[85]

It is doubtful whether Harris is justified in drawing this conclusion from Kelsen and it may be that Kelsenian analysis of the change of a basic norm can only help the legal scientist pronouncing dispassionately after the event.[86] So, we must ask; what does Kelsen mean by "effective," for his basic norm is based upon this? How satisfactory a test is efficacy? What is meant by saying that norms, to be effective, must be obeyed or applied "by and large?"[87] How does one compute the number of opportunities to obey the law? What of "dead-letter" laws or laws only

[83] *Cf. ante*, 310.

[84] See, for example, F.M. Brookfield (1969) 19 *University of Toronto Law J.*, pp. 326, 342–344; *cf.* Harris, *op. cit.*, pp. 125–127.

[85] *Op. cit.*, p. 132. Eekelaar finds another justification by treating the court structure as an "institutionalised substitute" for investigating attitudes of the population and that this can survive the collapse of the old constitution: see *Oxford Essays in Jurisprudence* (Simpson ed., 1973), pp. 29–41. For a discussion of the continuity of law where there is a change of constitution without revolution, see Finnis, *op. cit.*, pp. 60 *et seq.*

[86] See Dias [1968] C.L.J. 233; *cf.* Harris, *op. cit.*, p. 123. This is supported by Guest who also rejects Harris's view (1) because it involves a *petitio principii*, namely, that a legal science is presumed "socially useful" in that it provides guidance for judges and therefore cannot simply be claimed to provide "suggestive force" for judges and ground that it is a legal science; (2) Kelsen's pure theory excludes any reference to values in a political or moral sense and, in the absence of these there is no other "socially useful" function for a court to perform merely upholding or rejecting the validity of the laws of the new regime (1980) Acta Jur. 18–23).

[87] *The Pure Theory of Law*, p. 214; (1965) 17 Stan.L.Rev. 1142.

selectively enforced?[88] How many times is the law disobeyed by a motorist who drives for ten miles through a built-up area exceeding the speed-limit throughout his journey?[89] How many opportunities not to murder or steal does one get in a given period? Is motive for disobedience relevant? Are some laws more important than others? A man, for example, may never break a contract, pay all his taxes, heed the highway code but murder the head of state. Questions such as these suggest that effectiveness is a crude, unscientific test and yet it is crucial to Kelsen. Are we, therefore, to dismiss Kelsen's basic norm or can a more meaningful test be formulated? Harris's reformulation would relate the number of commands, permissions and authorisations issued by a legislator to the number of occasions that stipulated sanctions have been or are likely to be applied: "if there is a socially significant ratio between the official acts and the acts of disobedience, and it can be predicted that this ratio will continue to obtain for a reasonable length of time, the meaning-contents of the commands, permissions and authorisations are by and large effective norms".[90] But "socially significant" is vague, perhaps, purposely so. Would it involve, for example, attributing different weight to different "offences"? Would greater importance be attached to significant constitutional laws?[91] And, there are further difficulties: on this test, as indeed on Kelsen's, one might argue that the legal system in Southern Rhodesia under the Smith regime was the pre-U.D.I. system, for the majority of norms remained in force and there might have been a certain amount of disobedience to those newly instituted, leaving on a ratio test the balance in favour of the pre-U.D.I. system.[92]

This analysis has raised some of the difficulties inherent in Kelsen's theory of the basic norm. It may be thought to demonstrate that Kelsen is only useful to the legal scientist, and not the judge, and only in a residual case, and, further, that the kingpin of the whole structure rests upon the shaky foundation of a loose concept, *viz.*, effectiveness. It may be asked whether in this respect Kelsen really furthers our understanding of the legal order.[93]

---

[88] See, for example, the study by La Fave, *Arrest: The Decision to take a Suspect into Custody* (1965).
[89] *Cf.* Raz., *op. cit.*, p. 203.
[90] *Op. cit.*, p. 124; *cf.* Raz, *op. cit.*, pp. 203–205.
[91] See Hart, *The Concept of Law*, pp. 112–113.
[92] *Cf.* Raz's suggestion, *op. cit.*, p. 205.
[93] For a very searching if inconclusive exploration of the problems and obscurities relating to the basic norm, see Julius Stone, "Mystery and Mystique in the Basic Norm" (1963) 26 M.L.R. 34 and, further, *Legal System and Lawyers' Reasonings*, pp. 123–131. Kelsen's *Stanford Law Review* article is an attempted answer to some of the problems posed by Stone. See *post*, 289. Further criticism of the basic norm may be found in Raz, *The Authority of Law* (1979), Chap. 7. He argues that Kelsen's doctrine of the unity of a legal system fails (i) because not all laws which belong to one chain of validity are part of one legal system (if state A grants its colony, state B, independence (*semble*) on Kelsen's view state B would still be part of the same legal system as state A, though this would normally not be the case); (ii) because one can only identify the legal system with the help of the basic norm, whereas the basic norm can be identified only after the identity of the legal system has been established. *Cf.* A. Wilson (1982) 27 Am.J. of Jurisprud. 46.

## International Law

We have seen how Austin relegated international law to the realm of positive morality, contrary to the universally accepted usage of modern states and lawyers.[94] Kelsen seeks to overcome this difficulty by demonstrating how state laws can[95] be dovetailed into the international order of norms so as to form one monistic system.[96] There is no logical reason why monism should not postulate the superiority of municipal law, but for ideological reasons Kelsen is not prepared to countenance this. But quite apart from any possible objection as to the application of the principle of effectiveness,[97] this approach seems to be based on an illusory search for unity,[98] and to disregard the realities of the situation.[99] Furthermore, it has led Kelsen to modify national basic forms. "The reason for the validity of the national legal order . . . is no longer a norm presupposed in juristic thinking but a positive norm of international law,[1] and the "presupposed norm" now becomes one of international law. But does international law need a basic norm? We have seen that, in spite of its difficulties, and within a limited sphere, the basic norm did serve a useful function in a national legal context. It was argued that in a post-revolutionary situation the basic norm might provide guidance to a legal scientist. Can it really be supposed though, that similar guidance is needed in international society? Can international society undergo a

---

[94] *Ante,* 249–250.

[95] *What is Justice?* pp. 283–287; *The Pure Theory of Law,* pp. 328–344; (1960) 48 Geo.L.J. 627 and 27 Am.J. of Jurisprud. 64, 73–84.

[96] Kelsen is well aware that in existing society a dualistic pattern is still retained. He is, however, hopeful that monism will prevail: it is, thus, merely a heuristic suggestion. From the point of view of legal science the choice is irrelevant (it is a political question outside the purview of the pure theory of law), but "from the point of view of political ideology the choice is important" (*General Theory of Law and State,* p. 398). See McBride, 43 N.Y.U.L.R. 53, 70–71, and Hughes, 59 Calif.L.Rev. 695, 711–713.

[97] *Cf. ante,* 307 and *post,* 337.

[98] Thus Kelsen states that the task of natural science is to describe reality in one system of the laws of nature, and that of the jurist is to comprehend all human laws in one system of rules of law: *What is Justice?,* p. 287. Note the influence of Kantian philosophy, *ante,* 255.

[99] Hart points out that Kelsen fluctuates between two positions: (1) that international and all municipal systems *logically* must form a single unified system; (2) that *in fact* they form a single system. As to (1) Kelsen's argument depends mainly on his view that there can be no conflict between valid laws. But not only is this incorrect in regard to laws belonging to different systems, but even within the same system it would seem that conflicting laws can co-exist though obedience to both may be impossible. In any event the argument fails to establish the necessary unity of international and municipal law. As to (2), Kelsen relies on his principle of effectiveness to establish that only as result of a norm of international law can the legal order of a national state be legitimised. But even if international law did purport to confer validity on state laws, this would not prove that the latter actually derive their validity from the former, for this would depend uponrecognition by courts within their particular system (*Essays in Jurisprudence and Philosophy* (1983), p. 309). The above must not, however, be confused with the quite different question whether the validity of international law itself is to be treated as overriding national laws: this cannot depend exclusively on recognition or otherwise by national courts.

[1] *The Pure Theory of Law,* p. 215. See *post,* 346.

revolution? It is difficult to conceive of circumstances in which this could happen, short of one state or bloc capturing world power so conclusively that it could dictate new rules of international law to the rest of the subjugated world.[2] But practical realities do not seem to interest Kelsen as much as scientific unity and logical precision, and he accordingly postulates the basic norm of international law as "coercion of state against state ought to be exercised under the conditions and in the manner that conforms with the custom constituted by the actual behaviour of states."[3] What does this add to the positive norms of international law? To quote Professor Hart, "it says nothing more than that those who accept certain rules must also observe a rule that the rules ought to be observed,"[4] a wholly unnecessary, if not spurious, assumption.

Why does Kelsen insist upon the need for monism? The answer follows from Kelsen's view of the logical impossibility of more than one basic norm. In a dualistic system there would be as many basic norms as systems. There would be an insoluble *logical* contradiction,[5] which could only be resolved by some norm higher than the collective basic norms of the national legal orders, *viz.*, an international legal order. So France and Germany might both claim to legislate for Alsace-Lorraine, and only international law could provide a solution. However, this is not a logical question at all, but simply one of how legal systems are in fact constructed. There is no reason why the basic norm of a national legal order should not take account of the international obligations accepted by that order. Is it not true, for example, that international obligations are in the United Kingdom "customarily recognised as constitutional from time to time"?[6]

## The Rule of Recognition: A Comparison

There are superficial similarities between the *Grundnorm* and Hart's rule of recognition.[7] The rule provides authoritative criteria for identifying primary (and, presumably, other secondary) rules. How are these rules of recognition to be ascertained? Hart points out that such rules are often not expressly stated, but can be *shown* by the way in which particular rules are identified by the courts and other officials. Whether a primary

---

[2] *Cf.* the systems theory in international relations, whereby patterns of interaction between states lead to a self-regulating system which lasts so long as it can handle conflict and then give way to successive self-regulating systems. See, for example, Rosecrance, *Action and Reaction in World Politics* (1963).

[3] *The Pure Theory of Law*, p. 216, *cf. post*, 338. Does this amount to much more than might is right?

[4] *The Concept of Law*, p. 236 and *post*, 384.

[5] See *What is Justice*, pp. 284–285.

[6] *Ante*, 317.

[7] See *The Concept of Law* (revised ed., 1994), Chaps 5 and 6 and *post*, 342. See also Hart's own analysis of the differences between Kelsen and himself at pp. 292–293. And see Paulson, (1993) 6 *Ratio Juris* 227.

rule is "valid" really amounts to saying no more than that it passes all the tests provided by the appropriate rule of recognition.[8]

But in what sense can the rules of recognition themselves by regarded as "valid"?[9] Hart appears to recognise that such rules may themselves be formed on a hierarchical pattern and that, therefore, the validity of one or more of these rules may depend upon some higher rule of recognition, but this still leaves open the Kelsenite question as to the status of any ultimate rule since the only point is whether it is accepted by those who generate the system. There is, therefore, no assumption of validity, but its acceptance is simply factual. Should we then call the basic norm of the system either law or fact? In a sense, avers Hart, it is both. The rule does provide criteria of validity within the system and, therefore, it is worth calling such a rule, law: there is, however, also a case for calling it fact insofar as it depends for its existence upon actual acceptance. This fact of acceptance may be looked upon from two points of view, namely, from the point of view of the external statement of fact that the rule exists in the actual practice of the system, and also from the internal statements of validity which may be made by those in an official capacity who actually use it to identify law.[10]

Hart also points out that, although the notions of validity and efficacy may be closely related in a legal system, they are by no means identical. Their close relationship is demonstrated by the fact that if there is so little efficacy in a whole system of law, it would really be pointless to attempt to assess what actual rights and duties might exist there under or the validity of particular rules.

As to the question whether every system of law must be referable to some basic norm, Hart rejects Kelsen's view that this is an essential presupposition of all legal systems. All that it means, where a system lacks a basic norm, is that there will then be no way of demonstrating the validity of individual rules by reference to some ultimate rule of the system. Hart points out that this is not so much a necessity as a luxury found in advanced social system.[11] In simpler forms of society we may

---

[8] For discussion as to whether Hart believes in a rule or rules of recognition see *post*, 344. Raz's view is that "there is no reason to suppose that every legal system has just one rule of recognition" (*The Authority of Law* (1979), p. 95). He points to distinct rules of recognition imposing obligations on the courts to treat custom and precedent as sources of law. Raz argues that Kelsen's theory of the basic norm is unable to identify the legalsystem in such a case because there is no way of knowing whether there may be one or two basic norms, and therefore one or two legal systems in the same legal territory (*ibid.*, pp. 128–129).

[9] R. Sartorius claims that it is a rule of positive law (see in (ed.) R. Summers, *More Essaysin Legal Philosophy* (1971), p. 157). Harris (1971) C.L.J. 103, 117 describes it as a "social phenomenon". But if it is to be regarded solely as a fact, Hart would seem to be guilty of deriving "ought" propositions from it.

[10] R. Sartorius, *op. cit.*, argues that the flaw in Hart's approach is to seek one single concept of a valid law, whereas it is really a "cluster concept". But surely there must always be a core question as to whether a particular rule does qualify as forming part of a legal system?

[11] But, it may be argued, if the existence of a rule of recognition is not necessary for a legal system to exist, then it cannot be a necessary condition for the existence of valid law.

have to wait and see whether a rule gets accepted as a rule or not. This does not mean that there is some mystery as to why rules in such a society are binding, which a basic rule, if only we could find it, would resolve. The rules of a simple society, like the rule of recognition found in a more advanced system, are binding if they are accepted and function as such.[12]

Thus, Hart argues, there is no reason why we should insist that international law must have a basic norm. Such an assertion depends upon a false analogy with municipal law. International law, by contrast, may consist of a set of separate primary rules of obligation which are not united in this particular way. Indeed, the insistence upon the need for a basic norm, within the context of such a system as modern international law, often leads to a rather empty repetition of the fact that society does observe certain standards as obligatory. Thus, Hart refers to the rather empty rhetorical form of the so-called basic norm of international law to the effect that "states should behave as they have customarily behaved".[13] As for the rule regarding the binding force of treaties, this is merely one of the "set" of rules accepted as binding. Of course, if the rule was generally accepted that treaties might bind not merely the parties thereto but other states, then treaties would have a legislative operation and the established form of treaty-making might have to be recognised as in itself one of the criteria of validity. But international law has not yet reached this stage.

### International Law and Sanctions

Hart makes pertinent observations also on the present status of international law.[14] He does not accept the contention that this status is a mere matter of words. He points out that the extension of general terms may involve a question of principle, the credentials of which need to be inspected.

In the first place he makes the valuable point that the role of coercion may be entirely different in municipal law from international relations. In the municipal sphere, in a reasonably well-regulated state, such is the position of human vulnerability and the approximate equality of citizens, that physical sanctions are generally likely to prevail, and no combination of malefactors is likely to be so strong as to be able to resist the

---

[12] The position in medieval law provides an illustration. Thus, Pollock and Maitland (*History of English Law*, vol. 1, p. xcv), after asserting that law may be taken to be the sum of the rules administered by courts of justice, proceed as follows: "We have not said that it must be, or that it always is, a sum of uniform and consistent rules . . . administered under one and the same system. This would, perhaps, be the statement of an ideal accomplished in any nation. Certainly it would not be correct as regards the state of English legal institutions, not only in modern but in quite recent times. Different and more or less conflicting systems of law, different and more or less competing systems or jurisdiction, in one and the same region, are compatible with a high state of civilisation, with a strong government, and with an administration of justice well enough liked and sufficiently understood by those who are concerned."

[13] *Op. cit.*, p. 236.

[14] *ibid.*, Chap. 10.

organised power of the state. In answer to this it may be said that, in many countries, the operation of the law is exceedingly inefficient and the over-powerful citizen or corporation may be able to evade or resist or secure the perversion of actual legal rules. Moreover, in some instances, such as the Mafia in Sicily, the actual legal system may be virtually controlled by a secret or private organisation.[15] These points, however valid, really only go to the actual existence of particular legal systems; they do not alter the fact that experience shows that within developed social communities it is quite possible to apply legal sanctions with considerable regularity and consistency with very small risk to the peace and order of the community. This situation, however, by no means holds in regard to international relations, for since sanctions would have to be applied to whole nations rather than to individuals, there may be enormous risks involved including the possibility of war. It is therefore manifest that the question of sanctions cannot be approached in the same way as they have been in municipal law. thus, there seems to be a certain fallacy in the reasoning which regards international law as a kind of "primitive" system destined ultimately to develop on the same lines as municipal legal systems have done in advanced communities, with virtually self-operating impersonal acceptance of enforcement by way of physical sanctions in the last resort.[16]

Even so, this does not mean that the fact that sanctions may not be capable of being invoked in the same manner as in national affairs renders it futile to attempt to regulate international affairs by systematic legal rules. Such rules may be, and are regarded as, obligatory. There is a general pressure upon states to conform to these rules and actual claims are based upon them. There is sufficient evidence to show there is value in attributing the title of law to the rules governing the international community.

## Law and Fact

The relation of Kelsen's logical structure to the actual facts of particular states is by no means clear. Certainly Kelsen aims at presenting necessary form divorced from content, but, nevertheless, his whole argument is clearly aimed at a structure[17] which can be shown to fit the facts. Does this mean that his structure represents the form that any legal system

---

[15] And see further M. Kramer, *In Defense of Legal Positivism* (1999), pp. 92–101.
[16] Contrast M. Barkun, *Law Without Sanctions* (1968) (and see *ante*, 35) with R. Schwartz and J. Miller (1964) 70 Am. J. Sociology 159 who suggest that damages and mediation nearly always precede the introduction of police in legal history because of the need to build certain cultural foundations before a central regime of control (as reflected in policing) can develop.
[17] On the general difficulty of distinguishing structure and content, see A. J. Ayer, *Problem of Knowledge*, pp. 234–236.

*must* take, without being condemned to outer darkness as to being a legal order at all? Kelsen does seem to imply the universality of his system, yet much of it, such as his hierarchy of norms, as he himself admits,[18] is not relevant to anything but an advanced political state. Does it really apply to primitive society, or to an absolute theocratic monarchy, or to medieval feudal society? Moreover, it is very hard to grasp exactly to what extent Kelsen admits the relevance of fact at all. We are not concerned with how any particular system works, but with the ultimate fabric of any system. So that whether a judge individualises a statutory norm does not rest on examining English or German law, but on a consideration of the general logic of the situation. But then in deciding whether this *is* the general structure, must one not compare it with actual systems? And if the fact of effectiveness is relevant to the choice of the basic norm, why are facts irrelevant to other stages of the analysis? Kelsen, unfortunately, nowhere examines specifically the link between fact and law[19] save to say, somewhat darkly, that the relation of an act to a norm is that between an act and its *meaning*, and that the legal norm is the specific *meaning* of a norm-creating act.[20]

### Non-Legal Norms

Kelsen tells us that even if racketeers enforce a "tax" on night-clubs by coercion, this is not a legal norm. The reason is that this can only be created by persons considered authorities under the constitution. So to be legal a norm must form part of the official hierarchy of norms. But what of bodies like trade associations, which possess rules and sanctions, which the law neither prohibits nor enforces? These are presumably not legal norms, yet they not only resemble them closely but may be said to be lawful in so far as the state does not prohibit them. Nor does this analysis enable Kelsen to distinguish a wicked regime from a gunman-type situation. That there is a difference is clear. It is, as Kramer explains, that a gunman always issues his orders to a "highly limited set of people for a highly limited stretch or time": by contrast any legal regime, however evil, will use various sorts of norms that "typically apply to indefinitely numerous people for long periods of time".[21] In practice, and based on

---

[18] See *What is Justice?*, p. 246. *Cf.* McBride, 43 N.Y.U.L.R. 53, 70: "Kelsen's theory is most plausible against the background reality of the modern state, perhaps most especially the modern state of Continental Europe, with its legal system built upon the principle of codification and, one may add, written constitutions."

[19] By this is meant that the fails to clarify the relation of his general theory to the facts of actual legal systems. Of course, in other respects, Kelsen frequently discusses fact and law, *e.g.* acts creating norms (*General Theory*, p. 114); the principle of effectiveness (p. 118); judicial ascertainment of facts (p. 135), etc.

[20] *What is Justice?*, p. 214. *Cf. The Pure Theory of Law*, p. 102.

[21] *In Defense of Legal Positivism* (1999), p. 95.

historical experience (Hitler, Stalin, Pol Pot, Idi Amin, etc.), the line may not be as easy to draw.[22]


## CONCLUSION

Of Kelsen, Laski famously remarked that "granted its postulates I believe the pure theory to be unanswerable but ... its substance is an exercise in logic, not in life".[23] To some extent, as we have shown, there is truth in this dictum, but it certainly does less than justice to the impressive display of learning, searching analysis and striking insights ranging over the whole field of law which characterise Kelsen's juristic output.[24] But Raz is dismissive: "The basic norm replaces the sovereign, otherwise nothing has changed."[25] This chapter, and the extracts to follow, show that this is far from the truth.


## H. KELSEN
### The Pure Theory of Law
### (1934–1935)[26]

### I

The Pure Theory of Law is a theory of positive law. As a theory it is exclusively concerned with the accurate definition of its subject-matter. It endeavours to answer the question, What is the law? but not the question, What ought it to be?[27] It is a science[28] and not a politics of law.

That all this is described as a "pure" theory of law means that it is concerned solely with that part of knowledge which deals with law, excluding from such knowledge everything which does not strictly belong to the subject-matter law. That is, it endeavours to free the science of law from all foreign elements. This is its fundamental methodological principle.[29] It would seem a self-evident one. Yet a glance at the traditional science of law in its nineteenth and twentieth century

---

22  I. Stewart (1998) 51 C.L.P. 181, 189 points out that Kelsen excludes "nothing" on moral grounds: "He accepts that the concept [of law] can embrace an extermination camp operated according to such norms." And he adds "appalling things have been done in the name of positive law".

23  *Grammar of Politics* (4th ed.), p. vi.

24  On different phases of Kelsen's work, see S. Paulson in (ed.) L. Gianformaggio, *Hans Kelsen's Legal Theory* (1990), p. 11. See also S. Paulson (1992) 12 Ox. J. L. Studies 265.

25  *The Concept of Legal System* (1980), p. 95.

26  [From vols 50 and 51 L.Q.R.]

27  [*Cf.* Austin, *ante*, 294.]

28  [On Kelsen's use of the word "science" see *ante*, 13.]

29  [Some supporters of Kelsen argue for the scientific character of his approach on the ground that his theory consists of generalisations based on juridical experience. The theory is therefore scientific because empirical, and "pure" because it disregards value-judgments, in common with all the sciences. (See, *e.g.* N. Bobbio, *Teoria Generale del Diritto* (1955), pp. 46–48.) But this latter remark seems less applicable to the social than to the physical sciences, and in any event it does not seem beyond question why the science of *law* should not deal with *actual* values, as opposed at any rate to *a priori* values.]

developments shows plainly how far removed from the requirement of purity that science was. Jurisprudence, in a wholly uncritical fashion, was mixed up with psychology and biology, with ethics and theology. There is to-day hardly a single social science into whose province jurisprudence feels itself unfitted to enter, even thinking, indeed, to enhance its scientific status by such conjunction with other disciplines. The real science of law, of course, is lost in such a process.[30]

The Pure Theory of Law seeks to define clearly its objects of knowledge in these two directions in which its autonomy has been most endangered by the prevailing syncretism of methods. Law is a social phenomenon. Society, however, is something wholly different from nature, since an entirely different association of elements. If legal science is not to disappear into natural science, then law must be distinguished in the plainest possible manner from nature. The difficulty about such a distinction is that law, or what is generally called law, belongs with at least a part of its being to nature and seems to have a thoroughly natural existence. If, for instance, we analyse any condition of things such as is called law—a parliamentary ruling, a judicial sentence, a legal process, a delict—we can distinguish two elements. The one is a sensible act in time and place, an external process, generally a human behavior; the other is a significance attached to or immanent in this act or process, a specific meaning. People meet together in a hall, make speeches, some rise from their seats, others remain seated; that is the external process. Its meaning: that a law has been passed. A man, clothed in a gown, speaks certain words from an elevated position to a person standing in front of him. This external process means a judicial sentence. One merchant writes to another a letter with a certain content; the other sends a return letter. This means that have concluded a contract. Someone, by some action or other, brings about the death of another. This means, legally, murder. . . .

These external circumstances, since they are sensible, temporospatial events, are in every case a piece of nature and as such causally determined. But as elements of the system nature, they are not objects of specifically juristic knowledge, are, indeed, not legal matter at all. That which makes the process into a legal (or illegal) act is not its factuality, not its natural, causal existence, but the objective significance which is bound up with it, its meaning. Its characteristically legal meaning it receives from a norm whose content refers to it. The norm functions as a schema of meaning. It itself is born of a legal act which in its turn receives its meaning from another norm. That a certain condition of fact is the execution of a death sentence and not a murder, this quality, which is not perceptible to the senses, is arrived at only by a mental process: by confronting the act with the penal statute book and penal administration. That the above-mentioned correspondence meant the conclusion of a contract resulted solely from the fact that this circumstance fell under certain rulings in the civil statute book. That an assembly of persons is a parliament and that the result of their activities is a law is only to say that the whole condition of fact corresponds to definite occurrence coincides with the content of some norm which is presupposed as valid.

---

[30] [The impossibility of excluding all considerations of values or political ideology from the structure of law, however formalised, or indeed from any theory of jurisprudence, has been strenuously urged by Kelsen's critics. For an analysis of the implicit valuation elements and factual assumptions which are allegedly to be found within Kelsen's Pure Theory, see Julius Cohen, "The Political Element in Legal Theory: A Look at Kelsen's Pure Theory" (1978) 88 Yale L.J. 1. Cohen concludes that "Kelsen has fashioned a special pair of lenses through which the detached observer is invited to see what purport to be the structural elements and framework of any legal order. The picture received by this observer is distorted, however, because the viewing lenses are so constructed as to block from vision one of the theory's essential structural components—the valuational element" (p. 35). *Cf. ante,* 43, 50.]. Would Kelsen have been equally critical of the "law and . . . movement of to-day"? On this see E. Rubin (1997) Wisconsin L.R. 521.]

In defining the law as norm, and in restricting legal science (whose function is different from that of the legislative and executive organs) to knowledge of norms, we at the same time delimit law from nature and the science of law, as a normative science, from all other sciences which aim at explaining causal, natural processes. In particular, we delimit it from one science which sets itself the task of examining the causes and effects of these natural processes which, receiving their designation from legal norms, appear as legal acts.[31] If such a study be called sociology, or sociology of law, we shall make no objection. Neither shall we say anything here of its value or its prospects. This only is certain, that such legal-sociological knowledge has nothing to do with the norms of the law as specific contents. It deals only with certain processes without reference to their relation to any valid or assumed norms. It relates the circumstances to be examined not to valid norms but to other circumstances, as causes to effects. It inquires by what causes a legislator is determined in constituting these and not other norms, and what effects his ordinances have had. It inquires in what way economic facts and religious views actually influence the activities of the Courts, and for what motives men make their behavior conform to the law or not. For such an inquiry law is only a natural reality, a fact in the consciousness of those who make, or of those subjects to, the norms. The law itself, therefore, is not properly the subject of this study, but certain parallel processes in nature. In the same way the physiologist, examining the physical or chemical processes which condition or which accompany certain emotions, does not comprehend the emotions themselves. The emotions are not comprehensible in chemical or physiological terms. The Pure Theory of Law, as a specific science of law, considers legal norms not as natural realities, not as fact in consciousness, but as meaning-contents. And it considers facts only as the content of legal norms, that is, only as determined by the norms. Its problem is to discover the specific principles of a sphere of meaning.

. . . What is here chiefly important is to liberate law from that association which has traditionally been made for it—its association with morals. This is not of course to question the requirement that law ought to be moral, that is, good. That requirement is self-evident. What is questioned is simply the view that law, as such, is a part of morals and that therefore every law, as law, is in some sense and in some measure moral . . .

II

To free the theory of law from this element is the endeavour of the Pure Theory of Law. The Pure Theory of Law separates the concept of the legal completely from that of the moral norm and establishes the law as a specific system independent even of the moral law.[32] It does this not, as is generally the case with the traditional theory, by defining the legal norm, like the moral norm, as an imperative, but as an hypothetical judgment expressing a specific relationship between a conditioning circumstance and a conditioned consequence. The legal norm becomes the legal maxim—the fundamental form of the statute law. Just as

---

[31] [Thus though Kelsen would not deny that legal rules may have an actual causal effect on the minds of human beings and so affect their behaviour, he regards this as a sociological and not a juristic manner.

[32] [For Kelsen's curious contention that legal and moral norms cannot conflict because there is no collision between the two—the jurist and the moralist simply ignore morality of positive law as a system of valid norms: see *The Pure Theory of Law,* pp. 374–75. Kelsen's main argument seems to be that to allow the co-existence of a valid legal rule and a moral principle which conflict would involve a logical impossibility. Hart has demonstrated the fallacies in this reasoning: see "Kelsen Visited" in *Essays in Jurisprudence and Philosophy* (1983), pp. 286, 301–308. For the view that Kelsen's position is *logically* sound see M. Detmold, *The Unity of Law and Morality* (1984), p. 54. *Cf.* on Kelsen's view as to the unity of international and municipal law, *ante,* 321.]

natural law links a certain circumstance to another as cause to effect, so the legal rule links the legal condition to the legal consequence. In the one case the connecting principle is causality: in the other it is imputation. The Pure Theory of Law regards this principle as the special and peculiar principle of law. Its expression is the Ought. The expression of the causality principle is Necessity. The law of nature runs: If A is, then B must be. The legal rule says: If A is, then B ought to be. And thereby it says nothing as to the value, the moral or political value of the relationship. The Ought remains a pure *a priori* category for the comprehension of the empirical legal material.[33] In this respect it is indispensable if we are to grasp at all the specific fashion in which positive law connects circumstances with one another. For it is evident that this connexion is not that of cause and effect. Punishment does not follow upon a delict as effect upon a cause. The legislator relates the two circumstances in a fashion wholly different from causality. Wholly different, yet a connexion as unshakeable as causality.[34] For in the legal system the punishment follows always and invariably on the delict even when in fact, for some reason or other, it fails of execution. Even though it does not so fail, it still does not stand to the delict in the relation of effect to cause. When we say: If there is tort, then the consequence of tort (punishment) shall (*i.e.* ought to) follow, this Ought, the category of law, indicates only the specific sense in which the legal condition and the legal consequence are held together in the legal rule. The category has a purely formal character. Thereby it distinguishes itself in principle from any transcendental notion of law. It is applicable no matter what the content of the circumstances which it links together, no matter what the character of the acts to which it gives the name of law. No social reality can be refused incorporation in this legal category on account of its contentual structure.... [Vol. 50, pp. 477–485]

## IV

The law, or the legal order, is a system of legal norms. The first question we have to answer, therefore, is this: What constitutes the unity in diversity of legal norms? Why does a particular legal norm belong to a particular legal order? A multiplicity of norms constitutes a unity, a system, an order, when validity can be traced back to its final source in a single norm. This basic norm constitutes the unity in diversity of all the norms which make up the system. That a norm belongs to a particular order is only to be determined by tracing back its validity to the basic norm constituting the order. According to the nature of the basic norm, *i.e.* the sovereign principle of validity, we may distinguish two different kinds or

---

[33] [In Kelsen's jurisprudence the "ought" category is necessary in order to comprehend the empirical legal material. The Pure Theory, therefore, shows how a science of law is possible on the analogy of natural science. The propositions of the pure Theory, though in the grammatical form of ought, are nonetheless descriptive (see I. Stewart, "The Basic Norm as Fiction" (1980) Jur.Rev. 199, 204–205). This descriptive quality of the Pure Theory itself must not be confused with what Kelsen calls rules of law "in a descriptive sense," which are the legal rules formulated by the science of law. But the contention that there are descriptive ought-sentences is far from clear. One could think that the descriptive ought is something like Hart's inverted commas use (*The Language of Morals* (1952)) (a mention, not a use of the term "ought") but Kelsen rejects this (see Golding (1961) 47 A.R.S.P.). See also Hart, "Kelsen Visited" in *Essays In Jurisprudence and Philosophy* (1983).

[34] [This statement has been very much criticised. Thus Olivecrona says of it ironically: "A mystery it is and a mystery it will remain for ever" (*Law as Fact* (1939), p. 21). It will be seen from what follows in this paragraph that kelsen is here involved in the language of Kantian metaphysics. A rather more acceptable account of the normative proposition will be found in Kelsen's *General Theory of Law and State* (1946).]

orders, or normative systems. In the first such system the norms are valid by virtue of their content, which has a directly evident quality compelling recognition. This contentual quality the norms receive by descent from a basic norm to whose content their content is related as particular to universal. The norms of morals are of this character. Thus the norms: Thou shalt not lie, Thou shalt not deceive, Thou shalt keep thy promise, etc. derive from a basic norm of honesty. From the basic norm: Thou shalt love thy fellow-men, we can derive the norms: Thou shalt not injure they fellow, Thou shalt accompany him in adversity, etc. The question as to what, in a particular system of morals, is the basic norm, is not here under consideration. What is important is to recognize that the many norms of a moral system and already contained in its basic norm, exactly as particulars in a universal, and that all the individual norms can be derived from the basic norm by an operation of thought, namely, by deduction from universal to particular.

With legal norms the case is different. These are not valid by virtue of their content. Any content whatsoever can be legal; there is no human behavior which could not function as the content of a legal norm. A norm becomes a legal norm only because it has been constituted in a particular fashion, born of a definite procedure and a definite rule. Law is valid only as positive law, that is, statute (constituted) law. Therefore the basic norm of law can only be the fundamental rule, according to which the legal norms are to be produced; it is the fundamental condition of law-making. The individual norms of the legal system are not to be derived from the basic norm by a process of logical deduction. They must be constituted by an act of will, not deduced by an act of thought. If we trace back a single legal norm to its source in the basic norm, we do so by showing that the procedure by which it was set up conformed to the requirements of the basic norm. Thus, if we ask why a particular act of compulsion—the fact, for instance, that one man has deprived another of his freedom by imprisoning him—is an act of law and belongs to a particular legal order, the answer is, that this act was prescribed by a certain individual norm, a judicial decision. If we ask, further, why this individual norm is valid, the answer is, that it was constituted according to the penal statute book. If we inquire as to the validity of the penal statute book, we are confronted by the State's constitution, which has prescribed rules and procedure for the creation of the penal statute book by a competent authority. If, further, we ask as to the validity of the constitution, on which repose all the laws and act which they have sanctioned, we come probably to a still older constitutional and finally to an historically original one, set up by some single usurper or by some kind of corporate body. It is the fundamental presupposition of our recognition of the legal order founded on this constitution that that which the original authors declared to be their will should be regarded as valid norm. Compulsion is to be exercised according to the method and conditions prescribed by the first constitutional authority, or its delegated power. This is the schematic formulation of the basic norm of a legal order...

(a) This analysis of the function of the basic norm brings to light also a special peculiarity of the law—the law regulates its own growth and its own making. The unity of the legal order is a law-*making* unity. The law is not a system of equal, side-by-side norms: it is a hierarchy with different layers. Its formal pattern is roughly the following.

At the highest point of the individual State's legal order is the constitution—in the material sense—the essential function of which is to determine the organs and procedure for the setting up of general law, to determine legislation. The next stage consists of the general norms, set up by legislation, whose function, in turn, is to determine not only the organs and procedure (Courts and administrative tribunals) for the individual norms, but also the content of the latter. The general norm, which links an abstract condition of fact to an equally abstract consequence, if it is to have any meaning, needs to be individualized. It must be known definitely whether there is present *in concreto*[35] a condition of fact which the general norm *in abstracto* regulates, and for this concrete case a concrete act of compulsion must be prescribed and carried out—this also according to the abstract general norm. The agent in this is the judicial decision, the judicial power. The judicial power is by no means of a purely declaratory nature, such as the terms "laying down" and "ascertaining" the law suggest, as if in the statute, that is, the general norm, the law were already prepared and complete, simply waiting for the Courts to find it. The function of laying down the law is a properly constitutive one, it is a making of law in the real sense of the word. The relationship between the concrete condition of fact (and the discovery of its correspondence with the abstract condition) and the concrete legal consequence is specifically set up by the judicial decision. Just as at the general stage condition and consequence are joined by the statute, so at the individual stage they are joined by the judicial decision. The judicial decision is itself an individual legal norm.[36] It is the individualization or concretization of the general, abstract norm, the individual stage of the law-making process. This conclusion is hidden only from those who see in the general norm the repository of all law, wrongly identifying law with statute.

(b) Administration, no less than judicial decision, can be shown to be concretization of statute law. Indeed, a considerable part of that which we normally call administration is not to be distinguished functionally at all from that which we call judicial decision or finding of the Courts,[37] in so far as public policy is pursued technically, in both cases, in an identical fashion, namely, achieving the desired condition of affairs by attaching to its contradictory an act of compulsion in short, by making the desired social behavior legally obligatory. It makes no essential difference whether honour is protected by the assessment of damages in Court, or whether safety in the streets is ensured by the punishment of recklessness in administrative tribunals. To speak in the one case of the judiciary and in the other of the administration is to emphasize only a technical difference, the purely historical position of the Judge, namely, his independence—a characteristic generally, though by no means always, lacking to the administrative organ. Essential identity, however, is evident in this, that in each case public policy is realized indirectly. A functional distinction between judiciary and administration is present only when the State organ realizes the purposes of the State directly, as, for instance, when it itself builds the schools, drives the trains, administers hospitals. This kind of direct administration is indeed essentially different from

---

[35] [Hence the phrase, the "concretisation" of law. Ebenstein claims that this enables Kelsen to overcome "traditional weaknesses of both continental and Anglo-American legal theories, and to provide, perhaps for the first time, the structure of a unified legal theory that integrates legal phenomena of diverse legal systems into a whole" (59 Calif. L.R. 617, 644). But this is to underestimate the contribution of Bentham.]

[36] [The ascertainment of the facts by the tribunal is part of the constitutive process by which the norm is created, for in the world of law there are no "absolute" facts, but only facts as ascertained by a competent organ: see H. Kelsen, *General Theory of Law and State,* pp. 135–136.]

[37] [This statement is criticised by E. Bodenheimer (see *Jurisprudence,* p. 240) on the ground that administration involves the discretionary exercise of power, whereas law is a limitation upon the exercise of such power. But this criticism seems misconceived, in so far as it ignores the further point in Kelsen's analysis, that such administrative exercise of power may itself by referable to higher norms in the legal hierarchy, and which may, therefore, control the norms on a lower level. It is in this way that one legal norm may operate as a limitation upon another such norm. There is nothing in Kelsen's view, therefore, which prevents the administrative activity of the Government taking place within the framework of rules or legal standards, if the legal system in fact provides such operative framework. This may be done either by means of the ordinary courts, or by means of a special administrative court or tribunal, such as the French *Conseil d'Etat,* or by means of an official such as the Scandinavian Ombudsman or the British.]

judicial administration which is by its nature committed to an indirect pursuit of its, that is to say the State's, ends. If administration and judiciary, then, are to rank as fundamentally different, it can only be on the basis of the direct character of the former. This is to say that a correct view of the system of legal functions must draw a different line of demarcation from the customary one, which, legislation apart, breaks up the legal apparatus into a number of relatively isolated groups of tribunals which exercise for the most part similar functions. The correct view of the difference in function, the substitution for judiciary and administration of direct and indirect administration, would not be without its effects on the organization itself.

(c) In certain spheres of law, as for instance in civil law, the concretization of the general norms does not follow directly from the act of an official State instrument, such as is the judicial decision. In the case of the civil law, which the Courts have to apply, there is interposed between the statute and the decision the legal transaction, which with respect to the conditioning circumstance, has an individualizing function. Directed by the statute, the parties set up concrete norms for their mutual behavior,[38] an offence against which constitutes the condition of fact to be determined by the judicial decision. To this condition the judicial decision attaches the penal consequence.

The final stage of this law-making process, which began with the formation of the constitution, is the carrying out of the compulsive act, the penal consequence. . . .                                              [Vol. 51, pp. 517–522]


## H. KELSEN
### General Theory of Law and State
### (1946)


*Law as a coercive order*


The evil applied to the violator of the order when the sanction is socially organized consists in a deprivation of possessions—life, health, freedom, or property. As the possessions are taken from him against his will, this sanction has the character of a measure of coercion. This does not mean that in carrying out the sanction physical force must be applied. This is necessary only if resistance is encountered in applying the sanction. This is only exceptionally the case, where the authority applying the sanction possesses adequate power. A social order that seeks to bring about the desired behavior of individuals[39] by the enactment of such measures of coercion is called a coercive order. Such it is because it threatens socially harmful deeds with measures of coercion, decrees such measures of coercion. As such it presents a contrast to all other possible social orders—those that provide reward rather than punishment as sanctions, and especially those that enact no sanctions at all, relying on the technique of direct motivation. In contrast to the orders that enact coercive measures as sanctions, the efficacy of the others rests not on coercion but on voluntary obedience. Yet this contrast is not so distinct as it might at first sight appear. This follows from the fact that the technique of reward, as a technique of indirect motivation, has its place between the technique of indirect motivation through punishment, as a technique of

---

[38]  [Thus a contract is a legal norm, an individualisation of the more general norm under which it is made.]

[39]  [Kelsen has shifted his ground in *The Pure Theory of Law* (see p. 10). As Raz (*op. cit.*, p. 62) notes: "the intention to affect someone's behaviour is replaced by the intention to create a norm ... [which] presupposes the existence of norms and conventionalised activities, and cannot serve as their ultimate explanation." Hence, Raz argues "Kelsen's doctrine applies only to legislation within the framework of normative systems".]

coercion, and the technique of direct motivation, the technique of voluntary obedience. Voluntary obedience is itself a form of motivation, that is, of coercion, and hence is not freedom, but it is coercion in the psychological sense. If coercive orders are contrasted with those that have no coercive character, that rest on voluntary obedience, this is possible only in the sense that one provides measures of coercion as sanctions whereas the other does not. And these sanctions are only coercive measures in the sense that certain possessions are taken from the individuals in question against their will, if necessary by the employment of physical force.

In this sense, the law is a coercive order.

If the social orders, so extraordinarily different in their tenors, which have prevailed at different times and among the most different peoples, are called legal orders, it might be supposed that one is using an expression almost devoid of meaning. What could the so-called law of ancient Babylonians have in common with the law that prevails today in the United States? What could the social order of a negro tribe under the leadership of a despotic chieftain—an order likewise called "law"—have in common with the constitution of the Swiss Republic? Yet there is a common element, that fully justifies this terminology, and enables the word "law" to appear as the expression of a concept with a socially highly significant meaning. For the word refers to that specific social technique of a coercive order which, despite the vast differences existing between the law of ancient Babylon and that of the United States of today, between the law of the Ashantis in West Africa and that of the Swiss in Europe, is yet essentially the same for all these peoples differing so much in time, in place, and in culture: the social technique which consists in bringing about the desired social conduct of men through the threat of a measure of coercion which is to be applied in case of contrary conduct. What the social conditions are that necessitate this technique, is an important sociological question. I do not know whether we can answer it satisfactorily. Neither did I know whether it is possible for mankind to emancipate itself totally from this social technique. But if the social order should in the future no longer have the character of a coercive order, if society should exist without "law," then the difference between this society of the future and that of the present day would be immeasurably greater than the difference between the United States and ancient Babylon, or Switzerland and the Ashanti tribe.[pp. 18–19]

## THE LEGAL NORM

### *Legal norm and rule of law in a descriptive sense*

If "coercion" in the sense here defined is an essential element of law, then the norms which form a legal order must be norms stipulating a coercive act, *i.e.* a sanction. In particular, the general norms must be norms in which a certain sanction is made dependent upon certain conditions, this dependence being expressed by the concept of "ought." This does not mean that the law-making organs necessarily have to give the norms the form of such hypothetical "ought" statements. The different elements of a norm may be contained in very different products of the law-making procedure, and they may be linguistically expressed in very different ways. When the legislator forbids theft, he may, for instance, first define the concept of theft in a number of sentences which form an article of a statute, and then stipulate the sanction in another sentence, which may be part of another article of the same statute or even part of an entirely different statute. Often the latter sentence does not have the linguistic form of an imperative or an "ought" sentence but the form of a prediction of a future event. The legislator frequently makes use of the future tense, saying that a thief "will be" punished in such and such a way. He then presupposes that the question as to who is a thief has been answered somewhere else, in the same or in some other statute. The phrase "will be punished" does not imply the prediction of a future event—the legislator is no prophet—but an "imperative" or a "command," these terms taken in a figurative sense. What the norm-creating authority means is that the sanction "ought" to be executed against the thief, when the conditions of the sanction are fulfilled.

It is the task of the science of law to represent the law of a community, *i.e.* the material produced by the legal authority in the law-making procedure, in the form of statements to the effect that "if such and such conditions are fulfilled, then such and such a sanction shall follow." These statements, by means of which the science of law represents law, must not be confused with the norms created by the law-making authorities. It is preferable not to call these statements norms, but legal rules. The legal norms enacted by the law creating authorities are prescriptive; the rules of law formulated by the science of law are descriptive. It is of importance that the term "legal rule" or "rule of law" be employed here in a descriptive sense.[40]

### Rule of Law and Law of Nature

The rule of law, the term used in a descriptive sense, is a hypothetical judgment attaching certain consequences to certain conditions. This is the logical form of the law of nature, too. Just as the science of law, the science of nature describes its object in sentences which have the character of hypothetical judgments. And like the rule of law, the law of nature, too, connects two facts with one another as condition and consequence. The condition is here the "cause," the consequence the "effect." The fundamental form of the law of nature is the law of causality. The difference between the rule of law and the law of nature seems to be that the former refers to human being and their behavior, whilst the latter refers to things and their reactions. Human behavior, however, may also be the subject-matter of natural laws, insofar as human behavior, too, belongs to nature. The rule of law and the law of nature differ not so much by the elements they connect as by the manner of their connection. The law of nature establishes that if $A$ is, $B$ is (or will be). The rule of law says: If $A$ is, $B$ ought to be. The rule of law is a norm (in the descriptive sense of that term). The meaning of the connection established by the

---

[40] [It is clear that there is a distinction between legal norms as laid down by law-creating authorities, and rules of law as formulated by the juristic science of law. The former can be said to be prescriptive, and the latter descriptive. Some confusion, however, has been caused by Kelsen's description of the statements of the science of law as being "rules of law in a descriptive sense". Ross criticises Kelsen as putting forward the view that it is possible to conduct a science of law as being itself normative, *i.e.* that its conclusions will be normative statements and not descriptive statements. (See *On Law and Justice*, p. 10). Hart, however, has pointed out that though Kelsen's curious terminology is not beyond criticism, it does take account of an important distinction which is worth preserving. This is the fact that the statements of a jurist in relation to the laws of the legal system he is dealing with, do not have a "simple one-to-one correspondence" with the laws of the system in question. The jurist's exposition may have a consistency and order not present in the original, for the jurist does not just interpret the rules of the law-creating authorities, but seeks in effect a rational reconstruction of the law of a particular system. This is why Kelsen regards the science of law as being in a sense both normative and descriptive. (See Hart, *Essays in Jurisprudence and Philosophy* (1983), p. 286.) Hart has since claimed that this interpretation of Kelsen's thought is incorrect; he now thinks that Kelsen was seeking to distinguish between statements by the jurist which do or do not (as the case may be) involve acceptance of the shared standard of behaviour which are embodied in legal rules: see *Essays in Jurisprudence and Philosophy* (1983), pp. 14–15. But it is difficult to read this distinction, however valid in itself, into Kelsen's text. See further E. Bulygin, *Contemporary Philosophy* (1982), vol. 3, p. 127.

law of nature between two elements is the "is," whereas the meaning of the connection between two elements established by the rule of law is the "ought." The principle according to which natural science describes its object is causality; the principle according to which the science of law describes its object is normativity.[41]

Usually, the difference between law of nature and norm is characterized by the statement that the law of nature can have no exceptions, whereas a norm can. This is, however, not correct. The normative rule "If someone steals, he ought to be punished," remains valid even if in a given case a thief is not punished. This fact involves no exception to the ought statement expressing the norm; it is an exception only to an "is" statement expressing the rule that if someone steals, he actually will be punished. The validity of a norm remains unaffected if, in a concrete instance, a fact does not correspond to the norm. A fact has the character of an "exception" to a rule if the statement establishing the fact is in a logical contradiction to the rule. Since a norm is no statement of reality, no statement of a real fact can be in contradiction to a norm. Hence, there can be no exceptions to a norm. The norm is, by its very nature, inviolable. To say that the norm is "violated" by certain behavior is a figurative expression; and the figure used in this statement is not correct. For the statement says nothing about the norm: it merely characterizes the actual behavior as contrary to the behavior prescribed by the norm.

The law of nature, however, is not inviolable. True exceptions to a law of nature are not excluded. The connection between cause and effect established in a law of nature describing physical reality has the character of probability only, not of absolute necessity, as assumed by the older philosophy of nature. If, as a result of empirical research, two phenomena are considered to be in a relation of cause and effect, and if this result is formulated in a law of nature, it is not absolutely excluded that a fact may occur which is in contradiction to this law, and which therefore represents a real exception to the law. Should such a fact be established, then the formulation of the law has to be altered in a way to make the new fact correspond to the new formula. But the connection of cause and effect established by the new formula has also only the character of probability, not that of absolute necessity. Exceptions to the law are not excluded.

If we examine the way in which the ideal of causality has developed in the human mind, we find that the law of causality has its origin in a norm. The interpretation of nature has originally a social character. Primitive man considers nature to be an intrinsic part of his society. He interprets physical reality according to the same principles that determine his social relations. His social order, to him, is at the same time the order of nature. Just as men obey the norms of the social order, things obey the norms emanating from superhuman personal beings. The fundamental social law is the norm according to which the good has to be rewarded, the evil punished. It is the principle of retribution which completely dominates primitive consciousness. The legal norm is the prototype of this principle. According to this principle of retribution, primitive man interprets nature. His interpretation has a normative-juristic character. It is in the norm of retribution that the law of causality originates and, in the way of a gradual change of meaning, develops. Even during the nineteenth century, the law of causality was conceived of as a norm, the expression of the divine will. The last step in this emancipation of the law of causality from the norm of retribution consists in the fact that the former gets rid of the character of a norm and thereby ceases to be conceived of as inviolable.[42]                                    [pp. 45–47]

---

[41] [Where Kelsen speaks of two different *principles,* we may if we like refer to two types of propositions used for different purposes, *i.e.* to assert facts or to prescribe conduct.]

[42] *Cf.* H. Kelsen, *Society and Nature,* pp. 233 *et seq.* [*ante,* 97.]

*The basic norm of a legal order*

### The Basic Norm and the Constitution

The derivation of the norms of a legal order from the basic norm of that order is performed by showing that the particular norms have been created in accordance with the basic norm. To the question why a certain act of coercion—*e.g.* the fact that one individual deprives another individual of his freedom by putting him in jail—is a legal act, the answer is: because it has been prescribed by an individual norm, a judicial decision. To the question why this individual norm is valid as part of a definite legal order, the answer is: because it has been created in conformity with a criminal statute. This statute, finally, receives its validity from the constitution, since it has been established by the competent organ in the way the constitution prescribes.

If we ask why the constitution is valid, perhaps we come upon an older constitution. Ultimately we reach some constitution that is the first historically and that was laid down by an individual usurper or by some kind of assembly. The validity of this first constitution is the last presupposition, the final postulate, upon which the validity of all the norms of our legal order depends. It is postulated that one ought to behave as the individual, or the individuals, who laid down the first constitution have ordained. This is the basic norm of the legal order under consideration. The document which embodies the first constitution is a real constitution, a binding norm, only on the condition that the basic norm is presupposed to be valid. Only upon this presupposition are the declarations of those to whom the constitution confers norm-creating power binding norms. It is this presupposition that enables us to distinguish between individuals who are legal authorities and other individuals whom we do not regard as such, between acts of human beings which create legal norms and acts which have no such effect. All these legal norms belong to one and the same legal order because their validity can be traced back—directly or indirectly—to the first constitution. That the first constitution is a binding legal norm is presupposed, and the formulation of the presupposition is the basic norm of this legal order. The basic norm of a religious norm system says that one ought to behave as God and the authorities instituted by Him command. Similarly, the basic norm of a legal order prescribes that one ought to behave as the "fathers" of the constitution and the individuals—directly or indirectly—authorized (delegated) by the constitution command. Expressed in the form of a legal norm: coercive acts ought to be carried out only under the conditions and in the way determined by the "fathers" of the constitution or the organs delegated by them. This is, schematically formulated, the basic norm of the legal order of a single State, the basic norm of a national legal order. It is to the national legal order that we have here limited our attention. Later, we shall consider what bearing the assumption of an international law has upon the question of the basic norm of national law.

### The Specific Function of the Basic Norm

That a norm of the kind just mentioned is the basic norm of the national legal order does not imply that it is impossible to go beyond that norm. Certainly one may ask why one has to respect the first constitution as a binding norm. The answer might be that the fathers of the first constitution were empowered by God. The characteristic of so-called legal positivism is, however, that it dispenses with any such religious justification of the legal order. The ultimate hypothesis of positivism is the norm authorizing the historically first legislator. The whole function of this basic norm is to confer law-creating power on the act of the first legislator and on all the other acts based on the first act. To interpret these acts of human beings as legal acts and their products as binding norms, and that means to interpret the empirical material which presents itself as law as such, is possible only on the condition that the basic norm is presupposed as a valid norm. The basic norm is only the necessary presupposition of any positivistic interpretation of the legal material.

The basic norm is not created in a legal procedure by a law-creating organ. It is not—as a positive legal norm is—valid because it is created in a certain way by a legal act, but it is valid because it is presupposed to be valid; and it is presupposed to be valid because without this pre-supposition, no human act could be interpreted as a legal, especially as a norm-creating act.

By formulating the basic norm, we do not introduce into the science of law any new method. We merely make explicit what all jurists, mostly unconsciously, assume when they consider positive law as a system of valid norms and not only as a complex of facts, and at the same time repudiate any natural law from which positive law would receive its validity. That the basic norm really exists in the juristic consciousness is the result of a simple analysis of actual juristic statements. The basic norm is the answer to the question: how—and that means under what condition—are all these juristic statements concerning legal norms, legal duties, legal rights, and so on, possible?                              [pp. 116–117]

### Change of the Basic Norm[43]

It is just the phenomenon of revolution which clearly shows the significance of the basic norm. Suppose that a group of individuals attempt to seize power by force, in order to remove the legitimate government in a hitherto monarchic State, and to introduce a republican form of government. If they succeed, if the old order ceases, and the new order begins to be efficacious, because the individuals whose behavior the new order regulates actually behave, by and large, in conformity with the new order, then this order is considered as a valid order. It is now according to this new order that the actual behavior of individuals is interpreted as legal or illegal. But this means that a new basic norm is presupposed. It is no longer the norm according to which the old monarchical constitution is valid, but a norm according to which the new republican constitution is valid, a norm endowing the revolutionary government with legal authority. If the revolutionaries fail, if the order they have tried to establish remains inefficacious, then, on the other hand, their undertaking is interpreted, not as a legal, a law-creating act, as the establishment of a constitution, but as an illegal act, as the crime of treason, and this according to the old monarchic constitution and its specific basic norm.

### The Principle of Effectiveness

If we attempt to make explicit the presupposition on which these juristic considerations rest, we find that the norms of the old order are regarded as devoid of validity because the old constitution and, therefore, the legal norms based on this constitution, the old legal order as a whole, has lost its efficacy; because the actual behavior of men does no longer conform to this old legal order. Every single norm loses its validity when the total legal order to which it belongs loses its efficacy as a whole. The efficacy of the entire legal order is a necessary condition for the validity of every single norm of the order. A *conditio sine qua non,* but not a *conditio per quam.* The efficacy of the total legal order is a condition, not the reason for the validity of its constituent norms. These norms are valid not because the total order is efficacious, but because they are created in a constitutional way. They are valid, however, only on the condition that the total order is efficacious; they cease to be valid, not only when they are annulled in a constitutional way,

---

[43] [This passage was relied upon in a number of the so-called "Grundnorm" cases. See *ante,* 311, n. 44 and 317, n. 82.]

but also when the total order ceases to be efficacious. It cannot be maintained that, legally, men have to behave in conformity with a certain norm, if the total legal order, of which that norm is an integral part, has lost is efficacy. The principle of legitimacy is restricted by the principle of effectiveness.[pp. 118–119]

### The Reason of Validity of National and International Law

In order to answer the question whether international law and national law are different and mutually independent legal orders, or form one universal normative system, in order to reach a decision between pluralism and monism, we have to consider the general problem of what makes a norm belong to a definite legal order, what is the reason that several norms form one and the same normative system. . . .

. . . If the national legal order is considered without reference to international law, then its ultimate reason of validity is the hypothetical norm qualifying the "Fathers of the Constitution" as a law-creating authority. If, however, we take into account international law, we find that this hypothetical norm can be derived from a positive norm of this legal order: the principle of effectiveness. It is according to this principle that international law empowers the "Fathers of the Constitution" to function as the first legislators of a State. The historically first constitution is valid because the coercive order erected on its basis is efficacious as a whole. Thus, the international legal order, by means of the principle of effectiveness, determines not only the sphere of validity, but also the reason of validity of the national legal orders. Since the basic norms of the national legal orders are determined by a norm of international law, they are basic norms only in a relative sense. It is the basic norm of the international legal order which is the ultimate reason of validity of the national legal orders, too.

A higher norm can either determine in detail the procedure in which lower norms are to be created, or empower an authority to create lower norms at its own discretion. It is in the latter manner that international law forms the basis of the national legal order. By stipulating that an individual or group of individuals who are able to obtain permanent obedience for the coercive order they establish are to be considered as a legal and legitimate authority, international law "delegates" the national legal orders whose spheres of validity it thereby determines.                                                          [pp. 366–368]

### The basic norm of international law

Since national law has the reason of its validity, and hence its "source" in this sense, in international law, the ultimate source of the former must be the same as that of the latter. Then the pluralistic view cannot be defended by the assumption that national and international law have different and mutually independent "sources." It is the "source" of national law by which that law is united with international law, whatever may be the "source" of this legal order. Which is the source, then, that is, the basic norm of international law?

To find the source of the international legal order, we have to follow a course similar to that which led us to the basic norm of the national legal order. We have to start from the lowest norm within international law, that is, from the decision of an international court. If we ask why the norm created by such a decision is valid, the answer is furnished by the international treaty in accordance with which the court was instituted. If, again, we ask why this treaty is valid, we are led back to the general norm which obligates the States to behave in conformity with the treaties they have concluded, a norm commonly expressed by the phrase *pacta sunt servanda*. This is a norm of general international law, and general international law is created by custom constituted by acts of States. The basic norm of international law, therefore, must be a norm which countenances custom as a norm-creating fact, and might be formulated as follows: "The States ought to behave as they have customarily behaved." Customary international law, developed on the basis of this norm, is the first stage within the international legal order.[44] The next stage is formed by the norms created by international treaties. The validity of these norms is dependent upon the norm *pacta sunt servanda*, which itself is a norm belonging to the first stage of general international law, which is law created by custom constituted by acts of States. The third stage is formed by norms created by organs which are themselves created by international treaties, as for instance decisions of the Council of the League of Nations, or of the Permanent Court of International Justice.          [pp. 369–370]

## H. KELSEN
### Professor Stone and the Pure Theory of Law
### (1965)[45]

... I have always and not only in the second edition of my *Reine Rechtslehre*.[46] clearly distinguished between the basic norm presupposed in juristic thinking as the constitution in a legal-logical sense and the constitution in a positive legal sense, and I have always insisted that the basic norm as the constitution in a legal-logical sense—not the constitution in a positive legal sense—is *not* a norm of positive law, that it is not a norm "posited," *i.e.* created by a real act of will of a legal organ, but a norm *presupposed in juristic thinking.*[47]

It is as a norm presupposed in juristic thinking that the basic norm (*if* it is presupposed) is "at the top of the pyramid of norms of each legal order." It is "meta-legal" if by this term is understood that the basic norm is not a norm of positive law, that is, not a norm created by a real act of will of a legal organ. It is "legal" if by this term we understand everything which has legally relevant functions, and the basic norm presupposed in juristic thinking has the function to found the *objective* validity of the subjective meaning of the acts by which the constitution of a community is created. In this respect the theory of the basic norm is—to a certain extent—similar to the natural-law doctrine according to which a positive legal order is valid if it corresponds to the natural law. The natural law is not considered to be "meta-legal," though it is not *positive* law. But there are also essential differences between the doctrine of the basic norm and the natural-law doctrine. ...

The main difference is that the *content* of the positive legal order is completely independent of the basic norm from which only the *objective validity* of the norms of the positive legal order, not the content of this order, can be derived; whereas according to the natural-law doctrine a positive legal order is valid only if and insofar as its content corresponds to the natural law. Hence there can be no conflict between a positive-legal order and its basic norm, whereas from the point of view of a positivistic theory of law a conflict between positive law and what is supposed to be natural law is quite possible ...

[44] *[Cf.* Lauterpacht, *Development of International Law by International Court* (2nd ed., 1958), Chap. 28. See the *Franconia* case (*R. v. Keyn* (1876) 2 Ex. D. 63; but *cf. Chung Chi Cheung v. R.* [1939] A.C. 160). *Cf.* Nelson in 35 M.L.R. 52.]

[45] [From (1965) 17 Stan. L.R. 1130. The article is written in reply to Stone's writings on Kelsen, notably his "Mystery and Mystique in the Basic Norm" in (1963) 26 M.L.R. 34, and his chapter in *Legal Systems and Lawyers' Reasonings*.]

[46] [Now translated as *The Pure Theory of Law* (1967), by Max Knight.]

[47] [By which Kelsen means that the basic norm is not the ought propositions "*of* the constitution, but rather an ought proposition *about* the constitution. As such it is not a legal norm in the usual sense of being the construct of an organ of the system; rather, it is a construct of juristic thought which is necessary if we are to regard the system as giving rise to valid norms" (*per* G. Hughes in 58 Calif. L.Rev. 695, 704).]

I do not maintain that the basic norm "guarantees" the efficacy of the legal order to which it refers. What I say is that the basic norm refers only to a coercive social order which is by and large effective. That means: we presuppose the basic norm only if there exists a coercive social order by and large effective. I say in my *Reine Rechtslehre*: "[The] basic norm refers only to a constitution which is the basis of an effective coercive order. Only if the actual behavior of men corresponds, by and large, to the subjective meaning of the acts directed at this behavior, their subjective meaning is considered also as their objective meanings."[48] And I say further: "The reason for the objective validity of a legal order is ... the presupposed basic norm according to which one ought to obey a constitution which actually is established and by and large effective; and consequently one ought also to obey the norms created in conformity with the constitution and by and large effective."[49] Since—according to my theory—the basic norm refers only to a coercive order which is by and large effective, and since the basic norm is adapted to this coercive order and not the coercive order to the basic norm, it is *in this sense* that in the basic norm the actual establishment of the norms of the coercive order by real acts of will and the efficacy of these norms are made the condition of the objective validity of the coercive order. Hence the basic norm does not "guarantee" the efficacy of the legal order; it does nothing to make this order effective...

In view of the specific function of the basic norm presupposed in juristic thinking I call it "constitution in a legal-logical sense" in contra-distinction to the "constitution in the sense of positive law." It is to the constitution in the sense of positive law that the basic norm refers. I distinguish these two concepts as clearly as possible...

As essential point of my theory of the basic norm ... is that it is not necessary to presuppose the basic norm, that only *if* we presuppose it can we consider a coercive order which is by and large effective as a system of *objectively valid* norms. Consequently, the foundation of the objective validity of the legal norms is conditional, conditioned by the presupposition of the basic norm...

The problem that leads to the theory of the basic norm—as I explained in my *Reine Rechtslehre*—is how to distinguish a legal command which is considered to be objectively valid, such as the command of a revenue officer to pay a certain sum of money, from a command which has the same subjective meaning but is not considered to be objectively valid, such as the command of a gangster. The difference consists in that we do not consider the subjective meaning of the command of a gangster—as we consider the subjective meaning of the legal command of a revenue officer—as its objective meaning because we do not presuppose in the former case—as we presuppose in the latter case—a basic norm. A Communist may, indeed, not admit that there is an essential difference between an organization of gangsters and a capitalistic legal order which he considers as the means of ruthless exploitation. For he does not presuppose—as do those who interpret the coercive order in question as an objectively valid normative order—the basic norm. He does not deny that the capitalistic coercive order is the law of the State. What he denies is that this coercive order, the law of the State, is objectively valid. The function of the basic norm is not to make it possible to consider a coercive order which is by and large effective as law, for—according to the definition presented by the Pure Theory of Law—a *legal* order is a coercive order by and large effective; the function of the basic norm is to make it possible to consider this coercive order as an *objectively* valid order.[50]...          [pp. 1141–1144]

---

[48]  [*Cf. The Pure Theory of Law*, pp. 46–47.]
[49]  [*ibid.*, pp. 212–213.]
[50]  [See also (1965) 17 Stan.L.R. 1147–1153, for Kelsen's answers to Stone's seven specific questions formulated in (1963) 26 M.L.R. 34.]

## H. KELSEN
## The Pure Theory of Law
### (1967)[51]

*Norm and norm creation*

Those norms, then, which have the character of legal norms and which make certain acts legal or illegal are the objects of the science of law. The legal order, which is the object of this cognition is a normative order of human behavior—a system of norms regulating human behavior. By "norm" we mean that something *ought* to be or *ought* to happen, especially that a human being ought to behave in a specific way. This is the meaning of certain human acts directed toward the behavior of others. They are so directed, if they, according to their content, command such behavior, but also if they permit it, and—particularly—if they authorize it. "Authorize" means to confer upon someone else a certain power, specifically the power to enact norms himself. In this sense the acts whose meaning is a norm are acts of will. If an individual by his acts expresses a will directed at a certain behavior of another, that is to say, if he commands, permits, or authorizes such behavior—then the meaning of his acts cannot be described by the statement that the other individual *will* (future tense) behave in that way, but only that he *ought* to behave in that way. The individual who commands, permits, or authorizes *wills*; the man to whom the command, permission or authorization is directed *ought to*. The word "ought" is used here in a broader than the usual sense. According to customary usage, "ought" corresponds only to a command, while "may" corresponds to a permission, and "can" to an authorization. But in the present work the word "ought" is used to express the normative meaning of an act directed toward the behavior of others; this "ought" includes "may" and "can." If a man who is commanded, permitted, or authorized to behave in a certain way asks for the reason of such command, permission, or authorization, he can only do so by saying: Why "ought" I behave in this way? Or, in customary usage: Why may I or why can I behave in this way?

"Norm" is the meaning of an act by which a certain behavior is commanded, permitted, or authorized. The norm, as the specific meaning of an act directed toward the behavior of someone else, is to be carefully differentiated from the act of will whose meaning the norm is; the norm is an *ought*, but the act of will is an *is*. Hence the situation constituted by such an act must be described by the statement: The one individual wills that the other individual ought to behave in a certain way. The first part of this sentence refers to an *is*, the existing fact of the first individual's act of volition; the second part to an *ought*, to a norm as the meaning of that act. Therefore it is incorrect to assert—as is often done—that the statement: "An individual ought" merely means that another individual wills something; that the *ought* can be reduced to an *is*.

The difference between *is* and *ought* cannot be explained further. We are immediately aware of the difference. Nobody can deny that the statement: "something is"—that is, the statement by which an existent fact is described—is fundamentally different from the statement: "something ought to be"—which is the statement by which a norm is described. Nobody can assert that from the statement that something is, follows a statement that something ought to be, or vice versa.

This dualism of is and ought does not mean, however, that there is no relationship between *is* and *ought*. One says: an *is* conforms to an *ought*, which means that something is as it ought to be; and one says: an *ought* is "directed" toward an *is*—in other words: something ought to be. The expression: "an *is* conforms to an

---

[51] [Translated by Max Knight from the second edition of *Reine Rechtslehre* (1960).]

*ought*" is not entirely correct, because it *is* not the is that conforms to the *ought*, but the "something" that one time is and the other time ought to be—it is the "something" which figuratively can be designated as the content of the is or as the content of the ought.

Put in different words, one can also say: a certain something—specifically a certain behavior—can have the quality of is or of ought. For example: In the two statements, "the door is being closed" and "the door ought to be closed," the closing of the door in the former statement is pronounced as something that is, in the latter as something that ought to be. The behavior that is and the behavior that ought to be are not identical, but they differ only so far as the one is and the other ought to be. Is and ought are two different modi. One and the same behavior may be presented in the one or the other of the two modi. Therefore it is necessary to differentiate the behavior stipulated by a norm as a behavior that ought to be from the actual behavior that corresponds to it. We may compare the behavior stipulated by the norm (as content of the norm) with the actual behavior; and we can, therefore, judge whether the actual behavior conforms to the norm, that is, to the content of the norm.

The behavior as it actually takes place may or may not be equal to the behavior as it ought to be. But equality is not identity. The behavior that is the content of the norm (that is, the behavior that ought to be) and the actual behavior (that is, the behavior that is) are not identical, though the one may be *equal* to the other. Therefore, the usual way to describe the relation between an actual behavior and a norm to which the behavior corresponds: the actual behavior is the behavior that—according to the norm—ought to be, is not correct. The behavior that is cannot be the behavior that ought to be. They differ with respect to the modus which is in one case the is, in the other the ought.

Acts whose meaning is a norm can be performed in various ways. For example, by a gesture: The traffic policeman, by a motion of his arms, orders the pedestrian to stop or to continue; or by a symbol: a red light constitutes a command for the driver to halt, a green light, to proceed; or by spoken or written words, either in the imperative form—be quiet!—or in the form of an indicative statement—I order you to be silent. In this way also permissions or authorizations may be formulated. They are statements about the act whose meaning is a command, a permission, an authorization. But their meaning is not that something is, but that something ought to be. They are not—as they linguistically seem to be—statements about a fact, but a norm, that is to say, a command, a permission, an authorization.

A criminal code might contain the sentence: Theft is punished by imprisonment. The meaning of this sentence is not, as the wording seems to indicate, a statement about an actual event; instead, the meaning is a norm: it is a command or an authorization, to punish theft by imprisonment. The legislative process consists of a series of acts which, in their totality, have the meaning of a norm. To say that acts, especially legislative acts, "create" or "posit" a norm, is merely a figure of speech for saying that the meaning or the significance of the act or acts that constitute the legislative process, is a norm. It is, however, necessary to distinguish the subjective and objective meaning of the act. "Ought" is the subjective meaning of every act of will directed at the behavior of another. But not every such act has also objectively this meaning; and only if the act of will have also the objective meaning of an "ought" is this "ought" called a "norm." If the "ought" is also the objective meaning of the act, the behavior at which the act is directed is regarded as something that *ought* to be not only from the point of view of the individual who has performed the act but also from the point of view of the individual at whose behavior the act is directed, and of a third individual not involved in the relation between the two. That the "ought" is the objective meaning of the act manifests itself in the fact that it is supposed to exist (that the "ought" is valid) even if the will ceases to exist whose subjective meaning it is—if we assume that an individual ought to behave in a certain way even if he does not know of the act whose meaning is that he ought to behave in this way. Then the "ought" as the objective meaning of an act, is a valid *norm* binding upon the addressee, that is, the individual at whom it is directed. The ought which is the subjective meaning of an act of will is also the objective meaning of this act, if this act has been invested with this meaning, if it has been authorized by a norm, which therefore has the character of a "higher" norm.

The command of a gangster to turn over to him a certain amount of money has the same subjective meaning as the command of an income-tax official, namely that the individual at whom the command is directed ought to pay something. But only the command of the official, not that of the gangster, has the meaning of a valid norm, binding upon the addressed individual. Only the one order, not the other, is a norm-positing act, because the official's act is authorized by a tax law, whereas the gangster's act is not based on such an authorizing norm. The legislative act, which subjectively has the meaning of *ought*, also has the objective meaning—that is, the meaning of a valid norm—because the constitution has conferred this objective meaning upon the legislative act. The act whose meaning is the constitution has not only the subjective but also the objective meaning of "ought," that is to say, the character of a binding norm, if—in case it is the historically first constitution—we presuppose in our juristic thinking that we ought to behave as the constitution prescribes... [pp. 4–8]

### Positive and negative regulations: commanding, authorizing, permitting

The behavior regulated by a normative order is either a definite action or the omission (nonperformance) of such an action. Human behavior, then, is either positively or negatively regulated by a normative order. Positively, when a definite action of a definite individual or when the omission of such an action is commanded. (When the omission of an action is commanded, the action is forbidden.) To say that the behavior of an individual is commanded by an objectively valid norm amounts to the same as saying the individual is obliged to behave in this way. If the individual behaves as the norm commands he fulfills his obligation—he obeys the norm; if he behaves as the norm commands he fulfills his obligation—he obeys the norm; if he behaves in the opposite way, he "violates" the norm—he violates his obligation. Human behavior is positively regulated also, when an individual is authorized by the normative order to bring about, by a certain act, certain consequences determined by the order. Particularly an individual can be authorized (if the order regulates its own creation) to create norms or to participate in that creation; or when, in case of a legal order providing norms or to participate in that creation; or when, in case of a legal order providing for coercive acts as sanctions, an individual is authorized to perform these acts under the conditions stipulated by the legal order; or when a norm permits an individual to perform an act, otherwise forbidden—a norm which limits the sphere of validity of a general norm that forbids the act. An example for the last-mentioned alternative is self-defense: although a general norm forbids the use of force of one individual against another, a special norm permits such use of force in self-defense. When an individual acts as he is authorized by the norm or behaves as he is permitted by a norm, he "applies" the norm. The judge, authorized by a statute (that is, a general norm) to decide concrete cases, applies the statute to a concrete case by a decision which constitutes an *individual* norm. Again, authorized by a judicial decision to execute a certain punishment, the enforcement officer "applies" the individual norm of the judicial decision. In exercising self-defense, one applies the norm that permits the use of force. Further, a norm is also "applied" in rendering a judgment that an individual does, or does not, behave as he is commanded, authorized or permitted by a norm.

In the broadest sense, any human behavior determined by a normative order as condition or consequence, can be considered as being authorized by this order and in this sense as being positively regulated. Human behavior is regulated negatively by a normative order if this behavior is not forbidden by the order without being positively permitted by a norm that limits the sphere of validity of a forbidding norm, and therefore is permitted only in a negative sense. This merely negative function of permitting has to be distinguished from the positive function of permitting—"positive," because it is the function of a positive norm, the meaning of an act of will. The positive character of a permission becomes particularly apparent when the limitation of the sphere of validity of a norm that forbids a certain conduct is brought about by a norm that permits the otherwise forbidden conduct under the condition that the permission has to be given by an organ of the community authorized thereto. The negative as well as positive function of permitting is therefore fundamentally connected with the function of commanding. A definite human behavior can be *permitted* only within a normative order that *commands* different kinds of behavior.

"To permit" is also used in the sense of "to entitle (*berechtigen*)." If *A* is commanded to endure that *B* behaves in a certain way, it is said that *B* is permitted (that is, entitled) to behave in this way. And if *A* is commanded to render a certain service to *B*, it is said that *B* is permitted (that is, entitled) to receive the service of *A*. In the first example, then, the sentence "*B* is permitted to behave in a certain way" says the same as the sentence: "*A* is commanded to endure that *B* behaves in a certain way." And in the second example, the sentence: "*B* is permitted to receive a certain service from *A*" is commanded to render a service to *B*." The quality of *B*'s behavior "to be permitted" is merely the reflex of the quality of *A*'s" behavior to be commanded." This kind of "permitting" is not a function of the normative order different from its function of "commanding."[pp. 15–17]

### The reason for the validity of a legal order

The norm system that presents itself as a legal order has essentially a dynamic character. A legal norm is not valid because it has a certain content, that is, because its content is logically deducible from a presupposed basic norm, but because it is created in a certain way—ultimately in a way determined by a presupposed basic norm. For this reason alone does the legal norm belong to the legal order whose norms are created according to this basic norm. Therefore any kind of content might be law. There is no human behavior which, as such, is excluded from being the content of a legal norm. The validity of a legal norm may not be denied for being (in its content) in conflict with that of another norm which does not belong to the legal order whose basic norm is the reason for the validity of the norm in question. The basic norm of a legal order is not a material norm which, because its content is regarded as immediately self-evident, is presupposed as the highest norm and from which norms for human behavior are logically deduced. The norms of a legal order must be created by a specific process. They are posited, that is, positive, norms, elements of a positive order. If by the constitution of a legal community is understood the norm or norms that determine how (that is, by what organs and by what procedure—through legislation or custom) the general norms of the legal order that constitute the community are to be created, then the basic norm is that norm which is presupposed when the custom through which the constitution has come into existence, or the constitution-creating act consciously performed by certain human beings, is objectively interpreted as a norm-creating fact; if, in the latter case, the individual or the assembly of individuals who created the constitution on which the legal order rests, are looked upon as norm-creating authorities. In this sense, the basic norm determines the basic fact of law creation and may in this respect be described as the constitution in a logical sense of the word ... in contradistinction to the constitution in the meaning of positive law. The basic norm is the presupposed starting point of a procedure: the procedure of positive law creation. It is itself not a norm created by custom or by the act of a legal organ; it is not a positive but a presupposed norm so far as the constitution-establishing authority is looked upon as the highest authority and can therefore not be regarded as authorized by the norm of a higher authority.

If the question as to the reason for the validity of a certain legal norm is raised, then the answer can only consist in the reduction to the basic norm of this legal order, that is, in the assertion that the norm was created—in the last instance— according to the basic norm ...

The question of the reason for the validity of a legal norm belonging to a specific national legal order may arise on the occasion of a coercive act; for example, when one individual deprives another of his life by hanging, and now the question is asked why this act is legal, namely the execution of a punishment, and not murder. This act can be interpreted as being legal only if it was prescribed by an individual legal norm, namely as an act that "ought" to be performed, by a norm that presents itself as a judicial decision. This raises the questions: Under what conditions is such an interpretation possible, why is a judicial decision present in this case, why is the individual norm created thereby a legal norm belonging to a valid legal order and therefore ought to be applied? The answer is: Because this individual norm was created in applying a criminal law that contains a general norm according to which (under conditions present in the case concerned) the death penalty ought to be inflicted. If we ask for the reason for the validity of this criminal law, then the answer is: the criminal law is valid because it was created by the legislature, and the legislature, in turn, is authorized by the constitution to create general norms. If we ask for the reason of the validity of the constitution, that is, for the reason of the validity of the norms regulating the creation of the general norms, we may, perhaps, discover an older constitution; that means the validity of the existing constitution is justified by the fact that it was created according to the rules of an earlier constitution by way of a constitutional amendment. In this way we eventually arrive at a historically first constitution that cannot have been created in this way and whose validity, therefore, cannot be traced back to a positive norm created by a legal authority; we arrive, instead, at a constitution that became valid in a revolutionary way, that is, either by breach of a former constitution or for a territory that formerly was not the sphere of validity of a constitution and of a national legal order based on it. If we consider merely the national order, not international law, and if we ask for the reason of the validity of the historically first constitution, then the answer can only be (if we leave aside God or "nature") that the validity of this constitution—the assumption that it is a binding norm—must be *presupposed* if we want to interpret (1) the acts performed according to it as the creation or application of valid general legal norms; and (2) the acts performed in application of these general norms as the creation or application of valid individual legal norms. Since the reason for the validity of a norm can only be another norm, the presupposition must be a norm: not one posited (i.e. created) by a legal authority, but a presupposed norm, that is a norm presupposed if the subjective meaning of the constitution-creating facts and the subjective meaning of the norm-creating facts established according to the constitution are interpreted as their objective-meaning. Since it is the basic norm of a legal order (that is, an order prescribing coercive acts), therefore this norm, namely the basic norm of the legal order concerned, must be formulated as follows. Coercive acts sought to be performed under the conditions and in the manner which the historically first constitution, and the norms created according to it, prescribe. (In short: One ought to behave as the constitution prescribes.) The norms of a legal order, whose common reason for their validity is this basic norm are not a complex of valid norms standing co-ordinatedly side by side, but form a hierarchical structure of super- and sub-ordinate norms... [pp. 198–201]

### The basic norm as transcendental-logical presupposition

To understand the nature of the basic norm it must be kept in mind that it refers directly to a specific constitution, actually established by custom or statutory creation, by and large effective, and indirectly to the coercive order created according to this constitution and by and large effective; the basic norm thereby furnishes the reason for the validity of this constitution and of the coercive order created in accordance with it. The basic norm, therefore, is not the product of free invention. It is not presupposed arbitrarily in the sense that there is a choice between different basic norms when the subjective meaning of a constitution-creating act and the acts created according to this constitution are interpreted as their objective meaning. Only if this basic norm, referring to a specific constitution, is presupposed, that is, only if it is presupposed that one ought to behave according to this specific constitution—only then can the subjective meaning of a constitution-creating act and of the acts created according to this constitution be interpreted as their objective meaning, that is, as objectively valid legal norms, and the relationships established by these norms as legal relations....[52] [p. 201]

### The basic norm of international law

We shall now also consider the international legal order in relation to national legal orders; and we shall assume—as it is frequently assumed—that international law is valid for a state only if its government on the basis of an effective constitution has recognized international law; then our answer given so far to the question as to why law is valid, is still the same: the reason for the validity of law is a presupposed basic norm referring to an effective constitution. For in this case, international law is only a part of the national legal order, regarded as sovereign—and the reason for the validity of the national legal order is the basic norm referring to the effective constitution. The basic norm, as the reason for the international law, recognized on the basis of the constitution.

The situation is different, however, if international law is not regarded as part of the national legal order, but as a sovereign legal order, superordinated to all national legal orders, limiting them in their spheres of validity; if, in other words, one does not assume the primacy of the national legal orders, but the primacy of the international legal order. The latter does, in fact, contain a norm that represents the reason for the validity of the individual national legal orders. Therefore the reason for the validity of the individual national legal order can be found in positive international law. In that case, a positive norm is the reason for the validity of this legal order, nor a merely presupposed norm. The norm of international law that represents this reason for the validity usually is described by the statement that, according to general international law, a government which, independent of other governments, exerts effective control over the population of a certain territory, is the legitimate government; and that the population that lives under such a government in this territory constitutes a "state" in the meaning of international law, regardless of whether this

---

[52] [By insisting that the validity of the basic norm is a presupposition Kelsen excludes it from the category of propositions that may be verified. By investing his rules of recognition with the criterion of acceptance, Hart clothes his concept of the ultimate source of law with more meaningful purpose and reality. See, further, Hughes in 59 Calif.L.Rev. 695, 699–703.]

government exerts this effective control on the basis of a previously existing constitution or of one established by revolution. Translated into legal language: A norm of general international law authorizes an individual or a group of individuals, on the basis of an effective constitution, to create and apply as a legitimate government a normative coercive order. That norm, thus legitimizes this coercive order for the territory of its actual effectiveness as a valid legal order, and the community constituted by this coercive order as a "state" in the sense of international law—regardless of whether the government came to power in a "legitimate" way (in the sense of the previous constitution) or by revolution. According to international law, this power is to be regarded as *legal* power. This means that international law legitimizes a successful revolution as a law-creating procedure. If a positive norm of international law is recognized as the reason for the validity of a national legal order the problem of the basic norm is shifted, because the reason for the validity of the national legal orders, then, is no longer a norm only presupposed in juristic thinking but a positive norm of international law; and then the question arises as to the reason for the validity of the international legal order to which the norm belongs on which the validity of the individual national legal order is founded—the norm in which this legal order finds its direct, although not its ultimate, reason for the validity. This reason of validity, then, can only be the basic norm of international law, which, therefore, is the indirect reason for the validity of the national legal order. As a genuine basic norm, it is a presupposed—not a positive norm. It represents the presupposition under which general international law is regarded as the set of objectively valid norms that regulate the mutual behavior of states. These norms are created by custom, constituted by the actual behavior of the "states," that is, of those individuals who act as governments according to national legal orders. These norms are interpreted as legal norms binding the states, because a basic norm is presupposed which establishes custom among states as a law-creating fact. The basic norm runs as follows: "States—that is, the government of the states—in their mutual relations ought to behave in such a way"; or: "Coercion of state against state ought to be exercised under the conditions and in the manner, that conforms with the custom constituted by the actual behavior of the states."[53] This is the "constitution" of international law in a transcendental-logical sense.[54]

One of the norms of international law created by custom authorizes the states to regulate their mutual relations by treaty. The reason for the validity of the legal norms of international law created by treaty is this custom-created norm. It is usually formulated in the sentence: *pacta sunt servanda*.

The presupposed basic norm of international law, which institutes custom constituted by the states as a law-creating fact, expresses a principle that is the basic presupposition of all customary law: the individual ought to behave in such a manner as the others usually behave (believing that they ought to behave that way), applied to the mutual behavior of states, that is, the behavior of the individuals qualified by the national legal orders as government organs.[55]

No affirmation of a value transcending positive law is inherent in the basic norm of international law, not even of the value of peace guaranteed by the general international law created by custom and the particular international law created by treaty. International law and—if its primacy is assumed—the subordinated national legal orders are not valid "because" and "insofar as" they realize the value that consists in peace; they may realize this value if and so far as they are valid; and they are valid if a basic norm is presupposed that institutes

---

[53] *Cf.* § 42b–d.
[54] *Cf.* § 34d.
[55] The theory held by many authors that the norm of *pacta sunt servanda* is the basis of international law is to be rejected because it can be maintained only with the aid of the fiction that the custom established by the conduct of states is a tacit treaty.

custom among states as a law-creating fact regardless of the content of the norms thus created. If the reason for the validity of national legal orders is found in a norm of international law, then the latter is understood as a legal order superior to the former and therefore as the highest sovereign legal order. If the states—that is the national legal orders—are nevertheless referred to as "sovereign," then this "sovereignty" can only mean that the national legal orders are subordinated *only* to the international legal order.                                        [pp. 214–217]

### The hierarchical structure of the legal order

#### The Constitution

The peculiarity of the law that it regulates its own creation. ... This can be done by a norm determining merely the procedure by which another norm is to be created. But it can be done also by a norm determining, to a certain extent, the content of the norm to be created. Since, because of the dynamic character of law, a norm is valid because, and to the extent that, it had been created in a certain way, that is, in a way determined by another norm, therefore that other norm is the immediate reason for the validity of the new norm. The relationship between the norm that regulates the creation of another norm and the norm created in conformity with the former can be metaphorically presented as a relationship of super- and subordination. The norm which regulates the creation of another norm is the higher, the norm created in conformity with the former is the lower one. The legal order is not a system of co-ordinated norms of equal level, but a hierarchy of different levels of legal norms. Its unity is brought about by the connection that results from the fact that the validity of a norm, created according to another norm, rests on that other norm, whose creation in turn, is determined by a third one. This is a regression that ultimately ends up in the presupposed basic norm. This basic norm, therefore, is the highest reason for the validity of the norms, one created in conformity with another, thus forming a legal order in its hierarchical structure ...

Considering, only a national legal order, the constitution represents the highest level of positive law. "Constitution" is understood here in its material sense, that is, we understand by constitution the positive norm or norms which regulate the creation of general legal norms. The constitution may be created by custom or by a specific act performed by one or several individuals, that is, by a legislative act. In the latter case it is always formulated in a document and hence called a "written" constitution, in contradistinction to the "unwritten" constitution brought about by custom. The material constitution may consist partly of norms of written and partly of unwritten law. The unwritten norms of the constitution may be codified; and if this codification is the work of a law-creating organ and therefore acquires binding force, it becomes a written constitution.

The constitution in the material sense must be distinguished from the constitution in the formal sense, namely a document called "constitution," which, as written constitution, may contain not only norms regulating the creation of general norms (that is, legislation), but also norms concerning other politically important subjects; and, besides regulations according to which the norms contained in this document may be abolished or amended—not like ordinary statutes, but by a special procedure and under more rigorous conditions. These regulations represent the constitutional form, and the document to whose content these regulations refer, represents the constitution in a formal sense, which may include any desired content. The purpose of the regulations which render more difficult the abolition or amendment of the content of the constitution in a formal sense is primarily to stabilize the norms designated here as "material constitution" and which are the positive-legal basis of the entire national legal order.

In a modern legal order, the creation (regulated by the material constitution) of general legal norms has the character of legislation. The constitutional regulation of legislation determines the organs authorized to create general norms—statutes and ordinances. If the courts should be regarded as authorized to apply customary law also, they must be authorized by the constitution to do so in the same way as they must be authorized to apply statutes. In other words: the constitution must institute as a law-creating fact the custom constituted by the habitual behavior of the individuals subject to the national legal order—the "subjects." If the application of customary law by courts is considered to be legitimate although the written constitution contains no such authorization, then the authorization cannot be considered to proceed from an unwritten custom-created constitution[56] but must be *presupposed*, in the same way that it must be presupposed that the written constitution has the character of an objectively binding norm if the statutes and ordinances issued in accordance with it are regarded as binding legal norms. Then the basic norm (the constitution in the transcendental-logical sense) institutes not only the act of the legislator, but also custom as law-creating facts.

The constitution of the state, as a written constitution, can appear in the specific form of a constitution, that is, in norms that may not be abolished or amended as ordinary statutes but only under more rigorous conditions. But this need not be so. It is not so if there is no written constitution, if the constitution is created by custom and is not codified; then, even norms which have the character of a material constitution may be abolished or amended by simple statutes or by customary law.

It is possible that the organ specifically and formally authorized to create, abolish, or amend statutes having the character of a constitution is different from the organ authorized to create, abolish, or amend ordinary statutes. For example, the former function may be rendered by an organ different from the latter organ in composition and electoral procedure, such as a constituent national assembly. But usually both functions are performed by the same organ.     [pp. 221–223]

*Public and private law*

Until this day it has not been possible to achieve an entirely satisfactory definition of the difference. According to the majority view we are confronted here with a classification of legal relationships: private law represents a relationship between co-ordinated, legally equal-ranking subjects; public law, a relationship between a super- and a subordinated subject, that is, between two subjects of whom one has a higher legal value as compared with that of the other. The typical public-law relationship is that between state (or government) and subject (in German, characteristically, *Untertan.*) Private-law relationships are called simply "legal relationships" in the narrower sense of the term, to juxtapose to them the public-law relationships as "power relationships" or relationships of "dominion." In general, the difference between law and a nonlegal, or at least a half legal, power, and particularly, between law and state. A closer analysis of the higher value attributed to certain subjects, of their superordination over others, discloses that we are confronted here with a differentiation between law-creating facts. And the decisive difference is the same as that which is the basis for the classification of forms of government. The legal plus-value assigned to the state—that is, to its organs in relation to the subjects—consists in that the legal order concedes to individuals qualified as officials (or at least to some of them) the power to obligate the subjects by a unilateral expression of their will (commands). A typical example of a public-law relationship is the one established by an administrative order, that is, an individual norm issued by an administrative organ obligating legally the addressee to behave in conformity with the order. A typical example of

---

[56] [*Cf. The Pure Theory of Law*, p. 226.]

a private-law relationship is the one established by a legal transaction, especially the contract (that is, the individual norm created by the contract), by which the contracting parties are legally obligated to a mutual behavior. Whereas here the subjects participate in the creation of the norm that obligates them—this is, indeed the essence of contractual law creation—the subject obligated by the administrative order under public law has no part in the creation of the norm that obligates him. It is the typical case of an autocratic norm creation, whereas the private-law contract represents a typically democratic method of law-making. Therefore the sphere of legal transactions is characterized as the sphere of private autonomy.

### The Ideological Character of the Dualism of Public and Private Law

If the decisive difference between private and public law is comprehended as the difference between two methods of creating law; if the so-called public acts of the state are recognized as legal acts just as the private legal transaction; if, most of all, it is understood that the acts constituting the law-creating facts are in both cases only the continuations of the process of the creation of the so-called will of the state, and that in the administrative order just as much as in the private legal transaction only the individualization of general norms are effected—then it will not seem so paradoxical that the Pure Theory of Law, from its universalistic viewpoint, always directed toward the whole of the legal order (the so-called will of the state), sees in the private legal transaction just as much as in an administrative order an act of the state, that is, a fact of law-making attributable to the unity of the legal order. By doing so, the Pure Theory of Law "relativizes" the contrast between private and public law "absolutized" by the traditional science of law, changes it from an extra-systematic difference, that is, a difference between law and nonlaw or between law and state, to an intra-systematic one. The Pure Theory proves to be a true science by dissolving the ideology connected with the absolutizing of the difference in question.[57] ...     [pp. 280–282]

### The identity of State and law

#### The State as a Legal Order

A cognition of the state free of ideology, and hence of metaphysics and mysticism, can grasp its essence only by comprehending this social structure as an order of human behavior. It is usual to characterize the state as a political organization. But this merely expresses the idea that the state is a coercive order. For the specifically "political" element of this organization consists in the coercion exercised by man against man, regulated by this order—in the coercive acts prescribed by this order. These are precisely the coercive acts which the legal order attaches to certain conditions stipulated by it. As a political organization, the state is a legal order. But not every legal order is a state. Neither the pre-state legal order of primitive society, nor the super- (or inter-) state-international legal order represents a state. To be a state, the legal order must have the character of an organization in the narrower and specific sense of this word, that is, it must establish organs who, in the manner of division of labor, create and apply the norms that constitute the legal order; it must display a certain degree of centralization. The state is a relatively centralized legal order.

This centralization distinguishes the state as a legal order from the primitive pre-state order and the super-state order of general international law. In neither order are the general legal norms created by a central legislative organ but by way of custom, which means that the creation of general legal norms is decentralized.

---

[57] [For the Marxist attitude see *post*, 1141.]

Neither the pre-state nor the super-state legal order establishes courts authorized to apply the general norms to concrete cases, but authorizes the individuals subjected to the legal order themselves to render this function and, particularly, to execute, by way of self-help, the sanctions prescribed by the legal order. According to primitive law, it is the members of the murdered man's family who take blood revenge against the murderer and his family, which means, they are authorized to carry out the primitive punishment; it is the creditor himself who can satisfy his claim against the debtor by taking some property of the debtor and holding it in pawn. It is the government of the individual state which, according to general international law, is authorised to resort to war or take reprisals against a law-violating state, which means: against the subjects of the state whose government has violated the law. True, the individuals who in the pre-state and in the super-state community create (by custom) or apply the law and execute the sanctions, are legal organs and thus organs of the legal community; but they are not functioning in the manner of division of labor and therefore not centralized organs like a government, a legislature, and courts under a national legal order. The legal order of primitive society and the general inter-national law order are entirely decentralized coercive orders and therefore not states.

If the state is comprehended as a social community, it can be constituted only by a normative order. Since a community can be constituted by only *one* such order (and is, indeed, identical with this order), the normative order constituting the state can only be the relatively centralized coercive order which is the national legal order.

In traditional theory the state is composed of three elements, the people of the state, the territory of the state, and the so-called power of the state, exercised by an independent government. All three elements can be determined only juridically, that is, they can be comprehended only as the validity and the spheres of validity of a legal order.

The state's population is the human beings who belong to the state. If it is asked why an individual together with other individuals does belong to a certain state, no other criterion can be found than that he and the others are subject to a certain, relatively centralized, coercive order. All attempts to find another bond that holds together and unites in one unit individuals differing in language, race, religion, world concept, and separated by conflicts of interests, is doomed to failure. It is particularly impossible to demonstrate the existence of some sort of psychic interaction which, independent of any legal bond, unites all individuals belonging to a state in such a way that they can be distinguished from other individuals, belonging to another state, and united by an analogous-interaction as two separate groups. It is undeniable that no such interaction exists uniting all individuals belonging to one state, and only them; and it is undeniable that individuals belonging to different states may be connected spiritually much closer than those belonging to the same state. For they belong to this state only legally. They certainly may have a psychic relation to their state, as the saying goes; they may love it, even deify it, and be prepared to die for it. But they belong to it even if they do not feel that way, if they hate it, even betray it, or are indifferent to it. The question whether an individual belongs to a state is not a psychological but a legal question. The unity of individuals constituting a state's population can only be seen in the fact that the same legal order is valid for these individuals, that their behavior is regulated by the same legal order. The state population is the personal sphere of validity of the national legal order.

The state territory is a certain delimited space. It is not a delimited piece of the earth's surface, but a three-dimensional space which includes the space below the ground and the space above the territory enclosed by the so-called frontiers of the state. It is obvious that the unity of this space is not a natural, geographic one. The same state territory may include areas separated by the ocean, which is not the territory of *one* state, or by the territory of another state. No natural science, but only legal cognition can answer the question what criteria determine the frontiers of the space which is that of one state territory, what constitutes its unity. The so-called state territory can only be defined as the spatial sphere of validity of a national legal order...

It is almost self-evident that the so-called state power which is exercised by a government over a state's population within a state territory is not simply the power which some individual actually has over another individual consisting in the former's ability to induce the latter to behave as the first one desires. Many such actual power relationships exist without the one who has such power over another being regarded as an organ of the state. The relationship designated as state power is distinguished from other power relationships by the fact that it is legally regulated, which means that the individuals who exercise this power in their capacity as members of a state government are authorized by a legal order to exercise this power by creating and applying legal norms—that the state power has normative character. The so-called state power is the validity of an effective national legal order. That the government exerting the state power must be independent means that it must not be bound by any other national legal order; that the national legal order is inferior, if to any other legal order at all, only to the international legal order.

In the exercise of the state's power one usually sees the manifestations of a power which one considers as such an essential attribute of the state that one speaks of states as of "powers," even if they are not so-called "great powers." The "power" of a state can show itself only in the specific means of power which are at the disposal of a government; in the fortresses and prisons, the guns and gallows, the individuals uniformed as policemen and soldiers. But these fortresses and prisons, these guns and gallows, are dead objects; they become tools of state power only so far as they are used by a state government or by individuals according to orders directed to them by the government, only so far as the policemen and soldiers obey the norms that regulate their behavior. The power of the state is no mystical force concealed behind the state or its law; it is only the effectiveness of the national legal order.

Thereby the state whose essential elements are population, territory and power is defined as a relatively centralized legal order, limited in its spatial and temporal sphere of validity, sovereign or subordinated only to international law, and by and large effective.

## H. KELSEN
### The Function of a Constitution
(1986)[58]

The law is a system of norms, and norms are the meaning of acts of will that are directed toward the conduct of others. These acts of will are acts of will of human beings or of suprahuman beings—as with the acts of will of God, or, as in the case of so-called natural law, of Nature. However, only norms that are the meaning of human acts of will are to be considered as legal norms—more exactly, as norms of a body of positive law. These have the characteristic of regulating their own creation and application.

Acts of will that are directed toward the conduct of others are, primarily, commands. But not every command is a norm, and not every norm is a command. A norm may also be an authorisation to issue commands. If a robber demands that I give him my money, *i.e.* of his command, is not a norm. Nor do I violate any norm if I refuse to comply with his command.

---

[58] [This was originally written for a conference in Vienna in 1964, it is translated by Iain Stewart and reproduced from R. Tur and W. Twining, *Essays on Kelsen*.]

The subjective meaning of his act of will, that I *ought* to give him my money, does not become its objective meaning—that is, it is not interpreted as a binding norm, such as for example a command addressed to me by a tax official that I ought to hand over a specified sum of money. Why is the meaning of the act of will the *ought*, in the one case also the objective meaning of the act—that is, a binding, valid norm—but in the other case not? To put it differently: what is the basis of the validity of the norm, which exists in the one case but not in the other? The answer is: because in the one case—that of the command by the tax official—the act, the meaning of which is an ought, is authorised by a valid norm, but in the other case it is not. By virtue of this norm authorising the act, the subjective meaning of the act becomes also its objective act, the subjective meaning of the act becomes also its objective meaning—a binding, valid norm. The authorising, higher norm is the basis of the validity of the authorised, lower norm.

The idea that the basis of the validity of a lower norm is the validity of a higher norm appears to lead to an infinite regress. For the higher, authorising norm is itself the subjective meaning of an act of will directed toward the conduct of others; and only if this act too is authorised by a still higher norm is its subjective meaning also its objective meaning—that is, a binding, valid norm. A simple example may clarify this point: A father addresses to his son the individual norm, "Go to school." The son asks his father, "Why should I go to school?" That is, he asks why the subjective meaning of his father's act of will is its objective meaning, *i.e.* a norm binding for him—or, which means the same thing, what is the basis of the validity of this norm. The father responds: "Because God has commanded that parents be obeyed—that is, He has authorized parents to issue commands to children." The son replies: "Why should one obey the commands of God?" What all this amounts to is: why is the subjective meaning of this act of will of God also its objective meaning—that is, a valid norm? or, which means the same thing, what is the basis of the validity of this general norm? The only possible answer to this is: because, as a believer, one presupposes that one ought to obey the commands of God. This is the statement of the validity of a norm that must be presupposed in a believer's thinking in order to ground the validity of the norms of a religious morality. This statement is the basic norm of a religious morality, the norm which grounds the validity of all the norms of that morality—a "basic" norm, because no further question can be raised about the basis of its validity. The statement is not a positive norm—that is, not a norm posited by a real act of will—but a norm presupposed in a believer's thinking.

### Law and Morality

Let us now take an example from the domain of law. The distinction between law and morality consists in the fact that the law is a coercive order—that is, that the law seeks to bring about a specific mode of human conduct by attaching to the opposite mode of conduct, as sanction, a coercive act, the forcible taking away of life, of freedom, or of economic or other value. If someone steals, he ought to be imprisoned—by force if necessary. By this norm, the law prohibits theft. Morality too seeks to bring about a specific mode of human conduct, and morality too provides for sanctions. But these sanctions are the approbation of moral conduct and the disapprobation of immoral conduct, not coercive acts—nor do these sanctions serve as the means by which moral conduct ought to be brought about.

The general legal norm, "If someone steals, he ought to be imprisoned" is, to begin with, only the subjective meaning of an act of will of the legislator. This norm is applied through the judicial decision that Smith, who has stolen a horse from Jones, ought to be imprisoned for one year. This judicial decision is interpreted as a binding, valid, individual norm. Yet this norm too is, to begin with, only the subjective meaning of an act of will of the judge directed toward the conduct of an executive organ. If we interpret this subjective meaning also as the objective meaning—that is, as a binding norm—and hence understand a person performing that act as a "judge"—we do so because that act is authorised by a general norm, contained in a statute: "If someone steals, the judge competent to hear the case ought to punish him with imprisonment." The validity of the lower, individual norm is grounded by the validity of the higher, general norm. And the judge, in fact, so grounds his judgment that it conforms to a valid general legal norm that authorises him.

However, a general norm contained in a statute—as, indeed, the whole statute—is, to begin with, itself (as we have noted) only the subjective meaning of the act of will of a person, or of the majority of the persons forming a legislative body. The essential function of a legislator is the positing of general norms that determine the procedure of the law-applying organs, in particular the courts, and the content of the individual norms to be posited by these organs. To be sure, a "statute" may also contain things other than such general sense from "statute" in the material sense—or, more precisely, "statute-*form*" from "statute"—that is, a specific procedure from the essential function of that procedure, the creation of general norms.

If one asks why the subjective meaning of the legislator's act is also its objective meaning, *i.e.* a general norm; why the person performing that act is a "legislator"; in other words, what is the basis of the validity of the norm posited by the legislator's act; the answer is: because the act, the subjective meaning of which is the general norm, is authorised by the *constitution*. In this authorising of specific persons to create general norms lies the essential function of a constitution. If one distinguishes various forms of state—such as monarchy, aristocracy and democracy—the decisive criterion is that the constitution authorises in the first case a single specifically qualified individual, in the second a relatively limited group of specifically qualified individuals, and in the third the (as it is sometimes inexactly put) whole people—more correctly, a popular assembly or a popularly elected parliament—to create general norms.

True, the document that one calls "the Constitution" usually also contains other provisions than this kind of authorisation. Thus one must distinguish between constitution in the formal sense and constitution in the material sense—more correctly, between constitution-*form* and constitution. Constitution-form is a particular procedure in which a constitution created in the material sense, whatever the way in which it has come into existence, can be passed or amended. This procedure is distinct, essentially if not always by this alone, from the ordinary procedure of legislation, in that the coming into existence of a valid resolution—that is, an act of will passing or amending the constitution—is bound by constraining conditions. The aim of such constraint is to lend the greatest possible stability to the authorisation to create general legal norms, *i.e.* to the form of the state. Occasionally a constitution—that is, the document so named—contains the provision that the norms regulating the procedure of legislation must not be altered at all, or not in such a way as to alter the form.

If one asks what is the basis of the validity of a given constitution, the answer may be that that constitution came into existence through amendment of a preceding constitution, and that this amendment was made in the way that constitutional amendments on the basis of the preceding constitution have to be made. Thus one can refer back to a historically first constitution. This historically first constitution too is, to begin with, the subjective meaning of an act of will or a number of acts of will; and if one asks why the subjective meaning of the act creating the constitution is also its objective meaning—that is, a valid norm—or, in other words, what is the basis of the validity of this norm, the answer is: because one presupposes, as jurist, that one ought to conduct oneself as the historically first constitution prescribes. That is the basic norm. This basic norm authorises the individual or the sum of individuals who laid down the historically first constitution to posit norms that represent the historically first resolution of an assembly, the basic norm authorises the individuals forming that assembly; if the historically first constitution arose by way of custom, the basic norm authorises this custom—or, more correctly, it authorises the individuals whose conduct forms the custom giving rise to the historically first constitution.

## Norm and Justice

This is the basic norm of the legal order that is founded ultimately upon the historically first constitution. It is the "basic" norm, because no further question can be raised about the basis of its validity; for it is not a posited but a pre-supposed norm. It is not a positive norm, posited by a real act of will, but a norm presupposed in juristic thinking. It represents the ultimate basis of the validity of all the legal norms forming the legal order. Only a norm can be the basis of the validity of another norm.

To grasp the essence of the basic norm, one must above all keep in mind that it refers directly to a particular constitution that has in fact been laid down, whether created by custom or by formal statement. That it to say, it refers to the facts in which the norms of the constitution are posited, which norms are the subjective meaning of these facts—yet indirectly it refers to the general and individual norms of the legal order which are in fact posited in conformity with the constitution, *i.e.* the basic norm refers indirectly to the facts whose subjective meaning these norms are. That means that the basic norm refers only to an effective constitution—that is, to a constitution in conformity with which statutes, and judicial and admin-istrative decisions in conformity with statute, are in fact made.

The basic norm is thus not a product of free invention. It refers to particular facts existing in natural reality, to an actually laid down and effective constitution and to the norm-creating and norm-applying facts in fact established in con-formity with the constitution. Nevertheless, what content this constitution or the national legal order built on its foundation has, be that order just or unjust, does into come into question, nor whether that legal order in fact guarantees relative peace within the community constituted by it. In the presupposing of the basic norm, no value transcending positive law is affirmed.

Inasmuch as only the presupposing of the basic norm makes it possible to interpret the subjective meaning of the facts in which the constitution is laid down and of the facts established in conformity with the constitution as their objective meaning—the norms which are the subjective meaning of these facts as objec-tively valid legal norms—the basic norm as presented in legal science may be characterised (if a concept from the Kantian theory of knowledge may be applied here by analogy) as the transcendental-logical condition of the judgments with which legal science describes law as objectively valid order.

Just as Kant asks how it is possible to have an interpretation, free from all metaphysics, of the facts given to our senses, in terms of laws of nature for-mulated by natural science, so a pure theory of law has asked how it is possible to have an interpretation of the subjective meaning of certain facts as a system of objectively valid legal norms, describable in legal propositions, without recourse to metalegal authorities such as God or Nature. The epistemological answer of a pure theory of law is, on the condition that one presupposes the basic norm: one ought to conduct oneself as the constitution prescribes, that is, in conformity with the subjective meaning of the act of will creating the constitution, the commands of the creator of the constitution. The function of this basic norm is to ground the objective validity of a positive legal order, *i.e.* the norms, posited by human acts of will, of a by and large effective coercive order—that is, to interpret the sub-jective meaning of these acts as their objective meaning.

The basic norm may be termed "constitution in the transcendental-logical sense," as distinct from the constitution in the positive-legal sense. The latter is the constitution posited by human acts of will, whose validity is grounded by the presupposed basic norm.

The basic norm may, but need not, be presupposed. What ethics and legal science say about it is: only if it is presupposed can the subjective meaning of acts of will directed toward the conduct of others be interpreted also as their objective meaning, these meaning-contents be interpreted as binding moral or legal norms. Since this interpretation is conditioned by the presupposing of the basic norm, it must be granted that ought-propositions can be interpreted as objectively valid moral or legal norms only in this conditioned sense.

To the assumption of a norm not posited by a real act of will but only pre-supposed in juristic thinking, one can validly object that a norm can be the meaning only of an act of will and not of an act of thinking, that there is an essential correlation between "ought" and "willing." One can meet this objection only by conceding that, along with the basic norm, presupposed in thought, one must also think of an imaginary authority whose (figmentary) act of will has the basic norm as its meaning.

With this fiction, the assumption of the basic norm turns out to be contra-dictory to the assumption that the constitution, whose validity is grounded by the basic norm, is the meaning of an act of will of a supreme authority, over which there can be no higher authority. Thus the basic norm becomes a genuine fiction in the sense of Vaihinger's philosophy of "as if." A fiction in this sense is char-acterised by its not only contradicting reality but also containing contradiction within itself.[59] For the assumption of a basic norm—such as, for instance, the basic norm of a religious moral order, "One ought to obey the commands of God," or the basic norm of a legal order, "One ought to conduct oneself as the historically first constitution determines"—not only contradicts reality, since no such norm exists as the meaning of an actual act of will, but also contains con-tradiction within itself, since it represents the authorisation of a supreme moral or legal authority, and hence it issues from an authority lying beyond that authority, even though the further authority is merely figmentary.

For Vaihinger a fiction is an aid to thinking, of which one avails oneself if the aim of one's thinking cannot be reached with the material available. The aim of one's thinking in presupposing the basic norm is: to ground the validity of the norms forming a positive moral or legal order; that is, to interpret the subjective meaning of the acts positing these norms as their objective meaning, *i.e.* as valid norms, and the acts in question as acts positing norms. This object can be attained only by way of a fiction. Therefore one has to keep in mind that the basic norm in the sense of Vaihinger's "as if" philosophy is not a hypothesis—as I myself have occasionally characterised it—but a fiction, which is distinct from a hypothesis in that it is or should be accompanied by an awareness that reality does not cor-respond to it.

### Hierarchy of Norms

The relation between a higher and a lower norm lies in the validity of one norm grounding, in one way or another, the validity of another norm. A norm is related to another norm as higher to lower if the validity of the latter is grounded by the validity of the former. If the validity of the lower norm is grounded by the validity of the higher norm, in that the lower norm was created in the way prescribed by the higher norm, the higher norm, as it relates to the lower, has the character of a constitution; thus the essence of "constitution" consists in the regulating of the creation of norms. Then a statute—which regulates the procedure in which the

---

[59] This sentence summarizes Hans Vaihinger, *The Philosophy of "As If"* (2nd ed., 1935), pp. 97–100.

law-applying organs, in particular the courts, create individual norms—is a "constitution" in relation to these organs' procedure, just as the "constitution" in the more narrowly specific sense of the word is a constitution in relation to the procedure of legislation and the constitution in the transcendental-logical sense is a constitution in relation to the historically first constitution, the constitution in the positive-legal sense.

In the manner, the concept "constitution" is relativised. Seen from the viewpoint of the basic norm, both a positive moral order and a positive legal order are a generative framework, inasmuch as the basic norm only determines by whom the norms of the moral or legal order ought to be posited—that is, only the highest norm-positing authority is determined, without determining the content of the norms that this authorised authority is to posit. The norms that are posited by the highest moral or legal authority—God, or the creator of the constitution— authorised by the basic norm can themselves authorise further authorities to posit norms and thereby determine or not determine the content of the norms to be posited. Seen from the viewpoint of the highest moral or legal authority authorised by the basic norm, the structure of the positive norms forming the moral or legal order is not necessarily merely a generative framework.

In the sphere of morality this is quite evident, since the highest moral authority never authorises another, lower authority to posit norms with any content the latter may like. The norm proclaimed by Paul, "One ought to obey the authorities," certainly does not mean that one ought to obey even a command of the authorities that offends against certain norms posited directly by God, such as "You shall have no other god but me." In the sphere of law it is, as a rule, just the same, since the constitution usually does not confine itself to determining the procedure for creating general legal norms—legislation, as it is called—but very often also at least negatively determines the content of future statutes, by precluding certain contents—such as the limitation of freedom of expression or freedom of religion, or the taking into consideration of certain inequalities, such as that of race.

However, the general norms posited by the legislator always determine not only the procedure of the organs that are to apply these norms, but also the content of these norms, so that a positive legal order, too, at least as seen from the viewpoint of the statutes, is not merely a generative framework. A legal order of the latter character is conceivable, however: the legal order of Plato's ideal state authorised the judges, without their being bound by predetermined general norms, to decide individual cases according to their own discretion.

In any case, a positive legal order represents a system not of co-ordinate but of superordinate and subordinate norms—that is, a hierarchy of norms, whose highest tier is the constitution, which is grounded as valid by the presupposed basic norm, and whose lowest tier is the individual norms positing a particular concrete mode of conduct as obligatory. In this way the validity of the higher norm regulating the creation of the lower norm always grounds the validity of that lower norm.

The function of a constitution is the grounding of validity.     [pp. 111–119]

## J. RAZ
### The Purity of the Pure Theory
### (1981)

Kelsen's theory is, as is well known, doubly pure. It is free of sociological and psychological investigations and it separates law from morality.[60] The first purity has attracted much criticism and is generally regarded as having been completely

---

[60] *Cf., e.g. The Pure Theory of Law* (2nd ed.) p. 1 (referred to as *PTL*).

discredited. The criticism is based on one or the other of two quite separate objections. First is the objection that the content of the law cannot be established without regard to the actions and intentions of legal institutions, be they legislative or adjudicative.[61] Second, there is the objection that the law and its significance cannot be appreciated unless one studies it in its social context, with an emphasis on its actual effects in practice. Both objections are familiar and I will not discuss them in detail. Let me though make a couple of observations about the second one.

It is beyond doubt part of the task of legal philosophy to explain the methods by which the existence and content of the law are ascertained. If it is true that they cannot be ascertained without regard to the practices and manifested attitudes of legal institutions then the first objection is—as I believe it to be—an important valid objection to Kelsen's theory. It is less clear that the second objection is an objection at all. Kelsen did not deny the possibility of sociological jurisprudence. He was content to maintain four theses. First, that beside sociological jurisprudence there is also an independent inquiry, normative jurisprudence, whose subject is different. Normative jurisprudence is the study of legal norms, *i.e.* the study of how people ought to behave according to law. It is not an inquiry into how they actually do behave according to law. It is not an inquiry into how they actually do behave. Second, normative jurisprudence is no less empirical than sociological jurisprudence, since it is concerned exclusively with *positive* law, *i.e.* law as the product of social custom and of the activity of legislative and adjudicative institutions. Thirdly, normative jurisprudence enjoys in an important way a logical priority over sociological jurisprudence. The very definition of the subject matter of sociological jurisprudence presupposes an understanding of law as provided by its normative study, since sociology of law is the study of those aspects of human behaviour which are related to the law. Here "the law" must be normatively interpreted. Fourthly, normative jurisprudence is presupposed by sociology in another important way as well. The explanation of human behaviour related to law has to take account of the way people's beliefs about the law, normatively understood, affect their behaviour.[62]

I think that Kelsen was essentially right in all four theses. They show that he was not hostile to sociological jurisprudence, though admittedly his own interests did not take him that way. Though these views have since been independently explored and developed by both social scientists and philosophers, I do believe that Kelsen has anticipated many of the arguments used by other thinkers and that we can still benefit from his explanation of the relations between the normative and the sociological study of the law. Both his emphasis on the explanatory importance of people's beliefs concerning what they are normatively required to do and his insistence on the autonomy and distinctness of normative concepts are a valuable and lasting contribution to a subject which has been for years dominated by reductive attempts to provide eliminative definitions of normative terms in favour of non-normative, descriptive ones.

II

Kelsen's semantic anti-reductivism is of course intimately connected with the other purity of Kelsen's theory: its being free of moral elements. Here the antagonists were not the sociological theorists but the natural lawyers. The opposition to natural law was a major pre-occupation of Kelsen and he wrote

---

[61] *Cf.* H. L. A. Hart, "Kelsen Visited" 10 U.C.L.A. Law Rev. 109 (1963) and *Essays in Jurisprudence and Philosophy* (1983), Chap. 14.

[62] See for a detailed discussion Kelsen's *General Theory of Law and State*, pp. 162–178 (referred to as *GT*).

extensively on the subject throughout his life. His views place him in the historic tradition of legal positivism.

Three major theses have been traditionally associated with legal positivism.[63] First is the reductive semantic thesis which proposes a reductive analysis of legal statements according to which they are non-normative, descriptive statements of one kind or another. Second is the contingent connection thesis according to which there is no necessary connection between law and moral values. Third is the sources thesis which claims that the identification of the existence and content of law does not require resort to any moral argument.

The three theses are logically independent and one is free to accept any one of them while rejecting the others. They were however collectively endorsed by many leading positivists such as Bentham, J. Austin, O. W. Holmes and Alf Ross among others. Where does Kelsen stand on these issues? The question is of the utmost importance to the understanding of his theory of law. In many ways it is the most important set of problems that any philosophy of law has to face since it raises the problem of the double aspect of law, its being a social institution with a normative aspect. The supreme challenge for any theory of law is to do justice to both facts of the law.

Kelsen's solution is to reject the reductive semantic thesis and to embrace the contingent connection and the sources theses. Kelsen regards the law as positive law. It is based on social sources identifiable without any reference to moral argument. On this Kelsen never had any doubt. He never wavered in his endorsement of the two aspects of the thesis. The existence or non-existence of a legal system as a whole is a matter of social fact. It depends entirely on its efficacy in the society in question. Moreover, the test determining for every individual rule whether it belongs to a legal system in force in a certain country is equally a matter of social fact. It turns on whether or not it was posited in the appropriate way: whether or not it can be traced to an authorised social source.

Equally firm is Kelsen's belief in the contingent connection thesis. Kelsen insists that (1) to claim that there is a necessary connection between (the content of) law and morals either presupposes absolute moral values to which the law necessarily conforms or assumes that all the divers relativistic moralities have some values in common and that the law conforms to those. He further argues that (2) there are no absolute moral values and there is no common content to all the relativistic moralities. Hence he concludes that there is no necessary connection between law and morals.[64]

Kelsen's departure from the traditional positivist view is in his rejection of the semantic reductive thesis. Reductive positivists have variously argued that legal statements are statements about commands, or predictions of the likelihood of sanctions, or of courts' decisions, etc. Kelsen is adamant in rejecting all reductive analyses of legal statements. He holds that that "a norm . . . is 'valid' means that it is binding—that an individual ought to behave in in the manner determined by the norm" (*PTL* 193). Kelsen regards legal statements as fully normative statements. This view of his, as has been often noted, is difficult to reconcile with his acceptance of the sources and of the contingent connection thesis which lead him to say at the same time that juristic value judgments are judgments which can be tested objectively by fact.[65] It is in his handling of the tension between his non-reductive semantic views and the sources and contingent connection thesis that one finds his most original contribution to the general theory of law. It is this tension which leads directly to his best known doctrine, that of the basic norm.

---

[63]  *Cf.* my discussion of these problems in *Practical Reason and Norms* (1975), 5.3. and *The Authority of Law* (1979), essay 3. See also H. L. A. Hart, "The Separation of Law and Morals" in Harvard Law Rev. (1958). [*Essays in Jurisprudence and Philosophy*, Chap. 2.]
[64]  *Cf. PTL*, pp. 63–65.
[65]  *What is Justice?*, p. 227 (referred to as *WJ*).

## III

Before we turn to an examination of this aspect of Kelsen's contribution it has to be conceded that Kelsen's own espousal of the two positivist theses leaves a lot to be desired. Kelsen's defence of the sources thesis is largely dependent on the view that the "scientific" study of law would not be possible if the identification of law turned on moral argument.[66] But this argument is clearly fallacious. The study of law must be adjusted to its object. If its object cannot be studied "scientifically" then its study should not strive to be scientific. One can learn from the nature of an object how it should be investigated but one cannot postulate that the object has a certain character because one wishes to study it in a certain way.

Nor is Kelsen's defence of the contingent connection thesis more convincing. Not only has he failed to establish that there are no absolute values, nor even that there is no common ground to all relativistic moralities, he has failed to perceive the nature of the problem and addressed himself to the wrong question. Four elements contribute to this failure. First, from a relativistic point of view the right question for a person to ask is whether the morality which he shares does lead to the conclusion that there is a necessary connection between law and *this* morality, *i.e.* whether *this* morality is such that all legal systems whatever they may be do necessarily enshrine some of the values which it proclaims. For a relativist this question is of practical and theoretical importance. Clearly an affirmative answer to it does not require an affirmative answer to Kelsen's question whether there are common values to *all* relativistic moralities, which are respected by all legal systems.

Second, the question whether the law by its content necessarily conforms to moral values is not the only pertinent question to ask. Another is whether obedience to law is always morally required regardless of the content of the law. Possibly it is required because it is expected by others or because it will reciprocate their obedience. After all, Kelsen regards law as existing only if efficacious. I do not wish to maintain that this fact gives rise to any moral obligation. But it must be acknowledged that if it does, it will show a necessary connection between law and morals which does not depend on the content of the law.

Third, Kelsen's discussion is coloured by his conception of natural law as a theory which maintains that unjust laws are not valid laws at all. But many natural law theories do not conform to this view. Consider three prominent recent examples. Both Fuller in *The Morality of Law* (Cambridge 1964), Dworkin in *Taking Rights Seriously* (London 1977) and Finnis in *Natural Law and Natural Rights* (Oxford 1980) maintain that there is a necessary connection between law and morality. But none of them denies that there may be valid unjust laws.[67]

Finally, Kelsen here as elsewhere considers only conclusive moral force and neglects the possibility of a connection between law and morality which lends a prima facie moral character which may be overridden by conflicting moral considerations.

When we examine the views of the three prominent authors I mentioned, we find they tend to emphasise a connection between law and morality resting on various content-independent features of the law which does not exclude the possibility of valid unjust laws and which endows the law with only a prima facie moral force. Kelsen's arguments for the contingent connection thesis are inadequate against such theories. The inadequacy of Kelsen's argument does not, of course, mean that the views he thus tried to justify are themselves misconceived.

---

[66] *Cf. GT*, p. 5.

[67] Incidentally while all three reject the contingent connection thesis, only Dworkin rejects the sources thesis. Fuller's and Finnis's writings are consistent at least with a weak version of the sources thesis. For a distinction between a weak and a strong version of this thesis see my *The Authority of Law* (1979), essay 3.

But it is not my intention here to examine these theses.[68] Instead let us return to the question of their compatibility with a non-reductive semantic view of the analysis of legal statements. The question is crucial to the success of the second purity of the pure theory, its purity from moral elements. This purity seems to be guaranteed by the sources and contingent connection doctrines. But isn't that purity undermined by the views that legal statements are ordinary normative statements just like moral statements?

## IV

I have already mentioned that Kelsen's rejection of semantic reductivism was a departure from traditional positivist views. Another legal philosopher who shares his anti-reductivism is H.L.A. Hart, and it may help clarify Kelsen's position to briefly describe Hart's first.

As is well known, Hart distinguishes two kinds of statements standardly made by the use of deontic sentences, which he calls internal and external statements.[69] External statements are statements about people's behaviour and attitudes and need not concern us. Hart's notion of internal statements is fraught with difficulties. I will outline without detailed textual argument my understanding of it when applied to the law and I will refer to such statements as legal statements.[70] The law is for Hart an immensely complex social practice or set of practices. In part the meaning of legal statements can be given a truth-conditional analysis. Legal statements are true if and only if certain relations obtain between them and the complex legal practices. But it would be wrong to say that legal statements are just statements about the existence of those practices. The truth-conditional analysis does not exhaust the meaning of legal statements. To understand them one must also understand their standard uses and what they express. Their typical use is to provide guidance by criticizing, commending, demanding, advising, approving, etc. and they express acceptance by the speaker of standards of behaviour towards conformity with which the statement is used to guide its addressee.

This view of legal statements is meant to accommodate both their social-factual and their normative aspects. The factual aspect is captured by a truth conditional analysis. The normative one is accounted for by an explanation of the illocutionary force of the statements, and by the fact that they express not only the speaker's beliefs but also his practical attitude, his willingness to be guided by certain standards.

One would expect Kelsen to propound a view of legal statements rather like Hart's since Hart's account shares three of the most important features of Kelsen's doctrine of the law and of legal discourse. First, the existence of law can be objectively ascertained by reference to social facts. Hence Hart says, and one would expect Kelsen to agree, that legal statements are either true or false and that their truth conditions are their relations to complex social practices. Second, Hart, like Kelsen, regards legal statements as having a normative dimension which cannot be reduced to an assertion of any social facts. Third, Hart's account of the narrative dimension in terms of the illocutionary and expressive force of

---

[68] In *The Authority of Law* I have defended the sources thesis. Regarding the contingent connection issue one has to be more specific. I have argued that whatever moral character the law has is not enough to establish a prima facie obligation to obey the law. This leaves open the possibility of a necessary connection between law and morals of a lesser force.

[69] *Cf.* Hart, *The Concept of Law* (1961), pp. 57–59, 88–90, 291. For a discussion of Hart's anti-reductivism see G. Baker, "Defeasibility and Meaning" in Hacker and Raz (eds.), *Law, Morality and Society*. Essays in Honour of H. L. A. Hart (1977), p. 26.

[70] A similar analysis can be applied to his views of moral statements of duties but not to other normative statements.

legal statements avoids any reference to moral facts and does not presuppose the existence of moral values. Since Kelsen denies the existence of absolute moral values one might have expected him to provide an analysis of legal discourse along lines similar to Hart's.

Despite these similarities Kelsen's view of legal statement is radically different from Hart's because Kelsen advances a cognitivist interpretation of all normative discourses. He rejects expressive explanations such as Hart's.

For him a normative statement, be it legal, moral, or other, expresses a practical attitude only in that it expresses a belief in the existence of a valid norm (and a norm constitutes a value *WJ* 179). Hence the normative aspect of legal statements is not to be explained by their illocutionary force nor by the fact, taken by itself, that they express an acceptance of a standard of behaviour. It has to be explained by the fact that such statements state or presuppose the existence of a value or a norm, *i.e.* a normatively binding standard and not merely a social practice.

This understanding of Kelsen's position is not without its difficulties. He says, for example, that "there is not, and cannot be, an objective criterion of justice because the statement: something is just or unjust, is a judgment of value ... and these value judgments are by their very nature subjective in character, because based on emotional elements of our mind, on our feelings and wishes. They cannot be verified by facts, as can statements about reality. Ultimate value judgments are mostly acts of preference." (*WJ* 295). This passage suggests a non-cognitive interpretation of moral statements. But for the most part Kelsen adopts a cognitive view and regards every normative statement, legal or otherwise, as a statement of a binding norm or of the value it institutes. Such a semantic view is of course consistent with value-scepticism. It will merely lead the sceptic to the belief that all normative statements are false. Kelsen, however, is not a sceptic. He is a subjectivist or a relativist. Normative statements can be true or false. It is merely that their truth depends on the existence of relativistic rather than absolute values: "relativistic ... positivism does not assert that there are no values, or that there is no moral order, but only that the values in which men actually believe are not absolute but relative values." (*WJ* 179).

Unfortunately Kelsen's version of relativism is the familiar and incoherent one by which relativism is the non-relativist position that each person's values apply only to himself and each society's values to itself.[71] It is, of course, Kelsen's semantic doctrine rather than his theory of morals that I am concerned with. But the troubles with this kind of relativistic morality infect the interpretation of moral statements. It seems to suggest the oddity that sincere moral statements of a person about his own conduct are always true. Since he believes that there is a norm that he ought to perform a certain action, there is, in virtue of the relativistic morality, such a norm and his statement is true. Insincere moral statements about oneself are always false. The person does not believe that there is such a norm and therefore it does not exist and the statement is false. Normative statements about other people would be on this view true if and only if they accord with those other people's beliefs about themselves. Thus it is true that a racist should behave in a racist way.

None of this is acceptable and Kelsen does not explicitly draw such conclusions. He simply avoids talking of truth as applied to moral statements though he has no alternative account consistent with the rest of his doctrine. I believe that it is possible to provide a coherent relativist account of morality and that it can serve as a basis for a cognitivist interpretation of moral statements. But this is obviously not a task for this occasion. All that one can derive from Kelsen himself is the view that normative statements should be given a cognitivist interpretation, that they state the existence of duties, rights, powers or permissions and do not

---

[71]   *Cf., e.g. PTL*, pp. 59–69.

merely express the speaker's attitude. Whatever other speech-acts are performed in normative discourse the one speech act common to it is that of stating what is the case.

## V

Legal statements are normative statements in the sense and in the same way that moral statements are normative. This is as we saw the gist of Kelsen's semantic anti-reductivism. The implication of this persistent emphasis is that legal statements are "ought"-statements not to be confused with "is"-statements. The threat that this view poses to the purity of one's theory of law is evident. If legal statements are as normative as ordinary moral ones, if they are moral statements, then the law and its existence and content, which is what legal statements state, seem to be essentially moral facts. But the study of moral facts and their identification cannot be pure of moral considerations and arguments.

Kelsen's solution is threefold. First, he points out that the existence of law can be established and its content ascertained without the use of normative statements. The law can be described in sociological terms as a power structure in a society, etc. Such a description is not synonymous with a normative description of the law. If it were then it would amount to a reductive analysis of the normative factual basis of the law, all the social practices which Hart regards as constituting the existence of law. What will be left out is the claim that these social facts are "objectively valid": That they give rise to rights and duties and to other normative consequences. Some people have the appropriate moral beliefs and they regard the law as a normative system and describe it using legal statements. Those who do not share those moral views deny that the law is normative. But they can acknowledge its existence as a social fact.

But this first answer to the problem is not enough. It shows the possibility of a pure study of law as a complex social fact but it does not by itself establish the possibility of a pure study of law as a *normative* system. Therefore, Kelsen reinforces the first move with a second one. People have many moral beliefs. It is likely that for any individual in a society some of his moral beliefs coincide with the law and some diverge from it. But imagine a man whose moral beliefs are identical with the law. He does not add nor detract one *iota* from it. Furthermore, assume that his moral beliefs all derive from his belief in the moral authority of the ultimate law-making processes. For him, in other words, his belief in the validity of all and only the legal norms is not haphazard result of chance but a logical consequence of one of his beliefs. Let us call this person the legal man. Legal science, says Kelsen, studies the law as a normative system but without committing itself to its normativity. Basically the legal statements of legal science are conditional legal statements: If the legal man is right, they say, then this is what you ought to do: "The Pure Theory", he says, "describes the positive law as an objectively valid normative order and states that this interpretation is possible only under the condition that a basic norm is presupposed according to which the subjective meaning of the law-creating acts is also their objective meaning. The Pure Theory thereby characterizes this interpretation as possible, not necessary, and presents the objective validity of positive law only as conditional—namely conditional by the presupposed basic norm." (*PTL* 217/8). Therefore all the legal statement of legal science are hypothetical (*PTL* 71).

My legal man is one who endorses the basic norm and all that follows from it and nothing else. Scientific legal statements, being conditional statements of the form "if the legal man is right then one ought to ..." or "if the basic norm is valid one ought to ...," etc., are value-neutral. They are free of any moral presuppositions. By using them legal science can both be pure and describe the law as a normative system.

The problem with this second answer is that though it allows legal science to describe the law as a normative system it does not allow it to use categorical statements for they state that the law is a system of valid norms. It merely enables legal science to state what the law is *if it is valid*. This may be all that legal scholars need do. But it is not all that legal practitioners, barristers and solicitors, do. They do not merely talk about the law. They use it to advise clients and to present arguments before courts. Kelsen does not distinguish between the scholar and the practitioner. His analysis of legal discourse is meant to apply to both. But the practitioner does not state what the law is if it is valid. He states that it is valid. Yet if legal theory is pure such statements cannot be moral statements. They cannot be full-blooded normative statements. Kelsen requires a value neutral interpretation of categorical legal statements. He solves this problem by making his third move. Legal scientists, he says, do not merely describe what the law is if the basic norm is valid. They do actually presuppose the basic norm themselves. They assume its validity. "The basic norm really exists in the juristic consciousness" (*GT* 116). Kelsen sometimes draws obscurely on a distinction between positing and presupposing the basic norm (*PTL* 204n) to suggest that legal scientists (by which he refers to practitioners as well) presuppose but do not posit it as do people who actually believe in the moral validity of the law. This terminological distinction is not a happy one. His idea seems to be that not all scientific legal statements are hypotheticals of the type analysed above. Some or most are categorical statements based on a presupposition of the basic norm as a fiction.[72] Categorical legal statements are therefore of two types which I have called elsewhere committed and detached.[73] Committed statements are those of ordinary people who use normative language when stating the law because they believe or purport to believe in its binding force. Detached statements are typical of legal science which assumes the point of view of the legal man without being committed to it. It describes the law in normative statements but this is a description from a point of view which is not necessarily accepted by the speaker. He talks as if he accepts the basic norm and this pretense is what Kelsen refers to as presupposing the basic norm as a fiction. Detached statements state the law as a valid normative system; they do not merely describe what would be valid if the basic norm is valid. But they do so from a point of view, that of the legal man, to which they are not committed. Therefore, legal science is pure of moral commitment despite its use of normative language.

## VI

I have ascribed to Kelsen the view that there are three types of legal statements:

(1)   Statements conditional on the validity of the basic norm, which are normally uncommitted since their normative force depends on the unasserted condition: if the basic norm is valid then...

(2)   Detached statements, which are also morally uncommitted since they are statements from a point of view. They state what rights and duties there are on the assumption that the basic norm is valid but without commitment to that assumption.

(3)   Committed statements, which are ordinary moral statements about what ought to be done, what rights and duties people have because of the law.

Legal theory contains statements of the first two kinds only and is therefore pure.
    It has to be admitted, of course, that this is more a reconstruction than a straightforward interpretation. Kelsen does not distinguish clearly between the

---

[72]   *Cf.* "On the Pure Theory of Law" in Israel L.Rev. vol. 1, p. 6. [And see *ante*, 356].
[73]   *Cf.* Raz, *The Authority of Law* (1979), essay 8, and see also essay 7.

three classes and he himself confessed to confusing the last with the other two on occasion (*PTL* 204n., 218n.). Worse still, while I believe that he was generally aware of the distinction between the committed statements and the others, he appears completely unaware of the difference between the detached statements and those conditional on the validity of the basic norm. Here I think it is fair to accuse him of confusion and equivocation. He does shift from one position to the other without noticing the difference. I have tried to separate the strands of thought as clearly as I can. But such a reconstruction is bound to remain tentative and controversial.

Interpretation apart, the question arises how illuminating are these distinctions. I ask "how illuminating" and not "are they true" for it is clearly a programme for a explanation rather than a full explanation that Kelsen provides. We may approach the problem by comparing Kelsen (or should I say the reconstructed Kelsen?) with Hart.

Committed statements are essentially the same as Hart's internal statements with two important differences. First, Kelsen's is a cognitivist whereas Hart's is a non-cognitivist interpretation of the normativity of a statement. For Kelsen such statements are normative because they express a belief in the validity of a norm. For Hart they are normative because they express an attitude of willingness to be guided in a certain way. Second, Kelsen tends to identify all normative attitudes and beliefs as moral ones. Hart takes pains to explain that moral reasons are only one type of reason for accepting rules and for having the kind of practical attitude manifested in internal statements.

I will disregard the first difference for the moment. The second is sometimes thought to explain why Hart need not resort to Kelsen's distinction between committed and detached statements. All that Hart has to establish to be consistent with its own doctrine of the separation of law and morals[74] is that ordinary legal discourse does not commit one to a moral approbation of the law. Ordinary legal discourse consists of internal statements and those though expressing a practical attitude of acceptance of the law as a guide for behaviour do not necessarily express acceptance on moral grounds. Even if one accepts that the interpretation of legal discourse has to be freed only of moral evaluation and not of other kinds of normative evaluation Hart's position is still difficult to maintain. The crucial point is that much legal discourse concerns the rights and duties of others. While one can accept the law as a guide for one's own behaviour for reasons of one's own personal preferences or of self-interest one cannot adduce one's preferences or one's self interest by themselves as a justification for holding that other people must, or have a duty to act in a certain way. To claim that another has to act in my interest is normally to make a moral claim about his moral obligations.

There are to be sure reasons on which claims about other people's duties and rights can be based which are neither moral reasons nor the speaker's self interest or preferences. But none of them nor any combination of them is likely to explain the widespread use of normative language in legal discourse. I find it impossible to resist the conclusion that most internal or committed legal statements, at any rate those about the rights and duties of others, are moral claims.[75]

This conclusion creates a dilemma. Either all legal statements are statements expressing moral endorsement of the law or not all legal statements are internal statements as understood by Hart or committed statements à la Kelsen. Hart rejects the first horn of the dilemma and he is surely right to do so. Clearly many legal statements do not express a moral position either way. This fact need not be

---

[74]   *Cf.* Hart, *The Concept of Law*, Chap. IX and "The Separation of Law and Morals" in (1958) 71 Harvard Law Rev. [and *Essays in Jurisprudence and Philosophy*, p. 49.]
[75]   I am not saying that people who make such statements have the moral beliefs they express. They may be insincere.

disputed by natural lawyers and is indeed accepted by Finnis.[76] Hart is therefore bound to conclude that not all legal statements are internal. They cannot plausibly be said to be external statements since these are not normative statements but statements about other people's actions and beliefs. Hart has no alternative account. Kelsen has his doctrine of detached statements which provides the framework for a solution to the dilemma by explaining a class of statements which are normally made by the use of normative language, which are not about behaviour or beliefs but about rights and duties and which are nonetheless not committed and not internal statements.

## VII

I have said in my introductory remarks that Kelsen's most celebrated doctrine, that of the basic norm, is a direct result of the purity of the theory of law. Let me conclude by commenting on the connection between the theses. First, the ground for the doctrine of the basic norm is prepared by Kelsen's cognitivist interpretation of legal statements. A person who believes that one should behave in accordance with a certain social practice does not have an attitude which inclines him to demand conformity to and criticize deviation from the practice. He is so inclined to behave because he believes in the validity of norms requiring such behaviour.

Norms can be divided into two types. Some are dynamically derivative while others are not. A norm is dynamically derivative if its validity depends on the occurrence of an action which creates it. Actions can create norms if they are authorized to do so by some other norms. Those other norms may themselves be derivative ones. But any normative system must contain at least one non-derivative norm and all its derivative norms must be subsumed under non-derivative norms. But these conclusions are immediate results of Kelsen's principle of the autonomy of the normative, of his insistence that "ought" cannot be derived from "is", values cannot be derived from facts.

Laws are, as we have emphasized before, positive norms. That is, they are all dynamically derivative norms. But this means that the legal system will not be complete unless it also contains a non-derivative, *i.e.* a non-positive, norm which authorizes, directly or indirectly, all the positive laws of the system. That norm is the basic norm, *i.e.* a norm authorizing the creation of the historically first constitution and thus indirectly of all the other norms of the system.[77]

I have said that the basic norm has to be non-derivative, non-positive. This calls for further explanation. Individuals who do not regard the law as normatively valid do not, of course, believe in the validity of the basic norm at all. Those who accept the validity of the law may still not believe in its basic norm. Some may, for example, believe that many but not all of its norms are intuitively self-evident. Some but not all of the others may be believed by them to have been authorized by divine command and the rest to be binding because it was their parents' will that they should obey them. Such people while accepting the validity of all the law do not attribute it to the basic norm described by the theory of laws. Others may believe in the moral validity of some but not all the laws of the system. They too do not believe in the validity of the basic norm (which authorizes all the laws). They derive the validity of those laws they believe in from some other norm(s) which do not entail the validity of the laws they do not believe to be valid.

The point is that norms relativistically understood are always to be looked at

[76] See *Natural Law and Natural Rights*, pp. 234–237.
[77] *Cf.* J. Harris, "Kelsen's Concept of Authority" in (1977) Cambridge L.J. 353: S. Paulson, "Material and Formal Authorization in Kelsen's Pure Theory" in (1980) Cambridge L.J. 172.

from the point of view of some person or group and that every person or group is likely to believe in more or less than the validity of all positive law. Very few people are like the legal man postulated above. But legal men are the only ones likely to accept the Kelsenian basic norm as their ultimate non-derivative norm. Despite this the basic norm is the key to the scientific understanding of the law. The reason is that legal theory to remain pure cannot study the law in so far as it is embedded in the moral beliefs of one person or another. That would violate the sources thesis by making the identification of the law dependent on a particular set of moral beliefs. To be pure, legal theory must strictly adhere to the sources thesis and identify the law by social facts only. Hence to describe it normatively it must non-committally or fictitiously accept the basic norm of the legal man, *i.e.* the Kelsenian basic norm, for it is the only one to give validity to the *empirically established* law and to nothing else. This, then, is the sense in which the basic norm is the scientific postulate of legal thought.

This claim clarifies the dual role of law-creating facts in the law. On the one hand they establish the character of law as a social fact. All the norms created and identified in certain ways, which are by and large efficacious, constitute a complex social practice by which members of the society guide and co-ordinate their actions. This is the function of law-creating facts as establishing the membership of certain norms in a system which is socially practised. On the other hand those facts transmit normative force from the authorizing norm to the authorized one. Since the authorizing norm is valid and since it endows those acts with law-creating status the norm they are meant to create is also valid. This is the role of law-creating acts as conferring validity, transmitting binding force from one norm to another.

Moreover, it is not accidental that law-creating facts fulfill both roles. Legal theory is the normative study of a social normative system. Therefore, given its purity it represents as norms only those rules which belong to the effective social order. In other words it is the character of law-creating acts as criteria for membership in a socially effective system which qualifies them to serve as facts transmitting validity from one norm to another.

Once more we can improve our understanding of Kelsen's meaning by comparing it with Hart's. Hart's focus of interest is on the character of law as complex social practice. He describes the existence conditions of social rules and then he turns to normative social systems and introduces the notion of criteria of validity as a test of membership in a social practice tying legal rules indirectly to the complex practice. He is not specifically interested in the descent of normative force from one norm to another. Validity for him indicates just membership in a system established in a certain way. It has little to do with binding normative force.

Therefore from Hart's point of view there is no difference between the role of legislative acts and the social practice which establishes the existence of a rule of recognition. Both are relevant as establishing the membership of certain rules in a legal system. Not so for Kelsen: he emphasizes the fact that a legislative act not only establishes membership, it also confers normative force on the norm created. But the social practice which ties the ultimate legal rules to social reality, while it too is relevant to establish membership of the rule in an effective legal system (and also to establish the effectiveness of the system) does not fulfill the other role of transmitting normative force. To assume otherwise is to regard law as consisting of derivative laws only, which is, for Kelsen, a logical impossibility. If the judicial practices which according to Hart establish the existence of the rule of recognition were also to endow it with normative status this could only be in virtue of yet another norm which would then become itself the ultimate rule of the system.

I believe that this argument correctly reflects our unreflective thinking about the law. Judges regard the fact that a statute was enacted by Parliament as a reason to regard it as binding and to hold the litigants to be bound by it. But they do not necessarily regard the judicial practice of enforcing Parliamentary enactments as a reason for enforcing them, *i.e.* as a reason for accepting the rule of recognition as binding. They may accept the rule of recognition because they believe in parliamentary democracy or in some law and other argument, etc. But those norms which make them accept the binding force of the rule of recognition are not themselves part of the law. From the point of view of the study of law the ultimate rule is the rule of recognition directing the courts to apply Parliamentary legislation. The judicial practice of following the rule identifies it as part of a system effective in that society and helps establish the social existence of the whole system. Hart is right about this and Kelsen is guilty of overlooking or oversimplifying many of the facts which establish the social character of the law. But Kelsen is right in pointing out that these judicial social practices do not confer binding force on the ultimate legal rules and are not generally believed to do so. In this they differ from other law-creating acts. From the point of view of a pure study of law the validity of ultimate legal rules is simply (non-committally) assumed. [pp. 442–459]

REFERENCES

Alexy, Robert. 1989. On Necessary Relations between Law and Morality. *Ratio Juris* 2: 168–84.
——. 1992. *Begriffund Geltung des Rechts*. Freiburg: Karl Alber Verlag.
Austin, John (1885). *Lectures on Jurisprudence*, 2 vols. London: John Murray.
Beyleveld, Deryck, and Roger Brownsword (1986) *Law as a Moral Judgment*.
——. 1989. Normative Positivism: The Mirage of the Middle-Way. *Oxford Journal of Legal Studies* 9: 463–512.
——. 1992. The Implications of Natural-Law Theory for the Sociology of Law. In *Post-Modern Law*. Ed. Anthony Carty, 126–40.
Bryce, James. 1901. *Studies in History and Jurisprudence*.
Bulygin, Eugenio. 1982. Norms, Normative Propositions, and Legal Statements. In *Contemporary Philosophy. A New Survey*, vol. 3. Ed. Guttorm Fløistad, 127–52.
——. 1990. An Antinomy in Kelsen's Pure Theory of Law. *Ratio Juris* 3: 29–45.
D'Entrèves, Alessandro Passerin. 1962. 1970. *Natural Law*, 2nd edn., 173–84.
Dreier, Ralf. 1981. *Recht-Moral-Ideologie*. Frankfurt: Suhrkamp.
Duff, R. A. 1980. Legal Obligation and the Moral Nature of Law. *Juridical Review* 25 (N.S.): 61–87.
Dworkin, Ronald. 1978. *Taking Rights Seriously*.
Eckmann, Horst. 1969. *Rechtspositivismus und sprachanalytische Philosophie*.
Guastini, Riccardo. 1991. Problemi epistemologici del normativismo. In *Analisi e diritto. 1991*. Ed. Paolo Comanducci and Riccardo Guastini, 177–92.
Hacker, P. M. S. 1977. Hart's Philosophy of Law. In *Law, Morality and Society. Essays in Honour of H. L. A. Hart*. Ed. P. M. S. Hacker and Joseph Raz, 1–25.
Hart, H. L. A. 1957–58. Positivism and the Separation of Law and Morals. *Harvard Law Review* 71: 593–629.
——. 1961. *The Concept of Law*. Oxford: Clarendon.
——. 1982a. Legal Duty and Obligation. In H. L. A. Hart. *Essays on Bentham*, 127–61.
——. 1982b. Commands and Authoritative Reasons. In H. L. A. Hart. *Essays on Bentham*, 243—68.
Hoerster, Norbert. 1986. Kritischer Vergleich der Theorien der Rechtsgeltung

von Hans Kelsen und H. L. A. Hart. In *Untersuchungen'zur Reinen Rechtslehre*. Ed. Stanley L. Paulson and Robert Walter, 1–19.

——. 1993. Positivisten im Vergleichstest. In *Frankfurter Allgemeine Zeitung* 118:13, 24 May 1993.

Kant, Immanuel. 1781 and 1787. *Kritik der reinen Vernunft*. (References employ the standard "A" and "B" pagination.)

——. 1783. *Prolegomena*. (Reference is to section number.)

——. 1797. *Die Metaphysik der Sitten, 1. Teil: Metaphysische Anfangsgründe der Rechtslehre*. (Reference is to standard pagination established by the *Aka-demie* edition of *Kants gesammelte Schriften*; quotation translated by Bonnie Litschewski Paulson and Stanley L. Paulson.)

Kelsen, Hans, 1923. *Hauptprobleme der Staatsrechtslehre*.

——. 1925. *Allgemeine Staatslehre*.

——. 1928. *Die philosophischen Grundlagen der Naturrechtslehre und des Rechtspositivismus*. Charlottenburg (Berlin): Pan-Verlag Rolf Heise. Trans. Wolfgang H. Kraus under the title *Natural Law Doctrine and Legal Positivism*. In Kelsen. 1945. *General Theory of Law and State*, 398–445. Cambridge, Mass.: Harvard University Press.

——. 1934. *Reine Rechtslehre*. Vienna and Leipzig: Deuticke Verlag. Trans. Bonnie Litschewski Paulson and Stanley L. Paulson under the title *Introduction to the Problems of Legal Theory*. Oxford: Clarendon, 1992.

——. 1941–42. The Pure Theory of Law and Analytical Jurisprudence. *Harvard Law Review* 55: 44–70. Reprinted in Kelsen. 1957. *What is Justice?*, 266–87, 390 (notes). Berkeley, Calif.: University of California Press.

——. 1955–56. A "Dynamic" Theory of Natural Law. *Louisiana Law Review* 16: 597–620. (Reprinted in Kelsen. 1957. *What is Justice?*, 174–97. Berkeley, Calif.: University of California Press.)

——. 1960. *Reine Rechtslehre*, 2nd edn.

——. 1979. *Allgemeine Theorie der Normen. General Theory of Norms*. Ed. Kurt Ringhofer and Robert Walter. Vienna: Manz Verlag. Trans. Michael Hartney. 1991. *General Theory of Norms*. Oxford: Clarendon.

Korematsu v. United States, *United States Reports*, 323 (1944), 214–48.

Lyons, David. 1982. *Moral Aspects of Legal Theory*, 64—101.

MacCormick, Neil. 1978. *Legal Reasoning and Legal Theory*.

——. 1981. *H. L. A. Hart*.

Martin, Michael. 1987. *The Legal Philosophy of H. L. A. Hart. A Critical Appraisal*.

Merkl, Adolf Julius. 1931. Prolegomena einer Theorie des rechtlichen Stufenbaues. In *Gesellschaft, Staat und Recht*. Ed. Alfred Verdross, 252–94. Vienna: Springer. (Reprinted in *Die Wiener rechtstheoretische Schule*, vol. 1. Ed. Hans Klecatsky et al., 1311–61.

Nino, Carlos Santiago. 1978. Some Confusions around Kelsen's Concept of Validity. *Archiv für Rechts- und Sozialphilosophie* 64: 357–77.

Oladosu, Adejare. 1991. H. L. A. Hart on Legal Obligation. *Ratio Juris* 4: 152–76.

Paulson, Stanley L. 1992a. Kelsen's Legal Theory: the Final Round. *Oxford Journal of Legal Studies* 12: 265–74.

——. 1992b. The Neo-Kantian Dimension of Kelsen's Pure Theory of Law. *Oxford Journal of Legal Studies* 12: 311–32.

——. 1992c. Kelsen senza Kant. *Rivista internazionale di filosofia del diritto* 69: 404–17.

Raz, Joseph. 1976. Critical Study. Kelsen's General Theory of Norms. *Philosophia* 6: 495–504.

———. 1979. *The Authority of Law*. Oxford: Clarendon.

———. 1980. *The Concept of a Legal System*, 2nd edn. Oxford: Clarendon.

———. 1981. The Purity of the Pure Theory. [*Ante.*, xxx.]

———. 1990. *Practical Reason and Norms*, 2nd edn.

Sartorius, Ralf. 1987. Positivism and the Foundations of Legal Authority. In *Issues in Contemporary Legal Philosophy. The Influence of H. L. A. Hart*. Ed. Ruth Gavison, 43–61. Oxford: Clarendon.

Schauer, Frederick. 1991. *Playing by the Rules*. Oxford: Clarendon.

Shiner, Roger. 1992. *Norm and Nature*. Oxford: Clarendon.

Walochow, Wilfrid J. 1989. The Weak Social Thesis. *Oxford Journal of Legal Studies* 9: 23–55.

Xenophon. 1990. *Memorabilia*, I. ii. 40–46. Trans. Hugh Tredennick and Robin Waterfield, in Xenophon, *Conversations of Socrates*. London: Penguin.

# 6

## MODERN TRENDS IN ANALYTICAL JURISPRUDENCE

Whatever boundaries we impose on this chapter must necessarily be arbitrary. The chapter discusses Hohfeld's classic on fundamental legal conceptions—now more than three-quarters of a century old—because of the intrinsic interest of his ideas and the influence he continues to wield to-day.[1] But the principal focus of the chapter is on analytical jurisprudential thinking of the last 50 years. Hart's *Concept of Law* published in 1961, was a landmark monograph and remains a beacon for all who pursue scholarship in this area. The posthumous "Postscript" of 1994 would have rekindled interest were that necessary: it has certainly stimulated new debate and scholarship.[2] Hart's work (and that of his followers and critics) is central to this chapter.

In earlier editions of this book we included an extract from Robert Summers' article, "The New Analytical Jurists".[3] The jurisprudence he wrote about is no longer "new", and the extract is no longer featured. But we are justified in reflecting on what he wrote in 1966. Jurists, he noted, were performing "a wider variety of analytical activities than did most of their predecessors". He divided their activities into four main categories:

(i) analysis of the existing conceptual framework of and about law;
(ii) construction of new conceptual frameworks with accompanying terminologies;
(iii) rational justification of institutions and practices, existing and proposed; and
(iv) "purposive implication", the tracing out of what the acceptance of social purposes "implies" in terms of social arrangements and social ordering.

All four of these types of analytical jurisprudence persist, but to get an insight into the real character of contemporary legal philosophy we need to do no more than consult Neil MacCormick's article, "Contemporary Legal Philosophy: the Rediscovery of Practical Reason", published in

---

[1] *Post*, 569. And see Hart's explanation of legal limits on sovereignty (*The Concept of Law*, p. 66).
[2] Most obviously two Special Issues of *Legal Theory* (1998), vol. 4(3),(4) and J. Coleman, *Hart's Postscript* (2001).
[3] (1966) 41 New York Univ. L. Rev. 861, 865–877.

1983,[4] and in many ways the parallel of Summers' article, or consult the pages of the vibrant new Journal *Legal Theory*.

Some characteristics of contemporary legal philosophy to which he draws attention, in particular the "rediscovery" of practical reason, notably in the writings of Joseph Raz,[5] may be gathered from MacCormick, as well as in the extracts from Raz himself. One result of Raz's pursuit of reason for actions is to direct our attention, when looking at a concept like obligation, to the kinds of reasons we address when contemplating an actual or supposed obligation to act. This, as we shall see, constitutes a break in legal thinking. Austin would have pursued these reasons no further than "the threat of evil",[6] and even Hart (Austin's most trenchant contemporary critic[7]) sought the reasons (as we shall see) in "external" serious social pressure.[8]

In the extract from Raz's article "The Problem About The Nature of Law", reproduced in Chapter 2,[9] we see how he extends this line of argument to the problem of separating "law" from other norms, such as morality. This has, of course, been integral to the positivist pursuit. Does Raz offer any new insight? He shows that there is a difference between there being some sound reasons for conduct being legally obligatory and its actually being so. When we are considering whether "to do X" should be an obligation, we are at the "deliberative" phase of practical reasoning. Once an authoritative decision is taken that "to do X" is obligatory, further deliberation is excluded. Raz is right to draw attention to a significant distinction within practical reasoning between what has already been decided and what reasons there are for deciding one way or the other problems that are as yet not settled. MacCormick sees this as "unquestionably the best defence yet offered"[10] for the positivistic thesis on the conceptual independence of law from morality. It certainly appears fruitful, and there is no doubt that it has opened up a new avenue of enquiry. But what is an authoritative decision? This raises all the old questions about validity and about whether positivists have been able to discover a measuring-rod for distinguishing valid law from non-law or non-valid law. It also ignores the question as to whether further deliberation is indeed precluded or overridden by legal authoritative legal pronouncement. Whether or not civil disobedience can be justified, we would surely not wish to deny individuals autonomy of thought about the moral propriety of complying with law.[11]

The search for what it is that separates law from other normative phenomena remains a positivist project, even amongst those who identify

---

[4]  *Post*, 396.
[5]  Notably in *Practical Reason and Norms* (2nd ed., 1990).
[6]  *Ante*, 215.
[7]  *Post*, 335.
[8]  *Post*, 339.
[9]  *Ante*, 69.
[10]  (1983) 10 J.L.S. 1, 6.
[11]  And opening up the question of the moral basis of the obligation to obey the law: see generally William Edmundson, *The Duty To Obey The Law* (1999), and *post*, 405, 575.

with, what has come to be called, "inclusive legal positivism"[12] or "incorporationism".[13] And, it is a feature of contemporary jurisprudence that this search has taken jurists into new terrains. The issue of adjudication, peripheral to jurisprudence when Hart and Fuller had their celebrated debate in the *Harvard Law Review*,[14] is now central. Dworkin's critique of the model of positivism represented by Hart's *Concept of Law* began as a questioning of its theory of adjudication.[15] Dworkin was concerned, and rightly so, with the inadequacies of positivistic explanations of how disputes were determined when, as is so often the case, we "run out of rules". Dworkin's response was to construct a theory of law out of a theory of adjudication.[16] He shows that judges use, and must use, moral considerations, in addition to rules found in legislation and case law. He does not, however, claim that the validity of legal principles depends on their morality, and this distinguishes his thinking from natural law theorising.[17] Even so, some categorise him as a natural lawyer.[18] Dworkin argues that these moral considerations are integral to the moral theory justifying the enacted and case law binding on the judges. But, surely not all the considerations a judge uses in his deliberations and reasoning constitute the law? Dworkin seems to assume they do, though he offers no explanation as to why this should be so. To assume the law consists just of rules is clearly wrong—and Dworkin was right to draw attention to this failing in positivism—but there is no reason why a positivist theory should not be constructed to embrace standards other than rules. Indeed, MacCormick, in *Legal Reasoning and Legal Theory*, has shown the feasibility of such a project.[19]

Contemporary analytical jurisprudence—and not just in the English-speaking world—owes much to Hart.[20] It was he who shook English jurisprudence out of its lethargy in the 1950s. It was he who placed theorising about law back into the mainstream of philosophy. The significance of Hart's contribution also lies in his application of philosophy to substantive legal issues, such as causation,[21] to practices like punishment,[22] and to questions of moral philosophy such as the legitimacy of

---

[12] W. Waluchow, *Inclusive Legal Positivism* (1994); (2000) 6 *Legal Theory* 45.
[13] J. Coleman, 11 J. Legal Stud. 139 (1982) (also in *Markets, Morals and the Law* (1988) p. 3), (1998) 4 *Legal Theory* 381, and *The Practice of Principle* (2001). See also *post*, 490.
[14] *Post*, 414 and 417.
[15] In what is now Chap. 2 of *Taking Rights Seriously* (1977) (first published in 1967).
[16] *Post*, 1391.
[17] *Post*, 347.
[18] And see Dworkin, (1982) 34 Univ. of Florida L. Rev. 165.
[19] Published in 1978: see also *post*, 1579.
[20] The best critical introduction to whom is N. MacCormick, *H.L.A. Hart* (1981). See also M. Martin, *The Legal Philosophy of H.L.A. Hart* (1987) and M. Bayles, *Hart's Legal Philosophy* (1992). On H.L.A. Hart's life see N. Lacey, *A Life of H.L.A. Hart* (2004).
[21] With A. Honoré, *Causation In The Law* (2nd ed., 1985).
[22] *Punishment and Responsibility* (1968).

legal intervention into private morality.[23] The work of Raz,[24] Lyons,[25] MacCormick,[26] Coleman,[27] Campbell,[28] Waluchow,[29] Schauer[30] and many others builds on Hart's thought. Nor is analytical jurisprudence today confined, as perhaps it once was, to positivists, as the work of Dworkin (considered in this chapter and elsewhere in this book[31]), of Finnis,[32] of Duncan Kennedy,[33] of Unger,[34] of G. Cohen[35] and of Lukes,[36] all of whom are discussed elsewhere, amply demonstrates.

Positivism itself is not as easy to pigeon-hole as it once was. It is easy enough to identify two central tenets: the so-called "social thesis" (what counts as law in a given society is a matter of social fact); and the "separability thesis" (there is no necessary connection between law and morality).[37] But contemporary positivists differ on the best interpretation of these two theses. There is now a widely-accepted gulf between inclusive legal positivism (or incorporationism) which "allows that substantive moral principles can count as part of a community's binding law in virtue of their status as moral principles provided the relevant rule of recognition includes a provision to that effect"[38] and exclusive legal positivism, principally associated with Raz, which refuses to allow legal status to be determined by moral argument. Hart himself, perhaps implicitly in *The Concept of Law*, and now explicitly in its "Postscript",[39] allies himself with inclusive legal positivism or "soft positivism", as he calls it. The debate is returned to later in this chapter[40] and extracts will give the reader the flavour of this contemporary debate.

Both forms of positivism may be contrasted with Dworkin's "interpretivism" (where the rule of recognition plays no role). If *The Concept of Law* was the most significant contribution to jurisprudence in the 1960s— Jules Coleman goes further and describes it as "the most important and

---

[23] *Law, Liberty and Morality* (1963); *The Morality of The Criminal Law* (1965). And *post*, 409.

[24] *The Concept of A Legal System* (2nd ed., 1980); *Practical Reason and Norms* (1975, revised ed. 1990); *The Authority of Law* (1979); *Ethics in the Public Domain* (1994).

[25] *Moral Aspects of Legal Theory* (1993).

[26] *Legal Reasoning and Legal Theory* (1978); *Legal Right and Social Democracy* (1982); *Questioning Sovereignty* (1999).

[27] "Negative and Positive Positivism" in (1982) 11 J. Legal Studies 139; "Reason and Authority" in (ed.) R. George, *The Autonomy of Law* (1996).

[28] *The Legal Theory of Ethical Positivism* (1996); (1998) 51 C.L.P. 65.

[29] *Inclusive Legal Positivism* (1994).

[30] (1998) 51 C.L.P. 223; (1994) 24 Canadian J. of Philosophy 495; "Positivism Through Thick and Thin" in (ed.) B. Bix, *Analyzing Law* (1998), p. 65; "Positivism As Pariah" in (ed.) R. George, *The Autonomy of Law* (1996), p. 31.

[31] *Post*, Chap. 8.

[32] *Post*, 126.

[33] *Post*, see (1979) 28 Buffalo L.R. 209.

[34] *Post*, 1271.

[35] *Post*, 1170.

[36] *Post*, 1175.

[37] See J. Raz, for example, *The Authority of Law* (1979).

[38] *Per* J. Coleman in (ed.) R. George, *The Autonomy of Law* (1996), pp. 287–288.

[39] *The Concept of Law* (1994), pp. 250–254. And see B. Bix (1999) 12 Canadian J. of Law and Jurisprudence 17.

[40] *Post*, 385.

influential book in the legal positivist tradition"[41]—its natural successors have been Dworkin's *Taking Rights Seriously* and *Law's Empire*.[42] Hart demonstrated the need for students of the concept of law to appreciate the insights of analytical, particularly linguistic, philosophy. Dworkin has placed the issues of jurisprudence back—where they were in Bentham's writings—in the realm of moral and political philosophy.[43] His contributions to jurisprudence are matched by his contributions to the development of a liberal political theory.[44] It is his view that the right to equal concern and respect is the fundamental principle of moral theory (and of American constitutional law), and that utilitarianism is no substitute for a theory committed to "taking rights seriously". Dworkin's views have proved contentious. One of his sharpest critics is Hart. It is the brunt of Hart's argument that if someone's liberty is restricted he is not being treated as an equal.[45] Dworkin does not think that this usually happens, and that it occurs only when a person's convictions and values are condemned by others.[46] Dworkin's political theory—in particular his thinking on justice and equality—is considered in the next chapter; his interpretivism is considered in Chapter 8.[47]

## HART'S CONCEPT OF LAW

So much jurisprudential ink has been spilt trying to define law that the student may be surprised to find that Hart eschews this task. In his inaugural lecture, published as "Definition and Theory In Jurisprudence" and extracted in Chapter 2,[48] as well as in this chapter,[49] he turns his back on a tradition which seemed to believe that definitions could solve the difficulties to which the words embodying the concepts (such as "right" and "corporation") gave rise. The "growth of theory on the back of definition," to which he drew attention, is all too obvious in the writings of Austin,[50] a jurist whom Hart singled out for attack. Hart believed (the influence of linguistic philosophy[51] is plain) that a more fruitful approach would be to elucidate the conditions to which true statements are made in legal contexts about "rights," "corporations," etc. This project was

[41] (1998) 4 *Legal Theory* 381.
[42] Published in 1977 and 1986 respectively.
[43] And see W. Twining (1979) 95 L.Q.R. 557.
[44] See "Liberalism" in (ed.) S. Hampshire, *Public and Private Morality* (1978), *Freedom's Law* (1996) and *Sovereign Virtue* (2000).
[45] "Between Utility and Rights" in (ed.) A. Ryan, *The Idea of Freedom* (1979). More recent critiques are P. Neal (1995) 1 *Legal Theory* 205 and E. Sherwin (1995) 1 *Legal Theory* 227.
[46] "Is Wealth a Value?" in *A Matter of Principle* (1985), Chap. 12.
[47] *Post*, 717.
[48] *Ante*, 59.
[49] *Post*, 444.
[50] Thus Austin is forced to conclude that much we would regard as law is not so having initially framed a definition of law. See *ante*, 243.
[51] Some of these influences are discussed in N. MacCormick, *H. L. A. Hart* (1981), pp. 14–16.

pursued in *Causation In The Law*,[52] and in *The Concept of Law*. There is no definition of law or of a legal system as such in the *Concept*. The aim is elucidation, elucidation of concepts like rule and obligation, which have puzzled generations of legal thinkers. In the preface Hart quotes J. L. Austin's remarks that we may use "a sharpened awareness of words to sharpen our awareness of phenomena".[53] This is the goal of *The Concept of Law*. The book is offered as an "essay in descriptive sociology",[54] but this description is as likely to mislead as to guide. Certainly, it ignores questions about power, conflicts of interest, the symbolic dimensions of law's authority, its relationship to culture and class and many other matters of interest to sociologists of law. It is rather an essay in analytical jurisprudence, in conceptual analysis which, for all its faults, remains one of the most significant post-war texts in jurisprudence. We offer no extracts because we believe the whole book should be read by every student of the subject.

### An Outline of Hart's Jurisprudence

For Hart the legal system is a system of social rules. The rules are "social" in two senses: first in that they regulate the conduct of members of societies (they are "guides to human conduct and standards of criticism of such conduct")[55]; secondly, in that they derive from human social practices.[56] They are not the only social rules. There are, for example, rules of morality. Like rules of morality, laws are concerned with obligations: they make certain conduct "obligatory". But unlike rules of morality they have, what MacCormick calls, "a systemic quality"[57] which hinges on the inter-relationship of two types of rules, called by Hart "primary rules" and "secondary rules".

As we saw in Chapter 4, Hart objected to Austin's command theory on the grounds that it failed to encompass the "variety of laws".[58] His theory distinguishes between primary duty-imposing rules, such as the rules of the criminal law or the law of tort, and secondary power-conferring rules such as the laws that facilitate the making of contracts, wills, trusts, marriages, etc., or which lay down rules governing the composition and powers of courts, legislatures and other "official" bodies. These secondary rules relate in various ways to the primary ones: it is in this kind of relationship that the systemic quality of law is to be found.

According to Hart there are three kinds of secondary rule. There are rules which confer competence on officials to pass judgment in cases of

---

[52] Together with A. Honoré (1st, ed. 1959; 2nd ed. 1985).
[53] *ibid.*, p. v.
[54] *ibid. cf.* J. Gibbs (1968) 2 Law & Soc. Rev. 429. See also Edgeworth, 6 *Legal Studies* 115. Hart was undoubtedly familiar with Weber's *On Law in Economy and Society* (see Lacey, pp. 230–231). Weber is discussed at *post*, 839.
[55] *The Concept of Law* ("Postscript"), p. 249.
[56] On which see M.N. Smith (2006) 12 *Legal Theory* 265.
[57] *op. cit.*, n. 51.
[58] See *The Concept of Law*, Chap. 3 and *ante*, 267.

alleged wrongs and also to enforce the law, for example by ordering the payment of damages or by depriving someone of his liberty. Hart calls these rules "rules of adjudication". There are rules which regulate the process of change by conferring the power to enact legislation in accordance with specified procedures. These rules Hart designates "rules of change". Rules of change have additionally a lower-order or private dimension. These are rules which confer on ordinary individuals the power to produce changes in the legal relationships they have with others. Examples have already been given.[59] Thirdly, there is what Hart calls the "rule of recognition." What this does is to determine the criteria which govern the validity of the rules of the system. The rule of recognition (or rules, Hart is equivocal) is one of the more puzzling and troublesome features of Hart's jurisprudence.

This constitutes the skeleton of the legal system. But a legal system can only be said to "exist" if it is effectively in force. There are, according to Hart, "two minimum conditions necessary and sufficient for the existence of a legal system." These are that "those rules of behaviour which are valid according to the system's ultimate criteria of validity must be generally obeyed, and its rules of recognition specifying the criteria of legal validity and its rules of change and adjudication must be effectively accepted as common public standards of official behaviour by its officials."[60] The first condition has to be satisfied by private citizens and they may obey for any reason. The second condition must also be satisfied by the officials of the system and they must regard the secondary rules as "common standards of official behaviour and appraise critically their own and each other's deviations and lapses."[61] They must accept these rules (or at least the rule of recognition) and observe them from, what Hart calls, "the internal point of view."[62]

A system of rules which is in this sense effectively in force in a territory is, according to Hart, the central case of a legal system.[63] But there are other cases and much of Hart's analysis is an attempt to show the parallels between these and the standard, mature, stable legal system, and the differences. There are "primitive" forms of human social community where a common set of primary standards is observed but where power-conferring secondary rules have not developed. Hart attempts to show how the shortcomings suffered by such a pre-legal community are cured by the development of secondary power-conferring rules.[64] Because of the absence of these rules there is also missing in pre-legal societies concepts such as "power," "official," "legislature" which members of modern states take for granted. International law provides an analogous case. It

---

[59] *Ante*, 377.
[60] *The Concept of Law*, p. 116.
[61] *ibid.*, p. 117.
[62] This concept is discussed at pp. 56–58 and 88–90 and see *post*, 379–382.
[63] *ibid.*, p. 99.
[64] A. Skillen, *Ruling Illusions* (1977) refers to this, not inappropriately, as "white man's magic" (pp. 102–107).

lacks a central organ of adjudication with compulsory powers; it does not have (other than through multilateral treaties) a method for changing the rules to govern relationships between states; furthermore, there is no rule of recognition.[65]

Austin, we have seen, regarded neither primitive law nor international law as "law."[66] Hart does not agree. He draws a distinction between a "set" of rules and a "system." The most significant difference Hart puts like this: "In the simpler form of society we must wait and see whether a rules gets accepted as a rule or not; in a system with a basic rule of recognition we can say before a rule is actually made that it *will* be valid *if* it conforms to the requirements of the rule of recognition."[67] But, despite differences of form and structure, Hart detects essential similarities of content and function between simpler and complex cases. These similarities make it proper to think of "primitive law" and "international law" as sufficiently analogous to the more central case of the developed, modern municipal legal system to make it proper to describe them as "law." As far as content is concerned, both "primitive" societies and the international order contain among their primary rules elementary restrictions on violence, theft, breach of promise, etc. The explanation for this may be sought in terms of social function. As Hart puts it: "given survival as an aim, law and morals should include a specific content."[68]

This draws attention to another aspect of what Hart conceives to be part of legal order. He sees a core of good sense in natural law. If society is not to be a suicide club the legal orderings of human social communities must "naturally" embody a certain number of basic prohibitions, what he calls a "minimum content of natural law." This has been considered in Chapter 3.[69] Such limitations on conduct are common requirements of law and morality. There is, thus, an overlap between "law" and "morality." They are, nonetheless, concepts which Hart wishes to keep distinct. He distinguishes legal and moral obligations in terms of four "cardinal"[70] features of morality, each of which distinguish those "principles, rules and standards of conduct which are most commonly accounted 'moral'" from law: they are importance (some rules of law are, by contrast, of relative unimportance); immunity from deliberate change; the voluntary character of moral offences; and the "form" of moral pressure. Hart, as a positivist, does not believe that law is derived from morality, for, whatever the historical influence may be in the given case, there is no higher order to which law looks to take its authority. Furthermore, despite his espousal of a "minimum content of natural law," Hart is not saying that there is any necessary conceptual or definitional link between the legal and the moral. He does, however,

---

[65] See *post*, 384.
[66] *Ante*, 298.
[67] *The Concept of Law*, p. 100.
[68] *ibid.*, p. 193.
[69] *Ante*, 123–126.
[70] Hart, *op. cit.*, note 67, p. 173

acknowledge that the ultimate basis for preferring the positivist thesis, which insists on a clear differentiation of law and morals, is itself a moral one.[71] "A concept of law," he argues, "which allows the invalidity of law to be distinguished from its immorality, enables us to see the complexity and variety" of issues such as those that confront persons called upon to obey evil laws or those that German courts had to answer after the second world war.[72] Hart's differences with the naturalists come out well in his "debate" with Fuller.[73]

It was Hart's view that some laws, such as the Nazi decree at the centre of his debate with Fuller, were morally deficient, but law nonetheless. He argued that the creation of retroactive law was a lesser evil to tackle such a problem than the application of the morally suspect rule. But for Fuller it was the height of moral confusion for a court to refuse to apply something it admitted was law. However, in Hart's defence it may be said that he is distinguishing two questions: the identification of law and obligation to obey law so identified. Hart denied that the existence of law entailed an absolute obligation of obedience. Of course, in holding this position Hart is limiting himself to a small category of cases. Critics may argue that Hart is committed to the view that it is the judge's personal convictions about the law which determine its moral deficiency. An answer to this, though hardly satisfactory in the context of Nazi Germany or it may be feared other situations where the question is raised, is that the judge may claim that "the relevant moral criteria that are being transgressed are society's own professed moral standards," so that he is not using "public power for private ends because the ends sought are not private purposes ... but rather serve the coherence of public purposes."[74]

### The "Internal Aspect" of Law

It is at this stage that further reference needs to be made to Hart's discussion of, what he calls, the "internal" aspect of law. This constitutes a radical break with the thought of his positivist predecessors Austin and Bentham and also sharply differentiates Hart's thinking from that of his near-contemporary Kelsen. For Kelsen, as we have seen, there is a separate category of human thought (the "ought") radically distinct from the "is" and, therefore, from human psychology.[75] Hart's view is that normativity hinges on "human attitudes to human action."[76] Law, Hart

---

[71] See also his debate with Fuller, *post*, 414, 417.

[72] Hart, *op. cit.*, note 67, pp. 208–209.

[73] *Post*, 414. Hart now admits that the rule of recognition "may incorporate as criteria of legal validity conformity with moral principles or substantive values" (see *Concept of Law* ("Postscript"), p. 250).

[74] Per Belliotti, *Justifying Law* (1992), p. 54. See also the discussion *ante*. It is also worth asking whether the West German court which tried the grudge informer was part of the same legal system which tried her husband. Need the later legal system recognise the decisions of the earlier one? (And see *The Concept of Law*, pp. 118–120). For the view that positivism is authoritarian see D. Dyzenhaus (1992) 37 Amer. J. Jurisp. 83.

[75] *Ante*, 308.

[76] Per N. MacCormick, *op. cit.*, note 51, p. 25.

points out, depends not only on the external social pressures which are brought to bear on human beings, but also on the inner point of view that such beings take towards rules conceived as imposing obligations. In the case of a society with no more than a set of primary rules, it is necessary for its members not only to obey those rules but also consciously to view them as common standards of behaviour, violations of which are to be criticised, such criticisms being regarded as legitimate both by the offender and other members. In other words, in pre-legal societies an internal point of view on the part of its members is necessary for the preservation of group cohesion and solidarity. In legal systems, however, certainly in stable, mature ones, it is not necessary, says Hart, for citizens to possess an internal point of view. It is sufficient if the officials of the legal system have this view, though it is clearly desirable that citizens also experience it.[77]

Hart's explanation of social rules is thus dependent on a hermeneutic approach.[78] The hermeneutic approach is concerned with understanding the significance of human actions to those who do them and with how they interpret the actions of others. Hart introduces the internal aspect of rules to distinguish rules from habits. By contrast with those, like Austin, who stress the importance of "habits," what Hart is denying is the possibility of explaining rules solely by reference to external patterns of behaviour. To use an example of MacCormick's,[79] there is a difference between stopping one's car at red traffic lights and playing a car radio whilst stationary at the lights. To an outside observer there is little to differentiate the two activities, but to the insider the distinction lies in the different patterns of thought involved. In the case of stopping at red traffic lights, not doing so is considered to be a lapse in behaviour which is susceptible to criticism and such criticism is regarded as proper by others, indeed in most cases by the deviant motorist himself. This is not the case with failures to play car radios. Hart makes these points about criticism and its legitimacy before he introduces the concept of the internal point of view. They are, he says, included within it or at the very least fully understandable only by reference to it.

Accordingly, it is worth pondering on what Hart conceives this internal point of view to be. What is necessary, he writes, is "there should be a critical reflective attitude to certain patterns of behaviour as a common standard, and that this should display itself in criticism (including self-criticism), demands for conformity, and in acknowledgements that such criticism and demands are justified, all of which find their characteristic expression in the normative terminology of 'ought,' 'must' and 'should,'

---

[77] It may be essential where a society is in the throes of a revolution or has recently undergone major constitutional change.

[78] *Cf. ante*, 8. See further B. Rix (1999) 52 S.M.U. Law Rev. 167 and S. Perry in (ed.) A. Marmor, *Law and Interpretation* (1995), p. 97.

[79] MacCormick, *op. cit.*, note 51, pp. 30–31.

'right' and 'wrong.' "[80] But what comes first: criticism or attitude? Criticism is said to depend on the attitude but attitude is explained by reference to criticism and its justification. There is a circularity here which requires, but does not receive, further attention and explanation. Further, as MacCormick points out, reference to distinctive language like "ought," "must," etc., as part of the explanation of what is entailed in the critical reflective attitude does not assist, because such language is also a distinctive feature of situations where the speaker is not invoking any social rule. MacCormick gives the example of the vegetarian who says that eating meat is wrong.[81] But what this indicates is not that Hart is mistaken to introduce the internal viewpoint, for doing so constitutes a great advance on theories which concentrate on habits or regularities of behaviour, but rather that his analysis of the internal aspect may be incomplete. What is missing, MacCormick persuasively suggests, is an elucidation of "what is denoted by rules being generally *'accepted,'* *'supported'* by criticism, supported by *'pressure'* for conformity and so on."[82] He believes that such an elucidation must be by reference to a volitional element: "a wish or will that the pattern by upheld, a preference for conforming to non-conforming conduct."[83] On what are these wishes based? In part the answer may well be feelings that the individuals have, feelings of being bound, so that they want others to experience these same feelings. Hart, in believing that the internal aspect is often "misrepresented" as a "mere matter of feelings"[84] (which misrepresentation does often occur), may himself have underestimated the importance of the "emotional." In later writings[85] Hart has distinguished two types of statement (committed and detached) expressing an internal point of view. Both types of statement are of law, not about law. Committed statements are those made by persons who accept the rules; detached statements are made by persons who speak as if they accepted rules but do not commit themselves. A contemporary text on Roman law exemplifies this. But this distinction hardly seems very convincing. "A speaker's belief in the truth or correctness of a statement does not affect its meaning."[86] It may pertain to their force. Nor is the committed/detached distinction unique to normative discourse: scientists can make both a committed and a detached statement about a particular scientific theory.

That this is a problem which concerned Hart is evident from a new defence in his "Postscript". Responding to a criticism of Dworkin, he maintains that nothing in *The Concept of Law* would "preclude a non-participant external observer from describing the ways in which

---

[80] Hart, *op. cit.*, note 67, p. 57.
[81] MacCormick, *op. cit.*, note 51, p. 32.
[82] *ibid.*, p. 34.
[83] *ibid.*,
[84] Hart, *op. cit.*, note 67, p. 57.
[85] *Essays in Jurisprudence and Philosophy* (1983), p. 14; *Essays on Bentham* (1982), pp. 153–155. See also Raz, *The Authority of Law* (1979), pp. 153–157.
[86] *Per* M. Bayles, *op. cit.*, p. 55. See also P. Milton (1984) 47 M.L.R. 751, 754.

participants view the law from ... an internal point of view".[87] The descriptive legal theorist does not share the participants' acceptance of the law because he has this internal viewpoint but, stresses Hart, he must "*understand* what it is to adopt the internal point of view",[88] thought this does not require him to endorse it. But whilst this observer may understand it is necessary, it is difficult to see how he can understand what is involved. All the more so because Hart now apparently accepts that the internal perspective includes a belief that "there are *moral* reasons for conforming to the law's requirements and a *moral* justification of its use of coercion."[89] But supposing there are not—does Hart's theory enable the observer to keep sufficient distance to offer moral criticism of participants or indeed the system?[90]

## The Rule of Recognition

To understand the significance for Hart of the rule of recognition we must first examine Hart's criticisms of the Austinian view of sovereignty. Thus, he points out that a mere "habit of obedience" cannot explain the *continuity* of law, that is to say, the fact that obedience is rendered not merely to the initial ruler, but to his successor upon the demise of that ruler. First, and most significantly, because "habits are not normative; they cannot confer rights or authority on anyone"[91]; and secondly, because habits of obedience to one individual cannot, though "accepted rules" can, refer to a class of future successive legislators as well as the current one, or render obedience to them likely. So, as Hart maintains, "habitual obedience to one legislator neither affords grounds for the statement that his successor has the right to make law, nor for the factual statement that he is likely to be obeyed."[92] There is also the problem of accounting for the *persistence* of law[93]: why are Acts of Parliament passed in the nineteenth century still law today? The concept of habitual obedience cannot explain why: the citizens of today cannot be said habitually to obey a sovereign long since dead. Substitute for the "too simple notion" of habits of obedience the notion of "currently accepted fundamental rules specifying a class or line of persons whose word is to constitute a standard of behaviour for the society, *i.e.* who have the *right* to legislate"[94] and we have a more convincing explanation.

---

[87] Hart, *op. cit.*, n. 67, p. 242.
[88] *ibid.* But what if there are competing views within participants?
[89] *ibid.*, p. 243. A conclusion which (surprisingly) is not far from that adopted by Finnis (see *Natural Law and Natural Rights* (1980), pp. 3–18).
[90] It has been argued (by Holton (1998) 17 *Law and Philosophy* 597) that the internal point of view involves moral motivation. I share the doubt of A. Hatzistavrou (in Freeman and Harrison, *Law and Philosophy* (2007), p. 118) that this is so. See also S. Shapiro (1998) 4 *Legal Theory* 469, 489–492.
[91] *ibid.*, pp. 59–60.
[92] *ibid.*, p. 60.
[93] *ibid.*, pp. 61–66.
[94] *ibid.*, p. 62

There is also the problem of legal limitations on the sovereign.[95] Austin's theory could not accommodate these: sovereignty subject to legal limitations was for him a contradiction in terms.[96] Sovereigns laid down duties: how could they be subject to them? Hart points out that it is a misconception to view legal limitations as legal duties. They are, rather, legal disabilities.[97] " 'Limits' here implies not the presence of duty but the absence of legal power."[98] Restrictions on legislative power are "parts of the rule conferring authority to legislate and they vitally concern the courts, since they use such a rule as a criterion of the validity of purported legislative enactments coming before them."[99] Legislation, in these terms, which infringes such limitations is void.

This leads us to consider the rule of recognition. The rule (or rules—we will consider which shortly) provides authoritative criteria for identifying valid law within a particular legal system. How then is the rule of recognition to be ascertained? Hart points out that such a rule is often not expressly stated, but can be shown by the way in which particular rules (Hart says "primary" rules)[1] are identified by the courts and other legal officials. It is a form of social practice.[2] But this raises the first problem about it. As a practice it is presumably observable, but what could we be expected to observe in a court? Even if external behaviour were observable, we must not forget that the rule also has an internal aspect. Harris is led to the conclusion that the rule of recognition must be "an abstraction, a pure norm, arrived at inductively from observations of what lawyers do, but not itself witnessable."[3]

Whatever its juridical status, Hart tells us that the rule of recognition is ultimate and as an ultimate rule it can "neither be valid nor invalid."[4] Hart compares it to the metre bar in Paris, the ultimate test of the correctness of all measurement in metres, which we assume is itself correct. For Hart the only point is whether the rule of recognition is accepted as such by those who operate the system.

It is by no means clear what the nature of the rule of recognition is. As a secondary rule it ought to be power-conferring[5] but it does not confer a power as such on anyone. Hart also suggests that it may be a secondary rule in a weaker sense of being "about" primary rules.[6] But, if its function is identification then this is unnecessarily restrictive for it would need to be "about" other secondary rules as well. It should not be forgotten that most secondary rules confer law-making powers on private individuals.[7]

---

[95] *ibid.*, pp. 66–71.
[96] *Ante*, 253.
[97] Note the influence of Hohfeldian terminology, *post*, 396 and 569.
[98] Hart, *op. cit.*, note 67, p. 69.
[99] *ibid.*, p. 69.
[1] For the problem with this see *post*, 383–384.
[2] See W. Waluchow, *Inclusive Legal Positivism* (1994), p. 235.
[3] *Law and Legal Science* (1979), p. 62.
[4] Hart, *op. cit.*, note 67, p. 108.
[5] See *ibid.*, p. 81.
[6] *ibid.*, p. 94.
[7] *Ante*, 376.

This has led some, Raz,[8] MacCormick[9] as well as Hart himself, to suggest that the rule of recognition, despite ostensible associations with power-conferring secondary rules, is in reality duty-imposing. Intuitively this looks right: judges (presumably defined by rules of adjudication, validated by a rule of recognition, thus showing the essential circularity[10] of Hart's arguments) *have to* recognise as law that which satisfies certain authoritative standards. It is, therefore, puzzling that Hart should write that the word "obey" does not describe well "what judges do when they apply the system's rule of recognition and recognise a statute as valid law and use it in the determination of disputes."[11] It may not matter over much how we characterise the rule of recognition: as a rule of some "third" type, as an atypical secondary rule, even as a typical primary rule (without a sanction stipulated). Indeed, if it is social practice and nothing more it is questionable, to say the least, whether it is a rule at all.[12]

But should we be referring to "rule" or "rules" of recognition?[13] Hart seems to take two positions. Sometimes he makes it apparent that there is indeed one rule of recognition: in the United Kingdom this is "what the Queen in Parliament enacts is law."[14] But what of the other sources of law in the United Kingdom, what, for example, of the force of precedent? As a rule (if that is what it is, for it looks like a statement of fact) it is anyway too simple. What does "the Queen in Parliament" mean? What does "enacts" mean? An ultimate rule should not need to be interpreted by reference to (presumably) lower rules. It may be that Hart is merely saying that "what the Queen in Parliament enacts is law" is the actual practice of the British legal system. But if so, is there any point stipulating an additional rule to state this? Hart criticises Kelsen for doing as much in postulating a *Grundnorm* for international law.[15]

Hart also takes another position. At a number of places in *The Concept of Law* he describes the rule of recognition as specifying various criteria of validity and ranking them in order of precedence.[16] The rule of recognition is identified with the ranking of criteria. He further notes that where there are "several criteria ranked in order of relative subordination and primacy one of them is *supreme*."[17] In these terms "what the Queen in Parliament enacts is law" is supreme, but is neither sole (there are other authoritative sources) nor ultimate (the rule of recognition is the ultimate rule). This position has something in common with Kelsen's distinction between the constitution in the positive legal sense (the ultimate

---

[8] *The Concept of a Legal System* (1980), pp. 197–200.

[9] MacCormick, *op. cit.*, note 51, p. 105.

[10] And see Kramer (1988) 8 O.J.L.S. 401. Kramer refers to the rule of recognition as a "rule of misrecognition organised around a disrupted blindness" (p. 422).

[11] Hart, *op. cit.*, note 67, p. 113.

[12] *Cf.* Munzer, *Legal Validity* (1972).

[13] In *Essays on Bentham* he argues for a single rule of recognition (p. 155, n. 77). But in the "Postscript", there is reference once again to "rules" (p. 240).

[14] For example on p. 115.

[15] *Ante*, 323.

[16] For example, pp. 95, 100–101, 103.

[17] *op. cit.*, note 67, p. 105.

constitutional norms) and the constitution in the legal-logical sense (the *Grundnorm*), part of the function of which is to rank the ultimate constitutional norms.[18] And it takes a more plausible position than the previous one. But it is vague, and, not surprisingly, the rule is "very seldom expressly formulated as such."[19] Sometimes Hart seems to suggest that it embodies nothing but a ranking of criteria: at other times he indicates that other elements are included as well, such as rules of change.[20] Could the rule of recognition be more adequately formulated? In doing so is it not possible that one would end up writing a constitutional textbook? And if one did, one would not, of course, be stating a rule.

In the "Postscript", Hart has re-addressed the rule of recognition. In doing so he has offered new insights, some of which are really quite surprising. First, responding to Dworkin's criticism that he offers plain-fact positivism[21]—this would suggest that the criteria of legal validity can be reduced to some kind of "pedigree"[22] test—Hart retorts that the rule of recognition "may incorporate as criteria of legal validity conformity with moral principles or substantive values".[23] Secondly, he insists that the criteria provided by the rule of recognition may consist in "substantive constraints on the content of legislation"[24] (he uses examples in the U.S. Constitution but the articles in the European Convention on Human Rights now incorporated into U.K. law[25] are equally apposite). Thirdly, he rejects the idea that the rule of recognition's function is to provide for certainty to the exclusion of other values. The rule of recognition, he insists, may have a "debatable 'penumbra' of uncertainty".[26] However, as he acknowledges, it is a question of real moment how much uncertainty can be tolerated if there is to be "any significant advance from a decentralized regime of custom-type rules".[27] But is this only an empirical question or are other questions involved (whose uncertainty? how relevant is the perspective of the outside observer? how is uncertainty to be squared with the internal point of view?). Too much uncertainty and there will be very little difference between a mature system and a society with a set of rules.[28]

Hart sees the rule of recognition as a luxury[29] found in advanced social

---

[18] *Ante*, 316.

[19] Hart, *op. cit.*, note 67, p. 101.

[20] *ibid.*, p. 95. See also the discussion of desuetude on p. 103.

[21] See *Law's Empire* (1986), pp. 6–11. Hart prefers instead to call his variant of positivism "soft positivism".

[22] See Dworkin, *Taking Rights Seriously* (1977)

[23] *The Concept of Law*, p. 250.

[24] *ibid.*

[25] By the Human Rights Act 1998.

[26] *Op. cit.*, n. 67, p. 251.

[27] *ibid.*, p. 252.

[28] Hart does not consider whether there can be uncertainty in the rules of adjudication or rules of change.

[29] Hart, *op. cit.*, note 67, p. 103. But is it value diminished by acknowledgement now that it can be imbued with uncertainty?

systems, rather than as a necessity. Hart thus rejects the idea of Kelsen that a basic norm is an essential presupposition of all legal systems. In simpler forms of society we may have to wait and see whether a rule gets accepted or not. The rules of such a society are binding if they are accepted by the community but, of course, they would not be rules if they were not accepted.

Thus, says Hart, there is no reason at all why we should insist that there should be a basic norm in the international legal order.[30] Such an assertion depends, he claims, on a false analogy with municipal law. The insistence on the need for a basic norm often leads, as it does with Kelsen, to the rather empty repetition of the mere fact that society does observe certain standards as obligatory. Thus, Hart refers to the rather empty rhetorical form of the so-called basic norm of international law to the effect that "states should behave as they have customarily behaved."[31] This seems to be no more than an involved way of asserting the fact that there is a set of rules which are accepted by states as binding rules. Hart describes this as "mere useless reduplication."[32] He does not believe that there is a basic rule providing general criteria of validity for the rules of international law.[33]

### Is Law A System of Rules?

Hart's description of a legal system in terms of a union of primary and secondary rules provides a tool of analysis for much that has puzzled both jurist and political theorist. At the same time it may be wondered whether too much is claimed for this new view of old problems. There are times when Hart would appear to have moved little from Austin's command theory. Thus he writes: "So long as the laws which are valid by the system's tests of validity are obeyed by the bulk of the population this surely is all the evidence we need in order to establish that a given legal system exists."[34] Further, he concedes that there is more to a legal system than a union of rules. In particular, he stresses the "open texture" of rules,[35] as well as the distinctive relationship of law to morality and justice.

Hart's introduction of the "open texture" of rules is a recognition that (of course) legal rules cannot be expected to provide for every factual situation that may arise. Hart explains the problem with a simple

---

[30]  For Hart (*cf.* Austin, *ante*) international law is "law", though it is not a legal system (and see Bayles, *op. cit.*, p. 76).

[31]  As *per* Kelsen. See Hart, *op. cit.*, note 67, p. 236.

[32]  *ibid.*

[33]  On the rule of recognition and shifts in Hart's understanding of this from the original text to the revised edition in 1994 see J. Dickson (2007) 27 Ox. J.L.S. 373. For problems that Hart's analysis raises within a federal context, particularly in the U.S, see Greenawalt (1987) 85 Michigan L. Rev. 621 and (1988) 1 Ratio Juris. 40.

[34]  *ibid.*, p. 114.

[35]  See pp. 124–136, 272–273.

example (a rule that no vehicle may be taken into the park[36]). There is here a "core of certainty" (cars are clearly included) but a "penumbra of doubt" (there are situations where the application of the rule is uncertain—does it cover bicycles, roller skates, would it proscribe the mounting of a tank on a plinth to commemorate a battle?).[37] This is to be explained by two "handicaps" that the rule-maker (a human being rather than a god) labours under: "relative ignorance of fact" and relative "indeterminacy of aim".[38] It follows inevitably, according to Hart, that judges must use their discretion and make new law in penumbral situations. And this use of discretion is viewed positively by Hart (he draws a contrast between this conception which offers flexibility and one where formalism reigns[39]). There are, as Bix points out,[40] aspects of the "open texture" problem which derive from the nature of language (it lacks mathematical precision)—it is this upon which Hart primarily focuses— but aspects also related to the nature of rules and to suggestions as to the best ways of constructing dynamic systems of rules. Whether it follows from "open texture" that judges have (or should have) discretion to make law is not a question addressed by Hart. This omission may be attributable to a lower degree of concern or interest in judicial lawmaking then[41] (as opposed to now[42]) and in England (as contrasted with the United States). Hart was, however, clear that a judge could use moral standards in legislating in gaps in legal rules but that it did not follow from this that these standards were already there in the rules for the judge to find.[43]

Hart has had a number of critics, most notably Dworkin.[44] He has criticised Hart for representing law as a system of rules and for suggesting that, at certain points, the judges use their discretion and play a legislative role. Dworkin has argued (and he has not been alone)[45] that a conception of law as a system of rules fails to take account of, what he calls, "principles." He also maintains that judges do not have strong discretion, believing that even in "hard cases" there is "one right answer."[46]

Principles, he argues, are to be distinguished from rules in a number of ways. Principles, such as that no man may profit from his own wrong,

---

[36] *ibid.*, p. 126. A useful discussion of "open texture" is D. Lyons (1999) 18 Law and Philosophy 297.

[37] See (1958) 71 Harvard L.R. 593.

[38] *op. cit.*, p. 128.

[39] *ibid.*, pp. 129–130.

[40] *Law, Language and Legal Indeterminacy* (1993), pp. 22–25.

[41] Though a debate erupted in the late 1940s between Denning L.J. and Viscount Simonds. See *Seaford Court Estates v. Asher* [1949] 2 K.B. 481 and *Magor and St Mellons RDC v. Newport Corp.* [1952] A.C.189. *Shaw v. DPP* [1962] A.C.220 is almost contemporaneous with the *Concept*.

[42] An interest which has increased with the Human Rights Act 1998.

[43] *Op. cit.*, n. 21b, pp. 614–615 and *cf.* Dworkin, *post*, 1343.

[44] Hart now concedes that in the *Concept* he devoted far too little attention to adjudication, legal reasoning and principles (p. 259).

[45] See also R. Sartorius, *Social Policy and Judicial Legislation* (1971) and G. Hughes 77 Yale L. J. 411.

[46] Dworkin's thesis is further considered later in this chapter and in Chap. 18. On strong discretion see Waluchow (1983) 33 Phil. Q. 321.

differ from rules "in the character of the discretion they give"[47] for, while rules are applicable in an all-or-nothing fashion, principles state "a reason that argues in one direction but [do] not necessitate a particular decision. . . . All that is meant, when we say that a particular principle is a principle of our law, is that the principle is one which officials must take into account, if it is relevant, as a consideration inclining in one direction or another."[48] Further, principles have a dimension of weight or importance that rules lack. Rules, by contrast, are functionally important. Principles can conflict, and often do: if rules clash, a further rule is needed to regulate the conflict *(e.g.* if law and equity conflict, it is provided that equity prevails).[49] A further difference is that the force of a principle may become attenuated over a period of time: its strength may become eroded. Not so with rules: to use Dworkin's phrase, when they have served their use they are "torpedoed."[50]

That the differences between rules and principles can be over-emphasised is manifest in any detailed examination of the common law.[51] Hart himself in his "Postscript" has rightly raised important questions.[52] Do valid rules always determine the outcome of a case? No, Hart points out, for another rule may be judged more important.[53] That rules are not "all-or-nothing" is, Hart shows, demonstrated by the very example Dworkin uses to point to the importance of "principles" (*Riggs v. Palmer* [54]): a very clear rule was there defeated (in this instance) by a well-entrenched principle.[55] These rules survive to be used in subsequent cases where, in the first instance, they are regarded as more important than the other rule, and, in the second example, where they are considered more important than a competing principle. Nevertheless, Hart concedes he was wrong to neglect the role in legal reasoning played by non-conclusive principles, though he adds that he did discuss "variable legal standards"[56] and did explain why some areas of conduct were suitable for regulation not by such standards but by near-conclusive rules.[57]

Dworkin argues that positivist models of the judicial process, such as Hart's, cannot accommodate principles, and that it is this which makes them employ the concept of discretion.[58] And then "we can no longer speak of [the judge] being bound by standards, but must speak rather of

---

[47]  *Taking Rights Seriously* (1978), p. 24.
[48]  *ibid.*, p. 26.
[49]  See for an example of this *Walsh v. Lonsdale* (1882) 21 Ch.D. 9.
[50]  Dworkin, *op. cit.*, note 47, p. 40.
[51]  And see N. MacCormick, *Legal Reasoning and Legal Theory* (1978).
[52]  As Raz (1972) 81 Yale L.J. 823, 832–834 and Waluchow (1985) 5 Ox J.L.S. 187, 189–192 had already done.
[53]  *Op. cit.*, p. 261.
[54]  (1889) 22 N.E. 188: see Dworkin, *Taking Rights Seriously*, p. 23 and *Law's Empire*, pp. 15 *et seq.*
[55]  A recent discussion of the principle is *J v. S-T* [1997] 1 F.L.R. 402.
[56]  *Op. cit.*, p. 263.
[57]  So legal systems have specific rules (*e.g.* against murder) and not just principles upholding the sanctity of human life. *cf.* his minimum content of natural law at p. 194.
[58]  An excellent critique is L. Alexander and K. Kress in (ed.) A. Marmor, *Law and Inter pretation* (1995), p. 279 and *post*, 821.

what standards he 'characteristically uses.' "[59] This, Dworkin maintains, casts doubt on the positivist contention that law must be identified by some ultimate test of validity, such as Hart's rule of recognition. Though Hart, in a little-noticed note,[60] accepts permissive as well as mandatory sources of law, it is hardly surprising that the use which judges make of principles cannot be explained by this rule of recognition. That rule gives us the capacity to identify a law (*i.e.* a rule which *must* be applied in given situations), and principles are standards which are to be considered as inclining in one direction or another. But there is no reason why an ultimate test should not be formulated by which rules and principles could be identified. For example, "in the absence of binding statute and governing precedent courts must take into account principles to be found in legislation and the decisions of courts." It is not difficult to find support for the principles which Dworkin cites in the *dicta*, if not the *rationes decidendi*, of earlier decisions.[61] Further, it would seem that Dworkin himself comes close to accepting something like a master rule, because he distinguishes between settled law in which principles are embedded from unsettled law which provides the "hard cases" which are to be decided by the principle so derived.[62] Dworkin's strongest argument for principles binding judges is that if they don't, then neither do rules. Statutes and prior decisions are the main sources of rules but judges are only required to apply these because of the principles of legislative supremacy and *stare decisis*. It is these principles that make rules binding. Thus, a system of rules that judges have a duty to apply "the law" is not possible unless principles also bind the judges.[63]

It is perfectly possible to construct, as MacCormick has done, a positivist theory of law and adjudication which incorporates principles. It is MacCormick's view that principles do belong within the genus "law" and "interact with the rules, underpin them, hedge them in, qualify them, [and] justify the enunciation of new rulings as tested out by consequentialist arguments."[64] He sees the law as like a caterpillar tractor, "an endless belt which is continuously moving through time."[65] He disagrees with Dworkin who believes that the law is gapless.[66] There are, he avers, gaps, these being filled in "by extrapolation from what is already there."[67] Further, MacCormick denies that judges may exercise, what Dworkin calls, "strong discretion."[68] There are considerable constraints

---

[59] *ibid.*, p. 34, quoting *The Concept of Law*, p. 147.
[60] Hart, *op. cit.*, note 67, p. 294. Unfortunately, this is not developed in the text.
[61] Thus all the principles discussed in *Henningsen v. Bloomfield Motors* (1960) 161 A. (2d) 69 (one of the cases Dworkin uses, *op. cit.*, pp. 23–24) can be found in earlier decisions. See "Postscript", p. 266.
[62] *Cf.* Hart (1976) 51 *New York University Law Rev.* 549.
[63] *op. cit.*, note 47, pp. 29 *et seq.* See also Bayles, *op. cit.*, p. 167.
[64] *Legal Reasoning and Legal Theory* (1978), p. 244.
[65] *ibid.*, p. 246.
[66] See *post*, 719.
[67] MacCormick, *op. cit.*, note 64, pp. 246.
[68] *ibid.*, p. 251.

on what the judges may do.[69] No other decision-makers are compelled to expose their reasoning processes in the way that judges are. But Mac-Cormick does not agree with Dworkin that the limited discretion judges have can be characterised as "weak," with all that that implies. There is, MacCormick demonstrates and we shall see, a residual area of "pure practical disagreement."[70]

Hart's "Postscript" contains an attempt to incorporate principles within a positivist framework.[71] As MacCormick maintained,[72] Hart too now insists that "there is nothing in the non-conclusive character of principles nor in their other features to preclude their identification by pedigree criteria".[73] And there are examples where this has happened, not least the principle that "no man shall profit from his own wrong". Is Dworkin's criticism therefore, Hart asks, rather the more modest claim that "there are many legal principles that cannot be so [identified] because they are too numerous, too fleeting, or too liable to change or mod-ification, or have no feature which would permit their identification as principles of law by reference to any other test than that of belonging to that coherent scheme of principles which both best fits the institutional history and practices of the system and best justifies them"?[74] Is what is required then a criterion which would enable principles to be identified by reference to their content, rather than their pedigree? Hart seems to be saying that he and Dworkin are closer than either of them thought, perhaps suggesting that he ought to have concentrated less attention in the "Postscript" on Dworkin and more perhaps (ironically) on Raz.

But major differences with Dworkin remain, and the "Postscript" continues to address these. As Hart puts it:

> "The main difference between my view and Dworkin's here is that whereas I ascribe the general agreement found among judges as to the criteria for the identification of the sources of law to their shared acceptance of *rules* providing such criteria, Dworkin prefers to speak not of rules, but of 'consensus' and 'paradigms' and 'assumptions' which members of the same interpretive com-munity share."[75]

Hart's "officials" are not engaged in "constructive" interpretation as Dworkin's judges are: they are not engaged in a project of seeing law in its "best possible moral light". Is it that the projects which Hart and Dworkin pursue are so very different? Hart's *Concept* does not purport to provide a theory of adjudication. True, this is addressed more in the "Postscript", but it is in this that Hart himself most fully articulates his project (and the differences he perceives to exist with Dworkin). Whereas

---

[69] See also M. D. A. Freeman (1973) *Current Legal Problems*, p. 166 and see *post*, 1533.
[70] *op. cit.*, note 64, p. 251.
[71] Hart, *The Concept of Law*, ("Postscript"), pp. 263–268.
[72] *Ante*, 389.
[73] Hart, ("Postscript"), *op. cit.*, p. 264.
[74] *ibid.*, p. 265.
[75] *ibid.*, p. 266.

he sees legal theory as general and descriptive and morally neutral, he locates Dworkin's jurisprudence within a particular (Anglo-American) culture.[76]

## RAZ AND REASONS FOR ACTION

Of all Hart's successors Joseph Raz would generally be regarded as the most significant. Whilst it is impossible to do justice to the range[77] and complexity of his thought, some comments on his approach and his distinctive contribution to contemporary thinking about law are called for.

Raz is categorised (by others, for example Coleman[78] and Waluchow[79]) as an "exclusive legal positivist".[80]

He himself offers the "social thesis" as what he considers to be the core of legal positivism.[81] The main justification of the social thesis lies in "the character of law as a social institution".[82] What is law is a matter of social fact. The tests, Raz argues, for the identity and existence of a legal system contain three elements; efficacy, institutional character and sources. And in his view most positivists (those whom we may now call "inclusive legal positivists") emphasise efficacy and institutionality as the "only conditions"[83] concerning the social foundation of law. Raz rejects this "weak" social thesis in favour of a "strong" one which insists that the "existence and content of every law is fully determined by social sources".[84] The "weak" thesis is, Raz maintains, insufficient to characterise legal positivism and is "compatible" with a statement like "Sometimes the identification of some laws turns on moral arguments" which is "on the borderline of positivism".[85] Though some have so argued,[86] Raz is clear that the sources thesis is not about "the pursuit of certainty".[87] It does not distinguish between ways of establishing the law with certainty and those open to doubt, but between "non-evaluative and evaluative

---

[76] On Hart's methodological positivism see S. Perry (1998) 4 *Legal Theory* 427 and *post*, 510. Dworkin's distinct but related criticism of Hart (and others) in terms of "semantic sting" is considered in Chap. 7.

[77] This includes ethical and political thought as well as philosophy generally, reflected in respectively *Ethics In The Public Domain* (1994), *The Morality of Freedom* (1986) and *Engaging Reasons* (1999).

[78] *The Practice of Principle* (2001), p. 105.

[79] *Inclusive Legal Positivism* (1994); see also (2000) 6 *Legal Theory* 45.

[80] In *Inclusive Legal Positivism*, pp. 103–119.

[81] *The Authority of Law* (1979), p. 38.

[82] *ibid.*, p. 42.

[83] *ibid.*, p. 45.

[84] *ibid.*, p. 46.

[85] *ibid.*, p. 47. An example of this "borderline" is Hart's restatement in his "Postscript" that a system of law might incorporate within ultimate criteria of validity "principles of justice or substantive moral values" (p. 247).

[86] For example, G. Postema in (ed.) R. George, *The Autonomy of Law* (1996), p. 79.

[87] (1998) 4 *Legal Theory* 1, 8.

criteria".[88] It is about "finality".[89] For others, in particular Campbell, Raz's strong thesis can be seen as "prescription" to legislatures and judges rather than as "an analysis".[90] As he puts it:

> "We may interpret Raz's 'sources thesis' [as] contending that 'a jurisprudential theory is acceptable only if itstest for identifying the content of law and determining its existence depends exclusively on facts of human behaviour capable of being described in value-free terms, and applied without resort to moral argument'".[91]

Campbell is thus able to endorse the sources thesis as consistent with his own Ethical Positivism.[92]

Raz takes no view on whether judges should make new law. His point is that it is just clearer, as well as closer to the way we think and talk about the law, to separate the application of the law from the making of new law. He is thus able to conclude that whilst law is autonomous, *i.e.* it is possible to identify the content of law without recourse to moral reasoning, legal reasoning is not autonomous *i.e.* moral reasoning does (and should) play a part in saying how judges should decide cases according to law.[93]

Raz maintains that it is in the very nature of law and legal systems that they necessarily claim justified practical authority over a population.[94] It follows that a legal system must be the sort of institution logically capable of possessing authority, and also that legal directives must at least purport to have a special status.[95] Legal directives occupy a mediating role between people and "the right reasons"[96] which apply to them. They must "occupy, as all authority does, a mediating role between the precepts of morality and their application by people in their behaviour".[97] Authoritative legal directives provide both first-order reasons to do or refrain from doing what they specify and second-order reasons which exclude "dependent reasons", right reasons (including moral reasons) which would otherwise apply. In accepting the authority of the legal directive, we accept that we cannot act directly on the excluded dependent reasons. So "the authority's directives become our reasons".[98] We accept authority because we understand that its directives "yield benefits they

---

[88]  *ibid.*
[89]  *ibid.* This does not mean "nonrevisability" (see *ibid.*, n. 30).
[90]  *The Legal Theory of Ethical Positivism* (1996), p. 3.
[91]  *ibid.*, p. 85, and quoting J. Raz, *Practical Reason and Norms* (1990), pp. 39–40.
[92]  See *The Legal Theory of Ethical Positivism* (1996).
[93]  *Op. cit.*, note 90, pp. 4–6. He is responding to Postema, *op. cit.*, note 10.
[94]  *Cf.* H. Hurd (1991) 100 Yale L.J. 1611 and L. Alexander (1990) 18 *Philosophical Topics* 5.
[95]  Though, ironically, Raz doubts whether there is ever an obligation to obey the law based on the legitimate authority of its directives. See *The Authority of Law* (1979), p. 233, and *post*, 408.
[96]  *Ethics In The Public Domain* (1994), p. 214.
[97]  *ibid.*, pp. 225–226.
[98]  *Practical Reason and Norms* (1990), p. 193.

are meant to bring only if we do rely on them rather than on our own independent judgment of the merits of each case".[99]

How does this analysis differ from Hart's? For Hart, one can only speak of something as a rule in a community if there is a critical reflective attitude towards it,[1] if, in other words, it is social "practice".[2] But there are rules which are not practices (how many observe the 30 m.p.h. speed limit?), and Raz adds Hart's practice theory of norms cannot distinguish social rules and "widely accepted reasons",[3] as well as depriving rules of their normative character. Raz concedes that an analysis of legal rules has to make reference to a social practice, but the reason he gives for this is that they are legal rules, and not just rules. Raz, as we have seen,[4] defines rules in terms of the role they play in practical reasoning.

Nor does Raz entirely reject the internal point of view. What he substitutes for it he calls "statements from a point of view" or "detached normative statement".[5] These are found whenever a person "advises or informs another on his normative situation in contexts which make it clear that the advice or information is given from a point of view or on the basis of certain assumptions which are not necessarily shared by the speaker".[6] Raz gives the example of the orthodox but ill-informed Jew who asks his friend (a Catholic who is expert in Rabbinical Law) whether he should (for example, eat the bacon which has been served to the two of them in a restaurant). The Jew is asking what he should do according to his religion, not his friend's religion. The friend may personally think he should eat the bacon, but he knows he is being asked what is expected according to the norms of the Jewish religion. The Catholic friend is not "endorsing" Rabbinical law, rather asserting what is the case from the relevant point of view.[7] The same, Raz points out, applies to the lawyer who in effect says to his client "if you accept the law as valid, you should do x". But this is surely to miss an important distinction between friends and lawyers.

## RIGHTS

Thinking about rights ("rights-talk") is a pervasive concern of modern analytical jurisprudence. This section discusses two questions relating to

---

[99] *ibid.* See further *post*, 408, in relation to whether there is an obligation to obey the law.
[1] *Ante*, 340.
[2] But see Hart's response to Dworkin's criticism in *The Concept of Law* (1994), pp. 254–259.
[3] *Op. cit.*, note 22, p. 53. And see *post*, 461.
[4] They are "exclusionary reasons" (see pp. 49–84).
[5] *Op. cit.*, note 98, pp. 153–157.
[6] *ibid.*, p. 156.
[7] *ibid.*, pp. 156–157.

rights. The relationship between justice and rights is considered in a later chapter.[8]

## The Nature of Rights

There are two competing theories as to the nature of rights: one emphasises will or choice; the other interest or benefit. Each appears in "various manifestations and a long-running inconclusive series of test matches"[9] has been fought between them.[10]

The will theory, notably propagated by Hart,[11] is subscribed to by those who view the purpose of law as being to grant the widest possible means of self-expression to the individual, the maximum degree of individual self-assertion. The theory is closely related to ideas of sovereignty,[12] so that the only way reconciling conflicting wills is by postulating a superior will which can overcome all opposition. It is also closely related to ideas of moral individualism.[13] The theory identifies the right-bearer by virtue of the power that s/he has over the duty in question. S/he can waive it, extinguish it, enforce it or leave it unenforced. This decision is his/her choice. "Individual discretion is the single most distinctive feature of the concept of 'rights'."[14]

There are a number of difficulties with this view.[15] It would seemingly allow all rights to be waived. Most of us, however, believe that our duties not to kill or torture cannot be set aside by our potential victims releasing us from our duties. This suggests that Hart's account of the nature of rights is morally, if not also conceptually, inadequate. A further difficulty focuses on a procedural problem. As Gerber puts it: "the substantive right is one thing, and having a right is to claim it is another".[16] Some rights-holders lack the standing to bring their grievances forward. Children, for example, do not have the "right" to sue. There is a service available to them: they may sue through their "next friend" (usually a

---

[8]   Of course, one cannot entirely separate discussion about the nature of rights from their political justification. This is recognised by N. MacCormick (see in (ed.) M. Cohen, *Ronald Dworkin and Contemporary Jurisprudence* (1983), p. 182) who comments that anyone who wishes to give rights the kind of primacy that Dworkin wishes to give them in a political theory must think harder than Dworkin has thought about their nature" (p. 193).

[9]   *Per* N. MacCormick, *Legal Rights and Social Democracy* (1983), p. 154. M. Kramer, N. Simmonds and H. Steiner, *A Debate Over Rights* (1998) offers the best recent discussion about different conceptions of rights. Also useful is L. Wenar (2005) 33 *Phil and Public Affairs* 223.

[10]  There was a third view, which related rights to power. It was found in seventeenth-century writers like Spinoza and Hobbes and was standard to nineteenth-Century positivist accounts as well (*e.g.* in Austin). A variant is the realist explanation that rights are expectations. But see Hart, *Essays in Jurisprudence and Philosophy* (1983), p. 28.

[11]  See (1955) 64 Phil. Rev. 175; *Essays on Bentham* (1982), Chap. VII.

[12]  See Austin's exposition of this, *ante* 251; Bentham's at *ante*, 22.

[13]  And see J.S. Mill, *On Liberty* (1859).

[14]  *Per* R. Flathman, *The Practice of Rights* (1976).

[15]  Hart conceded that it fails to offer an adequate account of all legal rights, let alone moral ones. See *op. cit.*, note 10 (*Essays*).

[16]  "Rights" (1976) 62 A.R.S.P. 329, 333.

parent). But what if that person refuses to assist, or is the alleged duty bearer? These difficulties cast no doubt over the existence of the right, merely over an analysis which ties such rights to choice.

MacCormick used the question of children's rights to challenge the will theory.[17] The theory would argue in relation to children's rights that it is sufficient if some person acting on the child's behalf has the relevant powers over the duty in respect of the child. But, as indicated, that person is usually the parent, and s/he has the duty as well. The fact that powers are also given to others (local authorities, for example) does not assist, because these powers do not constitute the rights. They protect rights which are already there. This, says MacCormick, confuses substantive rights with ancillary remedial provisions: "It is unduly anglo-centric to erect the brocard 'ubi remedium ibi ius' into an analytic truth."[18]

The attribution of rights to animals, trees,[19] sea-shores, etc.—now common with concern for animal life and the environment prominent—also causes difficulties for the will theory, for what will can animals, let alone mountain peaks have? In truth, these issues cause the interest theory just as great a headache. Can animals or trees "benefit" from having a right conferred upon them? At best, someone other than the alleged holder of the right thinks that the tree does, or would, benefit. Surely, though, Flathman is right to say of such rights talk that it is "no more than inflated rhetoric",[20] and that it makes more sense to talk of good and bad treatment of animals, trees, etc., or good and bad policies towards the environment. That humans have duties towards animals (for example, under cruelty legislation) does not confer rights on them. The duty is in respect of the animal, not towards it.

The interest (or benefit) theory is first found in the writings of Bentham, and was adopted by Jhering.[21] It is today espoused by MacCormick,[22] Raz,[23] Lyons,[24] Campbell[25] and others. It argues that the purpose of rights is not to protect individual assertion but certain interests. Rights are said to be benefits secured for persons by rules regulating relationships. One version of the benefit theory says that X has a right whenever he stands to benefit from the performance of a duty (of course in utilitarian terms all duties are designed to promote some benefit). Another (found in MacCormick, Raz and Campbell) says that X can have a right (whether in moral theory or within a legal system) whenever the protection or the advancement of an interest of his is recognised (by moral theory or the legal system, as the case may be) as a reason for imposing

---

[17] *Legal Rights and Social Democracy* (1982), pp. 154–166.
[18] *ibid.*, p. 157.
[19] See C. Stone, *Should Trees Have Standing?* (1974).
[20] *Op. cit.*, note 77, p. 73. Further criticisms are found in T. Campbell, *The Left and Rights* (1983), pp. 87–92 and (1985) 5 *Legal Studies* 10.
[21] Who is discussed, *post*, 662.
[22] In (eds.) P. Hacker and J. Raz, *Law, Morality and Society* (1977).
[23] In (ed.) R.G. Frey, *Utility and Rights* (1985), p. 42.
[24] (1969) 6 Amer. Phil.Q. 173.
[25] *Op. cit.*, note 20 (*The Left*), pp. 92–102.

obligations, whether they are actually imposed or not. This has the advantage of enabling us to talk of rights in advance of determining exactly who has the duty, or needing to spell out in detail what is comprised in the duty.

The particular strength of the interest theory is that it covers all types of rights (the so-called socio-economic rights such as health care, education, a minimum income) as well as "liberties". The will theory is happier with the latter, What the interest theory does not explain is why rights should be tied to benefit is the first place. Can X's interests be advanced by a rule without that rule conferring on him/her rights? A parent's interests may be advanced by the rule limiting the contracts that a minor child may make, but no rights are conferred on the parent by that rule. Despite problems such as these, the interest theory remains the most convincing explanation of what having a right entails.

### Hohfeld's Analysis of Rights

There are clearly different types of "right". The concept is used ambiguously. Hohfeld (1879–1918) was not the first jurist to note this,[26] but his account (in two articles published in 1913 and 1917[27]) was the most rigorous and remains today, despite its faults, the source to which most (and not just jurists) return.[28]

The sentence "X has a right to R is, of course, different from 'X has a book'. The former is a normative statement, the latter a descriptive one. The 'truth' of normative statements may only be established by reference to rules (legal or otherwise). But 'X has a right to R' may, Hohfeld showed, be used to depict a number of different ideas which in everyday discourse, including legal discourse, were easily confused. His articles point to examples of sloppy judicial reasoning.[29] He sought through a schema to clarify different kinds of 'legal relations'. He did so by relating concepts to their 'correlatives' and 'opposites'[30] or class complements.[31]

He shows that the sentence "X has a right to R" may mean that Y (or indeed everyone) has a duty to let X do R, so that X has a claim against Y. The claim (not itself a particularly good term to stipulate since it

---

[26] Bentham distinguished rights and liberty; Austin made a few tentative and exploratory suggestions; Windscheid distinguished right and power; Terry and Salmond also began to analyse the concepts involved. This is explored in detail by J. Singer (1982) Wisc. L. Rev. 1975.

[27] (1913) 23 Yale L.J. 16; (1917) 26 Yale L.J. 710 (also *Fundamental Legal Conceptions As Applied in Judicial Reasoning* (1919). See *post*, 510.

[28] Amongst recent analyses and critiques of Hohfeld the following may be noted: A Halpin (2003) 16 Can. J. Law & Jurisprudence 41; V. Brown (2005) 58 C.L.P. 343; P. Jaffey (2006) 12 *Legal Theory* 137; A Halpin (2007) 13 *Legal Theory* 23.

[29] See, *e.g. S.S. Mogul v. McGregor* (1889) 23 Q.B.D. 59 and *Quinn v. Leathem* [1901] A.C. 495.

[30] The term "opposites" may be objected to. Kocourek says it is illogical "That which is not a right could be an elephant, star or angel" (*Jural Relations* (1927)). Thus, "contradictory" is often preferred.

[31] *Per* J. Stone, *Legal Systems and Lawyers' Reasonings* (1964), p. 139.

suggests something asserted but not necessarily recognised) is the right *stricto sensu*.[32]

The sentence may, however, and usually does, mean that X is free to do or refrain from doing something. It is not a question of what Y must do (or not do), but of what X may do. Hohfeld called this "right" a "privilege"[33]: others have preferred to call it a "liberty".[34] Privilege confers a special position and accurately captures some "privileges" (for example, the rule that a judge does no legal wrong in speaking slander when acting in a judicial capacity). However, exceptions on account of status are only one type of privilege: that we can do whatever the law allows us to do translates into Hohfeldian terminology as a privilege to do whatever is not a breach of duty.[35] Other "privileges" are legally granted for example, the Abortion Act 1967 permits doctors in specified circumstances to perform abortions that would otherwise be unlawful.

The word "right" is also sometimes used where what is meant is "power".[36] X has a power when s/he has the ability to change legal relationships, for example by making a contract or a will. Powers are usually parasitic on claim-rights and privileges: the owner of property may sell it because s/he has title to it (that is a complex of rights *stricto sensu*, privileges and, indeed, powers). But powers may also exist independently of other sorts of rights: for example, a trustee with a duty not to transfer trust property to another (and so no privilege or claim-right to transfer it) has the power to effect such a transfer if the purchaser acts without notice and in good faith.

Finally, the term "right" is sometimes used to describe the absence of a power—an immunity. Where Y lacks the power to produce a change in X's legal relations, X has an immunity.

The undoubted value of Hohfeld's analysis, whatever its limitations, should not blind us to the fact that there are common features shared by

---

[32] On the relationship between claims and rights see M.A. Stewart, *Law, Morality and Rights* (1983), particularly the articles by A. White and N. MacCormick. See also A. White, *Rights* (1984), Chap. 8. White's views have stimulated a lively debate, samples of which are MacCormick (1982) 1 Law & Phil. 337, S. Stoljar (185) 4 Law & Phil. 101 and A. Halpin (1991) 10 Law & Phil. 271.

[33] He himself sometimes uses the term wrongly: he talks of the "privilege of self-defence" (p. 33), but must mean the "right of self-defence". The "natural rights" Hobbes believes we have in a state of nature would be characterised by Hohfeld as privileges.

[34] See, *e.g.* Glanville Williams in (ed.) R.S. Summers, *Essays In Legal Philosophy* (1968), p. 121. The reason is that privilege suggests special favour to an individual or narrow class. It is Williams's contention that "privilege" is better conceived as a "privilege not". So if A has no right that B pays him £5, B is at liberty *not to* pay £5 (he has a "privilege not" or "liberty not").

[35] But many legal privileges are not absences of duty: Parliamentary privilege, for example, is immunity from an action in defamation. There are examples also where a defendant is absolved from, what would otherwise be, his duty, but where it would be inaccurate to characterise this as privilege (an instance is the *volenti nonfit iniuria* plea) There are also situations where a person may be privileged because he has a duty to do what he had done (consider the qualified privilege defence in defamation).

[36] See, further, A.R. White, *op. cit.*, note 94, Chap. 10.

all these types of rights. What MacCormick calls "normative security"[37] can be achieved in a number of ways. What Hohfeld has demonstrated are the separate ways in which this can be done.

There are many problems with Hohfeld's analysis. I point to a few major difficulties.

First, he purports to analyse fundamental legal concepts, but he has no concept of law, nor does he attempt to define what it is that gives his conceptions their "legal character".

Secondly, there is no adequate explication of what legal relations are. There is no discussion of the role that legal concepts play.[38] Though there is no real examination of the question, Hohfeld seems to assume that the word "right" denotes some entity.[39]

Thirdly, most, if not all, of Hohfeld's examples are drawn from private law. This may account for the cursory, and inadequate, treatment he gives to the concept of "duty". Whilst Hohfeld is correct to state that every right *stricto sensu* implies the existence of a correlative duty, not every duty implies a correlative right. Non-correlative duties do not seem to have a place in Hohfeld's scheme. This suggests that Hohfeld would find it difficult to explain whole areas of law, most obviously criminal law. By his failure to analyse "duty" Hohfeld misses the point that duties are not all of one type. There are prohibitions backed up by sanctions (the criminal law provides the paradigm of this), but there are also different types of regulation and many civil law duties. These, for example the duty to take reasonable care in the law of negligence, are related to issues of liability in ways Hohfeld does little to explain. Fourthly, other concepts are also explained inadequately. For example, power is described in terms of control. But control itself is not further explicated or discussed. And right *stricto sensu* is described in terms of claim, but claiming itself is far from an uncontentious or unambiguous activity.[40] For example, does *a* right imply a claim,[41] or imply a right *to* claim[42]?

Despite these faults, it is generally agreed that Hohfeld has uncovered longstanding confusions and offered valuable analytical clarification. His schema remains a starting-point for much contemporary rights analysis. It has been found useful by moral philosophers, by anthropologists,[43] by comparative lawyers, as well as by jurists.[44] Its value essentially lies in its enabling us to reduce any legal transaction (or moral relationship) to relative simplicity and precision, and to recognise its universality.

---

[37] His analysis of these ways, and of the essentially unitary concept of rights, is enlightening: see *op. cit.*, note 32.

[38] On this see A.W.B. Simpson (1964) 80 L.Q.R. 535 and A. Ross, "Tu-Tu" (*post*, 1074).

[39] Hohfeld, *op. cit.*, note 90, p. 30. On denotation see *ante*, 33.

[40] See, further, White, *op. cit.*, note 32, Chap. 18.

[41] See, *e.g.* M. Golding (1968) 52 Monist 521, 530–532.

[42] See, *e.g.* J. Feinberg (1966) 3 Amer.Phil.Q. 137, 143.

[43] Notably Hoebel (*post*, 1103).

[44] For the influence on Realism, the CLS movement and feminist jurisprudence see J. Balkin (1990) 44 Univ. of Miami L. Rev. 1119. Balkin suggests Hohfeld was the first legal semiotician (on semiotics see *post*, 1418).

## HUMAN RIGHTS

Central to much legal thinking today are human rights. Of course, this is not novel. In the U.S. it was taken to be "self-evident" in 1776 that all were "endowed by their Creator with certain inalienable rights";[45] in France 13 years later we were told that "men are born and remain free and equal in rights".[46] Such statements were not accepted by all: Bentham was an early critic, dismissing them as "nonsense upon stilts".[47] The human rights claimed today go beyond those then argued for, economic and social rights, for example, rights to life's necessities and to health care, the so-called "second generation rights". And they include children's rights, which was certainly not envisaged in the late eighteenth century.[48] Many who accept human rights do not believe second generation rights are included,[49] and few accept children's rights as human rights[50] (though the U.N. Convention on the Rights of The Child of 1989 is the most ratified of international treaties).

Amartya Sen points to a number of questions that a theory of human rights must address.[51]

i.   what kind of a statement does a declaration of human rights make?
ii.  what is it that makes human rights important?
iii. as rights, what obligations are entailed?
iv.  how are human rights best promoted? Must legislation (for example an instrument like the European Convention on Human Rights) be the primary way of implementing human rights? Indeed, is it a necessary pre-condition?
v.   is it reasonable to argue that the second generation rights are human rights?
vi.  how can arguments for human rights be defended (or challenged)? Given cultural diversity and pluralism in practice,[52] can it really be said that human rights are universal? Or are they invoked to impose Western ("capitalistic") values on the rest of the world?

Sen summarises his answers to these questions as follows.

---

[45]   U.S. Declaration of Independence. For the influence of Locke see *ante*, 107. See also M. Zuckert (2005) 22(1) *Social Philosophy and Policy* 27. See for a full account J. Mahoney, *The Challenge of Human Rights* (2007).
[46]   Note "men". This led a feminist actress, Olympe de Gouges to write the *Declaration of the Rights of Women and Citizenesses*: see S. Schama, *Citizens* (1989), 498.
[47]   In *Anarchical Fallacies* (1792).
[48]   See M. Freeman, *The Moral Status of Children* (1997), p. 47.
[49]   On second generation rights see W. Felice, *The Global New Deal: Economic and Social Human Rights in World Politics* (2003) and T. Pogge, *World Poverty and Human Rights* (2002). Critics include M. Ignatieff, *Human Rights as Politics and Idolatry* (2001) and O. O'Neill, *Towards Justice and Virtue* (1996).
[50]   See e.g. essays by Griffin, Brighouse and Arneil in (eds.) D. Archard and C. Macleod, *The Moral and Political Status of Children* (2002) or M. Guggenheim, *What's Wrong With Children's Rights* (2005).
[51]   (2004) 32 *Philosophy and Public Affairs* 315.
[52]   Cf. B. Barry, *Culture and Equality* (2001) and P. Kelly, *Multiculturalism Reconsidered* (2002). See also B. Parekh, *Rethinking Multiculturalism* (2000).

1.  Human rights can be seen as primarily ethical demands. They are not principally "legal", "proto-legal" or "ideal-legal" commands. [They] can, and often do, inspire legislation [but] this is [not] a constitutive characteristic of human rights.
2.  The importance of human rights relates to the significance of the freedoms that form the subject matter of these rights ... To qualify as the basis of human rights, the freedom to be defended or advanced must satisfy some "threshold conditions" of (i) special importance and (ii) social influenceability.
3.  Human rights generate reasons for action for agents who are in a position to help in the promoting or safeguarding of the underlying freedoms. The ... obligations primarily involve the duty to give reasonable consideration to the reasons for action and their practical implications ... The reasons for action can support both "perfect" obligations [and] "imperfect" ones ... Imperfect obligations are correlative with human rights ... as perfect obligations are. In particular, the acceptance of imperfect obligations goes beyond voluntary charity or elective virtues.
4.  The implementation of human rights can go well beyond legislation, and a theory of human rights cannot be sensibly confined within the juridical model ... for example, public recognition and agitation (including the monitoring of violations) can be part of the obligations—often imperfect—generated by the acknowledgement of human rights. Also, some recognized human rights are not ideally legislated, but better promoted though other means, including public discussion, appraisal and advocacy...
5.  Human rights can include significant and influenceable economic and social freedoms. If they cannot be realized because of inadequate institutionalization, then, to work for institutional expansion or reform can be a part of the obligations generated by the recognition of these rights. The current unreliability of any accepted human right, which can be promoted though institutional or political change, does not, by itself, convert that claim into a *non*-right.[53]
6.  The universability of human rights relates to the ideas of survivability in unobstructed discussion—open to participation by persons across national boundaries. Partisanship is avoided not so much by taking either a *conjunction*, or *an intersection*, of the views respectively held by dominant voices in different societies across the world ... but through an *interactive* process, in particular by examining what would survive in public discussion, given a reasonably free flow of information and uncurbed opportunity to discuss differing points of view.[54]

---

[53] Hohfeld's term: see *post*, 570
[54] *Op. cit.*, note 51, 319–320.

Human rights are thus seen by Sen as "prouncements in social ethics, sustainable by open public reasoning".[55] And he emphasizes that "the understanding and viability of human rights are ... intimately linked with the reach of public discussion, between persons and across borders".[56] Human rights are rights to which we are entitled by virtue of being human: they are held irrespective of gender and age—hence the importance of recognizing children's rights as human rights. We have a right not to be assaulted, and so do children. Thus, the corporal punishment of children violates their human rights.[57] That there is subjectivity inherent in human judgement does not mean we enter the world of the arbitrary. There are values that must be upheld. An obvious example is the sanctity of human life,[58] though debates over decisions about the beginning and the end of life (about embryo research and abortion and euthanasia) show how difficult it is to make these ethical judgements in "hard cases".[59]

What, then, is involved in making "judgement"? Those who are part of a community tend to uphold similar values. The debates over "universal" human rights versus alleged abuses in the name of culture and tradition can be understood as conflicts between different communities of judgement. The role of community in judgement thus needs to be explored. The writings of Kant offer insight.[60] For Kant the core of what makes judgement possible is our "common sense" shared by other judging subjects. It is this shared sense that allows us to exercise an "enlarged mentality" by imagining judgements from the standpoints of others.[61] For Kant the ground for our "common sense" is the identical cognitive faculties of imagination and understanding that all human beings share. The common sense is thus universal: so in exercising the enlarged mentality we place ourselves in the shoes of every other person. Judgements are thus universally valid. Hannah Arendt develops this by suggesting the common sense is not based in universally-shared cognitive faculties, but in shared community. She argues that the capacity to judge is "the ability to see things not only from one's own point of view but in the perspective of all those who happen to be present". For Arendt, the claims for validity are not universal, as they were for Kant, but tied to the community of judging subjects involved in the exercise of the "enlarged mentality".[62]

The conception of "enlarged mentality" is a helpful framework for understanding that subjectivity does not have to mean arbitrariness. Also, by basing judgement in real community Arendt forces us to ask

---

[55] *ibid.*, 355–356.
[56] *ibid.*, 356.
[57] See S. Bitensky, *Corporal Punishment of Children—A Human Rights Violation* (2006).
[58] See R. Dworkin, *Life's Dominion* (1993).
[59] See e.g. *Airedale NHS Trust v. Bland* [1993] A.C. 789; *Re A* [2001] Fam, 147; *Pretty v. UK* [2002] 2 FLR 45.
[60] In particular, *Critique of Judgment* (1987, originally 1790).
[61] *ibid*, & 35, 150–151.
[62] *Between Past and Future* (1961), p. 221.

about judgement: good judgement for and according to whom? For Kant, with his transcendental universality, such a question was unnecessary. But Arendt's reliance on actual community offers us a way to exploit the Kantian framework where there are doubts about a universality of judgement.

But whose standpoints are to be considered, and by whom? What is meant by "community"? If the common sense essential to judgement is not that of Kant's transcendental world of all human beings with faculties of imagination and understanding in common, what is it? How does the concept of the "enlarged mentality" work in a diverse, contested and fragmented social world? We need to understand the relationship between the universal and the particular in human judgement. This is particularly significant with debates about the universality of human rights. Take a cultural practice like female genital mutilation (FGM, sometimes called female circumcision).[63] We condemn such a practice in the name of universality—others condone it in the name of culture.[64] Our claim to normative universality—it would be foolish to claim descriptive universality—is challenged by others as merely the imposition of a particular Western conception on those who have different conceptions of core human values. Feminists know all too well how false our claims to universality have been, with a universal concept like citizenship clearly so gender-specific right up to modern (and arguably post-modern) times.[65]

How, then, is one to justify claims of abuses of human rights? What is the basis for such claims? With reference to which community is it made? Is it to the community of all 6 billion plus of us, the community to which we all belong because we are human? Does being "human" mean the same to all mankind? Or, are we necessarily invoking, even here, a Western conception of what being "human" is? Should we be looking to the particular community in which the abuses are taking place? And, if so, is there any greater reason to envision that community as monolithic, so that it only has one relevant shared "common sense"? Why should we do this when practices alleged to be abuses frequently take place where there are multiple overlapping communities with different "common senses"? Or should we say that there is a world community, a social world constituted by communication and actions such as ratification of international conventions? And, is it not possible to express such norms in universal terms and yet apply them in ways responsive to local context? An example might be a human right norm on the minimum age for marriage, which is sensitive to different understandings of the concept of "child" in different cultures.[66]

There is another danger in these debates, that it pits "us" against

---

[63] See S.A. James (1994), 8 Bioethics 1.
[64] See the debate between D. Coleman (1996) 96 Columbia L.R. 1093 and L. Volpp (1996) 96 Columbia L.R. 1573 and (2001) 101 Columbia L.R. 1181.
[65] See U. Vogel in U. Vogel and M. Moral (eds.), *The Frontiers of Citizenship* (1991); C. Pateman, *The Sexual Contract* (1988).
[66] See e.g. *Mohamed v Knott* [1969] 1 Q.B.1.

"them". There are people in *our* communities who do not accept human rights ideals—who accept the legitimacy of torture,[67] for example—and there are people in communities which reject such ideals who happily embrace them. Not all Germans in the years of the Nazis were Nazis: some risked their lives to save Jews from the Holocaust. What is it, then, that enables some people to judge, not only differently from, but in opposition to their communities. Arendt addressed this question too. She thought that we judged as a member of a community "guided by our community sense". But in the final analysis we were, she thought, members of a world community. We have "cosmopolitan existence". She invoked the idea of the "world citizen", the "world spectator".[68]

There is ambivalence here and many issues are raised. I pick up a couple only. What do we mean when we say an entire community (a few dissidents apart) is wrong? We all know that Nazism was wrong. But how do we know this? Are we saying their common sense was distorted, that it is characterised by bad judgement, or a failure to exercise judgement? From what standpoint do we make such a claim? How do we exercise our judgement? The assumption has been made that our judgements are grounded in local communities, but most communities are not homogeneous. We are exposed to overlapping communities, and these differ in their "common senses", at least in some respects. How then do we exercise our enlarged mentality when different judgements appear valid depending upon which community's common sense we have reference to? Are we to choose from different common senses of different communities, and, if so, how?

In forming a judgement we have to consider the perspectives of others, their "standpoints". Arendt claims that an "enlarged mentality" is an indispensable condition of right judgement; one's community sense makes it possible to enlarge one's mentality. What is meant by "community" here? Is it, as with Kant, one of all humanity? It would be difficult to conclude that the common sense which makes judgement possible is universal. What enables us to judge is membership in a community of other judging subjects who share a common sense that makes their judgements, and thus their inherent claims for the community, possible. This makes us ask what kind of common sense (or shared community) is necessary to make possible taking other people's *different* standpoints into account. For Arendt, the project of the enlarged mentality is an encounter with difference, but it is one that presupposes some commonality sufficient for imagining a different standpoint. The question of what has to be shared to understand difference is a large one: many disciplines can contribute to our appreciation of it. Expanding the base of one's common sense is important, but an effort still needs to be made to attempt to consider the standpoints of others. This is the exercise of the enlarged mentality, which in turn makes communication, which is so

---

[67] On torture see D. Sussman (2005) 33 *Philosophy and Public Affairs* 1.
[68] *Lectures on Kant's Political Philosophy* (1982), p.76

often blocked, possible. Arendt puts it thus: "one can communicate only if one is able to think from the other person's standpoint; otherwise one will never meet him, never speak in such a way that he understands".[69]

"Common sense"—the shared understandings that make the enlarged mentality and communication possible—is not static. It shifts over time, and in the course of encountering alternative "common senses". Think of the way "common sense" about slavery, about black people, women, children and the disabled has changed. In each case it has taken the efforts of moral entrepreneurs[70] to create new common senses. None of those engaged in work to achieve new common senses have been entirely successful. There are more slaves in the world today than when slavery was abolished in the U.S. after the Civil War.[71] The impetus for shift usually begins with a minority and is often identified with what we often call "informed opinion".[72] But where does the minority acquire its different "common sense"? In part from other communities of judgement to which they have recourse, at least in their imagination. And there *are* alternative communities (the churches, the ideals of law even where it is not the reality, the universities, the media where it is independent).[73] There are also political movements like feminism. The challenger to common sense in *extremis* will cut him/herself off from the community to whom s/he would ordinarily appeal for criteria of shared judgement and possible confirmation of the validity of his/her judgement.

In disputes about human rights, what we see are competing communities claiming that they provide the appropriate framework for judging. The greater the capacity to form links between competing frameworks, the greater is the possibility of claiming validity across communities. If we want to see our vision of human rights prevail across communities—in places where our judgement is not currently shared (Zimbabwe or Myanmar, for example)—we must engage in dialogue. Our aim must be the enlargement of a shared common sense. Human rights must not be seen as a foreign imposition, a tool of power: rather as an element of shared common sense. It is necessary to participate in dialogue that seriously engages local perspectives. It is necessary to open channels of communication.

But can we go further than this? Is humanitarian intervention justified when a state is in flagrant breach of human rights? Where there are very severe human rights violations, can forcible intervention be justified? Genocide, torture and apartheid are often invoked as examples. Countries which use the death penalty, by contrast, are heavily criticized, but there is no sustained campaign for intervention, even where it is used against children (as in Iran, and the U.S. only recently) or religious minorities (as in China). The debate, rekindled by the war on Iraq, came

---

[69]  *ibid*, 74
[70]  See H. Becker, *Outsiders* (1963).
[71]  Estimates vary between 12 and 26 million: many are children.
[72]  See A.V. Dicey, *Law and Public Opinion in England in the Nineteenth Century* (1914).
[73]  See H.L.A. Hart (1958) 71 Harvard L.R. 593, and *post*, 414.

sharply into focus in 2008 when the military dictatorship in Myanmar obstructed world relief efforts after a devastating cyclone. The argument against intervention rests on deference to sovereignty. It can be traced to Grotius who argued that "by forming sovereign states and giving themselves laws, human beings assert their moral autonomy".[74] But what if this autonomy is denied them, as it was to the black people of South Africa or the Jews of Germany under Nazism? Can such cases be distinguished from the many other states where there are major breaches of human rights?[75] The argument against intervention may also be prudential; it may make a bad situation worse. This has clearly happened in Iraq: as a result the case for humanitarian intervention has weakened. But it will not go away.[76]

## THE OBLIGATION TO OBEY THE LAW

For long there was considerable discussion about whether there was moral obligation to obey an unjust law.[77] This was seen at its starkest in the Hart-Fuller debate about Nazi law (the well-known "grudge informer" case posed the dilemma clearly[78]) and in disputes about the role of the judge in apartheid South Africa.[79] But more recently the question has been posed as to whether there is a moral obligation to obey law at all.[80] Few, if any, would argue that there is a duty to obey the law whatever the circumstances[81], so that the discussion tends to be couched in terms of a prima facie (or presumptive) obligation.[82] But even this has been questioned.

The question can be traced back as far as Plato.[83] The first modern articulation, however, was in the writings of W. D. Ross.[84] He argued:

[74] See M. Nussbaum, *Frontiers of Justice* (2006), p. 256. Grotius argues this in *On the Law of War and Peace*. See also Kant's *Perpetual Peace*.

[75] Nussbaum says such reasons are the primary ones for not intervening (by economic sanction) where there is "brutal and oppressive discrimination on grounds of sex" (*ibid*, p. 260). And see C. Mackinnon, *Are Women Human?* (2006), 276 (an essay entitled "Women's September 11th").

[76] See, further, on human rights, J. Griffin, *On Human Rights* (2008).

[77] See, *e.g.* Aquinas, *ante*, 142.

[78] Discussed by H. O. Pappe (1960) 23 M. L. R. 260 and see *ante*, 124. And see R. Alexy in (ed.) D. Dyzenhaus, *Recrafting The Rule of Law* (1999), p. 15 and *post*, 374. See also Radbruch's post-war papers (reproduced in (2006) 26 Ox. J.L.S. 1 and 13), and *post*, 421 and S. Paulson (2006) 26 Ox. J.L.S. 17.

[79] D. Dyzenhaus, *Hard Cases In Wicked Legal Systems* (1991); R. Wacks (1984) 101 South African L. J. 266, 295; J. Dugard (1971) 88 South African L. J. 181.

[80] M. B. E. Smith (1973) 82 Yale L. J. 950; R. Sartorius, *Individual Conduct and Social Norms* (1975); J. Raz, *The Authority of Law* (1979), p. 233; A. J. Simmons, *Moral Principles and Political Obligations* (1979); K. Greenawalt, *Conflicts of Law and Morality* (1987). W. Edmundson (2004) 10 *Legal Theory* 215, and *post*, 574.

[81] Although when Lord Chancellor in the 1970s Lord Hailsham espoused such a view.

[82] See, *e.g.* P. Singer, *Democracy and Disobedience* (1973).

[83] In the *Crito*.

[84] *The Right and The Good* (1930), p. 27.

"the duty of obeying the laws of one's country arises partly ... from the duty of gratitude for the benefits one has received from it; partly from the implicit promise to obey which seems to be involved in permanent residence in a country whose laws we know we are *expected* to obey, and still more clearly involved when we ourselves invoke the protection of its laws ... and partly (if we are fortunate in our country) from the fact that its laws are potent instruments for the general good."[85]

Twenty-five years later, Hart addressed the question. Invoking, what came to be known as, "the principle of fair play", he argued that:

"when a number of persons conduct any joint enterprise according to rules and restrict their liberty, those who have submitted to these restrictions when required have a right to a similar submission from those who have benefitted by their submission."[86]

By 1964, Rawls could assume "as requiring no argument" that "at least in a society such as ours" (that is the U.S.) there was a moral obligation to obey the law. He added that it could "of course, be overridden in certain cases by other more stringent obligations."[87]

It was M. B. E. Smith in 1973 who first dared to problematise the question[88] (though Fuller had anticipated this when in response to Hart he had asked how positivists could speak of there being a "moral dilemma" about whether to obey a morally bad law[89]). He argued that "although those subject to a government often have a prima facie obligation to obey particular laws (*e.g.* when disobedience has seriously untoward consequences or involves an act that is *malum in se*[90]), they have no prima facie obligation to obey all its laws".[91] Smith, returning to the subject in 1996[92], summarised, what he takes to be, a broad area of agreement between those who reject the duty of obedience.

First, there is an acknowledgement of the existence of legitimate authority. But authority is analysed "without reference to a duty of obedience".[93] But if a government has legitimate authority its citizens are virtually always obligated not to interfere with enforcement of its commands.[94]

Secondly, doubters have criticised the arguments set out to support the duty to obey the law. These are discussed a little later.

Thirdly, they draw attention to the many regulations of a modern state

---

[85]  (1955) 64 Philosophical Rev. 175, 185.
[86]  See for a similar view J. Rawls in S. Hook (ed.), *Law and Philosophy* (1964), p. 3.
[87]  *ibid.* See also *A Theory of Justice* (1971).
[88]  See *op. cit.*, note 80. He returned to the question in (ed.) D. Patterson, *A Companion To Philosophy of Law and Legal Theory* (1996), p. 465.
[89]  (1958) 71 Harvard L. Rev 630, 656 (*post*, 414). He observed: "It is like saying I have to choose between giving food to a starving man and being mimsy with the borogoves".
[90]  *Op. cit.*, note 80, p. 951.
[91]  *ibid.*
[92]  *Op. cit.*, note 88.
[93]  *ibid.*, p. 467.
[94]  Thus argued by K. Greenwalt, *op. cit.*, note 80, p. 55.

which, however important for the smooth running of society, can be broken without any suggestion that doing so is immoral. Smith quotes Devlin's reference to "many fussy regulations whose breach it would be pedantic to call immoral".[95]

Fourthly, they point to its redundancy. Every normative theory to be plausible, they argue, must "contain proscriptions against assault, reckless endangerment, fraud, breach of serious promises ... whose conjunction arguably specifies each important moral interest that we are bound to respect".[96] Thus whether or not it provides specifically for obedience to the law, "it will imply trivially that there is a prima facie duty to obey whenever disobedience puts an important moral interest at risk".[97] It is the strength of these independent moral reasons that "determines the strength of the reason to obey".[98] Thus, for example, marital rape has always been morally wrong: it is no more wrong now that it has been belatedly criminalised than it was before.

How then is an obligation to obey the law justified? A number of arguments have been put forward. One standard argument situates obligation in consent.[99] It is, of course, very difficult, if not impossible, to find express consent,[1] so that the argument usually cites implied consent: the action of voting, or accepting the benefits of living in a state, or remaining (rather than emigrating). But this is not how citizens would interpret their actions. And what are the alternatives? Nor is it clear why even if voting for example could be held to constitute consent that this would lead to an obligation to obey the laws, even, it may be added, those made by a Parliament for which one has voted. And would it mean that those who do not have the vote (children, prisoners) would not have an obligation to obey the law?

Others put the case in consequentialist terms. They ask us to consider the bad consequences for a society in which people disobeyed the law. To Hobbes, a classical source for this argument, "perpetual war of every man against his neighbour"[2] would be the likely result.[3] In a similar way those who object to civil disobedience often invoke the so-called "domino effect": interestingly, what empirical evidence there is suggests that in times of concerted civil disobedience, for example, when civil rights agitation was at its strongest in the American South this did not lead to a weakening of bonds to comply with ordinary criminal legislation.[4]

Another argument often put forward is the "free-rider" one, that is it is

---

[95] *The Enforcement of Morals* (1965), p. 27.
[96] *Op. cit.*, note 89, p. 468.
[97] *ibid.*
[98] *ibid.*
[99] In effect the social contract argument (see *ante*, 105) and by analogy in Rawls (*post*, 583).
[1] Even where there is emigration by a cohesive group (*e.g.* those who sailed to America on the "Mayflower").
[2] In *Leviathan*, 20 (pp. 144–145 of Tuck edition, 1996) and *ante*, 143.
[3] To T. Honoré the problem is the "attitude of disobedience" that it inculcates (see *Making Law Bind* (1987), p. 115).
[4] See *op. cit.*, note 82.

wrong for those who have benefitted from the state not to respond with obedience to the law. The analogy is sometimes drawn—by Plato for example[5]—with the duty of gratitude owed by children to their parents.

There is also the fairness or reciprocity argument, found in Hart (already quoted from[6]) and Rawls.[7] Rather than emphasising a duty to the state, this bases the case for an obligation to obey in a duty to one's fellow citizens.

Of these who have argued against an obligation to obey Raz has put the strongest case.[8] For Raz, we have a moral reason to comply with the law when we believe we will make the best moral choice by following the law rather than our own conscience. Thus, for example, a parent will comply with the law instructing her to have her child vaccinated against measles, mumps and rubella if she thinks the legislature with access to the best scientific knowledge has come to the best decision, but not otherwise.

The most difficult case occurs when we are required by law to do what morality forbids. This problem is addressed most fully and thoughtfully in Hurd's *Moral Combat*.[9] Hurd argues that the law cannot require us to do what morality forbids. She claims that the law can serve, at most, as a "theoretical authority"[10] about the content of our antecedently existing moral obligations. She disputes the claim which credits law with "practical authority"[11] (and hence the moral power to compel us to do what morality would otherwise prohibit us from doing); also the claim that law can at least be thought to possess "influential authority",[12] (and hence the moral power to compel us to do what morality would otherwise prohibit us from doing); also the claim that law can at least be thought to possess "influential authority"[13]—"a kind of theoretical authority that derives from the expertise of lawmakers to discern socially optimal arrangements".[14]

Those who criticise these views often point to the anarchy[15] they suppose will result from each acting as his own decision-maker rather than deferring to the law-giver, or criticise those who think they can come to a more morally right conclusion than the legislature. That we will inevitably have our own self-interests and prejudices and biases cannot be denied, but for Raz[16] can only be a factor in a calculation and cannot as such lead to an inevitable conclusion that submission to legal authority is the appropriate conclusion.

---

[5] In *Crito*, 50d–51d.
[6] *Ante*, 406.
[7] In *A Theory of Justice* (1971).
[8] *Op. cit.*, note 80.
[9] (1999).
[10] See Chap. 6.
[11] In Chap. 3.
[12] See Chap. 4.
[13] In Chap. 5.
[14] *ibid.*, p. xiii.
[15] See, *e.g.* Honoré, *op. cit.*, note 3.
[16] *Op. cit.*, note 80.

## THE LEGAL ENFORCEMENT OF MORALITY

Debates about the legal enforcement of morality can be found in Victorian England.[17] These were rekindled in the middle of the last century by the publication of the Wolfenden report on Prostitution and Homosexuality[18] and led to the Hart-Devlin debate,[19] and continue today with the challenge of new (or newer) moral problems, such as gay marriages,[20] surrogacy,[21] cloning[22] and assisted suicide.[23]

It was John Stuart Mill's thesis that legal coercion could only be justified for the purpose of preventing harm to others,[24] but even he accepted some paternalism.[25] Mill's thesis was attacked by the great Victorian judge, Stephen, in his *Liberty, Equality and Fraternity*.[26] Though the debate never died, it became a live issue again in the United Kingdom in the late 1950s when the Wolfenden report observed that there was a realm of private life which was not the law's business.[27] Lord Devlin, a leading judge, attacked this thesis in a lecture in 1959, and returned to the theme a number of times.[28]

Devlin argued that there is a public morality which provides the cement of any human society, and that the law, he argued especially the criminal law, must regard it as a primary function to maintain this public morality. Whether in fact in any particular case the law should be brought into play by specific criminal sanctions should depend upon the state of public feeling. Conduct which arouses a widespread feeling of reprobation, a mixture of "intolerance, indignation and disgust",[29] deserves to be suppressed by legal coercion in the interests of the integrity of society. For this purpose, Lord Devlin has recourse to the common law jury ideal, the notion that the "man in the jury-box" supplies an

---

[17] Mill, *On Liberty* (1859) is the classic statement of the liberal position. R. Wacks, *Law, Morality and the Private Domain* (2000) may also be consulted.

[18] (1957) Cmnd. 247. It is worth comparing the *Report of Advisory Committee on Drug Dependence: Cannabis* (1968).

[19] Devlin's views can be traced back to Durkheim (on whom see *post*, 843), though there is no evidence that Devlin was knowingly deriving any such assistance (see W. Thomas (1994) 32 Amer. Crim. L. Rev. 49).

[20] See the debate between J. Finnis and A. Koppelman in (1997) 42 Amer. J. of Jurisprud. 51, 97. See also J. Finnis (1994) 69 Notre Dame L. Rev. 1049.

[21] See D. Satz (1992) 21 Phil. and Public Affairs 107.

[22] See J. Robertson (1998) 76 Texas L. Rev. 1371; M. Nussbaum and C. Sunstein (eds.), *Clones and Clones* (1998).

[23] See R. Weir (1992) 20 *Law, Medicine and Health Care* 116, and, in particular now, J. Martel (2001) 10 Soc. & Legal Studies 147. See the symposium at (2008) 106 (8) Michigan L.R. for contemporary concerns. See particularly S. D. Smith (2008) 106 Michigan L.R. 1571.

[24] See J. Riley, *Mill on Liberty* (1998) for a detailed exposition. See also J. Feinberg, *Harm To Others* (1984).

[25] The liberty principle does not apply to children or "barbarians" in "backward states of society".

[26] First published in 1873 (the edition cited is edited by R. J. White in 1967).

[27] *Op. cit.*, note 18, para. 62.

[28] His essays are collected in *The Enforcement of Morals* (1965).

[29] *ibid.*, p. 17 (see also p. viii). Legal thinking has begun to engage the emotions: see, for example, K. Abrams and H. Keren (2008) 95 California L.R. 319.

adequate standard of current morality for the purpose of assessing the limits of legal intervention. The jury after all does not (or should not) give a snap judgment; its verdict is the outcome of argument and deliberation and it will, of course, have received guidance from an experienced judge. And, as for reliance on feeling, this was the ordinary man's best guide where a choice had to be made between a number of reasonable conclusions.[30] He therefore stigmatised as "an error of jurisprudence" Wolfenden's view that there is some single principle explaining the division between crime and sin, such as that based on Mill's notion of what may lead to harmful consequences to third persons. Devlin concluded that if vice were not suppressed, society would crumble: "The suppression of vice is as much the law's business as the suppression of subversive activities".[31]

This thesis received some implicit support from a contemporary case (the so-called *Ladies' Directory* case[32]) and has had more recent support from the House of Lords in the *Brown* case which condemned consensual and private sado-masochistic practices.[33] It was, however, strenuously opposed by Hart.[34]

Hart outlined,[35] in the first place, "the types of evidence that might conceivably be relevant to the issue". One could examine "crude historical evidence", look at disintegrated societies and enquire whether disintegration was preceded by a malignant change in their common morality, considering further any "causal connection". Such a survey would have formidable difficulties for, even supposing, which is most unlikely, that moral decadence was responsible for the decline of Rome[36] (for example), would such evidence be persuasive in considering modern societies? Hart puts his faith rather in the evidence of social psychology.[37] Depending upon one's ideology, the way of viewing the alternatives to the maintenance of a common morality could take one of two forms. One view would be "permissiveness": one would show how this led to a weakening of individual capacity for self-control and contributed to an increase in violence and dishonesty. Or one could look at this from the perspective of "moral pluralism". Would this lead to antagonism, to a society in the state of nature as depicted by Hobbes,[38] or rather to mutual tolerance, to co-existence of divergent moralities? What evidence there is suggests the latter, and Hart himself believes that modern Britain

---

[30] *ibid.*, p. ix.
[31] *ibid.*, pp. 13–14.
[32] [1962] A.C. 74 (rediscovering the crime of conspiracy to corrupt public morals).
[33] [1994] 1 A.C. 212.
[34] See especially *Law, Liberty and Morality* (1963).
[35] (1967) 35 Univ. of Chicago L. Rev. 1, 11–13.
[36] For the view that moral decadence was not among the causes of the decline of the Roman Empire, see A. H. M. Jones, *The Decline of The Ancient World* (1966), Chaps 24 and 26.
[37] *Op. cit.*, note 35, pp. 12–13.
[38] See *Leviathan*, Pt 1, Chap. 13 ("... the life of man, solitary, poor, nasty, brutish, and short").

exemplified this trend rather than anything approaching the Hobbesian picture.

Having removed the foundations of Devlin's thesis thus, Hart set about attempting to demolish the structure erected upon them. He dismissed as fantastic the notion that all morality forms "a single seamless web",[39] so that deviation from any one part would almost inevitably produce destruction of the whole. The mere fact that conventional morality may change in a permissive direction does not mean that society is going to be destroyed or subverted.[40] Again, Lord Devlin assumed a degree of moral solidarity in society, which may have existed in earlier periods of our history, but which is hardly discernible today.[41] Hart pointed out that the real solvent to social morality is not the failure of the law to endorse its restrictions, but rather the operation of the critical discussion. He also addressed the dangers to democracy which might result if free discussion were prohibited or curtailed on account of its impact on prevalent social morality. That the moral notions of the majority are matters to which the legislature must pay close account seems beyond question, but what Mill had in mind was that the idea that the majority had the moral right to dictate how everyone else should live needed to be rejected.[42] It is therefore important that public indignation should be subjected to rational and critical appraisal.[43]

Nevertheless, Hart accepted the need for the law to enforce some morality. The real area of dispute is thus where the line should be drawn. Mill drew it at "harm to others". Hart extended the role of the law by his acceptance of "paternalism", in addition to Mill's reliance on harmful consequences to others.[44] So, where Devlin justified *R. v. Donovan*[45] as enforcement of morality, Hart saw the decision as a concession to paternalism. Hart never defined paternalism, and Devlin was accordingly critical of its vagueness.[46] "What, also, I did not foresee was that some of the crew who sail under Mill's flag of liberty would mutiny and run paternalism up the mast."[47] Although Devlin was unable to distinguish paternalism and the enforcement of morals, there is a distinction which centres on the decision-making process of those who are subject to the law. Paternalism may thus intervene to stop self-inflicted harm such as

---

[39] *Op. cit.*, note 34.

[40] *Op. cit.*, note 35, pp. 9–10.

[41] But *cf.* S. Marcus, *The Other Victorians* (1967). S. Ranulf's view that the middle classes have a monopoly of moral indignation may be the key (*Moral Indignation and Middle Class Psychology* (1938), pp. 1–95). See also J. Gusfield, *Symbolic Crusade* (1963).

[42] *Op. cit.*, note 17.

[43] And see R. Dworkin, *Taking Rights Seriously* (1977), Chap. 10 and *Sovereign Virtue* (2000), Chap. 5.

[44] *Op. cit.*, note 34, pp. 30–34.

[45] [1934] 2 K. B. 498 (consent negatives crime of assault). See now *R. v. Brown*, *op. cit.*, note 33.

[46] Paternalism would prevent a person doing harm to himself rather than to others, so consent as negativing assault is irrelevant to paternalism, since there is no question of self-injury: see M. Bayles in (eds.) Pennock and Chapman, *The Limits of Law* (1974), p. 185. On paternalism and contract see S. V. Shiffrin (2000) 29 Phil. and Public Affairs 205.

[47] *Op. cit.*, note 28, p. 132.

the results of drug-taking or cigarette smoking (in the latter case by banning advertising, for example) or requiring the use of seat belts,[48] not because of a wish to enforce conventional morality, but because of doubts as to the capacity of the "victim" to make a rational decision, especially where s/he is mentally disturbed (according to conventional morality[49]) or physically ill.[50]

But Hart went further than this. He admitted, with Devlin, that some shared morality is essential to society, what he called "universal values".[51] If *any* society is to survive, if any legal system is to function, there must be rules prohibiting, for example, murder. But how is murder to be defined? Is abortion[52] or mercy-killing[53] or separating conjoined twins where one cannot live as a result murder?[54] The standard case remains uncontroversial, but the marginal one is no nearer solution. Hart further argued, in a later formulation,[55] that rules essential for a *particular* society (monogamy might be an example) might also be enforced. "For any society there is to be found ... A central core of rules or principles which constitutes its pervasive and distinctive style of life". For Hart it then became "an open and empirical question whether any particular moral rule is so organically connected with the central core that its preservation is required as a vital bastion".[56]

The defence of liberty in Mill and in Hart is not made subject to what that liberty is used for. It is true that Mill believed that a better society would emerge,[57] but in his view it was none of society's business how valuable an individual's activities were, so long as they were not harmful. Stephen was critical of this: "it is one thing however to tolerate vice so long as it is inoffensive, and quite another to give it a legal right not only to exist, but to assert itself in the face of the world as an 'experiment in living' as good as another, and entitled to the same protection from law."[58]

Contemporary perfectionist thinkers have picked up this insight. Thus, George in *Making Men Moral* argues that someone "who has good

---

[48] But *cf. op. cit.*, note 46, p. 184 (Paternalism no justification since fining or imprisoning the actors simply inflicts further injury on them).

[49] *Cf.* R. D. Laing, *The Divided Self* (1960); E. Goffman, *Asylums* (1961).

[50] *Cf.* C. L. Ten (1969) 32 M.L.R. 648, 660–661. On "harm" see B. Mitchell, *Law, Morality and Religion in a Secular Society* (1967); Riley, *op. cit.*, note 24, pp. 98–99; L. Alexander (1994) 7 Canadian J. of Law and Jurisp. 199.

[51] *Op. cit.*, note 64, p. 71. See also *The Concept of Law* (1994), pp. 193–200, discussed *ante*, 123.

[52] The exchange of views between Macedo and George and Wolfe (1997) 42 Amer. J. Jurisprudence 1, 31 may be noted. See also R. Dworkin, *Life's Dominion* (1993); S. Stroud (1996) 25 Phil and Public Affairs 140; E. Harman (1999) 28 Phil. and Public Affairs 310.

[53] See House of Lords' Select Committee on Medical Ethics, H.L. Paper 21 (1993–1994) and M. Otlowski, *Voluntary Euthanasia and the Common Law* (1997).

[54] See *Re A* [2000] 4 All E.R. 961.

[55] *Op. cit.*, note 35, p. 10.

[56] *ibid.*, p. 11.

[57] *Op. cit.*, note 17, p. 11–12.

[58] *Op. cit.*, note 26, p. 37.

reasons to believe that a certain act is immoral may support the legal prohibition of that act for the sake of protecting public morals without necessarily violating a norm of justice or political morality".[59] Perfectionism, he claims, "enables us to distinguish truly important liberties that government must always respect (and should often affirmatively act to protect and promote) from relatively unimportant liberties that may legitimately be limited for the sake of social and economic equality and other important goals and ideals."[60] And Raz shows that the perfectionist can also support a thesis not dissimilar from that espoused by Mill.

Raz's first premise is that "the main purpose of government" is "to assist people ... to lead successful and fulfilling lives" and that people's lives are successful and fulfilling to the extent that they are "spent in whole-hearted and successful engagement in valuable activities and relationships".[61] His second premise is that for most inhabitants of the industrialised world "the good life is a successful autonomous life", so that a perfectionist government is bound "to be sensitive to the need of people to be free in the sense of being capable of leading successful autonomous lives".[62] Raz argues that "not all the constraints imposed by coercion are a restriction of the autonomy of the coerced. An autonomous life is valuable only to the extent that it is engaged in *valuable* activities and relationships".[63] And, "given their duty to promote the well-being of people should they not take action to make sure that attractive options are available and that meaningless and worthless options are eliminated?".[64] Raz concludes that autonomy together with liberty impose severe limits on state moral paternalism.[65] It also leads us to conclude that there are activities which the state should not only permit but also endorse. For example, whilst earlier debates centred upon the decriminalisation of homosexual activities, the implication of Raz's liberal perfectionism is that we should make marriage an available option for gay couples.[66]

Many more questions can be asked about the legal enforcement of morality. Of what significance is it that such legislation does not work or makes bad worse? The experience of Prohibition in the United States and of back-street abortions are frequently-cited examples.[67] Arguing against legal moralism in this way is to offer prudential arguments. These are

---

[59] (1993), p. 190.

[60] *ibid.* On perfectionism see J. Chan (2000) 29 Phil. and Public Affairs 5.

[61] "Liberty and Trust" in (ed.) R. George, *Natural Law, Liberalism and Morality* (1996), p. 113.

[62] *ibid.*

[63] *ibid.*, p. 120.

[64] *ibid.*, p. 114.

[65] For a critique of Raz's perfectionism in relation to morals legislation see C. Wolfe in *op.cit.*, note 52, p. 131.

[66] But *cf.* J. Finnis, *ibid.*, pp. 7–9 distinguishing decriminalisation of adult homosexual acts from recognising homosexual marriages (Finnis puts "marriages" in quotes).

[67] On prohibition see A. Sinclair, *Prohibition: An Era of Excess* (1968). There was a campaign to introduce it in Britain: A. E. Dingle, *The Campaign for Prohibition in Victorian England* (1980).

important but must be separated from the ethical arguments we have been addressing. It is also sometimes argued that forcing someone to be "good" when they do not wish to do so in no way improves that person's life (though it may well improve the life of the community).[68] Dworkin makes this point: "Suppose someone who would lead a homosexual life does not out of fear of punishment. If he never endorses the life he leads as superior to the life he would otherwise have led, then his life has not been improved ... by the paternalistic constraints he hates."[69] Further, "we would not improve someone's life, even though he endorsed the change we brought about, if the mechanisms we used to secure the change lessened his ability to consider the critical merits of the change in a reflective way."[70]

---

## H. L. A. HART
### Positivism and the Separation of Law and Morals
### (1958)[71]

The third[72] criticism of the separation of law and morals is of a very different character; it certainly is less an intellectual argument against the Utilitarian distinction than a passionate appeal supported not by detailed reasoning but by reminders of a terrible experience. For it consists of the testimony of those who have descended into Hell, and, like Ulysses or Dante, brought back a message for human beings. Only in this case the Hell was not beneath or beyond earth, but on it; it was a Hell created on earth by men for other men.

This appeal comes from those German thinkers who lived through the Nazi regime and reflected upon its evil manifestations in the legal system. One of these thinkers, Gustav Radbruch, had himself shared the "positivist" doctrine until the Nazi tyranny, but he was converted by this experience and so his appeal to other men to discard the doctrine of the separation of law and morals has the special poignancy of a recantation. What is important about this criticism is that it really does confront the particular point which Bentham and Austin had in mind in urging the separation of law as it is and as it ought to be. These German thinkers put their insistence on the need to join together what the Utilitarians separated just where this separation was of most importance in the eyes of the Utilitarians; for they were concerned with the problem posed by the existence of morally evil laws.

Before his conversion[73] Radbruch held that resistance to law was a matter for the personal conscience, to be thought out by the individual as a moral problem, and the validity of a law could not be disproved by showing that its requirements

---

[68] See, *e.g.* by John Finnis (1994) 45 Mercer L. Rev. 687.

[69] *Sovereign Virtue* (2000), p. 218.

[70] *ibid.*

[71] [From (1958) 71 Harv. L. Rev. 593–629, copyright @ 1958, by the Harvard Law Review Association.]

[72] [Hart had earlier dealt with other criticisms: the confusion between the "command" theory and the separation of law and morals; and the linking of that separation with "formalism".]

[73] [*Cf.* E. Wolf (1958) 3 Natural L. F. 1, who suggests that the seeds of post-war Radbruch were clearly detectable in his pre-Nazi-era writings. Radbruch warned of "a renewed threat of barbarity" in 1932 and in 1933 branded Nazi criminal law as "terroristic" (see A. Kaufmann (1988) 9 Cardozo L. Rev. 1629, 1633). And see Alexy, *post*, 426.]

were morally evil or even by showing that the effect of compliance with the law would be more evil than the effect of disobedience. Austin, it may be recalled, was emphatic in condemning those who said that if human laws conflicted with the fundamental principles of morality then they cease to be laws, as talking "stark nonsense."[74] These are strong ... words, but we must remember that they went along—in the case of Austin and, of course Bentham—with the conviction that if laws reached a certain degree of iniquity then there would be a plain moral obligation to resist them and to withhold obedience. We shall see, when we consider the alternatives, that this simple presentation of the human dilemma which may arise has much to be said for it.

Radbruch, however, had concluded from the ease with which the Nazi regime had exploited subservience to mere law—or expressed, as he thought, in the "positivist" slogan "law as law" (*Gesetz als Gesetz*)—and from the failure of the German legal profession to protest against the enormities which they were required to perpetrate in the name of law, that "positivism" (meaning here the insistence on the separation of law as it is from law as it ought to be) had powerfully contributed to the horrors.[75] His considered reflections led him to the doctrine that the fundamental principles of humanitarian morality were part of the very concept of *Recht* or Legality and that no positive enactment or statute, however clearly it was expressed and however clearly it conformed with the formal criteria of validity of a given legal system, could be valid if it contravened basic principles of morality. This doctrine can be appreciated fully only if the nuances imported by the German word *Recht* are grasped. But it is clear that the doctrine meant that every lawyer and judge should denounce statutes that transgressed the fundamental principles not as merely immoral or wrong but as having no legal character, and enactments which on this ground lack the quality of law should not be taken into account in working out the legal position of any given individual in particular circumstances. The striking recantation of his previous doctrine is unfortunately omitted from the translation of his works, but it should be read by all who wish to think afresh on the question of the interconnection of law and morals.

It is impossible to read without sympathy Radbruch's passionate demand that the German legal conscience should be open to the demands of morality and his complaint that this has been too little the case in the German tradition. On the other hand there is an extraordinary naïveté in the view that insensitiveness to the demands of morality and subservience to state power in a people like the Germans should have arisen from the belief that law might be law though it failed to conform with the minimum requirements of morality. Rather this terrible history prompts inquiry into why emphasis on the slogan "law is law" and the distinction between law and morals, acquired a sinister character in Germany, but elsewhere, as with the Utilitarians themselves, went along with the most enlightened liberal attitudes. But something more disturbing than naïveté is latent in Radbruch's whole presentation of the issues to which the existence of morally iniquitous laws give rise. It is not, I think, uncharitable to say that we can see in his argument that he has only half digested the spiritual message of liberalism which he is seeking to convey to the legal profession. For everything that he says is really dependent upon an enormous overvaluation of the importance of the bare fact that a rule

---

[74] [*Cf. Bentham, ante*, 248.]

[75] [But, according to Kaufmann, *op.cit.* "there is no doubt that law and jurisprudence under National Socialism were anti-positivist" (p. 1644). According to one jurist, Larenz, writing in 1934, positivism was "a manifestation of intellectual foreign infiltration," of liberalism: according to another, Stolleis, it was deeply rooted in the "starry-eyed dualism of the 'sein and sollen' of, *inter alia*, Kelsen. Larenz's writings still constitute leading textbooks in Germany today (see Reimann (1988) 9 Cardozo L. Rev. 1651, 1653–1654). See more generally I. Müller, *Hitler's Justice* (1991) which casts doubts on whether the Nazi era was aberrant.]

may be said to be a valid rule of law, as if this, once declared, was conclusive of the final moral question: "Ought this rule of law to be obeyed?" Surely the truly liberal answer to any sinister use of the slogan "law is law" or of the distinction between law and morals is, "Very well, but that does not conclude the question. Law is not morality; do not let it supplant morality."

However, we are not left to a mere academic discussion in order to evaluate the plea which Radbruch made for the revision of the distinction between law and morals. After the war Radbruch's conception of law as containing in itself the essential moral principle of humanitarianism was applied in practice by German courts in certain cases in which local war criminals, spies, and informers under the Nazi regime were punished. The special importance of these cases is that the persons accused of these crimes claimed that what they had done was not illegal under the laws of the regime in force at the time these actions were performed. This plea was met with the reply that the laws upon which they relied were invalid as contravening the fundamental principles of morality. Let me cite briefly one of these cases.[76]

In 1944 a woman, wishing to be rid of her husband, denounced him to the authorities for insulting remarks he had made about Hitler while home on leave from the German army. The wife was under no legal duty to report his acts, though what he had said was apparently in violation of statutes making it illegal to make statements detrimental to the government of the Third Reich or to impair by any means the military defense of the German people. The husband was arrested and sentenced to death, apparently pursuant to these statutes, though he was not executed but was sent to the front. In 1949 the wife was prosecuted in a West German court for an offense which we would describe as illegally depriving a person of his freedom (*rechtswidrige Freiheitsberaubung*). This was punishable as a crime under the German Criminal Code of 1871 which had remained in force continuously since its enactment. The wife pleaded that her husband's imprisonment was pursuant to the Nazi statutes and hence that she had committed no crime. The court of appeal to which the case ultimately came held that the wife was guilty of procuring the deprivation of her husband's liberty by denouncing him to the German courts, even though he had been sentenced by a court for having violated a statute, since, to quote the words of the court, the statute "was contrary to the sound conscience and sense of justice of all decent human beings."[77] This reasoning was followed in many cases which have been hailed as a triumph of the doctrines of natural law and as signalling the overthrow of positivism. The unqualified satisfaction with this result seems to me to be hysteria. Many of us might applaud the objective—that of punishing a woman for an outrageously immoral act—but this was secured only by declaring a statute established since 1934 not to have the force of law, and at least the wisdom of this course must be doubted. There were, of course, two other choices. One was to let the woman go unpunished; one can sympathize with and endorse the view that this might have been a bad thing to do. The other was to face the fact that if the woman were to be punished it must be pursuant to the introduction of a frankly retrospective law and with a full consciousness of what was sacrificed in securing her punishment in this way. Odious as retrospective[78] criminal legislation and punishment may be, to have pursued it openly in this case would at least have had the merits of candour. It would have made plain that in punishing the woman a choice had to be made between two evils, that of leaving her unpunished and that of sacrificing a very precious principle of morality endorsed by most legal systems. Surely if we have learned anything from the history of morals it is that the thing to

---

[76] Judgment of July 27, 1949, Oberlandesgericht, Bamberg.

[77] [It would seem, however, that this case discussed by Hart and Fuller was not in fact decided on the basis that the earlier Nazi laws were to be treated as invalid.

[78] [Both Fuller and Radbruch would have preferred retrospective legislation.]

do with a moral quandary is not to hide it. Like nettles, the occasions when life forces us to choose between the lesser of two evils must be grasped with the consciousness that they are what they are. The vice of this use of the principle that, at certain limiting points, what is utterly immoral cannot be law or lawful is that it will serve to cloak the true nature of the problems with which we are faced and will encourage the romantic optimism that all the values we cherish ultimately will fit into a single system, that no one of them has to be sacrificed or compromised to accommodate another. . . .

It may seem perhaps to make too much of forms, even perhaps of words, to emphasize one way of disposing of this difficult case as compared with another which might have led, so far as the woman was concerned, to exactly the same result. Why should we dramatize the difference between them? We might punish the woman under a new retrospective law and declare overtly that we were doing something inconsistent with our principles as the lesser of two evils; or we might allow the case to pass as one in which we do not point out precisely where we sacrifice such a principle. But candour is not just one among many minor virtues of the administration of law, just as it is not merely a minor virtue of morality. For if we adopt Radbruch's view, and with him and the German courts make our protest against evil law in the form of an assertion that certain rules cannot be law because of their moral iniquity, we confuse one of the most powerful, because it is the simplest, forms of moral criticism. If with the Utilitarians we speak plainly, we say that laws may be law but too evil to be obeyed. This is a moral condemnation which everyone can understand and it makes an immediate and obvious claim to moral attention. If, on the other hand, we formulate our objection as an assertion that these evil things are not law, here is an assertion which many people do not believe, and if they are disposed to consider it at all, it would seem to raise a whole host of philosophical issues before it can be accepted. So perhaps the most important single lesson to be learned from this form of the denial of the Utilitarian distinction is the one that the Utilitarians were most concerned to teach: when we have the ample resources of plain speech we must not present the moral criticism of institutions as propositions of a disputable philosophy.[pp. 615–621]

## L. L. FULLER
### Positivism and Fidelity to Law—a Reply to Professor Hart
### (1958)[79]

Most of the issues raised by Professor Hart's essay can be restated in terms of the distinction between order and good order. Law may be said to represent order *simpliciter*. Good order is law that corresponds to the demands of justice, or morality, or men's notions of what ought to be. This rephrasing of the issue is useful in bringing to light the ambitious nature of Professor Hart's undertaking, for surely we would all agree that it is no easy thing to distinguish order from good order. When it is said, for example, that law simply represents that public order which obtains under all governments—democratic, Fascist, or Communist—the order intended is certainly not that of a morgue or cemetery. We must mean a functioning order, and such an order has to be at least good enough to be considered as functioning by some standard or other. A reminder that workable order usually requires some play in the joints, and therefore cannot be too orderly, is enough to suggest some of the complexities that would be involved in any attempt to draw a sharp distinction between order and good order.

For the time being, however, let us suppose we can in fact clearly separate the concept of order from that of good order. Even in this unreal and abstract form

[79] [From (1958) 71 Harv. L. Rev. 630–672, copyright @ 1958, by the Harvard Law Review Association.]

the notion of order itself contains what may be called a moral element. Let me illustrate this "morality of order" in its crudest and most elementary form. Let us suppose an absolute monarch, whose word is the only law known to his subjects. We may further suppose him to be utterly selfish and to seek in his relations with his subjects solely his own advantage. This monarch from time to time issues commands, promising rewards for compliance and threatening punishment for disobedience. He is, however, a dissolute and forgetful fellow, who never makes the slightest attempt to ascertain who have in fact followed his directions and who have not. As a result he habitually punishes loyalty and rewards disobedience. It is apparent that this monarch will never achieve even his own selfish aims until he is ready to accept that minimum self-restraint that will create a meaningful connection between his words and his actions.

Let us now suppose that our monarch undergoes a change of heart and begins to pay some attention to what he said yesterday when, today, he has occasion to distribute bounty or to order the chopping off of heads. Under the strain of this new responsibility, however, our monarch relaxes his attention in other directions and becomes hopelessly slothful in the phrasing of his commands. His orders become so ambiguous and are uttered in so inaudible a tone that his subjects never have any clear idea what he wants them to do. Here, again, it it apparent that if our monarch for his own selfish advantage wants to create in his realm anything like a system of law he will have to pull himself together and assume still another responsibility.

Law, considered merely as order, contains, then, its own implicit morality. This morality of order must be respected if we are to create anything that can be called law, even bad law. Law by itself is powerless to bring this morality into existence. Until our monarch is really ready to face the responsibilities of his position, it will do no good for him to issue still another futile command, this time self-addressed and threatening himself with punishment if he does not mend his ways.

There is a twofold sense in which it is true that law cannot be built on law. First of all, the authority to make law must be supported by moral attitudes that accord to it the competency it claims. Here we are dealing with a morality external to law, which makes law possible. But this alone is not enough. We may stipulate that in our monarchy the accepted "basic norm" designates the monarch himself as the only possible source of law. We still cannot have law until our monarch is ready to accept the internal morality of law itself.

In the life of a nation these external and internal moralities of law reciprocally influence one another; a deterioration of the one will almost inevitably produce a deterioration in the other. . . .

What I have called "the internal morality of law" seems to be almost completely neglected by Professor Hart. He does make brief mention of "justice in the administration of the law," which consists in the like treatment of like cases, by whatever elevated or perverted standards the word "like" may be defined. But he quickly dismisses this aspect of law as having no special relevance to his main enterprise.

In this I believe he is profoundly mistaken. It is his neglect to analyze the demands of a morality of order that leads him throughout his essay to treat law as a datum projecting itself into human experience and not as an object of human striving. When we realize that order itself is something that must be worked for, it becomes apparent that the existence of a legal system, even a bad or evil legal system, is always a matter of degree. When we recognize this simple fact of everyday legal experience, it becomes impossible to dismiss the problems presented by the Nazi regime with a simple assertion: "Under the Nazis there was law, even if it was bad law." We have instead to inquire how much of a legal system survived the general debasement and perversion of all forms of social order that occurred under the Nazi rule, and what moral implications this mutilated system had for the conscientious citizen forced to live under it.

It is not necessary, however, to dwell on such moral upheavals as the Nazi regime to see how completely incapable the positivistic philosophy is of serving the one high moral ideal it professes, that of fidelity to law. Its default in serving this ideal actually becomes most apparent, I believe, in the everyday problems that confront those who arc carnestly desirous of meeting the moral demands of a legal order, but who have responsible functions to discharge in the very order toward which loyalty is due.

Let us suppose the case of a trial judge who has had an extensive experience in commercial matters and before whom a great many commercial disputes are tried. As a subordinate in a judicial hierarchy, our judge has of course the duty to follow the law laid down by his supreme court. Our imaginary Scrutton has the misfortune, however, to live under a supreme court which he considers woefully ignorant of the ways and needs of commerce. To his mind, many of his court's decisions in the field of commercial law simply do not make sense. If a conscientious judge caught in this dilemma were to turn to the positivistic philosophy what succour could be expect? It will certainly do no good to remind him that he has an obligation of fidelity to law. He is aware of this already and painfully so, since it is the source of his predicament. Nor will it help to say that if he legislates, it must be "interstitially," or that his contributions must be "confined from molar to molecular motions."[80] This mode of statement may be congenial to those who like to think of law, not as a purposive thing, but as an expression of the dimensions and directions of state power. But I cannot believe that the essentially trite idea behind this advice can be lifted by literary eloquence to the point where it will offer any real help to our judge; for one thing, it may be impossible for him to know whether his supreme court would regard any particular contribution of his as being wide or narrow.

Nor is it likely that a distinction between core and penumbra would be helpful. The predicament of our judge may well derive, not from particular precedents, but from a mistaken conception of the nature of commerce which extends over many decisions and penetrates them in varying degrees. So far as his problem arises from the use of particular words, he may well find that the supreme court often uses the ordinary terms of commerce in senses foreign to actual business dealings. If he interprets those words as a business executive or accountant would, he may well reduce the precedents he is bound to apply to a logical shambles. On the other hand, he may find great difficulty in discerning the exact sense in which the supreme court used those words, since in his mind that sense is itself the product of a confusion.

Is it not clear that it is precisely positivism's insistence on a rigid separation of law as it is from law as it ought to be that renders the positivistic philosophy incapable of aiding our judge? Is it not also clear that our judge can never achieve a satisfactory resolution of his dilemma unless he views his duty of fidelity to law in a context which also embraces his responsibility for making law what it ought to be?

The case I have supposed may seem extreme, but the problem it suggests pervades our whole legal system. If the divergence of views between our judge and his supreme court were less drastic, it would be more difficult to present his predicament graphically, but the perplexity of his position might actually increase. Perplexities of this sort are a normal accompaniment of the discharge of

---

[80] *Southern Pac. Co. v. Jensen* (1997) 244 U.S. 205 at 221 (Holmes J., dissenting), paraphrasing *Storti v. Commonwealth* (1901) 178 Mass. 549 at 554; 60 N. E. 210 at 211 (Holmes C.J.), in which it was held that a statute providing for electrocution as a means of inflicting punishment of death was not cruel or unusual punishment within the Massachusetts Declaration of Rights, Mass. Const., Pt First, Art. XXVI, simply because it accomplished its object by molecular, rather than molar, motions.

any adjudicative function; they perhaps reach their more poignant intensity in the field of administrative law.

One can imagine a case—surely not likely in Professor Hart's country or mine—where a judge might hold profound moral convictions that were exactly the opposite of those held, with equal attachment, by his supreme court. He might also be convinced that the precedents he was bound to apply were the direct product of a morality he considered abhorrent. If such a judge did not find the solution for his dilemma in surrendering his office, he might well be driven to a wooden and literal application of precedents which he could not otherwise apply because he was incapable of understanding the philosophy that animated them. But I doubt that a judge in this situation would need the help of legal positivism to find these melancholy escapes from his predicament. Nor do I think that such a predicament is likely to arise within a nation where both law and good law are regarded as collaborative human achievements in need of constant renewal, and where lawyers are still at least as interested in asking "What is good law?" as they are in asking "What is law?"...                                         [pp. 644–648]

...Professor Hart castigates the German courts and Radbruch, not so much for what they believed had to be done, but because they failed to see that they were confronted by a moral dilemma of a sort that would have been immediately apparent to Bentham and Austin. By the simple dodge of saying, "When a statute is sufficiently evil it ceases to be law," they ran away from the problems they should have faced.

This criticism is, I believe, without justification. So far as the courts are concerned, matters certainly would not have been helped if, instead of saying, "This is not law," they had said, "This is law but it is so evil we will refuse to apply it." Surely moral confusion reaches its height when a court refuses to apply something it admits to be law, and Professor Hart does not recommend any such "facing of the true issue" by the courts themselves. He would have preferred a retroactive statute. Curiously, this was also the preference of Radbruch. But unlike Professor Hart, the German courts and Gustav Radbruch were living participants in a situation of drastic emergency. The informer problem was a pressing one, and if legal institutions were to be rehabilitated in Germany it would not do to allow the people to being taking the law into their own hands, as might have occurred while the courts were waiting for a statute.

As for Gustav Radbruch, it is, I believe, wholly unjust to say that he did not know he was faced with a moral dilemma. His postwar writings repeatedly stress the antinomies confronted in the effort to rebuild decent and orderly government in Germany....

...The situation is not that legal positivism enables a man to know when he faces a difficult problem of choice, while Radbruch's beliefs deceive him into thinking there is no problem to face. The real issue dividing Professors Hart and Radbruch is: How shall we state the problem? What is the nature of the dilemma in which we are caught?

I hope I am not being unjust to Professor Hart when I say that I can find no way of describing the dilemma as he sees it but to use some such words as the following: On the one hand, we have an amoral datum called law, which has the peculiar quality of creating a moral duty to obey it. On the other hand, we have a moral duty to do what we think is right and decent. When we are confronted by a statute that we believe to be thoroughly evil, we have to choose between those two duties.

If this is the positivist position, then I have no hesitancy in rejecting it. The "dilemma" it states has the verbal formulation of a problem, but the problem it states makes no sense. It is like saying I have to choose between giving food to a starving man and being mimsy with the borogoves. I do not think it is unfair to the positivistic philosophy to say that it never gives any coherent meaning to the moral obligation of fidelity to law. This obligation seems to be conceived as sui generis, wholly unrelated to any of the ordinary, extralegal ends of human life. The fundamental postulate of positivism—that law must be strictly severed from morality—seems to deny the possibility of any bridge between the obligation to obey law and other moral obligations. No mediating principle can measure their respective demands on conscience, for they exist in wholly separate worlds.

While I would not subscribe to all of Radbruch's postwar views—especially those relating to "higher law"—I think he saw, much more clearly than does Professor Hart, the true nature of the dilemma confronted by Germany in seeking to rebuild her shattered legal institutions. Germany had to restore both respect for law and respect for justice. Though neither of these could be restored without the other, painful antinomies were encountered in attempting to restore both at once, as Radbruch saw all too clearly. Essentially Radbruch saw the dilemma as that of meeting the demands of order, on the one hand, and those of good order, on the other. Of course no pat formula can be derived from this phrasing of the problem. But, unlike legal positivism, it does not present us with opposing demands that have no living contact with one another, that simply shout their contradictions across a vacuum. As we seek order, we can meaningfully remind ourselves that order itself will do us no good unless it is good for something. As we seek to make our order good, we can remind ourselves that justice itself is impossible without order, and that we must not lose order itself in the attempt to make it good.[81]                                    [pp. 655–657]

## GUSTAV RADBRUCH
### Statutory Lawlessness and Supra-Statutory Law[81a]
(1946)

*Translated by Bonnie Litschewski Paulson and Stanley L. Paulson*

### I.

By means of two maxims, "An order is an order" and "a law is a law", National Socialism contrived to bind its followers to itself, soldiers and jurists respectively. The former tenet was always restricted in its applicability; soldiers had no obligation to obey orders serving criminal purposes.[82] "A law is a law", on the other hand, knew no restriction whatever. It expressed the positivistic legal thinking that, almost unchallenged, held sway over German jurists for many decades. "Statutory lawlessness" was, accordingly, a contradiction in terms, just as "supra-statutory law" was.[83] Today, both problems confront legal practice time and time again. Recently, for example, the *Süddeutsche Juristen-Zeitung* published and commented on a decision of the Wiesbaden Municipal Court [handed down in November of 1945], according to which the "statutes that declared the property of the Jews to be forfeited to the State were in conflict with natural law, and null and void the moment they were enacted".[84]

---

[81] [See also *The Morality of Law* (1969), *ante*, 124, and 157.]
[81a] [From 26 Ox.J. of Legal Studies 1 (2006)].
[82] Military Criminal Code of 1940, § 47.
[83] [Translating "*Unrecht*" as "lawlessness" here—not as "injustice", "wrong", or "evil", among other possibilities—and "*Recht*" as "law"—not as "justice" or "right"—underscores the legal context of the sharp distinction Radbruch draws between the two terms. Better reflecting the "positivistic legal thinking" he mentions, the phrases themselves might read "statutory (or positive-law) lawlessness" and "supra-statutory (or supra-positive) law"]
[84] Heinz Kleine, in the *Süddeutsche Juristen-Zeitung* 1 (1946) 36.

## II.

In the criminal law, the same problem has been raised, particularly in debates and decisions within the Russian Zone.

1. A justice department clerk named Puttfarken was tried and sentenced to life imprisonment by the Thuringian Criminal Court in Nordhausen for having brought about the conviction and execution of the merchant Göttig by informing on him. Puttfarken had denounced Göttig for writing on the wall of a WC that "Hitler is a mass murderer and to blame for the war". Göttig had been condemned not only because of this inscription, but also because he had listened to foreign radio broadcasts. The argument made at Puttfarken's trial by the Thuringian Chief Public Prosecutor, Dr. Friedrich Kuschnitzki, was reported in detail in the press.[85] Prosecutor Kuschnitzki first takes up the question: Was Puttfarken's act a violation of law?

> The defendant's contention that his belief in National Socialism had led him to inform on Göttig is legally insignificant. Whatever one's own political convictions, there is no legal obligation to denounce anyone. Even during the Hitler years, no such legal obligation existed. The decisive question is whether the defendant acted in the interests of the administration of justice, a question presupposing that the judicial system is in a position to administer justice. *Fidelity to statutes, a striving toward justness, legal certainty—these are the requirements of a judicial system.* And all three are lacking in the politicized criminal justice system of the Hitler regime.
>
> Anyone who informed on another during those years had to know—and did in fact know—that he was delivering up the accused to arbitrary power, not consigning him to a lawful judicial procedure with legal guarantees for determining the truth and arriving at a just decision.
>
> With respect to this question, I subscribe fully to the opinion given by Professor Richard Lange, Dean of the Law Faculty of the University of Jena. So well known was the situation in the Third Reich that one could say with certainty: Any person called to account in the third year of the war for writing "Hitler is a mass murderer and to blame for this war" would never come out alive. Someone like Puttfarken certainly could not have had a clear view of just *how* the judiciary would pervert the law, but he could have been sure *that* it would.
>
> No legal obligation to inform on anyone can be drawn from section 139 of the Criminal Code either. It is true that, according to this provision, a person who obtains reliable information of a plan to commit high treason and fails to give timely notice of this plan to the authorities is subject to punishment. It is also true that Göttig had been condemned to death by the Appeal Court at Kassel for *preparing to commit high treason.* In a legal sense, however, there had certainly been no such preparation to commit high treason. After all, Göttig's brave declaration that "Hitler is a mass murderer and to blame for the war" was simply the naked truth. Anyone declaring and spreading this truth threatened neither the Reich nor its security, but sought only to help rid the Reich of its destroyer and thus to rescue it—in other words, the opposite of high treason. Scruples of legal form must not be allowed to obfuscate this plain fact. Furthermore, it is at least questionable whether the so-called Führer and Chancellor of the Reich should ever have been regarded as the legal head of state at all, and therefore questionable whether he was protected by the provisions on high treason. In any event, the defendant had not reflected at all on the legal implications of informing on Göttig, and, given his limited understanding, he could not have done so. Puttfarken himself has never declared that he informed on Göttig because he saw Göttig's inscription as an act of high treason and felt obliged to report it to the authorities.[86]

The Chief Public Prosecutor then addresses the question: Did Puttfarken's act render him culpable?

---

[85]  *Thüringer Volk* (Weimar), 10 May 1946.
[86]  Ibid. [Emphasis in original.]

Puttfarken essentially admits that he intended to send Göttig to the gallows, and a series of witnesses have confirmed his intention. *This is premeditated murder, according to section 211 of the Criminal Code.* That it was a court of the Third Reich that actually condemned Göttig to death does not argue against Puttfarken's having committed the crime. *He is an indirect perpetrator.* Granted, the concept of the indirect commission of a crime, as it has been developed in Supreme Court adjudication, usually looks to other cases, chiefly those in which the indirect perpetrator makes use of instruments lacking in will or the capacity for accountability. No one ever dreamed that a German court could be the instrument of a criminal. Yet today we face just such cases. The Puttfarken case *will not be the only one.* That the Court observed legal *form* in declaring its pernicious decision cannot argue against Puttfarken's indirect commission of the crime. Any lingering hesitancy on this score is cleared away by article 2 of the Thuringian Supplementary Law of 8 February 1946. Article 2, in order to dispel doubts, offers the following rendition of section 47, paragraph 1, of the Criminal Code: "Whoever is guilty of carrying out a criminal act, either by himself or through another person, even if that other person acted lawfully, shall be punished as perpetrator". This does not establish new, retroactively effective substantive law; it is simply an authentic interpretation of criminal law in force since 1871.[87]

After a careful weighing of the pros and cons, I myself am of the opinion that there can be *no* doubt that this is a case of murder committed indirectly. But let us suppose—and we must take this contingency into account—that the Court were to arrive at a different opinion. What would come into question then? If one rejects the view that this is a case of murder committed indirectly, then one can hardly escape the conclusion that the *judges who condemned Göttig to death, contrary to law and statute, are themselves to be regarded as murderers.* The accused would then be an *accomplice to murder* and punishable as such. Should this view, too, raise serious misgivings—and I am not unmindful of them—there remains the Allied Control Council Law No. 10 [of 20 December 1945]. According to article 2, paragraph 1(c),[88] the accused would be guilty of a crime against humanity. Within the framework of this statute, the question is no longer whether the national law of the land is violated. Inhuman acts and persecution for political, racial, or religious reasons are, without qualification, subject to punishment. According to article 2, paragraph 3,[89] the criminal is to be sentenced to such punishment as the court deems just.

[87] In his edition of the Criminal Code in its Thuringian rendition (Weimar: Landesverlag Thuringen, 1946), 13, Prof. Richard Lange states that "in those cases where the perpetrator has misused the judicial system to pursue his own criminal purposes (deception during litigation, political denunciation), much uncertainty has arisen about the concept of the indirect commission of a crime. Therefore, article 2 of the Supplementary Law of 8 February 1946 makes clear that the indirect commission of a crime is punishable even if the instrument that is employed has itself acted lawfully or in compliance with its official duty."

[88] [Control Council Law No. 10, article 2, paragraph 1(c): "*Crimes against Humanity.* Atrocities and offenses, including but not limited to murder, extermination, enslavement, deportation, imprisonment, torture, rape, or other inhumane acts committed against any civilian population, or persecutions on political, racial or religious grounds whether or not in violation of the domestic laws of the country where perpetrated".]

[89] [Ibid, article 2, paragraph 3: "Any persons found guilty of any of the crimes above mentioned [in article 2, paragraph 1] may upon conviction be punished as shall be determined by the tribunal to be just. Such punishment may consist of one or more of the following:

(a) Death.
(b) Imprisonment for life or a term of years, with or without hard labour.
(c) Fine, and imprisonment with or without hard labour, in lieu thereof.
(d) Forfeiture of property.
(e) Restitution of property wrongfully acquired.
(f) Deprivation of some or all civil rights.

Any property declared to be forfeited or the restitution of which is ordered by the Tribunal shall be delivered to the Control Council for Germany, which shall decide on its disposal."]

Even capital punishment.[90]

I might add that as a jurist I am accustomed to confining myself to a purely legal evaluation. But one is always well advised to stand, as it were, *outside* the situation and view it in the light of ordinary common sense. Legal technique is, without exception, merely the instrument the responsible jurist uses in order to arrive at a legally defensible decision.[91]

Puttfarken was condemned by the Thuringian Criminal Court not as an indirect perpetrator of the crime, but as an accomplice to murder. Accordingly, the judges who condemned Göttig to death, contrary to law and statute, had to be guilty of murder.

2. In fact, the Chief Public Prosecutor of Saxony, Dr J.U. Schroeder, announces in the press the intention of enforcing the principle of criminal "responsibility for inhuman judicial decisions", even when such decisions are based on National Socialist statutes:

> The legislation of the National Socialist state, on the basis of which death sentences like those cited here were pronounced, *has no legal validity whatsoever.*
>
> National Socialist legislation rests on the so-called *"Enabling Act"* [of 24 March 1933], which was passed without the constitutionally required two-thirds majority. Hitler had forcibly prevented the Communist representatives from participating in the parliamentary session by having them arrested, in spite of their immunity. The remaining representatives, namely from the Centre Party, were threatened by Nazi storm troopers (the SA) and thereby compelled to vote for the emergency powers.[92]
>
> A judge can never administer justice by appealing to a statute that is not merely unjust but *criminal*. We appeal to *human rights* that surpass all written laws, and we appeal to the inalienable, immemorial law that denies validity to the criminal dictates of inhuman tyrants.
>
> In light of these considerations, I believe that judges must be prosecuted who have handed down decisions incompatible with the precepts of humanity and have pronounced the death sentence for trifles.[93]

## III.

Positivism, with its principle that "a law is a law", has in fact rendered the German legal profession defenceless against statutes that are arbitrary and criminal. Positivism is, moreover, in and of itself wholly incapable of establishing the validity of statutes. It claims to have proved the validity of a statute simply by showing that the statute had sufficient power behind it to prevail. But while power may indeed serve as a basis for the "must" of compulsion, it never serves as a basis for the "ought" of obligation or for legal validity. Obligation and legal

---

[90] Criminal liability according to Allied Control Council Law No. 10 is not discussed in what follows, for German courts do not have primary jurisdiction here. See article 3, paragraph 1(d). ["Each occupying authority, within its Zone of Occupation, shall have the right to cause all persons so arrested and charged, and not delivered to another authority as herein provided, or released, to be brought to trial before an appropriate tribunal. Such tribunal may, in the case of crimes committed by persons of German citizenship or nationality against other persons of German citizenship or nationality, or stateless persons, be a German Court, if authorized by the occupying authorities."]

[91] *Thüringer Volk*, above n 5 [emphasis in original].

[92] Also requiring discussion here would be the extent to which the "normative force of the factual" [Georg Jellinek] makes valid law out of systems that come to power by way of revolution. And my colleague Walter Jellinek has kindly pointed out that it would be inaccurate to suggest that the two-thirds majority was achieved only by eliminating the Communists.

[93] *Tägliche Rundschau* (Berlin), 14 March 1946 [emphasis in original]. On criminal responsibility for unlawful judicial decisions, see also Friedrich Buchwald in his notable work, *Gerechtes Recht* (Weimar: Panses Verlag, 1946) at 3–8.

validity must be based, rather, on a value inherent in the statute. To be sure, *one* value comes with every positive law statute without reference to its content: Any statute is always better than no statute at all, since it at least creates legal certainty. But legal certainty is not the only value that law must effectuate, nor is it the decisive value. Alongside legal certainty, there are two other values: purposiveness[94] and justice. In ranking these values, we assign to last place the purposiveness of the law in serving the public benefit. By no means is law anything and everything that "benefits the people". Rather, what benefits the people is, in the long run, only that which law is, namely, that which creates legal certainty and strives toward justice. Legal certainty (which is characteristic of every positive-law statute simply in virtue of the statute's having been enacted) takes a curious middle place between the other two values, purposiveness and justice, because it is required not only for the public benefit but also for justice. That the law be certain and sure, that it not be interpreted and applied one way here and now, another way elsewhere and tomorrow, is also a requirement of justice. Where there arises a conflict between legal certainty and justice, between an objectionable but duly enacted statute and a just law that has not been cast in statutory form, there is in truth a conflict of justice with itself, a conflict between apparent and real justice. This conflict is perfectly expressed in the Gospel, in the command to "obey them that have the rule over you, and submit yourselves", and in the dictate, on the other hand, to "obey God rather than men".[95]

The conflict between justice and legal certainty may well be resolved in this way: The positive law, secured by legislation and power, takes precedence even when its content is unjust and fails to benefit the people, unless the conflict between statute and justice reaches such an intolerable degree that the statute, as "flawed law", must yield to justice. It is impossible to draw a sharper line between cases of statutory lawlessness and statutes that are valid despite their flaws. One line of distinction, however, can be drawn with utmost clarity: Where there is not even an attempt at justice, where equality, the core of justice, is deliberately betrayed in the issuance of positive law, then the statute is not merely "flawed law", it lacks completely the very nature of law. For law, including positive law, cannot be otherwise defined than as a system and an institution whose very meaning is to serve justice. Measured by this standard, whole portions of National Socialist law never attained the dignity of valid law.

The most conspicuous characteristic of Hitler's personality, which became through his influence the pervading spirit of the whole of National Socialist "law" as well, was a complete lack of any sense of truth or any sense of right and wrong. Because he had no sense of truth, he could shamelessly, unscrupulously lend the ring of truth to whatever was rhetorically effective at the moment. And because he had no sense of right and wrong, he could without hesitation elevate to a statute the crudest expression of despotic caprice. There is, at the beginning of his regime, his telegram offering sympathy to the Potempa murderers,[96] at the end, the hideous degradation of the martyrs of 20 July 1944.[97] The supporting theory had been provided by the Nazi ideologue, Alfred Rosenberg, writing in response to

[94] [The German "*Zweckmäßigkeit*" is often translated, respectably, as "utility" or "expediency". In the present context, however, any suggestion of utilitarianism would be misleading, as would the connotation of opportunism that attaches to "expediency". "Purposiveness" has the virtue of stemming directly from "purpose", thereby underscoring Radbruch's point.]

[95] [*The Holy Bible*, King James Version, 1611, Hebrews 13:17 and Acts 5:29 respectively.]

[96] [In 1932, five Nazi storm troopers were condemned to death by a court in Upper Silesia for the brutal murder of a Communist in the village of Potempa. Under pressure from the Nazis, their sentence was commuted to life imprisonment. After Hitler came to power, they were pardoned.]

[97] [Wehrmacht officers and others, arrested following their failed attempt to assassinate Hitler on 20 July 1944, were tortured, viciously humiliated in a sham trial, and executed.]

the Potempa death sentences: People are not alike, and murders are not alike; the murder of the pacifist Jaurès[98] was properly judged in France in a different light than the attempt to murder the nationalist Clemenceau;[99] for it is impossible to subject the patriotically motivated perpetrator to the same punishment as one whose motives are (in the view of the National Socialists) inimical to the people.[1] The explicit intention from the very beginning, then, was that National Socialist "law" would extricate itself from the essential requirement of justice, namely, the equal treatment of equals. It thereby lacks completely the very nature of law; it is not merely flawed law, but rather no law at all. This applies especially to those enactments by means of which the National Socialist Party claimed for itself the whole of the state, flouting the principle that every political party represents only a part of the state. Legal character is also lacking in all the statutes that treated human beings as subhuman and denied them human rights, and it is lacking, too, in all the caveats that, governed solely by the momentary necessities of intimidation, disregarded the varying gravity of offences and threatened the same punishment, often death, for the slightest as well as the most serious of crimes. All these are examples of statutory lawlessness.

We must not fail to recognize—especially in light of the events of those twelve years—what frightful dangers for legal certainty there can be in the notion of "statutory lawlessness", in duly enacted statutes that are denied the very nature of law. We must hope that such lawlessness will remain an isolated aberration of the German people, a never-to-be-repeated madness. We must prepare, however, for every eventuality. We must arm ourselves against the recurrence of an outlaw state like Hitler's by fundamentally overcoming positivism, which rendered impotent every possible defence against the abuses of National Socialist legislation.[2]                                                                                  [pp 1–8]


## R. ALEXY
### A Defence of Radbruch's Formula
#### (1999)[3]


The problem of dealing with a past devoid of the rule of law has twice confronted the courts in Germany in a century which is now drawing to a close: in 1945 after National Socialism was crushed and in 1989 after the collapse of the German Democratic Republic. In both cases the following question had to be answered. Should one regard as continuing to be legally valid something which offended against fundamental principles of justice and the rule of law when it was legally valid in terms of the positive law of the legal system which had perished. To use a handy though imprecise formulation, can something be illegal today which in the past was legal? After 1945 German courts answered "yes" to this question, and the Federal Court of Justice has followed this tradition after 1989 especially in its

---

[98] [Jean Jaurès, an eloquent politician known as an intellectual champion of socialism, was assassinated in Paris in 1914 by a fanatical nationalist, Raoul Villain. Villain was taken into custody pending trial, but acquitted in 1919 by jurors who reportedly felt he was a patriot who had done France a favour by getting rid of the antiwar Jaurès.]

[99] [Georges Clemenceau, a Radical Nationalist politician, survived an attempt on his life made in 1892 by a rival political group, taking revenge for his repudiation of their leader, General Boulanger, a convicted traitor who had committed suicide in 1891. The Boulangist who failed in his attempt to assassinate Clemenceau was unceremoniously executed.]

[1] *Völkischer Beobachter* (Munich) [publication of the National Socialist Party], 26 August 1932.

[2] Buchwald, too, argues for supra-statutory law in his book, above n 14, at 8–16. And compare Walter Roemer, *Süddeutsche Junsten-Zeitung* 1 (1946) 9–11.

[3] [From D. Dyzenhaus, *Recrafting the Rule of Law; The Limits of Legal Order* (1999).]

decisions in regard to the so-called wall shootings. The Federal Constitutional Court forged ahead in this course in cases of National Socialist injustice and affirmed it in cases concerning the injustice committed by the German Democratic Republic. Radbruch's formula formed the jurisprudential core of the judges' reasoning. In what follows, the first task will be to present this formula. Then its practical significance will be illustrated through two examples. Finally, we will ask whether the formula can stand up to jurisprudential critique.

## 1. The formula

Gustav Radbruch presented his famous formula under the immediate impression of twelve years of National Socialism. It reads:

> "The conflict between justice and legal certainty should be resolved in that the positive law, established by enactment and by power, has primacy even when its content justice reaches an intolerable level that the law is supposed to give way as a 'false law' [*unrichtiges Recht*] to justice. It is impossible to draw a sharper line between the cases of legalized injustice and laws which remain valid despite their false content. But another boundary can be drawn with the utmost precision. Where justice is not even aimed at, where equality—the core of justice—is deliberately disavowed in the enactment of a positive law, then the law is not simply 'false law', it has no claim at all to legal status".[4]

It is easy to see that this formula is composed of two parts. In the first part, the claim is that positive law loses its legal validity when its contradiction with justice reaches an "intolerable level". We can call this the "intolerability formula". In the second part, positive laws are denied legal status when in their enactment equality, which Radbruch says is the core of justice, is "deliberately disavowed". We can call this the "disavowal formula". The intolerability formula has an objective character. It is attuned to the level of injustice.[5] In contrast, there is something subjective about the disavowal formula: the purpose or intentions of the legislators. One can think of cases in which both formulae lead to different results. One can easily imagine a legislator who in fact strives for equality as the core of justice, but nevertheless brings about something which is intolerably unjust, just as one who is bent on bringing about injustice might fail and purpose should coincide when in issue is intolerable injustice. In this respect one can speak of an "overlapping" of both formulae.[6] Judicial reasoning has first and foremost applied the intolerability formula. In favour of this is that an "intention to warp justice" is very difficult to prove in doubtful cases. In this chapter, the intolerability formula is the focus.

Remarkable about Radbruch's formula is that it does not require any complete coincidence between law and morality. It allows enacted and effective law—Radbruch speaks of the "law established by enactment and by power"—to be valid even when it is unjust and it does not even require that the law as a whole orient itself to morality. It is much more the case that it builds into law an outermost limit. In general, law is that which is appropriately enacted and appropriately enacted and socially effective norms lose their legal character or their legal validity. Hence, one can express Radbruch's formula concisely:

---

[4] G. Radbruch, "Gesetzliches Unrecht und übergesetzliches Recht", in G. Radbruch, *Gesamtausgabe*, in A. Kaufmann (ed.) (1990), vol. 3, p. 89. Radbruch's famous essay was first published in 1946 in the first volume of the *Süddeutschen Juristen-Zeitung*, pp. 105–108.

[5] More precisely, two aspects should be distinguished within the framework of the intolerability formula. The first concerns the weighing, the second the threshold.

[6] S.L. Paulson, "Radbruch on Unjust Laws: Competing Earlier and Later Views?" (1995) 15 *Oxf. J. of Legal Studies* 489 at 491. [See also *ante*, 421].

appropriately enacted and socially effective norms lose their legal character or their legal validity when they are extremely unjust.

Even shorter:

Extreme injustice is no law.[7]

Whoever supports this thesis has ceased to be a legal positivist. When a positivist wants to establish what law is, he inquires only into what is appropriately enacted and socially effective. Though these are ideas which can be very differently interpreted and evaluated, as the many forms of legal positivism show, nothing more will be said on this issue here. Of interest in this chapter is only that for the positivist nothing about legal character or validity turns upon the content of the norm. The great legal positivist Hans Kelsen expressed this idea in a much cited formulation: "Hence any content whatsoever can be legal".[8] This is the positivist thesis of the separation of law and morality, in short, the positivist separation thesis. Even the anti-positivist takes into account appropriate enactment and social effectiveness if he wishes to be regarded as in his right mind. Radbruch's formula is clear evidence of this. But for the anti-positivist who adopts the formula there is nevertheless a limit, that of extreme injustice. In this way substantive correctness is imported as a limiting criterion into the concept of law. The concept of law is not filled out by morality but it is limited by morality. This is clearly only a partial connection of law and morality but it is a connection. Whoever advocates Radbruch's formula therefore supports the anti-positivist connection thesis.[9]

The conflict about Radbruch's formula is a philosophical conflict because it is a conflict about the concept of law. It speaks volumes about the character of legal philosophy that this conflict over its foundational concept—the concept of law— has at the same time direct practical consequences. We will take such consequences into account before we ask whether the better argument speaks for or against anti-positivism in the form of Radbruch's formula. And this can be done through two examples.

## II. Practical significance

The first example is a 1968 decision of the Federal Constitutional Court concerning Decree 11 in regard to the Reich's Citizenship Law of 25 November 1941. Section 2 of this decree reads:

"A Jew loses German nationality

(a) with the coming into force of this decree when he has his usual residence abroad at the time of the coming into force of this decree,
(b) when he at a later date takes up his usual residence abroad at the time when he changes his usual residence to abroad."

The occasion of the Federal Constitutional Court's decision was whether a Jewish lawyer, who had emigrated to Amsterdam shortly before the Second World War, had lost his German nationality in accordance with this rule. The outcome of a matter concerning an inheritance turned on this point. The lawyer had been

---

[7] Radbruch comes close to this formulation when he says that "horribly" unjust laws can be denied validity; see G. Radbruch, *Vorschule der Rechtsphilosophie*, in G. Radbruch, *Gesamtausgabe* (A. Kaufmann (ed.), 1990), vol. 3, p. 154.
[8] H. Kelsen, *Reine Rechtslehre* (2nd ed., 1960), p. 201.
[9] R. Alexy, *Begriff und Geltung des Rechts* (2nd ed., 1994), pp. 15 *et seq.* and pp. 52 *et seq.*

deported from Amsterdam in 1942. There was no news about his fate beyond that, so it had to be accepted that he had lost his life in a concentration camp.

The Federal Constitutional Court decided that the lawyer had not lost his German nationality because Decree 11 in regard to the Reich's Citizenship Law was from the outset void. The core of its reasoning reads:

> "Hence the Federal Constitutional Court has affirmed the possibility of depriving National Socialist 'legal' decrees of their legal validity because they so evidently contradict fundamental principles of justice that the judge who applied them or recognised their legal consequences would pronounce injustice instead of law (BVerfGE 3, 58 (119); 6, 132 (198)).
> Decree 11 offends these fundamental principles. In it the contradiction with justice has reached so intolerable a level that it must be regarded as void from the outset (see BGH, RzW 1962, 563; BGHZ 9, 34 (44); 10, 340 (342); 16, 350 (354); 26, 91 (93)))".

This is a classical anti-positivist argument. An appropriately enacted norm, one which was socially effective for the duration of its validity, is denied validity or— on this point the decision is not unequivocal—its character as law, because it offends suprapositive law. While Radbruch was not in fact mentioned by name, one finds his name nevertheless in earlier decisions of the Federal Constitutional Court on which the Court in this decision expressly relied. In any case more significant is that Radbruch's formulation of the "intolerable level" of the "contradiction" with "injustice" is applied. The decision on nationality is thus a paradigmatic case of the application of Radbruch's formula.

Expatriates often had no desire to get their old citizenship back. But generally in the case of property things were different. This was the issue in a decision of the Great Panel of the Federal Court of Justice for Civil Matters, which should rank with the decision on nationality. Once again the outcome of the proceedings turned on the validity of Decree 11 in regard to the Reich's Citizenship Law, this time on section 3, paragraph 1, provision 1, which reads:

> "The property of Jews who have lost their German nationality on the basis of this Decree becomes the property of the Reich with the loss of nationality."

A Jewish woman who emigrated to Switzerland in 1939 had left securities in a deposit in a German bank. During the entire period of National Socialist rule and also thereafter this deposit remained entered in the books of the bank in the name of the emigrant. After the end of the war she again took up domicile in the Federal Republic of Germany. Presently she demanded that the securities in the deposit be restored to her. The question was whether she had lost her property on the basis of the immediate expropriation in terms of section 3, paragraph 1, provision 1 of Decree 11. The Federal Court of Justice answered "no" to this question and therefore confirmed her demand for restitution. The details of its reasoning are complex but the core reads as follows:

> "§3 of Decree 11 under the Reich's Citizenship Law is to be regarded as from the outset void because of its iniquitous content which contradicts the foundational requirements of every order based on the rule of law".

Following this anti-positivist solution the emigrant could demand her property back simply because she had never lost it. From the standpoint of legal positivism some retroactive or correcting regulation was required if she were to have any title to claim restitution. Whether she could demand the property back would hinge then on the discretion of the legislature. The decision for or against legal positivism therefore can have immense practical significance for the victim of a tyrannical regime.

The second example of the practical significance of Radbruch's formula comes from the judicial decisions in regard to the deaths of fugitives on the border formerly internal to Germany. The Federal Court of Justice confirmed the guilt of simple border soldiers in its first judgment on wall shootings in November 1992, a good two years after reunification. Two years later in 1994 it decided that higher and the highest German Democratic Republic officials, among them the last Minister of Defence of the German Democratic Republic, Army-General Keßler, were criminally responsible for the killings on the border. It found them guilty of being the indirect cause of manslaughter. Again two years later, in October 1996, the Federal Constitutional Court declared this line of adjudication to be in accordance with the Constitution. Here only the leading decision is examined— the first judgment on wall shootings by the Federal Court of Justice.

This judgment concerned a twenty-year-old fugitive, who on 1 December 1984 at about 3.15 a.m. attempted to get over the border structure with a four-metre-long ladder. Two soldiers of the border patrol of the German Democratic Republic, one about twenty the other about twenty-three years old, caught sight of the fugitive about 100 metres away, as he prepared to cross the 29-metre-wide border strip. In the middle of the strip stood a 2.5-metre-tall alarm fence and at its end stood a 3.5-metre-high border wall. Neither calls nor warning shots could stop the fugitive. As he leant his ladder against the border wall and quickly ascended, it became clear to the two soldiers that only directed fire stood any chance of preventing his flight. They shot several bursts of fire at the fugitive. Though they aimed at his legs, they knew that there was the possibility that he would be killed especially because of their sustained fire. But even at this price they were determined to prevent his flight. The fugitive was hit a few seconds after they opened fire, at the moment his hand reached the top of the wall. He died within hours.

In 1992 the Berlin Provincial Court found both soldiers jointly guilty of manslaughter and sentenced the younger one to imprisonment in a young offender's facility for a year and six months and the older to a prison term of one year and nine months.[10] The execution of both punishments was deferred pending probation. In its first wall shooting decision, the Federal Court of Justice rejected the appeals against this judgment and confirmed the convictions though not the reasoning behind them.

In accordance with the rules of the treaty on the restoration of German unity the general principle was valid for both soldiers that their deed was punishable only if it was punishable in terms of the valid law governing at the time and in the place it was done. The crucial question was thus whether they had a permission or justification in terms of the law then in force in the German Democratic Republic. In issue as their ground of justification was section 27 of the 1982 Border Law of the German Democratic Republic. In the present case, section 27, paragraph 2, provision 1 was significant:

"The use of firearms is justified to prevent the directly imminent carrying out or the continuation of a criminal act which, in the circumstances, appears to be a felony."

The fugitive's crossing of the border was directly imminent and the soldiers fired to prevent him from that. According to the interpretation of the criminal law— both the dominant theory and the practice—of the German Democratic Republic it was a felony to attempt to break through the border as the fugitive had done. Hence all the preconditions of section 27, paragraph 2, provision 1 were in evidence. Even the remaining preconditions of section 27 were fulfilled. Fire was

---

[10] LG Berlin, NStZ 1992, 492 (493). Army-General Keßler has incurred the most severe punishment so far, as he was sentenced to seven years and six months; see BVerfGE 95, 96 (97).

only opened after milder measures did not work (section 27, paragraph 1, provision 2). In this case the fugitive could only be stopped by fire. He was called back and a warning shot was fired (section 27, paragraph 3). Finally, section 27, paragraph 5 had to be observed:

"When firearms are used the life of the person is if possible to be spared."

Even this norm was respected since it does not require that one may not in any way threaten life. It only says that "if possible" life is to be spared. The flight could not have been prevented at all without firing at the fugitive and, given that he was seconds away from succeeding, single shots would not have been as sure. When the prevention of the flight is understood as a justificatory ground in the sense of section 27, paragraph 2, it follows that section 27, paragraph 5 was also not violated.

The attempt to convict the border soldiers was undertaken by interpreting section 27 of the Border Law of the former German Democratic Republic in the light shed in the present by the principles of the rule of law. The judgment of the Berlin Provincial Court, which convicted both soldiers in the first instance, is an example of this. It held that the soldiers should have complied with the fundamental principle of proportionality, which meant that the soldiers should not have opened continuous fire. In addition, the aim of preventing a criminal act which did not endanger the life of another could never justify the killing of a person, since life is the most prized legal value.

One should welcome the fact that the Federal Court of Justice did not adopt this reasoning, at least in the first part of its judgment which is the part of interest here. Whoever interprets the former law of the German Democratic Republic in the light shed in the present by principles of the rule of law is pursuing a covert kind of retroactivity which is worse than an open one. The question whether the punishment today of both soldiers offends the proposition *Nullum crimen sine lege* or *Nulla poena sine lege* would be evaded. In this regard, the Berlin Provincial Court got the positive law wrong. For not only the wording of the positive law makes up the positive law in force at the time; there is also the interpretative practice of the time. If one applies this standard, then the deed of both soldiers, as the Federal Court of Justice effectively and in full detail showed, was justified by section 27, paragraph 2, provision 1 of the Border Law of the German Democratic Republic. The deed was thus legal in terms of the positive law valid at that time. Since a retroactive law which declared the deed as punishable today did not exist, both soldiers could be punished only if the justificatory ground in section 27, paragraph 2, provision 1 did not apply. The Federal Court of Justice brought Radbruch's formula into play on exactly this point:

"It is much more the case that a justificatory ground taken from the time of the deed can only be disregarded because of its offence to a higher order of law when in it is manifested a patently gross offence to the fundamental tenets of justice and humanity; the offence must be so weighty that it violates the legal convictions of all nations in regard to people's worth and dignity (BGHSt 2, 234, 239). The contradiction between positive law and justice must be so intolerable that the law has to give way to justice as a false law (Radbruch, SJZ 1946, 105, 107)."

The last sentence is an almost word for word repetition of Radbruch's intolerability formula. The Court then explained that the scope of application of Radbruch's formula was not limited to National Socialist injustice:

"In these formulations (see also BVerfGE 3, 225, 232; 6, 132f., 198f.) the attempt was made to define the worst violations of the law after the end of the National Socialist regime of violence. The transfer of these perspectives to the present case is not easy, because the killing of people on the internal German border cannot be equated with National Socialist mass murder. All the same, the insight achieved at that time remains valid that in judging deeds done at the command of the state one has to take into account whether the state has crossed the outer limits which are ordained to it by general convictions in any country".

Thus everything turns on the question whether the deaths on the internal German border amounted to an extreme injustice in Radbruch's sense. This is very controversial. The Federal Court of Justice answered in the affirmative with a detailed justification in the guarantees of the rights to life (Article 6) and mobility (Article 12) of the International Covenant on Civil and Political Rights of 19 December 1966, which, as it said, were drawn on as "guiding principles". This reasoning will not be reiterated here, since the issue is the presentation of the way in which Radbruch's formula works in practice. And this is shown with great clarity in the sentence with which the Federal Court of Justice removed from both border soldiers the justification in terms of the positive law of the former German Democratic Republic:

> "The justification stipulated by the law of the German Democratic Republic, described in §27 of the Border Law, had for this reason from the outset no validity in the interpretation which is defined by the actual relations on the border".

## III. *The Aspiration and the Limits of Law*

Radbruch's formula excludes certain contents from entering into the content of law, namely extreme injustice. In this way it restores a necessary connection between law and morality, that is, between the law as it is and the law as it ought to be. Appropriately enacted and socially effective law does not, to be sure, have to be just or right in order to be law, but it must not cross the threshold of extreme injustice. If this occurs, its legal character or validity as law is lost. This is a denial of the positivist thesis that there is a complete separation of law and morality and a profession of the anti-positivist connection thesis.

### 1. *A Conceptual Framework*

The conflict over legal positivism seems to be a conflict with no end, and that means it is a philosophical debate. In such disputes which are at once endless, acute and stubborn, one can surmise that all the participants are right in one or other aspect or in regard to one or other assumption. Our next task will be to cast a glance over these aspects or assumptions and here four distinctions are useful.

**(a) Norm and procedure.** The first distinction is between the legal system as a system of norms and the legal system as a system of procedures. As a system of *procedures* the legal system is a system of interactions dependent on rules and guided by rules by means of which norms are enacted, grounded, interpreted, applied and executed. As a system of *norms* the legal system is a system of results or products of the procedures provided for producing norms. This distinction approximates Fuller's between the law as "activity"[11] in the sense of a "purposive effort that goes into the making of law and the law that in fact emerges from that effort",[12] hence, the law as "product"[13] or "results".[14] It is obvious that the understanding of law as a system of procedures or activities is more suitable to an

---

[11] L.L. Fuller, *The Morality of Law* (1969), pp. 106, 119.
[12] *ibid.*, p. 193.
[13] *ibid.*, p. 106.
[14] *ibid.*, p. 119.

anti-positivist position than the exclusive focus on norms as the results of such procedures.

**(b) Observer and participant.** The second distinction is between the observer and participant perspectives. This dichotomy maps onto Hart's distinction between an "external" and an "internal" point of view.[15] Hart's distinction is clearly in need of interpretation.[16] Here we will interpret it with the help of the concepts of argumentation and of correctness: the *participant perspective* engages one who within a legal system takes part in argumentation about what it requires, forbids and permits and in addition about what it enables. The judge stands at the centre of the participant perspective. When other participants, including legal academics, lawyers, and citizens who concern themselves with the legal system, bring forth arguments for or against the particular meaning of laws, then they refer ultimately to what a judge would decide when he wanted to make a correct decision. The *observer perspective* engages one who asks not what the correct decision is in a particular legal system, but what the actual decision in a particular system will be. Again it is easy to recognise that the observer perspective is more suitable for the positivist and the participant perspective for the anti-positivist.

**(c) Classification and qualification.** The third distinction concerns the two different kinds of connection between law and morality. The first kind will be defined as "classificatory", the second as "qualificatory". One has to do with a *classificatory* connection when one maintains that norms or systems of norms which fail to meet a particular moral criterion fail to be legal norms or legal systems. Radbruch's formula creates such a connection since it excludes legal norms containing extreme injustice from the class of legal norms (or of valid legal norms). One has to do with a merely *qualificatory* connection when one maintains that norms or systems of norms which fail to meet a particular moral criterion could indeed be legal norms or legal systems, but are legally defective legal norms or legally defective legal systems. It is crucial that the defect asserted is a legal one and not merely moral.

The concept of a qualificatory connection is tightly bound up with the claim to correctness, since if the law necessarily raises a claim to correctness, then there necessarily exists a qualificatory relationship between law and morality.[17] Fuller's "internal" or "inner morality of law" as a "morality of aspiration"[18] resembles in a crucial respect the thesis of the claim to correctness. The incomplete fulfilment of the eight "principles of legality" which, according to Fuller, define the "inner morality of law", do not lead in general to a loss of legal character or legal validity.[19] It has therefore no classificatory meaning but rather the result is a qualification of the law or legal system as "bad".[20] Thus Fuller's theory is a classic example of theory which essentially depends on qualificatory connections.

The qualificatory connection does not imply any classificatory one.[21] It is however easier to justify the latter when the former exists than when it does not.

---

[15] H.L.A. Hart, *The Concept of Law* (1994), p. 89.

[16] See N. MacCormick, *Legal Reasoning and Legal Theory* (1978), pp. 275 *et seq.*

[17] See R. Alexy, "Law and Correctness" in M. Freeman (ed.), *Legal Theory at the End of the Millennium* (1998), pp. 214 *et seq.*

[18] L. Fuller, *The Morality of Law*, note 11 above, p. 43.

[19] *ibid.*, pp. 39, 41 *et seq.*

[20] *ibid.*, p. 39. In contrast, one has to do with a classificatory connection when Fuller says that "a total failure" in the fulfilment of any one of his eight principles of legality "does not simply result in a bad system of law; it results in something that is not properly called a legal system at all"; *ibid.*

[21] See N. MacCormick, "Natural Law and the Separation of Law and Morals", in R.P. George (ed.), *Natural Law Theory* (1992), pp. 112 *et seq.* and p. 130.

The justification of Radbruch's formula will thus begin with the justification of the qualificatory connection.

**(d) Analytical and normative arguments.** The fourth distinction is that between analytical and normative arguments for and against legal positivism. An *analytical* argument is presented when one shows it to be the case that the inclusion of moral elements in the concept of law is conceptually or linguistically necessary, impossible or merely possible. In contrast, the separation or connection thesis is supported by a normative argument when it is proposed that the inclusion or exclusion of moral elements is necessary to fulfil certain norms, such as the prohibition on retroactivity, or to realise certain values, such as human rights.[22]

As we have already seen, Radbruch's formula has to do with a classificatory connection. That the issue here cannot be decided on analytical grounds alone is demonstrated by the fact that neither of the following two sentences contains a contradiction.[23]

(1)  The Norm N is appropriately enacted and socially effective and therefore law even if it contains extreme injustice.
(2)  The Norm N is appropriately enacted and socially effective but not law because it contains extreme injustice.

Because of the vagueness and ambiguity of the expression "law" (*Recht*), a decision on the correctness of Radbruch's formula is ultimately possible only on the basis of normative arguments. These lead to completely different results depending on whether one adopts the observer or the participant perspective.

*2. The Observer*

To answer the question whether Radbruch's formula is acceptable from the observer standpoint we will return to Decree 11 in regard to the Citizenship Law of the Reich of 25 November 1941, which deprived the Jew who had emigrated of citizenship and property. Imagine a contemporary observer of the National Socialist legal system, a foreign jurist who was composing a yearly report on the National Socialist legal system for a law journal in his homeland. How would he at the end of 1941 describe the case presented above of the emigrant whose securities section 3, paragraph 1, provision 1 of that Decree declared to be the property of the German Reich? It would be the case that anyone in his homeland would understand without any further explanation the proposition:

(1)  A lost ownership of the securities in accordance with German law.

---

[22]  One could suggest that whoever justifies the positivistic thesis of the separation of law and morality with moral and hence normative arguments ceases to be a positivist. On this interpretation, it would be the case that any use of a moral argument in the framework of a theory of law turns the theory into an anti-positivist one. One reason that speaks against such an extremely strict definition of legal positivism is that hardly any positivist would survive. A much more weighty consideration is that the crucial difference is flattened between authors who claim that a norm loses its legal character or validity when it violates a moral criterion and authors who claim that nothing about legal character or validity turns on any moral criterion. Both supporters and opponents of Radbruch's formula could then be equally characterised as anti-positivists when they adduced for their position any non-positivist, normative and in this sense moral argument, for example, that of legal certainty. This mode of conceptual argument would be confusing.
[23]  Hart suggests that "the positivist might point to a weight of English usage" that sentences like (1) contain no contradiction; see H.L.A. Hart, *The Concept of Law*, note 15 above, p. 209. The argument is then to be extended to sentences like (2). Hart's argument is then compelling: "Plainly we cannot grapple adequately with this issue if we see it as one concerning the proprieties of linguistic usage".

But this is not the case with the following proposition:

(2)   A did not lose ownership of the securities in accordance with German law.

When no further information is given with this second proposition, he is either giving false information or confusing. The reason is that one can use the expression "law" in a way which serves only the value neutral identification of appropriately enacted and socially effective norms together with their consequences. Only this use is appropriate for the observer perspective. It serves clarity and truth of speech. A lawyer who had to advise a Jew at the end of 1941 and neglected Decree 11 would be in gross dereliction of duty. An appeal to Radbruch's formula would not help him in any way. Naturally, he could conclude his opinion with the following remark:

(3)   She has lost her property in accordance with regulations which are now valid in Germany, but which amount to extreme injustice and are therefore not law. After the collapse of National Socialism we will ensure that the loss of property is declared to be invalid.

With this, the position of the mere observer is relinquished and one takes up in anticipation the position of a participant in a discourse about how to classify legally the expropriation after the collapse of the dictatorship. With this change of perspective, the expression "law" takes on a different meaning.

## 3. The Correctness Argument

Properly understood the real question in the debate about Radbruch's formula is whether it is acceptable from the standpoint of a participant in a legal system. Here one has to distinguish between participants in legal procedures in an iniquitous state and participants in procedures which begin to come to terms with the former injustice after the collapse of the system. The question of whether the law necessarily raises a claim to correctness plays a decisive role in an explication of what it means to be a participant in a legal system. The thesis that the law necessarily raises such a claim can be called the "correctness argument". The correctness argument makes up the basis of the justification of Radbruch's formula.

The correctness argument maintains as valid that individual legal norms, individual legal decisions, and also whole legal systems necessarily raise a claim to correctness. This can be demonstrated by examples in which there is an explicit negation of the claim to correctness. Here only one is dealt with. It concerns the first provision of a new constitution for state X, in which a minority suppresses the majority. The minority would like to enjoy the advantages of the suppression of the majority while being honest about it. Their constitutional assembly thus decides on the following as the first provision of the constitution:

X is a sovereign, federal and unjust Republic.

Something is flawed in this constitutional provision, but the question is in what the flaw consists. One could immediately think of a conventional flaw. The provision doubtless offends conventions about the composition of constitutional texts but that in itself does not explain the flaw. For example, a 100-page catalogue of fundamental rights would also be most unusual and unconventional, but despite its unusualness it would not partake in the slightest of what makes the provision about injustice senseless. The same goes when one accepts that there is a moral flaw. From the standpoint of morality it makes no difference if the rights of the majority, at whose denial the provision about injustice aims, are expressly withheld in a second provision. But from the standpoint of what is flawed there is a real difference. The provision about injustice is not merely immoral it is also somehow crazy. One could perhaps think that there is just a political flaw in the provision about injustice. There is such a flaw here, but even that does not explain its flawed nature completely.[24] A constitution can contain much that is politically inappropriate and in this sense technically flawed without it looking as odd as our first provision. Neither the conventional, nor the moral, nor the technical flaws can explain the absurdity of the provision about injustice. This results, as is so often the case with the absurd, from a contradiction. A contradiction comes about because a claim to correctness is necessarily bound up with the act of giving a constitution, and in such cases it is above all a claim to justice. This claim, implicit in the act of giving a constitution, contradicts the explicit content of the provision about injustice. Such contradictions between the content of an act and the necessary presuppositions of its fulfilment can be called "performative contradictions".[25]

The claim to correctness determines the character of law. It excludes understanding law as a mere command of the powerful. Built into the law is an ideal dimension, an "aspiration" in Fuller's sense. This still tells us nothing definitive about Radbruch's formula. But it is clear that the law is not indifferent to its content.

The claim to correctness comprises the eight formal principles which, according to Fuller, define the inner or internal morality of law. But it goes further, including substantive justice[26] and thus what Fuller terms the external morality of law.[27] This connection of formal or procedural aspects with those of a material or substantive kind permits it to take into account the institutional as well as the ideal character of law.[28]

### 4. The Injustice Argument

The correctness argument does not by itself suffice to ground Radbruch's formula. While the mere non-fulfilment of the claim to correctness does lead to legal defectiveness, it does not strip a norm or a legal act of its legal character or legal validity. Thus further arguments are required in order to ground Radbruch's formula as a limit of law. The bundle of all these arguments can be called "the injustice argument". It is composed of seven arguments which are in essence normative and which sometimes are made up of several strands.

**(a) The Clarity Argument.**   The first argument to be dealt with is the clarity argument. Hart gave it its classic formulation:

> "For if we adopt Radbruch's view, and with him and the German courts make our protest against evil law in the form of an assertion that certain rules cannot be law because of their moral iniquity, we confuse one of the most powerful, because it is the simplest, forms of moral criticism. If with the Utilitarians we speak plainly, we say that laws may be law but too evil to be obeyed ...; when we have the ample resources of plain

---

[24] R. Alexy, "Bulygins Kritik des Richtigkeitsarguments", in E. Garzón Valdés, W. Krawietz, G.H. v. Wright and R. Zimmerling (eds.), *Normative Systems in Legal and Moral Theory. Festschrift for Carlos E Alchourrón and Eugenio Bulygin* (1997), pp. 243 *et seq.*

[25] In this regard, see R. Alexy, "Law and Correctness", note 17 above, pp. 209 *et seq.*

[26] *ibid.*, pp. 214 *et seq.* One can show this to be the case since justice is nothing other than correctness in regard to distribution and commutation and law certainly concerns distribution and commutation.

[27] L. Fuller, *The Morality of Law*, note 11 above, pp. 44, 96, 132, 224.

[28] See in this regard N. MacCormick, "Natural Law and the Separation of Law and Morals", note 16 *et seq* above, pp. 114 ff.

speech we must not present the moral criticism of institutions as propositions of a disputable philosophy".[29]

This objection has a certain force but it is not decisive. A positivist concept of law which rejects the inclusion of any moral elements is indeed *ceteris paribus* simpler than a concept of law which contains moral elements, and simplicity prima facie implies clarity. Still it is not the case that every increase in complexity brings a corresponding increase in unclarity. There is little to fear in the way of confusion on the part of jurist or citizen when the formula "Extreme injustice is no law" is built into the concept of law. Confusion could also come about when courts or legal philosophers say to them that the most extreme injustice can be law. It is true that unclarity can come about because of cases like the wall shootings in which the line between extreme and less than extreme injustice is not easy to draw. Still this is not a problem for the clarity argument, only for the legal certainty argument. The clarity argument concerns itself exclusively with the question whether confusion results when moral elements in particular are included in the concept of law.

One should agree with Hart that clarity is a "sovereign virtue in jurisprudence".[30] However one should not agree with his attribution to positivism of the "ample resources of plain speech" and to anti-positivism the "propositions of a disputable philosophy".[31] Anti-positivism can also be formulated in plain speech and positivism can also be seen as a disputable philosophy. In the conflict between positivism and anti-positivism both camps confront each other on fundamentally equal terms. That positivism cannot even claim for itself a presumption of correctness is demonstrated by the fact that the law necessarily raises a claim to correctness. This speaks more for than against the inclusion of certain criteria of correctness in the concept of law. Hence, the clarity argument is not a knockdown one in this respect.

**(b) The Efficacy Argument.** Radbruch put forward the view that legal positivism had made "both jurists and the people defenceless against just such arbitrary, cruel and criminal statutes" It had "disempowered every capacity to resist National Socialist legislation". His new[32] formula was supposed to provide jurists "with weapons against a recurrence of such an unjust state". In these quotations the future is as much a concern as the past. In respect of the past, we find two theses in Radbruch: a causal thesis and an exoneration thesis.[33] The causal thesis maintains that positivism eased the National Socialist takeover of power in 1933. The exoneration thesis argues that the unjust judgments given by judges of the Third Reich on the basis of unjust laws could "not lead to an attribution of personal responsibility ... just because they were educated in the spirit of positivism".[34] There are serious objections to both theses,[35] but these will not be pursued here. The acceptability of Radbruch's formula as a thesis of legal philosophy does not depend on Radbruch's conjectures about legal history, whether these are right or wrong. Rather, it depends on whether it, at an altogether

[29] H.L.A. Hart, "Positivism and the Separation of Law and Morals", in H.L.A. Hart, *Essays in Jurisprudence and Philosophy* (1983), pp. 77 *et seq.* [And *ante*, 414.]
[30] *ibid.*, p. 49.
[31] *ibid.*, p. 78.
[32] For the relationship between Radbruch's legal philosophy after 1945 to his (in effect) positivistic stance before 1933, see S.L. Paulson, "Radbruch on Unjust Laws", n. 6 above, p. 489.
[33] S.L. Paulson, "Lon L. Fuller, Gustav Radbruch, and the 'Positivist' Theses" (1994) 13 *Law and Philosophy* 313 at 314.
[34] G. Radbruch, "Die Erneuerung des Rechts" in A. Kaufmann (ed.), *Gesamtausgabe* (1990), vol. 3, p. 108.
[35] See in this regard, S.L. Paulson, n. 33 above, p. 314.

general level, contributes somewhat to preventing the worst sort of injustice, thus whether it is effective. This is the future directed aspect of the arming "against a recurrence of such an unjust state".

Hart accused Radbruch of "extraordinary naïvety".[36] One could hardly take seriously that an anti-positivist concept of law "is likely to lead to a stiffening of resistance to evil".[37] The objection about inefficacy is in good part completely justified. It makes little substantive difference to a judge in an unjust state whether he relies on Hart and refuses to apply an extremely unjust law on *moral* grounds or, with Radbruch, does the same by calling on *legal* grounds. In both cases he has to reckon with personal costs and the preparedness to take these on board depends on factors other than the concept of law.

Nevertheless, there are differences from the perspective of efficacy. The first becomes clear when one focuses on legal practice rather than the individual judge who measures legalised injustice against his conscience. When there exists in legal practice a consensus that the fulfilment of certain minimal requirements of justice is a necessary condition for the legal character or validity of the rules of the state, then anchored in legal practice is the capacity to provide resistance to the acts of an unjust state by dint of arguments which are juridical as well as moral. In this respect it is true that one should not be under any illusions about the prospects for success of such resistance. A fairly successful unjust regime is in the position quickly to destroy the consensus of legal practice by individual intimidation, changes in personnel, and rewards for conformity. But it is after all thinkable that a weaker unjust regime will not succeed, at least in its beginning phase. This is a relatively limited effect, but still an effect, which we can call the "effect on practice".

Once an unjust state is successfully established, legal concepts can no longer do much work. As the German judicial decisions after 1945 and after 1989 show, they can make a substantive difference only after the collapse of such a state. But somehow there is a delicate and not unimportant effect of the anti-positivist concept of law which can successfully work against legislated wrongs even in a successfully established unjust state. We can call this the "risk effect".

For a judge or official in an unjust state his own situation will look different depending on whether he has reason to interpret it in accordance with a positivistic or an anti-positivistic concept of law. Take for example a judge who confronts the question whether he should impose a terroristic prison sentence which falls within the scope of the legislated injustice. He is neither saint nor hero. He is as little concerned about the fate of the accused as he is greatly concerned by his own. On the basis of historical experience, he cannot exclude the possibility that the unjust state will collapse and he wonders about what would then happen to him. Suppose that he must accept that an anti-positivistic concept of law will prevail or be generally accepted, according to which the norm on which he based his terroristic judgment is not law. It follows that he undertakes a relatively high risk of not being able to justify himself later and thus of being prosecuted. The risk is diminished if he can be sure that his conduct will be judged later in accordance with a positivistic concept of law. The risk does not disappear altogether, because a retroactive law can be enacted on the basis of which he could be deemed responsible, but it is still not equivalent. Given the problems for the rule of law created by retroactive penal statutes it is quite likely that no such law will pass, and if it does pass, he can still defend himself on the basis that he acted in accordance with the positive law of the time. This makes it clear that a prevalent or general acceptance of an anti-positivist concept of law increases the risks for the individual in an unjust state who goes along with or participates in unjust acts which are covered by statute. It may follow that even for those who see no reason

---

[36]  H.L.A. Hart, "Positivism and the Separation of Law and Morals", n. 29 above, p. 74.
[37]  H.L.A. Hart, *The Concept of Law*, n. 15 above, p. 210.

to refrain from participating in injustice, or who would think such participation valuable, an incentive is established or strengthened to refrain from participation in injustice or at least to modify it. In this way, the prevalent or general acceptance of an anti-positivist concept of law can have positive effects even in an unjust state. In sum, one can say that from the perspective of keeping legislated injustice at bay the anti-positivist concept of law in some respects at least has the advantage over the positivist.

**(c) The Legal Certainty Argument.** A third argument against the anti-positivist concept of law supposes that it endangers legal certainty. In point of fact this argument affects those varieties of anti-positivism which propose a complete coincidence of law and morality and thus say that any injustice leads to the loss of legal character. And when one accords anybody the authority to decide not to follow laws if this is what his judgment about justice requires then the legal certainty argument becomes even stronger—an anarchism argument. We do not have to go further into this, since no anti-positivist who is worth taking seriously has put forward such views.[38] For Radbruch legal security is a value of the highest order. His reference to the "heavy" and "frightful dangers for legal certainty" show that he knew what was at stake. Radbruch's formula is not the result of a natural law intuition or an emotional reaction to National Socialism. Rather, it is the result of a careful balance of three elements which according to Radbruch make up the idea of law, which—as in the case of the claim to correctness—is implicated in the concept of law. The three elements are justice, purposiveness and legal certainty. In 1932 it was the case for judges, though not citizens, that the balance was achieved through giving legal certainty an "unconditional precedence" over justice and purposiveness. In order to get to his famous formula after 1945, Radbruch had to make only a minor adjustment in the system. It establishes a "hierarchy", which corresponds to Radbruch's older positivist understanding, in which purposiveness was at "the bottom" and legal certainty generally preceded justice. Only in the extreme case of intolerable injustice does the relationship reverse. When there exists such a thing as extreme injustice then this way of conceiving the relationship of legal certainty and justice is not only acceptable but mandatory. To give legal certainty precedence even in the case of extreme injustice could not be reconciled with the claim to correctness, which includes justice as well as legal certainty.

**(d) The Relativism Argument.** At this stage everything turns on the question whether there is such a thing as extreme injustice. Hart remarked that nothing followed for the concept of law from the fact that moral principles are "rationally defensible" or "discoverable".[39] We shall not attempt to decide this issue here.[40] In any case, the converse is right. If all judgments about justice were nothing more than mere expressions of emotions, decisions, preferences, interests or ideologies, in short, if the thesis of radical relativism and subjectivism were correct, little could be said in favour of the anti-positivist concept of law. Radbruch's formula would then be nothing other than an empowerment of the judge to decide against the law in cases in which his subjective convictions are particularly intensively

---

[38] This may be the reason why Hart speaks of a "danger of anarchy" which older authors like Bentham and Austin "may well have overrated"; H.L.A. Hart, *The Concept of Law*, n. 15 above, p. 211.

[39] H.L.A. Hart, "Positivism and the Separation of Law and Morals", n. 29 above, p. 84.

[40] Radbruch thought otherwise; "Doubtless, if the purpose of law and the means towards its achievement could be scientifically and clearly ascertained the conclusion would be inevitable that the validity of positive law must cease to exist which deviates from the natural law which science once recognised, just as the exposed error gives way to the revealed truth. No justification is conceivable of the validity of demonstrably false law."

affected. Hence, anti-positivism presupposes at least a rudimentary non-relativist ethic.

It is not possible to discuss here the problem of the justification of moral judgements or the objectivity of moral knowledge. Radical relativism can be opposed here only by means of a thesis and its illustration using two examples. The thesis states that judgments about extreme injustice are genuine judgments, capable of a rational justification and in so far possessing a cognitive and objective character.[41] Both examples are those already presented—the decisions on National Socialist injustice and on the killings on the internal German border.

The Federal Constitutional Court justified its application of Radbruch's formula in the decision about loss of nationality by saying that:

> "the attempt to destroy physically and materially certain parts of one's own population, including women and children, in accordance with 'racial' criteria"

"intolerably" contradicts justice and so amounts to an extreme injustice. This example is decisive. Naturally one can ask the further question why the destruction of parts of one's own population on a racial basis is extreme injustice. This question would however approach what Radbruch called "wilful scepticism". Here we should accept that there is a core area of human rights such that harm to it amounts to extreme injustice.[42]

If this is right then in principle the relativism objection is rebutted. Naturally nothing has yet been said about the degree or scope of the rebuttal. The wall shooting cases show this clearly. In contrast to the destruction of Jews in the Third Reich, there is a serious controversy about whether the killings on the internal German border amount to extreme injustice. The mere fact of this controversy shows that in this case the question whether there was extreme injustice cannot be decided by appeal to evidence but only with the help of arguments. In this regard the issue is not confined to the killing of people on a border. In addition, there is the fact that the killing took place because the fugitive wanted to leave a country in which he had to conduct his whole life in accordance with the will of the political leadership under circumstances which he did not desire and which he apparently detested. Even this might not amount to extreme injustice. But if one considers as a third factor that in the political system which the fugitive wanted to escape there was no possibility of changing the relationships through free public discussion and a political opposition, then there is something to be said for classifying as extreme injustice the killing of for the most part young men at the Berlin wall and on the border strips which until 1989 divided Germany.

Fuller objected that Radbruch's recourse to some or other "higher law" was superfluous.[43] Fuller's target here was what Radbruch defined as "suprapositive law" and specified primarily as human rights. Fuller suggested bringing into play as a substitute for such substantive standards his inner or internal morality of law, that is, his principles of legality:

> "To me there is nothing shocking in saying that a dictatorship which clothes itself with a tinsel of legal form can so far depart from the morality of order, from the inner morality of law itself, that it ceases to be a legal system".[44]

---

[41] See R. Alexy, *A Theory of Legal Argumentation* (1989), p. 177.

[42] For an attempt to ground such acceptance, see R. Alexy, "Discourse Theory and Human Rights" (1996) *9 Ratio Juris.*, 209.

[43] L.L. Fuller, "Positivism and Fidelity to Law" (1957/58) 71 *Harvard Law Rev.* 630 at 659.

[44] *ibid.* at 660.

Fuller applied this expressly to "the invalidity of ... statutes",[45] and, like Radbruch, he worked with a threshold which had to be crossed—"so far depart". One can therefore speak of a Fullerian version of Radbruch's formula. This version has the advantage that Fuller's principles of legality, for example, the requirement of publicity, the prohibition on retroactivity and the requirement of compliance with law[46] offer the relativism objection a much smaller target than Radbruch's substantive standards which are directly oriented to justice. In addition, it is generally true that extreme injustice is bound up with extreme harm to principles of the rule of law. However, the "overlapping" of substantive justice and of the formal requirements of the rule of law which Fuller observed is not strong enough to make Radbruch's formula superfluous. Decree 11 under the Reich's Citizenship Law of 25 November 1941, the topic of both of the cases set out above on National Socialist injustice, was enacted on the basis of an enabling provision contained in section 3 of the Reich's Citizenship Law of 15 September 1935 and was published in the appropriate fashion. The Reich's Citizenship Law, which expressly reserved citizenship to those of "German or substantively related blood", thus setting the stage directly for Decree 11, was unanimously approved by the Reichstag. Decree 11 is clear and determinate and it was followed by the official organs of the Third Reich. It does contain certain retroactive elements, because when it came into force it removed the citizenship and property of Jews who had emigrated before it came into force. But that is a relatively weak form of retroactivity. It consists simply in its being coupled to a set of circumstances at a particular point of time and with particular legal consequences, which obtained and persisted in the past. Taken by itself, this does not amount to a nullity.

Finally, nullity results not from the form of the regulation but from its substance, from its extreme injustice. Fuller's criteria can therefore complement but not replace Radbruch's formula. This is true also of section 27, paragraph 2 of the German Democratic Republic's Border Law, which was the focus of the wall killing cases.

**(e) The Democracy Argument.** The democracy argument is closely related to the legal certainty and to the relativism argument. It states that lurking in the anti-positivist concept of law is the danger that the judge in answering the call of justice will oppose the decisions of the legislature, which gets its legitimacy from democracy. Since in addition this results in an intrusion of the judicial branch into the legislative, the objection can also be formulated as one about the separation of powers. This objection comes up empty when, as in the cases discussed here, the law of dictators is in issue, who know neither democracy nor the separation of powers. But the objection also loses its force at a more general level. Radbruch's formula pertains only to extreme injustice. It works only in a core area. The controls on harms to basic rights exercised by constitutional courts in democratic constitutional states have a content which goes much further. If one wants to present a democracy or separation of powers argument against Radbruch's formula, one must therefore renounce any judicially controlled accountability of the legislature to the basic rights.

**(f) The Lack of Necessity Argument.** Radbruch, Fuller[47] and Hart[48] agreed that a retroactive law is to be recommended over the application of Radbruch's formula. One could go a step further and say that Radbruch's formula, at least in the period after the collapse of an unjust regime, is unnecessary because the new legislature has the power to override legal injustice by means of a retroactive law.

---

[45] *ibid.*
[46] See L.L. Fuller, *The Morality of Law*, note 11 above, p. 39.
[47] L.L. Fuller, "Positivism and Fidelity to Law", note 43 above, p. 661.
[48] H.L.A. Hart, "Positivism and the Separation of Law and Morals", note 29 above, p. 76.

However, this would be no solution if one takes into account the possibility that the new legislature—for whatever reason—is altogether inactive or not sufficiently active. The case discussed above of the Jewish emigrant's deposit of securities shows this with great clarity. If it were left up to the legislature whether she could get restitution of her property, and the legislature remained inactive, she would endure a violation of her rights based on extreme injustice. There are thus cases, required by the claim to correctness, in which Radbruch's formula is necessary to protect fundamental rights. In the actual case, a restitutory statute had been enacted. It provided for a limited period in which demands for restitution could be validated and the emigrant who had returned to Germany had failed to make a timeous claim. The Federal Court of Justice swept this limitation aside with Radbruch's formula and thus prevented the denial through the restitutory law of restitution to the emigrant. This example shows that respect for the rights of the citizen requires Radbruch's formula.

**(g) The Candour Argument.**  The candour argument asserts that Radbruch's formula leads to a circumvention in criminal cases of the fundamental principle *nulla poena sine lege*. Hart illustrates this argument through the case decided by the Superior Provincial Court Bamberg in 1949 of a woman who wanted to get rid of her husband and thus denounced him to the authorities in 1944 for having made insulting remarks about Hitler. The husband was sentenced to death, but this was not carried out and he was sent to frontline service. The Superior Provincial Court held that, although the conduct of the woman did not violate the law of the Third Reich, it was to be classified as a violation of the law because it "offended against the sense of justice and reasonableness of all right thinking people". It thus convicted her of deprivation of liberty. Hart objected in the following way:

> "There were, of course, two other choices. One was to let the woman go unpunished; one can sympathize with and endorse the view that this might have been a bad thing to do. The other was to face the fact that if the woman were to be punished it must be pursuant to the introduction of a frankly retrospective law and with a full consciousness of what was sacrificed in securing her punishment in this way. Odious as retrospective criminal legislation and punishment may be, to have pursued it openly in this case would at least have had the merits of candour".[49]

The candour argument is the strongest argument against Radbruch's formula but it is not a knockdown one.

The simplest path to its rescue would consist in narrowing its scope of application. One could say that it indeed leads to the conclusion that statutes which justify extreme injustice can never be law or achieve legal validity, but this does not mean that the trust of the actor in positive law should not be protected. The principle *Nulla poena sine lege* must be exclusively connected to this end and must take its bearings solely from enacted and effective norms whatever their content of injustice. The practical significance of Radbruch's formula would then, in order to protect the actor, be limited by the principle *Nulla poena sine lege*.

However, it is better to take the opposite path which consists in a narrowing of the principle *Nulla poena sine lege* by Radbruch's formula. This narrowing is obviously susceptible to limits for two reasons. The first reason is that Radbruch's formula has an exclusively negative character. It does not create new bases of criminality but only destroys particular grounds of justification in an iniquitous regime. The second reason arises out of the distinction between the prescription of the *lex scripta* and the *ius praevium*. Radbruch's formula cannot by definition offend against the prescription of the *ius praevium*—that the act must be

---

49   H.L.A. Hart, "Positivism and the Separation of Law and Morals", note 29 above, p. 76.

punishable before it is undertaken. According to the formula, it is the justificatory ground of an iniquitous regime that is from the outset a nullity. Thus applying Radbruch's formula does not retroactively change the legal situation, it just determines what at the time of the act the legal situation was. Of course from the perspective of the sheer facts of the matter there is a change, and just in this lies the critical bite of Radbruch's formula. This change means that the prescription of the *lex scripta* is not upheld which secured trust in the appropriately enacted and socially effective law which existed at that time. The core of Hart's accusation of lack of candour is thus that Radbruch reduced the principle of *Nulla poena sine lege* to the prescription of the *ius praevium* and thus concealed the harm to the prescription of the *lex scripta*. In this way the fact is concealed that there is a choice between "the lesser of two evils". The impression is created that:

> "all the values we cherish ultimately will fit into a single system, that no one of them has to be sacrificed or compromised to accommodate another".[50]

One can in fact abuse Radbruch's formula in this way. The potential of abuse, however, never entails necessity. In Radbruch himself one finds no simulated harmony. The opposite is the case for he talks of antinomies, conflicts and "frightful dangers". Radbruch was clear that his formula involved a choice between two evils and he did not make the slightest attempt to conceal this. That judicial decision-making can take this line is shown especially by the judgment of the Federal Constitutional Court about the wall shootings. Despite some false steps, it is clear that in the end the question is whether it is preferable to incur the cost of a loss in legal certainty or a loss in substantive justice. When it is not diluted by unnecessary extra features, the application of Radbruch's formula cannot be accused of lack of candour.

With this we are at the close of our review of the seven arguments. They showed that many perspectives come into play in the conflict over Radbruch's formula. Most of the objections can be deprived of their force. Against this background, one is weighing the trust of an actor who is active in an unjust state in an enduring justification on the basis of legislated injustice, a basis which supports his deeds, against the rights of the victim and indeed, because of the risk effect, also against the future victim. As a result, everything speaks in favour of not preserving any protection for the trust of the actor, if the threshold of extreme injustice is crossed. Radbruch's formula can thus also be accepted within the domain of criminal law.[51]                              [pp. 15–38]

---

[50] *ibid.*, p. 77.

[51] Radbruch's formula results in the deed being in violation of the law. The question of individual responsibility, without which the issue of punishment does not arise, is not thereby answered. In its first wall shooting judgment, the Federal Court of Justice described this pressing problem as "very difficult" but then decided simply on the obviousness to the young border soldiers of the injustice because of its extreme character. This conclusion is problematic. The Federal Constitutional Court explicitly contested this conclusion. It reasoned that the extreme character of injustice not always implies its obviousness for everybody. But the Court then sat on the fence since it allowed the Federal Court of Justice's conclusion to stand that there was subjective evidence simply on the basis of objective extreme injustice. There is something to be said for holding that many young border soldiers, because of their upbringing and their environment, lacked the potential to cultivate the capacity to appreciate clearly the extreme injustice of their act which would be required to confirm their guilt. It would follow that in spite of the violation of the law brought about by Radbruch's formula, they were not just to be punished in a mild way but acquitted. Something different is required in the case of their superiors. In the meantime the Federal Court of Justice has decided the case of the shooting of an armed deserter on the Berlin border in this fashion.

## H. L. A. HART
### Definition and Theory in Jurisprudence
(1954)[52]

Long ago Bentham issued a warning that legal words demanded a special method of elucidation and he enunciated a principle that is the beginning of wisdom in this matter though it is not the end. He said we must never take these words alone, but consider whole sentences in which they play their characteristic role. We must take not the *word* "right" but the sentence "You have a right" not the *word* "State" but the sentence "He is a member or an official of the state." His warning has largely been disregarded and jurists have continued to hammer away at single words. This may be because he hid the product of his logical insight behind technical terms of his own invention "Archetypation," "Phraseoplerosis," and the rest; it may also be because his further suggestions were not well adapted to the peculiarities of legal language which as part of the works of "Judge & Co" was perhaps distasteful to him. But in fact the language involved in the enunciation and application of rules constitutes a special segment of human discourse with special features which lead to confusion if neglected. Of this type of discourse the law is one very complex example and sometimes to see its features we need to look away from the law to simpler cases which in spite of many differences share these features. The economist or the scientist often uses a simple model with which to understand the complex; and this can be done for the law. So in what follows I shall use as a simple analogy the rules of a game which at many vital points have the same puzzling logical structure as rules of law. And I shall describe four distinctive features which show, I think, the method of elucidation we should apply to the law and why the common mode of definition fails.

1. First, let us take words like "right" or "duty" or the names of corporations not alone but in examples of typical contexts where these words are at work. Consider them when used in statements made on a particular occasion by a judge or an ordinary lawyer. They will be statements such as "A has a right to be paid £10 by B." "A is under a duty to fence off his machinery." "A & Company, Ltd have a contract with B." It is obvious that the use of these sentences silently assumes a special and very complicated setting, namely the existence of a legal system with all that this implies by way of general obedience, the operation of the sanctions of the system, and the general likelihood that this will continue. But though this complex situation is assumed in the use of these statements of rights or duties they do not *state* that it exists. There is a parallel situation in a game. "He is out" said in the course of a game of cricket has as its proper context the playing of the game with all that *this* implies by way of general compliance by both the players and the officials of the game in the past, present and future. Yet one who says "He is out" does not *state* that a game is being played or that the players and officials will comply with the rules. "He is out" is an expression used to appeal to rules, to make claims, or give decisions under them; it is not a statement *about* the rules to the effect that they will be enforced or acted on in a given case nor any other kind of statement *about* them. The analysis of statements of rights and duties as predictions ignores this distinction, yet it is just as erroneous to say that "A has a right" is a prediction that a court or official will treat A in a certain way as to say that "He is out" is a prediction that the umpire is likely to order the batsman off the field or the scorer to mark him out. No doubt, when someone has a legal right a corresponding prediction will normally be justified, but this should not lead us to identify two quite different forms of statement.

2. If we take "A has a right to be paid £10 by B" as an example, we can see what the distinctive function of this form of statement is. For it is clear that as

[52] [(1954) 70 L. Q. R. 37: also now in *Essays in Jurisprudence and Philosophy (1983)*.]

well as presupposing the existence of a legal system, the use of this statement has also a special connection with a particular rule of the system. This would be made explicit if we asked "Why has A this right?" For the appropriate answer could only consist of two things: first, the statement of some rule or rules of law (say those of Contract), under which given certain facts certain legal consequences follow; and secondly, a statement that these facts were here the case. But again it is important to see that one who says that "A has a right" does not *state* the relevant rule of law; and that though, given certain facts, it is correct to say "A has a right" one who says this does not state or describe those facts. He has done something different from either of these two things: he has drawn a conclusion from the relevant but unstated rule, and from the relevant but unstated facts of the case. "A has a right" like "He is out" is therefore the tail-end of a simple legal calculation: it records a result and may be well called a conclusion of law. It is not therefore used to predict the future as the American Realists say; it refers to the present as their opponents claim but unlike ordinary statements does not do this by describing present or continuing facts. This it is—this matter of principle—and not the existence of stray exceptions for lunatics or infants that frustrates the definition of a right in factual terms such as expectations or powers. A paralysed man watching the thief's hand close over his gold watch is properly said to have a right to retain it as against the thief, though he has neither expectation nor power in any ordinary sense of the words. This is possible just because the expression "a right" in this case does not describe or stand for any expectation or power, or indeed anything else, but has meaning only as part of a sentence the function of which as a whole is to draw a conclusion of law from a specific kind of legal rule.

3. A third peculiarity is this: the assertion "Smith has a right to be paid £10" said by a judge in deciding the case has a different status from the utterance of it out of court, where it may be used to make a claim, or an admission and in many other ways. The judge's utterance is official, authoritative and, let us assume, final; the other is none of these things, yet in spite of these differences the sentences are of the same sort: they are both conclusions of law. We can compare this difference in spite of similarity with "He is out" said by the umpire in giving his decision and said by a player to make a claim. Now of course the unofficial utterance may have to be withdrawn in the light of a later official utterance, but this is not a sufficient reason for treating the first as a prophecy of the last for plainly not all mistakes are mistaken predictions. Nor surely need the finality of a judge's decision either be confused with infallibility or tempt us to *define* laws in terms of what courts do, even though there are many laws which the courts must first interpret before they can apply. We can acknowledge that what the scorer says is final; yet we can still abstain from defining the notion of a score as what the scorer says. And we can admit that the umpire may be wrong in his decision though the rules give us no remedy if he is and though there may be doubtful cases which he has to decide with but little help from the rules.

4. In any system, legal or not, rules may for excellent practical reasons attach identical consequences to any one of a set of very different facts. The rule of cricket attaches the same consequence to the batsman's being bowled, stumped, or caught. And the word "out" is used in giving decisions or making claims under the rule and in other verbal applications of it. It is easy to see here that no one of these different ways of being out is more essentially what the word means than the others, and that there need be nothing common to all these ways of being out other than their falling under the same rule, though there *may* be some similarity or analogy between them. But it is less easy to see this in those important cases where rules treat a *sequence* of different actions or states of affairs in a way which unifies them. In a game a rule may simply attach a single consequence to the successive actions of a set of different men—as when a team is said to have won a game. A more complex rule may prescribe that what is to be done at one point in a sequence shall depend on what was done or occurred earlier: and it may be

indifferent to the identity of the persons concerned in the sequence so long as they fall under certain defining conditions. An example of this is when a team permitted by the rules of a tournament to have a varying membership is penalised only in the third round—when the membership has changed—for what was done in the first round. In all such cases a sequence of action or states of affairs is unified simply by falling under certain rules; they *may* be otherwise as different as you please. Here can be seen the essential elements of the language of legal corporations. For in law the lives of ten men that overlap but do not coincide may fall under separate rules under which they have separate rights and duties and then they are a collection of individuals for the law; but their actions may fall under rules of a different kind which make what is to be done by any one or more of them depend in a complex way on what was done or occurred earlier. And then we may speak in appropriately unified ways of the sequence so unified, using a terminology like that of corporation law which will show that it is *this* sort of rule we are applying to the facts. But here the unity of the rule may mislead us when we come to define this terminology. It may cast a shadow: we may look for an identical continuing thing or person or quality *in* the sequence. We may find it—in "corporate spirit." This is real enough; but it is a secret of success not a criterion of identity.

These four general characteristics of legal language explain both why definition of words like "right," "duty," and "corporation" is baffled by the absence of some counterpart to "correspond" to these words, and also why the unobvious counterparts which have been so ingeniously contrived—the future facts, the complex facts or the psychological facts—turn out not to be something in terms of which we can define these words although to be connected with them in complex or indirect ways. The fundamental point is that the primary function of these words is not to stand for or describe anything but a distinct function; this makes it vital to attend to Bentham's warning that we should not, as does the traditional method of definition, abstract words like "right" and "duty," "State," or "corporation" from the sentences in which alone their full function can be seen, and then demand of them so abstracted their genus and differentia.

Let us see what the use of this traditional method of definition presupposes and what the limits of its efficacy are, and why it may be misleading. It is of course the simplest form of definition, and also a peculiarly satisfying form because it gives us a set of words which can always be substituted for the word defined whenever it is used; it gives us a comprehensible synonym or translation for the word which puzzles us. It is peculiarly appropriate where the words have the straightforward function of standing for some kind of thing, or quality, person, process, or event, for here we are not mystified or puzzled about the general characteristics of our subject-matter, but we ask for a definition simply to locate within this familiar general kind or class some special subordinate kind or class. Thus since we are not puzzled about the general notions of furniture or animal we can take a word like "chair" or "cat" and give the principle of its use by first specifying the general class to which what it is used to describe belongs, and then going on to define the specific differences that mark it off from other species of the same general kind. And of course if we are *not* puzzled about the general notion of a corporate body but only wish to know how one species (say a college) differs from another (say a limited company) we can use this form of definition of single words perfectly well. But just because the method is appropriate at this level of inquiry, it cannot help us when our perplexities are deeper. For if our question arises, as it does with fundamental legal notions because we are puzzled about the general category to which something belongs and how some general type of expression relates to fact, and not merely about the place within that category, then until the puzzle is cleared up this form of definition is at the best unilluminating and at the worst profoundly misleading. It is unilluminating because a mode of definition designed to locate some subordinate species within some familiar category cannot elucidate the characteristics of some anomalous category; and it is misleading because it will suggest that what is in fact an anomalous category is after all some species of the familiar. Hence if applied to legal words like "right," "duty," "State," or "corporation" the common mode of definition suggests that these words like ordinary words stand for or describe some thing, person, quality, process, or event; when the difficulty of finding these becomes apparent, different contrivances varying with tastes are used to explain or explain away the anomaly. Some say the difference is that the things for which these legal words stand are real but not sensory, others that they are fictitious entities, others that these words stand for plain fact but of a complex, future, or psychological variety. So this standard mode of definition forces our familiar triad of theories into existence as a confused way of accounting for the anomalous character of legal words.

How then shall we define such words? If definition is the provision of a synonym which will not equally puzzle us these words cannot be defined. But I think there is a method of elucidation of quite general application and which we can call definition, if we wish. Bentham and others practised it, though they did not preach it. But before applying it to the highly complex legal cases, I shall illustrate it from the simple case of a game. Take the notion of a trick in a game of cards. Somebody says "What is a trick?" and you reply "I will explain: when you have a game and among its rules is one providing that when each of our players has played a card then the player who has put down the highest card scores a point, in these circumstances that player is said to have 'taken a trick'." This natural explanation has not taken the form of a definition of the single word "trick": no synonym has been offered for it. Instead we have taken a sentence in which the word "trick" plays its characteristic role and explained it first by specifying the conditions under which the whole sentence is true, and secondly by showing how it is used in drawing a conclusion from the rules in a particular case. Suppose now that after such an explanation your questioner presses on: "That is all very well, that explains 'taking a trick'; but I still want to know what the word 'trick' means just by itself. I want a definition of 'trick'; I want something which can be substituted for it whenever it is used. "If we yield to this demand for a single word definition we might reply: "The trick is just a collective name for the four cards." But someone may object: "The trick is not just a name for the four cards because these four cards will not always constitute a trick. It must therefore be some entity to which the four cards belong." A third might say: "No, the trick is a fictitious entity which the players pretend exists and to which by fiction which is part of the game they ascribe the cards." But in so simple a case we would not tolerate these theories, fraught as they are with mystery and empty of any guidance as to the use made of the word within the game: we would stand by the original two-fold explanation; for this surely gave us all we needed when it explained the conditions under which the statement "He has taken a trick" is true and showed us how it was used in drawing a conclusion from the rules in a particular case.

If we turn back to Bentham we shall find that when his explanation of legal notions is illuminating, as it very often is, it conforms to this method though only loosely...

...They are not paraphrases but they specify some of the conditions necessary for the truth of a sentence of the form "You have a right." Bentham shows us how these conditions include the existence of a law imposing a duty on some other person: and moreover, that it must be a law which provides that the breach of the duty shall be visited with a sanction if you or someone on your behalf so choose. This has many virtues. By refusing to identify the meaning of the word "right" with any psychological or physical fact it correctly leaves open the question whether on any given occasion a person who has a right has in fact any expectation or power; and so it leaves us free to treat men's expectations or powers as what in general men will have if there is a system of rights, and as part of what a system of rights is generally intended to secure. Some of the improvements which should be made on Bentham's efforts are obvious. Instead of characterising a right in terms of punishment many would do so in terms of the remedy. But I would prefer to show the special position of one who has a right by mentioning not the remedy but the choice which is open to one who has a right as to whether the corresponding duty shall be performed or not. For it is, I think, characteristic of those laws that confer rights (as distinguished from those that only impose obligations) that the obligation to perform the corresponding duty is made by law to depend on the choice of the individual who is said to have the right or the choice of some person authorised to act on his behalf.[53]

I would, therefore, tender the following as an elucidation of the expression "a legal right": (1) A statement of the form "X has a right" is true if the following conditions are satisfied:

   (a) There is in existence a legal system.
   (b) Under a rule or rules of the system some other person Y is, in the events which have happened, obliged to do or abstain from some action.
   (c) This obligation is made by law dependent on the choice either of X or some other person authorised to act on his behalf so that either Y is bound to do or abstain from some action only if X (or some authorised person) so chooses or alternatively only until X (or such person) chooses otherwise.

(2) A statement of the form "X has a right" is used to draw a conclusion of law in a particular case which falls under such rules.[54]                    [pp. 41–49]

---

[53] [For a criticism of the "will-theory" underlying Hart's view, see D. N. MacCormick in *Law, Morals, and Society* (Hacker and Raz eds.), Chap. 11. His main point is that this theory does not account for an important area of rights which cannot be waived by the right-holder, such as human rights protected under a Bill of Rights. MacCormick argues for a modified version of the "interest theory," on the basis that rights concern the interests of individuals, for which normative protection is provided by the law. See also 62 A. R. S. P. 305 and *ante*, 353–354.]

[54] This deals only with a right in the first sense (correlative to duty) distinguished by Hohfeld. But the same form of elucidation can be used for the cases of "liberty," "power," and "immunity," and will, I think, show what is usually left unexplained, *viz.*: why these four varieties, in spite of differences, are referred to as "rights." The unifying elements seems to be this: in all four cases the law specifically recognises the *choice* of an individual either negatively by not impeding or obstructing it (liberty and immunity) or affirmatively by giving legal effect to it (claim and power). In the negative cases there is no law to interfere if the individual chooses to do so or abstain from some action (liberty) or to retain his legal position unchanged (immunity); in the affirmative cases the law gives legal effect to the choice of an individual that some other person shall do or shall abstain from some action or that the legal position of some other person shall be altered. Of course, when we say in any of these four senses that a person has a right we are not referring to any *actual* choice that he has made but either the relevant rules of law are such that *if* he chooses certain consequences follow, or there are no rules to impede his choice *if* he makes it. If there are legal rights which cannot be waived these would need special treatment.

[A. W. B. Simpson, in "The Analysis of Legal Concepts" (1964) 80 L. Q. R. 535, criticises Hart's suggestion that the meaning of legal concepts can be given by showing how they function in particular sentences where conclusions are drawn from rules. Simpson argues that this form of elucidation is of very limited value because it is very far from exhaustive of the type of questions which may be legitimately asked in relation to legal concepts. However, some of the questions which he regards as unanswered by this method, hardly seem to be matters of great seriousness for jurisprudence, such as the question why we should use the word "possession" rather than the expression "old cheese." Other questions, such as the fact that Hart's elucidation does not enable us to see the common ground between, *e.g.* possession in English and Roman law, seem misconceived, since there is no reason why both the similarities and also the differences in the concept of possession as employed in Roman and English law should not be expounded on the lines indicated by Hart.]

## N. MACCORMICK
**Contemporary Legal Philosophy: The Rediscovery of Practical Reason**
(1983)

There must have been occasions on which even—or especially—those most actively engaged in philosophising about the law have had doubts, not to say (as the case of the unfrocked parson in *Decline and Fall*) Doubts. In their bluntest form the doubts concern whether there is any more need for a philosophy of law than for a philosophy of bus-driving. Lawyers convey houses, and bus drivers convey people. Both will do it regardless of any philosophical fuss; law is what lawyers do and bus driving is what bus drivers do; by all means inquire into the sociology of the bargain-driving and the bus-driving professionals, or of their impact (we hope not a literal impact) upon the surrounding community; by all means line them up in their respective places in the class-struggle (thereby securing a place in the pantheon of critical law or critical transport) but do not delude yourself that there is any useful or interesting job for philosophy in either case.

There being philosophical precedent of the highest authority for confuting imaginary doubts through real meditation, let me at least imagine such a doubt as that adumbrated above and see if I can meditate it away. This may prove an effective method for achieving my present appointed task, namely to give a view—I shall not pretend to a thorough conspectus—of significant contemporary development in the philosophy of law. My view acknowledges it as one essential task of legal philosophy to supply an epistemology of law, a theory, that is, as to the possibility of genuine knowledge in the legal sphere. But this is not the only task. Another, which grows out of the epistemological task, is to elucidate the nature and working of practical reason. Perhaps the most exciting development of the past decade or so has been in the rediscovery of practical reason, a recognition that general analyses of practical reasoning, practical discourse or practical reasonableness have much to offer to our understanding of the particular cases law and legal activity. I shall try to show this in what follows.

At the heart of the doubt raised in the opening paragraph is the notion of law as behaviour, law as what lawyers do. If this is as obviously correct as it sometimes seems, then indeed the understanding of law is surely best furthered by simply empirical inquiries, and will only be befuddled (as J. P. Gibbs has argued[55]) by the substitution of exercises in conceptual analysis for the necessary patient and painstaking investigation of the facts. On reflection, however, this is not so much a ground for doubting the need for a philosophy of law as one particular case of a legal philosophy. The conception of law as behaviour is the defining tenet of those philosophies of law to which (perhaps confusingly) the name "realist" has been attached. In its toughest, Scandinavian, version built upon Hägerström's work, such a conception of law belongs in a set of ontological tenets according to which belief in the existence of values, norms, and normative positions such as "right" or "duty" is necessarily false; false because there is only one world and that a material one. Such beliefs have causes and have effects, available and calling for empirical study; but as to their content, they do not even lack truth-value but are actually false.[56]

This epistemological theory walks necessarily in step with an ontological theory; claims to knowledge of what is actually non-existent are necessarily

---

[55] J. P. Gibbs, "Definitions of Law and Empirical Questions" (1968) 2 *Law and Society Rev.* 429.

[56] For recent views of Hägerström, see N. E. Simmonds, "The Legal Philosophy of Axel Hägerström" (1976) *Jur. Rev.* 210; G. D. MacCormack, "Hägerström on Rights and Duties" (1971) *Jur. Rev.* 59; J. Bjarup, *Reason, Emotion and Law; Studies in the Philosophy of Axel Hägerström* (1982). [On Hägerström, see *post*, 1036.]

groundless claims and a theory of what there is thus sets limits on, without fully determining, a theory of knowledge; in turn attempts to define and then to acquire possible knowledge lead into problems of method. The issue may be characterised as "empiricism—for and against"; but even this is in a way misleading, since what is in issue is at least as much the question what *are* genuine modes of observation, linked to the question what *is* available to be in relevant modes observed.

Even to pursue the theme this far is to be forced to recognise the implicit falsehood in the caricature opposition of philosophical and sociological inquiry set up in jest in my opening paragraph. For what is obvious is that the problems (of ontology, of epistemology, of methodology) which flow from any questioning of the conception of law as behaviour and its underpinning presuppositions are not different problems for, but problems common to, the philosophy of law, the sociology of law and legal scholarship itself. What is more, though by dictionary definition theories of what there is, how it is knowable and how to pursue knowledge of it are "philosophical" theories, this can in no sense justify any special arrogation of empire over them to any one group of soi-disant professionals—philosophy is an activity, not a trade. It follows, and is also true, that the greatest of mistakes is to suppose that crucial intellectual differences divide those who profess jurisprudence or the philosophy of law from those who profess either sociology of law or legal scholarship. The rivalries as between different ontological (and, as we shall see, deontological) assumptions or theories are rivalries which include in grouped warring camps sets of "philosophers," "sociologists" and "lawyers" internally differentiated not by differences of theory but by differences of focus of study, externally differentiated from other like sets by deep differences of deep theory.

To have said all this has been to have adopted by implication a substantial part of Richard Tur's recently stated thesis as to the essentially epistemological task of jurisprudence.[57] Basic to jurisprudence as a taught subject in law curricula, he argued, is the engagement of students in the inquiry whether there is legal knowledge and, if there is, what makes it possible and what it is knowledge *of*. (It should not be thought that such a question has no practical significance. If there is no such thing as legal knowledge, then once this truth is sufficiently disseminated, it will become a form of fraud for anyone to continue to conduct examinations in law on the basis that people can fail the exam for giving wrong answers; or if what is knowable in the field demarcated as "law" turns out to be a great deal different than traditional legal scholarship has supposed, the old books had better be burnt and a new start made. We might recall here that just this was the aim of "American realists," who as academic lawyers belong at any rate broadly in the same camp as the Scandinavians occupy philosophically and the judicial behaviouralists sociologically.)

Tur himself both owes a freely acknowledged debt to Kelsen in his case for jurisprudence as epistemology of law, and is, along with J. W. Harris and Alida Wilson, a notable upholder of the Kelsenian tradition in contemporary juristic debate in the U. K.[58] The special significance of that tradition is the way in which it represents the possibility of a genuine and objectively scientific study of norms, such that within the genus of the normative one can postulate specific differences for identifying state legal orders, in terms of dynamic character, monopolistic authorisation of coercive sanctions, a defined spatial sphere of validity, and relatively centralised organisations within the given spatial sphere. The Kelsenian project of elucidating the presuppositions required for any objective cognition of

---

[57] R. H. S. Tur, "What is Jurisprudence?" (1978) 28 *Philosophical Quarterly* 149; *cf*. N. MacCormick, "On Analytical Jurisprudence," in *Conceptions Contemporains du Droit* (ed. P. Trappe, 1982), pp. 29–41.

[58] See Tur, *op. cit.*; A. Wilson, "The Imperative Fallacy in Kelsen's Theory" (1981) 44 M. L. R. 270; J. W. Harris, *Law and Legal Science* (1979).

legal norms has been carried a step further by Harris's proposal to abandon the conception of a *Grundnorm* as the ultimate non-positive norm of a system of positive norms, reclassifying it as a "basic fiat" for the pursuit of legal science.[59] His point is that what we here have to do with is a methodological postulate for elaborating a certain form of knowledge, not a suprapositive norm for establishing a political constitution.

Not least among the merits of this proposal is that it exhibits the full fallaciousness of the fallacy so well beloved at least of jurisprudence finalists that *Grundnorm* and "rule of recognition" are more or less the same idea put in different languages. Recent scholarship having made the anglophone juristic community well aware of the true nature of Kelsen's theory as to the transcendental presuppositions required for knowledge claims in the world of the ought, we are in a position to appreciate that the rule of recognition plays no part in Hartian theory as that of the *Grundnorm* in Kelsenian. It does not follow, however, that there is no functional analogue in Hartian theory for the *Grundnorm*, understood as that which grounds the possibility of objectively meaningful and veridical normative discourse.

It is perhaps useful to recall how Karl Olivercrona, grounding himself in the realism of Hägerström, dismissed as a "great mystery" Kelsen's postulation of a world of the ought over and beyond the world of the is.[60] If the principle of cause and effect is the sole governing principle of every objective science, paralleled by the "principle of imputation,"[61] then indeed a conception of law as behaviour is the only one acceptable within the temple of science. This being the realist riposte to Kelsen's ambition for a "normative science," we ought to consider Hart's riposte to realism. What then was Hart's rejoinder to conceptions of law as behaviour? It was, of course, that such conceptions were vitiated by adherence to a purely external point of view in the study of legal and social rules; this is unacceptable because it necessarily misses the vital "internal aspect" of our response to rules.[62] From the standpoint of a linguistic analysis of human normative discourse, one cannot but see such discourse as involving and expressing standing common attitudes to conduct held by human beings as members of social groups constituted by their common adherence to common standards of conduct and criticism of conduct.

One interpretation of this view (J. W. Harris's) is that it is a more refined version of behaviourism, correlating the linguistic with the other overt behaviour of human beings.[63] In my opinion (argued for elsewhere) this is a misinterpretation of the view.[64] At any rate, the Hartian theory of the "internal aspect" of rules can and should be taken as leading on into a "hermeneutic"[65] or, as Anthony Kronman calls it in his recent study of Max Weber, an "exegetical"[66] approach to the understanding of normative discourse. The point is that we must attend to the data of our own and others' imputed *consciousness* in making sense of "the world of the ought." On this view, conceptual inquiries into normative terms or concepts and the uses we make of them stand not in contrast with, but as a variety of, empirical inquiry. That the only available data are immediately available data revealed by our self-awareness as conscious acting subjects engaged in intelligble

---

[59] Harris, *Law and Legal Science*, 70.

[60] K. Olivecrona, *Law as Fact* (first ed., 1939), p. 21. [And see *ante*, 329.]

[61] See H. Kelsen, *The Pure Theory of Law* (trans. M. Knight 1967), Chap. 2.

[62] See H. L. A. Hart, *The Concept of Law* (1961), pp. 55–56, 86–88, discussed in MacCormick, *H. L. A. Hart* (1981), Chaps 3 and 4 [and *ante*, 380–381].

[63] Harris, *Law and Legal Science*, pp. 52–57.

[64] MacCormick, *Hart*, Chaps 3 and 4.

[65] The first application of this description to Hart's work is by P. M. S. Hacker, "Hart's Philosophy of Law" in *Law, Morality and Society* (eds. P. M. S. Hacker and J. Raz, 1977), p. 9; see also MacCormick, *Hart, passim*.

[66] Anthony T. Kronman, *Max Weber* (1983), pp. 4–5, 34–36.

interaction with other like subjects does not make them less respectable or genuine than those amassed by "external" observation.[67]

In this view, the presupposition under which normative discourse is intelligible is that human beings are capable of consciously orienting their conduct towards fulfilment of preconceived patterns of conduct for whose observance they have a standing attitude of serious preference. The possibility of there being true or false normative statements such as ones about people's rights or duties or the wrongs they have done is a possibility conditioned by the existence of common or shared standards among members of groups with attitudes which remain relatively constant in time. The truth-conditions of the statements are presupposed, but not asserted, in the making or checking of the statements. Hence there can be genuine knowledge of and about norms, but not as timeless and universal prescriptions of the right, simply as local and temporal elements in the communal life of human groups or "societies." The case of a state legal system is simply a special case involving rules about conduct as well as rules about conduct, the latter being "valid" (this itself a normative predicate) in terms of the former.[68]

The upshot of the Kelsenian and the Hartian theses as to the possibility of genuine knowledge *of* norms as well as *about* norms is much the same despite all the serious differences of philosophical pedigree and method in the establishment of the theses. Both establish the possibility of judging what is legally right or legally obligatory subject to the caveat that every such judgment has to be relativised as to time, place and relevant population. Both deny that such judgments require or presuppose any judgment of what is morally right, and Kelsen denies the possibility of any objective judgment in the latter case while Hart remains non-committal on that point.[69]

The general theories, sharing the form of positivism which they do share, have of course formed the background for a great deal of more detailed analytical studies of terms and concepts in use among lawyers.[70] They have separately led to separate and mutually independent representation of legal facts as "institutional facts,"[71] and to complementary analyses of legal institutions, the form of which is also illuminating for the understanding of social and moral institutions on a wider front.[72] Such work has also continued the tradition of both drawing on and

---

[67]  Compare T. L. S. Sprigge. "The Importance of Subjectivity" (1982) 25 *Inquiry* 143.

[68]  These general observations can be supported by a reading of the following works by H. L. A. Hart: *The Concept of Law* (1961), Chaps 1–7; "Definition and Theory in Jurisprudence" (1954) 70 L. Q. R. 37, and "Bentham on Legal Rights," *Oxford Essays in Jurisprudence (Second Series)* (ed. A. W. B. Simpson, 1973), Chap. 3. [MacCormick's most recent views on Hart are found in (1994) 14 O.J.L.S. 1].

[69]  For Kelsen's value-scepticism, see *What is Justice* (1957), Chap. 1; on Hart's position, see MacCormick, *Hart*, Chap. 4.

[70]  One can here only gesture towards citing some examples, such as those provided by *Oxford Essays in Jurisprudence* (ed. A. G. Guest, 1961), *Oxford Essays in Jurisprudence (2nd Series)* (ed. A. W. B. Simpson, 1973), *Law, Morality and Society* (ed. P. M. S. Hacker and J. Raz, 1977) *Perspectives in Jurisprudence* (ed. E. Attwooll, 1977), most of the essays in which symposia bear out the point. Work such as Patrick Atiyah's *Promises, Morals and Law* (1981) indicates the value of extended concentration on particular legal and moral institutions, with which compare Charles Fried's *Contract as Promise* (1981).

[71]  See MacCormick, "Law as Institutional Fact" (1974) 90 L. Q. R. 102 and "On Analytical Jurisprudence," in *Conceptions Contemporains du Droit* (ed. P. Trappe, 1982), pp. 29–41; O. Weinberger "Das Recht als Institutionelle Tatsache" (1980) 11 *Rechtstheorie* 427 and "Jenseits von Positivismus and Naturrecht," in *Conceptions Contemporains (cit. sup.)* pp. 43–56 at pp. 45–47.

[72]  *Cf.* H. Rottleuthner, *Rechtstheorie und Rechtssziologie* (1981), pp. 57–61.

feeding back to the philosophy of language.[73] And at the same time there have been important critical refinements of the basic theories, most notably through the work of Joseph Raz in the discovery that a theory of norms calls both for the elucidation of principles for individuation of norms,[74] and *a fortiori* for a clearer specification of the grounds for distinguishing different types of norm according to their normative rather than their supposed or asserted social functions.[75]

The idea of a "normative function" is explained by reference to formal aspects of practical reason, that is to say, by reference to the types of reasons which norms constitute as elements in practical deliberation. Of the greatest interest in this line of inquiry is Raz's suggestion that, as well as having first order reasons for acting in certain ways, we also have second order reasons—reasons for acting or not acting upon other reasons. To the latter class belong so-called "exclusionary reasons", namely, reasons for excluding from deliberation some range of otherwise sound reasons bearing upon present options. A case in point is that of a promise to do something or other. At the time for keeping the promise, there may well be reasons for not performing the act as promised, which on their own merit would outweigh whatever reasons (apart from the promise) now tell in favour of doing that act. But the "obligatory" character of promise-keeping means that the given balance of first-order reasons is simply excluded from relevant deliberation while at the same time amounting to a sufficient first-order reason for acting.[76]

It remains controversial whether this analysis applied to concepts such as "rule" or "obligation" or "power" is as convincing as it is intricate.[77] But it has (like some other attempts) shifted the discussion of concepts like obligation on to the ground where they belong within a hermeneutic[78] study concerned with the kinds of reasons one is addressing when (for example) one contemplates an actual or supposed obligation to act, as distinct from those cases in which one is deliberating, under no constraint of obligation, about what it is best to do all things considered. This cannot but be more satisfactory than the oddly "external" analysis of obligation offered by Hart, in terms of the existence of "serious social pressure" as definitive of "rules of obligation."[79]

The most recent development in this line of argument by Raz has applied it to the problem of the conceptual demarcation of "law" from other things.[80] What is the difference between there being some sound and relevant reasons why some line of conduct should be legally obligatory and its actually being so? A possible answer is that while we are considering whether there should be such and such an obligation, we remain at a purely deliberative phase of practical discourse. A characteristic of legislative and judicial processes however is that they provide for a transition from "deliberative" to "executive" stages. Once an authoritative decision is taken that such and such is (or is not) obligatory, then *pro loco et*

---

[73] Particularly influential have been J. L. Austin's *How to do Things with Words* (1962), with which compare W. Twining and D. Miers, *How to do Things with Rules* (2nd ed., 1982), J. Searle, *Speech Acts* (1969) and L. Wittgenstein, *Philosophical Investigations* (1953). Except by Bernard Jackson, comparatively little has been done to absorb lessons from contemporary linguistic theory in the structuralist mode; see B. S. Jackson, "Structuralisme et 'Sources du Droit'" (1982) 27 A. P. D. 147; *Structuralism and Legal Theory*, (1979).

[74] See J. Raz, *The Concept of A Legal System* (2nd ed., 1981).

[75] Raz, "On the Functions of Law" in *Oxford Essays in Jurisprudence* (2nd Series).

[76] See in general, Raz, *Practical Reason and Norms* (1975); also "Promises and Obligations," *Law, Morality and Society.*

[77] For an acute critique of the concept of "exclusionary reasons", see K. M. Campbell, *The Concept of Rights* (Oxford University, D. Phil. Thesis, 1979).

[78] Albeit Raz does not himself so describe his work, I believe the appellation "hermeneutic" to be appropriate; and see MacCormick, *Hart*, Chap. 5.

[79] *Cf.* Hart, *Concept of Law*, pp. 86–88.

[80] J. Raz, "The problem about the Nature of Law" (1982) 3 *Contemporary Philosophy* 107. [And *ante*, 63.]

*tempore*, further deliberation is excluded or overridden from having direct practical bearing. Characteristically, the appeal to law, to legal rights or duties, is an appeal to that which has been so decided or settled. Of course, there may still be dispute or deliberation as to the proper interpretation or application of what has been settled and a variety of reasons may be canvassed for or against one or another interpretation (reasons of the same kind as must come into the account where there is an absence of settled law relevant to the problem within an established jurisdiction). But there is a significant distinction within our practical reasoning as between what has already been decided and what reasons there are for deciding one way or the other points as yet unsettled.

Whether or not this argument has sufficient power to sustain the traditional positivistic thesis as to the conceptual independence of law from morality, it is unquestionably the best defence yet offered for that thesis. It is also of value in establishing a ground independent of the actual or supposed concerns of professional lawyers for differentiating those among lawyers' concerns which are concerns about law from those that are not. The law is, in one trivial sense, what lawyers do; but not all that lawyers or judges do is the law, and some of it is quite as possibly illegal as much of it is manifestly non-legal.

Raz's general thesis about the reasons why practical reasoners sometimes have reasons for resort to laws and rules which exclude or restrict open ended deliberation is strikingly and quite independently corroborated by Robert Alexy's "*Theorie der juristischen Argumentation*."[81] Drawing widely from British and American moral philosophy in the analytic style, from Perelman's studies in rhetoric, from Haberma's theory of discourse and from other modern German philosophies. Alexy sets himself to establish as exhaustively as possible the rules and forms of argument which can be postulated as governing practical discourse in all its forms. The upshot is that we can establish a set of governing conditions for the "discourses" to which reasonable appeal may be made in order to justify actions and decisions of any sort. To satisfy these conditions is to accept as excluded many physical and psychological possibilities of action or decision— such are "discursively impossible"; the trouble, however, is that too little is excluded. In any given situation of choice, there may be a plurality of options open, all of which are "discursively possible" or justifiable by rational argument.[82]

This being so, it follows that reasonable persons have reason to wish for the existence of an authoritative process of decision making both as to common rules of social conduct and as to the right application of these rules; in short they have reason to favour the existence of a legal system, provided that it is constituted in a "discursively possible" (rationally justifiable) way, allowing, for example, for democratic election of the legislature, independence of judiciary from executive, and so forth.[83] More explicit than other current theories of legal reasoning, Alexy thus establishes the thesis (he calls it the *Sonderfallthese*) that legal reasoning both in the legislative and *a fortiori* in the adjudicative phases is (when properly conducted) simply a special case of general practical reasoning.[84] Among the special characteristics of legal reasoning is that within it grounds and procedures of argument are more restricted and clearly defined than in general practical discourse. Hence it can more frequently yield a single determinate outcome to a practical dilemma than the latter. Even so, there remain hard cases in which more than one solution may be "discursively possible" even within the special constraints of legal discourse; in such cases one is inevitably thrown back

---

[81] [1978: translated by Adler and MacCormick as *Theory of Legal Argumentation* (1988).]

[82] Alexy, *Theorie*, pp. 356–359; MacCormick, "Legal Reasoning and Practical Reason", pp. 279–280.

[83] Alexy, *op. cit.*, pp. 349–351; MacCormick, *op. cit.*, pp. 281–282; see also Alexy (1981) 12 *Rechtstheorie, Beiheft* 2.

[84] Alexy, *Theorie*, p. 263.

upon the resources of general practical discourse. Although it is proper for, or rather incumbent on, courts and advocates to proceed into general practical discourse when the resources of specifically legal discourse fail them, this would not justify claiming general practical discourse as a part of legal discourse or of law; for this would invert the genus/species relationship.[85] The justified demand that advocates and judges observe the general requirements of general practical discourse, even as a matter of fulfilling the duties of their legal station, does not rest upon the assumption that these requirements are themselves legal requirements (if they were, we might suppose them subject to being changed legislatively).

We might take this as indicating a ground of objection to two of the most controversial points in Ronald Dworkin's approach to legal theory, namely to his claim that in a developed legal system there are always adequate materials fully to justify a final decision of any litigable question[86] and his related claim that for every legal question there is a right answer (not excluding the remote possibility of a "tie judgment"[87]). As to the first of these claims, it can be rejoined that it is true that there will always be grounds and modes of argument which it will be proper for adjudicators and advocates to deploy as justifying their favoured conclusion to a disputed point of law, however hard the case; but that this does not close the question whether there are serious reasons for restricting our conception of "law" to a restricted special class of those grounds and procedures which are not common to all forms of reasonable practical discourse. As to the second, if it is true that the special justifying reasons for establishing specialised legal institutions and specialised procedures of discourse, namely to avoid so far as may be the relative indeterminacy of general practical discourse, then it cannot be assumed that there are single determinate solutions uniquely right and reasonable for hard cases. This will be so sometimes, for example, when canons of legal interpretation leave it open that the decision to a case may legally be either *d* or not *d*, but when one of these is unreasonable in terms of general practical discourse (was that what the majority thought in *Junior Books*?[88]). But if general practical discourse is in its nature less determinate than legal discourse (this being the justifying grounds, as distinct from the historical origin, of the existence of specialised legal institutions), it cannot always be so. Sometimes choices must be made as between equally reasonable views. Here we come into the realm of what John Farago well describes as "Intractable Cases."[89]

In that light, one might be tempted to join Alexy with Raz as a defender on the ramparts of legal positivism. This would not be so much wrong as irrelevant. The fundamentally Kantian aspects of Alexy's subordination of legal rationality to general practical rationality might in any event justify the opposite conclusion. In this regard, his work is comparable with the differently angled Kantian line stated with incomparable clarity in W. D. Lamont's *Law and Moral Order*,[90] which exhibits respect for the *form* of law as foundational for reasonable moral judgment, positive law being on the other hand essentially concerned to give concrete embodiment to practical requirements of respect for persons.

Yet, as I say, the point is not so much wrong as irrelevant. For the drawing of lines which enable us to differentiate state law from other varieties of non-state law present even in and beyond "state-societies," to say nothing of law in non-

---

[85] Alexy, *op. cit.*, pp. 346–348.
[86] R. Dworkin, *Taking Rights Seriously* (1978), Chap. 4.
[87] *Op. cit.*, Chap. 13; also, "No Right Answer?" in *Law, Morality and Society*, Chap 3.
[88] *Junior Books & Co. Ltd v. Veitchi Co. Ltd* [1982] 3 All E. R. 201.
[89] J. M. Farago, "Intractable Cases: the Role of the Uncertainty in the Concept of Law" (1980) 55 N. Y. Univ. Law Rev. 195; and see also Farago, "Judicial Cybernetics: the Effects of Self-Reference in Dworkin's Rights Thesis" (1980) Valparaiso Univ. Law Rev. 371.
[90] (1981).

state state societies,[91] and generally to differentiate legal discourse in all its forms from non-legal is both a subordinate task to that of understanding the concept of legality and in any event a task as imperatively to be addressed by "natural lawyers" as by "positivists." In fact, once the discussion is cast in terms of the place of law within a general view of practical reason, it ceases to make any serious sense to suppose that there is a choice to be made between being a "positivist" or a "natural lawyer" (except as a kind of sentimental attachment to a given historical tradition, rather like opting for Sabinianism or Proculianism) in terms of its being a choice which will determine some crucial differentiation of one's legal theory, granting revelation as to the nature of law and as to whether or not unjust laws count as law.

In fact, not the least significant aspect of the remarkable impact Ronald Dworkin's work has had upon the recent pursuit of legal philosophy has been in effect and substance to place questions about practical reasoning in legal contexts at the head of the agenda. For the response to his critique of Hartian jurisprudence with its stress upon the character of legal rules and obligations as based in social practices[92] has necessarily been by way of refining of our understanding not only of the social but even more of the practical character of the normative dimension of human thought. It may or may not be sound to suppose that all legal or social principles concern rights as distinct from policies which concern collective goals[93]; but it is obviously imperative to an adequate testing of Dworkin's case to investigate more fully our notion of what it is to have reasons of principle or reasons of policy for the courses we propose whether in a context of state law or of the law of (for example) a university, trade union or voluntary association. Nor is Dworkin's the only model for critical evaluation in this line: one may compare with it Robert Summers' investigation of the relationship and competition between "goal reasons" and "rightness reasons" as "reasons of substance" contrasting with "authority reasons" in common law systems,[94] in respect of which a point open to speculation is how either or both of Dworkin's and Summers' suggestions might be compared with Max Weber on "formal" versus "substantive" rationality, to which might be added the question whether in Weber himself the distinction of "purpose rationality" and "value rationality" in conduct has anything to offer in the way of further specifying a content for "substantive rationality."[95]

It certainly cannot be adequate, as I once thought it was, to lump together every appeal to general practical reasonableness or substantive grounds of decision in hard cases under the category of "consequentialist reasoning."[96] For as Bernard Rudden has shown, consequences are of various sorts,[97] and it now seems that once we start trying to disentangle logical from behavioural consequences and longer run outcomes of decisions, we return to problems of evaluation in

---

[91]  Compare M. Krygier, "*The Concept of Law* and Social Theory" (1982) 2 O.J.L.S. 155, and G. D. MacCormack "'Law' and 'Legal System'" (1979) 42 M. L. R. 285, for two views on the problem of "law" in non-state societies.

[92]  See Dworkin, *Taking Rights Seriously*, Chap. 2; also N. E. Simmonds "Practices and Professor Dworkin" (1978) *Jur. Rev.* 142; "Practice and Validity" [1979] C. L. J. 361–372.

[93]  Dworkin, *Taking Rights Seriously*, Chap. 4; criticised in MacCormick, *Legal Reasoning and Legal Theory* (1978), excursus to Chap. 9; also in T. D. Perry "Dworkin's Transcendental Idea" in *Midwest Studies in Philosophy VII*, pp. 255–270.

[94]  R. S. Summers, "Two Types of Substantive Reasons: The Core of a Theory of Common Law Justification" (1978) 63 Cornell Law Rev. 707.

[95]  *Max Weber on Law in Economy and Society* (ed. M. Rheinstein, 1954), pp. 1–2, 61–64.

[96]  MacCormick *Legal Reasoning and Legal Theory*, Chaps 5 and 6; but see now also MacCormick "Legal Decisions and their Consequences: from Dewey to Dworkin" (1983) N. Y. Univ. Law Rev. 58, 239–258.

[97]  B. Rudden, "Consequences" (1979) *Jur. Rev.* 193.

which "rightness reasons" (or, perhaps, "value rationality") and "goal reasons" (or, perhaps, "purpose rationality") remain locked in competition. And at this point specialist legal philosophical debate merges with the general debate among political and legal philosophers about justice and about the general contest between deontological and utilitarian theories of the right.[98]

It would be as wrong to exaggerate as to underplay the influence of Dworkin in focussing discussion upon problems of practical reason; indeed, in a sense it has been a side effect rather than an aim of the "Rights Thesis" to have promoted this concern. A great deal of the other work here discussed has taken shape quite independently of the Dworkinian enterprise and has in fact addressed the topic of practical reason more directly than Dworkin has. It has had other fore-runners in Chaim Perelman[99] and Joseph Esser[1] for example; and to the extent that it has in most cases had Kantian overtones, whether direct, as in W. D. Lamont's case, or mediated through Kelsenian thought as in other cases, it could be said to have involved a rediscovery of Lon Fuller's theories on the formal properties of legal order, as distinct from its instrumental character.[2]

The problem with a Kantian line of thought (and this problem Lamont at least supposes to rest on a misunderstanding) is that one may conclude that it tells us how to be rational in practical deliberation without showing whether one should be so. One way of dealing with that would be to follow John Finnis down the Thomist or Aristotelian line and to work forward from the simple self-evidence of certain basic values as goods of human existence.[3] If this can be so presented as to avoid J. L. Mackie's problem of "queerness"[4]—an existential or ontological queerness about the objective existence of values as such—then the answer can well be as Finnis presents it; namely, that practical reasonableness is one basic good among others (life, the pursuit of knowledge, sociability or friendship aesthetic experience, play and religion in Finnis's lists) with the special function of giving order and structure to our pursuit individually and communally of whatever else is of value.[5]

To grant the first steps of that argument is to be convinced by the main outline of what follows from it, though not necessarily with all the details of the conclusions. That is, one will necessarily find this that principles of practical reasonableness generate conceptions (not necessarily exactly Finnis's ones) of justice and the common good. And one will certainly find that the plurality of incommensurable goods means that it is possible for more than one individual or societal life-plan to be genuinely reasonable and soundly adjusted to individual or common good. The plurality of reasonable possibilities and the consequent need for determining upon one or another of them thus generate within this as within Alexy's thesis the need for allocation of authority both to common rules and at least to adjudicative but also in complex social orders to executive and legislative organs of communities.[6]

---

[98] As for example in J. Rawls, *A Theory of Justice* (1972); R. Nozick, *Anarchy, State and Utopia* (1974); Dworkin, *Taking Rights Seriously*; C. Fried, *Right and Wrong* (1978); R. Posner, *The Economics of Justice* (1981); V. Haksar, *Equality, Liberty and Perfectionism* (1979);

[99] Initiated in Ch. Perelman and L. Olbrechts-Tyteca, *La Nouvelle Rhétorique* (1958), and continued most recently in *Logique Juridique: Nouvelle Rhétorique* (1976) and *L'Empire Rhétorique* (1977).

[1] J. Esser, *Vorverstännis und Methodenwahl in der Rechtsfindung* (1970); discussed in L. V. Prott, "Updating the Judicial 'Hunch': Esser's Concept of Judicial Predisposition" (1978) 27 Am. Jo. Comp. Law 461.

[2] L. L. Fuller, *The Morality of Law* (Revised ed., 1969).

[3] See J. Finnis, *Natural Law and Natural Rights* (1980), Chaps 2–4.

[4] J. L. Mackie, *Ethics; inventing Right and Wrong* (1977), pp. 38–41.

[5] Finnis, *op. cit.*, Chap. 5.

[6] Finnis, *op. cit.*, Chaps 6–10.

Where there are authoritative institutions of this sort there have to be regulated procedures for the exercise of authority. What satisfies such procedures is valid ("formally valid"); and validity is at least a necessary condition for ascription of authority or obligatory character to purportedly authoritative determinations of general or particular issues for decision. Hence, although moral values supply the justifying reasons for the existence of endorsement of procedures of validation, it is a standing risk that the individuals in charge of such procedures may abuse them to the detriment of moral values. Hence validity and moral value are not in this theory (or, as Finnis shows, in most mainstream natural law theories) either equivalent or concurrent conditions of each other. The validity of a legal rule or decision hence may constitute a strong prima facie reason in favour of obeying it; but it is never conclusive of that issue; the moral disvalue of a rule or decision will not necessarily render it *ipso jure* null and void.[7]

Again we discover the fatuity of caricature oppositions as between natural law and legal positivism based upon a supposed conflict over the legal status of unjust laws. In and of itself, that is on both views a non-issue. The strength of the natural law tradition as represented by Finnis is in its insistence that some valid laws can indeed be corruptions of law.[8] They can be so in the sense of arising from an abuse of legal processes, "abuse" being necessarily defined in terms of an *essential* aspiration of genuine or "focal" legal enterprises towards realisation of a just and reasonable social ordering in the common good.[9] Here must be noted in parallel the aspirational character of the "inner morality of law," the "rule of law" in a procedural sense, as delineated by Lon Fuller. It remains a contested issue whether an aspiration to justice is to be treated as essential to or definitive of the legal enterprise in all its manifestations, or is to be distinguished as a specially urgent demand issued in the name of critical morality[10] and deriving its urgency from the constant exposure of human beings to possible unjust exercises of the power of modern states organised under and in the name of "law." But that difference of opinion is relatively less urgent than the questions what is unjust and where or how lines of resistance to injustice ought to be drawn. On anyone's view, unjust things will be done in the name and forms of law, and the critique of them is relatively little affected by resolving whether or not these represent a corruption of law in its ideal essence or simply an abuse of public power. The definitional view can indeed help judges to second-guess legislatures as to the justice and thus the lawfulness of what they propose; but that can be a two sided weapon where judicial wisdom is not necessarily sounder than legislative.[11]

These my most recent assertions about the critical role of natural law theory or the parallel exercises in "critical morality" offered by those whose self-definition is as "legal positivists" may in turn provoke objection from the standpoint of "critical law."[12] May it not be objected that the key fact about legal philosophy in all its current modes is its uncritical character? Can we not generalise to the whole of legal philosophy Karl-Ludwig Kunz's attack upon analytical legal philosophy for being in its fruits no better than a mode of legitimating under the title "law" (*Recht* with its even more telling ambiguities) whatever is done under the name and authority of a state?[13]

The most telling reply to this is by protest against arrogation of the term "critical" solely to the ideological stance or group of stances adopted by "critical

---

[7] *ibid.*, Chap. 11.

[8] *ibid.*, Chaps 1, 12.

[9] *ibid.*

[10] A term resurrected by H. L. A. Hart from nineteenth-century thinkers, in *Law, Liberty and Morality* (1963); *cf.* MacCormick, *Hart*, Chap. 4.

[11] *Cf.* Lord Lloyd, "Do we need a Bill of Rights" (1976) 39 M. L. R. 1; A. J. M. Milne "Should we have a Bill of Rights" (1977) 40 M. L. R. 389.

[12] *Cf.* R. Geuss, *The Idea of a Critical Theory: Habermas and the Frankfurt School* (1981).

[13] K. L. Kunz, *Die Analytische Rechtstheorie: Eine "Rechts" theorie ohne Recht?* (1977).

theorist." One can play the arrogation of labels game in a variety of ways, after all. Consider F. A. Hayek's distinction[14] between "critical rationalism" and "constructivist rationalism," under which "critical theorist" turn out to be uncritically and irrationally "constructivist". There is much to be said for Hayek's view that, as with the development of a system of common law, the role of reason in human affairs is best addressed to the continual adjustment and correction and analogical development of an inherited system of what he calls "rules of just conduct," a system which was not and could never have been the product of a single designing intelligence. The point about collective wisdom is that it is dis-seminated among the collectivity and cannot be aggregated into a single pro-gramme or package as constructivists would wish. The strength of this argument is, of course, independent of the particular political proposals which Hayek derives from it.

The same goes for Finnis's somewhat conservative implied judgment of the by-and-large soundness of existing legal institutions in western democracies, as judged by his principles. Is this, if in error because the principles are unsound or because they are misapplied? If it is true for example that there cannot be a "common good" in a society divided by class,[15] then it must be true that the aspiration to Finnisian or Thomist legality is incapable of fulfilment in a capitalist society. The same would be true of the aspiration to fraternity built into the Rawlsian theory of justice, and adopted by those who adapt Rawls to the pur-poses of a social democratic conception of justice and critical morality.[16]

This, however, is the very question. How can "common goods" be identified and squared with goods for the individuals who comprise a community? No one answer to this question is intrinsically more "critical" than any other; but *what* is to be criticised is a function of the answer given. A philosophical concern with legality and with rights either descriptive/analytical or normative/critical in thrust does not in itself pre-determine that, nor should it.

The point is well taken in Tom Campbell's recent *The Left and Rights*, where he faces up to the issue whether "rights" is intrinsically and necessarily a bourgeois or capitalist concept and hence to be wholly eschewed by socialist thinkers. His conclusion is to differentiate the capitalist conception of the rights people have and the necessary means of their fulfilment from a social conception, the latter being what he commends. In his words:

> Socialist rights are most positive, less dependent on the activation of the right-holder, more directed towards the protection and furtherance of those concerns which express the needs of active and creatively productive social beings than is the case with capitalist rights. Socialist rights are more organisational than political in that they inform the co-operative social effort rather than represent demands to be disputed and traded-off against each other. They are devices to secure the benefits which can be derived from harmonious communal living, not protections for the individual against the predations of others.[17]

The ambition here stated to secure "harmonious communal living" seems substantially the same as Finnis's "common good," nor is the stress on the good of human sociability fundamentally different. The difference lies in the conception of the rights which ought to be accorded to people in order to secure such goals. That difference is in turn at least in part explicable as a difference about social facts—about the kinds of relations which obtain between persons in present-day non socialist societies and about possibilities of other forms of community. Here

[14] F. A. Hayek, *Law, Legislation and Liberty* (1973), vol. 1, pp. 29–31.
[15] *Cf.* W. J. Chambliss and R. B. Seidman, *Law, Order and Power* (1971).
[16] Rawls, *A Theory of Justice*, 105–108; MacCormick, *Legal Right and Social Democracy* (1982) Chaps 1, 5.
[17] T. Campbell, *The Left and Rights* (1983), p. 213.

yet again one arrives at a point of necessary interlocking of philosophical and sociological concerns.

But the point at which one arrives poses its own problems. Is the possibility of different forms of society a matter to be determined by purely speculative "factual" inquiry, or are forms of life in part constituted by the modes of "practical discourse" in which humans can, and choose to engage? Do forms of life determine modes of discourse, or *vice versa?*[18] Such a question, I think, poses an unreal alternative. As Zenon Bankowski and David Nelken have pointed out in relation to my account of legal reasoning, it is true that the sustenance of such a group of professionals who practice it, and that those practitioners are or have been socialised into the discourse which they practice.[19] The "form of life" preexisted and moulded its present practitioners who in turn sustain it. One could not imagine it radically changed save by changing the form of life. Yet in turn the possibility of change exists within the system, to the extent that people see and show good reason for changing it. That every form of practical reasoning has necessarily a social context does not show that it cannot in turn be a cause of changes in the context. All it means is that change will be incremental and substitutional rather than radically revolutionary. Somewhat like Hayek, I am of the view that this is the desirable process of change. I can be shown to be wrong in that, if I am wrong, only by some appeal to practical reasons for greater and more sudden change. And, if such reasons are offered, they will fall to be judged by their soundness or weight, by the new form of life they offer me, not by the form of life by which I suppose them to have been generated.

Finally, let it be asked whether judgment of the soundness or weight of such reasons belongs within the scope of what is knowable. Are these matters of faith and conviction, or matters of knowledge? Do practical judgments in their character as such have truth value? Does reason in the governance of will play the same role as reason in the governance of speculative or factual inquiry? I cannot myself answer these questions. I can see the attractiveness of the Finnisian view under which judgments of absolute and relative value are capable of being true or false in their own right as such. Yet I remain upon the whole more persuaded of the alternative view that values are in the last resort functions of attitude rather than objects of cognitive apprehension. That we can subject them to the discipline of reason is not the same as supposing that they can be established by reasoning. And so I tentatively conclude that the sphere of normative knowledge is restricted more or less as legal positivists have demarcated it; restricted, that is, to knowledge of and within socially established norm-systems. Raz's line between matters decided at the "executive" stage and matters still under deliberation is here the crucial line. Law and laws are knowable as matters of "institutional fact" and not otherwise. But they are understandable only within the broader perspective of a study of practical reasoning in all its stages, and capable of sound implementation only under the guidance of practical reason. The philosophy of law must include, but is not exhausted by, legal epistemology.

As this paper commenced with an imaginary doubt, so it concludes with a real one. The real doubt is not about the value of a philosophy of law, but is rather of the kind which is a spur to its continuing pursuit. One line of inquiry to which it ought to give a stimulus is that of the study of reasoning in matters of fact. Behind one's doubt as to the ontological standing of non-positive norms and values perhaps lies an unstated contrast between the certainty of factual knowledge and the more tentative character of evaluation, with its consequential need for

---

[18] *Cf.* Aulis Aarnio, *On Legal Reasoning*, (1977), pp. 126–129; *Legal Points of View: Six Essays on Legal Philosophy* (1978), p. 162. A Peczenik, "Right and Wrong in Legal Reasoning" in *Conceptions Contemporains du Droit*, pp. 57–75.

[19] Z. Bankowski and D. Nelken, "Discretion as a Social Problem" in *Discretion and Welfare* (eds. M. Adler and S. Asquith, 1980), pp. 247–268 at 263–265.

decisions in circumstances of uncertainty. Especially in legal contexts, the standing of this background assumption about facts needs further consideration.

It is not true that, in law at least, only questions of law have to be decided, and decided on a judgment of the weight of non-demonstrative arguments. Exactly the same goes for questions of fact and evidence. There is less of a contrast than we are inclined to suppose. Just as we need reasonable processes for authoritative rulings on law, so we need reasonable processes for authoritative determinations about facts—or "truth certifying procedures," as they have been called.[20] Recent controversies about the nature of probabilistic reasoning in evidentiary matters (notably among Sir Richard Eggleston, Jonathan Cohen and Glanville Williams) are reminders of the difficulty and the controversial quality of this aspect of reasoning.[21] As William Twining has rightly put it, we have to "take facts seriously" too.[22] Does the necessary existence of social practices of fact-certification lead to the conclusion that what we take to be reality is only a social construct?[23] Or does the possibility that we should seriously entertain that belief about "reality" as a true belief require us to suppose that it either is or is not anchored in a real reality beyond all social constructs? If so, it will be at best a qualified truth. As to this aspect of reasoning, just as to practical reasoning, there is no feasible disentanglement of philosophical and sociological inquiries or hypotheses.

In this paper I have attempted to survey some main lines of current work in the philosophy of law. It seems to me that what is most exciting in recent work has been the rediscovery of practical reason as a focal topic for the philosophy of law. I have tried to show how work on it relates to and has grown out of concern for essentially epistemological questions about the possibility of and the limits of legal knowledge, and how it must be complemented (and is, albeit in too small a degree complemented) by reflection on fact-finding processes, and on the question whether these also engage practical reason rather than being matters of pure speculation. This view of the subject of course exhibits my own value judgment about that which is most worthy of our attention. Of the reasonableness of the value judgment, and thus of the principles for selection of the matters discussed, I must leave it to others to judge. [pp. 1–15]

## J. RAZ
**Practical Reason and Norms**
(1990)

### *Criticism of the practice theory*

The practice theory[24] suffers from three fatal defects. It does not explain rules which are not practices; it fails to distinguish between social rules and widely accepted reasons; and it deprives rules of their normative character. Let us consider these points one by one.

Rules need not be practised in order to be rules. It may be true that certain

---

[20] By Zenon Bankowski in "The Value of Truth: Fact-Scepticism Re-Visited" (1981) I *Legal Studies* 257–266.

[21] See R. Eggleston, *Evidence, Proof and Probability* (1978); J. Cohen, *The Probable and the Provable* (1977) G. Williams, "The Mathematics of Proof" (1979) Crim. Law Rev. 297, 340; J. Cohen, "The Logic of Proof" (1980) Crim. Law Rev. 91; G. Williams, "A Short Rejoinder", p. 103.

[22] W. Twining, "Taking Facts Seriously," in *Essays on Legal Education* (ed. N. Gold, 1981); "The Rationalist Tradition in Evidence Scholarship" in *Well and Truly Tried* (eds. E. Campbell and L. Waller, 1981); and see the symposium edited by Twining *Facts in Law* (1983).

[23] *Cf.* P. Berger and T. Luckmann, *The Social Construction of Reality* (1966).

[24] [The standard example of which is Hart's *Concept of Law*.]

types of rules must be practised. A legal rule is not a legal rule unless it is part of a legal system which is practised by a certain community. But this is necessary because it is a *legal* rule, and not because it is a rule. Likewise a rule is not a social rule unless it is practised by a certain community, but it may still be a rule. Moral rules are perhaps the clearest example of rules which are not practices. For example, many believe that it is a rule that promises ought to be kept. It may be true that this rule is practised in their communities, but what they believe when they believe that this is a rule is not that it is a practice. Nor is it a necessary condition for the correctness of their belief that the rule is practised. For one may believe that it is a rule that promises ought to be kept even if one is not, and has never been, a member of a community which practised the rule. Similarly, a person may believe in the validity of a rule that one ought to be a vegetarian even though he knows no other vegetarians.

One may be tempted to regard the cases I have referred to as cases of personal rules, but this is unlikely to solve our problem. We have not considered what the explanation of personal rules might be. It seems fairly clear, however, that to be useful at all the notion of a personal rule must mean more than simply a rule in the validity of which a person believes. If the conditions which must be satisfied before a person can be said to have a personal rule are more stringent than those on the basis of which a belief in the validity of a rule can be ascribed to him, then it is possible for a person to believe in the validity of a rule which is not his personal rule. A person may believe that a rule is valid even though he does not observe it. If so then on many occasions when a person believes in the validity of a moral rule the rule he believes in may not actually be his personal rule. Moreover, a man who follows a rule normally regards this fact as irrelevant to the correctness of his belief in the validity of the rule. We would not be surprised to hear him explain that he believes that it is a rule that such and such or that he believes that there is such a moral rule and therefore he has decided to try and follow it, or to make it his practice to follow it. Nor would we be surprised to hear him apologize and explain that despite his belief that there is such a moral rule he has never succeeded in behaving accordingly. We cannot refute him by saying that, since he is not actually following the rule, since it is not his personal rule, he must be wrong in thinking that it is a moral rule. Nor can we say that he is mistaken if it is neither his rule nor a social rule. He may admit to that and confess that neither he nor anybody he knows follows the rule, but regard this as proof of human imperfection and still believe in the validity of the moral rule. This argument does not imply that avowal of belief by a person is a sufficient condition for ascribing the belief to him. A person may sincerely declare that he believes in the validity of a rule and be mistaken. All I am arguing for is that the condition for ascribing the belief may not depend on his following the rule in practice. His belief may manifest itself, for example, in feelings of guilt and regret, and these may exist even though he invariably fails to follow the rule.

Nor can we escape from the problem by equating the holding of a personal rule with belief in the validity of the rule. If we do this it will be true, at the cost of trivializing the notion of a personal rule, that whenever a person believes in the validity of a rule it is his personal rule. Yet when he asserts that there is a rule he is not asserting that he believes in its validity. This view is no more plausible than the thesis that when a person asserts that it is raining what he is stating is that he believes it is raining.

These arguments do not, and are not designed to, prove that there are rules which are not practised. It may be that the person in my example is mistaken in believing that there are such rules, and he may be mistaken because the rules are not practised. He may be mistaken in thinking that there can be rules which are not practised. But even if he is wrong his belief is intelligible. He may be mistaken but he is not perserve or irrational or misusing language. This means that even if we believe that there can be a rule only if it is practised the word "rule" does not mean "a practice", and hence the explanation of what a rule is cannot be in terms of the practice theory. At best the practice theory is part of a substantive moral theory explaining when rules are valid or binding. It forms no part of the analysis of the concept of a rule.

The second major defect of the practice theory is its failure to distinguish between practised rules and accepted reasons. According to the practice theory, whenever a reason is believed in, followed and acted on by the relevant person or group, then they have a rule. If my first argument against the practice theory is sound, it follows that we can distinguish between a rule and a reason (which is not a rule) regardless of whether they are acted on and followed in practice. This suggests that there must be a distinction between the practice of acting on a general reason and that of following a rule. This distinction is in fact reflected in the way we interpret our practices. We do not regard every practice of acting on a general reason as acting on a rule. The practice theory fails to draw this distinction and it thereby fails to capture the essential features of rules.

Consider the case of Jack. Jack believes that he ought to read all of Iris Murdoch's novels and he does usually read them not long after publication. If he fails to read one of her novels within a year of its publication he tends to reproach himself for the omission. Yet he does not think of himself as having a rule that he should read all her novels. He does have other rules. He is a vegetarian and he cleans his teeth every evening. He does this because he believes that these are good rules to have. But he does not read Murdoch because of a belief in any rule.

Consider a community in which almost everybody believes that babies should be breast-fed or that children should be encouraged to learn to read when they are three years of age. This is generally done and people tend to reproach mothers who do not breast-feed or parents who do not teach their three-year-old children to read. Yet people in the community do not regard these as rules. They merely think that they are good things to do. They do regard it as a rule, for example, that people should go to church on Sunday. Somehow they think differently of this, though the difference is not reflected in their practice (except that they would talk of a rule only in the latter case). Warnock in *The Object of Morality* makes the same point using the following example: "Consider the situation of the spectator of a cricket match, ignorant of the game, and trying to work out what rules the players are following. He will find for instance that, when six balls have been bowled from one end, the players regularly move round and six balls are then bowled from the other end; deviations from this, he will observe, are adversely criticised. He will probably find also that, when a fast bowler is replaced by a slow one, some persons who were previously stationed quite close to the batsman are moved further away, some, probably, a lot further away; and he will find that, if this is not done, there is adverse criticism. But if he concludes that, in so acting, the players are following rules, he will of course be right in the first case, and wrong in the second. There is *no* rule that a slow bowler should not operate with exactly the same field setting as a fast one; this is indeed scarcely ever done, and it would nearly always be regarded as wrong to do it, but that is because, quite independently of any rules, it is something which there is nearly always good reason not to do" (pp. 45–46). The practice theory is at fault for failing to recognize and explain this distinction.

The third major defect of the practice theory is that it deprives rules of their normative character. We have already mentioned that a rule is a reason for action. The fact that rules are normally stated by using normative terms (and in trying to refute the practice theory I am arguing, among other things, that it can only be stated in such terms) indicates that they are operative reasons. A practice as such is not necessarily a reason for action. It may be, provided that there is reason for all to behave as everyone does (to drive on the left, or follow the common rules of etiquette, etc.) or if a certain person has, generally or in particular circumstances, reason to conform to the practice (in order not to be rejected by his neighbours or not to lose his job, etc.). But the practice theory fails to account generally for the normative character of rules. At best it could claim to explain conventional rules, namely those social rules which are maintained because people believe that all have a reason to behave as everyone does. Ultimately it fails to explain even those.

To appreciate this point we should return to Hart's analysis of social rules. His fourth condition is that members of the relevant community use expressions such as "it is a rule that one ought to ..." to justify their own actions, and to justify demands and criticisms addressed to others. But what is it that they are actually saying when stating that one should have behaved in a certain way because it is a rule that ...? There are three possible interpretations. According to the first they are not stating anything; they are acting. They are performing the speech act of criticizing (or demanding or justifying). The way Hart presents his analysis suggests that he does not accept this explanation, and surely he is right. For on this interpretation citing a rule does nothing to explain the demand or criticism, a view which is clearly wrong. Moreover, this interpretation does not apply at all to those cases in which one explains one's own or another person's action by saying that it was done because of a rule.

According to the second interpretation the statements under consideration invoke the practice as (an incomplete) reason for action. "I did it because of the rule" means I did it because everybody does. "Do it because of the rule" means do it because everybody does. There is no denying that sometimes that is what one intends to convey by making such a statement. This is the case when the rule is a conventional rule or when the speaker intends to appeal to reasons which his hearers may have for conforming to the rule, of the kind mentioned above (fear of public disapproval, etc.). But rules are invoked in other circumstances as well. When one explains a demand by reference to the rule that promises ought to be kept, one may intend to intimate that the hearer had better keep his promise or else he will have to take the consequences. But more often than not this is not the speaker's intention. And since at least sometimes this second interpretation fails, it always fails to explain what is stated, because what is stated is the same on all normal occasions on which such sentences are used. Though of course the speaker may have on occasion an additional point which he intends to convey, this cannot be part of what is stated. It is merely what is intimated or implied by the fact that he made the statement.

The third interpretation seems to be the one Hart has in mind. According to this interpretation, sentences of the form "it is a rule that x ought to o" and of the form "x ought to o" are standardly used to make the same statement. In other words, to state that it is a rule that one ought to o is to state that one ought to o. One can use either sentence to make this statement except that one can properly use the "it is a rule" formulation only if the appropriate practice exists. To state that it is a rule ..., is not to state that there is a practice. It is to assert that one ought to behave in this way, but one is entitled to use this sentence to make the assertion only if the practice exists. Both sentences are used to make the same statement with the use of the "it is a rule" sentence presupposing that the practice exists. This seems to me to be Hart's interpretation of the use of these sentences to make statements "from the internal point of view." They can, according to his theory, also be used to make statements "from the external point of view" which means statements that the practice exists.[25]

On this interpretation rule sentences are used to make normative statements. They are not, however, statements of a reason. They are merely statements that there is a reason. But there is a more serious drawback to this view. According to it the fact that there is a rule is irrelevant to the normative import of the statement. Saying "it is a rule that one ought, etc.," is rather like saying "one ought,

---

[25] [As to which see *ante*, 379.]

etc., and besides, though this is irrelevant from the point of view of practical reason, there is a practice of a certain kind." To be sure, mentioning the rule is not entirely irrelevant. In so far as it implies the existence of a practice it indicates that the speaker is not alone in his view; it is, therefore, an important rhetorical device. But it is irrelevant for practical reasoning. We must, therefore, reject the practice theory and look for an alternative. [pp. 53–58]

## J. RAZ
### Authority, Law and Morality
(1994)[26]

The main purpose of this essay is to defend the sources thesis against some common misunderstandings and to provide one reason for preferring it to the other two. The argument turns on the nature of authority, which is the subject of the first section. In the second section some of the implications of this analysis are shown to be relevant to our understanding of the law. Their relation with the three theses is then examined. The connection between law and authority is used to criticize Dworkin's support of the coherence thesis, as well as the incorporation thesis advocated by Hart and others. The rejection of these views leads to the endorsement of the sources thesis. [. . .] Throughout, the argument is exploratory rather than conclusive.

### I. Authority and Justification

Authority in general can be divided into legitimate and *de facto* authority. The latter either claims to be legitimate or is believed to be so, and is effective in imposing its will on many, over whom it claims authority, perhaps because it claim to legitimacy is recognized by many of its subjects. But it does not necessarily possess legitimacy. Legitimate authority is either practical or theoretica (or both). The directives of a person or institution with practical authority are reasons for action for their subjects, whereas the advice of a theoretical authority is a reason for belief for those regarding whom that person or institution has authority. Though the views here expressed apply to theoretical authorities as well, unless otherwise indicated

I shall use "authority" to refer to legitimate practical authority. Since our interest is in the law we will be primarily concerned with political authorities. But I shall make no attempt to characterize the special features of those, as opposed to practical authorities in general or legal features of those, as opposed to practical authorities in general or legal authorities in particular.

The distinction between reasons for action and reasons for belief may be sufficient to distinguish between practical and theoretical authorities, but it is inadequate to distinguish between authorities and other people. Anyone's sincere assertion can be a reason for belief, and anyone's request can be a reason for action. What distinguishes authoritative directives is their special peremptory status. One is tempted to say that they are marked by their authoritativeness. This peremptory character has other led people to say that in accepting the authority of another one is surrendering one's judgment to him, that the acceptance of authority is the denial of one's moral autaomy, and so on. Some have seen in these alleged features of authority a good deal of what often justifies submitting to authority. Many more derived from such reflections prove that acceptance of authority is wrong, or even inconsistent with one's status as a moral agent. Elsewhere[27] I have developed a conception of authority which accounts for its

---

[26] [From J. Raz, *Ethics in the Public Domain* (1994).]
[27] "Authority and Justification" (1985) 14 *Philosophy and Public Affairs* 3.

peremptory force while explaining the conditions under which it may be right to accept authority. Let me briefly repeat the main tenets of this conception of authority. Its details and the arguments in its support cannot be explored here.

Consider the case of two people who refer a dispute to an arbitrator. He has authority to settle the dispute, for they agreed to abide by his decision. Two features stand out. First, the arbitrator's decision is for the disputants a reason for action. They ought to do as he says because he says so. But this reason is related to the other reasons which apply to the case. It is not just another reason to be added to the others, a reason to stand alongside the others when one reckons which way is better supported by reason. The arbitrator's decision is meant to be based on the other reasons, to sum them up and to reflect their outcome. He has reason to act so that his decision will reflect the reasons which apply to the litigants. I shall call reasons of the kind which apply to the arbitrator dependent reasons. I shall also refer to his decision as a dependent reason for the litigants. Notice that in this second sense a dependent reason is not one which does in fact reflect the balance of reasons on which it is based. It is one which is meant to, *i.e.* which should, do so.

This leads directly to the second distinguishing feature of the example. The arbitrator's decision is also meant to replace the reasons on which it depends. In agreeing to obey his decision, the disputants agreed to follow his judgment of the balance of reasons rather than their own. Henceforth his decision will settle for them what to do. Lawyers say that the original reasons merge into the decision of the arbitrator or the judgment of a court, which, if binding, becomes *res judicata*. This means that the original cause of action can no longer be relied upon for any purpose. I shall call a reason which displaces others a pre-emptive reason.

It is not that the arbitrator's word is an absolute reason which has to be obeyed come what may. It can be challenged and justifiably disobeyed in certain circumstances. If, for example, the arbitrator was bribed, was drunk while considering the case, or if new evidence of great importance unexpectedly turns up, each party may ignore the decision. The point is that reasons that could have been relied upon to justify action before his decision cannot be relied upon once the decision is given. Note that there is no reason for anyone to restrain their thoughts or their reflections on the reasons which apply to the case, nor are they necessarily debarred from criticizing the arbitrator for having ignored certain reasons or for having been mistaken about their significance. It is merely action for some of these reasons which is excluded.

The two features, dependence and pre-emptiveness, are intimately connected. Because the arbitrator is meant to decide on the basis of certain reasons, the disputants are excluded from later relying on them. They handed over to him the task of evaluating those reasons. If they do not then reject those reasons as possible bases for their own action, they defeat the very point and purpose of the arbitration. The only proper way to acknowledge the arbitrator's authority is to take it to be a reason for action which replaces the reasons on the basis of which he was meant to decide.

The crucial question is whether the arbitrator's is a typical authority, or whether the two features picked out above are peculiar to it, and perhaps a few others, but are not characteristic of authorities in general. It might be thought, for example, that the arbitrator is typical of adjudicative authorities, and that what might be called legislative authorities differ from them in precisely these respects. Adjudicative authorities, one might say, are precisely those in which the role of the authority is to judge what are the reasons which apply to its subjects and decide accordingly, *i.e.* their decisions are merely meant to declare what ought to be done in any case. A legislative authority, on the other hand, is one whose job is to create new reasons for its subjects, *i.e.* reasons which are new not merely in the sense of replacing other reasons on which they depend but in not purporting to replace any reasons at all. If we understand "legislative" and "adjudicative" broadly, so the objection continues, all practical authorities belong to at least one of these kinds. It will be conceded, of course, that legislative authorities act for reasons. But theirs are reasons which apply to them and which do not depend on, *i.e.* are not meant to reflect, reasons which apply to their subjects.

The apparent attractiveness of the above distinction is, however, misguided. Consider an Act of Parliament imposing on parents a duty to maintain their young children. Parents have such a duty independently of this Act, and only because they have it is the Act justified. Further argument is required to show that the same features are present in all practical authorities. Instead, let me summarize my conception of authority in three theses:

> The dependence thesis: All authoritative directives should be based, among other factors, on reasons which apply to the subjects of those directives and which bear on the circumstances covered by the directives. Such reasons I shall call dependent reasons.
>
> The normal justification thesis: The normal and primary way to establish that a person should be acknowledged to have authority over another person involves showing that the alleged subject is likely better to comply with reasons which apply to him (other than the alleged authoritative directives) if he accepts the directives of the alleged authority as authoritatively binding, and tries to follow them, than if he tries to follow the reasons which apply to him directly.[28]
>
> The pre-emption thesis: The fact that an authority requires performance of an action is a reason for its performance which is not to be added to all other relevant reasons when assessing what to do, but should replace some of them.

The first and the last theses generalize the features we noted in the arbitration example. The normal justification thesis replaces the agreement between the litigants which was the basis of the arbitrator's authority. Agreement or consent to accept authority is binding, for the most part, only if conditions rather like those of the normal justification thesis obtain.

The first two theses articulate what I shall call the service conception of authority. They regard authorities as *mediating* between people and the right reasons which apply to them, so that the authority judges and pronounces what they ought to do according to right reason. The people on their part take their cue from the authority whose pronouncements replace for them the force of the dependent reasons. This last implication of the service conception is made explicit in the pre-emption thesis. The mediating role of authority cannot be carried out if its subjects do not guide their actions by its instructions instead of by the reasons on which they are supposed to depend. No blind obedience to authority is here implied. Acceptance of authority has to be justified, and this normally means meeting the conditions set in the justification thesis. This brings into play the dependent reasons, for only if the authority's compliance with them is likely to be better than that of its subjects is its claim to legitimacy justified. At the level of general justification the pre-empted reasons have an important role to play. But once that level has been passed and we are concerned with particular action, dependent reasons are replaced by authoritative directives. To count both as independent reasons is to be guilty of double counting.

This is the insight which the surrender of judgment metaphor seeks to capture. It does not express the immense power of authorities. Rather it reflects their limited role. They are not there to introduce new and independent considerations (though when they make a mistake and issue the wrong decrees they do precisely that). They are meant to reflect dependent reasons in situations where they are

---

[28]  The normal justification thesis specifies only the reasons for recognizing an authority. It says nothing on the reasons against doing so. These exist to various degrees depending on the nature of the case. They determine how strong the case for recognizing the authority has to be. It must be sufficient to overcome the reasons to the contrary.

better placed to do so. They mediate between ultimate reasons and the people to whom they apply.

## II. Authority and the Law

I will assume that necessarily law, every legal system which is in force anywhere, has *de facto* authority. That entails that the law either claims that it possesses legitimate authority or is held to possess it, or both. I shall argue that, though a legal system may not have legitimate authority, or though its legitimate authority may not be as extensive as it claims, every legal system claims that it possesses legitimate authority. If the claim to authority is part of the nature of law, then whatever else the law is it must be capable of possessing authority. A legal system may lack legitimate authority. If it lacks the moral attributes required to endow it with legitimate authority then it has none. But it must possess all the other features of authority, or else it would be odd to say that it claims authority. To claim authority it must be capable of having it, it must be a system of a kind which is capable in principle of possessing the requisite moral properties of authority. These considerations, I shall argue, create a weighty argument in favour of the sources thesis. Let us review them step by step.

The claims the law makes for itself are evident from the language it adopts and from the opinions expressed by its spokesmen, *i.e.* by the institutions of the law. The law's claim to authority is manifested by the fact that legal institutions are officially designated as "authorities", by the fact that they regard themselves as having the right to impose obligations on their subjects, by their claims that their subjects owe them allegiance, and that their subjects ought to obey the law as it requires to be obeyed (i.e. in all cases except those in which some legal doctrine justifies breach of duty). Even a bad law, is the inevitable official doctrine, should be obeyed for as long as it is in force, while lawful action is taken to try and bring about its amendment or repeal. One caveat needs be entered here. In various legal systems certain modes of conduct are technically unlawful without being so in substance. It is left to the prosecutorial authorities to refrain from prosecuting for such conduct, or to the courts to give absolute discharge. Where legally recognized policies direct such authorities to avoid prosecution or conviction, the conduct should not be regarded as unlawful except in a technical sense, which is immaterial to our considerations.

Does the fact that the law claims authority help us understand its nature in any way, beyond the sheer fact that the law makes this claim? If of necessity all legal systems have legitimate authority, then we can conclude that they have the features which constitute the service conception of authority. But it is all too plain that in many cases the law's claim to legitimate authority cannot be supported. There are legal systems whose authority cannot be justified by the normal justification thesis or in any other way. Can it not be argued that, since the law may lack authority, a conception of authority cannot contribute to our understanding of what it is, except by showing what it claims to be? This conclusion is at the very least premature. It could be that, in order to be able to claim authority, the law must at the very least come close to the target, *i.e.* that it must have some of the characteristics of authority. It can fail to have authority. But it can fail in certain ways only. If this is so, there are features of authority that it must have. If so, we can learn from the doctrine of authority something about the nature of law.

Note that nothing in this suggestion assumes that all the necessary features of the law are necessary features of every practical authority. The law may well have others. Indeed, I am already assuming that the law does have others, since it is not necessary that every person who has legitimate authority claims to have it, as the law necessarily does. All that we are trying to establish is whether some necessary characteristics of law are necessary characteristics of authority, which the law must have if it is to be capable of claiming authority.

I suggested above that only those who can have authority can sincerely claim to have it, and that therefore the law must be capable of having authority. This claim is so vague that, even if correct, it cannot be more than a gesture towards an argument. What might that be? Consider the fact that the law is a normative system. If it were not, it would be incapable of having practical authority. If the law were a set of propositions about the behaviour of volcanoes, for example, then it would not only lack authority over action, it would be incapable of having such authority. The statement that a normative system is authoritatively binding on us may be false, but at least it makes sense, whereas the claim that a set of propositions about volcanoes authoritatively determines what we ought to do does not even make sense.

But cannot one claim that a person X has authority which it would make no sense to attribute to X? The claim makes sense because we understand what is claimed, even while we know that it is not merely false but is necessarily, or conceptually, false. For example, what cannot communicate with people cannot have authority over them. Trees cannot have authority over people. But someone whose awareness of what trees are is incomplete, a young child, for example, can claim that they do have authority. He is simply wrong. Similarly, even if he is aware of the nature of trees, he may make an insincere claim to that effect. Perhaps he is trying to deceive a newly arrived Martian sociologist. Notice, however, that one cannot sincerely claim that someone who is conceptually incapable of having authority has authority if one understands the nature of one's claim and of the person of whom it is made. If I say that trees have authority over people, you will know that either my grasp of the concepts of authority or of trees is deficient or that I am trying to deceive (or, of course, that I am not really stating that trees have authority but merely pretending to do so, or that I am play-acting, etc.).

That is enough to show that since the law claims to have authority it is capable of having it. Since the claim is made by legal officials wherever a legal system is in force, the possibility that it is normally insincere or based on a conceptual mistake is ruled out. It may, of course, be sometimes insincere or based on conceptual mistakes. But at the very least in the normal case the fact that the law claims authority for itself shows that it is capable of having authority.

Why cannot legal officials and institutions be conceptually confused? One answer is that while they can be occasionally they cannot be systematically confused. For given the centrality of legal institutions in our structures of authority, their claims and conceptions are formed by and contribute to our concept of authority. It is what it is in part as a result of the claims and conceptions of legal institutions. This answer applies where the legal institutions themselves employ the concept of authority. But there may be law in societies which do not have our concept of authority. We say of their legal institutions that they claim authority because they claim to impose duties, confer rights, etc. Not having the concept they cannot be confused about it, though we can be confused in attributing the claim of authority to them.

The argument of the last four paragraphs has established, first, that one can fail to have authority because one is incapable of possessing authority (though even those capable of having authority may fail to have it), second, that since the law claims authority it is capable of having authority. There are two kinds of reason for not having authority. One is that the moral or normative conditions for one's directives being authoritative are absent. Typically, this will be either because the normal justification, explained above, is unavailable or because, though available, it is insufficient to outweigh the conflicting reasons which obtain in this particular case. The second kind of reason for not having authority is that one lacks some of the other, non-moral or non-normative, prerequisites of authority, for example, that one cannot communicate with others.

It is natural to hold that the non-moral, non-normative conditions for having authority are also the conditions of the ability to have authority. A person's authority may be denied on the ground that he is morally incompetent or wicked. But such facts do not show that he is incapable of having authority in the way that trees are incapable of having authority. Nazi rules may not be authoritatively binding, but they are the sort of thing that can be authoritatively binding, whereas statements about volcanoes cannot. Most arguments about the authority of governments and other institutions revolve around their moral claim to the obedience of their subjects. The existence of the non-moral qualifications is taken for granted. The argument does not start except regarding persons and institutions who meet those other conditions. That is why they are thought of as the conditions which establish capacity to possess authority.

If this view is correct then, since the law necessarily claims authority, and therefore typically has the capacity to be authoritative, it follows that it typically has all the non-moral, or non-normative, attributes of authority. The remainder of my argument, however, does not depend on this strong conclusion. We will concentrate on two features which must be possessed by anything capable of being authoritatively binding. These two features will then be used to support the sources thesis.

It is convenient to concentrate attention on instructions or directives. The terms are used in a wide sense which can cover propositions, norms, rules, standards, principles, doctrines, and the like. In that sense the law is a system of directives, and it is authoritative if and only if its directives are authoritatively binding. Likewise, whoever issues the directives has authority if and only if his directives are authoritatively binding because he makes them, that is (1) they are authoritative, and (2) part of the reason is that he made them.

The two features are as follows. First, a directive can be authoritatively binding only if it is, or is at least presented as, someone's view of how its subjects ought to behave. Second, it must be possible to identify the directive as being issued by the alleged authority without relying on reasons or considerations on which directive purports to adjudicate.

The first feature reflects the mediating role of authority. It is there to act on reasons which apply to us anyway, because we will more closely conform to those reasons if we do our best to follow the directives of the authority than if we try to act on those reasons directly. Hence, though the alleged authoritative instruction may be wrongly conceived and misguided, it must represent the judgment of the alleged authority on the reasons which apply to its subjects, or at least it must be presented as the authority's judgment. Otherwise it cannot be an authoritative instruction. If fails not because it is a bad instruction, but because it is not an instruction of the right kind. It may be an instruction given for some other occasion, or in jest, or an order or threat of a gangster who cares for and considers only his own good. Strictly speaking, to be capable of being authoritative a directive or a rule has actually to express its author's view on what its subjects should do. But given that this element is one where pretence and deceit are so easy, there is little surprise that appearances are all one can go by here, and the concept of *de facto* authority, as well as all others which presuppose capacity to have authority, are based on them. If the rule is presented as expressing a judgment on what its subjects should do, it is capable of being authoritative.

The second feature too is closely tied to the mediating role of authority. Suppose that an arbitrator, asked to decide what is fair in a situation, has given a correct decision. That is, suppose there is only one fair outcome, and it was picked out by the arbitrator. Suppose that the parties to the dispute are told only that about his decision, *i.e.* that he gave the only correct decision. They will feel that they know little more of what the decision is than they did before. They were given a uniquely identifying description of the decision and yet it is an entirely unhelpful description. If they could agree on what was fair they would not have needed the arbitrator in the first place. A decision is serviceable only if it can be identified by means other than the considerations the weight and outcome of which it was meant to settle.

This applies to all decisions, as much to those that a person takes for himself as to those taken for him by others. If I decide what would be the best life insurance to buy, it is no good trying to remind me of my decision by saying that I decided to buy the policy which it is best to buy. It means that I have to decide again in order to know what I decided before, so the earlier decision might just as well never have happened. The same applies to the subjects of any authority. They can benefit by its decisions only if they can establish their existence and content in ways which do not depend on raising the very same issues which the authority is there to settle.

Can it not be objected that my argument presupposes that people know the normal justification thesis, and the others which go with it? To be sure such an assumption would not be justified. Nor is it made. All I am assuming is that the service conception of authority is sound, *i.e.* that it correctly represents our concept of authority. It is not assumed that people believe that it does.

It is worth noting that a set of conditions rather like the pair I have argued for can be derived from a much weaker assumption than that of the service conception of authority explained above. I will call this the alternative argument. Its premiss is nothing more than the claim that it is part of our notion of legitimate authority that authorities should act for reasons, and that their legitimacy depends on a degree of success in doing so. Even those who reject the service conception of authority will accept conditions similar to the two I have argued for if they accept that legitimacy depends on (a degree of) success in acting for reasons. It is obvious that this weak assumption is enough to hold that only what is presented as someone's view can be an authoritative directive.

Instead of the second condition, that directives be capable of independent identification (i.e. independent of the reasons they should be based upon), two weaker conditions can be established. I will assume that authorities make a difference, *i.e.* the fact that an authority issued a directive changes the subjects' reasons. It follows that the existence of reasons for an authority to issue a directive does not by itself, without the directive having actually been issued, lead to this change in the reasons which face the subjects. Therefore, the existence of reasons which establish that a certain directive, if issued, would be the right one to have issued cannot show that such a directive exists and is binding. Its existence and content, in other words, cannot depend exclusively on the reasons for it. The existence and content of every directive depend on the existence of some condition which is itself independent of the reasons for that directive. Moreover, that further condition cannot simply be that that or some other authority issued another directive. Often the existence of one law is a reason for passing another. But we have just established that the existence of a law cannot depend simply on the existence of reasons for it, on reasons showing that it would be good if people behaved in the way it prescribes, or that it would be good if the law required them to do so. Therefore, the existence of one directive, though it may show that another is desirable or right, cannot by itself establish its existence.

### III. The coherence thesis

The previous section argued that, even though the law may lack legitimate authority, one can learn quite a lot about it from the fact that it claims legitimate authority. It must be capable of being authoritative. In particular it must be, or be presented as, someone's view on what the subjects ought to do, and it must be identifiable by means which are independent of the considerations the authority should decide upon.

It is interesting to note that legal sources meet both conditions. To anticipate and simplify, the three common sources of law, legislation, judicial decisions, and custom, are capable of being sources of authoritative directives. They meet the non-moral conditions implied in the service conception of authority. Legislation can be arbitrary, and it can fail to comply with the dependence thesis in many ways. But it expresses, or is at least presented as expressing, the legislator's judgment of what the subjects are to do in the situations to which the legislation applies. Therefore, it can be the product of the legislator's judgment on the reasons which apply to his subjects. The same is true of judicial decisions. Judges may be bribed. They may act arbitrarily. But a judicial decision expresses a judgment on the legal consequences of the behaviour of the litigants. It is presented as a judgment on the way the parties, and others in the same circumstances, ought to behave. Similarly with custom. It is not normally generated by people intending to make law. But it can hardly avoid reflecting the judgment of the bulk of the population on how people in the relevant circumstances should act. Source-based law can conform to the dependence thesis. It therefore conforms to the first of our conditions which are entailed by the fact that the law claims authority.

Legal sources also conform with the second of our two conditions, since they are capable of being identified in ways which do not rely on the considerations they are meant to decide upon. An income-tax statute is meant to decide what is the fair contribution of public funds to be borne out of income. To establish the content of the statute, all one need do is to establish that the enactment took place, and what it says. To do this one needs little more than knowledge of English (including technical legal English), and of the events which took place in Parliament on a few occasions. One need not come to any view on the fair contribution to public funds.

As was noted above, all three rivals, the coherence, the incorporation, and the sources theses, are united in attributing a special significance to source-based law. The preceding simplified account illustrates the way central features of the law can mesh in with and acquire a special significance from the service conception of authority and the two necessary features of law which it entails. It does not follow that these are the reasons normally given for the centrality of source-based law. The coherence thesis represents an account which is at the very least indifferent to the considerations outlined above. I have identified it as the view that the law consists of source-based law together with the morally best justification of the source-based law. This may look an unholy mixture of disparate elements. But it need not be. In the hands of its best advocate, R. M. Dworkin, it embodies a powerful and intriguing conception of the law.

Dworkin's conception of the law, expressed in various articles over many years, is not easy to ascertain. Some points of detail which are nevertheless essential to its interpretation remain elusive. Many readers of his celebrated "Hard Cases" (1975) took it to express a view of law which can be summarized in the following way:

> To establish the content of the law of a certain country one first finds out what are the legal sources valid in that country and then one considers one master question: Assuming that all the laws ever made by these sources which are still in force, were made by one person, on one occasion, in conformity with a complete and consistent political morality (i.e. that part of a moral theory which deals with the actions of political institutions), what is that morality?

The answer to the master question and all that it entails, in combination with other true premises is, according to this reading of Dworkin, the law. The master question may fail to produce an answer for two opposite reasons, and Dworkin complicates his account to deal with both. First, there may be conflicts within a legal system which stop it from conforming with any consistent political morality. To meet this point Dworkin allows the answer to be a political morality with which all but a small number of conflicting laws conform. Second, there may be more than one political morality meeting the condition of the master question (especially once the allowance made by the first complication is taken into account). In that case Dworkin instructs that the law is that political morality which is, morally, the better theory. That is, the one which approximates more closely to ideal, correct or true morality.

In his "Reply to Seven Critics" (1977) Dworkin returns to the question of the nature of law. He gives what he calls too crude an answer, which can be encapsulated in a different master question:

> To establish the content of the law of a certain country one first finds out what are the legal sources valid in that country and then one considers one master question: What is the least change one has to allow in the correct, sound political morality in order to generate a possibly less than perfect moral theory which explains much of the legal history of that country on the assumption that it is the product of one political morality?

That (possibly less than perfect) political morality is the law. Both master questions depend on an interaction of two dimensions. One is conformity with ideal morality, the other ability to explain the legal history of the country. The new master question differs from its predecessor in two important respects. First, its fit condition concerns all the legal history of the country. Acts of Parliament enacted in the thirteenth century and repealed fifty years later are also in the picture. They also count when measuring the degree to which a political morality fits the facts. The earlier test refered only to law still in force. Only fitting in with them counted. Second, the new master question gives less weight to the condition of fit. It is no longer the case that the law consists of the political morality which fits the facts best, level of it) now provides only a sort of flexible threshold test. Among the (presumably numerous) political moralities which pass it, the one which is closest to correct morality is the law.

I hesitate to attribute either view to Dworkin. The articles are not clear enough on some of the pertinent points, and his thought may have developed in a somewhat new direction since these articles were written. Luckily, the precise formulation of the master question does not matter to our purpose. Enough of Dworkin's thought is clear to show that its moving ideas are two. First, that judges' decisions, all their decisions, are based on considerations of political morality. This is readily admitted regarding cases in which sourcebased laws are indeterminate or where they conflict. Dworkin insists that the same is true of ordinary cases involving, say, simple statutory interpretation or indeed the decision to apply statute at all. This does not mean that every time judges apply statutes they consider and re-endorse their faith in representative democracy, or in some other doctrine of political morality from which it follows that they ought to apply these statutes. It merely means that they present themselves as believing that there is such a doctrine. Their decisions are moral decisions in expressing a moral position. A conscientious judge actually believes in the existence of a valid doctrine, a political morality, which supports his action.

If I interpret Dworkin's first leading idea correctly and it is as stated above, then I fully share it. I am not so confident about his second leading idea. It is that judges owe a duty, which he sometimes calls a duty of professional responsibility, which requires them to respect and extend the political morality of their country. Roughly speaking, Dworkin thinks that morality (i.e. correct or ideal morality) requires judges to apply the sourcebased legal rules of their country, and, where these conflict or are indeterminate, to decide cases by those standards of political morality which inform the source-based law, those which make sense if it is an expression of a coherent moral outlook.

Notice how far-reaching this second idea is. Many believe that the law of their country, though not perfect, ought to be respected. It provides reasonable constitutional means for its own development. Where reform is called for, it should be accomplished by legal means. While the law is in force it should be respected. For most, this belief depends to a large degree on the content of the law. They will deny that the laws of Nazi Germany deserved to be respected. Dworkin's obligation of professional responsibility is different. It applies to every legal system simply because it is a legal system, regardless of its content. Furthermore, it is an obligation to obey not merely the letter of the law but its spirit as well. Judges are called upon to decide cases where source-based law is indeterminate, or includes unresolved conflicts, in accordance with the prevailing spirit behind the bulk of the law. That would require a South African judge to use his power to extend apartheid.

Problems such as these led to the weakening of the element of fit in the second formulation of the master question. But then they also weaken the duty of professional responsibility. There is an attractive simplicity in holding that morality requires any person who joins an institution to respect both its letter and its spirit. If this simple doctrine does not apply to judges in this form, if their respect for their institution, the law, is weakened from its pure form in the first master question to that of the second, then one loses the theoretical motivation for such a duty, at least if it means more than saying that one ought to respect the legal institutions of a particular country because their structure and actions merit such respect, or to the extent that they do.

These are some of the doubts that Dworkin's second leading idea raises. My formulations of the two leading ideas (and of the doubts concerning the second) are mere sketches. They are meant to outline an approach to law which gives source-based law a special role in the account of law on grounds other than those explained in the previous section. It is easy to see that Dworkin's conception of law contradicts the two necessary features of law argued for above. First, according to him there can be laws which do not express anyone's judgment on what their subjects ought to do, nor are they presented as expressing such a judgment. The law includes the best justification of source-based law, to use again the brief description given in the coherence thesis of which Dworkin's master questions are different interpretations. The best justification, or some aspects of it, may never have been thought of, let alone endorsed by anyone. Dworkin draws our attention to this fact by saying that it requires a Hercules to work out what the law is. Nor does Dworkin's best justification of the law consist of the implied consequences of the political morality which actually motivated the activities of legal institutions. He is aware of the fact that many different and incompatible moral conceptions influenced different governments and their officials over the centuries. His best justification may well be one which was never endorsed, not even in its fundamental precepts, by anyone in government. Much of the law of any country may, according to Dworkin, be unknown. Yet it is already legally binding, waiting there to be discovered. Hence it neither is nor is presented as being anyone's judgment on what the law's subjects ought to do.

Second, the identification of much of the law depends, according to Dworkin's analysis, on considerations which are the very same considerations which the law is there to settle. This aspect of his theory is enhanced by his second master question, but it makes a modest appearance in the first as well. Establishing what the law is involves judgment on what it ought to be. Imagine a tax problem on which source-based law is indeterminate. Some people say that in such a case there is no law on the issue. The court ought to ask what the law ought to be and to decide accordingly. If it is a higher court whose decision is a binding precedent, it will have thereby made a new law. Dworkin, on the other hand, says that there is already law on the matter. It consists in the best justification of the source based law. So in order to decide what the tax liability is in law, the court has to go into the issue of what a fair tax law would be and what is the least change in it which will make source-based law conform to it. This violates the second feature of the law argued for above.

It is important to realize that the disagreement I am pursuing is not about how judges should decide cases. In commenting on Dworkin's second leading idea I expressed doubts regarding his view on that. But they are entirely irrelevant here. So let me assume that Dworkin's duty of professional responsibility is valid and his advice to judges on how to decide cases is sound. We still have a disagreement regarding what judges do when they follow his advice. We assume that they follow right morality, but do they also follow the law or do they make law? My disagreement with Dworkin here is that, in saying that they follow pre-existing law, he makes the identification of a tax law, for example, depend on settling what a morally just tax law would be, *i.e.* on the very considerations which a tax law is supposed to have authoritatively settled.

For similar reasons Dworkin's theory violates the conditions of the alternative argument, the argument based on nothing more than the very weak assumption that authorities ought to act for reasons and that the validity of authoritative directives depends on some degree of success in doing so. This assumption leads to the same first condition, *i.e.* that the law must be presented as the law-maker's view on right reasons. As we have just seen, Dworkin's argument violates this condition. He also violates the other condition established by the alternative argument, that the validity of a law cannot derive entirely from its desirability in light of the existence of other laws. Dworkin's theory claims that at least some of the rules which are desirable or right in view of the existence of source-based law are already legally binding.

Dworkin's theory, one must conclude, is inconsistent with the authoritative nature of law. That is, it does not allow for the fact that the law necessarily claims authority and that it therefore must be capable of possessing legitimate authority. To do so it must occupy, as all authority does, a mediating role between the precepts of morality and their application by people in their behaviour. It is this mediating role of authority which is denied to the law by Dworkin's conception of it.

## *IV. The Incorporation Thesis*

The problem we detected with the coherence thesis was that, thought it assigns source-based law a special role in its account of law, it fails to see the special connection between source-based law and the law's claim to authority, and is ultimately inconsistent with the latter. It severs the essential link between law and the views on right action presented to their subjects by those who claim the right to rule them. In these respects, the incorporation thesis seems to have the advantage. It regards as law source-based law and those standards recognized as binding by source-based law. The approval of those who claim a right to rule is a prerequisite for a rule being a rule of law. Thus the law's claim to authority appears to be consistent with the incorporation thesis.[29]

I should hasten to add that many of the supporters of the incorporation thesis do not resort to the above argument in its defence. Nor do they interpret the centrality of source-based law to their conception of law in that way. They regard

[29] Works recommending the incorporation thesis include Philip Soper, "Legal Theory and the Obligation of a Judge: The Hart-Dworkin Dispute" (1977) 75 *Law Review* 511–512; Jules L. Coleman, "Negative and Positive Positivism" (1982) 11 *Journal of Legal Studies* 139, 160, 162; D. Lyons, "Moral Aspects of Legal Theory", in (eds.) P. A French *et al.* (1982) 7 *Midwest Studies in Philosophy* 237.

it as supported by and necessary for some version of a thesis about the separability of law and morals. Jules Coleman, for example, is anxious to deny that there is "a necessary connection between law and morality".[30] He mistakenly identifies this thesis with another: "The separability thesis is the claim that there exists at least one conceivable rule of recognition and therefore one possible legal system that does not specify truth as a moral principle as a truth condition for any proposition of law."[31] If this were a correct rendering of the separability thesis stated by Coleman in the first quotation above, the incorporation thesis entails separability. But Coleman's rendering of his own separability thesis is mistaken. A necessary connection between law and morality does not require that truth as a moral principle be a condition of legal validity. All it requires is that the social features which identify something as a legal system entail that it possess moral value. For example, assume that the maintenance of orderly social relations is itself morally valuable. Assume further that a legal system can be the law in force in a society only if it succeeds in maintaining orderly social relations. A necessary connection between law and morality would then have been established, without the legal validity of any rule being made, by the rule of recognition, to depend on the truth of any moral proposition.

Supporters of the incorporation thesis may admit that, while it is not sufficient to establish the separability thesis, at least it is necessary for it, and is therefore supported by it. The separability thesis is, however, implausible. Of course the remarks about orderly social relations do not disprove it. They are much too vague and woolly to do that. But it is very likely that there is some necessary connection between law and morality, that every legal system in force has some moral merit or does some moral good even if it is also the cause of a great deal of moral evil. It is relevant to remember that all major traditions in Western political thought, including both the Aristotelian and the Hobbesian traditions, believed in such a connection.[32] If the incorporation thesis seems much more secure than the separability thesis, it is because if seems to be required by the fact that all law comes under the guise of authority, together with the considerations on the nature of authority advanced in the previous sections. The law is the product of human activity because if it were not it could not be an outcome of a judgment based on dependent reasons, that is, it could not provide reasons set by authority.

There may, of course, be other cogent reasons for favouring the incorporation thesis. They will not be explored here. Instead I will argue that the thesis ought to be rejected, and that the support it seems to derive from the argument about the nature of authority is illusory. In fact the incorporation thesis is incompatible with the authoritative nature of law. To explain the point let us turn for a moment to look at theoretical authority.

Suppose that a brilliant mathematician, Andrew, proves that the Goldbach

---

[30] Coleman, "Negative and Positive", *op. cit.*, p. 140.

[31] *ibid.*, p. 141.

[32] The following are some of the authors who advocated versions of the necessary connection thesis which are all compatible with the incorporation thesis: H. L. A. Hart, *The Concept of Law* (1961), Chap. 9 (on the minimum content of natural law); L. Fuller, *The Morality of Law* (1964), and "Forms and Limits of Adjudication" (1978) 92 *Harvard Law Review*; J. M. Finnis, *Natural Law and Natural Rights* (1980). I have discussed this approach in *Practical Reason and Norms*, pp. 162–170. It has been considered by P. Soper in "Legal Theory and the Obligation of a Judge: The Hart-Dworkin, Dispute" (1977) 75 *Michigan Law Review* and by D. Lyons in "Moral Aspects of Legal Theory", pp. 223, 226—though surprisingly he advances, albeit tentatively, the view that the facts which determine the existence and content of law do not guarantee it any moral value (p. 251). This, as I said, seems implausible. What does appear true is that the necessary connection between law and morality which is likely to be established by arguments of the kind canvassed by the above-mentioned authors is a weak one. It is insufficient *e.g.* to establish a prima facie obligation to obey the law.

hypothesis, that every integer greater than two is the sum of two prime numbers, is true if and only if the solution to a certain equation is positive. Neither he nor anyone else knows the solution of the equation. Fifty years later that equation is solved by another mathematician and the truth of the Goldbach hypothesis is established. Clearly we would not say that Andrew proved the hypothesis, even though he made the first major breakthrough and even though the truth of the hypothesis is a logical consequence of his discovery. Or suppose that Betty is an astrophysicist who demonstrates that the big bang theory of the origin of the universe is true if and only if certain equations have a certain resolution. Again, their resolution is not known at the time, and is discovered only later. It seems as clear of Betty as it was of Andrew that she cannot be credited with proving (or disproving) the big bang theory even though the truth (or falsity) of the theory is entailed by her discovery. Now imagine that Alice tells you of Andrew's discovery, or that Bernard tells you of Betty's. Alice and Bernard are experts in their respective fields. They give you authoritative advice. But Alice does not advise you to accept the Goldbach hypothesis. She merely advises belief in it if the relevant equation has a positive solution. The fact that the truth of the hypothesis is entailed by her advice is neither here nor there. The same applies to Bernard's advice based on Betty's work.

All this is commonplace. Nor is it difficult to understand why one cannot be said to have advised acceptance of a particular proposition simply on the ground that it is entailed by another proposition acceptance of which one did advise. People do not believe in all that is entailed by their beliefs. Beliefs play a certain role in our lives in supporting other beliefs, in providing premises for our practical deliberations. They colour our emotional and imaginative life. More generally, they are fixed points determining our sense of orientation in the world. Many of the propositions entailed by our beliefs do not play this role in our lives. Therefore they do not count amongst our beliefs. One mark of this is the fact that had people been aware of some of the consequences of their beliefs, rather than embrace them they might have preferred to abandon the beliefs which entail them (or even provisionally to stick by them and refuse their consequences, *i.e.* embrace inconsistencies until they found a satisfactory way out). This consideration explains why we cannot attribute to people belief in all the logical consequences of their beliefs. It also explains why a person cannot be said to have advised belief in a proposition he does not himself believe in. (Though it is possible to advise others to take the risk and act as if certain propositions are true even if one does not believe in them and equally possible to advise believing in a proposition if it is true.)

Advice shares the mediating role of authoritative directives. It too is an expression of a judgment on the reasons which apply to the addressee of the advice. Because the advice has this mediating role it can include only matters on which the adviser has a view, or presents himself as having one (to cover cases of insincere advice). Since a person does not believe in all the consequences of his beliefs he does not, barring special circumstances, advise others to believe in them either.

The analogy with authority is clear and hardly needs further elaboration. The mediating role of authority implies that the content of an authoritative directive is confined to what the authority which lends the directive its binding force can be said to have held or to have presented itself as holding. It does not extend to what it would have directed, given a chance to do so, nor to all that is entailed by what it has directed. It will by now be clear why the incorporation thesis must be rejected if the law does necessarily claim authority. The main thrust of the incorporation thesis is that all that is derivable from the law (with the help of other true premises) is law. It makes the law include standards which are inconsistent with its mediating role, for they were never endorsed by the law-making institutions on whose authority they are supposed to rest. The mistake of the incorporation thesis is to identify being entailed by the source-based law with being endorsed by the sources of law.

Law is a complex social institution, and some of its complexities help mask the incorporation thesis's mistake. When thinking of a piece of advice or of an authoritative directive we tend to think of them as having one author. In the law, as in other hierarchical institutions, matters are complicated in two respects. First, authoritative directives are typically issued by institutions following an elaborate process of drafting and evaluation. Second, they are often amended, modified, and their content amplified and changed by a succession of subsequent legislative, administrative, and judicial actions. A convention of reference sometimes exists which allows one to refer to a statute, or to the original judicial decision, when citing a legal rule, even though they are no more than the starting-point in the development of the rule, which is in a very real sense the product of the activities of several bodies over a period of time.

These complications mean, of course, that the rule as it is now may include aspects which cannot be attributed to its original creator. They are part of the rule because they are attributable to the author of a later intervention. For example, typically successive judicial interpretations change or add to the meaning of statutes. Likewise, though we attribute beliefs and intentions to institutions and corporations on the basis of the beliefs and intentions of their officials, the attributing functions may sometimes sanction holding a corporate body to have had a belief or an intention which none of its officials had. This is not the place to inquire into the rules of attributions invoked when we talk of the intentions or beliefs of states, governments, corporations, trade unions, universities, etc. All that is required for our present purposes is that attribution is made in a restrictive way which does not allow one to attribute to such a body all the logical consequences of its beliefs and intentions. Restrictions to all the foreseen or foreseeable consequences are the ones most common in the law. This is enough to show that the incorporation thesis receives no sustenance from the institutional complexities of the law, since it insists that the law includes all the logical consequences of source-based law.

In disputing the incorporation thesis I am not denying two other points which are asserted by D. Lyons in the most thoroughgoing defence of this position. First, I agree with him that judges who work out what is required by, for example, the due process provision of the American constitution are engaged in interpreting the constitution. Lyons is mistaken, however, in thinking that it follows from that that they are merely applying the law as it is (at least if they succeed in discovering the right answer). Judicial interpretation can be as creative as a Glen Gould interpretation of a Beethoven piano sonata. It is a mistake to confuse interpretation with paraphrase or with any other mere rendering of what the interpreted object is in any case. Second, Lyons is quite right to think that there is more to the law than is explicitly stated in the authoritative texts. Authorities can and do direct and guide by implication. It does not follow, however, that they imply all that is entailed by what they say, let alone all that is entailed by it with the addition of true premisses. The limits of the justifiable imputation of directives are no wider, I have argued above, than the limits of the imputation of belief.

### V. *The Sources Thesis*

The last section established that not all the moral consequences of a legal rule are part of the law.[33] But it leaves open the possibility that some are: that some moral consequences of a legal rule can be attributed to the author of that legal rule as representing its intention or meaning and thus being part of the law. I will not

---

[33] By the same reasoning it also established that not all the factual consequences of a rule of law are part of the law.

present a refutation of this possibility. The purpose of the present section is more modest. It argues that the authoritative nature of law gives a reason to prefer the sources thesis. It leaves open the possibility that additional considerations lead to a complex view of the law lying between the incorporation and the sources theses.

Let us distinguish between what source-based law states explicitly and what it establishes by implication. If a statute in country A says that income earned abroad by a citizen of A is liable to income tax in A, then it only implicitly establishes that I am liable to such tax. For my liability is not stated by the statute but is inferred from it (and some other premises). Similarly, if earnings abroad are taxed at a different rate from earnings at home, the fact that the proceeds of export sales are subject to the home rate is implied rather than stated. It is inferred from this statute and other legal rules on the location of various transactions.

The two examples differ in that the statement that I am liable to tax at a certain rate is an applied legal statement depending for its truth on both law and fact. The statement that export earnings are taxed at a certain rate is a pure legal statement, depending for its truth on law only (i.e. on acts of legislation and other law-making facts). The sources thesis as stated at the beginning of this chapter can bear a narrow or a wide interpretation. The narrow thesis concerns the truth conditions of pure legal statements only. Pure legal statements are those which state the content of the law, *i.e.* of legal rules, principles, doctrines, etc. The wide thesis concerns the truth conditions of all legal statements, including applied ones. It claims that the truth or falsity of legal statements depends on social facts which can be established without resort to moral argument.

The fact that the law claims authority supports the narrow sources thesis because it leads to a conception of law as playing a mediating role between ultimate reasons and people's decisions and actions. To play this role the law must be, or at least be presented as being, an expression of the judgment of some people or of some institutions on the merits of the actions it requires. Hence, the identification of a rule as a rule of law consists in attributing it to the relevant person or institution as representing their decisions and expressing their judgments. Such attribution need not be on the ground that this is what the person or institution explicitly said. It may be based on an implication. But the attribution must establish that the view expressed in the alleged statement is the view of the relevant legal institution. Such attributions can only be based on factual considerations. Moral argument can establish what legal institutions should have said or should have held but not what they did say or hold.

We have already traced one source of resistance to this conclusion to the assumption that if attribution is on factual rather than moral grounds then it must be a non-controversial, easily established matter which requires at most the application of a procedure of reasoning having the character of an algorithm to some non-controversial simple facts. The assumption that only moral questions can resist easy agreement or solution by algorithmic procedures has nothing to recommend it, and I in no way share it. The case for saying that attribution of belief and intention to their author is based on factual criteria only does not rest on the false claim that such attributions are straightforward and non-controversial. A second source of resistance, also noted above, derives from overlooking the greater complexity involved in attributing views or intentions to complex institutions whose activities spread over long stretches of time, and the tendency to think that nothing more is involved in these cases than is involved in attributing beliefs or intentions to individuals.

But there is a third difficulty with the view I am advocating which must be addressed now. One may ask: if an authority explicitly prohibited *e.g.* unfair discrimination, is not the fact that certain cases display unfair discrimination evidence enough for attributing their prohibition to the authority? Two considerations are usually brought to support the view that these reasons are sufficient to determine the content of the law on such matters. I shall try to rebut this view by showing that these supporting considerations are mistaken. First is the claim that the only alternative view holds that the law is determined only regarding cases which the law-maker actually contemplated and had in mind when making the law. This, let it be conceded right away, is not merely false but very likely an incoherent view. Second (and it does not matter that this point may be incompatible with the first), it is sometimes said that the only alternative view assumes that the law-makers intend their particular view of what is unfair discrimination to become law even if they are wrong.

Suppose that the fathers of the constitution outlawed cruel punishment. Suppose further that it is beyond doubt that they thought that flogging is not cruel, and finally, that in fact (or in morals) it is cruel. Are we to assume that the law-makers' intention was to exclude flogging from the scope of the constitutional prohibition of cruel punishments? Would not the correct view be that in making cruelty a bench-mark of legality the law-makers intended their own judgment to be subject to that criterion, so that, though believing flogging not to be cruel, they expressed the view that if it is cruel it is unlawful?

Both points have a *déjà vu* aspect. They depend on the unimaginative assumption that either the law is determined by the thoughts actually entertained by the law-maker when making the law or it must include all the implications of those thoughts. Since it must be granted, and I do grant, that it is not the first, the second is supposed to be the case. This was the structure of Lyons's argument regarding the explicit content thesis. As he saw it, either the law is confined to its explicit content or it contains all its implications. Since Hart rejects the second alternative he was saddled by Lyons with the first. Since Lyons sees, as everyone must, that the first is wrong, he embraces the second. The two considerations explained above are the psychological variants of Lyons's linguistic dichotomy. They contrast not actual language with its implications but actual thoughts with their implications.

The answer to both arguments is the same: the dichotomy is a false one. There are other possibilities. Sometimes we know of a person that, for example, if only he realized that certain forms of psychological abuse are cruel, would not be so indifferent to them. At others we know that if he were convinced that they are cruel he would find some other way to justify them. He would come to believe that cruelty is sometimes justifiable. In attributing such views to people, one does not endorse either of the two unacceptable views mentioned above. Naturally it is often impossible to impute any such view to a person. The question whether he would have maintained his intention to prohibit cruel punishment had he known that capital punishment is cruel (assuming for a moment that it is) may admit of no answer.

Furthermore, and this is often overlooked, the sources thesis by itself does not dictate any one rule of interpretation. It is compatible with several. It is compatible, for example, with saying that, if it is known that the law-makers prohibited cruel punishment only because they regarded flogging as not cruel, then that law does not prohibit flogging. It is also compatible with the rule that the law is confined in such cases to the intention expressed by the law-maker. This is to prohibit cruel punishment. Since, by this rule of interpretation, no more specific intention is attributable to the law-maker, the law gives discretion to the courts to forbid punishments they consider cruel (this reflects the lack of specificity in the law) and instructs them to forbid those which are cruel. Which of these, or of a number of alternative interpretations, is the right one varies from one legal system to another. It is a matter of their own rules of interpretation. One possibility is that they have none on this issue, that the question is unsettled in some legal systems. The only point which is essential to the sources thesis is that the character of the rules of interpretation prevailing in any legal system, *i.e.* the character of the rules for imputing intentions and directives to the legal authorities, is a matter of fact and not a moral issue. It is a matter of fact because it has to sustain conclusions of the kind: "That is in fact the view held by these institutions on the moral issues in question."

Two further points have to be made to avoid misunderstanding. First, none of the above bears on what judges should do, how they should decide cases. The issue addressed is that of the nature and limits of law. If the argument here advanced is sound, it follows that the function of courts to apply and enforce the law coexists with others. One is authoritatively to settle disputes, whether or not their solution is determined by law. Another additional function the courts have is to supervise the working of the law and revise it interstitially when the need arises. In some legal systems they are assigned additional roles which may be of great importance. For example, the courts may be made custodians of freedom of expression, a supervisory body in charge both of laying down standards for the protection of free expression and adjudicating in disputes arising out of their application.

Second, it may be objected that relying on the mediating role of authority becomes an empty phrase when it comes to legal rules which have evolved through the activities of many hands over a long time. The fact that we implicitly or explicitly endorse rules of attribution which sanction talk of the intention of the law where that intention was never had by any one person does not support the argument from the mediating role of the law. It merely shows it to be a formalistic, hollow shell. This objection, like some of the earlier ones, seems to betray impatience with the complexities, and shortcomings, of the world. Every attribution of an intention to the law is based on an attribution of a real intention to a real person in authority or exerting influence over authority. That intention may well relate to a small aspect or modification of the rule. If the intention of the law regarding the rule as a whole differs from that of any single individual, this is because it is a function of the intentions of many. Sometimes, but by no means always, this leads to reprehensible results. Be that as it may, the view propounded here will in such circumstances highlight the indirect and complex way in which the law has played its mediating role.

All the arguments so far concern the narrow sources thesis only. Nothing was said about its application to applied legal statements. I tend to feel that it applies to them as well, since they are legal statements whose truth value depends on contingent facts as well as on law. If one assumes that contingent facts cannot be moral facts, then the sources thesis applies here as well. That is, what is required is the assumption that what makes it contingently true that a person acted fairly on a particular occasion is not the standard of fairness, which is not contingent, but the "brute fact" that he performed a certain action describable in value-neutral ways. If such an assumption is sustainable in all cases, then the sources thesis holds regarding applied legal statements as well.

The considerations adumbrated above dispel some of the misunderstandings which surround the sources thesis. First, it does not commit one to the view that all law is explicit law. Much that is not explicitly stated in legal sources is nevertheless legally binding. Second, the sources thesis does not rest on an assumption that law cannot be controversial. Nor does it entail that conclusion. Its claim that the existence and content of the law is a matter of social fact which can be established without resort to moral argument does not presuppose nor does it entail the false proposition that all factual matters are non-controversial, nor the equally false view that all moral propositions are controversial. The sources thesis is based on the mediating role of the law. It is true that the law fails in that role if it is not, in general, easier to establish and less controversial than the underlying considerations it reflects. But this generalization is exaggerated and distorted when it turns into the universal, conceptual dogmas of the explicit content or the non-controversiality theses.

The sources thesis leads to the conclusion that courts often exercise discretion and participate in the law-making process. They do so when their decisions are binding on future courts (even where the decisions can be modified or reversed under restrictive conditions) and where their decisions do not merely reflect previous authoritative rulings. Saying this does not mean, however, that courts in exercising their discretion either do or should act on the basis of their personal views on how the world should be ideally run. That would be sheer folly. Naturally judges act on their personal views, otherwise they would be insincere. (Though the fact that these are their views is not their reason for relying on them. Their reasons are that those propositions are true or sound, for whatever reason they find them to be so.) But judges are not allowed to forget that they are not dictators who can fashion the world to their own blueprint of the ideal society. They must bear in mind that their decisions will take effect in society as it is, and the moral and economic reasons they resort to should establish which is the best or the just decision given things as they are rather than as they would be in an ideal world.

Finally, the sources thesis does not presuppose a non-naturalist ethical position. Even if a certain social fact entails certain moral consequences it can still be a source of law. It is a source of law as the social fact it is, and not as a source of moral rights and obligations. It is a source of law under its naturalistic rather than under its moral decription.                                                              [pp. 211–235]

### STEPHEN PERRY
### Law and Obligation
### (2005)[34]

#### I. Introduction

In this article I discuss the ancient question of whether or not there is a general moral obligation to obey the law. The question of political obligation, as I shall call it, is a central issue not just for political philosophy but also for jurisprudence, It is with jurisprudential aspects of the question that I will be particularly concerned here. I concentrate instead on clarifying the question itself and on elucidating the relationship between the concept of obligation as it applies to law and other important concepts in jurisprudence, including the concept of authority and, to some extent, the concept of law itself.

The concept of "obedience" involves, among other things, doing what somebody else tells you to do. Although the idea of doing what somebody else tells you to do is clearly a significant dimension of our concept of law, our notion of what *a* law is nonetheless cannot be reduced to the idea of either an order or a command. This was made abundantly clear by H.L.A. Hart in his critique of John Austin's theory of law.[35] An order can be issued by someone who neither has nor claims to have the authority to issue the order. Commands have the color of authority, but a command cannot include the commander within its scope, it cannot have normative content other than the imposition of an obligation. Writers of both a positivist and an antipositivist bent have put forward theoretical claims that could barely have been expressed in the limited theoretical vocabulary that was available to Anglo-American jurisprudence in the period before Hart wrote. These claims include, for example, the following: law includes principles as well as rules; law claims moral authority for itself; the organizing principle of law is the coordination of social activity. The fact that law can have normative content other than the imposition of obligations is now as universally obvious to theorists as it always was to lawyers. And theorists now take for granted that law can come into existence by means other than the deliberate prescription or enactment of

---

[34] [From (2005) 50 American Journal of Jurisprudence 263]
[35] H.L.A. Hart, *The Concept of Law*, 2d ed. (1994); hereafter referred to as *CL*.

obligation-imposing norms (although there is deep disagreement over how this can be so).[36] But despite all this the idea of one person telling another person what to do has, quite understandably, continued to draw much attention from legal philosophers. Now, however, this idea is discussed not with a view to giving us an exhaustive characterization of what a "law" is, but rather with a view to showing how, if at all, political authority can be justified.

It is a fundamental aspect of our concept of law that somebody tells somebody else what to do. It may or may not be fundamental to the concept that the person doing the telling is in a position to use coercive force to back up his demands and is prepared to do so. But whatever the truth may be regarding this latter point, it cannot be denied that law involves (among many other things) one person or group of persons, under authority or color of authority, telling another person or group of persons what to do.[37] To tell another person what to do under authority or color of authority is to impose, or at least to attempt to impose, an obligation on that other person. It is thus quite understandable that the ideas of authority and obligation are often treated by contemporary legal theorists as essentially two sides of the same coin.[38] Suppose for a moment that the content of a particular legal system consisted, apart from any foundational rules or arrangements such as a rule of recognition, entirely of obligation-imposing directives that had been deliberately issued *as* obligation-imposing directives by some organ or agent of government. If the government possessed legitimate authority, then it would have a normative power to obligate those over whom it held authority; persons who fell within the scope of a governmental directive would be bound by it, which is just to say that they would have an obligation to obey it. A government which claims to have legitimate authority claims, at the very least, to possess a power to obligate its subjects. This important point has a similarly important corollary. Since the exercise of such a power by an entity as powerful as a government is capable of affecting peoples' lives in very significant ways and possibly against their will, governments are claiming not just practical authority in some general sense but *moral* authority.[39] The normativity of the law is, in other words, moral normativity, which means, among other things, that when governments or their agents attempt to impose obligations they are attempting to impose moral obligations.

Joseph Raz has argued, correctly, in my view, that every legal system claims that it possesses legitimate authority in the sense described above, i.e., it claims to possess a moral power systematically to obligate its subjects by issuing morally binding directives.[40] In fact he makes the stronger argument that such a claim to authority is part of the nature of law, and here again I believe that he is correct. Of course any given legal system may fail, either partly or entirely, to have such

[36] Some writers emphasize that laws or legal norms can be customary in nature. Hart himself thought that a customary legal norm, which he called the rule of recognition, lay at the foundation of every legal system. Some writers, including Jules Coleman and Ronald Dworkin, argue that the content of at least some laws can or must be determined by reference to moral considerations.

[37] Where groups are involved, it is of course possible, as Hart pointed out, that the group doing the telling overlaps or coincides with the group being told what to do. See Hart, *CL*, at 73–78.

[38] See, e.g., Joseph Raz, *The Morality of Freedom*, 1986, 24 (hereafter referred to as *MF*).

[39] Raz has made this point, and variations on it, many times. For a recent statement see e.g. Raz, "Incorporation by Law," *Legal Theory* 10 (2004) 1, 6.

[40] See e.g. Raz, *Ethics in the Public Domain*, 1994, 199. (Hereafter referred to as *EPD*)

moral authority, but in order to be a legal system it must necessarily claim to have it. It is of course no easy matter to spell out with any degree of exactitude what it means to say that a legal system "claims" authority, let alone what it means to say that "law" claims authority. Raz has suggested that the law's claim to authority is manifested by certain characteristic beliefs and attitudes on the part of officials,[41] and he has suggested further that while it is a useful habit to personify the law, in the end what the "law" requires, claims or authorizes is a matter of what the organs of government, and in particular the courts, require, claim or authorize.[42] There is obviously much more to be said about what it means to say that the "law" claims authority (or indeed to say that the "law" does anything).[43] I am not entirely convinced, for example, that such locutions are only metaphors and that jurisprudence can do without a moral personification of the community of the kind that has been discussed by Ronald Dworkin.[44] But I cannot take up such issues here, and for present purposes I follow Raz in referring very loosely and more or less interchangeably to the law, the state, the government, and lawmakers and officials generally as claiming authority.

In section III of this paper I discuss the arguments of Joseph Raz, who attempts to elucidate the conditions under which governments possess the systematic moral power to impose obligations on their citizens and, hence, to elucidate the conditions under which citizens have, if they ever do have, a general moral obligation to obey the law.                                    [pp 263–266]

### III. *Raz on Political Authority and Political Obligation*

Raz defends a theory of political authority which he calls the service conception. The basic idea is contained in the so-called normal justification thesis, which holds that one person is a (practical) authority over another if the second will do better in complying with the reasons that apply to him if he defers to the judgment of the first person than if he tries to act on his own judgment of what ought to be done.[45] Political authority is, according to Raz, just a special case of practical authority thus understood. Political authority in its most central manifestations involves the government or one of its agents issuing a directive which claims to impose a moral obligation, and a directive of this kind is, for Raz, the central case of law. The normal way to show that the alleged obligation exists is to show that the normal justification thesis applies. If it does, then the person or persons who fall within the scope of the directive have an obligation to obey it. If they have an obligation to obey every directive which the government issues, then they have a general moral obligation to obey the law. As this summary suggests and as Raz has acknowledged, the service conception of political authority focuses on "the authoritative imposition of duties."[46] Raz holds that "all the other functions authorities may have are ultimately explained by reference to the imposition of duties."[47] This claim touches on some of the questions about the justification of authority that I raised in the preceding section, and I will return to it briefly later.

---

[41]   Ibid., 199–200. He also seems to suggest that attitudes and beliefs of those subject to law may also be relevant in this regard. See, e.g., ibid., at 199: "I will assume that necessarily law, every legal system which is in force everywhere, has *de facto* authority. That entails that the law either claims that it possesses legitimate authority or is held to possess it, or both."

[42]   Raz, *MF*, 70.

[43]   For another approach to this issue, see the interesting discussion in Timothy Endicott, "The Subsidiarity of Law and the Obligation to Obey," *American Journal of Jurisprudence* 50 (2005) 233–48.

[44]   Ronald Dworkin, *Law's Empire*, 1986, 167–75.

[45]   See e.g. Raz, *EPD*, 198; *MF*, 53.

[46]   Raz, *MF*, 44.

[47]   Ibid.

For the time being, however, I wish to take the service conception of authority on its own terms.

Raz is skeptical about the existence of a general obligation to obey the law. He does not think that there is any legal system in which the normal justification thesis can be shown to hold for every person and for every law which the system has in fact generated. But he does not deny that in reasonably just legal systems at least some people have an obligation to obey at least some laws just because they are the law. According to the service conception of authority, they have such obligations when the normal justification thesis applies. As this suggests, Raz does not regard the legitimacy of political authority as an all-or-nothing matter. A government can have partial authority, both in the sense that only some of its laws are ever justified and in the sense that any given law can be justified for some people but not for others. As he writes, "the normal justification thesis invites a piecemeal approach to the authority of governments, which yields the conclusion that the extent of governmental authority varies from individual to individual to individual, and is more limited than the authority governments claim for themselves in the case of most people."[48] Raz does not think that this is a morally untenable situation, however, because even governments which do not possess authority or which possess authority only partially can do a great deal of moral good.

I will return to the question of partial authority later. First, however, I want to discuss a certain conceptual dimension of the service conception of authority. Even though, as a practical matter, no legal system ever possesses the full authority it claims, it must, according to Raz, be *capable* of possessing such authority. If that were not the case then the officials and institutions which claim authority would be conceptually confused, and while they can occasionally be confused they cannot be confused systematically. This is because the claims and conceptions of officials "are formed by and contribute to" the concept of authority itself.[49] It might be added that, because of the centrality of the concept of authority to the concept of law, those same claims by officials are formed by and contribute to the concept of *law*. If officials were as confused as they would have to be if they were wrong in thinking that the law is capable of having the full moral authority it claims, then the very idea of law would not make sense. Because the concepts of law and authority are used by officials to describe their own practice of claiming systematically and comprehensively to impose obligations on others, and because those same officials believe that they not only claim to impose obligations in this way but actually succeed in doing so, something would have gone seriously wrong with the concepts if there could not, in fact, be any such systematically-obligating practice.

In order for a legal system to be capable of possessing the full authority that it claims, it must, according to Raz, *in fact* possess certain non-moral properties, such as the attribute of being able to communicate.[50] More importantly for present purposes, however, it must also be capable of possessing, in principle if not in fact, the moral property of comprehensively and systematically obligating in just the way that it claims to do. Fortunately for the concept of law, the normal justification thesis saves the day. Even though it never justifies *in practice* all the obligations that the law claims to impose, it shows that, in principle, those obligations are at least capable of being justified. If, implausibly, each and every person would happen to comply better with the reasons that apply to him if he were to obey each and every law on each and every occasion to which it applies, a general obligation to obey would exist. This is enough to show that officials are not confused in making the claims about their practice that they make, and this is

[48] Raz, *MF*, 80.
[49] Raz, *EPD*, 201.
[50] Raz, *EPD*, 199–204.

so even though they are invariably mistaken, at least to some degree, in making those claims. In principle they could be right, and this is enough to rescue the concept of law from confusion.

I believe that Raz is correct to make the conceptual claims that he does about the concepts of authority and law, and that is one reason why the question of whether or not there can be a general obligation to obey the law is central not only to political theory but also to jurisprudence. But I have some doubts as to whether these difficulties can be avoided quite as easily as Raz suggests. The service conception of authority succeeds, I believe, in showing how the law can give rise to reasons for action that people would not otherwise have. But it is nonetheless not entirely clear to me that it can bear all the moral and conceptual weight Raz tries to place on it. To put the difficulty in a nutshell, the service conception of authority may not be the law's conception of authority. The reason for this is that the reasons for action that are underwritten by the normal justification thesis do not seem to be, so far as the law's own self-understanding is concerned, the right kind of reasons. To show this, I want to focus on one type of case that Raz discusses at length, namely, the type of case in which one person has authority over another because the first possesses more expertise about some subject than the second.[51] Consider the following example. Suppose that we all have moral reason not to engage in action that would endanger the survival of a certain species of fish, for example cod. It doesn't matter for present purposes what the basis of the underlying moral reason is, but suppose it is the preservation of the food supply for future generations. Cod fishermen therefore have an underlying moral reason not to overfish. They may, however, lack the knowledge that would permit them to continue to fish without rapidly depleting the cod stocks. Suppose the government, following appropriate consultation, correctly determines that cod stocks can be sustained indefinitely if cod fishermen follow certain rules. These rules might impose quotas, or they might require that cod only be taken in certain months or if they are of a certain size. Raz's idea is that, if the government issues directives giving effect to these rules, the directives *replace*, for the fishermen, their underlying moral reason not to endanger the survival of cod. Raz maintains that the directives are, for the fishermen, new moral reasons. They have these reasons because they are more likely to do what they ought to do if they act on the directives than if they try to figure out for themselves how to avoid endangering cod. Notice that even though the directives are said to give rise in this way to new moral reasons, the directives are justified because they reflect the underlying moral reasons of conservation that we assumed apply independently to the fishermen.

In giving this example, I assumed that the government was correct in its assessment of what was required to preserve fish stocks. What if this assumption does not hold? Raz argues that the directives will still bind the fishermen, provided the government is more likely to be correct than they are, across some specified range of cases, about what right reason requires. If Raz is right about this, then legal directives can be binding even when they are substantively mistaken or unjust. Much depends, obviously, on how the appropriate range of cases is to be specified. Perhaps it concerns all matters pertaining to cod, or all matters pertaining to fishing, or all matters pertaining to conservation. There are some difficult issues here, but let me set them aside.[52] The important point for present purposes is that, according to Raz, the law makes a general claim that it is *always*, in *all* types of cases, more likely to get matters right than its subjects are. Of course, as Raz says, this claim is extremely unlikely to be correct as an empirical matter, but it is *conceivable* that it might be correct. If it were correct, then all law

---

[51]  See, e.g., ibid., 332.
[52]  I have discussed some of these issues in Perry, "Second-Order Reasons, Uncertainty and Legal Theory," *Southern California Law Review* 62 (1989) 913.

would be, according to Raz, obligatory in just the way that it claims to be. It is important to emphasize that this claim to comprehensive obligatoriness on the part of the law is *systemic*. The claim is not that each and every directive, considered one by one, correctly reflects the appropriate underlying reasons. The claim is, rather, that each and every directive is obligatory because it belongs to a system of content-independent directives that is, taken as a whole, morally authoritative.

The first question that I wish to raise about this very elegant set of arguments is this. Even if it is true that, in a broad range of cases, the normal justification thesis gives rise to new reasons for action, it is far from clear that those reasons are, as the law itself insists, obligations. Suppose that I will, in fact, do better in complying with the cod reasons that apply to me if I follow the government's directives regarding quotas, catch size, etc. than if I try to figure these matters out for myself. It seems correct to say that I have a new reason, and even a new moral reason, that I did not have before. Moreover this new reason is, as Raz says, exclusionary or preemptive in character, because in order to avoid the double-counting of reasons, I have to act on the directive alone and not simply take it into account in my assessment of what the underlying reasons require. Granting all this, what basis is there for saying that the directive is not only an exclusionary (moral) reason for me, but that it is also an *obligation*? All that Raz seems to say about this issue is that I have an obligation *because* my reason for action is an exclusionary reason, i.e., because it preempts the reasons that the new reason is supposed to replace.[53] If this were so, however, then presumably all exclusionary reasons would be obligations, including e.g. decisions (which Raz has elsewhere argued, correctly in my view, to be exclusionary reasons).[54] But this is to use the term "obligation" in a rather weak sense, and, more importantly, in a sense which does not fully capture the sense of obligation that is implicitly presupposed by the law's claim to authority.

One reason for saying that the service conception of authority does not fully capture the law's understanding of obligation is the following. On the service conception of authority, we do not seem to have any ground for regarding the government as anything other than a moral resource that is, so to speak, just there for me. Indeed Raz says that, in expertise cases like the cod example, "the law is like a knowledgeable friend."[55] But the law is not just informing or advising me that I ought to do X, and thereby giving me (if it happens to be a practical authority for me in the relevant area) a new exclusionary reason to do X. The law not only tells me what do in the sense of informing me what to do; it tells me what to do in the sense of *commanding* me what to do. Friends do not ordinarily issue commands to one another, but a knowledgeable friend can nonetheless inform me what to do and thereby give me, in accordance with the normal justification thesis, a new exclusionary (and possibly moral) reason that I did not have before. If this is all that Raz means by saying that I come under a new obligation, then the law is certainly capable of giving me obligations. But the law claims that I have an obligation to do X because it has commanded me to do X, and the obligation that arises from a command appears to be different in kind from the obligation that I might come under as a result of being given good advice by a friend. In commanding me, the law purports to exercise a power to obligate me. If the law's command and the friend's advice gave rise to obligations in the same way, presumably we would have to say that the friend, in giving her advice, has likewise (perhaps unknowingly) exercised a power to obligate me. It seems very odd, however, to say that the friend has done any such thing. If, on the other hand, the friend's advice gives rise to an obligation without involving the exercise

---

[53] *MF*, 60.

[54] Raz, *Practical Reason and Norms*, 1975, 65–71.

[55] Raz, *EPD*, 332.

of a normative power, then it would seem that the normal justification thesis does not fully capture the sense of the law's claim to obligate by commanding. It is also worth mentioning the following, related point. The law may well be correct in telling me what I have moral reason to do, but why does this give it the normative power to demand of me that I comply with that reason, let alone back up that demand with coercion? There may be a way to close this gap, but it is not immediately evident what it is.

Even if Raz is correct that any reasons for action which are generated by the normal justification thesis are properly characterized as obligations, there is another way in which this sense of obligation does not fully capture the understanding of obligation presupposed by the law. This can be brought out by asking the following question: To whom, if to anyone, are these obligations owed? Recall that Raz says that, in the expertise cases, "the law is like a knowledgeable friend." Perhaps in the right circumstances one has an obligation to do as one's friend advises, but surely one does not owe that obligation to the *friend*. One owes it, if to anyone, to oneself; one has an obligation to oneself to get the matter right, so to speak. The law, however, does not look on the situation that way. Not only does it regard me as being under an obligation, it regards me as owing that obligation to the government or community or state. I do not simply have the obligation in the air or owe it solely to myself. Relatedly, legal authorities regard themselves as having a right to demand compliance with the law (which is not the same thing as having a right to *enforce* the law), just as parents have a right to demand compliance with commands they issue to their children. In both cases, it seems correct to say that there is a duty owed to the parent in the one case, and the appropriately characterized collective entity in the other case.

A final reason to think that the law's conception of authority may not be that of the service conception has to do with the scope of the authority that the law claims for itself. Take the cod example once again. The law regards me as bound by its directives on cod even if I am the world's greatest living expert on the subject. Similarly, the state of New Jersey regards me as bound by its directives on cod even if I would comply much better with the cod-reasons that apply to me if I were to follow the laws of Massachusetts instead. In short, the law does not allow for the kinds of exceptions that seem to be unavoidably built into the normal justification thesis itself. If the law's conception of authority were that of the service conception, then it would presumably acquiesce gracefully, like a friend, whenever it was clear that someone else knew more than it does. But that is never the attitude the law takes. This difficulty can be put in another way. Raz is quite right to insist that the law's claim to moral authority is both comprehensive and systemic. The law does not claim that it gets the matter right now and then or from time to time; it insists that it gets the matter right all the time, in all types of cases, and for everyone. In other words, the law's own self-understanding insists that its authority is an all-or-nothing matter. As Finnis puts the point, the law presents itself as a seamless web.[56] But, I wish to suggest, precisely because the service conception of authority permits obligations to arise in a piecemeal fashion, it cannot be the conception of authority that inheres in the concept of law.

Let me say something, finally, about the set of questions that I raised in the preceding section. I argued there that because governments claim to do much more than impose obligations, it is not necessarily sufficient to justify the legitimacy of political authority in its entirety to show that governments can have the moral power to impose obligations. Raz of course recognizes that governments do much more than impose obligations, but as I noted earlier he argues that "all the other functions that authorities may have are ultimately explained by

---

[56] Finnis, "The Authority of Law in the Predicament of Contemporary Social Theory," *Notre Dame Journal of Law, Ethics and Public Policy* 1 (1984) 115.

reference to the imposition of duties."[57] I will assume that when Raz says that all the functions of authorities besides the imposition of obligations can be "explained" by reference to the imposition of duties, he means, at least in part, "justified." The justification of the authority to confer powers, create permissions, etc., must clearly be dealt with on a case by case basis, so it will be helpful to consider a concrete example, such as the contracts case that was briefly discussed in the preceding section. At the end of section II, I considered two possible ways in which the power to impose obligations, which is clearly a central case of governmental authority, might be related to the justification of other governmental powers. One possibility is that the justification of the power to impose obligations is generalizable to these other powers. There is, however, no obvious way to generalize the normal justification thesis so that it could justify a power to confer e.g., a power to contract, so let me set that possibility aside. The other possibility I mentioned is that the possession of the power to impose an obligation might directly figure in the justification of other governmental powers. This approach sounds much more promising, and I would like to discuss its application to the contracts case in some detail. For purposes of this discussion, I will assume that the normal justification thesis is, as Raz argues, the normal way to justify governmental authority to impose an obligation.

Suppose the government passes a law which claims to confer a power to contract on its subjects. It can only do this if it has the moral power to confer such a power (and hence only if its subjects have a liability to have such powers conferred upon them.) How might the government's power to confer a power be justified by reference to the power to impose obligations (which for present purposes I will assume the government has)? Suppose that two persons purport to exercise their newfound powers to contract, and hence come to regard themselves as under new mutual obligations to one another. (They are only *actually* under such obligations if the contract law was justified, which is what we are trying to determine.)[58] The mere exercise by private citizens of the power to contract does not seem in any way to implicate the *government's* power to impose obligations, so it would appear that the government's moral power to impose a power can only be justified by reference to its power to impose obligations if contractual obligations are legally enforceable. Suppose that one of the parties breaks his contract and the other party successfully sues him in court and obtains an award of damages. In issuing this award of damages the government, through the court, does clearly claim to impose a moral obligation on the contract-breaker. I assume it is Raz's view that the normal way to show that the contract-breaker in fact has this moral obligation is to invoke the normal justification thesis. The normal justification thesis only applies if the contract-breaker would better comply with the reasons that apply to him if he were to obey the damages award than if he were to act on his own judgment of what to do in these circumstances. The "reasons that apply to him" must presumably be, in this context, his obligation to comply with his contract (and the reasons which flow from that obligation when he broke it). Of course he only has these reasons if the government had the power to confer the power to contract on him in the first place, which is what we are trying to determine. The argument must therefore presumably be that the justification of the government's power to confer the power requires us to look ahead, so to speak, to the fact that the government will enforce contracts and can be

[57] *MF*, 44.

[58] It is possible that their contractual obligations coincide with obligations that they would have anyway because contract law simply reproduces their independent moral power to promise. In that case, the question of whether or not the contract law is morally justified is not answered by showing that it confers a new moral power, but rather by showing that it is a new ground for a moral power that already exists. For present purposes, we can ignore this complication.

shown, under the normal justification thesis, to have the moral authority to do so. This would all seem to be perfectly in order even though the reasons for action to which the normal justification thesis will eventually apply—namely, the obligation to comply with contracts and the associated obligation to rectify the situation if one does not—would not exist unless the government had the moral power to confer a power. This latter point suggests that the justification of the government's power to confer the power cannot look *solely* to the government's power to impose obligations, but I assume that Raz would not take issue with this. As was noted in section II, a person cannot hold a moral power to create a power unless the existence of the latter power would be morally valuable, and presumably the relevant value or values figure in some way in the justification of the former power as well. Raz, of course, has made important contributions to the literature on the values that are served by the possession of powers to promise and contract.[59] My suggestion is that these values should, in one way or another, also figure in the justification of the power to confer the power to contract.

The example suggests that one reason—there of course may be others—that the power to impose obligations is the central case of political authority is that the justification of the other normative powers that governments claim for themselves normally involves, and perhaps even requires, appeal to the power to impose obligations. The example is only an example, of course, and while it may be suggestive in this regard, it would be necessary to examine these various other powers one by one in order to establish this point in a more definitive way. Even if, however, it could be shown to be true that the justification of the full range of the government's claimed moral authority—its power to confer powers, create permissions, etc.—requires appeal to the power to impose obligations, the example suggests that such powers cannot be justified *solely* by reference to the power to impose obligations. This point may well be an obvious one, but the emphasis on obligation means that it often gets overlooked in jurisprudence (even if not in the philosophy of contract, the philosophy of torts, etc.). [pp 276–286]


JULES L COLEMAN
**Beyond the Separability Thesis: Moral Semantics and the Methodology of
Jurisprudence**
(2007)[60]


*In Defence of Descriptive Jurisprudence*


In this section, we turn our attention to theory construction in jurisprudence. A philosophical jurisprudence is an account or theory of the nature of law. Perhaps the most important if not yet fully formed debates in contemporary jurisprudence are methodological. Some of these concern the place of conceptual analysis; others explore the extent to which law should be approached as a code or a system of rules; and others still focus on whether jurisprudence should be pursued as a project in ideal theory. All of these raise extremely important issues, and I have some thoughts about many if not all of them. In many cases, my main thought is that the debate needs to be more precisely structured and the issues at stake better clarified.

I want to focus on yet another way in which law and morality might be related: this time in the context of the methodology of theory construction.

---

[59]  See Raz, "Promises and Obligations," in *Law, Morality and Society: Essays in Honour of H.L.A. Hart*, ed. P.M.S. Hacker and J. Raz 1977, 210, 226–28; Raz, *MF*, 86–87.
[60]  [From 27 Oxford Journal of Legal Studies 581]

### A. Is Jurisprudence Normative or Descriptive?

All theories have a revisionist component and ambition, and if we read "normative" too broadly we will be hard pressed to find a debate worth having. The first task therefore is to formulate the underlying issues clearly and precisely. We should do so in a way that not only illustrates the stakes, but enables us to appreciate the attractions of both positions.

Let us begin with the following characterizations of descriptive and normative jurisprudence. Descriptive jurisprudence claims that law can be analysed entirely in terms of its formal features. Normative jurisprudence denies this. It claims that any theory of law must make reference to material features of law or to the substantive value of living under law.

It follows that someone who defends descriptive jurisprudence is resisting the charge of those who say that it is impossible adequately to characterize law in terms of its formal features alone, and so the defence of descriptive jurisprudence is best seen as a possibility theorem. In a way, putting the project this way is too weak since those who defend descriptive jurisprudence do so because they advocate it as well; and they advocate it because they believe that there is some value in the kind of understanding of law that emerges. I am reasonably confident that this is the view of the two advocates of a descriptive jurisprudence whose work I know best—Hart and me.

I do not reject the possibility of pursuing a normative jurisprudence however. I think Raz's approach to law embeds his account within a substantive theory of legitimate authority and that account which has the consequence of yielding the Sources Thesis is, to my mind, extremely illuminating of law. In defending descriptive jurisprudence, I should not be read as rejecting normative jurisprudence or underestimating its value. Some of it, like Raz's, is very important, and of general philosophical interest.

On the other hand, someone engaged in normative jurisprudence need not reject the possibility of a descriptive jurisprudence. I have no reason to think that Raz, for example, thinks that trying to characterize law in terms of its formal features—as Hart does—is an impoverished or unilluminating project; and I have even less reason to believe that he thinks it sets an impossible task for itself. There is no reason why someone pursuing a normative jurisprudence must make it part of his account to reject the very possibility of a descriptive jurisprudence.

One preliminary problem we have in asking whether jurisprudence is normative or descriptive, then, is that we may have no reason for thinking that it cannot be both. So what I want to do is to formulate the dispute narrowly and in doing so focus only on those versions of normative jurisprudence that reject not merely the value of descriptive jurisprudence, but the very possibility of it. My aim is to defend descriptive jurisprudence against the most sophisticated arguments against it. In defending descriptive jurisprudence I hope that I will also give the reader some insight into its value and richness.

### B. Battle Lines Being Drawn

Descriptivism holds that an adequate theory of law need not refer to material features of law or to the important values exhibited by law or the desirable effects of living under law. Normative jurisprudence will have none of this. It holds that an adequate theory of law must refer to either the content of law (here and there) and especially to the value of being governed by law.

Normative jurisprudents have a number of different kinds of reasons for thinking that an adequate theory of law must refer to material features of law or to the substantive value of living under law. Two of these are particularly salient for our current purposes. The first of these is suggested by some of the considerations we explored in the previous section of this article. The idea is that one cannot account for the normative force of law other than by reference to the substantive content of the law. Since any adequate account of law must explain the normative force of law, and only the content of law can explain its force, any theory of law would have to refer to material features of law: that is, what the law requires.

One consequence of this line of argument is that it ties the defence of a normative jurisprudence to a particular account of the normative force of law. Defeat that account of the normative force of law and you defeat normative jurisprudence. The second line of argument is more promising and less obviously vulnerable. The thought is that, given the significant value of law, it is impossible to provide a sufficiently rich or robust characterization of law that did not make reference to its value. How can something of such importance and value in our social lives be characterized in a purely formal way?

One way of defending a descriptive jurisprudence would be to reject the underlying substantive claim about law on which the normativist appears to rely. If normative jurisprudence is a consequence of the view that governance by law is morally valuable or attractive, then one way of defending descriptive jurisprudence would involve rejecting the claim that governance by law is especially valuable or desirable.

Others may be inclined to adopt this approach but I would warn against doing so. In any case, it is not a line of argument available to me. After all, in rejecting the separability thesis, I pretty much accepted the central claim of the "value" view: namely, that being governed by law exhibits a number of moral ideals and expresses allegiance to a number of principles of political morality, including the principle of the rule of law itself.

## C. *Two Bad Inferences*

There are two implicit inferences in the arguments as we have outlined them, neither of which can be sustained. One inference appears to be that, in order to defend a normative jurisprudence, one needs to defend first a normative substantive feature of law. In other words, there is no defending a normative methodology absent an underlying normative theory of law. This inference is called into question by the popularity of so-called normative positivism: a positivist theory of law warranted by normative considerations, versions of which are held by reputable legal philosophers including, on my reading anyway, Tom Campbell, Jeremy Waldron, Jerry Postema, and dare I say, Jeremy Bentham. Frankly, I have never been persuaded by this line of argument, in part because it seems unduly pessimistic about the capacity of philosophy to uncover a sufficient number of illuminating and "defining" necessary truths about law. But my scepticism is of no matter here. Whatever the motivation there is certainly a burgeoning group of normative positivists: those who defend a broadly speaking positivistic conception of law on normative grounds.

The second inference is that one can only defend a descriptive jurisprudence if one has a view about law that it is in some sense morally neutral or that governance by law is not necessarily desirable or valuable. To be sure, many who defend a descriptive jurisprudence do so because they reject the view that law is necessarily valuable or because the content of law is essential to understanding the role of law in the realm of reasons.

Still, just as one can defend a "positivist" conception of law on normative grounds, the fact that governance by law is necessarily valuable—if true—is perfectly compatible with a descriptivist methodology. That is the claim I defend here. I have no interest in whether there are normative considerations that would favour a positivist conception of law; there may well be, but whether they are there or not it is of no moment to me. I want to defend descriptive jurisprudence and in this context that means establishing the consistency of a descriptivist methodology with the claim that governance by law is necessarily valuable or desirable.

## D. From Criterialism to Interpretivism

The most important purveyor of normative jurisprudence is Ronald Dworkin. His most well-known argument in favour of normative jurisprudence is the infamous semantic sting argument presented in *Law's Empire*. The argument is designed not merely to undermine descriptivism, but also to lay the foundation for his own substantive (law-as-integrity) and methodological (interpretivism) theories that occupy the remainder of the book.

According to Dworkin, many if not all of the most influential jurisprudential views take the project of jurisprudence to be semantic. On his reading, they take a jurisprudence to be a theory of the meaning of "law". In addition, all such theories adopt a criterialist semantics: that is, they take the semantic content of law to be fixed by widely shared criteria that determine the application conditions of "law".

We do Dworkin no favour by holding him to his formulation of the projects of jurisprudence. No theory of law in the past 50 years takes itself to be an account of the meaning of the word "law". The theories Dworkin has in mind are better described as efforts to provide an analysis of the concept of law, not the concept-word, "law". They take the burden of jurisprudence to be providing an account of the concept of law. The semantic sting is the following argument:

(1) There are jurisprudential views that take the project of jurisprudence to be determining the semantic content of the concept of law.
(2) These theories adopt a criterialism about semantic content.
(3) According to criterialism, the content of a concept is given by a set of widely, nearly universally shared criteria specifying the proper use of the concept.
(4) Because the content of the concept of law is fixed by shared criteria, meaningful disagreement about the criteria for the proper application of the concept of law is not possible.
(5) However, meaningful disagreement among lawyers about the criteria of legality in their community is a salient and familiar feature of legal practice. Therefore,
(6) Criterialism cannot account for this important and common feature of legal practice. Therefore,
(7) Criterialism fails as a theory of the semantic content of law and therefore
(8) All jurisprudential views that are criterialist fail as well.

The aim of the semantic sting is to establish that law cannot be a criterial concept. If the content of a criterial concept is given by shared criteria, then such concepts cannot admit of disagreement about what those criteria are. Disagreement about the criteria is incoherent if what makes them the criteria is that they are shared. A salient feature of legal practice for Dworkin is the extent of disagreement about the criteria of law. Therefore, law cannot be a criterial concept. The semantic sting is nested in a disjunctive syllogism designed to establish that law is an interpretive concept.

(1) Jurisprudential theories are either accounts of the semantic content of the concept of law or else they are interpretive theories.
(2) The semantic sting demonstrates the inadequacy of semantic theories. Therefore,
(3) The only potentially adequate theories of law are interpretive.

According to Dworkin a theory of law is a constructive interpretation, not of the concept of law, but of law itself. Constructive interpretations have two dimensions: fit and value. There is a good deal of controversy as to how fit and value operate together (or "fit" as one might say) but on my reading the best understanding is that in a constructive interpretation one ascribes a value to law and this value helps pick out which features of law are salient and which less so. Those that are picked out by the relevant value must be made to fit with one another and be seen in doing so as an expression of the underlying value attributed to law. It follows from the fact that law is an interpretive concept that the method by which we construct the content of the concept calls for substantive principles of political morality.

Many commentators take "fit" to be another way of talking about consistency or coherence and in doing so treat Dworkin as having some form of coherentist picture in mind. I take fit to be a much stronger condition than coherence or consistency. By my lights, we can talk about the relative tightness/looseness or extent of fit; and so I am inclined to think of fit in "inferential" terms in roughly the same way that Quine talks about inferential relations in the "web of belief". The greater the scope, richness and strength of the inferential relations among the elements of law, the tighter and stronger the fit will be.

If sound, the argument establishes that jurisprudential inquiry is an exercise in political philosophy and it does so by beginning with premises of a very general sort about the nature of concepts. It does not assume that law is valuable or desirable. Instead it establishes that law is a certain kind of concept: interpretive. And then it offers up a distinctive theory of interpretive concepts that is a form of constructivism. The content of the concept is constructed by attributing a value (in this case) to law; and that value guides us in identifying the salient features of law that figure in and are essential elements of the concept of it.

Even if we set aside the limited menu of options available for understanding concepts (criterial or interpretive), we are left with an argument that plays on a hidden ambiguity and then rests on a simple but profound confusion.

The ambiguity concerns the notion of shared criteria. There is a well-known distinction between individual and community-wide criterialism. Disagreement about the criteria for the proper application of a term is incompatible only with individual criterialism, but no philosopher of language thinks that the criteria of "law" or the concept to which it refers are shared in the sense of each competent speaker of the language having access to them. Individual criterialism is a plausible account of "sow", but not of "law". If there is any version of criterialism that could be an account of "law" it would be a community wide version of it that relies on the division of linguistic labour; and any community wide criterialism would allow for precisely the sort of disagreement about the criteria for applying the concept that Dworkin claims is inconsistent with criterialism.

Ori Simchen and I have argued elsewhere that there is no version of criterialism that is applicable to "law". In other words, the semantic sting is targeted at a form of criterialism that no one believes could be appropriate for terms like "law", and as the new theory of reference long ago taught us, there is no plausible form of criterialism in the offing anyway.[61]

The confusion on which the argument rests is profound. Criterialism is defined in (4) above and the evidence against it is provided in (5). However, (4) and (5) are talking about different criteria. The relevant criteria in (4) are those for the proper application of the concept; the criteria in (5) are those specifying the test of legality in a particular jurisdiction. This is the confusion between the criteria of law (in this or that jurisdiction) i.e. (5) and the criteria of the concept of law or of the term "law" i.e. (4). Establishing the fact (if it is one) that lawyers often disagree about the grounds or criteria of law in their community has no bearing whatsoever on the question of whether competent speakers of the language

---

[61] For fuller discussions see J. L. Coleman and Ori Simchen, "Law" (2003) 9 *Legal Theory* 1–41.

(including lawyers) disagree about the criteria for properly applying the concept. To see this simply notice that, if lawyers disagree about what makes something law in their community, then that is perfectly compatible with it being the case that among the criteria of the concept law that people share is the following: whether or not a given norm is part of the law of a jurisdiction is one of the things about which competent lawyers are prone to disagree. That they disagree is one of the criteria for the application of the concept that everyone agrees upon! The evidence that Dworkin brings to bear regarding disagreement in legal practice about the criteria of legality is basically a non-sequitur with regard to the issues at stake in the semantic sting.

The semantic sting seeks to make the case for interpretivism—that is a form of normative jurisprudence—by undermining the descriptivist alternative to it. But the argument fails at every turn. Without citing a single proponent of the view it identifies alternatives to interpretivism as having a semantic project in mind. Again without proper citation it identifies the semantic project with a form of criterialism that no one holds. It then develops an argument that if it applied at all would only apply against the form of criterialism that no one thinks is plausible or applicable. And to top it off, the argument it offers against criterialism is based on citing disagreement about the criteria of legality and not the criteria for properly applying the term or concept of law (or legality). If descriptivism is impossible and must give way to a normative jurisprudence it cannot be because it is otherwise vulnerable to the semantic sting.

## E. *The Value of Law and the Scope of Disagreements*

More conventional arguments for a normative jurisprudence begin with the assumption that I not only do not challenge, but also in fact accept, namely that governance by law is necessarily valuable. The simplest version of this argument takes it that the value of law is sufficiently rich and robust that we could not characterize law without making reference to it. A somewhat more complex version of the argument draws attention to the scope of disagreement about what the value(s) of being governed by law is (are). Here the thought is that any theory of law will be contestable because of the inherently controversial nature of the claim of value it makes. The correct theory of law will necessarily adjudicate among these conflicting claims about the value of law. And only a normative theory can do that.

It may be helpful to illustrate the strategy of argument indirectly, that is, without arguing directly for the claim that law is necessarily valuable in the way the argument on offer claims that it is. Why? Well, for one thing, we may want to motivate the case for a normative jurisprudence by showing how a similar methodology is called for in the case of concepts in the social neighbourhood of law, for example, justice, equality, liberty, and even morality. Certainly those defending a normative jurisprudence find the analogy with these political concepts apt.

Though different theorists might disagree about the specific or precise value of justice, equality or liberty, no one could seriously doubt that all are political values. An account of equality that does not explain the value of equality is, well, not an adequate account of equality. In general, an account of justice, equality or liberty must refer to their value—or so the normativist about political concepts would allege. According to those advocating normative jurisprudence, the same considerations apply in the case of law. An adequate account of the concept of law must proceed by assigning a contestable political value to law or to one of its cognate terms, e.g. "the rule of law", or "legality". The underlying idea is that we cannot provide an adequate account of any essentially evaluative concept in purely formal terms.

We can imagine several lines of response. One might deny that law is an essentially evaluative concept in the way that, for example, justice or equality is. Even if the latter concepts cannot be analysed in terms of their formal properties alone, the same may not be true of law. Second, one can argue that even justice and morality can be analysed in terms of their formal properties. No less an authority on these matters than Kant held precisely that view. Third, one can allow that law is essentially evaluative and show that the best way of explaining is not only the value it has, but also the scope of theoretical disagreement about it is provided by a descriptive and not a normative jurisprudence.

There is in fact something to be said for all three lines of response, but the second and third hold out the greatest philosophical interest; and the third in particular is the line I want ultimately to press. Let us not dismiss the first line of response too quickly. According to it, we simply deny that the analogy of law with justice, equality or morality is apt. Even if none of the former could be characterized formally that is no reason to think that the same would be true of law.

Someone pursuing this line need not argue that living under law is not valuable; his claim is the more modest one that whether or not legal governance is valuable depends on the particulars of the legal system and the availability of alternative means of regulating human affairs. Being governed by law is sometimes, perhaps, even often, desirable, but it is not necessarily so. Certainly law is not intricately and richly engaged with value in the way that, say, morality is. It is one thing to suggest that morality cannot be characterized in terms of its formal properties alone; another to claim that the same is true of law. The analogy with liberty may be more apt. After all, it is not obvious that liberty is necessarily valuable; and whether it is certainly depends on what we take liberty to be.

If liberty is defined as the absence of constraints or the existence of options or some such thing, then while we can imagine many circumstances under which having liberty is good for those who have it, we can also imagine a number of circumstances under which it is neither necessarily good for those who possess liberty so understood nor for those unable to constrain the exercise of it by them. If we are looking for a political concept that is analogous to law, liberty is more apt than either justice or morality is. An adequate account of liberty must possess the resources necessary to explain why liberty is valuable when it is, but such an account should also possess the resources adequate to explain why it is dangerous when it is. The same is true of law.

Because my entire strategy is to defend a descriptive jurisprudence even on the assumption that law is necessarily valuable or desirable, I see no point in pursuing this line of argument further. The better argument is always to give the opposition the premises they need and show that even armed with all the machinery they claim to need, the conclusion they seek fails to materialize. This brings me to the second line of defence.

The second line of response allows that some normative concepts, such as morality, are richly and intricately related to fundamental and important human values in ways many and varied. It is indeed impossible to separate morality from value. Nevertheless, one can give an adequate account of the concept of morality that makes no reference to contestable evaluative claims, or so philosophers as diverse as Plato, Kant and William Frankena, among others, have argued.

On Frankena's account, to use one of the more recent examples, the concept of morality picks out a set of norms that restrict our behaviour as it pertains to other human beings. Moral norms are categorical in the sense that they apply to a person regardless of how she feels or what she believes. They are universalizable in that they apply in the same way to everyone in relevantly similar circumstances; and they are supreme in the sense that the obligations or duties they impose win out when in conflict with other kinds of obligations or normative claims. We can understand Frankena to be offering an account of the application conditions of the term "moral",—the conditions that must be satisfied for a norm to count as a moral rule, yet nothing in this account of the concept of morality commits one to endorsing the content of any of the rules that satisfy the application-conditions of the concept.

Alas, for every Plato, Kant, and Frankena, there is an Aristotle or MacIntyre who believe that the ways in which morality is important to our lives is so rich and varied that it possesses no formal features adequate to capture its place in the human experience. Again this line of argument threatens to become more rhetorical than anything else, but I would not want to hang a defence of descriptive jurisprudence on such a controversial foundation. A truly persuasive descriptive jurisprudence still awaits us.

I want to build such a case in three parts. We begin with common ground on which this descriptivist at least and the normativist agree: namely that law is an essentially normative concept, by which I mean that being governed by law necessarily exhibits important moral virtues or expresses important ideals and embodies important political virtues. The first step in my argument is the claim that we need to formulate an adequacy condition on a theory of law as follows: any theory of law must have the resources adequate to explain why being governed by law is necessarily and importantly valuable or desirable.

It does not follow from the fact that an adequate account of law must be able to explain law's value that the value we associate with law must be part of the account. In fact, quite the contrary would seem to be the case. Here's why. Governance by law is valuable. One can argue for the value of governance by law from the point of view of any number of otherwise incompatible political theories: libertarianism, utilitarianism, egalitarianism and so on. The value of being governed by law may differ depending on the political theory. Part of what distinguishes these theories is that they associate different values with governance by law, and the fact that they are likely to identify some different features of law as essential to law having the value that it does.

So we want an account of law that has the resources not only to explain the value of legal governance but one that is thin enough to allow for law to be differentially valuable from the point of view of substantially different kinds of political theories. And that would seem to suggest that the value of law is not internal to our concept of it, but resides instead in the relevant political theories.

This is step 2 of my argument and it is composed of two different but related claims: first, the most persuasive accounts of the concept of law are those most compatible with the widest range of different political theories all of whom take governance by law to be necessarily valuable. Second, if an adequate account of law must make reference to the values (as opposed to the values being external to the concept and instead part of the relevant political theory), we are going to run into a number of familiar philosophical problems. For example, we will have a hell of a time explaining the possibility of meaningful disagreement using the same concept because there is some reason to think that a utilitarian and a libertarian are not using the same concept of law. Why? Because the theory of the concept on offer in each case attributes a different value to law that shapes the relevant conception. We need a plateau of agreement about the value intrinsic to law. If we do not have that, there is a real question about whether we can have meaningful disagreements. Moreover, it may turn out that only one theorist—the one with the right account of the value of law—is talking about law; other theorists may be saying true or false things but not about law; and so on.

Step 2 expresses what I think of as a meta-principle. If law is valuable it will be diversely valuable depending on the views one has in political philosophy; and so the last thing one would want to do is to tie a contestable value to law in order to explain what law is. Doing so would make it impossible to explain the differing values and importance of law within different political philosophies. What we want in a theory of law is *not* the value that law exhibits, but factors that very different theories can point to that are both essential to law and help us to understand the value law has from the point of view of the relevant theory. Take the idea that law consists in rules for example. This is a feature of law that can figure in a number of different kinds of accounts of the value of law from different philosophical perspectives.

This last remark brings us to the final step in my argument. Step 3 involves explicitly showing how a descriptivist methodology would work. Suppose that we take law to be valuable by which we mean that governance by law is necessarily desirable. What is the connection between this fact about law and the concept of law or the nature of law? The right answer to this question—according to the descriptivist—is this: an explanation of why law is desirable must make reference to at least some of law's essential features. If it is true that law is desirable but we cannot make sense of this by reference to some list of its essential features, then that list is incomplete or we have an inadequate account of what law is. The key point for a descriptivist is that to understand why law is desirable under certain circumstances, we are going to know much more than what we can read off the concept or infer from law's nature. We are going to know more about human beings—their interests, the constitutive elements of their welfare, what they want to accomplish jointly and severally, and so on.

In other words, some set of law's essential features must figure in an account of the value of law. But the value of law itself would not be read off this or any other list of those of law's features that are part of the concept of it. Instead, any account of the value of law must rely on a number of facts about persons, their projects and goals and so on, none of which are part of the concept of law. We do not determine the content of the concept of law by beginning with an account of the value of law. Rather we explain the value of law in terms of the interplay between features of the concept and facts about persons that are not part of the concept.

## 4. Conclusion

It may be old fashioned to worry about the relationship between law and morality. All the new problems in jurisprudence have to do with objectivity, determinacy, the nature of reference and so on. Much of my most recent work, including especially my article "Law" with Ori Simchen, would suggest that I too think the days of worrying about the relationship between law and morality are passé. They are only to the extent that the issues focus almost entirely on the separability thesis. There are extremely fresh and important issues about the relationship of law to morality that remain underdeveloped and inadequately appreciated. Some of these—like the question whether law calls for a moral semantics—turn out to shed significant light on some of the oldest problems in jurisprudence—how law creates content-independent moral reasons for acting— as well as some of the most intriguing and relatively new ones—what does it mean to think of law as a point of view. What was once old is new again. That may be as good a characterization of philosophy as I can find.        [pp 597–608]

### J. COLEMAN
### Inclusive Legal Positivism
### (2001)[62]

Despite their differences, the shared emphasis on the conventionality of law distinguishes legal positivism from a family of views that claims that the existence and content of criteria of legality are not a matter of convention or social fact, but

---

[62] [From J. Coleman, *The Practice of Principle* (2001).]

of substantive moral argument instead.[63] Ronald Dworkin is the leading contemporary advocate of this kind of view.[...]

According to Dworkin, there are four fundamental tenets of positivism: (1) the rule of recognition—the claim that wherever there is law there is a "master rule" that specifies the conditions necessary and sufficient for membership in the category "law"; (2) the model of rules—the claim that every norm that falls within the category "law" must be a rule; (3) the separability thesis—the claim that the substantive value or moral merit of a norm cannot be a condition of its legality; and (4) the discretion thesis—the claim that in a wide range of so-called hard cases there are no right answers compelled by the applicable law, and that judges in such cases exercise a limited "lawmaking" or quasi-legislative power.

The argument is that countenancing moral principles as binding legal sources—and not merely as discretionary standards—undermines each of these tenets. If moral principles can be legally binding, then they are legal standards; but principles are not rules, and so the model of rules—the claim that all legal standards are rules—cannot be sustained. If certain moral principles are legally binding, they are binding as principles, and therefore in virtue of their status as principles, which is to say that their claim to legal authority depends on their substantive merits; but if the substantive morality or merit of a principle is (or can be) a condition of legality (at least for some legally binding norms), then the separability thesis—the claim that morality cannot be a condition of legality—must likewise fall. So too the rule of recognition—the claim that all and only rules that satisfy the criteria set forth in a master rule are law—since at least some norms are binding as law in virtue of their substantive merits, and not in virtue of the fact that they satisfy conditions set out in any master rule. Finally, the need and opportunity for discretion is reduced as the number of legally authoritative standards is increased; in the limiting case it evaporates altogether.[64]

[...]

The importance of "The Model of Rules I" lies in its having provoked alternative explanations of the place of moral argument in legal discourse. Legal positivists have been forced to explain, in a way that is consistent with positivism's basic tenets, the apparent fact that moral principles can sometimes be binding legal sources.[...] I want to focus on the responses that have come to characterize the two main competing camps within the legal positivist tradition: exclusive legal positivism and inclusive legal positivism.

The central tenet of exclusive legal positivism is the claim that the criteria of legality must be *social sources*. Membership in the category "law" cannot depend on a norm's content or substantive merit. Something's being a law cannot depend on its being the case that it *ought* to be the law. The question is how and in what ways exclusive legal positivism can accommodate or respond to Dworkin's

---

[63] Dworkin invariably characterizes the positivist claim that legality is a matter of convention or social fact as the very different claim that legality is a matter of "hard facts", by which he means uncontroversial or noncontestable facts. While there is a sense in which every positivist endorses the former claim, no positivist need be committed to the latter.

[64] Of course, even as discretion owing to the availability of legally binding resources decreases (as the set of available resources increases), the possibility of discretion owing to vagueness increases (as the set of controversial moral predicates legally binding on officials increases). The same predicates that reduce discretion on one front increase it on another: a consequence of Dworkin's own view that moral predicates are controversial and contestable. To defeat the positivist view of discretion, Dworkin has to do more than show that the set of available legal resources on which a judge can draw goes beyond rules. Of course, no positivist really limits the set of resources binding on officials in the way Dworkin claims positivist do. The debate, then, has to be resolved on grounds having more to do with the structure of legal justification than with the set of binding legal sources.

observation that at least some moral principles are binding law in virtue of their substantive merits and *not* their social source. Can exclusive legal positivism explain cases in which morality is apparently incorporated into law?

The first thing to note is that what Dworkin has offered by way of a challenge to legal positivism is not a fact, but an interpretation of a fact. The relevant fact that needs to be explained or interpreted is that moral norms often figure as standards to which judges appeal in resolving legal disputes. Dworkin's interpretation is that judges appeal to these norms because they are binding on them, binding as law, and law because of their merits—because, in other words, they express an appropriate dimension of justice or fairness. It is not incumbent on legal positivism to provide in its own terms an account that embraces these interpretive claims of Dworkin's; for example, the legal positivist need not show (though doing so would be one possible way of answering Dworkin) how moral principles can be binding law in virtue of their merits. What legal positivism must account for in terms of its own basic commitments is simply the fact that moral norms figure importantly in adjudication.

In considering the range of strategies available to an exclusive legal positivist, we should begin by noting that he need not claim that every time a judge appeals to a moral principle he is doing so for the same reason. In other words, moral principles can figure in legal argument in different ways at different times. Thus, it is always open to exclusive legal positivism to claim that at least sometimes when judges appeal to moral principles, they are exercising discretion in the strong sense: appealing to standards that—contra Dworkin—are not binding on them, that are instead optional. This is not the only resource available to the exclusive legal positivist, however. He could argue that when moral principles figure in law, they are sometimes (or always) binding law—just as Dworkin claims they are. However the exclusive positivist would deny Dworkin's claim that such principles could be binding *law* because of their merits. Exclusive legal positivism is committed to the view that if moral principles are law, it is in virtue of their pedigree or social source, not their content.

By employing an important distinction of Joseph Raz's, the exclusive legal positivist can also argue that sometimes moral principles can be binding on officials without being part of the law of a community. Raz distinguishes between standards that are *binding on officials* and standards that are *part of a community's law*. Every standard that is part of the community's law is binding on officials, but not every standard that is binding on officials is part of the community's law. In a conflicts-of-law case, for example, a judge in the United States may be required to apply the law of another country. He may have no freedom to do otherwise. Yet the fact that the law of the other country—say, France—might be binding on an American official is not a reason for claiming that the law of France is part of the law of the United States, or that the law of the United States incorporates the law of France. The fact that judges of one country may be bound to apply the law of another does not eliminate the distinction between those two legal systems; nor does the legally mandated application by judges of the standards of a particular trade, business, or social group eliminate the distinction between the law and these other normative systems regulating behavior within a given society. Thus, even if Dworkin were right that moral principles can sometimes be legally binding, it would not follow that such standards are *part of the community's law*.

Raz's strategy also suggests a more sophisticated understanding of discretion. Because moral standards can sometimes be binding on officials without being part of the community's law, the positivist is not committed to the claim that whenever a judge appeals to a moral principle she is thereby applying a discretionary norm—in the sense of a norm she is free to ignore. Some extra-legal norms may be binding on officials, yet without being discretionary in the worrisome sense of being optional.

The exclusive legal positivist believes that moral standards may bind officials, but without being law (they may bind the way the law of France can be binding on US judges); that moral standards may be binding *as* law (though only in virtue of being identified by their social source); and finally, that moral standards may be nonbinding, and enter into legal argument as discretionary standards. Exclusive legal positivism thus admits of a variety of different possible roles for moral principles in legal argument. Moreover, all of these roles are consistent with the tenets Dworkin ascribes to legal positivism, with the exception of the model of rules—the claim that all legal standards are rules. This conclusion is of little concern, however, since no legal positivist has ever actually held that all legal standards are rules. This includes Raz and myself as well as Hart—who explicitly denied the claim long before Dworkin attributed it to him.

It is time to turn our attention to inclusive legal positivism. The first thing to note is that it shares with exclusive legal positivism a commitment to the conventionality of the criteria of legality. My own version of this claim encompasses the range of views detailed in the previous lecture under the rubric of the conventionality thesis. I have no reason to believe that Raz, for example, understands the conventionality of the criteria of legality along the same lines (though other exclusive legal positivists—for example, Scott Shapiro—do). All that matters at this point is that for positivists of whatever variety, the existence of the criteria of legality in any community depends on social facts—and not on moral arguments. The criteria of legality are in this sense conventional.

If what unites exclusive and inclusive legal positivism is a commitment to the conventionality of the criteria of legality, what distinguishes them is a difference over what can count as a criterion of legality. The exclusive legal positivist claims that all criteria of legality must state social sources. The inclusive legal positivist denies that, and allows that sometimes the morality of a norm can be a condition of its legality. Inclusive legal positivism thus rests on a distinction between the *grounds* and the *content* of the criteria of legality. The grounds of the criteria must be a social fact (a convention among officials), but the criteria themselves need not *state* social facts. By contrast, the exclusive legal positivist claims both that the rule of recognition must be a social rule, *and* that the criteria of legality set forth in it must be social sources.

Because inclusive legal positivism allows that some moral principles can be legally binding in virtue of their merits or value, not their source or pedigree, the inclusive legal positivist is prepared to accept more of Dworkin's suppositions than is the positivist who insists that the legality of moral principles depends entirely on their source.

Unlike Dworkin, however, the inclusive legal positivist holds that *whether or not morality is a condition of legality in a particular legal system depends on a social or conventional rule, namely the rule of recognition*. If the rule of recognition asserts that morality is a condition of legality, then morality is a condition of legality in that system. If the rule of recognition incorporates no moral principles, however, then no such principles figure in the criteria of legality.

The distinction between inclusive and exclusive legal positivism may now be stated succinctly: whereas both share positivism's basic commitment to the conventionality of legality, the inclusive legal positivist claims that positivism imposes no additional constraints on the content of those criteria, while the exclusive legal positivist maintains that legality must be a matter of social source, not content.[65]

It is important that we be as clear about what inclusive legal positivism is not as about what it is. Just about everybody gets right the basic premise of inclusive legal positivism, which is its rejection of the pedigree or social-source constraint

---

[65] Which is not to say that there are no constraints on the criteria of legality. The criteria are expressed in a rule of recognition that is a social rule. Thus, the criteria must be capable of supporting convergent behaviour among officials. This is a conceptual constraint, imposed not by any commitment of positivism but by the concept of a social rule.

on legality. On the other hand, it is a mistake to think that in rejecting the pedigree standard, the inclusive legal positivist is committed to the claim that wherever there is law, the rule of recognition makes morality a condition of legality. Inclusive legal positivism is the claim that positivism *allows* or *permits* substantive or moral tests of legality; it is not the view that positivism *requires* such tests. A legal system with only pedigree criteria of legality is surely a legal system, and inclusive legal positivists have no reason to think otherwise.

Another mistake is to think that whenever moral principles are law, the inclusive legal positivist must claim that this is because the rule of recognition in that a community makes morality a condition of legality. Again, not so. Inclusive legal positivism is the claim that positivism allows or permits such explanations of legal validity: not the view that positivism requires such explanations. It may well be that in a particular community all the moral principles that are law are law in virtue of their social sources. Such a legal community is surely possible, and again inclusive legal positivists have no reason to think otherwise.

Inclusive legal positivism is a theory of possible sources of legality. It says, in effect, that a positivist can accept not just that moral principles can sometimes figure in legal argument; not just that such principles can be binding on officials; but that sometimes they can be binding on officials because they are legally valid or part of the community's law, and—most significantly—that they may even be part of the community's law *in virtue of their merits*—provided the rule of recognition in that community has such provisions.

All inclusive legal positivists agree that morality can be a condition of legality. However, there are notable differences between my version of inclusive legal positivism and the versions offered by various other theorists. One such point of difference concerns the theoretical motivations for inclusive legal positivism, and the criteria by which theories of law are to be evaluated. One might naturally infer from Wil Waluchow's excellent book on inclusive legal positivism that he believes part of the motivation of inclusive legal positivism to be its *descriptive accuracy*.[66] He notes that many constitutions and federal charters have clauses that on their face appear explicitly to make morality a condition of legality. The "due process" and "equal protection" clauses of the United States Constitution, and its prohibition of "cruel and unusual" punishments, are typical of the kind of moral language one often finds in written constitutions. Facially, such clauses suggest that morality can be a condition of legality. Inclusive legal positivism explicitly allows just that. Thus, Waluchow at least implicitly suggests that inclusive legal positivism is more descriptively accurate than a theory that excludes morality from the conditions of legality; and in virtue of that, inclusive legal positivism enjoys something of an epistemically privileged status.[67] To reject it would be to suffer a loss of descriptive accuracy, which we should be willing to accept only for the most compelling reasons.

I reject this line of argument. Of course, no one denies that descriptive accuracy is a virtue of a theory. But the dispute between exclusive and inclusive legal positivists cannot be resolved on descriptive grounds, for the simple reason that the dispute is not a descriptive one. It is an interpretive dispute. Any jurisprudential theory that can explain what I have called the "surface syntax" of constitutional clauses that make reference to morality can be a descriptively accurate theory. The question is not whether exclusive or inclusive legal

---

[66] Waluchow, *Inclusive Legal Positivism* (1994).
[67] This is surely the understanding that leads Waluchow to refer to such clauses in the Canadian Charter as "Charter Challenges". See *Inclusive Legal Positivism*, Chap. 5. I am not certain that Waluchow would accept this characterization, but it is clearly the prevailing understanding of his view. *cf.* Stephen Perry, "Varieties of Legal Positivism" (July 1996) 9 *Canadian Journal of Law and Jurisprudence* 361–381.

positivism satisfies this criterion of descriptive accuracy; rather, the question is which view provides the *best explanation or interpretation* of the fact that moral language appears in constitutional clauses. Should we understand these clauses as incorporating morality into law? Should we read them as doing so in virtue of their substantive merits? These are interpretive questions and are, as I see it, to be answered in whatever way provides the best comprehensive understanding of legal practice. We cannot settle on a view about the criteria of legality without considering how that view affects the overall theory of law being developed. In this sense, any particular claim about the criteria of legality must be assessed holistically.

In fact, Raz has articulated a coherent and tenable way of understanding the relevant kinds of constitutional clauses without abandoning his exclusive legal positivist stance. His solution is to read clauses like the equal protection clause as directing officials to engage in substantive moral argument in order to determine *whether valid laws ought to be enforced* or are binding on officials. On Raz's view, enactments that come before the court to be evaluated under the equal protection standard are law, provided they satisfy the pedigree requirements; the equal protection clause does not go to the *legality* of such enactments, but rather, directs judges to engage in moral argument in order to determine whether the laws ought to be *enforced* or treated as binding.

I don't mean to defend this view as natural or perspicuous. It is neither. But our evaluation of it should be made in light of the whole picture. As we will see in the next lecture Raz is driven to this way of interpreting clauses like the equal protection clause by his account of law's claim to practical authority. If the best account of legal authority requires interpreting these sorts of clauses as Raz does, then however unintuitive or unnatural his interpretation may seem, it may yet be part of the best overall view of the matter available to us. As we will see in the following lectures what drives the dispute between inclusive and exclusive legal positivism concerns the way we are to understand law's claim to practical authority. The deep issue is whether that claim, properly understood, imposes constraints on the conditions of legality or not.

In denying that "morality" clauses should be interpreted as incorporating morality into law in virtue of its merits, the exclusive legal positivist is not arguing that we must trade off or abandon *descriptive accuracy* in favor of a better account of legal authority. Rather, exclusive legal positivists are arguing that we must trade off a degree of simplicity or intuitive appeal in one part of our account in exchange for a certain comprehensive understanding of law—of its conventionality and the role it plays in our practical lives. The defense of exclusive legal positivism rests on the claim that the most attractive comprehensive understanding available to us precludes interpreting "morality clauses" in a way that credits the surface syntax.

Similarly, in defending inclusive legal positivism, I am arguing that it too can provide a comprehensive understanding of law, its conventionality, and the role it plays in our practical lives; and that it can do so in a way that credits the surface syntax. Allowing for the possibility that morality can figure in legal practice in the way it appears to do is indeed a reason to prefer inclusive legal positivism—but only if the understanding of law it provides is otherwise compelling. It is not, on its own, the basis of a "challenge" that has to be met by exclusive legal positivists. Crediting the surface syntax has nothing to do with descriptive accuracy, and is thus inadequate to ground an "epistemically privileged" status for inclusive legal positivism.

I differ from other inclusive legal positivists not only about the motivations of the inclusive legal positivist project and the criteria for assessing its success, but, more importantly, about how to understand the nature of the objections exclusive legal positivists have made to that project. On a certain natural reading of Hart's discussion of the relationship between primary rules and the rule of recognition, the *function* of the rule of recognition is to solve a problem of "dissensus".[68] In a regime of primary social rules of obligation, there is likely to be disagreement about which social rules are those to which one ought to conform, and (on this reading of Hart) the rule of recognition exists to solve this problem of disagreement. Imagine, for example, living under a system of custom in which everyone is committed to acting according to custom, but where there are disagreements about what the custom *is*. To co-ordinate our behavior in a way that would enable us to secure the benefits of social life, we might well need a meta-rule to pick out or identify what the custom is. In the case of such a system of primary social rules, dissensus may require a "legal solution" in the form of the rule of recognition: a rule that creates a mark distinguishing those primary rules to which one ought to conform from other putative rules. Thus, the rule of recognition must be understood as existing in order to solve a problem of *inadequate consensus*.

Some inclusive legal positivists have interpreted the objections of exclusive legal positivists in the light of this rather natural reading of Hart. If the point of a rule of recognition is to solve a problem of dissensus, then no rule of recognition can impose criteria of legality that re-create that same problem. If the rule of recognition requires that individuals appeal to their beliefs about what morality requires in order to determine whether a putative norm is law (and thus constitutes the standard of conduct to which they are to comply) then the rule of recognition merely re-creates the problem it was designed to solve.

This reading of the exclusive legal positivist objection is bolstered by a similar, but in the end mistaken, interpretation of the well-known "arbitrator" example: Two people disagree about what fairness requires of them in their dealings with one another, and so they submit their dispute to the judgment of an arbitrator. If the arbitrator just tells them, "Do what is fair", then the arbitrator has only recreated the original problem. Some advocates of inclusive legal positivism have understood the problem to be that like the arbitrator, a rule of recognition that makes morality a condition of legality threatens simply to re-create a problem of dissensus or disagreement that the rule of recognition is designed to solve. Because it is the function of the rule of recognition to facilitate or create consensus about what ought to be done, it must set forth criteria of legality that are up to that task. This means it must set forth criteria that make the legality of a norm a matter of its social source, not its content.

Having interpreted the example in this way, it has struck some as natural to respond in the following way: to be sure, a rule of recognition must be capable of resolving dissensus to an extent sufficient to facilitate social co-operation. This constraint may be enough to rule out certain robust forms of inclusive positivism—those, in particular, that allow morality to be a sufficient condition of legality. Since sufficiency clauses merely direct individuals back to their divergent beliefs about how they ought to act, such clauses cannot facilitate or create consensus within a group about how its members are to act. On the other hand, there is no reason to suppose that less robust inclusive clauses preclude co-ordination or co-operative activity. In particular, necessity clauses—which require a more modest application of moral argument—may nevertheless be compatible with the rule of recognition's co-ordinating function. Thus, necessity clauses can withstand the exclusive legal positivist challenge (as these theorists understand it), and this has led them to defend what I take to be a truncated version of inclusive legal positivism.

We can enumerate three components in this line of response to exclusive legal positivism: (1) an interpretation of the role of a rule of recognition as designed to solve a problem of dissensus or controversy about what the obligation-imposing

---

[68]  The passages that give rise to this misreading are to be found in Chap. 5 of *The Concept of Law*. [And see *ante*, 382].

primary rules are; (2) a related understanding of the exclusive legal positivist objection, according to which no criteria of legality are permissible unless they are capable in principle of solving the problem of controversy or inadequate consensus; (3) the claim that this constraint rules out only certain more robust forms of inclusive legal positivism (in particular, sufficiency clauses of the sort my version of inclusive legal positivism permits). At the same time, the relevant constraint does not preclude less demanding moral criteria of legality—in particular those represented by necessity clauses.

Though each of these claims has a surface plausibility, none withstands scrutiny. The rule of recognition can of course solve a problem of dissensus, in this or that legal system, about what the obligation-imposing rules are. It does not follow, however, that this is its essential function—that in order for there to be law, there must be a rule of recognition that solves a problem of controversy. We can imagine, for example, a situation in which everyone agrees about what morality requires, but desires to have their shared moral-political commitments expressed in concrete legal institutions, as a way of fully expressing or realizing those commitments—and as a way of making those abstract commitments more concrete. In order that there be law, there must be a rule of recognition that states the criteria of legality; but the rule need not exist to solve any problem at all, let alone one of dissensus.

Turning to the second claim in the above line of argument—namely, the interpretive claim that the exclusive legal positivist objects to moral criteria of legality because such criteria merely re-create the problem the rule of recognition is designed to solve—we see that this claim too is mistaken. This interpretation is grounded in a misunderstanding of the arbitrator example, the point of which is *conceptual*. The "arbitrator" who tells us to do what is fair is not just failing to resolve our dispute, and thus failing to perform his putatively essential function— rather, the "arbitrator" is failing to *arbitrate*. His failure is not, in other words, practical or pragmatic—it is conceptual. He exercises no practical authority because he does not create reasons for acting, but merely directs us back to the dependent reasons for acting we already have. In order for him to *be* an arbitrator, he must provide us with reasons that replace—not merely ones that *restate*—the dependent reasons that apply to us.

To see in greater relief how the point of the arbitrator example differs from the way many inclusive legal positivists have understood it, we need only consider what an exclusive legal positivist would say about a case in which there is no disagreement about what morality requires. Here the rule of recognition that says, "X is law if and only if it expresses a requirement of morality" does not (indeed, cannot) re-create a problem of dissensus (there is no dissensus to re-create). Nevertheless, an exclusive legal positivist like Raz would have the *same* objection to inclusive legal positivism he has always had: moral criteria of legality vitiate law's claim to authority, because they cannot create reason for acting that replace the ones we already have. Raz claims that the function of law is to mediate between persons and reasons. The problem with an inclusive rule of recognition, as he sees it, is that law valid under it cannot, as a conceptual matter, perform its function. This has nothing to do with matters of degree or the extent of the dissensus.

Turning finally to the third claim above, we see that it represents a version of inclusive legal positivism that is in fact unconnected to the critique that is supposed to motivate it. If the point of defending the possibility of necessity clauses only (among morality conditions of legality) is to accommodate the exclusive legal positivist's objection, then this is a misguided retreat, based entirely on a misunderstanding of the objection. Moreover, since it robs inclusive legal positivism of its ability to answer Dworkin's original objection, this truncated form of positivism strikes one as both unhelpful and unmotivated.

Moreover, this line of argument on behalf of necessity clause only versions of inclusive legal positivism confuses a conceptual argument with an empirical one. If there is widespread agreement about what we morally ought to do, then a sufficiency clause should be possible, by these theorists' own lights. By the same token, it is easy to imagine social facts that are as likely to confound, confuse, and generate controversy as is any morality clause; such social-source criteria would have to be excluded. Whether or not a given set of criteria can solve a problem of dissensus for a given society, in other words, is logically independent of whether the criteria are social facts, or specify morality as a necessary or sufficient condition of legality. It is an *empirical* question what a given society happens to find confounding, confusing, or controversial. It is simply a mistake to base a conceptual claim about possible criteria of legality on an empirical generalization (no matter how well founded) about how controversial morality usually is. The question is whether there are criteria of legality that are *in principle* incapable of guiding conduct; not whether under particular conditions—even ones we might regard as typical—certain criteria would be sufficiently controversial to prevent co-ordination.

Finally, even if the rule of recognition exists to solve a problem of dissensus, this should not be understood as a problem of the *degree* of dissensus. That, of course, is precisely why I emphasize the conceptual difference between the *existence* conditions of a rule of recognition (and of law and legal authority more generally) and the *efficacy* of this or that rule of recognition, or of a legal practice based upon it. I fear that alternative understandings of inclusive legal positivism are the result of a misdiagnosis of the problem—if any—law exists to solve, a misunderstanding of the concerns many exclusive legal positivists have had about the available remedies, and a prescription for a return to health that treats the wrong problem, if it treats anything at all.

Controversy is *not* the issue for the exclusive legal positivist; only natural but serious confusions have led some inclusive legal positivists to think otherwise. The issue is one of the compatibility of certain criteria of legality with the *conceptual possibility* of legal authority, not the *de facto* possibility of legality.[69] And that is why I have continued to defend the most "robust" forms of rules of recognition, in which morality can be a sufficient condition of legality. If such clauses can withstand what are in fact the objections Raz and others have made—and not merely the objections that have been wrongly attributed to them—then any weaker version of the rule of recognition will withstand criticism as well.

While inclusive legal positivism is able to accommodate a claim like Dworkin's that our actual legal system incorporates morality into the criteria of legality, inclusive legal positivism is *not* the view that this is *in fact* the most apt characterization of our existing legal system—or of legal practice generally. It is simply the view that if such criteria of legality ever, often, or even always figure in legal practice, positivism can provide an explanation that is coherent and plausible. Inclusive legal positivism thus makes no claim as to the underlying merits of Dworkin's "observations" concerning the most apt way of characterizing the role of morality in adjudication, nor is it committed to a particular interpretation of our actual legal practice. Positivism can *grant* all of Dworkin's observations; however, it must maintain that the criteria of validity are criteria of validity in virtue of the practice among officials; that is, it must uphold some version of the conventionality thesis.

It is here that Dworkin wants to exert pressure. If the concern of the exclusive legal positivist is not morality's controversiality, that certainly is Dworkin's concern. By allowing morality to be a condition of legality, he argues, inclusive legal positivism is rendered incompatible with the conventionality thesis. The conventionality thesis is, I have argued, the central tenet of all plausible forms of

---

[69] For a fuller discussion of these issues, see my "Constraints on the Criteria of Legality" (2000) 6/2 *Legal Theory* 171–183.

legal positivism—including my own. Thus, it is especially important that we be capable of responding to Dworkin's objection that inclusive legal positivism is inconsistent with it.

In "The Model of Rules II" Dworkin argues that if there is a rule of recognition, it must be a "normative", not a social, rule.[70] The difference is a matter of existence conditions. Normative rules need not be practiced in order to impose obligations; their existence as regulative rules depends on the substantive arguments that can be mustered on their behalf. In contrast, the existence of social rules depends on their being practiced. Inclusive legal positivism—at least in the form I have developed it, which includes the version of the conventionality thesis outlined in the last lecture—requires both that the rule of recognition be a social rule *and* that the rule may incorporate principles that impose substantive moral criteria of legal validity. Dworkin argues, in effect, that these two requirements are incompatible.

The argument is this: Moral principles are inherently controversial. Judges will disagree about which principles satisfy the demands of morality, and about what the principles require. Since the rule of recognition is a social rule, it is partially constituted by or supervenient on a convergence of behavior—the convergence is an existence condition of the rule of recognition. Convergence, however, is undermined by the disagreement that would attend any rule that makes morality a condition of legality. Thus, inclusive legal positivism is incompatible with the conventionality thesis.

As I have emphasized elsewhere, Dworkin's argument misses the important difference between what the rule is and what falls under it. Judges may agree about what the rule *is* but disagree with one another over what the rule *requires*. They could not disagree in every case or even in most cases, since such broad and widespread disagreement would render unintelligible their claim to be applying or following the same rule. Nevertheless, judges can disagree in some significant set of controversial cases, without in the process abandoning their agreement about what the rule is. It hardly follows from the fact that judges disagree about some of the demands of morality that they also disagree about whether the rule governing their behaviour requires that they resolve disputes by determining what morality demands. In short, some disagreement about a rule's requirements is not incompatible with the rule's conventionality.

Dworkin has responded to this argument by labeling the distinction between content and application "doubtful". While this is clearly intended to disparage the argument, it is not obvious what point Dworkin means to make. It is plainly wrong to suggest that there is in general no meaningful distinction between application and content. Sometimes you and I may disagree about what the rule we are supposed to be following is; at other times we know perfectly well what the rule is, but disagree about what it requires of us. Dworkin's only substantive point

---

[70] While the distinction between normative and social rules is clear enough, it is misleading to refer to one kind of rule as normative and the other as social. Both after all are normative rules in the only important sense: that is, they both purport to provide reasons for action and to impose obligations. One has to be careful not to be misled into thinking that social rules cannot be normative. They surely can be, ...

Dworkin has shifted among a variety of related but distinct positions. At times he denies that the concept of law entails the existence of anything like a rule of recognition; other times he allows that there might well be a rule that sets out criteria of legality (a broadly speaking rule of recognition), but asserts that such a rule must be a normative rule, not a social rule. In the end I think the best interpretation of his view is this: he does not deny that there are criteria of legality. Like Raz, he sees no reason to think that the existence of such criteria must be explained in terms of a duty-imposing rule (of any sort) that sets them out, that makes them criteria of legality. Unlike Raz, who thinks that these criteria are conventional and depend on the practice of officials, Dworkin thinks they are normative in that they figure in the best interpretation of the practice of judges.

seems to be that we can always describe the same disagreement alternately as a disagreement about the rule or a disagreement about its application. But even that seems to presuppose, rather than to undermine, the legitimacy of the distinction. Does Dworkin mean that the distinction can do no work? That is simply false. Even if it did turn out to be logically possible to describe any disagreement about a rule as a disagreement either about its content or about its application, it hardly follows that the two kinds of descriptions would be equally apt all the time.[71]

Law's conventionality does not, of course, require that every disagreement about the rule of recognition is most aptly characterized as a disagreement in application. Some disagreements are best thought of as disagreements about how the law should be extended.[72] But the best or most apt way of characterizing a disagreement is not simply up for grabs. Which characterization is most apt is a determination to be made on the basis of our intuitive grasp of the case, on grounds of theoretical coherence, simplicity, consilience, and the like, or (when these kinds of considerations are in conflict) on the proper balance of all of these factors.

It is as though Dworkin were to insist that in every case, no matter what the circumstances or how far-fetched it would be, we must exercise the option (supposing it really is one) of interpreting disagreements as disagreements of content. If there were some reason to do that, we should certainly have to grant Dworkin his conclusion that the rule of recognition must be a "normative", and not a social, rule. But there is no reason to do that; or at least none that Dworkin has proposed. So not only does he apparently presuppose a distinction he has labeled "doubtful"—he also chooses the side of the distinction that supports his position, and does so without offering any theoretically motivated reason for doing so.

On the other hand, if we accept this perfectly natural and common distinction, by treating some disagreements concerning the rule of recognition as "application" rather than as "content" disagreements, we gain many theoretical advantages. We may coherently maintain both that moral principles can be law in virtue of their merits, and the conventionality thesis; this in turn, I have argued, offers the noteworthy advantage of enabling us to explain the possibility of law by appealing to social facts. Again, I insist that one has to choose among incompatible but equally coherent interpretations by appealing to the norms that govern theory construction, which are themselves grounded in the theoretical interest in securing as full and comprehensive an understanding of legal practice as possible.

Dworkin's argument cuts no ice against the conventionality thesis; there is no reason to think that a social rule cannot also be controversial in some of its applications. However, we might reformulate the objection so that it no longer makes a conceptual point about the consistency of inclusive legal positivism and the conventionality thesis, but rather, a practical point about the effectiveness of a rule of recognition that incorporates morality into law's validity conditions. Arguably, law is of practical significance because it guides or purports to guide human conduct. It might be thought that the motivation for insisting on the conventionality of law is to explain how law can perform this function. But the more controversial the rule of recognition, the less able it is to provide guidance— how can individuals conform to the law's demands when they cannot determine

---

[71] Sometimes the context will reveal to us which description is apt and why. Sometimes there may be no way of knowing independently of offering theoretical considerations on behalf of one interpretation or the other. For my part, I nowhere claim that all disagreements are best understood as disagreements in the application of the rule of recognition.

[72] I would never say, and did not say, that the disagreement in the rule of recognition evidenced by *Madison v. Marbury* 5 *U.S.* (1803) (I Cranach) 137 was a disagreement in the application of the rule.

reliably what behavior those demands require? If the rule of recognition invites dispute and controversy, the motivation for insisting on its conventionality evaporates. We are left with the more natural explanation of any test that makes morality a condition of legality: namely, that a rule that imposes moral criteria is itself a normative or moral rule.

This formulation of the objection fails to grasp the theoretical purpose of the conventionality thesis. The point of the conventionality thesis is to explain how law is possible; it is motivated by the need to explain law's *existence*, not its *efficacy*. Of course, law must exist if it is to be efficacious; but there is a special problem in explaining law's existence, and the conventionality thesis purports to solve it. The claim that law is made possible by a rule of recognition that supervenes on convergent behavior accepted from an internal point of view is a conceptual claim. It does not matter, for this purpose, whether or not the rule of recognition is controversial, as long as it is a rule. The positivist will, of course, readily grant the point that a rule of recognition's *efficacy* diminishes with its controversiality, and no positivist denies that controversy matters in this way. But the conventionality thesis is unaffected by the possibility (or actuality) of controversial provisions in the rule of recognition, provided at least some of these are plausibly understood as what I have called "application disagreements". Even if Dworkin is right and we could (logically) treat all application disagreements as content disagreements (and vice versa), there are strong theoretical reasons for not doing so.

Philosophy helps us understand the practices in which we are engaged, largely by clarifying the concepts that figure importantly in them. The distinctive philosophical method is conceptual analysis. A philosophical account of a concept is a contestable conception of it that is responsive to a set of interests or concerns. Depending on the concept at issue, these concerns can be either practical or theoretical; often they are both. In the method adopted and developed here conceptual analysis aims to produce the *thinnest* conception that is adequately responsive to the theoretical and practical concerns that motivate inquiry. At the beginning of Part II I argued that our concept of law should help us understand at least two central concerns about legal practice: the possibility of legal authority and the kind of normativity that is distinctive of it, while providing a plausible interpretation of the role of moral principle in legal argument.

Of course, a variety of theories of law, or conceptions of the concept, can be responsive to these concerns. Differing accounts must be evaluated against the relevant norms of theory construction: elegance, simplicity, and, most importantly, the breadth and depth of the understanding each provides. This means that a theory that can provide a single answer to both of the two fundamental questions of jurisprudence is, other things equal, a stronger theory than one whose answers are consistent but not mutually confirming. (Either kind of theory, of course, is preferable to one whose answers are inconsistent, or which leaves the central questions and concerns unattended.)

Properly understood, inclusive legal positivism of the sort I advocate—and the sort I take Hart to articulate as well—claims that a very thin conception of law— one that posits only the conventionality thesis—is adequate to explain the possibility of legal authority. The absence of further substantive constraints on the conditions of legality does not undermine the possibility of law resting on conventional practice—that is the point of meeting Dworkin's controversiality objection. It remains to answer the exclusive legal positivist who claims, in effect, that the conventionality thesis is not enough, and that we must add a social-source constraint on the conditions of legality in order adequately to explain law's distinctive normativity. [pp. 103–119]

## S. PERRY
### Hart's Methodological Positivism
(1998)[73]

To understand H.L.A. Hart's general theory of law, it is helpful to distinguish between *substantive* and *methodological* legal positivism. Substantive legal positivism is the view that there is no necessary connection between morality and the content of law. Methodological legal positivism is the view that legal theory can and should offer a normatively neutral description of a particular social phenomenon, namely law. Methodological positivism holds, we might say, not that there is no necessary connection between morality and law, but rather that there is no connection, necessary or otherwise, between morality and legal theory. The respective claims of substantive and methodological positivism are, at least on the surface, logically independent. Hobbes and Bentham employed normative methodologies to defend versions of substantive positivism,[74] and in modern times Michael Moore has developed what can be regarded as a variant of methodological positivism to defend a theory of natural law.[75]

In the first edition of *The Concept of Law*[76] Hart offered an extended defense of what has become an extremely influential version of substantive legal positivism. The core of the substantive theory is the fairly straightforward idea that law consists of a union of two types of rules: (i) secondary (meaning second-order) rules, which are rules that have been accepted as binding by judges and other officials, and (ii) primary rules, which are rules that have been identified as valid by a particular secondary rule called the rule of recognition.[77] At a methodological level, however, Hart's views are somewhat less easy to discern. In the Postscript to the second edition, responding in large part to the challenge of Ronald Dworkin's interpretivist approach to legal theory, Hart has made some of his methodological pre-suppositions more explicit.

In a section of the Postscript entitled "The Nature of Legal Theory," Hart describes the type of theory that he had intended to provide in writing *The Concept of Law*. The theory is supposed to be both general and descriptive. "It is *general* in the sense that it is not tied to any particular legal system or legal culture, but seeks to give an explanatory and clarifying account of law as a complex social and political institution with a rule-governed (and in that sense 'normative') aspect" (239). The theory is *descriptive* "in that it is morally neutral and has no justificatory aims: it does not seek to justify or commend on moral or other grounds the forms and structures which appear in my general account of law" (240). Hart notes that legal theory thus conceived "is a radically different enterprise" from Dworkin's conception, which is said to be in part evaluative and justificatory—that is, it is not purely descriptive—and also to be addressed to a particular legal culture—that is, it is not general. Hart goes on to observe that "[i]t is not obvious why there should be or indeed could be any significant conflict between enterprises so different as my own and Dworkin's conceptions of legal theory" (241).

---

[73] [From 4 *Legal Theory* 427.]

[74] On Bentham, *see* particularly Gerald Postema, *Bentham and the Common Law Tradition* (1986), pp. 328–336.

[75] Michael S. Moore, "Law as a Functional Kind" in *Natural Law Theory* 188 (Robert P. George ed., 1992).

[76] H.L.A. Hart *The Concept of Law* (1961). In this essay, all citations are to the second edition (1994), and are given by parenthetical page references in the text.

[77] As other commentators have observed, Hart draws the distinction between primary and secondary rules in at least two different ways. See P.M.S. Hacker, "*Hart's Philosophy of Law*" in *Law, Morality and Society: Essays in Honour of H.L.A. Hart*, pp. 1, 19–21 (P.M.S. Hacker & J. Raz eds., 1977).

Hart's claim in the Postscript that he had intended to provide in *The Concept of Law* a theory that is both general and descriptive is very good evidence that he meant to adopt a framework of methodological positivism. I shall argue that in developing his substantive theory Hart in fact combines elements of two distinct methodological approaches, which we can call the descriptive-explanatory method and the method of conceptual analysis. Of these, only the first can appropriately be said to involve a form of methodological positivism. The second, when understood and analyzed in its own terms, turns out in all significant respects to be Dworkin's interpretivism under a different name. The two different strains in Hart's methodological thought produce tensions in his substantive theory, and to resolve these it is necessary to opt for one or the other of the two methodologies. The descriptive-explanatory approach is appropriate if one intends to do science, but for jurisprudence, which is a branch of philosophy, the most appropriate procedure is conceptual analysis. When jurisprudence is understood in this way, and gives up trying to borrow inappropriate elements from the descriptive-explanatory approach, it can be seen that particular theories of law must be offered from the internal point of view and must be defended, in part, by resort to moral argument. The result is the complete abandonment of methodological positivism.

## I. The generality of legal theory

Hart maintains that his theory is general in the following sense. It is supposed to describe an institution that, "in spite of many variations in different cultures and in different times, has taken the same general form and structure" (240). This immediately raises the question of how we know or could come to know that these manifold social practices are in fact manifestations of *the same* institution, namely law.[78] A related question—perhaps at bottom it is the same question— concerns the status of propositions asserting that law *necessarily* does (or does not) possess such-and-such an attribute. Consider, for example, the soft positivist claim—one element of Hart's substantive positivist theory—that the criteria for identifying the content of law can in some legal systems be partly moral in nature, but are not necessarily so in all legal systems. What kind of necessity is at issue here, and to what domain of actual or possible practices does it apply?

There seem to be two main possibilities concerning how we could come to know which (actual or possible social practices are instances of law. The first supposes that what does and does not count as law is determined by applying the scientific method to come up with a so-called descriptive-explanatory theory.[79] The idea would be to study those social practices that we call law, but from an external perspective. Taking a certain kind of familiar social practice—for example, those practices Hart refers to as "modern municipal legal systems"—as a tentative starting point, a theory of this kind would develop its own internal descriptive categories. These categories would not necessarily correspond to what "we"—participants, in some appropriately loose sense, in modern municipal legal systems—have in mind, either explicitly or implicitly, in speaking of "law." To the extent that a descriptive-explanatory theory used the term "law," it would have to be regarded as a term of art. Its meaning and extension would be determined by the relative explanatory power of accepting one way of categorizing and describing social practices over another, where "explanatory power" would in

---

[78] *Cf.* John Finnis, *Natural Law and Natural Rights* (1980), pp. 1–6.

[79] *See, e.g.* W.J. Waluchow, *Inclusive Legal Positivism* (1994), pp. 19–29. Waluchow clearly believes that Hart is a proponent of the descriptive-explanatory method. (*ibid.* at pp. 14–15). In Stephen R. Perry, *"The Varieties of Legal Positivism"* (1996) 9 CAN J. L. & JURIS. 361, I criticize Waluchow's application of the descriptive-explanatory approach to jurisprudence in general.

turn depend on such standard metatheoretical criteria as the following: predictive power, coherence, range of phenomena explained, degree of explanatory unity, and the theory's simplicity or elegance. It thus might turn out that the initial examples of law on which we tend to focus at a pretheoretical stage—modern municipal legal systems, let's say—are, from the perspective of the best descriptive-explanatory theory, just a minor variant within a wider class of social practices. The theory might, for example, regard the difference between modern municipal legal systems and instances of so-called primitive law as theoretically insignificant because a taxonomy of the social world that ignored that distinction turned out to have greater explanatory power.

The second possibility concerning how we could come to know which actual or possible social practices constitute "law" would require us to analyze our own concept of law. We would inquire into the manner in which we conceptualize our own social practices so as, presumably, to clarify the concept and to come to a better understanding of the practices themselves. The notion of "necessity" involved in such statements as "Law necessarily does (or does not) possess such and such a characteristic" would then be conceptual rather than scientific necessity.

There are a number of indications, in both the original text of *The Concept of Law* and in the Postscript, that might be taken to suggest that Hart intended to adopt something like a descriptive-explanatory methodology. He says in the Preface, for example, that the book can be regarded as "an exercise in descriptive sociology." In the Postscript he speaks of a "descriptive jurisprudence" in which an "external observer" takes account of or describes the internal viewpoint of a participant without adopting or sharing that viewpoint (pp. 242–243). At many other points, however, Hart states, as the title of his book in fact suggests, that his primary methodology is conceptual analysis. In the Preface he writes that "[t]he lawyer will regard the book as an essay in analytical jurisprudence, for it is concerned with the clarification of the general framework of legal thought." (He then goes on to say that the book may *also* be regarded as an essay in descriptive sociology.) The main features of Hart's substantive theory of law are said to be "the central elements in the concept of law and of prime importance in its elucidation" (p. 17). And in the Postscript he formulates the main thesis of substantive legal positivism in terms of conceptual rather than scientific or empirical necessity: "[T]hough there are many different contingent connections between law and morality there are no necessary conceptual connections between the content of law and morality" (p. 268).

I will argue that while it is possible to discern elements of the descriptive-explanatory method in Hart's approach to doing legal theory, there are good reasons for believing that he does not in fact employ that method, or at least that he does not employ it in anything like a pure form. The most important such reason is that Hart adopts the particular characterization of law that he does, expressed in terms of a union of two types of rules, on the basis of evaluative judgments that have nothing to do with the metatheoretical criteria for assessing theories that were discussed above. I will also argue that there are good reasons for believing that the most fundamental aspect of Hart's primary methodology is conceptual analysis. The type of conceptual analysis he advocates is meant to be based on an external rather than an internal perspective, and in that respect resembles the descriptive-explanatory method. For present purposes, however, the details of Hart's particular conception of conceptual analysis are not of paramount importance. Our concern is with Hart's claim that his theory of law is "general." It is clear enough what "generality" would mean in a pure descriptive-explanatory theory: the theory would apply to whatever range of social practices that its own categories of description, derived on the basis of their explanatory power, picked out. But what does it mean to say that legal theory is general when your methodology is some form of conceptual analysis?

It is worth emphasizing that Hart's starting-point in elucidating the concept of law is not an assumed pretheoretical knowledge of criteria that are capable of picking out, from among the social practices that have existed somewhere, sometimes, in the history of the world, those that constitute "law." As he says in the Postscript, "[t]he starting-point for this clarificatory task is the widespread common knowledge of a modern municipal legal system which on page 3 of this book I attribute to any educated man" (240). At the specified point in the text Hart lists as follows the "salient features" of a legal system that an educated person might be expected to be able to identify:

> "They comprise (i) rules forbidding or enjoining certain types of behaviour under penalty; (ii) rules requiring people to compensate those whom they injure in certain ways; (iii) rules specifying what must be done to make wills, contracts or other arrangements which confer rights and create obligations; (iv) courts to determine what the rules are and when they have been broken, and to fix the punishment or compensation to be paid; (v) a legislature to make new rules and abolish old ones."

Hart is clearly not saying that a social arrangement that failed to possess all these features could not be a legal system. In fact, according to his substantive positivist theory, which defines law in terms of a union of two types of rules, only features (i) and (iv) appear to be necessary for the existence of law. Rather, Hart's rationale for beginning with the salient features of a modern municipal legal system would seem to be this. He is pointing to these features as (possibly conceptually contingent) attributes of a certain type of social institution that is, *for us*, a clear central case of *our* concept of law. He will then focus on that type of institution as he undertakes the task of clarifying that concept. Once this task has been accomplished and we have a more satisfactory grasp of our own concept, we will be in a better position to say whether or not various other types of social practice—for example, so-called primitive legal systems, international law, historical practices of one kind or another, contemporary foreign practices quite different from our own, etc.—are instances of law, that is, instances of law according to our own lights. As Joseph Raz puts the point, "[t]here is nothing wrong in interpreting the institutions of other societies in terms of our typologies. This is an inevitable part of any intelligent attempt to understand other cultures."[80]

What the process of conceptual analysis involves will be examined in greater detail. For the moment, I wish only to emphasize the following point. Although the clarified concept of law that is supposed to emerge from Hart's process of theorizing will in one sense be general—once we have the concept, we can use it to elucidate radically different foreign or historical practices and classify them as being, from our perspective, law, non-law, or perhaps something in-between— there is nonetheless a clear sense in which the genesis of the enterprise is "local." Hart begins with the knowledge that he takes to be common to educated persons in modern societies of an institution that holds a central place within those societies. A modern municipal legal system, as described by Hart, is a relatively specific type of institution that is located within the framework of a fairly recent historical innovation, namely the state. Hart does not claim that all instances of what we would and should call law are in all respects like modern municipal legal systems, but even so his project of conceptual clarification takes this local manifestation of the concept as its starting-point.

One might quarrel with the characterization of "modern municipal legal systems" in general as "local," but Hart clearly begins with the institutions most familiar to his readers—in chapter 1 of *The Concept of Law* he discusses the knowledge that English people will have of the English legal system—and then

---

[80] Joseph Raz, *The Authority of Law*, (1979), p. 50.

assumes that in other countries "there are legal systems which are broadly similar in structure in spite of important differences" (3). At a certain point, as we encounter foreign institutions that are more and more different from our own, this assumption might come to beg the question. But the concern here is with a question of judgment that arises in the process of investigation rather than with a denial of the idea that legal theory must begin locally: how much do the practices of foreign societies or cultures have to differ from our own before we ought to regard them as something other than mere variants on our own practices?

Once we see that the starting-point of Hart's legal theory is local in the way just described, the distance between his jurisprudential methodology and Ronald Dworkin's begins to lose the appearance of an unbridgeable gulf. Dworkin's theoretical point of departure is the "collective" identification of "the practices that count as legal practices in our own culture": "We have legislatures and courts and administrative agencies and bodies, and the decisions these institutions make are reported in a canonical way."[81] This collective and rather rough-and-ready singling out of familiar institutions as the initial focus of jurisprudential inquiry is very much reminiscent of Hart's reliance on the knowledge that he says any educated person will possess of his own legal system and of others that are plainly similar to his own. The following description that Dworkin gives of this process of identification also seems to be very much in the spirit of Hart's enterprise, at least if we replace the phrase "the interpretive problem" by "the task of conceptual clarification":

> "It would be a mistake ... to think that we identify these institutions through some shared and intellectually satisfying definition of what a legal system necessarily is and what institutions necessarily make it up. Our culture presents us with legal institutions and with the idea that they form a system. The question which features they have, in virtue of which they combine as a distinctly legal system, is part of the interpretive problem."[82]

In Sections VI and VII I argue that, if we press hard enough on the notion of conceptual analysis, the result is not far removed from what Dworkin means by interpretation. For the moment, however, my concern is with the related issues of where legal theory starts and how general it is. Dworkin's starting-point is a set of institutions that he says is presented to us as a system by our culture; at other points in *Law's Empire* he speaks of interpreting our *legal* culture. While Dworkin clearly does not associate "our" legal culture with the legal system of any single country, Hart is probably right when he asserts in the Postscript that the initial scope of Dworkin's theorizing is limited to something like Anglo-American law (240). Even so, all that really seems to be at stake here is a difference of opinion about the following question: To what extent should we assume, on the basis of superficial resemblance alone and in advance of actually formulating a theory of law, that foreign institutions really are similar, in every respect that might turn out to be theoretically relevant, to those institutions that in our own societies we call "law"?

Dworkin is more cautious than Hart in the implicit answer that he gives to this question, but that by itself is hardly indicative of a deep methodological divide between the two. Both theorists begin locally; they just have different views on what should count as local. Where Dworkin begins with common law systems, Hart's point of departure is the broader notion of a modern municipal legal system. Perhaps Hart can be understood as bracketing the common law with the civil law and then treating this single category of system as his starting-point, since most clear instances of a modern municipal legal system either derive

---

[81] Ronald Dworkin, *Law's Empire* (1986), p. 91.
[82] *ibid.*

directly from, or were significantly influenced by, one or the other of these two traditions. But the common law and civil law have the same historical roots: they are two strands within a larger historical tradition. Whether one begins one's theorizing with the common law or with the broader tradition of which it is a part might conceivably have an influence on the content of one's substantive theory, but regarded strictly from the point of view of methodology this does not seem to be a matter of great significance. The underlying issue is, in Dworkin's words, "[w]hich [historical] changes are great enough to cut the thread of continuity"?[83] This question is undoubtedly an important one, but it arises *within* a methodological approach in which the need to begin locally is already a given.

Both Hart and Dworkin go on to suggest that we can make use of the theories of law that each will develop from his respective starting-point to make sense of social practices that truly are different from our own. Naturally, a difference of opinion about the scope of the starting-point also represents a difference of opinion about which foreign practices should be treated as truly different from our own. Dworkin initially excludes Nazi Germany from the scope of his theorizing, for example, but holds that we can use the theory of law he ultimately develops to see that there is a sense in which the Nazis had law as well as a sense in which they did not. Hart, on the other hand, assumes from the outset, apparently as a pretheoretical matter, that the Nazis really did, by our lights, have law. For the reasons already given, however, that difference should not, without more, be taken as an indication that Hart's theoretical project is radically different from Dworkin's. Of course I have not shown that their projects are not in the end radically different because I have only addressed the issues of starting-point and generality. I have said nothing about Hart's claim that his theory of law, unlike Dworkin's, is "descriptive," and it is to that issue that we must now turn.

## II. The descriptiveness of legal theory

Hart says in the Postscript that his theory of law is meant to be descriptive in the following sense: "[The theory] is morally neutral and has no justificatory aims: it does not seek to justify or commend on moral or other grounds the forms and structures which appear in my general account of law" (240). To assess this set of claims it will be helpful to look at the substantive content of Hart's theory in somewhat greater detail than we have so far done. The two minimum conditions that Hart specifies as necessary and sufficient for the existence of a legal system are (i) the acceptance of certain types of secondary social rules by officials, the most important of which is a rule of recognition laying down criteria of validity for so-called primary rules, and (ii) general compliance on the part of the population at large with the primary rules these criteria identify as valid (pp. 116–117). Of these two conditions, it is the first that lies at the core of Hart's theoretical account of law. Law, he says, "may most illuminatingly be characterized" as the union of primary and secondary rules (p. 94), a union that, borrowing a phrase from Austin, he further describes as "the key to the science of jurisprudence" (p. 81). Occasionally Hart puts his point in terms of the rule of recognition in particular, rather than in terms of secondary rules generally: "[It is] the ... complex social situation where a secondary rule of recognition is accepted and used for the identification of primary rules of obligation ... which deserves, if anything does, to be called the foundations of a legal system" (p. 100).

The rule of recognition is said by Hart to be a social (or customary) rule. Such rules are constituted both by a regular pattern of conduct and by "a distinctive normative attitude" that Hart refers to variously as the phenomenon of "acceptance" (p. 255) and as the rule's "internal aspect" (p. 56). The internal

---

[83] *ibid.*, pp. 69–70.

aspect concerns the fact that "if a social rule is to exist, some at least must look upon the behaviour in question as a general standard to be followed by the group as a whole" (p. 56). The point of view of such persons is referred to by Hart as the "internal" point of view; it is the point of view of one who accepts the rule as a guide to conduct and as a standard of criticism both for himself and for others in the group (p. 89). It is important to note that those who take up the internal point of view adopt an attitude of *shared* acceptance (p. 102), and they look upon the rules as standards that are "essentially common or public" (p. 116). Their acceptance takes the form of "a reflective critical attitude" to the relevant pattern of conduct, and is given characteristic expression through the use of normative terminology such as "ought," "must," and "should" (pp. 56–57). In the case of certain social rules, including in particular the rule of recognition, the terminology of "obligation" takes hold: "Rules are conceived and spoken of as imposing obligations when the general demand for conformity is insistent and the social pressure brought to bear upon those who deviate or threaten to deviate is great" (p. 86).

The notion of a rule of recognition is the cornerstone of Hart's theory of law. In a given legal system this rule exists simply because it is accepted by officials (in the sense of "acceptance" that emerges from Hart's characterization of social rules in general), so that its existence is said to be "a matter of fact" (p. 110). The theory thus characterizes law in purely factual, non-normative terms. Clearly this aspect of the theory is part of what Hart has in mind when he writes in the Postscript that he had intended to provide a theory of law that is descriptive. Hart also seems to be suggesting, however, that it is not just his particular theory that possesses this attribute, but the general enterprise in which he is engaged. Legal theory, or at least the type of legal theory that Hart has opted to pursue, is itself descriptive in character. In other words, Hart appears to be claiming to be a methodological as well as a substantive legal positivist.

The most straightforward understanding of methodological positivism would look to what I earlier called the descriptive-explanatory method. Legal theory is, on this view, a form of scientific enterprise the point of which is to advance, from an external viewpoint, descriptive, morally neutral theories of the social world. A particular theory adopts the characterization of empirical phenomena that it does because the theory's proponents believe that characterization has explanatory power. As was noted in the preceding section, explanatory power is most plausibly understood as referring to metatheoretical criteria for assessing scientific theories: predictive power, theoretical simplicity, and so on. On the descriptive-explanatory interpretation of Hart's methodology, the reason for equating "law" (understood now as a term of art internal to the theory) with social systems based on a rule of recognition would be that one has grounds for believing that such a characterization has explanatory power in the sense just described.

There is something to be said for the descriptive-explanatory interpretation of Hart's methodology. For one thing, it is consistent with Hart's avowedly external theoretical perspective; as he says repeatedly, his theory is intended to take account of the internal point of view, but not to be offered from that point of view. For another, this interpretation offers a sensible understanding of the *sort* of claim Hart seems to be making when he places the notion of a rule of recognition at the center of his theory of law. Hart's assertion that all instances of the type of institution that he initially sets out to study—*viz.* modern municipal legal systems—contain a rule of recognition is, on the face of it, an empirical rather than a conceptual claim. Empirical claims are exactly what one would expect to find in a descriptive-explanatory theory. Moreover, Hart appears to treat this particular empirical claim as *novel*. Seen in that light, the claim does not seem to be plausibly regarded as an analysis of the concept of law (*i.e.* it does not seem to be plausibly regarded as figuring in our shared conceptualization of the practices that *we* call law). On a descriptive-explanatory approach, however, there is no necessary reason why the theory's categories should track the concepts of the participants in the social practices under study.

There are, however, serious problems with the descriptive-explanatory reading of Hart's methodology. As we have seen, the substantive theory he advances characterizes the phenomenon of "law" in terms of the notion of a rule of recognition. On a descriptive-explanatory approach the reason for adopting such a characterization would be its explanatory power in a scientific sense. But Hart does not give us any reason to believe that his theory of law is superior, in terms of explanatory power thus understood, to what he calls radically external theories. He does not argue that theories of the latter kind, which look at social phenomena in purely behavioristic terms and treat the internal point of view as epiphenomenal at best, must necessarily be deficient in predictive power, for example. Nor does he make such an argument about the possible class of theories that take Hart's own notion of acceptance as their basic explanatory category and treat the distinction between primary and secondary rules as theoretically unimportant. Hart does invoke the notion of explanatory power, but not in the ordinary scientific sense. He is interested, rather, in the power of a theory to elucidate concepts: "We accord this union of elements [*i.e.* primary and secondary rules] a central place because of their explanatory power in elucidating the concepts that constitute the framework of legal thought" (p. 81). Because the social practices under study are our own, the apparent claim is that Hart's theory will clarify our understanding of our own conceptual framework.

Hart offers, in effect, two answers to the question of why secondary rules generally, and the rule of recognition in particular, are of key importance in legal theory. The first is an elaboration of the idea just discussed—namely that at least one goal of legal theory is conceptual clarification. Hart argues that both the idea of a social rule and the associated notion of the internal point of view are required to analyze the basic concepts of obligation and duty. But there is, he says, a range of other legal concepts, such as authority, state, official, legislation, jurisdiction, validity, and legal power, that must be analyzed by reference to the internal point of view of a particular type of social rule, namely secondary rules that have been accepted by a certain subgroup within society ("officials") (pp. 98–99). Hart's critique of Austin's theory of law as orders backed by threats is, in essence, that it does not have the internal resources to elucidate these concepts. However, the concepts of authority, state, legislation, etc., are *our* concepts, where "we" must be understood as referring to participants in—or at least the subjects of—modern municipal legal systems. These are, in other words, the notions that we use to conceptualize certain of our own practices. This lends support to the suggestion that, when he speaks of conceptual analysis, Hart has in mind the clarification of the conceptual framework that we apply to certain aspects of our own social behavior. This is not, however, a standard goal of descriptive-explanatory theory. A radically external theory that transcended or ignored the participants' conceptualization of their own practice might well have greater explanatory power in the usual scientific sense. Degree of conceptual clarification appears, in fact, to be the sole basis by which Hart would judge the success of particular theories of law. Conceptual analysis is apparently an end in itself, and not just an extra criterion of adequacy that has been conjoined with explanatory power as ordinarily understood.

The second answer that Hart gives to the question of why the rule of recognition should have a key role to play in legal theory concerns certain defects that he says are associated with a simple regime of primary rules. Such a regime is said to be, as compared to a system containing secondary rules, uncertain, static, and inefficient (pp. 91–94). This list of defects is best understood as a reference back to an earlier statement by Hart that "[t]he principal functions of the law as a means of social control are ... to be seen in the diverse ways in which the law is used to control, to guide, and to plan life out of court" (p. 40). As Hart puts the point in the Postscript, the "primary function of the law [is] guiding the conduct of its subjects" (p. 249). While a regime of primary rules guides conduct, it does not do so *well*. A system containing secondary rules (of recognition, change, and adjudication) is better at this task because it is more certain, the content of the rules can be deliberately changed, and the rules can be more efficiently enforced (pp. 94–99). Thus, secondary rules, according to Hart, remedy the defects of a simple regime of primary rules.

This second argument for the centrality in legal theory of secondary rules is not coterminous in scope with the first argument. The first argument is that the notion of a secondary rule is necessary for the analysis of certain specific legal concepts, such as authority, legislation, and legal power. The second argument is that the notion of a secondary rule is necessary for the proper analysis of the more general concept of *law*. Thus, even if the first argument is correct in its claim about the concepts of authority, legislation, and so forth, it leaves open the possibility that the overarching category of "law" should abstract from the distinction between primary and secondary rules. As was suggested earlier, it is at least conceivable that the primary theoretical indicator of "law" might be the general phenomenon that Hart describes as the acceptance of social rules. The significant feature of those systems of rules that counted as law might then be, not whether they contained secondary rules, but rather whether they were backed by serious rather than trivial social pressure. On an understanding of law along those lines, social systems based on the union of primary and secondary rules would count as law, but so would certain systems consisting of primary rules alone.[84] Hart's second argument is intended to show that systems of the former type are in fact the paradigm of law, and not just a special case.

The statement that a regime of primary rules has defects, like the statement that these defects are remedied by the introduction of a rule of recognition and other secondary rules, is an evaluative claim. The values in question relate, as I have said, to the guidance of conduct, which means that they have a normative dimension. The descriptive-explanatory method assesses theories by means of criteria that are properly called evaluative, such as predictive power and simplicity, but the values in question are applicable to all scientific theories, and they are not normative in character. Moreover, Hart is making evaluative claims not about theories but about the very social practices he is studying. It does not, however, seem consonant with the descriptive-explanatory method (*i.e.* with the scientific method) that the descriptive categories adopted by a particular theory should be based on evaluative judgments of this kind. Hart's theoretical enterprise thus cannot plausibly be regarded as grounded in that method, or at any rate in a pure version of it.

The nature of the two arguments that Hart advances for the centrality in legal theory of the notion of a secondary rule—that this notion is required for the analysis of specific legal concepts such as authority and legislation, and that it is required for the analysis of the general concept of law—enable us to reach the following two conclusions about his methodology in legal theory. First, he has not adopted anything like a pure descriptive-explanatory approach; he is not doing science in the usual sense. Second, his main methodological technique is conceptual analysis, by which he means the clarification or elucidation of our manner of conceptualizing our own social practices. We must, of course, inquire

---

[84] In speaking of regimes of primary social rules that are backed by physical sanctions administered by the community at large rather than by officials, Hart says that "we shall be inclined to classify [such] rules as a primitive or rudimentary form of law" (p. 86). The characterization of such a regime as "primitive" is pretheoretical and potentially question-begging. By itself, it cannot bear the weight of a fundamental theoretical demarcation between the simpler social arrangement and systems based on a union of primary and secondary rules. It is for that reason that Hart requires the argument that a regime of primary rules is in certain respects defective.

more closely into what this technique involves, and one way to do this is to return to Hart's claim in the Postscript that his intent was to provide a theory of law that is "descriptive." What does this term mean when it is applied to conceptual analysis?

One thing the term "descriptive" might mean in the context of conceptual analysis is that the concept of law—either the concept that emerges from Hart's theorizing or, to the extent that this turns out to be different, our general, shared concept—has a certain type of content: it picks out social practices as "law" on the basis of purely factual, non-normative criteria. As was noted earlier, this is clearly a claim that Hart does wish to make, at least so far as his own theory is concerned. The particular conceptualization of law that he defends characterizes law in terms of two types of rules, which are in turn characterized by reference to various kinds of social fact.[85] Understood in that way, however, the claim that legal theory is descriptive is not methodological in nature. It is simply a claim about the content of the concept of law. It is a claim, in effect, that that concept is not thick; it picks out social practices on the basis of purely factual criteria, rather than, say, mixed moral and factual criteria. It is, in effect, just a way of stating the main thesis of substantive legal positivism.

But when Hart writes in the Postscript that his aim was to provide a "descriptive" theory of law, he seems to be making a claim about methodology and not just about the content of his own theory; he is, in effect, holding himself out to be both a methodological and a substantive legal positivist. The methodological claim is not, presumably, that the concept of law is *necessarily* non-thick—that we could not have a concept of law that included normative or moral considerations among its identifying criteria—because there is no good reason to think that such a claim is true. The more plausible way to understand the methodological claim is that Hart is simply setting out to *describe* the conceptual scheme that we apply to certain of our own social practices (those that can be identified on a pretheoretical basis as "modern municipal legal systems"). Such a project can presumably be carried out in a morally neutral manner whether the relevant concepts turn out to be thick or non-thick. On this view, Hart is simply describing the content of the relevant concepts and the relationships between them, whatever that content and those relationships turn out to be. This interpretation of Hart's methodological positivism is also consistent with the external perspective from which the theory is clearly meant to be offered. The idea is to describe and elucidate our conceptual scheme from the outside, as it were. In that way the theorist can remain neutral with respect to such questions as whether the social practice in question is justified, valuable, in need of reform, and so forth. He or she can simply describe what is there.

I believe that the interpretation of Hart's methodology that was sketched in the preceding paragraph captures fairly accurately Hart's own understanding of what is involved in doing legal theory. He intends to engage in conceptual analysis, but from the outside rather than the inside. It is important to emphasize that this is not just an application of the descriptive-explanatory method of ordinary science.

---

[85] The point here is that Hart claims that law *as a general type of institution* is identifiable solely by reference to various kinds of social fact; thus, the general concept of law is non-thick. But, as Hart makes clear in the Postscript, he does not think that each valid law within a legal system must be identifiable solely in social terms; the rule of recognition can adopt moral as well as social criteria of validity. This soft or incorporationist version of positivism is to be contrasted with the sources thesis defended by Raz, which holds that all laws must be identifiable as such solely by reference to social facts and without resort to moral argument. It will not be necessary, for purposes of this essay, to decide between these two versions of positivism. For the best recent discussion of incorporationism, *see* Jules L. Coleman, *"Reason and Authority"* in The Autonomy of Law: Essays on Legal Positivism (R. George ed., 1995), p. 287. On the sources thesis, *see* Joseph Raz, [*ante*, 391–392].

The starting-point of inquiry is the participants' own conceptualization of their practice, and from the perspective of the descriptive-explanatory approach that is an arbitrary limitation. Beyond that, Hart seems not to be particularly interested in the predictive power of his theory, or in other aspects of explanatory power in the usual scientific sense. Most importantly, his characterization of the general concept of law relies on evaluative judgments that simply have no place in the descriptive-explanatory methodology. Hart is engaged in a particular type of conceptual analysis that can appropriately be described as descriptive, but which is nonetheless distinct from the standard methodology of science. At this point it becomes necessary to inquire more closely into the nature of external conceptual analysis, as we might call this approach. That is the task we undertake in the following four sections.

### III. Description versus elucidation: the problem of normativity

In work published subsequent to *The Concept of Law*, Hart has written as follows: "For the understanding of [not only law but any other form of normative social structure] the methodology of the empirical sciences is useless; what is needed is a 'hermeneutic' method which involves portraying rule-governed behavior as it appears to its participants, who see it as conforming or failing to conform to certain shared standards."[86] Hart's rejection of the "methodology of the empirical sciences" might be read narrowly, as a rejection of behaviorist or radically empiricist methods of inquiry that forbid the theorist from taking account of mental states and attitudes.

In light of the discussion in the preceding section, however, I believe the better view is that Hart is simply not employing the scientific method at all, at least in anything like the usual sense. He has not set out to offer a descriptive-explanatory theory, the adequacy of which is to be judged by standard metatheoretical criteria such as predictive power. Instead, he has deliberately invoked the notion of *verstehen* from the hermeneutic tradition in the philosophy of social science, which suggest that his theoretical goal is to understand how the participants in a social practice regard their own behavior. But Hart does not want to go as far as those hermeneuts who, like Peter Winch, think that the theorist has no choice but to "join the practice" and theorize about it from the participants' point of view.[87] Hart's project involves "clarifying" or "elucidating" the participants' conceptual framework, but from an external perspective. This can, perhaps, be viewed as a hybrid methodology. As in the hermeneutic tradition Hart aims to understand how the participants regard their own behavior, but he hopes to achieve this understanding by taking up an external, observational stance reminiscent of that adopted by pure descriptive-explanatory theories.

That this is the best interpretation of Hart's claim to be doing descriptive legal theory, and hence the best way to make sense of his methodological positivism, is suggested by the following passage from the Postscript. The passage is long, but worth quoting in full:

> "[Dworkin's] central objection [to descriptive legal theory] seems to be that legal theory must take account of an internal perspective on the law which is the viewpoint of an insider or participant in a legal system, and no adequate account of this internal perspective can be provided by a descriptive theory whose viewpoint is not that of a participant but that of an external observer. But there is in fact nothing in the project of a descriptive jurisprudence as exemplified in my book to preclude a non-participant external observer from describing the ways in which participants view the law from such an internal point of view. So I explained in this book at some length that participants

[86]  H. L. A. Hart, *Essays in Jurisprudence and Philosophy* (1983), p. 13.
[87]  Peter Winch, *The Idea of a Social Science* (1958).

manifest their internal point of view in accepting the law as providing guides to their conduct and standards of criticism. Of course a descriptive legal theorist does not as such himself share the participants' acceptance of the law in these ways, but he can and should describe such acceptance, as indeed I have attempted to do in this book. It is true that for this purpose the descriptive legal theorist must *understand* what it is to adopt the internal point of view and in that limited sense he must be able to put himself in the place of an insider; but this is not to accept the law or endorse the insider's internal point of view or in any other way to surrender his descriptive stance." (p. 242)

In this passage Hart emphasizes the theorist's role in *describing* such facts as that participants accept rules as guides to conduct and standards for criticism. It is, of course, quite possible to describe social phenomena in a more or less value-neutral fashion, as Hart wishes to do. But it is worth bearing in mind that any given social phenomenon can be accurately described in an indefinitely large number of ways. Descriptions will differ from one another, for example, in the level of generality at which the practice is described (e.g., descriptions of individuals one by one, versus generalizations about all individuals in the relevant group). Different descriptions will individuate practices and sub-practices in different ways. There will also be differences in degree of selectivity, as every description inevitably fails to include some attributes of the object being described. Descriptions thus differ from one another with respect to what and how much they leave out, or, to put the point more positively, they differ insofar as they focus on or highlight different aspects of what is being observed. Thus, in observing one and the same social practice one onlooker—call him Oliver—might call attention to the existence and motivating force of punitive sanctions, while another—call him Herbert—might emphasize that at least some people are moved to act because they accept the practice, internalize it, and treat it as a guide to proper conduct. Some descriptions, taking what Hart calls an extreme external point of view (89), will characterize a social practice behavioristically, without reference to anyone's mental states. Other descriptions, like Hart's, will bring in the participants' attitudes and reasons for action. And so on.

Most of these possible descriptions will be of absolutely no interest to us, scientifically, philosophically, or otherwise. A set of descriptive statements is not, by itself, a *theory* of any kind, and that is so even if the statements are in certain respects general (*i.e.* apply to more than one occasion, or to more than one person). In ordinary science, a set of statements becomes a theory by making (preferably testable) predictions and/or by conceptualizing the world in a novel or abstract way. Hart, however, is not apparently interested in predictive power, and the whole point of his approach is to describe existing conceptualizations rather than to create new ones. To find a set of descriptive statements that constitutes the basis of a meaningful (non-scientific) theory, it is first of all clear that we must be observing the practice with a particular purpose in mind. Hart's purpose is, as I have said, to offer an external analysis of the participants' conceptualization of their practice, which means looking at that conceptualization from the outside.[88] Thus, Hart's particular descriptive account of law, focusing as it does on the phenomenon of acceptance, presumably becomes transformed into a theory because, as Hart emphasizes at a number of points throughout *The Concept of Law*, the account is supposed to "elucidate" or "clarify" the concepts that participants use: "We accord this union of elements a central place because of their explanatory power in elucidating the concepts that constitute the framework of legal thought" (p. 81).

It bears emphasis yet again that this notion of elucidation cannot simply be another term for explanatory power in the scientific sense. If that were the case,

---

[88] "For the observer may, without accepting the rules himself, assert that the group accepts the rules, and thus may from the outside refer to the way in which *they* are concerned with them from the internal point of view" (p. 89).

then Hart's theory would have to compete in the forum of predictive power with, for example, theories of social behavior that abstracted from the participants' own conceptualization of what they were doing and used different categories of description altogether. Of course, one of Hart's claims is that behaviorists and radical empiricists are wrong to insist that mental states and attitudes should as a matter of methodological principle be excluded from theories of social behavior, but it does not follow that there cannot be behaviorist theories, let alone that a behaviorist theory could not have greater explanatory power in the scientific sense than Hart's theory. Hart, however, does not even address this issue, and that must be because he understands "elucidation" in a very different way. At this point we must therefore inquire more closely into what Hart means by this notion, asking in particular whether the goal of conceptual elucidation is consistent with a background methodological framework that insists on accurate external description.

Scientific theories are capable of transforming the way that we look at the world; they can lead us to reject old conceptual schemes and to adopt new ones. But Hart does not purport to be offering a scientific theory, at least not in the usual sense, and in any event the object of his descriptive efforts is itself an existing conceptual scheme. Because a primary goal of description is presumably accuracy, one would have thought that the external observer should simply describe what is there, confusions, obscurities, and all. The description should, so to speak, be passive, mirroring whatever the observer finds; the aim should not be to transform, even in so apparently an innocuous way as by "clarification," that which is being observed. Thus, if, as Hart claims, participants in modern municipal legal systems, or at least some of those participants, are unclear what they mean when they speak of rules, obligations, authority, sovereignty, and so on, an accurate external description should surely just report that fact. If different people have different understandings of the relevant concepts, that fact too should simply be reported. Naturally, I do not mean to deny that an observer's external description of even a very familiar social practice like law could not give rise to new knowledge. For example, Hart would claim that the statement that all modern municipal legal systems possess a rule of recognition is an empirical observation.[89] If it is an empirical observation it is a novel one, and if it is true we have learned something. But producing new empirical knowledge is not the same thing as analyzing, elucidating, or clarifying a concept. The latter terms all suggest that Hart is employing a methodological technique that goes beyond, and perhaps is in some tension with, the passive external description of an existing conceptual scheme.

Let us suppose Hart is right in thinking that the statement "All modern municipal legal systems possess a rule of recognition" is a straightforward empirical observation. Even if that is so, Hart's theoretical claim that all instances of *law* possess a rule of recognition is not empirical in character, or at least it is not merely empirical. It is a conceptual claim of some kind that has, presumably, been produced by Hart's technique of conceptual analysis. Because this conceptual claim is, like its empirical counterpart, also novel, it is natural to ask whether the technique that produced it is consistent with the goal of accurate

---

[89]   Hart would claim this because he holds (i) that the term "modern municipal legal system" has a generally agreed-upon pretheoretical meaning and extension, and (ii) that statements about the existence of a rule of recognition are simply statements of fact. I shall suggest in Section V, however, that to support the claim that even a particular legal system possesses a rule of recognition requires normative argument; *a fortiori*, the same would be true of the claim that all modern municipal legal systems possess such a rule. A less controversial example of how external observation could produce new knowledge might be the empirical demonstration or refutation of the claim that, say, all modern municipal legal systems permit greater penalties to be imposed for completed crimes, as opposed to attempts.

external description. Has the theory, through "clarification," in some way transformed the concept that it was supposed to be describing from the outside? A rule of recognition is not, after all, one of those "salient features" of a modern municipal legal system that Hart says would be known to any educated person. Indeed, the originality of Hart's substantive theory of law might be said to consist in part in the claim to have brought to light a previously unnoticed empirical fact about modern municipal legal systems, namely that they all contain a rule of recognition. But that means, among other things, that Hart cannot respond to the concern that he has, in clarifying our concept of law, effectively transformed it by maintaining that he is simply picking out a known feature of modern legal systems that is, as it were, particularly salient. Pushing this point a bit further, it is not immediately clear how drawing attention to a hitherto unnoticed empirical fact could even figure in a piece of conceptual analysis, external or otherwise.

It will be helpful at this point if we ask just why Hart thinks that external conceptual analysis is a theoretically fruitful enterprise in the first place. Put slightly differently, in what respect does he believe that the concept of law stands in need of clarification or elucidation? Hart's response to this question begins to take shape early on in *The Concept of Law*, when he discusses the suggestion that nothing more is required by way of an answer to the question "What is law?" than an enumeration of those features of a modern municipal legal system that are, according to Hart, already known to most educated persons. (Such an enumeration is, of course, a good example of passive external description). This suggestion will not do, he says, because it fails to throw any light on what it is about law that has always puzzled legal theorists (5). As to what the sources of puzzlement are, Hart points to "three recurrent issues": "How does law differ from and how is it related to orders backed by threats? How does legal obligation differ from, and how is it related to, moral obligation? What are rules, and to what extent is law an affair of rules?" (13).

The point to notice here is that all three of these issues are aspects of, or involve possible solutions to, a more general problem, which we might label the problem of the normativity of law. In speaking of the normativity of law, I mean to refer to two facts: first, legal discourse is pervaded by such normative terms as "obligation," "right," and "duty"; and second, legal authorities and officials—metaphorically speaking, the law itself—purport by their actions of legislation, adjudication, and so on to place us under obligations that we would not otherwise have. Hart, possibly speaking loosely, expresses this latter point in terms not of purported but actual obligation: "The most prominent general feature of law at all times and places is that its existence means that certain kinds of human conduct are no longer optional, but in *some* sense obligatory" (p. 6, *cf.* p. 82). In speaking of the *problem* of the normativity of law, I mean to refer to a congeries of questions of the following kind: How is the concept of legal obligation to be analyzed? How is the concept of legal obligation related to that of moral obligation? What does it mean to claim authority over someone? Can law in fact give rise to obligations, either moral or of some other type, that people would not otherwise have? Clearly, Hart's "three recurrent issues" belong to this congeries.[90]

It is plausible to think that the provision of an account of the normativity of law is a central task of jurisprudence, if not the central task. In speaking of an "account" of the normativity of law I am being deliberately vague, so as to subsume such disparate views as, on the one hand, the natural law thesis that every law properly so-called is morally binding and, on the other hand, the Holmesian thesis that legal obligation is an empty concept. Whatever the nature

---

[90] This point is obvious in the case of the last two issues. It holds true of the first issue as well because Hart's concern there is with Austin's reductive analysis of the concept of legal obligation (*i.e.* with the analysis of legal obligation in terms of orders backed by threats).

of the particular account that a theorist offers, however, the central questions he or she must confront are these: Does law affect persons' reasons for action in the way that it claims to, namely by giving them obligations that they would not otherwise have? If law does so affect persons' reasons, what is the philosophical character of the resulting obligations and under what circumstances do they arise? It is because of this focus on the (apparent) reason-givingness of law that jurisprudence can plausibly be thought to be a *philosophical* discipline: it is, in effect, a branch of practical philosophy (*i.e.* the philosophy of practical reason). Hart is thus on strong ground in apparently placing the problem of the normativity of law at the heart of his own theoretical project. It is, moreover, very plausible to think that an inquiry into the normativity of law is, at least in part, a *conceptual* inquiry. Most people subject to modern municipal legal systems would probably identify as central to their experience of law the law's claim to authority—its claim, that is, to place us, through the actions of officials, under obligations that we would not otherwise have. (Many persons, but by no means all, would go on to add that the law succeeds in this endeavor.) The idea that the law purports to bind us by exercising authority over us is thus very plausibly regarded as an element of the concept of law. Hart implicitly makes this claim, and here, too, he is on very strong ground.

Viewed in methodological terms, then, Hart's project appears to be to clarify, from an external perspective, our shared concept of law, focusing in particular on the idea that law purports to bind us through authoritative acts. The substantive theory itself falls into three related parts. First, there is the general account of obligation, which Hart analyzes in terms of social rules. Second, there is the account of the family of legal concepts like authority, state, legislation, validity, and legal power, which Hart analyzes in terms of a particular type of social rule, namely secondary rules accepted by officials. Third, there is the analysis of the concept of law itself. Here Hart's account is that law is the union of secondary rules, and in particular the rule of recognition, with those primary rules that the rule of recognition identifies as valid. To arrive at a better understanding of what Hart has in mind when he speaks in general of analyzing or elucidating concepts, it will be helpful to examine in turn each of these three specific instances of analysis.

### *IV. External conceptual analysis: obligation*

As already mentioned, Hart analyzes obligation, including legal obligation, in terms of social rules. A social rule exists when (some appropriate but unspecified proportion of) the members of a group accept a general pattern of behavior as a common standard of conduct for all members of the group. Deviations from the pattern are regarded as justifying demands for conformity and warranting criticism that is typically expressed in the normative language of "right," "ought," "should," etc. (pp. 55–57). In the Postscript, Hart has made clear that his account is meant to apply only to *conventional* rules—that is, rules for which the general conformity of the group constitutes at least part of the reason for individuals' acceptance of the relevant pattern as a common standard of conduct (pp. 255–256).

A social rule is spoken of as giving rise to an *obligation* when the social pressure underlying the rule is particularly serious or insistent (86). Hart mentions two other characteristics of obligation that he says "go naturally together with this one." First, "[t]he rules supported by this serious pressure are thought important because they are believed to be necessary to the maintenance of social life or some highly prized feature of it" (p. 87). Hart gives the examples of rules that restrict the free use of violence, require honesty, and enforce promises. "Secondly, it is generally recognized that the conduct required by these rules may, while benefitting others, conflict with what the person who owes the duty may wish to do" (p. 87). Hart goes on to observe that obligations are thus commonly thought of as involving sacrifice or renunciation. Even so, those who accept an obligation-imposing rule need not do so because they regard it as morally binding. Acceptance can also be based on "calculations of long-term interest; disinterested interest in others; an unreflecting inherited or traditional attitude; or the mere wish to do as others do" (p. 203, *cf.* p. 257).

The essence of Hart's response to the problem of the normativity of law is thus to point to the phenomenon of acceptance, where acceptance need not be grounded in moral reason. The majority (or some other appropriate minimal proportion) of a group's members regard a general pattern of conduct from the internal point of view, meaning they regard the conduct as a general standard that is binding or obligatory for everyone in the group. It is in these terms that Hart wishes to account for the normativity of social rules, and law involves a special case of a social rule, namely the rule of recognition. It is, however, not entirely clear whether Hart believes that acceptance of a social rule gives rise to an *actual* obligation for the relevant group's members. He plainly does not think that acceptance creates a moral obligation, but at various points he can be understood as suggesting that it gives rise to what might be called a social obligation. The basis and character of such an obligation would be rather mysterious, however,[91] and in any event the focus of Hart's theory is clearly on the external descriptive statement that people *regard themselves* as obligated by the rule.

We must now ask the following question: To what extent can this external descriptive account of obligation be conceived as an analysis or elucidation of our common concept? Typically, the philosophical analysis of a concept attempts to make explicit what the theorist claims is in some sense already implicit in our common understanding. This can take the form of drawing attention to propositions that the theorist argues are either implicitly pre-supposed or necessarily entailed by the concept's having the content that it has. It can also take the form of an attempt to show that, properly understood, the concept is equivalent in either meaning or use to some other concept or concepts. Sometimes such an analysis will be explicitly and trivially semantic—for example, the statement that the concept "bachelor" comprehends the concept "unmarried"—but in interesting cases it will amount to a more ambitious philosophical attempt to *reduce* one concept to a logical configuration of others. Austin, for example, famously advanced a reductive analysis of obligation that Hart, in an equally famous critique, thoroughly demolished. The precise nature of a reduction is controversial, but perhaps we can say that it consists in an attempt to make explicit an alleged implicit equivalence in meaning between the concept being analyzed and the concepts to which it is ostensibly being reduced.

Finally, conceptual analysis can take the form of argument, within an established intellectual and cultural tradition, about the meaning and significance of the concept and its relationship to other concepts.[92] Sometimes such argument will be normative in character. But this does not involve us in any confusion because, as Joseph Raz points out, in the case of certain concepts "there is an interdependence between conceptual and normative argument."[93] Raz's example is authority, but the point is equally true of obligation. In fact, in the legal context, the two concepts are closely intertwined, as it is by means of the exercise of authority that the law claims to create new obligations. I will have something to say in the following section about the nature of legal authority. For now, it will suffice to point out that an analysis of the concept of obligation might well take

---

[91] *See* Ronald Dworkin, "The Model of Rules II" in *Taking Rights Seriously* (rev. ed., 1977), p. 46.

[92] *Cf.* Joseph Raz, *The Morality of Freedom* (1986), pp. 63–64.

[93] *ibid.*, p. 63.

the form of normative argument attempting to establish the conditions under which obligations are not just claimed to exist but really do exist (focusing, perhaps, on obligations of a particular sort, such as conventional obligations, or obligations ostensibly created by authority). An alternative analysis might be similarly normative but with a skeptical outcome, arguing that there are no obligations of the kind in question.

Hart's externally oriented, descriptive account of obligation cannot be said to offer an analysis of that concept in any of the senses discussed in the preceding two paragraphs. It does not offer a normative argument as to when, if ever, social rules really do create obligations, as opposed to the perception of obligations. Certainly the descriptive statement that people *regard* themselves and others as obligated by a general practice cannot, without more, tell us if and when they are in fact so obligated. If, on the other hand, we try to interpret Hart as offering either a semantic or a reductive analysis of obligation, the account is plainly deficient. If the members of the relevant group regard themselves as obligated in the sense of obligation that is supposedly being analyzed, then the account is circular. If they regard themselves as obligated in some different sense then, as Hart does not specify what that different sense is, the account is incomplete. In any event the only plausible candidate for that different sense would be moral obligation, and Hart is clear that those who adopt the internal point of view do not, or at least do not have to, regard themselves as obligated morally.

As it happens, Hart's account of obligation does not suffer from circularity or incompleteness, but that is because it cannot be regarded as a proper analysis. At its core it is simply a descriptive statement that (a certain proportion of) members of the relevant group regard themselves and all others in the group as obligated to conform to some general practice. This statement uses rather than analyzes the concept of obligation. In the original text of *The Concept of Law* Hart in effect maintains that officials regard themselves and all other officials as obligated, in that unanalyzed sense, by the general practice that constitutes the rule of recognition. To those who so regard themselves, this presumably does not come as news. If they or others want to know whether they are in fact under such an obligation, and if so why, enlightenment is not forthcoming. Precisely because Hart's account of obligation is descriptive and external, it cannot be said to have succeeded in clarifying or elucidating the concept in any significant way.

In the Postscript, Hart specifies that social rules must be understood as conventional practices. This means that members of the group (have reason to) regard themselves as obligated, at least in part, precisely because there is general conformity to the pattern of conduct that constitutes the social rule. We have here the beginning, but only the beginning, of one possible philosophical analysis of the concept of legal obligation. A complete analysis would need to tell us why and under what conditions the mere fact of general conformity to a pattern of conduct can help to create a reason for action, amounting to an obligation, for individuals to conform their own conduct to the pattern. While there are well-known philosophical accounts of conventionalism that attempt to answer these questions, the thesis that law is underpinned by a conventional rule is nonetheless a controversial one. Dworkin famously disputed it in "The Model of Rules II," for example.[94] This particular debate between Hart and Dworkin is philosophical in nature, not empirical. As I will argue more fully in the following sections, normative argument, probably of a moral and political nature, will be required to settle it. For now, I simply wish to draw attention to two points. First, the thought that such a debate might be required to settle an important question in legal theory suggests that more is at issue here than the neutral description of a social practice. Second and relatedly, such a debate seems best construed as taking place not between two outside observers but rather between two insiders,

---

[94] Dworkin, *op. cit.*, note 91, pp. 53–54, 59–61.

participants in the practice who disagree, on philosophical rather than on empirical grounds, about the practice's fundamental nature.

Recall that Hart was originally motivated to produce his theories of obligation, authority, and law by puzzles concerning the normativity of law. The essence of the problem of the normativity of law is philosophical: Docs law in fact obligate us in the way that it purports to do? This is an issue that arises within the philosophy of practical reason, and it would seem inevitable that its resolution will require normative and probably moral argument. An external description of the practice, to the effect that people *regard* themselves and others as obligated, is not likely to succeed in elucidating either the general concept of obligation or the specific claim that the law creates new obligations that would not otherwise exist.

## V. External conceptual analysis: authority

The second part of Hart's substantive theory of law is the account he gives of such concepts as authority, legislation, and validity. These concepts must be understood, Hart argues, by reference to secondary social rules. The basic idea is that officials accept, and thereby regard themselves as obligated by, the rule of recognition and certain other secondary rules that Hart calls *rules of change and rules of adjudication* (pp. 91–99). All of these are second-order rules—that is, they are rules about (primary) rules. Rules of change confer authority on legislatures and perhaps courts to create new primary rules and repeal or amend old ones. Rules of adjudication confer authority on courts to determine whether a primary rule has been broken. The rule of recognition provides authoritative criteria for identifying primary rules as valid, and imposes a duty on courts and perhaps other officials to apply those rules. Hart notes that close connections exist among these various types of secondary rule. The rule of recognition will necessarily make reference to any rules of change, and a rule of adjudication, conferring jurisdiction on courts, will in effect be a primitive form of a rule of recognition. Hart clearly regards the rule of recognition as the most fundamental secondary rule in a legal system.

As in the case of Hart's account of obligation, it is not clear that his account of the concepts of authority, validity, and so on is in any significant sense properly designated an *analysis*. This is so, at least, as long as he insists on sticking with an external, purely descriptive theoretical perspective. To see this, notice first that Hart maintains that statements *about* rules of recognition, to the effect either that they exist or that they possess or fail to possess value of some kind, are necessarily external in character (pp. 107–110). But there is no reason why participants in a social practice should have to hold a particular external view of their practice, or indeed any external view of it at all. As Hart notes, "[f]or the most part the rule of recognition is not stated, but its existence is *shown* in the way in which particular rules are identified, either by courts or other officials or private persons and their advisers" (p. 101). All that need necessarily be the case, apparently, is that a certain subgroup within the larger society—the so-called officials—regard themselves as bound by a rule that the externally observing theorist, but not necessarily the officials themselves, can characterize as both a social rule and as a rule of recognition. Neither officials nor others within the larger group require the general concept of either type of rule, which consequently need not enter—indeed, given Hart's insistence that statements about rules of recognition are necessarily external, perhaps cannot enter—into whatever conceptualization of their practice that they hold. The *idea* of a rule of recognition appears to be an external theoretical notion, an instance of which has, from outside the practice, been observed within it. But simply to make such an observation does not, without more, constitute a clarification or elucidation of the participants' own conceptual scheme.

This is not to deny that participants, upon being told by the friendly neighborhood legal theorist that their practice contains a rule of recognition, would not learn something about themselves. But they would come by that knowledge, and in the process master the new concept of a rule of recognition, *qua* external observers of their own practice. Their new knowledge could therefore not be said to elucidate or clarify—to offer an analysis of—their internal conceptual scheme. Of course, the natural response at this point is to argue that, even though the participants did not previously possess the concept of a rule of recognition, that concept was implicitly presupposed by their internal concepts of authority, validity, legal power, etc. Even though the participants might not have realized it, their internal conceptual scheme had already committed them to the idea of a rule of recognition. When this commitment is made explicit, the conceptual scheme is thereby clarified or elucidated. This is a perfectly reasonable characterization of how conceptual clarification might take place. The difficulty, however, is that the claim that the participants' existing conceptual scheme implicitly presupposes the idea of a rule of recognition looks more like an internal than an external statement. It is not a passive description offered from without, but rather an active clarification offered from within. As for the possible suggestion that statements about rules of recognition can be both external descriptions and internal clarifications, that might well be true. But if, as Hart states, the primary purpose of his theorizing is conceptual clarification, then for theoretical purposes it is the internal statement that matters, not the external one. If Hart's theory is to succeed in achieving this purpose, then it must be an an internal rather than an external theory.

Consider once again the debate between Dworkin and Hart that was mentioned briefly in the preceding section. Hart argues that law is underpinned by a conventional social rule, whereas Dworkin maintains that the foundation of law might be a concurrent rather than a conventional normative practice. A concurrent normative practice is one in which the members of a group "are agreed in asserting the same, or much the same, normative rule, but they do not count the fact of agreement as an essential part of their grounds for asserting that rule."[95] In the case of convention, the fact of agreement does count as an essential part of the case for accepting the rule. How would the debate to settle the question of whether law is a conventional or a concurrent normative practice proceed? One might begin by looking to the reasons that officials and others actually give, or would be prepared to give, for accepting the authority of law. This would be an empirical and a descriptive enterprise, and one that could be carried on from an external perspective. Moreover, it is at least conceivable that the members of the community under study might be in substantial and explicit agreement that theirs was a conventional practice in the sense just defined. If so, Hart could claim at least a limited victory in the debate. He would have succeeded in giving an external, purely descriptive account of a social practice that was, as advertised, conventional in character. At least in the special circumstances envisaged, the suggestion of the preceding paragraph that Hart must "go internal" seems to be mistaken.

Notice, however, that Hart could only claim this limited victory in the unlikely event that there existed substantial explicit agreement among participants that theirs was, in fact, a conventional social practice. In that case, the idea of a rule of recognition—understood explicitly to be a conventional, second-order social rule—would already figure in their conceptualization of that practice. They would already possess, internally, the concept of a rule of recognition, although probably not under that name. Their conceptual scheme would therefore not stand in need of clarification or elucidation.

If, however, we assume with Hart that there *is* a need for clarification, and in

---

[95] Dworkin, *op. cit.*, note 91, p. 53.

particular a need to make people aware of a previously unacknowledged conceptual commitment to a rule of recognition, then by hypothesis there is no substantial explicit agreement that the practice is a conventional one. The empirical data underdetermine the theory. Not only does this appear to be the situation that Hart is implicitly assuming to be the case, but it represents by far the most plausible supposition about the way things actually are. Some people will simply not accept the authority of law. Others will do so because they believe that law is a conventional normative practice in something like Hart's sense. Yet others will believe, with Dworkin, that law is a concurrent normative practice. Many, perhaps the vast majority, will accept the authority of the law without any very clear sense of why they are doing so. And all of this will typically be as true of officials as it is of citizens in general. In light of these facts, Hart's limited victory seems out of reach.

Hart is undoubtedly correct that an important task of legal theory is making clear our implicit conceptual commitments and presuppositions. But the need for clarification only exists if there is confusion, uncertainty, or disagreement of some kind within the internal conceptualization of the practice. Clarification cannot be achieved by an external description, which if it is to be accurate must either mirror the facts of confusion, uncertainty, and disagreement or—and this would be to give up the game altogether—simply avoid the issue by omitting any reference to these facts. (Recall that all descriptions are to a greater or lesser degree selective.) Conceptual clarification is, unavoidably, an internal enterprise. At this point it might perhaps be argued that it does not really matter whether Hart's theory is offered from an internal or an external perspective. What matters is that the theory is *descriptive* in Hart's specific sense of being "morally neutral and [without] justificatory aims" (p. 240). The suggestion is, in other words, that Hart is just making clear our conceptual commitments without either commending or condemning them, in a manner that does not involve moral or normative argument.

If the suggestion of the preceding paragraph were correct, then elucidation of the relevant concepts would have to be essentially uncontroversial. If an instance of conceptual analysis were to be characterizable as simply descriptive and without a normative aspect, it would have to be, once offered, more or less uncontestable; it would simply point out what was there to be seen but had not, for some reason, been previously noticed. The analysis in question would presumably have to take the form of a demonstration that the concepts of authority, validity, legislation, and so on all contain (no doubt implicitly) the notion of a rule of recognition as part of their meaning, or, perhaps, that the use of any of these concepts normally presupposes the existence of a rule of recognition. But both of these claims seem false on their face.

What is *perhaps* true is that the majority of the concepts with which Hart is concerned here, such as legislation, validity, and sovereignty, are all analyzable, in some fairly straightforward and uncontroversial sense, in terms of the concept of *authority*. Authority, in fact, appears to be both the linchpin in this family of concepts and the one whose analysis is key to arriving at a satisfactory philosophical theory of law. This is because, as Hart implicitly recognizes in allowing the problem of the normativity of law to shape his initial theoretical inquiry, it appears to be a core aspect of our concept of law that law claims authority over us. It is part of our concept of law, in other words, that those "in authority" claim to be able by their actions to create obligations for us that we would not otherwise have. But the concept of (political or legal) authority is *not* straightforwardly and uncontroversially analyzable in terms of the notion of a Hartian rule of recognition (*i.e.* in terms of a social or conventional rule). For one thing, an account of authority that appeals to a concurrent rather than to a conventional normative practice is, at the very least, arguable. In this context, then, it seems inevitable that conceptual analysis will involve more than just semantic or reductive analysis, or the making explicit of normatively neutral presuppositions.

Dworkin maintains that in order to show that law is a concurrent normative practice rather than a conventional one, he would need to appeal to "controversial principles of political morality."[96] He would have to argue, in other words, that law's claim to authority must be understood by reference to some independent moral principle rather than by reference to a convention, where the argument to that effect would itself be moral in nature. This seems basically correct. Authority is in fact Joseph Raz's prime example of a concept whose analysis properly involves normative argument, although he would probably not go so far as Dworkin in saying that such argument must be a matter of political morality. I will have something to say about Raz's own analysis of the concept of authority in Section VII. For now I wish only to point out that our main philosophical reason for wishing to analyze this concept must surely be our interest in knowing what kinds of reason for action the law claims systematically to create, as well as our associated interest in knowing whether or not it in fact creates them. This is the heart of the philosophical problem of the normativity of law, which as we have seen is one of Hart's points of departure in formulating his theory.

Nonetheless, in the first edition of *The Concept of Law*, Hart ultimately ignores both these questions by simply *describing*, from an external perspective, the phenomenon of acceptance. He says that people could accept a rule for any of a number of reasons, including moral belief and self-interest, but implies that these reasons are irrelevant to legal theory. He thereby refuses to look behind the brute social fact of acceptance in order to ask whether and under what circumstances that acceptance is justified. It is, however, only by means of such an inquiry that a solution to the problem of the normativity of law will be found. As was noted in the preceding section, the descriptive statement that people *regard* themselves as obligated by a general practice cannot, by itself, tell us whether or not the practice really does obligate them.

In the Postscript, Hart in effect begins to offer the outline of an internal account of authority when he says that part of the reason for accepting the rule of recognition is the very fact of its general acceptance. For the reasons given earlier, this cannot be a simple empirical observation about the reasons that either officials or other people might say they have for accepting the authority of law. It must be, at least in part, a philosophical theory about the reasons they really do (or at least might in principle) have, whether they acknowledge it at present or not. The process of conceptual clarification consists precisely in making clear what these reasons are, and that is why Raz is right to say that normative argument is involved. As it happens Hart's theory is incomplete, because he does not say why general conformity could be part of a reason for accepting a rule. There are, of course, well-known answers to this question: General conformity to some practice can solve a co-ordination problem or serve as a guide to what ought independently to be done.[97] General conformity can also make a type of activity that would otherwise be futile—that would be futile, in other words, if undertaken by one person or a few individuals only—morally worthwhile.[98]

The larger problem with Hart's inchoate internal theory is not its incompleteness in this sense, but rather that it cannot offer an account of the law's claim to

---

[96]  *ibid.*, pp. 60–61.
[97]  See Coleman, in (ed.) R. George, *The Autonomy of Law* pp. 287 and 300–302.
[98]  *Cf.* Raz, *op. cit.*, note 92, pp. 247–248. Of course, in this type of case general conformity is only a necessary condition for the existence of a reason for action, and not a sufficient condition; the activity must also be morally worthwhile for independent reasons.

authority over *everyone.*[99] Hart says that the rule of recognition is a practice defined by the attitudes of officials and no one else; although others in society might also share the internal point of view, it is possible to imagine extreme cases where the rule of recognition is accepted only by officials (p. 117). But a social rule cannot in general give convention-based reasons for action to anyone other than those who belong to the conforming group. The upshot is that the rule of recognition, understood as a conventional practice among officials, can in general give only officials conventional reasons. The general citizenry over whom the law claims authority, or at least those who do not personally accept the rule of recognition as a convention applicable to them, have no such reasons. (Of course, they might have other reasons to obey the law, such as self-interest or independent principles of morality, but these reasons are not claimed to be systematically generated by the rule of recognition.) It is part of our concept of law, however, that law claims authority over everyone, thereby ostensibly obligating them in ways that they would not otherwise be obligated, whether they accept the institutions of the law or not. The theory of the rule of recognition, far from being the sole possible basis for analyzing the concept of authority, thus turns out to be incapable, at least in the form presented by Hart, of providing any viable analysis of that concept. Beyond purporting to impose a duty of enforcement on officials, all the rule of recognition does is set out formal criteria of validity for other rules. As Jules Coleman points out, "[V]alidity is truth preserving [but] it is not authority preserving."[1]

## VI. *External conceptual analysis: law*

The third part of Hart's substantive theory of law is the account he gives of the nature of law itself. The basic claim of that account is, as we have seen, that every legal system contains secondary rules and, in particular, a rule of recognition. Hart argues that the notion of a rule of recognition lies at the core of the concept of law, presumably meaning by this *our* concept. I noted in Section II that even if the argument discussed in the preceding section were correct, to the effect that the concepts of authority, validity, etc., must be analyzed in terms of the notion of a rule of recognition, it would not, without more, entail that that notion is central to the concept of law.

To establish this latter proposition Hart therefore offers the following argument (pp. 91–99). He claims that a regime of primary rules is, as compared to a system containing a rule of recognition and other secondary rules, defective in certain respects: more particularly, such a regime is uncertain, static, and inefficient in the application of social pressure. Primary rules might be capable of guiding conduct—this being, according to Hart, the central function of law (pp. 39–40, 249)—but they do not do so well. The defects of a regime of primary rules are, however, remedied by the introduction of secondary rules. The status and content of primary rules—meaning now rules that are identified by the rule of recognition as valid—can be more readily determined, and the rules can be changed deliberately and enforced by centrally imposed sanctions. Hart states that consideration of these remedies "show[s] why law may most illuminatingly be characterized as a union of primary rules of obligation with . . . secondary rules" (p. 94).

As was noted in Section II, this defense of the thesis that the concept of law must be understood by reference to the notion of a secondary rule appeals to evaluative judgments. A regime of primary rules is said to be defective, and its

---

[99] *Cf.* Coleman, op. cit., note 85, pp. 298, 302. See also Jules L. Coleman and Brian Leiter, *"Legal Positivism" in A Companion to Philosophy and Legal Theory* (D. Patterson ed., 1996), pp. 241, 247–248.

[1] Coleman, *op. cit.,* note 97, p. 298.

defects are said to be remedied by the introduction of secondary rules. Because these judgments are concerned with the guidance of conduct, they are not just evaluative but normative. It is, moreover, the very social practices under study that are being evaluated. By contrast, the metatheoretical criteria that figure in the descriptive-explanatory method are non-normative, and they are used to evaluate only theories, not the subject matter of theories. The fact that Hart appeals to normative judgments does not mean, of course, that the concept of law which rests on those judgments ceases to be descriptive. Hart's concept has the content that it has quite independently of the character of the theorizing he employs to defend it, and, as we saw in Section II, his concept identifies social practices as instances of law on the basis of purely factual, non-normative criteria.

For similar reasons, Hart's reliance on normative judgments at the level of methodology does not call into question the status of his theory as a version of substantive legal positivism. What does seem to be called into question, however, is Hart's claim to be a methodological positivist. Insofar as he defends a particular theoretical characterization of law by appealing to the idea that secondary rules remedy the defects of regimes of primary rules, Hart cannot plausibly maintain that he is simply describing an existing conceptual scheme. He is opting for one conceptualization of social practices over others on the basis of normative argument.

The discussion in the preceding two sections suggests that Hart fails to achieve his goal of elucidating the concepts of obligation and authority, and thus fails to come to grips with the problem of the normativity of law, because he insists on simply describing the phenomenon of acceptance rather than inquiring into the conditions under which acceptance might be justified. That insistence on Hart's part is rooted in his commitment to methodological positivism. It might therefore be thought that, by implicitly abandoning methodological positivism in the development of his general theory of law, Hart has positioned himself to offer an account of the concept of law that is philosophically more satisfactory than those he offers of obligation and authority. That turns out not to be the case, however. The problem is that a satisfactory account of the concept of law must rest on a satisfactory account of the law's claim to authority (*i.e.* the claim that actions by those possessing authority give us obligations we would not otherwise have). Although Hart appears to abandon methodological positivism in the final stages of constructing his general theory of law, the accounts of obligation and authority upon which the theory builds are themselves developed, as we have seen, in accordance with the precepts of methodological positivism. The ultimate theory cannot transcend this starting-point.

A philosophically satisfactory analysis of the concept of legal authority, and hence a philosophically satisfactory analysis of the concept of law that takes the law's claim to authority seriously (as Hart's theory at least purports to do), must be offered from the internal point of view. Such a theory will try to make sense of law to *us*—that is, to those who engage in or are subject to law—by offering an account of whether and how the law's claim to authority over us might be justified. It will do this by attributing a point or function to law and showing how law's serving that function either does give us, or could under certain conditions give us, reasons for action of a specified type. In specifying one type of reason for action over another the theory will attempt to refine our initial, rough, and partially unclear conceptualization of our own practice. In Hart's terms, "the framework of legal thought" will thereby be clarified or elucidated. It is only in this way—looking at the practice from the participants' point of view, and employing normative argument—that conceptual clarification can take place.

This is not to deny that our conceptual scheme, as it exists at any given time, can be neutrally described from the outside. But such a description must faithfully mirror all confusions and disagreements. It does not clarify anything, and it is not a philosophical theory. A philosophical theory has the capability of clarifying, but it can only do so from the inside. Substantive legal positivism is one such clarifying theory—more precisely, it is a family of related theories but there are others, such as Dworkin's theory of law as integrity. Skeptical theories, which argue that law has no point or function and is incapable of giving us reasons for action that we would not otherwise have, are also possible. The philosophy of law consists of a debate among proponents of different such accounts that takes place, in effect, within the social practice of law itself.

Now it might seem that, by attributing the function of guiding conduct to certain social practices and then offering an account of law that is based on judgments about how well various of those practices serve this function, Hart has, despite his claim to be offering an external theory, effectively joined the internal debate. The difficulty with this suggestion is that Hart makes no attempt, at least in the main text of *The Concept of Law*, to show how law's serving the function of guiding conduct could give anyone a reason for action. The explanation for why he makes no such attempt is, presumably, that he insists on describing the phenomenon of acceptance from an external point of view, without considering whether and under what conditions such acceptance might be justified. And the reason that Hart insists on limiting his theory in this way is his initial commitment to methodological positivism. Thus, even if Hart implicitly abandons methodological positivism in the later stages of his theory, his commitment to it at the earlier stages prevents him from offering a theory of law of the kind discussed in the two preceding paragraphs.

Because Hart makes no attempt to show how law's having the function of guiding conduct could give anyone a reason for action, his attribution of this particular function to law, together with the associated judgments about the remedying effects of secondary rules, are best understood as being offered from an external rather than an internal perspective. Hart construes the guidance of conduct as a form of "social control" (p. 40). The theorist, looking at the practice from the outside, is in a position to assess the (moral) value of social control, to determine which social practices are best able to achieve such control, and to make the judgment that control is only possible if a sufficient number of people internalize legal rules by adopting the internal point of view. But this is to look at the phenomenon of acceptance in a completely instrumental fashion. From the theory's external perspective, it does not matter why people accept the rule of recognition and/or the legal system generally, nor does it matter whether it is possible to justify such acceptance *to them* (*i.e.* as individuals). All that matters is that they accept it. It is to look at the social practice in question as a kind of invisible hand. The benefits of social control, if any, will be achieved as long as there is sufficient acceptance. The actual reasons for acceptance, and the possibility or impossibility of justifying that acceptance to individuals, are irrelevant. At one point Hart writes that to mention the fact that members of a group look upon a general pattern of conduct from the internal point of view "is to bring into account the way in which the group regards its own behaviour" (p. 90). But to bring into account the way in which the group regards its own behavior is not enough simply to describe their adoption of the internal point of view. We must inquire into their reasons, actual or possible, for adopting that point of view, and this is precisely what Hart refuses to do.

The argument supporting Hart's general theory of law, on the interpretation of the theory that was advanced in the preceding paragraph, has normative elements. This interpretation supposes that Hart has implicitly abandoned methodological positivism, or at least has abandoned the goal of offering a description of social practices that in no way depends on normative argument, but that he has nonetheless retained methodological positivism's external stance. A theory of law that takes this form is perfectly possible, and is indeed properly characterized as a philosophical theory. Let me call theories like this, which attribute a point or function to social practices from the outside, *external theories*. External philosophical theories can co-exist with internal theories, which attribute a point or function to social practices from the participants' point of view. (There is no reason why a point cannot be ascribed to a social practice both internally and externally.) What an external theory cannot do, however, is claim to offer an analysis or elucidation of the participants' own conceptualization of their practice, which, in the case of law, means an elucidation of our shared concept of law. Only internal theories can do that. If a concept of law can appropriately be said to emerge from Hart's theory, it must be regarded as Hart's concept, not ours.

Moreover, an external theory like Hart's must compete with other external theories, which will conceptualize and perhaps individuate social practices in yet different ways. These theories will either attribute a different point or function to those practices (but always from an external perspective), or else will advance a different view of how social control, say, is best achieved. Holmes' theory of law, for example, can be regarded as an external theory which holds that social control is most readily maintained, not by the internalization of norms, but rather by coercion and the threat of punishment.[2] Holmes thus rejects the law's internal conceptual scheme, based on the notions of authority, obligation, and so on, as empty and a sham. As this is an external, normative critique of law, it is not touched by Hart's demolition of Austin's attempt to offer a reductive analysis of these concepts. A different kind of external theory, this time based on a natural law view, would argue that the point or function of law is, when viewed from the outside, to achieve justice, and thus only those social practices (of such-and-such an institutional character) that are in fact just are properly called law. The nature of the philosophical debate among proponents of different external theories is not entirely clear. Perhaps it is a form of pure political theory. At any rate, what it cannot be is a debate about how our shared concept of law should be clarified or elucidated.

### VII. Internal conceptual analysis

If we take seriously Hart's apparent goal of analyzing *our* framework of legal thought and *our* concept of law, then we must give up methodological positivism completely. This means abandoning not only the aspirations of methodological positivism to normatively untainted description, but also its external perspective. A philosophical theory that has the goal of clarifying the way we conceptualize our social practices must attempt, from our own point of view, to make those practices transparent to us. In the case of law, this means showing that the law's claim to authority over us is always justified, showing that it is justified only under certain conditions (which might not always hold), or showing that it is never justified. In this section I offer a brief overview of this approach to doing legal theory.

A philosophical analysis of the concept of law can be regarded as an attempt to understand the nature of the social practice of law because the concept is very much bound up with our understanding of the practice, and in particular with our understanding of the way in which we take that practice to affect our reasons for action. As Raz has observed, "The concept of law ... plays a role in the way in which ordinary people as well as the legal profession understand their own and other people's actions."[3] Raz goes on to note that "the culture and tradition of which the concept is a part provide it with neither sharply defined contours nor with a clearly identifiable focus"; it is thus the task of legal theory to identify, from among various and sometimes conflicting ideas, "those which are central

---

[2]  *Cf.* Stephen R. Perry, "Holmes versus Hart: The Bad Man in Legal Theory" in *The Legacy of Oliver Wendell Holmes: The Path of the Law and its Influence* (S.J. Burton ed.).
[3]  *See* Raz, (1985) 68 Monist 195, p. 321.

and significant to the way the concept plays its role in people's understanding of society."[4] Raz elaborates on some of the methodological implications of this conception of legal theory in the following passage:

"[I]t would be wrong to conclude ... that one judges the success of an analysis of the concept of law by its theoretical sociological fruitfulness. We are not free to pick any fruitful concepts. It is a major task of legal theory to advance our understanding of society by helping us understand how people understand themselves."[5]

All this seems correct. [...] But it does not show the precise sense in which philosophical theories that set out to clarify the concept of law are properly called internal. The claim I wish to make is that the "internality" of such a theory derives from the fact that it attempts to clarify the conceptual framework of the law by, among other things, addressing the problem of law's normativity. Such a theory either argues that law does not and cannot give rise to obligations that we would not otherwise have, in which case it is a skeptical theory, or else it attempts to make clear the conditions under which the law's claim to authority could be justified. A theory of the former kind argues, in effect, that law does not have any point or function, at least when viewed from an internal perspective. A theory of the latter kind attributes a function to law and then attempts to show how that function's being served could give those subject to law reasons for action they would not otherwise have. In specifying a particular type of reason for action, it proposes a clarifying refinement of the law's conceptual framework. Typically, this will take the form of a normative analysis of the concept of legal obligation. Generally speaking, a conception of the person as a practical reasoner will be at least implicit in such a theory, as it must claim that those subject to law are capable of acting upon reasons of the specified type. A skeptical theory attempts to show, in effect, that law could never be justified. A non-skeptical theory attempts to show the opposite. In both cases the concern is with justification from the point of view of those who are subject to law: the question is whether law could give *them* (moral) obligations they would not otherwise have. It is in that sense that these theories are internal.[6]

As I have argued elsewhere, the methodology for legal theory that is outlined in the previous paragraph is, in all essential respects, Dworkin's interpretivism.[7] Space precludes an extended discussion, but let me go over some of the main points. Dworkin is, in the first instance, concerned with social practices that manifest a special "interpretive attitude." This attitude has two components:

"The first is the assumption that the practice ... does not simply exist but has value, that it serves some interest or purpose or enforces some principle—in short, that it has some point—that can be stated independently of just describing the rules that make up the practice. The second is the further assumption that the requirements of [the practice]— the behavior it calls for or judgments it warrants—are not necessarily or exclusively what they have always been taken to be but are instead sensitive to its point."[8]

In cases where the interpretive attitude holds, participants conceptualize their practice in a certain way. They assume that the practice at least potentially has

---

[4] *ibid.*

[5] *ibid.*, pp. 321–322. [And *ante*, 82.]

[6] *Cf.* Finnis, *op. cit.*, note 78, pp. 14–15: "If there is a point of view in which legal obligation is treated as at least presumptively a moral obligation ..., a viewpoint in which the establishment and maintenance of legal as distinct from discretionary or statically customary order is regarded as a moral ideal if not a compelling demand of justice, then such a viewpoint will constitute the central case of the legal viewpoint."

[7] *See* Perry, *op. cit.*, note 2, pp. 121–135.

[8] Dworkin, *op. cit.*, note 91, p. 47. [And *post*, 717.]

*requirements*, meaning that it gives rise, or could give rise, to reasons for action for them. It thus makes sense that Dworkin speaks of "interpretive concepts" as well as of the interpretation of practices. He is concerned with practices whose associated concepts are, as was suggested earlier to be the case with law, intimately bound up with the way participants understand their own actions. The interpretive attitude is constituted by the following assumptions: first, the relevant social practice has a point or value; and second, the manner in which the practice affects reasons for action depends on what that point or value is taken to be. These are also the assumptions that underpin a non-skeptical internal theory of law.

Different "justifications" or "interpretations" of a social practice are, according to Dworkin, associated with different attributions of a point or value to it; in the case of law, these amount to different theories of law. The term "justification" is somewhat ambiguous, but let me suggest that in the present context it refers to a proposal concerning how to make the best possible moral sense of a practice, from the participants' point of view. In Dworkin's terminology, one tries to put the practice in the best possible moral light. This involves showing how the practice, construed in terms of a certain point or function that might plausibly be attributed to it, could under specified conditions give rise to moral obligations for participants that they would not otherwise have. The idea is to make moral sense of the practice by showing people why and under what circumstances they might have reason to comply with it. A skeptical theory will argue that they could never have such reason, but, as Dworkin quite rightly insists, skeptical theories must establish their conclusions by means of moral argument.

It should be noted that offering an internal justification for a practice does not commit a theorist to saying the practice is "justified" in any absolute sense, so that it should not be changed or abolished. A non-skeptical justification tries to make the best moral case that can be made for a social practice. But the fact that such a case can be made, and that the practice should in consequence be regarded as reason-creating, does not mean that it should not be replaced by an even better reason-creating practice. Thus, it does not follow from the fact that an internal justification can be offered for tort law that tort law should not be replaced by, say, a social compensation scheme.[9]

I am suggesting, then, that a "justification" in Dworkin's sense is concerned with illuminating the *conditions* under which an existing type of institution could give rise to obligations. It is not *directly* concerned with showing that such obligations do in fact arise, although the more unlikely it is that the posited conditions can exist—or rather, the more difficult it is to bring those conditions into existence—the less morally plausible the proposed justification will be. Thus, Dworkin's own substantive theory of law as integrity does not claim that law necessarily gives rise to what he calls associative obligations. Rather, the claim is that law's point or function is to justify state coercion by creating a certain kind of community, namely one that is based on the political ideal of integrity. This is best understood as a claim about our *concept* of law. Associative political obligations are said to arise in fact only when the conditions of integrity are met. These are, roughly, that members of the community reciprocally accept that they have special responsibilities toward one another, and that they plausibly suppose

---

[9]  *Cf.* Jules L. Coleman, *Risks and Wrongs* (1992), pp. 401–405.

that their community's practices manifest an equal concern toward all members.[10]

It is worth noting that nothing in Dworkin's interpretivism, understood strictly as a philosophical methodology for studying social practices, turns on the use of the word "interpretation" or on the meaning the word bears in other contexts. Thus, nothing turns on whether legal practice can be treated as a "text" in the sense of some more general theory of interpretation. It is possible to make all the methodological claims about legal theory that Dworkin wishes to make without bringing in the idea of interpretation at all, as I showed earlier in my characterization of internal theories. It is true that Dworkin himself maintains that there are connections between interpretivism, understood in the narrow methodological sense, and the interpretation of works of art. But those claims are severable from the case that can be made for the use of the interpretivist methodology in legal theory. It has thus been suggested, plausibly enough, that the goal of artistic interpretation is not to put objects of art in the best possible aesthetic light,[11] but it does not follow that the goal of a certain kind of legal theory is not to put the practices of law in the best possible moral light.

Raz's theory of law is an internal theory in the sense I have outlined here. It is worth briefly elaborating on this point, because as a version of substantive legal positivism the theory bears some resemblance to Hart's, yet it rests on quite different methodological premises. Raz characterizes the function of law, in terms reminiscent of Hart, as the guidance of conduct by means of publicly ascertainable rules.[12] But Raz, unlike Hart, offers normative argument to show how law's serving this function could give people reasons for action. This argument is initially offered as an analysis of the concept of authority. However, because Raz recognizes that it is part of the concept of law that the law claims legitimate authority for itself—meaning that courts, legislatures, and other legal institutions claim to create, through the issuing of directives, obligations that people would not otherwise have—the normative argument he advances ultimately figures in his analysis of the concept of law itself.

Raz offers what he characterizes as a normative-explanatory account of the concept of authority.[13] According to this account, which Raz labels the service conception, the law's conceptual claim to possess legitimate authority must be understood in terms of the following thesis. The normal way to establish that one

---

[10] Dworkin, *op. cit.*, note 8, pp. 197–202. The theory of law as integrity is meant to address what Dworkin calls "the puzzle of legitimacy." (*ibid.*, pp. 190–195). It is possible to imagine "external" accounts of law's legitimacy, which could well be associated with the kind of external philosophical theory that was discussed in the preceding section. These would argue for the moral legitimacy of state coercion without supposing that those subject to coercion have an obligation to comply. *See, e.g.* Robert Ladenson, "*In Defence of a Hobbesian Conception of Law*" (1980) 9 PHIL. & PUB. AFF. 134. But for Dworkin legitimacy is intimately concerned with the question, "Do citizens have genuine moral obligations just in virtue of law?" Dworkin, *op. cit.*, note 8, p. 191. Dworkin's substantive theory of law can thus be interpreted as an attempt to outline the conditions under which the law's conceptual claim to authority is justified. For Dworkin, however, that claim must be construed in a broader sense than I have construed it elsewhere in this essay. Essentially following Raz, I have supposed that the law's claim to authority is a claim that citizens are obligated by (and only by) the specific acts of those *in authority*. But Dworkin must suppose that law's claim to obligate is broader than this, as his substantive theory argues that citizens are obligated not only by the specific acts of authorities but by the best justification of the settled law. Indeed, it is precisely because Dworkin maintains that the *concept* of law involves the moral idea of "best justification" that his substantive theory is not a positivist one. (He does not become a positivist simply because, recognizing that the conditions of integrity might not be met in practice, he accepts that actual legal systems do not necessarily obligate.)

[11] Andrei Marmor, *Interpretation and Legal Theory* (1992), pp. 52–53.

[12] Raz, *op. cit.*, note 92, pp. 50–52.

[13] *See* Raz, *op. cit.*, note 80, pp. 295–305; Raz, *The Morality of Freedom* (1986) pp. 38–105.

person has authority over another involves showing that the latter is likely better to comply with the reasons for action that apply to him if he follows the former's directives than if he acts on his own judgment (the normal justification thesis). Let me call the reasons that apply to a person underlying reasons. To the extent that the underlying reasons are moral in nature, the law's claim to have legitimate authority will be a moral claim. If the law has legitimate authority in the sense explained, then its directives will be reasons for action in their own right, excluding direct reliance on the underlying reasons. According to Raz, the directives of a legitimate authority *replace* the underlying reasons, and hence are what he calls exclusionary or preemptive reasons for action. This is why the law claims to create obligations or duties, and not just reasons to be weighed in the balance against other reasons. On the question of whether political authority ever is legitimate, Raz concludes that "while [this] argument does confer qualified and partial authority on just governments it invariably fails to justify the claims to authority which these governments make for themselves."[14]

Raz's argument for the service conception of authority is moral in nature. If it is right, then the anarchist thesis that the state could never have the moral authority it claims is wrong. The theory sets out moral conditions of legitimacy that Raz holds are implicit in the concept of law and that must be met if the law is to give rise to obligations that people would not otherwise have. Raz's theory of law is thus also a political philosophy that is in direct competition with, among others, Dworkin's integrity theory (itself both a theory of law and a political philosophy). I am not concerned here to mediate this dispute, but simply to point it out and say something about its nature. The two theories yield rival normative analyses of the concept of legal obligation; in consequence, they also yield rival accounts of how our concept of law should be elucidated and further refined. Raz argues that the law claims to create, in accordance with the normal justification thesis, exclusionary reasons; Dworkin, that it claims to create associative obligations. There is controversy about the appropriate normative and conceptual analysis of legal obligation even among positivists. Thus, Bentham's normatively defended version of positivism makes the conceptual claim that legal directives add to, rather than replace, the reasons for action people already have.[15] Deciding among these various theories is not just a matter of determining which succeeds in better describing a pre-existing but partially implicit conceptualization of a social practice. There is no such conceptualization that, as Hart would apparently have it, can simply be described. This is philosophically contested ground, and the disagreement must ultimately be settled by moral and political argument intended to show which theory makes the best moral sense of the social practice we call law. In this way legal theory inevitably incorporates political philosophy.

### VIII. Conclusion

Hart makes two very important methodological points in *The Concept of Law*. The first is that a philosophical theory of law involves conceptual analysis, meaning the clarification or elucidation of the concept of law and of "the general framework of legal thought." The second is that a philosophical theory should attempt to come to grips with certain puzzling issues concerning the normativity of law (pp. 5–13). I take this second point to mean that a philosophical theory of law should address the problem of the normativity of law. But Hart's own substantive theory does not offer a satisfactory conceptual analysis, nor does it truly come to grips with law's normativity. The reason for this, I have argued, is that Hart is also committed to methodological positivism, which holds that a theory of law should offer external descriptions of legal practice that are "morally neutral

---

[14] Raz, *op. cit.* note 13, p. 78.
[15] *See* Postema, *Bentham and the Common Law Tradition* (1986), pp. 323–327.

[and] without justificatory aims" (p. 240). Hart's own theory of law, being external, is admittedly without justificatory aims: it does not try to show participants how the social practice of law might be justified to them. But the theory is not, I have argued, morally neutral. Even so it does not offer a solution to the problem of the normativity of law in the way that, say, Raz's theory does. One reason for this is precisely that the theory is external; another is that it rests on a purely descriptive account of the concepts of obligation and authority. As far as these latter concepts are concerned, Hart is content simply to make the observation that officials and perhaps others accept the rule of recognition, meaning they *regard* it as obligation-imposing. This is to describe the problem of the normativity of law rather than to offer a solution.

The substantive difficulties that Hart's theory faces thus have methodological roots. The related philosophical goals of analyzing the concept of law and addressing the problem of the normativity of law are plausible and appropriate ones for legal theory, but they cannot be accomplished by taking an external, purely descriptive approach. Hart seems to have borrowed the idea of a purely descriptive theory from the methodology of science, which is a very different kind of theoretical enterprise from philosophy. The result, from a methodological perspective, is an unsatisfactory hybrid. Of course, I do not mean to deny that it is possible to describe a social practice in a more or less neutral fashion and from an external point of view. As was noted in Section III, there are indefinitely many descriptions that can be offered of any given practice, although most of them are entirely lacking in interest or theoretical significance. If there is conceptual confusion, lack of clarity or disagreement within the practice, an accurate external description must simply report that fact; it cannot offer clarification.

Descriptions that are offered in accordance with the descriptive-explanatory method are potentially of scientific interest, but they will not necessarily track the participants' own conceptualization of their practice, nor will they offer an elucidation of that conceptualization that speaks to them as participants. Descriptive-explanatory theories are not philosophical in nature and, in particular, they do not address the problem of the normativity of law. External philosophical theories are possible, as we saw in Section VI, and Hart's general account of law can be understood in these terms. But such theories, although grounded in normative argument, also do not come to grips with the normativity of law. The predominant tradition in Anglo-American legal theory, from Hobbes and Bentham through Coleman, Dworkin, Finnis, Postema, and Raz (but excluding Austin and Waluchow along the way), has always supposed that the provision of an account of law's normativity has been a central task of jurisprudence. Hart professes to take that task seriously, but his commitment to methodological positivism prevents him from following through.                    [pp. 427–467]

## M. KRAMER
### How Moral Principles can Enter the Law
### (2000)[16]

In recent times [...] the debate between the proponents of the two principal species of legal positivism has gained new vigor. Specifically, some champions of Exclusive Legal Positivism have sophisticatedly challenged the Inclusive Legal

---

[16] [From 6 *Legal Theory* 83.]

Positivists' claim that moral principles can figure among the criteria by which the officials of a legal system ascertain the law. The present essay attempts to parry the most formidable of those recent challenges.[17]

This article's riposte endeavors to defend one variety of Inclusive Legal Positivism, while casting doubt on another variety. As will be seen, a notable salutary consequence of the recent attacks against the Inclusivist position is that they reveal an important divide within that position. Instead of seeking to straddle that divide, the first main section of this article will clearly opt for one side as opposed to the other. What will be defended here as Inclusive Legal Positivism is the view that consistency with a moral principle can be a *necessary* condition for the status of a norm as a legal norm. By contrast, this article in its first chief section distances itself from the view that correctness as a moral principle can be a *sufficient* condition for the status of a norm as a legal norm.

The latter view, designated by Jules Coleman as "Incorporationism,"[18] should thus be distinguished from the doctrine that is labeled herein as "Inclusive Legal Positivism." Coleman has developed his Incorporationist stance in reaction to Ronald Dworkin's broadsides against the legal-positivist model of law-ascertainment. In particular, he has sought to counter Dworkin's contention that legal positivists are unable to acknowledge that judges sometimes invoke moral principles as binding legal precepts. Incorporationism, which carves out just such a role for moral principles, is Coleman's answer to Dworkin—an accommodation of Dworkin's strictures shorn of his insistence that the process of law-ascertainment *must* involve a reliance on moral standards. Hence, given that the present essay looks askance at Coleman's position, it will have to come up with an alternative response to Dworkin's critique of positivism. Such a response will form my essay's second major section. As will become apparent, my discussion in that section does not reject Incorporationism outright. A more fruitful approach than wholesale rejection is the imposition of stringent limits on the range of circumstances to which Incorporationism pertains.

In venturing to uphold Inclusive Legal Positivism by distinguishing it from Incorporationism and by deflecting a powerful blow that has been launched against it, this essay reaffirms the doctrine advocated by H.L.A. Hart. Although Hart never distinguished clearly between Incorporationism and Inclusive Legal Positivism, all of his remarks on my general topic quite plainly align him with the latter theory. Whenever he readily acknowledged that the criteria for law-ascertainment in any particular legal system can include moral principles, he had in mind criteria that constitute restrictions on law-making power. That is, he had in mind the role of moral principles as hurdles that pose necessary conditions for the status of norms as legal norms.[19] Thus, my defense of Inclusive Legal Positivism is effectively an insistence that Hart correctly adumbrated the soundest way of developing his own legacy.

---

[17] My focus will lie chiefly on Scott Shapiro, "On Hart's Way Out" (1998) 4 LEGAL THEORY 469. For a couple of other recent contributions to the debate, from the camp of Exclusive Legal Positivism, see Scott Shapiro, "The Difference that Rules Make", in Brian Bix (ed.), Analyzing Law 33, 56–61; Brian Leiter, (1998), pp. "Realism, Hard Positivism, and Conceptual Analysis" (1998) 4 LEGAL THEORY 533.

[18] For Coleman's latest defense of his position, see *The Practice of Principle* [and *ante*, 498]. The doctrine espoused by Coleman was first propounded by Philip Soper, "Legal Theory and the Obligation of a Judge: The Hart/Dworkin Dispute" (1977) 75 MICHIGAN LAW REVIEW 473, 509–515.

[19] *op. cit.*, note 18, p. 496.

## I. *Of elbow room and scope restrictions*

Scott Shapiro has mounted a singularly powerful and subtle critique of Incorporationism and Inclusive Legal Positivism. He does not attempt to show that either of those doctrines is starkly incoherent or false, but instead attempts to show that neither of them is compatible with the claim that legal norms provide reasons for officials and citizens to act in specified ways. Most of his attention is focused on Incorporationism, which he aptly takes to be the thesis that there are no general constraints on the possible content of the criteria for law-ascertainment in any jural regime. Incorporationists maintain that the Rule of Recognition in any regime is conventional, and they further maintain that the conventions involved can take any number of routes. In particular, the criteria that make up some regime's Rule of Recognition can establish that moral correctness is a sufficient condition for the status of norms as legal norms. According to the Incorporationists, the Rule of Recognition can in principle consist completely of criteria that determine legality by reference to moral content rather than by reference to any procedural or historical touchstones.

Shapiro argues that, when officials adhere to an Incorporationist Rule of Recognition, the legal norms that they ascertain and affirm are not reasons for the decisions that they reach. Instead, those reasons reside entirely in the Rule of Recognition itself. If the criteria for law-ascertainment render moral worthiness a sufficient condition for the status of norms as laws, then the norms validated as laws under such criteria do not constitute any further grounds—any grounds beyond those supplied by the law-ascertaining criteria themselves—for official decisions. Given that the Incorporationist Rule of Recognition already directs judges and other officials to reach decisions through the application of moral principles, and given that the content of those moral principles is not subject to alternation by the will of the judges or other officials, those principles when validated as legal norms do not add any determinative force to that which is already present in the Rule of Recognition itself. At most, they are explications of what is already required by the Rule of Recognition. Any decisions to which they point have already been ordained by the criteria in that overarching rule. Thus, when an Incorporationist judge invokes a moral principle as a legal norm solely because of its content, he "is simply using it to figure out what the rule of recognition requires." Though the moral principles validated as legal norms may serve as heuristic indicators of the implications of the Rule of Recognition, they are no more than indicators. They do not amount to any partly independent bases for official decisions.

A non-Incorporationist Rule of Recognition, by contrast, does indeed engender laws that are themselves reasons for officials to reach certain outcomes as opposed to others. Under the criteria in such a rule, correctness as a moral principle is never sufficient to qualify a norm as a legal norm. In every instance, that is, the status of legality ensues from something other than a norm's content. As a consequence, the decision to which a legal norm leads in any specific context is not preordained by the Rule of Recognition under which the norm has been validated as a law. That decision follows from the content of the norm, which is not predetermined by the Rule of Recognition (since the tests for legality in that overarching rule are not content-focused). Precisely on account of this lack of predetermination, each legal norm constitutes a partly independent reason for an official to arrive at the rulings that the norm requires. Were the content of the norm different from what it is—as it easily could have been, even within the confines of a single Rule of Recognition—the results for which the norm calls would be different. Hence, the fact that any given law does have some particular content is a basis for decisions that goes beyond the basis contained in the Rule of Recognition itself. Because that content is not preordained by the Rule of Recognition, it plays a genuinely determinative role rather than a merely heuristic role. Whereas the outcomes required by an Incorporationist Rule of Recognition *R1* will remain the same regardless of any moral principles that are validated as laws under *R1*, the outcomes required by a non-Incorporationist Rule of Recognition *R2* will hinge crucially on the norms that are validated as laws (on content-independent grounds) under *R2*. Unlike the moral principles validated as laws by an Incorporationist Rule of Recognition, then, the laws validated under a non-Incorporationist Rule of Recognition make a real difference by dint of their interposition between the ultimate criteria of law-ascertainment and the concrete decisions of adjudicators and administrators. The substance of those laws will weigh against some outcomes and in favor of others.

What is the importance of this distinction between the Incorporationist and non-Incorporationist Rules of Recognition? Shapiro contends that the distinction is of the utmost importance because of the basic role that is ascribed to law by Hart and most other legal positivists: the role of presenting people with norms that guide and direct their conduct. Moral principles validated as laws under an Incorporationist Rule of Recognition cannot perform such a role. Legal norms that do not constitute any reasons for or against specific decisions are thereby devoid of any capacity for affecting the practical reasoning of the officials who might invoke the norms. Such norms in this context are empty shells, rather than considerations that should enter into a rational balancing of the factors that favor or disfavor particular outcomes. Under an Incorporationist Rule of Recognition *R1*, *R1* alone is what decisively affects the practical reasoning of officials. It alone poses veritable reasons-for-action. Moral principles validated as laws under *R1* might serve as heuristic aids for the task of finding out exactly what *R1* requires, but, with *R1* in place, they do not themselves require anything. Officials whose reasons-for-action derive from *R1* do not gain any further reasons-for-action from the moral principles that they apply thereunder. Their rational deliberations therefore assign no weight to those principles—which means that the principles in themselves cannot guide and direct the officials' law-ascertaining activities at all. And because those principles cannot perform any guiding role in connection with the officials' ascertainment of the law, they likewise cannot perform any such role in connection with the behavior of ordinary citizens. Whether citizens are directly familiar with the nature of officials' law-ascertaining endeavors, or whether they gain their familiarity through intermediaries such as lawyers and the press, the moral principles validated as laws under *R1* will present the citizens with no reasons-for-action that have not already been presented to them by *R1* itself. As reason-giving guides to conduct, then, those principles/laws are utterly redundant.

Such is the gist of Shapiro's critique of Incorporationism. Now, although the second half of my article will raise some doubts about the devastatingness of his critique, the basic correctness of his arguments against Incorporationism is not in question here. On the contrary, the soundness of those arguments is one principal factor underlying my extremely wary attitude towards Incorporationism. Strikingly in contrast with those impressive arguments, however, is his effort to wield his critique against Inclusive Legal Positivism after having wielded it against the Incorporationist doctrine. When his target shifts to the Inclusivist thesis that conformity with a moral principle can be a necessary condition (as opposed to a sufficient condition) for the status of a norm as a legal norm, his critique becomes otiose. His attack on Inclusive Legal Positivism appears to broach two chief objections, neither of which succeeds.

Shapiro first submits or appears to submit that Inclusive Legal Positivism runs afoul of the same general difficulties that beset Incorporationism. Asking whether Hart could legitimately have adopted the Inclusivist position—as opposed to the Incorporationist position—Shapiro declares that "he could not and for much ... the same reasons that felled [Incorporationism]."[20] He goes on to affirm: "Because

---

[20]  *ibid.*, p. 501.

someone who is guided by a rule of recognition that makes morality a necessary condition of legal validity can be neither epistemically nor motivationally guided by a rule supposedly validated by it, we must conclude that Hart cannot coherently embrace ... inclusive legal positivism." Shapiro then straightaway remarks that "this arguments is similar, but not identical, to the objection that was made against [Incorporationism]. The claim made here is not that a rule supposedly validated by an inclusive rule of recognition that made morality a necessary condition on legality cannot make a practical difference. The problem is that such a rule cannot make a practical difference *in the way that* rules are supposed to make practical differences."[21] We shall shortly explore the claim advanced in this last quotation. Before turning to that claim, however, this article should counter any lingering suggestion that Inclusive Legal Positivism plunges into the same pitfalls from which Incorporationism suffers.

Shapiro's key insight in his critique of Incorporationism is that an Incorporationist Rule of Recognition will preordain any concrete decisions reached thereunder, and that it will therefore render superfluous (except as heuristic aids) any intermediate moral principles that it validates as legal norms. Those norms and those concrete decisions cannot be other than what they are, inasmuch as they emerge under the away of a Rule of Recognition that calls for the application of correct moral principles. Everything is fixed from the outset, as long as that Rule of Recognition endures. And precisely because the content and implications of the legally incorporated moral principles are fixed from the outset, those principles themselves do not furnish any reasons for officials to arrive at certain decisions. Nor do they furnish any reasons for citizens to adjust their behavior in certain ways. Both for officials and for citizens, the reasons-for-action created by the law in an Incorporationist regime are created entirely by the regime's Rule of Recognition. Intermediate legal norms play no determining role whatsoever.

As Shapiro contends, an Incorporationist legal system is static in that its Rule of Recognition settles everything in advance. As he appositely states, there is no "elbow room" in such a system.[22] That is, insofar as judges adhere to an Incorporationist Rule of Recognition, there is no room for them to adopt intermediate legal norms or to reach concrete legal decisions other than those norms and decisions that are morally requisite. Very different indeed is any Inclusivist Rule of Recognition. Far from preordaining all laws and decisions *ab initio*, such a Rule of Recognition leaves an abundance of elbow room. Although it demands that laws and decisions be consistent with specified moral precepts, the congruence between the laws/decisions and the precepts is merely a threshold condition rather than a content-settling feature. Because that congruence can be adequately achieved through any of myriad diverse measures, the Inclusivist Rule of Recognition does not in itself select among those measures. That selection comes about through statutes and judicial doctrines and other legal norms, which consequently do provide reasons for officials to arrive at certain decisions and to eschew alternative decisions.

Let us ponder, for example, the Inclusivist Rule of Recognition depicted by Shapiro. Suppose that judges are empowered and obligated to apply any Congressional enactment unless it is "grossly unfair."[23] Suppose further that a minimum wage of one dollar per hour in the present-day United States would be grossly unfair to workers, and that a minimum wage of twelve dollars per hour (for menial work) would be grossly unfair to employers, and that minimum-wage levels between those two figures will not be grossly unfair. Against this background, Congress enacts a law requiring every employer to pay at least *eight* dollars per hour to every employee. In the aftermath of the enactment, the

[21] *ibid.*, p. 502 (emphasis in original).
[22] *ibid.*, 498.
[23] *ibid.*, 501.

decisions of adjudicative and executive officials and the effects on citizens' behavior will diverge quite notably from the corresponding decisions and effects that would be taking place if Congress had instead enacted a law requiring every employer to pay at least *four* dollars per hour. Because of the statute requiring at least eight dollars, and only because of that statute, the officials are empowered and obligated to treat the eight-dollar level as the minimum acceptable hourly wage. Their Inclusivist Rule of Recognition in itself does not single out that level at all. Rather, the only relevant inference derivable from their Rule of Recognition is that the minimum wage in the current American economy has to lie somewhere between one dollar and twelve dollars per hour. The eight-dollar level is in no way preordained. Had Congress passed a statute specifying six dollars, the minimum hourly wage would accordingly have been at the six-dollar level; and it would have been at the nine-dollar level if a statute specifying nine dollars had been passed. Precisely because the Inclusivist Rule of Recognition allows these and numerous other significant variations in the level of the statutory requirement, it does not predetermine specific outcomes. Those outcomes ensue instead from the changeable legislation that Congress enacts. Hence, unlike an Incorporationist Rule of Recognition, an Inclusivist Rule of Recognition is not static. Legal norms validated under it can play a guiding and directing role. This point applies, of course, not only to the particular example of minimum-wage laws, but also to the whole range of matters that might be regulated by statutes or other legal norms.

Although Shapiro does not explicitly acknowledge the point made in my preceding paragraph, and although he puts forth one or two pronouncements that may seem to bespeak a contrary view, he probably does not disagree with anything that has just been said. As was intimated four paragraphs ago, the gravamen of his argument against Inclusive Legal Positivism is quite different from his critique of Incorporationism. Here his complaint is not that legal norms validated under an Inclusivist Rule of Recognition will fail to constitute any reasons for officials' concrete decisions. His complaint, rather, is that the reasons constituted by those norms do not partake of the exclusionary or peremptory force that is characteristic of genuinely authoritative directives. He states his accusation forthrightly, with reference to the example of the minimum-wage statute:

> "Can the minimum-wage rule ... motivationally guide a judge? The answer to this question is ... 'no.' Recall that a rule motivationally guides conduct when it is taken as a peremptory reason for action; it follows that a rule cannot motivationally guide if the agent is required to deliberate about the merits of applying the rule. As the application of the minimum-wage rule depends, pursuant to the inclusive rule of recognition, on the employer first assessing whether the rule is grossly unfair, he cannot treat the rule as a peremptory reason for action and hence cannot be motivationally guided by it."[24]

Shapiro recapitulates his argument in a passage that has already been partly quoted herein: "The problem is that [an Inclusivist Rule of Recognition] cannot make a practical difference *in the way that* rules are supposed to make practical differences: if the agent is required to determine whether the rule ought to be followed on the merits, then it can count neither as an epistemic tool for authoritative designation nor as a peremptory reason for action."[25]

Shapiro presumes that, if ascertaining the existence of a legal norm will perforce involve some moral judgments, then the norm cannot amount to a peremptory reason for action. Such a position, based on Geoffrey Warnock's and Joseph Raz's conception of norms as exclusionary reasons (a conception that

---

[24]  *Ibid.* at 501.
[25]  *ibid.,* at 502.

Hart appropriated in his discussion of laws as peremptory reasons for action), has disregarded Raz's observations concerning possible restrictions on the scope of any particular reason's exclusionary or peremptory force. On the one hand, by virtue of being an exclusionary reason, a legal norm disallows certain considerations as legitimate bases for decisions or actions. The excluded considerations no longer properly count as factors that should be deemed to weigh against or for the mode of conduct which the norm requires or forbids. On the other hand, an exclusionary reason will almost never be of such overriding importance that it disallows *all* countervailing factors as legitimate bases for decisions and actions. In almost every instance, the peremptory sway of a norm is limited. As Raz writes: "It should be remembered that exclusionary reasons may vary in scope; they may exclude all or only some of the reasons which apply to certain practical problems. There may, for example, be some scope-affecting considerations to the effect that though Colin's promise [to act only in furtherance of the well-being of his son] apparently purports to exclude all the reasons not affecting his son's interests it does not in fact validly exclude consideration of justice to other people."[26] As long as an exclusionary reason removes *some* factors from a balance of considerations that can be legitimately acted upon, it need not remove *all* such factors. Restrictions on the scope of a peremptory reason are fully compatible with its nature as such a reason, as Leslie Green has remarked:

> "Such reasons may be both prima facie, in the sense that they are not conclusive about what ought to be done, and at the same time categorical. The fact that they exclude and not merely outweigh reasons for not-ς-ing makes them categorical; the fact that they may not exclude all contrary reasons makes them prima facie. Thus the force of such commitments depends ... [on] the scope of the reasons against ς-ing which they exclude."[27]

A legal norm can partake of peremptoriness even if it disqualifies only some countervailing concerns, rather than all countervailing concerns, as reasons for legitimately acting at variance with the norm's demands. Its peremptoriness consists in the fact that it does disqualify certain counterbalancing considerations. The fact that the norm does not disqualify certain other counterbalancing considerations is a matter that affects only the *scope*, and not the *existence*, of its peremptoriness.

Let us now re-examine the scenario that Shapiro discusses. The non-exclusion of gross unfairness—the non-exclusion of it as a factor that will militate against the status of a norm as a legal norm—is perfectly consistent with the exclusion of numerous other factors. For instance, a judge will be neither authorized nor obligated to depart from the terms of a minimum-wage statute simply because he thinks those terms are unfair (as opposed to grossly unfair). Though the gross unfairness of the statute is an operative consideration that must be taken into account by the judge as he gauges the statute's legal force, the mere unfairness of the statute is not such a consideration. It is excluded by the Rule of Recognition, which instead makes gross unfairness the pertinent touchstone. Even more plainly excluded as a basis for the judge's decisions is the mere unwisdom of the statute. A judge who regards the minimum-wage statute as inadvisable but not as grossly unfair is forbidden to nullify the statute on the basis of his judgment about the legislature's unwisdom. (Indeed, even if he does view the statute as grossly unfair, his invalidation of it must be premised solely on that ground and not on the ground of the legislature's unwisdom.) His Rule of Recognition, which obligates him to give effect to duly enacted statutes unless they are grossly unfair, will have disallowed him from acting upon his view of the statute's sheer imprudence. Insofar as he adheres to that Rule of Recognition, he does not let statutory

---

[26] Joseph Raz, *Practical Reason and Norms* (2nd ed., 1990), p. 40. [And *ante*, 461.]
[27] Leslie Green, *The Authority of the State* (1988), p. 39.

imprudence count as a factor that will incline him to strike down statutory mandates. He does not permit his views about the unwisdom of an enactment to inflect his official decisions about the enactment's jural status.

Hence, Shapiro errs when he submits that the legal norms validated under an Inclusivist Rule of Recognition cannot guide people's behavior in a peremptory fashion. Those norms do exclude a range of factors as legitimate reasons for failing to abide by the norms' requirements. To be sure, they do not exclude *all* such factors; for example, within the Rule of Recognition portrayed by Shapiro, gross unfairness is not excluded as a reason for nullifying legislative enactments. However, as we have seen, the peremptory force of a legal norm is fully compatible with the fact that not all concerns and considerations have been ruled out as bases for invalidating the norm. The noncomprehensiveness of a law's exclusionary sway is a restriction on the *scope* of that sway rather than a negation of its very *existence* and *nature* as such.

Shapiro's critique is warranted in application to Incorporationism, but not in application to Inclusive Legal Positivism. Although the guiding and directing role of law is stymied when a norm's correctness as a moral precept is a sufficient condition for the status of the norm as a law, that guiding and directing role is not thwarted at all when a norm's conformity to moral precepts is a *necessary* condition for the status of the norm as a law. Shapiro's onslaughts have left Inclusive Legal Positivism unscathed.

## II. Incorporationism revisited

Given that Incorporationism suffers from the shortcomings that Shapiro has deftly highlighted, we might wonder why anyone has been led to adopt the Incorporationist position. Why have Coleman and Philip Soper been prepared to take the view that a legal system might be structured by a Rule of Recognition which effectively establishes that correctness as a moral precept is sufficient to render a norm legally binding? Why have they been prepared to accept that such a test for legal bindingness might even be the only such test in a particular legal regime? Plainly both of these theorists have been replying to the anti-positivist strictures of Dworkin, who has maintained (especially in *Taking Rights Seriously*) that positivists cannot adequately account for the salience of moral principles in adjudication. Although some of Dworkin's objections have been aimed at the doctrine that I herein designate as Inclusive Legal Positivism, his most famous criticisms are those to which Incorporationism is a riposte.

[...]According to Dworkin, positivism is belied by the fact that judges sometimes apply moral principles as binding laws even though the principles lack any clear-cut origins in statutes or administrative decisions or judicial opinions. Now, a natural response for somebody confronted with such a line of criticism is to contend that the positivist model of law can perfectly well accommodate the alleged tendency of judges to treat moral principles as legal norms. What Coleman and others have argued is that the sheer conventionality of the Rule of Recognition does not perforce impose any constraints on the substance of that rule's criteria. "There is nothing in [the general notion of the Rule of Recognition] that imposes any constraints on the conditions of validity. The Incorporationist sees no reason for assuming that these conditions cannot in principle include criteria making moral value or merit a condition of legality, at least for some norms. For the Incorporationist, what matters in the rule of recognition is not the criteria of validity set forth, but its existence conditions."[28] As Coleman reiterates: "The key move for the Incorporationist is the claim that positivism imposes no constraint on the criteria of validity. Whether a particular rule of recognition does

---

[28]  Coleman (1998) 4 *Legal Theory* 381, 406–407.

so depends on the practice of officials."[29] Incorporationists, then, are quite willing to suggest that the processes of law-ascertainment in any given regime might render moral worthiness the lone sufficient condition for legal validity. [...]

Coleman's pronouncements on the elasticity of the criteria in the Rule of Recognition are excessively far-reaching statements of a thesis that should more confinedly be about the potential focus of such criteria on moral correctness. We therefore have to ask whether an Incorporationist Rule of Recognition can generate enough regularity to enable the existence of a legal system. This question is a key component of our broader inquiry into the adequacy of the Incorporationist reply to Dworkin. Let us straightaway note that this question concerning regularity does indeed pertain to the *existence* of legal systems and not merely to their *efficiency*. Coleman sometimes draws too sharp a distinction between effectiveness and existence, as in the following passage:

> "We need to distinguish between law's possibility and its efficacy. Positivists insist on law's conventionality as essential to our understanding its possibility. The claim that law is made possible by a rule of recognition that supervenes on a practice accepted from an internal point of view is a conceptual claim; it states possibility or existence conditions. It does not matter, for these purposes, whether the rule of recognition is controversial and, if so, how controversial it is.
>
> On the other hand, a rule of recognition's efficiency varies with its controversiality. No positivist believes that it does not matter whether the rule of recognition is controversial. It is just that if controversy matters, it matters from the point of view of law's efficacy, not from the point of view of law's possibility."[30]

Unquestionably, the concepts of efficiency and existence are neither intentionally nor extensionally equivalent—which is why we can correctly talk about inefficient legal systems. Instead of having to hold that such institutions are not legal systems at all, we can rightly hold that they are legal systems which do not operate very well. Nevertheless, although the states of efficiency and existence are plainly not identical, they are not separable to quite as great an extent as Coleman implies in the passage above.

A fairly substantial degree of regularity is essential not just for the efficiency of a legal regime, but also for its very existence as such. Severe disaccordance among the countless decisions of officials will not only disrupt the smoothness of their regime's workings, but will also deprive those workings of the minimum of cohesion that is necessary for any scheme of governance-through-legal-norms. A jural system in its operations obtains as a jural system only by partaking of consistency in considerable measure. For an expression of this point, we can resort to a comment made by Coleman just a couple of pages before the passage quoted above: "Judges may agree about what the [Rule of Recognition] is but disagree with one another over what the rule requires—especially in controversial cases. They could not disagree in every case or even in most cases, as such broad and widespread disagreement would render unintelligible their claim to be applying or following the same rule."[31] Hart advanced a basically similar observation, with reference to the need for officials to uphold the various norms of their legal regime:

> "Individual courts of the system though they may, on occasion, deviate from [its] rules must, in general, be critically concerned with such deviations as lapses from standards, which are essentially common or public. This is not merely a matter of the efficiency or health of the legal system, but is logically a necessary condition of our ability to speak of the existence of a single legal system. If only some judges acted 'for their part only' on the

---

[29] *ibid.*, p. 407.
[30] *op. cit.*, note 28, p. 412.
[31] *ibid.*, p. 410.

footing that what the Queen in Parliament enacts is law, and made no criticisms of those who did not respect this rule of recognition, the characteristic unity and continuity of a legal system would have disappeared. For this depends on the acceptance, at this crucial point, of common standards of legal validity. In the interval between these vagaries of judicial behaviour and the chaos which would ultimately ensue when the ordinary man was faced with contrary judicial orders, we would be at a loss to describe the situation. We would be in the presence of a *lusus naturae* worth thinking about only because it sharpens our awareness of what is often too obvious to be noticed."[32]

In short, a legal system must pass a certain threshold of regularity in its workings, if it is to exist as a legal system at all. Above that threshold, the system will be functional and efficient to a greater or a lesser extent. Below that threshold, however, it will be nonexistent—i.e., nonexistent as a legal system—rather than merely inefficient. Lon Fuller was quite correct to insist as much.[...]

Will an Incorporationist Rule of Recognition yield enough cohesion and uniformity to render possible the existence of a legal system? Clearly, any answer to this question must rely on one or two general empirical premises, however uncontroversial they might be. Unlike Shapiro's critique of Incorporationism—a critique with which this article has not yet entirely finished—my discussion of the operational regularity or irregularity of Incorporationist law-ascertaining criteria is not purely conceptual, even though it can aptly proceed at a high level of abstraction. (Specifically, my discussion will rest on an empirical premise relating to the ineliminability of widespread disagreement about the appropriateness of various ways of dealing with non-routine moral problems.) Moreover, the question posed here will oblige us to clarify the contours of an Incorporationist Rule of Recognition. We should first consider an uncompromisingly robust version which establishes that moral worthiness is the *lone* sufficient condition for the status of any norm as a legal norm; in a jural system that is oriented toward such a criterion, every legal judgment is a moral judgment through and through. Then we should consider a milder Incorporationist Rule of Recognition which establishes that moral worthiness is a sufficient condition for the status of any norm as a legal norm only in hard cases that cannot be resolved by reference to legal norms from other sources. As will be seen, Incorporationism of this milder variety should not be rejected out of hand.

In a regime where judges and other officials adhere to the robust version of the Incorporationist Rule of Recognition, their ostensible law-ascertaining activities will very likely partake of too little regularity to be properly classifiable as law-ascertainment. Such a Rule of Recognition instructs officials to handle every case by applying the moral norms that produce the optimal result in the circumstances. Although a system along these lines will leave some room for officials to pursue a certain degree of consistency among their decisions, there are ample reasons for thinking that the consistency in practice will be meager.[33] Let us ponder two main aspects of the situation.

First, because *ex hypothesi* there are no sources of law other than the realm of moral principles, any touchstones for official decision-making that stem from alternative sources cannot be treated systematically as authoritative. In other words, such touchstones cannot systematically amount to reasons-for-action which carry weight that is independent of their substantive worthiness. If officials do systematically ascribe content-independent weight to determinative standards (including, of course, standards other than moral principles that the officials deem to be worthy), then they are not adhering to a robustly Incorporationist Rule of Recognition. They are instead adhering to ordinary law-ascertaining criteria— i.e., non-Incorporationist criteria—and are simply upholding those criteria on the

---

[32] Hart, *Concept, op. cit.*, pp. 112–113.

[33] My view here is largely similar to that presented in Joseph Raz, *op. cit.*, note 26 pp. 137–141.

basis of the moral precepts that would be validated and applied directly as laws by a truly Incorporationist regime. If a robustly Incorporationist Rule of Recognition is at all distinctive, and if it is therefore more than just a misleadingly labeled motivational platform for an ordinary Rule of Recognition, it must involve the systematic invocation and application of moral principles on content-dependent grounds. Officials in a robustly Incorporationist regime focus chiefly or exclusively on the appropriate substantive resolutions of cases, rather than on formal or procedural earmarks. To be sure, as has been avouched above, many of the officials in such a regime will still undoubtedly endeavor to attain at least a modicum of consistency in their rulings, in the way of typical moral agents. Expectations that might be bred by past decisions will form part of the context wherein any present decisions are made. Nevertheless, if the officials' Rule of Recognition is genuinely and comprehensively Incorporationist, any consistency among their judgments cannot derive from systematic attentiveness to the manner in which the norms applied by their judgments have been brought into existence. Precisely on account of this aspect of any uncompromisingly Incorporationist regime, the consentaneity among the multifarious determinations of the officials therein will almost certainly be low.[34]

Second is a point emphasized not only by Hart but also by the great early modern philosophers who depicted a "state of nature" that anteceded the political institutions of full-fledged societies. Although one key feature of societies-with-governments that distinguishes them from acephalous societies is the existence of mechanisms for authoritative dispute resolution, another such feature is the existence of publicly ascertainable legal norms by reference to which the dispute resolution can proceed. A robustly Incorporationist regime will possess the first of these features but not the second. As a result, it will suffer from the severe problems of uncertainty and irregularity that have been highlighted by Hart and others in relation to primitive societies. Perhaps those problems can remain within manageable limits in a very small and static and highly homogeneous social unit, where moral attitudes are widely shared. However, in any large and dynamic and heterogeneous society, the problems of moral disunity are bound to be grave indeed unless they are overmastered through the erection of a publicly ascertainable set of norms to regulate conduct. Thus, since a comprehensively Incorporationist Rule of Recognition renders every legal judgment a moral judgment, and since a regime structured by such a Rule of Recognition will therefore not subordinate any moral dissension to publicly ascertainable legal norms, it almost inevitably will be a shuddersomely fractionated regime in which the officials reach numerous clashing decisions and send out numerous clashing signals. To be sure, as has already been granted, the officials will very likely make some efforts to co-ordinate their decisions. However, they will not be adhering to a fully Incorporationist Rule of Recognition unless they focus primarily on substantive moral issues. In connection with those issues, the need for co-ordination is just one ancillary consideration among many. Thus, the officials' adherence to a thoroughly Incorporationist Rule of Recognition virtually ensures that their mode of governance will lack the regularity essential for the existence of a legal system.

[. . .]

In sum, at least within a large and complex society, a comprehensively Incorporationist Rule of Recognition will very likely fail to secure the degree of regularity that is prerequisite to the functionality of a legal system. Though it might conceivably lead to a legal system that is woefully inefficient, it will much more probably lead to nothing at all that can qualify as governance-through-law. Precisely because such a Rule of Recognition is so unsuitable for enabling and sustaining the existence of a regime of law, the adoption of it by officials is exceedingly unlikely. If Incorporationist criteria for law-ascertainment play any

---

[34] This paragraph has been aimed principally against Philip Soper, *op. cit.*, note 18, p. 512.

fill the gaps as they please. If any official were to decide difficult cases by adverting to factors other than moral precepts, he would be criticized by his fellow officials for failing to comply with his adjudicative duties. Hence, his reliance on those precepts when tackling hard cases is not something that he is legally at liberty to eschew.

Of course, the likelihood of intractable disagreements among the officials about the appropriate outcomes in hard cases is overwhelmingly high. Their shared adherence to a mildly Incorporationist Rule of Recognition does not prevent them from diverging markedly in their selection and application of moral principles for dispatching difficult disputes. While concurring with one another about the intension of their Rule of Recognition, they persistently differ with one another (in hard cases) about its extension. Nevertheless, in hard cases with no uniquely correct solutions, all the moderately Incorporationist officials will be acting in accordance with their Rule of Recognition as long as the moral principles that they invoke and the outcomes that they favor are within the range of acceptable principles and outcomes. In any hard case where a uniquely correct solution is available, by contrast, only those officials who opt for the correct solution are acting strictly in accordance with the criteria in their Rule of Recognition. However, given that all the officials are credibly endeavoring in good faith to abide by those criteria (if indeed they are so endeavoring), and given that the unique correctness of the optimal solution is indemonstrable, the fact that some officials plump for suboptimal outcomes is not indicative of any breaches of duties. Although those officials might not be in strict compliance with the mildly Incorporationist instruction in their Rule of Recognition, they are not in violation of that instruction, either. Between strict conformity and outright transgression is the space occupied by their bona fide efforts.

In the foregoing respects, then, a moderate version of Incorporationism can remain unscathed by various difficulties, some of which would bedevil a robust version of Incorporationism. A mildly Incorporationist Rule of Recognition will not lead to disruptive levels of irregularity in the ascertainment of laws; nor in most circumstances will it bring forth legal norms that fail to provide guidance; nor will it leave officials legally free to decide hard cases in whatever manner they please. Having glanced at these important strengths of the moderate Incorporationist stance, we should now seek to choose between it and Exclusive Legal Positivism.

Considerable circumspection is advisable here. An effort to choose between an Exclusivist theory and a mild Incorporationist theory is always prone to degenerate into an exercise in arid terminological stipulations. Both the Exclusivist theorist and the mild Incorporationist theorist readily maintain that judges within some legal systems invoke moral precepts to resolve the points of contention in hard cases, which cannot be resolved on the basis of legal norms that derive from ordinary legislative/judicial/administrative sources. Theorists from both camps likewise readily accept that, within legal systems of the sort just mentioned, the resort to moral principles by judges in difficult cases is legally obligatory rather than discretionary. What is at issue, then, is neither the determinative role of moral precepts in hard cases nor the legal mandatoriness of that role within some jural systems. What is at issue, rather, is the status of the precepts which perform that role. Are those precepts legal norms when they are applied by judges to the facts of hard cases for the purpose of resolving the disputes therein? Or are they non-legal norms that stop up gaps in the law without having been components thereof? Are they laws that belong to the system wherein they are applied, or are they similar to the rules of sporting associations and the laws of foreign jurisdictions which might be invoked by judges in certain unusual cases?

Plainly, we cannot settle this matter by reference to the most obvious aspect of the applied moral principles that renders those principles akin to laws: their status within a legal system as binding standards that judges bring to bear when assessing people's conduct in order to resolve disputes. After all, as has just been remarked, the Exclusive Legal Positivists are wholly willing to endorse such a characterization of the moral principles' status. We therefore have to shift our focus to some other aspect of the moral principles—an aspect that pertinently distinguishes them from the rules of clubs and sporting associations and the laws of foreign jurisdictions. If we can indeed single out some such feature of the principles, we shall have grounds for favoring a modest Incorporationist theory over an Exclusivist theory.

Consider, then, the significance of the fact that the correctness of the moral precepts that are to be invoked in hard cases is not brought about by anyone's deliberate acts and is not susceptible to alteration through deliberate acts. Shapiro himself emphasizes this characteristic of morality in the course of his critique of Incorporationism. Of key importance here is that the tenor of correct moral principles does not lie within the deliberate control of anyone who is outside the legal system in which the principles are applied as binding standards of conduct. In this respect, those principles are notably different from the rules of clubs or sporting associations and the laws of foreign jurisdictions. In their substance, such rules and foreign laws do indeed lie entirely within the deliberate control of people other than the officials in the legal system *L* where the rules and foreign legal norms are invoked. People who run the clubs and sporting associations determine which rules are operative therein, and they can modify those rules deliberately through amendments thereto. Much the same can be said *mutatis mutandis* about the officials in foreign legal regimes, who determine which laws are operative therein and who can modify those laws through such techniques as repealing, amending, and overruling. Exactly because the foreign laws and the rulers of the clubs and associations are subject to the control of people outside *L*, the occasional application of those rules and laws within *L* should not be regarded as the incorporation of them into *L*'s matrix of legal norms. Instead, the application of them is a way of showing due respect for the norms that have been chosen and formulated in systems of authority that exist alongside *L*. As a means of showing such respect, the effectuation of those norms within *L* tends to highlight their separateness from *L*'s own norms. Given that the ground for invoking and applying foreign laws and associations' rules is their origin in external structures of authority that merit some recognition as such, the process of invoking and applying those rules/laws will have rested on a justification that underscores the fact that they belong to systems other than *L*. (Of course, some of the people in charge of clubs and sporting associations might also be legal officials. Nonetheless, each such person in his public capacity as an official is distinct from himself in his private capacity as a leader of a club or an association. The public and private roles remain separate, even if they are both occupied by a single person.)

Before contrasting the posture of clubs' rules and foreign laws with the posture of moral principles in hard cases, we should look at a further potential source of binding norms: custom. Few if any legal theories deny that customary norms have the status of full-fledged laws when invoked as such by judges. Indeed, one of the most prominent charges leveled by Hart against John Austin was that the latter theorist could not come up with any adequate explanation of the legal status of some customary norms.[37] Now, to a limited extent the reasons for ascribing binding force to customary norms are similar to the reasons for ascribing such force to the rules of clubs and the laws of foreign jurisdictions. That is, the officials in *L* who draw upon customary norms are thereby exhibiting due regard for the practices from which those norms are distilled. Nevertheless, the

---

[37] Hart, *Concept*, at 44–48. I have argued elsewhere that Austin's theory can accommodate the role of custom much more resourcefully than Hart suggests. See my *Legal Theory, Political Theory, and Deconstruction, Against Rhadamanthus* (1991), pp. 106–07.

dissimilarities between customary norms and foreign laws (or associations' rules) are more significant than the resemblances. Those dissimilarities warrant the difference between one's readiness to classify certain customary precepts as legal-norms-belonging-to-$L$ and one's reluctance so to classify any foreign laws or associations' rules. In the first place, the statutory/judicial/administrative laws of foreign jurisdictions and the codified rules of associations derive from the decisions of people who occupy positions of authority. Likewise, those laws and rules are subject to deliberate alteration through standard procedures undertaken by the people in the authoritative positions. By contrast, the precepts of custom emerge and develop gradually instead of being brought into existence through discrete and authoritative acts. Moreover, unlike the laws of foreign countries and the formal rules of sporting associations, customary precepts are not subject to deliberate and abrupt modification through set procedures. Nor do they issue from clear-cut channels of authority; rather, they are immanent in practices that are typically carried on in the absence of any formal hierarchies or authoritative pronouncements.

In these key respects, the norms generated by custom diverge strikingly from foreign laws and sporting associations' rules. Those laws and rules are highly malleable products of institutions that are counterparts (at least rough counterparts) of the legal system $L$ wherein the rules and laws are applied as binding norms from the outside. By contrast, customary precepts are not highly malleable and are not attributable to any authoritative decisions handed down and ratified through institutional mechanisms broadly akin to those in $L$. Hence, whereas the substance of the foreign laws and associations' rules is controlled by the directives of authorities outside $L$, the substance of customary precepts is not really within anyone's effective control. Since the tenor of the customary precepts is due to diffuse patterns of behavior rather than to focused decisions, and since the practices in which the precepts unfold are not authoritative institutions that are formal counterparts of $L$, the application of those precepts within $L$ should be seen as the incorporation of them into $L$'s assemblage of legal norms. Though the customary precepts are immanent in practices, they do not belong to any authoritative institutions outside $L$. Thus, when they receive formal recognition within $L$ as binding norms, they are not borrowings from another system in which they have an authoritatively established status. Until that point of formal recognition, they are free-floating—i.e., free of any institutional affiliation that has been authoritatively set. They are consequently available for incorporation into $L$. Plainly, that free-floating condition and that consequent availability for incorporation will not be characteristic of foreign laws or associations' rules. (Of course, a free-floating condition is hardly in itself sufficient to confer the status of a law on each norm that informs the authoritative utterances of officials. For instance, the fact that judges rely on the free-floating rules of grammar and diction does not mean that those rules are legal norms. Unlike statutes and judicial doctrines and certain customary and moral norms, grammatical rules do not serve as justificatory bases for official decisions. When judges have to explain why they are deciding a case one way as opposed to another, they do not invoke grammatical rules such as the rule against split infinitives. Instead, they have to invoke some statute[s], judicial doctrine[s], customary norm[s], moral norm[s], or other decision-determining standard[s]. As has already been fleetingly remarked about the moral principles that are applied in hard cases, the most obvious features of those principles that weighs in favor of our classifying them as laws is that they are indeed decision-determining standards.)

Along lines that are relevant here, principles of positive morality and principles of critical morality are much closer to customary precepts than to foreign laws or associations' rules. Indeed, moral principles of both types—especially the principles of critical morality—diverge more sharply from the aforementioned laws and rules than do customary precepts. Let us first ponder the status of positive moral standards. Positive morality consists in a mixture of customary beliefs/ practices and widespread convictions. With regard to the component of positive morality that comprises a large array of customary precepts, the status of moral principles is manifestly at one with the status of norms that are grounded in custom. Therefore, given that customary norms are available for incorporation into *L*'s laws, the same will obviously be true of positive moral precepts. With regard to the component of positive morality that comprises people's widely shared convictions about right and wrong, the posture of moral principles is even more clearly detached from any authoritative institutional origins. Individual convictions, no matter how pervasively they may be harbored, are not the products of formal enactments or authoritative decrees. The patterns or networks of those convictions do not belong to any system, regardless of how widespread the convictions are. People's staunchest beliefs about right and wrong are free-floating in the sense defined above. Ergo, the moral principles encapsulating those beliefs are available for incorporation into *L*'s matrix of laws.

If the principles of positive morality can become subsumed into the overall array of *L*'s legal norms—as has just been argued—then *a fortiori* a parallel conclusion is warranted in connection with the principles of critical morality. By definition, they are principles that possess their morally binding force independently of their having been upheld by anyone. Their soundness as moral principles does not depend at all on their having gained acceptance within any set of institutions; their status as precepts of critical morality derives from their intrinsic tenor and not from their influence or roles (if any) in some formal system of authority. Their status as critical precepts certainly cannot be terminated by anybody's decisions or enactments. It is not within anyone's control. Hence, if officials in *L* draw upon the principles of critical morality for the purpose of resolving hard cases, they are not doing so out of any perceived need to show regard for some coexistent system of formal authority. Instead, the officials are drawing on those principles as norms whose validity transcends any recognition of them in other systems. A condition of free-floatingness, in the sense defined above, is inherent in the posture of critical moral precepts as such. When those precepts are invoked and applied in *L*, they are not borrowings from some other institutional structure to which they really belong. Even more straightforwardly than customary standards, they have been available to enter *L*'s matrix of legal norms as full-fledged elements thereof.

Should we conclude, then, that any recourse to moral principles by the judges in a mildly Incorporationist regime is an application of pre-existent law? Such an inference would be precipitate, for it elides the difference between the following two types of hard cases: those in which there are uniquely correct ways of ranking the applicable moral principles, and those in which there are no uniquely correct rankings. In hard cases of the former sort, a mildly Incorporationist Rule of Recognition will have fixed the content of the prevailing law. Because that Rule of Recognition empowers and obligates officials to resort to moral principles in hard cases, and because *ex hypothesi* any questions about the bearing of those principles on the facts of certain hard cases can be answered in uniquely correct ways, the officials dealing with those cases have to pursue the uniquely correct routes if they are to decide the cases in accordance with their Rule of Recognition.

In a hard case *H* where the applicable moral principles can be ranked acceptably in more than one way, a mildly Incorporationist Rule of Recognition will not have fixed the content of the prevailing law. An irreducible and significant quantum of leeway will remain. In any such case, then, the ultimate resolution does not ensue simply from the balance of moral principles. Although the officials' recourse to moral precepts will probably help to narrow the range of acceptable outcomes, it will still leave key matters open—because the ranking of those precepts is open, to some extent. Accordingly, while the balance of moral norms invoked by judges to settle the points at issue in *H* may become the prevailing law that governs those points, it cannot accurately be presented as the pre-existent law thereon. Notwithstanding that the repertory of laws for hard cases under a mildly Incorporationist Rule of Recognition will encompass moral precepts, the pre-existent law for the controversy in *H* is indeterminate.

At any rate, what the second half of this article has sought to establish is that a moderate version of Incorporationism is preferable both to Exclusive Legal Positivism and to a thoroughgoing version of Incorporationism. Unlike the latter doctrine, the moderate variant of Incorporationism duly acknowledges the indispensability of uniformity and regularity in anything that counts as a legal system. Unlike Exclusive Legal Positivism, moreover, the position advocated herein can distinguish pertinently between the status of customary norms and the status of foreign laws (and of sporting associations' rules) when those norms and laws are given effect within any particular legal system. The basis for such a distinction leads to the conclusion that moral principles drawn upon by mildly Incorporationist judges in hard cases are sometimes laws of the system wherein they are invoked and applied. In insisting on that very point, a mild version of Incorporationism is superior to Exclusive Legal Positivism. When Incorporationism is confined within appropriate limits—quite severe limits—it proves to be a redoubtable doctrine indeed.                                    [pp. 83–108]

### SIR NEIL MACCORMICK
### A Very British Revolution?
### (1999)[38]

*Introduction: the sovereignty dispute*

Was there a revolution in Britain in 1972? Was the constitution then overthrown, not by violence but by stealth, when the Heath Government procured the enactment by a narrow majority of the European Communities Act 1972? Was the referendum of 1975 a belated democratic legitimation of a revolution already accomplished? Or did the revolution remain on hold until the House of Lords finally decided in *Factortame v. Secretary of State for Transport*[39] that traditional parliamentary sovereignty had been abandoned, and a later Act of Parliament might be disapplied to honour a commitment to European Community law confirmed by the earlier? Or is there some other way to account for what happened when, in accordance with the provisions of section 2 (1) and (4) of the European Communities Act 1972, and in the light of the ruling of the European Court of Justice concerning the incompatibility of the fisheries provisions in the Merchant Shipping Act 1988 with Community law, the House set aside the 1988 Act's provisions? Is talk of revolution exaggerated, overdramatic? Did the United Kingdom succeed in joining the European Community without undergoing a revolution in the process?

[...] Sir William Wade has put his high authority behind the "revolution thesis", but his argument has been countered in vigorous fashion by Trevor Allan.

---

[38] [From N. MacCormick, *Questioning Sovereignty* (1999).]

[39] See *Factortame v. Secretary of State for Transport* [1991] A. C. 603; Lord Bridge's dictum at pp. 658–9 has been noted as particularly significant: "If the supremacy within the European Community of Community law was not always inherent in the E.E.C. Treaty, ... it was certainly well established in the jurisprudence of the European Court of Justice long before the United Kingdom joined the Community. Thus, whatever limitation of its sovereignty Parliament accepted when it enacted the European Communities Act 1972 was entirely voluntary. Under the terms of the Act of 1972 it has always been clear that it was the duty of a United Kingdom court, when delivering final judgment, to override any rule of national law found to be in conflict with any directly enforceable rule of Community law."

Sir William, of course does not wish to portray bloodshed and violence and tumbrels rolling to the guillotine, but only a "technical revolution" in the legal sense.[40] A change, he points out, was made in the fundamental rules of the constitution of a kind that the constitution as understood in 1972 could not have authorized. For in 1972, the constitution had as its fundamental rule that Parliament is sovereign, in the sense that Parliament at any time can enact any norm it chooses as valid law, save a norm that would bind a successor Parliament. Dicey[41] says that as a "merely legal conception", sovereignty is "the power of law-making unrestricted by any legal limit". Wade says that "the rule was that an Act of Parliament in proper form had absolutely overriding effect, except that it could not fetter the corresponding power of future Parliaments".[42] For the sake of the subsequent argument, I shall re-express this in the present tense and in Hohfeldian categories[43] as follows: "Parliament has an unrestricted and general power to enact valid law, subject to only two disabilities, namely, a disability to enact norms disabling Parliament on any future occasion from enjoying the same unrestricted and general power, and a disability to enact laws that derogate from the former disability." This rule, according to Wade, existed as a practice of the judges, and was itself changeable only through decision by the judges.

Wade's thesis is that the House of Lords in its *Factortame*[44] decision in 1991, especially in the account given of it in the speech of Lord Bridge of Harwich, connived at overturning that fundamental constitutional rule, since it treated the legal change made by the Parliament that enacted the 1972 Act as one which imposed a restriction on the later Parliament that enacted the 1988 Act. If the decision did not itself overturn the fundamental rule, it indicated that the rule had already been overturned. Either way, a change of a fundamental kind had occurred in the way in which judges interpreted the legislative power of Parliament after accession to the European Communities. Judges now interpret Parliament's powers in terms different from those that were previously in use among the judiciary.

This change was one that could not have been itself legally warranted under the former understanding of the constitution. Accordingly, it could only have come about by a judicial decision to change the constitution or to acquiesce in a change made by the 1972 Parliament, despite the fact that the decision to make the change lacked authority in or under the constitution as that had long been understood up to the moment at which the change was made. Had the legislation been differently drafted, it might have been possible to achieve continuity, but given the terms of the 1972 Act, no pretence that a mere change in statutory interpretation was all that had happened could disguise the radical breach that had in fact occurred. Adopting terminology from H. L. A. Hart (himself a prior debtor to Professor Wade), Wade characterizes the revolutionary change he detects as a change in the "rule of recognition" that lacked the authority of the rule of recognition in use prior to the change.[45] What rule of recognition the judges subscribe to is a question itself of political fact. Since the facts have changed in a fundamental way, not derivable from the previously observed rule, a revolution must simply be acknowledged to have occurred. Hart himself had

---

[40] See Sir W. Wade, "Sovereignty—Revolution or Evolution?" (1996) 112 *Law Quarterly Review* 568–75 at 574.

[41] A. V. Dicey, *An Introduction to the Study of the Law of the Constitution* (10th ed., 1960), p. 27.

[42] "Sovereignty", at p. 574.

[43] [On Hohfeld see *ante*, 396 and *post*, 569.]

[44] [1991] A. C. 603 at 658–659.

[45] See "Sovereignty" at p. 574 "[The rule quoted above at note 5] is a rule of unique character, since only the judges can change it. It is for the judges, and not for Parliament, to say what is an effective Act of Parliament. If the judges recognize that there must be a change, as by allowing future Parliaments to be fettered, this is a technical revolution."

argued, partly by reference to a justly celebrated contribution by Wade[46] to an earlier debate about sovereignty, that the existence of an "ultimate rule of recognition" cannot itself be validated by any other rule or norm of law, but can only exist through a "complex and normally concordant practice" among judges and other officials. Its existence can thus only be a matter of social fact.[47]

Trevor Allan's response shows that there is no escape in such a debate from the deepest questions of legal philosophy. He criticizes Wade's approach as one based on a thin conception of the ultimate rules of constitutional law, for it suggests that the development of these rules is a process not subject to arguments of fundamental legal principle, but only to the influence of political considerations.[48] Ultimate constitutional rules belong to common law not to statute law. This does not diminish, but reinforces, the need for recourse to arguments of legal principle, including the principles necessary to and inherent in democratic constitutionalism. Such principles become decisively important when fundamental questions arise for decision in the light of developments such as the (ultimately political) decision of the United Kingdom to join the European Communities. The House of Lords may indeed have failed to explore such reasons as fully as it might and should have done in the *Factortame* decision. But the deficiencies of the decision in any event "suggest the influence of an inadequate positivist jurisprudence".[49] In the light of his own Dworkinian interpretivist approach to constitutional questions, developed in *Law, Liberty and Justice*,[50] it can fairly be inferred that Allan sees the baneful influence of "inadequate positivist jurisprudence" as pervading also Sir William's argument for the conclusion that the old constitution has been overthrown by acts of an essentially, albeit technically, revolutionary kind.

### The foundations of a constitution

The debate is one that goes to the fundamentals of an understanding of law. It poses sharply the issue of how it is possible to change a constitution in its fundamentals, while still acting in a constitutional and lawful manner and spirit. It thus demands some satisfactory account, necessarily a theoretical account, of what the foundations of a legal-constitutional order are, and how it is possible for these foundational elements in some way to regulate their own amendment or change. Wade having pitched his argument on the ground of Hart's theoretical account of these fundamentals, we do well to start there. As will be seen, particular attention must be given to the two Hartian ideas of "rules of change" and "rules of recognition"...

According to Hart any viable human community must live under shared rules that regulate at least interpersonal violence and some administration of the things that are necessary for human survival. These essential "primary rules" establish mutual obligations of mutual forbearance and limited mutual assistance. A simple regime of pure "primary rules of obligation" would, however, be too static and inefficient for large-scale technologically innovative societies. Such societies must

---

[46] See H. W. R. Wade, "The Legal Basis of Sovereignty", *Cambridge Law Journal* (1955), 172–94.

[47] See Hart, *The Concept of Law* (1994), chs. 6 and 10; the acknowledgment of Wade's piece is at p. 295.

[48] See T. R. S. Allan, "Parliamentary Sovereignty: Law, Politics, and Revolution", *Law Quarterly Review*, 113 (1997), 443–52, arguing that the emergence of judicial review of Acts of Parliament for conformity to European Community law is an evolution within constitutional law, justifiable by an appropriate interpretation of the relationship between democracy and sovereignty.

[49] *ibid.*, 448.

[50] Allan, *Law, Liberty, and Justice* (1993). [Or Dworkin see *Post*, 717].

by some means have developed institutions that can change the law legislatively and that can administer it judicially. These institutions depend more on power-conferring than on obligation-imposing rules. In summary, law in such societies takes the form of a "union of primary and secondary rules".[51] Primary rules concern the obligations imposed by law on persons in society in favour of others or in the public interest. Secondary rules concern the institutional organization and regulation of the making and enforcement of other rules. The secondary rules can be summarized (in alphabetical order) as:

1. "rules of adjudication", the substantial cluster of rules that constitute courts and empower judges to hear and determine trials and disputes, concluding them by the issuance of enforceable orders;
2. "rules of change", being (*a*) rules that constitute legislators or legislative bodies with power to enact general rules for the guidance of the population, and (*b*) rules that enable private persons to vary their rights and duties, by varying the incidence or application of primary rules that impose obligations;
3. a "rule of recognition" that establishes criteria for identifying which rules are valid members of the legal system maintained by the legal officials whose roles are regulated by rules of adjudication and rules of change. This rule depends on a complex but normally concordant practice of those officials whereby they appeal to the same rules as the rules of law that must be used and observed in their society. In healthily democratic societies, this shared practice also engages the active assent of citizens in general, but this is not necessary as a minimum condition for the existence of a legal system.

This idea of law as a "union of primary and secondary rules" has a pleasing simplicity and clarity, at any rate at first sight. Yet there are problems concerning the relationship among secondary rules of the three kinds. In particular, it is difficult in a concrete situation to see just what is the difference between a "rule of change", at any rate that concerning the highest acknowledged power of change, and the "rule of recognition", at any rate, that part of it which states the highest recognized criterion for the validity of law. This point has particular significance in the context of the present debate. Earlier, I summarized Wade's understanding of the doctrine of parliamentary sovereignty (pre-1972) in these terms:

"Parliament has an unrestricted and general power to enact valid law, subject to only two disabilities, namely, a disability to enact norms disabling Parliament on any future occasion from enjoying the same unrestricted and general power, and a disability to enact laws that derogate from the former disability."

Wade considers this to be, in Hartian terms, a "rule of recognition" for the United Kingdom; more cautiously, one might say that it is or was the "supreme criterion of validity" within the rule of recognition. This seems at first sight to put Hart's idea quite properly to use, for indeed when Hart applied his own theory to the British constitution as an illustrative example he stated that in England (*sic*) the "supreme criterion" of recognition within the "rule of recognition" recognized by English lawyers and in particular by English judges was this: "Whatever the Queen in Parliament enacts is law."[52]

The two formulae apparently say almost exactly the same thing. Looked at one

---

[51] The essential reference for all this is *Concept of Law*, ch. 5 [And *ante*, 382].

[52] *Concept of Law*, 148. There are in English law (to which Hart confines his remarks) other subordinate criteria: what is established by way of delegated legislation is also law, and so are precedents of the higher courts. As between these other criteria, there are some priority rankings to settle which prevails in case of conflict; but necessarily rules authenticated by reference to the supreme criterion override all others.

way, they state or assume that Parliament has (unrestricted) power to enact any rule into law. Looked at in the other way, they state that a rule is a rule of law if it is enacted by Parliament (and, as the Wade formula brings out, not superseded by any rule enacted by Parliament at a later date). On closer inspection certainly, the formula I ascribed to Wade is explicitly about the power to enact laws (the power to change law, that is), whereas the Hartian formula puts it the other way round, and is explicitly about ascribing the status "law" to whatever (in the way of a rule) Parliament enacts, or has enacted. It is perhaps a little uncertain whether Wade himself intends to express his point in terms of the power of Parliament to enact rules in an unrestricted way, or in terms of the overriding effect that the occurs recognize to be inherent in whatever Parliament enacts. However that may be, for present purposes we may take it that there are on either Wade's or Hart's view two aspects of the situation. Parliament has unrestricted power of enacting laws; the laws it enacts have to be recognized as binding by the judges.

If there really is a difference between a rule of change and a rule of recognition, the Wade formula as I stated it seems to be a rule of change, the Hart formula, of recognition. But is there a difference? Are we not simply dealing with two ways of saying the same thing? If there is a difference, there may also be a question why in Hart's scheme of things the rule of recognition is said to be the ultimate rule of a legal system. One might on the face of it argue as well that constitutions are ultimately about power and about any limits to which power can be subjected. The present popular concern is surely about the power question. Are not the deepest constitutional questions, indeed, those of law-making power? That is what is really at stake in the issue of the survival of sovereignty. Who has the final say? Parliament or Brussels? Why turn this round and look for the last answers in practices of recognition?

To see why it might be of value to differentiate two faces of essentially the same idea, postulating a distinction between rules of change and of recognition, two rules rather than one, it is necessary to reflect further on the idea of a constitution in which powers of legislation and adjudication are separated. This separation of powers is, of course, an idea that belongs to the framework of a constitutional state, to one species, we have seen, of institutional normative order rather than to the whole genus "law". But clearly it is the framework relevant to the present debate. Wherever such a constitution exists, by deliberate adoption at a foundational moment or by the curious process we see to have been involved in the United Kingdom, there has to be some way of ensuring that the different powers the constitution confers are exercised in a coherent way over time. For this, there has to be some reciprocal understanding among those who exercise different powers about the conditions and effects of their exercise.

A legislature in a constitutional state would fail to fulfil the function of making laws if those who administer the law fail to regard and to use as law the output of the legislature in the form of enacted rules of law. The judiciary in a constitutional state would fail to function as such if there were no executive arm ready to enforce and implement their judgements and decrees. And yet commonly, at least in their details, the organization and powers of the Courts are laid down in legislation, as are the details of the administrative law through which the executive arm has to operate. So there is a mutual interdependence. This is inevitable given that, although such a constitution achieves a certain (at least partial) separation of powers, the powers so separated are the powers of the same state that has to act with at least a minimal degree of coherence and integrity to be a functioning state at all.

In short, contemplating such a state, we need to differentiate those aspects of a constitution that confer powers, including conditions and restrictions on powers, and those that regulate the exercise of powers conferred. According to the model of a democratic, constitutional state, there have to be rules that confer powers of legislation on a legislature with a defined composition and structure elected by citizens through the use of voting rights enshrined in the constitution. There have to be rules that confer power to conduct the executive government, with power under appropriate legislation to raise (by taxation), and to spend, public money for public purposes. And there have to be rules that establish courts and empower the judges who sit in them to determine controversies of right and to preside over the trial of persons accused of crimes.

Explicitly or implicitly, those who hold the power to judge and decide cases according to law, must be provided with, or must develop through constitutional interpretation, norms that quantify their obligation to determine cases "according to law". What counts as law, and what is the rank order, or hierarchy, of validity-criteria? The point is that there must be a shared sense of its being obligatory to implement valid laws, and a shared understanding of what counts as valid law, and of the circumstances in which rules valid under higher-ranking criteria of validity override other rules.

An appropriate understanding or adaptation of Hart's structural account of "legal system" does thus differentiate the power-conferring "rules of change", "rules of executive empowerment" (omitted by Hart) and "rules of adjudication" from the duty-imposing "rule of recognition", with its structured hierarchy of legal sources, alias "criteria of recognition". Here then we have identified a necessary condition for coherence in a workable constitution for a law-state. There has to be reciprocal matching between the criteria for recognizing valid law, and the criteria for validly exercising the power to enact law (including any special procedures required for validity of a legislative change that changes provisions of the constitution itself). This necessary reciprocal reference belongs to what some consider the inevitable self-referential quality built into systems as such.[53] It is partly dependent on convention and inevitably subject to a process of evolution over time. It involves discussion and interpretation by journalists, scholars, and citizens as well as by legislature, executive, and courts over time, the courts' interpretations carrying the especially authoritative stamp characteristic of states that abide by the rule of law. The evolutionary character of constitutional law and doctrine is particularly marked where, as in the United Kingdom, there is no single written instrument (perhaps with an appendix of valid amendments up to date) that contains the fundamental empowering rules and such limits on the powers.

So it is not only possible but necessary to draw a distinction between the rule of recognition and the rule(s) of change in a constitution. The doctrine of the sovereignty of Parliament is not itself a "rule", but indeed a "doctrine" with two aspects. On the one hand, it concerns Parliament's power of change. According to the doctrine in question this is a power conferred by [a rule of] common law, the power being unrestricted except under the two conditions (the two "disabilities") noted above. On the other hand, it either concerns or cross-refers to the judges' obligation (also a common law obligation) to implement any validly enacted Act of Parliament as a highest source of law. But when we think of a constitution, or of the British constitution analytically, in the manner of Hart's conception of law, the "doctrine" reappears in our ideal reconstruction of the constitution as two distinct "secondary rules". And it is arguable, though only on one reading of his text, that Wade has conflated the two, thereby generating the problem of the apparent constitutional impossibility of the process of accession by the United Kingdom to the E.C.

---

[53] See G. Teubner, *Law as an Autopoietic System.* (1993), 19–24.

*Changing the rule of recognition*

Having brought matters to this stage, we can now face up to one critical question about the interaction and reciprocal referencing of the "rule of change" that empowers a supreme legislature and the "rule of recognition" itself. The question is: can the legislature amend the rule of recognition by adding to it new criteria of recognition of valid law? Must the courts recognize and give effect to legislation that purports to bring this about? Is any special legislative process called for in this case?

There can be no all-purpose theoretical answer to this question. Certainly, nothing in the general theory of law should exclude the possibility of such change. If the rule of recognition is a central part of constitutional law, and if constitutions are amendable, then surely it is a question for the interpretation of any particular constitution whether amendment of the rule of recognition is permitted (empowered) and, if it is, by what process and procedure. Assuming the United Kingdom constitution to have at its centre the elegant simplicity of the doctrine of parliamentary sovereignty (in tandem, perhaps, with the Rule of Law), the answer would seem obvious. "Yes. Parliament's powers include power to enact changes to the rule of recognition, but they do not include the power to change it in such a way as to disable Parliament from reversing in the future any such change that it makes." With great respect to Wade, it cannot be true that only the judges can change the rule of recognition, though certainly they have the last word on the question whether and how any change that Parliament may purport to make should have effect.

If we looked at historical precedents such as those involved in the Reform Acts and the Parliament Acts, we would note that changes connected with the power of change, concerning the composition of Parliament and of the electorate, have always required express legislative change. For example, *Nairn v University of Saint Andrews*,[54] upheld the proposition that a major and controversial change in the composition of the electorate, admitting women to the vote, could not be deemed to have been achieved merely by implication. So legislation that enabled Universities to adopt schemes for admitting women to degrees did not impliedly confer voting rights on women graduates, even though, at that time, University graduates as such were entitled to a vote in the University constituencies. This decision has been sharply criticized from a feminist standpoint, but the proposition that major changes require express enactment has a certain rough common sense about it.

Bearing that in mind, let us now examine the provisions of section 2(1) of the European Communities Act 1972:

> "All such rights, powers, liabilities, obligations and restrictions from time to time created or arising by or under the Treaties ... as in accordance with the Treaties are without further enactment to be given legal effect or used in the United Kingdom shall be recognized and available in law, and be enforced, allowed, and followed accordingly; and the expression 'enforceable Community right' and similar expressions shall be read as referring to one to which this section applies."

Coupled with that is the provision in section 2(4) that such obligations take effect so as to override "any enactment passed or to be passed" by the United Kingdom Parliament.

---

[54] *Nairn v University of St Andrews* [1909] A. C. 147, at p. 161: "It would require a convincing demonstration to satisfy me that Parliament intended to effect a constitutional change so momentous and far-reaching by so furtive a process" (*per* Lord Loreburn L.C.)

One should not impute to the draftsman or to Parliament intimate acquaintance with Hart's jurisprudence, far less an intent to refer to it, but one may nevertheless linger a little on the word "recognized" in section 2(1). Here Parliament instructs all persons and all officials of the state, and plainly not least the judiciary, that a new source of law is henceforward to be recognized. This is the force of: "obligations [etc. that are] created ... by ... the Treaties and that in accordance with the Treaties are without further enactment to be given legal effect." How obligations so recognized are to be ranked in competition with other sources is stated in 2(4). They have a ranking superior to Acts of Parliament passed or to be passed. Parliament in so enacting clearly envisages that its own powers (derived from what Hart calls a "rule of change") do extend to making a change in the criteria of what are to be recognized as legal rights and obligations in the United Kingdom constitution (that is, in what Hart calls the "rule of recognition").

This is done without conferring a new power of legal change on any agency internal to the constitution. The power of legal change with which this criterion of recognition meshes is not itself a power conferred by or in the United Kingdom constitution, however elastic the concept of "unwritten constitution" may be. It is (explicitly) the "Treaties" that confer the power of legal rule making (the power of change) whose output the Act obligates all and sundry in the United Kingdom to recognize.

Obviously, section 2(1) is not itself an entire "rule of recognition" as Hart intended the term. A rule of recognition may, and usually does, contain more than one criterion of validity of law, though when more than one criteria are included they are then ranked in priority. Clearly, section 2(1) inserts a new criterion of recognition into an already functioning rule of recognition, and section 2(4) indicates its ranking above other criteria. Previously, the recognized sources of law for the United Kingdom were, in rank order, Acts of Parliament, acts of delegated legislation so far as interpreted to be *intra vires*, and precedents of the higher courts, themselves ranked hierarchically. Henceforward they are to include "enforceable Community rights" in the sense defined, and these are to supersede the provisions of Acts of Parliament "passed or to be passed". So the criterion of being obligatory under the Treaties assumes hierarchical superiority over parliamentary enactment (perhaps one ought to expand the phrase, "being obligatory under the Treaties within the domains of legitimate activity of the Communities as interpreted by the European Court of Justice").

The issue raised by Wade therefore transforms itself. Had Parliament power to amend the rule of recognition as it purported to do by section 2 of the 1972 Act? On the prevalent reading of the constitution as of that date, to which of course Sir William Wade speaks with high authority, Parliament could enact into law whatever it thought fit to do, except for any provision that would bind its successors. Clearly, that would have ruled out any attempt to make a change in the rule of recognition that would itself be entrenched against future repeal by Parliament. On one interpretation of the 1972 Act, it achieved or purported to achieve just this impermissible effect. If we read section 2(4) as extending the superior validity of Community obligations over Acts of Parliament "to be passed" in future so as to rule out legislation expressly repealing sections 2(1) and 2(4) of the 1972 Act, this would clearly amount to an irrevocable transfer of power. That would convert Parliament into a subordinate legislature within some larger sovereign entity.[55]

---

[55] Dicey, of course, thought such a transfer was possible. Indeed, he considered it to have occurred historically to each of the former Parliaments of England and of Scotland when in 1707 they transferred their separate sovereignties to a new sovereign, the Parliament of Great Britain.

But the very fact that this interpretation would carry such an implication is a reason for rejecting it and seeking an alternative interpretation consistent with Parliament's decision to enter the European Community by a constitutionally legitimate process, given the understanding of the constitution that was prevalent in 1972. The alternative, and preferable, interpretation is that the 1972 Act made a valid change in the rule of recognition, as it purported to do, but with the implied condition that Parliament retained its power to reverse that change. That is, there is an implied condition that it could repeal section 2(1) and 2(4) if in future it should choose to do so. This is in fact generally held to be the case. The constitution remains a customary constitution, and one can say with reasonable confidence that this power of repeal, that is of unilateral and valid secession from the EC, subsists in the constitution of the United Kingdom and is exercisable by an Act of Parliament expressly enacted to that end.

This cannot blind one, however, to the magnitude of the change that was brought to light through the drawn-out soap-opera of the *Factortame* case. The pre-1972 doctrine of parliamentary sovereignty entailed as an unquestioned corollary a doctrine of implied repeal expressible in terms of the brocard *lex posterior derogat priori*, or "Where two laws are incompatible, the later repeals the earlier to the extent of the incompatibility." Acts of Parliament being supremely valid law, if there were an incompatibility between any two Acts, or parts of them, the more recent expression of Parliament's will necessarily cancelled the earlier. If the change to the rule of recognition has been validly enacted in the sense suggested, the *lex posterior* principle must be considered overridden in relation to matters of Community law.

If this were not so, the upshot would be remarkable. Any post-1972 Act found on proper interpretation to be in conflict with any enforceable Community right would have to be held to have repealed section 2(1) to the extent necessary for the validity of the legislation in question. A case in point would be the provisions of the Merchant Shipping Act 1988 that were attacked in *Factortame*. The position would yield the following dilemma. Either the attacked provisions are valid in Community law, in which case the Spanish fishermen lose their case alike in United Kingdom law and in E.C., law; or the attacked provisions are invalid in Community law, in which case, because they conflict with an enforceable Community right, they impliedly repeal section 2(1) of the 1972 Act. In the latter case, they are valid for the purposes of domestic law after all, and the Spanish fishermen lose their case so far as concerns any United Kingdom court. But the United Kingdom will be found to be in breach of its Treaty obligations, that is, in breach of Community law. No doubt Parliament could and perhaps would subsequently enact laws to rectify the British breach of Community law, possibly making retrospective provision to secure the Spanish fishermen the fruits in the United Kingdom of their enforceable Community right. But that would involve precisely the kind of process that the doctrine of "direct effect" in E.C., law is supposed to eliminate. It would fail to square with the arrangements to which Parliament resolved to sign up in 1972.

In the light of all that, we face some incentive to discover an alternative interpretation of the constitution that will make more reasonable sense of the decision taken by Parliament in 1972, confirmed by referendum in 1975, and subsequently upheld in the teeth of quite determined "Euro-sceptic" opposition. Can such an interpretation be found? I believe so. What this interpretation says is that Parliament did in 1972 have the power it then exercised to amend the rule of recognition by adding a new criterion of validity at the highest sub-constitutional level. By doing so, it excluded future application of the "*lex posterior*" principle in relation to sections 2 (1) and (4) of the 1972 Act. That did not, however, involve disabling Parliament, or purporting to disable Parliament, from repealing in future the change then being made to the rule of recognition. It would follow that Parliament has power to reamend the rule of recognition, but is only to be interpreted as exercising this power if it enacts legislation with that express purport. That is, it requires legislation expressly repealing sections 2(1) and 2(4).

Why might the second interpretation be preferable? First, it might be said that changing a fundamental article of the constitution is a weighty matter, not lightly undertaken. Here one might indeed point to the circumstances of the passage of the 1972 Act, with the attendant controversy that led up to and was only finally dispelled or at any rate stilled by the referendum of 1975. Then further, one might point to the fact that the 1988 Act was enacted on the understanding, by no means unreasonable, that it did a lawful thing. That is, in relation to the fisheries issue, it provided a means (contravening no enforceable Community right) to protect the domestic fisheries industry by upholding the rights of the United Kingdom in respect of Fisheries Quotas allowed within the Common Fisheries Policy. This understanding turned out false because of the European Court of Justice's interpretation of the Common Fisheries Policy in the light of the Four Freedoms, according to which the Spanish fishermen did suffer infringement of an enforceable Community right on account of the material sections of the Act. It would be a perverse conclusion indeed if an Act passed with the intention to implement Community law must be assumed to have impliedly repealed the 1972 Act just as soon as it turned out that the scheme devised to protect British fishermen did not implement but contravened Community law.

Taking the opposite line on this does not involve denying that Parliament has both right and power to decide that the issue of fisheries is a make-or-break issue, and thereupon to resolve by explicit legislation to revoke wholly or in part the United Kingdom's reception of enforceable Community rights as binding and applicable domestically. Of course, this could not be done without provoking a major crisis in the Community (and Union), and most probably the European Court of Justice would hold any unilateral legislation to this effect invalid and of no effect in the perspective of Community law. In turn, the courts in the United Kingdom would then face the question whether to uphold European law at the cost of a revolution in United Kingdom law, or to uphold United Kingdom law at the cost of a revolution in Community law. These are grave choices, and it is possible to envisage circumstances in which by deliberate political decision and with a clear democratic mandate a parliamentary majority would force just such a choice by deliberate legislation directed to that very end. What would be extraordinary, however, would be if the doctrine of implied repeal, coupled with the principle that later acts derogate from earlier ones, were judged to have forced this choice upon Parliament through a concatenation of unforeseen judicial decisions in 1989–91.

There can be no doubt of the magnitude of the legal and constitutional change that was involved when the United Kingdom acceded to the European Community. So long as that accession remains in force, the legal systems of the United Kingdom interact with a "new legal order" of a supranational kind, and incorporate into their own legal order(s) norms that are valid in that other legal order and accordingly (under section 2(1)) valid domestically as well. These norms are themselves subject to highest-level interpretation by the European Court of Justice, with its doctrine of the "primacy" or "supremacy" of Community law over the several laws of the member states. While the jurisprudence of the ECJ has been subjected to considerable controversy, and the United Kingdom government has sought to attack the Court's position,[56] it ought to be acknowledged that the crucial decisions about "new legal order" and "direct effect" were all in place prior to the UK's accession. To impute to Parliament in 1972, or to the electorate in the 1975 referendum, ignorance of the E.C., constitution as elaborated through the Court's decisions is to suppose a quite astonishing ineptitude on the part of those who led the Parliamentary and Referendum campaigns against accession.

---

[56] See the White Paper, *A Partnership of Nations*, Cm. 3181 (1996).

Such an imputation cannot be squared with any reasonable practice of ascertaining legislative intent against a background of known (in this case, notorious) contemporary circumstances.[57]

Given the system that is now in place, with the parallel existence and interaction of domestic and Community law, the interpretation proposed above secures for the overall system both coherence and integrity.[58] It achieves this far better than if we adhered to the alternative that says there can be piecemeal amendment and alteration to the rule of recognition in respect of enforceable Community rights, casting doubt on the extent of their domestic enforceability on a case-by-case basis. This would be all the more deleterious given the normative framework within which the European Court of Justice operates. That framework would require it to hold that all community obligations remained binding within the United Kingdom notwithstanding the opinion of British judges that inconsistent Acts of Parliament enacted after 1972 must prevail as a matter of domestic law.

### Pedigree, principle, and grundnorm

Trevor Allan has written slightingly of "an inadequate positivist jurisprudence". By implication, he suggests that any attempt to build a better understanding of constitutional law and theory on foundations constructed from Hart's theory of legal system is foredoomed to failure. He works from within a similar intellectual framework to that of Ronald Dworkin, and Dworkin in turn has doubted the whole idea of a legal theory that judges what counts as a valid proposition of law by reference to its "pedigree".[59]

The present chapter exhibits, I believe, the weakness as well as the strength of the attack on positivism and its concern with "pedigree". In any question about the effects of the UK's accession to the European Community, we are bound to consider what is to be the status so far as concerns the Courts of the United Kingdom of enforceable community rights. (To be exact, what is the status of any "such ... obligations ... from time to time created ... by ... the Treaties ... as in accordance with the Treaties are without further enactment to be given legal effect or used in the United Kingdom"?) When the United Kingdom resolved to accede to the Community, its decision had to entail that such obligations were to be "recognized and available in law, and be enforced, allowed, and followed accordingly", for that was the very character of the Community to which the country had decided to accede.

In turn, the character of that decision requires it to be accompanied by a decision on the issue how obligations with that "pedigree" (in general, "enforceable Community rights") are to stand in relation to legal norms with the distinct pedigree of being contained in Acts of Parliament. Again, the character of the Community to be joined entails that they must override provisions in Acts of Parliament to the extent of any inconsistency. And then the question arises whether it lies within the power of Parliament to enact legislation that will effect this fundamental alteration to pedigree-ranking of legal sources in the United Kingdom. Whatever be the merit of any one or another answer to that question, the question cannot be posed, let alone answered, without inquiry into what one might call the institutional rules of the constitution. These in turn are made intelligible through some general theory of legal systems and the constitutional framework of a state within the rule of law. There certainly were and are flaws in Hart's account of legal structures and in Sir William Wade's deployment of that account in relation to the present controversy. But the answer is not to abandon

---

[57] This is the very point that Lord Bridge of Harwich made so forcefully in *Factortame*.
[58] On "integrity", see R. Dworkin, *Law's Empire* (1986), Chap. 7. [And *post*, 724.]
[59] See R. Dworkin, *Taking Rights Seriously*, (1978), Chap. 2.

the enterprise on which they embarked, nor to indulge in put-downs about "inadequate positivist jurisprudence". It is to try to achieve a more thorough and satisfactory analysis that gets to the root of the problem about "pedigree tests", that is in more sober language, "criteria of recognition", and the extent of constitutional power to change those criteria within this legal system as it exists now.

On the other hand, it would be absurd to engage in some kind of a mock battle with the interpretive approach advocated by Allan and Dworkin, on the ground of some factitious—and factious—clash of schools or camps within jurisprudence. It is obvious that one can make no headway whatever with the attempt to understand a constitutional order in terms of the Hartian or similar structural accounts unless one engages in interpretive argument. That has to draw on what one takes to be the implicit principles of a constitutional order of the kind in question, interacting with a supranational community whose constitution is likewise to be interpreted in the light of the principles one takes to animate it. Our understanding of the kind of enterprise Hart was embarked on, and to which he made so large contributions, is indeed transformed when we reconsider it in the light of lessons taught by Dworkin, Allan, Guest,[60] and others of their cast of mind. But this is not, in my view, a transformation that makes redundant the foundational work that went before. The present debate brings this point out with remarkable clarity.

A further remark is necessary with a view to associating the name and achievement of Kelsen with the attempt to reach a synthesis of competing juristic tendencies at this apex-point of legal deliberation. He, after all, gave much thought to identifying the highest point in constitutional order, and the process (if any) of constitutional change to which it is subject. The foregoing discussion of the reciprocal interaction of the highest-level "rule of change" with the "rule of recognition" suggested a way of reading, or rationally reconstructing, actual constitutions, whether written or unwritten, in a theoretically intelligible way. The upshot is that it seems difficult to acquiesce in the idea that, however, you look at it, any constitution can be identified with, or said to yield a single highest-level rule to which all else is in some way subordinate.

From some points of view, most crucial is the dynamic aspect of a constitution, and the way it both empowers and yet sets conditions on legitimate change up to and including change in the constitution itself at its highest level. From other points of view, the question may be one of attempting to make sense of changes that have been made or at least attempted. Here, the critical questions focus on the "rule of recognition", that is on new criteria of validity and how they mesh with pre-existing ones, and, in particular, what are now the obligations of the courts as they seek to do justice "according to law". Understanding a constitution is not understanding any single rule internal to it as fundamental; it is understanding how the rules interact and cross-refer, and how they make sense in the light of the principles of political association that they are properly understood to express. If there is a fundamental obligation here, it is an obligation toward the constitution as a whole. It is the obligation to respect a constitution's integrity as a constitution, an obligation that has significance both in moments of relative stasis and in more dynamic moments. These are moments when, in response to changing circumstances, legislators or the people in a referendum make amendments, or judges engage in interpretative adjustment of principles and doctrines in a way that may produce great constitutional change but that does not thereby amount to radical or revolutionary discontinuity.

This, I think, shows that Kelsen was right in thinking that any fundamental norm underlying the whole of legal order has to be conceived as external to the constitution itself. The constitution is a totality of interrelated rules or norms that is historically given and yet dynamic in providing for the possibility of its own

---

[60] See S. Guest, *Ronald Dworkin* (1997).

change by processes for which it itself makes provision. However, there is no reason to follow Kelsen in treating this as a mere presupposition or transcendental hypothesis. Surely a working constitution requires this to be the kind of shared custom or convention held among those who treat the constitution as foundational of normative order. That is, then, a common social practice, and it is a practice that necessarily involves shared membership in what Dworkin calls a "community of principle", not a mere chance overlap of practical attitudes among those who hold power.[61] The idea of a *Grundnorm*, it is submitted, should be adapted to this sense. It is rewarding to see that out of the fierce dialectic of thesis and counter-thesis, a rewarding synthesis can be created from ideas developed by three of the most powerful and insightful jurisprudential thinkers of the century now ending.

### Sovereignty now

The conclusion of this chapter, in relation to its opening question, is in the negative. There was not in 1972 a revolution in the United Kingdom, not even in a technical legal sense. The constitutional changes that were made in 1972 are capable of being read as changes that involved the use of the "power of change" to add a new "criterion of recognition" to the rule of recognition. Unless this were interpreted as precluding later re-amendment of the rule of recognition by the same process, there would be no constitutional objection in terms of the constitution of 1972. Nothing forces such an interpretation, and it ought not to be accepted. There is therefore no legal discontinuity, no usurpation of power under the guise of legality.

In a less technical usage, the change made in 1972 was momentous enough to invite the label "revolutionary", and *Factortame* does indeed dramatize the point. For the time being, sovereign power has effectively been transferred in relation to certain matters to the European Community and its organs. It nevertheless remains true, when one examines constitutional questions solely in the perspective of English law or (at least *pro tempore*) Scots law, that one can say this with confidence: The power of unilateral reversal of the change of 1972 remains vested in Parliament by the constitutional law of the United Kingdom. Yet at the same time, the very transfer of powers achieved in 1972 introduces a new player into the interpretative scene, the European Court of Justice. So far as concerns obligations arising under the Treaties, the ultimate power of interpretation of the powers transferred by the United Kingdom and other member states, and of interpreting what counts as their valid implementation, rests with the European Court of Justice.

Under the constitutional case-law developed by the ECJ, the law of the European Community is a distinct legal system of a new type, neither international law nor state law, that enjoys "primacy" or "supremacy" over the laws of the member states. As Lord Bridge noted, this was an established doctrine before the United Kingdom resolved to join the Community. It carries the implication that Community law as a distinct system applies to all member states, and thus to the United Kingdom, and that in the perspective of this law the obligations of the member states to respect Community institutions are determined by Community law, not national law. It is therefore a question of Community law whether the overriding effect of Community norms over norms of national law includes or does not include fundamental constitutional provisions including those that could be interpreted as preserving a unilateral power of secession.        [pp. 79–94]

---

[61] See *Law's Empire*, ch. 6.

# W. N. HOHFELD
**Fundamental Legal Conceptions as Applied in Judicial Reasoning**
(1923)[62]

One of the greatest hindrances to the clear understanding, the incisive statement, and the true solution of legal problems frequently arises from the express or tacit assumption that all legal relations may be reduced to "rights" and "duties," and that these latter categories are therefore adequate for the purpose of analyzing even the most complex legal interests, such as trusts, options, escrows, "future" interests, corporate interests, etc. Even if the difficulty related merely to inadequacy and ambiguity of terminology, its seriousness would nevertheless be worthy of definite recognition and persistent effort toward improvement; for in any closely reasoned problem, whether legal or non-legal, chameleon-hued words are a peril both to clear thought and to lucid expression. As a matter of fact, however, the above mentioned inadequacy and ambiguity of terms unfortunately reflect, all too often, corresponding paucity and confusion as regards actual legal conceptions. That this is so may appear in some measure from the discussion to follow.

The strictly fundamental legal relations are, after all, *sui generis*; and thus it is that attempts at formal definition are always unsatisfactory, if not altogether useless. Accordingly, the most promising line of procedure seems to consist in exhibiting all of the various relations in a scheme of "opposites" and "correlatives," and then proceeding to exemplify their individual scope and application in concrete cases. An effort will be made to pursue this method:

| Opposites | { | right | privilege | power | immunity |
|---|---|---|---|---|---|
| | { | no-right | duty | disability | liability |
| | | | | | |
| Correlatives | { | right | privilege | power | immunity |
| | { | duty | no-right | liability | disability |

*Rights and Duties.* As already intimated, the term "rights" tends to be used indiscriminately to cover what in a given case may be a privilege, a power, or an immunity, rather than a right in the strictest sense...

Recognizing, as we must, the very broad and indiscriminate use of the term "right," what clue do we find, in ordinary legal discourse, toward limiting the word in question to a definite and appropriate meaning? That clue lies in the correlative "duty," for it is certain that even those who use the word and the conception "right" in the broadest possible way are accustomed to thinking of "duty" as the invariable correlative.[63] As said in *Lake Shore & M. S. R. Co. v. Kurtz*[64]:

"A duty or a legal obligation is that which one ought or ought not do to. 'Duty' and 'right' are correlative terms. When a right is invaded, a duty is violated,"[65]

---

[62] [From (ed. Cook, 1923), Chap. 1.]

[63] [A useful illustration of the practical value of Hohfeldian analysis may be found in J. W. Harris, 87 L. Q. R. 31. Harris distinguishes four concepts of duty and finds a failure to appreciate that the concept can be used differently at the root of the confusion between trusts and powers.]

[64] (1894) 10 Ind. App. 60.

[65] See also *Howley Park Coal, etc., Co. v. L. & N. W. Ry.* [1913] A. C. 11, 25. (*Per* Viscount Haldane L. C at 27: "There is an obligation (of lateral support) on the neighbour, and in that sense there is a correlative right on the part of the owner of the first piece of land"; *per* Lord Shaw: "There is a reciprocal right to lateral support for their respective lands and a reciprocal obligation upon the part of each owner.... No diminution of the right on the one hand or of the obligation on the other can be effected except as the result of a plain contract...").

In other words, if X has a right against Y that he shall stay off the former's land, the correlative (and equivalent) is that Y is under a duty toward X to stay off the place. If, as seems desirable, we should seek a synonym for the term "right" in this limited and proper meaning, perhaps the word "claim" would prove the best. The latter has the advantage of being a monosyllable . . .[66]

*Privileges and "No-Rights."*[67] As indicated in the above scheme of jural relations, a privilege is the opposite of a duty, and the correlative of a "no-right." In the example last put, whereas X has a *right* or *claim* that Y, the other man, should stay off the land, he himself has the *privilege* of entering on the lead; or, in equivalent words, X does not have a duty to stay off. The privilege of entering is the negation of a duty to stay off. As indicated by this case, some caution is necessary at this point; for, always when it is said that a given privilege is the mere negation of a *duty*, what is meant, of course, is a duty having a content or tenor precisely *opposite* to that of the privilege in question. Thus, if, for some special reason, X has contracted with Y to go on the former's own land, it is obvious that X has, as regards Y, both the privilege of entering and the *duty of entering*. The privilege is perfectly consistent with this sort of duty—for the latter is of the *same* content or tenor as the privilege;—but it still holds good that, as regards Y, X's privilege if entering is the precise negation of a duty *to stay off*. Similarly, if A has not contracted with B to perform certain work for the later, A's privilege of *not* doing so is the very negation of the duty of *doing* so. Here again the duty contrasted is of content or tenor exactly opposite to that of the privilege.[68]

Passing now to the question of "correlatives," it will be remembered, of course, that a duty is the invariable correlative of that legal relation which is most properly called a right or claim. That being so, if further evidence be needed as to the fundamental and important difference between a right (or claim) and a privilege, surely it is found in the fact that the correlative of the latter relation is a "no-right," there being no single term available to express the latter conception. Thus, the correlative of X's right that Y shall not enter on the land is Y's duty not to enter; but the correlative of X's privilege of entering himself is manifestly Y's "no-right" that X shall not enter.

In view of the considerations thus far emphasized, the importance of keeping the conception of a right (or claim) and the conception of a privilege quite distinct from each other seems evident; and, more than that, it is equally clear that there should be a separate term to represent the latter relation. No doubt, as already indicated, it is very common to use the term "right" indiscriminately, even when the relation designated is really that of privilege; and only too often this identity of terms has involved for the particular speaker or writer a confusion or blurring of ideas. . . .

. . . On grounds already emphasized, it would seem that the line of reasoning pursued by Lord Lindley in the great case of *Quinn v. Leathem*[69] is deserving of comment:

"The plaintiff had the ordinary *rights* of the British subject. He was at *liberty* to earn his living in his own way, provided he did not violate some special law prohibiting him from so doing, and provided he did not infringe the rights of other people. This *liberty* involved *the liberty* to deal with other persons who were

---

[66] [Hart has shown that claims can be defined as a power to enforce a duty coupled with the power to abolish the duty. See *Definition and Theory in Jurisprudence*, p. 16.]

[67] [See further Glanville Williams, "The Concept of a Legal Liberty" in Summers (ed.), *Essays in Legal Philosophy* (1968), p. 121. Williams, and many contemporary writers, prefer "liberty" to "privilege" as they believe the latter is tinged with political connotation of something specially granted, whereas in fact most "rights" are privileges or liberties.]

[68] [For the argument that privilege is not the negation of duty. See White (1978) 41 M. L. R. 299.]

[69] [1901] A. C. 495 at 534.

willing to deal with him. *This liberty* is *a right* recognized by law; its *correlative* is the general *duty* of every one not to prevent the free exercise of this *liberty* except so far as his own liberty of action may justify him in so doing. But a person's *liberty* or *right* to deal with others is nugatory unless they are at liberty to deal with him if they choose to do so. Any interference with their liberty to deal with him affects him."

A "liberty" considered as a legal relation (or "right" in the loose and generic sense of that term) must mean, if it have any definite content at all, precisely the same thing as *privilege*; and certainly that is the fair connotation of the term as used the first three times in the passage quoted. It is equally clear, as already indicated, that such a privilege or liberty to deal with others at will might very conceivably exist without any peculiar concomitant rights against "third parties" as regards certain kinds of interference.[70] Whether there should be such concomitant rights (or claims) is ultimately a question of justice and policy; and it should be considered, as such, on its merits. The only correlative logically implied by the privileges or liberties in question are the "no-rights" of "third parties." It would therefore be a *non sequitur* to conclude from the mere existence of such liberties that "third parties" are under a *duty* not to interfere, etc. Yet in the middle of the above passage from Lord Lindley's opinion there is a sudden and question-begging shift in the use of terms. First, the "liberty" in question is transmuted into a "right"; and then, possibly under the seductive influence of the latter word, it is assumed that the "correlative" must be "the general duty of every one not to prevent," etc.

Another interesting and instructive example may be taken from Lord Bowen's oft-quoted opinion in *Mogul Steamship Co. v. McGregor.*[71]

"We are presented in this case with an apparent conflict or antimony between two rights that are equally regarded by the law—the right of the plaintiffs to be protected in the legitimate exercise of their trade, and the right of the defendants to carry on their business as seems best to them, provided they commit no wrong to others."

As the learned judge states, the conflict or antimony is only apparent; but this fact seems to be obscured by the very indefinite and rapidly shifting meanings with which the term "right" is used in the above quoted language. Construing the passage as a whole, it seems plain enough that by "the right of the plaintiffs" in relation to the defendants a legal right or claim in the strict sense must be meant; whereas by "the right of the defendants" in relation to the plaintiffs a legal privilege must be intended. That being so, the "two rights" mentioned in the beginning of the passage, being respectively claim and privilege, could not be in conflict with each other. To the extent that the defendants have privileges the plaintiffs have no rights; and, conversely, to the extent that the plaintiffs have rights the defendants have no privileges ("no-privilege" equals duty of opposite tenor). [pp. 35–44]

...*Powers and Liabilities.* As indicated in the preliminary scheme of jural relations, a legal power (as distinguished, of course, from a mental or physical power) is the opposite of legal disability, and the correlative of legal liability. But what is the intrinsic nature of a legal power as such? Is it possible to analyze the conception represented by this constantly employed and very important term of legal discourse? Too close an analysis might seem metaphysical rather than useful; so that what is here presented is intended only as an approximate explanation, sufficient for all practical purposes.

A change in a given legal relation may result (1) from some superadded fact or group of facts not under the volitional control of a human being (or human beings): or (2) *from* some superadded fact or group of facts which are under the

---

[70] Compare *Allen v. Flood* [1898] A. C. 1.
[71] (1889) 23 Q. B. D. 59.

volitional control of one or more human beings. As regards the second class of cases, the person (or persons) whose volitional control is paramount may be said to have the (legal) power to effect the particular change of legal relations that is involved in the problem.

The second class of cases—powers in the technical sense—must now be further considered. The nearest synonym for any ordinary case seems to be (legal) "ability,"—the latter being obviously the opposite of "inability," or "disability." The term "right," so frequently and loosely used in the present connection, is an unfortunate term for the purpose,—a not unusual result being confusion of thought as well as ambiguity of expression. The term "capacity" is equally unfortunate; for, as well have already seen, when used with discrimination, this word denotes a particular group of operative facts, and not a legal relation of any kind.

Many examples of legal powers may readily be given. Thus, X, the owner of ordinary personal property "in a tangible object" has the power to extinguish his own legal interest (rights, powers, immunities, etc.), through that totality of operative facts known as abandonment; and—simultaneously and correlatively— to create in other persons privileges and powers relating to the abandoned object—*e.g.* the power to acquire title to the latter by appropriating it. *Similarly*, X has the power to transfer his interest to Y—that is, to extinguish his own interest and concomitantly create in Y a new and corresponding interest. So also X has the power to create contractual obligations of various kinds. Agency cases are likewise instructive. By the use of some *metaphorical* expression such as the Latin, *qui facit per alium, facit per se*, the true nature of agency relations is only too frequency obscured. The creation of an agency relation involves, *inter alia*, the grant of legal powers to the so-called agent, and the creation of correlative liabilities in the principal. That is to say, one party, P, has the power to create agency powers in another party, A,—for example, the power to convey P's property, the power to impose (so-called) contractual obligations on P, the power to discharge a debt owing to P, the power to "receive" title to property so that it shall vest in P, and so forth. In passing, it may well be to observe that the term "authority," so frequently used in agency cases, is very ambiguous and slippery in its connotation. Properly employed in the present connection, the word seems to be an abstract or qualitative term corresponding to the concrete "authorization,"—the latter consisting of a particular group of operative facts taking place between the principal and the agent. All too often, however, the term in question is so used as to blend and confuse these operative facts with the powers and privileges thereby created in the agent. A careful discrimination in these particulars would, it is submitted, go far toward clearing up certain problems in the law of agency....

...Passing now to the field of contracts, suppose A mails a letter to B offering to sell the former's land, Whiteacre, to the latter for ten thousand dollars, such letter being duly received. The operative facts thus far mentioned have created a power as regards B and a correlative liability as regards A. B, by dropping a letter of acceptance in the box has the power to impose a potential or inchoate obligation *ex contractu* on A and himself; and, assuming that the land is worth fifteen thousand dollars, that particular legal quantity—the "power *plus* liability" relation between A and B—seems to be worth above five thousand dollars to B. The liability of A will continue for a reasonable time unless, in exercise of his power to do so, A previously extinguishes it by that series of operative facts known as "revocation." These last matters are usually described by saying that A's "offer" will "continue" or "remain open" for a reasonable time, or for the definite time actually specified, unless A previously "withdraws" or "revokes" such offer. While, no doubt, in the great majority of cases no harm results from the use of such expressions, yet these forms of statement seem to represent a blending of non-legal and legal quantities which, in any problem requiring careful reasoning, should preferably be kept distinct. An offer, considered as a series of physical and mental operative facts, has spent its force and become *functus officio* as soon as such series has been completed by the "offeree's receipt." The real question is therefore as to the *legal effect*, if any, at that moment of time. If the latter consist of B's power and A's correlative liability, manifestly it is those *legal relations* that "continue" or "remain open" until modified by revocation or other operative facts. What has thus far been said concerning contracts completed by mail would seem to apply, *mutatis mutandis*, to every type of contract. Even where the parties are in the presence of each other, the offer creates a liability against the offerer, together with a correlative power in favour of the offeree. The only distinction for present purposes would be in the fact that such power and such liability would expire within a very short period of time. . . .

. . . In view of what has already been said, very little may suffice concerning a *liability* as such. The latter, as we have seen, is the correlative of power, and the opposite of immunity (or exemption). While no doubt the term "liability" is often loosely used as a synonym for "duty," or "obligation," it is believed, from an extensive survey of judicial precedents, that the connotation already adopted as most appropriate to the word in question is fully justified. . . .

. . . *Immunities and Disabilities*. As already brought out, immunity is the correlative of disability ("no-power), and the opposite, or negation, of liability. Perhaps it will also be plain, from the preliminary outline and from the discussion down to this point, that a power bears the same general contrast to an immunity that a right does to a privilege. A right is one's affirmative claim against another, and a privilege is one's freedom from the right or claim of another. Similarly, a power is one's affirmative "control" over a given legal relation as against another; whereas an immunity is one's freedom from the legal power or "control" of another as regards some legal relation.[72]

A few examples may serve to make this clear. X, a landowner, has, as we have seen, power to alienate to Y or to any other ordinary party. On the other hand, X has also various immunities as against Y, and all other ordinary parties. For Y is under a disability (*i.e.* has no power) so far as shifting the legal interest either to himself or to a third party is concerned; and what is true of Y applies similarly to every one else who has not by virtue of special operative facts acquired a power to alienate X's property. If, indeed, a sheriff has been duly empowered by a writ of execution to sell X's interest, that is a very different matter: correlative to such sheriff's power would be the *liability* of X—the very opposite of immunity (or exemption). It is elementary, too, that as against the sheriff, X might be immune or exempt in relation to certain parcels of property, and be liable as to others. Similarly, if an agent has been duly appointed by X to sell a given piece of property, then, as to the latter, X has, in relation to such agent, a liability rather an immunity. . . .

. . . In the latter part of the preceding discussion, eight conceptions of the law have been analyzed and compared in some detail, the purpose having been to exhibit not only their intrinsic meaning and scope, but also their relations to one another and the methods by which they are applied, in judicial reasoning, to the solution of concrete problems of litigation. Before concluding this branch of the discussion a general suggestion may be ventured as to the great practical importance of a clear appreciation of the distinctions and discriminations set forth. If a homely metaphor be permitted, these eight conceptions,—rights and

---

[72] [For an example of the distinction see *Broome v. D P P* [1974] A. C. 587 discussed in (1975) L. Q. R. 173 (Goodwin-Gill) and *cf. Kavanagh v. Hiscock* [1974] Q. B. 600. For examples of immunities consider the immunity of trade unions to actions in tort (Trade Union and Labour Relations Act 1974, s. 14) and of the Post Office in regard to its public duty to provide services (Post Office Act 1969, s. 9; and see *Gouriet v. Post Office Workers* [1977] 3 All E. R. 70 at 79).]

duties, privileges and no-rights, powers and liabilities, immunities and disabilities,—seem to be what may be called "the lowest common denominators of
the law." Ten fractions (1–3, 2–5, etc.), may, *superficially*, seem so different from
one another as to defy comparison. If, however, they are expressed in terms of
their lowest common denominators, (5–15, 6–15, etc.), comparison becomes easy,
and fundamental similarity may be discovered. The same thing is of course true as
regards the lowest generic conceptions to which any and all "legal quantities"
may be reduced.

Reverting, for example, to the subject to powers, it might be difficult at first
glance to discover any essential and fundamental similarity between conditional
sales of personalty, escrow transactions, option agreements, agency relations,
powers of appointment, etc. But if all these relations are reduced to their lowest
generic terms, the conceptions of legal power and legal liability are seen to be
dominantly, though not exclusively, applicable throughout the series. By such a
process it becomes possible not only to discover essential similarities and illuminating analogies in the midst of what appears superficially to be infinite and
hopeless variety, but also to discern common principles of justice and policy
underlying the various jural problems involved. An indirect, yet very practical,
consequence is that it frequently becomes feasible, by virtue of such analysis, to
use as persuasive authorities judicial precedents that might otherwise seem altogether irrelevant. If this point be valid with respect to powers, it would seem to be
equally so as regards all of the other basic conceptions of the law. In short, the
deeper the analysis, the greater becomes one's perception of fundamental unity
and harmony in the law.[73]                                                  [pp. 50–64]

### WILLIAM A. EDMUNDSON
### The Duty to Obey the Law
### (2004)

#### *Positive Accounts and Rebuttals*

The preponderance of the recent literature on the duty to obey the law consists of
positive accounts of the duty, responsive criticism, and rejoinders. The positive
accounts typically acknowledge the influence of John Simmons's 1979 book,
*Moral Principles and Political Obligations*, which built so impressive a negative
case that it is no exaggeration to say that the literature of the intervening quarter-
century has largely consisted of efforts to overcome or deflect Simmons's
objections.

It may be helpful to contrast "primitive" and "derived" positive accounts.
Derived accounts seek to justify the duty by tying it to a wider and perhaps less
controversial moral principle or cluster of moral principles. Primitive accounts,
on the other hand, seek to defend the duty as morally freestanding: Primitive
accounts may but need not locate the duty within a wider constellation of moral
principles, with which they may conflict. Instances of primitive accounts include
the "conceptual argument", which represents moral obligatoriness as essential to

---

[73] [For a critical but sympathetic appraisal of Hohfeld's scheme, see M. Radin, "A
Restatement of Hohfeld" in (1938) 51 Harv. Law. Rev. 1141. Less sympathetic critical
accounts are Finnis, 4 Adelaide L. Rev. 377 and Attwooll in, *Perspectives in Jurisprudence* (Attwooll ed., 1977), p. 79. See also MacCormick's criticism of Hohfeld's
reduction of rights to "atomic relationships" without residue. He points out that though
legislation may establish a whole set of such relationships no particular set would be
equivalent to the right actually established. (See Hacker and Raz (eds.) *Law, Morals and
Society*, pp. 206–207).

the existence of a legal system.[74] Certain hierarchical accounts of society and law's role in giving society its proper shape could be considered as primitive accounts of the duty to obey the law—I have in mind F.H. Bradley's "My Station and Its Duties" and resonances of Edmund Burke's or Hegel's organic visions of civil society. Also perhaps belonging in the primitive category are defenses that appeal to the presumptive correctness of moral intuition: Mark Murphy's recent defense of the duty by appeal to what he calls the "conscience principle" is an example.[75] Another way to take such accounts is as amplifications of an adequacy condition applicable to other, derived accounts.

Any discussion of a derived theory naturally falls into two parts. The first is an elaboration of the more general principle. The second is an evaluation of the prospects of assimilating political obligation to the general principle. Within the category of the derived, it may also be helpful to observe a distinction between "unary" and "mixed" accounts. Unary derived accounts approach the problem of defending the duty as a problem of deriving the duty from a single, more general moral principle whose validity is less dubious than that of the duty to obey the law. Derived mixed accounts do not restrict themselves to a single moral principle. Unary derived accounts can be further divided into three subcategories: *natural-duty* accounts, *volitional* accounts, and *associative* accounts. Briefly, natural duties are predicated upon nothing more than the personhood of the duty-bearer; volitional duties are predicated upon some voluntary act or preference of the duty-bearer; and associative duties are predicated upon the duty-bearer's perhaps unchosen and unwanted association with some proper subset of all persons. Other divisions are possible. Simmons and Wellman distinguish natural-duty accounts, associative accounts, and transactional accounts, each having further subdivisions.[76] Green divides the leading positive accounts into two major categories: voluntarist theories and nonvoluntarist theories.[77] > I claim no particular advantage for the scheme of classification I use here, other than the possibility that organizing the field in a different way may highlight important linkages.

Mixed derived accounts might conceivably draw upon elements from any combination within or across the three subcategories, but in fact advocates of mixed theories have not found it fruitful to exploit all such possibilities. In what immediately follows, I will outline some of the principal unary derived accounts. I will conclude by considering several noteworthy mixed theories.

## A. Natural Duty Accounts

Rawls described natural duties in this way:

> in contrast with obligations, it is characteristic of natural duties that they apply to us without regard to our voluntary acts. Moreover, they have no necessary connection with institutions or social practices; their content is not, in general, defined by the rules of these arrangements. ... A further feature of natural duties is that they hold between people irrespective of their institutional relationships; they obtain between all as equal moral persons. In this sense the natural duties are owed not only to definite individuals, say to those cooperating together in a particular social arrangement, but to persons generally. This feature in particular suggests the propriety of the adjective "natural."[78]

---

[74] Simmons 2001a, 72.

[75] M. Murphy, *Philosophical Anarchisms*.

[76] A. John Simmons, *Political Obligation and Authority*, *in* BLACKWELL GUIDE TO SOCIAL AND POLITICAL PHILOSOPHY (Robert L. Simon, ed., 2002); Christopher H. Wellman, *Political Obligation and the Particularity Requirement*, 10 LEGAL THEORY 97–115 (2004).

[77] Green, 5.

[78] RAWLS, *supra* note 18, at 114–115.

I have discussed Rawl's shifting view of political obligation elsewhere;[79] here it will suffice to say that his mature view was that political obligation, insofar as it purports to be universally borne, must be defended as deriving from a natural duty to support and comply with just institutions.[80] There are other natural-duty theories as well, but recent discussion has been dominated by a general objection, termed the "particularity problem," which has been made to any natural-duty account of political obligation and which some view as the most serious difficulty for any defense of political obligation.[81] John Simmons, who has pressed the objection, puts it this way:

> Political obligations are felt to be obligations of obedience and support owed to one particular government or community (our own), above all others. Citizens' obligations are special ties, involving loyalty or commitment to the political community in which they were born or in which they reside. More general duties with possible political content, such as duties to promote justice, equality, or utility, cannot explain (or justify, or be) our political obligations, for such duties do not necessarily tie us either to one particular community or to our own community.[82]

Rawls's natural duty to support just institutions, for example, is one that everyone—wherever and however situated—is supposed to owe toward existing, sufficiently just institutions—wherever and however situated. But the fact is that people believe they have special ties to their own states (however flawed) and not to others (however just). Natural-duty theory cannot dismiss this attitude without doing violence to what is a settled conviction of many reflective and reasonable people, and therefore the theory must instead somehow reconstruct it. The most promising lines of reconstruction for the natural duty theorist, however, are ones that seem to invoke things like consent or receipt of benefits—invocations that would lead to a mixed theory. The pursuit of a unary natural-duty theory of political obligation, the objection concludes, is a dead end. The objection is equally apt with respect to the duty to obey or to more encompassing notions of political obligation; it seems odd to say that one owes to persons generally a duty to obey the law, and odder still if we were to understand that duty to encompass the laws of (sufficiently just) states generally.

Jeremy Waldron has offered a general answer to the particularity objection on behalf of natural-duty accounts: he begins by noting a qualification in Rawls's statement of the natural duty and a related objection arising from that qualification.[83] Rawl's duty to support and comply with just institutions is restricted to those that "apply to us," and the objection[84] is that no sense can be given to the restriction without turning to ideas of consent or fair play. (The companion duty to help *create* just institutions is not qualified in this way but is instead qualified by the condition that the cost to the actor be minimal.) Preliminarily, Waldron notes that all will agree that there is a natural duty not to undermine just institutions existing elsewhere and argues that theories of "acquired" obligation (including consent and fair-play theories) cannot well explain why this should be so.

Waldron distinguishes between "range-limited" and range-unlimited principles of justice, and, as to the former, between two categories of person—insiders and outsiders. Range-limited principles are principles intended to do justice between a limited set of persons, for example, Hobbes's children or New Zealanders.

---

[79]  William A. Edmundson, *Introduction, in* THE DUTY TO OBEY THE LAW: SELECTED PHILO-SOPHICAL READINGS (William A. Edmundson, ed., 1999b).

[80]  RAWLS, *supra* note 18, at 114–117, 333–355.

[81]  Wellman, *supra* note 78.

[82]  A. JOHN SIMMONS, MORAL PRINCIPLES AND POLITICAL OBLIGATIONS (1979), at 250.

[83]  Waldron, *supra* note 18.

[84]  SIMMONS, *supra* note 85, at 151.

"Insiders" are simply those within the range of "conduct, claims, and interests" with which the relevant principle—or its administering institution—purports to deal[85]—they need not be volunteers or in any other sense beneficiaries. Waldron cites three conditions that must be satisfied if range-limited principles of justice are to be effective: (1) insiders must accept the demand of the relevant range-limited principle; (2) insiders must accept the demand that they accept the administering institution's administration of the principle; and (3) insiders and outsiders must refrain from undermining the administering institution. Waldron claims that his account of these demands makes sense of the Rawlsian proviso that the actor's duty to support just institutions is limited to those that "apply to him" and at the same time explains "much of" the specialness of an actor's relationship to his own national institutions—conceding that there is a somewhat atavistic residue of "patriotic affect" that escapes. Waldron's position is that "an organization that is just, effective, and legitimate (in the sense of being singled out as *the* salient organization for this territory) has *eo ipso* a claim on our allegiance.[86] With reference to Simmons's objection that others "cannot simply force institutions on me, no matter how just, and force on me a moral bond to do my part,"[87] Waldron responds that because the pursuit of substantive justice is morally imperative, at some point "the theorist of natural duty must stop treating [the] question, 'Can an organization simply impose itself on us, morally . . .?' as an objection and simply insist that the answer is yes."[88]

Although the particularity worry has dominated much recent discussion, the intuition from which it springs is not beyond question, and the absence after a decade of a compelling rejoinder to Waldron suggests that the worry may be overwrought.[89] John Simmons insists that "political obligations, properly understood, must bind us to one particular community or government in a way that is special [i.e., a way that arises from special relationships with certain others and are owed to these others and not to humankind generally]; if an obligation or duty is not "particularized" in this way, it cannot be what we ordinarily think of as a political obligation."[90] But it is not obvious why the particularly intuition should be any more sacrosanct than the prereflective intuition that political obligations exist—an intuition that Simmons himself repeatedly warns against taking at face value.[91] It may turn out that our political obligations are more cosmopolitan than we suppose prior to reflection. Simmons concedes that dual and multiple citizenship are held by many but doubts "whether one can satisfy all of the *possible* demands of obedience and support to more than one state simultaneously."[92] The doubt seems hyperbolic, however, it is a common-place occurrence for pro tanto duties to come into conflict without ceasing *ipso facto* to be genuine duties.

On Waldron's account, the range of a range-limited principle is determined with reference to its "point and justification,"[93] and so need not be limited in range to a geographical area; and a "territory," as he uses the term, need not correspond to any conventional boundary but may be "any area within which conflicts must be settled if any stable system of resource use is to be possible among the inhabitants."[94] The possibility arises that more than one institution may impose rules that apply to persons within a geographical area, and—because

---

[85] Waldron, *supra* note 18, at 279–280.
[86] *Id*. at 27.
[87] SIMMONS, *supra* note 85, at 148.
[88] Waldron, *supra* note 18, at 27.
[89] *Cf*. Mason, *supra* note 20, at 436–437; Wellman, *supra* note 78, at 101–105.
[90] Simmons, *supra* note 78, at 29.
[91] *Id*. at 20, 23.
[92] *Id*. at 29; emphasis in original.
[93] Waldron, *supra* note 18, at 280 of reprint.
[94] *Id*. at 281 of reprint.

Yet another problem for instrumentalist theories is what could be called the "harmless disobedience" difficulty, often put with reference to what have been termed "stop-sign-in-the-desert" examples, which are devised to show that there is nothing even pro tanto wrong with disobeying the law when there is a vanishingly low chance of harm and a palpable benefit to be gained.[11] Unless obedience is itself a morally compelling end, such theories are open to the objection that perfect and universal obedience is as a matter of fact not necessary to achieve plausible social ends—such as order, harmony, or substantive justice. A standard first move made to avoid the harmless-disobedience difficulty is to insist upon the necessity of social coordination to achieve a range of morally compelling ends[12]—but this move is generally agreed to fail for the simple reason that schemes of social coordination are typically able to tolerate nonconformity in small amounts. What has become the standard fallback move for such theories is the invocation of a fair-play duty, which condemns even harmless noncompliance as unfair to (or disrespectful of the equal worth of) those who do comply with socially beneficial rules. Theories that avail themselves of this move could be considered as mixed rather than pure theories or possibly as pure fair-play theories.

### Contractarian or Hypothetical-Consent Theories

Despite their voluntaristic flavor, accounts of this type are now widely thought to be properly classified as natural-duty theories.[13] Because such accounts are designedly insensitive to what Simmons calls "the eccentricties of individual uptake,"[14] their emphasis falls heavily upon what one ought to consent to rather than upon what one has in fact consented to. Moreover, because such theories typically invoke a highly idealized choice situation—such as Rawls's celebrated "original position"—their relevance to the constrained circumstances in which citizens would actually exercise or withhold their consent is questionable.[15]

Rawls's contractarian defense of the natural duty to support and comply with just institutions in *A Theory of Justice* has been so influential as to occupy the field.[16] Space will not permit a detailed examination of Rawls's view here; but the difficulties attending a contractarian account of the duty to obey are fairly obvious. For one, it is unclear what could rationally compel assent to a comprehensively applicable duty when it is well known that even just states may adopt silly and unjust laws. For another, the merits of the content independence that is supposed to characterize the duty to obey is controversial,[17] and thus it is difficult to understand why rational assent to the duty would be compelled, especially in the absence of any assurance that the state's judgment is generally superior to the citizen's.[18] To the extent that contractarian arguments take on a consequentialist flavor, they must overcome the "harmless disobedience" difficulty that attends the latter; and to the extent that the principle of fairness is invoked to avoid the difficulty, that principle must be reconstructed on a contractarian foundation if the overall account is to be unary rather than mixed.[19]

---

[11]  Smith, *supra* note 26.

[12]  *Cf.* Finnis, *supra* note 109; TONY HONORÉ, MAKING LAW BIND (1987), at 56–66.

[13]  Simmons, *supra* note 78; David Schmidtz, *Justifying the State*, 101 ETHICS 89–102 (1990); Cynthia Stark, *Hypothetical Consent and Justification*, 97 J. PHIL. 313–334 (2000); Cushing, *supra* note 50.

[14]  Simmons 2001a, 148.

[15]  Simmons, *supra* note 78.

[16]  Rawls, *supra* note 18; *cf.* Simon Cushing, *Rawls and "Duty-Based" Accounts of Political Obligation*, 99 APA NEWSL. ON PHIL. & L. 71–77 (1999); Lefkowitz, *supra* note 27, at 412–415.

[17]  *See, e.g.*, Alexander, *supra* note 38; Moore, *supra* note 62; Hurd, *supra* note 62.

[18]  Raz, *supra* note 112; CHRISTOPHER MORRIS, AN ESSAY ON THE MODERN STATE (1998).

[19]  *Cf.* WILLIAM A. EDMUNDSON, AN INTRODUCTION TO RIGHTS (2004), at 114–118.

*Fair-Play Accounts*

These accounts are inspired by H.L.A. Hart's celebrated *duty of fair play*, that is, the duty to cooperate that falls upon those who benefit from the cooperative sacrifices of others.[20] As Rawls expressed the idea:

> when a number of persons engage in a mutually advantageous cooperative venture according to rules, and thus restrict their liberty in ways necessary to yield advantages to all, those who have submitted to these restrictions have a right to a similar acquiescence on the part of those who have benefitted from their submission.[21]

Coordinate to the "right to acquiescence" is a duty on the part of the beneficiaries to submit to the rules. In Rawls's contractarian scheme, the principle of fair play would be adopted by suitably situated and qualified choosers and would hence count as a natural duty. Nonetheless, particular fair-play duties do not count as natural duties, Rawls concluded, because applications of the principle presuppose the knowing and presumably voluntary acceptance of benefits. The qualification led Rawls to abandon his erstwhile[22] hope of deriving universally borne political obligations from the principle of fairness. Simmons has elaborated this qualification and its implications for a fair-play account of the duty to obey.[23] A fairness principle that presupposes voluntary participation in a cooperative social venture and the willing acceptance of benefits deriving therefrom would be of limited use in the defense of a duty to obey the law. Although such a defense could fairly easily satisfy particularity worries (transborder "spillover" effects aside), it would fail to establish a duty universally borne except in the rare instance of smaller, well-integrated communities. In larger states, it is unlikely that all will regard themselves as willing cooperators.[24] Even if a cooperation condition were dispensed with, there remains the difficulty that public goods such as police protection and national defense are ones whose receipt noncooperators have no real choice about; and as to such "nonexcludable" goods, a principle of fair play that requires acceptance of benefits over and above mere receipt is unsatisfiable.[25]

A fair-play defense of the duty to obey thus faces a dilemma. A broader, nonvoluntaristic conception of the principle is vulnerable to Robert Nozick's notorious "classical music" counterexample:[26] Even if I enjoy the classical music my neighbors cooperatively broadcast by sacrificing one day a year at the community turntable, why should I have to pitch in? But a narrower, voluntaristic conception fails to generate a universally borne duty.[27] A number of philosophers[28] have treated the dilemma. Klosko, for example, contesting Rawls's and Simmons's voluntaristic formulation of the fairness principle, has emphasized the role of "presumptively beneficial goods"—a concept intended to track Rawls's primary goods, which are (unlike piped music) irrebuttably taken to be valued by any rational agent. I have discussed these efforts and Simmons's counters to them elsewhere and will not recapitulate that discussion here. It will perhaps be enough to say that the running dispute between Klosko and Simmons as to the proper general formulation of a binding principle of fairness turns upon appeals to one's intuitive response to a number of hypothetical state-of-nature situations that

---

[20] H.L.A. Hart, *Are There Any Natural Rights?* 64 PHIL. REV. 175–191 (1955).

[21] Rawls, *supra* note 18, at 112.

[22] John Rawls, *Legal Obligation and the Duty of Fair Play, in* LAW AND PHILOSOPHY, 3–18 (Sidney Hook, ed., 1964).

[23] Simmons, *supra* note 85, Simmons, *supra* note 25.

[24] Simmons, *supra* note 85.

[25] *Id*; Wolff, *supra* note 50.

[26] Robert Nozick, ANARCHY, STATE, AND UTOPIA (1974).

[27] Simmons, *supra* note 85; Wolff, *supra* note 50.

[28] Klosko, *supra* note 17; Arneson, *supra* note 17; Dagger, *supra* note 11.

involve undoubted benefits that cooperators bestow upon an "outsider" who prefers self-provision. Even if (as I think) Klosko has the better of the argument as to the general formulation of the fair-play principle, the problem remains that far from all of the goods in the bundle the state provides are presumptively beneficial, and thus the duty generated fails to be comprehensively applicable.

[pp 228–238)]

# 7

# THEORIES OF JUSTICE

## INTRODUCTION

Some of the earliest thinking about justice is found in Aristotle. It was he who distinguished "corrective justice" and "distributive justice".[1] The law of tort is often justified in terms of corrective justice. Seen in this way its objective is to do justice between the parties without taking account of larger distributive issues in society as a whole.[2] Whether this can be done is debatable—but this debate must be reserved for later in this chapter.[3] Most contemporary writing about justice is about distributive justice, about the appropriate distribution of goods. In the *Nicomachean Ethics*, Aristotle puts forward the view that goods should be distributed to individuals on the basis of their relative claims.[4] Such an idea is but a framework for examining different conceptions of justice: thus goods might be distributed according to needs[5] or desert[6] or moral virtue[7], etc.

## RAWLS AND DISTRIBUTIVE JUSTICE

One of the most interesting modern attempts to defend principles of justice is found in John Rawls's *A Theory of Justice*,[8] as now reformulated in *Political Liberalism*.[9] One cannot think about justice, one commentator observed,[10] without taking a position in Rawls's *Theory of Justice*.

---

[1] *Nicomachean Ethics*, Book V, paras 3:1131a–4:1132b. On the concept of justice itself see J. Waldron (2003) 9 *Legal Theory* 269.

[2] And see S. R. Perry (1992) 77 Iowa L.R. 449 and L. Weinrib, *The Idea of Private Law* (1995), pp. 56–144. W. Lucy, *Philosophy of Private Law* (2007).

[3] *Post*, 629.

[4] And see A. Beever (2004) 10 *Legal Theory* 33.

[5] *Cf.* Marx, *post*, 1150. See also D. Miller, *Social Justice* (1976), Chap. IV and M. Walzer, *Spheres of Justice* (1983), pp. 25–26 and 75–76.

[6] See D. Miller, *op. cit.*, n. 5, Chap. III, and J. Lucas (1972) 47 Philosophy 229–248.

[7] As commonly within the natural law tradition: see, *ante*, Chap. 3.

[8] First published in 1972 a revised edition was published in 1999: see the extract, *post*, 566. On Rawls' life and work see T. Pogge, *John Rawls: His Life and Theory of Justice* (2007).

[9] Published in 1993: see the extract, *post*, 643.

[10] R. A. Putnam in (eds.) M. Nussbaum and J. Glover, *Women, Culture and Development* (1995), p. 303.

The conception of justice for which Rawls argues demands:

(i)   the maximisation of liberty, subject only to such constraints as are essential for the protection of liberty itself;[11]

(ii)  equality for all, both in the basic liberties of social life and also in distribution of all other forms of social goods, subject only to the exception that inequalities may be permitted if they produce the greatest possible benefit for those least well off in a given scheme of inequality ("the difference principle"); and

(iii) "fair equality of opportunity"[12] and the elimination of all inequalities of opportunity based on birth or wealth.[13]

Rawls's theory differs from utilitarianism in three significant ways. First, utilitarians can accept inequalities, social arrangements in which some benefit at the expense of others, provided the benefits (or pleasures) exceed the costs (or pains), so that the outcome is the maximisation of overall welfare level ("the greatest happiness of the greatest number"). This may be thought unjust.[14] Secondly, while utilitarians defend liberty and political rights, they have no objection to limiting liberty or restricting political rights, provided doing so would promote greater well-being. Rawls's first principle (the equal maximum liberty principle) means that there are some rights, freedom of speech and association, the right to vote and stand for public office, liberty of conscience and freedom of thought, freedom of the person and the right to hold personal property, freedom from arbitrary arrest, which every system must respect. These are rights that may not be sacrificed to increase the aggregate welfare level. Thirdly, Rawls's conception of benefits is different from utilitarianism, which is concerned with welfare. Rawls, by contrast, defines benefits in terms of "primary goods"[15]: liberty and opportunity, income and wealth and the bases of self-respect.[16] These need not be considered desirable in themselves, but they give persons the opportunities rationally to further their own autonomy.[17] Rawls does not stipulate how primary goods should be used by individuals: he implies that they may use them as they choose, provided in doing so they do not undermine just institutions.

To arrive at these principles of justice Rawls uses a "refurbished"[18] version of the social contract argument.[19] He claims that his principles are those that "free and rational persons concerned to further their own interests would accept in an initial position of equality as defining the

---

[11]   In *Political Liberalism* "a fully adequate scheme of equal basic liberties" replaces "the most extensive total system" of *A Theory of Justice* (see p. 291).

[12]   See p. 60; *cf.* pp. 302–303.

[13]   Rawls does not espouse egalitarianism, rather qualified egalitarianism.

[14]   See D. Lyons, *The Forms and Limits of Utilitarianism* (1965); D. Miller, *op. cit.*, n. 5, pp. 30–40.

[15]   *Op. cit.*, n. 8, s. 15 and, for a restatement, *op. cit.*, n. 9, pp. 178–190.

[16]   *Op. cit.*, n. 8, pp. 92, 303 and 440.

[17]   On the relationship between rights and autonomy see D. Richards (1981) 92 Ethics 3.

[18]   *Per* N. MacCormick (1973) 89 L.Q.R. 393.

[19]   On the sources of the social contract argument see, *ante*, 105.

terms of their association".[20] This argument has only superficial similarities with the tradition of Hobbes, Locke and Rousseau. The function of the social contract in their theories is to justify the legitimacy of government and hence our obedience to it by claiming that we, or our forebears, agreed to establish a particular political structure. Rawls does not make any such claims: there is no historical or quasi-historical pact in his writing; nor does he use contractarianism to justify obedience to laws or governments.[21] What he sets out to show is that certain moral principles are binding upon us because they would be accepted by people like us in the "original position". As contrasted with naturalism,[22] Rawls does not assume the principles of justice can be found through the use of reason or in nature. Nor does he think they can be found empirically or in intuition or within religion. What Rawls hunts out are mutually acceptable ground rules.

He thus conducts a thought experiment. He imagines a hypothetical forum of individuals subject to a "veil of ignorance".[23] This precludes them from knowing more or less everything about their own selves, their conditions, so that they are incapable of distorting principles to serve their own or other special interests. They would be ignorant of their own views on the "good life". They would not know their status, social position, class, colour, religion, degree of intelligence or strength. They would not even know at what time or in what place they are living. They would not know to which generation they belong, or the stage of civilisation of their society. They would know that everyone, themselves included, has in some degree the characteristics mentioned. What they are ignorant of is "their own particular aggregation of them".[24] Thus constrained, the parties draw up the principles not by using moral reasoning, nor by effecting compromises between competing moral stands. Rather, as Lyons puts it:

> "moral notions enter into the contract argument by suggesting constraints on prudential reasoning (it must not be skewed to serve special interests, for example) and on the results (which must be general principles, applying to all societies)."[25]

---

[20] In *Political Liberalism* (p. 22) the "original position" is described as a "device of representation".

[21] Though he does defend a somewhat narrow defence of civil disobedience (see ss. 55, 57 and 59) which P. Singer, *Democracy and Disobedience* (1973) cogently criticises (pp. 86–92). See also G. Klosko (1994) 23 Philosophy and Public Affairs 251, and D. Lyons (1998) 27 Philosophy and Public Affairs 31.

[22] *Ante*, Chap. 3.

[23] And see, *post*, 633. See also *op. cit.*, n. 8, p. 79.

[24] Per N. MacCormick, *op. cit.*, n. 18, p. 395. "Sex" was omitted from *A Theory of Justice* but Rawls tells us that it was always his intention that the parties in the original position would not know the sex of those they represent (see (1997) 64 Univ. of Chicago L.R. 765).

[25] *Ethics And The Rule of Law* (1984), p. 140.

This aims at guaranteeing that the worst conditions one might find oneself in is the least undesirable of the alternatives. Given this connecting link, Rawls reasons that his principles would be preferred to others, since they favour the least advantaged members of society. It should be pointed out, however, that one can buy into the "original position" and still not be convinced by Rawls's principles, and the converse (being convinced by the principles but not the method of arriving at them) also applies.

*Political Liberalism* is an attempt to refine the thesis of *A Theory of Justice*, in large part in response to criticisms levelled at the first book.

We are now offered a political conception of justice (as distinguished from a comprehensive religious, philosophical or moral conception of the good). Political liberalism accepts the "fact of reasonable pluralism",[26] the fact that a diversity of reasonable yet conflicting and irreconcilable religious, philosophical and moral doctrines may be affirmed by citizens in the free exercise of their capacity for a conception of the good.

Political liberalism also emphasises the "fact of oppression",[27] the fact that "a continuing shared understanding on one comprehensive religious, philosophical or moral doctrine can be maintained only by the oppressive use of state power".[28]

Despite these two facts, Rawls argues that citizens in a constitutional democracy who hold opposing, even irreconcilable, conceptions of the good can find a shared basis of reasonable political agreement through "an overlapping consensus"[29] concerning a political conception of justice. Such a political conception of justice would provide fair terms of social co-operation on the basis of mutual respect and trust that the members of the society might reasonably be expected to endorse. And it would have priority over the state's pursuit of conceptions of the public good,[30] so that "justice" may be said to precede and to constrain the good.

In *Political Liberalism*, Rawls postulates a four-stage sequence whereby the two principles of justice are incorporated into the institutions and policies of a constitutional democracy.[31]

The first stage is the "original position", followed by constitutional, legislative and judicial stages.[32]

At the constitutional stage, the general structure of government and the political process are embodied in the constitution. So are the equal basic liberties of the first principle of justice. The second principle of justice is not, however, on Rawls's view, a constitutional *sine qua non* for a constitutional democracy. It is his view that the history of successful constitutions suggests that principles to regulate economic and social

---

[26] *Op. cit.*, n. 9, pp. 36 and 144. But see as to this J. Kraus (1999) 5 Legal Theory 45.
[27] *ibid.*, p. 37.
[28] *ibid.*
[29] *ibid.*, pp. 133 *et seq.*
[30] *ibid.*, pp. 6, 223 and 295.
[31] *ibid.*, pp. 174–176.
[32] *ibid.*, pp. 336–340 (see also *A Theory of Justice*, pp. 194–201).

inequalities, and other distributive principles, are generally not suitable as constitutional restrictions.[33] Rawls is, of course, referring largely to the American experience.[34]

The second principle of justice is incorporated only at the legislative stage, and then only insofar as it is accepted by citizens. Rawls thus has a dualist conception of constitutional democracy, with what the "People" will initially as a "higher law" than what subsequently emanates from legislative bodies.[35]

At the judicial stage, this dualism is protected by the courts, one role of which is to protect the higher law against challenges and encroachments by ordinary legislation. Rawls is thus committed to the institutions of judicial review as a necessary feature of a constitutional democracy.[36]

Rawls does not see the political conception of justice "as a method of answering the jurist's questions", though he believes it may provide "a guiding framework, which if jurists find it convincing, may orient their reflections, complement their knowledge and assist their judgment".[37] There is a nod here in the direction of those concerned with constitutional interpretation in the United States, but the issues he raises have implications for those concerned with democracy and adjudication elsewhere too.

The theme is taken up be Cass Sunstein in *The Partial Constitution.*[38] He puts forward a theory of "deliberative democracy". This requires governments to provide public-regarding reasons concerning the common good for its actions, and prohibits it from furthering only the "naked preference"[39] of private groups or individuals. "Deliberative democracy" has four core commitments. First, a belief in political deliberation with decisions reflecting public-regarding reasons.[40] Decisions should not merely protect *status quo* neutrality or "prepolitical" private rights.[41] Secondly, it entails a commitment to citizenship and to widespread political participation by the citizenry.[42] The development of the concept of citizen's charters in Britain in the 1990s is far from what Rawls and Sunstein envisage—these were designed by government and not by the people. A true commitment to citizenship implies not just a sphere of autonomy outside the state's interference,[43] but property rights

---

[33] *ibid.*, p. 337.

[34] Particularly of the so-called *Lochner* era (see *Lochner v. New York* (1905) 198 U.S. 45). Heightened judicial protection was given to substantive economic liberties through Due Process clauses. And see C. Sunstein (1987) 87 Columbia L.R. 873 and J. Fleming (1993) 72 Texas L.R. 211.

[35] *Op. cit.*, n. 9, pp. 231–234. See also B. Ackerman, *We The People* (1991).

[36] *ibid.*, pp. 233 and 240.

[37] *ibid.*, p. 368.

[38] Published in 1993.

[39] *Op. cit.*, n. 9, pp. 25–37.

[40] *ibid.*, pp. 133–141.

[41] *ibid.*, pp. 3–7 and 40–67.

[42] *ibid.*, pp. 135–136.

[43] *Cf.* Nozick, *post*, 595.

and social programmes that attack poverty[44] and the inclusion within citizenship of groups previously excluded on the basis of "morally irrelevant characteristics"[45] such as race, gender, sexual orientation, disability and, perhaps, age (to what extent do we recognise the citizenship of children?[46]). Rawls and Sunstein might detect some incoherence in New Labour's "social inclusion" policies, but the commitment to citizenship more closely approximates to theirs. There is, thirdly, a commitment to agreement as a regulative ideal for politics[47]: the goal is agreement among equal citizens through deliberation concerning public-regarding reasons, not conclusions which note the different perspectives of "disagreeable people".[48] The final commitment is to political equality. This prohibits not just disenfranchisement but also disparities in political influence held by different social groups.[49] It does not entail economic equality, but it does rule out poverty and discrimination, and does require rough equality of opportunity, including in particular educational opportunity.

Rawls's theory of justice—as originally conceived in the book of that name—had (and continues to have) an enormous impact, but it was subjected to a number of criticisms.[50]

The device of the "original position" attracted much criticism. Sandel showed that Rawls's account of this and the status of the descriptive premises was far from clear.[51] This makes it both easier to attack (there are, for example, inconsistencies), and to defend. Perhaps the most basic criticism asks why people who are not in the "original position" should adopt principles chosen by those who were.[52] Rawls's answer is that the conditions and constraints embodied in the "original position" constitute a model of procedural fairness, and so should be acceptable to everyone.[53] But what if there is a bias in the "original position" so that principles are not chosen fairly? To Marxists and some feminists[54] such bias is inevitable. Fisk,[55] for example, argues that it is impossible to abstract man from his material circumstances. Rawls's view of humans is that they are by nature free and rational beings.[56] But to Fisk "once the facts of my

---

[44] *Op. cit.*, n. 38, p. 139.
[45] *ibid.*, pp. 136 and 259–261.
[46] See M. Freeman, *The Moral Status of Children* (1997).
[47] *Op. cit.*, n. 9, p. 137.
[48] *Cf.* C. Eisgruber (1990) 43 Stanford L.R. 275.
[49] *Op. cit.*, n. 8, p. 137.
[50] The best collection remains N. Daniels, *Reading Rawls* (1975). See also B. Barry, *The Liberal Theory of Justice* (1973), R. P. Wolff, *Understanding Rawls* (1977) and T. Pogge, *Realizing Rawls* (1989).
[51] *Liberalism and the Limits of Justice* (1982), pp. 24–46.
[52] See T. Nagel (1973) Phil. Rev. 220; R. Dworkin (1973) 40 Univ. of Chicago L.R. 500 (both in Daniels, *op. cit.*, n. 50, at pp. 1 and 16).
[53] But why should commitment to procedural fairness constitute a justification? See D. Lyons in Daniels, *op. cit.*, n. 50, p. 141.
[54] See particularly S. M. Okin, *Justice, Gender and the Family* (1989), Chap. 5 (who nevertheless thinks "the original position" is a "brilliant" idea).
[55] In Daniels, *op. cit.*, n. 50, p. 53.
[56] *Op. cit.*, n. 8, p. 253.

historical situation are clear to me, then the life plans it would be rational for me to choose are considerably restricted".[57] Fisk applies this reasoning to numerous facets of Rawls's thought. Thus, Rawls says that persons in the "original position" will agree that there should be freedom of thought. But Fisk retorts:

> "The thoughts one takes an interest in defending are one's own rarely in more than the sense that one is willing to defend them ... They are ..., by and large, inculcated by institutions. And these institutions are strengthened by people defending these very thoughts."[58]

Liberals also detect bias in the "original position". Nagel[59] believes it contains a kind of bias to be found in all contractarian theories. Since parties in the "original position" must reach a unanimous choice, Rawls assumes that the "thin" theory of primary social goods is a sufficient basis for them to act in choosing a conception of justice. The theory is "thin" because parties do not know their full conception of the good, but only that wealth and self-respect,[60] for example, are desirable. If differing "full" conceptions of the good were allowed, no unanimity in principles would result. But, as Nagel points out, "the suppression of knowledge required to achieve unanimity is not equally fair to all the parties, because the primary goods are not equally valuable in pursuit of all conceptions of the good".[61] For example, Rawls's model contains a "strong individualistic bias ... The original position seems to presuppose not just a neutral theory of the good, but a liberal, individualistic conception according to which the best that can be wished for someone is the unimpeded pursuit of his own path".[62]

A number of questions may also be asked about the principles of justice.

Firstly, to what do the principles of justice apply? Rawls' answer is clear. He sees justice as a virtue—indeed, the first virtue—of social institutions.[63] His theory of justice is a normative blueprint for institutions. The same principles do not apply to individuals. As Letsas explains: "People can be cruel, insensitive, mean, generous or caring. But only the basic structure of society can be just or unjust".[64] But is this an unnecessarily limited conception of justice, one particularly open to challenge in a world where individuals feel bound to assist the relief of famine and to offer succour to victims of disasters particularly in the developing world? Liam Murphy has argued that the view—it may be

---

[57] *Op. cit.*, n. 55, p. 57.
[58] *ibid.*, p. 59.
[59] *Op. cit.*, n. 52.
[60] The argument that this should extend to health is made forcefully by N. Daniels, *Just Health* (2008), p. 46
[61] *ibid.*, p. 9.
[62] *ibid.*, pp. 9–10. See also Sandel, *op. cit.*, n. 51, pp. 59–65 and his comment (p. 28) that the "thin theory of the good is too thick to be fair".
[63] *Op. cit.*, note 8, p. 6.
[64] In M. Freeman and R. Harrison, (eds.) *Law and Philosophy* (2007), p. 49, 51.

characterised as dualistic—is indeed unduly limited. He maintains that "all fundamental normative principles that apply to the design of institutions apply also to the conduct of people". The refusal to extend principles of justice to personal conduct is "*prima facie* deficient".[65] The utilitarian would, of course, apply the same principles to individuals as to institutions.

The "difference principle" has provoked lively debate. To Rawls, the principle represents "an agreement to regard the distribution of natural talents as a common asset and to share in the benefits of this distribution whatever it turns out to be".[66] He sees the distribution of natural talents as a "collective asset" with the result that the "more fortunate are to benefit only in ways that help those who have lost out".[67] But, so Nozick argues, to regard people's natural assets as common property contradicts all that deontological liberalism affirms in emphasising the inviolability of the individual and the distinction between persons.[68] Is this right? It can be argued that the distribution of natural talents as a common asset does not violate the difference between persons, because it is not "*persons* but only 'their' *attributes*" that "are being used as means to others' wellbeing".[69] Nozick, however, seems to have anticipated this defence. He argues: "Whether any coherent conception of a person remains when the distinction is so pressed is an open question. Why we, thick with particular traits, should be cheered that (only) thus purified men within us are not regarded as means is also unclear."[70] Sandel constructs another defence for Rawls. Rawls, he argues, "might deny that the difference principle uses me as a means to others' ends, not by claiming that my *assets* rather than my *person* are being used, but instead by questioning the sense in which who share in 'my' assets are properly described as 'others'".[71] But, as Sandel concedes, this commits Rawls to an intersubjective conception of the self, and Rawls clearly rejects such a notion.

Another attempt to explicate the "difference principle" is suggested by Scanlon. In his view the argument for this principle starts from the idea that "as equal participants in a system of social co-operation, the members of a society have a prima facie claim to an equal share in the benefits it creates".[72] But will the wealthy co-operate? What appeal has the "difference principle" to them? Miller[73] is convinced that Rawls must have in mind a society which has only moderate class conflict, no ruling

---

[65] (1999) 27 *Phil and Public Affairs* 251, 279.
[66] *Op. cit.*, n. 8, p. 101.
[67] *ibid.*, p. 179.
[68] *Anarchy, State and Utopia* (1974), p. 228. On Nozick see, *post*, 595.
[69] *Per* Sandel, *op. cit.*, n. 51, p. 78.
[70] *Op. cit.*, n. 68, p. 228. But on this view Rawls's subject would resemble the Kantian transcendent (or disembodied) subject he set out to avoid.
[71] *Op. cit.*, n. 51, p. 79.
[72] *What We Owe To Each Other* (1998), p. 228.
[73] In Daniels, *op. cit.*, n. 50, p. 206.

class,[74] and no class-differentiated basic desires. This he sees as, at the very least, a controversial, and, more likely, a false set of assumptions.

The priority which Rawls gives to liberty must also be addressed. Rawls claims that a person in the "original position" will choose the "basic liberties"[75] in priority to any distribution of income, wealth and power because he knows that, by so doing, he will have the best chance of obtaining for himself the primary goods and of pursuing whatever other ends fit within his life-plans. Upon the forfeit of liberty, there is no guarantee that he would value any increase in wealth (to take one example) that this might bring. But it may be that different cultures put different values on liberty and wealth. Think of the experiences of countries like Singapore, Malaysia and South Korea, or of the contrast between the Soviet Union (where there were few liberties in practice) and Russia (where there is *glasnost* and starvation).

And what happens when basic liberties conflict? How, if at all, are they to be reconciled? Scanlon[76] has pointed to the conflict between two criteria Rawls uses in discussing restrictions on the system of liberties. On the one hand, liberty is to be restricted only for the sake of protecting the overall system of liberties. On the other hand, a "principle of common interests" is employed, according to which institutions are ranked by how effectively they guarantee the conditions necessary for all equally to further their aims, or how efficiently they advance shared ends that will similarly benefit everyone.[77] But do the two criteria agree with each other?

It is Hart's view[78] that the "principle of common interests" breaks down in important cases. He has also shown how Rawls underestimates the difficulty of balancing conflicting liberties. He maintains that some "criteria" of the value of different liberties must be invoked in the resolution of conflict between them. But Rawls tends to write as if the system of basic liberties were "self-contained", so that conflict within it could be adjusted without appeal to any other value than liberty and its extent.

Another problem relates to the rationale for giving liberty priority over other social goods. Rawls argues that once a certain level of well-being has been attained in a society, even its least well-off members will prefer increments in their liberty to an increase in other social goods. So, those in the "original position" will not allow liberty to be traded off for other social goods. But why? Is there any reason why a surrender of liberties made to secure a large increase in material welfare should be permanent?

---

[74] This is discussed, *post*, 1161.
[75] These are not specified exactly but include the list, *ante*, 584. A criticism is Hart, *Essays In Jurisprudence and Philosophy* (1983), Chap. 10: Rawls responds in *Tanner Lectures on Human Values* (1982), vol. iii, p. 1. One basic liberty (or so it is generally assumed) not addressed is reproduction. That this is not unproblematic is addressed by P. Dasgupta (1994) 23 Philosophy and Public Affairs 99.
[76] (1973) 121 Univ. of Penn. L. Rev. 1020 (part is reproduced in Daniels, *op. cit.*, n. 50, p. 206).
[77] *Op. cit.*, n. 8, p. 97.
[78] *Op. cit.*, n. 75, p. 233.

Why shouldn't people when affluence is achieved restore the liberties? Since parties in the "original position" are ignorant of the character and strength of their desires,[79] do they have a disposition to give a determinate answer to the question of which position (one prioritising liberty or one not doing so) it would be in their interests to choose? It is doubtful that they are.

Yet another problem concerns the compatibility of the first principle demand for equal liberty and the second principle justification for inequalities (even significant ones) in wealth and liberty. Is it not the case that inequalities in wealth and power always produce inequalities in basic liberty? This is, of course, a question of empirical social theory. Our historical experience is, as Rawls acknowledges,[80] that they do.[81] Rawls tries to circumvent this problem by introducing a distinction between liberty and worth of liberty. "Liberty", represented by the complete system of the liberties of equal citizenship, continues to be distributed in accordance with the first principle: the new social good, "the worth of liberty" to persons or groups is "proportioned to their capacity to advance their ends within the framework the system defines",[82] that is in accordance with the second principle. In this way, Rawls is able to argue that unequal wealth does not cause inequality of liberties, only inequality of the worth of liberty: "[s]ome have greater authority and wealth and therefore greater means to achieve their aims".[83] But is it useful to talk about something as a "liberty" when the majority is not in a position effectively to exercise it? What Rawls is doing is arbitrarily excluding economic factors from the category of constraints defining liberty.[84] Surely persons in the "original position" have equally good reason for choosing equality with regard both to liberty and "worth of liberty".

It might be thought that these are problems surmounted in the restatement of *Political Liberalism*. But it is doubtful whether this is so. The "original position" does not (with one exception[85]) occupy the prominent status it has in *A Theory of Justice*. Instead, Rawls tends to argue from the perspective of *this* world, and thereby to explain why persons committed to social co-operation will find overlapping consensus in the principles of justice. The "original position" is still there, though it may be speculated whether it remains of significance: if overlapping consensus is reached because people in the real world want it, there seems no need to construct justice in the "original position". Unless it is argued that

---

[79] See Hart, *Essays In Jurisprudence and Philosophy* (1983), p. 235.
[80] *Op. cit.*, n. 8, p. 226.
[81] For example, the right of free speech may be shared but the rich have greater access to the media and control over it and thus are in a position to have their opinions more readily advanced with the result that it is their interests which are promoted. And see C. MacKinnon, *Only Words* (1992), Chap. 3.
[82] *Op. cit.*, n. 8, p. 204.
[83] *ibid.*
[84] See further N. Daniels in *op. cit.*, n. 50, pp. 253 and 260.
[85] *Op. cit.*, n. 9, pp. 310–311 (using the "original position" to counter Hart's argument that the original position is too feeble to support the priority of the basic liberties).

overlapping consensus is a product of the "original position". But could Rawls arrive at such a conclusion without clothing the formerly naked participants so as to make them much like people who have experienced our world? This would rob the "device of representation" of any meaningful function.

Nor can it be said that the recasting of "justice as fairness" as a political theory overcomes the identified problems with the principles of justice. The bias against the maximisation of aggregate welfare, the predisposition to require that inequalities work to everyone's advantage are still present. It is impossible to apply the difference principle without using normative judgements about equality.[86] For example, unequal wage rates can only be justified if they are to everyone's advantage and the higher paying positions are open to all. But what does equal pay mean? Is equality to be related to the unit of need, or production, or effort, or the value of the work (and, if so, to whom?). Without a normative judgement as to the appropriate measurement of equality, the second of Rawls's principles is impossible to operationalise.

Nothing Rawls says in *Political Liberalism* encourages a belief that this problem is solved. The political version of justice articulated in it is no more neutral to competing moral theories than was the moral version of justice in *A Theory of Justice*. The emphasis now on real people and overlapping consensus makes the difference principle even harder to sustain. Can we believe that consensus could actually be achieved once people were aware of the normative ambiguities within equality?

These difficulties may explain a shift to the idea of public reason in public debate as the mechanism for allowing competing views to coexist.[87] Rawls's idea of public reason is that, in debating issues of basic political structure, we are limited to reasons that flow from our overlapping consensus about social co-operation. We cannot appeal to reasons we draw from our religious philosophies or other comprehensive moral systems, because to do so would undermine commitment to the over-lapping consensus. There must be a common currency of political debate. But can we avoid using comprehensive moral arguments in political debate? Consider debates in the recent past about the role of the state, privatisation, the relative merits of direct and indirect taxation, economic regulation. Are these not issues of basic political structure? Could they be debated without the disputants expostulating on the merits of free enterprise, of corporatism or socialism? Rawls seems to believe that reference to comprehensive moral values is permissible only when it affirms the overlapping consensus. Thus, he says, Martin Luther King was able to appeal to *Brown v. Board of Education*[88] (the Supreme Court case which ordered desegregation of schools), "to the political values expressed in the Constitution correctly understood". But what was

---

[86]  See P. Westen (1982) 95 Harvard L.R. 537, and *Speaking of Equality* (1990).
[87]  *Op. cit.*, n. 9, pp. 212–254.
[88]  (1954) 349 U.S. 483. And see *op. cit.*, n. 9, p. 250.

contained in this decision was still contentious when King preached and made his famous speeches: if it hadn't been, the civil rights movement would have been unnecessary or at least more easily winnable.[89]

Rawls supports the idea of public reason by drawing an analogy to rules of evidence and relevance for decisions by officials such as judges. The rules of hearsay evidence and that which requires a defendant in a criminal trial to be proved guilty beyond reasonable doubt are not the same rules of evidence used by a scientific society or a church council discussing a theological doctrine or a university faculty discussing educational policy.[90] It does not really assist Rawls's aim of distinguishing the political from the moral. Positivists[91] may be able to distinguish legal and moral argument—they have criteria to do so—but Rawls has no similar criteria to distinguish political and moral argument. At best he seems to suggest that what counts as political argument is what persons in the "original position" would construct as such. This is a normative argument but it hardly offers descriptive criteria.

Most recently, Rawls has extended his arguments to cover international law.[92] He has attempted to show how the "law of peoples" can be developed from a generalisation of liberal ideas of justice, and how it extends to non-liberal as well as to liberal societies. He argues that the idea of the "original position" can be used to model the agreement of representatives of both liberal and non-liberal societies on a "law of peoples" that respects basic human rights and is universal in its reach. From the device of representation of liberal societies ("the original position"), he believes familiar principles, including principles of human rights, will emerge. Additionally, he purports to show how well-ordered but non-liberal, hierarchical societies may also come to endorse these principles. However, some of the worst violators of human rights in the recent past were well-ordered hierarchical societies, the Soviet Union, South Africa, Chile under Pinochet. And some of the worst excesses of human rights violations, such as ethnic cleansing in Bosnia and Rwanda, took place in unstable societies where even state boundaries are in doubt.[93] It will be observed that in the international context Rawls pays no attention to the second of his principles. His "law of peoples" has no egalitarian distributive principle of any sort.[94] This commits Rawls to a laisser-faire global economic order and to demonstrate (ironically) that in the international context his conception of justice is little different from

---

[89] See the pessimism of D. Bell (1992) 24 Connecticut L.R. 363 and comments by Greene and Delgado (pp. 499, 527). For the view that *Brown* was a "Cold War imperative" see M. Dudziak (1988) 41 Stanford L. Rev. 61.

[90] And see W. Twining, *Rethinking Evidence* (1990).

[91] For example, Hart, *The Concept of Law* (1994), pp. 167–180.

[92] *The Law of Peoples* (1999). An earlier version is in (eds.) S. Shute and S. Hurley, *On Human Rights* (1993), p. 41, and *post*, 650. *The Law of Peoples* is discussed by S. Freeman (2006) 23 *Social Philosophy and Policy* 167, S. Macedo (2004) 72 Fordham L.R. 1721 and C. Beitz (2000) 110 Ethics 669.

[93] See C. Mackinnon in *On Human Rights, op. cit.*, n. 92, p. 83.

[94] See T. Pogge (1994) 23 Philosophy and Public Affairs 195, 196.

that of Nozick.[95] But why should representatives prefer an inegalitarian law of peoples over more egalitarian alternatives? Rawls is right in part to believe that the "great social evils in poorer societies are likely to be oppressive government and corrupt elites",[96] but, as Pogge observes, "relative poverty breeds corruptibility and corruption",[97] and it is "by no means entirely homegrown".[98]

## NOZICK: JUSTICE AS ENTITLEMENT

Robert Nozick's *Anarchy, State and Utopia*[99] is one of the most provocative essays in political philosophy in recent times. In it he revives the claim long associated with John Locke[1] and Herbert Spencer[2] that a "minimal state limited to the narrow functions of protection against force, theft, fraud, enforcement of contracts, and so on, is justified; and that the minimal state is inspiring as well as right".[3] He develops a conception of justice which he calls "entitlement theory",[4] according to which economic goods arise already encumbered with rightful claims to their ownership. Philosophies which espouse distributivism (or worse redistributivism) are misconceived. Nozick extols the virtues of eighteenth-century individualism and nineteenth-century capitalism[5]—and it may be thought to have captured the character of the Thatcher-Reagan era. Even so, it came as a profound shock to many.

First, Nozick seeks to justify the minimal state against the individualist anarchist who holds that "when the state monopolizes the use of force in a territory and punishes others who violate its monopoly, and when the state provides protection for everyone by forcing some to purchase protection to others, it violates moral side constraints on how individuals may be treated", thus concluding that the state itself is "intrinsically immoral".[6] Nozick responds with a thought experiment. He asks us to imagine individuals in a state of nature with rights (natural rights, of

---

[95] And see, *post*.

[96] *Op. cit.*, n. 92, p. 77.

[97] *Op. cit.*, n. 94, p. 213.

[98] *ibid.*, p. 214. See further T. Pogge, *World Poverty and Human Rights* (2002), and T. Pogge (2005) 19 *Ethics and international Affairs* 55.

[99] Published in 1974. It is said to be the "*locus classicus*" of contemporary libertarian argument on behalf of a minimal state" (B. Fried (1995) 24 Philosophy and Public Affairs 226). On the questions raised by Nozick see B. Fried (2005) 22 *Social Philosophy and Policy* 221.

[1] *Ante*, 145.

[2] *Post*, 837.

[3] *Op. cit.*, n. 99, p. ix.

[4] *ibid.*, pp. 149–182.

[5] It seems oblivious to nineteenth-century critiques of abstract individualism and most twentieth-century social science. Its principal method is "state of nature" theory, drawing substantive political conclusions from how abstractly conceived "rational" individuals, removed from any specific social context, would behave in imagined situations. See S. Lukes, "State of Nature" in *Essays in Social Theory* (1977), Chap. 11.

[6] *Op. cit.*, n. 99, p. 51. On moral side constraints see *ibid.*, pp. 28–35.

course) who act in their own interests and generally do "what they are morally required to do", and then to trace how associations would arise to protect their rights and how a dominant association within a territory would emerge which would have two essential features of the state: it would exercise monopoly over the use of force, and afford universal protection to rights in the territory. To Nozick what is attractive in this scenario is that the state "grows by an invisible-hand process and by morally permissible means, without anyone's rights being violated".[7]

Nozick then proceeds to defend the minimal state against arguments for a more extensive state. First, that the state is necessary, or is the best instrument, to achieve distributive justice. Against this Nozick puts forward his "entitlement theory" of justice: under this a person's holdings are just if acquired through just original acquisition or just transfer, or through the rectification of injustices in the first two senses. He claims that "if each person's holdings are just, then the total set (distribution) of holdings is just".[8] In the light of this, Nozick concludes that no state is justified in applying a principle or principles which aim at some end-results and specify some patterned distribution. The "entitlement theory" by contrast is "historical"[9] and so is unlikely to upset any pattern. Nozick then sets out to attack the case for state action to promote equality.[10] In his view the state should confine itself to enforcing contracts, prohibiting thefts and taking such other measures to secure holdings to those entitled to them.

In the final part of the book, Nozick offers a speculative Utopia, "a system of diverse communities, organised along different lines and perhaps encouraging different types of characters, and different patterns of abilities and skills".[11] The only possible framework for such a system is the minimal state which "best realizes the utopian aspirations of untold dreamers and visionaries".[12] He concludes that such a state "treats us as inviolate individuals, who may not be used in certain ways by others as means or tools or instruments or resources: it treats us as persons having individual rights with the dignity that this constitutes ... It allows us, individually and with whom we choose, to choose our life and realize our ends ... aided by the voluntary co-operation of other individuals possessing the same dignity".[13] He ends: "How *dare* any state or group of individuals do more. Or less."[14]

Nozick's book challenges[15] the whole concept of distribution. There is

---

[7]  *ibid.*, p. 119.
[8]  *ibid.*, p. 153.
[9]  "Whether a distribution is just depends upon how it came about" (*ibid.*)
[10]  He is particularly critical of B. Williams' well-known article "The Idea of Equality", *ibid.* in (eds.) P. Laslett and W. G. Runciman, *Philosophy, Politics and Society* (1962), p. 110.
[11]  *Op. cit.*, n. 99, p. 317.
[12]  *ibid.*, p. 333.
[13]  *ibid.*, pp. 333–334.
[14]  *ibid.*, p. 334.
[15]  And has provoked a wide range of critical comment, *e.g.* J. Paul, *Reading Nozick* (1981), J. Wolff, *Robert Nozick* (1991), T. Campbell, *Justice* (2nd ed., 2001), Chap. 3.

"no such meaningful concept as the goods of society but only the goods of particular individuals and society has no prima facie right to shuffle those around between individuals."[16] Nozick forces to ask not how distribution can be other than equal (Rawls's premise), but why should there be distribution at all. This is clearly an important question for all concerned with social and economic justice. For Nozick, "taxation of earnings from labor is on a par with forced labour",[17] making the government imposing such taxes into a "part owner" of the person taxed.[18] Forced labour is, of course, anathema to Nozick, as it is to most people. But is a system of income tax in any way comparable? Hart asks: "How can it be right to lump together, and ban as equally illegitimate things so different in their impact on individual life as taking some of a man's income to save others from some great suffering, and killing him or taking one of his vital organs for the same purpose?[19] Taxing is different from forced labour and slavery in terms of the burden it imposes and the gravity of restrictions.

When we look to Nozick for an argument justifying why the imposition of taxes constitutes a violation of rights we find none. His objection to taxation is rooted in his belief in the absolutely inviolable character of property rights. Judith Jarvis Thomson[20] for one doubts whether such a belief can be defended. She asks what it is, at the margins, which sustains the moral invincibility of a property claim, and, conversely, what it is that justifies the infringement of a property right when we are morally persuaded to avoid it (for example, taking a drug belonging to another to save a child's life).[21] Property claims are to be sustained, she argues, when, in addition to having acquired title to an object in suitable ways, we value that object highly: such claims may be overridden when a life will be lost in the absence of an infringement of rights. This demonstrates, so she argues, that rights are derivative from human interests and needs, which in turn suggests that the constraints which rights impose upon redistribution are not as inflexible as Nozick's conception of them leads him to believe.[22]

As indicated above, Nozick's book is in three parts. The first justifies the minimal "right-watchman" state against anarchists. But does Nozick succeed? Can a minimal state arise out of a state of nature without itself transgressing the rights of persons? Can it be shown that the dominant agency's procedures of adjudication and enforcement are morally

---

[16] *Per* C. Fried (1983) 1(1) Soc. Phil. and Policy 45, 49.
[17] *Op. cit.*, n. 99, p. 169. On taxation and the minimal state see J. Macey (2006) 23 *Social Philosophy and Policy* 255, 258–265. See also L. Murphy and T. Nagel, *The Myth of Ownership: Taxes and Justice* (2002).
[18] ibid., p. 172. But see E. Abramson (1981) 23 Arizona L.R. 753.
[19] *Essays in Jurisprudence and Philosophy*, p. 206.
[20] In J. Paul (ed.), *op. cit.*, n. 15, pp. 130–147.
[21] On whether there is a distinctly feminine "ethic of care", so that males and females might respond differently to this dilemma, see C. Gilligan, *In A Different Voice* (1982), pp. 25–32.
[22] Thomson's conception of rights is teleological: Nozick's is deontological.

superior to those of its competitors? If not, their elimination is ethically suspect.[23] Nozick does not provide any independent epistemic criteria for assessing the procedures of the emergent dominant agency. He argues that independent agencies may be prohibited provided their clients are suitably compensated. But, as Mack convincingly demonstrates, the introduction of a compensation principle is inconsistent with the general framework of deontic rights defended in *Anarchy, State and Utopia*.[24] He "identifies the compensation principle with an incipient utilitarianism by condoning rights violations in circumstances where the subject's well being is enhanced".[25] But to abandon the compensation principle would jeopardise the anti-anarchist project in Part I.

There is, however, a more basic question relating to that project. Nozick's objective is to explain historically the emergence of the state. But is that necessary, for what is important is not how it emerged—often a matter of historical conjecture—but the moral character of its present activities. It would be enough to justify the minimal state in the present "time-frame"[26]: earlier moral indiscretions are of secondary importance.

The second part of the book is concerned with arguments against the extensive state. It contains Nozick's defence of libertarian capitalism. He leaves many questions unanswered, and makes a number of assumptions which do not seem to stand up to examination. First, where do persons get their rights from? The many references to Kant[27] suggest their logical basis is deontic rather than teleological. But the process by which their bearers obtain their authority is not articulated. We are told it is an historical process. The initial act of appropriation confers unlimited rights of use and disposition. But, "while *some* historical method is the moral superiority of *any* teleological method of initial acquisition, Nozick has difficulty in specifying precisely which of several possible methods is to be preferred".[28] Though there is some ambivalence, he comes close to accepting Locke's labour theory of property acquisition.[29] Locke required that a limit be placed upon the amount of a resource that could be extracted from nature by anyone: "enough and as good" had to be left for others to secure. Nozick reformulates this limit in terms of a certain welfare baseline, though he declines to give attention to where baseline needs should be fixed.[30] As O'Neill points out, the transition from "A mixed his labour with X" (the classic Lockean formulation) to "A is entitled to (has the right to control) X" requires justification.[31] Nozick believes that we should "hold onto the notions of earning, producing,

[23]   See R. L. Holmes in J. Paul (ed.), *op. cit.*, n. 15, pp. 57–67.
[24]   *ibid.*, pp. 169–90. See also his "Nozick's Anarchism" in *Nomos* (1978), vol. xix, pp. 43–62, where he argues that a protective association does not amount to statehood.
[25]   *Per* J. Paul, "Introduction" in *op. cit.*, n. 15, p. 7.
[26]   To this effect see E. F. Paul in *op. cit.*, n. 15, pp. 270–285.
[27]   *Op. cit.*, n. 15, pp. 30–34.
[28]   *Per* J. Paul, *op. cit.*, n. 15, p. 18.
[29]   *Ante*, 109. Nozick's discussion is at pp. 174–178 of *Anarchy, State and Utopia*.
[30]   *Op. cit.*, n. 99, p. 177.
[31]   *Op. cit.*, n. 15, pp. 305–322 and 314.

entitlement, desert and so forth".[32] But, of course, "holding on" is insufficient. What is required is an argument. After all, as O'Neill says, "why should not labouring be a way of losing one's labour, of improving what is "in the common state?"[33] Locke's starting-point was that the Earth is common property: Nozick, by contrast, sets out to explain how what is unowned can become private property.

He offers little in the way of a positive foundation for his view. Instead, he attacks opposing theses. He argues that these are universally self-refuting: they attempt to realize either a particular distributive structure (*e.g.* equality), or a formula which assigns quantities of economic goods to particular individuals based on some characteristic possessed by them (*e.g.* merit, need). Nozick argues that if goods are distributed in accordance with some example of either of these principles, the distribution realised ($D_1$) will in all probability be supplanted in due course by another ($D_2$), by virtue of a voluntary economic transaction that people engage in subsequent to $D_1$. Any revision to $D_1$ will require an imposed reversal of the decisions made by individuals after the initial distribution. This means that people are given goods for their own use but not permitted to use them, except when by their choice the distributive *status quo* is maintained. To Nozick, this seemingly paradoxical result is an inevitable attribute of all patterned or end-result distributive systems. But Nozick is question-begging. He is assuming that the recipients of goods under $D_1$ are thereby given absolute rights of use and disposition, when it is precisely such rights that have to be established.[34] Nor, as Jeffrey Paul maintains, can it be argued that "the liberties of the recipients are infringed by the continuous reimposition of some distributive pattern, because, *ex hypothesis*, their freedom to rescind the desired pattern of distribution, $D_1$, is a freedom implicitly forbidden by $D_1$".[35] Since Nozick can offer no argument to support the freedom to "flout such distributive formulae he cannot", Paul notes, "reject distributivism for inhibiting it".[36]

Nozick's principal argument against distributionist theories of justice rests on their failure, as he sees it, to cohere with his ideal of individual liberty. The right to property is an expression of the right to liberty. But for Nozick the right to liberty is defined by reference to the right to property. How is this circular reasoning to be explained? Reiman suggests that it rests on the assumption that large-scale ownership has the same relationship to the liberty of others as small-scale. This ignores the fact that "property accumulation has threshold effects on liberty, such that small appropriations might nurture it while large doses can be fatal".[37]

---

[32] *Op. cit.*, n. 99, p. 155.
[33] *Op. cit.*, n. 15, p. 316.
[34] See O'Neill, *op. cit.*, n. 15. See also T. Nagel, *op. cit.*, n. 15, pp. 191–205 and C. C. Ryan, *ibid.*, pp. 323–343.
[35] J. Paul, *op. cit.*, n. 15, p 19.
[36] *ibid.*
[37] J. Reiman (1981) 92 Ethics 85, 91.

Nozick claims that private property increases freedom: his critics can justifiably claim that it inhibits it.[38] If, it can be argued, after a certain size, property holdings constitute a threat to the liberty of others, then "a morally sound concept of rights of ownership would have to be designed to prevent the unwanted threshold effect".[39] Indeed, if, as Nozick says, property rights derive from the right to liberty, and if it is the case that large-scale property accumulation has negative effects on liberty, then the right to liberty would, contrary to Nozick's thesis, demand redistributive theories of justice. Nozick's error—a not uncommon one—is to assume that it is possible to "define the conditions of freedom for single individuals prior to considering the conditions of freedom for all individuals."[40]

There are many more questions. How is the minimal state to be controlled? How is it to be kept minimal? How are the economically advantaged to be stopped acquiring political power? The minimal state and an alert citizenry are supposed to stop this happening. How is destitution to be prevented and relieved? Nozick's answer, naïve in the extreme, points to the free operation of the market, voluntary associations and private philanthropy.

The central flaw in Nozick's arguments is the "abstractness of the individualism they presuppose".[41] The individuals who conduct Nozick's thought experiment are neutered in the sense that they are de-psychologised, taken out of their culture and environment. Nozick assumes that it is possible to isolate people in this way, whereas in reality people are constituted by the societies into which they are socialised and live. Lukes rightly observes of this abstract individualism that it is a "distorting lens which satisfies the intellect while simplifying the world". He continues with remarks which this section may conclude: "Nozick's world not only excludes the ever-growing role of the state within contemporary capitalism; it is also radically pre-sociological, without social structure, or racial or cultural determinants of, and constraints upon, the voluntary acts and exchanges of its component individuals".[42]

## CAPABILITIES AND THE FRONTIERS OF JUSTICE

Another approach to social justice is to emphasize human capabilities. This is associated particularly with the economist Amartya Sen[43] and the philosopher Martha Nussbaum. For Nussbaum, on whom I will

---

[38] For example, G. Cohen in J. Arthur and W. Shaw (eds.), *Justice and Economic Distribution* (1978) and D. Zimmerman (1981) 10 Philosophy and Public Affairs 121. See also Campbell, *op. cit.*, n. 15, pp. 62–63.

[39] *Op. cit.*, n. 15, p. 91.

[40] *ibid.*, p. 94. Rawls's method (the "original position" and "veil of ignorance"), *ante*, 525, is different, but the *principles* which emerge may be subject to similar criticisms.

[41] Per Lukes, *op. cit.*, n. 5, p. 193.

[42] *ibid.*, pp. 193–194.

[43] "Capability and well-being" in (ed.) M. Nussbaum and A. Sen, *The Quality of Life* (1993), pp. 30–53.

concentrate, there are core human entitlements that should be respected and implemented by all governments "as a bare minimum of what respect for human dignity requires".[44] She lists central human capabilities—what people are actually able to do and to be. These are:[45]

1. Life: of normal length.
2. Bodily health: good health (including reproductive health); adequate nourishment, adequate shelter.
3. Bodily integrity: freedom of movement; security against assault (including sexual assault and domestic violence); opportunities for sexual satisfaction and choice in matters of reproduction.
4. Senses, Imagination and Thought. Being able to use the senses, to imagine, think and reason. Being able to use imagination and thought in connection with experiencing and producing works and events of one's own choice, religious, literacy, musical etc. Being able to use one's mind in this way, protected by guarantees of freedom of expression and freedom of religious exercise.
5. Emotions. Being able to have attachments to things and people outside ourselves, to love, to grieve, to experience longing, gratitude, justified anger.
6. Practical Reason. Being able to form a conception of the good, and to engage in critical reflection about the planning of one's life. This entails liberty of conscience and protection of religious observance.
7. Affection. Being able to live with and toward others, to recognize and show concern for other human beings, to engage in various forms of social interaction, to be able to imagine the situation of another. Protecting this means protecting institutions that constitute and nourish such forms of affection, and also protecting freedom of assembly and political speech. It also entails having the social bases of self-respect and non-humiliation, being able to be treated as a dignified being whose worth is equal to that of others. Inherent in this is the absence of discrimination on grounds of race, sex etc.
8. Other species. Being able to live with concern for and in relation to animals, plants, and the world of nature.
9. Play. Being able to laugh, play and enjoy recreational activities.
10. Control over One's Environment, both political and material. Thus, being able to participate effectively in political choices that govern one's life; and being able to hold property and seek enjoyment on an equal basis with others, and freedom from unwarranted search and seizure.

The list is similar to Finnis' basic goods of human flourishing,[46] though more extensive. It has close links also with Rawls'.[47] Nussbaum says "it is

---

[44] *Frontiers of Justice* (2006), p. 70.
[45] *ibid*, pp. 76–78 (the latest formulation).
[46] *Ante*, 127.
[47] *Ante*, 584.

a species of a human rights approach" and is thus "fully universal".[48] Even so there is respect for pluralism. The list is "open-ended".[49] The items on the list ought to be specified in a "somewhat abstract and general way".[50] So, different countries can give effect to capabilities differently: she gives the example of anti-Holocaust legislation in Germany and compares this with the U.S. which protects Holocaust denial unless there is an imminent threat of public disorder.[51] Following Rawls she argues also that the list can be seen as a "module" which can be "endorsed by people who otherwise have very different conceptions of the ultimate meaning and purpose of life".[52] She also emphasizes that the goal is "capability and not functioning".[53] So, in relation to health, people should be given "ample opportunities to lead a healthy lifestyle, but the choice should be left up to them; they should not be penalized for unhealthy choices".[54] This view is controversial: debates often focus on the smoker with lung cancer, the alcoholic in need of a liver transplant. However, the major liberties that protect pluralism are "central" items: freedom of speech, of association and of conscience.[55]

The interest in Nussbaum's most recent work lies in the way it addresses issues of social justice as they affect those with physical and mental disabilities, the developing world and non-human animals. Rawls' theory, hypothesising a contact for mutual advantage among approximate equals, cannot accommodate questions of social justice posed by unequal parties. And so, she asks, how can we extend equal rights of citizenship (health care, education, political rights and liberties) to those with disabilities. And how can we do so to all citizens of the world? And how can we bring our treatment of animals into our notions of social justice? She surprisingly (or should we be surprised) does not explore another section of the population deprived of the rights and dignity we associate with social justice, namely children. Are animals really more important?

Nussbaum aims to globalize the theory of justice. She focuses on the three problem areas because she says they have been "resistant".[56] But so, of course, have inequalities of race, sex and sexual orientation, though progress has been made in all three. She can argue for social justice for those with disabilities because the capabilities approach starts from conception of the person as a social animal "whose dignity does not derive entirely from an idealized rationality".[57] Because social contract theories are premised on the nation state, they cannot, according to

---

[48]  *Op. cit.*, note 44, p. 78.
[49]  *ibid.*
[50]  *ibid.*
[51]  *ibid*, p. 79.
[52]  *ibid.*
[53]  *ibid.*
[54]  *ibid*, p. 80.
[55]  *ibid.*
[56]  *ibid*, p. 92.
[57]  *ibid.*

Nussbaum, adequately address justice which talks to the inequalities between the richer and poorer countries. To solve this:

> "We must appreciate the complex interdependencies of citizens in different nations, the moral obligations of both individuals and nations to other nations, and the role of transnational entities ... in securing to people the most basic opportunities for a fully human life".[58]

Thirdly, because social contractual theories start from the allegedly crucial importance of human rationality, they deny justice to animals. Nussibaum responds, as many others have done, by recognizing animal intelligence and by rejecting the idea that "only those who can join in the formation of the social contract are full-fledged subjects of a theory of justice".[59] Because the capabilities approach emphasizes "a continuum of types of capability and functioning",[60] it can offer guidance superior to both utilitarianism and social contract theories.

## JUSTICE AS RIGHTS

For both Rawls and Nozick, there is a clear relationship between justice and rights but it is Ronald Dworkin who can be said most clearly to ground justice in rights.

In one sense there is nothing new in this: the idea that political morality and social choice were to be governed by considerations of the rights of individuals has its heritage in the writings of Locke[61] and Kant,[62] as well as in the literature and constitutions of the American and French revolutions. The emphasis has not gone unchallenged. Bentham was a trenchant critic, particularly of natural rights.[63] So was Marx.[64] Today, one of the central conflicts in legal, moral and political philosophy is between those who espouse rights-based theories and those, utilitarians in particular, who put forward goal-based theories.[65]

The distinction is easy enough to state. A requirement is rights-based when generated by a concern for some individual interest, and goal-based when propagated by the desire to further something taken to be of interest to the community as a whole.[66] The rights-based approach does not deny that the interest of a particular individual is not also shared by others (in the case of human rights, all) in the community, but it would

---

[58] *ibid*, p. 93.
[59] *ibid*.
[60] *ibid*.
[61] *Ante*, 107. See further K. M. McClure, *Judging Rights* (1996).
[62] *Ante*, 113. A modern parallel is A. Gewirth, *Reason and Morality* (1977).
[63] Which he called "nonsense upon stilts". A contemporary critic is M.-A. Glendon, *Rights Talk* (1991).
[64] See "On The Jewish Question": see also *post*, 1148, 1152. T. D. Campbell, *The Left And Rights* (1983), pp. 92–102 may also be consulted.
[65] See H. L. A. Hart in (ed.) A. Ryan, *The Idea of Freedom* (1979).
[66] See R. Dworkin, *Taking Rights Seriously* (1978).

claim that the interest of each individual *qua* individual is sufficient to generate the moral requirement.

Whether the distinction between the two approaches can also be drawn is rather more dubious. Many of the ideals with which we associate rights are dependent upon, indeed may be constituted by, the existence and maintenance of certain inherent public goods. So the right to freedom of speech[67] would have diminished value in an intolerant society. To Raz,[68] it is a "public good, and inherently so, that this society is a tolerant society, that it is an educated society, that it is infused with a sense of respect for human beings, etc. Living in a society with these character-istics is generally of benefit to individuals".

It is part of the philosophy of those who espouse rights-based theories to insist on the pre-eminence of rights. Rights are valuable commodities,[69] important moral coinage.[70] In Feinberg's words[71]:

> "A world without rights, no matter how full of benevolence and devotion to duty, would suffer an immense moral impoverishment ... A world with claim-rights is one in which all persons, as actual or potential claimants, are dignified objects of respect".

Not surprisingly, he concludes that "no amount of love or compassion, or obedience to higher authority, or *noblesse oblige*, can substitute for those values".

To Dworkin rights are "trumps".[72] They are grounded in a principle of equal concern and respect. So for a judge to make a mistake about a legal right is "a matter of injustice".[73] Further, the whole institution of rights rests on the conviction that "the invasion of a relatively important right" is a "grave injustice".[74] Dworkin sees rights as trumps over some back-ground justification for political decisions that state a goal for the com-munity as a whole. Thus, to use one of his well-known, if controversial, examples, "if someone has a right to publish pornography, this means that it is for some reason wrong for officials to act in violation of that right, even if they (correctly) believe that the community as a whole would be better if they did".[75] An individual thus has a right when there is a good reason for conferring upon him or her a resource or opportunity, even though there are considerations relating to the public interest which would argue against this being done. Nevertheless, Dworkin is prepared

---

[67] The classic exposition of which is J. S. Mill, *On Liberty* (1859), Chap. 2.
[68] "Right-Based Moralities" in (ed.) R. G. Frey, *Utility and Rights* (1985), pp. 42 and 46–47. See also J. Raz, *Ethics In The Public Domain* (1994), Chap. 3.
[69] R. Wasserstrom (1964) 61 J Philosophy 628, 629.
[70] But *cf*. A. Buchanan "What's So Special About Rights?" (1984) 2(1) Social Policy and Philosophy 61.
[71] "Duties, Rights and Claims" (1966) 3 Am. Phil. Q. 137.
[72] *Op. cit.*, n. 66, p. ix.
[73] *ibid.*, p. 130.
[74] *ibid.*, p. 199.
[75] *A Matter of Principle* (1985), Chap. 17; *cf*. R. Langton (1993) 22 Philosophy and Public Affairs 293.

to concede that interference in the life of an individual, where there would otherwise be a right, is justified where "special grounds" can be found.[76] But what is meant by saying that the public interest generally is not advanced by recognising a particular individual's rights?

There are, Dworkin notes,[77] two distinct senses in which a community may be said to be better off as a whole despite the fact that certain of its members are distinctly worse off. It may be better off in a *utilitarian* sense (the average or collective level of welfare in the community is improved even though the welfare of some falls), or in an *ideal* sense (because "it is more just, or in some way closer to an ideal society, whether or not average welfare is improved"). For example, a policy of affirmative action might be pursued to reduce social tensions or to make the community more equal and therefore more just.[78]

Rights, Dworkin states, are not "gifts" from God. Their institution is "a complex and troublesome practice that makes the Government's job of securing the general benefit more difficult and more expensive, and it would be a frivolous and wrongful practice unless it served some point".[79] For Dworkin, anyone who professes to "take rights seriously" must accept the ideas of human dignity and political equality.[80] He argues in favour of a fundamental right to equal concern and respect, and against any general right to liberty. The right to equal concern and respect is a final and not merely "a prima facie right"[81]—one person's possession or enjoyment of it does not conflict with another's. But will it serve as the foundation of a right-based *moral* theory? Dworkin puts it forward as a fundamental *political* right: governments must treat citizens with equal concern and respect.[82] But, as Mackie points out, "this cannot be what is morally fundamental".[83] The right to be treated in a certain way rests on a prior "right to certain opportunities of living".

Why does Dworkin reject a general right to liberty? It would seem for two reasons: first, he believes it cannot explain or justify the discrimination we would want to make between legitimate and illegitimate restrictions of freedom; and, secondly, because the right (or supposed right) is commonly used to support a right to the free use of property.[84] But, as far as the first reason is concerned, we can discriminate by examining how closely a certain freedom ties in with a person's "vital

---

[76] *Op. cit.*, n. 66, p. 188. Government has "a reason for limiting rights if it plausibly believes that a competing right is more important". But there must be a "compelling reason" (p. 200).

[77] *ibid.*, p. 232.

[78] This is discussed *post*, 609.

[79] *Op. cit.*, n. 66, p. 198.

[80] "Anyone who claims that citizens have rights must accept ideas very close to these" (p. 199).

[81] *Per* J. L. Mackie, "Can There Be a Right-Based Moral Theory?" in (ed.) R. French *et al. Studies in Ethical Theory* (1978), vol. 3.

[82] *Op. cit.*, n. 66, pp. 177–183. It is a "postulate of political morality" (p. 272).

[83] *Op. cit.*, n. 81.

[84] For example by Locke, *ante*, 107 and Nozick, *ante*, 595.

available".[2] And equality of "enjoyment" is relative to individual tastes and goals. Equality of resources, on the other hand, is measurable.

At the centre of any attractive theoretical development of equality of resources is the idea of an economic market. We are asked to indulge in a thought experiment (not unlike Rawls's). There are shipwreck survivors on a desert island which has "abundant resources and no native population",[3] and in which likely rescue is many years away. The assumption is that in these circumstances "no division of resources is an equal division if, once the division is complete, any immigrant would prefer someone else's bundle of resources to his own bundle".[4] Dworkin denotes this the "envy test".[5] It is an economic, not a psychological, test. Resources are distributed in an imaginary auction. Each participant/immigrant is given an equal number of tokens (Dworkin suggests clamshells) and bids for goods on the island. The bidding continues until no one envies anyone else's bundle of goods. In this way, "people decide what sorts of lives to pursue against a background of information about the actual cost their choices impose on other people and hence on the total stock of resources that may fairly be used by them".[6] The equality principle thus is used both to explain the envy test and to ensure that everyone comes to the auction as an equal. It also "creates the conditions for the conduct of the auction".[7]

Both Rawls and Dworkin have to grapple with the gambler, the person who plays his luck and may end up better off as a result (or, of course, worse off). Dworkin distinguishes between "option luck" and "brute luck".[8] The former—the gambler's luck—is, he believes, integral to personal liberty and is consistent with an equality of resources. Brute luck is, however, not a matter of choice. As examples of the difference Dworkin contrasts buying shares which increase in value and being struck by a falling meteorite. Dworkin would not limit risk-taking (save to prevent for example the total forfeiture of liberty by selling oneself into slavery[9]). So "resources gained through a successful gamble should be represented by the opportunity to take the gamble at the odds in force, and comparable adjustments [should be] made to the resources of those who have lost through gambles".[10] Brute luck, on the other hand, is not consistent with equality of resources: it is not an exercise of liberty. The problem is amenable to solution through insurance, or at least it is in many standard cases. You can insure your house against fire but not yourself against being born disabled or even against succumbing to a disability (acquiring multiple sclerosis, for example).

---

[2]  *Op. cit.*, n. 97, p. 191.
[3]  (1981) 10 Philosophy and Public Affairs 283, 285.
[4]  *ibid.*
[5]  *ibid.*
[6]  *ibid.*, p. 288.
[7]  *ibid.*
[8]  *ibid.*, p. 293.
[9]  See *ibid.*, p. 295. This concession to paternalism is reminiscent of Mill, *op. cit.*, p. 364.
[10]  *Op. cit.*, n. 97, p. 295.

Dworkin believes he has an answer. Insurance can cope with both kinds of luck: at least it can in his imaginary auction. For here, Dworkin hypothesises, insurance against disability will be available "at whatever level of coverage the policy holder chooses to buy".[11] Nor is there any "reason to think", so he argues, "that a practice of compensating the handicapped on the basis of such speculation would be worse, in principle, than the alternatives, and it would have the merit of aiming in the direction of the theoretical solution most congenial to equality of resources".[12] The immigrant—to return to Dworkin's model participant—will thus be compensated for brute bad luck by means of a levy of a compulsory insurance premium, and this, so Dworkin argues, will give him the same resources as those who do not suffer this fate. Dworkin, we should remind ourselves, has ruled out rooting justice in an equality of welfare, largely on the basis of its being impracticable. But resources (unlike welfare) are a means to an end, not an end in themselves. Whether justice is achieved depends upon how resources are used. Would not new disadvantaged minorities emerge?

And the protection of minorities is, as Dworkin acknowledges, central to any theory of justice. The reason is simple: majoritarianism can so easily lead to the trampling on the rights of minorities.[13] Dworkin is eager to protect these and to do so through the principle of equal concern and respect. He discussed this extensively in the context of affirmative action. His discussion hinged initially[14] on two well-known cases (*Sweatt* and *DeFunis*).[15] Sweatt was an African-American refused admission to the University of Texas Law School because (at that time) Texas state law provided that only whites could attend. DeFunis was a Jew whom the University of Washington Law School rejected but who would have been accepted had he been "a black or Filipino"[16] (test scores and college grades were lower for African-Americans and Hispanics because an affirmative action programme worked in their favour). Dworkin supports the Supreme Court decision in favour of *Sweatt* on the grounds that his exclusion violated his constitutional rights, but is happy with the policy pursued by the University of Washington, maintaining that no fundamental right of DeFunis was infringed.

What matters, Dworkin says, is whether persons are treated as equals with the same respect and concern as anyone else. But surely neither Sweatt nor DeFunis were so treated: in *Sweatt's* case this is self-evident, but is *DeFunis's* case really any different? His academic achievements are not being given equal weight with those of other races. Dworkin's response is that no one has a right to a Law School place and so it is

[11] *ibid.*, p. 296.
[12] *ibid.*, p. 299.
[13] And see R. Nordahl, "Rousseau in Dworkin" (1997) 3 Legal Theory 317.
[14] He also discusses the case of *Regents of the University of California v. Bakke* (see *A Matter of Principle, op. cit.*, n. 66, Chaps 14 and 15). He further addresses affirmative action in *Sovereign Virtue* (2000) Chaps 11 and 12.
[15] *Op. cit.*, n. 66.
[16] *ibid.*, p. 223.

he logically must accept the conclusion that all prospective purposive agents, equally and as such, have rights to freedom and well-being."[30]

The force of this logic is difficult to counter.[31] We must surely accept that when we wish to deny someone a right in the name of a greater social goal or higher moral ideal that we must justify our actions to him or her. But how would such a person understand our reasoning if we deny him/ her those interests s/he requires to be able to appreciate the force of our arguments (at the very least freedom of thought and expression)?

## FEMINISM AND JUSTICE

Feminist jurisprudence is considered in a later chapter.[32] Much of what is said in this section ties in closely with themes adumbrated there. Even so the distinctive contribution of feminism to justice should not be overlooked. Though herself sympathetic to Rawls's heuristic device upon which she believes she can build, Okin has offered a major critique of his theory of justice, in particular its failure to address justice within the family and the selection of primary goods.[33] She is critical also of a range of theories of justice.[34]

Other feminists, notably Carol Gilligan, have detected, what they call, a "different voice".[35] This is to draw attention to a contrast between an ethic of justice and rights and an ethic of care and relationship. Gilligan believes this is gender-related with the former associated with male thinking processes, the latter with female ones. As Lyons explains this,[36] those who view the self as "separated" from others are more likely to voice a morality of justice, and those who see the self as "connected" to others to express a morality of care.[37] The implications of Gilligan's thesis are tantalising. It could, of course, be used to justify confining women within the private sphere, and to explain (however inadequately) why theories of justice have so little penetrated the family, as well as to argue for greater participation of women in the public arena (and, then, to express disappointment when nothing of moment changes).

Of importance also is Carole Pateman's *The Sexual Contract*,[38] in

---

[30] The arguments are set out in more detail at pp. 45–55 and at pp. 197–202, and defended at pp. 67–78.

[31] Critiques are found in *Nomos* (1981), vol. xxiii (Friedman, p. 148; Morris, p. 158 and Golding, p. 165). Gewirth replies in *op. cit.*, n. 29, pp. 67–78.

[32] *Post*, Chap. 16.

[33] S. M. Okin, *Justice, Gender and the Family* (1989), and *post*, 695.

[34] See in particular her critiques of communitarianism (Chap. 3) and libertarianism (Chap.4).

[35] *In A Different Voice* (1982).

[36] "Two Perspectives: On Self, Relationships and Morality" in (eds.) C. Gilligan, J. V. Ward and J. M. Taylor, *Mapping The Moral Domain* (1988), p. 15. See also J. Tronto, *Moral Boundaries* (1993).

[37] On the "connection thesis" see West, *post*, 1323.

[38] Published in 1988.

particular her excavation of the social contract. She argues that the sexual subordination of women in marriage is both required by, and is an effect of, the social contract. The social contract to make civil society and the state could not have come into being, she argues, without a sexual contract which subordinates women in marriage.[39] To Pateman, Locke must be interpreted as more than a critique of patriarchalism[40]: rather, he must be seen as an advocate of its relocation. He separated political right from paternal right such that "masculine right over women is declared non-political"[41] but is left intact. Pateman argues that the liberal foundation of free and equal men in civil society required that patriarchalism be relocated from the political to the private domain. That may be so, but it is not clear why liberalism today requires a social contract. Indeed, it may be argued that not only liberalism, but also women's subordination, can be sustained without recourse to such a device.[42]

Locke required Pateman's corrective. On one level, Locke's separation was of the paternal from the political, but it can also be seen as a separation of the private from the public, for the public sphere embraces all social life except the domestic. An important result of this conception of public and private is that the public world (or civil society) is categorised as separate from the domestic sphere. The principles of association governing the two spheres are quite distinct: the public is governed by liberal criteria (rights, property, equality); the private is based on natural ties of sentiment and blood and marriage relationships—there is no free individualism here, rather natural subordination. By conceptualising civil society as removed from domestic life, the need to examine the latter disappears, and only re-emerges when inequalities of gender are scrutinised by feminist thinkers.[43]

Liberal feminism was for long dominant.[44] It was rooted in the belief that women are rights-bearing, autonomous human beings, and in this are no different from men. Accordingly, they should have equal opportunities and for example receive equal pay. Critics were concerned that an assimilationist theory of equality was being adopted that would benefit women only if they acted like men. The limitations of the strategy soon became apparent[45] and the feminist approach to justice, rather as its

---

[39] As Wendy Brown explains, "the sexual contract is where patriarchalism *lives* in the political and legal order ordinarily understood as its supersession" (*States of Injury* (1995), p. 136).

[40] And thus of Filmer.

[41] *Op. cit.*, n. 38, p. 90.

[42] Nor is the status of women outside marriage explained.

[43] Even the earliest of feminist thinkers (Mary Wollstonecraft and John Stuart Mill, for example): see Jane Rendall, *The Origins of Modern Feminism* (1985).

[44] A good illustration is Herma Hill Kay (1985) 1 Berkeley Women's Law J.1. And see *post*, 1230.

[45] And is well-illustrated in Deborah Rhode, *Speaking of Sex* (1997).

approach to questions of jurisprudence more generally, became more radical.

A good example is found in the writings of Iris Marion Young.[46] It is her view that it is "a mistake to reduce social justice to distribution".[47] Rather, she suggests, social justice means "the elimination of institutionalized domination and oppression".[48] Such a shift brings out "issues of decision making, division of labor, and culture that bear on social justice but are often ignored in philosophical discussions".[49] Typically, as we have seen, theories of justice have no room for a concept of social groups: Young believes that where there are social group differences, and, as an inevitable concomitant, some groups are privileged and others oppressed, "social justice requires explicitly acknowledging and attending to those group differences in order to undermine oppression".[50] This is a theory of justice that addresses injustice.[51] Distributive issues remain important but "the scope of justice extends beyond them to include the political as such, that is, all aspects of institutional organization insofar as they are potentially subject to collective decision".[52] But oppression and domination are "the primary terms for conceptualizing injustice".[53]

Whilst liberal feminists emphasise "sameness", Young focuses on difference. It is a denial of difference that contributes to social group oppression. Young argues for "a politics that recognizes rather than represses difference".[54] Oppression can result from tyranny but most is the result of "everyday practices of a well-intentioned liberal society".[55] It results from "often unconscious assumptions and reactions of well-meaning people in ordinary interactions, media and cultural stereotypes, and structural features of bureaucratic hierarchies and market mechanisms—in short the normal processes of everyday life".[56] Young's theory extrapolates from the experiences of oppressed groups (and not just women) and from the assumption that "basic equality in life situation for all persons is a moral value".[57]

There are five faces of oppression: exploitation; marginalization; powerlessness; cultural imperialism; and violence. To explain exploitation

---

[46] Notably *Justice and The Politics of Difference* (1990). See also *Intersecting Voices: Dilemmas of Gender, Political Philosophy and Policy* (1997). Tom Campbell, *Justice* (2001), Chap. 9 is a useful account.

[47] *Justice and The Politics of Difference* (1990), p. 15. See also A. Heller, *Beyond Justice* (1987).

[48] *ibid.* For an examination of Young's thesis within the context of foetal rights see Rachel Roth, *Making Women Pay* (2000).

[49] *ibid.*, p. 3.

[50] *ibid.*

[51] And see A. Sarat and T. R. Kearns, *Justice and Injustice in Legal Theory* (1996).

[52] *Op. cit.*, n. 46, p. 8. For example, how apposite is the distributive paradigm when it comes to addressing issues within the family or questions of reproduction and of sexuality? She discusses these issues in *Intersecting Voices, op. cit.*, n. 23, Chap. 5.

[53] *Op. cit.*, n. 46, p. 9.

[54] *ibid.*, p. 10.

[55] *ibid.*, p. 41.

[56] *ibid.*

[57] *ibid.*, p. 14.

she draws upon Marx[58]: "the central insight expressed in the concept of exploitation ... is that ... oppression occurs through a steady process of the transfer of the results of the labor of one social group to benefit another".[59] Exploitation enacts a structural relation between social groups. In Marx's analysis the mediating principle is class:[60] for Young it is gender (this has two aspects—the transfer of the fruits of material labour to men and the transfer of nurturing and sexual energies to women[61]), and race.

Marginalization is "perhaps the most dangerous form of oppression".[62] Marginals are "people the system of labor cannot or will not use".[63] This is the fate of, but not only of, "racially marked groups".[64] Distributive justice may address material deprivation, but there is injustice beyond distribution. "The provision of welfare itself produces new injustice by depriving those dependent on it of rights and freedoms that others have" and "even when material deprivation is somewhat mitigated by the welfare state, marginalization is unjust because it blocks the opportunity to exercise capacities in socially defined and recognized ways".[65] The concept, if not its implications, have been recognised in Britain by New Labour with its establishment of a Social Exclusion Unit. Somewhat astonishingly though, one of the intellectual architects of New Labour, Anthony Giddens, has assimilated the form of exclusion identified here with, what he calls, "voluntary exclusion", that is a withdrawal of affluent groups from public institutions.[66] Part of marginalization is designation as appropriate subjects for "patronizing, punitive, demeaning, and arbitrary treatment by the policies and people associated with welfare bureaucracies. Being a dependent in our society implies being legitimately subject to the often arbitrary and invasive authority of social service providers and other public and private administrators, who enforce rules with which the marginal must comply".[67] The premise is that we must distinguish the "deserving" from the "undeserving" so that we need to establish whether someone cannot work or will not work. But we could provide an unconditional basic income[68] or other unconditional benefits,[69] though whether our societies would find this acceptable is debatable.[70]

---

[58] And see *post*, 1140–1141.
[59] *Op. cit.*, n. 46, p. 49.
[60] And see the criticism *post*, 1140–1141.
[61] As analysed by Christine Delphy, *Close To Home* (1984) and Ann Ferguson, *Blood At The Root* (1989).
[62] *Op. cit.*, n. 46, p. 53.
[63] *ibid.*
[64] *ibid.* Others include the mentally ill and the homeless.
[65] *ibid.*, p. 54.
[66] *The Third Way* (1998), p. 103. *Critiques of which are A.* Carling (1999) 3 Imprints 217 and A. Callinicos (1999) 236 New Left Rev. 79.
[67] *Op. cit.*, n. 46, p. 54.
[68] See P. van Parijs (1991) 20 Philosophy and Public Affairs 101 and his *Real Freedom For All* (1995) and H. Steiner, *An Essay on Rights* (1994).
[69] Rawls's "difference principle" (*ante*, 590) allocates primary goods unconditionally.
[70] See, further, J. Wolff (1998) 27 Philosophy and Public Affairs 97.

Powerlessness is a form of oppression which, says Young, is experienced by non-professionals. The powerless lack "authority, status, and sense of self".[71] They lack also autonomy and respect. The privilege of professional respectability is seen starkly in the dynamics of racism and sexism. Young argues that in daily intercourse "women and men of color must prove their respectability. At first they are often not treated by strangers with respectful distance or deference. Once people discover that this woman or that Puerto Rican man is a college teacher or a business executive, however, they often behave more respectfully ... Working-class white men, on the other hand, are often treated with respect until their working-class status is revealed".[72]

To experience cultural imperialism[73] is "to experience how the dominant meanings of a society render the particular perspective of one's own group invisible at the same time as they stereotype one's group and mark it out as the Other".[74] Another feminist to identify this force of oppression is Nancy Fraser[75] who, following Charles Taylor,[76] talks of the "politics of recognition". Demands for welfare or health care rights are examples of redistributive claims: "efforts to win public acceptance of gay and lesbian households exemplify a politics of recognition".[77] The challenge, Fraser argues, is to combine just claims for redistribution and recognition so that each supports rather than undermines the other. The injustice of cultural imperialism is that "the oppressed group's own experience and interpretation of social life finds little expression that touches the dominant culture, while that same culture imposes on the oppressed group its experience and its interpretation of social life".[78]

Finally, there is the oppression of systematic violence: sexual assault, domestic violence, racist attacks, institutional racism by the police. Young asks: "Given the frequency of such violence in our society, why are theories of justice usually silent about it?"[79] And she observes: "What makes violence a phenomenon of social injustice, and not merely an individual moral wrong, is its systematic character, its existence as a social practice".[80] It is the daily knowledge shared by all members of oppressed groups that they are liable to violation that constitutes the oppression of violence.

The question may be asked as to whether if rights and economic

[71] *Op. cit.*, n. 46, p. 57.
[72] *ibid.*, p. 58.
[73] The term was coined by Maria Lugones and Elizabeth Spelman (1983) 6 Women's Studies International Forum 573.
[74] *Op. cit.*, n. 46, pp. 58–59.
[75] (1995) 212 New Left Rev. 68.
[76] See C. Taylor and A. Gutmann (eds.) *Multiculturalism: Examining The Politics of Recognition* (1994), p. 25.
[77] *Per* Elizabeth Kiss, "Justice" in (eds.) A. Jaggar and I. M. Young, *A Companion To Feminist Philosophy* (1998), pp. 487, 497. And see C. A. Ball (1997) 85 Georgetown Law J. 1871.
[78] *Op. cit.*, n. 46, p. 60.
[79] *ibid.*, p. 61.
[80] *ibid.*, p. 62.

resources were justly distributed these forms of injustice would still arise. Indeed, it is difficult to envision any of these faces of oppression being extirpated in the absence of redistributive justice. But it may be doubted whether this in itself would remove any of the categories of oppression Young lists. They call for structural and cultural changes: some of these might follow in the wake of redistributive policies.[81] For example, equal pay might lead to an improvement in the status of women and this to less (even ultimately no) domestic violence. But will equal pay be achieved in the absence of cultural change?[82]

A growing body of feminist moral theory[83] (of which Young's is an excellent example) has challenged the paradigm of moral reasoning as defined by the discourse of justice and rights. As Young notes:

"This 'ethics of rights' corresponds poorly to the social relations typical of family and personal life, whose moral orientation requires not detachment from but engagement in and sympathy with the particular parties in a situation; it requires not principles that apply to all people in the same way, but a nuanced understanding of the particularities of the social context, and the needs particular people have and express within it".[84]

Young's critique of impartiality is situated within her defence of difference. She argues that the ideal of impartiality in moral theory "expresses a logic of identity that seeks to reduce differences to unity. The stances of detachment and dispassion that supposedly produce impartiality are attained only by abstracting from the particularities of situation, feeling, affiliation and point of view".[85] Though this critique on one level seems extravagant (it would seem to require the rejection of rules altogether), its core reveals an important truth (that the logic of identity denies or represses difference). And she argues, following postmodernist thinkers[86] such as Adorno,[87] Derrida[88] and Irigaray,[89] that:

"Difference ... names both the play of concrete events and the shifting differentiation upon which signification depends. Reason, discourse, is already inserted in a plural heterogenous world that outruns totalizing comprehension. Any identifiable something presupposes a something else against which it stands as background, from which it is differentiated. No utterance can have meaning unless it stands out differentiated from another. Understood as different, entities, events, meanings, are neither identical nor opposed. They can be likened in certain respects, but similarity is never sameness, and the similar

[81] *Cf.* M. D. A. Freeman "Legal Ideologies, Patriarchal Precedents and Domestic Violence" in M. D. A. Freeman, *State, Law, and the Family* (1984), p. 51.

[82] And see R. Nelson and W. Bridges, *Legalizing Gender Inequality* (1999).

[83] The work of Carol Gilligan, Marilyn Friedman (*e.g. What Are Friends For? Feminist Perspectives on Relationships and Moral Theory* (1993)) and Noel Noddings, *Caring* (1986).

[84] *Op. cit.*, n. 46, p. 96.

[85] *ibid.*, p. 97. See also K. B. Jones, *Compassionate Authority* (1993), Chap. 4.

[86] On postmodernism see, *post*, Chap. 17.

[87] *Negative Dialectics* (1973).

[88] *Writing and Difference* (1978).

[89] *The Speculum of the Other Woman* (1985); see also *The Ethics of Sexual Difference* (1993).

of affirmative action. Affirmative action challenged "the primacy of a principle of nondiscrimination and the conviction that persons should be treated only as individuals and not as members of groups".[14] She is critical of two liberal assumptions: that a hierarchical division of labour is unproblematic (and therefore just) and a distribution of positions should be according to merit. As far as merit is concerned, "a class of powerful people establishes normative criteria, some of which have the function of affirming its own power and enforcing the organizational system that makes it possible".[15] In contrast to this ideology, she claims that decisions that establish and apply criteria of qualification should be made democratically.

But for Young discrimination in itself is not the problem. Rather it is the oppression associated with it. Equality (which she defines as "the participation and inclusion of all groups in institutions and positions"[16]) can be better served by differential treatment. And discrimination "tends to present the injustice groups suffer as aberrant, the exception rather than the rule".[17] Discrimination like injustice more generally is embedded within structure. For Young then the focus is on how decisions get made, as much, if not more, as the context of those decisions. So workplace decisions should be made democratically. Her assumption is that decisions so made would produce structures based on fairness and justice, rather perhaps as Fuller assumed that compliance with the principles associated with the "internal morality of law" would produce sub-stantively good legal systems.[18] Can we be sure in either case? Young retains her substantive conception of justice in tandem with the procedural mechanisms just depicted. This may be an acknowledgement that those put into decision-making positions may not necessarily share her views on justice, oppression and domination.

### ECONOMIC THEORIES OF LAW AND JUSTICE

Over 100 years ago, Holmes wrote that the man of the future would be "the man of statistics and the master of economics".[19] The economic analysis of law took another 70 years to develop but in the last 40 years, at least in the United States,[20] has come to dominate thinking about law,

---

[14] *Op. cit.*, n. 46, p. 192.
[15] *ibid.*, p. 212.
[16] *ibid.*, p. 195.
[17] *ibid.*, p. 196.
[18] *Ante*, 121.
[19] (1897) 10 Harv. L.R. 457, 469.
[20] A. M. Polinsky, *An Introduction to Law and Economics* (1989); R. Posner, *Economic Analysis of Law* (5th ed., 1998), *The Economics of Justice* (1983); A. W. Katz (ed.), *Foundations of the Economic Approach to Law* (1998). Useful English-based books are P. Burrows and C. Veljanovski, *The Economic Approach to Law* (1981) and A. Ogus and C. Veljanovski, *Readings in The Economics of Law and Regulation* (1984).

and not just in the more obvious commercial areas.[21] On one level it is a scientific alternative to utilitarianism.[22]

One of the problems with utilitarianism is the lack of a method for calculating the effect of a decision or policy on the total happiness of a relevant population. It offers no reliable technique for measuring change in the level of satisfaction of one individual relative to a change in the level of satisfaction of another. How is one person's happiness to be compared with another's?[23] Problems such as this had led economists to attempt to make utility arguments more rigorous.

The concept of value employed by economists is a truism: a thing has value (utility) for a person when that person values it. How much value a thing has for a given person is said to be "measured" by the maximum that person would be willing to pay for it, or the minimum the person would be willing to take to give it up.

Economists support this by two arguments. A concrete illustration may be drawn from their justification of private property rights. There are, they argue, costs (disutilities) when there is non-ownership of a scarce good. So, when the total cost of these "external" disutilities is greater than the cost involved in creating a system of ownership rights, then that system of property rights is justified by considerations of economic utility. The soundness of this argument depends on accepting the dominant guiding principle as that of minimising costs. The second argument concerns "alternative transactions", that is the ways in which people deal with resources used for the production of goods. Ownership rights, it is argued, stabilise these transactions.

The arguments turn on concepts like efficiency, superiority, optimality, allocation and distribution. The thought of Pareto (1848–1923)[24] has been particularly influential. The most basic notion in the economic analysis of law is efficiency or "Pareto optimality". A situation is said to be "Pareto-optimal" if it is impossible to change it without making at least one person believe he is worse off than before the change. A change is "Pareto-superior" when at least one person believes he is better off by it, while no one believes he is worse off. The definitions of "optimality" and "superiority" do not depend on objective assessments of good, but on subjective ones. Whether persons believe they will be better off, worse off, or the same, under a proposed change, and how much, is measured by their willingness to pay for the change, and how much.

The "Pareto superiority" standard only applies where there are no losers. But most social policies and most rules produce both winners and

[21] A. T. Kronman and R. Posner, *The Economics of Contract* (1979), B. Ackerman, *The Economic Foundations of Property Law* (1975), S. Shavell, *Economic Analysis of Accident Law* (1987), F. Easterbrook and D. Fischel, *The Economic Structure of Corporate Law* (1991).

[22] *Ante*, 248. On the relationship between economic analysis, efficiency notions and utilitarian moral theory see J. Coleman (1980) 8 Hofstra L.Rev. 509. On Bentham as a precursor of economic theories of justice see R. Posner (1998) 51 C.L.P. 425.

[23] See S. Scheffler (ed.), *Consequentialism and its Critics* (1988).

[24] See J. Coleman (1980) 68 Calif L.Rev. 221.

losers. If government were to act only where no one was made worse off, there would be very little it could do. Are the Pareto standards therefore of much value? Are they likely to appeal to a policy-oriented lawyer?

This is a reason why economists have offered the Kaldor-Hicks test[25] as a form of analysis which purports to justify government actions even when some persons are left worse off. It requires not that no one be made worse off by a change in the allocation of resources, but only that the increase in value be sufficiently large that the losers could be fully compensated. The Kaldor-Hicks test enables us to evaluate social policies and legal rules that produce winners and losers. The difference between "Pareto-superiority" and "Kaldor-Hicks efficiency" is "just the difference between *actual* and *hypothetical* compensation".[26] If compensation were actually paid to losers, the "Kaldor-Hicks efficient move" would become a "Pareto-superior" one.

The question must be asked why compensation is not paid, if it could be. The reasons given are two-fold. First, some losers deserve to lose. Coleman gives the example of policies implemented to break up inefficient monopolies.[27] Secondly, it may be very costly to compensate losers. The Kaldor-Hicks test assumes that compensation is to be costlessly rendered. But there will be transaction costs, so that the payment of compensation will not be costless. Why losers should be happy with an explanation that they could have been compensated but were not is left open.

The Kaldor-Hicks approach has a number of limitations. First, unlike "Pareto efficiency", "there is no sense of voluntarism". The efficient solution is "coercively imposed after some third-party determination of costs and benefits".[28] Secondly, because losers of "efficient" legal reforms go uncompensated for their losses, "the criterion is capable of generating quite drastic, capricious and inequitable redistributions of wealth".[29] Thirdly, it is often claimed that this approach "obviates the need to make inter-personal comparisons of utility".[30] But, as Veljanovski explains, "this is as much an interpersonal comparison as one that weighs the gains and losses on the basis of some normative and/or ethical value judgment regarding the relative 'worthiness' of individuals".[31] The approach assumes that the worth of a £1 is the same to everyone, clearly a false assumption.

A concept thus far missing from this discussion is justice. The omission is a reflection of the absence of thinking about distributive justice in the writings of economists. But Posner, the most influential thinker in the law

---

[25]  See N. Kaldor (1939) 49 Econ. J. 549; J. R. Hicks (1939) 49 Econ. J. 696 and (1940) 7 Economics 105.
[26]  *Per* J. L. Coleman (1984) 94 *Ethics* 649.
[27]  And see C. G. Veljanovski, *The New Law-and-Economics: A Research Review* (1982), p.37.
[28]  *ibid.*, p. 40.
[29]  *ibid.*
[30]  *ibid.*
[31]  *ibid.*

and economics movement, has addressed this issue.[32] He makes both a descriptive and a prescriptive claim about the economics of justice. The descriptive claim is that the "common law is best explained as if the judges were trying to maximise economic welfare".[33] Until recently, according to Posner, judges did not employ sophisticated economic analysis because they had no knowledge of it.[34] This may explain why much of the ideological underpinning of classical common law doctrine was laissez-faire-based.[35] The prescriptive claim is about wealth maximisation.[36]

The distribution of wealth determines in part both the economic value and the optimal allocation of resources in an economy. Thus, "to say that a situation is allocatively efficient is to say only that all the . . . gains from trade have been exhausted, given the *initial* distribution of wealth among individuals".[37] Under wealth maximisation, judges are to decide cases according to principles which will maximise society's total wealth. Posner argues that wealth maximisation exemplifies both utility and autonomy.[38] Whereas telling judges to maximise utility offers them very little guidance—utility whether as welfare or happiness is both difficult to discover and to measure—expecting them to maximise wealth is something they can do.[39] Money is easier to measure than utility. It is also, Posner claims, better than an approach based on autonomy because it allows for government action the consent for which it would be impractical to obtain in advance, but which would be forthcoming because, since it maximises social welfare, nearly everyone would have consented to it if asked, since it would leave almost everyone better off in the long term.[40]

There are problems with equating justice with wealth maximisation, and they are not problems necessarily associated with utilitarianism or an autonomy-based approach. Take the following example drawn from Veljanovski. If wealth was concentrated in a few who bought Rolls-Royces and caviar, "allocative efficiency [would] be consistent with the poor starving and the economy's productive activity [being] channelled into the manufacture of those luxury items".[41] On the other hand, with a more equitable distribution of wealth, productive efforts would go into

[32] See particularly *The Economics of Justice* (1983).
[33] *ibid.*, p. 4.
[34] The oft-cited exception is Judge Learned Hand's "BPL" formula for determining whether an act or omission had been negligent (*United States* v. *Carroll Towing Co.* (1947) 159 F. (2d) 169 discussed by S. Gilles (1994) 80 Virginia L.R. 1015. According to Posner, Hand's reasoning made explicit the otherwise implicit economic meaning of negligence.
[35] But for a sophisticated analysis see G. Calabresi and A. D. Melamed (1972) 85 Harvard L.R. 1089 and (1997) 106 Yale L.J. 2081.
[36] On the meaning of "wealth" see Posner, *The Problems of Jurisprudence* (1996), p. 356. It is to this normative claim that Dworkin responds (see *post*, 659).
[37] *Per* C. G. Veljanovski in (eds.) A. Ogus and C. G. Veljanovski, *Readings in the Economics of Law and Regulation* (1984), p. 22. (Emphasis added).
[38] *The Economics of Justice* (1983), p. 115.
[39] See further R. Posner (1979) 8 Journal of Legal Studies 103.
[40] See R. Posner (1986) 99 Harvard L.R. 1431 (part of a debate with Robin West: see (1985) 99 Harvard L.R. 384 and (1986) 99 Harvard L.R. 1449).
[41] *Op. cit.*, n. 37, p. 22.

the generation of more of the basic needs of everyday life. This means that there are an "infinite number of allocatively efficient outcomes that differ only with respect to the distribution of welfare among individuals in society".[42] Expressed in this way, efficiency is "little more than a *technocratic principle of unimprovability*; there is no rearrangement of society's productive activity or allocation of goods and services that will improve the economic welfare of society *given the distribution of wealth* upon which market transactions are based".[43] What this amounts to is a recognition that allocative efficiency in itself is not capable of generating any social welfare function. As Veljanovski concedes, normative economics needs a theory of distributive justice which will enable the analyst to rank "efficient outcomes in terms of their ethical attractiveness".[44] But economists have been reluctant to commit themselves to this type of thinking. They see justice as a notion which defies scientific analysis and they find it difficult to set up a social welfare function which is consistent with the assumptions about efficiency which are so central to their thinking.

This leads to one of the commonest criticisms of economic theories of law and justice. It is said[45] that the analysis merely reflects a particular ideology and since that ideology is perceived to be capitalistic and free market in orientation, it is seen to be an apologia for conservatism. This criticism says that the linchpin of the analysis is that what is efficient depends upon what people are willing to pay but this in turn is dependent upon what they are capable of paying: in other words, the more wealth one has, the more one is likely to increase it. The economic analysis is attacked not just because it lends itself to this pattern of distribution but because, as Coleman put it,[46] "it is that economic analysis requires and sanctions such patterns of distribution under the guise of pursuing the presumably desirable goal of efficiency".

There is some truth in this criticism. Thus, Posner advocates that in order for courts to promote efficiency they should assign entitlements by "mimicking" the market. Clearly, this involves assigning rights to resources to those parties who would have purchased them in an exchange market.

The criticism can be extended further. Again, Coleman makes the point forcibly:

"If rights are assigned in this way, the richer not only get richer, but because their newly acquired entitlements increase their wealth further, they are in an even better position to increase their wealth again by securing more rights on the grounds that their doing so is required by efficiency. Thus, efficiency not

---

[42]  *ibid.*
[43]  *ibid.*, pp. 22–23.
[44]  *ibid.*, p. 23.
[45]  A good example of this is C. E. Baker (1975) 5 Philosophy and Public Affairs 3.
[46]  (1984) 94 *Ethics* 649, 662.

only depends on prior wealth inequalities; pursuing efficiency leads inevitably to further inequities."[47]

It may, however, be argued that this inequality is an incident of the market, not of the economic analysis of law and justice. In these terms the ideology argument is no more (or less) an objection to economic analysis of law and justice than it is of markets generally. The critic may respond that, even if the idea of an efficient market outcome makes sense when there is an equal initial distribution, once resources are reallocated through trade or the political process disputes will arise "in which continuing to promote efficiency will serve only to redistribute wealth further in the direction of the already well-to-do".[48] Proponents respond that in markets "rational exchanges are made only when they are to the advantage of both parties".[49] Thus, Coleman makes the point that there is "nothing in economic analysis ruling out the making of compensatory lump-sum payments by those who gain entitlements to the losers". And so, as he claims, "the gain in efficiency need not create a snowball effect in favour of those who retain rights on efficiency grounds".[50] He is thus led to the conclusion that there is no bias favouring one economic group in the economic analysis of law.

This may be a logical conclusion, but how close to the realities of the world is it? What is envisaged is an abstract economic man. Do human beings actually behave in this way? And for how long can perfect competition and voluntary exchange last? People in the real world are not always able to assess what is in their rational self-interest and then act upon it. In the real world people's needs change; there are accidents, inventions. There is also altruism, a concern for the community, an interest in the environment. The economic argument says that any change in allocation or distribution which does not move things toward the economic ideal is unjustified. But are there not other goals than economic ones, for example social goals?

One of the earliest (and still sharpest) critics of the law and economics project was Leff.[51] He argued that the basic intellectual technique of the economic analysis of law is "the substitution of definitions for both normative and empirical propositions".[52] He saw the move to the economic analysis of law as "an attempt to get over, or at least to get by, the complexity thrust upon us by the Realists".[53] In Posner's *Economic Analysis of Law*, he detected a book in which it is "apparently plausible to declare 'it may be possible to deduce the basic formal characteristics of

---

[47] *ibid.* But see Note (1993) 107 Harvard L.R. 442, suggesting that there may be significant incentive effects for poor people as well.

[48] *ibid.*, p. 663.

[49] *ibid.*

[50] *ibid.*, p. 664.

[51] (1974) 60 Virginia L.R. 451.

[52] *ibid.*, p. 457. And *cf.* J. Gibbs (1968) 2 Law & Soc. Rev. 429.

[53] Leff, *op. cit.*, n. 51, p. 459. On the Realists *see post*, Chap. 10.

law itself from economic theory ...' *and then do it in a two-page chap-ter*".[54] His comment—rather sarcastically—was "what bliss". Leff's point is that the economic analysis of law is a gross over-simplification. It (he refers to Posner, but what he says may be generalised) centres round a "single-element touchstone ... 'What people want' is presented in such a way that while it is in form empirical it is almost wholly non-falsifiable by anything so crude as fact".[55] The basic propositions of the economic analysis of law are not, says Leff, empirical propositions at all. Rather they are "generated by 'reflection' on an 'assumption' about choice under scarcity and rational maximization".[56] Leff takes concepts like "effi-ciency" and "value" and comments that they have no meaning beyond "since people are rationally self-interested, what they *do* shows what they value, and their willingness to pay for what they value is proof of their rational self-interest". And, of course, "nothing merely empirical could get in the way of such a structure because it is definitional. That is why the assumption can predict how people behave: in these terms there is no other way they can behave".[57] Seen thus, the economic analysis of law is allowing normative propositions to be expressed in descriptive form, "slipping in" ought propositions almost surreptitiously.[58] Amartya Sen observed in 1985 that "We want a canonical form that is uncomplicated enough to be easily usable in theoretical and empirical analysis. But we also want an assumption structure that is not fundamentally at odds with the real world, nor one that makes simplicity take the form of naivety".[59]

Another critic is Ronald Dworkin. According to Dworkin, Posner "cannot claim a genuine Pareto justification for common law decisions, in either hard or easy cases. His relaxed version of Paretianism is only utilitarianism with all the warts. The voyage of his essay ends in the one traditional theory he was formerly most anxious to disown".[60] Dworkin questions whether efficiency should be the goal of law[61]—today "the vast majority of law and economics scholarship assumes without hesitation that [this is] the goal of law"[62]—and whether wealth is a value.[63] For Dworkin it is unclear "why" social wealth is a "worthy goal".[64] Is it because it is the "only" component of social value?[65] Or one component of social value amongst others?[66] Or is it because it is an instrument of value, so that "improvements in social wealth are not valuable in

[54]   *ibid.*, p. 459.
[55]   *ibid.*, p. 456.
[56]   *ibid.*, p. 457.
[57]   *ibid.*
[58]   And for doubts as to how well it is being done see R. Markovits (1993) 78 Iowa L.R. 327.
[59]   (1985) L.J. of Law, Economics and Organisation 341.
[60]   *A Matter of Principle* (1985), p. 283.
[61]   *ibid.*, Chap. 13.
[62]   *Per* J. Hanson and M. Hart, "Law and Economics" in (ed.) D. Patterson, *A Companion to Philosophy of Law and Legal Theory* (1996), p. 312.
[63]   *Op. cit.*, n. 60, Chap. 12.
[64]   *ibid.*, p. 240.
[65]   *ibid.*
[66]   *ibid.*

themselves, but valuable because they may or will produce other improvements that are valuable in themselves?".[67] What if slavery is the most efficient wealth maximisation system? Or if wealth creation were optimised by a system of apartheid?[68]

Economic models are also indicted for their lack of realism. It may be thought offensive to reduce the value of human life to monetary computations.[69] Thus, famously, and on more than one occasion, Posner has argued for a market in adoptions.[70] As he himself admits "economists like to think about the unthinkable".[71] Defenders however will point to the implicit monetary value we put on human life in virtually everything we do. Even so, it may be questioned whether a single kind of valuation, which imposes commensurability where none exists, assists our reasoning processes or distorts them.[72]

Realism may also be lacking from a model of decision making which assumes that people make decisions that are rational (both in relation to ends and means).[73] Ellickson has challenged the law and economics school to take on board the insights of psychology and sociology to inject "more realism about both human frailties and the influence of culture".[74] An example is the work of the cognitive psychologists, Daniel Kahneman and Amos Tversky. They found that people are myopic in their decisions, may lack skill in predicting their future tastes, and can be led to erroneous choices by fallible memory and incorrect evaluation of past experiences.[75] And, as Coleman points out, irrational ideas or prejudices will often persist over time.

## GLOBAL JUSTICE

It is commonly held that the scope of obligations of justice extends no further than membership in a common political community. The idea can be traced back to Thomas Hobbes, if not earlier, and persists. Hobbes argued that, whilst we are able to find true principles of justice by moral reasoning, "actual justice cannot be achieved except within a sovereign

---

[67] *ibid.*, pp. 240–241.
[68] Posner wrote that apartheid was wrong but only because it was "unlikely that ostracism, expulsion, or segregation of a productive group would actually increase a society's wealth" (*op. cit.*, n. 38, p. 85).
[69] See G. Calabresi and P. Bobbitt, *Tragic Choices* (1978).
[70] E. Landes and R. Posner (1978) 7 J. Legal Studies 323; R. Posner (1987) 67 Boston University L.R. 59. A critique is M. Kelman (1979) 55 S. Cal. L. Rev. 669. On the politics/economics of sex see L. R. Hirshman and J. E. Larson, *Hard Bargains* (1998).
[71] *The Economic Analysis of Law* (3rd ed., 1986), p. 141.
[72] See C. Sunstein (1993) 92 Michigan L.R. 779.
[73] See the Special Issue *of Legal Theory* on "Rationality" (1997), vol. 3(2).
[74] (1989) 65 Chicago-Kent L.R. 23, 25. See also his *Order Without* Law (1991), in particular Chap. 10.
[75] D. Kahneman (1997) 3 Legal Theory 105. See also O. Bar-Gill (2008) 92 Minnesota L.R. 749, and R. Epstein (2006) 73 University of Chicago L.R. 111 and R. Epstein (2008) 92 Minnesota L.R. 803.

state".[76] Rawls in *The Law of Peoples*, as already discussed,[77] was unable to overcome this assumption. But the facts of global injustice are well-known. Just to take one straightforward example, nine million people in the developing world die each year from infectious diseases—the same diseases claim 200,000 lives in the developed world.[78] Are there standards of justice that are globally significant? As Kukathas puts the question: "if individuals have basic rights in virtue of their humanity", are these "rights they hold as against the whole world"?[79]

Thomas Nagel, in an important recent article, argues they do not.[80] People, he claims, are in a justice relationship only if they belong to the same state. He is thus in a justice relationship with the Californian who picks his lettuce and the New Yorker who irons his shirts but not with the Brazilian who grows his coffee or the Philippine worker who assembles his computer.[81] Nagel believes he "owes nothing beyond humanitarianism to those with whom he shares no state".[82] He explains:

> "What creates the link between justice and sovereignty is something common to a wide range of conceptions of justice: they all depend on the coordinated conduct of large numbers of people, which cannot be achieved without law backed up by a monopoly of force ... At least among sizable populations, it cannot be provided by voluntary conventions supported solely by the mutual recognition of a common interest".[83]

But, as Cohen and Sabel point out, though states remain "essential players", increasingly rule making takes place in global settings that "even if established by states ... conduct their activities of making, elaborating, and applying rules activities with some de facto decision making independence from their creators".[84] And "even when rule-making and applying bodies lack their own independent power to impose sanctions through coercion, they have the capacity to encourage conduct by providing incentives and permitting the imposition of sanctions".[85] Global politics is "not an occasional matter of sparse agreements", but is "enduring and institutionally dense".[86] They make reference to the activities of the I.L.O.[87] and W.T.O. They could add the W.H.O.

But Nagel is convinced that treaties which set up trade rules have a

---

[76] See T. Nagel (2005) 33 *Phil and Public Affairs* 113, 114.
[77] *Ante*, 594.
[78] See World Health Organisation, *Changing History* (2004). A Maddison, *The World Economy: A Millennial Perspective* (2001) is worth consulting: the gaps have grown. So is J. Stiglitz, *Globalization and Its Discontents* (2001).
[79] C. Kukathas (2006) 23(1) *Social Philosophy and Policy* 1. This issue of Social Philosophy and Policy is devoted to "Justice and Global Politics". So is *Nomos* vol. 41 (1999).
[80] See *ante*, note 76.
[81] *ibid*, p. 141.
[82] Thus put by J. Cohen and C. Sabel (2006) 34 *Phil and Public Affairs* 147, 163.
[83] See *ante*, note 76, p. 115.
[84] See *ante*, note 82, p. 165.
[85] *ibid*.
[86] *ibid*, p. 166.
[87] This has "core labour rights". See B. Langille (2005) 16 European Journal of International Law 409. See, further, A.M Slaughter, *A New World Order* (2004).

"quite different moral character from contracts between self-interested parties within a sovereign state". They are "pure" contracts and "nothing guarantees the justice of their results".[88] They compare, he says, with contracts favoured by libertarians—the obligations they create and are and need not be underwritten by any kind of socioeconomic justice.[89]

To Julius, Nagel is "right about the shirt but wrong about the coffee".[90] "The world is governed from many capitals but indivisible in its injustice".[91] He sees Nagel's claim about states as "a piece of empirical political sociology".[92] But is the sociology "false", he asks. He cites the example of torture being carried out by the U.S.,[93] and asks "Do these people act in my name?"[94] He asks whether the laws of antebellum U.S. were enacted in the name of the slaves. Nagel, he notes, considering a similar objection about colonialism, says it might be sidestepped by adopting a sufficiently "broad interpretation of what it is for a society to be governed in the name of its members".[95] Julius asks us to consider a "hypothetical naked tyranny" (not difficult given their plenitude). In this tyranny:

"People do what the tyrant tells them to do so that he will not kill them. Though no one imagines there is any moral reason to obey him, it is hard to agree that the society is not unjust if people are going hungry as they build his pleasure palaces".[96]

Julius maintains that Nagel "cannot find injustice in [these people's] situation".[97]

## CORRECTIVE JUSTICE

It is in discussions about the rationale of tort law that we see corrective justice most clearly. Theories of distributive justice do not address the goals of tort law adequately. Courts do not use the law of tort to correct distributive imbalances, though they may sometimes appeal to considerations of distributive justice to fortify conclusions reached by other routes.[98] Even if they wanted to do so they would find distributive considerations inappropriate where the interests protected were persons' lives

---

[88] See *ante*, note 76, p. 141.
[89] *ibid.*
[90] (2006) 34 *Phil and Public Affairs* 176, 178.
[91] *ibid*, p. 176
[92] *ibid*, p. 182.
[93] See P. Sands, *Lawless World* (2006), Chap. 9
[94] Above, n. 90, p. 182.
[95] *Op. cit.*, note 76, p. 129, n. 14.
[96] *Op. cit.*, note 90, p. 183. Do we need hypotheticals when there is Zimbabwe in 2008? See *The Guardian*, July 5, 2008, p. 1.
[97] *ibid*, p. 183.
[98] See, *e.g.* Lord Steyn's judgment in *McFarlane* v. *Tayside Health Board* [2000] 2 A.C. 59. But note his comment that "tort law is a mosaic in which the principles of corrective justice and distributive justice and distributive justice are interwoven" (at 73).

or bodies. The most fundamental objection, though, is that distributive justice operates on a global level and tort law locally, between two persons. We do not think if A negligently injures B that C, D and E should assist B to restore A's *status quo ante*.[99] The causation requirement of tort law is also problematic for the distributive approach. It requires that recoverable losses be caused by human agency, so that a child born with special needs as a result of a doctor's negligence may recover considerable damages by way of compensation, but not one born with similar needs because of a genetic problem. Tort theorists who want tort law to achieve distributive justice—so that cases like these are not distinguished—advocate the abolition of tort law and its replacement by social compensation schemes.[1]

Attempts to explain tort law in terms of corrective justice is more promising. The underlying premise is that tort law should do justice between the parties, ignoring any larger distributive issues in the community as a whole. Corrective justice imposes an obligation on the tortfeasor to compensate his victim for the harm he has done: the victim has a correlative right to recover for his losses.[2] There are causation problems: space precludes their consideration here.[3] There is also the problem of separating the concerns of corrective and distributive justice. This is not a problem insofar as tort law is directed towards the protection of life and bodily integrity, for it is clear that these interests belong to the victim and no one else (it is not therefore subject to considerations of distributive justice). But where the interest which is the subject of protection is property (in its broadest sense), considerations of distributive justice are inevitable. The danger is that a corrective justice-based theory of tort law will collapse into a distributive theory.

There are arguments accordingly posited to demonstrate the independence of corrective justice from background conceptions of distributive justice. One is offered by Benson. "A person who, through an external manifestation of will, has brought something under his or her present and exclusive control prior to others is, relative to those others, entitled to it in corrective justice".[4] Another by Coleman. He discounts a deviation in holdings from an ideally just distribution when is not too great. This is particularly so where the existing system of property contributes to individual well-being and social stability.[5] These justifications, respectively Kantian and functional,[6] may not convince. But it may

---

[99] L. A. Alexander (1987) 6 Law and Philosophy 1, 6–7; J. Coleman, *Risks and Wrongs* (1992).
[1] S. Sugarman, *Doing Away With Personal Injury Law* (1989), pp. 127–152; C. Ham *et al.* *Medical Negligence: Compensation and Accountability* (1988).
[2] See generally S. Perry (1992) 77 Iowa L. Rev. 449.
[3] See R. W. Wright (1985) 73 California L. Rev. 1735 (see in particular the so-called NESS test).
[4] (1992) 77 Iowa L. Rev. 515, 543.
[5] *Op. cit.*, n. 99.
[6] And see J. Coleman, *The Practice of Principle* (2001).

nevertheless be thought that tort law can be explained in corrective justice terms.[7]

A number of thinkers have tried to do this. Some focus on the agency of the tortfeasor. Thus for Weinrib (for whom corrective justice is the "structure of immediate interaction for Kantian moral persons"[8]) if A's wrongful exercise of agency results in harm to the person or property of B, A has a duty in corrective justice to compensate B (and B has a correlative right to be compensated).[9] Others have focused on the victim's loss. As between a faulty injurer and an innocent victim, it is argued that it is morally preferable that the injurer should bear the loss. As Perry explains this treats corrective justice as a form of "localized distributive justice".[10] But why, he asks, should only the person who has injured the victim pay him compensation: others, equally at fault, who have for-tuitously avoided injuring anyone could equally be required to contribute towards the compensation. This was recognised by Coleman who advo-cated an "at-fault pool" under which all guilty of faulty driving would be required to pay into a pool to compensate victims, in proportion to the degree of fault and regardless of whether they had caused an accident.[11]

Perhaps we should persevere with localized distributive justice. Fletcher did so.[12] From a Rawlsian starting-point[13] premised upon the right of all to the "maximum amount of security compatible with a like security for everyone else",[14] he argues that someone who imposes on another a risk deemed unacceptable is under an obligation to compensate for loss. Compensation is "a surrogate for the individual's right to the same security as enjoyed by others".[15] But why not share the victim's loss amongst all those who engaged in the risky behaviour? Does it matter that they didn't cause any injury? That they didn't cause *this* injury?

If these approaches to corrective justice are not convincing, is there another route? Perry,[16] looking for a moral link between one person's conduct and another's loss, finds it, following Honoré,[17] in responsibility. If A chooses to act in a certain way, he should be fully responsible for any harms he causes (and, though this is not relevant here, whatever gains result should be his too[18]). This view is premised upon choice and leads to a conclusion that there should be strict liability.[19] But how real is choice?

---

[7] There are, of course, other theories, not considered here, in particular economic theories (see *e.g.* S. Shavell, *Economic Analysis of Tort Law* (1987).

[8] In (eds.) R. G. Frey and C. W. Morris, *Liability and Responsibility* (1991), pp. 290, 314.

[9] *The Idea of Private Law* (1995), pp. 56–144. This is criticised by S. Perry, *op. cit.*, n. 56, pp. 478–488.

[10] *ibid.*, pp. 470–475.

[11] (1974) 71 Journal of Philosophy 473, 484–488.

[12] (1972) 85 Harvard L. Rev. 537.

[13] *Ante*, 583.

[14] *Op. cit.*, n. 12, p. 550.

[15] *ibid.*

[16] In (ed.) D. Patterson, *A Companion To Philosophy of Law and Legal Theory* (1996), pp. 57, 75. See also S. Perry (1997) 26 Philosophy. and Public Affairs 351.

[17] (1988) 104 L.Q.R. 530.

[18] Hence the libertarian conclusion (see, *e.g.* Nozick, *ante*, 597) that taxation is wrong.

[19] See R. Epstein (1973) 2 J. of Legal Studies 151, 158–160.

Perhaps rather we should be looking to control: could the actor have foreseen and avoided causing the harm to the victim that he did? However, even if he could have avoided the harm by acting differently, it does not follow that he should have acted differently. It is impossible to act without subjecting others to risk. The modern law of negligence recognises this by providing that foreseeability is a necessary but not a sufficient condition of liability. What is also required is that the loss is "wrongful".[20] For Coleman a loss is "wrongful" if it results from conduct which is wrongful or infringes one of the victim's rights. The English courts do not use this language, but in adding to foreseeability and proximity the requirement that "the situation should be one in which the court considers it fair, just and reasonable that the law should impose a duty of a given scope upon the one party for the benefit of the other"[21] it may be thought to reach a similar conclusion albeit within the language of policy.

---

### JOHN RAWLS
**A Theory of Justice**
(Revised edition, 1999)

In working out the conception of justice as fairness one main task clearly is to determine which principles of justice would be chosen in the original position. To do this we must describe this situation in some detail and formulate with care the problem of choice which it presents. ... It may be observed, however, that once the principles of justice are thought of as arising from an original agreement in a situation of equality, it is an open question whether the principle of utility would be acknowledged. Offhand it hardly seems likely that persons who view themselves as equals, entitled to press their claims upon one another, would agree to a principle which may require lesser life prospects for some simply for the sake of a greater sum of advantages enjoyed by others. Since each desires to protect his interests, his capacity to advance his conception of the good, no one has a reason to acquiesce in an enduring loss for himself in order to bring about a greater net balance of satisfaction. In the absence of strong and lasting benevolent impulses, a rational man would not accept a basic structure merely because it maximised the algebraic sum of advantages irrespective of its permanent effect on his own basic rights and interests. Thus it seems that the principle of utility is incompatible with the conception of social co-operation among equals for mutual advantage. It appears to be inconsistent with the idea of reciprocity implicit in the notion of a well-ordered society. ...

I shall maintain instead that the persons in the initial situation would choose two rather different principles: the first requires equality in the assignment of basic rights and duties, while the second holds that social and economic inequalities, for example inequalities of wealth and authority, are just only if they result in compensating benefits for everyone, and in particular for the least advantaged members of society. These principles rule out justifying institutions on the grounds that the hardships of some are offset by a greater good in the aggregate. It may be expedient but it is not just that some should have less in

---

[20] Coleman's conclusion, *op. cit.*, n. 99.
[21] *Per* Lord Bridge in *Caparo Industries* v. *Dickman* [1990] 2 A.C. 605 at 617.

order that others may prosper. But there is no injustice in the greater benefits earned by a few provided that the situation of persons not so fortunate is thereby improved. The intuitive idea is that since everyone's well-being depends upon a scheme of co-operation without which no one could have a satisfactory life, the division of advantages should be such as to draw forth the willing co-operation of everyone taking part in it, including those less well situated. Yet this can be expected only if reasonable terms are proposed. The two principles mentioned seem to be a fair agreement on the basis of which those better endowed, or more fortunate in their social position, neither of which we can be said to deserve, could expect the willing co-operation of others when some workable scheme is a necessary condition of the welare of all. . . .

The problem of the choice of principles, however, is extremely difficult. I do not expect the answer I shall suggest to be convincing to everyone. It is, therefore, worth noting from the outset that justice as fairness, like other contract views, consists of two parts: (1) an interpretation of the initial situation and of the problem of choice posed there, and (2) a set of principles which, it is argued, would be agreed to. One may accept the first part of the theory (or some variant thereof), but not the other, and conversely. The concept of the initial contractual situation may seem reasonable although the particular principles proposed are rejected. To be sure, I want to maintain that the most appropriate conception of this situation does lead to principles of justice contrary to utilitarianism and perfectionism, and therefore that the contract doctrine provides an alternative to these views. Still, one may dispute this contention even though one grants that the contractarian method is a useful way of studying ethical theories and of setting forth their underlying assumptions.

Justice as fairness is an example of what I have called a contract theory. Now there may be an objection to the term "contract" and related expressions, but I think it will serve reasonably well. Many words have misleading connotations which at first are likely to confuse. The terms "utility" and "utilitarianism" are surely no exception. They too have unfortunate suggestions which hostile critics have been willing to exploit; yet they are clear enough for those prepared to study utilitarian doctrine. The same should be true of the term "contract" applied to moral theories. As I have mentioned, to understand it one has to keep in mind that it implies a certain level of abstraction. In particular, the content of the relevant agreement is not to enter a given society or to adopt a given form of government, but to accept certain moral principles. Moreover, the undertakings referred to are purely hypothetical: a contract view holds that certain principles would be acceptable in a well-defined initial situation.

The merit of the contract terminology is that it conveys the idea that principles of justice may be conceived as principles that would be chosen by rational persons, and that in this way conceptions of justice may be explained and justified. The theory of justice is a part, perhaps the most significant part, of the theory of rational choice. . . .                                                        [pp. 12–15]

### The Original Position and Justification

I have said that the original position is the appropriate initial *status quo* which insures that the fundamental agreements reached in it are fair. This fact yields the name "justice as fairness." It is clear, then, that I want to say that one conception of justice is more reasonable than another, or justifiable with respect to it, if rational persons in the initial situation would choose its principles over those of the other for the role of justice. Conceptions of justice are to be ranked by their acceptability to persons so circumstanced. Understood in this way the question of justification is settled by working out a problem of deliberation: we have to ascertain which principles it would be rational to adopt given the contractual situation. This connects the theory of justice with the theory of rational choice.

If this view of the problem of justification is to succeed, we must, of course, describe in some detail the nature of this choice problem. A problem of rational decision has a definite answer only if we know the beliefs and interests of the parties, their relations with respect to one another, the alternatives between which they are to choose, the procedure whereby they make up their minds, and so on. As the circumstances are presented in different ways, correspondingly different principles are accepted. The concept of the original position, as I shall refer to it, is that of the most philosophically favored interpretation of this initial choice situation for the purposes of the theory of justice.

But how are we to decide what is the most favored interpretation? I assume, for one thing, that there is a broad measure of agreement that principles of justice should be chosen under certain conditions. To justify a particular description of the initial situation one shows that it incorporates those commonly shared presumptions. One argues from widely accepted but weak premises to more specific conclusions. Each of the presumptions should by itself be natural and plausible; some of them may seem innocuous or even trivial. The aim of the contract approach is to establish that taken together they impose significant bounds on acceptable principles of justice. The ideal outcome would be that these conditions determine a unique set of principles; but I shall be satisfied if they suffice to rank the main traditional conceptions of social justice.

One should not be misled, then, by the somewhat unusual conditions which characterize the original position. The idea here is simply to make vivid to ourselves the restrictions that it seems reasonable to impose on arguments for principles of justice, and therefore on these principles themselves. Thus it seems reasonable and generally acceptable that no one should be advantaged or disadvantaged by natural fortune or social circumstances in the choice of principles. It also seems widely agreed that it should be impossible to tailor principles to the circumstances of one's own case. We should insure further that particular inclinations and aspirations, and persons' conceptions of their good do not affect the principles adopted. The aim is to rule out those principles that it would be rational to propose for acceptance, however little the chance of success, only if one knew certain things that are irrelevant from the standpoint of justice. For example, if a man knew that he was wealthy, he might find it rational to advance the principle that various taxes for welfare measures be counted unjust; if he knew that he was poor, he would most likely propose the contrary principle. To represent the desired restrictions one imagines a situation in which everyone is deprived of this sort of information. One excludes the knowledge of those contingencies which sets men at odds and allows them to be guided by their prejudices. In this manner the veil of ignorance is arrived at in a natural way. This concept should cause no difficulty if we keep in mind the constraints on arguments that it is meant to express. At any time we can enter the original position, so to speak, simply by following a certain procedure, namely, by arguing for principles of justice in accordance with these restrictions.

It seems reasonable to suppose that the parties in the original position are equal. That is, all have the same rights in the procedure for choosing principles; each can make proposals, submit reasons for their acceptance and so on. Obviously the purpose of these conditions is to represent equality between human beings as moral persons, as creatures having a conception of their good and capable of a sense of justice. The basis of equality is taken to be similarity in these two respects. Systems of ends are not ranked in value; and each man is presumed to have the requisite ability to understand and to act upon whatever principles are adopted. Together with the veil of ignorance, these conditions define the principles of justice as those which rational persons concerned to advance their interests would consent to as equals when none are known to be advantaged or disadvantaged by social and natural contingencies.                    [pp. 15–17]

*Two Principles of Justice*

I shall now state in a provisional form the two principles of justice that I believe would be chosen in the original position. . . .

The first statement of the two principles reads as follows.

First: each person is to have an equal right to the most extensive basic liberty compatible with a similar liberty for others.

Second: social and economic inequalities are to be arranged so that they are both (a) reasonably expected to be to everyone's advantage, and (b) attached to positions and offices open to all. . . .

By way of general comment, these principles primarily apply, as I have said, to the basic structure of society. They are to govern the assignment of rights and duties and to regulate the distribution of social and economic advantages. As their formulation suggests, these principles presuppose that the social structure can be divided into two more or less distinct parts, the first principle applying to the one, the second to the other. They distinguish between those aspects of the social system that define and secure the equal liberties of citizenship and those that specify and establish social and economic inequalities. The basic liberties of citizens are, roughly speaking, political liberty (the right to vote and to be eligible for public office) together with freedom of speech and assembly; liberty of conscience and freedom of thought; freedom of the person along with the right to hold (personal) property; and freedom from arbitrary arrest and seizure as defined by the concept of the rule of law. These liberties are all required to be equal by the first principle, since citizens of a just society are to have the same basic rights.

The second principle applies, in the first approximation, to the distribution of income and wealth and to the design of organizations that make use of differences in authority and responsibility, or chains of command. While the distribution of wealth and income need not be equal, it must be to everyone's advantage, and at the same time, positions of authority and offices of command must be accessible to all. One applies the second principle by holding positions open, and then, subject to this constraint, arranges social and economic inequalities so that everyone benefits.

These principles are to be arranged in a serial order with the first principle prior to the second. This ordering means that a departure from the institutions of equal liberty required by the first principle cannot be justified by, or compensated for, by greater social and economic advantages. The distribution of wealth and income, and the hierarchies of authority, must be consistent with both the liberties of equal citizenship and equality of opportunity.

[The] two principles (and this holds for all formulations) are a special case of a more general conception of justice that can be expressed as follows:

All social values—liberty and opportunity, income and wealth, and the bases of self-respect—are to be distributed equally unless an unequal distribution of any, or all, of these values is to everyone's advantage.

Injustice, then, is simply inequalities that are not to the benefit of all. . . .

As a first step, suppose that the basic structure of society distributes certain primary goods, that is, things that every rational man is presumed to want. These goods normally have a use whatever a person's rational plan of life. For simplicity, assume that the chief primary goods at the disposition of society are rights and liberties, powers and opportunities, income and wealth. [. . .] These are the social primary goods. Other primary goods such as health and vigor, intelligence and imagination, are natural goods; although their possession is influenced by the basic structure, they are not so directly under its control. Imagine, then, a hypothetical initial arrangement in which all the social primary goods are equally distributed: everyone has similar rights and duties, and income and wealth are evenly shared. This state of affairs provides a benchmark for judging improvements. If certain inequalities of wealth and organizational powers would make everyone better off than in this hypothetical starting situation, then they accord with the general conception.

Now it is possible, at least theoretically, that by giving up some of their fundamental liberties men are sufficiently compensated by the resulting social and economic gains. The general conception of justice imposes no restrictions on what sort of inequalities are permissible; it only requires that everyone's position be improved. We need not suppose anything so drastic as consenting to a condition of slavery. Imagine instead that men forego certain political rights when the economic returns are significant and their capacity to influence the course of policy by the exercise of these rights would be marginal in any case. It is this kind of exchange which the two principles as stated rule out; being arranged in serial order they do not permit exchanges between basic liberties and economic and social gains. The serial ordering of principles expresses an underlying preference among primary social goods. When this preference is rational so likewise is the choice of these principles in this order.

In developing justice as fairness I shall, for the most part, leave aside the general conception of justice and examine instead the special case of the two principles in serial order. The advantage of this procedure is that from the first the matter of priorities is recognised and an effort made to find principles to deal with it. One is led to attend throughout to the conditions under which the acknowledgement of the absolute weight of liberty with respect to social and economic advantages, as defined by the lexical order of the two principles, would be reasonable. Offhand, this ranking appears extreme and too special a case to be of much interest; but there is more justification for it than would appear at first sight. ... Furthermore, the distinction between fundamental rights and liberties and economic and social benefits marks a difference among primary social goods that one should try to exploit. It suggests an important division in the social system. Of course, the distinctions drawn and the ordering proposed are bound to be at best only approximations. There are surely circumstances in which they fail. But it is essential to depict clearly the main lines of a reasonable conception of justice; and under many conditions anyway, the two principles in serial order may serve well enough. When necessary we can fall back on the more general conception.

The fact that the two principles apply to institutions has certain consequences. Several points illustrate this. First of all, the rights and liberties referred to by these principles are those which are defined by the public rules of the basic structure. Whether men are free is determined by the rights and duties established by the major institutions of society. Liberty is a certain pattern of social forms. The first principle simply requires that certain sorts of rules, those defining basic liberties, apply to everyone equally and that they allow the most extensive liberty compatible with a like liberty for all. The only reason for circumscribing the rights defining liberty and making men's freedom less extensive than it might otherwise be is that these equal rights as institutionally defined would interfere with one another.

Another thing to bear in mind is that when principles mention persons, or require that everyone gain from an inequality, the reference is to representative persons holding the various social positions, or offices, or whatever, established by the basic structure. Thus in applying the second principle I assume that it is possible to assign an expectation of well-being to representative individuals holding these positions. The expectation indicates their life prospects as viewed from their social station. In general, the expectations of representative persons depend upon the distribution of rights and duties throughout the basic structure.

When this changes, expectations change. I assume, then, that expectations are connected: by raising the prospects of the representative man in one position we presumably increase or decrease the prospects of representative men in other positions. Since it applies to institutional forms, the second principle (or rather the first part of it) refers to the expectations of representative individuals. ... [N]either principle applies to distributions of particular goods to particular individuals who may be identified by their proper names. The situation where someone is considering how to allocate certain commodities to needy persons who are known to him is not within the scope of the principles. They are meant to regulate basic institutional arrangements. We must not assume that there is much similarity from the standpoint of justice between an administrative allotment of goods to specific persons and the appropriate design of society. Our common sense intuitions for the former may be a poor guide to the latter.

Now the second principle insists that each person benefit from permissible inequalities in the basic structure. This means that it must be reasonable for each relevant representative man defined by this structure, when he views it as a going concern, to prefer his prospects with the inequality to his prospects without it. One is not allowed to justify differences in income or organizational powers on the ground that the disadvantages of those in one position are outweighed by the greater advantages of those in another. Much less can infringements of liberty be counterbalanced in this way. Applied to the basic structure, the principle of utility would have us maximize the sum of expectations of representative men (weighted by the number of persons they represent, on the classical view); and this would permit us to compensate for the losses of some by the gain of others. Instead, the two principles require that everyone benefit from economic and social inequalities. It is obvious, however, that there are indefinitely many ways in which all may be advantaged when the initial arrangement of equality is taken as a benchmark. How then are we to choose among these possibilities? The principles must be specified so that they yield a determinate conclusion.          [pp. 52–56]

### The Veil of Ignorance

The idea of the original position is to set up a fair procedure so that any principles agreed to will be just. The aim is to use the notion of pure procedural justice as a basis of theory. Somehow we must nullify the effects of specific contingencies which put men at odds and tempt them to exploit social and natural circumstances to their own advantage. Now in order to do this I assume that the parties are situated behind a veil of ignorance. They do not know how the various alternatives will affect their own particular case and they are obliged to evaluate principles solely on the basis of general considerations.[22]

It is assumed, then, that the parties do not know certain kinds of particular facts. First of all, no one knows his place in society, his class position or social status; nor does he know his fortune in the distribution of natural assets and abilities, his intelligence and strength, and the like. Nor, again, does anyone know his conception of the good, the particulars of his rational plan of life, or even the special features of his psychology such as his aversion to risk or liability to optimism or pessimism. More than this, I assume that the parties do not know the particular circumstances of their own society. That is, they do not know its economic or political situation, or the level of civilization and culture it has been able to achieve. The persons in the original position have no information as to which generation they belong. These broader restrictions on knowledge are

[22]  The veil of ignorance is so natural a condition that something like it must have occurred to many. The closest express statement of it known to me is found in J. C. Harsanyi, "Cardinal Utility in Welfare Economics and in the Theory of Risk-Taking." *Journal of Political Economy*, vol. 61 (1953). Harsanyi uses it to develop a utilitarian theory [...].

appropriate in part because questions of social justice arise between generations as well as within them, for example, the question of the appropriate rate of capital saving and of the conservation of natural resources and the environment of nature. There is also, theoretically anyway, the question of a reasonable genetic policy. In these cases too, in order to carry through the idea of the original position, the parties must not know the contingencies that set them in opposition. They must choose principles the consequences of which they are prepared to live with whatever generation they turn out to belong to.

As far as possible, then, the only particular facts which the parties know is that their society is subject to the circumstances of justice and whatever this implies. It is taken for granted, however, that they know the general facts about human society. The understand political affairs and the principles of economic theory; they know the basis of social organization and the laws of human psychology. Indeed, the parties are presumed to know whatever general facts affect the choice of the principles of justice. There are no limitations on general information, that is, on general laws and theories, since conceptions of justice must be adjusted to the characteristics of the systems of social co-operation which they are to regulate, and there is no reason to rule out these facts. It is, for example, a consideration against a conception of justice that in view of the laws of moral psychology, men would not acquire a desire to act upon it even when the institutions of their society satisfied it. For in this case there would be difficulty in securing the stability of social co-operation. It is an important feature of a conception of justice that it should generate its own support. That is, its principles should be such that when they are embodied in the basic structure of society men tend to acquire the corresponding sense of justice. Given the principles of moral learning, men develop a desire to act in accordance with its principles. In this case a conception of justice is stable. This kind of general information is admissible in the original position.                                                     [pp. 118–119]

### Background Institutions for Distributive Justice

The main problem of distributive justice is the choice of a social system. The principles of justice apply to the basic structure and regulate how its major institutions are combined into one scheme. Now, the idea of justice as fairness is to use the notion of pure procedural justice to handle the contingencies of particular situations. The social system is to be designed so that the resulting distribution is just however things turn out. To achieve this end it is necessary to set the social and economic process within the surroundings of suitable political and legal institutions. Without the proper arrangement of these background institutions the outcome of the distributive process will not be just. Background fairness is lacking. I shall give a brief description of these background institutions as they might exist in a properly organised democratic state that allows private ownership of capital and natural resources. These arrangements are familiar, but it may be useful to see how they fit the two principles of justice. Modifications for the case of a socialist regime will be considered briefly later.

First of all, I assume that the basic structure is regulated by a just constitution that secures the liberties of equal citizenship (as described in the preceding chapter). Liberty of conscience and freedom of thought are taken for granted, and the fair value of political liberty is maintained. The political process is conducted, as far as circumstances permit, as a just procedure for choosing between governments and for enacting legislation. I assume also that there is fair (as opposed to formal) equality of opportunity. This means that in addition to maintaining the usual kinds of social overhead capital, the government tries to insure equal chances of education and culture for persons similarly endowed and motivated either by subsidizing private schools or by establishing a public school system. It also enforces and underwrites equality of opportunity in economic activities and in the free choice of occupation. This is achieved by policing the conduct of firms and private associations and by preventing the establishment of monopolistic restrictions and barriers to the more desirable positions. Finally, the government guarantees a social minimum either by family allowances and special payments for sickness and employment, or more systematically by such devices as a graded income supplement (a so-called negative income tax).

In establishing the background institutions the government may be thought of as divided into four branches.[23] Each branch consists of various agencies, and activities thereof, charged with preserving certain social and economic conditions. These divisions do not overlap with the usual organization of government but are to be understood as different functions. The allocation branch, for example, is to keep the price system workably competitive and to prevent the formation of unreasonable market power. Such power does not exist as long as markets cannot be made more competitive consistent with the requirements of efficiency and the facts of geography and the preferences of households. The allocation branch is also charged with identifying and correcting, say by suitable taxes and subsidies and by changes in the definition of property rights, the more obvious departures from efficiency caused by the failure of prices to measure accurately social benefits and costs. To this end suitable taxes and subsidies may be used, or the scope and definition of property rights may be revised. The stabilization branch, on the other hand, strives to bring about reasonably full employment in the sense that those who want to work can find it and the free choice of occupation and the deployment of finance is supported by strong effective demand. These two branches together are to maintain the efficiency of the market economy generally.

The social minimum is the responsibility of the transfer branch. ... The essential idea is that the workings of this branch takes needs into account and assigns them an appropriate weight with respect to other claims. A competitive price system gives no consideration to needs and therefore it cannot be the sole device of distribution. There must be a division of labor between the parts of the social system in answering to the common sense precepts of justice. Different institutions meet different claims. Competitive markets properly regulated secure free choice of occupation and lead to an efficient use of resources and allocation of commodities to households. They set a weight on the conventional precepts associated with wages and earnings, whereas the transfer branch guarantees a certain level of well-being and honors the claims of need. ... Certain precepts tend to be associated with specific institutions. It is left to the background system as a whole to determine how these precepts are balanced. Since the principles of justice regulate the whole structure, they also regulate the balance of precepts. In general, then, this balance will vary in accordance with the underlying political conception.

It is clear that the justice of distributive shares depends on the background institutions and how they allocate total income, wages and other income plus transfers. There is with reason strong objection to the competitive determination of total income, since this ignores the claims of need and an appropriate standard of life. From the standpoint of the legislative stage it is rational to insure oneself and one's descendants against these contingencies of the market. Indeed, the difference principle presumably requires this. But once a suitable minimum is provided by transfers, it may be perfectly fair that the rest of total income be settled by the price system, assuming that it is moderately efficient and free from monopolistic restrictions, and unreasonable externalities have been eliminated. Moreover, this way of dealing with the claims of need would appear to be more effective than trying to regulate income by minimum wage standards, and the like.

---

[23] For the idea of branches of government, see R. A. Musgrave, *The Theory of Public Finance* (New York, McGraw-Hill 1959), Chap. 1.

It is better to assign to each branch only such tasks as are compatible with one another. Since the market is not suited to answer the claims of need, these should be met by a separate arrangement. Whether the principles of justice are satisfied, then, turns on whether the total income of the least advantaged (wages plus transfers) is such as to maximize their long-run expectations (consistent with the constraints of equal liberty and fair equality of opportunity).

Finally, there is a distribution branch. Its task is to preserve an approximate justice in distributive shares by means of taxation and the necessary adjustments in the rights of property. Two aspects of this branch may be distinguished. First of all, it imposes a number of inheritance and gift taxes, and sets restrictions on the rights of bequest. The purpose of these levies and regulations is not to raise revenue (release resources to government) but gradually and continually to correct the distribution of wealth and to prevent concentrations of power detrimental to the fair value of political liberty and fair equality of opportunity. For example, the progressive principle might be applied at the beneficiary's end.[24] Doing this would encourage the wide dispersal of property which is a necessary condition, it seems, if the fair value of the equal liberties is to be maintained. The unequal inheritance of wealth is no more inherently unjust than the unequal inheritance of intelligence. It is true that the former is presumably more easily subject to social control; but the essential thing is that as far as possible inequalities founded on either should satisfy the difference principle. Thus inheritance if permissible provided that the resulting inequalities are to the advantage of the least fortunate and compatible with liberty and fair equality of opportunity. ... Fair equality of opportunity means a certain set of institutions that assures similar chances of education and culture for persons similarly motivated and keeps positions and offices open to all on the basis of qualities and efforts reasonably related to the relevant duties and tasks. It is these institutions that are put in jeopardy when inequalities of wealth exceed a certain limit; and political liberty in likewise tends to lose its value, and representative government to become such in appearance only. The taxes and enactments of the distribution branch are to prevent this limit from being exceeded. Naturally, where this limit lies is a matter of political judgment guided by theory, good sense and plain hunch, at least within a wide range. On this sort of question the theory of justice has nothing specific to say. Its aim is to formulate the principles that are to regulate the background institutions.

The second part of the distribution branch is a scheme of taxation to raise the revenues that justice requires. Social resources must be released to the government so that it can provide for the public goods and make the transfer payments necessary to satisfy the difference principles. This problem belongs to the distribution branch since the burden of taxation is to be justly shared and it aims at establishing just arrangements. Leaving aside many complications, it is worth noting that a proportional expenditure tax may be part of the best tax scheme.[25] For one thing, it is preferable to an income tax (of any kind) at the level of common sense precepts of justice, since it imposes a levy according to how much a person takes out of the common store of goods and not according to how much he contributes (assuming here that income is fairly earned). Again, a proportional tax on total consumption (for each year say) can contain the usual exemptions for dependents, and so on; and it treats everyone in a uniform way (still assuming that income is fairly earned). It may be better, therefore, to use progressive rates only when they are necessary to preserve the justice of the basic structure with respect to the first principle of justice and fair equality of opportunity, and so to forestall accumulations of property and power likely to undermine the corresponding institutions. Following this rule might help to signal an important distinction in questions of policy. And if proportional taxes should also prove

[24] See Meade, *Efficiency, Equality and the Ownership of Property*, pp. 56f.
[25] See Nicholas Kaldor, *An Expenditure Tax* (London, George Allen and Unwin, 1955).

more efficient, say because they interfere less with incentives, this might make the case for them decisive if a feasible scheme could be worked out. As before, these are questions of political judgment and not part of a theory of justice. And in any case we are here considering such a proportional tax as part of an ideal scheme for well-ordered society in order to illustrate the content of the two principles. It does not follow that, given the injustice of existing institutions, even steeply progressive income taxes are not justified when all things are considered. In practice, we must usually choose between several unjust, or second best, arrangements; and then we look to nonideal theory to find the least unjust scheme. Sometimes this scheme will includes measures and policies that a perfectly just system would reject. Two wrongs can make a right in the sense that the best available arrangement may contain a balance of imperfections, an adjustment of compensating injustices.

The two parts of the distribution branch derive from the two principles of justice. The taxation of inheritance and income at progressive rates (when necessary), and the legal definition of property rights, are to secure the institutions of equal liberty in a property-owning democracy and the fair value of the rights they establish. Proportional expenditure (or income) taxes are to provide revenue for public goods, the transfer branch and the establishment of fair equality of opportunity in education, and the like, so as to carry out the second principle. No mention has been made at any point of the traditional criteria of taxation such as that taxes are to be levied according to benefits received or the ability to pay.[26] The reference to common sense precepts in connection with expenditure taxes is a subordinate consideration. The scope of these criteria is regulated by the principles of justice. Once the problem of distributive shares is recognized as that of designing background institutions, the conventional maxims are seen to have no independent force, however appropriate they may be in certain delimited cases. To suppose otherwise is not to take a sufficiently comprehensive point of view. It is evident also that the design of the distribution branch does not presuppose the utilitarian's standard assumptions about individual utilities. Inheritance and progressive income taxes, for example, are not predicated on the idea that individuals have similar utility functions satisfying the diminishing marginal principle. The aim of the distribution branch is not, of course, to maximize the net balance of satisfaction but to establish just background institutions. Doubts about the shape of utility functions are irrelevant. This problem is one for the utilitarian, not for contract theory.

So far I have assumed that the aim of the branches of government is to establish a democratic regime in which land and capital are widely though not presumably equally held. Society is not so divided that one fairly small sector controls the preponderance of productive resources. When this is achieved and distributive shares satisfy the principles of justice, many socialist criticisms of the market economy are met. But it is clear that, in theory anyway, a liberal socialist regime can also answer to the two principles of justice. We have only to suppose that the means of production are publicly owned and that firms are managed by workers' councils say, or by agents appointed by them. Collective decisions made democratically under the constitution determine the general features of the economy, such as the rate of saving and the proportion of society's production devoted to essential public goods. Given the resulting economic environment, firms regulated by market forces conduct themselves much as before. Although the background institutions will take a different form, especially in the case of the distribution branch, there is no reason in principle why just distributive shares cannot be achieved. The theory of justice does not by itself favor either form of regime. As we have seen, the decision as to which system is best for a given people depends upon their circumstances, institutions, and historical traditions.

---

[26] For a discussion of these tax criteria, see Musgrave, *The Theory of Public Finance*, Chaps. IV and V.

the conceptions of the good associated with existing doctrines and thus improve the likelihood of securing an overlapping consensus.

This is not how justice as fairness proceeds; to do so would make it political in the wrong way. Rather, it elaborates a political conception as a freestanding view working from the fundamental idea of society as a fair system of co-operation and its companion ideas. The hope is that this idea, with its index of primary goods arrived at from within, can be the focus of a reasonable overlapping consensus. We leave aside comprehensive doctrines that now exist, or that have existed, or that might exist. The thought is not that primary goods are fair to comprehensive conceptions of the good associated with such doctrines, by striking a fair balance among them, but rather fair to free and equal citizens as those persons who have those conceptions.

The problem, then, is how to frame a conception of justice for a constitutional regime such that those who support, or who might be brought to support, that kind of regime might also endorse the political conception provided it did not conflict too sharply with their comprehensive views. This leads to the idea of a political conception of justice as a freestanding view starting from the fundamental ideas of a democratic society and presupposing no particular wider doctrine. We put no doctrinal obstacles to its winning allegiance to itself, so that it can be supported by a reasonable and enduring overlapping consensus.[pp. 38–40]

### Three Features of an Overlapping Consensus

There are at least four objections likely to be raised against the idea of social unity founded on an overlapping consensus on a political conception of justice. I begin with perhaps the most obvious of these, namely, that an overlapping consensus is a mere modus vivendi. . . .

Some will think that even if an overlapping consensus were sufficiently stable, the idea of political unity founded on an overlapping consensus must still be rejected, since it abandons the hope of political community and settles instead for a public understanding that is at bottom a mere modus vivendi. To this objection, we say that the hope of political community must indeed be abandoned, if by such a community we mean a political society united in affirming the same comprehensive doctrine. This possibility is excluded by the fact of reasonable pluralism together with the rejection of the oppressive use of the state power to overcome it. The substantive question concerns the significant features of such a consensus and how these features affect social concord and the moral quality of public life. I turn to why an overlapping consensus is not a mere modus vivendi.

A typical use of the phrase "modus vivendi" is to characterize a treaty between two states whose national aims and interests put them at odds. In negotiating a treaty each state would be wise and prudent to make sure that the agreement proposed represents an equilibrium point: that is, that the terms and conditions of the treaty are drawn up in such a way that it is public knowledge that it is not advantageous for either state to violate it. The treaty will then be adhered to because doing so is regarded by each as in its national interest, including its interest in its reputation as a state that honors treaties. But in general both states are ready to pursue their goals at the expense of the other, and should conditions change they may do so. This background highlights the way in which such a treaty is a mere modus vivendi. A similar background is present when we think of social consensus founded on self- or group interests, or on the outcome of political bargaining: social unity is only apparent, as its stability is contingent on circumstances remaining such as not to upset the fortunate convergence of interests.

That an overlapping consensus is quite different from a modus vivendi is clear from our model case. In that example, note two aspects: first, the object of consensus, the political conception of justice, is itself a moral conception. And second, it is affirmed on moral grounds, that is, it includes conceptions of society and of citizens as persons, as well as principles of justice, and an account of the political virtues through which those principles are embodied in human character and expressed in public life. An overlapping consensus, therefore, is not merely a consensus on accepting certain authorities, or on complying with certain institutional arrangements, founded on a convergence of self- or group interests. All those who affirm the political conception start from within their own comprehensive view and draw on the religious, philosophical, and moral grounds it provides. The fact that people affirm the same political conception on those grounds does not make their affirming it any less religious, philosophical, or moral, as the case may be, since the grounds sincerely held determine the nature of their affirmation.

The preceding two aspects of an overlapping consensus—moral object and moral grounds—connect with a third aspect, that of stability. This means that those who affirm the various views supporting the political conception will not withdraw their support of it should the relative strength of their view in society increase and eventually become dominant. So long as the three views are affirmed and not revised, the political conception will still be supported regardless of shifts in the distribution of political power. Each view supports the political conception for its own sake, or on its own merits. The test for this is whether the consensus is stable with respect to changes in the distribution of power among views. This feature of stability highlights a basic contrast between an overlapping consensus and a modus vivendi, the stability of which does depend on happenstance and a balance of relative forces. . . .

## An Overlapping Consensus not Indifferent or Skeptical

I turn to a second objection to the idea of an overlapping consensus on a political conception of justice: namely, that the avoidance of general and comprehensive doctrines implies indifference or skepticism as to whether a political conception of justice can be true, as opposed to reasonable in the constructivist sense. This avoidance may appear to suggest that such a conception might be the most reasonable one for us even when it is known not to be true, as if truth were simply beside the point. In reply, it would be fatal to the idea of a political conception to see it as skeptical about, or indifferent to, truth, much less as in conflict with it. Such skepticism or indifference would put political philosophy in opposition to numerous comprehensive doctrines, and thus defeat from the outset its aim of achieving an overlapping consensus.

We try, so far as we can, neither to assert nor to deny any particular comprehensive religious, philosophical, or moral view, or its associated theory of truth and the status of values. Since we assume each citizen to affirm some such view, we hope to make it possible for all to accept the political conception as true or reasonable from the standpoint of their own comprehensive view, whatever it may be. Properly understood, then, a political conception of justice need be no more indifferent, say, to truth in philosophy and morals than the principle of toleration, suitably understood, need be indifferent to truth in religion. Since we seek an agreed basis of public justification in matters of justice, and since no political agreement on those disputed questions can reasonably be expected, we turn instead to the fundamental ideas we seem to share through the public political culture. From these ideas we try to work out a political conception of justice congruent with our considered convictions on due reflection. Once this is done, citizens may within their comprehensive doctrines regard the political conception of justice as true, or as reasonable, whatever their view allows.

Some may not be satisfied with this; they may reply that, despite these protests, a political conception of justice must express indifference or skepticism. Otherwise it could not lay aside fundamental religious, philosophical, and moral questions because they are politically difficult to settle, or may prove intractable. Certain truths, it may be said, concern things so important that differences about them have to be fought out, even should this mean civil war. To this we say first that questions are not removed from the political agenda, so to speak, solely because they are a source of conflict. We appeal instead to a political conception of justice to distinguish between those questions that can be reasonably removed from the political agenda and those that cannot. Some questions still on the agenda will be controversial, at least to some degree; this is normal with political issues.

To illustrate: from within a political conception of justice let us suppose we can account both for equal liberty of conscience, which takes the truths of religion off the political agenda, and the equal political and civil liberties, which by ruling out serfdom and slavery take the possibility of those institutions off the agenda. But controversial issues inevitably remain: for example, how more exactly to draw the boundaries of the basic liberties when they conflict (where to set "the wall between church and state"); how to interpret the requirements of distributive justice even when there is considerable agreement on general principles for the basic structure; and finally, questions of policy such as the use of nuclear weapons. These cannot be removed from politics. But by avoiding comprehensive doctrines we try to bypass religion and philosophy's profoundest controversies so as to have some hope of uncovering a basis of a stable overlapping consensus.

Nevertheless, in affirming a political conception of justice we may eventually have to assert at least certain aspects of our own comprehensive religious or philosophical doctrine (by no means necessarily fully comprehensive). This will happen whenever someone insists, for example, that certain questions are so fundamental that to insure their being rightly settled justifies civil strife. The religious salvation of those holding a particular religion, or indeed the salvation of a whole people, may be said to depend on it. At this point we may have no alternative but to deny this, or to imply its denial and hence to maintain the kind of thing we had hoped to avoid. . . .

A third objection is the following: even if we grant that an overlapping consensus is not a modus vivendi, as I have defined it, some may say that a workable political conception must be general and comprehensive. Without such a doctrine on hand, there is no way to order the many conflicts of justice that arise in public life. The deeper the conceptual and philosophical bases of those conflicts, the objection continues, the more general and comprehensive the level of philosophical reflection must be if their roots are to be laid bare and an appropriate ordering found. It is useless, the objection concludes, to try to work out a political conception of justice expressly for the basic structure apart from any comprehensive doctrine. . . .

This partially comprehensive view might be explained as follows. We do best not to assume that there exist generally acceptable answers for all or even for many questions of political justice. Rather, we must be prepared to accept the fact that only a few questions we are moved to ask can be satisfactorily resolved. Political wisdom consists in identifying those few, and among them the most urgent.

That done, we must frame the institutions of the basic structure so that intractable conflicts are unlikely to arise; we must also accept the need for clear and simple principles, the general form and content of which we hope can be publicly understood. A political conception is at best but a guiding framework of deliberation and reflection which helps us reach political agreement on at least the constitutional essentials and the basic questions of justice. If it seems to have cleared our view and made our considered convictions more coherent; if it has narrowed the gap between the conscientious convictions of those who accept the basic ideas of a constitutional regime, then it has served its practical political purpose.

This remains true even if we cannot fully explain our agreement: we know only that citizens who affirm the political conception, and who have been raised in and are familiar with the fundamental ideas of the public political culture, find that, when they adopt its framework of deliberation, their judgments converge sufficiently so that political co-operation on the basis of mutual respect can be maintained. They view the political conception as itself normally sufficient and may not expect, or think they need, greater political understanding than that.

Here we are bound to ask: how can a political conception of justice express values that, under the reasonably favorable conditions that make democracy possible, normally outweigh whatever other values are likely to conflict with them? One reason is this. As I have said, the most reasonable political conception of justice for a democratic regime will be, broadly speaking, liberal. This means that it protects the familiar basic rights and assigns them a special priority; it also includes measures to insure that all citizens have sufficient material means to make effective use of those basic rights. Faced with the fact of reasonable pluralism, a liberal view removes from the political agenda the most divisive issues, serious contention about which must undermine the bases of social co-operation.

The virtues of political co-operation that make a constitutional regime possible are, then, very great virtues. I mean, for example, the virtues of tolerance and being ready to meet others halfway, and the virtue of reasonableness and the sense of fairness. When these virtues are widespread in society and sustain its political conception of justice, the constitute a very great public good, part of society's political capital. Thus, the values that conflict with the political conception of justice and and its sustaining virtues may be normally outweighed because they come into conflict with the very conditions that make social cooperation possible on a footing of mutual respect.

The other reason political values normally win out is that severe conflicts with other values are much reduced. This is because when an overlapping consensus supports the political conception, this conception is not viewed as incompatible with basic religious, philosophical, and moral values. We need not consider the claims of political justice against the claims of this or that comprehensive view; nor need we say that political values are intrinsically more important than other values and that is why the latter are overridden. Having to say that is just what we hope to avoid, and achieving an overlapping consensus enables us to do so.

To conclude: given the fact of reasonable pluralism, what the work of reconciliation by public reason does, thus enabling us to avoid reliance on general and comprehensive doctrines, is two things: first, it identifies the fundamental role of political values in expressing the terms of fair social co-operation consistent with mutual respect between citizens regarded as free and equal; and second, it uncovers a sufficiently inclusive concordant fit among political and other values seen in a reasonable overlapping consensus. . . .

## Steps to Constitutional Consensus

The last difficulty is that an overlapping consensus is utopian: that is, there are not sufficient political, social, or psychological forces either to bring about an overlapping consensus (when one does not exist), or to render one stable (should one exist).

There are two stages. The first stage ends with a constitutional consensus, the second with an overlapping consensus. The constitution at the first stage satisfies certain liberal principles of political justice. As a constitutional consensus, these principles are accepted simply as principles and not as grounded in certain ideas of society and person of a political conception, much less in a shared public conception. And so the consensus is not deep. . . .

How might a constitutional consensus come about? Suppose that at a certain time, because of various historical events and contingencies, certain liberal principles of justice are accepted as a mere modus vivendi, and are incorporated into existing political institutions. This acceptance has come about, let us say, in much the same way as the acceptance of the principle of toleration came about as a modus vivendi following the Reformation: at first reluctantly, but nevertheless as providing the only workable alternative to endless and destructive civil strife. Our question, then, is this: how might it happen that over time the initial acquiescence in a constitution satisfying these liberal principles of justice develops into a constitutional consensus in which those principles themselves are affirmed?

At this point, a certain looseness in our comprehensive views, as well as their not being fully comprehensive, may be particularly significant. To see this, let us return to our model case. One way in which that example may be atypical is that two of the three doctrines were described as fully general and comprehensive: a religious doctrine of free faith and the comprehensive liberalism of Kant or Mill. In these cases the acceptance of the political conception was said to be derived from and to depend solely on the comprehensive doctrine. But how far in practice does the allegiance to a principle of political justice actually depend on the knowledge of or the belief in its derivation from a comprehensive view rather than on seeming reasonable in itself or as being viewed as part of a pluralist view, which is the third doctrine in our model case?

There are several possibilities. Distinguish three cases: in the first the political principles are derived from a comprehensive doctrine; in the second they are not derived from but are compatible with that doctrine; and in the third, they are incompatible with it. In everyday life we have not usually decided, or even thought much about, which of these cases hold. To decide among them would raise highly complicated questions; and it is not clear that we need to decide among them. Most peoples' religious, philosophical, and moral doctrines are not seen by them as fully general and comprehensive, and these aspects admit of variations of degree. There is lots of slippage, so to speak, many ways for liberal principles of justice to cohere loosely with those (partially) comprehensive views, and many ways within the limits of political principles of justice to allow for the pursuit of different (partially) comprehensive doctrines.

This suggests that many if not most citizens come to affirm the principles of justice incorporated into their constitution and political practice without seeing any particular connection, one way or the other, between those principles and their other views. It is possible for citizens first to appreciate the good those principles accomplish both for themselves and those they care for, as well as for society at large, and then to affirm them on this basis. Should an incompatibility later be recognised between the principles of justice and their wider doctrines, then they might very well adjust or revise these doctrines rather than reject those principles....

Our next task is to describe the steps whereby a constitutional consensus on certain principles of basic political rights and liberties and on democratic procedures becomes an overlapping consensus as earlier defined.

What are the forces that push a constitutional consensus toward an overlapping consensus, even supposing a full overlapping consensus is never achieved but at best only approximated? I mention some of these forces as they relate to depth, breadth, and how specific, or how narrow, the class of conceptions in the focus.

As for depth, once a constitutional consensus is in place, political groups must enter the public forum of political discussion and appeal to other groups who do not share their comprehensive doctrine. This fact makes it rational for them to move out the narrower circle of their own views and to develop political conceptions in terms of which they can explain and justify their preferred policies to a wider public so as to put together a majority. As they do this, they are led to formulate political conceptions of justice. These conceptions provide the common currency of discussion and a deeper basis for explaining the meaning and implications of the principles and policies each group endorses.

Again, new and fundamental constitutional problems inevitably arise, even if only occasionally. Consider, for example, the Reconstruction amendments following the crisis of the Civil War. Debate over those and other fundamental amendments forced competing groups to work out political conceptions that contained fundamental ideas in the light of which the constitution as so far understood could be changed. A constitutional consensus at the level of principles viewed apart from any underlying conception of society and citizen—each group having its own reasons—is a consensus taken literally. It lacks the conceptual resources to guide how the constitution should be amended and interpreted.

A last reason relates to depth. In a constitutional system with judicial review, or review conducted by some other body, it will be necessary for judges, or the officers in question, to develop a political conception of justice in the light of which the constitution, in their view, is to be interpreted and important cases decided. Only so can the enactments of the legislature be declared constitutional or unconstitutional; and only so have they a reasonable basis for their interpretation of the values and standards the constitution ostensibly incorporates. Plainly these conceptions will have an important role in the politics of constitutional debates.

Let us next look at considerations relating to breadth. The main one is that a purely political and procedural constitutional consensus will prove too narrow. For unless a democratic people is sufficiently unified and cohesive, it will not enact the legislation necessary to cover the remaining constitutional essentials and basic matters of justice, and conflict will arise about these. There must be fundamental legislation that guarantees liberty of conscience and freedom of thought generally and not merely of political speech and thought. Equally there must be legislation assuring freedom of association and freedom of movement; and beyond this, measures are required to assure that the basic needs of all citizens can be met so that they can take part in political and social life.[28]

About this last point, the idea is not that of satisfying needs as opposed to mere desires and wants; nor is it that of redistribution in favor of greater equality. The constitutional essential here is rather that below a certain level of material and social well-being, and of training and education, people simply cannot take part in society as citizens, much less equal citizens. What determines the level of well-being and education below which this happens is not for a political conception to say. One must look to the society in question. But that does not mean that the constitutional essential itself is not perfectly clear: it is what his required to give due weight to the idea of society as a fair system of co-operation between free and equal citizens, and not to regard it, in practice if not in speech, as so much rhetoric.

The main point under breadth, then, is that the rights and liberties and procedures included in a constitutional consensus cover but a limited part of the fundamental political questions that will be debated. There are forces tending to amend the constitution in certain ways to cover further constitutional essentials, or else to enact the necessary legislation with much the same effect. In either case, groups will tend to develop broad political conceptions covering the basic structure as a whole in order to explain their point of view in a politically consistent and coherent way.

Finally, how specific is the consensus, or how wide is the range of the liberal conceptions defining it? Here there are two considerations. One concerns the range of views that can plausibly be elaborated from the fundamental ideas of society and person found in the public culture of a constitutional regime. Justice

---

[28] On this last see Frank Michelman, "Welfare Rights in a Constitutional Democracy," *Washington University Law Quarterly* (Summer 1979), esp. pp. 680–685.

as fairness works from the fundamental ideas of society as a fair system of cooperation together with the conception of the person as free and equal. These ideas are taken as central to the democratic ideal. Are there other ideas equally central, and if there are, would they give rise to ideals and principles markedly different from those of justice as fairness? We might conjecture that, other things equal, a political conception elaborated from such central ideas would certainly be typical of the focal class of an overlapping consensus, should such a consensus ever be reached.

The second consideration is that different social and economic interests may be assumed to support different liberal conceptions. The differences between conceptions expresses, in part, a conflict between these interests. Let us define the relevant interests for each conception as those that it would encourage and be supported by in a stable basic structure regulated by it. The width of the range of liberal conceptions will be determined by the degree of opposition among these interests. . . .

In order for justice as fairness to specify the center of the focal class, it would seem the following two conditions must hold:

(a)  it is correctly based on more central fundamental ideas; and
(b)  it is stable in view of the interests that support it and are encouraged by it.

Thus, if the liberal conceptions correctly framed from fundamental ideas of a democratic public culture are supported by and encourage deeply conflicting political and economic interests, and if there be no way of designing a constitutional regime so as to overcome that, a full overlapping consensus cannot, it seems, be achieved.

I have outlined in this and the previous section how an initial acquiescence in a liberal conception of justice as a mere modus vivendi could change over time first into a constitutional consensus and then into an overlapping consensus. In this process I have supposed that the comprehensive doctrines of most people are not fully comprehensive, and this allows scope for the development of an independent allegiance to the political conception that helps to bring about a consensus. This independent allegiance in turn leads people to act with evident intention in accordance with constitutional arrangements, since they have reasonable assurance (based on past experience) that others will also comply. Gradually, as the success of political co-operation continues, citizens gain increasing trust and confidence in one another. This is all we need say in reply to the objection that the idea of overlapping consensus is utopian.                                    [pp. 145–168]

### JOHN RAWLS
### The Law of Peoples
### (1993)[29]

*Extension to hierarchical societies*

The extension of liberal ideas of justice to the law of peoples proceeds in two stages, each stage having two steps. The first stage is that of ideal theory: the extension of the law of peoples to well-ordered liberal societies only. The second step of ideal theory is more difficult: It requires us to specify a second kind of society—a hierarchical society, as I shall say—and then to state when such a society is well ordered. Our aim is to extend the law of peoples to these well-ordered hierarchical societies and to show that they accept the same law of peoples as liberal societies do. Thus, this shared law of well-ordered peoples, both

---

[29]  [See *On Human Rights* (eds., Stephen Shute and Susan Hurley, Basic Books)]

liberal and hierarchical, specifies the content of ideal theory. It specifies the kind of society of well-ordered peoples all people should want and it sets the regulative end of their foreign policy. Important for us, it has the obvious corollary that nonliberal societies also honor human rights.

To show all this we proceed thus. First, we state three requirements for any well-ordered hierarchical regime. It will be clear that satisfying these requirements does not entail that a regime be liberal. Next, we confirm that, in an original position with a veil of ignorance, the representatives of well-ordered hierarchical regimes are reasonably situated as well as rational, and are moved by appropriate reasons. In this case also, the original position is a device of representation for the adoption of law among hierarchical peoples. Finally, we show that in the original position the representatives of well-ordered hierarchical societies would adopt the same law of peoples that the representatives of liberal societies do. That law thus serves as a common law of a just political society of well-ordered peoples.

The first of the three requirements for a hierarchical society to be well ordered is that it must be peaceful and gain its legitimate aims through diplomacy and trade, and other ways of peace. It follows that its religious doctrine, assumed to be comprehensive and influential in government policy, is not expansionist in the sense that it fully respects the civic order and integrity of other societies. If it seeks wider influence, it does so in ways compatible with the independence of, and the liberties within, other societies. This feature of its religion supports the institutional basis of its peaceful conduct and distinguishes it from leading European states during the religious wars of the sixteenth and seventeenth centuries.

A second fundamental requirement uses an idea of Philip Soper. It has several parts. It requires first, that a hierarchical society's system of law be such as to impose moral duties and obligations on all persons within its territory.[30] It requires further that its system of law be guided by a common good conception of justice, meaning by this a conception that takes impartially into account what it sees not unreasonably as the fundamental interests of all members of society. It is not the case that the interests of some are arbitrarily privileged, while the interests of others go for naught. Finally, there must be sincere and not unreasonable belief on the part of judges and other officials who administer the legal order that the law is indeed guided by a common good conception of justice. This belief must be demonstrated by a willingness to defend publicly the state's injunctions as justified by law. Courts are an efficient way of doing this.[31] These aspects of legal order are necessary to establish a regime's legitimacy in the eyes of its own people. To sum up the second requirement we say: The system of law is sincerely and not unreasonably believed to be guided by a common good conception of justice. It takes into account people's essential interests and imposes moral duties and obligations on all members of society.

This second requirement can be spelled out further by adding that the political institutions of a well-ordered hierarchical society constitute a reasonable consultation hierarchy. They include a family of representative bodies, or other assemblies, whose task is to look after the important interests of all elements of society. Although in hierarchical societies persons are not regarded as free and equal citizens, as they are in liberal societies, they are seen as responsible members of society who can recognize their moral duties and obligations and play their part in social life.

With a consultation hierarchy there is an opportunity for different voices to be heard, not, to be sure, in a way allowed by democratic institutions, but appropriately in view of the religious and and philosophical values of the society in question. Thus, individuals do not have the right of free speech as in a liberal society; but as members of associations and corporate bodies they have the right

---

[30] See Soper, *A Theory of Law* (1984), pp. 125–147.
[31] *Ibid.* p. 112, 118.

at some point in the process of consultation to express political dissent and the government has an obligation to take their dissent seriously and to give a conscientious reply. That different voices can be heard is necessary because the sincere belief of judges and other officials has two components: honest belief and respect for the possibility of dissent. Judges and officials must be willing to address objections. They cannot refuse to listen to them on the grounds that they think those expressing them are incompetent and cannot understand. Then we would not have a consultation hierarchy but a purely paternalistic regime.

In view of this account of the institutional basis of a hierarchical society, we can say that its conception of the common good of justice secures for all persons at least certain minimum rights to means of subsistence and security (the right to life), to liberty (freedom from slavery, serfdom, and forced occupations) and (personal) property, as well as to formal equality as expressed by the rules of natural justice (for example, that similar cases be treated similarly). This shows that a well-ordered hierarchical society also meets a third requirement: it respects basic human rights.

The argument for this conclusion is that the second requirement rules out violations of these rights. For to satisfy it, a society's legal order must impose moral duties and obligations on all persons in its territory and it must embody a reasonable consultation hierarchy which will protect human rights. A sincere and reasonable belief on the part of judges and other officials that the system of law is guided by a common good conception of justice has the same result. Such a belief is simply unreasonable, if not irrational, when those rights are infringed.

There is a question about religious toleration that calls for explicit mention. Whereas in hierarchical societies a state religion may be on some questions the ultimate authority within society and control government policy on certain important matters, that authority is not (as I have said) extended politically to other societies. Further, their (comprehensive) religious or philosophical doctrines are not unreasonable: They admit a measure of liberty of conscience and freedom of thought, even if these freedoms are not in general equal for all members of society as they are in liberal regimes. A hierarchical society may have an established religion with certain privileges. Still, it is essential to its being well-ordered that no religions are persecuted, or denied civic and social conditions that permit their practice in peace and without fear. Also essential, and this because of the inequality of religious freedom, if for no other reason, is that a hierarchical society must allow for the right of emigration. The rights noted here are counted as human rights.

An institutional basis that realizes the three requirements can take many forms. This deserves emphasis, as I have indicated only the religious case. We are not trying to describe all possible forms of social order consistent with membership in good standing of a reasonable society of peoples. Rather, we have specified three necessary conditions for membership of a reasonable society of peoples and then shown by example that these conditions do not require a society to be liberal.

[...]

Hierarchical societies are well-ordered in terms of their own conceptions of justice. This being so, their representatives in an appropriate original position would adopt the same principles as those sketched above that would be adopted by the representatives of liberal societies. Each hierarchical society's interests are understood by its representatives in accordance with or as presupposed by its conception of justice. This enables us to say in this case also that the original position is a device of representation.

Two considerations confirm this. The first is that, in view of the common good conception of justice held in a hierarchical society, the parties care about the good of the society they represent, and so about its security as assured by the laws against war and aggression. They also care about the benefits of trade and assistance between peoples in time of need. All these help protect human rights. In view of this, we can say that the representatives of hierarchical societies are rational. The second consideration is that they do not try to extend their religious and philosophical doctrines to other peoples by war or aggression, and they respect the civic order and integrity of other societies. Hence, they accept—as you and I would accept—the original position as fair between peoples and would endorse the law of peoples adopted by their representatives as specifying fair terms of political co-operation between them and other societies. Thus, the representatives are reasonably situated and this suffices for the use of the original position as a device of representation in extending the law of peoples to hierarchical societies.

Note that I have supposed that the parties as representatives of peoples are to be situated equally, even though the conception of justice of the hierarchical society they represent allows basic inequalities between its members. For example, some of its members are not granted equal liberty of conscience. There is, however, no inconsistency in this: A people sincerely affirming a nonliberal conception of justice may still think their society should be treated equally in a just law of peoples, even though its members accept basic inequalities among themselves. Though a society lacks basic equality, it is not unreasonable for that society to insist on equality in making claims against other societies.

About this last point, two observations. One is that although the original position at the first level, that of domestic justice, incorporates a political conception of the person rooted in the public culture of a liberal society, the original position at the second level, that of the law of peoples, does not. I emphasize this fact, since it enables a liberal conception of justice to be extended to yield a more general law of peoples without prejudging the case against nonliberal societies.

This leads to a second observation: the law of peoples might have been worked out by starting with an all-inclusive original position with representatives of all the individual persons of the world.[32] In this case the question of whether there are to be separate societies and of the relations between them, will be settled by the parties behind a veil of ignorance.

Hence I think it best to follow the two-level bottom-up procedure, beginning first with the principles of justice for the basic structure of domestic society and then moving upward and outward to the law of peoples. In so doing our knowledge of how peoples and their governments have acted historically gives us guidance in how to proceed and suggests questions and possibilities we might not otherwise have thought of. But this is simply a point of method and settles no questions of substance. These depend on what can actually be worked out.

One might well be skeptical that a liberal social contract and constructivist idea of justice can be worked out to give a conception of the law of peoples universal in its reach and also applying to nonliberal societies. Our discussion of hierarchical societies should put these doubts to rest. I have noted the conditions under which we could accept the law of liberal peoples we had sketched as sound and justified. In this connection we considered whether the law was stable with repect to justice, and whether, on due reflection, we could accept the judgments that its principles and precepts led us to make. If both these things hold, we said, the law of liberal peoples as laid out could, by the criteria we can now apply, be accepted as justified.

Parallel remarks hold for the wider law of peoples including well-ordered hierarchical societies. Here I simply add, without argument or evidence, but hoping it seems plausible, that these societies will honor a just law of peoples for much the same reasons liberal peoples will do so, and that both we and they will find the judgments to which it leads acceptable to our convictions, all things considered. I believe it is of importance here that well-ordered hierarchical

[32] Brian Barry, in his splendid *Theories of Justice* (1989), discusses the merits of doing this (pp. 183–189).

societies are not expansionist and their legal order is guided by a common good conception of justice ensuring that it honors human rights. These societies also affirm a peaceful society of peoples and benefit therefrom as liberal societies do. All have a common interest in changing the way in which politics among peoples—war and threats of war—has hitherto been carried on.

We may therefore view this wider law of peoples as sound and justified. This fundamental point deserves emphasis: There is nothing relevantly different between how, say, justice as fairness is worked out for the domestic case in *A Theory of Justice*, and how the law of peoples is worked out from more general liberal ideas of justice. In both cases we use the same fundamental idea of a reasonable procedure of construction in which rational agents fairly situated (the parties as representatives of citizens in one case and of peoples or societies in the other) select principles of justice for the relevant subject, either their separate domestic institutions or the shared law of peoples. As always, the parties are guided by the appropriate reasons as specified by a veil of ignorance. Thus, obligations and duties are not imposed by one society on another; instead, reasonable societies agree on what the bonds will be. Once we confirm that a domestic society, or a society of peoples, when regulated by the corresponding principles of justice, is stable with respect to justice (as previously defined), and once we have checked that we can endorse those principles on due reflection, then in both domains the ideals, laws, and principles of justice are justified in the same way.

### Human rights

A few of the features of human rights are. First, these rights do not depend on any particular comprehensive moral doctrine or philosophical conception of human nature, such as, for example, that human beings are moral persons and have equal worth, or that they have certain particular moral and intellectual powers that entitle them to these rights. This would require a quite deep philosophical theory that many if not most hierarchical societies might reject as liberal or democratic, or in some way distinctive of the Western political tradition and prejudicial to other cultures.

We therefore take a different tack and say that basic human rights express a minimum standard of well-ordered political institutions for all peoples who belong, as members in good standing, to a just political society of peoples. Any systematic violation of these rights is a serious matter and troubling to the society of peoples as a whole, both liberal and hierarchical. Since they must express a minimum standard, the requirements that yield these rights should be quite weak.

Recall that we postulated that a society's system of law must be such as to impose moral duties and obligations on all its members and be regulated by what judges and other officials reasonably and sincerely believe is a common good conception of justice. For this condition to hold, the law must at least uphold such basic rights as the right to life and security, to personal property, and the elements of the rule of law, as well as the right to a certain liberty of conscience and freedom of association, and the right to emigration. These rights we refer to as human rights.

Next we consider what the imposition of these duties and obligations implies, including (1) a common good conception of justice and (2) good faith on the part of officials to explain and justify the legal order to those bound by it. For these things to hold does not require the liberal idea that persons are first citizens and as such free and equal members of society who hold those basic rights as the rights of citizens. It requires only that persons be responsible and cooperating members of society who can recognize and act in accordance with their moral duties and obligations. It would be hard to reject these requirements (a common good conception of justice and a good faith official justification of the law) as too strong for a minimally decent regime. Human rights, understood as resulting from these requirements, could not be rejected as peculiarly liberal or special to our Western tradition. In that sense, they are politically neutral.

To confirm this last point, I consider an alleged difficulty. Many societies have political traditions that are different from Western individualism in its many forms. In considering persons from a political point of view, these traditions are said to regard persons not as citizens first with the rights of citizens but rather as first being members of groups: communities, associations, or corporations.[33] On this alternative, let's say associationist, view, whatever rights persons have arise from this prior membership and are normally enabling rights, that is, rights that enable person to perform their duties in the groups to which they belong. To illustrate with respect to political rights: Hegel rejects the idea of one person one vote on the grounds that it expresses the democratic and individualistic idea that each person, as an atomic unit, has the basic right to participate equally in political deliberation.[34] By contrast, in the well-ordered rational state, as Hegel presents it in *The Philosophy of Right*, persons belong first to estates, corporations, and associations. Since these social forms represent the rational interests of their members in what Hegel views as a just consultation hierarchy, some persons will take part in politically representing these interests in the consultation process, but they do so as members of estates and corporations and not as individuals, and not all individuals are involved.

The essential point here is that the basic human rights as we have described them can be protected in a well-ordered hierarchical state with its consultation hierarchy; what holds in Hegel's scheme of political rights holds for all rights. Its system of law can fulfill the conditions laid down and ensure the right to life and security, to personal property and the elements of the rule of law, as well as the right to a certain freedom of conscience and freedom of association. Admittedly it ensures these rights to persons as members of estates and corporations and not as citizens. But that does not matter. The rights are guaranteed and the requirement that a system of law must be such as to impose moral rights and duties is met. Human rights understood in the light of that condition cannot be rejected as peculiar to our Western tradition.

Human rights are a special class of rights designed to play a special role in a reasonable law of peoples for the present age. Recall that the accepted ideas about international law changed in two basic ways following World War II, and this change in basic moral beliefs is comparable to other profound historical changes. War is no longer an admissible means of state policy. It is only justified in self-defense and a state's internal sovereignty is now limited. One role of human rights is precisely to specify limits to that sovereignty.

Human rights are thus distinct from, say, constitutional rights, or the rights of democratic citizenship, or from other kinds of rights that belong to certain kinds of political institutions, both individualist and associationist. They are a special class of universal application and hardly controversial in their general intention. They are part of a reasonable law of peoples and specify limits on the domestic institutions required of all peoples by that law. In this sense they specify the outer boundary of admissible domestic law of societies in good standing in a just society of peoples.

Human rights have these three roles:

1. They are a necessary condition of a regime's legitimacy and of the decency of its legal order.

---

[33] See R. J. Vincent in T. Nardin (ed.), *Traditions of International Ethics* (1992), pp. 262–265.

[34] See *The Philosophy of Right* (1821), sedim 308.

2.  By being in place, they are also sufficient to exclude justified and forceful intervention by other peoples, say by economic sanctions, or in grave cases, by military force.
3.  They set a limit on pluralism among peoples.                        [pp. 60–71]

## R. NOZICK
### Anarchy, State and Utopia
### (1974)

The fundamental question of political philosophy, one that precedes questions about how the state should be organized is, whether there should be any state at all. Why not have anarchy. Since anarchist theory, if tenable, undercuts the whole subject *of political* philosophy, it is appropriate to begin political philosophy with an examination of its major theoretical alternative. Those who consider anarchism not an unattractive doctrine will think it possible that political philosophy *ends* here as well. Others impatiently will await what is to come afterwards. Yet ... archists and anarchists alike, those who spring gingerly from the starting point as well as those reluctantly argued away from it, can agree that beginning the subject to political philosophy with state-of-nature theory has an *explanatory* purpose. [...]

More to the point, especially for deciding what goals one should try to achieve, would be to focus upon a nonstate situation in which people generally satisfy moral constraints and generally act as they ought. Such an assumption is not wildly optimistic; it does not assume that all people act exactly as they should. Yet this state-of-nature situation is the best anarchic situation one reasonable could hope for. Hence investigating its nature and defects is of crucial importance to deciding whether there should be a state rather than anarchy. If one could show that the state would be superior even to this most favored situation of anarchy, the best that realistically can be hoped for, or would arise by a process involving no morally impermissible steps, or would be an improvement if it arose, this would provide a rationale for the state's existence; it would justify the state.[pp. 4–5]

The night-watchman state of classical liberal theory, limited to the functions of protecting all its citizens against violence, theft, and fraud, and to the enforcement of contracts, and so on, appears to be redistributive. We can imagine at least one social arrangement intermediate between the scheme of private protective associations and the night-watchman state. Since the night-watchman state is often called a minimal state, we shall call this other arrangement the *ultraminimal state*. An ultramininal state maintains a monopoly over all use of force except that necessary in immediate self-defence, and so excludes private (or agency) retaliation for wrong and exaction of compensation; but it provides protection and enforcement services *only* to those who purchase its protection and enforcement policies. People who don't buy a protection contract from the monopoly don't get protected. The minimal (night-watchman) state is equivalent to the ultraminimal state conjoined with a (clearly redistributive) Friedsmanesque voucher plan, financed from tax revenues. Under this plan all people, or some (for example, those in need), are given tax-funded vouchers that can be used only for their purchase of a protection policy from the ultraminimal state.

Since the night-watchman state appears redistributive to the extent that it compels some people to pay for the protection of others, its proponents must explain why this redistributive function of the state is unique. If some redistribution is legitimate in order to protect everyone, why is redistribution not legitimate for other attractive and desirable purposes as well? What rationale specifically selects protective services as the sole subject of legitimate redistributive activities?                                    [pp. 26–27]

A system of private protection, even when one protective agency is dominant in a geographical territory, appears to fall short of a state. It apparently does not provide protection for everyone in its territory, as does a state, and it apparently does not possess or claim the sort of monopoly over the use of force necessary to a state. In our earlier terminology, it apparently does not constitute a minimal state, and it apparently does not even constitute an ultraminimal state.

These very ways in which the dominant protective agency or association in a territory apparently falls short of being a state provide the focus of the individualist anarchist's complaint *against* the state. For he holds that when the state monopolizes the use of force in a territory and punishes others who violate its monopoly, and when the state provides protection for everyone by forcing some to purchase protection for others, it violates moral side constraints on how individuals may be treated. Hence, he concludes, the state itself is intrinsically immoral. The state grants that under some circumstances it is legitimate to punish persons who violate the rights of others, for it itself does so. How then does it arrogate to itself the right to forbid private exaction of justice by other non-aggressive individuals whose rights have been violated? *What* right does the private exacter of justice violate that is not violated also by the state when it punishes? When a group of persons constitute themselves as the state and begin to punish, *and forbid others from doing likewise*, is there some right these others would violate that they themselves do not? By what right, then, can the state and its officials claim a unique right (a privilege) with regard to force and enforce this monopoly? If the private exacter of justice violates no one's rights, then punishing him for his actions (actions state officials also perform) violates his rights and hence violates moral side constraints. Monopolizing the use of force then, on this view, is itself immoral, as is redistribution through the compulsory tax apparatus of the state. Peaceful individuals minding their own business are not violating the rights of others. It does not constitute a violation of someone's rights to refrain from purchasing something for him (that you have not entered specifically into an obligation to buy). Hence, so the argument continues, when the state threatens someone with punishment if he does not contribute to the protection of another, it violates (and its officials violate) his rights. In threatening him with something that would be a violation of his rights if done by a private citizen, they violate moral constraints.

To get to something recognizable as a state we must show (1) how an ultraminimal state arises out of the system of private protective associations; and (2) how the ultraminimal state is transformed into the minimal state, how it gives rise to that "redistribution" for the general provision of protective services that constitutes it as the minimal state. To show that the minimal state is morally legitimate, to show it is not immoral itself, we must show also that these transitions in (1) and (2) *each* are morally legitimate. In the rest of Part I of this work we show how each of these transitions occurs and is morally permissible. We argue that the first transition, from a system of private protective agencies to an ultraminimal state, will occur by an invisible-hand process in a morally permissible way that violates no one's rights. Secondly, we argue that the transition from an ultraminimal state to a minimal state morally must occur. It would be morally impermissible for persons to maintain the monopoly in the ultraminimal state without providing protective services for all, even if this requires specific "redistribution." The operators of the ultraminimal state are morally obliged to produce the minimal state. ... We argue that no state *more* powerful or extensive than the minimal state is legitimate or justifiable; ... [pp. 51–53]

The principle of compensation requires that people be compensated for having certain risky activities prohibited to them. It might be objected that either you have the right to forbid these people's risky activities or you don't. If you do, you needn't compensate the people for doing to them what you have a right to do; and if you don't, then rather than formulating a policy of compensating people for

your unrightful forbidding, you ought simply to stop it. In neither case does the appropriate course seem to be to forbid and then compensate. But the dilemma, "either you have a right to forbid it so you needn't compensate, or you don't have a right to forbid it so you should stop," is too short. It may be that you do have a right to forbid an action but only provided you compensate those to whom it is forbidden.                                                                                    [p. 83]

A protective agency dominant in a territory does satisfy the two crucial necessary conditions for being a state. It is the only generally effective enforcer of a prohibition on others' using unreliable enforcement procedures (calling them as it sees them), and it over-sees these procedures. And the agency protects those nonclients in its territory whom it prohibits from using self-help enforcement procedures on its clients, in their dealing with its clients, even if such protection must be financed (in apparent redistributive fashion) by its clients. It is morally required to do this by the principle of compensation, which requires those who act in self-protection in order to increase their own security to compensate those they prohibit from doing risky acts which might actually have turned out to be harmless, for the disadvantages imposed upon them.

We noted ... that whether the provision of protective services for some by others was "redistributive" would depend upon the reasons for it. We now see that such provision need not be redistributive since it can be justified on other than redistributive grounds, namely, those provided in the principle of compensation. (Recall that "redistributive" applies to reasons for a practice or institution, and only elliptically and derivatively to the institution itself.) To sharpen this point, we can imagine that protective agencies offer two types of protection policies: those protecting clients against risky private enforcement of justice and those not doing so but protecting only against theft, assault, and so forth (provided these are not done in the course of private enforcement of justice). Since it is only with regard to those with the first type of policy that others are prohibited from privately enforcing justice, only they will be required to compensate the persons prohibited private enforcement for the disadvantages imposed upon them. The holders of only the second type of policy will not have to pay for the protection of others, there being nothing here to compensate these others for. Since the reasons for wanting to be protected against private enforcement of justice are compelling, almost all who purchase protection will purchase this type of protection, despite its extra costs, and therefore will be involved in providing protection for the independents.

We have discharged our task of explaining how a state would arise from a state of nature without anyone's rights being violated. The moral objections of the individualist anarchist to the minimal state are overcome. It is not an unjust imposition of a monopoly; the *de facto* monopoly grows by an invisible-hand process and *by morally permissible means*, without anyone's rights being violated and without any claims being made to a special right that others do not possess. And requiring the clients of the *de facto* monopoly to pay for the protection of those they prohibit from self-help enforcement against them, far from being immoral, is morally required by the principle of compensation. ...[pp. 113–115].

What is the explanation of how a *minimal* state arises? The dominant protective association with the monopoly element is morally required to compensate for the disadvantages it imposes upon those it prohibits from self-help activities against its clients. However, it actually might fail to provide this compensation. Those operating an ultraminimal state are morally required to transform it into a minimal state, but they might choose not to do so. We have assumed that generally people will do what they are morally required to do. Explaining how a state could arise from a state of nature without violating anyone's rights refutes the principled objections of the anarchist. But one would feel more confidence if an explanation of how a state *would* arise from a state of nature also specified reasons why an ultraminimal state would be transformed into a minimal one, in addition to moral reasons, if it specified incentives for providing the compensation or the causes of its being provided in addition to people's desire to do what they ought. We should note that even in the event that no nonmoral incentives or causes are found to be sufficient for the transition from an ultraminimal to a minimal state, and the explanation continues to lean heavily upon people's moral motivations it does not specify people's objective as that of establishing a state. Instead, persons view themselves as providing particular other persons with compensation for particular prohibitions they have imposed upon them. The explanation remains an invisible-hand one.                                                           [p. 119]

## RONALD DWORKIN
## A Trump Over Utility
### (1981)[35]

This essay considers the question of how the right to moral independence might be defended, both in its abstract form and in the more concrete conception we discussed in considering public display of pornography. This question is important beyond the relatively trivial problem of obscenity itself, the right has other and more important applications, and the question of what kinds of arguments support a claim of right is an urgent question in political theory.

Rights (I have argued elsewhere)[36] are best understood as trumps over some background justification for political decisions that states a goal for the community as a whole. If someone has a right to moral independence, this means that it is for some reason wrong for officials to act in violation of that right, even if they (correctly) believe that the community as a whole would be better off if they did. Of course, there are many different theories in the field about what makes a community better off on the whole; many different theories, that is, about what the goal of political action should be. One prominent theory (or rather group of theories) is utilitarianism in its familiar forms, which suppose that the community is better off if its members are on average happier or have more of their preferences satisfied. Another, and in certain ways different, theory is the theory we found in the Williams strategy,[37] which argues that the community is better off if it provides the most desirable conditions for human development. There are of course many other theories about the true goal of politics, many of them much more different from either of these two theories than these are from each other. To some extent, the argument in favour of a particular right must depend on which of these theories about desirable goals has been accepted; it must depend, that is, on what general background justification for political decisions the right in question proposes to trump. In the following discussion I shall assume that the background justification with which we are concerned is some form of utilitarianism, which takes, as the goal of politics, the fulfilment of as many of peoples' goals for their own lives as possible. This remains, I think, the most influential background justification, at least in the informal way in which it presently figures in politics in the Western democracies.

Suppose we accept then that, at least in general, a political decision is justified if it promises to make citizens happier, or to fulfill more of their preferences, on average, than any other decision could. Suppose we assume that the decision to prohibit pornography altogether does, in fact, meet that test, because the desires

[35] [From "Is There A Right to Pornography?" (1981) 1 O.J.L.S. 177. Now also in *A Matter of Principle* (1985) ch. 17. See for a critique R. Langton (1990) 19 Phil. and Public Affairs 331.]

[36] Dworkin, *Taking Rights Seriously*.

[37] [The reference is to the Williams Report on Obscenity and Film Censorship, Cmnd. 7772 (1979).]

and preferences of publishers and consumers are outweighed by the desires and preferences of the majority, including their preferences about how others should lead their lives. How could any contrary decision, permitting even the private use of pornography, then be justified?

Two modes of argument might be thought capable of supplying such a justification. First, we might argue that, though the utilitarian goal states one important political ideal, it is not the only important ideal, and pornography must be permitted in order to protect some other ideal that is, in the circumstances more important. Second, we might argue that further analysis of the grounds that we have for accepting utilitarianism as a background justification in the first place—further reflection of why we wish to pursue that goal—shows that utility must yield to some right of moral independence here. The first form of argument is pluralistic: it argues for a trump over utility on the ground that though utility is always important, it is not the only thing that matters, and other goals or ideals are sometimes more important. The second supposes that proper understanding of what utilitarianism is, and why it is important, will itself justify the right in question.

I do not believe that the first, or pluralistic, mode of argument has much prospect of success, at least as applied to the problem of pornography. But I shall not develop the argument now that would be necessary to support that opinion. I want instead to offer an argument in the second mode, which is, in summary, this. Utilitarianism owes whatever appeal it has to what we might call its egalitarian cast. [. . .] Suppose some version of utilitarianism provided that the preferences of some people were to count for less than those of others in the calculation how best to fulfill most preferences overall either because these people were in themselves less worthy or less attractive or less well loved people, or because the preferences in question combined to form a contemptible way of life. This would strike us as flatly unacceptable, and in any case much less appealing than standard forms of utilitarianism. In any of its standard versions, utilitarianism can claim to provide a conception of how government treats people as equals, or, in any case, how government respects the fundamental requirement that it must treat people as equals. Utilitarianism claims that people are treated as equals when the preferences of each, weighted only for intensity, are balanced in the same scales, with no distinctions for persons or merit. The corrupt version of utilitarianism just described, which gives less weight to some persons than to others, or discounts some preferences because these are ignoble, forfeits that claim. But if utilitarianism in practice is not checked by something like the right of moral independence (and by other allied rights) it will disintegrate, for all practical purposes, into exactly that version.

Suppose a community of many people including Sarah. If the constitution sets out a version of utilitarianism which provides in terms that Sarah's preferences are to count for twice as much as those of others, then this would be the unacceptable, non-egalitarian version of utilitarianism. But now suppose that the constitutional provision is the standard form of utilitarianism, that is, that it is neutral towards all people and preferences, but that a surprising number of people love Sarah very much, and therefore strongly prefer that her preferences count for twice as much in the day-to-day political decisions made in the utilitarian calculus. When Sarah does not receive what she would have if her preferences counted for twice as much as those of others, then these people are unhappy, because their special Sarah-loving preferences, are unfulfilled. If these special preferences are themselves allowed to count, therefore, Sarah will receive much more in the distribution of goods and opportunities than she otherwise would. I argue that this defeats the egalitarian cast of the apparently neutral utilitarian constitution as much as if the neutral provision were replaced by the rejected version. Indeed, the apparently neutral provision is then self-undermining because it gives a critical weight, in deciding which distribution best promotes utility, to the views of those who hold the profoundly un-neutral (some would say anti-utilitarian) theory that the preferences of some should count for more than those of others.

The reply that a utilitarian anxious to resist the right to moral independence would give to this argument is obvious: utilitarianism does not give weight to the truth of that theory, but just the fact that many people (wrongly) hold that theory and so are disappointed when the distribution the government achieves is not the distribution they believe is right. It is the fact of their disappointment, not the truth of their views, that counts, and there is no inconsistency, logical or pragmatic, in that. But this reply is too quick. For there is in fact a particularly deep kind of contradiction here. Utilitarianism must claim [...] truth for itself, and therefore must claim the falsity of any theory that contradicts it. It must itself occupy, that is, all the logical space that its content requires. But neutral utilitarianism claims [...] that no one is, in principle, any more entitled to have any of his preferences fulfilled than anyone else is. It argues that the only reason for denying the fulfillment of one person's desires, whatever these are, is that more and more intense desires must be satisfied instead. It insists that justice and political morality can supply no other reason. This is [...] the neutral utilitarian's *case* for trying to achieve a political structure in which the average fulfillment of preferences is as high as possible. The question is not whether a government can achieve that political structure if it counts political preferences like the preferences of the Sarah lovers[38] or whether the government will in fact then have counted any particular preference twice and so contradicted utilitarianism in that direct way. It is rather whether the government can achieve all this without implicitly contradicting that case.

Suppose the community contains a Nazi, for example, whose set of preferences includes the preference that Aryans have more and Jews less of their preferences fulfilled just because of who they are. A neutral utilitarian cannot say that there is no reason in political morality for rejecting or dishonoring that preference, for not dismissing it as simply wrong, for not striving to fulfill it with all the dedication that officials devote to fulfilling any other sort of preference. For utilitarianism itself supplies such a reason: its most fundamental tenet is that peoples' preferences should be weighed on an equal basis in the same scales, that the Nazi theory of justice is profoundly wrong, and that officials should oppose the Nazi theory and strive to defeat rather than fulfill it. A neutral utilitarian is in fact barred, for reasons of consistency, from taking the same politically neutral attitude to the Nazi's political preference that he takes to other sorts of preferences. But then he cannot make the case just described in favor of highest average utility computing taking that preference into account.

I do not mean to suggest, of course, that endorsing someone's right to have his preference satisfied automatically endorses his preference as good or noble. The good utilitarian, who says that the push-pin player is equally entitled to satisfaction of that taste as the poet is entitled to the satisfaction of his, is not for that reason committed to the proposition that a life of push-pin is as good as a life of poetry. Only vulgar critics of utilitarianism would insist on that inference. The utilitarian says only that nothing in the theory of justice provides any reason why the political and economic arrangements and decisions of society should be any closer to those the poet would prefer than those the push-pin player would like. It is just a matter, from the standpoint of political justice, of how many people prefer the one to the other and how strongly. But he cannot say that about the conflict between the Nazi and the neutral utilitarian opponent of Nazism, because the correct political theory, his political theory, the very political theory to which he appeals in attending to the fact of the Nazi's claim, does speak to the conflict.

---

[38]  Though there are obvious dangers of a circle here. See Dworkin, "What is Equality? Part I Equality of Welfare," in 10 *Philosophy and Public Affairs* 3.

It says that what the neutral utilitarian prefers is just and accurately describes what people are, as a matter of political morality, entitled to have, but that what the Nazi prefers is deeply unjust and describes what no one is entitled, as a matter of political morality, to have. But then it is contradictory to say, again as matter of political morality, that the Nazi is as much entitled to the political system he prefers as is the utilitarian.

The point might be put this way. Political preferences, like the Nazi's preference, are on the same level—purport to occupy the same space—as the utilitarian theory itself. Therefore, though the utilitarian theory must be neutral between personal preferences like the preferences for push-pin and poetry, as a matter of the theory of justice, it cannot, without contradication, be neutral between itself and Nazism. It cannot accept at once a duty to defeat the false theory that some peoples' preferences should count for more than other peoples' and a duty to strive to fulfill the political preferences, of those who passionately accept that false theory, as energetically as it strives for any other preferences. The distinction on which the reply to my argument rests, the distinction between the truth and the fact of the Nazi's political preferences, collapses, because if utilitarianism counts the fact of these preferences it has denied what it cannot deny, which is that justice requires it to oppose them.

We could escape this point, of course, by distinguishing two different forms or levels of utilitarianism. The first would be presented simply as a thin theory about how a political constitution should be selected in a community whose members prefer different kinds of political theories. The second would be a candidate for the constitution to be so chosen; it might argue for a distribution that maximised aggregate satisfaction of personal preferences in the actual distribution of goods and opportunities, for example. In that case the first theory would argue only that the preferences of the Nazi should be given equal weight with the preferences of the second sort of utilitarian in the choice of a constitution, because each is equally entitled to the constitution he prefers, and there would be no contradiction in that proposition. But of course the neutral utilitarian theory we are now considering is not simply a thin theory of that sort. It proposes a theory of justice as a full political constitution, not simply a theory about how to choose one, and so it cannot escape contradiction through modesty.

Now the same argument holds (though perhaps less evidently) when the political preferences are not familiar and despicable, like the Nazi theory, but more informal and cheerful, like the preferences of the Sarah lovers who think that her preferences should be counted twice. The latter might, indeed, be Sarahocrats who believe that she is entitled to the treatment they recommend by virtue of birth or other characteristics unique to her. But even if their preferences rise from special affection rather than from political theory, these preferences nevertheless invade the space claimed by neutral utilitarianism and so cannot be counted without defeating the case utilitarianism provides. My argument, therefore, comes to this. If utilitarianism is to figure as part of an attractive working political theory, then it must be qualified so as to restrict the preferences that count by excluding political preferences of both the formal and informal sort. One very practical way to achieve this restriction if provided by the idea of rights as trumps over unrestricted utilitarianism. A society committed to utilitarianism as a general background justification which does not in terms disqualify any preferences might achieve that disqualification by adopting a right to political independence: the right that no one suffer disadvantage in the distribution of goods or opportunities on the ground that others think he should have less because of who he is or is not, or that others care less for him than they do for other people. The right of political independence would have the effect of insulating Jews from the preference of Nazis, an those who are not Sarah from the preferences of those who adore her.

The right of moral independence [...] can be defended in a parallel way.

Neutral utilitarianism rejects the idea that some ambitions that people might have for their own lives should have less command over social resources and opportunities than others, except as this is the consequence of weighing all preferences on an equal basis in the same scales. It rejects the argument, for example, that some peoples' conception of what sexual experience should be like, and of what part fantasy should play in that experience, and of what the character of that fantasy should be, are inherently degrading or unwholesome. But then it cannot [...] count the moral preferences of those who do hold such opinions in the calculation whether individuals who form some sexual minority, including homosexuals and pornographers, should be prohibited from the sexual experiences they want to have. The right of moral independence is part of the same collection of rights as the right of political independence, and it is to be justified as a trump over an unrestricted utilitarian defense of prohibitory laws against pornography, in a community of those who find offense just in the idea that their neighbors are reading dirty books, in much the same way as the latter right is justified as a trump over a utilitarian justification of giving Jews less or Sarah more in a society of Nazis or Sarah lovers.

It remains to consider whether the abstract right to moral independence, defended in this way, would nevertheless permit restriction of public display of pornography in a society whose preferences against that display were backed by the mixed motives [...]. This is a situation in which the egalitarian cast of utilitarianism is threatened from not one but two directions. To the extent to which the motives in question are moral preferences about how others should behave, and these motives are counted, then the neutrality of utilitarianism is compromised. But to the extent to which these are the rather different sort of motives we reviewed, which emphasize not how others should lead their lives, but rather the character of the sexual experience people want for themselves, and these motives are disregarded, the neutrality of utilitarianism is compromised in the other direction, for it becomes unnecessarily inhospitable to the special and important ambitions of those who then lose control of a crucial aspect of their own self-development. The situation is therefore not an appropriate case for a prophylactic refusal to count any motive whenever we cannot be sure that that motive is unmixed with moralism, because the danger of unfairness lies on both sides rather than only on one. The alternative [...] is at least better than that. This argues that restriction may be justified even though we cannot be sure that the preferences people have for restriction are untinged by the kind of preferences we should exclude, provided that the damage done to those who are affected adversely is not serious damage, even in their own eyes. Allowing restrictions on public display is in one sense a compromise; but it is a compromise recommended by the right of moral independence, once the case for that right is set out, not a compromise of that right.

### Hart's objections

There are then, good grounds for those who accept utilitarianism as a general background justification for political decisions also to accept [...] a right of moral independence in the form that I argued [...] would support or permit the major recommendations of the Williams Report. I shall end this essay by considering certain objections that Professor H. L. A. Hart has made[39] to a similar argument that I made [...] about the connection between utilitarianism and these rights.[40]

---

[39]  Hart, "Between Utility and Rights," 79 *Col. L. Rev.* 828, 836ff (1980).
[40]  See Dworkin, *Taking Rights Seriously.* Introduction, Chap. 12. and Appendix 357–358. See also Dworkin, "Liberalism" in Hampshire (ed.) *Public and Private Morality*, Cambridge University Press 1978, and Dworkin, "Social Science and Constitutional Rights: the Consequences of Uncertainty," 6 J. L. & Educ. 3 (1977).

Hart's objections show what I think is a comprehensive misunderstanding of this argument, which my earlier statement, as I now see, encouraged, and it might therefore be helpful, as insurance against a similar misunderstanding now, to report these objections and my reasons for thinking that they misconceive my argument.

I suggested, in my earlier formulation, that if a utilitarian counts preferences like the preferences of the Sarah lovers, then this is a "form" of double-counting because, in effect, Sarah's preferences are counted twice, once on her own account, and once through the second-order preferences of others that incorporate her preferences by reference. Hart says that this is a mistake, because in fact no one's preferences are counted twice, and it would *under*count the Sarah lovers' preferences, and so fail to treat them as equals, if their preferences in her favor were discarded. There would be something in this last point if votes rather than preferences were in issue, because if someone wished to vote for Sarah's success rather than his own, his role in the calculation would be exhausted by this gift, and if his vote was then discarded he might well complain that he had been cheated of his equal power over political decision. But preferences (as these figure in utilitarian calculations) are not like votes in that way. Someone who reports more preferences to the utilitarian computer does not (except trivially) diminish the impact of other preferences he also reports; he rather increases the role of his preferences overall, compared with the role of other peoples' preferences, in the giant calculation. So someone who prefers Sarah's success to the success of people generally, and through the contribution of that preference to an unrestricted utilitarian calculation secures more for her, does not have any less for himself— for the fulfillment of his more personal preferences—than someone else who is indifferent to Sarah's fortunes.

I do not think that my description, that counting his preferences in favor of Sarah is a form of double counting, is misleading or unfair. But this description was meant to summarize the argument, not to make it, and I will not press that particular characterization. [. . .] Hart makes more substantial points about a different example I used, which raised the question of whether homosexuals have the right to practice their sexual tastes in private. He thinks I want to say "that if, as a result of [preferences that express moral disapproval of homosexuals] tipping the balance, persons are denied some liberty, say to form some sexual relations, those so deprived suffer because by this result their concept of a proper or desirable form of life is desposed by others, and this is tantamount to treating them as inferior to or of less worth than others, or not deserving of equal concern and respect."[41]

But this misstates my point. It is not the result [. . .] of the utilitarian calculation that causes or achieves the fact that homosexuals are despised by others. It is rather the other way round: if someone is denied liberty of sexual practice in virtue of a utilitarian justification that depends critically on other peoples' moralistic preferences, then he suffers disadvantage in virtue of the fact that his concept of a proper life is already despised by others. Hart says that the "main weakness" in my argument—the feature that makes it "fundamentally wrong"— is that I assume that if someone's liberty is restricted this must be interpreted as a denial of his treatment as an equal. But my argument is that this is not inevitably or even usually so, but only when the constraint is justified in some way that depends on the fact that others condemn his convictions or values. Hart says that the interpretation of denial of liberty as a denial of equal concern is "least credible" in exactly the case I discuss, that is, when the denial is justified through a utilitarian argument, because (he says) the message of that justification is not that the defeated minority or their moral convictions are inferior, but only that they are too few to outweigh the preferences of the majority, which can only be

⁴¹  Hart *supra*, note 39, p. 842.

achieved if the minority is in fact denied the liberty it wishes. But once again this ignores the distinction I want to make. If the utilitarian justification for denying liberty of sexual practice to homosexuals can succeed without counting the moralistic preferences of the majority in the balance (as it might if there was good reason to believe what is in fact incredible, that the spread of homosexuality fosters violent crime) then the message of prohibition would, indeed, be only the message Hart finds, which might be put this way: "It is impossible that everyone be protected in all his interests, and the interests of the minority must yield, regrettably, to the concern of the majority for its safety." There is (at least in my present argument) no denial of treatment as an equal in that message. But if the utilitarian justification cannot succeed without relying on the majority's moralistic preferences about how the minority should live, and the government nevertheless urges that justification, then the message is very different and, in my view, nastier. It is exactly that the minority must suffer because others find the lives they propose to lead disgusting, which seems no more justifiable, in a society committed to treating people as equals, than the proposition we earlier considered and rejected, as incompatible with equality, that some people must suffer disadvantage under the law because others do not like them.

Hart makes further points. He suggests, for example, that it was the "disinterested" political preferences of liberals that tipped the balance in favor of repealing laws against homosexual relationships in 1967 in England, and asks how anyone could object that counting *those* preferences at that time offended anyone's rights to be treated as an equal. But this question misunderstands my point in a fundamental way. I do not argue—how could anyone argue?—that citizens in a democracy should not campaign and vote for what they think is just. The question is not whether people should work for justice, but rather what test we and they should apply to determine what is just. Utilitarianism holds that we should apply this test: we should work to achieve the maximum possible satisfaction of the preferences we find distributed in our community. If we accepted this test in an unrestricted way, then we would count the attractive political convictions of the 60s liberals simply as data, to be balanced against the less attractive convictions of others, to see which carried the day in the contest of number and intensity. Conceivably the liberal position would have won this contest. Probably it would not have.

But I have been arguing that this is a false test, which in fact undermines the case for utilitarianism, if political preferences of either the liberals or their opponents are counted and balanced to determine when justice requires. That is why I recommend, as part of any overall political theory in which utilitarianism figures as a background justification, rights to political and moral independence. But the liberals who campaigned in the interests of homosexuals in England in the 60's most certainly did not embrace the test I reject. They of course *expressed* their own political preferences in their votes and arguments, but they did not *appeal* to the popularity of these preferences as providing an argument in itself for what they wanted, as the unrestricted utilitarian argument I oppose would have encouraged them to do. Perhaps they appealed instead to something like the right of moral independence. In any case they did not rely on any argument inconsistent with that right. Nor is it necessary for us to rely on any such argument to say that what they did was right, and treated people as equals. The proof is this: the case for reform would have been just as strong in political theory even if there had been very few or no heterosexuals who wanted reform, though of course reform would not then have been practically possible. If so, then we cannot condemn the procedure that in fact produced reform on the ground that that procedure offended anyone's right to independence.

Hart's misunderstanding here was no doubt encouraged by my own description of how rights like the right to moral independence function in a constitutional system, like that of the United States, which uses rights as a test of the legality of legislation. I said that a constitutional system of this sort is valuable when the community as a whole harbors prejudices against some minority or convictions that the way of life of that minority is offensive to people of good character. In that situation, the ordinary political process is antecedently likely to reach decisions that would fail the test we have constructed, because these decisions would limit the freedom of the minority and yet could not be justified, in political theory, except by assuming that some ways of living are inherently wrong or degrading, or by counting the fact that the majority thinks them so as itself part of the justification. Since these *repressive* decisions would then be wrong, for the reasons I offer, the constitutional right forbids them in advance.

Of course the decision for reform that Hart describes would not—could not— be a decision justified only on these offending grounds. Even if the benign liberal preferences figured as data rather than argument, as I think they should not, no one would be in a position to claim the right to moral or political independence as a shield against the decision that was in fact reached. But someone might have been led to suppose, by my discussion, that what I condemn is any political process that would allow any decision to be be taken if peoples' reasons for supporting one decision rather than another are likely to lie beyond their own personal interests. I hope it is now plain why this is wrong. *That* position would not allow a democracy to vote for social welfare programs, or foreign aid, or conservation for later generations. Indeed, in the absence of an adequate constitutional system, the only hope for justice is precisely that people will vote with a disinterested sense of fairness. I condemn a political process that assumes that the fact that people have such reasons is itself part of the case in political morality for what they favor. Hart's heterosexual liberals may have been making the following argument to their fellow citizens. "We know that many of you find the idea of homosexual relationships troubling and even offensive. Some of us do as well. But you must recognize that it would deny equality, in the form of moral independence, to count the fact that we have these feelings as a justification for penal legislation. Since that is so, we in fact have no justification for the present law, and we ought, in all justice, to reform it." Nothing in this argument counts the fact that either the liberals or those they address happen to have any particular political preferences or convictions as itself an argument: the argument is made by appeal to justice not to the fact that many people want justice. There is nothing in that argument that fails to treat homosexuals as equals. Quite the contrary. But that is just my point.

I shall consider of the remaining objections Hart makes together. He notices my claim, that the rights people have depend on the background justification and political institutions that are also in play, because the argument for any particular right must recognize that right as part of a complex package of other assumptions and practices that it trumps. But he finds this odd. It may make sense to say, he remarks, that people *need* rights less under some forms of government than others. But does it make sense to say that they *have* less rights in one situation rather than another? He also objects to my suggestion [...] that rights that have long been thought to be rights to liberty, like the right of homosexuals to freedom of sexual practice or the right of pornographers to look at what they like in private, are in fact (at least in the circumstances of modern democracies) rights to treatment as an equal. That proposition, which Hart calls "fantastic," would have the consequence, he says, that a tyrant who had forbidden one form of sexual activity or the practice of one religion would actually eliminate the evil rather than increase it if he broadened his ban to include all sex and all religions, and in this way removed the inequality of treatment. The vice in prohibitions of sexual or religious activity, he says, is in fact that these diminish liberty, not equal liberty; adding a violation of equality to the charge makes equality an empty and idle idea with no work to do.

These different objections are plainly connected, because they suppose that whatever rights people have are at least in large part timeless rights necessary to protect enduring and important interests fixed by human nature and fundamental to human development, like interests in the choice of sexual partners and acts and choice of religious convictions. That is a familiar theory of what rights are and what they are for [. . .]. I did say that this theory is unlikely to produce a defense of the right I have been considering, which is the right of moral independence as applied to the use of pornography, because it seems implausible that any important human interests are damaged by denying dirty books or films. But that is not much of an argument against the general fundamental-interests theory of rights, because those who accept that theory might be ready to concede (or perhaps even to insist) that the appeal to rights in favor of pornographers is an error that cheapens the idea of rights, and that there is nothing in political morality that condemns the prohibition of pornography altogether if that is what will best fulfill the preferences of the community as a whole.

My aim is to develop a theory of rights that is relative to the other elements of a political theory, and to explore how far that theory might be constructed from the exceedingly abstract (but far from empty) idea that government must treat people as equals. Of course that theory makes rights relative in only one way. I am anxious to show how rights fit into different packages, so that I want to see, for example, what rights should be accepted as trumps over utility if utility is accepted, as many people think it should be accepted, as the proper background justification. That is an important question because at least an informal kind of utilitarianism has for some time been accepted in practical politics. It has supplied, for example, the working justification of most of the constraints on our liberty through law that we accept as proper. But it does not follow from this investigation that I must endorse [. . .] the package of utilitarianism together with the rights that utilitarianism requires as the best package that can be constructed. In fact I do not. Though rights are relative to packages, one package might still be chosen over others as better, and I doubt that in the end any package based on any familiar form of utilitarianism will turn out to be best. Nor does it follow from my argument that there are no rights that any defensible package must contain—no rights that are in this sense natural rights—though the argument that there are such rights, and the explanation of what these are, must obviously proceed in a rather different way from the route I followed in arguing for the right to moral independence as a trump over utilitarian justifications.

But if rights figure in complex packages of political theory, it is both unnecessary and too crude to look to rights for the only defense against either stupid or wicked political decisions. No doubt Hitler and Nero violated whatever rights any plausible political theory would provide; but it is also true that the evil these monsters caused could find no support even in the background justification of any such theory. Suppose some tyrant (an Angelo[42] gone even more mad) did forbid sex altogether on penalty of death, or banned all religious practice in a community whose members were all devout. We should say that what he did (or tried to do) was insane or wicked or that he was wholly lacking in the concern for his subjects which is the most basic requirement that political morality imposes on those who govern. Perhaps we do not need the idea of equality to explain that last requirement. [. . .] But neither do we need the idea of rights.

We need rights, as a distinct element in political theory, only when some decision that injures some people nevertheless finds prima facie support in the claim that it will make the community as a whole better off on some plausible account of where the community's general welfare lies. But the most natural source of any objection we might have to such a decision is that, in its concern with the welfare or prosperity or flourishing of people on the whole, or in the fulfillment of some interest widespread within the community, the decision pays

---

[42] [The reference is to Shakespeare's *Measure for Measure*.]

insufficient attention to its impact on the minority; and some appeal to equality seems a natural expression of an objection from that source. We want to say that the decision is wrong, in spite of its apparent merit, because it does not take the damage it causes to some into account in the right way and therefore does not treat these people as equals entitled to the same concern as others.

Of course, that charge is never self-validating. It must be developed through some theory about what equal concern requires, or, as in the case of the argument I offered, about what the background justification itself supposes that equal concern requires. Others will inevitably reject any such theory. Someone may claim, for example, that equal concern requires only that people be given what they are entitled to have when their preferences are weighted in the scales with the preferences, including the political and moral preferences, of others. In that case (if I am correct that the right to sexual freedom is based on equality) he would no longer support that right. But how could he? Suppose the decision to ban homosexuality even in private is the decision that is reached by the balance of preferences that he thinks respects equality. He could not say that, though the decision treats homosexuals as equals, by giving them all that equal concern for their situation requires, the decision is nevertheless wrong because it invades their liberty. If some constraints on liberty can be justified by the balance of preferences, why not this one?[43] Suppose he falls back on the idea that sexual freedom is a fundamental interest. But does it treat people as equals to invade their fundamental interests for the sake of minor gains to a very large number of other citizens? Perhaps he will say that it does, because the fundamental character of the interests invaded have been taken into account in the balancing process, so that if these are outweighed the gains to others, at least in the aggregate, were shown to be too large in all fairness to be ignored. But if this is so, then deferring to the interests of the outweighed minority would be giving the minority more attention than equality allows, which is favoritism. How can be then object to the decision the balancing process reached? So if anyone really does think that banning homosexual relationships treats homosexuals as equals, when this is the decision reached by an unrestricted utilitarian balance, he seems to have no very persuasive grounds left to say that that decision nevertheless invades their rights. My hypothesis, that the rights which have traditionally been described as consequences of a general right to liberty are in fact the consequences of equality instead, may in the end prove to be wrong. But it is not, as Hart says it is, "fantastic."                                                              [pp. 199–212]

## R. DWORKIN
### What is Equality? Part 2: Equality of Resources
### (1981)[44]

#### I. THE AUCTION

[...] I shall assume that equality of resources is a matter of equality in whatever resources are owned privately by individuals. Equality of political power, including equality of power over publicly or commonly owned resources, is therefore treated as a different issue, reserved for discussion on another occasion. This distinction is, of course, arbitrary on any number of grounds. From the standpoint of any sophisticated economic theory, an individual's command over public resources forms part of his private resources. Someone who has power to influence public decisions about the quality of the air he or she breathes, for

---

[43] See Dworkin, *Taking Rights Seriously, op. cit.*, pp. 266–272.
[44] [From (1981) 10 *Philosophy and Public Affairs* 283: now also in *Sovereign Virtue* (2000), Chap. 2].

example, is richer than someone who does not. So an overall theory of equality must find a means of integrating private resources and political power.

Private ownership, moreover, is not a single, unique relationship between a person and a material resource, but an open-textured relationship many aspects of which must be fixed politically. So the question of what division of resources is an equal division must to some degree include the question of what powers someone who is assigned a resource thereby gains, and that in turn must include the further question of his right to veto whatever changes in those powers might be threatened through politics. [. . .]

I argue that an equal division of resources presupposes an economic market of some form, mainly as an analytical device but also, to a certain extent, as an actual political institution. That claim may seem sufficiently paradoxical to justify the following preliminary comments. The idea of a market for goods has figured in political and economic theory, since the eighteenth century, in two rather different ways. It has been celebrated, first, as a device for both defining and achieving certain community-wide goals variously described as prosperity, efficiency, and overall utility. It has been hailed, second, as a necessary condition of individual liberty, the condition under which free men and women may exercise individual initiative and choice so that their fates lie in their own hands. The market, that is, has been defended both through arguments of policy, appealing to the overall, community-wide gains it produces, and arguments of principle that appeal instead to some supposed right to liberty.

But the economic market, whether defended in either or both of these ways, has during this same period come to be regarded as the enemy of equality, largely because the forms of economic market systems developed and enforced in industrial countries have permitted and indeed encouraged vast inequality in property. Both political philosophers and ordinary citizens have therefore pictured equality as the antagonist or victim of the values of efficiency and liberty supposedly served by the market, so that wise and moderate politics consists in striking some balance or trade-off between equality and these other values, either by imposing constraints on the market as an economic environment, or by replacing it, in part or altogether, with a different economic system.

I shall try to suggest, on the contrary, that the idea of an economic market, as a device for setting prices for a vast variety of goods and services, must be at the center of any attractive theoretical development of equality of resources. The main point can be shown most quickly by constructing a reasonably simple exercise in equality of resources, deliberately artificial so as to abstract from problems we shall later have to face. Suppose a number of shipwreck survivors are washed up on a desert island which has abundant resources and no native population, and any likely rescue is many years away. These immigrants accept the principle that no one is antecedently entitled to any of these resources, but that they shall instead be divided equally among them. (They do not yet realize, let us say, that it might be wise to keep some resources as owned in common by any state they might create.) They also accept (at least provisionally) the following test of an equal division of resources, which I shall call the envy test. No division of resources is an equal division if, once the division is complete, any immigrant would prefer someone else's bundle of resources to his own bundle.[45]

Now suppose some one immigrant is elected to achieve the division according to that principle. It is unlikely that he can succeed simply by physically dividing the resources of the island into $n$ identical bundles of resources. The number of each kind of the nondivisible resources, like milking cows, might not be an exact multiple of $n$, and even in the case of divisible resources, like arable land, some

---

[45] D. Foley, "Resource Allocation and the Public Sector," *Yale Economic Essays* 7 (Spring 1967); H. Varian, "Equity, Energy and Efficiency, *Journal of Economic Theory* (Sept. 1974): 63–91.

land would be better than others, and some better for one use than another. Suppose, however, that by a great deal of trial and error and care the divider could create *n* bundles of resources, each of which was somewhat different from the others, but was nevertheless such that he could assign one to each immigrant and no one would in fact envy anyone else's bundle.

The distribution might still fail to satisfy the immigrants as an equal distribution, for a reason that is not caught by the envy test. Suppose (to put the point in a dramatic way) the divider achieved his result by transforming all the available resources into a very large stock of plovers' eggs and pre-phylloxera claret (either by magic or trade with a neighboring island that enters the story only for that reason) and divides this glut into identical bundles of baskets and bottles. Many of the immigrants—let us say all but one—are delighted. But if that one hates plovers' eggs and pre-phylloxera claret he will feel that he has not been treated as an equal in the division of resources. The envy test is met—he does not prefer any one's bundle to his own—but he prefers what he would have had under some fairer treatment of the initially available resources.

A similar, though less dramatic, piece of unfairness might be produced even without magic or bizarre trades. For the combination of resources that composes each bundle the divider creates will favor some tastes over others, compared with different combinations he might have composed. That is, different sets of *n* bundles might be created by trial and error, each of which would pass the envy test, so that for any such set that the divider chooses, someone will prefer that he had chosen a different set, even though that person would not prefer a different bundle within that set. Trades after the initial distribution may, of course, improve that person's position. But they will be unlikely to bring him to the position he would have had under the set of bundles he would have preferred, because some others will begin with a bundle they prefer to the bundle they would have had in that set, and so will have no reason to trade to that bundle.

So the divider needs a device that will attack two distinct foci of arbitrariness and possible unfairness. The envy test cannot be satisfied by any simple mechanical division of resources. If any more complex division can be found that will satisfy it, many such might be found, so that the choice amongst these would be arbitrary. The divider needs some form of auction or other market procedure in order to respond to these problems. I shall describe a reasonably straightforward procedure that would seem acceptable if it could be made to work, though as I shall describe it it will be impossibly expensive of time. Suppose the divider hands each of the immigrants an equal and large number of clamshells, which are sufficiently numerous and in themselves valued by no one, to use as counters in a market of the following sort. Each distinct item on the island (not including the immigrants themselves) is listed as a lot to be sold, unless someone notifies the auctioneer (as the divider has now become) of his or her desire to bid for some part of an item, including part, for example, of some piece of land, in which case that part becomes itself a distinct lot. The auctioneer then proposes a set of prices for each lot and discovers whether that set of prices clears all markets, that is, whether there is only one purchaser at that price and all lots are sold. If not, then the auctioneer adjusts his prices until he reachers a set that does clear the markets.[46] But the process does not stop then, because each of the immigrants remains free to change his bids even when an initially market-clearing set of prices is reached, or even to propose different lots. But let us suppose that in time even this

---

[46] The process does not guarantee that the auction will come to an end in this way, because there may be various equilibria. I am supposing that people will come to understand that they cannot do better by further runs of the auction, and will for practical reasons settle on one equilibrium. If I am wrong, then this fact provides one of the aspects of incompleteness I describe in the next section.

leisurely process comes to an end, everyone declares himself satisfied, and goods are distributed accordingly.

Now the envy test will have been met. No one will envy another's set of purchases because, by hypothesis, he could have purchased that bundle with his clamshells instead of his own bundle. Nor is the choice of sets of bundles arbitrary. Many people will be able to imagine a different set of bundles meeting the no-envy test that might have been established, but the actual set of bundles has the merit that each person played, through his purchases against an initially equal stock of counters, an equal role in determining the set of bundles actually chosen. No one is in the position of the person in our earlier example who found himself with nothing but what he hated. Of course, luck plays a certain role in determining how satisfied anyone is with the outcome, against other possibilities he might envision. If plovers' eggs and old claret were the only resources to auction, then the person who hated these would be as badly off as in our earlier example. He would be unlucky that the immigrants had not washed up on an island with more of what he wanted (though lucky, of course, that it did not have even less). But he could not complain that the division of the actual resources they found was unequal.

He might think himself lucky or unlucky in other ways as well. It would be a matter of luck, for example, how many others shared various of his tastes. If his tastes or ambitions proved relatively popular, this might work in his favor in the auction, if there were economies of scale in the production of what he wanted. Or against him, if what he wanted was scarce. If the immigrants had decided to establish a regime of equality of welfare, instead of equality of resources, then these various pieces of good or bad luck would be shared with others, because distribution would be based, not on any auction of the sort I described, in which luck plays this role, but on a strategy of evening out differences in whatever concept of welfare had been chosen. Equality of resources, however, offers no similar reason for correcting for the contingencies that determine how expensive or frustrating someone's preferences turn out to be.[47]

Under equality of welfare, people are meant to decide what sorts of lives they want independently of information relevant to determining how much their choices will reduce or enhance the ability of others to have what they want.[48] That sort of information becomes relevant only at a second, political level at which administrators then gather all the choices made at the first level to see what distribution will give each of these choices equal success under some concept of welfare taken as the correct dimension of success. Under equality of resources, however, people decide what sorts of lives to pursue against a background of information about the actual cost their choices impose on other people and hence on the total stock of resources that may fairly be used by them. The information left to an independent political level under equality of welfare is therefore brought into the initial level of individual choice under equality of resources. The elements of luck in the auction are in fact pieces of information of a crucial sort; information that is acquired and used in that process of choice.

So the contingent facts of raw material and the distribute of tastes are not grounds on which someone might challenge a distribution as unequal. They are rather background facts that determine what equality of resources, in these circumstances, is. Under equality of resources, no test for calculating what equality requires can be abstracted from these background facts and used to test them.

---

[47] See, however, the discussion of handicaps below, which recognizes that certain kinds of preferences, which people wish they did not have, may call for compensation as handicaps.

[48] See Part I of this essay (*Philosophy & Public Affairs* 10, No. 3 [Summer 1981]) for a discussion of whether equality of welfare can be modified so as to make an exception here for "expensive tastes" deliberately cultivated. I argue that it cannot.

The market character of the auction is not simply a convenient or ad hoc device for resolving technical problems that arise for equality of resources in very simple exercises like our desert island case. It is an institutionalized form of the process of discovery and adaptation that is at the center of the ethics of that ideal. Equality of resources supposes that the resources devoted to each person's life should be equal. That goal needs a metric. The auction proposes what the envy test in fact assumes, that the true measure of the social resources devoted to the life of one person is fixed by asking how important, in fact, that resource is for others. It insists that the cost, measured in that way, figure in each person's sense of what is rightly his and in each person's judgment of what life he should lead, given that command of justice. Anyone who insists that equality is violated by any particular profile of initial tastes, therefore, must reject equality of resources, and fall back on equality of welfare.

Of course it is sovereign in this argument, and in this connection between the market and equality of resources, that people enter the market on equal terms. The desert island auction would not have avoided envy, and would have no appeal as a solution to the problem of dividing the resources equally, if the immigrants had struggled ashore with different amounts of money in their pocket, which they were free to use in the auction, or if some had stolen clamshells from others. We must not lose sight of that fact, either in the argument that follows or in any reflections on the application of that argument to contemporary economic systems. But neither should we lose sight ... of the important theoretical connection between the market and the concept of equality in resources.

There are, of course, other and very different sorts of objection that might be made to the use of an auction, even an equal auction of the sort I described. It might be said, for example, that the fairness of an auction supposes that the preferences people bring to the auction, or form in its course, are authentic—the true preferences of the agent rather than preferences imposed upon him by the economic system itself. Perhaps an auction of any sort, in which one person bids against another, imposes an illegitimate assumption that what is valuable in life is individual ownership of something rather than more cooperative enterprises of the community or some group within it as a whole. Insofar as this (in part mysterious) objection is pertinent here, however, it is an objection against the idea of private ownership over an extensive domain of resources, which is better considered under the title of political equality, not an objection to the claim that a market of some sort must figure in any satisfactory account of what equality in private ownership is.

## II. THE PROJECT

Since the device of an equal auction seems promising as a technique for achieving an attractive interpretation of equality of resources in a simple context, like the desert island, the question arises whether it will prove useful in developing a more general account of that ideal. We should ask whether the device could be elaborated to provide a scheme for developing or testing equality of resources in a community that has a dynamic economy, with labor, investment, and trade. What structure must an auction take in such an economy—what adjustments or supplements must be made to the production and trade that would follow such an auction—in order that the results continue to satisfy our initial requirement that an equal share of the resources be available to each citizen?

Our interest in this question is three-fold. First, the project provides an important test of the coherence and completeness of the idea of equality of resources. Suppose no auction or pattern of post-auction trade could be described whose results could be accepted as equality in any society much more complex or less artificial than a simple economy of consumption. Or that no auction could produce equality without constraints and restrictions which violate independent principles of justice. This would tend to suggest, at least, that there is no coherent ideal of equality of resources. Or that the ideal is not politically attractive after all.

We might discover, on the contrary, less comprehensive gaps or defects in the idea. Suppose, for example, that the design for the auction we develop does not uniquely determine a particular distribution, even given a stipulated set of initial resources and a stipulated population with fixed interests and ambitions, but is rather capable of producing significantly different outcomes depending on the order of decisions, arbitrary choices about the composition of the initial list of options, or other contingencies. We might conclude that the ideal of equality of resources embraces a variety of different distributions, each of which satisfies the ideal, and that the ideal is therefore partially indeterminate. This would show limitations on the power of the ideal to discriminate between certain distributions, but would not for that reason show that the ideal is either incoherent or practically impotent. So it is worth trying to develop the idea of an equal auction as a test of the theoretical standing and power of the political ideal.

Second, a fully developed description of an equal auction, adequate for a more complex society, might provide a standard for judging actual institutions and distributions in the real world. Of course no complex, organic society would have, in its history, anything remotely comparable to an equal auction. But we can nevertheless ask, for any actual distribution, whether it falls within the class of distributions that might have been produced by such an auction over a defensible description of initial resources. Or, if it is not, how far it differs from or falls short of the closest distribution within this class. The device of the auction might provide, in other words, a standard for judging how far an actual distribution, however it has been achieved, approaches equality of resources at any particular time.

Third, the device might be useful in the design of actual political institutions. Under certain (perhaps very limited) circumstances, when the conditions for an equal auction are at least roughly met, then an actual auction might be the best means of reaching or preserving equality of resources in the real world. This will be true, particularly, when the results of such an auction are antecedently indeterminate in the way just described, so that any result the auction reaches will respect equality of resources even though it is not known, in advance, which result would be reached. In such a case it may be fairer to conduct an actual auction than to choose, through some other political means, one rather than another of the results that an auction might produce. Even in such a case it will rarely be possible or desirable to conduct an actual auction in the design our theoretical investigations recommend. But it may be possible to design an auction surrogate—an economic or political institution having sufficient of the characteristics of a theoretical equal auction so that the arguments of fairness recommending an actual auction were it feasible also recommend the surrogate. The economic markets of many countries can be interpreted, even as they stand, as forms of auctions. (So, too, can many forms of democratic political process.) Once we have developed a satisfactory model of an actual auction we can use that model to test these institutions, and reform them to bring them closer to the model.

Nevertheless our project is in the main, within the present essay, entirely theoretical. Our interest is primarily in the design of an ideal, and of a device to picture that ideal and test its coherence, completeness, and appeal. We shall therefore ignore practical difficulties, like problems of gathering information, which do not impeach these theoretical goals, and also make simplifying counterfactual assumptions which do not subvert them. But we should try to notice which simplifications we are making, because they will be of importance, particularly as to the third and most practical application of our projects, at any later stage, at which we consider second-best compromises of our ideal in the real world.

### III. Luck and Insurance

If the auction is successful as described, then equality of resources holds for the moment among the immigrants. But perhaps only for the moment, because if they are left alone, once the auction is completed, to produce and trade as they wish, then the envy test will shortly fail. Some may be more skillful than others at producing what others want and will trade to get. Some may like to work, or to work in a way that will produce more to trade, while others like not to work or prefer to work at what will bring them less. Some will stay healthy while others fall sick, or lightning will strike the farms of others but avoid theirs. For any of these and dozens of other reasons some people will prefer the bundle others have in say, five years, to their own.

We must ask whether (or rather how far) such developments are consistent with equality of resources, and I shall begin by considering the character and impact of luck on the immigrants' post-auction fortunes. I shall distinguish, at least for the moment, between two kinds of luck. Option luck is a matter of how deliberate and calculated gambles turn out—whether someone gains or loses through accepting an isolated risk he or she should have anticipated and might have declined. Brute luck is a matter of how risks fall out that are not in that sense deliberate gambles. If I buy a stock on the exchange that rises, then my option luck is good. If I am hit by a falling meteorite whose course could not have been predicted, then my bad luck is brute (even though I could have moved just before it struck if I had any reason to know where it would strike). Obviously the difference between these two forms of luck can be represented as a matter of degree, and we may be uncertain how to describe a particular piece of bad luck. If someone develops cancer in the course of a normal life, and there is no particular decision to which we can point as a gamble risking the disease, then we will say that he has suffered brute bad luck. But if he smoked cigarettes heavily then we may prefer to say that he took an unsuccessful gamble.

Insurance, so far as it is available, provides a link between brute and option luck, because the decision to buy or reject catastrophe insurance is a calculated gamble. Of course, insurance does not erase the distinction. Someone who buys medical insurance and is hit by an unexpected meteorite still suffers brute bad luck, because he is worse off than if he had bought insurance and not needed it. But he has had better option luck than if he had not bought the insurance, because his situation is better in virtue of his not having run the gamble of refusing to insure.

Is it consistent with equality of resources that people should have different income or wealth in virtue of differing option luck? Suppose some of the immigrants plant valuable but risky crops while others play it safer, and that some of the former buy insurance against uncongenial weather while others do not. Skill will play a part in determining which of these various programs succeed, of course, and we shall consider the problems this raises later. But option luck will also play a part. Does its role threaten or invade equality of resources?

Consider, first, the difference in wealth between those who play it safe and those who gamble and succeed. Some people enjoy, while others hate, risks; but this particular difference in personality is comprehended in a more general difference between the kinds of lives that different people wish to lead. The life chosen by someone who gambles contains, as an element, the factor of risk; someone who chooses not to gamble has decided that he prefers a safer life. We have already decided that people should pay the price of the life they have decided to lead, measured in what others give up in order that they can do so. That was the point of the auction as a device to establish initial equality of resources. But the price of a safer life, measured in this way, is precisely forgoing any chance of the gains whose prospect induces others to gamble. So we have no reason to object, against the background of our earlier decisions, to a result in which those who decline to gamble have less than some of those who do not.

But we must also compare the situation of those who gamble and win with that of those who gamble and lose. We cannot say that the latter have chosen a different life and must sacrifice gains accordingly; for they have chosen the same lives as those who won. But we can say that the possibility of loss was part of the life they chose—that it was the fair price of the possibility of gain. For we might have designed our initial auction so that people could purchase (for example) lottery tickets with their clamshells. But the price of those tickets would have been some amount of other resources (fixed by the odds and the gambling preferences of others) that the shells would otherwise have bought, and which will be wholly forgone if the ticket does not win.

The same point can be made by considering the arguments for redistribution from winners to losers after the event. If winners were made to share their winnings with losers, then no one would gamble, as individuals, and the kind of life preferred by both those who in the end win and those who lose would be unavailable. Of course, it is not a good argument, against someone who urges redistribution in order to achieve equality of resources, that redistribution would make some forms of life less attractive or even impossible. For the demands of equality (we assume in this essay) are prior to other desiderata, including variety in the kinds of life available to people. (Equality will in any case make certain kinds of lives—a life of economic and political domination of others, for example—impossible.) In the present case, however, the difference is apparent. For the effect of redistribution from winners to losers in gambles would be to deprive both of lives they prefer, which indicates, not simply that this would produce an unwanted curtailment of available forms of life, but that it would deprive them of an equal voice in the construction of lots to be auctioned, like the man who hated both plovers' eggs and claret but was confronted only with bundles of both. They both want gambles to be in the mix, either originally or as represented by resources with which they can take risks later, and the chance of losing is the correct price, measured on the metric we have been using, of a life that includes gambles with a chance of gain.

We may, of course, have special reasons for forbidding certain forms of gambles. We may have paternalistic reasons for limiting how much any individual may risk, for example. We may also have reasons based in a theory of political equality for forbidding someone to gamble with his freedom or his religious or political rights. The present point is more limited. We have no general reason for forbidding gambles altogether in the bare fact that in the event winners will control more resources than losers, any more than in the fact that winners will have more than those who do not gamble at all. Our initial principle, that equality of resources requires that people pay the true cost of the lives that they lead, warrants rather than condemns these differences.

We may (if we wish) adjust our envy test to record that conclusion We may say that in computing the extent of someone's resources over his life, for the purpose of asking whether anyone else envies those resources, any resources gained through a successful gamble should be represented by the opportunity to take the gamble at the odds in force, and comparable adjustments made to the resources of those who have lost through gambles. The main point of this artificial construction of the envy test, however, would be to remind us that the argument in favor of allowing differences in option luck to affect income and wealth assumes that everyone has in principle the same gambles available to him. Someone who never had the opportunity to run a similar risk, and would have taken the opportunity had it been available, will still envy some of those who did have it.

Nor does the argument yet confront the case of brute bad luck. If two people lead roughly the same lives, but one goes suddenly blind, then we cannot explain the resulting differences in their incomes either by saying that one took risks that the other chose not to take, or that we could not redistribute without denying both the lives they prefer. For the accident has (we assume) nothing to do with choices in the pertinent sense. It is not necessary to the life either has chosen that he run the risk of going blind without redistribution of funds from the other. This is a fortiori so if one is born blind and the other sighted.

But the possibility of insurance provides, as I suggested, a link between the two kinds of luck. For suppose insurance against blindness is available, in the initial auction, at whatever level of coverage the policy holder chooses to buy. And also suppose that two sighted people have, at the time of the auction, equal chance of suffering an accident that will blind them, and know that they have. Now if one chooses to spend part of his initial resources for such insurance and the other does not, or if one buys more coverage than the other, then this difference will reflect their different opinions about the relative value of different forms or components of their prospective lives. It may reflect the fact that one puts more value on sight than the other. Or, differently, that one would count monetary compensation for the loss of his sight as worthless in the face of such a tragedy while the other, more practical, would fix his mind on the aids and special training that such money might buy. Or simply that one minds or values risk differently from the other, and would, for example, rather try for a brilliant life that would collapse under catastrophe than a life guarded at the cost of resources necessary to make it brilliant.

But in any case the bare idea of equality of resources, apart from any paternalistic additions, would not argue for redistribution from the person who had insured to the person who had not if, horribly, they were both blinded in the same accident. For the availability of insurance would mean that, though they had both had brute bad luck, the difference between them was a matter of option luck, and the arguments we entertained against disturbing the results of option luck under conditions of equal antecedent risk hold here as well. But then the situation cannot be different if the person who decided not to insure is the only one to be blinded. For once again the difference is a difference in option luck against a background of equal opportunity to insure or not. If neither had been blinded, the man who had insured against blindness would have been the loser. His option luck would have been bad—though it seems bizarre to put it this way—because he spent resources that, as things turned out, would have been better spent otherwise. But he would have no claim, in that event, from the man who did not insure and also survived unhurt.

So if the condition just stated were met—if everyone had an equal risk of suffering some catastrophe that would leave him or her handicapped, and everyone knew roughly what the odds were and had ample opportunity to insure—then handicaps would pose no special problem for equality of resources. But of course that condition is not met. Some people are born with handicaps, or develop them before they have either sufficient knowledge or funds to insure on their own behalf. They cannot buy insurance after the event. Even handicaps that develop later in life, against which people do have the opportunity to insure, are not randomly distributed through the population, but follow genetic tracks, so that sophisticated insurers would charge some people higher premiums for the same coverage before the event. Nevertheless the idea of a market in insurance provides a counterfactual guide through which equality of resources might face the problem of handicaps in the real world.

Suppose we can make sense of and even give a rough answer to the following question. If (contrary to fact) everyone had at the appropriate age the same risk of developing physical or mental handicaps in the future (which assumes that no one has developed these yet) but that the total number of handicaps remained what it is, how much insurance coverage against these handicaps would the average member of the community purchase? We might then say that but for (uninsurable) brute luck that has altered these equal odds, the average person would have purchased insurance at that level, and compensate those who do develop handicaps accordingly, out of some fund collected by taxation or other compulsory process but designed to match the fund that would have been provided through premiums if the odds had been equal. Those who develop handicaps will then have more resources at their command than others, but the extent of their extra resources will be fixed by the market decisions that people would supposedly have made if circumstances had been more equal than they are. Of course, this argument does involve the fictitious assumption that everyone who suffers handicaps would have bought the average amount of insurance, and we may wish to refine the argument and the strategy so that that no longer holds. But it does not seem an unreasonable assumption for this purpose as it stands.

Can we answer the counterfactual question with sufficient confidence to develop a program of compensation of that sort? We face a threshold difficulty of some importance. People can decide how much of their resources to devote to insurance against a particular catastrophe only with some idea of the life they hope to lead, because only then can they decide how serious a particular catastrophe would be, how far additional resources would alleviate the tragedy, and so forth. But people who are born with a particular handicap, or develop one in childhood, will of course take that circumstance into account in the plans they make. So in order to decide how much insurance such a person would have bought without the handicap we must decide what sort of life he would have planned in that case. But there may be no answer, even in principle, to that question.

We do not need, however, to make counterfactual judgments that are so personalized as to embarrass us for that reason. Even if people did all have equal risk of all catastrophes, and evaluated the value and importance of insurance differently entirely due to their different ambitions and plans, the insurance market would nevertheless be structured through categories designating the risks against which most people would insure in a general way. After all, risks of most catastrophes are now regarded by the actual insurance market as randomly distributed, and so we might follow actual insurance practice, modified to remove the discriminations insurers make when they know that one group is more likely, perhaps for genetic reasons, to suffer a particular kind of brute bad luck. It would make sense to suppose, for example, that most people would make roughly the same assessment of the value of insurance against general handicaps, such as blindness or the loss of a limb, that affect a wide spectrum of different sorts of lives. [...]

We would, in any case, pay great attention to matters of technology, and be ready to adjust our sums as technology changed. People purchase insurance against catastrophes, for example, against a background of assumptions about the remedial medical technology, or special training, or mechanical aids that are in fact available, and about the cost of these remedies. People would seek insurance at a higher level against blindness, for example, if the increased recovery would enable them to purchase a newly discovered sight-substitute technology, than they would if that increased recovery simply swelled a bank account they could not, in any case, use with much satisfaction.

Of course, any judgments that the officials of a community might make about the structure of the hypothetical insurance market would be speculative and open to a variety of objections. But there is no reason to think, certainly in advance, that a practice of compensating the handicapped on the basis of such speculation would be worse, in principle, than the alternatives, and it would have the merit of aiming in the direction of the theoretical solution most congenial to equality of resources.

We might now remind ourselves of what these alternatives are. I said in Part I of this essay that the regime of equality of welfare, contrary to initial impressions, does a poor job of either explaining or guiding our impulse to compensate the severely handicapped with extra resources. It provides, in particular, no upper bound to compensation so long as any further payment would improve the welfare of the wretched; but this is not, as it might seem, generous, because it leaves the standard for actual compensation to the politics of selfishness broken by sympathy, politics that we know will supply less than any defensible hypothetical insurance market would offer.

Consider another approach to the problem of handicaps under equality of resources. Suppose we say that any person's physical and mental powers must count as part of his resources, so that someone who is born handicapped starts with less by way of resources than others have, and should be allowed to catch up, by way of transfer payments, before what remains is auctioned off in any equal market. People's powers are indeed resources, because these are used, together with material resources, in making something valuable out of one's life. Physical powers are resources for that purpose in the way that aspects of one's personality, like one's conception of what is valuable in life, are not. Nevertheless the suggestion, that a design of equality of resources should provide for an initial compensation to alleviate differences in physical or mental resources, is troublesome in a variety of ways. It requires, for example, some standard of "normal" powers to serve as the benchmark for compensation. But whose powers should be taken as normal for this purpose? It suffers, moreover, from the same defect as the parallel recommendation under equality of welfare. In fact, no amount of initial compensation could make someone born blind or mentally incompetent equal in physical or mental resources with someone taken to be "normal" in these ways. So the argument provides no upper bound to initial compensation, but must leave this to a political compromise likely to be less generous, again, than what the hypothetical insurance market would command.

Quite apart from these practical and theoretical inadequacies, the suggestion is troublesome for another reason. Though powers are resources, they should not be considered resources whose ownership is to be determined through politics in accordance with some interpretation of equality of resources. They are not, that is, resources for the theory of equality in exactly the sense in which ordinary material resources are. They cannot be manipulated or transferred, even so far as technology might permit. So in this way it misdescribes the problem of handicaps to say that equality of resources must strive to make people equal in physical and mental constitution so far as this is possible. The problem is, rather, one of determining how far the ownership of independent material resources should be affected by differences that exist in physical and mental powers, and the response of our theory should speak in that vocabulary.

It might be wise [. . .] to bring our story of the immigrants up to date. By way of supplement to the auction, they now establish a hypothetical insurance market which they effectuate through compulsory insurance at a fixed premium for everyone based on speculations about what the average immigrant would have purchased by way of insurance had the antecedent risk of various handicaps been equal. [. . .]

But now a question arises. Does this decision place too much weight on the distinction between handicaps, which the immigrants treat in this compensatory way, and accidents touching preferences and ambitions (like the accident of what material resources are in fact available, and of how many other people share a particular person's taste)? The latter will also affect welfare, but they are not matters for compensation under our scheme. Would it not now be fair to treat as handicaps eccentric tastes, or tastes that are expensive or impossible to satisfy because of scarcity of some good that might have been common? We might compensate those who have these tastes by supposing that everyone had an equal chance of being in that position and then establishing a hypothetical insurance market against that possibility.

A short answer is available. Someone who is born with a serious handicap faces his life with what we concede to be fewer resources, just on that account, than others do. This justifies compensation, under a scheme devoted to equality of resources, and though the hypothetical insurance market does not right the balance—nothing can—it seeks to remedy one aspect of the resulting unfairness. But we cannot say that the person whose tastes are expensive, for whatever reason, therefore has fewer resources at his command. For we cannot state (without falling back on some version of equality of welfare) what equality in the distribution of tastes and preferences would be. Why is there less equality of resources when someone has an eccentric taste that makes goods cheaper for others, than when he shares a popular taste and so makes goods more expensive for them? The auction, bringing to bear information about the resources that actually exist and the competing preferences actually in play, is the only true measure of whether any particular person commands equal resources. If the auction has in fact been an equal auction, then the man of eccentric tastes has no less than equal material resources, and the argument that justifies a compensatory hypothetical auction in the case of handicaps has no occasion even to begin. It is true that this argument produces a certain view of the distinction between a person and his circumstances, and assigns his tastes and ambitions to his person, and his physical and mental powers to his circumstances. That is the view of a person I sketched in the introductory section, of someone who forms his ambitions with a sense of their cost to others against some presumed initial equality of economic power, and though this is different form the picture assumed by equality of welfare, it is a picture at the center of equality of resources.

In one way, however, my argument might well be thought to overstate the distinction between handicaps and at least certain sorts of what are often considered preferences. Suppose someone finds he has a craving (or obsession or lust or, in the words of an earlier psychology, a "drive") that he wishes he did not have, because it interferes with what he wants to do with his life and offers him frustration or even pain if it is not satisfied. This might indeed be some feature of his physical needs that other people would not consider a handicap at all: for example, a generous appetite for sex. But it is a "preference" (if that is the right word) that he does not want, and it makes perfect sense to say that he would be better off without it. For some people these unwanted tastes include tastes they have (perhaps unwittingly) themselves cultivated, such as a taste for a particular sport or for music of a sort difficult to obtain. They regret that they have these tastes, and believe they would be better off without them, but nevertheless find it painful to ignore them. These tastes are handicaps; though for other people they are rather an essential part of what gives value to their lives.

Now these cases do not present, for particular people, borderline cases between ambitions and handicaps. The distinction required by equality of resources is the distinction between those beliefs and attitudes that define what a successful life would be like, which the ideal assigns to the person, and those features of body or mind or personality that provide means or impediments to that success, which the ideal assigns to the person's circumstances. Those who see their sexual desires or their taste for opera as unwanted disadvantages will class these features of their body or mind or personality firmly as the latter. These are, for them, handicaps, and are therefore suitable for the regime proposed for handicaps generally. We may imagine that everyone has an equal chance of acquiring such a craving by accident. We may then ask—with as much or as little intelligibility as in the case of blindness—whether people generally would purchase insurance against that risk, and if so at what premium and what level of coverage. It seems unlikely that many people would purchase such insurance, at the rates of premium likely to govern if they sought it, except in the case of cravings so severe and disabling as to fall under the category of mental disease. But that is a different matter. The important point, presently, is that the idea of an insurance market is available here, because we can imagine people who have such a craving not having it, without thereby imagining them to have a different conception of what they want from life than what in fact they do want. So the idea of the imaginary insurance auction provides at once a device for identifying cravings and distinguishing them from positive features of personality, and also for bringing these cravings within the general regime designed for handicaps.                                    [pp. 283–304]

## I.M. YOUNG
### Defining Injustice as Domination and Oppression
### (1990)[49]

Because distributive models of power, rights, opportunity, and self-respect work so badly, justice should not be conceived primarily on the model of the distribution of wealth, income, and other material goods. Theorizing about justice should explicitly limit the concept of distribution to material goods, like things, natural resources, or money. The scope of justice is wider than distributive issues. Though there may be additional nondistributive issues of justice, my concerns [...] focus on issues of decisionmaking, division of labor, and culture.

Political thought of the modern period greatly narrowed the scope of justice as it had been conceived by ancient and medieval thought. Ancient thought regarded justice as the virtue of society as a whole, the well-orderedness of institutions that foster individual virtue and promote happiness and harmony among citizens. Modern political thought abandoned the notion that there is a natural order to society that corresponds to the proper ends of human nature. Seeking to liberate the individual to define "his" own ends, modern political theory also restricted the scope of justice to issues of distribution and the minimal regulation of action among such self-defining individuals.[50]

While I hardly intend to revert to a full-bodied Platonic conception of justice, I nevertheless think it is important to broaden the understanding of justice beyond its usual limits in contemporary philosophical discourse. Agnes Heller[51] proposes one such broader conception in what she calls an incomplete ethico-political concept of justice. According to her conception, justice names not principles of distribution, much less some particular distributive pattern. This represents too narrow and substantive a way of reflecting on justice. Instead, justice names the perspectives, principles, and procedures for evaluating institutional norms and rules. Developing Habermas's communicative ethics, Heller suggests that justice is primarily the virtue of citizenship, of persons deliberating about problems and issues that confront them collectively in their institutions and actions, under conditions without domination or oppression, with reciprocity and mutual tolerance of difference. She proposes the following test of the justice of social or political norms:

> Every valid social and political norm and rule (every law) must meet the condition that the foreseeable consequences and side effects the general observance of that law (norm) exacts on the satisfaction of the needs of each and every individual would be accepted by everyone concerned, and that the claim of the norm to actualize the universal values of freedom and/or life could be accepted by each and every individual, regardless of the values to which they are committed.[52]

In the course of this book I shall raise some critical questions about the ideas of citizenship, agreement, and universality embedded in the radically democratic ideal which Habermas and Heller, along with others, express. Nevertheless, I

---

[49] [From Iris Marion Young, *Justice and the Politics of Difference* (1990).]
[50] See A. Heller, *Beyond Justice* (1987), Chap. 2; of. A. MacIntyre, *After Virtue* (1981), Chap. 17.
[51] A. Heller, *op. cit.*, Chap. 5.
[52] *Op. cit.*, note 51, pp. 240–241. [On Habermas, see *post*, 969.]

endorse and follow this general conception of justice derived from a conception of communicative ethics. The idea of justice here shifts from a focus on distributive patterns to procedural issues of participation in deliberation and decisionmaking. For a norm to be just, everyone who follows it must in principle have an effective voice in its consideration and be able to agree to it without coercion. For a social condition to be just, it must enable all to meet their needs and exercise their freedom; thus justice requires that all be able to express their needs.

As I understand it, the concept, of justice coincides with the concept of the political. Politics includes all aspects of institutional organization, public action, social practices and habits, and cultural meanings insofar as they are potentially subject to collective evaluation and decisionmaking. Politics in this inclusive sense certainly concerns the policies and actions of government and the state, but in principle can also concern rules, practices, and actions in any other institutional context.

The scope of justice, I have suggested, is much wider than distribution, and covers everything political in this sense. This coheres with the meaning of justice claims of the sort mentioned at the outset of this chapter. When people claim that a particular rule, practice, or cultural meaning is wrong and should be changed, they are often making a claim about social injustice. Some of these claims involve distributions, but many also refer to other ways in which social institutions inhibit or liberate persons.

Some writers concur that distribution is too narrow a focus for normative evaluation of social institutions, but claim that going beyond this distributive focus entails going beyond the norms of justice per se. Charles Taylor[53], for example, distinguishes questions of distributive justice from normative questions about the institutional framework of society. Norms of justice help resolve disputes about entitlements and deserts within a particular institutional context. They cannot evaluate that institutional context itself, however, because it embodies a certain conception of human nature and the human good. According to Taylor, confusions arise in theoretical and political discussion when norms of distributive justice are applied across social structures and used to evaluate basic structures. For example, both right and left critics of our society charge it with perpetrating injustices, but according to Taylor the normative perspective from which each side speaks involves a project to construct different institutional forms corresponding to specific conceptions of the human good, a project beyond merely articulating principles of justice.

From a somewhat different perspective, Seyla Benhabib[54] suggests that a normative social theory which evaluates institutions according to whether they are free from domination, meet needs, and provide conditions of emancipation entails going beyond justice as understood by the modern tradition. Because this broader normative social theory entails a critique of culture and socialization in addition to critiques of formal rights and patterns of distribution, it merges questions of justice with questions of the good life.

I am sympathetic with both these discussions, as well as with Michael Sandel's related argument for recognizing the "limits" of justice and the importance of conceptualizing normative aspects of the self in social contexts that lie beyond those limits.[55] But while I share these writers' general critique of liberal theories of distributive justice, I see no reason to conclude with Taylor and Sandel that this critique reveals the limits of the concept of justice which a normative social philosophy must transcend. I disagree to some extent, moreover, with Taylor's

---

[53] "The Nature and Scope of Distributive Justice" in *Philosophy and the Human Science* (1985).
[54] *Critique, Norm and Utopia* (1986), pp. 330–336.
[55] *Liberalism and the Limits of Justice* (1982)

and Benhabib's suggestion that such a wider normative social philosophy merges questions of justice with questions of the good life.

Like many other writers cited earlier in this chapter, Taylor assumes that justice and distribution are coextensive, and therefore that broader issues of institutional context require other normative concepts. Many Marxist theorists who argue that justice is a merely bourgeois concept take a similar position. Whether normative theorists who focus attention on issues of decisionmaking, division of labor, culture, and social organization beyond the distribution of goods call these issues of justice or not is clearly a matter of choice. I can give only pragmatic reasons for my own choice.

Since Plato "justice" has evoked the well-ordered society, and it continues to carry those resonances in contemporary political discussion. Appeals to justice still have the power to awaken a moral imagination and motivate people to look at their society critically, and ask how it can be made more liberating and enabling. Philosophers interested in nurturing this emancipatory imagination and extending it beyond questions of distribution should, I suggest, lay claim to the term justice rather than abandon it.

To a certain extent Heller, Taylor, and Benhabib are right that a postmodern turn to an enlarged conception of justice, reminiscent of the scope of justice in Plato and Aristotle, entails more attention to the definition of ends than the liberal conception of justice allows. Nevertheless, questions of justice do not merge with questions of the good life. The liberal commitment to individual freedom, and the consequent plurality of definitions of the good, must be preserved in any reenlarged conception of justice. The modern restriction of the concept of justice to formal and instrumental principles was meant to promote the value of individual self-definition of ends, or "plans of life," as Rawls calls them. In displacing reflection about justice from a primary focus on distribution to include all institutional and social relations insofar as they are subject to collective decision, I do not mean to suggest that justice should include all moral norms in its scope. Social justice in the sense I intend continues to refer only to institutional conditions, and not to the preferences and ways of life of individuals or groups.

Any normative theorist in the postmodern world is faced with a dilemma. On the one hand, we express and justify norms by appealing to certain values derived from a conception of the good human life. In some sense, then, any normative theory implicitly or explicitly relies on a conception of human nature[56]. On the other hand, it would seem that we should reject the very idea of a human nature as misleading or oppressive.

Any definition of a human nature is dangerous because it threatens to devalue or exclude some acceptable individual desires, cultural characteristics, or ways of life. Normative social theory, however, can rarely avoid making implicit or explicit assumptions about human beings in the formulation of its vision of just institutions. Even though the distributive paradigm carries an individualist conception of society, which considers individual desires and preferences private matters outside the sphere of rational discourse, it assumes a quite specific conception of human nature. It implicitly defines human beings as primarily consumers, desirers, and possessors of goods[57]. C. B. Macpherson[58] argues that in presupposing such a possessively individualist view of human nature the original liberal theorists hypostatized the acquisitive values of emergent capitalist social relations. Contemporary capitalism, which depends more upon widespread indulgent consumption than its penny-pinching Protestant ancestor, continues to presuppose an understanding of human beings as primarily utility maximizers[59].

---

[56] *Feminist Politics and Human Nature* (1983), pp. 18–22.
[57] *Op. cit*, note 53, pp. 180–182.
[58] *The Political Theory of Possessive Individualism* (1962).
[59] *Op. cit.*, note 56.

The idea of human beings that guides normative social theorizing under the distributive paradigm is an image, rather than an explicit theory of human nature. It makes plausible to the imagination both the static picture of social relations entailed by this distributive paradigm and the notion of separate individuals already formed apart from social goods. Displacing the distributive paradigm in favor of a wider, process-oriented understanding of society, which focuses on power, decisionmaking structures, and so on, likewise shifts the imagination to different assumptions about human beings. Such an imaginative shift could be as oppressive as consumerist images if it is made too concrete. As long as the values we appeal to are abstract enough, however, they will not devalue or exclude any particular culture or way of life.

Persons certainly are possessors and consumers, and any conception of justice should presume the value of meeting material needs, living in a comfortable environment, and experiencing pleasures. Adding an image of people as doers and actors[60] helps to displace the distributive paradigm. As doers and actors, we seek to promote many values of social justice in addition to fairness in the distribution of goods: learning and using satisfying and expansive skills in socially recognized settings; participating in forming and running institutions, and receiving recognition for such participation; playing and communicating with others, and expressing our experience, feelings, and perspective on social life in contexts where others can listen. Certainly many distributive theorists of justice would recognize and affirm these values. The framework of distribution, however, leads to a deemphasizing of these values and a failure to inquire about the institutional conditions that promote them.

This, then, is how I understand the connection between justice and the values that constitute the good life. Justice is not identical with the concrete realization of these values in individual lives; justice, that is, is not identical with the good life as such. Rather, social justice concerns the degree to which a society contains and supports the institutional conditions necessary for the realization of these values. The values comprised in the good life can be reduced to two very general ones: (1) developing and exercising one's capacities and expressing one's experience[61], and (2) participating in determining one's action and the conditions of one's action[62]. These are universalist values, in the sense that they assume the equal moral worth of all persons, and thus justice requires their promotion for everyone. To these two general values correspond two social conditions that define injustice: oppression, the institutional constraint on self-development, and domination, the institutional constraint on self-determination.

Oppression consists in systematic institutional processes which prevent some people from learning and using satisfying and expansive skills in socially recognized settings, or institutionalized social processes which inhibit people's ability to play and communicate with others or to express their feelings and perspective on social life in contexts where others can listen. While the social conditions of oppression often include material deprivation or maldistribution, they also involve issues beyond distribution [...]

Domination consists in institutional conditions which inhibit or prevent people from participating in determining their actions or the conditions of their actions. Persons live within structures of domination if other persons or groups can determine without reciprocation the conditions of their action, either directly or by virtue of the structural consequences of their actions. Thorough social and political democracy is the opposite of domination.[...]

I think the concepts of oppression and domination overlap, but there is

---

[60] *Democratic Theory: Essays In Retrieval* (1973).
[61] *Cf* C. Gould, *Rethinking Democracy* (1988) ch. 2; W. Galston, *Justice and the Human Good* (1980), pp. 61–69.
[62] (1979) 11 Phil. Forum 172

nevertheless reason to distinguish them. Oppression usually includes or entails domination, that is, constraints upon oppressed people to follow rules set by others. But each face of oppression also involves inhibitions not directly produced by relations of domination. As should become clear in that chapter, moreover, not everyone subject to domination is also oppressed. Hierarchical decision-making structures subject most people in our society to domination in some important aspect of their lives. Many of those people nevertheless enjoy significant institutionalized support for the development and exercise of their capacities and their ability to express themselves and be heard.          [pp. 33–38]

THE FACES OF OPPRESSION

*Exploitation*

The central function of Marx's theory of exploitation is to explain how class structure can exist in the absence of legally and normatively sanctioned class distinctions.[63] In precapitalist societies domination is overt and accomplished through directly political means. In both slave society and feudal society the right to appropriate the product of the labor of others partly defines class privilege, and these societies legitimate class distinctions with ideologies of natural superiority and inferiority.

Capitalist society, on the other hand, removes traditional juridically enforced class distinctions and promotes a belief in the legal freedom of persons. Workers freely contract with employers and receive a wage; no formal mechanisms of law or custom force them to work for that employer or any employer. Thus the mystery of capitalism arises: when everyone is formally free, how can there be class domination? Why do class distinctions persist between the wealthy, who own the means of production, and the mass of people, who work for them? The theory of exploitation answers this question.

Profit, the basis of capitalist power and wealth, is a mystery if we assume that in the market goods exchange at their values. The labor theory of value dispels this mystery. Every commodity's value is a function of the labor time necessary for its production. Labor power is the one commodity which in the process of being consumed produces new value. Profit comes from the difference between the value of the labor performed and the value of the capacity to labor which the capitalist purchases. Profit is possible only because the owner of capital appropriates any realized surplus value.

In recent years Marxist scholars have engaged in considerable controversy about the viability of the labor theory of value this account of exploitation relies on[64]. John Roemer[65], for example, develops a theory of exploitation which claims to preserve the theoretical and practical purposes of Marx's theory, but without assuming a distinction between values and prices and without being restricted to a concept of abstract, homogeneous labor. My purpose here is not to engage in technical economic disputes, but to indicate the place of a concept of exploitation in a conception of oppression.

Marx's theory of exploitation lacks an explicitly normative meaning, even though the judgment that workers are exploited clearly has normative as well as descriptive power in that theory[66]. C. B. Macpherson[67] reconstructs this theory of exploitation in a more explicitly normative form. The injustice of capitalist society consists in the fact that some people exercise their capacities under the control,

---

[63] [On Marx see *post*, 1140].
[64] See R. Wolff, *Understanding Marx* (1984), ch. 4.
[65] *A General Theory of Exploitation and Class* (1982)
[66] A. Buchanan, *Marx and Justice* (1982), ch. 3
[67] *Op cit.*, note 58, ch. 3.

according to the purposes, and for the benefit of other people. Through private ownership of the means of production, and through markets that allocate labor and the ability to buy goods, capitalism systematically transfers the powers of some persons to others, thereby augmenting the power of the latter. In this process of the transfer of powers, according to Macpherson, the capitalist class acquires and maintains an ability to extract benefits from workers. Not only are powers transferred from workers to capitalists, but also the powers of workers diminish by more than the amount of transfer, because workers suffer material deprivation and a loss of control, and hence are deprived of important elements of self-respect. Justice, then, requires eliminating the institutional forms that enable and enforce this process of transference and replacing them with institutional forms that enable all to develop and use their capacities in a way that does not inhibit, but rather can enhance, similar development and use in others.

The central insight expressed in the concept of exploitation, then, is that this oppression occurs through a steady process of the transfer of the results of the labor of one social group to benefit another. The injustice of class division does not consist only in the distributive fact that some people have great wealth while most people have little.[68] Exploitation enacts a structural relation between social groups. Social rules about what work is, who does what for whom, how work is compensated, and the social process by which the results of work are appropriated operate to enact relations of power and inequality. These relations are produced and reproduced through a systematic process in which the energies of the have-nots are continuously expended to maintain and augment the power, status, and wealth of the haves.

Many writers have cogently argued that the Marxist concept of exploitation is too narrow to encompass all forms of domination and oppression.[69] In particular, the Marxist concept of class leaves important phenomena of sexual and racial oppression unexplained. Does this mean that sexual and racial oppression are nonexploitative, and that we should reserve wholly distinct categories for these oppressions? Or can the concept of exploitation be broadened to include other ways in which the labor and energy expenditure of one group benefits another, and reproduces a relation of domination between them?

Feminists have had little difficulty showing that women's oppression consists partly in a systematic and unreciprocated transfer of powers from women to men. Women's oppression consists not merely in an inequality of status, power, and wealth resulting from men's excluding them from privileged activities. The freedom, power, status, and self-realization of men is possible precisely because women work for them. Gender exploitation has two aspects, transfer of the fruits of material labor to men and transfer of nurturing and sexual energies to women.

Christine Delphy[70], for example, describes marriage as a class relation in which women's labor benefits men without comparable remuneration. She makes it clear that the exploitation consists not in the sort of work that women do in the home, for this might include various kinds of tasks, but in the fact that they perform tasks for someone on whom they are dependent. Thus, for example, in most systems of agricultural production in the world, men take to market the goods women have produced, and more often than not men receive the status and often the entire income from this labor.

With the concept of sex-affective production, Ann Ferguson[71]; identifies another form of the transference of women's energies to men. Women provide men and children with emotional care and provide men with sexual satisfaction,

---

[68] *Op cit.*, note 65, pp. 44–49.
[69] A Giddens, *A Contemporary Critique of Historical Materialism* (1981), p. 42
[70] *Close To Home* (1984)
[71] *Blood At The Root* (1989), ch 4.

and as a group receive relatively little of either from men[72]. The gender socialization of women makes us tend to be more attentive to interactive dynamics than
men, and makes women good at providing empathy and support for people's
feelings and at smoothing over interactive tensions. Both men and women look to
women as nurturers of their personal lives, and women frequently complain that
when they look to men for emotional support they do not receive it[73]. The norms
of heterosexuality, moreover, are oriented around male pleasure, and consequently many women receive little satisfaction from their sexual interaction with
men[74].

Most feminist theories of gender exploitation have concentrated on the institutional structure of the patriarchal family. Recently, however, feminists have
begun to explore relations of gender exploitation enacted in the contemporary
workplace and through the state. Carol Brown argues that as men have removed
themselves from responsibility for children, many women have become dependent
on the state for subsistence as they continue to bear nearly total responsibility for
childrearing.[75] This creates a new system of the exploitation of women's domestic
labor mediated by state institutions, which she calls public patriarchy.

In twentieth-century capitalist economies the workplaces that women have
been entering in increasing numbers serve as another important site of gender
exploitation. David Alexander[76] argues that typically feminine jobs involve gender-based tasks requiring sexual labor, nurturing, caring for others' bodies, or
smoothing over workplace tensions. In these ways women's energies are expended
in jobs that enhance the status of, please, or comfort others, usually men; and
these gender-based labors of waitresses, clerical workers, nurses, and other
caretakers often go unnoticed and undercompensated.

To summarize, women are exploited in the Marxist sense to the degree that
they are wage workers. Some have argued that women's domestic labor also
represents a form of capitalist class exploitation insofar as it is labor covered by
the wages a family receives. As a group, however, women undergo specific forms
of gender exploitation in which their energies and power are expended, often
unnoticed and unacknowledged, usually to benefit men by releasing them for
more important and creative work, enhancing their status or the environment
around them, or providing them with sexual or emotional service.

Race is a structure of oppression at least as basic as class or gender. Are there,
then, racially specific forms of exploitation? There is no doubt that racialized
groups in the United States, especially Blacks and Latinos, are oppressed through
capitalist superexploitation resulting from a segmented labor market that tends to
reserve skilled, high-paying, unionized jobs for whites. There is wide disagreement
about whether such superexploitation benefits whites as a group or only benefits
the capitalist class[77], and I do not intend to enter into that dispute here.

However one answers the question about capitalist superexploitation of
racialized groups, is it possible to conceptualize a form of exploitation that is
racially specific on analogy with the gender-specific forms just discussed? I suggest
that the category of *menial* labor might supply a means for such conceptualization. In its derivation "menial" designates the labor of servants. Wherever there is
racism, there is the assumption, more or less enforced, that members of the
oppressed racial groups are or ought to be servants of those, or some of those, in
the privileged group. In most white racist societies this means that many white
people have dark- or yellow-skinned domestic servants, and in the United States

[72] *Sexism, Racism and Oppression* (1984), pp. 142–148.
[73] B. Easton (1978) 39 Socialist Review 11
[74] R. Gottlieb (1984) 16 Rev. of Radical Political Economy 143
[75] E. Boris and P. Bardaglio in I. Diamond (ed) *Families, Politics and Public Policy*
[76] D. Alexander (1987) (PhD dissertation).
[77] M. Reich, *Racial Inequality* (1981).

today there remains significant racial structuring of private household service. But in the United States today much service labor has gone public: anyone who goes to a good hotel or a good restaurant can have servants. Servants often attend the daily—and nightly—activities of business executives, government officials, and other high-status professionals. In our society there remains strong cultural pressure to fill servant jobs—bellhop, porter, chambermaid, busboy, and so on—with Black and Latino workers. These jobs entail a transfer of energies whereby the servers enhance the status of the served.

Menial labor usually refers not only to service, however, but also to any servile, unskilled, low-paying work lacking in autonomy, in which a person is subject to taking orders from many people. Menial work tends to be auxiliary work, instrumental to the work of others, where those others receive primary recognition for doing the job. Laborers on a construction site, for example, are at the beck and call of welders, electricians, carpenters, and other skilled workers, who receive recognition for the job done. In the United States explicit racial discrimination once reserved menial work for Blacks, Chicanos, American Indians, and Chinese, and menial work still tends to be linked to Black and Latino workers[78]. I offer this category of menial labor as a form of racially specific exploitation, as a provisional category in need of exploration.

The injustice of exploitation is most frequently understood on a distributive model. For example, though he does not offer an explicit definition of the concept, by "exploitation" Bruce Ackerman seems to mean a seriously unequal distribution of wealth, income, and other resources that is group based and structurally persistent[79]. John Roemer's definition of exploitation is narrower and more rigorous: "An agent is exploited when the amount of labor embodied in *any* bundle of goods he could receive, in a feasible distribution of society's net product, is less than the labor he expended"[80]. This definition too turns the conceptual focus from institutional relations and processes to distributive outcomes.

Jeffrey Reiman argues that such a distributive understanding of exploitation reduces the injustice of class processes to a function of the inequality of the productive assets classes own. This misses, according to Reiman, the relationship of force between capitalists and workers, the fact that the unequal exchange in question occurs within coercive structures that give workers few options[81]. The injustice of exploitation consists in social processes that bring about a transfer of energies from one group to another to produce unequal distributions, and in the way in which social institutions enable a few to accumulate while they constrain many more. The injustices of exploitation cannot be eliminated by redistribution of goods, for as long as institutionalized practices and structural relations remain unaltered, the process of transfer will re-create an unequal distribution of benefits. Bringing about justice where there is exploitation requires re-organization of institutions and practices of decisionmaking, alteration of the division of labor, and similar measures of institutional, structural, and cultural change.

*Marginalization*

Increasingly in the United States racial oppression occurs in the form of marginalization rather than exploitation. Marginals are people the system of labor cannot or will not use. Not only in Third World capitalist countries, but also in most Western capitalist societies, there is a growing underclass of people permanently confined to lives of social marginality, most of whom are racially

---

[78] A. Symanski (1983) 17 Rev. of Radical Political Economy 106.
[79] *Social Justice and the Liberal State* (1980), ch. 8.
[80] *Op cit*, note 65, p. 122.
[81] J. Reiman, 16 Phil and Public Affairs 3; *cf* A. Buchanan, *op cit*, note 66, pp. 44–49

marked—Blacks or Indians in Latin America, and Blacks, East Indians, Eastern Europeans, or North Africans in Europe.

Marginalization is by no means the fate only of racially marked groups, however. In the United States a shamefully large proportion of the population is marginal: old people, and increasingly people who are not very old but get laid off from their jobs and cannot find new work; young people, especially Black or Latino, who cannot find first or second jobs; many single mothers and their children; other people involuntarily unemployed; many mentally and physically disabled people; American Indians, especially those on reservations.

Marginalization is perhaps the most dangerous form of oppression. A whole category of people is expelled from useful participation in social life and thus potentially subjected to severe material deprivation and even extermination. The material deprivation marginalization often causes is certainly unjust, especially in a society where others have plenty. Contemporary advanced capitalist societies have in principle acknowledged the injustice of material deprivation caused by marginalization, and have taken some steps to address it by providing welfare payments and services. The continuance of this welfare state is by no means assured, and in most welfare state societies, especially the United States, welfare redistributions do not eliminate large-scale suffering and deprivation.

Material deprivation, which can be addressed by redistributive social policies, is not, however, the extent of the harm caused by marginalization. Two categories of injustice beyond distribution are associated with marginality in advanced capitalist societies. First, the provision of welfare itself produces new injustice by depriving those dependent on it of rights and freedoms that others have. Second, even when material deprivation is somewhat mitigated by the welfare state, marginalization is unjust because it blocks the opportunity to exercise capacities in socially defined and recognized ways. I shall explicate each of these in turn.

Liberalism has traditionally asserted the right of all rational autonomous agents to equal citizenship. Early bourgeois liberalism explicitly excluded from citizenship all those whose reason was questionable or not fully developed, and all those not independent[82]. Thus poor people, women, the mad and the feeble-minded, and children were explicitly excluded from citizenship, and many of these were housed in institutions modeled on the modern prison: poorhouses, insane asylums, schools.

Today the exclusion of dependent persons from equal citizenship rights is only barely hidden beneath the surface. Because they depend on bureaucratic institutions for support or services, the old, the poor, and the mentally or physically disabled are subject to patronizing, punitive, demeaning, and arbitrary treatment by the policies and people associated with welfare bureaucracies. Being a dependent in our society implies being legitimately subject to the often arbitrary and invasive authority of social service providers and other public and private administrators, who enforce rules with which the marginal must comply, and otherwise exercise power over the conditions of their lives. In meeting needs of the marginalized, often with the aid of social scientific disciplines, welfare agencies also construct the needs themselves. Medical and social service professionals know what is good for those they serve, and the marginals and dependents themselves do not have the right to claim to know what is good for them[83]. Dependency in our society thus implies, as it has in all liberal societies, a sufficient warrant to suspend basic rights to privacy, respect, and individual choice.

Although dependency produces conditions of injustice in our society, dependency in itself need not be oppressive. One cannot imagine a society in which some people would not need to be dependent on others at least some of the time: children, sick people, women recovering from childbirth, old people who have

---

[82]  C. Pateman, *The Sexual Contract* (1988), ch. 3
[83]  See N. Fraser (1987) 2 Hypatia 103.

become frail, depressed or otherwise emotionally needy persons, have the moral right to depend on others for subsistence and support.

An important contribution of feminist moral theory has been to question the deeply held assumption that moral agency and full citizenship require that a person be autonomous and independent. Feminists have exposed this assumption as inappropriately individualistic and derived from a specifically male experience of social relations, which values competition and solitary achievement[84]. Female experience of social relations, arising both from women's typical domestic care responsibilities and from the kinds of paid work that many women do, tends to recognize dependence as a basic human condition[85]. Whereas on the autonomy model a just society would as much as possible give people the opportunity to be independent, the feminist model envisions justice as according respect and participation in decisionmaking to those who are dependent as well as to those who are independent[86]. Dependency should not be a reason to be deprived of choice and respect, and much of the oppression many marginals experience would be lessened if a less individualistic model of rights prevailed.

Marginalization does not cease to be oppressive when one has shelter and food. Many old people, for example, have sufficient means to live comfortably but remain oppressed in their marginal status. Even if marginals were provided a comfortable material life within institutions that respected their freedom and dignity, injustices of marginality would remain in the form of uselessness, boredom, and lack of self-respect. Most of our society's productive and recognized activities take place in contexts of organized social co-operation, and social structures and processes that close persons out of participation in such social cooperation are unjust. Thus while marginalization definitely entails serious issues of distributive justice, it also involves the deprivation of cultural, practical, and institutionalized conditions for exercising capacities in a context of recognition and interaction.

The fact of marginalization raises basic structural issues of justice, in particular concerning the appropriateness of a connection between participation in productive activities of social co-operation, on the one hand, and access to the means of consumption, on the other. As marginalization is increasing, with no sign of abatement, some social policy analysts have introduced the idea of a "social wage" as a guaranteed socially provided income not tied to the wage system. Restructuring of productive activity to address a right of participation, however, implies organizing some socially productive activity outside of the wage system[87], through public works or self-employed collectives.

*Powerlessness*

As I have indicated, the Marxist idea of class is important because it helps reveal the structure of exploitation: that some people have their power and wealth because they profit from the labor of others. For this reason I reject the claim some make that a traditional class exploitation model fails to capture the structure of contemporary society. It remains the case that the labor of most people in the society augments the power of relatively few. Despite their differences from nonprofessional workers, most professional workers are still not members of the capitalist class. Professional labor either involves exploitative transfers to capitalists or supplies important conditions for such transfers. Professional workers

---

[84] See C. Gilligan, *In A Different Voice* (1982).
[85] *Cf* N. Hartsock, *Money, Sex and Power* (1983), ch. 10.
[86] "A Non-Contractual Society" in (eds.) M. Hanen and K. Nielsen, *Science, Morality, and Feminist Theory* (1987).
[87] See C. Offe, *Disorganized Capitalism* (1985), pp. 95–100.

are in an ambiguous class position, it is true, because, they also benefit from the exploitation of nonprofessional workers.

While it is false to claim that a division between capitalist and working classes no longer describes our society, it is also false to say that class relations have remained unaltered since the nineteenth century. An adequate conception of oppression cannot ignore the experience of social division reflected in the collo-quial distinction between the "middle class" and the "working class," a division structured by the social division of labor between professionals and nonprofes-sionals. Professional are privileged in relation to nonprofessionals, by virtue of their position in the division of labor and the status it carries. Nonprofessionals suffer a form of oppression in addition to exploitation, which I call powerlessness.

In the United States, as in other advanced capitalist countries, most workplaces are not organized democratically, direct participation in public policy decisions is rare, and policy implementation is for the most part hierarchical, imposing rules on bureaucrats and citizens. Thus most people in these societies do not regularly participate in making decisions that affect the conditions of their lives and actions, and in this sense most people lack significant power. At the same time, domination in modern society is enacted through the widely dispersed powers of many agents mediating the decisions of others. To that extent many people have some power in relation to others, even though they lack the power to decide policies or results. The powerless are those who lack authority or power even in this mediated sense, those over whom power is exercised without their exercising it; the powerless are situated so that they must take orders and rarely have the right to give them. Powerlessness also designates a position in the division of labor and the concomitant social position that allows persons little opportunity to develop and exercise skills. The powerless have little or no work autonomy, exercise little creativity or judgment in their work, have no technical expertise or authority, express themselves awkwardly, especially in public or bureaucratic settings, and do not command respect. Powerlessness names the oppressive situations Sennett and Cobb describe in their famous study of working-class men.[88]

This powerless status is perhaps best described negatively: the powerless lack the authority, status, and sense of self that professionals tend to have. The status privilege of professionals has three aspects, the lack of which produces oppression for nonprofessionals.

First, acquiring and practicing a profession has an expansive, progressive character. Being professional usually requires a college education and the acquisition of a specialized knowledge that entails working with symbols and concepts. Professionals experience progress first in acquiring the expertise, and then in the course of professional advancement and rise in status. The life of the nonprofessional by comparison is powerless in the sense that it lacks this orien-tation toward the progressive development of capacities and avenues for recognition.

Second, while many professionals have supervisors and cannot directly influ-ence many decisions or the actions of many people, most nevertheless have considerable day-to-day work autonomy. Professionals usually have some authority over others, moreover—either over workers they supervise, or over auxiliaries, or over clients. Nonprofessionals, on the other hand, lack autonomy, and in both their working and their consumer-client lives often stand under the authority of professionals.

Though based on a division of labor between "mental" and "manual" work, the distinction between "middle class" and "working class" designates a division not only in working life, but also in nearly all aspects of social life. Professionals and nonprofessionals belong to different cultures in the United States. The two

---

[88]  *The Hidden Injuries of Class* (1972).

groups tend to live in segregated neighborhoods or even different towns, a process itself mediated by planners, zoning officials, and real estate people. The groups tend to have different tastes in food, decor, clothes, music, and vacations, and often different health and educational needs. Members of each group socialize for the most part with others in the same status group. While there is some intergroup mobility between generations, for the most part the children of professionals become professionals and the children of nonprofessionals do not.

Thus, third, the privileges of the professional extend beyond the workplace to a whole way of life. I call this way of life "respectability." To treat people with respect is to be prepared to listen to what they have to say or to do what they request because they have some authority, expertise, or influence. The norms of respectability in our society are associated specifically with professional culture. Professional dress, speech, tastes, demeanor, all connote respectability. Generally professionals expect and receive respect from others. In restaurants, banks, hotels, real estate offices, and many other such public places, as well as in the media, professionals typically receive more respectful treatment than nonprofessionals. For this reason nonprofessionals seeking a loan or a job, or to buy a house or a car, will often try to look "professional" and "respectable" in those settings.

The privilege of this professional respectability appears starkly in the dynamics of racism and sexism. In daily interchange women and men of color must prove their respectability. At first they are often not treated by strangers with respectful distance or deference. Once people discover that this woman or that Puerto Rican man is a college teacher or a business executive, however, they often behave more respectfully toward her or him. Working-class white men, on the other hand, are often treated with respect until their working-class status is revealed.

I have discussed several injustices associated with powerlessness: inhibition in the development of one's capacities, lack of decisionmaking power in one's working life, and exposure to disrespectful treatment because of the status one occupies. These injustices have distributional consequences, but are more fundamentally matters of the division of labor. The oppression of powerlessness brings into question the division of labor basic to all industrial societies: the social division between those who plan and those who execute.

### Cultural Imperialism

Exploitation, marginalization, and powerlessness all refer to relations of power and oppression that occur by virtue of the social division of labor—who works for whom, who does not work, and how the content of work defines one institutional position relative to others. These three categories refer to structural and institutional relations that delimit people's material lives, including but not restricted to the resources they have access to and the concrete opportunities they have or do not have to develop and exercise their capacities. These kinds of oppression are a matter of concrete power in relation to others—of who benefits from whom, and who is dispensable.

Recent theorists of movements of group liberation, notably feminist and Black liberation theorists, have also given prominence to a rather different form of oppression, which following Lugones and Spelman[89] I shall call cultural imperialism. To experience cultural imperialism means to experience how the dominant meanings of a society render the particular perspective of one's own group invisible at the same time as they stereotype one's group and mark it out as the Other.

Cultural imperialism involves the universalization of a dominant group's experience and culture, and its establishment as the norm. Some groups have

---

[89]  6 Women's Studies International Forum 573 (1983).

exclusive or primary access to what Nancy Fraser[90] calls the means of interpretation and communication in a society. As a consequence, the dominant cultural products of the society, that is, those most widely disseminated, express the experience, values, goals, and achievements of these groups. Often without noticing they do so, the dominant groups project their own experience as representative of humanity as such. Cultural products also express the dominant group's perspective on and interpretation of events and elements in the society, including other groups in the society, insofar as they attain cultural status at all.

An encounter with other groups, however, can challenge the dominant group's claim to universality. The dominant group reinforces its position by bringing the other groups under the measure of its dominant norms. Consequently, the difference of women from men, American Indians or Africans from Europeans, Jews from Christians, homosexuals from heterosexuals, workers from professionals, becomes reconstructed largely as deviance and inferiority. Since only the dominant group's cultural expressions receive wide dissemination, their cultural expressions become the normal, or the universal, and thereby the unremarkable. Given the normality of its own cultural expressions and identity, the dominant group constructs the differences which some groups exhibit as lack and negation. These groups become marked as Other.

The culturally dominated undergo a paradoxical oppression, in that they are both marked out by stereotypes and at the same time rendered invisible. As remarkable, deviant beings, the culturally imperialized are stamped with an essence. The stereotypes confine them to a nature which is often attached in some way to their bodies, and which thus cannot easily be denied. These stereotypes so permeate the society that they are not noticed as contestable. Just as everyone knows that the earth goes around the sun, so everyone knows that gay people are promiscuous, that Indians are alcoholics, and that women are good with children. White males, on the other hand, insofar as they escape group marking, can be individuals.

Those living under cultural imperialism find themselves defined from the outside, positioned, placed, by a network of dominant meanings they experience as arising from elsewhere, from those with whom they do not identify and who do not identify with them. Consequently, the dominant culture's stereotyped and inferiorized images of the group must be internalized by group members at least to the extent that they are forced to react to behavior of others influenced by those images. This creates for the culturally oppressed the experience that W.E.B. Du Bois called "double consciousness"—"'this sense of always looking at one's self through the eyes of others, of measuring one's soul by the tape of a world that looks on in amused contempt and pity"[91]. Double consciousness arises when the oppressed subject refuses to coincide with these devalued, objectified, stereotyped visions of herself or himself. While the subject desires recognition as human, capable of activity, full of hope and possibility, she receives from the dominant culture only the judgment that she is different, marked, or inferior.

The group defined by the dominant culture as deviant, as a stereotyped Other, is culturally different from the dominant group, because the status of Otherness creates specific experiences not shared by the dominant group, and because culturally oppressed groups also are often socially segregated and occupy specific positions in the social division of labor. Members of such groups express their specific group experiences and interpretations of the world to one another, developing and perpetuating their own culture. Double consciousness, then, occurs because one finds one's being defined by two cultures: a dominant and a subordinate culture. Because they can affirm and recognize one another as

---

[90]  2 Hypatia 103 (1987).
[91]  *The Souls of Black Folk* (1969), p. 45.

sharing similar experiences and perspectives on social life, people in culturally imperialized groups can often maintain a sense of positive subjectivity.

Cultural imperialism involves the paradox of experiencing oneself as invisible at the same time that one is marked out as different. The invisibility comes about when dominant groups fail to recognize the perspective embodied in their cultural expressions as a perspective. These dominant cultural expressions often simply have little place for the experience of other groups, at most only mentioning or referring to them in stereotyped or marginalized ways. This, then, is the injustice of cultural imperialism: that the oppressed group's own experience and inter-pretation of social life finds little expression that touches the dominant culture, while that same culture imposes on the oppressed group its experience and interpretation of social life.

[...]

## *Violence*

Finally, many groups suffer the oppression of systematic volence. Members of some groups live with the knowledge that they must fear random, unprovoked attacks on their persons or property, which have no motive but to damage, humiliate, or destroy the person. In American society women, Blacks, Asians, Arabs, gay men, and lesbians live under such threats of violence, and in at least some regions Jews, Puerto Ricans, Chicanos, and other Spanish-speaking Americans must fear such violence as well. Physical violence against these groups is shockingly frequent. Rape Crisis Center networks estimate that more than one-third of all American women experience an attempted or successful sexual assault in their lifetimes. Manning Marable[92] catalogues a large number of incidents of racist violence and terror against blacks in the United States between 1980 and 1982. He cites dozens of incidents of the severe beating, killing, or rape of Blacks by police officers on duty, in which the police involved were acquitted of any wrongdoing. In 1981, moreover, there were at least five hundred documented cases of random white teenage violence against Blacks. Violence against gay men and lesbians is not only common, but has been increasing in the last five years. While the frequency of physical attack on members of these and other racially or sexually marked groups is very disturbing, I also include in this category less severe incidents of harrassment, intimidation, or ridicule simply for the purpose of degrading, humiliating, or stigmatizing group members.

Given the frequency of such violence in our society, why are theories of justice usually silent about it? I think the reason is that theorists do not typically take such incidents of violence and harrassment as matters of social injustice. No moral theorist would deny that such acts are very wrong. But unless all immor-alities are injustices, they might wonder, why should such acts be interpreted as symptoms of social injustice? Acts of violence or petty harrassment are committed by particular individuals, often extremists, deviants, or the mentally unsound. How then can they be said to involve the sorts of institutional issues I have said are properly the subject of justice?

What makes violence a face of oppression is less the particular acts themselves, though these are often utterly horrible, than the social context surrounding them, which makes them possible and even acceptable. What makes violence a phe-nomenon of social injustice, and not merely an individual moral wrong, is its systemic character, its existence as a social practice.

Violence is systemic because it is directed at members of a group simply because they are members of that group. Any woman, for example, has a reason to fear rape. Regardless of what a Black man has done to escape the oppressions of marginality or powerlessness, he lives knowing he is subject to attack or

[92] *Race, Reform and Rebellim* (1984), pp. 238–241.

harrassment. The oppression of violence consists not only in direct victimization, but in the daily knowledge shared by all members of oppressed groups that they are *liable* to violation, solely on account of their group identity. Just living under such a threat of attack on oneself or family or friends deprives the oppressed of freedom and dignity, and needlessly expends their energy.

Violence is a social practice. It is a social given that everyone knows happends and will happen again. It is always at the horizon of social imagination, even for those who do not perpetrate it. According to the prevailing social logic, some circumstances make such violence more "called for" than others. The idea of rape will occur to many men who pick up a hitch-hiking woman; the idea of hounding or teasing a gay man on their dorm floor will occur to many straight male college students. Often several persons inflict the violence together, especially in all-male groupings. Sometimes violators set out looking for people to beat up, rape, or taunt. This rule-bound, social, and often premeditated character makes violence against groups a social practice.

Group violence approaches legitimacy, moreover, in the sense that it is tolerated. Often third parties find it unsurprising because it happens frequently and lies as a constant possibility at the horizon of the social imagination. Even when they are caught, those who perpetrate acts of group-directed violence or harrassment often receive light or no punishment. To that extent society renders their acts acceptable.

An important aspect of random, systemic violence is its irrationality. Xenophobic violence differs from the violence of states or ruling-class repression. Repressive violence has a rational, albeit evil, motive: rulers use it as a coercive tool to maintain their power. Many accounts of racist, sexist, or homophobic violence attempt to explain its motivation as a desire to maintain group privilege or domination. I do not doubt that fear of violence often functions to keep oppressed groups subordinate, but I do not think xenophobic violence is rationally motivated in the way that, for example, violence against strikers is.

On the contrary, the violation of rape, beating, killing, and harrassment of women, people of color, gays, and other marked groups is motivated by fear or hatred of those groups. Sometimes the motive may be a simple will to power, to victimize those marked as vulnerable by the very social fact that they are subject to violence. If so, this motive is secondary in the sense that it depends on a social practice of group violence. Violence-causing fear or hatred of the other at least partly involves insecurities on the part of the violators; its irrationality suggests that unconscious processes are at work. [. . .]

Cultural imperialism, moreover, itself intersects with violence. The culturally imperialized may reject the dominant meanings and attempt to assert their own subjectivity, or the fact of their cultural difference may put the lie to the dominant culture's implicit claim to universality. The dissonance generated by such a challenge to the hegemonic cultural meanings can also be a source of irrational violence.

Violence is a form of injustice that a distributive understanding of justice seems ill equipped to capture. This may be why contemporary discussions of justice rarely mention it. I have argued that group-directed violence is institutionalized and systemic. To the degree that institutions and social practices encourage, tolerate, or enable the perpetration of violence against members of specific groups, those institutions and practices are unjust and should be reformed. Such reform may require the redistribution of resources or positions, but in large part can come only through a change in cultural images, stereotypes, and the mundane reproduction of relations of dominance and aversion in the gestures of everyday life.                                                                    [pp. 48–63]

## S. M. OKIN
### Justice as Fairness: For Whom?
(1989)[93]

I turn to Rawls's theory of justice as fairness, to examine not only what it explicitly says and does not say, but also what it *implies*, on the subjects of gender, women, and the family.

There is strikingly little indication, throughout most of *A Theory of Justice*, that the modern liberal society to which the principles of justice are to be applied is deeply and pervasively gender-structured. Thus an ambiguity runs throughout the work, which is continually noticeable to anyone reading it from a feminist perspective. On the one hand, as I shall argue, a consistent and wholehearted application of Rawls's liberal principles of justice can lead us to challenge fundamentally the gender system of our society. On the other hand, in his own account of his theory, this challenge is barely hinted at, much less developed. After critiquing Rawl's theory for its neglect of gender, I shall ask two related questions: What effects does a feminist reading of Rawls have on some of his fundamental ideas [. . .]; and what undeveloped potential does the theory have for feminist critique, and in particular for our attempts to answer the question, Can justice co-exist with gender?

Central to Rawls's theory of justice is a construct [. . .]. Rawls argues that the principles of justice that should regulate the basic institutions of society are those that would be arrived at by persons reasoning in what is termed "the original position." His specifications for the original position are that "the parties" who deliberate there are rational and mutually disinterested, and that while no limits are placed on the general information available to them, a "veil of ignorance" conceals from them all knowledge of their individual characteristics and their social position. Though the theory is presented as a contract theory, it is so only in an odd and metaphoric sense, since "no one knows his situation in society nor his natural assets, and therefore no one is in a position to tailor principles to his advantage." Thus they have "no basis for bargaining in the usual sense." This is how, Rawls explains, "the arbitrariness of the world ... [is] corrected for," in order that the principles arrived at will be fair. Indeed, since no one knows who he is, all think identically and the standpoint of any one party represents that of all. Thus the principles of justice are arrived at unanimously. [. . .] First, let us see how the theory treats women, gender, and the family.

### Justice for All?

Rawls, like almost all political theorists until very recently, employs in *A Theory of Justice* supposedly generic male terms of reference.[94] *Men, mankind, he*, and *his* are interspersed with gender-neutral terms of reference such as *individual* and *moral person*. Examples of intergenerational concern are worded in terms of "fathers" and "sons," and the difference principle is said to correspond to "the principle of fraternity."[95] This linguistic usage would perhaps be less significant if it were not for the fact that Rawls self-consciously subscribes to a long tradition of moral and political philosophy that has used in its arguments either such

---

[93] [From Susan Moller Okin, *Justice, Gender and the Family* (1989).]

[94] He no longer does this in more recent writings, where the language is gender-neutral. See, for example, "Kantian Constructivism in Moral Theory," *The Journal of Philosophy* 77, No. 9 (1980); "Justice As Fairness: Political Not Metaphysical," *Philosophy and Public Affairs* 14, No. 3 (1985). As will become apparent, this gender neutrality is to a large extent false, since Rawls does not confront the justice or injustice of gender, and the gendered family in particular.

[95] Rawls, *Theory*, pp. 105–6, 208–9, 288–89.

"generic" male terms or more inclusive terms of reference ("human beings," "persons," "all rational beings as such"), only to exclude women from the scope of its conclusions. [...] There is a blindness to the sexism of the tradition in which Rawls is a participant, which tends to render his terms of reference more ambiguous than they might otherwise be. A feminist reader finds it difficult not to keep asking, Does this theory of justice apply to women?

This question is not answered in the important passages listing the characteristics that persons in the original position are not to know about themselves, in order to formulate impartial principles of justice. In a subsequent article, Rawls has made it clear that sex *is* one of those morally irrelevant contingencies that are hidden by the veil of ignorance.[96] But throughout A *Theory of Justice*, while the list of things unknown by a person in the original position includes "his place in society, his class position or social status, ... his fortune in the distribution of natural assets and abilities, his intelligence and strength, and the like, ... his conception of the good, the particulars of his rational plan of life, even the special features of his psychology,"[97] "his" sex is not mentioned. Since the parties also "know the general facts about human society,"[98] presumably including the fact that it is gender-structured both by custom and still in some respects by law, one might think that whether or not they knew their sex might matter enough to be mentioned. [...]

The ambiguity is exacerbated by the statement that those free and equal moral persons in the original position who formulate the principles of justice are to be thought of not as "single individuals" but as "heads of families" or "representatives of families."[99] Rawls says that it is not necessary to think of the parties as heads of families, but that he will generally do so. The reason he does this, he explains, is to ensure that each person in the original position cares about the well-being of some persons in the next generation. These "ties of sentiment" between generations, which Rawls regards as important for the establishment of intergenerational justice—his just savings principle—, would otherwise constitute a problem because of the general assumption that the parties in the original position are mutually disinterested. In spite of the ties of sentiment *within* families, then, "as representatives of families their interests are opposed as the circumstances of justice imply."[1]

The head of a family need not necessarily, of course, be a man. Certainly in the United States, at least, there has been a striking growth in the proportion of female-headed households during the last several decades. But the very fact that, in common usage, the term "female-headed household" is used *only* in reference to households without resident adult males implies the assumption that any present male takes precedence over a female as the household or family head. Rawls does nothing to contest this impression when he says of those in the original position that "imagining themselves to be fathers, say, they are to ascertain how much they should set aside for their sons by noting what they would believe themselves entitled to claim of their fathers."[2] He makes the "heads of families" assumption only in order to address the problem of justice between generations, and presumably does not intend it to be a sexist assumption. Nevertheless, he is thereby effectively trapped into the public/domestic dichotomy

---

[96] Rawls, "Fairness to Goodness," *Philosophical Review* 84 (1975): 537. He says: "That we have one conception of the good rather than another is not relevant from a moral standpoint. In acquiring it we are influenced by the same sort of contingencies that lead us to rule out a knowledge of our sex and class."

[97] Rawls, *Theory*, p. 137; see also p. 12.

[98] *ibid.*, p. 137. Numerous commentators on *Theory* have made the objection that "the general facts about human society" are often issues of great contention.

[99] *ibid.*, pp. 128, 146.

[1] *ibid.*, p. 128; see also p. 292.

[2] *ibid.*, p. 289.

and, with it, the conventional mode of thinking that life within the family and relations between the sexes are not properly regarded as part of the subject matter of a theory of social justice.

Let me here point out that Rawls, for good reason, states at the outset of his theory that the family *is* part of the subject matter of a theory of social justice. "For us" he says, "the primary subject of justice is the basic structure of society, or more exactly, the way in which the major social institutions distribute fundamental rights and duties and determine the division of advantages from social co-operation." The political constitution and the principal economic and social arrangements are basic because "taken together as one scheme, [they] define men's rights and duties and influence their life prospects, what they can expect to be and how well they can hope to do. The basic structure is the primary subject of justice *because its effects are so profound and present from the start*" (emphasis added).[3] Rawls specifies "the monogamous family" as an example of such major social institutions, together with the political constitution, the legal protection of essential freedoms, competitive markets, and private property.[4] Although this initial inclusion of the family as a basic social institution to which the principles of justice should apply is surprising in the light of the history of liberal thought, with its dichotomy between domestic and public spheres, it is necessary, given Rawls's stated criteria for inclusion in the basic structure. It would scarcely be possible to deny that different family structures, and different distributions of rights and duties within families, affect men's "life prospects, what they can expect to be and how well they can hope to do," and even more difficult to deny their effects on the life prospects of women. There is no doubt, then, that in Rawls's initial definition of the sphere of social justice, the family is included and the public/domestic dichotomy momentarily cast in doubt. However, the family is to a large extent ignored, though assumed, in the rest of the theory.

### The Barely Visible Family

In Part 1 of *A Theory of Justice*, Rawls derives and defends the two principles of justice—the principle of equal basic liberty, and the "difference principle" combined with the requirement of fair equality of opportunity. [. . .]

In Part 2, Rawls discusses at some length the application of his principles of justice to almost all the institutions of the basic social structure that are set out at the beginning of the book. The legal protection of liberty of thought and conscience is defended, as are democratic constitutional institutions and procedures; competitive markets feature prominently in the discussion of the just distribution of income; the issue of the private or public ownership of the means of production is explicitly left open, since Rawls argues that his principles of justice might be compatible with certain versions of either.[5] But throughout all these discussions, the issue of whether the monogamous family, in either its traditional or any other form, is a just social institution, is never raised. When Rawls announces that "the sketch of the system of institutions that satisfy the two principles of justice is now complete,"[6] he has paid no attention at all to the internal justice of the family. In fact, apart from passing references, the family appears in *A Theory of Justice* in only three contexts: as the link between generations necessary for the just savings principle; as an obstacle to fair equality of opportunity (on account of the inequalities among families); and as the first school of moral development. It is in

---

[3] *ibid.*, p. 7.
[4] *ibid.*, pp. 7, 462–63. Later, he takes a more agnostic position about the compatibility of his principles of justice with socialist as well as private property economies (sec. 42).
[5] For a good discussion of Rawls's view of just property institutions, see Richard Krouse and Michael McPherson, "Capitalism, 'Property-Owning Democracy,' and the Welfare State," in *Democracy and the Welfare State*, ed. Amy Gutmann (1988).
[6] Rawls, *Theory*, p. 303.

the third of these contexts that Rawls first specifically mentions the family as a just institution—not, however, to *consider* whether the family "in some form" is a just institution but to *assume* it.[7]

Clearly, however, by Rawls's own reasoning about the social justice of major social institutions, this assumption is unwarranted. [...] The central tenet of the theory, after all, is that justice as fairness characterizes institutions whose members could hypothetically have agreed to their structure and rules from a position in which they did not know which place in the structure they were to occupy. The argument of the book is designed to show that the two principles of justice are those that individuals in such a hypothetical situation would agree upon. But since those in the original position are the heads or representatives of families, they are not in a position to determine questions of justice within families. As Jane English has pointed out, "By making the parties in the original position heads of families rather than individuals, Rawls makes the family opaque to claims of justice."[8] As far as children are concerned, Rawls makes an argument from paternalism for their temporary inequality and restricted liberty.[9] (This, while it may suffice in basically sound, benevolent families, is of no use or comfort in abusive or neglectful situations, where Rawls's principles would seem to require that children be protected through the intervention of outside authorities.) But wives (or whichever adult member[s] of a family are *not* its "head") go completely unrepresented in the original position. If families are just, as Rawls later assumes, then they must become just in some different way (unspecified by him) from other institutions, for it is impossible to see how the viewpoint of their less advantaged members ever gets to be heard.

[...] The "heads of families" assumption, far from being neutral or innocent, has the effect of banishing a large sphere of human life—and a particularly large sphere of most women's lives—from the scope of the theory.

During the discussion of the distribution of wealth, for example, it seems to be assumed that all the parties in the original position expect, once the veil of ignorance is removed, to be participants in the paid labor market. Distributive shares are discussed in terms of household income, but reference to "individuals" is interspersed into this discussion as if there were no difference between the advantage or welfare of a household and that of an individual.[10] This confusion obscures the fact that wages are paid to employed members of the labor force, but that in societies characterized by gender (all current societies) a much larger proportion of women's than men's labor is unpaid and is often not even acknowledged as labor. It also obscures the fact that the resulting disparities in the earnings of men and women, and the economic dependence of women on men, are likely to affect power relations within the household, as well as access to leisure, prestige, political power, and so on, among its adult members. Any discussion of justice *within* the family would have to address these issues. [...]

Later, in Rawls's discussion of the obligations of citizens, his assumption that justice is agreed on by heads of families in the original position seems to prevent him from considering another issue of crucial importance: women's exemption from the draft. He concludes that military conscription is justifiable in the case of defense against an unjust attack on liberty, so long as institutions "try to make sure that the risks of suffering from these imposed misfortunes are more or less evenly shared by all members of society over the course of their life, and that there

---

[7]  *ibid.*, pp. 463, 490. See Deborah Kearns, "A Theory of Justice—and Love; Rawls on the Family," *Politics (Australasian Political Studies Association Journal)* 18, No. 2 (1983): 39–40, for an interesting discussion of the significance for Rawls's theory of moral development of his failure to address the justice of the family.

[8]  English, "Justice Between Generations," *Philosophical Studies* 31, No. 2 (1977): 95.

[9]  Rawls, *Theory*, pp. 208–9.

[10]  *ibid.*, pp. 99, 149.

is no avoidable *class* bias in selecting those who are called for duty" (emphasis added).[11] The complete exemption of women from this major interference with the basic liberties of equal citizenship is not even mentioned.

In spite of two explicit rejections of the justice of formal sex discrimination in Part 1, then, Rawls seems in Part 2 to be heavily influenced by his "family heads" assumption. He does not consider as part of the basic structure of society the greater economic dependence of women and the sexual division of labor within the typical family, or any of the broader social ramifications of this basic gender structure. Moreover, in Part 3, where he takes as a given the justice of the family "in some form," he does not discuss any alternative forms. Rather, he sounds very much as though he is thinking in terms of traditional, gendered family structure and roles. The family, he says, is "a small association, normally characterized by a definite hierarchy, in which each member has certain rights and duties." The family's role as moral teacher is achieved partly through parental expectations of the "virtues of a good son or a good daughter." In the family and in other associations such as schools, neighborhoods, and peer groups, Rawls continues, one learns various moral virtues and ideals, leading to those adopted in the various statuses, occupations, and family positions of later life. "The content of these ideals is given by the various conceptions of a good wife and husband, a good friend and citizen, and so on."[12] Given these unusual departures from the supposedly generic male terms of reference used throughout the book, it seems likely that Rawls means to imply that the goodness of daughters is distinct from the goodness of sons, and that of wives from that of husbands. A fairly traditional gender system seems to be assumed.

Rawls not only assumes that "the basic structure of a well-ordered society includes the family *in some form*" (emphasis added); he adds that "in a broader inquiry the institution of the family might be questioned, and other arrangements might indeed prove to be preferable."[13] But why should it require a broader inquiry than the colossal task in which *A Theory of Justice* is engaged, to raise questions about the institution and the form of the family? Surely Rawls is right in initially naming it as one of those basic social institutions that most affect the life chances of individuals and should therefore be part of the primary subject of justice. The family is not a private association like a church or a university, which vary considerably in the type and degree of commitment each expects from its members, and which one can join and leave voluntarily. For although one has some choice (albeit a highly constrained one) about marrying into a gender-structured family, one has no choice at all about being born into one. Rawls's failure to subject the structure of the family to his principles of justice is particularly serious in the light of his belief that a theory of justice must take account of "how [individuals] get to be what they are" and "cannot take their final aims and interests, their attitudes to themselves and their life, as given."[14] For the gendered family, and female parenting in particular, are clearly critical determinants in the different ways the two sexes are socialized—how men and women "get to be what they are."

If Rawls were to assume throughout the construction of his theory that all human adults are participants in what goes on behind the veil of ignorance, he would have no option but to require that the family, as a major social institution affecting the life chances of individuals, be constructed in accordance with the two principles of justice. [. . .]                                                        [pp. 89–87]

The significance of Rawls's central, brilliant idea, the original position, is that it forces one to question and consider traditions, customs, and institutions from all

---

[11] *ibid.*, pp. 380–81.
[12] *ibid.*, pp. 467, 468.
[13] *ibid.*, pp. 462–63.
[14] Rawls, "The Basic Structure as Subject," p. 160.

points of view, and ensures that the principles of justice will be acceptable to everyone, regardless of what position "he" ends up in. The critical force of the original position becomes evident when one considers that some of the most creative critiques of Rawls's theory have resulted from more radical or broad interpretations of the original position than his own. The theory, in principle, avoids both the problem of domination that is inherent in theories of justice based on traditions or shared understandings and the partiality of libertarian theory to those who are talented or fortunate. For feminist readers, however, the problem of the theory as stated by Rawls himself is encapsulated in that ambiguous "he." [. . .] Rawls [. . .] fails entirely to address the justice of the gender system, which, with its roots in the sex roles of the family and its branches extending into virtually every corner of our lives, is one of the fundamental structures of our society. If, however, we read Rawls in such a way as to take seriously both the notion that those behind the veil of ignorance do not know what sex they are and the requirement that the family and the gender system, as basic social institutions, are to be subject to scrutiny, constructive feminist criticism of these contemporary institutions follows. So, also, do hidden difficulties for the application of a Rawlsian theory of justice in a gendered society.

I shall explain each of these points in turn. But first, both the critical perspective and the incipient problems of a feminist reading of Rawls can perhaps be illuminated by a description of a cartoon I saw a few years ago. Three elderly, robed male justices are depicted, looking down with astonishment at their very pregnant bellies. One says to the others, without further elaboration: "Perhaps we'd better reconsider that decision." This illustration graphically demonstrates the importance, in thinking about justice, of a concept like Rawls's original position, which makes us adopt the positions of others—especially positions that we ourselves could never be in. It also suggests that those thinking in such a way might well conclude that more than formal legal equality of the sexes is required if justice is to be done. As we have seen in recent years, it is quite possible to enact and uphold "gender-neutral" laws concerning pregnancy, abortion, childbirth leave, and so on, that in effect discriminate against women. The United States Supreme Court decided in 1976, for example, that "an exclusion of pregnancy from a disability-benefits plan providing general coverage is not a gender-based discrimination at all."[15] One of the virtues of the cartoon is its suggestion that one's thinking on such matters is likely to be affected by the knowledge that one might become "a pregnant person." The illustration also points out the limits of what is possible, in terms of thinking ourselves into the original position, as long as we live in a gender-structured society. While the elderly male justices can, in a sense, imagine themselves as pregnant, what is a much more difficult question is whether, in order to construct principles of justice, they can imagine themselves as women. This raises the question of whether, in fact, sex *is* a morally irrelevant and contingent characteristic in a society structured by gender.

Let us first assume that sex is contingent in this way, though I shall later question this assumption. Let us suppose that it is possible, as Rawls clearly considers it to be, to hypothesize the moral thinking of representative human beings, as ignorant of their sex as of all the other things hidden by the veil of ignorance. It seems clear that, while Rawls does not do this, we must consistently take the relevant positions of both sexes into account in formulating and applying principles of justice. In particular, those in the original position must take special account of the perspective of women, since their knowledge of "the general facts about human society" must include the knowledge that women have been and continue to be the less advantaged sex in a great number of respects. In considering the basic institutions of society, they are more likely to pay special attention to the family than virtually to ignore it. Not only is it potentially the first

---

[15] *General Electric* v. *Gilbert*, 429 U.S. 125 (1976), 136.

school of social justice, but its customary unequal assignment of responsibilities and privileges to the two sexes and its socialization of children into sex roles make it, in its current form, an institution of crucial importance for the perpetuation of sex inequality.

In innumerable ways, the principles of justice that Rawls arrives at are inconsistent with a gender-structured society and with traditional family roles. The critical impact of a feminist application of Rawls's theory comes chiefly from his second principle, which requires that inequalities be both "to the greatest benefit of the least advantaged" and "attached to offices and positions open to all."[16] This means that if any roles or positions analogous to our current sex roles—including those of husband and wife, mother and father—were to survive the demands of the first requirement, the second requirement would prohibit any linkage between these roles and sex. Gender, with its ascriptive designation of positions and expectations of behavior in accordance with the inborn characteristic of sex, could no longer form a legitimate part of the social structure, whether inside or outside the family. Three illustrations will help to link this conclusion with specific major requirements that Rawls makes of a just or well-ordered society.

First, after the basic political liberties, one of the most essential liberties is "the important liberty of free choice of occupation."[17] It is not difficult to see that this liberty is compromised by the assumption and customary expectation, central to our gender system, that women take far greater responsibility for housework and child care, whether or not they also work for wages outside the home. In fact, both the assignment of these responsibilities to women—resulting in their asymmetric economic dependence on men—and the related responsibility of husbands to support their wives compromise the liberty of choice of occupation of both sexes. But the customary roles of the two sexes inhibit women's choices over the course of a lifetime far more severely than those of men; it is far easier in practice to switch from being a wage worker to occupying a domestic role than to do the reverse. While Rawls has no objection to some aspects of the division of labor, he asserts that, in a well-ordered society, "no one need be servilely dependent on others and made to choose between monotonous and routine occupations which are deadening to human thought and sensibility" and that work will be "meaningful for all."[18] These conditions are far more likely to be met in a society that does not assign family responsibilities in a way that makes women into a marginal sector of the paid work force and renders likely their economic dependence upon men. Rawls's principles of justice, then, would seem to require a radical rethinking not only of the division of labor within families but also of all the nonfamily institutions that assume it.

Second, the abolition of gender seems essential for the fulfillment of Rawls's criterion for political justice. For he argues that not only would equal formal political liberties be espoused by those in the original position, but that any inequalities in the *worth* of these liberties (for example, the effects on them of factors like poverty and ignorance) must be justified by the difference principle. Indeed, "the constitutional process should preserve the equal representation of the original position to the degree that this is practicable."[19] While Rawls discusses this requirement in the context of class differences, stating that those who devote themselves to politics should be "drawn more or less equally from all sectors of society,"[20] it is just as clearly and importantly applicable to sex differences. The equal political representation of women and men, especially if they

[16] Rawls, *Theory*, p. 302.
[17] *ibid.*, p. 274.
[18] *ibid.*, p. 529.
[19] *ibid.*, p. 222; see also pp. 202–5, 221–28.
[20] *ibid.*, p. 228.

are parents, is clearly inconsistent with our gender system. The paltry number of women in high political office is an obvious indication of this. These levels of representation of any other class constituting more than a majority of the population would surely be perceived as a sign that something is grievously wrong with the political system. But as British politician Shirley Williams recently said, until there is "a revolution in shared responsibilities for the family, in child care and in child rearing," there will not be "more than a very small number of women ... opting for a job as demanding as politics."[21]

Finally, Rawls argues that the rational moral persons in the original position would place a great deal of emphasis on the securing of self-respect or self-esteem. They "would wish to avoid at almost any cost the social conditions that undermine self-respect," which is "perhaps the most important" of all the primary goods.[22] In the interests of this primary value, if those in the original position did not know whether they were to be men or women, they would surely be concerned to establish a thoroughgoing social and economic equality between the sexes that would protect either sex from the need to pander to or servilely provide for the pleasures of the other. They would emphasize the importance of girls' and boys' growing up with an equal sense of respect for themselves and equal expectations of self-definition and development. They would be highly motivated, too, to find a means of regulating pornography that did not seriously compromise freedom of speech. In general, they would be unlikely to tolerate basic social institutions that asymmetrically either forced or gave strong incentives to members of one sex to serve as sex objects for the other.

There is, then, implicit in Rawls's theory of justice a potential critique of gender-structured social institutions, which can be developed by taking seriously the fact that those formulating the principles of justice do not know their sex. At the beginning of my brief account of this feminist critique, however, I made an assumption that I said would later be questioned—that a person's sex is, as Rawls at times indicates, a contingent and morally irrelevant characteristic, such that human beings really can hypothesize ignorance of this fact about them. First, I shall explain why, unless this assumption is a reasonable one, there are likely to be further feminist ramifications for a Rawlsian theory of justice, in addition to those I have just sketched out. I shall then argue that the assumption is very probably not plausible in any society that is structured along the lines of gender. I reach the conclusions not only that our current gender structure is incompatible with the attainment of social justice, but also that the disappearance of gender is a prerequisite for the *complete* development of a nonsexist, fully human theory of justice.

Although Rawls is clearly aware of the effects on individuals of their different places in the social system, he regards it as possible to hypothesize free and rational moral persons in the original position who, temporarily freed from the contingencies of actual characteristics and social circumstances, will adopt the viewpoint of the "representative" human being. He is under no illusions about the difficulty of this task: it requires a "great shift in perspective" from the way we think about fairness in everyday life. But with the help of the veil of ignorance, he believes that we can "take up a point of view that everyone can adopt on an equal footing," so that "we share a common standpoint along with others and do not make our judgments from a personal slant." The result of this rational impartiality or objectivity, Rawls argues, is that, all being convinced by the same arguments, agreement about the basic principles of justice will be unanimous. He does not mean that those in the original position will agree about *all* moral or social

---

[21] Elizabeth Holtzman and Shirley Williams, "Women in the Political World: Observations," *Daedalus* 116, No. 4 (Fall 1987). Despite superficial appearances, the situation is no different in Great Britain.

[22] Rawls, *Theory*, pp. 440, 396; see also pp. 178–79.

issues—"ethical differences are bound to remain"—but that complete agreement will be reached on all basic principles, or "essential understanding." A critical assumption of this argument for unanimity, however, is that all the parties have similar motivations and psychologies (for example, he assumes mutually disinterested rationality and an absence of envy) and have experienced similar patterns of moral development, and are thus presumed capable of a sense of justice. Rawls regards these assumptions as the kind of "weak stipulations" on which a general theory can safely be founded.[23]

The coherence of Rawls's hypothetical original position, with its unanimity of representative human beings, however, is placed in doubt if the kinds of human beings we actually become in society differ not only in respect to interests, superficial opinions, prejudices, and points of view that we can discard for the purpose of formulating principles of justice, but also in their basic psychologies, conceptions of the self in relation to others, and experiences of moral development. A number of feminist theorists have argued in recent years that, in a gender-structured society, the different life experiences of females and males from the start in fact affect their respective psychologies, modes of thinking, and patterns of moral development in significant ways.[24] Special attention has been paid to the effects on the psychological and moral development of both sexes of the fact, fundamental to our gendered society, that children of both sexes are reared primarily by women. It has been argued that the experience of in-dividuation—of separating oneself from the nurturer with whom one is originally psychologically fused—is a very different experience for girls than for boys, leaving the members of each sex with a different perception of themselves and of their relations with others. In addition, it has been argued that the experience of *being* primary nurturers (and of growing up with this expectation) also affects the psychological and moral perspective of women, as does the experience of growing up in a society in which members of one's sex are in many ways subordinate to the other sex. Feminist theorists have scrutinized and analyzed the different experiences we encounter as we develop, from our actual lived lives to our absorption of their ideological underpinnings, and have filled out in valuable ways Simone de Beauvoir's claim that "one is not born, but rather becomes, a woman."[25]

What seems already to be indicated by these studies, despite their incompleteness so far, is that *in a gender-structured society* there is such a thing as the distinct standpoint of women, and that this standpoint cannot be adequately taken into account by male philosophers doing the theoretical equivalent of the elderly male justices depicted in the cartoon. The formative influence of female parenting on small children, especially, seems to suggest that sex difference is even more likely to affect one's thinking about justice in a gendered society than, for example, racial difference in a society in which race has social significance, or class difference in a class society. The notion of the standpoint of women, while not without its own problems, suggests that a fully human moral or political theory can be developed only with the full participation of both sexes. At the very least, this will require that women take their place with men in the dialogue in approximately equal numbers and in positions of comparable influence. In a society structured along the lines of gender, this cannot happen.

In itself, moreover, it is insufficient for the development of a fully human theory of justice. For if principles of justice are to be adopted unanimously by

[23] Rawls, "Kantian Constructivism," p. 551; *Theory*, pp. 516–17, 139–41, 149.

[24] Major books contributing to this thesis are Jean Baker Miller, *Toward a New Psychology of Women* (Boston: Beacon Press, 1976); Dorothy Dinnerstein, *The Mermaid and the Minotaur* (New York: Harper & Row, 1977); Nancy Chodorow, *The Reproduction of Mothering* (Berkeley: University of California Press, 1978); Carol Gilligan, *In a Different Voice* (Cambridge: Harvard University Press, 1982); Nancy Hartsock, *Money, Sex, and Power* (New York: Longman, 1983).

[25] Simone de Beauvoir, *The Second Sex* (1952), p. 301.

representative human beings ignorant of their particular characteristics and positions in society, they must be persons whose psychological and moral development is in all essentials identical. This means that the social factors influencing the differences presently found between the sexes—from female parenting to all the manifestations of female subordination and dependence—would have to be replaced by genderless institutions and customs. Only children who are equally mothered and fathered can develop fully the psychological and moral capacities that currently seem to be unevenly distributed between the sexes. Only when men participate equally in what have been principally women's realms of meeting the daily material and psychological needs of those close to them, and when women participate equally in what have been principally men's realms of larger scale production, government, and intellectual and artistic life, will members of both sexes be able to develop a more complete *human* personality than has hitherto been possible. Whereas Rawls and most other philosophers have assumed that human psychology, rationality, moral development, and other capacities are completely represented by the males of the species, this assumption itself has now been exposed as part of the male-dominated ideology of our gendered society.

What effect might consideration of the standpoint of women in gendered society have on Rawls's theory of justice? It would place in doubt some assumptions and conclusions, while reinforcing others. For example, the discussion of rational plans of life and primary goods might be focused more on relationships and less exclusively on the complex activities that he values most highly, if it were to take account of, rather than to take for granted, the traditionally more female contributions to human life.[26] Rawls says that self-respect or self-esteem is "perhaps the most important primary good," and that "the parties in the original position would wish to avoid at almost any cost the social conditions that undermine [it]."[27] Good early physical and especially psychological nurturance in a favorable setting is essential for a child to develop self-respect or self-esteem. Yet there is no discussion of this in Rawls's consideration of the primary goods. Since the basis of self-respect is formed in very early childhood, just family structures and practices in which it is fostered and in which parenting itself is esteemed, and high-quality, subsidized child care facilities to supplement them, would surely be fundamental requirements of a just society. On the other hand, those aspects of Rawls's theory, such as the difference principle, that require a considerable capacity to identify with others, can be strengthened by reference to conceptions of relations between self and others that seem in gendered society to be more predominantly female, but that would in a gender-free society be more or less evenly shared by members of both sexes.

These arguments have led to mixed conclusions about the potential usefulness of Rawls's theory of justice from a feminist viewpoint, and about its adaptability to a genderless society. Rawls himself neglects gender and, despite his initial statement about the place of the family in the basic structure, does not consider whether or in what form the family is a just institution. It seems significant, too, that whereas at the beginning of *A Theory of Justice* he explicitly distinguishes the institutions of the basic structure (*including* the family) from other "private associations" and "various informal conventions and customs of everyday life," in his most recent work he distinctly reinforces the impression that the family belongs with those "private" and therefore nonpolitical associations, for which he

---

[26] Brian Barry has made a similar, though more general, criticism of Rawls's focus on the value of the complexity of activities (the "Aristotelian principle") in *The Liberal Theory of Justice* (1973), pp. 27–30. Rawls leaves room for such criticism and adaptation of his theory of primary goods when he says that it "depends upon psychological premises [that] may prove incorrect" (*Theory*, p. 260).

[27] Rawls, *Theory*, pp. 396, 440.

suggests the principles of justice are less appropriate or relevant.[28] He does this, moreover, despite the fact that his own theory of moral development rests centrally on the early experience of persons within a family environment that is both loving and just. Thus the theory as it stands contains an internal paradox. Because of his assumptions about gender, he has not applied the principles of justice to the realm of human nurturance, a realm that is essential to the achievement and the maintenance of justice.

On the other hand, I have argued that the feminist *potential* of Rawls's method of thinking and his conclusions is considerable. The original position, with the veil of ignorance hiding from its participants their sex as well as their other particular characteristics, talents, circumstances, and aims, is a powerful concept for challenging the gender structure. Once we dispense with the traditional liberal assumptions about public versus domestic, political versus nonpolitical spheres of life, we can use Rawls's theory as a tool with which to think about how to achieve justice between the sexes both within the family and in society at large.[pp. 101–109]

# R. POSNER
## The Ethical and Political Basis of Wealth Maximization
### (1983)[29]

### The Consensual Basis of Efficiency

*Terminological Clarification*

Pareto superiority—the principle that one allocation of resources is superior to another if at least one person is better off under the first than under the second and no one is worse off—was thought, by Pareto himself, to solve the traditional problem of practical utilitarianism—that of measuring happiness across persons to determine a policy's effect on total utility. As is well known, the Pareto solution is apparent rather than real.[30] Since it is impossible to measure utility directly, normally the only way of demonstrating the Pareto superiority of a change in the allocation of resources is to show that everyone affected by the change consented to it. If A sells a tomato to B for $2 and no one else is affected by the transaction, we can be sure that the utility to A of $2 is greater than the utility of the tomato to him, and vice versa for B, even though we do not know how much A's and B's utility has been increased by the transaction. But because the crucial assumption in this example, the absence of third-party effects, is not satisfied with regard to *classes* of transactions, the Pareto-superiority criterion is inapplicable to most policy questions: for example, whether a free market in tomatoes is Pareto superior to a market in which there is a ceiling on the price. The removal of such a ceiling would result in a higher market price, a larger quantity produced, higher rents to owners of land specialized to the growing of tomatoes, a reduction in the output of substitute commodities, and many other effects. It would be impossible to identify, let alone to negotiate for the consent of, everyone affected by the move from a price-controlled to a free tomato market.

I have described the concept of Pareto superiority as an attempt to solve the

---

[28] *ibid.*, p. 8. The more recent development is connected with Rawls's endorsement of the public/private dichotomy in Charles Larmore, *Patterns of Moral Complexity* (1987). Rawls most explicitly indicates that the family belongs in the "private" sphere, to which the principles of justice are not intended to apply, in "Justice As Fairness: Political Not Metaphysical," p. 245n.27, and in "The Priority of Right and Ideas of the Good," *Philosophy and Public Affairs* 17, No. 4 (1988): esp 263.

[29] [From R. Posner, *The Economics of Justice* (1983).]

[30] For a recent statement see G. Calabresi and P. Bobbitt, *Tragic Choices* (1978), pp. 83–85.

utilitarian's problem of the interpersonal comparison of utilities. But it is also possible to locate Pareto ethics in the Kantian philosophical tradition. Consent, an ethical criterion congenial to the Kantian emphasis on treating people as ends rather than means, in a word, on autonomy, is the operational basis of Pareto superiority. It is not the theoretical basis, so long as Pareto superiority is viewed as a tool of utilitarian ethics. If the utilitarian could devise a practical utility metric, he could dispense with the consensual or transactional method of determining whether an allocation of resources was Pareto superior—indeed, he could dispense with Pareto superiority itself.

If one considers consent an ethically attractive basis for permitting changes in the allocation of resources on grounds unrelated to the fact that a consensual transaction is likely to increase the happiness of at least the immediate parties, one will be led, in the manner of Nozick and Epstein,[31] to an ethical defense of market transactions that is unrelated to their promotion of efficiency in either the Pareto or the wealth-maximization sense. To be sure, in a market free from third-party effects, forbidding transactions would reduce the wealth of society and at the same time would reduce liberty or autonomy; hence the goals of maximizing wealth and of protecting autonomy would coincide. But the assumption of no third-party effects is stringent, and when it is abandoned, a wedge between consent and wealth maximization appears. Suppose a company decides to close a factory in town A and open a new one in B, and in neither location are there significant pollution, congestion, or other technological externalities from the plant. The move may still lower property values in A and raise them in B, making landowners in A worse off and those in B better off. Therefore the move will not be Pareto superior. In this example the third-party effects are merely "pecuniary" externalities, meaning that they result simply from a change in demand rather than from the consumption of some scarce resource (such as clean air, in the case of pollution, which is a technological externality), or, stated otherwise, that they have no net effect on the wealth of society; but this fact is irrelevant from the Pareto-superiority standpoint. All that matters is that the plant move will make some people worse off—the landowners in A and doubtless others, such as workers who have skills specialized to the plant being closed and positive costs of relocating in B.

Yet the move must increase the wealth of society, since the plant owners are better off, and the pecuniary externalities cancel out. Accordingly, the wealth-maximization criterion would allow the move. And as Jules Coleman has pointed out,[32] so would the Kaldor-Hicks criterion (sometimes called "Potential Pareto Superiority"), which requires not that no one be made worse off by a change in allocation of resources but only that the increase in value be sufficiently large that the losers can be fully compensated.[33] Since the decrease in land values in A is matched by the increase in B, in principle (that is, ignoring transfer costs) the landowners in A could be compensated, and then no one would be worse off. But in the absence of compensation, not only is full consent to the plant move lacking, total utility may be lower than before the move, because there is no way of knowing whether the utility to the winners of not having to pay compensation exceeds the disutility to the losers of not receiving compensation.

The Kaldor-Hicks criterion is much criticized, even by economists, precisely because it does not ensure that utility will be maximized. Nevertheless, it is incorrect to state that the Pareto criterion is the only "normal professional sense"

---

[31]  See Robert Nozick, *Anarchy, State, and Utopia* (1974); Richard A. Epstein, "Causation and Corrective Justice: A Reply to Two Critics," 8 *J. Legal Stud.* 477, 488 (1979).

[32]  See Coleman, (1980) 68 California L. Rev 221, at 239–242.

[33]  See Nicholas Kaldor, "Welfare Propositions of Economics and Interpersonal Comparisons of Utility," 49 *Econ. J.* 549 (1939); J. R. Hicks, "The Foundations of Welfare Economics," 49 *Econ. J.* 696 (1939)

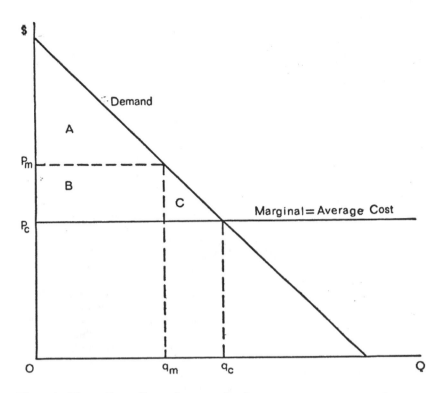

Figure 1. The welfare effects of monopoly. $Q$ = output; $q_m$ = monopoly output; $q_c$ = competitive output; $P_m$ = monopoly price; $P_c$ = competitive price. $A$ = part of consumer surplus kept by consumers; $B$ = part of consumer surplus appropriated by the monopolist; $C$ = welfare loss of monopoly.

of the term efficiency.[34] For example, when economists say that monopoly is inefficient, they mean inefficient in the Kaldor-Hicks or wealth-maximization, not the Pareto, sense. Figure 1 depicts the standard economic analysis of the welfare effects of monopoly. By reducing output and raising price, the monopolist transfers to himself the part of the consumer surplus labeled B in the figure. Part A remains with the consumers. Consumers lose the part labeled C, but the monopolist does not gain it. C is the traditional welfare loss of monopoly. The loss is clear from a wealth-maximization standpoint: the sum of consumer and producer surplus is less under monopoly than under competition (A + B compared to A + B + C). Thus a move from monopoly to competition would satisfy the Kaldor-Hicks or wealth-maximization criterion of Pareto superiority, because the monopolist would be worse off. And it would not be utility maximizing unless the utility of B + C to consumers exceeded the utility of B to the monopolist. Yet most economists would not hesitate to pronounce monopoly inefficient if it has the effects depicted in Figure 2. Indeed, most economists say Pareto but use Kaldor-Hicks in making welfare judgments.

[34] Ronald M. Dworkin, "Is Wealth a Value?" 9 *J. Legal Stud.* 191, 194 (1980).

*Wealth Maximization and the Principle of Consent*

The use of the word "efficiency" in the Kaldor-Hicks sense can be defended simply as an analytical convenience that enables issues of allocation to be discussed separately from issues of distribution. Kaldor himself defended it in this way, and he also offered an ethical argument that in retrospect seems naive. He argued that the government could always transform a wealth increase into a Pareto improvement by compensating the losers out of the gains to the winners. Whether or not it would do so was "a political question on which the economist, *qua* economist, could hardly pronounce an opinion."[35] Kaldor seems to have been suggesting that if the losers from some policy deserve compensation, the government will award it to them, and hence that a wealth increase will be transformed into a Pareto improvement unless there is some independent and compelling ethical reason for not following the Pareto principle. But this is a satisfactory approach only if it is assumed that the government makes decisions on ethical grounds. If instead government is viewed as an arena in which interest groups struggle for advantage with no regard for ethical considerations, it cannot be presumed that the failure to compensate people hurt by an efficient (in the Kaldor-Hicks sense) policy is ethically based.

There is, however, another way of harmonizing the Kaldor-Hicks or wealth-maximization approach, at least in some settings, with the Pareto approach. That is by reference to the idea of consent, the operational basis, of the Pareto criterion. The version of consent used here is ex ante compensation.[36] It is my contention that a person who buys a lottery ticket and then loses the lottery has "consented" to the loss so long as there is no question of fraud or duress; at least he has waived any objection to the outcome, assuming there was no fraud in the lottery. Many of the involuntary, and seemingly uncompensated, losses experienced in the market or tolerated by the institutions that take the place of the market where the market cannot be made to work effectively are fully compensated ex ante and hence are consented to in the above sense. Suppose an entrepreneur loses money as a result of a competitor's development of a superior product: since the entrepreneur's expected return includes a premium to cover the risk of losses due to competition, he was compensated for the loss ex ante. So were the landowners in A, in my previous example, at the time they bought the land: the probability that the plant would move was discounted in the purchase price they paid.[37]

The concept of ex ante compensation provides an answer to the argument that the wealth-maximization criterion, applied unflinchingly in market settings such as my plant-relocation example, would violate the principle of consent. A more difficult question is raised by the attempt to similarly base nonmarket but arguably wealth-maximizing institutions, such as the negligence system of automobile accident liability, on the principle. If a driver is injured by another driver in an accident in which neither was at fault, in what sense has the injured driver

---

[35] Kaldor, supra note 33, at 550.

[36] The argument that follows is sketched in Richard A. Posner, "Epstein's Tort Theory: A Critique," 8 *J. Legal Stud.* 457, 460, 464 (1979). A similar argument is made independently in Frank I. Michelman, "Constitutions, Statutes, and the Theory of Efficient Adjudication," 9 *J. Legal Stud.* 431, 438–440 (1980). Both arguments resemble a position taken by many welfare economists: that the Kaldor-Hicks criterion for deciding whether to undertake a public project satisfies the Pareto-superiority criterion provided there is a sufficient probability that an individual will benefit in the long run from such projects, though he may be a loser from a particular one. See A. Mitchell Polinsky, "Probabilistic Compensation Criteria," 86 *Q. J. Econ.* 407 (1972).

[37] A parallel but more difficult case, because of possible information costs, is that of the worker who loses his job (and incurs positive relocation costs) when the demand for his services collapses as a result of the development of a superior substitute for the product.

consented, or waived any objection, to not being compensated for his injury, which is the result under the negligence system?

To answer this question, we must consider the effect on the costs of driving of insisting on ex post compensation, as under a system of strict liability. By hypothesis the costs would be higher. Otherwise the negligence system would not be wealth-maximizing, and the issue of justifying wealth maximization by reference to the principle of consent would not arise. Would drivers be willing to incur higher costs in order to preserve the principle of ex post compensation? Presumably not. Any driver who wanted to be assured of compensation in the event of an accident, regardless of whether the injurer was at fault, need only buy first-party, or accident, insurance—by hypothesis at lower cost than he could obtain compensation ex post through a system of strict liability.

This point can be most easily grasped by imagining that everyone involved in traffic accidents is identical—is the same age, drives the same amount, and so forth. In these circumstances everyone will pay the same rates for liability and accident insurance. The difference between negligence and strict liability will be that under negligence, liability-insurance rates will be lower and accident-insurance rates higher because fewer accidents will give rise to liability, while under strict liability the reverse will be true. If, as I am assuming, negligence is the more efficient system, the *sum* of the liability and accident insurance premiums will be lower under negligence,[38] and everyone will prefer this.

I have used the example of negligence versus strict liability because it has been used to argue that the wealth-maximization approach is inconsistent with an approach based on notions of personal autonomy.[39] If a requirement of consent in the sense in which I am using the term is deemed an adequate safeguard of the autonomy interest, this argument must fail unless it is shown that a strict liability system would be cheaper than a negligence system.

My analysis may be questioned on the ground that the consent on which I am prepared, in principle at least, to justify institutions such as the negligence system is fictitious because it is not express.[40] But this objection founders precisely on the unavailability of a practical method for eliciting express consent, not so much to individual market transactions—though even there, as I have noted, the consent of third parties affected by those transactions often cannot feasibly be elicited—as to *institutions*, such as the negligence system or indeed the market itself. If there is no reliable mechanism for eliciting express consent, it follows not that we must abandon the principle of consent but that we should be satisfied with implied (or more precisely, perhaps, hypothetical) consent where it exists. Its existence can be ascertained by asking the hypothetical question whether, if transaction costs were zero, the affected parties would agree to the institution. The procedure resembles a judge's imputing the intent of parties to a contract that fails to provide expressly for some contingency.[41] Although the task of imputation is easier in the contract case, that case is still relevant in showing that implicit consent can be meaningful. The absence of an underlying contract affects one's confidence in making an inference of implicit consent but not the propriety of drawing such inferences.

To be sure, "A proposal is not legislation simply because all the members of the legislature are in favor of it."[42] But that is because there is a mechanism by which

---

[38] This assumes that all accident costs are reflected in insurance rates. Some accident-prevention costs (*e.g.*, the value of time lost in driving more slowly) are not. Presumably these costs would also be higher under strict liability if that is the less efficient liability rule.

[39] See Richard A. Epstein, "A Theory of Strict Liability," 2 *J. Legal Stud.* 151 (1973).

[40] Many economists use this procedure to make judgments of Pareto efficiency. For a recent example see Steven Shavell, "Accidents, Liability, and Insurance" (*Am. Econ. Rev.*).

[41] Epstein, supra note 2, at 496.

[42] An approach suggested in George P. Fletcher, "Fairness and Utility in Tort Theory," 85 *Harv. L. Rev.* 537 (1972).

will reflect some probability that the individual making the choice will turn out to be an unproductive member of society—perhaps one of Nozick's "utility monsters." The original-position approach thus obscures the important moral distinction between capacity to enjoy and capacity to produce for others. I prefer therefore to imagine actual people, deploying actual endowments of skill and energy and character, making choices under uncertainty. This is choice under conditions of natural ignorance rather than under the artificial ignorance of the original position.

### Limitations of Wealth Maximization as an Ethical Norm Founded on Consent

The argument that consent can supply an ethical justification for social institutions that maximize wealth requires qualification in two respects.

First, where the distributive impact of a wealth-maximizing policy is substantial and nonrandom, it is difficult to elicit or impute broad consent without actual compensation. I mentioned this possibility in connection with the choice between negligence and strict liability to govern traffic accidents, but it seemed unimportant there. Suppose, however, the issue were whether to substitute a proportionate for a progressive income tax. The substitution would increase the wealth of society if the increase in output (counting both work and leisure as output) by upper-bracket taxpayers, whose marginal tax rate would be lowered, exceeded the reduction in output caused by raising the marginal tax rate of lower-bracket taxpayers. But unless the net increase in output was sufficiently great to increase the after-tax incomes even of those taxpayers who would be paying higher taxes—and let us assume it was not—the lower-bracket taxpayers could hardly be assumed to consent to the tax change, even though it would be wealth maximizing.

I was first stimulated to investigate the ethical foundations of wealth maximization by the suggestion that it was too unappealing a value to ascribe to common law judges.[51] Yet it is precisely in the context of common law adjudication, as contrasted with the redistributive statutory domain illustrated by my tax example, that the consensual basis of wealth maximization is most plausible. The rules that govern the acquisition and transfer of property rights, the making and enforcement of contracts, and liability for accidents and for the kinds of naked aggression that were made crimes at common law are supported by a broad consensus and distribute their benefits very widely. For example, it is naive to think that refusing to enforce the leases poor people sign with richer landlords would make the poor better off. Landlords would charge higher rentals because of the greater risk of loss or would shift their property into alternative uses, with the result that the housing supply available to the poor would be smaller and the price higher. If from this example we generalize that the choice among common law rules usually does not have systematic distributive consequences, then it is reasonable to suppose that there is (or would be, if it paid people to inform themselves in these matters) general consent to those common law rules that maximize wealth. If so, a common law judge guided by the wealth-maximization criterion will be promoting personal autonomy at the same time.

Second, the initial assignment of property rights may seem a fertile area for generating conflicts between wealth maximization and consent. What if A's labor is worth more to B than to A? Then it would be efficient to make A the slave of B but this result would hardly comport with the principle of consent. I suggested in the last chapter that such cases are rare, but I would hesitate to say that they are nonexistent. One can imagine situations in which the costs of physical coercion were lower than the costs of administering employment or other contracts; in such

---

[51] See Neil K. Komesar, "Return to Slumville: A Critique of the Ackerman Analysis of Housing Code Enforcement and the Poor," 82 *Yale L. J.* 1175 (1973).

situations slavery might be wealth maximizing, but it presumably would not be consented to. There are modern examples, such as parental (and public) authority over children and military conscription. We do not use the term slavery to describe these examples, where it can be argued that efficiency in the sense of wealth maximization is allowed to override notions of autonomy. We reserve the term for those palpably exploitative forms of involuntary servitude that rarely can be justified on efficiency grounds. These distinctions suggest that efficiency as I have defined the term retains considerable moral force even when it is in conflict with notions of autonomy and consent.

## Implications for the Positive Economic Analysis of Law

### Why the Common Law Is Efficient

Scholars like myself who have argued that the common law is best explained as an effort, however inarticulate, to promote efficiency have lacked a good reason why this should be so. We may seem to be naive adherents of the outmoded "public interest" theory of the state.[52] This is the theory that the state operates, albeit imperfectly, to promote widely shared social goals—of which efficiency as I have defined it is one (we need not worry how important a one). The state promotes efficiency through providing or arranging for the provision of "public goods," goods that provide benefits not limited to those who pay for them and hence that are produced in suboptimal amounts by private markets. One of these public goods is a legal system that corrects sources of market failure such as externalities.

The public interest theory of the state is under severe attack from the proponents of the "interest group" or, more narrowly, "producer protection" theory of the governmental process,[53] which assigns primacy to redistribution as the object of public policy. The emphasis on redistribution results from treating government action as a commodity that is allocated in accordance with the forces of demand and supply. The characteristics that enable an industry or group to overcome free-rider problems and thereby outbid rival claimants for government protection and largesse have been studied, and the conclusion has been reached that compact groups generally outbid diffuse ones for government favor.

The interest group theory is an economic theory because it links government action to utility maximization by the people seeking such action. The public interest theory is a description rather than a theory because it does not show how utility maximizing by individuals results in government action that promotes the interest of such diffuse groups as the "public," consumers, taxpayers, or some other broad category. And the implication of the interest group theory that diffuse groups are likely to lose out in competition with more compact groups for government protection undermines the plausibility of the public interest theory even as description.

However, common law doctrines that satisfy the Pareto-superiority criterion in the form of the "principle of consent" (no common law doctrine would satisfy a literal interpretation of the Pareto criterion) are plausible candidates for survival even in a political system otherwise devoted to redistributive activities. A rule or institution that satisfies the principle of consent cannot readily be altered, at least by the tools (damages, injunctions) available to common law judges, in a way that will redistribute wealth toward some politically effective interest group. This is

---

[52] For a review of the rival theories of government discussed in this part of the chapter see Richard A. Posner, "Theories of Economic Regulation," 5 *Bell J. Econ. & Mgmt. Sci.* 335 (1974).

[53] The seminal paper in the economic theory of interest group politics (as distinct from theearlier political science theory) is George J. Stigler, "The Theory of Economic Regulation," 2 *Bell J. Econ. & Mgmt. Sci.* 3 (1971).

particularly clear in cases, such as the landlord-tenant case discussed earlier, where the parties to litigation have a preexisting voluntary relationship. Then all the court is doing is altering one term of a contract, and the parties can make offsetting changes in the remaining terms. Even if the dispute does not arise from a contract, the parties may be interdependent in a way that largely cancels any wealth effects from a change in the rule of liability. For example, in the nineteenth century, farmers were major customers of railroads, so it would not have made much sense then to attempt to transfer wealth from railroads to farmers or vice versa simply by broadening or narrowing the liability of railroads for damage to crops growing along railroad rights of way.

The potential for using the common law to redistribute wealth systematically is not great even in a case where there is no prior dealing among the parties to the redistribution. For example, it is hard to see how moving from a negligence system of automobile accident liability to a system of strict liability would increase the wealth of a compact, readily identifiable, and easily organizable group in the society. No one knows in advance whether he will be an accident victim. The principal effect of the move would simply be to reduce most people's wealth a little (always assuming that strict liability would indeed be less efficient than negligence in that setting).

This analysis does not deny the importance of interest groups in shaping public policy. The point is rather that by supporting the efficiency norm in areas regulated by common law methods, they are likely to promote their self-interest. By doing so they increase the wealth of the society, of which they will get a share; no alternative norm would yield them a larger share. To be sure, none of them will devote substantial resources to promoting the efficiency of the common law, because the benefits that each group derives will be small and because each will be tempted to take a free ride on the others. But for the efficiency norm to survive, few resources have to be devoted to promoting it; its distributive neutrality operates to reduce potential opposition as well as support.

This analysis implicitly treats judges simply as agents of the state and hence does not confront the difficulties that judicial independence from political control poses for any self-interest theory of judicial behavior. That is a problem in the economics of agency. The point of the present analysis is to relate the efficiency theory of the common law to the redistributive or interest group theory of the state, albeit some of the links in the chain are obscure. Also, the theory implies that where legislatures legislate within the area of common law regulation—legislate, that is, with respect to rights and remedies in torts, contracts, property, and related fields—they too will try to promote efficiency. It is not the nature of the regulating institution but the subjects and methods of regulation that determine whether the government will promote efficiency or redistribute wealth.[54]

The relationship of this analysis to my earlier ethical analysis should be clear. The principle of consent that I extracted from the Pareto-superiority criterion is another name for absence of systematic distributive effects. The probabilistic compensation discussed in connection with the negligence system of automobile accident liability allowed me to ignore ex post distributive effects in evaluating that system. By the same token, no group can hope to benefit ex ante from a change in the system (assuming the system is the most efficient one possible), and those who lose out ex post, being few and scattered, are not an effective interest group.

---

[54] In this analysis, the features of the judicial process that I have argued elsewhere (*e.g.*, Richard A. Posner, *Economic Analysis of Law* 404–405 [2d ed. 1977]) tend to suppress distributive considerations are thus viewed as effects rather than as causes of the judicial emphasis on efficiency.

*Is the Common Law Efficient or Utilitarian?*

Can one distinguish empirically between the efficiency theory of the common law and the theory that in the heyday of the common law the judges subscribed to the dominant ideology, which was utilitarianism? In the last chapter I showed that some influential figures in the legal scholarship of that period described the common law as utilitarian. It is unlikely that they meant utilitarian in contrast to economic. I know of no instances where utilitarian deviated from economic teaching and the common law followed the utilitarian approach. For example, income equality, protection of animals, and prohibition of begging are all policies advocated by Bentham, the most thorough-going utilitarian, yet there are no traces of these policies in the common law. Bentham also believed in imposing a legal duty to be a "good Samaritan," but the common law, perhaps on economic grounds, rejected such a duty.[55] Nor is there any trace in the common law of sympathy for the thief, rapist, or any other criminal who seeks to defend his crime on the ground that he derived more pleasure from the act than his victim suffered pain. Utilitarianism is a sufficiently flexible philosophy to accommodate arguments that allowing such a defense would not really maximize happiness in the long run, but this is just to say that enlightened utilitarianism incorporates the sorts of constraints that make wealth maximization an attractive ethical principle.

[pp. 88–107]

---

[55] Compare Jeremy Bentham, *Theory of Legislation* 189–190 (R. Hildreth ed. 1894), with William M. Landes & Richard A. Posner, "Salvors, Finders, Good Samaritans, and Other Rescuers: An Economic Study of Law and Altruism," 7 *J. Legal Stud.* 83, 119–127 (1978).

# 8

# DWORKIN AND INTERPRETIVISM

Ronald Dworkin is arguably the pivotal jurist of the last 40 years.[1] His corpus of work ranges from political and legal theory to commentary on major political issues of the day such as the appointment of Supreme Court justices.[2] He has written on abortion and euthanasia,[3] on affirmative action,[4] free speech,[5] liberty, equality and community,[6] and much else.

He first came to prominence as a critic of the model of positivism represented by H.L.A. Hart's orthodoxy: these criticisms were discussed in an earlier chapter.[7] His perspective has affinity with natural law, and in some of his earlier writing he appeared to identify with natural law thinking.[8] But we should not so categorise him: indeed, no pigeon-hole is appropriate. He is his own man, though he has enough followers to form a "school" of jurisprudence. It is with interpretivism that this is most associated.

## THE CRITIC OF POSITIVISM

As we have seen already, in his earliest writings[9] Dworkin challenged the most influential model of contemporary positivism,[10] which saw law as consisting of rules with gaps in those rules being filled by judicial discretion. Law, Dworkin argued, was more complicated than this. There were rules, but there were other standards as well, principles and policies. As a straightforward example of a principle, Dworkin cited "no man

---

[1] An account of his work until the mid 1990s is S. Guest, *Ronald Dworkin* (1997). This is a straightforward presentation of Dworkin's writings: it deliberately avoids engaging with criticisms of Dworkin.

[2] Often in the New York Review of Books.

[3] *Life's Dominion* (1993); *Sovereign Virtue* (2000), Chap. 14.

[4] *Sovereign Virtue* (2000), Chaps 11 and 12. See also *ante*, 609.

[5] *Freedom's Law* (1996) and *Sovereign Virtue* (2000) Chap. 10 On Dworkin and pornography see *ante*, 604.

[6] *Sovereign Virtue* (2000), Chaps 5. 3, 4, 5, and *post*.

[7] *Ante*, 386.

[8] "Natural Law Revisited" (1982) 34 Univ. of Florida L.R. 165

[9] *Ante*, 386.

[10] Represented by H.L.A. Hart in *The Concept of Law* (1961).

shall profit from his own wrong".[11] Policies, by contrast, set out "a goal to be reached, generally an improvement in some economic, political or social feature of the community".[12] We have already considered the differences Dworkin believed existed between rules and principles.[13] The differences, as he perceived them, may be exaggerated. But no one denies the significance of his criticism: even Hart in his "Postscript" admitted he had neglected the role in legal reasoning played by non-conclusive principles.[14] Dworkin argued that, in a standard positivist account of the judicial process such as Hart's, principles could not be accommodated: this is why in such accounts there is necessarily a resort to discretion. It should be noted that at this phase of his writing Dworkin is not separating law and morality, or at least doing so clearly. The principles to which he refers are to be found, just as rules are, in practice, in past official actions. "No man shall profit from his own wrong" may have its origins in morality (even in religion) but it owes its status to judicial pronouncements. He is not suggesting that principles are inherent in morality.

At the same time, Dworkin rejects the rule of recognition[15] as the pedigree test as to whether principles and other standards can be categorised as part of the legal system. He says such a rule would be an impossibility because such standards are "numberless" and "they shift and change so fast that the start of our list would be obsolete before we reach the middle". And, even if we succeeded, "we would not have a key for law because there would be nothing left for our key to unlock".[16]

We hear less of policies in later writings of Dworkin. But the distinction between principles and policies remains important. Principles relate to rights, whereas policies are about goals. "If rights are to be taken seriously, they must have a threshold weight against community goals".[17] Rights cannot be "trumped" by a competing community goal.[18] Judges are there to decide according to principle litigants' entitlements, not what serves the community best. Even when a judge appears to be appealing to policy, we should understand this as an "appeal to the competing rights of [for example] those whose security will be sacrificed, or whose just share of that resource will be threatened if the abstract right is made concrete".[19]

---

[11]  He illustrated this by reference to *Riggs v. Palmer* 22 NE 188 (1889).
[12]  *Taking Rights Seriously* (1977), p. 46.
[13]  *Ante*, 387–390.
[14]  The postscript is in the 1994 edition of *The Concept of Law*. See p. 263.
[15]  An interesting critique of Dworkin's views on the role of recognition is M. Kramer (1999) 5 *Legal Theory* 171.
[16]  *Taking Rights Seriously* (1977), p. 44.
[17]  See *ante*, 604.
[18]  *Taking Rights Seriously* (1977).
[19]  *ibid*, 100.

## Dworkin and "Hard Cases"

For Dworkin, judges are always constrained by the law: there is no law beyond the law. Dworkin's conception[20] of the dominion of law is of a gapless legal universe, where in every adjudication, even in the so-called "hard cases", there are controlling standards which judges are obligated to follow. The law is a seamless web, in which there is always a right answer.[21] Judicial decisions are "characteristically generated by principle" and "enforce existing political rights": litigants are therefore "entitled" to the judge's "best judgment" about what their rights are.[22] Dworkin admits that different judges can come to different conclusions "because a constitutional theory requires judgments about political and moral philosophy".[23] But, despite this, he maintains that judges may not rely on their own political views, but only on their beliefs in "the soundness of those convictions".[24]

Dworkin gives two reasons for objecting to judges acting as "deputy legislators".[25] First, it offends the democratic ideal that a community should be governed by elected officials answerable to the electorate. "The judge, not being elected, must not substitute his own will as against the legislature".[26] It is difficult to challenge such an ideal, but the reality is that in any complex society where, for example, there is ample use of subsidiary legislation, law-making by unelected officials is an inevitable consequence. In contrast, judges are subjected to more, and more rigorous, constraints on what they can do. His second objection to judicial originality is that "if a judge makes new law and applies it retroactively" to the litigation he is deciding, "the losing party will be punished, not because he has violated some duty he had, but rather a new duty created after the event".[27] This, Dworkin notes, has important implications for theories of legal obligation. However, in many (if not most) cases where judges have created new law, the person penalised could well have predicted that his activity would be characterised as a breach of duty. Does the person who skates on thin ice have a legitimate grievance when the point at which he falls in is not clearly marked, so that he is not given adequate warning that this may happen? This criticism is said by Guest to be "specious",[28] but is this so? Do those who indulge in elaborate tax avoidance schemes not do so knowing full well that a court may

---

[20] On the concept/conception distinction see *Law's Empire* (1985), 70–72, and Gallie (1965) 56 Proc. Aristotelian Soc. 167. Guest, n. 1, 29–32 is also helpful.

[21] But see *post*, 727.

[22] "The law may not be a seamless web, but the plaintiff is emitted to ask Hercules to treat it as if it were" n.16 above, 116. On right answers see TRS, Chap. 13.

[23] TRS, 117.

[24] *ibid*, 124. He concedes judges "cannot avoid politics" (1982) 60 Texas L.R. 527.

[25] Guest, n. 1 above, 175 adds a third reason: "judges speak judicially of their being 'bound by law'".

[26] *Per* Guest, n. 1 (1st edition, 1992), 172.

[27] In *Essays In Legal Philosophy* ((ed.) R. Summers, 1968), 43–44.

[28] N. 1 above, 175.

characterise their scheme as "evasion",[29] rather than avoidance? Does a person who throws blocks of concrete off a motorway bridge not knowingly take the risk that a court may impute such behaviour to be sufficiently blameworthy to be labelled "murder"?[30] Can a man who forces his wife to have sexual intercourse with him really complain when the courts say this constitutes rape, even though there has been marital rape immunity in existence for many centuries?[31]

To the positivist the "hard case" is peripheral. For Dworkin, however, their significance is as "pivotal cases testing fundamental principles, not as borderline cases calling for some more or less arbitrary line to be drawn".[32] This is, of course, how they are treated, as any glance at the decision-making processes of the highest courts in common law countries will reveal. So, what is the status of the "clear" case? Guest explains that "the assumption that a case is clear is the result of a process of reasoning and not the start".[33] Cases are "hard" where arguments exist as to what is the best understanding of the law: clear cases are those where no such doubts exist. Whether someone is "driving" a car may stimulate inter-pretational debate:[34] whether that person is over the "limit" is not nor-mally contestable. But the "core/penumbra", "hard case/clear case" is only of secondary importance to Dworkin and, indeed, nearly all cases that reach the stage of argument in court are "hard cases". Of greater significance is that Dworkin has focused our attention upon "the quality of the underlying legal argument justifying the invocation of the coercive powers of the state".[35]

## DWORKIN AND DISCRETION

Dworkin's challenge to positivism was considered in Chap. 6. A further question this raises is whether it is possible to eliminate judicial discre-tion, Critics, such as Greenawalt, have argued that the "denial of dis-cretion is wrong, or at least misleading", because it is based "on a peculiarly narrow notion of what it means to have discretion to make a choice".[36] It is inconsistent "with our ordinary understanding of judicial responsibilities for opinion; and it receives less support from opinions, briefs and critical legal writing than Dworkin ... suppose[s]."

But this is to misunderstand or misconstrue Dworkin. To suggest that judges have discretion is not to imply that they have licence to do what they will. It may be that in practice, in other words as a matter of

---

[29] And see *Ransom v. Higgs* [1974] 3 All E.R. 949, 969 *per* Lord Simon.
[30] *Cf R v. Hancock* [1986] 1 All E.R. 641.
[31] And see *R v. R* [1991] 3 W.L.R. 767. These points are also made by Hart in his "Post-script" (pp. 275–276).
[32] *Law's Empire*, 43.
[33] N. 1, above, 169.
[34] *R v. Price* [1968] 3 All E.R. 814; *Campbell v. Tormey* [1969] 1 All E.R. 961.
[35] *Per* Guest, n. 1, above, 171.
[36] (1975) 75 Columbia L.R. 359, 361.

description, some poor judges act as if they do. But the institution of judging offers the judge choice only within the constraints of judgment. The normative institution of judgment requires a decision to be justified by legal argument. Indeed, there are few decision makers compelled to explain their decisions as fully.

Dworkin offers a very full analysis of "discretion".[37] He distinguishes three senses of discretion, two "weak" and one "strong". Discretion in a strong sense occurs where a person "is simply not bound by the standards set by the authority in question".[38] Thus, the sergeant who is ordered to pick any five men for a patrol has strong discretion. But judges do not have such freedom to choose. Compare the sergeant, instructed to select his five most experienced men: he has discretion in the weak sense, just depicted, of judgement. There are criteria to which he, and we, can appeal to estimate experience. If he picks last week's recruits we can criticize him for exercising his judgement inappropriately. We can say—as we can say of judges—that he has come to a wrong decision. In many, if not most, cases judges have "weak" discretion of this nature. That is why the "hard case" is the norm, rather than the exception. There is another sense also in which discretion may be said to be "weak". It exists whether an official has the authority to make a decision: the sergeant in this sense has the discretion as to which experienced men he selects. Greenawalt argues that the line between unacceptable strong discretion and its weak acceptable sense is elusive. He claims that strong discretion exists if more than one decision is considered proper "by those to whom the decision—maker is responsible and whatever standards may be applicable either cannot be discovered by the decision-maker or do not yield clear answers to the questions that must be decided".[39] But are not these cases for the exercise of judgement?

## DWORKIN AND INTERPRETATION

It is central to Dworkin's project that to develop a theory of adjudication it is necessary to engage in a constructive interpretation of legal practice. But it is not simply the appropriate method for developing a theory of adjudication: it is also the method to be employed by the judge committed to law as integrity for deciding cases. Dworkin maintains that:

> "Judges who accept the interpretive ideal of integrity decide hard cases by trying to find, in some coherent set of principles about people's rights and duties, the best *constructive interpretation* of the political structure and legal doctrine of their community. They try to make that complex structure and record the best there can be".[40]

[37] TRS, 31–33.
[38] *ibid*, 32
[39] N. 36, above, 368.
[40] *Law's Empire*, 255.

"Constructive interpretation" is a methodology for interpreting social practices (he gives the example of the practice of courtesy), texts (and not just legal texts) and works of art. Dworkin employs this method to interpret legal practice. The distinctive feature of this is that it is "argumentative".[41] Dworkin distinguishes two ways of studying the argumentative aspect of legal practice. There is the "external point of view of the sociologist or historian", and the "internal point of view of those who make the claims".[42] To understand legal practice the internal participants' view must be embraced. *Law's Empire* "tries to grasp the argumentative character of our legal practice by joining that practice and struggling with the issues of soundness and truth participants face".[43]

Dworkin explains this by imagining a community which follows a set of rules called "rules of courtesy". Thus, this commonly says, "courtesy requires that peasants take off their hats to nobility".[44] The interpretive attitude has two assumptions: the practice does not just exist, but has value or purpose and it enforces some principle. The behaviour that the practice requires is sensitive to this purpose. "People", says Dworkin, "now try to impose *meaning* on the institution—to see it in its best light—and then try to restructure it in the light of that meaning".[45]

Two questions may be raised about this methodology. First in making the internal/external distinction, Dworkin is ignoring the fact that judges are "socially situated individuals who interpret the law for a particular purpose and bring a particular set of sociological and ideological predispositions to their understanding".[46] Dworkin appears to exclude "all sociological or ideological analysis—the very analysis of what the subject does bring to the object of understanding—as 'external critiques' that can tell us nothing about the nature of law".[47] Balkin comments: "So hermetically (and hermeneutically) sealed is Dworkin's universe that it becomes impossible to object that the concerns of judges occupy only one rather limited portion in the constellation of legal reality and the forms of legal understanding".[48]

Secondly, it may be questioned why one should want to see all social practices in their best light: after all, it may be said, some may have no redeeming features whatsoever. Why, for example, look at the practice of apartheid in its best light? Or at peasants doffing their hats to members of the nobility? Dworkin himself, needless to say, does not apply this method of constructive interpretation to positivism,[49] and certainly does

---

[41] *ibid*, 13.
[42] *ibid*.
[43] *ibid*, 14.
[44] *ibid*, 47
[45] *ibid*.
[46] *Per* J.M. Balkin (1993) 103 Yale L.J. 105, 134. And see *post* p. 1449.
[47] *ibid*.
[48] *ibid*.
[49] See C. Silver (1987) 6 *Law & Phil*. 381 ("Dworkin rarely asks whether an argument he calls positivistic is the best argument a Legal Positivist could make").

not do so to critical legal studies.[50] Constructive interpretation is a form of cultural understanding, but it is not the only one.

The process of constructive interpretation is made up of three analytical stages: the pre-interpretive stage, the interpretive stage and the post-interpretive stage.[51]

At the pre-interpretive stage, the participant identifies the rules and standards that tentatively constitute the practice. The equivalent stage in literary interpretation is identifying the text.[52]

At the interpretive stage, the interpreter "settles on some general justification for the main elements of the practice identified at the first analytic stage".[53]

The third stage is the post-interpretive or "reforming" stage, at which the participant "adjusts his sense of what the practice 'really' requires so as better to serve the justification he accepts at the interpretive stage".[54]

Of these three stages the interpretive is the pre-eminent. It is at this stage that the participant postulates the value of the practice. His proposal must satisfy two dimensions: it must be consistent with the data identified as constituting the practice at the pre-interpretive stage; and, in the light of his own convictions, he must choose a justification that he believes shows it in its best light.

Dworkin works through this interpretive process with the social practice of courtesy. And law, he says, is "an interpretive concept like courtesy".[55] What the law requires in a particular case thus rests ultimately on a constructive interpretation of legal practice. What, therefore, does it mean when we say that we must show a practice, in particular a legal practice, in its best light? Guest agrees that Dworkin is "less explicit" about this, though he is of the view that the idea is "central to his anti-positivist position that moral argument is an essential ingredient to legal argument".[56] It is, in Guest's opinion, "natural" to suppose that we must understand the social practices of law—ultimately, it seems, the licensing and constraining of governmental coercion[57]—in their most *moral* light. But why? Does this amount to anything more than asserting that the *status quo* is natural, so as to be beyond criticism? Guest concludes that Dworkin's definition is "peculiarly bourgeois" (by which it may be assumed he means "conservative"), but to assume, as he does, that the only opposition will come from committed anarchists is surely to underestimate the force of the objection.

---

[50] See Balkin, n. 46, above, 134–135 (n. 50).
[51] *Law's Empire*, pp. 65–68.
[52] Choosing, for example, between different versions of a Shakespeare play as it is found in different Folios.
[53] *Law's Empire*, p. 66.
[54] *ibid.*
[55] *ibid*, p87.
[56] N. 1, above, p. 28.
[57] *Law's Empire*, p. 93. This is as close as Dworkin comes to a definition of law.

## LAW AS INTEGRITY

Key to Dworkin's constructive interpretation of legal practice is his conception of law as integrity. Of the three rival theories of law which Dworkin constructs and compares (conventionalism,[58] pragmatism,[59] and "law as integrity"), it is, he argues, law as integrity which shows our legal practice in its best light. It offers a blueprint for adjudication which directs judges to decide cases by using the same methodology from which integrity was derived, namely constructive interpretation.[60]

Integrity is both a legislative and an adjudicative principle. It is as a legislative (or political) principle that Dworkin introduces the concept of integrity. He does this by means of discussion of "checkerboard solutions".[61] In Dworkin's view there are two commonly-accepted political values—justice and fairness.[62] "Fairness in politics is a matter of finding political procedures ... that distribute political power in the right way".[63] Justice ... "is concerned with the decisions that the standing political institutions ... ought to make. If we accept justice as a political virtue we want our legislators and other officials to distribute material resources and protect political liberties so as to secure a morally defensible outcome".[64] But for Dworkin there is a third political ideal—there as Neptune was before it was discovered—that of "integrity". This "requires government to speak with one voice, to act in a principled and coherent manner toward all its citizens, to extend to everyone the same substantive standards of justice or fairness it uses for some".[65] So, if government appeals to the principle that people are entitled to compensation from those who injure them by manufacturing defective cars, it must use the same principle in deciding whether a bank is liable for giving a negligent misstatement as well.

To justify his claim that integrity is a discrete political ideal, Dworkin demonstrates that it fits with, and provides a sound justification, of our political practices. We can, he maintains, explain why we are uncomfortable with checkerboard solutions only if we accept the ideal of integrity. A checkerboard statute is one which displays "incoherence in principle and that can be justified, if at all, only on grounds of a fair allocation of political power between different moral parties".[66] Given the division of opinion about abortion,[67] we could permit it for women

---

[58] See *Law's Empire*, Chap. 4: conventionalism is a restatement (seeing it in its best light?) of positivism. For a defence of conventionalism against Dworkin see N. Simmonds (1990) 49 C.L.J. 63.

[59] See *Law's Empire*, Chap. 5. This is close to Realism.

[60] "Law as integrity is different ... it is both the product of and the inspiration for constructive interpretation of legal practice" *Law's Empire*, 226.

[61] See *Law's Empire*, pp. 178–184 and *post*, 756–760.

[62] There is also procedural due process, but this is not particularly relevant here.

[63] *Law's Empire*, p.164.

[64] *ibid*, pp. 164–165.

[65] *ibid*, p. 165.

[66] *ibid*, p. 435 n.6.

[67] Between pro-choice liberals and pro-life conservatives.

born in even-numbered years but not for those born in odd-numbered ones. This may be accounted "fair"—each group in society has the abortion solution it wants. It is better than a "winner-takes-all" solution. But most of us would find such solutions abhorrent. Similarly, we cannot explain why checkerboard solutions are wrong if we focus just on considerations of justice. Of course, a checkerboard solution can never be a fully just one. At best it minimises injustices. But for Dworkin that many of us would prefer either of the alternative solutions (pro-choice or pro-life) to the checkerboard solution cannot be explained by reference to the ideal of justice. The explanation lies elsewhere in a third ideal, namely integrity. A state which adopts a checkerboard solution, for example to abortion, lacks integrity, because it must endorse principles to justify part of what it has done that it must reject to justify the rest.

Dworkin acknowledges that integrity can be flouted otherwise than by checkerboard solutions. It is, he concedes, a "flaw" in the American (for which read common law) legal system that we cannot integrate all our rules under one coherent scheme of principle. He also admits that integrity is not always more important than fairness and justice; lawmakers consequently should not always avoid breaches of integrity. And, occasionally, even a checkerboard solution may be justified. He gives the example of a legislature introducing no-fault compensation for defective manufacture of cars but finding it impossible to do so for other products. Integrity would condemn this, justice might favour it: this, says Dworkin, might be a case where justice is the more important consideration.[68]

The adjudicative principle of integrity "instructs judges to identify legal rights and duties ... on the assumption that they were all created by a single author—the community personified—expressing a coherent conception of justice and fairness".[69] A judge committed to integrity is required to decide particular cases by seeking a principle that "both fits and justifies some complex part of the legal practices, that ... provides an attractive way to see, in the structure of that practice, the consistency of principle integrity requires".[70]

To understand "fit" Dworkin employs the idea of the chain novel.[71] Imagine that a number of novelists agree to write one chapter each of a proposed novel. Or a number of writers are engaged on the project of a daily "soap". Or a musician in 2008 sets out to complete Schubert's "Unfinished Symphony". Clearly, there will be constraints of "fit" upon the author of the second chapter. The composer of the third movement of Schubert's Symphony could not write a foxtrot or employ bagpipes. These constraints will increase through each successive chapter. However, the concept of "fit" itself is by no means unproblematic. For

---

[68] *Law's Empire*, pp. 217–218. See, further, on "checkerboard statutes" D. Smith in (ed.) S. Hershovitz, *Exploring Law's Empire* (2006), 119.

[69] *Law's Empire*. 225.

[70] *ibid*, 228.

[71] *ibid*.

Dworkin, as Guest notes, the question of "fit" is itself an interpretive question.[72] Guest uses the example of the second chapter novelist deciding that the first chapter is a political tract about conservatism and accordingly continuing the novel as a political statement.

Stanley Fish, a persistent critic of Dworkin, takes issue with this.[73] He agrees with Dworkin that law, like any literary text, is a matter of interpretation, but goes on to argue that what is interpreted cannot be distinguished from the interpretation itself. On this view, the constraints on possible interpretations are not given by the item interpreted (the first chapter of the novel, the two movements of the Schubert symphony, the earlier case), but arise within the interpreting community, their expectations, their shared understandings. On this view what is required is the very external perspective of the sociologist which, we saw earlier,[74] Dworkin rejects. Not surprisingly, Dworkin has rejected as "extravagant"[75] Fish's claim that interpretation constitutes what is interpreted: this interpretation must fit into the existing body of legal materials.

It should not be thought that a judge committed to law as integrity is required to interpret laws in the light of the purpose which gave rise to them. On the contrary, he is required to "impose order over doctrine, not to discover order in the forces that created it. He struggles toward a set of principles he can offer to integrity, a scheme for transforming the varied links in the chain of law into a vision of government now speaking with one voice, even if this is very different from the voices of leaders past".[76]

Can "fit" be distinguished from the sorts of account of legal validity that one finds within positivism? Only, it seems, because Dworkin is compelled to conclude that what constrains interpretation is not historical legal material in some objective sense, but the judges' "convictions" about fit. These, Dworkin insists, are "political, not mechanical".[77] But, why do these convictions constrain judges? It cannot be because of the controls exercised by "significant others"[78] within the legal community. Such a sociological explanation is not open to Dworkin, nor would he wish to employ it. His answer is that the constraint upon judges arises from their personal need as individuals to integrate their convictions about "fit" with their convictions about whether their interpretation shows the interpreted practice in its best light.

"It is not the constraint of external hard fact or of interpretational consensus. But rather the structural constraint of different kinds of principle within a system of principle, and it is none the less genuine for that".[79]

---

[72] N. 1, above, 40

[73] (1982) 60 Texas L.R. 551; (1983) 62 Texas L.R. 299 (and see S. Fish, *Doing What Comes Naturally* (1990), Chaps 1, 2, 16. For a recent response see R. Dworkin, *Justice In Robes* (2006), 43–48. Guest defends Dworkin against Fish: see n.1, above, 40–42.

[74] *Ante*, 722.

[75] *A Matter of Principle* (1985), 176.

[76] *Law's Empire*, 273.

[77] *ibid*, 257.

[78] And *cf.* Llewellyn, *post*, 990.

[79] *Law's Empire*, 273.

It may be genuine, but is it really any constraint at all? And, what if there is conflict between convictions about fit and convictions as to which interpretation shows legal practices in their best light? These are not questions satisfactorily addressed by Dworkin. It may be that they are questions which cannot be answered within the legal-philosophical discourse of the "insider". Could it be that the answers need to be sought within the sociology of law that Dworkin rejects?[80]

## ONE RIGHT ANSWER?

In *Law's Empire* Dworkin states at the beginning of the book:

"In most hard cases there are right answers to be hunted by reason and imagination".[81]

At the end of the book he states:

"I have not drawn the conclusion that many readers think sensible. I have not said that there is never one right way, only different ways, to decide a hard case".[82]

Dworkin thus maintains that the process of adjudication inherent in the theory of "law as integrity" yields right answers to questions of law. *In Justice In Robes* (through the essay originally appeared in 1991), he says that his thesis about right answers in hard cases is "a very weak and commonsensical legal claim".[83] And it is a claim "made within legal practice rather than at some supposedly removed, external, philosophical level".[84] The best way of testing the claim is "to try to show what the right answer is in some particular hard case".[85] And he has done just this in a number of famous hard cases like the *Cruzan* decision.[86]

Dworkin does not say—though others may attribute this to him—that the right answer can necessarily be demonstrated to be such. It does not follow that if something cannot be demonstrated that it cannot be right. It is "insufficient"[87] to claim that there cannot be right answers merely because these answers cannot be proved or demonstrated. This criticism is thus fairly easy to dispose of. More difficult to counter is the criticism which asks how if the judge within the "law as integrity" model is to use his own political convictions to decide cases, and given that different judges will not necessarily have those same convictions, they can be

---

[80] See also R. Cotterrell, *The Politics of Jurisprudence* (1989), 180.
[81] viii–ix.
[82] At 412.
[83] *Justice In Robes* (2006), 41.
[84] *ibid.*
[85] *ibid.*
[86] He discusses this *ibid* at p. 42. See more fully *Life's Dominion,*.
[87] *Per* Guest, n. 1, above 1 p. 138.

expected to come to the same conclusion.[88] Given that integrity allows for disagreement about the law, can it yield a single right answer to difficult questions of law?

Dworkin's answer is not addressed to a method that would eliminate disagreement in law. Instead, what he offers is a reformulation of what is entailed in the claim that answers yielded by "law as integrity" are "right" answers. He asserts that "law as integrity" does not produce "objectively" right answers to questions of law. With this explanation he believes he has neutralised the critique based on, what he calls, "external scepticism".[89] External scepticism rejects the view that there are right answers "located in some 'transcendental reality' ".[90] It thus rejects the "absurd claim"[91] that answers yielded by integrity are "objectively" right answers to questions of law, so, "even if external scepticism is sound as a philosophical" position, it offers "no threat to our case for law as integrity or to Hercules' methods of adjudication under it".[92]

However, if the answers produced by "integrity" are not "objectively" right, in what other sense are they right? Dworkin's answer is that they are right because the judge as a participant in legal practice experiences them as right.[93] In this way Dworkin is able to postulate the existence of right answers, whilst at the same time admitting the possibility of disagreements amongst the judges as to what those right answers are. This may remove an apparent contradiction in Dworkin's thinking, but at what price? It will be remembered that Dworkin objected to the use of "strong" discretion by judges because retrospective legislation undercuts the rule of law. How, he argues, can citizens plan their activities if new duties may be imposed upon them after they have acted? But, it may be asked, is not Dworkin's defence of the right answer thesis open to the same objection? If different judges can come to different conclusions using their own political convictions, is it any solace to an aggrieved and surprised citizen to be told that the answer reached was "right" in the eyes of that judge? And, is that grievance not likely to be aggravated when Dworkin informs that citizen that a second judge could equally well

---

[88] "For every route Hercules took from the general conception to a particular verdict, another lawyer or judge who began in the same conception would find a different route and send in a different place" *per* Dworkin, *Law's Empire*, p.412.

[89] *Law's Empire*, pp. 78–85.

[90] *ibid*, p. 83

[91] *ibid*.

[92] *ibid*, pp. 266–267.

[93] "We might say ... the constraint is 'internal' or 'subjective'. It is nevertheless phenomologically genuine ... We are trying to see what interpretation is like from the point of view of the interpreter, and from that point of view the constraint he feels is as genuine as if it were uncontroversial, as if everyone felt it as powerfully as he does" (*Law's Empire*, p. 235). See also Dworkin in (eds) M. Brint and W. Weaver, *Pragmatism in Law and Society* (1991), pp. 359, 365–366, where he talks of "right or best or true or soundest" whilst admitting it is a waste of important energy to continue "grand debates" about whether there are right answers or only "useful or powerful or popular ones".

have come to a different conclusion and that too would have been right in the eyes of that second judge?[94]


## INTEGRITY AND LEGITIMACY

Part of Dworkin's case for integrity is that it captures our intuitions about checkerboard solutions. But his argument for integrity is more fundamental than this, and offers a justification of political obligation.

Thus, he argues that a:

> "Political society that accepts integrity as a political virtue thereby becomes a special form of community, special in a way that promotes its moral authority to assume and deploy a monopoly of coercive force".[95]

A state that "accepts integrity as a political ideal has a better case for legitimacy than one which does not".[96] Integrity insists that "each citizen must accept demands on him, and may make demands on others, that share and extend the moral dimension of any explicit political decisions".[97] It "fuses citizens' moral and political lives".[98]

Dworkin maintains that any argument for legitimacy must be able to account for the fact that political obligations are not consensual. He is critical of standard explanations like the social contract and its modern variants like Rawls's "original position".[99] He also dismisses justification of this in terms of "fair play".[1] He needs to explain why such obligation is special (why, for example, do "Britons" have any special duty to support the institutions of Britain?).[2] The explanation that Dworkin offers relies on the notion of community or fraternity. He argues that political obligation is a type of "associative obligation".[3] By this he means "the special responsibilities social practice attaches to membership in some biological or social group, like the responsibilities of family or friends or neighbors".[4] Associative obligations are

---

[94] Note that, under what Dworkin calls "a protestant attitude", each citizen is responsible for imagining what his or her society's public commitments to principle are, and what these commitments require in new circumstances (*Law's Empire*, p. 413, and also p. 190). This means in effect that everyone has to decide what the law is by reference to his or her own political convictions. But how can citizens be sure that their views coincide with others, let alone with judges? Can a society be run in this way? On Dworkin's "Protestantism" see G Postema (1987) 6 *Law and Phil.* 283.

[95] *Law's Empire*, p. 188.

[96] *ibid*, pp. 191–192.

[97] *ibid*, p.189.

[98] *ibid*. Jules Coleman observes a shift in Dworkin's philosophy from rights-based liberalism in TRS to "liberal community" in *Law's Empire* see (1995) 1 *Legal Theory* 33, 48–54.

[99] On this see *ante*, 584.

[1] See pp. 192–195.

[2] *ibid*, 193.

[3] *ibid*, 196.

[4] *ibid*.

"an important part of the moral landscape for most people, responsibilities to family and lovers and friends and union and office colleagues are the most important, the most consequential obligations of all".[5]

It may be worth pausing at this point to question whether Dworkin overplays his point by including within the range of responsibilities "union and office colleagues". He sees associative obligations (he sometimes uses the term "fraternal") as "special", in that they are confined to members of the group, and non-consensual, because we do not choose the obligations we owe to friends or colleagues. Associative obligations are defined by social practices which attach special obligations to membership within a particular social group.

A community's social practices give rise to "genuine" obligations only when two requirements are met. First, the community must be a "true" rather than a "bare" community. A "bare" community is transformed into a "true" community only when four conditions are met: (i) members of the group must regard the group's responsibilities as *special*, that is holding distinctly within the group; (ii) as *personal*, that is running from each member to each other member, not just to the group as a whole in some collective sense; (iii) as based on *concern* for the well-being of others in the group; and (iv) "members must suppose that the group's practices show not only concern but equal concern for all members. Fraternal obligations are in that secure conceptually egalitarian ... no one's life is more important than anyone else's."[6] Dworkin summarises these four conditions thus:

"The responsibilities a true community deploys are special and individualized and display a pervasive mutual concern that fits a plausible conception of equal concern".[7]

Dworkin relies on the notion of reciprocity to explain associative obligations. He claims that we have "a duty to honor our responsibilities under social practices that define groups and attach special responsibilities to membership, but this natural duty holds only when certain other conditions",[8] prominent amongst which is reciprocity, are met. Dworkin is, however, careful to distinguish this reciprocity from a relationship based on a *quid pro quo* exchange. What he has in mind is something "more abstract": thus "friend or family or neighbors need not agree in detail about the responsibilities attached to those forms of organisation", but they must show "roughly the same concern" for each other.[9] Dworkin is concerned to deflect the criticism that otherwise attracts to relating legitimacy to reciprocity by wedding reciprocity to

---

[5] *ibid.*
[6] *ibid*, p. 201.
[7] *ibid.*
[8] *ibid.*
[9] *ibid.*

social practices like friendship, but whether he has done this successfully may be disputed.

Perry[10] has rightly drawn our attention to some problems that the fourth condition (equal concern) poses in the context of the family. Dworkin himself discusses the examples of a culture that expects parents to choose husbands for their daughters, but not wives for their sons. This culture—and there are of course many real examples—accepts "in good faith" the equality of the sexes (in parenthesis we must add that this is unlikely to be so), but thinks that equality of concern obliges paternalism for daughters. Dworkin argues that girls in this culture owe their parents obligations of obedience, though he concedes that this obligation may be overridden by other moral considerations.[11] We know rather more about so-called arranged marriages—many of which are forced—and the retribution wreaked on disobedient daughters including the so-called "honour killings", now than was the case when *Law's Empire* was published. It may colour the way we read Dworkin. But even if we ignore what we now know, Dworkin is arguing that children can be obligated to obey their parents so long as parental power is exercised in accordance with "a conception of equal concern that is plausible and sincerely held".[12] But, as Perry points out, whether or not the claim is true, "equal concern" does not "here refer, as it does in the case of friendship, to an equal level of reciprocal concern that members of an associative relationship owe to one another".[13] He gives the example of a parent raising a child. The parent has an obligation to care for the child. Even if, as Perry says,[14] the child has an obligation to obey the parent—and this may be contested—the obligations are not reciprocal as those between two friends are.

This excursus into associative obligations is but a prelude to Dworkin's defence of political legitimacy. Dworkin argues that political obligation is an example of associative obligation. In his view political practice is a "bare" community which defines a nation state and imposes upon members of it obligations, including the obligation to obey the law, by virtue of membership of that nation "group". But to give rise to genuine obligations, a political community must be a "true" community. Only a community that endorses the ideal of integrity—"a community of principle"[15]—can claim the authority of a genuine associative community, and therefore claim moral legitimacy, that "its collective decisions are

---

[10] In (ed.) S. Hershovitz, *Exploring Law's Empire* (2006), Chap. 8.
[11] *Law's Empire*, pp. 204–205.
[12] *ibid.*
[13] N. 10, above, p. 89.
[14] *ibid*, p. 92.
[15] *Law's Empire*, p. 214.

matters of obligation and not bare power ... in the name of fraternity".[16]

Dworkin's account of associative obligations is surprisingly sketchy, given the importance attached to it.[17] It may be thought that, however convincing the account of associative obligations is in the context of friendship, its place in explaining political obligation has not been made out. This ultimately rests on coercion: neither friendship nor family does. Or is Dworkin committed to the view that a state which has to enforce its will upon recalcitrant citizens is not a "true" community? It would seem that a state which had to enforce laws by means of coercion was undercutting its own foundation, which rests on a relationship where there is obligation. But this is to assume that Dworkin has adequately accounted for associative obligations within groups such as family and friends. Some doubt has already been cast on this as far as family is concerned. But, more generally, do such associative obligations really rest on reciprocity?[18] Is this how members of a family or friends conceive of obligation? Do parents care for children so that children will care for them when they are elderly? What of the parent with a child who is not going to survive childhood or is so disabled that he will always need to be cared for? Can love or altruism be reduced to reciprocal obligation? Surely not. And it would seem that there are associative obligations where reciprocity is never in question. Can Dworkin explain the bonds which unite the Irish (think of St Patrick's Day parades in continents far from Ireland) or Jews fund-raising for Israel? It is different to see how he can account for those communities.[19]

## RIGHT ANSWERS AND WRONG ANSWERS

In the last chapter of *Law's Empire* Dworkin writes of Hercules's dilemma when he thinks "the best interpretation of the equal protection clause outlaws distinctions between the rights of adults and those of children that have never been questioned in the community, and yet he ... thinks that it would be politically unfair ... for the law to impose that view on a community whose family and social practices accept such distinctions as proper and fundamental".[20]

Can a "right answer" be at the same time a wrong answer? It is

---

[16] *ibid.* It may be thought strange that Dworkin should claim to find the answer to the puzzle of legitimacy in "fraternity", a concept with overtly chauvinist political connotations (on which see C. Pateman, *The Sexual Contact* (1988), pp. 78–82 and *The Disorder of Women* (1989), Chap. 2). See also J. Rawls, *A Theory of Justice* (1972), where fraternity is "the idea of not wanting to have greater advantage unless this is to the benefit of others who are less well off" (p. 105).

[17] He virtually admits this in *Law's Empire*, p. 197.

[18] A question now beginning to be explained: see J. Finch, *Family Obligations and Social Change* (1989); J. Eekelaar (1991) 11 Oxford Journal Legal Studies 340.

[19] For different accounts of "community" see M. Sandel, *Liberalism and the Limits of Justice* (1982). This emphasizes "self-identity". It is difficult to see how this can explain political obligation. Dworkin is critical of Sandel in *Sovereign Virtue*, p. 219.

[20] *Law's Empire*, p. 402.

interesting that this sentence has passed relatively unnoticed, perhaps because most readers of Dworkin would not question discrimination against children[21] any more than the communities of which they are a part. It may be easier to appreciate the problem, if we substitute "women" for "children", and place ourselves perhaps a generation ago. Would Hercules in this earlier time have had to allow his convictions that discrimination against women was wrong to be "trumped" by those of a community which did not question it? How would Hercules have responded to claims by women that they were "persons" and thus eligible to vote[22] or be admitted to legal practice?[23]

It is necessary to examine the status of children (or women) in relation to the community of principle which, as we have seen, can claim moral legitimacy in the name of "fraternity". Practices in relation to both women and children have been, and are, routinely justified by paternalism. As we have seen, Dworkin stresses that the conception of equal concern, a constructive feature of the community of principle, is not incompatible with paternalistic practices.[24] Dworkin uses the example, set out above, of a culture which believes parents can choose their daughters' husbands for them. Dworkin acknowledges that, if this "institution" of the family is "otherwise seriously unjust", it "cannot be justified in any way that recommends continuing it".[25] But serious injustice is exemplified by Dworkin as forcing family members to commit crimes in the interest of the family—he doesn't give an example, but so-called "honour killings" is a clear example. Whatever crime he has in mind, it would seem to compound the errors already perpetrated. What is the "interest" of the family? How does a culture think? And, most pertinently in this context, how is membership of a community tested? Dworkin does not question why certain persons, who he takes for granted are members of the group, need protection. But, perhaps they would not see themselves as members of the group. And, perhaps they need protection because of cultural practices of the past.[26] Even if they identify with the group and accept its practices, even those practices which hold them down, could this not be false consciousness rather than preference, the result of inculcation of a dominant ideology[27] over generations?

It is clear from Dworkin's discussion of the paternalistic family that he regards its female members as included within that community. But would they? Or is this a community defined by those who also define its practices? And, if the same applies to the wider community, as by definitional fiat it must, then, if we return to the moral dilemma posed in the conflict between the "right answer" and the answer deemed by the

[21] But see M. Freeman, *The Moral Status of Children* (1997).
[22] On the *Anthony* case see J. Hoff, *Law, Gender and Injustice* (1991) Chap. 5.
[23] As in *Bradwell v. Illinois* 83 US 130 (1873). And see K. Bartlett, *post*, 1360–1361.
[24] *Law's Empire*, p. 200.
[25] *ibid*, p. 205.
[26] See R. West (1990) 64 Tulane L. Rev. 659.
[27] See *post*, 1142.

"community" to be fair, we reach the conclusion that the community can fictively prescribe membership to those it denies participatory rights, and then in their name justify that exclusion.[28] And, furthermore, rely on the judiciary to legitimate their actions, for questioning the unquestioned exceeds the bounds of what Dworkin considers legitimate judicial activity.

---

**R. DWORKIN**
**Taking Rights Seriously**
(revised ed., 1978)

*The Rights Thesis*

*A. Principles and Policies*

Theories of adjudication have become more sophisticated, but the most popular theories still put judging in the shade of legislation. The main outlines of this story are familiar. Judges should apply the law that other institutions have made; they should not make new law. That is the ideal, but for different reasons it cannot be realized fully in practice. Statutes and common law rules are often vague and must be interpreted before they can be applied to novel cases. Some cases, moreover, raise issues so novel that they cannot be decided even by stretching or reinterpreting existing rules. So judges must sometimes make new law, either covertly or explicitly. But when they do, they should act as deputy to the appropriate legislature, enacting the law that they suppose the legislature would enact if seized of the problem.

That is perfectly familiar, but there is buried in this common story a further level of subordination not always noticed. When judges make law, so the expectation runs, they will act not only as deputy to the legislature but as a deputy legislature. They will make law in response to evidence and arguments of the same character as would move the superior institution if it were acting on its own. This is a deeper level of subordination, because it makes any understanding of what judges do in hard cases parasitic on a prior understanding of what legislators do all the time. This deeper subordination is thus conceptual as well as political.

In fact, however, judges neither should be nor are deputy legislators, and the familiar assumption, that when they go beyond political decisions already made by someone else they are legislating, is misleading. It misses the importance of a fundamental distinction within political theory, which I shall now introduce in a crude form. This is the distinction between arguments of principle on the one hand and arguments of policy on the other.

Arguments of policy justify a political decision by showing that the decision advances or protects some collective goal of the community as a whole. The arguments in favor of a subsidy for aircraft manufacturers that the subsidy will protect national defense, is an argument of policy. Arguments of principle justify a political decision by showing that the decision respects or secures some individual or group right. The argument in favor of anti-discrimination statutes, that a minority has a right to equal respect and concern, is an argument of principle. These two sorts of argument do not exhaust political argument. Sometimes, for

---

[28] Cf. K. Bartlett: "Feminists consider the concept of community problematic, because they have demonstrated that law has tended to reject existing structures of power" (1990) 103 Harvard L. Rev. 829, 841, and *post*, 1159.

example, a political decision, like the decision to allow extra income tax exemptions for the blind, may be defended as an act of public generosity or virtue rather than on grounds of either policy or principle. But principle and policy are the major grounds of political justification.

The justification of a legislative program of any complexity will ordinarily require both sorts of argument. Even a program that is chiefly a matter of policy, like a subsidy program for important industries, may require stands of principle to justify its particular design. It may be, for example, that the program provides equal subsidies for manufacturers of different capabilities, on the assumption that weaker aircraft manufacturers have some right not to be driven out of business by government intervention, even though the industry would be more efficient without them. On the other hand, a program that depends chiefly on principle, like an anti-discrimination program, may reflect a sense that rights are not absolute and do not hold when the consequences for policy are very serious. The program may provide, for example, that fair employment practice rules do not apply when they might prove especially disruptive or dangerous. In the subsidy case we might say that the rights conferred are generated by policy and qualified by principle; in the anti-discrimination case they are generated by principle and qualified by policy.

It is plainly competent for the legislature to pursue arguments of policy and to adopt programs that are generated by such arguments. If courts are deputy legislatures, then it must be competent for them to do the same. Of course, unoriginal judicial decisions that merely enforce the clear terms of some plainly valid statute are always justified on arguments of principle, even if the statute itself was generated by policy. Suppose an aircraft manufacturer sues to recover the subsidy that the statute provides. He argues his right to the subsidy; his argument is an argument of principle. He does not argue that the national defense would be improved by subsidizing him; he might even concede that the statute was wrong on policy grounds when it was adopted, or that it should have been repealed, on policy grounds, long ago. His right to a subsidy no longer depends on any argument of policy because the statute made it a matter of principle.

But if the case at hand is a hard case, when no settled rule dictates a decision either way, then it might seem that a proper decision could be generated by either policy or principle. Consider, for example, the problem of the recent *Spartan Steel* case.[29] The defendant's employees had broken an electrical cable belonging to a power company that supplied power to the plaintiff, and the plaintiff's factory was shut down while the cable was repaired. The court had to decide whether to allow the plaintiff recovery for economic loss following negligent damage to someone else's property. It might have proceeded to its decision by asking either whether a firm in the position of the plaintiff had a right to a recovery, which is a matter of principle, or whether it would be economically wise to distribute liability for accidents in the way the plaintiff suggested, which is a matter of policy.

If judges are deputy legislators, then the court should be prepared to follow the latter argument as well as the former, and decide in favor of the plaintiff if that argument recommends. That is, I suppose, what is meant by the popular idea that a court must be free to decide a novel case like *Spartan Steel* on policy grounds; and indeed Lord Denning described his own opinion in that case in just that way.[30] I do not suppose he meant to distinguish an argument of principle from an argument of policy in the technical way I have, but he in any event did not mean to rule out an argument of policy in that technical sense.

I propose, nevertheless, the thesis that judicial decisions in civil cases, even in hard cases like *Spartan Steel*, characteristically are and should be generated by principles not policy. That thesis plainly needs much elaboration, but we may

[29] *Spartan Steel & Alloys Ltd* v. *Martin & Co.* [1973] Q.B. 27.
[30] *ibid.*, at 36.

notice that certain arguments of political theory and jurisprudence support the thesis even in its abstract form. These arguments are not decisive, but they are sufficiently powerful to suggest the importance of the thesis, and to justify the attention that will be needed for a more careful formulation.

### B. Principles and Democracy

The familiar story, that adjudication must be subordinated to legislation, is supported by two objections to judicial originality. The first argues that a community should be governed by men and women who are elected by and responsible to the majority. Since judges are, for the most part, not elected, and since they are not, in practice, responsible to the electorate in the way legislators are, it seems to compromise that proposition when judges make law. The second argues that if a judge makes new law and applies it retroactively in the case before him, then the losing party will be punished, not because he violated some duty he had, but rather a new duty created after the event.

These two arguments combine to support the traditional ideal that adjudication should be as unoriginal as possible. But they offer much more powerful objections to judicial decisions generated by policy than to those generated by principle. The first objection, that law should be made by elected and responsible officials, seems unexceptionable when we think of law as policy; that is, as a compromise among individual goals and purposes in search of the welfare of the community among individual goals and purposes in search of the welfare of the community as a whole. It is far from clear that interpersonal comparisons of utility or preference, through which such compromises might be made objectively, make sense even in theory; but in any case no proper calculus is available in practice. Policy decisions must therefore be made through the operation of some political process designed to produce an accurate expression of the different interests that should be taken into account. The political system of representative democracy may work only indifferently in this respect, but it works better than a system that allows none-lected judges, who have no mail bag or lobbyists or pressure groups, to compromise competing interests in their chambers.

The second objection is also persuasive against a decision generated by policy. We all agree that it would be wrong to sacrifice the rights of an innocent man in the name of some new duty created after the event; it does, therefore, seem wrong to take property from the individual and hand it to another in order just to improve overall economic efficiency. But that is the form of the policy argument that would be necessary to justify a decision in *Spartan Steel*. If the plaintiff had no right to the recovery and the defendant no duty to offer it, the court could be justified in taking the defendant's property for the plaintiff only in the interest of wise economic policy.

But suppose, on the other hand, that a judge successfully justifies a decision in a hard case, like *Spartan Steel*, on grounds not of policy but of principle. Suppose, that is, that he is able to show that the plaintiff has a *right* to recover its damages. The two arguments just described would offer much less of an objection to the decision. The first is less relevant when a court judges principle, because an argument of principle does not often rest on assumptions about the nature and intensity of the different demands and concerns distributed throughout the community. On the contrary, an argument of principle fixes on some interest presented by the proponent of the right it describes, an interest alleged to be of such a character as to make irrelevant the fine discriminations of any argument of policy that might oppose it. A judge who is insulated from the demands of the political majority whose interests the right would trump is, therefore, in a better position to evaluate the argument.

The second objection to judicial originality has no force against an argument of principle. If the plaintiff has a right against the defendant, then the defendant has a corresponding duty, and it is that duty, not some new duty created in court, that justifies the award against him. Even if the duty has not been imposed upon him by explicit prior legislation, there is, but for one difference, no more injustice in enforcing the duty than if it had been.

The difference is, of course, that if the duty had been created by statute the defendant would have been put on much more explicit notice of that duty, and might more reasonably have been expected to arrange his affairs so as to provide for its consequences. But an argument of principle makes us look upon the defendant's claim, that it is unjust to take him by surprise, in a new light. If the plaintiff does indeed have a right to a judicial decision in his favor, then he is entitled to rely upon that right. If it is obvious and uncontroversial that he has the right, the defendant is in no position to claim unfair surprise just because the right arose in some way other than by publication in a statute. If, on the other hand, the plaintiff's claim is doubtful, then the court must, to some extent, surprise one or another of the parties; and if the court decides that on balance the plaintiff's argument is stronger, then it will also decide that the plaintiff was, on balance, more justified in his expectations. The court may, of course, be mistaken in this conclusion; but that possibility is not a consequence of the originality of its argument, for there is no reason to suppose that a court hampered by the requirement that its decisions be unoriginal will make fewer mistakes of principle than a court that is not.

## C. Jurisprudence

We have, therefore, in these political considerations, strong reason to consider more carefully whether judicial arguments cannot be understood, even in hard cases, as arguments, generated by principle. We have an additional reason in a familiar problem of jurisprudence. Lawyers believe that when judges make new law their decisions are constrained by legal traditions but are nevertheless personal and original. Novel decisions, it is said, reflect a judge's own political morality, but also reflect the morality that is embedded in the traditions of the common law, which might well be different. This is, of course, only law school rhetoric, but it nevertheless poses the problem of explaining how these different contributions to the decision of a hard case are to be identified and reconciled.

One popular solution relies on a spatial image; it says that the traditions of the common law contract the area of a judge's discretion to rely upon his personal morality, but do not entirely eliminate that area. But this answer is unsatisfactory on two grounds. First, it does not elucidate what is at best a provocative metaphor, which is that some morality is embedded in a mass of particular decisions other judges have reached in the past. Second, it suggests a plainly inadequate phenomenological account of the judicial decision. Judges do not decide hard cases in two stages, first checking to see where the institutional constraints end, and then setting the books aside to stride off on their own. The institutional constraints they sense are pervasive and endure to the decision itself. We therefore need an account of the interaction of personal and institutional morality that is less metaphorical and explains more successfully that pervasive interaction.

The rights thesis, that judicial decisions enforce existing political rights, suggests an explanation that is more successful on both counts. If the thesis holds, then institutional history acts not as a constraint on the political judgment of judges but as an ingredient of that judgment, because institutional history is part of the background that any plausible judgment about the rights of an individual must accommodate. Political rights are creatures of both history and morality: what an individual is entitled to have, in civil society, depends upon both the practice and the justice of its political institutions. So the supposed tension between judicial originality and institutional history is dissolved: judges must make fresh judgments about the rights of the parties who come before them, but these political rights reflect, rather than oppose, political decisions of the past. When a judge chooses between the rule established in precedent and some new rule thought to be fairer, he does not choose between history and justice. He rather makes a judgment that requires some compromise between considerations that ordinarily combine in any calculation of political right, but here compete.

The rights thesis therefore provides a more satisfactory explanation of how judges use precedent in hard cases than the explanation provided by any theory that gives a more prominent place to policy. Judges, like all political officials, are subject to the doctrine of political responsibility. This doctrine states, in its most general form, that political officials must make only such political decisions as they can justify within a political theory that also justifies the other decisions they propose to make. The doctrine seems innocuous in this general form; but it does, even in this form, condemn a style of political administration that might be called, following Rawls, intuitionistic.[31] It condemns the practice of making decisions that seem right in isolation, but cannot be brought within some comprehensive theory of general principles and policies that is consistent with other decisions also thought right. Suppose a Congressman votes to prohibit abortion, on the ground that human life in any form is sacred, but then votes to permit the parents of babies born deformed to withhold medical treatment that will keep such babies alive. He might say that he feels that there is some difference, but the principle of responsibility, strictly applied, will not allow him these two votes unless he can incorporate the difference within some general political theory he sincerely holds.

The doctrine demands, we might say, articulate consistency. But this demand is relatively weak when policies are in play. Policies are aggregative in their influence on political decisions and it need not be part of a responsible strategy for reaching a collective goal that individuals be treated alike. It does not follow from the doctrine of responsibility, therefore, that if the legislature awards a subsidy to one aircraft manufacturer one month it must award a subsidy to another manufacturer the next. In the case of principles, however, the doctrine insists on distributional consistency from one case to the next, because it does not allow for the idea of a strategy that might be better served by unequal distribution of the benefit in question. If an official, for example, believes that sexual liberty of some sort is a right of individuals, then he must protect that liberty in a way that distributes the benefit reasonably equally over the class of those whom he supposes to have the right. If he allows one couple to use contraceptives on the ground that this right would otherwise be invaded, then he must, so long as he does not recant that earlier decision, allow the next couple the same liberty. He cannot say that the first decision gave the community just the amount of sexual liberty it needed, so that no more is required at the time of the second.

Judicial decisions are political decisions, at least in the broad sense that attracts the doctrine of political responsibility. If the rights thesis holds, then the distinction just made would account, at least in a very general way, for the special concern that judges show for both precedents and hypothetical examples. An argument of principle can supply a justification for a particular decision, under the doctrine of responsibility, only if the principle cited can be shown to be consistent with earlier decisions not recanted, and with decisions that the institution is prepared to make in the hypothetical circumstances. That is hardly surprising, but the argument would not hold if judges based their decisions on arguments of policy. They would be free to say that some policy might be adequately served by serving it in the case at bar, providing, for example, just the right subsidy to some troubled industry, so that neither earlier decisions nor hypothetical future decisions need be understood as serving the same policy.

---

[31] See *A Theory of Justice*, Chap. 10.

Consistency here, of course, means consistency in the application of the principle relied upon, not merely in the application of the particular rule announced in the name of that principle. If, for example, the principle that no one has the duty to make good remote or unexpected losses flowing from his negligence is relief upon to justify a decision for the defendant in *Spartan Steel*, then it must be shown that the rule laid down in other cases, which allows recovery for negligent misstatements, is consistent with that principle; not merely that the rule about negligent misstatement is a different rule from the rule in *Spartan Steel*.

[pp. 82–88]

### Institutional Rights

The rights thesis provides that judges decide hard cases by confirming or denying concrete rights. But the concrete rights upon which judges rely must have two other characteristics. They must be institutional rather than background rights, and they must be legal rather than some other form of institutional rights. We cannot appreciate or test the thesis, therefore, without further elaboration of these distinctions.

Institutional rights may be found in institutions of very different character. A chess player has a "chess" right to be awarded a point in a tournament if he checkmates an opponent. A citizen in a democracy has a legislative right to the enactment of statutes necessary to protect his free speech. In the case of chess, institutional rights are fixed by constitutive and regulative rules that belong distinctly to the game, or to a particular tournament. Chess is, in this sense, an autonomous institution; I mean that it is understood among its participants, that no one may claim an institutional right by direct appeal to general morality. No one may argue, for example, that he has earned the right to be declared the winner by his general virtue. But legislation is only partly autonomous in that sense. There are special constitutive and regulative rules that define what a legislature is, and who belongs to it, and how it votes, and that it may not establish a religion. But these rules belonging distinctly to legislation are rarely sufficient to determine whether a citizen has an institutional right to have a certain statute enacted; they do not decide, for example, whether he has a right to minimum wage legislation. Citizens are expected to repair to general considerations of political morality when they argue for such rights.

The fact that some institutions are fully and others partly autonomous has the consequence mentioned earlier, that the institutional rights a political theory acknowledges may diverge from the background rights it provides. Institutional rights are nevertheless genuine rights. Even if we suppose that the poor have an abstract background right to money taken from the rich, it would be wrong, not merely unexpected, for the referees to a chess tournament to award the prize money to the poorest contestant rather than the contestant with the most points. It would provide no excuse to say that since tournament rights merely describe the conditions necessary for calling the tournament a chess tournament, the referee's act is justified so long as he does not use the word "chess" when he hands out the award. The participants entered the tournament with the understanding that chess rules would apply; they have genuine rights to the enforcement of these rules and no others.

Institutional autonomy insulates an official's institutional duty from the greater part of background political morality. But how far does the force of this insulation extend? Even in the case of a fully insulated institution like chess some rules will require interpretation or elaboration before an official may enforce them in certain circumstances. Suppose some rule of a chess tournament provides that the referee shall declare a game forfeit if one player "unreasonably" annoys the other in the course of play. The language of the rule does not define what counts as "unreasonable" annoyance; it does not decide whether, for example, a player who continually smiles at his opponent in such a way as to unnerve him, as the Russian grandmaster Tal once smiled at Fischer, annoys him unreasonably.

The referee is not free to give effect to his background convictions in deciding this hard case. He might hold, as a matter of political theory, that individuals have a right to equal welfare without regard to intellectual abilities. It would nevertheless be wrong for him to rely upon that conviction in deciding difficult cases under the forfeiture rule. He could not say, for example, that annoying behaviour is reasonable so long as it has the effect of reducing the importance of intellectual ability in deciding who will win the game. The participants, and the general community that is interested, will say that his duty is just the contrary. Since chess is an intellectual game, he must apply the forfeiture rule in such a way as to protect, rather than jeopardize, the role of intellect in the contest . . .

[pp. 101–102]

### The Common Law

#### 1. *Precedent*

One day lawyers will present a hard case to Hercules[32] that does not turn upon any statute; they will argue whether earlier common law decisions of Hercules' court, properly understood, provide some party with a right to a decision in his favor. *Spartan Steel* was such a case. The plaintiff did not argue that any statute provided it a right to recover its economic damages; it pointed instead to certain earlier judicial decisions that awarded recovery for other sorts of damage, and argued that the principle behind these cases required a decision for it as well.

Hercules must begin by asking why arguments of that form are ever, even in principle, sound. He will find that he has available no quick or obvious answer. When he asked himself the parallel question about legislation he found, in general democratic theory, a ready reply. But the details of the practices of precedent he must now justify resist any comparably simple theory.

He might, however, be tempted by this answer. Judges, when they decide particular cases at common law, lay down general rules that are intended to benefit the community in some way. Other judges, deciding later cases, must therefore enforce these rules so that the benefit may be achieved. If this account of the matter were a sufficient justification of the practices of precedent, then Hercules could decide these hard common law cases as if earlier decisions were statutes, using the techniques he worked out for statutory interpretation. But he will encounter fatal difficulties if he pursues that theory very far. It will repay us to consider why, in some detail, because the errors in the theory will be guides to a more successful theory.

Statutory interpretation . . . depends upon the availability of a canonical form of words, however vague or unspecific, that sets limits to the political decisions that the statute may be taken to have made. Hercules will discover that many of the opinions that litigants cite as precedents do not contain any special propositions taken to be a canonical form of the rule that the case lays down. It is true that it was part of Anglo-American judicial style, during the last part of the nineteenth century and the first part of this century, to attempt to compose such canonical statements, so that one could thereafter refer, for example, to the rule in *Rylands* v. *Fletcher*.[33] But even in this period, lawyers and textbook writers disagreed about which parts of famous opinions should be taken to have that character. Today, in any case, even important opinions rarely attempt that legislative sort of draftsmanship. They are reasons, in the form of precedents and

---

[32] [Hercules is discussed further at *post*, 792–793, 811 and 817–821. On the real "Hercules" see Balkin (1993) 103 Yale L. J. 105, 168.]

[33] [1866] L.R. 1 Ex. 265, *aff'd* (1868) L.R. 3 HL 330.

principles, to justify a decision, but it is the decision, not some new and state rule of law, that these precedents and principles are taken to justify. Sometimes a judge will acknowledge openly that it lies to later cases to determine the full effect of the case he has decided.

Of course, Hercules might well decide that when he does find, in an earlier case, canonical form of words, he will use his techniques of statutory interpretation to decide whether the rule composed of these words embraces a novel case.[34] He might well acknowledge what could be called an enactment force of precedent. He will nevertheless find that when a precedent does have enactment force, its influence on later cases is not taken to be limited to that force. Judges and lawyers do not think that the force of precedents is exhausted, as a statute would be, by the linguistic limits of some particular phrase. If *Spartan Steel* were a New York case, counsel for the plaintiff would suppose that Cardozo's earlier decision in *MacPherson* v. *Buick*,[35] in which a woman recovered damages for injuries from a negligently manufactured automobile, counted in favor of his client's right to recover, in spite of the fact that the earlier decision contained no language that could plausibly be interpreted to enact that right. He would urge that the earlier decision exerts a gravitational force on later decisions even when these later decisions lie outside its particular orbit.

This gravitational force is part of the practice Hercules' general theory of precedent must capture. In this important respect, judicial practice differs from the practice of officials in other institutions. In chess, officials conform to established rules in a way that assumes full institutional autonomy. They exercise originality only to the extent required by the fact that an occasional rule, like the rule about forfeiture, demands that originality. Each decision of a chess referee, therefore, can be said to be directly required and justified by an established rule of chess, even though some of these decisions must be based on an interpretation, rather than on simply the plain and unavoidable meaning, of that rule.

Some legal philosophers write about common law adjudication as if it were in this way like chess, except that legal rules are much more likely than chess rules to require interpretation. That is the spirit, for example, of Professor Hart's argument that hard cases arise only because legal rules have what he calls "open texture."[36] In fact, judges often disagree not simply about how some rule or principle should be interpreted, but whether the rule or principle one judge cites should be acknowledged to be a rule or principle at all. In some cases both the majority and the dissenting opinions recognize the same earlier cases as relevant, but disagree about what rule or principle these precedents should be understood to have established. In adjudication, unlike chess, the argument *for* a particular rule may be more important than the argument *from* that rule to the particular case; and while the chess referee who decides a case by appeal to a rule no one has ever heard of before is likely to be dismissed or certified, the judge who does so is likely to be celebrated in law school lectures.

Nevertheless, judges seem agreed that earlier decisions do contribute to the formulation of new and controversial rules in some way other than by interpretation; they are agreed that earlier decisions have gravitational force even

---

[34] But since Hercules will be led to accept the rights thesis, see pp. 115–116 [of *TRS*] his "interpretation" of judicial enactments will be different from his interpretation of statutes in one important respect. When he interprets statutes he fixes to some statutory language, as we saw, arguments of principle or policy that provide the best justification of that language in the light of the legislature's responsibilities. His argument remains an argument of principle; he uses policy to determine what rights the legislature has already created. But when he "interprets" judicial elements he will fix to the relevant language only arguments of principle, because the rights thesis argues that only such arguments acquit the responsibility of the "enacting" court.

[35] *MacPherson* v. *Buick Motor Co.* (1916) 217 N.Y. 382; (1916) 111 N.E. 1050.

[36] H.L.A. Hart, *The Concept of Law*, pp. 124–136.

when they disagree about what that force is. The legislator may very often concern himself only with issues of background morality or policy in deciding how to cast his vote on some issue. He need not show that his vote is consistent with the votes of his colleagues in the legislature, or with those of past legislatures. But the judge very rarely assumes that character of independence. He will always try to connect the justification he provides for an original decision with decisions that other judges or officials have taken in the past.

In fact, when good judges try to explain in some general way how they work, they search for figures of speech to describe the constraints they feel even when they suppose that they are making new law, constraints that would not be appropriate if they were legislators. They say, for example, that they find new rules immanent in the law as a whole, or that they are enforcing an internal logic of the law through some method that belongs more to philosophy than to politics, or that they are the agents through which the law works itself pure, or that the law has some life of its own even though this belongs to experience rather than logic. Hercules must not rest content with these famous metaphors and personifications, but he must also not be content with any description of the judicial process that ignores their appeal to the best lawyers.

The gravitational force of precedent cannot be captured by any theory that takes the full force of precedent to be its enactment force as a piece of legislation. But the inadequacy of that approach suggests a superior theory. The gravitational force of a precedent may be explained by appeal, not to the wisdom of enforcing enactments, but to the fairness of treating like cases alike. A precedent is the report of an earlier political decision; the very fact of that decision, as a piece of political history, provides some reason for deciding other cases in a similar way in the future. This general explanation of the gravitational force of precedent accounts for the feature that defeated the enactment theory, which is that the force of a precedent escapes the language of its opinion. If the government of a community has forced the manufacturer of defective motor cars to pay damages to a woman who was injured because of the defect, then that historical fact must offer some reason, at least, why the same government should require a contractor who has caused economic damage through the defective work of his employees to make good that loss. We may test the weight of that reason, not by asking whether the language of the earlier decision, suitably interpreted, requires the contractor to pay damages, but by asking the different question whether it is fair for the government, having intervened in the way it did in the first case, to refused its aid in the second.

Hercules will conclude that this doctrine of fairness offers the only adequate account of the full practice of precedent. He will draw certain further conclusions about his own responsibilities when deciding hard cases. The most important of these is that he must limit the gravitational force of earlier decisions to the extension of the arguments of principle necessary to justify those decisions. If an earlier decision were taken to be entirely justified by some argument of policy, it would have no gravitational force. Its value as a precedent would be limited to its enactment force, that is, to further cases captured by some particular words of the opinion. The distributional force of a collective goal, as we notice earlier, is a matter of contingent fact and general legislative strategy. If the government intervened on behalf of Mrs MacPherson, not because she had any right to its intervention, but only because wise strategy suggested that means of pursuing some collective goal like economic efficiency, there can be no effective argument of fairness that it therefore ought to intervene for the plaintiff in *Spartan Steel*.                                                                    [pp. 100–113]

## 2. *The Seamless Web*

Hercules' first conclusion, that the gravitational force of a precedent is defined by the arguments of principle that support the precedent, suggests a second. Since judicial practice in his community assumes that earlier cases have a *general* gravitational force, then he can justify that judicial practice only by supposing that the rights thesis holds in his community. It is never taken to be a satisfactory argument against the gravitational force of some precedent that the goal that precedent served has now been served sufficiently, or that the courts would now be better occupied in serving some other goal that has been relatively neglected, possibly returning to the goal the precedent served on some other occasion. The practices of precedent do not suppose that the *rationales* that recommend judicial decisions can be served piecemeal in that way. If it is acknowledged that a particular precedent it justified for a particular reason; if that reason would also recommend a particular result in the case at bar; if the earlier decision has not been recanted or in some other way taken as a matter of institutional regret; then that decision must be reached in the later case.

Hercules must suppose that it is understood in his community, though perhaps not explicitly recognized, that judicial decisions must be taken to be justified by arguments of principle rather than arguments of policy. He now sees that the familiar concept used by judges to explain their reasoning from precedent, the concept of certain principles that underlie or are embedded in the common law, is itself only a metaphorical statement of the rights thesis. He may henceforth use that concept in his decisions of hard common law cases. It provides a general test for deciding such cases that is like the chess referee's concept of the character of a game, and like his own concept of a legislative purpose. It provides a question— What set of principles best justifies the precedents?—that builds a bridge between the general justification of the practice of precedent, which is fairness, and his own decision about what that general justification requires in some particular hard case.

Hercules must now develop his concept of principles that underlie the common law by assigning to each of the relevant precedents some scheme of principle that justifies the decision of that precedent. He will now discover a further important difference between this concept and the concept of statutory purpose that he used in statutory interpretation. In the case of statutes, he found it necessary to choose some theory about the purpose of the particular statute in question, looking to other acts of the legislature only insofar as these might help to select between theories that fit the statute about equally well. But if the gravitational force of precedent rests on the idea that fairness requires the consistent enforcement of rights, then Hercules must discover principles that fit, not only the particular precedent to which some litigant directs his attention, but all other judicial decisions within his general jurisdiction and, indeed, statutes as well, so far as these must be seen to be generated by principle rather than policy. He does not satisfy his duty to show that his decision is consistent with established principles, and therefore fair, if the principles he cites as established are themselves inconsistent with other decisions that his court also proposes to uphold.

Suppose, for example, that he justify Cardozo's decision in favour of Mrs MacPherson by citing some abstract principle of equality, which argues that whenever an accident occurs then the richest of the various persons whose acts might have contributed to the accident must bear the loss. He nevertheless cannot show that that principle has been respected in other accident cases, or, even if he could, that it has been respected in other branches of the law, like contract, in which it would also have great impact if it were recognized at all. If he decides against a future accident plaintiff who is richer than the defendant, by appealing to this alleged right of equality, that plaintiff may properly complain that the decision is just as inconsistent with the government's behavior in other cases as if *MacPherson* itself had been ignored. The law may not be a seamless web; but the plaintiff is entitled to ask Hercules to treat it as if it were.

You will now see why I called our judge Hercules. He must construct a scheme of abstract and concrete principles that provides a coherent justification for all common law precedents and, so far as these are to be justified on principle, constitutional and statutory provisions as well. We may grasp the magnitude of this enterprise by distinguishing, within the vast material of legal decisions that Hercules must justify, a vertical and a horizontal ordering. The vertical ordering is provided by distinguishing layers of authority; that is layers at which official decisions might be taken to be controlling over decisions made at lower levels. In the United States the rough character of the vertical ordering is apparent. The constitutional structure occupies the highest level, the decisions of the Supreme Court and perhaps other courts interpreting that structure the next, enactments of the various legislatures the next and decisions of the various courts developing the common law different levels below that. Hercules must arrange justification of principle at each of these levels so that the justification is consistent with principles taken to provide the justification of higher levels. The horizontal ordering simply requires that the principles taken to justify a decision at one level must also be consistent with the justification offered for other decisions at that level.

Suppose Hercules, taking advantage of his unusual skills, proposed to work out this entire scheme in advance, so that he would be ready to confront litigants with an entire theory of law should this be necessary to justify any particular decision. He would begin, deferring to vertical ordering, by setting out and refining the constitutional theory he has already used. That constitutional theory would be more or less different from the theory that a different judge would develop, because a constitutional theory requires judgments about complex issues of institutional fit, as well as judgments about political and moral philosophy, and Hercules' judgements will inevitably differ from those other judges would make. These differences at a high level of vertical ordering will exercise considerable force on the scheme each judge would propose at lower levels. Hercules might think, for example, that certain substantive constitutional constraints on legislative power are best justified by postulating an abstract right to privacy against the state, because he believes that such a right is a consequence of the even more abstract right to liberty that the constitution guarantees. If so, he would regard the failure of the law of tort to recognize a parallel abstract right to privacy against fellow citizens, in some concrete form, as an inconsistency. If another judge did not share his beliefs about the connection between privacy and liberty, and so did not accept his constitutional interpretation as persuasive, that judge would also disagree about the proper development of tort.

So the impact of Hercules' own judgments will be pervasive, even though some of these will be controversial. But they will not enter his calculations in such a way that different parts of the theory he constructs can be attributed to his independent convictions rather than to the body of law that he must justify. He will not follow those classical theories of adjudication I mentioned earlier, which suppose that a judge follows statutes or precedent until the clear direction of these runs out, after which he is free to strike out on his own. His theory is rather a theory about what the statute or the precedent itself requires, and though he will, of course, reflect his own intellectual and philosophical convictions in making that judgment, that is a very different matter from supposing that those convictions have some independent force in his argument just because they are his.

[pp. 115–118]

## R. DWORKIN
### Law as Interpretation
(1982)[37]

In this essay I shall argue that legal practice is an exercise in interpretation not only when lawyers interpret particular documents of statutes, but generally. Law so conceived is deeply and thoroughly political. Lawyers and judges cannot avoid politics in the broad sense of political theory. But law is not a matter of personal or partisan politics, and a critique of law that does not understand this difference will provide poor understanding and even poorer guidance. I propose that we can improve our understanding of law by comparing legal interpretation with interpretation in other fields of knowledge, particularly literature. I also expect that law, when better understood, will provide a better grasp of what interpretation is in general.

*Law*

The central problem of analytical jurisprudence is this: What sense should be given to propositions of law? By propositions I mean the various statements lawyers make reporting what the law is on some question or other. Propositions of law can be very abstract and general, like the proposition that states of the United States may not discriminate on racial grounds in supplying basic services to citizens, or they can be relatively concrete, like the proposition that someone who accepts a check in the normal course of business without notice of any infirmities in its title is entitled to collect against the maker, or very concrete, like the proposition that Mrs $X$. is liable in damages to Mr $Y$. in the amount of $1150 because he slipped on her icy sidewalk and broke his hip. In each case a puzzle arises. What are propositions of law really about? What in the world could make them true of false?

The puzzle arises because propositions of law seem to be descriptive—they are about how things are in the law, not about how they should be—and yet it has proved extremely difficult to say exactly what it is that they describe. Legal positivists believe that propositions of law are indeed wholly descriptive; they are infact pieces of history. A proposition of law, in their view, is true if some event of a designated law-making kind has taken place, and otherwise not. This seems to work reasonably well in very simple cases. If the Illinois Legislature enacts the words, "No will shall be valid without three witnesses," then the proposition of law, that an Illinois will need three witnesses, seems to be true only in virtue of that historical event.

But in more difficult cases the analysis fails. Consider the proposition that a particular affirmative action scheme (not yet tested in the courts) is constitutionally valid. If that is true, it cannot be so just in virtue of the text of the Constitution and the fact of prior court decisions, because reasonable lawyers who know exactly what the Constitution says and what the courts have done may yet disagree whether it is true. (I am doubtful that the positivists' analysis holds even in the simple case of the will; but that is a different matter I shall not argue here).

What are the other possibilities? One is to suppose that controversial propositions of law, like the affirmative action statement, are not descriptive at all, but are rather expressions of what the speakers wants the law to be. Another is more ambitious: controversial statements are attempts to describe some pure objective or natural law, which exists in virtue of objective moral truth rather than historical decision. Both these projects take some legal statements, at least, to be

[37] [From 60 Texas L.R. 527. See also now Dworkin, *A Matter of Principle* (1985), p. 146.]

purely evaluative as distinct from descriptive: they express either what the speaker prefers—his personal politics—or what he believes is objectively required by the principles of an ideal political morality. Neither of these projects is plausible, because someone who says that a particular untested affirmative action plan is constitutional does mean to describe the law as it is rather than as he wants it to be or thinks that, by the best moral theory, it should be. He might, indeed, say that he regrets that the plan is constitutional and thinks that according to the best moral theory, it ought not to be.

There is a better alternative: propositions of law are not simply descriptive of legal history in a straightforward way, nor are they simply evaluative in some way divorced from legal history. They are interpretive of legal history, which combines elements of both description and evaluation but is different from both. This suggestion will be congenial, at least at first blush, to many lawyers and legal philosophers. They are used to saying that law is a matter of interpretation; but only, perhaps, because they understand interpretation in a certain way. When a statute (or the Constitution) is unclear on some point, because some crucial term is vague or because a sentence is ambiguous, lawyers say that the statute must be interpreted, and they apply what the call "techniques of statutory construction." Most of the literature assumes that interpretation of a particular document is a matter of discovering what its authors (the legislators, or the delegates to the Constitutional Convention) meant to say in using the words they did. But lawyers recognize that on many issues the author had no intention either way and that on others his intention cannot be discovered. Some lawyers take a more skeptical position. They say that whenever judges pretend they are discovering the intention behind some piece of legislation, this is simply a smoke screen behind which the judges impose their own view of what the statute should have been.

Interpretation as a technique of legal analysis is less familiar in the case of the common law, but not unfamiliar. Suppose the Supreme Court of Illinois decided, several years ago, that a negligent driver who ran down a child was liable for the emotional damage suffered by the child's mother, who was standing next to the child on the road. Now an aunt sues another careless driver for emotional damage suffered when she heard, on the telephone many miles from the accident, that her niece had been hit. Does the aunt have a right to recover for that damage? Lawyers often say that this is a matter of interpreting the earlier decision correctly. Does the legal theory on which the earlier judge actually relied, in making his decision about the mother on the road, cover the aunt on the telephone? Once again skeptics point out that it is unlikely that the earlier judge had in mind any theory sufficiently developed so as to decide the aunt's case either way, so that a judge "interpreting" the earlier decision is actually making new law in the way he or she thinks best.

The idea of interpretation cannot serve as a general account of the nature of truth of propositions of law, however, unless it is cut loose from these associations with the speaker's meaning or intention. Otherwise it becomes simply one version of the positivist's thesis that propositions of law describe decisions made by people or institutions in the past. If interpretation is to form the basis of a different and more plausible theory about propositions of law, then we must develop a more inclusive account of what interpretation is. But that means that lawyers must not treat legal interpretation as an activity *sui generis*. We must study interpretation as a general activity, as a mode of knowledge, by attending to other contexts of that activity.

Lawyers would do well to study literary and other forms of artistic interpretation. That might seem bad advice (choosing the fire over the frying pan) because critics themselves are thoroughly divided about what literary interpretation is, and the situation is hardly better in the other arts. But that is exactly why lawyers should study these debates. Not all of the battles within literary criticism are edifying or even comprehensible, but many more theories of interpretation have been defended in literature than in law, and these include theories that challenge the flat distinction between description and evaluation that has enfeebled legal theory. [pp. 527–30]

### III. Law and Literature

#### A. The Chain of Law

These sketchy remarks about literary interpretation may have suggested too sharp a split between the role of the artist in creating a work of art and that of the critic in interpreting it later. The artist can create nothing without interpreting as he creates; since he intends to produce art, he must have at least a tacit theory of why what he produces is art and why it is a better work of art through this stroke of the pen or the brush or the chisel rather than that. The critic, for his part, creates as he interprets; for though he is bound by the fact of the work, defined in the more formal and academic parts of his theory of art, his more practical artistic sense is engaged by his responsibility to decide which way of seeing or reading or understanding that work shows it as better art. Nevertheless there is a difference between interpreting while creating and creating while interpreting, and therefore a recognizable difference between the artist and the critic.

I want to use literary interpretation as a model for the central method of legal analysis, and I therefore need to show how even this distinction between artist and critic might be eroded in certain circumstances. Suppose that a group of novelists is engaged for a particular project and that they draw lots to determine the order of play. The lowest number writes the opening chapter of a novel which he or she then sends to the next number who adds a chapter, with the understanding that he is adding a chapter to that novel rather than beginning a new one, and then sends the two chapters to the next number, and so on. Now every novelist but the first has the dual responsibilities of interpreting and creating, because each must read all that has gone before in order to establish, in the interpretivist sense, what the novel so far created is. He or she must decide what the characters are "really" like; what motives in fact guide them; what the point or theme of the developing novel is; how far some literary devide or figure, consciously or unconsciously used, contributes to these, and whether it should be extended or refined or trimmed or dropped in order to send the novel further in one direction rather than another. This must be interpretation in a non-intention-bound style because, at least for all novelists after the second, there is no single author whose intentions any interpreter can, by the rules of the project, regard as decisive.

Some novels have in fact been written in his way (including the soft-core pornographic novel *Naked Came the Stranger*[38]), though for a debunking purpose, and certain parlor games for rainy weekends in English country houses have something of the same structure. But in my imaginary exercise the novelists are expected to take their responsibilities seriously and to recognize the duty to create, so far as they can, a single, unified novel rather than, for example, a series of independent short stories with characters bearing the same names. Perhaps this is an impossible assignment; perhaps the project is doomed to produce not simply a bad novel but no novel at all, because the best theory of art requires a single creator or, if more than one, that each have some control over the whole. (But what about legends and jokes?) I need not push that question further because I am interested only in the fact that the assignment makes sense, that each of the novelists in the chain can have some idea of what he or she is asked to do, whatever misgivings each might have about the value or character of what will then be produced.

Deciding hard cases at law is rather like this strange literary exercise. The

[38] P. Ashe, *Naked Came the Stranger* (1969).

similarity is most evident when judges consider and decide "common-law" cases; that is, when no statute figures centrally in the legal issue, and the argument turns on which rules or principles of law "underlie" the related decisions of other judges in the past. Each judge is then like a novelist in the chain. He or she must read through what other judges in the past have written not simply to discover what that judges have said, or their state of mind when they said it, but to reach an opinion about what these judges have collectively *done*, in the way that each of our novelists formed an opinion about the collective novel so far written. Any judge forced to decide a law suit will find, if he looks in the appropriate books, records of many arguably similar cases decided over decades or even centuries past by many other judges of different styles and judicial and political philosophies, in periods of different orthodoxies of procedure and judicial convention. Each judge must regard himself, in deciding the new case before him, as a partner in a complex chain enterprise of which these innumerable decisions, structures, conventions, and practices are the history; it is his job to continue that history into the future through what he does on the day. He *must* interpret what has gone before because he has a responsibility to advance the enterprise in hand rather than strike out in some new direction of his own. So he must determine, according to his own judgment, what the earlier decisions come to, what the point or theme of the practice so far, taken as a whole, really is.

The judge in the hypothetical case ... about an aunt's emotional shock, must decide what the theme is, not only of the particular precedent of the mother in the road, but of accident cases, including that precedent, as a whole. He might be forced to choose, for example, between these two theories about the "meaning" of the chain of decisions. According to the first, negligent drivers are responsible to those whom their behaviour is likely to cause physical harm, but they are responsible to the people for whatever injury—physical or emotional—they in fact cause. It this is the correct principle, then the decisive difference between that case and the aunt's case is just that the aunt was not within the physical risk, and therefore she cannot recover. On the second theory, however, negligent drivers are responsible for any damage they can reasonably be expected to foresee if they think about their behaviour in advance. If that is the right principle, then the aunt may yet recover. Everything turns on whether it is sufficiently foreseeable that a child will have relatives, beyond his or her immediate parents, who may suffer emotional shock when they learn of the child's injury. The injury trying the aunt's case must decide which of these two principles represents the better "reading" of the chain of decisions he must continue.

Can we say, in some general way, what those who disagree about the best interpretation of legal precedent are disagreeing about? I said that a literary interpretation aims to show how the work in question can be seen as the most valuable work of art, and so must attend to formal features of identity, coherence, and integrity as well as more substantive considerations of artistic value. A plausible interpretation of legal practice must also, in a parallel way, satisfy a test with two dimensions: it must both fit that practice and show its point or value. But point or value here cannot mean artistic value because law, unlike literature, is not an artistic enterprise. Law is a political enterprise, whose general point, if it has one, lies in coordinating social and individual effort, or resolving social and individual disputes, or securing justice between citizens and between them and their government, or some combination of these. (This characterization is itself an interpretation, of course, but allowable now because relatively neutral). So an interpretation of any body or division of law, like the law of accidents, must show the value of that body of law in political terms by demonstrating the best principle or policy it can be taken to serve.

We know from the parallel argument in literature that this general description of interpretation in law is not license for each judge to find in doctrinal history whatever he thinks should have been there. The same distinction holds between interpretation and ideal. A judge's duty is to interpret the legal history he finds, not to invent a better history. The dimension of fit will provide some boundaries. There is, of course, no algorithm for deciding whether a particular interpretation sufficiently fits that history not to be ruled out. When a statute or constitution or other legal document is part of the doctrinal history, the speaker's meaning will play a role. But the choice of which of several crucially different senses of speaker's or legislator's intention is the appropriate one cannot itself be referred to anyone's intention but must be decided by whoever must make the decision, as a question of political theory[39] in the common-law cases the question of fit is more complex. Any particular hypothesis about the point of a string of decisions ("These decisions establish the principle that no one can recover for emotional damage who did not lie within the area of physical danger himself.") is likely to encounter, if not flat counter-examples in some earlier case, at least language or argument that seems to suggest the contrary. So any useful conception of interpretation must contain a doctrine of mistake—as must any novelist's theory of interpretation for the chain novel. Sometimes a legal argument will explicitly recognize such mistakes: "Insofar as the cases of *A* v. *B* and *C* v. *D* may have held to the contrary, they were, we believe, wrongly decided and need not be followed here." Sometimes the doctrine of precedent forbids this crude approach and requires something like: "We held, in *E* v. *F,* that such-and-such, but that case raised special issues and must, we think, be confined to its own facts" (which is not quote so disingenuous as it might seem).

This flexibility may seem to erode the difference on which I insist, between interpretation and a fresh, clean-slate decision about what the law ought to be. But there is nevertheless this overriding constraint. Any judge's sense of the point or function of law, on which every aspect of his approach to interpretation will depend, will include or imply some conception of the integrity and coherence of law as an institution, and this conception will both tutor and constrain his working theory of fit—that is, his convictions about how much of the prior law an interpretation must fit, and which of it, and how. (The parallel with literary interpretation holds here as well).

It should be apparent, however, that any particular judge's theory of fit will often fail to produce a unique interpretation. (The distinction between hard and easy cases at law is perhaps just the distinction between cases in which they do and do not.) Just as two readings of a poem may each find sufficient support in the text to show its unity and coherence, so two principles may each find enough support in the various decisions of the past to satisfy any plausible theory of fit. In that case substantive political theory (like substantive considerations of artistic merit) will play a decisive role. Put bluntly, the interpretation of accident law, that a careless driver is liable to those whose damage is both substantial and foreseeable, is probably a better interpretation, if it is, only because it states a sounder principle of justice than any principle that distinguishes between physical and emotional damage or that makes recovery for emotional damage depend on whether the plaintiff was in danger of physical damage. (I should add that this issue, as an issue of political morality, is in fact very complex, and many distinguished judges and lawyers have taken each side.)

We might summarize these points this way. Judges develop a particular approach to legal interpretation by forming and refining a political theory sensitive to those issues on which interpretation in particular cases will depend; they call this their legal philosophy. It will include both structural features, elaborating the general requirement that an interpretation must fit doctrinal history, and substantive claims about social goals and principles of justice. Any judge's opinion about the best interpretation will therefore be the consequence of beliefs

---

[39] See Dworkin, *The Forum of Principle* in 56 N.Y.U.L. Rev. 469. [See now *A Matter of Principle* (1985), p. 33.]

other judges need not share. If a judge believes that the dominant purpose of a legal system, the main goal it ought to serve, is economic, then he will see in past accident decisions some strategy for reducing the economic costs of accidents overall. Other judges, who find any such picture of the law's function distasteful, will discover no such strategy in history but only, perhaps, an attempt to reinforce conventional morality of fault and responsibility. If we insist on a high order of neutrality in our description of legal interpretation, therefore, we cannot make our description of the nature of legal interpretation much more concrete than I have.

### B. *Author's Intention in Law*

I want instead to consider various objections that might be made not to the detail of my argument but to the main thesis, that interpretation in law is essentially political. I shall not spend further time on the general objection already noted: that this view of law makes it irreducibly and irredeemably subjective, just a matter of what particular judges think best or what they had for breakfast. Of course, for some lawyers and legal scholars this is not an objection at all, but only the beginnings of sceptical wisdom about law. But it is the nerve of my argument that the flat distinction between description and evaluation on which this skepticism relies—the distinction between finding the law just "there" in history and making it up wholesale—is misplaced here because interpretation is something different from both...

There is no obvious reason in the account I gave of legal interpretation to doubt that one interpretation of law can be better than another and that one can be best of all. Whether this is so depends on general issues of philosophy not peculiar to law any more than to literature; and we would do well, in considering these general issues, not to begin with any fixed ideas about the necessary and sufficient conditions of objectivity (for example, that no theory of law can be sound unless it is demonstrably sound, unless it would wring assent from a stone). In the meantime we can sensibly aim to develop various levels of a conception of law for ourselves, to find the interpretation of a complex and dramatically important practice which seems to us at once the right kind of interpretation for law and right as that kind of interpretation.

I shall consider one further, and rather different, objection in more detail: that my political hypothesis about legal interpretation, like the aesthetic hypothesis about artistic interpretation, fails to give an adequate place to author's intention. If fails to see that interpretation in law is simply a matter of discovering what various actors in the legal process—constitutional delegates, members of Congress and state legislatures, judges, and executive officials—intended. Once again it is important to see what is at stake here. The political hypothesis makes room for the author's intention argument as a conception of interpretation, a conception which claims that the best political theory gives the intentions of legislators and past judges a decisive role in interpretation. Seen this way, the author's intention theory does not challenge the political hypothesis but contests for its authority. If the present objection is really an objection to the argument so far, therefore, its claim must be understood differently, as proposing, for example, that the very "meaning" of interpretation in law requires that only these officials' intentions should count or that at least there is a firm consensus among lawyers to that effect. Both of these claims are as silly as the parallel claims about the idea or the practice of interpretation in art.

Suppose, therefore, that we do take the author's intention theory, more sensibly, as a conception rather than an explication of the concept of legal interpretation. The theory seems on firmest ground, as I suggested earlier, when interpretation is interpretation of a canonical legal text, like a clause of the Constitution, or a section of a statute, or a provision of a contract or will. But just as we noticed that novelist's intention is complex and structured in ways that embarrass any simple author's intention theory in literature, we must now notice that a legislator's intention is complex in similar ways. Suppose a delegate to a constitutional convention votes for a clause guaranteeing equality of treatment without regard to race in matters touching people's fundamental interests; but he thinks that education is not a matter of fundamental interest and so does not believe that the clause makes racially segregated schools unconstitutional. We may sensibly distinguish an abstract and a concrete intention here: the delegate intends to prohibit discrimination in whatever in fact is of fundamental interest and also intends not to prohibit segregated schools. There are not isolated, discrete intentions; our descriptions, we might say, describe the same intention in different ways. But it matters very much which description a theory of legislative intention accepts as canonical. If we accept the first description, then a judge who wishes to follow the delegate's intentions, but who believes that education is a matter of fundamental interest, will hold segregation unconstitutional. If we accept the second, he will not. The choice between the two descriptions cannot be made by any further reflection about what an intention really is. It must be made by deciding that one rather than the other description is more appropriate in virtue of the best theory of representative democracy or on some other openly political ground. (I might add that no compelling argument has yet been produced, so far as I am aware, in favor in deferring to a delegate's more concrete intentions, and that this is of major importance in arguments about whether the "original intention" of the Framers requires, for example, abolishing racial discrimination, or capital punishment.)

When we consider the common-law problems of interpretation, the author's intention theory shows in an even poorer light. The problems are not simply evidentiary. Perhaps we can discover what was "in the mind" of all the judges who decided cases about accidents at one time or another in our legal history. We might also discover (or speculate) about the psychodynamic or economic or social explanations of why each judge thought what he or she did. No doubt the result of all this research (or speculation) would be a mass of psychological data essentially different for each of the past judges included in the study, and order could be brought into the mass, if at all, only through statistical summaries about which proportion of judges in which historical period probably held which opinion and was more or less subject to which influence. But this mass, even tamed by statistical summary, would be of no more help to the judge trying to answer the question of what the prior decisions, taken as a whole, really come to than the parallel information would be to one of our chain novelists trying to decide what novel the novelists earlier in the chain had collectively written. That judgment, in each case, requires a fresh exercise of interpretation which is neither brute historical research nor a clean-slate expression of how things ideally ought to be.

A judge who believed in the importance of discerning an author's intention might try to escape these problems by selecting one particular judge or a small group of judges in the past (say, the judges who decided the most recent case something like his or the case he thinks closest to his) and asking what rule that judge or group intended to lay down for the future. This would treat the particular earlier judges as legislators and so invite all the problems of statutory interpretation including the very serious problem we just noticed. Even so, it would not even escape the special problems of common-law adjudication after all, because the judge who applied this theory of interpretation would have to suppose himself entitled to look only to the intentions of the particular earlier judge or judges he had selected, and he could not suppose this unless he thought that it was the upshot of judicial practice as a whole (and not just the intentions of some *other* selected earlier judge) that this is what judges in his position should do.

## IV. Politics in Interpretation

If my claims about the role of politics in legal interpretation are sound, then we should expect to find distinctly liberal or radical or conservative opinions not only about what the Constitution and laws of our nation should be but also about what they are. And this is exactly what we do find. Interpretation of the equal protection clause of the Constitution provides especially vivid examples. There can be no useful interpretation of what that clause means independent of some theory about what political equality is and how far equality is required by justice, and the history of the last half-century of constitutional law is largely an exploration of exactly these issues of political morality. Conservative lawyers argued steadily (though not consistently) in favor of an author's intentions style of interpreting this clause, and they accused others, who used a different style with more egalitarian results, of inventing rather than interpreting law. But this was bluster meant to hide the role their own political convictions played in their choice of interpretive style, and the great legal debates over the equal protection clause would have been more illuminating if it had been more widely recognized that reliance on political theory is not a corruption of interpretation but part of what interpretation means.					[pp. 540–549]

### RONALD DWORKIN
### Law's Empire
### (1986)

### The Interpretive Attitude

Perhaps this picture of what makes disagreement possible is too crude to capture any disagreement, even one about books. But I shall argue only that it is not exhaustive and, in particular, that it does not hold in an important set of circumstances that includes the oretical argument in law. It does not hold when members of particular communities who share practices and traditions make and dispute claims about the best interpretation of these—when they disagree, that is, about what some tradition or practice actually requires in concrete circumstances. These claims are often controversial, and the disagreement is genuine even though people use different criteria in forming or framing these interpretations; it is genuine because the competing interpretations are directed toward the same object or events of interpretation. I shall try to show how this model helps us to understand legal argument more thoroughly and to see the role of law in the larger culture more clearly. But first it will be useful to see how the model holds for a much simpler institution.

Imagine the following history of an invented community. Its members follow a set of rules, which they call "rules of courtesy", on a certain range of social occasions. They say, "Courtesy requires that peasants take off their hats to nobility," for example, and they urge and accept other propositions of that sort. For a time this practice has the character of taboo: the rules are just there and are neither questioned nor varied. But then, perhaps slowly, all this changes. Everyone develops a complex "interpretive" attitude toward the rules of courtesy, an attitude that has two components. The first is the assumption that the practice of courtesy does not simply exist but has value, that it serves some interest or purpose or enforces some principle—in short, that it has some point—that can be stated independently of just describing the rules that make up the practice. The second is the further assumption that the requirements of courtesy—the behavior it calls for or judgments it warrants—are not necessarily or exclusively what they have always been taken to be but are instead sensitive to its point, so that the strict rules must be understood or applied or extended or modified or qualified or limited by that point. Once this interpretive attitude takes hold, the institution of courtesy ceases to be mechanical; it is no longer unstudied deference to a runic order. People now try to impose *meaning* on the institution—to see it in its best light—and then to restructure it in the light of that meaning.

The two components of the interpretive attitude are independent of one another; we can take up the first component of the attitude toward some institution without also taking up the second. We do that in the case of games and contests. We appeal to the point of these practices in arguing about how their rules should be changed, but not (except in very limited cases) about what their rules now are; that is fixed by history and convention. Interpretation therefore plays only an external role in games and contests. It is crucial to my story about courtesy, however, that the citizens of courtesy adopt the second component of the attitude as well as the first; for them interpretation decides not only why courtesy exists but also what, properly understood, it now requires. Value and content have become entangled.

### How Courtesy Changes

Suppose that before the interpretive attitude takes hold in both its components, everyone assumes that the point of courtesy lies in the opportunity it provides to show respect to social superiors. No question arises whether the traditional forms of respect are really those the practice requires. These just *are* the forms of deference, and the available options are conformity or rebellion. When the full interpretive attitude develops, however, this assumed point acquires critical power, and people begin to demand, under the title of courtesy, forms of deference previously unknown or to spurn or refuse forms previously honored, with no sense of rebellion, claiming that true respect is better served by what they do than by what others did. Interpretation folds back into the practice, altering its shape, and the new shape encourages further reinterpretation, so the practice changes dramatically, though each step in the progress is interpretive of what the last achieved.

People's views about the proper grounds of respect, for example, may change from rank to age or gender or some other property. The main beneficiaries of respect would then be social superiors in one period, older people in another, women in a third, and so forth. Or opinions may change about the nature or quality of respect, from a view that external show constitutes respect to the opposite view, that respect is a matter of feelings only. Or opinions may change along a different dimension, about whether respect has any value when it is directed to groups or for natural properties rather than to individuals for individual achievement. If respect of the former sort no longer seems important, or even seems wrong, then a different interpretation of the practice will become necessary. People will come to see the point of courtesy as almost the converse of its original point, in the value of impersonal forms of social relation that, because of their impersonality, neither require nor deny any greater significance. Courtesy will then occupy a different and diminished place in social life, and the end of the story is in sight: the interpretive attitude will languish, and the practice will lapse back into the static and mechanical state in which it began.          [pp. 46–49]

... Creative interpretation is not conversational but *constructive*. Interpretation of works of art and social practices, I shall argue, is indeed essentially concerned with purpose not cause. But the purposes in play are not (fundamentally) those of some author but of the interpreter. Roughly, constructive interpretation is a matter of imposing purpose on an object or practice in order to make of it the best possible example of the form or genre to which it is taken to belong. It does not follow, even from that rough account, that an interpreter can make of a practice or work of art anything he would have wanted it to be, that a citizen of courtesy who is enthralled by equality, for example, can in good faith claim that courtesy actually requires the sharing of wealth. For the history or shape of a practice or object constrains the available interpretations of it, though the character of that constraint needs careful accounting, as we shall see. Creative interpretation, on the constructive view, is a matter of interaction between purpose and object.

A participant interpreting a social practice, according to that view, proposes value for the practice by describing some scheme of interests or goals or principles the practice can be taken to serve or express or exemplify. Very often, perhaps even typically, the raw behavioral data of the practice—what people do in what circumstances—will underdetermine the ascription of value: those data will be consistent, that is, with different and competing ascriptions. One person might see in the practices of courtesy a device for ensuring that respect is paid to those who merit it because of social rank or other status. Another might see, equally vividly, a device for making social exchange more conventional and therefore *less* indicative of differential judgments of respect. If the raw data do not discriminate between these competing interpretations, each interpreter's choice must reflect his view of which interpretation proposes the most value for the practice—which one shows it in the better light, all things considered.

I offer this constructive account as an analysis of creative interpretation only. But we should notice in passing how the constructive account might be elaborated to fit the other two contexts of interpretation I mentioned, and thus show a deep connection among all forms of interpretation. Understanding another person's conversation requires using devices and presumptions, like the so-called principle of charity, that have the effect in normal circumstances of making of what he says the best performance of communication it can be. And the interpretation of data in science makes heavy use of standards of theory construction like simplicity and elegance and verifiability that reflect contestable and changing assumptions about paradigms of explanation, that is, about what features make one form of explanation superior to another. The constructive account of creative interpretation, therefore, could perhaps provide a more general account of interpretation in all its forms. We would then say that all interpretation strives to make an object the best it can be, as an instance of some assumed enterprise, and that inter pretation takes different forms in different contexts only because different enterprises engage different standards of value or success. Artistic interpretation differs from scientific interpretation, we would say, only because we judge success in works of art by standards different from those we use to judge explanations of physical phenomena. [pp. 52–53]

## Stages of Interpretation

We must begin to refine constructive interpretation into an instrument fit for the study of law as a social practice. We shall need an analytical distinction among the following three stages of an interpretation, noticing how different degrees of consensus within a community are needed for each stage if the interpretive attitude is to flourish there. First, there must be a "preinterpretive" stage in which the rules and standards taken to provide the tentative content of the practice are identified. (The equivalent stage in literary interpretation is the stage at which discrete novels, plays and so forth are identified textually, that is, the stage at which the text of *Moby Dick* is identified, and distinguished from the text of other novels.) I enclose "preinterpretive" in quotes because some kind of interpretation is necessary even at this stage. Social rules do not carry identifying labels. But a very great degree of consensus is needed—perhaps an interpretive community is usefully defined as requiring consensus at this stage—if the interpretive attitude is to be fruitful, and we may therefore abstract from this stage in our analysis by presupposing that the classifications it yields are treated as given in day-to-day reflection and argument.

Second, there must be an interpretive stage at which the interpreter settles on some general justification for the main elements of the practice identified at the preinterpretive stage. This will consist of an argument why a practice of that general shape is worth pursuing, if it is. The justification need not fit every aspect or feature of the standing practice, but it must fit enough for the interpreter to be able to see himself as interpreting that practice, not inventing a new one. Finally, there must be a postinterpretive or reforming stage, at which he adjusts his sense of what the practice "really" requires so as better to serve the justification he accepts at the interpretive stage. An interpreter of courtesy, for example, may come to think that a consistent enforcement of the best justification of that practice would require people to tip their caps to soldiers returning from a crucial war as well as to nobles. Or that it calls for a new exception to an established pattern of defence: making returning soldiers exempt from displays of courtesy, for example. Or perhaps even that an entire rule stipulating deference to an entire group or class of persons must be seen as a mistake in the light of that justification.

Actual interpretation in my imaginary society would be much less deliberate and structured than this analytical structure suggests. People's interpretive judgments would be more a matter of "seeing" at once the dimensions of their practice, a purpose or aim in that practice, and the post-interpretive consequence of that purpose. And this "seeing" would ordinarily be no more insightful than just falling in with an interpretation then popular in some group whose point of view the interpreter takes up more or less automatically. Nevertheless there will be inevitable controversy, even among contemporaries, over the exact dimensions of the practice they all interpret, and still more controversy about the best justification of that practice. For we have already identified in our preliminary account of what interpretation is like, a great many ways to disagree.

We can now look back through our analytical account to compose an inventory of the kind of convictions or beliefs or assumptions someone needs to interpret something. He needs assumptions or convictions about what counts as part of the practice in order to define the raw data of his interpretation at the preinterpretive stage; the interpretive attitude cannot survive unless members of the same interpretive community share at least roughly the same assumptions about this. He also needs convictions about how far the justification he proposes at the interpretive stage must fit the standing features of the practice to count as an interpretation of it rather than the invention of something new. Can the best justification of the practices of courtesy, which almost everyone else takes to be mainly about showing deference to social superiors, really be one that would require, at the reforming stage, no distinctions of social rank? Would this be too radical a reform, too ill-fitting a justification to count as an interpretation at all? Once again, there cannot be too great a disparity in different people's convictions about fit; but only history can teach us how much difference is too much. Finally, he will need more substantive convictions about which kinds of justification really would show the practice in the best light, judgments about whether social ranks are desirable or deplorable, for example. These substantive convictions must be independent of the convictions about fit just described, otherwise the latter could not constrain the former, and he could not, after all, distinguish interpretation from invention. But they need not be so much shared within his community, for the interpretive attitude to flourish, as his sense of preinterpretive boundaries or even his convictions about the required degree of fit.                    [pp. 65–68]

## Integrity

### Agenda

We have two principles of political integrity: a legislative principle, which asks lawmakers to try to make the total set of laws morally coherent, and an adjudicative principle, which instructs that the law be seen as coherent in that way, so far as possible. Our main concern is with the adjudicative principle, but not yet. In this chapter I argue that the legislative principle is so much part of our political principle that no competent interpretation of that practice can ignore it. We measure that claim on the two dimensions now familiar. We ask whether the assumption, that integrity is a distinct ideal of politics, fits our politics, and then whether it honors our politics. If the legislative principle of integrity is impressive on both these dimensions, then the case for the adjudicative principle, and for the conception of law it supports, will already be well begun.

### Does Integrity Fit?

#### *Integrity and Compromise*

Integrity would not be needed as a distinct political virtue in a utopian state. Coherence would be guaranteed because officials would always do what was perfectly just and fair. In ordinary politics, however, we must treat integrity as an independent ideal if we accept it at all, because it can conflict with these other ideals. It can require us to support legislation we believe would be inappropriate in the perfectly just and fair society and to recognize rights we do not believe people would have there. We saw an example of this conflict in the last chapter. A judge deciding *McLoughlin* might think it unjust to require compensation for any emotional injury. But if he accepts integrity and knows that some victims of emotional injury have already been give a right to compensation, he will have a reason for deciding in favour of Mrs McLoughlin nevertheless.

Conflicts among ideals are common in politics. Even if we rejected integrity and based our political activity only on fairness, justice and procedural due process, we would find the first two virtues sometimes pulling in opposite directions. Some philosophers deny the possibility of any fundamental conflict between justice and fairness because they believe that one of these virtues in the end derives from the other. Some say that justice has no meaning apart from fairness, that in politics, as in roulette, whatever happens through fair procedures is just. That is the extreme of the idea called justice as fairness. Others think that the only test of fairness in politics is the test of result, that no procedure is fair unless it is likely to produce political decisions that meet some independent test of justice. That is the opposite extreme, of fairness as justice. Most political philosophers—and I think most people—take the intermediate view that fairness and justice are to some degree independent of one another, so that fair institutions sometimes produce unjust decisions and unfair institutions just ones.

If that is so, then in ordinary politics we must sometimes choose between the two virtues in deciding which political programs to support. We might think that majority rule is the fairest workable decision procedure in politics, but we know that the majority will sometimes, perhaps often, make unjust decisions about the rights of individuals. Should we tamper with majority rule by giving special voting strength to one economic group, beyond what its numbers would justify, because we fear that straight majority rule would assign it less than its just share? Should we accept constitutional constraints on democratic power to prevent the majority from limiting freedom of speech or other important liberties? These difficult questions arise because fairness and justice sometimes conflict. If we believe that integrity is a third and independent ideal, at least when people disagree about one of the first two, then we may well think that fairness or justice must sometimes be sacrificed to integrity.

## Internal Compromises

I shall try to show that our political practices accept integrity as a distinct virtue, and I begin with what I hope will strike you as a puzzle. Here are my background assumptions. We all believe in political fairness: we accept that each person or group in the community should have a roughly equal share of control over the decisions made by Parliament or Congress or the state legislature. We know that different people hold different views about moral issues that they all treat as of great importance. It would seem to follow from our convictions about fairness that legislation on these moral issues should be a matter not just of enforcing the will of the numerical majority, as if its view were unanimous, but of trades and compromises so that each body of opinion is represented, to a degree that matches its numbers, in the final result. We could achieve this compromise in a Solomonic way. Do the people of North Dakota disagree whether justice requires compensation for product defects that manufacturers could not reasonably have prevented? Then why should their legislature not impose this "strict" liability on manufacturers of automobiles, but not manufacturers of washing machines? Do the people of Alabama disagree about the morality of racial discrimination? Why should their legislature not forbid racial discrimination on buses but permit it in restaurants? Do the British divide on the morality of abortion? Why should Parliament not make abortion criminal for pregnant women who were born in even years but not for those born in odd years? This Solomonic model treats a community's public order as a kind of commodity to be distributed in accordance with distributive justice, a cake to be divided fairly by assigning each group a proper slice.

Most of us, I think, would be dismayed by "checkerboard" laws that treat similar accidents or occasions of racial discrimination or abortion differently on arbitrary grounds. Of course we do accept arbitrary distinctions about some matters: zoning, for example. We accept that shops or factories be forbidden in some zones and not others and that parking be prohibited on alternate sides of the same street on alternate days. But we reject a division between parties of opinion when matters of principle are at stake. We follow a different model: that each point of view must be allowed a voice in the process of deliberation but that the collective decision must nevertheless aim to settle on some coherent principle whose influence then extends to the natural limits of its authority. If there must be compromise because people are divided about justice, then the compromise must be external, not internal; it must be compromise about which scheme of justice to adopt rather than a compromised scheme of justice.

But there lies the puzzle. Why should we turn our back on checkerboard solutions as we do? Why should we not embrace them as a general strategy for legislation whenever the community is divided over some issue of principle? Why is this strategy not fair and reasonable, reflecting political maturity and a finer sense of the political art than other communities have managed to achieve? What is the special defect we find in checkerboard solutions? It cannot be a failure in fairness (in our sense of a fair distribution of political power) because checkerboard laws are by hypothesis fairer than either of the two alternatives. Allowing each of two groups to choose some part of the law of abortion, in proportion to their numbers, is fairer (in our sense) than the winner-take-all scheme our instincts prefer, which denies many people any influence at all over an issue they think desperately important.

Can we defend these instincts on grounds of justice? Justice is a matter of outcomes: a political decision causes injustice, however fair the procedures that produced it, when it denies people some resource, liberty, or opportunity that the best theories of justice entitle them to have. Can we oppose the checkerboard strategy on the ground that it would produce more instances of injustice than it would prevent? We must be careful not to confuse two issues here. Of course any single checkerboard solution of an important issue will produce more instances of injustice than one of the alternatives and fewer than the other. The community can unite over that proposition while disagreeing about which alternative would be more and which less just. Someone who believes that abortion is murder will think that the checkerboard abortion statute produces more injustice than outright prohibition and less than outright license; someone who believes women have a right to abortion reverses these judgments. So both have a reason of justice for preferring some other solution to the checkerboard one. Our question is whether we collectively have a reason of justice for not agreeing, in *advance* of these particular disagreements, to the checkerboard strategy for resolving them. We have a reason of fairness, as we just noticed, for that checkerboard strategy, and if we have no reason of justice against it, our present practice needs a justification we have not yet secured.

We are looking for a reason of justice we all share for rejecting the checkerboard strategy in advance even if we would each prefer a checkerboard solution on some occasions to the one that will be imposed if the strategy is rejected. Shall we just say that a checkerboard solution is unjust by definition because it treats different people differently for no good reason, and justice requires treating like cases alike? This suggestion seems in the right neighbourhood, for if checkerboard solutions do have a defect, it must lie in their distinctive feature, that they treat people differently when no principle can justify the distinction. But we cannot explain why this is always objectionable, so long as we remain on the plane of justice as I have defined it. For in the circumstances of ordinary politics the checkerboard strategy will prevent instances of injustice that would otherwise occur, and we cannot say that justice requires not eliminating any injustice unless we can eliminate all.

Suppose we can rescue only some prisoners of tyranny; justice hardly requires rescuing none even when only luck, not any principle, will decide whom we save and whom we leave to torture. Rejecting a checkerboard solution seems perverse in the same way when the alternative will be the general triumph of the principle we oppose. The internal compromise would have rescued some, chosen arbitrarily, from an injustice that others will be left to suffer, but the alternative would have been to rescue none. Someone may now say: nevertheless, though checkerboard solutions may be desirable for that reason on some occasions, we do better to reject their use out of hand in advance, because we have reason to think that in the long run more discrete injustice will be created than avoided through these solutions. But that would be a plausible prediction only for members of a constant and self-conscious majority of opinion, and if such a majority existed so would a self-conscious majority that would have the opposite opinion. So we have no hope of finding here a common reason for rejecting checkerboard solutions.

But perhaps we are looking in the wrong direction. Perhaps our common reason is not any prediction about the number of cases of injustice that the checkerboard strategy would produce or prevent, but our conviction that no one should actively engage in producing what he believes to be injustice. We might say: no checkerboard statute could be enacted unless a majority of the legislators voted for provisions they thought unjust. But this objection begs the main question. If each member of the legislature who votes for a checkerboard compromise does so not because he himself has no principles but because he wants to give the maximum possible effect to the principles he thinks right, then how has anyone behaved irresponsibly? Even if we were to accept that no legislator should vote for the compromise, this would not explain why we should reject the compromise as an *outcome*. For we can easily imagine a legislative structure that would produce compromise statutes mechanically, as a function of the different opinions about strict liability or racial discrimination or abortion among the various legislators, without any legislator being asked or required to vote for the compromise as a package. It might be understood in advance that the proportion of women who would be permitted an abortion would be fixed by the ratio of votes for permitting all abortions to total votes. If we still object, then our objection cannot be based on the principle that no individual should vote against his conscience.

So it seems we have no reason of justice for using the checkerboard strategy in advance, and strong reasons of fairness for endorsing it. Yet our instincts condemn it. Indeed many of us, to different degrees in different situations, would reject the checkerboard solution not only in general and in advance, but even in particular cases if it were available as a possibility. We would prefer either of the alternative solutions to the checkerboard compromise. Even if I thought strict liability for accidents wrong in principle, I would prefer that manufacturers of both washing machines and automobiles be held to that standard than that only one of them be. I would rank the checkerboard solution not intermediate between the other two but third, below both, and so would many other people. In some cases this instinct might be explained as reflecting the unworkability or inefficiency of a particular checkerboard solution. But many of those we can imagine, like the abortion solution, are not particularly inefficient, and in any case our instinct suggests that these compromises are wrong, not merely impractical.

Not everyone would condemn every checkerboard solution. People who believe very strongly that abortion is always murder, for example, may indeed think that the checkerboard abortion statute is better than a wholly permissive law. They think that fewer murders are better than more no matter how incoherent the compromise that produces fewer. If they rank the checkerboard solution last in other circumstances, in the case of strict liability for manufacturers, for example, they nevertheless believe that internal compromise is wrong, though for reasons that yield when the substantive issue is very grave. So they share the instinct that needs explaining. This instinct is likely to be at work, moreover, in other, more complicated rankings they might make. Suppose you think abortion is murder and that it makes no difference whether the pregnancy is the result of rape. Would you not think a statute prohibiting abortion except in the case of rape distinctly better than a statute prohibiting abortion except to women born in one specified decade each century? At least if you had no reason to think either would in fact allow more abortions? You see the first of these statutes as a solution that gives effect to two recognizable principles of justice, ordered in a certain way, even though you reject one of the principles. You cannot treat the second that way; it simply affirms for some people a principle it denies to others. So for many of us, our preferences in particular cases pose the same puzzle as our more comprehensive rejection of the checkerboard solution as a general strategy for resolving differences over principle. We cannot explain our hostility to internal compromise by appeal to principles of either fairness or justice as we have defined those virtues.

Astronomers postulated Neptune before they discovered it. They knew that only another planet, whose orbit lay beyond those already recognized, could explain the behavior of the nearer planets. Our instincts about internal compromise suggest another political ideal standing beside justice and fairness. Integrity is our Neptune. The most natural explanation of why we oppose checkerboard statutes appeals to that idea: we say that a state that adopts these internal compromises is acting in an unprincipled way, even though no single official who voted for or enforces the compromise has done anything which, judging his individual actions by the ordinary standards of personal morality, he ought not to have done. The state lacks integrity because it must endorse principles to justify part of what it has done that it must reject to justify the rest. That explanation distinguishes integrity from the perverse consistency of someone who refuses to rescue some prisoners because he cannot save all. If he had saved some, selected arbitrarily, he would not have violated any principle he needs to justify other acts. But a state does act that way when it accepts a Solomonic checkerboard solution; it is inconsistency in principle among the acts of the state personified that integrity condemns. [pp. 176–184]

## A large view

... Law as integrity denies that statements of law are either the backward-looking factual reports of conventionalism or the forward-looking instrumental programs of legal pragmatism. It insists that legal claims are interpretive judgments and therefore combine backward- and forward-looking elements; they interpret contemporary legal practice seen as an unfolding political narrative. So law as integrity rejects as unhelpful the ancient question whether judges find or invent law; we understand legal reasoning, it suggests, only by seeing the sense in which they do both and neither.

### Integrity and Interpretation

The adjudicative principle of integrity instructs judges to identify legal rights and duties, so far as possible, on the assumption that they were all created by a single author—the community personified—expressing a coherent conception of justice and fairness. We form our third conception of law, our third view of what rights and duties flow from past political decisions, by restating this instruction as a thesis about the grounds of law. According to law as integrity, propositions of law are true if they figure in or follow from the principles of justice, fairness, and procedural due process that provide the best constructive interpretation of the community's legal practice. Deciding whether the law grants Mrs McLoughlin compensation for her injury, for example, means deciding whether legal practice is seen in a better light if we assume the community has accepted the principle that people in her position are entitled to compensation.

Law as integrity is therefore more relentlessly interpretive than either conventionalism or pragmatism. These latter theories offer themselves *as* interpretations. They are conceptions of law that claim to show our legal practices in the best light these can bear, and they recommend, in their postinterpretive conclusions, distinct styles or programs for adjudication. But the programs they recommend are not themselves programs *of* interpretation: they do not ask judges deciding hard cases to carry out any further, essentially interpretive study of legal doctrine. Conventionalism requires judges to study law reports and parliamentary records to discover what decisions have been made by institutions conventionally recognized to have legislative power. No doubt interpretive issues will arise in that process: for example, it may be necessary to interpret a text to decide what statutes our legal conventions construct from it. But once a judge has accepted conventionalism as his guide, he has no further occasion for interpreting the legal record as a whole in deciding particular cases. Pragmatism requires judges to think instrumentally about the best rules for the future. That exercise may require interpretation of something beyond legal material: a utilitarian pragmatist may need to worry about the best way to understand the idea of community welfare, for example. But once again, a judge who accepts pragmatism is then done with interpreting legal practice as a whole.

Law as integrity is different: it is both the product of and the inspiration for comprehensive interpretation of legal practice. The program it holds out to judges deciding hard cases is essentially, not just contingently, interpretive; law as integrity asks them to continue interpreting the same material that it claims to have successfully interpreted itself. It offers itself as continuous with—the initial part of—the more detailed interpretations it recommends.          [pp. 225–227]

## Law: The Question of Emotional Damages

Law as integrity asks a judge deciding a common-law case like *McLoughlin*[40] to think of himself as an author in the chain of common law. He knows that other judges have decided cases that, although not exactly like his case, deal with related problems; he must think of their decisions as part of a long story he must interpret and then continue, according to his own judgment of how to make the developing story as good as it can be. (Of course the best story for him means best from the standpoint of political morality, not aesthetics.) We can make a rough distinction once again between two main dimensions of this interpretive judgment. The judge's decision—his postinterpretive conclusions—must be drawn from an interpretation that both fits and justifies what has gone before, so far as that is possible. But in law as in literature the interplay between fit and justification is complex. Just as interpretation within a chain novel is for each interpreter a delicate balance among different types of literary and artistic attitudes, so in law it is a delicate balance among political convictions of different sorts; in law as in literature these must be sufficiently related yet disjoint to allow an overall judgment that trades off an interpretation's success on one type of standard against its failure on another. I must try to exhibit that complex structure of legal interpretation, and I shall use for that purpose an imaginary judge of superhuman intellectual power and patience who accepts law as integrity.

Call him Hercules. In this and the next several chapters we follow his career by noticing the types of judgments he must make and tensions he must resolve in deciding a variety of cases. But I offer this caution in advance. We must not suppose that his answers to the various questions he encounters *define* law as integrity as a general conception of law. They are the answers I now think best. But law as integrity consists in an approach, in questions rather than answers, and other lawyers and judges who accept it would give different answers from his to the questions it asks. You might think other answers would be better. (So might I, after further thought.) You might, for example, reject Hercules' views about how far people's legal rights depend on the reasons past judges offered for their decisions enforcing these rights, or you might not share his respect for what I shall call "local priority" in common-law decisions. If you reject these discrete views because you think them poor constructive interpretations of legal practice, however, you have not rejected law as integrity but rather have joined its enterprise.

## Six Interpretations

Hercules must decide *McLoughlin*. Both sides in that case cited precedents; each argued that a decision in its favor would count as going on as before, as continuing the story begun by the judges who decided those precedent cases. Hercules must form his own view about that issue. Just as a chain novelist must find, if he can, some coherent view of character and theme such that a hypothetical single author with that view could have written at least the bulk of the novel so far, Hercules must find, if he can, some coherent theory about legal rights to compensation for emotional injury such that a single political official with that theory could have reached most of the results the precedents report.

He is a careful judge, a judge of method. He begins by setting out various

[40] [*McLoughlin v. O'Brian* [1983] 1 A.C. 410.]

candidates for the best interpretation of the precedent cases even before he reads them. Suppose he makes the following short list: (1) No one has a moral right to compensation except for physical injury. (2) People have a moral right to compensation for emotional injury suffered at the scene of an accident against anyone whose carelessness caused the accident but have no right to compensation for emotional injury suffered later. (3) People should recover compensation for emotional injury when a practice of requiring compensation in their circumstances would diminish the overall costs of accidents or otherwise make the community richer in the long run. (4) People have a moral right to compensation for any injury, emotional or physical, that is the direct consequence of careless conduct, no matter how unlikely or foreseeable it is that that conduct would result in that injury. (5) People have a moral right to compensation for emotional or physical injury that is the consequence of careless conduct, but only if that injury was reasonably foreseeable by the person who acted carelessly. (6) People have a moral right to compensation for reasonably foreseeable injury but not in circumstances when recognizing such a right would impose massive and destructive financial burdens on people who have been careless out of proportion to their moral fault.

These are all relatively concrete statements about rights and, allowing for a complexity in (3) we explore just below, they contradict one another. No more than one can figure in a single interpretation of the emotional injury cases. (I postpone the more complex case in which Hercules constructs an interpretation from competitive rather than contradictory principles, that is, from principles that can live together in an overall moral or political theory though they sometimes pull in different directions.) Even so, this is only a partial list of the contradictory interpretations someone might wish to consider; Hercules chooses it as his initial short list because he knows that the principles captured in these interpretations have actually been discussed in the legal literature. It will obviously make a great difference which of these principles he believes provides the best interpretation of the precedents and so the nerve of his postinterpretive judgment. If he settles on (1) or (2), he must decide for Mr O'Brian; if on (4), for Mrs McLoughlin. Each of the others requires further thought, but the line of reasoning each suggests is different. (3) invites an economic calculation. Would it reduce the cost of accidents to extend liability to emotional injury away from the scene? Or is there some reason to think that the most efficient line is drawn just between emotional injuries at and those away from the scene? (5) requires a judgment about foreseeability of injury, which seems to be very different, and (6) a judgment both about foreseeability and the cumulative risk of financial responsibility if certain injuries away from the scene are included.

Hercules begins testing each interpretation on his short list by asking whether a single political official could have given the verdicts of the precedent cases if that official were consciously and coherently enforcing the principles that form the interpretation. He will therefore dismiss interpretation (1) at once. No one who believed that people never have rights to compensation for emotional injury could have reached the results of those past decisions cited in *McLoughlin* that allowed compensation. Hercules will also dismiss interpretation (2), though for a different reason. Unlike (1), (2) fits the past decisions; someone who accepted (2) as a standard would have reached these decisions, because they all allowed recovery for emotional injury at the scene and none allowed recovery for injury away from it. But (2) fails as an interpretation of the required kind because it does not state a principle of justice at all. It draws a line that it leaves arbitrary and unconnected to any more general moral or political consideration.

What about (3)? It might fit the past decisions, but only in the following way. Hercules might discover through economic analysis that someone who accepted the economic theory expressed by (3) and who wished to reduce the community's accident costs would have made just those decisions. But it is far from obvious that (3) states any principle of justice or fairness. Remember the distinction between principles and policies [...] (3) supposes that it is desirable to reduce accident costs overall. Why? Two explanations are possible. The first insists that people have a right to compensation whenever a rule awarding compensation would produce more wealth for the community overall than a rule denying it. This has the form, at least, of a principle because it describes a general right everyone is supposed to have. I shall not ask Hercules to consider (3) understood in that way now, because he will study it very carefully in Chapter 8. The second, quite different, explanation suggests that it is sometimes or even always in the community's general interest to promote overall wealth in this way, but it does not suppose that anyone has any right that social wealth always be increased. It therefore sets out a policy that government might or might not decide to pursue in particular circumstances. It does not state a principle of justice, and so it cannot figure in an interpretation of the sort Hercules now seeks.

Law as integrity asks judges to assume, so far as this is possible, that the law is structured by a coherent set of principles about justice and fairness and procedural due process, and it asks them to enforce these in the fresh cases that come before them, so that each person's situation is fair and just according to the same standards. That style of adjudication respects the ambition integrity assumes, the ambition to be a community of principle. But [...] integrity does not recommend what would be perverse, that we should all be governed by the same goals and strategies of policy on every occasion. It does not insist that a legislature that enacts one set of rules about compensation today, in order to make the community richer on the whole, is in any way committed to serve that same goal of policy tomorrow. For it might then have other goals to seek, not necessarily in place of wealth but beside it, and integrity does not frown on this diversity. Our account of interpretation, and our consequent elimination of interpretation (3) read as a naked appeal to policy, reflects a discrimination already latent in the ideal of integrity itself.

We reach the same conclusion in the context of *McLoughlin* through a different route, by further reflection on what we have learned about interpretation. An interpretation aims to show what is interpreted in the best light possible, and an interpretation of any part of our law must therefore attend not only to the substance of the decisions made by earlier officials but also to how—by which officials in which circumstances—these decisions were made. A legislature does not need reasons of principle to justify the rules it enacts about driving, including rules about compensation for accidents, even though these rules will create rights and duties for the future that will then be enforced by coercive threat. A legislature may justify its decision to create new rights for the future by showing how these will contribute, as a matter of sound policy, to the overall good of the community as a whole. There are limits to this kind of justification [...]. The general good may not be used to justify the death penalty for careless driving. But the legislature need not show that citizens already have a moral right to compensation for injury under particular circumstances in order to justify a statute awarding damages in those circumstances.

Law as integrity assumes, however, that judges are in a very different position from legislators. It does not fit the character of a community of principle that a judge should have authority to hold people liable in damages for acting in a way he concedes they had no legal duty not to act. So when judges construct rules of liability not recognized before, they are not free in the way I just said legislators are. Judges must make their common-law decisions on grounds of principle, not policy; they must deploy arguments why the parties actually had the "novel" legal rights and duties they enforce at the time the parties acted or at some other pertinent time in the past. A legal pragmatist would reject that claim. But Hercules rejects pragmatism. He follows law as integrity and therefore wants an interpretation of what judges did in the earlier emotional damage cases that shows them acting in the way he approves, not in the way he thinks judges must decline to act. It does not follow that he must dismiss interpretation (3), as supposing that past judges acted to protect a general legal right to compensation when this would make the community richer. For if people actually have such a right, others have a corresponding duty, and judges do not act unjustly in ordering the police to enforce it. The argument disqualifies interpretation (3) only when this is read to deny any such general duty and to rest on grounds of policy alone.

### Expanding the Range

Interpretations (4), (5) and (6) do, however, seem to pass these initial tests. The principles of each fit the past emotional injury decisions, at least on first glance, if only because none of these precedents presented facts that would discriminate among them. Hercules must now ask, as the next stage of his investigation, whether any one of the three must be ruled out because it is incompatible with the bulk of legal practice more generally. He must test each interpretation against other past judicial decisions, beyond those involving emotional injury, that might be thought to engage them. Suppose he discovers, for example, that past decisions provide compensation for physical injury caused by careless driving only if the injury was reasonably foreseeable. That would rule out interpretation (4) unless he can find some principled distinction between physical and emotional injury that explains why the conditions for compensation should be more restrictive for the former than the latter, which seems extremely unlikely.

Law as integrity, then, requires a judge to test his interpretation of any part of the great network of political structures and decisions of his community by asking whether it could form part of a coherent theory justifying the network as a whole. No actual judge could compose anything approaching a full interpretation of all of his community's law at once. That is why we are imagining a Herculean judge of superhuman talents and endless time. But an actual judge can imitate Hercules in a limited way. He can allow the scope of his interpretation to fan out from the cases immediately in point to cases in the same general area or department of law, and then still farther, so far as this seems promising. In practice even this limited process will be largely unconscious: an experienced judge will have a sufficient sense of the terrain surrounding his immediate problem to know instinctively which interpretation of a small set of cases would survive if the range it must fit were expanded. But sometimes the expansion will be deliberate and controversial. Lawyers celebrate dozens of decisions of that character, including several on which the modern law of negligence was built...

Suppose a modest expansion of Hercules' range of inquiry does show that plaintiffs are denied compensation if their physical injury was not reasonably foreseeable at the time the careless defendant acted, thus ruling out interpretation (4). But this does not eliminate either (5) or (6). He must expand his survey further. He must look also to cases involving economic rather than physical or emotional injury, where damages are potentially very great: for example, he must look to cases in which professional advisers like surveyors or accountants are sued for losses others suffer through their negligence. Interpretation (5) suggests that such liability might be unlimited in amount, no matter how ruinous in total, provided that the damage is foreseeable, and (6) suggests, on the contrary, that liability is limited just because of the frightening sums it might otherwise reach. If one interpretation is uniformly contradicted by cases of that sort and finds no support in any other area of doctrine Hercules might later inspect, and the other is confirmed by the expansion, he will regard the former as ineligible, and the latter alone will have survived. But suppose he finds, when he expands his study in this way, a mixed pattern. Past decisions permit extended liability for members of some professions but not for those of others, and this mixed pattern holds for other areas of doctrine that Hercules, in the exercise of his imaginative skill, finds pertinent.

The contradiction he has discovered, though genuine, is not in itself so deep or pervasive as to justify a skeptical interpretation of legal practice as a whole, for the problem of unlimited damages, while important, is not so fundamental that contradiction within it destroys the integrity of the larger system. So Hercules turns to the second main dimension, but here, as in the chain-novel situation, questions of fit surface again, because an interpretation is *pro tanto* more satisfactory if it shows less damage to integrity than its rival. He will therefore consider whether interpretation (5) fits the expanded legal record better than (6). But this cannot be a merely mechanical decision; he cannot simply count the number of past decisions that must be conceded to be "mistakes" on each interpretation. For these numbers may reflect only accidents like the number of cases that happen to have come to court and not been settled before verdict. He must take into account not only the numbers of decisions counting for each interpretation, but whether the decisions expressing one principle seem more important or fundamental or wide-ranging than the decisions expressing the other. Suppose interpretation (6) fits only those past judicial decisions involving charges of negligence against one particular profession—say, lawyers—and interpretation (5) justifies all other cases, involving all other professions, and also fits other kinds of economic damage cases as well. Interpretation (5) then fits the legal record better on the whole, even if the number of cases involving lawyers if for some reason numerically greater, unless the argument shifts again, as it well might, when the field of study expands even more.

Now suppose a different possibility: that though liability has in many and varied cases actually been limited to an amount less than interpretation (5) would allow, the opinions attached to these cases made no mention of the principle of interpretation (6), which has in fact never before been recognized in official judicial rhetoric. Does that show that interpretation (5) fits the legal record much better, or that interpretation (6) is ineligible after all? Judges in fact divide about this issue of fit. Some would not seriously consider interpretation (6) if no past judicial opinion or legislative statement had ever explicitly mentioned its principle. Others reject this constraint and accept that the best interpretation of some line of cases may lie in a principle that has never been recognized explicitly but that nevertheless offers a brilliant account of the actual decisions, showing them in a better light than ever before. Hercules will confront this issue as a special question of political morality. The political history of the community is *pro tanto* a better history, he thinks, if it shows judges making plain to their public, through their opinions, the path that later judges guided by integrity will follow and if it shows judges making decisions that give voice as well as effect to convictions about morality that are widespread throughout the community. Judicial opinions formally announced in law reports, moreover, are themselves acts of the community personified that, particularly if recent must be taken into the embrace of integrity. These are among his reasons for somewhat preferring an interpretation that is not too novel, not too far divorced from what past judges and other officials said as well as did. But he must set these reasons against his more substantive political convictions about the relative moral value of the two interpretations, and if he believes that interpretation (6) is much superior from that perspective, he will think he makes the legal record better overall by selecting it even at the cost of the more procedural values. Fitting what judges did is more important than fitting what they said.

Now suppose an even more unpatterned record. Hercules finds that unlimited liability has been enforced against a number of professions but has not been enforced against a roughly equal number of others, that no principle can explain the distinction, that judicial rhetoric is as split as the actual decisions, and that this split extends into other kinds of actions for economic damage. He might expand his field of survey still further, and the picture might change if he does. But let us suppose he is satisfied that it will not. He will then decide that the question of fit can play no more useful role in his deliberations even on the second dimension. He must now emphasize the more plainly substantive aspects of that dimension: he must decide which interpretation shows the legal record to be the best it can be from the standpoint of substantive political morality. He will compose and compare two stories. The first supposes that the community personified has adopted and is enforcing the principle of foreseeability as its test of moral responsibility for damage caused by negligence, that the various decisions it has reached are intended to give effect to that principle, though it has often lapsed and reached decisions that foreseeability would condemn. The second supposes, instead, that the community has adopted and is enforcing the principle of foreseeability limited by some overall ceiling on liability, though it has often lapsed from that principle. Which story shows the community in a better light, all things considered, from the standpoint of political morality?

Hercules' answer will depend on his convictions about the two constituent virtues of political morality we have considered: justice and fairness. It will depend, that is, not only on his beliefs about which of these principles is superior as a matter of abstract justice but also about which should be followed, as a matter of political fairness, in a community whose members have the moral convictions his fellow citizens have. In some cases the two kinds of judgment—the judgment of justice and that of fairness—will come together. If Hercules and the public at large share the view that people are entitled to be compensated fully whenever they are injured by others' carelessness, without regard to how harsh this requirement might turn out to be, then he will think that interpretation (5) is plainly the better of the two in play. But the two judgments will sometimes pull in different directions. He may think that interpretation (6) is better on grounds of abstract justice, but know that this is a radical view not shared by any substantial portion of the public and unknown in the political and moral rhetoric of the times. He might then decide that the story in which the state insists on the view he thinks right, but against the wishes of the people as a whole, is a poorer story, on balance. He would be preferring fairness to justice in these circumstances, and that preference would reflect a higher-order level of his own political convictions, namely his convictions about how a decent government committed to both fairness and justice should adjudicate between the two in this sort of case.

Judges will have different ideas of fairness, about the role each citizen's opinion should ideally play in the state's decision about which principles of justice to enforce through its central police power. They will have different higher-level opinions about the best resolution of conflicts between these two political ideals. No judge is likely to hold the simplistic theory that fairness is automatically to be preferred to justice or vice versa. Most judges will think that the balance between the opinions of the community and the demands of abstract justice must be struck differently in different kinds of cases. Perhaps in ordinary commercial or private law cases, like *McLoughlin*, an interpretation supported in popular morality will be deemed superior to one that is not, provided it is not thought very much inferior as a matter of abstract justice. But many judges will think the interpretive force of popular morality very much weaker in constitutional cases like *Brown*,[41] because they will think the point of the Constitution is in part to protect individuals from what the majority thinks right. [pp. 238–250]

---

[41] *Brown v. Board of Education* (1954) 347 U.S. 483.

## A Provisional Summary

Judges who accept the interpretive ideal of integrity decide hard cases by trying to find, in some coherent set of principles about people's rights and duties, the best constructive interpretation of the political structure and legal doctrine of their community. They try to make that complex structure and record the best these can be. It is analytically useful to distinguish different dimensions or aspects of any working theory. It will include convictions about both fit and justification. Convictions about fit will provide a rough threshold requirement that an interpretation of some part of the law must meet if it is to be eligible at all. Any plausible working theory would disqualify an interpretation of our own law that denied legislative competence or supremacy outright or that claimed a general principle of private law requiring the rich to share their wealth with the poor. That threshold will eliminate interpretations that some judges would otherwise prefer, so the brute facts of legal history will in this way limit the role any judge's personal convictions of justice can play in his decisions. Different judges will set this threshold differently. But anyone who accepts law as integrity must accept that the actual political history of his community will sometimes check his other political convictions in his overall interpretive judgment. If he does not—if his threshold of fit is wholly derivative from and adjustable to his convictions of justice, so that the latter automatically provide an eligible interpretation—then he cannot claim in good faith to be interpreting his legal practice at all. Like the chain novelist whose judgments of fit automatically adjusted to his substantive literary opinions, he is acting from bad faith or self-deception.

Hard cases arise, for any judge, when his threshold test does not discriminate between two or more interpretations of some statute or line of cases. Then he must choose between eligible interpretations by asking which shows the community's structure of institutions and decisions—its public standards as a whole—in a better light from the standpoint of political morality. His own moral and political convictions are now directly engaged. But the political judgment he must make is itself complex and will sometimes set one department of his political morality against another: his decision will reflect not only his opinions about justice and fairness but his higher-order convictions about how these ideals should be compromised when they compete. Questions of fit arise at this stage of interpretation as well, because even when an interpretation survives the threshold requirement, any infelicities of fit will count against it, in the ways we noticed, in the general balance of political virtues. Different judges will disagree about each of these issues and will accordingly take different views of what the law of their community, properly understood, really is.

Any judge will develop, in the course of his training and experience, a fairly individualized working conception of law on which he will rely, perhaps unthinkingly, in making these various judgments and decisions, and the judgments will then be, for him, a matter of feel or instinct rather than analysis. Even so, we as critics can impose structure on his working theory by teasing out its rules of thumb about fit—about the relative importance of consistency with past rhetoric and popular opinion, for example—and its more substantive opinions or learnings about justice and fairness. Most judges will be like other people in their community, and fairness and justice will therefore not often compete for them. But judges whose political opinions are more eccentric or radical will find that the two ideals conflict in particular cases, and they will have to decide which resolution of that conflict would show the community's record in the best light. Their working conceptions will accordingly include higher-order principles that have proved necessary to that further decision. A particular judge may think or assume, for example, that political decisions should mainly respect majority opinion, and yet believe that this requirement relaxes and even disappears when serious constitutional rights are in question.

We should now recall two general observations we made in constructing the chain-novel model, because they apply here as well. First, the different aspects or dimensions of a judge's working approach—the dimensions of fit and substance, and of different aspects of substance—are in the last analysis all responsive to his political judgment. His convictions about fit, as these appear either in his working threshold requirement or analytically later in competition with substance, are political not mechanical. They express his commitment to integrity: he believes that an interpretation that falls below his threshold of fit shows the record of the community in an irredeemably bad light, because proposing that interpretation suggests that the community has characteristically dishonored its own principles. When an interpretation meets the threshold, remaining defects of fit may be compensated, in his overall judgment, if the principles of that interpretation are particularly attractive, because then he sets off the community's infrequent lapses in respecting these principles against its virtue in generally observing them. The constraint fit imposes on substance, in any working theory, is therefore the constraint of one type of political conviction on another in the overall judgment which interpretation makes a political record the best it can be overall, everything taken into account. Second, the mode of this constraint is the mode we identified in the chain novel. It is not the constraint of external hard fact or of interpersonal consensus. But rather the structural constraint of different kinds of principle within a system of principle, and it is none the less genuine for that.

No mortal judge can or should try to articulate his instinctive working theory so far, or make that theory so concrete and detailed, that no further thought will be necessary case by case. He must treat any general principles or rules of thumb he has followed in the past as provisional and stand ready to abandon these in favor of more sophisticated and searching analysis when the occasion demands. These will be moments of special difficulty for any judge, calling for fresh political judgments that may be hard to make. It would be absurd to suppose that he will always have at hand the necessary background convictions of political morality for such occasions. Very hard cases will force him to develop his conception of law and his political morality together in a mutually supporting way. But it is nevertheless possible for any judge to confront fresh and challenging issues as a matter of principle, and this is what law as integrity demands of him. He must accept that in finally choosing one interpretation over another of a much contested line of precedents perhaps after demanding thought and shifting conviction, he is developing his working conception of law in one rather than another direction. This must seem to him the right direction as a matter of political principle, not just appealing for the moment because it recommends an attractive decision in the immediate case. There is, in this counsel, much room for deception, including self-deception. But on most occasions it will be possible for judges to recognize when they have submitted an issue to the discipline it describes. And also to recognize when some other judge has not.

## Some Familiar Objections

### Hercules is Playing Politics

Hercules has completed his labours in *McLoughlin*. He declares that the best interpretation of the emotional damage cases, all things considered, is (5): the law allows compensation for all emotional injury directly caused by careless driving and foreseeable by a reasonably thoughtful motorist. But he concedes that in reaching that conclusion he has relied on his own opinion that this principle is better—fairer and more just—than any other that is eligible on what he takes to be the right criteria of fit. He also concedes that this opinion is controversial: it is not shared by all of his fellow judges, some of whom therefore think that some other interpretation, for example (6), is superior. What complaints are his arguments likely to attract? The first in the list I propose to consider accuses Hercules of ignoring the actual law of emotional injury and substituting his own views about what the law should be.

How shall we understand this objection? We might take it in two very different ways. It might mean that Hercules was wrong to seek to justify his interpretation by appealing to justice and fairness because it does not even survive the proper threshold test of fit. We cannot assume, without reviewing the cases Hercules consulted, that this argument is mistaken. Perhaps this time Hercules nodded; perhaps if he had expanded the range of his study of precedents further he would have discovered that only one interpretation did survive, and this discovery would then have settled the law, for him, without engaging his opinions about the justice of requiring compensation for accidents. But it is hardly plausible that even the strictest threshold test of fit will always permit only one interpretation, so the objection, understood this way, would not be a general objection to Hercules' methods of adjudication but only a complaint that he had misapplied his own methods in the particular case at hand.

We should therefore consider the second, more interesting reading of the objection: this claims that a judge must never rely on his personal convictions about fairness or justice the way Hercules did in this instance. Suppose the critic says, "The correct interpretation of a line of past decisions can always be discovered by morally neutral means, because the correct interpretation is just a matter of discovering what principles the judges who made these decisions intended to lay down, and that is just a matter of historical fact". Hercules will point out that this critic needs a political reason for his dictum that interpretations must match the intentions of past judges. That is an extreme form of the position we have already considered, that an interpretation is better if it fits what past judges said as well as did, and even that weaker claim depends on the special arguments of political morality I described. The critic supposes that these special reasons are not only strong but commanding; that they are so powerful that a judge always does wrong even to consider an interpretation that does not meet the standard they set, no matter how well that interpretation ties together, explains, and justifies past decisions.

So Hercules' critic, if his argument is to have any power, is not relying on politically neutral interpretive convictions after all. He, too, has engaged his own background convictions of political morality. He thinks the political values that support his interpretive style are of such fundamental importance as to eliminate any competing commands of justice altogether. That may be a plausible position, but it is hardly uncontroversial and is in no sense neutral. His difference with Hercules is not, as he first suggested, about whether political morality is relevant in deciding what the law is, but about which principles of morality are sound and therefore decisive of that issue. So the first, crude objection, that Hercules has substituted his own political convictions for the politically neutral correct interpretation of the past law, is an album of confusions.

### Hercules Is a Fraud

The second objection is more sophisticated. Now the critic says, "It is absurd to suppose that there is any single correct interpretation of the emotional injury cases. Since we have discovered two interpretations of these cases, neither of which can be preferred to the other on 'neutral' grounds of fit, no judge would be forced by the adjudicative principle of integrity to accept either. Hercules has chosen one on frankly political grounds; his choice reflects only his own political morality. He has no choice in the circumstances but to legislate in that way. Nevertheless it is fraudulent for him to claim that he has discovered, through his political choice, what the *law* is. He is only offering his own opinion about what it should be."

This objection will seem powerful to many readers, and we must take care not to weaken it by making it seem to claim more than it does. It does not try to reinstate the idea of conventionalism, that when convention runs out a judge is free to improve the law according to the right legislative standards; still less the idea of pragmatism that he is always free to do this, checked only by considerations of strategy. It acknowledges that judges must choose between interpretations that survive the test of fit. It insists only that there can be no best interpretation when more than one survives that test. It is an objection, as I have framed it, from within the general idea of law as integrity; it tries to protect that idea from corruption by fraud.

Is the objection sound? Why is it fraudulent, or even confusing, for Hercules to offer his judgment as a judgment of law? Once again, two somewhat different answers—two ways of elaborating the objection—are available, and we cannot do credit to the objection unless we distinguish them and consider each. The first elaboration is this: "Hercules" claim is fraudulent because it suggests that there can be a right answer to the question whether interpretation (5) or (6) is fairer or more just; since political morality is subjective there cannot be a single right answer to that question, but only answers." This is the challenge of moral skepticism ... I cannot escape saying something more about it now, but I will use a new critic, with a section of his own, to do so. The second elaboration does not rely on skepticism: "Hercules is a fraud even if morality is objective and even if he is right that the principle of foreseeability he settled on is objectively fairer and more just. He is a fraud because he pretends he has discovered what the law is, but he has only discovered what it should be." That is the form of the objection I shall consider here.

We ask of a conception of law that it provide an account of the grounds of law—the circumstances under which claims about what the law is should be accepted as true or sound—that shows why law licenses coercion. Law as integrity replies that the grounds of law lie in integrity, in the best constructive interpretation of past legal decisions, and that law is therefore sensitive to justice in the way Hercules recognizes. So there is no way Hercules *can* report his conclusion about Mrs McLoughlin's case except to say that the law, as he understands it, is in her favor. If he said what the critic recommends, that she has no legal right to win but has a moral right that he proposes to honor, he would be *misstating* his view of the matter. He would think that a true account of some situations—if he found the law too immoral to enforce, for example—but not of this one. A critic might disagree with Hercules at many levels. He might reject law as integrity in favor of conventionalism or pragmatism or some other conception of law. Or he might accept it but reach different conclusions about Hercules because he holds different ideas about the necessary requirements of fit, or different convictions about fairness or justice or the relation between them. But he can regard Hercules' use of "law" as fraudulent (or grammatically wrong) only if he suffers from the semantic sting, only if he assumes that claims of law are somehow out of order when they are not drawn directly from some set of factual criteria for law every competent lawyer accepts.

One aspect of the present objection, however, might be thought immune from my arguments against the rest. Even if we agree that Hercules' conclusions about Mrs McLoughlin are properly presented as conclusions of law, it might seem extravagant to claim that these conclusions in any way follow from integrity understood as a distinct political ideal. Would it not be more accurate to say that integrity is at work in Hercules' calculations just up to the point at which he has rejected all interpretations that fail the threshold test of fit, but that integrity plays no part in selecting among those that survive that test? Should we not say that his conception of law is really two conceptions: law as integrity supplemented, when integrity gives out, by some version of natural law theory? This is not a very important objection; it only suggests a different way of reporting the conclusions it no longer challenges. Nevertheless the observation that prompts it is too crude. For it is a mistake to think that the idea of integrity is irrelevant to Hercules' decision once that decision is no longer a matter of his convictions about fit but draws on his sense of fairness or justice as well.

The spirit of integrity, which we located in fraternity, would be outraged if Hercules were to make his decision in any way other than by choosing the interpretation that he believes best from the standpoint of political morality as a whole. We accept integrity as a political ideal because we want to treat our political community as one of principle, and the citizens of a community of principle aim not simply at common principles, as if uniformity were all they wanted, but the best common principles politics can find. Integrity is distinct from justice and fairness, but it is bound to them in that way: integrity makes no sense except among people who want fairness and justice as well. So Hercules' final choice of the interpretation he believes sounder on the whole—fairer and more just in the right relation—flows from his initial commitment to integrity. He makes that choice at the moment and in the way integrity both permits and requires, and it is therefore deeply misleading to say that he has abandoned the ideal at just that point.

### Hercules is Arrogant and Anyway a Myth

I shall deal much more briefly with two less important critics who nevertheless must be heard. I have been describing Hercules' methods in what some will call a subjective way, by describing the questions he must answer and judgments he must make for himself. Other judges would answer these differently, and you might agree with one of them rather than Hercules. We shall consider in a moment whether any of this means that neither Hercules nor any other judge or critic can be "really" right about what the law is. But Hercules' opinion will be controversial no matter how we answer that philosophical question, and his new critic seizes just on the fact of controversiality, untainted by any appeal to either external or internal skepticism. "Whether or not there are right answers to the interpretive questions on which Hercules" judgment depends, it is unfair that the answer of one judge (or a bare majority of judges on a panel) be accepted as final when he has no way to *prove*, against those who disagree, that his opinion is better."

We must return, for an answer, to our more general case for law as integrity. We want our officials to treat us as tied together in an association of principle, and we want this for reasons that do not depend on any identity of conviction among these officials, either about fit or about the more substantive principles an interpretation engages. Our reasons endure when judges disagree, at least in detail, about the best interpretation of the community's political order, because each judge still confirms and reinforces the principled character of our association by striving, in spite of the disagreement, to reach his own opinion instead of turning to the usually simpler task of fresh legislation. But even if this were not so, the present objection could not count as an objection to law as integrity distinctly, for it would apply in its full force to pragmatism or to conventionalism, which becomes pragmatism in any case hard enough to come before an appellate court. How can it be fairer for judges to enforce their own views about the best future, unconstrained by any requirement of coherence with the past, than the more complex but no less controversial judgments that law as integrity requires?

Another minor critic appears. His complaint is from a different quarter. "Hercules," he says, "is a myth. No real judge has his powers, and it is absurd to hold him out as a model for others to follow. Real judges decide hard cases much more instinctively. They do not construct and test various rival interpretations against a complex matrix of intersecting political and moral principles. Their craft trains them to see structure in facts and doctrine at once; that is what thinking as a lawyer really is. If they decided to imitate Hercules, trying in each case to secure some general theory of law as a whole, they would be paralyzed while their docket choked." This critic misunderstands our exercise. Hercules is useful to us just because he is more reflective and self-conscious than any real judge need be or, given the press of work, could be. No doubt real judges decide most cases in a much less methodical way. But Hercules shows us the hidden structure of their judgments and so lays these open to study and criticism. We must be careful to distinguish, moreover, two senses in which he might be said to have more powers than any actual judge could. He works so much more quickly (and has so much more time available) that he can explore avenues and ideas they cannot; he can pursue, not just one or two evident lines in expanding the range of cases he studies but all the lines there are. That is the sense in which he can aim at more than they: he can aim at a comprehensive theory, while theirs must be partial. But he has no vision into transcendental mysteries opaque to them. His judgments of fit and political morality are made on the same material and have the same character as theirs. He does what they would do if they had a career to devote to a single decision; they need, not a different conception of law from his, but skills of craft husbandry and efficiency he has never had to cultivate.

Now this critic trims his sails. "In any case Hercules has too much theory for easy cases. Good judges just know that the plain meaning of a plain statute, or a crisp rule always applied and never doubted in precedent, is law, and that is all there is to it. It would be preposterous, not just time-consuming, to subject these undoubted truths to interpretive tests on each occasion. So law as integrity, with its elaborate and top-heavy structure, is at best a conception for hard cases alone. Something much more like conventionalism is a better interpretation of what judges do in the easy ones." The distinction between easy and hard cases at law is neither so clear nor so important as this critic assumes, ... but Hercules does not need that point now. Law as integrity explains and justifies easy cases as well as hard ones; it also shows why they are easy. It is obvious that the speed limit in California is 55 because it is obvious that any competent interpretation of California traffic law must yield that conclusion. So easy cases are, for law as integrity, only special cases of hard ones, and the critic's complaint is then only what Hercules himself would be happy to concede: that we need not ask questions when we already know the answer.                                    [pp. 255–266].

**RONALD DWORKIN**
**Justice In Robes**
(2006)

*Law*

*Hart's Defense*

Law is a political concept: people use it to form claims *of* law, that is, claims that the law of some place or other prohibits or permits or requires certain actions, or provides certain entitlements, or has other consequences. An enormous social practice is built around making, contesting, defending, and ruling on such claims. But their character is elusive. What does the claim that "the law" requires something really mean? What in the world makes that claim true when it is true, and false when it is false? The law of England requires people to pay taxes periodically, and to pay damages if they break their contracts, except in certain circumstances. These propositions are true, English lawyers will tell you, because of what Parliament has enacted and what English judges have decided in the past. But why do these particular institutions (rather than, for example, an assembly of the presidents of major universities) have the power to make propositions of law true? Lawyers often claim, moreover, that some proposition of law is true—for instance, that Mrs. Sorenson is legally entitled to a share of damages from each of the drug companies—when no legislature or past judges have so declared or ruled. What else, beside these institutional sources, can make a claim of law true? Lawyers often disagree about whether some claim of law, including that one, is true, even when they know all the facts about what institutions have decided in the past. What in the world are they then disagreeing about? We want, moreover, to answer these questions not just for a particular legal system, like English law, but for law in general, whether in Alabama or Afghanistan, or anywhere else. Can we say anything, in general, about what makes a claim of law true wherever it is true? Can there be true claims of law in places with very different kinds of political institutions from those we have? Or no recognizable political institutions at all? Is there a difference, in England or anyplace else, between the claim that the law requires someone to perform contracts he signed and a prediction that officials will punish him if he does not? Or between that claim and the apparently different claim that he is morally obligated to perform his contracts? If a claim of law is different from both a prediction of consequences and a statement of moral obligation, how, exactly, is it different?

Hart set out to answer these ancient questions in *The Concept of Law*. . . . Hart thought that in every community in which claims of law are made the great bulk of the officials of the community all accept, as a kind of convention, some master rule of recognition that identifies which historical or other facts or events make claims of law true. These conventions might be very different from one legal system to another: in one place the master convention might identify legislatures and past judicial decisions as the source of true legal claims, while in another the convention might identify custom or even moral soundness as the source. What form the convention takes, in any particular community, is a matter of social fact: everything turns on what the bulk of the officials in that community happen to have agreed on as the master test. But it is part of the very concept of law that in every community some master convention exists and picks out what counts as law for that community.

Hart's sources thesis is controversial: my own view of what makes claims of law true when they are true is very different. What is now important, however, is not the adequacy of Hart's theory but its character. Ordinary, first-order legal practice may consist in competing value judgments: it will do so, Hart says in his Postscript, if the community's master rule of recognition uses moral standards as part of the test for valid claims of law. But his own theory, he insists, which describes ordinary legal argument, is not a normative or evaluative theory—it is not a value judgment of any kind. It is rather an empirical or descriptive theory that elucidates the concepts that that ordinary legal argument deploys. Hart's position is a special case of the standard Archimedean view that there is a logical divide between the ordinary use of political concepts and the philosophical elucidation of them.

His position is therefore open to the same objections we reviewed against Archimedeanism in general. First, it is impossible to distinguish the two kinds of claims—to distinguish the first-order claims of lawyers in legal practice from second-order philosophers' claims about how first-order claims are to be identified and tested—sufficiently to assign them to different logical categories. Hart's sources thesis is very far from neutral between the parties in Mrs. Sorenson's case, for example. No "source" of the kind Hart had in mind had provided that people in Mrs. Sorenson's position are entitled to recover damages on a market-share basis, or stipulated a moral standard that might have that upshot or consequence. So if Hart is right Mrs. Sorenson cannot claim that law is on her side. Indeed, the drug companies' lawyers made exactly the same argument in court as Hart made in his book. They said that her claim fails because nothing in the explicit law of the state, as identified by settled legal conventions, provides for such a claim. Mrs. Sorenson's lawyers argued to the contrary. They denied the sources thesis: they said that general principles inherent in the law entitled their client to win. So Hart's view is not neutral in the argument: it takes sides. It takes sides, in fact, in every difficult legal dispute, in favor of those who insist that the legal rights of the parties are to be settled entirely by consulting the traditional sources of law.

So the first difficulty of political Archimedeanism holds for Hart's legal version as well. So does the second difficulty. In what way is Hart's social sources theses supposed to be "descriptive"? Of course, as he and his defenders acknowledge, description is always itself a normative enterprise in *some* sense: any descriptive theory picks out one explanation of some phenomena as more revealing or salient or useful or something of the sort. Hart agreed that his analysis of law was normative in the sense in which any explanation of anything is normative: he meant that his theory is descriptive as opposed to morally or ethically evaluative. But as we noticed in the case of liberty, equality, and the rest, there are several modes of description, and we must ask in which of these modes he meant his theory to be descriptive. Though he and his followers have energetically protested that my criticism of their work is based on a misunderstanding of their methods and ambitions, it is difficult to find any helpful positive statements of what these methods and ambitions are, let alone any that explains their claim to a descriptive status. In a famously baffling phrase in the original version of *The Concept of Law*, he said that that book should be understood as "an exercise in descriptive sociology." But he did not elaborate that bare claim, and it is far from plain, as we shall see, what he could have meant by it.

We must, once again, exercise our own imagination. I earlier distinguished three ways in which someone might think that a conceptual analysis of a political concept is a descriptive enterprise, and we must consider each of these again, in this context. Is the sources thesis a semantic claim: does it aim to bring to the surface linguistic criteria that lawyers everywhere, or at least the bulk of them, actually follow when they make and judge claims of law? Hart did not mean, of course, to offer a simple dictionary definition or set of synonyms for any particular word or phrase. But it seems to me plausible that he meant to make a more ambitious philosophical claim, elucidating criteria of application that lawyers and others might recognize, after he had pointed them out, as the rules that they actually do follow in speaking about what the law requires or permits. I proposed that understanding of his enterprise in *Law's Empire*; I said that if my understanding was correct his enterprise was doomed because there are no shared criteria, even hidden ones, for endorsing or rejecting propositions of law, even among lawyers in particular jurisdictions let alone everywhere. In his Postscript, Hart vigorously denies that he intended any such thing; he says that I deeply misunderstood his project. I am battered but unbowed: I still think that my understanding of the enterprise in *The Concept of Law* is the best available.[42] Still, since Hart ridiculed this understanding of his project in his Postscript, we must look elsewhere.

Could he have thought that propositions of law form a kind of natural kind, like tigers and gold, so that discoveries might be made about them that could contradict what most people think about their truth or falsity? Just as we might discover that many animals labeled "Tiger" in zoos are not actually tigers, so, on this view, we might discover that, whatever people think, nothing is law that does not conform to the sources thesis. Deep discoveries about natural kinds do seem at once conceptual—tiger DNA can plausibly be called the essence of tigerhood—

---

[42] Others agree. See e.g. N. Stavropoulos (2001), Hart's Semantics in J. Coleman (ed.), *Hart's Postscript*, 59.

and descriptive. So this hypothesis, if we could accept it, would explain Hart's apparent belief that a conceptual investigation into law could be descriptive but not semantic. We need not pursue this, however, because Hart could not have thought that true claims of law form a natural kind. If liberty has no DNA, neither does law.

We are left with the third possibility I distinguished: that Hart's sources thesis is meant to be descriptive in the way of an empirical generalization of some sort. Some army of legal anthropologists might conceivably collect all the data that history can provide about the various occasions on which people have made, accepted, or rejected what we regard as claims of law. Some sociologist with a room-sized computer and a huge budget might hope to analyze that Everest of data, not to find the essence or nature of law, but simply to discover patterns and repetitions in the vast story. He might, most ambitiously, aim to identify laws of human nature: if he finds that people accept propositions of law only when the sources thesis endorses them, for example, he might hope to explain that remarkable fact through Darwinian principles, perhaps, or economic equations, or something of the sort. Or he might be much less ambitious—he might simply point out the regularity, which would certainly be interesting enough in itself, and not try to explain it.

Shall we understand Hart's Archimedeanism to be empiricial in either the more or less ambitious of these senses? There is an insuperable thresh-old objection: neither Hart nor his descendants have even so much as begun on the lifetime-consuming empirical studies that would be needed. They have not produced an anthill, let alone an Everest, of data. There is a further threshold objection, at least in Hart's own case. It would be exceedingly odd to refer to any such empirical study or generalization as aimed at discovering the concept or nature or very idea of law, and so odd to name a book supposedly reporting those dis-coveries *The Concept of Law*. Imagine an economist saying that Ricardo's laws lay bare the very concept of wage or profit, for example.

Behind these threshold difficulties lies a third and even greater embarrassment. If we conceive Hart's theories—or those of his descendants—as empirical gen-eralizations, we must concede at once that they are also spectacular failures. It would, I said, take a mountain of data to support the sources thesis as an empirical generalization, but it takes only a few counter-examples to refute it, and these are everywhere. There is now a lively debate in the United States about whether capital punishment is constitutional. The argument hinges on whether the Eighth Amendment to the Constitution, which prohibits "cruel and unusual punishments," incorporates some moral standard for appropriate punishments, which capital punishment might well be thought to fail, or whether, on the contrary, it incorporates no moral standard but instead prohibits only punish-ments that the statesmen and politicians who made the amendment—or the general public to which it was addressed—thought cruel. If we assume that capital punishment is in fact unacceptably cruel, but that almost no one thought it so in the eighteenth century, then lawyers who accept the first of these interpretations will think that constitutional law prohibits capital punishment and those who accept the second will think that it permits capital punishment. Those who argue for the first, or moral, reading plainly contradict the social sources thesis, since no social source has directed that the Eighth Amendment be read to incorporate morality. But, since no social source has ruled that morality is not relevant, those who argue against the moral reading also contradict that thesis.

Hart said that morality becomes relevant to identifying law when some "source" has decreed that morality should have that role, and he gave the abstract clauses of the American Constitution as examples. But he misunderstood the state of American constitutional law. There is no consensus either in favor of or against the moral reading of the Constitution: it is on the contrary a matter of fierce disagreement. I, among others, endorse the moral reading that Hart apparently has in mind.[43] But others, including Justice Antonin Scalia of the United States Supreme Court, and a notorious former judge, Robert Bork, denounce the moral reading as profoundly misjudged.[44] There is no convention for or against it, no basic rule of recognition from which either side could hope to support the propositions of constitutional law that it nevertheless claims to be true.

## The Value of Legality

### Legality

A fresh start? Political concepts are concepts of value, and political philosophers should aim to show, for each of them, more precisely where its value lies since political values are integrated rather than detached, this project must find the place of each value in a larger and mutually supporting web of conviction that displays supporting connections among moral and political values generally and then places these in the still larger context of ethics. This picture of political philosophy is not only wildly ambitious—it can only even be imagined in a cooperative way—but it is also very much against contemporary fashion. It is not in the spirit of modest value pluralism. It aims at a utopian and always unrealized goal—Plato's unity of value—instead.

We should try to approach the ancient puzzles of law in that way. We need to find, however, a political value that is linked to those puzzles in the right way. It must be a real value, like liberty, democracy, and the rest, and it must be widely accepted as a real value, at least if our project is to have any chance of influence. The value must nevertheless function, within our community, as an interpretive value—those who accept it as a value must nevertheless disagree about precisely what value it is, and must disagree, in consequence, at least to some degree, about which political arrangements satisfy it, or which satisfy it better and which worse. It must be a distinctly legal value so fundamental to legal practice that understanding the value better will help us better to understand what claims of law mean and what makes them true or false. We must be able to see, for example, how a specific conception of the value would generate the sources thesis, and how other conceptions would generate the very different theories of law that are also part of the literature of jurisprudence. We must be able to see how embracing one conception of the value rather than another would mean reaching one decision rather than another in Mrs. Sorenson's case.

It should now be clear what value that is: it is the value of legality—or, as it is sometimes more grandly called, the rule of law. Legality is a real value, and it is a distinctly legal value. Many people think, for instance, that the Nuremberg trials in which Nazi leaders were tried and sentenced after World War II offended legality even though they were justified by other political values—justice or expediency, for example. Legality is, moreover, a very popular value. It has been much more widely embraced, and over many more centuries, than the other values I discussed earlier, and it is very widely regarded as of even more fundamental importance than they are.

From the beginning, moreover, legality was an interpretive ideal, and it remains so for us. There are various ways to state the value abstractly. Legality is engaged, we might say, when political officials deploy the state's coercive power directly against particular persons or bodies or groups—by arresting or punishing them, for example, or forcing them to pay fines or damages. Legality insists that such power be exercised only in accordance with standards established in the right way before that exercise. But that abstract formulation is, on its own, almost

---

[43] See *Freedom's Law*.
[44] See the debate between Scalia and myself in A. Scalia, *A Matter of Interpretation*, (1997), 117 and see R. Dworkin 65 Fordham L.R. 1249 (1997).

entirely uninformative: it remains to be specified what kinds of standards satisfy legality's demands, and what counts as a standard's having been established in the right way in advance. People disagree markedly about those issues. Some say that the Nuremberg trials offended legality, whether or not they were finally justified by some other value. But others say that the trials protected or enhanced the true ideals of legality. People disagree now, along similar lines, about trials of deposed dictators for inhumane acts not condemned by local law when they acted, and about the trials of Balkan villains in international criminal courts. These different views represent a common adherence to the value of legality, but different conceptions of what legality is.

Nor can there be much doubt about the connection between the value of legality with the problem of identifying true or valid claims of law. Conceptions of legality differ, as I said, about what kinds of standards are sufficient to satisfy legality and in what way these standards must be established in advance; claims of law are claims about which standards of the right sort have in fact been established in the right way. A conception of legality is therefore a general account of how to decide which particular claims of law are true: Hart's sources thesis is a conception of legality. We could make little sense of either legality or law if we denied this intimate connection between conceptions of legality and the identification of true claims of law. We can sensibly think that though the law rejects Mrs. Sorenson's claim for damages according to market share, justice supports that claim. Or (less plausibly) the other way around: that though the law grants her that claim, justice condemns it. But it would be nonsense to suppose that though the law, properly understood, grants her a right to recovery, the value of legality argues against it. Or that though the law, properly understood, denies her a right to recovery, legality would nevertheless be served by making the companies pay.

We can rescue the important questions of legal philosophy from Archimedean obscurantism by attacking them in this different way. We understand legal practice better, and make more intelligible sense of propositions of law, by pursuing an explicitly normative and political enterprise: refining and defending conceptions of legality and drawing tests for concrete claims of law from favored conceptions. There is no question of taking theories of law constructed in that way to be merely "descriptive." They are conceptual, but only in the normative, interpretive sense in which theories of justice, as well as theories of democracy, liberty, and equality, are conceptual. They may be, like such theories, more or less ambitious. The more ambitious try to find support for their conceptions of legality in other political values—or rather, because the process is not oneway, they try to find support for a conception of legality in a set of other, related, political values, each of these understood in turn in a way that reflects and is supported by that conception of legality.

I offer my own book, *Law's Empire*, as a more elaborate example of what, I have in mind. I did not emphasize the word "legality" there, but I did appeal to the value: I said that a philosophical theory of law must begin in some understanding of the point of legal practice as a whole. I was not then so concerned with isolating and refining the other values that any persuasive account of law's point would implicate. But the more ambitious description of jurisprudence I have now described helps me better to understand, and I hope better to pursue, issues underdeveloped or ignored in the book. I said there, for example, that identifying true propositions of law is a matter of interpreting legal data constructively, and that a constructive interpretation aims both to fit and to justify the data. I warned that "fit" and "justification" are only names for two rough dimensions of interpretation, and that further refinement would require a more careful analysis of other, discrete political values through which to understand these dimensions more thoroughly, so that we might see, for example, how to integrate them in an overall judgment of interpretive superiority when they pull in opposite directions. The key political concepts that must be explored in that way, it now seems to me, are those of procedural fairness, which is the nerve of the dimension of fit, and substantive justice, which is the nerve of political justification. Understanding the concept of legality better, that is, means expanding the discussion of adjudication to include a study of these further values, and though it would be surprising if that further study did not alter our understanding of law in some way, it would also be surprising if our understanding of law did not produce at least somewhat different views of fairness and justice as well. A wide-ranging reinterpretation of political values leaves nothing wholly as it was.

## Jurisprudence Revisited

Can we interpret the leading traditions or schools of jurisprudence as reflecting (and therefore as different from another in respect of different conceptions of legality? That value insists that the coercive power of a political community should be deployed against its citizens only in accordance with standards established in advance of that deployment. What kind of standards? Established in what way? We attack these questions by proposing some reading of the value of legality—some putative point served by constraining the use of political power in that way—and this reading must implicate, as I have several times now said, other values that we recognize. If it is sufficiently ambitious, it will implicate a great many of them in what I called earlier a web of conviction. Nevertheless different conceptions will select different connected values as more important in that mix: conceptions will differ, we might say, in the importance each assigns to different values in creating the local magnetic field in which it places legality.

Schools or traditions of jurisprudence are formed by large differences in the character of those choices. Three important traditions have in fact been formed by the rival choices, as locally influential values, of the political values of accuracy, efficiency, and integrity. I shall explore each of these three traditions in that light, but I want particularly to emphasize, in advance, that I am not suggesting that any of the traditions I describe has chosen one of these three values as the exclusive key to legality, and disparaged or neglected all others. I claim that the legal positivist tradition emphasizes the relation between legality and efficiency, for example, but I do not mean that positivists have been insensitive to either good or fair government. Positivists differ among themselves, not only because they hold somewhat different views of what political efficiency means and why it is valuable, but also because they hold different views, reflected in the details of their positions, about the character and force of many other political ideals, and I shall mention some of the other values to which different positivists have appealed to shape and reinforce their dominant reliance on efficiency. My tripartite division distinguishes the centers of gravity of different groups or schools of theory; it is not meant to exhaust the complexity or explain the details of any one theory.

*Accuracy*. By accuracy I mean the power of political officials to exercise the state's coercive power in a substantively just and wise way. Legality promotes accuracy if official acts are more likely to be wise or just if they are governed by established standards than if they represent merely the contemporary judgment of some official about what would be just or wise. It is not immediately evident that that will always, or even usually, be the case. Plato said that legality would hinder accuracy if the officials whose power it restrained were people of great knowledge, insight, and character, because they would know more about the immediate case than those who had laid down laws in the past, and they would be sensitive to discrete aspects of the case that might require or justify some different treatment. But there are at least two possible reasons for thinking that nevertheless legality does improve accuracy. The first appeals to institutional, historical, or other contingent reasons for thinking that the judgment of past lawmakers, in spite of their distance from some immediate problem or issue, is nevertheless likely to be better than the contemporary official's instinct or decision. Plato endorsed legality, in spite of the reservation I just reported, for that sort of reason. Philosopher-kings are rarely in power, he said, and, particularly in a democracy, the people actually in charge are ill-informed, incompetent, corrupt, self-serving, or all of these. In those unfortunate circumstances, he said, it is better that officials be constrained to follow what was laid down in the past, because they cannot be trusted to make a good contemporary decision of their own. Political conservatives, like Burke and Blackstone, often defended legality in much the same way. They thought that established law was a repository of accumulated wisdom and clear thought, and was therefore more to be trusted than the decisions, particularly those made in the heat of some moment, of individuals of limited character, knowledge, and skill.

The second reason for supposing that legality improves accuracy is very different: it relies, not on any contingent reason for supposing that established standards are wiser and more just than fresh case-by-case rulings, but on a conception of legality that allows the tests for established standards to promote or even to guarantee that result. The medieval natural lawyers thought that good government meant government in accordance with God's will, that God's will was expressed in moral laws of nature, and that divinely inspired priests and rulers were reliable guides to that law. They were naturally attracted, therefore, to a conception of legality that emphasized these fortunate connections between legality and political virtue, and therefore to tests for law that include a requirement of moral worth or acceptability. There is nothing in the abstract concept of legality that excludes that connection, and if the true value of legality is identified only through a conception that formalizes it, then that conception will seem, for those who accept the sets of understandings into which it fits, irresistible. The natural law tradition, in its various forms and manifestations, is premised on that way of understanding why legality has the value it does.

*Efficiency.* Jeremy Bentham, the founder of at least the British form of legal positivism, was not, however, attracted to either of these two sets of assumptions. He did not suppose that old standards are good ones; on the contrary he was a restless, even radical, innovator. He did not believe that the moral law is evident in God's nature: he thought, on the contrary, that the very idea of natural rights is nonsense on stilts. His conception of legality's virtue lay not in accuracy but in efficiency. Political morality, he thought, lies in the greatest good of the greatest number, and that can best be secured, not by different coercive or policy decisions taken by different officials relying on their own immediate and diverse judgments, but by detailed policy schemes whose complex consequences can be carefully considered in advance, and which can be laid down in detail, preferably in elaborate statutory codes, and enforced to the letter. Only in that way can the massive problems of coordination that the government of a complex society confronts be solved. Legal positivism is a natural upshot of that understanding of legality true point and value. Efficiency is compromised or entirely undermined, he thought, when moral tests are included among the tests for law, because moral tests allow citizens and officials who disagree, often strenuously, about what morality requires to substitute their own judgment about what standards have been established: the consequent disorganization will produce not utility but chaos. So Bentham and his followers insisted that law is whatever and only what the sovereign ruler or parliament has decreed: law stops where decree ends. Only that understanding can protect law's efficiency.

Later positivists have been true to that faith: they all stress law's role in substituting crisp direction for the uncertainties of customary or moral imprecation. Hart wrote, much in the spirit of Thomas Hobbes, a positivist of an earlier era, that legality cures the inefficiencies of a mythical prelaw state of nature or custom. Joseph Raz argues that the nerve of legality is authority, and that authority is damaged or undermined unless its directives can be identified without recourse to the kinds of reasons for action that citizens have before authority has spoken. Authority cannot serve its purpose, he insists, unless its directives replace rather than only add to the reasons people already have.

Efficiency is not the only value that positivists take into account in forming their conceptions of legality. Bentham, for example, thought it important that the public retain a healthy sense of suspicion and even skepticism about the moral worth of their laws: they should understand the difference between law as it is and as it should be. He worried that if judges could properly appeal to morality in deciding what the law is, then this crucial line would be blurred: people might assume that whatever judges declare to be law cannot be very bad because it has passed that moral test. Liam Murphy, among contemporary legal positivists, has appealed to the importance of public vigilance in defending his own positivistic understanding of legality's value.[45] Hart was concerned, not just about efficiency, but about an independent aspect of political fairness. If a community's law can be determined simply by discovering what the pertinent social sources—the legislature, for instance—have declared, then citizens are put on fair warning about when the state will intervene in their affairs to help or obstruct or punish them. If, on the other hand, the decisions of those sources are subject to supplement or qualification by moral considerations and principles, citizens cannot as easily or with the same confidence know where they stand. In America, some constitutional lawyers are drawn to a version of positivism for an entirely different reason. If morality is acknowledged to be among the tests for law, then judges whose own moral opinions would then be decisive in constitutional cases have much greater power over ordinary citizens than if morality is understood to be irrelevant to their office. Particularly when judges are appointed rather than elected, and cannot be deposed by popular will, this aggrandizement of their power is undemocratic.[46]

So legal positivists can defend their conception of legality, which insists that morality is not pertinent to the identification of law, by showing how well legality so understood serves efficiency, and also these other values. That defense assumes, of course, particular conceptions of these other values, and these conceptions can and have been challenged. It might be argued that political efficiency means coordinating a population's behavior toward good goals, for example, rather than simply any goals, that fair warning is sufficiently given, at least in some contexts, by the promise or threat that moral standards will be applied in judging particular behavior, that the critical judgment of a populace is sharpened not diminished by a "protestant" understanding of law that allows it to disagree, in part on moral grounds, with official declarations of what the law requires, and that democracy means not just majority rule but majority rule subject to the conditions, which are moral conditions, that make majority rule fair. Positivism rejects these and other alternative understandings—that is, it not only selects which political values to emphasize in constructing an account of legality, but also interprets those other values, controversially in the light of its own conception of legality. There is nothing threateningly circular in this complex conceptual interaction; on the contrary it is exactly what the philosophical project of locating a political value like legality in a larger web of value requires.

*Integrity.* Efficiency of government, on any plausible conception of what that means, is plainly an important product of legality, and any plausible explanation of legality's value must emphasize that fact. No ruler, even a tyrant, survives for

---

[45] The Political Quesion of the Concept of J. Coleman (ed.), *Hart's Postscript.*
[46] I elaborate and criticize this argument from democracy to positivism in *Freedom's Law.*

long or achieves his goals, even very bad ones, if he altogether abandons legality for whimsy or terror. But there is another important value that legality might also be seen to serve, not in competition with efficiency, but sufficiently independent of it to provide, for those who take it to be of great importance, a distinctive conception of what legality is for. This is political integrity, which means equality before the law, not merely in the sense that the law is enforced as written, but in the more consequential sense that government must govern under a set of principles in principle applicable to all. Arbitrary coercion or punishment violates that crucial dimension of political equality, even if, from time to time, it does make government more efficient.

Integrity has been a popular ideal among political philosophers for centuries, and its connection with legality has often been noted. The connection is sometimes expressed in the rubric that under the rule of law no man is above the law; but the force of that claim, as the various discussions of it make plain, is not exhausted by the ideal that each law should be enforced against everyone according to its terms. That stipulation would be satisfied by laws that, by their terms, applied only to the poor, or exempted the privileged, and the philosophers who describe legality in this way have in mind substantial and not merely formal equality before the law. A. V. Dicey, for example, in his classic study of the British Constitution, draws the following distinction:

> We mean in the second place, when we speak of the rule of law ... not only that with us no man is above the law, but (what is a different thing) that here every man, whatever be his rank or condition, is subject to the ordinary law of the realm...

and he later refers to this as "the idea of legal equality."[47] F.A. Hayek makes much the same claim though, unsurprisingly, he associates it with liberty rather than equality. He wrote in a classic work:

> The conception of freedom under the law that is the chief concern of this book rests on the contention that when we obey laws, in the sense of general abstract rules laid down irrespective of their application to us, we are not subject to another man's will and are therefore free ... This, however, is true only if by "law" we mean the general rules that apply equally to everybody. This generality is probably the most important aspect of that attribute of law which we have called its "abstractness." As a true law should not name any particulars, so it should especially not single out any specific person or group of persons.[48]

If we associate legality with integrity in this way, then we will favor a conception of the former that reflects and enhances the association. We prefer an account of what law is, and of how it is to be identified, that incorporates the value—integrity—whose pertinence and importance we recognize. If one way of deciding Mrs. Sorenson's case will treat her as equal before the law, in the sense that integrity assumes, and another will not, then we prefer a conception of legality that encourages the first and discourages the second decision. I tried to construct such a conception of law in *Law's Empire*; I want to emphasize, that *Law's Empire* reports only one way in which integrity and legality can be understood in each other's terms, and readers who are dissatisfied with my own construction should not reject the general project for that reason.

I suppose I should, however, anticipate a different objection that someone might wish to make at this point. He might object that the correct decision in Mrs. Sorenson's case depends on what the law actually is, not on what we would like the law to be because we are attracted to some other ideal, like integrity. But, we

---

[47] A.V. Dicey, *Introduction to the Study of the Law of the Constitution*, 114.
[48] F.A. Hayek, *The Constitution of Liberty*, 1960, 153.

cannot identify the correct tests for deciding what the law really is without deploying and defending a conception of legality, and we cannot do that without deciding what, if anything, is really good about legality. Jurisprudence is an exercise in substantive political morality. Of course, we cannot successfully propose an analysis of legality that bears no relation to legal practice: a successful account of any value must be able to be seen as an account of *that* value as it exists and functions in a scheme of values we share. Just as a claim about Mrs. Sorenson's legal rights must fit the legal practice of the jurisdiction in which the case arises, so any claim about what legality is must fit legal practice more generally. But more than one conception of legality will fit well enough; that is why we have different judicial philosophies represented even on the same bench. The cutting edge of a jurisprudential argument is its moral edge.

*Interpretive Positivism*

The difficulties I have been describing in Hart's self-professed methodology, which insists that theories of law are descriptive and neutral, can all be cured by recasting his arguments in the interpretive mode I have been suggesting. We strive to understand legality by understanding what is distinctly important and valuable in it, and we are tempted, initially, by the idea that legality is important because it provides authority in circumstances when authority is needed. But that claim invites a further conceptual question. Authority, too, is a contested concept: we need an account of authority that shows what the value is in it. The key to that further question lies in the mix of other values that legal positivists have traditionally celebrated, and, particularly, in the efficiency that authority brings. As positivists from Hobbes to Hart have pointed out, and as history has amply confirmed, political authority makes policy and coordination possible, and though policy and coordination may not work to everyone's benefit, they often, perhaps even usually, do. We are guided by this larger matrix of ideas in settling on conceptions of the discrete concepts it engages: the concepts of legality, efficiency, and authority. We must settle on conceptions of each that allows it to play its part in the larger story.

So we adopt an "exclusive" positivist conception of legality, which insists that morality plays no role in identifying true claims of law, and we also adopt what Joseph Raz calls a "service" conception of authority, which insists that there is no exercise of authority except when what has been directed can be identified without recourse to reasons the directive is meant to resolve and replace.[49] We no longer suppose that these conceptual claims are neutral, Archimedean excavations of rules buried in concepts that everyone with a full grasp of the concept or a full knowledge of the language will recognize. We may still say, as positivists have, that we have identified the salient aspects of our concepts that help us best to understand ourselves or our practice or our world. But now we make explicit what is obscure in those unhelpful claims: we understand ourselves and our practices better in one particular way—by designing conceptions of our values that show what, on reflection, we find most valuable in them, each and in the whole. We make no pretense that our conclusions are uncontroversial or disengaged from concrete political decision. If our constructions show that most of what most people think about law is a mistake—if they show that the claims of law that both sides make in Sorenson's case are wrong because none of them respects the sources thesis—then that is not an embarrassment to us, any more than it would embarrass us if our conclusions about equality showed that most people have steadily misunderstood what equality really is.

That is, the best we can do for the central claims of legal positivism. It sounds tinny and artificial, because in fact it would not make our law more certain or

---

[49] J. Raz, Ethics in the Public Domain, 1994.

predictable or our government more efficient or effective if our judges were suddenly converted to legal positivism and explicitly and rigorously enforced the sources thesis. On the contrary, judges would then rely much less on claims of law than they now do. If I am right, American judges would be forced to declare that there is no law in America at all, except the bare, uninterpreted words of the Constitution.[50] Even if they somehow avoided that frightening conclusion, they would be forced to subvert rather than to serve legality, even on the positivist's conception of that virtue, because they would be forced to declare much too often that either the law said nothing about the matter in controversy, or that the law was too unjust or unwise or ineffective to enforce. Judges who thought it intolerable that Sorenson should have no remedy, for example, would be forced to declare that, in spite of the fact that the law favored the defendant, they would ignore the law and hence ignore legality and award her compensation. They would announce that they had a "discretion" to change the law (or, what comes to the same thing, to fill in gaps in the law they had discovered) through the exercise of a fresh legislative power that contradicts the most basic understanding of what legality requires.

So it may seem perverse, or at least ungenerous, for me to attribute to positivists such a self-defeating argument for their position. But we should now notice that when positivism was first proposed, and when it was an actual force among lawyers and judges rather than only an academic position, the political situation was very different. Bentham, for example, wrote in an age of simpler and more stable commerce and a more homogenous moral culture: he could plausibly hope, as he did, for statutory codifications that would rarely leave gaps or require controversial interpretation. In those circumstances judges wielding moral tests for law posed a distinct threat to utilitarian efficiency that could be avoided most simply by denying them any such power. Even in the earlier years of the last century, progressive lawyers shared Bentham's views: progress, they thought, was available through administrative agencies, acting under broad parliamentary mandates, issuing detailed regulations that could be applied and enforced by technicians. Or, in the United States, through detailed uniform codes compiled by a national law institute trained by academic lawyers and proposed for adoption by the several states. Once again, in this atmosphere, judges claiming power to distil moral principles from an ancient and unsuited common law seemed archaic, conservative, and chaotic. The danger of such a claim was brilliantly illustrated by the Supreme Court's 1904 *Lochner* decision, which held that the conception of liberty embedded in the Fourteenth Amendment made progressive legislation that limited the number of hours bakers could be asked to work each day unconstitutional.[51] Legal positivism, progressives thought, saved law from such reactionary morality.

Oliver Wendell Holmes's positivism was a working legal doctrine: he cited positivism in dissenting from Supreme Court decisions in which, in his view, justices had assumed an illegitimate power to make their own law by pretending to find principles embedded in the law as a whole. "The common law is not a brooding omnipresence in the sky," he declared in one famous dissent, "but the articulate voice of some sovereign or quasi sovereign that can be identified; although some decisions with which I have disagreed seem to me to have forgotten the fact."[52] The jurisprudential argument between positivism and older theories of law was at the center of the long controversy about whether federal judges, when they had jurisdiction only because the parties were from different states, were constitutionally obliged to enforce the common law of one of those states as that law had been declared by the state's own courts, or whether they

---

[50] See *Justice in Robes*, Chap. 7.
[51] *Lochner v New York* 198 U.S. 45 (1905).
[52] *Southern Pacific Co. v Jensen* 244 U.S. 205, 222, Holmes dissenting.

were permitted to decide differently by finding and applying principles of "general" law not recognized by any state court. In *Erie Railroad v. Tompkins*, the Supreme Court finally decided that there was no such thing as "general" law: there was only law as declared by particular states.[53] Justice Brandeis, for the Court, quoted another famous Holmes passage:

> Law in the sense in which courts speak of it today does not exist without some definite authority behind it ... the authority and only authority is the State, and if that be so, the voice adopted by the State as its own [whether it be of its Legislature or of its Supreme Court] should utter the last word.

Brandeis made plain the practical importance of this view of law: the contrary view, long followed by the federal courts, destroyed uniformity because it produced different results on the same issue in state and federal courts, encouraging out-of-state plaintiffs to bring suits in federal courts when that was to their advantage. Of course, the Court could have reached the same result—for those practical reasons—without embracing positivism, but the muscular rhetoric of that legal doctrine had great appeal because it allowed Holmes, Brandeis, Learned Hand,[54] and other "progressives" to paint their more conservative opponents as victims of an incoherent metaphysics. Changes in society's expectations of law and judges were well under way, however, even in the 1930s when they wrote, and with accelerating velocity in the decades that followed, that made positivism's general conception of legality steadily more implausible and self-defeating. Elaborate statutory schemes became increasingly important sources of law, but these schemes were not—could not be—detailed codes. They were more and more constructed of general statements of principle and policy that needed to be elaborated in concrete administrative and judicial decisions; if judges had continued to say that law stopped where explicit sovereign direction ran out, they would have had constantly to declare, as I said, that legality was either irrelevant to or compromised in their judgments.

In the 1950s, moreover, several Supreme Court justices began a new turn in American constitutional law that made jurisprudence a riveting issue of national politics. They began to interpret the abstract clauses of the Constitution, including the due process and equal protection clauses, as stating general moral principles that give individual citizens important rights against national and state governments, rights whose existence presupposed that law was not limited to deliberate enactment, and whose contours could only be identified through substantive moral and political judgment. That initiative suddenly reversed the political valence of the jurisprudential argument: conservatives became positivists who argued that the Court was making up new constitutional rights of racial equality and freedom in reproductive decisions, for example, and therefore subverting legality. Some of the liberals who approved the Court's direction then moved from positivism toward a different conception of legality that stressed the principled integrity of the American constitutional settlement. In the last decades, the most conservative Supreme Court justices have engineered a further change in valence: their initiatives increasingly require them to ignore much Supreme Court precedent, and they therefore find a better justification in conservative political principle than in any orthodox version of legal positivism.

When Hart wrote *The Concept of Law* he could no longer rely, as Bentham and Holmes could, on the contemporary appeal of the positivist conception of legality. Hart's account of positivism's efficiency is a Just-So story from an imagined ancient past: a supposed pre-historical transition from the chaos of primary-rule tribal inefficiency to the crisp authority of secondary rules embraced in a liberating

---

[53]   304 U.S. 64 (1938).
[54]   See *Freedom's Law*, Chap. 17.

and near-uniform explosion of consensus. Those who followed his lead have continued to write about authority, efficiency, and coordination. But they cannot confirm their claims in actual political practice either, and that may explain why they fall back, as Hart did, on self-descriptions that seem to isolate their theories from such practice. They say that they are probing the very concept or nature of law, which remains the same in spite of shifting features of political practice or structure, or that, in any rate, they offer only descriptive accounts of what that practice is, withholding any judgment about what it should be or become. That is the methodological camouflage that I have challenged in this essay. If, the self-description cannot be made both intelligible and defensible, then we must concentrate on the more comprehensible justification I tried to substitute—the substantive, positivist account of the value of legality that I have now described. It is a virtue of that description, I think, that it brings to the surface the appeal positivism had for lawyers and judges, and for scholars in substantive fields of law, in times past, when its conception of legality seemed more plausible than it now does.

## Concluding Thoughts

I have been emphasizing similarities between the concept of legality—as a foundation for legal philosophy—and other political concepts, and I shall close by noting an important difference. Legality is sensitive in its application, to a far greater degree than is liberty, equality, or democracy, to the history and standing practices of the community that aims to respect the value, because a political community displays legality, among other requirements, by keeping faith in certain ways with its past. It is central to legality that a government's executive decisions be guided and justified by standards already in place, rather than by new ones made up *ex post facto*, and these standards must include not only substantive laws but also the institutional standards that give authority to various officials to create, enforce, and adjudicate such standards for the future. Revolution may be consistent with liberty, equality, and democracy. It may, and often has been, necessary in order to achieve even a decent level of those values. But revolution, even when it promises to improve legality in the future, almost always involves an immediate assault on it.

So any even moderately detailed account of what legality requires in concrete terms in some particular jurisdiction must attend very carefully to the special institutional practices and history of that jurisdiction, and even a moderately detailed account of what it requires in one place will be different, and perhaps very different, from a parallel account of what it requires elsewhere. (Arguing and deciding about these concrete requirements in a particular community is the quotidian work of that community's practicing lawyers, at one level, and of its academic lawyers at another.) That is also true, to some more limited extent, about other political virtues: the concrete institutional arrangements that count as improving democracy or advancing equality or better protecting liberty in a country with one political demography and history may well be different from those that count in that way in another.

But though legality is evidently even more sensitive, in detail, to special features of political practice and history than these other virtues, it does not follow, for legality any more than for the others, that nothing of importance can or should be done to explore the value at a philosophical level that transcends most details of place. For just as we can explore the general concept of democracy by developing an attractive abstract conception of that concept, so we can also aim at a conception of legality of similar abstraction, and then attempt to see what follows, by way of concrete propositions of law, more locally. There is no bright-line conceptual or logical difference of the kind the Archimedeans want between jurisprudence so conceived and the more ordinary, day to day, concerns of lawyers and legal scholars I just mentioned. But there is nevertheless a sufficient difference in level of abstraction and in relevant skills to explain why the philosophical issues seem different, and are ordinarily in the hands of people with somewhat different training, from the more concrete ones.

Any attempt at an ecumenical conception of legality faces pressure from two directions. It must aim at sufficient content to avoid vacuity but also at sufficient abstraction to avoid parochialism.[55] I tried to steer the needed course between these dangers in *Law's Empire*: I said that legality is best served through a process of constructive interpretation along the lines, and responding to the two dimensions, mentioned above. My views have been sufficiently controversial to suggest that I escaped vacuity, but it is unclear how far I escaped parochialism. It is a frequent objection among British critics that my project is either parochial in inspiration—that it aims at no more than explaining the legal practice of my own country—or obviously parochial in result because we can somehow see, without much thought or research, that it fits only that one legal practice.[56] In fact, my account aims at very great generality, and how far it succeeds in that aim can only be assessed by a much more painstaking exercise in comparative legal interpretation than these critics have undertaken. I said, earlier, in discussing other political values, that we cannot tell in advance how far we might succeed in finding plausible conceptions of these that reconcile them with one another rather than leaving them, as they are so often declared to be, in conflict. We must do our best, and then see how far we have succeeded. We must take the same view of the different question of how much abstraction an informative account of legality can achieve. We must wait and see. [pp 168–185]

## GERALD J. POSTEMA
### Integrity: Justice in Workclothes
(2004)[57]

Integrity is an important value of political morality—perhaps the most immediately important such value governing law and its administration—although I fully agree with skeptics that a compelling case for integrity has not yet been offered. The aim of this essay is to construct a case for integrity, and in doing so provide an argument for the internalist approach to the moral force of precedent. I draw liberally on Dworkin's discussion of integrity, but my argument is not a reconstruction of Dworkin's. Indeed, at some crucial points my conception of integrity departs from Dworkin's, and my argument takes a rather different route from his. Nevertheless, both my conception of integrity and my argument for it remain akin to Dworkin's. . . .

I INTEGRITY: THE NOTION

*Integrity and the concept of law*

The value of integrity has a respected, if sometimes contested, place in interpersonal morality.[58] The question I want to address, however, is whether it should be placed alongside values like justice, fairness, liberty, equality, community, benevolence, and desert as an important constituent of *political* morality. More

---

[55] There are further conditions of success.
[56] This criticism is not confined to British critics: it appealed to Posner also: *Law and Legal Theory in England and America*, 1997.
[57] [From ed. Justine Burley. *Dworkin and His Critics*].
[58] For a critical discussion of the philosophical literature on integrity as a personal moral virtue see Cheshire Calhoun, "Standing for Something," *Journal of Philosophy*, vol. 92, 1995, pp. 235–60.

specifically, I am interested in whether integrity provides us with standards distinct from those provided by the other political values, standards by which we must assess our law and its interpretation and application.

To fix the notion of integrity, we must first consider some very general features of law, features of what Dworkin calls "the concept of law."[59] Broadly speaking, law is a pervasive social institution or practice which provides a framework of practical reasoning for individual citizens and for society as a whole acting through government officials. The distinctive feature of this framework is that officials and citizens alike seek to justify their actions by appeal to rules or principles drawn from past political decisions of the community, as recorded in the books and reflected in the practices of its law. So conceived, law serves at least two broad social goals: (1) to facilitate and coordinate the pursuit of both the common goals of the community and the goals of its members, and (2) especially where the exercise of coercion is involved, to constrain the community and its members to actions and policies consistent with public principles. The rules, precedents, and principles of law ground reciprocal obligations between the community and its members and define a framework by which the government is held accountable to citizens and citizens are held accountable to each other.

This concept of law defines integrity's career. Integrity gives specific content to the abstract legal notion that present official or private actions are warranted by the past through *principles* derived from past decisions. Integrity explains *how* past political decisions yield present practical directives. It also purports to provide rational support for this generative capacity by linking law's project, understood in terms supplied by integrity, to more fundamental values of political morality. That is, it purports to explain why such directives are normative for officials and citizens. So integrity claims to be more than merely a method or technique of practical reasoning specially adapted to law's distinctive tasks; it also claims to be a substantive value of political morality. Although distinct from other political values, it takes its moral focus and force from the service it renders more fundamental values, in particular justice and fidelity.

### The core idea of integrity

In this context, the core idea of integrity is coherence of action and of principle. To legitimate the actions of the community and its members, the principles drawn from past decisions and actions of the community must (in the ideal case) express a unified, common, and relatively comprehensive vision of justice for the community.[60] Integrity demands that, through its officials, the community act on a coherent set of principles of justice even when its citizens disagree about what the correct principles of justice are.[61] We can identify several important components of this core idea of integrity.

First, integrity is a norm of *unification* called forth by a more fundamental social *unity*. Dworkin insists that those who are bound by integrity must view the community as if it were a single individual moral agent.[62] This personification of the community, however, is not a deep feature of the notion of integrity; it is merely a heuristic device. Yet, as such, it gives expression to the important and deep assumption of the unity of the community. The demand for integrity arises only when the decisions and actions of a community and its members, viewed both synchronically and diachronically, are internally related, that is, as potentially in harmony or in conflict, as extending or qualifying each other, and as bearing on the meaning and affecting the practical force of each other. For only

[59] Dworkin, *Law's Empire*, p. 93.
[60] Ibid., p. 134.
[61] Ibid., p. 166.
[62] Ibid., pp. 167–75.

when this is the case can there arise an intelligible demand for their *unification* into a scheme that relates them to a common, albeit complex, set of themes, purposes, or principles. That is to say, integrity *assumes* there is some compelling moral reason for treating the various actions and decisions as unified in this way, namely, as internally related and thus needing unification. The reason will have to be one of political morality (as opposed to a metaphysical, epistemological, or prudential practical reason). Where we do not have sufficient reason to regard these actions and decisions as internally related—where we lack reason to treat their agents as forming a single community calling for unification—integrity has no place, just as considerations of loyalty and friendship have no place between strangers.

Second, integrity also calls for *internal justification*. Integrity maintains that the obligations, responsibilities, and rights of citizens and officials go beyond the explicit extension of the community's settled rules. It also maintains that past decisions and actions not only have "external effect" or causal traces, but also generate or bring to bear norms or principles drawn from those past decisions and actions and its settled rules.

Third, the principles sought by integrity are principles of *justice*. The concept of justice gives shape and direction to integrity's quest for principled unity of the community's past and present. "Justice," as I shall use it, is meant to include all that falls under the terms "justice," "fairness," and "due process," as Dworkin defined those terms in *Law's Empire*.[63] While relatively broad, this notion of justice is limited by the fact that our focus is on the integrity of law in the context of political society. Thus justice in and of the community is integrity's guiding star.

Fourth, integrity calls on officials and citizens to view their practice as the expression of a *coherent* set of principles, but the notion of coherence I use here is a deliberately weak one. It merely signifies an intelligibility, a unity of vision, under the notion of justice. It is not meant to invoke other, more precise or technical notions of coherence. In particular, it does not require that the principles must be reducible to a single master principle (monism) or a set of formally ranked principles. Nor does coherence suggest that the principles must each entail, imply, or justify each other. This kind of coherence can obtain among distinct and irreducible principles which may even conflict in specific cases from time to time. The "unification" that integrity seeks is just the weak constraint on a set of principles requiring them to fit together into an intelligible, practically and morally meaningful whole under the concept of justice.[64] Coherence of this sort is not a logical or quasi-logical notion like consistency or mutual entailment. Rather, it is a morally substantive notion and it is always judged, and must always be defended, on substantive grounds. Most importantly, integrity does not assume that coherence is desirable in itself such that the more coherent a set of principles is (as measured along one of the previously mentioned, more or less formal scales), the greater is the integrity of the practice in question. Finally, integrity regards coherence as an *ideal*, a normative *project*. Thus, our best efforts may only achieve an approximation of coherence. This is especially true of law. Oliver Wendell Holmes pressed this point against C. C. Langdell and the formalists of his day. Law, he maintained, "is always approaching and never reaching consistency. It is forever adopting new principles for life at one end, and it always

---

[63]  Ibid., pp. 176–8, 404–7.

[64]  I agree with Joseph Raz that this weak notion of coherence is the notion at the core of Dworkin's idea of integrity in *Law's Empire* (see pp. 165–7), despite some language in that work that suggests a stronger notion. For Raz's defence of this interpretation and references to *Law's Empire*, see Joseph Raz, "The Relevance of Coherence," in *Ethics in the Public Domain* (Oxford: Clarendon Press, 1994).

retains old ones from history at the other, which have not been absorbed or sloughed off. It will become entirely consistent only when it ceases to grow."[65]

Fifth, integrity is essentially *historical*. Integrity seeks to forge a common vision of justice from the past public decisions and actions of the community. The search for principles of justice undertaken in the name of integrity is historically situated; integrity takes past decisions and actions as its point of departure and normative compass. Our past practice bears the shape of our common life, while forcing us to address the question of what this shape is.

Sixth, integrity requires officials and citizens to seek *common, public* principles of justice in their common past. The exercise of practical reasoning disciplined by integrity is a common, public activity—an activity of the community as a whole and of its members regarding themselves as members.[66] In her 1997 Carus Lectures, Annette Baier spoke of the social nature of reasoning, especially practical reasoning, as "a commons of the mind."[67] Her metaphor is even more apt for the political past, as reported and recorded in the books and reflected in the practice of law. Past actions and decisions provide a kind of commons, a common resource and inheritance, available to each member, not for merely private purposes, however noble, but for the purpose of forging a common just future.

The present conception of integrity departs from Dworkin's original notion at this point. According to Dworkin, the attitude of integrity is "a protestant attitude that makes each citizen responsible for imagining what his society's public commitments to principles are, and what these commitments require in new circumstances."[68] This "protestant" attitude, while rightly highlighting individual responsibility, ignores the interactive, public character of the practical reasoning demanded by integrity.[69] Dworkin himself observes at one point that "the community as a whole and not just individual officials one by one must act in a principled way."[70] That is correct, I believe, but I would add that the community achieves integrity only when its members seek *as a community* to act from a coherent vision of justice.

*Integrity and regret*

Finally, integrity is hollow and fraudulent if it does not balance *respect* for past practice with a more self-critical attitude which I will call *regret*.[71] Integrity calls for responsible coherence of action and principle. This makes it a complex virtue, for it calls for coherence of principle, coherence of action with principle, *and* appropriate responses to departures from each. Integrity, or its failure, are often most evident in the manner in which we seek to restore equilibrium between action and principle. As Lynne McFall reminded us, "[a] person who admits to having succumbed to temptation has more integrity than the person who sells out,

---

[65] O. W. Holmes, *The Common Law*, ed. M. DeWolfe Howe, [1881]1963), p. 32.

[66] I have defended a notion of public, plural, practical deliberation in three papers: "Morality in the First Person Plural" *Law and Philosophy*, vol. 14, 1995, pp. 35–64; "Public Practical Reason: An Archeology," *Social Philosophy and Policy*, vol. 12, 1995, pp. 43–86 [hereinafter Postema, "An Archeology"]; "Public Practical Reason: Political Practice," in Ian Shapiro and Judith Wagner DeCew (eds.), *NOMOS XXXVII: Theory and Practice*, (1995).

[67] Annette Baier, *The Commons of the Mind*, 1997.

[68] Dworkin, *Law's Empire*, p. 413.

[69] For a more general criticism of Dworkin's theory of law and interpretation along these lines, see Gerald J. Postema, "'Protestant' Interpretation and Social Practices," *Law and Philosophy*, vol. 6, 1986, pp. 283–319.

[70] Dworkin, *Law's Empire*, p. 184.

[71] I use "regret" as a term of art. I intend it to encompass the capacities to acknowledge and take responsibility for mistakes and to take appropriate steps to correct and compensate for the wrongs they cause.

[and] then fixes the books. ...."[72] Integrity sometimes calls for recognizing violations of principle, resisting the temptation to abandon or rearticulate the principle to accommodate the violation, and responsibly acting to restore the equilibrium. Thus, when integrity calls on us to determine what our common past practice commits us to now and in the future, we must responsibly balance respect for our past practice with appropriate regret for it. We cannot simply hold fixed our principles and self-deceptive high ideals and refuse to take responsibility for actions that fail to conform to them; nor can we simply take the actions of the past as fixed—as coherent expressions of principle—and ask only what principles these actions serve. Integrity demands that we recognize the possibility of hypocrisy at both of these levels and that we act on sound judgment in response to it.

Dworkin's notion of integrity does not rule out this complexity, although sometimes his interpretive project of "showing the practice in its best light" seems to lose sight of the dimension of regret.[73] At times, Dworkin's "interpreter" seems more like an outside observer seeking a charitable *explanation* of the community's behavior than a member of that community taking responsibility with others for their practice. Dworkin's interpreter treats elements of the practice that do not fit the interpretation merely as others, "mistakes" perhaps, but not integral features of past practice with the same moral significance for the present as duly accounted for elements. However, this is not the attitude of a responsible participant in the practice, or member of the community whose practice it is, let alone that of a responsible official speaking and acting for that community. Nietzsche warned that "as long as the past must be described as something worthy of imitation, ... so long, at least, is the past in danger of being somewhat distorted, of being reinterpreted according to aesthetic criteria and so brought closer to fiction. ...."[74] Without regret, interpretation of our past becomes disengaged and aesthetic at best, and celebratory revisionist history at worst.

In the context of law, regret involves two related responses to problematic decisions, rules, or actions of the past. First, it involves isolating the offending items from the body of legal materials of the polity and limiting the influence of the offending items on the principles drawn from them in the name of integrity, thereby limiting their contribution to the guidance and justification of decisions and actions in the present.[75] This limiting of the normative influence of past decisions and rules can take a variety of more or less drastic forms, ranging from localizing their influence to some specific area of the law where its influence is less pernicious, to restricting the decisions to its narrowest terms (for example, to cases "on all fours" with it), to draining it of all normative force by reversing or overruling the decision. Second, regret also involves acknowledging, and in appropriate ways correcting and compensating for, the legacy of the offending rules or decisions in the body of law itself and in the lives of those who have suffered under them. Integrity calls for sensitive judgment to determine the just balance of respect and regret regarding the past, and in determining the appropriate response of regret in its two dimensions.

Insofar as regret calls for some form of localizing short of eliminating the

---

[72] Lynne McFall, "Integrity," *Ethics*, vol. 98, 1987, pp. 5–20, at p. 7.

[73] This may be true of Dworkin, *Law's Empire*, p. 257. See Raz, "The Relevance of Coherence," pp. 282, 298 (arguments against global coherence in law); ibid., pp. 299–303 (defense of local coherence).

[74] Friedrich Nietzsche, *On the Advantages and Disadvantages of History for Life*, trans. P. Preuss ([1874] 1980), p. 17.

[75] For purposes of illustration I assume here a mode of reasoning on the model of Dworkin's theory of interpretation. See Dworkin, *Law's Empire*, pp. 45–86. On that model, actions of the past exert their influence over present decisions beyond their "explicit extensions," through the principles drawn from (and justifying) the past decisions, which principles, then, guide deliberations in present cases.

normative influence of offending rules or decisions of the past it compromises to some extent the law's coherence. It may not be possible to integrate completely into an intelligible vision of justice elements of our recorded political past which nevertheless exert some normative force on present decisions. Where regret is indicated, what Raz calls the "global coherence" of law is likely to be compromised.[76] Raz is highly critical of accounts of law that insist on global coherence, while he recognizes the importance of some kinds of "local coherence."[77] However, in contrast to this notion of islands of local coherence in a globally noncoherent body of law, integrity admits islands of compromised coherence in a body of law that strives still for coherence. It is important to stress that these compromises of coherence do not pose a challenge to integrity. They are the product of regret which is an essential component of integrity. So the balance of respect and regret, and regret's determination of the kind and extent of isolation of offending rules and decisions of the past, are matters determined within and in the service of integrity. Because integrity is an important moral value, this balance is a moral balance; however, it is not a balance, all moral things considered, of concern for the past with other distinct morally relevant considerations. The principles in the name of which regret is exercised are drawn not from some account of morality considered independently of the past decisions, rules, and actions of the polity, but from principles embedded in them.

Thus complex integrity forces us to make room for the kind of deeply upsetting argument that Frederick Douglass made in his *Fourth of July Oration of 1852*,[78] "What have I, or those I represent to do with your national independence?" he asked.

> The existence of slavery in this country brands your republicanism as a sham, your humanity as a base pretense, and your Christianity as a lie. ... Are the great principles of political freedom and natural justice, embodied in the Declaration of Independence, extended to us? ... This Fourth of July is *yours* not *mine*. You may rejoice, I must mourn.[79]

The power of this argument comes directly from the fact that it appeals to principles historically professed, but only partially practiced. Integrity, however, requires that we view and take responsibility for our *whole* past, not just the agreeable parts. It requires that we establish coherence of action with professed principle, not by accommodating the violation by adjusting the principle, but by adjusting the practice and forcing it in new directions.

Joseph Raz recently criticized coherence theories of adjudication, and integrity theories to the extent they depend on coherence, for "idealiz[ing] the law out of the concreteness of politics."[80] "The reality of politics leaves law untidy," he argues.[81] Coherence theories, however,

> attempt to prettify it and minimize the effect of politics. ... But, in countries with decent constitutions, the untidiness of politics is morally sanctioned ... by the morality of authoritative institutions. There is no reason to minimize its effects, nor to impose on the courts duties which lead them to be less just than they can be.[82]

[76] Raz, "The Relevance of Coherence," p. 298.

[77] See ibid., pp. 282–98 (arguments against global coherence in law) and pp. 299–303 (defense of local coherence).

[78] F. Douglass, "Fourth of July Oration," in Herbert J. Storing (ed.), *What Country Have I? Politica Writings by Black Americans* ([1852]1970), p. 28.

[79] Ibid., pp. 31–2, 36.

[80] Raz, "The Relevance of Coherence," p. 298.

[81] Ibid.

[82] Ibid.

However apt Raz's criticism may be of simpler coherence theories of adjudication, it should be clear that his charge of "idealizing the law out of the concreteness of politics" cannot be laid at the door of a notion of integrity that demands a proper balance of respect and regret for the past. There is nothing pretty or idealized about the kind of argument Douglass mounted, an argument that calls for integrity of the more complex kind I have urged. Indeed, I will argue the complex integrity that I have described operates in and on the untidy reality of politics.

### In defense of integrity

Thus far I have only sketched a cartoon of the notion of integrity I wish to defend. Far more detail can be drawn in to make the picture complete, and in those details lie many devilish difficulties. Yet I propose to proceed boldly on the assumption that each of the devils can be met and ultimately subdued. My task is to try to defend the notion I have roughly sketched above, leaving to other hands the task of drawing in its details. Let me make clear, however, that my aim is to answer challenges to the intelligibility of integrity as a value of political morality. In the concluding section, I will argue for the relevance of this value to law, but my aim is not to defend in this essay an integrity theory of (the nature of) law, let alone Dworkin's own "law as integrity" theory. What I have to say here may be useful for that project, but it is not my project here. I will be satisfied if I can make a persuasive case for the moral importance of integrity.[83]

Integrity assumes, but does not itself demonstrate, the truth of three claims. First, integrity presupposes that the various actions and decisions of people have sufficient unity—that they are actions of a community—such that they call for the kind of normative unification that integrity sets as a project for the community's members. Second, integrity assumes that justice is public and political such that integrity's project is not individual, but communal. And third, integrity rests on the assumption that the community's past is normative for its present and future. Regarding the first assumption, the task is not to demonstrate its truth, but rather to identify those conditions that must obtain for it to be true in any particular group of people. This is a difficult and important task on which there has been very little work. However, I will not undertake this task here, as I suspect that the source of skepticism about the place of integrity in political morality lies elsewhere. Skepticism can be traced to the second and third assumptions. Thus my defense of integrity will focus on the political and historical character of integrity, and thus on its links to *justice* and *fidelity*, the two more fundamental values of political morality that integrity serves. My defense of integrity as an important value governing law will succeed if I can show (1) that justice is public and political in the way integrity assumes; (2) that, in communities meeting the conditions of unity presupposed by integrity, the past is normative for them in the complex way integrity describes; and (3) that law is governed by integrity so understood. These tasks structure the remainder of this essay.

---

[83] Thus the important objections that Raz raised against coherence theories of law and adjudication (see ibid., pp. 282–98), do not challenge my project here, first because the notion of coherence he has in mind is much stronger than the one I am using, and second because his most important arguments are directed against coherence theories of law and adjudication. At the conclusion of this essay, I will briefly consider possible extensions of Raz's arguments to the notion of integrity defended here.

## II Integrity and Justice

*Distinct but closely related*

Dworkin insists that integrity is an independent value of political morality, distinct from justice and fairness.[84] His claim does not rest on an argument that these values are rooted in fundamentally different moral concerns, as one might argue in the case of justice and benevolence.[85] Rather, he appeals to the possibility of conflict between them and the thought that in some cases it is right for integrity to prevail, but that in other cases the injustice of the decision or rule recommended by integrity may be so great that its moral claim is utterly defeated.

Many integrity skeptics argue against Dworkin that either integrity is simply parasitic on justice and so not a distinct virtue, or distinct but not a recognizable moral value at all.[86] Critics argue that although integrity requires principled consistency, the principles are either morally correct principles of justice, in which case integrity simply is justice, or they are morally objectionable and so cannot claim our allegiance. But this argument identifies integrity with a merely formal notion of justice or equality and does not apply to the richer notion of integrity described in the previous section. On the basis of this argument alone, then, it would be a mistake to conclude that there is no fundamental difference between integrity and justice.

Yet even Dworkin admits that these values are closely related on some deeper level:

> We accept integrity as a political ideal because we want to treat our political community as one of principle, and the citizens of a community of principle aim not simply at common principles, as if uniformity were all they wanted, but the best common principles politics can find. Integrity is distinct from justice and fairness, but it is bound to them in that way: integrity *makes no sense* except among people who want fairness and justice as well.[87]

According to Dworkin, the quest for integrity is linked closely to the pursuit of justice. What is the nature of this relationship?

*The circumstances of integrity*

Integrity, I shall argue, is justice in a certain guise: justice in political workclothes. But, if they are related in this way, how can justice override, let alone utterly

---

[84] See Dworkin, *Law's Empire*, op. cit., pp. 176–84.

[85] For example, one might argue that benevolence is concerned with promoting the overall good or well being of persons and lends itself easily to aggregating over persons and maximizing, while justice concerned with the way individuals are treated, or with the right distribution of resources and opportunities in a community, or the right sort of relationships among members of a community, values the typically resist aggregation and maximizing.

[86] See e.g., Alexander and Kress, "Against Legal Principles," p. 755 [and *post*]; Raz, "The Relevance Coherence," op. cit., pp. 296, 298 (maintaining that "[s]peaking with one voice ... is not an independent ideal with the moral force to lead us to endorse solutions less just than they need to be" but rather is just "a by-product of an ideal situation"); Denise Réaume, "Is Integrity a Virtue?" *University Toronto Law Review*, vol. 39, 1989, pp. 392–3 (rejecting Dworkin's assurance that consistency has independent value and stating that fairness, justice, and procedural due process require consistency). By see Raz, "The Relevance of Coherence," pp. 303–9 (giving reasons to doubt that integrity Dworkin understands it requires coherence or speaking with one voice).

[87] Dworkin, *Law's Empire*, p. 263 (emphasis added).

defeat, demands of integrity? Taking a cue from Jeremy Waldron, I suggest that the answer can be found in what he calls "the circumstances of integrity."[88] Recall that, according to Rawls and Hume, the circumstances of *justice* are those general features of human beings and their natural and social environments in which alone justice has a point—conditions in which alone justice is both necessary and possible.[89] There is a rough analogy between the circumstances of justice and the operating conditions of a thermostat. Thermostats regulate temperatures in a building, but they work only within a certain range of temperatures. Beyond that range, they cannot function and are liable to melt or freeze.[90] Where the circumstances of justice are not found, intelligible questions of justice do not arise and demands for justice lose their point. Where they are found, there is reason to press for justice and to hope that it might be achieved. Moreover, these circumstances broadly define the task that justice must perform. In Hume's familiar formulation, the circumstances of justice fall somewhere between a utopia, in which there is no scarcity of resources or conflict of interests regarding the use of the resources, and a dystopia of radical scarcity or radically opposed and irresolvable conflicts of interest.[91]

Likewise, Waldron suggests that the "circumstances of integrity" are conditions that make possible and define the practical task of integrity.[92] These circumstances also fall between utopian and dystopian extremes. In a community where officials and citizens hold basically the same views regarding justice, and their institutions largely conform to these views, integrity has no place. This is the utopian extreme relative to the circumstances of justice. The dystopian extreme can take one of three forms: (1) there may be no community among a scattered and divided group of people or at least not enough unity to warrant a search for a common framework of justice; or (2) there may be some hope for such community, but the rules, decisions, and standards of the community are not merely "untidy," but hopelessly and irremediably chaotic; or (3) while they may not be chaotic—indeed, they may be rationally ordered to a high degree and terrifyingly efficient—they are deeply and irremediably corrupt and unjust, not in merely this or that case but pervasively.

From this artlessly presented list a writer with Hume's literary skills could fashion a tale of social life in which integrity would no longer have a rational or moral point. It is not that in such conditions life would be devoid of integrity and be the worse for it, but rather that in such conditions there would no longer be reason to seek integrity. The moral of such a tale would suggest the essential circumstances of integrity—those conditions of human beings and their social and natural environments in which there would be a point to the pursuit of integrity. Among those conditions we would find the following. First, the people bound to integrity's quest live together in some sort of community with some degree of unity. Second, in this community members correctly regard it as appropriate to expect, indeed to demand, justice of their institutions and arrangements. Third, there is disagreement (possibly deep disagreement) in the community over what justice requires of citizens and their institutions. Thus, from the perspective of at least some citizens, existing institutions fail to meet standards of justice. Not only are standards of justice contested, but so are important institutions and

---

[88] See Jeremy Waldron, "The Circumstances of Integrity," *Legal Theory*, vol. 3, 1997, pp. 1–22.

[89] See David Hume, *Enquiries Concerning Human Understanding and Concerning the Principles of Morals*, ed. P. H. Nidditch (Oxford: Oxford University Press, 3rd edn. [1752]1975), pp. 183–92; John Rawls, *A Theory of Justice* (Cambridge, MA: Harvard University Press, 1971), pp. 126–30.

[90] This analogy is used by Robert Nozick for a different purpose. See Robert Nozick, *The Nature of Rationality* (Princeton, NJ: Princeton University Press, 1993), p. 35.

[91] See Hume, *Enquiries*, pp. 183–92.

[92] See Waldron, "The Circumstances of Integrity," pp. 5–9.

arrangements in the community, and the resulting contest is formulated in terms of contested principles of justice. Fourth, for most citizens, however, the injustice is not so extreme that they find no moral reason for seeking to preserve the community or for working for justice in it. Finally, while the multiplicity and diversity of convictions of justice have their disparate effects on the community's institutions, these institutions are not regarded by members as irremediably chaotic.

This is the soil into which integrity sends its roots. The tale, had we told it, would show that integrity is not only historical, but also essentially political. Integrity has an intelligible role and moral force where justice is both feasible and in dispute. When justice is no longer worth seeking, or is unfeasible, or when the claims of justice are clear to all members of the community, then integrity no longer has a mission. Integrity is a virtue in the real, untidy world of politics, but we should not confuse this world with the world of Realpolitik, for integrity disciplines politics with a conscience. It charges citizens to forge and act on a coherent, common vision of justice. They must practice politics with an eye fixed on the ideal of justice. As Waldron observes, "[Integrity] is a value whose job it is to come into play when the place properly assigned to justice in the life of a community—the role of determining a proper distribution of rights and duties, burdens and benefits, etc.—turns out to have been filled by disparate and competing conceptions of justice itself."[93]

Integrity makes sense only among people who want justice, but disagree about what justice requires. In this sense, integrity depends on and serves justice. But in this real world of politics it serves justice by displacing it. When people committed to justice in their community recognize that there is a sincere, reasonable, and principled disagreement about what justice requires, the pursuit of justice changes direction.[94] In the circumstances of integrity, justice is pursued obliquely: integrity replaces justice as the primary target. It requires members of a community to ask themselves: because as a community we aspire to justice, to what justice-approximating principles are we committed in virtue of our past collective decisions? Integrity is justice in political workclothes, with its sleeves rolled up.

### Justice and integrity in conflict

Despite this close relationship between justice and integrity, we can still explain the appearance of conflict between them. First, justice can appear to defeat, even extinguish, integrity's moral force in cases in which a community's practice falls below a threshold level of justice, such that there is no moral reason to seek integrity. In less extreme situations, even in normal, untidy politics, justice can appear to conflict with integrity when we think of justice abstracted from the real world of politics, and ignore the public dimension of justice.[95] In such circumstances, integrity may require one outcome and (idealized) justice another. Alexander and Kress object that integrity demands that we "abandon our moral principles,"[96] which of course is a price we may not pay. But their objection rests on a misunderstanding about what *justice itself* requires, for, in the circumstances of integrity, justice itself demands that we seek some common understanding of the requirements of justice. In those circumstances, Waldron rightly observes that, "at the level of discretion, the game is not one 'in which each tries to plant the flag of his convictions over as large a domain of power or rules as possible.'

---

[93] Ibid., p. 12.

[94] "[I]ntegrity—like fairness—is a political value that approaches issues of justice from an oblique angle—an angle defined functionally by the need to deal with the fact that various decisions to which our community has already committed itself have been made on the basis of disparate and conflicting conceptions of justice" (ibid.).

[95] I explain and defend the public dimension of justice in the following section.

[96] Alexander and Kress, "Against Legal Principles," p. 784 [and *post* 821].

Exercises of social power must claim legitimacy in relation to the community as a whole."[97] To pursue justice in the circumstances of integrity without regard to the rest of one's community is in effect to *abandon* justice, or at least to fail in a fundamental way to understand the nature of that pursuit. Far from recommending a form of "moral alienation," as Alexander and Kress fear,[98] integrity gives proper direction and discipline to the pursuit of justice.

My aim in this section has been to explore the relationship between justice and integrity. The key claim is that integrity comes into play as a significant moral value, as a moral imperative, when there is a point to seeking justice but there is serious disagreement about what justice requires—when there is reason to forge or at least work to approximate a common conception of justice and to work for institutions and arrangements in our community that conform to it. What reason might there be to forge such a common conception? One might maintain that it is required by a principle of treating each other as equals or according each other equal respect, or perhaps the reason is simply that we desire such a community. However, the more fundamental reason to pursue a common conception of justice is that it is required by structural features of justice itself. Or so, at least, I shall now argue.

### III The Public Character of Justice

My proposal for understanding integrity depends on the assumption that integrity is deeply linked to justice and that justice is essentially political in the sense that justice can only be achieved *in common*. Justice, I maintain, is not only a public good, but it is also a common product, a product of common deliberation and common action. And, I maintain, this is true not just contingently, in view of those features of the world that pursuers of justice must accommodate, but in virtue of the very structure and point of justice itself. If my case for the moral force of integrity is to succeed I must defend this assertion. I undertake to do so in this section.

#### The concept of justice in view

Before I begin, let me say that I do not claim that the thesis of the public and political character of justice holds for every use of the term justice. Over the centuries the term has permitted a wide variety of uses without loss of intelligibility. A systematic Aristotelian study of these uses might seek to identify a central or focal use and relate other legitimate uses to it as extensions in many directions from this common starting point. That, however, is not my task. Recognizing that there may be some uses of the generic notion that may not comport fully with my thesis[99] does not dissuade me from advancing the thesis for the exceedingly common and arguably most important use in our discussion of integrity and law. The justice I have in mind is the same justice we hope for and demand from law. It is the target we set for our law and the rule by which we measure it. To call it "legal justice," however, would narrow the notion too far, for the notion of justice I have in mind is not justice as defined by law, but justice that stands as the judge and measure of law.

---

[97] Waldron, "The Circumstances of Integrity," op. cit., p. 19 (quoting Dworkin, *Law's Empire*, op. cit., p. 211).

[98] See Alexander and Kress, "Against Legal Principles," pp. 784–5 [and *post* 821].

[99] For example, divine or cosmic justice, or justice between individuals in a "state of nature."

By this notion, justice is right order of, and a framework of public justification in, historical communities of rational, moral persons.[1] We can isolate three essential and closely interrelated components or dimensions of justice so understood. I shall assume as common ground the claim that justice defines right order for rational moral persons. Expressed abstractly, this idea is uncontested. More controversial is the claim that justice necessarily assumes some kind of relationship or community among rational, moral persons, and that it essentially defines a framework for public justification in such a community. These are the lemmas I need to establish if I am to offer a convincing argument for the claim that justice is essentially political.

### Justice in and of communities

Consider our common starting point: justice is right order of rational, moral persons. The first thing to note is that justice is not only right or rational order *of* rational, moral persons, but right order *for* them. That is, justice is a normative order, providing agents with prescriptive guides which recognize in their content and practical force that the agents are rational, moral persons. Moral persons are rational: they can order their desires and understand their natural environment enough to determine how best to fulfill those desires; they also have the self-control and deliberative capacities necessary to act effectively on this understanding. Moral persons are also social: they are dependent on each other for both material and moral survival. They must work together to satisfy their physical needs, and they depend on each other for the development and maintenance of a sense of self, of purpose, and of direction. In *The Republic*, Plato extends this notion of justice beyond the snapping point when he argues that justice is primarily a matter of relations among parts of the soul.[2] His insight is deep and important; however, his mistake was to apply this insight to the wrong entity. The insight is that justice is not merely an order imposed from the outside on otherwise unrelated parts, but is rather the proper order for things *of a kind*, thereby *constituting* the related parts as well as the whole. That is to say, justice is *constitutive* (or more modestly, partially constitutive) of rational, moral persons. By defining their relations to each other and thereby constituting the community of which they are members, justice is fundamental to the nature of rational, moral persons. Justice is right order of a certain kind of thing: of a community of rational, moral persons. It defines proper relations among members *regarded as members*.

We can put the same point in Humean terms. Justice arises as a problem and a project for rational creatures only insofar as they are materially and morally interdependent, that is, only insofar as they are related in certain ways and have the biological and psychological characteristics that make those relations necessary for survival. To speak of justice between creatures commits one to the view that they are already related, or at least potentially related, such that certain kinds of practical problems of social interaction arise and must be dealt with collectively. Justice presupposes a common stock of goods or bads that are the products of their life together which must be allocated individually. It also defines a structure of duties, rights, and responsibilities that governs interactions of individual members of the community. These essential features of justice are neatly summarized in Hume's image of a vault.[3] Benevolence, like a wall, can be built out of individual acts, no one of which is essential to the structure as a whole;

---

[1] By "right order" I mean a rationally defensible and morally imperative structure or arrangement, a moral blueprint, regarded not only in the abstract but also as realized in some community.

[2] Plato, *The Republic*, Book IV.

[3] See Hume, *Enquiries*, p. 305 (explaining that human well-being, raised by the social virtue of justice, may be compared to the building of a vault).

however, justice, like a vault, carefully defines the relationships among all the individual parts. On the strength of these relationships, the edifice stands secure. That kind of structure is not for every kind of social interaction or social setting among human beings, but in historical communities among rational, moral persons the vault must be constructed. Only when there is reason to rightly order a *community* of moral persons does the blueprint of justice become morally relevant.

Unfortunately, it has been easy for philosophers to ignore the fact that justice is by its nature always located in, and is a kind of ordering of, human communities. This is especially tempting for those who think that basic to all forms of injustice are inequalities that are arbitrary from a moral point of view—lacking positive moral justification.[4] This leads them to infer from differences between parties for which no moral justification can be found that the relatively disadvantaged party is the victim of injustice. This, they think, is true not only in historical communities where the differences are structured into patterns of treatment that affect access to common resources, benefits, or protections, and mark inequalities in the status of members of the community, but also between parties entirely unrelated, belonging to distant and unrelated societies—for example, people on physically and historically widely separated islands between which there is no communication. Mere differences in ability to meet basic needs or develop important human capacities (so-called "natural inequalities") are thought to be unjust inequalities, which ought to be corrected in the name of justice, if correction is possible. The relative advantages and disadvantaged are said to be unjust simply because they are morally arbitrary.

Sometimes arguments of this kind are advanced in defense of an egalitarian conception of justice. But we do not have to abandon egalitarianism to see the mistakes in this kind of argument. The argument rests on two confusions. The first is a confusion of justice with other grounds or kinds of moral consideration, such as humanitarian concern or benevolence. Justice is essentially comparative: it calls for a balancing of benefits or burdens—a proper and in some sense equal distribution of advantages and disadvantages. It also lays a special obligation on those who are better off to bear the burden of rectification. In contrast, benevolence or humanitarian concern are focused on human well-being and not on balancing or equalizing resources. To the extent that human beings have legitimate, serious needs and it is possible to meet them, we have reason, in the name of humanity, to undertake to meet them if it is possible. No special obligation lies on those who are better off in this respect, except for the fact that those who are better off may be able to sustain the loss better than others. In particular, no special claim to equalize the advantages and disadvantages, in the spirit of justice, lies against the advantaged parties. We can explain the intuitive moral pressure we feel when we learn of the needs of distant and unrelated people in moral terms other than justice.

The alleged injustice of "natural inequalities" also rests on a more fundamental confusion. It confuses *differences* with *inequalities*. This is a mistake even when the differences carry with them disadvantages for which there is no apparent moral justification. Differences are inequalities only when there is some relationship between the parties such that the difference is properly regarded as at least *prima facie* illegitimate, and so in need of legitimation. It is not enough to claim that there is no moral justification for the difference; the difference must be

---

[4]  An argument of this kind can be found in Brian Barry, *Theories of Justice* 1989, pp. 238–9. The idea that injustice can be best understood as an inequality between persons for which there is no moral justification is at the core of Rawls's "intuitive argument" for his principles of justice. See Rawls, *A Theory of Justice*, pp. 72–5. There is a helpful discussion of this argument in Will Kymlicka, *Contemporary Political Philosophy* 1990 pp. 55–8.

morally unjustified. A difference is *morally unjustified* only if moral justification is called for and found lacking, but not all differences call for justification. The "morally arbitrary" differences that strike us as unjustified are those that, in virtue of features of persons and their relationships, have a distinctive moral character. They are differences that make a *moral* difference when they should not. Mere differences can be identified in nonevaluative terms, but *inequalities* presuppose an evaluative standard and a context in which comparing the advantages and disadvantages of the parties against that standard is appropriate. These conditions are met just when there is a moral relationship between parties that calls for such comparative judgments. Such judgments are called for only when the parties can plausibly be regarded as members of the same community and the disadvantages of one party are relevantly compared to the advantages of the other in relation to some common stock against which both can legitimately make claims. In other words, justice insofar as it demands a kind of equality presupposes a moral relationship of mutual interdependence, that is, a community. For it is *as members* of such a community that each can make claims against the others by making claims against a common stock that is the product of their life together.

## Public justification

Justice, then, is right order of communities of rational, moral persons. It is also a framework of principles for public justification of their common institutions and social arrangements and for actions within these institutions and arrangements. For rational, moral persons who are members of the same community it is important not only that they *be* in the right kind of relationships, but also that they can *recognize* the relationships as right. This is because moral persons are concerned not only with the benefits of just arrangements, but with what those arrangements say publicly about the moral status of each member. Justice is not only normative, it is also expressive. It nourishes those who hunger for recognition as persons alongside other persons,[5] comembers of a common enterprise. Justice speaks to a critical need of moral persons, a need that exists alongside, and sometimes even outstrips in importance, the needs addressed by the specific goods that justice distributes.

Justice is not merely a result, an ordering that obtains in or among social elements; it is also a structure of principles that can be understood and applied to behavior. Even more than this, justice provides a lens through which all members sees themselves and the relations that bind them to comembers. It is no accident that this expressive and reflective device is a set of normative principles, for it is fundamentally as rational, moral persons, who can govern their actions and interactions by principles they publicly endorse, that they acknowledge each other. Their recognition of each other as rational moral persons takes the form of endorsement of a set of principles by which they justify their individual actions and common institutions. Thus this justification must be public—a matter of offering reasons *to each other*. Those who speak the language of justice are thereby committed to justifying the claims they make in the name of justice to comembers insofar as they are reasonable and willing to do the same. The mandate of justice is not only to set social arrangements in right order, but to make the rightness of that order manifest to every member of society.

Justice is also public in another way: to speak the language of justice is necessarily to speak to the community, or to individual members of it, in the name of the community. It is to speak of responsibilities and obligations, claims and commitments, of the community as a whole, and of individuals in their capacity

---

[5] For the centrality of mutual recognition to the moral enterprise, see Postema, "An Archaeology," pp. 76–85.

as members. Thus one speaks not for one's own part only, expressing a private preference for the ordering of relationships or the distribution of goods, but rather for the whole community, from a point of view common to members and available to them insofar as they regard themselves as members.

## Justice in progress

Thus far we have viewed justice statically, as if it were already in place, fully mature, in a more or less ideal "well-ordered society." However, as much as that perspective dominates our reflections about justice, it is not the practical reality we face as we move into the political arena, where we are as likely to struggle over what justice requires as over the best way to meet its demands. Thus we must also look at justice in its dynamic dimension, in the process of formation. I have argued that justice is public in the sense that it is a public good in the familiar economist's sense of that term, and so is enjoyed publicly, and in the sense that it provides a scheme of public justification, and so is deliberated about publicly. From these two premises we can draw the conclusion that justice is by its very nature *political*, and in that further sense public.[6] By this I mean that it is essential to justice that it be achieved only through the group efforts of members of political society working out its basic terms.

This is most evident from the fact that justice is a public good, for as such it can be achieved only through coordinated, collective action. In the world in which we live, we can secure the public good of justice only if we work in concert with others; we do so not only for the community, but also inevitably with the community. This simply follows from the fact that justice is a public good. Nothing in this, however, precludes the *imposition* of just order on a community, save the contingent fact that none of us is able to impose such order.

However, the fact that justice provides a framework for public justification, and so requires not merely right order but manifest right order, rules out the imposition of just social order even if it were empirically possible. It makes justice inseparable from politics, the product of common effort. This claim is not immediately evident, I admit. Were not the great legendary Lawgivers—individuals such as Solon, Lycurgus, Jehovah on Sinai—allegedly fashioners of just order? One might argue that Hobbes's proposal to let the Sovereign define for us the just and the unjust is not inconceivable, it is just politically unfeasible and morally risky. However, my claim is that the realities corresponding to these myths are conceivable only by ignoring that the rightness of the order must be manifest, or by implicitly assuming that justice is not reasonably in dispute, or is silent in the face of reasonable disputes. But each of these conditions is mistaken.

The myth of the Great Lawgiver imagines the apolitical creation of a just regime, but this is conceivable only if we focus exclusively on justice as right order. However, justice is *manifest* right order, a scheme of public principles by which members of the community can justify their actions and institutions to each other. Moreover, in the nonideal conditions of ordinary political life, that is, in the circumstances of integrity, what justice requires is itself reasonably in dispute. To ignore these conditions is to restrict justice to ideal conditions. But justice speaks even in the nonideal conditions of ordinary political life. Justice requires that its fundamental concerns be respected in the processes by which justice is deliberated even when the details of its substantive principles are reasonably in dispute. Justice addresses not only "well-ordered societies," but also societies in the circumstances of integrity, where justice is still in the process of formation.

---

[6] Burke seemed to have this sense of the term "political" in mind when he said, "Political arrangements, as it is a work for social ends, is only to be wrought by social means, there mind must conspire with mind." See Edmund Burke, *Reflections on the Revolution in France*, [1790]1969), p. 281.

Thus, in the circumstances of integrity, justice cannot be imposed. It is not enough that right order be established, it is equally important, from the point of view of justice itself, that right order be established through ordinary politics— through reasonable members of political society working together to forge a conception all can recognize as reasonable. As I noted earlier, if, in the circumstances of integrity, justice must be manifest to all reasonable persons, then we cannot regard the pursuit of justice as a game "in which each person tries to plant the flag of his convictions over as large a domain of power or rules as possible."[7] When one encounters reasonable challenges to one's principles of justice, one' is forced to shift deliberative as well as practical focus, to identify a basis from which to achieve something approaching agreement about the principles of justice in question. The struggle for justice takes a more oblique form. The door is opened for integrity.

### Integrity and the two faces of justice

This argument suggests that justice always has two sides or faces, one ideal and the other consensual. Between them there is always a tension. The key to understanding justice in its dynamic dimension is to keep this tension fully in mind. In "the circumstances of integrity," where there is a point to seeking justice but wide disagreement about what justice requires, integrity stands between "ideal justice" (justice *sans* politics) and mere convention or consensus (political agreement *sans* justice). Integrity keeps the essential tension clearly in focus. It tethers visions of justice to the historical circumstances of particular political societies, and equips politics in those societies for a common struggle for justice.

However, precisely because this tension is always manifest, those who seek justice may never be fully satisfied where the circumstances of integrity obtain. They seek an ideal that can be achieved only based on common agreement around principles of right social order. Yet the principles for which they fight are likely to appear either too ideal, and so unlikely to attract the requisite consensus, or too ad hoc or conventional, and so too accommodating to political demands of the moment. This explains, perhaps, why we are inclined to insist that integrity and justice can conflict, even as we admit, with some discomfort, that integrity must be preferred. The sense of conflict comes from our looking to justice sans politics, while our admission that integrity must, for the moment, be preferred gives due credit to the political side of justice.

Integrity, I have argued, simply is justice properly situated in politics, keeping the essential tension between the ideal and consensual dimensions of justice clearly in sight. The moral force of integrity lies, at least in part, in the need to approximate justice in the political circumstances in which we find ourselves. If we accept that justice issues genuine moral demands, then we must also accept that integrity does so as well, otherwise justice must remain silent in communities that fall short of well-ordered societies. Moreover, integrity is capable of issuing genuine moral demands, not because it is parasitic on justice as the notions of consistency or formal justice are said to be, but in the more complex way in which integrity focuses the pursuit of justice in the circumstances of integrity. We are bound to the complex discipline of integrity whenever we have reason to seek justice in the circumstances of integrity.

### IV Fidelity

We are now in a position to consider the link between integrity and fidelity. My thesis is that fidelity takes the shape of integrity in a community bound to pursue justice in the circumstances of integrity. Integrity focuses the pursuit of justice in a

---

[7] Dworkin, *Law's Empire*, p. 211.

specifically historical way, that is, through constructing principled accounts of the community's past decisions and actions. Integrity assumes that a community's past practice is normative for the community and its members. This assumption must be shown to be reasonable if we are to connect integrity as described and defended here to law, for it is the essentially historical character of law that integrity is said to justify.

One reason why it is reasonable to seek approximations of justice in the past political decisions of a community may be that, in the circumstances of integrity, we are more likely to achieve a degree of (at least temporary) principled agreement in this indirect way, than through some more direct approach. The focus of public debate regarding justice is more concrete and limited and so more likely to attract agreement. The past decisions, we might say, represent a form of moral capital in political society,[8] the appropriate exploitation of which over time can yield increasingly satisfying agreements of the right kind.

There may be some force in this argument—I do not dismiss it out of hand— but it appears too weak to bear the full weight of the case for the historical character of integrity. This case, I believe, rests more securely on the link between integrity and the political value of fidelity. Thus I will argue that fidelity takes the shape of integrity in a community bound to pursue justice in the circumstances of integrity.

### The notion of fidelity

Fidelity is a matter of keeping faith with a common past. Hume, a political conservative but still a child of the Enlightenment, maintained that, while "every thing be produc'd *in time*, there is nothing real, that is produc'd *by time*."[9] Against this Humean sentiment Dworkin asserts, in defense of the alleged "gravitational force" of legal precedent, that "the very fact of [the] decision, as a piece of political history, provides some reason for deciding other cases in a similar way in the future."[10] Anthony Kronman even more pointedly maintains that we are bound by past decisions "in the sense of being obligated to respect [the past] for its own sake ... just because it is the past we happen to have."[11] With this especially bold and unqualified assertion, Kronman seeks to highlight the intrinsic moral value of fidelity to the past against the overwhelmingly dominant modern view that the past at best has instrumental value. However, Kronman's thesis is implausible and fails to grasp the nature of the value of fidelity.

Kronman is right to resist the appeal of reducing the value of the past to its merely instrumental value for the future. He goes wrong when he suggests that this value is absolute, or theoretically primitive, or in some way *sui generis*. There is a clear sense in which fidelity has intrinsic value, but the value it accords to the past is not accorded to the past just considered in itself—"merely because it is the past," as Kronman puts it.[12] The moral and practical force of fidelity can be understood only insofar as it is related to other values we hold dear. Fidelity is not an instrumental value, if by this we mean that its value is a function of the value of the consequences it causally brings about, but it has its value only *in service* of other values. Fidelity is the mode in which we express our commitment to certain other values. Its value, then, is intrinsic, but not self-sufficient.

It is easy to misunderstand fidelity's evaluative valence because it is common

---

[8]  Govert Den Hartogh, Professor of Philosophy, University of Amsterdam, suggested this thought to me, although I do not think he is inclined to endorse the argument as a whole.

[9]  David Hume, *A Treatise of Human Nature*, ed. P. H. Nidditch [1739]1979), p. 509 (emphasis added).

[10]  Dworkin, *Taking Rights Seriously*, p. 113.

[11]  Anthony T. Kronman, "Precedent and Tradition," *Yale Law Journal*, vol. 99, 1990, pp. 1036–7.

[12]  Ibid., p. 1039.

for us to speak of fidelity to law, or to principle, or to the past. However, the moral value of fidelity is fundamentally an interpersonal (and possibly intra-personal) value. It arises from relationships of a certain sort and is directed towards parties to those relationships. Duties of fidelity are owed to people, not to theories, principles, rules, or events. Fidelity is a matter of keeping faith with our common past as the appropriate mode of keeping faith with each other as comembers of the community to which we are committed.[13] By "keeping faith with each other" I mean interacting on terms and in ways appropriate to the moral nature of the relationship among us. This is the thesis I shall here defend, but a further clarification is required before I do so.

Fidelity is a complex value; it recognizes that the past can be normative for us in a complex way. Fidelity calls for respect for the decisions and actions of the past, but this respect is tempered by what I earlier called regret. Fidelity demands a *critical* respect for the past. This is not a normative demand imposed from the outside; it is implied by the fact that fidelity serves other values, in particular, the fact that fidelity identifies the appropriate mode of keeping faith with others. If fidelity required only a straightforward and simple imitation of the past, it would confuse its usual mode with its more fundamental end: it would confuse mere conformity with the past, and fidelity to rules or events, with keeping faith with each other as comembers of a community to which we are committed. With this in mind we are in a position to consider an argument for fidelity so understood.

*Temporally extended values*

My argument begins with the notion of temporally extended values, which I borrow from Thomas Hill, Jr. "Some of our values," Hill observes, "are cross-time wholes, with past, present, and future parts united in certain ways ... [They are] 'organic unities'—i.e., wholes the value of which is not necessarily the sum of the values of the parts."[14] For goods of this kind, he continues, "[t]he value of any moment often depends on what came before and what we anticipate to follow. ... The past is seen as more than a time of accumulated debts and assets, and the future is valued as more than an opportunity for reinvesting and cashing in assets."[15] To illustrate his point, Hill considers how one might view the situation in which one negligently wronged another person. One might see that past action not simply as generating a duty to compensate the victim, but in a quite different way that links past, present, and future together as internally related components of a valued relationship.

> One may say, for example, that the *whole* consisting of your life and your relationship with [the victim] will be a better thing if you acknowledge the wrong and make efforts to restore what you have damaged. ... [T]he requirement [to compensate] is just what is required to bring about a valuable connected whole with past, present, and future parts—the best way to complete a chapter, so to speak, in two intersecting life-stories.[16]

While some values are temporally extended, other values are indifferent to time, or at least for them time is not fundamental. Pleasure, liberty, autonomy, and life itself do not seem to be temporally extended values. For example, autonomy is genetically temporal: it comes into being over time. It may even be epistemically temporal: it manifests its existence to others over time. Yet it does not appear to

---

[13] This is the thesis I set out in "On the Moral Presence of the Past," *McGill Law Journal*, vol. 36, 1991, p. 1170. My argument below revises in several respects the defence of the thesis found in that essay. I will not identify the changes here.

[14] T. Hill, Jr., *Autonomy and Self-Respect*, 1991, pp. 202–03.

[15] Ibid., p. 202.

[16] Ibid., p. 204.

be evaluatively temporal: its value does not seem tied up with its mode of coming to be or its manifestation to others.

In contrast, some goods are evaluatively temporal; the values they embody are temporally extended. The clearest examples of temporally extended values are found in human relationships, but they are familiar in intrapersonal contexts as well. Respect for oneself; or personal integrity, is one such value. Consider the following example.[17] Throughout her life, Jean's mother was always generous to people who had fallen on hard times. She provided food and clothing to them and sometimes even let them stay in her house until they could get back on their feet. After her mother's death, Jean resolved to actively support local efforts to find shelter for the homeless, in honor of her mother. On the anniversary of her mother's death, Jean realized with shame that her resolve had weakened to the point that it had completely slipped her mind over the past six months. Not only had the needs of some homeless people not been met, but also she had failed. Her resolve had turned omission into failure. During the year, she had reason to write out a check to the homeless shelter and to volunteer from time to time, not only because the needs of the homeless were great, but also because this need had a special significance to her life in virtue of her resolve and its meaning to her. The resolve had given a certain determinate shape to her life, and to her relationship with her mother; it gave her reasons rooted in the meaningfulness of living out that life over time. Personal integrity, as well as the shape of her relationship to her mother, imposed a demand on her which was continuous over time, because the self (and this relationship) had integrity only in and over time.

Temporally extended values are found even more clearly in interpersonal relationships. Hill offers a compelling illustration.[18] John and Mary are friends; they mutually value their friendship and the trust and respect for each other that are at its core. Recently, Mary has been the victim of insulting and abusive behavior by other people, and John worries that he also has said things that unintentionally may have insulted her. But Mary has not let on that she has been hurt, and he fears that he may make matters worse by creating what he regards as groundless suspicions. In view of the value of their friendship to both of them, he asks himself what response would best affirm the relationship he has and wishes to continue with her. Hill continues:

> Given their history together, it is important to him to do his part towards restoring the relationship if it indeed has been marred by perceived insults or suspicions. To be sure, he wants *future* relations of mutual trust and respect, but not at any price and not by just any means. Their history together is not irrelevant, for what he values is not merely a future of a certain kind but that their relationship over time be of the sort he values.[19]

Hill's example clearly shows that the value of friendship is temporally extended. Friendship connects people to each other over time, giving their interactions special moral significance to them. Loyalty gives expression to this moral significance. Fidelity to the past that friends share with each other is one very important way in which they recognize and manifest their regard for each other as friends. It is, of course, the mutual value of the friendship that gives friends reasons to keep faith with each other; it is in this soil that fidelity takes root. In the absence of this relationship, the same people would not have this reason to keep faith with each other. In this respect, as we have seen, fidelity is in the service of other values and to that extent presupposes them.

It is also worth noting another feature of this example of friendship. There are

---

[17] I have used this example in "On the Moral Presence of the Past," p. 1174. It is based on an example of Joseph Raz, *The Morality of Freedom*, pp. 385–6.
[18] See Hill, *Autonomy and Self-Respect*, pp. 204–5.
[19] Ibid., p. 205.

complex links between past actions, interactions, and events involving friends, on the one hand, and the friendship and its value to them, on the other. The value of friendship is temporally extended, as we have seen, and so it depends on the way the friends integrate their past, present, and future. Friends are committed to each other, but it would often be a mistake to regard the moral value of the friendship as the product of their commitment, on the model, say, of a promise or contract. The commitment is an expression of their recognition of the value of the relationship. Moreover, the relationship and its moral significance for the friends may have emerged over time through their interactions and shared experiences which, as Aristotle reminded us, enrich and are enriched by their common perception and common discourse.[20]

*Justice as a temporally extended value*

In our personal lives and in interpersonal relationships like friendship, the past makes its presence felt practically and morally in virtue of the fact that its significance for us lies in its relationship to a whole whose value is extended over time. The past is not merely the source of causal traces that we must now take into account in our practical or moral reasoning; rather, the past has evaluative or normative significance for present deliberation and action (as does the future), because the values that demand attention in our deliberation are temporally extended values that embrace and integrate the past, the present, and the future. From the perspective of temporally extended values, time's arrow points in more than one direction. More precisely put, the evaluative relationships among the parts of temporally extended value-wholes[21] are multidimensional, characterized by mutuality rather than unilateral determination. This is evident in the examples considered thus far, but it is also clear when we consider the value of a community that makes justice a fundamental aim. Here, again, fidelity finds a home, for fidelity in a vital, complex way links past, present, and future in communities aspiring to justice.

Justice is right order of historical human communities. It is temporally extended value because it gives public, moral shape to the temporally extended value of community for us. Let us consider first the value of community and then observe the way justice gives shape to this value.

The historical character of living communities, as opposed to abstractly conceived ones, is obvious and does not need to be demonstrated. However, to say that a community is historical is to say more than merely that it has a history— that it endures over a period of time and that events in it could be recorded should anyone find it interesting to do so. For in that limited sense, "flies of a summer" and the herd grazing in the field have a history.[22] The historical character of human communities is fundamentally different. It is a function of self-conscious common memory framed and informed by a sense of significance that gives the historical events a distinctively human value. This sense of significance is borne of decisions, aims, commitments, and practices that establish and nourish human relationships and give a meaningful structure to individual human lives.

Moreover, the value of community, and the values available to us in communities, are essentially historical values. In Burke's evocative image, society is a partnership extended over time "between those who are living, those who are

---

[20] See Aristotle, *Nicomachean Ethics*, Book 1, 1170b, 11. 11–2.
[21] Recall that Hill suggested that we conceive of temporally extended values as organic unities. See text accompanying note 64 above.
[22] "Flies of a summer" is, of course, Burke's famous phrase. See Burke, *Reflections on the Revolution in France*, op. cit., p. 193. Aristotle drew the contrast between cows sharing a pasture and human interactions that have an essential historical and common significance. See Aristotle, *Nicomachean Ethics*, p. 177 (Book 1, 1170b, 11. 11–4).

dead, and those who are to be born."[23] Like partners in an ongoing contractual relationship, generations are bound together in relations of mutual dependency.[24] One generation is dependent on preceding generations for the material, moral, and cultural resources that make possible human and autonomous lives. Without those resources not only would opportunities for a wide variety of meaningful pursuits be closed to us, but also we would not generally have the ability to judge our own goals as worthy of pursuit. At the same time, the previous generation is dependent on its successors for the achievement and preservation of the goals and projects that give their lives significance precisely by the fact that they transcend the limits of their biological existence. This dependency has many dimensions. Not only must the projects of the past be embraced by the present, or their accomplishments preserved, but they must be understood, interpreted, and given practical shape so that, in the new circumstances of the present, the projects of the past can be pursued intelligently. Past practice bears the stamp of our common life, but at the same time it forces us to address together the question of what this shape is and shall be. Our attempt to give it shape for the present and future depends on how we expect it to be received and followed in the future. Each generation bears this relationship of mutual dependency both to its predecessors and its successors. Each generation must look both to the past and to the future for the evaluative shape of its present actions. In this, Kronman observes, there is mutual vulnerability: we cannot force our ancestors to provide us with the material, moral, and cultural resources we need for a full and rich life; likewise, our ancestors cannot force us to embrace their projects (or their understanding of them), and we are in no better position with regard to the generations to come.[25]

Thus the values available to us and only realized in historical communities, including the value of community itself, are temporally extended values. These values are given distinctively moral shape by justice. In relatively large, non-intimate communities, justice is the structure in which partners recognize and respect each other as comembers. In virtue of its public dimension, justice is concerned with the messages we send to each other regarding our respective places in the community. The way we arrange our communal affairs, and distribute the benefits and burdens of common life, expresses our regard for each other as fellow members of the community. Justice gives a special focus to temporally extended value of community. Through it, we give expression to our regard for each other across generations and to our regard for current fellow members. In this way, the value of justice, too, is temporally extended.

Fidelity calls for keeping faith with the past as a way of keeping faith with each other. We can now see why this is important: fidelity gives explicit shape to the historical dimension of justice. We can also see why fidelity requires us to hold a complex attitude with regard to the past—a combination of respect and regret—for fidelity relates past, present, and future in the service of justice, that is, in the service of making the community over time an expression of justice. To accomplish this a certain way of understanding or interpreting the public and political actions of the community is needed. These actions must be regarded as committed to and directed towards establishing and maintaining justice. At the same time,

[23] Burke, *Reflections on the Revolution in France*, pp. 194–5.
[24] I follow Kronman's discussion here, see Kronman, "Precedent and Tradition," op. cit., pp. 1067–8. However, I describe the relations among generations in terms of mutual *dependency* rather than mutual *indebtedness* as Kronman does, because the latter begs the question of the normative upshot of the mutual dependence. I believe mutual dependency establishes the special historical character of communities; the value of communities to us both as individuals and as members of these communities is, then, temporally extended in a deep sense. In virtue of the temporally extended character of the values available to us in historical communities, fidelity imposes its normative demands on us. That is why we are "indebted."
[25] See ibid., p. 1067.

fidelity requires that the community take full responsibility for its actions and the arrangements it enforces. The arrangements must be recognizable as expressions of just and proper regard for each member as an equal member of the community, or at least as bona fide attempts to give concrete shape to that fundamental attitude. Respect for past practice, then, must always be in the service of the aspiration for justice, and hence never uncritical.

In communities aimed at justice, where not only the reality falls short of the standard, but the standard itself is in dispute, fidelity is integrity. Integrity is the form fidelity takes in the circumstances of integrity, that is, in a community committed to justice but divided over what justice requires. Integrity is the way members of such a community keep faith with each other and with their collective commitment to justice as the fundamental mode of their relationships. In such circumstances, only integrity can give expression to that fundamental common commitment.

## V Integrity and the Law

I have argued that fidelity takes the shape of integrity in a community bound to the pursuit of justice in the circumstances of integrity. It remains, finally, for me to show that law provides a natural medium in which to seek justice in the way integrity prescribes.

Integrity, as explained and defended here, need not be realized only in law. It is conceivable that other practices less formal and less formally institutionalized than law might also be bound by this important value of political morality. Yet these other practices are likely to look very much like less formal analogues of law, for law seems by its nature and its governing regulative idea to be committed to the discipline that integrity imposes on collective practical reasoning. Law is historical by its very nature. As Kronman says,

> ...respect for past decisions is not a characteristic of certain legal systems only. It is rather a feature of law in general, and whenever there exists a set of practices and institutions that we believe are entitled to the name of law, the rule of precedent will be at work, influencing, to one degree or another, the conduct of those responsible for administering the practices and institutions in question.[26]

Law is a framework of practical reasoning that anchors the public justification of decisions and actions to past communal decisions and actions. This is not exclusively true of reasoning from precedent, but it is most clearly and immediately evident there. Reasoning from precedent by analogy is not mere imitation, nor is it a matter of prediction, nor some version of formal consistency. It is an evaluatively informed assessment of the normative significance of the past decision for the instant case, as well as of the significance it might hold for the future. Reasoning from precedent is as much "forward-looking" as "backward-looking." That is to say, the values that govern precedent are temporally embedded in just the way I described integrity to be in the previous section. I need not pursue this argument any further here, as Alexander and Kress made the case well in their discussion of the practice of common-law reasoning.[27]

There is a further, stronger connection between law and integrity. Not only does legal argument tend to take the shape integrity recommends, but it *must* do so because the legitimacy of law in circumstances of integrity depends on its being manifestly governed by the aspiration to justice. The governing regulative idea of law is not merely consistency, order, or even authority. Any of these, without the

---

[26] Ibid., p. 1032.
[27] See Alexander and Kress, "Against Legal Principles," op. cit., pp. 745–52 (discussing legal principles in jurisprudential thought). [And see *post* 821].

manifest project of directing all resources towards justice—towards manifest right order in the community—is not worthy of our allegiance, has no legitimacy, and so at best can only command prudent compliance. Only if law is governed by the demands and discipline of integrity can it claim legitimacy where there is deep and fundamental disagreement about justice. If it is disciplined by integrity, public reasoning that purports to bind (and is likely to affect) all members of the society can be seen to be in the service of law's regulative idea, even when the demands of that regulative idea are in dispute.

Yet, despite all that has been said, it might still seem that law is an implausible focus for the discipline of integrity. In the circumstances of justice, there may be deep disagreements about justice, and we can expect them to be reflected in assessments of the law. Many citizens may judge the past actions of the community as reflected in the practices of law to be seriously, perhaps even pervasively, unjust. Why, then, should they be inclined to treat these practices as defining commitments of the community, as integrity counsels?

This is an important challenge, but it can be met. Recall that integrity has a point only in the circumstances of integrity. These circumstances include not only disagreement about what justice requires, but also the fact that it is reasonable for members to regard their community as aspiring to justice and that social and political arrangements are not irremediably unjust. If these circumstances do not obtain, then, like a thermostat in temperatures beyond its operative range, integrity no longer functions; it no longer makes any moral claim. In such circumstances it would be unreasonable to expect citizens to look to the law as the point of departure for the pursuit of a publicly defensible vision of justice. However, where the circumstances of integrity do obtain, it is reasonable for citizens to regard their community as aspiring to justice. Moreover, it is likely that the law will be the record of this aspiration, for, by virtue of its prominent place in the life of a community, it will be the primary locus of the community's efforts to realize the aspiration to justice. Integrity is valid and binding only in its distinctive circumstances, but where those circumstances obtain it commands the allegiance of all who aspire to justice.

This suggests one further objection to my linking of integrity to law. It might be argued that in circumstances of justice historic disputes regarding justice will inevitably leave their traces in the law. Different conceptions of justice have influenced substantial portions of the law at different times in history. Thus integrity's demand that law be seen as issuing from a coherent vision of justice seems extravagant and dishonest. Is it not better to acknowledge that, due to the history of political struggles, one set of principles underlies one part of the law, a different set underlies another part, and so on? A more honest account of the society's commitments rooted in its law would seem to be a kind of patchwork quilt. Does not coherence, in the unlikely event it could be achieved, simply mask the political reality of law, encouraging an exercise in self-deception rather than integrity?[28]

This complex objection is open to several different interpretations. The first understands the aim of constructing a coherent vision of justice from the community's past actions to be a kind of historical narrative or description. On this view, the requirement of coherence invites distortion of the real political history of law. But this objection merely rests on a misunderstanding of the task of practical deliberation disciplined by integrity. The aim is not to chronicle a community's past from some neutral observer's point of view, but rather to uncover in that past principles governing its actions in the present. In view of these quite different aims, it should not be surprising if the results are different.

---

[28] This argument was suggested to me by Raz's remarks in "The Relevance of Coherence," pp. 280, 298, but I do not claim that the paraphrase in the text exactly captures the main thrust of Raz's argument.

Second, the objector may be making a skeptical argument. On this reading the objection is that integrity's demand of coherence has no ground in moral or practical reason. There simply is no moral reason to act from principles that fit together in a coherent vision of justice, the skeptic might argue. So, if principles underlying one part of the law do not fit intelligibly with those underlying a different part, that is no matter for concern. This is a fundamental challenge to the claims of this essay, but it strikes me as utterly implausible. If we accept that law is fundamentally governed by the aspiration to justice, we cannot accept with equanimity an acknowledged and unresolvable incoherence, for incoherence undermines any attempt to do justice in a community. Of course, principles may fail to fit together intelligibly, not because they clash, but precisely because they *do not* conflict, as the principles of French and Iranian constitutional law, or the principles of mechanics and electronics, may be very different yet not in conflict. But that could be true only if the noncohering principles of law do not meet on the same logical, theoretical, or practical plane. That surely is not the case with the laws of any given political society.

Third, the objection might more plausibly take a distinctively moral form. The critic may point out that in our imperfect world where "the debris of past political struggles"[29] is preserved in the books and practices of law, we are forced to make compromises by a morality mindful of concrete circumstances and the limits of political feasibility. We only make the ideal the enemy of the good and feasible if we reject approximations to morally sound solutions because they reduce the coherence of law.[30] However, this argument does not challenge the notion of integrity that I have tried to defend. First of all, the notion of coherence I rely on is intentionally very weak.[31] Second, integrity, as I understand it, is a complex moral standard calling for a proper and defensible balance of respect and regret regarding past rules and decisions of a polity.[32] Regret, I have argued, accepts *in the name of integrity* certain compromises of coherence—pockets of incoherence in a body of law that nevertheless strives for coherence. As it stands, this objection does not undermine integrity's claim to moral force and relevance in the context of law.

But the moral objection might be pressed again, this time more pointedly. "[I]n countries with decent constitutions, the untidiness of politics is morally sanctioned ... by the morality of authoritative institutions."[33] These institutions are authorized to give direction to human affairs and to control social interaction through their deliberate decisions. Given the vagaries of politics, we have no reason to expect the decisions and actions of these institutions over time to fit neatly into a coherent system of rules and principles.[34] The moral basis for the authority of these institutions, and thus the grounds for accepting their less than coherent results, are typically traced to two different but arguably related sources: the need for coordination of human affairs and social interaction and the place of such institutions in a robust democracy.

A satisfying reply to this objection calls for a general discussion of fundamental issues of normative political (and especially democratic) theory. It is too late in this essay to address these issues fully. In lieu of such a discussion I will merely suggest what I believe the eventual outcome of that discussion will be and leave to another occasion a proper discussion of this important objection and the issues it raises. First, coordination arguments, as important as they are in this context, are

[29] This is Raz's phrase (ibid., p. 280).
[30] Again, an argument along these lines is suggested by Raz (ibid., pp. 296–7), but I am taking the argument out of its complex context and directing it by extension to my integrity thesis. My reply is aimed at the argument above, not Raz's.
[31] See pp. 802–804 in the text above.
[32] See pp. 804–806 in the text above.
[33] Raz, "The Relevance of Coherence," pp. 298–9.
[34] See ibid., pp. 284–5.

never sufficient grounds for legislative and adjudicative institutions. Taken alone, they give too much weight to considerations of social order and not enough to other important moral concerns like justice. Because we are likely to be talking about political societies in the circumstances of integrity, we must ground the legitimacy of authoritative institutions in an argument that includes both integrity and coordination. Similarly, a plausible theory of democracy will have to include integrity as a key commitment of democratic adjudicative institutions. Thus I agree that authoritative institutions can be morally justified and that this may involve morally sanctioning "untidy politics," at least up to a point. But this is not because integrity is supplanted, but because the moral case for the legitimacy of those institutions depends in part on their ability to meet the demands of integrity on the law.

Theorists who reject integrity as the governing idea of law's distinctive form of public practical reasoning—whether they be natural lawyers, positivists, or latter-day pragmatists—either reject justice as law's fundamental governing ideal, or they misunderstand what justice by its nature demands. Appeals to justice that are not given recognizable public content supplied by the law itself must either give us an account of the public resources they draw upon or stand convicted of mis-understanding the nature of their appeal, and thus failing in their appeal. For justice, as we have seen, is necessarily public. To make decisions of law in the name of justice is to make them in the name of the community as a whole. It is never sufficient for those empowered to make such decisions to do so on the basis of what they, for their own part only, regard as morally best. Authority has its important place in this approach, but always governed by and in the service of justice. Where justice is pursued in the circumstances of integrity, justice will require that officials vested with such authority be governed by the discipline of integrity. Authority freed from integrity's discipline is free to ignore politics, and the very circumstances that demand that we pursue justice indirectly, in the name of justice itself. Theories that refuse to recognize the demands and discipline of integrity deprive official decisions and actions of legitimacy at precisely the point at which it is needed most.                                                      [pp 293–315]

## SCOTT HERSHOVITZ
### Integrity and Stare Decisis
### (2006)[35]

Many think that stare decisis binds even the highest court in a jurisdiction to follow precedents that were decided incorrectly. Indeed, the view is commonly held by legal scholars[36] and judges[37] alike. But if that is what stare decisis really requires, it is puzzling. What could justify a principle that requires courts to make the same mistakes over and over again? Surely a better principle (one that most of us endorse) is that people should own up to their mistakes and seek *not* to repeat them. Could legal reasoning really be so different from everyday reasoning that principle requires courts to make mistakes repeatedly rather than correct them?

---

[35] [From (ed) Scott Hershovitz, *Exploring Law's Empire*]

[36] *See, e.g.*, L. Kornhauser, *An Economic Perspective on Stare Decisis*, 65 CHI.-KENT L.REV. 63, 65 (1989) (describing stare decisis as "a practice that, paradoxically, demands that a court adhere to a prior decision it considers wrong"); L. Alexander, *Constrained by Precedent*, 63 S. CAL. L. REV. 1, 4 (1989) ("I shall focus on those situations ... in which a subsequent court believes that, though a previous case was decided incorrectly, it must, nevertheless ... decide the case confronting it in a manner that it otherwise believes is incorrect").

[37] "[T]here is nothing to do except stand by the errors of our brethren of the week before, whether we relish them or not." B. CARDOZO, THE NATURE OF THE JUDICIAL PROCESS 150 (1921).

Horizontal stare decisis requires that a court follow its own precedents. This essay explores the mystery of horizontal stare decisis.

The view that stare decisis condemns courts to repeat their mistakes neither fits nor justifies our legal practice. Fit is problematic because, with some regularity, courts overrule precedents that they regard as mistaken. Justification is problematic because, as we shall see, the values most often cited in defense of stare decisis—efficiency and fairness—cannot underwrite a general practice of following incorrectly decided precedents.

The key to understanding the practice of stare decisis, I shall argue, lies elsewhere. Specifically, it lies in the virtue Ronald Dworkin calls integrity. Integrity is a value that is realized by patterns of behavior across time. The unique demand that integrity makes upon both individuals and courts is that they recognize that what they have done in the past affects what they ought to do now. Stare decisis, I aim to show, promotes integrity in judicial decision making.

I also aim to show that stare decisis is a broader practice than we traditionally conceive it. On an integrity-based view, stare decisis is the practice of engaging with history, not just by following precedents, but also by distinguishing them and, when appropriate, overruling them. Overruling a precedent, and sometimes even distinguishing one, are often thought of as acts that run counter to the demands of stare decisis. But if we think of stare decisis as a practice in which courts strive to exhibit integrity in decision making, then we can see that distinguishing and overruling precedents are ways that a court engages with its own history. As we shall see, a court with no concern for the integrity of its own decision making would not need to distinguish or overrule its precedents. It could simply ignore them. [103–104]

We started our inquiry with the question, "What justifies adherence to a decision known to be wrong?" We saw that this question is misleading because it does not accurately capture what stare decisis requires. So we asked a different question: "What justifies adherence to a precedent irrespective of its merit?" This question better captures the canonical formulation of stare decisis, but it still leaves us with an intractable problem. We can explain why lower courts ought to defer to the decisions of higher courts simply by invoking Raz's normal justification thesis. But we cannot find an analogue that explains why the highest court in a land should accord its own previous decisions similar deference. Neither efficiency nor fairness does the trick.

Fortunately, to justify stare decisis, we need not justify adhering to decisions irrespective of their merits. After all, courts do not do that. With some regularity, courts overrule precedents and limit their scope by distinguishing them. We can think of overruling and distinguishing as ways of breaching stare decisis. But we can also see overruling and distinguishing as part of the practice of stare decisis. On this broader view, the central demand of stare decisis is that courts engage with the past and act with integrity.

We owe our understanding of the special connection between law and integrity to the work of Ronald Dworkin. Dworkin was the first to recognize that integrity is central to understanding our legal institutions. This was no trivial observation, because (as we shall see below) integrity may not be a value for all institutions, perhaps not even all law-like ones.

Before we can explore the connection between stare decisis and integrity, we must get a fix on what integrity is. Providing a full account is too large an endeavor to take on here, but some preliminary efforts will help us to get an alternative account of stare decisis off the ground. According to Dworkin:

> We want our neighbors to behave, in their day-to-day dealings with us, in the way we think right. But we know that people disagree to some extent about the right principles of behavior, so we distinguish that requirement from the different (and weaker) requirement

that they act in important matters with integrity, that is, according to convictions that inform and shape their lives as a whole, rather than capriciously and whimsically.[38]

Acting with integrity does not require that one act correctly. Rather, it requires that one always act in accord with genuine convictions about what the right way to act is. Integrity may seem like a second-best sort of value, one to be pursued only when one cannot be confident of acting correctly. Indeed, Dworkin seems to invite this understanding of integrity by suggesting that we demand it of others because we know that we disagree about what is right. Integrity is not a second-best value, however, and our primary reason for demanding integrity in ourselves and others is not our inability to agree about what is right. Rather, we demand integrity because, whatever doubt we have about particular moral views, we are confident that the demands of morality are coherent.[39] We are also confident that morality does not demand that we act capriciously or whimsically in matters of importance. Thus, if we are striving to act morally, we will act with integrity.

Let me put the point another way. Someone who acts with integrity may nevertheless do something she ought not to do from time to time. But someone who acts without integrity, someone who acts incoherently or capriciously in matters of importance, simply cannot be acting morally except by happenstance. A lack of integrity signifies a lack of a commitment to act morally.

An individual displays integrity when her actions taken as a whole reflect a commitment to a coherent and defensible moral view. The moral view must be coherent because the demands of morality are coherent. However, commitment to an evil moral view is no virtue simply because the view is coherent. Thus, integrity also requires that one act in accord with a defensible moral view. Otherwise, acting with integrity would not be a way of striving to act morally.

Of course, a defensible moral view is not necessarily a true one. This is why Dworkin is right when he says that the demand that we act with integrity is weaker than the demand that we act morally. However, acting with integrity is part of striving to act morally, and that is the source of its value. We respect others for their integrity even when we disagree with their actions because we recognize their genuine commitment to acting morally.

Now we get to the important part for understanding stare decisis. Acting with integrity requires recognizing that what one has done in the past is relevant to what one ought to do now. Integrity requires a commitment to a moral view, and one can only display a commitment to a moral view by a pattern of behavior across time. Constantly shifting moral views are a sign of caprice, not integrity.

Importantly, refusing to change one's moral views in the face of persuasive reason to do so is also inconsistent with integrity. Remember that integrity is valuable because it is an aspect of striving to act morally. If you are genuinely striving to act morally, you will change your beliefs and behavior in response to persuasive argument or new evidence. A rigid refusal to change one's moral convictions in the face of new information is not a sign of integrity; it is a sign of obtuseness.

There are at least two situations in which integrity requires one to repudiate one's past. The first is when one's moral convictions undergo genuine change. Integrity requires acting in accord with one's new moral convictions. If a person's moral convictions are constantly shifting, we will not say that she acts with integrity even if she always acts in accord with her genuine moral convictions. This is because we doubt that she has any commitment to her moral views or to acting morally. But in the normal case, revisions in one's beliefs and behaviors are not only consistent with integrity, they are required by it.

---

[38]  R. Dworkin, Law's Empire 166 (1998).
[39]  I am using "morality" in its widest sense, in which the demands of morality are coextensive with the demands of reason.

One should also repudiate one's past when one's past behavior is inconsistent with the moral commitments one has made. This is an all too common occurrence for most of us. Integrity does not require that one repeat one's mistakes; rather, it requires correcting them to bring one's behavior in accord with one's moral commitments.

These remarks are, of course, only exploratory. A full consideration of the nature of integrity demands more space and attention than available here. However, we have made enough progress in understanding what integrity demands of individuals that we can turn our attention to what integrity requires of courts.

Courts are moral actors, and a court can display integrity in much the same way that an individual can. A court displays integrity when its decisions reflect a commitment to a coherent and defensible view of the rights and duties people have under the law. Such a commitment can only be displayed by a pattern of decisions across time. If a court's rulings change capriciously, if it fails to pay heed to its own pronouncements, we will doubt that it has any genuine commitment to the views it expresses. On the other hand, if the court takes seriously what it has said in the past and it displays consistency and coherence in action, we will believe that the court acts on the basis of genuine convictions about the content of the law.

Why should courts act with integrity? For insight, let us turn once again to Dworkin. He writes:

> Integrity becomes a political ideal when ... we insist that the state act on a single, coherent set of principles even when its citizens are divided about what the right principles of justice and fairness really are. We assume, in both the individual and political cases, that we can recognize other people's acts as expressing a conception of justice or decency even when we do not endorse that conception ourselves. This ability is an important part of our more general ability to treat others with respect, and it is therefore a prerequisite of civilization.[40]

We want the state (and, derivatively, its courts) to act in accord with a single, coherent set of principles for the same reason we want individuals to do so. We are confident that morality provides a coherent vision of what we owe to one another, and that that vision does not demand that the state or its agents act capriciously in matters of importance. If the state acts incoherently or capriciously in matters of importance, it cannot be acting morally except by happenstance. We may disagree about what morality requires of the state, but we want the state to strive to act morally. Acting with integrity is a sign that it does so.

Dworkin breaks down the demands of integrity into two principles: the principle of integrity in legislation and the principle of integrity in adjudication. The latter principle, he says, explains "why judges must conceive of the body of law they administer as a whole rather than as a set of discrete decisions they are free to make or amend one by one, with nothing but a strategic interest in the rest."[41] Stare decisis is a means by which we promote this sort of integrity in judicial decision making.

A court that considers itself bound by the principle of stare decisis recognizes that what it has done in the past affects what it ought to do now. Of course, integrity in judicial decision making is no more a matter of slavishly repeating past decisions, right or wrong, than it is for individuals. Just as individuals must sometimes repudiate their past, courts must do so as well. They must do so whenever their convictions about the content of the law undergo genuine change, and they must do so when they discover that their past decisions conflict with

---

[40] DWORKIN, *supra* note 38, at 166.
[41] DWORKIN, *supra* note 38, at 167.

their genuine commitments. Of course, if a court constantly shifts its views, we will doubt that it has any genuine commitment to them, and we will not regard it as acting with integrity. But, in the normal case, a court can overturn a precedent it regards as mistaken without doing any violence to its integrity, and indeed, integrity may demand that it do so.

There is good reason to think of stare decisis as a broader practice than simply following precedent. If a court seeking to act with integrity has previously announced a rule of law, it has three options: it can follow it, it can overrule it, or it can distinguish the case. Overruling and distinguishing are as much ways of engaging with the past as following is. They are ways of saying, "we recognize that our prior decision is relevant in deciding what we ought to do now, but for these reasons we are not following it here." A court that did not consider itself bound by stare decisis would not need to overrule or distinguish cases because it would not recognize what it had done in the past as relevant to what it ought to do now.

An example of such an institution may help to make the point clear. Up until a few years ago, allegations of student conduct violations at the University of Georgia were adjudicated by an organization called the Student Judiciary. The Student Judiciary heard cases running the gamut from trivial infractions like excessive noise in dorms to serious offenses such as DUI and sexual assault. Members of the Student Judiciary sat on panels as judges in what were essentially mini-trials to determine whether a student violated a rule and, if so, to impose an appropriate sanction. Sanctions ranged from reprimand to expulsion.

The Student Judiciary had no system of precedent. A panel would not consider the decision of a previous panel, even if a previous decision is precisely on point. Thus, no case law grew up around the conduct rules or their implementation. Each panel treated each case as if no others had preceded it.

The Student Judiciary shunned precedent for a variety of reasons. One reason is that it was seeking to avoid some of the accoutrements of real legal systems. It did not want to require student defendants to research previous decisions, nor did it want to expend resources cataloguing them. For the Student Judiciary, efficiency counseled against stare decisis.

The most important reason for shunning precedent, however, was the way the Student Judiciary conceived of its mission. It understood itself to share the educational aims of the broader university. The organization believed that its responsibility was to provide each student who appeared before a panel with the best educational experience it could. A system of precedent might have gotten in the way of tailoring each student's hearing and sanction to their individual educational needs. Without precedent, maximum flexibility was maintained. The system's rejection of stare decisis was so complete that decisions from prior cases were not even considered relevant, let alone dispositive.

Integrity was simply not a value the adjudicative practices of the Student Judiciary recognized. This is interesting, because the Student Judiciary was as court-like as an institution can be without being part of an actual legal system. The Student Judiciary administered a system of conduct rules of general application through adjudicatory bodies with judges and lawyer-like advocates. The Student Judiciary was even an organ of the state.[42]

I suspect that the Student Judiciary was, in fact, concerned with the integrity of its decision making. Stare decisis is not the only way to promote integrity. The Student Judiciary demanded that potential members participate in lengthy training, which promoted consistency and coherence in the decisions of its panels, and members received continuing education as well. Nevertheless, in the

---

[42]  *Red & Black Pub. Co., Inc. v. Board of Regents*, 427 S.E. 2d 257 (Ga. 1993) (holding that the Student Judiciary is subject to Georgia's Open Records Act, which applies to state agencies).

individual case, the Student Judiciary was designed to be unresponsive to claims that a prior decision bound it to a course of action. Thus, unlike a court that adheres to stare decisis, the Student Judiciary never had the need to distinguish or overrule one of its prior decisions.

In contrast to the Student Judiciary, a court that adheres to stare decisis is different not simply because it has a commitment to following its prior decisions, but because it has committed itself to the idea that what it has done in the past is relevant to what it ought to do now. Such a court answers to its precedents, by following them, distinguishing them, and, on occasion, overruling them. Following, distinguishing, and overruling are all part of the pursuit of integrity in adjudication.

This essay started with a question: could legal reasoning really be so different from everyday reasoning that principle requires courts to make mistakes repeatedly rather than correct them? Notwithstanding the traditional view of stare decisis, the answer is no. Stare decisis does not require a court to blindly follow incorrectly decided precedents. Nor does it require a court to stand by a precedent irrespective of its merit. What stare decisis does require is that courts engage with the past and act with integrity. They do this when they display a commitment to a coherent, defensible view of the content of the law.

Now that we have an expanded view of the practice of state decisis, it is reasonable to wonder whether efficiency and fairness might not play a role in justifying it after all. Neither efficiency nor fairness seemed promising as a justification for a practice of following past decisions irrespective of their merit. But the broader practice of engaging with the past by following, overruling, and distinguishing precedent may well be both fair and efficient. Whether it is either, of course, depends on how good a job courts do of it. The efficiency and fairness of stare decisis conceived broadly still depends, in part, on the efficiency and fairness of the decisions in particular cases.

The real place for efficiency and fairness in an explanation of stare decisis is not so much in justifying the practice, but in giving it its contour. This essay has not addressed the conditions under which a court ought to overturn one of its precedents. In any given case, the question of whether a court should follow a precedent depends crucially on matters of fairness and efficiency, and on a multitude of other values as well. The fact that courts bother to engage with precedent at all, however, is best explained by judicial aspirations to act with integrity.                                                                [113–118]

## JEREMY WALDRON
### The Rule of Law as a Theater of Debate
### (2004)[43]

The "right answer thesis," when it was introduced into his jurisprudence, was not there to vindicate the claims of any particular legal proposition. It was there, and Professor Dworkin argued for it, in order to counter the suggestion explicit in H. L. A. Hart's legal positivism that in hard cases the sources of law may run out, leaving the decision maker—usually a judge—to come up with a determination on some basis other than legal argument.[44] On Hart's positivist account, there may have to be an end to the process of *legal* argumentation, and if a decision is reached it may have to be reached on some other basis. But the case that Dworkin makes—a case that we will not examine here—is supposed to show that the

---

[43] [From ed. Justine Burley, *Dworkin and His Critics*]
[44] H. L. A. Hart, *The Concept of Law*, 2nd edn. (1994).

possibilities for the methods and processes of legal argumentation are much deeper and more extensive than that.[45] This position is expressed using the idea of "the right answer" and associating it with the thesis that even in a hard case one of the parties has a right to win.[46] But since Dworkin denies—that any alleged right answer is self-certifying as such, what we have is actually an account of how and why we should persist in arguing about the answer to hard cases, under-written by the notion of an objectively true outcome. We have, in short, a tech-nique for lawyers and judges—a technique that is supposed to be made compelling by Dworkin's account of how his ideal judge proceeds rather than by his account of where his ideal judge ends up.[47]

In interpreting his position this way, I have no particular investment in showing that Professor Dworkin really does or really does not believe in right answers to hard legal questions. As we have seen, he says he doesn't believe in one particular version of the right answer thesis—the transcendental strongbox account.[48] In other places, the thesis that there are right answers seems to be something that he does want to defend. But what he mainly wants to defend it from, I think, are denials that would have the consequence of crippling or blocking the procedures of legal argumentation. So Dworkin's repeated insistence that there can be right answers even though there is protracted disagreement among members of the community as to what these right answers are, is not, as it seems to be, an attempt to protect the right answer thesis from a particularly troubling objection. It is, rather, very close to the heart of the matter: if claims of objectivity and the persistence of argument were not associated in this way, the right answer thesis would not be doing the work that he wants it to do in his jurisprudence.

In *Law's Empire*, the right answer thesis is notable by its absence. I am not saying it is explicitly denied. But the book is mainly given over to an account of how lawyers and judges proceed and what justifies requiring them to proceed in that way. Again, how they proceed, Dworkin says, is by *arguing*, and the book "tries to grasp the argumentative character of our legal practice. . . ."[49]

> Legal practice, unlike many other social phenomena, is *argumentative*. . . . People who have law make and debate claims about what law permits and forbids that would be impossible—because senseless—without law and a good part of what their law reveals about them cannot be discovered except by noticing how they ground and defend these claims.[50]

Having said that, I should add that Professor Dworkin does not treat legal argumentation simply as an aesthetic. Another way he characterizes legal practice is in terms of its "propositional" character,[51] which reminds us that the argument is *about* something and about something that matters.[52] But there is less emphasis on objectivity in *Law's Empire* than there is in some of Dworkin's other writings. His tactic, in an interesting section on "external skepticism" is to defuse the debate about objectivity, rather than take one side in that debate and defend it.[53] Metaphysical issues, he says, should not be allowed to distract us from the

---

[45]  See especially "The Model of Rules I and 'Hard Cases'," in *Taking Rights Seriously*.
[46]  Ibid., p. 82.
[47]  For Hercules' "technique" see ibid., pp. 129–30.
[48]  See Dworkin, *Taking Rights Seriously*, p. 337.
[49]  Ronald Dworkin, *Law's Empire* (1986), p. 14.
[50]  Ibid., p. 13.
[51]  Ibid., p. 14.
[52]  *Law's Empire* opens with the words "It matters how judges decide cases" (ibid., p. 1).
[53]  Ibid., pp. 76–86.

practice of argumentation about law and justice, and it must not be allowed to infect our explication of the issues at stake in such argumentation.

The conception of law defended in *Law's Empire* is a particular account of the connection between the way we justify present exercises of power and the relation between past decisions that have been made in the community. The general idea of the rule of law, Dworkin says, is this: "Law insists that force not be used or withheld, no matter how useful that would be to ends in view, no matter how beneficial or noble those ends, except as licensed or required by individual rights and responsibilities flowing from past political decisions about when collective force is justified."[54] Now, it would not be hard to put a gloss on that which accorded with the rule-book conception—under the rule of law, force may not be used unless licensed in advance by antecedently posited rules (laid down in statutes or precedents, for example)—and that conception would justify the doctrine in terms of the importance of notice and predictability for those upon whom force is likely to be used. But Dworkin's gloss on the idea of law again emphasizes the *argumentative* character of the relation between present force and antecedent decisions. It isn't just a matter of pointing to a justification in the existing materials; it's a matter of arguing from those materials, arguing about their interpretation and arguing about the general principles that they (arguably) presuppose. He notes as a matter of fact that lawyers and judges tend to worry away at statutes and precedents long after they have exhausted any possible significance these could have as bases of predictability: "[O]ur judges actually pay more attention to so-called conventional sources of law like statutes and precedents than conventionalism allows them to do."[55] And he believes that it is the task of jurisprudence to explain this persistence in argumentation.

The explanation he offers—law as integrity—it is the idea of a certain sort of community, where people accept that they are bound together by reciprocal obligations that run deep and pervasively through their existing practices of mutual concern and respect. They treat particular obligations that they may have been found to have to one another in particular cases not as limited to those circumstances but "as derivative from and expressing a more general responsibility active throughout [their] association in different ways."[56] To honor this commitment, when any particular issue comes up for present decision, they are bound to delve relentlessly into the established terms of their association to ascertain how the present issue would best be decided in view of the deep commitments they think of themselves as having already taken on. That is what Professor Dworkin means by the rule of law—decision making in the context of that sort of practice. He believes it gives a distinctive flavor to a community's political culture:

> Politics has a different character for such a people. It is *a theater of debate* about which principles the community should adopt as a system, which view it should take of justice, fairness, and due process. ... Members of a community of principle accept that their political rights and duties are not exhausted by the particular decisions their political institutions have reached, but depend, more generally, on the scheme of principles those decisions presuppose and endorse.[57]

Of course, this "theater of debate" is likely to be characterized by disagreement. People will disagree about what principles our existing decisions presuppose, and they will disagree too about what would be attractive or eligible principles to consider for this role. And Professor Dworkin as always wants to resist any

---

[54] Ibid., p. 93.
[55] Ibid., p. 130.
[56] Ibid., p. 200.
[57] Ibid., p. 211.

skeptical claim that such disagreement makes the argument futile or inconsequential. Once again, if there is a role for the idea of "right answers" in *Law's Empire*, it is to block this move—that is, as before, to underwrite, with the idea of objectivity, the point of persisting with argument in the absence of consensus. Mostly, though, "law as integrity consists in an approach, in questions rather than answers."[58] Whatever its role in the book, the idea of objective right answers is not supposed to condemn as violations of the rule of law political arguments that in an objective sense *fail to get it right* about the principled relation between present issues and antecedent decisions. Instead it seems as though the demands of integrity are satisfied, on Dworkin's view, in the *attempt* to ascertain and work from deeper principles implicit in existing decisions.

> We want our officials to treat us as tied together in an association of principle, and we want this for reasons that do not depend on any identity of conviction among these officials, either about fit or about the more substantive principles an interpretation engages. Our reasons endure when judges disagree, at least in detail, about the best interpretation of the community's political order, because each judge still confirms and reinforces the principled character of our association by *striving* in spite of the disagreement, to reach his own opinion instead of turning to the usually simpler task of fresh legislation.[59]

The expressive value of integrity is confirmed, he says, "when people in good faith *try* to treat one another in a way appropriate to common membership in a community ... and to see each other as making *this attempt*, even when they disagree about exactly what integrity requires in particular circumstances."[60]

All of this argues, in my view, for a conception of the rule of law that is, in the last analysis, proceduralist rather than objectivist. A society ruled by law, according to Dworkin, is a society committed to a certain method of arguing about the exercise of public power. A society shows its allegiance to the rule of law by dint of its commitment to asking certain questions and approaching them in the right way. And it is distinguished, ultimately, from societies that lack such a commitment not by the substance of what it does—substantively respecting moral rights, for example—but by the procedures that it unflinchingly follows. "Law is not exhausted by any catalogue of rules or principles [or] ... by any roster of officials. ... Law's empire is defined by attitude, not territory or power or process."[61]

My characterization of Dworkin's account of the rule of law as a proceduralist conception may be misunderstood. In modern constitutional theory, terms like "proceduralism" and "legal process" are associated with views that confine constitutional review to procedural or quasi-procedural issues. According to John Hart Ely, for example, judges may review legislation for defects in the procedures involved in its enactment or in order to maintain the integrity of the democratic process; but they should not address issues of substance in exercising what is in fact quite a problematic power, from a democratic point of view.[62] Now Professor Dworkin is a critic of this view: he does not believe that procedural issues can be separated from substantive issues in the way that Ely implies, nor does he accept

---

[58] Ibid., p. 239. See also ibid., p. 412: "I have not devised an algorithm for the courtroom. No electronic magician could design from my arguments a computer program that would supply a verdict everyone would accept once the facts of the case and the text of all past statutes and judicial decisions were put at the computer's disposal."

[59] Ibid., p. 264 (my emphasis).

[60] Ibid., p. 190 (my emphasis).

[61] Ibid., p. 413.

[62] John Hart Ely, *Democracy and Distrust: A Theory of Judicial Review* (1981).

that there is a serious issue about the democratic status of judicial review that needs to be addressed in this way.[63] On Dworkin's theory, judges have no choice but to follow the instruction of the Constitution and address substantive issues of moral right. And a regime in which they are empowered to do this may well be a better democracy precisely because of their ability to address substantive as well as procedural issues in this way.[64] But none of this detracts from what I have referred to as the proceduralist aspect of Dworkin's own jurisprudence. In constitutional law, Dworkin's position is that important issues of rights must be dealt with through a set of procedures appropriate to their character as issues of principle, and this applies whether the issues themselves are issues about political procedures or not.

Reference to constitutional theory, however, does give us the opportunity to consider more closely the kind of procedures that Professor Dworkin has in mind in his conception of the rule of law. I have used the words "argument" and "argumentation" over and over again to refer to these procedures. But we need to pin things down a little. The complaint is often heard that Dworkin's proceduralism does not necessarily imply any commitment to participatory values. Allan Hutchinson is one of the severest critics on this score: "Despite paying lip-service to 'a theater of debate,' *Law's Empire* is about accepting and assuming political obligations and not about participating in the making of them. ... In *Law's Empire*, judges have been elevated to the rank of moral prophets and philosopher monarchs. For citizens, politics has become a spectator sport."[65] And Silas Wasserstrom says something similar about Dworkin's legalistic "theater of debate":

> Nor am I at all sure what the "theater of debate about which principles the community should adopt as a system" is supposed to be like, but I suspect it would not be very moving or dramatic, even for the community's few moral philosophers who attend or participate. ... I have no clear idea what the politics of the community of principle would be like, but I suspect its politics would be rather rarified and effete, and would involve very few ordinary citizens as active participants.[66]

I have my own doubts about Dworkin's commitment to democratic politics,[67] but I think this is a little unfair. Several times in *Law's Empire*, Dworkin indicates that it is the responsibility of each citizen, not just each judge, to try to figure out what integrity requires: in a community governed by the rule of law "each citizen has a responsibility to identify, ultimately, [a scheme of principle] for himself, as his community's scheme," and to organize his dealings with other citizens on that basis.[68] Indeed Professor Dworkin appears to think that one of the advantages of an American-style system of judicial review is that it actually improves the quality of debate among members of the public.

> When an issue is seen as constitutional, ... and as one that will ultimately be resolved by courts applying general constitutional principles, the quality of public argument is often

---

[63] Dworkin, "The Forum of Principle," in *A Matter of Principle*, pp. 33–71, pp. 57–69.

[64] See Dworkin, *Freedom's Law*, ch. 1. For a critique of this position, see Jeremy Waldron, "Judicial Review and the Conditions of Democracy," *Journal of Political Philosophy*, vol. 6, 1998, p. 335, and *Law and Disagreement*, ch. 13.

[65] Allan C. Hutchinson, "Indiana Dworkin and *Law's Empire*," *Yale Law Journal*, vol. 96, 1987, pp. 637–55, at p. 654. For "theater of debate," see Dworkin, *Law's Empire*, p. 211 and the passage cited at text accompanying note 4 above.

[66] Silas Wasserstrom, "The Empire's New Clothes," *Georgetown Law Journal*, vol. 75, 1986, pp. 199–314 at p. 265.

[67] See Waldron, *Law and Disagreement*, ch. 13.

[68] Dworkin, *Law's Empire*, pp. 190, 213.

improved, because the argument concentrates from the start on questions of political morality. ... When a constitutional issue has been decided by the Supreme Court, and is important enough so that it can be expected to be elaborated, expanded, contracted, or even reversed by future decisions, a sustained national debate begins, in newspapers and other media, in law schools and classrooms, in public meetings and around dinner tables. That debate better matches [the] conception of republican government, in its emphasis on matters of principle, than almost anything the legislative process on its own is likely to produce.[69]

He may or may not be right about this.[70] But so far as the characterization of his conception of the rule of law is concerned, it is evident that Dworkin does not think citizens are required to submit to oligarchic nonparticipatory determinations of what law, rights, and principles add up to. The discussion of civil disobedience that we studied in section II of this chapter makes that quite clear, and it indicates that the proceduralism of Dworkin's may not be regarded as a purely spectator sport.

We have seen that throughout Dworkin's writings, the idea that there are objective right answers to the conundrums that legality poses for us helps invigorate and keep open the legal and political processes that he favors. It is true that this gives a particular objectivist spin to Dworkin's theory of institutional competence, and sometimes he says things like this: "The best institutional structure is the one best calculated to produce the best answers to the essentially moral question of what the democratic conditions actually are, and to secure stable compliance with those conditions."[71] He uses this also as a basis for some skepticism about legislative procedures, which he says may not be "the safest vehicle for protecting the rights of politically unpopular groups."[72] But he is also sometimes willing to say that "[l]egislatures are guardians of principle too,"[73] and that if lawmakers ask themselves the right questions and proceed in the right, responsive to concerns about integrity and principle in their deliberations, then their procedures too are constitutive of the rule of law.[74]

I have mostly shied away from asserting that Dworkin's conception of the rule of law is unequivocally proceduralist. We have seen throughout that there are elements of the objectivist and the rule-book conception, and no doubt other conceptions too. It is a delicate exercise in triangulation, as it were, to see how a given conception responds to the interlocking concerns about settlement, process, and objectivity that are implicated in the rule of law ideal. All of them in various ways pay tribute to the needs and concerns of ordinary people and what they expect from their law.[75] What I have tried to do, however, is to emphasize those parts of Professor Dworkin's conception of legality that find respect for individuals and their rights in the manner in which we proceed in our legal system, not just in the notion of objective principles or in the reality of established settlements. The rule of law prevails in a community, according to Dworkin, when its "collective decisions [are] made by political institutions whose structure, composition, and practices treat all members of the community, as individuals with equal concern and respect."[76] A society committed to the rule of law in this sense may well use courts more than a society without such a commitment. But that is not merely because—and I think not mainly because—courts are more likely to get

[69] Dworkin, *Freedom's Law*, p. 345.
[70] For a critique, see Waldron, *Law and Disagreement*, pp. 289–91.
[71] Dworkin, *Freedom's Law*, p. 34.
[72] Ibid.
[73] Ibid., p. 31.
[74] See Dworkin, *Law's Empire*, pp. 167, 176, and 217–19.
[75] For an interesting discussion of the values associated with legality, see also Ronald Dworkin, "Hart's Postscript and the Character of Political Philosophy," pp. 24–8.
[76] Dworkin, *Freedom's Law*, p. 17.

things right. It is rather that courts are supposed to exhibit in their forms, structures, and procedures a determination to take seriously the issues of right that they are addressing. A society committed to the rule of law

> encourages each individual to suppose that his relations with other citizens and with his government are matters of justice, and it encourages him and his fellow citizens to discuss as a community what justice requires those relations to be. It promises a forum in which his claims about what he is entitled to have will be steadily and seriously considered at his demand.[77]

For these purposes, taking rights seriously is not so much a matter of getting rights right; it is a matter of conveying in the *way* in which we make our decisions that we understand that rights are involved. Personally, I believe that the same argument can be made, on certain favorable assumptions, for legislatures too: they too have their own way of respecting in their structures and procedures the equality of respect due to the opinions of ordinary men and women.[78] But I shall not try to persuade Professor Dworkin of that now. This chapter, as I said at the beginning, is supposed to be an exposition of his account of the rule of law, and it is intended to bring out proceduralist themes in that account that are in danger of being downplayed in a jurisprudential environment that continues to be obsessed with the right answer thesis.                                    [327–332]

## L. ALEXANDER AND K. KRESS
### The Arguments Against Legal Principles
### (1995)[79]

Notwithstanding their dominance in legal practice, the case for the existence of legal principles fails miserably. Our argument focuses on Dworkin's account of legal principles, which we believe to be the most careful account in the literature. Most other accounts of legal principles share the crucial flaw of Dworkin's, for they are based on the mistaken assumption that there can be norms that are not correct moral norms, that are not posited in canonical form like legal rules, but that arise out of the posited legal rules.[80]

### A. Past arguments against Dworkin's legal principles

#### 1. The Normative Unattractiveness of Legal Principles

One of the earliest arguments against legal principles is found in Alexander and Bayles's criticism of *Taking Rights Seriously*.[81] Alexander and Bayles point out that moral principles are morally attractive because they *are* our moral ideals. They are the very standards of moral attractiveness. Moral principles are what ideally should govern our conduct in all instances, both within the legal system and without.[82]

Legal *rules* can be morally attractive because they can be formulated to give

---

[77] Dworkin, "Political Judges and the Rule of Law," p. 32.

[78] See Waldron, *Law and Disagreement*, chs. 3–5 and 10–11. See also Jeremy Waldron, *The Dignity of Legislation* (1999).

[79] [From A. Marmor (ed.), *Law and Interpretation* (1995).]

[80] Joseph Raz's account avoids this flaw because he accepts as authoritative only posited principles. See Joseph Raz, "Legal Principles and the Limits of Law" in (1972) 81 *Yale L.J.* 823, 848. Raz's account, however, runs into the problem regarding whether principles can be enacted.

[81] See Alexander and Bayles, pp. at 271–278.

[82] *ibid.*, p. 277.

better guidance than the moral principles themselves.[83] How moral principles apply to particular cases will frequently be controversial. Having everyone individually determine how the moral principles apply may lead to moral errors, lack of co-ordination, and other ills. Thus, the resulting state of affairs is, in light of the moral principles themselves, morally inferior to the state of affairs emerging from clear, blunt, formal rules. This may be so even if the rules, because of their blunt, formal nature, produce morally incorrect results (in terms of the moral principles) in some particular cases. Indeed, this may be so even if there are better rules available than those actually in place, for there may be higher order rules that authorize the (non-ideal) lower-order rules and which themselves are ideal (or as near ideal as can be agreed upon and morally preferable to anarchy).

Moral principles have the virtue of moral correctness; legal rules have the virtues of being the creations of those with the authority to make law and of giving clear guidance. Legal principles, however, have none of these virtues. They are neither morally correct nor uncontroversial in application. Nor have they been promulgated by authorities whose power to create norms is rule-based, for they are not posited norms.[84] They represent the worst of all worlds. Alexander and Bayles concluded that Dworkin had made out no case for legal principles as appropriate norms.[85]

## 2. *Legal Principles and the Spurious Claims of Equality and Integrity*

In *Law's Empire* Dworkin continues to press the case for legal principles derived from the axes of fit and moral acceptability, but he buttresses the case for such legal principles by arguments appealing to "integrity". Integrity is Dworkin's name for a particular version of equality, namely, the equality that is manifested by acting in a "principled" way and applying the same legal principles to X that one has applied to Y. When one determines what are the most morally attractive principles that "fit" past legal decisions at the threshold level, and then applies those principles in the present, one is treating present litigants in a principled way and maintaining equality between them and past litigants. Dworkin also requires that the principles underlying various aspects of doctrine be consistently applied and fit coherently together into an overall scheme of principles expressing "a single and comprehensive vision of justice".[86]

[...] Dworkin's support of legal principles by reference to equality is confused. If "equality" is a value, it is not a free-standing one. Rather, it is theory-dependent. In other words, each moral theory—each set of moral principles—will generate its own conception of equality. And each moral theory will dictate the pursuit of equality through following the theory itself. Thus, there cannot be a coherent reason in terms of the true moral value of equality for ever departing from the requirements of the correct moral theory. The true moral value of

---

[83] *ibid.*, p. 272.

[84] Again, legal principles are not just those correct moral principles explicitly recognized as legally controlling in cases, legislation, and constitutions. Such a description of legal principles as enacted moral principles fails to account for the role legal principles are supposed to play in justifying the bulk of the legal materials, much of which may be morally incorrect. The claim that legal principles are enacted moral principles requires an ontology of legal rules, legally enacted moral principles, and moral principles that have not been legally enacted. This ontology depends upon an unlikely severability of moral principles from each other (so that some but not others can be legally enacted). In most moral theories of which we are aware, however, moral principles are far too interrelated to lend themselves to legal severance.

[85] Alexander and Bayles, *supra*, n. 81, pp. 277–278.

[86] Ken Kress, "Coherence and Formalism" in (1993) 16 *Harv. J. L. Pub. Pol'y* 639, 652–653 n. 46.

equality is internal to the correct moral theory, not a reason to depart from it in favour of morally incorrect legal principles.[87]

## 3. The Retroactivity of Legal Principles

In *Taking Rights Seriously* and thereafter, Dworkin argues that adjudicating by reference to legal principles protects legal rights against retroactive upsets. Legal positivists, who argue that legal rules exhaust the legal norms available in adjudication, must decide cases on grounds other than legal grounds whenever those cases are not covered by legal rules. That, argues Dworkin, leads to applying new legal rules—those formulated in cases without pre-existing legal rules—to transactions that arise before the legal rules are promulgated, which is akin to legislating retroactively. Legal principles, on the other hand, are already immanent in past decisions, define the legal rights to which those past decisions give rise, and can determine outcomes in cases not governed by legal rules.

Alexander and Bayles, along with others, argue that Dworkin's argument from retroactivity is both confused and question-begging.[88] It is confused because any moral arguments against retroactivity could be accommodated by judges through recourse to correct moral principles whenever the legal rules failed to resolve a case. (In other words, in deciding based on correct moral principles which party should prevail in a lawsuit, the parties' expectations, the extent of their reliance on those expectations, and the countervailing benefits of upsetting their expectations would be among the factors that correct moral principles would dictate be taken into account.)[89] It is question-begging because it assumes that legal rights exist and thus could be retroactively upset in cases not covered by legal rules, a proposition legal positivists would dispute.

Perhaps the most interesting criticism of the argument from retroactivity is a *tu quoque* response by Kress. Kress demonstrates that Dworkin's own theory of adjudication grounded in legal principles results in retroactive application of legal rights.[90]

Kress's argument builds upon the role of authoritative institutional acts, such as constitutions, statutes, and judicial decisions, within Dworkin's theory. Legally

[87] Although Dworkin is vague on this point, it appears that integrity serves both as a constraining principle on other moral principles and (ambiguously) as simply one moral principle among equals. In its capacity as just one principle among others, it would presumably be theory-dependent, just as are "justice" and "due process". In its role as a constraining principle on others, it would serve as a test that the other principles must meet. Integrity cannot coherently play both roles.

To meet the criticism in the text of integrity as a theory-independent test of moral principles, Dworkin might concede that integrity is theory-dependent and argue that it is just one of our liberal-egalitarian principles. The problem with such a rejoinder is that it leads to intractable theoretical difficulties through self-reference. Integrity (1) is part of correct moral theory (CMT). 1, when coupled with legal decisions that are inconsistent with CMT (morally incorrect legal decisions), requires us to adopt covering principles that are inconsistent with CMT. In other words, I requires us to change the covering moral principles of which it is itself a component. Thus I requires that it itself be changed. I requires ~1. Integrity, therefore, cannot be both theory-dependent *and* a test for selecting the principles that make up moral theories.

[88] See Alexander and Bayles, *supra*, n. 81, pp. 284–285.

[89] Reliance values, like equality, are theory-dependent, that is, internal to whatever moral theory is correct. No set of incorrect decisions, no matter how numerous, can ever give one reason to depart from applying correct moral principles. Incorrect decisions are, of course, part of the furniture of the world to which correct moral principles apply, and they can and certainly do affect how those principles apply (and whether the principles should be directly or indirectly applied). That is, incorrect decisions in the past can alter what are correct outcomes in the present. But incorrect decisions can never alter the principles by which correctness is gauged.

[90] *Op. cit.*, n. 86.

authoritative principles and the rights that they describe are, for Dworkin, a function of institutional history and moral-political theory. Outcomes in concrete cases at law are in turn a function of the application and elaboration of legal principles (and rights). Thus, by transitivity, correct outcomes are a function of institutional history (along with moral-political theory). This much is obvious. Differences in constitutional and statutory provisions, precedents, and administrative rulings result in varying legal rights and principles, that is, in different law.

Suppose that, as a consequence of a judicial decision, a change in legal rights occurs after the facts giving rise to a lawsuit but before the case is adjudicated. With only rare exceptions,[91] the case will be adjudicated on the basis of the legal rights existing at the time of trial (and final adjudication) and not on the basis of the legal rights that existed at the time of the events giving rise to the lawsuit. If one of the legal rights that changes in consequence of the judicial decision is dispositive of the lawsuit, then the litigant who would have won (based upon the law existing at the time of the underlying events) will lose, and the litigant who would have lost will win. This is nothing less than retroactive application of law.

The same result can be established more elegantly by first noticing that, in Dworkin's theory, the legal principles—the morally best principles, $T_1$, that meet or exceed the threshold of fit—will always be precisely at the minimum threshold of fit. This can be demonstrated by *reductio ad absurdum*. Suppose the legal principles $T_1$ exceed the threshold of fit. $T_1$ could then be "transformed" into a morally more attractive set of principles $T_2$ by replacing one or more morally unattractive principles $p_1$ of $T_1$ that fit the institutional history well with morally more attractive principles $p_2$ that fit less well, yet still leave $T_2$ over the threshold of fit. But then $T_2$ is a better set of principles than $T_1$ because it is morally better than $T_1$ yet exceeds the threshold of fit. This contradicts the assumption that $T_1$ was the morally best set of principles exceeding the threshold of fit. QED.

The same conclusion can be reached by a positive argument. If the alleged set of legal principles exceeds the threshold of fit, we can substitute principles, trading off fit for greater moral appeal until we reach the minimum threshold of fit and maximum moral appeal at that threshold. The set of principles reached at that point are the veridical legal principles.

Some may object that principles are not as abundant, nor as finely discriminable, as the proof requires. Dworkin is estopped from raising that objection. He argues that no Hartian master test for law could distinguish legal from non-legal principles based upon institutional support. *A fortiori*, he claims, no test of institutional support could "fix [a principle's] weight at a particular order of magnitude".[92] Besides the *ad hominem* against Dworkin, infinite differentiation of principles may be justified in several ways. Principles' weights may vary along a real-valued continuum. Natural, normative, or legal language may be rich enough to provide subtly differing articulations of principles and their weights. Normative considerations may require infinite discriminability. Mathematical construction may provide it. A metaphysical principle of sufficient reason may establish it. Even if principles were not infinitely divisible, but only finely so, this would only mean that the best set of principles may slightly exceed the threshold of fit but need not be precisely equal to it. Under this condition, the results to follow would still be true, although the proofs of them would be less elegant.

That Dworkinian legal principles are always at the threshold of fit entails that principles are continuously changing. Applying these new principles to events arising before the new principles become legally authoritative amounts to retroactive application of law. We shall elaborate upon these claims.

Suppose that the minimum threshold of fit in a given jurisdiction is 80 per cent

---

[91] The main exception is when courts apply law prospectively only, in any of a number of variations.

[92] Dworkin, p. 40.

of judicial decisions. (Ignore, for simplicity, enactments, regulations, judicial hierarchies, and so on. The argument is sound even with these added complications.) Suppose that there have been 100 decisions to date, and that there is only one judge.

We have just seen that Dworkinian legal principles will just meet the threshold. Since the threshold is 80 per cent, Dworkinian legal principles $T_1$ will fit 80 per cent of the cases. They will explain 80 and fail to explain 20 of the 100 cases.

Now suppose that 100 new decisions arise and the judge correctly applies Dworkinian legal principles $T_1$ in resolving the cases. $T_1$ fits 100 of the new cases, since it was followed in deciding them. There are now 200 decisions. $T_1$ fits 80 of the first 100, and 100 of the second 100. Thus, $T_1$ fits $180/200 = 90$ per cent of the total decisions. This exceeds the threshold of fit, 80 per cent, so $T_1$ can no longer be the Dworkinian legal principles by the result just proven since $T_1$ substantially exceeds the threshold of fit. We can construct a $T_2$ with 80 per cent fit and morally better principles, by trading off fit for moral appeal until we reach the threshold of fit.

For one or more principles, $T_2$ differs from $T_1$. This means that $T_2$ will decide some cases differently from how $T_1$ would. Litigants whose cause of action arises when $T_1$ is the set of legal principles, but whose cases are decided when $T_2$ is the set of legal principles, will be subject to retroactive application of law whenever the differences between $T_1$ and $T_2$ are relevant to their lawsuit. If a changed principle is dispositive, the litigant who would have won loses, and vice versa.

In fact, $T_1$ will cease to be at the threshold of fit before 100 decisions have been rendered, and the law will therefore change sooner. Principles continuously evolve in Dworkinian legal theory. (This may explain some of the woolly statements in chapter 11 of *Law's Empire* about a law beyond the law, and about the law working itself (morally?) pure.)

Susan Hurley rejects Kress's intervening case argument for retroactivity in Dworkin's theory.[93] Although her exposition is subtle and complicated, the essence of her objection can be conveyed simply.

Hurley argues, following a suggestion of Dworkin's, that precedent changes the truth value of legal propositions only when judges make mistakes, and never when they make correct decisions.[94] The retroactivity resulting from mistaken judicial decisions is not of substantial, abstract, theoretical import—although it is significant to theories that take consequences into account and to theories that are concerned with human limitations. It is also of no great practical moment. If intervening case retroactivity could be confined to when judges make mistakes, the damage would be limited.

Hurley issues the following "challenge": "How, on coherentist assumptions, could the precedential force of a decision ... change the law itself, as opposed to our *beliefs* about it, if that decision were *ex ante* correct?"[95]

It appears that Hurley has mistaken Kress's intervening-case argument. The intervening-case argument does not suppose that when a judge makes a correct decision, the truth of the proposition decided in that opinion has been changed by the judge. Rather, the position is that when the judge makes a correct decision, the judge may well increase the weight of the principles or propositions supporting that decision (not necessarily their truth value). As a ripple effect of the increase in the weight of those principles or propositions, the decision may change the truth value of some other (logically? theoretically? normatively?) related propositions, resulting in ripple-effect retroactivity for some litigant whose case depends upon those other propositions.

---

[93] Susan Hurley, "Coherence, Hypothetical Cases, and Precedent" in (1990) 10 Ox. J. Leg. Stud. 221.

[94] *ibid.*, p. 228 n. 40.

[95] Hurley, *supra*, n. 93, p. 247.

Thus, Hurley is mistaken when she writes: "suppose the decision was *ex ante* correct and settled [and the judge decides it correctly]. In this case there is change neither in the law nor beliefs about it, so no retroactivity problem can arise."[96] There may be no change respecting beliefs or the truth of the law respecting the decision, but principles (or policies) supporting the decision may gain weight or strength, thus leading to a change in the law respecting a related proposition.

Hurley, and by Hurley's reporting, Dworkin,[97] have fallen victim to the following fallacy. They have a myopic view of the possibilities for coherentist theories of legal reasoning. Their view of coherence theories of law is too crude, and misses the potential richness of coherentist methodology. They appear to presuppose or believe that within coherentist methodology, all that can be relevant to a proposition of law, either before or after a judge decides it, is its truth value. They forget, what each has noted elsewhere, that propositions of law, or at least the principles which support them, have a dimension of weight,[98] or they have forgotten the significance of this dimension for judicial decision-making. When the judge correctly decides a case in which the dispositive issue is P, and the judge so holds, the truth value of P does not change, but its weight or the weight of the principles underlying it does. This increase in weight is what makes possible the change in weight and in truth value of other principles in subsequent cases, which gives rise to dispositive ripple effects and retroactivity.

Hurley's interpretation of precedent is undesirable on independent grounds. It cannot explain how law evolved from a clean slate to its current state. More importantly, what justification can be given for a doctrine of precedent which operates only when judges make mistaken decisions? According to Hurley, Dworkin's claim is that when a judge makes a correct decision, that decision does not change the truth value of the dispositive proposition (or of any other). However, when a judge makes a mistake and holds that P when prior to the decision in fact not-P was true, then the doctrine of precedent will sometimes operate to make P true thereafter. This may be so, for example, when the competition between P and not-P is relatively fierce, with not-P barely edging out P, so that the additional values behind following precedents suffice to give P the edge after the decision. So it appears that, according to Hurley and Dworkin, precedent makes a difference only when judges make mistakes. What could possibly be the underlying moral justification for a doctrine which operates to give people a right to the same incorrect decisions that have previously been made but is ineffective to make any difference when a judge makes a correct decision?

Of course, there might be reasons of notice, efficiency, justified reliance, liberty, practical uncertainty, separation of powers, comparative justice, and the like, supporting a doctrine of precedent which will sometimes take a legally mistaken proposition, say P, and make it correct thereafter in consequence of a mistaken judicial decision supporting it. But such reasons will also have some effect in giving further support to a correct legal proposition P which is so decided by a judge.

We shall provide one further reason why the Hurley doctrine of precedent does not comport with legal practice. Suppose that Q is legally true, but has never been explicitly so decided. According to Hurley, when it is first explicitly decided, that adds no additional force or weight to the principles recommending Q. Nor, presumably, the second time Q is explicitly decided, nor the fifth, nor the hundredth. So let Q be explicitly decided in a hundred decisions. According to Hurley, the best theory of law will be precisely the same after a hundred decisions of Q as it was before Q was even once correctly or explicitly decided. But now let us suppose that three decisions or five or some moderate number come out

---

[96] *ibid.*, p. 249.
[97] *ibid.*, p. 248 and n. 40.
[98] *ibid.*, pp. 225, 240, 247; Dworkin, *supra*, n. 77, pp. 26–27.

explicitly rejecting Q. Where there are *one hundred* decisions embedding Q and three or one or a modest number rejecting Q, the best theory of law on a coherentist account will, all other things being equal, be more likely to include Q than it will when there are *no* decisions explicitly deciding Q and one or three or a moderate number proclaiming not-Q. The explicit decision that Q, particularly the repeated explicit decision that Q, has some force in withstanding a small number of incorrect decisions that not-Q. What better way is there to understand this phenomenon with a coherentist framework than that the explicit decision of Q increase the weight of Q and its underlying principles, and the principles which those principles support and rely on for support? What better way to explain this phenomenon within a coherentist framework than to say that decisions have ripple effects throughout the seamless web? And if this is correct, then Kress's retroactivity argument against Dworkin's coherentist methodology stands.

## B. New and conclusive arguments against legal principles: The arguments from weight and fit

### 1. The Argument from Weight

Legal principles, as we have said, are not the same as correct moral principles. They are, instead, incorrect moral principles, or just plain incorrect principles. But are there such things?

There are, of course, incorrect *rules*, norms posited by particular people at a particular time and with a particular canonical form and intentional structure that demarcates their extensions. Rules, correct or incorrect, are weightless. They either apply or don't apply, but they cannot be "weighted". (Actually, rules are not weightless; rather, they claim to have *infinite* weight where they apply.) Principles, however, are supposed to have (finite) weight. Indeed, weight is essential to their being principles, since they have neither canonical form nor dependence on particular persons' datable intentions to govern their application. Their application is a function of their weight.

An *incorrect* principle, in so far as it is a principle, must, therefore, have weight. How else could we determine in a particular case whether the incorrect principle outweighs competing principles? (If incorrect principles never outweigh competing principles, correct and incorrect, then they can never determine the outcome of any case, since competing principles are always available to govern the case. At a minimum, the entire set of morally correct principles is available.) But what weight will incorrect principles have, and how will such weight be determined? No set of past cases, no matter how large the set, can fix as a matter of logical entailment the weight in the context of a present case of any principle that would explain those past cases, as Quine's indeterminacy thesis demonstrates.

We can, of course, "assign" a weight to an incorrect principle by deciding a case in accord with it or against it. In doing so we are declaring that the incorrect principle $P_1$ shall outweigh correct principle $P_c$ in Case C. We are not *discovering* that it is the case, however, for there is nothing to discover. Our declaration that it is the case cannot be correct or incorrect. The weight of $P_1$ in case C does not determine the outcome in Case C; rather, the outcome in Case C determines the weight of $P_1$ in Case C.

Suppose one were to argue that we induce the weight in the same way we induce the incorrect principle, by looking at past cases. Assume, for example, that there have been N cases in which plaintiffs named Green have won even though correct principles $P_c$ would have dictated that they lose. Suppose we induce the existence of incorrect principle $P_G$, "plaintiffs named Green should be preferred". Suppose we have a new case with a plaintiff named Green where $P_c$ would dictate that Green lose. Does $P_C$ outweigh $P_G$ or does $P_G$ outweigh $P_C$? All we know is that $P_G$ outweighed $P_C$ in past cases $C_N$. This does not tell us whether $P_G$

outweighs $P_C$ in the present case. What other arguments might determine $P_G$'s weight in this case? Arguments about how this case ought (really) to come out? Those arguments will all be based on correct principles $P_C$. They will dictate that $P_G$ be followed from now on only when it is consistent with $P_C$, which means $P_G$ has no weight of its own, which means it does not exist. The argument for inducing the weight of incorrect principles mistakenly views the adjudicative enterprise as predictive, while in fact it is normative.

Suppose we do not induce the "correct" incorrect principle and its weight from past cases. Assume, instead, that we rely on the incorrect principle's *promulgation*. Take freedom of speech, for example. Suppose that there is no independent moral principle of freedom of speech. Rather, the freedom of speech we should endorse is the product of moral principles regarding liberty and anti-paternalism.

Now suppose the constitutional framers declare that "the principle of freedom of speech shall be recognized". There is no problem treating this as a *rule* (with infinite weight within the scope of its application), as Justice Black tried (unsuccessfully) to treat the first amendment.[99] But suppose we try to take the framers at their word and treat free speech as a principle, albeit an incorrect one. What weight do we give it when it conflicts with $P_C$? Not its real weight (for, being incorrect, what would its *real* weight be?). Its promulgation cannot help us here, for unless the framers tell us how it is to be applied in each possible case—in which case they have made it into a *rule*—all we know from its promulgation is its promulgation. We do not know *it*. Nor can we. What is *there* to know?

Incorrect principles have a problematic metaphysical status. Our argument is that determining their weight may be like assigning a property to "the ether"; it cannot be done correctly or incorrectly, since there is nothing in the world that is "the ether with (or without) the property".[1]

---

[99] See, *e.g. Kongisberg* v. *State Bar of California* (1961) 366 U.S. 36, 60–71 (Black, J., dissenting).

[1] T. R. S. Allan shares our intuitions about incorrect principles. He, too, argues that principles cannot exist without weight, and that Dworkin's legal principles, being morally incorrect, are always outweighed by correct principles: "It is important to see that the weight of a principle is a function of the relevant facts. It is the nature of a principle to argue in favour of a certain result, but not conclusively: it does not dictate a decision in the manner of a rule, which applies absolutely (subject only to stated or acknowledged exceptions). The weight of a principle can only be determined by the court seised of the particular case and acquainted with the proven facts ... A rule may be applied, at least in the case of statutes, by a process of definition. Where a set of circumstances fall within the ambit of the rule, as determined by its enacted terms, no further deliberation is normally required: the rule dictates a particular result. It is precisely the function of rules to foreclose such deliberation in advance of particular cases arising for decision. By contrast, a principle makes an appeal directly to reason. It follows that Hercules can only apply a principle he understands and shares and therefore values. Since the weight of a principle inevitably depends on all the circumstances of the case, its application is always a matter of judgment—necessarily personal judgment.

It is hard to see how Hercules could determine the weight of a principle whose results he thought unfortunate, perhaps pernicious. If he applied the principle to the extent he thought truly appropriate—ascertaining its weight—he would inevitably reject it altogether. He could not, then, discriminate between particular cases, distinguishing or following precedents in all their complexity, on the basis of a popular conception of principle he himself rejected. It follows that it makes no sense to attempt to compare principles one accepts with those one rejects, even if the latter are popular. The comparison would by wholly theoretical: it could gain no purchase on the particular facts of concrete cases." T. R. S. Allan, "Justice and Fairness in *Law's Empire*" and see (1993) 52 Cambridge L.J. 64, 69–71.

## 2. The Argument from Fit

If there are legal principles that are morally incorrect principles, then Dworkin's account of them is the best there is. Namely, the incorrect principles ($P_1$) that exist are those principles that "fit" above some threshold with past government actions and that are the morally best such principles, "best" being measured by normative distance to correct principles ($P_c$). But in fact, $P_1 = P_c$. Dworkin's case for legal principles is nothing more than a case for correct moral principles. Why?

Suppose there are in the past N cases, $C_N$, that have not been decided in accord with correct principles $P_C$. Of all the incorrect principles $P_1$ that would "fit" the past cases, there is one principle that "fits" perfectly and is also morally best. That is the principle that is coextensive with $P_C$ except for cases $C_N$ (where it dictates the results reached in $C_N$). Let us call this principle $P_C$–$C_N$.

It is clear that no set of incorrect principles $P_1$ fits better than $P_C$–$C_N$, since the latter exhibits 100 per cent fit. Nor is any set morally better, since $P_C$–$C_N$ will dictate exactly the same results in all future cases and hypothetical cases as $P_C$. Therefore, Dworkin would have to urge that we decide based on incorrect principle $P_C$–$C_N$.

Is there anything wrong with this? Well, $P_C$–$C_N$ is not an *elegant* principle. But why should that disqualify it *normatively*, as opposed to aesthetically, given that it scores highest on both the fit and moral dimensions?

$P_C$–$C_N$ might be condemned as arbitrary and ad hoc. That is true. But if so, *all* incorrect principles are arbitrary and ad hoc, constructed to "justify" mistaken decisions.[2]

Dworkin argues that a legal system that manifests ad hoc principles lacking integrity is unable to generate the associative bonds necessary for legal obligation and moral legitimacy. In Section E below we will address this claim.

$P_C$–$C_N$ might be condemned as failing to accord persons equal treatment in those future cases that are "like" cases $C_N$ but in which $P_C$–$C_N$ will have a "different" outcome (one in accord with $P_C$, not $C_N$). This objection is confused. Equality is in one sense completely dependent on substantive principles[3]; therefore, $P_C$–$C_N$ generates its own conception of equality. On the other hand, if the point is that true equality, that mandated by $P_C$, differs from $P_C$–$C_N$, the point is correct but supports $P_C$–$C_N$. The litigants in $C_N$ and in $P_C$–$C_N$ are being treated equally in the sense that our best view of what is just at the time is being applied to each of them. $C_N$ is in the past and cannot be undone. $P_C$–$C_N$ will produce all the true equality ($P_C$ equality) one can now achieve.[4]

Thus, the objections based on inelegance, ad hoc principles, and equality all fail to dislodge $P_C$–$C_N$ as the preferred incorrect principle $P_1$.

Finally, since the past is past, and since $P_C$–$C_N$ dictates exactly the same results in the future as $P_C$ does, there is no practical difference between $P_C$–$C_N$ and $P_C$. And since $P_C$–$C_N$ is the incorrect principle—$P_1$-that we are supposed to choose, $P_1 = P_C$. There are no incorrect principles of any practical (what other?) consequence.

---

[2] Dworkin sometimes treats his value of "integrity", reflecting the ideals of community and fraternity, as on a par with other values, such as justice, due process, etc., and sometimes treats it as a value capable of trumping other values. In the latter sense, integrity as the queen of values might urge the rejection of principles that, while more just, are too complex to form the basis of a "community of principle" relative to simpler though less just principles. We find such a view, resting as it does on the fragmentation of moral theory, to be objectionable.

[3] See Peter Westen, "The Empty Idea of Equality" in (1982) 95 Harv. L. Rev. 537.

[4] We cannot do better in terms of morally significant equal treatment than to treat everyone in accordance with our current best view of justice. A past injustice creates no reason, not even a very weak one, to commit a present injustice.

### C. A misleading analogy: legal principles and the methodology of reflective equilibrium

Some might argue that the case for legal principles rests on the case for employing the methodology of reflective equilibrium. In the moral realm, reflective equilibrium is championed as the correct epistemological method for discovering (constructing?) correct moral principles.[5] One moves between one's considered moral judgments regarding particular cases and more general moral principles that would account for such judgments, adjusting the principles and reconsidering particular judgments until the principles and judgments reach an equilibrium state. Could we not say by analogy that legal principles are those principles that are in equilibrium with (most of) the cases?[6]

The answer is no. First, in moral reflective equilibrium, it is considered judgments that we have to bring into reflective equilibrium with our principles (and vice versa). In law, it is authoritative legal acts that must be brought into equilibrium with a theory of justice.

Secondly, and relatedly, in the moral methodology of reflective equilibrium we consider everything that can possibly bear on our judgments (what we know about psychology, sociology, economics, and so forth). In constructing legal principles, however, we are limited to primary legal materials (decisions, statutes, and so forth) and, importantly, cannot consider more than a certain percentage of those materials to be mistaken (the threshold of "fit"). There is no such limitation on moral reflective equilibrium.

Finally, assume, as its proponents claim, that the method of reflective equilibrium does lead to correct moral principles. If so, the method would also lead to correct moral principles when applied to legal materials. For although those correct moral principles would not necessarily be consistent with any particular percentage of the primary legal materials—the method would presumably lead to dropping *all* morally misguided legal materials and supplanting them with morally correct notions that might have no legal pedigree—those moral principles *would* be consistent with our considered judgements *about* the primary legal materials.

Thus, reflective equilibrium does not support the use of morally incorrect legal principles.

The arguments from weight and fit are two sides of a single coin. For suppose one were to argue that all possible incorrect principles with all possible weights exist in some Platonic way. Then among those incorrect principles with Platonic existence would be an incorrect principle with a weight such that it would always be outweighed by correct moral principles except in those past cases that were decided inconsistently with correct moral principles. Indeed, that incorrect principle would be the morally best incorrect principle we could choose as well as one with total fit: it would be morally best because it is completely consistent with correct moral principles for all future cases, and it has total fit because it coheres with all past cases. But *that* "incorrect" principle is really identical for all practical purposes to correct moral principles and so is not a counter-example to the claim that incorrect principles do not, for practical purposes, exist in any way that matters. Either legal principles are just (correct) moral principles, or they are nothing.

---

[5]  See John Rawls, "Outline of a Decision Procedure for Ethics" in (1951) 60 *Phil. Rev.* 177; John Rawls, *A Theory of Justice* (1971), pp. 14–21 (esp. 19–21), 43–53, 578–82; Norman Daniels, "Wide Reflective Equilibrium, and Theory Acceptance" in (1979) 76 *J. Phil.* 256.

[6]  See Dworkin, *supra*, n. 77, pp. 159–166.

## D. Legal Principles and Agreement Among Competent Practitioners

One final objection to our case against legal principles goes as follows: Legal principles, like legal rules, are established through the practices and conventions of competent professionals. In cases where legal rules do not determine the results, those practices and conventions establish the governing legal principles and their weights. Legal principles and their weights are whatever competent practitioners would agree they were.[7]

We have several responses to this objection. First, the objection implies that when competent practitioners disagree about legal principles and their weights, there are no legal principles about which to agree or disagree. If legal principles and their weights are completely determined by professionals' conventions, then the absence of convention means the absence of legal principle. Professionals could never meaningfully disagree about what the legal principles are.[8]

When professionals do agree, however, they could be agreeing about legal principles, as this argument we are constructing has it, or they could be agreeing about moral principles and establishing a higher-order legal rule to govern the case based on those moral principles. How would we tell whether, when professionals agree about a case not determined by legal rules, they are agreeing about legal principles or establishing a higher-order legal rule based on their moral principles? We submit that so long as agreement is what constitutes legal principles and their weights, we will never be able to distinguish legal principles from higher-order legal rules. The argument from convention does not support legal principles.[9]

The argument we have just made against agreement among competent practitioners as establishing legal principles assumes that what practitioners are agreeing about is how particular cases ought to be resolved. At that level, we have argued, legal principles cannot be distinguished from higher-order legal rules. Suppose, however, it is argued that the objects of these agreements are not particular outcomes but are legal principles themselves (and their weights). In other words, what establishes legal principles just *is* agreement among competent practitioners about what those legal principles are.

This position has two variants, neither of which is tenable. On one, the practitioners *posit* the legal principles through their agreement. As we have already noted, however, legal principles cannot be posited.

The alternative is to argue that it is the practitioners' agreement about what the legal principles *are* that establishes them. This alternative, however, involves fatal self-reference. If the agreement establishes legal principles, how can the practitioners agree *about* legal principles?

---

[7] Owen Fiss, "Objectivity and Interpretation" in (1982) 34 *Stan. L. Rev.* 739, Dworkin, *Law's Empire*, Chap. 3 (discussing conventionalism).

[8] Conventionalist theories not requiring agreement or near agreement have been advocated in recent years. See *e.g.* Steven J. Burton, *An Introduction to Law and Legal Reasoning* (1985) (law is the coherent reconstruction of the practices and dispositions of the legal community); We have serious doubts that conventionalism can ever dispense with agreement. In any event, against these conventionalist theories, we would urge the normative superiority of following correct moral principles rather than conventional legal principles. We do not mean to imply that *moral* principles are not, at some deep level, matters of agreement. See Jurgen Habermas, *Legitimation Crisis* (1973); Rawls, *A Theory of Justice*, pp. 11–17. Legal principles that were matters of agreement at *that* level would be identical to (correct) moral principles. Therefore, if legal principles are distinct from correct moral principles, they must be so at a more superficial level; and at that level, disagreement undermines their existence.

[9] Dworkin would agree with us on this point. See Dworkin, *supra*, n. 77, pp. 120–139.

### E. Is There a Moral Argument for Extending Past Decisions Into the Future?

To this point we have argued that Dworkinian legal principles, which correspond to the reconstructive method of common law reasoning, represent an unattractive response to past mistaken decisions.

(1) Legal principles produce results different from those which correct moral principles produce.

(2) Legal principles do not have the indirect consequentialist virtues of determinate rules, which, though capable of producing morally incorrect results in particular applications, may produce on balance more morally correct results overall.

(3) Legal principles are not required for treating present and past litigants "equally"; the correct conception of equality is internal to correct moral theory and can never require departure from that theory.

(4) Legal principles produce retroactivity in the law.

(5) If legal principles differ from correct moral principles, the weight of legal principles will be indeterminate, which means the principles themselves will be indeterminate. Reconstructive methodology cannot yield determinate weight, nor can weight be posited or a matter of agreement.

(6) The method by which legal principles are derived requires fit. Fit is neither sufficient by itself to yield legal principles (because an indefinite number of different principles can fit any set of legal materials, no matter how extensive), nor is fit capable of constraining its necessary complement of moral acceptability. The best incorrect principles that fit past mistakes are morally correct principles with exceptions corresponding precisely to those mistakes. Such incorrect principles will be the practical equivalents of correct principles. Legal principles correctly derived will thus always collapse into moral principles.

(7) Legal methodology requires only posited legal materials and correct moral principles. In Dworkin's terms, it requires "pragmatism", though a pragmatism that shows a proper regard for the rule-of-law values of conventions. Legal principles will be either otiose (if they behave no differently from correct moral principles) or morally pernicious.

One consequence of our argument is that there is no reason to extend past morally incorrect decisions into the future by departing from correct moral principles. That is not to say that past morally incorrect decisions leave no traces, such as rules, reliance, and so forth. It is rather to say that morally correct decisions in the present will take proper account of the traces of past incorrect decisions.

The case for legal principles requires, therefore, an argument for *abandoning* correct moral principles in the present when they conflict with legal principles, not merely an argument that correct moral principles heed the past and its traces. We shall assume, contrary to points (5) and (6) above, that legal principles can be derived that have determinate weight and yet do not collapse into correct moral principles. What is the argument *for* them, given the powerful arguments against them?

In this section we will explicate and respond to the most powerful argument of this kind we know of: Dworkin's claim in *Law's Empire* that we must follow the past in the sense that our current governmental acts must manifest integrity.

Before we describe and criticize in detail Dworkin's argument that integrity is necessary for the associational bonds required for obligation and legitimacy, we wish to remark briefly on some connotations and implications of the term "integrity".

Dworkin obtains a patina of legitimacy by calling his theory "law as integrity", yet his opponents' "pragmatism" and "conventionalism". He also receives an unfair rhetorical advantage from illegitimately extending the analogy of integrity as a personal virtue to integrity as an institutional virtue. That is to say, integrity is a virtue in a person who acts consistently according to some set of principles.

Yet for Dworkin, integrity as an *institutional virtue* does not entail that the government act on the basis of consistent principles or motivations. Rather, integrity is a virtue of institutions in so far as the *interpreter* can imaginatively reconstruct or interpret the institutional history to reflect a set of principles, even if the governmental actors whose acts constitute the institutional practices acted from very different principles or motivations. Thus it may be that one governmental actor acted on the basis of right-wing motivations, another on the basis of moderate motivations, and a third from left-wing motivations. Nevertheless, all three acts can be said to display integrity if the interpreter can reinterpret those three acts as all flowing from a consistent set of principles which fit the acts reasonably well. This concern might be thought exaggerated, because one aspect of fit is fitting the justifications given by the governmental actors. But while that is one aspect of fit, it need not be the most important, and it appears that for Dworkin it is not a crucial or necessary aspect of fit.

In the personal realm, in contrast, an actor would not be said to be displaying integrity if his acts were motivated by very different sets of principles, even if they could be reconstructed so as to be seen to flow from a single set of principles. Thus, Dworkin obtains an unfair rhetorical advantage by the use of the term "integrity" when he transfers it from the personal to the institutional realm.

More importantly, "integrity" in its ordinary usage requires a natural law interpretation of pragmatism. We shall establish this claim in four stages.

First, integrity as a personal virtue surely requires—with a caveat to be discussed later—consistency in its underlying justifications. We would not call someone a person of integrity if some of her acts were based upon one set of principles and others were built upon inconsistent principles and still others were performed without justification at all (if that is possible). Moreover, the term "integrity" can only be applied to actors whose justifications, rationales, or motivations are intelligible to us. Thirdly, it appears that integrity requires not only consistent application of some set of principles but also that the set of principles is within some range of principles that are thought plausible. If the principles are thought silly, or worse yet incoherent, we would not call a person who follows them a person of integrity.

Finally, and most controversially, yet most importantly, a person who acts on the basis of one set of justifications while agreeing that a better justificatory scheme is available does not display integrity. Integrity demands not only action consistent with a set of principles, but also action based on the set of principles which one believes to be best. So, for example, an individual who has consistently followed principles of nepotism and becomes convinced that equal opportunity is preferable would lack integrity if he continued to follow nepotistic principles. Suppose he were to say: "You have now convinced me that equal opportunity is morally preferable to nepotism. Yet, I am a person of integrity. In order to maintain my integrity, I will continue to act on nepotistic justifications, even though I now agree that equality of opportunity is superior as a matter of morality and justice." Surely such a person lacks integrity. Integrity requires that one act on the basis of the principles which one believes to be best. Put differently, integrity entails natural law, that one act on correct moral principles.

[pp. 292–311]

# 9

# SOCIOLOGICAL JURISPRUDENCE AND THE SOCIOLOGY OF LAW

## INTRODUCTION

One of the most characteristic features of the twentieth-century jurisprudence was the development of sociological approaches to law.[1] The social sciences had an influence almost comparable to that of religions in earlier periods. Legal thought has tended to reflect the trends to be found in sociology. So long as functionalist, consensus-oriented approaches dominated the scene in sociology, sociological jurisprudence mirrored this prevailing paradigm. Roscoe Pound, the most influential of sociological jurists, was the leading representative of this approach. When conflict theories tended to dominate the sociological stage these we reflected in legal thinking too.

This is one of the reasons why it is difficult to identify a central proposition of sociological jurisprudence. Nevertheless, one can pinpoint a number of ideas in the thinking of those who adopt a sociological approach to the legal order. There is a belief in the non-uniqueness of law: a vision of law as but one method of social control.[2] There is a also a rejection of a "jurisprudence of concepts", the view of law as a closed logical order. The shortcomings of formal, logical analysis were noticed as new problems emerge for which existing law did not provide solutions.[3] Further, sociological jurists tend to be sceptical of the rules presented in the textbooks and concerned to see what really happens, "the law in action".[4] Sociological jurists also tend to espouse relativism. They reject the belief of naturalism that an ultimate theory of values can be found:[5] they see reality as socially constructed[6] with no natural guide to the solution of many conflicts. Sociological jurists believe also in the

---

[1] See R. Cotterrell (1998) 25 J. L. S. 171.

[2] See Ehrlich, *post*, 847. See also Packer, *The Limits of the Criminal Sanction* (1968); Black, *The Behavior of Law* (1976), Chap. 6.

[3] On the Continent it was Gény who drew attention to this in the context of the codes.

[4] So do the American Realists, *post*, 1013 and Critical Legal Theorists, *post*, Chap. 14.

[5] See Pound, *Interpretations of Legal History* (1923), Chap. 7; *cf.* Stammler's view of "natural law with a variable content", (*ante*, 87).

[6] *Cf.* Berger and Luckmann, *The Social Construction of Reality* (1966). See the discussion of this in relation to Critical Legal Studies, *post*, 1220. See also I. Hacking. *The Social Construction of What?* (1999).

importance of harnessing the techniques of the social sciences, as well as the knowledge culled from sociological research, towards the erection of a more effective science of law. Lastly, there is an abiding concern with social justice, though in what this consists, and how it is to be attained, views differ. Does law, for example, function as an instrument outside particular interests in some neutral way, as Pound thought, or is it the result of the operation of interests, as contemporary conflict jurists argue?[7] Upon the answer to this question much depends, including whether law can be used for the purposes of social engineering and, if so, to what effect.

It depends upon how one defines sociological jurisprudence as to how far back it goes. Hume, who provides one of the intellectual foundations of positivism, wrote of law as a developing social institution which owed its origin not to man's nature but to social convention.[8] Vico too rejected the fixed concept of human nature which had characterised social thought since Aristotle. In *The New Science* he argued that human society was historical, social institutions and human relationships are the product of action.[9] Montesquieu argued that law was the product of numerous factors, for example local manners, custom, physical environment: a good law, he maintained, conformed to the spirit of society.[10] The historical school of jurisprudence emphasised the dynamics of legal development and showed how law was closely related to its social context.[11] The contribution of Hegel, the first thinker to separate the state from civil society should also not be overlooked.[12] All of these have contributed to the growth of sociological jurisprudence. More significant, however, are Comte and the great sociologists, Weber and Durkheim. Nor should the contribution of Marx[13] be underestimated.

## COMTE AND SOCIOLOGY

The first serious attempt to apply the scientific method to social phenomena was made by Auguste Comte (1798–1857), who invented the

---

[7] See Quinney, *The Social Reality of Crime* (1970) and W. Chambliss and R. Seidman, *Law, Order and Power* (2nd ed., 1982).

[8] See his *Treatise on Human Nature* (1740). On Hume *cf. ante*, 114–116.

[9] Published in 1744. It is available in an English translation (T.G. Bergin and M.H. Frisch, eds., 1948). See also *ante*, 114. On Vico, see R. Brown, *The Nature of Social Laws* (1984), Chap. 6.

[10] See *The Spirit of the Laws* (1748). See *ante*, 114.

[11] Stone says of this that it "not only led the jurists towards the promised land; it also reduced the main forts of its existing occupants. It played the role of Moses, and, in part at least, of Joshua as well. But it was not to be under its own banner [*i.e.* the *Volksgeist*, *post*.] that the promised land was to be conquered and occupied (*Social Dimensions of Law*, p. 36).

[12] R. Fine and R. Vázquez in (ed.) M. Freeman, *Law and Sociology* (2006), p. 241.

[13] *Post*, Chap. 13.

term "sociology".[14] This was part of the powerful emphasis in the nineteenth century on science as the royal road to progress. Comte urged that there are four means of social investigation, namely, observation, experiment, comparison, and the historical method; and that it is the last which is specific to sociology. The data of this latter method were to be taken from observation and tested against the known laws of human nature.[15] This involved some advance on Bentham who confined his attention to the laws of human nature as a foundation of social science to the virtual neglect of history. John Stuart Mill at any rate so regarded it, and considered that, by means of this method, empirical generalisations could attain the status of laws and sociology thus become a science.

Unfortunately, Comte did not remain true to his own scientific approach, and in his later years deserted the empirical method for sweeping *a priori* affirmations, such as his view that there were invariable natural laws operating in the field of social activity. He laid down that mankind inevitably passes through three stages, *viz.*, the theological (where phenomena are explained in terms of superior beings), the metaphysical (where abstract entities like nature are held responsible) and the scientific or positive (at which stage man is content to observe phenomena). Such was his final dogmatism that he was led to formulate an authoritarian concept of the character of "positive society", and also to put forward a new Religion of Humanity, with an elaborate ritual aimed at achieving an effective means of social cohesion.[16]

## LAISSEZ FAIRE AND HERBERT SPENCER

The dissemination of the Darwinian evolutionary theory of natural selection gave a further impetus to this development, and enabled it to be linked with the ideology of laissez faire in economic and social affairs. Thus, for Herbert Spencer (1820–1903), evolution was the key to the understanding of human progress and legal and social development could best be left to evolve by a natural selection like biology.[17] Such a conclusion was regarded as scientific and not to be confused with the unscientific historicism derived from Herder or Hegel.[18]

[14] It is no longer thought, as it once was, that Comte was the founder of sociology, any more than Bentham by coining the words "international law" and "codification" founded respectively that discipline or that method. See W. Runciman, *Sociology in its Place* (1970), p. 1. M. Pickering, *Auguste Comte* (1993) situates his life and thought.

[15] According to Comte: "No real observation is possible except in as far as it is first directed, and finally interpreted, by some theory". He saw observation and laws as "indispensably connected" (*The Positive Philosophy* (English ed., 1896), vol. II, p. 243). On Comte's relation with 19th century statistics and social surveys, P. Halfpenny, *Positivism and Sociology* (1982) is useful.

[16] N. Timasheff, *An Introduction to the Sociology of Law* (1939), p. 45 claimed that the discipline of sociology "was born in the state of hostility to law".

[17] Hence the state existed only to further individual freedom: Comte, on the other hand, favoured a highly collectivist programme.

[18] *Cf. post*, 1077–1078.

Laissez faire was both an economic theory and a philosophy of action. Spencer's contribution was to apply the organic evolutionary idea in relation to society. He believed that by the great process of biological evolution, social evolution would arise as part of an automatic and independent process. Contrary to Bentham, Spencer desired to impress upon society the very small part that conscious direction could hope to achieve in altering the process of social evolution. Spencer failed to perceive the direction in which society was moving.[19] Spencer's opposition to social engineering is grounded in his concept of society. He defined this as a "thing" which grows, evolving from small "aggregations" so simple "in structure as to be considered structureless" in which there is "scarcely any mutual dependence of parts", to complex, differentiated structures in which the separate parts acquire mutual and functional dependence: society is a structure characterised by co-operation between parts and whole. The disturbance of this consensus undermines the equilibrium of the whole system. An example would be government interference with the workings of social or economic life.

## JHERING (1818–1892)

Jhering, by contrast with Bentham, placed great emphasis on the function of law as an instrument for serving the needs of human society.[20] In society there is an inevitable conflict between social interests and each individual's selfish interests. To reconcile this conflict the state employs both the method of reward, by enabling economic wants to be satisfied, and the method of coercion. There may be unorganised coercion,[21] as in the case of social conventions or etiquette, but law is specifically that form of coercion which is organised by the state. Jhering did not deny the existence of altruistic impulses, but recognised that these would not suffice without the coercive form of social control provided by law. The success of the legal process was to be measured by the degree to which it achieved a proper balance between competing social and individual interests. Jhering, however, gave very little indication of a scale of values with which to achieve this balance.[22]

---

[19] Spencer is, however, coming back into fashion. Donald Macrae (see his introduction to *The Man versus The State* (1969) attributes this to a backlash against the increasing power of the bureaucracy and "over-criminalisation" of the citizen by constant addition of regulative offences. And *cf.* the ideas of Nozick, *ante*, 595, 656.

[20] Bentham, despite his enthusiasm for law reform, remained a supporter of laissez faire, being wedded to the idea that once the legal system was overhauled and renovated, there would be little need for further legislative interference. Even so in his final blueprint (the *Constitutional Code* (1830)) there is provision for ministers of health, education, social security and transport (see R. Harrison, *Bentham* (1983), pp. 258–260). Instrumentalism is discussed fully by B. Tamanaha, *Law as a Means to an End* (2006).

[21] See M. Friedland, *Sanctions and Rewards in the Legal System* (1989).

[22] On Jhering see N. Duxbury (2007) 27 Ox. J.L.S. 23, who questions whether he was an interest theorist.

## Max Weber (1864–1920)

Further impetus was given to exploring the sociological foundations of law by Weber, Durkheim and Ehrlich. Weber was the first to develop a systematic sociology of law.[23] More than that, he was the first to see the sociology of law as central to sociological theory. His training was as a lawyer. His earliest writings resemble those of the German Historical School.[24] He later reacted against this. His primary concern was to understand the development and characteristics of Western society, the most distinctive feature of which in its developed form was capitalism. This led him in two directions: first, into historical and comparative studies of the world's major civilisations; secondly, into studies of the origins of capitalist development and "rationalism". The existence of rational legal order is a critical feature of capitalist society.

Weber emphasised the peculiarly "rational" quality of legal institutions in modern Western societies. He saw law[25] as passing through stages ranging from charismatic legal revelation through what he called "law prophets" to a "systematic elaboration of law and professionalised administration of justice by persons who have received their legal training in a learned and formally logical manner".[26] He did not suggest any evolutionary sequence: his stages were "ideal types" and "elements from each ... can be found in ancient as well as in modern legal practice, as Weber showed by a profusion of illustrations".[27]

This applies also to Weber's ideas concerning types of irrationality and rationality that characterise legal systems.[28] Legal irrationality, that is a failure to be guided by general rules, may be *formal*, as where decisions are determined by means beyond the control of reasoning (*e.g.* trial by ordeal or oracle), or *substantive*, where the decision-maker is guided only by reaction to the individual case (Weber thought this was exemplified by the cadi in the Moslem market-place, and some believe that "jury equity" can be similarly described). A legal system exhibited *substantive* rationality when it was guided by principles albeit of an ideological system other than that of the law itself, for example religion or justice. Such legal systems lacked the restraints of procedural formality and the sort of

---

[23] On Weber see R. Bendix, *Max Weber: An Intellectual Portrait* (1960). On his sociology of law, A. Hunt, *The Sociological Movement in Law* (1978), Chap. 5 is useful, as is A. Kronman, *Max Weber* (1983), which situates his sociology of law within his philosophy. See also R. Cotterrell, *Law's Community* (1995), Chap. 7 and W. T. Murphy, *The Oldest Social Science?* (1997), Chap. 2. A powerful critique of Weber is H. Berman (1987) 65 Washington University L.Q. 758.

[24] *Cf. post,* 1079 *et seq.*

[25] Weber's definition of law is Austinian. See S. Stoljar in *Studies in the Sociology of Law* (G. Sawer, ed.) (1961), p. 33. *cf.* A. Kronman, *Max Weber* (1983), pp. 28–31.

[26] M. Weber, *Law and Economy in Society* (M. Rheinstein, ed.) (1954).

[27] *Per* Bendix, *op. cit.,* p. 388. Berman, n. 19, above, emphasises that there are many important things the method of "ideal types" cannot grasp.

[28] But Weber's thesis fails to capture the huge diversity of regulatory practices of contemporary law and governance: see (2002) 29 (1) Journal of Law and Society 1–225 (Special Issue).

consistency that we associate with a system of judicial precedent. It attained *formal*, logical rationality when its rules were expressed by the use of abstract concepts created by legal thought itself and conceived of as constituting a complete system. Such legal systems, Weber claimed, were unique to modern Western civilisation. Formal rationality must be considered a leading characteristic of modern legal systems.[29]

Weber is concerned to discover how and why this process of rationalisation developed. Rational law is a product of the rationalism of Western culture. But what is this? Weber's own analysis is far from precise but in general he attributes the growth of "occidental rationalisation of law"[30] to developing bourgeois interests and the interests of absolutist states. But he rejects any suggestion that there is any specifically economic causation.[31] He also rejected the view that the reception of Roman law had played any part in the development of capitalism. In Weber's view, the most significant development was the growth of bureaucracy. Only this "has established the foundation for the administration of a rational law conceptually systematised".[32] Other factors also played a part. Weber stresses the contribution of legal professionals. Thus, for example, he saw English lawyers with a vested interest in retaining archaic formalistic features as the major impediment to rationalisation. England caused Weber acute problems.[33]

Another causal factor is the significance attached to natural law. Weber saw natural law in its revolutionary, rather than reactionary, guise.[34] Its role was to legitimate legal change and as such is a necessary factor in the rationalisation of law. It was, Weber thought, the absence of natural law which impeded the progress to rationalisation of both Chinese and Judaic law.[35]

Weber's discussion of the relationship between law and capitalism is interesting both in its own right and in relation to Marxism. Unlike Marx, Weber was not prepared to explain law as in any way "determined" by economic forces.[36] Law was relatively autonomous.[37] Though influenced by economic forces, it also influenced economic and other processes in society. "Economic situations", Weber wrote, "do not automatically give birth to new legal forms; they merely provide the

---

[29] Epitomised for Weber in the conceptual jurisprudence of the German Pandectists and the continental codes. As a sociologist Weber believed that his role was not to judge legal systems or their rules but only to understand them.

[30] *The Religion of China* (1951), p. 149.

[31] *Cf.* Marx's view. Weber was one of the earliest critics of Marx, and note Trubek's sharp comment that Weber avoided "the oversimplifications found in both the liberal and the Marxist accounts of law in his time, and, to some extent, in ours" ((1985) 37 Stanford Law Rev. 919, 922).

[32] *Economy and Society* (G. Roth and C. Witrich, eds.), p. 975.

[33] As to which see, *post*, 841–842.

[34] *Cf. ante*, 83.

[35] See *The Religion of China*, pp. 147–150.

[36] *Cf. post*, 1135, 1167.

[37] On relative autonomy see R. Miliband, *Marxism and Politics* (1977).

opportunity for the spread of legal technique if it is invented".[38] Though law is not determined by economic forces, it is perceived by Weber as being "crucially related"[39] to them. For example, Weber showed how modern rational capitalism needed not just a technical means of production but also a "calculable legal system".[40] The modern capitalist enterprise "rests primarily on *calculation* and presupposes a legal and administrative system, whose functioning can be rationally predicted".[41]

England was an enigma for Weber. It provided him with some proof of the non-determinant role of economic factors in the development of law (it was after all the first country to produce modern capitalism). On the other hand it did so with a legal system which fell far short of attaining formal rationality. How then is the English example to be explained: as an exception? If so, how is the exception to be explained? More generally, the question must be raised as to whether failure to fit England into his general thesis casts doubts on the validity of the Weberian thesis. Weber's comments on English law and institutions are interesting in themselves. He saw our methods of proof as "irrational". This applied to jury trial, the system of lay magistracy, the adversary system as well as the system of precedent. He also saw precedent as having undergone a profound change. A process of internal rationalisation had taken place. From "empirical justice" (or substantive irrationality) the system has moved (Weber does not explain how) to one where rational grounds come to be expected and general rules and principles develop. The result is a system based on general and abstract rules. So great has the change become that critics of the common law system, such as the American Realists,[42] could denigrate as formalism or a jurisprudence of concepts the belief that the system was logically complete, gapless and ready to apply to any given factual situation.

England, to quote Weber, "achieved capitalistic supremacy ... not because of but rather in spite of its judicial system".[43] If this seems to cast doubt on Weber's general theory of the inter-relationship between law and capitalism, he seeks to turn "this apparent contradiction to the advantage of his general theoretical position".[44] What would be fatal to a uni-causal theory is grist to Weber's multi-causal mill of history. It enables him to argue that the relationship he sets up between capitalism and rational law is "but one example and at the same time to be prepared to explain empirical departures" from this "posited general relationship

---

[38] *Law and Economy*, p. 131.
[39] Per A. Hunt, *The Sociological Movement in Law* (1978), p. 120.
[40] *The Protestant Ethic and the Spirit of Capitalism* (1930), p. 25.
[41] *Economy and Society*, p. 1394.
[42] *Post*, Chap. 10.
[43] *Law and Economy*, p. 231. Cf also Renner, *post*, 979, 1023. On Weber and the "England problem" see A. Kronman, *Max Weber* (1983), pp. 120–24. Ewing ((1987) 21 Law and Soc. Rev. 487) rejects the idea of the "England problem". She argues that Weber actually identified formal justice and guaranteed rights as the features of modern law that directly facilitated the rise of capitalism.
[44] Per A. Hunt, *op. cit.*, n. 39, p. 125. *cf.* D. Trubek (1972) 82 Yale L.J. 3.

by reference to specific conjunctures of other causal variables".[45] What starts as a threat to Weber's overall position ends as a strengthening of his pluralistic, multi-variate analysis. It should also be added that Weber was only defining the ideal-type of capitalistic law.

Weber was also interested in why people believed they had an obligation to obey the law. There were, he explained, different models of legitimate domination: the traditional, the charismatic, and the legal-rational. In the first, legitimacy is claimed for, and believed in by the sanctity of old unquestioned rules and powers. In the second, it vests in a leader, a Jesus or (unfortunately) a Hitler. The contrast between traditional and charismatic domination is brought out well in Jesus's statement: "It is written, but I say unto you". The third (legal-rational domination) rests on a belief in the legality of enacted rules and the right of those who have authority under such rules to issue commands. It is the third type of domination that particularly interests Weber. In the first two forms, authority vests in persons. But in the third, typified by the modern bureaucratic state, it resides in rules. The characteristic feature of legal-rational authority is formalistic impersonality: officials exercise their duties "without hatred or passion, and hence without affection or enthusiasm ... without regard to personal considerations".[46] Weber offers important insights into the relationship between law and domination, but domination cannot be explained in this simple reductionist way.

Weber is the most influential of sociologists. But how well do his categories serve those who study law and society today? One problem that concerns legal sociologists is the limits of the law? They want to know why anti-discrimination law[47] or rent control legislation[48] are less successful than their proposers intend. Does Weber's theory throw any light on this? He would suggest that laws would fail where the legal system was insufficiently autonomous or legal reasoning insufficiently legalistic. Can problems like racial discrimination be tackled by more narrowly drawn rules? To take a second example, the twentieth-century was characterised by an interventionist welfare state. The rules of such a system tend to be characterised by looseness and the emphasis is on discretion.[49] Weber's theory is incapable of embracing welfare state concepts. It seems irreversibly committed to a model of capitalism tied to laissez-faire economics.

---

[45] *ibid.*
[46] *Economy and Society*, n. 32 above, p. 225.
[47] See N. Glazer and K. Young, *Ethnic Pluralism and Public Policy* (1983).
[48] See D. Nelken, *The Limits of the Legal Process* (1983). But a study by Savelsberg of economic crime in West Germany supports Weber's central predictions ((1987) 21 Law and Soc. Rev. 525).
[49] *Cf.* Z. Bankowski and D. Nelken, "Discretion as a Social Problem" in *Discretion and Welfare* (S. Asquith and M. Adler, eds.) (1981), pp. 247–269. And see S. Feldman's article showing that Weber's insights can be applied to modern constitutional law questions: (1992) 16 Law and Social Inquiry 205.

## Emile Durkheim (1858–1917)

Durkheim, the great French sociologist, is another of the major figures of sociology to have taken a considerable interest in legal phenomena.[50] He was one of the earliest thinkers about the criminal process[51]: he wrote on punishment,[52] on the law of contract[53] and notably in *The Division of Labour in Society*, developed a typology of the evolution of the law which has had a profound influence on subsequent sociological and anthropological thought.

It was Durkheim's thesis that law was the measuring rod of any society. Law, he thought, "reproduces the principal forms of social solidarity".[54] According to Durkheim there are two basic types of societal cohesion (what he called solidarity): *mechanical* solidarity to be found in homogeneous societies and *organic* solidarity which was found in more heterogenous and differentiated modern societies which rest on functional inter-dependence produced by the division of labour. Linked to these forms of integration are two types of law *viz.*, repressive and restitutive. In a society based on mechanical solidarity law is essentially penal. With increased differentiation societal reaction to crime becomes a less significant feature of the legal system, and restitutive sanction becomes the main way of resolving disputes.

Durkheim's typology is rooted in *a priori* thinking and empirical data have cast doubt on it.[55] His assertion that small-scale societies lack a division of labour has been shown by anthropologists since Malinowski[56] to be over-simple. Schwartz and Miller found that "police are found only in association with a substantial degree of division of labour" while restitutive sanctions, damages and mediation exist in many societies which "lack even rudimentary specialisation".[57] According to Hunt "the rise of repressive law can be associated with the emergence of social stratification and state forms after earlier pre-state stages of development

---

[50] On Durkheim generally see Lukes, *Emile Durkheim* (1973). This pays little attention to Durkheim's legal thought. See Chap. 13. *cf.* Alpert, *Emile Durkheim and His Sociology* (1961) which does. And see S. Lukes and A Scull, *Durkheim and the Law* (1983) and F. Pearce, *The Radical Durkheim* (1989). See also R. Cotterrell, *Law's Community* (1995), Chap. 9 and R. Cotterrell, *Emile Durkheim: Law in a Moral Domain* (1999).

[51] See Taylor, Walton and Young, *The New Criminology* (1973), Chap 3. And in S. Lukes and A. Scull, Chap. 4.

[52] "Two Laws of Penal Evolution" (1973) 2 Econ. & Society 278.

[53] *Professional Ethics and Civic Morals* (1957). And in S. Lukes and A. Scull, Chap. 8. Durkheim's ideas were developed by G. Davy: see G. MacCormack (1980) 15 Irish Jurist 166.

[54] *The Division of Labour in Society* (1984), p. 68. According to Schluchter (2003) 19 European Sociological Review 537, 538, for Durkheim "Sociology is first of all a comparative sociology of law".

[55] See, generally, Diamond, *Primitive Law, Past and Present* (1972), and S. Moore, *Law as Process* (1987) and see now J. Gibbs (2003) 21 *Sociological Theory* 103.

[56] *See ante*, 324.

[57] (1964) 70 Am. J. Sociol. 159. Though Baxi (1974) 8 Law and Soc. Rev. 645 is critical of Schwartz and Miller's methodology. But Spitzer (1975) 9 Law and Soc. Rev. 613 and Wimberley (1973) 79 Am. J. Sociol. 78 come to similar conclusions to Schwartz and Miller.

which exhibit predominantly non-repressive forms of social regulation".[58] The majority of societies from which Durkheim took his data were not primitive at all but rather the ancient societies of Greece, Rome and Egypt. Durkheim, however, neglects the concept of the state.[59]

Recent opinion suggests, contrary to Durkheim's hypothesis, that repressive law diminishes in importance as we move away from modern nation states and that it is almost totally absent in the simplest societies. To Barnes "it is governmental action that is typically repressive".[60] Sheleff[61] claims that Durkheim's use of law as an index of social organisation is justified, but only if we reverse the relationship between types of law and types of solidarity. He notes that Durkheim appeals to Biblical evidence, arguing that in the Pentateuch there are very few non-repressive laws, and even these are not as "foreign to penal law as may appear at first glance, for they all bear the mark of religion".[62] It is, however, possible to see in the five books of Moses a set of religious and moral exhortations devoid of punitive backing plus a legal system embodying the notion of restitution.

The evidence from early modern Europe also undermines Durkheim's thesis. Lenman and Parker,[63] while conceding that there was barbarous punishment of certain crimes, point out that there was composition of others. The composition system was part of the tradition of community law which, in Durkheim's terms, exalted restitutory justice. It developed from the laws of the German tribes which invaded the Roman Empire. "State law", on the other hand, emphasised punitive justice and was "rooted", at least in part, in the legal system of the Empire and its Byzantine successor.[64] They show between the tenth and nineteenth centuries State law gradually displaced community law throughout Europe, very early in England[65] and much later in the Continent with the reception of Roman law. In Anglo-Saxon England, however, "local customary legal systems emphasised the settling of disputes through reconciliation rather than through punishment.[66] This pattern was reversed as the common law of the state replaced the legal systems of local feudal authorities and offences previously treated as civil wrongs were redefined as assaults on the King's peace. At the same time the ambit of the criminal sanction expanded to take in many prohibitions with no basis in customary law. Further, the criminal court became more punitive and "the State's control over the everyday life of its subjects,

---

[58] *The Sociological Movement in Law* (1978), p. 141.
[59] He regards it as important but refuses to analyse why it is important and what interests it serves.
[60] *Man*, vol. 1, pp. 168–169.
[61] (1975) European J. Sociology XVI 29.
[62] *ibid.*
[63] In V.A.C. Gatrell, B. Lenman and G. Parker, *Crime and the Law: The Social History of Crime in Western Europe Since 1500* (1980), p. 11.
[64] *ibid*, p. 44.
[65] From the time of Henry II.
[66] *Per* F. DuBow, quoted in Lukes and Cohen, *op. cit.*, p. 12.

through its machinery of laws, grew ever closer".[67] Lenman and Parker cast doubt also on Durkheim's thesis of the decline of repressive sanctions with the growth of the nineteenth century. "Instead of readjusting social relationships ... the penitentiary sought to reconstruct personalities. Furthermore, the norms for reconstruction were laid down by the state".[68] They note that early modern ecclesiastical tribunals had applied "Christian norms" in a similar way but they looked for a "public reconciliation between parties or individual wrong-doers and the community". The modern state, by contrast, "is at once impersonal and, in theory, infinitely demanding".[69]

Lukes and Scull believe that Durkheim "systematically"[70] underestimated the repressive aspects of modern law, in particular (i) the punitive dimension of civil law (recent trade union legislation and litigation[71] is testimony to this); (ii) the nature of modern criminal law itself, its expansion into new areas with the growth of the regulatory state and the "welfare sanction"[72]: they point out that sometimes such incursions are strengthened by the use of vicarious and thus collective responsibility; (iii) in non-liberal states "such expansion has often embraced individual private life and the economic sphere"[73] (they give as examples the South African pass laws and Communist states' penalties for economic crimes; (iv) "the nature and depth of 'repression' in both civil and criminal law is greater and more complex than may appear on the surface, involving stigmatization and the exclusion of alien elements in a process that can itself be understood in a quasi-Durkheimian manner as a way of reaffirming the collective identity of the group".[74]

To understand the greatest limitations in Durkheim's sociology of law it is necessary to look at his concept of law itself. For Durkheim, law was barely distinguishable from morality. He tended to see the law as derived from and expressive of a society's morality. He wrote of social solidarity as "a wholly moral phenomenon"[75] and saw law as an "external index which symbolised it". There is a close relationship between law and morality, but there are also conflicts between legal and moral rules and, indeed, between different moral principles. Durkheim tended to underestimate conflict. He did not concentrate on moral conflicts or the ways law and morality could come into conflict with each other. Durkheim presents a consensus view of the relationship between law and social

---

[67] *Op. cit.*, n. 63, p. 15.
[68] *ibid*, p. 44. See also M. Foucault, *Discipline and Punish* (1975) and M. Ignatieff, *A Just Measure of Pain* (1978) and in S. Cohen and A. Scull (eds.), *Social Control and the State* (1983).
[69] *ibid*.
[70] *Op. cit.*, p. 13.
[71] See R. Rideout (1997) 50 C.L.P. 361.
[72] See D. Garland (1981) 8 Brit. J. of Law and Soc. 29 and *Punishment and Modern Society* (1990).
[73] *Op. cit.*, p. 14.
[74] *Op. cit.*, n. 51. See E. Goffman, *Stigma* (1964) and in general the writings of the labelling school. (For example, H. Becker, *Outsiders* (1963).)
[75] *Post*, 891.

order which overestimates groupness and fails to explain why dispute-resolving institutions come into existence.[76]

Secondly, Durkheim focused on that part of the law which limits individual's activities, on criminal law and punishment, sanctions and obligations. This is not unreminiscent of the imperative school of jurisprudence. As with Austin,[77] for example, one problem of this is that it precluded any systematic inquiry into the facilitative aspects of law, the law concerned with powers, constituting relationships, defining practices. He recognised the existence of these aspects of law. Indeed, his discussion of contract[78] is both pertinent and prescient of twentieth-century developments. He shows how individual action is increasingly permeated by "contractual solidarity": the importance of contract increases with a division of labour. His argument is that contracts become more and more just until they move into the realm of "social equity".[79] He thought that "just contract" required that private ownership should not be misused: he was opposed to fixed rights of inheritance because, as he saw it, they conflicted with contractual solidarity. Twentieth-century developments have vindicated his ideas on contract. We have seen vast inroads on freedom of contract.[80]

Thirdly, and curiously for a legal sociologist, Durkheim has little understanding of legal processes, of how law is made, applied, enforced. He analyses "society" and its legal rules. He gives scant attention to the legal profession,[81] the police, the courts. He recognises, of course, the existence of state officials but he sees them as carrying out collective moral sentiments. These "interpreters" are "appliers"[82]: they add nothing as they translate "social representations" into law. This enables Durkheim to ignore questions about power, conflict of interests, the role of professions, bureaucracy and countless other questions which are central to contemporary sociologists of law.[83] The importance of Durkheim clearly lies rather more in opening up speculation about the relationship between law and social order than in the answers that he himself suggests.[84]

---

[76] See the discussion of consensus, *post*, 852–854.

[77] *Ante*, 267.

[78] See S. Lukes and A. Scull, *Durkheim and The Law* (1983), Chap. 8.

[79] *ibid.*

[80] In such fields as landlord and tenant, employment and consumer protection. On "just contracts" note the increasing tendency to refer to relative bargaining strength in legislation (*e.g.* Supply of Goods (Implied Terms) Act 1973; Unfair Contract Terms Act 1977). See also G. Gilmore, *The Death of Contract* (1974) and M. Trebilcock, *The Limits of Freedom of Contract* (1993).

[81] *Cf.* Weber, *ante*, 841.

[82] *Per* D. Garland, "Durkheim's Theory of Punishment: A Critique" in *The Power To Punish* (D. Garland and P. Young, eds.) (1983).

[83] See also the comment of Lukes and Scull, *op. cit.*, n. 78, p. 8: "Durkheim and the Durkheimians closed off most of the questions that have been central to the modern sociology of law, criminology, and the study of deviance".

[84] See also the very useful article by W.P. Vogt, "Obligation and Right: The Durkheimians and the Sociology of Law" in *The Sociological Domain* (P. Besnard ed.) (1983), p. 177.

## Eugen Ehrlich (1862–1922)

Ehrlich was an eminent jurist who was concerned to expound the social basis of law.[85] For him law is derived from social facts and depends not on state authority but on social compulsion. Law differs little from other forms of social compulsion, and the state is merely one among many associations, though it possesses certain characteristic means of compulsion. The real source of law is not statutes or reported cases but the activities of society itself. There is a "living law" underlying the formal rules of the legal system and it is the task of judge and jurist to integrate these two types of law. Commercial law, for instance, as embodied in statutes and cases, involves a constant attempt to try to keep up with commercial usage, for the "centre of legal gravity lies ... in society itself".[86] Hence great emphasis is placed on fact-studies, as against analytical jurisprudence, in exploring the real foundations of legal rules, their scope and meaning and potential development.[87]

In heterogeneous and pluralistic societies there will invariably be more than one living law. Ehrlich believed that the living law should rank in

---

[85] See D. Nelken (2007) 3 International Journal of Law in Context 189 and (2008) 9 Theoretical Inquiries in Law.

[86] E. Ehrlich, *Fundamental Principles of Sociology of Law* (1936), Foreword. Thus, Macaulay has demonstrated that in business conducted between manufacturers in Wisconsin relatively little attention is paid to detailed planning or legal sanctions and that the functions of contract are served by other devices. Two of the most effective norms, which are widely accepted, are the honouring of commitments and the "duty" to produce a good product and stand behind it. Not only is contract law not needed in many situations but its use is thought to have undesirable consequences. For, apart from the delay and possible loss of business, a carefully worked out relationship indicates a lack of trust and blunts the demands of friendship, "turning a co-operative venture into an antagonistic horse trade". There is, furthermore, a resulting loss of flexibility and the exposure to the costs of litigation: ((1963) 28 Am. Sociol. Rev. 55). For a study supporting this see H. Beale and T. Dugdale (1975) 2 Brit.J.Law & Soc. 45, and see also R. Lewis (1982) Brit.J.Law & Soc. 153. See, also, Nussbaum, in *Essays on Jurisprudence from the Columbia Law Review*, p. 184 and the writings of Underhill Moore. Moore "felt that the degree of deviation in the behaviour of the litigants from regular, overt, institutional behaviour provides the crucial index in terms of which decisions could be predicted. The grosser the deviation, the more likely it is that the claims of the deviant litigant will not be judicially allowed. For this reason Moore insisted that the focus of scientific legal analysis should be the comparison of the behaviour of the litigants with patterns of institutional behaviour". (Rumble, *American Legal Realism*, p. 163). A study of banking practices confirmed the hypothesis that the court in fact used as its standard the degree which litigants deviated from the institutional patterns of behaviour. Gross deviations were "not accorded by the court a legal consequence conforming to the institutional consequences which would have followed had the standard device been used" (50 Yale L.J. at p. 1250). See further J.H. Schlegel (1981) 29 Buffalo Law Rev. 195. On Ehrlich and "legal consciousness" see M. Hertogh (2004) 31 Journal of Law and Society 457. See also M. Hertogh, *Rediscovering Ehrlich*.

[87] In addition to this theoretical perspective. Ehrlich was one of the first to undertake empirical surveys to substantiate his thesis. Living in part of the Austro-Hungarian Empire where there were no less than nine different ethnic and religious groups, "he had his students investigate the 'practices and attitudes of nearby communities, using an original but rather primitive personal interview questionnaire.'" (Littlefield (1967) 19 Maine L. Rev. 1, 2). Partridge suggests that Ehrlich may have drawn an overgeneralised conclusion from a culturally diversified society which is not present in a more homogeneous one ((1961) 39 Australian J. of Phil, 201, 217).

order of priority the different claims and demands made upon the law by different people. Further, the legislator or jurist, in adjusting the formal law to match the living law, should balance these demands. He wrote that "when the jurist is asked to draw the line between the conflicting interests independently, he is asked by implication, to do it according to justice ... The catch phrase about balancing of interests[88] that is so successful at the present time is not an answer to this question, for the very question is: What is it that gives weight to the interests that are to be balanced? Manifestly, it is not the balancing jurist, writer or teacher, judge or legislator, but society itself ... Justice does not proceed from the individual, but arises in society".[89]

Ehrlich thus minimises the place of legislation as a formative factor in law, and in some ways may be regarded as a Savigny denuded of Hegelian *mystique*.[90] But there is far more in his approach than this, for he emphasises how law is distilled out of the interplay of social forces. That there is much truth in this viewpoint can hardly be denied. Thus the practices of the commercial world are often found to be embodied gradually in commercial law. Ehrlich recognised, however, that a legal system has an impetus of its own, a professional tradition which may operate for good or ill, and accordingly stressed the need for lawyers and judges to understand the social foundations of legal rules and thereby develop them. So, too, by insisting on the fact that law was not a unique phenomenon, he enabled us to attain a better grasp of those large spheres of activity which are becoming increasingly widespread in the modern state, where autonomous associations apply private "legal systems" of their own almost independently of the ordinary legal process of the courts, as, for instance, in the case of trade or professional associations or trade unions exercising disciplinary powers.[91] Ehrlich might be criticised for failing to appreciate the significant influence that state law has on the shaping and development of living law. Associations are not completely free to generate spontaneous living law. Their actions always take place in the shadow of the law.[92] For the student of jurisprudence perhaps Ehrlich's main failing was his neglect of a criterion by which legal norms could be distinguished from other norms operative in social life. It was

---

[88]  *Cf.* Pound, *post*, 849.
[89]  *Op. cit.*, p. 200. And see *post*, 850.
[90]  *Cf.* note 11 on p. 836, *ante* and *post*, 1079.
[91]  An excellent study which demonstrates this is S. Henry, *Private Justice* (1983). He examines discipline in industry and shows the integral links between private justice and formal law. See also Gurvitch's criticism of Ehrlich: "the law of societies is artificially impoverished by being confined to the spontaneous, as though it did not have its own abstract propositions in autonomous statutes of groups, and its own rules of decision elaborated in the functioning of boards of arbitration and similar bodies" (*Sociology of Law* (1947). pp. 121–122).
[92]  *Cf.* R. Mnookin and L. Kornhauser (1979) Yale L.J. 950 and H. Jacob (1992) 26 Law and Soc. Rev. 565.

the American Realist Felix Cohen who observed that "under Ehrlich's terminology, law itself merges with religion, ethical custom, morality, decorum, tact, fashion and etiquette".[93]

Ehrlich unduly belittled the primary role of legislation in creating new law. He also failed to realise that a grasp of underlying social phenomena may not in itself point the way to appropriate legislative or judicial solutions. The legal process may be invoked as in itself an educative factor.[94]

### ROSCOE POUND (1870–1964)[95]

The sociological approach to law struck a particularly responsive chord in the United States in the early part of the twentieth century. The expansive character of American society, its material wealth, and its devotion to scientific technology, all encouraged the belief that the basic problem was one of adequately controlling and distributing that wealth, and that the solution could best be attained by the application of the developing social sciences to the problems of man in society, just as man's physical environment could be harnessed by the proper use of the physical sciences. Hence, law as a form of social control, to be adequately employed in enabling just claims and desires to be satisfied, must be developed in relation to existing social needs, and must not be chary of relying upon the social sciences in studying the place of law in society, and the means of making it most effective in action.

It is in the writings of Roscoe Pound that the most influential exposition of American sociological jurisprudence is to be encountered.

### Social Engineering

For Pound, jurisprudence is not so much a social science as a technology, and the analogy of engineering is applied to social problems.[96] He is concerned primarily with the effects of law upon society and only to a lesser extent with questions about the social determination of law.[97] Emphasis is laid on the need to accumulate factual information and statistics and to this end Pound put forward a practical programme, in which the establishment of an adequately equipped Ministry of Justice

---

[93] *The Legal Conscience* (1960), p. 187. Ehrlich did suggest that the characteristic feature of the legal norm is that it is, within the group, of great importance, of basic significance" (*op. cit.*, pp. 167–168). But this hardly offers "a reliable distinction between legal and unlegal norms", *per* B. Z. Tamanaha in *Realistic Socio-Legal Theory* (1997), p. 95.

[94] Though doubt has been cast upon this by G. Rosenberg, *The Hollow Hope* (1991).

[95] A good intellectual biography of Pound is Wigdor, *Roscoe Pound: Philosophy of Law* (1974).

[96] For Pound social engineering was "descriptive of a neutral process rather than prescriptive of pragmatic reform. It meant only that law was shaped in accordance with social ends; it did not define particular ends or particular means of attaining them" (per Wigdor, *op. cit.*, p. 230).

[97] *Cf.* Ehrlich's approach *ante*, 847.

looms large. Little attention is paid to conceptual thinking. The creative role of the judiciary, on the other hand, is in the forefront, as is the need for a new legal technique directed to social needs. The call is for a new functional approach to law.

Pound took over Jhering's view of the law as a reconciler of conflicting interests, and gave it certain distinctive features. For Pound the law is an ordering of conduct so as to make the goods of existence and the means of satisfying claims go round as far as possible with the least friction and waste. Pound regards these claims as interests which exist independently of the law and which are "pressing for recognition and security". The law recognises some of these, giving them effect within defined limits. Pound attempted to expound and classify the categories of interests which are thus acknowledged in a modern democratic society. This seems to ignore the extent to which existing law is based on giving effect to vested rights. Further, it has been pointed out by Stone[98] that in an age of mass communication and mass persuasion considerable difficulty may be experienced in distinguishing what are the actual desires of the public or particular groups, in view of the operation of so many organised professional persuaders, both open and hidden. The public as a whole may both lack the means of articulating its desires, or their expression may be manipulated in a variety of ways.

How does Pound locate his interests? Social psychologists might look for basic drives or instincts and initially, this was the approach favoured by Pound. But the inadequacy of this method soon became apparent, for the social psychologists themselves could reach no unanimity on what the basic instincts were, and, further, it was clear that instinctual behaviour could not be eliminated from its environmental source.[99] Sociologists, on the other hand, might undertake empirical research designed to elicit the wants of society. But this too has problems. How should the question be phrased? Should one ask for attitudes or, in an effort to assimilate norms of decision with "living law", should one question behaviour or should one ask for opinions on existing law or frame questions in such a way as to elicit personal "injustices"?[1] And how should one weigh up expressions of wants against the practicalities of legal administration?[2] There are limits to effective legal action.

Pound's own approach was somewhat less fertile. He looks to actual assertions of claims in a particular society, especially as manifested in legal proceedings and legislative proposals, whether accepted or rejected.[3] As to the former, however, it may be said these will depend very much on the state of the law, and the extent to which the costs system may

---

[98] See *Human Law and Human Justice*, pp. 278–279, 282–284.

[99] Pound deferred to Dewey's advice. See, further, Dewey, *Human Nature And Conduct* (1922), Pt. II, secs. V, VI.

[1] *Cf.* Barton and Mendlovitz, *The Experience of Injustice as a Research Problem* (1960) 13 J. Legal Educ. 24.

[2] These questions are suggested by a reading of Cohen, Robson and Bates's *Parental Authority: The Community and the Law* (1958).

[3] See R. Pound, *Jurisprudence*, vol. 3, pp. 287–291.

discourage litigation on doubtful new points. The different way in which the law on privacy has developed in England and in the United States emphasises this distinction.[4] The failure of English law to develop more than a rudimentary corpus of social security case-law is a further example.[5] Patterson,[6] with some justice, has described Pound's catalogue of interests as a rationalisation of the actual. It must also be said that there are interests not only in the sense of what people want but in the sense of what may be good for them regardless of their actual desires. A good deal of social, and almost the whole of penal legislation, may be of this character.[7]

As to Pound's classification of interests, though this purports to be an objective statement of those existing desires which Western society, at least, wishes to protect, there is some force in the contention that it reads rather like a political manifesto in favour of a liberal and capitalist society, as well as suffering from excessive vagueness. Moreover it cannot be suggested that these categories of interests have ever been proved to exist, *de facto*, by scientific research; what they amount to really are no more than common-sense inferences deduced from different branches of the legal system itself, as symbolising the social purposes of the community. And the further question remains, what happens when these so-called interests conflict or, in other words, how do we evaluate them in due order of priority?[8]

## Values

Pound's answer is that every society has certain basic assumptions upon which its ordering rests, though for the most part these may be implicit rather than expressly formulated. Certain of these assumptions may be identified as the jural postulates of the legal system. Pound endeavoured to state what these were for Western society,[9] while recognising that they are not static, but may change as society develops new needs and new tensions. Postulates may indeed conflict,[10] but the success of any particular society will depend on the degree to which it is socially integrated and so accepts as common ground its basic postulates. Whether Pound's jural postulates correctly identified the legal values of twentieth-century

---

[4] See Westin, *Privacy and Freedom* (1967).

[5] Seen by Reich as "the new property" ((1964) 73 Yale L.J. 778).

[6] *Jurisprudence: Men and Ideas of the Law* (1953), p. 518.

[7] A striking example is the Obscene Publications Act 1959 (and, similarly, the Theatres Act 1968). Obscenity can be justified "as being for the *public good*" if it is in the interests of science, literature, art, etc., when it is quite clear that the majority of people would not wish these to be advanced.

[8] Another problem is that interests often cannot be secured unless they are able to depend on values. For example, if one regards racial equality as an interest, it is difficult to see how it can be made to work until integration and non-discrimination are accepted as postulates. See Barry, *Political Argument* (1965), pp. 124–126.

[9] See *post*, 899.

[10] Though none of Pound's do. See, *e.g.* Pound's careful rationalisation of the nascent postulate of "job-security".

America may be doubted. Value judgments may affect our choices and
conduct and should, as Pound urges, be factors which weigh in determining the current of judicial decisions. Also their relative value may be
assessed, as with Utilitarianism, by regard for the consequences, and
though these cannot be exactly predicted, social studies may provide
some clues.

Pound does not give much detailed attention to the way one conflicting
interest is to be compared with another, but he does indicate that if such
an interest is stated in its social aspect then so, too, must the other
interests, for otherwise there will be a built-in bias in favour of the social
as against the private view. Thus, suppose a court is considering whether
a factory, which is operating in a residential area, constitutes a nuisance.
If the court is considering the discomfort inflicted on adjoining residents,
this must be weighed against the individual interest of the factory owner
and not against the social interest of the factory, for instance, the
employment it offers.[11] Some support for this view may be found in the
English nuisance cases which hold that the fact that the defendant factory
owner is a public benefactor is irrelevant. This might have been appropriate in an individualist age, but it seems doubtful how far social
interests ought now to be ignored. Perhaps the appropriate answer is that
private interests should always be balanced one against the other and
then social interests should be evaluated separately, before a final balance
is sought between both types of factor.[12]

## A Consensus Model of Society

Pound sees law as adjusting and reconciling conflicting interests. It is an
instrument which controls interests according to the requirements of the
social order. But there is no doubt that for Pound law represents the
consciousness of the whole society. He sees the law as some "brooding
omnipresence in the sky"[13] operating outside of particular interests.

Pound is describing a society which is homogeneous, static and cohesive, one with shared values and traditions. Whatever society Pound
thought he was describing, it certainly was not the United States, nor, it
may be added, can British society be recognised in this model. A reading
of Platt on the origins of juvenile justice,[14] Gusfield on the temperance
movement and Prohibition,[15] Duster on drugs legislation[16] or Nelken on

[11]  See the Canadian case of *Bottom v. Ontario Leaf Tobacco Co.* [1935] 2 D.L.R. 699;
  another example is *W v. Egdell* [1990] Ch. 359.
[12]  For Pound's view that in "weighing" interests, the comparison must be made "on the
  same plane", whether this be private, public or social, see R. Pound, *Jurisprudence*, vol. 3,
  pp. 328–331 and *cf.* G. Sawer, *Law in Society* (1965), pp. 156–160.
[13]  *Cf.* Holmes, quoted *ante*, 268.
[14]  *The Child Savers* (revised ed., 1977).
[15]  *Symbolic Crusade* (1963).
[16]  *The Legitimisation of Morality* (1970) or P. Bean, *The Social Control of Drugs* (1974).

the Rent Acts[17] will dispel any doubt that laws are the result of a value consensus.

The consensus model long held the stage.[18] Today, however, it may be said that most writing in the sociology of law embraces a conflict paradigm.[19] Quinney has argued that the law consists of the interests of only "specific segments" of the population.[20] It does not represent, as Pound alleged, a compromise of diverse interests but rather supports some at the expense of others. Hills puts it thus: "the exponents of the interest-group approach emphasise the ability of particular groups to shape the legal system to serve their needs and safeguard their particular interests ... power, coercion and constraint rather than the sharing of common values, are the basic organising principles in the interest-group perspective".[21]

The difference between the approaches is basic. Law to Pound is a social force: to Quinney, for example, it is a social product. Even with those laws upon which there is a considerable (if not total) agreement, one may wonder if even these originated in conflict and, if so, how they became the object of consensus subsequently. Not all killing is murder[22] and until recently husbands could not be convicted of raping their wives.[23]

A difficulty with the conflict model is how to explain laws which appear to limit the activities of powerful groups. But it may be said that such laws (for example, factories legislation or anti-trust legislation) are inadequately and ineffectively enforced[24] and that some such legislation which at face would seem to constrain the powerful may in fact be in the interests of the most powerful: thus pollution legislation may be in the interests of large organisations who are thus enabled to knock out small

[17] *The Limits of the Legal Process* (1983).
[18] The views of Durkheim, Ross, Ehrlich and Pound are examples of it. See also Friedmann, *Law In A Changing Society* (1972). A good critique, using Durkheim as the model, is T. Campbell, *Seven Theories of Human Society* (1981), Chap. 7. See generally, the critique in Gouldner, *The Coming Crisis of Western Sociology* (1970).
[19] There is a danger in looking at these two models uncritically which Nelken identifies. He makes the correct observation that it "can lead to the ... error of identifying law so closely with the form of the society that it becomes difficult to examine the special role performed by legal institutions and conceptions as a repository of traditional and cultural meanings" (1982) 9. J.Law & Soc. 177, 184).
[20] *Crime and Justice In Society* (1969), p. 25. In his later writing he has rejected this terminology. Law is now, according to him, "the tool of the ruling class" (*Criminal Justice in America* (1974), p. 10).
[21] *Crime, Power and Morality* (1971), pp. 3–4.
[22] Some acts are labelled as "patriotism".
[23] See *R. v. R.* [1991] 4 All E.R. 481.
[24] See Carson, (1970) 10. B.J. Crim.83; 33 M.L.R. 396 and his study of safety on oil rigs, *The Other Price of Britain's Oil* (1981) and Pearce in Taylor and Taylor, *Politics and Deviance* (1972) and *Crimes of the Powerful* (1976).

competitors.[25] Morals legislation also causes problems for it is normally instigated by economically weak, middle-class crusaders.[26]

Whether the consensus or conflict model is the more accurate can only be determined by empirical research. There has been a considerable amount of this (Hall on theft,[27] Chambliss on vagrancy,[28] Schur on morals offences,[29] Thompson on the "Black Act"[30] are classic examples) and they give substantial support to the conflict model. Of course, class interests are not the only ones which influence the passage of legislation and the influence of professional organisations,[31] and bureaucracies such as governmental agencies[32] themselves *inter alia* play an important part in the passage of legislation.

If law is the outcome of group conflict, it becomes necessary to conceptualise that conflict. Is it better described in terms of a "power élite"[33] or are there many different groups with varying amounts of power, none of which is all-powerful?[34] Sociological jurists differ on this. Quinney, for example, once believed in pluralism[35] and now attempts to identify a ruling class élite.[36] Other writers (Dahrendorf is a notable instance[37]) prefer the more open, pluralistic model of conflict. Once again it is ultimately an empirical question of which view best fits reality.

## SOCIOLOGICAL JURISPRUDENCE SINCE POUND

Pound died in 1964, and, although his writings span sixty years, his seminal influence dates from his writings in the first third of the twentieth

---

[25] *Cf.* Kolko, *Railroads and Regulations 1877–1916* (1965), particularly pp. 144–151. But the legislation in practice may be directed against a different group from that supposed by the legislative entrepreneurs. An excellently-documented example of this is D. Nelken, *The Limits of The Legal Process* (1983). The Rent Acts were directed against "Rachmanism", exploitation and harassment of tenants by commercial landlords. The majority of those prosecuted were working-class home-owners involved in complex "domestic" disputes with their tenants.

[26] Becker, *Outsiders* (1963) describes them as "moral entrepreneurs".

[27] *Theft, Law and Society* (1952), Chap. 1.

[28] (1964) 12 *Social Problems* 67.

[29] *Crimes without Victims* (1965).

[30] *Whigs and Hunters* (1975). See also Hay *et al., Albion's Fatal Tree* (1975).

[31] Akers, 3 Law & Soc.Rev. 463; Roby, 17 *Social Problems* 83; Greenwood and Young, *Abortion in Demand* (1976).

[32] Becker, *Outsiders* (1963); Lindesmith, *The Addict and the Law* (1967); Dickson, 16 *Social Problems* 143. But for the view that neither model is explanatory and that an adequate theory of lawmaking must begin with an understanding of the structural constraints that exist in political, economic and structural relations see Chambliss and Zatz, *Making Law* (1993).

[33] See C. Wright Mills, *The Power Elite* (1956), *cf. ante*, 261.

[34] See A. Rose, *The Power Structure* (1967).

[35] *Crime and Justice in Society* (1969); *The Social Reality of Crime* (1970).

[36] *Critique of Legal Order* (1974).

[37] *Class and Class Conflict In Industrial Society* (1959).

century. It is all too easy to identify sociological jurisprudence with Pound.[38] But sociological jurisprudence neither begins nor ends with Pound, and it is valuable to identify some more recent trends in sociological thought.

Selznick, a leading American sociologist, has pin-pointed three stages in the sociology of law.[39] Pound, together with his continental progenitors, belong to the first stage, wherein the pioneer, communicates a perspective. So, Pound identified the task of the lawyer as "social engineer", formulated a programme of action, attempted to gear individual and social needs to the values of Western democratic society. The early Realist writings convey similar orientation.[40] Pound, and Holmes[41] too, was a "generaliser", a purveyor of "grand theory": he provides the theoretical context for an understanding of law in society. But he did little empirical research, though such work was undertaken by contemporaries. Their writings are characterised by a concern for substantive legal problems rather than the workings of legal institutions, and by a penchant for law reform, doubtless inherited from Pound and the Realists. Furthermore, the initiative for this empirical research was taken by lawyers, not sociologists, and often by practitioners rather than jurists. Perhaps as a result, conclusions and implications were framed in grandiose terms.[42]

The second stage was characterised by a concern for method. The skills of the academic lawyer and sociologist were synthesised: the jurist often suggested the field of activity and posed the questions: the sociologist collaborated in the research, adapting his techniques from the mainstream of sociological inquiry. The Chicago jury project was the result of one such collaboration.[43] At the same time the jurist trained himself in the techniques of sociology, the mechanics of social surveys, the use of statistics and other necessary technological skills. The jurists of this second generation were content to survey narrower problems and achieve less far-reaching conclusions.

---

[38] "Pound was the perfect type to direct the transmission of new learning to an intellectually rigid profession ... His legal theory was marred by its contradictions and ambivalence, but there was nothing ambivalent about his influence ... In the last analysis, his most important legacy was in the questions he posed rather than the answers he provided" (D. Wigoder, *Roscoe Pound, Philosopher of Law* (1974), p. 287).

[39] See "The Sociology of Law" in R. Merton, L. Broom and L. Cottrell (eds), *Sociology Today: Problems and Prospects* (1959).

[40] *Cf.* Llewellyn, *post*, 1011.

[41] *Post*, 986–988.

[42] So, Underhill Moore and Charles Callahan's research on traffic and parking regulations were described as contributions to psychological learning theory. See 53 Yale L.J. 1 as to which see J.H. Schlegel (1981) 29 Buffalo L.Rev. 195, 267–292.

[43] See H. Kalven and H. Zeisel, *The American Jury* (1966). Other examples are the Columbia Project for Effective Justice, see *ante*, 8, n. 52 and the study of the economies of personal injury litigation in (1961) 61 Colum. L.R. 1; empirical research on the legal profession (Carlin, *Lawyers on their Own* (1962); Smigel, *The Wall Street Lawyer* (1964), and see the contributions in Part 5 of Aubert *Sociology of Law* (1969), particularly those by Rueschemeyer and Dahrendorf); work on the police (Skolnick, *Justice Without Trial* (1966) and arrest (La Fave, *Arrest; The Decision to Take a Suspect into Custody* (1965)) and many other subjects.

## Talcott Parsons

But "grand theory" did not die with Pound. In Lasswell and McDougal[44] we find the same broad generalisations and "grand prospectus".[45] Others, Julius Stone for example, looked to Talcott Parsons as offering the type of model to which sociological jurists had to aspire.[46] Stone believed that one of the main faults of classical sociological jurisprudence was the treatment of particular problems in isolation. He argued that "the sociological jurist of the future will generally have to approach his problems though a vast effort at understanding the wider social context."[47] And he claimed that, whatever its faults, the Parsonian "social system" offered a model of what such jurists should hope to achieve. Stone saw that the problem sociological jurisprudence laboured with was its methodology of working outwards from legal problems to the relevant social science. Instead, he advocated "a framework of thought receptive of social data which will allow us to see 'the social system' as an integrated equilibration of the multitude of operative systems of values and institutions embraced within it".[48]

Parsons' functional approach has few supporters today. He saw the major function of the legal system as integrative. "It serves to mitigate potential elements of conflict and to oil the machinery of social intercourse. It is ... only by adherence to a system of rules that systems of social interaction can function without breaking down into overt or chronic convert conflict".[49] Parsons insisted on the analytical separation of the "legal system" and the "political system". This separation is facilitated by Parsons' assertion that the interpretive work of the courts is the central feature of the legal order: the legislature, the centre of the political system is there to formulate policy.[50]

This Parsonian model has been developed by Bredemeier.[51] He sees the legislature providing the courts with policy goals in return for interpretation, and with enforcement in exchange for legitimation. But what are these goals? Bredemeier, like Parsons and Stone, assumes a value consensus within society. The analytical distinction between legal and political systems is not easy to sustain: what of judicial decisions grounded overtly in policy? More fundamentally, should it be assumed that the legal system is integrative? There are occasions when far from being a contributive force to the good order of society, the legal system is

---

[44] See (1943) 52 Yale L.J. 203; (1952) 61 Yale L.J. 915.
[45] See H. Kalven in (eds.) Haber and Cohen, *The Law School of Tomorrow* (1968), p. 161. On Lasswell and McDougal see 7th edition of this book at pp. 679–681.
[46] See *Social Dimentions of Law and Justice* (1966), pp. 13–28. See also his *Law and the Social Sciences* (1966), pp. 29–49, and P. S. Cohen, *Modern Social Theory* (1972), pp. 96 et seq.
[47] (1966) 1 Israel L.R. 173, 176–177. *Cf. Social Dimensions,* n. 46, pp. 26–27.
[48] *Law and the Social Sciences* (1966), p. 27.
[49] "The Law and Social Control" in W. Evan, *Law and Sociology* (1962), pp. 57–58.
[50] For an attempt to apply Parsons see L. Mayhew, *Law and Equal Opportunity* (1968).
[51] "Law as an Integrative Mechanism" in (ed.) W. Evan, *Law and Sociology* (1962), p. 78.

clearly dysfunctional: for example, when the judiciary's ignorance of commercial practices drives business to arbitration or when court decisions cause industrial strikes, or litigation is prohibitively expensive. And, what is regarded as functional for one section of the community may be quite the reverse for another. There are too many problems with Parsonian type models for us to invest the hope in them that Stone did.

## Selznick

Selznick claimed in 1962 that the third stage had not yet been reached. It is the time when sociological jurisprudence will develop an "intellectual autonomy and maturity", when having learnt the necessary skills, the jurists can return to some of the theoretical questions posed at the outset, the function of law, the role of legality, the meaning of justice, and a sociology of law will emerge. Selznick, for example, has tried to understand legality from a sociological position.[52] The development of a sociology of law does suggest that Selznick's third stage has been reached. This is discussed in the next section.

Another of Selznick's concerns has been with attempting a *rapprochement* between sociology and natural law.[53] He claims that sociologists are wrong to separate fact and value since they deal with normative systems where values are central, and where what is involved consists of measuring actual social conditions against a "master ideal". The important ideals in the legal system, Selznick asserts, are justice and legality. In discussing the latter Selznick comes close to what Fuller advanced in *The Morality of Law*.[54] Fuller requires only certain formal procedural requirements: it is not clear whether Selznick would so limit himself or whether he would require some minimum substantive standards, rather like Hart's minimum content of natural law.[55] Rejecting cultural relativism he asserts that there are universal values: "such motivating forces as the search for respect including self-respect, for affection, and for surcease of anxiety; such potentialities as the union of sex and love, the enlargement of social insight and understanding, reason and aesthetic creativity".[56] He claims that "if there is to be a legal order, it must serve the proper ends of man".[57] Selznick, unlike Fuller does not cast doubt on the validity of a legal order which falls short in this way, but on its "maturity".

· There are a number of difficulties with this thesis. There are empirical problems: how does one determine a "universal value"? Are those he cites universal?[58] It may be doubted. Further, it must not be forgotten that

---

[52] See *Law, Society and Industrial Justice* (1969).
[53] (1961) 6 *Natural Law Forum* 84.
[54] *Ante*, 118.
[55] *Ante*, 123.
[56] *Op. cit.*, n. 52, p. 93.
[57] *ibid*, p. 102.
[58] *Cf.* Mead, *ante*, 225 and the discussion of Finnis, *ante*, 126 *et seq.*

greed, lust, aggressiveness are also motivating forces and, unfortunately, no less (or may be more) universal.[59]

In *Law, Society and Industrial Justice* Selznick seeks to show that legal orders are not unique to the political state. He sees law as a generic element in the structure of many different groups in society. Law, he claims, is "endemic in all institutions that rely for social control on formal authority and rule making".[60] So the normative structure of many private associations, churches, large corporations, trade unions, universities, can be described as law. What distinguishes law from social control is not the coercion involved but "the invocation of authority".[61] Selznick's ideas involve a welding together of ideas taken from Weber and Ehrlich[62] on the one hand and Hart and Fuller on the other. *Law, Society and Industrial Justice* can be said to be one of the first examples of the "third stage" of the sociology of law.[63]

## TOWARDS A SOCIOLOGY OF LAW

For much of the twentieth century the sociology of law was eclipsed by sociological jurisprudence. It was Pound, rather than Weber or Durkheim, who was the dominant figure. From the 1960s the term "sociological jurisprudence" was used less frequently, and what came to be known as socio-legal studies took its place. Advocates of socio-legal studies emphasise the importance of placing law in its social context, of using social-scientific research methods, of recognising that many traditional jurisprudential questions are empirical in nature and not just conceptual.[64] A pervasive theme is the gap between legal rules and actually lived social norms.[65] But this gap, often said to be between "law in the books" and "law in action", was too often only described and too rarely analysed. For Cotterrell, socio-legal studies was a "transition phase".[66] It had considerable impact: on the law, on legal education and

---

[59]  A point made by Gordis, in Cogley, *Natural Law and Modern Society* (1966), p. 257.
[60]  *Law, Society and Industrial Justice* (1969), p. 7.
[61]  *ibid. cf. ante*, 264.
[62]  Ehrlich maintained that the legal order of associations was the "most basic form of law" (*Principles of the Sociology of Law*, p. 37). Ehrlich relies on coercion as a distinguishing mark but this does not allow him to distinguish law from social control.
[63]  Described by Nonet as "jurisprudential sociology"; see (1976) 10 Law and Soc. Rev. 525. Insight into Selznick's thinking can be found in the interview he gave to Roger Cotterrell: see (2004) 31 Journal of Law and Society 291.
[64]  *Cf* J. Gibbs (1968) 2 Law and Soc. Rev. 429
[65]  A point made strongly by K. Llewellyn in the "points of departure" of the Realist movement (see *post*, 1012–1015).
[66]  *Law's Community* (1995), p. 296.

on law publishing. It helped focus greater attention on concepts like discretion[67], institutions such as tribunals[68], and different techniques of decision-making and conflict resolution, such as alternative dispute resolution.[69]

The shortcomings of socio-legal studies were identified by Lawrence Friedman. He wrote:

> "To many observers, the work done so far amounts to very little: an incoherent or inconclusive jumble of case studies. There is (it seems) no foundation; some work merely proves the obvious, some is poorly designed; there are no axioms, no 'laws' of legal behavior, nothing cumulates. The studies are at times interesting and are sporadically useful. But there is no 'science'; nothing adds up.... Grand theories do appear from time to time, but they have no survival power; they are nibbled to death by case studies. There is no central core."[70]

Socio-legal studies was largely lacking in any theoretical under-pinning[71]. The law—note this often defined narrowly[72]—and the legal system were treated as discrete entities, as unproblematic, and as occupying a central hegemonic position. There was rarely any attempt to relate the legal system to the wider social order or to the State. When reforms were suggested—and as progressive scholars reform was often the aim—they were to make the legal system operate more efficiently or effectively. And the emphasis was more on the "behaviour"[73] of institutions rather than on trying to understand legal doctrine.

This is not what the sociology of law is about, as those who remembered what Weber, Durkheim, Ehrlich had written were able to point out. For the sociology of law, as Campbell and Wiles explained in 1976:

> "the focus is no longer on the legal system, known and accepted, but on understanding the nature of social order through a study of law.... The goal is not primarily to improve the legal system, but rather to construct a theoretical understanding of that legal system in terms of the wider social structure".[74]

Much of the focus in contemporary writing is on what is involved in this "understanding". Should legal definitions be transformed into sociological categories or sociological insights into legal concepts? Can

---

[67] See A. K. Bottomley, *Decisions in The Penal Process* (1973); A. Pratt (1999) 8 Soc. & Legal Studies 199, N. Lacey in (ed) K. Hawkins, *The Uses of Discretion* (1992).

[68] See T. Prosser (1977) 4 Br. J. of Law and Soc. 39; N. Wikeley (2000) 63 MLR 475.

[69] See W. Twining (1993) 56 MLR 380; S. Silbey and A. Sarat (1989) 66 Denver University Law Review 437; J. Esser (1989) 66 Denver University Law Review 499; G. Douglas *et al* (2000) 63 MLR 177.

[70] (1986) 38 Stanford Law Review 763, 779.

[71] See also A. Hunt (1981) 8 Br. J of Law & Soc 47.

[72] See R. Cotterrell, *post*, 916. See also Hans and Vidmar, and Constable (1992) 16 Law and Social Inquiry 323, 353.

[73] See D. Black, *The Behavior of Law* (1976) and *post*, 862. But for the relationship of Black's work to Durkheim see Cotterrell, *op cit*, n. 3, ch. 9. A defence is M. P. Baumgartner in (ed) D. Patterson, *A Companion to Philosophy of Law and Legal Theory* (1996) ch. 28.

[74] (1976) 10 Law and Soc. Rev 547, 553.

the two approaches be combined? If the law has a limited sociological understanding of the world, does sociology have anything to offer the jurist to enable him better to appreciate it? As Nelken points out, there are dangers.[75] He, following Sarat and Silbey,[76] notes the concern of sociologists of law that they will be used ("the pull of the policy audience"), compromising academic social science and blunting the edge of political critique. Nelken's own concern, as will be seen in an extract from a recent paper of his,[77] is that "the introduction of different styles of reasoning can have ill effects for legal practice by misunderstanding and thus threatening the integrity of legal processes or the values they embody".[78]

But for Cotterrell the sociology of law is a "transdisciplinary enterprise and aspiration to broaden understanding of law as a social phenomenon".[79] He emphasises the centrality of the sociology of law for legal education and legal practice: "the methodology of sociological understanding of legal ideas is the deliberate *extension* in carefully specified directions of the diverse ways in which legal participants themselves think about the social world in legal terms".[80] Sociology, Cotterrell argues, offers insights into legal thinking and can transform legal ideas by reinterpreting them. He uses[81] the example of private purpose trusts. Cotterrell is aware that this could lead to sociology recreating law in its own image. On the contrary, he argues, when seen in this way it ceases to appear as "the invocation of a competing academic discipline with the aim of colonizing law".[82] It is rather "a necessary means of broadening legal understanding—the systematic and empirical understanding of a certain aspect of social life which is recognised as 'legal' ".[83]

But can sociology "climb out of its own skin and get inside the law to understand and explain the law's 'truth' "?[84] That is has difficulties in so doing are attributable only in part to its limitations. As Banakar has convincingly shown, "the fact that law secures its domination and authority through normative closure.... denies the commonality of discourses of sociology and law, posing unique[85] methodological problems for the sociology of law. The sheer institutional strength of the law hampers access to empirical material, questions the relevance of sociological insights into legal reasoning and ... raises doubts on the adequacy

---

[75] (1988) 25 Journal of Law and Soc. 407, 408.
[76] (1988) 10 Law and Policy 97.
[77] *ibid*, and *post* 929 and see his important article in (ed.) M. Freeman, *Law and Sociology* (2006), p. 16.
[78] *ibid*. See also D. Nelken "A Just Measure of Science" in (eds) M. Freeman and H. Reece, *Science In Court* (1998), p. 11.
[79] (1998) 25 Journal of Law and Soc. 171, 187 (and see *post*, 919).
[80] *ibid* p. 190.
[81] See (1993) 46 Current Legal Problems 75.
[82] *Op cit*, n. 16, p. 191.
[83] *ibid*.
[84] The question as posed by R. Banakar (2000) 27 Journal of Law and Soc. 273, 274.
[85] Medical Sociology is different.

of sociology to produce a knowledge which transcends its own reality".[86]

Nelken's response is that if we are "to bring sociology of law up against its limits",[87] its dependence on sociology must be recognised. And it becomes necessary to "examine more carefully how its reflexivity and that of law relate".[88] Nelken points to a range of writing in legal and social theory which sets out to analyse differences (and similarities) between sociological reflexivity and legal closure: Lyotard's "phrases in difference",[89] Luhmann's autopoiesis,[90] Murphy's law's estrangement.[91]

Cotterrell believes that the law can profit from sociologically-inspired resolutions, particularly where legal doctrine is rift by conflicting precedents. This is true, and it would be foolish for the lawyer today to ignore social insights. But, as Nelken points out, the introduction of such insights also has "the potential to distort or at least change legal ... practices rather than simply help them to sort out self-induced muddles".[92] If only we knew when social science could guide to the answer— and convince us it was the right one. Nelken may well be right that social insights function differently when they prise open legal closure—he cites Downs's discussion[93] of the so-called "battered women's syndrome" as a method of displacing law's myths about woman battering—than when they are used to provide closure.[94]

But, as Trubek points out "whatever social science *can* do for law, it *cannot* offer ... objectivist grounding for legal policy".[95] Not that this view is accepted by all legal sociologists.

Donald Black, for example, and pre-eminently, predicts the development of what he calls "sociological law" when lawyers reflexively internalise the conclusion that sociology is the best guide to legal outcomes.[96] According to Black, the sociology of law entails the adoption of an observer's perspective.[97] This requires detachment and is in striking contrast to what Cotterrell advocates. But Black would claim that its findings are of great relevance to participants in the legal system. It may challenge long-standing conceptions about law. "Official versions" of the intentions and purposes of particular statutes are not, as a result, granted automatic respect, but are instead subjected to critical scrutiny.[98] So too

---

[86] *Op cit*, n. 84 p. 284.

[87] *Op cit*, n. 75, p. 415.

[88] *ibid* p. 417.

[89] *The Differend: Phrases in Dispute* and *post*, 1421.

[90] (1992) 13 Cardozo L.R. 1419, and *post*, 877.

[91] *The Oldest Social Science?* (1997) (on which see A. Jacobson (1992) 26 Journal of Law and Soc. 260).

[92] *Op cit*, n. 75, p. 422.

[93] See Downs, *More Than Victims: Battered Women, the Syndrome Society and the Law* (1996).

[94] *Op cit*, n. 75, p. 422.

[95] (1990) 18 Florida State U.L.R 1 (and see *post*, 936).

[96] *Sociological Justice* (1989).

[97] *ibid.*, pp. 19–22.

[98] Examples are I. Brownlee (1998) 25 J. of Law and Soc. 313 (on criminal justice legislation); M. Lindsay (1998) 23 Law and Soc Inquiry 541 (on eugenics legislation); C. Augst (2000) 9 Soc. and Legal Studies 205 (embryo protection and "risk").

are the "conventional justifications of court procedures, and the legal representation of clients".[99] The sociology of law "even suggests new possibilities for manipulating legal systems deliberately in order to bring about desired results, techniques of social engineering likely to become highly controversial as well as highly effective".[1] It also puts into perspective "many of the most time-honoured notions of lawyers and legal scholars".[2] Thus, discretion is shown to be not random and capricious— though it may be doubted if anyone thinks it is—but rather highly regular and patterned ("constrained by the dictates of social laws"[3]). Black's sociology of law suggests also a different understanding of discrimination; that it is not exceptional but ubiquitous, and is not limited to the effects of social class or race. It is, says Black, "an aspect of the natural behavior of law, as natural as the flying of birds or the swimming of fish".[4]

In the late 1990's a new form of sociological jurisprudence was proclaimed: realistic socio-legal theory. To Brian Tamanaha, whose book is thus entitled,[5] this identifies and develops foundations[6] for social scientific study of law. He draws on philosophical pragmatism[7] to establish an epistemological foundation which specifies the nature of social science and its knowledge claims, and a methodological foundation which uses both behaviourism and interpretivism.[8] He contrasts his realistic approach to socio-legal theory with critical schools of socio-legal theory, in particular with the critical legal studies movement of which he is scornful.[9] Like Cotterrell, though for very different reasons, Tamanaha believes that legal theory and socio-legal studies have a lot to learn from one another. Unlike many sociologists of law, who took a definition of law from within jurisprudence,[10] Tamanaha insists that law should not be defined in ways that assume sociological connections but should be subject to investigation and proof.[11] *Normative* beliefs, such as that law is the central force in the maintenance of social order and social control is the central activity of law, have, he says, "masqueraded as *descriptions* of law, even within social scientific studies which have prided themselves on being purely descriptive".[12]

---

[99] Z. Bankowski and G. Mungham, *Images of Law* (1976).
[1] *Per* Baumgartner, *op. cit.*, n. 73, p. 413.
[2] *ibid.*
[3] *ibid.*
[4] *Op. cit.*, n. 73, pp. 21–22.
[5] *Realistic Socio-Legal Theory: Pragmatism and A Social Theory of Law* (1997).
[6] In the context of an emphasis on anti-foundationalism associated with critical legal studies and postmodernism.
[7] Tamanaha discusses this in Chap. 2.
[8] See *op. cit.*, n. 5, Chap. 3.
[9] *ibid.*, pp. 188–191.
[10] Weber and Malinowski both worked with definitions of law which could have been taken straight from Austin. See *ante*, 291 and *post*, 1085.
[11] *Op. cit.*, n. 5, pp. 105–128.
[12] *ibid.*, p. 130.

In a strong riposte to standard conceptual jurisprudence he expresses the view that:

> "What law is and what law does connot be captured in any single scientific concept. The project to devise a scientific concept of law was based upon a misguided belief that law comprises a fundamental category. To the contrary law is thoroughly a cultural construct, lacking any universal essential nature. Law *is* whatever we attach the label *law* to."[13]

He would appear to confront conceptual jurisprudence face on by denying that there is a concept of law. That he does not go this far is apparent from articles Tamanaha has published[14] and from a response to this very criticism[15] in a "Symposium" on his book.[16] There he says of theorizing about the concept of law that "we do it because law is a key social phenomenon that must be understood, analyzed and discussed, which could not begin nor be carried far without conceptual analysis".[17]

It is rather a recognition—though this is not novel[18]—that different phenomena fall under the concept "law". Law is a concept conventionally applied to a "variety of multifaceted, multifunctional phenomena: natural law, international law, primitive law, religious law, customary law, state law, folk law, people's law, and indigenous law.... From the state law of Massachusetts to the law of the Barotse....".[19] And, as Bix points out, Tamanaha implicitly "accepts and supports the idea of a concept of (Western) state law".[20]

Tamanaha insists, however, that there is not a "central case of law".[21] He cites the example of international law which has its own integrity and has been functioning as a form of law for at least two centuries but which remains under traditional conceptual analysis a "borderline form of law".[22] He is concerned that the central case approach to the concept of law fits,and was the product of, the ascendancy of state law that accompanied the rise of the state. His alternative conceptualisation of law is, he believes, better able to account for the proliferation of different kinds of law[23] than the traditional monotypical view of *the* concept of law".[24]

But how is one to evaluate whether one concept of law is better than another? Tamanaha offers the following evaluative criteria:

---

[13] *ibid.*, p. 128.
[14] (2000) 27 J. Law and Soc. 296 and (1995) 15 Oxford J. of L.S. 501.
[15] By Brian Bix (2000) 32 Rutgers L.J. 227, 229–230.
[16] (2000) 32 Rutgers L.J. 281.
[17] *ibid.*, p. 283.
[18] Austin recognises this: see *ante*, 295. So of course did Hart (*The Concept of Law* (1994), pp. 15–16) and does Finnis (note his emphasis on the "focal meaning" of law).
[19] *Op. cit.*, n. 15, p. 128.
[20] *Op. cit.*, n. 15, p. 229.
[21] *Op. cit.*, n. 16, p. 284.
[22] *ibid.*
[23] He does not include within this the implications of cyberspace on which see M. Radin and R.P. Wagner (1998) 73 Chicago-Kent Law Rev. 1595.
[24] *Op. cit.*, n. 16, p. 285.

"First, the concept must be coherent, or analytically ... sound, in the sense that, for example, it should not contain internal contradictions, or have gaps in crucial spots. Second, the concept must be consistent with, or 'fit', or be adequate to, the reality, phenomenon, or idea it purports to represent, describe, or define.... Third, the concept must have a use value in the sense that it will enhance our understanding or help us achieve our objectives."[25]

Hart, it will be remembered, described his text as an "essay in descriptive sociology".[26] But it contains no description of social practices drawn from any legal system.[27] Can conceptual jurisprudence have autonomy (or at least relative autonomy) from empirical reality? For Tamanaha it cannot. Thus one of the overriding objectives of his *Realistic Socio-Legal Theory* is to "bring into legal theory an infusion of insights from the social scientific study of law. Socio-legal theory is a practice of theorizing about law that incorporates aspects of both (conceptual and socio-legal) approaches to legal phenomena".[28] Sociological inquiries into "the practices that legal theories purport to analyze and explain (and describe and prescribe) are essential to the enterprise of legal theory, or at least to a legal theory that wants to be good at what it does".[29] Legal theory, however, can neither be "subsumed within" nor "dictated to" by legal sociology.[30]

Questions remain, one, taken up by Rubin, is:

"To say that 'truth' is what works or that theories are to be judged on the basis of their usefulness begs the basic question, for we still need to know the criteria for determining usefulness, for deciding what works and what does not. This opens all the questions that pragmatism seeks to preclude.... Something more is needed, some criterion to tell us how we recognise that a particular practice or social experience has generated something which we are willing to describe as truth, or knowledge."[31]

Does then the "realistic" aspect of Tamanaha's project depend upon the pragmatist theory of truth? It would seem so.[32] But for Tamanaha there is more to pragmatism than just what works. "What works" is part of what is involved. However, and here he quotes Putnam, "the model is a group of inquirers trying to produce good ideas and trying to test them to see which ones have value".[33] There is thus a community of investigators. There is also the material context or environment (including other persons). This is where "the strong strain of realism in pragmatist

---

[25] *ibid.*
[26] *Ante,* 376.
[27] Bix, *op. cit.,* n. 15, questions whether Hart's "claim" can be taken seriously (see p. 236).
[28] *Op. cit.,* n. 52, p. 287. He claims Hart, Posner (*The Problems of Jurisprudence* (1990)) and Dworkin (*Law's Empire* (1986)) as allies, but this is contentious.
[29] *ibid.,* p. 287.
[30] *ibid.,* p. 288.
[31] (2000) 32 Rutgers L.R. 241, 244. For another view of law and truth, see D. Patterson, *Law and Truth* (1996) (general theories of truth are irrelevant to social practice of law).
[32] Tamanaha concedes this (*op cit*) n. 16, p. 292. On pragmatism see S. Haack (2005) 50 Am. J. Jurisprudence 71.
[33] *Pragmatism: An Open Question* (1995) p. 71.

thought emerges.... The 'notion of reality independent of either of us....
lie at the base of the pragmatist definition of the truth. With some such
reality any statement, in order to be counted true, must agree".[34]

As far as criteria of usefulness are concerned, Tamanaha insists this
cannot be answered in abstract or general terms: it is a function of the
particular activity at hand. Where the activity is the social scientific study
of legal phenomena the criteria include:

1) whether the information is reliable and fits the facts of the matter
   about legal phenomena (i.e. do judges *in fact* treat people differently because of race?);

2) whether it fits within a meaningful framework of interesting
   questions about law ... for the community of socio-legal in vesti-
   gators; and

3) whether it enhances our ability to observe, understand, explain,
   describe, analyse, prescribe, critique and change legal practices to
   serve our interests, to make law better. What those interests might
   be, what it means to make law "better", cannot be determined by
   pragmatism itself. That determination must be made in the social
   arena by social actors as a matter of substantive policy choices".[35]

Much of interest emerges from Tamanaha's realistic socio-legal theory.
Most significantly, that law is a social practice amenable to social scientific study, and that legal theory and socio-legal theory have a lot to
learn from each other.[36] It has long been recognised that sociological
thinking about law would be considerably hampered without the insights
of analytical jurisprudence. But analytical jurisprudence can look to
sociology as well and has much to gain provided it uses the data
appropriately. Thus it is important for those studying the concept of law
to know why people obey (or don't obey) the law,[37] why people use extra-
legal norms and procedures to resolve disputes,[38] how other societies (not
those in Hart's central case, for example) deal with disputes.[39] So long as
it is recognised that analytical jurisprudence is not making empirical
claims.

## UNGER AND THE DEVELOPMENT OF MODERN LAW

A modern text in the tradition of Weber and Durkheim is Unger's *Law in
Modern Society*. He claims that "each society reveals through its law the

---

[34]  *Op cit* n. 16, pp 294–295, quoting W. James, *Pragmatism and the Meaning of Truth* (1975)
      p. 283.
[35]  *Op cit* n. 16, p. 297.
[36]  One of Tamanaha's best chapters is on the internal/external distinction, throwing light on
      a central problem in contemporary analytical jurisprudence (see ch. 6).
[37]  See T. Tyler, *Why People Obey The Law* (1990).
[38]  See R. Ellickson, *Order Without Law* (1991).
[39]  See B. Tamanaha, *Understanding Law In Micronesia* (1993).

innermost secrets of the manner in which it holds men together".[40] He distinguishes three types of law: customary law ("any recurring mode of interaction among individuals and groups, together with the more or less explicit acknowledgement by these groups and individuals that such patterns of interaction produce reciprocal expectations of conduct that ought to be satisfied");[41] bureaucratic or regulatory law ("a law deliberately imposed by government rather than spontaneously produced by society"),[42] and the legal order or legal system ("committed to being general and autonomous as well as public and positive").[43]

Unger describes the processes which have led to changes from customary to bureaucratic law and from this to a legal order and eventually will lead to, what he calls, a postliberal legal order.[44] Changes in a society's legal system are intimately related to changes both in its organisation and consciousness. Neither material[45] nor ideal[46] explanations are given priority.

The "legal order" is to be found in modern Western liberal societies. For it to exist no group must occupy a permanently dominant position or have an inherent right to govern. A second major condition for the emergence of a legal order is "a widespread belief in what might loosely be called natural law".[47] Group pluralism and the belief in higher law, justified by a transcendent religion combine to produce a legal order and "turn men's minds toward the rule of law ideal".[48] Unger develops this thesis through a comparison of modern Western legal history and the experience of Ancient Chinese culture and other civilisations including that of Greece, Rome, ancient India, Islam and Judaism. He shows how, by his criteria, Chinese society never succeeded in achieving a legal order.[49] The Jewish *halakhah*, he argues, seems to have come closer to a legal order than any other body of sacred law.[50]

Unger's study of the legal order is directed towards showing why citizens of liberal society find it both necessary to struggle for the rule of law and impossible to achieve it. The disintegration of traditional types of legality and legal thought reveals far-reaching changes in society and culture. Unger discusses the character of these changes through a comparison of different types of modern society. He sees "the state, a supposedly neutral overseer of social conflict, forever caught up in the

---

[40] *Law in Modern Society*, p. 47.
[41] *ibid.*, p. 49.
[42] *ibid.*, p. 51. *cf.* Weber, *ante*, 839.
[43] *ibid.*, p. 52.
[44] *ibid.*, pp. 193 *et seq.*
[45] As with Marxist explanations.
[46] As in natural law, *ante*, Chap. 3.
[47] *Op. cit.*, p. 76. But natural law surely was dominant rather in earlier stages of Western culture.
[48] *ibid.*, p. 83.
[49] *ibid.*, pp. 86–100.
[50] *ibid.*, p. 119. *Halakhah* is Jewish religious law and consists of the five books of Moses, prophetic injunctions, interpretation of the rabbis, as well as custom.

antagonism of private interests and made the tool of one faction or another".[51] In postliberal society this is recognised and the state takes on a welfare aspect.[52] There is also the recognition that other organisations have power which leads to the development of corporatism. Welfare emphases gives rise to policy-oriented legal reasoning, interest in substantive justice, general clauses in legislation. The generality of the legal order is undermined as is its autonomy. Postliberal society is moving, Unger claims, away from formality towards equity and solidarity. Equity is the intuitive sense of justice in the particular case: solidarity is "the social face of love; it is concern with another as a person rather than just respect for him as a bearer of formally equal rights and duties".[53] Unger believes "one is never permitted to take advantage of legal rights so as to pursue one's own ends without regard to the effect one may have on others. This ideal holds that the overriding collective interest is the interest in maintaining a system of social relations in which men are bound to act, if not compassionately, at least as if they had compassion for each other".[54]

The future[55] lies, Unger believes, in a return to a customary law or tribalist society or in the reassertion of communitarian concerns. The first offers a suppression of individual freedom because the existing order is sanctified: the second subversion of inequality and confidence in collective choices making possible "an ever more universal consensus about the immanent order of social life".[56]

No short summary can do justice to Unger's arguments or give any idea of the wealth of illuminating illustrative detail to be found in his treatise. His conclusions are at times reminiscent of Plato[57] and at others at Marx.[58] His style borders on the theological and his discussion of contemporary society is often over-abstract. But whether one agrees with his conclusions or not, and they are sure to provoke considerable controversy and debate, his book is one of the most stimulating essays of legal and social theory to have appeared for many years. His discussion of the evolution of law and its types, combining historical research and philosophical argument, makes *Law in Modern Society* a valuable contribution to our understand of legal culture.

---

[51] *ibid.* p. 181.
[52] *ibid.* pp. 192–193.
[53] *Op. cit.*, p. 206.
[54] *ibid.* p. 209.
[55] *ibid.* pp. 238–242.
[56] *ibid.* p. 240.
[57] At one point (p. 242) Unger compares the prospects ahead of us to alternative between the "City of Pigs" and "the Heavenly City". (*cf.* Plato, *Republic*, 372D).
[58] *Post*, Chap. 12.

## HABERMAS AND THE CENTRALITY OF LAW

Habermas's *Between Facts and Norms*[59] covers so much ground of legal and political theory that it is impossible to do it justice here.[60] Rather than attempt to extract from the book I include a recent article of Habermas's in which he summarises his major contributions to legal theory.[61]

The permanent tension in legal thinking between legal sociology and a philosophy of law (or justice) is captured by Habermas in the title "between facts and norms". The tension is one between facticity and validity.[62] As Cotterrell explains this:

> "Law's facticity is its character as a functioning system, ultimately coercively guaranteed. To understand this facticity is to understand social or political power working through law. Law's validity, however, ... is a matter of its normative character, its nature as a coherent system of meaning, as prescriptive ideas and values. Validity lies ultimately in law's capacity to make claims supported by reason, in a discourse that aims at and depends on agreement between citizens."[63]

Seeing law in this way is to acknowledge that the legal system must be "socially effective" and "ethically justified".[64]

It will be observed that in Habermas's use of the term "validity" is embraced the guarantee of law's legitimacy. It is more conventional to understand legitimacy as the acceptance of law by citizens,[65] and validity in terms of a test like the "rule of recognition".[66] Sociologists look to lawyers' and legal officials' views of what is authoritative as representing only one perspective (albeit a most important one) in considering how power is imposed through law.

Habermas argues that legal philosophy must recognise fundamental changes in the social environment of beliefs and values in which the law's claims to authority must ultimately be grounded. And validity and facticity "have parted company as incompatible".[67] What is needed is "an analysis equally tailored to the normative reconstruction and the

---

[59] Published in English translation in 1996. Literature on Habermas is enormous: S. White (ed.), *The Cambridge Companion To Habermas* (1995) is a useful source.

[60] (1999) 76 Denver University Law Review contains a colloquium in which aspects of Habermas's project are assessed. See also T. Campbell (1998) 51 CLP 65, 87–92, R. Cotterrell (1998) 51 CLP 367, 371–375, W. Forbath (1998) 23 Law & Soc. Inq. 969.

[61] *Post*, 969.

[62] *Op cit*, n. 59, p. 90.

[63] *Op cit*, n. 60, p. 371. And see Habermas, *op cit*, n. 59, pp. 14, 29–30.

[64] Habermas quotes from Ralf Dreier, *Recht-Moral-Ideologie* (1981) p. 198.

[65] See Cotterrell, *op cit*, n. 1, referring to Weber, *ante*, 839 and citing A. Hyde (1983) Wisconsin L. Rev 379 and C. McEwan and R. J. Maiman (1986) 8 Law and Policy 257. See also T. Tyler, *Why People Obey The Law* (1990).

[66] *Ante*, 382.

[67] *Op cit*, n. 59, p. 26.

empirical disenchantment of the legal system"[68] (as Cotterrell puts it, "to law as ideal and reality"[69]).

Habermas believes—surely incorrectly—that sociology has "devalued"[70] law, that it describes law in language that "neither seeks nor gains an entry into the intuitive knowledge of [legal] participants".[71] Luhmann's "systems theory"[72] is said to have gone the farthest along this axis—and that may be so. But Habermas's comment underestimates both classical legal sociology (Weber,[73] Durkheim,[74] Ehrlich[75]) and contemporary thinkers such as Cotterrell,[76] Nelken[77] and Tamanaha.[78] Cotterrell senses that it may be that Habermas "too readily assumes that legal sociology's concern is to emphasize law's facticity as governmental direction and not also to consider its validity—the conditions of its existence as a structure of reason and principle".[79]

Rather it may be thought that Habermas overplays the centrality of law to the organisation of today's complex societies. He imbues law with, what Tamanaha has called, an "heroic" quality.[80] How, Habermas asks

"can disenchanted, internally differentiated and pluralized lifeworlds be socially integrated if, at the same time, the risk of dissension is growing, particularly in the spheres of communicative action that have been cut loose from the ties of sacred authorities and released from the bonds of archaic institutions?"[81]

And he sees law as "what is left from a crumbled cement of society".[82] But law too is deprived of the metaphysical and religious support it earlier enjoyed and must find a new basis for legitimation. This is found in, what he calls, the discourse principle *viz*, "only those [legal] norms are valid to which *all persons possibly affected* would agree as participants in rational discourses".[83] Further, "the only law that counts as legitimate is one that could be rationally accepted by all citizens in a discursive process of opinion and will-formation".[84]

But is law essential to the integration of modern society?[85] Have societies collapsed for lack of law to act as an integrative mechanism? The

---

[68] *Ibid*, p. 66.
[69] *Op cit*, n. 60, p. 373.
[70] *Op cit*, n. 59, p. 48.
[71] *ibid*.
[72] *Post*, 877.
[73] *Ante*, 839.
[74] *Ante*, 843.
[75] *Ante*, 847.
[76] *Ante*, 860.
[77] *Ante*, 861.
[78] *Ante*, 862. Habermas ignores these contemporary legal sociologists.
[79] *Op cit*, n. 60, p. 374.
[80] (1999) 76 Denver University Law Rev. 989, 993.
[81] *Op cit*, n. 59, p. 26.
[82] 76 Denver University Law Review 937 (*post*, 969).
[83] *ibid*, p. 940 (and *post*, 971).
[84] *Op cit*, n. 59, p. 135.
[85] Similarities with Durkheim's thesis are clear: see *ante*, 843.

most egregious example of disintegration in recent times is surely the Soviet Union and, though the reasons for this are complex, it was not for lack of law.[86] Nor was this the case in its satellites, East Germany, Hungary or Czechoslovakia. True, in all these countries law may have failed to fill a vacuum.[87] In other societies which have disintegrated—in Africa for example—there has not been the tradition of legalism and much law under which they have operated was imposed by colonial powers. Ha-bermas has got it the wrong way round. It is not that law holds together societies that would otherwise collapse: rather that law is strong in well-ordered functioning societies.

Tamanaha is surely right to insist that

> "just about *everything* that doesn't break society apart contributes to social order: intersubjectivity, shared language, values, customs, conventions, beliefs, practices, habits of action, role orientations, organized complexes of action (institutional arrangements), associations, explicit co-ordination, shared knowledge, self-interested action, survival instinct, altruism, the market, the reinforcing effects of the successful conduct of affairs, spontaneous social organization, and more, including all those traits selected by evolution which have helped the human species thrive as social animals. . . . and, yes, also law."[88]

There are significant questions which must be asked and which Habermas ignores. Which laws (and whose laws) allegedly constitute the cement of society? Is it the law of property (which most people do not have)? Or family laws (largely irrelevant to most of society throughout most of history and hence, even where relevant, ignored)? Or criminal laws (used against the weak but rarely of use to them)? The old riposte to "law and order" whose law? and what order? seems especially apposite here.[89] Is Habermas's perspective one from the perspective of the economically powerful and/or legal functionaries? It certainly does not look like one "from below".[90] Perhaps Habermas should direct his attention not to the preservation of society through law, but to why societies disintegrate and to the status of law in such societies. If Habermas were right, one would expect law to play a much greater role in people's everyday lives than we know it does. The most effective laws conform to what people do anyway,[91] and there is, in general, profound ignorance of the law.[92]

We have seen how for Habermas the test for the legitimacy of law is the

---

[86] Eric Hobsbawm, *Age of Extremes* (1994) is of the view that the collapse can be explained in Marxist terms.

[87] Insights into which may be found in D. Shlapentokh (2000) 17 Social Philosophy and Policy 269.

[88] *Op cit*, n. 82, p. 995. See also Tamanaha (1995) 15 Ox. J. Legal Studies 969.

[89] *Cf* the Marxist view of law, *post*, 1145.

[90] For agreement see Tamanaha, *op cit*, n. 82, especially pp. 996–997. On questions of multiculturalism see C. Taylor, *Multiculturalism* (1994) (this includes a response by Habermas at p. 107).

[91] As Ehrlich argued (see *ante*, 847).

[92] See A. Podgorecki *et al., Knowledge and Opinion About Law* (1973).

discourse principle.[93] But the standard set out ("all persons possibly affected") is unattainable and, therefore, idealized. Habermas accepts this: he calls his discourse principle "counterfactual".[94] Can it therefore be empirical? And if it is, this would amount to a claim that the law is legitimate—certainly one fraught with danger.[95] And one anyway that Habermas would be hard put to justify. As Tamanaha points out: "To the extent that no real situation can ever meet the discourse principle, it is not clear that it can ever be usefully applied as a concrete standard with which to test real situations".[96] Inevitably then there are calls to substitute for unanimity majority agreement.[97] And it would seem to argue for the legitimacy of Western liberal democracies.[98] The discourse principle is procedural. The success of deliberative politics depends

"...on institutionalisation of corresponding procedures and conditions of communication, as well as the interplay of institutionalized deliberative processes with informally developed public opinions".[99]

In such a context law becomes the medium through which

"the structures of mutual recognition already familiar from simple interactions and quasi-natural solidarities can be transmitted, in an abstract but binding form, to the complex and increasingly anonymous spheres of a functionally differentiated society".[1]

Rather like Fuller,[2] Habermas assumes that through proper decision-making processes good outcomes will emerge. These outcomes should appeal to those least advantaged.[3] Any form of legitimation, Habermas argues, must appeal to "a posttraditional moral consciousness of citizens who are no longer disposed to follow commands, except for good reasons".[4] However, as Tamanaha points out the question is "whether the populace will agree with Habermas that legal norms are worthy of being followed solely because they are consistent with the discourse principle,

---

[93] See the sentence quoted at n. 83.
[94] *Postmetaphysical Thinking: Philosophical Essays* (1992), p. 47.
[95] See D. Dyzenhaus (1996) 46 Univ. of Toronto L.J. 129, 175.
[96] *Op. cit.*, n. 82, p. 1000.
[97] *E.g.* J. Bohman (1994) 28 Law and Soc. Rev. 897, 921.
[98] "Despite Habermas's impeccable critical pedigree, it is difficult to read his argument without sliding to the conclusion that our systems of liberal democracies and the rule of law, despite their flaws, for the most part are deserving of a substantial claim to legitimacy" (*per* Tamanaha, *op. cit.*, n. 82, p. 1001).
[99] *Op. cit.*, n. 59, p. 298.
[1] *ibid.*, p. 318.
[2] *The Morality of Law*, discussed *ante*, p. 118.
[3] Thus, in relation to women Habermas notes that liberal rights can only "empower women to shape their own lives autonomously" if democratic structures "also facilitate equal participation in the practice of civic self-determination, because only women themselves can clarify the 'relevant aspects' that define equality and inequality for a given matter" (*op. cit.*, n. 1, p. 420).
[4] *Op. cit.*, n. 82, p. 938 (and *post*, 969).

whether they will count this as a 'good reason' ".[5] This is not to deny the importance of the legitimacy of the procedure but for most people it is the outcome produced which counts.

A more fundamental objection to the discourse principle is the way it emphasises "the citizen who participates in political opinion- and will-formation".[6] Citizens must, he insists, "be willing to participate in the struggle over the public relevance, the interpretation and evaluation of their own needs, before legislators and judges can even know what it in each case means to treat like cases alike".[7] Though it is undeniable that in an ideal world there will be such participation, it hardly represents reality or even a realistic goal.[8] Tamanaha points also to the "alienating, excluding effect of, and the irony of, a theory which makes an extensive case for open and accessible discourse, but is presented in a form and manner that is comprehensible only to the initiated."[9]

The reference in the last paragraph to judges points to one other problem with Habermas's thesis. Can it really account for the common law? This, as we know, has caused legitimation problems for legal theorists. For long the declaratory theory of precedent was a convenient smoke-screen.[10] Dworkin's picture of a succession of Herculean judges creating law as "integrity"[11] is unlikely to satisfy historians of law. And others, including those who are sceptical,[12] can offer nothing very convincing. The central problem of modern legal theory for Habermas—the tension between facticity and validity—appears only with the separation of positive law and life-world forms upon the arrival of modernity. But is this separation realised in a common law system? Can Habermas explain the continued and pervasive operation of the customary forms and processes that are the common law system? The role of the judge in the common law world is different from in civilian countries and the latter are Habermas's model.[13]

## CRITICAL EMPIRICISM

With sociolegal studies' "maturity"[14] has come both reassessment and a call for socio-legal scholarship that is both critical and empirical.[15] But, as

[5] *Op cit*, n. 80, p. 1002.
[6] *Op cit*, n. 82, p. 942 (and *post*, 969).
[7] *ibid.*
[8] *Cf* Rousseau, *ante*, 147.
[9] *Op cit*, n. 80, p. 1003.
[10] *Post*, 1536. And note Lord Reid's comment *(post)* that we don't believe in fairy tales any longer.
[11] *Ante*, 724.
[12] *E.g.* D. Kennedy, *A Critique of Adjudication* (1997).
[13] See C. Kemp's excellent critique in (1999) 76 Denver University Law Rev. 961, 973–975. See also Forbath, *op cit*, n. 60.
[14] The American Law and Society Association has just celebrated its 25th anniversary.
[15] The earliest call came from Susan Silbey (see (1985) 9 Legal Studies Forum 7)

Trubek and Esser note,[16] "for those who equate empiricism with a value free search for objective knowledge, critical empiricism is a contradiction in terms". Law and Society studies is said to be going through a crisis. Three concerns are voiced. That what was once a vanguard movement is now an intellectual backwater. That it has lost its political "edge", "becoming little more than the handmaiden of policy-makers".[17] That it has lost its support base and that it is threatened by the rapid rise of other movements of legal thought, law and economics,[18] critical legal studies,[19] feminist jurisprudence,[20] and postmodernism.[21]

Critical empiricists claim to be developing a new approach to socio-legal scholarship. Silbey "envisions" and "proposes" a sociology of law to "study law as a social practice".[22] Sarat "offers a reorienting strategy for empirical research on law in action".[23] Brigham wants to "recast the study of impact into the framework of interpretive social science".[24] Those with these goals are not just lawyers and sociologists, but come also from the disciplines of anthropology (Merry[25] and Yngvesson[26]) and political science (Harrington,[27] Mather,[28] Villmoore[29]). They have produced empirical studies, analyses of legal concepts and theoretical explications. Their goal is to highlight "objects and spaces, in the world not previously recognised as significant".[30] As Silbey and Sarat put it:

"The task for those who seek to preserve that critical edge [in socio-legal studies] is to reconstitute and reimagine the subject of socio-legal research. This requires attention to epistemology and understanding, or how we can claim to know and what claiming to know can possibly mean.... [The task] is to locate and examine the knowledge and tradition we call law and society. [It is] suggested that it may be time to move our activity into places and spaces in the social environment we have not previously considered in order to reconceive the relationship between law and society."[31]

A couple of examples may be used to illustrate this new epistemology and focus. Yngvesson[32] has analyzed strategies of power in criminal complaint hearings. She shows how the ideology of relational complaints

---

[16] (1989) 14 *Law and Social Inquiry* 3, 4.
[17] *ibid.* p. 6.
[18] *Ante*, 620.
[19] *Post*, Chap. 14.
[20] *Post*, Chap. 15.
[21] *Post*, Chap. 16.
[22] (1985) 9 *Legal Studies Forum* 7
[23] (1985) 9 *Legal Studies Forum* 23, 24.
[24] (1985) 9 *Legal Studies Forum* 47
[25] (1986) Am. Ethnologist 253. See also *post*, n. 43.
[26] (1988) 22 Law and Society Rev. 409.
[27] (1989) 17 Int. J. Sociology of Law 41; (1988) 10 *Law and Policy* 293.
[28] (1980) 15 Law and Soc. Review 775 (with Yngvesson); (1994) 28 Law and Soc. Review 149 (with McEwen and Maiman)
[29] (1990) 15 *Law and Social Inquiry* 149.
[30] *Op. cit.*, n. 8, p. 14.
[31] (1987) 21 Law and Society Rev. 165 and *post*, 944 (this quotation being omitted).
[32] (1988) 22 Law and Society Rev. 409.

as "garbage" and of property matters as "crime" is reproduced in distinctions drawn by the court clerk between serious and trivial events, as he negotiates the withdrawal and dismissal of complaints brought by citizens.[33] Dismissals reproduce the separate spheres of community (held together by ongoing ties) and law (a sphere defined in terms of rights and entitlement), but are carried out through the "gentle violence" of dismissals "chosen" by the citizens themselves in the context of an ongoing relation with the court clerk. It is through this relationship that the dependence of citizens on the court is created (as well as the status of the clerk as the appropriate official for handling "garbage" produced). At the same time it empowers citizens as agents who "choose" and the clerk as an official who maintains the boundaries of law. Harrington and Merry[34] have shown how the concept of mediator neutrality and detachment emerge in diverse practices of selecting mediators who unselfconsciously "produce" a nonjudgmental stance in their approach to handling conflict. The mediator selection process becomes "a site for the ideological production of "neutrality" in the form of a detached stance",[35] rather as, in Yngvesson's research, the process of handling complaints by the court clerk becomes a site for the ideological production of "garbage" in the ongoing involvement of the clerk with trouble that "won't go away". These interpretive socio-legal studies draw on the work of Bourdieu,[36] particularly his analysis of "symbolic capital" and "symbolic violence". Symbolic capital and symbolic violence create and maintain "a lasting hold over someone" in "euphemized" form.[37] Symbolic violence is the "gentle, invisible form of violence, which is never recognized as such, and is not so much undergone as chosen, the violence of credit, confidence, obligation, personal loyalty, hospitality, gifts, gratitude, piety".[38] Such conduct is "intrinsically *equivocal*", and is concerned with what "holds together in practice". Analysis, he maintains and he is followed in this by Yngvesson and Harrington and Merry, must attend to this and not get lost in "self-mystifying demystification".[39] These examples show the ways in which this group of thinkers[40] have highlighted concepts like "ideology" and "process" and have thrown new light on the contours of disputing.

But its critics, even those broadly sympathetic to its goals, detect an underlying inconsistency. A reading of the group's literature suggests that the participants "retain and share a belief that social science can provide authoritative descriptions of the world. This belief keeps them from

---

[33]  Similar analyses of the ways the police sort cases can be found in R. Reiner, *The Politics of the Police* (2nd ed. 1993).

[34]  (1988) 22 Law and Society Rev. 709.

[35]  *ibid.* p. 730.

[36]  *Outline of a Theory of Practice* (1977).

[37]  *ibid.* p. 191.

[38]  *ibid.* p. 192.

[39]  *ibid.* p. 179.

[40]  Often referred to as the Amherst group because it is loosely organized round a seminar held there.

questioning the theme of universal scientism".[41] But Trubek and Esser claim, such a belief is inconsistent with elements of the interpretive model of action to which the group is committed. In addition, the critical empiricists perceive ideologies to be "objects of perception that can be described empirically",[42] but to take this idea to its conclusion—which is not done—would require it to include their own understanding of their own knowledge production. The implication of this is that "the values we advance, the perspectives we construct, and the evaluative criteria we apply are all historical; they are deeply implicated with one another; they hold together (though loosely) as webs of meaning; and they change over time and over space".[43]

These criticisms have provoked a lively debate in the pages of *Law and Social Inquiry*.[44] It has led Sarat to concede that the "group" is "struggling to do empirical work in a world stripped of a self-confident belief in the distinction between subjects and objects and between ways of representing the world and the world that is represented".[45] It acknowledges that it is "caught in a social process within which the most pressing question will always be the political one of deciding what counts as accurate, persuasive and authoritative".[46] Sarat does, however, concede that the rules of critical and empirical work have yet to be stated clearly— a judgment with which it is difficult not to agree. This will continue to raise question marks over "critical empiricism" but not to devalue the insights of an intriguing product.

## BOURDIEU AND HABITUS

Some reference has already been made to Pierre Bourdieu.[47] But it is perhaps his concept of "habitus" by which he is known best, and it is this which has most influenced legal thinkers. Habitus is:

> "The strategy-generating principle enabling agents to cope with the unforeseen and ever-changing situations ... a system of lasting and transposable dispositions which, integrating past experiences, function at every moment as a matrix of perception, appreciation and action and makes possible the achievement of infinitely diversified tasks."[48]

Bourdieu explains that legal practices—and not just legal practices—are "patterned"[49] by education, tradition and everyday experience of legal

[41] *Per* Trubek and Esser, *op. cit.*, n. 16, p. 35.
[42] *ibid.* p. 40.
[43] *ibid.*
[44] (1989) 14 *Law and Social Inquiry* (1) and (1990) 15 *Law and Social Inquiry* (1).
[45] (1990) 15 *Law and Social Inquiry* 155, 160.
[46] *ibid.* p. 162.
[47] The best introduction to his thinking is P. Bourdieu (1987) 38 Hastings L.J. 805.
[48] P. Bourdieu in P. Bourdieu and L.J.D. Wacquant, *An Invitation to Reflexive Sociology* (1992), p. 18.
[49] See R. Terdiman, *Introduction to Bourdieu*, p. 805.

custom and professional practice. They "operate as a learned yet deep structure of behaviour",[50] termed by Bourdieu "habitus".

" 'Habitus" is concerned with what actors, for example, legal professionals, judges, police officers, do. As Brubaker explains, it is a mediating concept connecting social structure with practical activity.[51] The "socialization effect of habitus materializes when examined in the context of the concept of field".[52] "Field" is Bourdieu's second conceptual tool. It is a way of examining structure and practices. The juridical field is "an area of norms and practices . . . that constitute the legal process within which lawyers operate".[53] The assumption is that legal conflicts are solved by applying legal norms (legislation, precedent, rules of procedure). According to Bourdieu, in a common law system "the law is jurisprudential (case law), based almost exclusively on the decisions of courts and the rule of precedent. Such a legal system gives primary to procedures, which must be fair".[54] That a set of social practices predominant in one area of human life, such as disputing, "can importantly influence practices, beliefs and norms in other areas of society"[55] is not unique to Bourdieu, but it is basic to his conception of law. Thus, he writes:

> "The law is the quintessential form of 'active' discourse, able by its own operation to produce its effects. It would not be excessive to say that it creates the social world, but only if we remember that it is this world which first creates the law".[56]

As he describes this process, law "transmutes regularity (that which is done regularly) into rule (that which must be done)", and thus imposes "a representation of normalcy".[57]

Chase, commenting on Bourdieu, believes it is "intuitive" that we take from our practices in one area of life "a sense of how to deal with other situations". [58] An explanation of why this should be is still required. It is a question that has exercised disciplines from anthropology to cognitive psychology. One attempt at an answer is in Balkin's recent book *Cultural Software*.[59] Balkin uses the term "cultural software" to refer to the shared understandings and ways of thinking that are communicated throughout society.[60] We are "cultural creatures"; we are "born with the ability to absorb and communicate previously developed culture".[61] We have finite

---

[50] *ibid.*
[51] (1985) 14 Theory and Society 723.
[52] According to J. Marshall in (eds.) M. Freeman, *Law and Sociology* (2006), p. 281.
[53] *ibid.*
[54] *Op. cit.*, note 47, p. 822.
[55] Per O. Chase, *Law, Culture and Ritual* (2005), p. 127.
[56] *Op. cit.*, note 47, p. 839.
[57] *ibid*, pp. 846–847.
[58] *Op. cit.*, note 55, p. 127.
[59] J.M. Balkin, *Cultural Software: A Theory of Ideology* (1998).
[60] *ibid*, pp. 13–19.
[61] *ibid*, p. 5.

memory and creativity. This is certainly one of the reasons why we use a concept or a cultural tool when confronted by a new situation. Balkin gives the example of democratic political concepts influencing the functioning of religious organisations.

AUTOPOIESIS AND LAW[62]

The autopoietic theory of law, associated with the German writers Niklas Luhmann and Gunther Teubner,[63] is adopted from biology. The word "autopoiesis" was coined by a biologist to describe the self-referential, self-replicating qualities of the typical biological system.[64] In most biological systems, the initial properties of a member of one generation are controlled by properties of members of the preceding generation. Since an autopoietic system can only use its own elements, it "constitutes the elements of which it consists through the elements of which it consists".[65] Such a system is operationally closed: "closure consists in the fact that all operations always reproduce the system".[66]

Luhmann claims that law is an autopoietic system and so is operationally closed. Law is distinguished from its environment as a set of normative, rather than cognitive expectations.[67] The autopoiesis of the legal system is normatively closed in that only the "legal system can bestow legally normative quality on its elements and thereby constitute them as elements".[68] This function appears to be much like Hart's rule of recognition[69] but there is an important difference. Hart's rule of recognition took as its referrent the behaviour of officials and was therefore part of the society: Luhmann's function is a part of the legal system and is distinctly separate from the society.

This raises the question of how a closed autopoietic legal system responds to developments in its larger social environment. Luhmann's initial answer to this is that the legal system, though normatively closed is cognitively open. "The norm quality serves the autopoiesis of the system, its self continuation in deference to the environment. The cognitive

---

[62] See "Unity of the Legal System" in G. Teubner, *Autopoietic Law* (1988), p. 12; (1992) 13 Cardozo L. Rev. 1419; (1989) 89 Northwestern L. Rev. 136 and see A. Jacobson (1989) 87 Michigan L. Rev. 1647 and H. Rottleutner (1989) 23 Law and Soc. Rev. 778.

[63] *Autopoietic Law* (1988); (1989) 23 Law and Soc. Rev. 728. Autopoietic Law has exponents in Britain as well, notably Michael King (1991) 18 J. Law and Soc. 303 and (with Christine Piper), *How The Law Thinks About Children* (1990) and (1993) 20 J. Law and Soc.; David Nelken, "Changing Paradigms in Sociology of Law" in G. Teubner, *Autopoietic Law* (1988), p. 191; and W. T. Murphy (1994) V *Law and Critique* 241.

[64] Maturana in 1970 being the first to use it in *Biology of Cognition*.

[65] *Per* Luhmann, "Unity", p. 14.

[66] *ibid.* p. 15.

[67] *ibid.* p. 19.

[68] *ibid.* p. 20.

[69] *Ante*, 382. *Cf* Luhmann: the system needs no "legitimation" by the social system (*op. cit.* 13 Cardozo L. Rev. at p. 1422).

quality serves the co-ordination of this process with the system's environment"[70] That this distinction was rather obscure[71] is now conceded by Luhmann, who has now introduced the notion of "structural coupling".[72] This is to be understood as channelling the extra-legal environment into the legal and vice versa. "Structural couplings are forms of simultaneous ... relations."[73] They "provide a continuous influx of disorder against which the system maintains or changes its structure".[74] In addition, Luhmann regards communication as the basis and the subject matter of the system. It is the "domain" in which the differentiation of the legal system becomes possible.[75] But Luhmann stresses that this does not require "a communication *of* the legal system *to* the society as a relation between sender and receiver. The legal system cannot communicate as a unity and the society has no address".[76]

The reader of this may wonder why because a theory is accepted in biology it should have any explanatory power in law. He or she may wonder also whether we are being offered "theory" or "metaphor"[77] If it is only a metaphor, why should everything be explained by it, particularly since it is taken from a realm far removed from law? It may occur also that this is a theory developed by someone with a civilian background. Perhaps it is easier to see the value of Luhmann's analysis when the legal system is codified—but such systems, it may be responded, are also not closed or self-replicating. The French Civil Code antedates the industrial revolution: its section on delicts is in five terse provisions. But the French judiciary has been able to fashion a corpus of law to respond to industrial, economic, social and technological developments. Can this really be explained by the notion of "structural couplings?" Perhaps the preoccupation with systems and boundaries can be attributed to German legal tradition. For, surely, it may be said, Anglo-American approaches to law, particularly in the twentieth century, have emphasized the continuum between law, politics, economics etc.[78] Why is the economic approach to law so attractive to so many?[79] Legal systems are characterized by durability and stability and often they are resistant to change. But occasionally radical changes occur? *Brown v. Board of*

---

[70]  *Op. cit.* n. 62, p. 20.
[71]  And see R. Lempert in G. Teubner, *op. cit.*, n. 62, p. 152.
[72]  See (1992) 13 Cardozo L. Rev. 1419, 1432.
[73]  *ibid.*
[74]  *ibid.* p. 1433.
[75]  *ibid.* p. 1434.
[76]  *ibid.*
[77]  And see S. Diamond (1992) 13 Cardozo L. Rev. 1763.
[78]  *Cf.* Shklar's remark, *ante*, 21, that law is not a "discrete entity".
[79]  See *ante*, 620. Described by Barnett as "a view that caught on like no other since realism" (97 Harv. L. Rev. 1223, 1229 (1984)).

*Education*[80] and *Roe v. Wade*[81] in the United States,[82] the sweeping away of the marital rape immunity and the *doli incapax* presumption in England.[83] These examples reflect the normative adaptability of the legal system to normative change within society. The autopoietic system is open to facts but these are values. We could dress them up as facts, but then what sense would there be in calling the system closed? Luhmann's answer is to invoke the structural coupling, to which reference has already been made. Structural coupling is non-causative in nature: changes in the moral environment do not cause normative adjustments in the system, because it remains an intra-system choice whether or not the change should be made. But does this convince the sceptic? Of course, it was ultimately the "choice" of judges to reject the "separate but equal" doctrine, to give women greater reproductive rights. But there were constraints[84] on these choices which to a large extent "caused" such changes. Statutes not infrequently refer explicitly to extra-legal norms: the Unfair Contract Terms Act 1977 refers to inequality of bargaining power, the Matrimonial Causes Act 1973 requires a court considering a clean break to consider whether the party upon whom it is to be imposed can adjust without undue hardship to it. Luhmann's likely response will separate facts and norms so that even a statute incorporating an extra-systemic standard can be described within autopoiesis theory. But formalism of this kind distorts—perhaps too high a price to pay to preserve a theory.

Any number of other questions may be asked. Does legislative history have a part to play in an autopoietic theory of statutory construction?[85] Do the findings of social science research have no part to play in the work of the courts?[86] For example, psychological evidence on the value of eyewitness testimony.[87] How does autopoiesis characterize custom, in particular mercantile custom? And, think of the Hart-Fuller debate in the context of autopoietic theory. As Sinclair[88] puts it: "Is there not something quite frightening about an autonomous legal system, subject only to its own operational constraints, but still the legal system defining legality for society?"[89] A final intriguing question concerns the origins of legal systems. If all legal systems are autopoietic, including the first ones, where did they come from and why did they emerge? Unless the first legal system was not autopoietic or not a legal system (by what test?), it seems

[80]   347 U.S. 483 (1954).
[81]   410 U.S. 113 (1973).
[82]   *R. v. R.* [1991] 4 All E.R. 481.
[83]   [1994] 3 All E.R. 190. But for the argument that Luhmann's systems theory prepares the ground for a genuinely sociological theory of human rights see G. Verschraegen (2002) 29 Journal of Law and Society 258.
[84]   On which see Dworkin, *ante*, 728.
[85]   See *Pepper* v. *Hart* [1992] 3 W.L.R. 1032. See *post*, 1417.
[86]   And see S. Herzberger (1993) 25 Connecticut L. Rev. 1067.
[87]   For example, G. Wells and E. Loftus, *Eyewitness Testimony: Psychological Perspectives* (1984).
[88]   (1992) 16 Legal Studies Forum 81, 97.
[89]   See also M. Rosenfeld (1992) 13 Cardozo L. Rev. 1681.

it must have had its source in the extra-legal environment, whether this was religion, morality, or power.

The reader may ponder whether autopoiesis is the ultimate[90] in sociological theories of law or an antidote to sociological jurisprudence.[91]

---

### R. VON JHERING
#### Law as Means to an End[92]

The decisive position which I shall constantly keep in mind in the following consideration is that of the *security* of the satisfaction of human wants; it shall be the standard by which I intend to measure all the phenomena of commerce.

Want is the band with which nature draws man into society, the means by which she realizes the two principles of all morality and culture. "Everybody exists for the world", and "the world exists for everybody". Dependent as he is upon his fellowmen through his need, and the more so as his need grows, man would be the most unhappy being in the world if the satisfaction of his need depended upon accident, and he could not count with all security upon the cooperation and assistance of his fellowmen. In that case the animal would be an object of envy to him, for the animal is so made by nature that when it comes into possession of the powers destined for it by nature it needs no such support. The realization of the mutual relations of man for her purpose; the elimination of accident; the establishment of the security of the satisfaction of human need as a basal form of social existence; the regulated, assured and substantial system of actions and methods which minister to this satisfaction, keeping equal step with the need—that is *commerce*.

The simplest form of satisfaction of a need, in man as in the animal, lies in his own power. But whereas in the animal, need and power coincide, this is not the case in man. It is this very disproportion between the two, this insufficiency of his own power, which is the cause by means of which nature forces him to be a man; namely, to look for man, and in association with others to attain those purposes to which he is alone unequal. In his necessity she refers him to the outside world and his fellows.                                    [pp. 75–76]

... we finally come upon the vital point in the whole organization of right. This consists in the preponderance of the *common* interest of *all* over the *particular* interests of one *individual; all* join for the common interests, only the *individual*

---

[90] It has been called a "purified sociology of law": Rottleuthner (1989) 23 Law and Soc. Rev. 779.

[91] The (1992) Cardozo Law Review, vol. 13(5) is a symposium devoted to Luhmann's legal sociology. A further useful critique of autopoiesis is James (1992) 19 J. Law and Soc. 271 (to which King replies at (1993) 20 J. Law and Soc. 143). Nobles and Schiff (in (ed.) M. Freeman, *Law and Sociology* (2006), p. 32) have examined the implications of Luhmann's system theory for jurisprudence, in particular for some of Dworkin's thinking. Luhmann offers, they say, a sociological explanation for long-running debates within jurisprudence over such questions as the source of law, its determinacy/indeterminacy, and the role of justice. "Hercules", they argue, provides a poor description of law "or at least one that might appeal to a sociologist concerned to accommodate the given world of law's vast number of operations within their descriptions" (p. 37). Their *A Sociology of Jurisprudence* (2006) also repays study.

[92] [Translated, I. Husik (1924).]

stands for the particular interest. But the power of all is, the forces being equal, superior to that of the individual; and the more so the greater their number.[93]

We thus have the formula for social organization of force, viz., preponderance of the force which is serviceable to the interests of all over the amount at the disposition of the individual for his own interest; the power being brought over to the side of the interest common to all.

The form in private law of a combination of several persons for the pursuit of the same common interest is *partnership*, and although in other respects the State is very different from partnership, the formula in reference to regulating force by interest is quite the same in both. Partnership contains the prototype of the State, which is indicated therein in all its parts. Conceptually as well as historically, partnership forms the transition from the unregulated form of force in the individual to its regulation by the State. Not merely in the sense that it contains a combination of several for the same purpose, and thereby makes possible the pursuit of aims which were denied to the power of the individual ... but in an incomparably greater measure in the sense that it solves the problem of creating the preponderance of power on the side of right. It does this by putting in place of the opposition of two particular interests fighting one another without an assured prospect of the victory of right, that between a common interest and a particular, whereby the solution comes of itself. In partnership all partners present a united front against the one who pursues his own interests at the expense of these common interests assigned by the contract, or who refuses to carry out the duties undertaken by him in the contract; they all unite their power against the one. So the preponderance of power is here thrown *on the side of right*, and partnership may therefore be designated as the mechanism of the *self-regulation of force according to the measures of right*.[94]                    [pp. 220–221]

## M. WEBER
### Economy and Society
### (1968)

*The Formal Qualities of Modern Law*

*1. Particularism in Modern Law*

[T]he specifically modern occidental type of administration of justice has arisen on the basis of rational and systematic legislation. However, its basic formal qualities

---

[93]  [Although a follower of Bentham, Jhering criticised his individualistic approach. Jhering insisted on the primacy of social purposes, and based this on the fact that men in their mutual relations gradually perceive that they will best further their own purposes by cooperation. Jhering referred to "social mechanics", as the means by which society achieved its social purposes. These means were divided between law, involving the use of organised coercion, and the voluntary processes of social life, which rely upon reward and the satisfaction of human needs, etc. Justice is achieved by the measure to which the common purposes of society are fulfilled. Unfortunately, however, as Stone points out, Jhering did not really provide an adequate criterion of justice. Indeed his arguments seem to lead to the inevitable conclusion that individual purposes must always yield to social purposes. But this hypothesis depends on the rather naïve assumption that in any case of conflict there will always be an acceptable consensus as to what the common interest requires. Moreover, it appears to ignore those areas where individual interest, such as freedom of speech, may possess a higher value than some common social purpose which would favour the suppression of discordant voices (*cf.* J. Stone, *Human Law and Human Justice*, Chap. 5).]

[94]  [For Jhering the task of bringing the legal order into closer touch with actual human needs was a matter for the legislature rather than part of the judicial function. See I. Jenkins, "Jhering", in (1960–1961) 14 Vanderbilt L. Rev. 169, 184–185.]

are by no means unambiguously definable. Indeed, this ambiguity is a direct result of more recent developments.

The ancient principles which were decisive for the interlocking of "right" and "law" have disappeared, especially the idea that one's right has a "valid" quality only by virtue of one's membership in a group of persons by whom this quality is monopolized. To the past now also belongs the tribal or status-group quality of the sum total of a person's rights and, with it, their "particularity" as it once existed on the basis of free association or of usurped or legalized privilege. Equally gone are the status and other special courts and procedures. Yet neither all special and personal law nor all special jurisdictions have disappeared completely. On the contrary, very recent legal developments have brought an increasing particularism within the legal system. Only the principle of demarcation of the various spheres has been characteristically changed. A typical case is that of commercial law, which is, indeed, one of the most important instances of modern particularism. Under the German Commercial Code this special law applies to certain types of contracts, the most important of which is the contract for acquisition of goods with the intention of profitable resale. This definition of commercial contract is entirely in accordance with a rationalized legal system; the definition does not refer to formal qualities, but to the intended functional meaning of the concrete transaction. On the other hand, commercial law also applies to certain categories of persons whose decisive characteristics consists in the fact that contracts are made by them in the course of their business. What is thus really decisive for the demarcation of the sphere of this type of law is the concept of "enterprise". An enterprise is a commercial enterprise when transactions of such peculiar kind are its constitutive elements. Thus every contract which "belongs" substantively, *i.e.* in its intention, to a commercial enterprise is under Commercial Code, even though, when regarded alone and by itself, it does not belong that category of transactions which are generically defined as commercial and even though, in a particular case, such a contract may happen to be made by a nonmerchant. The application of this body of special law is thus determined either by substantive qualities of an individual transaction, especially its intended meaning, or by the objective association of a transaction with the rational organization of an enterprise. It is not determined, however, by a person's membership in a status group legally constituted by free agreement or privilege, which was in the past the operative factor for the application of a special law.

Commercial law, then, inasmuch as its application is personally delimited, is a class law rather than a status-group law. However, this contrast with the past is but a relative one. Indeed, so far as the law of commerce and the law of other purely economic "occupations" are concerned, the principle of jurisdictional delimitation has always had a purely substantive character, which, while often varying in externals, has essentially been the same throughout. But those particularities in the legal system which constituted a definite status law were more significant both quantitatively and qualitatively. Besides, even the vocational special jurisdictions, so far as their jurisdictions did not depend upon the litigants' membership in a certain corporate body, have usually depended upon mere formal criteria such as acquisition of a license or a privilege. For example, under the new German Commercial Code, a person is characterized as a merchant by the mere fact that he is listed in the register of commercial firms. The personal scope of application of the commercial law is thus determined by a purely formal test, while in other respects its sphere is delimited by the economic purpose which a given transaction purports to achieve. The spheres of the special laws applicable to other occupational groups are also predominantly defined along substantive or functional criteria, and it is only under certain circumstances that applicability is governed by formal tests. Many of these modern special laws are also combined with special courts and procedures of their own.

Mainly two causes are responsible for the emergence of these particularistic laws. In the first place, they have been a result of the occupational differentation and the increasing attention which commercial and industrial pressure groups have obtained for themselves. What they expect from these particularistic arrangements is that their legal affairs will be handled by specialized experts. The second cause, which has played an increasingly important role in most recent times, has been the desire to eliminate the formalities of normal legal procedure for the sake of a settlement that would be both expeditious and better adapted to the concrete case. In practice, this trend signifies a weakening of legal formalism out of considerations of substantive expediency and thus constitutes but one instance among a whole series of similar contemporary phenomena.

## 2. The Anti-Formalistic Tendencies of Modern Legal Development

From a theoretical point of view, the general development of law and procedure may be viewed as passing through the following stages: first, charismatic legal revelation through "law prophets"; second, empirical creation and finding of law by legal honoratiores, *i.e.* law creation through cautelary jurisprudence and adherence to precedent: third, imposition of law by secular or theocratic powers: fourth and finally, systematic elaboration of law and professionalized administration of justice by persons who have received their legal training in a learned and formally logical manner. From this perspective, the formal qualities of the law emerge as follows: arising in primitive legal procedure from a combination of magically conditioned formalism and irrationality conditioned by revelation, they proceed to increasingly specialized juridical and logical rationality and systematization, sometimes passing through the detour of theocratically or patrimonially conditioned substantive and informal expediency. Finally, they assume, at least from an external viewpoint, an increasingly logical sublimation and deductive rigor and develop an increasingly rational technique in procedure.

[. . .]

Only the Occident has witnessed the fully developed administration of justice of the folk-community (*Dinggenossenschaft*) and the status-stereotyped form of patrimonialism; and only the Occident has witnessed the rise of the national economic system, whose agents first allied themselves with the princely powers to overcome the estates and then turned against them in revolution; and only the West has known "Natural Law", and with it the complete elimination of the system of personal laws and of the ancient maxim that special law prevails over general law. Nowhere else, finally, has there occurred any phenomenon resembling Roman law and anything like its reception. All these events have to a very large extent been caused by concrete political factors, which have only the remotest analogies elsewhere in the world. For this reason, the stage of law decisively shaped by trained legal specialists has not been fully reached anywhere outside of the Occident. Economic conditions have, as we have seen, everywhere played an important role, but they have nowhere been decisive alone and by themselves. To the extent that they contributed to the formation of the specifically modern features of present-day occidental law, the direction in which they worked has been by and large the following: To those who have interests in the commodity market, the rationalization and systematization of the law in general and the increasing calculability of the functioning of the legal process in particular, constituted one of the most important conditions for the existence of economic enterprise intended to function with stability and, especially, of capitalistic enterprise which cannot do without legal security. Special forms of transactions and special procedures, like the bill of exchange and the special procedure for its speedy collection, serve this need for the purely formal certainty of the guaranty of legal enforcement.

On the other hand, the modern and, to a certain extent, the ancient Roman, legal developments have contained tendencies favourable to the dilution of legal formalism. At a first glance, the displacement of the formally bound law of evidence by the "free evaluation of proof appears to be of a merely technical character. The primitive system of magically bound proof was exploded through the rationalism of either the theocratic or the patrimonial kind, both of which postulated procedures for the disclosure of the real truth. Thus the new system clearly appears as a product of substantive rationalization. Today, however, the scope and limits of the free evaluation of proof are determined primarily by commercial interests, *i.e.* by economic factors. It is clear that, through the system of free evaluation of proof, a very considerable domain which was once subject to formal juristic thought is being increasingly withdrawn therefrom. But we are here more concerned with the corresponding trends in the sphere of substantive law. One such trend lies in the intrinsic necessities of legal thought. Its growing logical sublimation has meant everywhere the displacement of dependence on externally tangible formal characteristics by an increasingly logical interpretation of *meaning* in relation to the legal norms themselves as well as in relation to legal transactions. In the doctrine of the continental "common law" this interpretation claimed that it would give effect to the "real" intentions of the parties; in precisely this manner it introduced an individualizing and relatively substantive factor into legal formalism. This kind of interpretation seeks to construct the relations of the parties to one another from the point of view of the "inner" kernel of their behaviour, from the point of view of their mental "attitudes" (such as good faith or malice). Thus it relates legal consequences to informal elements of the situation and this treatment provides a telling parallel to that systematization of religious ethics. Much of the system of commodity exchange, in primitive as well as in technically differentiated patterns of trade, is possible only on the basis of far-reaching personal confidence and trust in the loyalty of others. Moreover, as commodity exchange increases in importance, the need in legal practice to guarantee or secure such trustworthy conduct becomes proportionally greater. But in the very nature of the case, we cannot, of course, define with formal certainty the legal tests according to which the new relations of trust and confidence are to be governed. Hence, through such ethical rationalization the courts have been helpful to powerful interests. Also, outside of the sphere of commodity exchange, the rationalization of the law has substituted attitude-evaluation as the significant element for assessment of events according to external criteria. In criminal law, legal rationalization has replaced the purely mechanistic remedy of vengeance by rational "ends of punishment" of an either ethical or utilitarian character, and has thereby introduced increasingly nonformal elements into legal practice. In the sphere of private law the concern for a party's mental attitude has quite generally entailed evaluation by the judge. "Good faith and fair dealing" or the "good" usage of trade or, in other words, ethical categories have become the test of what the parties are entitled to mean by their "intention". Yet, the reference of the "good" usage of trade implies in substance the recognition of such attitudes which are held by the average party concerned with the case, *i.e.* a general and purely business criterion of an essentially factual nature, such as the average expectation of the parties in a given transaction. It is this standard which the law has consequently to accept.

The expectations of parties will often be disappointed by the results of a strictly professional legal logic. Such disappointments are inevitable indeed where the facts of life are juridically "construed" in order to make them fit the abstract propositions of law and in accordance with the maxim that nothing can exist in the realm of law unless it can be "conceived" by the jurist in conformity with those "principles" which are revealed to him by juristic science. The expectations of the parties are oriented towards the economic or the almost utilitarian *meaning* of a legal proposition. However, from the point of view of legal logic, this *meaning* is an "irrational" one. For example, the layman will never understand why it should be impossible under the traditional definition of larceny to commit a larceny of electric power. It is by no means the peculiar foolishness of modern jurisprudence which leads to such conflicts. To a large extent such conflicts rather are the inevitable consequence of the incompatibility that exists between the intrinsic necessities of logically consistent formal legal thinking and the fact that the legally relevant agreements and activities of private parties are aimed at economic results and oriented towards economically determined expectations. It is for this reason that we find the ever-recurrent protests against the professional legal method of thought as such, which are finding support even in the lawyers' own reflections on their work. But a "lawyers' law" has never been and never will be brought into conformity with lay expectation unless it totally renounce that formal character which is immanent in it. This is just as true of the English law which we glorify so much today, as it has been of the ancient Roman jurists or of the methods of modern continental legal thought. Any attempt to replace the antiquated "law of nature" by a new "natural law" aiming at "dispute settlement" in accordance with the average expectations of average parties would thus come up against certain immanent limitations. But, nevertheless, this idea does have some validity in relation to the realities of legal history. The Roman law of the later Republic and the Empire developed a type of commercial ethics that was in fact oriented towards that which is to be expected on the average. Such a view means that only a small group of clearly corrupt or fraudulent practices would be outlawed, and the law should not go beyond what is regarded as the "ethical minimum". In spite of the bona fides (which a seller had to display), the maxim of *caveat emptor* remained valid.

New demands for a "social law" to be based upon such emotionally coloured ethical postulates as "justice" or "human dignity", and directed against the very dominance of a mere business morality, have arisen with the emergence of the modern class problem. They are advocated not only by labour and other interested groups but also by legal ideologists. By these demands legal formalism itself has been challenged. Such a concept as economic duress, or the attempt to treat as immoral, and thus as invalid, a contract because of a gross disproportion between promise and consideration, are derived from norms which, from the legal standpoint, are entirely amorphous and which are neither juristic nor conventional nor traditional in character but ethical and which claim as their legitimation substantive justice rather than formal legality.

Status ideologies of the lawyers themselves have been operative in legal theory and practice along with those influences which have been engendered by both the social demands of democracy and the welfare ideology of monarchical bureaucracy. Being confined to the interpretation of statutes and contracts, like a slot machine into which one just drops the facts in order to have it spew out the decision (plus opinion), appears to the modern lawyer as beneath his dignity; and the more universal the codified formal statute law has become, the more unattractive has this notion come to be. The present demand is for "judicial creativeness", at least where the statute is silent. The school of "free law" has undertaken to prove that such silence is the inevitable fate of every statute in view of the irrationality of the facts of life; that in countless instances the application of the statutes as "interpreted" is a delusion, and that the decision is, and ought to be, made in the light of concrete evaluations rather than in accordance with formal norms.

For the case where the statute fails to provide a clear rule, the well-known Article 1 of the Swiss Civil Code orders the judge to decide according to that rule which he himself would promulgate if he were the legislator. This provision, the practical import of which should not be overestimated, however, corresponds formally with the Kantian formula. But in reality a judicial system which would practice such ideals would, in view of the inevitability of value-compromises, very often have to forget about abstract norms and, at least in cases of conflict, would have to admit concrete evaluations, *i.e.* not only nonformal but irrational law-findings. Indeed, the doctrine of the inevitability of gaps in the legal order as well as the campaign to recognize as fiction the systematic coherence of the law has been given further impetus by the assertions that the judicial process never consisted, or, at any rate never should consist, in the "application" of general norms to a concrete case, just as no utterance in language should be regarded as an application of the rules of grammar. In this view, the "legal propositions" are regarded as secondary and as being derived by abstraction from the concrete decisions which, as the products of judicial practice, are said to be the real embodiment of the law.

Use has also been made of the historical fact that for long periods, including our own, private parties have to a large extent been advised by professional lawyers and judges who have had technical legal training or that, in other words, all customary law is in reality lawyers' law. This fact has been associated with the incontrovertible observation that entirely new legal principles are being established not only *praeter legem* but also *contra legem* by judicial practice, for instance, that of the German Supreme Court after the entry into force of the Civil Code. From all these facts the idea was derived that case law is superior to the rational establishment of objective norms and that the expediential balancing of concrete interests is superior to the creation and recognition of "norms" in general. The modern theory of legal sources has thus disintegrated both the half-mystical concept of "customary law", as it had been created by historicism, as well as the equally historicist concept of the "will of the legislator" that could be discovered through the study of the legislative history of an enactment as revealed in committee reports and similar sources. The statute rather than the legislator has been thus proclaimed to be the jurists' main concern. Thus isolated from its background, the "law" is then turned over for elaboration and application to the jurists, among whom the predominant influence is assigned at one time to the practitioners and at others, for instance, in the reports accompanying certain of the modern codes, to the scholars. In this manner the significance of the legislative determination of a legal command is, under certain circumstances, degraded to the role of a mere "symptom" of either the validity of a legal proposition or even of the mere desire of such validity which, however, until it has been accepted in legal practice, is to remain uncertain. But the preference for a case law which remains in contact with legal reality—which means with the reality of the lawyers—to statute law is in turn subverted by the argument that no precedent should be regarded as binding beyond its concrete facts. The way is thus left open to the free balancing of values in each individual case.

In opposition to all such value-irrationalism, there have also arisen attempts to reestablish an objective standard of values. The more the impression grows that legal orders as such are no more than "technical tools", the more violently will such degradation be rejected by the lawyers. For to place on the same level such merely "technical rules" as a customs tariff and legal norms concerning marriage, parental power, or the incidents of ownership, offends the sentiment of the legal practitioners, and there emerges the nostalgic notion of a metapositive law above that merely technical positive law which is acknowledged to be subject to change. The old natural law, it is true, looks discredited by the criticisms levelled at it from the historical and positivist points of view. As a substitute there are now advanced the religiously inspired natural law of the Catholic scholars, and certain efforts to deduce objective standards from the "nature" of the law itself. The latter effort has taken two forms. In the *a-prioristic*, Neo-Kantian doctrines, the "right law", as the normative system of a "society of free men", is to be both a legislative standard for rational legislation and a source for judicial decisions where the law refers the judge to apparently nonformal criteria. In the empiricist, Comtean, way those "expectations" which private parties are justified to have in view of the average conception existing with regard to the obligations of others, are to serve as the ultimate standard, which is to be superior even to the statute and which is to replace such concepts as equity, etc., which are felt to be too vague.

[...]

### 3. Contemporary Anglo-American Law

The differences between Continental and Common Law methods of legal thought have been produced mostly by factors which are respectively connected with the internal structure and the modes of existence of the legal profession as well as by factors related to differences in political development. The economic elements, however, have been determinative only in connection with these elements. What we are concerned with here is the fact that once everything is said and done about these differences in historical developments, modern capitalism prospers equally and manifests essentially identical economic traits under legal systems containing rules and institutions which considerably differ from each other at least from the juridical point of view. Even what is on the face of it so fundamental a concept of Continental law as *dominium* still does not exist in Anglo-American law. Indeed, we may say that the legal systems under which modern capitalism has been prospering differ profoundly from each other even in their ultimate principles of formal structure.

Even today, and in spite of all influences by the ever more rigorous demands for academic training, English legal thought is essentially an empirical art. Precedent still fully retains its old significance, except that it is regarded as unfair to invoke a case from too remote a past, which means older than about a century. One can also still observe the charismatic character of lawfinding. In practice, varying significance is given to a decided case not only, as happens everywhere, in accordance with the hierarchical position of the court by which it was decided by also in accordance with the very personal authority of an individual judge. This is true for the entire common-law sphere, as illustrated, for instance, by the prestige of Lord Mansfield. But in the American view, the judgment is the very personal creation of the concrete individual judge, to whom one is accustomed to refer by name, in contrast to the impersonal "District Court" of Continental-European officialese. The English judge, too, lays claim to such a position. All these circumstances are tied up with the fact that the degree of legal rationality is essentially lower than, and of a type different from, that of continental Europe. Up to the recent past, and at any rate up to the time of Austin, there was practically no English legal science which would have merited the name of "learning" in the Continental sense. This fact alone would have sufficed to render any such codification as was desired by Bentham practically impossible. But it is also this feature which has been responsible for the "practical" adaptability of English law and its "practical" character from the standpoint of the public.

The legal thinking of the layman is, on the one hand, literalistic. He tends to be a definition-monger when he believes he is arguing "legally". Closely connected with this trait is the tendency to draw conclusions from individual case to individual case; the abstractionism of the "professional" lawyer is far from the layman's mind. In both respects, however, the art of empirical jurisprudence is cognate to him, although he may not like it. No country, indeed, has produced more bitter complaints and satires about the legal profession than England. The formularies of the conveyancers, too, may be quite unintelligible to the layman, as again is the case in England. Yet, he can understand the basic character of the English way of legal thinking, he can identify himself with it and, above all, he can make his peace with it by retaining once and for all a solicitor as his legal father confessor for all contingencies of life, as is indeed done by practically every English businessman. He simply neither demands nor expects of the law anything which could be frustrated by "logical" legal construction.

Safety valves are also provided against legal formalism. As a matter of fact, in the sphere of private law, both Common Law and Equity are "formalistic" to a considerable extent in their practical treatment. It could hardly be otherwise under the traditional spirit of the legal profession. But the institution of the civil jury imposes on rationality limits which are not merely accepted as inevitable but are actually prized because of the binding force of precedent and the fear that a precedent might thus create "bad law" in a sphere which one wishes to keep open for a concrete balancing of interests. We must forego the analysis of the way in which this division of the two spheres of *stare decisis* and concrete balancing of interests is actually functioning in practice. It does in any case represent a softening of rationality in the administration of justice. Alongside all this we find the still quite patriarchal, summary and highly irrational jurisdiction of the justices of the peace. They deal with the petty causes of everyday life and they represent a kind of kadi justice which is quite unknown in Germany. The Common Law thus presents a picture of an administration of justice which in the most fundamental formal features of both substantive law and procedure differs from the structure of Continental law as much as is possible within a secular system of justice, that is, a system that is free from theocratic and patrimonial powers. Quite definitely, English law-finding is not, like that of the Continent, "application" of "legal propositions" logically derived from statutory texts.

These differences have had some tangible consequences both economically and socially; but these consequences have all been isolated single phenomena rather than differences touching upon the total structure of the economic system. For the development of capitalism two features of Common Law have been relevant and both have helped to support the capitalistic system. Legal training has primarily been in the hands of the lawyers from among whom also the judges are recruited, *i.e.* in the hands of a group which is active in the service of propertied, and particularly capitalistic, private interests and which has to gain its livelihood from them. Furthermore and in close connection with this, the concentration of the administration of justice in London and its extreme costliness have amounted almost to a denial of access to the courts for those with inadequate means. At any rate, the essential similarity of the capitalistic development on the Continent and in England has not been able to eliminate the sharp contrasts between the two types of legal systems. Nor is there any visible tendency towards a transformation of the English legal system in the direction of the Continental under the impetus of the capitalist economy. On the contrary, wherever the two kinds of administration of justice and of legal training compete with one another, as for instance in Canada, the Common Law way has come out on top and has overcome the Continental alternative rather quickly. We may thus conclude that capitalism has not been a decisive factor in the promotion of that form of rationalization of the law which has been peculiar to the continental West ever since the rise of Romanist studies in the medieval universities.

### 4. *Law Justice and Corporative Tendencies in the Modern Legal Profession*

Modern social development, aside from the already mentioned political and internal professional motives, has given rise to certain other factors by which formal legal rationalism is being weakened. Irrational kadi justice is exercised today in criminal cases clearly and extensively in the "popular" justice of the jury. It appeals to the sentiments of the layman, who feels annoyed whenever he meets with formalism in a concrete case, and it satisfies the emotional demands of those under-privileged classes which clamour for substantive justice.

Against this "popular justice" element of the jury system, attacks have been directed from two quarters. The jury has been attacked because of the strong interest orientation of the jurors as against the technical matter-of-factness of the specialist. Just as in ancient Rome the jurors' list was the object of class conflict, so day the selection of jurors is attacked, especially by the working class, as favouring class justice, upon the ground that the jurors, even though they may be "plebeians", are picked predominantly from among those who can afford the loss of time. Although such a test of selection can hardly be avoided entirely, it also depends, in part at least, on political considerations. Where, on the other hand, the jurors' bench is occupied by working-class people, it is attacked by the propertied class. Moreover, not only "classes" as such are the interested parties. In Germany, for instance, male jurors can practically never be moved to find a fellow male guilty of rape, especially where they are not absolutely convinced of the girl's chaste character.

From the standpoint of professional legal training lay justice has been criticized on the ground that the laymen's verdict is delivered as an irrational oracle without any statement of reasons and without the possibility of any substantive criticism. Thus one has come to demand that the lay judges by subjected to the control of the legal experts. In answer to this demand there was created the system of the mixed bench, which, however, experience has shown to be a system in which the laymen's influence is inferior to that of the experts. Thus their presence has practically no more significance than that of giving some compulsory publicity to the deliberation of professional judges in a way similar to that of Switzerland, where the judges must hold their deliberation in full view of the public. The professional judges, in turn, are threatened, in the sphere of criminal law, by the overshadowing power of the professional psychiatrist, onto whom more and more responsibility is passed, especially in the most serious cases, and on whom rationalism is thus imposing a task which can by no means be solved by means of pure science.

Obviously all of these conflicts are caused by the course of technical and economic development only indirectly. Primarily they are rather consequences of the insoluble conflict between the formal and the substantive principles of justice, which may clash with one another even where their respective protagonists belong to one and the same social class. Moreover, it is by no means certain that those classes which are negatively privileged today, especially the working class, may safely expect from an informal administration of justice those results which are claimed for it by the ideology of the jurists. A bureaucratized judiciary, which is being planfully r?cruited in the higher ranks from among the personnel of the career service of the prosecutor's office and which is completely dependent on the politically ruling powers for advancement, cannot be set alongside the Swiss or English judiciary, and even less the (Federal) judges in the United States. If one takes away from such judges their belief in the sacredness of the purely objective legal formalism and directs them simply to balance interests, the result will be very different from those legal systems to which we have just referred. However, the problem does not belong to this discussion. There remains only the task of correcting a few historical errors.

Prophets are the only ones who have taken a really consciously "creative" attitude towards existing law; only through them has new law been consciously created. For the rest, as must be stressed again and again, even those jurists who, from the objective point of view, have been the most creative ones, have always and not only in modern times, regarded themselves to be but the mouthpiece of norms already existing, though, perhaps, only latently, and to be their interpreters or appliers rather than their creators. This subjective belief is held by even the most eminent jurists. It is due to the disillusionment of the intellectuals that today this belief is being confronted with objectively different facts and that one is trying to elevate this state of facts to the status of a norm for subjective judicial behaviour. As the bureaucratization of formal legislation progresses, the traditional position of the English judge is also likely to be transformed permanently and profoundly. On the other hand, it may be doubted whether, in a code country, the bestowal of the "creator's" crown upon bureaucratic judges will really turn them into law prophets. In any case, the juristic precision of judicial opinions will be seriously impaired if sociological, economic, or ethical argument were to take the place of legal concepts.

All in all the movement is one of those characteristic reactions against the dominance of "specialization" and rationalism, which latter has in the last analysis been its very parent. The development of the formal qualities of the law certainly shows some peculiarly antinomial traits. Rigorously formalistic and dependent on what is tangibly perceivable as far as it is required for security to do business, the law has at the same time become informal for the sake of business good-will where this is required by the logical interpretation of the intention of the parties or by the "good usage" of business intercourse, interpreted at some "ethical minimum."

The law is drawn into antiformal directions, moreover, by all those powers which demand that it be more than a mere means of pacifying conflicts of interest. These forces include the demand for substantive justice by certain social class interests and ideologies; they also include the tendencies inherent in certain forms of political authority of either authoritarian or democratic character concerning the ends of law which are respectively appropriate to them; and also the demand of the "laity" for a system of justice which would be intelligible to them; finally, as we have seen, anti-formal tendencies are being promoted by the ideologically rooted power aspirations of the legal professional itself.

Whatever form law and legal practice may come to assume under the impact of these various influences, it will be inevitable that, as a result of technical and economic developments, the legal ignorance of the layman will increase. The use of jurors and similar lay judges will not suffice to stop the continuous growth of the technical elements in the law and hence of its character as a specialists' domain. Inevitably the notion must expand that the law is a rational technical apparatus, which is continually transformable in the light of expediential considerations and devoid of all sacredness of content. This fate may be obscured by the tendency of acquiescence in the existing law, which is growing in many ways for several reasons, but it cannot really be stayed. All of the modern sociological and philosophical analyses can only contribute to strengthen this impression, regardless of the content of their theories concerning the nature of law and the judicial process.                                     [pp. 880–895.]

## E. DURKHEIM
### The Division of Labour in Society
### (1893)[95]

#### Laws as an Index of Social Solidarity

We have not merely to investigate whether, in [advanced] societies, there exists a social solidarity arising from the division of labour. This is a self-evident truth, since in them the division of labour is highly developed, and it engenders solidarity. But above all we must determine the degree to which the solidarity it produces contributes generally to the integration of society. Only then shall we learn to what extent it is necessary, whether it is an essential factory in social cohesion, or whether, on the contrary, it is only an ancillary and secondary condition for it. To answer this question we must therefore compare this social bond to others, in order to measure what share in the total effect must be attributed to it. To do this it is indispensable to begin by classifying the different species of social solidarity.

However, social solidarity is a wholly moral phenomenon which by itself does not lend itself to exact observation and especially not to measurement. To arrive

[95] [This translation is by W. D. Halls (1984).]

at this classification, as well as this comparison, we must therefore substitute for this internal datum, which escapes us, an external one which symbolises it, and then study the former through the latter.

That visible symbol is the law. Indeed, where social solidarity exists, in spite of its non-material nature, it does not remain in a state of pure potentiality, but shows its presence through perceptible effects. Where it is strong it attracts men strongly to each other, ensures frequent contacts between them, and redoubles the opportunities available to them to enter into mutual relationships. Stating the position precisely, at the point we have now reached it is not easy to say whether it is social solidarity which produces these phenomena or, on the contrary, whether it is the result of them. It is also a moot point whether men draw closer to one another because of its dynamic effects, or whether it is dynamic because men *have* come closer together. However, for the present we need not concern ourselves with elucidating this question. It is enough to state that these two orders of facts are linked, varying with each other simultaneously and moving in the same direction. The more closely knit the members of a society, the more they maintain various relationships either with one another or with the group collectively. For if they met together rarely, they would not be mutually dependent, except sporadically and somewhat weakly. Moreover, the sum of these relationships is necessarily proportioned to the sum of legal rules which determine them. In fact, social life, wherever it becomes lasting, inevitably tends to assume a definite form and become organized. Law is nothing more than the most stable and precise element in this very organization. Life in general within a society cannot enlarge in scope without legal activity similarly increasing in a corresponding fashion. Thus we may be sure to find reflected in the law all the essential varieties of social solidarity.

It may certainly be objected that social relationships can be forged without necessarily taking on a legal form. Some do exist where the degree of regulation does not attain such a level of consolidation and precision. This does not mean that they remain indeterminate; instead of being regulated by law they are merely regulated by custom. Thus law mirrors only a part of social life and consequently furnishes us with only incomplete data with which to resolve the problem. What is more, it is often the case that customs are out of step with the law. It is repeatedly said that customs temper the harshness of the law, correct the excesses that arise from its formal nature, and are occasionally inspired with a very different ethos. Might then customs display other kinds of social solidarity than those expressed in positive law?

But such an antithesis only occurs in wholly exceptional circumstances. For it to happen law must have ceased to correspond to the present state of society and yet, lacking any reason for continuing to exist, is sustained through force of habit. In that event, the new relationships that are established in spite of it, will become organised, for they cannot subsist without an effort of consolidation. Yet, being at odds with the old law, which persists, and not succeeding in penetrating the legal domain proper, they do not rise beyond the level of custom. Thus opposition is sparked off. But this can only occur in rare, pathological cases, ones which cannot continued without danger. Normally customs are not opposed to law; on the contrary, they form the basis for it. It is true that sometimes nothing else is built upon this basis. There may exist social relationships governed only by that diffuse form of regulation arising from custom. But this is because they lack importance and continuity, excepting naturally those abnormal cases just mentioned. Thus if types of social solidarity exist which custom alone renders apparent, these are assuredly of a very secondary order. On the other hand law reproduces all those types which are essential, and it is about these alone that we require to know.

Should we go further and assert that social solidarity does not consist entirely in its visible manifestations; that these express it only partially and imperfectly;

that beyond law and custom there exists an inner state from which solidarity derives; and that to know it in reality we must penetrate to the heart of it, and without any intermediary? But in science we can know causes only through the effects that they produce. In order to determine causes more precisely science selects only those results that are the most objective and that best lend themselves to quantification. Science studies heart through the variations in volume that changes in temperature cause in bodies, electricity through its physical and chemical effects, and force through movement. Why should social solidarity prove an exception?

Moreover, what remains of social solidarity once it is divested of its social forms? What imparts to it its specific characteristics is the nature of the group whose unity it ensures, and this is why it varies according to the types of society. It is not the same within the family as within political societies. We are not attached to our native land in the same way as the Roman was to his city or the German to his tribe. But since such differences spring from social causes, we can only grasp them through the differences that the social effects of solidarity present to us. Thus, if we neglect these differences, all varieties become indistinguishable, and we can no longer perceive more than that which is common to all varieties, *i.e.* the general tendency to sociability, a tendency which is always and everywhere the same and is not linked to any particular social type. But this residual element is only an abstraction, for sociability *per se* cannot be met with anywhere. What exist and what are really alive are the special forms of solidarity—domestic, occupational, national, that of the past and that of today, etc. Each has its own special nature. Hence general features can in any case only furnish a very incomplete explanation of the phenomenon, since necessarily they allow to escape what is concrete and living about it.

Thus the study of solidarity lies within the domain of sociology. It is a social fact which can only be known thoroughly through its social effects. If so many moralists and psychologists have been able to deal with this question without following this method it is because they have avoided the difficulty. They have divested the phenomenon of everything that is more specifically social about it, retaining only the psychological embryo from which it develops. It is indeed certain that solidarity, whilst being pre-eminently a social fact, is dependent upon our individual organism. In order to exist it must be sustained by our physical and psychological constitution. Thus, at the bare minimum, we can content ourselves with studying it from this viewpoint. But in that case we shall perceive only that aspect of it which is the most indistinct and the least special. Precisely speaking, this is not even solidarity itself, but only what makes it possible.

Moreover, such an abstract study cannot yield very fruitful results. For, so long as it remains in the state of a mere predisposition of our psychological nature, solidarity is something too tenuous to be easily understood. It remains an intangible virtuality too elusive to observe. To take on a comprehensible form that we can grasp, social outcomes must provide an external interpretation. Moreover, even in such an indeterminate state, it depends on social conditions, which explain it and consequently it cannot be detached from them. This is why a few sociological perspectives are not infrequently to be found among these purely psychological analyses. For example, some mention is made of the influence of the *gregarious* state on the formation of social feeling in general; or the main social relationships on which sociability depends most obviously are rapidly sketched out. Undoubtedly such additional considerations, introduced unsystematically as examples and randomly as they suggest themselves, are insufficient to cast much light on the social nature of solidarity. Yet at least they demonstrate that the sociological viewpoint must weigh even with the psychologists.

Thus our method is clearly traced out for us. Since law reproduces the main forms of social solidarity, we have only to classify the different types of law in order to be able to investigate which species of social solidarity correspond to them. It is already likely that one species of law exists which symbolizes the special solidarity engendered by the division of labour. Once we have done this, so as to judge what part the division of labour plays, it will be enough to compare the number of legal rules which give it expression to the total volume of law as a whole.

To undertake this study we cannot use the habitual distinctions made by jurisprudents. Conceived for the practice of law, from this angle they can be very convenient, but science cannot be satisfied with such empirical classifications and approximations. The most widespread classification is that which divides law into public and private law. Public law is held to regulate the relationships of the individual with the State, private law those of individuals with one another. Yet when we attempt to define the terms closely, the dividing line, which appeared at first sight to be so clear-cut, becomes blurred. All law is private, in the sense that always and everywhere individuals are concerned and are the agents. But, above all, all law is public, in the sense that it is a social function, and all individuals are, although in different respects, functionaries of society. The functions of marriage and parenthood, etc., are not spelt out or organized any differently from those of ministers and legislators. Not without reason did Roman law term guardianship a *munus publicum*. Moreover, what is the State? Where does it begin, where does it end? How controversial is this question is well known. It is unscientific to base such a fundamental classification on such an obscure and inadequately analysed idea.

In order to proceed methodically, we must discover some characteristic which, whilst essential to juridical phenomena, is capable of varying as they vary. Now, every legal precept may be defined as a rule of behaviour to which sanctions apply. However, it is clear that the sanctions change according to the degree of seriousness in which the precepts are held, the place they occupy in the public consciousness, and the role they play in society. Thus it is appropriate to classify legal rules according to the different sanctions which are attached to them.

These are of two kinds. The first consist essentially in suffering, or at least in some disadvantage imposed upon the perpetrator of a crime. Their purpose is to hurt him through his fortune, his honour, his life, his liberty, or to deprive him of some object whose possession he enjoys. These are said to be repressive sanctions, such as those laid down in the penal code. It is true that those which appertain to purely moral rules are of the same character. Yet such sanctions are administered in a diffuse way by everybody without distinction, whilst those of the penal code are applied only through the mediation of a well-defined body—they are organized. As for the other kind of sanctions, they do not necessarily imply any suffering on the part of the perpetrator, but consist merely in *restoring the previous state of affairs*, re-establishing relationships which have been disturbed from their normal form. This is done either by forcibly redressing the action impugned, restoring it to the type from which it has deviated, or by annulling it, *i.e.* depriving it of all social value. Thus legal rules must be divided into two main species, according to whether they relate to repressive, organized sanctions, or to ones that are purely restitutory. The first group covers all penal law; the second, civil law, commercial law, procedural law, administrative and constitutional law, when any penal rules which may be attached to them have been removed. [pp. 24–29]

## E. EHRLICH
### Principles of the Sociology of Law[96]

The impulses to create law which result from the distribution of power in society have their source in society. The frequently used word *Machtverhaältnisse* (distribution of power) indeed is not available as a scientific term because of its indefiniteness; we are using it here as referring to the distribution of power which is based on position in the state, on economic or on social position. Furthermore the legal proposition does not owe its existence to any consideration of the interests of individual classes or ranks, but of those of all social strata; and it is immaterial whether actual general interests are involved or merely imagined ones, as in the case of the superstitious belief in the existence of witches. Under this head comes the defence against external enemies and elemental forces. In the last analysis, at least in the judgment of those that act, the interests of individual strata of the population are general interests when popular opinion does not regard the interests of the other strata as worth taking into account, *e.g.* the interests of the slaves in Rome; up to the nineteenth century, quite generally, the interests of the unfree peasantry; in the Polish republic, and in ancient Hungary, usually, the interests of those who were not members of the nobility; and until late in the nineteenth century, the interests of the non-propertied classes. And for most modern men and women the interest of the utterly neglected and submerged perhaps is but little more than something to be protected against. In their opinion, the general interest includes protection of the social order against individuals who are beyond the pale of society. This protection may be effected by means of a part of the criminal law, police law, and procedural law. In reality all of this is a matter of the distribution of power. A decision rendered for the protection of the general interest may be said to be a decision based solely upon considerations of expedience. Wherever there is no doubt as to where the power lies in a state, or where the voice of popular consciousness speaks in no uncertain tones, the task of the jurist is a merely technical one. The content of the legal proposition is given by society. His function is merely to provide the wording of it and to find the means whereby the interests which are to be secured can be secured most effectively. This technical function however must not be underrated . . .

The decision as to the interests involved in a dispute is entrusted by the state to the jurist when it is clearly indicated neither by the general interest nor by the distribution of power in society as a whole. This situation may be brought about by various causes. In the first place very often the parties to the dispute are quite unaware of the great social interests involved in the decision; very often the latter are distributed among the various classes and ranks in such a manner as to place them above the struggles of class and rank; in many cases these social interests are too inconsiderable and insignificant to become involved in the dispute. Very often, too, the possessors of power, who are called upon to render the decision, are not at all involved in the conflict of interests. The most important cause however is the fact that the powers that are engaged in the struggle on behalf of the different interests counterbalance one another or that the influences that proceed from the groups that are most powerful politically, economically, or socially, are checked or thwarted by other social tendencies, which are based on religious, ethical, scientific, or other ideological convictions.

When the jurist is asked to draw the line between the conflicting interests independently, he is asked, by implication, to do it according to justice. This implies, in the first place, something negative. He is asked to arrive at a decision without any consideration of expediency and uninfluenced by the distribution of

---

[96] [Translated, W.L. Moll (1936). For a sympathetic critique and detailed discussion of Ehrlich's thought see Littlefield (1967) 19 Maine L. Rev. 1.]

power. In recent times, it is true, it has often been said that justice, too, is a matter involving questions of power. If the writer means to say that the idea of justice, on which the decision is based, must have attained a certain power in the body social at the time when it influences the judicial finding of norms or the activity of the state, he is indeed stating a truth, but it is a self-evident truth; and a self-evident truth does not require statement. But if he means to say that, under the cloak of justice, effect is always being given to the influence of political, social, or economic position, the statement is manifestly incorrect. A legal norm whose origin can be traced to such influences is usually stigmatized by that very fact as something unjust. Justice has always weighted the scales solely in favour of the weak and the persecuted. A just decision is a decision based on grounds which appeal to a disinterested person; it is a decision which is rendered by a person who is not involved in the conflict of interests, or which, even though it be rendered by a person involved in this conflict, nevertheless is such as a disinterested person would render or approve of. It is never based on taking advantage of a position of power. When a person who is in a position of power acts justly, he acts against his own interest, at any rate against his immediate interest, prompted by religious, ethical, scientific, or other ideological considerations; perhaps merely by considerations of prudent policy. The parties of political and social justice find their adherents chiefly among ideologists who are not personally interested in the political and social conflicts of interests. In this fact lies their strength and also their weakness.

But all of these are negative characteristics. Which are the positive characteristics of justice? The catch phrase about balancing of interests is not an answer to this question; for the very question is: What is it that gives weight to the interests that are to be balanced? Manifestly it is not the balancing jurist, writer or teacher, judge or legislator, but society itself. The function of the jurist is merely to balance them. There are trends caused by the interests that flourish in society which ultimately influence even persons that are not involved in these conflicting interests. The judge who decides according to justice follows the tendency that he himself is dominated by. Justice therefore does not proceed from the individual, but arises in society.

The rôle of the person rendering the decision is of importance only inasmuch as, within certain limitations, he can select the solution which corresponds most nearly to his personal feelings. But in doing this, he cannot disregard the social basis of the decision. If a Spartacus, favoured by fortune, had abolished slavery in antiquity, or if the socialists should abolish private property, let us say in a beleaguered city, as was done in Paris during the days of the Commune, these facts would have nothing to do with justice. And a judge who, in a decision which he renders, recognizes private property in means of production in spite of the fact that he is a socialist, or who admits the defence that the debt sued upon in a stock-exchange transaction is a gaming debt although in his opinion the setting-up of this plea is a breach of good faith, does not thereby contradict himself. In doing these things he is merely being guided by social tendencies against his own individual feeling in the matter. A rebellious slave, the government of a beleaguered city, like that of Paris during the Commune, can indeed proceed according to their individual feelings, but they can do so only because they have been removed from social influences by the force of circumstances. Justice is a power wielded over the minds of men by society.

It is the function of juristic science, in the first place, to record the trends of justice that are found in society, and to ascertain what they are, whence they come, and whither they lead; but it cannot possibly determine which of these is the only just one. In the forum of science, they are all equally valid. What men consider just depends upon the ideas they have concerning the ends of human endeavour in this world of ours, but it is not the function of science to dictate the final end of human endeavour on earth. That is the function of the founder of a religion, of the preacher, of the prophet, of the preacher of ethics, of the practical jurist, of the judge, of the politician. Science can be concerned only with those things that are susceptible of scientific demonstration. That a certain thing is just is no more scientifically demonstrable than is the beauty of a Gothic cathedral or of a Beethoven symphony to a person who is insensible to it. All of these are questions of emotional life. Science can ascertain the effects of a legal proposition, but it cannot make these effects appear either desirable or loathsome to man. Justice is a social force, and it is always a question whether it is potent enough to influence the disinterested persons whose function it is to create juristic and statute law.

But although science can teach us nothing concerning the end, once the end is determined, it can enlighten us as to the means to that end. The practical technical rules that perform this function are based on the results of pure science. There is no science that teaches men that they ought to be healthy, but practical medical science teaches men who desire to be healthy what they can do, to bring about the result. Practical juristic science is concerned with the manner in which the ends may be attained that men are endeavouring to attain through law, but it must utilize the results of the sociology of law for this purpose. The legal proposition is not only the result, it is also a lever, of social development; it is an instrumentality in the hands of society whereby society shapes things within its sphere of influence according to its will. Through the legal proposition man acquires a power, limited though it be, over the facts of the law; in the legal proposition a willed legal order is brought face to face with the legal order which has arisen self-actively in society.                                                              [pp. 198–203]

The sociology of law then must begin with the ascertainment of the living law.[97] Its attention will be directed primarily to the concrete, not the abstract. It is only the concrete that can be observed. What the anatomist places under the microscope is not human tissue in the abstract but a specific tissue of a specific human being; the physiologist likewise does not study the functions of the liver of mammals in the abstract, but those of a specific liver of a specific mammal. Only when he has completed the observation of the concrete does he ask whether it is universally valid, and this fact, too, he endeavours to establish by means of a series of concrete observations, for which he has to find specific methods. The same may be said of the investigator of law. He must first concern himself with concrete usages, relations of domination, legal relations, contracts, articles of association, dispositions by last will and testament. It is not true, therefore, that the investigation of the living law is concerned only with "customary law" or with "business usage." If one does any thinking at all when one uses these words— which is not always the case—one will realize that they do not refer to the concrete, but to that which has been universalized. But only the concrete usages, the relations of domination, the legal relations, the contracts, the articles of association, the dispositions by last will and testament, yield the rules according to which men regulate their conduct. And it is only on the basis of these rules that the norms for decision that the courts apply and the statutory provisions that alone have hitherto occupied the attention of jurists arise. The great majority of judicial decisions are based on the concrete usages, relations of possession,

---

[97] [Ehrlich's "living law" by no means corresponds with Pound's "law in action". The latter is confined to practices and usages of officials and citizens; the former refers to actual *norms* observed by citizens as members of groups or associations. For Pound, law reform should be primarily (if not necessarily) aimed at bringing the "law in books" into conformity with the law in action, whereas Ehrlich saw "norms for decisions" and "living law" as not necessarily in competition; the former were relevant to cases of dispute and conflict, while the latter prevailed under normal conditions. See D.Nelken, "Law in action or living law?" (1984) 4 *Legal Studies* 157, who argues that Ehrlich's approach, though underestimating the important of, and need for, legislative intervention, is a better focus for empirical research, being more firmly related to sociological theory.]

contracts, articles of association, and dispositions by last will and testament, that the courts have found to exist. If we would comprehend the universalizations, the reductions to unity, and the other methods of finding forms that the judge and the lawgiver employ, we must first of all know the basis upon which they were carried out. To this extent Savigny was right when he said that the law—and by law he means above all the legal proposition—can be understood only from its historical connection; but the historical connection does not lie in the hoary past, but in the present, out of which the legal proposition grows.

But the scientific significance of the living law is not confined to its influence upon the norms for decision which the courts apply or upon the content of statutes. The knowledge of the living law has an independent value, and this consists in the fact that it constitutes the foundation of the legal order of human society. In order to acquire a knowledge of this order we must know the usages, relations of domination, legal relations, contracts, articles of association, declarations by last will and testament, quite independently of the question whether they have already found expression in a judicial decision or in a statute or whether they will ever find it. The provisions contained in the German Commercial Code regulating stock exchanges, banks, publishing houses, and other supplementary provisions were full of gaps when they were enacted and, for the most part, have become antiquated. Modern commerce has meanwhile created an enormous number of new forms, which ought to be the subject matter of scientific study as well as those that have been enumerated in the statute. Very much that is of genuine value can be found on this point in the literature on the science of commerce that is blossoming forth so abundantly. A part of the order in the sphere of mining and navigation has been made accessible to legal science through mining law, maritime law, and the law of inland navigation, but for the most part this has long since become antiquated. The factory, the bank, the railroad, the great landed estate, the labour union, the association of employers, and a thousand other forms of life—each of these likewise has an order, and this order has a legal side as well as that of the mercantile establishment, which is being regulated in detail only by the Commercial Code. In addition there are countless forms in which the activity of these associations manifests itself outwardly, above all the contracts. In studying the manufacturing establishment, the legal investigator must pursue the countless, highly intricate paths that lead from the acceptance of the order to the delivery of the finished products to the customer.[98]

[pp. 501–503]

## R. POUND
### Philosophy of Law
(Revised ed. 1954)

### *The End or Purpose of Law*

At the end of the last and the beginning of the present century, a new way of thinking grew up. Jurists began to think in terms of human wants or desires or expectations rather than of human wills.[99] They began to think that what they had to do was not simply to equalize or harmonize wills, but, if not to equalize, at least to harmonize the satisfaction of wants. They began to weigh or balance and reconcile claims or wants or desires or expectations, as formerly they had

---

[98] [Ehrlich's concern is with the actual sociological and economic background to legal norms rather than with the mere statements of legal rules by legislators or courts. This savours more of the later Realist movement (though lacking some of its doctrinal extravagances) than of Pound's *a priori* catalogues of human interests and values.]

[99] [*Cf.* Jhering, *ante*, 880.]

balanced or reconciled wills. They began to think of the end of law, not as a maximum of self-assertion, but as a maximum satisfaction of wants. Hence for a time they thought of the problems of ethics, of jurisprudence, and of politics as chiefly one of valuing; as a problem of finding criteria of the relative value of interests. In jurisprudence and politics they saw that we must add practical problems of the possibility of making interests effective through governmental action, judicial or administrative. But the first question was one of the wants to be recognized—of the interests to be recognized and secured. Having inventoried the wants or claims or interests which are asserting and for which are asserting and for which legal security is sought, we were to value them, select those to be recognized, determine the limits within which they were to be given effect in view of other recognized interests, and ascertain how far we might give them effect by law in view of the inherent limitations upon effective legal action. This mode of thinking may be seen, concealed under different terminologies, in more than one type of jurist in the present century.

Three elements contributed to shift the basis of theories as to the end of law from wills to wants, from a reconciling or harmonizing of wills to a reconciling or harmonizing of wants. The most important part was played by psychology which undermined the foundation of the meta-physical will philosophy of law. Through the movement for unification of the social sciences, economics also played an important part, especially indirectly through the attempts at economic interpretation of legal history, reinforcing psychology by showing the extent to which law had been shaped by the pressure of economic wants. Also the differentiation of society, involved in industrial organization, was no mean factor, when classes came to exist in which claims to a minimum human existence, under the standards of the given civilization, became more pressing than claims to self-assertion. Attention was turned from the nature of law to its purpose, and a functional attitude, a tendency to measure legal rules and doctrines and institutions by the extent to which they further or achieved the ends for which law exists, began to replace the older method of judging law by criteria drawn from itself. In this respect the thought of the present is more like that of the seventeenth and eighteenth centuries than that of the nineteenth century. French writers have described this phenomenon as a "revival of juridical idealism." But in truth the social utilitarianism of today and the natural-law philosophy of the seventeenth and eighteenth centuries have only this in common: Each has its attention fixed upon phenomena of growth: each seeks to direct and further conscious improvement of the law.

In its earlier form social-utilitarianism, in common with all nineteenth-century philosophies of law, was too absolute. Its teleological theory was to show us what actually and necessarily took place in lawmaking rather than what we were seeking to bring about. Its service to the philosophy of law was in compelling us to give over the ambiguous term "right" and to distinguish between the claims or wants or demands, existing independently of law, the legally recognized or delimited claims or wants or demands, and the legal institutions, which broadly go by the name of legal rights, whereby the claims when recognized and delimited are secured. Also it first made clear how much the task of the lawmaker is one of compromise ... Conflicting individual wills were to be reconciled absolutely by a formula which had ultimate and universal authority. When we think of law as existing to secure social interest, so far as they may be secured through an ordering of men and of human relations through the machinery of organized political society, it becomes apparent that we may reach a practicable system of compromises of conflicting human desires here and now, by means of a mental picture of giving effect to as much as we can, without believing that we have a perfect solution for all time and for every place...[1]

---

[1] [Sociological jurisprudence relies on "valuations" but these are relative, not absolute in character.]

... Social utilitarianism has stood in need of correction both from psychology and from sociology. It must be recognized that lawmaking and adjudication are not in fact determined precisely by a weighing of interest. In practice the pressure of wants, demands, desires will warp the actual compromises made by the legal system this way or that. In order to maintain the general security we endeavour in every way to minimize this warping. But one needs only to look below the surface of the law anywhere at any time to see it going on, even if covered up by mechanical devices to make the process appear an absolute one and the result a predetermined one. We may not expect that the compromises made and enforced by the legal order will always and infallibly give effect to any picture we may make of the nature or ends of the process of making and enforcing them. Yet there will be less of this subconscious warping if we have a clear picture before us of what we are seeking to do and to what end, and if we build in the image thereof so far as we consciously build and shape the law.

Difficulties arise chiefly in connection with criteria of value. If we say that interests are to be catalogued or inventoried, that they are then to be valued, that those which are found to be of requisite value are to be recognized legally and given effect within limits determined by the valuation, so far as inherent difficulties in effective legal securing of interests will permit, the question arises at once. How shall we do this work of valuing? Philosophers have devoted much ingenuity to the discovery of some method of getting at the intrinsic important of various interests, so that an absolute formula may be reached in accordance wherewith it may be assured that the weightier interests intrinsically shall prevail. But I am sceptical as to the possibility of an absolute judgment. We are confronted at this point by a fundamental question of social and political philosophy. I do not believe the jurist has to do more than recognize the problem and perceive that it is presented to him as one of securing all social interests so far as he may, of maintaining a balance or harmony among them that is compatible with the securing of all of them. The last century preferred the general security. The present century has shown many signs of preferring the individual moral and social life.[2] I doubt whether such preferences can maintain themselves.

Social utilitarians would say, weigh the several interests in terms of the end of law. But have we any given to us absolutely? Is the end of law anything less than to do whatever may be achieved thereby to satisfy human desires? Are the limits any other than those imposed by the tools with which we work, whereby we may lose more than we gain, if we attempt to apply them in certain situations? If so, there is always a possibility of improved tools. The Greek philosopher who said that the only possible subjects of lawsuit were "insult, injury, and homicide" was as dogmatic as Herbert Spencer, who conceived of sanitary laws and housing laws in our large cities as quite outside the domain of the legal order. Better legal machinery extends the field of legal effectiveness as better machinery has extended the field of industrial effectiveness. I do not mean that the law should interfere as of course in every human relation and in every situation where someone chances to think a social want may be satisfied thereby. Experience has shown abundantly how futile legal machinery may be in its attempts to secure certain kinds of interests. What I do say is, that if in any field of human conduct or in any human relation the law, with such machinery as it has, may satisfy a social want without a disproportionate sacrifice of other claims, there is no eternal limitation inherent in the nature of things, there are no bounds imposed at creation to stand in the way of its doing so ...

... For the purpose of understanding the law of today I am content with a picture of satisfying as much of the whole body of human wants as we may with the least sacrifice. I am content to think of law as a social institution to satisfy social wants—the claims and demands and expectations involved in the existence

---

[2] [This seems to contradict the trend towards "collectivism" in twentieth-century society.]

of civilized society—by giving effect to as much as we may with the least sacrifice, so far as such wants may be satisfied or such claims given effect by an ordering of human conduct through politically organized society. For present purposes I am content to see in legal history the record of a continually wider recognizing and satisfying of human wants or claims or desires through social control; a more embracing and more effective securing of social interests; a continually more complete and effective elimination of waste and precluding of friction in human enjoyment of the goods of existence—in short, a continually more efficacious social engineering.[3]                                                    [pp. 42–47]

## R. POUND
### Outlines of Jurisprudence
(5th ed. 1943)[4]

*The Programme of the Sociological School*

Sociological jurists insist upon eight points:

(1) Study of the actual social effects of legal institutions, legal precepts and legal doctrines.
(2) Sociological study in preparation for law-making.
(3) Study of the means of making legal precepts effective in action.
(4) Study of juridical method.
(5) A sociological legal history; study of the social background and social effects of legal institutions, legal precepts, and legal doctrines, and of how these effects have been brought about.
(6) Recognition of the importance of individualized application of legal precepts—of reasonable and just solutions of individual cases.
(7) In English-speaking countries, a Ministry of Justice.
(8) That the end of juristic study, toward which the foregoing are but some of the means, is to make effort more effective in achieving the purposes of law.

## R. POUND
### Contemporary Juristic Theory
(1940)

*A Measure of Values*

Since Jhering showed us the difference between the legal institution we set up to secure a recognized claim or demand and the claim or demand itself, as it exists apart from the law,[5] we have known the claim or demand by the name of interest. The term has occasioned some confusion because it has easily been confused with an idea of advantage; the more so since Jhering's social utilitarianism made social advantage the criterion of value and treated it as something given, as something we know exactly as we know that a certain claim or demand exists *de facto* and is pressed upon lawmakers and courts for recognition. Everyone has an interest in, that is, makes a claim to the satisfaction of his desires. They are his interests as he

---

[3] [Here Pound displays his attachment to the nineteenth-century belief in evolutionary progress; nor is this surprising since the sociological creed is essentially an optimistic one which puts its faith in human perfectibility, especially in social relations.]
[4] [The programme in fact dates from 1911.]
[5] [See *ante* 880, but *cf.* 851.]

sees it, and his view of the matter cannot be ignored by telling him it is not to his advantage to want what he feels he wants and insists he ought to have. Very likely we can't give him what he claims or all that he claims, but it is because we have to consider the conflicting or overlapping claims of others, not because we decide he does not want it. We must, therefore, begin by ascertaining what are the claims and demands which press upon lawmakers and judges and administrative agencies for recognition and securing.

In the inventory with which we must begin it is convenient to classify the interests of which the legal order must take account as individual or public or social. All interests are those of individual human beings asserted by individuals. But some are claims or demands or desires involved in the individual life and asserted in title of that life. Others are claims or demands or desires involved in life in the politically organized society and asserted in title of that society. Others or the same in other aspects are claims or demands or desires involved in social life in civilized society and asserted in title of that life. Every claim does not necessarily go once and for all in one of these categories. The same claim may be asserted and may have to be looked at from different standpoints; it may be asserted in title of more than one aspect of life. Thus my claim to my watch may be asserted as an individual interest of substance when I sue someone, who walks off with it without my consent, either to recover possession of it or to obtain the money value as damages for converting it. But it may be looked at also as a social interest in the security of acquisitions and asserted as such when I persuade the district attorney to prosecute for larceny someone who has stolen it from me.

A mere sketch in broad lines of the scheme of interests which have pressed upon the legal order in the past will suffice for our purposes.[6] Individual interests are interests of personality or interests in the domestic relations or interests of substance. Interests of personality are those involved in the individual physical and spiritual existence; in one's body and life, *i.e.* security of his physical person and his bodily health, in free exertion of one's will, *i.e.* freedom from coercion, and from deception as to what one is tricked into doing by false representations, in free choice of location, in one's reputation, in freedom to contract and of entering into relations with others, in free industry, *i.e.* in freely employing himself or gaining employment in any occupation or activity for which he is or is considered qualified, and in free individual belief and opinion. It is enough to point out in passing that the interests in freedom of contract and in freedom of industry overlap or come into competition with claims of labouring men asserted through trade unions and have raised difficult questions for the courts.

Like difficult questions are raised by individual interests in the domestic relations. It is obvious that husband and wife have each a claim or demand which they make against the whole world that outsiders shall not interfere with the relation. Yet on a weighing of all the interests involved have been impelled to abrogate the action for alienation of affections by which that interest had been secured. The interest is still recognized but effective security is now denied. It is obvious too that the relation involves reciprocal claims or demands which each asserts against the other. The claims of the husband to the society of the wife and to her services for the benefit of the household, formerly well secured, are now deprived of all substantial security on a weighing in comparison with the individual interest of the wife in individual free self-assertion. But the claim or demand of the wife for support and maintenance is not only recognized but is secured in a variety of ways which make it one of the best secured interests known to the law. So it is with the interests involved in the relation of parent and child. Formerly the claims of the parent were given effect by privileges of correction, by

[6] [For a very full discussion of the classification and the content of the various interests which compete in a modern legal system, see especially, R. Pound, *Jurisprudence*, vol. 3. See also J. Stone, *Social Dimensions of Law and Justice*, pp. 175–176.]

control of the child's earnings, and by a wide authority of shaping the training and bringing up of the child in every phase. Everywhere today individual interests of the child and a social interest in dependents have been weighed against the claims of parents, and juvenile courts, courts of domestic relations, and family courts have greatly changed the balance of these interests.

By interests of substance we mean the claims or demands asserted by individuals in title of the individual economic existence. Claims with respect to property involve too many questions to make it worth while to do more than mention them in the present connection. It will be more useful for our immediate purpose to look at a group of interests in economically advantageous relations with others. Such relations may be social or domestic or official or contractual. If a man is wrongfully and maliciously expelled from a social club and injury to his social standing in the community may have a serious economic effect upon him. Yet other claims have to be considered and the courts cannot compel the members of the club to associate with him if they persist in refusing to do so. We have noted already how claims of the husband to the services of the wife in the household are no longer effectively secured either against outside interference with the relation or against the wife's refusal to perform. As to official relations, public interests have to be weighed and the older conception of property in a profitable office has been given up. But the most significant questions have arisen with respect to contractual relations. If A has a contract with B he makes a claim against the whole world that third persons shall not interfere to induce B to break the contract. Yet the third person may assert claims which have to be taken account of in this connection, and some of the hardest questions in labour law have turned on recognition of claims of labour organizations to induce breaking of contracts of employment and what should be regarded as giving a privilege to interfere with such contracts.

As to public interests, it will be enough to instance one type of question where difficult problems of weighing have arisen. How far is the dignity of the political organization of society an interest to be taken into account? When the political organization was struggling with kin organization and religious organization for the primacy in social control, the dignity of the state was a very serious matter. It was settled that the state could not be sued without its consent, that its debts could not be set off against its claims, that it was not estopped by what was done by its officials, and that its claims were not lost by official neglect to assert them nor barred by limitation. Other public interests, *e.g.* a claim to unimpaired efficiency of the political organization, entered into the reckoning. But the extent to which the rules just mentioned secure no more than the dignity of the state and the weight to be given to that interest today are controversial subject in public law.

One could devote a whole lecture to a catalogue of social interests. First we may put the general security, including claims to peace and order, the first social interest to obtain legal recognition, the general safety, long recognized under the maxim that the public safety is the highest law, the general health, the security of acquisitions and the security of transactions. The two last afford an excellent example of the overlapping and conflict of recognized interests. From the standpoint of the security of acquisitions a thief or one who wrongfully holds another's property should not be able to transfer to a third person a better title than he has. But from the standpoint of the security of transactions, people generally who have no knowledge or notice of the owner's claims and, acting in good faith, part with value in a business transaction with one in possession of the property ought to be protected. Possession ought to give a power of business transactions as to the thing possessed and apparently owned. This question as to the limits of what is called negotiability has been coming up all over the world and recent legislation has been giving greater effect to the security of transactions in comparison with the security of acquisitions. Closely related is the social interest in the security of social institutions, domestic, religious, political, and economic. According as one gives the chief weight to the individual claims of husband and wife or to the social interest in marriage as a social institution, he arrives at different results on the vexed questions of divorce legislation. According as he gives more weight to individual interests in free belief and opinion or to the social interest in the security of political institutions, he will reach different results as to legislation against and prosecutions for sedition. Other important social interests are an interest in the general morals, an interest in the use and conservation of social resources, and an interest in general progress, social, political, economic and cultural. Finally [. . .] there is the social interest in the individual life, the claim asserted in title of social life in civilized society that each individual be secure in his freedom, have secured to him opportunities, political, social and economic, and be able to live at least a reasonably minimum human life in society. Here again all manner of overlappings and conflicts are continually encountered. But perhaps enough has been said to bring out that every item in the catalogue requires to be weighed with many others and that no one can be admitted to its full extent without impairing the scheme as a whole.          [pp. 60–67.]

[. . .]

. . . What then is the practical measure of values which the law has been using where theories have failed it? Put simply it has been and is to secure as much as possible of the scheme of interests as a whole as may be with the least friction waste; to secure as much of the whole inventory of interests as may be with the least impairment of the inventory as a whole.[7] No matter what theories of the end of law have prevailed, this is what the legal order has been doing, and as we look back we see has been doing remarkably well.          [pp. 73–76]

[. . .]

While philosophers are debating whether a scheme of values is possible, lawyers and courts have found a workable one which has proved as adequate to its tasks as any practical method in any practical activity. Without putting it in that way they have treated the task of the legal order as an engineering task of achieving practical results with a minimum of friction and waste. We must not forget that law is not the only agency of social control. The household, the church, the school, voluntary organizations such as trade associations, professional associations, social clubs and fraternal organizations, each with their canons of conduct, do a greater or lesser part of the task of social engineering. But the brunt of the task falls on the legal order. The increasing secularization of social control, the disintegration of kin organization, loosening of the discipline of the household, loss of ground by the church and secularizing of education, have added immeasurably to what we expect of the law. It is the more idle to expect its task to be performed by some off-hand system of personal discretion applied to single cases as unique.

There is at any rate an engineering value in what services to eliminate or minimize friction and waste. It may be that an ethical value may be found in what gives the most effect to human demand with the least sacrifice. At any rate William James thought so. It may be that this adjustment of competing interests with a minimum of waste makes for civilization and has a philosophical value.

I am not offering this idea of social engineering as a cure-all to be taken over by political and juristic theory and used to solve all the difficult problems of the

---

[7]  [The problem here is to determine by what standard it is to be judged that one interest is to prevail over another. Social utility, for instance, may decree the extinction of criminal lunatics, but our sense of justice or morality may demand their preservation. Aristotle's theory of distributive justice breaks down because it fails to provide a standard of reference (*cf.* H. Kelsen, *What is Justice?*, pp. 127–128); Pound seems to consider that a ready test can be found, by assessing the resultant "friction and waste" involved in different solutions. But these are very intangible and even subjective conceptions as applied to human society.]

science of law of the world of today. What I have set forth is no more than a
description of how the legal order actually functions.                    [pp. 79–80]

## P. SELZNICK
### The Sociology of Law
### (1959)[8]

... The sociology of law may be regarded as an attempt to marshal what we know
about the natural elements of social life and to bring that knowledge to bear on a
consciously sustained enterprise, governed by special objectives and ideals. Thus
understood, legal sociology follows a pattern similar to that of industrial
sociology, political sociology, and educational sociology. With some prophetic
license, we can detect in all these efforts three basic stages of development.

The primitive, or missionary, stage is that of communicating a perspective,
bringing to a hitherto isolated area an appreciation of basic and quite general
sociological truths, such as the significance of group membership for individual
behaviour. This early phase characteristically includes much theoretical discussion and analysis of everyday experience. There may also be some organized
research, but what there is is mostly demonstrative in function, more valuable for
its educational effect than for anything else. In law, such demonstrative research
has not been particularly important, in part because of the role played by fact-
guided judicial decisions and by the writings of men with rich experience in legal
affairs. Although most of the theoretical work in this field has been done by
European social scientists, the task of communicating an elementary, not-very-
sophisticated sociological perspective has been accomplished largely by American
legal scholars who were influenced by European thought, and by some of the
more articulate appellate judges.

The second stage belongs to the sociological craftsman. It is a muscle-flexing
period marked by intellectual self-confidence, a zeal for detail, and an earnest
desire to be of service. At this stage the sociologist seeks more than the communication of a general perspective. He wants to explore the area in depth, to
help to solve its problems, and to bring to bear quite specific sociological techniques and ideas. There are a number of signs that the sociology of law is about to
enter this stage of development.

The third stage, as I envision it, is one of true intellectual autonomy and
maturity. This stage is entered when the sociologist goes beyond (without repudiating) the role of technician or engineer and addresses himself to the larger
objectives and guiding principles of the particular human enterprise he has elected
to study. He reasserts the moral impulse that marked the first stage of sociological
interest and influence. But the third stage is of a higher, more sophisticated level
than the first because the second stage has provided a sounder basis for critical
analysis...

In a broad sense, there is no real problem of articulating sociological inquiry to
the needs of legal development. *Sociology can contribute most to law by tending its
own garden.* Truly sound knowledge regarding basic human relations and institutions will inevitably find its way into legal doctrine. Truths so well founded that
no reasonable, educated man can deny them need no special means of communication beyond the ordinary channels of education. It is well to remember that,
although the law is abstract, its decision-making institutions deal with a concrete
and practical world. Recognition of basic truths about that world cannot be long
denied. Moreover, the legal order is becoming increasingly broad in scope,
touching more and more elements of society. This means that sociological

[8] [From Robert K. Merton, Leonard Broom, Leonard S. Cottrell Jr (eds.), *Sociology
Today: Problems and Prospects* (1959, Basic Books Inc., Publishers, New York).]

research addressed to the important characteristics of society, and to the basic changes in it, will automatically have legal relevance. This relevance, of course, goes beyond bare description. It includes making the law sensitive to the values that are at stake as new circumstances alter our institutions.

If this be true, if sociologists have only to mind their own business, why a special concern for sociology of law? Perhaps the most obvious answer is that two-way communication can bring to legal analysis more rapid and direct benefits from sociological research. But as soon as this communication begins, we see that the real problem and the real opportunity stem from the incomplete and tentative character of our knowledge. There are very few incontrovertible sociological truths. Most of what we know is tentative, not only in the sense that all scientific conclusions are tentative, but also in the sense that our research in many vital areas is still primitive and pioneering. Yet legal scholars are interested in this work, and properly so, because the very least it does is to challenge older images of man and society and offer new guides for the assessment of experience. This kind of knowledge, however, cannot be absorbed directly; it must be tested within the specific areas of legal interest; it must withstand the common-sense critiques of the practical lawyer. Such communication cannot take place effectively unless sociological inquiry is made directly relevant to legal problems.

But the sociology of law has an additional, and more profound, rationale than the communication of specific sociological knowledge regarding nonlegal phenomena. The law is itself a social phenomenon, an important agency of social control. The study of the law for itself, as a part of the natural order, is very much the sociologist's business. From this standpoint the sociology of law can contribute both to the science of society itself and to the self-knowledge of legal practitioners. Since self-knowledge and moral development are so intimately related, it is plain that here lies sociology's most important special contribution. This is the distinctive office of the third, most advanced stage of legal sociology.

### Stage II and its Problems

In the second stage of development of legal sociology the main effort is to apply sociological analysis to particular problems of legal doctrine and legal institutions.

The present outcropping of interest in law on the part of sociologists has been stimulated by a number of related developments. Probably most important is the rising self-confidence among sociologists—confidence in the ability of the field to cast new light on particular areas and to help in the solution of practical problems. Another stimulus has been the development and refinement of research methods, involving not merely statistical sophistication but the identification of characteristic social factors of proven researchability. This means that at least one brand of empiricism has been available for active service, ready to form the basis of large and quickly organized research operations.

Interest in law has also been encouraged by new work in the sociology of administration. These studies have restated some older problems regarding the interplay of formal systems of social control and the spontaneous behavior of men and groups. Some of us who have worked in that field have discovered that in studying formal organizations we were also studying legal systems. It is clear that what we were learning about the functions of formal rules, the interdependence of authority and consent, and similar matters was not really new from the larger perspective of legal sociology. [...]

Finally, recent years have seen a fresh approach to the relation between custom and law; today we regard the law as a more creative agency than earlier sociologists believed it to be. This new perspective has been largely stimulated and sustained by recent history in the field of race relations [...].

These developments promise a new and fruitful period of research and analysis. But we should take a close look at the characteristic avenues by which sociologists will enter the field. Perhaps we should speak of these as temptations, the better to mark out the probable risks and pitfalls.

An obvious temptation (although also an opportunity) is to offer research technique as the peculiar contribution of the sociologist. By technique I mean the apparatus of survey and experimental research, not the more common-sense historical and reportorial data-gathering that has been the main standby of sociological classics. It seems obvious to me that quantitative research can and must play an important role in legal sociology. Any continuing program of study in that field could easily keep a staff of survey technicians busy on fruitful projects. The subjective meaning of specific rules, such as the lawyer-client privilege, for clients as well as members of the bar; the social composition of the bench and of juror panels; the self-images of lawyers, their career lines and other matters affecting professional integrity; the quasi-legal claims and expectations of various classes of citizens—these and a host of other specific studies depend for their execution on sophisticated survey technique.

But a serious risk is entailed and should not be overlooked. If we emphasize technique, we inevitably design projects that are congenial to the skills at hand. To be sure, such projects often have a market value in that they promise information that seems to be of immediate practical use to a client. Yet we know from experience that technique-stimulated research is seldom effectively guided by significant theoretical concerns or even by matters of the greatest long-run importance to the client himself. Attempts to apply small-group theory to the study of juries may seem an exception, but in fact they are not. The study of small groups, beyond certain first principles, is one of the more weakly developed areas in sociology; if this work is pushed to the forefront in legal sociology, it will be less for the sound knowledge it can offer than for the opportunity it presents to apply sophisticated research technique.

Another approach involves a similar risk, although it also begins from a posture of strength. Here one emphasizes the fund of sociological ideas, rather than the availability of research methods. The plan is to draw upon this sociological armory in order to illuminate particular problems in the legal field, whether of doctrine or of institutional functioning ... The effect upon legal doctrines and institutions of a number of sociological phenomena, including socialization, value systems, stratification, collective behavior, and demographic trends, would be studied. But the main objective of this pedagogical device is to impress upon the student the force of sociological concepts and principles; it is not offered as a substitute for the autonomous, research-oriented organization of a field of inquiry. We cannot indiscriminately apply all our sociological ideas to legal studies; we must have a theoretical ground for supposing that some notions will be more important than others.

An indifferent appreciation of the entire sociological armory encourages intellectually low-level research, for two reasons. On the one hand, there is a natural tendency to choose those sociological concepts that are easiest to handle; since it is all sociology anyway if no theoretical ground exists for choosing the more difficult problems this solution will seem quite respectable. Yet the net result may be fact-fathering of a quite trivial nature. On the other hand, this same indifference may result in choosing problems of immediate interest to a client, whether or not the studies entail any advance in our general knowledge.

The alternative to those approaches is more painful. It involves a double intellectual commitment, to problems of greatest theoretical concern in sociology and to problems that are truly important to the legal order itself. In sociology, the roughly defined area we call "social organization" remains a challenging frontier. In this field we attempt to identify the essential characteristics of different types of society, to locate the key human relationships that give a social order its distinctive qualities, to discover how major groups interact and what stable arrangements result. Most of the truly great names in sociology have been identified with broad studies of this sort. At the same time, these problems are the hardest to handle and are most frequently shunned.

From the legal side, the important problems also suggest an emphasis on studies of social organization. For example, what are the limits of law as an instrument of social control? What are the capabilities of courts, as we know them and as they could be? How much does society require of these agencies? How much can legitimately be demanded? Roscoe Pound stated this problem more than a generation ago, and offered some answers.[9] But research has been wanting. This is the kind of problem that can be approached in many ways, but it surely demands both a broad theoretical perspective and an emphasis on societal needs and institutional potentialities. Thus an assessment of demands upon the legal systems depends on what is going on within major groups and in the relations among them. Whether modern economic institutions can autonomously safeguard their members against arbitrary treatment and undue loss of liberty depends on the nature of participation and the dynamics of internal control. The sociological answer to this question inevitably affects the role of the courts. The potential achievements and vulnerabilities of both legal and nonlegal institutions are a proper and even urgent subject for sociological inquiry...

### Stage III and its Problems

As we approach a more advanced stage of development, all the classic problems of legal philosophy emerge again. For at this point we should be ready to explore the meaning of legality itself,[10] to assess its moral authority, and to clarify the role of social science in creating a society based on justice.

In a consideration of these matters, the central fact is the role of reason in the legal order. Legality as we know it is based on a combination of sovereign will and objective reason. The word *reason* has an old-fashioned ring to it, but its long life is not yet over. Reason is an authoritative ideal, and the bearers of reason have, inevitably, a creative legal role. We see this, not only in the idea and practice of grounded judicial decision-making, but in the bast body of critical literature produced by legal scholars. Whatever the lawyer's commitment to legal positivism, to the belief that law is what the legislatures and the courts enunciate and enforce, there is at least an implicit recognition that not all law is on the same level. Some law is inferior because it contains the wrong mixture of arbitrary sovereign will, including majority will, and right reason. This is especially true of judge-made law, but legislatures can also make inferior laws. An inferior legality is manifested in the disposition of judges to give a narrow construction to statutes that depart from common-law principles, and in the ease with which judicial conclusions are modified or reversed. An inherent legality is doubtless much influenced by the derivation of a rule—whether from immediate political pressures or from a larger evolution consonant with underlying principles of legal order. I think that the quality of legality, and gradations in it, will be a primary preoccupation of the sociology of law in the future, as it has been in the past. In this work, moreover, we shall have to study the relation between reason and social consensus, for we shall not be satisfied with the assumption that community sentiment, as it bears on law, is basically nonrational.

Because reason is legally authoritative, scholarship has a direct significance for law that it does not have for other fields. This is indicated by the special role of law-review articles and legal treatises cited as authority by the courts. This work usually involves a critical restatement of common-law doctrine, but it also can

---

[9] Roscoe Pound, "The Limits of Effective Legal Action", Int. J. Ethics, 27 (1917), 150–67.
[10] [A beginning has been made. See *ante*, 857.]

and does locate new rights. The restatement aspect does give this work a special status, but there is no fundamental difference between sociological learning made legally relevant and the kind of analytical writing found in the law reviews. In any case, like any other inquiry, legal reasoning cannot but accept the authority of scientifically validated conclusions regarding the nature of man and his institutions. Therefore, inevitably, sociology and every other social science have a part in the legal order.

The underlying role of reason explains why legal scholarship and the sociology of law are mainly preoccupied with common law, and therefore with judicial behavior, rather than with legislation. It is true that somewhat more emphasis in legal training is now placed on legislation, reflecting the great growth of the legislative process. [...]

A concern for the role of reason must bring with it a certain disaffection with what has come to be known as legal realism. The hard-headed effort to base our notion of law on actual behavior is certainly congenial to a sociological orientation. But human behavior is a very subtle mixture of self-restraint and impulse, idealism and self-interest, *behavior* guided by a long-range end-in-view and *behavior* compelled by day-to-day pressures. We cannot accept as more than a passing polemical formula the aphorism that the law is what the judges say it is. Taken literally, this settles nothing, for if a consistency is found in judicial *behavior*, searching out the underlying premises of a normative system and upholding the essential ingredients of legality, then all nonpositivist interpretations of law are still available and the problems they raise are with us still.

The ideal of reason presumes that there are principles of criticism of positive law. It also presumes, as Lon Fuller has pointed out,[11] that there are principles of criticism of "living" law. Little is gained in any ultimate sense by looking beyond positive law to actual normative *behavior*. We must go on to seek out the foundations in reason for choosing among human norms those that are to be given the sanction of law. This will bring us, I cannot doubt, to an acceptance of some version of a doctrine of natural law, although it may not, and perhaps should not, be called that, given its historical associations. A modern naturalist perspective may be preferable, despite the still-unsettled question of whether an objective basis of normative order can be discovered, and despite the large differences between positivism and pragmatism, affecting the ideal of reason in law, regarding the subjective component of valuation and the role of will in judgment. But whatever the philosophical auspices, the search for principles on criticism based on social naturalism must go on. Law based on reason and nature summons man to his potentialities but sees those potentialities as something that science can identify; law based on reason and nature locates the weaknesses of the human spirit, such as pride, apathy, and self-abasement, and works to offset them. The natural order, as it concerns man, is compact of potentiality and vulnerability, and it is our long-run task to see how these characteristics of man work themselves out is the structure and dynamics of social institutions.

[pp. 115–127]

---

[11] Lon L. Fuller, "American Legal Realism," Univ. of Penn. Law Rev., 82 (1934). 453 *et seq.*

## A. HUNT
### Dichotomy and Contradiction in the Sociology of Law[12]
(1981)

*Contemporary Sociology of Law: Old Problems and New Variants*

There have been some significant theoretical developments in the sociology of law in the last few years. During the formative period of the sociology of law in the United States in the 1950's and early 1960's there existed a widespread consensus as to the nature of the project of the sociology of law. This consensus was formed around the interweaving of two apparently different traditions. Most pronounced and visible was the continuing dominance of the perspectives of American Realism organised around the problematic of examining the operational failures of the legal process to meet legal ideals operating with the presumption of the perfectability of the legal process to meet these ideals. Indeed it is important to place due emphasis upon the continuing impact of the Realist perspective. This is nowhere more apparent than in Trubek's proposed "new realism"[13] Harnessing yet again the realist aphorism of the contrast between "law in books" and "law in action", that is, between the ideal and reality, he seeks to harness this as an articulated methodology for checking reality against the ideal. Yet the original Realist unproblematic presumption was of the perfectability of law; they presumed some operational deficiency revealed through empirical study followed by scientifically informed reform, "social engineering", could be overcome such that "the gap" between reality and ideal could be narrowed or closed. The manner in which the relation between legal ideals and legal reality has been theorised, particularly by Trubek and Unger, is more sophisticated than the version offered by the early Realists. Yet nevertheless both the theoretical terms and their practical points of reference remain central to modern sociology, and, as I shall argue in a later section, are not any means distant from the concerns of contemporary Marxist writers.

Our discussion of contemporary liberal legal theory should properly start with Roberto Unger since he has rapidly come to exercise a powerful influence within recent legal history. His earlier and most generalised excursion into social theory in *Knowledge and Politics* is itself impressive if only for the breadth of its concerns and for its sweeping claims to provide an alternative to the classical tradition of social theory, which is taken as embracing almost every major form of social theory developed over the last three centuries.[14] It is important to note that Unger himself locates the problems of legal theory as "the immediate subject of my interest".[15] It is however in *Law in Modern Society* that he addressed problems of legal theory. In this text, despite the continued presence of an overarching concern with the development of "total criticism" he nevertheless takes his stand more firmly within the terrain of positions which are part of the partial criticism which in *Knowledge and Politics* he had argued were irremediably scarred by the antinomies inherent in liberal theory.[16] He now proposes to resolve the predicament of social and legal theory through an attempted integration of the two major contemporary competing paradigms, the instrumentalist or conflict perspective and the consensus perspective. Yet despite his commitment to a synthesis which

---

[12] [(1981) 8 Brit. J. Law & Soc. 47.]
[13] Trubek "Complexity and Contradiction in Legal Order" (1977) 11 *Law and Society Rev.* 529. [And see also the Critical Legal Studies movement, *post*, Chap. 14.]
[14] R. Unger, *Knowledge and Politics* (1975).
[15] *ibid*, p. 3.
[16] *ibid*, p. 7. His orientation to these competing paradigms is not dissimilar to that earlier advanced by Dahrendorf in which both are recognised as grasping different aspects of reality (Dahrendorf, *Class and Class Conflict in Industrial Society* (1959)).

overcomes the systematic deficiencies of both, his method of combination is inherently additive and non-synthetic; his general hypothesis is "that some social settings might best be understood in light of the doctrine of consensus and others from the perspective of the theory of instrumentalism".[17]

He proceeds to posit the existence of two types of law which embody the general characteristics of the two alternative theoretical perspectives. "Interactional law" is allied to consensus theory and "bureaucratic law" to instrumental theory. The strength of Unger's analysis, although I shall argue it is severely limited, resides in the break he effects with the normative integration theories of contemporary sociology of law within which law operates as a general and pervasive mechanism of societal integration through the linked processes of social control and socialisation buttressed by the legitimising properties of law. He effects this breach with normative integration theories through his emphasis on the conflict or tension between the two different "modes of order" which coexist within the contemporary legal order.

It should however be noted that this position is not particularly original. It is firmly and powerfully present in Weber's classic discussion of the tension between formal and substantive justice. It is only the more crude appropriations of Weber which emphasised a simpler and therefore more evolutionary thesis of the triumph of formal rationality in the legal order of capitalist society. But even though Weber's analysis rests on the problematic tension between formal and substantive rationality he nevertheless places unqualified priority upon formal rationality which he saw as the only alternative when confronted with the rising demand for substantive justice articulated in its most powerful form by the labour and socialist movement. Just so does Unger throw in his lot with legal rationality/ formalism. He identifies three functionally significant components of legal systems—formal, procedural and substantive; but of these three it is formalism which lies at the core of the development of modern Western rule of law. His emphasis is such that formalism in his analysis wholly subordinates the other components. The result is that he presents, as did Weber before him and as does Hayek today, the demand for substantive justice as the source of the dangerous erosion of formalism. As I will argue more generally, despite his apparent commitment to liberal political values he is led inexorably towards conservatism and pessimism which even his sociological version of Christian theology cannot disguise.

We find then in Unger a specific variant of the general dichotomy which lies at the heart of the tension inherent in the liberal doctrine of the rule of law. It is expressed as the tension between "collective values" and "bureaucratic welfare tyranny". Despite his apparent commitment to achieve synthesis he evades the challenges and thereby reinforces the fundamental conservatism of his position by the evasive observation that it is beyond the remit of his present enquiry.[18] However the general outline of the synthesis which he desires is clearly indicated. Yet his "solution" cannot be treated as one which marks a development in social theory which overcomes or supersedes the dualism. Rather his transcendental theology posits an immanent process of social transformation the resultant of which abolishes both the theoretical problem and the dichotomy within law. He relies upon the assertion of an immanent essentialism reconciling "individual freedom" and "community cohesion". "The more perfect this reconciliation becomes, the more does the society's emergent interactional law reveal the requirements of human nature and social existence".[19] Far from advancing a theoretical synthesis we return to the old "search for this latent or living law"

---

[17]  R. Unger *op. cit., supra*, n. 14, p. 127.
[18]  *ibid.* p. 129.
[19]  *ibid.* p. 264.

which seeks to "discover a universal given order in social life".[20] This question for an immanent or spontaneous normative order in large measure marks a return to an older and more conservative tradition epitomised in general by Durkheim's search for the "ideological community" and more particularly within the sociology of law by Ehrlich's espousal of "living law".[21] Yet the temptation should be avoided to immediately apply a conservative label to Unger's position. His claim, most explicit in *Knowledge and Politics*, to discern evidence of the realisation of his synthesis in the contemporary developments within the "Welfare-corporate state" and within actual socialist societies should caution us against too hurried political labelling. It is sufficient to note that Unger's attempt to resolve the general dichotomy in the social and legal order takes the form of a synthesis whose starting point is an essentially metaphysical concept of "community".

The pursuance of community is grounded in a general pessimism about the trajectory of modern legal development. Talcott Parsons's late and perceptive review of *Law in Modern Society* provides a very striking illustration of the contrast between two generations of sociological theorists.[22] Parsons notes important areas of agreement and convergence between his own position and that advanced by Unger. I am disposed to place considerable weight on what Parsons identifies as his fundamental disagreement which leads him to brand Unger's theoretical position as unacceptable. "Perhaps the main reason I am critical of Unger is that I do not share his—perhaps fashionable—pessimism about the drastic erosion of the rule of law".[23]

Parsons has been the embodiment of the most systematised commitment to a positive evaluation of the modern trajectory of the capitalist democracies. Unger can be read as representative of the more recent self-doubt and anxiety which finds its reverberations at all levels of political and social theory and which cuts across traditional political and theoretical boundaries. The pessimism to which Parsons refers finds its expression within both neo-conservative jurisprudence and contemporary Marxist debates about law.[24]

Donald Black presents an apparently sharp contrast to Unger's social philosophical theorisation. I confess at the outset to a deep-seated dislike for the rigid positivism and formalism which characterises his most general theoretical intervention *The Behavior of Law*.[25] Such a response is sufficient to discourage me from engaging in a general review of his work. Yet despite the profound difference in methodology and theoretical orientation between Black and Unger I will seek to demonstrate that there are two important continuities. Black presents his own specific formulation of the general dichotomy and, secondly, his position is marked by a pervasive pessimism about the role of law in modern capitalist democracies in spite of his apparent commitment to universalistic sociology purged of all concern with current policy objectives.[26]

Black has noted the continuing impact of the legal realist tradition; he rejects its prostitution of scientific method to the pursuit of policy objectives subsumed under the dichotomy between "law in books" and "law in action". But in seeking to impose a strict divide between "pure sociology of law" and "applied sociology of law" and thereby to break with the tradition imposed by legal realism, he

---

[20] *ibid.* p. 242.
[21] E. Ehrlich, *Fundamental Principles of the Sociology of Law* (1967).
[22] Parsons, "Review of Unger's *Law in Modern Society*" (1977) 12 *Law and Society Rev.* 133.
[23] *ibid.* p. 148.
[24] See, for example, F. A. Hayek, *Law, Legislation and Liberty* (3 volumes 1973, 1976 and 1979), and I. Jenkins, *Social Order and the Limits of Law* (1980).
[25] D. Black, *The Behavior of Law* (1976).
[26] Black, "The Boundaries of Legal Sociology" (1972) 81 *Yale Law Rev.* 1086.

actually bears witness to its influence by adopting its underlying positivism and behaviourism.[27] His injunction that "law consists in observable acts, not in rules"[28] replicated Oliver Wendell Holmes aphoristic characterisation of law as "the prophecies of what the courts will do in fact, and nothing more pretentious, are what I mean by the law".[29] The step that Black effects is to transform the pragmatic positivism of the early realists into a formalistic behaviouralist variant.

In order to locate the presence of the general dichotomy it is necessary to trace briefly Black's methodology. His starting point, as the title of the book indicates, is to treat law as a behavioral phenomenon, purged of all value judgments and ideals. Law "behaves" or varies in relation to other observable social phenomena or "dimensions". He posits two dimensions to be variation of law; the first is quantitative, reducible to "more law/less law". The second dimension is provided by "the style of law" which in turn corresponds to styles of social control. The styles of law are merely listed, no indication is given of where the classification is derived from, but it may be noted in passing that like many other typologies that have been advanced within the sociology of law, they have a scarcely concealed evolutionary implication in the transition from the "penal" style (*i.e.* primitive), through "compensatory" and "therapeutic" to (the more advanced) "conciliatory" style.[30] "Style of law" as the second dimension in the variation of law plays little part in the subsequent elaboration. The variations in styles of law are introduced in an arbitrary manner and are not systematically integrated within the body of the theory. The difficulty in quantifying "style" and the ever present danger that the identification of "style" may carry evaluative connotations probably explains the limited attention it receives.

The book thereafter is predominantly concerned to advance quantitatively expressed hypotheses concerning the behaviour of law. In the main they are couched in terms of variations of "more" or "less" law. He nowhere indicates how this quantification of law is to be undertaken. It is assumed without specification of any method of measurement that quantitative variations are self-evidently identifiable. Thus, to take just one example, in dealing with the relationship between law and stratification he advances the hypothesis that "law" varies directly with stratification' *i.e.* the more stratification a society has, the more law it has.[31] The startling evidence for this hypothesis is to repeat the well-trodden anthropological data about the limited role and extent of law in "simple" society. This taken with the assumption that is some self-evident sense "modern" society has more law. The spurious scientificity of his appeal to quantification does not however appear to permit any exploration of the relation between law and the variety of forms and degrees of stratification in "modern" society. Stripped of their scientism his hypotheses are sociological commonplaces distorted to fit universalistic pretensions. Black's purportedly sophisticated theoretical enterprise is nothing more and nothing less than systematic common sense; and no systematisation of common sense can turn it into good sense.

Yet behind the appeal to the quantification of legal phenomena we find lurking the general dichotomy between coercion and consent. The general couplets that run through his hypotheses of less/more law, undifferentiated/differentiated with the dichotomy between consensual and coercive characteristics of law. This emerges most explicitly in his reject of the Durkheimian equation between simple/undifferentiated society and repressive law.[32]

It is further manifest in his predilection for curvilinear hypotheses; for example

---

[27]   *ibid.* p. 1087.
[28]   *ibid.* p. 1091.
[29]   Holmes, "The Path of Law" (1897) 10 *Harvard Law Rev.* 461. [See *post*, 1007.]
[30]   Black, *op. cit., supra*, n. 25, p. 4.
[31]   *ibid.*, p. 13.
[32]   *ibid.* p. 37.

in positing the quantitative growth of law with social differentiation he posits a subsequent diminution of law "As social life evolves beyond interdependence to symbiosis ... law declines".[33] The complex symbiotic differentiation of modern society manifests itself not only, according to Black, in a decrease of law but a growing emphasis upon "conciliatory" in contrast to "penal", styles of law.

The variety of curvilinear hypotheses which is advanced provided evidence not only of the presence of the coercion/consent dichotomy but also of the deep social and political pessimism which underlies his apparently neutral and apolitical stance. His evolutionary perspective posits first an increase in the quantity of law and then its decrease; it is this decrease that he decrease as the "return to anarchy".[34] Black's predilection for quantitative behaviouralism commits him, since it constrains him to see the variance of law in terms of increases and decreases, to a cyclical vision of legal and social development. Such a cyclical element is as Eder argues the reintroduction of an archaic philosophy of history.[35] Far from the value-freedom whose shrine he prays before, Black's sociology of law is transparently ideological. It is but an ideological anxiety that besets liberal intellectuals and paves the way for neo-conservatism. "Encounters replace the social structures of the past, and people increasingly have closeness without permanence, depth without commitment".[36] The breakdown of community and the advance of social equality combine to produce conditions in which law tends to decrease; the result is the situational society in which there is no place for the rule of law and the values of liberal legalism. It is remarkable how, despite the sharp theoretical differences between them, the conclusions arrived at by both Black and Unger replicate the deep pessimism of the liberal intelligentsia in the United States.

David Trubek's project of developing a "new realism", referred to at the beginning of this section, marks the clearest and most explicit continuity which has stamped American sociology of law with much of the intellectual imprint of pre-War realism. It needs to be stressed that his "new realism" marks a significant attempt to be beyond the unproblematic treatment of "the gap between legal ideals and legal reality". His position is further significant in that it is marked by an explicit commitment to engage in a meaningful dialogue with the more recently emerging Marxist trend within American sociology of law. It is for this reason that my attention will be primarily focused upon his lengthy review article of Isaac Balbus" *Dialectics of Legal Repression*. I will not at this stage be concerned to comment on his critique of Balbus but rather to concentrate on the second half of his essay in which he advanced his "new realism".[37] With respect of Trubek's earlier writing I only want to draw attention to the extent which he more than any other contemporary writer in the field of the sociology is concerned with the theoretical lineage of the field; this concern has manifested itself in the extent to which he goes beyond the conventional deferential bow to the legacy of Max Weber.[38] He has sought to re-examine the Weberian legacy and this concern has its reverberations in the more recent essay.

The element which is "new" in Trubek's realism is the way in which he problematises "the gap" between legal ideals and reality by abandoning the assumption of the perfect ability of law; "the gap" is presented as itself being a necessary consequence of the structural characteristics of liberal democracy. "The gap between the ideals of law and its performance is a central and pervasive

[33] *ibid.* p. 40.
[34] *ibid.* p. 132.
[35] Eder, "Rationalist and Normative Approaches to the Sociological Study of Law" (1977) 12 *Law and Society Rev.* 138.
[36] Black, *op. cit.*, p. 135.
[37] Trubek, *op. cit., supra*, n. 13.
[38] Trubek, "Max Weber on Law and the Rise of Capitalism" (1972) 3 *Wisconsin Law Rev.* 720 and "Toward a Social Theory of Law" (1972) 82 *Yale Law J.* 1.

feature of legal existence".[39] Yet it is significant that, despite the abandonment of the simple-minded social engineering of the early Realists, its effects remain contagious such that despite the apparently greater sophistication of his "mediative perspective" his concern is still with "the cure" for the realist dichotomy, in that "law represents an effort to mediate fundamental conflicts"[40] but one which is doomed to remain imperfect.

Within this reworking of the problematic of legal realism and of mainstream sociology of law we find lurking the general dichotomy. Law in books/law in action is the manifestation of the opposition between ideal/reality; the central content of this opposition within liberal democracy is seen as that between the ideal of social equality and the persistence of structures of hierarchy and dominance. The polarity between equality and hierarchy is, of course, but another form of the opposition between consent and coercion.

There are two significant features to be found in the development of Trubek's attempt to overcome the simple opposition of ideal and reality, consent and coercion. The first concerns the methodology he proposes; it is this which ties him closest to the realist tradition but to which he gives a significantly idealistic inflection. This arises because he insists on giving methodological priority to ideals as the starting point against which legal reality is to be examined. "Such a system *must begin* with ideals basic to our society ... I propose that we examine law in terms of its contribution to these values".[41] And again: "A legal order in not and end in itself. The system must be justified by its contribution to more fundamental social ideals".[42] It should be noted that a very similar idealism is present in Unger's work and constitutes an important continuity, which is made explicit by Trubek's frequent citation of Unger. For Unger "the deepest root of all historical change is manifest or latent conflict between the view of the ideal and the experience of actuality".[43] Two negative consequences follow from such idealist positions. The first is that in giving priority to ideals, the ideals themselves are regarded as unproblematic, they form the taken for granted and uncontested presumption of society as a purposive and organic enterprise of Hegelian character bent on the realisation of ideals that march through the pages of history. No space is left for a critical examination of, for example, the ideological role of the ideal of equity in capitalist democracies. The second consequence of the idealist methodology is that it necessarily involves the positing of a conception of a universal human nature which is realised in the historical process. This is most explicit in Unger and is not disputed by Trubek. "The universal is human nature ... the particulars are the forms of social life and the individual personalities by which that humanity is represent".[44]

Trubek seeks to combine this methodology with theoretical elements appropriated from the Marxist tradition, and more particularly from the historical analysis of law developed by E. P. Thompson in *Whigs and Hunters* and his colleagues in parallel work.[45] Thompson's emphasis upon the complex and contradictory character of law clearly, from his explicit acknowledgements, made a considerable impact upon Trubek.

We reach, then, not a simple conclusion (law = class power) but a complex and contradictory one. On the one hand it is true that law did mediate class relations to the advantage of the rules. ... On the other hand, the law mediated these

---

[39]   Trubek, *op. cit., supra,* n. 13, p. 544.
[40]   *ibid.* p. 542.
[41]   *ibid.* p. 546.
[42]   *ibid.* p. 547.
[43]   Unger, *op. cit., supra,* n. 14, p. 157.
[44]   *ibid.* p. 261.
[45]   D. Hay *et al., Albion's Fatal Tree: Crime and Society in Eighteenth Century England* (1975). [There is an extract from *Whigs and Hunters, post,* 1181.]

relations through legal forms, which imposed, again and again, inhibitions upon the actions of the rulers.[46]

Thompson makes a more specific contribution to Trubek's position because it was *Whigs and Hunters* that "first suggested to me the perspective outlined in the essay"[47] which he identifies as "the mediative perspective" which asserts that "a significant feature of legal life in liberal capitalist societies is the simultaneous assertion and negation of basic ideals of equality, individuality, and community. The legal order neither guarantees these ideals, nor does it simply deny them: it does both".[48] Trubek does not adopt the specifically Marxist connotations of "mediation" which, for reasons he does not explain, he sees as closely related to the theory of alienation. Rather he proposes to adopt "the ordinary English language sense" which he identifies as "a communicative intervention aimed at reconciling or compromising conflicting ideas or interests".[49]

What Trubek has failed to notice that there is in "the ordinary English language sense" a second meaning to the word, and it is this one, which both Marx and Thompson employ, of mediation as the process of the forming a link or connection between different objects or processes.

This is not a semantic disputation; important consequences follow from the initial identification of the concept. My reservation about Trubek's mediation = conciliation is threefold: first, that it imports a consensual character to the process of mediation and, second, that it implies ends, and objectives of human agencies as constitutive of the process and, thirdly, that it carries unavoidably functionalist implications. What Trubek misses about the alternative definition of mediation, and which is developed in Marxist literature, is that all social activity involves processes in which "things" (whether they be artifacts, language, institutions, etc.) mediate between people and the social and natural environment in which they live *and* which have differential effects in transforming the nature of that relation. Applying this directly to problems of the sociology of law, one of the most important questions, which Marx asked (but it should be noted did not provide a direct answer) was: "the really difficult point to be discussed is how the relations of production as legal relations take part in the uneven development (of material production)".[50] Marx here poses the role of law as a process of "mediation" of legal relations as the form in which relations of production are operative and which have definite effects and consequences. It is this set of central issues which Marx and Thompson pose without importing the "solution" that is introduced by Trubek's identification of mediation as conciliation.

The above exploration of the concept "mediation" is not intended to teach lessens to Trubek about "ordinary English language" or to claim a privileged interpretation of Marx but it does serve to emphasise two points. First, the joining of a meaningful exchange between Marxists and non-Marxists involves certain problems which make it unwise to attempt simply borrowing or lifting from one theoretical tradition into another. It should be emphasised that this caution should be seen as applying not only to the adoption of elements of Marxism but likewise applies to the incorporation within Marxism from other traditions. An interesting example of the latter problem can be seen in the problems that arise when Marxists seek to make use of the Weberian concepts of legitimacy and domination; the difficulty arises from the way in which Weber's concepts are produced and thus linked to the analysis of the interpersonal relation between the rulers and ruled which is not directly compatible with the theoretical framework of class analysis. To avoid misunderstanding let me stress that I do not seek to

---

[46] Thompson, *op. cit.*, n. 45, p. 242.
[47] Trubek, *op. cit., supra*, n. 13, p. 543.
[48] *ibid.* p. 544.
[49] *ibid.* p. 543.
[50] K. Marx, *Grundrisse* (1969) 109.

place any barrier in the way of cross-fertilisation between disparate theoretical traditions but rather to enter a caution against the simple borrowing or transplanting of individual concepts.

The manner in which Trubek employs the concept of mediation as the equivalent of conciliation has one further interesting consequence. His general position does, as I have argued, provide evidence of the presence of the general dichotomy between coercion and consent as the underlying mode of theorisation of his sociology of law. Beyond this general presence Trubek gives a particular inflection through his equation of mediation and conciliation which emphasises the proximity of Trubek's position to the sociology of law of the 1950's and 1960's, with its central assumption of the normative integration or consensual character and function of law.

One significant point of differentiation between Trubek on the one hand and Unger and Black on the other is that there is no note or sign of the pessimism regarding the trajectory of law in contemporary capitalist democracies that has been pointed to in the case of both Unger and Black. Rather Trubek exhibits a much closer lineage with the liberal confidence in the effectivity of law. He holds out a continuing and renewed faith in the role of law in the contemporary period.                                                                                                    [pp. 53–61]


## R. COTTERRELL
### The Significance of a Concept of Law Not Restricted to State Law
### (1995)[51]

Important work has been done on the basis of concepts of law within each of the categories outlined above. Is it necessary, then, or indeed possible to make any general remarks about the relative utility of these approaches? It is hardly necessary to say that a definition of law does not prevent the researcher from studying other social phenomena outside the definition but seen, for certain purposes, to be relevant to legal analysis. Yet the usage of the term "law" in studies of regulation or social order is important since, like any such designation, it suggests an integrity in the object of study which separates it from other phenomena that may appear similar in certain respects.

To tie law to state law or lawyers' law imposes definite limits on the extent to which law can be envisaged in radically differing forms while yet retaining important continuities with what is presently familiar to the lawyer. To see law as wider than state law—as compassing so-called private legal systems[52] or forms of social order or social interaction in diverse groups, institutions, or associations, is to raise seriously the hypothesis that the problems of legal regulation with which lawyers and legislators concern themselves may arise in some form in many different kinds of normative system. These problems include those of the justifications of legal decision-making and of the authority-bases of adjudicative processes; of the conditions of legitimacy of legal orders; of the relationships between sources of legal authority; of the conditions of effectiveness of enforcement of law; of the interpretation, development, generalization, and systematization of rules; of the translation of goals and policies into regulatory form; of the relationship between rule and discretion as administrative devices, and between certainty and justice as legal ideals.

To assume that these and other problems within or about law are peculiar to lawyers' law is to make an unnecessarily restrictive assumption. The issues involved may undoubtedly be developed most fully and with most sophistication in relation to lawyers' law. Some of these problems may indeed be absent in some

---

[51]   [From R. Cotterrell, *Law's Community* (1995).]
[52]   *Social Structure and Law* (1990).

other normative systems. And the specification of which of these foci of analysis are central and which peripheral to legal study extending to normative orders other than state law will depend in part on the choice of a particular concept of law. Yet to widen the concept of law beyond the lawyer's view of it is to assert the sociological necessity of considering the possibility that legal thought or legal processes in various empirically analysable forms may be a relatively pervasive feature of social life rather than isolated phenomena of a narrow professional sphere.

Sociology of law may well be best served at the present stage of its development by a plurality of approaches to the problem of the concept of law. Indeed, it is implicit in what was said earlier about the variety of aims of writers in this field that this plurality is probably inevitable, quite apart from any question of its desirability. Yet increasing interest in both phenomenological and anarchist approaches to legal analysis suggests a reorientation towards a serious concern with non-state law systems of regulation in contemporary Western societies and with the processes of social rule formation quite apart from formal law-creating processes. If, however, the dominant concept of law in contemporary sociology of law remains the state law concept the danger is that the problems of lawyers' law may be seen as analytically distinct from those of other actual and potential regulatory systems. Thus the withering away of law can be foretold, by some writers, without serious consideration of the possibility that, like hydra heads, law and its problems and consequences may be chopped off in their most visible forms (as state law) only to remain or reappear in other regions of social life which they in fact pervade.

The problems of an uncompromising juridical pluralism that accords no theoretical primacy to state law have been clearly stated in the literature[53], and touched on above. The crucially important relationship between law and state is often treated only peripherally given such a conceptual approach, and the relationship between state law and other forms of normative order remains an unsolved problem. A useful concept of law today must surely treat lawyers' law as central, a primary focus of analysis. Yet if analysis is to be developed to explore fully the reach into society of law as both an instrument and formalization of power and as an ideological phenomenon, there seem good grounds for making central the hypothesis that legal thinking is not merely lawyers' thinking, and that the characteristics which sociology of law identifies in state legal institutions may not be unique to them.

One consequence of this might be to avoid utopian thinking that suggests without empirical demonstration that the features of state law and its institutions which sociology of law identifies will not be replicated in various ways in informal regulatory or adjudicatory processes, or in social systems (for example, regions, collectives, autonomous or semi-autonomous social organizations, or groups) smaller than those of the nation state which forms the typical unit of modern legal jurisdiction[54]. Another consequence might be to raise seriously the possibility that the experience of forms of social organization quite separate from the official state legal system may yield insights into problems of normative order that are typically considered only in relation to state or lawyers' law.[55] The experience of "simpler" legal orders of simpler social systems than that of the nation state may offer legal insights in a manner somewhat parallel to the insights into complex societies that

---

[53] *Sociologie Juridique* (1978), pp. 213 *et seq.*
[54] R. Dahl and E. R. Tufle, *Size and Democracy* (1974); K. Newton (1982) 30 Political Studies 190; M. Taylor, *Community, Anarchy and Liberty* (1982).
[55] This is, of course, the methodological assumption underlying Karl Llewellyn's "law jobs" theory which boldly encompasses the "law" of "a newly wedded couple, a newly formed partnership, a two child casual playgroup".

anthropologists have often claimed as one special justification for the study of relatively simple societies.

These kinds of considerations suggest links between aspects of the concerns of sociology of law and of sociology of organizations. Indeed, at one stage in the recent development of sociology of law influences from this other field of social research were manifest.[56] Interestingly a recent survey of problems of the field of sociology of organizations[57] has called for a reorientation of emphases to take account of the increasing importance of phenomenological perspectives and other recent developments in theory. Thus Peter Manning notes the failure of sociological studies to find a way of specifying in objective terms the nature of organizations and calls for a recognition of the importance of the conceptions of the organization held by those participating in it. Occupational culture is thus of great importance. It provides the image of the organization for those involved in it; "the framework around which organizational work is legitimated"[58]. It acts as a "grid or screen by which events are defined and also makes relevant internal rules"[59]

Using empirical data on police organization as a foundation for analysis, Manning identifies three elements which constitute occupational culture: principles (the most abstract statement of culture), working rules ("by which the principles are translated into the everyday negotiated bases for work")[60] and actual work practices. He goes so far as to set out a detailed code of such principles and rules for the occupational culture of the police he studied in London and in the United States. It is important to stress that an analysis in terms of the relation of rules and principles offers only one possible and partial approach to the problem of analysis of a structure of normative regulation. Yet the parallel with more familiar issues of legal theory seems obvious.

From an entirely different point of view it might be asked whether a sociology of law tied to lawyers' conventional definitions of law ties itself to a form of regulation that may be gradually decreasing in importance. Numerous forms of bureaucratic regulation and control seem to be developing or to have developed in close alliance with orthodox legal forms yet in substantial independence of the reach of analysis of the lawyer. Much of the analysis of rule and discretion in welfare provision, in prison regimes, and in regulation of the national economy and of particular public and private enterprises is concerned in various ways with this matter. Much social theory now foresees the gradual superseding of lawyers' law in its familiar forms by a variety of technological mechanisms of administration and control.

Whether such analyses have merit is not relevant here.[61] Neither can it be claimed that sociology of law can usefully consider all aspects of any such transformation and all the varied forms of control that have been discussed in recent critical literature.[62] Yet it can be argued that sociology of law must take sufficient account, as central to its project, of forms of regulation going far beyond the boundaries of state or lawyers' law: sufficient, that is, so as to be able to make assessments of the nature of changes in patterns of regulation fundamentally important to any judgement of the changing social significance of the lawyers' law of the state.

The conclusion to which these arguments lead is that, in general terms, a concept of law that treats state law as central to the concept of law in modern

---

[56] Particularly through the influence of writers such as Selznick and Evan.
[57] 33 Br. J. of Sociology 118.
[58] *ibid.*, p. 125.
[59] *ibid.*, p. 130.
[60] *ibid.*, p. 125.
[61] (1982) 9 J. of Law and Soc. 177.
[62] See especially Michel Foucault's various writings, T. Mathiesen, *Law, Society and Political Action* (1980), and J. Donzelot, *The Policing of Families* (1980).

industrialized societies, but treats certain other normative systems in these societies as directly comparable and closely related theoretically within a kind of regulatory continuum, is of particular utility for confronting contemporary problems posed by theory and empirical research in sociology of law. My view, then, is that the kinds of institutional concepts of law discussed earlier which avoid both exclusive concern with state law and also pure juridical pluralism, and treat state law as central to but not the exclusive concern of analysis of law in contemporary Western societies, are potentially fruitful.                  [pp. 32–37]

## R. COTTERRELL
### Why Must Legal Ideas be Interpreted Sociologically?
### (1998)[63]

#### I. Sociology of Law and Legal Ideas

A modern myth about sociological study of law survived until quite recently, encouraged from within legal philosophy and by some legal sociologists themselves. According to this myth an inevitable division of labour governed legal inquiry. While lawyers and jurists analysed law as doctrine—norms, rules, principles, concepts and the modes of their interpretation and validation, sociologists were concerned with a fundamentally different study: that of behaviour, its causes and consequences. Hence, the legal sociologist's task was solely to examine behaviour in legal contexts.[64] Sociology could contribute little to the understanding of legal ideas, abstracted from their effects on specific actions. In this sense sociology of law conducted inquiries peripheral or even *external* to law as lawyers understood it. Legal sociologists often avoided lawyers' disputes or theories about the nature of doctrine as such.[65] They studied primarily practices of dispute processing, administrative activity or law enforcement, or social forces operating on legislation, especially as a result of the actions of particular law-making or policy-advocating groups.

That this division of labour was in no way inevitable is clear from the briefest glance at the work of the classic founders of sociology of law. While Max Weber saw sociology's object as the study of social action, he treated the nature of legal ideas and the variety of types of legal reasoning as central to his sociological concern with law.[66] Émile Durkheim intended that the enterprise of understanding law as doctrine should itself become a field of sociology, so that lawyers' questions would eventually be reformulated through sociological insight.[67] For Eugen Ehrlich, the lawyer's understanding of law would be simultaneously subverted and set on surer foundations by means of sociological inquiry into popular

---

[63] [From 25 *Journal of Law and Society* 171.]

[64] See, for example, D. Black, *The Behavior of Law* (1976), treating legal sociology as the study of governmental social control. Correspondingly, Hans Kelsen wrote of sociology's role as that of inquiring "into the causes and effects of those natural events that ... are represented as legal acts." See H. Kelsen, *Introduction to the Problems of Legal Theory* (1992) 13. In his final work, he asserted that such a legal sociology "does not describe the law, but rather law-creating behaviour and law-observing or law-violating behavior. See H. Kelsen, *General Theory of Norms* (1991) 301.

[65] Vilhelm Aubert's work provides a significant exception. See, for example, V. Aubert, "The Structure of Legal Thinking" in *Legal Essays: A Tribute to Frede Castberg*, eds. J. Andenaes *et al.* (1963) 41–63; and C. M. Campbell, "Legal Thought and Juristic Values" (1974) 1 *Brit. J. of Law and Society* 13–30.

[66] M. Weber, *Economy and Society* (1968) Part 2, ch. 8.

[67] É. Durkheim, Letter to the Director of the *Revue néo-scholastique*, in É. Durkheim, *The Rules of Sociological Method and Selected Essays on Sociology and its Method* (1982) 260; É. Durkheim, *Textes 1: Élements d'une théorie sociale* (1975) 244.

understandings of legal ideas.[68] Leon Petrazycki considered that law should be studied as a variety of forms of consciousness and understanding.[69] Equally, numerous contributions to legal philosophy, including modern realist jurisprudence in Scandinavia, the United States of America, and elsewhere, showed that jurists had serious concerns with behaviour in legal contexts in their efforts to grasp the nature of legal ideas.

To remove a focus on legal doctrine from sociological inquiry would prevent legal sociology from integrating, rather than merely juxtaposing, its studies with other kinds of legal analysis. Without this focus, sociological observation of behaviour might influence policy expressed in legal doctrine; but this would amount not to a sociology of law but to a diversity of sociological information presented to legal policy-makers. The old claim that social science should be "on tap rather than on top" in legal inquiries reflected the idea that sociology and other social sciences were debarred from offering insight into the *meaning* of law (as doctrine, interpretation, reasoning, and argument). Hence, in so far as proponents of legal sociology accepted the myth of an inevitable division of labour, they were tempted to argue defensively that lawyers' debates on doctrine were trivial or mystificatory, and that real knowledge about law as a social phenomenon was gained only by observing patterns of judicial, administrative or policing activity, lawyers' work and organization, or citizens' disputing behaviour. Correspondingly, opponents of legal sociology hastened to dismiss it as unable to speak about *law* at all; fated to remain for ever "external" and thus irrelevant to legal understanding.                                                        [pp. 171–173]

## II. Is Sociology's "Truth" Powerless?

Criticisms of legal sociology's capacity to understand legal ideas have become more sophisticated, though they have not changed their fundamental character. It is now widely accepted that sociological inquiry is valuable and necessary in illuminating the social or historical processes that shape legal doctrine. [...]

The most powerful current critique of legal sociology—the one which this paper seeks to examine and respond to—does not deny that sociological inquiry can, in its own ways, explain aspects of legal doctrine. It argues rather that sociology has *no privileged way of approaching legal ideas*—no specially powerful insight which can prevail over others. Because of this, it has no way of plausibly claiming that its interpretations are better than those which lawyers themselves can give. It therefore becomes an open question why a sociological view should be adopted in preference to any other. In other words, the claim is no longer that law cannot be understood in sociological terms. It is: why should we want to do so? What is to be gained by doing so, especially for lawyers, or other participants (for example, litigants or just lay citizens) in legal processes?

These questions are sharpened with additional claims. It is sometimes suggested that sociology is an exceptionally weak and inadequate explanatory discourse. For example, it is claimed to have "an intriguing inability to constitute its field of study."[70] The concept of "the social" thus remains "remarkably unexamined" in socio-legal studies and, it is said, no longer provides a focus for them.[71] On the other hand, law is now seen by those sceptical of sociology's interpretive capacities as having an intellectual power and resilience which

---

[68]  E. Ehrlich, *Fundamental Principles of the Sociology of Law* (1936).
[69]  L. Petrazycki, *Law and Morality* (1955).
[70]  P. Fitzpatrick, "Being Social in Socio-Legal Studies" (1995) 22 *J. of Law and Society* 105–12, at 107.
[71]  id., p. 106.

protects it from social science's earlier "imperial confidence" that it could know law better than law knew itself.[72]

In a rich discussion of relationships between law and scientific (including social science) disciplines, David Nelken describes the efforts of these disciplines to tell "the truth about law" as being confronted now with law's own "truth".[73] What he means is that law has its own ways of interpreting the world. Law as a discourse determines, within the terms of that discourse, what is to count as "truth"—that is, correct understanding or appropriate and reliable knowledge—for specifically legal purposes. It resists scientific efforts to interpret it away (for example, in economic cost-benefit terms, psychological terms of causes and consequences of mental states, or sociological terms of conditioning social forces). None of these interpretations, it is claimed, grasps law's own criteria of significance.

When law borrows from scientific disciplines or practices it appears to do so as it sees fit, taking what it deems useful, on its own conditions, for its own purposes.[74] Concepts borrowed are often transformed, turned into "hybrid artifacts", tailored to legal use.[75] And law goes on the offensive. It provides its own explanations of the social world. It interprets social life in its own terms. Law is said to provide truth for itself, for its purposes, which cannot be swept away by sociology, but with which sociology's interpretations are fated merely to co-exist. Because of this, sociology cannot reshape legal understanding; it provides at best a resource of ideas from which law may borrow if it finds reasons to do so. In a different sense from before, social science is again "on tap, but not on top".

From the standpoint of sociology the problem is not merely that its insights can be made to seem irrelevant to legal understanding. It is not just the unpleasantness of rejection that dominates this scenario, but also the frustration of attempting the impossible. The argument goes as follows. As sociology tries to understand law, law disappears, like a mirage, the closer the approach to it. This is because as sociology interprets law, law is *reduced to sociological terms*. It becomes something different from what it (legally) is; or rather, from what, in legal thought, law sees itself as being. How can legal ideas be understood sociologically without, in the process, being turned into sociological ideas?[76] The "legal point of view", as Robert Samek called it in a neglected discussion of related themes,[77] disappears; subsumed into a sociological viewpoint and lost. It cannot be grasped sociologically because it is *not* sociological. It is a specifically *legal* point of view.

Legal sociology's potential is also challenged from another standpoint. For more than a decade, concern among progressive legal scholars has been less and less with how law is produced by society (the traditional outlook of legal sociology) and increasingly with the way "society" is produced by law.[78] Not only can law stand alone from sociology with its own basis of understanding, taking or leaving social scientific insights as it sees fit, but it is said to be able also to create the central objects of inquiry—the very ontological basis—of sociology itself. According to some influential scholars, law has no need, and no possibility, of

---

[72] D. Nelken, "Can There Be a Sociology of Legal Meaning?" in *Law as Communication*, ed. D. Nelken (1996) 107–28, at 108–9.

[73] Nelken, *op. cit.*, n. 72, p. 107.

[74] id., pp. 101–2.

[75] G. Teubner, "How the Law Thinks: Toward a Constructivist Epistemology of Law" (1989) 22 *Law and Society Rev.* 727–57, at 747.

[76] Nelken, *op. cit.*, n. 72; p. 112. For example, legal explanations of criminal conduct are interms of responsibility. When the matter is considered sociologically in terms of causation of patterns of criminal activity through social or economic conditions, legal questions of responsibility may sometimes be partly or even wholly displaced.

[77] R. Samek, *The Legal Point of View* (1974).

[78] D. Nelken, "Beyond the Study of 'Law and Society'? Henry's *Private Justice* and O'Hagan's *The End of Law*" [1986] *Am. Bar Foundation Research J.* 323–38, at 325.

doing more than creating its own normative understanding of its social environment.[79] But, in a more radical view, law is also seen as responsible, partly at
least, for *creating the social categories which sociology itself must work with.*
[pp. 173–176].

For these reasons a sharp line between the legal and the social can no longer be
drawn; a "more holistic understanding" is required.[80] Legal ideas constitute a
form of social knowledge in themselves. The often neglected point that legal
speculations once provided prototypes for early forms of social theory[81] acquires
a new significance.

Certainly, some scholars in sociology of law continue to ask for evidence of
law's ideological effects and to nurse doubts about law's capacity to influence
social consciousness.[82] The demands and doubts are unsurprising given that the
postulated direction of influence *from* legal ideas as shaping forces in social life fits
uneasily with legal sociology's traditional assumption that society shapes law, and
that effects of law on society are always specific matters for empirical study. But
newer approaches to the relationship between the "legal" and the "social" refuse
to see law and society as somehow separate or even competing spheres of influence. They more often treat as self-evident that law constitutes social life to a
significant degree by influencing the meanings of basic categories (such as property, ownership, contract, trust, responsibility, guilt, and personality) that colour
or define social relations. Hence, when the nature of socio-legal studies is considered, it is said to be no longer clear (and perhaps never was) whether the
enterprise is legal, social or a mixture of the two.[83] The field remains undefined;
conceptual clarity seems sacrificed to a need to avoid deep controversies about the
foundations of social scientific inquiries about law.[84]

What then should be made of the effort to understand legal ideas (elements of
legal doctrine and the reasoning and forms of interpretation that surround them)
sociologically? This paper argues that the main problems that are said to
undermine this effort are in fact, despite their apparent seriousness, solvable or
ultimately false. They do not stand in its way. But they do very properly demand
that the nature, aims,and methods of sociological inquiry be clarified. Nevertheless, the claim to be made here is not merely that the effort to understand legal
ideas sociologically is appropriate. My claim is that the *only* way to grasp these
ideas imaginatively as ideas about the organization of the social world is through
some form of sociological interpretation.

In the remainder of this paper an attempt is made to address the issues raised
above for sociological understanding of legal ideas by analysing the two main
apparent sources of difficulty to which these issues relate. The first of these is the
nature of law's own "truth"—its capacity to interpret the world in its own way.
What is this "truth" which, it is suggested, law produces or inhabits? What is to
be made of the claim that law knows itself better than sociology can know it? Can
we, indeed, speak of law "knowing" or "thinking" anything?[85] The second source
of difficulty is the need to clarify what is meant by the effort to gain "sociological
understanding". What kind of understanding is envisaged here? What is

---

[79]  N. Luhmann, "Closure and Openness: On Reality in the World of Law" in *Autopoietic
    Law: A New Approach to Law and Society*, ed. G. Teubner (1988) 335–48.
[80]  id., pp. 325, 338.
[81]  See D. R. Kelley, *The Human Measure: Social Thought in the Western Legal Tradition*
    (1990); W. T. Murphy, "The Oldest Social Science? The Epistemic Properties of the
    Common Law Tradition" (1991) 54 *Modern Law Rev.* 182–215; S. P. Turner and R. A.
    Factor, *Max Weber: The Lawyer as Social Thinker* (1994).
[82]  L. M. Friedman, "The Concept of Legal Culture: A Reply", in *Comparing Legal Cul-
    tures*, ed. D. Nelken (1997) pp. 33–9, at 37–9.
[83]  Fitzpatrick, *op. cit.*, n. 70, p. 105.
[84]  Compare Nelken, *op. cit.*, n. 72, p. 108.
[85]  Compare Teubner, *op. cit.*, n. 75.

sociology's "truth", or in Nelken's phrase, what kind of "truth about law" can sociology offer? Does this, for example, imply a need to subsume law as a discipline under the hegemony of another academic discipline, such as sociology?

I argue that no such implication is required. Indeed, it would entirely miss the point. Disciplinary boundaries should be viewed pragmatically; indeed, with healthy suspicion. They should not be prisons of understanding. The term "sociological" is necessary to keep firmly in mind certain definite foci in interpreting law, but these foci and their authoritative definition are not the property of any particular academic discipline. Participants in law—not just lawyers but all those who seek to use legal ideas for their own purposes, to promote or control the interests of others, or more generally for public purposes of direction or control—understand legal ideas in practical terms. The aim in what follows is to show that the most practical view of legal ideas is one informed by sociological insight. Legal ideas are properly understood sociologically.        [pp. 173–178]

### III. Does Law have its own way of seeing the World?

[. . .] The strongest current arguments for law's capacity to declare sociological understanding of legal ideas irrelevant are arguments emphasizing these kinds of indicators. In one way or another, these indicators make possible what Nelken terms "law's truth". When attempts are made to specify the indicators, however, they seem remarkably limited. They may amount to no more than a consistent focus in any context on marking a distinction between the "legal" and the "illegal"; right and wrong in terms of specifically legal definitions.[86] Otherwise, law might be said to be distinctively concerned with institutional rather than brute facts, and with considerations of authority, integrity, fairness, justice, acceptability, and practicability. It has to use "arbitrary cut-off points" in argument, and often chooses not to look behind its presumptions. It seeks to provide certainty and to relate to common sense. It may adopt or reject scientific (including social scientific) knowledge or reasoning in order to pursue these objectives. It gathers and presents facts in ways tailored to adjudicative needs.[87] It operates by means of practical reasoning and argumentation that may be more or less specific to its governmental, dispute processing or social control tasks. But any enumeration of characteristics of law's truth will miss the point for "what truth means for law is the result of its own processes."[88] "Ultimately," as Arthur Leff puts it, "law is not something we know but something that we do."[89] It is not grasped by description from "outside" but by working and thinking within it.
[pp. 179–180]

[. . .]

Thus law tends to become, in arguments about "law's truth", an abstract site of understanding removed from particular kinds of social locations [. . .].

From a sociological standpoint, however, it is an empirical question how far and in what forms this cohesion, distinctiveness or specificity may exist. Lawyers operating between different legal systems can experience different "truths" of law, and sometimes have difficulty in establishing a shared discourse. Even within the same system, outlooks on almost all matters legal may sometimes differ radically as between different participants in legal processes. As Balkin suggests, there may be much disagreement on matters of method no less than on the interpretation of particular matters of doctrine. And it contributes little to envisage all these actual or potential disagreements as part of an ongoing conversation on the justice or

---

[86] N. Luhmann, "The Coding of the Legal System" in *State, Law and Economy as Autopoietic Systems*, ed. G. Teubner and A. Febbrajo (1992), pp. 145–185.
[87] See, generally, Nelken, *op. cit.*, n. 72, pp. 99–100.
[88] *ibid.*, p. 103.
[89] Quoted *ibid.*, p. 99.

integrity of law. Such a conversation may exist only because the structure of political power forces those who wish to have access to or protection from that power to adjust their claims and arguments. It may force them to press these claims and arguments in ways that distort the particular legal "truth" which they would otherwise wish to express.

Law's basic "truth" may be merely the *provisional, pragmatic consensus* of those legal actors who are perceived at any given time to be supported by the highest forms of authority within the legal system of the state. Another way of putting the matter would be that there is no "law's truth", no single legal point of view, but only the different—sometimes allied, sometimes conflicting—viewpoints expressing the experience, knowledge, and practices of different legal actors and participants. What links all of these as "legal" in some official sense is their varied relationships with matters of government and social control and with institutionalized doctrine bearing on these matters.

Undoubtedly law is presented professionally as a more or less unified, specialized discourse. But, as Balkin notes, it is an intellectually vulnerable, open discourse, liable to invasion by many kinds of ideas, including sociological ones. Ultimately, it is given discursive coherence and unity only because its intellectual insecurity, its permanent cognitive openness, is stabilized by *political fiat*. The political power of the state which guarantees the decisions of certain official legal interpreters, puts an end to argument, determines which interpretive concepts prevail, asserts favoured normative judgments as superior to all competing ones, and guarantees normative closure by the threat of official coercion.[90] The *voluntas*, or coercive authority, of law, centralized by political structures and organized through legal hierarchies, stabilizes and controls potentially unlimited, often competing and conflicting, elaborations of *ratio*—reason and doctrinal principle—in a host of diverse sites and settings of legal argument and interpretation.

Seen in sociological perspective, this is the nature of law's truth as a unified, distinctive discourse; a contingent feature of particular social environments. Sociological interpretation both reveals law's character and is, like many other forms of knowledge, available to enrich law's debates, colour its interpretations, and strengthen or subvert the strategies of control to which legal discourse is directed. Sociological insight is simultaneously inside and outside legal ideas, constituting them and interpreting them; sometimes speaking through them and sometimes speaking about them; sometimes aiding, sometimes undermining them. Thus a sociological understanding of legal ideas does not reduce them to something other than law. It expresses their social meaning *as law* in its rich complexity.

At the same time law defines social relations and influences the shape of the very phenomena that sociology studies. Thus legal and other social ideas interpenetrate each other. A line between law and society is, as has been seen, no longer capable of being sharply drawn. Law constitutes important aspects of social life by shaping or reinforcing modes of understanding of social reality. It would be remarkable if the power of law as officially guaranteed ideas and practices could have no such effects. One might indeed wonder what law as an expression of power is for, if not for this. But a sociological perspective makes it possible to *observe and understand* this effect of legal discourses and situate it in relation to the social effects of other kinds of ideas and practices. Law constitutes society in so far as it is, itself, an aspect of society, a framework and an expression

---

[90]  Thus, as Robert Cover puts it, the problem that requires a court to make an authoritative legal ruling is not that the law is unclear but that there is *too much law*. Courts (and especially the ultimate courts of appeal in a legal system) exist "to suppress law, to choose between two or more laws, to impose upon law a hierarchy." See R. Cover, "The Supreme Court 1982, Foreword: *Nomos* and Narrative" (1983–4) 97 *Harvard Law Rev.* 4–68, at 40.

of understandings that enable society to exist. A sociological perspective on legal ideas is necessary to recognize and analyses the intellectual and moral power of law in this respect. To interpret legal ideas without recognizing, through socio-logical insight, this dimension of them would be to understand them inadequately. It would be to treat them as less significant and less complex than they are made to appear in a broader sociological perspective.

### IV. What is a Sociological Perspective?

Is it, however, really necessary to invoke the word "sociological" here? Why privilege sociology? Nelken[91] argues that sociology is sometimes presented as supreme only by downgrading law's disciplinary status. He doubts that sociology can ultimately transcend its own methods of argument and style. The legal sociologist may stand too close to sociology to understand law. And, in any case, why should a sociological, rather than, for example, an economic or psychological viewpoint be favoured?[92] Why should sociology impose *its* understandings? On the other hand, if it does not do so, its analyses of law can be criticized as being parasitic on law's own definitions of "the legal".[93]

But most of these problems surely disappear once it is recognized that use of the word "sociological" does not imply adherence to the distinct methods, the-ories or outlook of the academic discipline called sociology. It is appropriate to claim that a sociological perspective is indispensable in orienting oneself, whether for practical (participatory) or theoretical purposes, to contemporary law as a social phenomenon. But the term "sociological" must be taken in a methodolo-gically broad and, at the same time, theoretically limited sense. This rejects any implication of attachment to a specific social scientific or other discipline. Sociological understanding of legal ideas is *transdisciplinary* understanding.[94] But it is properly termed sociological because it consistently and permanently addresses the need to reinterpret law *systematically and empirically* as a *social* phenomenon. This terminology also suggests, however, that a legal outlook can itself be sociological, involving a systematic, empirical view of the social world, though it need not be so. As noted earlier, sociological understanding is simul-taneously inside and outside legal ideas.

The essence of a sociological interpretation of legal ideas lies in three postu-lates. First, law is to be seen as an entirely *social* phenomenon; law as a field of experience is to be understood as an aspect of social relationships in general, as wholly concerned with the co-existence of individuals in social groups. Secondly, the social phenomena of law must be understood *empirically* (through detailed examination of variation and continuity in actual historical patterns of social coexistence, rather than in relation to idealized or abstractly imagined social conditions). And thirdly, they must be understood *systematically*, rather than anecdotally or impressionistically; the aim is to broaden understanding from the specific to the general. It is to be able to assess the significance of particularities in a wider perspective; to situate the richness of the unique in a broader theoretical context and so provide orientation for its interpretation.        [pp. 180–183]

Approaches to legal inquiry that are set up as in some way *opposed* to socio-logical perspectives are, *to the extent that they are presented in this competitive way*, often ultimately more restricted forms of understanding of law as a social phenomenon to the extent that they actually exclude sociological insight in certain ways. Otherwise, most productively, these other approaches are best seen as allied

---

[91] Nelken, *op. cit.*, n. 72, p. 125; Nelken, *op. cit.*, n. 72, p. 115.
[92] id. (1994), p. 125.
[93] C. Pennisi, "Sociological Uses of the Concept of Legal Culture" in *Comparing Legal Cultures*, ed. D. Nelken (1997) 105–18, at 107.
[94] Cotterrell, *Law's Community* (1995), ch. 3.

with and (in so far as they seek to offer social insight) even appropriately organized by means of a (perhaps implicit) sociological perspective. They should be treated as specialized co-workers with sociological inquiry.

Equally, sociological inquiry needs to be open and receptive to a variety of forms of legal inquiry that are not generally thought of as sociological. It must recognize their special power and merit and draw from and interact with them. Sometimes, indeed often, these forms of inquiry produce sociological insights while declaring justifiably that their ideas and approaches are directed to quite different purposes, and founded on quite different bases, from those that they associate with sociological studies.                                        [pp. 184–185]

## V. How Should Legal Ideas be Interpreted?

The term "sociology of law" remains useful as a label for identifying a vitally important body of research on legal processes and as an important focus of self-identification for scholars committed to extending this research. But it is a somewhat unsatisfactory and misleading term when it is used to refer to the sociological study of legal ideas. It often suggests a sub-discipline or a specialism, a branch of sociology or a distinct compartment of legal studies. In considering the interpretation of legal ideas it would be better to speak of sociological perspectives or insights, or sociological understanding or interpretation.

*Sociological* interpretation of legal ideas is not a particular, specialized way of approaching law, merely co-existing with other kinds of understanding. Sociology of law in this particular context is a transdisciplinary enterprise and aspiration to broaden understanding of law as a social phenomenon. It certainly insists on its criteria of the social, the systematic, and the empirical, reflecting—as will be further illustrated subsequently—the conviction that these criteria are inscribed in some sense and in some degree in participant understandings of the nature of law itself as a social phenomenon. It seeks to go beyond many such understandings. But sociology of law is otherwise *inclusive* rather than exclusive. Sociological insight is found in many disciplinary fields of knowledge and practice.

If sociological inquiries about law have an intellectual or moral allegiance, then this is to law itself—that is, to its enrichment through a radical broadening of the perspectives of the varied participants in legal processes, practices, and forms of knowledge. Sociological inquiry is critical because it insists that the legal perspectives of many of these participants (whether lawyers or non-lawyers) are *insufficiently* systematic and theoretically informed or sensitive to empirical variation, and have *too narrow* an awareness of law's social character. But it is also constructive because it cannot merely condemn existing legal ideas without also asking at all times how law might be *reinterpreted* and so re-imagined and reshaped consistently with its social character, when understood better in a broader sociological perspective.

It should be clear that the discussion above of sociological understanding of legal ideas takes for granted the need to reject the familiar dichotomy between internal and external views of law, or between insider and outsider perspectives. This dichotomy is familiar within legal philosophy. Its assertion is a device that accompanies the false assertion of the uniqueness of "law's truth". As Nelken properly points out,[95] the internal-external distinction is, for the most part, merely a feature *internal* to lawyers' thinking. It reflects especially a professional self-image in terms of a special kind of reasoning and understanding.[96] When legal thinking is understood sociologically, the distinction disappears between internal (legal participant) views of law and external (for example, social scientific observers') views. It is replaced by a conception of partial, relatively narrow or

---

[95] Nelken, *op. cit.*, n. 72, pp. 111–2.
[96] Cotterrell, *op. cit.*, n. 94, ch. 5.

specialized participant perspectives on (and in) law, confronting and being confronted by, penetrating, illuminating, and being penetrated and illuminated by, broader, more inclusive perspectives on (and in) law as a social phenomenon.

It might be asked what happens to justice and legal values in sociological understanding. Can a sociological understanding of legal ideas address questions of justice? The answer is, clearly, yes. It was noted earlier that sociological insight should both inform and interpret legal ideas. The question of whether sociology is "inside" or "outside" law becomes redundant. It is both inside and outside; and so the inside-outside demarcation is meaningless in this context.[97] The line between law and society, and thus between legal and sociological interpretation becomes indistinct. Law constitutes society in certain respects; social understanding informs law in certain ways. But in so far as sociological interpretation of legal ideas relates them to the entire context of social relationships in general it focuses attention on the patterning of those relationships, which is the specific concern of justice.

Justice is a perception of social relations in balance. It is one aspect of a sense of social cohesion or integration.[98] The radical broadening of perspective which sociological interpretation seeks makes it possible to enrich understandings of the social conditions of justice. The consistent focus of sociological inquiry on the social, the systematic, and the empirical provides the essential dimensions of this enriched understanding. Sociological inquiry cannot abolish disagreement as to what justice demands in any particular situation. But it can reveal the meaning of justice claims in a broader perspective by systematically analysing the empirical conditions that provide postulates underlying these claims.

If sociological interpretation of legal ideas is to be characterized in these ways, can we say anything concrete and specific about its *methods*? As noted earlier, settled methodology is the unifying feature which, according to Jack Balkin, law so crucially lacks. Can such a settled methodology be attributed to sociological inquiry?

The answer must recognize a crucial claim made earlier. This is that, if sociological inquiry about legal ideas is to be treated as having any specific intellectual allegiance, it is to law as a social phenomenon, not to an academic discipline of sociology or to any other social science discipline. Hence the sociological understanding of legal ideas reflects methodologically law's own fragmentary and varied methodological characteristics as understood by those who participate in or are affected by legal practices. This is inevitable because of the interdependence of legal and sociological understanding referred to earlier. Sociological interpretation extends legal analysis; it broadens the perspectives of legal participants.

It does not necessarily *replace* those perspectives or *contradict* them by the use of a specific methodology foreign to the diverse methods already used by legal participants. If it did so *generally* this would be to replace law with sociology; to fall into the trap which, as noted earlier, has been said by some commentators to ensnare all sociological attempts to grasp law's truth. Thus, the methodology of sociological understanding of legal ideas is the deliberate *extension* in carefully specified directions of the diverse ways in which legal participants themselves think about the social world in legal terms. It seeks radically to extend the already partially systematic and empirical characteristics of this legal thinking, and thereby sets out to transform legal ideas by reinterpreting them.

An illustration may help to clarify this argument. The English law of trusts has developed a strange impasse in one narrow and somewhat arcane area of legal doctrine. While property can be held on trust by trustees to benefit individuals or

---

[97] See R. Cotterrell, "Law and Community: A New Relationship?" (1998) 51 *Current Legal Problems*, 367.

[98] Compare É. Durkheim, *The Division of Labour in Society* (1984) 77.

groups of individuals in a wide variety of ways, English law, unlike some other common law jurisdictions, has declared that property may not be held on trust for abstract non-charitable purposes—for example, to promote press freedom, or sport outside an educational context.

When it is asked why English law takes this particular stance on private purpose trusts and how the law in this area should be developed in the light of the precedents, answers are not particularly straightforward. The cases refer to particular private purpose trusts as illustrations, and offer various reasons for a tradition of judicial hostility to them. The matter is dealt with by the courts partly by looking at what has been decided in the past, partly by detailing technical problems that would be faced by law if private purpose trusts were to be declared generally valid (for example, problems of enforcement), and partly by offering policy arguments about the social or economic rights and wrongs of allowing particular kinds of trusts to be set up.

Legal thinking in this area is empirical up to a point, looking at what has been decided and the specific judicially stated circumstances in which particular decisions were taken. It considers how law in this area has been and can be enforced. It tries also to be systematic, seeking general principles which can unite the judicial approaches taken (but it ultimately admits failure, declaring that cases in which some private purpose trusts have been upheld are anomalous). It is also aware of the nature of the law in this field as an expression of social relations. Thus, it considers policy; for example, the social and economic pros and cons of restrictions on alienation of property and of particular kinds of testamentary freedom. But legal analyses do not seem to remove the deep-rooted controversies surrounding the law in this area. Commentators take a variety of positions on the issues, some supporting the general legal hostility to private purpose trusts, others declaring it unjustified. And the controversy has continued for decades. In other jurisdictions matters have been dealt with by legislative reform.

A sociological approach to doctrine in this area attempts to extend established methods of legal thought in new, relatively unfamiliar ways.[99] First, it puts the development of doctrine into a far wider historical context, noting the changing social and economic contexts in which trust law as a whole has developed. By this means it suggests that the institution of the trust has been thought of in ways that have changed radically over time. This change becomes recognizable when attention shifts from the development of a particular line of precedents, as in orthodox legal analysis, to changing patterns of legal ideas about the nature of trusting relationships seen as interrelated with broader social, economic, and moral ideas. Thus, the inquiry broadens the idea of law as a social phenomenon by treating legal ideas as an aspect of social ideas in development. This is not to reduce the former to the latter, but to see each as inseparable from the other.

Similarly, empirical inquiry is broadened beyond the observation of previous decisions to include much wider observation of the particular social contexts and implications of these decisions. It considers their relation with other legal developments in areas that may be legally distinct from but socially interconnected with the area of private purpose trusts, viewed as an area of legally structured social relationships. Thus, sociological inquiry seeks a broader, systematic view of the law by reinterpreting the relationships of ideas which the lawyer identifies. It puts them into an intellectual context that allows the identification of other relationships and other connections. And these in turn help to explain the law as it stands and point to ways of rethinking and developing it.

When sociological inquiry is used in the ways outlined above it ceases to appear

---

[99]   R. Cotterrell, "Some Sociological Aspects of the Controversy Around the Legal Validity of Private Purpose Trusts" in *Equity and Contemporary Legal Developments*, ed. S. Goldstein (1992) 302–34; R. Cotterrell, "Trusting in Law: Legal and Moral Concepts of Trust" (1993) 46 *Current Legal Problems* 75–95.

as the pursuit of a methodology alien to law, or the invocation of a competing academic discipline with the aim of colonizing law. It is seen as the radical extension and reflexivity of legal participants' understanding of law. Viewed in this way, it appears as a necessary means of broadening legal understanding the systematic and empirical understanding of a certain aspect of social life which is recognized as "legal".

It procedes from participant understandings, but because it seeks to *systematize* legal understanding beyond the needs of particular participants, it goes beyond their perspectives. For example, it certainly does not reject—but does not treat (for its purposes) as adequate—personal or anecdotal accounts of legal experience, particular narratives which cannot be generalized. Because it treats very seriously the requirement that systematizations of legal or social knowledge must be grounded in *empirical* observation, it resists speculations that it considers as taking inadequate account of empirical variation. And because it emphasizes law's character as a *social* phenomenon, it examines law's social character far more extensively and broadly than most participants need to do. Hence, for example, it is led to extend its conception of the legal as a social phenomenon beyond the forms of law familiar to lawyers or some other categories of legal participants.[1]

Viewed in this way the enterprise of sociological interpretation of legal ideas is not a desirable supplement but an essential means of legal understanding. Legal ideas are a means of structuring the social world. To appreciate them in this sense and to recognize their power and their limits, is to understand them sociologically. [pp. 187–92]

## D. NELKEN
### Blinding Insights? The Limits of a Reflexive Sociology of Law
### (1998)[2]

What is law for sociology? And what is sociology to law? Above all, what is sociology of law—and more generally any other study of "law and"—good for? From its emergence as a topic of academic enquiry there has been division and sometimes competition between those approaches to the sociological understanding of law whose main aim is to reveal what law is unable (or unwilling) to see, and those whose goal is to help law see more clearly. The first approach relates law to its wider historical and social environment, and to competing and overlapping disciplines and practices, and has little difficulty in showing how legal actors often have little grasp of the factors which shape the "inputs" and "outcomes" of their decisions. The second presupposes most of these constraints and seeks to improve the quality of decision making in terms which can be used by legal actors. Where the first type of scholarship deliberately transforms legal definitions into sociological categories,[3] the second seeks to translate sociological

---

[1] Some sociological theories of legal pluralism offer the clearest examples here. They often suggest a vast *diversity* of legal knowledge, consciousness, authority, and experience which tends to be obscured by the orthodox typical focus of lawyers' practice and legal education on uniform law applied by official national and state courts.

[2] [From 25 *Journal of Law and Society* 407.]

[3] All the major textbooks, including Roger Cotterrell's magisterial synthesis of the field, reconceptualize legal phenomena in terms of issues such as social order, social control, regulation, dispute processing, governmentality, desert, distribution, power, symbolism, ideology, or rationality, rather than the doctrinal definitions of lawyers or administrative categories.

insights into legal concepts.[4]

How do these approaches relate? Is there a way of combining them? More precisely, how far can the methods useful for showing the limits of law's sociological understanding of the world also be used for helping law to overcome those limits? Whereas we should expect there to be much common ground[5] there have always also been scholars who have argued that a synthesis is neither possible nor desirable. Typically the concern of many sociologists of law has been that the "pull of the policy audience",[6] or the limitations of practical decision making in legal settings, would compromise the proper development of academic social science or blunt the edge of political critique. But there is also an opposite worry—and it is this which will be my topic in this paper. Here the charge is that the introduction of different styles of reasoning can have ill effects for legal practice by misunderstanding and thus threatening the integrity of legal processes or the values they embody.[7] In particular, the introduction of "social scientism" will either succeed all too easily in making law more of a policy science than is really good for it, as is claimed by many adhering to the "law and literature" movement,[8] or else, even in failing, will produce a "hybrid" monstrosity which is neither law or social science, as asserted by autopoieticists such as Gunther Teubner.[9]                                                                      [pp. 407–408]

Cotterrell's recent paper contains some novel arguments, in particular, regarding the commensurability of legal discourses and sociological methods and the utility of sociological insights in legal processes. But it is best understood as the strongest statement yet of his new-found conviction that the social study of law can contribute most to the understanding of law by weakening its own ties to sociology.

Is this new account useful as a description or even as an aspiration for anything which could plausibly still be described as sociology of law? Cotterrell is not greatly concerned about this label. But a more important difficulty that is raised is the basis for defining what count as sociological insights (since Cotterrell speaks of gathering them wherever they may be found) and how to measure success in understanding the social aspects of law once we have broken free of "any particular academic discipline".[10] Reflexivity in the sense of self-criticism, the recognition that truths are partial and that there is still far to go, will not be enough to establish if any progress is being made.

But, in any case, it is not so easy to become un-disciplined. The "paradox" of sociology's weakness constituting its strength means that it is not even that clear

---

[4] This classification is put forward by John Monahan and Laurens Walker in their leading United States casebook, *Social Science in Law* (1994): "we here view social science as an analytic tool in the law, familiarity with which will heighten the lawyer's professional effectiveness and sharpen the legal scholar's insights. The principal alternative to the insider perspective on the relation of social science to law is the 'law and society' or sociology of law approach which seeks to understand the functioning of law as a social system." Variations on this distinction are captured in other classifications such as sociology of law versus socio-legal studies, "law and society" versus sociological jurisprudence, and so on.

[5] This is occupied in Britain by the deliberately ecumenical socio-legal association, or the "law in context" series of textbooks which is dedicated to "broadening the study of law from within".

[6] A. Sarat and S. Silbey, "The Pull of the Policy Audience" (1988) 10 *Law and Policy* 97.

[7] L. Tribe, "Trial by Mathematics: Precision and Ritual in the Legal Process" (1971) 84 *Harvard Law Rev.* 1329; M. Constable, *The Law of the Other* (1994); D. Nelken "A just measure of science" in *Science in Court*, eds. M. Freeman and H. Reece (1998).

[8] See, for example, J. Boyd White, *When Words Lose their Meaning* (1984).

[9] G. Teubner, "How the Law Thinks: Toward a Constructivist Epistemology of Law" (1989) 23 *Law and Society Rev.* 727; when law "enslaves" science it produces hybrid creatures having "unclear epistemic status and unknown social consequences".

[10] *ibid.*, p. 177.

whether in what he now prefers to call "a sociological perspective on legal theory" Cotterrell is really asking us to abandon sociology or still seeking to make ever stronger claims on its behalf. It would indeed be paradoxical if the author of the leading British textbook in the sub-discipline, a textbook actually criticized for being over-concerned with professional sociological respectability,[11] turned his back on all that he had achieved.[12] In fact, Cotterrell continues to make explicit reference to the sociological perspective and to mobilize a working idea of what constitutes social insight which is firmly situated within the boundaries of academic sociology. Many times his argument comes close to the near tautology of claiming that only sociology can satisfactorily explain the way law is constituted by and reconstitutes social ideas, even though the larger case he is advancing is that it is legal discourses *as such* which are and must be concerned with such insights when deciding cases or otherwise intervening in social life.[13] Other disciplinary approaches, such as law and literature, are swiftly, and not entirely convincingly, despatched as self-evidently poor competitors to sociology,[14] just as he has criticized other recent approaches to legal discourse for being insufficiently concrete about the specifics of place, authors, and empirical evidence.[15] Most significant, his arguments in favour of law's need for social insight often rely exactly on the external understanding of law produced by disciplinary protocols rather than participants' experiences; thus he rejects Dworkin's idea of law as an ongoing conversation about integrity because, he argues, justice must primarily be treated as the result of a discussion shaped by the constraints of power.[16] Nor is his call for sociology of law to swear intellectual allegiance to law assumed to be in any way inconsistent with a continuing requirement to "radically extend" lawyers' views[17] or to "transform legal ideas by reinterpreting them".[18]

My reservations about some aspects of the way Cotterrell has reformulated the task of a social study of law must, however, be understood against the background of overwhelming agreement with most of what he is trying to do (indeed, he generously cites some of my recent work). I also worry about the dangers of false dichotomies such as that between merely "taking problems" as defined by law or policy makers and "making problems" to fit an academic discipline.[19] I too am convinced that sociology of "law" needs to deal with legal doctrine and not limit itself to providing a "sociology of courts and lawyers", and I have used the overworked phrase "changing paradigms" to point to new developments capable of redirecting studies into law and society.[20] Like Cotterrell, and at about the same time, I concluded that legal and sociological discourses needed to be

---

[11]  S.S. Silbey, "Loyalty and Betrayal: Cotterrell's Discovery and Reproduction of Legal Ideology" (1991) 16 *Law and Social Inquiry* 80.

[12]  Near the beginning of his recent article *ante*, 747, Cotterrell says that existing types of sociological studies of the "law in action" remain of central importance. Apparently we are not forced to choose between the approaches represented by the two stages of his thinking despite their different implicit assessments of sociology's disciplinary strengths or their different ideas of appropriate methodologies for producing social insight.

[13]  Cotterrell, *ante*, 916, pp. 177, 181. He avoids tautology by asserting that sociology can also help legal discourses to extend and systematize their implicit social insights. But this begs the question why they need to go in this rather than another direction.

[14]  *ibid.*, p. 183.

[15]  R. Cotterrell, *The Sociology of Law* (1992, 2nd ed.) at 308–9.

[16]  Cotterrell, *ante*, 916, pp. 180–1.

[17]  *ibid.*, p. 191.

[18]  *ibid.*, p. 190.

[19]  D. Nelken. "The 'Gap Problem' in the Sociology of Law: A Theoretical Review" in *Windsor Yearbook of Access to Justice* (1981) 35; and "Law in Action or Living Law? Back to the Beginning in Sociology of Law" (1984) 4 *Legal Studies* 152.

[20]  D. Nelken, "Beyond the Study of Law and Society" (1986) *Am. Bar Foundation J.* 323; and "Changing Paradigms in the Sociology of Law" in *Autopoietic Law: A New Approach to Law and Society*, ed. G. Teubner (1987) 191.

confronted.[21] We both think that the notion of reflexivity may be the key to further progress in understanding the relationship between law and sociology, but are cautious about embracing autopoietic ideas of self-referential recursivity.

Yet it is over the question of reflexivity where we also most differ (at least in terms of what we now choose to emphasize). Cotterrell increasingly stresses the need to free social insights from the limits of academic sociology so as to help law reflexively overcome its blind spots; I think we should worry just as much about how to further sociology's own reflexivity.[22] The programme I have proposed for what I call the second generation of "law in context" work is, therefore:

> to seek an account of law which contextualises the bounded and practical rationalities of legal and other actors and the process of legal reproduction *without assuming that they could or should have adopted the place, point of view or practice of the discipline which produces this account.* Even for social scientists, law's lack of awareness, or selective awareness of its context, must be treated as an intrinsic, if changing, feature of its social reproduction, rather than as simply the origin of corrigible errors to be excised by the expert or political activist.[23]

In the rest of this paper I shall therefore try to clarify what may be at stake in these different ways to employ the idea of reflexivity. Deliberately over-simplifying, we could say that where Cotterrell presently seeks the aim of increasing legal reflexivity by requiring sociology to go beyond its limits as an academic subject, I suggest that sociology of law should try better to understand its limits as a way of seeing. Where he argues that sociology has the capacity to transform legal discourses despite their claims to autonomy, I am more interested in noting the way law (necessarily) transforms other discourses. Finally (and as a consequence) we disagree over how easy it is to use "social insights" in deciding what solutions are appropriate in legal disputes.                    [pp. 412–414]

Those who see sociology's task as revealing what law cannot or will not see have the relatively straightforward though important job of showing how legal solutions frequently fail to grasp social problems. But Cotterrell wants us to go further. His goal is to reveal and systematize law's proto-social ideas so as ensure that legal solutions are better shaped by social insights. By treating legal ideas "as an aspect of social ideas in development" so as to clarify the socio-political contexts and implications of past and present decision making,[24] Cotterrell believes that sociologically inspired resolutions can be crafted even, or especially, where legal doctrine faces only conflicting precedents (as in his example of the confused status of private-purpose trusts in English law). Perhaps. But what if, as I have been arguing, the introduction of social insights also has the potential to distort or at least change legal practices rather than simply help them to sort out self induced muddles?

Once again, the problems I am raising have nothing to do with the untenable

---

[21] D. Nelken "Criminal law and criminal justice; some notes on their irrelation" in *Criminal Law and Justice*, ed. I. H. Dennis (1987) 139. I first came to see the need to give attention to what I called "irrelation" as I reviewed the difficulties of synthesizing insights about crime and criminal justice into criminal law. I have tried to produce more wide-ranging analyses (in D. Nelken, "The truth about Law's Truth" in *European Yearbook for the Sociology of Law*, eds. A. Febbrajo and D. Nelken (1990) 87–163; "The Loneliness of Law's Meta-Theory" in *Plural Legalities: Critical Legal Studies in Europe*, eds. R. de Lange and K. Raes (1991) 172; "Are disputes between Law and Science resolvable?" in *Proceedings of the Bologna International Conference on Sociology of Law*, ed. V. Ferrari (1991).

[22] For a fuller discussion of five kinds of reflexivity, see D. Nelken, "Reflexive Criminology?" in *The Futures of Criminology*, ed. D. Nelken (1994) 7.

[23] Nelken, (1996) 19 Socio-Legal Newsletter 12.

[24] Cotterrell, *ante*, 916, pp. 190–1.

claim that law is free of outside influence (whether cognitive or normative). The differences between the ways law reaches closure and sociology advances its own reflexivity does not mean that social insights, ideas or facts do not or cannot enter the reproduction of legal cognition. In different settings, such as the university, courts, tribunals, or regulatory policy-making bodies, and at various stages of legal and administrative processes, those who take or influence decisions may have their ideas changed by education, policy discussions, political action or activism, legal advocacy, lobbying or media reports. Present or future legal and other decision makers may be informed by, presuppose or actually seek out assistance in obtaining such insights.

In this sense, Cotterrell is obviously right to argue that social insights do and should influence the crafting of legal solutions to social issues. We are indeed all legal realists now; Anglo-American legal scholarship regularly produces a sort of interdisciplinary bricolage. No serious discussion of the present and future of, say, public law, negligence or family law could be carried on in Britain without some reference to social considerations.[25] The puzzle that concerns us here, however, is whether there is a way of guiding this process which could tell us when and in what way social insights *must* shape legal decision making and the likely effect of introducing such insights. Our undoubted ability to describe and perhaps even explain the rise and fall of different forms of social knowledge in legal processes works well enough after the event, but does not provide us with a metric or even a rule of thumb for deciding what to do in particular cases. In general, social insights seem to function differently when they serve to open up legal closure than when they are used to provide closure. Can we ensure social insights get into law in a way which reflects their sociological sense but also respects the differences and integrity of different discourses and practices?[26]

Until quite recently Cotterrell admitted that "it is still very much an open question how far any productive dialogue or integration of normative legal theory with empirical legal theory is possible"[27] even though he went on to insist that a synthesis was essential because legal doctrine itself cannot explain legal change or grasp the social reality it needs to handle. More recently he explained that "in one sense law and sociology as forms of professional practice are similar in scope yet wholly opposed in method and aims".[28] Faced with these differences, some authors propose that we uproot social science insights from the methods which generate them,[29] but this, of course, begs the question of what happens when we separate an approach from its methodology. Cotterrell's new arguments about the similarities between law and sociology, on the other hand, seems to be suggesting that their methods are not after all that different:

> The sociological understanding of legal ideas reflects methodologically law's own frag-
> mented and varied methodological characteristics as understood by those who participate
> in or are affected by legal practices.[30]

---

[25] See the chapters by D. Oliver, B. Hepple, and M. Freeman in *Law and Opinion at the End of the Twentieth Century*, ed. M. Freeman (1997).

[26] For an important illustration of such difficulties, see the discussion of the use of "battered women's syndrome" as a method of displacing law's "myths" about wife battering in D. Downs, *More than Victims: Battered Women, the Syndrome Society and the Law* (1996).

[27] R. Cotterrell, *The Politics of Jurisprudence* (1989) 232. I have been arguing that we need to draw a sharper distinction than Cotterrell does between "dialogue" and "integration".

[28] Cotterrell, *op. cit.*, n. 15, p. 5. At p. 6 he added "law is a practical craft of systematic control of social relations and institutions. Sociology is a scientific enterprise that seeks systematic knowledge of them", though, once again, he went on to suggest that these dividing lines would have to give way eventually.

[29] Rubin, *op. cit.*, n. 7.

[30] Cotterrell, *op. cit.*, n. 13, p. 27.

But is this convincing? An alternative view would suggest, on the contrary, that for social insight to be effective in shaping legal discourses (for better or worse) it is neither *necessary nor sufficient* for them to have much in common. Donald Black, for example, has repeatedly claimed that his rigorously external behaviourist interpretation of legal behaviour (like the long-standing tradition of behaviourist prediction of judicial decision making) may be highly useful to lawyers in planning their litigation strategies. Indeed, he predicts the evolution of what he calls "sociological law", as lawyers reflexively internalize the finding that sociology provides the best guide to legal outcomes.[31] Conversely, even if we were to concede that the interpretative search for social insight is, as Cotterrell claims, more like law (and vice versa) than the methodology pursued by any other discipline, this does not guarantee that social insights can therefore be well-integrated; indeed it may be an explanation of their relative *lack* of integration. In many legal processes, what law calls for is precisely forms of knowledge/power which are in fact *different* and thus supplemental to its own.

Cotterrell himself has repeatedly argued that "law" seeks to borrow from other disciplines mainly when it is undergoing crises in which it is unable to maintain at least the appearance of discursive self-sufficiency.[32] But how is this claim to be reconciled with his more voluntaristic vision of the possibility of bringing social insights at will to help law achieve better understanding of its tasks? He suggests that the adoption of sociological insights is the most "practical" of approaches for participants in legal processes—but we must, of course, ask: most practical for whom, and why? It is no doubt possible to provide a sociological analysis of the significance of the different precedents concerning the status of private-purpose trusts which relates this to deeper social conflicts and contradictions. But can any proposal to resolve these clashes be anything other than a political choice to close down some alternative interpretations in favour of others?

What is really involved in going from dialogue to integration? How can context become pretext? What happens when we switch from explaining the "truth about law" to co-producing "law's truth"?[33] Why choose law?[34] What if the Rortian project of changing moral vocabularies[35] is better carried on in other spheres?[36] For George Gurvitch—no simple-minded believer in the separate worlds of "is" and "ought"—it was, none the less, essential to differentiate between the "art" of sociological jurisprudence and the "scientific" project of sociology of law.[37] Part of the difficulty here has to do with the relationship between theory and practice, or, rather, between, on the one hand, the practices of academic explanation and critique and, on the other, those of legal decision making, myth making, rule following, and participation in rituals.[38] The attempts by Stanley Fish to prove that theory is irrelevant to practice are probably exaggerated[39] (much depends on how far anyone really believes that theory can "guide" practice). But Pierre Bourdieu has shown convincingly how easy it is for free-ranging theorizing to

---

[31]  D. Black, *Sociological Justice* (1989) 102.

[32]  Cotterrell, *op. cit.*, n. 97, p. 55.

[33]  Nelken, *op. cit.* (1990), n. 21.

[34]  Not everybody (for example, second- and third-wave feminists) would necessarily welcome law becoming more effective in its grasp of reality.

[35]  R. Rorty, *Contingency, Irony and Solidarity* (1989).

[36]  Compare the careful discussion of the interrelationship but also necessary differences between the projects of critique, utopianism, and reform in N. Lacey, "Normative Reconstruction in Socio-Legal Theory" (1996) 5 *Social and Legal Studies* 131.

[37]  Gurvitch's caution on the "necessity of detaching the sociology of law from the teleogical art of jurisprudence" (Gurvitch, *op. cit.*, n. 46, p. 134) is all the more significant because his ambitions for sociology of law are otherwise so much in line with those of Cotterrell.

[38]  Compare Cotterrell, *op. cit.*, n. 15: "some of the myths and mysteries of law must be carried with us as we try to subject it to the questioning gaze of science" (1st ed., p. 331).

[39]  See, for example, M. Rosenfeld, *Just Interpretations* (1998) at 34–45.

misconstrue the temporal and constrained logic of practical reason and everyday decision making.[40] Certainly, a sociological perspective also reveals similarities in the way that both sociology and law warrant their truth claims and make them stick.[41] But if we follow Cotterrell's call to integrate social insights into law, we must at least accept that interpretation in practical contexts is itself already "application" (and thus a species of "violence").[42] The successful adoption of our interpretations necessarily depends on and becomes part of law's legitimation—because only law is allowed to give binding interpretations.[43] But this is not what Cotterrell means by talking about allegiance to law.

It seems to me that Cotterrell's latest formulation of its task well illustrate how a reflexive sociology of law has to struggle with three interrelated dilemmas. The first is the choice between *techne* and *physis* or, as he puts it, between "sociology as engineering" and "sociology as enlightenment". Cotterrell says he has now definitely opted for the latter, and this probably explains the repeated use of the word "insight". But while he argues that "science" is only an aspiration, it is still *this* which is the aspiration. Despite some gestures towards the postmodern,[44] he continues to be attached to the power of sociology's truth to resolve problems which befuddle legal doctrine by helping law overcome "partial perspectives". But where does this power come from? Sociology of law's guiding paradigm assumes that a better understanding of social "context" can provide the clue to the "fit" law has had and should have in the future.[45] But Cotterrell (like Roberto Unger before him[46]) increasingly wants to transcend the impression of "false necessity" which can be the legacy of social science in pursuit of a vision of how law could help create a new social and communal order: law as a *transformer* of context.

One person's vision can be another's nightmare. Where does Cotterrell's vision come from and what grounds it? The second dilemma faced by sociology of law is that between criticism and completion of law's work. Cotterrell is uninterested in merely deconstructing law—and, equally, law would have little to gain by borrowing a deconstructed method from sociology.[47] Does this mean that social insights are to be brought in to help provide the determinacy which law is unable to achieve by itself? The source of Cotterrell's vision, however, is more an ideal of what law should become in the future than what it is now: social theory and social insight, therefore, are to play their role as part of "internal" or "immanent" critique. But if allegiance is to an ideal of law not to law as it is now, how far can a process of critique and of broadening law's understanding also provide the means for legal closure?

Perhaps law is itself only one part of a larger project of social change. On whose terms? The final dilemma is that between the responsibilities of expertise, and the duty, rather, to give "voice" to the experiences and wishes of social participants, especially those whose voices law ignores. This issue was brought to the fore by Susan Silbey's review of Cotterrell's textbook,[48] but is an increasingly favoured methodological trend within the United States "law and society" and

---

[40] P. Bourdieu, *The Logic Of Practice* (1990).

[41] S. Fuchs and S. Ward, "What is Deconstruction and where and when does it take place? Making Facts in Science, Building Cases in Law" (1994) 59 *Am. Sociological Rev.* 481.

[42] A. Sarat and T.R. Kearns, *Law's Violence* (1992).

[43] Monahan and Walker (*op. cit.*, n. 19) would have judges instruct juries as to established social scientific facts in the same way as they now instruct them with respect to binding principles of law.

[44] Cotterrell, *op. cit.*, n. 15, at p. 310 argues that we should "not be constrained even by visions of truth".

[45] Nelken, *op. cit.* (1986), n. 40.

[46] R. M. Unger, *What Should Legal Analysis Become?* (1996).

[47] D. E. Litowitz, *Postmodern Philosophy and Law* (1997).

[48] Silbey, *op. cit.*, n. 11.

critical legal scholars' movements. Cotterrell (but not only Cotterrell) has difficulty in identifying the specific "historical subject" whose interests could provide him with his standpoint and yardstick for change; he offers instead a role for the expert as mediator of knowledge claims. On the one hand. Cotterrell invites us to respect "local, partial perspectives" rather than replace them. The broader perspective which seeks to interpret these knowledge must itself be "grounded in, enriched and validated by them".[49] On the other hand, he recognizes that "social knowledge" about law is shaped by ideology but argues that sociology of law can help unmake ideology by revealing law's fragilities and strengths.[50] The danger, of course, is that if "particular narratives which cannot be generalized"[51] are first obliged to satisfy the protocols of sociological understanding, we risk (as much as law) betraying the lived experience of individuals who have declining faith in experts and yet cannot manage without them.[52]

Both sociology and law risk becoming technocratic and imposing their truth on social actors; each also claims to have the potential to resist these trends. Is law or sociology better equipped to be the bulwark against the further spread of technocratic means-end rationality? Is law or sociology more suited to protecting the local and the pluralist? Which is more in touch with the common sense of social actors? In the end, I may only be offering a further note of caution concerning the dangers which Cotterrell warns about when discussing the blinkers of academic sociology. Sociology of law is obliged to pay allegiance (if we must use this language) to both law *and* sociology. Law's style as a social practice, even perhaps its social function, is to blur the dilemmas it faces. But sociology's insights may also obscure even as they reveal. Sociology of law has as its primary task to expose law's dilemmas, but also—as far as it can—to recognize its own.[pp. 421–426]

## DAVID M. TRUBEK
### Back to the Future: The Short Happy Life of the Law and Society Movement
(1990)[53]

*Critiques of the Original Law and Society Understanding*

The original law and society understanding was flawed at its inception, for it rested on contradictory premises about the nature of both law and social science. These contradictions were not fully apparent at the time, but have become clearer in recent years. As a result, some scholars in the law and society tradition have begun to distance themselves from the original understanding and to construct elements of an alternative vision of the socio-legal enterprise. Many still hold on to the original faith, but its heyday has passed.

### A. Society as a System

The law and society movement is largely responsible for bringing the idea of "society as a system" into modern American legal thought. The notion that society must be seen as an interdependent set of elements, with law as one of these elements, represented a major advance in legal thought. The original understanding of systematicity, though, has been criticized and revised.

This understanding was formed at a time when the social sciences in America

---

[49] Cotterrell, *op. cit.*, n. 15, at pp. 310.
[50] id., pp. 311–12.
[51] Cotterrell, *op. cit.*, n. 97, p. 191.
[52] Z. Bauman, *Legislators and Interpreters* (1987).
[53] [See (1990) 18 *Florida State University Law Review* 1]

were under the influence of structural-functionalism.[54] This school's view of the social system contained two key ideas that have been questioned: social integration and functional necessity. For the structural-functionalists, society is a tightly integrated system of inter-related elements or structures. These structures exist because they perform functions: One can explain various structures, including those of ideas, by discovering their function. To this extent, functional analysis is a useful and unavoidable form of social thought.

But under the sway of objectivist notions, scholars suggested that observed functions may also be objectively necessary. The 1950's and 1960's necessitarian strain in systems thinking allowed this body of thought to be easily transformed from a set of analytic statements into justifications for existing institutional arrangements in American society.

Critics, however, have brought both pillars of the analytic structure into question. Scholars have challenged this notion of a tight societal integration, asserting that various aspects of society are tied together in a looser and more tenuous way. The critics have further questioned the functional necessity of existing structures. They have replaced functional analysis with geneological investigations which show that social structures and legal institutions are shaped by purpose and interest, not by the invisible hand of objective necessity.[55] These investigations do not give up on the effort to situate legal doctrines, ideas, and institutions within a broader framework of social explanation. Nor do they abandon functionalism completely. Rather, they relax necessitarian assumptions and thus allow analysts to question the objective necessity of particular arrangements which have developed in any given society.[56]

A good example of legal post-functionalist systems thinking can be seen in recent feminist critiques of law. These analyses use structural explanations of male domination as both analytical and critical tools. Feminists have highlighted ways in which bodies of legal doctrine and systems of legal thought constitute and maintain patriarchal relationships where women are subordinated to (and defined by) men. This account includes a notion of structure (or system): patriarchy or male domination is conceived of as a patterned structure made up of inter-related elements. This idea of "structure" or system is loosened and relativized, especially in the work of recent, explicitly post-structuralist feminist critics. Post-structuralist feminists recognize structure while denying that it reflects objective necessity or manifests normative validity.[57] ...

## B. *Objectivism: The Idea of a Positive Social Science*

The original understanding of systematicity was connected to an objectivist epistemology. Society was perceived as an object, like the solar system, with invariant relationships and determinate regularities. In this context, social science could be imagined as a neutral technique to grasp the regularities that govern the operations of this object. Thus, the original law and society understanding

---

[54] See, generally, *Toward a General Theory Of Action* (T. Parsons & E. Shils eds. 1951); A. Gouldner, *The Coming Crisis Of Western Sociology* (1970) (containing an overview of Talcott Parsons's ideology); C. Mullins, *Theories and Theory Group In Contemporary American Sociology* 66–67 (1973) (stating that structural functionalism was the majority view in sociology from 1951–68).

[55] Gordon, *Critical Legal Histories*, 36 Stan. L. Rev. 57, 70–71 (1984).

[56] Roberto Unger has written a sweeping and comprehensive critique of objectivist/necessitarian modes of social analysis. *See* R. Unger, *Social Theory: Its Situation and Its Tasks* (1987).

[57] See, *e.g.* C. MacKinnon, *Toward a Feminist Theory of The State* (1989); Scales, *The Emergence of Feminist Jurisprudence: An Essay* (1986) 95 Yale L. J. 1373 and *post*, 1300; West, *Jurisprudence and Gender* (1988) 55 U. Chi. L. Rev. 1 [and see *post*, 1320.]

employed a concept of science and scientific method that was modeled on prevailing views of how natural science worked.

It is no surprise that law and society initially accepted a positivist notion of social science. This view of social knowledge was widespread in the social sciences in the 1950's and 1960's. Moreover, it was attractive to the legal academic culture. Post-Realist legal thought can be seen as a series of evasions, efforts to deny the normative crisis generated by Realism's deconstructive onslaughts. As Joseph Singer has pointed out, most post-Realist scholars sought some substitute for the normative authority of the lost doctrinal tradition.[58] Where legal process theorists offered neutral procedures as the answer, law and society promised objective knowledge produced by a positive science of society.

Positive science, like procedure, answers the question of normative thought by evading it. It society were a system obeying objective laws, and if positive science could identify those laws and unearth the social policies that were consistent with them, then policy formation would once again be grounded on a neutral and objective basis. While the idea of a positive science of society seems to us one of the most problematic features of the original understanding, it may have seemed particularly attractive to the lawyers of the Imperial epoch.

In recent years, many critics have questioned the positivist account of objectivity in social knowledge.[59] Some have sought to develop an alternative view, which I shall call "discursivity."[60] This view of the social disciplines starts with the recognition that social knowledge does not mirror an objective reality that is somehow "out there", but is instead part of the process through which social relations are formed and reformed. The understanding of social science as a discursive practice has begun to influence the social disciplines and to enter into the thinking of some law and society scholars.

To embrace discursivity is to recognize that social life is a network of relations invested with differentials of power. These relationships are constituted linguistically (or "discursively"): the very concepts we use to describe and explain society contribute to the constitution of social relations. As a result, we cannot separate our studies and understandings of social life from social life itself: as social "scientists", we cannot detach ourselves and our knowledges from society in the way astronomers separate themselves from the solar system. It follows that when we construct an account of society, we do not simply mirror social relations, but rather contribute either to their reproduction or transformation.

The recognition of discursivity changes our whole understanding of the relationship between law and the social disciplines. If social knowledge is discursive, it cannot produce unproblematic maps of social relations or uncontested, factually-based answers to questions of social policy. This recognition means that whatever social science *can* do for law, it *cannot* offer ... objectivist grounding for legal policy. ... If legal culture accepts the critique of objectivism and the concept of discursive social knowledge, the original understanding will be drawn into question, and the nature and purpose of the alliance between law and the social disciplines will have to be reexamined.

### C. Disengagement from Law and Politics

The third feature of the original understanding was the idea that law and society as a scholarly project should be disengaged from both legal doctrine and politics. At least *some* of the founders saw a need to make law and society an autonomous

---

[58] Singer (1988) 76 Calif. L. Rev. 465, 518–528.

[59] For a general discussion of objectivism, see R. Unger. *See also* Trubek & Esser (1989) 14 Law and Soc. Inquiry 3. pp. 12–13.

[60] I take the term "discursivity" from E. Laclau & C. Mouffe, *Hegemony and Socialist Strategy* 2–5 (1985). For a discussion of discursivity in law and society research, see (1988) 51 Law and Cont. Problems.

enterprise, disengaged from both the traditional pursuit of legal knowledge and direct programmatic involvement. This double disengagement was needed to carry out the original law and society research program: the application of the methods of positive science to the study of both society and law as systems.

Disengagement from law was also needed because studying "law" at the time meant the examination of doctrine and the interpretation of rules and texts. Law and society sought to constitute a different kinds of "law" as the object of study— law as system and behavior would join law as doctrine and idea as legitimate objects for study. To accomplish this task, the movement had to disengage from academic law as then practiced. Disengagement from politics, at least provisionally, was also needed. Having adopted an objectivist concept of social knowledge, law and society needed to present itself as independent from and neutral towards any particular group interest or social vision. It sought knowledge of social laws and regularities which—it was thought—were independent of values and programs.

For those who accept discursivity, however, disengagement is both undesirable and ultimately impossible. If social knowledge constitutes rather than mirrors social relations, its producers have a responsibility for the social impact of the knowledges they construct. Moreover, in this view, social knowledge is inherently programmatic: if we are to understand society, we must imagine how it might be transformed. Thus, it makes no sense to speak of the production of knowledge independent of projects that either reproduce or transform social life.

There are additional reasons to question disengagement today. The original rationale for it was both practical and epistemological. As we come to question its epistemological foundations, so should we interrogate its practical bases. These were founded in a perceived need to insulate a fledgling enterprise from the older doctrinal tradition in the law. Perhaps such protectionism was needed in the days when law and society was an infant industry. But much has changed since 1964. The law and society movement has taken hold. And legal academic culture has changed radically: the doctrinal tradition has crumbled, and eclectic policy science has become the norm, not the exception. We are all legal realists today.[61]

### D. Law as a Univocal Source of Normative Guidance

...Many law and society scholars viewed law as an unproblematic source of normative inspiration. Remember that a staple product of the early law and society movement was the gap study, a research project that took some understanding of the law as a normative starting point and then measured its impact of "penetration."[62]

This tendency to accept the law as a clear source of legitimate authority can be seen with stark clarity in the work of some "law and development" scholars. The law and development movement was a sort of export branch of Imperial legal culture. In the 1960's, American legal academics, encouraged by massive grants from foundations and government agencies, turned to the study of the role of law in Third World "development". Some law and society scholars participated in the law and development effort.

The law and development movement took the value of modern law to be self evident. "Modern law" usually meant the codes or new statutory enactments which third would governments had imported from other, presumably more advanced, nations. Usually, these codes or statutes set forth norms that had little relation to everyday life in the countries of Africa, Asia, and Latin America. Law

---

[61] See Tushnet, *Post-Realist Legal Scholarship (1980)* Wis. L. Rev. 1383.
[62] Sarat, *Legal Effectiveness and Social Studies of Law: On the Unfortunate Persistence of a Research Tradition* (1985) 9 Legal Stud. F. 23, 24–30. See also Friedman, *Legal Culture and Social Development* (1969) 4 Law & Soc'y Rev. 29, 43.

and development scholars assumed that adoption and implementation of these (often imported) modern laws marked development or progress. And they treated as a "problem" the fact that social relations in Third World countries did not conform to these newly enacted norms. This equation of legal standards with progress, and the definition of non-compliance as a problem, led these scholars to spend a considerable amount of time thinking about how we could develop a way to measure—and thus increase—the "penetration" of so-called modern law.

Compressed in that single word are a whole set of assumptions and attitudes that have come under attack. Critics have challenged the following assumptions: that any body of law contains a single set of principles or rules whose impact can be unproblematically measured; that law emanates from some central source and then is implanted in society; that modern law (whatever that is) is normatively desirable or historically inevitable; and, finally, that the social scientific task of measuring "penetration" is a progressive task. It does not require much sophisticated feminist analysis to see how the use of the term "penetration" crystallized the hegemonizing, dominating, and patriarchal nature of imperial legal culture is the 1960's.

One of the most significant developments in American legal culture has been the questioning of the whole idea that law contains a univocal set of normative standards, whether of an explicit statutory or vaguer higher law nature, which can serve as an unproblematic guideline for social criticism and transformation. ... The law and society movement, like all Post-Realist movements in legal thought, was an effort to evade the corrosive effect of Legal-Realism's demolition of ideas of univocality and higher law. But this recognition was suppressed, and to some degree evaded, when the original law and society understanding was constructed in the 1960's.

In recent years, substantial bodies of scholarship, including critical legal studies, feminist critiques of law, and critical race theory, have brought to light the complex and contradictory nature of legal doctrine, thus undermining the idea of univocality.[63] These studies show that legal doctrine contains alternative normative strands which suggest very different social visions. [...]

### E. *The Progressive Nature of Law and Society Knowledge*

The architects of the law and society movement wanted to create a field or discipline that was disengaged from politics. Yet they were confident that this project would contribute to the progressive political agenda that they ... favored. Of all the contradictions of the original law and society understanding, this idea that liberal values would be automatically fostered by a neutral science of law in society seems to be the most perplexing. Yet it was a central, albeit unarticulated, premise of a significant portion of the work produced in the formative period of the law and society movement.

The Imperial Age was dominated by three major reform impulses that took hold within the American establishment: (1) the rights explosion led by the Warren Court; (2) the civil rights efforts of the Kennedy and Johnson Administrations; and (3) the War on Poverty and other Great Society programs designed to increase economic opportunity. A review of the early volumes of the *Law and*

---

[63] For an excellent introduction to this form of analysis, see Gordon, *Unfreezing Legal Reality: Critical Approaches to Law* (1987) 15 Fla. St U.L. Rev. 195. See also R. Unger, *The Critical Legal Studies Movement* (1986); Crenshaw, *Race, Reform, and Retrenchment: Transformation and Legitimation in Antidiscrimination Law* (1988) 101 Harv. L. Rev. 1331. Kennedy, *Form and Substance in Private Law Adjudication* (1976), 89 Harv. L. Rev. 1685. This mode of analysis was not unknown to the founders of law and society. *See* Macaulay, *Private Legislation and the Duty to Read—Business Run by IBM Machine, The Law of Contracts and Credit Cards* (1966) 19 Vand. L. Rev. 1051, 1056–69.

*Society Review* confirms the extent to which the research conducted and the results reported were thought to advance the liberal legal agenda of the day. [...]

Needless to say, events in law and politics have overtaken this naive equation of neutral, objective science with progressive politics. In the legal academy a competing academic project—law and economics—has arisen. This movement, presented as an objective social science, rests on a more conservative political agenda. Law and economics' efforts have proven more successful in legal culture than the more hesitant efforts of law and society scholars to merge science and progressive politics. In the world of national politics, the liberal coalition has collapsed and liberal self-confidence has been sapped. We have learned that many of the bold pronouncements and commitments of the 1960's were largely symbolic. Many were never implemented, despite the countless gap studies. Law and society scholars began to learn that it takes more than a study to close the gap between promise and fulfilment in American life.

### Post-Imperial Legal Culture

We now live in a Post-Imperial Age. The main difference between the legal culture of our day and the epoch in which the law and society idea took shape and the "original understanding" was formed is not the disappearance of all the ideas that dominated legal culture in the Imperial Era, but the fact that they are no longer hegemonic.

...As the power of Imperial legal culture has waned, new ways of thinking about law have become possible. As a result, we can speak of an emerging "countervision". This countervision, though, has not led to a new "understanding", let alone generated a new "paradigm". It is still more the rejection of prevailing ideas from the Imperial Age than an alternative conceptualization of law, society, and scholarship. Nonetheless, it could be a starting point.

### A. The Emergent Countervision

Where the Imperial Jurists thought law could be easily and consciously deployed as the instrument of a unified and transformative will, some today see law as fragile, contradictory, fragmentary, and dispersed. Where Imperial legal culture was objectivist, positing that scholarship could point toward a "correct" answer to legal questions, the countervision accepts discursivity and recognizes that scholarship is an arena of struggle in which various visions compete. Where Imperial lawyers saw clear distinctions between law and society, knowledge and politics, an authoritative normative tradition and (sometimes) recalcitrant social structures, those who embrace the countervision blur these distinctions, recognize contradiction, and seek to cope with a complex and contradictory situation.

### 1. Law as Fragile

As the result of over two decades of gap studies, impact studies, and implementation research, we have come to doubt the independent power of law to reshape social arrangements. The law and society movement has helped us see the fragility of law's grasp of social life. Laws are rarely clear cut, so that while "law" may be thought of as the command of the sovereign, it is often damn hard to figure out just what the sovereign wants! More importantly, the resistances to messages encoded in law are often incredibly powerful. Even when new laws seem relatively clear, those who work with these laws on a day-to-day basis find the message diluted, if not reversed, by interpretative struggles, outright denial, and avoidance. It is this sense of fragility that gives the Post-Imperial Jurist her sense of marginality.

## 2. A Contradictory, Multi-vocal, Normative Tradition

It turns out that the sovereign more often than not speaks with a forked tongue. While the Critical Legal Studies movement has done more than anyone to document and explain the normative contradictions embedded in most complex bodies of legal doctrine, many Post-Imperial lawyers understand—at some level—that there are always competing precedents, alternative interpretations, and radically different social visions in our legal tradition. At least since Duncan Kennedy demonstrated how private law doctrine oscillates between rules and standards, formality and informality, and individualist and altruist visions of law and society, we have been forced to recognize the complex and contradictory nature of American law.[64]

The reasons given for this fact, and the ideas people have about what to do with or about it, are varied. Some, longing for an imagined past in which law was univocal, might seek newer and better interpretive methods which would fix legal meaning once and for all. But others revel in the openness and play which contradiction permits. For those of this persuasion, the fluidity of law is not a problem to be solved, but an opportunity to be seized. Thus, for example, Roberto Unger and others in the Critical Legal Studies tradition find in this situation opportunities for radical scholarship and practice. They call for "deviationist" doctrinal work in which alternative readings of the legal tradition are to be produced in an effort to further alternative moral visions and political projects.[65]

## 3. Legal Culture as Fragmentary

The more the post-modernist ideas advance within legal culture, the more we begin to see law not as a set of determinate commands, or even as contradictory-yet-structured sets of rules, principles, and visions, but rather as a series of fragments which are deployed through a wide range of localized processes or practices. It is no accident that legal culture is beginning to pay attention to what anthropologists call "practice theory", a body of thought that sees culture as bits and pieces of myth, metaphor, and idea which are deployed in moments of practice.[66] This anthropological vision fits very well with the contemporary jurists' understanding of the phenomenology of legal decision-making.[67]

## 4. Law and Legal Ideology Dispersed in Society

Imperial Jurists saw law as powerful, univocal, and ultimately coherent. At the same time, they imagined law as a unified system made up of a hierarchy of constitutional norms, statutory rules, judicial interpretations, and common law principles. The law, in short, was the law. Not only has Post-Imperial legal culture questioned law's power, univocality, and coherence, it also has come to see law as dispersed throughout social life.[68] We see this view in the notion of law as ideology, now a major subject for investigation by law and society scholars. When we conceive of law as ideology, we understand that law may affect social life not by the imposition of a transformative Will, but by reinforcing widely-held notions

---

[64] See Kennedy (1976) 89 Harv. L. R. 1685. [And see *post*, 1210–1212].

[65] R. Unger, *The Critical Legal Studies Movement* (1986).

[66] For an application practice theory to legal studies, see Coombe, 14 Law and Social Inquiry, 69, at 111–21.

[67] See Kennedy, *Freedom and Constraint in Adjudication: A Critical Phenomenology*, 36 J. Legal Educ. 518 (1986).

[68] I do not simply refer to ideas like Eugen Ehrlich's famous "living law", the idea of a local and customary law more powerful than statutes and codes. E. Ehrlich, *Fundamental Principles of the Sociology of Law* (1936). These ideas have been with us for a long time, although the law and society movement did a lot to bring Ehrlich's insights into mainstream American legal culture. [*See also ante*, 894.]

of what is possible or imaginable. Law as ideology is not necessarily just on the books or in "action"; it is everywhere in social life where action is imagined or not imagined, taken or not taken.

The view of law as "dispersed" reframes the question of the power of law. If the law reflects and reinforces ideologies that emanate from many sources, then it may not be a powerful tool to change society—as the Imperial Jurists imagined—but may rather have a powerful grip *on* society.

The question of whether law is a straitjacket, or just another complex and contradictory arena for struggle, depends on how we see power and ideology. While from some perspectives the ideological view of law makes it seem like a solid bulwark for the *status quo*, the law seems open and manipulable from others. This latter view is the message of "practice theory". If law, albeit ideological, is neither unified nor structured, and if our legal culture is a series of fragments whose significance is determined through multiple, often low level, and frequently local practices of interpretation and decision, then attention naturally turns to the many sites and moments of practice, and the opportunities for transformative action they provide.

## 5. Law and Legal Scholarship as Arenas of Struggle

The idea that both law and legal scholarship are "arenas of struggle" appears in the literatures of Post-Imperial legal culture and is a central feature of the emerging countervision. Even if they have abandoned the Imperial epoch's vision of law as a univocal source of progressive values and a privileged instrument for social change, those who embrace this vision have not given up on law as a site for transformative action. These anti-Imperial Scholars still believe that law makes a difference and that struggles in and about the law are worthwhile. But they have no illusions that the law contains immanent principles of freedom and equality which can and will be worked pure, thus guaranteeing emancipation. On the contrary, they expect and often find in the law strands of the same racism, sexism, and elitism that they are struggling against in social life.[69] Yet at the same time, many do not see in the law a rigid structure of oppression, hierarchy, and domination. Because the law is fragile, contradictory, fragmented, and dispersed, it guarantees nothing. But, by the same token, nothing is impossible. Victories in law do not necessarily lead to changes elsewhere, but they are victories all the same.

## 6. Living in the Contradiction

Those who see law as fragile, contradictory, fragmentary, and dispersed have blurred the clean lines between law and society that marked Imperial legal culture and influenced the original understanding. Further, they have obscured the distinction between the construction of social knowledge and the transformation of society. Some may see these people as confused and muddle-headed, but I do not. The emerging countervision is a way of living with, and taking advantage of, a series of contradictions that exist in our culture. We live in a society that believes in law and whose legal tradition contains many progressive values. We live in a society that believes in the power of knowledge and the authority of scholarship. At the same time, ours is a society in which hierarchies of class, race, and gender persist and influence the operations of the law and the production of scholarship. For those scholars who embrace progressive values and grasp the contradictions in our society, there is room for maneuver. Legal doctrine can be deployed for

---

[69] D. Bell, *And We Are Not Saved: The Elusive Quest For Racial Justice* (1987); C. MacKinnon, *Feminism Unmodified* (1987); Austin, *Sapphire Bound!* (1989) Wis. L. Rev. 539 (minority feminist scholarship).

normative argument, legal studies can foster progressive visions, legal victories can advance worthy causes. But everything is partial, tentative, and limited. Imperial Jurists might denounce this stance as hesitant and confused, but then look what a mess they have left us!                                    [pp. 31–46]

## SUSAN S. SILBEY AND AUSTIN SARAT
### Critical Traditions in Law and Society Research
### (1987)[70]

At first glance, the conjunction of the words "critical" and "traditions" in the title of this paper seems something of a paradox: Whereas "traditions" signifies connection, stability over time, regularized practice, and continuity, "critical" suggest interpretation and challenge, distance and change. The paradox dissipates, however, in the recognition that criticism occurs within a context provided by tradition and that critique is at least partially constituted by that which it seeks to resist, reform, or revise. Critique is not fully or completely opposed to tradition; instead it suggests that while there is participation in a shared context, it is participation at a distance.

Law and society has always imagined itself to be a critical enterprise, outside of the mainstream of legal discourse, participating at a remove while offering an alternative epistemology and sociology of law.[71] Its focus has been de-centering, concerned not with what the law *is* but with what the law *does*.[72]

Our claim is broad but simple: Legal institutions cannot be understood without seeing the entire social environment. At the same time that we have been insisting on bringing sociology to law, we have done less well attending to the forces that frame our descriptions of legal institutions and their environments. We have not done very well at promoting a sociology of the sociology of law. It is to this enterprise that we will turn our attention....

### *Epistemological Foundations*

Much contemporary social theory argues forcefully, and persuasively, we think for the indeterminism of the social world.[73] The concepts, texts, and situations we both live with and observe do not exist outside the very systems of thought we construct. This, in some very simple sense, challenges our scientific claims and our ability to maintain and advance a rigorous, disciplined knowledge producing enterprise. Or does it? We worry that too much recent social theory and criticism, theory and criticism to which we are quite sympathetic, goes too far in leading, against its better instincts, to a dangerous reductionism.

But first let us reemphasize our sympathy for the indeterminist position. This position suggests that[74]

> "each move to fix meaning fails because no essential or necessary meaning adheres to either the expressions [we use] or the things they signify.... The search for such meaning leads back to contingent social practices rather than to objective 'reality'. These social practices embody contingent choices concerning how to organize the thick texture of the world.... What gets called 'knowledge' is the ... effect of social power institutionalized in [socially constructed] ... representational conventions"

---

[70] [From *Law & Society Review*, volume 21, Number 1]
[71] See Friedman (1986) 38 Stanford L. Rev. 763
[72] See Trubek (1984) 36 Stanford L. Rev. 575
[73] See Foucault, *The Archaeology of Knowledge* (1972); Derrida, *Writing and Difference* (1978), p. 278; Unger, *Knowledge and Politics* (1975).
[74] *Per* G. Peller, 73 Calif. L. Rev 1151, 1168–70.

In *Philosophy and the Mirror of Nature*, Richard Rorty writes in a similar vein, describing recent philosophical developments from the point of view of what he calls an anti-Cartesian and post-Kantian revolution. Put simply, he argues that we must abandon the notion of knowledge as an accurate representation of some externally existing reality. He suggests that we cease imagining constraints on what can count as knowledge, since justification is "a social phenomenon, rather than a transaction between 'the knowing subject' and 'reality'[75]" Rorty reminds us that "investigations of the foundations of knowledge or morality or language or society may be simply apologetics, attempts to externalize a ... contemporary language-game, social practice, or self-image".[76] The search for rationality and objectivity, he claims, is a self-deceptive effort to universalize the discourse of particular cultures. Thus Rorty tries to edify rather than systematize to help "readers, or society as a whole, break free of outworn vocabularies and attitudes, rather than ... provide 'grounding' for the intuitions and customs of the present".[77]

Of course, much of this argument is familiar. Because the world is socially constructed does not mean that the world is not consequential. While it may be impossible to separate ourselves from our subjects (hence the earlier suggestion of a distance not a separation), it is equally impossible to demonstrate or know fully that from which we are separate. But in our rush to maintain a critical edge by challenging accepted paradigms and in our inability to separate the world from consciousness, we do not want to argue that there is no world separate from consciousness. This is an old problem.

From Zeno to Hume, skeptics have had to come to terms with a world whose consequences they encounter but whose existence they cannot demonstrate. One is reminded of a story in which Boswell was bemoaning his inability to refute Berkeley's ingenious sophistry and the apparent necessity for axiomatic, non-demonstrable first principles. Johnson responded by kicking a stone so hard that he himself bounced off it, saying, as he did, "I refute it thus."

Once created, the social world becomes something like that stone: wholly out there, not easily moved, and something we bounce off all the time. Laws may be human creations and thus apparently malleable, contradictory, and indeterminant, subject to interpretation and reformation. But to the defendant who goes to jail, the law is certainly less malleable and less subject to reinterpretation and more like something one bounces against. We butt up against the law all the time. Law creates the difference between marrying and just living together, not a very large difference, some might say, until you try to walk away. Because of court decisions black people lose their jobs and white persons are put in their place, and people are executed instead of spending their lives in prison.

Just as critics may give in to an unfortunate temptation to equate empirical science with positivism and determinism and then to condemn all empirical science in order to eschew any association with positivism and determinism, defenders of the faith in science may lose more than they realize if they dismiss critics like Rorty as people who deny that there is a "there" out there, as naive philosophical radicals, or as nihilists. The critics are none of these.

Surely the import of contemporary theory is not that there is no "there" out there but rather that our ability to know what is there is limited. If there are no determinative ways to know the world separate from our socially created representational systems, then what matters most is what counts as knowledge, what styles of work are welcomed and supported, what styles are rejected, and what gloss must be put on our work to satisfy those upon whose material largesse we are most dependent. It matters whether what counts as knowledge is created in

---

[75] *Philosophy and The Mirror of Nature* (1979) p. 9.
[76] *ibid.* pp. 9–10
[77] *ibid.* p. 12.

professional discourse or in supermarkets and whether it is created by men or by women.

Critical theorists especially are telling us that not only are meaning and knowledge a product of social power, but that this is a process that is not entirely knowable. There are great silences and omissions; many voices are unheard, not well understood, and even subjugated. Indeed, a strong claim is made for indeterminacy because, it is argued, the social world may be uncontrolled, not simply uncontrollable. Even if we succeed in opening our vision to recognize and include subjugated knowledge, this should not then blind us to the inevitability of a hard-fought struggle between dominant and dominated discourses.

We have been describing, somewhat elliptically, three basic positions. The first says that there is a physical and social world ordered by rules and norms that are knowable and independent of human intervention. This is the science in social science. The second builds upon the first but notices the interaction of observer and the world; it says that the world out there is known as well as constructed through collective human action. Finally there is third, postmodern or post-structural position that celebrates the infinite openness attached to a radically constructivist vision. It suggests the insufficiency of locating, and possibly predicting, action or knowledge based upon groups, classes, genders, or institutions because the categories and locations are themselves problematic. Indeed, the poststructural innovation deconstructs the last universal institution—language—and highlights the nonreferential, contradictory, and indeterminant character of language itself.

### The Emergence of Law and Society

This brief comment on some modern critical thought brings us to an unsettling conclusion or, better, to an unsettling beginning. To maintain a critical distance from our present project, we would be compelled to demonstrate regularly the indeterminacy of our analysis of indeterminacy. Given this conclusion, is it nonetheless possible to extract some instruction about how to proceed? We think so. We hear two relatively clear messages. First, we are asked to notice the location and historicity of the communities within which social construction takes place,[78] for example, to notice the institutional locations of law and society research; second, we are urged to guard against turning these bounded observations of law into universals. This approach urges attention to the specific situations, institutions, and struggles out of which the field of law and society emerged. Law and society research has roots far deeper and older than the American realists, origins that lie within the modern conception of law itself.

The distinction between law and society derives from European political struggles in which the distinction between civil society and the state was postulated and then used to keep the state in its place.[79] For medieval Europeans the merger of law and society was an excuse for hierarchical oppression, so they tried to separate the two. For Americans, the rule of law is linked to these notions of the separation of law from state and society. Because it suggests rationalized ordering, law is viewed as something at once state produced but yet able to control the state.[80] While in the European context law carries the burden of being part of a hierarchy, in the American context the sense of hierarchy and oppression is absent. Instead there is a persistent notion of external and neutral regulation, and as a result we carry the burden of demonstrating that law and hierarchy have a relationship.

The immediate forebearers of the law and society movement, the legal realists,

---

[78]  M. Foucault *Power / Knowledge* (1980).
[79]  See the Writings of John Locke [discussed *ante*, 107].
[80]  See F. Hayek, *The Constitution of Liberty* (1960)

challenged contemporary social and political elites, yet they never challenged the predominant faith in law. Instead they sought to mobilize legal authority for particular political projects, following quite consistently the liberal tradition they inherited. Rather than waning, confidence in law was high.[81] Thus as an heir of the realists, the law and society movement, while proclaiming itself the carrier of a new vision, evolved within a tradition that was largely hopeful about law and the possibilities for social change and reform through law.[82]

In some ways the major emphasis and innovation of the law and society movement was not so much an interest in the social forces that produced law, although certainly there was some of this, but rather an interest in how law operated upon social phenomena. With a self-consciously empirical commitment, itself a predictable move within the mainstream intellectual currents of the late nineteenth and early twentieth centuries, scholars explored the consequences and implementation of law and found, much to their surprise, the ineffectiveness of law—the gap between the law on the books and the law in action.[83]

The law and society field proclaimed itself a counter-hegemony; it stood, we were told, at the margins. But, some might ask, at the margins of what? Surely we were not marginal in efforts to combine scientific method and administration that became so central a part of political science and sociology in the 1960s and 1970s and has become today so important a part of economics. If we were marginal, it was only within law schools. The claim to a position outside mainstream legal thought is, however, a very narrow and particular claim; law and society is neither intellectually marginal nor culturally deviant. While we thought we were producing a new understanding of law, the bite was never all that critical because we never tried to undo liberal claims about the relationship between law and society. If there was a distinction between law and society and mainstream legal scholarship, it was not in the observation that law was not autonomous but in the degree of emphasis each placed upon different sides of the divide. If the law schools overestimated the determinacy of law, the law and society movement underestimated its consequences.[84]

Even today this difference persists between what might be the emerging new orthodoxy of critical legal studies and law and society research. For advocates of critical legal studies, law is a central cultural and social institution; their paradigm suggests too strong an influence of law on social behavior and too large a role for law in the construction of the social world. In contrast the law and society tradition often provides too small a role for law in constituting social life. By looking at hard cases in the administration of law, we were drawn all too frequently to instances when law failed. Law in its daily life was basically not analyzed. We looked at the ways in which consumer protection laws were enforced,[85] but we did not look at the ways in which they buying and selling of goods took account of and accounted for its legal regulation.[86] We looked at violations of law but not at instances of law-abidingness.[87]

Earlier we said that we butt up against the law all the time. We misspoke. We do not trip on the law. In the ways in which we have been studying law, we hardly ever encounter it; however, others trip over it all the time. The law has a very different presence in our lives and the lives of the less privileged. The work of the Law and Society Association has contributed to demonstrating and explicating this inequality. But in the formulation of our subject, we nevertheless discuss it as

---

[81] *Op. cit.* n. 72.

[82] See A. Sarat (1985) 9 Legal Studies Forum 23

[83] [As with Pound, *ante*, 835 and Llewellyn, *post*, 1013.]

[84] See R. Abel (1973) 26 Stanford Law Rev. 175

[85] See S. Silbey (1981) 15 Law and Soc. Rev. 849; Silbey and Brittner (1982) 4 Law and Policy Q. 399.

[86] Silbey (1984) Am. Bar Foundation Research J. 429

[87] [But see now T. Tyler, *Why People Obey the Law* (1990).]

if it were a universal: "The law". We know that the law does not work for us in the same ways it does for people in Jamaica Plain or the Hopi Indians. Why, therefore, do we talk about "the law". Because we have been busy problematizing the relationship between law and society, we neglected to make problematic the idea of law itself. We looked for the connections between law and society as if the two were separate and singular. They are not. "The law" is a fiction, but laws are real. Similarly, "society" is a fiction. We invent these fictions. We cannot escape them. As scholars and critics we must work hard to distance ourselves from them.

Our tradition invests law and society with the very reifying rigidity that we imagine ourselves to be overturning. Law and society scholarship has not been simply concerned with the autonomy of law or the lack thereof; it advances a discourse of universality, elides its own sources, denies its own history and location, and speaks as if there were no perspectives.

## Conclusion

We end, as we began, with a paradoxical statement: Criticism arises from both a greater commitment to and a greater distance from one's tradition. To be critical bespeaks a desire to be faithful to a tradition by refusing to accept its imperfections. This requires an unwillingness to rest content with primary orienting norms and a willingness to invert what is central so that the marginal, invisible, or unheard becomes a voice and a focus. However, fidelity also requires more than unmasking and debunking; it demands a willingness to construct anew.

It might sound like we are praising critical legal studies,[88] and, to a degree, we are. These critics remind us of our own critical impulses. We need, however, to keep these impulses alive by directing our energies to law as it is found not just in legal doctrine or in the routine but difficult problems of legal implementation. We need likewise to resist the temptation to give in to depression and sadness. Because our work has undermined a technocratic or reformist confidence in law, we are liberated to see our subject with fewer illusions and greater clarity. We must be both critical and empirical.

For those of us in the law and society tradition, this means that we pay special attention to ways of proceeding. From the science in law and social science, we get an insistence of generalization and understanding in its largest exploratory sense. A critic's inversion of this leads to research that is intensive rather than extensive and that sees things in their singularity rather than assimilating them to general categories. Such an inversion emphasizes particularity and specificity, something that might be called the "authenticity of dailiness". The turn to the particular and the idiosyncratic celebrates varying forms of law. It means an awareness that the rule of law is itself a particular kind of fiction. With this awareness, it becomes possible to understand the remarkable growth and power of the ethnography of American law.[89] It is indeed truly radical in a legal order that proclaims its fidelity to the rule of law that scholars go to the periphery—to small towns, to rural places, to working class neighborhoods—to look at the way people in these places come to terms with and often resist the penetration of official legal norms as they construct their own local universe of legal values and behavior. This is only possible is a post-Vietnam, post-Watergate, post-law and society America, where our highest legal aspirations have been sullied and where there is indeed a clear picture of the inefficacy of many attempts at central legal control. We need to stop trying quite so hard to come to terms with the ineffectiveness and to start studying what legal life is like in the vast interstices of law.

Finally, the law and society tradition, in its effort to understand the

---

[88]  [On which see *post*, Chap. 14.]

[89]  See C. Greenhouse (1982) 17 Man 58; D. Engel (1983) Amer Bar Foundation Research J 803; S. Merry (1979) 12 Law and Soc. Rev. 891

contribution of legal institutions to social process, focuses primarily upon the law. To invert this aspect, attention needs to be paid to social processes themselves, no matter what their geographical location. The risk has to be taken and the courage has to be mustered to immerse ourselves in the study of social transactions and social processes. If we take as our subject the constitutive effect of law we cannot be content with literary theory applied to legal doctrine. We must instead study families, schools, work places, social movements, and, yes, even professional associations to present a broad picture in which law may seem at first glance virtually invisible. We will find in these efforts instances that both confirm and contradict the dominant discourse; we will also find instances that will require us to reimaging the discourse in a different way. We would then understand law not as something removed from social life, occasionally operating upon and struggling to regulate and shape social forms, but as fused with and thus inseparable from all the activities of living and knowing. We would, as critics, hear new voices and move our tradition to encapsulate them . . .                              [pp 165–173]

## NIKLAS LUHMANN
**Operational Closure and Structural Coupling: The Differentiation Of The Legal System**
(1992)[90]

. . . The description of a system as autopoietic, as autonomous, as operationally closed, refers to the network of its operations and not to the totality of all empirical conditions, that is, the world. The question is not how a system can maintain itself without any environmental support. Rather, it is what kind of operations enable a system to form a self-reproducing network which relies exclusively on self-generated information and is capable of distinguishing internal needs from what it sees as environmental problems.

The answer is no longer a disguised tautology but an obvious one. The unity of the system is produced by the system itself. The methodological task becomes to "unfold" (as logicians would say) this tautology, and this has to be done by empirically identifying the operations which produce and reproduce the unity of the system (for example, the biochemical processes within a living cell) . . .[p. 1420]

A description of the legal system as an autopoietic system would require us to say that the states of the system are exclusively determined by its own operations. The environment can eventually destroy the system, but it contributes neither operations nor structures. The structures of the system condense and are confirmed as a result of the system's own operations, and the operations are in turn recursively reproduced by structural mediation. In this sense, the system is a structure-determined system. But how can the society tolerate, or even promote, the emergence of such a degree of autonomy within itself? It is obvious that the legal system uses communication as its own basal operation and that it uses language, although employing special terminology. It is also obvious that we find a flow of communication crossing the boundaries of the legal system (which, of course, does not mean that the legal system can communicate as a collective actor on its own behalf). On the other hand, we could hardly think of a legal system as being unable to recognize its own boundaries, as an arbitrarily designed analytic

---

[90] [From (1992) 13 Cardozo L. Rev. 1419]

object of outside observers. Such a system would be unable to distinguish between the legal and the external consequences of a legal decision, to mention a famous and controversial issue.[91] It would be unable to find reasons for staying with precedents, for distinguishing, or for overruling. It would even be unable, as we shall see, to separate conceptual (internal) issues and interest (external) issues. As a social system within the societal system, it reproduces society by communication. There is no sense in separating law and society as if these were two different objects, and not even good sense in treating the society as the environment of the legal system. The legal system itself is an inseparable part of the societal system— it does not simply depend on external sources for social support and legitimation, but is an inextricable part of the network that reproduces the society by recursively connecting communication with communication. Nevertheless, the legal system is a closed system, producing its own operations, its own structures, and its own boundaries by its own operations; not by accepting any external determination nor, of course, any external delimitation whatsoever. To put it even more pointedly, just because the legal system operates as part of the social network of societal operations, there is no sense in looking for external sources of determination and delimitation. As part of the societal system, the legal system is a self-organizing, self-determining system . . .

As in all cases of operational closure, the problem is *how to define the operation that differentiates the system and organizes the difference between system and environment* while maintaining reciprocity between dependence and independence. This indeed is a most difficult question; it is the core problem of a theory of the legal system.                                                                 [pp. 1424–1425]

Within the traditional framework of functionalism and division of labor one would tend to point to a specific function, and this remains part of the truth. The function of the legal system may be defined as producing and maintaining counter-factual expectations in spite of disappointments.[92] The communication of this intention to maintain one's own expectations even if they are not fulfilled (that is, to refuse to learn from facts) uses the symbols of normativity, for example, the world "should". But this does not suffice for closing the system because there are many nonlegal norms, and the concept of function itself suggests looking for functional equivalents and asking the question of whether learning would not be the better (or at least a functionally equivalent) way to equip the system with stable expectations . . . Nowadays, people look for moral rules or values to found the legal system in nonlegal norms—the famous Jellinek-Weber-Habermas line of "legitimation,"[93] or the American discussion of moral aspiration versus original intent as a guideline for an interpretation of the constitution. My advice would be to unask such questions—or to "deconstruct" them—and to replace them with the question of how the system organizes its own closure, its own social autonomy, and its own immunity in fulfilling its function.

Legal reasoning uses the distinction between norms and facts, between normative and cognitive expectations. It has to know in which respects it is supposed to learn (did somebody kill another woman?) and in which respects not (should she have been killed?). Legal reasoning would not get along very well by confusing these questions. In this sense, the system is normatively closed and cognitively open at the same time. But the legal system has to anticipate (that is, to know in advance of every specific operation) which norms are legal norms and which norms are simply opinions in its environment, for example, beautiful images of

---

[91]   See Bernard Rudden, "Consequences" (1979) 24 Jurid. Rev 193; Neil MacCormick "On Legal Decisions and Their Consequences: From Dewey to Dworkin" (1983) 58 N.Y.U.L. Rev. 239

[92]   For further elaboration, see Niklas Luhmann, *A Sociological Theory of Law* (1985), pp. 22–49.

[93]   See *e.g.* Jurgen Habermas, *Legitimation Crisis* (Thomas McCarthy trans., 1977)(1973).

economic *and* ecological rationality. In other words, the legal system has to organize the legal validity of norms, validity represented as a circulating symbol, moved by legislation and contract, and with continually shifting contents. The recursive autopoietic network of reproducing normative expectations with reference to normative expectations uses the distinguishing mark of legal validity. Acceptable legal reasoning has to restrict itself to legal norms (including norms of moral standards referred to by legal norms, professionally sound practice, and so on.[94] This is how closure is recognized—or "observed"—in the system (every legal theorist will immediately recognize H.L.A. Hart's secondary rules of recognition).[95] However, this does not quite satisfactorily explain how closure is produced in the first place.

The structure that actually organizes the autopoiesis of the system as an unavoidable outcome of its own operations is the system's binary code; that is, the continuous necessity of deciding between legal right and wrong. This code is a strictly internal structure. To declare something illegal does not mean that it belongs to the environment of the system. We have to differentiate the distinction between self-reference and external reference on the one hand, and legal and illegal on the other. Moreover, the code of the system is not a norm; this assumption would only lead to the paradoxical question of whether the distinction between legal and illegal is *itself* legal or illegal. The code is simply a rule of attribution and connection. If the question arises whether something is legal or illegal, the communication belongs to the legal system, and if not then not. There is no further sanction and no natural or societal sorting of topics and communications as belonging or not to the legal system; it is a purely factual matter. The question of legality is or is not picked up in communication, and by this very fact the communication takes part in the recursive network of legal communication.[96] Nobody, not even the legal system, can refuse to ask the question. It may, of course, be possible to avoid asking the question by suppressing communication. The legal system can expand or shrink according to societal violence; but this does not change the rule of attribution and connection, it simply changes its range of application.

Identifying itself by its binary code, and distinguishing itself from its environment by the specificity that code, the legal system knows of no fundamental norm (*Grundnorm*) representing its unity within the societal system. There is no way to introduce the unity of the system into the system. The system is an open-ended, ongoing concern structurally requiring itself to decide how to allocate its positive or negative value. The bifurcation necessitates decisions and thereby further operations, and decisions require the construction of normative rules (programs) to connect them in a network for reproducing decisions. Norms, then, are purely internal creations serving the self-generated needs of the system for decisional criteria without any corresponding "similar" items in its environment. Nothing else is meant by "autopoiesis". Historically, there is no beginning except an always renewed reconstruction of the past. Logically, there are no apriorities, but simply a circular, reciprocal conditioning of the code and programs. Only the programs have a normative status and convey a normative quality to concrete expectations. They serve the function of the system. The closure of the system is produced by realizing the structural difference of the code and programs, and this difference along gives legal norms a distinctive flavor.

---

[94] See Neil MacCormick, *Legal Reasoning and Legal Theory* (1978) (proposing for this refined positivistic approach the brand name of "institutional theory of law").

[95] See H.L.A. Hart, *The Concept Of Law* (1961). [And see *ante*, 375.]

[96] See Niklas Luhmann, "Communication about Law in Interaction Systems", in Advances in Social Theory and Methodology: Toward as Integration of Micro- and Macro-Sociologies (eds. K. Knorr-Cetina & V. Cicoural (1981), p. 234.

Normative closure means, above all, that morality as such has no legal rele-vance—neither as code (good/bad, good/evil), nor in its specific evaluations. The law provides ample space for immoral behavior. *Non omne quod licet hon-estum est.*[97] This is not simply a moral weakness of the law, but a condition of free and unrestrained development of moral communication. Such was the common opi-nion in the eighteenth and nineteenth centuries, and it was the unavoidable consequence of religious and moral pluralism produced by the printing press. Of course, this does not prevent the legal system from incorporating moral con-straints as legal constraints; but this has to be done within the system and has to be checked by the usual references to legal texts, precedents, or rulings that limit the realm of legal argument.[98] Even theories that dare to asset that all legal decisions in so-called "hard", and even "easy", cases need a moral justification maintain that looking for "grounds drawn from outside the law" is, "indeed, ... *required* by law."[99] Whatever import one claims for external references, these references are aspects of internal operations. The system has to take care of itself.

The daily problem of closed social systems is how to connect internal and external references by internal operations. At the operational level this problem is solved by distinguishing norms form facts; that is, in terms of internal structures, distinguishing normative from cognitive expectations. The distinction of nor-mative and cognitive expectations, and this hold true for any distinction, has to be *made*; in our case, it has to be made *by the legal system*. It cannot be found in the natural or created world. It is not a "categorical" property of the world. This means that even "facts" that are relevant for the legal system are not facts for everybody. Facts are constructions, statements about the world, and careful sociological investigations show that scientific facts and facts which serve as components of legal or political-administrative decision making differ in remarkable ways.[1] In other words, knowledge has different "credibility profiles"[2] inside and outside the legal system. Legal facts are made to fit the legal frame-work; they have to facilitate as far as possible the deductive use of legal norms. They have to support the presentation of legal validity by conveying the impression that, given the rules, the decision follows from the facts of the case. They have to be certified facts.

At the level of juridical doctrine, the same problem can be formulated in terms of concepts and interests. We are used to thinking of analytic jurisprudence and interest-orientation as two different, competing schools of legal thought. The interest approach was born, at least in Germany, by inventing an opponent called *Begriffjurisprudenz* (Conceptual Jurisprudence). Roscoe Pound copied this polemical style.[3] The tribal rules of the academic system favor such distinctions of schools and controversies. The legal system operates under different conditions of autopoietic reproduction. It has to combine internal and external references and, to the extent that generalizations are useful, may refer to well-tried concepts and

---

[97] Dig. 50. 17. 144 (Paulus, Ad Edictum 62) ("Not everything which is lawful is honor able").

[98] See Neil MacCormick, "Why Cases Have Rationes and What These Are", in *Precedent in Law* (ed. Lawrence Goldstein, 1987) pp. 155, 166–182.

[99] David Lyons, "Justification and Judicial Responsibility" (1984) 72 Cal. L. Rev. pp. 178, 186, 188, (introducing further distinctions to "make this conclusion less paradoxical").

[1] See Expert Evidence: Interpreting Science In The Law (Roger Smith & Brian Wynne eds. 1989) [hereinafter Expert Evidence].

[2] Brian Wynne's term. Brian Wynne, *Establishing the Rules of Laws: Constructing Expert Authority*, in Expert Evidence, *supra* n 19.

[3] See Roscoe Pound, *Mechanical Jurisprudence* (1908) 8 Colum. L. Rev. 605.

to well-known interests. There is no contradiction is using both references simultaneously. Concepts articulate the self-referential aspects of legal decisions; interests, on the other hand, are environmental facts to be taken as given. The task of the system as formulated by the system consists of distinguishing interests protected by the law from interests to be suppressed and combatted.[4]

This distinction cannot be derived from the environment of the system, nor can it be "seen" as an inherent quality of systems. The distinction must be constructed by the internal operations. This is not to say that the dividing line separating protected from suppressed interests can be drawn arbitrarily. The guarantee of "justice" is not the correspondence with external qualities or interests, but the consistency of internal operations recognizing and distinguishing them. It is this requisite of consistency which, under conditions of sufficient complexity, leads to the elaboration of concepts.

Concepts are also internal operators referring to *internal* differences, or at least this has to be presupposed. Even if a concept—like the bona fides of the Romans—has moral connotations in everyday language, these do not become part of the law except by explicit reference. In other words, bona fides is not a "source of law".[5] The same holds true for terms that are used in legal texts but also have scientific meanings (often more than one) outside the law. If a concept is used explicitly as citation, it refers to environmental norms, rules, and customs as facts that must be proven.

At the level of single cases, there may be a choice between giving priority to the urgency of interests or to the purity of legal concepts, but the system as such cannot choose in this way. If its decisions are presented as evaluations of interests, this amounts to understating conceptual issues and neglecting for the time being the control of consistency. If the reasons given are conceptual ones, this will be a disguised way of *favoring* or *disfavoring* certain interests more than others. In theoretical terms, the ultimate problem always consists of combining external and internal references, and the real operations which produce and reproduce such combinations are always internal operations. *Nothing else is meant by closure....*                              [pp. 1426–1431]

The emergence of closed systems requires a specific form of relations between system and environments; it presupposes such forms and is a condition of their possibly as well. The theory of "open systems" describes these forms with the categories of *input* and *output*. This model postulates a causal chain in which the system itself services as the connecting part linking input and outputs. The theory of autopoietic systems replaces the input/output model with the concept of *structural coupling*. It renounces the idea of an overarching causality (admitting it, of course, as a construct of an observer interested in causal attributions), but retains the idea of highly selective connections between systems and environments.

---

[4] See Roscoe Pound, *Jurisprudence* (1959). He writes: "A legal system attains the ends of the legal order (1) by recognizing certain interests individual, public, and social; (2) by defining the limits within which those interests shall be recognized and given effect through legal precepts ...". *ibid.* at 16. So some (or almost all?) interests are left without protection, or are even repressed. This positive/negative distinction can, of course, not be deduced from the interests a such, for even bad interests are interests. A theory which looks exclusively at interests cannot give good reasons for this distinction except by saying that the legal system has an interest in distinguishing protected and unprotected interests. See Philipp Heck, *Gesetzesauslegung und Interessenjurisprudenz* (1914), *reprinted in* Philipp Heck, Dax Problem Der Rechtsgewinnung 102 (1968); Benjamin Cardozo, *The Nature of the Judicial Process* 112 (1921) ("One of the most fundamental interests is that the law shall be uniform and impartial").

[5] See Antonio Carcaterra, Intorno Ai Bonaei Fidei Iudicia (1964); Yan Thomas, *La langue du droit romain: Problèmes et méthodes.* 19 Archives De Philosophie du Droit 103 (1974) (asking for more refined semiotic analyses of this question).

The structural coupling of system and environment does not contribute operations (or any other components) for the reproduction of the system. It is simply the specific form in which the system presupposes specific states or changes in its environment and relies on them. Walking presupposes the gravitational forces of the earth within very narrow limits, but gravitation does not contribute any steps to the movement of bodies. Communication presupposes awareness states of conscious systems, but conscious states cannot become social and do not enter the sequence of communicative operations as a apart of them; they remain environmental states for the social system. Structural couplings are forms of simultaneous (and therefore, not causal) relations. They are analogical, not digital, coordinations.

The system in its normal dealings does not observe its structural couplings, but it has to contend with perturbations, irritations, surprises, and disappointments channeled by its structural couplings. It must also assimilate and accommodate such ambiguities. But perturbations are purely internal constructs because they appear only as deviations from expectations; that is, in relation to the structure of the system. The environment does not contain perturbations or anything that in a semantical sense is similar to them. Nor is there any transmission of perturbations from the outside into the system. The twin concepts of closure and structural coupling exclude the idea of information "entering" the system from the outside. Even in the case of cognitive expectations this is impossible because selections of information are always internally constructed, and cognitive expectations are nothing but specific forms to be prepared for irritations (surprises, unpredictabilities).[6] But without structural coupling there would be no perturbation and the system would lack any chance to learn and transform its structures. Hence, structural coupling, together with sufficient internal complexity, is a necessary precondition for building up regularities to construct order from noise or redundancy from variety. Communication never becomes thought, but without being continually irritated by communication, an individual would not become a socialized individual; it would remain dependent upon its flow of perceptions, that is, dependent upon structural couplings and internally constructed regularities of another type.

In this way, structural couplings provide a continuous influx of disorder against which the system maintains or changes its structure. Memory depends upon this tendency towards entropy. Memory is not a storage of past facts (the past can never be present), but a form for mediating order and disorder—very frequently by forgetting, in other cases by constructing a spatial or temporal order to dissolve incompatibilities. However, this would not be possible if structural couplings did not exclude most of the environmental facts from immediate relevance. Structural coupling presupposes and organizes decoupling. Communication (which is to say, society) is coupled to consciousness, but not to the immense mass of physical, chemical, and biological facts. These facts can prevent communication and they can destroy it, but they cannot irritate communication. In this sense, coupling has to be conceived as a difference, as a form with two sides: an internal side that admits irritation and an external side to which the system remains indifferent. Structural couplings arise with systems; they are not physical, chemical, biological facts that exist before systems emerge (although these facts as such preexist as preadaptive advances for the emergence of systems).

---

[6] This responds to a remark of William Evan, that the theory of autopoietic systems does not explain how information (expectations, demands) is transmitted to the legal system. William M. Evan, *Social Structure And Law: Theoretical And Empirical Perspectives* 42 (1990). There is normal communication as the operation of the societal system, to be sure, but no contribution of external sources to what the closed system can handle as information.

Applying this complex conceptual apparatus at the level of societal differentiation, and in particular to the differentiation of a legal system, we immediately see the structural coupling of social communication reproducing society on the one hand, and special legal meanings as normative projections claiming legal validity—the legal code and the special programs (laws, regulations, contracts)— on the other. Communication is the "domain" in which the differentiation of a legal system becomes possible. This does not (and cannot!) require a communication *of* the legal system *to* the society as a relation between sender and receiver. The legal system cannot communicate as a unity and the society has no address. However, by operating within its own boundary, the legal system reproduces itself and the societal system without making this simultaneity a topic of communication, without using it as an argument in pleading before the court, and, of course, without needing any "legitimation" by the societal system. It happens as an unavoidable fact *because* (not although!) the legal system reproduces itself under the condition of operational closure.

Given the fact of the structural coupling of the societal system and its legal system, further structural couplings can evolve between the legal system and other functional subsystems. All subsystems use the same domain, "communication". They could not be subsystems of the societal system on the basis of other types of operations—say biological or conscious ones—but this does not solve all the problems of coupling and decoupling which arise in the relations between the subsystems.... Under the regime of functional differentiation, the societal system loses its integrative capacity. Reduced to its mechanism of structural coupling, it continues to autopoietically reproduce itself by communication. But language as such contains and spreads the possibility of refusing all kinds of proposals. Under these conditions, the social order requires autopoietic closure, self-organization, and autonomy of the most important function system as well as the development of new forms of structural coupling for the relations between these systems.

The economic system depends on the codes of property and money. Without a clear divide between having and not having property rights, no transaction would be possible. Nevertheless, the economic and the legal consequences of a transaction are completely different because they occur in different systems in different recursive networks under different criteria and concrete conditions. The economic and the legal systems are and remain separate, and both operate under the condition of operational closure; but this needs a specific mechanism of structural coupling, above all in the form of property and contract.[7]

There is much historical evidence that, beginning in the fourteenth century, the legal system adapted to these requirements and enlarged—slowly, and with many scruples—the permitted degrees of freedom in property and contract. The core meaning of property has included since Bartolus,[8] in addition to defense and use and enjoyment (*usus, fruitio*), the right of disposal (*disposition*). The same improbabilities deform and generalize the institution of contract; contract was the most important legal invention of Roman civil law, providing a legal instrument not only for solving actual conflicts, but for regulating and avoiding them. During the transition from stratification, based on real estate, to functional differentiation, the society created needs, motives, and legitimation for enlarging the scope

---

[7] Other important requisites include corporate law—which, during the eighteenth and nineteenth centuries, became independent from political privileges and monopolies—and patent law, and, last but not least, the banking system. The latter provided a sufficient separation and recoupling of money and other (real) property for the credit mechanism which the economy needed: the capacity to pay even without sufficient wealth.

[8] Bartolus was a twelfth century Italian jurist and commentator on Roman law.

of employing property and the scope of possible contracts with legal protection. The limitations of access to courts which the traditions of civil law and common law arranged under the names of *action* and writ vanished, and finally—in England only in the nineteenth century—contracts became legally valid, even with "consideration", on the basis of private will.[9]

Modern concepts of property and contract do not integrate or even differentiate the legal and economic systems. As mechanisms of structural coupling, they organize the reciprocal irritation of the systems and influence, in the long run, the natural drift of structural developments in both systems. In particular, the regulatory state presupposes this connection and uses it as a medium of political intervention into both systems by limiting once again the degrees of freedom for using property and contact.

If we look for a parallel mechanism coupling the legal system and the political system, we find it in the form of constitutions—in the modern sense—emerging from revolutionary movements during the second half of the eighteenth century. The historical innovation, the mutation of legal forms, had been occasioned by concrete political circumstances and by the possibilities they provide for an instrumental use of conceptual variations.[10] This has been "favored" by the modern concept of the "state", which suggests a unity of political and legal "sovereignty". This unity makes if difficult to see the distinction, but the political system and the legal system are separate, operationally closed, autopoietic systems. A political operation as such never has legal relevance if not endowed with it by the legal system and vice versa. Otherwise no political discourse, no political bargaining, and no policy planning would be possible without immediate legal effects. The constitution separates the systems and provides for their structural coupling. The ultimate paradoxes and tautologies of the legal system (that law is whatever the law arranges to be legal or illegal) can be unfolded by reference to the political system (for example, the political will of the people giving itself a constitution), and the paradoxes and tautologies of the political system (the self-inclusive, binding, sovereign power) can be unfolded by reference to the positive law and by supercoding the legal system with the distinction of constitutional and unconstitutional legality.[11] ...                                     [pp. 1431–1437]

One of the most frequent objections to the theory of autopoietic system in general, and its application to legal systems specifically, states that this theory—if it is a theory at all[12] does not care for empirical verification.[13] This criticism needs two comments. First, the repertoire of empirical methods in present day sociology is very limited and completely inadequate for objects like the legal system; that is, self-observing objects with highly structured complexity. Restricting the access to objects by available empirical methods—and I take this denotation in its usual meaning—would simply mean not seeing the society and its legal system as it constructs and presents itself. It requires going out of the market and leaving the business to others—to mass media and to sociological writers. This should not be the last word. Secondly, one can look for new combinations of (1) well-known

---

[9]  For the common law, see Patrick S. Atiyah, *The Rise and Fall of Freedom of Contract* (1979); Morton J. Horwitz, *The Transformation Of American Law, 1780–1860* (1977).

[10]  See e.g., Conceptual Change And The Constitution, (Terence Ball and John G. A. Pocock eds., 1988); *Political Innovation And Conceptual Change* (Terence Ball *et al.* eds., 1989).

[11]  For the decisive invention of the term "unconstitutional" during the eighteenth century, see Gerald Stourzh, *Constitution: Changing Meanings of the Term from the Early Seventeenth to the Late Eighteenth Century*, in *Conceptual Change And The Constitution, supra* n. 28 at 35.

[12]  Within the context of American sociology, this level of theorizing is sometimes called "metatheoretical".

[13]  See e.g., Evan, *supra* n. 26, at 46.

and uncontroversial (maybe obvious or even trivial) facts; and (2) theoretical descriptions which present the obvious in unusual illumination. The distinction between operational closure and structural coupling is one of these theoretical instruments. In other words, given the structure of its domain, sociology cannot reduce its concept of social reality to self-created data. We may even doubt whether there is any correlation between empirical research and social reality, except by the methodologically unguided "active interpretation" of results.

If these considerations suggest (to repeat, for the present situation) a primacy of refined theoretical research, they do not exclude empirical research. We have outlined a hypothesis indicating relations between a transition from stratification to functional differentiation and the intervention of new or the reformulation of old mechanisms of structural coupling during the transition period. There could be many similar suggestions, for example, concerning the forms of deparadox-ification of the legal system's self-description[14] or the replacement of the unified notion of *iurisdictio* by the separation and circular recombination of legislation and jurisdiction as a condition for the transition from natural law to positive law as the dominant form of self-validation of the legal system. There could be many empirical projects exploring the sensitivity (or limits thereon) of the autopoiesis of the legal system to social and political changes. There are no fundamental incompatibilities between the theory of self-referential systems and empirical research, but there is an uncomfortable tension between theoretical conceptions and the present possibilities of empirical research. Instead of rejecting theory as unverifiable, critics should see the insufficiencies on both sides. [pp. 1438–1439]

## ROGER COTTERRELL
### Law and Social Theory
### (2006)[15]

The relationship between legal studies and social theory has been ambivalent and often difficult. Why is this so? What is the value of social theory in legal studies today and why is law an important social phenomenon for social theory to consider? This chapter addresses these questions and considers recent challenges to the projects of social science and social theory. It also introduces the special problems posed for theoretical studies of law by globalization and the growth of transnational law.

What can social theory contribute to legal studies? And what place does law have as a concern of social theory? Three or four decades ago, when "law-and-society" (sociolegal) studies were first becoming a lively, popular focus for research, defining the relations of law and social theory meant mainly locating law's place in the theoretical traditions of the academic discipline of sociology, and asking what those traditions might offer the study of law. Now, however, social theory is not the preserve of any particular academic discipline. It has to be defined in terms of its objectives rather than particular traditions that have shaped it.

### Law in Classic Social Theory

Social theory is systematic, historically informed and empirically oriented theory seeking to explain the nature of "the social". And the social can be taken to mean the general range of recurring forms, or patterned features, of interactions and relationships between people. The social is the ongoing life of human beings lived

---

[14] See Niklas Luhmann, *The Third Question: The Creative use of Paradoxes in Law and Legal History* (1988) 15 J. L. & Soc. 153.

[15] [From *Law, Culture and* Society]

alongside and in relation to others; the compendium of institutions, networks, patterns and structures of collective life resulting from human coexistence. So, it is the collective life of human groups and populations, but also the life of individuals insofar as this is shaped by their relation to those populations or groups. The social is a realm of solidarity, identity and cooperation, but also of power, conflict, alienation and isolation; of stable expectations, systems, custom, trust and confidence, but also of unpredictable action, unforeseen change, violence, disruption and discontinuity.

Described in these expansive terms, the social seems bewilderingly general as an object or field of study. Debates about its nature and significance are fundamental today in assessing the significance of social theory itself. And the essence of the social has been seen in social theory in radically different ways. For example, in Max Weber's (1968) classic sociological writings it appears as a limited number of distinct types of social action combined in innumerable ways to give rise to what we recognize as "capitalism", "bureaucracy", "domination" and all the other seemingly solid structures of the social world. Sometimes the social has been seen in terms of an evolution of human relations—for example in Marcel Mauss" (1990) famous analysis of the significance of gift relationships. Its essence has also been found in different types of cohesion of human populations (Durkheim 1984) or sociality or bonding between the members of social groups (Gurvitch 1947). Sometimes it has been understood as categories or institutional forms in terms of which individuals interrelate—for example, in Georg Simmel's (1971) analyses of "the stranger", "the metropolis", "fashion", "conflict", "exchange" and other phenomena.

The object that has served—implicitly or explicitly—as the primary focus for most social theory is *society*, conceived as a unified totality in some sense, so that the study of how that totality exists could be distinct from, though related to, the study of politics, law, the economy or other more specific kinds of social action or experience. Society in this sense is "the sum of the bonds and relations between individuals and events—economic, moral, political—within a more or less bounded territory governed by its own laws" (Rose 1996: 328). Even where social theory has not treated society directly as its object, its characterizations of the social assume that social phenomena cohere in a significant way: that social life forms a fabric of some kind; that it has continuity and scale and that particular exemplifications of the social relate to larger patterns, even if their exact limits or boundaries may be variable or hard to specify. The social includes class, race and gender relations, and specifically economic relations, for example, but social theory assumes it must treat all of these as components or aspects of more general patterns or features of human interaction, and that its consistent focus must be on that generality. The social is always assumed to be in some sense intelligible as a unity.

In the classic social theory of the late nineteenth and early twentieth century, "society" was mainly typified by the politically organized and territorially bounded society of the modern Western nation state. Given this position, it is not surprising that a strong sensitivity to law is found in the most ambitious and influential contributions to this theory—the work of Emile Durkheim, Weber and Karl Marx. The reach of society could be seen as paralleling the jurisdictional reach of nation state legal systems. As social theory examined the general social relations and structures comprising society, it encountered modern law as a society-wide system of definition and regulation of these relations and structures. In a sense, law and social theory competed in characterizing modern society, but law could be treated in social theory as exemplifying certain structures and patterns fundamental to this society.

So, for Durkheim, the substance of modern law (particularly contract, commercial, property and criminal law) and its processes expressed the particular characteristics of modern social solidarity, by which he meant the manner in which modern society was integrated and given a sense of unity despite its increasing complexity, changeability and diversity. A study of the development of law across the centuries could show how the structures of solidarity allowing modern society to cohere had gradually formed (Durkheim 1984). His conclusion was that the only value system that could integrate modern societies—and so must be the moral foundation of all modern law—would be one requiring universal respect for the autonomy and human dignity of every individual citizen (Durkheim 1975a; Cotterrell 1999; 103–47).

In a completely different way and using different methods, Weber also securely linked the study of law with the study of the social in its modern forms. Modern law exemplified a kind of rationality mirroring and running parallel with the rationalization of other aspects of life in the West. While formal legal rationality was a distinctive mode of thought and practice, it could be seen as part of a far wider rationalization of the modern world. The study of legal rationality's development and its interrelations with other varieties of rationality (especially in economic action, administration and politics) could, in Weber's view, provide major insights into the nature of the social in the unique forms it had taken in the West (Weber 1968: Part 2, Chapter 8).

Marx, seeking to analyse the nature and destiny of capitalism, saw law as in one sense superstructural, a product rather than an engine of capitalism's trajectory as a mode of production and as the overall structure of the social in the modern West. But he emphasized law's role in defining social relations, repressing class unrest and helping to constitute the ways of thinking—above all in terms of property and contract—that serve as fundamental ideological supports of capitalist social relations (Cain and Hunt 1979). Thus, like Durkheim and Weber, Marx saw a need to take account of the development of law to identify the way it produced particular ideas, ways of reasoning or forms of practice at certain stages in history.

So, each of these writers saw law as essential in transforming the social—establishing foundations of modern society, however differently they might characterize this modernity in their work.

These brief comments may be enough to illustrate two points: that the concept of *modernity* has often, in practice, been inseparable from that of society in the vision of social theory and that law was often treated in classic social theory as, in some way, a crucial marker, component or agent of the coming into being of the modern world. More recent social theorists have often treated the emergence of a certain kind of legal system as crucial in this sense. Talcott Parsons, for example, saw the emergence of a "general legal system"—cutting across all traditional special statuses and providing a universal system of rights and obligations—as "the most important single hallmark of modern society" (Parsons 1964: 353). But we shall see later that the concepts of modernity and society, so central to social theory, are at the heart of debates surrounding it as an enterprise today.

Leaving aside these debates for the moment, what has social theory in its classic or traditional forms been able to offer legal studies? If social theory is abstract and broad in scope, law as a practice, and often as a field of study, has been said, by contrast, to be wedded to the "method of detail" (Twining 1974), focused on particularity and immediate problem-solving. Social theory in general has claimed that philosophical analyses, reflections on historical experience and systematic empirical observations of social conditions can be combined to explain the nature of society. Social theorists' considerations of law are coloured by this amalgam of philosophical, historical and observational orientations. As a by-product of its general concerns, social theory has often assessed law's capacities, limits, conditions of existence and sources of authority and power.

Its attraction for some legal scholars has been that its perspectives on law have been much wider than those the legal specialist alone could usually be expected to command. So, social theory has been called on in sociolegal studies to escape the limits of law's method of detail as well as to counter narrow social scientific empiricism. The promise has always been to *broaden* social perspectives on law. The corresponding risk has always been that the broad perspective loses the richness and specificity of particular experiences or practices of "the legal". The method of detail may need supplementing but has its value nonetheless.

Despite these claims for social theory's usefulness to legal studies and the prominent presence of law in the classics of social theory, the link between legal studies and social theory has usually been tenuous. That various changes in both law and social theory are bringing about a greater mutual dependence will be a main argument later in this chapter. Nevertheless, until quite recently, the relationship could be characterized as predominantly one of disinterest or token acknowledgment.

Despite the example set by the classic writers, social theorists have often doubted whether law is important enough or sufficiently identifiable as a distinct social phenomenon to deserve special consideration in any theory of the social. Could most of what needs to be analysed be treated in terms of concepts such as administrative action, state coercion, social norms, social control, ideology, reciprocity, conformity and deviance, bureaucratic norms or custom? Law, as such, might not need theorizing: that could be left to jurists for their own purposes. The term "law" would remain for the social theorist only a common-sense label that might usefully designate clusters of phenomena to be explained theoretically without essential reference to it. In any event, law's identity and significance vary considerably between different societies. And general conceptions or definitions of law are dominated by juristic perceptions which most social theorists have not sought to upset.

For example, social theorists have rarely adopted the radical reformulations of the concept of law associated with what is now called social scientific legal pluralism (Griffiths 1986; Merry 1988). Legal pluralism in this sense explicitly denies that juristic conceptions of law are universally adequate and adopts some wider conception of law that can embrace, for various analytical purposes, phenomena that the lawyer would not recognize as legal—for example, private or "unofficial" norm systems of various kinds. Among major social theorists only Georges Gurvitch stands out as having radically rejected juristic conceptions of law in favour of an intricate, fully elaborated theory of legal pluralism integrated into his broader social theory. Significantly Gurvitch reached this position on the basis of his early sociolegal and philosophical inquiries (Gurvitch 1935; 1947), rather than as a by-product of his later general sociological theory.

Indeed, in contrast to social theorists, it is those social scientists who see law as central to their research careers, and tend to refer to themselves as "law-and-society" or sociolegal scholars, who have most often embraced legal pluralist perspectives. But many sociolegal scholars have been content to follow social theory's general lead, paying homage to the broad insights about law to be found in classic social theory but otherwise mainly using "law" as a pragmatic umbrella term for clusters of social phenomena analysed in terms of concepts familiar in their parent social science disciplines.

Just as social theory has tended to avoid law while considering its social manifestations, so lawyers and legal scholars have mainly avoided social theory. And certainly, from a juristic standpoint, the usefulness of a theory of the social may not seem obvious: the social might be viewed as what law itself creates as its own jurisdiction, the structure of the social being simply the regulatory structure that law provides. In this sense the social is the taken-for-granted locus and environment of legal practice. And, undoubtedly, from a juristic viewpoint, law seems endlessly resourceful in defining and adjusting its reach and the nature of the relations it regulates: the social is what law treats as such.

*Law and Contemporary Social Change*

What is happening to change this typical relationship of disinterest? Relevant changes in the situation of law and legal studies, on the one hand, and of social theory, on the other, have often been associated with the idea of the passing of modernity and its replacement with the postmodern. "Post" implies that the new can only be understood as related to and, in some sense, a supplement or reaction to what preceded it, but also that modernity's features can now be identified with finality, so that what follows is distinct from them.

According to Jean-François Lyotard's celebrated dictum, the most profound exemplification of postmodernity is a loss of faith in "grand narratives" (Lyotard 1984: 37) in a fluid, rapidly changing, intensely self-questioning and uncertain (Western) world: the coming of "a new age of radical rootlessness and doubt" (Douzinas and Warrington 1991: 9). This applies not only to comprehensive systems of thought such as Marxism and the great religions, but to general theories of "society" as a stable, integrated totality, to political ideologies of all kinds and to the very idea of "science" as the progressive unveiling of truth. All are said to flounder on the rocks of patent social contingency and indeterminacy.

The result is a new privileging of "local knowledge" (Geertz 1983) and a perception of the failure or pointlessness of all attempts to generalize broadly about social change or social phenomena. The tendency in such circumstances might be to abandon social theory altogether. A new focus on the local and the specific, on the instability of social structures and institutions, and the exhilarating or frightening rootlessness of individual lives casts doubt on the usefulness of treating society as an object sufficiently solid to theorize (Rose 1996; Bauman 1992: 190). The dialectic of order/change and structure/agency in traditional sociological analyses of society does not seem to capture the sense of radical fluidity that postmodern thought associates with contemporary human coexistence in the most highly developed nations of the world.

The idea that it is no longer useful to theorize society has sometimes led into more general but very opaque claims about "the death of the social" (Baudrillard 1983: Chapter 2). The doomsday scenario here is that social theory loses its integrity, having lost its object. It is replaced with a host of competing discourses—especially literary, feminist, psychoanalytic, economic and cultural theory—that focus on human relations no longer considered in terms of any explicit overall conception of the social.

More concrete ideas bearing directly on the destiny of law can also be mentioned. The social is sometimes claimed to be disappearing as a specific primary field of government intervention, and enterprises organized around it (such as social work, social welfare, sociology and socialism) are losing prestige (Simon 1999: 144–7). A further claim is that the social as a field distinct from the political is atrophying. From one viewpoint, the social has become merely a population mass, silent and inert, no longer the active source of political energies but merely a passive recipient of governmental actions (Baudrillard 1983: 19–25). A consequence would seem to be that legal interventions can hardly look for effective legitimation or direction from this source.

From another viewpoint, an individualization of lifestyles puts in issue the stability of many social institutions (for example, traditional family, employment and gender relations) but creates unprecedented opportunities for a radical remaking of the social through the spontaneous choices of individuals in relation to their own lives (for example, Beck and Beck-Gernsheim 2002). Thus, politics is potentially transformed, its focus shifted towards the local and the personal but also, very importantly, towards the global (as in many environmental, security and health concerns widely shared across national boundaries). Meanwhile, politics in nation states becomes increasingly moribund in the traditional public sphere. Indeed, in a revitalized politics, lines between public and private, and national and global, might eventually become meaningless (Beck 1992: Chapter 8; 2000: Chapter 2). The primary implication for legal studies would seem to be that the horizon and appropriate methods of regulation are changing in very fundamental ways.

The importance of this recent theorizing is certainly not to undermine the social as a category. Indeed, many theorists—including some, such as Jean Baudrillard, who have dramatically declared the social's demise—continue to refer to "society" without apparent embarrassment (Smart 1993: 55–6). For legal studies, the importance of these writings is to show that the nature of the social cannot be assumed as unproblematic. Law may define the social as it regulates it, but it does so under conditions that the social itself provides. Law presupposes a conception of the social that defines not only its technical jurisdiction, but also the arena in which its interventions require rational integration, and the general source of its legitimation and cultural meanings. It follows that, as the identity, coherence and shape of the social are questioned, assumptions about the nature and efficacy of law are also put in issue.

In contemporary social theory, Michel Foucault's work provides one of the most important vehicles for reconsidering the nature and scope of law in terms of fundamental long-term changes in the character of the social. It raises the question of whether law has failed to keep step with these changes and become marginalized as a result, increasingly giving way to other kinds of regulation and control. Foucault's works describe processes by which new kinds of knowledge and power have arisen, reinforcing each other to create what he calls disciplinary society (Foucault 1977: 216). The prison, the asylum, the school, the medical clinic and other particular institutional sites have been primary foci for the gradual emergence of constellations of knowledge/power in which technical norms, expertise, training and surveillance combine to regulate populations and define the place of individuals as autonomous, responsible subjects.

In lectures towards the end of his career, Foucault elaborated the general implications for law of his earlier studies. He sharply contrasts the majesty of law with the "art of government" focused on administering social life (Foucault 1991: 92). Law is, in his view, the expression of sovereign power: what is most important about it is that it demands obedience and requires that all affronts to the sovereignty it embodies be punished. The essence of law is, therefore, coercion. Foucault contrasts, with law's "occasional or discontinuous interventions in society", something he sees as very different: "a type of power that is disciplinary and continuously regulative and which pervasively, intimately and integrally inhabits society" (Fitzpatrick 1992: 151). This is an autonomous, expert form of governing, focused specifically on regulating economy and population and relying on "multiform tactics" and a range of techniques, expertise and information united only by a need for "wisdom and diligence" (Foucault 1991: 95, 96).

Foucault calls this pervasive regulatory activity "governmentality" rather than government, to emphasize that it goes beyond and uses a far wider range of techniques than government in the usual political sense, and its sites of operation are not restricted to what is usually thought of as the public sphere but relate to all aspects of life. Nevertheless, the rise of governmentality marks a stage in the development of the state, from the "state of justice" and law, through the "administrative state" of regulation and discipline organized territorially, to the "governmental state" which aims at guaranteeing security and is "essentially defined no longer [exclusively] in terms of its territoriality ... its surface area, but in terms of the mass of its population with its volume and density ..." (Foucault 1991: 104).

Significantly, law's destiny is left vague. Perhaps ultimately it is for jurists and sociolegal scholars to sort this out. The state's stages of development are cumulative so that eventually legal, administrative and governmental state forms coexist. Some writers see Foucault as claiming that law is progressively replaced by technical and disciplinary norms, and charge him with propounding a narrow view of law, apparently ignoring its current scope and character (Hunt 1993: Chapter 12). Others argue that Foucault well recognizes law's nature and scope in contemporary society (Ewald 1990) and sees only its old regulatory supremacy as undermined. His claim, undoubtedly, is that law has been reduced from its grandly sovereign status to a position alongside many other regulatory techniques, no more than a "tactic" of government to be used or not used, as appropriate (Foucault 1991: 95).

From another point of view, the key debate around Foucault and law is about law's *potential*. In the newly recognized complexity and indeterminacy of society, does action through and on law provide an important means of navigating the social and the many decentred locations of power which Foucault's work emphasizes (as suggested, for example, by Munro 2001), or is it increasingly a distraction as a focus for solving or campaigning on important social issues (Smart 1989), being tied to forms of state action and political projects that are increasingly remote from many regions of the social?

The ambiguous implications of Foucault's work show that social theory's changing images of the social destabilize established ideas of law, pointing in different directions towards new conceptualizations. A broad, loosened conception of law might see it metamorphosing into diverse regulatory strategies, forms and tactics attempting to mirror the fluidity, contingency and indeterminacy of the social (Rose and Valverde 1998). Law might seem an indefinite aspect of a range of tactics of governance operating in contexts—for example, schools, religious practices, rural traditions, campaigns to protect local industries (Cooper 1998)—often distanced from the direct operation of state agencies.

In this context, new unifying principles arise, focused, for example, on the control of risk, so that risk emerges as a major category for making sense of the normative implications of contingency (Beck 1992). Perceptions or calculations of risk can then be seen to operate as signals to alert or set in motion regulatory processes and provide their focus (see, for example, Ericson and Haggerty 1997). Equally, they can be rallying points for political and legal action (Franklin 1998).

By contrast, conceptions of law that in some way emphasize its autonomy or distinct identity rather than its tactical flexibility might see it as in crisis, overburdened with regulatory tasks for which it is unsuitable (Teubner (ed.) 1987). Or they might emphasize as somewhat remarkable the fact that, in such conditions of complexity, the legal system copes; that it pours out rules and decisions despite the ever-increasing diversity of social life and the rapidity of social change.

Autopoiesis theory, developed as a form of social theory by the sociologist Niklas Luhmann (1995), can be seen in this context as a particularly inventive way of conceptualizing how law copes with changes in the nature of the social without losing its special identity in the process, and becoming—as Foucault seems to suggest—just part of a continuum of regulatory tactics. Autopoiesis theory seeks to explain how law retains a distinctive character and stability in complex societies, at the same time as it addresses an ever-increasing range of problems thrown up by the fluidity and complexity of the social. The theory also suggests why legal interventions often produce unforeseen and unintended social consequences and why law often seems persistently unresponsive to demands emerging from the social.

In Luhmann's formulation, law is cognitively open but normatively closed, insofar as it has become an autopoietic (self-observing, self-producing and self-reproducing) system of communication (Luhmann 1992a). This means that, like other social systems of communication (such as the economy, the polity and science), law is necessarily open to information from its environment but, no less necessarily, it reads this information only in its own discursive terms. Law processes information solely for the purposes of applying its unique normative coding of legal/illegal in terms of which all its decisions must be made. Similarly, other systems interpret legal rules and decisions in terms of their own system codings, for example the criteria of efficient/inefficient in the case of the economy.

As social theory, autopoiesis theory clearly pictures law in the way it so often appears to jurists—as a self-founding discourse unfazed by circularity in its reasoning and invocations of authority. It shows how law can operate in this way and explains sociologically why it does. The theory claims that the increasing complexity of the social gives rise, in an evolutionary process, to the gradual differentiation of society into a number of specialized systems of communication, of which law is one. The legal system is thus not defined in terms of rules and institutions—as, for example, in Talcott Parsons' (1977: 174–6) earlier theory of social differentiation as a response to complexity—but by its distinctive discourse of legality and illegality.

Hence, law can pervade the spaces of the social. As discourse it can exist anywhere and everywhere and the thematization of issues as legal (Luhmann 1981) can occur in contexts not restricted to the formal legal institutions of the nation state. Thus, autopoiesis theory can accommodate the idea of an emerging "global law without a state" (Teubner (ed.) 1997), or of law's presence in the private realms that social theorists have identified as contemporary sites of a new politics and of the transformation of the social.

Nevertheless, the theory suffers, as many critics have pointed out, from an almost impenetrable abstraction. Attempts to use it in empirical sociolegal research have had limited success although it has provided a striking way of emphasizing, for example, legal discourse's perceived deafness or incomprehension when sometimes faced in court with the discourses of social welfare in cases involving children (King and Piper 1995). Despite being among the most sophisticated and rigorous recent contributions to social theory and having had its legal implications extensively elaborated (for example, Teubner 1993; Přibáň and Nelken (eds) 2001), autopoiesis theory stands some way apart from many of the themes this chapter has stressed. It has not extensively examined the changing character of the social in concrete terms in relation to law, and it has not indicated how contemporary legal change can be interpreted in the light of social theory. It leaves relatively unexplored the details of the discursive character that it attributes to developed law. And the theory explains little about how autopoietic law will actually respond to what the social may throw up as regulatory problems. Its concern seems only to affirm that law will seek to address these matters always from its own point of view with its own discursive resources.

## Foundations of Legal Authority

Autopoiesis theory attempts to bypass one question that has long been a major focus for social theory: What is the source and foundation of law's authority, the legitimacy that enables it to demand respect and command obedience? For Luhmann, the issue of law's legitimacy has been replaced by that of function: the question is simply about efficiency—whether law can effectively fulfil its social task of producing decisions according to its own criteria of legality/illegality. But one might still want to ask how functional success is to be judged and recognized. In fact, much recent social theoretical writing wrestles with questions about law's "grounds", its ultimate bases of authority or legitimacy.

Durkheim's classic social theory assumed that law and morality are inseparable and that morality is law's "soul". Since he understood morality as the normative structure of society, his social theory makes the strong claim that law finds all its meaning, authority and effectiveness ultimately in this moral structure. Without such a grounding it becomes mere force or empty words (Cotterrell 1999). In a sense, Weber's social theory turned these Durkheimian claims upside down. Modern law, having lost its "metaphysical dignity" with the discrediting of natural law theories, is revealed, in his view, as no more than "the product or the technical means of a compromise of interests" (Weber 1968: 874–5). Law needs no moral authority. Instead, its rules and procedures, in their abstract formality, can themselves become a means of *giving* authority, as in the political authority of the rule of law as a legitimation of government. Weber's work is thus one of the clearest sources of the familiar idea of legitimacy through legality or procedure (Cotterrell 1995: Chapter 7).

Interestingly, the broad problems, if not the substance, of both Durkheim's and Weber's opposing positions are strongly present in recent writing on law in social theory and in invocations of social theory in legal studies. Postmodern ideas about the collapse of grand narratives might suggest that the authority or validity of all large-scale structures of knowledge has been put in question. But it could be argued that some kind of Weberian legitimacy through legality remains the only possibility of stable authority in the postmodern social environment. Contemporary law—explicitly constructed, particular and local in scope, and ever-changing—might seem the quintessentially postmodern form of knowledge or doctrine: not in any sense a grand narrative, but the perfect pragmatic embodiment of contingency, impermanence, artificiality, transience and disposability; its doctrine continually adapted, amended, cancelled, supplemented or reinterpreted to address new problems.

Hence, postmodern writing on law has often emphasized law's simultaneous moral emptiness and social power in a world that has lost faith in other discourses (Goodrich 1990). And autopoiesis theory's unconcerned recognition that the very essence of legal discourse is circular reasoning has some affinities with claims informed by postmodern perspectives (Cotterrell 2003: Chapter 9): for example, that law's self-founded authority acts powerfully to disguise the incoherences of concepts such as "society" and "nation", even though legal thinking itself presupposes these concepts (Fitzpatrick 2001).

Not unrelated to these lines of thought is a stress, in much recent sociolegal writing, on law's constitutive power (for example, Brigham 1996)—its ability actually to create the social (not just for immediate regulatory purposes but also in the wider consciousness of all who participate in social life) by shaping over time such general ideas as property, ownership, responsibility, contract, rights, fault and guilt, as well as notions of interests, identity and community. To be theoretically coherent, the idea of law as constitutive in this sense—with antecedents stretching back to Marx's emphasis on law's ideological power—must ultimately either presuppose some notion of law as self-founding or recognize that law and the social are *mutually* constituting, that law gains its meaning and ultimate authority from the social at the same time as it shapes the social through its regulatory force. In other words, law is an aspect or field of social experience, not some mysteriously external force acting on it.

This last conclusion might reopen Durkheimian questions about the social bases of law's authority and imply that the social is more coherent, stable and susceptible to theorization than many writings on postmodernity assume. This is what Jürgen Habermas' influential social theory claims. He presents an image of society as made up partly of systems (for example, economic, political and legal systems), such as Luhmann describes, and partly of what Habermas calls the "lifeworld". The lifeworld is the environment of everyday social experience in which customs, cultures, moral ideas and popular understandings are formed and reproduced. The lifeworld provides experiential "background knowledge" (Habermas 1996: 23) with the aid of which people interpret each other's conduct and communicative actions. It is also the source of solidarity and legitimations necessary to the maintenance of the various systems that make up society. Yet it is continually colonized, invaded and transformed by these systems. So, for Habermas, the social exists in the interplay of system and lifeworld.

In contrast to all postmodern portrayals of contingency, indeterminacy and moral vacuity as characteristics of contemporary life, Habermas pursues the Enlightenment project of the discovery of reason in law, society and nature. He sees law not as self-grounding but as deriving its authority from reason—what he calls a communicative rationality, dependent for its adequate development on certain ideal conditions under which agreement between persons pursuing opposed or divergent interests becomes possible. Law, for Habermas, is the only medium that can link the lifeworld and the various systems of complex modern societies. Law, as a system itself, depends on the lifeworld for its authority and significance. The Durkheimian aspect of Habermas' thought is thus his insistence that law must be rooted in and express lifeworld sources of social solidarity. He sees law as having the main responsibility to coordinate contemporary societies, participating in both the instrumental rationality that pervades social systems and the consensus-oriented communicative rationality that the maintenance of lifeworld solidarity requires.

In his major work on legal theory (Habermas 1996), he insists that law and morality are distinct, though both derive from the same ultimate founding principle of communicative rationality. The conditions for this rationality to flourish include certain specified basic rights which can only be secured through legal processes. These processes, in turn, presuppose and must be designed to support democratic structures. Law and democracy are thus inseparably interwoven.

Habermas' ideas on law have been much discussed in sociolegal literature perhaps mainly because they clearly affirm law's relation to reason and the possibility of law's rational justification in the face of postmodern doubts. But these ideas have significantly shifted location over time. From components of an empirically oriented social theory focused notably on conditions of legitimate government in capitalist societies (Habermas 1975), they have turned into a more speculative legal philosophy. Interestingly, Habermas (1987: 249) has criticized Foucault's view of power as "utterly unsociological" but the same might be said of some of his own very abstract, general discussions of communicative rationality.

Perhaps the most thought-provoking feature of Habermas' recent work is the fact that law has come to assume a very central position in his picture of society. Law might seem in some images of postmodernity to be the epitome of contemporary valid knowledge, but in Habermas' entirely different outlook it appears, potentially at least, to epitomize essential social processes of consensus formation; its interpretive procedures hold out possibilities for developing communicative rationality. Law's procedures are the devices by which rationally-oriented communicative action becomes practically possible on a society-wide basis. From a certain standpoint, then, the significance of law for social theory is affirmed in the most unambiguous terms. Law is the foundation of central structures of social life; a set of processes and procedures on which society's very integrity depends.

## Law Beyond Nation States

I suggested earlier that law had often been able to avoid entanglement with social theory because it could take the nature of the social for granted. Law constitutes in regulatory terms what it treats as the social but it has to *presuppose* an overall conception of the social in which its regulatory actions can make sense. For a long time, Western legal thought presupposed the political society of the modern nation state as its overall conception of the social.

The growth of transnational regulation and regulatory aspirations (in human rights, commerce and finance, intellectual property, environmental protection, information technology and many other areas) creates new incentives for legal studies to draw on the resources of social theory. This is because it potentially disturbs long-standing presuppositions about law's stable relation to the political society of the nation state. Social theory's efforts to understand the social as extending beyond the bounds of society in this sense, or as shaped by powerful transnational forces, are presently organized mainly around the portmanteau concept of globalization. But law does not figure prominently in theories of globalization, perhaps because it is usually seen as following rather than actively shaping the transnational extension of the social. Globalization is often described in terms of particular forms of this extension such as the harmonization of markets, the transformation of culture (understood, for example, as traditions, basic values or beliefs), or the effects of new communication technologies. Law's role, even where seen as vital in these developments, is usually thought of as purely technical. Relatively few writers (cf. Teubner (ed.) 1997; Santos 2002) see the need for theories of 'global law' or legal transnationalization. Law in its traditional forms is widely assumed to be endlessly adaptable, capable of relating to the social wherever legal practice encounters it.

I think that some of the most important future relations of legal studies and social theory will, however, focus on the need to understand the changing character of law as it participates in developments currently associated with globalization. How far is social theory (which so often assumed the political society of the nation state as the social) helpful as law increasingly relates to a social realm demarcated in other terms?

As has been seen, debates inspired by Foucault's work address the nature of contemporary regulation (with its intricate, if somewhat indeterminate, links to the law created by sovereign power) and the complexity of networks of power in the social. These debates have great relevance for attempts to understand the nature and social contexts of transnational regulation. It will surely be necessary to ask whether, at some point, transnational regulatory forms can presuppose, to use Foucault's terms, the "cutting off of the king's head" (Foucault 1979: 88–9)— in other words, the freeing of regulatory strategies from the coercive demands of national sovereign power. It will be necessary to consider how far transnational social spaces can be created in which dispersed but pervasive power can be used not merely to discipline individuals, but also to create possibilities for their autonomy—the dual aspects of this power that are analysed in Foucault's work. In related ways, Ulrich Beck's writings (for example, Beck 1992; 2000) identify, in terms of individualization and risk, new regulatory problems but also new foci of liberating political action that can, as he stresses, relate as much to transnational as national arenas.

An engagement between legal studies and social theory beyond the nation state focus does not depend entirely on posing new sociolegal questions. It can also be a matter of presenting old ones in new contexts. Some of the most important old questions are about the way law secures authority through responsiveness to the experience or understandings of the population it regulates. Durkheim, always concerned with these issues, offered an important theory of democracy that has been largely unrecognized in sociolegal studies. He understood democracy, as an ideal practice, to be less a matter of popular representation than of sensitive, informed deliberation by means of which understandings, issues and values rooted in widespread everyday social experience can be recognized and translated into effective regulation (Cotterrell 1999: Chapters 10 and 11).

Durkheim's concerns about the moral groundings of law have not become irrelevant. But they are much more difficult to address when the social can no longer easily be thought of simply as a unified national political society. It has become hard to assume or specify a basis of moral cohesion in such a society, given what social theory has taught about the diversity, fluidity and contingency of the social. And the wider terrain of the social over which transnational regulation now operates might seem even more obviously culturally diverse, variable, fragmented and indefinite in scope.

Communitarian writings have explored what moral bonds are possible and necessary in complex modern societies but, despite efforts to ground their analyses in the traditions of social theory (Selznick 1992), they tend to be vague about the extent of existing moral consensus in these societies (Bauman 1993: 44–5) and risk lapsing into nostalgia for old forms of social solidarity or moralistic exhortations to recover values. Some alternative approaches have sought a pre-social "ethics of alterity" as a basis of moral evaluation of the social (Bauman 1989: Chapter 7; 1993: 47–53) and, by extension, a means of morally evaluating contemporary law (for example, Cornell 1992).

A different way forward might be to accept the concept of community as a potentially useful replacement for or supplement to that of (national) society, and to accept the need for solidarity in communities as the moral justification for regulating them. But community would need to be seen as existing in varied forms: in instrumental relationships such as those that provide the basis of commerce; in affective relationships of friendship, love or care; in relations based on shared beliefs or ultimate values; and in traditional relations based on shared environments or historical experiences. On such a view, the social is structured by the fluid, intricate interweaving of different types of community, whether this interweaving constitutes the society of the nation state, or particular groups or patterns of human interaction in this society, or networks of interaction, interests or concerns extending across nation state borders. On this view, law is the regulation and expression of communities.

Old questions about law's bases of authority or legitimacy remain very important as the social seems increasingly "globalized", unless a view such as Luhmann's is adopted, suggesting that law's successful functioning is all that matters. Even if function is everything, it is still necessary to ask what ultimate conditions can ensure that law's regulatory functions are fulfilled. Habermas (1996: 33) writes that coercive law "can preserve its socially integrating force only insofar as the addressees of legal norms can understand themselves, taken as a whole, as the rational *authors* of those norms" (emphasis in original). Whatever view is taken of his ideas about communicative rationality, this restatement of an old problem has new urgency as law extends its reach beyond national frontiers, and national law-making is more generally seen as driven by transnational forces.

If democracy, as Habermas claims, can in some conditions provide a sense of popular authorship of law in the political societies of nation states, where is such a sense to be found in the social realms addressed by transnational regulation or by national law subject to transnational pressures? How is Durkheim's democratic deliberation about the social to be achieved transnationally to create regulation that promotes solidarity? Marxist writings have properly emphasized—sometimes in debate with Foucault (Poulantzas 1978: 76–92)—law's sources in organized power and the nature of its coercive and persuasive force (Jessop 1980). But questions about its *moral authority* remain. As the nature of the social changes, sociolegal research is challenged to consider these questions anew, perhaps long before they become dilemmas disrupting law's everyday practice of the method of detail.                                                                    [pp 15–28]

## JÜRGEN HABERMAS
### Between Facts and Norms: An Author's Reflections
(1999)[16]

What an author has actually said in and with a book, is up to interpretation. An intelligent reader will almost always know better than the author himself. The author only knows what he *intended* to say. With *Droit et Democratie* I think I have made specific contributions to six topics:

I.   The form and function of modern law;
II.  The relation between law and morality;
III. The relation between human rights and popular sovereignty;
IV.  The epistemic function of democracy;
V.   The central role of public communication in mass-democracy;
VI.  The debate about competing paradigms of law.

### I. The Form and Function of Modern Law

The first topic—form and function of modern law—issues from a sociological controversy about the function of modern law. The question is whether modern law is just a means for the exercise of administrative or political power or whether law still functions as a medium of social integration. In this regard I side with Emile Durkheim and Talcott Parsons against Max Weber: Today legal norms are what is left from a crumbled cement of society; if all other mechanisms of social integration are exhausted, law yet provides some means for keeping together complex and centrifugal societies that otherwise would fall into pieces. Law stands in as a substitute for the failures of other integrative mechanisms—markets and administrations, or values, norms, and face-to-face communications. This integrative capacity can be explained by the fact that legal norms are particularly functional in virtue of an interesting combination of formal properties: Modern law is cashed out in terms of subjective rights; it is enacted or positive as well as enforced or coercive law; and though modern law requires from its addressees nothing more than normconformative behavior, it must nevertheless meet the expectation of legitimacy so that it is at least open to the people to follow norms, if they like, out of respect for the law. It is easy to see why this legal form fits the requirements of modern societies:

Modern law is supposed to grant an equal distribution of *subjective rights* for everybody. Such liberties function as a protective belt for each person's pursuit of her own preferences and value-orientations and thereby fits the pattern of decentralized decision-making (which is in particular required for market-societies).

Modern law is *enacted* by a political legislators and confers with its form a binding authority to flexible programs and their implementation. It thus fits the particular mode of operation of the modern administrative state.

Modern law is *enforced* by the threat of state sanctions and grants, in the sense of an average compliance, the "legality" of behavior. It thus fits the situation of pluralist societies where legal norms are no longer embedded in an encompassing ethos shared by the population as a whole.

Modern law grants, however, stability of behavioral expectations only on the condition that people can accept enacted and enforceable norms at the same time as *legitimate* norms that *deserve* intersubjective recognition. Law thus fits to a posttraditional moral consciousness of citizens who are no longer disposed to follow commands, except for good reasons.

---

[16] [From (1999) 76 *Denver University L. R.* 937.]

## II. The Relation Between Law and Morality

The second topic—the relation between law and morality—issues from the controversy between legal positivism and natural rights theories about the question, how to explain the specific validity of law. Both positions face well-known and complementary difficulties. To put it in a nutshell: positivists, on one side, conceive legal norms as binding expressions of the superior will of political authorities. Like legal realists, who treat legal norms just as the result of policydecisions, positivists cannot explain how legitimacy can spring from sheer legality. Both positivists and realists (including proponents of the CLS movement) refuse to recognize any claim to legitimacy stronger than the kind of legal validity that terminates in formally correct enactment and efficient enforcement. Proponents of natural right theories, on the other side, derive the legitimacy of positive law immediately from a higher moral law. Positive law here figures as the lowest level in a hierarchy of laws, the top of which is occupied by natural law, which is explained in metaphysical or religious terms. Even if we leave problems of foundationalism aside, such an assimilation of law to morality blurs important differences between the two. Whereas moral norms primarily tell us, what we *ought* to do and what we *owe* each other, modern law is in the first place designed for the distribution of individual *liberties*—for the determination of private spheres where everybody is free to do what one wants to do. Moral rights, on the other hand, are derivative from other people's *duties* towards us, whereas in law, rights are duties, since legal duties only result from mutual constraints of equally granted liberties.

The complementary weaknesses of both positions leads us to the conclusion that legitimacy of law must not be assimilated to moral validity, nor should law be completely separated from morality. Law is best understood as a functional *complement* of a weak posttraditional morality, which is, beyond in-stitutionalization, only rooted in the conscience of the individual person. From an observer's point of view, modern law can therefore compensate for the uncertainties of moral conscience that usually works well only in the context of face-to-face contacts; whereas coercive law has an impact far beyond that. At the same time, positive law does not lose all moral content, at least not as long as it meets the legitimacy requirement.

## III. The Relation Between Human Rights and Popular Sovereignty

The third topic—the relation between human rights and popular sovereignty— issues from a longstanding controversy about the source of legitimacy. Because of the positivity of law, we must distinguish here the role of *authors* who make (and adjudicate) law, from that of *addressees* who are subjects of established law. The autonomy of the person, which in the moral domain is all of one piece, so to speak, appears in the legal domain only in the dual form of private *and* public autonomy. These two elements—the liberties of the subject of private law and the political autonomy of citizens—must be mediated in such a way that the one form of autonomy is not impeded by the other one. This is to say that legal persons can be autonomous only insofar as they can understand themselves, in the exercise of their civic rights, as authors of just those norms, which they are supposed to obey as addressees. However, this intuition has never been quite convincingly explicated in Political Theory.

The republican tradition, which goes back to Aristotle and the political humanism of the Renaissance, has always given the public autonomy of citizens' priority over the prepolitical liberties of private persons. Liberalism, on the other hand, has always invoked the danger of tyrannical majorities and postulated the priority of the rule of law, as guaranteed by negative freedoms. Human rights were supposed to provide legitimate barriers that prevented the sovereign will of the people from encroaching on inviolable sphere of individual freedom. But both views are one-sided. The rule of law, expressed in the idea of human rights, must neither be merely imposed on the sovereign legislator as an external barrier, nor be instrumentalized as a functional requisite for the democratic process. In order to articulate this intuition properly, it helps to view the democratic process from the standpoint of discourse theory.

At this point I cannot summarize the complex arguments for the interdependence of both, human rights and popular sovereignty. Let me only make two remarks. The first suggestion is to conceive human rights as what is necessary for the legal institutionalization of the democratic process of self-legislation. That is, however, prima facie plausible only for those civil rights—the rights of communication and participation—that empower citizens to exercise their political autonomy. The suggestion is less plausible for the classical human rights that guarantee citizens' private autonomy. So it is further suggested to analyze the very grammar of the legal language which citizens must speak when they of the legal language which citizens must speak when they wish to act *as* citizens. In other words, the legal code as such must be available as soon as we would wish to legally institutionalize a democratic process. We know from the analysis of the legal form, however, that we cannot establish any kind of legal order without creating placeholders for legal persons who are bearers of individual rights— whichever right these may be. But providing subjective rights means per se to provide a guarantee for private autonomy. This then is the core of the argument: Without basic rights that secure the private autonomy of citizens, there also would not be any medium for the legal institutionalization of the conditions under which these citizens could make use of their public autonomy. Thus private and public autonomy mutually presuppose each other in such a way that neither human rights nor popular sovereignty can claim primacy over its counterpart.

### IV. The Epistemic Function of Democracy

The fourth topic—the epistemic function of democracy—issues from the question why we may expect the legitimacy of law to emerge from the democratic process at all. The discourse-approach explains the legitimacy-generating force of the process with a democratic procedure that grounds a presumption of the rational acceptability of outcomes. Norms owe their legitimacy to a kind of recognition that is based on rationally motivated agreement. This assumption is stated in terms of the discourse principle: "Only those norms are valid to which all persons possibly affected could agree as participants in rational discourses." The contractarian tradition up to Rousseau and Kant has also referred to "reason" as a post-metaphysical base for legal and political orders. This mentalist conception of reason is now translated, however, in pragmatist terms and spelled out in terms of practices of reason-giving, *i.e.* as conditions for deliberation. Rational discourse is supposed to be public and inclusive, to grant equal communication rights for participants, to require sincerity and to diffuse any kind of force other than the forceless force of the better argument. This communicative structure is expected to create a deliberative space for the mobilization of the best available contributions for the most relevant topics.

"Deliberation" is broadly understood here and covers a wide range of reasons. Depending on empirical, technical, prudential, ethical, moral or legal reasons we distinguish different types of rational discourse and corresponding forms of communication. The rational acceptability of legal norms does not depend only, and not even primarily on moral considerations, but on other kinds of reasoning as well, including processes of fair bargaining. Compromises form, after all, the core of politics. Anyway, this encompassing notion of "deliberation" is to pave the way for a process-conception of legitimation. Legitimation depends on an appropriate legal institutionalization of those forms of rational discourse and fair bargaining that ground the presumption of the rational acceptability of outcomes. Deliberative politics is thus wedded to a complex notion of procedural legitimacy. There are three different kinds of procedures intertwined in the democratic process: first, the purely cognitive procedures of (various forms of) deliberation; secondly, decision procedures that link decisions to preceding deliberations (in normal cases the majority rule); finally, legal procedures which specify and regulate in a binding manner the material, social and temporal aspects of opinion— and will-formation processes.

## V. The Central Role of Public Communication in Mass-Democracy

The fifth topic—the central role of public communication—is an obvious implication of the discourse-approach. From a normative point of view, structural features of political communication are more important than individual properties, such as the capacity for rational choice or good intentions or appropriate motivations. Public communication must be inclusive and selective at the same time; it must be channeled in such a way, that relevant topics come up, interesting contributions and reliable information come in, and good arguments or fair compromises decide on what comes out. This view is sufficiently abstract to bridge the gap between the normative idea of self-legislation and the stubborn facts of complex societies.

In virtue of the discourse-approach we can now disconnect the idea of popular sovereignty from its traditional bearer, "the people", which is a notion too concrete for present circumstances. On the normative level, another conception takes the place of the "sovereignty of the people": the communicative freedom of citizens, which is supposed to issue in a public use of reason. Collective actors of civil society who are sufficiently sensitive and inclusive, can both be instrumental for the perception problems of society-wide relevance, translate them into public issues and thus generate, through various networks, the "influence" of public opinions. But such "influence" is transformed into "power" only by an interaction of the informal and diffuse communications flows of the public sphere at large with formally organized opinion- and will-formation processes first embodied in the parliamentary and the judiciary complex. "Communicative power" is produced according to the democratic procedures of elected and deliberating bodies and then, in accordance with legislative programs and court decisions, transformed into the "administrative power" of the executive agencies, available for the purpose of implementation. This is, of course, only the normatively prescribed image from which the real circuit of power widely deviates. But it is an image that allows us at least to connect the normative self-understanding or constitutional democracy with its real practices.

## VI. The Debate About Competing Paradigms of Law

The last topic—the introduction of a new, proceduralist paradigm of law—issues from the hopeless competition between the two received legal paradigms, the liberal and the welfare-state paradigm. The *liberal paradigm* counts on an economic society that is institutionalized through private law, above all through property rights and contractual freedom, and thus left to the spontaneous workings of the market. If, however, the legal capacity of private persons to own, acquire or sell property is supposed to guarantee social justice, then everybody must enjoy equal opportunities for making effective use of equally distributed legal powers. Since capitalist societies generally do not meet this requirement, proponents of the *welfare-state paradigm* argue for compensating growing inequalities in economic power, property, income and living conditions. Private law must be substantially specified and social rights must be re-introduced. On the other hand, unintended effects of welfare-paternalism indicate limitations of this alternative, too. It turns out that the traditional debate on deregulated markets versus state regulations is too narrowly focused on private autonomy, while the internal relation between *private and public* autonomy drops out of the picture. Between the two received paradigms, the only controversial issue is whether private autonomy is best guaranteed straightaway by negative freedoms, or whether the conditions for private autonomy must be secured through the provision of welfare entitlements.

One way out of this impasse is indicated by a third, a *proceduralist paradigm* that crystallizes neither around the private competitor on markets nor around the private client of welfare bureaucracies, but has its focus on the citizen who participates in political opinion- and will-formation. For private legal subjects cannot enjoy equal liberties if they themselves do not in advance exercise their civic autonomy in common in order to specify, which interests are at stake and which standards of evaluation are justified in the light of which cases should be treated alike and different cases differently. Citizens can only arrive at fair regulations for their private status if they make an appropriate use of their political rights in the public domain. They must be willing to participate in the struggle over the public relevance, the interpretation and evaluation of their own needs, before legislators and judges can even know what it in each case means to treat like cases alike. In highly differentiated societies with an intransparent diversity of interests, it is an epistemic requirement for the equal distribution of liberties for everybody that those citizens affected and concerned first get themselves the chance to push their cases in the public, and articulate as justify those aspects which are relevant for equal treatment in typical situations. Briefly, the private autonomy of equally entitled citizens can be secured only insofar as citizens actively exercise their civic autonomy. [pp. 937–942]

## MAURICIO GARCÍA VILLEGAS
### On Pierre Bourdieu's Legal Thought
(2004)

Pierre Bourdieu showed remarkably little interest in the study of law. His thought in this area is fragmentary and incomplete. Disciples, followers, and commentators of Bourdieu manifest the same lack of interest regarding the legal phenomena. In the United States, for example, although references to his work are common in studies of law and society[17], in depth analyses on Bourdieu's legal thought by either sociologists or jurists are absent. In France, scholars interested in his legal contributions are no more than a handful of academics, who try to apply his theory to the study of specific legal areas in a somewhat hit-and-miss

---

[17] Above all in those that take a cultural approach: this is the case of Legal Consciousness Studies (on this see Mauricio GARCIA VILLEGAS, "Symbolic Power Without Symbolic Violence?", *Florida Law Review*, 55 (1), 2003, p. 157–189: ID., "Symbolic Power Without Symbolic Violence?, Critical Comments on Legal Consciousness Studies in USA", *Droit et Société*, 53, 2003, p. 137–161).

fashion[18]. Should we then conclude that Bourdieu's ideas are not important to the study of law? I think not. The fact that the law is a marginal topic in Bourdieu's work can better be explained by the uncertain nature of the communications amongst French sociologists and jurists and the relative marginality of the sociolegal perspective in France than by the importance of Bourdieu's legal ideas to the two disciplines. Bourdieu himself recognized on several occasions that he had not dedicated the time and effort to this subject that its importance warranted.

In this essay I propose to discuss Bourdieu's contribution to the sociology of law from a comparative perspective, taking advantage of my position as an external observer to the French sociolegal debate. The principal idea that I wish to develop here is the following: Bourdieu's contribution to theorizing legal phenomena needs to be understood through an explication of the disciplinary debates amongst sociologists and lawyers in France; these debates both locate his theory and enable us better to understand the scope and type of discourse that he employs. The paper is divided into three parts. In the first section, I discuss some ideas that I believe are fundamental to the writings of Bourdieu on law. In the second part, I try to locate his thought within the theory of law and in social theory and to show its sociological roots and its sociolegal limitations. Finally, I will discuss the disciplinary squabbling amongst French sociologists and jurists, comparing their situation to that of colleagues in other countries, and I will explain how these misunderstandings had a significant influence on Bourdieu's work.

## *I. Bourdieu and the Law*

A complete exegesis of Bourdieu's legal thought would require the explication of a series of theoretical assumptions proper to his social theory that I lack the space to embark upon in these pages. I will limit myself to the explanation of one point that I consider essential to Bourdieu's conception of the legal field as well as better to understand the French debate that his thought on the question of law has provoked. This point concerns Bourdieu's attempt to construct a theory of legal practice that could transcend the subject/object dichotomy.

In Bourdieu, culture cannot be understood outside the economic conditions in which subjects act. Cultural tastes are never disinterested and can only be understood by starting from a theory of symbolic power[19]. Culture is a set of

---

[18]   In the United States, Patricia Ewick and Susan Silbey, *The Common Place of Law: Stories from Everyday Life*, Chicago, University of Chicago Press, 1998. In theoretical studies of sociology of law, Bourdieu is frequently cited to justify a theoretical framework (see for instance: Ruth Margaret Buchanan, "Context, Continuity, and Difference in Poverty Law Scholarship", *University of Miami Law Review*, 48, 1994, p. 999–1062; Michael W. McCann, *Rights at Work: Pay Equity Reform and the Politics of Legal Mobilization*, Chicago, University of Chicago Press, 1994; Sally Engle Merry, *Getting Justice and Getting Even: Legal Consciousness among Working-Class Americans*, Chicago, University of Chicago Press, 1990). For a general assessment see Mauricio Garcia Villegas, "Symbolic Power Without Symbolic Violence?", *op. cit.* In France, perhaps the best known repository of the ideas of Bourdieu on the legal field is Dezalay (Yves Dezalay, Austin Sarat and Susan Silbey, "D'une démarche contestataire à un savoir méritocratique. Élément pour une histoire sociale de la sociologie juridique américaine", *Actes de la recherche en sciences sociales*, 78, 1989, p. 79–90; Yves Dezalay and David Trubek, "La restructuración global y el derecho", *Pensamiento Jurídico*, 1, 1997 p. 5–41);

[19]   According to Swartz, interpreting Bourdieu: "If his theory of practices extends the idea of interest to culture, then his theory of symbolic power extends culture to the realm of interest with the claim that all forms of power require legitimation" (David Swartz, *Culture and Power : The Sociology of Pierre Bourdieu*, Chicago, University of Chicago Press, 1997, p. 89).

dispositions internalized by individuals through a process of socialization that constitute schemas of perception and understanding of the world. These internalized dispositions work only to the extent that there is a certain correspondence with the hierarchical order that they represent. According to Bourdieu, "*il existe une correspondance entre les structure sociales et les structures mentales, entre les divisions objectives du monde social—notamment en dominants et dominés dans les différent champs—et les principes de vision et division que les agents leur appliquent*"[20]. This correspondence fulfills essential political functions in society. Thus symbolic systems are not only tools of knowledge but, first and foremost, instruments of domination. A central objective of Bourdieu's work is to show how culture and social class correlate. In general terms Bourdieu's sociological theory asks the following question: how is it possible that hierarchically based systems of domination persist and reproduce themselves through social practices ? Bourdieu views society as a stratified and differentiated space in which individuals struggle to defend positions and interests. Now, domination, more than something linked to the use of physical violence, is articulated through, and experienced through, the use of symbolic violence. The ones who are dominant in society do not achieve that position merely through possession of economic capital. They also attain it thanks to the cultural capital that they possess and to the close connection between these two forms of capital. This articulation operates in such a way that the symbolic systems—through which we establish classifications and determine the essential categories of social inclusion and exclusion—have both a cognitive/social organization function[21] and also a political function of domination. The law is a good example of symbolic system.

The law is a social field—set of objective and historical relations between positions of social actors who struggle for power or capital—in which participants struggle over the appropriation of the symbolic power that is implicit in legal texts[22]. Thus, the law becomes a form *par excellence* of symbolic power—and of symbolic violence—given the possibilities possessed by its practitioners to create institutions and with them historical and political realities through a simple exercise of naming[23]. The internal dynamic of the field is associated with the question of domination. The potential of the law to establish classifications that are essential to the social order—legal/illegal, just/unjust, true/false—entails enormous political power. Legal authority is the privileged form of power, especially in terms of legitimate symbolic violence—monopolized by the State— which the State both produces and practices[24]. The use of the symbolic is an inherently violent practice to the extent to which it imposes meaning on the world and on social relations in which economic and political power lose their original arbitrary and exclusive connotation and appear as something normal and acceptable.

But the law can not be reduced to a tool for political domination. In understanding the symbolic force of law or its legitimizing effect, we must avoid both those materialistic accounts that see only power relations in the explanation of law, as well as idealistic ones that explain it through the general recognition of the universal values expressed in its norms. "We can no longer ask whether power

[20] Pierre BOURDIEU, *La noblesse d'État. Grandes écoles et esprit de corps*, Paris, Minuit, 1989, p. 7.

[21] The cognitive structures which social agents implement in their practical knowledge of the social world are internalized "embodied" social structure (see Pierre BOURDIEU, *La distinction : critique sociale du jugement*, Paris, Minuit, 1979).

[22] Pierre BOURDIEU, "The Force of Law: Toward a Sociology of the Juridical Field", *Hastings Law Journal*, 38 (5), 1986, p. 814–853 (p. 817–818).

[23] *Ibid.*, p. 839.

[24] This idea of symbolic power is also usefully explored by Georges BALANDIER, *Le pouvoir sur scenes*, Paris, Balland, 1992: and Harry PROSS, *Violencia social de los simbolos*, Barcelona. Anthropos, 1989.

comes from above or from below", says Bourdieu with reference to the debate between critical and doctrinal explanations of law[25]. Bourdieu counters the materialistic accounts, acknowledging the existence of an autonomous social universe capable of the production and reproduction, by the logic of its specific functioning, of a legal corpus relatively independent of external constraints[26]. However, he also recognizes that, the legal field has a smaller degree of autonomy than others, such as the artistic or the literary fields, given the essential role it plays in social reproduction.

Since the law is a social field in which a great deal of social and symbolic capital resides, it is not surprising that inside the field there are fierce clashes among its members for the possession, and distribution, of this capital. From this point of view, the theoretical debates inside the legal academy—for instance between formalists and anti-formalists in the early 20th century in United States, or between *iuspositivism* and *iusnaturalism* in 20th century-Europe—seek to consolidate a specific possession-position-distribution of the symbolic capital that is at play both inside and outside the field. Inside the legal field, actors located in different positions and endowed with different dispositions, fight for the chance to pronounce the final word about the meaning and ultimate scope of the law. Such a struggle is not only intellectual but also political, given the fact that the most legal debate has direct implications for the distribution of power and goods that occurs in the political field. Controlling the law is important to social control[27]. This is why the struggle also takes place outside the field.

The conventional idea that the legal culture of countries, with its debates, its authors, its schools and internal movements, is sufficient to explain the origin, evolution and actual status of the legal traditions and legal practices found therein is seen to be problematic. That explanation ignores the strong connections that exist between the culture and the social and material conditions in which it prospers. "*Il n'est pas trop de dire qu'il* fait *le monde social, mais à condition de ne pas oublier qu'il est fait par lui*[28]." Structures limit and mold perceptions, discourses, and practices from which social reality is constructed. The subject is as much of the world as the world is subjectivized, says Bourdieu. In short, the internal struggle among legal actors for the appropriation of symbolic power has not been independent of the political context in which it has taken place. Connections between the political and the legal field are multiple and mutually constitutive.

This does not mean, as some theories of the law have led us to believe, that knowledge of the material conditions in which the legal discussion takes place is sufficient to know the outcome. The legal field in its majesty, its rites, and its shrines is not amenable to being reduced merely to existing economic forces. It is not just a reflection of the material world[29]. Neither is the law pure erudition that can be detached from the social conditions in which it is found. These extremes ignore the existence of law understood as a social field that is relatively independent of external demands—the logic of which is determined, according to Bourdieu, by two factors:

> [...] *d'une part, par les rapports de force spécifiques qui lui confèrent sa structure et qui orientent les luttes de concurrence ou, plus précisément, les conflits de compétence dont il est*

---

[25] Pierre BOURDIEU, "The Force of Law: Toward a Sociology of the Juridical Field", *op. cit.*, p. 841.

[26] *Ibid.*, p. 816.

[27] So, for example, the legal delimitation of the right to property is also a response to poverty and social marginality.

[28] Pierre BOURDIEU, *op. cit.* note 25, p. 839.

[29] Evgency PASHUKANS, *Law and Marxism: A General Theory*, London, Ink Links, 1978.

*le lieu et, d'autre part, par la logique interne des œuvres juridiques qui délimitent à chaque moment l'espace des possibles, et, par là, l'univers des solutions proprement juridiques*[30].

## II. Social Theory and Legal Theory in the Writings of Bourdieu

The core concepts of Bourdieu's conception of law are found in his text "La force du droit", published in 1986[31], although elements appear scattered throughout his entire output[32]. One of the difficulties with this article is derived from the fact that in it Bourdieu utilizes critical arguments against legal theorists and sociologists alike, with the aim of making his diatribe against the jurists and the legal system more effective. In the course of outlining his legal conception, Bourdieu attacks both sociological and legal theories of law, and both conservative and progressive legal approaches. As a result it is difficult neatly to classify his thought. No legal perspective is privileged in the discussion: Felix Cohen and the realists appear in opposition to Kelsen and the positivists just as Kelsen and Luhmann are opposed to Althusser, and to E. P. Thompson, and that in a presentation of the juridical debate that seems to render all of them inadequate. This suggests that his theory both distances itself from the sociolegal currents or traditions, and also tries to attain a broader scope than that of a simple sociological critique of the legal science of jurists.

What Bourdieu terms a "rigorous science of law" (*une science rigoureuse du droit*) as opposed to a "legal science" (*science juridique*) is a critical explication of law from the field of sociology, that is to say, a *critical sociology of law*[33]. Above all, Bourdieu distances himself from the critical or progressive currents of legal thought that dominated France over much of the 20th century. Here I am referring basically to two: materialist perspectives, whether of a marxist (Althusser) or anthropological (Levi-Strauss) cast, and "social" or "communitarian" perspectives. Materialist approaches in large part found a home in the movement *Critique du droit*, created at the end of the seventies. The second, which I may term "social", found initial expression in the *Free Law Movement* represented by Eugen Ehrlich and Kantorowitz in Germany, and later in the work of Gurvitch in France[34]. According to this perspective, the law should be an expression of the interests and the existing patterns in communities; the official law then should be constructed "from below," out of the social realm.

The fact that Bourdieu's ideas on law could have some influence on the legal thought of lawyers, or so-called *science juridique* (legal science) could be important but it does not seem to be the essential point. It is true that very often, when

---

[30]  Pierre BOURDIEU, *op cit*, note 25, p. 816.

[31]  See note 25.

[32]  Above all in some chapters contained in Pierre BOURDIEU, *Choses dites*, Paris, Minuit, 1987, especially: "De la régle aux stratégies", "La codification" and "Espace social et pouvoir symbolique"; Pierre BOURDIEU, "Habitus, code et codification", *Actes de la recherche en sciences sociales*, 64, 1986, p. 40–44; and ID., "Les juristes, gardiens de l'hypocrisie collective", in François CHAZEL and Jacques COMMAILLE (sous la dir.), *Normes juridiques et régulation sociale*, Paris, LDGJ, 1991, p. 95–99.

[33]  In the sociology of law it is important to distinguish between at least two types of approaches. Some authors attempt to integrate law as one aspect of the general explication of the workings of society. This view was adopted by the classical sociological theorists and may be termed *sociology of law*. The second approach sets itself the task of explicating the law from a sociological perspective. The authors who are mining this vein generally consider themselves to be working in a current that is critical of formalist legal dogma. This second approach can be called *sociolegal theory*. On this see the classic distinction made by Renato Treves between "sociology in law" and "sociology on law" (Renato TREVES, "Two Sociologies of Law", *European Yearbook in Law and Society*, 1977).; see also Jacques COMMAILLE, "Sociologie juridique", in Denis ALLAND and Stéphane RIALS (sous la dir.), *Dictionnaire de la culture juridique*, Paris, PUF, 2003.

[34]  See Pierre BOURDIEU, *op cit*, note 25, English version p. 84.

Bourdieu refers to the law, he treats specific problems of legal theory—such as legal interpretation—but this does not mean that his aim is to construct a theory of law. Bourdieu wanted above all to construct a sociological explanation of law that was consistent with his theory of social fields, and particularly with his concept of *habitus*. Therefore, Bourdieu's theory should not be read, or at least not exclusively, from the starting point of legal science but rather from a sociological perspective. Stated more specifically, jurists who become interested in Bourdieu's work should first immerse themselves in his social and critical theory of rules and habitus, and from there explain subjects such as symbolic violence and the "hypocrisy" of jurists[35]. Only in this way can his pejorative statements about law and lawyers be assessed in their correct proportions. So, for example, Jacques Caillosse—in the article published in this journal—questions the coherency of Bourdieu's discourse in the following passage: "*Si l'opposition entre règles et régularités dont Bourdieu fait gros usage n'est en tant que telle en rien discutable, jusqu'où est-elle totalement compatible avec la réflexion qu'il esquisse par ailleurs sur la fatalité de l'interprétation juridique?*" There would be, according to Caillosse, "*une représentation démiurgique du Droit et du Législateur, totalement incompatible avec la théorie de l'interprétation*". Similarly, Violaine Roussel—essay also published in this volume—considers that Bourdieu's idea of formalization of the norms supposes a rigidity in legal practice that does not actually exist and thus should not be contrasted to the flexibility of habitus. It seems to me that the problem with these interpretations lies in the fact that they do not start from Bourdieu's social theory: they do not take into consideration the different meanings that Bourdieu gives to the word *norm* or *rule*: as social regularity or as legal norm.

The meaning of concepts such as rule, norm and habitus in Bourdieu's *théorie de la pratique* is a central point in his work, and for this reason it merits a detailed treatment. Let's begin by examining the following passage from *Choses dites*:

> *Le jeu social est réglé, il est le lieu de régularitès. Les choses s'y passent de façon régulière; les héritiers riches se marient réguliérement avec les cadettes riches [...]. Je peux dire que toute ma réflexion est partie de là: comment des conduites peuvent-elles être réglées sans être le produit de l'obéissance à des règles?*[36]

Bourdieu's idea was to construct a "model of the game which will not be the mere recording of explicit norms or a statement of regularities [...]". His purpose was to account for socially regular actions which cannot be explained, either as the result of obedience to rules, or as brute causality. Bourdieu rejects the notion of norm—understood as legal or moral commandment—with the intention of "*échapper aux naïvetés les plus grossières du juridisme qui tient les pratiques pour le produit de l'obéissance des normes*"[37]. Frédéric Ocqueteau and Francine Soubiran-Paillet are correct in suggesting that the rejection of rules – understood as commands that produce obedience – as an explanation of certain social regularities is a rejection that ought to be interpreted in the context of the ethnological debate that Bourdieu unleashed during the 1970s in his *Esquisse d'une théorie de la*

---

[35] Speaking of an article of Bourdieu (Pierre BOURDIEU, "Les juristes, gardiens de l'hypocrisie collective", *op. cit.*).

[36] Pierre BOURDIEU, *Choses dites, op. cit.*, p. 81.

[37] Pierre BOURDIEU. *Esquisse d'une théorie de la pratique*, précédé de *Trois études d'ethnologie kabyle*, Genève, Droz. 1972, p. 171.

*pratique*[38], and in which the concept of habitus was central[39]. In other terms Bourdieu's solution for this intermediate model between rules and norms was the concept of habitus. The habitus is

> [...] *un système de dispositions durables, structures structurées prédisposées à fonctionner comme structures structurantes, c'est-à-dire en tant que principe de génération et de structuration de pratiques et de représentation qui peuvent être objectivement "réglées" et "régulières" sans être en rien le produit de l'obéissance à des règles, objectivement adaptées a leur but sans supposer la visée consciente des fins et la maîtrise expresse des opérations nécessaires pour les atteindre et, étant tout cela, collectivement orchestrées sans être le produit de l'action organisatrice d'un chef d'orchestre*[40].

The concept of habitus then—always viewed within this sociological perspective of explication of social practices and their regularities—is intended to move beyond the institutionalized epidermis that makes up the legal rules by which persons behave or do not behave in a certain manner. As Jacques Bouveresse wrote: "As the habitus is not necessarily of a mental nature (there are forms of habitus which are simply corporeal) it is independent of any distinction between the conscious or unconscious, and it is not less independent of distinctions like that between the product of a simple causal constraint and an action that is "free" in that it escapes any constraints of this nature[41]." The habitus is then an intermediate concept between rules – in the legal sense – and causality or rules in a physical sense.

The pejorative sense in which Bourdieu often uses terms such as rule or norm finds its explanation in his structural theory of practice (*théorie structurelle de la pratique*) where he attempts to connect culture, structure, and practice. Norms are accorded this treatment, in the first place, because they are seen as obstacles to real knowledge of social practices, or in Bourdieu's own words for the knowledge of "the immanent principle to practice" that is to say, habitus. In the second place, the meaning and scope of norms is generally monopolized by jurists, the owners par excellence of symbolic violence in the society, through the so-called *science du droit*. For this reason Bourdieu speaks more disparagingly of lawyers than, for example, sports figures.

However, as outlined above, Bourdieu himself was careful not go too far in his condemnation of the legal sphere: "*La réaction contre le juridisme en sa forme ouverte ou masquée ne doit pas conduire à faire de l'habitus le principe exclusif de toute pratique, bien qu'il n'y a pas de pratique qui n'ait l'habitus à son principe*[42]." The legal rules are a type of substitute that intervenes when the habitus is incapable of fulfilling its regulatory functions. The law is, then, the exception whereas habitus is the rule[43]. Exceptions arise in moments of crisis in the habitus: "*On peut poser en loi générale que plus une situation est dangereuse, plus la pratique*

---

[38] Pierre BOURDIEU, *Outline of a Theory of Practice*, New York, Cambridge University Press, 1977.

[39] According to Ocqueteau and Soubiran-Paillet, in this debate Bourdieu attempts to differentiate his position from those of Radcliffe-Brown and Malinowski. For Radcliffe-Brown norms are what ensures order in society, and Malinowski's interest lay in individual choices and the way individuals act to achieve their own interests (Frédéric OCQUETEAU and Francine SOUBIRAN-PAILLET, "Champ juridique, juristes et règle de droit: une sociologie entre disqualification et paradoxe", *op. cit.*; chapters published in English in *Outline of a Theory of Practice*).

[40] Pierre BOURDIEU, *Esquisse d'une théorie de la pratique, op. cit.*, p. 175.

[41] Jacques BOUVERESSE, "Rules, Dispositions, and the Habitus", in Richard SHUSTERMAN (ed.), *Bourdieu: A Critical Reader*, Oxford, Blackwell, 2000, p. 53.

[42] Pierre BOURDIEU, *Esquisse d'une théorie de la pratique, op. cit.*, p. 25.

[43] This of course is particularly clear in those societies in which there is no developed legal order, such as, for example, among the Kabyle people.

*tend à être codifiée. Le degré de codification varie comme le degré de risque*[44]." Here we see the virtue of codifying a rule which is that it allows, like all rationalization, "*une économie d'invention, d'improvisation, de création*"[45]. But the form or the codification does not operate simply through its technical efficiency in clarifying or rationalizing, according to Bourdieu:

> *Il y a une efficacité proprement symbolique de la forme. La violence symbolique, dont la réalisation par excellence est sans doute le droit, est une violence qui s'exerce, si l'on peut dire, dans les formes, en mettant des formes. Mettre des formes, c'est donner à une action ou à un discours la forme qui est reconnue comme convenable, légitime, approuvée [...]. La force de la forme [...] est cette force proprement symbolique qui permet à la force de s'exercer pleinement en se faisant méconnaître en tant que force et en se faisant reconnaître, approuver, accepter, par le fait de se présenter sous les apparences de l'universalité – celle de la raison ou de la morale*[46].

Hence, for Bourdieu, the law is not reducible to a question of interests—as Weber or Marx thought—just as interests are not reducible to law. Hence, the first lines in his article "La force du droit", in which Bourdieu tries to construct a relatively autonomous legal sphere between the positivist formalism of Hans Kelsen, in which the subjective view dominates, and the materialism of Louis Althusser, in which the objectivist perspective does. As I said before, we are here assessing Bourdieu's challenge to construct a theory of legal practice that could transcend the subject/object dichotomy. It is:

> [...] *un univers social relativement indépendant par rapport aux demandes externes, à l'intérieur duquel se produit et s'exerce l'autorité juridique, forme par excellence de la violence symbolique légitime dont le monopole appartient à l'État et qui peut s'assortir de l'exercice de la force physique*[47].

While Bourdieu is interested in the law as a social field in which an important part of the mechanisms of social production and reproduction are defined and executed, Caillosse is interested in the law itself and the possibilities of constructing a science of law. In his analysis of Bourdieu, Caillosse emphasizes, among other points, one that, in my view, is somewhat secondary : his pejorative view of lawyers and of their claims to possess their own rational and politically neutral truth. Caillosse could be correct in his complaint about Bourdieu's negative bias in that it is true that the law is something more than a symbolic pantomime maintaining the political power of certain social interests. However, in my view Bourdieu's emphasis is more rhetorical than analytical; Bourdieu is trying to deconstruct the myths of the so-called *science juridique*, insofar as the law is a bastion of symbolic violence that allows the reproduction of the structure of social domination and the perception of the legitimacy of that process.

The above does not mean that Bourdieu's conceptualization of the law is invulnerable to criticism. The theory of Bourdieu can be challenged either as a critical theory or as a flawed critical theory. My reservations, which I think I share with Professor Caillosse, address the second point; that is, they refer to the inadequacies of its critical proposition. Although as stated above, the sociological theory of Bourdieu on law has great explantory power and represents a significant advance over both materialist and communitarian critical theories, it has also important limitations. The emphasis on symbolic efficacy of law as an expression of legitimated state violence gives one the impression that the law is part of a hegemonic monolithic institutional order and that the fissures in this order are

---

[44]  Pierre BOURDIEU, *Choses dites, op. cit.*, p. 96.
[45]  *Ibid.*, p. 103.
[46]  *Ibid.*
[47]  Pierre BOURDIEU, "La force du droit", *op. cit.*, p. 3; English version p. 816.

insignificant. This view of the state and of law has obscures the emancipatory potential which occasionally arises in the discourse on rights[48].

This statist and monopolistic outlook on the law is closely linked to French history and to the relationship of law and political power in that history. Since the French Revolution the law is conceived of as a matter of legislation, a fact which led to a clear separation between, on the one hand, legal doctrine aiming at being formalistic and "scientific," and on the other hand, legal critique or sociolegal perspective, being political and ideological. Critical or anti-formalistic perspectives in France, and to a lesser extend on the European continent, usually dismiss legal autonomy and overestimate the sociological and political dimension of law.

In the Anglo-Saxon tradition, the role of the judge encouraged an interpretivist and political understanding of law. Whereas, in England and USA the term *law* relates to political power and does not necessarily include a concept of *right*—see for instance John Locke or the American Declaration of Independence—, in Europe terms like *droit, recht, diritto, derecho* had a larger meaning, including what was right. This is why critical view in Europe tends to get rid of the *law* in order to highlight rights as social rights not legal rights.

For anti-formalists and socio-legal movements in France – as well as in Latin American countries – law was seen as *political power* that ought to be denounced and replaced by another power and another law. This conception is part of a long European tradition rooted in the beginnings of the absolute monarchy in France at the dawn of the 17th century[49]. According to this, the law is the expression of state sovereignty embodied in the monarch. The French Revolution did not break with this tradition. On the contrary, it accentuated it by proposing the idea— initially put forward by Sieyès and later by Robespierre – of popular sovereignty. The writings of Rousseau, interpreted by Sieyès, did not leave much room for political critique through law.

In short, Bourdieu's critique of law should be understood as an attack on a particular type of political domination through law that had a particularly successful moment in French political and institutional history. That model, nowadays, is in crisis, in France and throughout the world, or at least it no longer has the force that it once had. This does not necessarily mean that domination is less effective; simply that it utilizes multifaceted and frequently opposed conditions. In the specific case of the law, Bourdieu's theory does not enable us to understand the intricate problems of inter-legality and legal pluralism that occur in contemporary societies as an outgrowth of the confluence of national, local and transnational orders that can be and often are mutually exclusive. Bourdieu had a view of the legal field that was too nationally rooted, as authors like Dezalay and Garth have assumed the task of disproving through their own Bourdieu's theory of social fields.

## III. Bourdieu's Approach to the Disagreements between Lawyers and Sociologists

One of the first surprises for researchers new to the sociolegal debate in France is the enormous importance that disciplinary differences between jurists and sociologists assume in this country. In general terms, these disagreements have been fueled by political-cultural factors: opposing perceptions of the world owing

---

[48] See Michael McCANN and Tracy MARCH, "Law and Everyday Forms of Resistance: A Socio-Political Assessment", in Austin SARAT and Susan SILBEY (eds.), *Studies in Law, Politics, and Society*, London, JAI Press, 1995; Michael McCANN, "Resistance, Reconstruction, and Romance in Legal Scholarship", *Law and Society Review*, 26 (4), 1992, p. 733–749: Boaventura DE SOUSA SANTOS, "Oppositional Postmodernism and Globalization", *Law and Social Inquiry*, 23 (1), 1998, p. 121–139.

[49] On this point, see for instance Jean VAN HOUTTE, "La sociologie du droit ou les limites d'une science", *Droit et Société*, 3, 1986, p. 171–186.

to the social and institutional emphases of the two profession; differentiation between lawyers and sociologists in terms of hierarchal social status which leads to conflicting political opinions, etc.[50]. Of course this does not happen only in France; different cultural and political sensibilities characterize the legal and sociological communities in other countries as well. However, what in other countries is a difference in the focus, in France is almost antipathy. I will use Bourdieu's social theory to assess this point.

The clash between lawyers and sociologists in France may be associated with the type of legal doctrine created out of the French Revolution, and the strength with which lawyers exert the monopoly of legal interpretation inside this legal doctrine. Let me explain. In each legal tradition different protagonists of the legal debate—judges, legislators, and professors—have attained different positions and amount of power. The contrast between Common Law and Civil Law jurisdictions is rooted in the political and social history of England and the continent. Since 1200 England has possessed a unified legal system called, for this reason, common law. This is even more important if we take into consideration the fact that France reached the stage of one code of laws for the whole realm just before the Revolution of 1789 and Germany accomplished the same task in the 19th century[51]. Codification on the continent was the response, brought about by the Enlightenment, to a great need for rationalization and organization. English lawyers never felt such a need. Since feudal times the King of England had been able to organize and centralize judicial practice so the local jurisdiction and feudal courts diminished in importance.

In France, efforts aiming at the consolidation of a unified legal system came about with the creation of the absolutist state in the 16th century[52]. But the French legal system was not really unified until the end of the Revolution, when the Civil Code was put in place. Since the Revolution, legislation is alleged to be the source of the legal system whereas the role of the judiciary is relegated to the task of mechanical application. Not only did the law acquire a great deal of formality and rationality but also there was a clear separation between the political function of creation – corresponding to the legislators – and the technical function of adjudication, which was supposed to be driven by free value judgment[53]. This is why the legal mainstream never accepted the limitation on the autonomy of the law vis-à-vis social facts and political powers. The main debate vexing legal scholars pitted scholars supporting legal positivism against those advocating natural law. It was framed to answer the question of whether or not the legal system was autonomous from fundamental values, not from social values or constitutional values.

In short, the dominance of professors and lawmakers in the process of fostering autonomy in the French legal system favored a formalistic type of legal science, divorced from practice, and self-sufficient. This in turn accentuated the importance of the symbolic capital earned by protagonists in the legal field, individuals whose fate was closely tied to that of the dominant interests. This particular historical formation not only created a type of legal critique that reduced law to political manipulation, as explained above, but also established epistemological

---

[50] André-Jean ARNAUD, *Le droit trahi par la sociologie*, Paris, LGDJ, coll. "Droit et Société. Recherches et travaux", 1998; Jacques COMMAILLE, "La sociologie du droit en France. Les ambiguités d'une spécialisation", *Sociologia del diritto*, 16 (2), 1989, p. 19–42.

[51] R. C. VAN CAENEGEM, *Judges, Legislators and Professors: Chapters in European Legal History*, Cambridge, Cambridge University Press, 1987, p. 94.

[52] Perry ANDERSON, *El Estado Absolutista*, Madrid, Siglo Veintiuno Editores, 1979.

[53] A different development took place in America over the course of the 19th century, with the consolidation of the idea that judges make a significant portion of the law. The explanation of this trend had to do with the history of judges in America and their relation to political power. On this point see R. C. VAN CAENEGEM, *Judges, Legislators and Professors*, *op. cit.*

barriers to communication between sociologists and lawyers. It is important to bear in mind that Bourdieu writes in this very particular French context, and therefore it is also important to understand his theory from that context.

## Conclusion

In this essay I have tried to bring a historical and comparative perspective to the debates on law and society in France and particularly to the assessment of Bourdieu's conception of the legal field within this debate. My first point has been that such an assessment should be contextualized in the disciplinary disputes and prejudices reigning between sociologists and lawyers, which have been determined by the history of legal doctrine and legal formalism in France. Because Bourdieu's view of the law did not escape this disciplinary dustup, it is useful to put his thought in context, beginning from the particular features of the legal field that he had in mind.

In the second place, criticisms of Bourdieu's thought on law are often launched from the theory of law (*jurisprudence*) and thus tend to underestimate the importance of his social theory and especially his idea of habitus, to the comprehension and correct appraisal of his contribution on legal phenomena.

In the third place, the sociolegal debate in France frequently hides a deeper and more fundamental debate between *consensus* and *conflict* theories, which likewise implicates a division between progressive and conservative theories. Generally speaking, the true debate on the sociological meaning of law—and this is what Bourdieu's work takes up, and not a science of law—is determined by theoretical presuppositions on social theories, *i.e.* the author's position on a theoretical spectrum on which these two theories are at the extremes[54]. So, for example, lawyer's reservations about the idea that the law is a particularly efficient form of symbolic violence exerted legitimately by the state, originate—mostly unconsciously—in a sort of consensus, or liberal, conception of society rather than in a legal conception.

Finally, the critical and disciplinary emphasis in Bourdieu's thought on the law obscures the political complexity of law in contemporary society and, particularly, the ambiguous nature of rights as tools for social emancipation. Although they generally operate to bolster state legitimacy (symbolic efficacy) they also have the potential to be appropriated by social movements and to serve as a political weapon against hegemonic power. Bourdieu's lack of acknowledgement of this complexity is closely linked to the French history of rights and the political role that they have filled. Nevertheless, Bourdieu's critical theory represents an advance in comparison to other critical theories, which, in France, have basically been related to the work of Durkheim or Marx. Pierre Lascoumes, for example, has argued that those countries in which legal sociology developed under the influence of Durkheim—such as France, Belgium, and Spain—created a positivist legal sociology that little by little lost its independence from law[55]. On the other hand, the countries influenced by Max Weber's legal sociology—Anglo-Saxon countries, Germany, and Italy—put more stress on interpretation and were more flexible in epistemological terms, which facilitated its development. The scholarly work of Pierre Bourdieu may represent a third path—closer perhaps to Weber than to Durkheim—with the potential to move the studies of law and society ahead. But of course these ideas deserve more time to be developed.

---

[54] On the concept of theoretical presupposition see Jeffrey ALEXANDER, *Twenty Lectures*, New York, Columbia University Press, 1987.

[55] Jacques COMMAILLE, "The Law and Science: Dialectics Between the Prince and the Maidservant", *Law and Policy*, 10 (2/3), 1983, p. 253–265.

# 10

# AMERICAN REALISM

## The "Revolt Against Formalism"[1]

In the nineteenth and in the early years of the twentieth century, laissez-faire was the dominant creed in America. This creed was associated, in the intellectual sphere, with a certain attachment to what has been called "formalism" in philosophy and the social sciences. This was marked by a reverence for the role of logic and mathematics and *a priori* reasoning as applied to philosophy, economics and jurisprudence, with but little urge to link these empirically to the facts of life. Yet empirical science and technology were increasingly dominating American society and with this development arose an intellectual movement in favour of treating philosophy and the social sciences, and even logic itself, as empirical studies not rooted in abstract formalism. In America this movement was associated with such figures as William James and Dewey in philosophy and logic, Veblen in economics, Beard and Robinson in historical studies, and Mr. Justice Holmes in jurisprudence.[2] It is important to note that this movement[3] was especially hostile to the so-called British empirical school derived from Hume, and to which Bentham, Austin and Mill adhered. For while it is true that these thinkers were positivist and anti-metaphysical they were for the anti-formalists not empirical enough, since they were associated with *a priori* reasoning not based on actual study of the facts, such as Mill's formal logic and his reliance on an abstract "economic man," Bentham's hedonic calculus of pleasures and pains, and the analytical approach to jurisprudence derived from Austin.[4] They were particularly critical of the ahistorical approach of the English utilitarians. Nor, unlike the sociologists of Pound's persuasion, were they interested

---

[1] See the admirable account of this development in Morton G. White's *Social Thought in America: The Revolt Against Formalism*. The case for formalism is put by E. Weinrib (1988) 97 Yale L.J. 949 (and *The Idea of Private Law* (1995)); R. Summers, *Form and Function in a Legal System* (2006); and A. Scalia, *A Matter of Interpretation* (1997).

[2] "It is fair to say that 'the revolt against formalism' was an important part of the general intellectual climate that fostered [the Realists'] approach," *per* Twining, *Karl Llewellyn and the Realist Movement* (1973), p. 9. For literary parallels see Hopkins (1983) 4 Pace L. R. 29 (written in 1931).

[3] See J. Diggins, *The Promise of Pragmatism* (1994) for an assessment.

[4] Thus Holmes said of Austin's definition of law (*ante*, 291) that it was "not satisfactory from a philosophical point of view" (see H. C. Shriver, *Holmes: Notices and Letters* (1936), p. 21).

to borrow from Bentham such abstract analyses of society as his doctrine of conflicting human interests. What these writers in their various fields were concerned to emphasise was the need to enlarge knowledge empirically, and to relate it to the solution of the practical problems of man in society. Hence pragmatism attempted to link truth with practical success in solving problems, and in its more developed form of instrumentalism, Dewey further emphasised the empirical approach by treating knowledge as a kind of experience arising out of human activity creating a problem, and which is attained when the problem is solved. Again Veblen emphasised the importance of studying institutions empirically and especially the connection between economic institutions and other aspects of culture. The new historians stressed the economic forces in social life and the need to study history as a pragmatic means of controlling man's future. All of these currents of thought played a vital role in the gradual movement of the United States from a highly individualist to a form of collective society in the first half of the twentieth century.

## MR JUSTICE HOLMES[5]

Both in his writings in his long tenure as a Justice of the Supreme Court, Holmes played a fundamental part in bringing about a changed attitude to law. His emphasis on the fact that the life of the law was experience[6] as well as logic,[7] and his view of law as predictions of what courts will decide,[8] stressed the empirical and pragmatic aspect of law.[9] He believed,

---

[5] Valuable insights are in R. Gordon, *The Legacy of Oliver Wendell Holmes, Jr.* (1992). Recent historians of pragmatism have doubted whether Holmes's prediction theory of law was ever seriously influenced by the writings of James or Peirce, indeed whether he understood the full impact of their philosophical theories. See Thayer, *Meaning and Actions* (1968), p. viii and *cf.* Fisch and Robin, *Studies in the Philosophy of Peirce*, pp. 3–32. Thayer points out, however, that Holmes found more interest in and sympathy for Dewey's outlook than in that of James or Peirce. Holmes's "Olympian figure" has been said to preside, like some brooding omnipresence, over all discussions of American legal realism; (Twining, *op. cit.*, pp. 15–16). "For the pragmatists, the pattern of all inquiry—scientific as well as moral—is deliberation concerning the relative attraction of various concrete alternatives," *per* R. Rorty, *The Consequences of Pragmatism* (1982), p. 164. On Peirce and Law see R. Kevelson, *Peirce and Law* (1991), particularly the essay by R. Summers at p. 153. See also R. Lipkin (1993) 67 Tulane L.R. 1561.

[6] For a discussion of what Holmes meant by experience, see Wiener, *Evolution and the Founders of Pragmatism* (1949), Chap. 8.

[7] *The Common Law* (1881), p. 1. See further S. Haack (2007) 20 Ratio Juris 1.

[8] See *post*, 821.

[9] "It is largely to Holmes's emphasis on public policy that American legal thought owes its 'pragmatic' casts," *per* Golding (1979) 5 *Social Theory and Practice* 183, 184. Holmes was always somewhat ambivalent in his attitude towards theory. Despite his doubt that "there is any more exalted form of life than that of a great abstract thinker" (*ibid.*, p. 224), he preferred to leave "twisting the tail of the Cosmos" to his friend James. "Anything that will discourage men from believing general propositions I welcome only less than anything that will encourage them to make them" (*Holmes-Laski Letters*, I, 579), sums up his attitude. In law he reiterated that general propositions do not decide cases and stressed the practical aspects of law "as a business" (*Collected Legal Papers*, pp. 170–171), at the same time advising reliance on a science which will measure "the

as he wrote to William James in 1868, that "law as well as any other series of facts in this world may be approached in the interests of science."[10] For him, too, legal history was to be studied primarily as a first step towards a deliberate reconsideration of the worth of rules developed historically. "It is revolting to have not better reason for a rule than that so it was laid down in the time of Henry IV."[11] Also law must be strictly distinguished from morals, for the lawyer is concerned with what the law *is*, not what it *ought* to be. Yet here may be discerned something of a paradox, for Holmes also never tired of asserting how "policy" governed legal development, especially in the form of the "inarticulate" convictions of those engaged in creating law.[12] The answer to this is that Holmes felt that the development of law could be justified scientifically, for the "true science of law ... consists in the establishment of its postulates from within upon accurately measured social desires instead of tradition."[13] In this respect Holmes apparently relied more on practical than on pure science, the lawyer trained in economics and statistics,[14] though he nowhere clearly indicated how an objectively sound "policy" was to be attained. However this was far more likely to be achieved when the real basis of legal rules was openly avowed rather than remaining inarticulate or suppressed. Holmes, it would seem, accepted the possibility of scientific valuation in law, but he did not go so far as Dewey in the view that the *choice* between different values can also be verified scientifically.[15] For Holmes, the arbiter of this choice could, in the last resort, only be naked force.[16]

---

relative worth of our different social ends" (p. 226). "Very likely it may be that with all the help that statistics and every modern appliance can bring us there never will be a commonwealth in which science is everywhere supreme. But it is an ideal, and without ideals what is life worth?" (p. 242). But he also noted that: "We have too little theory in the law" and that "the world is governed today (more) by Kant than by Bonaparte" (*The Path of the Law* (1897) 10 Harv. L. Rev. 457, 478). On pragmatism see S. Haack (2005) 50 Am. J. Jurisprudence 71.

[10] See M. Howe, *Holmes; The Shaping Years* (1957), p. 257.
[11] *Collected Legal Papers*, p. 187.
[12] Tushnet has argued that Holmes's position on the character of public policy in the development of the law underwent a change as a result of his experience as a state supreme court judge. His original position was that there was an "organic" connection between legal development and social sentiment: the law was a reflection of public opinion (see also A. V. Dicey, *Law and Public Opinion in England During the Nineteenth Century* (1914), p. 1). This conception of public policy was subsequently rejected and replaced by the view that legal change is due to specific appeals to public policy made by individual judges in the deciding of cases and then only incrementally ((1977) 63 Virginia Law Rev. 975, 1044–1052). But *cf.* Golding, *op. cit.*, at pp. 201–202.
[13] *ibid.*, pp. 225–226. Holmes was also a leading exponent of judicial restraint. According to Tushnet (1977) 63 Virginia Law Rev. 975 this was a deliberate strategy adopted by him to get other judges to appeal to public policy.
[14] Of whom Brandeis later provided the prototype. On the "Brandeis brief," see A. T. Mason, *Brandeis and the Modern State*, Chap. VI.
[15] See Morton G. White, *op. cit.*, Chap. XIII.
[16] "I believe that force, mitigated so far as may be by good manners, is the *ultima ratio*": *Pollock-Holmes Letters*, II, p. 36.

## THE AMERICAN LEGAL SYSTEM

Holmes's view of law as "prediction" placed both litigation and the professional lawyers in the centre of the legal stage. His emphasis on what courts may do, rather than on abstract logical deduction from general rules, and on the inarticulate ideological premises which may underlie the decisions of courts,[17] focused attention of the empirical factors which underlie a legal system. There was much in the American system which made this new approach seem especially acceptable to American lawyers. For not only was the Austinian analysis based on sovereignty singularly ill-adapted to the complexities of the federal constitution, but the function of the Supreme Court acting as a censor of legislation and deciding what were effectively political issues; the divergence of legal rules and decisions in different states, and even in the same state or court (having regard to a far laxer rule of precedent in America than in England); the large extent to which American courts were manifestly engaged in the process of generating new law, and the vast congeries of courts involving a numerous judiciary, many of whom were elected politicians, and of very varying calibre; all these matters seemed to lend force to Holmes' vigorous insistence on a fresh and more empirical attitude to the legal process. And for those who were progressively minded Holmes' reliance on practical social science seemed to point the way to future progress, and his dissenting judgments, especially in the *Lochner*[18] and *Abrams*[19] cases, were thought to point the way to a more rational and scientific application of the constitution to the actual social needs of a highly industrialised society.[20]

## THE "REALIST" MOVEMENT IN LAW

The general intellectual movement in favour of "realism" as against formalism reached its heyday by the end of the 1920s. Much of the characteristic tendencies of the sociological school, especially its reliance on interrelated social sciences, can be seen as reflections of Holmes's views on law. Realists were the first lawyers to undertake empirical social scientific research into laws and legal institutions, though many of their assumptions were naive and what they produced is generally thought to suffer from a reliance on crude empiricism.[21] Again, legal writers occasionally could be found who to some extent echoed Holmes's view of law

---

[17] See *The Common Law*, pp. 35–36.
[18] (1904) 198 U.S. 74. On which see C. Sunstein (1987) 87 Columbia L.R. 873.
[19] (1919) 250 U.S. 616.
[20] On Holmes's influence on the legal profession see R. Gordon, *The Legacy of Oliver Wendell Holmes Jr* (1992).
[21] See Llewellyn's comment (1956) 8 J. Legal Educ. 399, 400–401. And see now the articles by J. Schlegel in (1979) 28 Buffalo Law Rev. 459 on Clark and Douglas and in (1979) 29 Buffalo Law Rev. 195 on Underhill Moore. Moore is also discussed by Verdun-Jones and Cousineau (1978) 1 Int.J. of Law and Psych. 375.

as being what courts may decide. Indeed, Gray[22] went so far as to assert that even a statute is not law until a court interprets it. But Gray, and also Salmond, for whom law was law because the courts in fact observe it,[23] remain analytical jurists, with little interest in the social foundations of law, and its relation to other social disciplines. Thus, despite Holmes's great influence both as part of the general movement and as the outstanding American jurist of his day, it was not until towards the end of his career that a legal movement under the designation of "legal realism" began to manifest itself.

### Fact-skeptics and Rule-skeptics

Frank insists that there are really two[24] groups of realists, "rule-skeptics," as he calls them, who regard legal uncertainty as residing principally in the "paper" rules of law and who seek to discover uniformities in actual judicial behaviour, and "fact-skeptics," who think that the unpredictability of court decisions resides primarily in the elusiveness of facts.[25] The former, he suggests, make the mistake of concentrating on appellate courts, whereas it is to the activities of trial courts that attention needs

---

[22] For insight into Gray, in particular his analysis of the state, see D. N. MacCormick (1981) 66 Cornell L.R. 973. He notes some similarities with Kelsen's theory of the state (pp. 980–984). On Kelsen see *ante*, Chap. 5.

[23] Salmond defined law as the rules recognised and acted upon by courts of justice: see *Jurisprudence* (11th ed.), p. 17. *cf.* Pollock and Maitland, *The History of English Law*, vol. 1, p. xcv: "... law may be taken for every purpose, save that of strictly philosophical enquiry, to be the sum of the rules administered by courts of justice."

[24] It has been suggested that there are in fact *three* categories of skeptics. In his *American Legal Realism* (1968), Rumble detects, "opinion-skepticism" in the writings of a number of the Realists, notably Llewellyn, Felix Cohen and Bingham. The idea is better known in Judge Hutcheson's phrase as the "judicial hunch" (see (1929) 14 Cornell L.Q. 274). Though somewhat exaggerated and not a little naive, there is some truth in the belief that judicial reasoning is *ex post facto* decision making, mere rationalisation "intended to make the decision seem plausible, legally decent, legally right ... legally inevitable" (Llewellyn, *Jurisprudence*, p. 58). Whilst "opinion-skepticism" is an undoubted undercurrent in Realist thought (in spite of the cogent criticism of the Realist sympathiser, E. S. Robinson), to endow the idea with a separate label is to inflate its importance and invite similar divisive speculations. On Frank see N. Duxbury (1991) 18 J.L.S. 175. Duxbury's *Patterns of American Jurisprudence* (1995) is an invaluable source of information on realism (see pp. 65–159). See also B. Leiter in (eds.) M. Golding and W. Edmundson, *Blackwell Guide to Philosophy of Law and Legal Theory* (2005) pp. 6–66.

[25] Frank never defined "fact skepticism." Cahn, a great admirer of Frank, described it as "an integral doctrine with three associated prongs": "it criticises our capacity to ascertain the transactions of the past, it distrusts our capacity to predict fact-findings and value judgments of the future; and, finally, it discloses the importance of the personal element in all processes of choice and decision." (Preface to Frank, *Courts on Trial*, p. ix.). Both Cahn (*Confronting Injustice*, pp. 321–322) and Rumble stress the relationship of fact-skepticism to Frank, the law-reformer. If a tribunal decides on the basis of facts other than the actual facts (are facts finite?), then improvements must be made to the fact-finding process. Rumble believes this to be the theme of *Courts on Trial* (1949), whilst the earlier, and better-known, *Law and The Modern Mind* (1930) concentrates on the unpredictability of the tribunal's reaction to found facts, whatever the *real* facts. But can the thinking process really be compart mentalised in this way, and do not one's reactions to possible found facts often colour those facts which one will find? (*American Legal Realism*, pp. 109–111.)

most to be directed.[26] No doubt there is force in this contention, for it is familiar enough to find that nice points of law often dissolve away before decisions "on the facts," quite apart from the fact that the majority of cases involve no disputed law at all. Also, the facts may affect the actual decision as to the law, since courts often "wrench" the law in order to make it fit what they conceive to be the merits of a case, not always with adequate regard to the wider implications of their decision. But at the same time it is difficult not to feel that Frank makes an over-elaborated case about what in essence has never been far from the thoughts of the legal profession, *viz.*, that you can never anticipate with certainty which way a court or jury will jump on issues of fact, and that innumerable factors combine to promote such uncertainty and render it ineradicable.[27] In stressing this thesis, Frank effectively makes the points that the text-book approach, which treats the law as no more than a collection of abstract rules, is grossly misleading and that much of legal uncertainty is inherent and not due to deliberate mystification. But it must be said that Frank adds little to his contentions by a curious affection for an implausible application of psycho-analysis, whereby he seeks to attribute the search for legal certainty to the need for a Father-figure,[28] the infallible judge, nor by his reliance on the principle of indeterminacy in modern physics as showing the impossibility of attaining certainty in the legal sphere.[29]

### Llewellyn on Institutions and "Law-Jobs"[30]

The functional approach to law adopted by Llewellyn is well brought out by his treatment of law as an institution. For Llewellyn an institution is an organised activity which is built around a job or a "cluster" of jobs. In the case of a major institution, its "job-cluster" is fundamental to the continuance of the society or group in which it operates. The institution of law in our society is an extremely complex one, consisting not only of a body of rules organised around concepts and permeated by a large number of principles. In addition there are certain elaborated techniques

---

[26] See particularly Frank's searching criticisms of the American trial systems in *Courts on Trial* (1949). See J. Frank, "Cardozo and the Upper-Court Myth" (1948) 13 *Law and Contemporary Problems* 369.

[27] Lundstedt (*Legal Thinking Revised*, p. 394) describes Frank's *Law and the Modern Mind* as a "more amusing than indicative of fruitful thought." For a more sympathetic appraisal of Judge Frank's contribution, see E. Cahn in (1957) 66 Yale L.J. 824 and in *Confronting Injustice* (1967), pp. 265–324.

[28] Frank did not test his belief empirically, but that has been done, indirectly, by Ladinsky and Silver (1967) Wis.L.Rev. 128. They comment: "Public acquiescene to judicial actions in the realm of policy-making hardly seems to be a function of the 'priestly' image promulgated by Lerner or Frank ... public support seems more a matter of acquiescence or ignorance ... of respect for the judiciary as one kind of government official rather than as a distinctive office embodying unique functions and status" (pp. 167–168).

[29] *Cf. ante*, 7.

[30] See further W. L. Twining, *Karl Llewellyn and the Realist Movement* (1973), pp. 175–184 and *Globalisation and Legal Theory* (2000), pp. 75–82. and A. Hunt, *The Sociological Movement in Law* (1978), Chap. 3. See also *post*, 1016.

such as the use of precedent, and over and above all these matters is an ideology, consisting of a body of far-reaching values and ideals which, though to a large extent implicit rather than expressly avowed, may, nevertheless, form an immensely influential part of the institution of law as a whole. Apart from all these, there is also a host of practices, some very flexible, and others quite rigid, which determine how certain things within the legal system may or may not be done. All such matters control in various ways the activities of what Llewellyn calls the "men-of-law."

An institution has jobs to do, and the important thing is to see that these jobs are well and effectively carried out. A functioning institution is something which is rooted in the life of the community and has to be constantly tested by the needs of that community; and moreover, the results of its working have to be open to inquiry. Much of Llewellyn's interest has been centred upon what he calls the ways in which in various types of community the "law-jobs" are actually carried out.

"Law-jobs,"[31] are Llewellyn's way of describing the basic functions of the law, which, for him, are two-fold: "to make group survival possible," but, additionally, to "quest" for justice, efficiency and a richer life. To this end he lists "law-jobs" as the disposition of "trouble-cases" (his study of they Cheyenne[32] was focused on this function of law, which Llewellyn believed was common to all systems at whatever stage of development); "preventive channeling," the reorientation of conduct and expectations to avoid trouble;[33] the provision of private law activity by individuals and groups, such as the autonomy inherent in a law of contract; and "the say," the constitutional provision of procedures to resolve conflict, much in the manner of Hart's "rules of adjudication."[34] The first three jobs describe "bare bones" law, but out of them may emerge, though Llewellyn gives no indication how, the additional "questing" phase of the legal order. For Llewellyn the problem was thus finding the best ways to handle "legal tools to law-job ends."[35]

Llewellyn sees these "law-jobs" as universal. He puts forward his theory of them as a general framework for the functional analysis of law. What this overlooks are dimensions of structure and power[36] which are

---

[31] See *post*, 1016.

[32] Llewellyn and Hoebel, *The Cheyenne Way* (1941), the theme of which was to demonstrate that primitive law can be understood in terms of the functions common to it and to advanced systems. And see *post*, 1086 and 1103.

[33] So one of the keys to the Uniform Commercial Code, of which Llewellyn towards the end of his life was a prime mover, is the facilitating of commercial practices through custom, usage and agreement; see Twining, *Karl Llewellyn and the Realist Movement*, Chaps 11, 12; and Wiseman (1987) 100 Harv.L.Rev. 465.

[34] See *The Concept of Law* (1994), pp. 96–98.

[35] Llewellyn set this to verse. See his *Semi-Ballade on the Glorious Quest*, in *Jurisprudence* (1962), n. 214. According to Twining (*Karl Llewellyn and the Realist Movement*, p. 181) "the law-jobs theory is both vague and contains an element of tautology." He stresses that despite this it has been found useful in the initial stages of the Chicago Arbitration Project. For another view of the basic techniques of law see Summers (1971) 59 Calif.L.Rev. 733 and (1974) 58 Cornell L. Rev. 1.

[36] On power see *post*, 1163.

different in different societies. The fault is common to functionalist
theories.[37] The quest for universality leads Llewellyn to concepts of a high
level of abstraction. He also leaves us with numerous questions unanswered. What, for example, is the relationship between the different "law-
jobs"? He tells us that the disposition of trouble-cases is the most
important function of law. Is this conclusion logically required by his
theory or is it merely an inference drawn from Llewellyn's experience of
complex, judge-oriented common law systems?

This brings one to his notion of a "craft" as a minor institution. A craft
in this sense consists of a kind of "know-how" among a body of specialists who are engaged in performing certain of the jobs within the
framework of an institution. It consists of an organised and continuous
body of skills developed by specialists and handed down from generation
to generation by a process of education and practical example. The
practice of the law is the practice of a set of crafts, and of these one of the
most important is what is frequently called juristic method.

### The Common Law Tradition

In Llewellyn's book, *The Common Law Tradition*, Llewellyn develops this
idea of a craft in considerable detail, as applied to the juristic method of
the common law. This book may be described as a kind of handbook of
the craft both of judging and of advocacy within the framework of the
common law tradition, though applied especially to appellate cases.
There is a certain irony in the thesis of this book, coming from one who
has long been identified, though not altogether correctly, with the notion
of the large measure of unpredictability in the decisions of the court. The
aim of the book is to deal with what it describes as a "crisis of confidence
within the Bar," concerning especially the question whether there is a
reasonable degree of "reckonability" in the work of U.S. appellate
courts. Llewellyn begins by pointing out that the profession in America is
exceedingly worried because it is believed that the courts have moved
away from a basis of stable decision-making, in favour of deciding cases
on the basis of their sentiments, and then simply seeking for *ex post facto*
justification in their judgments.[38]

On the contrary, argues Llewellyn, there is a large measure of predictability in case-law, and this he attributes to the general craft of
decision-making in the common law tradition. Llewellyn examines in
detail what he calls "a cluster of factors" which tend to have a major
steadying influence in producing stability in the work of the courts. These

---

[37] *Cf.* the discussion of Parsons, *ante*, 856.
[38] *Cf.* his address to the Conference of Chief Justices in 1959, in *Jurisprudence* (1962), p.
215.

include[39] such matters as "law-conditioned officials"; known doctrinal techniques; the limiting of issues; the adversary arguments of counsel; and so on. But especially, in this book. Llewellyn emphasises the importance of what he calls the general "period style"[40] employed by the courts. This cluster remains a hypothesis. Llewellyn makes no attempt to test empirically any of his steadying factors. He gives no indication of how an assessment could be made of the relative weight of each, nor, indeed, how each can be used for predictive purposes.[41] Llewellyn's discussion of "period style" is, nonetheless, of particular interest. In the common law, says Llewellyn, the practice of the courts has fluctuated between two types of style which he names the Grand Style and the Formal Style. The Grand Style is based essentially on an appeal to reason, and does not involve a slavish following of precedent; regard is paid to the reputation of the judge in deciding the earlier case, and principle is consulted in order to ensure that precedent is not a mere verbal tool, but a generalisation which yields patent sense as well as order. Policy under this style, comes in for explicit examination. Under the so-called Formal Style, on the other hand, the underlying notion is that the rules of law decide the cases; policy is for the legislature, not for the courts, and therefore this approach is authoritarian, formal and logical. The Grand Style is also characterised by resort to, what Llewellyn calls, "situation sense"; the Formal Style, on the other hand, is not so concerned with social facts. Further, the Grand Style is concerned with providing guidance for the future far more than is the Formal Style.

Llewellyn does not assert that these styles are ever found in their absolute purity at any given moment; there tends rather to be a movement from one period to another between these two opposite poles.[42] Thus, the Grand Style he regards as characteristic of the creative period of American law in the early part of the nineteenth century; thereafter there was a rapid move in the latter half of that century in America towards an increasingly Formal Style. Llewellyn argues that in recent time the American appellate courts have been moving steadily back towards the earlier type of Grand Style, and it is this tendency which has misled the legal profession into thinking that there is a higher measure of

---

[39] See *op. cit.*, p. 19. Rumble, *op. cit.*, pp. 51–53 has a useful discussion of these steadying factors. He stresses Llewellyn's emphasis of the role a judge is expected to play in the American judicial system as the most important of the fourteen factors. (See *The Common Law Tradition*, pp. 46–47.)

[40] See *post*, p. 1021.

[41] Judicial behaviouralism subsequently attempted this. See the comments in Becker, *Political Behaviouralism and Modern Jurisprudence: A Working Theory and Study in Judicial Decision-Making* (1964), pp. 63–64. See also *post*, 1001.

[42] "Concepts like Grand Style and Formal Style are best treated as relatively simple theoretical models, more suited for painting a broad picture than for detailed analysis" (*per* Twining, *Karl Llewellyn and the Realist Movement*, p. 214).

unpredictability in their decisions than there was in the previous more formal period.[43] This Llewellyn attributes to a misconception as to the ways in which the court uses precedent and the tremendous "leeways" which are afforded by the system of precedent, whatever particular period style may be in operation. Under any style of precedent there are multiple techniques by which opposite or conflicting results may be reached, and the only question really is whether the court will employ a style which will produce a more effective and just outcome, and one more adapted to the social needs of the period, or will try to immunise itself to some degree against the changing pattern of the society in which the court has its being.

There are however, two rather curious and unexpected features in Llewellyn's last book which do deserve some comment. According to Llewellyn, it is a feature of the Grand Style, which he warmly approves, that the courts proceed to arrive at decisions in relation to what he calls "situation sense." It is exceedingly difficult to grasp exactly what the author has in mind by this concept. No doubt he was particularly concerned with the importance of not dealing so much with a unique situation, but a situation seen as a "type," and therefore, providing a rule or principle for the future. It appears to involve "true understanding" of the facts and "right evaluation" of them.[44] Llewellyn does not think that "situation sense" depends on personal preference. On the other hand Llewellyn is not prepared to commit himself to a comprehensive value system, so cannot invoke reference to objectively verifiable categories. Unlike Dworkin,[45] Llewellyn did not believe in "one single Right Answer."[46] If, as Llewellyn is suggesting, there is more than one reasonable solution, how is it to be judged? It should be "something which can be hoped, or thought, to look reasonable to any thinking man."[47] In other words "people by the use of reason can at least narrow the range of their disagreements."[48] Under the Grand Style, Llewellyn seems to be saying that insight and wisdom is developed whereby the judges will achieve a kind of reasonable criterion, though not one which can be specifically formulated, and so arrive at a wide measure of agreement as to what are the appropriate legal solutions both worthy of approval by the community and likely, in fact, to be approved by the community. This may or may not be true in relation to particular periods or particular legal systems, but it seems a very far cry from the scientific realism which has so long been regarded as one of the animating influences of the realist

---

[43] The Supreme Court under Chief Justice Warren is thought to have exemplified this approach. See the excellent critique of this in Bickel. *The Supreme Court and the Idea of Progress* (1970). On appellate courts, generally, see Keeton's account of creativity in the law of torts in roughly the same period (*Venturing to do Justice* (1968)).

[44] *Cf. The Common Law Tradition*, p. 127.

[45] Though to understand this see *ante*, 727.

[46] *The Common Law Tradition*, pp. 24–5, 226–32.

[47] *ibid.*, p. 277.

[48] Twining, *Karl Llewellyn and the Realist Movement*, p. 219.

movement. It savours, indeed, far more of Savigny[49] than of social science. Moreover, Llewellyn does not seem to face up to the fact than in many communities, certainly including his own, there may be vital issues involving conflicts of values between different groups and interests in the community; how, then, can there be any objective core of insight which can produce decisions appropriate to reconcile all this welter of confusion?[50] It may well be that a more honest decision will be produced by a judge who approaches the question in the spirit of the Grand Style rather than looking at the matter through the spectacles of formalism. All the same, Llewellyn seems unduly optimistic when he claims that what he calls "the law of the singing reason" will tend to produce a rule yielding regularity, "reckonability" and justice altogether.[51] It is fair to add, however, that Llewellyn does not put his case higher than saying that the Grand Style is likely to produce a greater proportion of such decisions than any other style.

The second rather curious feature of this book is that the author confines his evidence almost exclusively to the material which appears from the actual decisions of appellate courts. True, he recognises that these do not disclose the whole truth of what he calls "the fact of life," but he does insist that these provide adequate material for revealing the techniques of the courts, especially if one employs his chosen procedure, not of examining cases according to their subject matter, but in the order they happen to be reported in the volumes of reports relating to particular courts. But he insists we must learn to read these cases, not for what they decide, but for their "flavor." Do not look, he urges, to "what w?s held" but look to "what was bothering and helping the court." In a sense, therefore, the wheel seems to have gone full circle, for we now find Llewellyn virtually ignoring subjective factors; concentrating entirely on the actual decisions of the court as opposed to extrinsic factors; and, nevertheless, urging that far from being irrational and uncertain, if one understands the proper technique of reading opinions, it is possible to show that there is an exceptionally high measure of "reckonability" in American appellate decisions. Despite all this, Llewellyn is far from having renounced any of his earlier enthusiasms. In fact he argues strongly that his last book is still as much based upon the realistic technique of the past as any of his previous contributions. The fervour of the movement has not disappeared; all that is changed is the field of operations. It may have been necessary before to spend a good deal of time attacking opposing views; now the important thing is to get down to the actual study of the material, and the opinions in court judgments are

---

[49] As to whom see *post*, 1079.

[50] Twining, *Karl Llewellyn and the Realist Movement*, pp. 221–227, is extremely helpful here.

[51] Note also the "law of fitness and flavor." "The work of the job in hand, and even more of the job at large, must fit and fit into the body and flavor of the law" (*Common Law Tradition*, p. 222). This "law" counters any activist tendencies. But on "activism" *cf.* Twining (1971) 87 L. Q. R. 398, 400–401.

just as important a form of material as any other. With this view, at any
rate, even the most orthodox common lawyer is hardly likely to dissent.

It is a little disarming to find that what started as a rather revolutionary
movement has ended up fundamentally as an appeal for a common-sense
approach to law. What Llewellyn claims to have attempted and to some
extent achieved is to establish a jurisprudence which may serve the needs
of the ordinary student of law, the ordinary practitioner and the ordinary
judge. In this process, a good many myths have to be eliminated, and, in
particular, both the myth that certainty can be achieved under a legal
system, or its opposite, that predictability is unattainable.[52] On the contrary, urges Llewellyn, in his final work, the common law system produces, in his view, a remarkably high measure of predictability so that a
skilled lawyer proceeding on the basis discussed in this book ought, in
Llewellyn's view, to average correct predictions in eight out of ten cases.
Here, again, is reassurance enough for the orthodox.

## Scientific and Normative Laws

Is it a valid criticism of the realists that they ignore the purely normative
character of legal rules and seek to replace those by scientific statements
laying down uniformities of human conduct?[53] Legal rules are norms of
conduct which are in themselves neither true nor false.[54] Yet the realist
seems to be seeking to prove their truth or falsity in relation to the criteria
of actual human behaviour. This is not an easy point to deal with,
especially as it concerns a logical distinction of the kind to which the
realist, with his addiction to brute fact, remains profoundly indifferent.
The realist does not deny the normative character of legal rules. What he

---

[52] That Llewellyn regards rules as playing a very significant role in the formulation and
development of law is sufficiently testified by his activity as one of the chief draftsmen of
the new Uniform Commercial Code which is being rapidly adopted in the majority if the
States of the Union. This Code has embodied to a noteworthy degree the approach of
what Llewellyn has called the "Grand Style," and so providing a fabric of rules which
will give the court the opportunity to apply "Situation-sense" to shape the deciding rule
and to enable the court to re-test the rules in the light of reason as it evolves from the
situation. Moreover, the Code's first canon of construction is: "This Act shall be liberally
construed and applied to promote its underlying purposes and policies." See Ment-
schikoff (Llewellyn's widow) (1964) 27 M.L.R. 107, 108: "The extent to which [the
U.C.C.] reflects Llewellyn's philosophy of law and his sense of commercial wisdom and
need is startling." See also Twining, *Karl Llewellyn and the Realist Movement*, Chaps 11
and 12.

[53] This criticism is more valid in relation to Frank and some of the earlier writings of
Llewellyn, but there is no doubt that later Realism as exemplified by mature Llewellyn
took cognisance of the normative character of legal rules. See, for example, Llewellyn,
*post*, 1015, and in *The Common Law Tradition*.

[54] *Ante*, 24–27.

says is that these norms do not provide the complete answer to the actual behaviour of courts, legal officials or those engaged in legal transactions.[55] If we are to understand the actual working of law in human society it is not enough simply to peruse a collection of the relevant legal norms for these tell us little about actual "legal behaviour," in the sense of how legal business is in fact transacted. Of course, a follower of Kelsen might say that this is outside the field of true legal science, but he cannot and indeed would not deny that it is a legitimate field of inquiry in itself. The Kelsenite, therefore, concentrates on his norms, the realist on his facts of society, each regarding the other's activity patronisingly as a peripheral study on the fringe of his own central sphere. Yet, it may be suggested, both equally represent essential aspects of the legal process if an overall picture is to be taken of law, which is both an intellectual conception and a function of human society.

## REALISM: AN ASSESSMENT

In an authoritative recent history of American Realism Laura Kalman[56] concludes that it failed. To the off-quoted adage that "we are all realists now,"[57] she says it is "a truism to refer to it as a truism."[58] It was, she argues, essentially a conservative movement. She concedes its contributions broadened the curriculum but it "left representation of the wealthy at its heart"[59] and "enabled both the casebook and the case method to survive."[60] The "realists who called themselves realists"[61] did little to "integrate law with social science or organize casebooks along factual lines."[62] By the 1960s they had made a positive contribution to legal education but "the appellate opinion still lay at the core of legal education"[63] (though not, of course, at the centre of legal practice).[64] She sees realism as much like its companion, the New Deal. It may have seemed revolutionary, but there was no revolution, or, as Gilmore has put it, "the revolution may have been merely a palace revolution, not much more

---

[55] Admittedly the realist predilection, following Holmes, to treat rules of law as *predictions* of what the court may do, seems to go counter to this. But this is because the realist is here thinking of the viewpoint of the lawyer advising his client, rather than of the norm prescribed by the judge, or laid down for his guidance; see W. H. Wilcox (1981) 66 Cornell L.Rev. 1058 and W.L. Twining, *post*, 1029.

[56] *Legal Realism At Yale, 1927–1960* (1986).

[57] See, *e.g.* J. Singer, "Legal Realism Now" (1988) 76 California L. Rev. 465, 503.

[58] *Op. cit.*, n. 56, p. 229.

[59] *ibid.*, p. 230. On the conservatism of the Realists see also B. Ackerman, *Reconstructing American Law* (1984), where he said it was "profoundly conservative, not radically iconoclastic" (p. 5).

[60] *ibid.*

[61] By which she means those of the 1920s and 1930s, not later generations.

[62] *Op. cit.*, n. 56, p. 229.

[63] *ibid.*

[64] Where settlement out of court, of new alternative methods of dispute resolution, was the goal.

than a changing of the guard."[65] To Kalman, realism was not intellectually significant and "pedagogically, it had not fulfilled its promise."[66] Gilmore too concludes critically that they "no more proposed to abandon the basic tenets of Langdellian jurisprudence that the Protestant Reformers of the fifteenth and sixteenth centuries proposed to abandon the basic tenets of Christian theology."[67] Realists, concludes Kalman, pointed to "the role of idiosyncracy in law"[68] whilst retaining a belief in the rule of law: accordingly, they attempted to make it more efficient and more certain. And so, she argues, they failed to confront their own most arresting message that "all law is politics."[69]

This is a message that the Critical Legal Studies movement was to take up.[70] But how fair is this assessment? More sympathetic recent assessments have been made by Singer[71] and Horwitz.[72] To Singer, "legal realism has fundamentally altered our conceptions of legal reasoning and of the relationship between law and society."[73] The realists were, he believes, "remarkably successful both in changing the terms of legal discourse and in undermining the idea of a self-regulating market system."[74] He sees all major current schools of jurisprudential thought as "products"[75] of legal realism.

Horwitz is more fulsome in his praise. Like Singer, he locates Realism within its historical context. Horwitz see "the most important legacy of Realism" as its "challenge to the orthodox claim that legal thought was separate and autonomous from moral and political discourse."[76] Their attack on deductive legal reasoning constituted, he argues, the realists' most "original and lasting contributions to legal thought."[77] Legal Realism is seen as "the culmination of early-twentieth-century assaults on legal fundamentalism and, in particular, on late-nineteenth-century categorical thinking."[78] The importance of stressing that legal clarifications and categories were "not natural but constructs"[79] is highlighted. And here the influence of pragmatism was important. The way to determine whether a legal classification was good or not depended on the purposes for which the category was created, not on some measure of whether it fitted or reflected a pre-existing natural category ... Just as

---

[65] *The Ages of American Law* (1977), p. 87.

[66] *Op. cit.*, n. 56, p. 230.

[67] *Op. cit.*, n. 65. See also B. Bix, *Jurisprudence: Theory and Context* (2006), pp. 167–168.

[68] *Op. cit.*, n. 56, p. 231 (see also pp. 6–7).

[69] *ibid.*

[70] *See post*, Chap. 12. And see "Round and Round the Bramble Bush: From Legal Realism to Critical Legal Scholarship" (1982) 95 Harvard L. Rev. 1669 and M. Tushnet (1982) 15 J.S.P.T.L. 20.

[71] *Op. cit.*, n. 57 (a review of Kalman).

[72] *The Transformation of American Law 1870–1960* (1992), Chap. 7.

[73] *Op. cit.*, n. 57, p. 467.

[74] *ibid.*

[75] *ibid.*

[76] *Op. cit.*, n. 72, p. 193.

[77] *ibid.*, p. 199.

[78] *ibid.*, p. 200.

[79] *ibid.*

pragmatism had attacked the essentialist claims of philosophical idealism by insisting on a functionalist and consequentialist truth, so did the Realists treat the value of concepts and categories in terms of the results that they produced."[80] The hostile attitude towards abstractions may be one of realism's breakthroughs.[81]

And, though Kalman indicts the conservatism of the Realist movement, the same critique was applied to the legal institutions of capitalism. To quote Horwitz once more: "The Realists of the 1920s and 1930s pursued their attack on the legitimacy of the market with a degree of insight, brilliance and social passion that has never been equalled since."[82] They emphasized that the market was neither natural nor neutral, but rather a social construct, which could therefore be judged only in terms of its social consequences.[83] Legal Realists were also the first systematically to challenge the public-private dichotomy in law[84] as conceived within classical liberalism. "A picture of a decentralized, comprehensive, and self-regulating market lay at the core of all efforts to define the public-private distinction. Just as the analogous division between public and private law pre-supposed that voluntary relations of market exchange would usually make coercive regulatory intervention unnecessary, the more general separation of activities into public and private spheres was also driven by a conception of a neutral, apolitical, and above all, self-regulating economic realm."[85] It was the radical realist critique which through this reasoning came to articulate the conception of all law as public law.

Not all Realists stood for all these ideas. But gradually many of these insights did pervade legal thinking generally. Later "schools," in particular the Critical Legal Studies movement, feminists and post-modernists[86] owe considerable debts to the Realists, though it is not always acknowledged how much they can trace to the Realist movement. That the "Critics" and the others transcend the Realist critique and offer new challenges cannot be in doubt—but it was the Realists who did much of the initial spade-work.

---

[80] *ibid.*
[81] And see the work of Hohfeld, discussed *ante*, 396.
[82] *Op. cit.*, n. 72, p. 195.
[83] Most notably Robert Hale on whom see B. Fried, *Robert L. Hale and Progressive Legal Economics* (1994). And see D. Ross, *Origins of American Social Science* (1990), pp. 174 and 419–20.
[84] See Singer, *op. cit.*, n. 37, pp. 477–496; Horwitz, *op. cit.*, n. 72, pp. 206–208.
[85] *Per* Horwitz, *ibid.*, p. 206.
[86] Respectively discussed in Chaps 14, 15 and 16.

POST-REALISM

*Jurimetrics*

Realism has indirectly engendered two movements themselves closely related: Jurimetrics and Judicial Behaviouralism. Neither of these movements has had much impact in this country, but in the United States they continue to be felt.

In one sense, they take over where realism left off, for, whilst the realists had some inspired ideas, developed a number of theoretical models, and urged us to exploit the social and technological sciences, these later movements are firmly established within the mainstream of the social sciences, and use techniques associated with them.

Jurimetrics was introduced into legal vocabulary by Lee Loevinger in 1949.[87] It stands for the scientific investigation of legal problems, especially by the use of computers and by symbolic logic.[88] There have been experiments with computers to investigate such questions as the different ways in which a judge and a jury may decide the same case, the effect that the formulation of the legal rule as to insanity may have on jury verdicts, the reliability and credibility of testimony, and, more especially, the particularly realist preoccupation with the prediction of judicial decisions.[89] Work has also been done on the question how far patterns of consistency or regularity may be shown to exist in relation to a large number of judicial decisions in a particular legal field. It has even been suggested that the day may come when defendants will be given the choice of trial with the aid of a computer.[90]

These developments have not occurred without vigorous resistance, especially by those who think there are dangerous ideological but political implications in allowing legal inquiries to be conducted by machines rather than by judges or administrators. Defenders of jurimetrics respond that its aim is not to eliminate reason or philosophy from jurisprudence or to find a substitute for necessary values which are an intrinsic part of law making. All that this particular type of investigation is concerned with is those matters which are capable of being subjected to quantitative or probability assessments, and which can produce results capable of being scientifically verified or tested.

Fears remain, fuelled by experiments with rather sweeping, even dangerous, claims. For example, Beutel in *Experimental Jurisprudence* (published in 1957), while conceding that, for the present, problems involving moral and social value—judgements cannot be effectively

---

[87] (1949) 33 Minn. L. Rev 455.
[88] A valuable introduction is Kayton (1964) 33 Geo. Wash. L.Rev. 287. On the use of mathematical techniques in the trial process see L. Tribe (1971) 84 Harv. L.Rev. 1329 and *cf.* R. Lempert (1977) 75 Michigan L.Rev. 1021.
[89] See C. Tapper, *Computers and the Law* (1992). See also B. Ackerman, *Reconstructing American Law* (1984), particularly pp. 66–67.
[90] By Reed Lawlor (1967) 13 Practical Lawyer 3, 10.

subjected to the technique of experimental jurisprudence, nevertheless cast his eye towards a distant future when methods of scientific prediction may be so developed that they may take over the direction and control of what "some now call human values and that this power may be turned scientific purposes".[91] Under such conditions, new scientific methods will be called for,[92] and it will be necessary for the overwhelming mass of people to hand over matters which they cannot understand to able scientists who can alone understand and be entrusted with the new types of governmental and legal devices. But, as Lasswell wrote, "whoever controls information (enlightenment) is likely to control public order".[93] These are real lessons here for lawyers.

### Judicial Behaviouralism

Judicial Behaviouralism developed in the 1960s. Its roots are in realism (and to some extent sociological jurisprudence) and political science. From realism it took the *faith* that judicial behaviour was predictable and the *aim* of developing means of predicting decisions. From political science it took such techniques as scaling and small group psychology.

It developed, according to Glendon Schubert, because the realists failed to deliver what they promised.[94]

> "Legal research remains today at the primitive level of development, as a science, that generally characterized political science one or two generations ago. By and large, legal method is no more in phase with modern science that it was in the days of Austin."[95]

And he pinpoints two deficiencies in Realist thought, one in their theory, the other in their methods. "Science requires both theoretical methods for which operationalized hypotheses can be inferred and methods for testing such hypotheses with data derived from empirical observations."[96] He excepted Realists[97] like Herman Oliphant[98] from his critique, but not its major figures.

---

[91] At p. 51.

[92] Leading works on this are Hans Baade, *Jurimetrics* (1963) and F. Beutel, *Experimental Jurisprudence* (1957).

[93] (1967) 21 Rutgers L.Rev. 645, 676. Enlightenment is one of Lasswell's eight value categories, which the legal process is expected to maximise.

[94] More from Llewellyn than Frank. See, for example, Llewellyn's criticism of Frank's emphasis on unpredictability in *Jurisprudence*, p. 101 (written in 1931), and his own demonstration of "reckonability" in *The Common Law Tradition*.

[95] (1966) 34 Geo. Wash. L.Rev. 593, 600–601.

[96] *ibid.* See also his *Judicial Behavior* (1964), pp. 1–18 and Becker, *Political Behavioralism and Modern Jurisprudence*, Pt. II.

[97] On the relationship between Realism and behaviouralism see Ingersoll (1966) 96 *Ethics* 253.

[98] See W. Rumble, *American Legal Realism* (1968), pp. 159–161, 171–173. See also the writings of Felix Cohen and his functional model with its declaration of war on empirically unverifiable concepts (*The Legal Conscience* (1960)). M. Golding ((1981) 66 Cornell L.Rev. 1032) is of the opinion that Cohen's work represents the realist movement's best theoretical work.

It is possible to argue that Llewellyn's cluster of steadying factors could be the type of theoretical model that Schubert has in mind. But it is difficult to think Llewellyn so intended it. Nor did Llewellyn tell us how to use his "model", or how to differentiate the effect of different factors. But, even if the Realists developed models, they did not draw hypotheses from them, and certainly there was no attempt at empirical verification of any such hypothesis. Llewellyn's *Common Law Tradition* is not research in the same genre as Schubert's.

The behaviouralists start with two advantages: the heritage of Realist questioning, and their own technical expertise as social scientists. Their work tends to concentrate on multiple courts and majority decisions.[99] They thus limit themselves to contentious appellate decisions.[1] There have been attempts to correlate attitudes and backgrounds with voting records, and to trace the development of blocs, the emergence of leadership and interaction, and bargaining problems. And there has been a certain amount of prediction. But, unlike the Realists, they have not been concerned to help the practitioner, and, accordingly, find prediction after the event—what Nagel termed *post diction*[2]—equally satisfying. Not many lawyers are likely to share this view.

Schubert has been concerned with motivations behind judicial decisions, particularly with *attitude*. It is his thesis that judges do not agree or disagree because they reason in similar or different ways, but because they have similar or dissimilar attitudes. This seems to ignore their common training and environment, the "taught tradition" and institutional factors such as *stare decisis*. Schubert's method of discovering a judge's attitudes is similarly suspect. By looking at their previous decisions he believes he can elicit their reactions to fact-patterns, and draws the hypothesis that a recurrence of fact-patterns will stimulate a similar response. But this is to reduce the judge to little more than a conveyor belt to which materials are fed and identical products emerge. It is also to adopt an over-mechanical concept of causation: a judge may be a Catholic of Irish ancestry and may have consistently decided labour disputes in favour of trade unions, but neither Schubert, nor any other behaviouralist, has shown that he so decided *because* of his religion or ethnic origin. Furthermore,[3] the facts upon which Schubert concentrates are not the "facts" at all, but a distillation he finds in the judicial opinion. These are not *the* facts, but the facts the judge found *significant*. To find the actual fact sources, the behaviouralists should learn from Jerome Frank[4]—and study the briefs, oral arguments, minutes of case conferences, etc. These are, it is true, other methods of eliciting a judge's

---

[99] By excluding unanimous decisions a veil is drawn over the divergences that may lie behind such decisions. The approach also gives undue weight to dissenting judgments. And see, further, L. Fuller (1966) 79 Harv. L.Rev. 1604, 1609–1611.

[1] *Cf.* the views of J. Frank, *ante*, 989.

[2] (1965) 63 Mich. L.Rev. 1411, 1422.

[3] Fuller is ironically critical of the conservative nature of the extra-curial influences chosen by the researches (see (1966) 79 Harv. L.Rev. 1604, 1608–1609).

[4] *Post*, 990.

attitude—Nagel, for example, sent them questionnaires.[5] But there is no reason to believe that these would any more successful. Further, as both Fuller[6] and Stone[7] point out, the behaviouralists puts consistency at the premium as if the judicial process where a formalized game of "Snap". Stone quotes a Japanese scholar foreseeing with zest "the day ... when the courts will use [an electronic machine] in arriving at their decisions".[8] Will the role of the behaviouralists seeking to explain what judges will decide if they act consistently with past decisions merge with that of the appellate judge whose concern is *justice?*[9]

Attitude correlation is not the only approach of the behaviouralists. Another common method is to relate social background to decision making, for example, to test whether prior judicial experience as a first instance judge makes an appellate judge more likely to favour judicial restraint or *stare decisis*. Schmidhauser[10] tested the *a priori* assertion that there was indeed, such a correlation by looking at a large number of U.S. Supreme Court decisions where precedent was overruled, and then establishing a propensity to overrule score for each judge. On scaling them he found that judges with lower court experience had a greater propensity to overrule than judges without such experience. He also found that, contrary to expectations, dissenting judges had the lowest propensity to overrule, and drew the conclusion that the stereotype of a dissenter was a "tenacious advocate of traditional doctrine". These conclusions are interesting, but limited. No causal link is demonstrated. The dangers lurks—as with behaviouralism generally—of losing sight of the normative character of law.

With their political science background, judicial behaviouralists may be forgiven for thinking that judges are policy makers, and nothing else. But, just as it would be wrong to ignore the political element in decision making, it is equally facile to see judges as politicians, and nothing else. Future behaviouralists may rescue the "ought" of law and appreciate its underlying rationale.[11]

---

[5] See "Off-The-Bench Judicial Attitudes" in (ed.) G. Schubert, *Judicial Decision-Making* (1963).

[6] *Op. cit.*, n. 3, p. 1616.

[7] *Social Dimensions of Law and Justice* (1966), p. 693.

[8] *ibid.*, pp 693–694 and *Law and Social Sciences* (1966), pp 82–83.

[9] Nor should it be forgotten that the court can fashion the judge's conception of his/her role. "Role theory indicates how broad is the area of similarity in the behaviour of judges, because of the structural factors of the role", *per* James (1968) 30 J. of Politics 186.

[10] (1959) 3 Midwest J. of Political Science 1.

[11] Judicial behaviouralism hardly developed in Britain (see L Baum's criticism (1977) 7 B. J. of Polit. Sci. 511) of British political scientists' lack of interest in the courts). See, however, D. Robertson (1982) 12 Br. J. of Polit. Sci. 1.

### Pragmatism In Law

As already noted, Realism was influenced by philosophical pragmatism.[12] With the decline of Realism an echo of this pragmatism has re-emerged as "pragmatism in law".[13] One of today's self-proclaimed legal pragmatists is Richard Posner.[14] He is "interested in pragmatism as a disposition to ground policy judgments on facts and consequences rather than on conceptualisms and generalities.[15] In his words, to be pragmatic is to be "instrumental" "forward looking", "empirical", "skeptical", "antidogmatic".[16] It is not, in his view, incompatible to subscribe to pragmatism as well as espousing an economic analysis of law. Thus, law and economics "epitomizes the operation in law of the ethic of scientific inquiry, pragmatically understood ... Economics is the instrumental science par excellence".[17]

Posner's pragmatism can be illustrated by examining his theory of adjudication. The pragmatist judge is looking for the best decision having in mind present and future needs and "so does not regard the maintenance of consistency with past decisions as an end in itself but only as a means for bringing about the best results in the present case".[18] Precedent is thus a source of information and a limited constraint on freedom of decision, but it is not where the judge will get "the rule of decision for the truly novel case".[19]

Nor will the judge be assisted by recourse to philosophy, even perhaps to philosphical pragmatism.[20] So Posner argues: "Philosophical pragmatists and their opponents go at each other hammer and tongs over such questions as whether language reflects reality, whether free will is compatible with a scientific outlook, and whether such questions are even meaningful. I am not interested in such issues".[21] Posner now insists that moral theory has little to offer law and recommends instead that judges and jurists should seek assistance in economists' empirical tools.

This has led to a somewhat acrimonious argument with Dworkin.[22] A fulcrum of this disputation is the U.S Supreme Court decision on the

---

[12] *Ante*, 985.
[13] See R. Warner, "Legal Pragmatism" in (ed.) D. Patterson, *A Companion To Philosophy of Law and Legal Theory* (1996), p. 385. The *Cardozo Law Rev.*, vol. 18(1) is a Special Issue source on "The Revival of Pragmatism".
[14] *The Problematics of Moral and Legal Theory* (1999), Chap. 4.
[15] *ibid.*, p. 227.
[16] *Overcoming Law* (1995), p. 11. This is defended (against Dworkin) at (1997) 29 Arizona State L.J. 377, 384–386.
[17] *Overcoming Law, op. cit.*, p. 15. And see *ante*, 620.
[18] (1996) 18 Cardozo L.Rev. 1, 5.
[19] *ibid.*
[20] T. Grey (1996) 18 Cardozo L.R. 21 has argued the case for pragmatism in legal theory being independent of pragmatism in philosophy. See also M. Rosenfeld (1996) 18 Cardozo L.R. 97, 103–110.
[21] *Op. cit.*, n. 14, p. 227: he cites R. Rorty.
[22] One example of which is in (1997) 29 Arizona State L.J. 353 (Dworkin), 377 (Posner), 431 (Dworkin). Interesting insights (including historical analogies) are found in A. Hutchinson and S. Archer (2001) 54 C.L.P. 19.

right to assisted suicide.[23] Dworkin had been one of the authors of "The Philosophers' Brief", the arguments of which the Supreme Court rejected,[24] and subsequently attacked the Court for failing to "understand fully the philosophical dimension of adjudication and the ethical responsibilities of judges in interpreting the Constitution".[25] But for Posner, Dworkin was wrong to insist that judges have recourse to moral theory. And the Supreme Court was right to distance itself from moral debates about the right to die. Courts carry out their institutional roles best when they anchor policy judgments in facts and consequences, rather than, what he calls, conceptualisms and generalities.

But when a philosophical question arises in connection with a legal issue—as it clearly did in the right to assisted suicide cases—it is "continuous" with legal argument.[26] Luban[27] uses the example of *Jones* v. *Barnes*.[28] A convicted robber asked his assigned counsel to raise issues on appeal in addition to those counsel had chosen to focus on. Counsel refused, the appeal failed and the convicted man sought *habeas* relief, arguing that he had received ineffective assistance of counsel. The majority ruled against him. Its reasoning was overtly paternalistic. Questions of tactics are properly left to lawyers, not clients, because lawyers know better than clients what is in the client's best interests; to hold otherwise "would disserve the very goal of vigorous and effective advocacy".[29] The dissenting judges replied with a direct argument against paternalism which could have come straight from Kant or Mill. Said Justice Brennan "today's ruling denegrates the values of individual autonomy and dignity . . . The role of the defense lawyer should be above all to function as the instrument and defender of the client's autonomy and dignity".[30] As Luban points out, both the majority and the minority could have couched their arguments in pragmatic terms but this would have evaded the issue of principle which both sides rightly addressed— and that issue of principle is a philosophical issue that invites philosophical questions about the nature of autonomy and dignity.[31]

## *Legal Process*

It is Duxbury who points to a tradition of American jurisprudence known as "legal process" as a post-realist tradition.[32] Whilst conceding that it is inappropriate strictly to characterize it as such—for it paralleled

---

[23] *Washington v. Glucksberg* (1997) 521 U.S. 702.
[24] *New York Rev. of Books*, March 27, 1997, pp. 41–47.
[25] *Per* Hutchinson and Archer, *op. cit.*, n. 22, p. 23.
[26] *Per* D. Luban (1996) 18 Cardozo L.R. 43, 58.
[27] *ibid.*, p. 59.
[28] (1983) 463 U.S. 745.
[29] *ibid.*, p. 754.
[30] *ibid.*, p. 763.
[31] See further J. Hampton (1992) 39 UCLA L.Rev. 1659, M. Galanter and D. Luban (1993) 42 Am. U.L. Rev. 1393, D. Dolinko (1986) 33 UCLA L.Rev. 1063.
[32] (1993) 15 Cardozo L.Rev. 601.

if it did not pre-date the advent of realism—it was "only as legal realism began to wane that the process tradition came to acquire a distinctive reality".[33]

At the centre of "the legal process" is the belief that law is a purposive process. Accounting to Henry Hart and Albert Sacks[34] the very purpose of legal institutions is to maximise the total satisfaction of valid human desires.[35] Successful pursuit of this goal demands an efficient legal system. According to Hart and Sacks, there will only be such a system if most issues of social ordering are left to the autonomy of individuals and groups. The law should only intervene when required and then it should only be the legal institution (whether in the particular case this be the legislation or the courts) which is competent to do so. Although Hart and Sacks comment upon the competence of all law-making bodies, it is their reflections on the courts which are central to the legal process tradition. Courts have "the power of reasoned elaboration"[36] and are therefore expected to reach decisions on the basis of rationally defensible principles. A decision could not be a good decision unless supported by principle. Why this should be so—pragmatists for example could easily defend a decision which was unprincipled but had good consequences—was not elaborated upon by Hart and Sacks.

One who attempted to do so was Herbert Wechsler. In a famous article published in 1959[37] he argued that in the first half of the twentieth century (particularly during the "New Deal" era), the U.S. Supreme Court had paid little attention to principles. By the 1950s, he conceded, "good" decisions were being made—he cites *Brown v. Board of Education*.[38] But even decisions like this one were unsatisfactory because they were insufficiently principled. Thus, the Supreme Court should have invalidated segregation of schools not because segregation harmed black children (on which he anyway questioned the evidence) but on the basis of a principle, neutral as between blacks and whites, such as that the state ought not to impede freedom of association.[39] It was all very well applauding the Court for deciding *Brown v. Board of Education* the way it did but activist courts could equally well come to decisions of which one disapproved.[40] But if neutral principles governed, adjudication was more likely to command respect whether one liked the conclusions or not.

As Duxbury points out, "this faith in principle marks off the legal process tradition from realist tradition in American jurisprudence".[41] The

---

[33] *Per* N. Duxbury, "Post-Realism and Legal Process" in (ed.) D. Patterson, *op. cit.*, n. 13, pp. 291, 296.
[34] *The Legal Process* (Tentative ed. 1958) (ed. by Eskridge and Frickey, 1994).
[35] The influence of Pound is very clear (see *ante*, 897).
[36] *Op. cit.*, n. 34, p. 161.
[37] (1959) 73 Harvard L. Rev. 1.
[38] (1954) 347 U.S. 483. This ordered the desegration of schools "with all deliberate speed".
[39] Wechsler was not convinced that this was the principle at stake here.
[40] *Lochner v. New York* 198 U.S. 74 (emphasising liberty of contract), today best known for Holmes J.'s dissent (*ante*, 988).
[41] *Op. cit.*, n. 33, p. 300.

Realist recognized indeterminacy,[42] but gave few clues as to how it was to be constrained or eliminated. The process thinkers see such constraint on indeterminacy as lying within the force of principle. This is not a complete or, some would say,[43] even a satisfactory answer. Principles themselves may be indeterminate or may conflict.

"Legal process" may be seen as a bridge between realism—to which perhaps it was a response—and the writings of Ronald Dworkin and "law as integrity".

---

## O. W. HOLMES
### The Path of the Law
#### (1897)[44]

Take the fundamental question, What constitutes the law? You will find some text writers telling you that it is something different from what is decided by the courts of Massachusetts or England, that it is a system of reason, that it is a deduction from principles of ethics or admitted axioms or what not, which may or may not coincide with the decisions. But if we take the view of our friend the bad man[45] we shall find that he does not care two straws for the axioms or deductions, but that he does want to know what the Massachusetts or English courts are likely to do in fact. I am much of his mind. The prophecies of what the courts[46] will do in fact, and nothing more pretentious, are what I mean by the law.[47]     [pp. 172–173]

---

[42] On indeterminacy see L.B. Solum (1987) 54 Univ. of Chicago L. Rev. 462. A. D'Amato has called indeterminancy "the key issue in legal scholarship today" ((1990) 85 Northwestern Univ. L.Rev. 148).

[43] In particular the critical legal theorists: see ch. 14.

[44] [From (1897) 10 Harv. L.Rev. 457–478.

It should not be forgotten that this statement was made in the context of legal education. This extract has been described by Llewellyn as the "internationally-cited goblin-painting of realism" (*The Common Law Tradition*, p. 511).]

[45] [On the significance of the "bad man" for legal theory, see Twining (1973) 58 Cornell L.R. 275. He shows that "when Holmes advised his audience to adopt the standpoint of the Bad Man, he was not seriously urging them to use the Bad Man as an ethical model, rather, he was suggesting that they look at law from the perspective of a citizen who is concerned with predicting the consequences of his actions" (p. 282).]

[46] [Even if "courts" here is wide enough to cover administrative or other tribunals, there are many classes of matters which in a modern state remain largely in the field of administration and negotiation, and are hardly ever the subject of litigation. This no doubt accounts for Llewellyn's expansion of the idea to cover, "officials." (But see his Foreword to the revised edition (1951) of *The Bramble Bush*, pp. 8–9). But it remains true that even in such cases negotiations may be conducted and decisions reached with one eye on what a court might conceivably decide. Nor is this a form of prediction which interests only "the bad man" in Holmes's sense.]

[47] For the strikingly similar sentiments of Jhering, see Zweigert and Siehr (1971) 19 Am.J.Comp.L. 215, 228. Striking similarities between this and the labelling perspective in deviancy theory have been noted by Gibbs in Scott and Douglas, *Theoretical Perspectives on Deviance* (1972).]

## J. FRANK
### Law and the Modern Mind
(English ed., 1949)

Actually, these so-called realists have but one common bond, a negative characteristic already noted: skepticism as to some of the conventional legal theories, a skepticism stimulated by a zeal to reform, in the interest of justice, some courthouse ways. Despite the lack of any homogeneity in their positive views, these "constructive skeptics," roughly speaking, do divide into two groups; however, there are marked differences, ignored by the critics, between the two groups.

The first group, of whom Llewellyn is perhaps the outstanding representative, I would call "rule skeptics." They aim at greater legal certainty. That is, they consider it socially desirable that lawyers should be able to predict to their clients the decisions in most lawsuits not yet commenced. They feel that, in too many instances, the layman cannot act with assurance as to how, if his acts become involved in a suit, the court will decide. As these skeptics see it, the trouble is that the formal legal rules enunciated in courts' opinions—sometimes called "paper rules"—too often prove unreliable as guides in the prediction of decisions. They believe that they can discover, behind the "paper rules," some "real rules" descriptive of uniformities or regularities in actual judicial behavior, and that those "real rules" will serve as more reliable prediction-instruments, yielding a large measure of workable predictability of the outcome of future suits. In this undertaking, the rule skeptics concentrate almost exclusively on upper-court opinions. They do not ask themselves whether their own or any other prediction-device will render it possible for a lawyer or layman to prophesy, before an ordinary suit is instituted or comes to trial in a trial court, how it will be decided. In other words, these rule skeptics seek means for making accurate guesses, not about decisions of trial courts, but about decisions of upper courts when trial-court decisions are appealed. These skeptics cold-shoulder the trial courts. Yet, in most instances, these skeptics do not inform their readers that they are writing chiefly of upper courts.

The second group I would call "fact skeptics." They, too, engaging in "rule skepticism," peer behind the "paper rules." Together with the rule skeptics, they have stimulated interest in factors, influencing upper-court decisions, of which, often, the opinions of those courts give no hint. But the fact skeptics go much further. Their primary interest is in the trial courts. No matter how precise or definite may be the formal legal rules, say these fact skeptics, no matter what the discoverable uniformities behind these formal rules, nevertheless it is impossible, and will always be impossible, because of the elusiveness of the facts on which decisions turn, to predict future decisions in most (not all) lawsuits, not yet begun or not yet tried. The fact skeptics, thinking that therefore the pursuit of greatly increased legal certainty is, for the most part, futile—and that its pursuit, indeed, may well work injustice—aim rather at increased judicial justice. This group of fact skeptics includes, among others, Dean Leon Green, Max Radin, Thurman Arnold,[48] William O. Douglas (now Mr. Justice Douglas), and perhaps E. M. Morgan.

Within each of these groups there is diversity of opinion as to many ideas. But I

---

[48] [But Arnold was a critic of Frank and realism generally. For Arnold the law was an important symbol, an ideal of government. "The ideal of a judiciary which discovers its principles through the enlightened application of established precedents dramatizes that most important conception that there is a rule of law above men" (24 U.Chi.L.Rev. 634). The Realist had seen this but had regarded it as a defect in the law. But "the escape of the law from reality constitutes ... its greatest strength." (*The Symbols of Government* (1935), p. 44).]

think it can be said that, generally, most of the rule skeptics, restricting themselves to the upper-court level, live in an artificial two dimensional legal world, while the legal world of the fact skeptics is three-dimensional. Obviously, many events occurring in the fact skeptics' three-dimensional cosmos are out of sight, and therefore out of mind, in the rule skeptics' cosmos.

The critical anti-skeptics also live in the artificial upper-court world. Naturally, they have found less fault with the rule skeptics than with the fact skeptics. The critics, for instance, said that Llewellyn was a bit wild yet not wholly unsound, but the men like Dean Green grossly exaggerated the extent of legal uncertainty (*i.e.* the unpredictability of decisions). To my mind, the critics shoe the wrong foot: Both the rule skeptics and the critics grossly exaggerate the extent of legal certainty, because their own writings deal only with the prediction of upper-court decisions. The rule skeptics are, indeed, but the left-wing adherents of a tradition. It is from the tradition itself that the fact skeptics revolted.

As a reading of this book will disclose, I am one of the fact skeptics. The point there made may be summarized thus: If one accepts as correct the conventional description of how courts reach their decisions, then a decision of any lawsuit results from the application of a legal rule or rules to the facts of the suit. That sounds rather simple, and apparently renders it fairly easy to prophesy the decision, even of a case not yet commenced or tried, especially when as often happens, the applicable rule is definite and precise (for instance, the rule about driving on the right side of the road). But particularly when pivotal testimony at the trial is oral and conflicting, as it is in most lawsuits, the trial court's "finding" of the facts involves a multitude of elusive factors: First, the trial judge in a non-jury trial or the jury in a jury trial must learn about the facts from the witnesses; and witnesses, being humanly fallible, frequently make mistakes in observation of what they saw and heard, or in their recollections of what they observed, or in their court-room reports of those recollections. Second, the trial judges or juries,[49] also human, may have prejudices—often unconscious unknown even to themselves—for or against some of the witnesses, or the parties to the suit, or the lawyers.

Those prejudices, when they are racial, religious, political, or economic, may sometimes be surmised by others. But there are some hidden, unconscious biases of trial judges or jurors—such as, for example, plus or minus reactions to women, or unmarried women, or red-haired women, or brunettes, or men with deep voices or high-pitched voices, or fidgety men, or men who wear thick eyeglasses, or those who have pronounced gestures or nervous tics—biases of which no one can be aware. Concealed and highly idiosyncratic, such biases—peculiar to each individual judge or juror—cannot be formulated as uniformities or squeezed into regularized "behavior patterns." In that respect, neither judges nor jurors are standardized.

The chief obstacle to prophesying a trial-court decision is, then, the inability, thanks to these inscrutable factors, to foresee what a particular trial judge or jury will believe to be the facts. Consider, particularly, the perplexity of a lawyer asked to guess the outcome of a suit not yet commenced: He must guess whether some of the witnesses will persuasively lie, or will honestly but persuasively give unaccurate testimony; as, usually, he does not even know the trial judge or jury who will try the case, he must also guess the reactions—to the witnesses, the parties and the lawyers—of an unknown trial judge or jury.

These difficulties have been overlooked by most of those (the rule skeptics included) who write on the subject of legal certainty or the prediction of decisions.

---

[49] [Research since Frank wrote has shown that jury verdicts are not as unpredictable as he suggested. There is, for instance, a high coincidence between jury verdicts and the decision a judge would have arrived at without a jury. See Kalven and Zeisel, *The American Jury* (1966).]

They often call their writings "jurisprudence"; but, as they almost never consider juries and jury trials, one might chide them for forgetting "jurisprudence."

Moreover, most of them overlook another feature, not revealed in the conventional description of how courts decide cases, a feature unusually baffling: According to the conventional description, judging in a trial court is made up of two components which, initially distinct, are logically combined to produce a decision. Those components, it is said, are (1) the determination of the facts and (2) the determination of what rules should be applied to those facts. In reality, however, those components often are not distinct but intertwine in the thought processes of the trial judge or jury. The decision is frequently an undifferentiated composite which precedes any analysis or breakdown into facts and rules. Many a time, for all anyone can tell, a trial judge makes no such analysis or breakdown when rendering his decision unaccompanied by an explanation. But even when he publishes an explanation, it may be misdescriptive of the way in which the decision was reached...

Shutting their eyes to the actualities of trials, most of the lawyers who write for other lawyers or for laymen about the courts are victims of the Upper-Court Myth. They have deluded themselves and, alas, many non-lawyers, with two correlated false beliefs: (1) They believe that the major cause of legal uncertainty is uncertainty in the rules, so that if the legal rules—or the "real rules" behind the "paper rules"—are entirely clear and crisp, the doubts about future decisions largely vanish. (2) They believe that, on appeals, most mistakes made by trial courts can be rectified by the upper courts. In truth, as noted above, the major cause of legal uncertainty is fact-uncertainty—the unknowability, before the decision, of what the trial court will "find" as the facts, and the unknowability after the decision of the way in which it "found" those facts. If a trial court mistakenly takes as true the oral testimony of an honest but inaccurate witness or a lying witness, seldom can an upper court detect his mistake; it therefore usually adopts the facts as found by the trial court. It does so because the trial court saw and heard the witnesses testify, while the upper court has before it only a lifeless printed report of the testimony, a report that does not contain the witnesses' demeanor, which is often significantly revealing...

With this perspective, we get new light on the doctrine of following the precedents ... That doctrine ... may have less practical importance to the ordinary man than its more ardent advocates accord it. Yet no sane informed person will deny that, within appropriate limits, judicial adherence to precedents possesses such great value that to abandon it would be unthinkable...

However, even when properly and conscientiously utilized, the practice of following the precedents cannot guarantee the stability and certainty it seems to promise to some of those who confine their scrutiny to upper-court decisions. For, in an upper court, ordinarily no fact-finding problem exists, as the facts are beyond dispute, having already been found by the trial court. The usual questions for the upper court are, then, these: Do the facts of the case now before the court sufficiently resemble those of an earlier case so that the rule of that case is applicable? If there is such a resemblance, should that rule now be applied or should it be modified or abandoned? Although able lawyers cannot always guess how an upper court will answer those questions, the educated guesses of those lawyers are good in the majority of instances. When, in a trial court, the parties to a suit agree on the facts, so that the facts are undisputed, that court faces only those same questions; and again, usually, able lawyers can guess the answers.

But, to repeat, in most cases in the trial courts the parties to dispute about the facts, and the testimony concerning the facts is oral and conflicting. In any such case, what does it mean to say that the facts of a case are substantially similar to those of an earlier case? It means, at most, merely that the trial court regards the facts of the two cases as about the same. Since, however, no one knows what the trial court will find as the facts, no one can guess what precedent ought to be or will be followed either by the trial court or, if an appeal occurs, by the upper court. This weakness of the precedent doctrine becomes more obvious when one takes into account the "composite" factor, the intertwining of rules and facts in the trial court's decision.

This weakness will also infect any substitute precedent system, based on "real rules" which the rule skeptics may discover, by way of anthropology—*i.e.* the mores, customs, folkways—or psychology, or statistics, or studies of the political, economic, and social backgrounds of judges, or otherwise. For no rule can be hermetically sealed against the intrusion of false or inaccurate oral testimony which the trial judge or jury may believe.[50]                                        [pp. vii-xiv]

## K. LLEWELLYN
### Some Realism About Realism
### (1931)[51]

*Real realists*

What, then *are* the characteristics of these fermenters? One thing is clear. There is no school of realists. There is no likelihood that there will be such a school. There is no group with an official or accepted, or even with an emerging creed. There is no abnegation of independent striking out. We hope that there may never be. New recruits acquire tools and stimulus, not masters, nor overmastering ideas. Old recruits diverge in interests from each other. They are related, says Frank, only in their negations, and in their skepticisms, and in their curiosity.

There is, however, a *movement* in thought and work about law. The movement, the method of attack, is wider than the number of its adherents. It includes some or much work of many men who would scorn ascription to its banner. Individual men, then. Men more or less interstimulated—but no more than all of them have been stimulated by the orthodox tradition, or by that ferment at the opening of the century in which Dean Pound took a leading part. Individual men, working and thinking over law and its place in society. Their differences in point of view, in interest, in emphasis, in field of work, are huge. They differ among themselves well-nigh as much as any of them differs from, say, Langdell. Their number grows. Their work finds acceptance.

What one does find as he observes them is twofold. First (and to be expected) certain points of departure are common to them all. Second (and this, when one can find neither school nor striking likenesses among individuals, is startling) a cross-relevance, a complementing, an interlocking of their varied results "as if

[50] [One aspect of Frank, often neglected, is that of Frank—the law reformer. He made a number of constructive proposals which taken together would go some way towards reducing fact-uncertainty. Rumble, *op. cit.*, pp. 126–130 gives a useful summary of some of Frank's ideas. His views on legal education are particularly pertinent. Reading only appeal court opinions was like "future horticulturists studying solely cut flowers." Instead, students should observe at first hand the operations of trial and appellate courts, the actions of legislatures and administrative agencies. Law schools ought to conduct legal clinics Case-books should contain the complete record of the whole case.]

[51] [From (1931) 44 Harv.L.Rev. 1222, © 1931, by the Harvard Law Review Association. Now reprinted in K. Llewellyn, *Jurisprudence* (1962), p. 42, with a few textual amendments, which have been embodied in those portions of the text quoted in this volume. The interesting background to this article is described by Twining in *Karl Llewellyn and the Realist Movement*, Chap. 5. But newly uncovered private correspondence throws a rather different light on the exchange: see Hull (1987) Wisconsin L.Rev. 921. Hull has gone on to argue that Llewellyn "deliberately rewrote the public version of the intellectual history of the movement to conceal Pound's vital role in it." (1989) Duke L.J. 1302, 1306.]

they were guided by an invisible hand." A third thing may be mentioned in passing: a fighting faith in their methods of attack on legal problems; but in these last years the battle with the facts has proved so much more exciting than any battle traditionalism that the fighting faith had come (until the spring offensive of 1931 against the realists) to manifest itself chiefly in enthusiastic labor to get on.

But as with a description of an economic order, tone and color of description must vary with the point of view of the reporter. No other one of the men would set the picture up as I shall. Such a report must thus be individual. Each man, of necessity, orients the whole to his own main interest of the moment—as I shall orient the whole to mine: the workings of case-law in appellate courts. Maps of the United States prepared respectively by a political geographer and a student of climate would show some resemblance; each would show a coherent picture; but neither's map would give much satisfaction to the other. So here. I speak for myself of that movement which in its sum is realism; I do not speak of "the realists"; still less do I speak *for* the participants or any of them. And I shall endeavor to keep in mind as I go that the justification for grouping these men together lies not in that they are *alike* in belief or work, but in that from certain common points of departure they have branched into lines of work which seem to be building themselves into a whole, a whole planned by none, foreseen by none, and (it may well be) not yet adequately grasped by any.

The common points of departure are several.

(1)  The conception of law in flux, of moving law, and of judicial creation of law.

(2)  The conception of law as a means to social ends and not as an end in itself; so that any part needs constantly to be examined for its purpose, and for its effect, and to be judged in the light of both and of their relation to each other.

(3)  The conception of society in flux, and in flux typically faster than the law, so that the probability is always given that any portion of law needs re-examination to determine how far it fits the society it purports to serve.

(4)  The *temporary* divorce of Is and Ought for purposes of study.[52] By this I mean that whereas value judgments must always be appealed to in order to set objectives for inquiry, yet during the inquiry itself into what Is, the observation, the description, and the establishment of relations between the things described are to remain *as largely as possible* uncontaminated by the desires of the observer or by what he wishes might be or thinks ought (ethically) to be. More particularly, this involves during the study of what courts are doing the effort to disregard the question what they ought to do. Such divorce of Is and Ought is, of course, not conceived as permanent. To men who begin with a suspicion that change is needed, a permanent divorce would be impossible. The argument is simply that no judgment of what Ought to be done in the future with respect to any part of law can be intelligently made without knowing objectively, as far as possible, what that part of law is now doing. And realists believe that experience shows the intrusion of Ought-spectacles *during the investigation of the facts* to make it very difficult to see what is being done. On the Ought side this means an insistence on informed evaluations instead of armchair speculations. Its full implications on the side of Is-investigation can be appreciated only when one follows the contributions to objective description in business law and practice made by realists whose social

---

[52]  [The influence of Weber's *wertfrei* social science is apparent. But, on the possibility of developing a value-free sociology as a myth see A. Gouldner, 9 *Social Problems* 199–213.]

philosophy rejects many of the accepted foundations of the existing economic order.[53]

[...]

(5) Distrust of traditional legal rules and concepts insofar as they purport to *describe* what either courts or people are actually doing.[54] Hence the constant emphasis on rules as "generalized predictions of what courts can do." This is much more widespread as yet than its counterpart: the careful severance of rules *for* doing (precepts) from rules *of* doing (practices).

(6) Hand in hand with this distrust of traditional rules (on the descriptive side) goes a distrust of the theory that traditional prescriptive rule-formulations are *the* heavily operative factor in producing court decisions. This involves the tentative exploration of the theory of rationalization for what light it can give in the study of opinions. It will be noted that "distrust" in this and the preceding point is not at all equivalent to "negation in any given instance."

(7) The belief in the worthwhileness of grouping cases and legal situations into narrower categories than has been the practice in the past.[55] This is connected with the distrust of verbally simple rules—which so often cover

---

[53] [This starting-point is at once the most controversial and difficult of Llewellyn's credo. It is not accepted by all Realists (see, *e.g.* H. Yntema (1960–61) 14 Vand. L.R. 317, 323–325). Together with point (5), it was the principal bone of contention with Pound, though Stone believes the controversy to have been illusory. (*Social Dimensions*, pp. 64–67). "It is certainly now clear," he writes, "that [Llewellyn] was asking *not for the observor to ignore the actor's ideals, but for the observor to put aside his own*, so that accurate observation and description should not be interfered with." (*ibid.*, pp. 64–65). And, in an article he wrote in 1939 ("One 'Realist's View of Natural Law for Judges," in *Jurisprudence*, p. 111), Llewellyn confirms that lawyers are concerned with values "applicable to a given going society," though from the point of view of the jurist this "ought" becomes an "is." See, further, on this question, Friedrich, 74 *Ethics* 201. Llewellyn's view of natural law has the relativist ring of Stammler about it. He distinguishes a lawyer's natural law from a philosopher's. The latter is concerned with the right ordering of any human society, the lawyer with principles "applicable to a given going society." A lawyer's natural law is an effort to bring the philosopher's Natural Law to bear in lawyer-like actual regulation "on legal problems in a particular society. It afford[s] a concrete guide to the making of proper positive law." See for elucidation Twining, *Karl Llewellyn and the Realist Movement*, pp. 187–8.]

[54] [The so-called Free-Law School of the Continent is to be distinguished from the Realists, since the former did not so much distrust rules, but asserted that there are many gaps in the law which the courts may fill by exercising a free discretion. This did not prevent there being a large area where the rules as formulated exercised a substantially effective control. See H. Kantorowicz (1934) Yale L.J. 1240. *cf.* Frank, *Law and the Modern Mind*, pp. 301–306. For an appraisal of the Free-Law School see, Foulkes (1969) 55 *Archiv für Rechts-und-sozialphilosophie* 367. For the view that the free law movement is the source of American Realism see J. Herget and S. Wallace (1987) 73 Virginia Law Rev. 399. Their comparative appendix (pp. 440–52) shows real parallels. The conduit seems to have been Roscoe Pound.]

[55] [The quest for narrower, more significant, categories is always a sound *first* approach to wide categories which are not giving satisfaction-in-use. But, of course, once satisfactory narrower categories have been found and tested, the eternal quest recurs, for wider synthesis—but one which really stands up in use. With this advice in mind, the framers of the Uniform Commercial Code often substitute narrower categories for a broad one. But the reverse is also occasionally true. For example, trust receipts, chattel mortgages, *etc.* are replaced by the umbrella, "security." See Twining, O'Donovan, Paliwala in Jolowicz (ed.), *The Division and Classification of the Law*, pp. 10, 24. On the success of this see the interesting article on Llewellyn and merchant rules by Z. Wiseman (1987) 100 Harv.L. Rev. 465.]

dissimilar and non-simple fact situations (dissimilarity being tested partly by the way cases come out, and partly by the observer's judgment as to how they ought to come out[56]; but a realist tries to indicate explicitly which criterion he is applying in any particular instance).[57]

(8) An insistence on evaluations of any part of law in terms of its effects, and an insistence on the worthwhileness of trying to find these effects.

(9) Insistence on *sustained and programmatic attack* on the problems of law along any of these lines. None of the ideas set forth in this list is new. Each can be matched from somewhere; each can be matched from recent orthodox work in law. New twists and combinations do appear here and there. What is as novel as it is vital is for a goodly number of men to pick up ideas which have been expressed and dropped, used for an hour and dropped, played with from time to time and dropped—to pick up such ideas and set about *consistently, persistently, insistently to carry them through*...

The first, second, third and fifth of the above items, while common to the workers of the newer movement, are not peculiar to them. But the other items (4, 6, 7, 8 and 9) are to me the characteristic marks of the movement. Men or work fitting those specifications are to me "realistic" whatever label they may wear. Such, and none other, are the perfect fauna of this new land. Not all the work cited below fits my peculiar definition in all points. All such work fits most of the points.

Bound, as all "innovators" are, by prior thinking, these innovating "realists" brought their batteries to bear in first instance on the work of appellate courts. Still wholly within the tradition of our law, they strove to improve on that tradition.

(a) An early and fruitful line of attack borrowed from psychology the concept of *rationalization* already mentioned. To recanvass the opinions, viewing them no longer as mirroring the process of deciding cases, but rather as trained lawyers' arguments made by the judges (after the decision has been reached), intended to make the decision seem plausible, legally decent, legally right, to make it seem, indeed, legally inevitable—this was to open up new vision. It was assumed that the deductive logic of opinions need by no means be either a *description* of the process of decision, or an *explanation* of how the decision was reached. Indeed over-enthusiasm has at times assumed that the logic of the opinion *could* be neither; and similar over-enthusiasm, perceiving case after case in which the opinion is clearly almost valueless as an indication of how that case came to decision, has worked at times almost as if the opinion were equally valueless in predicting what a later court will do.

But the line of inquiry via rationalization has come close to demonstrating that in any case doubtful enough to make litigation respectable the available authoritative premises—*i.e.* premises legitimate and impeccable under the traditional legal techniques—are at least two, and that the two are mutually contradictory as applied to the case in hand. Which opens the question of what made the court select the one available premise rather than the other. And which raises the greatest of doubts as to *how far* that supposed certainty in decision which derives merely or even chiefly from the presence of accepted rules really goes.

---

[56] [A striking illustration of this comes out in the writings of Willard Hurst. See particularly his study of the Wisconsin lumber industry, *Law and Economic Growth* (1964), and see the comment in Stone (1966) 1 Israel L.R. 173, 192.]

[57] On this see Jolowicz (ed.), *The Division and Classification of the Law*. Jolowicz advocates factual classification and enlisting the help of social scientists and economists.

(b) A second line of attack has been to discriminate rules with reference to their relative significance. Too much is written and thought about "law" and "rules," lump-wise. Which part of law? Which rule? Iron rules of policy, and rules "in the absence of agreement"; rules which keep a case from the jury, and rules as to the etiquette of instructions necessary to make a verdict stick—if one can get it; rules "of pure decision" for hospital cases, and rules which counsellors rely on in their counselling; rules which affect many (and which many, and how?) and rules which affect few. Such discriminations affects the traditional law curriculum, the traditional organisation of law books, and, above all, the orientation of study: to drive into the most important fields of ignorance.

(c) A further line of attack on the apparent conflict and uncertainty among the decisions in appellate courts has been to seek more understandable statement of them by grouping the facts in new—and typically but not always narrower—categories. The search is for correlations of fact-situation and outcome which (aided by common sense) may reveal *when* courts seize on one rather than another of the available competing premises. One may even stumble on the trial of *why* they do. [. . .] If so, the rules—viewed as statements of the course of judicial behavior—as *predictions* of what will happen—need to be restated. Sometimes it is a question of carving out hitherto unnoticed exceptions. But sometimes the results force the worker to reclassify an area altogether. Typically, as stated, the classes of situations which result are narrower, much narrower than the traditional classes. The process is in essence the orthodox technique of making distinctions, and reformulating—but undertaken systematically; exploited consciously, instead of being reserved until facts which refuse to be twisted by "interpretation" force action. The departure from orthodox procedure lies chiefly in distrust of, instead of search for, the widest sweep of generalization words permit. Not that such sweeping generalizations are not desired—*if they can be made so as to state what judges do or ought to do.*

All of these three earliest lines of attack converge to a single conclusion: *there is less possibility of accurate prediction of what courts will do than the traditional rules would lead us to suppose* (and what possibility there is must be found in good measure outside these same traditional rules). [pp. 1233–1241]

## K. LLEWELLYN
### My Philosophy of Law
(1941)[58]

There was a time when law was the concern of philosophers, and was conceived as a part of philosophy. There has been concern more recently, among the social scientists, with law as a social science. Lawyers know law as a craft, and as a profession; they know it also as a body of rules; they have rarely bothered to figure out the relation between these phases. Statesmen have known law as one key-aspect of society, as a guide, as a tool, as a limiting obligation—but rarely have they wrestled with how these all fit together. In truth, law is each of these things which have been mentioned, and it is more things, as well; and one large portion of the disputes among jurisprudes loses much of its meaning and if the phases of law which are peculiarly dear to one and another of the combatants are put each into relation with law as a whole.

That whole is most fruitfully viewed as a going institution, and a necessary institution, in society. And a going institution is of course never made up of rules

---

[58] [From *My Philosophy of Law*, published by Boston Law Co.]

alone, nor of ideals alone. It may contain rules as one of its parts. In the case of our own law, the institution contains as one of its parts a tremendous and tremendously important body of rules,[59] organized (quite loosely) around concepts and shot through with principles.[60] Indeed, companioning these rules and principles of "law" proper, there are other rules and other concepts: the formulated techniques of "precedent," of "construction," and the like, to guide manipulation of the first. But over and above these, the going institution of our law contains an ideology and a body of pervasive and powerful ideals which are largely unspoken, largely implicit, and which pass almost unmentioned in the books. It contains also a host of sometimes vagrant, sometimes rigid practices, of ways of doing what is done, without such things as rules would have no meaning in life. And *it contains* also a host of men, who are an integral working portion of the whole, and are not simply persons "subject to" some thing outside them which one can know as "law." To see this is not to see men running and ruling, wild and arbitrary. It is to see them running and ruling in courses somewhat channeled, with ideas and ideals somewhat controlled. They are the men of *law*, the *law*-men. That makes a difference.

To expand the field of jurisprudence in this fashion out beyond the rules, the imperatives and the norms, has seemed to some bewildering. To shift the focus of emphasis off of the rules has seemed to others wayward and even dangerous. The position taken here is that such expansion and shift are a sound road out of prior confusion, on through any bewilderment, into a deeper simplicity; and that they are a sound road out of prior inadequate guidance and pseudo-certainty, through and beyond any danger, on into deeper, clearer, and more effective ways of guidance and truer certainty. The wider view of rules-in-their-setting yields rules both righter, and more effective. It then continues to illumine such better rules as not being the whole of law, but only one characteristic and crucial part of that whole. It insists, for each tomorrow, on the need for looking at that tomorrow's law-*consumer*.

To begin, the viewing of law as a going institution provides two vitally servicable points of orientation which freshen eyes and give a cross-check on what may be there to see. For, first, a going institution has jobs to do, and its function is to get them done effectively and well. This gives a pole of purpose and value of measure by. And, secondly, a going institution has results in life, and must be tested by them; and those results are capable of inquiry. The measure of the institution is, then, the measure of how its results check in fact, in regard to the actual doing of its jobs.

The jobs on which law is focussed are not indeed accomplished wholly by law, nor will they ever be. For all that, they are well seen as peculiarly *law*-jobs, because law represents a phase and a machinery in their accomplishment which is peculiarly conscious, is often critical in its points of incidence, and is the area of action and thought in which conflicts and needed corrections come peculiarly to attention, with best hope of better solutions.

The lines of "law-job" around which it seems especially useful to group legal phenomena for study are five:

1. The disposition of the trouble-case: a wrong, a grievance, a dispute. This is garage-repair work or the going concern of society, with (as case-law shows) its continuous effect upon the remaking of the order of that society.
2. The preventive channeling of conduct and expectations so as to avoid trouble, and together with it, the effective reorientation of conduct and expectations in similar fashion. This does not mean merely, for instance,

---

[59] [Note the emphasis on rules, *cf. ante*, 1013.]
[60] [Llewellyn's language is remarkably prescient of Dworkin's.]

new legislation; it is, instead, what new legislation (among other things) is about, and is for.

3. The allocation of authority and the arrangement of procedures which mark action as being authoritative; which includes all of any constitution, and much more.

4. The positive side of law's work, seen as such, and seen not in detail, but as a net whole: the net organization of the society *as a whole* so as to provide integration, direction, and incentive.

5. "Juristic method," to use a single slogan to sum up the task of so handling, and of so building up effective traditions of handling, the legal material and tools and people developed for the other jobs—to the end that those materials and tools and people are kept doing their law-jobs, and doing them better, until they become a source of revelation of new possibility and achievement.

In the doing of each of these law-jobs one can distinguish a bare-bones aspect which runs no further than the keeping of a society (or indeed of any group) together and alive; and, in addition, two ideal aspects. The one ideal aspect has to do with efficiency of operation. The other has to do with the realization of man's aspirations.

Around the law-jobs (which are inherent in the nature of any group, big or little) there develop (in any group) activities. When these activities become distinct enough to be recognizable as such, the stuff of law has thereby become observable as such. When men specialize in such activities, the men of law become recognizable, both the men and the stuff show, as distinguishing marks, a more-or-less regularity of action, and show felt standards, more or less articulate, as to the manner and direction of such action. It is ill-advised to take either the practices or the standards, to take either the men or the practices-and-standards, as being alone somehow the substance of law. The going institution takes them in, all together. "Precept" and "principle," *e.g.* to be part of a legal system, must be somehow actually at work in that system, and only in and through men and ideas *held* by men can they be at work. Practice, again, is the bony structure of a legal system. Yet practice is no part of *law* except as it comes wrapped in and is measured constantly against the held norm or felt ideal. Men are the life blood of a legal system, yet men are not even of it, save as bedded in a context of tradition, both existent and becoming, which shapes the men even as it is being shaped by them.

Out of the conjunction of activities and men around the law-jobs there arise the crafts of law, and so the craftsmen. Advocacy, counselling, judging, law-making, administering—these are major groupings of the law-crafts. But mediation, organization, policing, teaching, scholarship, are others. At the present juncture, the fresh study of these crafts and of the manner of their best doing is one of the major needs of jurisprudence. On the spotting and successful communication of the subtler craft traditions depends any finer flowering. We have too long left the detail of the finer traditions to be gathered in the dark; too many of the aspiring miss them; those who do come to grasp them reach the point of true grasp and skill unduly late, and without reckonable uniformity.

Among other things, only a clear perspective of the crafts of the quite different tasks of different crafts leads to a clear view of the manifold nature of legal rules themselves. Rules are measures based on ideals, practices, standards of commands, measures cast into verbal form, authoritative verbal form, with sharp-edged consequences. They add thus a tremendous power at once of communication, of rigidification over time, and of flexibility. They are a well-nigh indispensable precondition to any degree of standardization of law-work across space and the generations. They stand with such relative conspicuousness to observation, they accumulate so easily, they can be gathered so conveniently, and they are so easy to substitute for either thought or investigation, that they have drawn the attention of jurisprudes too largely to themselves: to the rules—as if rules stood and could stand alone. A first evil has been the attribution to the rules of many results, *e.g.* of court decision—which rest instead on phases of judicial tradition. Not the least of that tradition is the ideal of justice to be reached, an ideal equipped with a whole set of *janus-faced* techniques for handling rules to keep them out of the way of justice. Reckonability of result here lies only sometimes in the rules; it lies with some consistency in the tradition. The crass instance is the "correctness," both in doctrine and in sense, of either emasculating a silly statute by treating it as in "derogation," or of expanding a wise but ill-drawn statute as "remedial." The polite convention that the results in both cases are drawn from the rule alone produces conflicting doctrine on the correct method of handling statutes, which proceeds in other cases, where an answer right in substance, is not quite so clear, to lead to trouble. The same holds of the equally multiform and mutually inconsistent "correct" doctrines on how to handle precedent, principle, or standard. But let this situation be seen as a problem in the ways of a going institution, and the craft of judging must at once come in for study. The quest becomes then one for guidance, first, as to when a court will use some particular one of such "correct" techniques rather than any other; and second, as to when it ought to.

This discrimination between when it will and when it ought to, is the discrimination between rules for counselors and rules for judges. The counselor's basic need is accurate prediction; the judge's is clear guidance as to how to decide. A well-built rule can indeed under certain conditions serve both needs at once. First, if judges would abdicate their duty of serving justice, an accurate statement of past judicial practice could tell them how to decide. But judges will not ignore justice consistently, even if accepted jurisprudential theory tells them to—as once it did. Second, if there is a clear, and plainly wise, and plainly applicable rule, it can be followed by a court, and it will be, and a counselor can predict that rather accurately. But our prevailing stock of rules contains many which are either not so clear, or not so plainly wise, or far from plain as to when they apply.

Confusion between prediction—"rules" of law for counselors and ought-rules of law for judges is a product of a case-law system, confused by stubborn doctrine that what courts have done, courts must continue (without regard to reason) to do. It is significant that few writers have ever felt happy with a straight "what the courts will do" approach to statute law, and that no American writer feels happy with a straight "what the official will do" approach to persons into whose action the courts' *established tradition* of search for justice cannot be smuggled. Nonetheless, to see the division of the crafts, as between the counselor and the judge, is to see the need of the one for hard-eyed prediction, and the need of the other for light on how to decide. Again, to see that division of the crafts and to see how wide the differences in these two needs gape today in fact, in too many areas, is to be led to perception that with the right kind of rule, there need be no such cleavage. For, as has been mentioned, wherever a rule is clear, and plainly wise, and plainly applicable, a judge not only can follow it, but it can be predicted that he will. This is the type of case leading to a deeper simplicity which arises out of the seeming initial complexity, when one begins to size up traditional "simple" doctrine against the going institution. The varied phases of the institution do at first force differentiation—say, as between prediction-rules and ought-rules. They force examination of each, separately, for its nature and for its justification; and for a while things seem to have been made complex. But out of such analysis emerges a new and clearer line of synthesis: To see that the kind of rule can do both jobs at once and to see further what the elements of such a right rule are, is to see also that no rule which does not do both at once can be a right rule.

At no point does a proper emphasis upon the nature of a craft of law come more helpfully than in the troubled area of the administrative agency. The health of work in law, on the part of the determining or acting official, does not lie, and never will lie, in our civilization, in regularity of practice, in the sense of conformity merely to an external pattern, whether the pattern be one of words or of any other kind. The health of such action lies in regularity of conformance to a sound and knowable reason, within limits set by the tradition. The reason must be sound because the reason needs retesting as events proceed. The reason must be knowable, because our polity has grown too complex for "juristic instinct" alone to serve the needs of the far-flung indirect contacts of a nation. It must be knowable, too, because only the knowable and articulated reason moves almost automatically into being rechecked, retested, by and against events as they proceed. Arnold's turning of prosecutor's direction into a discretion which guides both staff and public, and which he and his staff can be held to answer for in terms of their reasons, is an instance. But reason, openness and even-handedness are as essential in the quasi-executive and quasi-legislative aspects as in the quasi-judicial. That once perceived, one recurs to the more purely judicial phase of matters legal (or administrative) with fresh understanding of what type of "political intrusion" upon "judicial" work means "judicial" statesmanship, what kind means outrage.

It should be clear enough what this approach to jurisprudence as centered on the going institution of the law means to the relation of jurisprudence as a discipline to other disciplines, and to the relation of the various branches of jurisprudence to each other. The social pre-science of the law (for it is not yet a science) is the study of how the institution does in fact go round, and how it does in fact draw upon and react upon the society of which it is a part. Among other things that science sets out (or seeks to) are the conditions under which rules work and to which they are subject in their work; and on such inquiry doctrine must rest, to become effective. The quest to determine sound goals, and to evaluate measures in the light of them, flows from concern with what the institution of law is for. "Straight" analytical work is a familiar part of the exploration and ordering of the doctrinal phase; but functional analysis adds a new dimension to it. For instance, to integrate the kind and degree of remedy into the concept of "right" (*e.g.* specific versus substituted versus wholly indirect remedy) would seem to offer as much new value for clarification and incisive grasp as did the Hohfeld subdivision. The crafts, again, when the going institution is the focus, are seen each as a distinct field of effort and study, but not as self-contained; each is a feeder of, and is fed by, the rules; but rules and craft together are seen in terms of the law-jobs, and their results cry to be checked against the jobs they should be doing.

On the more technical phases of work with doctrine, the approach by way of the going institution bears directly, and it bears simply enough. For one who has come to doubt that any but the most sweetly drawn of rules, any but a singing principle, can do its work by almost mystical direct appeal to all decent-minded men alike—such as one must go hunting for what it is that aids the work of the less perfect of rules, concepts, standards, principles, as they operate by way of men who are but men, trained well or ill, and surely the heterogeneous fashion, in the various crafts. The subtle osmosis of meaning into law-terms from terms taken out of life; the astounding absence of fixed verbal form in those rules of common law which yet are commonly dealt with as if deduction from them gave a sure technique; the ways of American legal thinking, at work always with the core of an idea, neglectful, even distrustful, of an idea's fuzzed edges—yet, always with a document, often with a statute, at work to nail down the very corners of a word; the unspoken ways in which "fields" of law come to be staked out, mostly by nobody, which yet limit the bearing and implication of any rule of principle or concept; the inarticulate but powerful ways in which such ideas as "balance" and "wholeness" work themselves unmistakably into each last type of doctrinal development; the never failing insertion of an implicit preamble of purpose into the construction of any statute—these are enough to illustrate the lines of inquiry, on the technical side.

More and more it grows clear that the goal of *technical* study is better rules for decision which will make unnecessary much of the elaborately two or seven-faced techniques now current in our efforts to make case-to-case sense out of jumbled rules. The goal of technical study is thus the reduction of its own field of operation. Not its elimination; for rules of law fully plain to every plain man are a will-o'-the-wisp. But confusion, expense, delay, uncertainty, and too frequent injustice in outcome are in most important measure a reducible fruitage of our present inadequate techniques of rules. Reduction, moreover, turns on such technical results as can be given wide democratic appeal at least within the crafts. The results must work out into a form readily communicable, readily grasped. But if the present prospect holds, approach by way of seeing the going institution whole is leading to precisely that. The synthesis which seems ahead seems likely to be simple, because it will rest four-square upon law's bedrock, and will not budge from that.

Two more instances, much misunderstood, may clinch the point. Reaching into the law-jobs takes one at first out into the whole baffling field of the ways and nature of society. Yet one finds shortly that it has simplified his seeing; for any group, whether a family, a close corporation, or a school, proves to be faced with the basic law-jobs; so that one can see the jobs and their meaning without the complex machinery and ideology of the State being thrown like a forest across the line of vision. Then the technical ways of law gain pattern because their function can be seen, and each detailed device invites its check-up against experience. So also, on the purely technical side, inquiry into what else there is, say, to the judging craft, beside the rules, seems at first blush to lead into all the vagaries of individual psychology and so into hopeless additional complication. But shortly there emerge at least three clusters of factor: those which distinguish Jones from Smith—factors which seemed at first to stand out, but which prove rapidly to be the least vital part of the problem. Second, there is the cluster of common human and professional factors in the judges, that great realm of workable predictability which rests in their being not only men, but American, and not only Americans, but American lawyers. And third, there is the cluster which goes to their being judges, and of the American tradition, and in or about the present time. And these two latter clusters of factor prove, as one examines the cases and the rules, to give the wherewithall for getting far closer to accurate prediction than do any but the rarest rules alone. Watch them closely enough, moreover, and they begin to give guidance on a point mentioned above: what rules work very well, what rules not so well; what lines of argument work very well, so well at times as to mislead a judge—and what the answers are to the misleading arguments. The answers prove in turn to cluster along the lines of the best-built rules. But the lines of the best-built rules prove in their turn to cluster along two lines of non-rule factor in the picture; it is when the rule is clear both in application and in reason, and when the reason also makes sense in the application, that it talks alike to Jones and Smith, the men, to Jones and Smith, *JJ*. It is when it talks alike to all of these that the results fully, and with certainty and justice combined, transcend the persons of Arthur Jones and Edward Smith, the individuals. It is then, too, that the citizen can understand, and truly honor, those results—facing them neither in blind faith, nor with frustration before the barrier of technique, nor with cynicism, but with a right sense that it is his law, of which he is a right part.

The art of building such rules I hold that jurisprudence can recapture and spread, on a democratic scale, among the craftsmen. A long haul it may be, but a good haul to get back and shoulders into. In accomplishing this, jurisprudence also places itself in the world. For sound sociology of law is the precondition to sound legal technique. And a sound sociology plays not alone, as Timasheff suggests, between the two poles of power and ethics, but between six poles which I

prefer to call Might, Right, Skills, Rules, Results, and Law's People. And such a
sociology is not limited to the idea of law given by the State.     [pp. 183–197]

## K. LLEWELLYN
### The Common Law Tradition
(1960)

*The general period-style and its promise*

There is a further cluster of conditioning and steadying factors in the work of the
appellate courts (and commonly at the same time of other branches of legal work)
which has been curiously disregarded. It is the general and pervasive manner over
the country at large, at any given time, of going about the job, the general
outlook, the ways of professional knowhow, the kind of thing the men of law are
sensitive to and strive for, the tone and flavor of the working and of the results. It
is well described as a "period-style"; it corresponds to what we have long known
as period-style in architecture or the graphic arts or furniture or music or drama.
Its slowish movement but striking presence remind me also of shifting "types" of
economy ("agricultural," "industrial," *e.g.*) and of the cycles or spirals many
sociologists and historians discover in the history of political aggregations or of
whole cultures.

Thus, for instance, the outlook and manner of Mansfield, or of Marshall, Kent,
Cowen, Parker, Tilghman, Gibson, are in no wise peculiar to these giants; both
are shared unmistakably by most of the lesser men of the period. The type-
thinking of the time is to view precedents as welcome and *very* persuasive, but it is
to test a precedent almost always against three types of reason before it is
accepted. The reputation of the opinion-writing judge counts heavily (and it is
right reason to listen carefully to the wise). Secondly, "principle" is consulted to
check up on precedent, and at this period and in this way of work "principle"
means no mere verbal tool for bringing large-scale order into the rules, it means a
broad generalization which must yield patent sense as well as order, if it is to be
"principle." Finally, "policy," in terms of prospective consequences of the rule
under consideration, comes in for explicit examination by reason in a further test
of both the rule in question and its application. The tone and mark consist in an
as-of-courseness, in the constant questing for better and best law to guide the
future, but the better and best law is to be built on an out of what the past can
offer; the quest consists in a constant re-examination and reworking of a heritage,
that the heritage may yield not only solidity but comfort for the new day and for
the morrow.

This is the Grand Style of the Common Law. I am referring to a way of
thought and work, not to a way of writing. It is a way of on-going renovation of
doctrine, but touch with the past is too close, the mood is too craft-conscious, the
need for the clean line is too great, for the renovation to smell of revolution or,
indeed, of campaigning reform. Of the judges named above, Mansfield and
Gibson stand out from the others in that in each an impatience to build *fast*
sometimes stirs strongly enough to permit breaks with the past that jar the
rhythm of the law and of the work. To that degree and on those occasions they
are out of key with the Grand Style at its peak. There will of course always be an
opposition, and some of it will be factious and fractious; and contemporary
criticism and abuse are inherent in the controversy which produces law. But some
of the sparks caused by Mansfield and Gibson, great judges though both were,
were struck by a brusqueness of manner and language toward men and toward
tradition which is no part of that grace in work which is the Grand Style as its
best. For let me repeat: "style" refers in this connection not to literary quality or
tone, but to the manner of doing the job, to the way of craftsmanship in office, to

a functioning harmonization of vision with tradition, of continuity with growth, of machinery and purpose, of measure with need. This can conceivably work out into florid words or into ponderous Elizabethan euphuism; if so, I am prepared to be laden with the language if I may have the thing. But it is worthy of note (and it is perhaps some evidence that style grips in one first more phases of man and culture than we always realize) that work in the Grand Style has, historically, tended into simplicity of verbal form and of sentence and paragraph structure, in combination with a certain pungency.

It will also be obvious that in this reference to the early nineteenth-century work in this country I have in mind something greater, deeper, and of more far-reaching implication than the "formative" character of the early American era as discussed by Roscoe Pound. His other phrasing, "our classic period," comes much closer to what is here in mind. With "formative" his eye was on the effective creation of needed doctrine—by selection, by modification, by invention. That was indeed in process, in say 1820–1860, and the Grand Style is peculiarly apt to such a task. But the matter goes much further: the Grand Style is *always* the best style, even though the cabin of doctrine may seem for the moment complete, with only chinks and leaks left to attend to.

On reckonability of result, three points cry for attention: first, the Grand Style is the best device ever invented by man for drying up that free-flowing spring of uncertainty, conflict between the seeming commands of the authorities and the felt demands of justice. Second, when a frozen text happens to be the crux, to insist that an acceptable answer shall satisfy the reason *as well as* the language is not only to escape much occasion for divergence, but to radically reduce the degree thereof . . . Third, the future-directed quest for ever better formulations for guidance, which is inherent in the Grand Style, means the on-going production and improvement of rules which make sense on their face, and which can be understood and reasonably well applied, even by mediocre men. *Such* rules have a fair chance to get the same results out of very different judges, and so in truth to hit close to the ancient target of "law and not men." . . .

The Formal Style is of peculiar interest to us because it set the picture against which all modern thinking has played—call it, as of the last eighty or ninety years, "the orthodox ideology." That picture is clean and clear: the rules of law are to decide the cases; policy is for the legislature, not for the courts, and so is change even in pure common law. Opinions run in deductive form with an air or expression of single-line inevitability. "Principle" is a generalization producing order which can and should be used to prune away those "anomalous" cases or rules which do not fit, such cases or rules having no function except, in places where the supposed "principle" does not work well, to accomplish sense—but sense is no official concern of a formal-style court.

Langdell's dazzling contract-construct is the American archetype of such a set of principles: without consideration, no legal obligation on a promise; consideration is *only* a bargained-for detriment (this planes off, for example, all enforcement via reliance, and all matters already past when a promise is made); the detriment can move *only* from the promisee (this chops off all enforcement by beneficiaries); an offer requires communication in order to be capable of acceptance (this prunes away the old sensible "unknown reward" cases); acceptance must be by *either* a promise *or* "an act," the very promise *or* the very act "called for" by the "master of the offer"—a jealous master, who has no desire to close a deal (this puts the ax to any expectation of alternative or even reasonable modes of acceptance, glorifies last-minute revocation in the continuing performance cases, and crowns verbal ribbon-matching between communications with a kind of ponderous dignity). Sense, the ways of men with words, the ways of businessmen in dealing, these are irrelevant and literally inadmissible: they do not get into the hall, to be heard or considered. Generations of law students were introduced to their profession by way of these strange ideas, and courts have in consequence made actual decisions in their image, sometimes with a touch of patent Parkeian pleasure as the pretty little puzzle-pieces lock together to leave for hundreds of good business promises no legal container but the garbage can. But in the ideal of the Formal Style, as has been said, thus to prune away anomaly is to vindicate Principle: large-scale Order. And it is a good judge's business to steel himself against emotion, and against deflection by sense or sense of justice which may run counter to "the law," lest such should lead him to neglect of his stern duty; in the titans of the style there develops a perverse drive for the "strong" opinion dear to Parke.[61] Finally, even as the common law is thus moved with sweat toward a simpler and more peacefully life-remote structural system, the disturbing statute (inconsistently with "Policy for the Legislature") is dealt with as an enemy invader.

This deeply etched and reversed picture or idea-pattern did not, as the labor injunction cases and the familiar Constitutional cases remind us, in fact bar out innovations of doctrine as far-reaching as they could be sudden; far less did it bar out those more gradual and less noticed cumulative changes which have been with us throughout our history. But it did, in its devotees (and that means by say 1885 practically the bar and bench entire) drive *conscious* creation all but underground, make change and growth things to be ignored in opinions, and to be concealed not only from a public but from a self. Meanwhile, the available doctrine material (then even more grievously afflicted than today with preindustrial concepts and flavor, while major reformatory statues were being knocked out again and again)—that material lagged further and further behind conditions which were remodeling with increasing speed, and the urge for felt right which no judge of conscience can ever wholly escape tended more and more into clash with prevailing doctrine and with the death's-head duties of the prevailing pattern of judicial ideal. It is true that widespread public revolt put on the bench a great body of State court judges to replace many whose feeling for justice had merged in peace with obsolete or otherwise unhappy doctrine. But note: whatever their political or economic or social outlook, these new appellate judges, too, had grown up in and into the formal-style picture of how to go about their work. Pound's famous American Bar Association speech of 1906 had sounded warnings and blown the charge, but it had died out on the inert resistant air.[62] What was left in the State courts at large was an astounding decrease in reckonability of result: judges who wanted to go right, and did not know how to; other judges who more often than not, though felt justice cried loud, could yet deafen their ears as they remembered duty to "the law," but who nevertheless with frequent, persistent, and almost random irregularity jumped "legal" traces and coursed to fulfilment of their other duty by way of bad logic, or by distortion of authority or fact, or by main strength. The effects not only on reckonability but on "the law," during the early decades of the twentieth century, were devastating.

Such generalizations as the foregoing can offer light and perspective; they cannot offer basis for conclusion to any particular, re either jurisdiction or era. What, for example, is true in general of Massachusetts, New York, Ohio, and Pennsylvania in the first half of the nineteenth century holds much less for Illinois

---

[61] I have not myself come across this in print, but Pound used to quote Parke roughly thus: A strong opinion was one in which by the employment of pure legal reasoning one arrived inescapably at a conclusion which no layman could possibly have foreseen.

[62] The Causes of Popular Dissatisfaction with the Administration of Justice; (1937) 40 Am.L.Rev. 729; (1906) 20 J. Am. Jud. Soc. 178.

It is extraordinary to contrast the tone of this with Pound's Justice According to Law, III (1914) 14 Colum. L. Rev. 103—culminating (at 115): "For a time there was need of propogandist agitation. It was necessary that the public, the legal profession and the courts be made to recognise that our legal system was to be re-examined, many of its fundamental principles recast, and the whole readjusted to proceed along new lines. *This task of awakening has been achieved.*" (emphasis added). [On Pound see *ante*, 849.]

until the advent of Breese in 1857; and in New York the Supreme Court can show the Grand Style in perfection in the same volume in which the Court for the Correction of Errors is bogged in wordy senators. Similarly, the Formal Style, which had begun to lose control of the New York Court of Appeals, before 1920, continued to dominate the Supreme Court of Maryland (both in manner of writing and manner of deciding) for more than a generation thereafter; and while the Supreme Court of Massachusetts were in 1939 still writing largely in the strict Formal Style, there can be no question that their process of actual deciding had already materially departed therefrom; indeed, even in 1939 Chief Justice Field was casting the Opinions of the Justices in a manner strongly reminiscent of the Grand Style, and within a few years thereafter the Formal Style had completely lost control of the law opinions, too. No, a "prevailing" style does not mean a uniformity...

It is of course when this type of contract ceases to seem idiosyncratic that "change of style" has begun. This showed in the New York Court of Appeals and in the Second Circuit before 1920; the work of Burch and Mason showed clearly in Kansas by 1905. Long before the movement became characteristic of the Supreme Court of the United States its mark had become clear upon the State courts in general; the Supreme Court—save for some dissenters—was indeed amazingly slow in responding to the tide. During the last three decades it has become clear that the Formal Style, though still of influence and moment, has yet lost its grip. It offers still one of the standard styles for the writing of opinions, but I do not believe that it anywhere wholly dominates opinion-writing style today, nor do I believe that in any of our appellate courts it retains its ancient aspect of a deep, unquestioned, and powerful faith. Today's typical appellate judge is interested first of all in getting the case decided *right*—within the authorities; and however he writes, it is the goal of rightness which gives the main drive and direction to his labors. The danger, as has been said above, has become one of giving too little attention to continuity and to guidesomeness of legal doctrine.

What now of the effects of this shift on reckonability of outcome?

(i)   *Re statutes*, the gain has been great. Today's appellate courts have long made their peace with the legislatures. Today, nine times out of ten, or better, legislative policy is not resisted, but is accepted cheerfully, and the courts work with it. This obviously aids prediction of result.

Not yet, however, has the Grand Style of statutory treatment been recaptured. The courts do not yet regularly and as of course face up to their job of integrating the particular statute into the doctrinal whole; and while the sound principle "where the reason stops, there stops even the enacted rule (*lex*)" is receiving attention half the time or more, often even when the statutory language makes it difficult, yet the courts at large are still caught in the theories of the '90's on the equally important matter of implementing the clear purposes of a statute with the full resources of a court or the matter of recognizing a clear and broad statutory policy in an apt area even though that area is not embraced by the literal language.

(ii)  *Re the bar:* To the degree that the appellate courts have—as they have— resorted to conscious consideration of right and wisdom in order to guide choice between or among the permissible doctrine possibilities, a tool for producing much more reckonable regularity has been added to their actual working kit. But to the degree that such consideration fails to be unmistakable on the face of the opinion, most of the bar remains in the dark about what is happening, and accordingly is troubled in prediction. Moreover, *occasional* display of process and reason in *occasional* opinions does not do the necessary work for the bar in general, as contrasted with the really good appellate lawyer. For the bar in general, in the first place, does not read the current legal reports, as such. Most of the bar *read* (I am not saying "note" or "skim") almost exclusively the cases whose *subject matter* is of interest to the individual reading lawyer, and so will never see most of such indications as have been referred to. In the second place, the bar in general reads to discover what the last authoritative statement or decision is about "the law" of a point; it does *not* read to get light on how the court is, in general, going about its perplexing job of deciding tough cases. And in the third place, the bulk of the bar reads still with the spectacles of "orthodox ideology," so that a court's remarks about the reason and wisdom of the decision just do not come through. At best: "*mere* dicta."

It is of first importance to observe that any such general ignorance and confusion of the bar does more than yield worry and distress, does more than undermine that confidence in the law and in the appellate bench which every lawyer needs for his soul's health. It also drives into a vicious circle. For it produces appeals based not on sound judgment but on wild speculation, therefore vastly too many appeals, half or more of them those footless, "foredoomed" ones of which Cardozo wrote. These proceed to heap waste-work on the appellate court until that court's time gives out and the full job which is the court's function must, in most instances, be scanted or passed over. Meantime, an American advocate's nature being to acquire belief in his cause, the appealing lawyer finds himself once again kicked in the teeth "without ground"; the slow bleeding of his faith *and* of his judgment continues—fertilizing a new crop of footless appeals.

(iii) *Re the judges themselves:* Meantime the inarticulateness of the vast body of appellate judges about how they do their work and why—their inarticulateness even to themselves—leaves them man by man somewhat soul-troubled, albeit their consciences are clear. This tells against reckonability of result; case by case, a trouble man is less certain in his action than a man who, like James Stephen's salmon, "is all one piece from his head to his tail." There obviously results some waste of effort, some waste of energy in internal friction, and especially an unevenness in operation which lessens predictability for the most skilled observer, whether at the bar or outside.

But the biggest single effect of the inarticulateness is that it tends to focus the court's known duty to justice—to what is right and fair—on the particular case and on the particular parties who happen to be in hand. This is a better way of going at decision than to discard the earthy concreteness of the case and to ignore the starry-eyed or knave-fool equities; but it is for all that a half-baked technique and one which strains towards both discontinuity and unwisdom. The wise place to search thoroughly for what is a right and fair solution is *the recurrent problem situation* of which the instant case is *typical.* For in the first place this presses, this drives, toward formulating a solving *and guiding rule*; and to address oneself to the rule side of the puzzle is of necessity both to look back upon the heritage of doctrine and also to look forward into prospective consequences and prospective further problems—and to account to each. In that work, the tang of the case at bar gives feel and flavor, and stimulates the imagination; but the immediate equities fall into a wider, paler frame which renders it much easier both to feel and to see how much and what parts of them are typical and so are proper shapers of policy, how much and what part on the other hand is too individual for legal cognizance or appeals rather to sentimentality than to the sensitivity and sense proper to a legal-governmental scheme. It is not to appellate courts that our policy commits the pardoning power, nor yet the dispensing power, to be exercised along any lines which cannot be put into a form significantly general.

It seems to me obvious at sight that this order of approach to the problem of deciding an appellate case *must* materially raise the level of reckonability, make results more even, make the operating factors easier to foresee and forefeel, make the ways of handling prior doctrine stand forth, make the new formulations so reached increase in adequacy both of content and of phrasing. It seems to me no less obvious at sight that this same order of approach *must* at the same time raise the level of wisdom of result. At the moment it is a procedure employed from time to time by every court, employed consistently by none that I have studied.

Some of what has just been said may suggest heavy uncertainty of result to be today's condition. I mean no such suggestion. I hold that from the beginning of this century to say 1950, there occurred in the State supreme courts a rise in reckonability of result (and, let me add, of wisdom of result as well) which resembles the percentage rise in national production. It was, as I see it, an outgrowth of groping, not of plan; it was uncoordinated; it just happened, over fifty years of cumulative drift, with many men worried and independently at work. In process, as an impact on the particular case, such a change is irregular and unreckonable; but its net can and slowly has thrust the whole of operation up into a higher and much more even plateau of forecastability. I do not spot heavy influence of any particular leading figures unless it be Cardozo. I incline to believe, moreover, that until rather recently the ferment among the intellectuals which was discussed at the outset of this paper has been of minor moment. Today, taking the close of the trial as a base line, my judgment (this is much more than a guess or a "guestimate") is that a skilled man careful of the lines of factor here discussed ought even in the present state of our knowledge to average correct prediction of outcome eight times out of ten, and better than that if he knows the appeal counsel on both sides or sees the briefs.[63]                              [pp. 35–45]

*Reckonability of result*

### Theory of Rules

Before we again pick up the forecasting problem, let us make quick audit of the last assertion: Are the lines of inquiry we have been exploring indeed available to ordinary lawyers? Or do these leads or devices go dumb or incoherent in the absence of some peculiar psychological or other technical training, or in the absence of some elaborate and inaccessible data, or in the absence of some intransmissible native knack? I submit that the signs to be looked for, though wholly understandardized, are nonetheless as gross and unmistakable as road signs, and that there are obvious and valuable procedures of interpretation and use which are wellnigh as simple and communicable as the driving of a nail. Road signs *can* be hammered on the thumb; but for daily living the signs suffice to guide most folk and the process to rough-carpenter boards into some utility. I submit that the average lawyer has only to shift his focus for a few hours from "*what* was held" in a series of opinions to what those opinions suggest or show about *what was bothering and what was helping the court* as it decided. If he will take that as his subject matter, I submit that the average lawyer can provide himself, and rather speedily, with the kit of coarse tools we have been discussing and with evidence too, of his own ability to use that kit to immediate advantage.

Is the effort worth while? Leave intellectual curiosity on one side, and the fun that comes from sudden novel cross-lighting of scenes otherwise too familiar for notice. Look, if you will, to bald practicality: does this proposed way of reading opinions, this proposed focus on the *How* of the court's deciding, substantially increase the reader's forecasting power, as contrasted with a forecasting based merely on a search for the prevailing doctrine, or with a forecasting based chiefly

---

[63] [See table on p. 1028. *post.*]

on feel, hunch, or guess, or with a forecasting based on some unanalyzed cross-play of those two? For the ordinary lawyer I submit that there can be no question as to the gain in predictive power. Spend a single thoughtful weekend with a couple of recent volumes of reports from your own supreme court, read this way, and you can never again, with fervor or despair, make that remark about never knowing where an appellate court will hang its hat. Spend five such weekends, and you will be getting a workable idea of the most local geography of hat-racks.

Neither can there be question for most of the better appellate lawyers, that these approaches, based as they are on the best practice, make conscious and clear, and thus available even on bad days, values which in the absence of a good day may otherwise fail to come to bear. I speak not, naturally, of the genius or near-genius whose intuition regularly and almost on contact with a case strikes for the jugular, for that point and aspect which will catch and move the court; such a man has little need for these cruder forms of intellectual apparatus. For all except such, however, the point is clinched by certain propositions from the theory of rules:

### The function of rules is guidance

#### Rules are Not to Control, but to Guide Decision

This is a fundamental truth which is inherent in the duty of a court to introduce into its work some touch of reason and some feeling for sense and fairness, in terms of the type-situation. Where the rule rates high in wisdom and is also technically clear and neat, the guidance is indeed so cogent as, in effect, to be almost equivalent to control or dictation; so, also, when the measure is technically well designed and the rule is a legislative product of unmistakable policy and is too fresh off the griddle for modifying circumstance to have supervened. But in such case the near-control is not because those rules are rules of law, but because of the particular kind of rule of law they happen—rather unusually—to be. So that it is of the essence to distinguish among rules of law, both in regard to what may be expected of them and in regard to what should be.          [pp. 178–180]

RESTATEMENT OF GRAND STYLE AND FORMAL STYLE AS
THEORETICAL MODELS [By W. L. Twining][64]

| Model of legal rule | *Grand Style* | *Formal Style* |
|---|---|---|
| | To produce effects z or for reasons z or to remedy mischief z | If x, then y |
| Principle | A general proposition embodying a policy; its function is to guide, but not to control interpretation | A rule of a general kind which may be used as the basic premise of a syllogism |
| Diagnosis of a problem involving a question of law | The scope of x is doubtful | The scope of the rule is clear, but its application is doubtful |
| Court's conception of its role | (1) To resolve the doubt according to wisdom, justice and situation sense within the leeways accorded by the authoritative sources (2) To provide guidance for the future | To discover and declare the applicable rule and to apply it to the facts of this particular case |
| Sources which may be invoked in justification | (1) Authoritative sources such as states and cases (2) Principle (see above) (3) Policy, situation sense and "reason" (4) Social research findings (*e.g.* Brandeis brief) | (1) Authoritative sources such as statutes and cases (2) Principle (see above) (3) "Logic?" |
| Typical techniques of interpretation | (1) Mischief rule (statutes) (2) Interpretation of cases in light of situation sense and policy rationales | (1) Literal rule (statutes) (2) "Simple cites"; dogmatic assertion of ratio decidendi, heavy reliance on language of court in prior case |
| Aesthetics | Functional beauty (fitness for purpose) | Elegantia |
| Other indicia | (1) *e.g.* cessante ratione, cessat ipsa lex (2) Open acknowledgement of law-making function, albeit interstitial, etc. | *e.g.* (1) "It is with great reluctance that I must conclude..." (2) "This is a court of law, not of morals" (3) Declaratory theory of judicial function, etc. |

[64] (See *Karl Llewellyn and The Realist Tradition* (1973), p. 213.)

## W. TWINING
### The Significance of Realism
(1973)[65]

... The realist movement should be viewed, in first instance, not as a school of jurisprudence but as an historical phenomenon. The starting point should be to identify the concerns of particular individuals at particular moments in time ... It is apparent that the intellectual roots of the realist movement were rather complex. From the many strands that became entangled with each other, perhaps four sets of questions can be singled out as having been of particular concern to leading figures at Harvard, Yale and Columbia law schools during the period of the rise of the realist movement: (1) What should law schools be teaching, by what methods? (2) What should be the scope and methods of legal research? Is an empirical science of law possible and, if so, how can it be developed? (3) How far are legal institutions, concepts, principles, and rules adequately performing their proper role in a rapidly changing American society? In particular, what is the actual and potential role of courts, especially appellate courts, as agencies of legal change? (4) What is the relationship between law as a discipline and other social sciences such as economics, sociology, psychology and anthropology? How can communication and co-operation between law and social sciences be extended?

These were, of course, not the only questions that were of concern during this period, individuals differed in the priority they attached to them and the issues were not always posed so starkly or in identical terms. However, such questions did represent a dominant focus of attention, and certain general points can be made about them. First, these are not, in first instance, "ultimate" or "philosophical" questions. One of the safer generalizations that can be made about realists from Corbin (or Gray) to Llewellyn or Douglas or Moore is that they did not look on themselves as philosophers. It is to their credit that they perceived that there was some connection between legal philosophy and the problems of legal education, legal research and legal literature, but their primary concern was more with the latter than the former. Yet much of the secondary literature, especially that which has emanated from England, pictures "the realists" as legal philosophers who gave imperfect answers to philosophical questions about the nature of law rather than as scholar-teachers who made valuable contributions to the discussion of a medley of less fundamental issues. While it may be a valid exercise to subject the views of any writer to philosophical scrutiny, such an exercise may have a distorting effect unless it is made clear that philosophical questions were tangential to his concerns. A second point is that realist movement grew up in the atmosphere of the "revolt against formalism." For many American jurists, from Holmes to McDougal, the major irritant was an approach and attitude to law of which Langdell and his followers became the chief symbol. A shared enemy provided a unifying element, but there was divergence both in the grounds for attack and even more so in the remedies proposed by way of alternative. Thus Holmes, Gray and Frank all in different ways provided rationalizations for the practising lawyer's scepticism of the cloistered, library-bound academic. But in so far as they had any constructive alternative to offer, their solutions tended to be rather different. At Yale in the period immediately after 1913, Corbin, Hohfeld and Cook while sharing with their opponents a tendency to concentrate on appellate court judgments, used the weapons of analytical jurisprudence to show that the "over-logical" adherents of the deductive model of judicial reasoning (whoever they might be) had been indulging in "pseudo-logic." Their "constructive" contributions, of which Corbin's work on contracts is the outstanding example, tended to be at a less general level. The Scientists and the Prudents at

---

[65] [From W. Twining, *Karl Llewellyn and the Realist Movement* (1973)]

Columbia followed in the footsteps of Pound and Holmes in maintaining that law should not be treated as an autonomous, self-contained discipline, but should be set clearly and consistently in its social and economic context. But while the Scientists took their first faltering steps outside the library and, in the view of many, fell flat on their faces, the Prudents combined a traditional interest in vocational training with a more complacent view than the Scientists of the problems of integrating law and the social sciences. Thus a united front was not maintained against the common enemy, and after the Columbia crisis[66] the realist movement became too fragmented for generalization to be fruitful. That realism began to be treated as a single phenomenon *after* the crucial split is best seen as one of the ironies of history. It may be another that the lawyers wooed the social scientists before the latter were ready for them.

Analytical treatment of the ideas of leading realists presents some problems. Much of their work, including some of the best, was not intended as a contribution to general jurisprudence and it is not easy to isolate passages which are potentially of general significance or lasting value from those which were mainly directed to ephemeral or parochial concerns. In the literature of legal realism are to be found intelligent discussions of such topics as the nature and function of law, classification, the relationship between law and the physical and social sciences, the nature and functions of legal concepts, legal reasoning, interpretation of statutes and cases, corporate personality, the role of fictions, symbols, ritual and myths in law, the nature of judicial processes, as well as of topics which are not commonly associated with "Jurisprudence." One less to be learned from viewing the realist movement in its historical context is that analytical treatment of ideas and theories associated with "realism" must start with particular writings of named individuals.                                    [pp. 375–377]

... There is much more to the literature of realism than the writings of a few individuals. There is first of all a mass of detailed studies which could be considered to be to a greater or lesser extent applications of "a realist approach." There is also a great deal of writing about realism, or provoked by it. Even their most severe critics have acknowledged that many realists were stimulating and provocative. Professor Hart has suggested that some of the American literature on realism can be illuminatingly read as a debate.[67] The suggestion is a good one, but it may be more appropriate to see the position in terms of a series of debates on a variety of issues. Unfortunately the standards of debate in modern jurisprudence have tended to fall short of those of the medieval disputation. Llewellyn, who felt strongly that he had been regularly misrepresented and misunderstood, had some scathing things to say about polemical jurisprudence:

"Though

    (a)  jurisprudes are mostly lawyers, so trained in the rhetoric of controversy, with
       (i)  its selective, favorable posing of issues, and
      (ii)  its selection, coloring, argumentative arrangement of facts, and
    (iii)  its use of epithet and innuendo, and
    (iv)  its typical complete distortion of the advocate's vision, once he has taken a case, so that he ceases to even take in any possibility which would work against him (as especially in the prevalent "romantic" type of advocacy), that
    (b)  it has proved necessary to police their work as advocates by

---

[66] [See as to this W. Twining, *Karl Llewellyn and the Realist Movement, op. cit.,* pp. 51–55. 103–104.]

[67] *The Concept of Law* (1961), p. 250.

(i) forcing them to define issues by a careful system of phrased pleading, served back and forth with opportunity for answer, under the supervision of a responsible and authoritative tribunal, and

(ii) limiting their arguments to the issues so drawn, and

(iii) confining the "facts" to which they can resort to a record, and

(iv) barring guilt by association, or by imputation, or without proof of particular offense, etc., yet

(c) in Jurisprudence every man

(i) states his own issue, misstates the other man's issue, beclouds the or-any issue, evades the or-any issue, etc., uncontrolled by procedure or by answer, or by authority (and cases where a jurisprude has stated an issue fairly are museum-pieces), and

(ii) use his rhetoric also without control, and

(iii) is free to dream up "facts" even by anonymous imputation, and

(iv) consequently always rides his strawman down.

(d) Where as in law one party always loses, or each must yield something, in Jurisprudence there is thus Triumphant Victory for All. This makes for comfort, if not for light".[68]

Anyone approaching the polemical literature on realism would be wise to heed this warning and to be selective in what he chooses to read. The cruder misrepresentations are best ignored, as are some of the wilder statements of some people who have been labelled as "realists." Thus it is best to discount as misleading allegations that "the" realists favoured totalitarianism or unfettered official discretion or that they denied the very existence of rules or that they espoused extreme versions of economic determinism, moral nihilism or psychological behaviourism. It should be abundantly clear that Karl Llewellyn never espoused such views; if passages supporting such interpretations are to be found in the writings of one or more individuals who might reasonably be identified as "realists," it would not be difficult to show that they were untypical or peripheral to the main concerns of the core members of the realist movement. "Debate" at this level tends quickly to deteriorate into a sterile form of witch-hunt.

While individual realists have often been the victims of misrepresentation, even this kind of misunderstanding has had some positive aspects. The process of exposing errors has stimulated critics to clarify their own ideas. Fuller and Kennedy, for example, in discussing realism have made interesting contributions to the perennial debate between Natural Law and Positivism.[69] John Dickinson, Karl Olivecrona and H. L. A. Hart are among those who have done work of lasting value in the process of showing why it is inadequate to define law in terms of predictions, or what is wrong with the belief that "talk of rules is a myth" or why the notion of "legal right" cannot be elucidated simply in terms of brute fact.[70] It is of relatively minor importance that it is not always easy to identify passages in which these ideas were clearly expounded, for exposure of error can be illuminating irrespective of whether it has in fact been prevalent or has not even been subscribed to by a single prominent person. Jurisprudence seems to need its Aunt Sallies.

Those who have a taste for disputation can find some illuminating material on some issues which might still be considered to be "live." As already indicated, the

[68] *Law in Our Society*, pp. 86, n. 87.

[69] See, especially, W. B. Kennedy, "Functional Nonsense and the Transcendental Approach" in (1936) 5 *Fordham L. Rev.* 272; "More Functional Nonsense" in (1937) 6 *Fordham L. Rev.* 75; "Realism, What Next?" in (1938) 7 *Fordham L. Rev.* 203; and L. Fuller, *The Law in Quest of Itself* (1940).

[70] *e.g.* J. Dickinson, "Legal Rules: Their Function in the Process of Decision" in (1931) 79 *U. Pa. L. Rev.* 833; "Legal Rules: their Application and Elaboration" in (1931) *U. Pa. L. Rev.* 1052; K. Olivercrona, *Law as Fact* (1962), pp. 213–215; H. L. A. Hart, "Definition and Theory in Jurisprudence" in (1954) 70 L.Q.R. 37.

scepticism of practitioners about the systematizing inclinations of some academic lawyers is dramatized by Holmes's attacks on Langdell and his colleagues; Frank articulated other aspects of the practitioner's dissatisfaction in his attack on "appellate court-itis." Dickinson, Wechsler and Dworkin are among those who, in different ways, have subtly defended the need for principled decision-making and the Rule of Law in face of the view that judicial creativity is both inevitable and desirable.[71] Llewellyn's typology of the Grand Style and the Formal Style pinpoints a recurrent strain which is not confined to the work of judges. While the case for the Grand Style has been made with force and eloquence, the defenders of the Formal Style have tended to be less articulate. Partial defences have been made in terms of "judicial restraint" and "neutral principles"; students of the English scene in particular have had in recent years to face the question whether emphasis on judicial law-making may not sometimes be a form of conservative politics masquerading as radical jurisprudence.[72] But a fully argued case, perhaps in terms of the functions of formalism, has yet to be made in the modern context.

In respect of empirical investigation of the law in action, realists have had to face attacks on more than one front. On the one hand, many lawyers take the view that such enquiries should be left to social scientists, thereby raising questions as to whether, and, if so, when, it is desirable or feasible to treat law as an autonomous discipline rather than as part of the behavioural sciences; on the other hand, charges of "barefoot empiricism" and "naive realism" have been levelled against some realists who, like Llewellyn and Frank, were sometimes prepared to rely on common sense, experience and intuition as sources of information and insight. Related to this is the fact that espousal by Cook, Moore and other various versions of "the scientific analogy" produced a variety of sceptical reactions from within the realist movement as well as from without. Realists were largely pioneers in the development of an empirical science of law and the "debate" in this area even now remains at a relatively unsophisticated level.

Debate and disputation no doubt have a useful role to perform in the development of juristic thought. But as one hacks one's way through the tangled undergrowth of confused and confusing jurisprudential controversy one is left with a strong impression that a great deal of it has been artificial and unnecessary, as well as repetitive. A puzzling question is why has realism been so controversial? Granted the dangers of generalizing about "the realists," if there is one thread that runs consistently through the work of American jurists from Holmes through Pound and the pioneers of the realist movement to Lasswell and McDougal and beyond it is this: that there is more to the study of law than the study of a system of rules; that for most purposes legal doctrine should be seen in the context of legal processes. This surely deserves to be a truism; it is demonstrably part of "the neglected obvious," but it is hardly the stuff of persistent controversy. Few jurists, few practising lawyers, and few academic lawyers have consciously and openly opposed the proposition that it is desirable to adopt a broad perspective and consider the law in its social context. The uncontroversial nature of the core of realism is illustrated by the current ambivalence towards the realist movement of many American law teachers, who sometimes speak of "realism" as a passing phase while acknowledging its continued vitality. Their attitude can best be expressed by adapting a well-known incantation: "Realism is dead; we are all realists now."

---

[71] J. Dickinson, *op. cit.*, n. 49; see further his major work, *Administrative Justice and the Supremacy of Law in the United States* (1927). H. Wechsler, "Toward Neutral Principles of Constitutional Law" in (1959) 73 *Harv. L. Rev.* 1 and see R. Dworkin, "Is Law a System of Rules?" in *Essays in Legal Philosophy* (R. Summers ed., 1968).

[72] R. Stevens, "The Role of a Final Appeal Court in a Democracy: The House of Lords Today" in (1968) 28 M.L.R. 509; L. Jaffe, *English and American Judges as Lawnmakers* (1969).

While there may be pockets of resistance to the development of a "contextual approach," for most law teachers in the United States and elsewhere in the common law would the crucial question is not Whether? but How? Here Karl Llewellyn's evaluations of the realist movement come into their own. For he maintained that its main contribution was not to be found in the more general ideas, but rather in their determination to apply in a "sustained and program matic" way ideas which had been made almost commonplace by Holmes and Pound at the level of abstract theory, but the practical implications of which had not been fully realized.[73] ... [pp. 379–382]

Llewellyn's final evaluation of the achievements of the realist movement would appear to have been that there was relatively little new or controversial about the beliefs shared by most of its members, that their occasional overstatements at a theoretical level were of minor significance, and that the chief characteristic of the movement was that its members wished to try to act on their beliefs, especially in research and teaching, in a more sustained and systematic way than the great majority of their predecessors had done. Thus his argument appears to be that the realist movement should be judged primarily by its fruits, especially by the extent, the quality and the value of the research and writing it inspired, rather than by the worthwhileness or originality of its contributions to legal theory. Thus the Columbia casebooks, empirical research projects, reforms in legal education, changes in the style and orientation of contributions to law reviews, the Uniform Commercial Code, and the resurgence of the Grand Style were better indicia of the achievements, and failures, of the realist movement than its contributions to jurisprudence for the hundred. In short, the suggestion is that the main achievement of the movement was to concertize sociological jurisprudence.

Llewellyn's suggestion is attractive. It should be obvious that the realist movement and the work of individual realists would of necessity feature prominently in a balanced general appraisal of developments in the United States in legal education, legal research and legal literature during the period 1920 to 1970.

If it is fair to say that the main achievement of the realist movement was to concretize sociological jurisprudence, then no study of their work should be confined to discussions of very general topics. Perhaps the most important lesson to be learned from a study of realism is a partial answer to the question: What difference can it make in practice to adopt a sociological (or realist or contextual) approach to law? One simple way to set about obtaining an elementary answer is to compare and contrast examples of legal "products" in the making of which formalist and contextual ideas have been operative. Of course, any attempt to chart the "influence" of the movement with precision could easily lure the unwary into crude or subtle pitfalls of the "post hoc, proper hoc" variety. The chapters of the Uniform Commercial Code illustrate some of the difficulties of relating general ideas to particular legal artifacts. This kind of enquiry is elusive, but it is not impossible, at least at a common-sense level. Thus it is both feasible and useful even for undergraduates to undertake elementary analysis along these lines. For instance, judicial opinions can be compared and analysed in terms of the Grand Style and the Formal Style or similar, more refined, models; it is illuminating to compare and contrast the Sale of Goods Act, 1893 with Article 2 of the Uniform Commercial Code, the approaches of Corbin and Williston and Pollock to, *e.g.* the Statute of Frauds, or Salmond on *Torts* with Atiyah's, *Accidents, Compensation and the Law*. Casebooks based on Langdell's prototype can be compared and contrasted with compilations of "Cases and Materials" such as those prepared at Columbia in the 1930s or at Yale in the early 1960s. It is interesting to consider the work of Willard Hurst in juxtaposition to that of writers who have narrower conceptions of legal history. Further examples can easily be culled from the literature of international or comparative law, or, indeed,

---

[73] Especially *Jurisprudence* (1931), p. 57.

from almost any other field of legal endeavour. Even in quite elementary exercises of this kind it is, of course, important to keep asking to what extent differences between "approaches" or particular pieces of work can be explained in terms of operative ideas which could be categorized as "jurisprudential." The answers will not always be obvious. And this, too, may help to drive home the lesson that jurisprudence need not be a subject apart.

If law students are able to do such elementary exercises in comparative analysis, it should not be beyond the capacity of legal scholars to undertake this type of enquiry in a more sustained manner on a broader front. Here, as elsewhere, substantial progress will be unlikely without adequate support from theory. In this respect there are limitations on the value of the literature of realism. In so far as it is a fair verdict that the most worthwhile achievements of the realist movement were at the "applied" level, this involves an admission that it made a relatively insignificant theoretical contribution to the development of a systematic sociology of law... [pp. 383–384]

In the next phase of Anglo-American jurisprudence lawyers will continue to look at the social scientists and to others for assistance. There are indications that social science has more to offer us today than it had in the twenties and thirties; similarly philosophers have in recent years provided jurists with some usable techniques of conceptual analysis. But it is important to guard against the tendency to allow vague calls for interdisciplinary co-operation to perform the role of a ritual incantation—a hopelessly optimistic prayer for a *deus ex machina*. One of the main lessons to be drawn from the story of the realist movement is that it is easy to ignore or to underestimate the difficulties, theoretical and practical, of sustained interdisciplinary work. It is easy for inflated optimism to be replaced by sour disillusion; it is difficult to strike a balance between professional self-confidence and willingness to seek help from outside. Anglo-American legal culture has its share of chauvinists and masochists—those who would go it alone and those who would reject most of the rich intellectual heritage of the law. Such extreme views could easily provoke some futile polemics, but they represent in exaggerated form two broad alternative strategies for developing a contextual approach to law: the one approach emphasises broadening the study of law from within, building a long tradition of humanistic scholarship by lawyers and jurists. The other emphasises the value of looking at law from without, through the spectacles of one or more disciplines. Jurisprudence is broad enough to accommodate both strategies and many variations on them.

In the interpretation presented in this book, the leading American realists by and large chose the strategy of broadening the study of law from within. Law was their primary discipline and they were proud of it. As sociologists or psychologists or anthropologists or economists or philosophers they were, at best, intelligent amateurs. They have most to teach those who wish to treat law as their primary discipline, while keeping it steadfastly in its place as one of the great humane studies. From this point of view a primary function of Jurisprudence, and of jurists, is to serve as a conduit, to channel into the intellectual milieu of the law, concepts, techniques, insights and information from neighbouring fields. Seen thus, "traditional" Jurisprudence still has an important role to perform.

In developing working theories and usable hypotheses there will be some of us who will feel attracted simultaneously by thinkers as seemingly diverse as, for example, Bentham and Llewellyn. Both are products of the intellectual milieu of the common law and they have more in common than may at first appear. In so far as there are differences, one of the problems is to strike a balance between the systematic generalizing tendencies of a Bentham or a Lasswell and the sensitivity to the nuances of the particular of a Karl Llewellyn. Where a healthy balance can be struck, perhaps there lies the best hope for the preservation and exploitation of what is worthwhile in the common law tradition. [pp. 386–387]

# 11

# THE SCANDINAVIAN REALISTS

Despite the unfortunate ignorance in the common law world both of the working of the legal systems in the Scandinavian countries, and of their legal literature, common lawyers slowly became aware of a significant movement in legal thought in these countries. As our knowledge of the methods and concepts of Scandinavian law increased, the writings of these jurists became more meaningful. The relative insularity of the Scandinavian countries, geographical isolation, immunity from international commerce, together with early national formulations of law, meant that Roman law had little impact on their civilisations. In their substantive law and, though less so, in their legal science, they remained outside the main legal families of the world.[1] Their law is less codified than the rest of Europe and, as a result, more judge-orientated. This comes out particularly in the writings of Ross[2] and, to a lesser extent, in those of Olivecrona.[3] The Scandinavian penchant for social welfare is apparent in the writings of Lundstedt, though he himself would never had admitted that his philosophy was tarnished by ideology. Perhaps, above all, the jurists' rejection of metaphysics comes out in the rather down-to-earth Scandinavian approach to crime and its treatment.

The movement looks to Hägerström[4] as its spiritual father, but the protagonists best known in Britain are Olivecrona and Ross. Their writings aroused considerable interest perhaps because they seem to be in line with the empirical traditions in English philosophy and jurisprudence, and also to have some affinities to the sociological approach which grew in influence.

---

[1] On which see David and Brierley, *Major Legal Systems of the World* (1968), pp. 41–45, 89, 96. There is no doubt in the mind of Sundberg that the Scandinavian systems are heavily influenced by Civil law (*Scandinavian Studies in Law* (1969), p. 179).

[2] *Post*, 1065.

[3] *Post*, 1057.

[4] See *Inquiries into the Nature of Law and Morals* (1953). And see *post*, 1052. See also his *Philosophy and Religion* (1964). Phalen (1884–1931) was the co-founder of the Uppsala school. For the view that Scandinavian realism is also the "heir" of Comte's positivist sociology (*ante*, 838) see Hall, *Foundations of Jurisprudence* (1973), p. 57. A valuable discussion of the Uppsala school of legal thinking is F. Schmidt (1978) 22 *Scandinavian Studies in Law* 151.

## AXEL HÄGERSTRÖM (1868–1939)

*"No one of [Lundstedt, Olivecrona and Ross] is wholly self-contained. To understand them, or effectively criticise them, one must constantly return to Hägerström. They presume the substantial truth of his subtle and detailed analysis."*[5]

A few comments on Hägerström's approach will, therefore, help to set the jurists in perspective.[6]

Hägerström was not a lawyer, but a philosopher whose attention was directed to law and ethics as particularly fertile sources of metaphysics. He dedicated his life to exposing speculative ideas and myths by which man is exploited by man. He wanted to establish a real legal science which could be applied to the reorganisation of society in just the same way as the natural sciences had been used to transform the natural environment. To do this, legal science had to be emancipated from mythology, theology and metaphysics. It is the aim of philosophy, Hägerström contended, to liberate the human mind from the phantoms of its own creation. Legal thinking and language abound with such sham concepts. For someone who wanted, as Hägerström did, to destroy transcendental metaphysics, where better to start than law?[7] Rights, duties, property, will of the state were all mere word-play but legal thinking without them was, so it seemed, unthinkable. The fallacy had to be explained, an objective theory of knowledge had to be erected. Legal philosophy for Hägerström as, indeed, it became for his followers, is a sociology of law without empirical investigation, but built instead upon conceptual, historical and psychological analysis. Much of his writing is, accordingly, a critique of the errors of juristic thought. Austin, with his command theory and such concepts as the "will of the state,"[8] and Kelsen's neo-Kantian reduction of the dualism of existence and validity

---

[5] *Per* J. Passmore (1961) 36 *Philosophy* 143. The debt to Hägerström is less evident in the writings of Ross than the other two, but is marked nonetheless. For an attempt to trace Scandinavian Realism earlier than Hägerström to early legal thinking in Denmark, see K. Illum (1968) 12 *Scandinavian Studies in Law* 51, 57, where the writings of Ørsted (1778–1860) are cited as evidence of the realist tendency. Ørsted rejected natural law in the sense of a complete integral system of law. It was useless for deciding disputes. The modern Scandinavians go further: for them natural law theories are meaningless.

[6] See, further, Olivecrona (1959) 3 *Scandinavian Studies in Law* 125 and *Law as Fact* (2nd ed.), pp. 174–177, 227–233; Passmore, *op. cit.*; Broad (1951) 26 *Philosophy* 99, For an assessment of Hägerström, see N. E. Simmonds (1976) Jur. Rev. 210. In his view Hägerström can be regarded as a "founder of modern philosophy".

[7] These views are expressed most pungently in his *Philosophy and Religion* (1964). "We must destroy metaphysics if we ever wish to pierce through the mist of words which has arisen out of feelings and associations and to proceed 'from sounds to things'" (p. 74). Hägerström's reasons for rejecting metaphysics as meaningless were not that of the logical positivists (*viz.* that they cannot be verified), but because they are self-contradictory statements and (*pace* Hegel whom Hägerström followed) all self-contradictory statements are meaningless according to the law of contradiction.

[8] *Op. cit.*, n. 6, pp. 20–35.

into the category of *Sollen*, into, that is, metaphysics, come in for particular censure.[9] So do factual explanations of the concept of a right.[10]

A short discussion of this will demonstrate Hägerström's method. He first reviews the attempts that have been made to discover the empirical basis of a right. He dismisses each as unsuccessful: "the factual basis which we are seeking cannot be found . . . either in *protection guaranteed*[11] or *command issued*[12] by an external authority." He concludes that there are no such facts. The "idea" has nothing to do with reality: its content is some kind of supernatural power with regard to things and persons. Hägerström next sought a psychological explanation, and found it in the feeling of strength and power associated with the conviction of possessing a right: "one fights better if one believes that one has right on one's side."[13] Hägerström takes this discussion no further. But it is clear from his writings that, though rights may not exist, they are useful tools of thought. It is at this point that the jurists take up the analysis. Ross, for example, in *Tu-Tu*,[14] accepts implicitly Hägerström's analysis and shows how statements about rights made in a legal context may have realistic meaningful content.

Hägerström also investigated the historical bases of the idea of a right. To this end he made extensive studies of Greek and, more particularly, Roman law and history.[15] His studies were conceived to demonstrate that the framework of the *jus civile* was a system of rules for the acquisition and exercise of supernatural powers. He was puzzled why, for example, the buyer claimed the *res mancipi* as his before the ceremony of *mancipatio*[16] was over. Hägerström's explanation was that the buyer's statement was not true; that, in effect, he used the formal words to make the *res mancipi* his property: the words and gestures had a magical effect, the act was a ritual. He believed, and there is an element of truth in his belief, that modern law is equally a ritualistic exercise. One thinks of the legal oath, the black cap, the wedding ring or the coronation ceremony. But, as Pollock wrote,[17] ritual is to law as a bottle is to liquor: you cannot drink

---

[9] *Op. cit.*, n. 6, p. 257. On the dualism see Ross, *On Law and Justice*, p. 11 and Kelsen, *ante*, 305.

[10] See MacCormack, *Judicial Review* (1971), p. 59. Sundby (1968) 13 Nat. L. Forum 72 deals with contemporary Scandinavian analyses of "right," but is useful in relating this to Hägerström.

[11] The state only steps in if the right of property is violated, so right of property (*cf.* novel disseisin) is a prerequisite of protection. Can a *sine qua non* of protection be identical with the fact of protection? See Olivecrona (1959) 3 *Scandinavian Studies in Law* 128.

[12] Can powers, for example, to sell or transfer be explained in this way? Hägerström thinks not.

[13] *Op. cit.*, n. 4, p. 5.

[14] *Post*, 1074. On the relationship between Hägerström and *Tu-Tu*, see Olivecrona, *op. cit.*, pp. 177 *et seq.*

[15] See, *Der römische Obligationsbegriff* (2 vols, 1927, 1941), parts of which are translated in *Inquiries into the Nature of law and Morals*. The work as a whole has never been translated. His writings met a hostile reception from Roman law scholars, see MacCormack (1969) 4 *Irish Jurist* 153 and 37 *Tijdschrift voor Rechtsgeschiedenis* 439.

[16] See B. Nicholas, *Roman Law* (1962), p. 63.

[17] Quoted in Passmore (1961) 36 *Philosophy* 143, 156.

the bottle, but equally you cannot cope with liquor without the bottle. There is a danger in assimilating legal with ritual symbols, for ritual can only be understood if the *beliefs* underlying it are investigated, but legal symbols perform a *function* and are not just concerned with beliefs.[18] Hägerström's ideas were based on Greek and Roman sources, but modern research, in attacking the assumptions embedded in the anthropology of Tyler and Frazer's *Golden Bough*, has cast doubt on Hägerström's understanding of the role of magic in less complex societies.[19] The influence of Hägerström's thesis is nonetheless apparent in Olivecrona's analysis of legal language, in his discussion of what he calls "performatives," legal words which are used to produce certain desired results, usually a change in legal relationships.[20] Thus, "I do" said, during a marriage ceremony, influences people to regard a man and a woman in a different light from the way it treated them prior to the ceremony. In Olivecrona's words: "it is the language of magic."[21]

Two examples have been used to show Hägerström's influence. Others may be briefly noted: Hägerström's emphasis on law as rules about force comes out in the writings of both Olivecrona and Ross,[22] and Olivecrona's concept of "independent imperatives"[23] must be understood against the background of Hägerström's thoughts on the derivation of duties. These will be discussed in those contexts.[24]

## LAW AS FACT[25]

The Scandinavian Realists,[26] resemble other modern schools in their positivist outlook and in their desire to eliminate metaphysics. For them law can be explained only in terms of observable facts, and the study of such facts, which is the science of law, is, therefore, a true science like any other concerned with facts and events in the realm of causality.[27] Thus, all such notions as the binding force or validity of law, the existence of legal rights and duties, the notion of property are dismissed as mere fantasies

---

[18] See MacCormack (1969) 4 *Irish Jurist* 153, 167.

[19] *ibid.*, p. 154 and 37 *Tijdschrift voor Rechtsgeschiedenis* 439.

[20] See his *Legal Language and Reality* (in Essays in Honor of Pound, ed. Newman), p. 151; and *Law as Fact* (2nd ed.), Chaps 8 and 9.

[21] *Legal Language and Reality*, p. 175.

[22] *Post*, 1062 and 1065.

[23] *Post*, 1059.

[24] On which see Passmore, *op. cit.*, p. 143 and *post*, 880, n. 15. For the view that Hägerström abandoned the task of serious analysis of an important dimension of language and led his followers into a "blind alley" see Hart, *Essays in Jurisprudence and Philosophy* (1983), p. 13.

[25] "The problem we all face is not whether to be realistic, but how, not whether to portray law as fact rather than fiction, but what counts as a fact, and what, therefore, as a factual portrayal of it," *per* D. N. MacCormick (1974) 90 L.Q.R. 102, 103.

[26] According to Ross the term "Realism" is a "battle-cry" rather than an explanatory word.

[27] *Cf. ante*, 6.

of the mind,[28] with no actual existence other than in some imaginary metaphysical world. If then those notions are dismissed as mere metaphysical will-o'-the-wisps, what is left for the legal scientist?

Apparently nothing but predictions as to judicial behaviour, apart from various kinds of psychological pressures which, for various reasons not necessarily material, do in fact, human nature being what it is, exert an influence on human conduct, and given certain conditions promote that regularity of behaviour with which we associate a legal system. Does this mean that the normative element of legal rules is thus entirely eliminated? Not altogether, for Olivecrona propounds the view that rules of law are what he terms "independent imperatives," that is propositions in imperative form (as opposed to statements of fact) but not issuing, like commands, from particular persons.[29] It would seem, however, that Olivecrona attaches little importance to this analysis, since for him laws "exist" only in the sense that words are to be found written on pieces of paper, or intermittently stored or present in human minds or memories, and the real significance of these words is merely in the factual circumstance that these words are a link in the chain of physical causation, producing certain courses of behaviour on the part of human beings.[30] Lundstedt,[31] on the other hand, rejects everything normative, which he apparently identifies with the metaphysical. Legal rules are no more than "labels" which, torn from their context of legal machinery, are merely meaningless scraps of paper. In that context these "labels" may influence action, though the causal connection is extremely complicated. It may be "quite practical" to speak of legal rules in common parlance (though there is really no *need* to do so) and there is no reason why ordinary practising lawyers should not use this form of words. But legal writers concerned with *actual* and not imaginary connections should refrain from arguing that, *because* of a certain rule, a legal duty is imposed. For this is to support a metaphysical or normative link which no amount of observation can establish as a fact.[32] He rejected legal duties (a duty is only a *term* for an effect upon man of maintaining divers rules of law applicable to certain actions) and legal rights. Thus, "a so-called right of property is only the legally risk-free possibilities to the owner of acting at

[28] Bentham had long before propounded a similar view: see *Of Laws in General* (ed. Hart) (1970), pp. 251–253.

[29] *Cf. ante*, 257 and see *post*, 1059.

[30] Olivecrona thus adopts the causal theory of language. See F. Waismann, *The Principles of Linguistic Philosophy* (1965), Chap. VI. Olivecrona distinguishes two types of legal language: technical (or hollow) and performative. The former is passive, describing a state of affairs. Thus, in the statement: "X is the owner of Blackacre", "owner" has no counterpart in the sensible world but it is a "signal" invested with a social function because people have learnt to react to [it] in a particular manner" (Arnholm, 6 *Scandinavian Studies in Law* 9). The latter is used to produce certain desired results; it is Hägerström's magic (*cf. ante*, 857). On this point see *Law as Fact* (2nd ed.), Chaps 8 and 9.

[31] On Lundstedt, see C. Munro (1981) Jur. Rev. 55. He believes Lundstedt's reputation as the most extreme of the Scandinavian Realists is not altogether deserved and calls for a more sympathetic appraisal of his Jurisprudence.

[32] See Lundstedt, pp. 301 *et seq.*

will as to a certain thing." This position which is advantageous to the owner is "nothing but a *consequence* of the maintenance of certain rules of law."[33] Lundstedt saw rights and duties as nothing more than conclusions from rules of law. A good illustration is his analysis of *Rylands v. Fletcher.*[34] What the court actually did in this case, Lundstedt avers, was decide what the rule as to damages should be for cases in which something dangerous had escaped from land. The fact that it reasoned in terms of an obligation on the property-owner was illusory, superfluous and, because it mystifies, also harmful.[35] Thus, as Campbell has stated, while "Kelsen ... offered an account of law stated purely in terms of *Sollen*, Lundstedt ... tried to present an account purely in terms of *Sein*,"[36] thereby throwing the baby out with the bath water.[37]

## ROSS'S THEORY OF LAW

Ross's theory is the most readily acceptable of the trio of Scandinavians referred to here.[38] He emphasises the normative character of legal propositions but prefers the term "directives" or quasi-commands[39] to Olivecrona's "independent imperatives." But Ross points out that a distinction must be drawn between two kinds of legal knowledge, *viz.*, the law actually in force (for instance, a rule contained in a statute), and sentences in a textbook where the law in force is stated. Only the former are prescriptive; the latter, so far as they intend to afford knowledge of what is actually the law, consist of assertions or descriptions. They are propositions not *of* law, but *about* the law. The doctrinal study of law, that is the study of the rules of an actual legal system, is normative in the

---

[33] "Law and Justice" (1950), quoted in Munro, *op. cit.*, n. 31, p. 58.

[34] (1868) L.R. 3 H.L. 330.

[35] See *Legal Thinking Revised* (1956), pp. 64–66.

[36] See (1958) 21 M.L.R. p. 566.

[37] *Cf.* Jerome Hall, *op. cit.*, pp. 378–380. This attitude is also connected with the fallacy that meaning equals "naming," so that if such words as law, state, right, property, are not names corresponding to physical entities, they are meaningless. This ignores the *functional* use of many words, which neither Olivecrona nor Ross overlooked: *cf. ante*, 33 and see *post*, 1045 and 1074.

[38] See *On Law and Justice* (1958) and *Directives and Norms* (1968). For a criticism of the views expressed in the earlier work, see Arnholm (1957) 1 *Scandinavian Studies in Law* 11. Useful comments on the later work are found in MacCormack, *Juridical Review* (1970), p. 33.

[39] In *On Law and Justice*, Ross explains his preference for "directive" over "independent imperatives." Bearing in mind that these were directed to judges (*cf. post*, 1041), the choice of language reflected their range of application. One cannot command a judge or other legal authority. The shift in *Directives and Norms* to quasi-commands may partly be explained by Ross's widening of the concept (as explained, *post*, 1042), and also by his analysis of the logic of imperatives (*i.e.* deontic logic): rules of law are but one species of the genus directive; they are impersonal and heteronomous. Ross draws a useful diagrammatic summary of the types of directive in *Directives and Norms*, p. 60.

sense that it is *about* norms, but it actually consists of assertions.[40] These assertions state or purport to state what is "valid law" and one of the first problems of jurisprudence is to elucidate this concept. Ross does not seek, as Lundstedt does, to reduce all law to sociological phenomena. On the contrary his conclusion is the more reasonable one that "valid law" means an abstract set of normative ideas which serve as a scheme of interpretation for the phenomena of law in action (*e.g.* the actual physical activities involved in a transaction of sale).[41]

But from here Ross moved to a position which, as formulated in *On Law and Justice*, was narrow and less tenable. As such it was criticised in the first two editions of this book.[42] Ross formerly held that the validity of law could properly be considered only from one point of view, *viz.*, as a scheme of interpretation enabling us to comprehend, and within such limits as are practicable, to predict the activities of judges. Accordingly, he asserted that a legal norm such as a statutory rule was primarily a directive not to the population at large, but to the judge. In his later *Directives and Norms*, he shifted his ground somewhat and countered some of this criticism. He now differentiates a logical and psychological point of view. Legal rules are rules about the exercise of force and as such are directed to officials. Their observance is based on "the experience of validity." A statutory prohibition against murder is *implied* in the rule directing the courts and other administrative agencies to deal with any case of murder brought before them in the requisite manner. Logically, then, the rule of substantive law, or primary rule, has no independent existence. But, and here lies the new emphasis, "from a psychological point of view ... there do exist two sets of norms." For "rules addressed to citizens are felt psychologically to be independent entities which are grounds for the reactions of the authorities." It follows, therefore, that these primary rules must be seen as "actually existing norms, in so far as they are followed with regularity and experienced as being binding".[43] What Ross now suggests, therefore, is that there is "no need" to describe two sets of directives, one to the population at large and the other to the courts, for the former can be understood from the latter. "To know these (secondary) rules is to know everything about the existence and content of law."[44] This may be so, but it is still to miss a whole dimension of laws. It cannot really be supposed that laws are made to measure the behaviour

---

[40] In *Directives and Norms*, Ross distinguishes indicative and directive speech. (Note how he now investigates language by investigating speech, and see on this Hare, 78 *Mind* 464). He warns that whilst directives may be in the imperative mood, or make use of deontics (*e.g.* ought, duty), they may also be expressed in the indicative and give the false impression that they are descriptions of fact (*e.g.* "whoever kills another man is imprisoned for five years to life"). See also Kelsen's distinction between norms and normative statements (*ante*, 310, n. 43) and see the discussion of Bentham, *ante*, 253. Of course in a system where text-book writers are authoritative,), a statement in a textbook may very well be normative. Ross does not deny this. See *On Law and Justice*, p. 46.

[41] *ibid.*, p. 18.

[42] See Lloyd, *Introduction to Jurisprudence* (2nd ed.), pp. 294–296.

[43] *Directives and Norms*, pp. 90–92, and see *post*, 1073.

[44] *ibid.*, p. 91; *post*, 1073.

of officials: law is a means of social control and as such is aimed at the public generally. It is also to pass over the reasons why the behaviour posited in the primary directive is generally obeyed. As Ross remarked in *On Law and Justice*, "the more effectively a rule is complied with in extra-judicial life, the more difficult it is to ascertain whether the rule possesses validity, because the courts have that much less opportunity to manifest their reactions."[45]

Ross now recognises the social dimensions of law. What he is saying in *Directives and Norms* is that, as a matter of juristic precision, it is possible to reduce all laws to directions to officials. But, he is admitting that this is not how society functions. A reference to the psychological existence of two sets of directives is a recognition that the behaviour and feelings of *all* members of society are the "social facts" required to determine the existence of rules of law. Ross thus now accepts what he earlier scorned in Olivecrona as "psychological realism,"[46] for Olivecrona has never given officials the pre-eminence that Ross formerly did. But, when Ross refers to "all members of society," it must be noted that he qualifies this by limiting his norm to those to whom it applies. "Thus the directive that shops are to be closed at a certain hour relates only to those members of society who are shopkeepers."[47] But how is such a rule to be distinguished from a rule which is valid for society generally even though it regulates the behaviour of a limited class? This is a problem not solved by Ross. To suggest, as he might, that the distinguishing criterion is enforceability by the courts and other agencies is to return to the analysis of *On Law and Justice*; hardly a satisfactory solution.[48]

Neither in *On Law and Justice* nor in *Directives and Norms* has Ross limited himself to a purely behaviouristic interpretation of judicial or social activity. With reference to the judge, Ross has insisted that "a behaviouralist interpretation ... achieves nothing,"[49] but one must take into consideration his "ideological" or "spiritual" life.[50] Analysis which began to look close to an American Realist position[51] thus comes to resemble the elucidation of an "internal attitude" which we associate with Hart.[52] As with Hart, the external aspect of law is described as the outwardly observable and regular compliance with a pattern of action. But

---

[45] Ross, *On Law and Justice*, p. 36.

[46] *ibid.*, p. 71.

[47] *Directives and Norms*, p. 83; *post*, 1069.

[48] Ross's legal theory of prediction is cogently criticised by Lauridsen (1976) 20 *Scandinavian Studies in Law* 179. He shows that the answer to the question whether theft is punishable inevitably leads into an endless chain of descriptions.

[49] *Op. cit.*, p. 88.

[50] *On Law and Justice*, p. 37, and see *post*, 1070.

[51] *ibid.*, p. 73. Ross, however, attributes a "behaviouristic" realism to Holmes on the ground that he refers to predictions of what courts *do*, and claims greater virtue for his own interpretation involving a synthesis of psychological and behaviouristic views (*i.e.* both the external conduct of the judge and his normative ideology). But what Holmes was emphasising was what judges *do*, as contrasted with what they *say*, not with what they *think*, and here Holmes and Ross seem to be on common ground (*cf. ante*, 1007).

[52] *Ante*, 379.

this is not sufficient: there must also be a feeling of compulsion to observe the behaviour prescribed, what he describes as an "experience of validity." But, though, Ross's "verbal reactions of disapproval" look very like Hart's "critical reflective attitude," their "internal aspects" do not coincide. Hart's criticism of Ross, voiced in a review of *On Law and Justice* still stands, for the type of distinction upon which Hart insists is one used to divide "two radically different types of statement for which an opportunity is afforded whenever a social group conducts its affairs by rules."[53] Ross has not reached this conclusion in spite of an analysis which seeks an understanding of directives through speech.

Ross's equation of validity and social facts causes a large number of problems. It involves a reduction of questions of validity to questions of existence. For Ross law exists if it is effectively followed and actually adhered to. Law is valid if it is felt by judges to be binding. But how are we to discover this? We could look to judicial judgments but we have no way of knowing what we find there is not rationalisation. Judges might observe laws out of fear or indifference. It may be questioned also whether Ross does not treat validity of laws and feelings of obligation in the wrong sequence. Can one identify valid laws by feelings of "feeling bound" which, it might be thought, result from the very obligations those laws impose? Another problem occurs when there are no judicial opinions. The more effective a law the less opportunities a judge will have to pronounce on it. This leads to the conclusion that the more Ross's primary directives are complied with, the more difficult it will be to ascertain whether they possess validity—a strange conclusion, indeed.

## THE "VERIFIABILITY" PRINCIPLE

There are similarities between the views of Hägerström and those of the logical positivists of the Vienna circle.[54] But, according to Olivecrona,[55] there are also important differences. In particular Hägerström had different reasons from the logical positivists for rejecting metaphysics. His main reason was that metaphysical statements are self-contradictory.

Ross was particularly influenced by logical positivism. Thus in *On Law and Justice* he wrote that "there is only one world and one cognition. All science is ultimately concerned with the same body of facts, and all scientific statements about reality—that is, those which are not purely

[53] (1959) Cam. L.J. 233, 237. This review is now in *Essays in Jurisprudence and Philosophy* (1983), p. 161. Hart now concedes he said something misleading. He now agrees that the normative vocabulary of "ought", "must", "duty", etc., can be used not just in statements expressing the internal point of view, but also in "detached" statement by, for example, lawyers. There are thus three kinds of statement: internal, external and detached (p. 14). And see *ante*, 381.

[54] This point is also made by Simmonds, *op. cit.*, n. 6, p. 211. Both Hägerström and the logical positivists have a profound awareness of the misleading properties of the surface forms of language and both are ethical non-cognitivists (on this see *ante*, 262, n. 91).

[55] Personal communication.

logical—mathematical—are subject to experimental test."[56] He regarded the doctrinal study of law as "an empirical social science."[57] Olivecrona and Lundstedt were not so influenced.

Nevertheless, Ross is open to the criticisms that have been levelled at early logical positivism. The view that meaning is given by factual verifiability and that therefore any proposition which is not verifiable is meaningless or nonsense has difficulties.[58] For, as Urmson observed, the word "nonsense" is itself a highly metaphysical concept, and it came to be realised that this just would not do, not the least reason being that the proposition about verifiability turned out itself to be metaphysical and therefore "nonsense" on the logical positivist interpretation.[59] It is a pity that Ross neglected the later works of Wittgenstein, in which he exposes the errors, which he earlier shared with others, in attributing a single function to language, to which all propositions must conform in order to make sense at all. In his posthumously published writings,[60] Wittgenstein was at pains to remove this illusion and to demonstrate the infinitely varied uses of language, and the different types of meaning which may be secreted in different usages. This approach was employed mainly as a solvent of various perennial philosophical problems, but for the present purpose it may be invoked in order to reveal the fallacy in some of the earlier realist thinking. For the normative use of language is as perfectly legitimate as the empirical, and serves to direct our attention to a class of propositions which are not used as statements of empirical fact, but as guides to human conduct framed in imperative form.[61] It is this class of proposition that is the proper subject-matter (*inter alia*) of ethics and theology, as well as of jurisprudence. That such propositions may be related to empirical facts does not imply that the latter can be substituted for the former. For to do this is to overlook the fundamental distinction between "ought" and "is," and to engage in what Moore has stigmatised as the "naturalistic fallacy."[62] This does not mean, however, as the Scandinavian writers thought, that we must thereby acknowledge a special realm of existence for "ought" statements, distinct from that of empirical statements, at any rate unless we recognise that the word "exist" may be used in divers senses, as, for instance, when Kelsen equates it with validity.[63] What is involved here is a particular use of language, and this use can only be understood, as Wittgenstein demonstrated, by examining the actual ways in which this usage is effected.

[56] Ross, *On Law and Justice*, p. 67.
[57] *ibid.*, p. 40.
[58] The best-known statement in English of the logical positivist viewpoint is contained in A.J. Ayer, *Language, Truth and Logic* (2nd ed., 1946).
[59] J. O. Urmson, *Philosophical Analysis* (1956), pp. 168–178.
[60] See especially *Philosophical Investigations* (1953). For a brief exposition, G.J. Warnock, *op. cit.*, Chap. 6. For a fuller account, see Pears, *Wittgenstein* (1971), Pt II. Also helpful are Kenny, *Wittgenstein* (1973) and Ayer, *Wittgenstein* (1985).
[61] *Cf. ante*, 11.
[62] *See ante*, 12.
[63] *Cf. ante*, 308.

Indeed the more extreme of the Realists hardly seem to have faced up to the implications of their desire to banish all conceptual thinking as meaningless, since, as Jerome Hall has pointed out, this must affect the use of "ideas" in every sphere of thought, and in particular in the realm of legal theory itself. Thus they seem to be faced with the same dilemma as that which confounded the logical positivists, namely, how to answer the question why their own theory, which can only exist in the realm of ideas, and is, therefore, in that sense, metaphysical, is not also "nonsense."[64]

However, it must be recorded that later Realist writings demonstrate a healthy and sophisticated appreciation of the problems and uses of legal language. Both Olivecrona and Ross stress the multiple uses of language. In the words of MacCormack: "The multiple function of language and the psychological realities of beliefs and feelings are the main elements in the explanation offered by Olivecrona and Ross of legal rules and their validity and of legal rights."[65] In particular, two points may be stressed. They do not conceive of their task as that of laying bare the existing meaning of some word or expression, but rather of shaping concepts to direct our lives. Legal enactments are directives, geared to influence behaviour.[66] Secondly, both have emphasised the different types of legal language: thus Ross distinguishes different categories of speech: the indicative, the directive and the emotive, and shows how legal regulation makes use of all three.[67] And, Olivecrona differentiates two types of legal language: the technical and the performative,[68] one passive, one creative. Both of these writers emphasise that legal rights and duties and property do not stand for any objects in the sensible world, yet that sentences in which these words occur do have certain functions. Thus, the lessons of the later Wittgenstein and of J.L. Austin are not lost on Olivecrona or Ross, even if their earlier writings betray a certain naïveté.

ORIGIN OF LAW

It is characteristic of the realist approach that in discussing the origin of law Olivecrona states that though the making of new "imperatives" presupposes a legal system already in being, we cannot trace law to its ultimate historical origin, since however far back we go there is always

---

[64] See Jerome Hall, *op. cit.*, pp. 378–380.
[65] (1970) Jur. Rev. 33, 38.
[66] The influence of Von Wright, particularly his *Norm and Action* (1963) should be noted.
[67] *Directives and Norms*, p. 34.
[68] The expression is that of J.L. Austin (in his *How to do Things with Words*).

some social organisation in existence.[69] Thus, for him the origin of law is purely a question of factual and historical origins, of the growth "out of customary, magico-religious rules found in ancient societies."[70] But the jurist, except as a legal historian, is more concerned with the source of legal validity either of particular rules or of the legal system itself, rather than of the historical origin of law in the mists of time. It is this question that Olivecrona rejects as metaphysical, and therefore as meaningless, and thereby seeks to deprive us of a form of conceptual thought and of linguistic usage, the normative, which mankind has found to be so utterly indispensable that it would be singular to discover that it is meaningless and had no distinctive usage in human life and affairs.


## "Reductionism" and Legal Concepts

It should be added that Ross also is involved in another fallacy once associated with logical positivism, that of assuming that concepts can always be reduced by analysis to a series of factual propositions to which they are equivalent, and for which they can be substituted.[71] Hence it was thought at one time that all the so-called fictional entities of philosophy (such as the "physical" table we see and which had been stigmatised as a mere "logical construction") could be spirited away by this process. Unfortunately it later became apparent that this form of reductionism would not even work in regard to such simple everyday concepts as "England" or "France," for instance, in such a sentence as "England declared war in 1939."[72] So, too, it will be found that no amount of conversion into factual statements will altogether eliminate the hard core of such concepts as rights and property, for the very good reason that

[69] *Law as Fact* (1st ed., 1939), pp. 72–74. The so-called second edition published in 1971 is not a second edition at all, but a reworking of certain of the themes of the first. The second edition is an altogether "bigger" book, surveying what Olivecrona regards as the common roots of positivism and natural law and using historical analysis, both Roman and Nordic, to explain law. Some of the differences are described by MacCormack in (1974) 60 A.R.S.P. 393. The particular passage referred to in the note will not be found in the 1971 edition, but the problem of "establishing a constitution" is discussed at pp. 96–105, where the problems of disentangling law from religion are delineated in a Roman context. See also (1964) 18 Rutgers L. Rev. 794, 807, where he suggests that natural law concepts (*e.g.* the will of the people or the word of the Founding Fathers) are at the root of all law. But, even this suggests that some social organisation is in existence. It was, for example, received ideals and beliefs inherited from their countries of emigration which endowed certain people (*viz.*, the Founding Fathers) with authority to rule.

[70] *Law as Fact* (2nd ed.), p. 103. Olivecrona's views on magic are criticised by MacCormack (1974) 60 A.R.S.P. 393, 408–410.

[71] *Cf.* J. O. Urmson, *op. cit.*, Chap. 10. A good example of this approach is in Ross, "*Tu-Tu*," *post*, 1074, and see his remarks that statements concerning valid law at present time "must be understood as referring to hypothetical future decisions (by courts and administrative agencies) under certain conditions" (*On Law and Justice*, p. 41). The statement that "In Denmark women have the right to vote" is said to be quite comparable to the statement "Switzerland is a mountainous country".

[72] See this example worked out, in Urmson, *op. cit.*, pp. 151–152. But for a criticism, see B. Russell, *My Philosophical Development*, pp. 221–225. Olivecrona agrees with this.

such reduction ignores the normative factors.[73] Hence, quite apart from the practical inconvenience of doing without this vital form of legal shorthand (for who would prefer to propound a whole interlocking array of legal rules, or even perhaps the whole legal system, in order to avoid speaking of "rights" or "property"?), no amount of factual analysis is capable of providing a total substitute for this form of speech.[74] This, indeed, is another aspect of Moore's so-called "naturalistic fallacy."[75]

## FEATURES OF LAW

Despite the rejection of metaphysics, Olivecrona still engages in a search for the characteristic features of law. For him these are to be discerned in certain factual circumstances. Thus they are connected with a *de facto* organisation of persons, the state, which is ready to apply the laws and which possesses a monopoly of force[76] for this purpose. Legislation operates by reason of the legislators occupying key positions, which enable them to bring psychological pressures upon the population as a whole. These pressures largely derive from the use of certain "formalities" in the act of legislation, which play a vital causal role in producing the psychological reaction essential to compliance.[77] What Olivecrona is thus mainly concerned to show is that there is nothing mystical about the working of a legal system, and that there is no need to rely on fictitious entities or concepts such as the state, or the binding validity of law. Here again, however, like Lundstedt, he seems to confuse the two notions of normative and metaphysical. It may be that Olivecrona's description of psychological pressures is correct, though it is put forward, somewhat ironically for an empiricist, merely as an *a priori* assertion, without any factual evidence or proof that it may not be a gross over-simplification of the actual working of what Lundstedt never tires of describing as the immensely complex legal

---

[73] *Cf.* Wisdom's view that we cannot pass by deductive argument from one *type* of statement to another. Here he quotes Butler's saying: "Everything is what it is and not another thing." See the discussion in D. Pole, *The Later Philosophy of Wittgenstein* (1958), pp. 116–120.

[74] Olivecrona is also in general agreement with this. See *Law as Fact* (2nd ed.), Chaps 8 and 9. The assumptions that the other Realists agreed with Ross is easy to understand for there has been very little discussion between Ross and the others.

[75] *Ante,* 12.

[76] Bobbio and Catania have suggested that the view that law consists of rules about force is to be ascribed to Kelsen but Olivecrona shows that Kelsen's view (now found in *What is Justice?*, p. 257) first appeared in 1941 after Olivecrona's *Law as Fact* was published (1976) *Rivista internazionale di filsofia del diritto* 548).

[77] *Law as Fact* (1st ed.), Chap. 2, and see also (2nd ed.), pp. 3–96. But, how do people become acquainted with legislation? Very few actually witness the "formalities" of law-making. With this problem in mind Olivecrona has introduced what he calls "a secondary imperative sign," *viz.,* publication in an official gazette (something unknown in common law countries) and through intermediate reliable sources, the press and media. "Its psychological significance depends on the public's taking it for granted that a text which is said to be a law has really passed through the constitutional formalities" (see 18 Rutgers L. Rev. 794, 806). See Ross's criticism of this as "psychological realism" (*On Law and Justice*, pp. 71–74). Milgram's experiments, referred to *ante,* 264, appear to support Olivecrona's general thesis.

machinery. Thus, even if we may agree with Olivecrona's view of the necessity of force as the ultimate background to law, we may hesitate without evidence to accept his rather naîve explanation as to the way it influences human conduct.[78] Again his notion of the state as an "organisation" of persons hardly seems to avoid all suspicion of conceptual thinking. Also his insistence on "formality" in law seems more appropriate to a modern democratic state, but Olivecrona has specifically limited himself to the typical situation in modern western society.[79]

## LAW AND MORALS

Without going as far as Hobbes, who argued that law and morals were identical,[80] the Scandinavians[81] have sought to reverse the general notion of moral standards as being embodied in law by the idea that it is moral ideas that are themselves largely determined by law.[82] Admittedly there are some moral feelings which are natural phenomena, such as love and compassion,[83] but these are insufficiently strong to produce the restraints necessary for civilised life. Law is, therefore, the primary factor in influencing moral standards, especially by its use of force. It is the regular use of force and the propaganda associated with it that establish moral standards. For instance, the general attitude to other persons' property is unthinkable independently of law and legal machinery, and if sanctions were removed man's morals would undergo a profound change.[84]

Of course, to ask which came first historically, law or moral standards, is rather like inquiring which came first, the chicken or the egg. No doubt laws have frequently created fresh moral standards,[85] and in the case of

[78] *Law as Fact* (1st ed.), pp. 143 *et seq.*

[79] See *Law as Fact* (2nd ed.), pp. 1, 271. *cf.* Weber's views on legal rationalism *ante*, 839.

[80] See *Leviathan*, *cf. ante*, 146. See also the determinist view of Savigny and the historical school, and its de-mysticised restatement in Ehrlich, and the classical Marxist viewpoint upturned in the Soviet concept of "parental law". The writings of Olivecrona are also in striking contrast to those of the American sociologist, W. G. Sumner, whose philosophy was summed up in his classic *Folkways* (1906) in the telling phrase: "Legislation cannot make mores". Of course, few today accept this extreme conservative thesis. But the Scandinavian philosophy goes to the opposite extreme; not only can legislation make mores, but it is the prime mover in any change of sentiment or morality. It is this that is being criticised in this section.

[81] But Ross parts company with them here: see *On Law and Justice*, pp. 59–64.

[82] Lundstedt had similar views on justice (*Legal Thinking Revised*, pp. 159–170): law was one of the principal factors that moulded and refined feelings of justice.

[83] *Cf.* Jhering's four levers of social motion, *Law as a Means to an End*, *ante*, 880.

[84] *Law as Fact* (1st ed.), pp. 136–140.

[85] See the problems encountered in "Westernisation" programmes. In Turkey, for example, wholesale introduction of western commercial law moulded commercial behaviour successfully, but the introduction of Western family law affected personal relationships but little (see K. Lipstein (1956) 6 *Annales de la Faculté de Droit d'Istanbul* 10). Similarly, the attempt to impose a minimum age of marriage amongst Yemenite Jews in Israel foundered. (See Dror, 33 Tulane L. Rev. 749: there is an extract in Aubert, *Sociology of Law* (1969), p. 90.) Another well documented example is Massell (2 Law & Soc. Rev. 179) discussing the Bolshevik attack on traditional Moslem culture. Note the tenacity of "living law" (*cf. Ehrlich, ante*, 847, n. 86) in family relationships. A good general account is L. Friedman, *Law and Society*, Chap. 11.

some fundamental parts of the moral code, such as those relating to murder or theft, legal prohibitions go back to so early a period that it is difficult to disentangle legal, moral and religious decrees. Nonetheless, if we view society at any particular stage of its development, we do find a moral sense urging particular standards of conduct as right or just, even though the law may take a contrary or neutral view. It is just this severance between law and morals that the empiricists since Hume have been desirous of emphasising.[86] True, as Olivecrona might urge, the development of moral standards is unthinkable (at any rate in civilised society) save in a context of an existing legal system, with force regularly applied to maintain at least a basic standard of social conduct, but this is very different from asserting that every change or improvement in moral standards primarily derives from law, and not the other way round. For instance, when we contemplate modern society we see that improvements of a moral order, such as penal reform, often derive not so much from society as a whole, and certainly not from the impetus of its existing legal system, but from the energies of an enlightened minority, which brings relentless pressure on the recalcitrant majority. The force behind such movements may be of various kinds, moral, religious or rational. Olivecrona would attribute law reform to enlightened self-interest.[87] But the moral force *initiating* the reform may be quite selfless, as in the case of the great penal reformers, and indeed some reforms may even, at least at first, be thought socially harmful, though morally desirable, as in the case of the more lenient treatment of certain types of offenders.[88]

## LEGAL IDEOLOGY—THE METHOD OF JUSTICE v. SOCIAL WELFARE

For Lundstedt, all other jurists save himself, his mentor Hägerström[89] and perhaps his pupil Olivecrona have followed the road of legal ideology, or the method of justice.[90] This means that they have relied in one way or another on a material objective law, underlying the actual legal system, and depending on the common sense of justice to develop the law and to fill the gaps in the legal system. This is condemned both as metaphysical nonsense, and as an attempt to invoke natural law or justice to supply an objective valuation in what, for the Realists, can only be purely subjective, since for them value judgements depend purely on

---

[86] See *ante*, 24.

[87] *Op. cit.*, p. 167. Recent sociological studies do suggest that behind many enlightened reforms are the self-interests of the moral entrepreneurs. See, *e.g.* A. Platt, *The Child Savers* (revised ed., 1977) or J. Gusfield, *Symbolic Crusade* (1963).

[88] It has recently been argued that law has an expressive function. See C. Sunstein (1996) 144 Univ. of Penn. L. Rev. 2021 and L. Lessig (1995) 62 Univ. of Chicago L. Rev. 943. See also N. Scott Arnold (2000) 17(1) Soc. Phil. and Policy 87.

[89] There existed between Hägerström and Lundstedt what can only be described as a "God-to-Prophet" relationship. See Schmidt (1978) 22 *Scandinavian Studies in Law* 151, 160.

[90] Lundstedt was one of the intellectual leaders of the Swedish Social Democratic party, so presumably also had an ideology, even if he was not aware of it.

individual feelings and emotions, and are incapable of scientific objectivity. Lundstedt directs an impassioned onslaught on many of those modern thinkers whose thought might, by the uninitiated, be believed to resemble his own, as, for instance, the utilitarians, the sociological jurists, and the American Realists. For Lundstedt, jurisprudence must be a *natural* science, based on observation of facts and actual connections, and not on personal evaluations or metaphysical entities. Yet science has not so far progressed sufficiently in this field to enable us to establish or demarcate these connections with precision. Hence the need for what he calls "constructive" jurisprudence, which has to work practically on the hypothesis of certain social evaluations, such as that legal activities are indispensable for the existence of society, and that their aim must be to produce the most frictionless functioning of the legal machinery.[91] How then does this differ, for instance, from the Benthamite or the Poundian approach? According to Lundstedt, because he proceeds not on an ideological basis, as, for instance, by seeking for "justice," but on arguments based solely on social realities, that is, on people as they are actually constituted. The "social welfare" method[92] which he propounds is, therefore, so he asserts, quite distinct from such common ideas as the needs of society or of social policy, as it means nothing but what is *actually considered* useful to men in society, with the way of life and aspirations that they have at a particular time. This implies the encouragement in the best possible way of what people in general *actually* strive to attain, and not what they ought to strive for. As knowledge increases legal activities may eventually be able to be based on a legal science which has a more or less complete knowledge of the facts, and which can establish social valuations on this foundation.[93]

Lundstedt's notion of "social welfare" appears to be very abstract. He links it to "security," "security in enterprise activities," "security in the economic transactions of everyday life." It comprises, he says,[94] the general spirit of enterprise and its postulate, a general sense of security as concerns enterprise activities as well as other modes of action not harmful from a social point of view. Thus it seems to amount to everything that is good for the common production of wealth and the common exchange of commodities. Despite his political affiliations, this led him to some rather conservative conclusions. Thus, writing of tort and contract he could see "little room" for equity or justice. The rules of contract and tort existed, he believed, "for the very purpose of promoting the 'common transactions' in the community."

One may, indeed, ask whether this outlook does not itself involve a number of personal valuations which are no less vulnerable than those of anyone else, on Lundstedt's view, *e.g.* why should we aim at social

---

[91] Lundstedt, *op. cit.*, pp. 131–136.
[92] For an attack on what he calls "the chimera of social welfare", see A. Ross, *On Law and Justice*, pp. 295–296; *cf.* pp. 360–363.
[93] *Legal Thinking Revised*, p. 128.
[94] *Legal Thinking Revised*, p. 138.

welfare at all? But apart from this, Lundstedt's devotion to *actual* aspirations presumably adds up to the dominant views of the bulk of society, and seems to leave but little, if any, scope for the reforming impulses of a minority in advance of the sluggish opinions of the mass, or, indeed, scope for the possibility of moral pluralism.

Lundstedt's views on criminal law and punishment (thought by Schmidt to be his most original contribution to legal science[95]) fit in with his views on social welfare. He urges that the individual case must be seen from the perspective of the interests of society. He is opposed to individualising treatment, a believer rather in general prevention. Penalties are to "break down the criminal." That the potential offender fears punishment is a subordinate factor. What is important is that the criminal law appeals to public morality. To be effective it must influence morals so that certain acts become condemnable. When this happens the criminal justice system will succeed in its aim of repressing crime.

Further, although Lundstedt castigates Pound's jural postulates severely as "nothing more than phrases heaped upon phrases without the possibility of finding any line of thought,"[96] it is difficult to see why Lundstedt's own hypothesis as to the basis of the legal system are not equally *a priori*, drawn as they are not from sociological research, but from personal reflection and individual evaluations. If it is true that Pound discusses law "in complete abstraction from our experience of it,"[97] might this criticism not equally apply to the formulation of the "social welfare" method? It must be borne in mind that, in any event, in natural and any other science, hypotheses are only available in so far as they can be and are tested against verifiable observations. In both instances the test of these various hypotheses seems still to come, and the reader may remain for the time being equally impressed (or unimpressed) before either set of unverified dogmatic hypotheses.

### SCANDINAVIAN AND AMERICAN REALISM

It has been shown that the Scandinavian Realists share with sociological jurists[98] like Pound a weakness for *a priori* assertions, while at the same time insisting on the need for basing the law on the needs of social life. But the Scandinavians link this attitude with varying degrees of hostility to all conceptual thinking, which they stigmatise as metaphysical or ideological. The American Realists, on the other hand, are not much interested in general theorising about law, and although they may share with the Scandinavians the feeling that rules do not decide cases, they do

---

[95] *Op. cit.*, p. 162.
[96] *ibid.*, p. 349.
[97] *ibid.*, p. 350.
[98] "While Pound was interested in general movements of thought and in grand generalisation, the Realists (American) advanced in pointed elucidations." J. Hall, in (1958) 44 Virg.L.Rev. 323.

not altogether reject the normative aspect of legal rules.[99] What they are mainly interested in is the practical working of the judicial process, whereas the Scandinavians are more concerned with the theoretical operation of the legal system as a whole. Moreover, although the Scandinavians are the most extreme of empiricists, it is the Americans who primarily stress the need for factual studies in working out proper solutions for legal problems, and the Scandinavians who appear to rely mainly on argument of an *a priori* kind to justify particular legal solutions or development.[1] Altogether it may be said that the Scandinavian movement, for all its positivism, remains essentially in the European philosophical tradition, whereas the American bears many of the characteristics of English empiricism.[2]

---

### AXEL HÄGERSTRÖM
**Inquiries into the Nature of Law and Morals**
(1953)[3]

*What idea has one in one's mind in making a declaration of intention in the sphere of private law, in so far as one is thinking of coming into existence of rights and duties in connexion with it?*

In answering the above question it is convenient first to enquire what is understood by "rights" and "duties" in a *law* within the sphere of private law. Certainly such a law expresses in an imperative form the idea of "rights" and "duties." Such a law is undoubtedly of decisive importance in giving effect to a "declaration of intention" in accordance with the content of the declaration. This is true also of customary law, which is also regarded as determining "rights" and "duties" as something which ought to happen, although in this case there are no propositions expressed in a certain form.

In order to answer the latter question it is necessary to enquire what the "legislator" has in view when he brings about the occurrence of a certain pronouncement concerning "rights" and "duties," which has the character of a law. This is the same as to enquire what he knows concerning the consequence of such a pronouncement. It is plain that what he knows, from his knowledge of the effectiveness of the legal system, no matter what may be the cause of that effectiveness, is the following. He knows that what is described, either in laws within the sphere of private law or by some other method with the same content, as the rights and duties arising in certain situations, will in fact come into existence in the actual world. It will come into existence there in such a way that the

---

[99] Perhaps this is why Lundstedt declares that Holmes' view of law, as predictions of what courts will do, "has no bearing on legal science, though it may stimulate a legal ideologist to reflection" (*op. cit.*, p. 391). But see also his list of criticisms (p. 393), all of which seem to turn on an alleged failure to analyse or understand certain basic conceptions. Even the last of these, the lack of a "positive method" based on social welfare, seems to argue against the pragmatical attitude of the Americans, in favour of a unified approach which is regarded as justifiable *a priori*.

[1] But for a discussion of investigations inspired by the sociological method, see T. Eckhoff, "Sociology of Law in Scandinavia" in (1960) 4 *Scandinavian Studies in Law* 29.

[2] A full comparison is M. Martin, *Scandinavian and American Legal Realism* (1997). See also G. Alexander (2002) 50 Am. J. Comparative Law 131.

[3] [The date of the translation, by C. D. Broad.]

"possessor of the right" in most cases receives the advantages to which he is "entitled" as against the person who is "under the obligation" to act. This effect of legislation within the sphere of private law on the whole always happens. If the "possessor" of the right needed *generally* to have recourse to a legal action, and if the person who is "under the obligation" needed *generally* to be compelled by that means, it would be impossible to maintain the system of actions-at-law itself.

But the "legislator" also knows something further. He knows that anyone who fulfils the requirements of procedural law, especially as regards establishing the facts presupposed in the substantive law, will in general get a judgment against the defendant, which will in the last resort be enforced. Here it is a matter of complete indifference whether the facts in question *really* existed or not. Although in law "rights" and "duties" are attached to the *existence* of certain facts, anyone who can fulfil the requirements of the courts, especially as regards proofs, enjoys advantages which are at least equivalent to those which should accrue to the person who is described as "possessing a right." This, of course, does not prevent a person, whose case is supported by the actual facts to which he appeals, from getting satisfaction through a lawsuit. But in the lawsuit the question is simply whether or not the legal requirements in regard to the facts are satisfied. It may happen that the defendant has already satisfied the plaintiff's demands. If so, this operates only in the following way. The fulfilment, in regard to just this fact, of the requirements of the courts in the matter of proof concerning relevant facts, causes the plaintiff to lose his case.

But this makes plain what the idea of "rights" and "duties," which is expressed in the imperative form in every law within the sphere of private law, is really about, in so far as the "legislator" had in mind something which he really knew would be actualized by means of the law. It is always a thought of the above-mentioned actual order of things; *i.e.* the idea that, when certain facts exist, a person will as a rule enjoy certain advantages as against a certain other person or persons. But it is also an idea of something else, *viz.*, that legal proof in court, of the facts which the law regards as relevant, gives to a person the power, ultimately backed by compulsion, of getting at least an equivalent for the advantages which, according to the law, he should enjoy if the facts are as stated. It is evident, however, that the law becomes ineffective, *if* the person whom it designates as the possessor of a right against another person or persons neither receives the advantages in question gratuitously nor is able to fulfil the requirements of the courts. In that case the right amounts to nothing. This is of course presupposed in the law. On the other hand, the law has an effect, which does not agree with its text, if a person can in a lawsuit fulfil the legal requirements of proof without the alleged facts really existing. But even this effect follows from the law's own content. For even laws within the sphere of private law necessarily refer to legal processes, and give effective rules for them.

All this, however, holds only on the assumption that the "legislator," in giving an imperative expression to certain ideas of "rights" and "duties," has in mind what he really can *know* to be the consequences of doing so. Another question is this. Does the legislator *believe* that he is *merely* bringing about such actual conditions; and does he therefore mean by "rights" and "duties" *only* what has been alleged above? But the following at least is now clear. Suppose that a private individual makes a "declaration of intention" within the sphere of private law, with the object of bringing about the legal consequences corresponding to it, and that he believes that it will have this effect through actual law or through custom having the force of law. Such a person, in giving expression in imperative form to the idea of certain rights and duties coming into existence, has the following belief. He believes himself to know (and he therefore always has in view of making his declaration) that an actual situation of the kind contemplated will come into existence in accordance with the idea thus imperatively expressed. He must therefore, like the legislator himself, mean by the "rights" and "duties," which he says will come into being, just such a factual situation. It is only necessary to make the following reservation here. A private individual cannot be sure that just *his* case may not be one of the exceptional cases in which recourse to the courts is necessary, either because of the recalcitrance or the importance of the party who is under the obligation, or because of difference of opinion about the meaning of the declaration, or for some other reason. So the most that can be said here is that he means such a *de facto* set of order of things as would ensure, *either* that what is called a "right" will in fact be obtained from the party who is under the "obligation," *or* that the party who owns the "right" would acquire a power of the kind described through a process of law. But, just as with the legislator, so here with the "declaration of intention" within the sphere of private law, the question remains whether there is not something *further* in what is understood by "rights" and "duties."

Before entering upon this question, we must investigate what the judge understands by "rights" and "duties," when he makes a decision on the basis of law or custom. Suppose he decides in the plaintiff's favour by recognizing that a certain "right" belongs to the latter. He cannot possibly mean by this that the plaintiff *actually* will obtain, if necessary by legal compulsion, so far as possible an equivalent for the advantages which belong to him, according to law or custom, if the facts appealed to in the case are as alleged. For the plaintiff will obtain this equivalent only *through* the judge's decision. So the judge cannot make the actuality of the plaintiff's obtaining this equivalent the ground for his decision. Suppose that the judge, as is natural, understands by a "right" what the legislator understands by it according to the view stated above, *viz.*, a certain actual state of affairs, to which there corresponds as an alternative a power, backed by compulsion, as described above. Then he can merely proclaim that the plaintiff ought to have the disputed "right," and, no doubt, in such a way that the opposing party 'ought; to be subjected to a certain compulsion. If he uses the expression "is entitled," he is merely expressing the *idea* of a right, not his *knowledge* of its existence. But he causes it to be realized *through* such an utterance in accordance with the ideal content of the law.

Here, for the sake of clearness, we raise the following question. What investigation does a judge, in a case in private law, make the basis of his decision? We ask first what it is that he investigates in view of the law or custom in the sphere of private law. This question will be treated, however, only from the point of view of a judge who understands the following by what the law (or custom having the force of law) calls a "right" or a "duty," He is assumed to understand by this something which *can* occur in the actual world, *i.e.* a certain social state of affairs, which includes, as an alternative, a power conditioned by the rules of procedure in the courts. Here again the first question to be asked is whether he applies the legal "ought" to the actual case. The answer is a decided No! For the law's utterance "It *shall* be so!" is merely a phrase, which does not express any kind of idea, but serves as a psychological means of compulsion in a certain case. But it is only from ideas that any logical conclusion can be drawn. On the other hand, the ideal content of the law is of course used in the case in question. And it is only for *psychological* associative reasons, and not for *logical* ones, that the result which he reaches by this application presents itself to him as an ought.

Next we can raise the following question. "Rights" and "duties," founded on law or on custom having the force of law, cover two alternatives, *viz.* (i) a direct action by one party for the benefit of the other, in accordance with the law or custom, or (ii) a power conditioned by the rules of procedure, of one party to set the law in motion against the other, whereby an equivalent can be obtained for the latter's neglect to perform the action. This power is either expressly stated in the law or tacitly understood in the custom to belong to the plaintiff, on condition that he can establish the facts which he alleges in his suit. But with *which* of these alternatives is the judge concerned, in so far as he seeks to realize the ideal content of the law in the case before him? Suppose that there is no doubt about the facts. Suppose, further, that the plaintiff asserts, and the defendant does not deny, that the defendant has not so far fulfilled, by his own free actions, the legal conditions which (in the plaintiff's opinion) are contemplated by the law as applied to the present case. Suppose, finally, that the defendant denies that the meaning of the law is what the plaintiff asserts it to be, though he does not contest the facts alleged by the plaintiff. On these suppositions, the judge of course investigates the case only from the point of view of the second alternative, *viz.*, the legal position as regards the law administered by the courts. He can do nothing concerning the first alternative. Supposing that the plaintiff has the law on his side, the judge would be talking nonsense if he decided that the plaintiff has a right in the former sense. The ideal content of the law cannot be realized in that way.

But take the case now that plaintiff and defendant agree on the meaning of the law as applied to the present case, and that the judge accepts their interpretation, but, that they disagree as to the facts relevant to the case, even, *e.g.* as to whether the defendant has not already fulfilled his obligations to the plaintiff. Then the judge would investigate the case according to the rules of the courts concerning evidence and the burden of proof. This implies that, here too, if the plaintiff wins, it can only be the second alternative that comes into the question; there can be no question of adjudging to the plaintiff a right in the sense of something that exists prior to the suit.

So the conclusion is as follows. Whether the dispute is concerned with the ideal content of the law or custom or with facts, a judge whose conception of "rights" and "duties" is determined by what he knows can be actualized in the physical world, he can never take account in his decision of "rights" existing prior to the legal process. It is plain that it is here assumed that the case at issue really is of such a kind that it really could be decided exactly in accordance with established rules of law or custom. If this is not so, the judge himself functions as a legislator for the case. But we are not concerned with that.

We come now to our original question. Does not the "legislator" in the sphere of private law, and also the private individual who makes a "declaration of intention" within that sphere, after all really mean by "rights" and "duties" something more than a certain actual social state of affairs? It does seem as if commonsense draws a distinction between having a "right" and *enjoying* it, and between *being* under an "obligation" and that obligation being fulfilled even under compulsion. Still more does it seem to distinguish between having a "right" and being able to win in a lawsuit in consequence of the rules of evidence and the rules concerning the burden of proof. This difference shows itself also in the common view of a lawsuit as a means of actualizing in the physical world "rights" and "duties" which existed before the suit was undertaken. Here it is held that the possibility of suing is something which belongs to the person who has the "right" as a consequence or a function of his right in the primary sense. In the same way, it is held that the subjection of the person who is under an "obligation" to the compulsion of the court is a consequence of his "obligation" in the primary sense. If the notion of a "right" includes as one alternative under it the possibility, under certain circumstances, of acquiring by process of law an equivalent to the advantage to which one is entitled; and if the notion of a "duty" includes under it as one alternative being subject to compulsion by the courts; then it is clear that these cannot be a *consequence* of the existence of a "right" or a "duty" respectively. For, in that case, neither could exist without that which is said to be an effect of it. But an effect is always something other than its cause. But what does a "right" or a "duty" mean, if empowerment by the courts or subjection to them, as the case may be, is regarded as a consequence of its existence? It is plain that it would by no means follow from the existence of a "right" that there is a power to compel by process of law the party who is under an "obligation", unless the notion of the "right" included that power, and unless the notion of being under an "obligation" included being subject to this power. But the power and the subjection would here exist quite independently of any occurrence in actual life. It is clear that it need not manifest itself even as an actual power given by the courts. For, according to the commonsense view, one can have a "right" without the conditions required for obtaining such a power being fulfilled. It may be, *e.g.* that one cannot prove the existence of the facts required, when the burden of proof rests with oneself. Compare the state of affairs here with the situation which arises if "right" and "duty" have the meaning previously suggested. According to that view, they are related to actual circumstances in the following way. A "right" means that he who possesses it either (i) will obtain from the party who is under the corresponding "obligation" the advantage to which he is "entitled," or (ii) will acquire from the courts a power of compulsion, provided that he fulfils their requirements, particularly in the matter of proving the facts which the law explicitly states or which custom tacitly implies as conferring the "right."[4] It is then clear that there is nothing whatever left of "rights" or "duties," if *neither* of the two alternatives are fulfilled. It is true, no doubt, that it always holds good that, *if* this or that condition were fulfilled in the actual world, the "right" or the "duty" would become something actual. Such a connexion is expressed imperatively in a law, and is thought of by anyone who relies upon custom, as that which ought to happen. But it is also part of the idea thus presented, to which the ought is attached, that, if the conditions for exerting compulsion by process of law are not fulfilled and yet the action demanded is not performed, then the "right" comes to nothing. But, according to the usual way of looking at it, as soon as the facts exist which are connected in law or custom with the occurrence of a "right" or a "duty" within the sphere of private law, the "right" or the "duty" in question becomes a reality, even if the person who has the "right" neither actually enjoys the advantage attaching to it without recourse to the courts nor is able to fulfil the conditions required in order to obtain an equivalent by process of law.

It is, therefore, clear that the "legislator" in the sphere of private law *also* thinks that the effect of a legal enactment concerning "rights" and "duties" is the coming into existence of a power (and a state of subjection to that power) which falls outside the physical world. As regards juridical "obligation" in particular, this is supposed to be present in the "obliged" party, be it noted, quite regardless of whether he does or *can* fulfil it, and even of whether he actually feels any obligation whatever to perform the action which is said to be his "duty." The actual enjoyment of the advantages, to which one is said to be "entitled" as against the person who is under the "obligation," now becomes a mere exercise of the supernatural "right" which one has. This "exercise" issues from the "right"; but the latter exists independently, even if it cannot be exercised because of natural obstacles. Conversely, the action which is "obligatory" is merely a fulfilment of the duty which exists independently of it. The authority who applies the law thus comes to be in the position that he can actually declare that the plaintiff *has* a certain right and the defendant a certain duty; and he can make this declaration, *as a true statement*, the basis for decisions concerning executive coercion. Even if the "legislator" *also* understands by "rights" and "duties" a certain social state of affairs which he aims at realizing, as we have shown to be the case, yet the idea of "rights" and "duties" as supernatural powers and bonds is present and active throughout. The latter is connected with the former point of view in such a way that the contemplated social state of affairs is regarded as a consequence of the existence of these rights and duties. And the very names "rights" and "duties" are based on this. But in this way legislation is supposed to be armed with a power of acting directly in the supernatural world, and by means of such action producing effects in the physical world.

Moreover, if the idea of "rights" and "duties," which is expressed in a legal

---

[4] Similar remarks apply, *mutatis mutandis*, to the person who is under an obligation.

imperative in the sphere of private law, has this supernatural meaning, then a person who makes a "declaration of intention" within that sphere, in the knowledge that it will be effective through law or custom having the force of law, will have the same idea of "rights" and "duties." He too will think of the social state of affairs, which is to arise, as a mere consequence of supernatural relationships of power.

Before going further in this matter, we would point out that the supposed supernatural power or obligation, as the case may be, is a logical absurdity. It is held to refer to a reality which is elevated above the physical world. Yet, on the other hand, every "right" is supposed to have as its *object* an advantage which belongs to the physical world, and every "duty" is supposed to have as its object a certain way of acting in that world.                          [pp. 315–324]

## K. OLIVECRONA
### Law as Fact
(1st ed., 1939)

*The Binding Force of Law*

If we discard the superstitious idea that the law emanates from a god, it is obvious that every rule of law is a creation of men. The rules have always been established through legislation, or in some other way, by ordinary people of flesh and blood. In other words, they are produced by natural causes. On the other hand, they have natural effects in that they exert a pressure on the members of the community. The rules of law are a natural cause—among others—of the actions of the judges in cases of litigation as well as of the behaviour in general of people in relation to each other. The law-givers and other people who are in a position to lay down rules of law may actually influence the conduct of the members of the community. But that is certainly all they can do.[5]

We can never escape the conclusion that the law is a link in the chain of cause and effect.[6] It has, therefore, a place among the facts of the world of time and space. But then it cannot at the same time belong also to another world. The law cannot on the one hand be a fact (which it undoubtedly is) with natural causes and natural effects and on the other hand something outside the chain of causes and effects. To maintain the contrary involves pure superstition. The meaning must be—if there is any real meaning at all—that the law is endowed with a supernatural power.[7] Otherwise the words are empty, being used according to a secular habit without a real thought behind them.

Every attempt to maintain scientifically that law is binding in another sense than that of actually exerting a pressure on the population, necessarily leads to absurdities and contradictions. Here, therefore, is the dividing-line between

---

[5] [An interesting outcome of the stress upon law as a means of exerting influence on human behaviour by affecting the motives of individuals, has been to direct attention to the various ways in which legislation may be made effective by being translated into changes in social behaviour. One difficulty is that modern laws are so complex that they are not suited to affect directly any people outside official circles, and therefore the influence upon the formation of motives must tend to be indirect rather than direct. For an attempt to explore the various levels at which this may occur, see an article by P. Stjernquist in *Legal Essays to Castberg* (1963), p. 153.]

[6] [Olivecrona does not here seek to deny the distinction between a physical law of nature and a normative rule, but makes the point that the latter may itself operate as a physical cause of the conduct of human beings. But other Scandinavian realists, such as Lundstedt, go much further in attempting to eliminate the normative element of law altogether as a metaphysical fiction. *Cf. ante*, 1039.]

[7] [*Cf.* the influence of Hägerström, *ante*, 1036 and 1053–1054.]

realism and metaphysics, between scientific method and mysticism in the explanation of the law. The "binding force" of the law is a reality merely as an idea in human minds. There is nothing in the outside world which corresponds to this idea.[8]                                                                    [pp. 16–17]

### The Content of a Rule of Law

Thus the content of a rule of law of this type[9] is an idea of an imaginary action by a judge in an imaginary situation. We might add at once, however, that a rule of law is never intended to be regarded in isolation. It is always connected with other rules and its meaning does not emerge unless this connexion is observed. The rule about condemning the murderer to death is not only related to the law of procedure where the actions leading up to the judgment are pictured. Many more rules come into play. The accused must have attained a certain age, he must have been of sound mind when he committed the crime, and so on. Thus the picture of the imagined situation in which judgment should be given is very rich in detail. Many rules must be put together in order to make complete the picture of the situation and of the action desired.

With this qualification the content of the rules of law may be defined as *ideas of imaginary actions by people* (*e.g.* judges) *in imaginary situations*. The application of the law consists in taking these imaginary actions as models for actual conduct when the corresponding situations arise in real life.[10]                            [p. 29]

### A Rule of Law is not a Command in the Proper Sense[11]

The imperative theory has been so thoroughly criticised by previous authors that there is no need to discuss it at length here. We have only to confront the theory with obvious social facts. Its innermost meaning is to range law among the facts of the actual world. The commands, if there be any commands, are of course natural facts.[12] The theory, therefore, has the aim we pursue in this treatise. Only, the facts are misinterpreted when the rules of law are said to be commands in the proper sense of the word.

A command presupposes one person who commands and another to whom the command is addressed. In true appreciation of this fact, the imperative theory has endeavoured to point out from whom the "commands" emanate. Generally this has not been said to be any single individual. It would be hard indeed to maintain that the immense bulk of rules contained in the law of a modern state are the commands of any single human being. Such a being would undoubtedly require superhuman qualities. It is for this reason that the commands are ascribed to the *state*.

---

[8]  [But this does not exclude the normative *form* of the legal proposition. On the fallacy of regarding meaning as a kind of naming of objects, see *ante*, 39. *cf. Law as Fact* (2nd ed., 1971) pp. 110–112 where the view is expressed that investigations into the meaning of "binding force" are "futile".]

[9]  [*e.g.* that a murderer should be condemned to death.]

[10]  [Later Olivecrona writings are not so judge-orientated. See, for example, *Legal Language and Reality*, p. 180 and *post*, 885, where the content of a rule is now its effect on everybody, not just judges.]

[11]  [See further *Law as Fact* (2nd ed., 1971), pp. 120–126, and, particularly, his discussion of what Hare calls "the constative fallacy", the temptation to reduce imperatives to indicatives (pp. 125–126).]

[12]  [This may be so in Austin's case, since he looked to the *fact* of habitual obedience as the ultimate source of law, as well as accepting the view that it was the mental state of the commander that gave an expression the characteristic of a *command*. But another view is that stress is here laid simply on the imperative *form* of the legal proposition, and Olivecrona himself seems to favour this view.]

It is, however, impossible to maintain that the "state" properly speaking, could issue commands. The state is an organisation. But organisation cannot, as such, be said to command. If this is maintained, the expression is at best a loose one for the fact that commands are given by individuals active within the organisation. Only in this sense is the statement at all reasonable. [pp. 35–36]

### The Rules of Law as "Independent Imperatives"

Though not real commands, the rules of law, as has already been said, are given in the imperative form. The ideas about certain actions in certain situations, which form the contents of the rules, are not narratively described in the rules. The text of the law does not say that the law-givers or some other persons actually have conceived such and such imaginations in their minds. This would be absurd. The ideas are *imperatively* expressed. Whatever words are used, the meaning of a rule is always: this action *shall* be performed under such and such circumstances, this right *shall* arise from such and such facts, this official *shall* have this or that power, etc.

Now, does not this mean that the rules are, after all, commands? No, it does not. The term "command" may, of course, be used by everybody according to his own pleasure, provided that the meaning is made clear. What is important is not the terminological question. But different *things* must be kept apart if the real nature of the law is to be made clear. Such imperative statements as are found, *e.g.* in the law, must be carefully distinguished from commands in the proper sense. They are something else. The imperative theory has neglected this distinction. For this reason it has been driven to unrealistic constructions in order to make the realities of the law fit in with the assumption that the rules are commands in the proper sense of the word.

A command in the proper sense implies a personal relationship. The command is given by one person to another by words or gestures meant to influence the will. Now the same kind of words are also used in many connexions where no personal relations whatever exist between the person who commands and the receiver of the command. The words can nevertheless have a similar, if not identical, effect. They function independently of any person who commands. We may in this case speak of "*independent imperatives*," in order to get a convenient term.

As an example of independent imperatives may be cited the Decalogue. It cannot be said that Moses is commanding us to do this or that. Nor is this supposed to be so. The words are said to be the commands of God. In reality the Decalogue is a bundle of imperative sentences, formulated several thousand years ago and carried through the centuries by oral tradition and in writing. They are nobody's commands, though they have the form of language that is characteristic of a command.

The rules of law are of a similar character.[13] [pp. 42–43]

### Ordinary Legislation

From the traditional standpoint the act of legislating implies something inexplicable, though this is not always clearly realised. It is, however, inexplicable how the draft, or bill, can be lifted into another sphere of reality through being promulgated as a law. The draft is only a set of fictive articles, put before the

---

[13] [See Passmore's account of Hägerström on the origin of "duties". When we take an act to be our duty, we believe it is objectively our duty, quite irrespective of the fact that someone has commanded it. The reason for this, according to Hägerström, is that in our early years we are commanded by parents, teachers, etc. We come to do things not because we are commanded to do them by a particular person, but because the action comes to be regarded as commanded by its very nature. (1961) 36 *Philosophy* 143.]

legislative authorities for their consideration. The promulgated law, on the other hand, contains "binding" rules, *i.e.* it has a supernatural force. Thus the draft has undergone a profound change through the act of promulgation. The law is in essence something entirely different from the bill. And this change has been brought about by a vote in an assembly, or by the signing of a paper by a person in a prominent position.

This mysticism, and the scholasticism which follows in its wake, obviously has its origin in the idea of the binding force of the law. Once this idea is discarded as superstitious, there is nothing inexplicable about the act of legislating. It may be difficult to give a full explanation of its effect, since the matter is rather complicated, but the explanation will deal with facts only.

Legislating has an *actual* effect of supreme importance to the community. The draft had no significance for social life beyond that of being an object of discussion and formal proceedings. It was not a wheel in the machinery of the state. But the law is. The officials take it as a model for their actions and are virtually compelled to do so. The general public must take it into consideration as a barrier against some activities and a furtherance of others. The actual pressure of the law is there as soon as the draft has been promulgated.

The effect of the act of law-giving is in no way of a mystical character. It is only a question here of cause and effect in the natural world, on the *psychological* level.[14] The purpose of the law-givers is to influence the actions of men, but this can only be done through influencing their minds. How the influence works on the individual mind is a question of psychology. For the purpose of this treatise we need only point out the general conditions which make law-giving possible as an effective instrument of governing society, the basic elements in the structure of society which are a prerequisite to the functioning of the law-giving apparatus.

Under ordinary circumstances legislation takes place in accordance with the rules of the constitution. Its effect results in the first place from the general reverence in which the constitution is held and the habitual obedience to its rules. We find an attitude of this kind at least in every civilised country of the Western type (and no others need be considered here, for the sake of brevity). Everywhere there exists a set of ideas concerning the government of the country, ideas which are conceived as "binding" and implicitly obeyed. According to them certain persons are appointed to wield supreme power as kings, ministers, or members of parliament, etc. From this their actual power obtains. The general attitude towards the constitution places them in key-positions, enabling them to put pressure on their fellow-citizens and generally to direct their actions in some respects.

I do not want here to inquire into the causes which have led to this attitude, or the causes which have brought those particular persons into power. That is a question for history and social psychology to answer. Here it is enough to point to the actual situation as it undoubtedly exists in every country where it is not temporarily suspended during a revolution. The attitude is not, of course, endowed with any intrinsic self-supporting stability. It must be sustained through an unremitting psychological pressure on the members of the community. For the holders of the key-positions to maintain themselves in their places it is above all necessary that they actually use the power conferred on them through the

[14] [*Cf.* B. De Jouvenel, *Sovereignty*, on the extent to which men are ruled by "compulsive images" (pp. 296–298).]

psychological situation in the country, and use it with a certain determination.[15]

The attitude towards the constitution has a double significance. First, it causes people positively to accept duly promulgated laws as "binding" upon everybody and take them without reflection or opposition as patterns for their conduct. Secondly, the power to legislate is monopolised by those who are designated as law-givers in the constitution. The minds of the people are so to speak shut off in every other direction. Nobody else can secure attention or obedience in the field reserved for the law-givers by the constitution. To put up a competition with them in their field is in most cases meaningless.

Thus, the effect of the attitude towards the constitution is first, that the constitutional law-givers gain access to a psychological mechanism, through which they can influence the life of the country; secondly, that only they gain access to this mechanism and that everybody else is debarred from using it or building up another of the same kind.[16] I use the term "mechanism" on purpose as being, in my opinion, the appropriate one, since the reactions of people in this respect generally follow very definite lines and may be foretold with great accuracy. The attitude of the public is—under normal circumstances—so rigid and uniform that the psychological effect of the act of legislating takes place smoothly, without any special effort on the part of the law-givers. We are so familiar with this situation that it seems to be a part of the order of the universe like the rising and the setting of the sun. Therefore, we do not reflect on the simple fact that the effect of legislation is conditioned by the psychological attitude which we ourselves and the millions of other people maintain. Because of this attitude the law-givers can play on our minds as on a musical instrument.

Besides the attitude of mind among the general public, another basic condition is required for the process of legislating to be effective. This is organisation. There must be a body of persons, ready to apply the laws, if necessary with force, since it would be clearly impossible to govern a community only by directly influencing the minds of the great masses through law-giving. We shall have to return to this matter later on. The organisation that wields force, the state organisation, is largely composed of persons who are trained automatically to execute the laws which are promulgated in the constitutional form, irrespective of their own opinion of their advisability.[17] The organisation is therefore like a vast machinery, so regularly and certainly does it function. The law-givers sit in the centre of the machinery as before a switchboard, from where they direct the different wheels.

The real significance of the act of legislating is now apparent. The draft is not

---

[15] [Even if it be admitted that law has to be explained in terms of facts, it may still be necessary, as Durkheim has pointed out, to distinguish between social facts and psychological facts. The individual has not only a psychic life of his own but is born into a social world, and while we may have recourse to psychology to explain the features of the individual's psychic life, in the realm with which sociology is concerned the "facts" of social life may appear on quite a different level of abstraction from that of individual psychology. It may be said then, that one of the important points overlooked by Olivecrona's approach, is that law exists not just as a set of ideas in the consciousness of individual citizens, but that it exists and persists as a social institution, and that if we are to seek a factual substratum to law, it should be sought not so much in the psychic reactions of individuals, but in the social character of institutions. *cf.* E. E. Evans-Pritchard, *Social Anthropology* (1951), p. 45; J. Beattie, *Other Cultures* (1964), pp. 26–28, 73.]

[16] [Thus for Olivercrona the "legality" of a revolution is established when the revolutionaries have effectively seized hold of this mechanism and used its pressures to remove the reverence for the old régime in favour of their own. *cf.* Austin's theory of habitual obedience. The latter looks at it from the point of view of the obedient citizen transferring his allegiance; the former, from the point of view of the legislator, bringing the citizens into an appropriately receptive state of mind.]

[17] [This ignores the discretion which it is impossible to eliminate and which all officials have.]

lifted into another sphere of reality but it simply made the object of certain formalities which have a peculiar effect of a psychological nature. The formalities are the essential thing. The legislative act consists in nothing but these. The same statements as those contained in a law, if made by the same persons without observing the constitutional form, are of no avail.[18]                    [pp. 51–56]

### The Actual use of Force in the State Organisation

In every community force is consistently applied through the officials of the state, more particularly in three forms;—police measures against disturbances, infliction of punishment and execution of civil judgments. In all three cases physical violence or coercion is the ultimate expedient. It is used not only to disperse dangerous mobs if need be and to keep the peace generally. It is also an unavoidable instrument in the regular application of criminal and civil law. In criminal law, actual violence against the person of the criminal is used in the form of the death penalty and imprisonment. Even in civil law physical violence is sometimes used against a person, as *e.g.* when a tenant is ejected from the premises by means of force and when imprisonment for debt[19] takes place. Generally, however, violence against a person is not needed in civil matters. Nevertheless, it must not be forgotten that physical force is the basis of execution in these cases too. Thus the goods of the debtor are seized by force if he does not deliver them peacefully when they are required in order to pay his debt. Physical force is restored to in administrative law, also, when necessary. In the whole field therefore, the provisions of the law are ultimately carried out by physical force or violence.[20]

Actual violence is, however, kept very much in the background. The more this is done, the smoother and more undisturbed is the working of the legal machinery. In this respect many modern states have been successful to an extent which is something of a miracle, considering the nature of the man.[21] Under suitable conditions the use of violence in the proper sense is so much reduced that it passes almost unnoticed.

Such a state of things is apt to create the belief that violence is alien to the law or of secondary importance. This is, however, a fatal illusion. One essential condition for reducing the application of violence to this extent is that there is to hand an organised force of overwhelming strength in comparison to that of any possible opponents. This is generally the case in every state organised on modern lines. Resistance is therefore known to be useless. Those who are engaged in applying force in criminal and civil matters of the ordinary kind are few in number, it is true. But they are thoroughly organised and they are in each case concerned with only a single individual, or a few individuals.          [pp. 124–125]

### Law Chiefly Consists of Rules about Force

Thus the traditional ways of defining the relations between law and force must be discarded. It is impossible to maintain that law in a realistic sense is guaranteed or protected by force. The real situation is that law—the body of rules summed up as law—consists chiefly of rules *about* force,[22] rules which contain patterns of conduct for the exercise of force.

---

[18]  [This is not necessarily so. In Rome under the Dominate the will of the Emperor was law however expressed. Custom as a source of law has proved a problem to Olivecrona.]

[19]  [Imprisonment for civil debt was abolished in Great Britain in 1970 (Administration of Justice Act 1970). It remains, however, for maintenance defaulters and tax defaulters.]

[20]  [See also *Law as Fact* (2nd ed., 1971), pp. 271–273.]

[21]  [Olivecrona's is essentially a Hobbesian view of man and society. See *Leviathan, ante*, 143.]

[22]  [See, too A. Ross, *On Law and Justice* (1958), pp. 52–58.]

It must be kept in mind, of course, that at the same time the rules contain patterns of conduct for the private citizens. But these patterns, or rules, are only another aspect of the rules about the use of force, and those rules are the deciding factor. The citizens have to make their behaviour confirm to them. Rules about "rights" and "duties" which are not also rules for the use of overwhelming force are of little avail in actual life. Rather than accept the traditional classification of rules as primary and secondary I should therefore like to call the rules about force primary rules and the rules for the conduct of private citizens secondary rules.[23] This would not be quite exact, however. In reality the rules of civil and criminal law are at one and the same time rules for the private citizens as well as for the use of force by the officials. It is only a question of different aspects of the same rules. But we are justified in defining law as rules about force, since everything turns upon the regular use of force.[24]

Outside civil and criminal law, in administrative law, there is a vast amount of rules which are not directly concerned with the use of force (*e.g.* rules about education, health, communications, etc.). Sometimes force is necessary even in this field, though on the whole the rules are applied by the officials in other ways. But all these rules presuppose an organised force behind them and they presuppose that force is used according to the rules of civil and criminal law. However important they may be in our time, they must therefore be regarded as an addition to that central body of rules which consists of the rules about force. It might be added that the constitution consists of rules which indirectly concern the use of force, in that they regulate the laying down of rules of civil and criminal law. [pp. 134–135]

### Our Moral Standards and the Law

In so far as thoughts of unlawful acts enter the mind and appear attractive, they are more effectively counteracted by the involuntary moral impulse than by cold calculations about the risks. An unconditional: "You shall not!" rings in our ears. "This is low! It is detestable!" Such independent imperatives and expressions of value beat down the tendencies to unlawfulness. And these ideas and the feelings which accompany them are to a very large extent—though not, of course, exclusively,—a consequence of the "administration of justice" through regular infliction of punishment and extraction of damages.

It might, however, be suggested that the relations between the law and the moral ideas are the very opposite of this—*i.e.* that the moral ideas are the primary factor and that the law is inspired by them. In fact this is the position generally taken up by jurisprudence and legal philosophy. The principal rules of law are represented as being based on "justice." This means either that they are founded on an abstract norm, existing by itself *in nubibus*, or that the law is founded on our *ideas* about justice. Both these ways of stating the case are incorrect.

It is hardly necessary specifically to refute the contention that the law is based on abstract justice. This view is too openly superstitious. The only question which

---

[23] [*Cf.* Kelsen's view, *ante*, 311.]

[24] [Schulz, *Principles of Roman Law*, pp. 20–24, 158, 196–197, points out that much of a society's organisation may consist of non-legal customs, and instances, in Roman law, restraints on *patria potestas* and testation, marriage customs, etc. The realistic view is to equate these with law as kinds of psychological pressures which are all causally effective. Olivecrona, however, also relies on the sanctionist criterion of organised force as differentiating legal from other norms and denies that law can be based on the state, which itself presupposes the law (pp. 40–41). Elsewhere, he asserts that the specific feature of legal rules in their relation to a state organisation, which, by a monopoly of force, can establish new imperatives and ensure general obedience. See his essay on "Law as Fact" in *Interpretations of Modern Legal Philosophy* (1947), p. 555.]

need be discussed is whether the *ideas* of justice are the primary factor in regard to the law or whether they are fashioned by the law...

...The first question is how the moral standards of every single individual are fashioned and what is the influence of the use of force according to the rules of law in this respect. Everybody grows up in a community where a legal machinery has existed since times immemorial. The question concerns the influence of this machinery and its rules on our moral ideas. The second question concerns the part played by moral ideas in the formation of new rules added to the already existing body of rules of law. To being with, the first question only will be discussed.

With regard to this question it seems obvious that it must be answered in the sense indicated above. Our upbringing makes this unavoidable. The character is necessarily formed under the influence of our surroundings, especially in earlier years: The society where we live puts its stamp on our ideas. But among the forces working within society the law is without doubt one of the foremost. The law certainly cannot be a projection of some innate moral convictions in the child or adolescent, since it existed long before he was born. When he grows up and becomes acquainted with the conditions of life he is subjected to its influence. The first indelible impressions in early youth concerning the relations to other people are directly or indirectly derived from the law. But the effect is not only to create a fear of the sanctions and cause the individual to adjust himself so as to be able to live without fear. The rules also have a positive moral effect in that they cause a deposit of moral ideas in the mind.

The rules of law are independent imperatives. In that form they are communicated to young and old. You shall not steal!—of this type are the rules concerning our behaviour. Now these imperatives are (so to speak) absorbed by the mind. We take them up and make them an integral part of our mental equipment. A firm psychological connexion is established between the idea of certain actions and certain imperative expressions, forbidding the actions or ordering them to be done. The idea of committing, *e.g.* theft is coupled with the idea of an imperative: you shall not! Then we have a moral command with "binding force". We speak of a moral command when an independent imperative has been completely objectivated and therefore is regarded as binding without reference to an authority in the outer world. The chief imperatives of the law are generally transformed in that way. Only when this is the case is the law really firmly established.

A moral influence of the law is required for its effectivity only in respect of a limited number of fundamental rules, and only in these cases is such an influence possible. For the rest it is enough that the idea of a moral obligation to abide by the law as such is sustained and that it is not damaged by unreasonable laws or arbitrary jurisdiction.

Several things explain how the rules of law can thus be absorbed by the whole people. The suggestive effect of the imperatives is enormous when there is power behind them—here the majestic power of the state, working relentlessly according to the rules about sanctions. This power is surrounded by august ceremonies and met with a traditional and deep-rooted reverence. All this combines to make a profound impression on the mind, causing us to take the fundamental "commands" of the law to heart as objectively binding. We do it all the more readily since we understand, at least instinctively, the necessity of these rules for the maintenance of peace and security.

The absorption of the imperatives cannot, of course, be effected under all circumstances. On the contrary, it is possible only under specific conditions, which ought to be thoroughly studied. Broadly speaking the first requirement is that the rules appear as reasonable to most people, *i.e.* as furthering ends which are generally recognised as desirable. Otherwise the rules will have no moral effect or may even arouse moral indignation. Also it is necessary that the application of sanctions is regular and fairly impartial.

It seems impossible not to admit that those are, in brief words, the relations between law and the moral standards of the individual. The law is the primary factor. The individual is caught in its grip from the earliest stage in life and his moral ideas are developed under its influence. The law—including the regular use of force according to the rules—is not, of course, an isolated factor. There is never a single cause for such a complicated thing as our moral ideas. The causes are necessarily manifold. Above all, the use of force must be associated with propaganda, preparing the minds for the reception of the imperatives, and there must be a direct inculcation of the imperatives through parents, teachers, superiors etc. What is suggested here is merely that the use of force is one of the chief factors in the moulding of our moral standards, and not the other way round.[25] [pp. 151–156]

# A. ROSS
## On Law and Justice
### (1958)

### *Analysis of the Concept "Valid Law"*

Let us imagine that two persons are playing chess, while a third person looks on.

If the onlooker knows nothing about chess he will not understand what is going on. From his knowledge of other games he will probably conclude that it is some sort of game. But he will not be able to understand the individual moves or to see any connection between them. Still less will we have any notion of the problems involved in any particular disposition of the pieces on the board... [p. 11]

... Human social life ... acquires the character of community life from the very fact that a large number (not all) of individual actions are relevant and have significance in relation to a set of common conceptions of rules. They constitute a significant whole, bearing the same relation to one another as move and countermove. Here, too, there is mutual interplay, motivated by and acquiring its significance from the common rules of the social "game." And it is the consciousness of these rules which makes it possible to understand and in some measure to predict the course of events.

I will now examine more closely what a rule of chess actually is, and in what way it is possible to establish what the rules are which govern the game of chess.

I have in mind here the primary rules of chess, those which determine the arrangement of the pieces, the moves, "taking," and the like, and not rules of chess theory.

As to the latter a few remarks will suffice. Like other technological rules they obviously are of the nature of hypothetical theoretical pronouncements. They assume the existence of the primary rules of chess and indicate the consequences in which different openings and gambits will lead in the game, judged in relation to the chance of winning. Like other technological rules their directive force is conditioned by an interest—in this example the interest in the winning of the game. If a player does not have this interest, then the theory of the game is without importance to him.

[25] [For a useful discussion of Olivecrona on law and morals, see J. Merrills (1969) 19 U. Toronto L.J. 46. The criticism is voiced that Olivercrona's account distorts the view of law by failing to consider what Hart has called the internal aspect of rules of law. Morality is instrumental in achieving acceptance of the rules of law from this internal point of view. This is overlooked by Olivecrona. It may be suggested, however, that both Olivecrona and his critic have adopted over-simplistic models of law and morality, and that the relationship between them is more interactional. Olivecrona has not discussed this question in the second edition of *Law as Fact*.]

The primary rules of chess, on the other hand, are directives. Although they are formulated as assertions about the "ability" or "power" of the pieces to move and "take," it is clear that they are intended to indicate how the game is to be played. They aim directly, that is, unqualified by any underlying objective, to motivate the player; they tell him, as it were: This is how it is played.

These directives are felt by each player to be socially binding; that is to say, a player not only feels himself spontaneously motivated ("bound") to a certain method of action but is at the same time certain that a breach of the rules will call forth a reaction (protest) on the part of his opponent. And in this way they are clearly distinguished from the rules of skill contained in the theory. A stupid move can arouse astonishment, but not a protest.

On the other hand, the rules of chess are not tinged with morality; this is the result of the fact that normally no one really wants to break them. The wish to cheat at a game must be due to the fact that a player has an aim other than merely to win according to the rules of the game; for example, he may want to be admired or to win a sum of money which is at stake. This latter aim is often present at a game of cards, and it is well known that the demand for honourable play here takes on a moral value.

How is it possible then to establish which rules (directives) govern the game of chess?

One could perhaps think of approaching the problem from the behaviourist angle—limiting oneself to what can be established by external observation of the actions and then finding certain regularities. But in this way an insight into the rules of the game would never be achieved. It would never be possible to distinguish actual custom, or even regularities conditioned by the theory of the game, from the rules of chess proper. Even after watching a thousand games it would still be possible to believe that it is against the rules to open with a rook's pawn.[26]

The simplest thing, perhaps, would be to go by certain authoritative rulings, for example, rulings given at chess congresses, or information contained in recognised textbooks on chess. But even this might not be sufficient, since it is not certain that such declarations are adhered to in practice. Sometimes games are played in fact in many varying ways. Even in a classic game like chess variations of this kind can occur (for example, the rule about "taking" *en passant* is not always adhered to). This problem of what rules govern "chess" must therefore, strictly speaking, be understood to refer to the rules which govern an actual game between two specific persons. It is their actions, and theirs alone, which are bound up in a significant whole and governed for both of them by the rules.

Thus we cannot but adopt an introspective method. The problem is to discover which rules are actually felt by the players to be socially binding, in the sense indicated above. The first criterion is that they are in fact effective in the game and are outwardly visible as such. But in order to decide whether rules that are observed are more than just customary usage or motivated by technical reasons, it is necessary to ask the players by what rules they feel themselves bound.

Accordingly we can say: a rule of chess "is valid" means that within a given fellowship (which fundamentally comprises the two players of an actual game) this rule is effectively adhered to, because the players feel themselves to be socially bound by the directive contained in the rule. The concept of validity (in chess) involves two elements. The one refers to the actual effectiveness of the rule which can be established by outside observation. The other refers to the way in which the rule is felt to be motivating, that is, socially binding.

There is a certain ambiguity in the concept "rule of chess." The rules of chess

---

[26] [For a discussion of the relevance of games as a model see G. Hughes (1968) 77 Yale L.J. 475 reprinted in *Law, Reason and Justice* (ed. Hughes 1969), pp. 101, 104–107.]

have no reality and do not exist apart from the experience of the players, that is, their ideas of certain patterns of behaviour and, associated therewith, the emotional experience of the compulsion to obey. It is possible to abstract the meaning of an assertion purely as a thought content ("2 and 2 make 4") from the apprehension of the same by a given person at a given time; and in just the same way it is also possible to abstract the meaning of a directive ("the king has the power of moving one square in any direction") from the concrete experience of the directive. The concept "rule of chess" must therefore in any accurate analysis be divided into two: the experienced ideas of certain patterns of behaviour (with the accompanying emotion) and the abstract content of those ideas, the norms of chess.

Thus the norms of chess are the abstract idea content (of a directive nature) which makes it possible, as a scheme of interpretation, to understand the phenomena of chess (the actions of the moves and the experienced patterns of action) as a coherent whole of meaning and motivation, a game of chess; and, along with other factors, within certain limits to predict the course of the game.

The phenomena of chess and the norms of chess are not mutually independent, each of them having their own reality; they are different sides of the same thing. No biological-physical action is as such regarded as a move of chess. It acquires this quality only by being interpreted in relation to the norms of chess. And conversely, no directive idea content has as such the character of a valid norm of chess. It acquires this quality only by the fact that it can, along with others, be effectively applied as a scheme of interpretation for the phenomena of chess. The phenomena of chess becomes phenomena of chess only when placed in relation to the norms of chess and vice versa.

The purpose of this discussion of chess has undoubtedly become clear by now. It is a pointer toward the statement that the concept "valid norm of chess" may function as the model for the concept "valid law" which is the real object of our preliminary considerations.

The law too may be regarded as consisting partly of legal phenomena and partly of legal norms in mutual correlation.

Observing the law as it functions in society we find that a large number of human actions are interpreted as a coherent whole of meaning and motivation by means of legal norms as the scheme of interpretation. A purchases a house from B. It turns out that the house is full of termites. A asks B for a reduction in the purchase price, but B will not agree. A brings an action against B, and the judge in accordance with the law of contract orders B to pay to A a certain sum of money within a given time. B does not do this. A has the sheriff levy upon the personal property of B which is then sold in auction. This sequence of events comprises a whole series of human actions, from the establishment of the law of contract to the auction. A biological-physical consideration of these actions cannot reveal any causal connection between them. Such connections lie within each single individual. But we interrupt them with the aid of the reference scheme "valid law" as legal phenomena constituting a coherent whole of meaning and motivation. Each one of these actions acquires its legal character only when this is done. A's purchase of the house happens by word of mouth or with the aid of written characters. But these become a "purchase" only when seen in relation to the legal norms. The various actions are mutually motivating just like the moves in chess. The judge, for example, is motivated by A's and B's parts in the deal (and the further circumstances in connection with it, the condition of the house), and by the precedents establishing the law of contract. The whole proceeding has the character of a "game," only according to norms which are far more complicated than the norms of the game of chess.

On the basis of what has been said, the following hypothesis is advanced: The concept "valid (Illinois, California, common) law" can be explained and defined in principle in the same manner as the concept "valid (for any two players) norm of chess." That is to say, "valid law" means the abstract set of normative ideas which serve as a scheme of interpretation for the phenomena of law in action, which again means that these norms are effectively followed, and followed because they are experienced and felt to be socially binding.[27]

This conclusion may perhaps be thought commonplace, and it may seem that a vast apparatus of reasoning has been employed to this end. This might be true if the problems were approached by a person with no preconceived notions. But it would not be true for an historical approach. By far the greater part of all writers on jurisprudence up to the present have maintained that the concept "valid law" cannot be explained without recourse to the metaphysical. The law according to this view is not merely an empirical phenomenon. When we say that a rule of law is "valid" we refer not only to something factual, that can be observed, but also to a "validity" of a metaphysical character. This validity is alleged to be a pure concept of reason of divine origin or existing *a priori* (independent of experience) in the rational nature of man. And eminent writers on jurisprudence who deny such spiritual metaphysics have nevertheless been of the opinion that the "validity" of the law can only be explained by means of specific postulates.

Seen in this light our preliminary conclusion will, I trust, not be called commonplace. This analysis of a simple model is calculated to raise doubts as to the necessity of metaphysical explanations of the concept of law. Who would ever think of tracing the valid norms of chess back to an *a priori* validity, a pure idea of chess, bestowed upon man by God or deduced by man's eternal reason? The thought is ridiculous, because we do not take chess as seriously as law—because stronger emotions are bound up with the concepts of law. But this is no reason for believing that logical analysis should adopt a fundamentally different attitude in each of the two cases. [pp. 13–18]

## A. ROSS
### Directives and Norms
### (1968)

*A norm is to be defined as a directive which corresponds in a particular way to certain social facts*

... It is not possible to define the concept "norm" (in a way useful to the social sciences) so that it denotes either simply a kind of meaning content (which includes all or only some directive), or simply a set of social facts. Both approaches must founder as too one-sided. We must then further conclude that a definition is required which integrates both aspects of the matter in the concept "norm." On this basis, I put forward the following definition: *a norm is a directive which stands in relation of correspondence to social facts*, the nature of the relation to be specified subsequently. The only directives which can stand in the required relation are the impersonal directives with the exclusion of the autonomous moral directives; that is, those directives which have been called ... "quasi-commands" and "constitute rules based on mutual agreement."

Before I undertake the task of specifying what relation of correspondence is relevant I want to stress the fundamental adequacy of the definition. The norm is said to be a directive, in the sense of a meaning content; to this extent the definition is adequate with regard to the use according to which a norm can be *followed or complied with*, felt to be *binding*, and *logically* related to the other norms so that they together constitute a *system of norms*. But according to the definition a directive is a norm only if it corresponds to certain social facts, in a

---

[27] By the judge and other legal authorities applying the law. [This is no longer Ross's view as to the range of directives. See *ante*, 1041 and *post*, 1073–1074.]

way to be specified. To say that a norm "exists" means, then, that these facts exist; and to this extent the adequacy of the definition is secured with regard to that use of "norm" which requires that norms can exist, and that statements to this effect form part of the description of societies.

Now, in undertaking the task of specifying how directives are related to social facts, I assume provisionally that we are concerned only with generally formulated directives, or rules.[28] It is, then, barely questionable that the fundamental condition for the existence of a norm must be that *in the majority of cases the pattern of behaviour presented in the directive (s–b) is followed by the members of the society*. If a rule is not effective in this sense, then it would be misleading to say that it "exists," if such a statement is meant to be part of a description of social facts.

That a pattern of behaviour is on the whole *followed* does not mean that every member of the society generally acts in the same way in given circumstances. Usually the description of *s* is so qualified that the norm will concern only certain categories of the members of the society. Thus the directive that shops are to be closed at a certain hour relates only to those members of society who are shopkeepers.

That the pattern is *on the whole* followed involves a certain vagueness which makes it difficult to decide in some circumstances whether or not a norm exists.

This condition, however, is not of itself sufficient to provide an adequate definition. For it is necessary for the establishment of a norm that it be followed not only with external regularity, that is with observable conformity to the rule, but also with the consciousness of following a rule and being bound to do so.[29] If this requirement is not met (I shall subsequently return to the question of what it implies) then many patterns of social behaviour which differ essentially from those traditionally called norms would be included under the concept. I have in mind the following types of observable regularities of behaviour.

*Patterns Biologically or Physically Based*

Man's biological make-up and the general economy of nature effect conformity of behaviour in many ways. Most of us sleep during the night and are awake in daytime; we turn on the light when it becomes dark and wear more clothes when it is cold; we carry an umbrella or a raincoat if it looks like rain.

*Technical Patterns*

As we have mentioned earlier, some directives are offered as advice or directions for the most efficient performance of certain tasks and achievements of certain goals. When faced with similar tasks, people will to a great extent act uniformly and follow directions which are warranted by technology and tradition. This is especially true of professional undertakings. Bricklayers are trained in the time-honoured methods of building a wall or a chimney, gardeners learn how to graft and plant cuttings, tailors are taught the traditions of their profession.

*Folkways (habits which lack binding force)*

Because of uniform interests and traditions uniform habits grow up in the life of people. In certain circles, under certain circumstances, it is usual to celebrate Christmas with a Christmas tree and gifts; to eat at set hours; to dance at the local inn on Saturday night; to get engaged before being married; to wear a wedding ring; to serve mustard with boiled cod; to have children baptized and confirmed.

[28] [*Cf. Directives and Norms* (1968), para. 22.]
[29] H. L. A. Hart, *The Concept of Law* (1994).

These patterns, without changing their substance, may become customs of a normative character merely by being deeply established.

These three and perhaps other classes of behaviour patterns are characterized by external conformity or regularity, without being internalized, that is, without being experienced as binding. This much, I believe, is commonly agreed. But agreement comes to an end when the question is raised of what is meant by calling a pattern of behaviour "binding."[30] Two answers have commonly been given. Some writers have attached importance to the condition that the rule of action is experienced internally as *valid* ("binding" means arousing a feeling of obligation). Others have regarded as the decisive feature the external fact that violation of a rule is regularly met by a reaction (sanction) on the part of other members of society, the individual agent feeling himself in a position of coercion: either he follows the rule, or runs the serious risk of being exposed to punishment of some kind ("binding" means "*coercing*").

On the former account, the criterion of a pattern of behaviour's having binding force lies in mental experiences and reactions either of the agent himself or of a spectator. A person who is in situation *s* (that is, a situation in which behaviour *b* is expected, in accordance with the supposed pattern) feels a special prompting or impulse to act according to the pattern. This impulse does not appear as a manifestation of his needs and interests; it may, indeed, conflict with these. Even though there exist no external hindrances to acting in violation of the pattern, and although his interests prompt him to act differently, the agent, under the influence of this impulse, does not feel free to do so. He feels himself to be subject to a peculiar kind· of "compulsion," but not a compulsion in the usual sense of a pressure stemming from the threat of sanctions—a threat of having inflicted on him some evil, which provides an incentive to act based on his interests and fears. The "compulsion" that constitutes "binding force" resembles the compulsion which arises out of the threat of sanctions in so far as the agent does not feel free, but rather feels under pressure to act in a way which conflicts with the way he would *like* to act. But it differs from external compulsion in that the impulse which prevents him from following his desires is not itself experienced as a manifestation of any need or interest; that is, it is not rooted in the fear of some evil or the desire for some good. For this reason, the compelling impulse has a stamp of intelligibility and mystery, as if it did not arise from his own nature but was a dictate coming to him from outside.

This peculiar experience of being bound is manifested verbally in deontic words and phrases. Asked why he is acting against his own interest the agent will give answers such as "because it is my *duty* to do so," "because it is the *right* thing to do," "because I *ought* to do it whether I like it or not." ...

What the agent experiences immediately, a witness may experience by imagining himself in the agent's place. For him the impulse manifests itself as the *expectation* that the pattern in question will be followed. This "expectation" is not, however, theoretical (like that expressed in "rain is to be expected later in the day") but constitutes a *demand* (a deontic term).[31] It shows itself verbally as an expression of *approval or disapproval* according to whether the demand is satisfied: he did *right*, or *wrong*, he *ought* not to have acted in that way. Verbal reactions of disapproval are often accompanied by adverse feelings, ranging from cool reserve to anger and indignation, and these emotions may be so strong that they lead to acts of violence, such as lynching. Although reactions of this kind are, we may suppose, produced mainly by the violation of the interests of the one who reacts, they may also be disinterested and caused by pure moral indignation. It is

---

[30] [*Cf.* Olivecrona, *ante*, 1057.]
[31] [*Cf.* Bentham, *ante*, 253.]

another question whether moral indignation can always be assumed to conceal hidden motives of self-interest (*e.g.* envy).[32]

I shall call any experience of obligation, rightness, wrongness, approval, or disapproval, the *experience of validity*. It must be made clear that this term designates certain psychological phenomena; "validity" is nothing but the peculiar characteristic of these experiences. When I speak of the "experience of validity," then, I am not referring to a recognition of "validity" in the sense ... of a property inherent in moral principles, which cognitivists claim to exist and non-cognitivists deny. But it is not accidental that the word "validity" is used to characterize these psychological experiences; for it is just the false interpretation of these experiences which has given rise to the idea of an objective quality of validity accessible to cognition.

According to the rival account of the "binding" character of a behaviour pattern, what distinguishes a binding norm from non-binding conformity, or internal regularity from external conformity, is a set of observable facts: if the pattern of behaviour is violated, there regularly follows a reaction on the part of the society. This reaction comes either from individuals acting spontaneously or from the institutionalized organs of society created for this purpose (the police, the courts, and executive authorities). This is Geiger's view. According to him, as we have seen, $s \rightarrow b$ expresses an existing norm if the pattern $s_1 \rightarrow r$ is regularly followed, where $s_1$ stands for $s$ & $\sim b$ ($s \rightarrow b$ is violated) and $r$ signifies a reaction which has the character of a sanction. A norm exists, on this view, if compliance with its directed pattern of behaviour is guarantied by *threat of coercion*. The experience of the norm as "binding" is the internal reflection of this external fact.[33]

To some extent the two views lead to the same results. For the emotional and perhaps physical reactions of disapproval will in themselves constitute a sanction. The crucial question must then be one of approach: can the existence of a system of sanctions and, hence, of a normative system, be discovered merely by external observation of behaviour?

The answer is that it cannot. Not any disagreeable reaction is a sanction. The notion of a sanction is intimately connected with the feeling of disapproval. A merely external record of behaviour must lead to unacceptable results, by abstracting from the meaning of the reaction and its mental background. A person who earns a certain income is regularly met with the requirement to pay a certain sum to the Inland Revenue. Why do we not interpret this demand as a sanction (a fine) which shows the existence of a norm forbidding the earning of such an income?[34] Why are customs duties not considered to be sanctions against imports, or the coercive measures taken with regard to the insane interpreted as sanctions against becoming insane: These and similar questions are not answerable on behaviouristic premisses; and this proves that a behaviouristic account of what it is for a norm to exist cannot be sustained.

The inadequacy of the account is especially obvious in the case of legal norms. Since legal sanctions are applied according to the decisions of the courts, the existence of a legal norm would have to be derived from an observed regularity in court decisions. But external observation is not sufficient for establishing such a regularity. For a long period of time a judge may display a certain typical reaction; he may, for example, regularly impose penalties for criminal abortion. But the pattern of reaction may change suddenly, if a new law has been passed. Nor

---

[32] *Cf.* Svend Ranulf, *The Jealousy of the Gods and Criminal Law at Athens* (1933–1934), vol. I–II; *Moral Indignation and Middle Class Psychology* (1938).

[33] "That a norm is binding means: it is probable that either people comply with it or that violation of it calls forth an adverse reaction." Theodor Geiger, *Vorstudien zu einer Soziologie des Rechts* (1947), p. 165, *cf.* pp. 26, 32 *et seq.*, 47, 157 *et seq.*

[34] [*Cf. ante*, 312–313.]

can regularity be ascertained by recourse to the observation of a more general pattern of behaviour, *viz.* "obeying the legislator." For it is not possible, from the observation of behaviour alone, to identify the "legislator" who is being obeyed. External observation alone might lead us to believe that it is certain individuals who are obeyed, that is, those persons named as members of the legislature. But one day there is a general election and the composition of the legislative changes. And so we go on, perhaps right up to the constitution; but even the constitution may be changed. A behaviourist interpretation, then, achieves nothing. For the *change* in the judge's behaviour can be understood and predicted only by taking into account ideological facts, that is, only by assuming the existence of those feelings of validity, or ideology, which motivate the judge's decisions. Only on the hypothesis of the allegiance which judge feels towards the constitution, its institutions and the traditionally recognized sources of law, is it possible to interpret changing judicial reactions as a coherent whole—as regularities constituted by an ideology. . . .

The future behaviour of the courts, as we have seen, cannot be predicted on the basis of past decisions alone. Judicial regularity is not external, habitual and static, but rather internal, ideological and dynamic.

There is another reason why the sanction theory will not do. As we have seen, according to that theory, the criterion for the existence of the norms $s \rightarrow b$ is that the pattern $s_1 \rightarrow r$ is regularly followed. But in this case, what kind of regularity is it supposed to be? Does the formula $s_1 \rightarrow r$ itself signify a mere habit without binding force, or a pattern of behaviour which itself has a normative character? The latter must be the case: People are *expected* to disapprove of contraventions of a norm. That $s_1 \rightarrow r$ is binding is especially obvious when $r$ is taken to be the reaction of the courts to violations of legal norms. Geiger agrees with this. If, however, $s_1 \rightarrow r$ is itself a norm, that is, a pattern of behaviour which is binding, then the theory entails the existence of a third norm, $s_2 \rightarrow r$ according to which sanctions are to be applied against whoever violates the second norm ($s_1 \rightarrow r$) which itself demands the application of sanctions against whomever violates the first norm ($s \rightarrow b$)—and so *ad infinitum*. Any norm requires as its basis an infinite chain of norms. A pattern of behaviour is said to be a norm, to be binding, only if it is backed up by sanctions. But the coercive measures themselves are taken in accordance with norms which have also to be backed up by sanctions applied in accordance with norms—and so on to infinity. A model which thus implies an infinite regress cannot be adequate as a description of reality.

I have dwelt at length on Geiger's theory of sanctions, because we have to understand why it is unsound before we can see what social facts are referred to when we speak of the existence of a legal norm, or its being in force. The opinion is widely held that what constitutes the existence of a legal norm is the fact of the physical power behind the law, a power that will be exercised against offenders by the police, the courts and executive agencies. It is said that the law consists of rules which will be maintained, if the need arises, by means of physically coercive force—the use of violence. On this view, a law like the one which requires a buyer to pay the stipulated price depends in turn upon another rule which requires coercive sanctions to be used against the buyer who refuses to comply voluntarily. What is the nature of these secondary sanction-demanding norms? If it is said that they are themselves legal rules we land in the infinite regress mentioned already: secondary rules presuppose third level rules which presuppose fourth level rules, etc.[35] If it is said, on the other hand, that the secondary rules are not themselves legal rules, we have on our hands the paradox that the rules which govern the judge's exercise of his office are not legal rules. In addition to these complications, the theory has the unfortunate consequence that large parts of what is normally considered the law are denied to be of a legal nature and are excluded from the

---

[35] [*Cf.* Bentham, *ante*, 252 and see comment in n. 44, p. 286.]

province of the law. For it is a fact that there can be no enforcement of much of constitutional law, administrative law, and procedural law, in so far as these concern the competence and obligations of the highest organs of the state. Such is the case especially where there exists no judicial review of legislation.[36]

These complications and unacceptable consequences disappear, if we take the position that legal rules are not rules *maintained by* the exercise of coercion but rules *about* its exercise; they are rules which are in general not enforced but followed voluntarily, that is, in virtue of the feelings of validity which endows the rules with binding force. Legal rules are directed at those in authority, the organs of the state, and their source of effectiveness is the allegiance of officials towards the constitution and the institutions derived from it, together with the non-violent sanctions of disapproval and criticism which are implied in this attitude. Legal rules govern the structure and functioning of the legal machinery. By "legal machinery" I mean the whole set of institutions and agencies through which the *actes juridiques* and the factual actions we ascribe to the state are undertaken. It includes the legislature, the courts, and the administrative apparatus, to which belong the agencies of enforcement (especially the police and the military). To know these rules is to know everything about the existence and content of the law. For example, if one knows that the courts are directed by these laws to imprison whoever is guilty of manslaughter, then, since imprisonment is a reaction of disapproval and, consequently, a sanction, one knows that it is forbidden to commit manslaughter. This last norm is implied in the first one directed to the courts; logically, therefore, it has no independent existence. The upshot is that, in describing a legal order, there is no need to employ a double set of norms, one demanding of citizens a certain type of behaviour (*e.g.* not to commit manslaughter), and the other prescribing for the agencies of the legal machinery under what conditions coercive sanctions are to be applied (*e.g.* if manslaughter has been committed). At times, those drafting statutes employ the device of formulating a legal rule as a directive to the courts, leaving it to the citizen to infer what conduct is required of him. The criminal code is drawn in exactly this way. Nowhere is it stated in so many words that manslaughter is prohibited. The prescription against this and other crimes is, rather, inferred from the appropriate rules of the criminal code which are directed to the judge. The Danish Criminal Code, section 237, thus simply states that "he who kills another man shall be sentenced for manslaughter to imprisonment from 5 years and into lifetime." More commonly, however, another device is employed. *Primary* rules (or substantive law) state how citizens are obliged to behave. It is impossible to infer from these rules alone how a judge is to decide in the case of a violation. According to the circumstances of the case, the judge may specify as a sentence some punishment (whose kind and severity is left unspecified by the primary law), or enjoin some performance or payment for damages. For this reason a set of *secondary* rules (the law of sanctions) is required to specify what sanctions may be exacted of those who violate the substantive law, and to make more precise the conditions under which various sanctions may be applied. Such rules are directed to the judge, instructing him how to decide different types of case. They are often expressed in terms of the *legal effects* that arise out of violations of substantive law; for example, when it is said that the legal effect of overdue delivery is to give the buyer a right to claim damages. This rule in fact amounts to a directive to the judge, requiring him to hold for the plaintiff when he sues in appropriate circumstances.

Are we to conclude from this that there are two sets of legal norms, one addressed to the citizens stating their obligations, and another addressed to judges, directing them to decide certain cases in certain ways?

From a logical point of view, we must answer in the negative: there exists only

---

[36] *On Law and Justice*, pp. 52 *et seq.*

one set of rules, namely, the so-called "secondary" rules which prescribe how cases are to be decided, which, that is, basically prescribe the conditions under which violent coercion is to be exercised. For we have seen that primary norms, logically speaking, contain nothing not already implied in secondary norms, whereas the converse does not hold.[37]

From a psychological point of view, however, there do exist two sets of norms. Rules addressed to citizens are felt psychologically to be independent entities which are grounds for the reactions of the authorities. If we apply our definition of the existence of a norm, primary rules must be recognized as actually existing norms, in so far as they are followed with regularity and experienced as being binding. It is immaterial to the question of the existence of these rules that they are, in addition, sanctioned by the threat of coercion and consequently obeyed from mixed motives, both interested (fear of sanctions) and disinterested (respect for law and order). Confusion on this point might lead to the mistaken objection that our logical thesis that there exists only one set of norms implies that the law is obeyed solely from fear of sanctions.[38]                    [pp. 82–92]

## A. ROSS
## Tû-tû
### (1956)[39]

...We find the following phrases, for example, in legal language as used in statutes and the administration of justice:

1.  *If a loan is granted, there comes into being a claim;*
2.  *If a claim exists, then payment shall be made on the day it falls due,*

which is only a roundabout way of saying:

3.  *If a loan is granted, then payment shall be made on the day it falls due.*

That "claim" mentioned in (1) and (2), but not in (3), is obviously, like "tû-tû," not a real thing; it is nothing at all, merely a word, an empty word devoid of all semantic reference. Similarly, our assertion to the effect that the borrower becomes "pledged" corresponds to the allegorical tribe's assertion that the person who kills totem animals becomes "tû-tû."[40]

We too, then, express ourselves as though something had come into being between the conditioning fact (juristic fact) and the conditional legal consequence, namely, a claim, a right, which like an intervening vehicle or causal connecting link promotes an effect or provides the basis for a legal consequence. Nor, really, can we wholly deny that this terminology is associated for us with more or less indefinite ideas that a right is a power of incorporeal nature, a kind of inner, invisible dominion over the object of the right, power manifested in, but nevertheless different from, the exercise of force (judgment and execution) by means of which the factual and apparent use and enjoyment of the rights is effectuated.

In this way, it must be admitted, our terminology and our ideas bear a considerable structural resemblance to primitive magic thought concerning the invocation of supernatural powers which in their turn are converted into factual effects. Nor can we deny the possibility that this resemblance is in reality rooted in

---

[37]  *Op. cit.*, pp. 45–46, *cf.* pp. 66–69.
[38]  *Op. cit.*, pp. 68 *et seq.*
[39]  [From (1957) 70 Harv.L.Rev. 812. Copyright © 1957 by the Harvard Law Review Association.]
[40]  [Earlier in this article Ross has explained that amongst the Noisulli Islanders the belief is held that *(inter alia)* if a man encounters his mother-in-law he is "Tû-Tû" and if he does not undergo purification a terrible calamity will befall the whole community.]

tradition, which, bound up with language and its power over thought, is an age-old legacy from the infancy of our civilization. But after these admissions have been made, there still remains the important question, whether sound, rational grounds may be adduced in favour of the retention of a "tû-tû" presentation of legal rules, *i.e.* a form of circumlocution in which between the juristic fact and the legal consequence there are inserted imaginary rights. If this question is to be answered in the affirmative, the ban on the mention of rights must be lifted. Now I do maintain that this question must be answered in the affirmative, and shall proceed to show why, taking as my point of departure the concept of ownership.

The legal rules concerning ownership could, without doubt, be expressed without the use of this term. In that case a large number of rules would have to be formulated, directly linking the individual legal consequences to the individual legal facts. For example:

if a person has lawfully acquired a thing by purchase, judgment for recovery shall be given in favour of the purchaser against other persons retaining the thing in their possession;

if a person has inherited a thing, judgment for damages shall be given in favour of the heir against other persons who culpably damage the thing;

if a person by prescription has acquired a thing and raised a loan that is not repaid at the proper time, the creditor shall be given judgment for satisfaction out of the thing;

if a person has occupied a *res nullius* and by legacy bequeathed it to another person, judgment shall be given in favour of the legatee against the testator's estate for the surrender of the thing;

if a person has acquired a thing by means of execution as a creditor and the object is subsequently appropriated by another person, the latter shall be punished for theft,

and so on, bearing in mind, of course, that in each case the formula might be far more complicated.

An account along these lines would, however, be so unwieldy as to be practically worthless. It is the task of legal thinking to conceptualize the legal rules in such a way that they are reduced to systematic order and by this means to give account of the law in force which is as plain and convenient as possible. This can be achieved with the aid of the following technique of presentation.

On looking at a large number of legal rules on the lines indicated it will be found that it is possible to select from among them a certain group that can be arranged in the following way:

$$
\begin{array}{cccccc}
F_1\text{--}C_1 & F_2\text{--}C_1 & F_3\text{--}C_1 & \cdot & F_p\text{--}C_1 \\
F_1\text{--}C_2 & F_2\text{--}C_2 & F_3\text{--}C_2 & \cdot & F_p\text{--}C_2 \\
F_1\text{--}C_3 & F_2\text{--}C_3 & F_3\text{--}C_3 & \cdot & F_p\text{--}C_3 \\
\cdot & \cdot & \cdot & & \cdot \\
\cdot & \cdot & \cdot & & \cdot \\
\cdot & \cdot & \cdot & & \cdot \\
F_1\text{--}C_n & F_2\text{--}C_n & F_3\text{--}C_n & \cdot & F_p\text{--}C_n
\end{array}
$$

(Read: the conditioning fact $F_1$ is connected with the legal consequence $C_1$ etc.) This means that each single one is a certain totality of conditioning facts $(F_1\text{--}F_p)$ is connected with each single one of a certain group of legal consequences $(C_1\text{--}C_n)$; or, that it is true of each single $F$ that is connected with the same group of legal consequences $(C_1 + C_2 \ldots + C_n)$, or that a *cumulative plurality of legal consequences is connected to a disjunctive plurality of conditioning facts.*

These $n \times p$ individual legal rules can be stated more simply and more manageably in the figure:

$$\left.\begin{array}{c} F_1 \\ F_2 \\ F_3 \\ \cdot \\ \cdot \\ \cdot \\ F_P \end{array}\right\} \rightarrow O \left\{\begin{array}{c} C_1 \\ C_2 \\ C_3 \\ \cdot \\ \cdot \\ \cdot \\ C_N \end{array}\right.$$

where $O$ (ownership) merely stands for the systematic connection that $F_1$ as well as $F_2$, $F_3 \ldots F_p$ entail the totality of legal consequences $C_1$, $C_2$, $C_3 \ldots C_n$. As a technique of presentation this is expressed then by stating in one series of rules the facts that "create ownership," and in another series the legal consequences that "ownership" entails.

It will be clear from this that the "ownership" inserted between the conditioning facts and the conditioned consequences is in reality a meaningless word—a word without any semantic reference whatever, serving solely as a tool of presentation. We talk as if "ownership" were a causal link between $F$ and $C$, an effect occasioned or "created" by every $F$, and which in its turn is the cause of a totality of legal consequences. We say, for example, that:

(1) If A has lawfully purchased an object ($F_2$), ownership of the object is thereby created for him.

(2) If A is the owner of an object, he has (among other things) the right of recovery ($C_1$).

It is clear, however, that (1) + (2) is only a rephrasing of one of the presupposed norms ($F_2$–$C_1$), namely, that purchase as a conditioning fact entails the possibility of recovery as a legal consequence. The notion that between purchase and access to recovery something was "created" that can be designated as "ownership" is nonsense. Nothing is "created" as the result of A and B exchanging a few sentences legally interpreted as "contract of purchase." All that has occurred is that the judge will now take this fact into consideration and give judgment for the purchaser in an action for recovery...[41]          [pp. 144–148]

---

[41] [Ross describes words like ownership as "without meaning, *i.e.* without any semantic reference, and serve a purpose only as a technique of presentation" (p. 149). But *cf. ante*, 33 as to this theory of meaning. Also, it is possible within the context of a legal system to eliminate a corporation by reducing it to a set of rules relating to individuals? This is something like the well-known and ineffectual "bracket-theory". That a corporation has rights and duties distinct from those of individuals is a perfectly meaningful assertion in law. Nor, it should be noted, does this entail the existence *de facto*, of a corporate "entity". Ross's view that legal concepts have no semantic reference is also less tenable when one gives the notion of semantic reference a rather wider ambit. For instance we say that Jones is the owner of that motor-car, does this not have a semantic reference in the fact that it will normally be associated with certain attitudes and behaviour both of Jones himself in relation to the motor-car, and also to attitudes and behaviour of other persons in relation to that article? (*cf.* U. Scarpelli, *op. cit.*, p. 91). For further criticisms, see A. W. B. Simpson, "The Analysis of Legal Concepts" in (1964) 80 L. Q. R. 534.]

# 12

# HISTORICAL AND ANTHROPOLOGICAL JURISPRUDENCE

## The Romantic Reaction

Two principal movements emerged as a reaction to the natural law thinking of the eighteenth century. One was the school of legal positivism; the other, by way of contrast, relied upon a mystic sense of unity and organic growth in human affairs. The Romantic Movement was itself part of a surge of the human mind against the classical and rationalistic standards of the eighteenth century in favour of feeling and imagination, and this impact was felt especially in the realm of art and literature. Its influence in the sphere of thought was equally pervasive. The impulses stirring in both fields emerged strikingly in Rousseau, whose writings revealed not only a new literary style but also a belief in the mysterious entity of the collective.[1] An even profounder attachment to the organic roots of society was evinced by Edmund Burke,[2] who, by emphasising the national foundations of the mysterious forces which move society, gave the organic approach its link with nationalism that became so prominent a feature during the nineteenth century.

## Herder and Hegel

But it was in Germany that this new movement was to find the most fertile soil. The Germans have been described as "the people of the romantic counter-revolution against the rationalism of the Enlightenment—of ... the mystical uprising against intellectual clarity."[3]

The most formidable and influential among the founders of this new

---

[1] See *The Social Contract, ante*, 147. See further J. Miller, *Rousseau: Dreams of Democracy* (1984)

[2] *Cf. ante*, 116–117.

[3] E. Heller, *The Ironic German* (1958), pp. 156–157. See also P. Geyl, *Debates with Historians*, pp. 4–8 and also F.M. Barnard, *Herder's Social and Political Thought* (1965).

movement was Herder,[4] who rejected the universalising tendencies of the French *philosophes* and stressed the unique character of every historical period, civilisation and nation. Every nation possesses its own individual character and qualities and none is intrinsically superior to others.[5] Any attempt to bridge these innumerable manifestations under the general command of a universal natural law based on reason was inimical to the free development of each national spirit (*Volksgeist*) and could result in imposing a crippling uniformity.[6] Herder, however, unlike his follower Hegel, viewed the bureaucratic state with unqualified antipathy; the state "robbed men of themselves," and was a substitution of machinery for life.[7]

Hegel, on the other hand, extolled the state as transcending individualistic interest.[8] Conflict between these could only be overcome by the conscious direction of the state. Far from advocating an authoritarian régime, Hegal regarded the state as the means of securing national freedom and strongly attacked the Prussian State of his day for leaving no free play to individuals or to groups.[9] Nevertheless, every developed state, at least in an ideal sense, was an absolute end-in-itself, enjoying total sovereignty and autonomy as regards its neighbours.[10] Hegel did not foresee the chauvinist force of nationalism, which was to develop in the course of the nineteenth century, and which ignored all his stress on freedom as the very essence of the state. Thus, by exploiting his fame while distorting his philosophy, a doctrine emerged based on glorification of an authoritarian state, viewed as an organic entity superior to the individuals comprised in it and dedicated to a national policy with war as an instrument of national achievement.[11]

---

[4] For a recent illuminating account of Herder's thought, see I. Berlin, *Vico and Herder* (1976). Similar ideas are to be found in Montesquieu's *The Spirit of the Laws* published in 1748. On Montesquieu, see Stark, *Montesquieu—Pioneer of the Sociology of Knowledge* (1960). On the relationship between the thought of Montesquieu and Rousseau and later thought surrounding the French Revolution see N. Hampson, *Will and Circumstance* (1983).

[5] Berlin, *op. cit.*, pp. 163, 181.

[6] *ibid.*, p. 175. See Also N. Hampson, *The Enlightenment* (1968), pp. 239–243.

[7] *ibid.*, p. 162.

[8] See S. Avineri, *Hegel's Theory of the Modern State* (1972), p. 101. R. Plant in *Hegel* (1973) argues that his thought was dominated by the ideal of restructuring society on a harmonious, reciprocating basis, restoring a sense of community. A critical influence was a rather romanticised picture of the Athenian *polis*.

[9] Avineri, *op. cit.*, pp. 49, 57, 126, 151.

[10] *ibid.*, pp. 200–201.

[11] *ibid.*, pp. 240–241. Avineri's book must be taken as a definitive refutation of the long-standing idea that Hegel favoured an absolute authoritarian state of which Prussia afforded the model.

## THE GERMAN HISTORICAL SCHOOL[12]

To Herder, perhaps influenced by Vico,[13] is principally due a new approach to history as the life of communities, rather than concerned with the exploits of kings, statesmen, generals and other so-called great men. But Herder's particular originality and influence was due to his belief that different cultures and societies developed their own values rooted in their own history, traditions and institutions, and that the quality of human life and its scope for self-expression resided precisely in this plurality of values, each society being left free to develop in its own way.[14]

Out of this ferment of ideas there arose the great German historical school of the nineteenth century, one of whose early off-shoots was the historical school of jurisprudence associated with the name of Savigny.

## F. K. von SAVIGNY (1779–1861)[15]

Savigny rejected natural law. To him a legal system was part of the culture of a people. Law was not the result of an arbitrary act of a legislator but developed as a response to the impersonal powers to be found in the people's national spirit. This *Volksgeist* "a unique, ultimate and often mystical reality"[16] was, Savigny believed, linked to the biological heritage of a people.

Savigny successfully used his *Volksgeist* theory to reject the French Code and the move to codification in Germany.[17] As a result German law remained, until 1900, Roman law adapted to German conditions with the injection of certain local ideas. But Savigny was not just a theorist. As a historian he set himself the task of studying the course of development of Roman law from ancient times till its existing state as the foundation of the civil law of contemporary Europe. This led him to hypothesise that all law originated in custom and only much later was created by juristic activity. He concedes that "in the earliest time to which authentic history

---

[12] The social and philosophical context of which is explored by H. Schnädelbach, *Philosophy in Germany 1831–1933* (1984). See also H. S. Reiss, *The Political Thought of the German Romantics* (1955).

[13] See I. Berlin, *op. cit.*, p. 147. On Vico see *ante*, 114, 836.

[14] *ibid.*, p. 153.

[15] See H. Kantorowicz, "Savigny and the Historical School of Law" (1937) 53 L.Q.R. 326; Stone, *Social Dimensions of Law and Justice* (1966), pp. 86–89, 101–111.

[16] *Per* Stone, *op. cit.*, p. 102.

[17] Savigny's hostility was qualified rather than absolute. He believed, as against Thibaut, that attempts to codify were premature, and would be an obstacle to the natural development of law through the *Volksgeist*. But codification would be a proper course of action when experts (jurists, historians, linguists, and perhaps, judges) discovered, and were able to announce, *that* law which resided in the collective consciousness. Codification *was* then desirable. Savigny, it should be noted, was the Prussian Minister of Legislation. Hegel opposed customary unwritten law and his view on English common law as "an Augean stable" resembles Bentham's. Hegel asserted that English law needed a scientific remodelling and codification. See Avineri, *op. cit.*, pp. 186, 210–215.

extends, the law will be found to have already attained a fixed character, peculiar to the people, like their language, manners, and constitution."[18]

Rather like Spengler[19] a century later, Savigny sees a nation and its state as an organism which is born, matures and declines and dies. Law is a vital part of this organism. "Law grows with the growth, and strengthens with the strength of the people, and finally dies away as the nation loses its nationality."[20] Nations and their law go through three developmental stages. At the outset of a nation there is a "political" element of law: there are principles of law which are not found in legislation but are part of "national convictions" (*Volksglauben*). These principles are "implicitly present in formal symbolic transactions which command the high respect of the population, form a grammar of the legal system of a young nation, and constitute one of the system's major characteristics."[21] In its middle period law retains this "political" element to which is added the "technical" element of juristic skill. This period is the apogee of a people's legal culture and is the time when codification is feasible. It is desirable only so that the legal perfection of the period can be preserved for posterity. With the decline of a nation law no longer has popular support and becomes the property of a clique of experts. In time even this skill decays. Ultimately, there is loss of national identity.

## THE *VOLKSGEIST*—SOME PROBLEMS

The writers of this persuasion seem to assume that every "People" is in some way an identifiable entity, with a corporate conviction or will of its own. This approach later crystallised in Gierke's theory of the "real" personality of corporate bodies, and his desire to establish the superiority of Germanic law, as against Roman law, in countenancing this view.[22] We are thus, in the first place, required to accept that collective groups possess some kind of metaphysical personality distinct from the members comprised in the group, a view which recalls the old fallacy that words are names of "things," and that there must be a distinct entity denoted by every word.[23] But, more than this, it is implied that the notion of a "people" is a perfectly definite one that can be applied to specific groups which possess this mysterious collective consciousness. This appears to postulate a degree of unity of thought and action in particular nations, races, or the inhabitants of political units, of which there is little evidence

---

[18] *Of the Vocation of Our Age for Legislation and Jurisprudence* (1831) (transl, Haywood), p. 24.
[19] *The Decline of the West* (1923) (transl. C.F. Atkinson, 1928).
[20] *ibid.*, p. 27.
[21] L. Pospisil, *Anthropology of Law* (1971), p. 142.
[22] See his celebrated *Das deutsche Genossenschaftsrecht, passim.*
[23] *Cf. ante*, 33. And see Lloyd, *Unincorporated Associations* (1938), Chap. 1.

in human history.[24] And it seems to ignore the role and effects of conquest by war; the position of enslaved and servile populations; and the control of nations and empires by ruling minorities, and the manner in which these latter may impose new patterns on their subjects (whether in the spirit of a "creative minority" in Toynbee's sense,[25] or of a "power *élite*" in that of Wright Mills[26] is immaterial). Nor does this theory deal adequately with the introduction of alien law and custom by peaceful penetration, as in the case of a Western code being adopted in such a country as modern Japan. Savigny was much exercised by the remarkable phenomenon of the so-called "Reception of Roman Law" into Germany in the sixteenth century, which he regarded as "the greatest and most remarkable action of a common customary law in the beginning of the modern age."[27] His explanation of this, however, as having being adopted into the popular consciousness of the German People is hardly convincing, and is really little more than a legal fiction. That "to probe the spirit of the German *Volk* Savigny went straight back to Roman law" is perhaps the strangest of paradoxes in Savigny's thought.[28]

## Legislation and *Juristenrecht*

It must be admitted that the historical school had at least, if in a most confusing manner, grasped the important truth that law is not an abstract set of rules simply imposed on society, but is an integral part of that society, having deep roots in the social and economic habits and attitudes of its past and present members. Moreover, equally acceptable is the view that judges and lawyers generally, as forming part of the society in which they live and have their being, reflect many, if not all, the basic habits and attitudes of their society, so that the development of the law, so far as it rests in their hands, will probably conform in a broad and general way to the patterns of behaviour which are widely approved or at least accepted in that society. But this is far from saying that the judge, in reaching a decision or framing a rule, is acting as a mere organ of the people's consciousness. A great deal of law, for one thing, is highly technical, and a legal profession, like any other compact body, develops an impetus of its own which may lead it in many directions, and by no means only in that one which would be approved or even understood by the popular consciousness. "Could it be pretended (remarks Sir Carleton Allen) that a pious faith in the sanctity of seisin burns in the bosom of the

---

[24] See also the point made by Stone (*Social Dimensions*, pp. 162–163) that the consciousness of people can no longer be regarded as an inviolable inner spirit since it is a prey to mass-suggestion by propaganda and mass media, and these are usually concentrated in an élite.

[25] See A *Study of History*, vol. III, pp. 239 *et seq*, and vol. XII, p. 305.

[26] See C. Wright Mills, *The Power Elite* (1956). More generally see T.B. Bottomore, *Elites and Society* (1964). See also the Marxist view of society, *post*, Chap. 12.

[27] *System of Modern Roman Law* (transl. W. Holloway), p. 63.

[28] See J. Dawson, *The Oracles of the Law* (1968), pp. 451–452.

Commonwealth suffusing all its members with a healthy glow?"[29] Again, the judge, though he may be representative of his country and age, nevertheless has a creative function in developing the law, which cannot be exercised by merely imagining how society as a whole would decide the question before him, even assuming society is capable of forming any view at all.[30] And to assert that in some inexplicable and metaphysical manner the judge's thought somehow "connects" on each occasion with the People's mind is the merest subterfuge. Even Savigny recognises that owing to the complexity of developed law the precise details of decisions are a specifically juristic task beyond the scope of the popular consciousness. But the gap is not bridged by simply postulating an automatic correlation between lawyers' law and popular consciousness (or perhaps one should say, in more modern phraseology, *sub*-consciousness). Nor can this be laid down even as a *desideratum*, for on many issues public opinion may be non-existent, hopelessly divided or unascertainable, and on some matters at least the judge must be expected to set a higher standard than one which is in fact observed or accepted by the mass of the community.[31] This is to say nothing of the view, already discussed, that law is itself the moulder of custom rather than the reverse.[32]

As for legislation, Savigny seemed greatly to underrate its significance for modern society.[33] A progressive society, as Maine later pointed out, has to keep adapting the law to novel social and economic conditions,[34] and legislation has proved in modern times the essential means of attaining this end, however imperfectly. And with this objective, those who exercise the legislative authority have frequently, while paying heed if not lip-service to public opinion, to provide a lead in many directions where the public is confused or undecided, and even in some cases where there may be widespread hostility to a proposed reform.


### SIR HENRY MAINE (1822–1888)


In England the historical approach, divested of its mystical adherence to the *Volksgeist*, made important advances in the pioneering hands of Sir

---

[29] *Law in the Making* (7th ed.), p. 114.
[30] *Cf.* Lloyd, *Public Policy* (1953), Chap. 7. Judges do, however fashion such concepts as that of the "reasonable man" to create the appearance that they are deciding cases in accordance with common morality.
[31] Lloyd, *Public Policy, op. cit.*, pp. 126–127.
[32] Savigny admitted it was impossible to avoid some statutory legislation, but said this should only be when "higher political progress" demanded a change in the law, or to resolve doubts, or where a positive provision is required (*e.g.* the period for prescription).
[33] *Ante*, 1048.
[34] See his *Ancient Law*. Maine did not admire judicial legislation in English law, and favoured codification. But he was essentially and "evolutionist."

Henry Maine.[35] Maine opposed to rationalising theories of natural law and the utilitarian schools[36] a serious endeavour to study the nature and development of early law both in its actual historical context, and also as illuminated by the study of undeveloped societies in the contemporary world. In practice this meant for Maine principally the early law of Greece, Rome and the Old Testament, supplemented by the native law of India. Maine treated India as "the great repository of ancient juridical thought," insisting that it included "a whole world of Aryan institutions, Aryan customs, Aryan laws, Aryan ideas, in a far earlier stage of growth and development than any which survive beyond its borders."[37] Insufficient research into these, as well as a failure to distinguish clearly between different stages in the development of early law and custom, led Maine into some intuitive generalisations, which though brilliantly formulated and expounded, find little support among present-day legal historians and anthropologists. This applies particularly to his notion of early law passing through three consecutive phases of royal judgments, aristocracies as repositories of custom, and finally an Age of Codes.[38]

Maine was also a man of his time, and the impact of biological evolutionary theory[39] was such that his work on legal development was set within a unilinear evolutionary framework.[40] He justified this in terms of the "stability of human nature,"[41] a concept akin to that found in naturalist writers such as Maritain[42]. But, as Pospisil has noted, Maine's contribution to jurisprudence lies not so much in his specific conclusions as in "the empirical, systematic, and historical methods he employed to arrive at his conclusions, and in his striving for generalizations firmly

[35] Maine's background, life and some of his ideas are traced in George Feaver, *From Status to Contract* (1969). An appraisal of Maine, in the context of Victorian evolutionary sociology has been made by J.W. Burrow, *Evolution and Society* (1966), (Chap. 5 is devoted to Maine). There are fascinating insights into the relationship between Maine's thought and that of contemporaries in S. Collini *et al.*, *That Noble Science of Politics* (1983), particularly pp. 145–148, 209–246.

[36] Maine was not, however, opposed to the principles of Utilitarianism, merely its exposition in the writings of Bentham and Mill. He was opposed to their deductive method, their lack of scientific analysis. His opposition to natural law and, more significantly its social contract manifestations, was based on what he regarded as their unhistorical nature. See, further, Burrow, *op. cit.*, p. 28 and Collini *et al.*, *op. cit.*, p. 215. Mill was apparently an admirer of Maine though he reproved him for his criticisms of Bentham and Austin (*ibid.*, pp. 145–147).

[37] In *Observation of India*, pp. 209, 211, quoted in Collini *et al.* at p. 211.

[38] See *post*, 1102. See also the point made by Burrow (*op. cit.*, p. 178) that Maine's "method of comparative philology proved a blind alley; historical explanation continued to do duty as analytic ones; while Maine's emphasis on common racial origins narrowed his horizon without validating his method." Maine's reasons for investigating India, but not other undeveloped societies, was common Aryan origins of its peoples and of those of Europe.

[39] See E.D. Elliott (1985) 85 Columbia L.R. 38; and A. Hutchinson and S. Archer (2001) 54 C.L.P.

[40] Maine did, however, note in *Early Law and Custom* (1883) that "there is nothing in the recorded history of society to justify the belief that ... the same transformations of social constitution succeeded one another everywhere, uniformly if not simultaneously" (pp. 218–219).

[41] *Ancient Law* (1905 ed.), p. 112.

[42] *Ante*, 150.

based on the empirical evidence at his disposal ... He blazed a scientific trail into the field of law, a field hitherto dominated by philosophizing and speculative thought."[43]

LAW AND ANTHROPOLOGY[44]

One of Holmes's many pieces of advice was to the effect that "if your subject is law, the roads are plain to anthropology," and it was "perfectly proper to regard and study the law simply as a great anthropological document."[45] Yet until the early part of the twentieth century it was common to view "law" in a rigid and narrow way.[46] Primitive peoples[47] without formal legal codes, courts, policemen or prisons were thought to lack anything that might be dignified by the appellation "law." It was conceded that they had custom, which, it was assumed, was a characteristic of early or tribal society. And often custom was conceived of as absolutely rigid, complete conformity being enforced by the overwhelming power of group sentiment, amply fortified by religion and magic.[48] Nor was it doubted that in some way "custom" was inferior to "law."

Even in the twentieth century anthropologists using a folk rather than an analytic concept of law[49] have been inclined to deny that simpler

---

[43] *Anthropology of Law* (1971), p. 150. Leading American writers Wigmore and Corbin worked within an evolutionary theory paradigm.

[44] Good discussions of the two disciplines are C. Geertz, *Local Knowledge* (1983), Chap. 8; R.R. French in (ed.) D. Patterson, *A Companion To Philosophy of Law and Legal Theory* (1996), Chap. 27; W. Twining (1973) 7 Law and Soc. Rev. 561; and F. Snyder (1981) 8 Br. J. of Law and Soc. 141. See also (ed.) M. Freeman, *Law and Anthropology* (forthcoming, 2009). A useful reader is S.F. Moore, *Law and Anthropology—A Reader* (2004).

[45] (1889) 12 Harv. L. Rev. 443.

[46] Further, surprisingly little attention has been given to the questions why and how legal systems in pre-industrial societies differ. An interesting recent exploration of this is K.S. Newman, *Law and Economic Organization* (1983). She adopts a Marxist approach to these questions and sees the key as lying in economic organization.

[47] The tendency today is to refer to such societies more neutrally, as, for example, "tribal" or "stateless" or "segmentary lineage" societies. "Tribal" or "stateless" will be used normally in this chapter, and throughout the book, but "primitive law" and "primitive societies" will be retained where the reference is to classical anthropology, where this terminology was consistently used. *cf., e.g.* the terminology used by Maine and Malinowski with that used by Gluckman or Bohannan.

[48] See such writers as Frazer, Durkheim and Hobhouse. On Hobhouse, see L. Pospisil. *Anthropology of Law* (1971), p. 179. See A.S. Diamond, *Primitive Law* (2nd ed.). Also Hoebel, *Law of Primitive Man* (1954), pp. 257–260: and Gluckman, *Judicial Process among the Barotse* (1967), pp. 264–267. The latter two writers consider Diamond goes too far in his criticism of Maine, by seeking to make a clear separation between the social phenomena of law and religion in early society. See also J. Stone, *Social Dimensions of Law and Justice*, pp. 134–135.

[49] *Cf.* R. Abel (1973–74) 8 Law and Soc.Rev. 217.

societies had law.[50] Radcliffe-Brown defined law, after Austin and Pound,[51] as "social control through the systematic application of the force of politically organised society."[52] His pupil, Evans-Pritchard, utilised this conceptual framework in his studies of the Nuer of the Sudan. They had "no law" for although "there are conventional compensations for damage, adultery, loss of limb and so forth, ... there is no authority with power to adjudicate on such matters or to enforce a verdict."[53] Malinowski, whose studies of the Trobriand Islands were some of the earliest and most influential participant observations of a primitive society, was critical of this type of ethnocentrism.[54] It was wrong, he claimed, to define the forces of law in terms of "central authority, codes, courts, and constables."[55] The Trobrianders' society was orderly even though these were lacking. He accounted for this in terms of "reciprocity, systematic incidence, publicity and ambition."[56] Thus, by means of a primitive "stop-list," a failure to comply with a man's economic obligation, for example to make a customary payment, would result in the economic support of the community being withheld from the defaulter, who would thus be left helpless and alone. Malinowski's "minimal definition" of law was intended to be of universal application. But to model a definition of law on Trobriand ethnography is as ethnocentric as to base it on the English legal system.[57] Malinowski's description of social order in terms of felt reciprocities and interdependencies glosses over the normative element in it. As Hamnett writes, this implies "an automatic adherence to *practice*."[58] But customary law is not a statement of practice. It is rather a "normatively clothed set of abstractions from practice."[59] It envelopes the concept of a rule with, what Hart calls, an "internal aspect," and is not merely convergent habitual behaviour.[60]

A different approach from Malinowski's is to be found in Max

---

[50] Consider Hart's distinction between a "set" of rules and a legal system, *ante*, 336. MacCormack has argued that the need to distinguish between the concepts of "law" and "legal system" is underlined by the appropriateness of the term "law" as applied to certain rules accepted as binding in a tribal society, even though there be no legal "system" in any of the varied sense of that term deployed by modern jurists. (See G. MacCormack "Law" and 'Legal System' " (1979) 42 M.L.R., 285.

[51] *Cf. ante*, 897.

[52] "Primitive Law" in *Encyclopaedia of the Social Sciences* (1933), p. 202, reprinted in *Structure and Function in Primitive Society* (1952), Chap. 12.

[53] *The Nuer* (1940), p. 162. Shortly afterwards he acknowledged the existence of law among the Nuer: "there is machinery for settling disputes and a moral obligation to conclude them sooner or later" ("The Nuer of Southern Sudan" in *African Political Systems* (1940) (Fortes and Evans-Pritchard, eds.), p. 278).

[54] By concentrating on function rather than form and giving priority to ideological categories of the actors themselves, Malinowski was able to escape, partly at least, ethnocentric misuse of Western legal ideas. See Roberts, *Order and Dispute* (1979) pp. 190–191.

[55] *Crime and Custom in Savage Society* (1926), p. 14.

[56] *ibid.*, pp. 67–68.

[57] Malinowski recognised that customary law was often breached in Trobriand society. His views on the extent to which sanctions might be employed against defaulters changed at different periods. See I. Schapera, in *Man and Culture* (Firth, ed., 1957). p. 139.

[58] *Social Anthropology and Law* (1977), p. 7.

[59] *ibid* See also his *Chieftainship and Legitimacy* (1975), p. 14.

[60] *Ante*, 379.

Gluckman's studies of the Barotse.[61] The Lozi, he states, have "law as a set of rules accepted by all normal members of the society as defining right and reasonable ways in which persons ought to behave in relation to each other and to things, including ways of obtaining protection for one's rights."[62] Law is also a specific social fact. It "influences the behaviour of both Lozi judges and public"[63] and it "will be distinguished by observers, and distinguished by the people, from other types of social fact."[64] Faller's studies of the Basoga follow Gluckman's approach.[65]

A common approach today is to focus not on law as such but on methods of handling disputes.[66] Definitional questions are sidestepped and attention concentrated on the institutions and techniques for resolving conflict, whether or not these deserve to be designated as "legal." The "behaviouristic lens of legal realism"[67] and the interest of political scientists and sociologists in the problems of conflict resolution have been pervasive influences.[68] The collaboration of Llewellyn and Hoebel in *The Cheyenne Way* is a particularly fruitful result of this orientation.[69] It not only "raised new problems and set new standards in the analysis of tribal law"[70] but it served as a model for examining how "law-jobs" were handled in a particular society. Hoebel, indeed, described "Primitive Law" as "the henchman of Legal Realism."[71] The analysis of "trouble cases" in *The Cheyenne Way* has been described as "law's principal gift to anthropology."[72] Others have been influenced by Realism. Pospisil, after examining "the important attributes, functions and processes of law" in "tribal" and "civilised" societies, concludes "there is no basic qualitative difference" between them.[73] Law, he believes, "manifests itself in the form of a decision passed by a legal authority."[74] This perspective has also been

---

[61] *The Judicial Process among the Barotse* (1955): *The Ideas in Barotse Jurisprudence* (1965).
[62] *The Judicial Process among the Barotse*, p. 229.
[63] *ibid.*, p. 352.
[64] *ibid.*, p. 265.
[65] *Law Without Precedent* (1969) and in *Social Anthropology and Law* (Hamnett, ed, 1977), p. 53.
[66] Twining (1973) 7 Law and Soc. Rev. 561, 564. According to Cain and Kulcsar (16 Law and Soc.Rev. 375) there is now a "growth industry" in such studies. For examples of this, see 15 Law and Soc. Rev. 3–4, a double issue devoted to the subject. See also Snyder (1981) 8 Brit. J. Law & Soc. 141, 144–151.
[67] Hoebel, *Anthropology—The Study of Man* (4th ed., 1972), p. 500.
[68] For example, Aubert's articles in 7 *Journal of Conflict Resolution* 26 and 11 *Journal of Conflict Resolution* 40. A good introduction to these developments is S. Vago, *Law and Society* (1981), Chap. 6.
[69] On this, see Twining, *Karl Llewellyn and the Realist Movement* (1973), Chap. 8, See also 31 M.L.R. 165, and (1973) 7 Law and Soc. Rev. 561. On Hoebel more generally, see Pospisil, 7 Law and Soc.Rev. 537.
[70] Per Gluckman, *The Judicial Process among the Barotse*, p. 1.
[71] *The Political Organisation and Law-Ways of the Comanche Indians* (Memoirs of the American Anthropological Association, No. 54) (1941). p. 48.
[72] By Twining (1973) 7 Law and Soc. Rev. 579.
[73] *Anthropology of Law* (1971), p. 341.
[74] *ibid.*, p. 342.

a stimulus towards theories of dispute institutions in society, such as is found in the writings of Richard Abel.[75]

There are limitations[76] in this approach. All becomes "subordinated to the analysis of procedures, strategies and processes."[77] The study of substantive concepts and rules is of secondary importance and no real attention is given to definitions of law. There is also the danger that courts and decision processes of complex modern societies will be the models against which to measure simpler ones. Some tribal societies have courts which we would have no difficulty in recognising as such. Hoebel has described the tribal council of an American Indian pueblo sitting in a judicial capacity as one such example.[78] But what of such ordered proceedings as the Eskimo song-contest[79] or "drumming the scandal" amongst the Tiv?[80] Gluckman's studies of the judicial process among the Barotse have led him to conclude that this corresponds with more than it differs from the judicial process in Western society. But he is dealing with a society which is sufficiently developed to possess established judicial tribunals. He has been concerned to posit what he regards as minimum requirements of procedure to characterise a particular conflict resolution as a judicial process and he rejects both the song-contest and "drumming the scandal" as not legal.[81] There is a danger that, in searching for "adequate" categories, Gluckman may be guilty of cultural solipsism, in taking the Barotse, who have had more contact with Western "civilisation" as the norm and rejecting as pre-legal, proceedings which do not meet their standards.

Another important question is the relationship between courts and norms. Do stated norms influence the actions and decisions of participants in settlement processes? Comaroff and Roberts, in a useful paper,[82] have studied the approach to this question among the Tswana. They note no obvious relationship between the clarity with which abstract norms are articulated, the way in which they are employed and their importance in decision-making. The invocation of norms is directly related to their utilisation in argument. In the vast majority of cases Tswana judges isolate a single issue within a dispute and hand down a decision in relation to that issue which makes "no explicit reference"[83] to any norm.

---

[75] "A Comparative Theory of Dispute Institutions in Society" in (1973–74) 8 Law and Soc. Rev. 217.
[76] Apart from the pitfalls inherent in Realism. See *ante*, 996.
[77] *Per* Synder, *op. cit.*, p. 145.
[78] "Keresan Pueblo Law" in *Law in Culture and Society* (L. Nader, ed., 1969), p. 92.
[79] See Hoebel, *The Law of Primitive Man* (1954), pp. 93–99.
[80] See Bohannan, *Justice and Judgment among the Tiv* (1957), for example at pp. 142–144.
[81] See "The Ideas of Barotse Jurisprudence" in *Politics, Law and Ritual in Tribal Society* (1965), and his new edition of *The Judicial Process among the Barotse*, containing a long reappraisal in the light of criticism of the book.
[82] "The Invocation of Norms in Dispute Settlement: The Tswana Case" in Hamnett (ed.), *Social Anthropology and Law*, p. 77. See also now their book, *Rules and Processes: The Cultural Logic of Dispute in an African Context* (1981).
[83] *ibid.*, p. 107.

Norms are invoked by judges when they find it necessary to "distinguish or adjudicate between a plurality of paradigms of argument."[84]

A concentration on processes of settling disputes tends to give us a pathological picture of the societies being described. Much law, we know if facilitative[85] and the social order is a complex programme for living together,[86] a means of promoting interaction. An important question, therefore, is in what ways, if at all, legal behaviour is different from behaviour which is non-legal or other than legal. What is the relationship between law and custom and social control? Law in our own society is just one aspect of social control.

Hoebel states that "law is more than custom and less than social control."[87] Custom consists of social norms, and social norms are sanctioned. Behaviour in accord with these norms is rewarded; that at variance with it is regarded as deviant and often responded to punitively. Social control encompasses these rewards and punishments.[88] These sanctions may be very effective.[89] Yet, as Hoebel notes, "their simple effectiveness does not make law of them."[90] The law, he argues, "consists of social norms, *plus*."[91] Ordinary day-to-day social control does not always work. And it is then that the law is invoked. For psychological penalties, physical or economic ones are substituted. Hoebel distinguishes law from general social norms in three ways. "The real *sine qua non* of law in any society is the legitimate use of physical coercion."[92] The other distinguishing marks are the invocation of authority and an element of regularity or consistency.[93] Law, accordingly, shares a number of characteristics with custom. Both consist of social norms. They have an element of regularity in common: "that which is normally done (the *is*) and that which is expected to be done (the *ought*)."[94] Like custom, law is sanctioned.

Jurists and anthropologists are not agreed on the relationship between custom and law.[95] Law grows with societal complexity, with the decline in the importance of primary groups such as the family, with the breakdown of organised religion, with industrialisation and bureau-cratisation. In many of the tribal societies studied by anthropologists custom is sufficient for the needs of that society. It is all too easy to assume that because we need legal regulation that so must "less happy or civilised peoples." Yet too much anthropology has started from a Western framework into

---

[84]  *ibid.*, 5 pp. 107–108.
[85]  *Ante*, 268.
[86]  See Fuller, *post*, 1111.
[87]  Radcliffe-Brown, *op. cit.*, n. 52, p. 503.
[88]  On social control see C.K. Watkins, *Social Control* (1975), Chap. 1.
[89]  See Weber's comment that "social sanctions can be a more severe punishment than any legal penalty" (*Law in Economy and Society.*)
[90]  *Anthropology: the Study of Man* (4th ed., 1972), p. 519.
[91]  *ibid.*, p. 504.
[92]  *ibid.*
[93]  *Cf. ante*, 40.
[94]  *ibid.*, p. 518.
[95]  *Cf.* Bohannan and Diamond, *post*, 1121, 1124.

which the mechanics of tribal societies have been fitted. Gluckman's attempt to use the "reasonable man" concept in a Barotse context is one example of this[96]; Llewellyn and Hoebel's explanation of Cheyenne law in Western pigeon-holes is another.[97] Does it really help us to understand the legal and pre-legal processes of less developed societies to introduce a Hohfeldian pattern of jural relations, as Hoebel did?[98] By contrast there is an increasing recognition that we may learn more about law and organisation in developed Western societies by studying its equivalent in simpler societies. Barkun's study of segmentary lineage societies and international systems is a good example of this.[99] Edmund Leach's Munro lectures throwing light on the relationship between custom, law and terrorist violence in the contemporary world is another.[1] And Fuller argues most persuasively that we can further our understanding of law through a study of custom.[2]

It is a common view, represented here by the extract from Bohannan,[3] that what begins as custom becomes redefined in legal institutions and is then turned upon the social conflicts which custom cannot resolve. Laws, Bohannan contends, result from "double institutionalisation." He recognises that this conception of the law-custom relationship is inadequate where there is more than one culture (*e.g.* colonial societies) or more than one centre of power, as in international relations or stateless societies. This view has been attacked by Stanley Diamond, one of a growing number of Marxist anthropologists. To Diamond custom represents order: law is "the antonym and not the synonym of order."[4] He sees law as "cannibalising" the institutions which it purports to reinforce. He draws particular attention to the repressive process by which governments have gained sovereignty over peoples in Africa. Like all Marxists Diamond idealises primitive society: the cleavage into classes being akin, in Marxist thought, to the Fall of Man.

In the last thirty years anthropologists studying legal processes have placed greater emphasis on economic factors, in particular on forms of domination and questions of social inequality.[5] They have found Marxism a fertile source of theoretical concepts and of explanation. Some have made use of Marxist theories of law but most have not. In general the thrust of those using Marxist theories has been to use the theories and concepts for the study of legal processes. An abiding concern in Marxist

---

[96] *Post,* 1109.

[97] See the comment in Hall "Methods of Sociological Research in Comparative Law" in *Legal Thought in the U.S.A. under Contemporary Pressure* Hazard and Wagner, eds., 1970), p. 156.

[98] *Post,* 1103.

[99] *Law Without Sanctions* (1968).

[1] *Custom, Law and Terrorist Violence* (1977).

[2] *Post,* 1111.

[3] *Post,* 1121.

[4] (1971) 38 *Social Research* 42. Also in *The Rule of Law* (1971) (Wolff, ed.) and Black and Mileski, *The Social Organisation of Law* (1973), p. 318.

[5] An interesting example is Dwyer, "Law Actual and Perceived: The Sexual Politics of Law in Morocco" (1979) 13 Law and Soc. Rev. 739.

approaches is the relationship between the development of capitalism and processes of legal change. In *Capitalism and Legal Change: An African Transformation*,[6] Snyder discusses the ways in which the subsumption of African peasants within capitalist relations of production has influenced legal ideas within what was a pre-capitalist social formation. He shows, rather in the manner of Renner,[7] how, despite the apparent continuity of simple legal concepts, there was a profound transformation of concrete legal forms. In a recent article he argues that "customary" law has been used as an ideology of colonial domination.[8] Fitzpatrick, by contrast, argues that in contemporary underdeveloped countries one of the functions of law is to conserve the traditional mode of production, despite economic forces which would encourage its dissolution. He stresses the ways in which state law is used to restrict the formation of indigenous classes and attempts to demonstrate how pre-capitalist law constitutes pre-capitalist modes of production, and is constituted by it.[9]

The novelty of approaches such as these, apart from using an explicitly Marxist analysis, is that, as one would expect, attention is given to the role of the state in less developed communities. Fitzpatrick for example has examined the establishment of village courts in Papua New Guinea and concluded that, contrary to the official version of why these were established, they are in effect an extension of state apparatuses of social control into rural villages. He also found that they enhanced the formation of class alliances.[10]

The scope and nature of legal anthropology has changed and broadened considerably in the recent past. The concerns of the legal anthropologist are now similar to those whose concern is general social theory and the sociology of law. Roberts, in an important article,[11] picked out what he considered to be the distinctive contribution of the legal anthropologist. This lies in research methods and in an emphasis on modes of dispute settlement, the litigant's perspective in disputes and informal alternatives to courts, matters certainly neglected by mainstream jurisprudence and only recently considered by sociologists of law. The importance of a focus on dispute processes is considered in the next section.

---

[6] (1981).

[7] See *post*, 1155 and 1191.

[8] "Colonialism and Legal Form: The Creation of 'Customary Law' in Senegal" (1981) 19 J. of Legal Pluralism 44.

[9] *Law and State in Papua New Guinea* (1980); "Law, Modernization and Mystification" in S. Spitzer (ed.), *Research in Law and Sociology* (1980).

[10] "The Political Economy of Dispute Settlement in Papua New Guinea" in C. Sumner (ed.), *Crime, Justice and Underdevelopment* (1981). See also A. Paliwala, *ibid.*

[11] (1976) 39 M.L.R. 663, 676–679.

## Dispute Processes

Growing out of the anthropology of law is a vast new literature on dispute processes. As indicated already the influence of Realism[12] played a part in this redirection but it reflected also changes taking place elsewhere in anthropological study.[13] The methods developed by anthropologists, such as case method or situational analysis, once used in traditional anthropological settings, were soon adapted to study dispute processes in the United States and other developed countries.

Not only is there a shift from organisation to process but this is accompanied also by one from groups to networks of individuals. Attention is no longer concentrated on officials[14] but emphasis is given to the actions of parties to disputes and their perceptions of action.[15] For example, Starr's research in Turkey showed how, in disputing, rural villagers formulated strategies to maintain honour or compete for scarce resources.[16]

There is also work being done on the life-history of disputes, on the effect of pre-dispute relations between the parties on subsequent public confrontation. An example of this is Barbara Yngvesson's study of a Swedish fishing village.[17] She contrasted social processes in conflicts involving community members with those involving people defined as "outsiders." In the former a period of "cooling" was characteristic, a time during which the consequences of formal reactions were considered. She has since suggested that such periods of "bracketed structural time" form part of dispute processes more generally, including within the setting of an American court.[18]

Out of such studies attempts have been made to theorise about dispute processes. There are a number of attempts at typologies. Roberts, drawing on Bohannan's stark dichotomy of "law and war,"[19] has suggested "fighting" and "talking."[20] He argues that to "be successful, bilateral negotiation must be seen as the 'right' way of resolving a dispute: the ready disposition to talk and the conciliatory gesture must represent approved responses."[21] Talking, on the other hand, has little chance of success "where honour demands retaliation to an assumed wrong and where conciliatory approaches are likely to be identified as

---

[12] *Ante*, 1086.
[13] See L Nader and B. Yngvesson in *Handbook of Social and Cultural Anthropology* (J.J. Honigman, ed., 1973). On the relationship between dispute systems and culture see O.G. Chase, *Law, Culture and Ritual* (2005).
[14] *Cf.* the Realist approach, *ante*, 1007.
[15] The importance of this to rule-based theories of law, such as Hart's, cannot be under estimated. See *ante*, 390.
[16] *Dispute and Settlement In Rural Turkey: An Ethnography of Law* (1978).
[17] (1976) 3 Amer. Ethnologist 353 and in Nader and Todd (eds.), *The Disputing Process in Law in Ten Societies* (1978).
[18] In P.H. Gulliver (ed.), *Cross-Examination: Essays in Memory of Max Gluckmann* (1978).
[19] In Introduction to *Law and Welfare* (1967), p. xiii.
[20] *Order and Dispute* (1979), Chap. 9.
[21] *ibid.*, p. 166.

signs of weakness."[22] To Brenda Danet there are seven types of dispute process: physical violence, appeals to the supernatural and the use of magical procedures and avoidance or ostracism as relatively non-verbal modes of processing disputes: shaming, reconciliation rituals, verbal contests and settlement-directed talking as relatively verbal modes.[23] Koch differentiated six procedures based on the presence or absence of a third party and the mode of its intervention and, secondly, the nature of the outcome. (Avoidance, negotiation and coercion were dyadic procedures; mediation, arbitration and adjudication were triadic.)[24]

Once anthropologists turned their attention away from "stateless" societies to their own more complex Western world,[25] their concerns also shifted. A striking feature of contemporary anthropological research into legal processes has been the concentration on the problem of differential access to justice and alternative informal dispute resolution mechanisms associated with, what has come to be known as, "delegalisation." A good example of the former is Galanter's exploration of why, as he puts it, "the 'haves' have come out ahead."[26] Part of the answer lay in the various alternatives to the court system. Delegalisation is thought to have obvious benefits but anthropologists working largely though not exclusively within a Marxist framework have questioned these. Thus, Abel[27] has shown that delegalisation presupposes equality between social actors, a high degree of normative consensus and the existence of adequate informal controls. He concluded that in capitalist societies where these conditions did not exist delegalisation was detrimental to the interests of the weak.[28] This is, of course, an implicit recognition of the value of the "rule of law,"[29] an ideal usually rejected by Marxist thinkers.

Legal anthropologists have also turned their attention to systems of alternative legal culture in industrialised countries. Greenhouse[30] examined southern Baptists in the United States "who specifically eschew the courts because they believe that an adequate Christian life can only be led by following the law of God".[31] Merry's studies of small claims courts

---

[22] *ibid.*

[23] "Language In The Legal Process" (1980) 14 Law and Soc.Rev. 445.

[24] "The Anthropology of Law and Order" in S. Tax and L.G. Freeman (eds.), *Horizons of Anthropology* (1977), pp. 307–311. See also K.F. Koch *et al*, (1976) 10 Law and Soc.Rev. 443.

[25] This was not entirely from choice. The end of near-end of colonialism blocked many openings in the "third world".

[26] (1974) 9 Law and Soc. Rev. 95; (1975) 9 Law and Soc.Rev. 347; (1999) Wisc. L.Rev.

[27] "Delegalisation: A Critical Review of Its Ideology, Manifestations and Social Consequences" sequences" in Blankenberg *et al.*, *Alternative Rechtsformen und Alternativen zum Recht* (1976), p. 165. See also B. de Sousa Santos (1980) 8 *International Journal of the SoCiology of Law* 379.

[28] For an analysis of the Family Court ideal within this critical context see M.D.A. Freeman, "Questioning The Delegalization Movement in Family Law: Do We Really Want A Family Court?" in J. Eekelaar and S. Katz (eds.), *The Resolution of Disputes in Family Law* (1984).

[29] But see the interesting reflections of E.P. Thompson in *Whigs and Hunters* (1977), reproduced in part *post*, 1181.

[30] *Praying For Justice: Task, Order and Community in an American Town* (1986).

[31] *Per* R.R. French, *op. cit.*, note 44, p. 401.

and mediation in the United States has thrown light on popular legal conceptions of concepts such as legal consciousness and legal discourse.[32] Engel has done innovative work on the way parents of children with special needs use myths and narratives.[33] There has been work too on legal language[34] (speech styles, speech and power, rule-talk and relationship-talk[35]), on legal documents[36] (for example on the cultural characteristics of documents), and on relationships between ordinary and judicial culture. A particularly interesting example of this is the work of Lawrence Rosen on Islamic justice[37]. He found that the discretion of the Qadi judge "lies not in the development of a body of doctrine which is consistent with ... itself, but rather in the fit between the decisions of the Muslim judge and the cultural concepts and social relations to which they are inextricably tied".[38]

Where once the focus was external (a good example was the way Gluckman used the "reasonable man" concept in Barotse society),[39] legal anthropology today focuses on local understandings of law and legal practice from the perspective of the insider.[40]

## LEGAL PLURALISM

Legal pluralism[41] is a species of normative pluralism. Normative pluralism is an everyday experience for all of us (the rules of the road, of grammar, of our workplace, etc.). Legal pluralism refers to "legal systems, networks or orders co-existing in the same geographical space".[42] A good example was found in colonial South America where three legal systems could be found operating in parallel: there was the law of Spain imposed by the Spanish conquerors and administered though colonial governors, the laws of the indigenous Indian populations, and also the

---

[32] *Getting Justice and Getting Even: Legal Consciousness Among Working Class Americans* (1990).

[33] (1993) 27 Law and Soc. Rev. 785.

[34] J. Conley and W. O'Barr, *Rules Versus Relationships: The Ethnography of Legal Discourse* (1990).

[35] *Cf.* C. Gilligan, *In A Different Voice* (1982) *post*, 1289.

[36] B. Messick, *The Calligraphic State: Textual Domination and History In A Muslim Society* (1993).

[37] *The Justice of Islam* (2000).

[38] *The Anthropology of Justice: Law As Culture In Islamic Society* (1989), p. 18 (a study of Morocco). Another example is A. Griffiths (1998) 23 Law and Soc. Inquiry 587 (on Botswana).

[39] *Ante*, 1109.

[40] The influence of Clifford Geertz is significant. And see R.R. French (1996) 30 Law and Soc. Rev. 417.

[41] A good introduction to which is D. Galligan, *Law In Modern Society* (2007), Chap. 9.

[42] *Per* W. Twining, *Globalisation and Legal Theory* (2000), p. 83.

law of the Church through the Inquisition.[43] A generation ago it stood for state legal pluralism (the typical colonial country had a plural legal system). Now it tends to be assumed that "the idea of a pluralistic legal system is impossible".[44] Rather, it is usually now thought that in all societies there is a plurality of legal orders with "official" state law as only one of these. This

"... new legal pluralism moves away from questions about the effect of law on society or even the effect of society on law toward conceptualizing a more complex and interactive relationship between official and unofficial forms of ordering. Instead of mutual influences between separate entities, this perspective sees plural forms of ordering as participating in the same social field."[45]

An excellent example of this is Santos's study of the squatter settlement of Pasargada in Rio de Janeiro.[46] He "unthinks" the state and state law as privileged units of analysis by demonstrating that both are reproduced and legitimated through various tangential methods. He examines thirteen local dispute settlements in Pasargada. Within the narrative of the case records are rhetoric, bureaucracy and violence—which Santos identifies as structural features of law.[47] These features shape local legal experience. This unofficial legal system, however, does not challenge the criteria of the formal legal system, nor its legal ideologies.[48] Rather it "exists congruently within an elitist state legalism, never claiming to compete with it beyond the borders of the squatter settlement".[49] It is what Moore has called, a "semi-autonomous social field".[50] Santos explains that:

"Despite its repressive policy of community control, the state has tolerated a settlement it defines as illegal, and, by that continuing tolerance, it has allowed the settlement to acquire a status we may call a legal or extralegal. This may be explained by the fact that Pasargada and its law, as they presently exist, are probably functional to the interests of the power structure in Brazilian society. By disposing of secondary conflicts among the oppressed classes, Pasargada

---

[43]  See L. Benton, *Law and Colonial Cultures: Legal Regimes in World History* (2002). Although there was no doubt where the real power lay, there were disputes about boundaries, which matters fell within which jurisdictions. For other discussions of legal pluralism see A. Griffiths in (eds.) R. Banakar and M. Travers, *An Introduction To Law and Social Theory* (2002), S. Roberts (2005) 68 MLR1 and B. de Sousa Santos (2006) 40 Law and Society Review 39 (on Mozambique). On legal pluralism in medieval Europe see R.C. Van Caenegen, *European Law in the Past and the Future* (2002). On global legal order see W. Twining, *Globalization and Legal Theory* (2000) and W. Twining (2005) 1 International Journal of Law in Context 5, and L. Friedman (2001) 37 Stanford Journal Int Law 347.

[44]  *Per* J. Vanderlinden (1989) J. Legal Pluralism 149, 154.

[45]  *Per* S. E Merry (1989) 22 Law and Soc. Rev. 869, 873.

[46]  *Toward A New Common Sense: Law, Science and Politics In the Paradigmatic Tradition* (1995), Chap. 3. And see E. Darian-Smith (1998) 22 Law and Soc. Inquiry 81 and Santos's response (at p. 121).

[47]  *ibid.*, p. 112.

[48]  Which are based on property and class. On ideology see *post*, 1141.

[49]  *Per* Darian-Smith, *op. cit.*, n. 46, p. 105.

[50]  S.F. Moore (1973) 7 Law and Soc. Rev 719; see also her *Law As Process* (1978).

law not only relieves the official courts and officers of legal aid of the burden of hearing *favela* cases, but also reinforces the socialization of Pasargadians in a legal ideology that legitimates and consolidates class domination. By providing Pasargadians with peaceful means of dispute prevention and settlement, Pasargada law neutralizes potential violence, enhances the possibility of orderly life, and thus instills a respect for law and order that may carry over when Pasargadians go into town and interact with official society."[51]

But the very concept of legal pluralism has difficulties.[52] Twining draws attention to a number.[53] First, conceptual problems arise about when, where and how to draw distinctions between legal and non-legal phenomena, and between legal orders, systems, traditions and cultures. Secondly, very few orders or systems of norms are complete, self-contained or impervious. Thirdly, co-existing normative and legal orders interact in complex ways. "Sometimes they compete or conflict, sometimes they sustain or reinforce each other; often they influence each other through interaction, imposition, imitation and transplantation".[54] Fourthly, there is a tendency to "romanticise"[55] pluralism. Pluralism may be progressive: it may also be quite the reverse.[56] Fifthly, it is wrong to conflate "normative pluralism" with "the idea of a pluralistic approach to or the bringing of multiple perspectives to bear on a phenomenon".[57]

There is a lot of criticism of the concept of legal pluralism.[58] Teubner, noting how it appeals to post-modernists,[59] observes that they give vague answers to the connections between the social and legal fields: "interpenetrating, intertwined, integral, superposed, mutually constitutive, dialectical". It is, he comments, "the very charm of postmodernism".[60] Teubner's answer is to subject the concept of legal pluralism to autopoietic analysis. But does this advance our understanding of legal pluralism?[61] Tamanaha fiercely attackes legal pluralist approaches because they

---

[51] *Op. cit.*, n. 46, p. 236.
[52] See G. Woodman (1998) 42 J. Legal Pluralism 21.
[53] *Op. cit.*, n. 43, pp 85–86.
[54] *ibid.*, p. 85.
[55] On this he cites Santos (*op. cit.*, n. 46), but it may be that this is a trap into which Santos himself falls.
[56] See the "debate" between D. Coleman and L. Volpp in (1996) 96 Columbia L. Rev. 1093, 1573, and S.M. Okin, *Is Multiculturalism Bad For Women?* (1999), and *post*, 1244. And see A. Griffiths' case study on Kwena women's rights in (eds.) J. Cowan, M.B. Dembour and R. Wilson, *Culture and Rights* (2001), pp. 102–126, questioning whether the UN Convention on the Elimination of All Forms of Discrimination Against Women (1979) is adequate to relieve the local circumstances of women. She shows how peasant women are often precluded from entering the form of marriage envisaged by the Convention. On children, rights and culture see H. Montgomery, *ibid*, pp. 80–101, questioning whether the UN Convention on the Rights of the Child (1989) gives children rights they do not want.
[57] *Op. cit.*, n. 43, p. 86. Twining's sixth point—whose concern is legal pluralism?—is of less importance here.
[58] For example, B. Tamanaha (1993) 20 J.L.S. 192; Santos, *op. cit.*, n. 46, pp. 114–117.
[59] See *post*, Chap. 15.
[60] (1992) 13 Cardozo L.Rev. 1443, 1443–1444.
[61] Twining's criticism, *op. cit.*, n. 57, p. 87 may be noted.

confuse the idea of law.[62] How is law distinguished in a pluralist view from other normative systems? What makes a social rule system legal? Does not legal pluralism confer the label "law" too "promiscuously" on rule systems or normative orders?[63] A theory of legal pluralism could lead to a position in which drawing a clear line between state and society, even between the public and the private, becomes problematic.[64]

---

## F.K. VON SAVIGNY
### System of Modern Roman Law[65]
(1840)

In the general consciousness of a people lives positive law and hence we have to call it people's law (*Volksrecht*). It is by no means to be thought that it was the particular members of the people by whose arbitrary will, law was brought forth; in that case the will of individuals might perhaps have selected the same law, perhaps however and more probably very varied laws. Rather is it the spirit of a people living and working in common in all the individuals, which gives birth to positive law, which therefore is to the consciousness of each individual not accidentally but necessarily one and the same. Since therefore we acknowledge an invisible origin of positive law we must as to that origin, renounce documentary proof: but this defect is common to our and every other view of that origin, since we discover in all peoples who have ever presented themselves within the limits of authentic history an already existing positive law of which the original generation must lie beyond those limits. There are not wanting proofs of another sort and suitable to the special nature of the subject-matter. Such a proof lies in the universal, uniform recognition of positive law and in the feeling of inner necessity with which its conception is accompanied. This feeling expresses itself most definitely in the primeval assertion of the divine origin of law of statutes; a more manifest opposition to the idea of its arising from accident or the human will is not to be conceived. A second proof lies in the analogy of other peculiarities of peoples which have in like manner an origin invisible and reaching beyond authentic history, for example, social life and above all speech. In this is found the same independence of accident and free individual choice, the same generation from the activity of the spirit of the people working in common in each individual; in speech too from its sensible nature, all this is more evident and recognizable than in law. Indeed the individual nature of a particular people is determined and recognized solely by those common directions and activities of which speech as the most evident obtains the first place.

The form however in which law lives in the common consciousness of a people is not that of abstract rules but as the living intuition of the institutions of law in their organic connexion, so that whenever the necessity arises for the rule to be conceived in its logical form, this must be first formed by a scientific procedure from that total intuition. That form reveals itself in the symbolical acts which display in visible shape the essence of the jural relation and in which the primitive laws express themselves more intelligibly and thoroughly than in written laws.

In this view of the origin of positive law, we have at present kept out of sight

---

[62] *Op. cit.*, n. 58, p. 193.

[63] A question asked by R. Cotterrell (1998) 51 C.L.P. 367, 380.

[64] *ibid.*, p. 379, citing S. Henry, *Private Justice* (1983). But perhaps drawing such lines should be. problematic (and see S. Boyd, *Challenging The Public/Private Divide* (1997)).

[65] [English translation by W. Holloway (1867).]

the progress of the life of a people in time. If we now look also at this operation upon law we must above all ascribe to it an establishing force. The longer the convictions of law live in a people, the more deeply they become rooted in it. Moreover law will develop itself by use and what originally was present as a mere germ will by practice assume a definite shape to the consciousness. However in this way the changing of law is also generated. For as in the life of single men, no glimpse of complete passiveness can be perceived, but a continual organic development, so is it with the life of peoples and with each single element of which that concrete life is composed. Thus we find in speech a constant gradual shaping and development and in like manner in law. This gradual formation is subject to the same law of generation from inner power and necessity, independent of accident and individual will, as its original arising was. But the people experiences in this natural process of development, not merely a change in general, but it experiences it in a settled, regular series of events and of these each has its peculiar relation to the expression of the spirit of the people in which the law is generated. This appears in the clearest and strongest manner in the youth of a people for then the connexion is more intimate, the consciousness of it is more generally diffused and is less obscured by the variety of individual cultivation. Moreover in the same degree in which the cultivation of individuals becomes heterogeneous and predominant and in which a sharper division of employment, of acquirements, and of ranks produced by these, enters, the generation of law which rests upon the common consciousness becomes more difficult; and this mode of generation would disappear altogether if new organs for that purpose were not formed by the influence of these self-same new circumstances; these organs of legislation and the science of law of which the nature will be immediately explained.

This new development of law may have an entirely different relation to the originally existing law. New institutions of law may be generated by it, the existing law transformed or it may be entirely swept away if it has become foreign to the thought and need of the age.

## People (Volk)

The generation of law has been preliminarily posited in the people as the active, personal subject. The nature of this subject will not be more accurately defined. If in the examination of the jural relation, we remove by abstraction, all its special content, there remains over as a common nature, the united life of a plurality of men, regulated in a defined manner. We might naturally be led to stop short at this abstract conception of a plurality and regard law as its discovery, without which the external freedom of no individual could subsist, but such an accidental meeting of an undefined multitude is a conception both arbitrary and entirely wanting in truth: and even if they found themselves so met together, the capacity for producing law would be entirely wanting since with a need the power of at once supplying it, is not given. In fact we find so far as history informs us upon the matter, that wherever men live together, they stand in an intellectual communion which reveals as well as establishes and develops itself by the use of speech. In this natural whole is the seat of the generation of law and in the common intelligence of the nation penetrating individuals, is found the power of satisfying the necessity above recognized.

The boundaries however of individual nations are certainly undefined and wavering and this state of doubt also shows itself in the unity or variety of the law engendered in them. Thus as to kindred races it may appear uncertain whether they are to be regarded as one people or as several; in like manner we also frequently find in their law not an entire consonance, probably however an affinity.

Even where the unity of a people is undoubted,[66] within its limits are often found inner circles which are included in a special connexion side by side with the general union of the people, as cities and villages, guilds and corporations of every sort which altogether form popular divisions of the whole. In these circles again a special generation of law may have its seat as particular law, side by side with the general law of the nation which by that particular law is on many sides complete or altered.

When we regard the people as a natural unity and merely as the subject of positive law, we ought not to think only of the individuals comprised in that people at any particular time; that unity rather runs through generations constantly replacing one another, and thus it unites the present with the past and the future. This constant preservation of law is effected by tradition and this is conditioned by, and based upon, the not sudden but ever gradual change of generations. The independence of the life of individuals, here asserted of law, appertains first to the unchanged continuation of the rules of law: it is secondly too the foundation of the gradual formation of law and in this connexion we must ascribe to it a special importance.

This view in which the individual people is regarded as the generator and subject of positive or practical law may appear too confined to some who might be inclined to ascribe that generation rather to the general spirit of humanity than to that of a particular people. On closer examination these two views do not appear conflicting. What works in an individual people is merely the general human spirit which reveals itself in that people in a particular manner. The generation of law is a fact and one common to the whole. This is conceivable only of those between whom a communion of thought and action is not only possible but actual. Since then such a communion exists only within the limits of an individual people so here also can practical law alone be created, although in its production, the expression of a generative principle common to men in general, is perceived, but not the peculiar will of individual peoples, of which perhaps no single trace might be found in other peoples. For this product of the people's mind is sometimes entirely peculiar to a single people, though sometimes equally present in several peoples. [pp. 12–17]

### Customary law

This name may easily mislead us into the following course of thinking. When anything whatever needed to be done in a jural relation, it was originally quite indifferent what was done; accident and arbitrary will anyhow settled the decision. If the same case presented itself a second time, it was easier to repeat the same decision that to deliberate upon a new one and with each fresh repetition, this procedure of necessity appeared more convenient and more natural. Thus after a while such a rule would become law as had originally no greater claim to prevail than an opposite rule and the cause of origin of this law was custom alone. If one looks at the true bases of positive law, at the actual substance of it, he will see that in that view, cause and effect are exactly reversed. That basis has its existence, its reality in the common consciousness of the people. This existence is an invisible thing; by what means can be recognize it? We do so when it reveals

---

[66] [Savigny nowhere faces up to the questions, What is a People? and, what are the criteria for determining its degree of unity, natural or artificial? Later writers put a greater emphasis on *racial* unity, but again the meaning of race was either evaded or deliberately obscured. Spengler in *The Decline of the West* stresses that a *Volk* is neither a political, linguistic nor zoological unit but a "spiritual" unit. A *Volk* is not held together by "mere units of physical origin." No *Volk*, he insisted, "was ever yet stirred to enthusiasm for *this* ideal of 'blood-purity'" ((1982) (trans. C.F. Atkinson), vol. 2, p. 165). See also Baker, *Race* (1974), pp. 53–55 on the meaning of *Volk*.]

itself in external act when it steps forth in usage, manners, custom; in the uniformity of a continuing and therefore lasting manner of action we recognize the
belief of the people as its common root and one diametrically opposite to bare
chance. Custom therefore is the badge and not a ground of origin of positive law.
However this error which converts custom into a ground of origin has also an
ingredient of truth which must now be reduced to its proper dimensions. Besides
those bases universally recognized in the consciousness of a people and
undoubted, there are many determinations as to details which have in themselves
a less certain existence; they may obtain such an existence, by being through
constant practice brought more definitely to the consciousness of the people
itself...

## Legislation

...If we enquire first as to the contents of written law, they are already determined by the mode of derivation of the law-giving power; the already present
people's law supplies those contents or what is the same thing, written law is the
organ of people's law. If one were to doubt that, one must conceive the lawgiver
as standing apart from the nation; he however rather stands in its centre, so that
he concentrates in himself their spirit, feelings, needs, so that we have to regard
him as the true representative of the spirit of the people. It is also entirely erroneous to regard this position of the legislator, as dependent upon the different
arrangement of the legislative power in this or that constitution. Whether a prince
makes the law or a senate or a larger collection of people formed by election or
perhaps the agreement of several such powers is furnished for legislation, the
essential relation of the legislator to the people's law is not at all changed and it is
again owing to the error of the conception censured above, if some believe that
real people's law is only contained in the laws made by selected representatives...

The influence of legislation upon the progress of law is more important than
upon its original formation. If through changed manners, views, needs, a change
in the existing law becomes necessary or if in the progress of time entirely new
legal institutions are necessary, these new elements may indeed be introduced into
the existing law by the same innate invisible power which originally generated the
law. It is however precisely here that the influence of legislation may become most
obviously beneficial, nay indispensable. Since those operative principles only enter
gradually, there of necessity arises an interval of uncertain law and this uncertainty is brought to an end by the expression of the law.[67]...

Lastly into the history of every people, enter stages of development and conditions which are no longer propitious to the creation of law by the general
consciousness of a people. In this case this activity, in all cases indispensable, will
in great measure of itself devolve upon legislation...

## Juristic law[68]

It is a natural consequence of the development of nations that as culture progresses, special activities and acquirements should separate and thus form separate occupations for the different classes. Thus also law, originally the common
property of the collective people, by the more extended relations of active life is
developed in so special a manner that it can no longer be mastered by the

---

[67] [The modern reader may well ask himself how such social legislation as Factories Acts,
Public Health Acts, Town Planning Acts, etc., could ever come into being by the process
here envisaged. The answer is that in an age of *laissez faire* their exclusion would be
regarded as wholly laudable.]

[68] [On the importance of this "technical element" see *ante*, 1081–1082.]

knowledge uniformly spread among the people. Then is formed a special order of persons skilled in law who as an actual part of the people, in this order of thought represent the whole. The law is in the particular consciousness of this order, merely a continuation and special unfolding of the people's law. It leads hence-forth a double life; in outline it continues to live in the common consciousness of the people, the more minute cultivation and handling of it, is the special calling of the order of jurists . . .

### Relation Between Sources of Law

From the previous exposition it follows that originally all positive law is people's law and that side by side with this spontaneous generation, comes legislation (often even in early times) enlarging and propping it up. Then by the progressive development of the people, legal science is added; thus in legislation and the science of law, two organs are furnished to people's law, each of which simul-taneously leads its independent life. If lastly in later times, the law-forming energy departs from the people as a whole, it continues to live in these organs. Then since the largest and most important parts of the old people's law have been incor-porated into legislation and legal science, that law shows itself very little in its original shape but merely appears through their medium. Thus it may happen that people's law may be almost hidden by legislation and legal science in which it lives on, and that the true origin of existing positive law, may be easily forgotten and misunderstood. Legislation especially, in its external influence has such a preponderance, that the delusion easily arises that it is the sole true ground of origin of law and that all others must be considered in the subordinate position of a mere supplement or adjunct to it. Law however is never in a healthy condition, unless these law-forming powers work harmoniously together, none of them isolating itself from the others: and since legislation and legal science are the continuous product of individual consciousness and reflexion, it is also of importance that correct views of the origin of positive law, and of the true con-nexion of the powers co-operating in that production, should obtain and assert the mastery.                                                    [pp. 28–42]

### SIR HENRY MAINE
### Ancient Law
### (1859)

### Themistes[69]

The earliest notions connected with the conception, now so fully developed, of a law or rule of life, are those contained in the Homeric words "Themis" and "Themistes." "Themis," it is well known, appears in the later Greek pantheon as the Goddess of Justice, but this is a modern and much developed idea, and it is in a very different sense that Themis is described in the Iliad as the assessor of Zeus. It is now clearly seen by all trustworthy observers of the primitive condition of mankind that, in the infancy of the race, men could only account for sustained or periodically recurring action by supposing a personal agent. Thus, the wind blowing was a person and of course a divine person; the sun rising, culminating, and setting was a person and a divine person; the earth yielding her increase was a person and divine. As, then, in the physical world, so in the moral. When a king

---

[69] [For a detailed criticism of Maine's theory of early law, see A.S. Diamond, *Primitive Law* (2nd ed., 1950); Pospisil, *Anthropology of Law* (1971), pp. 143–150; and Redfield (1950) 3 Western Pol. Q. 574.]

decided a dispute by a sentence, the judgment was assumed to be the result of direct inspiration.[70]...

Even in the Homeric poems we can see that these ideas are transient. Parities of circumstance were probably commoner in the simple mechanism of ancient society than they are now, and in the succession of similar cases awards are likely to follow and resemble each other. Here we have the germ or rudiment of a custom, a conception posterior to that of Themistes or judgments. However strongly we, with our modern associations, may be inclined to lay down *a priori* that the notion of a Custom must precede that of a judicial sentence, and that a judgment must affirm a custom or punish its breach, it seems quite certain that the historical order of the ideas is that in which I have placed them.[71]

### Customary Law

The important point for the jurist is that aristocracies were universally the depositaries and administrators of law. They seem to have succeeded to the prerogatives of the king, with the important difference, however, that they do not appear to have pretended to direct inspiration for each sentence. The connection of ideas which caused the judgments of the patriarchal chieftain to be attributed to superhuman dictation still shows itself here and there in the claim of a divine origin for the entire body of rules, or for certain parts of it, but the progress of thought no longer permits the solution of particular disputes to be explained by supposing an extra-human interposition. What the juristical oligarchy now claims is to monopolise the *knowledge* of the laws, to have the exclusive possession of the principles by which quarrels are decided. We have in fact arrived at the epoch of Customary Law. Customs or Observances now exist as a substantive aggregate, and are assumed to be precisely known to the aristocratic order or caste. Our authorities leave us no doubt that the trust lodged with the oligarchy was sometimes abused, but it certainly ought not to be regarded as a mere usurpation or engine of tyranny. Before the invention of writing, and during the infancy of the art, an aristocracy invested with judicial privileges formed the only expedient by which accurate preservation of the customs of the race or tribe could be at all approximated to. Their genuineness was, so far as possible, insured by confiding them to the recollection of a limited portion of the community.

The epoch of Customary Law, and of its custody by a privileged order, is a very remarkable one. The condition of jurisprudence which it implies has left traces which may still be detected in legal and popular phraseology. The law, thus known exclusively to a privileged minority, whether a caste, an aristocracy, a priestly tribe, or a sacerdotal college, is true unwritten law. Except this, there is no such thing as unwritten law in the world. English case-law is sometimes spoken of as unwritten, and there are some English theorists who assure us that if a code of English jurisprudence were prepared we should be turning unwritten law into written—a conversion, as they insist, if not of doubtful policy, at all events of the greatest seriousness. Now, it is quite true that there was once a period at which the English common law might reasonably have been termed unwritten. The elder English judges did really pretend to knowledge of rules, principles, and distinctions which were not entirely revealed to the bar and to the lay-public. Whether all the law which they claimed to monopolise was really unwritten, is exceedingly questionable; but at all events, on the assumption that there was once a large mass of civil and criminal rules known exclusively to the judges, it presently ceased to

---

[70] [But see Maine's *Early Law and Custom*, p. 163, where he admits that such judgments are doubtless drawn from pre-existing custom.]

[71] [This notion of custom may be compared with the Roman and modern civilian idea of case law as creative of a kind of customary law: *cf*. Jolowicz, *Roman Foundations of Modern Law*, pp. 36–37.]

be unwritten law. As soon as the Courts at Westminster Hall began to base their judgments on cases recorded, whether in the year-books or elsewhere, the law which they administered became written law. At the present moment a rule of English law has first to be disentangled from the recorded facts of adjudged printed precedents, then thrown into a form of words varying with the taste, precision, and knowledge of the particular judge, and then applied to the circumstances of the case for adjudication. But at no stage of this process has it any characteristic which distinguishes it from written law. It is written case-law, and only different from code-law because it is written in a different way.

From the period of Customary Law we come to another sharply defined epoch in the history of jurisprudence. We arrive at the era of Codes, those ancient codes of which the Twelve Tables of Rome were the most famous specimen. In Greece, in Italy, on the Hellenised seaboard of Western Asia, these codes all made their appearance at periods much the same everywhere, not, I mean, at periods identical in point of time, but similar in point of the relative progress of each community. Everywhere, in the countries I have named, laws engraven on tablets and published to the people take the place of usages deposited with the recollection of a privileged oligarchy. It must not for a moment be supposed that the refined considerations now urged in favour of what is called codification had any part or place in the change I have described. The ancient codes were doubtless originally suggested by the discovery and diffusion of the art of writing. It is true that the aristocracies seem to have abused their monopoly of legal knowledge, and at all events their exclusive possession of the law was a formidable impediment to the success of those popular movements which began to be universal in the western world. But, though democratic sentiment may have added to their popularity, the codes were certainly in the main a direct result of the invention of writing. Inscribed tablets were seen to be a better depository of law, and a better security for its accurate preservation, than the memory of a number of persons however strengthened by habitual exercise.                                    [pp. 10–13]

The movement of the progressive[72] societies has been uniform in one respect. Through all its course it has been distinguished by the gradual dissolution of family dependency, and the growth of individual obligation in its place. The Individual is steadily substituted for the Family, as the unit of which civil laws take account. The advance has been accomplished at varying rates of celerity, and there are societies not absolutely stationary in which the collapse of the ancient organisation can only be perceived by careful study of the phenomena they present. But, whatever its pace, the change has not been subject to reaction or recoil, and apparent retardations will be found to have been occasioned through the absorption of archaic ideas and customs from some entirely foreign source. Nor is it difficult to see what is the tie between man and man which replaces by degrees those forms of reciprocity in rights and duties which have their origin in the Family. It is Contract. Starting, as from one terminus of history, from a condition of society in which all the relations of Persons are summed up in the relations of Family, we seem to have steadily moved towards a phase of social order in which all these relations arise from the free agreement of Individuals...

The word Status may be usefully employed to construct a formula expressing the law of progress thus indicated, which, whatever be its values, seems to me to be sufficiently ascertained. All the forms of Status taken notice of in the Law of Persons were derived from, and to some extend are still coloured by, the powers and privileges anciently residing in the Family. If then we employ Status, agreeably with the usage of the best writers, to signify these personal conditions

---

[72] [Maine regarded these as exceptional. "The natural condition of mankind (if that word 'natural' is used) is not the progressive condition. It is the condition not of changeableness but of unchangeableness. The immobility of society is the rule; its mobility is the exception" (*Popular Government*, p. 170).]

only, and avoid applying the term to such conditions as are the immediate or remote result of agreement, we may say that the movement of the progressive societies has hitherto[73] been a movement *from Status to Contract.* [pp. 180–182]

### E. A. HOEBEL
### The Law of Primitive Man
### (1954)

*The Functions of Law*

Law performs certain functions essential to the maintenance of all but the most simple societies.

The first is to define relationships among the members of a society, to assert what activities are permitted and what are ruled out, so as to maintain at least minimal integration between the activities of individuals and groups within the society.

The second is derived from the necessity of taming naked force and directing force to the maintenance of order. It is the allocation of authority and the determination of who may exercise physical coercion as a socially recognized privilege-right, along with the selection of the most effective forms of physical sanction to achieve the social ends that the law serves.

The third is the disposition of trouble cases as they arise.

The fourth is to redefine relations between individuals and groups as the conditions of life change. It is to maintain adaptability.[74]

Purposive definition of personal relations is the primary law-job. Other aspects of culture likewise work to this end, and, indeed, the law derives its working principles (jural postulates) from postulates previously developed in the nonlegal spheres of action. However, the law's important contribution to the basic organization of society as a whole is that the law specifically and explicitly defines relations. It sets the expectancies of man to man and group to group so that each knows the focus and the limitations of its demand-rights on others, its duties to others, its privilege-rights and powers as against others, and its immunities and liabilities to the contemplated or attempted acts of others.[75] This is the "bare-bones job," as Karl Llewellyn likes to call it. It is the ordering of the fundamentals of living together.

No culture has a specific starting point in time; yet in the operation of the first function it is as though men were getting together and saying to each other, "Look here! Let's have a little organization here or we'll never get anywhere with this mess! Let's have a clear understanding of who's who, what we are to do, and how we are going to do it!" In its essence it is what the social-contract theorists recognized as the foundation of social order.

---

[73] [It is to be noted that Maine qualifies this celebrated dictum by the word "hitherto." Certainly since his day the movement has been away from freedom of contract towards an increasingly collectivist society, though not one which can be readily brought within the category of status as understood in earlier ages.

[74] *Cf.* K. N. Llewellyn, "The Normative, the Legal, and the Law-jobs: The Problem of Juristic Methods" (1940) 49 *Yale Law Journal* 1355–1400. See also Llewellyn and Hoebel, *The Cheyenne Way*, Chap. xi.

[75] [Hoebel is following Hohfeld's terminology; *cf. ante*, 510. The use of contemporary technical terms when describing primitive societies is criticised by Sawer, as this in itself tends to give tribal law the appearance of a degree of definition which it does not have, and thereby begs the very question to be decided, *i.e.* to what extent legal institutions and concepts in our sense are reproduced in undeveloped forms of society; see G. Sawer, *Law in Society*, pp. 43–47.]

The second function of the law—the allocation of authority to exercise coercive physical force—is something almost peculiar to things legal.

Custom has regularity, and so does law. Custom defines relationships, and so does law. Custom is sanctioned, and so is law. But the sanctions of law may involve physical coercion. Law is distinguished from mere custom in that it endows certain selected individuals with the privilege-right of applying the sanction of physical coercion, if need be. The legal, let it be repeated, has teeth that can bite. But the biting, if it is to be legal and not mere gangsterism, can be done only by those persons to whom the law has allocated the privilege-right for the affair at hand.[76]

We have seen that in primitive law authority is a shifting, temporary thing. Authority to enforce a norm resides (for private wrongs) with the wronged individual and his immediate kinsmen—but only for the duration of time necessary to follow through the procedural steps that lead to redress or punishment of the culprit. In primitive law the tendency is to allocate authority to the party who is directly injured. This is done in part out of convenience, for it is easier to let the wronged party assume the responsibility of legal action. It is also done because the primitive kinship group, having a more vital sense of entity, is naturally charged with a heavier emotional effect. In any event, when the community qua community acknowledges the exercise of force by a wronged person or his kinship group as correct and proper in a given situation, and so restrains the wrongdoer from striking back, then law prevails and order triumphs over violence.

We have also found in our studies of primitive societies that in a limited number of situations authority is directly exercised by the community on its own behalf. It takes the form of lynch law in some instances where clear procedures have not been set up in advance, as in the Comanche treatment of excessive sorcery and Shoshone treatment of cannibalism. Lynch law among primitives, however, is not a backsliding from, or detouring around, established formal law as it is with us. It is a first fitful step toward the emergence of criminal law in a situation in which the exercise of legal power has not yet been refined and allocated to specific persons. It is a blunt crude tool wielded by the gang hand of an outraged public.

Yet lynch law is rare among primitives. Even the simplest of them have crystalized standards as to what constitutes criminal behaviour, and the exercise of public authority is delegated to official functionaries—the chieftain, the council of chiefs, and the council of elders.

Power may sometimes be personal, as is the power of the bully in the society of small boys, and as was to some extent the power of William the Conqueror. But personal tyranny is a rare thing among primitives. Brute force of the individual does not prevail. Chiefs must have followers. Followers always impose limitations on their leaders. Enduring power is always institutionalized power. It is *transpersonalized*. It resides in the office, in the social status, rather than in the man. The constitutional structures of the several tribes examined in this book have all clearly revealed how political and legal authority are in each instance delimited and circumscribed.

This point is emphasized only to dispel any residue of the hoary political philosophies that assumed without basis in fact that primitive societies existed under the rule of fang and claw.

However, the personal still obtrudes. An "office" although culturally defined is, after all, exercised by an individual. And who that individual is at any moment certainly makes a difference. There is leeway in the exercise or non-exercise of power just as there are limits. A man may be skilled in finding the evidence and the truth in the cases he must judge and in formulating the norms to fit the case in

---

[76] [On the relationship between law and custom *cf. ante*, 1088.]

hand—or he may be all thumbs. He may be one who thirsts for power and who will wield all he can while grasping for more. Or he may shrink from it. Power defined through allocation of legal authority is by its nature trans-personalized, yet by the nature of men it can never be wholly depersonalized. A Franklin Roosevelt is not a Warren Harding.                                    [pp. 275–278]

The third function of law calls for little additional comment ... Some trouble cases pose absolutely new problems for solution. In these cases the first and second functions may predominate. Yet this is not the situation in the instance of most legal clashes in which the problem is not the formulation of law to cover a new situation but rather the application of pre-existing law. These cases are disposed of in accordance with legal norms already set before the issue in question arises. The job is to clean the case up, to suppress or penalize the illegal behavior and to bring the relations of the disputants back into balance, so that life may resume its normal course. This type of law-work has frequently been compared to work of the medical practitioner. It is family doctor stuff, essential to keeping the social body on its feet. In more homely terms, Llewellyn has called it, "garage-repair work on the general order of the group when that general order misses fire, or grinds gears, or even threatens a total breakdown."[77] It is not ordinarily concerned with grand design, as is the first law-job. Nor is it concerned with redesign as is the fourth. It works to clean up all the little social messes (and the occasional big ones) that recurrently arise between the members of the society from day to day.

Most of the trouble cases do not, in a civilized society, of themselves loom large on the social scene, although in a small community even one can lead directly to a social explosion if not successfully cleaned up. Indeed, in a primitive society the individual case always holds the threat of a little civil war if procedure breaks down, for from its inception it sets kin group against kin group—and if it comes to fighting, the number of kinsmen who will be involved is almost always immediately enlarged. The fight may engulf a large part of the tribe in internecine throat-cutting. Relatively speaking, each run-of-the-mill trouble case in primitive law imposes a more pressing demand for settlement upon the legal system than is the case with us.

While system and integration are essential, flexibility and constant revision are no less so. Law is a dynamic process in which few solutions can be permanent. Hence, the fourth function of law: the redefinition of relations and the reorientation of expectancies.

Initiative with scope to work means new problems for the law. New inventions, new ideas, new behaviors keep creeping in. Especially do new behaviors creep in, nay, sweep in, when two unlike societies come newly into close contact. Then the law is called upon to decide what principles shall be applied to conflicts of claims rooted in disparate cultures. Do the new claims fit comfortably to the old postulate?[78] Must the newly realized ways of behaving be wholly rejected and legally suppressed because they are out of harmony with the old values? Or can they be modified here and altered there to gain legal acceptance? Or can the more difficult operation of altering or even junking old postulates to accommodate a new way be faced? Or can fictions be framed that can lull the mind into acceptance of the disparate new without the wrench of acknowledged junking of the old? What *is* it that is wanted? The known and habitual, or the promise of the new and untested? Men may neglect to turn the law to the answer of such questions. But they do not for long. Trouble cases generated by the new keep marching in. And the fourth law-job presses for attention.

Recapitulation of just one Cheyenne case will throw the process into focus. The acquisition of horses greatly altered all Plains Indian cultures. One important

---

[77] Llewellyn, "The Normative, the Legal, and the Law-jobs", p. 1375.
[78] [This refers to the basic jural postulates of the particular society.]

Cheyenne basic postulate ran,[79] "Except for land and tribal fetishes, all material goods are private property, but they should be generously shared with others." When it came to horses, this led some men to expect that they could freely borrow horses without even the courtesy of asking. For horse owners this got to the point of becoming a serious nuisance, as in the cases of Pawnee and Wolf Lies Down.[80] Wolf Lies Down put his trouble case to the members of the Elk Soldier Society. They got his horse back for him with a handsome free-will offering of additional "damages" from the defendant to boot. The trouble case was neatly disposed of. But the Elk Soldiers did not stop there. There was some preventive channeling of future behaviour to be done. Hence the "Now we shall make a new rule.[81] There shall be no more borrowing of horses without asking. If any man takes another's goods without asking, we will go over and get them back for him. More than that, if the taker tries to keep them, we will give him a whipping." Here was the fourth function of law being performed. The lines for future conduct re horses were made clear.

Work under Function IV[82] represented social planning brought into focus by the case of the instant and with an eye to the future.

The problem of reorienting conduct and redirecting it through the law when new issues emerge is always tied to the bare-bones demand of basic organization and the minimal maintenance of order and regularity. It may also shade over into work colored by a greater or lesser desire to achieve more than a minimum of smoothness in social relations. When this becomes an important aspect of law-work, a special aspect of law-ways activity may be recognized? The creation of techniques that efficiently and effectively solve the problems posed to all the other law-jobs so that the basic values of the society are realized through the law and not frustrated by it.

The doing of it has been called by Llewellyn "Juristic Method." It is the method not only of getting the law-jobs done but doing them with a sure touch for the net effect that results in smoothness in the doing and a harmonious wedding of what is aspired to by men and what is achieved through the law. It is the work not just of the craftsman but of the master craftsman....

Skill in juristic method may be the unique quality of a great judge or chief who judges for his people. In which case you may have a single man, or occasional men, cropping up to soften hard-shell legalism. Or it may become an institutional quality of a whole system in which a tradition of method is to keep one eye on the ultimate social goals of men and another on the working machinery to see that it is steering towards those goals. For juristic method, while it works on the immediate grievance to see that "justice" receives its due, also looks beyond to discern as far as possible the ultimate effect of the social policy that the *ratio decidendi* will produce. It weighs and balances the "rights" of the individual in *this particular case* against the need for order per se and the far-running needs of the group as a whole. It recognizes that regularity exists not only for the sake of regularity, which is no *Ding an sich*, but as a means to social and individual existence. But it also knows that absolute regularity is impossible in social physiology. It seeks as best it may to keep the working law flexible enough to allow leeway at the points where leeway will not cause the social fabric to part at the seams, and at the same time it seeks to maintain sufficient stiffness in the fibre of the law so that it will not lose its binding effect....

---

[79]  [As formulated by Hoebel. Hoebel is not explicit about his technique of identifying these principles and about his method of selection. See Moore, "Law and Anthropology" in *Biennial Review of Anthropology* (1969), p. 263.]

[80]  [See pp. 146–149 of Hoebel's book.]

[81]  [Llewellyn and Hoebel, *The Cheyenne Way* (1941), p. 128, admit this promulgation of a "new law" is truly a "rare occurrence."]

[82]  [See *ante*, 1103.]

Admittedly it would be hard, if not impossible, to scale a society on a measure of juristic method. Yet, grossly perceived, it can be seen to exist among primitives, often in large degree, and I venture to state in larger degree than in the archaic law of some of the Mediterranean civilizations, and in England after the Common Law had hardened and before Equity had been created to counteract its unreasonable effects.

If ever Sir Henry Maine fixed an erroneous notion on modern legal historians, it was the idea that primitive law, once formulated, is stiff and ritualistic (and by implication weak in juristic method).[83] ... In most primitive trouble cases the situation is surprisingly fluid, but flowing within channels that are built by the preexisting law and moving to a reasonably predictable settlement. The channels, however, shift and bend like the course of a meandering river across the bed of a flat flood plain, though flowing ever in a given direction. Men are at work on the law.

The very fact that the bulk of the substance and procedure of primitive law emerges through case action involving claim and counterclaim, pleading and counterpleading, tends to keep legal behavior relatively close to the prevailing social values. Which way a new issue will go will depend not alone upon the facts but also upon the skill of the litigants in framing the issue and arguing the relevance of their respective positions to the prevailing social ideas of right conduct and group well-being—or upon persuasiveness in argument that a new orientation of values is in order to meet changed conditions, even though the tough man and his kinsman, though "wrong," may sometimes make his position stick with naked force. Thus, the wise claimant argues his case not in terms of "this is good for me" but rather by maintaining "this is what we all want and should do." If he is a primitive advocate, it is more likely than not that he will also insist, if he can, that this is the way it has been from time immemorial. But the past certainly has no inflexible grip on primitive law.

Fiction[84] is one of the great devices of juristic method by means of which men fit new legal norms into old principles so as to reorient conduct without the need to junk long-standing postulates. Except for the universal practice of adoption, whereby outsiders are identified *as if* they are actually kinsmen, primitive men do not have to rely too heavily on the subterfuge of fiction to achieve legal change. Nevertheless, when the need is there many tribes have had recourse to its use.

An outstanding example may be found in adoptive marriage among the patrilinal groups of Indonesia. The important value for these people is to maintain the unbroken continuity of the paternal lineage. To do this, a family without sons adopts their daughter's husband as a "son" with the effect that her children remain within their clan and their inheritance will remain within their line.[85]

[pp. 279–284]

Thus far ... we have been concerned with the functions of law in their universal aspects. Do these lead to universal principles of content? Yes, but among the highly diversified cultures of the primitive world they are few and very generalized for the most part.

The one assumption of overwhelming importance underlying all primitive legal and social systems is the postulation of magico-religious forces as being superior to men, and also that spirit beings have emotional intelligence similar to man's. Its effect on the law systems is variable. It is strongest in its consequences among those people whose religion emphasizes the role of ancestral spirits, and where the anger of spirits is believed to jeopardize the well-being of the entire society. The

---

[83] Maine, *Ancient Law*, esp. Chaps ii and iv.

[84] "Any assumption which conceals, or affects to conceal, the fact that a rule of law has undergone alteration, its letter remaining unchanged, its operation being modified." Maine, *Ancient Law*, p. 25.

[85] Ter Haar, *Adat Law in Indonesia*, pp. 175–176.

sins that arouse such anger are almost certainly taken up by the law as crimes. Almost universally, excessive abuse of personal control of supernatural powers (sorcery out of hand) is treated as a crime. On the other hand, appeal to the supernatural to solve problems of evidence through use of oracles, divination, conditional curse or oath is a very nearly universal legal device.

Homicide within the society is, under one set of conditions or another, legally prohibited everywhere. Likewise, it is universally recognized as a privilege-right under certain circumstances, either in self-defence against illegal, extreme assault (including sorcery) or as a sanction for certain illegal acts.

Virtually every society assumes the relative social inferiority of women (the Ifugao are one exception) and allows male relatives and husband demand-rights and privilege-rights, powers and immunities, in relation to their female relatives and wives that do not find their equivalents on behalf of the women as against the males. Thus it appears to be universal on the primitive level (and general on the civilized level) that the husband may kill the adulterous wife caught *inflagrante delicto*. For the wife to enjoy such a privilege-right is most rare.

Law universally supports the principle of relative exclusiveness in marital rights. Adultery seems always to be punishable under the law, although just what constitutes adultery will be variable as marriage and kinship forms vary. The right to life and the right to wife are legal fundamentals. All legal systems, primitive and civilized, assume the importance of the kinship group, and all support it as a medium of inheritance of property rights.

All legal systems give cognizance to the existence of rights to private property in some goods; but among primitives land is legally treated as belonging directly or ultimately to the tribe or the kinship group; it is rarely sustained legally as an object of private property.[86]

When the law-jobs get done, these norms inevitably become the common denominator of legal culture. But the functions of law, whatever the norms they may give rise to in any particular society, are what constitute the crucial universal elements of the law. Any one or half-hundred societies may select one rule of law and not another—the range is wide—but none can ignore the law-jobs. In the last analysis, that the law-jobs get done is more important than how they are done. Their minimal doing is an imperative of social existence. Their doing with juristic finesse is an achievement of high skill.[87]　　　　　[pp. 285–287]

---

[86]　[*Cf.* M. Mead, *ante*, 225.]

[87]　[For an assessment of Hoebel's contribution to the anthropology of law see Pospisil (1973) 7 Law and Soc. Rev. 537. His greatest and most lasting impact on the discipline is said to be his introduction into the discipline of the "case method" of study. It is however a restricted view not readily applicable in "trouble-less" cases. It places an overemphasis on conflict and suffers from similar defects as Realism, from which it was taken. See Holleman (1973) 7 Law and Soc. Rev. 585. Limitations of the case method are also discussed by Gluckman in 7 Law and Soc. Rev. 611. He remarks "one cannot even record what law does without recording what law is" (p. 616). Hoebel recognised this: legal rules were "guides for action, and more often than not the real norms of behaviour coincide with them" (*The Law of Primitive Man*, p. 30).]

## M. GLUCKMAN
### Judicial Process among the Barotse
(revised ed. 1967)

*The Reasonable Man*[88]

It is perhaps now reasonable time that I gave the Lozi[89] phrase for "a reasonable man." It is clear from the texts and from my discussion of the preceding cases that in practice judges do not often use such a phrase explicitly, but that the reasonable man is usually implicitly present when they contrast reported behaviour with the norms of behaviour of particular positions. One *general* phrase in Lozi is *mutu yangana: mutu* = person, and *ngana* = mind, wisdom, intelligence, intellect, reason, sense, commonsense. From the many contexts in which I have heard *mutu yangana* used, I consider it is best translated as "a man of sense," with the meaning that Jane Austen brought out in *Sense and Sensibility* . . . It includes the idea of "having sound principles." This is made clearer in the more common general Lozi phrase used in contexts where people are being judged: *mutu yalukile*, of which "an upright man" is probably the best English rendering. "*—Lukile*" is an adjective from the verbal root *kuluka*, "to go straight," "to stand upright." "Straightforwardness," "uprightness," "decency," "principle," "virtue," are therefore the qualities which the Lozi demand of people. This demand includes both sense or reasonableness (*ngana*) and uprightness (*kuluka*)....

That *muti yalukile*, an upright man, embraces both sense and uprightness is apparent if we recall the cross-examination and judgments in cases cited. In "The Case of the Biassed Father"[90] the village headman would have behaved sensibly and uprightly if he had been impartial in settling the dispute between his sons and his nephews, as would SAYWA in "The Case of the Violent Councillor" had he not backed his own children. Reference to any of the praises or reprimands bestowed by judges emphasizes this partial identification. However, the identification is only partial, and *mutu yangana* and *mutu yalukile* are distinguished. For though the judges assess behaviour, in considering evidence, by the standard of the upright man, and urge this standard on litigants, the law only demands "reasonable" behaviour—the standard of "the sensible man." Hence the upright man does not have mistresses, but the law only requires that a man should not neglect his wives while he pursues mistresses, and allows him mistresses if they be not married to others...

Lozi judges do not make continual explicit use of the general phrase for a reasonable man because in most cases they are giving judgments on the behaviour of persons occupying specific social positions in multiplex relations—they are chiefly concerned with relationships of status. Therefore the judges more often work explicitly with the phrases, "a good husband," "a sensible induna," and so on. Indeed, they often use the term for the social position without using the qualificative. This in itself states the norms of customary behaviour and reasonable fulfilment of obligations. The emphatic use of terms defining social position is very common in praising people. For example, Lozi rarely speak of a woman as an industrious gardener without adding, "*Kimusalf*" ("she's a wife"), or, *"Kimwana"* ("she's a child"), since gardening is so important a duty of women. Similarly, when it became known how much Nyambe, the son of NAWALA Mutondo, had brought back from Johannesburg for his kin, people said of him: "*Kimwana, uezize*"—"he's a child, he has done [what he ought to have done]."

---

[88] [For a critical analysis of the "reasonable man" in Gluckman, see Epstein (1973) 7 Law and Soc. Rev. 643.]
[89] [A people of Barotseland in Northern Rhodesia (Zambia): see *op. it.*, p. 1.]
[90] [The cases referred to by Gluckman are described in detail in the book.]

This phrase, "*Uezize,*" ("he [or she] has done") is often used on its own of a man who has fulfilled his obligations, beyond reasonable demands. Similarly, Lozi says, "He's a chief—an induna—a headman—a subject," for political positions; "He's a fisherman—a herdsman—a servant," for employees; "He's a magician—a smith—a potter—a carver," for specialists; and so forth.

Judges also use this common practice of reference, and in doing so they are setting up the differentiated standard of the reasonable and perhaps even upright incumbent of a particular social position. Recall what ALULEYA said to one nephew in "The Case of the Biassed Father": "You, B, I see you are really a man, because you said, 'My brothers, do not leave home.' And you went to your father to adjust matters. You should have persisted more, but your behaviour when you returned to Loziland shows you are really a man." "A man" here means one who tries to see that a family dispute is argued out and settled.

Again, in "The Case of the Man who Helped his Mother-in-Law Cross a Ford" a judge praised a girl who said she could not live with her husband after he saw her two maternal uncles' wives naked and slept with one of them. He told her husband: "I support your wife; she is a good girl, a true woman [wife]. If our children were the same, we would have children." Here the girl is praised because she recognizes her duties to her maternal uncles, so she is "a child," and these conflict with her duties as a woman and wife of their wives' seducer, so she is "a woman."

This usage is not, of course, peculiar to the Lozi. We have it in phrases such as, "he's a man—a gentleman—a sportsman—a king," and so on. In both cultures it implies approbation of a person showing the qualities and conforming to the norms demanded of a certain social position; or in the negative—as "*hasimulena yo,*" "he is not a chief,"—it states disapprobation of a person who has failed to show these qualities, or has exhibited contrary qualities, and has violated the appropriate norms. Note how in "The Case of the Eloping Wife" the judges said of her insults to her father: "Now your father has no child" ... "Find another father." But this sort of phrase, common though it be in everyday usage presumably everywhere, is of great sociological importance because it covers the whole social process of judging people against norms, and it is therefore very significant when it is used in the judicial process, as among the Lozi. It is their "reasonable person" differentiated by sex and in manifold social positions.

In addition to these phrases for the reasonable incumbent of a social position, the Lozi also apply the verb "*kuutwahala,*" "to be understandable," "to be obvious," "to be reasonable," to the whole of evidence or to particular actions. *Kuutwahala* is a derivative of *kuutwa,* to hear or understand, which is also used frequently by judges, *Kukolwahala,* to be credible, from *kukolwa* (to believe) is similarly used. -*Lukile,* right, is also applied to actions and to evidence; but I did not record this use of -*ngana,* sensible, without a noun of social position. Again, the Lozi do not always use these phrases explicitly—at least they do not appear often in my necessarily abbreviated records and I do not recall their frequent use. Unfortunately, while I was in the field I was not yet on the look-out for them. But I noted their appearance sufficiently often to be able to cite them as established legal concepts, and to say that they are always implicitly present in the judges' statement of norms against the recapitulation of witnessed or reported actions. These phrases too are commonly used outside the courts.

The judges therefore use in this aspect of their work a process and standards that are common throughout the society. They are setting up minimum standards which people ought to observe, if they are not to be punished, for various social positions. These are not always ideal standards, for Lozi ethics demands fulfilment of obligations beyond the basic reasonable norm, and generous refusal to insist on rights. The concept of "reasonable" measures the range of allowed departure from the highest standards of duty and absolute conformity to norm, and the minimum adherence which is insisted on. Professors Llewellyn and

Hoebel drew attention to this important problem in their *The Cheyenne Way: Conflict and Case Law in Primitive Jurisprudence*, when they wrote: "... one phenomenon of law, as of institutions in general, which has received altogether too little attention save in relation to bills of rights and the due process clause, is the two *ranges of leeway* of man's conduct which are a part of any legal or social system—the range of permissible leeway and the range of actively protected leeway."[91] Curiously, though Professor Llewellyn is a jurist, he did not suggest taking over the legal concept of "reasonable standards" to handle this problem, though I hope I have already shown how these standards among the Lozi cover both "the range of permissible leeway, and the range of actively protected leeway." Indeed, it seems to me that "the reasonable man" is more precisely the man who conforms reasonably to the customs and standards of his social position, clearly he corresponds closely with the concept of "the *rôle* of a particular *status*," which has become so important in current anthropology and sociology. The rôle of a status—for which I prefer the term (social) position to avoid the plural "statuses"—is that series of actions which a person ought to perform, and which his fellows are entitled to expect from him. Professors Parsons and Shils thus speak of the expectations of the rôle ... This qualification is important, for it sets those standards of conformity in meeting the demands of one's rôle which courts will enforce for a particular situation. The situations which confront people vary greatly, particularly at times when major social changes are occurring. Many rôles, defined in general terms such as "a husband must care for his wife," remain constant; but in all the variety of actual, and even changing, situation, the concept of "reasonableness" enables judgments to be passed on actions in terms of new as well as of established standards.[92] ...                    [pp. 125–129]

## L. L. FULLER
### Human Interaction and the Law
### (1969)[93]

This neglect of the phenomenon called customary law has, I think, done great damage to our thinking about law generally. Even if we accept the rather casual analysis of the subject offered by the treatises, it still remains true that a proper understanding of customary law is of capital importance in the world of today. In the first place, much of international law, and perhaps the most vital part of it, is essentially customary law. Upon the successful functioning of that body of law world peace may depend. In the second place, much of the world today is still governed internally by customary law. The newly emerging nations (notably in India, Africa, and the Pacific) are now engaged in a hazardous transition from systems of customary law to systems of enacted law. The stakes in this transition from systems of customary law to systems of enacted law. The stakes in this transition—for them and for us—are very high indeed. So the mere fact that we do not see ourselves as regulating our conduct toward fellow countrymen by customary law does not mean that it is of no importance to us as world citizens.

The thesis I am going to advance here is, however, something more radical than a mere insistence that customary law is still of considerable importance in the world of today. I am going to argue that we cannot understand "ordinary" law

---

[91] At p. 23.

[92] [On the contribution of Gluckman to anthropological thought see Handelman, in *Freedom and Constraint* (Aronoff, ed., (1976), p. 7. On his contribution to jurisprudence see G. MacCormack (1976) Jur.Rev. 229.]

[93] [From (1969) 14 Am. J. Jurisprud. 1.]

(that is, officially declared or enacted law) unless we first obtain an understanding of what is called customary law.[94]

In preparing my exposition I have to confess that at this point I encountered a great frustration. This arises from the term "customary law" itself. This is the term found in the titles and the indices, and if you want to compare what I have to say with what others have said, this is the heading you will have to look under. At the same time the expression "customary law" is a most unfortunate one that obscures, almost beyond redemption, the nature of the phenomenon it purports to designate. Instead of serving a neutral pointer, it prejudges its subject; it asserts that the force and meaning of what we call "customary law" lie in mere habit or usage.

Against this view I shall argue that the phenomenon called customary law can best be described as a *language of interaction*. To interact meaningfully men require a social setting in which the moves of the participating players will fall generally within some predictable pattern. To engage in effective social behavior men need the support of intermeshing anticipations that will let them know what their opposite numbers will do, or that will at least enable them to gauge the general scope of the repertory from which responses to their actions will be drawn. We sometimes speak of customary law as offering an unwritten "code of conduct." The word "code" is appropriate here because what is involved is not simply a negation, a prohibition of certain disapproved actions, but also the obverse side of this negation, the meaning it confers on foreseeable and approved actions, which then furnish a point of orientation for ongoing interactive responses. Professors Parsons and Shils have spoken of the function, in social action, of "complementary expectations"[95]; the term "complementary expectations" indicates accurately the function I am here ascribing to the law that develops out of human interaction, a form of law that we are forced—by the dictionaries and title headings—to call "customary law." ...        [pp. 2–3]

The first of these objections[96] is that customary law in primitive societies may lay down rules that have nothing to do with human interaction. There may be offenses against deities and spirits; a man may be punished, even by death, for an act committed out of the presence of other persons where that act violates some taboo. The answer to this is, I suggest, that animistic views of nature may vastly extend the significance one man's acts may have for his fellows ... The extent to which one man's beliefs and acts will be seen as affecting his fellows will depend upon the degree to which men see themselves as parts, one of another, and upon their beliefs about the intangible forces that unite them. Within the extended family the distinction between other-regarding and self-regarding acts will assume an aspect very different from what it has in our own society, composed, as that society is, largely of strangers with a strong disbelief in the supernatural.

A further objection to the conception of customary law as a language of interaction may be stated in these terms: Any such conception is much too rationalistic and attributes to customary law a functional aptness, a neatness of purpose, that is far from the realities of primitive practice. Customary law is filled with ritualistic routines and pointless ceremonies; these may cater to a certain instinct for drama, but they can hardly be said to serve effective communication or the development of stable expectations that will organize and facilitate interaction.

In answer I would assert, on the contrary, that a significant function of ritual is precisely that of communication, of labelling acts so that there can be no mistake as to their meaning ... Certainly among a people who have no state-kept official records to show who is married to whom, the elaborate wedding ceremonies

---

[94] [This thesis is also presented by M. Barkun in *Law Without Sanctions* (1968).]
[95] Talcott Parsons and Edward Shils, *Toward a General Theory of Action* (1951), p. 64.
[96] [*i.e.* to treating customary law as a language of interaction.]

found in some customary systems can be said to serve a purpose of communication and clarification.

To illustrate the points I have been making with regard to ritualism, and, more generally, with regard to the communicative function of customary practices, I should like to refer briefly to a development that appears to be occurring in the diplomatic relations of Russia and the United States. Here we may be witnessing something like customary law in the making. Between these two countries there seems to have arisen a kind of reciprocity with respect to the forced withdrawal of diplomatic representatives. The American government, for example, believes that a member of the Russian embassy is engaged in espionage, or, perhaps I should say, it believes him to be *over*engaged in espionage; it declares him *persona non grata* and requires his departure from this country. The expected response, based on past experience, is that Russia will acquiesce in this demand, but will at once counter with a demand for the withdrawal from Russia of an American diplomatic agent of equal rank. Conversely, if the Russians expel an American emissary, the United States will react by shipping back one of Russia's envoys.

Here we have, for the time being at least, a quite stable set of interactional expectancies; within the field covered by this practice each country is able to anticipate with considerable confidence the reactions of its opposite number. This means that its decisions can be guided by a tolerably accurate advance estimate of costs. We know that if we throw one of their men out, they will throw out one of ours.

It should be noticed that the practice is routinized and contains (at least latently) ritualistic and symbolic qualities. Suppose, for example, that the American authorities were confronted with this dilemma: the Russians have declared *persona non grata* a high-ranking member of the American embassy in Moscow, and it turns out to be difficult to find an appropriate counterpart for return to Russia. We may suppose, for example, that the Soviet representatives of equal rank with the expelled American are persons Washington would like very much to see remain in this country. In this predicament it could cross the minds of those responsible for the decision that they might, in order to preserve a proper balance, return to Russia five men of a lower rank than the expelled American, or perhaps even that the expulsion of ten filing clerks would be the most apt response.

Now I suggest that any responsible public official would reflect a long time before embracing such an alternative. Its danger would lie in the damage it would inflict of the neat symbolism of a one-to-one ratio, in the confusion it might introduce into the accepted meaning of the acts involved. This is a case where both sides would probably be well-advised to stick with the familiar ritual since a departure from it might forfeit the achieved gains of a stable interactional pattern.

The illustration just discussed may seem badly chosen because it represents, one might say, a very impoverished kind of customary law, a law that confers, not a reciprocity of benefits, but a reciprocity in expressions of hostility. But much of the customary law of primitive peoples, it should be recalled, serves exactly the same function. Open and unrestricted hostilities between tribes often become in time subject to tacit and formalized restraints and may, in the end, survive only as a ritualistic mock battle.[97] Furthermore, in the diplomatic practice I have described here there may be present a richer reciprocity than appears on the surface. At the time of the *Pueblo* incident it was suggested that Russia and the United States may share an interest in being moderately and discreetly spied on by one another. We don't want the Russians to pry out our military secrets, but we want them to know, on the basis of information they will trust, that we are not planning to mount a surprise attack on them. This shared interest may furnish

---

[97] There is thus less paradox than might at first appear in the title of Paul Bohannan's anthology, *Law and Warfare—Studies in the Anthropology of Conflict* (1967).

part of the background of the ritualistic and patterned exchange of diplomatic discourtesies that seems to be developing between the two countries....[pp. 5–8]

...How much of what is called customary law really deserves the epithet "law"? Anthropologists have devoted some attention to this question and have arrived at divergent responses to it, including one which asserts that the question is itself misconceived, since you cannot apply a conception interwoven with notions of explicit enactment to a social context where rules of conduct come into existence without the aid of a lawmaker. Among those who take the question seriously the answer proposed by Hoebel has perhaps attracted the most attention; it will repay us to consider it for a moment. Hoebel suggests that in dealing with stateless or primitive societies

> ...law may be defined in these terms: A social norm is legal if its neglect or infraction is regularly met, in threat or in fact, by the application of physical force by an individual or group possessing the socially recognized privilege of so acting.[98]

There are, I suggest, a number of difficulties with this solution. First, it seems to define "law" by an imperfection. If the function of law is to produce an ordered relationship among the members of a society, what shall we say of a system that works so smoothly that there is never any occasion to resort to force or the threat of force to effectuate its norms? Does its very success forfeit for such a system the right to be called by the prestigious name of "law"?

Again, can it always be known in advance whether the infraction of some particular norm will be visited with forceful reprisal? The seriousness of the breach of any rule is always in some measure a function of context. One might be inclined to hazard a guess that few societies would regularly punish with violence infractions of the rules of etiquette. Suppose, however, that a peacemaking conference is held by delegations representing two tribes on the verge of war; a member of one delegation uses an insulting nickname in addressing his opposite number; the result is a bloody and disastrous war. Is it likely that his fellow tribesmen would be content to visit on the offender some moderate measure of social censure? If this illustration seems contrived, it may be observed that in our free society it is an accepted legal principle that a man incurs no liability for expressing to another a low opinion of his intelligence and integrity. If a lawyer trying a case in court were to take advantage of this freedom in addressing the judge, he might very well find himself escorted forcibly from the courtroom to serve a jail sentence for contempt.

Perhaps the basic objection to Hoebel's proposal is that it ignores the *systematic* quality of primitive law. The law of the tribe or extended family is not simply a chart of do's and don'ts; it is a program for living together. Some parts of the program may achieve articulation as distinct "norms" imposing specially defined "sanctions." But the basic logic of customary law will continue to inhere in the system as a whole. Lévi-Strauss may seem at times to drive this quality of primitive social orders to the point of caricature,[99] but if so, his efforts have provided a wholesome antidote to the tendency to assume that any customary system can be reduced to a kind of code book of numbered paragraphs, each paragraph standing forth as a little law complete in itself.

A recent controversy among anthropologists is worthy of consideration in this connection. In his famous book, *The Judicial Process among the Barotse of Northern Rhodesia*, Max Gluckman suggested that a key element of Barotse legal reasoning lay in the concept of "the reasonable man." The fact that this concept also plays a role in more "advanced" systems argued, so Gluckman concluded,

[98] E. Adamson Hoebel, *The Law of Primitive Man* (1954), p. 28.
[99] See Claude Lévi-Strauss, *The Savage Mind* (1962, English trans. 1966).

for a certain unity in legal reasoning everywhere. This conclusion was rather emphatically rejected by a number of his professional colleagues.[1]

Perhaps it may help to clarify the issues by considering a rule of law, familiar to every reader, that is at least customary in origin. I refer to "the rule of the road" by which (over most of the world) one passes the oncoming vehicle on the right. Now it would seem redundant and even absurd to introduce into this context anything like the concept of the reasonable man; I pass on the right, not because I am a reasonable man, but because it is the rule. But suppose a situation is encountered in which the presuppositions underlying the rule no longer hold. For example, one is driving in a parking lot, without marked lanes, where other vehicles are coming and going, backing and turning. Or, driving on a regular highway, one encounters an approaching vehicle careering back and forth across the road apparently out of control. In situations like these what is demanded is plainly something like the judgment and concern of "the reasonable man"; in such a context the rule of the road can furnish at most a kind of presumptive guide as to what to do when other factors in the situation offer no clear solution.

Primitive society, like vehicular traffic, is run by a system of interlocking roles. When one man steps out of his role, or a situation arises in which a familiar role forfeits some or all of its meaning, then adjustments will have to be made. There can be no formula to guide these adjustments beyond that of "reasonableness"— exercised in the light of the demands of the system as a whole. ... [pp. 10–12]

...If we permit ourselves to think of "contract law" as the "law" that the parties themselves bring into existence by their agreement, the transition from customary law to contract law becomes a very easy one indeed. The difficulty then becomes, not that of subsuming the two kinds of law under one rubric, but of knowing how to draw a clear line of division between them. We may say of course (using the jargon I have inflicted on the reader here) that in the one case the relevant interactional expectancies are created by words; in the other, by actions.

But this is too simple a view of the matter. Where words are used, they have to be interpreted. When the contract falls within some general area of repetitive dealings, there will usually exist a body of "standard practice" in the light of which verbal ambiguities will be resolved. Here, in effect, interactional regularities in the world outside the contract are written into the contract in the process of interpretation. In commercial law generally it is often difficult to know whether to say that by entering a particular field of practice the parties became subject to a governing body of customary law or to say that they have by tacit agreement incorporated standard practice into the terms of their contract.

The meaning of a contract may not only be determined by the area of practice within which the contract falls, but by the interactions of the parties themselves after entering their agreement. If the performance of a contract takes place over a period of time, the parties will often evidence by their conduct what courts sometimes call a "practical construction" of their agreement; this interpretation by deeds may have control over the meaning that would ordinarily be attributed to the words of the contract itself. If the discrepancy between the parties' acts and the words of their agreement becomes too great to permit the courts to speak of a "practical construction," they may hold that the contract has been tacitly modified or even rescinded by the manner in which the parties have conducted themselves towards one another since entering the agreement.

Generally we may say that in the actual carrying out of a complex agreement between friendly parties, the written contract often furnishes a kind of framework for an ongoing relationship, rather than a precise definition of that relationship. For that definition we may have to look to a kind of two-party customary law implicit in the parties' actions, rather than to the verbal formulations of the

---

[1] Llewellyn, *op. cit., supra*, pp. 82–162, 387–398. (Gluckman's answer to critics on this point will be found in the second reference.) [And see *ante*, 1109.]

contract; if this is true of contracts that are eventually brought to court, it must be much more commonly so in situations where the parties make out without resort to litigation.

If the words of a contract have to be interpreted in their interactional context, or in the light of the actions taken under them by the parties, the actions that bring customary law into existence also have to be interpreted sometimes almost as if they were words. This problem of interpretation is at once the most crucial and most neglected problem of customary law, intrinsically difficult, it is made more so by inept theories about the nature of customary law; such as those explaining it as an expression of "the force of habit" that "prevails in the early history of the race."

The central problem of "interpretation" in customary law is that of knowing when to read into an act, or a pattern of repetitive acts, an obligatory sense like that which may attach to a promise explicitly spelled out in words. All are agreed that a person, a tribe, or a nation does not incur an obligation—"legal" or "moral"—simply because a repetitive pattern can be discerned in his or its actions. All would probably also agree that the actions which create customary law must be such as enter into *interactions*, though a complication ensues when we recall that under some circumstances inaction can take on the qualities of action, as when it becomes appropriate to call it "acquiescence" or "forbearance." Beyond this we encounter almost a vacuum of ideas.

Into this vacuum there is projected at least one articulate attempt at formulating a test. This is found in the doctrine of *opinio necessitatis*. According to this principle (which still enjoys some esteem in international law) customary law arises out of repetitive actions when and only when such actions are motivated by a sense of obligation, in other words, when people behave as they do, not because they want to, or because they act unreflectively, but because they believe they have to act as they do. This seems a curiously inept solution. In clear cases of established customary law, it becomes a tautology; in situations where customary law is in the process of being born, it defaults. ...                                    [pp. 14–16]

The familiar phenomenon of the spread of customary law from one social context to another suggests a further distinction between customary law and contract law that deserves critical examination here. It may be said that a contract binds only the parties to it, while customary law normally extends its rules over a large and at times somewhat unclearly defined community. The first observation is that while this spread of customary law is a common occurrence it is by no means inevitable. Something that can be called two-party customary law can and does exist; it is, again, only linguistic prejudice that makes us hesitant about this employment of the word "law."

Where customary law does in fact spread we must not be misled as to the process by which this extension takes place. It has sometimes been thought of as if it involved a kind of inarticulate expression of group will; the members of *Group B* perceive that the rules governing *Group A* would furnish an apt law for them; they therefore take over those rules by an act of tacit collective adoption. This kind of explanation abstracts from the interactional processes underlying customary law and ignores their ever-present communicative aspect. Take, for example, a practice in the field of international relations, that of offering a twenty-one-gun salute to visiting heads of state. By a process of imitation this practice seems now to have become fairly general among the nations. One may say loosely that its appeal lies in the appropriateness of a resounding boom of cannon as a way of signalizing the arrival of a distinguished visitor. But why twenty-one guns, instead of sixteen or twenty-five? It is apparent that once the pattern of twenty-one became familiar, any departure from it could generate misapprehension; spectators would spend their time, not in enjoying the grandeur of cannon roar, but in counting booms, attributing all sorts of meanings—intended and unintended—to any departure from the last allocation. Generally we may say that where *A* and *B* have become familiar with a practice, obtaining between *C* and *D*, *A* is likely to adopt this pattern in his actions towards *B*, not simply or necessarily because it has any special aptness for their situation, but because he knows *B* will understand the meaning of his behavior and will know how to react to it.

As for the proposition that a contract binds only those who made it, who actively and knowingly assented to its terms, a mere glance at modern contracting practice is sufficient to reveal how unreal and purely formal this proposition can become. Only a tiny fraction of the "contracts" signed today are actually negotiated or represent anything like an explicit accommodation of the parties' respective interests. Even contracts drafted by lawyers, and in theory specially fitted to the parties' situation, are apt to be full of traditional or "standard" clauses borrowed from other contracts and from general practice. These clauses are employed for a great variety of reasons—because the lawyer is in a hurry, or because he knows from the precedents how the courts will construe them, or because the interests at stake are insufficient to justify the fee that would be appropriate to a more careful, specially tailored phrasing.

But the realities of contracting practice are much farther removed from the picture of a "meeting of minds" than is suggested by a mere reference to standard clauses. In fact, the overwhelming majority of contracts are embodied in printed forms, prepared by one party to serve his interests and imposed on the other on a take-it-or-leave-it basis...

There remains for discussion one further distinction that can be made between contract law and customary law. This lies in the notion that a contract comes into effect at once, or when the parties stipulate it shall, while custom becomes law only through a usage observed to have persisted over a considerable period.

This is, again, too simple a view of the matter. The notion that customary law comes into effect gradually and only over a considerable period of time comes about, in part because of mistaken implications read into the word "customary," and in part because it is true that normally it takes some time for reciprocal interactional expectancies to "jell." But there are circumstances in which customary law (or a phenomenon for which we have no other name) can develop almost overnight. ... [pp. 16–18]

As for the notion that a contract binds at once, and before any action has been taken under it, this is again a misleading simplification, especially when the matter is viewed historically....

It appears likely that in all legal systems the enforcement of the executory bilateral contract is a development that comes quite late.[2] ... with the development of something like a market economy. ... [p. 19]

I have treated both customary law and contract law as interactional phenomena. I have viewed them as arising out of interaction and as serving to order and facilitate interaction. Can anything like this be asserted of enacted law, as typified, for example, by the statute? Can we regard enacted law itself as dependent on the development of "stable interactional expectancies" between lawgiver and subject? Does enacted law also serve the purpose of ordering and facilitating the interactions of citizens with one another?...

Let us test the question whether enacted law serves to put in order and facilitate human interaction by inquiring how this conception applies to some actual branches of the law ... consider the law embraced under the following headings: contract, agency, marriage and divorce, property (both private and public), and the rules of court procedure ... they facilitate human interaction as traffic is facilitated by the laying out of roads and the installation of direction signs. To say that these branches of law would be unnecessary if men were more disposed to act morally is like saying that language could be dispensed with if only men were

---

[2] [It developed in English law only in the seventeenth century. See Milsom, *Historical Foundations of the Common Law* (1981), Chap. 12.]

intelligent enough to communicate without it. The fact that the branches of law just listed include restraints as well as enabling provisions detracts in no sense from their facilitative quality; there is no more paradox here than there is in the proposition that highway traffic can be expedited by signs that read, "NO LEFT TURN," "STOP, THEN ENTER."

An interactional theory of law can hardly claim acceptance, however, simply because it seems apt when applied to certain branches of the law, such as contracts, property, agency, and marital rights. The law of crimes, for example, presents a quite different test, for here an interactional view encounters an environment much less congenial to its premises. There would, for example, be something ludicrous about explaining the rule against murder as being intended to facilitate human interaction by removing from men's confrontations the fear that they may kill one another. Murder, we are likely to say, is prohibited because it is wrong, not because the threat of it can detract from the potential richness of man's relations with his fellows.

Viewed from a historical perspective, however, the matter assumes a very different aspect. Students of primitive society have seen the very inception of the concept of law itself in limitations on the blood feud. A member of *Family A* kills a member of *Family B*. In a primitive society the natural response to this act is for the members of *Family B* to seek revenge against *Family A*. If no limits are set to this revenge, there may ensue a war to the death between the two families. There has, accordingly, grown up in many primitive societies a rule that blood revenge on the part of *Family B* must, in the case supposed, be limited to one killing, though the injured family is regarded as being entitled as of right to this degree of counterkill. A later development will normally prohibit blood revenge and require instead compensation in the form of "blood money" for the life of the man whose life was taken. Here, plainly, the law of murder serves to regulate interaction and, if you will, to facilitate interaction on a level more profitable for all concerned than killing and counterkilling.

Today the law against murder appears on the surface to have become entirely divorced from its interactional origins; it is seen as projecting its imperative, "thou shalt not kill," over the members of society generally and without regard to their interrelations. But what has in fact happened is that interactional issues that were once central have, as the result of legal and moral progress, been pushed to the periphery, where they remain as lively as ever. The most obvious example is offered by the plea of self-defence; a man is still legally privileged to kill an aggressor if this is necessary to save his own life. But how shall we interpret "necessary" in this context? How far can we expect a man to run some risk to his own life in order to avoid taking the life of another? Again, there is the question of reducing the degree of the offense when a man kills in "hot blood," as when he comes upon another making love to his wife. Finally, there are the disputed issues of killing to prevent a felony or to stop a fleeing felon. In all these much-debated cases the rule against homicide may be modified, or punishment reduced, by a reference to the question: what can reasonably be expected of a man in these interactional situations?

... There are, certainly, some manifestations of law which cannot readily be forced into this frame of thought. Perhaps the most significant of these lies in that portion of the criminal law relating to what have been called "crimes without victims." ...

It is no accident ... that it is in this area ... that the grossest failure of law have everywhere occurred. ...

We should begin by asking ourselves why the law fails so notably in this general area of "crimes without victims." The usual answer is that you cannot enforce morality by law. But this is not so. Keeping promises may be a moral obligation, yet the law can and does successfully force people to keep their promises. Not only that, but the legal enforcement of promises, far from weakening the moral sense of obligation, tends to strengthen it. Suppose, for example, a situation where men associated in some business enterprise are discussing whether they ought to perform a disadvantageous contract. Those who believe they are morally bound to do so are in a position to remind their less principled associates that if the contract is broken they will all be brought to court and will subject themselves, not only to the cost, but also to the opprobrium of an adverse judgment. There are areas of human concern, then, where the cliche that you can't make men act morally by law does not hold. These are, I believe, precisely the areas where the law's sanctions reinforce interactional expectancies and facilitate a respect for them.

In dealing with primitive systems a distinction is sometimes taken between wrongs and sins.[3] A wrong is an act that inflicts a palpable damage on the fabric of social relations; a sin is thought to work a more diffuse harm by spreading a kind of corruption. Typically in primitive societies wrongs and sins are dealt with by different standards and different procedures, formalized "due process" being not uncommonly relaxed in the case of sins. While I would not recommend a resort to sorcery or ostracism as a way of dealing with modern sins, I think we might profitably borrow from primitive society some of the wisdom displayed in the basic distinction between wrongs and sins. Perhaps we might also add to that wisdom the insight that the best way for the law to deal with at least some modern sins is to leave them alone.... [pp. 20–23]

It is time now to turn to what may seem the more basic question: Does enacted law itself depend for its existence on the development of "stable interactional expectancies" between lawgiver and subject?...

The law does not tell a man what he should do to accomplish specific ends set by the lawgiver; it furnishes him with base lines against which to organize his life with his fellows. A transgression of these base lines may entail serious consequences for the citizen—he may be hanged for it—but the establishment of the base lines is not an exercise in managerial direction. Law provides a framework for the citizen within which to live his own life, though, to be sure, there are circumstances under which that framework can seem so uncomfortably lax or so perversely constrictive that its human object may believe that straightforward managerial direction would be preferable.

If we accept the view that the central purpose of law is to furnish base lines for human interaction, it then becomes apparent why the existence of enacted law as an effectively functioning system depends upon the establishment of stable interactional expectancies between lawgiver and subject. On the one hand, the lawgiver must be able to anticipate that the citizenry as a whole will accept as law and generally observe the body of rules he has promulgated. On the other hand, the legal subject must be able to anticipate that government will itself abide by its own declared rules when it comes to judge his actions, as in deciding, for example, whether he has committed a crime or claims property under a valid deed. A gross failure in the realization of either of these anticipations—of government toward citizen and of citizen toward government—can have the result that the most carefully drafted code will fail to become a functioning system of law.... [p. 24]

...The first observation is that this form of law[4] is at home completely across the spectrum of social contexts, from the most intimate to those of open hostility. That the family cannot easily organize itself by a process of explicit bargaining does not mean there will not grow up within it reciprocal expectancies of the sort that, on a more formal level, would be called "customary law." Indeed, the family could not function without these tacit guidelines to interaction; if every interaction had to be oriented afresh and ad hoc, no group like the family could succeed in the discharge of its shared tasks. At the midrange, it should be observed that

---

[3] See, *e.g.* Henry Maine, *Ancient Law* (10th ed., 1884), pp. 359–361.

[4] [*i.e.* customary law.]

the most active and conspicuous development of customary law in modern times lies precisely in the field of commercial dealings. Finally, while enemies may have difficulty in bargaining with words, they can, and often do, profitably half-bargain with deeds. Paradoxically the tacit restraints of customary law between enemies are more likely to develop during active warfare than during a hostile stalemate of relations; fighting one another is itself in this sense a "social" relation since it involves communication.

That customary law is, as I have expressed it, "at home" across the entire spectrum of social contexts does not mean that it retains the same qualities wherever it appears. On the contrary, it can change drastically in nature as it moves from one end of the spectrum to the other. At the terminal point of intimacy customary law has to do, not primarily with prescribed acts and performances, but with roles and functions. The internal operations of a family, kinship group, or even tribe, may demand, not simply formal compliance with rules, but an allocation of authority, and a sense of trusteeship on the part of those who make decisions and give directions. In the middle area, typified by arm's length commercial dealings, customary law abstracts from qualities and dispositions of the person and concentrates its attention on ascribing appropriate and clearly defined consequences to outward conduct. Finally, as we enter the area of hostile relations, a decided change in the general "flavor" of customary law takes place. Here the prime desideratum is to achieve—through acts, of course, not words—the clear communication of messages of a rather limited and negative import; accordingly there is a heavy concentration on symbolism and ritual.

The influence of social context should be borne in mind, I suggest, in weighing against one another the sometimes conflicting views of anthropologists as to the nature of customary law. It is interesting in this connection to compare two works that have become classics: Malinowski, *Crime and Custom in Savage Society* (1926), and Gluckman, *The Judicial Process Among the Barotse of Northern Rhodesia* (1955, 2d ed. 1967).

Malinowski sees the central principle of customary law in a reciprocity of benefits conferred; he even suggests, in one incautious moment, that the sanction which insures compliance with the rules of customary law lies in a tacit threat that if a man does not make his contribution, others may withhold theirs. Though Gluckman is for the most part careful in limiting his generalizations to the particular society he studied, he seems to see as a central concept of customary law generally that of "the reasonable man." "The reasonable man," for Gluckman, is the man who knows his station and its responsibilities and who responds aptly to the shifting demands of group life. Simplifying somewhat we may say that the central figure for Manilowski is essentially a trader, albeit one who trades on terms largely set by tradition rather than by negotiation. For Gluckman it is the conscientious tribesman with a sense of trusteeship for the welfare of the group.

When we observe, however, the internal economic and kinship organizations of the two societies studied, it becomes apparent why the two scholars should arrive at such divergent conceptions of the model of man implicit in customary law. Malinowski begins his account by observing that the human objects of his study, who live dispersed on different islands, are "keen on trade and exchange." The first concrete situation he discusses involves two village communities on the same island at some distance from each other, the one being located on the coast, the other inland. Under a "standing arrangement" between the two, the coastal village regularly supplies the inland village with fish, receiving in return vegetables. The "trade" between the two is not, of course, the product of explicit bargaining, and indeed at times each of the villages will seek, not to give short measure, but to put the other to shame by outproducing it.

Among Gluckman's Barotse, on the other hand, economic production and consumption are organized largely on a kinship basis. The cases before the *kuta* studies by Gluckman were chiefly cases that might be described as involving the internal affairs of an extended family, though those affairs included some property disputes. Something of the range of the cases studied is suggested by sampling of the titles Gluckman assigns to them: "The Case of the Cross-Cousin Adultery," "The Case of the Wife's Granary," "The Case of the Urinating Husband," "The Case of the Headman's Fishdams (or) the 'Dog-in-the-Manager' Headman." The atmosphere of the arguments and decisions, reported so vividly by Gluckman, reminds one of what might be expected in a court of domestic relations, mediating the tangled affairs of the family and, occasionally and reluctantly, exercising a power to put them straight by judicial fiat.

The two systems of customary law studied by Malinowski and Gluckman operated, it is plain, in quite different social contexts, though this does not mean that a Malinowski might not find elements of reciprocity or exchange among the Barotse, or that a Gluckman could not find apt occasion to apply the concept of "the reasonable man" among the Trobrianders. I would suggest generally that if we seek to discover constancies among the different systems of customary law we shall find them in the interactional processes by which those systems come into being, rather than in the specific product that emerges, which must of necessity reflect history and context.[5]...                                   [pp. 31–33]

## PAUL BOHANNAN
### The Differing Realms of the Law
### (1965)[6]

#### *Double Institutionalization*

Law must be distinguished from traditions and fashions and, more specifically, it must be differentiated from norm and from custom. A norm is a rule, more or less overt, which expresses "ought" aspects of relationships between human beings. Custom is a body of such norms—including regular deviations and compromises with norms—that is actually followed in practice much of the time.

All social institutions are marked by "customs" and these "customs" exhibit most of the stigmata cited by any definition of law. But there is one salient difference. Whereas custom continues to inhere in, and only in, these institutions which it governs (and which in turn govern it), law is specifically recreated, by agents of society, in a narrower and recognizable context—that is, in the context of the institutions that are legal in character and, to some degree at least, discrete from all others.

Just as custom includes norms, but is both greater and more precise than norms, so law includes custom, but is both greater and more precise. Law has the additional characteristic that it must be what Kantorowicz calls "justiciable,"[7] by which he means that the rules must be capable of reinterpretation, and actually must be reinterpreted, by one of the legal institutions of society so that the conflicts within nonlegal institutions can be adjusted by an "authority" outside themselves.

It is widely recognized that many peoples of the world can state more or less precise "rules" which are, in fact, the norms in accordance with which they think they ought to judge their conduct. In all societies there are allowable lapses from

---

[5]  [Fuller's view of law in terms of the facilitation of human interaction has influenced two "law and development" scholars, Meagher and Smith, *Law and the Development Practitioner* (1974).]

[6]  [In 67 *American Anthropologist*, No. 6, Pt II, pp. 33–42; extract taken from the reprint in *Law and Warfare* (Bohannan ed., (1967).]

[7]  [In *The Definition of Law* (1958), p. 76.]

such rules, and in most there are more or less precise rules (sometimes legal ones) for breaking rules.

In order to make the distinction between law and other rules, it has been necessary to introduce furtively the word "institution." I use the word in Malinowski's sense.[8]

A legal institution is one by means of which the people of society settle disputes that arise between one another and counteract any gross and flagrant abuses of the rules (as we have considered them above) of at least some of the other institutions of society. Even ongoing society has legal institutions in this sense, as well as a wide variety of nonlegal institutions.

In carrying out the task of settling difficulties in the nonlegal institutions, legal institutions face three kinds of tasks: (1) There must be specific ways in which difficulties can be disengaged from the institutions in which they arose and which they now threaten and then be engaged within the process of the legal institution. (2) There must be ways in which the trouble can now be handled within the framework of the legal institution, and (3) There must be ways in which the new solutions which thus emerge can be re-engaged within the processes of the non-legal institutions from which they emerged. It is seldom that any framework save a political one can supply these requirements.

There are, thus, at least two aspects of legal institutions that are not shared with other institutions of society. Legal institutions—and often they alone—must have some regularized way to interfere in the malfunctioning (and, perhaps, the functioning as well) of the nonlegal institutions in order to disengage the trouble-case. There must, secondly, be two kinds of rules in the legal institutions—those that govern the activities of the legal institution itself (called "adjectival law" by Austin, and "procedure" by most modern lawyers), and those that are substitutes or modifications or restatements of the rules of the nonlegal institution that has been invaded (called "substantive law").[9]

Listed above are only the minimal aspects that are all shared by all known legal institutions....

Seen in this light, a fairly simple distinction can be made between law and custom. Customs are norms or rules (more or less strict, and with greater or less support of moral, ethical, or even physical coercion) about the ways in which people must behave if social institutions are to perform their tasks and society is to endure. All institutions (including legal institutions) develop customs. Some customs, in some societies, are reinstitutionalized at another level: they are restated for the more precise purposes of legal institutions. When this happens, therefore, law may be regarded as a custom that has been restated in order to make it amenable to the activities of the legal institutions. In this sense, it is one of the most characteristic attributes of legal institutions that some of these "laws" are about the legal institutions themselves, although most are about the other institutions of society—the familial, economic, political, ritual, or whatever.

One of the reddest herrings ever dragged into the working of orderly jurisprudence was Malinowski's little book called *Crime and Custom in Savage Society* ... It has had an undue and all but disastrous influence on the rapprochement between anthropology and jurisprudence. Malinowski's idea was a good one; he claimed that law is "a body of binding obligations regarded as right by one party and acknowledged as the duty by the other, kept in force by the specific mechanism of reciprocity and publicity inherent in the structure of ... society." His error was in equating what he had defined with the law. It is not law that is "kept in force by ... reciprocity and publicity." It is custom, as we have defined it here. Law is, rather, "a body of binding obligations regarded as right by one party and acknowledged as the duty by the other" *which has been re-*

---

[8]  *The Dynamics of Culture Change.*
[9]  [*Cf.* Hart's classification of primary and secondary rules, *ante*, 376.]

*institutionalized within the legal institution so that society can continue to function in an orderly manner on the basis of rules so maintained.* In short, reciprocity is the basis of custom; but the law rests on the basis of this double institutionalization. Central in it is that some of the customs of some of the institutions of society are restated in such a way that they can be "applied" by an institution designed (or, at very least, utilized) specifically for that purpose.

One of the best ways to perceive the double institutionalized norms, or "laws," is to break up the law into smaller components, capable of attaching to persons (either human individuals or corporate groups) and so to work in terms of "rights" and their reciprocal duties or "obligations." In terms of rights and duties, the relationships between law and custom, law and morals, law and anything else, can be seen in a new light. Whether in the realm of kinship or contract, citizenship or property rights, the relationships between people can be reduced to a series of prescriptions with the obligations and the correlative rights that emanate from these presumptions. In fact, if it is not carried too far and unduly formalized, thinking in terms of rights and obligations of persons (or role players) is a convenient and fruitful way of investigating much of the custom of many institutions.[10] Legal rights are only those rights that attach to norms that have been doubly institutionalized; they provide a means for seeing the legal institutions from the standpoint of the persons engaged in them.

The phenomenon of double institutionalization of norms and therefore of legal rights has been recognized for a long time, but analysis of it has been only "justiciability" of the law. It would be better to say that legal rights have their material origins (either overly or covertly) in the customs of nonlegal institutions but must be *overtly restated* for the specific purpose of enabling the legal institutions to perform their task.

A legal right (and, with it, a law) is the restatement, for the purpose of maintaining peaceful and just operation of the institutions of society, of some, but never all, of the recognized claims of the persons within those institutions; the restatement must be made in such a way that these claims can be more or less assured by the total community or its representatives. Only so can the moral, religious, political, and economic implications of law be fully explored.

Law is never a mere reflection of custom, however. Rather, law is always out of phase with society, specifically because of the duality of the statement and restatement of rights. Indeed, the more highly developed the legal institutions, the greater the lack of phase, which not only results from the constant reorientation of the primary institutions, but also is magnified by the very dynamic of the legal institutions themselves.[11]

Thus, it is the very nature of law, and its capacity to "do something about" the primary social institutions, that creates the lack of phase. Moreover, even if one could assume perfect legal institutionalization, change within the primary institutions would soon jar the system out of phase again. What is less obvious is that if there were ever to be perfect phase between law and custom, then society could never repair itself, grow and change, flourish or wane. It is the fertile dilemma of law that it must always be out of step with society, but that people must always (because they work better with fewer contradictions, if for no other reason) attempt to reduce the lack of phase. Custom must either grow to fit the law or it must actively reject it; law must either grow to fit the custom, or it must ignore or suppress it. It is in these very interstices that social growth and social decay take place.

Social catastrophe and social indignation are sources of much law and resultant changes in custom. With technical and moral change, new situations appear that must be "legalized." This truth has particular and somewhat different

---

[10] [See Hohfeld, *ante*, 569; Hoebel, *ante*, 1103.]
[11] *Legal Systems and Lawyers' Reasonings* (1964), Chap. 1, Pt 1.

applications to developed and to less highly developed legal systems. On the one hand, in developed municipal systems of law in which means for institutionalizing behaviour on a legal level are already traditionally concentrated in political decision-making groups such as legislatures, nonlegal social institutions sometimes take a very long time to catch up with the law. On the other hand, in less developed legal systems, it may be that little or no popular demand is made on the legal institutions, and therefore little real contact exists or can be made to exist between them and the primary institutions.[12] Law can become one of the major innovators of society, the more effective the greater a people's dependence on it....                                                                                                  [pp. 45–50]

## S. DIAMOND
### The Rule of Law versus the Order of Custom
### (1971)[13]

We must distinguish the rule of law from the authority of custom. In a recent effort to do so (which I shall critically examine because it is so typical), Paul Bohannan contends that laws result from "double" institutionalization. He means by this no more than the lending of a specific force, a cutting edge, to the functioning of "customary" institutions: marriage, the family, religion. But, he tells us, the laws so emerging assume a character and dynamic of their own. They form a structured, legal dimension of society; they do not merely reflect, but interact with given institutions. Therefore, Bohannan is led to maintain that laws are typically out of phase with society and it is this process which is both a symptom and cause of social change. The laws of marriage, to illustrate Bohannan's argument with the sort of concrete example his definition lacks, are not synonymous with the institution of marriage. They reinforce certain rights and obligations while neglecting others. Moreover, they subject partners defined as truant to intervention by an external, impersonal agency whose decisions are sanctioned by the power of the police.

Bohannan's sociological construction does have the virtue of denying the primacy of the legal order, and of implying that law is generic to unstable (or progressive) societies, but it is more or less typical of abstract efforts to define the eternal essence of the law and it begs the significant questions. Law has no such essence but a definable historical nature.

Thus if we inquire into the structure of the contemporary institutions which, according to Bohannan, stand in a primary relation to the law, we find that their customary content has drastically diminished. Paul Radin made the point as follows: "A custom is, in no sense, a part of our property functioning culture. It belongs definitely to the past. At best, it is moribund. But customs are an integral part of the life of primitive peoples. There is no compulsive submission to them. They are not followed because the weight of tradition overwhelms a man ... a custom is obeyed there because it is intimately intertwined with a vast living network of interrelations, arranged in a meticulous and ordered manner."[14] And, "What is significant in this connection," as J. G. Peristiany indicates, "is not that common values should exist, but that they should be expressed although no common political organization corresponds to them."[15]

No contemporary institution functions with the kind of autonomy that permits us to postulate a significant dialect between law and custom. We live in a law-

---

12  *Social Dimensions of Law and Justice* (1965), Chap. 2, s. 17.
13  [From (1971) 38 *Social Research* 42.]
14  Paul Radin, *The World of Primitive Man* (1953), p. 223.
15  J. G. Peristiany, *The Institutions of Primitive Society* (1956), p. 45.

ridden society; law has cannibalized the institutions which it presumably reinforces or with which it interacts.

Accordingly, morality continues to be reduced to or confused with legality. In civil society we are encouraged to assume that legal behavior is the measure of moral behavior, and it is a matter of some interest that a former Chief Justice of the Supreme Court proposed, with the best of intentions, that a federal agency be established in order to advise government employees and those doing business with the government concerning the legal propriety of their behavior. Any conflict of interest not legally enjoined would thus tend to become socially or morally acceptable; morality becomes a technical question. Efforts to legislate conscience by an external political power are the antithesis of custom: customary behavior comprises precisely those aspects of social behavior which are traditional, moral, and religious, which are, in short, conventional and non-legal. Put another way, custom *is* social morality.[16] The relation between custom and law is, basically, one of contradiction, not continuity.

The customary and legal orders are historically, not logically related. They touch coincidentally; one does not imply the other. Custom, as most anthropologists agree, is characteristic of primitive society, and laws of civilization. Robert Redfield's dichotomy between the primitive "moral" order and the civilized "legal" or "technical" order remains a classic statement of the case.

"The dispute," writes William Seagle, "whether primitive societies have law or custom, is not merely a dispute over words. Only confusion can result from treating them as interchangeable phenomena. If custom is spontaneous and automatic, law is the product of organized force. Reciprocity is in force in civilized communities too but at least nobody confuses social with formal legal relationships."[17] Parenthetically, one should note that students of primitive society who use the term "customary law" blur the issue semantically, but nonetheless recognize the distinction.

It is this overall legalization of behavior in modern society which Bohannan fails to interpret. In fascist Germany, for example, laws flourished as never before. By 1941, more edicts had been proclaimed than in all the years of the Republic and the Third Reich. At the same time, ignorance of the law inevitably increased. In a sense, the very force of the law depends upon ignorance of its specifications, which is hardly recognized as a mitigating circumstance. As Seagle states, law is not definite and certain while custom is vague and uncertain. Rather, the converse holds. Customary rules must be clearly known; they are not sanctioned by organized political force, hence serious disputes about the nature of custom would destroy the integrity of society. But laws may always be invented, and stand a good chance of being enforced: "Thus, the sanction is far more important than the rule in the legal system ... but the tendency is to minimize the sanction and to admire the rule."[18]

In fascist Germany, customs did not become laws through a process of "double institutionalization." Rather, repressive laws, conjured up in the interest of the Nazi Party and its supporters, cannibalized the institutions of German society. Even the residual customary authority of the family was assaulted: children were encouraged to become police informers, upholding the laws against their kin. "The absolute reign of law has often been synonymous with the absolute reign of lawlessness."[19]

Certainly, Germany under Hitler was changing society, if hardly a progressive one, but it was a special case of the general process in civilization through which the organs of the state have become increasingly irresistible. It will be recalled that

---

[16] Sydney P. Simpsom and Julius Stone, *Law and Society in Evolution* (1942), Bk. 1, p. 2.
[17] William Seagle, *The History of Law* (1946), p. 35.
[18] *ibid.*, pp. 19–20.
[19] *ibid.*

Bohannan takes the domination of law over custom to be symptomatic of changing societies. But the historical inadequacy of his argument lies exactly here: he does not intimate the overall direction of that change and therefore fails to clarify the actual relation between custom and law. Accordingly, the notion that social change is a function of the law, and vice versa, implies a dialectic that is out of phase with historical reality.

Plato, it deserves note, understood this well enough when he conceived the problem of civilization as primarily one of injustice, which he did not scamp by legalistic definition. His remedy was the thorough restructuring of society. Whether we admire his Utopia or not, The Republic testifies to Plato's recognition that laws follow social changes and reflect prevailing social relationship, but are the cause of neither. Curiously, this view of the relationship between law and society accords with the Marxist perspective on the history of culture. Customary societies are said to precede legal societies, an idea which, semantics aside, most students of historical jurisprudence would accept. But Marxists envision the future as being without laws as we know them, as involving a return to custom, so to speak, on a higher level, since the repressive, punitive and profiteering functions of law will become superfluous. Conflicts of economic and political interest will be resolved through the equitable reordering of institutions. Law, for the Marxists and most classical students of historical jurisprudence, is the cutting edge of the state—but the former, insisting on both a historical and normative view of man, define the state as the instrument of the ruling class, anticipating its dissolution with the abolition of classes and the common ownership of the basic means of production. Whatever our view of the ultimate Marxist dynamic, law is clearly inseparable from the state. Sir Henry Maine equates the history of individual property with that of civilization: "Nobody is at liberty to attack several property and to say at the same time that he values civilization. The history of the two cannot be disentangled. Civilization is nothing more than the name of the ... order ... dissolved but perpetually reconstituting itself under a vast variety of solvent influences, of which infinitely the most powerful have been those which have, slowly, and in some parts of the world much less perfectly than others, substituted several property for collective ownership."[20] In the words of Jeremy Bentham, "Property and law are born together and die together."

Law, thus, is symptomatic of the emergence of the state; the legal sanction is not simply the cutting edge of institutions at all times and in all places. The "double institutionalization" to which Bohannan refers needs redefinition. Where it does occur, it is an historical process of unusual complexity and cannot be defined as the simple passage of custom into law. It occurs, as we shall see, in several modes. Custom—spontaneous, traditional, personal, commonly known, corporate, relatively unchanging—is the modality of primitive society; law is the instrument of civilization, of political society sanctioned by organized force, presumably above society at large, and buttressing a new set of social interests. Law and custom both involve the regulation of behavior but their characters are entirely distinct; no evolutionary balance has been struck between developing law and custom, whether traditional or emergent.                    [pp. 42–47]

... In the transition from primitive to political society the means of control and integration employed were, in a wider sense, "all ... deliberately conceived and (executed): they are agencies of an assimilation conscious of itself and of the message which it carries."[21] Finally, we are led to ask, as did Nadel about the Nupe: "What did the taxpaying law abiding citizen receive in return for allegiance to king and nobility? Was extortion, bribery, brutal force, the only aspect under which the state revealed itself to the populace? The people were to receive, theoretically, on the whole, on thing: security—protection against external and

[20]    Henry Maine, *Village Communities and Miscellanies* (1859), p. 230.
[21]    S. F. Nadel, *A Black Byzantium* (1942), p. 144.

internal enemies, and general security for carrying out the daily work, holding markets, using the roads. We have seen what protection and security meant in reality. At their best, they represented something very unequal and very unstable. This situation must have led to much tension and change within the system and to frequent attempts to procure better safeguards for civil rights.[22]

The struggle for civil rights, then, is a response to the imposition of civil law. With the destruction of the primitive base of society, civil rights have been defined and redefined as a reaction to drastic changes in the socioeconomic structure, the rest of caste and class systems, imperialism, modern war, technology as a means of social exploitation, maldistribution and misuse of resources, racial hatred. The right to socially and economically fruitful work, for example, which did not come into question in primitive society or in a traditional sector of an early state (and therefore was not conceived to be a stipulated right) becomes an issue under capitalism. The demand implies a need for profoundly changing the system and indicates that our sense of the appropriately human has very ancient roots indeed. However, we are reminded by the struggle for civil rights, that legislation alone has no force beyond the potential of the social system that generates it. From the study of proto-states we also learn that the citizen must be constantly alert to laws which seek to curb his rights in the name of protection or security. Restrictive legislation is almost always a signal of repressive institutional change, but is, of course, not the cause of it...

The major focus of the defense of the citizen as a person can only be on procedure or, as we call it in our society, due process. [pp. 69–70]

...For example, the only way dissidents in Russia can defend themselves against summary punishment and make their cases universally understandable is by calling attention to abuses of procedure. The spirit of the laws, mummified in the excellent constitution of 1936, is irrelevant, abstract. The tribunal that discharges the intentions of the state can discard, suspend, reinterpret, and invent laws at will. The court, not the constitution, is the primary legal reality. And the politically inspired charge of insanity, which can remove dissidents from the body politic altogether, is the ultimate etatistic definition of the person—a non-being incapable of autonomy. And that, I should note, is foreshadowed in the consummate anti-Socratic Platonism of the Laws, the heavenly city brought to earth, wherein the ordinary citizen is "to become, by long habit, utterly incapable of doing anything at all independently."

Procedure is the individual's last line of defense in contemporary civilization, wherein all other associations to which he may belong have become subordinate to the state. The elaboration of procedure then, is a unique, if fragile, feature of more fully evolved states, in compensation, so to speak, for the radical isolation of the individual. In the proto-states, the harshness of rudimentary procedure was countered by the role of the kinship units which, as we recall, retained a significant measure of functional socioeconomic autonomy and, therefore, of local political cohesion.

But "law has its origin in the pathology of social relations and functions only when there are frequent disturbances of the social equilibrium."[23] Law arises in the breach of a prior customary order and increases in force with the conflicts that divide political societies internally and among themselves. Law *and* order is the historical illusion; law versus order is the historical reality.

In the tradition of Rousseau, Lévi-Strauss, in a moment of candor, declares, "We must go beyond the evidence of the injustices and abuses to which the social order gives rise, and discover the unshakable basis of human society ...

---

[22] Nadel, "Nupe State and Community" in *Africa*, vol. VIII, p. 287.
[23] Seagle, *op. cit.*, p. 36.

Anthropology shows that base cannot be found in our own civilization, ours is indeed perhaps the one furthest from it."[24]

The progressive reduction of society to a series of technical and legal signals, the consequent diminution of culture, *i.e.* of reciprocal, symbolic meanings, are perhaps the primary reasons why our civilization is the one least likely to serve as a guide to "the unshakable basis of human society."          [pp. 70–72]

---

[24]  Claude Lévi-Strauss, *A World on the Wane* (1961), p. 390.

# 13

## MARXIST THEORIES OF LAW AND STATE

Marxism[1] is a system of sociology, a philosophy of man and society and a political doctrine. It is unique in that no other body of social thought became the doctrine of an important political movement and ultimately the orthodoxy of ruling parties in much of the world. In this chapter Marx's own thought and later developments in Marxist thought are surveyed.

It is Marx's lasting contribution to social thought that he viewed human societies as systems,[2] but more controversial is his view of the interrelationship of the parts of those systems. He attached primacy to the economic system. This was the "base" or "infrastructure" and everything else, political institutions, laws, religion, ethics, was "super-structural."[3] His theory of law and state might be described crudely as an economic theory of law and state. Secondly, and this is why Marxist thought proved so attractive to critics of social systems, he saw societies as inherently unstable systems. Furthermore, he sought the cause of social change in the internal contradictions and conflicts in social systems.

Marx was a materialist. Materialistic views of the world were common in the eighteenth century, being espoused by such thinkers as Descartes, Diderot and Feuerbach. But, according to Marx, they conceived of the world and man in purely mechanical terms, which allowed no scope for an explanation of development. If the world were a machine it could only do what it was made to do and not develop any new quality.[4] Marx found the principle of development he was looking for in Hegelian dialectics.

---

[1] On which see Avineri, *The Social and Political Thought of Karl Marx* (1968), McLellan, *Karl Marx—His Life and Thought* (1973), Bottomore, *The Sociological Theory of Marx* (1973), Lichtheim, *Marxism* (1961), Plamenatz, *German Marxism and Russian Communism* (1954), Wood, *Karl Marx* (1981). Texts will be found in editions by Lawrence and Wishart and Penguin. Useful collections are McLellan, *The Thoughts of Marx* (1971), Bottomore and Rubel, *Marx—Selected Writings on Sociology and Social Philosophy* (1956), Feuer, *Marx and Engels—Basic Writings on Politics and Philosophy* (1960). Collections of legal writings are M. Cain and A. Hunt, *Marx and Engels on Law* (1979) and P. Phillips, *Marx and Engels on Law and Laws* (1980). A valuable introduction is H. Collins, *Marxism and Law* (1982). So is Vincent (1993) 20 J.L.S. 371.
[2] *Cf.* the approach, using very different premises, of Parsons, referred to *ante*, 856.
[3] *Post*, 1134.
[4] Marx's critique of existing materialism is to be found in his *Concerning Feuerbach* (see *Early Writings* (Penguin ed., 1975), pp. 421–423).

## DIALECTICS, HEGEL AND MARX

For Hegel[5] history was a process in which the Absolute progressively unfolded itself, revealing more of its true nature in later periods than in earlier. The dialectic was the clue to this development. From the Greek (meaning argument or debate), the dialectic is the theory of union of opposites. The idea is to be found in Plato who regarded contradictions as obstacles to arriving at the truth and used the dialectic to rid himself of them. To Hegel, however, "the power of the negative", as he called it, was at the root of everything. There was always a tension between any present state of affairs and what it was becoming. But it was only through this tension that any progress towards truth was possible. For Marx, Hegel's chief attraction lay in his "philosophy's apparent ability to become the key to the realisation of idealism in reality, thus eliminating the dichotomy Kant bequeathed to the German philosophical tradition".[6]

The attraction of the dialectic for Marxists lies in its showing that phenomena do not exist in isolation and must be studied in their movement and development, and in depicting society as full of contradictions.[7] So they can draw the conclusion from the former that capitalism is a transient phase of human development and from the latter develop such concepts as alienation.[8]

Marx's dialectic was different from Hegel's.[9] Marx rejected Hegel's idealist philosophy and substituted materialism. A combination of Hegel's dialectic and a materialist theory of knowledge produced *dialectical materialism*, and this, applied to human relations within society, particularly to their evolution and development, Marx called *historical materialism*.[10] Marx explained his dialectical method in an Afterword in 1873 to the second edition of Volume 1 of *Capital*. It was, he claimed, "not only different from the Hegelian, but its direct opposite. To Hegel the life process of the human brain, *i.e.* the process of thinking, which, under the name of 'the idea', he even transforms into an independent subject, is the demiurgos of the real world, and the real world is only the

---

[5] And see *ante*, 1078. Hegel substituted for the familiar idealist notion of a higher reality beyond the actual world, the doctrine of a higher reality in the shape of what a thing is capable *of becoming* when it has realised its full potentialities. This has some resemblance to Aristotle, *cf. ante*, 137. On the Hegelian dialectic, see A. Wood, *Karl Marx* (1981), Chap. XIII; Jordan, *The Evolution of Dialectical Materialism* (1967).

[6] *Per* Avineri, *Social and Political Thought of Marx* (1968), pp. 8–9. *cf. ante*, 305–306.

[7] For Hegel, the law of contradiction produced, in the form of thesis and antithesis, a solution by way of synthesis on a higher level. This he applied to opposing forces in nature or society. Marx seized on this approach towards history and society, particularly with reference to the "class-conflict".

[8] Alienation arises as a *result* of something and is always *from* something. Thus, for Marxists, in capitalism man is alienated from the products of his activity since these belong to the capitalist; he is also alienated from his productive activity itself; he is also alienated from his essential nature and from other men.

[9] On the differences see A. Wood, *Karl Marx* (1981), Chap. XIV.

[10] Marx never in fact used the expression. He referred to the "materialist conception of history" (McLellan, *Marx* (1975), p. 38).

external, phenomenal form of "the idea". With me, on the contrary, the ideal is nothing else than the material world reflected by the human mind and translated into forms of thought ... With Hegel [the dialectic] is standing on its head. It must be turned right side up again if you would discover the rational kernel within the mystical shell."[11] Nevertheless, Marx "respected Hegel as a great thinker and considered his dialectic a valuable instrument for investigating the world".[12]

## MARX AND HEGEL'S POLITICAL PHILOSOPHY

Marx believed that Hegel's political philosophy "set the seal of approval upon a reality basically defective and distorted".[13] So, Hegelian philosophy could not be reformed without reforming reality itself. "The philosophers have only *interpreted* the world", wrote Marx in commenting upon the eleventh thesis on Feuerbach, "the point is to *change* it."[14]

Hegel depicted civil society as the clash of social forces, to be transcended by the universality of the state.[15] The state was abstracted from those forces, social and historical, which created and conditioned it. Marx asserts by contrast that the separation of civil society and state which Hegel formulated as a matter of principle is in fact only a historical phenomenon, the causes of which can be analysed. It is furthermore necessarily ephemeral. For Marx, Hegel's discussion of the state "ignores the social context of human relationship at the same time as it rationalises existing social organisation".[16] The state is discussed without reference to the individuals whose role it directs. Hegel's mediation of the two by means of political representation was, Marx believed, misconceived. The delegates of civil society in a representative assembly enjoy their status because they are members of a political organisation and not because they legitimise the particular interests of civil society. "Political institutions, despite their claim to universality and generality, only mask the particularistic, egoistic interest of civil society."[17] "The anatomy of this civil society," Marx wrote in his *Contribution to the Critique of Political Economy*, "has to be sought in political economy".[18]

These problems are also to be found in Hegel's treatment of bureaucracy.[19] To Hegel, the bureaucracy was the "universal class",[20] a paradigm of mediation between civil society and the state. Marx saw this as

---

[11] Quoted from Feuer, *op. cit.*, pp. 186–187.
[12] *Per* McLellan, *Karl Marx—Life and Thought* (1973), p. 124.
[13] *Per* Avineri, *op. cit.*, p. 16.
[14] In *Early Writings* (Penguin ed.), p. 423.
[15] See Avineri, *Hegel's Theory of the Modern State* (1972), pp. 141–154, and *cf. ante*, 904. See also F. Dallmayr (1989) 10 Cardozo L. Rev. 1337.
[16] *Per* Avineri, *Social and Political Thought of Marx*, p. 17.
[17] *ibid.*, p. 19.
[18] *Post*, 1167.
[19] On which see Avineri, *Hegel's Theory of the Modern State*, pp. 155–161.
[20] *Philosophy of Right*, p. 205.

illusory: the bureaucracy merely used the name of the general interest to further its own. It was an "institutional licence for sectional interests".[21]

For Hegel a person's private position determined his political status. For Marx this status was determined by his property relations and "class differences of civil society become political differences".[22] The state's claim to appear as the general interest was therefore nothing more than a mask for class interests. Those who lack property and need work ("the class of concrete labour") was "less a class of civil society than the basis on which the spheres of civil society rest and move".[23] Civil society could not function without the labouring classes, though these had hitherto been conceived of as marginal to it. Hegel's mistake, so Marx believed, was to ignore the human subject. It was only natural, Avineri comments, that "the modern state should be reduced accordingly to the private individual isolated from his social context".[24] It was "the riddle of modern constitutions (Marx tells us) as well as of Hegel's philosophy, especially his philosophy of law and religion", to treat man not as a subject but to identify him with his "predicate, class".[25] It was vital to Marxian philosophy to unveil this seeming mystification.

## THE MATERIALIST CONCEPTION OF HISTORY

The basic premise underlying the Marxian conception of history is that the "nature of individuals depends on the material conditions determining their production". What individuals are "coincides with their production, both with *what* they produce, and with *how* they produce".[26] To understand man and his history, therefore, it is necessary to understand his productive activity. "Self-creation through labour" is the "primary factor in history and ideas and concepts—political, philosophical or religious—through which men interpret this activity [are] secondary".[27]

Marx sees the principle governing all human relations to be found in the common end that all men pursue, *viz.* production of means to support life and exchange of things produced. There are two factors in production: "productive forces", the instruments of production including labour and implements as well as the knowledge and skills of those who produce and the "productive relations" between men.[28] The two are related so that as one changes so does the other. The exact relationship between the two

---

[21] *Per* Avineri, *Social and Political Thought of Marx*, p. 23.
[22] *Early Writings* (Penguin ed.), pp. 141–142 (*Critique of Hegel's Doctrine of the State*).
[23] Quoted by Avineri, in *Social and Political Thought of Marx*, p. 26.
[24] *ibid.*
[25] Quoted *ibid.*, p. 27.
[26] Marx and Engels, *The German Ideology*, p. 31.
[27] McLellan, *Marx* (1975), p. 38.
[28] Materialism "epitomised and under-scored the significance for historical and social explanation of generalisations about causality" (McBride, *The Philosophy of Marx* (1977), p. 80).

is not altogether clear. Marx speaks of the "determination" of the organisation of labour as the means of production. He also says of social or economic relations that they "correspond" to the productive forces. The different views are similar to the different positions taken on the relationship of base and superstructure.[29] Does Marx therefore hold an exclusively "technological" theory of history?[30] There are certainly texts which support such a position. For example, in *The German Ideology*, Marx tells us that "the aggregate of productive powers accessible to men conditions the state of society". In *The Poverty of Philosophy* he says that "a change in men's productive forces necessarily brings about a change in their relations of production". But it is also apparent that for Marx productive forces, whilst the most prominent factor determining production relations, are not the sole factor. The economic structure of a society depends on the productive forces it possesses, but only against a background which includes the historical circumstances and social forms in which these powers happened to be acquired. Another reason for hesitating to call Marx's theory of history "technological" is the wide range of things that he includes among society's productive forces. He even refers to "the revolutionary class itself"[31] and to modes of "cooperation"[32] as productive powers. But the latter example seems to threaten the entire project of explaining social forms in terms of productive forces since "they appear simply to identify what is to be explained with part of what is to do the explaining".[33] It might, however, be possible to distinguish those features of co-operative relationships which are productive powers from others which are not. If we do this we are left with a theory both less simple and also less tidy than that presented by a casual reading of Marx. It seems that Marx's theory of the relationship between production and society is technological in the weak sense that its aim is to explain production relations or social forms in terms of productive powers.

Marx sets out "a scientific account of social change".[34] Like other contemporaries he made sweeping historical generalisations.[35] He traced productive relations through a number of stages. In the "beginning" these were co-operative. Social revolutions take place as new inventions result in the newly-discovered productive forces coming into conflict with existing relations of production. "In acquiring new productive forces men change their mode of production; and in changing their mode of production they change all their social relations. The hand-mill gives you

---

[29] *Post*, 1134.
[30] G. Cohen, *Karl Marx's Theory of History* (1978); Shaw, *Marx's Theory of History* (1978). *cf.* S. Hook, *Toward the Understanding of Karl Marx* (1933); Walker, *Marx* (1978). See also Kolakowski, *Main Currents*, vol. 1, Chap. XIV.
[31] In *The Poverty of Philosophy*.
[32] In *The German Ideology*.
[33] *Per* Wood, *op. cit.*, p. 73.
[34] *Per* Bottomore and Rubel, *Karl Marx* (Pelican ed., 1963), p. 36.
[35] See Lichtheim, *Marxism* (1964), p. 141. *cf.* Maine, *ante*, 1100.

society with a feudal lord: the steam-mill, society with the industrial capitalist".[36] Marx sees "the Asiatic, the ancient, the feudal and the modern bourgeois methods of production as so many epochs in the progress of the economic formation of society".[37] History is conceptualised as a history of class struggles. The particular structure of the classes at any time is determined by the mode of production. It is the contradictions within the system, which furthermore cannot be resolved within its framework, that lead to higher stages of development.[38] He saw the contradictions within capitalism leading to increasingly acute conflict which only a revolution could resolve. Thus, and here Marx assumed the prophetic role, would the working class acquire political hegemony and found first a socialist, then a classless communist, society. Only then did he believe man's essence would be realised.

## BASE AND SUPERSTRUCTURE

Marx distinguished between the economic structure of society (the "base" or "infrastructure") and the "superstructure" which rose upon this "real foundation". To Marx the key was "the mode of production of material life conditions" and this, he wrote in a celebrated passage in the Preface to *A Contribution to the Critique of Political Economy* in 1859, "conditions the social, political and intellectual life process in general. It is not the consciousness of men that determines their being, but, on the contrary, their social being that determines their consciousness".[39] The meaning of the "superstructure" and its precise relationship to the base have proved extremely contentious.

First, what is the superstructure? As Williams points out,[40] it is used in three senses: (i) the legal and political forms which express existing real relations of production; (ii) forms of consciousness which express a particular class view of the world; (iii) a process in which, over a whole range of activities, men become conscious of a fundamental economic conflict and fight it out. These different senses direct our attention respectively to institutions, forms of consciousness and political and cultural practices. Marx was attacking "areas" of thought and activity, so that the common abstraction of base and superstructure is, somewhat ironically, persistence of a mode of thought that he attacked, though, it must be conceded, that he gave considerable warrant for this. Two points must, however, be noted. First, Marx was fighting against idealist modes

---

[36] Marx, *The Poverty of Philosophy*, p. 122.

[37] Marx, *Critique of Political Economy, post*, 1168. "All these states have one fundamental feature in common: they are all 'class states'". (Miliband, *Marxism and Politics* (1977), p.74.)

[38] Marx's theory of social change presupposes a tendency for human productive powers to expand and an inability (in class or pre-class society) within production relations to accommodate this expansion.

[39] See *post*, 1168.

[40] *Marxism and Literature* (1977), pp. 76–77.

of thought then dominant,[41] and in particular against the idea of law as autonomous, as playing a causal role in the historical process. Marx insisted that "revolution" was not "made by law". Secondly, as Engels pointed out, the economic basis of a struggle could be dulled in consciousness. It was (and is) all too easy for a legal system to be projected as independent of its economic content in the course of professional development, so that the connection between them can become obscured.[42]

The key passage to an understanding of the base-superstructure relationship is Marx's Preface to *A Contribution to the Critique of Political Economy*.[43] Certainly, the language used in this passage is suggestive of the economic determinism of which critics accuse Marxism.[44] So are some other passages. Thus, for example, Marx and Engels write of law having "just as little an independent history as religion."[45] Engels, in his famous letter to Conrad Schmidt, observes that economic relations are "reflected" in legal principles: "the jurist imagines he is operating with *a priori* propositions, whereas they are really only economic reflections".[46] Marx in *The Poverty of Philosophy* says of legislation that it "never does more than proclaim, express in words, the will of economic relations",[47] and in volume 1 of *Capital* juridical relations are said to be "but the reflex of the real economic relation" which "determines the subject-matter comprised in each ... juridical act".[48]

Thus described, the law appears as subsidiary to economic relations, indeed derivative from them. It is conceived as lacking in autonomy[49] and, therefore, for example, in any social engineering[50] potential. The view that law follows, and never leads, is a common nineteenth-century belief.[51] If there were no more to Marx's explication of base and superstructure than this, it would be easy to criticise his crude concept of causality. The determinism would be rigid, even mechanistic. But the writings of Marx and Engels are replete with suggestions which fill out the simple analysis just depicted. Thus, in *Capital* Marx concedes that

---

[41] In particular that associated with Hegel (see *ante*, 954).

[42] A good illustration of this is Engels, *The Housing Question* (in Cain and Hunt at p. 55): "The more intricate [a] legal system becomes, the more is its mode of expression removed from that in which the usual economic conditions of the life of society are expressed. It appears as an independent element which derives the justification for its existence and the substantiation of its further development not from the economic relations and from its own inner foundations or, if you like, the 'concept of the will'. People forget that their right derived from their economic conditions of life, just as they have forgotten that they themselves derive from the animal world". See also Marx and Engels, *The German Ideology, post*, 1168–1169.

[43] *Post*, 1167.

[44] Observe words like "constitutes ... real foundation", "conditions", "but a legal expression for the same thing". See *post*, 1168, 1169.

[45] *The German Ideology, post*, 1169.

[46] Extracted in Cain and Hunt, *op. cit.*, at p. 57.

[47] Extracted in Cain and Hunt, *op. cit.*, at p. 59.

[48] Lawrence and Wishart edition (1970), p. 89.

[49] *Post*, 1138.

[50] *Ante*, 849.

[51] See Savigny and the *Volksgeist, ante*, 1079.

"same economic base" will show "infinite variations and gradations in appearance which can be ascertained only by analysis of the empirically given circumstances" (he lists "natural environment, racial relations, external historical influences").[52] Elsewhere he refers to the importance of "tradition" playing a dominant role in primitive modes of production and of "regulation and order" themselves being "indispensable elements of any mode of production, if it is to assume social stability and independence from mere change and arbitrariness".[53] Engels talks of ideology[54] influencing the economic base and, within certain limits, modifying it. He gives this example[55]: "The basis of the right of inheritance is an economic one, provided the level of development of the family is the same. It would, nevertheless, be difficult to prove ... that the absolute liberty of the testator in England[56] and the severe and very detailed restrictions imposed on him in France are due to economic causes alone. But in their turn they exert a very considerable effect on the economic sphere, because they influence the distribution of property". Marx stresses that laws "stabilise" relations of distribution and this has an effect on production which "requires" to be determined in each specific instance.[57] Engels (in a letter to Borgius) argued that "race" was itself an economic factor (not a remark that can easily be taken at face value). But he continued to argue that legal development (*inter alia*), though based on economic development, reacted upon political, philosophical, religious and other developments and "also upon the economic basis". He explained: "One must not think that the economic situation is *cause, and solely active*, whereas everything else is only passive effect. On the contrary, inter-action takes place on the basis of economic necessity, which *ultimately* always asserts itself".[58]

In all this there are hints of a more elaborate analysis of base and superstructure than appears in the deceptively simple passage from the *Critique of Political Economy*. This is not surprising for, to put it at its most obvious, why did Marx and Engels write so voluminously if ideas were incapable of changing the world? Engels (in the Schmidt letter already referred to) admits as much: "Why do we fight for the political dictatorship of the proletariat if political power is economically impotent?"[59] Yet in the final analysis the "*ultimately* determining factor in history is the production and reproduction of real life".[60] Engels claimed that neither he nor Marx had ever asserted "more than this". Those, he

---

[52] Vol. III, p. 772.
[53] *ibid.*, p. 793.
[54] Including law.
[55] Letter to Conrad Schmidt (1890), extracted in Cain and Hunt, *op. cit.*, pp. 57–58.
[56] This was changed in 1938 (see now Inheritance (Provision for Family and Dependants) Act 1975). But there is still greater freedom in England than in countries which operate with systems of community of property and rights of inheritance.
[57] *Grundrisse* (Penguin ed., 1969), p. 98.
[58] Parts of this letter are extracted in Cain and Hunt, *op. cit.*, p. 58.
[59] *Op. cit.*, n. 55, at p. 58.
[60] *Per* Engels in letter to J. Bloch (1890), extracted in Cain and Hunt, *op. cit.*, p. 56.

believed, who "twisted" their language to suggest that the economic factor was the "*only* determining one" were transforming the proposition into a "meaningless, abstract, absurd phrase". The superstructure, he maintained, exercised influence upon the course of historical struggles and "in many cases" determined their "form" in particular.[61]

The problems do not, however, end with exegesis, however satisfactory this may be. More basic questions need to be asked. Are infrastructure and superstructure separate constructs? Plamenatz[62] pointed out long ago that property affected production and that a system of property could have an influence on what was produced and how. Even more significantly, he suggested that it was impossible to define relations of production without using moral or normative concepts. Is it possible to understand capitalistic enterprise without using concepts found within company legislation and case law?[63] To this "problem of legality"[64] Cohen has retorted by trying to substitute for the language of rights that of powers.[65] He so conceives the economic structure that it is free of all "superstructural encumbrances".[66] He attempts a *rechtsfrei*[67] description of productive relations and then purports to show how they, so described, may be said to explain property relations.[68] But is it possible to conceive of the economic structure non-normatively? The actors within an economic structure are identified in normative terms. A slave is a "non-person", a "res" lacking in certain rights. A landowner is a "person" in whom is vested a complex bundle of rights,[69] which we call "ownership". It is no more feasible to describe a slave or landowner non-normatively than a court or an official, as we saw in relation to definitions of law posited by Holmes[70] or Llewellyn.[71] Further, can the economic structure of production relations be reduced to a set of *de facto* powers? As Lukes points out,[72] what counts as an agent's abilities and inabilities will be

---

[61] *ibid.* See also R. Miliband, *Marxism and Politics* (1977) arguing that it is "apposite and meaningful to treat the 'economic base' as a starting-point, as a matter of the *first instance*" and that we can still "attribute to political forms and forces whatever degree of autonomy is judged in any particular case to be appropriate" (p. 8).

[62] *Man and Society* (1963), vol. 2, pp. 274–292. See also H. Acton, *The Illusion of the Epoch* (1955).

[63] For example, the separateness of the corporate entity as established in *Salomon's* case [1897] A.C. 22.

[64] So called by G.A. Cohen, *Karl Marx's Theory of History* (1978), p. 217.

[65] See Proc. of Artist Soc. Supp. (1970), vol. 44, pp. 121–124; in C. Abramsky and B. Williams (eds.), *Essays in Honour of E.H. Carr* (1974); and in *op. cit.*, n. 65, especially in Chaps III and VIII.

[66] He does not state where power comes from. It could, of course, come from the law, but this would defeat his analysis. More likely it emanates from force (*e.g.* military) or ideology (*cf post*, 1170).

[67] *ibid.*, p. 225.

[68] See *post*, 1171.

[69] Using "rights" in its generic sense. Many of the "rights" are "privileges", "powers" and "immunities" (see Hohfeld, *ante*, 569).

[70] See his "bad man" definition, *ante*, 1007.

[71] "What officials do about disputes", said Llewellyn. But what is an "official"? See, further, Hart, *The Concept of Law* (1994), Chap. 7.

[72] "Can the Base be distinguished from the Superstructure?" in D. Miller and L. Siedentop (eds.), *The Nature of Political Theory* (1983), p. 111.

"closely dependent upon how that agent is conceived". Further, "what counts as enabling or constraining is never a simple matter of fact but is always relative to background assumptions and judgments, some of them normative".[73] As Collins points out,[74] it is rules which define reciprocal expectations. Property-owners do, of course, have powers, for example, the power to exclude trespassers from their land but they have such powers because the trespassers have (in Hohfeld's language) no-rights and because a legal system provides remedies.[75] Cohen's response to this is to affirm its accuracy as a matter of fact in a period when there is a stable social formation but to argue that in a period of transformation it is extra-legal power that counts, not the exercise of legal rights, and only later does this power become consolidated as the new legal position. In Collins's words "the base is divorced from legal rights, which are only created subsequently in order to stabilize and protect the new relations of production".[76] What is missing in this defence is an explanation of why, if naked extra-power is effective, a legal superstructure should be created. What is it that should impel the powerful to translate their power into legal form? Part of the answer to this may lie in the concept of ideology, to which later reference is made.[77] But we are still left wondering whether base and superstructure can be separated.[78]

Some light on the relationship between base and superstructure is also thrown by legal historians.[79] Most economic historians have taken the view that law is a "dependent variable, symptom rather than determinant of the means and ends of the economic process".[80] This conclusion is consistent with an analysis of law in terms of the base-superstructure metaphor. Weber recognised, however, that the relationship between law and economy is problematic, that the law may affect the economy.[81] Hartwell agrees: "legal institutions have some autonomy of their own which, in varying degrees, makes them exogenous variables in any process of economic change".[82] Perhaps the most interesting study of the relationship between law and economy is Horwitz's *The Transformation*

---

[73] *ibid.*, p. 112.
[74] *Marxism and Law* (1982), pp. 78–79. The original insight, though not in relation to this problem, comes from Hart (see *The Concept of Law*, Chaps 4–5 and *ante*, 394).
[75] See, in relation to this, Hart's analysis of rights (*ante*, 444).
[76] *Op. cit.*, note 74, p. 83.
[77] *Post*, 1141.
[78] Cohen has defended his position in "Reply to Four Critics" in *Analyse und Kritik* (1983), vol. 5, pp. 212–219.
[79] An excellent discussion of this genre is D. Sugarman, "Perspective and Practice in Law and History: A Prologue to the Study of the Relationship between Law and Economy from a Socio-Historical Perspective" in B. Fryer *et al., Power and the State* (1981), pp. 70–106. See also D. Sugarman and G.R. Rubin in G.R. Rubin and D. Sugarman (eds.), *Law, Economy and Society* (1984), pp. 1–123.
[80] *Per* D. Landes, quoted in D. Sugarman, *op. cit.*, at p. 72. P. Mathias (*The First Industrial Nation* (1969), pp. 36–37) says "non-legal criteria were the prime determinants of change".
[81] *Ante*, 840. See also R.B. Ferguson "Commercial Expectations and the Guarantee of Law" in G.R. Rubin and D. Sugarman (eds.), *op. cit.*, pp. 192–208.
[82] *The Industrial Revolution and Economic Growth* (1971), p. 256.

*of American Law 1780–1860*.[83] Horwitz traces the influence of economy on law whilst at the same time showing how the law helped to forge a major change in the economy. He argues that there was a radical break with pre-capitalist society and its law after 1790, and that in the period 1790–1860 the American courts "engineered the facilitation and legitimation of industrial capitalism".[84] He demonstrates the ways in which judges were able to mould the law so as to promote emergent mercantile interests at the expense of other weaker groups in the community. The result was a profound redistribution of power and wealth. He argues that the very conception and function of law changed. From being a static set of principles reflecting customary ideas of justice and practice derived from natural law, the law became more functional, more instrumental. The idea of property changed: in the eighteenth century it represented the power to prevent others interfering with enjoyment; it came in the course of the nineteenth century to be seen as a power to develop property regardless of injurious consequences to others. Common law rules which obstructed demands for economic growth were repudiated: he cites the development of fault in negligence and thus a lower level of duty and less liability than had been the case earlier. The judiciary was seeking to accommodate "the new insistence of entrepreneurial groups that certainty and predictability of legal consequences were essential for economic planning".[85] He charts many other changes, for example in contract law the growth of the doctrine *caveat emptor* reflecting the needs of business for certainty. He shows how the new law favoured commerce at the expense of labour and consumers, how the law in effect came to ratify the inequalities produced by the market system. At the heart of these changes, he argues, was an alliance between the legal profession and the mercantile classes. In showing as he does how the law actively participated in economic growth, in demonstrating the role it played in capitalist accumulation and in redistributing wealth and political power, Horwitz has provided us with a well-documented case study of the relationship between base and superstructure and one which suggests the active role played by the superstructure in redesigning the economic base.[86]

---

[83] Published in 1977. On Horwitz see Sugarman (1980) 7 Brit. J. Law & Soc. 297 and W. Holt (1982) 23 Will and Mary L. Rev. 663–723.

[84] *Per* Sugarman, *op. cit.*, n. 80, p. 74.

[85] *Op. cit.*, note 83, p. 81.

[86] But note he does concentrate on reported cases. To what extent are these congruent with business practice? *cf. ante*, 848.

THE QUESTION OF CLASS

Marx saw history as the history of class struggles. But he neither invented the concept "class"[87] nor does he offer much in the way of systematic analysis of it.[88] He rejected the theory that classes are distinguished merely by wealth and poverty. He also rejected a definition of classes in terms of their sources of revenue. In *Capital*[89] he writes that there are three large classes in capitalist society, wage labourers, capitalists and landowners. His reason for distinguishing these three is that he regards the conflicts of interest between them as fundamentally more historically important than conflicts within them, or conflicts between them and less potent classes (such as the peasantry and the petty bourgeoisie).[90] But he qualifies this by adding that in England (where capitalism had then reached its most developed form) stratification does not appear in pure form; there were "middle and intermediate strata". He saw a process, however, whereby those landowners would be squeezed out and two classes would remain; bourgeoisie and proletariat. In *The Communist Manifesto* these are "two great hostile camps".[91]

Marx's position is complicated by his recognition of a new middle class and his characterisation of a group like farm labourers to an intermediate position between peasants and proletariat. Indeed, he viewed peasants as a reactionary group and was reluctant to identify them with the urban proletariat upon which he pinned his faith. The intelligentsia[92] also caused Marx problems. So did what he called the *Lumpenproletariat*, the drop-outs of society. Though very different Marx saw the potential for each to be reactionary, selling its services to the bourgeoisie.

Marx's position on class is thus neither clear nor simple. He was, of course, not describing a static society and his view was that, despite variations that then existed, the capitalists and the proletariat were essentially the only classes in developed capitalist society. Marx also stressed that a class did not really exist until it became conscious of itself as such. Thus he said of the proletariat that it was "not yet sufficiently developed to constitute itself into a class" and that it was not yet a "class for itself".[93] Classes are not, then, "given" along with a system of production relations: they arise out of such a system when shared interests in

---

[87] "No credit is due to me for discovering the existence of classes in modern society nor yet the struggle between them", wrote Marx in 1852. Early formulations are those of Ferguson and Miller, eighteenth-century Scottish historians.

[88] McLellan, *The Thought of Marx* (1971), p. 151.

[89] *Capital*, vol. III, p. 832.

[90] *Per*, Wood, *op. cit.*, p. 90. See also E. Hobsbawm: "classes are merely special cases of social relations of production" (*Pre-Capitalist Economic Formations* (1965), p. 11).

[91] In Feuer (ed.), *op. cit.*, p. 49.

[92] *The German Ideology*, p. 21. They made "the perfecting of the illusion of the class about itself their chief source of livelihood".

[93] *The Poverty of Philosophy*, pp. 140, 195. Similarly with revolutionary consciousness, Marx argued that its existence guaranteed that a revolution was bound to happen. See Avineri, *The Social and Political Thought of Marx* (1968), p. 144. Marx's views of the acquisition of class consciousness mark out his thinking from that of Weber.

a common situation lead to the development of political movements and class ideologies which promote those interests.[94]

It is often said by way of criticism of Marx that he over-emphasised the significance of economic class both as an explanation of historical trends and as an indicator of individual conduct.[95] Certainly there would appear to be other possible dimensions of stratification. In a patriarchal society women will be treated as inferior.[96] In a racist society discrimination is practised against people of a different racial origin. It can hardly be contested that the oppression of women associated with male supremacy antedates capitalism,[97] persisted in "socialist" countries and that such patterns of dominance are to be found outside the nuclear family in communal living.[98] Marxists often interpret sex discrimination[99] and racism in Britain and other Western European countries in terms of the ideological needs of European colonialism. Racism is seen to serve the interests of capitalism. One commentator described British race relations legislation as "education of the lesser capitalists in the ways of enlightened capital" for "now that immigration laws[1] were turning immigrants into migrants ... it was necessary to counter the social and political cost of racial friction".[2]

## MARX AND IDEOLOGY

The concept of ideology does not begin with Marx nor is it unique to Marxism.[3] It is central to Marxian understanding of law. Indeed, some of the most interesting recent developments in Marxist theory have taken place in the concept of ideology. The concept has a number of different meanings: (i) a system of beliefs characteristic of a class or group; (ii) a system of illusory beliefs, false ideas, false consciousness (that is, as opposed to true or scientific knowledge); (iii) the general process of the

---

[94] Marx wrote: "Separate individuals form a class only insofar as they have to carry on a common struggle against another class".

[95] Dahrendorf, *Class and Class Conflict in our Industrial Society* (1959).

[96] There is a huge literature on this. Good examples are E. Zaretsky, *Capitalism, The Family and Personal Life* (1976); M. Barrett, *Women's Oppression Today* (1988). But *cf.* F. Engels, *The Origins of the Family, Private Property and the State*, as to which see R. Delmar in J. Mitchell and A. Oakley (eds.), *The Rights and Wrongs of Women* (1976), p. 271. See also Young, *ante*, 614–617.

[97] See H. Hartmann (1976) 1 *Signs* 137. She argues that the emergence of capitalist production systematically alters pre-existing patterns of sexual exploitation. The development of capitalist industry served to intensify the subordination of women by increasing male dominance in the economic and political spheres which were separated from the "home". G. Lerner argues that patriarchy was the first exploitative labour system (*The Creation of Patriarchy* (1986)).

[98] Abrams and McCulloch, *Communes, Sociology and Society* (1976), Chap. 5.

[99] See J. Mitchell, *Women's Estate* (1971).

[1] A reference to the Immigration Act 1971.

[2] Sivanandan, "Race, Class and the State" (1976) 17 *Race and Class*, 347, 362.

[3] On the history of the concept see G. Lichtheim, *The Concept of Ideology and Other Essays* (1967); M. Seliger, *Ideology and Politics* (1976).

production of meanings and ideas.[4] There is no concentrated treatment of ideology in the works of Marx and Engels.[5] Marx's position involved a rejection of Hegel.[6] In Hegel, human beings appear as the creators of their own history but in conditions only partly disclosed to them in terms of their own consciousness: conditions, as Giddens says,[7] that can only be understood retrospectively. Marx rejected the latter claim and held that social analysis "can discern and help to actualise immanent tendencies in contemporary social development".[8] After Marx the diagnosis of ideology became a mode of penetrating beyond the consciousness of human actors, of uncovering the "real foundations" of their activity and using this for the purpose of social transformation.

Marx's fullest discussion of ideology is in *The German Ideology*.[9] Marx uses the imagery of the *camera obscura*, of the world turned upside down. "If in all ideology men and their circumstances appear upside down as in a camera obscura, this phenomenon arises just as much from their historical life-process as the inversion of objects on the retina does from their physical life-process".[10] It is not simply, according to Marx, that things have to be set right side up again. In addition, we have to discover through empirical, historical study the circumstances which have led to the formation of different kinds of ideology. Also in *The German Ideology*, Marx asserts that ideologies express or justify the interests of dominant classes. The connection between the two is supplied by "the demystifying of ideology"[11] that the *camera obscura* image suggests— history should not be written within the constraints of the ideas of the dominant class. It is Marx's claim that historians and social analysts who do not examine the "material" basis of ideology end up ensnared in the "illusions of that epoch". And they fall prey as well to "false consciousness".[12] False consciousness is a major obstacle to revolution: until the proletariat develops class consciousness and demystifies their bourgeois ideological framework, there can be no revolution.

It is clear where the "ruling class" gets its common perception of its interests. Its members have similar processes of socialisation and similar experiences of productive activities. But how does this dominant ideology get transmitted to the rest of the population? Further, if social being determines social consciousness, then why shouldn't each class form its own system of belief in the accordance with its particular interests?

---

[4] See R. Williams, *Marxism and Literature* (1977).

[5] One of the clearest presentations and defences of Marx's views on ideology is found in G. Lukács's *History and Class Consciousness* (1923, English translation, 1971).

[6] See *ante*, 1130–1131.

[7] *Central Problems in Social Theory* (1979), p. 166.

[8] *ibid.*

[9] In Chap. 1. See Cain and Hunt, *Marx and Engels on Law* (1979), Chap. 4 for a valuable collation of texts on ideology. The clearest treatment of Marx and ideology is M. Seliger, *The Marxist Conception of Ideology* (1977).

[10] As quoted in Giddens, *op. cit.*, n. 7, p. 167.

[11] *Per* Giddens, *op. cit.*, n. 7, p. 16.

[12] Engels's term. "False consciousness" is the adoption by the subordinate classes of the dominant ideology.

Marx's answer is in terms of the class which is the ruling material force being at the same time the ruling intellectual force. Marx's two views of ideology are clearly in potential conflict. It is the second theory that all classes share in the system of belief imposed by the dominant class which raises the most problems. It is clear how Marxists think a common culture is transmitted from dominant to subordinate classes.

The fullest modern exposition of this is by Althusser.[13] He argues that there are a vast number of institutions involved in one way or another in the dissemination of ideology and these are state ideological apparatuses. He distinguishes these from the "repressive state apparatus". Althusser lists these "Ideological State Apparatuses" as "the religious ISA (the system of different churches), the educational ISA (the system of the different public and private 'Schools'), the family ISA, the legal ISA, the political ISA (the political system, including the different Parties), the trade union ISA, the communications ISA (press, radio and television, etc.), the cultural ISA (literature, the Arts, sports, etc)". To call all these "state" ideological apparatuses at the very least confuses class and state power, even though, as Miliband puts it, the "state is in *all* respects the ultimate sanctioning agency of class power".[14] The dominant class (assuming for this purpose that there is one)[15] under the protection of the state has vast resources, considerably greater than those of the subordinate classes, to bring its own weight to bear on "civil society".

A good example of such a class using the law in this way is Hay's account of criminal law processes in eighteenth-century England.[16] It is Hay's view that "the criminal law, more than any other social institution" made it possible to govern the country without a police force or large army.[17] He is concerned with an apparent paradox: the century witnessed both an enormous expansion in the number of capital offences, but at the same time there was a weak and declining enforcement of the law, frequent acquittal of defendants on technical grounds as well as frequent pardons or commutations of the death sentence. Contemporary reformers argued, to little avail, that property could be better protected and crime more effectively controlled by a more serious commitment to the detection of crime and to certain but graded punishments. This, says Hay, though seemingly irrational, is explicable if we adopt the perspective that the social function of the criminal law was not the management of crime but the sustenance of the moral authority of the gentry and the creation of a complex and richly articulated system of social relationships of personal dependency that constituted the structure of power. "The law was important as gross coercion; it was equally important as ideology. Its

[13] "Ideology and Ideological State Apparatuses" in *Lenin and Philosophy* (1972). I. Balbus (1977) 11 Law and Society Review 571 may also be consulted.

[14] *Marxism and Politics* (1977), p. 55.

[15] *Cf. post*, 1163.

[16] "Property, Authority and the Criminal Law", in D. Hay *et al.* (eds.), *Albion's Fatal Tree* (1977), pp. 17–64. In eighteenth-century England, the landed gentry was a clear ruling élite.

[17] *ibid.*, p. 56.

majesty, justice and mercy helped to create the spirit of consent and submission, the 'mind-forged manacles', which Blake saw binding the English poor".[18] Hay sees the functions and strength of ideology as twofold. First, "its effectiveness lies ... in its very elasticity, the fact that men are not required to make it a credo, that it seems to them a product of their own minds as their own experience ... The courts dealt in terror, pain and death, but also in moral ideals, control of arbitrary power, mercy for the weak. In doing so they made it possible to disguise much of the class interest of the law.[19] Secondly, an additional strength of an ideology is its "generality", for: "provided that its depths are not explored too often by too many, it remains a reservoir of belief throughout the society and flows into the gaps made by individual acts of protest".[20]

Hay goes some way towards showing how dominant ideology was transmitted to the subordinate classes of eighteenth-century England. But as a general thesis doubt has been cast on the dominant ideology notion, in particular on its transmitting capacity, by Abercrombie, Hill and Turner.[21] They show that it is typically the case that the subordinate classes do not believe the dominant ideology and that this has far more significance for the integration and control of the dominant class itself. It is their argument that the apparatuses of transmission of belief are not very efficient in reaching the subordinate classes. They go on to suggest that the importance of dominant ideology has declined as a way of securing coherence of the dominant class as well. They point out that the economic functioning of today's form of capitalism is not dependent on the existence of a dominant class which retains capital within the family structure since monopoly firms are not family firms.

The debate on ideology and law continues. One of the most interesting discussions is Sumner's *Reading Ideologies*.[22] He observes that legal ideology contains more than just capitalist economic ideology. Law reflects the ideologies of different fractions within the bourgeoisie and the ideologies of other classes. It also reflects the ideologies of occupational groups, minority groups and the ideologies related to family structure, political representation, etc. He sees law as an ideological form of the fullest complexity but argues it is not equally pluralistic: it is basically a reflection of class inequality, expressing the ideologies of the dominant class. He concludes: "the legal system is first and foremost a means of exercising political control available to the propertied, the powerful and the highly educated. It is the weapon and toy of the hegemonic bloc of classes and class fractions whose rough consensus it sustains. As such, it

---

[18] *ibid.*, p. 49.

[19] *ibid.*, p. 55.

[20] *ibid.* For an attempt to see family law as ideology see M.D.A. Freeman, "Legal Systems, Patriarchal Ideologies and Domestic Violence" in S. Spitzer and R. Simon (eds.), *Research in Law, Deviance and Social Control* (1982), vol. 4, pp. 131–162.

[21] *The Dominant Ideology Thesis* (1980).

[22] *Reading Ideologies: An Investigation into the Marxist Theory of Ideology and Law* (1979).

lies hidden beneath a shroud of discourse, ritual and magic which proclaim the Wisdom and Justice of The Law".[23]

## THE STATE AND LAW

Some of Marx's views on the state have already been referred to.[24] His early ideas evolved by way of criticism of Hegel. Essentially his aim in these writings was to stress the gap that existed between civil society and the state. The state was viewed as the "most characteristic institution of man's alienated condition".[25] The state was merely a political abstraction. In his later writings he concentrated more on an analysis of the function of the state in society. Indeed, "whereas in his earlier writings he had tended to emphasise the gap between the state and society, he later considered the state as part of society".[26] The state was then seen as an instrument of class oppression. ("The executive of the modern state is but a committee for managing the common affairs of the whole bourgeoisie", he noted in *The Communist Manifesto*.)[27] These two views are different but, as McLellan emphasises, they are by no means incompatible.

Marx traced the origin of the state, as he did other social institutions, to the division of labour. He saw the state as in contradiction to the real interests of all members of society. It was an "illusory community serving as a screen for the real struggles waged by classes against each other".[28] At each stage of production in history there was a political organisation which corresponded to that stage and which supported the interests of the then dominant class. "The state", Marx wrote, "acts as an intermediary in the formation of all communal institutions and gives them a political form. Hence there is the illusion that law is based on will, that is, on will divorced from its real basis, on free will".[29]

Sometimes, Marx notes, the state may be representative not of the whole of a class but only of a section of that class. He cites the example of the financiers in France under Louis-Philippe. One class can also control the state for the benefit of another class. Marx saw this as the case in England when the Whigs did this on behalf of the middle class. Marx also thought that the state could play an independent role in backward countries and in absolute monarchies in the transition between feudal

---

[23] *ibid.*, p. 277. An interesting discussion of law and ideology is in E. Genovese's *Roll, Jordan, Roll* (1976), pp. 25–49 and in Part III of *Fruits of Merchant Capital* (1983) (written with E. Fox-Genovese). Collins, *Marxism and Law* (1982), Chap. 3 is also useful. And see R. Cotterrell (1988) 15 J.L.S. 5, 9.

[24] *Ante*, 1131. On the materialist view of the State see Holloway and Picciotto, *State and Capital* (1978), Chap. 1 and B. Jessop, *The Capitalist State* (1982). A very useful collection of materials, Marxist and non-Marxist is D. Held *et al.*, *States And Societies* (1983).

[25] McLellan, *The Thought of Karl Marx* (1971), p. 179.

[26] *ibid.*, p. 181.

[27] (Penguin ed., 1975), p. 82.

[28] Per McLellan, *The Thought of Karl Marx* (1971), p. 182.

[29] *Grundrisse*, p. 48.

and bourgeois classes. Marx also doubted whether the state was necessarily an instrument of class domination in certain Asiatic, paternalistic
societies (India, China and Russia) where "the despot ... appears as the
father of all the numerous lesser communities, thus revealing the common
unity of all". But generally Marx saw the state functioning as an
instrument of class oppression, as in North America, "where the state ...
was from the start subordinated to bourgeois society and production".[30]

Thus, there are two views of the state in Marx: one sees it as the
"instrument" of a ruling class and a "secondary" view sees it as "independent from and superior to all social classes, as being the dominant
force in society rather than the instrument of a dominant class".[31] What
Marx called "Bonapartism" was the extreme manifestation of the state's
independent role in Marx's own lifetime. Miliband argued that for Marx
the Bonapartist state remained the "protector of an economically and
socially dominant class" even if it was "politically" independent from any
given class.[32] He later reformulated this distinction in terms of a difference between the state acting autonomously *on behalf* of the ruling class
and its acting *at the behest* of that class. The latter he described as "a
vulgar deformation of the thought of Marx".[33]

It is in the writings of Poulantzas that we get the fullest exploration of
the concept of the autonomy of the state. He coined the expression
"relative autonomy of the state".[34] This phrase tries to capture the idea
that whatever autonomy the state might have (and it might be substantial) it remained for all practical purposes the state of the ruling class.
There has been considerable discussion by Marxists about the nature of
the constraints and pressure which cause the state to serve the needs of
capital, and general agreement that the state is decisively constrained by
forces external to it, constraints that originated in the national and
international capitalist context in which it operates.[35] Marxists and
pluralists agree that the state is reactive rather than pro-active: it appears
to be the "historical subject" but in reality is the object of forces and
processes at work in society.

This view is now under attack. A good example is Theda Skocpol's
*States and Social Revolution*, who argues that the Marxist tradition, in
seeing the state's function in terms of the containment of class conflict,
fails to treat the state "as an autonomous structure—a structure with a
logic and interests of its own not necessarily equivalent to, or fused with,
the interests of the dominant class in society".[36] The degree of autonomy
enjoyed by the state is dependent on the hegemony of the dominant class:
where the class is truly all-powerful in economic, political, social and

[30] *Pre-Capitalist Economic Formations*, p. 69.
[31] *Per* R. Miliband, "Marx and the State" in *The Socialist Register* (1965), p. 283.
[32] *ibid.*, p. 285.
[33] "Poulantzas and the Capitalist State" in 82 *New Left Rev.* 83.
[34] *Political Power and Social Classes*.
[35] A point on which democratic pluralists agree, though they differ as to the pressures,
    attributing these to competing interest groups. See *post*, 1162.
[36] (1979), p. 27.

cultural terms, and so free from effective challenge, it is likely that the state will also be subject to its hegemony. Where, on the other hand, such hegemony is strongly challenged, the autonomy of the state is likely to be substantial. Indeed, where there is intense competition and resulting political instability, the state may assume authoritarian forms and free itself from constitutional checks and balances. But in most "late" capitalist societies capital has had to reach an accommodation with organised labour and the state is left with considerable autonomy.

What is this autonomy for? Classical Marxism responded to this question in over-simplistic terms. It said it was to protect the existing social order and the dominant class as the main, if not sole, beneficiary of that social order. This leaves out of account other very powerful impulses to state action generated from within the state by people in charge of decision-making power. The state makes possible the exercise of power: it is also the source of status. Those holding powerful positions in the state may be as interested in power, status and privilege as in the interests of capital. They will not express themselves in terms of personal interest, rather in terms of "national interest" and those who seek state power usually find it easy to convince themselves and others that their achievement of power is synonymous with the "national interest". And, on the whole, those in charge of the state have believed that the "national interest" is intimately connected with the health of capitalist enterprise. This is not to say that there is always congruence between state power and class interests. For example, the state needs revenue: it cannot obtain all it requires from the subordinate classes and so must levy taxes on capital. Similarly, with reform and regulation (laws on restrictive practices, controls on pollution, etc): capital may be irritated by such legislation and arguably the state would not undertake such measures if it were under the thumb entirely of capitalist concerns. But the state, in addition to autonomy, is concerned with pressure from below and with maintaining an efficient and viable labour force.

It is, however, necessary to avoid reductionism. The relationship between state power and class interests is best conceived neither in terms of the state as representing class interests, nor in terms of the "primacy of politics" ("state reductionism"). There is, as Miliband argues,[37] a partnership involved. Skocpol contests this: in her view the state is "for itself" and against all classes and groups in society. History demonstrates that even this is not true. Even governments of the Left have accommodated to the interests of capital,[38] and business interests, though antagonistic to socialist governments, have understood that even these seek to maintain the existing social order and to defend their class interests where these are conceived to be in the national interest.[39] And, in any case, capital knows

---

[37] "State Power and Class Interests" in 110 New Left Review 57.
[38] Allende's Chile was an exception, and it was soon overthrown.
[39] And see on this R. Miliband's *The State in Capitalist Society* (1969).

that only a small part of the state changes hands: the civil service, police, judiciary, military remain virtually intact.

Marx's views on law are not set out separately in any treatise and must be pieced together from his writings.[40] There is no definition of law as such in Marx. Both he and Engels concentrate their attention rather on how law is created. They are interested in ideology and law as a manifestation of this. But Marx cannot fail to be interested in law for capitalist society is characterised by private property and this is nothing more than a bundle of legal rights relating to the use and disposition of things. Capital in such a society is private property. This, Marx tells us, enables its owner to buy the labour of another and use it to create surplus value. The worker is exploited for he does not receive his full value of the labour power.

For Marx one of the main functions of law is to obscure power relationships. Thus, the legal form will refer to the right to enter freely into contracts but in the absence of equality of bargaining power, this freedom is illusory. The legal form is an ideological cloak. The law, of course, may pretend to neutrality. Phrases such as "equality before the law" are common. But, says Engels, "the power given to one party by its different class position, the pressure it exercises on the other—the real economic position of both—all this is no concern of the law ... That the concrete economic situation compels the worker to forego even the slightest semblance of equal rights—this again is something the law cannot help".[41] The law thus serves to legitimate and mystify.

## Marx and Justice, Morality and Human Rights

There is an essential paradox in the writings of Marx and Engels on the questions of justice and morality. On the one hand, it is claimed that morality is a form of ideology and that any given morality always arises out of a particular stage of the development of productive forces and relations and so is relative to a particular mode of production and particular class interests. On this premise Marx is forced to concede that capitalist exploitation is not unjust (though slavery under capitalism would be), and does not violate the rights of workers. The Marxian critique of capitalism is not moral but scientific. On the other hand, Marxist writings are full of moral judgments. Both Marx and Engels leave us in no doubt as to their hatred of a capitalist system and the effects this has on workers.[42] Nevertheless, Marx stresses that morality

---

[40] The best attempt to do this is M. Cain and A. Hunt, *Marx and Engels on Law* (1979). See also R. Kinsey (1978) 5 Brit. J. Law & Soc. 202.

[41] Quoted, *ibid.*, p. 142.

[42] F. Engels, *The Condition of the Working Class in England* is the best example. Marx in *Capital* (vol. 1) endorses this view. He wrote: "The moral degradation caused by the capitalist exploitation of women and children has been so exhaustively depicted by F. Engels ... that I need only mention the subject ... But the intellectual desolation artificially produced by converting immature human beings into mere machines for the fabrication of surplus value ... finally compelled even the English Parliament to make elementary education a compulsory condition".

has no independence, no history. The communists, Marx and Engels wrote in *The German Ideology*, "do not preach morality at all". Marx scorned the anarchist Proudhon's appeal to an ideal of justice. In *Capital* he asks: what opinion "should we have of a chemist who, instead of studying the actual laws of the molecular changes in the composition and discomposition of matter ... claimed to regulate [them] by means of 'eternal ideas', of 'naturalité' and 'affinité'? Do we really know any more about 'usury' when we say it contradicts justice 'éternelle' ... than the fathers of the church did when they said it was incompatible with ... 'la volonté éternelle de Dieu'?" Marx was impatient with those who put forward utopias as spurs to working-class action. The working class, he wrote, "have no ready-made utopias to introduce *par décret du peuple*".[43] Instead, emancipation would come through struggle, a series of historic processes. The working class "have no ideals to realize, but to set free elements of the new society with which old collapsing bourgeois society itself is pregnant".[44] But Marx had no doubt that this new society was a "higher" form of society, "*human* society or associated humanity".[45] Marx divided this higher form into two phases, a lower and a higher (it was Lenin who christened these respectively socialism and communism). The former abolishes exploitation but not yet exchange: the latter represents Marx's ultimate ideal.

Marx's descriptions of post-capitalist society are extremely thin. What is clear is that the ideal society would be one in which, under conditions of abundance, human beings could achieve self-realisation in a new form of social unity. In *Capital*, he describes production in such a society as consisting in "socialised man ... rationally regulating ... interchange with Nature ... instead of being ruled by it as the blind forces of Nature".[46] It is a society of true freedom, with alienation overcome and the realisation of human nature.

The paradox is reflected in the writings of later Marxist writers. Kautsky spoke with scorn of "Ethical Socialism".[47] For him moral tenets arose from "social needs" and "all morality is relative", "the moral rules alter with the society, yet not uninterruptedly and not in the same fashion

---

[43] Engels also decried attempts to specify details about communism. It was impossible to do so without falling into "utopianism or empty phrase-making" (quoted in Lukes, "Marxism, Morality and Justice" in (ed.) G.H.R. Parkinson, *Marx and Marxisms* (1982), pp. 177–206).

[44] *The Civil War in France*, in *Selected Works*, vol. 1, p. 523.

[45] In *Theses on Feuerbach, Collected Works*, vol. 5, p. 8 (10th thesis).

[46] Vol. III, pp. 799–800. See also *Grundrisse* (Penguin, 1973), p. 488 ("rich individuality which is as all-sided in its production as in its consumption, and whose labour also therefore appears no longer as labour".).

[47] Ethical Socialists tried to wed Marxism and Kantianism. They said that even if the Marxian philosophy of history were true and socialism inevitable, it would not follow that socialism must therefore be accepted as good and worth striving for. Some further value judgments were required, based on grounds other than historical materialism. They argued that the Kantian ethic could provide the missing link by showing that the socialist order was one where society has no other end than to treat the human person as an end in himself (see L. Kolakowski, *Main Currents of Marxism*, vol. 2, Chap. XII).

and degree as the social needs".[48] Plekhanov "saw no need to supply moral grounds for joining a movement certain to succeed".[49] And Lenin said there was in Marxism "not a grain of ethics from beginning to end" since "theoretically, it subordinates the 'ethical standpoint' to the 'principle of causality', in the practice it reduces to the class struggle".[50] Morality, for Lenin, was what served to "destroy the old exploiting society". He added: "We do not believe in an eternal morality, and we expose the falseness of all the fables about morality".[51] All these writers, it goes without saying, continued to attack the exploitative conditions of industrial capitalism.

Can this paradox be resolved or is Marxism self-contradictory? There are a number of possible approaches. One would focus on the question of tactics (the use of moral concepts gives comfort to the "class enemy"). But, as Lukes notes, "at best this is an argument about what it is appropriate to say and write ... not about what is right to believe".[52] Another approach would emphasise relativism. Is the Marxist view of morality "a self-consistent attack on non-relativist ethics"?[53] This interpretation is incompatible with what Marxists have written. It is also difficult to understand how their criticism of industrial capitalism and projections of something better can be made compatible with ethical relativism. A third approach would focus on the alleged "abstractness" of morality. The approach preferred by Lukes (it is submitted justifiably) is to look at the aspects of morality which Marx, and subsequent Marxists, have singled out as ideological and relative to class interests and particular modes of production. The most obvious aspect of moral appraisal that meets this criterion is justice.

Marx's view of justice emerges most clearly in *Capital* and the *Critique of the Gotha Programme*. In *Capital*[54] he writes of the content of justice as corresponding to the mode of production so that "slavery on the basis of capitalist production is unjust; likewise fraud in the quality of commodities". In the *Gotha* critique, Marx asks: "What is a just distribution?" His response is: "Do not the bourgeoisie assert that the present-day distribution is 'just'? And is it not, in fact, the only 'just distribution on the basis of the present-day mode of production'?"[55] For Marx and Engels then, judgements about justice are not made by reference to abstract or formal principles independent of the existing mode of production: they do not postulate an ideal against which social reality can be measured and, if need be, adjusted.[56] Lukes interprets Marx to be saying

---

[48] *Ethics and the Materialist Conception of History, op. cit.*, pp. 17, 192, 184.

[49] *Per* Lukes, *op. cit.*, n. 43, p. 189.

[50] *Collected Works*, vol. I, p. 421.

[51] *Collected Works*, vol. XXXI, pp. 291–294.

[52] *Op. cit.*, n. 43, p. 195.

[53] *ibid.*

[54] Vol. III, Chap. 21, pp. 333–334.

[55] As quoted by Lukes, *op. cit.*, n. 43, p. 197. T. Campbell, *Justice* (2001) is a useful account on Marx on justice.

[56] *Cf.* the goal of naturalism (see Chap. 3, *ante*).

that "justice" is a juridical concept the role of which is to govern juridical relations. "The principles of *Recht* do not provide a set of independent rational standards by which to measure social relations, but must themselves always in turn be explained as arising from and controlling those relations".[57] Marx's objection to "Right" (*Recht*) is that it "by its very nature can consist only in the application of a common standard".[58] In the higher phase of communism, however, Marx talks of the "narrow horizon of bourgeois right" being "crossed in its entirety".[59] By this Marx seems to mean not that there will be no more bourgeois right, but that there will be no more right, that is no more legal and moral rules.[60] The communist ideal of "From each according to his ability, to each according to his needs" would, on this interpretation, not be such a rule (abilities and needs would be infinite and so not specifiable with any precision in advance).

By examining justice and *Recht* in this way it is possible to see why Marx, and later Marxists, should have come to reject morality, and to predict its withering away under communism. But this is not to say that Marxism rejects morality totally: indeed, in part Marxism is a morality— it is a doctrine about fundamental human goods and how they come to be realised.[61] What is it, then, that distinguishes the narrow sense of morality, rejected by Marxism, from morality in this wider sense? To Mackie[62] this narrow sense of morality is "a system of a particular sort of constraints on conduct—one whose central task is to protect the interests of persons other than the agent and which present themselves to an agent as checks on his natural inclinations or spontaneous tendencies to act". Mackie argues that this form of morality is needed to tackle a problem inherent in the human condition viz. that "limited resources and limited sympathies together generate competition leading to conflict and in absence of what would be mutually beneficial co-operation.[63] But it is, of course, a distinctive feature of Marxism that it denies that these are universal features of the human predicament: quite the contrary, it argues

---

[57] *Op. cit.*, n. 43, p. 198. *Recht* is a word for which there is no direct English translation. Hart notes that it (or the French *droit*) seems "to hover uncertainly between law and morals". He contends that it does "mark off an area of morality (the morality of law) which has special characteristics. It is occupied by the concepts of justice, fairness, right and obligation" ("Are There Any Natural Rights?" in (1955) 64 Philosophical Rev.

[58] *Gotha Programme*, quoted by Lukes, *op. cit.*, p. 199. To us this is a strange argument since this characteristic is one of the more obvious features of law. It may be argued that this amounts to an argument that any social system operating through general rules is inequitable.

[59] And see *post*, 1154.

[60] Pashukanis, *post*, 1160 seems to adopt a similar view of *Recht*, encompassing law and morality.

[61] See C. Taylor, "Marxism and Empiricism" in (eds.) B. Williams and A. Montefiore, *British Analytical Philosophy* (1966). *cf.* A. Heller, "The Legacy of Marxian Ethics To day" in Praxis International, vol. 1, p. 346 (1982).

[62] *Ethics: Inventing Right and Wrong* (1977), p. 106.

[63] *ibid.*, p. 111. For a similar view, and for the part which law plays in promoting such co-operation, see Hart, *The Concept of Law* (1994), pp. 193–200 ("the minimum content of natural law") and see *ante*, 123.

that they are historically determined and specific to class societies. Neither limited resources nor limited sympathies nor conflicts of interest are endemic to the human condition. Indeed, to assume they are is an ideological error, ideological in that it serves to buttress class-based societies. Thus, as Lukes says, "Marxism's distinctive attitude to morality is explained and the paradox within it removed. Prevailing moralities (in the narrower sense, as part of *Recht*) provide part of the ideological cement of class societies and all moralities in this sense purport to accommodate interests to the mutual advantage of all . . . Morality (as the fundamental human good) requires abandoning a condition which requires morality (as part of *Recht*). The good consists in eliminating the conditions of morality and the circumstances of justice".[64]

Marx's view of morality is thus internally consistent. The paradox may be resolved. But, as Lukes rightly asks, is the Marxian theory of morality "plausible"?[65] He gives a number of reasons for believing it is not. At root they all attack the narrowness of the Marxian analysis of social antagonism. Conflict cannot necessarily be reduced to class conflict.[66] Even if communism can eliminate class divisions there is no reason to believe that it can also rid society of conflict. For in part conflict results from the fact a complex society consists of a large number of individuals. Marxists do not satisfactorily explain why individuals should sacrifice their autonomy for the sake of supposed social unity.[67]

Can Marxists, therefore, believe in human rights? Some contemporary Marxists are prepared to use the language of "human rights".[68] The true question is whether they can do so whilst remaining faithful to Marxism. A convincing case that they cannot do so is put by Lukes.[69] In *On the Jewish Question* Marx wrote of "the so-called *rights of man*" as "simply the rights of a *member of civil society*, that is, of egoistic man, of man separated from other men and from the community". He saw "liberty" as founded not upon the relations between man and man but "rather upon the separation of man from man. It is the right of such separation". Its practical application was the right of private property.[70] To Marx and Engels all that "basic laws" would do is furnish principles for the regulation of conflicting claims and thus serve to promote class compromise and delay revolutionary change. Upon the attainment of communism the concept of human rights would be redundant because the conditions of social life would no longer have need of such principles of constraint.[71] It

---

[64] *Per* Lukes, *op. cit.*
[65] *ibid.*
[66] See *ante*, 1141 and F. Parkin, *Marxism and Class Theory: A Bourgeois Critique* (1979).
[67] One attempt to do so is by Rosa Luxemburg, on whom L. Kolakowski, *op. cit.*, n. 30, vol. 2, Chap. III and N. Geras, *The Legacy of Rosa Luxemburg* (1976), pp. 133–94.
[68] For example, G.A. Cohen in (1981) 126 *New Left Review* 12. *cf.* Rawls, *ante*.
[69] "Can a Marxist Believe in Human Rights?" in (1982) Praxis International, vol. 1, p. 334.
[70] *Karl Marx: Early Writings* (ed. T.B. Bottomore, 1963), pp. 24–26.
[71] See *ante*, 1151.

is also clear (particularly in the writings of Trotsky)[72] that in the struggle to attain communism concepts like human rights could be easily pushed aside—and were.[73]

## THE "WITHERING AWAY" OF THE STATE

To Marx the state and law were temporary phenomena. Revolution was inevitable and this would be bound to break the power of the state. With the abolition of classes the power of the state would disappear and governmental functions be transformed into simple administrative ones. The typical manifestations of the state including bureaucracy and a judiciary would disappear. Engels referred to the state "withering away",[74] Marx himself always referred to its "abolition" (*Aufhebung*).[75] Running through all Marx's writings is a connection between universal suffrage and abolition of the state.[76] Thus in *The Communist Manifesto* proletarian rule is linked to the attainment of universal suffrage: "the first step in the revolution of the working class is to raise the proletariat to the position of ruling class, to win the battle of democracy".[77] According to Avineri, "dialectically, the state that would really carry out its universal potential must end with communism and consequently with its own abolition, since 'public power will lose its political character'. The ultimate realisation of the Hegelian idea of the state as universal power implies, according to Marx, that "once the state is truly universal, it ceases to exist as a differential organism".[78]

Marx's conception of the future role of the "state" is to be found in his comments on the Paris Commune and his *Critique of the Gotha Programme*. Marx approved of the Commune's proposals to have all officials including judges elected by universal suffrage,[79] and paid the same wages as workmen. "Instead of deciding once every three or six years which member of the ruling class was to misrepresent the people in parliament,

---

[72] See L. Trotsky, J. Dewey and G. Novack, *Their Morals and Ours: Marxist versus Liberal Views on Morality* (4th ed., 1979). See further, L. Kolakowski, *op. cit.*, note 67, partic. pp. 509–512 discussing Trotsky's *The Defence of Terrorism*.

[73] Interesting admissions are K. Cavooki, "The Attainment of Human Rights in Socialism" in (1982) Praxis International, vol. 1, p. 365; L. Kopelev, *No Jail For Thought* (1979), pp. 31–34. With socialism's demise this is now accepted by all.

[74] See *post*, 1189. On recent Marxist theories of the State see Jessop (1977) 1 Cambridge J. of Econ. 353.

[75] Avineri, *The Social and Political Thought of Karl Marx* (1968), noted the two different terms derive from different intellectual traditions. Engels *Absterben* is a "biological simile". Marx's *Aufhebung* is "a philosophical term with clear dialectical overtones" (p. 203).

[76] This is found as early as his critique of Hegel's *Philosophy of Right*.

[77] *Op. cit*, n. 27, p. 102.

[78] *Op. cit.*, n. 75, p. 207.

[79] His approval of the fact that delegates were bound by formal instructions of constituents and were recallable is reminiscent of the ideas of Rousseau. See Colletti, *From Rousseau to Lenin* (1972), Pt III and R. Wokler, "Rousseau and Marx" in D. Miller and L. Siedentop (eds.), *The Nature of Political Theory* (1983), pp. 219–246.

universal suffrage was to serve the people constituted in Communes, as individual suffrage serves every other employer in search for the workmen and managers of his business".[80] Marx also noted approvingly that the Commune was the first revolution in which the working class was openly acknowledged as the only class capable of "social initiative" by the bulk of the Parisian middle class. The Commune's failure also taught Marx that workers' movements would have to develop politically if a subsequent uprising was to be successful. The seeds of Marx's concept of the dictatorship of the proletariat[81] are here.

In the Gotha critique[82] Marx points to "a period of revolutionary transformation" between capitalist and communist society. In this period "the state can be nothing but the revolutionary dictatorship of the proletariat".[83] McLellan points out that the word "dictatorship" did not have the same connotation for Marx as it does today. He associated it principally with the Roman office of "*dictatura*", where all power was legally concentrated in the hands of a single man during a limited period in a time of crisis.[84] The Gotha programme contained, according to Marx, nothing but the "old familiar democratic litany".[85] It called for state-aided workers' co-operatives rather than the revolutionary transformation of society. Even with the abolition of the division of labour and consequent disappearance of the state, communist society in its first stage would still be stamped "in every respect, economically, morally and intellectually with the birthmarks of the old society from whose womb it emerges".[86] "Right can never be higher than the economic structure of society and its cultural development conditioned thereby".[87] Only after some considerable time would full communism be achieved, "the narrow horizon of bourgeois right to be crossed in its entirety".[88] Then society could "inscribe on the banners: from each according to his ability, to each according to his needs".[89]

Marx foretold that revolution would come as the result of a severe economic crisis.[90] His materialist view of history would seem to indicate that the most advanced industrial countries should experience revolution

[80] *The Civil War in France*, p. 211.
[81] Though *The Communist Manifesto*, a quarter of a century earlier, contains similar ideas.
[82] The Gotha programme of 1875 was an attempt to accommodate revolutionary politics to the Prussian state and Bismarck's policy of uniting Germany under Prussian hegemony.
[83] "Critique of Gotha Programme" in *Selected Works*, vol. II, p. 30.
[84] *The Thought of Marx* (1971), pp. 202–203.
[85] *Op. cit.*, n. 83, at p. 30.
[86] *ibid.*, p. 24.
[87] *ibid.*
[88] *ibid.*
[89] *ibid.* A similar idea had been expressed by the French socialist Louis Blanc a quarter of a century earlier. There are echoes of this today in A. Sen, *Inequality Reexamined* (1992) (equality of opportunity based on functioning of human capacities). On the problems Marx's aphorism caused jurists in East Germany see I. Markovits (1978) 45 U. of Chic. L. Rev. 612, 632.
[90] *Selected Works* (1850), vol. I, p. 231. In his later writings Marx conceived of the possibility of a successful revolution in countries where the majority of the population were peasants.

first. Yet he thought that in these (he cited the United States, England and the Netherlands) communism could come about by peaceful means.[91] But in the year before his death he hinted that Russia might prove the starting-point of the revolution.[92] He thought the Russian system of community development of land could serve as the starting-point for communist development.[93] As early as *The Communist Manifesto* he had set out a programme to be implemented by the dictatorship of the proletariat upon its take-over.[94] It is a fairly modest list of proposals and does not include nationalisation of industry as such.

### OTHER MARXISMS

The writings of Marx have proved a powerful and pervasive influence on subsequent social and legal thought. The pervasiveness of Marx's influence is only matched by the variety of the forms which Marxism has taken. Three of these are sketched in this section.

#### *Karl Renner*

Renner's *Institutions of Private Law and their Social Functions*[95] is an attempt to utilise the Marxist system of sociology for the construction of a theory of law. He set out to demonstrate that in spite of the stability of legal concepts, like property or contract, their social functions had undergone profound transformation. The illusion of conservatism, immutability, uniformity is created but in reality considerable adaptation has taken place. Renner believed that to understand a legal concept one had to penetrate its economic base. Furthermore, he stressed the importance of history. His particular interest was in the changing functions of the legal institution of private property and in the need to explain the functions fulfilled by legal institutions at particular points in time.

Thus, he shows how in medieval society ownership symbolised a unit of which the family farm was typical. Then the place of production and consumption was the same and the legal conception of ownership represented its economic base. When, however, ownership of a complex of things (now called "capital") no longer coincides with the base of personal work, it becomes a source of a new power of command. Renner shows how the capitalist exercises a quasi-public authority over those

---

[91] Quoted in McLellan, *The Thought of Marx* (1971), p. 201.
[92] *Selected Works*, vol. I, p. 24. (Preface to 2nd Russian edition of *The Manifesto of the Communist Party*, 1882.)
[93] Discussed in Berman, *Justice in the USSR* (1963).
[94] See McLellan, *op. cit.*, note 91, pp. 219–220.
[95] Published in English in 1949, with an introduction by Kahn-Freund. Useful additional discussion are R. Kinsey, "Karl Renner on Socialist Legality" in D. Sugarman (ed.), *Legality, Ideology and the State* (1983), pp. 11–42; Robson in *Perspectives in Jurisprudence* (Attwoll, ed.) (1977), p. 221; Tigar and Levy, *Law and the Rise of Capitalism* (1977), pp. 303–309.

who are tied to him by a contract of service. The juristic institution has not changed but its function has. The owner of certain things can now use his ownership to control other persons and ownership becomes the centre of number of complementary legal institutions, like sale, loan, tenancy, hire and contract of service. The latter is called a contract and emphasises "will" but the real expression of the capitalist's power is not in the contract but the internal rules regulating conditions of work. Renner shows how in time the complementary legal institutions assume the real function of ownership and this itself becomes an empty legal form. In this way the concept of private ownership has become transformed into an institution of public law.

The awakening of the interest of lawyers and criminologists[96] in Marx led to rekindled interest in Renner's book. Renner's ideas about the relationship of property and society, though dating from the early years of the last century, are as apt today as they were then. The twentieth century witnessed considerable inroads into property to protect tenants, employees and consumers but the power of property remains, and the question of control has not altered significantly.[97]

To some, Renner's views will seem out of line with Marx. For Marx law was part of the superstructure.[98] Renner would appear to be suggesting that legal *forms* can remain unchanged despite economic transformations in society. Renner had, however, read Marx and perhaps understood him better than many of those who attribute a straightforward economic determinism to him. Renner noted that infrastructure and superstructure were "metaphors" and that they served "only to illustrate the connection, not to define in exact terms".[99] He also observed that "the mechanism by which economy as the causal factor brings about the effect of law is obscure and unexplored".[1] For Renner the law might thus itself become an active agent in reshaping social conditions. Renner's book repays study as the first, and still the most detailed, study of the relationship of law and economy.[2] It shows the relationship to be more subtle and complicated than a superficial reading of Marx would indicate. Renner's study is significant for demonstrating the part which legal culture has played in economic development. He shows, for example, how the English doctrine of estates contributed towards a more rapid shift from feudal to capitalistic relations than was the case on the Continent where the Roman law concepts of property contained, as a matter of principle, the element of eternity.

---

[96] See Taylor, Walton and Young, *The New Criminology* (1973).
[97] This point is well made by Robson, *op. cit.*
[98] *Cf. ante*, 1134 *et seq.*
[99] *Institutions of Private Law*, p. 55.
[1] *ibid.*, p. 56.
[2] A celebrated non-Marxist study of the relationship is Weber's *Law in Economy and Society* (1954). For a Marxist critique of Weber, see Walton in *The Sociology of Law* (Carlen, ed., 1976), p. 7. *cf.* Hunt, *The Sociological Movement in Law* (1978), Chap. 5.

## Antonio Gramsci

Gramsci,[3] the founder of the Italian Communist Party, developed his most important ideas whilst he languished in prison under Mussolini. His *Prison Notebooks* were published posthumously and only appeared in English in 1971. They reveal Gramsci to be one of the liveliest and creative of Marxist thinkers.[4]

An interesting and novel construct in Gramsci's thought is that of "ideological hegemony".[5] He believed that class domination resulted as much from popular consensus engineered in civil society as from physical coercion or its threat by the state apparatus. This was, he thought, particularly the case in advanced capitalist societies where the media, mass culture, education and the law take on a new role.[6] It followed that the existing order was strengthened and perpetuated by certain "super-structural" phenomena and that therefore the struggle for liberation required the creation of a "counter-hegemonic" world-view. For Gramsci revolution is not an event but a process and, what he calls, "consciousness transformation" is integral to it. Previously Marxists had focused on economic relations in society. Gramsci widened horizons to embrace politics, culture and ideology. He stressed the complex interrelationship of each and urged that no aspect of "bourgeois culture" was immune from the class struggle. Unlike most Marxists Gramsci thought the participation of socialists in bourgeois institutions desirable.[7]

## Pashukanis

Of Soviet jurists the one to command attention and respect is Pashukanis, who wrote in the 1920s and was a victim of a Stalinist purge in 1937.[8]

---

[3] Useful discussions are Anderson (1976–1977) 100 *New Left Rev.* 5; Boggs, *Gramsci's Marxism* (1976) and see, in particular now, M. Cain, "Gramsci, The State and the Place of Law" in *Legality, Ideology and the State* (D. Sugarman, ed., (1983), pp. 95–118. See also C. Baci-Glucksman, *Gramsci and the State* (1980). B. Jessop, *Theories of the Capitalist State* (1982), Chap. 4, is useful on Gramsci and neo-Gramscianism.

[4] Gramsci's concepts, notably "hegemony", are being employed with increasing frequency by scholars in many disciplines. See for example, Nairn, *The Break-up of Britain* (1977), pp. 132–137, Thompson, *Whigs and Hunters* (1975), Chap. 10, Beirne, *Fair Rent and Legal Fiction* (1977), p. 79, Williams, *Marxism and Literature* (1977).

[5] On it see Hunt in *The Sociology of Law* (Carlen, 1976), pp. 35, 42. There is a full discussion of its history and uses in Anderson, *op. cit*, note 3.

[6] *Viz.* that of "an educator" (*Prison Notebooks*, p. 260).

[7] Against Gramsci's point that the bourgeois state induces obedience through ideological hegemony, it may be said that this is in fact the case with all ruling ideologies including communist ones. *cf.* Poulantzas, *Political Power and Social Classes* (1973), p. 217.

[8] A critical re-assessment is M. Head, *Evgeny Pashukanis—A Critical Reappraisal* (2008). Useful discussions of Pashukanis are R. Warrington "Pashukanis and the Commodity Form Theory" in *Legality, Ideology and the State* (D. Sugarman, ed., (1983), pp. 43–68; Sharlet, *Soviet Union* (1974), vol. I, No. 2, p. 103; Fuller, 47 Mich.L.Rev. 1157; Arthur, *Critique No. 7* (1976–1977), Redhead, *Critique No. 9* (1978). On January 20, 1937 *Pravda* declared him an enemy of the people. He disappeared without trace, trial or confession (see R. Sharlet, "Stalinism and Soviet Legal Culture" in *Stalinism: Essays In Historical Interpretation* (R.C. Tucker, ed., (1977).

Pashukanis viewed legal theory as an historical enquiry: first, in that an understanding of bourgeois forms of law required an historical approach to the question of law because law was a result of a specific stage of social development only; and, secondly, he saw the task of Marxist legal theory as being to demonstrate the transient nature of law. Law exists, he wrote, "for the sole purpose of being utterly spent".[9] He made no pretence to develop an objective theory of law: his jurisprudence was designed to meet the political end of Bolshevism. Pashukanis saw his theory as being sociological.[10] He prided himself on his theory's sound link with reality.[11]

His theory of law, the Commodity-Exchange Theory, saw contract as the foundation of all law.[12] Law arises out of the needs of the commodity form of production. "The commodity is the cell form of legal relations because capitalist society consists of producers of commodities".[13] Commodities produced are then exchanged. All law is directed towards oiling this process of commodity exchange between subjects who act as "guardians" of commodities and are created by law to enable the commodity production form of society to function. Thus labour law was nothing more than a series of employment contracts, family law derived from a contractual view of marriage and even criminal law rested on a kind of bargain between the state and the citizen, whereby equivalent punishments were meted out for particular acts and the criminal bought off the blood feud or "paid for his crime". For Pashukanis the commodity form of exchange historically precedes (and, indeed, is logically prior to) the legal system which emerges from it. Only with the full development of the commodity form is there the possibility of a full developed abstract legal form at all. Commodity production develops through trade and law grows as trade increases in importance. As exchange develops so also disputes increase and a legal system has to develop to cope with these conflicts. Pashukanis states that: "It is disputes, conflicts of interest, which create the legal form, the legal superstructure".[14]

There are a number of problems with the commodity form theory.[15] Most obviously, it must be said that Pashukanis's argument that commodity exchange both antedates (historically) and is logically prior to law

---

[9] *Law and Marxism*, p. 133.

[10] *Op. cit.*, n. 21, p. 107.

[11] He was critical of normative theories such as Kelsen (*ante*, Chap. 5) and condemned natural law (*cf. ante*, Chap. 3) and will theories (*cf. ante*, Chap. 4) because they did not correspond to reality (*op. cit.*, n. 21, p. 145). He was also critical of Renner who he said was unable "to comprehend the concept of law in its actual workings" (*ibid.*, p. 56).

[12] In a striking phrase he referred to all law as "commercial law". The spirit of Maine seems to live on in Pashukanis. *cf. ante*, 1082. B. Edelman, *Ownership of the Image* (1979) argues that it is on the basis of this that the "genius" of Pashukanis can be recognised (p. 24). See also I. Balbus (1977) 11 Law and Soc. Rev. 571. Balbus's ideas owe a lot to Pashukanis.

[13] *Per* R. A. Warrington, *op. cit.*, n. 8, p. 48.

[14] *Op. cit*, n. 9, p. 93. A superficial similarity with early American Realism may be detected, *cf. ante*, 986.

[15] Head, *op. cit.*, n. 8, discuss fully criticisms that have been made of this: see pp. 213–218.

is unacceptable. How can property exist prior to law? Is it possible to define or analyse property relations without using legal concepts? Pashukanis certainly thinks it is. For example, he writes of the concept of theft arising before the concept of property.[16] But theft involves the appropriation of property.

Secondly, Pashukanis's theory concentrates on the exchange of commodities as if this were all capitalism was about. But, as Warrington stresses,[17] "capitalism is a process of production, and exchange is merely a part of that process". Legal theory should therefore be as much concerned with production as with exchange. Pashukanis ignores this process. Further, "not only does Pashukanis apparently ignore the central influence of production on law", but "his legal theory is not based on capitalist commodity production at all".[18] He seems to assume that a nascent legal form of pre-capitalist commodity production "expands" as the commodity form of production develops into the dominant world form. But, of course, commodity production itself has undergone enormous changes. Thirdly, Pashukanis argues (in part following Marx[19]) that "just as the market almost ignores use values and concentrates on the socially embodied labour-time in a commodity, where equivalent amounts of labour-time are exchanged, so law operates in a similar manner.[20] The law, Pashukanis argues, deals only with the formal equality of citizens[21] and ignores the substantive inequalities[22] between them. But does it? It may[23] have done in the nineteenth century but how is one to reconcile Pashukanis's view with Rent Acts, consumer protection legislation, legislation protecting employees against unfair dismissal or discrimination on grounds of race or gender?[24] Is Pashukanis confusing the "legal" and the "economic"?[25] He certainly seems to be ignoring the effects that the law can have on the economic structure.[26] A fourth puzzle with Pashukanis's emphasis on the relationship between commodity form and legal form is why the capitalist class uses law, when it could use brute force[27] (that, after all, in Marxist terms, is the form in which they are ultimately grounded). To this Head responds that this is to ignore "the ideological function of law in mystifying the real class relations in

---

[16] *ibid.*, p. 167. *cf.* H. Kelsen, *The Communist Theory of Law* (1955), p. 93 and Warrington, *op. cit*, n. 8, p. 52.

[17] *Per* Warrington, *ibid.*, p. 53.

[18] *ibid.*

[19] Marx's distinction between use value and exchange value.

[20] *Per* Warrington, *op. cit*, p. 55.

[21] *i.e.* the analogue of the exchange value.

[22] *i.e.* the analogue of the use value.

[23] But *cf.* now P. Atiyah, *The Rise and Fall of Freedom of Contract* (1979), Pt II.

[24] Though it must be conceded that such legislation does not always achieve what its form suggests it might. For example, 33 years after the Equal Pay Act 1970 came into operation the percentage of female earnings to male is barely higher than it was when the legislation was implemented.

[25] *Ante*, 1134.

[26] *Ante*, 1138–1139.

[27] But *cf.* Thompson on the rule of law, *post*, 1181. Also useful is D. Hay's "Property, Authority and the Criminal Law" in *Albion's Fatal Tree* (1975), pp. 17–63.

capitalist society but also, more profoundly, the very basis of capital accumulation in the 'free' (unfettered) purchase and consumption of labour power as a commodity".[28] Fifthly, if law is so central, one ought to have expected Pashukanis to believe not in revolution but in legal reformism, though as an orthodox Bolshevik this was far from his thoughts.[29] Head answers this too: he says Pashukanis regarded the law as "secondary", though influential, in social relations derived from economic relations.[30]

Pashukanis believed that law reached its highest point of development under capitalism. Indeed, there were no other legal norms besides those of bourgeois law. Law was therefore a peculiarly capitalist problem. It followed that there was no law before capitalism and no such law as proletarian law and that the Soviet Union, in so far as it needed to use law, would have to use bourgeois law. This was all the more so during a period like that of the New Economic Policy (a period of mixed economy starting in 1921). To say that there was no law prior to capitalism is, of course, to assert that all social managements prior to the commodity form of society were not law-based. This is a totally untenable position: feudalism, for example, embodied a highly elaborate legal structure (tenure, for example, is a legal concept).[31] To be consistent Pashukanis would have had to deny this just as he denied that slavery[32] was a legal relation (he said it required no specifically legal formulation).[33]

Pashukanis believed that law would ultimately wither away to be replaced by administration. In a socialist community private law disappeared, being swallowed up in the public sector, which was conceived as purely administrative, consisting not of fixed rules but only of guides to administrative discretion.[34] Further, as man became a "group creature" and there was complete identity of interest, morality too would disappear since this was also founded upon a concept of exchange. Pashukanis is not entirely consistent. He argues that criminal law is a requirement of capitalist society only and becomes "utterly meaningless if the principle of the equivalent relation disappears from it".[35] But he seems also to have envisaged a penal system lacking "any element of antagonism"[36] emerging with the complete disappearance of classes.

---

[28] *Op.cit*, p. 221. He quotes Pashukanis at pp. 139–140. See also *post*, 1199.
[29] See further, P. Beirne and R. Sharlet's Introduction to *Pashukanis: Selected Writings on Marxism and Law* (1980). And see Pashukanis, *op. cit.*, p. 98, where he argues that law cannot be beneficial to the revolutionary process.
[30] *Ibid.*
[31] It would be interesting to see what he would have had to say about feudal concepts of property in English land law immediately prior to the property legislation of 1925 (when England was a leading capitalist country). See also H. Collins, *Marxism and Law* (1982), p. 82.
[32] On slavery see *ante*, 1137.
[33] *Op. cit*, n. 9, p. 110.
[34] Pashukanis was committed to the "plan" (see Kamenka and Tay in 21 Univ. of Toronto L.Rev.). *cf.* Binns, *Capital and Class No. 10* (1980).
[35] *Op. cit*, p. 176.
[36] *ibid.*, p. 175.

However, if penal systems are one result of commodity societies, it is difficult to see how he can justify the necessity for them in a post-capitalist society.[37]

Pashukanis's commitment to the ultimate disappearance of law is the logical conclusion of his commodity form theory. To be coherent this theory had to postulate that only societies based on commodity production had legal systems or any need for them. Accordingly, in his view, so long as the Soviet Union needed law (a fact that the N.E.P. recognised) it had to use bourgeois law and, furthermore, could not develop since it had reached its apogee under capitalism (despite the fact that the Soviet Union had barely emerged from feudalism). Pashukanis's thesis that law would gradually wither away with the attenuation of bourgeois society was unacceptable to an increasingly authoritarian state, as well as in the process of rapid industrialisation, and, though he tried muddled recantations,[38] his demise was inevitable.

## MARXIST THEORIES OF LAW AND STATE—A CRITIQUE

Criticism of Marx's theories takes two distinct lines. First, there are those which quarrel with Marxian analyses of society and his predictions of what a revolution would achieve. Secondly, there are those which point to the non-applicability of the theory to contemporary society.

Arguments of the first type point to the overemphasis in Marx of the significance of economic class,[39] and to the fact that there are other dimensions of stratification, like race and sex and other struggles that cannot be grasped through class theory such as ecology and disarmament. As has been pointed out,[40] the Marxist response is to view such inequality and oppression as in the interests of capitalism or at least a section of it. The dialectical interpretation is also criticised. Why should it end with socialism? A point made ever more forcefully with the collapse of the Soviet Union.[41] Is Marx's picture of primitive society idealised? Was not Hobbes's description of the life of man in the state of nature as "solitary, poor nasty, brutish and short" more accurate?[42] Anthropological evidence, furthermore, has shown that private property and institutions like contract are to be found in societies which Marx would, in every other sense, have regarded as "primitive".[43] Historians have shown capitalistic attitudes and practices in pre-industrial society as early

---

[37] But it is clear that Pashukanis's attention (rather like Hohfeld, *ante*, 396, 569) was on civil law and his discussion of criminal law rather a clumsy afterthought).

[38] P. Beirne and R. Sharlet publish these in their *Selected Writings on Marxism and Law* (1980). A rigorous defence is Norrie (1982) 10 Int. J. of Soc. of Law 419.

[39] Weber was one of Marx's earliest critics on this score.

[40] *Ante*, 1141.

[41] See the symposium in (2003) 20(1) Social Philosophy and Policy. See also R. Dahrendorf, *Reflections on The Revolution in Europe* (1990).

[42] In *Leviathan* (1651).

[43] Pospisil. *Kapauku Papuan Economy* (1963).

as the ninth century, and that the ideology of capitalism had rural origins.[44] Further, feudalism has been shown not to be as static as Marx assumed. It has also been demonstrated that in England changes within it came from feudal lords and not from a class challenge to them.[45]

Marx's view of law can also be seen as over-simplified. Even if some law does exist to exploit the workers and to promote the interests of the "ruling class",[46] it can be argued that law has many other functions as well. Indeed, Marx (and contemporary Marxists) accept this. They argue that the ideological functions of law are just as important to the maintenance of social order as its repressive functions.[47] Indeed, some law restrains oppression. This is recognised by some Marxists as, for example, in E.P. Thompson's defence of the rule of law.[48] He accepts that law mediates class relations to the advantage of the "ruling class" but he sees that in many cases it has also imposed restraints on that class. Law mystifies class rule, but its rhetoric and the rules themselves are not just a sham, as some Marxists including Marx and Engels themselves, alleged. "People are not as stupid" as some suppose them to be, says Thompson.[49] Thompson detects real differences, often glossed over, between brute force and the rule of law. The latter he sees as an unqualified good. And, as Beirne and Quinney put it, "To deny or to belittle this good is a desperate error of intellectual abstraction, a self-fulfilling error that disarms us before power and that discards a whole inheritance of struggle *about* law.[50] Thompson's contribution to the debate about law is a particularly valuable one.[51] But what he seems to assume is that "the rule of law" itself is some abstract concept that can be abstracted from its historical context. This clearly is not the case: what Soviet jurists referred to as "socialist legality"[52] and Dicey[53] or Thompson as the "rule of law" are not functional equivalents: the rule of law assumes different forms.[54]

Even so the tendency is for Marxists to argue that where law inhibits oppression it does so, not for altruistic reasons, but to further the

[44]  Hallam "The Medieval Social Picture" in *Feudalism, Capitalism and Beyond* (Kamenka and Neale. eds., (1975)) p. 29.
[45]  West, "On the Ruins of Feudalism—Capitalism?" in *ibid.*, p. 51.
[46]  An excellent critique of the class instrumentalism within Marxism (in the context of law) see H. Collins, *Marxism and Law*, Chap. 2.
[47]  See also Gramsci, *ante*, 1157.
[48]  In *Whigs and Hunters* (1977), p. 258 and *post*, 1013.
[49]  *Post*, 1015. On the influence of Thompson for South African constitutional developments see Corder (1994) 57 M.L.R. 491, 527.
[50]  *Marxism and Law* (1982), p. 100.
[51]  See M.D.A. Freeman, "Questioning the Delegalisation Movement in Family Law" in J. Eekelaar and S. Katz, *The Resolution of Family Conflict* (1984), p. 7.
[52]  Defined as "the rigorous and undeviating adherence to and execution of Soviet laws by all state agencies, public organizations, persons in authority and citizens" (Strogovich, *Soviet Law and Government*, vol. 4(4), p. 13).
[53]  See his *Introduction to the Study of the Law of the Constitution* (1st ed., 1885) and R. Cosgrove, *The Rule of Law: A.V. Dicey, Victorian Jurist* (1980) on which see D. Sugarman (1983) 46 M.L.R. 102.
[54]  See further, in relation to Thompson, S. Redhead, "Marxist Theory: The Rule of Law and Socialism" in (ed.) P. Beirne and R. Quinney, *op. cit*, p. 328. See also Thompson's "Trial by Jury" in his *Writing By Candlelight* (1980), p. 99.

interests of the "ruling class" or a segment of it. A good illustration of this is the literature, beginning with Marx himself,[55] explaining the origins of nineteenth-century factory legislation.[56] Law sometimes functions purely as a regulator. At other times it serves to enhance security or moral standards or the family. Yet it can be asked, whose social or moral standards are being secured and why the monogamous, patriarchal society is deemed deserving of protection. Legislation enforcing moral standards causes particular problems, for the middle classes seem to have a "monopoly of moral indignation"[57] and much "morals legislation" seems to emanate from campaigns of those who would appear to be economically not very powerful.[58] A bureaucracy like the police, a government agency or a professional organisation like the British Medical Association is also instrumental in the passage and enforcement of legislation.[59]

Laws which are (or appear to be) against the interests of the "ruling class" also cause Marxist problems. As Chambliss put it "laws are passed which reflect the interests of the general population and which are antithetical to the interests of those in power".[60] Reference has been made to this problem in an earlier chapter.[61] Marxists give a variety of answers. Bonger[62] in 1916 explained the paradox by suggesting another *viz.*, that even the powerless had some power. This concession to pluralism does not meet with the approval of most contemporary Marxists. To Tigar[63] such laws are a bribe, a small concession to buy off the demand for more fundamental changes. To Hepburn, "laws which appear inimical to a particular interest or segment of the capitalist élite may be seen as a symbolic means of internal self-regulation or as vehicles designed to protect the greater interests of the élite by restricting those individual members whose reckless, public and harmful activities may alienate a large section of the powerless".[64]

This leads to yet another problem: what is meant by the "ruling class"? It is argued by Dahl,[65] Rose[66] and Polsby,[67] for example, that the power structure in contemporary society is a complex of power centres, a pluralist congeries, which makes shifting compromises and

---

[55] See *Capital*.

[56] For example, the writings of W.G. Carson. A good example is contained in *Crime, Criminology and Public Policy* (R.G. Hood, ed., (1974), p. 107.

[57] The term is Ranulf's (*Moral Indignation and Middle Class Psychology* (1938)).

[58] See Duster, *The Legislation of Morality* (1970); Sinclair, *Prohibition—An Era of Excess* (1962).

[59] Greenwood and Young, *Abortion In Demand* (1976), Becker, *Outsiders* (1963), Roby (1969) 17 *Social Problems* 83, Dickson (1968) 16 *Social Problems* 56.

[60] *Crime and the Legal Process* (1969), p. 10.

[61] *Ante*, 852–854.

[62] *Criminality and Economic Conditions* (1916).

[63] "Socialist Law and Legal Institutions" in *Law Against the People* (Lefcourt, ed., 1973). See also Wolfe, *The Seamy Side of Democracy* (1973).

[64] "Social Control and the Legal Order" (1977) 1 *Contemporary Crises* 77, 85.

[65] *Who Governs?* (1961); *Pluralist Democracy in the United States* (1967).

[66] *The Power Structure* (1967).

[67] *Community Power and Political Theory* (1963).

accommodations but which does not coalesce into a monolithic all-powerful ruling élite. Pluralists deny that any one interest can marshal the power regularly to impose its will upon the larger society through decisive control over governmental decision-making. Dahl points to the difficulties of identifying the ruling élite as a well-defined group.[68] Marxists like Miliband attempt to make such an identification. In *The State in Capitalist Society*[69] he argues that the state includes not just the executive and legislative branches of government, but the civil service, local government, the judiciary, military and the police. He sees the "state system" as the interaction of these institutions. In these terms he tries to explain why an anti-capitalist government[70] (he gives as an example the Labour government of 1945) failed to achieve a socialist society. He attributes this to the fact that it had to work with other members of the system selected and socialised by class background and political pressures under the old régime. Griffith's assertion that the judiciary supports the *status quo* and associates the public interest with the policies of the Conservative party is to similar effect.[71] Griffith, however, does not define the *status quo* and ignores the very many cases where the judiciary has overturned it. The American Supreme Court under Warren was doing just this much of its time.

Ultimately the Marxist-pluralist dispute[72] revolves about which model best fits empirical reality. But this in itself is no easy investigation for the disputants are not agreed upon what they are investigating. Few questions illustrate better the elusiveness of "facts" in the social sciences and the impossibility of *wertfrei* investigation.[73] Recent writing has tried to clarify the concept of power.[74] Thus, from the one-dimensional view that élites have power to influence policy, Bachrach and Baratz[75] have developed the idea that power should be measured not solely by positive actions which achieve desired objectives in a controversy but also by the ability to keep the controversy from surfacing in the first place. Power

---

[68]  An interesting question was raised as to whether there was a ruling class in the USSR See Nove (1975) 27 *Soviet Studies* 615; Hirszowicz (1976) 28 *Soviet Studies* 262; Kusiv (1976) 28 *Soviet Studies* 274.

[69]  (1969), Chap. 3.

[70]  *ibid.*, pp. 96 *et seq.*

[71]  *The Politics of the Judiciary* (5th ed., 1995).

[72]  Useful critiques are Mankoff (1970) 17 *Social Problems* 418, Cunningham (1976) 39 *Science and Society* 385.

[73]  See Gouldner, *For Sociology* (1973), Chap. 1.

[74]  See, in addition to works cited here, Lukes, *Power—A Radical View* (1976). A rather different view is presented in the writings of the French philosopher, Michel Foucault. Power, he argues, is not a thing which some groups can exclusively have and exercise against other powerless people. In his view power is dispensed throughout the body politic. He is accordingly less concerned with its function than with its techniques and procedures, the mechanisms and apparatuses of regulation involved. See, particularly, his *Discipline and Punish* (1977) and *Madness and Civilization* (1975). There are good critiques of Foucault by Ignatieff in *Social Control and The State* (S. Cohen and A. Scull, eds.) (1983), pp. 79–95 and by Smart in *The Power to Punish* (D. Garland and P. Young, eds.) (1983), pp. 62–83.

[75]  (1962) 56 Am.Pol.Sci.Rev.947; (1963) 57 Am.Pol.Sci.Rev.632. Also in *Power and Poverty* (1970).

involves not just "decisions" but "non-decisions" in areas where interest is in maintaining the *status quo*. But how is one to determine empirically the existence of a non-decision?[76] This seems a problem in which the Scandinavian realists[77] would revel.

It may be possible to establish the existence of a ruling class élite in a particular society at a particular time. At the moment, as Rock has commented in a perceptive article, little more than "anthropomorphic conspiracy theory" is to be found.[78] What he writes of deviancy theory can be generalised. "The perspective offers no understanding of law as a complex and variegated rule-system whose origins are frequently as mysterious to élites as to the governed. It offers no vision of a legal system as a series of constraints upon law-giver and ruled alike. It does not refer to legitimacy and authority other than in the context of manipulation and mystification. It does not provide for the elaborate patterns of accommodation that characterise many situations of social control. The law-giver is an Olympian figure endowed with a rationality, an innocence of unintended consequences, and a clear self-interestedness ... Such a legislator is a strange creature to discover in sociological analysis. He lacks plausibility, if only because it is difficult to conceive of a powerful group which is utterly emancipated from the common-sense ideas that prevail amongst the powerless ... But the origins of such a caricatured figure are quite intelligible. He is the natural outcome of an analysis which lacks a sense of history, a sensitivity to institutional patterns, and a range which is wider than the narrow focus upon encounters between deviants and officials".

The other line of attack on Marx points to his failure to predict twentieth-century developments. Since he is seen as some kind of a prophet this attack, if accurate, is legitimate. Thus, Dahrendorf[79] points to the decomposition of capital, the managerial revolution described by Burnham[80] and Berle and Means[81] which has split off ownership of the means of production from their control.[82] In fact only a tiny proportion of the population hold shares in private corporate enterprises.[83] Is there any evidence that business policy has changed as a result of the change in personnel? Dahrendorf also refers to the decomposition of labour,

---

[76] *Cf.* Wolfinger (1971) 65 Am.Pol.Sci.Rev. 1063; Nadel (1975) 37 J. of Politics 2.

[77] *Ante*, Chap 11. *cf.* Russell's question: "Are there negative facts?" (See Urmson, *Philosophical Analysis*, p. 68).

[78] "Sociology of Deviancy and Conceptions of Moral Order" (1974) 14 Brit.J. of Criminology.

[79] *Class and Class Conflict In Industrial Society* (1959).

[80] *The Managerial Revolution* (1941).

[81] *The Modern Corporation and Private Property* (1932). *cf.* Nichols, *Ownership, Control and Ideology* (1969).

[82] The importance of the ownership/control debate can be exaggerated. The real question is not one of form but rather of function. The importance is what consequences attach to having control within an organisation. A thoughtful analysis of power in these terms is G. Therborn, *What Does The Ruling Class Do When It Rules?* (1978) (more succinctly in *Classes, Power and Conflict* (A. Giddens and D. Held, eds., (1982), pp. 224-248).

[83] See Westergaard and Resler, *Class in a Capitalist Society* (1975), p. 156. See table at p. 158.

divisions between skilled and unskilled workers, often between indigenous workers and immigrants, the plurality of status and skill groups, as
well as the new middle class.[84] There are arguably now divisions between
those in employment and the unemployed. There are also factors that
mitigate class cleavage; the extension of the suffrage, the introduction of
social welfare benefits, a certain amount of income redistribution through
taxation. Inequalities undoubtedly remain.

---

### HEGEL
### Philosophy of Right

(Translated T.M. Knox)

*The Idea of the State*

The state in and by itself is the ethical whole, the actualization of freedom; and it
is an absolute end of reason that freedom should be actual. The state is mind on
earth and consciously realizing itself there. In nature, on the other hand, mind
actualizes itself only as its own other, as mind asleep. Only when it is present in
consciousness, when it knows itself as a really existent object, is it the state. In
considering freedom, the starting-point must be not individuality, the single self-
consciousness, but only the essence of self-consciousness; for whether man knows
it or not, this essence is externally realized as a self-subsistent power in which
single individuals are only moments. The march of God in the world, that is what
the state is. The basis of the state is the power of reason actualizing itself as will.
In considering the Idea of the state, we must not have our eyes on particular states
or on particular institutions. Instead we must consider the Idea, this actual God,
by itself. On some principle or other, any state may be shown to be bad, this or
that defect may be found in it; and yet, at any rate if one of the mature states of
our epoch is in question, it has in it the moments essential to the existence of the
state. But since it is easier to find defects than to understand the affirmative, we
may readily fall into the mistake of looking at isolated aspects of the state and so
forgetting its inward organic life. The state is no ideal work of art; it stands on
earth and so in the sphere of caprice, chance, and error, and bad behaviour may
disfigure it in many respects. But the ugliest of men, or a criminal, or an invalid,
or a cripple, is still always a living man. The affirmative, life, subsists despite his
defects, and it is this affirmative factor which is our theme here.

*The Particular State*

The state in its actuality is essentially an individual state, and beyond that a
particular state. Individuality is to be distinguished from particularity. The former
is a moment in the very Idea of the state, while the latter belongs to history. States
as such are independent of one another, and therefore their relation to one
another can only be an external one, so that there must be a third thing standing
above them to bind them together. Now this third thing is the mind which gives
itself actuality in world-history and is the absolute judge of states. Several states
may form an alliance to be a sort of court with jurisdiction over others, there may
be confederations of states, like the Holy Alliance for example, but these are

---

[84] Marx was not unaware of some of these divisions. *cf. ante*, 1140.

always relative only and restricted, like "perpetual peace". The one and only absolute judge, which makes itself authoritative against the particular and at all times, is the absolute mind which manifests itself in the history of the world as the universal and as the genus there operative. [p. 279]

## K. MARX
### Critique of Hegel's Philosophy of Right
### (1843)[85]

Since it is of the essence of bureaucracy to be the "state as formalism", so its aim implies this also. The real aim of the state thus appears to bureaucracy as an aim against the state. The spirit of bureaucracy is therefore the "formal spirit of the state". Thus it makes the "formal spirit of the state" or the real lack of spirit by the state into a categorical imperative. Bureaucracy counts in its own eyes as the final aim of the state. Because it makes its "formal" ends into its content, it enters into conflict everywhere with "real" ends. It is therefore compelled to claim the formal for its content and its content as the formal. The aims of the state are transformed into the aims of the bureaux and the aims of the bureaux into the aims of the state. Bureaucracy is a circle from which no one can escape. Its hierarchy is a hierarchy of knowledge. The apex entrust the lower circles with insight into the individual while the lower circles leave insight into the universal to the apex, so they deceive each other reciprocally.

Bureaucracy constitutes an imaginary state beside the real state and is the spiritualism of the state. Thus every object has a dual meaning, a real one and a bureaucratic one, just as knowledge is dual, a real and a bureaucratic (it is the same with the will). But the real thing is treated according to its bureaucratic essence, its other-worldly spiritual essence. Bureaucracy holds in its possession the essence of the state, the spiritual essence of society, it is its private property. The general spirit of bureaucracy is secret, mystery, safeguarded inside itself by hierarchy and outside by its nature as a closed corporation. Thus public political spirit and also political mentality appear to bureaucracy as a betrayal of its secret. The principle of its knowledge is therefore authority, and its mentality is the idolatry of authority. But within bureaucracy the spiritualism turns into a crass materialism, the materialism of passive obedience, faith in authority, the mechanism of fixed and formal behaviour, fixed principles, attitudes, traditions; as far as the individual bureaucrat is concerned, the aim of the state becomes his private aim, in the form of a race for higher posts, of careerism.

## K. MARX
### Preface to Contribution to Critique of Political Economy
### (1859)[86]

I was led by my studies to the conclusion that legal relations as well as forms of State could neither be understood by themselves, nor explained by the so-called general progress of the human mind, but that they are rooted in the material conditions of life, which are summed up by Hegel after the fashion of the English and French writers of the eighteenth century under the name *civil society*, and that the anatomy of civil society is to be sought in political economy. The study of the latter which I had begun in Paris, I continued in Brussels where I had emigrated

---

[85] [From McLellan, *Early Texts*, p. 69.]
[86] [This passage and that from *German Ideology* are translated by T.B. Bottomore, and taken from Bottomore and Rubel, *Karl Marx, Selected Writings In Sociology and Social Philosophy* (1961).]

on account of an expulsion order issued by M. Guizot. The general conclusion at which I arrived and which, once reached, continued to serve as the guiding thread in my studies, may be formulated briefly as follows: In the social production which men carry on they enter into definite relations that are indispensable and independent of their will; these relations of production correspond to a definite state of development of their material powers of production. The totality of these relations of production constitutes the economic structure of society—the real foundation, on which legal and political superstructures arise and to which definite forms of social consciousness correspond. The mode of production of material life determines the general character of the social, political, and spiritual processes of life. It is not the consciousness of men that determines their being, but, on the contrary, their social being determines their consciousness. At a certain stage of their development, the material forces of production in society come in conflict with the existing relations of production, or—what is but a legal expression for the same thing—with the property relations within which they had been at work before. From forms of development of the forces of production these relations turn into their fetters. The occurs a period of social revolution. With the change of the economic foundation the entire immense superstructure is more or less rapidly transformed. In considering such transformations, the distinction should always be made between the material transformation of the economic conditions of production which can be determined with the precision of natural science, and the legal, political, religious, aesthetic or philosophical—in short, ideological—forms in which men become conscious of this conflict and fight it out. Just as our opinion of an individual is not based on what he thinks of himself, so can we not judge of such a period of transformation by its own consciousness; on the contrary, this consciousness must rather be explained from the contradictions of material life, from the existing conflict between the social forces of production and the relations of production. No social order ever disappears before all the productive forces for which there is room in it have been developed; and new, higher relations of production never appear before the material conditions of their existence have matured in the womb of the old society. Therefore, mankind always sets itself only such problems as it can solve; since, on closer examination, it will always be found that the problem itself arises only when the material conditions necessary for its solution already exist or are at least in the process of formation. In broad outline we can designate the Asiatic, the ancient, the feudal, and the modern bourgeois modes of production as progressive epochs in the economic formation of society. The bourgeois relations of production are the last antagonistic form of the social process of production; not in the sense of individual antagonisms, but of conflict arising from conditions surrounding the life of individuals in society. At the same time the productive forces developing in the womb of bourgeois society create the material conditions for the solution of that antagonism. With this social formation, therefore, the prehistory of human society comes to an end.                    [pp. 67–69]

### K. MARX AND F. ENGELS
### The German Ideology
### (1845–1846)

Since the State is the form in which the individuals of a ruling class assert their common interests, and in which the whole civil society of an epoch is epitomized, it follows that the State acts as an intermediary for all community institutions, and that these institutions receive a political form. Hence the illusion that law is based on will, and indeed on will divorced from its real basis—on *free* will. Similarly, law is in its turn reduced to the actual laws.

Civil law develops concurrently with private property out of the disintegration of the natural community. Among the Romans the development of private property and civil law had no further industrial and commercial consequences, because their whole mode of production remained unchanged. Among modern peoples, where the feudal community was disintegrated by industry and trade, a new phase began with the rise of private property and civil law, which was capable of further development. The first town which carried on an extensive trade in the Middle Ages, Amalfi, also developed at the same time maritime law. As soon as industry and trade developed private property further, first in Italy and later in other countries, the perfected Roman civil law was at once taken up again and raised to authority. When, subsequently, the bourgeoisie had acquired so much power that the princes took up their interests in order to overthrow the feudal nobility by means of the bourgeoisie, there began in all countries—in France in the sixteenth century—the real development of law, which in all countries except England proceeded on the basis of the Roman Code. Even in England, Roman legal principles had to be introduced for the further development of civil law (especially in the case of personal movable property). It should not be forgotten that law has not, any more than religion, an independent history. [pp. 228–229]

### F. ENGELS
### The Housing Question[87]

At a certain, very primitive stage of the development of society, the need arises to bring under a common rule the daily recurring acts of production, distribution and exchange of products, to see to it that the individual subordinates himself to the common conditions of production and exchange. This rule, which at first is custom, soon becomes *law*. With law organs necessarily arise which are entrusted with its maintenance—public authority, the state. With further social development, law develops into a more or less comprehensive legal system. The more intricate this legal system becomes, the more is its mode of expression removed from that in which the usual economic conditions of the life of society are expressed. It appears as an independent element which derives the justification for its existence and the substantiation of its further development not from the economic relations but from its own inner foundations or, if you like, from "the concept of the will". People forget that their right derived from their economic conditions of life, just as they have forgotten that they themselves derive from the animal world. With the development of the legal system into an intricate, comprehensive whole a new social division of labour becomes necessary; an order of professional jurists develops and with these legal science comes into being. In its further development this science compares the legal systems of various peoples and various times not as a reflection of the given economic relationships, but as systems which find their substantiations in themselves. The comparison presupposes points in common, and these are found by the jurists compiling what is more or less common to all these legal systems and calling it *natural right*. And the stick used to measure what is natural right and what is not is the most abstract expression of right itself, namely, *justice*. Henceforth, therefore, the development of right for the jurists, and for those who take their word for everything, is nothing more than a striving to bring human conditions, so far as they are expressed in legal terms, ever closer to the ideal of justice, *eternal* justice. And always this justice is but the ideologised, glorified expression of the existing economic relations, now from their conservative, and now from their revolutionary angle. The justice of the Greeks and Romans held slavery to be just; the justice of the bourgeois of 1789 demanded the abolition of feudalism on the ground that it was unjust. For the Prussian Junker even the miserable District

[87] [From Marx and Engels, *Selected Works*, vol. III, pp. 365–366.]

Ordinance is a violation of eternal justice. The conception of eternal justice, therefore, varies not only with time and place, but also with the persons concerned, and belongs among those things of which Mülberger correctly says, "everyone understands something different". While in everyday life, in view of the simplicity of the relations discussed, expressions like right, wrong, justice, and sense of right are accepted without misunderstanding even with reference to social matters, they create, as we have seen, the same hopeless confusion in any scientific investigation of economic relations as would be created, for instance, in modern chemistry if the terminology of the phlogiston theory were to be economic conditions suffers increasingly. All the more so the more rarely it happens that a code of law is the blunt, unmitigated, unadulterated expression of the domination of a class—this in itself would offend the "conception of right". Even in the *Code Napoléon* the pure, consistent conception of right held by the revolutionary bourgeoisie of 1792–96 is already adulterated in many ways, and in so far as it is embodied in the Code, has daily to undergo all sorts of attenuations owing to the rising power of the proletariat. This does not prevent the *Code Napoléon* from being the statute book which serves as the basis of every new code of law in every part of the world. Thus to a great extent the course of the "development of law" simply consists in first attempting to eliminate contradictions which arise from the direct translation of economic relations into legal principles, and to establish a harmonious system of law, and then in the repeated breaches made in this system by the influence and compulsion of further economic development, which involves it in further contradictions. (I am speaking here for the moment only of civil law.)

The reflection of economic relations in the form of legal principles is likewise bound to be inverted: it goes on without the person who is acting being conscious of it; the jurist imagines he is operating with *a priori* propositions, whereas they are really only economic reflections; everything is therefore upside down. And it seems to me obvious that this inversion, which, so long as it remains unrecognised, forms what we call *ideological outlook*, influences in its turn the economic basis and may, within certain limits, modify it. The basis of the right of inheritance is an economic one, provided the level of development of the family is the same. It would, nevertheless, be difficult to prove, for instance, that the absolute liberty of the testator in England and the severe and very detailed restrictions imposed upon him in France are due to economic causes alone. But in their turn they exert a very considerable effect of the economic sphere, because they influence the distribution of property.

### G.A. COHEN
### Karl Marx's Theory of History
(1978)

*Base and Superstructure, Power and Rights*

*The Problem of Legality*

In this section we venture a solution to a difficulty which arises for historical materialism, which may be called "the problem of legality".

The problem: if the economic structure is constituted of *property* (or *ownership*) relations, how can it be distinct from the legal superstructure which it is supposed to explain?[88] For

---

[88] See Plamenatz, *German Marxism*, Chap. II, section 1, which is criticised in my "On Some Criticisms, I", section (5).

the property relations of men belong to the sphere of their *legal* relations: property is first of all a legal institution. To say that the key to understanding historical phenomena must be sought in the property relations of men means saying that this key lies in the institutions of law.[89] ...

But how can they fail to be mixed up when the economic structure is *defined* in legal terms? And is not such a definition mandatory, since the structure of an economy is (or at least includes) a structure of ownership? ...

The problem, which has two connected parts, is (i) to formulate a non-legal interpretation of the legal terms in Marx's characterization of production relations, in such a way that (ii) we can coherently represent property relations as distinct from, and explained by, production relations.

Our solution proceeds as follows. First, we display ownership as a matter of enjoying rights. Then, for each ownership right we formulate what will be called a "matching power". Next, we similarly describe production relations which "match" property relations. Finally, we show how production relations, thus identified, may be represented as explaining property relations.

Though Marx uses the terms "property", "owns", etc., when he characterizes production relations, we thought it advisable to dispense with them, and spoke instead of various combinations of the sorts of rights owners typically enjoy. The offending concept in our provisional characterization of the economic structure is the concept of a right.

Now we can transform any phrase of the form "the right to ø" into a phrase which denotes a power by dropping the word "right" and replacing it by the word "power". Let us call the power the new phrase denotes a power which *matches* the right denoted by the original phrase. If *x* has power *p* and power *p* matches right *r*, we may say that, roughly speaking, the content of the power he has is the same as the content of right *r*, but we cannot infer that he also has right *r*. Possession of powers does not entail possession of the rights they match, nor does possession of rights entail possession of the powers matching them. Only possession of a *legitimate* power entails possession of the right it matches, and only possession of an *effective* right entails possession of its matching power. One might say that the power to ø is what you have in *addition to* the right to ø when your right to ø is effective, and that the right to ø is what you have *in addition to* the power to ø when your power to ø is legitimate.

This does not mean that a man cannot have a power which matches an ineffective right he has. For example: a man has the right to travel, but a gang of hoodlums do not want him to. They would prevent him from travelling, and they are too strong to be restrained by the legitimate authorities, who are weak. But the man has a stronger gang at his disposal, which is able to defeat the gang that would block his movement. He has the right to travel *and* the power to travel, even though his right to travel is ineffective.

We are using "power" as follows: a man has the power to ø if and only if he is able to ø, where "able" is non-normative. "Able" is used normatively when "He is not able to ø" may be true even though he is ø-ing, a logical feature of legal and moral uses of "able". Where "able" is non-normative, "He is ø-ing" entails "He is able to ø".                                                                    [pp. 217–220]

We now have a way of excising legal terms from the description of production relations. We can construct *rechtsfrei* production relations which match property relations in just the way powers match rights. We proceed to illustrate the use of the method. The method works only if the *rechtsfrei* characterizations of production relations it supplies do not alter the intent of the claims Marx made about production relations using a legal vocabulary.

Consider the contrasting relations of production, described in legal terms, ...

[89] [*Per* Plekhanov, *The Marxist View*, p. 35.]

which distinguish the ideal-typical slave from the ideal-typical proletarian. ... Neither owns any means of production. Marx differentiates them by pointing out that whereas the proletarian owns his labour power, the slave does not. Unlike the latter, the former has the right to withhold it.

Our programme enjoins us to translate as follows: the proletarian has the power to withhold his labour power, while the slave does not.

Objection: The reason the slave is said to lack this power is that if he does not work he is likely to be killed, and he will certainly die. But a similar fate awaits the withholding proletarian, since he loses his means of subsistence. Therefore the proletarian is also unable to withhold his labour power. Therefore the descriptions of the production relations of slaves and proletarians no longer contrast when they are purged of legal terms in accordance with our programme.

Reply: It is relevant that the withholding slave is liable to be killed and the proletarian is not, but we shall not rely on this difference. We concede that the withholding proletarian dies. But note that he may be able to withhold his labour power from a given capitalist, including his current employer, without fear of death. The slave cannot withhold his labour power from his particular master and still live.

The proletarian is constrained to offer his labour power not to any particular capitalist, but to some capitalist or other. If he wishes to survive, he must present himself on the labour market to the capitalist class, and he is forced to serve that class. This accords well with Marx's frequent statement that the proletarian is owned not by any given capitalist, but by the capitalist class as a whole.[90] The matching non-legal statement of his position is true.

That is how to carry out the programme in one important case. It is impossible to demonstrate the viability of the programme except on a case-by-case basis, but we submit that it will generate the appropriate results quite generally.

[pp. 222–223]

*Bases Need Superstructures*

Production relations are functionally explained by the development of the productive forces. Property relations are, in turn, functionally explained by production relations: legal structures rise and fall according as they promote or frustrate forms of economy favoured by the productive forces. Property relations have the character they do because production relations require that they have it.

In human society might frequently requires right in order to operate or even to be constituted. Might without right may be impossible, inefficient, or unstable. Powers over productive forces are a case in point. Their exercise is less secure when it is not legal. So, for efficiency and good order, production relations require the sanction of property relations. Hence men fight, successfully, to change the law so that it will legitimate powers they either have or perceive to be within their grasp, and lawmakers alter the law to relieve actual or potential strain between it and the economy...

If production relations require legal expression for stability, it follows that the foundation requires a superstructure. This seems to violate the architectural metaphor, since foundations do not normally need superstructures to be stable. We must be careful if we are looking for a visual image to go with the metaphor. One slab resting on another would be inappropriate. One correct picture is the following.

Four struts are driven into the ground, each protruding the same distance above it. They are unstable. They sway and wobble in winds of force 2. Then a

---

[90] See "Wage-Labour and Capital", p. 83; *Grundrisse*, p. 464; *Capital*, vol. i pp. 168, 574, 613–614; "Results", p. 1032; *Theories of Surplus Value*, vol. i, pp. 229, 349; Engels, "Principles of Communism", Question 7.

roof is attached to the four struts, and now they stay firmly erect in all winds under force 6. Of this roof one can say: (i) it is supported by the struts, and (ii) it renders them more stable. There we have a building whose base and super-structure relate in the right way.

The picture does not display the claim that the base explains the character of the superstructure. One has to add a caption which says that when and because struts would otherwise be unstable a roof which secures them tends to be imposed. Non-metaphorically: the property relations are as they are because their being so is conductive to the initiation or maintenance of the production relations (demanded by the productive forces).

In law-abiding society, men's economic powers match the rights they have with respect to productive forces. Do they have the rights because they have the powers, or do they have the powers because they have the rights? The question is ambiguous.

Consider a man who has a right $r$. Since society is law-abiding, his right is effective. So he will also have power $p$, which matches $r$. Moreover, he has $p$ *because* he has $r$. Society being law-abiding, he can only have $p$ as a result of having $r$. The same is true with respect to all economic powers and all economic agents. So we can say: in law-abiding society men have the powers they do because they have the rights they do.

That seems to refute the doctrine of base and superstructure. But the above analysis, though correct, is incomplete. Historical materialism takes the analysis further, and it is in fact compatible with the truths of the last paragraph. For it says that right $r$ is enjoyed because it belongs to a structure of rights, which obtains *because* it secures a matching structure of powers. The content of the legal system is dictated by its function, which is to help sustain an economy of a particular kind. Men do get their powers from their rights, but in a sense which is not only allowed but demanded by the way historical materialism explains rights by reference to powers.

Now some texts which show that Marx and Engels affirmed a functional account of the relation between base and superstructure. Here is what Marx told the jury at the trial of the Rhenish Democrats in 1849:

> Society is not founded upon the law; this is a legal fiction. On the contrary, the law must be founded upon society, it must express the common interests and needs of a society—as distinct from the caprice of individuals—which arise from the material mode of production prevailing at the given time. This Code Napoléon, which I am holding in my hand, has not created modern bourgeois society. On the contrary, bourgeois society, which emerged in the eighteenth century and developed further in the nineteenth, merely finds its legal expression in this Code. As soon as it ceases to fit the social conditions, it becomes simply a bundle of paper.[91]

*Capital* articulates the idea that the base needs a superstructure:

> ... regulations and order are themselves indispensable elements of any mode of production, if it is to assume social stability and independence from mere chance and arbitrariness ... [92]

Since the base needs a superstructure, it "creates" one:

---

[91] "Speech at the Trial of the Rhenish District Committee of Democrats", p. 232.
[92] *Capital*, vol. iii p. 774.

> ... every form of production creates its own legal relations, forms of government etc. The crudity and the shortcomings of the bourgeois conception lie in the tendency to see but an accidental reflective connection in what constitutes an organic union.[93]

Bases need superstructures, and they get the superstructures they need because they need them: this is what is meant by saying that the two are *organically* connected.

The fact that production relations require the order law supplies may lead to misperceptions of the historical process ... Engels makes a similar point:

> Since in each particular case the economic facts must assume the form of juristic motives in order to receive legal sanction; and since, in so doing, consideration has of course to be given to the whole legal system already in operation, the juristic form is, in consequence, made everything and the economic content nothing.[94]

We saw that law can look more fundamental than the economy, when the underlying functional explanation of law is ignored (p. 232). The role of force in history is open to similar misconstrual. Engels' main criticism of the "force theory" is that it mistakes the fact that force functions to sustain economic structures as a proof that force is more basic than the economy. When he protests "that force is only the means, and that the aim is economic advantage"[95] he is asserting, in crude terms, a functional connection between base and superstructure. Another primitive formulation:

> Every socialist worker, no matter of what nationality, knows quite well that force only protects exploitation, but does not cause it; that the relation between capital and wage-labour is the basis of his exploitation, and that this was brought about by purely economic causes and not at all by means of force.[96]

The statement is primitive because it does not accommodate the fact, known to Engels, that force figures considerably among the *immediate* causes of economic power, just as rights do. Indeed, effective rights are effective partly because of the force behind them.

An important Preface sentence says:

> At a certain stage of their development, the material productive forces of society come into conflict with the existing relations of production, or—what is but a legal expression for the same thing—with the property relations within which they have been at work hitherto.[97]

We can now say that when productive forces "come into conflict" with property relations it is because the forces conflict with the production relations those property relations formulate and protect. The solution is either a change in production relations in violation of the law, with the law later falling into line, or a change in law which facilitates a change in production relations. History is full of both solutions. [pp. 231–234]

---

[93] *Grundrisse*, p. 88.
[94] "Ludwig Feuerbach and the End of Classical German Philosophy", p. 397. Engels is allowing that the *way* the economic content expresses itself legally depends in part on the already existing legal system. This is an aspect of the "relative autonomy" of the superstructure.
[95] *Anti-Dühring*, p. 221.
[96] *ibid.*, pp. 211–12.
[97] *Critique of Political Economy*, p. 21 [and *ante*, 1167].

## S. LUKES
### Can the Base be Distinguished From the Superstructure?
(1983)[98]

Can the economic structure, or base, be distinguished from the superstructure? This is a basic question, for unless it can, the explanations promised by historical materialism ... will fail. I shall consider the question by presenting ... the answer advanced by G.A. Cohen.[99]

In the first place, Cohen's own account of his programme is insufficiently radical. For he speaks of the "proletarian" and the "slave", "landowners" and "capitalists" as having or lacking (non-normative) powers. But in speaking thus, he is not speaking non-normatively, since the actors in question are not identified in a non-normative fashion. A slave, for example, is a slave just because he lacks certain rights, just as a landowner by definition possesses certain rights. Statements attributing powers to occupants of roles such as these are plainly not *rechtsfrei*, at least where they have or lack these powers in virtue of their roles. So, to carry out Cohen's programme systematically, one must eliminate all reference to features of the actors and their roles that refer to or presuppose rights and, more generally, ownership relations. Unless this is done, one will not have excluded from the economic structure "the legal, moral and political relationships of men". The principle of a *rechtsfrei* conception of the economic structure must be applied rigorously.

In reply to this, it might be claimed, as Cohen does, that the economic structure consists in production relations which relate terms that do not belong to the structure itself (though they do belong to the economy). On this account, one could describe the structure as relating variables, just like the structure of a bridge or an argument: the economic structure is a form whose proper description makes no reference to the persons or productive forces related together by it, and indeed necessary for it to exist. But the relations in question hold by virtue of the rights and obligations attaching to the roles occupied by persons so related: as Cohen himself says, "The structure may be seen not only as a set of relations but also as a set of roles". Therefore, a proper description of the structure will not, as Cohen rightly says, make specific reference to the specific *role-occupants*, but it can scarcely avoid reference to their normatively-defined roles. To this, of course, Cohen will reply that such roles *can* be identified non-normatively ... We shall come to this claim shortly. Only if it can be sustained, will Cohen's programme have been carried out rigorously.

But, in the second place, we must ask: can it be carried out at all? Recall that the aim is to identify an economic structure of production relations, as a set of *de facto* powers, which will in turn explain the superstructure of law, morality, etc., as a set of rights and obligations. Let us, then, look more closely at this purged or purified "matching" economic framework of "powers or abilities" and "inabilities or constraints".

I propose here to offer three arguments. The first two attack Cohen's project indirectly; only the third meets it head on. The former, if accepted, put in question the idea that the economic structure, conceived as a set of "powers and constraints", could be described in a single, determinate, objective and rationally incontestable manner. If this is doubted, then the "hardness" of the economic structure (and thus of historical materialism itself) is no longer easy to believe in: how it is conceived will be relative to perspectives that are, in turn, not normatively neutral. The latter puts in question Cohen's claim that norms can be seen as

---

[98] [From D. Miller and L. Siedentop, *The Nature of Political Theory*.]
[99] [*Ante*, 1137 and 1170.]

bringing about and sustaining relations of production while remaining no part of their content.

First, then, what count as an agent's abilities and inabilities will be closely dependent upon how that agent is conceived (which only strengthens the first point made above). If the agent (whether individual or collective) is conceived in a sufficiently "substantial" way, then that agent's abilities will appear to be very narrowly circumscribed; if conceived sufficiently abstractly, they may appear to be very wide indeed. Consider the question: ... did the British Labour Government in 1929 have the power, or ability, to avert (or at least better manage) the economic crisis? Here again, the answer depends upon how that Government is conceived—as irremediably constituted by given traditions of thought and action, or as capable of alternative strategies in a time of crisis. Or, to take Cohen's own example, different conceptions of contemporary British workers yield different answers to the question of what powers they have (to withhold labour collectively, to escape individually, to overthrow capitalism, to build socialism) and how much of such powers they have. Moreover, if the agents in question are defined in terms of their *roles*, that is *eo ipso* to define their abilities and inabilities, assuming of course that they act in accordance with their roles. But in terms of *which* roles should they be defined, and how role-determined should they be taken to be?

Second, what counts as enabling or constraining is never a simple matter of fact but it is always relative to background assumptions and judgements, some of them normative. To attribute abilities to agents is to accept as possibly true a set of conditionals, most of them counterfactual, of the form "under conditions C, agent A will do or be x". and to attribute an inability is to rule some such conditionals out. But a deep question is: what are to be included in the conditions specified in the antecedent? Until that is answered, attributions of abilities and inabilities remain indeterminate. But it cannot be answered in a definitive and rationally incontestable manner.

Consider Cohen's own example of the slave's alleged inability to withhold his labour power. Under certain interpretations of C, this is plainly false, even on pain of death, of some, even perhaps of most slaves (as the history of slave rebellions demonstrates). If, however, one includes in C the condition that the slave behaves "reasonably" or "normally" (that is, that he conforms to yet-to-be-specified norms of reasonableness), then Cohen's claim may well be true. Here I merely wish to draw attention to the fact that not merely is the latter interpretation not normatively neutral, but the choice between them is not so either. Accordingly, no Cohenite description of the economic structure of slavery could be normatively neutral. So, to sum up these two arguments, I have suggested that if it is sought to describe the base in terms of abilities and inabilities, powers and constraints, then (1) which description is appropriate will always be contestable and (2) this will be so partly on normative, that is moral and political, grounds.

Third, it is worth focusing directly on one type of enabling and constraining condition, namely *norms*.

In general, enabling and constraining conditions may be external or internal to agents. Thus some physical factors are plainly external and some psychological factors plainly internal. Within a certain range, however, whether they are external or internal will itself depend on how the agent is conceived, where the boundaries of the self or the collectivity in question are drawn.

Norms are distinctive in being both external and internal, and in a particular way. They confront individuals as externally given but they can only be generally effective in enabling and constraining them in so far as they are (in H.L.A. Hart's phrase) "internally accepted".[1] Of course, I may be induced to comply with a custom or convention or moral principle or legal rule by the fear of the sanction that would be brought to bear in the case of my non-compliance, but no set of

---

[1] [*Cf. ante*, 379.]

norms stably regulating the behaviour of adults could rely on this mechanism alone. For such regulations to be generally effective, there must exist a high degree of intersubjective acceptance of rules, and of the purposes the rules are taken to serve (though an individual need not believe, in any given case, that his compliance will lead to the fulfilment of that purpose). In short, a stable system of enablements and constraints, to be effective, requires that I and relevant others are generally motivated by certain kinds of shared (teleological) reasons for acting and not acting.[2] These give such enablements and constraints their distinctively normative character.

Now, it is essential to Cohen's programme that such enablements and constraints be identifiable in non-normative terms, that is in abstraction from what gives them their distinctively normative character. The programme, he claims, "says what production relations are, not what maintains them". He cites the case of an illegal squatter who secures his dominion over a tract of land by having retainers who use force illegally on his behalf, or by perpetrating a myth that anyone who disturbs his tenure of the land will be damned to eternal hellfire. What that squatter has *in common with* a legal owner of similar land, whose tenure is protected by law, is that both have the *power to use their land*. This, so the argument runs, is the content of the production relation in question, in the one case sustained by force and myth, in the other by the law. So the relations embodying normative enablements and constraints are, on Cohen's argument, abstractable from the norms that may have brought them about and maintain them in being. Is this so?

Consider the basic economic relationship of contract. If any relation of production is central to the economic structure of capitalism, this must be it. Can it be described in the manner proposed?

Interestingly, Durkheim took Herbert Spencer to be asserting just this—that economic life consisted in "the spontaneous accord of individual interests, an accord of which contracts are the natural expression", society being "merely the stage where individuals exchanged the products of their labour, without any properly social influence coming to regulate this exchange". To this Durkheim replied that "in the play of these relations themselves ... social influence makes itself felt. For not everything in the contract is contractual". By this he meant that "a contract is not sufficient unto itself, but is possible only thanks to a regulation of the contract which is originally social". Recall that Durkheim defined the social in terms of externality, constraint, and generality (throughout society), plus independence (of individual circumstances); and that he saw the law, in particular, and norms, in general, as paradigmatically social phenomena. Contract law "determines legal consequences of our acts that we have not determined ... We co-operate because we wish to, but our voluntary co-operation creates duties for us that we did not desire". Contract law is not "simply a useful complement of individual agreements; it is their fundamental norm".[3] Durkheim is here making two points (which he did not distinguish from one another): that contract law, together with a whole network of customary and conventional norms, combine to define the social practice of contracting; and that other such laws and norms regulate contractual behaviour, rendering certain actions possible and proscribing others on pain of sanctions. In short, the relation of contract is, in this double sense, essentially norm-governed. Does not this fundamental objection apply to both Marx and Spencer—or at least to Cohen's Marx and Durkheim's Spencer?

But, it may be asked, is there not a *rechtsfrei* relationship here, abstractable from the norms that govern it, in either sense?

How would we go about describing it? Cohen's answer is: in terms of the

---

[2] See G. H. von Wright, *Explanation and Understanding* (1971), pp. 145 *et seq.*

[3] E. Durkheim, *The Division of Labour in Society* (1933), pp. 203, 211, 215, 214 (amended translation: S.L.). [And see *ante*, 843.]

abilities and inabilities of the contracting partners. But abilities and inabilities to do ... what? The performance of contractual obligations is normally described in a vocabulary (paying wages, supplying services, buying and selling, honouring debts) which *already presupposes* the institution of contract and its regulating norms, as well as a whole network of supporting informal norms. In this sense, the norms that define the practice of contracting enter into the description of the activities involved in that practice. To this, it may be replied that a thin "behavioural" description of such activities (*e.g.* handing over money of a certain value, performing certain tasks, etc.) could suffice in the description of the abilities and inabilities. But the trouble is here that such thin "behavioural" descriptions would underdetermine the appropriate thick, normatively-loaded descriptions: only some payments of money by certain persons in certain ways would count as "payment of wages", only certain kinds of task performance as the supplying of a contracted service. Recall that Cohen's non-normative relations of production are intended to be "matching". But how could the "thin" non-normative descriptions of transactions and dependencies between agents succeed in identifying *just those* transactions and dependencies which the normative relations involve unless the normative description were already, implicitly or explicitly, presupposed?

Suppose, however, that we overlook this difficulty, arising from the first sense in which contracts are norm-governed. What about the second sense: the sense in which laws and conventions supply agents with certain kinds of *reasons* for acting and not acting, thereby enabling people to do what they otherwise would not, and preventing them from doing what they otherwise would? Can one describe contractual relationships in terms of abilities and inabilities in a way that abstracts from the operation of such reasons?

An ability and an inability, as we have already seen, are explicable as sets of conditionals, most of them counterfactual. In a pure, non-normative relationship of power-say, of simple coercion—my ability to secure an outcome may be stated as a set of conditionals of the following type: "If I order my slave to sweep the floor, making threat *t*, he will do so" or "If I threaten workers with redundancy, they will come into line". But what of normative power-relationships? Here a whole new range of counterfactual conditionals enters the story, of the following type: "If I offer employment at the going rate for the job, the workers will accept the offer" or "If I break the agreement thus made, they will come out on strike". In these cases the enablements and constraints *consist* in internally accepted norms and would not exist if attitudes changed. The normative beliefs in question enter irreducibly into the description of the powers and constraints linking the contracting parties. In other words, the norms, both informal and formal (the pay norm and the legal obligation to pay it once agreed), *are* what enables and constrains the parties—enabling the employers to secure the work on the terms agreed, but not if the terms are broken, by giving the parties certain reasons for acting as they do.

Let us return to the illegal squatter and the legal landowner. I can sum up the two points just made concerning norm-governed economic relationships by observing that (1) both squatter and proprietor can, it is true, keep people off their land; (2) the proprietor, unlike the squatter, can in addition secure the respect of people for his title to the land (*e.g.* should he wish to bequeath it); and (3) he can do so only by virtue of the reason-giving prevalent legal norms governing ownership of property and informal norms governing what landholders may legitimately lay claim to. From all of which I conclude that one cannot identify the powers and constraints embodied in norm-governed economic relationships independently of the norms which, in both senses, govern them.

Is there any interpretation of Cohen's purportedly purified economic structure, allegedly purged of all normative, superstructural encumbrances, that escapes the foregoing objections?

So far as I can see, there are only two possibilities. On the one hand, Cohen's proposal may be a purely linguistic one—a proposed translation manual converting all statements about rights and obligations into statements couched in a purged vocabulary of "matching" powers and constraints.

There are, however, two decisive objections to this interpretation. First, it will not serve Cohen's purpose, since the objectionable normative elements would all survive, albeit convertly, in the identified economic structure: the purging would be solely at the linguistic level. But second, this is plainly not Cohen's intention anyway. His aim, after all, is coherently to "represent property relations as distinct from, and explained by, production relations".[4] He believes that his proposed *rechtsfrei* characterizations refer to a set of relations distinct from and explanatory of those referred to by talk of rights and duties in the normal sense. Thus, he explains away Marx's own continued adherence to legal terminology when speaking of the relations of production by remarking that

> there was no attractive alternative. Ordinary language lacks a developed apparatus for describing production relations in a *rechtsfrei* manner. It does have a rich conceptual system for describing property relations, strictly so called. Given the poverty of the vocabulary of power, and the structural analogies between powers and rights, it is convenient to use rights-denoting terms with a special sense, for the sake of describing powers.[5]

In short, Cohen clearly believed that his proposed *rechtsfrei* terms (and Marx's allegedly special use of *rechtsvoll* terms) identify relations distinct from, if structurally analogous to, those that rights-denoting terms normally identify.

The only alternative possibility I can see is that Cohen's economic structure, composed of powers and constraints, is intended to *exclude* all those that are norm-governed. But to this interpretation too there are two decisive objections. The first is that this would result in a hopelessly impoverished, indeed scarcely coherent, conception of the economic structure. The second objection is that, in any case, it is doubtful that this *is* Cohen's Marx: that is, that Cohen's programme of identifying a non-normative economic structure is to be understood in this way. For, in answering the possible objection that he is merely expounding the so-called "force-theory", condemned by Engels, Cohen remarks, as we have seen, that "our definition of production relations does not stipulate how the powers they unfold are obtained or sustained. The answer to that question does involve force, but also ideology and the law. The programme says what production relations are, not what maintains them".[6]

I have argued that these two are the only remaining interpretations of Cohen's general programme of purging the economic structure of superstructural encumbrances, that neither does the job; and that neither squares with Cohen's intentions. There is, however, a third and final possibility: to reduce the generality of the programme. That is, one could read it as an attempt to purge the economic structure only of specifically legal elements, narrowly defined, as distinct from those pertaining to custom, convention, and morality. (It is, after all, formulated in response to the so-called "problem of legality".) Interestingly enough, this interpretation fits rather well the historical cases that Cohen cites to illustrate how his programme enables one to explain changes in property relations—the free circulation of labour in violation of the law of settlement which was eventually scrapped, the admitting of those of low status to the clothing industry in violation of a law eventually repealed, the formation of illegal unions leading to their eventual legal recognition, and the process leading to the early factory legislation: "the struggle led to fairly well recognized practices, and then the law broke its

---

[4] *Karl Marx's Theory of History*, p. 219.
[5] *ibid.*, p. 224.
[6] *ibid.*, p. 223.

silence and gave the facts legal form". In all these cases, informal norm-governed practices (responding, it is true, to developing productive forces, which they in turn facilitate) eventually acquire legal form.

But this, less general, interpretation of Cohen's programme once more encounters two decisive objections. It does not square with Cohen's general objective of finding "a method of conceiving of the economic structure which excludes from it the legal, moral and political relationships of men". And second, therefore, it does not succeed in distinguishing the base from the superstructure, in the manner required. At the most, it distinguishes an expanded (norm-governed) "base" from a diminished (narrowly legal) "superstructure".[pp. 110–118]

## K. MARX AND F. ENGELS
### The German Ideology
### (1845–1846)[7]

Out of this very contradiction between the interest of the individual and that of the community the latter takes an independent form as the *State*, divorced from the real interests of individual and community, and at the same time as an illusory communal life, always based, however, on the real ties existing in every family and tribal conglomeration—such as flesh and blood, language, division of labour on a larger scale, and other interests—and especially, as we shall enlarge upon later, on the classes, already determined by the division of labour, which in every such mass of men separate out, and of which one dominates all the others. It follows from this that all struggles within the State, the stuggle between democracy, aristocracy, and monarchy, the struggle for the franchise, etc., etc., are merely the illusory forms in which the real struggle of the different classes are fought out among one another.                                                                                       [p. 191]

If power is taken as the basis of right, as Hobbes, etc., do, then right, law, etc., are merely the symptom, the expression of *other* relations upon which State power rests. The material life of individuals, which by no means depend merely on their "will", their mode or production and form of intercourse, which mutually determine each other—this is the real basis of the State and remains so at all the stages at which division of labour and private property are still necessary, quite independently of the *will* of individuals. These actual relations are in no way created by the State power; on the contrary they are the power creating it. The individuals who rule in these conditions, besides having to constitute their power in the form of the State, have to give their will, which is determined by these definite conditions, a universal expression as the will of the State, as law—an expression whose content is always determined by the relations of this class, as the civil and criminal law demonstrates in the clearest possible way.   [pp. 191–192]

## K. MARX
### Preface to The Critique of Political Economy
### (1859)[8]

At a certain stage of their development, the material productive forces of society come in conflict with the existing relations of production, or—what is but a legal expression for the same thing—with the property relations within which they have been at work hitherto. From forms of development of the productive forces these relations turn into their fetters. Then begins an epoch of social revolution. With a change of the economic foundation the entire immense superstructure is more or

---

[7] [From McLellan, *The Thought of Marx*, p. 191.]
[8] [From McLellan, *The Thought of Marx*, p. 208.]

less rapidly transformed. In considering such transformations a distinction should always be made between the material transformation of the economic conditions of production, which can be determined with the precision of natural science, and the legal, political, religious, aesthetic or philosophical forms in which men become conscious of this conflict and fight it out.

## K. MARX AND F. ENGELS
### The German Ideology
(1845–1846)

The ideas of the ruling class are in every epoch the ruling ideas: *i.e.* the class which is the ruling *material* force of society is at the same time its ruling *intellectual force*. The class which has the means of material production at its disposal, consequently also controls the means of mental production, so that the ideas of those who lack the means of mental production are on the whole subject to it. The ruling ideas are nothing more than the ideal expression of the dominant material relations, the dominant material relations grasped as ideas; hence of the relations which make the one class the ruling one, therefore, the ideas of its dominance. The individuals composing the ruling class possess among other things consciousness, and therefore think. Insofar, therefore, as they rule as a class and determine the extent and compass of an historical epoch, it is self-evident that they do this in its whole range, hence among other things rule also as thinkers, as producers of ideas, and regulate the production and distribution of the ideas of their age: thus their ideas are the ruling ideas of the epoch. For instance, in an age and in a country where royal power, aristocracy and bourgeoisie are contending for domination and where, therefore, domination is shared, the doctrine of the separation of powers proves to be the dominant idea and is expressed as an "eternal law".

## E. P. THOMPSON
### Whigs and Hunters
(1975)

*The Rule of Law*

From these perspectives concern with the rights and wrongs at law of a few men in 1723 is concern with trivia. And the same conclusion may be reached through a different adjustment of perspective, which may coexist with some of the same arguments. This flourishes in the form of a sophisticated, but (ultimately) highly schematic Marxism which, to our surprise, seems to spring up in the footsteps of those of us in an older Marxist tradition. From this standpoint the law is, perhaps more clearly than any other cultural or institutional artefact, by definition a part of a "superstructure" adapting itself to the necessities of an infrastructure of productive forces and productive relations. As such, it is clearly an instrument of the *de facto* ruling class: it both defines and defends these rulers' claims upon resources and labour-power—it says what shall be property and what shall be crime—and it mediates class relations with a set of appropriate rules and sanctions, all of which, ultimately, confirm and consolidate existing class power. Hence the rule of law is only another mask for the rule of a class. The revolutionary can have no interest in law, unless as a phenomenon of ruling-class power and hypocrisy; it should be his aim simply to overthrow it. And so, once again, to express surprise at the Black Act or at partial judges is—unless as confirmation and illustration of theories which might easily be demonstrated without all this labour—simply to expose one's own naivety.

So the old middle ground of historiography is crumbling on both sides ... And does it matter a damn who gave Parson Power his instructions; which forms brought "Vulcan" Gates to the gallows; or how an obscure Richmond publican managed to evade a death sentence already determined upon by the Law Officers, the First Minister and the King?

I am disposed to think that it does matter ... But to show this must involve evacuating received assumptions—that narrowing ledge of traditional middle ground—and moving out onto an even narrower theoretical ledge. This would accept, as it must, some part of the Marxist-structural critique; indeed, some parts of this study have confirmed the class-bound and mystifying functions of the law. But it would reject its ulterior reductionism and would modify its typology of superior and inferior (but determining) structures.

First, analysis of the eighteenth century (and perhaps of other centuries) calls in question the validity of separating off the law as a whole and placing it in some typological superstructure. The law when considered as institution (the courts, with their class theatre and class procedures) or as personnel (the judges, the lawyers, the Justices of the Peace) may very easily be assimilated to those of the ruling class. But all that is entailed in "the law" is not subsumed in these institutions. The law may also be seen as ideology, or as particular rules and sanctions which stand in a definite and active relationship (often a field of conflict) to social norms; and, finally, it may be seen simply in terms of its own logic, rules and procedures—that is, simply *as law*. And it is not possible to conceive of any complex society without law.

We must labour this point, since some theorists today are unable to see the law except in terms of "the fuzz" setting about inoffensive demonstrators or cannabis-smokers. I am no authority on the twentieth century, but in the eighteenth century matters were more complex than that. To be sure I have tried to show, in the evolution of the Black Act, an expression of the ascendancy of a Whig oligarchy, which created new laws and bent old legal forms in order to legitimize its own property and status; this oligarchy employed the law, both instrumentally and ideologically, very much as a modern structural Marxist should expect it to do. But this is not the same thing as to say that the rulers had need of law, in order 'to oppress the ruled, while those who were ruled had need of none. What was often at issue was not property, supported by law, against no-property; it was alter-native definitions of property-rights: for the landowner, enclosure—for the cot-tager, common rights; for the forest officialdom, "preserved grounds" for the deer; for the foresters, the right to take turfs. For as long as it remained possible, the ruled—if they could find a purse and a lawyer—would actually fight for their rights by means of law; occasionally the copyholders, resting upon the precedents of sixteenth-century law, could actually win a case. When it ceased to be possible to continue the fight at law, men still felt a sense of legal wrong: the propertied had obtained their power by illegitimate means.

Moreover, if we look closely into such an agrarian context, the distinction between law, on the one hand, conceived of as an element of "superstructure", and the actualities of productive forces and relations on the other hand, becomes more and more untenable. For law was often a definition of actual agrarian *practice*, as it has been pursued "time out of mind". How can we distinguish between the activity of farming or of quarrying and the rights to this strip of land or to that quarry? The farmer or forester in his daily occupation was moving within visible or invisible structures of law: this merestone which marked the division between strips; that ancient oak—visited by processional on each Rogation Day—which marked the limits of the parish grazing; those other invisible (but potent and sometimes legally enforceable) memories as to which parishes had the right to take turfs in this waste and which parishes had not; this written or unwritten custumal which decided how many stints on the common land and for whom—for copyholders and freeholders only, or for all inhabitants?

Hence "law" was deeply imbricated within the very basis of productive relations, which would have been inoperable without this law. And, in the second place, this law, as definition or as rules (imperfectly enforceable through institutional legal forms), was endorsed by norms, tenaciously transmitted through the community. There were alternative norms; that is a matter of course; this was a place, not of consensus, but of conflict. But we cannot, then, simply separate off all law as ideology, and assimilate this also to the state apparatus of a ruling class. On the contrary, the norms of foresters might reveal themselves as passionately supported values, impelling them upon a course of action which would lead them into bitter conflict—with "the law".

So we are back, once again, with *that* law: the institutionalized procedures of the ruling class. This, no doubt, is worth no more of our theoretical attention; we can see it as an instrument of class power *tout court*. But we must take even this formulation, and see whether its crystalline clarity will survive immersion in scepticism. To be sure, we can stand no longer on that traditional ground of liberal academicism, which offers the eighteenth century as a society of consensus, ruled within the parameters of paternalism and deference, and governed by a "rule of law" which attained (however imperfectly) towards impartiality. That is not the society which we have been examining; we have not observed a society of consensus; and we have seen the law being devised and employed, directly and instrumentally, in the imposition of class power. Nor can we accept a sociological refinement of the old view, which stresses the imperfections and partiality of the law, and its subordination to the functional requirements of socio-economic interest groups. For what we have observed is something more than the law as a pliant medium to be twisted this way and that by whichever interests already possess effective power. Eighteenth-century law was more substantial than that. Over and above its pliant, instrumental functions it existed in its own right, as ideology; as an ideology which not only served, in most respects, but which also legitimized class power. The hegemony of the eighteenth-century gentry and aristocracy was expressed, above all, not in military force, not in the mystifications of a priesthood or of the press, not even in economic coercion, but in the rituals of the study of the Justices of the Peace, in the quarter-sessions, in the pomp of Assizes and in the theatre of Tyburn.

Thus the law (we agree) may be seen instrumentally as mediating and reinforcing existent class relations and, ideologically, as offering to these a legitimation. But we must press our definitions a little further. For if we say that existent class relations were mediated by the law, this is not the same thing as saying that the law was no more than those relations translated into other terms, which masked or mystified the reality. This may, quite often, be true but it is not the whole truth. For class relations were expressed, not in any way one likes, but *through the forms of law*; and the law, like other institutions which from time to time can be seen as mediating (and masking) existent class relations (such as the Church or the media of communication), has its own characteristics, its own independent history and logic of evolution.

Moreover, people are not as stupid as some structuralist philosophers suppose them to be. They will not be mystified by the first man who puts on a wig. It is inherent in the especial character of law, as a body of rules and procedures, that it shall apply logical criteria with reference to standards of universality and equity. It is true that certain categories of person may be excluded from this logic (as children or slaves), that other categories may be debarred from access to parts of the logic (as women or, for many forms of eighteenth-century law, those without certain kinds of property), and that the poor may often be excluded, through penury, from the law's costly procedures. All this, and more, is true. But if too much of this is true, then the consequences are plainly counterproductive. Most men have a strong sense of justice, at least with regard to their own interests. If the law is evidently partial and unjust, then it will mask nothing, legitimize nothing, contribute nothing to any class's hegemony. The essential precondition for the effectiveness of law, in its function as ideology, is that it shall display an independence from gross manipulation and shall seem to be just. It cannot seem to be so without upholding its own logic and criteria of equity; indeed, on occasion, by actually *being* just. And furthermore it is not often the case that a ruling ideology can be dismissed as a mere hypocrisy; even rulers find a need to legitimize their power, to moralize their functions, to feel themselves to be useful and just. In the case of an ancient historical formation like the law, a discipline which requires years of exacting study to master, there will always be some men who actively believe in their own procedures and in the logic of justice. The law may be rhetoric, but it need not be empty rhetoric. Blackstone's *Commentaries* represent an intellectual exercise far more rigorous than could have come from an apologist's pen.

I do not know what transcultural validity these reflections may have. But they are certainly applicable to England in the eighteenth century. Douglas Hay, in a significant essay in *Albion's Fatal Tree*, has argued that the law assumed unusual pre-eminence in that century, as the central legitimizing ideology, displacing the religious authority and sanctions of previous centuries. It gave way, in its turn, to economic sanctions and to the ideology of the free market and of political liberalism in the nineteenth. Turn where you will, the rhetoric of eighteenth-century England is saturated with the notion of law. Royal absolutism was placed behind a high hedge of law; landed estates were tied together with entails and marriage settlements made up of elaborate tissues of law; authority and property punctuated their power by regular "examples" made upon the public gallows. More than this, immense efforts were made (and Hay has explored the forms of these) to project the image of a ruling class which was itself subject to the rule of law, and whose legitimacy rested upon the equity and universality of those legal forms. And the rulers were, in serious senses, whether willingly or unwillingly, the prisoners of their own rhetoric; they played the games of power according to rules which suited them, but they could not break those rules or the whole game would be thrown away. And, finally, so far from the ruled shrugging off this rhetoric as a hypocrisy, some part of it at least was taken over as part of the rhetoric of the plebian crowd, of the "free-born Englishman" with his inviolable privacy, his *habeas corpus*, his equality before the law. If this rhetoric was a mask, it was a mask which John Wilkes was to borrow, at the head of ten thousand masked supporters.

So that in this island and in that century above all one must resist any slide into structural reductionism. What this overlooks, among other things, is the immense capital of human struggle over the previous two centuries against royal absolutism, inherited, in the forms and traditions of the law, by the eighteenth-century gentry. For in the sixteenth and seventeenth centuries the law had been less an instrument of class power than a central arena of conflict. In the course of conflict the law itself had been changed; inherited by the eighteenth-century gentry, this changed law was, literally, central to their whole purchase upon power and upon the means of life. Take law away, and the royal prerogative, or the presumption of the aristocracy, might flood back upon their properties and lives; take law away and the string which tied together their lands and marriages would fall apart. But it was inherent in the very nature of the medium which they had selected for their own self-defence that it could not be reserved for the exclusive use only of their own class. The law, in its forms and traditions, entailed principles of equity and universality which, perforce, had to be extended to all sorts and degrees of men. And since this was of necessity so, ideology could turn necessity to advantage. What had been devised by men of property as a defence against arbitrary power could be turned into service as an apologia for property in the face of the propertyless. And the apologia was serviceable up to a point: for these "propertyless", as we have seen, comprised multitudes of men and women who themselves enjoyed, in fact, petty property rights or agrarian use-rights whose definition was inconceivable without the forms of law. Hence the ideology of the great struck root in a soil, however shallow, of actuality. And the courts gave substance to the ideology by the scrupulous care with which, on occasion, they adjudged petty rights, and, on all occasions, preserved properties and forms.

We reach, then, not a simple conclusion (law = class power) but a complex and contradictory one. On the one hand, it is true that the law did mediate existent class relations to the advantage of the rulers; not only is this so, but as the century advanced the law became a superb instrument by which these rulers were able to impose new definitions of property to their even greater advantage, as in the extinction by law of indefinite agrarian use-rights and in the furtherance of enclosure. On the other hand, the law mediated these class relations through legal forms, which imposed, again and again, inhibitions upon the actions of the rulers. For there is a very large difference, which twentieth-century experience ought to have made clear even to the most exalted thinker, between arbitrary extra-legal power and the rule of law. And not only were the rulers (indeed, the ruling class as a whole) inhibited by their own rules of law against the exercise of direct un-mediated force (arbitrary imprisonment, the employment of troops against the crowd, torture, and those other conveniences of power with which we are all conversant), but they also believed enough in these rules, and in their accom-panying ideological rhetoric, to allow, in certain limited areas, the law itself to be a genuine forum within which certain kinds of class conflict were fought out. There were even occasions (one recalls John Wilkes and several of the trials of the 1790s) when the Government itself retired from the courts defeated. Such occa-sions served, paradoxically, to consolidate power, to enhance its legitimacy, and to inhibit revolutionary movements. But, to turn the paradox around, these same occasions served to bring power even further within constitutional controls.

The rhetoric and the rules of a society are something a great deal more than sham. In the same moment they may modify, in profound ways, the behaviour of the powerful, and mystify the powerless. They may disguise the true realities of power, but, at the same time, they may curb that power and check its intrusions. And it is often from within that very rhetoric that a radical critique of the practice of the society is developed: the reformers of the 1790s appeared, first of all, clothed in the rhetoric of Locke and of Blackstone.

These reflections lead me on to conclusions which may be different from those which some readers expect. I have shown in this study a political oligarchy inventing callous and oppressive laws to serve its own interests. I have shown judges who, no less than bishops, were subject to political influence, whose sense of justice was humbug, and whose interpretation of the laws served only to enlarge their inherent class bias. Indeed, I think that this study has shown that for many of England's governing élite the rules of law were a nuisance, to be manipulated and bent in what ways they could; and that the allegiance of such men as Walpole, Hardwicke or Paxton to the rhetoric of law was largely humbug. But I do not conclude from this that the rule of law itself was humbug. On the contrary, the inhibitions upon power imposed by law seem to me a legacy as substantial as any handed down from the struggles of the seventeenth century to the eighteenth, and a true and important cultural achievement of the agrarian and mercantile bour-geoise, and of their supporting yeomen and artisans.

More than this, the notion of the regulation and reconciliation of conflicts through the rule of law—and the elaboration of rules and procedures which, on occasion, made some approximate approach towards the ideal—seems to me a cultural achievement of universal significance. I do not lay any claim as to the abstract, extra-historical impartiality of these rules. In a context of gross class inequalities, the equity of the law must always be in some part sham. Trans-planted as it was to even more inequitable contexts, this law could become an instrument of imperialism. For this law has found its way to a good many parts of the globe. But even here the rules and the rhetoric have imposed some inhibitions upon the imperial power. If the rhetoric was a mask, it was a mask which Gandhi and Nehru were to borrow, at the head of a million masked supporters...

I am insisting only upon the obvious point, which some modern Marxists have overlooked, that there is a difference between arbitrary power and the rule of law. We ought to expose the shams and inequities which may be concealed beneath this law. But the rule of law itself, the imposing of effective inhibitions upon power and the defence of the citizen from power's all-intrusive claims, seems to me to be an unqualified human good. To deny or belittle this good is, in this dangerous century when the resources and pretensions of power continue to enlarge, a desperate error of intellectual abstraction. More than this, it is a self-fulfilling error, which encourages us to give up the struggle against bad laws and class-bound procedures, and to disarm ourselves before power. It is to throw away a whole inheritance of struggle *about* law, and within the forms of law, whose continuity can never be fractured without bringing men and women into immediate danger...

It is true that in history the law can be seen to mediate and to legitimize existent class relations. Its forms and procedures may crystallize those relations and mask ulterior injustice. But this mediation, through the forms of law, is something quite distinct from the exercise of unmediated force. The forms and rhetoric of law acquire a distinct identity which may, on occasion, inhibit power and afford some protection to the powerless. Only to the degree that this is seen to be so can law be of service in its other aspect, as ideology. Moreover, the law in both its aspects, as formal rules and procedures and as ideology, cannot usefully be analysed in the metaphorical terms of a superstructure distinct from an infrastructure. While this comprises a large and self-evident part of the truth, the rules and categories of law penetrate every level of society, effect vertical as well as horizontal definitions of men's rights and status, and contribute to men's self-definition or sense of identity. As such law has not only been imposed *upon* men from above: it has also been a medium within which other social conflicts have been fought out. Productive relations themselves are, in part, only meaningful in terms of their definitions at law: the serf, the free labourer; the cottager with common rights, the inhabitant without; the unfree proletarian, the picket conscious of his rights; the landless labourer who may still sue his employer for assault. And if the actuality of the law's operation in class-divided societies has again and again, fallen short of its own rhetoric of equity, yet the notion of the rule of law it itself an unqualified good.

This cultural achievement—the attainment towards a universal value—found one origin in Roman jurisprudence. The uncodified English common law offered an alternative notation of law, in some ways more flexible and unprincipled—and therefore more pliant to the "common sense" of the ruling class—in other ways more available as a medium through which social conflict could find expression, especially where the sense of "natural justice" of the jury could make itself felt. Since this tradition came to its maturity in eighteenth-century England, its claims should command the historian's interest. And since some part of the inheritance from this cultural moment may still be found, within greatly changed contexts, with the United States or India or certain African countries, it is important to reexamine the pretensions of the imperialist donor...

If we suppose that law is no more than a mystifying and pompous way in which class power is registered and executed, then we need not waste our labour in studying its history and forms. One Act would be much the same as another, and all, from the standpoint of the ruled, would be Black. It is because law *matters* that we have bothered with this story at all ... If I judge the Black Act to be atrocious, this is not only from some standpoint in natural justice, and not only from the standpoint of those whom the Act oppressed, but also according to some ideal notion of the standards to which "the law", as regulator of human conflicts of interest, ought to attain. For "the law", as a logic of equity, must always seek to transcend the inequalities of class power which, instrumentally, it is harnessed to serve. And "the law" as ideology, which pretends to reconcile the interests of all degrees of men, must always come into conflict with the ideological partisanship of class.

We face, then, a paradox. The work of sixteenth- and seventeenth-century jurists, supported by the practical struggles of such men as Hampden and Lilburne, was passed down as a legacy to the eighteenth century, where it gave rise to a vision, in the minds of some men, of an ideal aspiration towards universal values of law. One thinks of Swift or of Goldsmith, or, with more qualifications, of Sir William Blackstone or Sir Michael Foster. If we today have ideal notions of what law might be, we derive them in some part from that cultural moment. It is, in part, in terms of that age's own aspiration that we judge the Black Act and find it deficient. But at the same time this same century, governed as it was by the forms of law, provides a text-book illustration of the employment of law, as instrument and as ideology, in serving the interests of the ruling class. The oligarchs and the great gentry were content to be subject to the rule of law only because this law was serviceable and afforded to their hegemony the rhetoric of legitimacy. This paradox has been at the heart of this study.[9]                    [pp. 259–269]

## K. MARX
### The Civil War in France
### (1871)[10]

The Paris Commune, was, of course, to serve as a model to all the great industrial centres of France. The communal *régime* once established in Paris and the secondary centres, the old centralised Government would in the provinces too, have to give way to the self-government of the producers. In a rough sketch of national organisation which the Commune had no time to develop, it states clearly that the Commune was to be the political form of even the smallest country hamlet, and that in the rural districts the standing army was to be replaced by a national militia, with an extremely short term of service. The rural communes of every district were to administer their common affairs by an assembly of delegates in the central town, and these district assemblies were again to send deputies to the National Delegation in Paris, each delegate to be at any time revocable and bound by the *mandat impératif* (formal instructions) of his constituents. The few but important functions which still would remain for a central government were not to be suppressed, as has been intentionally misstated, but were to be discharged by Communal, and therefore strictly responsible agents. The unity of the nation was not to be broken, but, on the contrary, to be organised by the Communal Constitution and to become a reality by the destruction of the State power which claimed to be the embodiment of that unity independent of, and superior to, the nation itself, from which it was but a parasitic excrescence. While the merely repressive organs of the old governmental power were to be amputated, its legitimate functions were to be wrested from an authority usurping pre-eminence over society itself, and restored to the responsible agents of society. Instead of deciding once in three or six years which member of the ruling class was to misrepresent the people in Parliament, universal suffrage was to serve the people, constituted in Communes, as individual suffrages serves every other employer in the search for the workmen and managers in his business. And it is well known that companies, like individuals, in matters of real business generally

---

[9]  [Critiques of this are H. Merri (1980) 7 Brit. J. of Law & Soc. 194 and B. Fine, *Democracy and The Rule of Law* (1984), pp. 169–189.
[10]  [From McLellan, *The Thought of Marx*, pp. 193–194.]

know how to put the right man in the right place, and, if they for once make a mistake, to redress it promptly. On the other hand, nothing could be more foreign to the spirit of the Commune than to supersede universal suffrage by hierarchic investiture. [pp. 193–194

## K. MARX
### Critique of the Gotha Programme
(1875)[11]

What we have to deal with here is a communist society, not as it has *developed* on its own foundations, but, on the contrary, just as it *emerges* from capitalist society; which is thus in every respect, economically, morally and intellectually, still stamped with the birth marks of the old society from whose womb it emerges. Accordingly, the individual producer receives back from society—after the deductions have been made—exactly what he gives to it. What he has given to it is his individual quantum of labour. For example, the social working day consists of the sum of the individual hours of work; the individual labour time of the individual producer is the part of the social working day contributed by him, his share in it. He receives a certificate from society that he has furnished such and such an amount of labour (after deducting his labour for the common funds), and with this certificate he draws from the social stock of means of consumption as much as costs the same amount of labour. The same amount of labour which he has given to society in one form he receives back in another.

Here obviously the same principle prevails as that which regulates the exchange of commodities, as far as this exchange of equal values. Content and form are changed, because under the altered circumstances no one can give anything except his labour, and because, on the other hand, nothing can pass to the ownership of individuals except individual means of consumption. But, as far as the distribution of the latter among the individual producers is concerned, the same principle prevails as in the exchange of commodity equivalents: a given amount of labour in one form is exchanged for an equal amount of labour in another form.

Hence, *equal right* here is still in principle—*bourgeois right*, although principle and practice are no longer at loggerheads, while the exchange of equivalents in commodity exchange only exists *on the average* and not in the individual case.

In spite of this advance, this *equal right* is still constantly stigmatised by a bourgeois limitation. The right of the producers is *proportional* to the labour they supply; the equality consists in the fact that measurement is made with an *equal standard*, labour.

But one man is superior to another physically or mentally and so supplies more labour in the same time, or can labour for a longer time; and labour, to serve as a measure, must be defined by its duration or intensity, otherwise it ceases to be a standard of measurement. This *equal* right is an unequal right for unequal labour. It recognises no class differences, because everyone is only a worker like everyone else; but it tacitly recognises unequal individual endowment and thus productive capacity as natural privileges. *It is, therefore, a right of inequality, in its content, like every right.* Right by its very nature can consist only in the application of an equal standard; but unequal individuals (and they would not be different individuals if they were not unequal) are measurable only by an equal standard in so far as they are brought under an equal point of view, are taken from one *definite* side only, for instance, in the present case, are regarded *only as workers* and nothing more is seen in them, everything else being ignored. Further, one worker is married, another not; one has more children than another, and so on and so forth. Thus, with an equal performance of labour, and hence an equal share in the

11 [*ibid.*, pp. 222–224.]

social consumption fund, one will in fact receive more than another, one will be richer than another, and so on. To avoid all these defects, right instead of being equal would have to be unequal.

But these defects are inevitable in the first phase of communist society as it is when it has just emerged after prolonged birth pangs from capitalist society. Right can never be higher than the economic structure of society and its cultural development conditioned thereby.

In a higher phase of communist society, after the enslaving subordination of the individual to the division of labour, and therewith also the antithesis between mental and physical labour, has vanished; after labour has become not only a means of life but life's prime want; after the productive forces have also increased with the all-round development of the individual, and all the springs of co-operation wealth flow more abundantly—only then can the narrow horizon of bourgeois right be crossed in its entirety and society inscribe on its banners: From each according to his ability, to each according to his needs!      [pp. 222–224]

## F. ENGELS
### Anti-Dühring

(Quoted and translated in M. Oakshott, Social and Political Doctrines of Contemporary Europe)

### The State

The state, therefore, has not existed from all eternity. There have been societies which managed without it, which had no conception of the state and state power. At a certain stage of economic development, which was necessarily bound up with the cleavage of society into classes, the state became a necessity owing to this cleavage. We are now rapidly approaching a stage in the development of production at which the existence of these classes has not only ceased to be a necessity, but is becoming a positive hindrance to production. They will fall as inevitably as they arose at an earlier stage. Along with them, the state will inevitably fall. The society that organizes production anew on the basis of the free and equal association of the producers will put the whole state machine where it will then belong: in the museum of antiquities, side by side with the spinning-wheel and the bronze axe.      [pp. 129–130]

### "Withering Away" of the State

The proletarian seizes the state power and transforms the means of production in the first instance into state property. But in doing this, it puts an end to itself as the proletariat, it puts an end to all class differences and class antagonisms, it puts an end also to the state as the state. Former society, moving in class antagonisms, had need of the state, that is, an organization of the exploiting class, at each period for the maintenance of its external conditions of production; that is, therefore, for the forcible holding down of the exploited class in the conditions of oppression (slavery, villeinage or serfdom, wage-labour) determined by the existing mode of production. The state was the official representative of society as a whole, its embodiment in a visible corporation; but it was this only in so far as it was the state of that class which itself, in its epoch, represented society as a whole: in ancient times, the state of the slave-owning citizens; in the Middle Ages, of the feudal nobility; in our epoch, of the bourgeoisie. When ultimately it becomes really representative of society as a whole, it makes itself superfluous. As soon as there is not longer any class of society to be held in subjection; as soon as, along with class domination and the struggle for individual existence based on the former anarchy of production, the collisions and excesses arising from these have also been abolished, there is nothing more to be repressed, which would make a special repressive force, a state, necessary. The first act in which the state really comes forward as the representative of society as a whole—the taking possession of the means of production in the name of society—is at the same time its last independent act as a state. The interference of the state power in social relations becomes superfluous in one sphere after another, and then ceases of itself. The government of persons is replaced by the administration of things and the direction of the process of production. The state is not "abolished", it *withers away*. It is from this standpoint that we must appraise the phrase "free people's state"—both its justification at times for agitational purposes, and its ultimate scientific inadequacy—and also the demand of the so-called anarchists that the state should be abolished overnight.                                   [pp. 130–131]

### LENIN
### State and Revolution
(1917)

*(Quoted and translated in M. Oakeshott op. cit.)*

It may be said without fear of error that of this argument of Engels', which is so singularly rich in ideas, only one point has become an integral part of socialist thought among modern Socialist Parties, namely, that according to Marx the state "withers away"—as distinct from the anarchist doctrine of the "abolition of the state". To emasculate Marxism in such a manner is to reduce it to opportunism for such an "interpretation" only leaves the hazy conception of a slow, even, gradual change, of absence of leaps and storms, of absence of revolution. The current, widespread, mass, if one may say so, conception of the "withering away" of the state undoubtedly means the slurring over, if not the repudiation, of revolution.

Such an "interpretation" is the crudest distortion of Marxism, advantageous only to the bourgeoisie; in point of theory, it is based on a disregard for the most important circumstances and considerations pointed out, for example, in the "summary" of Engels' argument we have just quoted in full.

In the first place, Engels at the very outset of this argument says that, in assuming state power, the proletariat by that "puts an end to the state ... as the state". It is not "good form" to ponder over what this means. Generally, it is either ignored altogether, or it is considered to be a piece of "Hegelian weakness" on Engels' part. As a matter of fact, however, these words briefly express the experience of one of the great proletarian revolutions, the Paris Commune of 1871. As a matter of fact, Engels speaks here of the "abolition" of the *bourgeois* state by the proletarian revolution, while the words about its withering away refer to the remnants of the *proletarian* state *after* the socialist revolution. According to Engels the bourgeois state does not "wither away", but is "*put an end to*" by the proletariat in the course of the revolution. What withers away after the revolution is the proletarian state or senior-state.

Secondly, the state is a "special repressive force", Engels gives this splendid and extremely profound definition here with complete lucidity. And from it follows that the "special repressive force" for the suppression of the proletariat by the bourgeoisie, for the suppression of the millions of toilers by a handful of the rich, must be superseded by a "special repressive force" for the suppression of the bourgeoisie by the proletariat (the dictatorship of the proletariat). This is precisely what is meant by putting an end to "the state as the state". This is precisely the "act" of taking possession of the means of production in the name of society. And it is obvious that such a substitution of one (proletarian) "special repressive force" for another (bourgeois) "special repressive force" cannot possibly take place in the form of "withering away".

Thirdly, in regard to the state "withering away", and the even more expressive and colourful "ceasing of itself", Engels refers quite clearly and definitely to the period *after* the state as "taken possession of the means of production in the name of society", that is, *after* the socialist revolution. We all know that the political form of the "state" at that time is the most complete democracy. But it never enters the head of any of the opportunists who shamelessly distort Marxism that Engels here speaks of *democracy* "withering away", or "ceasing of itself". This seems very strange at first sight; but it is "unintelligible" only to those who have not pondered over the fact that democracy is *also* a state and that, consequently, democracy will also disappear when the state disappears. Revolution alone can "put an end" to the bourgeois state. The state in general, *i.e.* most complete democracy, can only "wither away".

Fourthly, after formulating his famous proposition that "the state withers away", Engels at once explains concretely that this proposition is directed equally against the opportunists and the anarchists. In doing this, however, Engels puts in the forefront the conclusion deduced from the proposition, the "state withers away", which is directed against the opportunists.

One can wager that out of every 10,000 persons who have read or heard about the "withering away" of the state, 9,990 do not know, or do not remember, that Engels did not direct the conclusions he deduced from this proposition against the anarchists *alone*. Of the remaining ten, probably nine do not know the meaning of "free people's state" or why an attack on this watchword contains an attack on the opportunists ... The conclusion drawn against the anarchists has been repeated thousands of times, vulgarized, dinned into people's heads in the crudest fashion and has acquired the strength of a prejudice; whereas the conclusion drawn against the opportunists has been hushed up and "forgotten!" ...

Fifthly, this very same work of Engels', of which everyone remembers the argument about the "withering away" of the state, also contains a disquisition on the significance of violent revolution. Engels' historical analysis of its role becomes a veritable panegyric on violent revolution. This "no one remembers"; it is not good form in modern Socialist Parties to talk or even think about the importance of this idea, and it plays no part whatever in their daily propaganda and agitation among the masses. And yet, it is inseparably bound up with the "withering away" of the state into one harmonious whole ...[12]    [pp. 131–133]

## K. RENNER
### The Institutions of Private Law and their Social Functions
### (1949)[13]

*The Economic and Social Functions of the Legal Institutions*

We propose to examine only the economic and social effect of the valid norm as it exists, so long as the norm does not change.

Those acquainted with socialist literature will at once perceive that we have taken as our subject the mutual relations between law and economics. The traditional Marxist school conceives the economic relations as the substructure and the legal institutions as the superstructure. "Substructure" and "superstructure" are metaphors, borrowed from architecture; it is obvious that they serve only to illustrate the connection, not to define it in exact terms. The superstructure,

---

[12] [For an account of the evolution of Lenin's thought on state and law, see E. H. Carr, *The Bolshevik Revolution* (1966), Pt I, pp. 238, 256.]
[13] [Translated with Introduction by O. Kahn-Freund.]

according to Marx's well-known formula,[14] comprises not only law but also ethics and culture, in fact every ideology. This terminology must therefore apply to many facts other than those relevant to the law, whose structures are completely different and must be separately defined. The relation between the philosophy of an age and the economic substructure of that age is obviously determined by key concepts quite different from those of legal norm, exercise of a right, and the like. We must desist, therefore, from attempting to give a general exposition of the Marxist concept of superstructure. We must recognise that each of these social phenomena, which in their general aspects are quite aptly illustrated by Marx's metaphor, requires a specific investigation. We attempt this investigation in regard to law.

Our previous explanations have made it clear that the relation is not merely one of cause and effect. It would be no solution of our problem to say that the economic structure generates the norm. Such an assumption could apply only to one of the fields of learning, that concerned with the creation of laws. Yet the mechanism by which economy as the causal factor brings about the effect of law, is obscure and unexplored. It probably would not become intelligible by any ultimate abstraction, such as the application of the primitive categories of cause and effect ... In the second province, that of positive legal analysis, the concepts of cause and effect generally mean little; the main concern here is obviously that of motive, means and ends, and the appropriate method of explanation is teleological, not causal. If we were to describe the superstructure of law in the third field (that of the economic and social efficacy of the norms) as exclusively the effect of the social and economic substructure, our conclusions would be proved to be absurd by the very facts to which they refer.

It is mere platitude to say that laws can influence economy sufficiently to change it and can therefore be considered as causes of economic results. Marx, of course, was the last person to deny this. "The influence of laws upon the conservation of the relations of distribution and consequently their influence upon production must be specifically determined".[15] Laws are made with the intention of producing economic results, and as a rule they achieve this effect. Social life is not so simple that we can grasp it, open it and reveal its kernel like a nut, by placing it between the two arms of a nutcracker called cause and effect. Although he was much occupied with legal problems, Marx never found time to "determine the influence of the laws" (as above); yet he saw the problem clearly as is proved in particular by the following methodological hint: "The really difficult point to be discussed here, however, is how the relations of production as relations of the law enter into, a disparate development. An instance is Roman civil law in its relations to modern production".[16] We make use of this hint in the formulation of our problem: (1) Law which continues unchanged in relation to changing economic conditions; (2) Changed economic conditions in relation to the new norms and the new law. Our study, however, will be concerned with the first part of the problem only.

We start with a definite legal system based upon a definite economic foundation as it appears at a given moment of history. All economic institutions are at the same time institutions of the law. All economic activities are either, like sale and purchase, acts-in-the-law, or, like farming one's own land, the mere exercise of a right; or if neither, like the work of a mill-hand at his loom, even though they are extra-legal activities, they are nevertheless performed within definite legal conditions. We see that the act-in-the-law and the economic action are not identical.

---

[14] [See *ante*, 1134.]
[15] *Neue Zeit*, p. 744.
[16] *ibid.*, p. 779.

The process of eating has a physiological, and economic and a volitional aspect but it is not an act of will with the qualities of an act-in-the-law. Yet the conditions under which it takes place are determined to some extent by the law.

The circulation of goods in a capitalist society is mediated by sale and purchase and by ancillary contracts: these are transactions for which the law of obligations provides various forms. Production, however, is not in itself an act-of-the-law. It can be the mere exercise of the right of ownership, as in the case of the peasant. In the capitalist factory, however, the legal aspect of production is more complicated. For the capitalist, production is the exercise of his right of ownership, since factory and machines are his property. For the worker it is the fulfilment of a legal obligation which has been established by the contract of employment. In so far as it is the latter, it is an act-in-the-law; in so far as it is the former, it is the mere exercise of a right. Thus a simple economic category is equivalent to a combination of various legal categories, there is no point-to-point correspondence. A number of distinct legal institutions serves a single economic process. They play a part which I will call their economic function.

Yet every economic process which in theory is an isolated unit is only part of the whole process of social production and reproduction. If the economic function is related to this whole, it becomes the social function of the legal institution.

A comprehensive exposition of the functions fulfilled by the legal institutions at every stage of the economic process has been given in *Das Kapital*, Marx's principal work. No other investigator, either before or after him, was more aware of their importance for even the most minute details of this process. We shall see that no other economic theory gives so much insight into the connections between law and economics. Marx's predecessors and successors either refused to recognise the problem or could not do it full justice.

If we regard a social order as static and confine our attention to a certain moment of history, then the legal norms and the economic process merely appear as mutually conditioned and subservient to one another. Within the economic structure economic process and legal norm appear as the same thing: the former seen as an external, technico-natural event, the latter as an inherent relation of will, seen from the point of view of individual will-formation. We call the external, technico-natural process the substratum of the norm. This sounds very plausible. But we can no more study the laws of gravity from a stone in a state of rest than we can learn the art of cooking from the cook who was pricked by the Sleeping Beauty's spindle. All that we can observe is that in a state of rest legal and economic institutions, though not identical, are but two aspects of the same thing, inextricably interwoven. We must define and describe this co-existence.

This observation, however, only stresses the fact that they are mutually determined. We must study the process in its historical sequence, the gradual transition of a social order from a given stage to the next. The inherent laws of development can only be revealed if the events are seen in motion, in the historic sequence of economic and legal systems. If we examine two consecutive periods, chosen at random, we may obtain results which, though they apply to these particular periods of transition, cannot claim to be generally valid. To decide the function of the law in general, we have to study inductively all social orders as they appear in the course of history, from the most primitive to the most highly developed. By this method we obtain the general categories of the social order and at the same time the general functions of the law.

This procedure is legitimate in spite of the fact that every individual stage of development has its specific nature and is subject to its peculiar laws. Marx frequently refers to general principles of this kind, declaring them to be justified. "All periods of production have certain characteristics in common . . . production in general is an abstract concept, but a reasonable one in that it really establishes and emphasizes what is common, and thus saves us repetition". ". . . a unity brought about by the fact that the subject, mankind, and the object, nature, are always the same".[17] Yet Marx disparages these general abstractions in economics often enough to fortify our objections against them. One of his reasons was the tendency of economists, which still exists, to regard the categories of the capitalist order as eternal and sacrosanct. Another reason lies in the limitations of his own task, *viz*, to explore and describe one individual period only. "Yet it is the very difference from what is general and common which is the essential element of a particular development". If Marx had concentrated upon the definition of peculiar characteristics of one epoch as he found them, he might have given a description in the manner of a research student, but the laws of social development would have remained hidden from him. Marx, however, seeks to explain the specific historical phenomenon alongside with previous individual forms as being merely an individual manifestation of the general principle. In this way he discovers inherent connections within the development.

The following may serve as an example: "Surplus labour is a general social phenomenon as soon as the productivity of human labour power exceeds the immediate needs of life, but its appearance in the feudal epoch differs from that in the capitalist epoch—in the former it is villeinage, in the latter surplus value".

We cannot dispense in our enquiry with a general survey of the functions performed by the legal institutions. Every individual functions which is historically determined is correlated to the whole and can only be clearly understood within its context. A diagrammatic exposition of the functions at least clears the field. A concrete detail cannot be demonstrated otherwise than by relating it to the general whole. "A phenomenon is concrete because it integrates various determining factors, because it is a unity of multiplicity. If it is thought out, it appears as the product and result of an integrating process" . . .      [pp. 55–60]

. . . I maintain that Karl Marx deliberately set out to observe and describe each and every phenomenon of the capitalist epoch, correlating these to a continuous development of human society on the basis of an inherited legal system, rigid, retarded and fossilised. Those who expect from his critique of political economy a guide for economic behaviour, or an analysis of subjective valuations, or something similar, are therefore bound to misunderstand him. Only if the great historical drama is approached as he approached it, only then is it revealed in a true light: a society of small commodity producers has overcome feudal restrictions by dint of hard struggle, and at least establishes a system wherein the producer freely disposes over his means of production. It is now declared that everyone shall own his means of production, that everyone shall be free to exchange the fruits of his labours for those of everyone else, it is ordained that everybody shall peacefully enjoy and keep his own as he has saved it from the ruins of the feudal system. The law leaves to every individual the use of his means of production, permitting him to work as he finds expedient. As the product of everybody's labours automatically becomes his property, the law may safely do so. The law also leaves it to every individual to provide for his descendants, and it may safely do so: for the father's property forms a fund of subsistence for the inheriting children. This plain and simple regulation of property merely attempts legally to stabilise[18] the existing living conditions of society.

## 1. Change of Functions and Change of Norms

But now we find the peaceful enjoyment of one's own property developing into the draconic control of alien labour-power, and giving rise to a new regulation of

---

[17] *Neue Zeit*, vol. 21, p. 712.
[18] The bourgeois revolution was so much easier because there was no necessity to form new social groups or to redistribute possessions, apart from the liberation of peasants. Fundamentally it proclaimed only two commandments; a material one, that everyone should keep what he had, and a personal one, that everyone should mind his own business.

labour, more sever and in its initial stages more cruel than any regulation of feudal times or of the time of the pharaohs—we need only mention child labour. Thus peaceful enjoyment of one's own object becomes constant appropriation of the proceeds of the labour of others; it becomes title to surplus value, distributing the whole of the social product as profit, interest and rent among an idle class, and limiting the working class to the mere necessities of existence and procreation. In the end it reverses all its original functions. The owner has now no longer even detention of his property; it is deposited at some bank, and whether he is a labourer or working capitalist, the owner cannot dispose of his own. He may not even be acquainted with the locality of the concern in which he has invested his property. Yet one function of capital is indestructibly linked up with his person, the function of appropriating the products of alien labour; and month by month the bank messenger delivers to the owner of the revenue of his economic property.

This vast process of change, with all its accompanying phenomena, is unfolded before the eyes of Karl Marx; he exposes it as the problem of our time, as the vital question of the whole of human society in our present era. His thoughts cover the whole of human society and at the same time they concentrate upon the inherent and most secret principles of its existence; in his thoughts he is in advance of the overwhelming majority of our generation.

He has made it clear to us that property in the capitalist epoch fulfils functions quite different from those which it fulfilled in the era of simple commodity production, and partly opposed to these. He has made it clear that property has become antisocial, intrinsically opposed to the real interests of society. Yet all property is conferred by the law, by a conscious exercise of the power of society. When society was in control it endowed the individual with the power of disposal over corporeal things; but now the corporeal object controls the individuals, labour-power, even society itself—it regulates the hierarchy of power and labour, the maintenance and procreation of society. Mankind has become tributary to its own creation.

The norm is the result of free action on the part of a society that has become conscious of its own existence. The society of simple commodity producers attempts to stabilise its own conditions of existence, the substratum of its existence, by means of the norm. But in spite of the norm, the substratum changes, yet this change of the substratum takes place within the forms of the law; the legal institutions automatically change their functions which turn into their very opposite, yet this change is scarcely noticed and is not understood. In view of all this the problem arises whether society is not bound to change its norm as soon as it has become conscious of the change in its functions.

## 2. Complementary Institutions Displace the Principal Institution

An urgent demand for a human society that acts in freedom and in full consciousness, that creates its norms in complete independence: this is socialism. The very word expresses this. The passing of man from the realm of necessity to the realm of freedom cannot be conceived otherwise than an a marshalling of the organized will of society against the paltry presumptuousness of the individual, so that the object that has become the master of man may again be subjected to the control of society. Common will can achieve this only by a direct, controlled and well-aimed regulation of the relations among men and between man and nature, so that every person and every object may have its functions openly established and may fulfil them in a straightforward manner.

Utopians indulged in dreams and speculations as to how this could be achieved, fanatics of law and philosophy felt themselves obliged to preach fantastic remedies. It was thought that completely new legal institutions would have to be fashioned and the old ones abolished by decree, in order to bring about something that man had never known before. The socialists of this period, the

Messianic era of socialism, failed to recognise that it is above all the way of experience which can lead to the new, that even the state of the future is conditioned by the past and that it cannot be otherwise. This era has long since passed away, nowadays we rely on empirical fact, and rightly so. But the socialists, and also unfortunately their leading group, the Marxists, disdain to apply this experience in the realm of the law and the state. They fail to comprehend and to investigate scientifically, how far it is true that the new society is already preformed in the womb of the old, even in the field of the law. May it not be true that here also new life is already completely developed in the mother's womb, waiting only for the liberating act of birth?

Some vista of the future, some answers to the questions which we have raised, must have occurred to anyone who has accompanied us on our journey through economics, who has joined in our study with critical regard to the sufferings of mankind. Every society requires a regulation of power and labour. Why do we not set out to create it directly? Why do we not appoint skilled teachers to be masters of our apprentices, why does society accept blindly everyone who takes over an enterprise by the chance of birth or inheritance, although he may be totally unfit to instruct? Why does not society select the best-qualified agriculturist to succeed into a farm that has become vacant, instead of the rich city man who buys it as a hobby, or instead of the fortuitous heir who may be no good? If hereditary appointments are now abolished as insufferable in the case of the most unimportant public office, why is it that the fortuitous heir may still succeed into an important economic enterprise which is responsible for the good or bad fortune of a thousand workers, and, maybe, for the adequate supply of certain goods for the whole of society? Anyone can see that society is in immediate need of a regulation of appointments. Our expositions have shown that the real successor who serves the economic functions of a concern is appointed by contract of employment, so that the heir need only play the part of the possessor of a title to surplus value without performing any function. We have seen that even to-day property is supplemented by complementary institutions which take over its real functions. Should we not come to the conclusion that the process of change towards a new legal order has already begun, that the complementary institutions already pre-shaped in the framework of the old order will become the principal institutions so that the institution which has previously played the principal part can be abolished, without any disturbance of the economic process, in so far as it not longer serves a useful social purpose?

Feasible as this idea seems, it nevertheless comes up against the most rampant prejudices. It would mean that the contract of employment would become the principle institution of the social regulation of labour, but this institution was during the last century denounced as the source of all social suffering. We are asked to revolutionise our conceptions completely. But we have already met two decisive reasons for changing this opinion. We have seen that the contract of employment, like all legal forms, is in itself neither good nor evil, that the value of the legal form is solely determined by the social function fulfilled by the legal institution. We have seen that it is not the legal form of the contract of employment but its connection with the institution of property which makes the former an instrument of exploitation. Secondly, experience has shown us that the contract of employment even to-day has developed into the established "position" and has to a large extent become socialised and made secure by means of manifold social rights.

### 3. Complementary Institutions of Public Law Force the Private Law Institutions into the Background

A second and probably even more important phenomenon becomes apparent and must be considered by the intelligent observer.

Property is a matter of private law. The whole body of our legal doctrine is based upon this fact. We distinguish between private and public law as the two principal branches of our legal analysis, as we understand it. The normative content of our existing laws fully justifies this division and we cannot avoid making this distinction. Our observations, however, have led us to recognise that every legal order must grant to everybody a private sphere into which the common will does not intrude. After the victory of a liberalist philosophy with its concepts of natural rights, to which the victory of the bourgeoisie over the feudal system corresponded in practice, a theory of constitutional law was evolved which set limits to the powers of the state, affecting even the public law. Public law may not transgress these limits; within them the individual is free and not subject to the control of the state. Here he is no longer a citizen of the state but simply a human being who enjoys freedom of thought and religion, freedom of convictions which the states may not touch. We hold this freedom of the individual in high esteem. It is not a present of nature and its was gained as a precious good of civilisation only after severe social and political struggle; and no thinking socialist would dream of surrendering it.[19] As far as we can judge looking into the future, material goods will also belong to this sphere, not only family portraits and other articles of sentimental value, but also the bulk of goods intended for consumption, household utensils, perhaps even the home itself. There will always be a private "*suum*", a sphere of one's "legal own", even with regard to rights *in rem*, no matter what social order men may give themselves.

But contemporary property, capital as the object of property, through *de jure* private, has in fact ceased altogether to be private. No longer does the owner make use of property in a technical way; the tenement house serves a number of strangers and the railway serves all and sundry. Property in its technical aspect has been completely estranged from the owner. The Roman civil lawyer believed that *dominus rei suae legem dicit*. As far as ownership of capital is concerned, this pronouncement is no longer true: it is society that disposes of capital and prescribes the laws for its use. It may be maintained at least that the object has ceased to be private and is becoming social. An army of a thousand miners, an army with its own generals, commissioned and non-commissioned officers, all of them employees, have complete technical control of the mine; they search its depths and bring its treasures to light, securing not only its continuity but also its very existence; and they stake their own lives for this purpose. Evidently it is a more provocative fiction that this army should be regarded as a disconnected crowd of strangers, and the share-holders, who may not even know where their property is situated, as the real owners. Language, indeed, revolts against such abuse.

What is it that makes this abuse nevertheless apparently tolerable? Public law has for a long time recognised that where the whole of society is in principle concerned with an object, it can no longer be treated as a matter that is merely private. So it comes about that private law is supplemented by rules of public law relating to the object; a process that was cautions and tentative in the beginning but soon became more decided and in the end was developed in full consciousness.

In the liberal epoch the state considered every interference with the economic system and therefore with private law as contrary to reason and natural law; accordingly it refrained from it completely and merely exercised the restricted functions of protection and administration of justice. But since the middle of the last century the state is no longer content merely to hold the mace and the scales, it begins to take an active part in administration. New norms are made year by

---

[19] This has not prevented Bolshevism from again establishing the omnipotence of the state, from stringently curtailing human freedom in the spiritual sphere. I think this is a disastrous retrogression. It is not justifiable to surrender achievements of civilisation even if they are branded as introductions of the enemy, the hated bourgeoisie.

year in increasing numbers in the form of statutes, orders and instructions of the administrators of the state. Administrative law develops into a special branch of legal analysis, and economic administration soon becomes the most extensive part within this branch. Grievances arise out of the application of the law of property and the contract of employment to the factory, and therefore administrative law must step in. Regulations relating to the normal working day, factory inspection, and protection of women and children are institutions of public law which increasingly supplement these institutions of private law. Insurance against sickness, accident and old age follow suit, public labour exchanges replace the private labour market, and so on. In the end the relations of labour are as to nine parts regulated by public law, and the field of influence of private law in restricted to the remaining tenth.

When we were dealing with the functions of capital, we nearly always had occasion to refer to complementary institutions of public law and to emphasise that these are new creations; in the main they were introduced or at least perfected only after the death of Karl Marx.

Thus we are led to surmise that a two-fold development is taking place: first, that the complementary institutions of private law have deprived the owners of their technical disposal over their property; and secondly, that the common will has subjected property to its direct control, at least from the point of view of the law. Elements of a new order have been developed within the framework of an old society. So it may not be necessary to clamour for prophets whose predictions of the future will flow from esoteric qualities of the soul. It may well be that there is no need to proclaim premiums for those who would draft the new legal constitution of a reasonable social order: perhaps the truth is that we can simply deduce the law of the future from the data supplied by our experience of to-day-and yesterday.

Should this be so, and we have good reason to believe it, our only problem would be to burst the shell which still obstructs the new development; to set free the complementary and supplementary institutions and to use them straightforwardly in accordance with their present and real functions, freed from restriction; to elevate them, the previous handmaidens of property, into the principal institutions; and to liberate them from the fetters of traditional property, which has lost its functions and has itself become a restrictive force.

Our observations have shown, however, that this cannot be the automatic result of a change of functions, that new norms are required to achieve it. For there can be no doubt that only a norm can break another norm. The norm, however, is a conscious act of will performed by society.

### 4. Legal Doctrine and the Tasks of Society

If society has become conscious of the changes in the functions of property and its contradictory effects, the question arises whether it must not change the norm. If it has surrounded property with so many barriers that these have gained the specific and paramount importance of a legal construction *sui generis*, should it not set free this new construction from the obstructions caused by its origin? Or has it surrendered so much of its autonomy that it can no longer perform this last step or dare not do so? Does society still enjoy freedom of will, the power to create new norms? Even if it disposes of the instruments of legislation, if its legal title to free legislation is beyond dispute, the question still remains: is society still able to control technically the forces of development which have been set free? Society is sovereign as the legislator, but is it equally sovereign in practice? Or can it achieve in practical life only what it must? We have already become acquainted with the external limits which restrict the efficacy of the norm. If the law changes its functions, does this enforce a change of norms as well? Why do the norms not change equally automatically? If a change in functions is always also the cause of a change in norms, why is it that this cause cannot equally take effect in the quiet way of facts? How is the law determined by economics?

We have seen that the economic substratum dislocates the functions of the norm, that it reverses them; but the norm itself remains indestructible. The capital function also remains indestructible, and all development serves only its perfection. Therefore it may seem as if the crudest change of function does not react on this nebulous creation, this immaterial formula, those imperatives which apparently have no existence or only modestly vegetate in the documents of the statutes. Does it mean that the norms are indestructible, eternal, changeless, or at least determined by no other power than their own?

Given that, like all else under the sun, norms have their causes, wherein do these lie? Given that they enjoy a real existence, what are its characteristics, what is the mode of their existence and how do they change? Given that their origin lies in the conditions of life of the human race, that they are nothing more than a means of preserving human society, what part do they actually play in the existence and development of our own generation?

These are open questions of jurisprudence. The time has come to engage in an attempt at their solution. [pp. 292–300]

## E. PASHUKANIS
### Law and Marxism
### (1978)

A further objection to our conception of the tasks of general legal theory is that the underlying abstractions are regarded as exclusive to bourgeois law. Proletarian law—we are told—should find alternative general concepts, and the search for such alternatives should be the task of the Marxist theory of law.

At first sight, this objection appears to be a very serious one. Yet it rests on a misunderstanding. In raising a demand for new general concepts specific to proletarian law, this line appears to be revolutionary par excellence. In reality, however, this tendency proclaims the immortality of the legal form, in that it strives to wrench this form from the particular historical conditions which had helped bring it to full fruition, and to present it as capable of permanent renewal. The withering away of certain categories of bourgeois law (the categories as such, not this or that precept) in no way implies their replacement by new categories of proletarian law, just as the withering away of the categories of value, capital, profit and so forth in the transition to fully-developed socialism will not mean the emergence of new proletarian categories of value, capital and so on.

The withering away of the categories of bourgeois law will, under these conditions, mean the withering away of law altogether, that is to say the disappearance of the juridical factor from social relations.

The transition period—as Marx showed in his "Critique of the Gotha Programme"—is characterised by the fact that social relations will, for a time, necessarily continue to be constrained by the "narrow horizon of bourgeois right".[20] It is interesting to analyse what constitutes, in Marx's view, this narrow horizon of bourgeois right (*Recht*). Marx presupposes a social order in which the means of production are socially owned and in which the producers do not exchange their products. Consequently, he assumes a higher stage of development than the "new economic policy" which we are presently experiencing.[21] He sees

---

[20] Marx, "Marginal Notes to the Programme of the German Workers' Party", in Marx and Engels, *Selected Works* (1970), vol. III, p. 19. [and *ante*, 1151.]

[21] [That is "New Economic Policy": The N.E.P. was introduced in 1921 and established a mixed economy with a free market. It ended in 1928 with the establishment of the first Five Year Plan.]

the market as having been already replaced by an organised framework, such that in no way.

> does the labour employed on the products appear here as *the value* of these products, as a material quality possessed by them, since now, in contrast to capitalist society, individual labour no longer exists in an indirect fashion but directly as a component part of the total labour.[22]

Nevertheless, Marx says, even when the market and market exchange have been completely abolished, the new communist society will of necessity be

> in every respect, economically, morally and intellectually, still stamped with the birth marks of the old society from whose womb it emerges.[23]

This becomes evident in the principle of distribution as well, according to which

> the individual producer receives back from society—after the deductions have been made—exactly what he gives to it.[24]

Marx stresses that in spite of the radical transformation of form and content

> the same principle prevails as that which regulates the exchange of commodities, as far as this is exchange of equal values ... a given amount of labour in one form is exchanged for an equal amount of labour in another form.[25]

To the extent that the relation of the individual producer to society still retains the form of the exchange of equivalents, it also retains the form of law (*Recht*), for "right" (*Recht*) by its very nature can consist only in the application of an equal standard".[26] However, as this makes no allowance for the natural inequality of individual talent, it is "a right of inequality, in its content, like every right".[27] Marx does not mention that there must be a state authority which guarantees the enforcement of these norms of "unequal" right by its coercion, thus retaining its "bourgeois limit", but that goes without saying. Lenin concludes:

> Of course, bourgeois right in regard to the distribution of *consumer* goods inevitably presupposes the existence of the *bourgeois state*, for right is nothing without an apparatus capable of enforcing the observance of the standards of right.

It follows that under communism there remains for a time not only bourgeois right, but even the bourgeois state, without the bourgeoisie![28]

Once the form of equivalent exchange is given then the form of law—the form of public, or state authority—is also given, and consequently this form persists even after the class structure has ceased to exist. The withering away of law, and with it, of the state, ensues, in Marx's view, only after "labour has become not only a means of life but life's prime want",[29] when the productive forces grow

---

[22] Marx, "Marginal Notes", *op. cit.*, p. 17.
[23] *ibid.*
[24] *ibid.*
[25] *ibid.*, p. 18.
[26] *ibid.*
[27] *ibid.*
[28] Vladimir Il'ich Lenin, "The State and Revolution", Chap. 5 in V. I. Lenin, *Selected Works* (1966), p. 335. [*Ante*, 1190.]
[29] Marx, "Marginal Notes", *op. cit.*, p. 19.

together with the all-round development of the individual, when everyone works spontaneously according to their abilities...

Thus Marx conceives of the transition to developed communism not as a transition to new forms of law, but as a withering away of the legal form as such, as a liberation from that heritage of the bourgeois epoch which is fated to outlive the bourgeoisie itself.

At the same time, Marx reveals that the fundamental condition of existence of the legal form is rooted in the very economic organisation of society. In other words, the existence of the legal form is contingent upon the integration of the different products of labour according to the principle of equivalent exchange. In so doing, he exposes the deep interconnection between the legal form and the commodity form. Any society which is constrained, by the level of development of its productive forces, to retain an equivalent relation between expenditure and compensation of labour, in a form which even remotely suggests the exchange of commodity values, will be compelled to retain the legal form as well. Only by starting from this fundamental aspect can one understand why a whole series of other social relations assume legal form. To draw the inference from this, however, that there must always be laws and courts, since not even with the greatest possible economic provision would there be an end to all offences against the person, would simply mean taking secondary, minor aspects for the main, fundamental one. Even progressive bourgeois criminology has become convinced that the prevention of crime may properly be viewed as a medical-educational problem. To solve this problem, jurists, with their "evidence", their codes, their concepts of "guilt", and of "full or diminished responsibility", or their fine distinctions between complicity, aiding and abetting, instigation and so on, are entirely superfluous. And the only reason this theoretical conviction has not yet led to the abolition of penal codes and criminal courts is, of course, that the overthrow of the legal form is dependent, not only on transcending the framework of bourgeois society, but also on a radical emancipation from all its remnants.

The critique of bourgeois jurisprudence from the standpoint of scientific socialism must follow the example of Marx's critique of bourgeois political economy. For that purpose, this critique must, above all, venture into enemy territory. It should not throw aside the generalisations and abstractions elaborated by bourgeois jurists, whose starting point was the needs of their class and of their times. Rather, by analysing these abstract categories, it should demonstrate their true significance and lay bare the historically limited nature of the legal form.

Every ideology dies together with the social relations which produced it. This final disappearance is, however, preceded by a moment when the ideology, suffering the blows of the critique directed at it, loses its ability to veil and conceal the social relations from which it emanated. The exposure of the roots of an ideology is a sure sign of its imminent end.                              [pp. 61–64]

Only when bourgeois relations are fully developed does law become abstract in character. Every person becomes man in the abstract, all labour becomes socially useful labour in the abstract,[30] every subject becomes an abstract legal subject. At the same time, the norm takes on the logically perfected form of abstract universal law.

The legal subject is thus an abstract owner of commodities raised to the

---

[30] "For a society of commodity producers, whose general social relation of production consists in the fact that they treat their products as commodities, hence as values, and in this material (*sachlich*) form being their individual, private labours into relation with each other as homogeneous human labour, Christianity with its religious cult of man in the abstract, more particularly in its bourgeois development, *i.e.* in Protestantism, Deism, etc., is the most fitting form of religion". (Marx, *Capital*, vol. I, *op. cit.*, p. 172).

heavens. His will in the legal sense has its real basis in the desire to alienate through acquisition and to profit through alienating. For this desire to be fulfilled, it is absolutely essential that the wishes of commodity owners meet each other halfway. This relationship is expressed in legal terms as a contract or an agreement concluded between autonomous wills. Hence the contract is a concept central to law. To put it in a more high-flown way: the contract is an integral part of the idea of law. In the logical system of juridical concepts, the contract is merely a form of legal transaction in the abstract, that is, merely one of the will's concrete means of expression which enable the subject to affect the legal sphere surrounding him. Historically speaking, and in real terms, the concept of the legal transaction arose in quite the opposite way, namely from the contract. Outside of the contract, the concepts of the subject and of will only exist, in the legal sense, as lifeless abstraction. These concepts first come to life in the contract. At the same time, the legal form too, in its purest and simplest form, acquires a material basis in the act of exchange. Consequently the act of exchange concentrates, as in a focal point, the elements most crucial both to political economy and to law. In exchange, Marx says, "the content of this juridical relation (or relation of two wills) is itself determined by the economic relation".[31] Once arisen, the idea of the contract strives to attain universal validity. The owners of commodities were of course proprietors even before they acknowledged one another as such, but in a different, organic, non-legal sense. "Mutual recognition" is nothing more than an attempt to rationalise, with the aid of the abstract formula of the contract, the organic forms of appropriation based on labour, occupation and so on, which the society of commodity producers finds in existence at its inception. Considered in the abstract, the relationship of a person to a thing is totally devoid of legal significance. The jurists sense this when they try to construe the institution of private property as a relationship between subjects, in other words, between people. Yet they conceive of this relationship in a purely formal, and, moreover, in a negative way, as a universal prohibition, which excludes everybody but the owner from using and disposing of the object. This interpretation may be adequate for the practical purposes of dogmatic jurisprudence, but it is quite useless for theoretical analysis. In these abstract prohibitions, the concept of property loses any living meaning and renounces its own pre-juridical history.

If, then, development began from appropriation, as the organic, "natural" relationship between people and things, this relation was transformed into a legal one as a result of needs created by the circulation of goods, primarily, that is, by buying and selling. Hauriou points out that, at first, trade by sea and by caravan did not create the need for property to be safe-guarded. The distance separating the people involved in exchange from each other was the best protection against any claims. The establishment of permanent markets created the necessity for settling the question of right of disposal over commodities, and hence for property law.[32] The property title *mancipatio per aes et libram* in ancient Roman law shows that is arose simultaneously with the phenomenon of domestic exchange. Similarly, inheritance has only been established as a property title since the time when civil intercourse became interested in such a transfer.[33]

Writing of exchange, Marx says that one owner of commodities may appropriate another's commodity in exchange for his own only with the consent of the other commodity-owner.[34] This is exactly the notion which the representatives of the doctrine of natural law tried to express by attempting to give property a basis in the form of a primitive contract. They are right—not, of course, in the sense that such a contractual act did take place at some historical point in time, but in

---

[31]  *ibid.*, p. 178.
[32]  Maurice Hauriou, *Principles de droit public*, p. 286.
[33]  *ibid.*, p. 287.
[34]  Marx, *Capital*, vol. I, *op. cit.*, p. 178.

that natural or organic forms of appropriation assume a juridical "rationale" in the reciprocal transactions of appropriation and alienation. In the act of alienation, abstract property right materialises as a reality. Any other employment of an object is related to some concrete form of its utilisation as a means of production or consumption. If, however, the object has a function as an exchange value, it becomes an impersonal object, a purely legal object, and the subject disposing of it becomes a purely legal subject. The contrast between feudal and bourgeois property can be explained by their different approach to circulation. Feudal property's chief failing in the eyes of the bourgeois world lies not in its origin (plunder, violence), but in its inertia, in the fact that it cannot form the object of a mutual guarantee by changing hands through alienation and acquisition. Feudal property, or property determined by estate, violates the fundamental principle of bourgeois society: "the equal opportunity to attain inequality". Hauriou, one of the most astute bourgeois jurists, quite rightly emphasises reciprocity as the most effective security for property, which can be brought about with the minimum use of external force. This mutuality, which is ensured by the laws of the market, lends property the quality of an "eternal" institution. In contrast to this, the purely political security vouchsafed by the coercive machinery of state amounts to nothing more than the protection of specified personal stocks belonging to the owners—an aspect which has no fundamental significance. In the past, the class struggle has often resulted in a reallocation of property, the expropriation of usurers and large landowners.[35] Yet these upheavals, extremely unpleasant though they may have been for those groups and classes who were their victims, did not shake the foundations of private property, the economic framework linking economic units through exchange. The same people who had rebelled against property had no choice but to approve it next day when they met in the market as independent producers. That is the way of all non-proletarian revolutions. It is the logical consequence of the ideals of the anarchists. Whilst they do, of course, reject the external characteristics of bourgeois law—state coercion and the statutes—they preserve its inner essence, the free contract between autonomous producers.

Thus, only the development of the market creates the possibility of—and the necessity for—transforming the person appropriating things by his labour (or by robbery) into a legal owner. There is no clearly defined borderline between these two phases. The "natural" changes into the juridicial imperceptibly, just as armed robbery blends quite directly with trade.                                           [pp. 120–124]

To the extent that society represents a market, the machinery of state is actually manifested as an impersonal collective will, as the rule of law, and so on. Every buyer and seller is . . . a legal subject par excellence. The autonomous will of those engaged in exchange is an indispensable precondition wherever the categories of value and exchange value come into play. Exchange value ceases to be exchange value, the commodity ceases to be a commodity, if exchange ratios are determined by an authority situated outside of the internal laws of the market. Coercion as the imperative addressed by one person to another, and backed up by force, contradicts the fundamental precondition for dealings between the owners of commodities. In a society of commodity owners, and within the limits of the act of exchange, coercion is neither abstract nor impersonal—hence it cannot figure as a social function. For in the society based on commodity production, subjection to one person, as a concrete individual, implies subjection to an arbitrary force, since it is the same thing, for this society, as the subjection of one owner of commodities to another. That is also why coercion cannot appear here

---

[35] This gives rise to Engels' remark: "It is thus entirely true that for 2,500 years private property could be protected only by violating property rights". (Friedrich Engels, "The Origin of the Family, Private Property and the State" in Marx and Engels, *Selected Works* (1970), vol. III, p. 281.)

in undisguised form as a simple act of expediency. It has to appear rather as coercion emanating from an abstract collective person, exercised not in the interest of the individual from whom it emanates—for every person in commodity-producing society is egoistic—but in the interest of all parties to legal transactions. The power of one person over another is brought to bear in reality as the force of law, that is to say as the force of an objective, impartial norm.

Bourgeois thought, which takes the framework of commodity-production for the eternal and natural framework of every society, therefore, regards abstract state power as an appurtenance of any and every society.

This is most naïvely expressed by the theoreticians of natural law, who based their theory of power on the idea of the intercourse between autonomous and equal personalities and imagined that, in so doing, they were proceeding from the principles of social intercourse as such. In fact, all they have developed, in various keys, is the theme of a power representing the connecting link between autonomous owners of commodities. This explains the fundamentals of this doctrine, which were evident as early as Grotius.[36] For the market, what really matters is that the commodity owners should engage in exchange; the power structure is something secondary and derived, externally imposed on the existing commodity owners. This is why the theoreticians of natural law do not regard state power as a phenomenon which arose historically and is therefore bound up with forces at work in the society in question, but think of it rather in an abstract and rationalistic manner. In intercourse between commodity owners, the necessity for authoritarian coercion arises whenever the peace is disturbed or a contract not fulfilled voluntarily. the doctrine of natural law therefore reduces the function of state power to keeping the peace, and sees the state's sole determining feature as being the instrument of law. After all, in the market, one owner of commodities is a commodity owner by the consent of the others, and all of them are commodity owners through their collective will. That is why the theory of natural law deduces the state from the contract between isolated individuals. This is the entire theory in skeleton form, which admits of the most diverse concrete variations, depending on the historical position, or the political sympathies and dialectical abilities of any one author. It allows of republican as well as monarchist deviations, and of altogether the most varying degrees of democratic and revolutionary "-isms".

On the whole, though, this theory was the revolutionary banner under which the bourgeoisie fought out its revolutionary struggles against feudal society. That also decided the fate of the theory. Since the bourgeoisie became the ruling class, the revolutionary past of natural law has begun to arouse apprehension, and the prevailing theories cannot wait to consign it to oblivion. Of course the theory of natural law does not stand up to any kind of historical or socialist critique, for the picture it paints in no way corresponds to reality. Yet the odd thing is that the juridicial theory of the state which superseded the natural law theory of the state, and which dispensed with the doctrine of the inherent and inviolable rights of people and citizens, thus acquiring the label "positive", distorts actual reality just as much as its predecessor. It is forced into this distortion, because every *juridical* theory of the state must of necessity posit the state as an independent power separated from society. It is this which constitutes the *juridical* nature of the theory.

Although in fact the activity of state organisations goes on in the shape of decrees and edicts emanating from individuals, juridical theory assumes firstly, that the state, not individuals, issues these orders, and secondly, that these orders are subordinate to the general norms of the code which, in turn, expresses the will of the state.

On this point, the theory of natural law is not one whit more fanciful than any of the juridical theories of the state, even the most positive of them, for the

---

[36] [*Cf. ante,* 105–106.]

substantive element in the doctrine of natural law was that it posited, in addition to the various forms of mutual personal dependence (from which this doctrine abstracts), another form of dependence—on the impersonal collective will of the state.

Yet just this construct also forms the basis of the legal theory of the "state as a person". The element of natural law in the juridical theory of the state lies much deeper than was apparent to the critics of the doctrine of natural law. It lies in the very concept of *public* authority, that is, of an authority which belongs to no one in particular, stands above *everyone*, and addressed itself to *everyone*. In using this concept to orient itself, juridical theory inevitably loses touch with actual reality. The difference between the doctrine of natural law and most recent legal positivism consists only in the fact that the former is much more clearly aware of the logical connection between abstract state power and the subject in the abstract. It grasped the necessary connection between these mystically veiled relations of commodity-producing society and hence provided an example of classical clarity of construction. In contrast to this, would-be legal positivism is undecided even about its own logical premises.

The constitutional state (*Rechtsstaat*) is a mirage, but one which suits the bourgeoisie very well, for it replaces withered religious ideology and conceals the fact of the bourgeoisie's hegemony from the eyes of the masses. The ideology of the constitutional state is even more convenient than religious ideology, because, while it does not entirely reflect objective reality, it is still based on this reality. Power as the "collective will", as the "rule of law", is realised in bourgeois society to the extent that this society represents a market. From this point of view, even police regulations can figure as the embodiment of the Kantian idea of freedom limited by the freedom of others.

The free and equal owners of commodities who meet in the market are free and equal only in the abstract relation of appropriation and alienation. In real life, they are bound by various ties of mutual dependence. Examples of this are the retailer and the wholesaler, the peasant and the landowner, the ruined debtor and his creditor, the proletarian and the capitalist. All these innumerable relationships of actual dependence form the real basis of state structure, whereas for the juridical theory of the state it is as if they did not exist. Further, the life of the state consists of the struggle between various political forces, between classes, parties, all manner of groupings; it is here that the real mainsprings of the machinery of state lie hidden. To juridical theory they are just as incomprehensible as the relationships mentioned above. The jurist may well be able to show a greater or lesser flexibility and ability to adapt to the facts; he can, for example, also take into account, besides statute law, the unwritten rules which have gradually arisen in the course of state practice, but that does not alter anything in principle in his fundamental approach to reality. A certain discrepancy between legal truth and truth to which historical and sociological research aspires is unavoidable. This is due not only to the fact that the dynamic of social life overturns rigidified legal forms and that, as a result, the jurist is condemned always to complete his analysis far too late; even if he does remain up to date with the facts in his assertions, he renders these facts differently than the sociologist. For, so long as he remains a jurist, he starts from the concept of the state as an autonomous force, set apart from all other individual and social forces. From the historical and political point of view, the resolutions of an influential class or party organisation have a significance as great, and sometimes greater, than the decisions of parliament or of any other state organisation. From the legal point of view, facts of the first kind are, as it were, non-existent. In contrast to this, one can, by ignoring the legal standpoint, see in every parliamentary resolution not an act of state, but a decision reached by a particular group or clique (acting in accordance with individual-egoistic or class-orientated motives, like every other collective.) The extreme normativist Kelsen concludes from this that the state exists only in theory, as a closed system of norms or obligations. Such immateriality in the object of the theory of constitutional law must indeed alarm the practical jurists. For they sense, if not with their reason, then with their instinct, the undoubted practical validity of their concepts, precisely in this wicked world and not in the sphere of pure logic alone. The "state" of the jurists is linked, despite its "ideological nature", to an objective reality, just as the most fantastic dream is still based on reality.

This reality is primarily the machinery of state itself, with all its material and personal elements.                                                      [pp. 143–148]

One must, therefore, bear in mind that morality, law and the state are forms of bourgeois society.

The proletariat may well have to utilise these forms, but that in no way implies that they could be developed further or be permeated by a socialist content. These forms are incapable of absorbing this content and must wither away in an inverse ratio with the extent to which this content becomes reality. Nevertheless, in the present transition period the proletariat will of necessity exploit this form inherited from bourgeois society in its own interest. To do this, however, the proletariat must above all have an absolutely clear idea—freed of all ideological haziness—of the historical origin of these forms. The proletariat must take a soberly critical attitude, not only towards the bourgeois state and bourgeois morality, but also towards their own state and their own morality. Phrased differently, they must be aware that both the existence and the disappearance of these forms are historically necessary.[37]                                           [p. 160]

Historically, the origin of criminal law is associated with the custom of blood vengeance. Undoubtedly these two phenomena are genetically very close to one another. However, vengeance *really becomes vengeance* only because it is followed by fines and sentences; here too it is only the subsequent stages of development (as is often to be observed in the history of mankind) which render comprehensible the implications contained in the preceding forms. If one approaches the same phenomenon from the opposite end, one can see nothing in it but the struggle for existence, a purely biological fact. For the criminologists, fixated on a later epoch, blood vengeance is synonymous with the *jus talionis*, that is, with the principle of equivalent requital, whereby the possibility of further vengeance is excluded if the injured party or his clan have avenged the offence . . .

Vengeance first begins to be regulated by custom and becomes transformed into retribution according to the rule of the *jus talionis*: "an eye for an eye, a tooth for a tooth", at the time when, apart from revenge, the system of compositions or of expiatory payment is adopted. The idea of the equivalent, this first truly juridical idea, itself originates in the commodity form. Felony can be seen as a particular variant of circulation, in which the exchange relation, that is the contractual relation, is determined retrospectively, after arbitrary action by one of the parties. The ratio between offence and retribution is likewise reduced to this exchange ratio. That is why Aristotle, when speaking of equalisation in exchange as a form of justice, divided this into two sub-species, equalisation by voluntary and by involuntary acts. In the process, he considers the economic relations of buying, selling, loans, and so forth as the former, and all forms of crime which entail a punishment as their equivalent at the latter. He is also the author of the definition of crime as an involuntarily concluded contract. Punishment emerges as an equivalent which compensates the damage sustained by the injured party. As we know, this idea was also adopted by Hugo Grotius. Naïve as these constructs may seem at first sight, they conceal a much finer feeling for the legal form than is to be found in the eclectic theories of modern jurists. In the examples of

---

[37] Does this mean, then, that "there will be no morality in the society of the future"? Not at all, if one understands morality in the wider sense as the development of higher forms of humanity, as the transformation of man into a species-being (to use Marx's expression)

vengeance and punishment, we can observe with particular clarity the imperceptible nuances by which the organic and biological is related to the juridical. This fusion is heightened by the fact that man is not able to renounce the interpretation of the phenomena of animal life to which he is accustomed, that is the juridical (or ethical) interpretation. In the actions of animals, man unintentionally finds the significance which was actually only projected onto them by subsequent development, that is, by the historical development of humanity.

Self-defence is one of the most natural phenomena of animal life. It is completely irrelevant whether we find it only as an individual reaction of a lone creature or as a reaction of a collective. According to the evidence of scholars who study the life of bees, the bees guarding the entrance to the beehive attack and sting any be not belonging to the swarm if it attempts to gain entry to the hive in order to steal honey. Moreover, if a be from another swarm has already gained access to the hive, it is killed the instant it is discovered. It is not unusual, in the animal world, to find cases where the reaction is separated by a certain interval of time from the action causing it. The animal does not respond immediately to the attack, but delays this until a later, more suitable time. Self-defence here becomes vengeance in the trust sense of the word. And since, for modern man, vengeance is inextricably linked with the idea of equivalent retribution, it therefore comes as no great surprise that Ferri, for example, wishes to assume the existence of a "juridical" instinct in animals.[38]

In fact, the juridical idea, or the idea of the equivalent, is first clearly delineated and objectively realised at that level of economic development where this form becomes common as equalisation in exchange. This certainty does not occur in the animal world, but in human society. It is entirely unnecessary to this process for expiatory payment to have completely supplanted vengeance. It is precisely in cases where restitution has been refused as something dishonourable (a view prevalent for a long while among primitive peoples), and where the carrying out of personal revenge was regarded as a solemn duty, that the act of vengeance acquires a new nuance which it did not have when it was not yet an alternative. Now, the idea of vengeance as the only adequate retribution is projected onto it. The renunciation of restitution in money form emphasises, so to speak, that the shedding of blood is the only equivalent for blood already shed. Vengeance is transformed from a purely biological phenomenon into a juridical institution by being linked with the form of equivalent exchange, exchange according to values. [pp. 168–70]

---

[38] Enrico Ferri, *Sociologia criminale* (Russian translation with a preface by Drill), vol. II, p. 37.

# 14

# CRITICAL LEGAL STUDIES

Critical legal studies (C.L.S.) burst on the scene in the United States in the late 1970s with a series of conferences.[1] It grew out of a dissatisfaction with current legal scholarship. It was more a ferment than a movement with those who identified as "crits" a diverse group perhaps united only by their commitment to a more egalitarian society. Off-shoots are critical feminist jurisprudence, critical race theory, the Lat-Crit movement and other examples of outsider jurisprudence, such as "queer jurisprudence".[2]

Like realism, with which it is often compared, it was sceptical of orthodoxy.[3] It built upon insights from social and critical philosophy, literary theory and elsewhere. It drew on the radical political culture of the 1960s generation. It "asserts the inescapability of commitment and rejects the aspirations of the preceding intellectual climate's search for value neutrality."[4] There is a shared concern with the "politics of law."[5] In one sense it is a continuation of the Realists' project,[6] but its objectives are much wider. The Realists were firmly within the camp of liberalism: the C.L.S. movement was more radical an attempt to escape the "crippling choice"[7] between liberalism and Marxism. Like the Realists C.L.S. rejects formalism,[8] but the Realists saw legal reasoning as autonomous or distinct and C.L.S. scholars certainly reject the enterprise of presenting a

---

[1] These began in 1977. The initiative came from a group of jurists including Abel, Horwitz, Kennedy, Trubek, Tushnet and Unger dissatisfied with the Law and Society Association, which they thought had become too closely identified with empiricism and behaviourism. In Britain, the Critical Legal Conference was formed in 1984. And see A. Thurschwell in (ed.) J. Protevi, *A Dictionary of Continental Philosophy* (2006).

[2] On which see F. Valdes (1995) 83 California Law Rev. 3. For some comparisons see F. Valdes (1999) 53 Univ. of Miami L. Rev. 1265. See *post*, Chap. 17.

[3] And see J.A. Standen (1986) 79 Virginia L.Rev. 983, and J.S. Russell (1986) 18 Ottawa L.Rev. 1.

[4] *Per* J. Boyle (1985) 133 Univ. of Penn. Law Rev. 685.

[5] See D. Kairys (ed.), *The Politics of Law* (1982; 3rd ed., 19).

[6] On the relationship between Realism and C.L.S. see Note (1982) 95 Harv. L.Rev. 1669, 1670–1686. On the historical background more generally see J. Schlegel (1984) 36 Stanford L.Rev. 391.

[7] *Op.cit.*, n. 5, p. 16 (1982 ed.). But are C.L.S.'s criticisms of Marxism well-founded? For a view that they are not see S. Sciaraffa (1999) 5 *Legal Theory* 281.

[8] See G.Fletcher (1982) 90 Yale L.J. 970; O.Fiss (1982) 34 Stanford L.Rev. 739. See also M. Tushnet (1981) 90 Yale L.J. 1205 who argues that most legal scholars would privately accept the view that legal rules have no objective content, but are unprepared to make a public acknowledgement for fear of undermining the whole enterprise of liberal legal theory (p. 1206). But is this a view that would command support in Britain?

value-free model of law. A major difference between critical and orthodox (including for these purposes Realist) legal thought is then that,
though the latter rejects formalism, it maintains the existence of a viable
distinction between legal reasoning and political debate. Critical legal
thought does not countenance this distinction. Crits believed there is no
distinctive mode of legal reasoning. Law is politics. It does not have an
existence outside of ideological battles within society.[9]

### CRITICAL LEGAL STUDIES AND LIBERALISM'S CONTRADICTIONS

A central thrust of C.L.S.'s attack was against legal liberalism, a tradition
they associate not just with the positivism of Hart, Kelsen and Raz but
also with the writings of Dworkin, Rawls, Nozick, Finnis, Fuller and
much else besides. What do the Crits object to in legal liberalism?

According to Mark Kelman (whose *A Guide to Critical Legal Studies*[10]
is probably the best introduction to the subject), liberalism in the eyes of
Crits is "a system of thought that is simultaneously beset by internal
*contradiction* ... and by systematic *repression* of the presence of these
contradictions."[11] There are, he claims, three central contradictions: (i)
that between "a commitment to mechanically applicable rules as the
appropriate form for resolving disputes ... and a commitment to situa-
tion-sensitive, ad hoc standards,"[12]; (ii) "the contradiction between a
commitment to the traditional liberal notion that values or desires are
arbitrary, subjective, individual and individuating while facts or reason
are objective and universal *and* a commitment to the ideal that we can
know social and ethical truths objectively ... or to the hope that one can
transcend the usual distinction between subjective and objective in
seeking moral truth"[13]; (iii) "the contradiction between a commitment to
an intentionalistic discourse, in which all human action is seen as the
product of a self-determining individual will, and determinist discourse,
in which the activity of nominal subjects merits neither respect nor
condemnation because it is simply deemed the expected outcome of
existing structures."[14]

The implications of each of these contradictions may be examined
further by concentrating on some leading C.L.S. essays. The first contradiction regarding rules and standards may be illustrated by reference
to the leading C.L.S. thinker, Duncan Kennedy. His "Form and Substance in Private Law Adjudication" is unquestionably one of the seminal
pieces of C.L.S. literature.[15] Central to this article is the question: what

---

[9]  See R. Gordon (1981) 90 Yale L.J. 1017; D. Kennedy (1976) 89 Harvard L.R. 1685; R.
     Unger (1983) 96 Harvard L.R. 561.
[10]  Published by Harvard University Press in 1987.
[11]  *ibid.*, p. 3.
[12]  *ibid.*, and Chap. 1.
[13]  *ibid.*, and Chap. 2.
[14]  *ibid.*, and Chap. 3.
[15]  (1976) 89 Harvard L.R. 1685. See also his *A Critique of Adjudication* (1997).

degree of formal realizability should legal norms have? He explains it thus:

> "The extreme of formal realizability is a directive to an official that requires him to respond to the presence together of each of a list of easily distinguishable factual aspects of a situation by intervening in a determinate way. Ihering used the determination of legal capacity by sole reference to age as a prime example of a formally realizable definition of liability.[16] ... At the opposite pole from a formally realizable rule is a standard.... A standard refers directly to one of the substantive objectives of the legal order. Some examples are good faith, due care, unconscionability, unjust enrichment, and reasonableness."[17]

The problem of form derives from the belief that there are good reasons for thinking that it is better for legal norms to have a higher degree of formal realizability (that is, to be cast as rules). There are, however, good counter-reasons for believing that they are better cast as standards. The virtues of the rule form are that it confines official discretion[18] and that it provides citizens with a clear advance warning of the circumstances in which public power may be deployed, thus giving them both choice and security.[19] But the rule form also has its vices. If the age example is used, then that protecting minors from improvident contracts can be seen to protect those who are as mature as adults and therefore do not need protection and to fail to protect those chronologically of age who lack the maturity to make rational decisions. The rule is there to implement a substantive purpose, but it does not always succeed. The virtues and vices of standards are a mirror image of those of rules. The choice could therefore be said to come down to a question of which form most effectively carries out the substantive purpose. This would ask an empirical question.[20] No doubt this is the conventional approach to the dilemma. But it is not Kennedy's.

For Kennedy the two positions (pro-rules and pro-standards) are "an invitation to choose between sets of values and visions of the universe."[21] The formal arguments about the use of rules or standards is thus related to substantive ideals about the proper ordering of society. The jurisprudential position that favours rules is linked with one substantive ethical view (individualism): the jurisprudential view that favours standards with another (altruism). Individualism is bracketed with liberalism and the belief that all values are subjective: altruism with collectivism and the belief that justice consists of order directed to the achievement of shared ends. The pre-Civil War period was characterised, Kennedy

---

[16] See also J. Boyle, *Critical Legal Studies* (1992), p.XIX. (The U.S. Constitution says the President must be 35, but does this refer to calendar age or the level of maturity expected of a person in the eighteenth century at 35?).

[17] *Op.cit.*, n. 15, pp. 1687–1688.

[18] See K.C. Davis, *Discretionary Justice* (1969).

[19] See H.L.A. Hart, *Punishment and Responsibility* (1968).

[20] What Kennedy calls (*op. cit.*, n. 15) "a positivist investigation of reality" (p. 1712).

[21] *ibid.*

argues, by altruism, to be succeeded in the classical period by individualism.[22] The modern era is an age of contradiction: though it is dominated by considerations of morality and policy, the conflict between individualism and altruism remains. The judge is thus constantly presented with a political choice. The modern jurist has contradictory pulls:

> "The explanation of the sticking points of the modern individualist and altruist is that both believe quite firmly in both of these sets of premises, in spite of the fact that they are radically contradictory. The altruist critique of liberalism rings true for the individualist who no longer believes in the possibility of generating concepts that will in turn generate rules defining a just social order. The liberal critique of anarchy or collectivism rings true for the altruist, who acknowledges after all we have not overcome the fundamental dichotomy of subject and object. So long as others are, to some degree, independent and unknowable beings, the slogan of shared values carries a real thrust of a tyranny more oppressive than alienation in an at least somewhat altruistic liberal state."[23]

Kennedy's dichotomy can be over-emphasised and, as a result, misinterpreted. As Kelman points out,[24] he is not saying that individualists will inevitably favour the rule form for any legal norm and altruists the standard form. He would not, and should not, subscribe to a claim about human social life that asserts something to be inevitable. And, secondly, Kennedy himself gives examples of rule-like norms that have been consistently promoted by those holding altruistic principles, for example progressive income tax laws and standards that can promote individualist values, such as, the negligence standard. Kelman suggests that Kennedy be interpreted as positing an "aesthetic" connection between form and substance.[25] He states "the rule *form* may always tend to appeal to the *substantive* individualist because its formal virtues match up aestethically with the virtues he is inclined to admire."[26] But, as Altman argues,[27] this will not do. What is the aesthetic connection, if any, between the rule form with its doctrine of fair opportunity and the individualist virtue, as Kennedy conceives it, of self-reliance? The connection may be logical: it is difficult to see any aesthetic link. Altman believes that the best interpretation of "Form and Substance" construes Kennedy "as postulating the relatively modest logical connections between form and substance. Individualism provides general but feasible reasons for choosing rules over standards, while altruism provides general but defeasible reasons for choosing the opposite."[28]

---

[22] He discusses this more fully in "Toward an Historical Understanding of Legal Consciousness: the Case of Classical Legal Thought in America, 1850–1940 in *Research in Law and Sociology* (ed. S. Spitzer, 1980), vol. 3, p. 3.

[23] *Op.cit.*, n. 15, p. 1774.

[24] *Op.cit.*, n. 10, p. 17. See also A. Altman, *Critical Legal Studies: A Liberal Critique* (1990), p. 111.

[25] *Op.cit.*, n. 10, pp. 59–61.

[26] *ibid.*, p. 59.

[27] *Op.cit.*, n. 24, p. 112.

[28] *ibid.*, p. 114.

But, it may well be asked, whether at root the Kennedy critique of the first contradiction of liberalism stands up to critical examination. The model of liberalism attacked has a straw-man feel about it. It is significant, for example, that the work of Neil MacCormick is ignored by Kennedy, Kelman and Altman. But a reading of this opens up a more sophisticated picture of liberal legalism than the over-rigid dichotomy and their supposedly ethical associations depicted here.[29] Are rules and standards really in polar opposition? Or is MacCormick not right to indicate that "it takes a rule to make a standard legal," and "may take a standard to make a rule satisfactorily workable?"[30] Can rules be interpreted without standards? Are all rules alike and "mechanically applicable?" The "two" in the "two witnesses for a will" rule[31] requires nothing more than the ability to count, but what is a witness depends on a valuation of the importance to be attached to considerations like sight and hearing and these require judgement and interpretation. Indeterminacy becomes more apparent when one takes a rule like that which lays down that in matters relating to a child's upbringing the child's welfare is paramount.[32] This "rule" has to be seen as a concretisation of standards (the residential status quo is good[33] and should be favoured), presumptions and assumptions (babies need mothers,[34] older boys fathers) and all sorts of values (discipline is good for children,[35] the tenets of Scientology bad).[36] It is difficult to imagine any rule requiring judicial interpretation which is so determinate that its proper application is decidable without regard to background standards or values. Of course, the premise underlying the critique of liberalism is that legalism itself is necessarily bad, but MacCormick for one is unhappy with its designation as a vice, rather than a virtue.[37]

The second of liberalism's contradictions—the facts-values distinction, the reason-desire separation, Kelman illustrates by reference to Unger's *Knowledge and Politics*,[38] perhaps the seminal early C.L.S. work, and to the writing of Heller.[39] In a nutshell the problem is identified as liberalism's positivist method failing to meet its normative needs, the difficulties it confronts when applying empirical methodology to human desire.[40] "Since there is no objective good, only preference satisfaction has any

---

[29] See his *Legal Reasoning and Legal Theory* (1978), many of the essays in *Legal Rights and Social Democracy* and "The Ethics of Legalism" in (1989) 2 *Ratio Juris* 184. See also "Reconstruction after Deconstruction: Closing In On Critique" in *Closure or Critique: New Directions in Legal Theory* (A. Norrie ed., 1993), p. 142 and *Rhetoric and The Rule of Law* (2005).

[30] "Reconstruction After Deconstruction", *op. cit.*, n. 29, p. 145.

[31] Wills Act 1837, s.9.

[32] Children Act 1989, s.1.

[33] *Re W* (1983) F.L.R. 492.

[34] *Cf. Re A* [1991] 2 F.L.R. 394.

[35] *May v. May* [1986] 1 F.L.R. 325.

[36] *Re B and G* [1985] F.L.R. 134.

[37] See "The Ethics of Legalism", *op.cit.*, n. 29.

[38] (1974). This is discussed by Kelman, *op.cit.*, n. 10, Chap. 2.

[39] See, in particular, (1984) 36 Stanford L. Rev. 127, particularly pp. 172–181.

[40] And see Kelman, *op.cit.*, n. 10, p. 73.

claim; thus good social systems simply accurately aggregate private preferences (for example through markets and voting systems)."[41] In earlier chapters we have seen how utilitarians and economists tackle this: utilitarians[42] by claiming that we are morally bound to seek the maximisation of utility—we don't simply desire to do so; the economists[43] by avoiding the problem. Yet, as Kelman says, most liberals would find the Coasean[44] description of our practices quite inadequate. Do women have the right not to be raped only because it is "society's *factual* judgment"[45] that they would probably purchase the right from would-be rapists were it assigned to them in the first place?[46] But, exponents of C.L.S. would contend, values are not merely matters of taste. Rather, they can be considered as universal maxims to govern human relationships, practices and laws.

The third contradiction invokes the long-standing conflict between free will and determinism. Liberal discourse is said to privilege intentionalist discourse (which pictures human action in phenomenological, forward-looking, free-will-oriented terms), just as it privileges a commitment to the Rule of Law, individualism and value subjectivity.[47] Determinist discourse, by contrast, pictures conduct in backward-looking, amoral terms, with conduct simply a last event in a chain of connected events so pre-determined as to merit neither respect nor condemnation. Kelman illustrates this by reference (but no exclusively so) to the criminal law.[48] He shows through a series of examples the ways in which orthodox criminal law, premised on liberalism and therefore on free will, often uses determinist discourse.

In Kelman's *Stanford* article, he examines the importance to criminal law of the stage that precedes legal analysis. He argues that "legal argument has two phases: interpretive construction and rational rhetoricism, and that the former, a vital step which undercuts the authority of the latter, goes virtually unexamined."[49] An example is that the result of a case may depend on whether the defendant's act is set in a broad or narrow time-frame. The issue has come to a head with a series of cases where battered women have murdered their husbands and the scope of the provocation defence has been tested.[50] If a broad time-frame is used,

---

[41]  *ibid.*

[42]  *Ante*, 248.

[43]  *Ante*, 620.

[44]  Some empirical evidence of this is R. Ellickson, *Order Without Law: How Neighbors Settle Disputes* (1991). And see *ante*, 627.

[45]  *Op.cit.*, n. 10, p. 68.

[46]  See, further, G. Schwartz (1979) Wisconsin L.Rev. 799, 804–808.

[47]  *Op.cit.*, n. 10, p. 86 and Chap. III.

[48]  And see also his "Interpretive Construction in the Substantive Criminal Law" (1981) 33 Stanford L.Rev. 591, and *post*, 1244.

[49]  33 Stanford L.Rev. 591 at 591–592.

[50]  See *R. v. Thornton* [1992] 1 All E.R. 306, *R. v. Ahluwalia* [1992] 4 All E.R. 889 (and *Nicolson and Sanghvi* (1993) Crim. L.R. 728). On abuse excuses see the Symposium in (1996) 57 Univ. of Pittsburgh L. Rev. and also M. Stoker (1999) 16 Soc. Phil. and Pol. 175.

she may have defences of provocation, even self-defence: in a narrow time-frame she has committed murder. There is no meta-theory to tell us which is the appropriate time-frame; the decision accordingly is "ara-tional".[51] Kelman argues that this interpretive construction hides the fact that the criminal law is taking a political, and perhaps also a moral, decision—to take an intentionalist (free will) or determinist view of the defendant. He writes:

> "Often, conduct is deemed involuntary (or determined) rather than freely willed (or intentional) because we do not consider the defendant's earlier decisions that may have put him in the position of apparent choicelessness. Conversely, conduct that could have been viewed as freely willed or voluntary if we looked only at the precise moment of the criminal incident is sometimes deemed involuntary because we open up the time frame to look at prior events that seem to compel or determine the defendant's conduct at the time of the incident. The use of 'time-framing' as interpretive *method* blocks the perception that intentionalist or determinist issues could be substantively at stake. If one has somehow convinced oneself that the narrow time-framed focus is the appropriate *technique* for interpreting criminal law material, there is simply no background data one can use, either to provide the grist for a determinist account or to locate a prior sphere of choice in a seemingly constricted world."[52]

Nor, he points out, is this limited to "hard cases", because narrow time-framing "fends out" the possibility of undertaking determinist analyses.[53]

## RULES AND REASONING

As noted already, one characteristic of C.L.S. is its rejection of formal-ism. Formalism has tended to be the fall back position of liberal legal thinking when forced to confront the question: how can a legal system give the kinds of neutral decisions expected of it. Formalists, as C.L.S. characterise them,[54] circumvent this problem by insisting that the judge is not imposing his values (or anyone else's) but merely interpreting the words of the law. Hart, by separating "core" and "penumbra"[55] could be taken to admit the problem by his concession that the judge had to have recourse to discretion in interpreting the "penumbra" of legal rules. Fuller's response[56]—that judges were to seek out the purpose behind the rule—does not satisfy Crits any more because, they argue, that "pur-pose" is equally indeterminate. Who knows what Parliament (or

---

[51] *Per* J. Boyle, *op.cit.*, n. 16, p. XXVII.
[52] *Op. cit.*, n. 49, p. 594.
[53] The analysis pursued here may be equally applicable in other areas of legal doctrine (tort and divorce being the most obvious examples).
[54] See, *e.g.* R. Unger, *Knowledge and Politics* (1975), pp. 83–103.
[55] See *The Concept of Law* (1994), pp. 124–136; 71 Harvard L.Rev. 593 and *ante*, 414. And see F. Cohen (1935) 35 Columbia L.Rev. 809 for an early (Realist) critique of this view.
[56] 71 Harvard L.Rev.630 (1958) and *ante*, 417.

Congress) intends?[57] Nor, they would argue, does Dworkin satisfactorily answer this question.[58]

In the C.L.S. view, formalism relies on a new kind of essentialism—the belief that there are essential meanings to words. But one theme in C.L.S. writing is to connect adjudication to legislation and to ask the same questions about the legitimacy of the exercise of state power in relation to judicial activity as has been asked for millennia about the operation of power by other state institutions. Legal decisions, on this view, are no more neutral than the decisions of a legislature or an executive. Political choices are equally involved. The public/private law distinction is exposed as chimerical. The Realists said as much,[59] and Kelsen saw this too,[60] but the theme is more fully developed within C.L.S. writing. If the view that there is a line between private and public law is a myth,[61] the rules of private law cannot be deduced from the interplay of free market forces. Contract law[62] as much as administrative law, property law as much as environmental law, has to be chosen. There is nothing natural or neutral about it. Arguments about deregulation and privatisation are exposed for the shams that they are. Those who wish to deregulate the free market or privatise the family are only expressing a preference for one set of regulation, usually one less susceptible to scrutiny and control, over another.[63] A free market could be one in which workers had decision-making power, a deregulated family could be one which developed power and choices on children, but these are not usually the models envisaged by their advocates. Kennedy on Blackstone's *Commentaries* and Clare Dalton on the deconstruction of contract doctrine illustrate those themes.

The next extract from Peter Gabel is both a development of this work and a step-up from it. The analysis goes beyond legal doctrine to examine legal processes within the dynamics of social theory.[64] For Gabel, legal thought is part of a larger practice of turning concepts or social roles into things, the practice of "reifying."[65] Each person experiences himself as a thing-like function of "the system."[66] "Thus, a 'small businessman' experiences himself as a 'small businessman' 'a secretary' as a 'secretary,' a 'child' as a child."[67] "One is never, or almost never, a person; instead

[57] Nor is this problem alleviated by the courts' greater willingness to consult extrinsic material. See *Pepper v. Hart* [1993]1 All E.R. 42.

[58] See *Law's Empire* (1986). See also D. Kennedy, *A Critique of Adjudication* (1997), pp. 119–130.

[59] L.Jaffe (1937) 51 Harvard L.Rev.201, Hale (1943) 43 Columbia L.Rev.603.

[60] *The Pure Theory of Law* (1967), p. 280–284.

[61] D. Kennedy (1982) 130 Univ. of Pennsylvania L.Rev. 1349.

[62] See C. Dalton (1985) 94 Yale L.J. 997.

[63] See F. Olsen (1985) 18 U. Mich. J.L. Rev. 835; M.Freeman (1985) 38 C.L.P. 153.

[64] The influences of Marxism and of Sartre (in particular *The Critique of Dialectical Reason* (1976)) are clear.

[65] On which see P. Berger and T. Luckmann, *The Social Construction of Reality* (1967); R.D. Laing, *The Politics of Experience* (1967).

[66] *Research in Law and Sociology* (1980), vol. III, p. 28.

[67] *ibid.*

one is successively a 'husband,' 'bus passenger,' 'small businessman,' 'consumer' and so on."[68] Social roles appear to have an objective character. In Gabel's view, legal reasoning is a system in which "one manipulates concepts that share exactly this reified and apparently thing-like quality."[69] So long as we know and remember this, it may not matter overmuch. But once this knowledge is forgotten or glossed over the abstractions are taken on as beliefs about an objective reality. And at this point we can believe ourselves "actually to be living in a world of rights-holders, legal subjects and formal equality."[70] The reification of legal concepts becomes a way of legitimating the status quo.

Gabel's views are not subscribed to by many within the C.L.S. movement. To many his emphasis on repression and alienation, on the lack of "connectedness" in society is misplaced (is there an unalienated existence outside, beyond or underneath social role and reified concept?). Gabel "tries to capture both the objective structures of apparent necessity and the subjective moments shaped by those structures."[71] He presents legal doctrine "as though it is both infinitely manipulable and firmly constrained by the reified metaphors of common sense and legal consciousness."[72] There may be important implications in this in trying to understand the judicial role: how real, for example, is judicial choice even within areas of "weak discretion."[73] But there is no doubt that the chief merit in Gabel's writing is in showing the power of reification in legal (as well as social) thought.

## CRITICAL LEGAL STUDIES AND LEGAL PRACTICE

One of the reasons why C.L.S. could not fail to have had an impact is that its protagonists have concerned themselves with the problems of legal practice. Practitioners who felt able to ignore debates about the rule of recognition or the morality of law—"these did not concern *them*"—had to grapple with the issues confirmed by the "Crits." Perhaps only the Realists of earlier schools and now Dworkin can have locked theory so much into practice.

Critical legal theorists believe that the lessons of critique can radicalise law practice. Thus, Gabel and Harris argue that "the very public and political character of the legal arena gives lawyers, acting together with clients and fellow legal workers, an important opportunity to reshape the way that people understand the existing social order and their place within it".[74] Their objective is "to show the way that the legal system

---

[68] *ibid.*
[69] *Per* J. Boyle, *op.*, n. 16, p. xvii.
[70] *ibid.*, pp. XVII-XVIII.
[71] *Per* J. Boyle (1985) 133 Univ. of Pennsylvania L.Rev. 685, 719–720.
[72] *ibid.*, p. 735.
[73] *Cf.* R. Dworkin *ante*, 721.
[74] (1982–83) XI *Rev. of Law and Social Change* 369, 370.

works at many different levels to shape popular consciousness towards accepting the legitimacy of the status quo, and to outline the ways that lawyers can effectively resist these efforts in building a movement for fundamental social change."[75] They use several examples, most graphically the notorious trial of a rape victim who shot and killed her assailant.

Inez Garcia had two trials.[76] The first succeeded in that she was not convicted of first-degree, but only of second-degree, murder. But to achieve this required psychiatric testimony that she was unconscious of what she was doing. "Politically" this defence degraded Garcia. Her true feelings come out in the following "I took my gun, I loaded it, and I went after them ... I am not sorry that I did it. The only thing that I am sorry about is that I missed [the second assailant]."[77] And earlier in the trial, she had reacted angrily to the judge's decision to disallow testimony about the emotional trauma of rape, screaming at the judge: "Why don't you just find me guilty? Just send me to jail ... I killed the fucking guy because he raped me!"[78]

There was a retrial[79] at which she was represented by a radical-feminist attorney, Susan Jordan.[80] The task Jordan faced was "to translate the male-oriented rule of self-defence into a form that would capture the real experience of a woman facing possible attack by a man."[81] Jordan was able to confront the cultural myths about rape (that women invite, encourage, like rape, that it is their fault) by creative use of *voir dire*. The jury, so constructed, "was able to view the rape not as a sexual act caused by male-female flirting, but rather as a violent assault."[82] The authors comment[83]:

"The two trials of Inez Garcia demonstrate that in the right circumstances it is possible to win a case with a political approach when a more conventional approach would fail ... With a male attorney in her first trial in effect apologizing for her action and the anger that produced it, Garcia was separated from the movement supporting her, and indeed from her own self. In pleading 'impaired consciousness' she was forced to deny the legitimacy of her own action and simultaneously the legitimacy of 'unreasonable' rage that women throughout the country were expressing in response to their social powerlessness in relation to men. The form of the first trial turned Garcia into a isolated object of the legal system, a mere 'defendant' requesting mercy from a 'masculine' legal structure ... The most important feature of the second trial was that it reversed the power relations upon which the first trial was premised. The defence both affirmed the validity of Garcia's action, and allowed Jordan

[75] *ibid.*
[76] The first trial is discussed in C. Garry and A. Goldberg, *Street Fighter in the Courtroom* (1977), pp. 217–241. It is reported as *People v. Garcia* at 126 Cal. Rptr, 275, Cert. denied (1975) 426 U.S. 911. There is no law report of the retrial.
[77] See Garry and Goldberg, *op. cit.*, n. 76, p. 236.
[78] *ibid.*, p. 231.
[79] Because of an improper jury direction.
[80] See Schneider and Jordan (1978) 4 Women's Rights L. Rep. 149. See also Donovan and Wildman (1980–1981) 14 Loy. L.A. L. Rev. 435.
[81] *Op. cit.*, n. 74, p. 382.
[82] *ibid.*, p. 383.
[83] *ibid.*, pp. 383–384.

to join Garcia as co-advocate for a vast popular movement, to speak to the jury not as a State-licensed technician 'representing' an abstract 'defendant,' but as a woman standing together with another woman. Together, the two women were able to put the act of rape itself on trial and to address the jurors ... about the true meaning of being a woman ... The effect of this was to transform the courtroom into a popular tribunal ... This shift in the vectors of power within the room also allowed the jurors to escape their own reification, to discover themselves as politically responsible for making a human, rather than a merely formal decision based on an application of existing law. Thus, the conduct of the second trial ... served to expand the power of the movement from which the political basis of the case derived, and to delegitimate the apparent necessity of existing legal consciousness ... Breaking through the sedimented authoritarian forms of legal proceedings in an overtly political case has radical implications ... it signifies that the existing order is *merely possible*, and that people have the freedom and power to act upon it."[84]

Gabel and Harris use two other high-visibility political cases, the *Chicago 8* Trial[85] and one of the early children's rights cases, *Tinker v. Des Moines School District*,[86] but they admit that the strategies described here are only relevant in such situations. For, "if there is one thing that critical legal scholars are agreed about it is that social change is not a matter of clever legal argument deployed by elite lawyers, but rather a process of democratic organisation and mobilization in which law will play a necessary part."[87] But C.L.S. subscribes neither to the liberal view that law can be a principal instrument of social change[88] nor to the Marxist view that marginalises law and lawyers to a "superstructural fringe",[89] rendering it largely irrelevant to political change. The C.L.S. position is more complex, reflecting a recognition of the complexity of law itself. As Boyle indicates, "it may be necessary to combine an exhaustive analysis of legal doctrine with a theoretical understanding of the hegemonic power of the law and a series of micro-phenomenological accounts of its application."[90]

C.L.S. has had an impact on legal education too, as the extract from Duncan Kennedy's polemic, "Legal Education as Training for Hierarchy" reveals.[91] The word "hierarchy" is vague and, according to Kennedy, deliberately so.[92] Kennedy could have substituted a concept like "class" or "domination" with their relatively clear meanings.

---

[84] See also D. Kennedy (1985) 63 Texas L. Rev. 1377.

[85] *United States v. Dellinger* 472 F.2nd 340: *Cert.* denied 410 U.S. 970 (1973).

[86] (1969) 393 U.S. 503. The case centred on whether freedom of expression extended to school children who wished to protest against the Vietnam War by wearing armbands.

[87] *Op. cit.*, n. 16.

[88] *Cf., e.g.* Pound's view of social engineering (*ante*, 849).

[89] *Op. cit.*, n. 16. On the Marxist position, see *ante*, 1134.

[90] *Op. cit.*, n. 16. He cites the work of Regina Austin on employee abuse as a paradigmatic example of this work (see (1988) 41 Stanford L. Rev. 1).

[91] See also his article on the political significance of the structure of the law curriculum (1983) 14 Seton Hall L.Rev.1. Further reference may be made to Toni Pickard (1983) 33 U.T.L.J. 279, and to A. Thomson in *Critical Legal Studies* (P. Fitzpatrick and A. Hunt (eds.), 1987), p. 183.

[92] See his *Legal Education and The Reproduction of Hierarchy: A Polemic Against The System* (1983), p. 80. See also *post*, 1267.

Instead, he wants to tell us what he feels intuitively is wrong with the system, how it separates subjects, ranks different law schools, (de)grades students. He says its a "typical American phenomenon,"[93] but much of what he says is increasingly recognisable is the United Kingdom too. It is an analysis which employs a mixture of social theories, with the influences of realism, of Foucault,[94] of feminism all at times apparent and at others submerged. It is an essay which premises "liberation from the constraints of hierarchy, the process of bondage, through the conscious practice of group self-determination."[95] but, it has to be said, it is one short on concrete proposals—though paying the law school janitor the same as the law school professors[96] would not be difficult to justify in some cases.


LEGAL THEORY AND SOCIAL THEORY

One of the principal advances of C.L.S. is to demonstrate the need to integrate legal theory within social theory. Drawing on Habermas,[97] Marcuse,[98] Mannheim,[99] Gramsci,[1] critical legal theorists have attempted to introduce into discourse about law the insights and models of analysis of social theory, in particular the relativity of truth to any given social or historical group. In this view, reality is not a product of nature, but is socially constructed.[2] Social arrangements are not unproblematic, inexorable givens: what we see as the social order is merely where "the struggle between individuals was halted and truce lines were drawn up."[3]

Critical legal theorists are not the only thinkers about law to be convinced by its social contingency.[4] But the novelty of their thinking lies in their attempts to identify the role played by law and legal reasoning[5] in the processes through which a particular social order comes to be seen as

---

[93] *ibid.*, p. 84.
[94] With Foucault, Kennedy shares a scepticism of the value of "global, totalitarian theories" (such as Marxism) (*Power/Knowledge* (1980), p. 80).
[95] *Op. cit.*, n. 92, p. 97.
[96] *ibid.*, p. 79.
[97] *Knowledge and Human Interest* (1972); *Legitimation Crisis* (1975); *The Philosophical Discourse of Modernity* (1990). See D. Held, *Introduction To Critical Theory* (1980) and W. T. Murphy (1989) 42 C.L.P. 135.
[98] See *Reason and Revolution* (1942); *One-Dimensional Man* (1964).
[99] *Ideology and Utopia* (1936); *Essays on the Sociology of Knowledge* (1952).
[1] See *Prison Notebooks* (1971) and *ante*, 1157.
[2] See P. Berger and T. Luckmann, *The Social Construction of Reality* (1966). See also *ante*, 5.
[3] *Per* A. Hutchinson and P. Monahan (1984) 36 Stanford L. Rev. 199, 216.
[4] See, *e.g.* L. Friedman (1969) 4 Law and Soc. Rev. 29, whose exploration of "legal culture" is an attempt to discover "those values and attitudes in society which determine what [processual and institutional] structures are used and why; which rules work, and which do not, and why" (p. 35).
[5] For example, Gabel, *ante*, 1216 and *post*, 1236. Note Gabel's argument that the supposed neutrality and objectivity of legal reasoning is more than a lawyer's imperative: it is a prerequisite for the legitimacy of the liberal state.

inevitable. Legal discourse is a discourse that concerns the basic terms of social life.[6] By identifying and overturning existing forms of legal consciousness, exponents of critical legal studies hope to emancipate the individual. "By demonstrating that social life is much less structured and much more complex, much less impartial and much more irrational, than the legal process suggests, the interests served by legal doctrine and theory will surface."[7]

An example is Mark Tushnet's article "Corporations and Free Speech."[8] It is an examination of some U.S. Supreme Court cases that have constricted the ability of the State to regulate the "speech" of corporations.[9] He finds a common link in the cases in the idea that speech is a commodity that can be bought and sold. The court has been, he argues, applying the deep structure of capitalism to a particular area of constitutional law. Tushnet's explanation lies at the level of consciousness.[10] But what is the relationship between capitalism and consciousness? To speak of "capitalism" as a well-defined social order comes close to denying the social contingency thesis to which, it has been argued, C.L.S. is committed.[11] But, as we have seen, Kennedy, for one, is not prepared to relate the law inexorably to "any aspect of the social totality." He maintains that "the outcomes within the law have no inherent logic."[12]

Out of this theorising has come understanding of the status quo and, just occasionally, blueprints for different social orderings. A notable example is found in the writings of Roberto Unger.[13] In his article entitled "The Critical Legal Studies Movement,"[14] he offers, what he calls, "a structure of no-structure."[15] He describes his programme as "super-liberalism," "the building of a social world less alien to a self that can always violate the generative rules of its own mental or social constructs and put other rules and other constructs in their place."[16] This represents

---

[6] See R. Unger (1983) 96 Harvard L.Rev. 561, 576–83 (also published as *The Critical Legal Studies Movement* (1986)) and *post*, 1271.

[7] *Op. cit.*, n. 4, p. 217.

[8] In D. Kairys (ed.), *op. cit.*, n. 5, p. 253.

[9] For example, *Central Hudson Gas and Electricity Corp. v. Public Services Commission* (1980) 447 U.S. 557 (striking down a regulation prohibiting an electric utility company from advertising to promote energy use).

[10] There is considerable controversy within C.L.S. over the nature (and origins) of legal consciousness. See R. Gordon, *post*, 1235. See also Unger, *op. cit.*, n. 6, p. 564. Some with neo-Marxist views like Gabel and Abel explain law in terms of stages of capitalist development. But Kennedy (see (1980) *Research in Law and Sociology* 3) and Unger (*op.cit.*, n. 6) depict the resolution of legal doctrine as an endless conflict between opposing and unassimilable world views. See the discussion between Gabel and Kennedy, "Roll Over Beethoven" in (1984) 36 Stanford L.Rev. 1.

[11] See *ante*, 1220. See also *ante*, 1161.

[12] See *op. cit.*, n. 9, p. 50 and *post*, 1267.

[13] It is impossible to do justice to Unger is work within political and social theory and this discussion concentrates on his seminal article, subsequently published in book form. But see, in addition, *Social Theory: Its Situation and Task* (1987) and the three-volume *Politics: A Work In Constructive Social Theory* as well as *Passion: An Essay on Personality* (1984).

[14] *Op. cit.*, n. 6.

[15] *ibid.*, p. 666.

[16] *ibid.*, p. 602.

an effort to make "social life" resemble what "politics" is like in liberal democracies, "a series of conflicts and deals among more or less transitory and fragmentary groups."[17] He is concerned to protect freedom better and, in this venture, he sees a crucial role for law and legal thought. He has specific proposals: a "rotating capital fund"[18] to finance projects and effect a "decentralisation of production and exchange." The legal counterpart to this is "the disaggregation of the consolidated property right."[19] But, so as not to throw out the baby with the bathwater, Unger accepts that some regime of rights is necessary if his blueprint is to succeed. He, therefore, suggests the creation of four types of rights: immunity rights which establish the "nearly absolute claim of the individual to security against the state, other organisations and other individuals."[20] Secondly, "destabilization" rights, admitted by Unger himself to be "novel and puzzling," which entitle individuals to demand the disruption of established institutions and forms of social practice that have achieved the "very sort of insulation and have contributed to the very kind of crystallized plan of social hierarchy and division that the entire constitution wants to avoid."[21] Thirdly, market rights which give a "conditional and provisional claim to divisible portions of social capital."[22] They are a substitute for existing absolute property rights. Finally solidarity rights ("the legal entitlements of communal life")[23]: these foster mutual reliance, loyalty and communal responsibility.

Subsequent works have further developed this project. In *Passion*,[24] Unger addressed the situation of the self in modern society. In *Politics*,[25] political institutions were reconstructed to reflect this refined sense of self. In *What Should Legal Analysis Become?*,[26] the role of law and lawyers in this society is a central focus.

*Passion* is about "sympathy". This is based on the "opportunity for discovery and self-expression".[27] Solidarity, which had been key to his earlier writing, is now shown to result from the empowerment experienced by self-assertion. People feel a sense of affinity with others within a community that they feel they have helped to create. This is why the idea of "sympathy" must be understood both as constitutive of, and constituted by, radical democracy.[28] Passion may seem to work at odds with "reason", but Unger sees them as complementary. Reason is important but it is not the motivating force of political action. The "rational actor" is a myth and passion (or emotions) is an essential ingredient of

---

[17] *ibid.*, p. 661.
[18] *ibid.*, p. 596.
[19] *ibid.*, p. 597.
[20] *ibid.*, p. 599.
[21] *ibid.*, p. 600.
[22] *ibid.*
[23] *ibid.*
[24] *Passion: An Essay on Personality* (1984).
[25] *Politics: A Work In Constructive Legal Theory* (1987) (2 vols).
[26] (1996). And post, 1271.
[27] *Op. cit.*, n. 13, p. 28.
[28] *ibid.*, pp. 8–15.

participatory democracy. Law is thus the expression of passion, and critical legal politics must be founded on passion.

In *Politics*, Unger turns to the demand for participatory government. Society belongs to us, and so do its laws. We are not constrained by so-called metaphysical foundations and so can change society. There are no social or legal "truths", nothing to stop our changing and reshaping society and its laws.[29] Unger is encouraged by modern social thought which has "an image of man that emphasises both his content-bound predicament and his context-smashing capabilities".[30] But if law is going to be changed by those who feel oppressed by it, there must be "radical democracy". Much of the second volume of *Politics* is taken up with models of such democracy: democratic pluralism is a key to all of these. Unger sees rights, even entrenched rights, as essential for radical participatory democracy. There is a problem here for if rights are entrenched, they are features of society and its laws which are changeable. Unger's response—which hardly seems convincing—is that such rights have to be understood to express an "attitude" rather than to define "structures". And in a participatory democracy we rule, not the structures.

*What Should Legal Analysis Become?* is in two parts. The first is a critique of dominant trends in legal scholarship which, he argues, has not contributed to serious social reform. Thus, for example, he refers to one "dirty little secret of contemporary jurisprudence" as its discomfort with democracy. This, he says,

> "...shows up in every area of contemporary legal culture: in the ceaseless identification of restraints upon majority rule, rather than of restraints upon the power of dominant minorities, as the overriding responsibility of judges and jurists; in the consequent hypertrophy of countermajoritarian practices and arrangements; in the opposition to all institutional reforms, particularly those designed to heighten the level of popular political engagement, as threats to a regime of rights; in the equation of rights of property with the rights of dissent; in the effort to obtain from judges, under the cover of improving interpretation, the advances popular politics fail to deliver; in the abandonment of institutional reconstruction to rare and magical moments of national refoundation; in the single-minded focus upon the higher judges and their selection as the most important part of democratic politics; in an ideal of deliberative democracy as most acceptable when closest in style to a polite conversation among gentlemen in an eighteenth-century drawing room; and, occasionally, in the explicit treatment of party government as a subsidiary, last-ditch source of legal evolution, to be tolerated when none of the more refined modes of legal resolution applies. Fear and loathing of the people always threaten to become the ruling passions of this legal culture."[31]

And, as can be seen, this is pertinent and biting, even savage.

The second part of the book is a prescription, a positive programme, but, it may be thought, a somewhat vague or elusive one. Legal analysis,

---

[29] See vol. 1,pp. 18–35, 135–137.
[30] *ibid.*, p. 192.
[31] *Op. cit.*, n. 26, pp. 72–73.

he argues, has the potential "to become a master tool of institutional imagination in a democratic society".[32] So he looks to an ideal of commitment "to make adjudication serve the larger goal of advancing the power of a free people to govern themselves".[33] Unger is surely right to believe that jurisprudence should develop conceptions of constitutionalism, legislation and adjudication which embody the democratic idea. But can this be done by *legal* analysis? Does the legal analyst, as Dworkin, Habermas[34] and Unger himself have done, not have to become a social scientist and/or a theorist of culture? Can jurisprudence get to democracy through law? Or is "democratic jurisprudence", as Waldron has suggested,[35] an oxymoron?


CONCLUSION

Like a meteor the Crits appeared, shone brightly for a short time and have gone. To Duxbury,[36] writing in 1995, they were in decline, to Tamanaha in 2000 they were a "dead horse".[37] To him, and to many others, they failed to live up to their promise as a transformative approach to law. It is now generally agreed they exaggerated the indeterminacy of law.[38] Perhaps also they underplayed the "critical". The most recent writings of Duncan Kennedy[39] and Roberto Unger[40] are rather conventional when compared with their work at the height of the Crits' movement.

Undoubtedly, they spawned other movements: critical race theory, critical feminist jurisprudence, LatCrit, critical race feminism, outsider jurisprudence more generally.[41] Ward, I believe, is right to observe that C.L.S. has lived on to take a "more directed"[42] set of paths. He identifies three: one is that just referred to (feminist and race theory). A second is the reconstructive liberalism, particularly associated with Roberto Unger.[43] The political import of this is an effective decentralisation of power. Similar theorising is found in Habermas, though there is no evidence that it was this "critical" thought which influenced him. Unger was considered earlier in this chapter, Habermas in an earlier one.[44]

---

[32] *ibid.*, p. 26.
[33] *ibid.*, p. 115.
[34] *Ante*, 969.
[35] (1998) 98 Columbia Law Rev. 510.
[36] *Patterns of American Jurisprudence* (1995), pp. 426–428.
[37] (2000) 27 J. Law and Soc. 296.
[38] T. Endicott, *Vagueness In Law* (2000) whilst presenting an indeterminacy thesis distances himself from C.L.S. and similar movements.
[39] *Critique of Adjudication* (1997).
[40] *What Should Legal Analysis Become?* (1996).
[41] *See post*, Chap. 17.
[42] *An Introduction to Critical Legal Theory* (1998), p. 157.
[43] *Ante*, 1221–1224.
[44] On Unger see J. W. Harris (1989) 52 M.L.R. 42 and J. Finnis in J. Eekelaar and J. Bell (eds.), *Oxford Essays In Jurisprudence* (3rd series, 1987), pp. 146—165.

The third direction is towards theories of language. Literary theory is of particular interest because it offers support to their belief in interpretive indeterminacy.[45] Ward singles out Allan Hutchinson.[46] "We are never not in a story",[47] argues Hutchinson, because "history and human action only take on meaning and intelligibility within their narrative context and dramatic settings".[48] We are all living our lives like actors in a performance, and lawyers are merely trained to play a particular role. Once we understand this theatricality or pretence, we are ready to "debunk the elite fables of law",[49] realise our constitutive role in the actual performance and play a more assertive role. This shift in critical focus has, Hutchinson argues, "produced a more urgent appreciation of the relation between language and social action".[50]

---

### ROBERT GORDON
### Law and Ideology
### (1988)[51]

For the Crits, law is inherently neither a ruling-class game plan nor a repository of noble if perverted principles. It is a plastic medium of discourse that subtly conditions how we experience social life. Crits therefore tend to take the rhetoric of law very seriously and to examine its content carefully.

To get a picture of the way Crits think, consider all the habitual daily invocations of law in official and unofficial life—from the rhetoric of judicial opinions through advice lawyers give to clients, down to all the assertions and arguments about legal rights and wrongs in ordinary interactions between police and suspects, employers and workers, creditors and debtors, husbands, wives and neighbors, or television characters portraying such people. Sometimes these ways of speaking about law (*legal discourses*, let's call them) appear as fancy technical arguments, sometimes as simple common sense. ("An employer has the right to control what happens on his own property, doesn't he?") In whatever form, they are among the discourses that help us to make sense of the world, that fabricate what we interpret as its reality. They construct roles for us like "Owner" and "Employee," and tell us how to behave in the roles. (The person cast as "Employee" is subordinate. Why? It just is that way, part of the role.) They wall us off from one another by constituting us as separate individuals given rights to protect our isolation, but then prescribe formal channels (such as contracts, partnerships, corporations) through which we can reconnect. They split up the world into categories that filter our experience—sorting out the harms we must accept as the hand of fate, or as our own fault, from the outrageous injustices we may resist as wrongfully forced upon us. Until recently, for instance, an employer's sexual advances didn't occupy any legal category. They were a kind of indignity that a woman had to interpret as something her own dress and manner had invited, or as an inevitable occupational risk, given natural male aggression

---

[45] See J. B. White, *Justice As Translation* (1990).
[46] *Dwelling On The Threshold* (1988). See also (2001) 21 *Legal Studies* 65.
[47] *ibid.*, p. 13.
[48] *ibid.*
[49] *ibid.*, p. 21.
[50] *ibid.*, p. 148.
[51] [From Tikkun, vol. 3, (No. 1).]

(and the statistical frequency of creeps), one that could get her fired unless she gave in or had incredible tact. Now such advances have the legal name of "sexual harassment," This doesn't always improve the practical situation of the victims—since vindicating legal rights costs money, emotion, smooth working relations, the chance of promotion, and maybe even one's career—but for many men and women the feminist politics that forced the change in legal categories has completely changed how they interpret and feel about the behavior.

Some of the basic points the Critics want to make about legal discourses are as follows:

*These are discourses of power.* Law is not, of course, uniquely the tool of the powerful. Everyone invokes the authority of law in everyday interactions, and the content of laws registers many concessions to groups struggling for change from below, as well as to the wishes of the politically and economically dominant. But to be able to wield legal discourses with facility and authority or to pay others (lawyers, legislators, lobbyists, etc.) to wield them on your behalf is a large part of what it means to possess power in society. Legal discourses therefore tend to reflect the interests and the perspectives of the powerful people who make most use of them.

*Whether actually being used by the powerful or the powerless, legal discourses are saturated with categories and images that for the most part rationalize and justify in myriad subtle ways the existing social order as natural, necessary, and just.* A complaint about a legal wrong—let's say the claim that one is a "victim of discrimination"—must be framed as a complaint that there has been a momentary disturbance in a basically sound world, for which a quick fix is available within the conventional working of existing institutions. A black applicant to professional school, whose test scores are lower than those of a competing white applicant, asks for admission of grounds of "affirmative action." Everybody in that interaction (including the applicant) momentarily submits to the spell of the worldview promoted in that discourse, that the scores measure an "objective" merit (though nobody really has the foggiest idea *what* they measure besides standardized test-taking ability) that would have to be set aside to let him in. A middle-aged widow buys a cheap promotional package of lessons at a dance studio. The studio hooks her on flattery and attention, then gets her to sign a contract for 4,000 hours of dance instruction. To break her contract, she will have to struggle to make a case that her situation is grotesquely exceptional—the result of serious fraud, and, even if she wins, she and her lawyers will have participated in and reinforced the law's endorsement of "normal" marketplace relations as unproblematically voluntary, informed, noncoercive, and efficient.

Thus legal discourses—in conjunction with dozens of other nonlegal discourses—routinely help to create and maintain the ordinary inequities of everyday social life: the coercions, dominations, and dependencies of daily relations in the marketplace, the workplace, and the family; the ordering of access to privilege, authority, wealth, and power by hierarchies of class, race, gender, and "merit."

*Yet legal discourses have the legitimating power they do because they sketch pictures of widely shared, wistful, inchoate visions of an ideal*—a society of dealings between genuinely free and independent equals, one so ordered that we could cooperate with others without having to worry that they would hurt or enslave us, so structured as continually to open to question the legitimacy of its hierarchies. Thus law is always a source of images and ideals that challenge and urge us to revise current arrangements as well as justifying them. The problem is that, in the ordinary uses of law, the revisionary images are realized in scattered fragments and otherwise muted and repressed.

So the big premise of the C.L.S. method, the *raison d'être* of its scholarship and local political tactics, is that the deployment of ordinary legal discourse is a form of political practice, and one with *unnecessarily* conservative consequences. If we experience a sense of stasis and paralysis about the possibilities for social change, we owe our passivity in part to the character of these pervasive discourses. C.L.S. people believe that when you take legal discourse apart and see how it works, you can start to reinterpret it and to gain the energy and motivation to engage in local political action that in turn can help to change the social context that the discourse has hardened. Since most of the Crits were academics in law schools, they first picked on the targets that were closest to them, the standard ways that other law teachers wrote, taught, and talked about, the first-year legal subjects, such as Torts, Contracts, and Property.

Their first problem was to figure out how legal training produces its mind-numbing paralysis—how even left-liberal students trained by left-liberal teachers end up drained of energy and hope for social change. One big reason, of course, is that graduates of the elite schools are lavishly rewarded in money and social status for going into large-firm corporate law practice and tend over time to adjust their ideals to their situations. Graduates of less elite schools think themselves lucky to get any legal job on any terms that are offered. But both types of lawyers tend to excuse their passivity with the gloomy thought that nothing can change anyway, and that conclusion—so the Crits speculate—they owe in part to the conservatizing elements in academic-legal discourse.

Those elements take a number of different forms. There is a traditional kind of law teaching, perfected around the 1950s and still probably the dominant one, that is very elusive because it never makes any of its premises or assumptions explicit. The teacher creates confusion by slashing up the reasoning of the judges who decide the cases assigned for classroom reading and also the reasoning of the students, but ends up suggesting that there's a delicate, complex balance-point, a moderate centrist position, that a smart, sensible, *professional* lawyer can settle on. Such a teacher presents a centrist politics as if it were a craft. There is now a fresh set of discourses urging the natural necessity of conservative or mildly reformed social arrangements; this is the economic analysis of law by scholars such as Guido Calabresi of Yale and Richard Posner of Chicago—far more intellectually formidable than the old style of legal theory and increasingly influential among policymakers and scholars. Legal economists assert that disputes about particular legal arrangements (*e.g.*, decisions about whether polluters should have to pay homeowners to pollute the air, or homeowners pay polluters not to pollute) and may be resolved through value-neutral comparisons of alternative solutions as more or less "efficient."

Fighting, as they saw it, fire with fire, the Crits responded to long articles in elite law journals with longer articles in elite law journals. Streetwise radical lawyers have always mocked the Crits for "footnote activism." using up political energy in pedantic swiping at mandarin doctrines, but from the C.L.S. point of view, the strategy made sense: they were matching a local discourse of power and constraint—one that had some discernible impact on their own and their students' lives—with a discourse of resistance. It is a modest form of political action simply to try to reduce the authority of those people who control the local situation and thus to create a little extra space for your own projects, your counterinterpretations of the same discourses. Through this work, the Crits hoped to develop a set of critical insights and demolition rhetorics that they and others could pick up and use on all sorts of legal discourses, not just those of other scholars. [...]

Here are some of the methods the Crits have deployed against mainstream legal discourses:

*Trashing* This sixties-evoking phrase covers a big miscellaneous grab bag of techniques designed to dent the complacent message embedded in legal discourse, that the system has figured out the arrangements that are going to make social life about as free, just, and efficient as it ever can be. The trasher tries to show how discourse has turned contingency into necessity and to reveal the repressed alternative interpretations that are perfectly consistent with the discourse's stated premises. Trashing techniques are used sometimes simply to attack the discourses on their own terms—to show their premises to be contradictory or incoherent and their conclusions to be arbitrary or based on dubious assumptions or hidden rhetorical tricks. The C.L.S. critiques of legal economics, for instance, have borrowed from and added to the multidisciplinary critiques of the neoclassical economic model of human beings as rational self-interested maximizers of their satisfactions: critiques that the model is vacuous (it tells you that people "want" *everything* they get); that when the model is given concrete content, it is obviously wrong (people are often irrational or altruistic) and too narrow (people want self-worth and the esteem of others as well); that there are fatal ambiguities in the notion of choosing selves (personalities are divided in their desires, desires change over time, short-term desires are often destructive to long-term selves); that the individualism of the model is a culturally and historically specific image of human conduct (a product of certain modern market cultures), that the model falsely claims it is universal; and so forth. Crits by no means reject economic analysis as valueless: they teach it and make regular use of it in their work (although the economists do not reciprocate). But by showing that the agile interpreter can justify as economically efficient virtually any imaginable scheme of social arrangements, the critique helps to deprive technocracy of its mystery; its pretense that science, magically substituting for agonizing political and ethical choices, dictates that if we want to remain prosperous we must endure all the miscellaneous injustices now in place and even invent new ones. The Critics' message is that the economic-efficiency analysis of legal practices isn't a science, it's just a very manipulable rhetoric, often a useful rhetoric which highlights problems and possible consequences that one wouldn't otherwise notice, but a myopic rhetoric, too, which systematically obscures from view—has no way even to *talk* about—the violence, coercion, irrationality, cultural variety, solidarity, and self-sacrifice of lived experience.

*Deconstruction* The Crits do not believe, however, that their trashing reveals a random chaos or that what lies behind the seeming order of legal decisions is just pure power (or personal whim). There is *a patterned chaos*, and the aim of critical scholarship is in part to uncover the patterns. Some of their best work is a familiar kind of left-wing scholarship, unmasking the often unconscious ideological bias behind legal structures and procedures, which regularly makes it easy for business groups to organize collectively to pursue their economic and political interests but which makes it much more difficult for labor, poor people, or civil rights groups to pursue theirs. Other work aims at laying bare "structures of contradiction" that underlie fields of law. Contract law in the Critics' view, for example, draws regularly for its inspiring assumptions upon two diametrically opposed visions of social life. One is a stark neo-Hobbesian world of lonely individuals, predatory and paranoid, who don't dare associate with each other except through formal contracts that strictly limit their obligations. The other is a world in which trustful co-operation is the norm and people assume indefinite open-ended responsibilities to others with whom they deal regularly and who have come to rely on them. Both sets of images, and the regimes of legal obligation they recommend, are potentially available in every legal decision about a contract. Yet the legal system persistently gives one of the regimes (the rule-bound, formal, individualistic one in this case) an arbitrarily privileged position and partially suppresses the other or reserves it for the deviant or exceptional case.

*Genealogy* Still another way to heighten awareness of the transitory, problematic, and manipulable ways legal discourses divide the world is to write their history. The Crits have turned out a lot of history of legal categories. They have focused their attention, for instance, on the mid-nineteenth century moment, when the business corporation, once an entity created only to serve the "public" ends of the commonwealth, was reclassified as "private" and thus free as any individual to do what its managers pleased in the market, while the city corporation was reclassified as the "public" agent of the legislature and its managers' legal powers from then on were strictly confined. Crits also write social history revealing that even the most basic legal concepts, such as "private property," have never had any definite, agreed-upon content but have, on the contrary, always been fiercely struggled over, so that any conventional stability the concepts may now seem to possess represents nothing more than a temporary truce that could be unsettled at any moment.

Such techniques owe much to standard liberal and radical analysis. But in the hands of Critics they add up to a style and method of critique that is quite distinctive. Consider the case of pickets who want to demonstrate in a shopping mall and are kicked off the mall by the owner. Lawyers usually approach this situation as one involving a conflict between two opposing "rights," the property right of the owner to exclude unwanted visitors or behavior and the demonstrators' right to free speech. Judicial decisions suggest that the way to resolve the conflict is to ask whether the mall is "public" or "private" in character (the more "private" it is, the greater the right to exclude). The Crit begins by asking why labeling the mall as "property" should give the right to exclude pickets in the first place and goes through the standard justifications for property rights. The efficiency rationale says that owner control will yield the highest valued uses of the property. But it is not at all clear that the shoppers do not value diverse viewpoints at the mall, that they are only there to buy and not to converse and socialize, or that their decisions to shop at this mall or go elsewhere are likely to any important extent to depend on being free from pickets.

Anyway, the "taste" of owner and shoppers, if real, to be free from exposure to political speech may be one (like the "taste" for not serving or sitting next to blacks at lunch counters) that should not be entitled to recognition, rendering the whole "efficiency" calculus irrelevant. The privacy rationale for exclusion has much less appeal when the owner is a bodiless corporation that lets hordes of strangers swarm over "its" property daily. Crits examine the private versus public distinction, what it means, and why any of those meanings should be dispositive. How "private," for instance, is the owner's decision to exclude pickets, once he asks the cops and courts for injunctions, fines, and jails to back it up? History lends a hand here, pointing out that common law traditionally prescribed social obligations to propertyholders (such as public access to inns and common carriers) in return for the protections of public force and the privileges of corporate status. Some argue that the picket's right of access ought to turn on how "public" the property is in the sense of how many links it has to state agencies—zoning privileges, tax exemptions, police services—a bundle of attributes only arbitrarily related to the crucial issue of the appropriate sites of political debate.

This brief sketch of one Critical approach certainly does not demand the conclusion that the correct, legal solution is to allow pickets, although all Crits probably would favour that result. One can examine just as skeptically the scope of "free speech" rights, which as currently interpreted would allow demonstrators no access at all even to platforms *intended* for public political discussion, such as newspapers, unless they first purchase a controlling shareholders' interest. All the approach is meant to do is to show that when legal discourse identifies the shopping mall as "private property," it sets up a powerful mystifying charm that sends the pickets scrambling to find a stronger counter-charm—"free speech." When you pick the discourse apart, you may find that calling the mall "private property"—even if you completely accept all the standard justifications for private property—tell you virtually nothing about whether owners should be able to exclude pickets.

Trashing, deconstruction, and history have the very real utility of exposing the vulnerability of the routine justifications of power, of enabling people to spot the structural defects and to challenge many of the rationales they hear advanced for especially ugly legal practices. But nobody can be content just to trash, and in the second phase of C.L.S. many Crits find themselves trying to do the intellectual spadework, and often some of the political organizing as well, for various concrete projects of reconstruction. Some of these, notably that of the Harvard theorist Roberto Mangabeira Unger, are on the grand scale—a thousand-page reimagination of democracy, with detailed architectural sketches of political, economic, and social life as it might become. Most are much less ambitious and take the form of activism regarding low-income housing policy, legal regulation of pornography and rape, immigration reform, welfare and social security policy, delivery of legal services, labor law and specifically university labor practices, and always, naturally, law school politics.

If one of the effects of law is to constrict our ability to imagine alternative social arrangements, then it should be possible to liberate social imagination by dredging up and then working to flesh out some of the alternatives that are already present but have been suppressed in legal discourse. Historians have recently been revising the "republican" view of the purpose of politics as that of facilitating self-development through participation in community self-governance—a periodic rival to the dominant liberal view that the end of politics is only to facilitate the individual pursuit of self-interest. Several Crits have begun to ask how republican ideology might influence the redesign of legal institutions—cities, corporations, workplaces, local administrative agencies. Others have followed what Unger calls the method of "doctrinal deviation," taking a set of practices that have been routinely applied in one social field and imaginatively transferring them to another. Economic democracy is one example. Another is William Simon's program of "downward professionalization." In detailed studies of welfare administration, Simon makes the case (backed up by the historical example of the New Deal-era social workers) for entrusting the kind of broad discretionary decision making habitually given by judges and corporate managers to street-level welfare workers, arguing that such a regime could be superior in terms of both efficiency and humanity than the current regime of mechanized administration. Still other Crits are making use of feminist theory and phenomenology to try to evoke richer and fuller descriptions of intersubjective experience that can be found in the abstract and impoverished categories of law and legal economics, to try to recapture the selves from which they claim legal discourses have alienated us, as well as exposing the techniques of alienation.

To return now to where I began: What is it about C.L.S. that makes people so angry? As American critical movements in law go, it has stung the sharpest of any since the Legal Realism of the 1920s and 1930s, which C.L.S. much resembles in its evident delight in showing up the manipulability, vacuity, and arbitrarily conservative conclusions of legal discourses. The other main challenge to mainstream legal thought has been the movement to study law in its social context, which has repeatedly shown how power politics and cultural variation prevent formal legal rules from being enforced and applied in real life the way legal theories and doctrines predict they will be. But lawyers who make their livings expounding formal legal doctrine have been mostly impervious to demonstrations of its limited relevance. It has taken rowdies invading the heart of their own citadel to make them sit up. Still, why such fury?

For one thing, for all the use it makes of conventional academic argument, C.L.S. is a radical movement and of the left, and that's enough in itself to make some fellow lawyers see Red. The public attacks on C.L.S. make up a fascinating collage of what Americans tend to think a left-wing movement must be about, with bits and pieces pulled from the French Revolution (Burke-Carlyle-Dickens version), vulgar Marxism, Soviet Stalinism, sixties anarchism. In these bizarre fantasies, Crits are Bolshevik saboteurs who will take over if you allow any in your faculty or firm, dangerous (in the Age of Reagan, yet), "nihilist" subverters of the "rule of law," infantile but basically harmless hippie/yippies—or all of these at once. The attackers automatically suppose—obviously without bothering to read any of their work—that Crits must believe law to be nothing more than the result of ruling-class domination or the personal and political whims of judges, and that the Crit program must be, after a violent seizure of the state, to "socialize the means of production."

But there are more sophisticated opponents, too. After all, the Crits really are out to reduce the legitimacy and authority of their elders in the intellectual legal establishment; and those elders, no fools, realize that and despise them for it, the more so because the Crits are not always kind or polite. Along with the academic trashing techniques I've described go ruder ones—satire, savage mockery, even sometimes scatology and a sort of juvenile thumb-nosing irreverence. [...]

Some opponents see C.L.S. as a threat to liberal freedoms, those maintained by the "rule of law." If every "right" is seen as contingent, up for grabs, capable of being flipped inside out through reinterpretation in the twinkling of an eye, what will we rely on to save us from the "fascists" or the "mob"? There are hard questions ... but a brief Critical answer might run like this: Legal "rights" are shorthand symbols for social practices that we collectively maintain. We value the symbols because of the latent utopian promises they hold out to us—promises of a world where we could freely and safely choose our associations with others without fear of domination by arbitrary authority. Yet, in any actual version of the legal code and its application, such promises will be realized only partially, occasionally, in fragments. The pretense that legal rules have an objective fixed set of meanings, above and beyond political choice, may sometimes help to keep monsters fenced in: If you live in Chile or Poland, or belong to a habitually trampled group in this country, you want to appeal as often as you can to rights and legal principles transcending those recognized by the dominant political forces. But the pretense of the objectivity of law also harmfully mystifies social life, encouraging people to think that the practices codified in law have fixed and frozen what they can hope to achieve, that so long as their rights are protected they can't complain, and discouraging them from political action aimed at transforming the content of rights so as to realize the emancipatory potential of law. A commitment to legalism can never substitute for a commitment to the ideals law distortedly symbolizes. As the Czech dissident Vaclav Havel writes in *The Power of the Powerless* (1985) after insisting at length on the importance of a politics of legalism aimed at embarrassing state authorities into giving some real content to the legal rituals that sustain their legitimacy:

> [E]ven in the most ideal of cases, the law is only one of several imperfect and more or less external ways of defending what is better in life against what is worse. ... Establishing respect for the law does not automatically ensure a better life, for that, after all, is a job for people and not for laws and institutions. It is possible to imagine a society with good laws that are fully respected but in which it is impossible to live. Conversely one can imagine life being quite bearable even where the laws are imperfect and imperfectly applied. ... Without keeping one's eyes open to the real dimensions of life's beauty and misery, and without a moral relationship to life, this struggle [for legality] will sooner or later come to grief on some self-justifying system of scholastics.

### R. W. GORDON
### New Developments in Legal Theory
### (1982)[52]

If what is important about law is that it functions to "legitimate" the existing order, one starts to ask *how* it does that. And for the purposes of this project, one does not look only at the undeniably numerous, specific ways in which the legal system functions to screw poor people—though it is always important to do that too, to point out as often and as powerfully as possible—but rather at all the ways in which the system seems at first glance basically uncontroversial, neutral, acceptable. This is Antonio Gramsci's notion of "hegemony," *i.e.* that the most effective kind of domination takes place when both the dominant and dominated classes believe that the existing order, with perhaps some marginal changes, is satisfactory, or at least represents the most that anyone could expect, because things pretty much have to be the way they are.[53] So Gramsci says, and the "critical" American lawyers who have accepted his concept agree, that one must look closely at these belief-systems, these deeply held assumptions about politics, economics, hierarchy, work, leisure, and the nature of reality, which are profoundly paralysis-inducing because they make it so hard for people (including the ruling classes themselves) even to *imagine* that life could be different and better.

   Law, like religion and television images, is one of these clusters of belief—and it ties in with a lot of other nonlegal but similar clusters—that convince people that all the many hierarchical relations in which they live and work are natural and necessary. A small business is staffed with people who carry around in their heads mixed clusters of this: "I can tell these people what to do and fire them if they're not *very* polite to me and quick to do it, because (a) I own the business; (b) they have no right to anything but the minimum wage; (c) I went to college and they didn't; (d) they would not work as hard or as efficiently if I didn't keep after them; a business can't run efficiently without a strong top-down command structure; (e) if they don't like it they can leave," etc.—and the employees, though with less smugness and enthusiasm, believe it as well. Take the ownership claim: the employees are not likely to think they can challenge that because to do so would jeopardize their sense of the rights of ownership, which they themselves exercise in other aspects of life ("I own this house, so I can tell my brother-in-law to get the hell out of it"); they are locked into a belief-cluster that abstracts and generalizes the ownership claim.

   Now, the point of the work (usually called anti-positivist or interpretive) that some of the "critical" lawyers are doing[54] is to try to describe—to make maps of—

---

[52] [From D. Kairys (ed.). *The Politics of Law.*]

[53] See Antonio Gramsci. *Selections from the Prison Notebooks* (Quinton Hoare and Geoffrey Nowell-Smith eds and trans., (1971), pp. 195–196. 246–247. [And *ante*, 1157.]

[54] See, *e.g.* Kennedy. Isaac D. Balbus, "Commodity Form and Legal Form: An Essay on the Relative Autonomy of the Law" (1977) 11 *Law & Society Review* 571; Thomas C. Heller. "Is the Charitable Exemption from Property Taxes an Easy Case? General Concerns About Legal Economics and Jurisprudence" in *Essays on the Law and Economics of Local Governments* (ed. Daniel Rubinfeld, 1979), pp. 183–251: A. I. Katz, "Studies in Boundary Theory: Three Essays in Adjudication and Politics" (1979) 28 *Buffalo Law Review* 383; Roberto Unger, *Knowledge and Politics* (1975).

some of these interlocking systems of belief. Drawing here on the work of such "structuralist" writers as Lévi-Strauss and Piaget, they claim that legal ideas can be seen to be organized into structures, *i.e.* complex cultural codes. The way human beings experience the world is by collectively building and maintaining systems of shared meanings that make it possible for us to interpret one another's words and actions. Positive social scientists (who would include both liberal and Marxist "instrumentalist" legal theorists) are always trying to find out how social reality objectively works, the secret laws that govern its action: they ask such questions as, "Under what economic conditions is one likely to obtain formal legal rules?" Anti-positivists assert that such questions are meaningless, since what we experience as "social reality" is something that we ourselves are constantly constructing; and that this is just as true for "economic conditions" as it is for "legal rules." If I say, "That's a bus taking people to work," I'm obviously doing much more than describing a physical object moving through space; my statement makes no sense at all except as part of a larger cultural complex of shared meanings: it would mean little or nothing to you if your culture were unfamiliar with bus technology, with "work" as an activity performed in a separate place outside the family compound, or indeed with "work" as distinct from "play" of "prayer."

"Law" is just one among many such systems of meaning that people construct in order to deal with one of the most threatening aspects of social existence: the danger posed by other people, whose co-operation is indispensable to us (we cannot even have an individual identity without them to help define it socially), but who may kill us or enslave us. It seems essential to have a system to sort out positive interactions (contracts, taxation to pay for public goods) from negative ones (crimes, torts, illegal searches, unconstitutional seizure of property). In the West, legal belief-structures, together with economic and political ones, have been constructed to accomplish this sorting out. The systems, of course, have been built by elites who have thought they had some stake in rationalizing their dominant power positions, so they have tended to define rights in such a way as to reinforce existing hierarchies of wealth and privilege.

Even more important, such system building has the effect of making the social world as it is come to seem natural and inevitable. Though the structure are built, piece by interlocking piece, with human intentions, people come to "externalize" them, to attribute to them existence and control over and above human choice; and, moreover, to believe that these structures must be the way they are. Recall the example given earlier of the person who works in a small business for the "owner" of the business. It is true that the owner's position is backed up by the ultimate threat of force—if she does not like the way people behave on her property, she can summon armed helpers from the state to eject them—but she also has on her side the powerful ideological magic of a structure that gives her the "rights" of an "employer" and "owner," and the worker the "duties" of an "employee" and "invitee" on the "owner's property." The worker feels he cannot challenge the owner's right to eject him from her property if she does not like the way he behaves, in part because he feels helpless against the force she can invoke, but also because in part he accepts her claim as legitimate: he respects "individual rights of ownership" because the powers such rights confer seem necessary to his own power and freedom; limitations on an "owner's" rights would threaten him as well. But the analogy he makes is possible only because of his acquiescence in a belief-structure—liberal legalism—that abstracts particular relationships between real people (this man and the woman he "works for"; this man and the brother-in-law he wants to eject from his house) into relations between entirely abstract categories of "individuals" playing the abstract social roles of "owner," "employee." etc. This process of allowing the structure we ourselves have built to mediate relations among us so as to make us see ourselves as performing abstract roles in a play that is produced by no human agency is what is usually called (following Marx and such modern writers as Sartre and Lukács) reification.[55] It is a way people have of manufacturing necessity: they build structures, then act as if (and genuinely come to believe that) the structures they have built are determined by history, human nature, economic law.

Perhaps a promising tactic, therefore, of trying to struggle against being demobilized by our own conventional beliefs is to try to use the ordinary rational tools of intellectual inquiry to expose belief-structures that claim that things as they are must necessarily be the way they are. There are many varieties of this sort of critical exercise, whose point is to unfreeze the world as it appears to common sense as a bunch or more of less objectively determined social relations and to make it appear as (we believe) it really is: people acting, imagining, rationalizing, justifying.

One way of accomplishing this is to show that the belief-structures that rule our lives are not found in nature but are historically contingent; that have not always existed in their present. ... This discovery is extraordinarily liberating, not (at least not usually) because there is anything so wonderful about the belief-structures of the past, but because uncovering those structures makes us see how arbitrary our categories for dividing up experience are, how nonexhaustive of human potentiality. Another useful exercise is just simple empirical disproof of the claim of necessity. When it is asserted that strict, predictable rules of private property and free contract are necessary to protect the functioning of the market, maintain production incentives, etc., it can be shown that the actual rules are not at all what they are claimed to be, that they can be applied quite differently in quite different circumstances, sometimes "paternalistically," sometimes strictly, sometimes forcing parties to share gains and losses with each other, and sometimes not at all.[56] Or it may be asserted that certain hierarchical ways of organizing are necessary for efficient realization of economies of scale. One can use historical (nineteenth-century, worker-organized steel production) or comparative (Japanese, for instance) examples to demonstrate that "efficient" production can occur under all sorts of conditions.[57] Or one can try to show that even at the level of theory, the claim of necessity is, on its own terms, incoherent or contradictory; this approach is currently being practised on the various forms of "legal economics" that claim that certain regimes of leal rules are "efficient".[58] One can bring similar critiques to bear on claims that things must be the way they are because of some long-term logic of historical change ("modernization," "what is, after all, an inevitable consequence of social life in industrialized societies," "the price of living in a modern pluralistic society," "an inevitable consequence of the declining rate of profit under monopoly capitalism," etc.). It turns out that these theories of development cannot be applied to the concrete histories of particular societies without being so qualified, refined, or partially repudiated that they lose all their force as determining theories—at best, they are only helpful insights or ways of organizing thinking about the world.

---

[55] See generally P. Gabel, *Research in Law and Sociology* (ed. S. Spitzer), vol. 3 [*post*, 1073].

[56] See, *e.g.* Duncan Kennedy, "Form and Substance in Private Law Adjudication," (1976) 89 *Harvard Law Review* 1685; Karl Klare, "Contracts, Jurisprudence and the First-Year Casebook," (1979) 54 *New York University Law Rev.* 876. *Cf.* James B. Atleson, "Work Group Behavior and Wildcat Strikes: The Causes and Functions of Industrial Civil Disobedience" (1973) 34 *Ohio State Law J.* 750.

[57] See, *e.g.* Katherine W. Stone, "The Origin of Job Structures in the Steel Industry" (1974) 6 *Review of Radical Political Economy* 61.

[58] See, *e.g.* Mark Kelman, "Choice and Utility" (1979) *Wisconsin Law Review* 769, Kelman, "Consumption Theory, Production Theory and Ideology in the Coase Theorem" (1979) 52 *Southern California Law Review* 669; Thomas C. Heller, *op. cit.*, Morton J Horwitz, "Law and Economics; Science or Politics?" (1980) 8 *Hofstra Law Rev.* 905; Duncan Kennedy and Frank I. Michelman, "Are Property and Contract Efficient" (1980) 8 *Horstra Law Rev.* 711.

If we start to look at the world this way—no longer as some determined set of "economic conditions" or "social forces" that are pushing us around but rather as in the process of continuous creation by human beings, who are constantly reproducing the world they know because they (falsely) believe that have no choice—we will obviously bring a very different approach to the debate over whether legal change can ever effect real ("social and economic") change, or whether law is wholly dependent on the real, "hard" world of production. For if social reality consists of reified structures, "law" and "the economy" are *both* belief-systems that people have externalized and allowed to rule their lives. Moreover, if the critiques of legal belief-structures are accurate—that even in their theoretically ideal forms they are contradictory and incoherent, and that in practical application they depart constantly from the ideal in wildly unpredictable fashion—it follows that no particular regime of legal principles *could* be functionally necessary to maintain any particular economic order. Similarly, no given economic order can be thought of as requiring for its maintenance any particular bunch of legal rules, except of course those that may be part of the *definition* of that economic order, as "private property" of some sort is to most people's definition of capitalism.

So—if one were to adopt this approach—one would no longer be inclined to look for "scientific" or "positivist" explanations of how the world works in large-scale theories of historical interrelations between states, societies, and economies (one would actually be trying to knock down such theories). It may be that the place to look is somewhere quite different—in the smallest, most routine, most ordinary interactions of daily life in which some human beings dominate others and they acquiesce in such domination. It may be, as Foucault's work suggests,[59] that the whole legitimating power of a legal system is built up out of such myriad tiny instances.

I do not want to give the impression that everyone in the critical legal-studies movement has adopted the approaches I have just described. On the contrary, these approaches are hotly debated. Some of those who most fiercely dispute the validity of these approaches do so in part on political grounds. I will mention a few of the criticisms and briefly respond to them.

One criticism is that the view that law and the economy as we know them are structures inside people's heads is a form of "idealism"; it assumes that the world can be changed merely by *thinking* about it differently. This charge is, I think, both true and not true. It is true in that the belief it criticizes is indeed that the main constraints upon making social life more bearable are these terrible, constricting limits on imagination; and that these structures are as obdurate as they are because they are collectively constructed and maintained—we *have* to use them to think about the world at all, because the world makes no sense apart from our systems of shared meanings. But the charge is not true if it means to imply that we believe that all constraints on human action are imaginary, alienated ideas of "false necessity." Obviously there are many constraints on human social activity—scarcities of desired things, finite resources of bodies and minds, production possibilities of existing and perhaps all future technologies, perhaps even ineradicable propensities for evil—that any society will have to face. What is false is to think that these constraints somehow necessarily dictate that we must have some specific set of social arrangements that we are already familiar with, in history or in our own time; that the human race can live only within its real constraints in a few specific ways (*e.g.* that it *must* choose between liberal capitalism and state socialist dictatorship).

The notion that there are no objective laws of social change is in one way profoundly depressing. Those who have come to believe it have had to abandon the most comforting hopes of socialism: that history was on its side, and that

---

[59] See especially Michel Foucault, *Discipline and Punish: The Birth of the Prison.*

history could be accelerated through a scientific understanding of social laws. It no longer seems plausible to think than organization of the working class or capture of the state apparatus will *automatically* bring about the conditions within which people could begin to realize the utopian possibilities of social life. Such strategies have led to valuable if modest improvements in social life, as well as to stagnation, cooptation by the existing structures, and nightmare regimes of state terror. Of course, this does not mean that people should stop trying to organize the working class or to influence the exercise of state power; it means only that they have to do so pragmatically and experimentally, with full knowledge that there are no deeper logics of historical necessity that can guarantee that what we do now will be justified later. Yet, if the real enemy is us—*all* of us, the structures we carry around in our heads, the limits on our imagination—where can we even begin? Things seem to change in history when people break out of their accustomed ways of responding to domination, by acting as if the constraints on their improving their lives were not real and that they could change things: and sometimes they can, though not always in the way they had hoped or intended; but they never knew they could change them at all until they tried.

[pp. 286–292]

### PETER GABEL
### Reification in Legal Reasoning
### (1980)[60]

Legal reasoning is an inherently repressive form of interpretive thought which limits our comprehension of the social world and its possibilities. This interpretive thought emerges within consciousness at moments of uncertainty about the legitimacy of the concrete world within which we find ourselves, and its function is to institutionalize—with the help of such overpowering psychological symbols as robed judges, quasi-ecclesiastical schools, the Profession, and the Tribunal— the boundaries of a legitimate rationality. It is therefore incorrect to say, as does the instrumentalist, that legal rules and principles directly serve the interests of the dominant class by bringing about certain consequences in the socioeconomic order. Legal outcomes have only the most marginal effect on the movement of socioeconomic processes and social actors who have been conditioned to accept the apparent necessity of these processes do not require anything so abstract as "legal rules" to shape and direct their daily conduct. It is closer to the truth to say that it is action which has an "instrumental" effect on legal thought, as social actors of every class seek to legitimate to themselves the experiential world within which they come to know themselves and their relations with others, under definite historical conditions.

This is not to deny the reality of class domination; it only emphasizes that legal domination arises within the consciousness of every person as a sort of legitimating repression, much like what is called a "resistance" in psychoanalysis. Legal thought originates, of course, within the consciousness of the dominant class because it is in this class's interest to bring it into being, but it is accepted and interiorized by everyone because of the traumatic absence of connectedness that would otherwise erupt into awareness. This is why the legal form becomes "fetishized" as Balbus[61] has put it: people "believe in" the legal order because the legal order substitutes as harmonious abstract world for the concrete alienation that characterizes their lived experience. Thus, while legal thought represses, it also reassures; it is, so to speak, the superego of the public self at the level of social interpretation.

---

[60] [From *Research in Law and Sociology*, vol. 3].
[61] (1977) 11 Law and Soc. Rev. 571, 582.

The character of this repressive thought is accurately described by the word "reification," which is properly understood as a certain sort of distortion of meaning that occurs within communication. This distortion is sometimes called the "fallacy of misplaced concreteness" because when we "reify," we draw an abstraction from a concrete milieu and then mistake the abstraction for the concrete. (An example is the well-known expression "law is a means of social control," which suggests that "the law" is substantial, like a fence.) The "mis-placed-concreteness" characterization is descriptively accurate, but it lays insufficient emphasis on the intersubjective and paradoxical meaning of reified communication. For in reification we do not simply make a kind of private error about the true nature of what we are talking about; we participate in an unconscious conspiracy with others whereby everyone knows of the fallacy, and yet denies that the fallacy exists. More specifically, in a reified communication the speaker: (1) misunderstands by asserting that an abstraction is concrete; (2) understands that he misunderstands or knows that the communication is "false"; and (3) denies both to himself and to the listener that he knows either of these things by the implied assertion that the communication is "true," or concrete. Thus, reification is not simply a form of distortion, but also a form of unconscious coercion, which, on the one hand, separates the *communicated* or *socially apparent* reality from the reality of experience and, on the other hand, denies that this separation is taking place. The knowledge of the truth is both repressed and "contained in" the distorted communication simultaneously.

An example relevant to the development of "legal reification" can be found in any first-grade classroom. It is 8:29 and children are playing, throwing food, and generally engaging in relatively undistorted communication. At 8:30, the teacher (who is replacing the father and who, in later years, will be replaced by the judge) calls the class to attention: it is time for the "pledge of allegiance." All face front, all suffer the same social rupture and privation, all fix their eyes on a striped piece of cloth. As they drone on, having not the slightest comprehension of the content of what they are saying, they are nonetheless learning the sort of distorted or reified communication that is expressed in the legal form. They are learning, in other words, that they are all abstract "citizens" of an abstract "United States of America," that there exists "liberty and justice for all," and so forth—not from the content of the words, but from the ritual which forbids any rebellion. Gradually, they will come to accept these abstractions as descriptive of a concrete truth because of the repressive and conspiratorial way that these ideas have been communicated (each senses that all the others "believe in" the words and therefore they must be true), and once this acceptance occurs, any access to the paradoxically forgotten memory that these are mere abstractions will be sealed off. And once the abstractions are reified, they can no longer be criticized because they signify a false concrete.

And yet this false concrete that emerges within reified communication is not merely a *conception* of reality, not merely an "ideological representation"; the pledge of allegiance is itself a living sequence during which a ritual of the Other is enacted through everyone. Each child enacts a humility, as does the teacher, who is merely playing the role of sovereign; each draws the act down upon himself; each institutes in every gesture (even in the modulation of the vocal chords) an obedience to "a presence that is everywhere elsewhere",[62] such that the represented world is also realized in the body, such that the social body of a collectivity becomes the expression of a *gap* that gives reality the feel of pseu-doreality, in which each movement is lived in the as-if. The terrible truth of reification is that it is alive within each of us as the haunted embodiment of an alienated desire, such that representational "communication" is itself the expression of an alienated communion in which everyone is other to himself, knows this, and can do

---

[62] R. D. Laing, *The Politics of Experience* (1967), p. 84.

nothing, or almost nothing, about it. And because appearance floods reality in this way, intimating a "reality" that is already an absence to itself, it becomes impossible to divorce the false consciousness that signifies a false concrete from the false concrete itself. There is a dim and intuitive comprehension that something is very wrong, but this comprehension is the only trace of itself, like the "other side" of a mobius strip.

...I investigate the way that the alienated communion of a group "legalizes" itself in representational thought. My discussion of alienation will be limited to a brief introductory description of the organization of groups within capitalism, and of the way in which living within these groups feels in many ways like the way children feel when they are "passivized" by the pledge of allegiance. The better part of the essay describes the way that "the law" emerges within our alienated culture as a kind of quasi-religious belief-system which simultaneously compensates for our feelings of loss within these alienated groups and conceals these feelings from us.

### *Law as a denial of a collective feeling of illegitimacy, and an affirmation of the law-like nature of the normal*

I take it as given at the outset of this essay that human relationships within contemporary capitalism are characterized by a traumatic absence of connectedness that does not wish to become conscious of itself. The source of this absence of connectedness is the passivity, impotence, and isolation generated by the structure of groups, as those groups are themselves organized by the movement of capital. Within these groups, no one is normally aware of his or her sense of unconnectedness, passivity, impotence, and isolation, because this felt reality is *denied* by the socially communicated reality. Each person denies to the other that he or she is suffering, because this collective denial has been made a condition of what social connection there is. One cannot assert that the pledge of allegiance is insane and still remain "with" one's friends and family—so we forget that this pledging is insane and reinforce the collective coercion.

Within these alien collectivities, each person experiences himself as a thing-like function of "the system", understood as the semi-autonomous structure which constitutes the group's inertia. Each person experiences himself this way because each person is recognized in this way by everyone else, and human beings are such that they experience themselves as they are recognized.[63] Thus, a "small businessman" experiences himself as a "small businessman," a "secretary" as a "secretary," a "child" as a "child." These role-experiences are thing-like in that each is subject to rigid determinations within the group's socially defined and socially communicated structure. Thus, within an American family, a child must experience himself as a child because he is treated as a child within the family system which constitutes each of its subjects. Yet to say that each person experiences himself as thing-*like* is to express the meaning of alienation: each actor is passivized within a role that denies him recognition as a connected, active, potentiated, and intersubjective *person*. One is never, or almost never, a person; instead, one is successively a "husband," "bus passenger," "small businessman," "consumer," and so on.[64]

The experiential starting point for understanding the function of "the law" in this milieu is to recognize, to sense, that this thing-like quality that pervades each of these groups is felt as *illegitimate*. Even as we are passivized into imprisoning roles, and even as this reification is denied by each of us to the other, there is a collective tendency to explode the whole thing. This is true within the smallest sub-group (two people talking in a room), and it is true within the totality within

---

[63] G. W. F. Hegel, *The Phenomenology of Mind* (1967).

[64] *Cf.* Laing, *op. cit.*, n. 62.

which each sub-group is situated. Although each sub-group does have a semi-autonomy from the entire group (from "capitalism"), it is nonetheless situated within the living totality that is capitalism, and in fact each sub-group is given its fundamental determination from the totalizing effect of the movement of capital. Thus, one cannot discover the final intelligibility of the way clerical workers chat in the halls, or the way businessmen expound over lunch, without situating each tone and gesture within the organization of the entire human group. The clerical workers *secret themselves* from their bosses, and this is what it means to move into the hall and "gossip." The bosses *talk too loud* at lunch in order to reinstitute their nervous privilege to do so. Each "alienation" is expressive of the totalizing movement of an internal class-struggle, and this class-struggle as a whole is felt as illegitimate, because each person is able to experience himself only as thing-like, as passivized within a role. And because this sense of illegitimacy is always threatening to erupt into awareness, there is a need for "the law."

The function of "the law" is to give each of us the impression that the system operates according to a normative law. The law is a denial, at the level of social interpretation, of our collective experience of illegitimacy. Through the law we tell ourselves, through the collective terror and coercion that I have described, that what is, ought to be—that the system follows a law. This profound tautology expresses what I mean when I say that the function of law is legitimation.

### The phenomenology of the legal opinion

When I say that the law represents the system as if the system followed a normative law, I mean that the law is an instance of the *system* thinking itself, the word "thinking" being used in an active, transitive sense.[65] When a judge engages in legal reasoning, he is, of course, a person who is thinking. But he is a person passivized within a role, fulfilling what is often called "the judicial function," and his thought corresponds itself to the movement of the system as a whole. Precisely to that extent that the "small businessman" has become a "small businessman," the "secretary" a "secretary," and so on—precisely, that is, to the extent that intersubjectivity has been reduced to a series of interlocking roles and functions—to that extent the judge's legitimating thought becomes a sort of carapace which fits itself over those roles in order to *think* them legitimatively. In other words, we might say that it is capital that engages in legal reasoning through the judge, precisely because it is capital which totalizes the objectified interpersonal relations which legal reasoning interprets. One could say that the judge is dissociated or "decentred" from his own subjectivity by virtue of his own alienation, and so he is reduced to performing a certain "thinking function" whereby he represents what is as if it were "legal."

. . .

**2.** *The Reification of Legal Concepts as a Way of Legitimating the Status-quo* In order to grasp the way that the judge derives legal concepts from his apprehension of the social field, we must remember that his intention is to adjudicate a dispute in such a way that the system will be restored to a normal and legitimated equilibrium in the realm of thought. He has, in other words, an unconscious *legitimating intention* and it is towards-legitimating-the-system that he has apprehended the events leading up to the dispute as a disequilibrated fact-situation in the first place. In order now to conceptualize the fact-situation "legally," he must abstract legitimating concepts from the normal movement of the facts, concretize the abstractions, and then re-describe the facts with the aid of these abstractions. This is exactly what it means to apply the law to the facts. Simultaneously, the facts become lawful and the law becomes factual.

---

[65] *Cf.* J.-P. Sartre, *Critique of Dialectical Reason* (1976).

Since the law as a generality is supposed to apply to everyone in "the society," the primary legal abstractions drawn from any fact-situation must be universal. Within the operational reasoning of the physical world (the laws of physics), an example of such a universal abstraction is the concept "particle" because it signifies the movement of anything whatsoever, to the extent that the movement of the whole of the material world is apprehended as being made up of parts. An atom, a photon, an electron—all of these can be abstracted to higher levels of universality by the concept "particle." Within legal reasoning as it is applied to the social world, the equivalent to this concept is the concept "party." The bailee, the tort-feasor, the executor, the trustee—all of these abstractions share the universal abstract feature of being "parties in dispute." The "party" is the abstract universal "particle" of the social field, and signifies simply that the social field is comprised of "legal parts" that are, at this highest level of generality, identical to one another.

In order to legalize the normal movement of the social field, each party must be conceptualized as possessing certain universal normative "properties" signifying that the way people do function together normally is also the way people should function together normally. These properties are called "rights" and "duties." Within any fact-situation of whatever kind, each party is presumed to have a "right" to the other's normal functioning (*e.g.*, prompt delivery of the goods, driving at normal speed), and each party is also resumed to have a "duty" to function normally toward the other. If we continue to think of the judge as a "legitimation scientist" who observes the "data" that makes up the social field, we can say that he conceptualizes what he sees as a mass of moving "parties," all identical, all linked to one another through the bonding permitted by the rights and duties possessed by each party. And in so doing, he reifies the interaction of the parties as legitimate a priori, since it appears to him that the parties interact because they *ought* to. From within the legitimating gaze, a party delivers goods on time, or a party remains within the speed limit, or a party disposes of net income properly, *because* he has a duty to do so and *because* the other has a right to it. Once the abstractions are concretized, it appears that this is simply how parties interact, or more precisely, it appears that parties do interact the way they should. "Is" and "ought" are fused in the very way that the social field is conceptualized.

Within any particular fact-situation, the legal party is reconceptualized in terms of the particular function that he or she (perhaps "it" would be the correct pronoun) is obliged to perform. Suppose, for example, that party A is in dispute with party B because B delivered some goods five days late (A would not transfer money to B, B is upset, etc.) The system is in disequilibration and the judge is asked to state its law, which, as we can now begin to see, is nothing more than the legitimating conceptual representation of its normal functioning. He asks first: "What was B's duty?" This is derived by abstracting a concept from B's normal function within the system, reifying the concept in such a way that the function becomes "what B is," and then describing what B does in normative terms as identical to what B ought to do. Thus a "party" of the type B is conceptualized as a "seller," a concept which simply freezes this party's function as it is dictated by the movement of the commodity; this function is then factualized as what sellers do (the common-sense may be, in this case, that sellers deliver goods on time); and then this factualized normal function receives a normative articulation ("sellers have a duty to deliver goods on time"). When a "seller" fails to deliver goods on time to a "buyer," then the buyer's "right" has been "violated." In analyzing the facts this way, all that the judge actually does is to restate the facts in terms of their lawful attributes, such that what happened in the facts appears as a violation of a law immanent to them. And through this restatement, normal equilibration of the seller-buyer world is restored in the realm of thought.

It follows from this that a "rule of law" is merely the normative reification of function—it is a way of describing a normal practice that has been generated by pressures within the system in a legitimating conceptual form. The judge needs to construct such a rule because what he wants to do is to describe what this seller "should have done" by evaluating her factual conduct in relation to what all sellers "should be doing" within the system. This can only be accomplished by evaluating what this seller did in relation to what sellers as a generality (as performers of the "seller-function") actually do, and then re-presenting this evaluation in an "ought" form. For example, the actual rule that is to be applied in the case that we are looking at, the prompt-delivery rule, emerged as a rule receiving wide acceptance from the socio-economic relations of classical free-market capitalism. We can infer from the very fact that this rule was "accepted" and "made sense" that these socio-economic relations generated a normal practice in commodity-exchange transfers that favored the simultaneous transfer of goods for money. Faced with a systematic breakdown, the judge abstracts from this normal practice a legitimating rule that "applies" to all sellers: "Prompt delivery by the seller is a condition precedent to the buyer's duty to pay." When this rule is reified as a "law," the appearance is created that the "commodity-exchange transfer-function," as it is supposed to be performed by all sellers within the system, is *caused* by "the rights and duties of the parties." The judge can then deduce whether *this* seller did what she "ought" to do.

This process of reifying the rule turns the world as it is on its head, because it signifies that a norm of intersubjective action is "caused" by an ideological appearance that has been drawn from it. The process of deducing outcome from rule then becomes the process of signifying the causality of the law, of signifying that the social order is the consequence of a legal order that is immanent to it. [. . .]

*The "ontological" basis of legitimation; legal reasoning as a way of restoring the unalienated group in imaginary form*

*A. The Relationship between Legal Reasoning and Normative Political Theory*

No matter how much people experience their social relations between things, they do not forget that in reality these relations are only thing-like.[66] For this reason, a law which reifies and legitimates these relations must itself be legitimated by concepts which are abstracted from the subjectivity of those to whom the law applies. A person who asks why he has a legal duty to do something is not answered by being told "because it is your function to do it." Such an answer would suggest that he is actually a thing, which he knows is not the case. The only effective answer to such a question is to justify the duty by reference to a "human nature" which brought the duty into being, or, in other words, the law must appear to spring from normative assumptions about *who* "the parties" are as real people.

These normative assumptions are embodied in the abstractions of normative political theory. The activity of thinking up political theory is formally identical to the activity of thinking up legal reasoning. It consists in apprehending the system as a synthetic quasi-object (the presupposed norm), drawing abstractions from the movement of concrete social actors as they move in their normal functioning, reifying these abstractions, and then creating the appearance, through "political reasoning," that these abstractions have brought the world as it is into being. In political reasoning, the thinker's intention is to attribute a *normative subjectivity* to the members of a culture that is then reified as "human nature," in exactly the same way that legal reasoning reifies the duties of the seller as an ingredient or property of what might be called the "seller's nature." In each

---

[66] *Cf.* F. Jameson, *Marxism and Form* (1971), pp. 244–246.

case, we are dealing with a reifying thought, but political reasoning backs up legal reasoning by articulating the relationship between the seller as functioning-unit and the seller as human being, such that the "duty" corresponding to the seller's function seems to be ultimately derived from his own intentions. Of course, these "intentions" are actually those of the abstract and normative "subject" whose identity has been grafted as a reified fact onto the seller's being (thus, it is said that he entered the contract of his own "free will"); yet the seller feels these intentions as his (or, in other words, it "makes sense" to him to call them his intentions) because his identity as normative subject has been abstracted from his actual alienated functioning in the world (engaging in apparently voluntary transactions in a "private" market).

Thus, it makes sense, in the objective context of a freely competitive market, to describe the necessary systemic function of exchange as the consequence of an intentional interaction between two "free and equal" subjects. Seen as quasi-objects, the participants in an exchange *are* in a certain sense "free and equal"—that is, in the sense in which atoms as "mere facts" appear to the physicist as unattached and identical. The subjective concepts are abstracted from the concrete functioning of the participants, and once reified, they represent the functional interaction as the consequence of the participants' human nature as subjects. Similarly, it makes sense, in the objective context of the cooperative market that we now have, to describe the same exchange as the consequence of an intentional interaction between two "free and equal" subjects "acting in good faith." Seen as quasi-objects, the participants in an exchange today *do* "act in good faith" in the same sense that the bonded atoms in a molecule appear to the physicist as attached to one another. The subjective moral sentiment is abstracted from the objective functional reality, and reified, such that it appears that the necessity of objective co-operation in state-regulated monopoly capitalism is the consequence of the participants' subjective intentions. In both cases, the alienated intention which is forced upon the participants by the movement of the commodity and which mirrors their function, is replaced normatively in the abstract.

These are examples of the way that political theory is used within judicial opinions. In any historical period there are also full-blown works of political theory which subjectivize and naturalize the entire system of social relations from which they are abstracted. Thus, liberal political theory, as it emerged in the context of a developing competitive market, described the entire structure of market relations as the consequence of atomized and self-interested "free wills" (utilitarianism and social contract theory). Its conceptual structure made the facts of competitive capitalism "legitimately lawful" by allocating the responsibility for its law to an hypostasized "we" which supposedly brought the world as it was then into being. This "we" was an abstract collection of free wills who created an abstract "state" that created the laws by which social relations were to be governed. Today, liberal political theory has been modified to conform to the cooperative structure of contemporary capitalism. It is imagined that classical liberal theory was wrong in failing to include a moral component in each subject's free will that would limit liberty as license in the interests of a newly conceived notion of the general welfare. And it is through this new conception of a more moral "we" that the laws of corporate liberalism find their political justification. Seen in this way, a work of normative political theory is a kind of fantastic fable or myth describing the world as it is in a common-sense mythical form, and yet hiding its mythic quality beneath the false concretization of reified abstractions.

Now if we put this brief description of political reasoning together with the description of legal reasoning in the previous section, we can see each judicial opinion as a mythical narrative that restores the system's equilibration in the realm of thought by resolving a dispute according to the requirements of "human nature." The equilibrative tendency within the system is apprehended as the movement of a normative political "we," or in other terms, the intersubjective movement of socio-economic relations is abstracted as a political communion of normative subjects. Through the abstract "political process," "we" create the laws which govern "us." These laws define the "rights and duties" of normative subjects to one another, and are "applied" in the resolution of disputes between "parties." And through the collective fantasy of applying the law, the resolution of each dispute restores a disrupted communion to its lawful state. We are reminded that the system itself is the embodiment of our collective nature.

## B. *The Transposition of the Real into the Imaginary*

And yet this description of legal reasoning, which we should now call "politico-legal" reasoning, does not explain its efficacy, its psychological power. If the motive force behind this thought-process is the concealment of "a traumatic absence of connectedness that does not wish to become conscious of itself," it remains for us to understand how the experience of thinking this way provides a psychic gratification that temporarily alleviates the trauma when it threatens to erupt, through the dispute or breakdown, into awareness.

The solution to this dilemma is to be found in the ontological meaning for each person of *experiencing* the intersubjective movement of socio-economic relations as a political communion of normative subjects. This experience is captured in the psychoanalytic concept of a "wish fulfillment." Under the pressure of what Freud called the "return of the repressed," or of what we can here describe as the possibility of becoming aware of the social alienation that pervades our entire collective experience, we respond by imagining that we are actually disalienated in an harmonious socio-political connection that is also "the law." No matter what the particular content of the politico-legal thought (feudal/religious, capitalist/ liberal, etc.), its universal ontological feature is that it generates an imaginary feeling of "with-ness" by restoring the feeling of being-in-a-group in an imaginary way. In other words, there occurs something like what Freud called a "cathexis," whereby dammed up desire is partially and momentarily gratified through images that are signified in thought. These images are potentiated in such a way that they are able to allow us to experience, through an infinite number of historical forms, what life would be like in the absence of alienation. Thus, to imagine a society of "free and equal citizens" is to *experience*, however dimly, a feeling of collective spontaneity free of interpersonal domination; to imagine a world in which people have "moral obligations" to one another is to experience, however dimly, a feeling of reciprocal recognition and commitment. And even God's harshest commands, as they were embodied in the politico-legal ideology of feudalisms, allowed people to experience a feeling of genuine love through the image of possible salvation. It is the cathexis of these ideal images that provides what we might call the emotional correlate of reification: "belief" in the law derives not from mere indoctrination, but from a desire to reify, a desire to believe that the abstract is concrete, that the imaginary is real.

The reason that these ideal images can take an infinite number of historical forms is that our ontology, our social being, is indivisible. We do not want freedom and equality and recognition and justice in an additive fashion; it is, rather, that each of these words signifies an indivisible and whole way of being-in-a-group that will achieve concrete expression only with the elimination of alie-nation. In the ontological sense, freedom implies equality just as equality implies freedom, and both will be realized in the concrete when either is, neither before the other. There is no limit to the way that this sense of wholeness and sociality can be expressed, since the historical development of forms of social expression is nothing other than an infinite evocation of social being in the course of its becoming. Thus, from the ontological point of view, we can say that the judicial or political "ideologist," as a social theorist of the imaginary, has an infinite variety of images available to him in the construction of his legitimation thought.

From the socio-historical point of view, however, his options are strictly limited by what we could call formal and historical constraints. The "formal" constraint is one that I have emphasized consistently in the course of this essay—in order for politico-legal reasoning to "make sense," there must always be a relative correspondence in form between the imaginary social organization of the legitimating images and the social organization of the concrete socio-economic world from which these images are drawn. Thus, from a purely formal standpoint, for example, the legitimation of the feudal hierarchies required an ideology of Divine Right *or any formal equivalent* that could represent these hierarchies in an imaginary ideal way. The "historical" constraint on the development of politico-legal thought is what gives a relatively determinate *content* to the particular evocation of the ideal that is possible at a given historical moment. Because there must be an historical continuity to the development of ideological forms, the ideological tensions that are continually produced by formal disjunctions between a prevailing ideology and the transforming equilibration of the common-sense must be mediated by a thought that simultaneously conserves the existing forms and images while surpassing them toward new imaginary wholes. In this historical sense, the hierarchies of feudal life, for example, required an ideology of Divine Right *or any mediative equivalent* that could have adjusted the prior cosmology to a new social order.

As an historical figure, therefore, the ideologist is perhaps best seen as a kind of sleight-of-hand man or "bricoleur"[67] who seeks to fuse these ontological, formal, and historical dimensions of legitimating thought in the fabrication of a perpetual illusion that everyone wants to believe. The group conspires to create him in order to maintain its collective repression in the face of a perpetual terror that there will be a "breakdown of law," which is to say a breakdown of even the imaginary forms of social cohesion. The only antidote to this perpetual movement of unconscious conspiracy is the development of a concrete disalienating social movement that would make imaginary forms of social cohesion unnecessary. And one feature of the development of such a movement must be the delegitimation of the law altogether, which is to say the delegitimation of the notion that social life is created and enforced by imaginary ideas.                     [pp. 25–46]

## MARK KELMAN
### Interpretive Construction in the Substantive Criminal Law
### (1981)[68]

Legal argument has a standard, and putatively rational, form: It states overarching purposes to the legal system, and from those purposes it deduces answers to specific doctrinal dilemmas. This article examines the standard doctrinal arguments routinely made by judges and commentators on the substantive criminal law. I do not wish to challenge any results these commentators may reach, except insofar as it is important to challenge some universally held beliefs in order to counter claims that there are easy criminal law cases. Instead, I want to challenge the falsely complacent sense that the arguments, while grounded in politically controversial purposes, are deduced or derived in a rational and coherent fashion once the purposes are settled. I contend that legal argument has two phases, interpretive construction and rational rhetoricism, and that the former, a vital step which undercuts the rationality of the latter, goes virtually unexamined.

By interpretive construction, I refer to processes by which concrete situations are reduced to substantive legal controversy: It refers both to the way we construe

---

[67] C. Lévi-Strauss, *The Savage Mind* (1966).
[68] [From (1981) 33 Stanford L. R. 591.]

a factual situation and to the way we frame the possible rules to handle the situation. What then follows logically, if not chronologically, is rational rhetoricism—the process of presenting the legal conclusions that result when interpretive constructs are applied to the "facts." This rhetorical process is the "stuff" of admirable legal analysis: distinguishing and analyzing cases, applying familiar policies to unobvious fact patterns, and emphasizing the degree to which we can rely on the least controversial underlying values. These rhetorical techniques are so intellectually complex that there is a powerful tendency to elevate falsely the importance of intellect in actual legal decisionmaking, to fail to see the interpretive construction that makes the wise posturing possible. I will look behind (or unpack) this rhetoric to the selection of "relevant" categories and "relevant" facts. At the same time, I will try to understand the appeal of the well-argued case, an appeal clearly felt by so many of my colleagues and students.

[...]

### A general summary of interpretive constructs

Legal argument can be made only *after* a fact pattern is characterized by interpretive constructs. Once these constructs operate, a single legal result seems inevitable, a result seemingly deduced on general principle. These constructs appear both in conscious and unconscious forms in standard legal discourse. Before examining in detail how interpretive constructs reify substantive "textbook" law, it will be useful to examine them more precisely.

### A. Four Unconscious Interpretive Constructs

Unconscious interpretive constructs shape the way we view disruptive incidents, but they are never identified or discussed by judges or commentators. There are basically four forms of unconscious constructs, two dealing with "time-framing" and two dealing with problems of categorization. I discuss unconscious constructs before conscious ones because the former are often used to avoid issues inherent in the latter, issues that the legal analysts are most prone to be aware are controversial, perhaps insoluble, and highly politicized.

**1.** Broad and narrow time frames. We put people on trial. People exist over time; they have long, involved personal histories. We prosecute particular acts— untoward incidents—that these people commit. But even these incidents have a history: Things occur before or after incidents that seem relevant to our judgment of what the perpetrator did. Sometimes we incorporate facts about the defendant's personal history.[69] Other times, we incorporate facts about events preceding[70] or post-dating[71] the criminal incident. But an interpreter can readily focus solely on the isolated criminal incident, as if all we can learn of value in assessing culpability can be seen with that narrower time focus.

Most often, though not invariably, the arational choice between narrow and broad time frames keeps us from having to deal with more explicit political questions arising from one conscious interpretive construct—the conflict between intentionalism and determinism. Often, conduct is deemed involuntary (or determined) rather than freely willed (or intentional) because we do not consider the defendant's earlier decisions that may have put him in the position of apparent choicelessness. Conversely, conduct that could be viewed as freely willed or voluntary if we looked only at the precise moment of the criminal incident is

---

[69] For example, we incorporate facts about a defendant's personal history in raising the insanity defense.

[70] *e.g.* in raising the defense of duress.

[71] *e.g.* in raising the defense of abandonment.

sometimes deemed involuntary because we open up the time frame to look at prior events that seem to compel or determine the defendant's conduct at the time of the incident. The use of "time-framing" as interpretive *method* blocks the perception that intentionalist or determinist issues could be substantively at stake. If one has somehow convinced oneself that the incident, narrow time-framed focus is the appropriate *technique* for interpreting criminal law material, there is simply no background data one can use, either to provide the grist for a determinist account or to locate a prior sphere of choice in a seemingly constricted world. The interpretive "choice" between narrow and broad time frames affects not only controversial, doctrinally tricky legal cases, but also "easy" cases, because narrow time-framing fends off, at the methodological level, the possibility of doing determinist analyses.

**2.** Disjoined and unified accounts. A second unconscious interpretive construct relating to time involves the tension between disjoined and unified accounts of incidents. Many legally significant situations seem to require a somewhat broad time frame, at least in the sense that we feel we must look beyond a single moment in time and account, in some fashion, for some clearly relevant earlier moment. The earlier "moment" may be the time at which a defendant made some judgment about the situation she was in, some judgment that at least contributed to the ultimate decision to act criminally. For instance, the defendant negligently believes she must use deadly force to defend herself and then she intentionally kills someone, having formed that belief. Alternatively, the earlier moment may simply be the moment at which the defendant initiated the chain of events that culminated in criminal results. For instance, the defendant may shoot at X, but the bullet will miss X and then kill Y, an unforeseeably present bystander.

Once we agree to look at these earlier moments, we must decide whether to disjoin or unify the earlier moment with the later moment. We can treat all the relevant facts as constituting a single incident, or we can disjoin the events into two separate incidents.

Once this arational interpretive decision is made, the question of criminal culpability is forever biased. Is a negligent decision to kill followed by an intentional killing a negligent or intentional act? Is the person who misses X and shoots Y someone who commits two crimes—attempted murder of X plus, say, reckless homicide of Y—or one crime—an intentional murder of a person? Sometimes, unifying two arguably separate incidents allows us to avoid making a hard-to-justify assertion that the arguably second incident or decision was determined by the first. Often, other interests are at stake in separating or joining a series of incidents.

**3.** Broad and narrow views of intent. A third unconscious construct involves broad and narrow views of intent. Each time someone acts, we can say with fair confidence that, in the absence of some claim of accident, he intended to do precisely the acts that he has done. But we have difficulty categorizing those acts, because an individual set of acts may, in the observer's eyes, be an instance of a number of different categories of acts. For example, when the defendant intends to undertake certain deeds constituting a particular crime, it feels both misleading in significant ways, and perfectly proper in others, to assert that the defendant intended the particular crime. On one hand, it is odd to think of actors as viewing the world in criminal law categories when they act. On the other hand, it is equally odd to think of actors as focusing in their consciousness only on the most precise physical motions they undertake. Thus, when we talk of the requisite intent to commit assault *with intent* to commit murder, it is peculiar to think *either* that the defendant must have mentally focused his conduct on the broadly interpreted *crime* of murder (with all its complications, *e.g.*, that he must intend to act with malice, premeditation, nonprovocation, nonjustification, etc.), or that it is sufficient that he simply focused on the physical *motions* which would predicate the crime (*e.g.*, pulling the trigger on the gun, which we may deem murder if, in fact, he acted with what we call malice, nonprovocation, etc.).

Similarly, a defendant may perform suspicious acts not in themselves criminal or abandon a particular criminal attempt. We wonder whether the defendant, in the first case, can accurately be thought of as intending only the precise acts he committed or whether, in some broader sense, he *intended* some apter deeds which we would deem criminal acts. Likewise, in the second case, we wonder whether the defendant abandoned only the one criminal incident or abandoned the criminal category of which that incident is but an instance.

**4.** Broad and narrow views of the defendant. A fourth unconscious construct is that the interpreter may view defendants in broad or narrow terms. Each defendant is a unique individual, with a unique set of perceptions and capabilities. Every crime is committed in a unique setting. At the same time, every defendant has general human traits, and is thus a representative of the broader category of human beings. Similarly, the setting in which a crime is committed is an instance of those settings in which the crime is generally committed, and the features of the more general situation could be ascribed to the particular situation. By varying our interpretive focus, by particularizing at times and categorizing at others, substantive criminal law reaches all manner of results. Shifts in these perspectives underlie efforts to make doctrinal categories appear more cogent than they actually are.

## B. Conscious Interpretive Constructs

Just as unconscious constructs shape the way we view disruptive incidents, conscious constructs settle doctrinal issues while obscuring the nondeductive nature of legal discourse. I discuss two forms of conscious construction: the choice between intentionalistic and deterministic accounts of human conduct, and the choice between stating legal commands in the form of precise rules or vague ad hoc standards. While judges and commentators seem to be aware of these constructs, they discuss them only as *general* philosophical themes in the criminal law.

But I will argue that any consciously stated "grand" choices elevating intentionalism or rules, determinism or standards, as *the* solution to legal dilemmas is inevitably partial. The "victory" of one framework or the other is a temporary one that can never be made with assurance or comfort. Each assertion manifests no more than a momentary expression of feelings that remain contradictory and unresolved. Most significantly, arguments based on these explicitly political issues feel less "legal" than arguments grounded in traditional doctrinal categories. Perhaps more important for this article, I will also argue that the *un-self-conscious* assertion of the inexorability of applying one or the other poles in these controversies to a particular setting settles many doctrinal issues, though the problematic nature of chosen doctrine would become more apparent if the use of interpretive constructs surfaced. In this sense, these interpretive constructs function just like the four unconscious constructs. Though they are conscious political positions when employed at a general level, they may function as unreasoned presuppositions that solve cases while obscuring the dissonant, fundamentally nondeductive nature of legal disclosure.

**1.** Intentionalism and determinism. Intentionalism is the principle that human conduct results from free choice. An intentionalist interpretation of an incident gives moral weight to autonomous choice and expresses the indeterminacy of future actions.[72] Determinism, on the other hand, implies that subsequent

---

[72] For a fuller account of responsibility-demanding existentialist phenomenology, see H. Fingarette, *The Self in Transformation: Psychoanalysis, Philosophy and the Life of the Spirit* (1963), pp. 162–169.

behavior is casually connected to prior events. A determinist interpretation considers behavior by looking backward, and it expresses no moral respect or condemnation of these predetermined acts.

Most basic issues of the criminal law are issues of the applicability of an intentionalist model.[73] Notions of blameworthiness and deterrence are both based on the assumption that criminal actors make intentional choices. Of course, criminal jurisprudence *acknowledges* the plausibility of a determinist discourse, but it *acts* as if the intentionalist discourse is ultimately complete, coherent, and convincing.[74] It is quite apparent, however, that standard criminal law doctrine often interprets facts in deterministic modes. For example, duress, insanity, and provocation are determinist excuses for otherwise criminal conduct.

2. Rules versus standards. An overarching conflict within our legal system pertains to the form that legal pronouncements should take.[75] Our legal system bounces fitfully between "clearly defined, highly administrable, general rules"[76] and "equitable standards producing ad hoc decisions with relatively little precedential value."[77]

Rules seem, on the positive side, capable of uniform and nonprejudicial application. They define spheres of autonomy and privacy and sphere of duty by giving clear notice to citizens of the legal consequences of their conduct. The void-for-vagueness and strict construction doctrines both resonate in the rule-respecting liberal tradition. On the negative side, rules will inevitably be both over-and underinclusive according to the purposes reasonably attributable to the law.[78] This not only leads to random injustice when particular culpable parties are acquitted[79] and nonculpable parties are convicted,[80] but it enables people to calculate privately optimal levels of undesirable behavior that are within the precise confines of the law.[81]

Standards alleviate the problems of nonpurposive applications of legal commands to particular cases. On the other hand, they may be difficult to administer or may be enforced in a biased, unequal, and uncertain fashion. The use of standards in the criminal law is rampant. Whether we are talking about requirements of "malice" in homicide law, looking at regulatory statutes that are

---

[73] The standard text writers all must at some point refute the relevance of determinism to the criminal law. See, *e.g.*, G. Fletcher, *Rethinking Criminal Law* (1978), paras 6.4.3, 10.3.1; J. Hall, *General Principles of the Criminal Law* (1960), pp. 455–460; H.L.A. Hart, *Punishment and Responsibility* (1968), pp. 28–31, 179–185; H. Packer, *The Limits of The Criminal Sanction* (1968), pp. 74–75; G. Williams, *The Criminal Law: General Part* (1961), pp. 547–49.

[74] See, *e.g. State v. Sikora* (1965) 44 N.J. 453 at 470, 210 A.2d 193, 202.

[75] A fuller account of this conflict, assessing as central to our legal culture, is given by Kennedy, *Form and Substance in Private Law Adjudication* (1976) 89 Harv. L. Rev. 1685.

[76] *ibid.*, p. 1685.

[77] *ibid.*

[78] Take a simple example: a statutory rape law designed to protect innocent girls from the sexual pressures of the sophisticated. In its rule form, the age of consent is given as, say, 16. Some girls under 16 will be perfectly sophisticated, however, and some over 16 will not be.

[79] See, *e.g. Lewis v. Commonwealth* (1945) 184 Va. 69 and (1945) 34 S.E.2d 389 (defendant not guilty of disorderly conduct on a bus when disorderly conduct statute referred only to cars, trains, and cabooses); *Rex v. Bazeley* (1799) 168 Eng. Rep. 517 (when embezzlement was not contemplated by traditional legal category of larceny, bank teller who appropriated a note found not guilty because it was in his possession when he appropriated it).

[80] See, *e.g. R. v. Dudley & Stephens* [1884] 14 Q.B. 273 at 288.

[81] This problem is better recognized in private law than in criminal law. It is perhaps the dominant problem in tax law, where the courts affirm the rights of taxpayers to minimize tax liabilities as long as they follow the rules, *e.g. Gregory v. Helvering* (1935) 293 U.S. 465, but recharacterize transactions when taxpayers characterizations fall outside of what "the statute intended." *Knetsch v. United States* (1960) 364 U.S. 361 at 365.

openly vague in proscribing *unreasonable* restraints of trade,[82] or considering the use of discretion in prosecution and sentencing, it is difficult to deny that avoiding vagueness is more important as ideology than in practice. In any argument within our culture, *both* of these modes of framing legal commands are simultaneously appealing and unappealing; neither has killer force. Because neither position can dominate the other, legal arguments about the desirable form of legal commands are not just oscillating, unsettled, and unbalanced, but the choice of one resolution or the other ultimately feels like a product of whim—a reflection of one's most recent overreaction to the follies of the previously adopted form.

## II. Unconscious interpretive constructs

Having examined the interpretive constructs in general, I shall now apply the four unconscious constructs to doctrinally "hard" cases in the substantive criminal law. This part illustrates how each construct is used and how certain results are apparently mandated only after an unwarranted interpretation is made. I shall also try in this section to account for the appearance of particular constructs in particular fact situations. Though I am generally skeptical of accounts of construction, it is most often my belief that interpretive construction appears to enable the legal analyst to avoid dealing with fundamental political problems.

### A. Broad and Narrow Time Frames

**1.** Narrow time-framing. Generally speaking, narrow time frames buttress the traditionally asserted intentionalism of the criminal justice system. In a number of doctrinal areas, though, conduct is deemed to be involuntary or otherwise outside the responsibility of the defendant even though, if we interpret the relevant legal material as including earlier decisions (that is, if we broaden the time frame), we can interpret the *course* of conduct that culminates in criminal harm as chosen.

*Status versus conduct distinction.* The tensions of time-framing are evident in the status versus conduct distinction. In *United States v. Moore,*[83] Judge Wright, in dissent, argued that a statute proscribing narcotics possession should not apply to drug addicts, because possession merely manifests their status of being addicted. He contended that drug addicts cannot be deterred from or blamed for possessing narcotics *because* their addiction rendered them choiceless. Since punishment is inappropriate unless its deterrence or retributory aims are met, it is inapt here.

Fully addicted people truly may not be deterrable by the prospect of punishment at the *moment* when they decide to possess or use drugs. In Judge Wright's narrow view of the relevant legal material, the defendant may be nondeterrable because his then-pressing desire makes him oblivious to the costs imposed by state punishment. But once we broaden the time frame, we can see that even the particular use by the addict in *Moore* would have been less likely if addicts were punished. Assuming, as one must in applying deterrence theories, that actors calculate rationally and try to avoid pain, we know that if a person can be punished at *any* future time he uses drugs, not just in the pre-addiction period, he will be less prone to start using drugs. But, of course, if the person who ultimately came to trial had not made the initial uses, he would not have become an addict or made the particular use we are concerned with.

Precisely the same objection can be made to Judge Wright's argument that the status of addiction cannot be deemed blameworthy. Even if we should not blame people for *being* sick, we may well blame them for *becoming* sick. The addict may

---

[82] See, *e.g.* 15 U.S.C. § 45 (a) (1976; and Supp. III, 1979).
[83] 486 F.2d 1139 (DC Cir. 1973).

seem blameless in the narrow time frame, but in a broader time frame he may well be blameworthy. Certainly, it is not at all uncommon or bizarre for a parent to blame (and punish) a child who goes out of the house in a storm without adequate raingear for *getting* a cold, even though the same parent would punish the child for the "status" of *being* ill. Venereal disease is another clear case: That VD is generally considered a disease hardly precludes us from blaming its victims, because they *contracted* it through *earlier* voluntary acts.[84]

Judge Wright dismissed, in conclusory fashion, the possibility of using a broader time frame in assessing retributive demands.[85] Presumably, Judge Wright used a very *narrow* time frame here to reach the determinist result he would like to reach by using the very *broadest* one: I surmise that the judge actually believes that the initial "voluntary" drug uses are themselves determined by social and environmental pressures that predate those early uses. Despairing of the possibility of applying a very wide time focus and a more general determinism, he avoided this political confrontation by constructing the legal "material" in terms of the traditional *incident* focus, a focus which the majority implicitly rejected in the following conclusory terms:

> The gist of appellant's argument is that "the common law has long held that the capacity to control behavior is a prerequisite for criminal responsibility."
>
> It is inescapable that the logic of appellant's argument, if valid, would carry over to all other illegal acts of any type whose purpose was to obtain narcotics.[86]

It we take it as given that we *must* punish the people we are now punishing— and a lot of those people are stealing to obtain narcotics—then we must avoid Judge Wright's incident-based determinism. But this is simply a functionalist complacency, the belief that things are right because they are done: a world view hardly more or less acceptable than any other political assertion (*e.g.*, things can be presumed to be wrong, if done, because the world we see is pretty crummy), and hardly the outcome of piercing legal analysis.

*The voluntary act requirement.* Unconscious shifting between broad and narrow time frames also arises in applying the criminal law's voluntary act requirement. In *Martin v. State*,[87] police officers arrested the defendant at his home and took him onto a public highway, where the defendant used loud and profane language. He was convicted under a statute prohibiting public exhibition of a drunken condition. The appellate court reversed, holding that the defendant was involuntarily and forcibly carried to the public place by the arresting officers. The court concluded, uncontroversially, that an involuntary act cannot give rise to liability.[88] But in *People v. Decina*,[89] the court sustained the defendant's conviction

---

[84] In his concurring opinion in *Robinson v. California* (1962) 370 U.S. 660 at 676–78, Justice Douglas argued that it is unconstitutionally cruel and unusual to punish a person for being an addict, since addiction is an illness. But why are we morally duty-bound to treat, rather than to condemn, sick people, if we believe that having an illness is not an inevitably disconnected incident, but may be part of an historical process to which the ill person voluntarily contributed?

[85] Judge Wright noted that "there may have been a time in the past before the addict lost control when he made a conscious decision to use drugs. But imposition of punishment on this basis would violate the long-standing rule that [t]he law looks to the immediate, and not to the remote cause; to the actual state of the party, and not to the causes, which remotely produced it." '486 F.2d at 1243 (quoting *United States v. Drew*, 25 F. Cas. 913 at914(C.C.D. Mass. 1828).

[86] 486 F.2d at 1145.

[87] (1944) 31 Ala. App. 334 and 17 So. 2d 427.

[88] *ibid.* at 335 and 17 So. 2d at 427.

[89] 2 N.Y. 2d. 133 at 138; N.E.2d 799; (1956) 157 N.Y.S.2d 558.

for negligent homicide, though at the time his car struck the victims, he was unconscious as a result of an epileptic fit, not voluntarily operating the vehicle. The court held that the defendant was culpable because he had made a conscious decision to drive, knowing that an epileptic attack was possible.[90]

The hidden interpretive time-framing construct becomes visible when one tries to square *Martin* with *Decina*. In *Decina*, the court opened up the time frame, declaring that if the defendant commits a voluntary act at time one which poses a risk of causing an involuntary harm later—drives the car knowing he is a blackout-prone epileptic—then the second act—crashing while unconscious—will be deemed voluntary. But the defendant in *Martin*, as well, may have done *something* (voluntarily (before the police came) that posed a risk that he would get arrested and carried into public in his drunken state. While it is plausible that Martin was arrested on an old warrant and could not foresee that he would wind up in public on this occasion, it is quite possible that the defendant was arrested for activity he was engaging in his home: for instance, beating his wife.[91] Why did the court not consider saying that the voluntary act at time one (wife beating) both posed a risk of and caused a harmful involuntary act at time two (public drunkenness) and assessing the voluntariness of the alleged criminal act with reference to the wider time-framed scenario? It cannot be that the involuntary, harmful act at time two was unforeseeable: The probability of an epileptic blackout is almost certainly far lower than the probability of ending up in public after engaging in behavior likely to draw police attention. Arguments that we are less concerned with people "thinking ahead" to avoid public drunkenness than unconscious driving seem inadequate as well; the penalties for public drunkenness are presumably set lower to reflect the relative lack of gravity of the offense. Ultimately, the *Martin* finding of voluntariness "works" not because it is "right," but because all the hard points disappear in the initial interpretive construction of the potentially relevant facts. [591–605]

**2.** Broad time-framing. Much criminal law doctrine departs from the traditional incident focus and opens up the time frame. Broad time frame construction is most often used when deterministic discourse supplants the usual in-tentionalism. The substantive doctrines of duress, subjective entrapment, provocation and insanity are examples of such uses of broad time-framing. These doctrines describe how certain blameworthy acts are in fact blameless because rooted in or determined by factors that preceded the criminal incident. The question, of course, is why the broad time frame is selected in these cases, while it continues to be excluded as methodologically inappropriate in most other cases for no apparent reason.

Broad time-framing unrelated to determinism and intentionalism also occurs in other areas of the substantive criminal law. The time frame can be opened up to account for events both prior and subsequent to the criminal incident.

*Abandonment.* The basic decision to allow *any* abandonment defense allows a wide time-framed interpretive construction.[92] The defendant has already committed some act which, if interrupted by external forces, would constitute an offense, an attempt of some other substantive crime. Yet we judge the act

---

[90] *ibid.* at 139–140; 138 N.E.2d at 803–804; 157 N.Y.S.2d at 565.

[91] Courts do not examine whether the defendant's voluntary acts brought the police to his home just prior to the arrest. Instead, they unconsciously use a narrow time frame in assessing voluntariness.

[92] See, *e.g.* Model Penal Code 5.01 (4) (Tent. Draft No. 10, 1960), exculpating an actor who completely and voluntarily renounces an unconsummated criminal plan, even though he has already done enough so that were he interrupted by external forces, he would be guilty of contempt. *Cf. People v. Staples* 6 Cal. App. 3d 61, 85 Cal. Rptr. 589 (2d Dist. 1970) (denying that voluntary abandonment is a good defense).

innocent because of the defendant's *subsequent* failure to consummate the harm. Although many reasons for this widened time frame have been offered, none overcomes the fundamentally nonrational, interpretive aspect of the initial broadening of focus. Some deterrence-oriented theorists suggest that an abandonment defense provides incentives to avoid the consummation of harm.[93] But there are surely a number of "completed" crimes whose harm can be as effectively "undone" as can be abandoned attempt: An embezzler, for instance, may return money to victims unaware of their loss[94] and "undo" as much harm as the person who desists from an assault with intent to commit rape because the victim talks him out of continuing.[95]

Retributively oriented commentators note that abandonment makes us reassess our version of the defendant's blameworthiness or deviance.[96] Of course, if we admitted evidence of post-criminal conduct (whether remorse, restitution, condonation, or reform) into *every* trial, we would frequently change our views of the defendant's blameworthiness. Once more, the act of interpretation, the open time frame, *allows* the policy conclusion.

Broad time-framing is used in the abandonment area because the general rule-oriented nature of the criminal law has already stumbled in the less rule-like attempt area. Attempt law is generally problematic in our legal culture because it is inexorably less rule-like than the law of consummated harms; the actus reus of "attempting" refers not so much to particular proscribed acts[97] as to unavoidably noncategorizable acts which, in the particular case, seem to give evidence of the particular defendant's subjective disposition to act criminally. To commit rape is to force carnal knowledge of a woman; to attempt rape is to do sufficient acts to indicate that one *would* force carnal knowledge. Whether the requisite "sufficient" acts include the precise acts of undressing, fondling, cornering, isolating from public view, using force, and/or simply implying that force will be used is inevitably a case-by-case determination. I suspect that the use of a forward-looking broad time frame in considering the blameworthiness of an attempter is the predictable outcome of the breakdown of the rule-like form. The system demands all available information about defendant's blameworthiness, taken from as wide a period as possible, as soon as it departs from the rule-like form.

The attachment to overtly political Rule of Law ideals *precludes* a general broadening of time focus in the traditional consummated harm case; the idea is that blameworthiness must be conclusively presumed from the performance of one of the proscribed acts in one of the narrow time-framed blameworthy fashions. Once we allow ourselves to recognize the breakdowns in our inevitably imprecise conclusive presumptions, we see the strains of legalism. To recognize that we were probably thinking about the unremorseful, nonrestitutionary thief when we set out general penalties for larceny is to remind ourselves of the limit of the universalistic model. But we can avoid overtly political defenses of obviously inapt conclusive presumptions by implying that, as a matter of *method*, our factual inquiry simply does not go forward once a criminal act is complete.

The undefended, but deviant, broad time frame appears in constructing an abandonment defense because of the inevitable breakdown of pure legalist form in the attempt area. Since we *cannot* infer blame from a single act, because no such act is present in attempting, we move, at the very least, to more partial Rule of Law strictures: We try to infer a disposition to perform one of the still automatically blameworthy acts. But this does not imply, as Fletcher seems to believe,

---

[93] See, *e.g.* W. LaFave & A. Scott, *Handbook on Criminal Law* (1972), para. 60, at 450; G. Williams, *Criminal Law General Part* (1961), pp. 620–621.

[94] G. Fletcher, *Rethinking Criminal Law* (1978), 3.3.8 at 186.

[95] *ibid.*

[96] See *Le Barron v. State* (1966) 32 Wis. 2d 294 and 145 N.W.2d 79.

[97] G. Fletcher, *supra*, n. 94, 3.3.8 at 187–188.

the *logical* necessity of allowing an abandonment defense: Once one performs acts indicating a firm intention to commit blameworthy criminal acts, there is no rational reason not to treat the performance of these acts as conclusively presumed proof of criminal intent. Of course, such a conclusive presumption would be inaccurate, as all conclusive presumptions are; the abandoning defendant demonstrates that our presumption that defendants who have "attempted" are firmly resolved to commit crimes is sometimes wrong. But the remorseful consummated criminal would equally well demonstrate that conclusive presumptions about the need to incapacitate, reform, or blame a person because he has committed some crime can be inapt. The abandonment defense, then, appears not because a forward-looking broad time frame is logically better suited to attempt law, but because the always available policy attacks on rules (and conclusive presumptions) are allowed to sway only in an area where the rule-form is already weakened by the imprecision of the definition of the act upon which criminal liability is predicated.

*Consent.* Problems of time-framing also appear in deciding whether consent has been given to otherwise criminal acts. Assuming, arguendo, that no action is harmful which the *subject* assents to, we still can *identify* the supposedly consenting subject using either a broad or a narrow time frame. We can look into the subject's past or just at a single moment of assent. Should that moment be immediately before the act is performed? If the victim at one point did not assent to the harmful act but has assented to it right before the act is taken, has he assented to it? When Odysseus demands at one point to be bound up when the Sirens sing, and *later* demands to be released, which choice most fulfills his "desires"? When someone goes on a diet, do you give him the piece of chocolate cake he begs for if you are trying to do *his* will? That we have no ready rules of thumb—*e.g.*, "last statement counts," or "statements made under oath count"— can be seen not just from these sorts of explicitly ambivalent expressions over time, but by noting that we vary our definitions of assent to account for *implicit suppositions* of ambivalence over time. For instance, in ordinary commercial dealings, a simple nod and a grunted, "I'll take that box of strawberries for 59 cents" allows the other actor to consummate a sale without much fear of harming the buyer. But if someone grunts, "I wish you'd kill me," we do not take the remark as manifesting welfare-maximizing assent on which the would-be killer is entitled to act.

In terms of broadening the time frame backward, we must also determine whether the origins of preference formation should be considered. Does it matter if the assent follows threats or bribes (restricted determinism) or a warped childhood (fuller determinism)? Does it matter whether the subject chose these influences or that, ultimately, no one privately chooses the most basic influences? Is the subject we are interested in the developing person or only that person who actually developed?[98]

Just as significant—and perhaps more operationally significant to judicial efforts to define consent—is whether we open the time frame to account for beliefs held subsequent to the action, too. Do we require that the subject not regret or disown the earlier choice before we exculpate the defendant? It is perfectly plausible that a defendant be deemed guilty of a "harmful" assault if there is ultimately a complainant: that the harm may be revealed only *after* the fact. A philosophical scheme that denies the possibility that one can harm those who have consented to one's acts seems mechanically workable only if we define the consenting subject in the narrowest time frame, accounting only for preferences

---

[98] See, *e.g.* H. Gintis, *Consumer Behavior and the Concept of Sovereignty: Explanations of Social Decay* (1972) 62 Am. Econ. Rev. 267 (discussing the development in a capitalist society of taste for private appropriation of goods rather than for "community" and "meaningful work").

expressed by the subject at the moment of defendant's conduct. This definition of the consenting subject is hardly compelling, however, since it is unlikely that the victim dissociates himself into a disconnected series of assenters. More likely, the subject views himself as a person with a continuous personal identity, a person concerned about later reevaluation of current decisions and the impact of past pressures on choice.

Ultimately, the narrow time-framed view of consent serves a vital *ideological* function, though it produces rather trivial criminal law results. Narrow time-framing here may serve not so much to deny the criminality of otherwise culpable drug sellers, sex criminals, or prostitutes, but to buttress the ideological argument for the beneficence of untrammeled markets, to certify the wage-work trade and buyer-seller dealings as nonexploitative and harmonious, without regard to the historical, wide time-framed conditions in which these "deals" occur.[99] [611–616]

## V. Conclusion

I can interpret my own task of deconstructing rhetoric in three distinct, though not wholly incompatible, fashions. First, I can view the piece as a rather traditional legal realist's plea for the "politicization" of legal disclosure. One might view my arguments as having the following structure: The courts and commentators purport to solve the particular doctrinal dilemma, but their "solutions" use an unsupportable "interpretation" or "characterization" to make the case appear manageable. Had they been doing "good" legal analysis, they would instead "balance" the substantive policy concerns at stake to reach a well-reasoned result.

I have very limited sympathy for this account. First of all, this account fails to come to grips with a central and undeniable fact: Perfectly competent and intelligent commentators continue to mask so-called policy with a powerful residual conceptualism. The commentators I have cited are hardly Langdellians, the courts hardly premodern. I am dealing almost exclusively with the masters of realist thinking. Second, and quite related, I sense that the policy-balancing act that the traditional realist advocates *never* takes very full hold, both because it renders all legal outcomes highly ad hoc and because it makes legal discourse seem less distinct from nonlegal argument. Third, by failing to deconstruct the mechanisms needed to maintain the persistence of conceptualist solutions, traditional realists are unable to see that culture's *blindness* to its constructs is critical. Thought takes on a natural, apolitical, noncontingent quality unless it is subject to ordered deconstruction.

A second plausible account of my work is that I am attempting to account for the existence of interpretive construction, and that identifying the forms that characterization takes is just one important step towards understanding the process of interpretation at a broader level. At various points I have accounted for the appearance of a particular interpretive construct as manifesting a simple class conflict between those protecting the position that the legal system routinely allows them from sudden, incidental disruption, and those disfavored by the routine distortion of benefits that the legal system generates. Naturally, those disfavored by the ordinary legal distributions of economic power are most prone to use means generally considered criminal.

Interpretive construction could play very distinct roles in this class conflict. It is possible that each construction might correspond to the political program of a social class. I would call this view "construction determinism": a belief that the interpretive technique an analyst uses is itself a product of the social class he politically supports. Alternatively, each legal *result* could correspond to the

---

[99] For a more in-depth discussion of the relationship between single-moment choices and desires manifested over time in the context of traditional neoclassical welfare economics, see M. Kelman, *Choice and Utility* (1979) Wis. L. Rev. 769, 778–787.

political program of a social group, and interpretive construction may serve simply to *cover up* the result-oriented, overtly political nature of resolving disputes. I would call this view "result determinism": a belief that the "bottom line" of any case results from class conflict, and the interpretive technique is just a ruse to hide a primitive assertion of power to promote one's selfish interests behind a mask of legal deductions. Finally, it may be that maintaining the appearance (or illusion) of legal argument is a significant political program of any dominant social class, so that making formal arguments which do not refer to the unexplainable interpretation—that actually ground the arguments may sometimes be more vital than maintaining either the construction or particular results. I would call this "legal form determinsim": a belief that the preservation of the faith in an orderly, nonarbitrary distribution of political and economic benefits is more central to dominant classes than either the result of any particular case or the preservation of the dominance of any one construction.

Throughout the essay, I have proffered all these sorts of explanations. I argued, for instance, in Part IV, that the most basic task of dominant group is to identify criminality with disruption, with incidents that break the ordinary flow of distribution of burdens and benefits. My claim was that certain characterizations or constructions are most compatible with that end. In Part II, I frequently gave "result-oriented" explanations, made claims that an advocate of a certain position constructs the legal material simply to reach a desired result, and that the result is based on some *real* interest in winning a certain class of cases, either because they are significant to maintaining economic or political control or because they help solidify a certain ideological story that is helpful to maintaining domination. Finally, even in those cases when it seemed as if no one could possibly care about construction form or results in a particular setting, there is always the fallback claim that a legal system ought not to have gaps; it ought to look as if *every* case can be resolved by some similar "scientific" method.

A third account of my enterprise is that the interpretive constructs I note are not politically meaningful at all, but simply inexplicably unpatterned mediators of experience, the inevitably nonrational filters we need to be able to perceive or talk at all. If that were the case, my role would be largely aesthetic: I speak on behalf of those who no longer like to listen to people making arguments that mask a hidden structure of "nonarguments" with insistent, false rigor. In the preface to their property casebook, Professors Casner and Leach wrote that, "In order to move the student along the road of becoming a lawyer, he must be subjected to close analytical testing that rejects generalities or approximations. We think this must come at the beginning of his law study to get him to recognize and abhor superficiality."[1] I don't know whether to laugh or cry. When the unwarranted conceptualist garbage is cleared away, dominant legal thought is nothing *but* some more or less plausible common-wisdom banalities, superficialities, and generalities, little more on close analysis than a tiresome, repetitive assertion of complacency that we do pretty well, all considered, when you think of all the main concerns we've got to balance." Legal thought *does* have its rigorous moments, but these are largely grounded in weak and shifting sands. There is some substance, but we tend to run for cover when it appears.

In the criminal law, two substantive concerns recur. Intentional action and rule-like form are purportedly necessary to construct our, ordinary jurisprudence. But no one truly believes in absolute intentionalism in rules, though the departures from the polar positions are vague and weakly defended. We must avoid the issues in order to talk like lawyers, partly because we have so little to say about them that is not deeply contradictory and ambivalent. What is worse for the lawyer rhetoritician is that when we assert a bottom line, we are rarely very convincing. We rarely do more than restate some utterly nonlegal functionalist

[1] A. Casner & W. Leach, *Cases and Text on Property* (2nd ed. 1969, vol. vii).

preference, some pompous version of Pollyana's principles, or some equally nonlegal anger or contempt for a system which the comfortable beneficiaries of a rule structure cash in on their strengths and self-righteously condemn those marginalized in the most central social and collective decisions—the decisions about how rights, duties, and privileges are created and enforced. Rather than face our inability to speak, we hide the uses of standards and determinist discourses, or proclaim, loudly if not clearly, that when we are *obviously* using them, we are in an "exceptional" circumstance.

Most often, we avoid the issues altogether by constructing the legal material in terms of apparently well-established conceptualist dogma looking to concepts that, at some broad level, are doubtless "justified" (somewhere or other). As best I can tell, we do these interpretive constructions utterly un-self-consciously. I have never seen or heard anyone declare that they are framing time broadly or narrowly, unifying or disjoining an incident, broadly or narrowly categorizing a defendant's actual or required intent or a defendant's being or circumstances, let alone explain why they are doing it. It is illuminating and disquieting to see that we are nonrationally constructing the legal world over and over again; it is a privilege to discern some structure to this madness, a privilege one gets when a system feels unjust and unnatural. The outsider sees patterns that the insider committed to keeping the enterprise afloat, never sees, structuring the practices of others is a funny and fun form of dismissal.

One real conclusion, one possible bottom line, is that I've constructed a very elaborate, schematized, and conceptual piece of winking dismissal: Here's what they say, this is how far they have gotten. You know what? There's not much to it.                                                                                          [669–673]

## CLARE DALTON
### An Essay In The Deconstruction of Contract Doctrine
### (1985)[2]

*Doctrine, the cohabitation contract, and beyond*

Doctrinal arguments cast in terms of public and private, manifestation and intent, and form and substance, continue to exert a stranglehold on our thinking about concrete contractual issues. By ordering the ways in which we perceive disputes, these arguments blind us to some aspects of what the disputes are actually about. By helping us categorize, they encourage us to simplify in a way that denies the complexity, and ambiguity, of human relationships. By offering us the false hope of definitive resolution, they allow us to escape the pain, and promise, of continual reassessment and accommodation. . . .

I illustrate the poverty of traditional doctrinal arguments by examining the use of contract doctrine in recent cases involving the agreements of non-marital cohabitants. . . . Distinctions between private and public realms, between contracts implied-in-fact and contracts implied-in-law, play an important part in the decisions. Interpretive questions and questions about the basis for enforcement—about consideration—also loom large, reiterating the concern with private and public, but couching that concern in the competing terms of subjective and objective, form and substance.

Significantly, the opinions largely ignore the aspect of the public-private debate that appears in contract doctrine as the set of rules governing duress and unconscionability. The concerns of those doctrines—preventing oppression of both by the state—are nonetheless highly relevant. For at the heart of these cases lies the problem of power. It is only because the exercise of power in this context is

---

[2] [From (1985) 94 Yale L.J. 997.]

not seen as fitting the traditional rubrics of duress and unconscionability that courts are able to ignore and avoid it.

Once the convoluted play of doctrine in this area has been exposed, we can see that traditional doctrinal formulations are not the only means for understanding how and why decisionmakers reach their decisions. At this point, other inquiries become both possible and legitimate. In suggesting what some of those other inquiries might be, my conclusion points toward possible ways of expanding our thinking about the issues of contract law.

*The Cases*

State courts have increasingly confronted cases involving various aspects of the cohabitation relationship, and their decisions have attracted a fair amount of scholarly attention.[3] I focus on two such decisions: that of the California Supreme Court in *Marvin v. Marvin*,[4] and that of the Illinois Supreme Court in *Hewitt v. Hewitt*.[5]

In *Marvin*, Justice Tobriner addressed the question of whether the plaintiff Michelle Triola, who have lived with the defendant, Lee Marvin, for seven years, could recover support payments and half the property acquired in Lee Marvin's name over the course of the relationship. The court found that the plaintiff, in alleging an oral contract, had stated a cause of action in express contract, and further found that additional equitable theories of recovery might be applicable. On remand, the trial court found that there existed neither an express contract nor unjust enrichment, but awarded the plaintiff equitable relief in the nature of rehabilitative alimony. The court of appeals then struck this award on the theory that relief could be granted only on the basis of express contract or quasi-contract.

The alleged oral agreement provided that plaintiff and defendant would, while they live together, combine their efforts and earnings and share equally any property accumulated. They agreed to present themselves publicly as husband and wife. Triola also undertook to serve as the defendant's companion, homemaker, housekeeper, and cook. A later alleged modification to the contract provided that Triola would give up her own career in order to provide these services; in return, Marvin promised to support Triola for the rest of her life. The relationship ended when Marvin threw Triola out.

The plaintiff in *Hewitt* was in many respects a more sympathetic figure than Michele Triola. When she and Mr Hewitt were both college students, she became pregnant. He then proposed that they live together as man and wife, presenting

---

[3] For illustrative cases, see *Jones v. Daly* (1981) 122 Cal. App. 3d 500 and 176 Cal. Rptr. 130; *Donovan v. Scuderi*, 51 Md. App. 217, 443 A. 2d 121 (Ct Spec. App. 1982); *Kinnison v. Kinnison*, 627 P.2d 594 (Wyo. 1981); *see also* Blumberg, *Cohabitation Without Marriage: A Different Perspective* (1981) 28 UCLA L. Rev. 1125, 1125 n.2 (collecting cases). For illustrative articles, see Blumberg, *op. cit.*; Crutchfield, *Nonmarital Relationships and Their Impact on the Institution of Marriage and the Traditional Family Structure* (1980–1981) 19 J. Fam. L. 247; Deech, *The Case Against Legal Recognition of Cohabitation* (1980) 29 Int'l & Comp. L.Q. 480; Fineman, *Law and Changing Patterns of Behavior: Sanctions on Non-Marital Cohabitation* (1981) Wisc. L. Rev. 275; Case Comment, *Property Rights Upon Termination of Unmarried Cohabitation: Marvin v. Marvin* (1977) 90 Harv. L. Rev. 1708.

[4] (1976) 18 Cal. 3d 660; 557 P.2d 106; and 124 Cal. Rptr. 815. *Marvin* also generated a subsequent appeals court decision interesting in its own right. *See Marvin v. Marvin*, (1981) 122 Cal. App. 3d 871; 176 Cal. Rptr. 555.

[5] (1979) 77 Ill.2d 49; 394 N.E.2d 1204. The lower appeals court opinion in *Hewitt* (1978) 62 Ill. App. 3d 861; 380 N.E.2d 454 (reversing dismissal on grounds that public policy did not disfavor grant of mutually enforceable property rights to knowingly unmarried cohabitants in non-meretricious relationship), provides a perfect counterpoint to its Supreme Court successor.

themselves as such to their families and friends, and that he thereafter share his life, future earnings, and property with her. She borrowed money from her family to put him through professional school, worked with him to establish his practice, bore him three children and raised them, and otherwise fulfilled the role of a traditional wife. After over fifteen years he left her. She sought an equal division of property acquired during the relationship and held either in joint tenancy or in the defendant's name.

The appeals court ruled that she could have an equitable share of the property if she were able to prove her allegation of an express oral contract, although it did not preclude the possibility of alternative equitable theories of recovery in appropriate circumstances. The Supreme Court of Illinois reversed, basing its decision principally on considerations of public policy.

### Express and Implied Agreement

The opinions in the cohabitation cases indicate that the distinction between the intention-based express contract and the public institution of quasi-contract may be central to the question of whether to grant relief. ... Techniques for interpreting the express contract are indistinguishable from techniques used to determine the presence of a quasi-contractual relationship. If the interpretive techniques employed highlight factors external to the parties and their actual intentions, even express contracts seem very public. If, in contrast, the techniques used have as their stated goal the determination of the parties' intentions, then quasi-contracts appear no less private or consensual than express contracts. The cohabitation opinions employ both public-sounding and private-sounding arguments to reach a variety of conclusions. In some cases courts determine that the parties are bound by *both* real and quasi-contractual obligations, in others that they are bound by neither, in yet others that they are bound by one but not the other. The arguments do not determine these outcomes—they only legitimate them.

In these cases there is a common presumption that agreements between intimates are not contractual. While this model of association was developed in husband-wife and parent-child cases, non-marital cohabitants are assumed, for these purposes, to have the same kind of relationship. ... Express words are taken to be words of commitment but not of contract; conduct that in other circumstances would give rise to an implied-in-fact contract is instead attributed to the relationship.[6]

One possible explanation for this presumption against finding contracts is that it accords with the parties' intentions. It can be argued that cohabitants generally neither want their agreements to have legal consequences, nor desire to be obligated to one another when they have stopped cohabitating. It can further be presented as a matter of fact that their services are freely given and taken within the context of an intimate relationship. If this is so, then a subsequent claim of unjust enrichment is simply unfounded.

This intention-based explanation, however, coexists in the opinions—indeed sometimes coexists within a single opinion—with two other, more overtly public, explanations that rest on diametrically opposed public policies. The first suggests that the arena of intimate relationships is too private for court intervention

---

[6] In *Balfour*, Lord Justice Duke stated:
   It was said that a promise and an implied undertaking between strangers, such as the promise and implied undertaking alleged in this case would have founded an action on contract. That may be so, but it is impossible to disregard in this case what was the basis of the whole communications between the parties ... The basis of their communications was their relationship of husband and wife, a relationship which creates certain obligations, but not that which is here put in suit.
   *Balfour v. Balfour* [1919] 2 K.B. 571 at 576, *per* Duke L.J.

through contract enforcement to be appropriate. In *Hewitt*, for example, the Illinois Supreme Court suggests that "the situation alleged here was not the kind of arm's length bargain envisioned by traditional contract principles, but an intimate arrangement of a fundamentally different kind.[7]

While it has some intuitive appeal, the argument that intimate relationships are too private for court enforcement is at odds with the more general argument that all contractual relationships are private and that contract enforcement merely facilitates the private relationships described by contract. To overcome this apparent inconsistency, we must imagine a scale of privateness on which business arrangements, while mostly private, are still not as private as intimate arrangements. But then the rescue attempt runs headlong into the other prevailing policy argument, which separates out intimate arrangements because of their peculiarly public and regulated status. Under this view, it is the business relationship that by and large remains more quintessentially private.

According to this second argument, the area of non-marital agreements is too public for judicial intervention. The legislature is the appropriate body to regulate such arrangements; courts may not help create private alternatives to the public scheme. In *Hewitt*, the supreme court directly follows this appeal to the intimate nature of the relationship with an acknowledgement of the regulated, and hence public, character of marriage-like relations. With respect to intimate relations conceived as public, the judiciary can then present itself as either passive or active. The argument for passivity is that judges should "stay out" of an arena already covered by public law. The argument for activity is that judges should reinforce public policy by deterring the formation of deviant relationships, either because they fall outside the legislative schemes organizing familial entitlement and property distribution, or because they offend public morality.

Neither the private nor the public arguments for the absence of contract in this setting are conclusive. Both private and public counterarguments are readily available. If the absence of contract is presented as flowing from party intention, competing interpretations of intention can be used to argue the presence of contract. If, within a more public framework, the court categorizes the concerns implicated by the relationship as private, then an argument can be made that within the boundaries expressly established by legislation, the parties should be free to vary the terms of their relationship without interference by the state. If the focus is the place of cohabitation agreements within the publicly-regulated sphere of intimate relationships, then an argument can be made that certain kinds of enforcement in fact extend and implement public policy rather than derogate from it.

The availability of this range of intention-based and policy-based arguments makes possible virtually any decision. A court can find or not find a "real" contract. It can decide that enforcement of a real contract is or is not appropriate. It can decide that while real contracts should be enforced, there is no basis for awarding quasi-contractual relief in the absence of an expressed intention to be bound. It can decide that even in the absence of real contract, the restitutionary claim of the plaintiff represents a compelling basis for quasi-contractual relief. Further, the competing public and private strands of argument—each of which connects to both enforceability and non-enforceability arguments—can be used within the same opinion or other legal text, without the inconsistencies being so apparent as to undermine the credibility of the final result.

## Manifestation and Intent

Some identifiable, particular patterns do emerge from this overall confusion of public and private arguments. As with all agreements, for example, every aspect

---

[7] *Hewitt*, 77 Ill. 2d at 61; and 394 N.E.2d at 1209.

of a cohabitation agreement raises interpretive questions that will drive a court to search for the elusive correspondence between subjective intent and manifested form. Even this most private exercise of contractual interpretation thereby opens the doors to the imposition of public values, norms, and understandings. Two interpretive issues in particular recur in the cases. The courts repeatedly consider how to evaluate the relationships out of which the agreements arise. They also repeatedly consider how to evaluate the role of sex in these relationships and in these agreements. This section explores the very different ways in which the opinions treat these issues, within the range of options made available by current doctrine.

Courts frequently invoke the context of cohabitation relationships to avoid enforcing agreements arising out of them. The argument here is essentially that even if such agreements use language of promise, or commitment, or reciprocal obligation, that language must be understood, *in the intimate context in which it is employed*, as not involving any understanding that one party might use a court to enforce a duty forsaken, or a promise broken.

In theory, if the parties make perfectly clear their intention to be legally bound by their agreement, then their intention governs.[8] But this leaves open the question of when a court will find objective manifestations of such an intention to be bound. Will a written agreement be more susceptible to legal enforcement than an oral one? Will an agreement in which the reciprocal obligations relate to a particular piece of property or to a transaction that can be separated out, however artificially, from the affective context of the relationship convince a court that it has crossed the boundary between intimate unenforceability and business-like enforceability? These approaches all find some support in the cases, although their manipulability and their imperfect correspondence to questions of motivation and intention are obvious.

A second common theme employing notions of manifestation and intent is the specific role of sex in the parties' arrangements. The boundaries of this debate are set both by the tradition that precludes enforcement of prostitution contracts for reasons of public policy, and by the acknowledgement that even cohabiting parties may form valid contracts about independent matters. In the case of cohabitation agreements, the question therefore becomes whether the sex contemplated by the parties contaminates the entire agreement to the point where it is seen to fall within the model of the prostitution contract, or whether other features of the agreement can be seen as independent and enforceable.

Judges' differing interpretations of virtually identical agreements seem to depend quite openly on either their views of what policy should prevail or their own moral sense. Rarely does a judge even appear to make a thorough attempt to understand and enforce what the parties had in mind. For Justice Underwood in *Hewitt*, for example, nothing but "naivete" could explain the assertion that "there are involved in these relationships contracts separate and independent from the sexual activity, and the assumption that those contracts would have been entered into or would continue without that activity.[9]

Justice Tobriner in *Marvin*, on the other hand, rejects the idea that the sexual relationship between parties to a cohabitation contract renders the contract as a whole invalid. He explicitly uses the divide between object and subjective, form and substance, to carve out a much larger space for enforceable agreements than that envisaged by Underwood.[10] Tobriner's test has two components: Contracts between non-marital partners are enforceable unless they *explicitly* rest "upon the

---

[8] See *Balfour* [1919] 2 K.B. at 574, *per* Warrington, L.J. ("It may be, and I do not for a moment say that it is not, possible for such a contract as is alleged in the present case to be made between husband and wife. The question is whether such a contract was made.")

[9] 394 N.E.2d at 1209.

[10] *Marvin*, 18 Cal. 3d at 672; 557 P.2d at 114–115; 134 Cal. Rptr. at 823–824.

immoral and illicit consideration of meretricious sexual services."[11] Furthermore, such contracts are unenforceable only "*to the extent*" that they rest on this meretricious consideration.[12]

Tobriner is not so naive as to suppose that the Triola-Marvin agreement did not contemplate a sexual relationship. But he feels that the "subjective contemplation of the parties" is too "uncertain and unworkable" a standard.[13] He relies instead on formal criteria of intent—on the manifestations of agreement alleged by Triola—to determine if his two-part test of enforceability has been met. For the purposes of this analysis Tobriner describes the agreement as follows: "[T]he parties agreed to pool their earnings, . . . they contracted to share equally in all property acquired, and . . . defendant agreed to support plaintiff."[14] None of this strikes Tobriner as necessitating a conclusion that sex invalidates the agreement.[15]

Of course the formal criteria are themselves empty of significance until given meaning by judicial analysis. The very same language construed by Tobriner had been given very different effect in an earlier decision. In *Updeck v. Samuel*, a California District Court of Appeal considered the statement that the woman would make a permanent home for the man and be his companion as indicating precisely the sexual character of the relationship.[16] Unwilling or unable to disapprove *Updeck*, Tobriner is forced to distinguish this case in a fashion that directly undercuts the legitimacy of his stated reliance on form or manifestation. He argues that the *Updeck* agreement was found invalid because the Court "[v]iew[ed] the contract as calling for adultery."[17] But the very act of "viewing" the contract, or interpreting its terms, involves an explanation of substance. The court in *Updeck* supplied sexual substance, while Tobriner supplies economic substance. *Jones v. Daly*,[18] a case subsequent to *Marvin*, provides another striking illustration of the manipulability of form. In *Jones*, which involved a homosexual partnership, a California Court of Appeal denied relief on the ground that an agreement, in other respects almost identical to the *Marvin* agreement, contained the word "lover."

As the courts wrestle with these interpretive questions, we see them apparently infusing a public element, external to the parties' own view of their situation, into their assessment of cohabitation agreements. We also can see how this is a necessary result of the tension between manifestation and intent, of the way in which intent requires embodiment in manifested forms, even while the forms require an infusion of substance before they can yield meaning. Indeed, to accuse judges of moving from the private to the public sphere is only to accuse them of the inevitable. If there is force behind the accusation, it is not *that* they have made the transition *un-self-consciously*, and that the particular values, norms, and understandings they incorporate are different from the ones we would have

---

[11] *ibid.* at 669; 557 P.2d at 112; 134 Cal. Rptr. at 821.

[12] *ibid.*; 557 P.2d at 112; 134 Cal. Rptr. at 821 (emphasis in original). Severability as a device for rescuing the cohabitation agreement has proved popular. See *e.g. Rehak v. Mathis* (1977) 239 Ga. 541, 544; 238 S.E.2d 81, 82–83 (Hill, J., dissenting); *Donovan v. Scuderi*, 51 md. App. 217, 219; 443 A.2d 121, 123 (Ct Spec. App. 1982).

[13] *Marvin*, 18 Cal. 3d at 672; 557 P.2d at 114, 134 Cal. Rptr. at 823.

[14] *ibid.* at 674–75; 557 P.2d at 116, 134 Cal. Rptr. at 823.

[15] *ibid.*; 557 P.2d at 116, 134 Cal. Rptr. at 825.

[16] *Updeck v. Samuel* 123 Cal. App. 2d 264, 266, 267 P.2d 822, 824 (Dist. Ct App. 1954) (finding oral contract based on immoral consideration where both parties legally married to other spouses).

[17] *Marvin* 18 Cal. 3d at 671; 557 P.2d at 114, 134 Cal. Rptr. at 823. In *Marvin*, as in *Updeck*, the defendant was legally married to another spouse during at least a portion of the term of his contract with the plaintiff. *ibid.* at 667, 557 P.2d at 111; 134 Cal. Rptr. at 820.

[18] 122 Cal. App. 3d 500; 176 Cal. Rptr. 130 (Ct App. 1981).

favored, or different from the ones we think would correspond with those of one
or both of the parties to the agreement.

### Consideration: Its Substance

Consideration doctrine offers yet other opportunities for the conflation of public
and private, and the introduction of competing values, norms, and understandings into the resolution of these cohabitation cases. Just as in the area of
interpretation, the crucial additions are judicial conceptions of sexuality, and of
woman's role in her relationship with man. Two aspects of consideration doctrine
recur in the cases. Each illustrates the proposition that formal consideration
doctrine cannot be implemented without recourse to substance. Substance, here
as elsewhere, can be provided by assessments of objective value or by investigations into subjective intent. It is with respect to these substantive inquiries that
ideas about sexuality and relationship come to play so potentially important a
part.

The first use of consideration doctrine in this context shows up in the disin-
clination of courts to enforce contracts based on "meretricious" consideration.[19]
Courts frequently search beyond the express language of the agreement in order
to "find" that sex is at the heart of the deal—specifically that the woman is
providing sexual services in return for the economic security promised by the
man. Insofar as this investigation depends on divining what the parties had in
mind, consideration turns on subjective intent. For these purposes, it matters not
at all that "intent" has been derived from the judge's own feelings about such
relationships, even when the express language of the parties would appear to
point in an opposite direction.

The treatment of meretricious consideration also illustrates how consideration
may depend on a finding of objective value. When courts refuse to enforce contracts based on the exchange of sexual services for money, they are, for long-
standing policy reasons, declining to recognize sexual services as having the *kind*
of value that they will honor. This decision, based on an objective measure of
value, is no different from the decision that "nominal" consideration will not
support a contract. There, too, courts disregard intention in the name of a policy
that depends upon societal recognition of certain sorts of values and delegitimation of others.

The second aspect of consideration doctrine of interest in this context is the
traditional conclusion that the woman's domestic services cannot provide consideration for the promises made to her by the man. This is usually linked to the
idea that the relationship itself is not one the parties see as having a legal aspect.
The standard explanation is that the woman did not act in expectation of gain,
but rather out of affection, or that she intended her action as a gift.

Tobriner in the *Marvin* decision rejects this conclusion by recasting the issue as
one properly belonging in the selfish world of business. Unless homemaking
services are considered lawful and adequate consideration for a promise to pay
wages, the entire domestic service industry will founder. Just as plainly, such
services can provide the consideration for an agreement concerning property
distribution. Tobriner thus appeals to the substance of objective value: There is a
market in which domestic services receive a price; when intimates arrange that one
will deliver those same services to the other, that promise is therefore capable of
supporting a return promise.

Even as Tobriner uses ideas of objective value, however, his reasoning reveals
that the ultimate rationale for this aspect of consideration doctrine depends upon

---

[19] See *e.g. Hill v. Estate of Westbrook*, 95 Cal. App. 2d 599, 603; 213 P.2d 727, 730 (Dist. Ct
App. 1950); *Rehak v. Mathis* 239 Ga. at 543; 238 S.E.2d at 82; *Hewitt v. Hewitt* 77 Ill. 2d
at 58–59; 394 N.E.2d at 1208; *Donovan v. Scuderi* 51 Md. App. at 219; 443 A.2d at 123.

arguments of subjective intent. Like the promise in the *Michigan* case,[20] the services could constitute consideration if they were offered with the intention of bargain or exchange. It is only the altruistic context, revealing the beneficent intention, which invalidates them.

Thus, while one route of access into this issue threatens to expose the public determination of what value the law will and will not recognize, that route is apparently closed off by the reminder that it is private intention, not public power, that assigns value. But then the very public role abjured in the context of objective value is played out instead through the "finding" of intent according to criteria that are essentially and inevitably public rather than private.

## The Question of Power

Under duress and unconscionability doctrines, policing the "fair" exchange is tied irretrievably to asking whether each party entered into the contract freely, whether each was able to bargain in equally unconstrained ways, and whether the deal was a fair one. I suppose that any of us would find these questions even harder to answer in the context of intimate relationships than in other contexts—harder in that we would require a much more detailed account of the particulars before we could hazard an opinion, and harder in that even this wealth of detail would be likely to yield contradictory interpretations. Yet we acknowledge the important of these questions in the area of intimate relations; we do not imagine either that most couples wind up with a fair exchange, or that most couples have equal bargaining power vis-à-vis one another.

The doctrinal treatment of cohabitation agreements, however, like the treatment of contracts in general, usually pays little attention to questions of power and fairness. Duress and unconscionability are the exceptions that prove the rule. Those doctrines identify the only recognized deviations from the supposedly standard case of equal contracting partners. Intimate partners are conceived of as fitting the standard model. One consequence of this conception is that courts can justify the failure to enforce cohabitation arrangements as mere nonintervention, overlooking the fact that the superior position in which nonaction tends to leave the male partner is at least in part a product of the legal system.[21] Another is that courts can idealize the private world in which their "nonintervention" leaves the parties, disregarding the ways in which that world is characterized by inequality and the exercise of private power.[22] Yet another is that courts can talk blithely about the intentions of "the parties" in fashion that ignores the possibility that one party's intentions are being respected at the expense of the other's.

Not all of the cohabitation contract opinions ignore the issue of fairness and power. They are more likely to receive explicit attention when a judge frankly invokes "public policy" instead of relying exclusively on contract doctrine. They appear, for example, when the Illinois appeals court in *Hewitt* explains why enforcement of such agreements promotes rather than undermines the institution of marriage. When a judge casts his opinion in traditional doctrinal terms, using intention, for example, or consideration, then any sensitivity he has to questions of power and fairness must be translated—translated, for example, into a willingness to assume that the parties did intend to enter a relationship of reciprocal obligation or that the woman has provided services that require compensation. Frequently this involves construing the male partner's intentions *as if* he were the concerned and equal partner the law assumes him to be. Again, these devices

---

[20]   *Wisconsin & Mich. Ry. Co. v. Powers* (1903) 191 U.S. 379.
[21]   See, *e.g.* Taub & Schneider, *"Perspectives on Women's Subordination and the Role of Law"* in *The Politics of Law, op. cit.*, n. 11 at 117 and especially 118–124.
[22]   Taub & Schneider, *op. cit.*, at 122; *cf. Coppage v. Kansas* (1915) 236 U.S. 1, 15 (discussing employer-employee relationship).

parallel those used by courts across the range of contract decisions. But only when judges move outside the framework of traditional contract doctrine will they be in a position to grapple with the full range of problems posed by these disputes.

There are several ways to begin a richer examination of the cohabitation cases. First, we can learn from the truths underlying contract doctrine while rejecting the idea that that doctrine alone can lead us to correct answers. The dichotomies of public and private, manifestation and intent, form and substance, do touch on troubling questions that are central to our understanding of intimate relationships and the role of the state in undermining or supporting them. The problem with doctrinal rhetoric is twofold. First, it recasts our concerns in a way that distances us from our lived experience of them. Second, the resolution of the cases that the application of doctrine purports to secure offers us a false assurance that our concerns can be met—that public can be reconciled with private, manifestation with intent, form with substance.

Once we realize that doctrinal "resolutions" are achieved only by sleight of hand, consideration of the identified dichotomies helps us to explore more fully the cohabitation agreement. What is the nature of this relationship, or what range of cohabitation arrangements precludes us from making general statements about the nature of the relationship? To what extent do these relationships need protection from authority, and to what extent do they require nurturing by authority? To what extent do they reflect the shared expectations of their participants, and to what extent the imposition of terms by one party on another? How can we harbor intimacy within institutions that offer the flexibility to accommodate individual need, while at the same time providing a measure of predictability and stability? What stake does the society have in limiting the forms of association it will recognize? Given our dependence on our social and cultural context, what freedom does any of us have to reimagine the terms of human association?

Study of the play between public and private, objective and subjective, shows us that these dichotomies organize not only the strictly doctrinal territory of contract interpretation or consideration, but also the broader "policy" issues that are folded into the cases. Questions of judicial competence, for example, turn out to involve precisely the question of whether a private sphere can be marked off from the public sphere. Similarly, whether enforcement of cohabitation agreements is a pro-marriage or an anti-marriage position turns out to depend on questions of intention and power. Even as this analysis illuminates the policy dimension of the cases, it refutes the claim that the addition of policy considerations can cure doctrinal indeterminacy.

If neither doctrine nor the addition of policy can determine how decision-makers choose outcomes in particular cases, the next question is whether the opinions contain other material that illuminates the decision-making process. The dimension of these cohabitation cases that cries out for investigation is the images they contain of women, and of relationship. And since images of women and of relationship are the central concern of feminist theory, I have used that theory as the basis for my enquiry. This does not, of course, foreclose the possibility that other enquiries, in this or other settings, might prove equally possible and promising once doctrine is opened up to make room for them.

I am not claiming that judges decide cohabitation cases on the basis of deeply held notions about women and relationship in the sense that these notions provide a determinate basis for decision. For this to be true, attitudes toward women and relationship would have to be free from contradiction in a way that doctrine and policy are not. I believe instead that these notions involve the same perceived divide between self and other that characterizes doctrine, and are as internally contradictory as any doctrine studied in this Article. My claim, therefore, is only that notions of women and relationship are another source of influence, and are therefore as deserving of attention as any other dimension of the opinions. These notions influence how judges frame rule-talk and policy-talk; in a world of indeterminacy they provide one more set of variables that may persuade a judge to decide a case one way or another, albeit in ways we cannot predict with any certainty.

One introductory caveat is in order. To say that "the opinions" convey images of woman and relationship is to miss the distinction between images that appear to inhere in the doctrine as it has developed, and images woven into the texture of opinions seemingly at the initiative of a particular judge. I think this distinction is worth noting, even though in practice it cannot always be made. It becomes clearest, perhaps, when a judge struggles *against* images he sees embedded in the doctrine, and offers new images that in turn provide him with new doctrinal choices.

One powerful pair of contradictory images of woman paints the female cohabitant as either an angel or a whore. As angel, she ministers to her male partner out of noble emotions of love and self-sacrifice, with no thought of personal gain. It would demean both her services and the spirit in which they were offered to imagine that she expected a return—it would make her a servant. As whore, she lures the man into extravagant promises with the bait of her sexuality—and is appropriately punished for *her* immorality when the court declines to hold her partner to his agreement.

Although the image of the whore is of a woman who at one level is seeking to satiate her own lust, sex—in these cases—is traditionally presented as something women give to men. This is consistent both with the view of woman as angel, and with the different image of the whore as someone who trades sex for money. In either event, woman is a provider, not a partner in enjoyment. When a judge invokes this image, he supports the view that sex contaminates the entire agreement, and that the desire for sex is the only reason for the male partner's promises of economic support. If sex were viewed as a mutually satisfying element of the arrangement, it could be readily separated out from the rest of the agreement. In most cases, the woman's career sacrifices and childbearing and homemaking responsibilities would then provide the consideration for the economic support proffered by the man.

Marriage is often presented in the cases as the only way in which men and women can express a continuing commitment to one another. This suggests that when men do not marry women, they intend to avoid all responsibility for them. Women therefore bear the burden of protecting themselves by declining the irregular relationship. At the same time, the institution of marriage as an expression of caring is portrayed as so fragile that only the most unwavering support by the state will guarantee its survival. This could mean that other expressions of caring would entirely supplant marriage without vigilant enforcement of the socially endorsed forms of relationship, although that would be inconsistent with the portrayal of marriage as the only expression of commitment. Alternatively, it could mean that men and women would not choose to enter relationships of caring without pressure from the state.

These nightmarish images have much in common with what other disciplines tell us men think about women and relationship. The conception of women as either angels or whores is identified by Freud,[23] and supported by feminist accounts.[24] The evil power of female sexuality is a recurrent subject of myth and history.[25] The contrast of men fearing relationship as entrapping, and women

---

[23] S. Freud, "A Special Type of Choice of Object Made by Men" in *The Standard Edition of the Complete Psychological Works of Sigmund Freud* XI 165 (J. Strachey trans. & ed. 1957); S. Freud, *On the Universal Tendency to Debasement in the Sphere of Love* XI in *ibid.* at 179.

[24] See, *e.g.* A. Dworkin, *Woman Hating* (1974).

[25] *ibid.*, see especially pp. 31–46, 118–150.

fearing isolation, is the subject of Carol Gilligan's work in the psychology of moral development[26]; others have explored the origins of that difference in the context of psychoanalytic theory.[27] Raising these images to the level of consciousness and inquiry therefore seems to me an important aspect of undertaking this particular set of cases. It is also a way of stepping beyond the confines of current doctrine and beginning to think about other ways of handling the reciprocal claims cohabitants may make of one another.

*Epilogue*

The stories told by contract doctrine are human stories of power and knowledge. The telling of those stories—like the telling of any story—is, in one sense, an impoverishing exercise: The infinitely rich potential that we call reality is stripped of detail, of all but a few of its aspects. But it is only through this restriction of content that any story has a meaning. In uncovering the way doctrine orders, and thereby creates, represents, and misrepresents reality, I have suggested and criticized the particular meaning created by doctrinal stories, the particular limitations entailed in the telling of those stories.

My critique is in turn a story, which itself creates order and meaning. My story, too, is subject to the charge that it has reduced the richness of contract law and the multiplicity of its concerns to a few basic elements, that it misrepresents as much as it reveals. And, in fact, I do not believe that my story is the only one that can be told about contract doctrine. I insist only that it is *an* important story to tell.

My story reveals the world of contract doctrine to be one in which a comparatively few mediating devices are constantly deployed to displace and defer the otherwise inevitable revelation that public cannot be separated from private, or form from substance, or objective manifestation from subjective intent. The pain of that revelation, and its value, lies in its message that we can neither know nor control the boundary between self and other. Thus, although my story has reduced contract law to these few basic elements, they are elements that merit close scrutiny: They represent our most fundamental concerns. And the type of analysis I suggest can help us to understand and address those concerns.

By telling my story, I also hope to open the way for other stories—new accounts of how the problems of power and knowledge concretely hamper our ability to live with one another in society. My story both asks why those problems are not currently addressed by doctrine and traditional doctrinal analysis, and suggests how they might be. By presenting doctrine as a human effort at world-making, my story focuses fresh attention on those to whom we give the power to shape our world. My story requires that we develop new understandings of our world-makers as we create them, and are in turn created by them. This kind of inquiry, exemplified for me by feminist theory, can help us see that the world portrayed by traditional doctrinal analysis is already not the world we live in, and is certainly not the only possible world for us to live in. And in coming to that realization, we increase our chances of building our world anew.       [1095–1114]

---

[26]  C. Gilligan, *post*, 1189.
[27]  N. Chodorow, *The Reproduction of Mothering* (1978); D. Dinnerstein, *The Mermaid and the Minotaur* (1976).

## DUNCAN KENNEDY
### The Ideological Content of Legal Education
(1982)[28]

One can distinguish in a rough way between two aspects of legal education as a reproducer of hierarchy. A lot of what happens is the inculcation through a formal curriculum and the classroom experience of a set of political attitudes toward the economy and society in general, toward law, and toward the possibilities of life in the profession. These have a general ideological significance, and they have an impact on the lives even of law students who never practise law. Then there is a complicated set of institutional practices that orient students to willing participation in the specialized hierarchical roles of lawyers. Students begin to absorb the more general ideological message before they have much in the way of a conception of life after law school, so I will describe this formal aspect of the educational process before describing the ways in which the institutional practice of law schools bear on those realities.

Law students sometimes speak as though they learned *nothing* in school. In fact, they learn skills to do a list of simple but important things. They learn to retain large numbers of rules organized into categorical systems. They learn "issue spotting," which means identifying the ways in which the rules are ambiguous, in conflict, or have a gap when applied to particular fact situations. They learn elementary case analysis, meaning the art of generating broad holdings for cases so that they will apply beyond their intuitive scope, and narrow holdings for cases so that they won't apply where it at first seemed they would. And they learn a list of balanced, formulae, pro/con policy arguments that lawyers use in arguing that a given rule should apply to a situation despite a gap, conflict, or ambiguity, or that a given case should be extended or narrowed. These are arguments like "the need for certainty" and "the need for flexibility," "the need to promote competition" and the "need to encourage production by letting producers keep the reward of their labor."

One should neither exalt these skills nor denigrate them. By comparison with the first-year students' tendency to flip-flop between formalism and mere equitable intuition, they represent a real intellectual advance. Lawyers actually do use them in practice; and when properly, consciously mastered, they have "critical" bite. They are a help in thinking about politics, public policy, ethical discourse in general, because they show the indeterminacy and manipulability of ideas and institutions that are central to liberalism.

On the other hand, law schools teach these rather rudimentary, essentially instrumental skills in a way that almost completely mystifies them for almost all law students. The mystification has three parts. First, the schools teach skills through class discussions of cases in which it is asserted that law emerges from a rigorous analytical procedure called legal reasoning, which is unintelligible to the layperson but somehow both explains and validates the great majority of the rules in force in our system. At the same time, the class context and the materials present every legal issue as distinct from every other—as a tub on its own bottom, so to speak—with no hope or even any reason to hope that from law study one might derive an integrating vision of what law is, how it works, or how it might be changed (other than in any incremental, case-by-case, reformist way).

Second, the teaching of skills in the mystified context of legal reasoning about utterly unconnected legal problems means that skills are taught badly, unselfconsciously, to be absorbed by osmosis as one picks up the knack of "thinking like a lawyer." Bad or only randomly good teaching generates and then

[28] [Extracted from "Legal Education as Training for Hierarchy" in *The Politics of Law* (D. Kairys ed.).]

accentuates real differences and imagined differences in student capabilities. But it does so in such a way that students don't know when they are learning and when they aren't, and have no way of improving or even understanding their own learning process. They experience skills training as the gradual emergence of differences among themselves, as a process of ranking that reflects something that is just "there" inside them.

Third, the schools teach skills in isolation from actual lawyering experience. "Legal reasoning" is sharply distinguished from law practice, and one learns nothing about practice. This procedure disables students from any future role but that of apprentice in a law firm organized in the same manner as a law school, with older lawyers controlling the content and pace of depoliticized craft training in a setting of intense competition and no feedback.

### The formal curriculum: Legal rules and legal reasoning

The intellectual core of the ideology is the distinction between law and policy. Teachers convince students that legal reasoning exists, and is different from policy analysis, by bullying them into accepting as valid in particular cases arguments about legal correctness that are circular, question-begging, incoherent, or so vague as to be meaningless. Sometimes these are just arguments from authority, with the validity of the authoritative premise put outside discussion by professorial fiat. Sometimes they are policy arguments (*e.g.* security of transaction, business certainty) that are treated in a particular situation as though they were rules that everyone accepts but that will be ignored in the next case when they would suggest that the decision was wrong. Sometimes they are exercises in formal logic that wouldn't stand up for a minute in a discussion between equals (*e.g.* the small print in a form contract represents the "will of the parties").

Within a given subfield, the teacher is likely to treat cases in three different ways. There are the cases that present and justify the basic rules and basic ideas of the field. These are treated as cursory exercises in legal logic. Then there are cases that are anomalous—"outdated" or "wrongly decided" because they don't follow the supposed inner logic of the area. There won't be many of these, but they are important because their treatment persuades students that the technique of legal reasoning is at least minimally independent of the results reached by particular judges and is therefore capable of criticizing as well as legitimating. Finally, there will be an equally small number of peripheral or "cutting-edge" cases the teacher sees as raising policy issues about growth or change in the law. Whereas in discussing the first two kinds of cases the teacher behaves in an authoritarian way supposedly based on his objective knowledge of the technique of legal reasoning, here everything is different. Because we are dealing with "value judgments" that have "political" overtones, the discussion will be much more freewheeling. Rather than every student comment being right or wrong, all student comments get pluralist acceptance, and the teacher will reveal himself to be either a liberal or a conservative rather than merely a legal technician.

The curriculum as a whole has a rather similar structure. It is not really a random assortment of tubs on their own bottoms, a forest of tubs. First, there are contracts, torts, property, criminal law, and civil procedure. The rules in these courses are the ground rules of late-nineteenth-century laissez-faire capitalism. Teachers teach them as though they had an inner logic, as an exercise in legal reasoning, with policy (*e.g.* commercial certainty in the contracts course) playing a relatively minor role. Then there are second- and third-year courses that expound the moderate reformist program of the New Deal and the administrative structure of the modern regulatory state (with passing reference to the racial egalitarianism of the Warren Court). These courses are more policy oriented than first-year courses, and also much more ad hoc. Teachers teach students that limited interference with the market makes sense and is as authoritatively grounded in statutes as the ground rules of laissez-faire are grounded in natural law. But each problem is discrete, enormously complicated, and understood in a way that guarantees the practical impotence of the reform program. Finally, there are peripheral subjects, like legal philosophy or legal history, legal process, clinical legal education. These are presented as not truly relevant to the "hard" objective, serious, rigorous analytic core of law; they are a kind of playground or finishing school for learning the social art of self-presentation as a lawyer.

This whole body of implicit messages is nonsense. Teachers teach nonsense when they persuade students that legal reasoning is distinct, *as a method for reaching correct results*, from ethical and political discourse in general (*i.e.* from policy analysis). It is true that there is a distinctive lawyers' body of knowledge of the rules in force. It is true that there are distinctive lawyers' argumentative techniques for spotting gaps, conflicts, and ambiguities in the rules, for arguing broad and narrow holdings of cases, and for generating pro and con policy arguments. But these are *only* argumentative techniques. There is never a "correct legal solution" that is other than the correct ethical and political solution to that legal problem. Put another way, everything taught, except the formal rules themselves and the argumentative techniques for manipulating them, is policy and nothing more. It follows that the classroom distinction between the umproblematic, legal case and the policy-oriented case is a mere artifact: each could as well be taught in the opposite way. And the curricular distinction between the "nature" of contract law as highly legal and technical by contrast, say, with environmental law is equally a mystification.

These errors have a bias in favor of the center liberal program of limited reform of the market economy and pro forma gestures toward racial and sexual equality. The bias arises because law school teaching makes the choice of hierarchy and domination, which is implicit in the adoption of the rules of property, contract, and tort, look as though it flows from and is required by legal reasoning rather than being a matter of politics and economics. The bias is reinforced when the center liberal reformist program of regulation is presented as equally authoritative but somehow more policy oriented, and therefore less fundamental. The message is that the system is basically OK, since we have patched up the few areas open to abuse, and that it has a limited but important place for value-oriented debate about further change and improvement. If there is to be more fundamental questioning, it is relegated to the periphery of history or philosophy. The real world is kept at bay by treating clinical legal education, which might bring in a lot of information threatening to the cozy liberal consensus, as free legal drudge work for the local bar or as mere skills training.

It would be an extraordinary first-year student who could, on his own, develop a theoretically critical attitude toward this system. Entering students just don't know enough to figure out where the teacher is fudging, misrepresenting, or otherwise distorting legal thinking and legal reality. To make matters worse, the two most common kinds of left thinking the student is likely to bring with her are likely to hinder rather than assist in the struggle to maintain some intellectual autonomy from the experience. Most liberal students believe that the left program can be reduced to guaranteeing people their rights and to bringing about the triumph of human rights over mere property rights. In this picture, the trouble with the legal system is that it fails to put the state behind the rights of the oppressed, or that the system fails to enforce the rights formally recognized. If one thinks about law this way, one is inescapably dependent on the very techniques of legal reasoning that are being marshalled in defense of the status quo.

This wouldn't be so bad if the problem with legal education were that the teachers *misused* rights reasoning to restrict the range of the rights of the oppressed. But the problem is much deeper than that. Rights discourse is internally inconsistent, vacuous, or circular. Legal thought can generate equally plausible rights justifications for almost any result. Moreover, the discourse of rights imposes constraints on those who use it that make it almost impossible for it to function effectively as a tool of radical transformation. Rights are by their nature "formal," meaning that they secure to individuals legal protection for as well as from arbitrariness—to speak of rights is precisely *not* to speak of justice between social classes, races, or sexes. Rights discourse, moreover, simply presupposes or takes for granted that the world is and should be divided between a state sector that enforces rights and a private world of "civil society" in which atomized individuals pursue their diverse goals. This framework is, *in itself*, a part of the problem rather than of the solution. It makes it difficult even to conceptualize radical proposals such as, for example, decentralized democratic worker control of factories.

Because it is logically incoherent and manipulable, traditionally individualist, and willfully blind to the realities of *substantive* inequality, rights discourse is a trap. As long as one stays within it, one can produce good pieces of argument about the occasional case on the periphery where everyone recognizes value judgments have to be made. But one is without guidance in deciding what to do about fundamental questions and fated to the gradual loss of confidence in the convincingness of what one has to say in favor of the very results one believes in most passionately.

The alternative left stance is to undertake the Procrustean task of reinterpreting every judicial action as the expression of class interest. One may adopt a conspiracy theory in which judges deliberately subordinate "justice" (usually just a left liberal rights theory) to the short-run financial interests of the ruling class, or a much more subtle thesis about the "logic" or "needs" or "structural prerequisites" of a particular "stage of monopoly capitalism." But however one sets out to do it, there are two difficulties. The first is that there is just too much drek, too much raw matter of the legal system, and too little time to give everything you have to study a sinister significance. It would be a full-time job just to give instrumental Marxist accounts of the cases on consideration doctrine in first-year contracts. Just exactly why was it that late-nineteenth-century capitalism needed to render an uncle's promise to pay his nephew a handsome sum if he didn't smoke till age twenty-one, a legal nullity? Or was it the other way around: that capitalism *needed* such promises to be enforceable?

The second difficulty is that there is no "logic" to monopoly capitalism, and law cannot be usefully understood, by someone who has to deal with it in all its complexity, as "superstructural." Legal rules the state enforces and legal concepts that permeate all aspects of social thought constitute capitalism as well as responding to the interests that operate within it. Law is an aspect of the social totality, not just the tail of the dog. The rules in force are a factor in the power or impotence of all social actors (though they certainly do not determine outcomes in the way liberal legalists sometimes suggest they do). Because it is part of the equation of power rather than simply a function of it, people struggle for power through law, constrained by their limited understanding and limited ability to predict the consequences of their maneuvers. To understand law is to understand this struggle as an aspect of class struggle *and* as an aspect of the human struggle to grasp the conditions of social justice. The outcomes of struggle are not preordained by any aspect of the social totality, and the outcomes within law have no "inherent logic" that would allow one to predict outcomes "scientifically" or to reject in advance specific attempts by judges and lawyers to work limited transformations of the system.

Left liberal rights analysis submerges the student in legal rhetoric but, because of its inherent vacuousness, can provide no more than an emotional stance against the legal order. The instrumental Marxist approach is highly critical of law but also dismissive. It is no help in coming to grips with the particularity of rules and rhetoric because it treats them, a priori, as mere window dressing. These theories fail left students because they offer no base for the mastery of ambivalence. What is needed is to think about law in a way that will allow one to enter into it, to criticize it without utterly rejecting it, and to manipulate it without self-abandonment to *their* system of thinking and doing.

### Student Evaluation

Law schools teach a small number of useful skills. But they teach them only obliquely. It would threaten the professional ideology and the academic pretensions of teachers to make their students as good as they can be at the relatively simple tasks they will have to perform in practice. But it would also upset the process by which a hierarchical arrangement analogous to that of law school applicants, law schools, and law firms is established within a given student body.

To teach the repetitive skills of legal analysis effectively, one would have to isolate the general procedures that make them up, and then devise large numbers of factual and doctrinal hypotheticals where students could practice those skills, knowing what they were doing and learning in every single case whether their performance was good or bad. As legal education now works, on the other hand, students do exercises designed to discover that the "correct solution" to a legal problem might be, those exercises are treated as unrelated to one another, and students receive no feedback at all except a grade on a single examination at the end of the course. Students generally experience these grades as almost totally arbitrary—unrelated to how much you worked, how much you like the subject, how much you thought you understood going into the exam, and what you thought about the class and the teacher.

This is silly, looked at as pedagogy. But it is more than silly when looked at as ideology. The system generates a rank ordering of students based on grades, and students learn that there is little or nothing they can do to change their place in that ordering, or to change the way the school generates it. Grading as practised teaches the inevitability and also the justice of hierarchy, a hierarchy that is at once false and unnecessary. [pp. 44–51]

### R. M. UNGER
### The Spell of Rationalizing Legal Analysis
### (1996)[29]

*Legal thought and social democracy*

Why have law and legal doctrine failed to make the move from their characteristic focus upon the effective enjoyment of rights to the recognition and development of transformative institutional opportunity? Why have they worked in the belief that individual and collective self-determination depend upon empirical and defeasible conditions without turning more wholeheartedly to the legal analysis and construction of the contrasting practices and institutions capable of fulfilling these conditions? Why, therefore, have they not gone on to identify in these small and fragmentary alternatives the possible beginnings of larger alternatives: different institutional pathways for the redefinition and transformation of representative democracy, market economy, and free civil society? Why, in other words, have they failed to extend their rejection of the nineteenth-century idea that free polities and economies have a predetermined legal form, constitutive of freedom itself, into a more thoroughgoing rebellion against institutional fetishism?

[29] [From R. M. Unger, *What Should Legal Analysis Become?* (1996).]

The most important reasons for the arrested development of legal thought lie in the history of modern politics. Nevertheless, the simple attribution of the limits of contemporary legal thought to the constraints upon the political transformation of social arrangements is insufficient as explanation on several grounds.

The same period that saw the development of legal thought arrested also witnessed a connected series of radical reforms in the institutional and ideological context of political and economic life: the reforms labeled in Europe as social democracy and described in the United States as the New Deal. These changes had one of their points of focus and support in Keynesianism: a connected series of institutional and ideological innovations, freeing national governments from sound-finance doctrine and thus diminishing the dependence of public policy upon the level of business confidence. These were radical reforms because we cannot understand the force and shape of the major political, economic, and discursive routines of the contemporary industrial democracies—such as the political-business cycle—except by reference to them. They helped set the boundary conditions within which individuals and organized groups would, in the succeeding period, understand and defend their interests.

It is nevertheless true that, like any institutional settlement, the social-democratic compromise implied renunciation of a broader realm of conflict and controversy. National governments won the power and the authority to manage the economy countercyclically, to compensate for the unequalizing effects of economic growth through tax-and-transfer, and to take those investment initiatives that seemed necessary to satisfy the requirements for the profitability of private firms. In return, however, they had to abandon the threat radically to reorganize the system of production and exchange and thereby to reshape the primary distribution of wealth and income in society.

The refusal of legal analysis to move from the concern with rights enjoyment to the pursuit of institutional change may seem merely the legal counterpart to the foreclosure of broader conflict by the social-democratic settlement. The role of the practical legal reformer would be to continue and to complete the unfinished work of the social-democratic reformation. The task of the legal thinker would be to develop a theory of law that, freer of the nineteenth-century devotion to a predetermined private-law system, would do justice to social-democratic commitments. From this angle the reluctance to pass from the theme of effective rights enjoyment to the practice of institutional criticism appears to be a consequence of the renunciation of broader institutional experimentalism. Such a renunciation represented an essential term of the social-democratic compromise. Not until that compromise gets challenged and changed could we expect legal analysis to continue on the trajectory I earlier traced. As it has been challenged if at all mainly from the right, so the argument would conclude, there is little reason to expect such a forward impulse.

The trouble with this account of the sources of institutional conservatism in the practice of legal analysis is that it relies upon too static and one-sided a picture of institutional settlements and of their relation to legal thought. For one thing, there is no watertight division between the reconstructive moment of crisis and energy and the supposedly barren sequel. Not only have problems and alternatives touching on the design of institutions continued to appear, but it is also often hard to say which of the solutions considered is more faithful to the earlier, foundational compromise. For another thing, institutional change is not just a cause of reimagination; it is also a consequence. If we have indeed renounced a functionalist and evolutionary determinism in our understanding of institutional history, we must grant to our practices of social imagination such as legal analysis some power of productive apostasy and practical presentiment. Finally, the exculpatory picture fails to acknowledge the self-subversive and self-transformative capacities of a tradition of discursive practice such as that of legal analysis.

The history of legal thought over the last hundred years provides—I shall soon argue—a striking example of these capacities. Why have they fallen into disuse?

### The method of policy and principle

The failure to move from the moment of attention to rights enjoyment to the moment of institutional reimagination is more than the silent echo in law of political quiescence in society. It reveals the influence of a now canonical practice of legal analysis: one that enjoys increasing influence throughout the world but that has until now found its most elaborate development in American legal doctrine and theory. I shall call it rationalizing legal analysis, giving, for the purpose, specific content to the term "rationalizing." It is a style of legal discourse distinct both from the nineteenth-century rationalism and from the looser and more context-oriented analogical reasoning that continues to dominate, in the United States as elsewhere, much of the practical reasoning of lawyers and judges.

There is no such thing as "legal reasoning": a permanent part of an imaginary organon of forms of inquiry and discourse, with a persistent core of scope and method. All we have are historically located arrangements and historically located conversations. It makes no sense to ask "What is legal analysis?" as if discourse (by lawyers) about law had a permanent essence. In dealing with such a discourse, what we can reasonably ask is "In what form have we received it, and what should we turn it into?" In this book I argue that we now can and should turn it into a sustained conversation about our arrangements.

Rationalizing legal analysis is a way of representing extended pieces of law as expressions, albeit flawed expressions, of connected sets of policies and principles. It is a self-consciously purposive mode of discourse, recognizing that imputed purpose shapes the interpretive development of law. Its primary distinction, however, is to see policies of collective welfare and principles of moral and political right as the proper content of these guiding purposes. The generalizing and idealizing discourse of policy and principle interprets law by making sense of it as a purposive social enterprise that reaches toward comprehensive schemes of welfare and right. Through rational reconstruction, entering cumulatively and deeply into the content of law, we come to understand pieces of law as fragments of an intelligible plan of social life.

Within such a practice analogical reasoning is defined as the confused, first step up the ladder of rational reconstruction. The often implicit purposive judgements guiding the analogist point upward, for their authority and consistency, to more comprehensive ideas of policy and principle. The repeated practice of policy-oriented and principle-based analysis should, so the most ambitious and influential views of the practice teach, lead to ever higher standards of generality, coherence, and clarity in the rational representation of law.

The ideal conceptions representing law as an imperfect approximation to an intelligible and defensible plan are thought to be partly already there in the law. The analysts must not be thought to make them up. They are not, however, present in a single, unambiguous form, nor do they fully penetrate the legal material. Thus, legal analysis has two jobs: to recognize the ideal element embedded in law, and then to improve the law and its received understanding. Improvement happens by developing the underlying conceptions of principle and policy and by rejecting, from time to time and bit by bit, the pieces of received understanding and precedent that fail to fit the preferred conceptions of policy and principle. Too much pretense of discovering the ideal conceptions ready-made and fully potent within existing law, and the legal analyst becomes a mystifier and an apologist. Too much constructive improvement of the law as received understanding represents it to be, and he turns into a usurper of democratic power. In fact, because the apologetic mystification may be so insecurely grounded in the actual materials of law, both these countervailing perversions of rational reconstruction are likely to end in an unjustified confiscation of law-making power by the analyst.

In what vocabulary should we think of policy and principle or to what conceptions should we resort in trying to connect policies and principles to one another, and in preferring some to others? The major schools of legal theory in the age of rationalizing legal analysis can most usefully be understood as the contrasting operational ideologies of this analytic practice. Each school proposes a different way of grounding, refining, and reforming the practice. Thus, for example, one school may look to goals of allocational or dynamic economic efficiency while another may start from a view of the proper roles and responsibilities of the different institutions within a legal system. Nevertheless, the same argumentative structure recurs in all these theories: the purposive ideal conceptions of policy and principle, whatever their substance, are partly already there in the law, waiting to be made explicit, and they are partly the result of the improving work undertaken by the properly informed and motivated analyst.

### The diffusion of rationalizing legal analysis

The practice of legal analysis theorized in this manner now enjoys immense and increasing influence. It may dominate only a minor part of the practical discourse of lawyers and lower-court judges, preoccupied with preventing conflict, controlling violence, and negotiating compromise. It nevertheless is coming to occupy the central imaginative space in the way in which the judicial, legal-professional, and legal-academic elites talk about law and develop its practical, applied understanding. At a minimum, it preempts an alternative imagination of law from holding this space and exercising this influence.

Given its historical specificity, this style of legal discourse spreads unevenly throughout the world, and takes on in different places characteristics shaped by an earlier history of methods and ideas. It has received its most lavish elaboration in the contemporary United States, for reasons later to be explored, but its worldwide influence grows steadily. In this respect it is an event characteristic of an historical situation in which humanity finds itself united by a chain of analogies, in experiences, problems, and solutions, and anxious reformers of society and culture pillage and recombine practices and institutions from all over the world. It is in this way rather than by the cruel devices through which capital becomes hypermobile while labor remains imprisoned in the nation-state—or in blocs of homogeneous nation-states—that mankind is becoming truly one. Countries in which a more analogy-bound practice of legal reasoning continues to enjoy greater respect (for in all countries such a practice enjoys actual influence), or in which the project of nineteenth-century legal science clings to a life-in-death, soon become theaters for the conflict between the old doctrinalism and the new style of rational reconstruction in law.

A familiar difference of emphasis illustrates how, as it spreads through the world, the method adapts to the idiosyncratic compulsions born of the many histories it intersects. In the United States the continuing duality of common law and statutory law has repeatedly suggested the idea that the retrospective, reconstructive, and dynamic interpretation of law under the guidance of connected policy and principle has a broader and more persistent role to play in judge-made law than in the judicial construction of statutes. Only slowly have lawyers knocked these barriers down, claiming in statutory construction the same freedom to keep on reinterpreting and reconstructing that they attribute to the internal development of the common law.

In civil-law countries the path-dependent history of attitudes toward rational reconstruction in law followed a different course. The project of nineteenth-century legal science, which found its most systematic expression in the work of the German pandectists, was understood by its votaries to be the rescue and refinement of the old Roman-Christian common law of Europe. A struggle developed between two attitudes toward codification—codification as the taming of the power of the jurists by democracy and codification as the convenient summation of the jurists' doctrines. Where the first attitude prevailed, as in post-revolutionary France, there was a concerted attempt to uphold literalism in the interpretation of law. This literalism outlived its political roots and helped pre-empt pandectism, as it helps restrain today the full-fledged inauguration of rationalizing legal analysis. But where, in the late democratizing countries of most of Europe, private and academic jurists retained their law-shaping authority throughout the era of great codifications in the late nineteenth and the early twentieth centuries, codes were imagined by the jurists as the compressed expression of their science. Democratic institutions, where they existed, confirmed and corrected doctrines that predated them. In such a climate the road to rational reconstruction in legal analysis was open. No association between codification and literalism took hold. A long history prepared the reception of today's rationalizing legal analysis.

### *The antiexperimentalist influence of rationalizing legal analysis*

As it spreads through the world, rationalizing legal analysis helps arrest the development of the dialectic between the rights of choice and the arrangements that make individual and collective self-determination effective—a dialectic that is the very genius of contemporary law. The most important way in which it does so is by acquiescing in institutional fetishism. It represents the legally defined practices and institutions of society as an approximation to an intelligible and justified scheme of social life. It portrays the established forms of representative democracy, the regulated market economy, and civil society as flawed but real images of a free society—a society whose arrangements result from individual and collective self-determination. If these forms are never the only possible ones, at least they are, according to this point of view, the ones that history has vali-dated—a history marked by both the intractability of social conflicts and the scarcity of workable arrangements.

Rationalizing legal analysis works by putting a good face—indeed the best possible face—on as much of law as it can, and therefore also on the institutional arrangements that take in law their detailed and distinctive form. It must restrict anomaly, for what cannot be reconciled with the schemes of policy and principle must eventually be rejected as mistaken. For the jurist to reject too much of the received understanding of law as mistaken, expanding the revisionary power of legal analysis, would be to upset the delicate balance between the claim to dis-cover principles and policies already there and the willingness to impose them upon imperfect legal materials. It would be to conspire in the runaway usurpation of democratic power. Thus, deviations and contradictions become intellectual and political threats rather than intellectual and political opportunities, materials for alternative constructions.

A simple parable helps bring out the significance of these constraints for the suppression of the institutional imagination in legal thought and shows how contrasting practices of legal analysis may become self-fulfilling prophecies. Suppose two societies in one of which the institutional arrangements are perceived to be slightly more open to challenge and revision than in the other. In the marginally more open society the jurists say: "Let us emphasize the diversity and the distinctiveness of the present arrangements, their accidental origins and sur-prising variations, the better to criticize and change them, pillaging arrangements devised for other purposes and recombining them in novel ways." The practice of such a style of legal analysis over time will result in institutions that invite practical experimentalism, including experimentalism about the institutions themselves. Imagine, by contrast, a society in which the institutions seem marginally less open to revision. The jurists may say: "Let us make the best out of the situation by putting the best plausible face upon these arrangements, emphasizing their proximity to a rational and infinitely renewable plan. In the name of this rational reconstruction we may hope to make things better, especially for those who most need help: the people likely to be the victims of the social forces most directly in control of law-making." The sustained practice of this method will, however, help close down our opportunities for institutional experimentalism. It will do so both by turning away from actual experiments and by denying us a way of thinking and talking, collectively, about our institutional fate in the powerful and irreplaceable detail of law. Such is the world rationalizing legal analysis has helped make. [pp. 34–40]

### The historical context of an obsession

The limitations of rationalizing legal analysis find an omnipresent excuse in the constraints of the judicial role. Like its immediate predecessors, rationalizing legal analysis has been primarily meant for judges or for those who, as bureaucrats or as expert but unofficial legal analysts, stand, practically or mentally, in the place of judges. Even when contemporary theories of the "legal process" have turned the judiciary into but one of a system of legal agents, it has remained the first among equals, at the apex of the pyramid of "reasoned elaboration," just as legislation has been relegated to a residual status, a last-ditch instrument to be used when the powers of rational deliberation fail. Every proposal for the reform and redirection of legal analysis can be met by the objection: What could judges do with such a method? The conversation-stopping question "How should judges decide cases?" has remained the central question in the theory of law.

The query about the judicial decision deserves no such privilege. The privilege masks indefensible, antidemocratic precommitments, and its persistence helps arrest the progress of legal theory. In particular, the privilege has served as both cause and consequence of the failure of contemporary legal thought to move from its ever present concern with the effective enjoyment of rights to its undeveloped appreciation of the alternative institutional pathways for developing the exercise of rights in free societies. The judicial obsession has helped cast an anti-experimentalist spell upon legal thought, seducing it into the betrayal of its primary vocation in a democracy. We need to demote the question "How should judges decide cases?" to specialized and secondary status, as a question requiring special answers but leaving the field open for practices of legal analysis directed to other ends. The central end is the working out, in imagination and in practice, of the interaction between ideals or interests and institutions or practices through the detailed medium of law and legal thought. Before probing, however, the relation of rationalizing legal analysis to the exemplary status of the judge, it is useful to remember some puzzling features of the history of this status.

Dispute settlement has been, together with conquest and defense, the paramount source of government, for no aim has been more fundamental in the history of society than the effort to establish and sustain order, threatened by conflict, usurpation, and revenge. To our modern eyes, therefore, the early forms of government often appear to be judicial. This impression, however, conveys a half-truth: we conflate the inclusive practice of pacification and judgement by such protostate institutions with the specialized although ambitious work of modern judges. The most important point to understand about those early institutions is that they worked against a background of customary law, over parts of which sacred law or kingly intervention might be superimposed.

Customary law takes shape around a series of interlocking continuities: of law with the actual expectations and claims that people make upon one another according to the social roles they occupy; of normative standards with routinized behavior and belief; and of the acts by which people define what the law is with the acts by which they apply it in particular cases. The cumulative effect of these continuities is to naturalize society: by placing most social arrangements beyond the reach of effective challenge and revision, they become in practice the natural order of things. Even in late medieval Europe the emerging centers of government remained divided between *jurisdictio* and *gubernaculum*. *Jurisdictio* restated a common, customary law in the course of applying it. Princely *gubernaculum* intervened to manage crisis and dispose of resources and manpower without seeking to disturb the naturalized order of society. When such an enacted sense of naturalness has to coexist with an awareness of differences among ways of life in distinct societies, it turns into a richly defined conception of collective identity: Roman customs defining what it means to be a Roman.

Only fitfully and ambivalently did the common law of England or the *ius commune* of continental Europe develop in sharper contrast with social custom. Procedures emerged to conduct dispute settlement. Jurists started to think of their law as a product of history evolving in historical time. Societies began to assert greater powers to remake themselves through the artifice of their laws.

### Adjudication and rational reconstruction

Now look ahead to the work of modern judges and the place of the modern judiciary. The judicial application and elaboration of law take place against a backdrop in which law is recognized to be made, and is made in fact, by non-judicial agencies. In a democracy the political branches of government must count heavily among these lawmakers. Yet the power of the judges as elaborators of law seems to exceed what their occasional responsibilities as custodians of con-stitutionally entrenched individual rights can explain. Comparative historians of modern law have shown how, from around 1800, judges came to assume, even in continental Europe, greater responsibilities for the revisionary interpretation and reorganization of law. They did not remain the passive slaves to the original lawmakers that many of the radical reformers and democrats of the early nine-teenth century wanted them to be. Codification often slowed the growth of judicial power. The prestige of academic jurists and private jurisconsults modified it. It, nevertheless, continued. Today, in a country like Germany, the techniques of the interpretation of law have become much more similar to those of, say, American judges than the divergent histories of the two traditions might lead us to expect. Historians have nevertheless failed to explain why judges have con-tinued to climb the ladder of lawmaking power even where the traditional legal culture seems hostile to their claims.

We can find an answer in the reciprocal adaptation of institutional realities and spiritual preconceptions in these judge-promoting states. Rule-of-law ideals and administrative efficiency alike require that law be formulated as a body of rules and doctrines conferring typical, stable claims upon broad groups of role-occu-pants: citizens, taxpayers, consumers, and workers; creditors and debtors; spouses and children. Imagine that there are divisions among the interests and the ideologies producing this body of law but that the divisions are not so deep, nor the governing elites so fragmented and sectarian, that they cannot leave their agreements relatively incomplete and rely upon special cadres of officeholders to complete them. One way to understand rationalizing legal analysis and the sig-nificant judicial power that it both grants and conceals is to say that it serves as the instrument by which the lawmaking elites in the political branches of gov-ernment transfer the responsibility for completing their agreements to judges and other professional law appliers. The ostentatious devolution of power to law appliers, through the use of vague rules and standards, is simply the extreme case of an inveterate habit. However, the judges could not be effective in this work of making patent the hidden social logic of what may appear to be ramshackle compromises if they were to deploy the methods of the political branches. Nor, by deploying those methods, could they reconcile the responsibility of refining law with the task of respecting and securing rights in particular cases. Thus, rationalizing legal analysis, like its nineteenth-century predecessors, serves as the discursive tool of an institutional fix.

As the divisions and the alternatives presented in democratic politics sharpen, the expedient of treating the law as a series of incomplete agreements, with an inner logic capable of being made patent retrospectively, loses its purchase on reality. There is no developing rational scheme that different fragments of law may be seen to exemplify. Rather than being a problem for democracy, the absence of such a latent scheme is, in a sense, a precondition of democratic vigor, for democracy expands by opening social life up to conscious experimentation. For the same reason, the devolution of law-completing and law-reconstructive responsibility to an insulated band of experts in rational deliberation makes no sense. Such an expertise properly belongs to citizens. Any pluralistic and democratic society may have good reason to leave some of its agreements incomplete, but only a democracy in the grip of antidemocratic superstition will entrust to a cadre of juristic mystagogues the task of elaborating these agreements in the light of systematic conceptions of right or welfare supposedly latent in those bargains.

Reconsidered from this angle, rationalizing legal analysis and the connection it establishes between adjudication and the rational reconstruction of law appear to depend upon a telling combination of circumstances. There must be enough practical experimentalism about social life to make deliberate lawmaking the main source, rather than the marginal corrective, of social arrangements. However, there must not be so much democratic experimentalism as to render suspect the passage from the prospective history of law as compromise among contested interests and visions to its retrospective history as the systematic embodiment of connected policies and principles. Democracy and democratic experimentalism are what this transaction constrains. Such a society continues to cling to a powerful residue of the old naturalization of social life under the aegis of customary law—and of the latter-day counterpart to this naturalization in the idea of a self-evident system of arrangements and rights for free economic and political life.

Rationalizing legal analysis draws much of its force and meaning from the largely untested belief in a natural correspondence between the method of legal reasoning and the responsibilities of judicial decision. The institutional and ideological constraints upon the judicial role in a democracy and the effort to expound law as connected principle and policy seem to reinforce and to justify each other. Once we have decided that judges should apply a method of reasoned elaboration, and interpreted reasoned elaboration as the rationalizing reconstruction of law in the vocabulary of impersonal policy and principle, we can then assign to every other agent of the legal system—the administrative agency, the private rightholder, and the legislature—a suitably loosened variant of reasoned elaboration. At last, we come to the residual, reason-resistant practice of electoral party politics, the last refuge, rather than the first source, of law-making. The judge stands at the center of this imaginative system because he is supposed to be the embodiment of reason in law.

*Putting adjudication in its place*

A threshold objection to this exemplary link between legal reasoning and the judicial decision is that being a judge is an institutionally shaped role rather than a social activity with a permanent core and stable boundaries. It is a role whose contours vary from one society and from one time to another. A simple thought experiment makes the point. Should the work of settling disputes of right among individual litigants and the work of reorganizing organizational practices that frustrate the enjoyment of rights (as through complex enforcement) be carried out by the same institutional agent, as it now more or less is, or should it be divided up and assigned to two different agents? In one case, the judicial role, as now understood in the United States, might have to continue expanding. In the other case, it might have to contract. No methodological program can remain indifferent to the institutional setting of its execution.

Two realities sunk in historical variation and contingency—the practice of legal analysis and the situation of being a judge—cannot be made any less variable and contingent by being somehow superimposed, as if they naturally went together and belonged to each other. Yet this arbitrary equation helps shape the program of rationalizing legal analysis.

Once we recognize the strangeness of this familiar identification of legal reasoning with judicial decision we can also begin to appreciate its consequences. These fall into two broad classes, of which the second and less tangible is by far the more important. The first set of consequences is the exorbitant influence exercised on the practice of legal analysis by the ambitions and anxieties of a special cast of characters: the judges, the bureaucrats, and the private jurists. These jurists stand in the imaginative position of judges, or whisper, figuratively or literally, into their ears.

These characters want important work to do, as we all do when we are serious. They also want to reconcile the importance of their work with the limiting claims of democratic legitimacy and practical efficacy. Rationalizing legal analysis can be understood as simply the most recent solution to this problem. Because it is reconstructive and revisionary, and can result in the reinterpretation and reassignment of rights, it creates an opportunity for important work. Because it claims to interpret law, or to elaborate it under rational guidance, and because it avoids the reimagination and remaking of institutional arrangements, it respects practical limits to the power of experts and democratic limits to the authority of unelected officials and professionals. In all these respects, rationalizing legal analysis neatly parallels the forms of policy analysis and prescription deployed by policy experts in and out of office. It tracks the essential logic of the social-democratic compromise, with its hospitality to tax-and-transfer and its abandonment of structural challenge.

The trouble lies in subordinating what legal analysis can do for the republic and its citizens to what it can do for the jurists by reconciling their ambitions with their anxieties. The "status group" stands in the way of the more general mission, imprisoning a larger task within the confines of special concerns. This imprisonment will impose an intolerable cost if its effect is to arrest the democratic project. It will arrest the project if it denies us the instruments with which to identify and to resolve the unstable relation between assumptions about institutions and practices and definitions of interests and ideals. This unstable relation lies at the heart of each of the familiar programmatic positions—conservative, centrist, or progressive—in contemporary democratic politics.

Thus, we come to the second, more elusive and more important class of consequences of the single-minded fascination with judges in legal thought. The effect of this fascination is to usurp the imaginative field in which more constructive and reconstructive practices of legal analysis might develop. The standard of serviceability to judges imposes a paralyzing constraint upon the reinvention of legal analysis: any more ambitious and transformative style of analysis will seem merely to increase the already excessive powers of judges.

Leave analysis to the judges, the answer may go, and deal with the internal relation of interests and ideals to institutions and practices by all the other readily available varieties of political argument, outside legal discourse. The trouble is that this internal relation is played out most importantly when it is played out in detail. At the indispensable level of detail, it lives in the law. The law does not describe behavioral regularities and social arrangements; it selects those arrangements from which claims, backed by state power, will flow. Legal doctrine, in turn, relates these power-giving and power-denying arrangements to conceptions of human connection: pictures of the possible and desirable forms of association in the different domains of social experience.

If the large-scale institutional and imaginative alternatives expressed as comprehensive ideologies have lost their seductions, and the great transformative projects they put forward have collapsed in failure and disappointment, the alternatives continue to live in the small. Nowhere does institutional detail meet imaginative conceptions more fully, and nowhere does their meeting have greater importance for people's powers and incapacities, than in law and legal thought. The lawyers have control, intellectual as well as practical, over this vital stuff. We dare not abandon it to them lest they represent it in a way motivated by the self-regarding reconciliation of the desire to do important work with the need to avoid embarrassment in the eyes of democracy.

This relation among law, lawyers, and citizens is typical rather than anomalous. As state-oriented politics in the rich industrial democracies narrow in scope, as philosophy relinquishes the claim to subversive and reconstructive authority, the struggle over the fundamentals disappears from the central arenas of politics and philosophy. What was withdrawn from the main staging ground of politics and culture reappears, however, under the disguise of technical expertise, in the practice and discourse of the professions. For the democratic project to advance, the specialized disciplines and the professional practices must somehow return to the central conversation of the democracy the larger agenda they helped take away from it. They must return it enriched, and they must return it in a way recognizing the inevitability of specialized knowledge and technical expertise, while transforming the relation of experts to citizens.

The jurist, no longer the imaginary judge, must become the assistant to the citizen. The citizen rather than the judge must turn into the primary interlocutor of legal analysis. The broadening of the sense of collective possibility must become the controlling mission of legal thought.


### How should judges decide cases?


Suppose, then, that we treat the question "How should judges decide cases?" as a special question, requiring a special solution. Suppose, further, that in offering this special answer we take care to avoid the illusions of rationalizing legal analysis, its illusions about analogy, about arbitrariness, and about reform. We should define the method in a way that respects the human reality and the practical needs of the people who come into court without harnessing them to a glittering scheme for the improvement of law. We must be sure that our judicial practice leaves open and available, practically and imaginatively, the space on which the real work of social reform can occur. We must eschew dogma and accept compromise in our account of the practice as well as in our understanding of the society to which the practice contributes. We should try to remain close to what judicial decisions in contemporary democracies are actually like.

The view of legal analysis in an adjudicative setting I now offer deflates the vast intellectual and political hopes of rationalizing legal doctrine. It is less ambitious within adjudication, however, only because it is more ambitious outside it. Moreover, it has the virtue of realism: it describes the mass of actual judicial decisions much better than does the canon of rationalizing legal analysis. That it should be superior to its established rival even in this respect is striking when we remember the tendency of any discursive practice to become a self-fulfilling prophecy and the susceptibility of any discursive practice to be influenced by a prestigious conception of its work. The theory of it enters into the thing itself. That the program of rationalizing legal analysis should exercise some influence upon judicial practice, especially in the higher courts, is predictable; that this influence should nevertheless remain so limited is revealing.

The heart of most legal analysis in an adjudicative setting should and must be the context-oriented practice of analogical reasoning in the interpretation of statutes and past judicial decisions. This analogical reasoning must be guided by the attribution of purpose to the interpreted materials, an attribution that can often remain implicit in situations of settled usage but that must be brought out into the open whenever meanings and goals are contested. Purposes need to be explicated when they are contested in fact, in the larger experience of society and culture and in the life situations of the litigants, rather than merely by the advocates in court.

The practice of purposive analogical reasoning should, however, differ in two crucial respects from the method recommended by rationalizing legal analysis and its supporting cast of theories. First, it should acknowledge no drive toward systematic closure and abstraction: the conceptual ascent of purposive judgments toward prescriptive theory-like conceptions of whole fields of law and social life. Second, it should attempt to avoid any rigid contrast between the prospective and the retrospective genealogies of law: between law as it looks to those who struggle, in politics and public opinion, over its making and law as it looks after the fact to its professional and judicial interpreters. The purposes guiding the analogist must be just as eclectic in character as those motivating the contestants in original lawmaking. They range from the triumph of one group interest over another to the force of one set of anxieties in relation to a countervailing set of fears.

What matters is for the judge to form a view of these purposes that is continuous with the real world of discourse and conflict from which that fragment of law came. Moreover, the view should recognize the contestable and factional quality of each of the interests, concerns, and assumptions to which it appeals. They count not because they are the best and the wisest but because they won, and were settled, earlier down the road of lawmaking. Deference to literal meanings and shared expectations is simply the limiting case of a more general commitment to respect the capacity of parties and movements to win in politics, and to encode and enshrine their victories in law.

The transfer of this commitment to a system of judge-made law, such as the Anglo-American common law, presents special problems. For here there never was a moment before and beyond the rationalizing and retrospective discourse of specialized lawyers in each historical period. The key point is that a common law after democracy and within democracy must mean something different, and develop in a different way, from a common law outside and before democracy. To be tolerable within democracy a common law cannot represent the cumulative discovery and refinement of a natural and stable world of custom by a group of legal wise men. Nor can it be the basic system of private-law categories defining the necessary legal forms of free economies and societies. It exists on sufferance as a body of historical compromises that the people choose occasionally to revise. From the perspective of democratic beliefs and practices, we can no longer interpret the body of statutory law in the light of common-law ideas and analogies, nor acquiesce in the strict construction of statutes in derogation of common law. We should reinterpret the common law in the context of democratic experi-mentalism as a penumbra of arrangements and assumptions that the democracy has not yet disturbed and may not always need to displace. We strengthen its continuing vitality and authority by bringing to its case-by-case development the assumptions and analogies active in the political making, and the judicial construction, of statutory law. In this way we make it ours rather than expecting it, through its immanent development, "to work itself pure."

The context-oriented practice of analogical reasoning, with its respect for literal meanings and settled understandings, its refusal of conceptual ascent, its commitment to seek guidance in the mentalities and vocabularies of the real political world from which laws come, and its recognition of the contestable and fractional character of the interests and concerns at issue, is also an incomplete practice. It is incomplete even as a method of judicial decision. To understand why it is incomplete and to grasp the implications of its incompleteness we must recognize that two large ideals bear upon its work and modify its course. The first is an ideal of concern with the litigants as real people, with their vulnerabilities and expectations. The second is an ideal of commitment to make adjudication serve the larger goal of advancing the power of a free people to govern themselves. We are often lucky enough to serve these ideals by clinging to the standard methods of judicial decision. Sometimes, however, loyalty to the ideals requires us to break with this standard practice. From such a departure for the sake of the ideal of human concern arises the deviation of equity. From the departure for the sake of the ideal of popular self-government comes the deviation of judicial statecraft.

In every culture a large part of moral life consists in the claims and expectations people make upon one another by virtue of their respective roles. The role-dependence of our ideas of reasonable and fair behavior holds as much for chosen as for ascriptive roles. Although you would hardly guess it from the moral writings of the philosophers, role-related expectations are the major field on which behavioral routines meet prescriptive beliefs. They are therefore the primary residue of customary law in modern society.

In a democracy whose arrangements have some measure of reality, because it is neither prey to extreme inequalities nor subject to colonial rule, the law will usually conform to such preexisting claims and expectations. To be sure, the law may also be used to change them and therefore to resist them. In the conditions of democracy, however, that is most likely to happen when there is already a conflict of moral and political sensibilities, opening a space in which the legal initiative takes hold.

Thus, the standard contextualist and analogical method of judicial decision will usually be able to placate the role-based popular code of fairness. The judge succeeds in bringing moral expectations established in the social worlds of the litigants to bear upon the purposive practice of analogical judgements. At times the law will openly invite him to do so through its use of open-ended standards like reasonableness, unconscionability, and good faith, or through trade practice and commercial usage. More often he will be able to act without explicit invitation, as part of the justified effort to read and elaborate law in the context of the social and cultural worlds that produced it.

Sometimes, however, the judge and the litigants will not be so lucky. The modest, sensitive, good-faith interpretation of the law will result in the case at hand in a stark contrast between the legal mandate and the moral outcome. This contrast may be the direct and foreseeable result of the law that people wanted to make. They may, for example, have reformed family law in ways designed to overturn role-based expectations in present family life. Alternatively, there may be no way to bridge the gap between law and custom without threatening, or appearing to threaten, some part of the institutionalized structure of society.

The problem is then not that the division between custom and law was itself intended but rather that it cannot be escaped without dramatically expanding the stakes in the conflict. For example, if, out of respect for the ideal of human concern, we were to use the doctrine of economic duress in contract law to void all contracts concluded between members of different social classes, we would find ourselves with a roving mandate to subvert and reconstruct the social order.

There are circumstances in which judges may and should wield a fragment of such a mandate so that the political branches and the citizenry can do so as well; I discuss them soon under the exception of judicial state-craft. For the most part, however, such work lies beyond what judges can effectively or legitimately accomplish. If they insist upon undertaking it, they risk being driven by the need to reconcile ambition with modesty to a clumsy and haphazard reformism, as productive of mischief as of good.

There will, however, be situations in which a large gap does open up between law and custom. The gap may not be itself the legal project nor its foreseeable consequence. Judges can fashion an ad hoc remedy, leaving the institutional structure of society untouched and unthreatened. Here is the opportunity for equity. The microexceptionalism of equitable adjustment is the one-time remaking of rights in the context of roles, the anomalous sacrifice of law to custom. It is an attempt to diminish the quota of cruelty in everyday experience, and to do so not on an aggregate scale but in the dimension of an event and an encounter. The humanity of the judge responds to the humanity of the litigants. Such a stopgap should enjoy no afterlife and exert no influence. It makes an exception to standard judicial practice, but an exception properly included within a larger view of the practice.

The ideal of popular self-government usually finds its best judicial defense in the modesty of the standard practice for all the reasons explored in my earlier discussion of the infirmities of judicial van-guardism. The shamefaced Bonapartism of legal elites, claiming to defend the people from their own ignorance, anger, and selfishness, does not have an encouraging record. Even if it chooses wisely the line of democratic advance, it discovers more often than not that its shortage of power and legitimacy keeps it from dealing with the institutionalized structures from which most disadvantage and exclusion result; that the flight from ultimate causes is soon attended by their sanctification; that its benefits get misdirected to the undeserving segments of deserving groups; that its high-handedness and haphazardness help keep the disadvantaged disorganized and divided; and that the practical effects are often as paltry as the corrective intervention is noisy. Moreover, to use any particular case to push history forward may often violate the ideal of human concern as well as the ideal of popular self-government by subordinating the problems of the litigants to the ambitions of a black-robed providence.

The arguments of this book have nevertheless also shown there to be circumstances in which the judges may properly take it upon themselves to cut through a Gordian knot in the law with their swords of constructive interpretation. They may do so under the promptings of the ideal of popular self-government. The basic condition justifying these acts of judicial statecraft is that there be an entrenched impediment to the enjoyment of rights, especially the rights composing the system of popular self-government. To call the obstacle "entrenched" is to say that it resists challenge and defiance by the ordinarily available devices of political and economic action, and that its victims consequently find themselves unable to escape it by their own efforts. There are then two principal variants.

The obstacle may be one that is diffuse in the experience of certain groups although triggered by particular practices. The political branches of government fail to respond, often because the antidemocratic taint touches the arrangements concerning their formation, such as voting practices or access to the media. The remedy may be a bold remaking of law, whether constitutional law or ordinary law. Such an arrogation of tribunician power amounts to a gamble for support. The prospects for its efficacy as well as the case for its legitimacy (efficacy and legitimacy overlap) are therefore greatly strengthened when the reformers below

can appeal to a broad-based current of opinion in society. It is also reinforced
when the reformers act as the partners of organized movements in the depart-
ments of social life in which they intervene. The partnership of the American
federal judiciary with the civil-rights movements, and then, more tentatively, with
the feminist movement, during the heyday of progressive jurisprudence, provides
the most familiar examples.

Alternatively, the obstacle may be localized in the power structures of particular organizations or social practices. The corruption of the ideal of popular self-
government may seem less evident. In its more subtle and limited form it may
nevertheless be all the more insidious in sapping the capacity for individual as well
as collective self-determination. The solution then lies in the structural but episodic intervention of complex enforcement.

So long as we fail to establish a distinct branch of government to perform this
role, with more democratic accountability and greater investigative, technical,
financial, and administrative resources than the traditional judiciary now enjoys,
there will be no institutional agent well-suited to the performance of this mission.
Better an ill-suited agent, however, than none at all. Judges may often be the best
agents around. At least they may be the only willing agents.

They will then have to test how far their power and authority as well as their
wills and imaginations enable them to push the work of structural but episodic
intervention. They will need to do the job in full awareness of the constraints their
incongruity as agents imposes upon the execution of their self-appointed task.
They will have reason to be both skeptical and humble. They will understand, in
this variant of judicial statecraft as in the other, that it is one thing to call the
spirits and another for the spirits to come.                          [pp. 106–119.]

# 15

# FEMINIST JURISPRUDENCE

## Origins

Feminist jurisprudence emerged about thirty years ago.[1] Its origins can be explained in a number of ways. One sees it as an off-shoot of critical legal studies.[2] Many feminist legal theorists subscribed to the early principles of the CLS movement in the 1970s, including the "basic critique of the inherent logic of the law, the indeterminacy and manipulability of doctrine, the role of law in legitimating particular social relations, the illegitimate hierarchies created by law and legal institutions."[3] But women at CLS conferences were "ghettoised." In 1983 the CLS conference devoted a section of the conference to feminism specifically. A caucus of "Fem-Crits" emerged. Some of the earlier work in feminist jurisprudence reflects this, Olsen on the family and the market,[4] MacKinnon's comparison of sexism to classism and feminism to Marxism,[5] work on the "public" and the "private,"[6] analysis of the law's relationship to oppression, in particular to patriarchy.[7]

Feminist jurisprudence is also, necessarily, a development from the women's movement more generally. This emerged (more accurately re-emerged) in the late 1960s and early 1970s with the writing of Simone de Beauvoir,[8] Betty Freidan,[9] Germaine Greer,[10] Kate Millett,[11] Eva Figes[12]

---

[1] Through path-breaking classics like Mary Wollstonecraft's *A Vindication of the Rights of Women* (1792) and J.S. Mill and Harriet Taylor's *The Subjection of Women* (1869) long anti-date modern literature. For the claim that Bentham was proto-feminist see N. Lacey (1998)51 CLP 441.

[2] See *ante*, 1209. See C. Menkel-Meadow (1988) 38 J. Legal Ed. 61. On similarities and differences see D. Rhode (1990) 42 Stanford L. Rev. 617 and R. West (1986) 2 Wis. Women's L.J. 85.

[3] *Per* Menkel-Meadow *op. cit.* note 2, p. 63.

[4] (1983) 96 Harvard L. Rev. 1497.

[5] (1982) 7 *Signs* 515; (1983) 8 *Signs* 635. And see now *Toward A Feminist Theory of The State* (1989), Chap. 1.

[6] For example, N. Taub and E. Schneider in D. Kairys (ed.), *The Politics of Law* (1982, new ed. 1990). More fully see K. O'Donovan, *Sexual Divisions in Law* (1985).

[7] J. Rifkin (1980) 3 Harvard Women's L.J. 83; D. Polan in D. Kairys (ed.), *The Politics of Law* (1982, new ed. 1990).

[8] *The Second Sex* (1949): often considered to be the forerunner of contemporary feminism.

[9] *The Feminine Mystique* (1963).

[10] *The Female Eunuch* (1971).

[11] *Sexual Politics* (1970).

[12] *Patriarchal Attitudes* (1970).

and others.[13] To Ashe the development of feminist jurisprudence, on the heels of feminist sociology,[14] feminist philosophy[15] and feminist history[16] was a natural "extension of the engagement of female reflection and speech to one more area of discourse."[17] There was a large proliferation in the 1970s and 1980s in women's studies courses.[18]

The large number of women studying law—a phenomenon of the late 1960s onwards—also had its impact, as female students began to question a curriculum which neglected issues of central concern to women: rape,[19] domestic violence,[20] reproduction,[21] unequal pay,[22] sex discrimination,[23] sexual harassment.[24] Most of the leading writers in feminist jurisprudence were studying law at this time or later. Some who became practising lawyers undertook litigation on behalf of women and this litigation nourished both their scholarship and that of others.[25]

It is unimportant when the term "feminist jurisprudence" was first used. Some trace it to an intervention of Ann Scales at a Harvard conference in 1978.[26] Her article "Towards a Feminist Jurisprudence" was published in 1981[27]: Catharine MacKinnon's influential article "Feminism, Marxism, Method and the State: Toward Feminist Jurisprudence"

---

[13] Good accounts are H. Eisenstein, *Contemporary Feminist Thought* (1984); A. Jaggar, *Feminist Politics and Human Nature* (1983) and J. Mitchell and A. Oakley (eds.), *What is Feminism?* (1986). The context is well-described by M. Chamallas, *Introduction to Feminist Legal Theory* (2003).

[14] Good examples are J. Freeman, *The Politics of Women's Liberation: A Case Study of An Emerging Social Movement and its Relation To The Policy Process* (1975) and A. Oakley, *Women's Work: The Housewife, Past and Present* (1974).

[15] See C. Gould and M. Wartofsky, *Women and Philosophy: Towards a Theory of Liberation* (1976). And see now S. Walby, *Theorizing Patriarchy* (1990).

[16] See for example, the work of L. Gordon, *Women's Body: Women's Rights: A Social History of Birth Control* (1976), and *Heroes of Their Own Lives: The Politics and History of Family Violence* (1989), and C. Smart, *Regulating Womenhood* (1992).

[17] (1987) 38 Syracuse L. Rev. 1129, 1150.

[18] Producing a large number of readers including S. Ruth, *Issues In Feminism* (1980), and M. Evans, *The Women Question* (1982).

[19] See S. Estrich, *Real Rape* (1987). And what is seduction? Is it a form of fraud and should it, therefore, be tortious? See for this suggestion J. Larson (1993) 93 Columbia L. Rev. 374.

[20] See E. Stanko, *Intimate Intrusions* (1985); M. Pagelow, *Women-Battering* (1981).

[21] See M. Stanworth, *Reproductive Technologies* (1987). See also Z.R. Eisenstein, *The Female Body and the Law* (1988) (for the view that the pregnant body and the problem it poses should be at the centre of legal debate).

[22] See N. Dowd (1990) 32 Arizona L. Rev 431; L. Finley (1986) 86 Columbia L. Rev. 1118; D. Rhode (1988) Duke L.J. 1207; D. Rhode (1991) 100 Yale L.J. 1731.

[23] See Linda Blum, *Between Feminism and Labor* (1991).

[24] See C. MacKinnon, *Sexual Harassment of Working Women* (1979). See also T. Morrison, *Race-ing justice, En-gendering Power* (1992) on the Clarence Thomas affair. For the argument that it should be a tort, see Korn (1993) 67 Tulane L. Rev. 1363. An interesting perspective in L. May, *Masculinity and Morality* (1998), Chap. 6.

[25] Good examples are Elizabeth Schneider, Wendy Williams, Nadine Taub and Ruth Bader Ginsburg (appointed as a Supreme Court Justice in 1993). See also Ginsburg's article (1992) 67 N.Y. U.L. Rev 1185.

[26] See P. Cain (1989) 4 Berkeley Women's Law J. 191, 193. And see A. Scales herself in *Legal Feminism* (2006), p. 1 and 153.

[27] See 56 Indiana L.J. 375: see also 95 Yale L.J. 1373 and *Legal Feminism* (2006).

first appeared in 1983.[28] Feminist jurisprudence is a house with many rooms: in this it reflects the different movements in feminist thought. But what unites feminist legal theorists is a belief that society, and necessarily legal order, is patriarchal.[29]

It seeks to analyse the contribution of law in constructing, maintaining, reinforcing and perpetuating patriarchy and it looks at ways in which this patriarchy can be undermined and ultimately eliminated. Although there is much, and an increasing amount of grand theorising, what Carol Smart has called "scientific feminism,"[30] there remains a belief in the "desirability of the concrete."[31] This is one of the things that clearly demarcates feminist jurisprudence from mainstream legal theory.

### THE INQUIRIES OF FEMINIST JURISPRUDENCE

Clare Dalton has written of feminism that it is a "range of committed inquiry and activity dedicated first, to describing women's subordination—exploring its nature and extent; dedicated second, to asking both *how*—through what mechanisms, and *why*—for what complex and interwoven reasons—women continue to occupy that position; and dedicated third to change".[32] To engage in feminist legal thought is to use feminism to concentrate this inquiry and activity on the legal system. Like CLS, feminist jurisprudence inquires into the politics of law, but its particular focus is on the "law's role in perpetuating patriarchal hegemony."[33] The inquiry is feminist in that it is grounded in women's concrete experiences: the personal is the political.[34] The method of feminism is consciousness-raising, in Catharine MacKinnon's words,[35] "the collective critical reconstruction of the meaning of women's social experience, as women live through it." The goal is change, "revision," as Adrienne Rich puts it.[36] And she adds, "this is 'more than a chapter in cultural history; it is an act of survival.'"

There is a useful list of feminist inquiry into law in an essay by Heather

---

[28] (1983) 8 *Signs* 635 (a version of this is now Chap. 8 of *Toward a Feminist Theory of The State* (1989).

[29] See, *e.g.* L. Bender (1988) 38 J. Legal Educ. 3. But see *Cain, post* 1316.

[30] See (1992) 1 Soc. and Legal Studies 29. See also her *Feminism and the Power of The Law* (1989), Chap. 4.

[31] See M. Fineman in Fineman and Thomadsen (eds.), *At the Boundaries of Law: Feminism and Legal Theory*, p. xi. On feminism in relation to non-law areas see C. Weedon, *Feminist Practice and Poststructuralist Theory* (1987), p. 11.

[32] (1987) 3 Berkeley Women's L.J. 1, 2.

[33] *Per* H. Wishik (1985) 1 Berkeley Women's L.J. 64, 67.

[34] Said by Mari Matsuda to be "the primary tenet of feminist theory" (see 1986) 16 N. Mex. L.R., 613). The phrase "reflects the view that the realm of personal experience ... has always been trivialized, particularly for women" *per* E. Schneider (1986) 61 N.Y. Univ. L.R. 589.

[35] *Per* C. MacKinnon, (1982) 7 *Signs* 515.

[36] *On Lies, Secrets and Silence: Selected Prose* 1966–1978 (1980), p. 35.

Wishik.[37] She suggests seven questions that feminist jurisprudence poses. They are:

1. What have been and what are now all women's experiences of the "life situation" addressed by the doctrine, process or area of law under examination?
2. What assumptions, descriptions, assertions and/or definitions of experience—male, female or ostensibly gender neutral—does the law make in this area?
3. What is the area of mismatch, distortion or denial created by the differences between women's life experiences and the law's assumptions or imposed structures?
4. What patriarchal interests are served by the mismatch?
5. What reforms have been proposed in this area of law or women's life situation? How will these reform proposals, if adopted, affect women both practically and ideologically?
6. In an ideal world, what would this woman's life situation look like, and what relationship, if any, would the law have to this future life situation?
7. How do we get there from here?

It is important to realise, as Wishik notes, that "the analytic frames of patriarchal law are not the spaces within which to create visions of feminist futures."[38] Post modernism is also having an impact. Thus, as Dalton argues, "we can not only research what happens to women in the world shaped by law, law language and legal institutions, but challenge even the structure of legal thought as contingent and in some culturally specific sense 'male,' implying the need for more radical changes than the ameliorative amendations we have offered in the past."[39]

There are different feminist jurisprudences. In the second extract Cain offers a useful categorisation into four schools of thought: liberal, radical, cultural and postmodern. An early theme and pursuit for feminist thinkers about law was equality.[40] Cain takes this theme and shows how the different models perceive and tackle this problem. For liberals, equality amounts to equal opportunity. Radical feminists, such as Littleton and MacKinnon, focus on differences between women and men and support affirmative measures to challenge inequalities. Cultural feminists also emphasize difference, but view it more positively. They (thinkers such as Carol Gilligan and Robin West) use the rhetoric of equality to advocate change that supports the values (caring, relational connectedness) of this difference. Postmodern feminism[41] sees equality as

---

[37] (1985) 1 Berkeley Women's L.J. 64.
[38] *ibid.*, p. 77.
[39] *Op. cit.*, n. 32, p. 12.
[40] See H.H. Kay (1985) I Berkeley Women's Law J I see further A. Scales, *Legal Feminism* (2006), Chap. 4.
[41] See M.J. Frug (1992) 105 Harvard L.Rev. 1045: see also D. Cornell, *Beyond Accommodation* (1991) and J.Butler, *Gender Trouble* (1990).

a social construct and, since it is a product of patriarchy, one in need of feminist reconstruction, but it warns against searching for a new truth to replace an old one. It denies that there is a single theory of equality that will benefit all women. Some feminist critics of postmodernism see it as leading to doing nothing "even faster than traditional liberalism".[42] Cain herself wants feminists to turn away from debates about equality. She looks to legal theories that will support the process of self-definition, and to methods that will raise consciousness and give voice to the unknown in women's experiences.[43] A number of examples of this have now appeared.[44]

To Scales, in the first of the extracts, the underlying problem is the objectification of women, the "tyranny of objectivity." Feminism, she argues, proceeds from the principle that objective reality is a myth, with patriarchal myths as projections of the male psyche. She is critical of the U.S. Supreme Court's equal protection approach to sex discrimination (and would be equally so of the model adopted in the United Kingdom) because it makes maleness the norm of what is human, the goal being neutrality. It is, she argues, necessary to reconstruct the legal system. She points both to the significance, and the dangers, of Gilligan's *In a Different Voice*.[45] Gilligan, a developmental psychologist, has argued that women's moral development reflects a focus on responsibility and contextuality, whilst men's relies more heavily on rights and abstract justice. An "ethic of justice" is rooted in the value that everyone should be treated the same: an "ethic of care" rests on the premise of nonviolence, that "no one should be hurt."[46] Gilligan has been enormously influential,[47] though she has been criticised *inter alia* for her essentialism, her categorisation of a common female voice, rather than a plurality of different voices.[48] To Scales the danger of taking Gilligan's insight is to believe that a care-based and rights-based view are compatible. She is critical of what she calls, "incorporationism." This, she says, "represses contradictions"; it "usurps women's language in order to further define

---

[42] See A Scales, n. 40, above, p.40. See also C. Mackinnon (2007) 75 Chicago-Kent L. R 687, 710.
[43] See also J.Scott (1988) 14 Feminist Studies 33, and M.P.Lara, *Moral Textures* (1998).
[44] For example, P.Williams, *The Alchemy of Race and Rights* (1991); R.Austin (1989) Wisc L. Rev 539; M. Matsuda (1989) 87 Mich L.R. 2320. S. Estrich's *Real Rape, op. cit.*, n. 19, is a graphic illustration of the genre.
[45] (1982.) For a defence of its value to feminist jurisprudence see C. Menkel-Meadow (1985) 1 Berkeley Women's L.J. 39. See also L. Bender (1990) 15 Vermont L. Rev. 1. More generally see S. Benhabib, *Situating The Self* (1992), Chap. 5 and J. Tronto, *Moral Boundaries* (1993).
[46] Gilligan, *op. cit.*, n. 45, p. 174.
[47] An excellent critique is J. Williams (1989) 87 Michigan L. Rev. 797. An excellent challenge in the context of criminal law is K. Daly (1989) 17 Int.J.Soc.Law 1. For her influence see C. Menkel-Meadow (1985) 1 Berkeley Women's L.J. 39 and (1987) 42 University of Miami L. Rev. 29; M. Minow (1987) 9 Harv. Women's L.J. 1 (children's rights); K. Lahey and S. Salter (1985) 23 Osgoode Hall L.J. 543; J. Cohen (1990) 25 Tulsa L.J. 657.
[48] See, *e.g.* A. Harris (1990) 42 Stanford L.Rev. 581.

the world in the male image."[49] But inequality is not a legal mistake that can be undone by expressing examples of irrationality. "The injustice of sexism is not irrationality; it is domination."[50] Scales looks to a feminist jurisprudence which will focus on domination, disadvantage and disempowerment rather than one which examines differences between men and women.

To Robin West, in the third extract,[51] the failure of modern legal theory lies in its understanding of what it is to be a human being. Such theory is male because it assumes that individuals are essentially separate from one another. She argues, to the contrary, that women are connected to other human beings, especially through the biologically based activities of pregnancy, breast-feeding and heterosexual intercourse. West argues for a feminist jurisprudence that reconstructs legal concepts to take account of the realities of women's experiences. Not only is the "separation thesis" an obstacle to the development of feminist legal theory, but it constitutes a barrier to the demolition of patriarchy. West's "connectedness" thesis is essentialist[52]: other feminists[53] working within jurisprudence have criticised her reliance on a concept of "woman" that it is, they claim, abstracted from the experiences of white women.

## EQUALITY AND DIFFERENCE

The next extracts from MacKinnon and Littleton join a debate which has been central to feminist thinking since the 1970s[54]: one confronted also by policy-makers on this side of the Atlantic.[55] The early push by feminists was for equality with men. But increasingly questions began to be asked: do women want to be treated like men? does equality require different treatment? are there more important values than equality? At the root of these questions is the issue of how feminists should define and respond to sexual difference. Should difference be ignored or emphasised and, if

---

[49] See *post*, 1304.
[50] *Post*, 1304.
[51] *Post*, 1320.
[52] See P. Cain, *post*, 1316 and A. Harris (1990) 42 Stanford L.Rev. 581. See also D. Cornell (1990) 75 Cornell L.R. 644. Responses to essentialism are offered by E. Jackson (1993) 20 J.L.S. 398, 401 and J. Conaghan (2000) 27 J.L.S. 351, 366.
[53] See P. Cain (1989) 4 Berkeley Women's L.J. 199. A defence of essentialism is R. West (1989) *University of Chicago Legal Forum* 59. See also D. Fuss, *Essentially Speaking: Feminism, Nature and Difference* (1989).
[54] The materials in Part III of Weisberg, *Feminist Legal Theory: Foundations* (1993) provide the best collection of source materials on this subject. A good liberal statement of the problem is D. Kirp *et al, Gender Justice* (1986). For an account of difference from the perspective of the "different," rather than the dominant group, see M. Minow. *Making All The Difference* (1990).
[55] For the European dimension see More (1993) 1 Fem. Leg. Studies 45.

emphasised, what, if any, is the place of affirmative action[56] to assist the "different" to achieve functional equality? MacKinnon and Littleton (and also Cain, previously discussed) are critical of the traditional approach to equality. This traditional approach is perhaps best represented in a classic article by a liberal feminist, Wendy Williams.[57] Williams had argued that feminists have only two choices: either equality on the basis of similarities between the sexes or special treatment on the basis of sexual differences. She favoured the former, since difference always means women's difference, and this provides the basis for treating women worse as well as better than men. But an equal treatment approach only benefits women who meet male norms and not those who engage in female activities, childbearing and rearing most notably.

Littleton's critique of equality is based on its "phallocentrism."[58] She calls for a reconstruction of thinking about equality to transcend its enmeshment within the very gender system that feminists are resisting. She labels her model "equality as acceptance"[59]: to "accept" women's difference, society must do more than merely accommodate the difference. As Cain puts it,[60] what Littleton requires is the "centralization of 'women' (her identity, her specificity, her difference from men) in normative debates about how the world ought to be structured." Equality as acceptance focuses not on sources of differences, but on their consequences, the differences that difference makes.[61] To show how the acceptance model would work, Littleton constructs "gender complements" by matching a female-gendered difference to its male complement and then treating them equally in terms of compensation, status and opportunity for promotion into decision-making positions. Readers may find some of the consequences of this strange, like paying mothers the same wages and benefits as soldiers or not paying soldiers, and others may object that matching may reinforce stereotypes (Littleton conceded this), but it is her claim that the values upheld by phallocentrism will be challenged and changed as women achieve equal decision-making opportunities.

Catharine MacKinnon is probably the most influential of feminist legal scholars.[62] In the extract from *Feminism Unmodified* she argues that

---

[56] There is a thoughtful collection of articles on this in Social Philosophy and Policy (1991), vol. 8(2), particularly articles by Hill and Radin. See, further, the arguments of W. van Alstyne (1978) 46 University of Chicago L.R. 775 (it fails to alleviate and contributes to "racism, racial spoils system, racial competition and racial odium" (p. 778). And *cf.* R. Colker (1986) 61 N.Y.U.L.Rev. 1003 (*status quo* is not neutral, so neutral rules recreate non-neutrality).

[57] (1984–85) 13 N.Y.U. Rev. L. and Soc. Change 325; (1982) 7 Women's Rights L. Rptr. 175. See also W. Williams and N. Taub (1985) 37 Rutgers L. Rev. 825.

[58] *Post*, 1347.

[59] *ibid., post*, 1348.

[60] *Post*, 1314.

[61] See D. Rhode, *Justice and Gender* (1989), pp. 111 and 319.

[62] See *Feminism Unmodified* (1987), and *Toward A Feminist Theory of the State* (1989). See also *Women's Lives—Men's Laws* (2005) and *Are Women Human?* (2006). For a critique see E. Jackson (1992) 19 J.L.S. 195.

feminists should concentrate on identifying dominance. This treats gender equality issues as questions about the distribution of power, about male supremacy and female subordination. It is dominance, not difference, that is central to MacKinnon. This conceptualisation enables MacKinnon to broaden the focus of inquiry beyond the orthodox terrain of work conditions to take in violence, prostitution and pornography. She claims that the dominance approach is the authentic feminist voice: the difference approach, she argues, adopts the viewpoint of male supremacy on the status of the sexes; the dominance approach sees social inequalities from the standpoint of the subordination of women to men. MacKinnon's article is a clarion call for equal power for women.[63] But are all women always subordinate to men or always dominated by men in the same way? Is this also the experience of lesbians?[64] Does every fact related to women's experience "neatly and unreservedly" support her thesis of male dominance?[65] Does MacKinnon's thesis over-emphasise women's descriptions of subordination and play down descriptions of freedom?[66] Does it refuse to acknowledge the positive aspects of difference, for example those such as caring that are associated with motherhood? Is MacKinnon's answer to this satisfactory, that "women value care because men have valued [women] according to the care [they] give them?"[67] MacKinnon has been criticised for perpetuating a stereotype of women as victims,[68] and for embracing a deterministic vision of male-female relations.[69] Nor does she offer much by way of a blueprint as to how power should be used by women once they have acquired it,[70] though her own work on anti-pornography ordinances may offer a hint.[71]

## WOMEN AND IDEOLOGY

One debate within contemporary feminist jurisprudence relates to ideology and women's choices. The debate is an echo of one we

[63] And therefore for changes in the law that will end power inequalities, in such areas as sexual harassment, violence and pornography. On pornography see C. MacKinnon, n.62, above, Chaps 24–29. P. Cain, *post*, 1352. See more generally Littleton's comment, *post*, 1314–1315.

[64] See P. Cain (1989) 4 Berkeley Women's Law Journal 199. On lesbian jurisprudence see especially the work of Ruthann Robson, *Sappho goes to Law School* (1998) and (2002) 75 Temple U.L.R. 709 (on marriage).

[65] See K. Bartlett (1987) 75 Calif. L.Rev. 1559, 1565. See also F. Olsen (1989) 89 Columbia L.Rev. 1131.

[66] See S. Wildman (1990) 2 Yale J.L. and Feminism 435, 439.

[67] See *Feminism Unmodified, op. cit.*, note 62, p. 39, and *post*, 1342.

[68] See, for example, A. Harris (1990) 42 Stanford L.Rev. 581 pointing to literary works like Alice Walker's *The Color Purple* and Toni Morrison's *Beloved* which, instead of lingering on black women's victimisation and misery, though recognising pain, ultimately celebrates transcendence.

[69] See L. Finley (1988) 82 Nw. U.L.Rev. 352, 364.

[70] See K. Bartlett (1987) 75 Calif. L.Rev. 1559, 1565.

[71] See MacKinnon on pornography in *Feminism Unmodified, op. cit.*, note 62, Pt. III and *Only Words* (1993).

encountered in our discussion of Marx and ideology[72]. The argument that women suffer from "false consciousness", or that their choices are unconsciously determined by gender ideology, has tormented feminist theory. Though the problem arises in several contexts and is discussed by many theorists, it is to Catharine MacKinnon's claims regarding sexuality that it is frequently traced. Her claims arise in the context of a central argument of hers: that coercion is paradigmatic of heterosexual relations and constitutive of the social meaning of gender under gender inequality[73].

Abrams points to a range of criticisms that can be levelled at ideological determination claims[74]. She also explains the strategical advantages of ideological determination arguments. "By declining to acknowledge the possibility that women's choices regarding sexuality might be free from ideological determination, MacKinnon prevents women from exempting themselves from her analysis".[75] But it has problems too. It has the potential for distancing women who appreciate the argument put forward but cannot accept its implications. There is also the danger the arguments pose in contexts (abortion is a good example[76]) where women's agency is called into question[77]. And there are the barriers these arguments create to "remedial analysis"[78] which require of decision makers that they identify the range of factors that influence women's choices. Abrams concludes that:

"Feminist scholars and activists need alternative modes of discourse through which to analyze controversial choices made by women: forms of discourse that acknowledge the possibility that women may be influenced by the internalization of the very ideology that has subordinated them, yet avoid the claims of determination that alienate women, facilitate the misrepresentation of their decision making capacities and impede inquiry into contributing causal factors which may be more readily subject to remediation".[79]

## THE PUBLIC AND THE PRIVATE

It has been said that the dichotomy between the "public" and the "private" is "ultimately what the feminist movement is about"[80]. Nicola Lacey explains that:

[72] *Ante*, 1141: see C. MacKinnon, *Toward A Feminist Theory of the State* (1989), pp 13–36.
[73] See C. MacKinnon (1983) 8 Signs 65 and *op cit*, n. 71, pp. 172–183. Another example is J. Williams (1989) 87 Mich. L. Rev 797 (note her use of Gramsci, *ante*, 1157 at p. 829). See also A. Scales, n. 27, above, Chap. 7.
[74] See (1990) 24 Georgia L.R. 761.
[75] (1990) 24 Georgia L. Rev. 761, 775.
[76] See J.Braucher (1991) 25 Georgia L.Rev 595.
[77] As it long was in relation to the suffrage: see J.Rendall, *The Origins of Modern Feminism* (1985).
[78] *Op cit*, n. 75, p. 793.
[79] *ibid*, p. 795.
[80] By Carole Pateman in (eds) S.I.Benn and G.F.Gaus, *Public and Private in Social Life* (1983), p. 281. See also W. Kymlicka, *Contemporary Political Philosophy* (1990), pp. 247–62, S.M. Okin, *Justice, Gender and the Family* (1989), pp. 110–133.

"The ideology of the public/private dichotomy allows government to clean its hands of any *responsibility* for the state of the 'private' world and *depoliticises* the disadvantages which inevitably spill over the alleged divide by affecting the position of the 'privately' disadvantaged in the 'public' world".[81]

Too often those who point to a public/private dualism do so as if they are two discrete entities—that they are "out there", two almost natural realms—or even that they are fixed categories or value-free. What this ignores is the historical specificity of the conjunction, its relativity to time and place. Indeed, different concepts of the private are sometimes used in tandem, and indistinguishably. Thus, it is clear that, in talking of the family as "private", one is referring both to its being (supposedly) outside the authority of the state, and outside the scope of market relations. Neither is true.

The constructs of public and private should rather be seen as normative. Every concept of the "public" presupposes a corresponding delimitation of the "private". The language of privacy or intimacy acts as an "idealising lens"[82] to disguise and legitimate unequal spheres of men and women. Since power is deemed to be situated in the public arena, power relations in the domestic sphere can be ignored. It is as if they do not exist.

This has a number of consequences. One practical consequence is, as Lacey states, "the consolidation of the *status quo*: the *de facto* support of pre-existing power relations and distributions of goods within the "private sphere".[83] Domestic relations are thus left in the pre-liberal world, and power differentials, so central to family life, are overlooked. The political nature of the family, as the place where we learn (or learn in part) our gendered selves, is ignored. Women are depoliticised and their lives are marginalised—only in the last 30 years has domestic violence assumed any political importance[84] or abortion entered the political consciousness.[85] The emphasis instead is on "public" wrongs and women's injuries are often not recognised or compensated as injuries by the "public" legal culture.[86] There has been considerable debate on the question whether the state should intervene in family relations. But as Olsen[87] has demonstrated, the question is totally unreal, for non-intervention—no less than intervention—is a political act: it amounts to intervention to recognise and confirm the *status quo*, and it legitimises existing power relationships.

Liberals who favour autonomy for the private sphere often rest their

---

[81] *Unspeakable Subjects* (1998), p. 77.
[82] *Per* S. Benhabib, *Situating The Self* (1992), p. 109.
[83] *Op cit*, n. 81, p. 77.
[84] M.A. Fineman and R. Mykitiak, *The Public Nature of Private Violence* (1994).
[85] S. Sheldon, *Beyond Control—Medical Power and Abortion Law* (1997). See also C. Mackinnon, n. 62, above pp. 139–150, and A. Scales, n. 27, above, pp. 147–150.
[86] R. West (1987) 3 Wisconsin Women's Law Journal 81: but of D. Cornell, *Beyond Accommodation* (1991), pp. 21–36.
[87] (1985) 16 University of Michigan Journal of Law Reform 835.

case on freedom but, as Bill Jordan noted in *Freedom and the Welfare State*, this is often "the freedom of more powerful members (usually husbands in relation to wives, and parents in relation to children) to exercise this power without restriction".[88] By contrast, part of the modern history of the "public" has been an attempt to curb power, to protect against abuse and to introduce a measure of justice and equality. An equally important part has regulated and controlled, often in a discriminatory way. Intervention can be benign or intrusive, depending on perspective. In a valuable recent essay, Dorothy Chann[89] has shown that early twentieth-century state initiatives and reform campaigns in Canada, dealing with sex and venereal diseases, attempted to regulate women's sexual and reproductive lives in different ways, depending upon whether they were viewed as deviant, deviant but salvageable, or incorrigible, and how this in turn was related to factors such as class, race and familial status.

The private sphere is, of course, permeated by government (why can't gays inter-marry[90] or prospective adopters pay for children?) And, as Anita Allen points out, "To the extent that government is infused with patriarchal, heterosexual ideals, men and women's privacy rights are likely to reflect patriarchal, heterosexual ideals of a private sphere".[91]

## CULTURAL PLURALISM AND WOMEN'S RIGHTS

One problem that feminism has had to confront—it is addressed in the extract from Susan Moller Okin—is the right of minority cultures "to live according to their own value systems"[92] when these cultures appear to Western feminists to be detrimental to women. How should a Western legal system respond, for example, to polygamy or female genital mutilation? If it allows these practices it may legitimate gender inequalities. Much cultural behaviour takes place in the private sphere, so that the debate here is linked to that in the previous section.[93]

In an important article[94] Coleman cites disturbing examples to

---

[88] (1976), p. 60.

[89] In (ed) S. Boyd, *Challenging the Public/Private Divide: Feminism, Law and Public Policy* (1997), p. 62.

[90] They can in the Netherlands, Spain, Canada and in Massachusetts and California, and civil partnerships are permitted elsewhere.

[91] "Privacy" in (eds) A. Jaggar and I.M. Young, *A Companion to Feminist Philosophy* (1998), p. 456, 461. See also A. Allen and E. Mack (1990) 10 Northern Illinois Law Review 441. There is a vast literature on public/private dichotomies. Examples (not previously cited) are F. Olsen (1983) 96 Harvard Law Review 1497, K. O'Donovan, *Sexual Divisions In Law* (1985), R. Gavison (1992) 45 Stanford Law Review 1, M. Thornton (1991) 18 JLS 448, and J. Ursel, *Private Lives, Public Policy* (1992).

[92] *Per* M.F. Fresco in M.F. Fresco and P.J. van Tongeren (eds), *Perspectives on Minorities* (1991), p. 154.

[93] The private/public dichotomy is an artificial construction of liberal democracies and other cultures would not employ any such conception. See A.W. Musschenga in *op cit*, n. 91, p. 131.

[94] (1996) 96 Columbia Law Review 1093.

demonstrate the consequences of allowing cultural practices exemption from liberal rights and freedoms: the use of the so-called "cultural defence" can lead to women being denied protection that would be taken for granted by women within the dominant culture.[95] To take just one example drawn from Coleman's article: Should a man from Laos be able to invoke the Hmong custom of "marriage by capture" as a defence to a charge of rape in the U.S. court? The cultural defence, it may be argued, affords substantive equality between individuals by "individualising justice". The victim here had rejected certain aspects of her culture including "marriage by capture". But supposing she had not? Or to take a second example: English law outlaws female circumcision[96] and does not distinguish between girls and adult women. Is the law justified in refusing a Somali woman living in London the right to be circumcised when it allows her, for example, to consent to breast implants?[97] For Coleman cultural defences are "eerily reminiscent of the history of gender and racial apartheid".[98]

Coleman's article should be read in the context of Volpp's response.[99] Volpp argues that Coleman's approach looks only at whether the process is fair, not the outcome. Instead of an anti-discrimination principle, she prefers the principle of anti-subordination. This is colour conscious and considers the "concrete effects of government policy on people's substantive condition".[1] She points also to problems with Coleman's presentation of children and, especially, women as "victims". She takes the example of the practice of parent-child suicide (a mother kills her children and then takes her own life because of the "shame"[2] of her husband's infidelity). The woman is said to be a victim of her culture. But, argues Volpp, a "more sophisticated" reading of such a case is that "women are not subsumed by culture, but are in active negotiation with it".[3] She invokes the example of circumcision practices in which they are actively involved.

This debate inevitably throws up a conflict between women's interests and those of a racial or cultural group. It is an issue addressed by critical race theory.[4] For Volpp prioritising women's rights embraces gender consciousness at the expense of race consciousness.[5] But can it not be argued that allowing a cultural defence enables the rights of a group to prevail over the interests of female members of that group who are likely to have had little input into the formulation of its norms? To Volpp

---

[95] On which see A.O. Renteln, *The Cultural Defense* (2004).
[96] Since 1985: see now the Female Genital Mutilation Act 2003.
[97] See S. Sheldon and S. Wilkinson (1998) 12 Bioethics 263; K. Green and H. Lim (1998) 7 Soc & Legal Studies 365; L. Bibbings in J. Bridgeman and S. Millns, *Law and the Body Politics* (1995), p. 151.
[98] *Op cit*, n. 94, p. 1162.
[99] (1996) 96 Columbia Law Review 1573.
[1] *ibid.*, p. 1595.
[2] *Op cit*, n. 94, p. 1125.
[3] *Op cit*, n. 99, p. 1585.
[4] *Post*, 1491.
[5] *Op cit*, n. 99, p. 1580.

Coleman's thesis is premised on a view that the cultures of Asia and Africa "lag behind" the West. Just as "maleness" has long been the norm, so, it may be argued, Western culture is now the standard by which to judge morality.[6]

Okin's paper (extracted here) is the lead article in a published colloquium.[7] The responses, which cannot be reproduced here, repay study. Kymlicka's[8] may be found particularly interesting because it connects with a wider debate and with his thesis[9] about the need for minority groups to be afforded "external protections" (language rights, guaranteed political representation, compensation for historical injustice, etc.). These rights are very different from rights claimed by groups against their members to restrict choice in the name of cultural tradition or "integrity", but the former may well impact upon the latter. If external protection extends to funding ethnic media would it uphold the right of free speech in the name of liberalism or curtail it if it were used to propagate forced marriage or polygamy or genital mutilation in order to protect women?[10]

## FEMINIST LEGAL METHODS

Two of the extracts examine feminist legal methodology. Feminist theory challenges the positivist-empirical tradition, the assumption that through observation and measurement by an objective observer the truth about reality will emerge. Feminist legal methods, by contrast, are influenced by the interpretive or hermeneutic tradition[11] and by the methods of critical theory.[12] Nielsen explains the differences thus: "the positivists' goal is to predict and control, the hermeneutics' is to understand, and the critical theorists' approach is to emancipate—that is, to uncover aspects of society, especially ideologies, that maintain the *status quo* by restricting or limiting different groups' access to the means of gaining knowledge."[13] Postmodernism has also offered insights for those pursuing feminist legal theory. As Flax puts it, "contemporary feminists join other postmodern philosophers in raising important metatheoretical questions about the possible nature and status of theorizing itself."[14] Postmodernists reject the idea, so central to the liberal thinking of the Enlightenment,[15] that

---

[6] See C, Fluehr-Lobban (1998) 20 Anthro nn. 1.

[7] S.M. Okin, *Is Multiculturalism Bad for Women?* (1999).

[8] *ibid*, pp. 31–34.

[9] In *Multicultural Citizenship* (1995).

[10] See C. Mackinnon, *Only Words* (1993), ch.3.

[11] See *ante*, 8, 380. This can be traced to Weber and Alfred Schutz (*ante*, 9). See, further, B. Glaser and A. Strauss, *The Discovery of Grounded Theory* (1967).

[12] Associated in origin with the Frankfurt school.

[13] J. McCarl Nielsen (ed.) *Feminist Research Methods* (1990), p. 9. On the differences between the traditions see R. Bernstein, *Beyond Objectivism and Relativism* (1983).

[14] (1987) 12 *Signs* 621, 624.

[15] See A. Norrie, *Closure or Critique?* (1993), Chap. 1.

there is a self-contained "subject" separable from social reality.[16] It problematises the notion that "the human subject can be conceived of as a unitary agent of intervention in the social world."[17] The subject is in these terms, as Bartlett argues, a social construct, the product of "multiple structures and discourses,"[18] for example history, culture and language, beyond individual control. Essentialism[19] is necessarily rejected, whether it is that of patriarchy itself or the alternatives offered by cultural feminism. And, if objective truth is challenged, so of course are such manifestations of it as the law itself and criteria for legal legitimacy. If these too are social constructs, their supposed neutrality is deconstructed and the gender hierarchies endemic in them exposed. Latterly, there has come the realisation in some feminist writing, notably that of Martha Minow,[20] that the insights so gained can be turned on other forms of subordination based on factors other than gender (race, religion, ethnicity, handicaps, sexual preference, socio-economic class and age).

In "*Feminist Legal Methods*," Bartlett[21] seeks to identify the methods that make the study and practice of law characteristically "feminist." She emphasises *three*: asking the woman question, feminist practical reasoning and consciousness-raising. These methods, she shows, reveal things that traditional legal methods ignore. She then addresses the nature of the truth claims that these methods entail. Her essay moves through an evaluation of three theories of knowledge in feminist legal thinking, empiricism, standpoint epistemology and postmodernism to argue in favour of "positionality," a stance which acknowledges the existence, but also the contingency, of empirical truths, values and knowledge. The truth is seen as situated and partial. Because knowledge is located in social contexts and reflects different experiences, the key, she argues, lies "in the effort to extend one's limited perspective."[22] But are all other perspectives to be incorporated? Clearly not, but then we need standards of judgement, and these appear to be missing. Positionality is thus seen as a foundation for further knowledge and insight. It emerges from a belief, common to feminist writers exploring feminist epistemology, that through improved methodology will come not just better understanding but a greater ability to urge transformative practice.

Finley's essay[23] is an examination of the relationship between language, power and the law. She argues that legal language and reasoning is gendered: it is informed by men's experiences and derives from the

---

[16] See L. Alcoff (1988) 13 *Signs* 405, and see K. Bartlett, *post*, 1371. See also 1410.
[17] *Per* A. Barron in A. Norrie (ed.) *Closure or Critique, op. cit.*, note 15, p. 80.
[18] *Post*, 1372.
[19] But see A. Young (1990) 1 *Law and Critique* 201.
[20] (1988) 38 J. Legal Educ. 47 and *Making All the Difference* (1990).
[21] See *post*, 1359. On Bartlett, see S. Williams (1993) 8 Berkeley Women's L.J. 63, 100–102. Another strategy is story-telling: see K. Abrams (1991) 79 California L. R. 971.
[22] See *post*, 1375.
[23] *Post*, 1377.

powerful social position of men, relative to women. She emphasises, much as Olsen does,[24] the dualistic and polarised nature of this thinking, and stresses that the claim that law is patriarchal does not mean that women have been ignored by law, but the law's cognition of women is refracted through the male eye rather than through women's experiences and definitions. Her essay gives numerous examples of "malestream" law,[25] ranging from such obvious areas such as rape law with men's definition of sex[26] and labour law with its gendered meaning of work, to examples drawn from less conspicuous mainstream areas, such as tort[27] (note the way that damages for non-economic loss, pain and suffering and nervous shock are seen as marginal and expendable[28]). The "mainstreaming"[29] of feminist legal theory is, indeed, an increasingly noticeable characteristic, with work like that of Vandervelde[30] on the gendered origins of *Lumley v. Gye*,[31] Gross[32] on bankruptcy law (a *Gilligan*-difference approach being used to suggest that some women may adopt a different moral stance as regards past debts), Kornhauser on tax[33] and Charlesworth, Chinkin and Wright applying feminist analysis to international law[34] (why until recently were female genital mutilation,[35] population control, mail order bride practices, sex tourism outside the terrain of international human rights law?). Few areas of law "no matter how musty or arcane" have remained immune from feminist legal scholarship.[36] For Finley the answer does not lie in creating a new language—some French feminists have argued for this.[37] Instead, she proposes "critical engagements with the nature of legal language"[38] to bring women's experiences, perspectives and voices into law to empower

---

[24] See (1990) 18 Int. J. Soc. of Law 199 (see also in D. Kairys, *The Politics of Law* (2nd ed., 1990).

[25] The phrase is Cain's: see (1989) 4 Berkeley Women's L. J. 191.

[26] See *post*, 1378–1379. See also Duncan (1994) 2 Fem. Leg. Studies 3.

[27] On which see L. Bender (1988) 38 J. Legal Ed. 3, criticised by R. Posner (1989) *University of Chicago Legal Forum* 191, 213. See also M. Chamallas (1998) 146 Univ. of Pennsylvania L.R. 463 and L.N. Finley (2003) 53 Emory L.J. 1263.

[28] *Bourhill v. Young* [1943] A.C. 92 (note Lord Macmillan's reference to "elements of greater subtlety" and Lord Porter's to those not possessing the "customary phlegm," endorsed by Lord Bridge in *McLoughlin v. O'Brian* [1983] 1 A.C. 410.

[29] See C. Menkel-Meadow (1992) 23 *Pacific Law Journal* 1493.

[30] See (1992) 101 Yale L. J. 775.

[31] (1853)2 E. and B. 216.

[32] (1990) 88 Michigan L. Rev. 1506.

[33] (1987) 86 Michigan L. Rev. 465. See also Beck (1990) 43 Vanderbilt Law Rev. 317 and J. Grbich (1997) 5 Feminist Legal Studies 131.

[34] (1991) 85 American J. of International Law 615. See also K. Engle (1992) 26 New England L. Rev. 1509.

[35] On which see E. Dorkenoo and S. Elsworthy, *Female Genital Mutilation* (1992). See *post*, 1403.

[36] J. Conaghan (2000) 27 J.L.S. 351, 352.

[37] See L. Irigaray, *The Sex Which Is Not One* (1985) (the French original was published in 1973) and H. Cixous and C. Clérment, *The Newly Born Woman* (1986) (the French original in 1975).

[38] See *post*, 1386.

women and help legitimate these experiences. This has already had an impact: sexual harassment is beginning to be recognised,[39] the concept of rape has been broadened to take account of rape in marriage.[40] Other areas, such as tort, contract and property can be opened up to take account of the experiences of women, and in particular the "injuries" they suffer.[41]

These matters may belong to the "private",[42] but they are as much the concern of jurisprudence as the so-called public questions, which have been the predominant concerns of jurists (mainly male) and will still take up the bulk of this book.

---

## ANN C. SCALES
### The Emergence of Feminist Jurisprudence: An Essay
### (1986)[43]

We as lawyers have been trained to desire abstract, universal, objective solutions to social ills, in the form of legal rules or doctrine. Much of the history of feminist jurisprudence has reflected that tradition. It has been a debate, in the abstract, about appropriate rules. This essay uses the work of several non-legal authors to illustrate the impossibility of seeing solutions to inequality through that lens of abstraction. This essay concerns feminist efforts to live with, and ultimately to resist, abstraction itself.

*Where We've Been*

In this country, the engine of the struggle for equality has been Aristotelian: Equality means to treat like persons alike, and unlike persons unlike.[44] Under this model, when legal distinctions are made, the responsible sovereign must point to some difference between subjects which justifies their disparate treatment.[45] That was the model in *Reed v. Reed*,[46] the first equal protection case decided favorably in the Supreme Court for women. Under the expert guidance of Ruth Bader Ginsburg and the ACLU Women's Rights Project, the *Reed* Court held that the state of Idaho could not presumptively deny to women the right to administer estates. With respect to such activities, the Court saw that women and men are "similarly situated." That is, no demonstrable difference between the sexes justified treating them differently.

This is what Professor Catharine MacKinnon has called "the differences approach,"[47] and it worked extraordinarily well for Ginsburg and her legions.

---

[39] In the U.S. see MacKinnon, *Feminism Unmodified, op. cit.*, note 71, Chap. 9., and title VII of the Civil Rights Act 1964. On the VII of the Civil Rights Act 1964.

[40] In England see *R. v. R.* [1991] 3 W.L.R. 767, but there are similar developments elsewhere many ante-dating that in England. And see the discussion of *State v. Smith* in *post*, 1364–1365.

[41] See A. Howe on ways of making harms suffered by women legally cognisable (1987) 14 Int. J. of Sociology of Law 423, also in Fineman and Thomadsen, *op. cit.*, note 31, p. 148).

[42] See S. M. Okin, *Justice, Gender and The Family* (1989).

[43] [From 95 Yale Law Journal 1373].

[44] Aristotle, *Nicomachean Ethics V* (3) (D. Ross trans. 1925), pp. 112–114.

[45] This is what Charles Frankel has called "basic equality." See Frankel, *"Equality of Opportunity"* (1971) 81 *Ethics* 191, 194–96.

[46] (1971) 404 U.S. 71.

[47] C. MacKinnon, *Sexual Harassment of Working Women* (1979), p. 101.

Indeed, all was going swimmingly until the Court had to face situations where the sexes are not, or do not seem to be, similarly situated—situations involving pregnancy,[48] situations involving the supposed overpowering sexual allure which women present to men,[49] and situations involving the historical absence of women.[50] When the "differences approach" was applied in those cases, the plaintiffs lost. Aristotle would have been thrilled.

Feminist legal scholars have devoted enormous energies to patching the cracks in the differences approach. Which differences between the sexes are or should be relevant for legal purposes? How does one tell what the difference are? Does it matter whether the differences are inherent or the result of upbringing? Is it enough to distinguish between accurate and inaccurate stereotyped differences? Or are there situations where differences are sufficiently "real" and permanent to demand social accommodation?

In response to these questions, feminists have tried to describe for the judiciary a theory of "special rights" for women which will "fit"[51] the discrete, non-stereotypical, "real" differences between the sexes. And here lies our mistake: We have let the debate become narrowed by accepting as correct those questions which seek to arrive at a definitive list of differences. In so doing, we have adopted the vocabulary, as well as the epistemology and political theory, of the law as it is.

When we try to arrive at a definitive list of differences, even in sophisticated ways, we only encourage the law's tendency to act upon a frozen slice of reality. In so doing, we participate in the underlying problem—the objectification of women. Through our conscientious listing, we help to define real gender issues out of existence. Our aim must be to affirm differences as emergent and infinite. We must seek a legal system that works and, at the same time, makes differences a cause for celebration, not classification.

A new jurisprudence emerges as we cease to conduct the debate in prescribed legalistic terms. The equal/special rights debate, for example, reflects the circularity of liberal legal thinking. The rights formula, described in terms of constitutional fit, presumes a fixed reality of gender to which law must conform. The problem of sexual inequality, however, when understood as systematic domination, is not susceptible to that view. Our past reliance on rights/rule structuring has been disappointing, because we have been unable to see the solipsism of the male norm. Our tendency as lawyers to seek comprehensive rules in accordance with that norm is a dangerous learned reflex which defeats feminism's critique of objectification.

## The Tyranny of Objectivity

Underlying the Supreme Court's ruling in *Reed v. Reed*[52] was a perception that sexism is a distortion of reality. Once the Court made this discovery, it needed to

---

[48] *Geduldig v. Aiello* (1974) 417 U.S. 484 (exclusion of pregnancy from risks covered by state employees' insurance plan does not constitute sex discrimination under equal protection clause).

[49] For an analysis of how the image of "woman as temptress" excuses discrimination, see Aiken (1984) 7 N.Y.U. Rev. L & Soc. Change 357. Most illustrative of this phenomenon are *Dothard v. Rawlinson* (1977) 433 U.S. 321 (refusal to hire female prison guards allowed under Title VII as bona fide occupational qualification), and *Michael M v. Sonoma Country Super. Ct.* (1981) 450 U.S. 464 (constitutionality of California's statutory rape law sustained).

[50] *Rostker v. Goldberg* (1981) 453 U.S. 57 (upholding constitutionality of exclusion of women from draft registration).

[51] The "fit" metaphor probably had its origin in Tussman & tenBroek, "The Equal Protection of the Law" (1949) 37 Calif. L. Rev. 341, and is usually presented in terms of the famous Venn diagrams therein. *ibid.* at 347.

[52] (1971) 404 U.S. 71.

transform its discovery into a legalistic code, to construct an "objective" rule. And here lies the most difficult part of rule-making in our system as it is— phrasing the rule so that people believe that the rule is detached, so that it appears to transcend the results in particular cases.[53]

The philosophical basis of such an approach is "abstract universality."[54] In order to apply a rule neutrally in future cases, one must discern *a priori* what the differences and similarities among groups are. But because there are an infinite number of differences and similarities among groups, one must also discern which differences are relevant. To make this determination, one must first abstract the essential and universal similarities among humans;[55] one must have strict assumptions about human nature as such. Without such an abstraction, there is no way to talk about which differences in treatment are arbitrary and which are justified. Underlying this approach is the correspondence theory of truth: The sovereign's judgments are valid only when they reflect objective facts. Thus, somewhere in the nature of things there must be a list of sex differences that matter and those that do not. Notice, however, that abstract universality by its own terms cannot arrive at such a list. It has no "bridge to the concrete"[56] by which to ascertain the emerging and cultural qualities which constitute difference.

With nothing above ground, abstract universality constructed a dark tunnel to its tainted delusion. It made maleness the norm of what is human, and did so sub rosa, all in the name of neutrality.[57] By this subterranean system, the "relevant" differences have been and always will be those which keep women in their place.[58] Abstract universality is ideology, pure and simple. It is a conception of the world which takes "the part for the whole, the particular for the universal and essential, or the present for the eternal."[59] With the allegedly anonymous picture of humanity reflecting a picture males have painted of themselves, women are but male subjectivity glorified, objectified, elevated to the status of reality. The values of things "out there" are made to appear as if they were qualities of the things themselves. So goes the process of objectification: the winner is he who makes his world seem necessary.

Feminist analysis begins with the principle that objective reality is a myth. It recognizes that patriarchal myths are projections of the male psyche.[60] The most pernicious of these myths is that the domination of women is a natural right, a mere reflection of the biological family. The patriarchal paradigm of the will of the father informs rationality at every historical stage.

A legal system must attempt to assure fairness. Fairness must have reference to real human predicaments. Abstract universality is a convenient device for some philosophical pursuits, or for any endeavour whose means can stand without

---

[53] The equality of transcendence of results has been said to be the primary feature of neutrality in constitutional adjudication. Wechsler, "*Toward Neutral Principles of constitutional Law,*" (1959) 73 Harv. L. Rev. 1, 12 [and see, *ante*, 1006].

[54] Gould, "The Woman Question: Philosophy of Liberation and the Liberation of Philosophy" in *Women and Philosophy: Toward A Theory of Liberation* (C. Gould & M. Wartofsky eds. 1976), pp. 5–6.

[55] *ibid.* at 13.

[56] Gould, *supra* note 54 at 20.

[57] The most striking example is Justice Bradley's concurrence in *Bradwell v. Illinois* (1872) 83 U.S. (16 Wall.) 130, 14–42 (holding 14th Amendment's privileges and immunities clause did not entitle Myra Bradwell to bar membership).

[58] The cataloguing of differences along the lines described in the text is most evident in the pregnancy area, where the treatment of pregnancy demanded by women would impose an immediate financial burden on men. See, *e.g. General Electric Co v. Gilbert* (1976) 429 U.S. 125.

[59] Gould, *supra* note 54 at 21.

[60] MacKinnon, "An Agenda for Theory," (1982) 7 *Signs* 515 at 539, 541. Smith, "The Sword and Shield of Perseus: Some Mythological Dimensions of the Law," (1983) 6 J.L. & Psychiatry 235, 239.

ends, but it is particularly unsuited for law. Law is, after all, a social tool. It is only extrinsically important. Its actual value depends upon its success in promoting that which is intrinsically valuable. By inquiring into the mythic structure of objectivity, we see that abstract universality explicitly contradicts the ideal of a "government of laws, not men." Our task, therefore, is to construct a system which avoids solipsism, which recognizes that the subjectivity of the law-maker is not the whole of reality.

### A Call For Vigilance

It is imperative for jurisprudence to tap the power of the more radical versions of feminism. An effective contemporary feminist critique must be radical in the literal sense. It must go to the root of inequality. Without extraordinary subterranean vigilance, the radical potential of feminism will be undermined. Like other movements that presage revolutionary change, feminism faces a constant threat of deradicalization.

In *In A Different Voice*,[61] developmental psychologist Carol Gilligan observed that little girls and little boys appear to grapple with moral problems differently. Boys tend to make moral decisions in a legalistic way: they presume that the autonomy of individuals is the paramount value, and then employ a rule-like mechanism to decide among the "rights" of those individuals. Gilligan refers to this as the "ethic of rights" or the "ethic of justice." Girls, on the other hand, seem to proceed by the "ethic of care." They have as their goal the preservation of the relationships involved in a given situation. Their reasoning looks like equity: they expand the available universe of facts, rules, and relationships in order to find a unique solution to each unique problem.

Just as Gilligan's work has the potential to inspire us in historic ways,[62] it could also become the Uncle Tom's Cabin of our century. Lawyers are tempted to use Gilligan's work in a shallow way, to distill it into a neat formula. Her thesis is memorable, handy, and easy to over-simplify. Rightly or wrongly, many people feel that such an over-simplified version comports with their experience of the sexes. Moreover, generalizations taken from Gilligan provide accessible analogues to the law/equity split, and to the ethical positions competing in any legal dispute. All in all, Gilligan's work tempts one to suggest that the different voices of women can somehow be grafted onto our right-and rule-based legal system.[63]

One in a non-vigilant mode might be moved to think that we could have a system which in the abstract satisfies all the competing considerations; rules, rights, relationships, and equity. This is what I call the "incorporationist" view. Gilligan asserts that as a matter of personal moral development, the ability to integrate the ethics of care with the ethics of rights signals maturity. I think no one would disagree with such a goal in an emotional realm. Emotional and cognitive maturity have, however, come to mean very different things. In the majority culture, emotional maturity does not count as knowledge. The ad hoc evaluations we must undertake in the emotional realm cannot be acknowledged elsewhere. Such judgments are not "reliable;" only "objectivity" is reliable. We should be especially wary when we hear lawyers, addicted to cognitive objectivity as they are, assert that women's voices have a place in the existing system.

---

[61] C. Gilligan, *In A Different Voice* (1982).

[62] It has already helped support some excellent work in the area of alternative dispute resolution. See, *e.g.* Menkel-Meadow, "Toward Another View of Legal Negotiation: The Structure of Problem Solving," (1984) 31 U.C.L.A. L. Rev. 754, 763 n. 28 (Gilligan's theory supports argument that problem-solving, as opposed to adversarial, negotiation is preferable).

[63] See, *e.g.* Karst, "Women's Constitution," (1984) Duke L.J. 447, 484, 494–95 (urging that legal system should open up to "the voices of women").

Incorporationism presumes that we can whip the problem of social inequality by adding yet another prong to the already multi-pronged legal tests my students feel they must memorize. Incorporationism suffers from the same lack of vision as the "equal rights/special rights" debate. Both presume that male supremacy is simply a random collection of irrationalities in an otherwise rational coexistence. Both presume that instances of inequality are mere legal mistakes—a series of failures to treat equals as equals which we can fix if we can just spot, the irrationality in enough cases. As MacKinnon has demonstrated, however, from such viewpoints we cannot see that male supremacy is a complete social system for the advantage of one sex over another.[64] The injustice of sexism is not irrationality; it is domination. Law must focus on the latter, and that focus cannot be achieved through a formal lens. Binding ourselves to rules would help us only if sexism were a legal error.

A commitment to equality requires that we undertake to investigate the genderization of the world, leaving nothing untouched. The principles of objectivity, abstraction, and personal autonomy are at risk. In our search, we must look for the deeper causes and consequences of Gilligan's findings. Her work is empirical evidence for what feminist theory has already postulated: A male point of view focuses narrowly on autonomy, on the separation between self and others. That disjunction contains the roots of domination. In the terms of feminist theory, male reality manifests itself by negating that which is non-male. The male model defines self, and other important concepts, by opposing the concept to a negativized "other."[65] Male rationality divides the world between all that is good and all that is bad—between objective and subjective, light and shadow, man and women. For all of these dichotomies, the goodness of the good side is defined by what it is not.

Whereas the male self/other ontology seems to be oppositional, the female version seems to be rational.[66] The female ontology is an alternative theory of differentiation that does not define by negation nor require a "life and death struggle"[67] to identify value in the world. Instead, it perceives relationship as constitutive of the self. It perceives dichotomization as irrational.[68]

Male and female perceptions of value are not shared, and are perhaps not even perceptible to each other. In our current genderized realm, therefore, the "rights-based" and "care-based" ethics cannot be blended. Patriarchal psychology sees value as differently distributed between men and women: Men are rational, women are not. Feminist psychology suggests different conceptions of value: Women are entirely rational, but society cannot accommodate them because the male standard has defined into oblivion any version of rationality but its own. Paradigmatic male values, like objectivity, are defined as exclusive, identified by their presumed opposites. Those values cannot be content with multiplicity; they create the other and then devour it. Objectivity ignores context; reason is the opposite of emotion; rights preclude care. As long as the ruling ideology is a function of this dichotomization, incorporationism threatens to be mere co-optation, a more subtle version of female invisibility.

By trying to make everything too nice, incorporationism repress contradictions. It usurps women's language in order to further define the world in the male image; it thus deprives women of the power of naming. Incorporationism

---

[64] See C. MacKinnon, *Sexual Harassment of Working Women* (1979), p. 121.

[65] These ideas were first articulated in a feminist context by Simone de Beauvoir [in] *The Second Sex*.

[66] The term "self/other ontology" and the distinction between "relational" and "oppositional" ontologies are taken from Whitbeck, "A Different Reality: Feminist Ontology" in *Beyond Domination: New Perspectives On Women and Philosophy* (C. Gould ed. 1984), p. 64.

[67] *ibid.* at 69.

[68] *ibid.* at 76.

means to give over the world, because it means to say to those in power: "We will use your language and we will let you interpret it."

### Feminist method

Feminist thinking has evolved dramatically in the last twenty years, from an essentially liberal attack on the absence of women in the public world to a radical vision of the transformation of that world. The demand for "gender neutrality" which served valiantly in the legal struggles of the seventies has inevitably become a critique of neutrality itself, which proceeds by an admittedly non-neutral method. Explanations of our method usually provoke the charge of nominalism, such is the staying power of the ideal of objectivity. Feminist method would appear to be an easy target for that weapon. Feminism does not claim to be objective, because objectivity is the basis for inequality. Feminism is not abstract, because abstraction when institutionalized shields the *status quo* from critique. Feminism is result-oriented. It is vitally concerned with the oblivion fostered by lawyers' belief that process is what matters.

The next step for theory is therefore to demonstrate that feminist method leads to principled adjudication and a more orderly coexistence. Let us begin by reconsidering Carol Gilligan's results. The little boys' approach divides life into opposing camps. In a moral dilemma, this person or that person shall win, based upon some "essential" difference in their situations. One must be shown to be unworthy and wrong. One must be transformed into the "other."

Perhaps there is something in the paradigm of male infant development which teaches a harsh method of differentiation. Insofar as objectification is taught as the preferred way to see the world, we replicate the emotional substructure of domination. The children are thereby programmed, prepared to fall into the habit of objectification which is at the heart of woman-loathing. As adults, these people may have noble intentions, but it will be too late. At best, they will become incorporationists—people must co-opt the voices of the powerless, who can't let them speak for themselves because, by definition, "the other" is mute.

Compare the problem-solving method used by the little girls. Their habit of expanding the context, of following the connections among people and events, is descriptive of rationality. When given a situation with which to grapple, the girls do not insist upon uncovering an essence of the problem, but look rather for a solution that is coherent with the rest of experience.

If I am right that the "rights-based" and "care-based" approaches are incompatible, we must make a choice between adjudicative principles. The choice is not, however, between male and female hegemony. The choice is rather between a compulsion to control reality and a commitment to restrain hegemony. Do we want a system that brooks no disagreement or one that invites as many points of view as the varieties of existence require? The values of honesty and pragmatism require us to choose the relational model, because only it describes how we as language-users actually and responsibly perform according to truly meaningful criteria.

Law, like the language which is its medium, is a system of classification. To characterize similarities and differences among situations is a key step in legal judgments. That step, however, is not a mechanistic manipulation of essences. Rather, that step always has a moral crux.

Law needs some theory of differentiation. Feminism, as a theory of differentiation, is particularly well suited to it. Feminism brings law back to its purpose—to decide the moral crux of the matter in real human situations. Law is a complex system of communication; its communicative matrix is intended to give access to the moral crux. Finding the crux depends upon the relation among things, not upon their opposition. In any case, imperfect analogies are available; a case is similar or dissimilar to others in an unlimited variety of ways. The scope and limits of any analogy must be explored in each case, with social reality as our guide. This is a normative, but not illogical process. Any logic is a norm, and cannot be used except with reference to its purposes. Why should that be so hard to perceive, to teach, and to do?

Wittgenstein believed that his work with language was obvious, that he was supplying "observations which no one has doubted, but which have escaped remark only because they are always before our eyes."[69] It would also seem obvious that relational reasoning is law's soul, that law's duty is to enhance, rather than to ignore, the rich diversity of life. Yet this purpose is not obvious; it is obscured by the myth of objectivity which opens up law's destructive potential. Feminism inverts the logical primacy of rule over facts. Feminist method stresses that the mechanisms of law—language, rules, and categories—are all merely means for economy in thought and communication. They make it possible for us to implement justice without reinventing every wheel at every turn. But we must not let means turn into ends. When those mechanisms obscure our vision of the ends of law, they must be revised or ignored. Sometimes we must take the long route in order to get to where we really need to be.

In feminist thought, deciding what differences are relevant for any purpose does not require objectifying and destroying some "other." Feminism rejects "abstract universality" in favor of "concrete universality." The former conjures differences—it elevates more to dispositive principles and defines others out of existence—and makes maleness the norm. The latter reinterprets differences in three crucial ways. First, concrete universalism takes differences to be constitutive of the universal itself. Second, it sees differences as systematically related to each other, and to other relations, such as exploited and exploiter. Third, it regards differences as emergent, as always changing.[70]

In the past, two legal choices appeared to resolve claims of social injustice: Law could either ignore differences, thereby risking needless conformity, or it could freeze differences, thereby creating a menu of justifications for inequality. Concrete universality eliminates the need for such a choice. When our priority is to understand differences and to value multiplicity, we need only to discern between occasions of respect and occasions of oppression. Those are judgments we know how to make, even without a four-part test to tell us, for every future circumstance, what constitutes domination.

Domination comes in many forms. Its mechanisms are so insidious and so powerful that we could never codify its "essence." The description that uses no formula, but which points to the moral crux of the matter, is exactly what we need.

### Coping with equality

The problem of inequality of the sexes stands in complex relation to the problem of survival. Inequality in the sexual division of labor assures replication of the model of aggression. Pathological aggression accounts for inequality. If these connections are ever to be unpacked, if we are serious about survival, we need a radically more serious approach to equality. Law must embrace a version of equality that focuses on the real issues—domination, disadvantage and disempowerment—instead of on the interminable and diseased issue of differences between the sexes. I endorse the definition of equality proposed by MacKinnon:[71] The test in any challenge should be "whether the policy or practice in question

---

[69] L. Wittgenstein, *Philosophical Investigations* § 415 at 125.

[70] Gould, *supra* note 54 at 27.

[71] C. MacKinnon, *supra* note 64, at 117. Nearly identical standards could be applied to other historically disadvantaged groups.

integrally contributes to the maintenance of an underclass or a deprived position because of gender status."[72] MacKinnon contrasts this to the "differences approach," calling it the "inequality approach."[73] I would call the former "thinking like a lawyer," the latter, "thinking like a person."

That is not to say that the proposed standard will be easy to implement. It will require us to bring the very best of our humanness to bear. The critics appropriately worry, for example, that classifications designed to address the real problems of women (such as pregnancy legislation) will serve to reinforce stereotypes about women's place. The problem for feminist legal scholars, I think, is that we are unsure how to measure what about stereotyping is at issue in a given case. The notion of stereotyping connotes over-simplification, inattention to individual characteristics, lack of seriousness, and invariance. We use the concept of stereotyping without difficulty when the challenged practice is based upon an untrue generalization. All of the connotations of stereotyping are clearly implicated in negative ways. In such cases, both the differences approach and the inequality approach would prohibit the classification.

The inequality approach focuses upon two other sources of feminist discomfort: first, the need for a reliable approach to generalizations which are largely true (either because of biology or because of highly successful socialization); and second, the need to distinguish between beneficial and burdensome legislation.

Only the inequality approach attempts to reckon with true generalizations. Indeed, in that view, different treatment based upon unique physical characteristics would be "among the *first* to trigger suspicion and scrutiny."[74] In the past, biological differences have been used to show that classifications are not sex-based.[75] Thereby, the reasons for having antidiscrimination laws have been seen as the reasons to allow discrimination.[76] The inequality approach unravels the tautology. It makes no sense to say that equality is guaranteed only when the sexes are already equal. The issue is not freedom to be treated without regard to sex; the issue is freedom from systematic subordination because of sex.[77]

The inequality approach would also reach stereotypes which, though not biologically based, have largely made themselves true through a history of inequality.[78] Consider the situation in *Phillips v. Martin Marietta Corp.*,[79] where the company hired males with preschool age children, but would not hire women in that category. As a variation, suppose the trial court had found that women with small children did in fact have greater responsibilities, and therefore were, as a group, less well suited for the jobs in question. Such a finding would correspond to the facts of allocation of child-raising responsibility. The only challenge that will work in this scenario is one from an "exceptional" woman candidate for employment—a woman with preschool aged children whose job performance will not be impaired by her obligations to them. The policy will be deemed irrational as applied to her.

Compare the inequality approach, which is triggered not by irrationality, but by disadvantage. In our scenario, the inequality approach is superior because it reaches the worse injustice: The fact that women who fit the stereotype are

---

[72] *ibid.* at 102.

[73] See Williams, Women's Rights L. Rep. 75 at 197–200 (1982); Taub, Book Review (1980) 80 Colum. L. Rev. 1686, 1682–93 reviewing C. MacKinnon.

[74] See C. MacKinnon, *supra* note 64 at 118.

[75] See, *e.g. Michael M.* v. *Sonoma County Super. Ct.* (1981) 450 U.S. 464, 476 (upholding statutory rape law that presumes male is culpable aggressor because "consequences of sexual intercourse and pregnancy fall more heavily on the female than on the male").

[76] See C. MacKinnon, *supra* note 64 at 227.

[77] *See id.* at 117.

[78] *See id.* at 122–25.

[79] (1971) 400 U.S. 542 (*per curiam*) (reversing Court of Appeals' determination that policy was not sex-based).

precluded from advancement in our economic system: A challenge adjudicated by that standard would succeed on behalf of the unexceptional as well as the exceptional. Employers (and other employees who have carried a dis-proportionately lower burden in child-rearing) would then essentially have to compensate for the benefits they have derived from women's double burden. Such payment should include damages, and court-ordered advancement, day care, parents' leave, and reallocation of workers' hours and rewards. This redistribution of historical burdens and benefits may seem a sweeping remedy, but it is the only one which addresses the reality.

With respect to our second problem, the discernment of genuinely beneficial classifications, suppose that the same company offered a hiring preference for women with school age children, and provided some relief from the double burden. The offer undoubtedly "reinforces a stereotype," but what shall we make of the fact that the stereotype is in large part—if only contingently and temporarily—true? But true only because women carry a disproportionate burden of the child-caring responsibility in our society. Especially when women can elect to receive the benefits (as opposed to risking stigmatization by them), what is the objection to such a plan? Disadvantage has a way of replicating and reinforcing itself. To oppose the scheme is to be reduced to relying upon a groundswell of exceptional behaviors within the disadvantaged group itself. Historically, however, disadvantaged groups have been forced to rely upon surrogates to better themselves. That has not required that the groups thus assisted conform for all time to the surrogates' perceptions of them (or even to their own perceptions of themselves).

Beneficial classifications, therefore, seem necessary to the ultimate undoing of stubborn stereotypes. It is true that in our history, stereotypical differences, both real and imagined, have served primarily as convenient, "natural" justifications for imposition of burdens. It does not follow, however, that we cannot use differences progressively. Injustice does not flow directly from recognizing differences; injustice results when those differences are transformed into social and economic deprivation. Our task then, is to exercise our capacity for discernment in more precise ways. Allegedly beneficial classifications, even when they invoke a stereotype, must be measured against what is objectionable in stereotyping. Beneficial classifications, such as the employment preference in our example, will survive under the inequality approach if they do not have those characteristics. Insofar as the employment preference over-simplifies, it is an over-simplification in the service of a profound complexity, as is any well-drafted policy. The preference provides to individuals the opportunity to demonstrate their capacities when the stereotype is set aside. It evinces laudable seriousness toward the problem, especially insofar as the stereotype takes upon itself some of the burden of the past discrimination. Last, and perhaps most important, it is not invariant. By definition it points to the stereotype for the purpose of undoing it, as an example of how revised present arrangements can relieve centuries of disadvantage. When allegedly beneficial classifications do not have this form, or when once beneficial schemes cease to have it, the inequality approach would prohibit them.

Admittedly, the inequality approach would sometimes require that different standards be used for men and women. If that were not so, however, the approach would not be working. Its emphasis is upon enforced inferiority, not sex-differentiated treatment. When the aim is to discover the reality of domination, the standard to be applied depends upon the context. The inequality approach requires an investigation which must delve as deeply as circumstances demand into whether the challenged policy or practice exploits gender status. To worry in the abstract about which standard should be applied at what time is to replicate the fallacy of the differences approach.

In short, the inequality approach means that we have to think more broadly about what we want "equality" to mean. The traditional bases for differentiation between the sexes are socially-created categories, given meaning only by assigned biases. We create the relevant comparisons, and are free to do so de novo in light of social realities. Thus, in the preferential hiring situation, we would say that the right at stake, rather than the right to be treated without regard to sex, is the right not to have one's existence bifurcated because of sex. In the pregnancy situation, it is the right to have one's total health needs taken as seriously as are those of the other sex.

Logic is no obstacle to the implementation of the inequality approach. The obstacles are, rather, perception and commitment. When the fact of judicial manipulation has been so salient in the past, why should we now expect those responsible for implementing the law to be able to see, in any given situation, how women have been disadvantaged? Accustomed as judges are to looking for similarities and differences, they can not or will not make the assessments of deprivation and disempowerment.

My response to this, on optimistic days, is that we are more persuasive than we believe we are. If judges are supposed to accept guidance, we as practitioners and scholars ought to be able to provide it. There has been some progress, however modest.[80] Our duty is to be vigilant in assuring that what happens is real progress, and to guide the courts through our proposed transformation of adjudication.

At less optimistic moments, candor would compel me to admit that implementation of a feminist approach will ultimately depend upon significant changes in judicial personnel. Given what we have experienced, however, I feel comfortable with such an admission. It is time that feminist lawyers spoke openly about the politics of neutrality, instead of pretending that sexism were a legal mistake. We have, for example, squandered over a decade discussing what legal standard could have prevented the outrage of *Geduldig v. Aiello*.[81] But let's face it—the problem in that "analysis" (that no discrimination exists if pregnant women and pregnant men are treated the same) is not that the Supreme Court used the wrong legal standard. The problem was much more serious: It was that our highest court cavalierly allowed California to disadvantage women with respect to their reproductive capabilities. Our highest court endorsed a modern version of a centuries-old method of domination.

We must never forget *Geduldig*. Our Supreme Court got away with it because we allowed the question of pregnancy to be sequestered in our own minds from the question of domination. In our search for a liberal resolution, the real issue remained invisible, and our critique came dangerously close to consent. Our objections can no longer be oblique, for then they are lost. Keeping dissent hidden is an ancient tactic which renders the dissent trivial, abnormal, and disconnected from its roots. Due to the distribution of women in society, this has particularly been the case with feminism. Because each new feminist work or insight appears as if from nowhere, "each contemporary feminist theorist [is] attacked or dismissed ad feminam, as if her politics were simply an outburst of personal bitterness or rage."[82] Trust we must have that we can describe the issues; empowered we must be when our trust is violated.

The proposed inequality standard will not take root overnight. Developments in feminist theory take decades to manifest themselves in law. But it will happen;

---

[80] Taub cites *Califano* v. *Goldfarb* (1977) 430 U.S. 199, as an example of the Court's inability to see disadvantage to women. Taub, *supra* note 73 at 1691. In that case, the Court invalidated a social security benefits provision which disadvantaged the survivors of female workers. Only a plurality saw the scheme as discriminatory toward women. Since that time, however, a majority seems to have become adept at recognizing such discrimination against deceased workers. See *Wengler* v. *Druggists Mut. Ins. Co.* (1980) 446 U.S. 142, 152 (workers' compensation laws denying widower benefits on his wife's work-related death that are available to widows violates equal protection clause).

[81] (1974) 417 U.S. 484.

[82] A. Rich, *On Lies, Secrets and Silence* (1979), p. 11.

the difficulty of the process must not stop us from demanding that change, or from continuing the tradition that makes it possible.

## Feminist method revisited

The term "feminist jurisprudence" disturbs people. That is not surprising, given patriarchy's convenient habit of labelling as unreliable any approach that admits to be interested, and particularly given the historic *a priori* invalidation of women's experience. That longstanding invalidation also causes women, including feminist women, to be reluctant to make any claims beyond the formal reach of liberalism. Further, we are taught to ascribe the legal system's successes to the principle of detachment.

In the understandable rush to render feminism acceptable in traditional terms, it is sometimes suggested that we ought to advertise our insight as a revival of the Legal Realism in the 1930's. We are surely indebted to the Realists for their convincing demonstration that the law could not be described, as the positivists had hoped, as a scientific enterprise, devoid of moral or political content. The Realists' description of the influence of morality, economics, and politics upon law is the first step in developing an antidote for legal solipsism. In the end, however, the Realists did not revolutionize the law but merely expanded the concept of legal process. The Realists did not press their critique deeply enough; they did not bring home its implications. In the face of their failure, the system has clung even more desperately to objectivity and neutrality. "[T]he effect of the Realists was much like the role that Carlyle pronounced for Matthew Arnold: 'He led them into the wilderness and left them there.'"

Feminism now faces the charge leveled at Realism, that it destroys the citadel of objectivity and leaves nothing to legitimate the law. Our response to this state of affairs begins with an insight not exclusive to feminist thought: The law must finally enter the twentieth century. The business of living and progressing within our disciplines requires that we give up on "objective" verification at various critical moments, such as when we rely upon gravity,[83] or upon the existence of others, or upon the principle of verification itself. Feminism insists upon epistemological and psychological sophistication in law: Jurisprudence will forever be stuck in a post-realist battle of subjectivities, with all the discomfort that has represented, until we confront the distinction between knowing subject and known object.

Feminist method is exemplary of that confrontation. And because we do not separate the observer from the observed, "[f]eminism is the first theory to emerge from those whose interest it affirms."[84] Feminist method proceeds through consciousness raising. The results of consciousness raising cannot be verified by traditional methods, nor need they be. We are therefore operating from within an epistemological framework which denies our power to know. This is an inherently transformative process: It validates the experience of women, the major content of which has been invalidation.[85]

"Feminism criticizes this male totality without an account of our capacity to do so or to imagine or realize a more whole truth. Feminism affirms women's point of view by

[83]  See T. Kuhn, *The Structure of Scientific Revolutions* (2nd ed., 1970), p. 108 (abandonment by eighteenth-century scientists of attempt to explain gravity reflected "neither a decline nor a raising of standards, but ... the adoption of a new paradigm"). [and see *ante*, 27].

[84]  MacKinnon, "An Agenda for Theory", p. 543. Because feminism emerges from women themselves, we can largely avoid the old quandary of whether revolutionary consciousness arises from the masses or must be prompted by a revolutionary elite.

[85]  *See* MacKinnon, "An Agenda for Theory", *supra* note 84, at 536; MacKinnon, "Toward Feminist Jurisprudence" 8 *Signs* 635, 638.

revealing, criticizing, and explaining its impossibility. This is not a dialectical paradox. It is a methodological expression of women's situation. ... Women's situation offers no outside to stand on or gaze at, no inside to escape to, too much urgency to wait, no place else to go, and nothing to use but the twisted tools that have been shoved down our throats. If feminism is revolutionary, this is why."[86]

Consciousness raising is a vivid expression of self-creation and responsibility. To Wittgenstein's insight that perceptions have meaning only in the context of experience, feminism would add that perceptions have meaning only in the context of an experience that matters. Consciousness raising means that dramatic eye-witness testimony is being given; it means, more importantly, that women now have the confidence to declare it as such. We have an alternative to relegating our perception to the realm of our own subjective discomfort. Heretofore, the tried and true scientific strategy of treating non-conforming evidence as mistaken worked in the legal system. But when that evidence keeps turning up, when the experience of women becomes recalcitrant, it will be time to treat that evidence as true.[87]

The foundations of the law will not thereby crumble. Though feminism rejects the notion that for a legal system to work, there have to be "objective" rules, we admit that legality has (or should have) certain qualities. There must be something reliable somewhere, there must be indicia of fairness in the system, but neither depends on objectivity. Rather, we need to discard the habit of equating our most noble aspirations with objectivity and neutrality. We need at least to redefine those terms, and probably to use others, to meet our very serious responsibilities.

My admission that feminism is result-oriented does not import the renunciation of all standards. In a system defined by constitutional norms such as equality, we need standards to help us make connections among norms, and to help us see "family resemblances"[88] among instances of domination. Standards, however, are not means without ends: They never have and never can be more than working hypotheses. Just as it would be shocking to find a case that said, "the petitioner wins though she satisfied no criteria," so it must ultimately be wrong to keep finding cases that say, "petitioner loses though the criteria are indefensible." In legal situations, a case is either conformed to a standard or the standard is modified with justification. That justification should not be that "we like the petitioner's facts better;" rather, it is that "on facts such as these, the standard doesn't hold up."

The feminist approach takes justification seriously; it is a more honest and efficient way to achieve legitimacy. The feminist legal standard for equality is altogether principled in requiring commitment to finding the moral crux of matters before the court. The feminist approach will tax us. We will be exhausted by bringing feminist method to bear. Yet we must force law makers and interpreters to hear that which they have been well trained to ignore. We will have to divest ourselves of our learned reticence, debrief ourselves every day. We will have

---

[86] MacKinnon, "Toward Feminist Jurisprudence" *op. cit.* n. 85; at 637, 639.

[87] MacKinnon illustrates with reference to rape. Rape law has assumed that a single, objective state of affairs existed: A "rape" occurred or it didn't; consent was given or it wasn't. In fact, however, the reality is often split—"a woman is raped but not by a rapist," *ibid.* at 654—and in focusing on the accused's state of mind, the law concludes that the rape did not happen. The dilemma here involves more than questions of legal process. Deciding what presumptions should apply then requires a reexamination of law's presuppositions about sexuality itself, and then a decision as to what conditions of sexuality the law should enforce. The choice may come down to one between protecting the likelihood that men will mistakenly infer consent, on one hand, and encouraging women's access to the world without fear, on the other.

[88] L. Wittgenstein, *supra* note 69, § 67 at 32.

to trust ourselves to be able to describe life to each other—in our courts, in our legislatures, in our emergence together. [1373–1403]

## PATRICIA A. CAIN
### Feminism and the Limits of Equality
(1990)[89]

In this Essay, I will consider four schools of feminist thought: liberal, radical, cultural and postmodern. My initial purpose is to highlight and explain the disagreements over the meanings of equality that have occurred among feminist legal scholars influenced by these four schools of thought. I believe these disagreements reflect real differences of opinion about how "woman" is currently defined by male power and how she should be defined by feminists.

Specifically, I will propose that feminists in law concentrate on alternative legal arguments—that is, arguments based not on equality, but on other concepts that are better-tailored to accomplishment of the feminist goal of self-definition.

### Schools of Feminist Thought: Perspectives on "Woman" and "Equality"

*Liberal Feminism.* Liberal feminism is rooted in the belief that women, as well as men, are rights-bearing, autonomous human beings. Rationality, individual choice, equal rights and equal opportunity are central concepts for liberal political theory. Liberal feminism, building on these concepts, argues that women are just as rational as men and that women should have equal opportunity with men to exercise their right to make rational, self-interested choices. Early liberal feminists include Mary Wollstonecraft (1759–1799) and Harriet Taylor.

Today, liberal feminism is often associated with Betty Friedan and other founders of the National Organization of Women. Within the legal academy, it is a term associated with Ruth Bader Ginsburg, Herma Hill Kay, Wendy Williams and Nadine Taub. Liberal feminism is viewed as the dominant theory behind much of the post-*Reed v. Reed* constitutional litigation brought on behalf of women. This litigation was spearheaded by Ruth Bader Ginsburg, who was then a Professor of Law at Rutgers and subsequently at Columbia University.[90]

Liberal feminists have been criticized by more radical feminists for being concerned only with equal pay in the public sphere. Litigators, like Ruth Bader Ginsburg, have been charged as being short-sighted because they adopted an assimilationist theory of equality that would benefit women only if they acted like men.[91]

Let me spell out the critique a bit further. Remember that equality theory, as applied to gender, has been conceptually limited by the "similarly situated" requirement. If members of the dominant gender (men) enjoy rights that members of the nondominant gender (women) want, then the only way for women to obtain these rights under existing equal protection doctrine is to argue that, as to the right in question, women are similarly situated to men. If men are being paid X dollars for performing a job in the public sphere, then women should be entitled to the same pay for performing the same job. The equality argument is that women are workers just like men. It is this argument of similarity that makes it possible to expand women's rights. Radical feminists complain, however, that

---

[89] [From (1990) 24 Georgia Law Rev 803.]
[90] [Appointed a Supreme Court Justice in 1993.]
[91] Some feminists additionally criticize this early equality litigation because it included cases like *Craig* v. *Boren* (1976) 429 U.S. 190, in which men successfully argued for rights held by women: in *Craig*, the right to buy 3.2 per cent. beer.

to argue on the basis of women's similarity to men merely assimilates women into an unchanged male sphere. In a sense, the result is to make women into men.

The liberal feminist response to this is that early feminist litigation was concerned with breaking down male-created categories. The point was not to make women into men, but to expand the possibilities for female life-experience by freeing women from the limitations of the male-constructed category "woman." "Woman" was to be freed from the private domestic sphere, if she so chose.

The radical feminist rejoinder is: Yes, but on whose terms? The workplace remains male-constructed. The category "worker" is male-constructed. To force women from one male-constructed category to another is not a real victory, especially if the newly constructed female worker adopts the existing patriarchal view of the world.[92]

Wherever one comes out on this particular debate between liberal and radical feminists, it is important to understand both sides. Both sides agree that women should not be limited by male-constructed categories. Their disagreement is over which categories are most worthy of challenge. At this level, the disagreement is political and instrumental. The disagreement becomes substantive, however, when we shift the focus to the question of what should take the place of the male-constructed category "woman." Radical feminists fear that arguments couched in equal protection terms alleging the similarity between women and men may ultimately be harmful because such arguments endorse entrenched patriarchal values. The new category "woman" that emerges from such arguments is still male-constructed. This concern is valid. But if radical feminists think that liberal feminist legal scholars do not share this concern, they are mistaken.

As Wendy Williams, a liberal feminist, has recently explained, the problem with the presently constructed sex categories, male and female, is that they are defined as "discontinuous complementary poles."[93] Furthermore, the problem with antidiscrimination law is that it

> "requires that we be female or male ... before it will extend its protection. ... Thus discontinuity and complementarity are the prerequisites to remedies under the anti-discrimination laws: A person must *be* one sex, maintain the appearance (in clothing and effect) of that sex, and prefer sex with the 'opposite' sex. If a person has complied with the requirement that he or she be properly 'sexed,' the law will then provide partial protection against penalties for being of a sex."[94]

Williams does not embrace the law's definition of "woman" when she argues that a woman (as defined by the law) is the victim of sex discrimination. Yet, as much as she may be troubled by the law's construction of "woman," she is willing to use that construction to prevent even narrower definitions from limiting the possibilities of real women in the world today.

*Radical Feminism.* Radical feminism is not easily defined because it takes many forms. For my purposes, it will be sufficient to contrast radical feminist thought with liberal feminist thought. First, whereas liberal feminists emphasize the individual (men and women as individual human beings), radical feminists focus on women as a class, typically as a class that is dominated by another class known as men. Second, whereas liberal feminist equality arguments are based primarily on the similarities between men and women, radical feminists tend to build arguments that focus on the differences between men and women. These

---

[92] Martha Minow tells of a similar problem involving high-school girls, who, after being admitted to previously all-male Central High in Philadelphia, along with their male cohorts began to "look down upon the girls enrolled at Girl's High." Martha Minow, "Beyond Universality" (1989) U. Chi. Legal F. 115, 127–28.

[93] Wendy Williams, "First Generation" (1989) U. Chi. Legal F. 99 at 105.

[94] *ibid.* at 105–06 n. 16.

differences, argue radical feminists, have been constructed in such a way as to contribute to women's inequality.

Radical feminists in the legal academy include Catharine MacKinnon and Christine Littleton. Littleton has argued for a reconstructed concept of sexual equality which would recognize woman's difference from man.[95] She calls her model "equality as acceptance."[96] To "accept" woman's difference, society must do something more than merely accommodate the difference. I interpret Littleton's "equality as acceptance" thesis to require the centralization of "woman" (her identity, her specificity, her difference from man) in normative debates about how the world ought to be structured. Consider the current dilemma over pregnancy in the workplace. If women had participated equally in designing the workplace from the beginning, employers would not be asked to make accommodations for pregnancy. Instead, the workplace would have been structured so that pregnant workers were not viewed as different from the norm. To move from the male-modeled workplace that currently exists to one that fully accepts women will require some fundamental changes in the model itself. We will have achieved "equality as acceptance" only when woman's difference from man is costless.[97]

Catharine MacKinnon argues that because men have defined women as different, equality arguments cannot succeed.[98]

Recognizing that women as a class are different from men as the two sexes have been socially constructed, MacKinnon would abandon liberal equality arguments. In MacKinnon's view, "an equality question is a question of the distribution of power."[99] The most important difference between women and men is the difference in power. Men dominate women. Men take from women. Furthermore, men have been in control for so long that legal discourse completely ignores the reality of women's lives. Thus, equality theory, as a legal discourse, has focused on public sphere issues like pregnancy in the workplace—issues of import in male lives—rather than focusing on those long-silenced parts of female experience such as rape and other forms of sexual assault.

Using the rhetoric of domination and sexual subordination instead of equality, radical feminists in the MacKinnon camp argue for changes in laws that will end the inequality in power. Sex equality, in this view, affirmatively requires protecting women from such things as sexual harassment, rape and battering by men. An extension of this theory is used to justify a ban on pornography because pornography is thought to contribute to women's sexual subordination.

Some liberal feminists question parts of the radical feminist agenda on grounds that special protections for women often lead to inequality. The most serious disagreement between liberal and radical feminists is over pornography. Radical feminists, especially MacKinnon, support laws that will suppress pornography.[1] Pornography, in their view, is male-created, and defines "woman" as a sexual object. Liberal feminists agree that most pornography is male-created and that

---

[95] Christine Littleton, "Reconstructing Sexual Equality" [*post*, 1347].

[96] *ibid*, p 1312–1313. I endorse the rhetoric of "acceptance" as opposed to "accommodation" because "equality as accommodation" keeps man at the center and woman at the margin.

[97] See *ibid.* at 1323–25.

[98] [See *post*, 1338.]

[99] [*Post*, 1338.]

[1] See *Feminism Unmodified*, pp. 176–195.

male-created pornography defines "woman" as a sexual object.[2] But, argue liberal feminists, to allow the state to ban pornography is to give the state power to define acceptable sex. Since the current state is a creature of male power, there is no reason to believe the state will define acceptable sex in a way that is consistent with an individual woman's own definition of her sexual self. In the pornography debate, the radical feminists' reliance on equality theory as a class-based theory (pornography contributes to woman's inequality) clashes with the liberal feminists' commitment to individual liberty.

Some liberal feminists[3] (as well as postmodern feminists) also challenge the radical feminists' emphasis on "woman" as a class. They argue that radical feminists fail to take account of the many differences among women, focusing only on how all women are different from men. To focus on "woman" as a unitary category is to define her in some essential way, to claim that all women are alike in some essential way.

Radical feminists respond to this challenge by denying the existence of a female essence. Radical feminists embrace totally the claim that women are socially constructed.[4] They do not believe that by deconstructing her we will find some underlying true essence. Rather they believe that by challenging the male construction of the category "woman," we can begin to construct our own category. We may not be able to free ourselves from socially constructed categories, but a woman-defined "woman" is at least an improvement over the present state of affairs.

*Cultural Feminism.* Cultural feminists, like radical feminists, focus on woman's difference from man. Cultural feminists, however, unlike their radical sisters, embrace woman's difference. Carol Gilligan, for example, argues that women, because of their different life experiences, speak in a "different voice" from their male counterparts.[5] Gilligan identifies the female voice with caring and relationships. Woman's moral vision encompasses this different voice. Woman's difference is good.

Feminists in the Gilligan camp are interested in changing institutions to give equal weight to woman's moral voice. They argue that the category "woman" has not been so much misdefined by men, as it has been ignored and undervalued. Yes, women are nurturing. Yes, women value personal relationships. These attributes are to be valued. Using equality rhetoric, cultural feminists argue for material changes in present conditions that would support woman-valued relationships.

Martha Fineman, for example, has argued for a concept of equality that recognizes and values the special relationship between mother and child.[6] Similarly, Robin West has charged that all modern legal theory is "masculine" because it is based on a view of human beings as primarily distinct and

---

[2] Some liberal feminists worry, however, that laws used to suppress pornography will be used first against the less powerful members of society who produce pornography, specifically lesbians, who are attempting to create erotic images of women free from male-defined "woman-as-sexual-object" imagery. [Baehr (2008) 27 *Law and Philosophy* 193 explains that while feminism does not condemn prostitution or the objectification of women directly, it does strongly condemn and require the remedying of the effects those practices have on the distribution of public goods.]

[3] *e.g.* Wendy Williams, "First Generation" at 107–08.

[4] Catharine MacKinnon, *Toward a Feminist Theory*, p. 109.

[5] Carol Gilligan, *In a Different Voice* (1982).

[6] Martha Fineman, "Dominant Discourse, *Professional Language and Legal* Change in Child Custody Decisionmaking" (1988) 101 Harv. L. Rev. 727; Martha Fineman, "Implementing Equality: Ideology, Contradiction, and Social Change: A Study of Rhetoric and Results in the Regulation of the Consequences of Divorce" 1983 Wis. L. Rev. 789.

unconnected to each other. A properly constructed feminist jurisprudence would reflect the reality of women's lives—their essential connectedness.[7]

I have defined cultural feminism to include feminists who ascribe fully to the social construction thesis. In such cases, the only difference between radical and cultural feminists is that radical feminists have chosen to emphasize in their theory a negative aspect of "woman"—her sexual objectification—whereas, cultural feminists emphasize a positive aspect—her special bond to others.[8] Because their emphasis is different, radical and cultural feminists may contribute differently to the project of self-definition.[9]

Some cultural feminists, however, can be understood to support the concept that "woman," although currently constructed in a certain way, has a discoverable natural essence.[10] Whether viewed as natural or socially constructed, woman's capacity for caring and connection has provided substance for an interesting debate between radical feminist MacKinnon and cultural feminist Gilligan. Gilligan's work encourages us to value woman's view of herself and the world around her. MacKinnon, however, is suspicious of this "different voice." This voice, after all, has been constructed in response to the patriarchy. For those who subscribe to the social construction thesis, the voice is just another voice of the patriarchy. Alternatively, if there is such a thing as a natural or authentic "woman," how can we know that this is her voice? MacKinnon argues that until women cease to be victims of subordination they cannot speak for themselves.[11]

This argument has a certain Catch-22 effect. Woman-identified values, such as caring and connection to others, are suspect because they are values that women have created in response to the patriarchy. We value caring because that is what our oppressors have caused us to value (because we define ourselves in relation to our oppressors, we aren't really engaging in self-definition). But if all women are victims of the patriarchy, how can any woman ever claim knowledge of what is truly in woman's best interest? How can we know that any equality arguments will further the best interests of women?

There must be some way to free ourselves sufficiently from the patriarchy to engage in the project of self-definition. Feminist theorists outside the field of law have argued in favor of separatism at least as an interim step in creating a woman-defined "woman."[12] But legal theorists have been obsessed with equality, a concept which is inconsistent with separatism.

---

[7] Robin West, "Jurisprudence and Gender" (1985) 55 U. Chi. L. Rev. 1. [and *post*, xxx.]

[8] Although feminists in law tend to concentrate on the special bond between mother and child, other feminist theorists focus on the special bonds between adult women. See, *e.g.* Mary Daly, *Gyn/Ecology* (1978); Audre Lord, *Sister Outsider* (1984); Adrienne Rich, *On Lies, Secrets and Silence* (1979).

[9] Radical feminists can fight against the sexual objectification of woman without intentionally creating a positive concept of woman as sexual subject. And cultural feminists can fight to protect woman's special bond to others without intentionally adopting the definition of "woman" as archetypical nurturer. Yet, in both cases, legal arguments produce rhetoric that shape our future reality. Some forms of feminist argument may reshape our concept of men more than our concept of "woman," I have in mind MacKinnon's arguments that men have all the power and that men abuse women.

[10] I understand Robin West to take that position. Robin West, "Feminism, Critical Social Theory and Law" 1989 U. Chi. Legal F. 59, 84–96.

[11] Catharine MacKinnon, *Feminism Unmodified*, p. 39. See also Ellen DuBois, Mary Dunlap, Carol Gilligan, Catharine MacKinnon & Carrie Menkel-Meadow, "Feminist Discourse: Moral Values and the Law—A Conversation" (1985) 34 Buffalo L. Rev. 11.

[12] See, *e.g.* Radicalesbians, "The Woman Identified Woman" reprinted in *For Lesbians Only: A Separatist Anthology*, (Sarah L. Hoagland & Julia Penelope eds. 1988), p. 17; Marilyn Frye, "Some Reflections on Separatism and Power" reprinted in *For Lesbians Only: A Separatist Anthology, supra.*

*Postmodern Feminism.* Postmodern feminists eschew the idea of unitary truth, of objective reality. They readily admit that categories, especially gender categories, arc mere social constructs. Equality, too, is a social construct. It is true that these constructs, as products of the patriarchy, are in need of a feminist reconstruction. But postmodern feminism tells us to beware of searching for a new truth to replace the old. There simply is no such thing as the essential "woman." There is no such thing as the woman's point of view. There is no single theory of equality that will work for the benefit of all women. Indeed, there is probably no single change or goal that is in the best interest of all women.

Some would argue that the concept "postmodern feminism" is an oxymoron. It is a phrase that combines two concepts—postmodernism and feminism—that cannot logically coexist. For if postmodernism views the category "woman" as being so multifarious that it denies unitariness, how can it ever ascribe to be feminist, since feminism is a theory that focuses on the unitary category "woman"?

My own answer to this supposed conundrum is that postmodern feminism does not focus on the category "woman." Rather, it focuses on the situated realities of women, plural. Postmodern feminists question earlier feminist attempts to redefine the category "woman." Any definition, even one articulated by feminists, is limiting and serves to "tie the individual to her identity as a woman."[13] Furthermore, feminists who support any single definition of "woman" are viewed by postmodernists as tending toward essentialism.

One need not embrace postmodernism completely to criticize the tendency towards essentialism found in radical and cultural feminist writings. Wendy Williams, usually viewed as a liberal feminist, has raised concerns about the homogeneity of certain feminist concepts of "woman."[14] Similarly, Angela Harris has argued that the meta-theories of gender constructed by Catharine MacKinnon and Robin West rely on a concept of "woman" that has been abstracted from the experience of white women.[15] I have made a similar claim that the "woman" constructed by these theorists also appears to be heterosexual.[16] If feminists are fighting for maximum liberation, then equality arguments and theories aimed primarily at white heterosexual women will not accomplish that task.

At the same time, postmodern thought poses a certain dilemma. Any theory requires some degree of abstraction and generalization. Thus, if feminists embrace the particular situated realities of all individual women, plural, we will find it difficult to build a theory, singular, to combat oppression. As to the category "woman," postmodernism suggests that it is a fiction, a non-determinable identity. Linda Alcoff complains that whereas feminist definitions of "woman" tend toward essentialism, postmodernism tends toward nominalism.[17]

I am reluctant to classify any feminist theorists within the legal academy as purely postmodern, although a number of such scholars do incorporate postmodern themes in their writing. For example, strains of postmodern thought can be found in the critical feminist legal scholarship of Frances Olsen[18] and Deborah

---

[13] Linda Alcoff 13 *Signs* 305.

[14] Williams, "First Generation" *supra* note 3.

[15] "Race and Essentialism in Feminist Legal Theory" (1990) 42 Stan. L. Rev. 581.

[16] Patricia Cain, "Feminist Jurisprudence: Grounding the Theories" (1989–90) 4 Berk. Women's L.J. 191.

[17] *Supra* note 13, at 307.

[18] See, *e.g.* Frances Olsen, "The Sex of Law" *in The Politics of Law* 453, 458 (David Kairys ed. 1990); Frances Olsen, "Feminist Theory in Grand Style" (Book Review) (1989) 89 Colum. L. Rev 1147, 1169–77 (reviewing Catharine MacKinnon, *Feminism Unmodified*, (explaining, with approval, feminist objections to grand theory, yet defending Catharine MacKinnon's grand theory as politically useful); Frances Olsen, "The Family and the Market: A Study of Ideology and Legal Reform" (1983) 96 Harv. L. Rev. (challenging dichotomous thinking and embracing androgyny as a goal that allows for multiplicity and diffusiveness).

Rhode.[19] Both Ka(r)tharine Bartlett and Martha Minow have focused on the importance of multiple perspectives in the construction of reality.[20] Margaret Jane Radin, in writing about feminism and pragmatism, echoes the postmodern feminist's rejection of abstract universal theory in favor of practical solutions to concrete situations.[21]

Within the legal academy, the feminist theorists most closely aligned with postmodern feminism is Drucilla Cornell. Building on the work of deconstructionist Jacques Derrida and the psychoanalytic theories of Jacques Lacan and Julia Kristeva, Cornell shows us how we might reconstruct "woman" without resorting to essentialism or unitary concepts. She names her brand of feminism "ethical feminism" and contrasts it with liberal and radical feminism.[22] Rather than deriving what "woman" ought to be from the reality of what is, Cornell encourages us to create, with the help of allegory and myth, an "imaginative universal,"[23] a mythology of the feminine in which all women can find themselves. This appeal to myth carries with it a call for collective imagining, informed by women's realities, but not limited by them. Cornell's "ethical feminism" offers us the possibility of building a shared concept of "woman" that is always more than we are individually, and thus is never limiting.

## V. The future

I have identified the four schools of feminist thought, or feminisms. There are, of course, other ways to categorize these feminisms.[24] Whatever the categorization, the boundaries are never as fixed as the labels make them seem. And some feminists slip in and out of the various categories. I chose to draw the lines as I drew them to emphasize one aspect of the various feminisms: how they see the category "woman" as she is presently constructed by male society. Liberal feminists, according to my taxonomy, see "woman" defined primarily as someone confined to the private sphere.[25] Radical feminists see her as man's sexual object. Cultural feminists see her as caring and connected to others. Finally, postmodern feminists see her as so overly-determined that she is an absence, not a presence.[26]

These different perspectives reflect the variety of woman's experience. Since feminist theory is built from the real life experience of real women, our theories will necessarily be varied if they are to capture the breadth of that experience. Our theories are built to address the harms that we see. But our theories must not divide us. They must not prevent us from seeing the harms that others see.

What we experience shapes our view of the world. For feminist theorists, our

---

[19] See, *e.g.* Deborah Rhode, "Introduction: Theoretical Perspectives on Sexual Difference" in *Theoretical Perspectives on Sexual Difference* 1, 7–9 (Deborah Rhode ed. 1990); Deborah Rhode, "Feminist Critical Theories" (1990) 42 Stan. L. Rev. 617.

[20] See Katharine Bartlett, "Feminist Legal Methods" (1990) 103 Harv. L. Rev. 829; Martha Minow, "Beyond Universality" 1989 U. Chi. Legal F 115; Martha Minow, "Foreword: Justice Engendered" (1987) 101 Harv. L. Rev. 10.

[21] "If feminists largely share the pragmatist commitment that truth is hammered out piecemeal in the crucible of life and our situatedness, they also share the pragmatist understanding that truth is provisional and ever-changing." Margaret Jane Radin, "The Pragmatist and the Feminist" (1990) 63 S. Cal. L. Rev. 1699.

[22] Drucilla Cornell, "The Doubly-Prized World: Myth, Allegory and the Feminine" (1990) 75 Cornell L. Rev. 644.

[23] *ibid.* at 644.

[24] Rosemarie Tong, for example, makes the following classifications: liberal, Marxist, radical, psychoanalytic, socialist, existentialist and postmodernist.

[25] See Wendy Williams, "First Generation", *supra* note 3.

[26] Luce Irigaray, "This Sex Which is Not One" in *New French Feminisms* 99 (Elaine Marks & Isabelle de Courtivron eds. 1981).

experiences as women shape our understanding of male power. Our theories reflect that understanding. We begin from where we stand.

I began this Essay with the observation that feminist legal theorists have spent too much time debating equality and not enough time debating the meaning of self-definition for women. The equality debate has at times assumed *sub silentio* varying definitions of what "woman *is*" and what "woman *should be.*" The equality debate has also assumed *sub silentio*, at a minimum, that "woman" *is* and, perhaps further that "woman" *should be*, a working definition or category for law.

I propose that, in the future, feminist legal theorists be more explicit about their understanding of what "woman is" and what "woman should be." I believe this conversation about the meaning of "woman" is, at least for the moment, much more important to feminist theory than the development of any sort of abstract equality theory. To have the conversation is to engage in the process of self-definition. We must have the conversation before we can conclude whether "woman," however defined, is a category that ought to continue.

Some feminist legal theorists have already steered away from the equality debate and focused more directly on the question of self-definition. Robin West, in particular, has focused directly on the meaning of "self" for feminist theorists, warning us to beware of postmodernism's rejection of essentialism.[27] Ruth Colker's recent work grapples with the meaning of authentic existence for women.[28] And Drucilla Cornell encourages us to continue the search for the feminine employing myth as a necessary part of the process.[29] I believe this discussion of the meaning of self and questioning of who defines whom is a useful development for the future of feminist legal theory.

The challenge I pose to feminist legal theorists is a challenge to develop legal theories that will support the process of self-definition—theories that will support the conversation. By focusing on the process of self-definition, I mean to suggest that we more fully acknowledge the importance of feminist method in building our substantive theories.

I have suggested that consciousness raising is the cornerstone of feminist method. Consciousness raising is about giving voice to the unknown in women's experience. Consciousness raising makes available stories that are personal and private. Consciousness raising brings new understanding by making known the unknown. Legal theories to support consciousness raising would include not only theories that protect speech, but theories that encourage the right kind of listening, a listening that privileges (temporarily) the previously silenced.

Feminist theorists have made valuable contributions to law by adding a female perspective to legal discussions. But feminist theorists should not privilege one perspective over another. Our contributions are especially valuable, not because we speak from a female perspective, but because we speak from a previously-silenced perspective.

We should fashion feminist legal theories with a view to uncovering the silences.[30] At the same time, these theories should reflect our obligations to listen and to participate positively in the construction of another's self-identity. Our theories must not rely on definitions that limit another's self-conception. We must

---

[27] See Robin West, "Feminism, Critical Social Theory and Law", *supra* note 10 at 59.
[28] See, *e.g.* Ruth Colker, "Feminism, Theology, and Abortion" 77 Calif. L.R. 1011. Ruth Colker, "Feminism, Sexuality, and Self: A Preliminary Inquiry into the Politics of Authenticity" (Book Review) (1988) 68 B.U.L. Rev. 217 (reviewing Catharine MacKinnon, *Feminism Unmodified.*
[29] Drucilla Cornell, *ante*, note 22.
[30] See, *e.g.* Janet Halley, "The Politics of the Closet: Towards Equal Protection for Gay, Lesbian, and Bisexual Identity" (1989) 36 U.C.L.A. L. Rev. 915 (arguing that courts ought to strike down laws that penalize homosexuals so that we can speak and be heard in the political process).

be principled in our interactions with one another, yet we must also be always open to the truth of the other's story.

Feminist method, as I conceive it, is about being in the world in a way that embraces both our separateness and our connectedness with others. Similarly, self-definition is not solely an individual enterprise grounded in our separation from each other, nor solely a group project impervious to individual realities. Thus, we need to build feminist legal theories that support the telling of our individual truths, as well as theories that protect the space we share with others as we construct our identities. I believe it is time to recapture from the patriarchy such principles as individual autonomy, privacy,[31] free speech,[32] intimacy and association.[33]

I agree with the postmodern insight that there is no single, unitary definition of "woman." Indeed, it is precisely because there is no single definition of "woman," that our conversations about the meaning of "woman" become so important. I propose that we put substantive theories (such as equality) to one side until we have continued our conversations further.                              [803–823]

## ROBIN WEST
### Jurisprudence and Gender
### (1988)[34]

#### Introduction

What is a human being? Legal theorists must, perforce, answer this question: jurisprudence, after all, is about human beings. The task has not proven to be divisive. In fact, virtually all modern American legal theorists, like most modern moral and political philosophers, either explicitly or implicitly embrace what I will call the "separation thesis" about what it means to be a human being: a "human being," whatever else he is, is physically separate from all other human beings. I am one human being and you are another, and that distinction between you and me is central to the meaning of the phrase "human being." Individuals are, in the words of one commentator, "distinct and not essentially connected with one another."[35] We are each physically "boundaried"—this is the trivially true meaning of the claim that we are all individuals.

The first purpose of this essay is to put forward the global and critical claim

---

[31] Privacy, as it has been constructed by male liberal theory, keeps the state out of individual space in a way that privileges male power. Thus, Catharine MacKinnon criticizes judicial reliance on privacy doctrine in the abortion decisions, because it leaves many women privately pregnant with no access to needed abortions. See Catharine MacKinnon, *Feminism Unmodified.*

[32] The guarantee of free speech benefits those who have the power to draw listeners: those with the greatest access to the market of ideas. The construction of "woman" is a product of this market. Both government and corporate funding of speech, from National Endowment for the Arts grants to television commercials, impact seriously on the concept of "woman" in this society. We need a concept of free speech that recognizes existing inequalities in power and re-conceives the role of the "state" in providing access to listeners.

[33] Intimacy and association are values that need to be extended to protect those relationships that are essential to our constructions of self. These include same-sex couples as well as other relationships with non-biological families. See Kenneth Karst, "The Freedom of Intimate Association" (1980) 89 Yale L.J. 624, 635; Nancy Polikoff, "This Child Does Have Two Mothers: Redefining Parenthood to Meet the Needs of Children in Lesbian-Mother and Other Nontraditional Families" (1990) 78 Geo. L.J. 459.

[34] [From (1988) 55 Univ. of Chicago Law Review 1.]

[35] Naomi Scheman, "Individualism and the Objects of Psychology" in Sandra Harding and Merrill B. Hintikka eds., *Discovering Reality* (1983), pp. 225, 237.

that by virtue of their shared embrace of the separation thesis, all of our modern legal theory—by which I mean "liberal legalism" and "critical legal theory" collectively—is essentially and irretrievably masculine. The gap between the description of human nature assumed or explicated by legal theory and the description of women explicated by feminist theory reflects a very real political obstacle to the development of a "feminist jurisprudence:" feminists take women's humanity seriously, and jurisprudence does not, because the law does not. Until that fact changes, "feminist jurisprudence" is a political impossibility. The virtual abolition of patriarchy—a political structure that values men more than women—is the political precondition of a truly ungendered jurisprudence. But the gap between legal theory's descriptions of human nature and women's true nature also presents a *conceptual* obstacle to the development of feminist jurisprudence: jurisprudence must be about the relationship of human beings to law, and feminist jurisprudence must be about women. Women, though, are not human beings. Until that philosophical fact changes, the phrase "feminist jurisprudence" is a conceptual anomaly. Nevertheless, it does not follow that there is "no such thing" as feminist jurisprudence, any more than it follows from the dominant definition of a "human being" that there is no such thing as women. The second purpose of this paper is to explore and improve upon the feminist jurisprudence we have generated to date, in spite of patriarchy, and in spite of the masculinity of mainstream jurisprudence.

Finally, the conclusion suggests how a humanist jurisprudence might evolve, and how feminist legal theory can contribute to its creation.

### Masculine jurisprudence and feminist theory

The split in masculine jurisprudence between legal liberalism and critical legal theory can be described in any number of ways. The now standard way to describe the split is in terms of politics: "liberal legal theorists" align themselves with a liberal political philosophy which entails, among other things, allegiance to the Rule of Law and to Rule of Law virtues, while "critical legal theorists," typically left wing and radical, are skeptical of the Rule of Law and the split between law and politics which the Rule of Law purportedly delineates. Critical legal theorists are potentially far more sensitive to the political underpinnings of purportedly neutral legalistic constructs than are liberal legalists. I think this traditional characterization is wrong for a number of reasons: liberal theorists are not necessarily politically naive, and critical theorists are not necessarily radical. However, my purpose is not to critique it. Instead, I want to suggest another way to understand the divisions in modern legal theory.

An alternative description of the difference (surely not the only one) is that liberal legal theory and critical legal theory provide two radically divergent phenomenological descriptions of the paradigmatically male experience of the inevitability of separation of the self from the rest of the species, and indeed from the rest of the natural world. Both schools, as we shall see, accept the separation thesis; they both view human beings as materially (or physically) separate from each other, and both view this fact as fundamental to the origin of law. But their accounts of the subjective experience of physical separation from the other—an individual other, the natural world, and society—are in nearly diametrical opposition. Liberal legalists, in short, describe an inner life enlivened by freedom and autonomy from the separate other, and threatened by the danger of annihilation by him. Critical legal theorists, by contrast, tell a story of inner lives dominated by feelings of alienation and isolation from the separate other, and enlivened by the possibility of association and community with him. These differing accounts of the subjective experience of being separate from others, I believe, are at the root of at least some of the divisions between critical and liberal legal theorists. I want to review each of these experiential descriptions of separation in some detail, for I will ultimately argue that they are not as contradictory as they first appear. Each story, I will suggest, constitutes a legitimate and true part of the total subjective experience of masculinity.

I will start with the liberal description of separation, because it is the most familiar, and surely the most dominant. According to liberal legalism, the inevitability of the individual's material separation from the "other," entails, first and foremost, an existential state of highly desirable and much valued freedom: because the individual is *separate* from the other, he is *free* of the other.

This existential condition of freedom in turn entails the liberal's conception of value. Because we are all free and we are each equally free, we should be treated by our government as free, and as equally free. The individual must be treated by his government (and by others) in a way that respects his equality and his freedom. Ronald Dworkin puts the point in this way:

> "What does it mean for the government to treat its citizens as equals? *That is ... the same question as the question of what it means for the government to treat all its citizens as free, or as independent*, or with equal dignity."[36]                    [pp. 1–6]

Because of the dominance of liberalism in this culture, we might think of autonomy as the "official" liberal value entailed by the physical, material condition of inevitable separation from the other: separation from the other entails my freedom from him, and that in turn entails my political right to autonomy.

Autonomy, freedom and equality collectively constitute what might be called the "up side" of the subjective experience of separation. Autonomy and freedom are both entailed by the separation thesis, and autonomy and freedom both feel very good. However, there's a "down side" to the subjective experience of separation as well. Physical separation from the other entails not just my freedom; it also entails my vulnerability. Every other discrete, separate individual—because he is the "other"—is a source of danger to me and a threat to my autonomy. I have reason to fear you solely by virtue of the fact that I am me and you are you. You are not me, so by definition *my* ends are not your ends. Our ends might conflict. You might try to frustrate my pursuit of my ends. In an extreme case, you might even try to kill me—you might cause my annihilation.

Annihilation by the other, we might say, is the official *harm* of liberal theory, just as autonomy is its official value. Hobbes, of course, gave the classic statement of the terrifying vulnerability that stems from our separateness from the other.

We can call this liberal legalist phenomenological narrative the "official story" of the subjectivity of separation. According to the official story, we value the freedom that our separateness entails, while we seek to minimize the threat that it poses. We do so, of course, through creating and then respecting the state.

Now, Critical Legal Theory diverges from liberal legalism on many points, but one striking contrast is this: critical theorists provide a starkly divergent phenomenological description of the subjective experience of separation. According to our critical legal theorists, the separate individual is indeed, in Sandel's phrase, "epistemologically prior to the collective." Like liberal legalists, critical legal theorists also view the individual as materially separate from the rest of human life. But according to the critical theorist, what that material state of separation existentially entails is not a perpetual celebration of autonomy, but rather, a perpetual longing for community, or attachment, or unification, or *connection*. The separate individual strives to connect with the "other" from whom he is separate. The separate individual lives in a state of perpetual dread not of annihilation by the other, but of the alienation, loneliness, and existential isolation that his material separation from the other imposes upon him. The individual

---

[36] Ronald Dworkin, *A Matter of Principle* (1985), p. 191 [and see *ante*, 603].

strives through love, work, and government to achieve a unification with the other, the natural world, and the society from which he was originally and continues to be existentially separated. The separate individual seeks *community*—not autonomy—and dreads isolation and alienation from the other—not annihilation by him.

According to the critical theorist, while the dominant liberal culture insists we value autonomy and fear the other, what the individual truly desires, craves, and longs to establish is some sort of connection with the other, and what the individual truly dreads is alienation from him.

Let me now turn to feminist theory. Although the legal academy is for the most part unaware of it, modern feminist theory is as fundamentally divided as legal theory. One way to characterize the conflict—the increasingly standard way to characterize the conflict—is that while most modern feminists agree that women are different from men and agree on the importance of the difference, feminists differ over which differences between men and women are most vital. According to one group of feminists, sometimes called "cultural feminists," the important difference between men and women is that women raise children and men don't. According to a second group of feminists, now called "radical feminists," the important difference between men and women is that women get fucked and men fuck: "women," definitionally, are "those from whom sex is taken," just as workers, definitionally, are those from whom labor is taken. Another way to put the difference is in political terms. Cultural feminists appear somewhat more "moderate" when compared with the traditional culture: from a mainstream non-feminist perspective, cultural feminists appear to celebrate many of the same feminine traits that the traditional culture has stereotypically celebrated. Radical feminists, again from a mainstream perspective, appear more separatist, and, in contrast with standard political debate, more alarming. They also appear to be more "political" in a sense which perfectly parallels the critical theory-liberal theory split described above: radical feminists appear to the more attuned to power disparities between men and women than are cultural feminists.

I think this traditional characterization is wrong on two counts. First, cultural feminists no less than radical feminists are well aware of women's powerlessness vis-a-vis men, and second, radical feminism, as I will later argue, is as centrally concerned with pregnancy as it is with intercourse. But again, instead of arguing against this traditional characterization of the divide between radical and cultural feminism, I want to provide an alternative. My alternative characterization structurally (although not substantively) parallels the characterization of the difference between liberal and critical legalism. Underlying both radical and cultural feminism is a conception of women's existential state that is grounded in women's potential for physical, material connection to human life, just as underlying both liberal and critical legalism is a conception of men's existential state that is ground in the inevitability of men's physical separation from the species. I will call the shared conception of women's existential lives the "connection thesis." The divisions between radical and cultural feminism stem from divergent accounts of the subjectivity of the potential for connection, just as what divides liberal from critical legal theory are divergent accounts of the subjectivity of the inevitability of separation.

The "connection thesis" is simply this: Women are actually or potentially materially connected to other human life. Men aren't. This material fact has existential consequences. While it may be true *for men* that the individual is "epistemologically and morally prior to the collectivity," it is not true for women. The potential for material connection with the other defines women's subjective, phenomenological and existential state, just as surely as the inevitability of material separation from the other defines men's existential state. Our potential for material connection engenders pleasures and pains, values and dangers, and attractions and fears, which are entirely different from those which follow, for men, from the necessity of separation. Indeed, it is the rediscovery of the multitude of implications from this material difference between men and women which has enlivened (and divided) both cultural and radical feminism in this decade (and it is those discoveries which have distinguished both radical and cultural feminism from liberal feminism).

While radical and cultural feminists agree that women's lives are distinctive in their potential for material connection to others, they provide sharply contrasting accounts of the subjective experience of the material and existential state of connection. According to cultural feminist accounts of women's subjectivity, women value intimacy, develop a capacity for nurturance, and an ethic of care for the "other" with which we are connected, just as we learn to dread and fear separation from the other. Radical feminists tell a very different story. According to radical feminism, women's connection with the "other" is above all else invasive and intructive: women's potential for material "connection" invites invasion into the physical integrity of our bodies, and intrusion into the existential integrity of our lives. Although women may "officially" value the intimacy of connection, we "unofficially" dread the intrusion it inevitably entails, and long for the individuation and independence that deliverance from that state of connection would permit. Paralleling the structure above, I will call these two descriptions feminism's official and unofficial stories of women's subjective experience of physical connection.

In large part due to the phenomenal success of Carol Gilligan's book *In a Different Voice*, cultural feminism may be the most familiar of these two feminist strands, and for that reason *alone*, I call it feminism's "official story," "Cultural feminism" is in large part defined by Gilligan's book. Defined as such, cultural feminism begins not with a commitment to the "material" version of the connection thesis, but rather, with a commitment to its more observable existential and psychological consequences. Thus limited, we can put the cultural feminist point this way: women have a "sense" of existential "connection" to other human life which men do not. That sense of connection in turn entails a way of learning, a path of moral development, an aesthetic sense, and a view of the world and of one's place within it which sharply contrasts with men's.

Why are men and women different in this essential way? The cultural feminist explanation for women's heightened sense of connection is that women are more "connected" to life than are men because it is women who are the primary caretakers of young children. A female child develops her sense of identity as "continuous" with her caretaker's, while a young boy develops a sense of identity that is distinguished from his caretaker's. Because of the gender alignment of mothers and female children, young girls "fuse" their growing sense of identity with a sense of sameness with and attachment to the other, while because of the gender distinction between mothers and male children, young boys "fuse" their growing sense of identity with a sense of difference and separation from the other. This turns out to have truly extraordinary and far reaching consequences, for both cognitive and moral development. Nancy Chodorow explains:

> "[This means that] [g]irls emerge from this period with a basis for 'empathy' built into their primary definition of self in a way that boys do not ... [G]irls come to experience themselves as less differentiated than boys, as more continuous with and related to the external object-world and as differently oriented to their inner object-world as well."[37]

Women are therefore capable of a degree of physical as well as psychic *intimacy* with the other which greatly exceeds men's capacity. Carol Gilligan finds that:

[37] Nancy Chodorow, *The Reproduction of Mothering* (1978), 167.

"The fusion of identity and intimacy ... [is] clearly articulated ... in [women's] ... self-descriptions. In response to the request to describe themselves, ... women describe a relationship, depicting their identity *in* the connection of future mother, present wife, adopted child, or past lover. Similarly, the standard of moral judgment that informs their assessment of self is a standard of relationship, an ethic of nurturance, responsibility, and care ... [In] women's descriptions, identity is defined in a context of relationship and judged by a standard of responsibility and care. Similarly, morality is seen by these women as arising from the experience of connection and conceived as a problem of inclusion rather than one of balancing claims."[38]

Thus, according to Gilligan, women view themselves as fundamentally connected to, not separate from, the rest of life. This difference permeates virtually every aspect of our lives. According to the vast literature on difference developed by cultural feminists, women's cognitive development, literary sensibility, aesthetic taste, and psychological development, no less than our anatomy, are all fundamentally different from men's, and are different in the same way: unlike men, we view ourselves as connected to, not separate from, the other.

The most significant aspect of our difference, though, is surely the moral difference. According to cultural feminism, women are more nurturant, caring, loving and responsible to others than are men. This capacity for nurturance and care dictates the moral terms in which women, distinctively, construct social relations: women view the morality of actions against a standard of responsibility to others, rather than against a standard of rights and autonomy from others. As Gilligan puts it:

"The moral imperative ... [for] women is an injunction to care, a responsibility to discern and alleviate the 'real and recognizable trouble' of this world. For men, the moral imperative appears rather as an injunction to respect the rights of others and thus to protect from interference the rights to life and self-fulfillment."[39]

Cultural feminists, to their credit, have reidentified these differences as women's strengths, rather than women's weaknesses. Cultural feminism does not simply *identify* women's differences—patriarchy too insists on women's differences—it celebrates them. Women's art, women's craft, women's narrative capacity, women's critical eye, women's ways of knowing, and women's heart, are all, for the cultural feminist, redefined as things to celebrate. Most vital, however, for cultural feminism is the claim that intimacy is not just something women *do*, it is something human beings *ought* to do. Intimacy is a source of value, not a private hobby. It is morality, not habit.

To pursue my structural analogy to masculine legal theory, then, intimacy and the ethic of care constitute the entailed *values* of the existential state of connection with others, just as autonomy and freedom constitute the entailed values of the existential state of separation from others for men. Because women are fundamentally connected to other human life, women value and enjoy intimacy with others (just as because men are fundamentally separate from other human life men value and enjoy autonomy). Because women are connected with the rest of human life, intimacy with the "other" comes naturally. Caring, nurturance, and an ethic of love and responsibility for life is second nature. Autonomy, or freedom from the other, constitutes a value for men because it reflects an existential state of being: separate. Intimacy is a value for women because it reflects an existentially connected state of being.

Intimacy, the capacity for nurturance and the ethic of care constitute what we might call the "up side" of the subjective experience of connection. But there's a "down side" to the subjective experience of connection. There's danger, harm,

---

[38] Gilligan, *In a Different Voice*, pp. 159–160.
[39] Id. at 100.

and fear entailed by the state of connection as well as value. Whereas men fear annihilation from the separate other (and consequently have trouble achieving intimacy), women fear separation from the connected other (and consequently have trouble achieving independence). Gilligan makes the point succinctly: "Since masculinity is defined through separation while femininity is defined through attachment, male gender identity is threatened by intimacy while female gender identity is threatened by separation."[40] Separation, then, might be regarded as the official harm of cultural feminism.

It seems plausible that women are more psychically connected to others in the way Gilligan describes and for just the reason she expounds. Mothers raise children, and as a consequence girls, and not boys, think of themselves as continuous with, rather than separate from, that first all-important "other"—the mother. But this psychological and developmental explanation just raises—it does not answer—the background material question: why do women, rather than men, raise, nurture, and cook for children? What is the cause of *this* difference?

Although Gilligan doesn't address the issue, other cultural feminists have, and their explanations converge, I believe, implicitly if not explicitly, on a material, or mixed material-cultural, and not just a cultural answer: women *raise* children— and hence raise girls who are more connected and nurturant, and therefore more likely to be nurturant caretakers themselves—because it is women who bear children. Women are not inclined to abandon an infant they've carried for nine months and then delivered. If so, then women are ultimately more "connected"— physically, emotionally, and morally—to other human beings because women, as children were raised by women and women raise children because women uniquely, are physically and materially "connected" to those human beings when the human beings are fetuses and then infants. Women are more empathic to the lives of others because women are physically tied to the lives of others in a way which men are not. Women's moral voice is one of responsibility, duty and care for others because women's material circumstance is one of responsibility, duty and care for those who are first physically attached, then physically dependent, and then emotionally interdependent. Women think in terms of the needs of others rather than the rights of others because women materially, and then physically, and then psychically, provide for the needs of others. Lastly, women fear separation from the other rather than annihilation by him, and "count" it as a harm, because women experience the "separating" pain of childbirth and more deeply feel the pain of the maturation and departure of adult children.

[...] There are several reasons for the reluctance of American cultural feminists to explicitly embrace a material version of the connection thesis.

The major, reason for the resistance to material explanations of women's difference in American feminism is primarily strategic: American feminists of all stripes are wary of identifying the material fact of pregnancy as the root of moral, aesthetic, and cognitive difference.

[...]

If cultural feminism is our dominant feminist dogma, then this account of the nature of women's lives constitutes the "official text" of feminism, just as liberal legalism constitutes the official text of legalism.

These two "official stories" sharply contrast. Whereas according to liberal legalism, men value autonomy from the other and fear annihilation by him, women, according to cultural feminism, value intimacy with the other and fear separation from her. Women's sense of connection with others determines our special competencies and special vulnerabilities, just as men's sense of separation from others determines theirs. [...]

Against the cultural feminist backdrop, the story that radical feminists tell of women's invaded, violated lives is "subterranean" in the same sense that, against

---

[40]  Id. at 8.

the backdrop of liberal legalism, the story critical legal theorists tell of men's alienation and isolation from others is subterranean. According to radical feminism, women's connection to others is the source of women's misery, not a source of value worth celebrating. For cultural feminists, women's connectedness to the other (whether material or cultural) is the source, the heart, the root, and the cause of women's different morality, different voice, different "ways of knowing," different genius, different capacity for care, and different ability to nurture. For radical feminists, that same potential for connection—experienced materially in intercourse and pregnancy, but experienced existentially in all spheres of life—is the source of women's debasement, powerlessness, subjugation, and misery. It is the cause of our pain, and the reason for our stunted lives. Invasion and intrusion, rather than intimacy, nurturance and care, is the "unofficial" story of women's subjective experience of connection.

Thus, modern radical feminism is unified among other things by its insistence on the invasive, oppressive destructive implications of women's material and existential connection to the other. So defined, radical feminism (of modern times) begins not with the eighties critique of heterosexuality, but rather in the late sixties, with Shulamith Firestone's angry and eloquent denunciation of the oppressive consequences for women of the physical condition of pregnancy. Firestone's assessment of the importance and distinctiveness of women's reproductive role parallels Marilyn French's. Both view women's physical connection with nature and with the other as in some sense the "cause" of patriarchy. But their analyses of the chain of causation sharply contrast. For French, women's reproductive role—the paradigmatic experience of physical connection to nature, to life and to the other, and thus the core of women's moral difference—is also the cause of patriarchy, primarily because of men's fear of and contempt of nature. Firestone has a radically different view. Pregnancy is indeed the paradigmatic experience of physical connection, and it is indeed the core of women's difference, but according to Firestone, it is for that reason *alone* the cause of women's oppression. But it is nevertheless the radical argument—that pregnancy is a dangerous, psychically consuming, existentially intrusive, and physically invasive assault upon the body which in turn leads to a dangerous, consuming intrusive, invasive assault on the mother's self-identity—that best captures women's own sense of the injury and danger of pregnancy, whether or not it captures the law's sense of what an unwanted pregnancy involves, or why women should have the right to terminate it.

The radical feminist argument for reproductive freedom appears in legal argument only inadvertently or surreptitiously, but it does on occasion appear. It appeared most in the phenomenological descriptions of unwanted pregnancies collated in the *Thornburgh* amicus brief recently filed by the National Abortion Rights Action League.[41] The descriptions of pregnancy collated in that peculiarly non-legal legal document are filled with metaphors of invasion—metaphors, of course, because we lack the vocabulary to name these harms precisely. Those descriptions contrast sharply with the "joy" that cultural feminists celebrate in pregnancy, childbirth and child-raising. The invasion of the self by the other emerges as a source of oppression, not a source of moral value.

This danger, and the fear of it, is gender-specific. It is a fear which grips women, distinctively, and it is a fear about which men, apparently, know practically nothing.

Radical feminism of the eighties has focused more on intercourse than on pregnancy. But this may represent less of a divergence than it first appears. From the point of view of the "connection thesis," what the radical feminists of the eighties find objectionable, invasive, and oppressive about heterosexual intercourse, is precisely what the radical feminists of the sixties found objectionable,

---

[41] (1986) 476 U.S. 747.

invasive, and oppressive about pregnancy and motherhood. According to the eighties radical critique, intercourse, like pregnancy, blurs the physical boundary between self and other, and that blurring of boundaries between self and other constitutes a profound invasion of the self's physical integrity. That invasion—the "dissolving of boundaries"—is something to condemn, not celebrate.

Like pregnancy, then, intercourse is invasive, intrusive and violative, and like pregnancy it is therefore the cause of women's oppressed, invaded, intruded, violated, and debased lives. For both Dworkin and Firestone, women's potential for material connection with the other—whether through intercourse or pregnancy—constitutes an invasion upon our physical bodies, an intrusion upon our lives, and consequently an assault upon our existential freedom, whether or not it is also the root of our moral distinctiveness (the claim cultural feminism makes on behalf of pregnancy), or the hope of our liberation (the claim sexual liberationists make on behalf of sex). In their extremes, of course, both unwanted heterosexual intercourse and unwanted pregnancy can be life threatening experiences of physical invasion. An unwanted fetus, no less than an unwanted penis, invades my body, violates my physical boundaries, occupies my body and can potentially destroy my sense of self. What unifies the radical feminism of the sixties and eighties is the argument that women's potential for material, physical connection with the other constitutes an invasion which is a very real harm causing very real damage, and which society ought to recognize as such.

The material, sporadic violation of a woman's body occasioned by pregnancy and intercourse implies an existential and pervasive violation of her privacy, integrity and life projects. According to radical feminists, women's longings for individuation, physical privacy, and independence go well beyond the desire to avoid the dangers of rape or unwanted pregnancy. Women also long for liberation from the oppression of intimacy (and its attendant values) which both cultural feminism and most women officially, and wrongly, overvalue. Intimacy, in short, is *intrusive*, even when it isn't life threatening. An unwanted pregnancy is disastrous, but even a *wanted* pregnancy and motherhood are intrusive. The child *intrudes*, just as the fetus invades.

Similarly, while unwanted heterosexual intercourse is disastrous, even wanted heterosexual intercourse is intrusive. The penis occupies the body and "divides the woman" internally, to use Andrea Dworkin's language, in consensual intercourse no less than in rape. It preempts, challenges, negates, and *renders impossible* the maintenance of physical integrity and the formation of a unified self. The deepest unofficial story of radical feminism may be that intimacy—the official value of cultural feminism—is itself oppressive. Women secretly, unofficially, and surreptitiously long for the very individuation that cultural feminism insists women fear: the freedom, the independence, the individuality, the sense of wholeness, the confidence, the self-esteem, and the security of identity which can only come from a life, a history, a path, a voice, a sexuality, a womb, and a body of one's own.

Radical feminism, then, is unified by a particular description of the subjectivity of the material state of connection. According to that description, women dread intrusion and invasion, and long for an independent, individualized, *separate* identity. While women may indeed "officially" value intimacy, what women unofficially crave is physical privacy, physical integrity, and sexual celibacy—in a word, physical exclusivity. In the moral realm, women officially value contextual, relational, caring, moral thinking, but secretly wish that everyone would get the hell out of our lives so that we could pursue our own projects—we loathe the intrusion that intimacy entails. In the epistemological and moral realms, while women officially value community, we privately crave solitude, self-regard, self-esteem, linear thinking, legal rights, and principled thought.

Finally, then, we can schematize the contrast between the description of the "human being" that emerges from modern legal theory, and the description of women that emerges from modern feminism:

THE OFFICAL STORY  THE UNOFFICIAL STORY
(Liberal legalism and          (Critical legalism
cultural feminism)          and radical feminism)

|  | Value | Harm |  | Longing | Dread |
|---|---|---|---|---|---|
| LEGAL THEORY (human beings) | Autonomy | Annihilation; Frustration |  | Attachment; Connection | Alienation |
| FEMINIST THEORY (women) | Intimacy | Separation |  | Individuation Intrusion | Invasion; |

As the diagram reveals, the descriptions of the subjectivity of human existence
told by feminist theory and legal theory contrast at every point. First, and most
obviously, the "official" descriptions of human beings' subjectivity and women's
subjectivity contrast rather than compare. According to liberal theory, human
beings respond aggressively to their natural state of relative physical equality. In
response to the great dangers posed by their natural aggression, they abide by a
sharply anti-naturalist morality of autonomy, rights, and individual spheres of
freedom, which is intended to and to some extent does curb their natural
aggression. They respect a civil state that enforces those rights against the most
egregious breaches. The description of women's subjectivity told by cultural
feminism is much the opposite. According to cultural feminism, women inhabit a
realm of natural *inequality*. They are physically stronger than the fetus and the
infant. Women respond to their natural inequality over the fetus and infant not
with aggression, but with nurturance and care. That natural and nurturant
response evolves into a naturalist moral ethic of care which is consistent with
women's natural response. The substantive moralities consequent to these two
stories, then, unsurprisingly, are also diametrically opposed. The autonomy that
human beings value and the rights they need as a restriction on their natural
hostility to the equal and separate other are in sharp contrast to the intimacy that
women value, and the ethic of care that represents not a limitation upon, but an
extension of, women's natural nurturant response to the dependent, connected
other.

### Feminist jurisprudence

By the claim that modern jurisprudence is "masculine," I mean two things. First,
I mean that the values, the dangers, and what I have called the "fundamental
contradiction" that characterize women's lives are not reflected at any level
whatsoever in contracts, torts, constitutional law, or any other field of legal
doctrine. The values that flow from women's material potential for physical
connection are not recognized as values by the Rule of Law, and the dangers
attendant to that state are not recognized as dangers by the Rule of Law.

First, the Rule of Law does not value intimacy—its official value is autonomy.
The material consequence of this theoretical undervaluation of women's values in
the material world is that women are economically *impoverished*. The value
women place on intimacy reflects our existential and material circumstance;
women will act on that value whether it is compensated or not. But it is not.
Nurturant, intimate labor is neither valued by liberal legalism nor compensated
by the market economy. It is not compensated in the home and it is not compensated in the workplace—wherever intimacy is, there is no compensation.
Similarly, separation of the individual from his or her family, community, or
children is not understood to be a harm, and we are not protected against it. The
Rule of Law generally and legal doctrine in its particularity are coherent reactions
to the existential dilemma that follows from the liberal's description of the male

experience of material separation from the other: the Rule of Law acknowledges the danger of annihilation and the Rule of Law protects the value of autonomy. Just as assuredly, the Rule of Law is *not* a coherent reaction to the existential dilemma that follows from the material state of being connected to others, and the values and dangers attendant to that condition. It neither recognizes nor values intimacy, and neither recognizes nor protects against separation.

Nor does the Rule of Law recognize, in any way whatsoever, muted or unmuted, occasionally or persistently, overtly or covertly, the contradiction which characterizes women's, but not men's, lives: while we value the intimacy we find so natural, we are endangered by the invasion and dread the intrusion in our lives which intimacy entails, and we long for individuation and independence. Neither sexual nor fetal invasion of the self by the other is recognized as a harm worth bothering with. Sexual invasion through rape is understood to be a harm, and is criminalized as such, only when it involves some other harm: today, when it is accompanied by violence that appears in a form men understand (meaning a plausible threat of annihilation); in earlier times, when it was understood as theft of another man's property. But marital rape, date rape, acquaintance rape, simple rape, unaggravated rape, or as Susan Estrich wants to say "real rape"[42] are either not criminalized, or if they are, they are not punished—to do so would force a recognition of the concrete, experiential harm to identity formation that sexual invasion accomplishes.

Similarly, fetal invasion is not understood to be harmful, and therefore the claim that I ought to be able to protect myself against it is heard as nonsensical. The argument that the right to abortion mirrors the right of self defense falls on deaf ears for a reason: the analogy is indeed flawed. The right of self defense is the right to protect the body's security against annihilation liberally understood, not invasion. But the danger an unwanted fetus poses is not to the body's security at all, but rather to the body's integrity. Similarly, the woman's fear is not that she will die, but that she will cease to be or never become a self. The danger of unwanted pregnancy is the danger of invasion by the other, not of annihilation by the other. In sum, the Rule of Law does not recognize the danger of invasion, nor does it recognize the individual's need for, much less entitlement to, individuation and independence from the intrusion which heterosexual penetration and fetal invasion entails. The material consequence of this lack of recognition in the real world is that women are *objectified*—regarded as creatures who can't be harmed.

The second thing I mean to imply by the phrase "masculine jurisprudence" is that both liberal and critical legal theory, which is about the relation between law and life, is about men and not women. The reason for this lack of parallelism, of course, is hardly benign neglect. Rather, the distinctive values women hold, the distinctive dangers from which we suffer, and the distinctive contradictions that characterize our inner lives are not reflected in legal theory because legal theory (whatever else it's about) is about actual, real life, enacted, legislated, adjudicated law, and women have, from law's inception, lacked the power to make law protect, value, or seriously regard our experience. Jurisprudence is "masculine" because jurisprudence is about the relationship between human beings and the laws we actually have, and the laws we actually have are "masculine" both in terms of their intended beneficiary and in authorship. Women are absent from jurisprudence because women as *human beings* are absent from the law's protection: jurisprudence does not recognize us because law does not protect us. The implication for this should be obvious. We will not have a genuinely ungendered jurisprudence (a jurisprudence "unmodified" so to speak) until we have legal doctrine that takes women's lives as seriously as it takes men's. We don't have such legal doctrine. The virtual abolition of patriarchy is the necessary political condition for the creation of non-masculine feminist jurisprudence.

---

[42] Susan Estrich, *Real Rape* (1987).

It does not follow, however, that there is no such thing as feminist legal theory. Rather, I believe what is now inaccurately called "feminist jurisprudence" consists of two discrete projects. The first project is the unmasking and critiquing of the patriarchy behind purportedly ungendered law and theory, or, put differently, the uncovering of what we might call "patriarchal jurisprudence" from under the protective covering of "jurisprudence." The primary purpose of the critique of patriarchal jurisprudence is to show that jurisprudence and legal doctrine protect and define women. Its second purpose is to show how women—that is, people who value intimacy, fear separation, dread invasion, and crave individuation—have fared under a legal system which fails to value intimacy, fails to protect against separation, refuses to define invasion as a harm, and refuses to acknowledge the aspirations of women for individuation and physical privacy.

The second project in which feminist legal theorists engage might be called "reconstructive jurisprudence." The last twenty years have seen a substantial amount of feminist law reform, primarily in the areas of rape, sexual harassment, reproductive freedom, and pregnancy rights in the workplace. For strategic reasons, these reforms have often been won by characterizing women's injuries as analogous to, if not identical with, injuries men suffer (sexual harassment as a form of "discrimination;" rape as a crime of "violence"), or by characterizing women's longing as analogous to, if not identical with, men's official values (reproductive freedom—which ought to be grounded in a right to individuation—conceived instead as a "right to privacy," which is derivative of the autonomy right). This misconceptualization may have once been a necessary price, but it is a high price, and, as these victories accumulate, an increasingly unnecessary one. Reconstructive feminist jurisprudence should set itself the task of rearticulating these new rights in such a way as to reveal, rather than conceal their origin in women's distinctive existential and material state of being. The remainder of this article offers a schematization and criticism of the feminist jurisprudence we have generated to date, in spite of patriarchy and in spite of the masculinity of legal theory. I then suggest further lines of inquiry.

## *The Critique of Patriarchal Jurisprudence*

Structurally, the feminist attempt to describe and critique patriarchal jurisprudence by necessity tracks the methodological divisions in masculine jurisprudence, so I need to make one further diversion. Masculine jurisprudence is divided internally by a methodological issue which is as definitive and foundational as the substantive issues that divide liberal from critical legalism. Some legal theorists practice what might be called a "narrative" and "phenomenological" jurisprudential method, (hereinafter, simply narrative) and some practice what might be called an "interpretivist" method. Narrative and interpretive methodology have adherents in both liberal and critical legal literature. Thus, if we look at both two, but four major jurisprudential traditions in legal scholarship. Liberal legalism can be either interpretive or narrative, as can critical legal theory. Put differently, a narrative methodology can be either critical or liberal, as can interpretivism.

"Narrative legal theory," whether it be liberal or critical, moves methodologically from a description of justice, the state of nature, or of the "human being" which aims for some degree of generality if not universality, and then tells either a narrative *story* about how human beings thus described come to agree on the Rule of Law, or, alternatively, a phenomenological *description* of how it *feels* to be a person within a legal regime. To the narrative and phenomenological legal theorists, (whether critical or liberal) the *person*, the natural state, and the demands of justice are first, both historically and phenomenologically. Human beings create the Rule of Law from the state of nature to comply with the demands of justice and the narrative theorist tells how and why. "Interpretive" jurisprudence, whether liberal or critical, moves methodologically in the opposite direction. Interpretive theorists begin with an interpretation of law, or of a body of legal doctrine, or of the idea of law itself, and derive from that interpretation an account of justice. The methodological assumption of interpretive jurisprudence is that the legal text not only reflects, but to some degree even defines, what justice requires and hence what a person is. It is the purpose of interpretive jurisprudence to provide the best interpretation of the "justice" that the legal text has defined. Thus, the interpretivist tells the story of justice from the point of view of the rule of law, rather than the story of the emergence of "law" from the point of view of human beings under the constraints of justice. While to the narrative theorist, "we" create legal texts, to the interpretivists, the texts "create" as they define our moral commitments and hence our view of ourselves, and it is the theorist's special role to show exactly who it is that the texts have created.

Putting together substance and method, we can generate a four-boxed matrix: narrative liberal legalism, interpretive liberal legalism, narrative critical theory and interpretive critical theory.

|  | NARRATIVE | INTERPRETIVE |
|---|---|---|
| LIBERAL | Hobbes, Ackerman, Rawls | Blackstone R. Dworkin |
| CRITICAL | "Phenomenology Project" (rights) Unger, Gabel | D. Kennedy "Deconstruction Project" |

*The Narrative and Phenomenological Critique.* By "the critique of patriarchal jurisprudence" I mean four distinct projects, which parallel the matrix given above. First, *narrative* critical jurisprudence aims to provide, in a Hobbesian (or Ungerian) manner, the material, internal, phenomenological, subjective story of women's experience of the emergence and present reality of the Rule of Law. That story goes something like this. Prior to the advent of the "Rule of Law," we might hypothesize, women bore, breast fed, nurtured and protected children. Women did the nurturant work. As described above, women lived in a "natural web of hierarchy:" they were profoundly unequal to the infants they raised. While men responded to their condition of natural equality with mutual aggression, women responded to their condition of natural inequality with nurturance and an ethic of care. Women were at the same time profoundly unequal to men. Prior to the Rule of Law, women, and only women, were vulnerable to sexual invasion. Thus, inequality vis-a-vis both children and men, an ethic of care for the weak, and sexual vulnerability to the male, was women's natural state, while equality, mutual fear and suspicion was men's.

Then, on day two, came the Rule of Law. According to the Hobbesian story, the Rule of Law significantly improved the quality of men's lives: men's lives became longer, less nasty, less brutish (even if somewhat more alienated), and more productive. But not so for women: the same Rule of Law left women's natural lives intact, worsened her material condition, and reified her sexual vulnerability into a male right of access. The Rule of Law changed the conditions that uniquely pertained to women in the state of nature, but the change was for the worse: after the Rule of Law, women are still uniquely capable of intimacy, but newly unrecognized for their nurturant activity in a world that values autonomy and compensates individuated labor. Similarly, women remain uniquely vulnerable to invasion, but newly unprotected against that injury in a world that protects against other injuries. The narrative and phenomenological task for the critique of patriarchal jurisprudence is to tell the story and phenomenology of the human community's commitment to the Rule of Law from women's point of view. We need to show what the exclusion of women from law's protection has meant to both women and law, and we need to show what it means for the Rule of Law to exclude women and women's values.

The way to do this is to tell true stories of women's lives. The Hobbesian "story" of deliverance from the state of nature to the Rule of Law, as both liberal and radical legal scholars are fond of pointing out, does not purport to be history. But that doesn't make it fantasy. The Hobbesian story of the state of nature (and the critical story of alienation as well) is a synthesis of umpteen thousands of personal, subjective, everyday, male experiences. *Images* are generated from that synthesis, and those images, sometimes articulate, sometimes not, of what it means to be a human being then become the starting point of legal theory. Thus, for example, the Hobbesian, liberal picture of the "human being" as someone who treasures autonomy and fears annihilation from the other comes from men's primary experiences, presumably, of school yard fights, armed combat, sports, games, work, big brothers, and fathers. Similarly, the critical picture of the human being as someone who longs for attachment and dreads alienation comes from the male child's memory of his mother, from rejection experiences painfully culled from his adolescence, and from the adult male's continuing inability to introspect, converse, or commune with the natural world, including the natural world of others. When Peter Gabel says "Let me start by making a descriptive assertion [about human beings] ... which seems to me ... [to be] self-evidently true"[43] and then what follows is a descriptive statement which is self-evidently untrue of women, he is not simply "mistaken," he is mistaken in a particular (male) way and for a particular (male) reason. When Hobbes, Ackerman, Dworkin, Rawls and the rest of the liberal tradition describe the natural human predicament as one of natural equality and mutual antagonism, and describe human beings as inevitably separate and mutually self-interested, thus definitionally excluding pregnant women and breast-feeding mothers from the species, they also are mistaken in a particular way and for a particular reason. Gabel has confused his male experience of separation and alienation with "human" experience, and liberals have confused their male experiences of natural equality-and-through selfishness with "human" experience, and they have done so because women have not made clear that our day-to-day, lived experience—of intimacy, bonding, separation, sexual invasion, nurturance and intrusion—is incommensurable with men's. We need to flood the market with our own stories until we get one simple point across: men's narrative story and phenomenological description of law is not women's story and phenomenology of law. We need to dislodge legal theorists' confidence that they speak for women, and we need to fill the gap that will develop when we succeed in doing so.

Put phenomenologically, instead of narratively, feminist legal theorists need to show through stories the value of intimacy—not just to women, but to the community—and the damage done—again, not just to women, but to the community—by the law's refusal to reflect that value. We not only need to show that these values are missing from public life and not rewarded in private life, but we also need to show how our community would improve if they were valued. We need to show, (as Suzanna Sherry,[44] Lynne Henderson,[45] Martha Minow[46] and others have begun to do), that a community and a judiciary that relies on nurturant, caring, loving, empathic values rather than exclusively on the rule of reason will not melt into a murky quagmire, or sharpen into the dreaded spector of totalitarianism.

---

[43] Gabel, 62 Tex.L.Rev. at 1566.
[44] S. Sherry, (1986) 72 Va.L.Rev. 543 and (1986) 4 *Law and Inequality* 159.
[45] Henderson, "Legality and Empathy" (1987) 85 Mich.L.Rev. 1574.
[46] Martha Minow, "Foreword: Justice Engendered" (1987) 101 Harv.L.Rev. 10.

On a more local level, we need to show that a law school which employs, protects, and even *compensates* for these competencies will be a better law school. We needed to show, (as Martha Fineman has done in the area of custody decisions[47]), that a legal and economic system which values, protects and rewards nurturant labor in private life will make for a better community. We need to show that community, nurturance, responsibility, and the ethic of care are values at least as worthy of protection as autonomy, self-reliance, and individualism. We must do that, in part, by showing how those values have affected and enriched our own lives. Similarly, we need to show—and again, I think we need to do it with stories—how the refusal of the legal system to protect those values has weakened this community, as it has impoverished our lives.

From a radical point of view, we also need to explain, through stories, how physical invasion and intrusion harm women, and how they harm women distinctively. We need to explain, as Susan Estrich, Lynn Henderson and Diana Russell have begun to do, the danger and the harm of rape that is not seen as rape: invasive marital intercourse and invasive intercourse with "dates."[48] We need to explain how it feels to live entirely outside the protection of rape law: how it feels to be a wife in a state which defines rape as the "nonconsensual sexual intercourse by a man with a woman not his wife;" how it feels to be the person that another person has a legal right to invade without your consent. We need to provide stories rich enough to show that this harm is not the harm of annihilation protected by the Rule of Law, although it may accompany it. We need to show that the harm of invasive intercourse is real even when it does not look like the kind of violence protected by the Rule of Law. We need to show that invasive intercourse is a danger even when it cannot be analogized in any way whatsoever to male experience.

*The Interpretive Critique.* The purpose of the interpretive critique of patriarchal jurisprudence complements that of the narrative critique. As the narrative critique explores the Rule of Law from women's point of view, the interpretive critique aims to explore women from the point of view of the Rule of Law. The interpretive critique shows how patriarchal doctrine constructs, defines, and delimits women, just as interpretive masculine jurisprudence, both liberal and critical, aims to provide accounts of how doctrine constructs, defines, and delimits the human being. For although women—people who values intimacy and are harmed by invasion—have not been accorded the protection of the Rule of Law, we have hardly been ignored. Women are not constructed as human within this system, but we are nevertheless constructed as something else: as valueless, as objects, as children, or as invisible. The interpretive critique should aim to articulate what that something else might be. The interpretive critique is a lot like shining a light on darkness, or proving a negative—it involves looking at what lies between the images of legalism, instead of looking directly at legalism. The interpretive critique must deconstruct the images that authoritatively diminish women, sometimes down to nothing.

On the cultural side of the substantive divide, this means showing how legalism devalues women, but not valuing what women value. To name just a few examples, Martha Fineman has tried to show who and what a "mother" is understood to be in a legal system where nurturant labor is neither recognized nor

---

[47] Martha L. Fineman and Anne Opie, "The Uses of Social Science Data in Legal Policymaking: Custody Determination at Divorce" (1987) Wisc.L.Rev. 107; Martha L. Fineman, "A Reply to David Chambers" (1987) Wisc.L.R. 165; Martha L. Fineman, "Dominant Discourse, Professional Language and Legal Change" (1988) 101 Harv.L.-Rev. 727.

[48] Estrich, *Real Rape;* Henderson, Book Review (1988) Berkeley Women's L.J. 47; Diana E.H. Russell, *Rape in Marriage* (1982).

valued in custody disputes.[49] Other interpretive cultural feminists have tried to show what it means, objectively, not to be paid for housework, for child-raising, and for relational work in the workplace. On the radical side, this means showing what it means, to take just a few examples, Andrea Dworkin has begun to show who the "woman" is defined to be by the pornographer, and Catharine MacKinnon has begun to show how the First Amendment has defined the pornographer's definition of the woman.[50] Susan Estrich, Diana Russell, and others have begun to show what a "wife" *is* in a legal system which defines rape as the nonconsensual intercourse by a man with a woman, *not his wife*.[51] We need, I think, to do more of this: most notably, we need to understand how laws criminalizing abortion construct "motherhood" and how *Roe v. Wade*[52]—which constructs the right to abortion as the product of a need to balance medicinal privacy rights of doctors and patients against the right to life of a fetus—constructs the female. Henderson has done some of this work.[53] The matrix I foresee, with a sample of representative participants, looks like this:

### CRITIQUE OF PATRIARCHAL JURISPRUDENCE

|  | CULTURAL FEMINISM | RADICAL FEMINISM |
|---|---|---|
| Interpretive Jurisprudence | Sherry and Henderson (on judging) Fineman (motherhood) Dalton (midwives) | MacKinnon (first amend) A. Dworkin (pornography) Estrich (rape) |
|  | DECONSTRUCTION PROJECTS | |
| Narrative Jurisprudence | Littleton Fineman | NARAL (Abortion) MacKinnon (sex harass) Estrich (rape) |
|  | PHENOMENOLOGICAL PROJECTS (of romance, porn, etc.) | |

*Reconstructive Jurisprudence*

The goal of reconstructive feminist jurisprudence is to render feminist reform rational. We must change the fact that, from a mainstream point of view, arguments for feminist legal reform efforts are (or appear to be) invariably irrational. The moral questions feminist reforms pose are always incommensurable with dominant moral and legal categories. Let me put it this way: given present moral categories, women's issues are crazy issues. Arguments for reproductive freedom, for example, are a little insane: pro-choice advocates can't explain the difference between reproductive freedom and infanticide; or how this right can possibly be grounded in the Constitution; or how it is that women can claim to be "nurturant" and at the same time show blatant disregard for the rights and feelings of fetuses. In fact, my sense, drawn from anecdotal evidence only, is that the abortion issue is increasingly used in ethics as well as constitutional law classrooms to exemplify the "irrationality" of individual moral commitment. Rape reform efforts that aim to expand the scope of the defined harm are also perceived, I believe, as insane. Why would anyone possibly object to non-violent sex? Isn't sex always pleasurable? Feminist pornography initiatives are viewed as

---

[49] Martha L. Fineman, (1988) 101 Harv. L.Rev. 727.
[50] MacKinnon, "Feminism Unmodified" at 206–13.
[51] Estrich, *Real Rape*; Russell, *Rape in Marriage*.
[52] (1973) 410 U.S. 113.
[53] Henderson, (1987) 85 Mich.L.Rev. 1574.

irrational, and the surrogate motherhood issue is no better. There's an air of irrationality around each of these issues.

That air of irrationality is partly real and partly feigned. The reason for the air of irrationality around particular, substantive feminist legal reform efforts, I believe, is that feminist legal reforms are by necessity advocated in a form that masks rather than reflects women's true subjective nature. This is hardly surprising: language, of course, constrains our descriptive options. But whether or not surprising, the damage is alarming, and we need to understand its root. Arguments for reproductive freedom, for example, are irrational because the categories in which such arguments must be cast are reflective of men's, not women's, nature. This culture thinks about harm, and violence, and therefore self defense, in a particular way, namely a Hobbesian way, and a Hobbesian conception of physical harm cannot possibly capture the gender-specific subjective harm that constitutes the experience of unwanted pregnancy. From a subjective, female point of view, an abortion is an act of self defense, (not the exercise of a "right of privacy") but from the point of view of masculine subjectivity, an abortion can't possibly be an act of self defense: the fetus is not one of Hobbes' "relatively equal" natural men against whom we have a right to protect ourselves. The fetus is unequal and above all else dependent. That dependency and inequality is the essence of fetus-hood, so to speak. Self-defense doctrine with its Hobbesian background and overlay simply doesn't apply to such dependent and unequal "aggressors," indeed, the notion of aggression itself does not apply to such creatures.                                                              [pp. 6–28]

[...]

"Reconstructive feminist jurisprudence," I believe, should try to explain or reconstruct the reforms necessary to the safety and improvement of women's lives in direct language that is true to our own experience and our own subjective lives. The dangers of mandatory pregnancy, for example, are invasion of the body by the fetus and the intrusion into the mother's existence following childbirth. The right to abort is the right to defend against a particular bodily and existential invasion. The harm the unwanted fetus does is not the harm of annihilation, nor anything like it: it is not an assault, or a battery, or a breached contract, or an act of negligence. A fetus is not an equal in the state of nature, and the harm a fetus can do is not in any way analogous to that harm. It is, however, a harm. The fetus is an "other," and it is perfectly sensible to seek a liberal sounding "right" of protection against the harm the fetus does.                                          [p. 70]

[...] The goal of reconstructive feminist jurisprudence should be to provide descriptions of the "human being" underlying feminist legal reforms that will be true to the conditions of women's lives. Our jurisprudential constructs—liberalism and critical theory—might then change as well to account for true descriptions of women's subjectivity.

### Conclusion: toward a jurisprudence unmodified

The "separation thesis," is drastically untrue of women. What's worth noting by way of conclusion is that it is not entirely true of men either. First, it is not true materially. Men are connected to another human life prior to the cutting of the umbilical cord. Furthermore, men are somewhat connected to women during intercourse, and men have openings that can be sexually penetrated. Nor is the separation thesis necessarily true of men existentially. As Suzanna Sherry has shown, the existence of the entire classical republican tradition belies the claim that masculine biology mandates liberal values.[54] More generally, as Dinnerstein, Chodorow, French, and Gilligan all insist, material biology does not *mandate*

[54]  Sherry (1986) 72 Va.L.Rev. at 584.

existential value: men *can* connect to other human life. Men can nurture life. Men can mother. Obviously, men can care, and love, and support, and affirm life. Just as obviously, however, most men don't. One reason that they don't, of course, is male privilege. Another reason, though, may be the blinders of our masculinist utopian visionary. Surely one of the most important insights of feminism has been that biology is indeed destiny when we are unaware of the extent to which biology is narrowing our fate, but that *biology is destiny only to the extent of our ignorance.* As we become increasingly aware, we become increasingly free. As we become increasingly free, we, rather than biology, become the authors of our fate. Surely this is true both of men and women.

On the flip side, the "connection thesis" is also not entirely true of women, either materially or existentially. Not all women become pregnant, and not all women are sexually penetrated. Women can go through life unconnected to other human life. Women can also go through life fundamentally unconcerned with other human life. Obviously, as the liberal feminist movement firmly established, many women can and do individuate, speak the truth, develop integrity, pursue personal projects, embody freedom, and attain an atomistic liberal individuality. Just as obviously, most women don't. Most women are indeed forced into motherhood and heterosexuality. One reason for this is utopian blinders: women's lack of awareness of existential choice in the face of what are felt to be biological imperatives. But that is surely not the main reason. The primary reason for the stunted nature of women's lives is male power.

Perhaps the greatest obstacle to the creation of a feminist jurisprudence is that feminist jurisprudence must simultaneously confront both political and conceptual barriers to women's freedom. The political barrier is surely the most pressing. Feminists must first and foremost counter a profound power imbalance, and the way to do that is through law and politics. But jurisprudence—like law—is persistently utopian and conceptual as well as apologist and political: jurisprudence represents a constant and at least at times a sincere attempt to articulate a guiding utopian vision of human association. Feminist jurisprudence must respond to these utopian images, correct them, improve upon them, and participate in them as utopian images, not just as apologies for patriarchy. Feminism must envision a post-patriarchal world, for without such a vision we have little direction. We must use that vision to construct our present goals, and we should, I believe, interpret our present victories against the backdrop of that vision. That vision is not necessarily androgynous; surely in a utopian world the presence of differences between people will be cause only for celebration. In a utopian world, all forms of life will be recognized, respected and honored. A perfect legal system will protect against harms sustained by all forms of life, and will recognize life affirming values generated by all forms of being. Feminist jurisprudence must aim to bring this about and, to do so, it must aim to transform the images as well as the power. Masculine jurisprudence must become humanist jurisprudence, and humanist jurisprudence must become a jurisprudence unmodified. [pp. 70–72]

## CATHARINE A. MACKINNON
### Difference and Dominance: On Sex Discrimination
(1987)[55]

What is a gender question a question of? What is an inequality question a question of? These two questions underlie applications of the equality principle to issues of gender, but they are seldom explicitly asked. I think it speaks to the way gender has structured thought and perception that mainstream legal and moral

[55] [From *Feminism Unmodified; Discourses on Life and Law*.]

theory tacitly gives the same answer to them both: these are questions of sameness and difference. The mainstream doctrine of the law of sex discrimination that results is, in my view, largely responsible for the fact that sex equality law has been so utterly ineffective at getting women what we need and are socially prevented from having on the basis of a condition of birth: a chance at productive lives of reasonable physical security, self-expression, individuation, and minimal respect and dignity. Here I expose the sameness/difference theory of sex equality, briefly show how it dominates sex discrimination law and policy and underlies its discontents, and propose an alternative that might do something.

According to the approach to sex equality that has dominated politics, law, and social perception, equality is an equivalence, not a distinction, and sex is a distinction. The legal mandate of equal treatment—which is both a systemic norm and a specific legal doctrine—becomes a matter of treating likes alike and unlikes unlike; and the sexes are defined as such by their mutual unlikeness. Put another way, gender is socially constructed as difference epistemologically; sex discrimination law bounds gender equality by difference doctrinally. A built-in tension exists between this concept of equality, which presupposes sameness, and this concept of sex, which presupposes difference. Sex equality thus becomes a contradiction in terms, something of an oxymoron, which may suggest why we are having such a difficult time getting it.

Upon further scrutiny, two alternate paths to equality for women emerge within this dominant approach, paths that roughly follow the lines of this tension. The leading one is: be the same as men. This path is termed gender neutrality doctrinally and the single standard philosophically. It is testimony to how substance gets itself up as form in law that this rule is considered formal equality. Because this approach mirrors the ideology of the social world, it is considered abstract, meaning transparent of substance; also for this reason it is considered not only to be *the* standard, but *a* standard at all. It is so far the leading rule that the words "equal to" are code for, equivalent to, the words "the same as"—referent for both unspecified.

To women who want equality yet find that you are different, the doctrine provides an alternate route: be different from men. This equal recognition of difference is termed the special benefit rule or special protection rule legally, the double standard philosophically. It is in rather bad odor. Like pregnancy, which always calls it up, it is something of a doctrinal embarrassment. Considered an exception to true equality and not really a rule of law at all, this is the one place where the law of sex discrimination admits it is recognizing something substantive. Together with the Bona Fide Occupational Qualification, the unique physical characteristic exception under ERA policy, compensatory legislation, and sex-conscious relief in particular litigation, affirmative action is thought to live here.[56]

The philosophy underlying the difference approach is that sex *is* a difference, a division, a distinction, beneath which lies a stratum of human commonality, sameness. The moral thrust of the sameness branch of the doctrine is to make normative rules conform to this empirical reality by granting women access to what men have access to: to the extent that women are no different from men, we deserve what they have. The differences branch, which is generally seen as patronizing but necessary to avoid absurdity, exists to value or compensate women for what we are or have become distinctively as women (by which is meant, unlike men) under existing conditions.

My concern is not with which of these paths to sex equality is preferable in the long run or more appropriate to any particular issue, although most discourse on

---

[56] The exception to Title VII of the Civil Rights Act of 1964, 42 U.S.C. § 2000 e-(2)(e), permits sex to be a job qualification when it is a valid one.

sex discrimination revolves about these questions as if that were all there is. My point is logically prior: to treat issues of sex equality as issues of sameness and difference *is to take a particular approach*. I call this the difference approach because it is obsessed with the sex difference. The main theme in the fugue is "we're the same, we're the same, we're the same." The counterpoint theme (in a higher register) is "but we're different, but we're different, but we're different." Its underlying story is: on the first day, difference was; on the second day, a division was created upon it; on the third day, irrational instances of dominance arose. Division may be rational or irrational. Dominance either seems or is justified. Difference *is*.

There is a politics to this. Concealed is the substantive way in which man has become the measure of all things. Under the sameness standard, women are measured according to our correspondence with man, our equality judged by our proximity to his measure. Under the difference standard, we are measured according to our lack of correspondence with him, our womanhood judged by our distance from his measure. Gender neutrality is thus simply the male standard, and the special protection rule is simply the female standard, but do not be deceived: masculinity, or maleness, is the referent for both. Think about it like those anatomy models in medical school. A male body is the human body; all those extra things women have are studied in ob/gyn. It truly is a situation in which more is less. Approaching sex discrimination in this way—as if sex questions are difference questions and equality questions are sameness questions—provides two ways for the law to hold women to a male standard and call that sex equality.

I should say that it takes up a very important problem: how to get women access to everything we have been excluded from, while also valuing everything that women are or have been allowed to become or have developed as a consequence of our struggle either not to be excluded from most of life's pursuits or to be taken seriously under the terms that have been permitted to be our terms. It negotiates what we have managed in relation to men. Legally articulated as the need to conform normative standards to existing reality, the strongest doctrinal expression of its sameness idea would prohibit taking gender into account in any way.

Its guiding impulse is: we're as good as you. Anything you can do, we can do. Just get out of the way. I have to confess a sincere affection for this approach. It has gotten women some access to employment and education, the public pursuits, including academic, professional, and blue-collar work; the military; and more than nominal access to athletics. It has moved to change the dead ends that were all we were seen as good for and has altered what passed for women's lack of physical training, which was really serious training in passivity and enforced weakness. It makes you want to cry sometimes to know that it has had to be a mission for many women just to be permitted to do the work of this society, to have the dignity of doing jobs a lot of other people don't even want to do.

The issue of including women in the military draft[57] has presented the sameness answer to the sex equality question in all its simple dignity and complex equivocality. As a citizen, I should have to risk being killed just like you. The consequences of my resistance to this risk should count like yours. The undercurrent is: what's the matter, don't you want me to learn to kill ... just like you? Sometimes I see this as a dialogue between women in the afterlife. The feminist says to the soldier, "we fought for your equality." The soldier says to the feminist, "oh, no, *we* fought for *your* equality."

Feminists have this nasty habit of counting bodies and refusing not to notice their gender. As applied, the sameness standard has mostly gotten men the benefit

---

[57] *Rostker* v. *Goldberg* (1981) 453 U.S. 57. See also Lori S. Kornblum, "Women Warriors in a Men's World: The Combat Exclusion" (1984) 2 Law and Inequality 353.

of those few things women have historically had—for all the good they did us. Almost every sex discrimination case that has been won at the Supreme Court level has been brought by a man.[58] Under the rule of gender neutrality, the law of custody and divorce has been transformed, giving men an equal chance at custody of children and at alimony. Men often look like better "parents" under gender-neutral rules like level of income and presence of nuclear family, because men take more money and (as they say) initiate the building of family units.[59] In effect, they get preferred because society advantages them before they get into court, and law is prohibited from taking that preference into account because that would mean taking gender into account. The group realities that make women more in need of alimony are not permitted to matter, because only individual factors, gender-neutrality considered, may matter. So the fact that women will live their lives, as individuals, as members of the group women, with women's chances in a sex-discriminatory society, may not count, or else it is sex discrimination. The equality principle in this guise mobilizes the idea that the way to get things for women is to get them for men. Men have gotten them. Have women? We still have not got equal pay, or equal work, far less equal pay for equal work, and we are close to losing separate enclaves like women's schools through this approach.

Here is why. In reality, which this approach is not long on because it is liberal idealism talking to itself, virtually every quality that distinguishes men from women is already affirmatively compensated in this society. Men's physiology defines most sports,[60] their needs define auto and health insurance coverage, their socially designed biographies define workplace expectations and successful career patterns, their perspectives and concerns define quality in scholarship, their experience and obsessions define merit, their objectification of life defines art, their military service defines citizenship, their presence defines family, their inability to get along with each other—their wars and rulerships—defines history, their image defines god, and their genitals define sex. For each of their differences from women, what amounts to an affirmative action plan is in effect, otherwise known as the structure and values of American society. But whenever women are, by this standard, "different" from men and insist on not having it held against us, whenever a difference is used to keep us second class and we refuse to smile about it, equality law has a paradigm trauma and it's crisis time for the doctrine.

What this doctrine has apparently meant by sex inequality is not what happens to us. The law of sex discrimination that has resulted seems to be looking only for

---

[58]	David Cole, "Strategies of Difference: Litigating for Women's Rights in a Man's World" (1984) 2 Law & Inequality 33, 34, n. 4.

[59]	Lenore Weitzman, "The Economics of Divorce: Social and Economic Consequences of Property, Alimony and Child Support Awards" (1982) 28 U.C.L.A. Law Rev. 1118, 1251, documents a decline in women's standard of living of 73 per cent. and an increase in men's of 42 per cent. within a year after divorce.

[60]	A particularly pungent example comes from a case in which the plaintiff sought to compete in boxing matches with men, since there was no matches sponsored by the defendant among women. A major reason that preventing the woman from competing was found not to violate her equality rights was that the "safety rules and precautions [were] developed, designed, and tested in the context of all-male competition." *Lafler* v. *Athletic Board of Control* (1982) 536 F.Supp. 104, 107 (W.D. Mich.). As the court put it: "In this case, the real differences between the male and female anatomy are relevant in considering whether men and women may be treated differently with regard to their participating in boxing. The plaintiff *admits* that she wears a protecting covering for her breasts while boxing. Such a protective covering ... would violate Rule Six, Article 9 of the Amateur Boxing Federation rules currently in effect. The same rule *requires* contestants to wear a protective cup, a rule obviously designed for the unique anatomical characteristics of men." Id. at 106 (emphasis added). The rule is based on the male anatomy, therefore not a justification for the discrimination but an example of it. This is not considered in the opinion, nor does the judge discuss whether women might benefit from genital protection, and men from chest guards, as in some other sports.

those ways women are kept down that have *not* wrapped themselves up as a difference—whether original, imposed, or imagined. Start with original: what to do about the fact that women actually have an ability men still lack, gestating children in utero. Pregnancy therefore is a difference. Difference doctrine says it is sex discrimination to give women what we need, because only women need it. It is not sex discrimination not to give women what we need because then only women will not get what we need. Move into imposed: what to do about the fact that most women are segregated into low-paying jobs where there are no men. Suspecting that the structure of the marketplace will be entirely subverted if comparable worth is put into effect, difference doctrine says that because there is no man to set a standard from which women's treatment is a deviation, there is no sex discrimination here, only sex difference. Never mind that there is no man to compare with because no man would do that job if he had a choice, and of course he has because he is a man, so he won't.

Now move into the so-called subtle reaches of the imposed category; the *de facto* area. Most jobs in fact require that the person, gender neutral, who is qualified for them will be someone who is not the primary caretaker of a pre-school child. Pointing out that this raises a concern of sex in a society in which women are expected to care for the children is taken as day one of taking gender into account in the structuring of jobs. To do that would violate the rule against not noticing situated differences based on gender, so it never emerges that day one of taking gender into account was the day the job was structured with the expectation that its occupant would have no child care responsibilities. Imaginary sex differences—such as between male and female applicants to administer estates or between males aging and dying and females aging and dying—I will concede, the doctrine can handle.

What the sameness standard fails to notice is that men's differences from women are equal to women's differences from men. There is an *equality* there. Yet the sexes are not socially equal. The difference approach misses the fact that hierarchy of power produces real as well as fantasied differences, differences that are also inequalities. What is missing in the difference approach is what Aristotle missed in his empiricist notion that equality means treating likes alike and unlikes unlike, and nobody has questioned it since. Why should you have to be the same as a man to get what a man gets simply because he is one? Why does maleness provide an original entitlement, not questioned on the basis of *its* gender, so that it is women—women who want to make a case of unequal treatment in a world men have made in their image (this is really the part Aristotle missed)—who have to show in effect that they are men in every relevant respect, unfortunately mistaken for women on the basis of an accident of birth?

The women that gender neutrality benefits, and there are some, show the suppositions of this approach in highest relief. They are mostly women who have been able to construct a biography that somewhat approximates the male norm, at least on paper. They are the qualified, the least of sex discrimination's victims. When they are denied a man's chance, it looks the most like sex bias. The more unequal society gets, the fewer such women are permitted to exist. Therefore, the more unequal society gets, the *less* likely the difference doctrine is to be able to do anything about it, because unequal power creates both the appearance and the reality of sex differences along the same lines as it creates its sex inequalities.

The special benefits side of the difference approach has not compensated for the differential of being second class. The special benefits rule is the only place in mainstream equality doctrine where you get to identify as a woman and not have that mean giving up all claim to equal treatment—but it comes close. Under its double standard, women who stand to inherit something when their husbands die have gotten the exclusion of a small percentage of the inheritance tax, to the tune of Justice Douglas waxing eloquent about the difficulties of all women's economic situation.[61] If we're going to be stigmatized as different, it would be nice if the compensation would fit the disparity. Women have also gotten three more years than men get before we have to be advanced or kicked out of the military hierarchy, as compensation for being precluded from combat, the usual way to advance.[62] Women have also gotten excluded from contact jobs in male-only prisons because we might get raped, the Court taking the viewpoint of the reasonable rapist on women's employment opportunities.[63] We also get protected out of jobs because of our fertility. The reason is that the job has health hazards, and somebody who might be a real person some day and therefore could sue—that is, a fetus—might be hurt if women, who apparently are not real persons and therefore can't sue either for the hazard to our health or for the lost employment opportunity, are given jobs that subject our bodies to possible harm.[64] Excluding women is always an option if equality feels in tension with the pursuit itself. They never seem to think of excluding men.

The double standard of these rules doesn't give women the dignity of the single standard; it also does not (as the differences standard does) suppress the gender of its referent, which is, of course, the female gender. I must also confess some affection for this standard. The work of Carol Gilligan on gender differences in moral reasoning[65] gives it a lot of dignity, more than it has ever had, more frankly, than I thought it ever could have. But she achieves for moral reasoning what the special protection rule achieves in law: the affirmative rather than the negative valuation of that which has accurately distinguished women from men, by making it seem as though those attributes, with their consequences, really are somehow ours, rather than what male supremacy has attributed to us for its own use. For women to affirm difference, when difference means dominance, as it does with gender, means to affirm the qualities and characteristics of powerlessness.

Women have done good things, and it is a good thing to affirm them. I think quilts are art. I think women have a history. I think we create culture. I also know that we have not only been excluded from making what has been considered art; our artifacts have been excluded from setting the standards by which art is art. Women have a history all right, but it is a history both of what was and of what was not allowed to be. So I am critical of affirming what we have been, which necessarily is what we have been permitted, as if it is women's, ours, possessive. As if equality, in spite of everything, already ineluctably exists.

I am getting hard on this and am about to get harder on it. I do not think that the way women reason morally is morality "in a different voice." I think it is morality in a higher register, in the feminine voice. Women value care because men have valued us according to the care we give them, and we could probably use some. Women think in relational terms because our existence is defined in relation to men. Further, when you are powerless, you don't just speak differently. A lot, you don't speak. Your speech is not just differently articulated, it is silenced. Eliminated, gone. You aren't just deprived of a language with which to articulate your distinctiveness, although you are; you are deprived of a life out of which articulation might come. Not being heard is not just a function of lack of recognition, not just that no one knows how to listen to you, although it is that; it is also silence of the deep kind, the silence of being prevented from having anything to say. Sometimes it is permanent. All I am saying is that the damage of sexism is real, and reifying that into differences is an insult to our possibilities.

---

[61]  *Kahn* v. *Shevin* (1974) 416 U.S. 351, 353.

[62]  *Schlesinger* v. *Ballard* (1975) 419 U.S. 498.

[63]  *Dothard* v. *Rawlinson* (1977) 433 U.S. 321; see also *Michael M.* v. *Sonoma County Superior Court* (1981) 450 U.S. 464.

[64]  *Doerr* v. *B.F. Goodrich* 1979 484 F. Supp. 320 (N.D. Ohio); Wendy Webster Williams, "Firing the Woman to Protect the Fetus: The Reconciliation of Fetal Protection with Employment Opportunity Goals Under Title VII" (1981) 69 Georgetown L.J. 641.

[65]  Carol Gilligan, *In a Different Voice* (1982).

So long as these issues are framed this way, demands for equality will always appear to be asking to have it both ways: the same when we are the same, different when we are different. But this is the way men have it: equal and different too. They have it the same as women when they are the same and want it, and different from women when they are different and want to be, which usually they do. Equal and different too would only be parity. But under male supremacy, while being told we get it both ways, both the specialness of the pedestal and an even chance at the race, the ability to be a woman and a person, too, few women get much benefit of either.

There is an alternative approach, one that threads its way through existing law and expresses, I think, the reason equality law exists in the first place. It provides a second answer, a dissident answer in law and philosophy, to both the equality question and the gender question. In this approach, an equality question is a question of the distribution of power. Gender is also a question of power, specifically of male supremacy and female subordination. The question of equality, from the standpoint of what it is going to take to get it, is at root a question of hierarchy, which—as power succeeds in constructing social perception and social reality—derivatively becomes a categorical distinction, a difference. Here, on the first day that matters, dominance was achieved, probably by force. By the second day, division along the same lines had to be relatively firmly in place. On the third day, if not sooner, differences were demarcated, together with social systems to exaggerate them in perception and in fact, *because* the systematically differential delivery of benefits and deprivations required making no mistake about who was who. Comparatively speaking, man has been resting ever since. Gender might not even code as difference, might not mean distinction epistemologically, were it not for its consequences for social power.

I call this the dominance approach, and it is the ground I have been standing on in criticizing mainstream law. The goal of this dissident approach is not to make legal categories trace and trap the way things are. It is not to make rules that fit reality. It is critical of reality. Its task is not to formulate abstract standards that will produce determinate outcomes in particular cases. Its project is more substantive, more jurisprudential than formulaic, which is why it is difficult for the mainstream discourse to dignify it as an approach to doctrine or to imagine it as a rule of law at all. It proposes to expose that which women have had little choice but to be confined to, in order to change it.

The dominance approach centers on the most sex-differential abuses of women as a gender, abuses that sex equality law in its difference garb could not confront. It is based on a reality about which little of a systematic nature was known before 1970, a reality that calls for a new conception of the problem of sex inequality. This new information includes not only the extent and intractability of sex segregation into poverty, which has been known before, but the range of issues termed violence against women, which has not been. It combines women's material desperation, through being relegated to categories of jobs that pay nil, with the massive amount of rape and attempted rape—44 per cent. of all women—about which virtually nothing is done;[66] the sexual assault of children—38 per cent. of girls and 10 per cent. of boys—which is apparently endemic to the patriarchal family,[67] the battery of women that is systematic in one quarter to one

---

[66] Diana Russell and Nancy Howell, "The Prevalence of Rape in the United States Re visited" (1983) 8 *Signs: Journal of Women in Culture and Society* 689 (1983).

[67] Diana Russell, "The Incidence and Prevalence of Intrafamilial and Extrafamilial Sexual Abuse of Female Children" (1983) 7 *Child Abuse & Neglect* 133.

third of our homes,[68] prostitution, women's fundamental economic condition, what we do when all else fails, and for many women in this country, all else fails often,[69] and pornography, an industry that traffics in female flesh, making sex inequality into sex to the tune of eight billion dollars a year in profits largely to organized crime.

These experiences have been silenced out of the difference definition of sex equality largely because they happen almost exclusively to women. Understand: for this reason, they are considered *not* to raise sex equality issues. Because this treatment is done almost uniquely to women, it is implicitly treated as a difference, the sex difference, when in fact it is the socially situated subjection of women. The whole point of women's social relegation to inferiority as a gender is that for the most part these things aren't done to men. Men are not paid half of what women are paid for doing the same work on the basis of their equal difference. When they are hit, a person has been assaulted. When they are sexually violated, it is not simply tolerated or found entertaining or defended as the necessary structure of the family, the price of civilization, or a constitutional right.

Does this differential describe the sex difference? Maybe so. It does describe the systematic relegation of an entire group of people to a condition of inferiority and attribute it to their nature. If this differential were biological, maybe biological intervention would have to be considered. If it were evolutionary, perhaps men would have to evolve differently. Because I think it is political, I think its politics construct the deep structure of society. Men who do not rape women have nothing wrong with their hormones. Men who are made sick by pornography and do not eroticize their revulsion are not under-evolved. This social status in which we can be used and abused and trivialized and humiliated and bought and sold and passed around and patted on the head and put in place and told to smile so that we look as though we're enjoying it all is not what some of us have in mind as sex equality.

The second approach—which is not abstract, which is at odds with socially imposed reality and therefore does not look like a standard according to the standard for standards—became the implicit model for racial justice applied by the courts during the sixties. It has since eroded with the erosion of judicial commitment to racial equality. It was based on the realization that the condition of Blacks in particular was not fundamentally a matter of rational or irrational differentiation on the basis of race but was fundamentally a matter of white supremacy, under which racial differences became invidious as a consequence.[70] To consider gender in this way, observe again that men are as different from women as women are from men, but socially the sexes are not equally powerful. To be on the top of a hierarchy is certainly different from being on the bottom, but that is an obfuscatingly neutralized way of putting it, as a hierarchy is a great deal more than that. If gender were merely a question of difference, sex inequality would be a problem of mere sexism, of mistaken differentiation, of inaccurate categorization of individuals. This is what the difference approach thinks it is and is therefore sensitive to. But if gender is an inequality first, constructed as a socially relevant differentiation in order to keep that inequality in place, then sex inequality questions are questions of systematic dominance, of male supremacy, which is not at all abstract and is anything but a mistake.

---

[68] R. Emerson Dobash and Russell Dobash, *Violence against Wives: A Case against the Patriarchy* (1979).

[69] Kathleen Barry, *Female Sexual Slavery* (1979); Moira K. Griffin, "Wives, Hookers and the Law: The Case for Decriminalizing Prostitution" (1982) 10 *Student Lawyer* 18.

[70] *Loving* v. *Virginia* (1967) 388 U.S. 1, first used the term "white supremacy" in invalidating an antimiscegenation law as a violation of equal protection. The law equally forbade whites and Blacks to intermarry.

If differentiation into classifications, in itself, is discrimination, as it is in difference doctrine, the use of law to change group-based social inequalities becomes problematic, even contradictory. This is because the group whose situation is to be changed must necessarily be legally identified and delineated, yet to do so is considered in fundamental tension with the guarantee against legally sanctioned inequality. If differentiation is discrimination, affirmative action, and any legal change in social inequality, is discrimination—but the existing social differentiations which constitute the inequality are not? This is only to say that, in the view that equates differentiation with discrimination, changing an unequal *status quo* is discrimination, but allowing it to exist is not.

Looking at the difference approach and the dominance approach from each other's point of view clarifies some otherwise confusing tensions in sex equality debates. From the point of view of the dominance approach, it becomes clear that the difference approach adopts the point of view of male supremacy on the status of the sexes. Simply by treating the *status quo* as "the standard," it invisibly and uncritically accepts the arrangements under male supremacy. In this sense, the difference approach is masculinist, although it can be expressed in a female voice. The dominance approach, in that it sees the inequalities of the social world from the standpoint of the subordination of women to men, is feminist.

If you look through the lens of the difference approach at the world as the dominance approach imagines it—that is, if you try to see real inequality through a lens that has difficulty seeing an inequality as an inequality if it also appears as a difference—you see demands for change in the distribution of power as demands for special protection. This is because the only tools that the difference paradigm offers to comprehend disparity equate the recognition of a gender line with an admission of lack of entitlement to equality under law. Since equality questions are primarily confronted in this approach as matters of empirical fit—that is, as matters of accurately shaping legal rules (implicitly modeled on the standard men set) to the way the world is (also implicitly modeled on the standard men set)— any existing differences must be negated to merit equal treatment. For ethnicity as well as for gender, it is basic to mainstream discrimination doctrine to preclude any true diversity among equals or true equality within diversity.

To the difference approach, it further follows that any attempt to change the way the world actually is looks like a moral question requiring a separate judgment of how things ought to be. This approach imagines asking the following disinterested question that can be answered neutrally as to groups: against the weight of empirical difference, should we treat some as the equals of others, even when they may not be entitled to it because they are not up to standard? Because this construction of the problem is part of what the dominance approach unmasks, it does not arise with the dominance approach, which therefore does not see its own foundations as moral. If sex inequalities are approached as matters of imposed status, which are in need of change if a legal mandate of equality means anything at all, the question whether women should be treated unequally means simply whether women should be treated as less. When it is exposed as a naked power question, there is no separable question of what ought to be. The only real question is what is and is not a gender question. Once no amount of difference justifies treating women as subhuman, eliminating that is what equality law is for. In this shift of paradigms, equality propositions become no longer propositions of good and evil, but of power and powerlessness, no more disinterested in their origins or neutral in their arrival at conclusions than are the problems they address.

There came a time in Black people's movement for equality in this country when slavery stopped being a question of how it could be justified and became a question of how it could be ended. Racial disparities surely existed, or racism would have been harmless, but at that point—a point not yet reached for issues of sex—no amount of group difference mattered anymore. This is the same point at which a group's characteristics, including empirical attributes, become constitutive of the fully human, rather than being defined as exceptions to or as distinct from the fully human. To one-sidedly measure one group's differences against a standard set by the other incarnates partial standards. The moment when one's particular qualities become part of the standard by which humanity is measured is a millennial moment.

To summarize the argument: seeing sex equality questions as matters of reasonable or unreasonable classification is part of the way male dominance is expressed in law. If you follow my shift in perspective from gender as difference to gender as dominance, gender changes from a distinction that is presumptively valid to a detriment that is presumptively suspect. The difference approach tries to map reality; the dominance approach tries to challenge and change it. In the dominance approach, sex discrimination stops being a question of morality and starts being a question of politics.

You can tell if sameness is your standard for equality if my critique of hierarchy looks like a request for special protection in disguise. It's not. It envisions a change that would make possible a simple equal chance for the first time. To define the reality of sex as difference and the warrant of equality as sameness is wrong on both counts. Sex, in nature, is not a bipolarity; it is a continuum. In society it is made into a bipolarity. Once this is done, to require that one be the same as those who set the standard—those which one is already socially defined as different from—simply means that sex equality is conceptually designed never to be achieved. Those who most need equal treatment will be the least similar, socially, to those whose situation sets the standard as against which one's entitlement to be equally treated is measured. Doctrinally speaking, the deepest problems of sex inequality will not find women "similarly situated"[71] to men. Far less will practices of sex inequality require that acts be intentionally discriminatory.[72] All that is required is that the *status quo* be maintained. As a strategy for maintaining social power first structure reality unequally, then require that entitlement to alter it be grounded on a lack of distinction in situation; first structure perception so that different equals inferior, then require that discrimination be activated by evil minds who *know* they are treating equals as less.

I say, give women equal power in social life. Let what we say matter, then we will discourse on questions of morality. Take your foot off our necks, then we will hear in what tongue women speak. So long as sex equality is limited by sex difference, whether you like it or don't like it, whether you value it or seek to negate it, whether you stake it out as a grounds for feminism or occupy it as the terrain of misogyny, women will be born, degraded, and die. We would settle for that equal protection of the laws under which one would be born, live, and die, in a country where protection is not a dirty word and equality is not a special privilege.                                                                      [pp. 32–45]

---

[71]  *Royster Guano Co.* v. *Virginia* (1920) 253 U.S. 412, 415: "[A classification] must be reasonable, not arbitrary, and must rest upon some ground of difference having a fair and substantial relation to the object of the legislation, so that all persons similarly circumstances shall be treated alike." *Reed* v. *Reed* (1971) 404 U.S. 71, 76: "Regardless of their sex, persons within any one of the enumerated classes ... are similarly situated ... By providing dissimilar treatment for men and women who are thus similarly situated, the challenged section violates the Equal Protection Clause."

[72]  *Washington* v. *Davis* (1976) 426 U.S. 229 and *Personnel Administrator of Massachusetts* v. *Feeney* (1979) 442 U.S. 256 require that intentional discrimination be shown for discrimination to be shown.

## CHRISTINE A. LITTLETON
**Reconstructing Sexual Equality**
(1987)[73]

Feminist critique has illuminated the "male-dominated" or "phallocentric"[74] nature of every social institution it has examined, including law.

Although one more criticism of men's domination of the public discourse on equality might not be amiss, that is not the focus of this Article. Rather, the focus here is on a more insidious and complex form of male domination, which I term "phallocentrism." A history of almost exclusive male occupation of dominant cultural discourse has left us with more than incompleteness and bias. It has also created a self-referencing system by which those things culturally identified as "male" are more highly valued than those identified as "female," even when they appear to have little or nothing to do with either biological sex. By this process, "to be a man" does not simply mean to possess biologically male traits, but also to take on, or at least aspire to, the *culturally* male. Similarly social institutions within a male-dominated culture can be identified as "male" in the sense that they are constructed from the perspective of the culturally male. By use of the term "phallocentrism" I hope to capture this perspective—not the perspective of biological males, but the perspective to which the culture urges them to aspire, and by which the culture justifies their dominance....

Equality, belonging both to law and to language, provides its own case study of phallocentrism. Using feminist methodology's primary questions—"What has been women's concrete experience?" and "What has been left out?"[75]—feminist critique has examined the phallocentrism of equality as both a concept and a form of legal analysis. As a concept, equality suffers from a "mathematical fallacy"— that is, the view that only things that are the same can ever be equal. In legal analysis, courts routinely find women's "difference" a sufficient justification for inequality, constructing at the same time a specious "sameness" when applying phallocentric standards "equally" to men and women's different reproductive biology or economic position to yield (not surprisingly) unequal results for women.

This feminist critique of equality has cast doubt on the merits of another feminist enterprise—the as yet only partially successful attempt by feminist lawyers to have sex accepted as similar to, and coextensive with, race under constitutional and statutory guarantees of equality. "Equality," which has historically been the rallying cry of every subordinated group in American society, can no longer be embraced unambivalently by feminists.

Equality is enmeshed in, and ensnared by, the very gender system feminists are resisting. But I believe it is capable of having meaning beyond that system. To the extent that it is a social construct,[76] equality can be deconstructed and, at least theoretically, reconstructed as a means of challenging, rather than legitimating,

---

[73] [From (1987) 75 California L. Rev. 1274]

[74] "Phallocentric" or "phallologocentric" are terms coined by the French feminists of the "politique et psychoanalyse" school, which tends to view social institutions as created from the male viewpoint—*i.e.* as epistemologically "male." See New French Feminisms: An Anthology (E. Marks & I. de Courtivron eds. 1980), pp. 5, 36, [hereinafter French Feminisms]; L. Irigaray, *This Sex Which is Not One* (C. Porter trans. 1985), p. 163 ("Isn't the phallic tantamount to the seriousness of meaning?") (emphasis deleted). I adopt the term "phallocentric" as closest to describing the full content of feminist critique.

[75] See, *e.g.* C. Gilligan, *A Different Voice* at 5–23; Wishik [*ante*, 1288].

[76] I take this question to be broader than whether equality is a construct of unequal power, as Catharine MacKinnon claims. (1982) 7 *Signs* 515, 542.

social institutions created from the phallocentric perspective.[77] This possibility is so appealing, so evocative of the yearnings of so many of us, that the project of reconstructing sexual equality must at least be attempted, difficult and fraught with dangers as it appears.[78] ...

My proposal is easy to state, somewhat harder to fill with content, and even harder to implement. It is simply this: *The difference between human beings, whether perceived or real, and whether biologically or socially based, should not be permitted to make a difference in the lived-out equality of those persons.* I call this model of "equality as acceptance."[79] To achieve this form of sexual equality, male and female "differences" must be costless relative to each other. Equal acceptance cannot be achieved by forcing women (or the rare man) individually to bear the costs of culturally female behavior, such as childrearing, while leaving those (mostly men and some women) who engage in culturally male behavior to reap its rewards.

### Development of feminist legal theory

#### A. Legal Equality

Legal concern with sexual equality is very recent.[80] It developed primarily in response to powerful analogies between the situation of racial minorities, especially Blacks as a class, and the situation of women. Those analogies were and are highly problematic, both theoretically and historically, but they supported the claim that women must necessarily be included within the equality-of-persons norm embedded in the political and social framework of this society, and specifically articulated in the equal protection clause of the fourteenth amendment. ...

#### B. Feminist Responses

Feminist legal theory has been primarily reactive, responding to the development of legal racial equality theory. The form of response, however, has varied. One response has been to attempt to equate legal treatment of sex with that of race and deny that there are in fact any significant natural differences between women and men; in other words, to consider the two sexes symmetrically located with regard to *any* issue, norm, or rule. This response, which I term the "symmetrical" approach, classifies asymmetries as illusions, "overbroad generalizations," or

---

[77] "Deconstruction" in Critical Legal Studies circles denotes a method of analyzing legal materials. Using the internal contradictions within legal texts and between the texts and their referents, the analyst can demonstrate either intellectual incoherence, see, *e.g.* Dalton, *ante*, 1256 (discussing indeterminacy of contract rules), or political bias, see, *e.g.* Klare, "Judicial Deradicalization of the Wagner Act and the Origins of Modern Legal Consciousness 1937–1941" (1978) 62 Minn. L.Rev. 265 (discussing the judicial impact upon organized labor and its consequences).

[78] See Williams, "The Equality Crisis: Some Reflections on Culture, Courts and Feminism" (1982) 7 Women's Rts. L. Rep. 175, 198–200 (discussing dangers of seeing women as different from men).

[79] The model of equality as acceptance has a fairly specific content that distinguishes the term "acceptance" from its use by other equality theorists such as Karst, "Foreword: Equal Citizenship Under the Fourteenth Amendment" (1977) 91 Harv. L. Rev. In Karst's model of "equal citizenship," acceptance means only the absence of stigma. Leaving in place current hierarchies of value, Karst argues for the equal right of all citizens to aspire to whatever is socially valued. In contrast, the model of acceptance that I propose challenges those value hierarchies. It asserts that women have not simply been excluded from the "good life," but our potential contribution to the definition of that good life has also been ignored.

[80] See, *e.g. Reed* v. *Reed* (1971) 404 U.S. 71; *Frontiero* v. *Richardson* (1973) 411 U.S. 677; *Craig* v. *Boren* (1976) 429 U.S. 190.

temporary glitches that will disappear with a little behavior modification. A competing response rejects this analogy, accepting that women and men are or may be "different," and that women and men are often asymmetrically located in society.[81] This response, which I term the "asymmetrical" approach, rejects the notion that all gender differences are likely to disappear, or even that they should.

Symmetrical Models of Sexual Equality Feminist theorists frequently take the symmetrical approach to sexual equality, not as an ideal, but as the only way to avoid returning to separate spheres ideology. For example, in her highly compelling defense of symmetry in the law, Wendy Williams warns that "we can't have it both ways, we need to think carefully about which way we want to have it."[82]

There are two models of the symmetrical vision—referred to here as "assimilation" and "androgyny." Assimilation, the model most often accepted by the courts,[83] is based on the notion that women, given the chance, really are or could be just like men.[84] Therefore, the argument runs, the law should require social institutions to treat women as they already treat men—requiring, for example, that the professions admit women to the extent they are "qualified," but also insisting that women who enter time-demanding professions such as the practice of law sacrifice relationships (especially with their children) to the same extent that male lawyers have been forced to do.

Androgyny, the second symmetrical model, also posits that women and men are, or at least could be, very much like each other, but argues that equality requires institutions to pick some golden mean between the two and treat both sexes as androgynous persons would be treated.[85] However, given that all of our institutions, work habits, and pay scales were formulated without the benefit of substantial numbers of androgynous persons,[86] androgynous symmetry is difficult to conceptualize, and might require very substantial restructuring of many public and private institutions.[87] In order to be truly androgynous within a symmetrical framework, social institutions must find a single norm that works equally well for all gendered characteristics. Part of my discomfort with androgynous models is that they depend on "meeting in the middle," while I distrust the ability of any person, and especially any court, to value women enough to find the "middle." Moreover, the problems involved in determining such a norm for even one

---

[81] Asymmetries in areas such as responsibility for childrearing need not, of course, be attributed to nature, but rather to the complex combination of legal, social, and psychological incentives presented to women and men. Asymmetrists do not necessarily deny that sex differences are alterable, but they do reject the notion that equality must await their disappearance.

[82] Williams, *ante*, note 78, at 196 (emphasis added).

[83] See, *e.g. Hopkins* v. *Price Waterhouse* (1985) 618 F. Supp. 1109 (D.D.C.). The court had no difficulty deciding that a female candidate denied partnership in an accounting firm had been discriminated against where several of the partners criticized her for displaying "masculine characteristic[s]." *ibid.* at 1118.

[84] Harriet Taylor Mill, well ahead of her time, nonetheless urged only that legal restrictions on women's employment be abandoned, leaving in place the obvious "incompatibility" of motherhood and employment. Mill, "Enfranchisement of Women" in *Essays on Sex Equality* (A. Rossi ed. 1970), pp. 91, 103–104. Perhaps enfranchisement was only to apply to *single* women.

[85] For example, Wendy Williams describes the "equal treatment" response to the pregnancy in the workplace dilemma as androgynous because it promotes the "normalization" of pregnancy. Williams, *Equality's Riddle*, 15 NYU Rev. L. and Soc Change 325, 363.

[86] See *Blank* v. *Sullivan & Cromwell* (1975) 418 F. Supp. 1, 4 (S.D.N.Y.) (Hon. Constance Baker Motley's denial of motion to recuse for bias in sex discrimination case, based in part on "jurisdiction by necessity" argument).

[87] See, *e.g.* Rossi, "Sex, Equality: The Beginnings of Ideology" in *Beyond Sex-Role Stereotypes* (A. Kaplan & J. Bean eds. 1976), pp. 80, 87; Taub, (1985) 13 NYU Rev. Law & Soc. Change 381 (suggesting a restructuring of the way academic progress is measured).

institution are staggering. At what height should a conveyor belt be set in order to satisfy a symmetrical androgynous ideal?

Symmetry appears to have great appeal for the legal system, and this is not surprising. The hornbook definition of equal protection is "that those who are similarly situated be similarly treated,"[88] and many courts, following the Supreme Court's lead, have held that absent a showing of similarity, strict scrutiny is simply inapplicable.[89] Symmetrical analysis also has great appeal for liberal men,[90] to whom it appears to offer a share in the feminist enterprise. If perceived difference between the sexes is only the result of overly rigid sex roles, then men's liberty is at stake too.[91] Ending this form of sexual inequality could free men to express their "feminine" side, just as it frees women to express their "masculine" side.

**2.** Asymmetrical Models of Sexual Equality Asymmetrical approaches to sexual equality take the position that difference should not be ignored or eradicated. Rather, they argue that any sexually equal society must somehow deal with difference, problematic as that may be. Asymmetrical approaches include "special rights," "accommodation," "acceptance," and "empowerment."

The special rights model affirms that women and men *are* different, and asserts that cultural differences, such as childrearing roles, are rooted in biological ones, such as reproduction. Therefore, it states, society must take account of these differences and ensure that women are not punished for them. This approach, sometimes referred to as a "bivalent" model,[92] is closest to the "special treatment" pole of the asymmetrical/symmetrical equality debate. Elizabeth Wolgast, a major proponent of special rights, argues that women cannot be men's "equals" because equality by definition requires sameness.[93] Instead of equality, she suggests seeking justice, claiming special rights for women based on their special needs.

The second asymmetrical model, accommodation, agrees that differential treatment of biological differences (such as pregnancy, and perhaps breastfeeding) is necessary, but argues that cultural or hard-to-classify differences (such as career

---

[88]   Tussman & TenBroek, "The Equal Protection of the Laws" (1949) 37 Calif. L. Rev. 341, 344. Tussman & tenBroek also critiqued that formulation as begging the question, *ibid.* at 344–46, but their critique is less well-known than their restatement of the law.

[89]   See, *e.g. Rostker* v. *Goldberg* (1981) 453 U.S. 57; *Michael M.* v. *Superior Court* (1981) 450 U.S. 464 (both holding strict scrutiny inapplicable to classifications based on actual or legal differences between the sexes).

[90]   The least critical symmetrical approaches are found in the work of male legal theorists. Richard Wasserstrom, for example, envisions the sexually equal society as one in which biological sex is "no more significant than eye color," and in which asking whether a new baby is a boy or a girl is no more common than asking whether it has large or small feet. Wasserstrom, 24 U.C.L.A. Law Rev. 581, at 606. Wasserstrom does recognize a problem with his "assimilationist" ideal. "That term suggests the idea of incorporating oneself, one's values, and the like into the dominant group and its practices and values. I want to make it clear that no part of that idea is meant to be captured by my use of this term." *ibid.* at 604 n. 46. Unfortunately, his prescription of ignoring difference leaves unanalyzed and uncriticized the phallocentric value hierarchy that consistently disadvantages women. *ibid.* at 611. Despite his protestations, Wasserstrom's assimilationist ideal, as developed in the text of his article, is precisely the one he claims to reject.

[91]   Though both men and women are harmed in similar ways by the rigidity of sex stereotypes it is men's *liberty* interest that is infringed, not their *equality* interest. See *infra* Part III. And the liberty interest of men is hardly infringed to the same degree as most women's. See, *e.g.* M. Frye, *The Politics of Reality* (1983) (describing interlocking restrictions on women's lives).

[92]   See Scales, 56 Ind. L.J. 315 at 430–34; see also E. Wolgast, *Equality and the Rights of Women* (1980), pp. 61–63.

[93]   E. Wolgast, *supra* note 92, at 122 ("Consider, if both men and women are taught about the delivery of a baby, and both are taught to 'participate' in it, their roles will still be sex-differentiated. And similarly, there will be some sex-differentiation in parenthood.")

interests and skills) should be treated under an equal treatment or androgynous model. Examples of accommodation models include Sylvia Law's approach to issues of reproductive biology[94] and Herma Hill Kay's "episodic" approach to the condition of pregnancy.[95] These approaches could also be characterized as "symmetry, with concessions to asymmetry where necessary." The accommodationists limit the asymmetry in their models to biological differences because, like Williams, they fear a return to separate spheres ideology should asymmetrical theory go too far.

My own attempt to grapple with difference, which I call an "acceptance" model, is essentially asymmetrical. While not endorsing the notion that cultural differences between the sexes are biologically determined, it does recognize and attempt to deal with both biological and social differences. Acceptance does not view sex differences as problematic per se, but rather focuses on the ways in which differences are permitted to justify inequality. It asserts that eliminating the unequal consequences of sex differences is more important than debating whether such differences are "real," or even trying to eliminate them altogether.

Unlike the accommodationists, who would limit asymmetrical analysis to purely biological differences, my proposal also requires equal acceptance of cultural differences. The reasons for this are twofold. First, the distinction between biological and cultural, while useful analytically, is itself culturally based. Second, the inequality experienced by women is often presented as a necessary consequence of cultural rather than of biological difference. If, for instance, women do in fact "choose" to become nurses rather than real estate appraisers, it is not because of any biological imperative. Yet, regardless of the reasons for the choice, they certainly do not choose to be paid less. It is the *consequences* of gendered difference, and not its sources, that equal acceptance addresses. . . .

The focus of equality as acceptance, therefore, is not on the question of whether *women* are different, but rather on the question of how the social fact of gender asymmetry can be dealt with so as to create some symmetry in the lived-out experience of all members of the community. I do not think it matters so much whether differences are "natural" or not; they are built into our structures and selves in either event. As social facts, differences are created by the interaction of person with person or person with institution; they inhere in the relationship, not in the person. On this view, the function of equality is to make gender differences, perceived or actual, costless relative to each other, so that anyone may follow a male, female, or androgynous lifestyle according to their natural inclination or choice without being punished for following a female lifestyle or rewarded for following a male one.

As an illustration of this approach, consider what many conceive to be the paradigm difference between men and women—pregnancy. No one disputes that only women become pregnant, but symmetrical theorists analogize pregnancy to other events, in order to preserve the unitary approach of symmetrical theory. Such attempts to minimize difference have the ironic result of obscuring more fundamental similarities.

In *California Federal Savings & Loan Association* v. *Guerra (Cal. Fed.)*,[96] Lillian Garland, a receptionist at California Federal tried to return to her job after the birth of her child. The bank refused to reinstate her, and she sued under the California Fair Employment and Housing Act (FEHA). That law requires that employees temporarily disabled by pregnancy be given an unpaid leave of up to

---

[94] Law, "Rethinking Sex and the Constitution" (1984) 132 U. Pa. L. Rev. 955, 1007–13 (calling for equal treatment in all areas *except* reproduction, where an analysis based on an empowerment approach should be adopted).

[95] Kay, (1985) 1 Berkeley Women's L.J. 1, 27–37 (sex differences should be ignored, *except* during the time a female is actually pregnant).

[96] (1987) 107 S. Ct. 683.

four months, with guaranteed reinstatement in their original job or its equivalent. The bank in turn sued in federal court, claiming that the FEHA was preempted by Title VII of the Civil Rights Act of 1964, as amended by the Pregnancy Discrimination Act (PDA). The PDA requires only that employers treat pregnancy the same as any other disability. California Federal argued that the PDA prevented California from enforcing its pregnancy disability leave requirements against firms that did not provide these benefits for disabilities unrelated to pregnancy.

In addition to narrow questions of statutory interpretation, *Cal. Fed.* raised more fundamental questions about the meaning of equal employment opportunity for women. Citing the dangers of separate spheres ideology raised by "protectionist" legislation, the national ACLU filed an amicus brief arguing that the California law should be struck down, and that the remedy should provide for job-protected leave for all temporarily disabled employees, whatever the source of their disability. California feminist groups, such as Equal Rights Advocates, filed on the other side of the debate, arguing that the California law guaranteed equality of opportunity, and was thus consistent with federal law and policy.

Missing in these arguments, however, was any recognition that working men and women shared a more fundamental right than the right to basic disability leave benefits or job protection. The Coalition for Reproductive Equality in the Workplace (CREW) advanced the position that working women and men share a right to procreative choice in addition to an interest in disability leave. In order to ensure equal exercise of procreative rights, it argued, an employer must provide leave adequate to the effects of pregnancy.

> "The California statute eliminates barriers to equality in both procreation and employment faced by women who cannot afford to lose their jobs when they decide to become parents. Male employees who become fathers and female employees who become mothers are thus enabled to combine procreation and employment to the same extent."

This form of acceptance, unlike those that analogize pregnancy to disability, emphasizes the basic commonality of procreation as a human endeavor involving both women and men. By recognizing pregnancy as "different" from other causes of disability, it supports efforts to equalize the position of working women and men with respect to this fundamental right.

The foregoing asymmetrical models, including my own, share the notion that, regardless of their differences, women and men must be treated as full members of society. Each model acknowledges that women may need treatment different than that accorded to men in order to effectuate their membership in important spheres of social life; all would allow at least some such claims, although on very different bases, and probably in very different circumstances.[97]

A final asymmetrical approach, "empowerment," rejects difference altogether as a relevant subject of inquiry.[98] In its strongest form, empowerment claims that the subordination of women to men has itself constructed the sexes, and their differences. For example, Catharine MacKinnon argues:

> "[I]t makes a lot of sense that women might have a somewhat distinctive perspective on social life. We may or may not speak in a different voice—I think that the voice that we have been said to speak in is in fact in large part the 'feminine' voice, the voice of the victim speaking without consciousness. But when we understand that women are *forced* into this situation of inequality, it makes a lot of sense that we should want to negotiate, since we lose conflicts. It makes a lot of sense that we should want to urge values of care,

---

[97] For example, Kay argues that differential treatment must be strictly limited to pregnancy, breastfeeding, menstruation, and rape. (1985) 1985 U. Ill. L. Rev. 39, 81.

[98] This model has been articulated most fully by MacKinnon, and draws heavily on the work of radical feminist theorists such as Andrea Dworkin.

because it is what we have been valued for. We have had little choice but to be valued this way."[99]

A somewhat weaker version of the claim is that we simply do not and cannot know whether there are any important differences between the sexes that have not been created by the dynamic of domination and subordination. In either event, the argument runs, we should forget about the question of differences and focus directly on subordination and domination. If a law, practice, or policy contributes to the subordination of women or their domination by men, it violates equality. If it empowers women or contributes to the breakdown of male domination, it enhances equality.

The reconceptualization of equality as antidomination, like the model of equality as acceptance, attempts to respond directly to the concrete and lived-out experience of women. Like other asymmetrical models, it allows different treatment of women and men when necessary to effectuate its overall goal of ending women's subordination. However, it differs substantially from the acceptance model in its rejection of the membership, belonging, and participatory aspects of equality.

The Difference that Difference Makes. Each of the several models of equality discussed above, if adopted, would have a quite different impact on the structure of society. If this society wholeheartedly embraced the symmetrical approach of assimilation—the point of view that "women are just like men"—little would need to be changed in our economic or political institutions except to get rid of lingering traces of irrational prejudice, such as an occasional employer's preference for male employees. In contrast, if society adopted the androgyny model, which views both women and men as bent out of shape by current sex roles and requires both to conform to an androgynous model, it would have to alter radically its methods of resource distribution. In the employment context, this might mean wholesale revamping of methods for determining the "best person for the job." Thus, while assimilation would merely require law firms to hire women who have managed to get the same credentials as the men they have traditionally hired, androgyny might insist that the firm hire only those persons with credentials that would be possessed by someone neither "socially male" nor "socially female."

If society adopted an asymmetrical approach such as the accommodation model, no radical restructuring would be necessary. Government would need only insist that women be given what they need to resemble men, such as time off to have babies and the freedom to return to work on the same rung of the ladder as their male counterparts. If, however, society adopted the model of equality as acceptance, which seeks to make difference costless, it might additionally insist that women and men who opt for socially female occupations, such as child-rearing, be compensated at a rate similar to those women and men who opt for socially male occupations, such as legal practice. Alternatively, such occupations might be restructured to make them equally accessible to those whose behavior is culturally coded "male" or "female."

The different models also have different potential to challenge the phallocentrism of social institutions. No part of the spectrum of currently available feminist legal theory is completely immune to the feminist critique of society as phallocentric. We cannot outrun our history, and that history demonstrates that the terms of social discourse have been set by men who, actively or passively, have ignored women's voices—until even the possibility of women having a voice has

---

[99] *Feminist Discourse* (1985) 34 Buffalo L.R. 11, at 27.

become questionable.[1] Nevertheless, the models do differ with respect to the level at which the phallocentrism of the culture reappears.

Under the assimilationist approach, for example, women merit equal treatment only so far as they can demonstrate that they are similar to men. The assimilation model is thus fatally phallocentric. To the extent that women cannot or will not conform to socially male forms of behavior, they are left out in the cold. To the extent they do or can conform, they do not achieve equality *as women*, but as social males.

Similarly, empowerment and androgyny (an asymmetrical and a symmetrical approach, respectively) both rely on central concepts whose current meaning is phallocentrically biased. If "power" and "neutrality" (along with "equality") were not themselves gendered concepts, the empowerment and androgyny approaches would be less problematic. But our culture conceives of power as power used by men, and creates androgynous models "tilted" toward the male. As Carrie Menkel-Meadow put it, the trouble with marble cake is that it never has enough chocolate; the problem with androgyny is that it never has enough womanness. Similarly, empowering women without dealing with difference, like assimilation, too easily becomes simply sharing male power more broadly.[2]

Equality as acceptance is not immune from phallocentrism in several of its component concepts. However, the concepts are not necessarily entailed by the theory and may be replaced with less biased concepts as they reveal themselves through the process of equalization. For example, in discussing employment-related applications of the model, I use the measures already existing in that sphere—money, status, and access to decisionmaking. These measures of value are obviously suspect. Nevertheless, my use of them is contingent. Acceptance requires only that culturally coded "male" and "female" complements be equally valued; it does not dictate the coin in which such value should be measured. By including access to decisionmaking as part of the measure, however, the theory holds out the possibility that future measures of value will be created by women and men *together*. Thus, acceptance strives to create the preconditions necessary for sexually integrated debate about a more appropriate value system.

The various models of equality arise out of common feminist goals and enterprises: trying to imagine what a sexually equal society would look like, given that none of us has ever seen one; and trying to figure out ways of getting there, given that the obstacles to sexual equality are so many and so strong.

The perception among feminist legal thinkers that the stakes in the symmetrical vs. asymmetrical debate are high is correct. Difference indeed makes a difference. Yet, the frantic nature of the debate about difference between the sexes makes the divergent views within feminist legal thought appear as a deadly danger rather than an exciting opportunity. The label "divisive" gets slapped on before the discussion even gets underway.

We need to recognize difference among women as diversity rather than division, and difference between women and men as opportunity rather than danger . . .

---

[1] See H. Cixous, "*Sorties*" in French Feminisms pp. 90, 91–92 (excerpts); L. Irigaray,; *cf.* MacKinnon, *op. cit.* 337 ("That pornography chills women's expression is difficult to demonstrate empirically because silence is not eloquent.").

[2] Power as it has traditionally been exercised within a phallocentric culture is *male* power, even when exercised by women. Unless our conception of power is transformed by a recognition of difference, the empowerment of women runs the risk of becoming an improved form of assimilation.

*Making difference costless*

I have thus far constrained this speculative exercise to respond to equality's legal tradition, feminist critique of equality, and feminist critique of male power as a system. However, I also recognize the need to account for "different kinds of sexual difference." Thus, although I do not claim to offer a blueprint for specific application, I will attempt in this Part to lay out the foundation for the house that a reconstructed sexual equality may someday build.

*Differently Gendered Complements*

The problem of identifying gendered complements lies along two axes of difference. One axis measures the "source" of differences, ranging from the clearly biological to the clearly social (with a great deal of controversy in between). The other measures the degree of overlap between the sexes, and runs from more-or-less differences on one end to yes-or-no differences on the other.

For gender differences that are more-or-less, there is a significant degree of overlap between the sexes. Height is one of these. Not all women would have been disaffirmed by the too-high podium that was "built for a man," and not all men would have been affirmed by it. But more women than men in this society would have had the feminist lawyer's experience. Additionally, differences of the more-or-less variety are easier to deny, since there is always some woman over six feet or some man under five, and a great number of both in between. These differences are also easier to "match," because shorter and taller are both measures of the same concededly shared human characteristic of height.

For yes-or-no gender differences, there is no overlap at all. The primary example of this is, of course, pregnancy. No man can become pregnant, and most women can. However, women who have never had the capacity for pregnancy are not thereby made either biologically or socially male, even when the dominant culture has tended to view them as "not women." Thus, although it is useful for purposes of analysis to separate yes-or-no differences from more-or-less ones, they represent two poles of the same spectrum.

Disparate treatment analysis under Title VII allows individuals who are exceptions to the "rule" of their biological sex to be socially classed with the other sex. Thus, tall women must be treated the same as tall men, and short men the same as short women. As the podium example demonstrates, phallocentrism in such cases usually involves setting the norm by reference to the center of the male bell curve. When the norm is set by reference to the female bell curve, the same analysis applies; men who can type must be allowed into socially female secretarial positions...

Disparate impact analysis allows socially female women to bring equality claims if the job qualification containing the gendered norm is irrelevant to the applicant's ability to perform the job. No showing of direct intent to discriminate is required.[3] Under disparate impact doctrine, then, a woman can establish discrimination by demonstrating that women as a class are more severely affected than men by a facially neutral employment practice, such as a height requirement.[4] The employer can, however, justify the discriminatory impact by demonstrating that the practice is "job related" or necessary to the employer's

---

[3] *Griggs* v. *Duke Power Co.* (1971) 401 U.S. 424.

[4] The Court has stated that Title VII protects whites just as it protects non-whites, and men just as it protects women. See, *e.g. Newport News Shipbldg. & Dry Dock Co.* v. *EEOC* (1983) 462 U.S. 669, *Regents of the Univ. of Calif.* v. *Bakke* (1978) 438 U.S. 265, 308–09,n. 44. While disparate impact analysis should, therefore, theoretically be equally available to male plaintiffs, I am aware of no sex discrimination cases in which men have asserted this theory.

business. Moreover, the relevance of the practice is tested solely by reference to the way the job is already structured. Thus, even disparate impact analysis—as currently practised—does not allow for challenges to male bias in the structure of businesses, occupations, or jobs.

Equality as acceptance would support challenges to government and employer policies and practices that use male norms even when such norms are considered job-related, necessary to the business, or "substantially related to an important governmental interest." Unlike the more radical version of the model of androgyny referred to above, however, acceptance would not necessarily require the *elimination* of such norms. Acceptance could instead be achieved by inventing complementary structures containing female norms. For example, assume an employer successfully defends its 5/9″ minimum height requirement as necessary to the job of sorting widgets as they pass on a conveyor belt. Equality as acceptance could be achieved by restructuring the job itself—in this case, by changing the height of the conveyor belt or by adding a second belt. Alternatively, the employer could defend the requirement by demonstrating that equal job opportunities exist in the plant for applicants shorter than 5/9″. Acceptance would thus permit *de facto* sex segregation in the workplace, but *only* if the predominantly male and predominantly female jobs have equal pay, status, and opportunity for promotion into decisionmaking positions.

Yes-or-no differences do not yield so readily to matching. This has helped focus the "equal treatment/special treatment" debate on pregnancy—specifically, on the question of whether requiring employers to grant pregnancy leaves for women violates the equal rights of men, who can never take advantage of such leaves. If pregnancy were a more-or-less difference, such as disabling heart trouble or childcare responsibility, it would be easy for the current legal system to answer this question. Since it is a yes-or-no difference, however, the legal system runs in circles: the Supreme Court in *Geduldig* v. *Aiello*[5] said pregnancy is different, so women can be punished for it; the federal district court in *Cal. Fed.*[6] said pregnancy is not different, so women should not benefit from it; the Supreme Court, affirming the Ninth Circuit in *Cal. Fed.*,[7] said pregnancy is different, so men are not hurt by taking account of it.

I think that the appropriate unit of analysis in yes-or-no cases is *interaction* of the sexes rather than comparison. Even with rapidly developing reproductive technology, it is still necessary for some part of a woman to interact with some part of a man to produce a pregnancy. In that interaction, the gendered complements are pregnancy for the woman and fewer sperm cells for the man. Since pregnancy almost always results in some period of disability for the woman, making the sex difference costless with respect to the workplace requires that money, status, and opportunity for advancement flow equally to the womb-donating woman and the sperm-donating man (himself an equal contributor to the procreative act).[8]

Both average height and pregnancy lie near the biological pole of the source

---

[5] (1974) 417 U.S. 484.

[6] *California Fed. Sav. & Loan Ass'n* v. *Guerra* (1984) 33 Empl. Prac. Dec. (CCH) 34, 227, *rev'd* (1985) 758 F.2d 390 (9th Cir.), *aff'd,* (1987) 107 S. Ct. 683.

[7] (1987) 107 S. Ct. 683.

[8] Equality as acceptance does not itself dictate whether this acceptance should be accomplished by (1) female and male workers sharing the disadvantage that the workplace now visits on women alone—perhaps through requiring male employees to take on without extra pay some portion of the work of the absent female employees; (2) eliminating the disadvantage to women through some form of pregnancy leave rights; or (3) reshaping the structure itself so that no disadvantage arises at all—through more radical time-shifting, time-sharing work schedules or through elimination of the workplace-home dichotomy. While equality as acceptance would support arguments for all three, option (2) is probably the most viable currently.

axis; these differences are clearly biological. Their existence and degree of overlap are less problematic as an empirical matter than differences lying closer to the cultural pole. The clearly cultural differences, on the other hand, are more problematic, primarily because they are even more likely than biological differences to give rise to stereotypes that harm women. Arguments for ignoring difference are also more plausible with reference to the cultural axis. Because these differences are acquired, they can presumably be done away with, if not for us then for our children or grandchildren. This combination of danger and plausibility has led several sex equality theorists to place themselves toward the middle of the symmetrical vs. asymmetrical debate. I am, however, either brave or foolhardy enough to believe that even cultural differences can be made accessible to equality analysis.

Cultural differences of the more-or-less variety can be dealt with along the same general lines as biological differences that overlap. Under acceptance, marital dissolution decrees, for example, could value the contributions of the non-earner spouse (usually, but not always, the woman), take into account services in the home performed after divorce, and treat realistically the expenses necessarily incurred by the custodial parent. These measures would go further toward reducing the potentially devastating economic impact of divorce for women than current experiments, such as presumptions in favor of joint custody.[9]

Cultural differences of the yes-or-no variety are easier to identify than those of the more-or-less, but harder to deal with. Fortunately, there are relatively few of them (far fewer than there were a few decades ago). The most visible is employment in the armed services. Women are excluded from draft registration, and female volunteers are excluded from combat positions.

Just as gendered complements in the "biological" realm come from our current perceptions of biology, so must gendered complements in the "cultural" realm come from our current perceptions of culture. The traditional gender divide sets up "warrior" in its cultural sense directly opposite "mother" in its cultural sense. The "cult of motherhood" resembles the "glory of battle" in a number of ways. Both occupations involve a lot of unpleasant work, along with a real sense of commitment to a cause beyond oneself that is culturally gussied up and glamorized culturally to cover up the unpleasantness involved. Both involve danger and possible death. And, of course, the rationale most frequently given for women's exclusion from combat is their capacity for motherhood.

Making this gender difference less costly could mean requiring the government to pay mothers the same low wages and generous benefits as most soldiers. It could also mean encouraging the use of motherhood as an unofficial prerequisite for governmental office. As a paying occupation with continuing status perks, many more men might be induced to stay home and raise their children. Alternatively, but less likely, making difference costless could mean ceasing to pay combat troops.

For example, in *Personnel Administrator* v. *Feeney*,[10] the Supreme Court upheld Massachusetts' lifetime veteran's preference against an equal protection challenge, reasoning that Massachusetts had not intended that preference to lock women into lower-level and dead-end civil service positions, regardless of this obvious effect. Under an equality as acceptance model, a state's failure to provide equal preference for the gendered female complement to military service would be evidence of intentional discrimination. Thus, even without additional constitutional or statutory enactment, a change in the Court's underlying model of equality could alter the result in actual cases.

Matching gendered complements in order to equalize across cultural

---

[9] *Cf.* Bartlett & Stack, "Joint Custody, Feminism and the Dependency Dilemma" (1986) Berkeley Women's L.J. 9.

[10] 442 U.S. 256 (1979).

differences may sound like marching directly into the valley of the stereotypes. Those who consider Carol Gilligan's discovery of "a different voice" sexist are not likely to find this appealing. Nevertheless, allow me to make two disclaimers. First, almost all cultural differences are, or could easily be, "more or less." Lots of biological men exhibit socially female characteristics (for which they are all too often punished); at least as many biological women exhibit socially male ones (for which they are often rewarded, although they are simultaneously punished for not having the biological form to match); and many more women and men fall in the middle, exhibiting no readily identifiable "male" or "female" behavior patterns. Second, what is objectionable about stereotypes is not that they are *never* true, but rather that they are not *always* true. Demonstrating that not every women with children is primarily responsible for their care may help those women who do not have such responsibility to compete for certain jobs, but it does little to help those women struggling to hold down two jobs, only one of which is paid.

Disclaimers aside, what is relevant for this exercise is not the accuracy or inaccuracy of any set of gendered complements, but rather how the complements reward or punish those who are perceived to fall on one side or the other. Studies of sex-segregated work places tend to show that there is a high correlation between employer perceptions of gender differences and the segregation patterns themselves. These perceived gender differences, such as lifting strength and small-muscle dexterity, are of the more-or-less type, and tend to fall toward the middle of the "source" axis. Requiring individual testing alleviates segregation to some extent, but it only helps those women who do not fit the female stereotype (at the expense, of course, of those men who do not fit the male stereotype). However, the main problem was sex segregation is that promotion patterns and pay scales are determined by entry-level job classifications. Thus, those women who do fit the female stereotype (of say, low lifting strength and high small-muscle dexterity) are stuck. They are not harmed by the "female" job classification as such; they are harmed by the disparity in pay and opportunity for promotion that goes along with it. And the disparity in promotion opportunities continues the cycle of overvaluation of "male" characteristics and undervaluation of "female" ones, because employers will continue to select those biological men and women who are socially male.

If, alternatively, both "male" and "female" entry-level positions paid the same and offered the same promotion opportunities, individual testing would not matter so much. Indeed, assuming proportionate numbers of openings, applicants might well self-select into the classification that better utilizes their particular strengths and minimizes their particular weaknesses. If so, the segregation pattern would gradually break down unless employers actively and, legally speaking, "intentionally" sought to maintain it. Moreover, even if self-selection by individual skills did not occur, a better sex mix at the management level would eventually have a significant impact throughout the firm.

As Frances Olsen sets forth in *The Sex of Law*, we tend to think in dichotomies, and those dichotomies are both sexualized (with one side masculine and the other feminine) and hierarchicized (with one side in each pair superior).[11] She argues that the sexualization and hierarchicization should be attacked simultaneously, to the end of deconstructing the dichotomies themselves. While I do not disagree with this goal, I do think Olsen's strategy is impractical. Dichotomies that purport to describe gender differences are, I think, only likely to fall apart once they no longer accurately describe differences in pay scales, hiring patterns, or promotion ladders. Additionally, since we presently think in these dichotomies, we may as well use them to help us in our struggle to discard them.

The rigidity of sexualized dichotomies does appear to be gradually breaking down in many areas. With regard to the practical problem of implementation,

---

[11] Olsen (1990). 18 Int. J. Soc. Law 199.

however, the true breakdown of any particular male-female dichotomy is not a problem, but a benefit. It puts us one step closer toward eliminating them entirely.

Equality as acceptance provides a methodology for assuring that sexual differences do not take on the unnecessary consequence of sexual inequality. In order to apply that methodology, we must open inquiry into the identification, use, and meaning of such differences. Through a model of equal acceptance, the legal system, which has historically been a conduit through which perceived difference between both sexes has rationalized concrete disadvantage to one, may finally become an arena for reclaiming equality across difference.

*Conclusion*

As I look back on the argument made here on behalf of the model of acceptance, I perceive these major points: (1) in order to be faithful to feminist critique, a reconstructed equality norm must be capable of application across or beyond difference; (2) although no reconstruction undertaken under conditions of inequality can claim to be completely free from phallocentric bias, a reconstruction can increase equality and invite later, freer reconstructions by shifting the frame and moving the margin into the picture; (3) making difference costless (or even cost less) will shift the frame, allowing us to see ever more subtle forms of phallocentric bias while reducing the danger that difference will be used to recreate inequality; (4) the model of costless difference can be applied *within* contexts without impeding later efforts to apply it *across* contexts; and (5) much of the model's usefulness can be realized now, without waiting for major legislative or cultural change.

## KATHERINE T. BARTLETT
### Feminist Legal Methods
### (1990)[12]

In what sense can legal methods be "feminist"? Are there specific methods that feminist lawyers share? If so, what are these methods, why are they used, and what significance do they have to feminist practice? Put another way, what do feminists mean when they say they are doing law,[13] and what do they mean when, having done law, they claim to be "right"?

Feminists have developed extensive critiques of law and proposals for legal reform. Feminists have had much less to say, however, about what the "doing" of law should entail and what truth status to give to the legal claims that follow. These methodological issues matter because methods shape one's view of the possibilities for legal practice and reform. Method "organizes the apprehension of truth; it determines what counts as evidence and defines what is taken as verification.[14] Feminists cannot ignore method, because if they seek to challenge existing structures of power with the same methods that have defined what counts within those structures, they may instead "recreate the illegitimate power structures [that they are] trying to identify and undermine."[15]

Method matters also because without an understanding of feminist methods, feminist claims in the law will not be perceived as legitimate or "correct." Feminists have tended to focus on defending their various substantive positions or

---

[12] [From (1990) 103 Harv. L. Rev. 829]
[13] This article is primarily about "doing law" in the limited sense encompassed by the professional activities of practicing lawyers, lawmakers, law professors, and judges.
[14] MacKinnon 7 Signs 515, at 527.
[15] Singer, *Should Lawyers Care About Philosophy?* 1989 Duke L.J. 1752.

political agendas, even among themselves. Greater attention to issues of method may help to anchor these defenses, to explain why feminist agendas often appear so radical (or not radical enough), and even to establish some common ground among feminists.

As feminists articulate their methods, they can become more aware of the nature of what they do, and thus do it better... [pp. 830–831]

### Feminist doing in law

When feminists "do law," they do what other lawyers do: they examine the facts of a legal issue or dispute, they identify the essential features of those facts, they determine what legal principles should guide the resolution of the dispute, and they apply those principles to the facts. In doing law, feminists like other lawyers use a full range of methods of legal reasoning—deduction, induction, analogy, and use of hypotheticals, policy, and other general principles.

In addition to these conventional methods of doing law, however, feminists use other methods. These methods, though not all unique to feminists, attempt to reveal features of a legal issue which more traditional methods tend to overlook or suppress. One method, asking the woman question, is designed to expose how the substance of law may silently and without justification submerge the perspectives of women and other excluded groups. Another method, feminist practical reasoning, expands traditional notions of legal relevance to make legal decisionmaking more sensitive to the features of a case not already reflected in legal doctrine. A third method, consciousness-raising, offers a means of testing the validity of accepted legal principles through the lens of the personal experience of those directly affected by those principles...

### Asking the woman question

A question becomes a method when it is regularly asked. Feminists across many disciplines regularly ask a question—a set of questions, really—known as "the woman question,"[16] which is designed to identify the gender implications of rules and practices which might otherwise appear to be neutral or objective...

In law, asking the woman question means examining how the law fails to take into account the experiences and values that seem more typical of women than of men, for whatever reason, or how existing legal standards and concepts might disadvantage women. The question assumes that some features of the law may be not only nonneutral in a general sense, but also "male" in a specific sense. The purpose of the woman question is to expose those features and how they operate, and to suggest how they might be corrected.[17]

Women have long been asking the woman question in law. The legal impediments associated with being a woman were, early on, so blatant that the question was not so much whether women were left out, but whether the omission was justified by women's different roles and characteristics. American women such as Elizabeth Cady Stanton and Abigail Adams may seem today all too modest and

---

[16] See, *e.g.* Gould, "The Woman Question: Philosophy of Liberation and the Liberation of Philosophy" in *Women and Philosophy: Toward a Theory of Liberation* (C. Gould & M. Wartofsky eds. 1976), p. 5 (discussing the woman question in philosophy); Hawkesworth, "Feminist Rhetoric: Discourses on the Male Monopoly of Thought" (1988) 16 Pol., Theory 444, 452–56 (examining the treatment of the woman question in political theory). The first use of the term "woman question" is in S. De Beauvoir, *The Second Sex* (1957), p. xxvi.

[17] See Wishik, *ante*, 1287–1288.

tentative in their demands for improvements in women's legal status. Yet while social stereotypes and limited expectations for women may have blinded women activists in the eighteenth and nineteenth centuries, their demands for the vote, for the right of married women to make contracts and own property, for other marriage reforms, and for birth control challenged legal rules and social practices that, to others in their day, constituted the God-given plan for the human race.

Within the judicial system, Myra Bradwell was one of the first to ask the woman question when she asked why the privileges and immunities of citizenship did not include, for married women in Illinois, eligibility for a state license to practice law.[18] The opinion of the United States Supreme Court in Bradwell's case evaded the gender issue, but Justice Bradley in his concurring opinion set forth the "separate spheres" legal ideology underlying the Illinois law.

Women, and sometimes employers, continued to press the woman question in challenges to sex-based maximum work-hour legislation, other occupation restrictions, voting limitations, and jury-exemption rules. The ideology, however, proved extremely resilient.

Not until the 1970's did the woman question begin to yield different answers about the appropriateness of the role of women assumed by law. The shift began in 1971 with the Supreme Court's ruling on a challenge by Sally Reed to an Idaho statute that gave males preference over females in appointments as estate administrators.[19] Although the Court in *Reed* did not address the separate spheres ideology directly, it rejected arguments of the state that "men [are] as a rule more conversant with business affairs than ... women,"[20] to find the statutory preference arbitrary and thus in violation of the equal protection clause. This decision was followed by a series of other successful challenges by women arguing that beneath the protective umbrella of the separate spheres ideology lay assumptions that disadvantage women in material, significant ways.

Although the United States Supreme Court has come to condemn explicitly the separate spheres ideology when revealed by gross, stereotypical distinctions, the Court majority has been less sensitive to the effects of more subtle sex-based classifications that affect opportunities for and social views about women. The Court ignored, for example, the implications for women of a male-only draft registration system in reserving combat as a male-only activity.[21] Similarly, in upholding a statutory rape law that made underage sex a crime of males and not of females, the Court overlooked the way in which assumptions about male sexual aggression and female sexual passivity construct sexuality in limiting and dangerous ways.[22] ...

Feminists today ask the woman question in many areas of law. They ask the woman question in rape cases when they ask why the defense of consent focuses on the perspective of the defendant and what he "reasonably" thought the woman wanted, rather than the perspective of the woman and the intentions she "reasonably" thought she conveyed to the defendant.[23] Women ask the woman question when they ask why they are not entitled to be prison guards on the same terms as men; why the conflict between work and family responsibilities in women's lives is seen as a private matter for women to resolve within the family

---

[18] See *Bradwell* v. *Illinois* (1873) 83 U.S. (16 Wall.) 130.
[19] See *Reed* v. *Reed* (1971) 404 U.S. 71.
[20] Brief for Appellee at 12, *Reed* (No. 70-4).
[21] See W. Williams, 7 Women's Rights L. Rep. 175, at 181-90.
[22] See *ibid*.
[23] See S. Estrich, *Real Rape* (1987) pp. 92-104.

rather than a public matter involving restructuring of the workplace;[24] or why the right to "make and enforce contracts" protected by section 1981 forbids discrimination in the *formation* of a contract but not discrimination in its *interpretation*.[25] Asking the woman question reveals the ways in which political choice and institutional arrangement contribute to women's subordination. Without the woman question, differences associated with women are taken for granted and, unexamined, may serve as a justification for laws that disadvantage women. The woman question reveals how the position of women reflects the organization of society rather than the inherent characteristics of women. As many feminists have pointed out, difference is located in relationships and social institutions—the workplace, the family, clubs, sports, childrearing patterns, and so on—not in women themselves. In exposing the hidden effects of laws that do not explicitly discriminate on the basis of sex, the woman question helps to demonstrate how social structures embody norms that implicitly render women different and thereby subordinate.

Once adopted as a method, asking the woman question is a method of critique as integral to legal analysis as determining the precedential value of a case, stating the facts, or applying law to facts. "Doing law" as a feminist means looking beneath the surface of law to identify the gender implications of rules and the assumptions underlying them and insisting upon applications of rules that do not perpetuate women's subordination. It means recognizing that the woman question always has potential relevance and that "right" legal analysis never assumes gender neutrality... [pp. 836–843]

### Feminist practical reasoning

Some feminists have claimed that women approach the reasoning process differently than men do.[26] In particular, they say that women are more sensitive to situation and context, that they resist universal principles and generalizations, especially those that do not fit their own experiences, and that they believe that "the practicalities of everyday life" should not be neglected for the sake of abstract justice. Whether these claims can be empirically sustained, this reasoning process has taken on normative significance for feminists, many of whom have argued that individualized factfinding is often superior to the application of bright-line rules,[27] and that reasoning from context allows a greater respect for difference[28] and for the perspectives of the powerless.

As a form of legal reasoning, practical reasoning has many meanings invoked in many contexts for many different purposes. I present a version of practical reasoning in this section that I call "feminist practical reasoning." This version combines some aspects of a classic Aristotelian model of practical deliberation with a feminist focus on identifying and taking into account the perspectives of the excluded.

---

[24] See Dowd, "Work and Family: The Gender Paradox and the Limitations of Discrimination Analysis in Restructuring the Workplace" (1989) 24 Harv. C.R.-C.L. L. Rev. 79; Olsen, "The Family and the Market: A Study of Ideology and Legal Reform" (1983) 96 Harv. L. Rev. 1497; Taub, "From Parental Leaves to Nurturing Leaves" (1985) 13 N.Y.U. Rev. L. & Soc. Change 381; J. Williams, "Deconstructing Gender" 87 Michigan L. Rev 797; W. Williams, "Equality's Riddle" (1984) 13 NYU Rev. Law & Soc. Change 325.

[25] *Cf.* "The Supreme Court, 1988 Term—Leading Cases" (1989) 103 Harv. L. Rev. 137, 330.

[26] See C. Gilligan, *In a Different Voice*.

[27] Bartlett, "Re-Expressing Parenthood" (1988) 98 Yale L.J. 293, 321–26; Sherry, (1986) 72 Va. L.R. 543, at 604–613.

[28] See Minow & Spelman, "Passion for Justice" (1988) 10 Cardozo I., Rev. 37, 53; Scales, (1986) 95 Yale L.J. 1373 at 1388.

*Feminist practical reasoning.* Feminist practical reasoning builds upon the traditional mode of practical reasoning by bringing to it the critical concerns and values reflected in other feminist methods, including the woman question. The classical exposition of practical reasoning takes for granted the legitimacy of the community whose norms it expresses, and for that reason tends to be fundamentally conservative. Feminist practical reasoning challenges the legitimacy of the norms of those who claim to speak, through rules, for the community. No form of legal reasoning can be free, of course, from the past or from community norms, because law is always situated in a context of practices and values. Feminist practical reasoning differs from other forms of legal reasoning, however, in the strength of its commitment to the notion that there is not one, but many overlapping communities to which one might look for "reason." Feminists consider the concept of community problematic,[29] because they have demonstrated that law has tended to reflect existing structures of power. Carrying over their concern for inclusionism from the method of asking the woman question, feminists insist that no one community is legitimately privileged to speak for all others. Thus, feminist methods reject the monolithic community often assumed in male accounts of practical reasoning, and seek to identify perspectives not represented in the dominant culture from which reason should proceed.

Feminist practical reasoning, however, is not the polar opposite of a "male" deductive model of legal reasoning. The deductive model assumes that for any set of facts, fixed, pre-existing legal rules compel a single, correct result. Many commentators have noted that virtually no one, male or female, now defends the strictly deductive approach to legal reasoning.[30] Contextualized reasoning is also not, as some commentators suggest,[31] the polar opposite of a "male" model of abstract thinking. All major forms of legal reasoning encompass processes of both contextualization and abstraction. Even the most conventional legal methods require that one look carefully at the factual context of a case in order to identify similarities and differences between that case and others. The identification of a legal problem, selection of precedent, and application of that precedent, all require an understanding of the details of a case and how they relate to one another. When the details change, the rule and its application are likely to change as well.

By the same token, feminist methods require the process of abstraction, that is, the separation of the significant from the insignificant.[32] Concrete facts have significance only if they represent some generalizable aspect of the case. Generalizations identify what matters and draw connections to other cases. I abstract whenever I fail to identify every fact about a situation, which, of course, I do always. For feminists, practical reasoning and asking the woman question may make more facts relevant or "essential" to the resolution of a legal case than would more nonfeminist legal analysis...

Similarly, the feminist method of practical reasoning is not the polar opposite of "male" rationality. The process of finding commonalities, differences, and

---

[29] See Abrams, "Law's Republicanism" (1988) 97 Yale L.J. 1591, 1606–07 Sullivan, "Rainbow Republicanism" (1988) 97 Yale L.J. 1713, 1721.

[30] See, *e.g.* Bennett, "Objectivity in Constitutional Law" (1984) 132 U. Pa. L. Rev. 445, 495 ("'Mechanical' jurisprudence has no visible contemporary adherents."); Stick, "Can Nihilism Be Pragmatic?" (1986) 100 Harv. L. Rev. 332, 363–65 (asserting that outside a "core area," in which the application of legal rules is certain, "only the most unreconstructed logical positivist" accepts a strict deductive model of legal reasoning).

[31] See, *e.g.* Matsuda, "Liberal Jurisprudence and Abstracted Visions of Human Nature: A Feminist, Critique of Rawls's Theory of Justice" (1986) 16 N.M.L. Rev. 613, 618–24; Scales, *ante*, note 31 at 1376–78.

[32] *Cf.* K. Llewellyn, *The Bramble Bush* (1960), p. 48 (arguing that a concrete fact is significant because it is *representative* of a wider abstract *category* of facts").

connections in practical reasoning is a rational process. To be sure, feminist practical reasoning gives rationality new meanings. Feminist rationality acknowledges greater diversity in human experiences and the value of taking into account competing or inconsistent claims. It openly reveals its positional partiality by stating explicitly which moral and political choices underlie that partiality,[33] and recognizes its own implications for the distribution and exercise of power.[34] Feminist rationality also strives to integrate emotive and intellectual elements and to open up the possibilities of new situations rather than limit them with prescribed categories of analysis. Within these revised meanings, however, feminist method is and must be understandable. It strives to make more sense of human experience, not less, and is to be judged upon its capacity to do so.

*Applying the Method.*—Although feminist practical reasoning could apply to a wide range of legal problems, it has its clearest implications where it reveals insights about gender exclusion within existing legal rules and principles....

[An] example is the 1981 New Jersey Supreme Court case, *State* v. *Smith*.[35] In rejecting the defendant's marital-exemption defense in a criminal prosecution for rape, the court engaged in a multi-layered process of reasoning; it examined the history of the exemption, the strength and evolution of the common law authority, the various justifications offered by the state for the exemption, the surrounding social and legal context in which the defendant asserted the defense, and the particular actions of the defendant in this case that gave rise to the prosecution. This process of reasoning deserves close analysis because it differs markedly from the abstract, formalistic reasoning used by other courts considering related issues.

In his opinion for a unanimous court, Justice Pashman began with an examination of the source of the common law marital exemption to rape. It found the basis for the exemption "in a bare, extra-judicial declaration made some 300 years ago"[36] by Sir Matthew Hale: " 'But the husband cannot be guilty of a rape committed by himself upon his lawful wife, for by their mutual matrimonial consent and contract the wife hath given up herself in this kind unto her husband, which she cannot retract.' "[37] From this authority, the court determined that the common law exemption to rape "derived from the nature of marriage at a particular time in history."[38] At that time, marriages were "effectively permanent, ending only by death or an act of Parliament."[39] The court reasoned that the rule was stated "in absolute terms, as if it were applicable without exception to all marriage relationship,"[40] because marriage itself was not retractable at the time of Lord Hale. But things have changed. "In the years since Hale's formulation of the rule," the court observed, "attitudes towards the permanency of marriage have

---

[33] See Haraway, "Situated Knowledges: The Science Question in Feminism and the Privilege of Partial Perspective" (1988) 14 Feminist Stud. 575, 590.

[34] See Haraway, *supra* n. 37 at 590; Minow, 101 Harv. L. Rev. 10 at 65–66; see also Flax, 12 *Signs* 621 at 633 (describing the need to be sensitive to interconnections between knowledge and power); Minow & Spelman, (1988) 10 Cardozo L. Rev 37, at 57–60 (calling for "a direct human gaze between those exercising power and those governed by it"); Gabel & Harris, "Building Power and Breaking Images: Critical Theory and the Practice of Law" (1982–83) 11 N.Y.U. Rev. L. & Soc. Change 369, 375 (suggesting a focus on "counter-hegemonic" law practice that draws attention to issues of power distribution). [and see *ante*, 1217–1219].

[35] 85 N.J. 193, 426 A.2d 38 (1981). [See also the English case of *R.* v. *R.* [1992] 1 A.C. 199].

[36] 85 N.J. at 200, 426 A.2d at 41.

[37] *ibid.* (quoting I M. Hale, *History of the Pleas of the Crown* *629).

[38] *ibid.* at 201, 426 A.2d at 42.

[39] *ibid.* (citing H. Clark, *Law of Domestic Relations* (1968), pp. 280–282.

[40] *ibid.*

changed and divorce has become far easier to obtain.''[41] Moreover, even during Lord Hale's time, the court surmised, the rule may not have applied in all situations, as when a judicial separation was granted. The court drew from its historical analysis a tentative conclusion, but reserved the ultimate question in the case for fuller analysis: "The rule, formulated under vastly different conditions, need not prevail when those conditions have changed."[42]

The court then explored the major justifications "which might have constituted the common law principles adopted in this State,"[43] including the notion that the woman was the property of her husband or father, the concept that a husband and wife were one person, and the justification that a wife consents to sexual intercourse with her husband.[44] The court engaged in a detailed analysis of each justification. The property notion, it concluded, was never valid in this country in that rape statutes "have always aimed to protect the safety and personal liberty of women."[45] The marital unity concept could not now be valid, the court decided, given the other crimes against a wife, such as assault and battery, of which a husband could be convicted, and because in many other areas of the law the " 'principle' of marital unity was discarded in this State long before the commission of defendant's alleged crime."[46] The implied-consent justification, the court reasoned, is not only "offensive to our valued ideals of personal liberty," but is "not sound where the marriage itself is not irrevocable." The court noted that under the facts of this case—a year before the attack, a judge allegedly had ordered defendant to leave the marital home following another violent incident, the parties lived apart in different cities, the defendant broke into his wife's apartment at about 2:30 a.m., "over a period of a few hours, repeatedly beat her, forced her to have sexual intercourse and committed various other atrocities against her person," and caused her to require medical care at a hospital[47]—the husband could not claim that consent was implied.[48]

The *Smith* court's analysis is typical of many judicial opinions which "interpret" the common law and statutes by delving deeply into historical and policy considerations.[49] Thus, its use of practical reasoning has deep roots in American jurisprudence. I use it as an example because it demonstrates a conventional model upon which feminist practical reasoning can usefully build.

The *Smith* case helps to show, for example, how the particular facts of a case do not just present the problem to be solved, but also instruct the decisionmaker about what the ends and means of law ought to be. The circumstances of the estrangement, the middle-of-the-night break-in (two doors were broken to get inside), and defendant's repeated attacks and "atrocities" illustrate a kind of broken relationship that puts into perspective the interests a state might have in spousal reconciliation, in preventing false recriminations, or in marital privacy. Faced with the abstract question whether the marital exemption to rape should be available to husbands who have separated from their wives, more serene images come to the minds of most judges, even those who have experienced unhappy

---

[41] *ibid.*
[42] *ibid.*
[43] *ibid.* at 204, 426 A.2d at 43 (footnote omitted).
[44] See *ibid.* at 205, 426 A.2d at 44.
[45] *ibid.* at 204, 426 A.2d at 44.
[46] *ibid.* at 205, 426 A.2d at 44 (citing as examples the Married Women's Acts, abolition of spousal tort immunity, alienability of a wife's interest in property held in tenancy by the entirety, the rule allowing wife to use her own surname, and indictment of husband and wife for conspiracy).
[47] *ibid.* at 197, 426 A.2d at 40.
[48] See *ibid.* at 207, 426 A.2d at 45. The Virginia Supreme Court used similar reasoning to reach the same result. See *Weishaupt* v. *Commonwealth* (1984) 315 S.E.2d 847, 855.
[49] See M. Eisenberg, *The Nature of the Common Law* (1988), p. 196, n. 35.

marriages. The concrete facts of *Smith* present one picture that might not readily surface to inform decisionmakers about what legal rules are practical and wise.

The *Smith* case also illustrates how practical reasoning respects, but does not blindly adhere to, legal precedent. In contrast to courts that have followed more formalistic approaches, the *Smith* court saw itself as an active participant in the formulation of legal authority. Without ignoring the importance to law of consistency and tradition, the Court took an approach sensitive to the human factors that a more mechanical application of precedent might ignore.

Although the *Smith* case illustrates some of the attributes of a highly contextual, pragmatic approach to decisionmaking, feminist practical reasoning would pursue some elements further than the court did. For example, feminist practical reasoning would more explicitly identify the perspective of the woman whose interest a marital rape exemption entirely subordinates to that of her estranged husband. This recognition would help to demonstrate how a rule may ratify gender-based structures of power, and thus provide the court stronger grounds for finding the exemption inapplicable to the *Smith* facts. On the other hand, feminist practical reasoning would also require more explicit recognition of the interests that supported the exemption and that the court too summarily dismissed. For example, the court rejected without discussion the state's interest in the reconciliation of separated spouses that the marital rape exemption was intended in part to serve. It also failed to address the state's concern about the evidentiary problems raised in marital rape cases. The facts of the *Smith* case illustrate the weakness of these state interests. A more forthright analysis of them would have given a fuller picture of the issues, as well as guidance for other courts to which these factors may seem more significant.

A fuller, practical-reasoning approach would also have given greater attention to the "due process" notice interests of the defendant who, when he acted, may have thought his actions were legal. Despite the heinous nature of the defendant's actions in this case, practical reasoning requires the examination of all perspectives, including those that a court might ultimately reject. The *Smith* court examined some relevant factors in its due process analysis, such as whether the court's ruling would be unexpected, the relationship between the exemption and the rule to which the exemption applied, and the type of crime. It failed, however, to examine the role social conditioning plays in acculturating men to expect, and demand, sex. Such an examination, repeated in other cases, may help to identify the real problems society has to face in rape reform, and to challenge more deeply both male and female expectations about sex.

*Feminist Practical Reasoning: Method or Substance?*—The *Smith* case raises further questions about the relationship between feminist method and substance.

On the other hand, if one assumes that one neither can nor should eliminate political and moral factors from legal decisionmaking, then one would hope to make these factors more visible. If political and moral factors are necessarily tied into any form of legal reasoning, then bringing those factors out into the open would require decision-makers to think self-consciously about them and to justify their decisions in the light of the factors at play in the particular case.

Feminists, not surprisingly, favor the second set of assumptions over the first. Feminists' substantive analyses of legal decisionmaking have revealed to them that so-called neutral means of deciding cases tend to mask, not eliminate, political and social considerations from legal decisionmaking. Feminists have found that neutral rules and procedures tend to drive underground the ideologies of the decisionmaker, and that these ideologies do not serve women's interests well. Disadvantaged by hidden bias, feminists see the value of modes of legal reasoning that expose and open up debate concerning the underlying political and moral considerations.   By   forcing   articulation   and   understanding   of   those considerations, practical reasoning forces justification of results based upon what interests are actually at stake.

The "substance" of feminist practical reasoning consists of an alertness to certain forms of injustice that otherwise go unnoticed and unaddressed. Feminists turn to contextualized methods of reasoning to allow greater understanding and exposure of that injustice. Reasoning from context can change perceptions about the world, which may then further expand the contexts within which such reasoning seems appropriate, which in turn may lead to still further changes in perceptions. The expansion of existing boundaries of relevance based upon changed perceptions of the world is familiar to the process of legal reform. The shift from *Plessy* v. *Ferguson*[50] to *Brown* v. *Board of Education*,[51] for example, rested upon the expansion of the "legally relevant" in race discrimination cases to include the actual experiences of black Americans and the inferiority implicit in segregation. Much of the judicial reform that has been beneficial to women, as well, has come about through expanding the lens of legal relevance to encompass the missing perspectives of women and to accommodate perceptions about the nature and role of women. Feminist practical reasoning compels continued expansion of such perceptions.

### Consciousness-raising

Another feminist method for expanding perceptions is consciousness-raising.[52] Consciousness-raising is an interactive and collaborative process of articulating one's experiences and making meaning of them with others who also articulate their experiences. As Leslie Bender writes, "Feminist consciousness-raising creates knowledge by exploring common experiences and patterns that emerge from shared tellings of life events. What were experienced as personal hurts individually suffered reveal themselves as a collective experience of oppression."[53]

Consciousness-raising is a method of trial and error. When revealing an experience to others, a participant in consciousness-raising does not know whether others will recognize it. The process values risk-taking and vulnerability over caution and detachment. Honesty is valued above consistency, teamwork over self-sufficiency, and personal narrative over abstract analysis. The goal is individual and collective empowerment, not personal attack or conquest.

Elizabeth Schneider emphasizes the centrality of consciousness-raising to the dialectical relationship of theory and practice. The interplay between experience

---

[50] (1896) 163 U.S. 537.

[51] (1954) 347 U.S. 483.

[52] Catharine MacKinnon sees consciousness-raising as *the* method of feminism. MacKinnon, *ante*. Many feminist legal thinkers have emphasized the importance of consciousness-raising to feminist practice and method. See, *e.g.* Law, "Equality: The Power and Limits of the Law" (1986) 95 Yale L.J. 1769, 1784; Scales at 1401–02; Schneider, at 602–604. For historical perspectives in the American women's movement, see C. Hymowitz & M. Weissman, *A History of Women in America* (1978), pp. 351–55; and G. Lerner, *The Majority Finds Its Past* 1979, at 42–44.

[53] Bender, "A Lawyer's Primer on Feminist Theory and Tort" (1988) 38 L. Legal Educ. 3, 9; see also Z. Eisenstein, *Feminism and Sexual Equality: Crisis in Liberal America* (1984) pp. 150–57 (stressing the importance of building feminist consciousness out of sex-class consciousness); T. De Lauretis, *Alice Doesn't: Feminism, Semiotics, Cinema* (1984), p. 185 (describing consciousness-raising as "the collective articulation of one's experience of sexuality and gender—which has produced, and continues to elaborate, a radically new mode of understanding the subject's relation to social-historical reality"); J. Mitchell, *Woman's Estate* (1971), p. 61 (maintaining that through consciousness-raising, women proclaim the painful and transform it into the political).

and theory "reveals the social dimension of individual experience and the individual dimension of social experience" and hence the political nature of personal experience.[54]

Consciousness-raising operates as feminist method not only in small personal growth groups, but also on a more public, institutional level, through "bearing witness to evidences of patriarchy as they occur, through unremitting dialogues with and challenges to the patriarchs, and through the popular media, the arts, politics, lobbying, and even litigation."[55] Women use consciousness-raising when they publicly share their experiences as victims of marital rape, pornography, sexual harassment on the job, street hassling, and other forms of oppression and exclusion, in order to help change public perceptions about the meaning to women of events widely thought to be harmless or flattering.

Consciousness-raising has consequences, further, for laws and institutional decisionmaking more generally. Several feminists have translated the insights of feminist consciousness-raising into their normative accounts of legal process and legal decisionmaking. Carrie Menkel-Meadow, for example, has speculated that as the number of women lawyers increases, women's more interactive approaches to decisionmaking will improve legal process.[56] Similarly, Judith Resnik has argued that feminist judging will involve more collaborative decisionmaking among judges.[57] Such changes would have important implications for the possibilities for lawyering and judging as matters of collective engagement rather than the individual exercise of judgment and power.

The primary significance of consciousness-raising, however, is as meta-method. Consciousness-raising provides a substructure for other feminist methods—including the woman question and feminist practical reasoning—by enabling feminists to draw insights and perceptions from their own experiences and those of other women and to use these insights to challenge dominant versions of social reality.

Consciousness-raising has done more than help feminists develop and affirm counter-hegemonic perceptions of their experiences. As consciousness-raising has matured as method, disagreements among feminists about the meaning of certain experiences have proliferated. Feminists disagree, for example, about whether women can voluntarily choose heterosexuality, or motherhood; or about whether feminists have more to gain or lose from restrictions against pornography, surrogate motherhood, or about whether women should be subject to a military draft. They disagree about each other's roles in an oppressive society: some feminists accuse others of complicity in the oppression of women.[58] Feminists disagree even about the method of consciousness-raising; some women worry that it sometimes operates to pressure women into translating their experiences into positions that are politically, rather than experientially, correct.[59]

These disagreements raise questions beyond those of which specific methods are appropriate to feminist practice. Like the woman question and practical

---

[54] (1986) 61 N.Y.U. Law. Rev. 589 at 602–604. Hence the feminist phrase: "The personal is the political." MacKinnon's explanation of this phrase is perhaps the best: "It means that women's distinctive experience as women occurs within that sphere that has been socially lived as the personal—private, emotional, interiorized, particular, individuated, intimate—so that what it is to *know* the *politics* of woman's situation is to know women's personal lives." MacKinnon, *ante*, note 17, at 535.

[55] Bender, *supra*, note 56 at 9–10.

[56] See Menkel-Meadow, (1985) 1 Berkeley Women's L.J. 39, at 55–58.

[57] See Resnik, "On the Bias: Feminist Reconsiderations of the Aspirations for Our Judges" (1988) 61 S. Cal. L. Rev. 1877, 1942–43.

[58] See C. MacKinnon, at 198–205 (accusing women who defend first amendment values against restrictions on pornography of collaboration).

[59] See Colker, (1988) 68 B.U.L. Rev. 217 at 253–54 (noting that consciousness-raising may influence women to adopt "inauthentic" expressions of themselves).

reasoning, consciousness-raising challenges the concept of knowledge. It presupposes that what I thought I knew may not, in fact, be "right." How, then, will we know when we *have* got it "right"? Or, backing up one step, what does it mean to *be* right? And what attitude should I have about that which I claim to know? [pp. 849–867]

### Feminist knowing in law

A point—perhaps *the* point—of legal methods is to reach answers that are legally defensible or in some sense "right."

In this section, I explore several feminist explanations for what it means to be "right" in law. I look first at a range of positions that have emerged from within feminist theory. These include the three positions customarily included in feminist epistemological discussions: the rational/empirical position, standpoint epistemology, and postmodernism. In addition I examine a fourth stance called positionality, which synthesizes some aspects of the first three into a new, and I think more satisfactory, whole. I evaluate each position from the same pragmatic viewpoint reflected in the feminist methods I have described: how can that position help feminists, using feminist methods, to generate the kind of insights, values, and self-knowledge that feminism needs to maintain its critical challenge to existing structures of power and to reconstruct new, and better, structures in their place?

### The Rational/Empirical Position

Feminists across many disciplines have engaged in considerable efforts to show how, by the standards of their own disciplines, to improve accepted methodologies. These efforts have led to the unraveling of descriptions of women as morally inferior, psychologically unstable, and historically insignificant—descriptions these disciplines long accepted as authoritative and unquestionable.

Similarly, feminists in law attempt to use the tools of law, on its own terms, to improve law. Using the methods discussed in Part II of this Article, feminists often challenge assumptions about women that underlie numerous laws and demonstrate how laws based upon these assumptions are not rational and neutral, but rather irrational and discriminatory. When engaged in these challenges, feminists operate from a rational/empirical position that assumes that the law is not objective, but that identifying and correcting its mistaken assumptions can make it more objective.

When feminists challenged employment rules that denied disability benefits to pregnant women, for example, they used empirical and rational arguments about the similarity between pregnancy and other disabilities. Each side of the debate defended a different concept of equality, but the underlying argument focused upon which is the most rational, empirically sound and legally supportable interpretation of equality.

In other areas of the law, feminists have also operated from within this rational/empirical stance. Susan Estrich, for example, argues that the correction of certain factual inaccuracies can better achieve the purposes of rape law—to prevent rape, to protect women, and to punish rapists. Estrich contends, for example, that the assumption that women mean "yes" when they say "no" is false and that a rational rape law would define consent so that "no means no."[60]

All of these arguments from the rational/empirical stance share the premise

---

[60] S. Estrich, *supra*, note 23, at 102. Estrich argues also that rape law would be more rational if a negligence standard were applied to the defendant's intent. See *ibid.* at 92–104.

that knowledge is accessible and, when obtained, can make law more rational. The relevant empirical questions are often very difficult ones: if parents, usually men, who fall behind in their child support obligations face almost certain jail sentences, will they be more likely to make their child support payments on time?[61] If state law singles out pregnancy as the only condition for which job security is mandated, how much additional resistance to hiring women, if any, is likely to be created, and what impact on the stereotyping of women, if any, is likely to result?[62] The rational/empirical position presumes, however, that answers to such questions can be improved—that there is a "right" answer to get—and that once gotten, that answer can improve the law.

Some feminists charge that improving the empirical basis of law or its rationality is mere "reformism" that cannot reach the deeper gendered nature of law.[63] This charge unfortunately undervalues the enormous transformation in thinking about women that the empirical challenge to law, in which all feminists have participated, has brought about. Feminist rational/empiricism has begun to expose the deeply flawed factual assumptions about women that have pervaded many disciplines, and has changed, in profound ways, the perception of women in this society. Few, if any, feminists, however, operate entirely within the rational/empirical stance, because it tends to limit attention to matters of factual rather than normative accuracy, and thus fails to take account of the social construction of reality through which factual or rational propositions mask normative constructions.[64] Empirical and rational arguments challenge existing assumptions about reality and, in particular, the inaccurate reality conveyed by stereotypes about women. But if reality is not representational or objective and not above politics, the method of correcting inaccuracies ultimately cannot provide a basis for understanding and reconstructing that reality. The rational/empirical assumption that principles such as objectivity and neutrality can question empirical assumptions within law fails to recognize that knowability is itself a debatable issue. I explore positions that challenge, rather than presuppose, knowability in the following sections.

### Standpoint epistemology

The problem of knowability in feminist thought arises from the observation that what women know has been determined—perhaps overdetermined[65] by male culture. Some of the feminists most concerned about the problem of over-determination have adopted a "standpoint epistemology" to provide the grounding

---

[61] This was the principal research questions in D. Chambers, *Making Fathers Pay* (1979).

[62] See W. Williams, *ante*, note 27, at 355.

[63] Christine Littleton and Catharine MacKinnon, for example, associate rational/empirical efforts to open up more opportunities for women with "assimilationism" or "liberal feminism," which, in retaining its focus on individualism, provides no basis from which to challenge the way in which women's individuality has been determined by men rather than freely chosen, or to validate any of the choices that individuals make. See Littleton, (1989) 41 Stanford L. Rev. 751, at 754–763; C. MacKinnon, *Feminism Unmodified*, at 137.

[64] Feminists have made significant contributions to understandings about the social construction of reality. See, generally, S. de Beauvoir, *The Second Sex* (describing how men have defined women as other and created a myth of woman); S. Harding, *The Science of Feminism* (arguing that science is gendered); MacKinnon, *ante*, note 63 (arguing that gender is a social construct that embodies male sexual dominance).

[65] *Cf.* Alcoff, (1988) 13 *Signs* 405 at 416 (describing Derrida's and Foucault's view that "we are overdetermined ... by a social discourse and/or cultural practice"); J. Mitchell, *supra* note 53 at 99–122. Juliet Mitchell defines overdetermination as "a complex notion of 'multiple causation' in which the numerous factors can reinforce, overlap, cancel each other out, or contradict one another." (*Psychoanalysis and Feminism* (1974), p. 309.)

upon which feminists can claim that their own legal methods, legal reasoning, and proposals for substantive legal reform are "right."

Feminist standpoint epistemology identifies woman's status as that of victim, and then privileges that status by claiming that it gives access to understanding about oppression that others cannot have...

Feminists have located the foundation of women's subordination in different aspects of women's experiences. Feminist post-Marxists find this foundation in women's activities in production, both domestic and in the marketplace;[66] other emphasize women's positions in the sexual hierarchy,[67] in women's bodies,[68] or in women's responses to the pain and fear of male violence.[69]...

Standpoint epistemology has contributed a great deal to feminist understandings of the importance of our respective positioning within society to the "knowledge" we have. Feminist standpoint epistemologies question "the assumption that the social identity of the observer is irrelevant to the 'goodness' of the results of research," and reverse the priority of a distanced, "objective" standpoint in favor of one of experience and engagement.

Despite the valuable insights offered by feminist standpoint epistemology, however, it does not offer an adequate account of feminist knowing. First, in isolating gender as a source of oppression, feminist legal thinkers tend to concentrate on the identification of woman's true identity beneath the oppression and thereby essentialize her characteristics. Catharine MacKinnon, for example, in exposing what she finds to be the total system of male hegemony, repeatedly speaks of "women's point of view," of "woman's voice," of empowering women "on our own terms," of what women "really want," and of standards that are "not ours." Ruth Colker sees the discovery of women's "authentic self"[70] as a difficult job given the social constructions imposed upon women, but nonetheless, like MacKinnon, insists upon it as a central goal of feminism...

Although the essentialist positions taken by these feminists often have strategic or rhetorical value, these positions obscure the importance of differences among women and the fact that factors other than gender victimize women....

In addition to imposing too broad a view of gender, standpoint epistemologists also tend to presuppose too narrow a view of privilege. I doubt that being a victim is the only experience that gives special access to truth. Although victims know something about victimization that non-victims do not, victims do not have exclusive access to truth about oppression. The positions of others—co-victims, passive bystanders, even the victimizers—yield perspectives of special knowledge that those who seek to end oppression must understand.

Standpoint epistemology's claim that women have special access to knowledge also does not account for why all women, including those who are similarly situated, do not share the same interpretations of those situations—"a special explanation of non-perception."[71] One account argues that the hold of patriarchal ideology, which "intervenes successfully to limit feminist consciousness,"[72] causes "false consciousness." Although feminist legal theorists rarely offer this explanation explicitly, it is implicit in theories that associate with women certain

---

[66] See Hartsock, "The Feminist Standpoint: Developing the Ground for a Specifically Feminist Historical Materialism" in *Discoverying Reality: Feminist Perspectives on Epistemology, Metaphysics, Methodology, and Philosophy of Science* (S. Harding & M. Hintikka eds. 1983), p. 283.

[67] See MacKinnon, *ante*, note 63.

[68] See, generally, Z. Eisenstein, *The Female Body and the Law* (1988).

[69] See West, 5 Wisc. Women's L.J. 91.

[70] See Colker, 68 B.U. Law. Rev. 216 at 218.

[71] Charles Taylor uses this phrase in describing the general phenomenon of false consciousness. See C. Taylor, *Philosophy and the Human Sciences* (1985), p. 95.

[72] Z. Eisenstein, *Feminism and Sexual Equality* (1984), p. 153.

essential characteristics, variance from which connotes a distortion of who women really are or what they really want...

A final difficulty with standpoint epistemology is the adversarial we/they politics it engenders. Identification from the standpoint of victims seems to require enemies, wrongdoers, victimizers. Those identified as victims ("we") stand in stark contrast to others ("they"), whose claim to superior knowledge becomes not only false but suspect in some deeper sense: conspiratorial, evil-minded, criminal. You (everyone) must be either with us or against us. Men are actors—not innocent actors, but evil, corrupt, irredeemable. They conspire to protect male advantage and to perpetuate the subordination of women. Even women must choose sides, and those who chose badly are condemned.

This adversarial position hinders feminist practice. It impedes understanding by would-be friends of feminism and paralyzes potential sympathizers. Even more seriously, it misstates the problem that women face, which is not that men act "freely" and women do not, but that both men and women, in different but interrelated ways, are confined by gender. The mystifying ideologies of gender construction control men, too, however much they may also benefit from them. As Jane Flax writes, "Unless we see gender as a social relation, rather than as an opposition of inherently different beings, we will not be able to identify the varieties and limitations of different women's (or men's) powers and oppressions within particular societies."[73] In short, gender reform must entail not so much the conquest of the now-all-powerful enemy male, as the transformation of those ideologies that maintain the current relationships of subordination and oppression.

### Postmodernism

The postmodern or poststructural critique of foundationalism resolves the problem of knowability in a quite different way. While standpoint epistemology relocates the source of knowledge from the oppressor to the oppressed, the postmodern critique of foundationalism questions the possibility of knowledge, including knowledge about categories of people such as women. This critique rejects essentialist thinking as it insists that the subject, including the female subject, has no core identity but rather is constituted through multiple structures and discourses that in various ways overlap, intersect, and contradict each other. Although these structures and discourses "overdetermine" woman and thereby produce "the subject's experience of differentiated identity and ... autonomy,"[74] the postmodern view posits that the realities experienced by the subject are not in any way transcendent or representational, but rather particular and fluctuating, constituted within a complex set of social contexts. Within this position, being human, or female, is strictly a matter of social, historical, and cultural construction.[75]

Postmodern critiques have challenged the binary oppositions in language, law, and other socially-constituting systems, oppositions which privilege one presence—male, rationality, objectivity—and marginalize its opposite—female, irrationality, subjectivity. Postmodernism removes the grounding from these oppositions and from all other systems of power or truth that claim legitimacy on the basis of external foundations or authorities. In so doing, it removes external

---

[73] At 641. As Flax also writes, women cannot be "free of determination from their own participation in relations of domination such as those rooted in the social relations of race, class, or homophobia," while men are not. *ibid.* at 642.

[74] Coombe, "Room For Manoeuver: Toward a Theory of Practice in Critical Legal Studies" (1989) 14 Law & Soc. Inquiry 69, 85.

[75] See Fraser & Nicholson, (1989) 14 Law and Soc. Inquiry at 83–91; Rabine, "A Feminist Politics of Non-Identity" (1988) 14 Feminist Stud, 11, 25–26.

grounding from any particular agenda for social reform. In the words of Nancy Fraser and Linda Nicholson, postmodern social criticism "floats free of any universalist theoretical ground. No longer anchored philosophically, the very shape or character of social criticism changes; it becomes more pragmatic, ad hoc, contextual, and local."[76] There are no external, overarching systems of legitimation; "[t]here are no special tribunals set apart from the sites where inquiry is practiced." Instead, practices develop their own constitutive norms, which are "plural, local, and immanent."[77]

The postmodern critique of foundationalism has made its way into legal discourse through the critical legal studies movement. The feminists associated with this movement have stressed both the indeterminacy of law and the extent to which law, despite its claim to neutrality and objectivity, masks particular hierarchies and distributions of power. These feminists have engaged in deconstructive projects that have revealed the hidden gender bias of a wide range of laws and legal assumptions.[78] Basic to these projects has been the critical insight that not only law itself, but also the criteria for legal validity and legitimacy, are social constructs rather than universal givens.[79]

Although the postmodern critique of foundationalism has had some considerable influence on feminist legal theory, some feminists have cautioned that this critique poses a threat not only to existing power structures, but to feminist politics as well.[80] To the extent that feminist politics turns on a particular story of woman's oppression, a theory of knowledge that denies that an independent, determinate reality exists would seem to deny the basis of that politics. Without a notion of objectivity, feminists have difficulty claiming that their emergence from male hegemony is less artificial and constructed than that which they have cast off, or that their truths are more firmly grounded than those whose accounts of being women vary widely from their own. Thus, as Deborah Rhode observes, feminists influenced by postmodernism are "left in the awkward position of

---

[76] Fraser & Nicholson, *supra*, note 75 at 85.

[77] *ibid.* at 87.

[78] See, *e.g.* Dalton, 94 Yale. L.J. 997; Olsen, 96 Harv. L. Rev. 1487; Bender, 38 J. Legal. Educ. 3.

[79] Although feminist legal theory has taken seriously the postmodern critique of foundationalism, it has yet to make much sense or use of the postmodern critique of the subject. Marie Ashe has argued that the poststructural subject, defined as "a being that is maintained only through interactive exchanges within a social order," Ashe, "Mind's Opportunity: Birthing a Poststructuralist Feminist Jurisprudence" (1987) 38 Syracuse L. Rev. 1129, 1165, "appears utterly at odds with the notions of individual autonomy and personhood valued as fundamental in the liberal legal tradition." *ibid.* at 1151. The direction in which Ashe urges feminist jurisprudence should move, however, appears to turn on the existence of certain "real" experiences on the part of women who are pregnant and bear children, which are at odds, she suggests, with the reality assumed by law. In universalizing these experiences and speaking of the "inner discourses of mothers," Ashe seems to abandon the poststructural view. See "Law-Language of Maternity: Discourse Holding Nature in Contempt" (1988) 22 New Eng. L. Rev. 521. 527.

Drucilla Cornell has hinted at a concept of gender differentiation drawn from poststructural theory that might prove fruitful for feminist legal practice. Building on the importance of the excluded "Other" in the construction of women, she suggests that "what we are as subjects [can never be] fully captured by gender categories," that an interrelational intersubjectivity is more than the sum of its parts, and that immanent in the gender system is a "more than this" which has the potential for freeing us from the false choice between universality and absolute difference. See Cornell & Thurschwell, "Feminism, Negativity, Intersubjectivity" in *Feminism as Critique* (S. Benhabib & D. Cornell eds. 1987), pp. 143, 161–162.

[80] See, *e.g.* Bordo, "Feminism, Postmodernism, and Gender-Scepticism" in *Feminism/Postmodernism* (L. Nicholson ed. 1990), 133; Fraser & Nicholson, *supra* n. 75 at 83; Poovey, (1988) 14 Feminist Studies 51.

maintaining that gender oppression exists while challenging [their] capacity to document it."[81]

Feminists need a stance toward knowledge that takes into account the contingency of knowledge claims while allowing for a concept of truth or objectivity that can sustain an agenda for meaningful reform. The postmodern critique of foundationalism is persuasive to many feminists, whose experiences affirm that rules and principles asserted as universal truths reflect particular, contingent realities that reinforce their subordination. At the same time, however, feminists must be able to insist that they have identified unacceptable forms of oppression and that they have a better account of the world free from such oppression. Feminists, according to Linda Alcoff, "need to have their accusations of misogyny validated rather than rendered 'undecidable.'"[82] In addition, they must build from the postmodern critique about "how meanings and bodies get made," Donna Haraway writes, "not in order to deny meanings and bodies, but in order to build meanings and bodies that have a chance for life."[83]

To focus attention on this project of rebuilding, feminists need a theory of knowledge that affirms and directs the construction of new meanings. Feminists must be able to both deconstruct *and construct* knowledge . . .

### *Positionality*

Positionality is a stance from which a number of apparently inconsistent feminist "truths" make sense. The positional stance acknowledges the existence of empirical truths, values and knowledge, and also their contingency. It thereby provides a basis for feminist commitment and political action, but views these commitments as provisional and subject to further critical evaluation and revision.

Like standpoint epistemology, positionality retains a concept of knowledge based upon experience. Experience interacts with an individual's current perceptions to reveal new understandings and to help that individual, with others, make sense of those perceptions. Thus, from women's position of exclusion, women have come to "know" certain things about exclusion: its subtlety; its masking by "objective" rules and constructs; its pervasiveness; its pain; and the need to change it. These understandings make difficult issues decidable and answers non-arbitrary.

Like the postmodern position, however, positionality rejects the perfectibility, externality, or objectivity of truth. Instead, the positional knower conceives of truth as situated and partial. Truth is situated in that it emerges from particular involvements and relationships. These relationships, not some essential or innate characteristics of the individual, define the individual's perspective and provide the location for meaning, identity, and political commitment. Thus, as discussed above, the meaning of pregnancy derives not just from its biological characteristics, but from the social place it occupies—how workplace structures, domestic arrangements, tort systems, high schools, prisons, and other societal institutions construct its meaning.

Truth is partial in that the individual perspectives that yield and judge truth are necessarily incomplete. No individual can understand except from some limited perspective. Thus, for example, a man experiences pornography as a man with a particular upbringing, set of relationships, race, social class, and sexual preference, and so on, which affect what "truths" he perceives about pornography. A woman experiences pregnancy as a woman with a particular upbringing, race, social class, set of relationships, sexual preference, and so on, which affect what

---

[81] D. Rhode, (1990) 42 Stanford Law Rev. 617, 620.
[82] Alcoff, *supra*, note 65 at 419.
[83] Haraway, *supra*, note 33 at 580.

"truths" she perceives about pregnancy. As a result, there will always be "knowers" who have access to knowledge that other individuals do not have, and no one's truth can be deemed total or final.

Because knowledge arises within social contexts and in multiple forms, the key to increasing knowledge lies in the effort to extend one's limited perspective. Self-discipline is crucial. My perspective gives me a source of special knowledge, but a limited knowledge that I can improve by the effort to step beyond it, to understand other perspectives, and to expand my sources of identity. To be sure, I cannot transcend my perspective; by definition, whatever perspective I currently have limits my view. But I can improve my perspective by stretching my imagination to identify and understand the perspectives of others.

Positionality's requirement that other perspectives be sought out and examined checks the characteristic tendency of all individuals—including feminists—to want to stamp their own point of view upon the world. This requirement does not allow certain feminist positions to be set aside as immune from critical examination. When feminists oppose restrictive abortion laws, for example, positionality compels the effort to understand those whose views about the sanctity of potential human life are offended by assertion of women's unlimited right to choose abortion. When feminists debate the legal alternative of joint custody at divorce, positionality compels appreciation of the desire by some fathers to be responsible, co-equal parents. And (can it get worse?) when feminists urge drastic reform of rape laws, positionality compels consideration of the position of men whose social conditioning leads them to interpret the actions of some women as "inviting" rather than discouraging sexual encounter.

Although I must consider other points of view from the positional stance, I need not accept their truths as my own. Positionality is not a strategy of process and compromise that seeks to reconcile all competing interests. Rather, it imposes a twin obligation to make commitments based on the current truths and values that have emerged from methods of feminism, and to be open to previously unseen perspectives that might come to alter these commitments. As a practical matter, of course, I cannot do both simultaneously, evenly, and perpetually. Positionality, however, sets an ideal of self-critical commitment whereby I act, but consider the truths upon which I act subject to further refinement, amendment, and correction.

Some "truths" will emerge from the ongoing process of critical reexamination in a form that seems increasingly fixed or final. For feminists, the commitment to ending gender-based oppression has become one of these "permanent truths." The problem is the human inclination to make this list of "truths" too long, to be too uncritical of its contents, and to defend it too harshly and dogmatically.

Positionality reconciles the existence of reliable, experienced-based grounds for assertions of truth upon which politics should be based, with the need to question and improve these grounds. The understanding of truth as "real," in the sense of produced by the actual experiences of individuals in their concrete social relationships, permits the appreciation of plural truths. By the same token, if truth is understood as partial and contingent, each individual or group can approach its own truths with a more honest, self-critical attitude about the value and potential relevance of other truths.

The ideal presented by the positionality stance makes clear that current disagreements within society at large and among feminists—disagreements about abortion, child custody, pornography, the military, pregnancy, and motherhood, and the like—reflect value conflicts basic to the terms of social existence. If resolvable at all, these conflicts will not be settled by reference to external or pre-social standards of truth. From the positional stance, any resolutions that emerge are the products of human struggles about what social realities are better than others. Realities are deemed better not by comparison to some external, "discovered" moral truths or "essential" human characteristics, but by internal truths that make the most sense of experienced, social existence. Thus, social truths will emerge from social relationships and what, after critical examination, they tell social beings about what they want themselves, and their social world, to be.

In this way, feminist positionality resists attempts at classification either as essentialist on the one hand, or relativistic on the other. Positionality is both nonrelative and nonarbitrary. It assumes some means of distinguishing between better and worse understanding; truth claims are significant or "valid" for those who experience that validity. But positionality puts no stock in fixed, discoverable foundations. If there is any such thing as ultimate or objective truth, I can never, in my own lifetime, be absolutely sure that I have discovered it. I can know important and non-arbitrary truths, but these are necessarily mediated through human experiences and relationships. There can be no universal, final, or objective truth; there can be only "partial, locatable, critical knowledges."[84] no aperspectivity—only improved perspectives.

A stance of positionality can reconcile the apparent contradiction within feminist thought between the need to recognize the diversity of people's lives and the value in trying to transcend that diversity. Feminists, like those associated with the critical legal studies movement, understand that when those with power pretend that their interests are natural, objective and inevitable, they suppress and ignore other diverse perspectives. This understanding compels feminists to make constant efforts to test the extent to which they, also, unwittingly project their experiences upon others. To understand human diversity, however, is also to understand human commonality. From the positional stance, I can attain self-knowledge through the effort to identify not only what is different, but also what I have in common with those who have other perspectives. This effort, indeed, becomes a "foundation" for further knowledge.

Because of its linkage between knowledge and seeking out other perspectives, positionality provides the best foothold from which feminists may insist upon both the diversity of others' experiences, and their mutual relatedness and common humanity with others. This dual focus seeks knowledge of individual and community, apart and as necessarily interdependent. As others have noted, much of the recent scholarship that attempts to revive ideals of republicanism and the public virtue has given inadequate attention to the problem of whose interests are represented and whose are excluded by expressions of the "common" or "public" interest.[85] Positionality locates the source of community in its diversity and affirms Frank Michelman's conclusions about human commonality: "The human universal becomes difference itself. Difference is what we most fundamentally have in common."[86]

All three of the methods discussed in this Article affirm, and are enhanced by, the stance of positionality. In asking the woman question, feminists situate themselves in the perspectives of women affected in various ways and to various extents by legal rules and ideologies that purport to be neutral and objective. The process of challenging these rules and ideologies, deliberately, from particular, self-conscious perspectives, assumes that the process of revealing and correcting various forms of oppression is never-ending. Feminist practical reasoning, likewise, exposes and helps to limit the damage that universalizing rule and assumptions can do; universalizations will always be present, but contextualized reasoning will help to identify those currently useful and eliminate the others. Consciousness-raising links that process of reasoning to the concrete experiences

---

[84] Haraway, *supra*, note 33 at 584.

[85] See, *e.g.* Bell & Bansal, "The Republican Revival and Racial Politics" (1988) 97 Yale L.J. 1609 (1988); Young, "Impartiality and the Civic Public: Some Implications of Feminist Critiques of Moral and Political Theory" in *Feminism as Critique*, p. 66.

[86] Michelman, 100 Harv. L. Rev. 4, at 32. Michelman incorporates points made by Drucilla Cornell and Martha Minow.

associated with growth from one set of moral and political insights to another. Positional understanding enhances alertness to the special problems of oppressive orthodoxies in consciousness-raising, and the insights developed through collaborative interaction should remain open to challenge, and not be held hostage to the unfortunate tendency in all social structures to assume that some insights are too politically "correct" to question.

Positional understanding requires efforts both to establish good law and to keep in place, and renew, the means for deconstructing and improving that law. In addition to focusing on existing conditions, feminist methods must be elastic enough to open up and make visible new forms of oppression and bias. Reasoning from context and consciousness-raising are self-renewing methods that may enable continual new discoveries. Through critical practice, new methods should also evolve that will lead to new questions, improved partial insights, better law, and still further critical methods.

### Conclusion: feminist methods as ends

I have argued that feminist methods are means to feminist ends: that asking the woman question, feminist practical reasoning, and consciousness-raising are methods that arise from and sustain feminist practice. Having established the feminist stance of positionality, I now want to expand my claim to argue that feminist methods are also ends in themselves. Central to the concept of positionality is the assumption that although partial objectivity is possible, it is transitional, and therefore must be continually subject to the effort to reappraise, deconstruct, and transform. That effort, and the hope that must underlie it, constitute the optimistic version of feminism to which I adhere. Under this version, human flourishing means being engaged in the world through the kinds of critical yet constructive feminist methods I have described. These methods can give feminists a way of doing law that expresses who they are and who they wish to become.

This is, I contend, a goal central to feminism: to be engaged, with others, in a critical, transformative process of seeking further partial knowledges from one's admittedly limited habitat. This goal is the grounding of feminism, a grounding that combines the search for further understandings and sustained criticism toward those understandings. Feminist doing is, in this sense, feminist knowing. And vice versa.                                                                [pp. 849–888]

### LUCINDA M. FINLEY
### Breaking Women's Silence in Law: The Dilemma of the Gendered Nature of Legal Reasoning
### (1989)[87]

Language matters. Law matters. Legal language matters.

I make these three statements not to offer a clever syllogism, but to bluntly put the central thesis of this Article: it is an imperative task for feminist jurisprudence and for feminist lawyers—for anyone concerned about what the impact of law has been, and will be, on the realization and meanings of justice, equality, security, and autonomy for women—to turn critical attention to the nature of legal reasoning and the language by which it is expressed.

---

[87] [From (1989) 64 Notre Dame Law Rev. 886]

*The gendered nature of legal language is what makes it powerful and limited*

## Why Law is a Gendered (Male) Language

Throughout the history of Anglo-American jurisprudence, the primary linguists of law have almost exclusively been men—white, educated, economically privileged men. Men have shaped it, they have defined it, they have interpreted it and given it meaning consistent with their understandings of the world and of people "other" than them. As the men of law have defined law in their own image, law has excluded or marginalized the voices and meanings of these "others." Law, along with all the other accepted academic disciplines, has exalted one form of reasoning and called only this form "reason." Because the men of law have had the societal power not to have to worry too much about the competing terms and understandings of "others," they have been insulated from challenges to their language and have thus come to see it as natural, inevitable, complete, objective, and neutral.[88]

Thus, legal language and reasoning is gendered, and that gender matches the male gender of its linguistic architects.[89] Law is a patriarchal form of reasoning, as is the philosophy of liberalism of which law (or at least post-Enlightenment Anglo-American law) is part.

The claim that legal language and reasoning is male gendered is partly empirical and historical. The legal system, and its reasoning structure and language have been framed on the basis of life experiences typical to empowered white males. Law's reasoning structure shares a great deal with the assumptions of the liberal intellectual and philosophical tradition, which historically has been framed by men. The reasoning structure of law is thus congruent with the patterns of socialization, experience, and values of a particular group of privileged, educated men. Rationality, abstraction, a preference for statistical and empirical proofs over experiential or anecdotal evidence, and a conflict model of social life, corresponds to how these men have been socialized and educated to think, live, and work.

My claim that legal reasoning and language are patriarchal also has a normative component, in the sense that male-based perspectives, images, and experiences are often taken to be the norms in law. Privileged white men are the norm for equality law; they are the norm for assessing the reasonable person in tort law[90]; the way men would react is the norm for self-defense law;[91] and the male worker is the prototype for labor law.[92]

Legal language is a male language because it is principally informed by men's experiences and because it derives from the powerful social situation of men,

---

[88]  The critique of objectivity and neutrality as not what they claim to be but as partial, male-biased perspectives is a standard and crucial part of current feminist theory that has moved beyond being merely reformist to challenging the foundations of disciplines. I have developed it elsewhere, see Finley, "Transcending Equality"; and Finley, "Choice and Freedom: Elusive Issues in the Search for Gender Justice" (1987) 96 Yale L.J. 914.

[89]  Some feminist theorists say that in order to escape patriarchy, women need to create a new language all their own, emanating from their bodies/embodied selves. See, *e.g.* M. Daly, *Gyn/Ecology, The Meta-Ethics of Radical Feminism* (1978). Consider also French feminist theorists such as Luce Irigaray and Julia Kristeva. See *New French Feminisms: An Anthology* (I. de Courtivron & E. Marks eds. 1981).

[90]  See Bender, "A Lawyer's Primer on Feminist Theory and Tort" (1988) 38 J. Legal Educ. 3; Finley, "Break in the Silence: Including Women's Issues in a Torts Course" (1989) 1 Yale J.L. & Feminism 41.

[91]  See, *e.g. State* v. *Wanrow* (1977) 88 Wash. 2d 221, 559 P. 2d 548; Schneider, "Equal Rights to Trial for Women; Sex Bias in the Law of Self-Defense" (1980) 15 Harv. C.R.—C.L. L. Rev. 623.

[92]  See, *e.g.* J. Conaghan, "The Invisibility of Women in Labour Law: Gender-Neutrality in Model-Building" (1986) 14 Int. L.J. Soc. of L. 377.

relative to women. Universal and objective thinking is male language because intellectually, economically, and politically privileged men have had the power to ignore other perspectives and thus to come to think of their situation as the norm, their reality as reality, and their wives as objective. Disempowered, marginalized groups are far less likely to mistake their situation, experience, and views as universal.[93] Male reasoning is dualistic and polarized thinking because men have been able, thanks to women, to organize their lives in a way that enables them not to have to see such things as work and family as mutually defining. Men have acted on their fears of women and nature to try to split nature off from culture, body from mind, passion from reason, and reproduction from production.[94] Men have had the power to privilege—to assign greater value to—the side of the dichotomies that they associate with themselves. Conflict-oriented thinking, seeing matters as involving conflicts of interests or rights, as contrasted to relational thinking, is male because this way of expressing things is the primary orientation of more men than women. The fact that there are many women trained in and adept at male thinking and legal language does not turn it into androgynous language—it simply means that women have learned male language, as many French speakers learn English.

The claim that law is patriarchal does not mean that women have not been addressed or comprehended by law. Women have obviously been the subjects or contemplated targets of many laws. But it is men's understanding of women, women's nature, women's capacities, and women's experiences—women refracted through the male eye—rather than women's own definitions, that has informed law.

One notable example of a male judicial perspective characterizing women as men see them is the often-flayed U.S. Supreme Court decision in *Bradwell v. Illinois*,[95] in which Justice Bradley exalted the delicate timidity and biologically bounded condition of women to conclude that women were unfit for the rude world of law practice. Another example is the decision in *Geduldig v. Aiello*,[96] in which the Court cordoned off the female experience of pregnancy and called this experience unique, voluntary, and unrelated in any way to the workplace.

The legal definition of rape provides another example of the male judicial perspective. It is the male's view of whether the woman consented that is determinative of consent; it is men's view of what constitutes force against men and forms a resistance by men in situations other than rape that defines whether force has been used against a woman and a woman has resisted; it is men's definition of sex—penetration of the vagina by the penis—rather than women's experience of sexualized violation and violation that defines the crime.[97] The legal view of prostitution as a crime committed by women (and more recently also committed by men playing the woman's role in a sexual encounter with men) with no "victims" is another obvious example. The world "family" and the area of "family law" is yet another example. The norm of "family," the fundamental meaning of the term embedded in and shaped by law, is of a household headed by a man with a wife who is wholly or somewhat dependent on him. Other forms of family—especially those without a man—are regarded as abnormal. To a significant extent, the purpose of the discipline of family law is to sanction the formation of ideal families and to control and limit the formation and existence of these nonideal families, and thus to control the status and lives of women.

---

[93] See N. Hartsock, *Rethinking Modernism: Minority versus Majority Theories, Cultural Critique* (1987), No. 7, 187, 205; M. Matsuda, "When the First Quail Calls: Multiple Consciousness as Jurisprudential Method" (1987) 11 Women's Rts. L. Rep. 7.

[94] See, *e.g.* S. Griffin, *Woman and Nature: The Roaring Inside Her* (1978).

[95] (1873) 83 U.S. 442.

[96] (1973) 417 U.S. 484.

[97] See, *e.g.* S. Estrich, *Real Rape* (1987); MacKinnon, 8 *Signs* 635.

*The Power and Limitations of Male Legal Language*

Analysis of the way the law structures thought and talk about social problems is necessary to understand how the law can limit our understandings of the nature of problems and can confine our visions for change. A male-gendered way of thinking about social problems is to speak in terms of objectivity, of universal abstractions, of dichotomy, and of conflict. These are essentially the ways law talks about social problems.

Modern Anglo-American law talks about social problems within the individualistic framework of patriarchal Western liberalism, a theory that itself has been challenged by feminists as resting on a fundamentally male world view. This framework sees humans as self-interested, fundamentally set-apart from other people, and threatened by interactions with others.[98] To control the threat of those who would dominate you or gain at your expense, you must strive to gain power over them. This power can easily become domination because the point of its exercise is to protect yourself by molding another to your will.

As part of this individualistic framework, law is conceptualized as a rule-bound system for adjudicating the competing rights of self-interested, autonomous, essentially equal individuals capable of making unconstrained choices. Because of the law's individualistic focus, it sees one of the central problems that it must address to be enforcing the agreements made by free autonomous individuals, as well as enforcing a few social norms to keep the battle of human life from getting out of hand. It envisions another central task to be eliminating obvious constraints on individual choice and opportunity. The constraints are thought to emanate primarily from the state or from the bad motivations of other individuals. An individualistic focus on choice does not perceive constraints as coming from history, from the operation of power and domination, from socialization, or from class, race and gender. A final key task for individualistic liberal law is to keep the state from making irrational distinctions between people, because such distinctions can frustrate individual autonomy. It is not an appropriate task to alter structures and institutions, to help the disempowered overcome subordination, to eliminate fear and pain that may result from encounters masquerading as "freely chosen,"[99] to value nurturing connections,[1] or to promote care and compassion for other people.[2]

To keep its operation fair in appearance, which it must if people are to trust resorting to the legal method for resolving competing claims, the law strives for rules that are universal, objective, and neutral. The language of individuality and neutrality keeps law from talking about values, structures, and institutions, and about how they construct knowledge, choice, and apparent possibilities for conducting the world. Also submerged is a critical awareness of systematic, systemic, or institutional power and domination. There are few ways to express within the language of law and legal reasoning the complex relationship between power, gender, and knowledge. Yet in order for feminists to use the law to help effectuate change, we must be able to talk about the connection between power and knowledge. This connection must be acknowledged in order to demystify the "neutrality" of the law, to make the law comprehend that women's definitions have been excluded and marginalized, and to show that the language of neutrality itself is one of the devices for this silencing.

---

[98] See S. Harding, *The Science Question* p. 171. See also N. Hartsock, *Money, Sex and Power: Toward a Feminist Historical Materialism* (1983); A. Jaggar, *Feminist Politics and Human Nature* (1983).

[99] See, *e.g.* West, "The Difference in Women's Hedonic Lives: A Phenomenological Critique of Feminist Legal Theory (1987) 3 Wis. Women's L.J. 89.

[1] Tort law, for example, reluctantly and rarely allows recovery for emotional distress caused when a loved one is injured.

[2] See, *e.g.* Bender, *supra*, note 90.

The language of neutrality and objectivity can silence the voices of those who did not participate in its creation because it takes a distanced, decontextualized stance. Within this language and reasoning system, alternative voices to the one labeled objective are suspect as biased. An explicit acknowledgement of history and the multiplicity of experiences—which might help explode the perception of objectivity—is discouraged. To talk openly about the interaction between historical events, political change, and legal change is to violate neutral principles, such as adherence to precedent—and precedents themselves are rarely talked about as products of historical and social contingencies. For example, in the recent U.S. Supreme Court decision declaring a municipal affirmative action plan unconstitutional, *City of Richmond v. Croson*,[3] the majority talks in the language of neutrality, of color-blindness, and of blind justice[4] and it is the more classicly legal voice. The dissent, which cries out in anguish about the lessons of history, power, and domination, is open to the accusation that it speaks in the language of politics and passions, not law.

In legal language, experience and perspective are translated as bias, as something that makes the achievement of neutrality more difficult. Having no experience with or prior knowledge of something is equated with perfect neutrality. This way of thinking is evident in jury selection. A woman who has been raped would almost certainly be excluded as a juror in a rape trial—it is assumed that her lived experience of rape makes her unable to judge it objectively. Legal language cannot imagine that her experience might give her a nuanced, critical understanding capable of challenging the male-constructed vision of the crime. Yet someone with no experience of rape, either as victim, perpetrator, or solacer/ supporter of victim, is deemed objective, even though it may be just their lack of experience that leaves them prone to accept the biased myths about women's behavior that surround this crime.

Because it is embedded in a patriarchal framework that equates abstraction and universalization from only one group's experiences as neutrality, legal reasoning views male experiences and perspectives as the universal norm around which terms and entire areas of the law are defined. Examples of this phenomenon abound, and exposing them has been a central project of feminist jurisprudence. Thus, for example, my previous work, as well as that of several others,[5] has examined how talk about equality, couched in comparative language of sameness/ difference, requires a norm or standard for comparison—and that norm becomes white males. The more a non-white person can be talked about as the same as a white male, the more deserving she or he is to be treated equally to, or the same as, white males. This language not only uses white males as the reference-point, but it also exalts them. To be the same as white males is the desired end. To be different from them is undesirable and justifies disadvantage.

Many doctrinal areas of the law are also fundamentally structured around men's perspectives and experiences. The field of labor law uses a gendered meaning of work—as that which is done for wages outside your own home—as its focus. Thus, any talk about reforming labor law, or regulating work, will always leave unspoken, and thus unaffected, much of what women do, even women who

---

[3] (1989) 109 S. Ct. 706.

[4] Speaking of the meaning of images conveyed by the use of language, the law's metaphor for neutrality and justice—blindness—is a curious one considering the meaning of blindness in other contexts. Rather than equating blindness with an objective, whole,- universal view, in other language systems blindness means not being able to fully comprehend, being partial because not all senses are able to be employed. The parable of the blind men and the elephant, in which none can imagine the whole, is illustrative of the usual connotation of blindness.

[5] See, *e.g.* Finley, "Transcending Equality"; Littleton, "Equality and Feminist Legal Theory" (1987) 48 U. Pitt. L. Rev. 1043; Minow, "Learning to Live with the Dilemma of Difference: Bilingual and Special Education" (1985) 48 Law & Contemp. Probs. 157.

also "work" in the legal conventional sense.[6] Legal intervention in work—or the perception that no intervention is needed—assumes that workers are men with wives at home who tend to the necessities of life. It is only in this framework that we can even think of work and family as separate and conflicting spheres.[7]

Tort law defines injuries and measures compensation primarily in relation to what keeps people out of work and what their work is worth. It is in this framework that noneconomic damages, such as pain and suffering or compensation for emotional injuries, which are often crucial founts of recovery for women, are deemed suspect and expendable. In the language of criminal law, the paradigmatic criminal is a male, and women criminals are often viewed as doubly deviant.[8] Another example of the manifestation of the male reference-points is how self-defense law looks to male notions of threat and response to assess what is reasonable.[9] Contract law is built around the form of transactions that predominates in the male-dominated marketplace, and doctrines that are regarded as necessary to assist the weak (*i.e.*, helpless women), such as reliance and restitution, are subtly demeaned by the language as "exceptions," as deviations from the normal rules of contract.[10] All of this suggests that for feminist law reformers, even using the terms "equality," "work," "injury," "damages," "market," and "contract" can involve buying into, and leaving unquestioned, the male frames of reference. It also leaves unspoken, and unrecognized, the kinds of work women do, or the kinds of injuries women suffer.

The language of law is also a language of dichotomies, oppositions, and conflict. No doubt this is partly attributable to the fact that law so frequently is invoked in situations of conflict—it is called on to resolve disputes, to respond to problems that are deemed to arise out of conflicting interests. Another reason legal language is put in terms of opposing interests is due to its place within an intellectual tradition—Western liberal thought—that orders the world in dualisms: culture/nature, mind/body, reason/emotion, public/private. Law is associated with the "male" and higher valued side of each of these dualisms.[11] This means that law adopts the values of the privileged side of the dualisms, such as the self-interested, "rational" exchange values of the marketplace, or the shunning of emotion. It also means that legal language has few terms for comprehending in a positive, valuable way the content of the devalued sides of the dualisms—or those, such as women, who are associated with the devalued sides. For example, law's operation within a perceived dichotomy of public/private, and its preference for the public as the proper area for its concern, leaves law largely ignorant of and unresponsive to what happens to women within the private realm. Thus the "public" language of law contributes to the silencing of women.

---

[6] For an analysis of the gendered nature of labor law, see Conaghan, *supra*, note 94.

[7] The paradigm of the male worker is also evident in the structure of the social security system. See M. Abramovitz, *Regulating the Lives of Women—Social Welfare Policy from Colonial Times to The Present* (1988). It is also evident in the structure of unemployment insurance, which regards family or reproductive reasons for disengaging from employment as voluntary quits or as rendering a worker unavailable for work, as reasons to disqualify a worker from unemployment compensation. See Pearce, "Toil and Trouble: Women Workers and Unemployment Compensation" 10 *Signs:* (1985) J. Women in Cult. & Soc'y 439.

[8] See Chesney-Lind & Daly, "Feminism and Criminology (1987) 5 Just. Q. 497; Heidensohn, "Models of Justice: Portia or Persephone? Some Thoughts on Equality, Fairness and Gender in the Field of Criminal Justice" (1986) 14 Int'l J. Soc. of L. 287.

[9] See, *e.g.* State v. *Wanrow* (1977) 88 Wash. 2d 221, 559 P. 2d 548; Schneider, *supra*, note 91.

[10] See Dalton, "An Essay in the Deconstruction of Contract Doctrine, (1985) 94 Yale L.J. 997; Frug, "Re-Reading Contracts: A Feminist Analysis of a Contracts Casebook" (1985) 34 Am. U.L. Rev. 1065. [And see *ante*, 1093].

[11] For a discussion of the dualisms that structure liberal legal thinking, see A. Jaggar, *supra* note 98; F. Olsen, *The Sex of Law* in Kairys, *The Politics of Law* (1990)).

The conflict aspect of legal language—the way it talks about situations and social problems as matters of conflicting rights or interests—fosters polarized understandings of issues and limits the ability to understand the other side. It also squeezes out of view other ways of seeing things, nonoppositional possibilities for dealing with social problems. Since a language of conflict means that one side has to be preferred, there will always be winners and losers. In a polarized language of hierarchical dualisms set within a patriarchal system, it will often be women, and their concerns, that will lose, be devalued, or be overlooked in the race to set priorities and choose sides.

Another problematic instance of the language of conflicting rights is the law's approach to issues of women's reproductive freedom. These issues are being framed by the law as conflicts between maternal rights, such as the right to privacy and to control one's body, and fetal rights, such as the right to life, or the right to be born in a sound and healthy state. They are also framed as conflicts between maternal rights and paternal rights, such as the man's interest in reproductive autonomy. To talk about human reproduction as a situation of conflict is a very troublesome way to understand this crucial human event in which the well-being, needs, and futures of all participants in the event, including other family members, are inextricably, sensitively connected. Just because everything that happens to one participant can affect the other does not mean they are in conflict. It suggests, rather, that they are symbiotically linked. The fetus is not there and cannot exist without the mother. An action taken for the sake of the mother that may, in a doctor's but not the mother's view, seem to pose a risk to the fetus, such as her decision to forego a caesarean birth, or to take medication while pregnant, may actually be necessary (although perhaps also still presenting a risk of harm) for the fetus because without an emotionally and physically healthy mother there cannot be a sustained fetus or child.[12]

If we stop talking about reproductive issues as issues of opposing interests, but discuss them as matters where the interests of all are always linked, for better or worse, then there is much less risk that one person in the equation—the woman—will drop out of the discussion. Yet that is what often happens in dualistic, win-lose conflict-talk. As one commentator has said, "respect for the fetus is purchased at the cost of denying the value of women."[13] Legal discourse is frequently guided by the male-based medical perspective, which when matched with the erasing process of win-lose legal discourse, pushes the mother further into the recesses of invisibility. Dawn Johnsen offers an insightful analysis of how this process works: "[b]y separating the interests of the fetus from those of the pregnant woman, and then examining, often post hoc, the effect on the fetus of isolated decisions made by the woman on a daily basis during pregnancy, the state is likely to exaggerate the potential risks to the fetus and undervalue the costs of the loss of autonomy suffered by the woman."[14] A chilling example of the process of obliterating the woman occurred in a case in which a court ordered a caesarean section performed on a woman over her religious objections. The mother virtually disappeared from the text, and certainly her autonomy was of little concern to the court, as the judge wrote that all that stood between the fetus and "its independent existence, was, put simply, a doctor's scalpel."[15] The court did not even say an incision in "the mother." Just "a scalpel"—the mother was not mentioned as a person who would be cut by that scalpel, who would have to undergo risky

---

[12] For a work that seeks to approach abortion in terms of the connections between mother and fetus, see R. Goldstein, *Mother Love and Abortion: A Legal Interpretation* (1988).

[13] Farrel-Smith, "Rights-Conflict, Pregnancy and Abortion" in *Beyond Domination: New Perspectives on Women and Philosophy* (C. Gould ed. 1983), p. 27.

[14] Johnsen, "The Creation of Fetal Rights: Conflicts with Women's Constitutional Rights in Liberty, Privacy and Equal Protection" (1986) 95 Yale L.J. 599, 613.

[15] "In the Matter of Madyun Fetus" (1986) 114 Daily Washington L.Rep. 2233, 2240 (D.C. Super. Ct. July 26, 1986).

surgery. She was not mentioned as someone whose health and existence were necessary to the child's life; she was no more than an obstacle to the fetus' life.

The legal approach to the problem of pornography as if it presented a conflict between women's and men's interests in not being objectified and degraded, and the societal interest in free speech, is another example of unproductive conflict-talk which limits our understanding of a problem and of women's experiences. The equation of not being degraded and objectified with the diluted word "interest" is troubling. The very thought that an abstract principle like free speech could be considered more important than working against domination, violence, injury, and degradation, and redressing the needs of those who have suffered from these things, is also disturbing. Talking about the pornography issue as presenting an inherent conflict with free speech, and thus simply a matter of balancing the weights of the respective interests, leaves the meaning and scope to be given to "speech" undiscussed. The conflict-talk also leaves the framework of free speech law unexamined. Yet the terms of that framework define moral harm to the consumers of pornography, and not physical harm to the people who are used to make it or are victimized by it, as the appropriate focus of legal concern. The legal rhetoric also squeezes out from the debate the question whether there really is a conflict between "free speech" and women's civil rights.

The dichotomous, polarized, either/or framework of legal language also makes it a reductionist language—one that does not easily embrace complexity or nuance. Something either must be one way, or another. It cannot be a complicated mix of factors and still be legally digestible. The law has a hard time hearing, or believing, other languages. That is part of its power.

One of the other languages that the law does not easily hear is that associated with the emotions, with expression of bursting human passion and aspirations. Law is a language firmly committed to the "reason" side of the reason/emotion dichotomy. Indeed, the law distrusts injuries deemed emotional in character; it suspects them as fraudulent, as feigned, as not important. The inability to hear the voice of emotion to respond to thinking from the emotions, is one of the limitations of the legal voice. There are some things that just cannot be said by using the legal voice. Its terms, depoliticize, decharge, and dampen. Rage, pain, elation, the aching, thirsting, hungering for freedom on one's own terms, love and its joys and terrors, fear, utter frustration at being contained and constrained by legal language—all are diffused by legal language.

Examples of the "fit" problem can be found throughout law. How can we fit a woman's experience of living in a world of violent pornography into obscenity doctrine, which is focused on moral harm to consumers of pornography? How can women fit the reality of pregnancy into equality doctrine without getting hung up on the horns of the sameness-difference dilemma? How can women fit the difference between a wanted and an unwanted pregnancy into the doctrinal rhetoric of privacy and "choice"?[16] This rhetoric presumes a sort of isolated autonomy alien to the reality of a pregnant woman. How can women fit the psychological and economic realities of being a battered woman into criminal law, which puts the word "domestic" before "violence"? This choice of terminology reduces the focus on the debilitating effects of violence and increases attention to the fact that the setting is the home, an environment in which we are all supposedly free to come and go as we "choose." How can women fit the way incest victims repress what has happened to them until the memory is released by some triggering event in adulthood with the narrow temporal requirements of statute of limitations law? How can women fit the fact that this crime, and others of sexualized violence against women, so often happens behind closed doors with no "objective witnesses," into the proof requirements of evidentiary law? How, as Kristin Bumiller explores in her article, *Rape as a Legal Symbol: An Essay on*

---

[16] See, *e.g.* Ashe, "Zig-Zag Stitching" (1989) 13 Nova. L.J. 355.

*Sexual Violence and Racism,*[17] can we fit the experience of having what a woman thought was a pleasant social interaction but then crosses the invisible line to become threatening violence, into rape doctrine? Rape law focuses on sex, not on violence. It focuses on the woman's consent to sex, from the male point of view—and so it presumes that any indication of assent to social interaction is also assent to "do what the man wants."[18] How, as Lucie White asks in her paper, *Unearthing the Barriers to Women's Speech: Notes Toward a Feminist Sense of Procedural Justice,*[19] can a black mother on welfare ever convey her world to the welfare bureaucracy that is charging her with an overpayment because she followed its erroneous advice and spent an injury insurance check? What is important to this woman is that she did nothing wrong, and that she was able to buy her children Sunday shoes. But what is relevant to the state's welfare law is not her view of right and wrong, or her own understanding of what was necessary for her family—in her world, having Sunday shoes was essential to human dignity—but whether the items she bought with the insurance check fit the state's definition of "necessities" of life.

Legal language frames the issues, it defines the terms in which speech in the legal world must occur, it tells us how we should understand a problem and which explanations are acceptable and which are not. Since this language has been crafted primarily by white men, the way it frames issues, the way it defines problems, and the speakers and speech it credits, do not readily include women. Legal language commands: abstract a situation from historical, social, and political context; be "objective" and avoid the lens of nonmale experience; invoke universal principles such as "equality" and "free choice;" speak with the voice of dispassionate reason; be simple, direct, and certain; avoid the complexity of varying, interacting perspectives and overlapping multi-textured explanations; and most of all, tell it and see it "like a man"—put it in terms that relate to men and to which men can relate.

Feminist theory, on the other hand, which is not derived from looking first to law, but rather to the multiple experiences and voices of women as the frame of reference, tells us to look at things in their historical, social, and political context, including power and gender; distrust abstractions and universal rules, because "objectivity" is really perspectived and abstractions just hide the biases; question everything, especially the norms or assumptions implicit in received doctrine, question the content and try to redefine the boundaries;[20] distrust attributions of essential difference and acknowledge that experiences of both men and women are multiple, diverse, overlapping and thus difference itself may not be a relevant legal criterion; break down hierarchies of race, gender, or power; embrace diversity, complexity, and contradiction—give up on the need to tell "one true story" because it is too likely that that story will be the story of the dominant group;[21] listen to the voice of "emotion" as well as the voice of reason and learn to

---

[17] (1988) U. Miami L. Rev. 75.

[18] See S. Estrich, *supra* n. 97.

[19] See L. White, (1990) 38 Buffalo L. Rev. 1.

[20] For a discussion of how examining women's situations and then applying them to law requires changing disciplinary boundaries and creating wholly new disciplines, see Norwegian Law Professor Tove Stang-Dahl's description of the Women's Law progam at the University of Oslo in Norway. Stang-Dahl, "Taking Women as a Starting Point: Building Women's Law" (1986) 14 Int.L.J. Soc. of L. 239.

[21] For example, white feminists tend to tell a story of women's true situation that excludes the differing situations of poor women and women of color and women of different ethnic backgrounds. For developments of this critique of white feminism by other white feminists, see E. Spelman, *Inessential Woman: Problems of Exclusion in Feminist Thought* (1989); Kline, "Race, Racism and Feminist Legal Theory" (1989) 12 Harv. Women's L.J. 115.

value and legitimate what has been denigrated as "mere emotion."[22]

### Dealing with the dilemma of legal language

So, what's a woman do? Give up on law, on legal language entirely? Disengage from the legal arena of the struggle? Neither of these strategies is really an available option. We cannot get away from law, even if that is what we would like to do. Because law is such a powerful, authoritative language, one that insists that to be heard you try to speak its language, we cannot pursue the strategy suggested by the theorists from other disciplines such as the French feminists, of devising a new woman's language that rejects "phallologocentric" discourse.[23]

Nor can we abandon caring whether law hears us. Whether or not activists for women look to law as one means for pursuing change, the law will still operate on and affect women's situations. Law will be present through direct regulation, through nonintervention when intervention is needed, and through helping to keep something invisible when visibility and validation are needed.[24] Law will continue to reflect and shape prevailing social and individual understandings of problems, and thus will continue to play a role in silencing and discrediting women.

Since law inevitably will be one of the important discourses affecting the status of women, we must engage it. We must pursue trying to bring more of women's experiences, perspectives, and voices into law in order to empower women and help legitimate these experiences. But this is not as easy as it sounds, because there is no "one truth" of women's experiences, and women's own understandings of their experiences are themselves affected by legal categorizations.

There have been examples of promising word changes and consequent meaning changes in legal discourse. Consider the now widespread use of the term "sexual harassment," for what used to be considered a tort of invading individual dignity or sensibilities; the term "battering" for domestic violence. But even these language changes get confined by the legal frameworks into which they are placed. For example, the individualistic and comparative discrimination framework now applied to sexual harassment leaves some judges wondering about bisexual supervisors as a means to deny that discrimination is what is occurring.[25] The contract model of damages in discrimination law means that the dignity and personal identity values that tort law once recognized often go under-compensated.[26] And the use of the term "sexual assault" in place of "rape" in

---

[22] For examples of work that seeks to value the voice of caring, see C. Gilligan, *In A Different Voice* (1982); N. Noddings, *Caring—A Femine Approach to Ethics and Moral Education* (1984); S. Ruddick, *Maternal Thinking: Toward a Politics of Peace* (1989); Bender, *supra*; and Tronto, *Beyond Gender Difference to a Theory of Care*, 12 *Signs*: J. Women in Cult. & Soc'y 644 (1987).

[23] For examples of the French feminist theory, see L. Irigaray, *This Sex Which is Not One* (C. Porter trans. 1985), and *Speculum of the Other Woman* (G. Gill trans. 1985); H. Cixous, "Laugh of the Medusa" in *New French Feminisms*. Note that one of the French feminist language theorists, Julia Kristeva, proposes critical engagement with the existing language as a way to change it. See Nye, "Woman Clothed with the Sun" (1987) 12 *Signs* 664.

[24] For a discussion of these three ways in which law intervenes, even when it is not seeming to do so, see K. O'Donovan, *Sexual Divisions in Law* (1985) pp. 11–19; see also F. Olsen, "The Myth of State Intervention in the Family" (1985) 18 U. Mich. J.L. Ref. 835.

[25] See, *e.g.* Judge Bork's dissenting opinion in *Meritor Sav. Bank v. Vinson* (1985) 753 F.2d 141 (D.C. Cir.).

[26] See, *e.g.* Schoenheider, "A Theory of Tort Liability for Sexual Harassment in the Workplace" (1986) 134 U. Pa. L. Rev. 1461.

some rape reform statutes has not obviated the problems of "objective" male-perspectived judgments of female sexuality and consent.[27]

It is not my purpose to offer a simple, neat, for all times solution to the dilemma of legal language. Indeed, to even think that is possible would be contradictory to my message—it would be a capitulation to the legal ways of thinking that I seek to destabilize in order to expand. But I am not without solutions to the dilemma of the gendered nature of legal reasoning. This leads to self-conscious strategic thinking about the philosophical and political implications of the meanings and programs we do endorse. For example, just what are the implications of arguing either sameness or difference? If both have negative implications, then this should suggest the need to reframe the issue, to ask previously unasked questions about the relevance or stability of differences, or about the role of unexamined players such as employers and workplace structures and norms. Critical thinking about norms and what they leave unexamined opens up conversations about altering the norms and thus the vision of the problem. This leads to thinking about new ways of reasoning and talking. It leads to offering new definitions of existing terms; definitions justified by explorations of context and the experiences of previously excluded voices. Or, it leads to thinking about offering wholly new terms.

In addition to critical engagements with the nature of legal language, another promising strategy is to sow the mutant seeds that do exist within legal reasoning. Because legal reasoning can be sensitive to context, we can work to expand the context that it deems relevant. By pulling the contextual threads of legal language, we can work towards making law more comfortable with diversity and complexity, less wedded to the felt need for universalizing, reductive principles.

The law's oft-proclaimed values of equity and fairness can also work as mutating agents. The equity side of law counsels taking individual variations and needs into account. Arguments about when this should be done in order to achieve fairness must proceed with reference to context, to differing perspectives, and to differing power positions. The more we can find openings to argue from the perspective of those often overlooked by legal language, such as the people upon whom the legal power is being exercised, or those disempowered or silenced or rendered invisible by the traditional discourse, the more the opportunities to use the engine of fairness and equity to expand the comprehension of legal language.

## NICOLA LACEY
### The Feminist Challenge to Conventional Legal Scholarship
### (1998)[28]

Over the last fifteen years, a number of important intellectual movements such as "law in context", "socio-legal studies" and "critical legal studies" have begun to reshape the approach of legal education. Notwithstanding their influence, the orientation of most courses in law remains a broadly positivist one. By this I mean simply that legal education assumes the existence of a relatively discrete social phenomenon—law—and sees itself as imparting both knowledge of particular laws and techniques through which students can broaden and use this knowledge

---

[27] See, *e.g.* E. Sheehy, *Personal Autonomy and the Criminal Law: Emerging Issues for Women, Background Paper for the Canadian Advisory Council on the Status of Women* (Sept. 1987), 19–28; Bienen, "Rape III—National Developments in Rape Reform Legislation" (1980) 6 Women's Rts. L. Rep. 170; Dawson, "Legal Structures: A Feminist Critique of Sexual Assault Reform" (1985) 14 *Resources for Feminist Research* No. 3 at p. 42 (Nov. 1985); Boyle, "Sexual Assault and the Feminist Judge" (1985) 1 Can. J. Women & L. 99.

[28] [From N. Lacey. *Unspeakable Subjects* (1998).]

in intellectual and practical contexts. Furthermore, in so far as law courses reach beyond the description and analysis of law, they tend to do so by contextualising that analysis within a set of broadly liberal ideas which are thought to inform legal arrangements in modern societies such as Britain. I therefore want to single out a number of assumptions common to positivistic and liberal legal scholarship which are the target of feminist critique of the gender bias of law and legal methods. These various points are closely interwoven, but I think that it is useful to separate them out to get a sense of the range of arguments which have been influential in the development of feminist legal thought.

### The neutral framework of legal reasoning

A central tenet of both positivist scholarship and the liberal ideal of the rule of law is that laws set up standards which are applied in a neutral manner to formally equal parties. The questions of inequality and power which may affect the capacity of those parties to engage effectively in legal reasoning have featured little in either mainstream legal theory or legal education. These questions have, on the other hand, always been central to critical legal theory, and they find an important place within feminist legal thought. In particular, the work of social psychologist Carol Gilligan[29] on varying ways of constructing moral problems, and the relationship of these variations to gender, has opened up a striking argument about the possible "masculinity" of the very process of legal reasoning.

As is widely known, Gilligan's research was motivated by the finding of psychological research that men reach, on average, a "higher" level of moral development than do women. Gilligan set out to investigate the neutrality of the tests being applied: she also engaged in empirical research designed to illuminate the ways in which different people construct moral problems. Her research elicited two main approaches to moral reasoning. The first, which Gilligan calls the ethic of rights, proceeds in an essentially legalistic way: it formulates rules structuring the values at issue in a hierarchical way, and then applies those rules to the facts. The second, which Gilligan calls the ethic of care or responsibility, takes a more holistic approach to moral problems, exploring the context and relationships, as well as the values, involved, and producing a more complex, but less conclusive, analysis. The tests on which assessments of moral development have conventionally been made by psychologists were based on the ethic of rights: analyses proceeding from the ethic of care were hence adjudged morally underdeveloped. It was therefore significant that Gilligan's fieldwork suggested that these two types were gender-related, in that girls tended to adopt the care perspective, whilst boys more often adopted the rights approach.

Gilligan's assertion of the relationship between the two models and gender is a controversial one. Nonetheless, her analytical distinction between the two ethics is of great potential significance for feminist legal theory. The idea that the distinctive structure of legal reasoning may systematically silence the voices of those who speak the language of relationships is a potentially important one for all critical legal theory. The rights model is, as I have already observed, reminiscent of law: it works from a clear hierarchy of sources which are reasoned through in a formally logical way. The more contextual, care or relationship-oriented model would, by contrast, be harder to capture by legal frameworks, within which holistic or relationally-oriented reasoning tends to sound "woolly" or legally incompetent, or to be rendered legally irrelevant by substantive and evidential rules. Most law students will be familiar with the way in which intuitive judgements are marginalised or disqualified in legal education, which proceeds precisely by imbuing the student with a sense of the exclusive relevance of formal legal sources and technical modes of reasoning.

---

[29]  See C Gilligan, *In A Different Voice* (1982).

There are, however, several important pitfalls for feminist legal theory in some of the arguments deriving from Gilligan's research.[30] One way of reading the implications for law of Gilligan's approach is that legal issues, indeed the conceptualisation of legal subjects themselves, should be recast in less formal and abstract terms. But such a strategy of recontextualisation may obscure the (sometimes damaging) ways in which legal subjects are already contextualised. In the sentencing of offenders, or in the assumptions on which victims and defendants are treated in rape cases, for example, we have some clear examples of effective contextualisation which cuts in several political directions—not all of them appealing to feminists. In certain areas, it may be that legal reasoning is already "relational" in the sense espoused by many feminists, but that it privileges certain kinds of relationships: such as proprietary, object relations.[31] A general call for "contextualisation" may also be making naive assumptions about the power of such a strategy to generate real change given surrounding power relations: as the case of rape trials shows all too clearly, the framework of legal doctrine is not the only formative context shaping the legal process. The important project, then, is that of recontextualisation understood not as reformist strategy but rather as critique: in other words, the development of a critical analysis which unearths the logic, the substantive assumptions, underlying law's current contextualisation of its subjects, and which can hence illuminate the interests and relationships which these arrangements privilege.

### Law's autonomy and discreteness

Another standard assumption of mainstream legal scholarship is that law is a relatively autonomous social practice, discrete from politics, ethics, religion. An extreme expression of this assumption is found in Hans Kelsen's "pure" theory of law,[32] but weaker versions inform the entire positivist tradition. Indeed, this is what sets up one of positivism's recurring problems—that is, the question of foundations, of the boundaries between the legal and the non-legal; of the source of legal authority, and the relation between law and justice.[33]

This mainstream assumption, like the idea that legal method is discrete or distinctive, is challenged by feminist legal theory. Feminist theory seeks to reveal the ways in which law reflects, reproduces, expresses, constructs and reinforces power relations along sexually-patterned lines. In doing so, it questions law's claims to autonomy and represents it as a practice which is continuous with deeper social, political and economic forces which constantly seep through its supposed boundaries. Hence the ideals of the rule of law call for modification and reinterpretation. There are obvious, and strong, continuities here between the feminist and the marxist traditions in legal thought.[34]

### Law's neutrality and objectivity

As I have already mentioned, difference feminism has developed a critique of the very idea of gender neutrality, of gender equality before the law, in a sexually-patterned world. Feminist legal theory deconstructs law's claims to be enunciating truths, its pretension to neutral or objective judgement, and its constitution of a field of discrete and hence unassailable knowledge.

---

[30] For a useful discussion, see M. Frug, *Postmodern Legal Feminism* (1992) Ch. 3.
[31] For further discussion see J. Nedelsky, 1 Review of Constitutional Studies (1993); L. Irigaray *J' Aime A Toi* (1992).
[32] See *ante*, 255.
[33] For an extended analysis of this problem, see M. Davies, *Delimiting The Law* (1996).
[34] See H. Collins, *Marxism and Law* (1982).

This argument takes a number of forms in contemporary feminist legal theory. One derives from the Foucaultian critique of feminist writers such as Carol Smart.[35] The argument is that law, by policing its own boundaries via its substantive rules and rules of evidence, constitutes itself as self-contained, as a self-reproducing system.[36] There is, hence, a certain "truth" to this aspect of law. But by standing back so as to cast light on the point of view from which law's truth is being constructed, we can undermine law's claims to objectivity. Another, rather different, example is Catharine MacKinnon's well known epistemological argument.[37] In MacKinnon's view, law constructs knowledge which claims objectivity, but "objectivity" in fact expresses a male point of view. Hence "objective" standards in civil and criminal law—the "reasonable person"—in fact represent a position which is specific in not only gender but also class, ethnic and other terms. The epistemological assertion of "knowledge" or "objectivity" disguises this process of construction, and writes sexually specific bodies out of the text of law. The project of feminism is to replace them. The difficult trick is to do so without fixing their shape and identity within received categories of masculine and feminine. Hence not all feminists endorse the idea of abandoning "reasonableness" tests or the appeal to otherwise universal standards.[38]

### Law's centrality

In stark contrast to not only a great deal of positivist legal scholarship but also much "law and society" work, feminist writers have often questioned law's importance or centrality to the constitution of social relations and the struggle to change those relations. Clearly feminist views diverge here. Catharine MacKinnon, for example, is optimistic about using law for radical purposes; but many other feminists—notably British feminist Carol Smart—have questioned the wisdom of placing great reliance on law and of putting law too much at the centre of our critical analysis. Perhaps this is partly a cultural difference: the British women's movement has typically been relatively anti-institutional and oppositional. Yet even in the USA, where there is a stronger tradition of reformist legal activism, feminists associated with critical legal studies have been notably cautious about claims advanced in some critical legal scholarship[39] about law's central role in constituting social relations. Feminists have thus tended further towards a classical marxist orientation on this question than have their non-feminist critical counterparts. In terms of analytic focus, however, this has led feminists to address a range of social institutions—the family, sexuality, the political realm, bureaucracies—well beyond the marxist terrain of political economy. Feminists writers continue to be ambivalent about whether and how law ought to be deployed as a tool of feminist action, practice and strategy. To the extent that feminist critique identifies law as implicated in the construction of existing gender relations, how far can it really be used to change them, and do strategic attempts to use law risk reaffirming law's power?

### Law as a system of enacted norms or rules

Typically, feminist legal theory reaches beyond a conception of law as a system of norms or rules—statutes, constitutions, cases—and beyond "standard" legal officials, such as judges, to encompass other practices which are legally relevant or

---

[35] See in particular C. Smart, *Feminism and The Power of Law* (1989) Ch. 1; A. Bottomley and J. Conaghan (eds.), *Feminist Theory and Legal Strategy* (1993).
[36] *Cf.* the arguments of autopoietic theory: see G Teubner *Law As An Autopoietic System* (1993), and *ante* 877.
[37] See MacKinnon, *ante*, 1337.
[38] See for example, Cornell, *The Imaginary Domain* (1995) Ch. I.
[39] See for example Unger, 99 Harvard L Rev. 561 (1983).

"quasi-legal". For example, the Oslo School of Women's Law had its main focus on administrative and regulatory bodies such as social welfare agencies, the medical system and the family.[40] This reorientation is born of a very basic socio-legal insight: that the power and social meaning of law are determined not only at its legislative, doctrinal and judicial levels but also by a myriad non-legal or partially legal decisions about its interpretation and enforcement.

This institutional refocusing is also connected with post-structuralist ideas, and notably with Michel Foucault's reconceptualisation of power—a reconceptualisation which has important implications for law.[41] Foucault distinguished between sovereignty power—power as a property or possession; juridical power; and disciplinary power—the relational power which inheres in particular practices and which flows unseen throughout the "social body". His argument was that the later modern world was gradually seeing the growth of subtle, intangible, disciplinary power, at the expense of both the old sovereignty and modern juridical power. Foucault was therefore inclined to think that law was waning in importance as a form of social governance. Smart, however, uses his argument about power in a different way in relation to law: she points out that law itself embodies disciplinary power. For one of the distinguishing features of disciplinary power is its subtly normalising effect, and as soon as we look beyond a narrow stereotype of law as a system of rules backed up by sanctions, we begin to see that one of law's functions is precisely to distribute its subjects with disciplinary precision around a mean or norm.

For example, the way in which legal rules distribute social welfare benefits or allocate custody of children (on divorce or via adoption) reflects judgements about the right way to live; it expresses assumptions about "normality". A yet more spectacular example is that of the construction of gay and straight sexualities in criminal laws and in family and social welfare legislation. These "normalising" assumptions have a pervasive power which also structures the administration of laws (e.g. of social welfare benefits and policing policies) at the bureaucratic level, generating phenomena such as reluctance to prosecute in "domestic violence" cases, the oppressive policing of gay sexuality, and the discriminatory administration of welfare benefits. Feminist (like other critical) analyses are interested here not just in legal doctrine but also in legal discourse, *i.e.* how differently sexed legal subjects are constituted by and inserted within legal categories via the mediation of judicial, police or lawyers' discourse. The feminist approach therefore mounts a fundamental challenge to the standard ways of conceptualising law and the legal, and moves to a broader understanding of legally relevant spheres of practice.

### Law's unity and coherence

Readers of both student texts and legal cases will be familiar with the very high importance attached by lawyers and legal commentators to the idea (or ideal) of law as a unitary and a coherent system of rules or norms. It is an idea which informs legal theory in a number of ways. Once again, Kelsen provides a spectacular example: his Grundnorm had to be hypothesised precisely because otherwise it would have been impossible to interpret law as a coherent, non-contradictory normative field of meaning.[42] As a law student, one of the first things one is taught to do is to hone in on contradictory or inconsistent arguments. The idea of coherence as the idea(l) which lies at the heart of law finds its

---

[40] T. Stang Dahl, *Women's Law* (1986).
[41] See M. Foucault, *The Archaelogy of Knowledge* (1972), *Discipline and Punish* (1977); Smart, *op. cit.*, n. 35.
[42] [See *ante*, 306].

fullest expression in Ronald Dworkin's idea of "law as integrity",[43] but it is also voiced in procedurally-oriented ethical and political theories, notably in critical theory of the Frankfurt School.[44]

Feminist scholarship, like much other critical legal theory, is concerned to question this belief in law's coherence and to reconstruct the pretension to coherence as part of the ideology of both law and jurisprudence: as part of what helps to represent law as authoritative, adjudication as democratically legitimate and so on. The critical analysis of contradictions, and the unearthing of what have been called "dangerous supplements" and hidden agendas, takes place both at the level of doctrine and at that of discourse.[45]

To take some specific examples, the assertion within legal doctrine of particular questions or issues as within public or private spheres is contradictory, question-begging, under-determined: sexuality, for example, is public for some purposes and private for others.[46] The idea of the legal subject as rational and as abstracted from its social context is undermined by exceptions such as defences in criminal law, shifts of time-frame in the casting of legal questions, and an arbitrary division of issues pertaining to conviction and those pertaining to sentence.[47] In contract law, one could cite shifts between a freedom of contract model and a model which views contract as a long-term relationship within which, for example, loss occasioned by the parties' general reliance upon the contractual relationship can be recognised and compensated.[48] Nor are these incoherencies confined to the doctrinal framework: they mark also the discourse through which human subjects are inserted into that structure. For example, the rational and controlled male of legal subjectivity is also the rape defendant who is vulnerable to feminine wiles and who is, on occasion, incapable of distinguishing "yes" from "no". The unearthing of such contradictions is not just a matter of "trashing": it forms part of an intellectual and political strategy—of exposing law's indeterminacy, of emphasising its contingency, and of finding resources for its reconstruction in those doctrinal principles and discursive images which are less dominant yet which fracture and complicate the seamless web imagined by orthodox legal scholarship.

*Law's rationality*

Perhaps most fundamentally of all, it is argued that contradictions and indeterminacy in legal doctrine undermine law's supposed grounding in reason, just as the smuggling in of contextual and affective factors undermines law's apparent construction of the subject as a rational, self-interested actor. Furthermore, in so far as law is successful in maintaining its self-image as a rational enterprise, this is because the emotional and affective aspects of legal practice are systematically repressed in orthodox representations. Once one reads cases and other legal texts not only for their formal meaning but also as rhetoric, one sees how values and techniques which are not acknowledged on the surface of legal doctrine are in fact crucial to the way in which cases are decided.[49]

These, then, are the principal ways in which feminist legal theory has challenged the tenets of conventional jurisprudence and legal education, and it was my (then very vague) apprehension of these sorts of arguments which prompted me to start thinking seriously about feminist legal theory in the early 1980s. As I hope this brief account reveals, feminist theory engages with some highly complex

---

[43] See above, 724.
[44] *Between Facts and Norms* (1996), and *ante* 969.
[45] P. Fitzpatrick (ed.) (1991); *Dangerous Supplements*.
[46] See F Olsen 96 Harvard L.Rev. 1497 and *ante*, 1293. (1983).
[47] See M Kelman *ante*, 1244.
[48] See H Collins, *The Law of Contract* (1997).
[49] *Op. cit.*, n. 32.

questions: it is not surprising, therefore, that it is a rapidly moving field which constantly throws up new questions just as old ones appear to be nearing resolution. It is—like all intellectually challenging approaches—marked by vigorous contestation. ... What I hope to have achieved in this preliminary characterisation is to have communicated a sense of the intellectual vitality and ambition of feminist thought. I hope also to have suggested the extent to which feminist legal scholarship has to swim against a very strong current of intellectual convention—something which, for feminist scholars as well as students, is occasionally both exhausting and disorienting. [pp. 4–12].

Several arguments have been used to support the idea that feminist legal scholars should engage in the development of a feminist jurisprudence. Perhaps most obviously, it may be argued that feminist analysis and critique of laws and legal institutions is itself inevitably a theoretical enterprise which merits the denomination "jurisprudence". Furthermore, many of the "standard" jurisprudential questions are of explicit or implicit relevance for feminist enterprises. On the one hand, feminism poses certain distinctive theoretical questions of and about law: why are women excluded from certain areas of law: what happens when women are included; how does law construct the female subject in language; how can law be changed better to reflect women's interests and experience? These explicitly feminist questions of legal theory are located within broader categories of legal theoretical enterprise: sociological jurisprudence, discourse theory, the analysis of law's ideological functions. More controversially, it could be argued that feminist legal theory inevitably begs questions about the definition of law and the legal sphere which have been the stuff of analytical jurisprudence. Feminisms which move beyond a liberal framework to develop a more radical critique generally reject and regard as theoretically flawed the very enterprises of "objective" analysis and of normative jurisprudence which claims to reflect the ethical "view from nowhere". These arguments detect, among other things, a strong tendency towards legal closure in orthodox constructions of the jurisprudential enterprise. Yet there are strong reasons to assert that jurisprudence encompasses critical and interpretive tasks which are quite in tune with feminist theoretical thinking.

A second reason for thinking that feminists should engage in jurisprudence has to do with the power of orthodox theoretical thinking about law and the legal sphere. For example, the traditional stance of analytical jurisprudence, with its common emphasis on legal closure—the autonomy of law—has been a crucially important focus for feminist critique of the pretended "objectivity" and "neutrality" of "the legal point of view". Yet feminist scholars have in fact engaged in rather little direct debate with traditional jurisprudence, perhaps out of a conviction that it is too antediluvian to merit explicit attention, or out of an anxiety that such a debate would inevitably be constructed in terms of an agenda set by orthodoxy.[50] This is unfortunate, given that many of the beliefs about neutrality and autonomy criticised by feminists are bolstered by the traditional jurisprudential texts which constitute the core of many jurisprudence courses. It also arguably weakens the feminist position by giving rise to a tendency to lump all "traditional jurisprudence" together, condemning it in undifferentiated terms as "positivist", "essentialist", "gender blind", "masculinist" or "objectivist". Traditional jurisprudence, of course, encompasses a variety of theoretical projects and positions, which raise different kinds of problems from a feminist perspective, and not all of which are inevitably prone to either legal closure or genderblindness. A critical feminist jurisprudence which took on particular jurisprudential doctrines and positions might well strengthen the case for the general propositions which feminists wish to assert.

Thirdly, feminist legal scholarship's emphasis upon the importance of careful

---

[50] For two honourable exceptions, see M Davies, *Asking The Law Question* (1994) and V Kerruish, *Jurisprudence to Ideology* (1992).

analysis and critique of particular legal practices could be read as contributing to a shift away from a monolithic, universalising conception of the jurisprudential project, centred around a number of abstract questions such as "what is law?" or "what is distinctive about legal reasoning?", towards a more concrete and particularistic conception of jurisprudence. Should we allow orthodox scholars to appropriate the concept of jurisprudence, marginalising the more "applied", political theoretical enterprises around law, or should we rather assert the status of this work as properly within the scope of jurisprudence?

Finally, the most straightforward way in which feminist legal scholarship may engage in jurisprudence is in terms of a liberal feminism mainly concerned to develop an "immanent critique" of laws and legal practices. In other words, this feminist approach takes jurisprudence and the legal sphere on their own terms, and then holds up their actuality to contrast them with their own professed standards and ideals. This is the kind of analysis which argues for formal legal equality and equality of opportunity for women in law, and which has met with a substantial degree of success in many legal systems in modern times. Yet it is at precisely this point that ambivalence about feminist jurisprudence begins to surface. For the majority of feminist scholars working in this area today want to press beyond a liberal analysis to a more radical critique.[51]

The case against a feminist jurisprudence has been put most powerfully by Carol Smart. Smart notes the attractions of feminist jurisprudence:

> "The idea of a feminist jurisprudence is tantalizing in that it appears to hold out the promise of a fully integrated theoretical framework and political practice which will be transformative, unlike the partial or liberal measures of the past ... It promises a general theory of law which has practical applications. Because it appears to offer the combination of theory and practice, and because it will be grounded in women's experience, the ideal of a feminist jurisprudence appears to be a way out of the impasse of liberal feminist theories of law reform".[52]

But she sees the idea as giving rise to two problems:

> "We should ... consider whether the quest for a feminist jurisprudence is not falling into the trap of ... the 'androcentric standard' whereby feminists find they enter into a game whose rules are predetermined by masculine requirements and a positivistic tradition ... We need also to consider whether implicit in this quest is the tendency to place law far too much into the centre of our thinking."[53]

To take the latter point first, "grand" feminist theorising about law has, on this view, served women badly. Whilst Smart certainly does not reject theory itself, she is critical of the way in which the debate has too often remained at an abstract level, trapped within theoretical dichotomies such as equality versus difference, public versus private, which are partly of its own creation. Such theory, she argues, contributes little to our understanding of the subtle, multiple and concrete ways in which legal practices construct and sustain women's oppression. This

---

[51] The extent to which radical feminists such as Catharine MacKinnon can usefully exploit a quasi-liberal critique is just the kind of question which has given rise to the controversy which I shall analyse. The characterisation of MacKinnon's position as quasi-liberal is certainly not one which she herself would affirm: however, one could certainly argue that her law reform projects themselves take a paradigmatically liberal form, employing a concept of "harm" to women which might have been taken straight from John Stuart Mill. Her project could be also seen as engaging in the kind of philosophical closure implicit in much liberal discourse.

[52] *Op. cit.*, n. 35, p. 66; Smart draws the notion of the "androcentric standard" from Thornton (1986) 3 Australian J of Law and Soc. 5.

[53] *ibid.*, pp. 67–8.

could be seen as an instrumentalist argument against feminists spending time and effort on a project which offers little hope of political gain or enlightenment.[54] Smart's other argument might be taken to suggest a more fundamental objection to "grand" theory. What are the "masculine requirements" which taint the very notion of feminist jurisprudence? One view could be that the very project of abstract theorisation is unsatisfactory and indeed to be regarded with suspicion by feminists and other radicals. For the move from concrete to abstract becomes a means of assimilating and hence disguising the varied experiences of legal subjects: factors such as race and gender are rendered invisible by the move to abstraction; the voices of people of colour, poor people, women and other powerless groups are silenced. Theory may therefore serve precisely the mystifying objectification which it is a task of feminism to undermine and expose.

Smart wants to distinguish, however, between "grand" and "abstract" theory, her objection being to the former rather than the latter. On this view, "grand" theory is that which "totalises" or "universalises"—which claims to generate truths of general applicability. Any "total" theory of or about law may lead subtly to a "totalising" theory which represses difference, and even to "totalitarian" thinking and practice: any "normative" theory may lead towards "normalisation" and hence to repression. Alternatively, such "grand" theory may succeed only in offering accounts of the phenomena they purport to explain at so high a level of abstraction that they become banal or simplistic. I shall return below to the question of just what constitutes "grand" theory and whether "grandness" is distinct from "abstraction". Leaving that question aside for the moment, the main burden of Smart's argument is that legal theory as it traditionally conceives itself is ideological and hence effective in underpinning the very power of law:[55] its claims to truth, impartiality and objectivity, its place high up in the hierarchy of knowledges, which have been so damaging to women and other oppressed groups. Legal theory, in other words, participates in a strong form of legal closure which is inimical to a recognition of the politics of law.

### Interpreting the Debate

It would, of course, be possible to interpret the debate about feminist jurisprudence as a trivial disagreement which turns on semantics: can the term "jurisprudence" encompass critical and interpretive as opposed to analytic and prescriptive theoretical projects? To dismiss the debate in these terms would, I think, be a mistake. For it touches on a number of fundamental theoretical and political issues which are salient to contemporary feminism, and the very reason why the question of feminist jurisprudence is so problematic is connected to these deeper questions.

Most obviously, there is the question of what kind of theoretical enterprise feminism should engage in, and how far it should concern itself with law in the first place. Is the very idea of feminist theory of law one which implicitly acknowledges legal closure, the autonomy of the legal realm—a closure which is ultimately disempowering to feminism, whose main task is political critique? Is the idea of a feminist theory of law simply a contradiction in terms? Do we really have the power to construct the debate in our own terms—or is the jurisprudential enterprise inevitably loaded towards masculinist concepts and male interests, so that the construction of a feminist jurisprudence is, in Audre Lorde's famous phrase, a futile attempt to destroy the master's house with the master's tools? Even worse, does the project of constructing a feminist theory of law commit the almost unmentionable sin of essentialism, participating in the idea that law has

---

[54] Smart's main targets in this critique are MacKinnon and Gilligan.
[55] *Cf.* Kerruish, *op. cit.*, n. 50.

some fixed "essence", as opposed to being open to social and political recon-struction?[56] If legal theory does contain an irreducible core of essentialism, is this inevitable, or defensible on strategic grounds?

Secondly, there is a set of questions about the place in feminism for normative, reconstructive or utopian thinking, as opposed to negatively critical or "decon-structive" thinking. Does the idea of feminism as critique mean that we are always "trashing"—exposing sexism, bias, lack, absence—or is it the job of feminist legal scholars also to prescribe—to suggest legal reforms—or to imagine other possible legal worlds and processes, or indeed worlds without law? And if, as many feminists believe, there is this positive, reconstructive aspect to the feminist enterprise, does it need some kind of grounding or foundation?[57] This shades into a third important question, and brings the issue of philosophical closure into the argument. We must ask whether feminist thought should continue to be located firmly in the post-enlightenment modernism in whose terms (rights, calls for equality and so on) we have become familiar with feminist claims being couched. Alternatively, it might be argued that the critical potential of modernism and liberalism have been exhausted, and must now give way to a post-modernist, resolutely critical mode which utterly rejects philosophical closure and opens up legal discourse to the "play of difference", to the multiple possibilities raised by deconstructive critique. Yet even this way of putting the question is misleading, for it suggests that deconstruction, discourse theory, post-modernist fragmenta-tion and relativism necessarily go hand in hand. Whilst it is certainly true that this relationship is a familiar one, Drucilla Cornell has suggested that one can com-bine a deconstructive project with an ethical feminism significant aspects of which seem to belong firmly in the modernist tradition.[58] Ultimately, this brings us back to the question of what kind of theory feminism can and should engage in, refined in terms of possibly multiple combinations of modernist and post-modernist, critical and reconstructive, discourse-oriented and materialist, essentialist and social-constructionist projects. Should these dichotomies themselves be regarded as having any validity, and what combinations of project may be theoretically defensible or politically productive?

Fourthly, the questions already raised connect with a further important fem-inist preoccupation: that of the relationship between theory and practice. Fem-inism has generally been fiercely committed to the idea that theory and practice form inseparable parts of the political project: theory which is neither informed by the issues thrown up by practice nor likely to contribute to feminist praxis has been seen as an irrelevant and even elitist preoccupation, of no real theoretical or political validity. This commitment to the interrelation of theory and practice which feminism shares with many other radical discourses of course relates to feminist ambivalence about "grand" and, in some feminisms, all abstract theory, and marks a tendency in feminist thought which is resistant to philosophical closure. But recent debates have thrown up, as I shall try to show, some

---

[56] See Smart *op. cit.*, n. 35.
[57] See N. Fraser, *Unruly Practices* (1989); L. Nicholson (ed.), *Feminism/Postmodernism* (1990).
[58] Cornell, *Transformations* (1993) Ch. 4. Cornell's more recent work continues to develop a distinctive blend of modernist and post-modernist orientations. In *Beyond Accommoda-tion* (1991), Cornell aligns herself, with some reservations, with post-modernism; in *The Imaginary Domain* (1995) she defends a version of liberalism in the public sphere. This is, however, a liberalism which, though universalistic in its normative reach, resists any appeal to foundations. More generally, it would of course be a mistake to conflate the "textual turn" in contemporary social theory with a general post-modernist rejection of the possibility of coherent meta-narratives. For example, the work of Pierre Bourdieu, *Outline of a Theory of Practice* (1977)) combines a focus on discourse, social con-structionism and a rejection of universalism with a decisive rejection of the post-mod-ernism of other French social theorists such as Derrida and Lyotard.

intractable questions about the political and strategic defensibility of engaging in action informed by theory which falls short of feminist ideals: in Cornell's words, deciding to work for, for example, legal equality, whilst still knowing that this is something one will never be prepared to *settle for.*[59]

Fifth, the debate about feminist jurisprudence touches on important questions about the relationship of law to other institutions and structures of power. Is law a *relatively* autonomous field, change in which really holds out the hope of material gains for women? Or is law radically implicated with other powerful discourses and institutions in the social, political, cultural and economic realms? This question has a crucial bearing on the potential efficacy of feminist legal strategies. Finally, the debate about feminist jurisprudence raises questions about the relationship between feminism and other social critiques which present themselves as progressive—work in critical race theory, critical legal studies, marxist theory, post-structuralist and post-modernist analysis. In a sense, then, there is an important issue about closure within feminism—both in terms of how autonomous it is as a critical analysis, and in terms of how far it presupposes a foundationalist meta-ethics. The increasing recognition in modern feminist thought of the diversity and fragmentation of social experience and hence of the need to listen to the insights of women situated in a variety of locations relative to the many powerful sites of social oppression—class, race, sexuality—raises important questions about the power of a critique which draws on several sources of enlightenment and a common methodology. At the same time, the spectre of total fragmentation seems to threaten feminism's mission to speak in the voice of political outrage or advocacy[60]—a practice which at least superficially seems to pull feminism back in the direction of philosophical closure.

### Feminism, Law and Legal Theory

Some of the problems around which the debate about feminist jurisprudence has been centred seem as intractable as they do not just because of the complexity of the theoretical and political questions involved, but also because of a degree of slippage between those different questions. I shall illustrate this contention with some examples.

### What is "Grand Theory"?

The debate about the problematic nature of "grand" theory seems to me to be under-developed, with the result that some versions of the argument are in danger of abandoning important feminist legal theoretical projects along with analytical jurisprudence, "viewpointless" normative jurisprudence and crudely monolithic feminist theories. It is open to feminists to construct the jurisprudential project in interpretive and critical ways which are friendly to feminism and certainly not "grand" in the relevant sense. Indeed, Carol Smart's critique of the "quest for a feminist jurisprudence" itself employs concepts such as "patriarchy" and "phallogocentrism" which are themselves highly theorised, just as much of her work shows a strong commitment to engage in theoretical tasks of conceptualisation and analysis. Foucaultian discourse theory and Derridean deconstruction could be said to be every bit as "grandly theoretical" as any jurisprudential theory so far attempted. They too are universalistic at least at the level of method, and to the extent that they seek our attention they inevitably claim a persuasiveness which participates in some kind of validity claim. Of course, we may well want to criticise critical theories as themselves unduly abstract, apolitical or inaccessible.

---

[59] Cornell, *Transformations* (1993) Ch. 4.
[60] For a thought-provoking analysis of the pitfalls of this aspect of feminism, see W. Brown, *States of Injury* (1995).

But it seems unarguable that they have generated theoretical ideas which have been found to be powerful in developing feminist critiques of law.[61] This having been said, the question of just what makes a "grand theory" "grand" still needs clearer specification if we are to accept it as a generally negative denomination. And in seeking that clarification, we should be sensitive to the fact that, irrespective of the kinds of truth claims which they assert, the progressiveness and illuminating potential of theories is heavily context-dependent. For example, natural law theory's influence on liberation theology and positivism's basically constructionist stance and its critique of the authoritarian model of law and state implicit in some natural law theory constitute contributions with which many feminists would be sympathetic.

There are at least three elements to the idea of "grand" theory as a pejorative. The first objection is to theories which have pretensions to assert Truth (with a capital T!).[62] This may be "true" of all theories except for the most thoroughly deconstructive ones, but it is a relatively trivial "truth". For comprehensive theories of law can easily be reinterpreted as offering partial perspectives or insights—interpretations rather than "truths". In other words, whilst theories inevitably make an implicit claim to "truth" or "validity", it is up to us, the critical audience, to reconstruct the status of their claims, and in doing so to take on board such insights as they have rather than rejecting them in a wholesale way. If the core of the idea of grand theory lies in the status of its truth claims, this is perhaps something which feminism need not fear in any general way. For it may be argued that the very multiplicity of and controversy among "grand" theories purporting to have access to Truth or to give us the last word on reality are undermining to that status in a fairly effective way. The interpretivist reconstruct of such theories does indeed seem to be an important feminist move, but this should not rule out feminist jurisprudence. Furthermore, while *law's* pretensions to Truth or objective validity are clearly a central object of critique in feminist theory, it is not clear that feminist *jurisprudence* necessarily has to engage in the same pretensions. In this sense the burden of Smart's argument concerns feminist engagement with *law* rather than with *legal theory*.

The second theme which can be identified in the debate about "grand" theory is an objection to theories which are monolithic in the sense that they seek to reduce all aspects of women's oppression to one or two basic factors such as sexuality or, as in the case of early marxist feminism, a particular conception of class. This is indeed an important defect of some theories, but it does not apply to all theories which purport to have a broad scope. The search for a "universal" theory of law does not necessarily imply that it must be "universalising" or "totalising": it may in fact be eclectic, complex, pluralistic. For example, Tove Stang Dahl interprets the feminist jurisprudential project in a pluralistic and positive way, identifying a number of sites and modes of legal subordination of women, and engaging in a project of reconceptualisation of legal categories along feminist lines.[63]

Finally, a third objection is to the (high) degree of abstraction of "grand" theories. Again, this seems to me to be an important objection given that the move from concrete to abstract can indeed serve as a cover for the marginalisation or suppression of varying perspectives: abstraction can indeed serve totalisation. Yet this must be a question of degree. *Any* use of theoretical terms inevitably involves conceptualisation and hence a degree of abstraction; indeed this is an inevitable feature of the use of language. As we have already seen, Smart and other feminist theorists themselves clearly affirm the necessity for legitimacy

---

[61] See D. Rhode (1990) 42 Stanford L. Rev 617.
[62] *Cf.* Smart *op. cit.*, n. 35 pp. 71–2, 85–6.
[63] See *op. cit.*, n. 40. Her particular reconceptualisation is, I think, problematic, but much of her methodology is instructive.

of abstraction in the theoretical enterprise. The three aspects of "grand" theory, then, need to be looked at separately in the case of any candidate for the category.

### Against "Grand" Theory or Against "Centre-ing" Law?

It seems to me that the central object of Carol Smart's critique is not so much the idea of grand theory but rather her second concern—the importance which the project of feminist jurisprudence implicitly accords to law as a site of women's oppression and, most importantly, for feminist activism and reform. Smart has powerful arguments about the limitations of law as a feminist strategy. To the extent that we accept them, these arguments give us powerful political reasons not to expend too much energy on reconstructive legal theory. This is a very different issue from that of the status of theory itself. But Smart's political argument can be questioned. Her explicit acceptance of the importance of the critical project implicitly recognises, as the title of her book suggests, the importance of law as a means of entrenching, expressing and maintaining women's oppression. If law can be powerful in these ways, does not legal critique and change hold out some prospect of progress for women, even if not a panacea? The view that law is a relatively unimportant site for feminist intervention, and that we should be cautious in engaging with it, is itself informed by a set of theoretical views about the relative significance of different sites and modes of power, among which Smart emphasises the importance of law's claims to Truth and its high position in the "hierarchy of knowledges".[64] But this argument is not in itself sufficient to support the "de-centre-ing" of law in feminist theory and practice; this conclusion only follows if it is clear that *other* discourses or institutions exist or can be created which make a weaker claim to Truth than does law. Yet obvious possibilities such as institutions within the political sphere themselves engage in effective marginalising strategies which make them problematic in terms of feminist practice.

### The Problem of Induction from Theory to Practice

Whether or not it is appropriate to take a *general* position on the need for feminists to "de-centre" law in our approach to theory and practice, we need to avoid another potential slippage in the debate about feminist jurisprudence and legal reforms. This is a shift from a general argument about the need to "de-centre" law to a specific, and often powerful, critique of particular inductions from theory to practice in feminist legal scholarship. Perhaps the best example here is the debate around MacKinnon's and Dworkin's famous attempt to legislate against pornography by means of an ordinance which, among other things, sought to give individual women a civil right of action for the harms done to them by pornography as sex discrimination via the sexual objectification of women.[65] Smart, among others, has cogent criticisms of MacKinnon's induction from theory to practice.[66] Smart's critique has two dimensions: first, there is an argument about the kind of theory which MacKinnon develops—a monolithic, "grand" feminist jurisprudence which seeks to reduce all aspects of women's oppression to one dimension, and which treads dangerously close to a biologistic essentialism. The implication of this is something close to total hopelessness in terms of the prospects for feminist progress. On the other hand, there is a critique of MacKinnon's political strategy: even if we agreed with her analysis, would we want to affirm this particular kind of reformism?

Of course, this brings us back to the questions of the relation between theory

[64] Smart *op. cit*, n. 35, Ch. I.
[65] See *ante*, 1292.
[66] *Op. cit*, n. 35, Ch. 6.

and practice and between principle and strategy. The distinction which I have drawn between the two aspects of the critique of MacKinnon raises the converse possibility that even though we disagreed with her analysis, we might still see sense in her legal strategies. For example, despite its strategic dangers already discussed, one potential advantage of the anti-pornography campaign might well have been a contribution to opening up the legal process in a way which enables women to use it—both in the sense of having effective access to it, and in the sense of recognising the rights and claims it instantiates as responding to women's needs and therefore thinking of law as something which can be empowering to women as well as to men. More straightforwardly, I would argue that MacKinnon's campaign to have sexual harassment recognised as a legal wrong has been an important and in many ways effective feminist strategy.

I want to emphasise this distinction, because I think that it is most unlikely, given the centrally *political* impetus of feminism, that feminist lawyers will give up hope of the possibility of modest progress through legal change. What is more, it would be very unfortunate if we did give it up. As Smart herself argues, it would be a mistake to regard all legal reformist strategies as equally flawed. What we need is not an abandonment of the legal and political project, but rather the development of more sophisticated understandings of legal practices, their strengths and well as their evident and important limitations. This would include a theoretical understanding of how law relates to other powerful institutions and discourses. Doubtless this is an inelegantly eclectic view, but I would contend that feminist politics around law have room not only for critical analysis of the *status quo* but also for both pragmatic/strategic and utopian thinking and action. If I am right, it follows that we must be alive to the differences between strategy and ideal, and of the different ways in which they must be assessed.    [pp. 168–180]

## SUSAN MOLLER OKIN
### Is Multiculturalism Bad for Women?
(1999)[67]

Until the past few decades, minority groups—immigrants as well as indigenous peoples—were typically expected to assimilate into majority cultures. This assimilationist expectation is now often considered oppressive, and many Western countries are seeking to devise new policies that are more responsive to persistent cultural differences. The appropriate policies vary with context: countries such as England, with established churches or state-supported religious education, find it difficult to resist demands to extend state support to minority religious schools; countries such as France, with traditions of strictly secular public education, struggle over whether the clothing required by minority religions may be worn in the public schools. But one issue recurs across all contexts, though it has gone virtually unnoticed in current debate: what should be done when the claims of minority cultures or religions clash with the norm of gender equality that is at least formally endorsed by liberal states (however much they continue to violate it in their practices) [...]                                                      [p. 9]
    I think we [...] have been too quick to assume that feminism and multi-culturalism are both good things which are easily reconciled. I shall argue instead that there is considerable likelihood of tension between them—more precisely, between feminism and a multiculturalist commitment to group rights for minority cultures.                                                                   [p. 10]
    Demands for such group rights are growing—from indigenous native populations, minority ethnic or religious groups, and formerly colonized peoples (at

[67] [From J. Cohen, M. Howard and M. Nussbaum (eds), *Is Multiculturalism Bad for Women?* (1999).]

least when the latter immigrate to the former colonial state). These groups, it is argued, have their own "societal cultures" which—as Will Kymlicka, the foremost contemporary defender of cultural group rights, says—provide "members with meaningful ways of life across the full range of human activities, including social, educational, religious, recreational, and economic life, encompassing both public and private spheres."[68] Because societal cultures play so pervasive and fundamental a role in the lives of their members, and because such cultures are threatened with extinction, minority cultures should be protected by special rights. That, in essence, is the case for group rights.

Some proponents of group rights argue that even cultures that "flout the rights of [their individual members] in a liberal society"[69] should be accorded group rights or privileges if their minority status endangers the culture's continued existence. Others do not claim that all minority cultural groups should have special rights, but rather that such groups—even illiberal ones that violate their individual members' rights, requiring them to conform to group beliefs or norms—have the right to be "left alone" in a liberal society.[70] Both claims seem clearly inconsistent with the basic liberal value of individual freedom, which entails that group rights should not trump the individual rights of its members; thus I will not address the additional problems they present for feminists here.[71] But some defenders of multiculturalism confine their defense of group rights largely to groups that are internally liberal.[72] Even with these restrictions, feminists—everyone, that is, who endorses the moral equality of men and women—should remain skeptical. So I will argue. Most cultures are suffused with practices and ideologies concerning gender. Suppose, then, that a culture endorses and facilitates the control of men over women in various ways. Suppose, too, that there are fairly clear disparities in power between the sexes, such that the more powerful, male members are those who are generally in a position to determine and articulate the group's beliefs, practices, and interests. Under such conditions, group rights are potentially, and in many cases actually, antifeminist. They substantially limit the capacities of women and girls of that culture to live with human dignity equal to that of men and boys, and to live as freely chosen lives as they can.

Advocates of group rights for minorities within liberal states have not adequately addressed this simple critique of group rights, for at least two reasons. First, they tend to treat cultural groups as monoliths—to pay more attention to differences between and among groups than to differences within them. Specifically, they accord little or no recognition to the fact that minority cultural groups, like the societies in which they exist (though to a greater or lesser extent), are themselves *gendered*, with substantial differences in power and advantage between men and women. Second, advocates of group rights pay little or no attention to the private sphere. Some of the most persuasive liberal defenses of group rights urge that individuals need "a culture of their own," and that only within such a culture can people develop a sense of self-esteem or self-respect, as well as the capacity to decide what kind of life is good for them. But such arguments typically neglect both the different roles that cultural groups impose on their members and the context in which persons' senses of themselves and their capacities are

---

[68] Will Kymlicka, *Multicultural Citizenship: A Liberal Theory of Minority Rights* (1995), pp. 89, 76. See also Kymlicka, *Liberalism, Community, and Culture* (1989).

[69] Avishai Margalit and Moshe Halbertal, "Liberalism and the Right to Culture," *Social Research* 61, 3 (Fall 1994): 491.

[70] For example, Chandran Kukathas, "Are There Any Cultural Rights?," *Political Theory* 20, 1 (1992): 105–39.

[71] Okin, "Feminism and Multiculturalism: Some Tensions," *Ethics* 108, 4 (July 1998): 661–84.

[72] For example, Kymlicka, *Liberalism, Community, and Culture* and *Multicultural Citizenship* (esp. chap. 8).

first formed *and* in which culture is first transmitted—the realm of domestic or family life.

When we correct for these deficiencies by paying attention to internal differences and to the private arena, two particularly important connections between culture and gender come into sharp relief, both of which underscore the force of this simple critique of group rights. First, the sphere of personal, sexual, and reproductive life functions as a central focus of most cultures, a dominant theme in cultural practices and rules. Religious or cultural groups often are particularly concerned with "personal law"—the laws of marriage, divorce, child custody, division and control of family property, and inheritance.[73] As a rule, then, the defense of "cultural practices" is likely to have much greater impact on the lives of women and girls than on those of men and boys, since far more of women's time and energy goes into preserving and maintaining the personal, familial, and reproductive side of life. Obviously, culture is not only about domestic arrangements, but they do provide a major focus of most contemporary cultures. Home is, after all, where much of culture is practiced, preserved, and transmitted to the young. On the other hand, the distribution of responsibilities and power at home has a major impact on who can participate in and influence the more public parts of the cultural life, where rules and regulations about both public and private life are made. The more a culture requires or expects of women in the domestic sphere, the less opportunity they have of achieving equality with men in either sphere.

The second important connection between culture and gender is that most cultures have as one of their principal aims the control of women by men. Consider, for example, the founding myths of Greek and Roman antiquity, and of Judaism, Christianity, and Islam: they are rife with attempts to justify the control and subordination of women. These myths consist of a combination of denials of women's role in reproduction; appropriations by men of the power to reproduce themselves; characterizations of women as overly emotional, untrustworthy, evil, or sexually dangerous; and refusals to acknowledge mothers' rights over the disposition of their children.[74] Think of Athena, sprung from the head of Zeus, and of Romulus and Remus, reared without a human mother. Or Adam, made by a male God, who then (at least according to one of the two biblical versions of the story) created Eve out of part of Adam. Consider Eve, whose weakness led Adam astray. Think of all those endless "begats" in Genesis, where women's primary role in reproduction is completely ignored, or of the textual justifications for polygamy, once practiced in Judaism, still practiced in many parts of the Islamic world and (though illegally) by Mormons in some parts of the United States. Consider, too, the story of Abraham, a pivotal turning point in the development of monotheism.[75] God commands Abraham to sacrifice "his" beloved son. Abraham prepares to do exactly what God asks of him, without even telling, much less asking, Isaac's mother, Sarah. Abraham's absolute obedience to God makes him the central, fundamental model of faith for all three religions. [...]                                                                                     [pp. 11–14]

Many of the world's traditions and cultures, including those practiced within formerly conquered or colonized nation-states—which certainly encompasses most of the peoples of Africa, the Middle East, Latin America, and Asia—are quite distinctly patriarchal. They too have elaborate patterns of socialization, rituals, matrimonial customs, and other cultural practices (including systems of

---

[73] See, for example, Kirti Singh, "Obstacles to Womens" Rights in India," in *Human Rights of Women: National and International Perspectives*, ed. Rebecca J. Cook (1994), pp. 375–96, esp. pp. 378–89.

[74] See, for example, Arvind Sharma, ed., *Women in World Religions* (1987); John Stratton Hawley, ed., *Fundamentalism and Gender* (1994).

[75] See Carol Delaney, *Abraham on Trial* (1998).

property ownership and control of resources) aimed at bringing women's sexuality and reproductive capabilities under men's control. Many such practices make it virtually impossible for women to choose to live independently of men, to be celibate or lesbian, or to decide not to have children.

Those who practice some of the most controversial of such customs—clitoridectomy, polygamy, the marriage of children or marriages that are otherwise coerced—sometimes explicitly defend them as necessary for controlling women and openly acknowledge that the customs persist at men's insistence. In an interview with *New York Times* reporter Celia Dugger, practitioners of clitoridectomy in Côte d'Ivoire and Togo explained that the practice "helps insure a girl's virginity before marriage and fidelity afterward by reducing sex to a marital obligation." As a female exciser said, "[a] woman's role in life is to care for her children, keep house and cook. If she has not been cut, [she] might think about her own sexual pleasure."[76] In Egypt, where a law banning female genital cutting was recently overturned by a court, supporters of the practice say it "curbs a girl's sexual appetite and makes her more marriageable."[77] Moreover, in such societies, many women have no economically viable alternative to marriage.

In polygamous cultures, too, men readily acknowledge that the practice accords with their self-interest and is a means of controlling women. As a French immigrant from Mali said in a recent interview: "When my wife is sick and I don't have another, who will care for me? ... [O]ne wife on her own is trouble. When there are several, they are forced to be polite and well behaved. If they misbehave, you threaten that you'll take another wife." Women apparently see polygamy very differently. French African immigrant women deny that they like polygamy and say that not only are they given "no choice" in the matter, but their female forebears in Africa did not like it either.[78] As for child or otherwise coerced marriage: this practice is clearly a way not only of controlling whom the girls or young women marry but also of ensuring that they are virgins at the time of marriage and, often, of enhancing the husband's power by creating a significant age difference between husbands and wives.

Consider, too, the practice—common in much of Latin America, rural Southeast Asia and parts of West Africa—of pressuring or even requiring a rape victim to marry the rapist. In many such cultures [...] rapists are legally exonerated if they marry or (in some cases) simply offer to marry their victims. Clearly, rape is not seen in these cultures primarily as a violent assault on the girl or woman herself but rather as a serious injury to her family and its honor. By marrying his victim, the rapist can help restore the family's honor and relieve it of a daughter who, as "damaged goods," has become unmarriageable. In Peru, this barbaric law was amended for the worse in 1991: the codefendants in a gang rape now are all exonerated if just one of them offers to marry the victim (feminists are fighting to get the law repealed). As a Peruvian taxi driver explained: "Marriage is the right and proper thing to do after a rape. A raped woman is a used item. No one wants her. At least with this law the woman will get a husband."[79] It is difficult to imagine a worse fate for a woman than being pressured into marrying the man who has raped her. But worse fates do exist in some cultures—notably in Pakistan and parts of the Arab Middle East, where women who bring rape charges quite frequently are charged themselves with the serious Muslim offense of *zina*, or sex outside of marriage. Law allows for the whipping or imprisonment of such women, and culture condones the killing or pressuring into suicide of a raped woman by relatives intent on restoring the family's honor. ...][pp. 14–16]

---

[76] *New York Times*, 5 October 1996, A4. The role that older women in such cultures play in perpetuating these practices is important but complex and cannot be addressed here.
[77] *New York Times*, 26 June 1997, A9.
[78] *International Herald Tribune*, 2 February 1996, News section.
[79] *New York Times*, 12 March 1997, A8.

## Group Rights?

Most cultures are patriarchal, then, and many (though not all) of the cultural minorities that claim group rights are more patriarchal than the surrounding cultures. So it is no surprise that the cultural importance of maintaining control over women shouts out to us in the examples given in the literature on cultural diversity and group rights within liberal states. Yet, though it shouts out, it is seldom explicitly addressed.[80]

A paper by Sebastian Poulter about the legal rights and culture-based claims of various immigrant groups and Gypsies in contemporary Britain mentions the roles and status of women as "one very clear example" of the "clash of cultures."[81] In it, Poulter discusses claims put forward by members of such groups for special legal treatment on account of their cultural differences. A few are nongender-related claims; for example, a Muslim schoolteacher's being allowed to be absent part of Friday afternoons in order to pray, and Gypsy children's being subject to less stringent schooling requirements than others on account of their itinerant lifestyle. But the vast majority of the examples concern gender inequalities: child marriages, forced marriages, divorce systems biased against women, polygamy, and clitoridectomy. Almost all of the legal cases discussed by Poulter stemmed from women's or girls' claims that their individual rights were being truncated or violated by the practices of their own cultural groups. In a recent article by political philosopher Amy Gutmann, fully half her examples have to do with gender issues—polygamy, abortion, sexual harassment, clitoridectomy, and purdah.[82] This is quite typical in the literature on subnational multicultural issues. Moreover, the same linkage between culture and gender occurs in practice in the international arena, where women's human rights are often rejected by the leaders of countries or groups of countries as incompatible with their various cultures.[83]

Similarly, the overwhelming majority of "cultural defenses" that are increasingly being invoked in U.S. criminal cases involving members of cultural minorities are connected with gender—in particular with male control over women and children.[84] Occasionally, cultural defenses are cited in explanation of expectable violence among men or the ritual sacrifice of animals. Much more common, however, is the argument that, in the defendant's cultural group, women are not human beings of equal worth but rather subordinates whose primary (if not only) function is to serve men sexually and domestically. Indeed, the four types of cases in which cultural defenses have been used most successfully are: (1) kidnap and rape by Hmong men who claim that their actions are part of their cultural practice of *zij pojniam*, or "marriage by capture"; (2) wife-murder by immigrants from Asian and Middle Eastern countries whose wives have either committed adultery or treated their husbands in a servile way; (3) murder of children by Japanese or Chinese mothers who have also tried but failed to kill themselves, and who claim that because of their cultural backgrounds the shame of their

---

[80] See, however, Bhikhu Parekh's "Minority Practices and Principles of Toleration," *International Migration Review* (April 1996): 251–84, in which he directly addresses and critiques a number of cultural practices that devalue the status of women.

[81] Sebastian Poulter, "Ethnic Minority Customs, English Law, and Human Rights," *International and Comparative Law Quarterly* 36, 3 (1987): 589–615.

[82] Amy Gutmann, "The Challenge of Multiculturalism in Political Ethics," *Philosophy and Public Affairs* 22, 3 (Summer 1993): 171–204.

[83] Mahnaz Afkhami, ed., *Faith and Freedom: Women's Human Rights in the Muslim World* (1995); Valentine M. Moghadam, ed., *Identity Politics and Women: Cultural Reassertions and Feminisms in International Perspective* (1994).

[84] For one of the best accounts of this, and for legal citations for the cases mentioned below, see Doriane Lambelet Coleman, "Individualizing Justice through Multiculturalism: The Liberals' Dilemma," *Columbia Law Review* 96 (1996): 1093–1167.

husbands' infidelity drove them to the culturally condoned practice of mother-child suicide; and (4) in France—though not yet in the United States, in part because the practice was criminalized only in 1996—clitoridectomy. In a number of such cases, expert testimony about the accused's or defendant's cultural background has resulted in dropped or reduced charges, culturally based assessments of *mens rea*, or significantly reduced sentences. In a well-known recent case in the United States, an immigrant from rural Iraq married his two daughters, aged 13 and 14, to two of his friends, aged 28 and 34. Subsequently, when the older daughter ran away with her 20-year-old boyfriend, the father sought the help of the police in finding her. When they located her, they charged the father with child abuse and the two husbands and boyfriend with statutory rape. The Iraqis' defense is based in part on their cultural marriage practices.[85]

As the four examples show, the defendants are not always male, nor the victims always female. Both a Chinese immigrant man in New York who battered his wife to death for committing adultery and a Japanese immigrant woman in California who drowned her children and tried to drown herself because her husband's adultery had shamed the family relied on cultural defenses to win reduced charges (from first-degree murder to second-degree murder or involuntary manslaughter). It might seem, then, that the cultural defense was biased toward the male in the first case and the female in the second. But though defendants of different sexes were cited, in both cases, the cultural message is similarly gender-biased: women (and children, in the second case) are ancillary to men and should bear the blame and the shame for any departure from monogamy. Whoever is guilty of the infidelity, the wife suffers: in the first case, by being brutally killed on account of her husband's rage at her shameful infidelity; in the second, by being so shamed and branded such a failure by his infidelity that she is driven to kill herself and her children. Again, the idea that girls and women are first and foremost sexual servants of men—that their virginity before marriage and fidelity within it are their preeminent virtues—emerges in many of the statements made in defense of cultural practices.

Western majority cultures, largely at the urging of feminists, have recently made substantial efforts to preclude or limit excuses for brutalizing women. Well within living memory, American men were routinely held less accountable for killing their wives if they explained their conduct as a crime of passion, driven as they were by jealousy and rage over the wife's infidelity. Also not long ago, female rape victims who did not have completely celibate pasts or who did not struggle—even when to do so meant endangering themselves—were routinely blamed for the attack. Things have now changed to some extent, and doubts about the turn toward cultural defenses undoubtedly are prompted in part by a concern to preserve recent advances. Another concern is that such defenses can distort perceptions of minority cultures by drawing excessive attention to negative aspects of them. But perhaps the primary concern is that, by failing to protect women and sometimes children of minority cultures from male and sometimes maternal violence, cultural defenses violate women's and children's rights to equal protection of the laws.[86] When a woman from a more patriarchal culture comes to the United States (or some other Western, basically liberal, state), why should she be less protected from male violence than other women are? Many women from minority cultures have protested the double standard that is being applied on behalf of their aggressors.[87]

---

[85] *New York Times*, 2 December 1996, A6.
[86] See Coleman, "Individualizing Justice through Multiculturalism."
[87] See, for example, Nilda Rimonte, "A Question of Culture: Cultural Approval of Violence against Women in the Asian-Pacific Community and the Cultural Defense," *Stanford Law Review* 43 (1991): 1311–26.

## Liberal Defense

Despite all this evidence of cultural practices that control and subordinate women, none of the prominent defenders of multicultural group rights has adequately or even directly addressed the troubling connections between gender and culture or the conflicts that arise so commonly between feminism and multiculturalism. Will Kymlicka's discussion is, in this respect, representative.

Kymlicka's arguments for group rights are based on the rights of individuals and confine such privileges and protection to cultural groups that are internally liberal. Following John Rawls, Kymlicka emphasizes the fundamental importance of self-respect in a person's life. He argues that membership in a "rich and secure cultural structure,"[88] with its own language and history, is essential both for the development of self-respect and for giving persons a context in which they can develop the capacity to make choices about how to lead their lives. Cultural minorities need special rights, then, because their cultures may otherwise be threatened with extinction, and cultural extinction would be likely to undermine the self-respect and freedom of group members. Special rights, in short, put minorities on an equal footing with the majority.

The value of freedom plays an important role in Kymlicka's argument. As a result, except in rare circumstances of cultural vulnerability, a group that claims special rights must govern itself by recognizably liberal principles, neither infringing on the basic liberties of its own members by placing internal restrictions on them nor discriminating among them on grounds of sex, race, or sexual preference.[89] This requirement is of great importance to a consistently liberal justification of group rights, because a "closed" or discriminatory culture cannot provide the context for individual development that liberalism requires, and because otherwise collective rights might result in subcultures of oppression within and facilitated by liberal societies. As Kymlicka says, "To inhibit people from questioning their inherited social roles can condemn them to unsatisfying, even oppressive lives."[90]

As Kymlicka acknowledges, this requirement of internal liberalism rules out the justification of group rights for the "many fundamentalists of all political and religious stripes who think that the best community is one in which all but their preferred religious, sexual, or aesthetic practices are outlawed." For the promotion and support of *these* cultures undermines "the very reason we had for being concerned with cultural membership—that it allows for meaningful individual choice."[91] But the examples I cited earlier suggest that far fewer minority cultures than Kymlicka seems to think will be able to claim group rights under his liberal justification. Though they may not impose their beliefs or practices on others, and though they may appear to respect the basic civil and political liberties of women and girls, many cultures do not, especially in the private sphere, treat them with anything like the same concern and respect with which men and boys are treated, or allow them to enjoy the same freedoms. Discrimination against and control of the freedom of females are practiced, to a greater or lesser extent, by virtually all cultures, past and present, but especially by religious ones and those that look to the past—to ancient texts or revered traditions—for guidelines or rules about how to live in the contemporary world. Sometimes more patriarchal minority cultures exist in the midst of less patriarchal majority cultures; sometimes the reverse is true. In either case, the degree to which each culture is patriarchal and its willingness to become less so should be crucial factors in judgment about the justifications of group rights—once women's equality is taken seriously.

---

[88]  Kymlicka, *Liberalism, Community, and Culture*, p. 165.
[89]  *ibid.*, pp. 168–72, 195–98.
[90]  Kymlicka, *Multicultural Citizenship*, p. 92.
[91]  Kymlicka, *Liberalism, Community, and Culture*, pp. 171–72.

Clearly, Kymlicka regards cultures that discriminate overtly and formally against women—by denying them education or the right to vote or hold office—as not deserving special rights.[92] But sex discrimination is often far less overt. In many cultures, strict control of women is enforced in the private sphere by the authority of either actual or symbolic fathers, often acting through, or with the complicity of, the older women of the culture. In many cultures in which women's basic civil rights and liberties are formally assured, discrimination practiced against women and girls within the household not only severely constrains their choices but also seriously threatens their well-being and even their lives.[93] And such sex discrimination—whether severe or more mild—often has very powerful *cultural* roots.

Although Kymlicka rightly objects, then, to the granting of group rights to minority cultures that practice overt sex discrimination, his arguments for multiculturalism fail to register what he acknowledges elsewhere: that the subordination of women is often informal and private, and that virtually no culture in the world today, minority or majority, could pass his "no sex discrimination" test if it were applied in the private sphere.[94] Those who defend group rights on liberal grounds need to address these very private, culturally reinforced kinds of discrimination. For surely self-respect and self-esteem require more than simple membership in a viable culture. Surely it is *not* enough for one to be able to "question one's inherited social roles" and to have the capacity to make choices about the life one wants to lead, that one's culture be protected. At least as important to the development of self-respect and self-esteem is *our place within our culture*. And at least as pertinent to our capacity to question our social roles is *whether our culture instills in us and forces on us particular social roles*. To the extent that a girl's culture is patriarchal, in both these respects her healthy development is endangered.

## Part of the Solution?

It is by no means clear, then, from a feminist point of view, that minority group rights are "part of the solution." They may well exacerbate the problem. In the case of a more patriarchal minority culture in the context of a less patriarchal majority culture, no argument can be made on the basis of self-respect or freedom that the female members of the culture have a clear interest in its preservation. Indeed, they *might* be much better off if the culture into which they were born were either to become extinct (so that its members would become integrated into the less sexist surrounding culture) or, preferably, to be encouraged to alter itself so as to reinforce the equality of women—at least to the degree to which this value is upheld in the majority culture. Other considerations would, of course, need to be taken into account, such as whether the minority group speaks a language that requires protection, and whether the group suffers from prejudices such as racial discrimination. But it would take significant factors weighing in the other direction to counterbalance evidence that a culture severely constrains women's choices or otherwise undermines their well-being.[95] [. . .]   [pp. 17–23]

---

[92] Kymlicka, *Multicultural Citizenship*, pp. 153, 165.

[93] See, for example, Amartya Sen, "More Than One Hundred Million Women Are Missing," *New York Review of Books*, 20 December 1990.

[94] Will Kymlicka, *Contemporary Political Philosophy: An Introduction* (1990), pp. 239–62.

[95] [The book contains incisive critiques. See also L. Volpp [2001] 101 Columbia Law Review 1181].

# 16

## POSTMODERNIST JURISPRUDENCE

We have already seen strands of postmodernist thinking in the chapters on critical legal studies and feminist jurisprudence. Though both of these "schools" can be seen as "discrete", much of both of them had by the end of the 1980s become submerged in postmodernism.

### POSTMODERNISM AND MODERNISM

Postmodernism is "a notoriously ambiguous concept."[1] Since it is *post* modern, it seems it comes after the "modern," but is it a culmination of modernity, a phase in late modernity, a continuation of modernity by other means? And, as *modern* "it refers back and claims to overcome a historical period (modernity), or a system of thought and regime of knowledge (modern), or a cultural and artistic movement (modernism)."[2]

Both categorisations or periodisations were first used in the world of art and architecture, only later influencing philosophy, social theory, history, politics and ethics. Postmodernist jurisprudence is a late player on the postmodernist stage: there was little participation by jurists in the postmodernist movement until the late 1980s.

To understand postmodernism it is first necessary to grasp what is meant by modernism. But this too can be seen in different ways. One way of understanding modernism is to see it as "a rage against existing order."[3] Modernism is said to exalt "the attack on form, the belief that an ability to go beyond, to transcend, to break through, is the *raison d'être* of art and perhaps of life."[4] The Realist project was part of this.[5] Thus, they showed that the "form" of rights was different from what had been assumed,[6] and that the "form" of orthodox reasoning, particularly the case method of legal education, overlooked considerations of value and

---

[1] See C. Douzinas and R. Warrington, *Postmodern Jurisprudence* (1991), p. 14. An excellent account of the origins and themes of postmodernist jurisprudence is S. Feldman, *American Legal Thought from Premodernism to Postmodernism* (2000), Chap. 5.

[2] Douzinas and Warrington, *ibid.*, pp. 14–15.

[3] See J. Boyle (1991) 62 Univ. of Colorado L.Rev. 489, 501.

[4] *ibid.* And see also M. Berman, *All That Is Solid Melts Into Air* (1982).

[5] See D. Luban's "Legal Modernism" (1986) 84 Michigan L.Rev. 1656.

[6] See J. Singer (1982) Wisconsin L.Rev. 975

ignored social science data.[7] So too was some of the early "Crit" writing: for example, that challenging the public-private dichotomy.[8] There was a desire to get beyond form to function: a belief that by getting rid of "transcendental nonsense,"[9] access to the true functions of each rule would be opened. But, as Boyle points out:

> "After this critique of the limiting qualities of form comes a certain fear of the abyss. Wait a minute—if we trash this, what is left? Doesn't this lead to nihilism? Doesn't this even lead to fascism? And just as the early modernist artists were accused of fomenting fascism, of breaking down Western civilization, of undermining the cultural forms that uphold all that is good and just, so the legal realists were accused of exactly the same thing: of breaking down the structure of society, of preparing the way for some sort of awful anarchy or revolution."[10]

Looked at in this way postmodernism is the realisation that there is "no beyond," no place "outside of the forms."[11] And this can be celebrated as an "exhilarating moment of rapture" for it "defies the system, suspects all totalising thought and homogeneity and opens space for the marginal, the different and the 'other' ".[12] It stands for "flux, dispersal, plurality and localism."[13] There is "a cluster of styles, strategies, preoccupations, texts, readings, objects and performances."[14]

According to Jennifer Wicke, there are more than 31 flavours of postmodernism! And so, the "decision about what postmodernism is remains as fraught as ever."[15]

## THE DEATH OF THE SUBJECT

One important postmodernist theme invokes the instability or in-determinateness of the "subject"[16]: references are often made to the "death of the subject."[17] But this in itself seems to embrace different critiques. One emphasises the inadequacy of traditional social categories (women,[18] gays, blacks or African-Americans, consumers). Living in different

---

[7] See F. Cohen (1935) 35 Columbia L.Rev. 809, and see *ante*, 1215.

[8] See D. Kennedy (1982) 130 Univ. of Pennsylvania L.Rev. 1349; M. Horwitz (1982) 130 Univ. of Pennsylvania L.Rev. 1423; K. Klare (1982) 130 Univ. of Pennsylavania L.Rev. 1358; F. Olsen (1983) 96 Harvard L.Rev. 1497. See also, 1293–1294.

[9] In Felix Cohen's phrase (*op. cit.*, n. 7).

[10] *Op. cit.*, n. 3, pp. 502–503. And see E. Purcell, *The Crisis of Democratic Theory: Scientific Naturalism and The Problem of Value* (1973), pp. 159–178.

[11] *Op. cit.*, n. 3, p. 503.

[12] *Op. cit.*, n. 1, p. 15.

[13] *ibid.*

[14] *Per* Dale Jamieson (1991) 62 Univ. of Colorado L.Rev. 577, 578.

[15] (1991) 62 Univ. of Colorado L.Rev. 455, 456 and *post*, 1429.

[16] And see J. Schroeder (1992) 47 Univ. of Miami L. Rev. 1, and R. Coombe (1991) 69 Texas L.R. 1853. See also J. Schroeder, *The Vestal and The Fasces* (1998).

[17] For example by J. Lacan, *Ecrits: A Selection* (1977).

[18] And see the discussion of "essentialism" in Chap. 15. And see the discussion of "race", *post*, 1495–1496.

worlds simultaneously, social identity is said to be fractured, and there is no schematism or rule for reconciliation. Another penetrates deeper—into the psyche of the individual. In this image, individuals are themselves "sites of conflicting narratives and incommensurable points of view. To be a person is to be a more or less conventional location for the eddys and cross-currents of various words, images, pictures, and other representations that intersect in some way at some given point in metaphysical space."[19]

These two critiques find their sources similarly, in fragmentation and differences, rather than unity and university. The one is, however, clearly in tension with the other. The first deconstructs social categories, seeming to presuppose individual identity and agency with individuals as instigators of political change: the second, in rejecting individualism, rejects the individual as the fulcrum upon which change could take place.

## The "Subject" and The Legal System

One result of this approach is to shift the focus of jurisprudence from a study of the legal system and its properties (order, coherence, determinacy, etc.) to "the nature of the legal subject who apprehends the legal system and judges it to have these properties."[20] What Balkin has called "the nature of legal understanding," becomes central to "jurisprudential enquiry." Since the legal subject is socially constructed, the ways this social construction has led the legal subject to understand the legal system also becomes crucial. On this view, standard jurisprudential accounts misdescribe the nature of the legal system, ignoring its necessary connections to human understanding. And, equally importantly, it makes "the subject's contribution to the legal system invisible. It cuts off possible avenues of inquiry about the 'we' who understand the law, thus shielding the subject from intellectual scrutiny."[21]

As Balkin points out, even a theory of law such as Dworkin's which assumes legal understanding to be an interpretive activity confines this to the view of the subject making arguments within the legal system. Dworkin does not countenance jurisprudential critique of a legal

---

[19] *Op. cit.*, n. 14, p. 583–584.
[20] *Per* J. M. Balkin (1993) 103 Yale L.J. 105, 106. Schlag (and *see post*, 1440), has been at the forefront with Balkin of this trend. See Schlag (1987) 76 Geo. L. J. 37; (1990) 43 Stanford L.Rev. 167; (1991) 139 Univ. of Pennsylvania L.Rev.801 and (1991) 69 Texas L.Rev. 1627. See also M. Dan-Cohen (1992) 105 Harv. L.Rev 959; S. Winter (1990) 78 California L.Rev. 1441, R. Coombe (1989) 34 McGill L.J. 603 and (1991) 69 Texas L.Rev. 1853; D. Cornell (1988) 136 Univ. of Pennsylvania L.Rev. 1135.
[21] *Per* Balkin, *op. cit.*, n. 20, p. 109. See also Schlag (1991) 69 Texas L.Rev. 1627, at 1633, 1729.

interpreter's views on sociological, psychological or ideological grounds.[22] For Dworkin,

> "the legal subject makes her appearance at the beginning of legal theory only to be shielded, protected, isolated and forgotten thereafter. Once the legal subject has been installed as the interpreter and hence arbiter of the nature of law, psychological and ideological contributions to what she interprets are wholly beyond the bounds of jurisprudential scrutiny. All arguments must be directed instead to the nature of the object she constructs."[23]

The centrality of the "internal perspective" can be traced to Hart's *Concept of Law*.[24] But Balkin and others argue instead for a "critical perspective," "one that employs ideological critique to reflect on our internal experience of law."[25] This does not reject the internal perspective: it makes it a central object of study. A critical perspective:

> "takes seriously the contributions of subjectivity to the nature of law; it treats the sociology of knowledge as a full partner in the jurisprudential enterprise. Instead of taking for granted the primacy of the internal viewpoint of parti-cipants in the legal system, [it] asks how this internal experience comes about. It recognizes in the internal experience of legal norms an effect whose causes must be unearthed and reflected upon."[26]

It is Balkin's view, that our subjectivity affects the process of legal understanding in ways that conventional jurisprudential discourse either de-emphasises or, more commonly, ignores. He points to three dimen-sions of this.

First, subjects bring *"purposes"*[27] to their understanding of law: legal understanding is a "purposive *activity* of subjects."[28] Balkin sees the internal perspective as a plurality of such perspectives, taking account of the various activities that different participants engage in when "under-standing law." There is, the claims, "a network of overlapping and interconnected forms of legal understanding, in which hierarchical status and relationships of dependence are provisional and much less clear."[29] Secondly, judgements about the law rest on the "nature of the self," "they are ... shaped by the self's psychological needs."[30] Thirdly, sub-jectivity is important to the study of law because "legal understanding is also a source of power over the legal subject."[31] If we wish to understand

[22] See *A Matter of Principle* (1985), p. 177 ("skepticism brought to an enterprise from the outside ... which engages no arguments of the sort the enterprises requires ... can make no difference to our efforts to understand and improve interpretation, art and law"). And see *Law's Empire* (1986), pp. 85–90, and *ante*, 721.
[23] *Per* J. M. Balkin, *op. cit.*, n. 20, p. 110.
[24] *Ante*, 339. And see J. Raz (1992) 72 Boston Univ. L.Rev. 273, 292.
[25] *Op. cit.*, n. 20, p. 110.
[26] *ibid.*, pp. 110–111. See also B. Tamanaha, *Realistic Socio-Legal Theory* (1997), Chap. 6.
[27] *ibid.*, p. 112.
[28] *ibid.*
[29] *ibid.*
[30] *ibid.*, p. 113.
[31] *ibid.*

legal understanding, "we must recognise not only the effects that our understanding has on the objects we construct, but the effects that the act of understanding has on us."[32] Jurisprudence envisions power in political terms[33] and misses the power over the subject that arises from the act of understanding itself. Balkin maintains that "legal understanding is something that happens to us and changes us. It is a type of receptivity, of vulnerability, which affects us as much as it affects the law we attempt to understand. Legal understanding thus makes the legal subject a locus of ideological power."[34] An important consequence of this is that jurisprudence should properly study the legal subject, a striking omission in orthodox jurisprudential enquiry.

## LAWYERS, THEIR CLIENTS AND THEIR SCHOLARSHIP

Another thread to postmodernist jurisprudence is its challenge to the traditional understanding of the lawyer-client relationship. A good example of this is in the writing of Felstiner and Sarat.[35] Orthodoxy sees the relationship either as conceived by predefined roles or arising from the actions of autonomous individuals. They argue to the contrary that the relationship is "always constrained yet contingent ... limited yet subject to constant transformation through negotiation".[36]

Where traditional jurisprudence concentrates on doctrine, postmodernist jurists are more concerned to see law from the perspective of cultural and social studies. This is common, but not unique, amongst those who espouse "outsider jurisprudence".[37] A good example—not drawn from "outsider jurisprudence"—is Balkin's discussion of modern constitutionalism in which he explores the ways postmodern culture and technology have affected law as an institution. He asks:

> "What effect has the rise of mass media and the industrialization of symbolic forms had on the way that the public understands their legal rights and their ability to participate in the legal system? One might well invent, by analogy to the phenomenon of 'sound bites', the concept of 'law bites', or symbols of the legal system that have become the common cultural coin of the general public ... Mass broadcast of American police shows (and later *L.A. Law*) has apparently altered the public's perception of the criminal and civil justice system ... These symbolic representations of law become the common forms of discourse and benchmarks of expectation about law among the lay public".[38]

---

[32] *ibid.*
[33] From Austin's sovereign to Marx's dominant class.
[34] *Op.cit.*, p. 113.
[35] (1992) 77 Cornell L.R. 1447
[36] According to Feldman, *op. cit.*, note 1, above, p. 167.
[37] For example, Critical Race Theory (see Chap. 17).
[38] (1992) 90 Michigan L.R. 1966, 1978. See also S.E. Merry (1992) 37 New York Law School L.R. 209.

Feldman points out that "postmodern legal scholars frequently ignore modernist fences as they jump from place to place, from discipline to discipline, as if they were following a contingent and evolving path of hypertext links on the World Wide Web".[39]


## A POLITICAL AGENDA

Postmodernism can be seen as a strategy for liberating "suppressed narratives and voices drowned out by univocal projections of master narratives ..." Postmodern critique, it is argued, "illuminates the underside of master narratives, thereby exposing the subordination and marginality of alternative social visions whose relegation to the status of *exception* to the rule, *counter*-tradition or *minority* perspective can no longer be objectively justified."[40] A major theme in postmodernism is subversion, the commitment to undermine dominant discourse. Postmodernists believe that the potential for subversive struggle is particularly propitious given the discrediting of Marxism, the instabilities of late capitalism and the contradictions of the bureaucratic Welfare State. These faults and fissures are seen as a source of resistance and freedom.[41] Postmodernists "look to new forms of politics that go beyond emancipation because the 'enemies', if they exist at all, are no longer the bourgeoisie or the boss so much as the bureaucracy, centralized government and 'democratically' elected representatives."[42]

It is argued that change will be brought about through small-scale transformation. Boyle[43] maintains that, by increasing the plasticity of social structures, the state itself will be converted from a source of stability to a source of change: equality and rights discourse[44] play a fundamental role in reconstructing collective identities. Once the principle of equality is accepted in one sphere, there will be a demand for it in other areas too and the structures of late capitalism will be subverted from within. By "within" is meant from "below." The goals of postmodern politics are stated in terms of a radical and a plural democracy. According to Aronowitz[45] the contemporary state, reflecting the logic of modernity, is characterised by extreme centralising tendencies: it is colonising, totalising, bureaucratic. By way of contrast, the postmodern state is minimalist because radical democracy depends on the

---

[39] See Feldman, above, n. 1, p. 168. And see G. Edward White (1994) 6 Yale J. Law and Humanities 1.
[40] *Per* A.E. Cook (1992) 26 New England Univ. L.Rev. 751, 754. See also the discussion of Critical Race Theory in Chap. 17, *post*.
[41] See E. Laclau and C. Mouffe, *Hegemony and Socialist Strategy* (1985), pp. 36–37.
[42] *Per* P. Rosenau, *Post-Modernism and The Social Sciences* (1992), p. 146.
[43] (1985) 98 Harvard Law Rev. 1066.
[44] See Crenshaw, *post*, 1509. On the question of what kind of rights see the discussion of Unger, *ante*, 1221. See, further, Fudge and Glasbeek (1992) 1 *Social and Legal Studies* 45 and *cf.* Herman (1993) 2 *Social and Legal Studies* 25.
[45] "Postmodern and Politics" in A. Ross (ed.), *Universal Abandon? The Politics of Post modernism* (1988), p. 48.

proliferation of public spaces where social agents become increasingly capable of self-management.

Radical pluralism can amount to nothing more than unchecked relativism. Deconstruction does not necessarily lead to beneficent outcomes. Two strategies can be used to overcome this problem. One, associated with Habermas,[46] argues that through rational discourse, rational agreement can be reached which transcends the immediate interests of the participants, and only through reason can humanist values be preserved from harmful forces. But postmodernists reject the notion that politics can generate another meta-narrative or that consensus can be anything other than temporary. A second strategy is associated with the revival of pragmatism.[47] Pragmatism attracts postmodernists for several reasons. It rejects foundationalism: knowledge is radically contingent; the test of knowledge is efficacy; thinking is instrumental, functional, problem-solving. Secondly, in its contemporary re-interpretation at least, pragmatism is progressive, emancipatory and democratic. Pragmatists are concerned with the relationship of knowledge and power and the ways in which discourse, whether in science, politics or ethics, is linked to structures of domination. When pragmatists ask whether a particular practice works, "we must ask ourselves, 'works *for whom?*' Who benefits and who loses from existing political, economical and legal structures?"[48] As "cultural criticism",[49] which locates politics in the everyday experience of ordinary people, there are obvious attractions for postmodernists. On the other hand, a penchant for alluding to "common sense"[50]—all-to-easily identified with the *status quo*—means the commitment is far from wholehearted or universal. Further, there is a tendency for pragmatists to take the "standpoint"[51] of the outsider, thus losing sight of the point of view of the insider. And, as Morawetz states: "ultimately, all of us experience ourselves as insiders for whom objectivity, or rational deployment of strategies for arriving at what we regard as truth, matters."[52]

POSTMODERN LAW: POSTMODERN STATE

Postmodernism is also a response to, what Habermas called, the "legitimation crisis."[53] It is argued that the modern bureaucratic state has

---

[46] *The Theory of Communicative Action* (1984), vol. 2. See also *Between Facts and Norms* (1997), and *ante*, 969.

[47] See, in particular, R. Rorty, *Consequences of Pragmatism* (1982) and S.D. Smith (1990) 100 Yale L.J. 409; C. West, *The American Evasion of Philosophy* (1989); T. Grey (1989) 41 Stanford L.Rev. 787; M. Radin (1990) 63 S. California L.Rev. 1699 (and other articles in this symposium), P. Swan (1989) 12 Dalhousie L.J. 349. See also, *ante*, 1004.

[48] *Per* J. Singer (1990) 63 S. California L.Rev. 1821, 1841.

[49] *Per* C. West, *op. cit.*, n. 47, p. 213.

[50] And see Singer, *op. cit.*, n. 48, West, *op. cit.*, n. 42, and Radin, *op. cit.*, n. 42.

[51] And see Twining, *ante*, 1029 and Bartlett, *ante*, 1370.

[52] (1992) 141 Univ. of Pennsylvania L.Rev. 371, 445.

[53] On which see Habermas's book with the title.

become dysfunctional, either because it has "colonized other life-worlds,"[54] or because it has inappropriately interfered with the functioning of other subsystems.[55] The result has been inefficiencies in managing economic and social problems and the distortion of human relations.[56]

The postmodern alternative converts the state into an "absent structure" and makes possible "the autonomy of law as a system of social regulation."[57] There is a new emphasis on legal pluralism. This "decenters the state by pointing to the plurality of legal orders, both state and non-state existing in the same political space."[58] The state is not the only source of rules of law. We live in families, we work in offices and factories, we buy goods as consumers in the market, we may accept religious affiliations.[59] Santos points out that "as the state has become more problematic as a social actor, its 'absenteeism' has become more untenable."[60] The result, he argues, is that "the analytical focus must ... be on the state as contested terrain in which state and non-state, local and translational social relations interact, merge and conflict in dynamic and even volatile combinations."[61] Does this mean bringing the state back? In one sense, it does. But it brings it back to a "place" where it was not before. In recent years we have witnessed decentering by the state, in the growth, for example, of alternative dispute resolution and community policing.[62] In this way the state reproduces itself and, indeed, expands in forms which appear, but only appear, as non-state political forms.

Santos[63] argues that the modern idea of global rationality has disintegrated into a multitude of uncontrollable, irrational mini-rationalities. What is required is to reinvent these mini-rationalities so that they form a new totality. And the postmodern struggle of mini-rationalities will be different from that experienced during modernity because of the nature of postmodern knowledge. This is "situational, empathetic and participatory rather than objectively distanced": it is "local, but being local, it is also total."[64] Postmodern critical theory arises out of "emancipatory everyday practices."[65] Politics and the law in the postmodern transition is "the emergence of a new legal minimalism and of micro-revolutionary

---

[54] As Habermas puts it (see *The Theory of Communicative Action*, vol II, 1987).
[55] See G. Teubner, *Dilemmas of Law in the Welfare State* (1986)
[56] See J. Handler (1992) 26 *Law and Society Review* 697.
[57] *Per* B. de Sousa Santos (1992) 1 *Social and Legal Studies* 131, 132.
[58] *ibid.*, p. 133 and see, *ante*, 1093.
[59] And see A. Sachs (1992) 1 *Social and Legal Studies* 217, 225–226, referring to the religious laws of marriage of Catholics and Jews.
[60] *Op. cit.*, n. 57, p. 133.
[61] *ibid.*
[62] See R. Abel, *The Politics of Informal Justice* (1992) and the Dartmouth collection by M. Freeman (ed.), *Alternative Dispute Resolution* (1994). See also J. Black (2001) 54 C.L.P. 103.
[63] "The Postmodern Transition: Law and Politics" in A. Sarat and T. Kearns (eds.), *The Fate of Law* (1991), pp. 79–118 *and post*, 1465. See also *ante*, 1094–1095.
[64] *ibid.*, p. 100.
[65] *ibid.*, p. 102.

practices."[66] Because we are in an increasingly complex network of subjectivities, a proliferation of political and legal "interpretive communities" will emerge out of the struggle against the "monopolies of
interpretation."[67]

The political agenda will emphasise redistribution of economic
resources, as well as the distribution of "postmaterialist" goods such as a
better environment and peace and greater democratisation. It will lead to
the empowering of victimised groups. And law will be "decanonized," as
it proves ineffective, opening a "gap in social imagination." Social change
will follow as "autonomous subjectivities ... free themselves from the
prejudices of legal fetishism."[68]

This message and prescription will undoubtedly be attractive to many,
particularly those alienated by the shift to the Right in liberal democracies in the 1980s and those depressed by the failure of the alternatives,
whether socialist or social welfare corporatist. But the rejection of the
large narrative by postmodernists does not appeal to all feminists or to
exponents of, what is coming to be known, as "outsider jurisprudence".[69]

Thus, for example, Fraser and Nicholson[70] are critical of a "justice of
multiplicities." Referring to Lyotard's rejection of a common consciousness of social identity, they argue that "he rules out the sort of
critical social theory that employs general categories like gender, race and
class"[71] as being too reductive. But, they claim, you cannot understand
the full dimensions of the subordinate position of women without grand
narratives. The "smallish, localized narrative"[72] hampers rather than
promotes sisterhood."[73]

The Critical Race movement, as we shall see in the next chapter, also
reacts to this. This denies that the experience of black people can be
understood without discussing the large narratives of societal racism in
its historical context and its continuing structural manifestations. For
Patricia Williams, "the concept of rights ... is the marker of our citizenship, our relations to others".[74] Instead of deconstructing the myth of
rights, as Crits and postmodernists commonly do, Williams see such
deconstruction as threatening the tenuous empowerment that "people of
color" have experienced in the years since *Brown v. Board of Education*.[75]
She claims that "rights rhetoric has been and continues to be an effective
form of discourse for blacks".[76] Rights may disable or isolate white

---

[66] *ibid.*, p. 105.
[67] *ibid.*, p. 108.
[68] *ibid.*, p. 117.
[69] *See post*, Chap. 17.
[70] "Social Criticism Without Philosophy: An Encounter Between Feminism and Post modernism" in A. Ross (ed.), *op. cit.*, n. 45, p. 87 (quoting Lyotard).
[71] *ibid.*, pp. 88–89.
[72] *ibid.*, p. 89.
[73] See to similar effect Iris Marion Young, *ante*, 614 and more generally Seyla Benhabib, *Situating The Self (1992)*, Chap. 7.
[74] *The Alchemy of Race and Rights* (1991), p. 164.
[75] (1954) 347 U.S. 483; but see D.Bell, *And We Are Not Saved* (1987).
[76] *Op. cit.*, n. 74, p. 149.

people: for blacks the experience of rights-assertion is "both of solidarity and freedom ... a process of finding the self".[77]

## SEMIOTICS AND LEGAL THEORY

The aim of semiotic study is to understand the system of signs which creates meaning within a culture. It is to understand "the underlying structures that make meaning possible."[78] Language is central to the nature of law—that much was clear to the Scandinavian Realists, in particular Olivecrona.[79] But, as Jackson points out, they tended to see language "primarily in terms of the goals and intentions of authors."[80] The legal semiotician seeks to identify the "grammar" of legal discourse—"the acceptable moves available in the language game of legal discourse."[81] These, Balkin explains, "may occur at the level of permissible argument forms, modes of factual characterization, categories of social perception, or in many other ways. The semiotician traces the way the system produces meaning ... and tries to see the gaps or uncertainties within the structure, the many different levels at which rhetorical tropes[82] can occur, and the many possible ways of redescribing them."[83] Consider, for example the way the common law, in the rhetorical practice of judgment, resorts to "figures of artificial or legal reason:"[84] the "reasonable man", the "officious bystander," the opening of the "floodgates," "good faith," "justice," "honour," "immemorial usage."

It could be said that good legal analysis has always concerned itself with modes of legal argumentation. And to some extent it has. But legal semiotics goes beyond legal analysis as traditionally understood. "It systematizes and organizes the process of discovery in legal analysis."[85] For Balkin, though the comparison is more than a little unfair, the semiotician is like the algebraist, the conventional legal analyst the school child. Both can do sums, "but the former can explicate the more general principles which ensure the correctness of the latter's work, and may permit much more powerful insights."[86] Why, for example, do different choices of argument and characterisation occur in the way in which they do?

Legal semiotics is, as is the C.L.S. writing, interested in ideology. But the interest is a different one, and, it may be thought from the viewpoint of the practising lawyer or student, a more valuable one. As we have seen,

---

[77] *ibid.*, p. 160. See also the extract from Crenshaw, *post*, 1509.
[78] *Per* J.M. Balkin (1991) 69 Texas L.R. 1831, 1845.
[79] And see *ante*, 1039. See also Ross, *ante*, 1074.
[80] *Semiotics and Legal Theory* (1985), p. 4.
[81] *Op. cit.*, n. 20, p. 1845. See also Balkin (1990) 76 Virginia L. Rev. 199–201.
[82] That is repeatable forms of argument.
[83] *Per* Balkin, *op. cit.*, n. 20, p. 1845.
[84] *Per* Goodrich (1992) 1 *Social and Legal Studies* 7, 8.
[85] *Per* Balkin, *op. cit.*, n. 20, p. 1839.
[86] *ibid.*

the C.L.S. viewed ideology as a smokescreen: legal semiotics, however, takes the language of the law seriously. For the legal semiotican, "ideology is constituted in part by the very patterns of argument and factual characterization that persons within the legal culture adopt."[87] C.L.S. wants to demystify legal reasoning, by demonstrating its indeterminacy and its political character. The goal of demystification is to denude legal reasoning of its seeming naturalness and legitimacy. Legal semiotics' approach may be different but it assists in the general project of opening up the law. For example, it demonstrates that the same forms of argument repeat themselves. As Balkin points out,[88] this has three possible implications, though he himself is only happy with the third of these. First, it may suggest that legal discourse is "formulaic" and so does not determine the outcome of cases: that there is nothing inevitable about the results of cases. And, if legal reasoning does not decide cases, something else, politics or ideology, does. Secondly, demonstrating the formulaic character of legal reasoning may be thought to undermine its claims to authority and respect: thus legal semiotics was thought, by Boyle for example,[89] to facilitate the demystification or debunking of legal reasoning. You showed that law was merely a game with routinised moves that anyone could play: something else was going on behind this facade and it was this that really counted. Thirdly, the demonstration that legal reasoning was formulaic pointed to "an incredible similarity between legal argument and political argument. The basic forms of legal argument turned out to be amazingly similar to the basic forms of everyday moral and political discourse."[90] This asserts the independence of legal reasoning from political and moral argument, albeit the interpermeability of the respective discourses. These similarities may also be greater at some times than others, perhaps when what Llewellyn has described as the "grand style"[91] dominates. And there are important differences: for example, language in law is institutionally controlled[92] by legislation and precedent. The meaning of a word like "family"[93] can change overnight with a new ruling: in political and moral discourse this occurs over a period of time and is more imperceptible.[94]

Perhaps the most interesting postmodern account of law using semiotics is Peter Goodrich's *Languages of Law*.[95] Here semiotic method and French psychoanalytic theory[96] are used to unravel the forms and

---

[87] *ibid.*, p. 1840.

[88] *ibid.*, pp. 1841–1842.

[89] (1985) 34 Am. U.L.Rev. 1003, 1015, 1051–1052.

[90] *Op. cit.*, n. 20, p. 1842.

[91] See *ante*, 840.

[92] Jackson, *op. cit.*, n. 80, quotes Carzo to this effect (see p. 307).

[93] See *Dyson Holdings v. Fox* [1976] Q.B. 503. But see *Fitzpatrick v. Sterling Housing Association* [1999] 4 All E.R. 705.

[94] When did "gay" cease to mean joyful and become equated with homosexual?

[95] (1990) See also *ante*, 1416. On the importance of myth see P. Fitzpatrick. *The Mythology of Modern Law* (1992).

[96] In particular Lacan and Legendre.

appearances of the law and to show how its different forms legitimate the practice for the legal subject.

Part of Goodrich's project is to reconstruct the English common law. He sees this as a set of norms and practices which together constitute a simple, unified tradition. "To study the common law historically is to study it as tradition, as a plural set of practices which developed over long periods of time ... as a mixture of image and myth, oral memory and written text, custom and judicial legislation ... It is to study a body of texts and contexts in which fiction is as forceful as analysis, image is as significant as rule and the play of memory as strong as the logic of argument."[97] His aim is to deconstruct the myth of the common law: this involves a critique of the normative conception of legitimation, law and rights. The authority of law is linked to a "myth which structures the symbolic points of reference for all legal subjects and establishes an institutional order in which the truth is the foundation of legal discourse."[98] Goodrich locates the discourse of modern democracy within these traditions and myths of the common law. He understands the law of the constitutional state as legitimating discourse by virtue of its reliance on norms, rights and justice. By contrast he sees the system of constitutional democracy as based on a tradition which attempts to ground its legitimacy on the consent of the people: the paradox is that the people are absent and the agreement was never reached. In the mythic social contract "the sender and receiver of the message are one and the same; the contract separates the parties to the exchange simply so as to unite them indissolubly, textually, legally." And yet this paradox is at the root of law. "The contract is that which excludes, it is that which immunizes us against other discourses and precludes that we even think of any other law."[99]

Goodrich may be thought to be offering an unduly pessimistic view of constitutional democracy and the part the law plays within it. It is an explicit challenge to the modernist belief that legitimate action and the exercise of power can be distinguished, a riposte to the claim that civil society and its normative resources are the foundation for right. Goodrich, though, shows that in England at least, constitutionalism has been built on a rather narrow set of beliefs,[1] justified by a series of "legal symbols which are embedded in a closed and sterile symbolic field of endless repetition."[2] This may be so, but is all (or is British) democratic society nothing more than the effect of power relations? Is there no space for the individual, no opportunity for democratic participation? Is normative discourse really *only* mystificatory? Is the rule of law an

---

[97] *Op. cit.*, n. 84, p. 8.
[98] *Per* J. McCahery (1993) 2 *Social and Legal Studies* 397, 415.
[99] See, *op. cit.*, n. 84, p. 171.
[1] In *op. cit.*, n. 84, he quotes (at p. 11) a seventeenth-century historian, William Dugdale who refers the common law to a beginning "no less antient than the beginning of differences betwixt man and man, after the first peopling of this land; it being no other than pure and tryed reason or the absolute perfection of reason."
[2] *Op. cit.*, n. 98, p. 417. And see Goodrich, *op. cit.*, n. 84, particularly pp. 9–15.

insubstantial spectre?[3] Goodrich's work in uncovering forgotten practices, his raising of suppressed history, offers, it is true, "history of another possibility."[4] But can he step outside his history to do this? Is his account any "more free of forgettings that the project which he excoriates"?[5] This may be doubted. If Goodrich's project is to produce a more inclusive view of the law, to make law self-founding, then, ironically, it is itself predicated upon a version of closure[6] and can be seen as a variant of modernism, rather than an exploration of postmodernist disclosure. Or does it rather cast doubt on the possibility of transcending closure, perhaps even on the postmodernist project?

---

### JEAN FRANÇOIS LYOTARD
#### Answering the Question: What Is Postmodernism?
(1984)[7]

*A demand*

This is a period of slackening—I refer to the color of the times. From every direction we are being urged to put an end to experimentation, in the arts and elsewhere. I have read an art historian who extols realism and is militant for the advent of a new subjectivity. I have read an art critic who packages and sells "Transavantgardism" in the marketplace of painting. I have read that under the name of postmodernism, architects are getting rid of the Bauhaus project, throwing out the baby of experimentation with the bathwater of functionalism. I have read that a new philosopher is discovering what he drolly calls Judaeo-Christianism, and intends by it to put an end to the impiety which we are supposed to have spread. I have read in a French weekly that some are displeased with *Mille Plateaux* [by Deleuze and Guattari] because they expect, especially when reading a work of philosophy, to be gratified with a little sense. I have read from the pen of a reputable historian that writers and thinkers of the 1960 and 1970 avant-gardes spread a reign of terror in the use of language, and that the conditions for a fruitful exchange must be restored by imposing on the intellectuals a common way of speaking, that of the historians. I have been reading a young philosopher of language who complains that Continental thinking, under the challenge of speaking machines, has surrendered to the machines the concern for reality, that it has substituted for the referential paradigm that of "adlinguisticity" (one speaks about speech, writes about writing, intertextuality), and who thinks that the time has now come to restore a solid anchorage of language in the referent. I have read a talented theatrologist for whom postmodernism, with its games and fantasies, carries very light weight in front of political authority, especially when a worried public opinion encourages authority to a politics of totalitarian surveillance in the face of nuclear warfare threats.

I have read a thinker of repute who defends modernity against those he calls the neoconservatives. Under the banner of postmodernism, the latter would like,

---

[3] And *cf.* E.P. Thompson, *ante*, 1181.

[4] *Op. cit.*, n. 84, p. 17.

[5] *Per* Stanley Fish in A. Norrie (ed.), *Closure or Critique* (1993), p. 157.

[6] On closure see I. Stewart (1987) 50 M.L.R. 908 and (1990) 17 J.L.S. 273 and Norrie (ed) *Closure or Critique* (1993).

[7] [From J.F. Lyotard, *The Postmodern Condition: A Report on Knowledge* (1984).]

he believes, to get rid of the uncompleted project of modernism, that of the Enlightenment. Even the last advocates of *Aufklärung*, such as Popper or Adorno, were only able, according to him, to defend the project in a few particular spheres of life—that of politics for the author of *The Open Society*, and that of art for the author of *Ästhetische Theorie*. Jürgen Habermas (everyone had recognised him) thinks that if modernity has failed, it is in allowing the totality of life to be splintered into independent specialties which are left to the narrow competence of experts, while the concrete individual experiences "desublimated meaning" and "destructured form," not as a liberation but in the mode of that immense *ennui* which Baudelaire described over a century ago.

Following a prescription of Albrecht Wellmer, Habermas considers that the remedy for this splintering of culture and its separation from life can only come from "changing the status of aesthetic experience when it is no longer primarily expressed in judgments of taste," but when it is "used to explore a living historical situation," that is, when "it is put in relation with problems of existence." For this experience then "becomes a part of a language game which is no longer that of aesthetic criticism"; it takes part "in cognitive processes and normative expectations"; "it alters the manner in which those different moments *refer* to one another." What Habermas requires from the arts and the experiences they provide is, in short, to bridge the gap between cognitive, ethical, and political discourses, thus opening the way to a unity of experience.

My question is to determine what sort of unity Habermas has in mind. Is the aim of the project of modernity the constitution of sociocultural unity within which all the elements of daily life and of thought would take their places as in an organic whole? Or does the passage that has to be charted between heterogeneous language games—those of cognition, of ethics, of politics—belong to a different order from that? And if so, would it be capable of effecting a real synthesis between them?

The first hypothesis, of a Hegelian inspiration, does not challenge the notion of a dialectically totalizing *experience*; the second is closer to the spirit of Kant's *Critique of Judgment*; but must be submitted, like the *Critique*, to that severe reexamination which postmodernity imposes on the thought of the Enlightenment, on the idea of a unitary end of history and of a subject. It is this critique which not only Wittgenstein and Adorno have initiated, but also a few other thinkers (French or other), who do not have the honor to be read by Professor Habermas—which at least saves them from getting a poor grade for their neoconservatism.

## Realism

The demands I began by citing are not all equivalent. They can even be contradictory. Some are made in the name of postmodernism, others in order to combat it. It is not necessarily the same thing to formulate a demand for some referent (and objective reality), for some sense (and credible transcendence), for an addressee (and audience), or an addressor (and subjective expressiveness) or for some communicational consensus (and a general code of exchanges, such as the genre of historical discourse). But in the diverse invitations to suspend artistic experimentation, there is an identical call for order, a desire for unity, for identity, for security, or popularity (in the sense of *Öffentlichkeit*, of "finding a public"). Artists and writers must be brought back into the bosom of the community, or at least, if the latter is considered to be ill, they must be assigned the task of healing it.

There is an irrefutable sign of this common disposition: it is that for all those writers nothing is more urgent that to liquidate the heritage of the avant-gardes. Such is the case, in particular, of the so-called transavantgardism. The answers given by Achille Bonito Oliva to the questions asked by Bernard Lamarche-Vadel and Michel Enric leave no room for doubt about this. By putting the avantgardes through a mixing process, the artist and critic feel more confident that they can suppress them than by launching a frontal attack. For they can pass of the most cynical eclecticism as a way of going beyond the fragmentary character of the preceding experiments; whereas if they openly turned their backs on them, they would run the risk of appearing ridiculously neoacademic. The *Salons and the Académies*, at the time when the bourgeoisie was establishing itself in history, were able to function as purgation and to grant awards for good plastic and literary conduct under the cover of realism. But capitalism inherently possesses the power to derealize familiar objects, social roles, and institutions to such a degree that the so-called realistic representations can no longer evoke reality except as nostalgia or mockery, as on occasion for suffering rather than for satisfaction. Classicism seems to be ruled out in a world in which reality is so destabilized that it offers no occasion for experience but one for ratings and experimentation.

This theme is familiar to all readers of Walter Benjamin. But it is necessary to assess its exact reach. Photography did not appear as a challenge to painting from the outside, any more than industrial cinema did to narrative literature. The former was only putting the final touch to the program of ordering the visible elaborated by the quattrocento; while the latter was the last step in rounding off diachronies as organic wholes, which had been the ideal of the great novels of education since the eighteenth century. That the mechanical and the industrial should appear as substitutes for hand or craft was not in itself a disaster—except if one believes that art is in its essence the expression of an individuality of genius assisted by an elite craftsmanship.

The challenge lay essentially in that photographic and cinematographic processes can accomplish better, faster, and with a circulation a hundred thousand times larger than narrative or pictorial realism, the task which academicism had assigned to realism: to preserve various consciousnesses from doubt. Industrial photography and cinema will be superior to painting and the novel whenever the objective is to stabilize the referent, to arrange it according to a point of view which endows it with a recognizable meaning, to reproduce the syntax and vocabulary which enable the addressee to decipher images and sequences quickly, and so to arrive easily at the consciousness of his own identity as well as the approval which he thereby receives from others—since such structure of images and sequences constitute a communication code among all of them. This is the way the effects of reality, or if one prefers, the fantasies of realism, multiply.

If they too do not wish to become supporters (of minor importance at that) of what exists, the painter and novelist must refuse to lend themselves to such therapeutic uses. They must question the rules of the art of painting or of narrative as they have learned and received them from their predecessors. Soon those rules must appear to them as a means to deceive, to seduce, and to reassure, which makes it impossible for them to be "true." Under the common name of painting and literature, an unprecedented split is taking place. Those who refuse to reexamine the rules of art pursue successful careers in mass conformism by communicating, by means of the "correct rules," the endemic desire for reality with objects and situations capable of gratifying it. Pornography is the use of photography and film to such an end. It is becoming a general model for the visual or narrative arts which have not met the challenge of the mass media.

As for the artists and writers who question the rules of plastic and narrative arts and possibly share their suspicions by circulating their work, they are destined to have little credibility in the eyes of those concerned with "reality" and "identity"; they have no guarantee of an audience. Thus it is possible to ascribe the dialectics of the avant-gardes to the challenge posed by the realism of industry and mass communication to painting and the narrative arts. Duchamp's "ready made" does nothing but actively and parodistically signify this constant process of dispossession of the craft of painting or even of being an artist. As Thierry de Duve penetratingly observes, the modern aesthetic question is not "What is beautiful?" but "What can be said to be art (and literature)?"

Realism, whose only definition is that it intends to avoid the question of reality implicated in that of art, always stands somewhere between academicism and kitsch. When power assumes the name of a party, realism and its neoclassical complement triumph over the experimental avant-garde by slandering and banning it—that is, provided the "correct" images, the "correct" narratives, the "correct" forms which the party requests, selects, and propagates can find a public to desire them as the appropriate remedy for the anxiety and depression that public experiences. The demand for reality—that is, for unity, simplicity, communicability, etc.—did not have the same intensity nor the same continuity in German society between the two world wars and in Russian society after the Revolution: this provides a basis for a distinction between Nazi and Stalinist realism.

What is clear, however, is that when it is launched by the political apparatus, the attack on artistic experimentation is specifically reactionary: aesthetic judgment would only be required to decide whether such or such work is in conformity with the established rules of the beautiful. Instead of the work of art having to investigate what makes it an art object and whether it will be able to find an audience, political academicism possesses and imposes a priori criteria of the beautiful, which designate some works and a public at a stroke and forever. The use of categories in aesthetic judgment would thus be of the same nature as in cognitive judgment. To speak like Kant, both would be determining judgments: the expression is "well formed" first in the understanding, then the only cases retained in experience are those which can be subsumed under this expression.

When power is that of capital and not that of a party, the "transavantgardist" or "postmodern" (in Jencks's sense) solution proves to be better adapted than the antimodern solution. Eclecticism is the degree zero of contemporary general culture: one listens to reggae, watches a western, eats McDonald's food for lunch and local cuisine for dinner, wears Paris perfume in Tokyo and "retro" clothes in Hong Kong; knowledge is a matter for TV games. It is easy to find a public for eclectic works. By becoming kitsch, art panders to the confusion which reigns in the "taste" of the patrons. Artists, gallery owners, critics, and public wallow in the "anything goes," and the epoch is one of slackening. But this realism of the "anything goes" is in fact that of money; in the absence of aesthetic criteria, it remains possible and useful to assess the value of works of art according to the profits they yield. Such realism accommodates all tendencies, just as capital accommodates all "needs," providing that the tendencies and needs have purchasing power. As for taste, there is no need to be delicate when one speculates or entertains oneself.

Artistic and literary research is doubly threatened, once by the "cultural policy" and once by the art and book market. What is advised, sometimes through one channel, sometimes through the other, is to offer works which, first, are relative to subjects which exist in the eyes of the public they address, and second, works so made ("well made") that the public will recognize what they are about, will understand what is signified, will be able to give or refuse its approval knowingly, and if possible, even to derive from such work a certain amount of comfort.

The interpretation which has just been given of the contact between the industrial and mechanical arts, and literature and the fine arts is correct in its outline, but it remains narrowly sociologizing and historicizing—in other words, one-sided. Stepping over Benjamin's and Adorno's reticences, it must be recalled that science and industry are no more free of the suspicion which concerns reality than are art and writing. To believe otherwise would be to entertain an excessively humanistic notion of the mephistophelian functionalism of sciences and technologies. There is no denying the dominant existence today of techno-science, that is, the massive subordination of cognitive statements to the finality of the best possible performance, which is the technological criterion. But the mechanical and the industrial, especially when they enter fields traditionally reserved for artists, are carrying with them much more than power effects. The objects and the thoughts which originate in scientific knowledge and the capitalist economy convey with them one of the rules which supports their possibility: the rule that there is no reality unless testified by a consensus between partners over a certain knowledge and certain commitments.

This rule is of no little consequence. It is the imprint left on the politics of the scientist and the trustee of capital by a kind of flight of reality out of the metaphysical, religious, and political certainties that the mind believed it held. This withdrawal is absolutely necessary to the emergence of science and capitalism. No industry is possible without a suspicion of the Aristotelian theory of motion, no industry without a refutation of corporatism, of mercantilism, and of physiocracy. Modernity, in whatever age it appears, cannot exist without a shattering of belief and without discovery of the "lack of reality" of reality, together with the invention of other realities.

What does this "lack of reality" signify if one tries to free it from a narrowly historicized interpretation? The phrase is of course akin to what Nietzsche calls nihilism. But I see a much earlier modulation of Nietzschean perspectivism in the Kantian theme of the sublime. I think in particular that it is in the aesthetic of the sublime that modern art (including literature) finds its impetus and the logic of avant-gardes finds its axioms.

The sublime sentiment, which is also the sentiment of the sublime, is, according to Kant, a strong and equivocal emotion: it carries with it both pleasure and pain. Better still, in it pleasure derives from pain. Within the tradition of the subject, which comes from Augustine and Descartes and which Kant does not radically challenge, this contradiction, which some would call neurosis or masochism, develops as a conflict between the faculties of a subject, the faculty to conceive of something and the faculty to "present" something. Knowledge exists if, first, the statement is intelligible, and second, if "cases" can be derived from the experience which "corresponds" to it. Beauty exists if a certain "case" (the work of art), given first by the sensibility without any conceptual determination, the sentiment of pleasure independent of any interest the work may elicit, appeals to the principle of a universal consensus (which may never be attained).

Taste, therefore, testifies that between the capacity to conceive and the capacity to present an object corresponding to the concept, an undetermined agreement, without rules, giving rise to a judgment which Kant calls reflective, may be experienced as pleasure. The sublime is a different sentiment. It takes place, on the contrary, when the imagination fails to present an object which might, if only in principle, come to match a concept. We have the Idea of the world (the totality of what is), but we do not have the capacity to show an example of it. We have the Idea of the simple (that which cannot be broken down, decomposed), be we cannot illustrate it with a sensible object which would be a "case" of it. We can conceive the infinitely great, the infinitely powerful, but every presentation of an object destined to "make visible" this absolute greatness or power appears to us painfully inadequate. Those are Ideas of which no presentation is possible. Therefore, they impart no knowledge about reality (experience); they also prevent the free union of the faculties which gives rise to the sentiment of the beautiful; and they prevent the formation and the stabilization of taste. They can be said to be unpresentable.

I shall call modern the art which devotes its "little technical expertise" (*son "petit technique"*), as Diderot used to say, to present the fact that the unpresentable exists. To make visible that there is something which can be conceived and which can neither be seen nor made visible: this is what is at stake in modern painting. But how to make visible that there is something which cannot be seen? Kant himself shows the way when he names "formlessness, the absence of form," as a possible index to the unpresentable. He also says of the empty "abstraction" which the imagination experiences when in search for a presentation of the infinite (another unpresentable): this abstraction itself is like a presentation of the infinite, its "negative presentation." He cites the commandment, "Thou shalt not make graven images" (*Exodus*), as the most sublime passage in the Bible in that it forbids all presentation of the Absolute. Little needs to be added to those observations to outline an aesthetic of sublime painting. As painting, it will of course "present" something though negatively; it will therefore avoid figuration or representation. It will be "white" like one of Malevitch's squares; it will enable us to see only by making it impossible to see; it will please only by causing pain. One recognizes in those instructions the axioms of avant-gardes in painting, inasmuch as they devote themselves to making an illusion to the unpresentable by means of visible presentations. The systems in the name of which, or with which, this task has been able to support or to justify itself deserve the greatest attention; but they can originate only in the vocation of the sublime in order to legitimize it, that is, to conceal it. They remain inexplicable without the incommensurability of reality to concept which is implied in the Kantian philosophy of the sublime.

It is not my intention to analyze here in detail the manner in which the various avant-gardes have, so to speak, humbled and disqualified reality by examining the pictorial techniques which are so many devices to make us believe in it. Local tone, drawing, the mixing of colors, linear perspective, the nature of the support and that of the instrument, the treatment, the display, the museum: the avant-gardes are perpetually flushing out artifices of presentation which make it possible to subordinate thought to the gaze and to turn it away from the unpresentable. If Habermas, like Marcuse, understands this task of derealization as an aspect of the (repressive) "desublimation" which characterizes the avantgarde, it is because he confuses the Kantian sublime with Freudian sublimation, and because aesthetics has remained for him that of the beautiful.

### The postmodern

What, then, is the postmodern? What place does it or does it not occupy in the vertiginous work of the questions hurled at the rules of image and narration? It is undoubtedly a part of the modern. All that has been received, if only yesterday (*modo, modo*, Petronius used to say), must be suspected. What space does Cézanne challenge? The Impressionists'. What object do Picasso and Braque attack? Cézanne's. What presupposition does Duchamp break with in 1912? That which says one must make a painting, be it cubist. And Buren questions that other presupposition which he believes had survived untouched by the work of Duchamp: the place of presentation of the work. In an amazing acceleration, the generations precipitate themselves. A work can become modern only if it is first postmodern. Postmodernism thus understood is not modernism at its end but in the nascent state, and this state is constant.

Yet I would like not to remain with this slightly mechanistic meaning of the word. If it is true that modernity takes place in the withdrawal of the real and according to the sublime relation between the presentable and the conceivable, it is possible, within this relation, to distinguish two modes (to use the musician's language). The emphasis can be placed on the powerlessness of the faculty of presentation, on the nostalgia for presence felt by the human subject, on the obscure and futile will which inhabits him in spite of everything. The emphasis can be placed, rather, on the power of the faculty to conceive, on its "inhumanity" so to speak (it was the quality Apollinaire demanded of modern artists), since it is not the business of our understanding whether or not human sensibility or imagination can match what it conceives. The emphasis can also be placed on the increase of being and the jubilation which result from the invention of new rules of the game, be it pictorial, artistic, or any other. What I have in mind will become clear if we dispose very schematically a few names on the chessboard of the history of avant-gardes: on the side of melancholia, the German Expressionists, and on the side of *novatio*, Braque and Picasso, on the former Malevitch and on the latter Lissitsky, on the one Chirico and on the other Duchamp. The nuance which distinguishes these two modes may be infinitesimal; they often coexist in the same piece, are almost indistinguishable; and yet they testify to a difference (*un différend*) on which the fate of thought depends and will depend for a long time, between regret and assay.

The work of Proust and that of Joyce both allude to something which does not allow itself to be made present. Allusion, to which Paolo Fabbri recently called my attention, is perhaps a form of expression indispensable to the works which belong to an aesthetic of the sublime. In Proust, what is being eluded as the price to pay for this allusion is the identity of consciousness, a victim to the excess of time (*au trop de temps*). But in Joyce, it is the identity of writing which is the victim of an excess of the book (*au trop de livre*) or of literature.

Proust calls forth the unpresentable by means of a language unaltered in its syntax and vocabulary and of a writing which in many of its operators still belongs to the genre of novelistic narration. The literary institution, as Proust inherits it from Balzac and Flaubert, is admittedly subverted in that the hero is no longer a character but the inner consciousness of time, and in that the diegetic diachrony, already damaged by Flaubert, is here put in question because of the narrative voice. Nevertheless, the unity of the book, the odyssey of that consciousness, even if it is deferred from chapter to chapter, is not seriously challenged: the identity of the writing with itself throughout the labyrinth of the interminable narration is enough to connote such unity, which has been compared to that of *The Phenomenology of Mind.*

Joyce allows the unpresentable to become perceptible in his writing itself, in the signifier. The whole range of available narrative and even stylistic operators is put into play without concern for the unity of the whole, and new operators are tried. The grammar and vocabulary of literary language are no longer accepted as given: rather, they appear as academic forms, as rituals originating in piety (as Nietzsche said) which prevent the unpresentable form being put forward.

Here, then, lies the difference; modern aesthetics is an aesthetic of the sublime, though a nostalgic one. It allows the unpresentable to be put forward only as the missing contents; but the form, because of its recognizable consistency, continues to offer to the reader or viewer matter for solace and pleasure. Yet these sentiments do not constitute the real sublime sentiment, which is in an intrinsic combination of pleasure and pain: the pleasure that reason should exceed all presentation, the pain that imagination or sensibility should not be equal to the concept.

The postmodern would be that which, in the modern, puts forward the unpresentable in presentation itself; that which denies itself the solace of good forms, the consensus of a taste which would make it possible to share collectively the nostalgia for the unattainable; that which searches for new presentations, not in order to enjoy them but in order to impart a stronger sense of the unpresentable. A postmodern artist or writer is in the position of a philosopher: the text he writes, the work he produces are not in principle governed by pre-established rules, and they cannot be judged according to a determining judgment, by applying familiar categories to the text or to the work. Those rules and categories are what the work of art itself is looking for. The artist and the writer, then, are working without rules in order to formulate the rules of what *will have been done.* Hence the fact that work and text have the characters of an *event*; hence also, they always come too late for their author, or, what amounts to the same thing, their being put into work, their realization (*mise en oeuvre*) always begin too soon. *Post modern* would have to be understood according to the paradox of the future (*post*) anterior (*modo*).

It seems to me that the essay (Montaigne) is postmodern, while the fragment (*The Athaeneum*) is modern.

Finally, it must be clear that it is our business not to supply reality but to invent allusions to the conceivable which cannot be presented. And it is not to be expected that this task will effect the last reconciliation between language games (which, under the name of faculties, Kant knew to be separated by a chasm), and that only the transcendental illusion (that of Hegel) can hope to totalize them into a real unity. But Kant also knew that the price to pay for such an illusion is terror. The nineteenth and twentieth centuries have given us as much terror as we can take. We have paid a high enough price for the nostalgia of the whole and the one, for the reconciliation of the concept and the sensible, of the transparent and the communicable experience. Under the general demand for slackening and for appeasement, we can hear the mutterings of the desire for a return of terror, for the realization of the fantasy to seize reality. The answer is: Let us wage a war on totality: let us be witnesses to the unpresentable; let us activate the differences and save the honor of the name. [pp. 71–82]

## JENNIFER WICKE
### Postmodern Identity and the Legal subject
### (1991)[8]

Postmodernism has an alchemical sheen, the ability to conjoin with disparate words and impart a heady gloss to them, a *frisson* of difference, a catalyzing agency, the torque of the new. In just such a manner, the coming together of "postmodernism" and the Law, with its stern capital "L" intact, promises to be a dynamic coupling, postmodernism offering to put its delirious spin on the rigor and fixity of the body of law. Of course in this scenario postmodernism carries all the significations of glamour and seduction, the law remaining an unwilling or at least staid partner in this dalliance. While perhaps a consummation devoutly to be wished, the interpenetration of the two gives off theoretical sparks but also real tensions in praxis. In addressing postmodernism as it carves out the terrain of identity, and then following the collision of this logic with the formidable dominance of the subject of and under the law, I will be mapping a tension which may signal a misalliance between postmodernism and the legal subject, an aporia with political consequences. The two senses of a legal subject—as a subject area under the heading of the law and as the human subject constituted by legal discourse—both come into play in this tension with the importunities of postmodern identity, that term itself covering both the identity of the postmodern and what we could consider a newly-determined postmodern identity politics. I want to argue that the inevitable "postmodernizing" of legal discourse, which may have many local insights to offer, should not come in the guise of depoliticizing the discursive ammunition that the law provides the legal subject within the nets of postmodern hegemonic forms. In short, while embracing the postmodern insofar as it provides a critique of the self-evident field of Law, I will suggest also the ambivalence of this embrace; the costs of a shot-gun marriage between the two are too high— these bedfellows could make strange politics.

Postmodernism or postmodernity cannot be taken as a given in any cultural discourse ... The "postmodern" threatens to enter the triad "the Humanities, Postmodernism, and the Law" as a reified term with an unproblematized locus.

---

[8] [From (1991) 62 Univ. of Colorado L. Rev. 455.]

Such difficulties are rife in any foregrounding of postmodernity, in any context whatever, because the postmodern has a highly equivocal conceptual status, an uncertain provenance, and a variable and often conflictual set of interlocutors. There are more than thirty-one flavors of postmodernism, and the sorting out of the indices and differentia of these critical brands entails opening a theoretical Pandora's box. Postmodernism was the term that marked the eighties on the critical map, and the term is still fiercely clinging to its position in the intellectual and cultural wars as the nineties begin, although the decision about what post-modernism is remains as fraught as ever—one reason why postmodernism can maintain its franchise and even set up new outposts on criticism's terrain. Post-modernism names a debate in theory, a set of discourses and disciplines, a criterion of style in aesthetics, a historical period, and a way of life. The individual word, postmodernism, gets stretched as taut as an elastic band in trying to encompass these divergent directions.

Among the valences within this stressed term, the umbrella of postmodernism, are descriptions of decor and even room colors, architectural designs as different as Philip Johnson's AT&T Chippendale building and the 40 foot high seven dwarfs of the new Walt Disney World center, the dread of nuclear destruction and world annihilation, the internal movements of a film like *Blue Velvet*, the shift to a post-industrial economy taking place anywhere from 1945 to 1968, broad societal and economic shifts into a media or a consumer or a multinational phase, art by Longo, Schnabel, Fischl, Sherman, Kruger, Holzer, and Rosler, an anti-tele-ological presence within epistemology, an anaesthetization of feeling, the presence of the simulacrum in the form of the takeover of images, a set of rhetorical tropes, the decentering of the subject, Madonna in any of her endless incarnations, the collapse of cultural hierarchies, the end of Western metaphysics, the loss of the great Western meta-narratives of progress, reason, or revolution, or the "crisis in representation." Add to that the abbreviated form "post," which can be stuck promiscuously on nearly any phenomenon, theoretical or cultural, to heighten the vertigo with which one wanders when assaying the postmodern. A simplifying gesture might seem to be extirpating the word entirely, on the grounds that if it can mean all these things, then it is meaningless and should be dispatched to the rubbish heap of theory. Postmodernism won't just slink away into the night in that tame fashion, however, or wither away; while the elasticity of the term can in fact sometimes be a cover for sloppy or just mindless employment of it, it is equally true that where there is conceptual smoke there is conceptual fire. In other words, the multiple determinations of postmodernism have to do with very real critical debates with very real critical stakes, being staged around a volatile but nonetheless pressing and important term, whose very elusiveness is a sign that something productive may be going on. At the least, it is impossible to ignore these debates, and to dismiss them with a wave of the hand is to place oneself outside the semantic confines of a major moment in theory, which has had actual consequences—the postmodern as self-fulfilling critical prophecy.

In framing my remarks as postmodern, then, I necessarily elide a fragmented history and gloss over problems in formulating a singular postmodern; I do this not nonchalantly but with concern for the occlusions that will follow in my critical wake. Two primary assumptions about postmodernity animate what is to follow: first, that any serious consideration of postmodernity would have to stem from a historical periodization where the postmodern genuinely described a convergence of historical phenomena, at a specific, if loosely chosen time, and second, that postmodernism refers to a congeries of theoretical suppositions about the nature of language, texts, and human subjects within the lens of the social. Interestingly, the major articulations of the postmodern have arisen in camps that construe these two assumptions as antipathies. I'll trace out briefly that division, and then the claims which make my analysis eager to override those differences. This traversal requires the invoking of postmodernism as a series of "names," as theoretical designation sites, an unavoidably monadic way of getting at conceptual discriminations. Unfortunately, this inventory is the main way postmodernity has been assimilated within what we can call for convenience's sake "the humanities," so a rehearsal of how the postmodern came to be naturalized as a term may not be tangential to what concerns us.

Fredric Jameson's essay *Postmodernism and Consumer Society* is a touchstone here, for regardless of what flavor of postmodernism one is led to choose the route has to pass through his essay, at least in the international theorizing on postmodernity.[9] Jameson is the first to so succinctly state that postmodernism is a historical moment which expresses, in his words, "the logic of the culture of late capitalism." Jameson gets at postmodernity initially through the attempt to understand the aesthetic objects postmodernity necessarily produces, since for him all art and culture will stem from the material conditions of the society in which it is produced and received. Consequently, he starts with the bald fact of, say, Andy Warhol in painting; of John Cage or Philip Glass or The Clash; of the literary phenomenon of Thomas Pynchon's *Gravity's Rainbow*; of architecture like John Portman's Bonaventure Hotel or the Las Vegas-loving buildings of Venturi and Scott Brown. Jameson asks what differentiates these disparate objects or artifacts or styles from art which can be called modernist—from Joyce or Eliot, Mies van der Rohe, Corbusier, Schoenberg, and Picasso. He adduces two signal changes: one is the technique of pastiche as opposed to modernist parody, the setting of heterogeneous elements next to one another without any attempt to sort them out or give them different values, as parody obviously does. Part of this entails an important distinction for Jameson; he sees modernist art in a dialectic with mass culture, establishing its removal from it, while postmodern art abolishes the distinction between high and low and sets these two realms up against one another within the same work, without privileging one over the other. Postmodernist art will be a bricolage, a collection of scraps and fragments pasted together, hybridizing high art and mass culture, recycling images and narratives, determinedly unoriginal. These ways of talking about postmodern art have been highly influential, and in general in postmodern theory there is a kind of consensus that this art denies the primacy or sole power of an author as the origin of meaning, razes the distinction between originals and copies, creative texts and critical ones, and through pastiche, parody, allegory, and simulation celebrates the proliferation of sources and readings instead of the unified, pure text or artifact.

The implications for the humanities are evident—both the method and the object of postmodern study are irretrievably altered; ramifications for legal discourse are also clear, since the assumptions about the legal text shift accordingly. Not that the legal text now is shaped as either parody or pastiche, but rather that the legal text ceases to emanate from an origin point of timeless authority or as a singular transmission. Beyond the consideration of discrete legal texts as altered textual objects, the "postmodern" would invade an account of the Law *tout court*, to put it punningly; postmodern critical attitudes would direct attention to the filtering of legal discourse through electronic media, as in televised courtroom trials and even phenomena like the much-watched Congressional querying of Judge Bork. The ineluctably hybrid and multiple nature of contemporary discursive objects would invade even the more sacred precincts of legal thought and action; since legal discourse is not by and large self-consciously artistic, what is meant by this is the cultural framing by which and through which legal forms are perceived and acted out. None of these changes can be considered without taking into account the material, historical specificity of a vast societal change undergone in Western countries, at least, since World War II. Prescient varieties of

---

[9] Jameson, "Postmodernism and Consumer Society" in *Postmodernism and its Discontents* 13 (E. Kaplan ed., 1988). See also Jameson, *Postmodernism* (1990).

postmodern thought articulate the political effects of "late capitalism" and post-industrial society as these inflect all the aspects of modern society and its subjects.

Secondly, Jameson discerns a change in the *affect* the work of art evokes or envinces, from the anxiety or alienation of modernism's subject, nicely emblematized for Jameson in Edvard Munch's painting "The Scream," to what must be called the schizophrenic subject of postmodernism. Jameson is not using this term in a clinical sense, to say that we all have been made literally psychotic by the conditions of postmodernity, nor is he using it as a criticism, as a way of dismissing the present mode of being. "Schizophrenia" is instead the emergent psychic norm of the postmodern, a dystopia right out of a novel by Philip K. Dick, the consumer consciousness disintegrating into a succession of instants, condemned through the ubiquity of mass images and commodified information to live in a timeless now rather than the centering, full time of meaning and history. For Jameson's essay, this occasions the actual loss of history; instead, the historical is transformed into the nostalgic image since we have lost access to our history in the welter of competing images and the fragmentation of social life, so that no coherent communities or narratives of a shared history can exist side by side in its commodification, the theme park as history.

In fact, there are four basic features of the postmodern for Jameson: the lack of depth or distance in the art work, the building, or the image, and also in the criticism which would try to gain distance on its object; a weakening of the historical sense, both public and private; a new emotional tone called "intensities," which transforms the nature of our relation to objects; and the centrality of the new technologies of information and reproduction which are themselves linked to the new circumstance of global corporate capitalism—think of AT&T's logo of the shimmering, electrically alive globe, or the global penetration of the computer, say, in its use to keep track of police monitorings in South Africa. This last aspect points to a key tenet of Jameson's take on the postmodern: it is totalizing. Postmodernism is not transgressive for Jameson—it is embraced by the market, absorbed by advertisement, television, and film, an insider trader in postmodernism itself.

Jameson's postmodernism tends to homogenize the concept, making postmodernism hold too many contradictory phenomena. The workings of late capitalism, for example, are not at all monolithic, nor do they tend only in the direction of greater and greater control, surveillance, and hegemony, as Jameson would have it. These might seem to be quibbles, but they also amount to saying that Jameson's view of the postmodern is totalizing. That move has real consequences, because Jameson sees theory (in the form of cultural critique) as sidelined by postmodernism, paralyzed by its insidious grip. The nostalgic and despairing cast of Jamesonian postmodernism has had its effects, since it has become only too easy in light of it to overemphasize the impotence of the subject, or person, caught in its toils and to fail to recognize the many opportunities for refashioning and redesigning the cultural contours of postmodern forms. A flip side of this dread before the entrapping quandaries of the postmodern is the rather facile delight with which a critic like Gregory Ulmer enthuses over the pedagogic possibilities of the new electronic and computer media, finding in them an automatic destabilizing power, where the written word loses its supposed hegemony and is replaced with the delicious "difference" of electronic traces.[10] For both, culture has not disappeared; on the contrary, its realm has so expanded that it has become everything. In the society of the simulacrum, there are only pseudo-events, no longer any "real" ones. Jameson confronts this emptiness and

---

[10] "Difference" is Jacques Derrida's coinage for the force in and behind language that is oppositional to what he calls "logocentrism." Difference refers to the deferring and the differing aspects inherent in all language, where language is seen as the play of differences without a center, whether that center is figured as God, man, subject, authority, or Law.

longs for the lost social community that pre-dates such amnesia and exists now only in the glimpse of "utopia" conjured up within mass culture. Without dredging up such longings, it is possible to agree that postmodernity does resituate the cultural scene in all its parameters, and that the notion of the legal subject can be stretched beyond recognition by this new postmodern space.

A recent spectacular example of the implosion of postmodernity into the legal subject occurred in the Wisconsin trial of a man for the rape of only one of numerous personalities of a woman suffering, so the court was told, from multiple-personality disorder.[11] This rich scenario of the postmodernizing of legal subjectivity unfolded with Jamesonian melancholia in the nexus between the media and the courts, as the labile, fissured identity of a sort of folk-postmodernism, or postmodernism via the National Enquirer (as sensationalized "multible-personality disorder"), encountered the legal norms of self-hood and singular self-identity, as well as the legal subject in the mode of truth-telling and self-incrimination. The trial took place with great public attention to the media event of testimony being funneled through a shape-shifting identity on the part of the victim, only one of whose personalities and thus bodies had been raped, while the "others" remained unmolested by what would, had they been entirely present during the sex, in their cases have been consensual. Who "she" was, and the apparent impossibility of ascertaining a single, unified victim for the crime of rape, since the offended personality had agreed to sex but was considered to be too immature or troubled to be genuinely consenting, opened a mise-en-abyme in the notion of the legal subject, an abyss all too readily filled by the simulacral aspects of the trial. Played out in the tabloids, on tabloid TV, on "regular" television news, and in a host of media forms including National Public Radio, it produced a simulacral theater in which the public at large was asked to witness to the implausible fascinations and conundrums of this postmodern predicament. The defendant had to be tried simultaneously as a more traditional legal subject, in other words as a coherent psychic identity for whom the words "understanding" and "truth" had some fixed relevance. The spectacular display of the multiple personalities or the literalized (if technically erroneous) "schizophrenia" on display in the media-pervaded courtroom showed the difficulties inherent in introducing a postmodern identity definition into a courtroom still operating within another paradigm for the legal subject, on the basis of which the defendant was found guilty. A "postmodern identity" of this sort—kitschy, spurious, and the product of an unholy alliance with a self-promoting form of psychology—is not at all what postmodern theoreticians seek to propose, but rather a turbulence in the zone of culture pre-emptively tossed out a subject in pieces, a fluctuating subjectivity, and forced its apparition onto the cultural screen. Here the trial for rape was as much a trial of this problematic new cultural identity as it was for the assault which may or may not have happened; the discourse of the legal subject was asked, as it were, to confirm the status of an unprecedented legal identity. A boundary-line between the setting of the trial and such collective inquisition sites as the Oprah Winfrey show was blurred throughout the trial. The defendant's guilt was found to inhere in realizing that this woman was mentally ill and still proposing sex with her, a violation of the protective law surrounding such dealings with those assumed not to be in a position to defend themselves or their desires. The neutralization of identity into a quiver of self-inventoried alternative personalities leaves the legal subject in pieces as well, on one side of this divide only, the side where an alliance between a performative self and the multiple screening images of radio, television, and print can be effected. On the other, the legal subject remains in full force, the issue of "intention" still rigidly invoked. The imbalance of this encounter leaves lop-sided the engagement of postmodern

---

[11] *Wisconsin v. Peterson*, 90-CF-280 (Winnebago County Cir. Ct., Branch 4, dismissed January 17, 1991).

identity with the legal subject because it is so irresolvably bound up in a cultural staging. Postmodern theorizing helpfully can point out the fluid borders of such a staging and the ways they overlap with legal norms; nonetheless, to efface or erase the legal subject, however much predicated on an illusory unity, singularity, intentionality, would be an enormous political loss.

At the other remove from Jameson's melancholy in the face of the postmodern as he sees it, is the influential discussion of the postmodern conducted in the work of Jean-Francois Lyotard, especially in the slim volume *The Postmodern Condition: A Report on Knowledge*, where Lyotard's claims are entirely different; the crux of his book is that in postmodernity, the major narratives governing social experience since the Enlightenment have disappeared, and that the disappearance of these meta-narratives has left instead the liberating potential of local, interlocking language games, which replace the overall structures.[12] The monumental public narratives of evolution, progress, class struggle, or even Enlightenment have all dissolved for Lyotard into the play of atomized, technologically-assisted subjects, who do not connect with one another in any overarching way, such as, for example, by being members of a proletariat. Constructing political responses by way of reference to the teleological or progressive scenarios of the past is doomed and frivolously wrong-headed; there are no Manichean rents in the social fabric, but a closely-knit weave of intricate interconnections. In society, individuals are like billiard balls being played on random billiard tables in pool halls scattered randomly across a landscape, a Brownian motion of local determinations. Both the utopianism and the teleology inherent in the historicist postmodernism of a Jameson are avoided by Lyotard in favor of what might be called an avant-garde utopian gesture. The adhesive of the Lyotardian version of the postmodern has had remarkable sticking power, in that a typical summary of postmodernism involves recounting that it has made linear narratives of history obsolete, and transfigured the relationship of individual subject to social and historical narratives in correspondingly major ways.

I would go so far as to say that a large part of the debate about postmodernism has arisen in the attempt to *historicize* the discourses of poststructuralism, which have been very resistant to this process, or to deny the need for any complex historical consciousness at all, as is Lyotard's preference. Deconstructive wings of theory, for example, have gladly gone over to the postmodernism of Lyotard, because it announces the end of history, or at least the meaninglessness of historical narratives of rationality, progress, or struggle that we could tell one another and comprehend. Language games are all that are left, and however agonistic they may be, no larger accretion of collective identity on a historical terrain of struggle is to be expected, marking a signal failure in the articulation of the postmodern.

To step back and consider the problems of "postmodern identity" is to confront an immediate contradiction. Following out a post-structuralist logic would entail putting the concept of identity under heavy scrutiny, and, indeed, insofar as "identity" can be construed as analogous to a stable, univocal self, an innate or immanent nature, a fixed or self-evident being, postmodern thought has scoured those Augean stables and evacuated out any such stability. Postmodern identity comes with such certification of its fragmented, fractured nature, of its fissuring by the myriad social discourses which construct it, its elusive relation to self-presence, its foregone inconclusion, that to work one's way back out onto the relatively stable plane of an identity per se is perhaps inconceivable and undesirable. Nonetheless, and at the same time, while postmodernism eschews any essence or origin, any authoritative center or even fixed point of leverage, identity has come to be an increasingly pressing concern within formations of the postmodern. While the "postmodern" itself, as theory, cannot buttress an identity-

[12] J. F. Lyotard, *The Postmodern Condition* (G. Bennington trans., 1984) [and *ante*, 1421].

formation and remain internally consistent, postmodernity or postmodern sociohistorical conditions make a demand for the structures of identity to contest the fragmentation of civil society. "Postmodern identity" is to that extent an oxymoron; it is also a neologism for identity, a new way of saying that there is an identity peculiar to the postmodern, and peculiarly postmodern.

This has real repercussions for the intersection of law and postmodernism, whether that is on the turf of a change in the interpretive matrix of the law, or in the confrontation of legal discourse with changed social circumstances, the postmodernizing of law itself. The link must initially be teased out through the relation of the two words "identity" and "subject." Take the latter first. "Subject" has two valences for this discussion, one the more general meaning of a locus of subjectivity, the individual human subject, and the other the pinned or fixed object of subjection, a *subjected* one. Michel Foucault plays on these differences in his essay *The Subject in Power*, where he hypothesizes that a subject, formed out of its very subjections, becomes a subject by virtue of being made subject (to).[13] "Identity" does not have the neat internal play of ambiguity as a word, but the same doubleness holds good; an identity could be said to be the adopted agency of one who has been identified as the result of some social process—for example, a gay identity presupposing having been socially identified as gay, and then adopting that designation as a place from which to situate one's identity. An "identity" of this sort is connected to the "subject" in that identity is the self-chosen and usually communal expression of a subject position, making a particular subject-position active as a functioning social identity, with the understanding that both of these states takes place in the plural, not the singular. A footnote to this discussion would require pointing out that Foucault perhaps develops this understanding of the subject after repeated critiques of the impossibility of discerning an agent of change within his sociohistorical schema, which proposes the dispersal of power relations to such an attenuated degree that revolution, change, or resistance is difficult to hypothesize or explain.

The Lyotardian version of postmodernism tunnels into this aspect of identity and subjects it to philosophical critique. In the most attenuated sense, the grounds for collective identity are swept away with the meta-narratives, so that "class" no longer serves as an identity marker of any predictive force, for example, and subjects are instead bundles of activated discursive shards, where there is never to be any one exclusive or overpowering identity. Thus, for Lyotard, there is always room to maneuver on the speech-activated board of culture and never any entirely hegemonic counter-force to confront. The exception to this is what Lyotard has come to see as the circumstances of the "third-world," whose sad job it is simply to "survive," while our first-world, postmodern task is to creatively multiply the features of our worlds. The forces arrayed against third-world survival are not enumerated or explored in Lyotardian postmodernism, presumably because these might threaten to look remarkably like relics of the disintegrated meta-narratives, and even the split between first and third worlds, in Lyotard's fuzzy terminology, would need to be theorized in some interlinking fashion. Barring this connection, the grounds on which identities form are murky at best. The strength of Lyotard's post-Enlightenment discourse has, however, truly set an agenda within postmodernism, which reverberates to the perceived conceptual inadequacy in both political and philosophical categories of the subject. "Local determination" is the arresting catch-phrase for a society configured as interlocking, often antagonistic micro-identities. Lyotard does turn attention, in *Le Difference*,[14] to larger situations of injustice, and he post-modernly characterizes these in linguistic terms; proper names act as signifiers for *differends*, circumstances of injustice which fall

---

[13] Michel Foucault's later essays and interviews turn on these questions. See "The Subject in Power" in *Art After Modernism* (M. Tucker & D. Godine ed., 1984), p. 417.

[14] J. F. Lyotard, *The Difference* (G. van Don Abeel trans., 1988).

outside prior genres of discourse and reduce their sufferers to silence or to coded names. "Auschwitz" is Lyotard's main example of such a *differend*, a name which for witnesses of and to the Holocaust signals the injustice for which reparations are sought outside of "normal" channels or genres of legal discourse, since these cannot contain the enormity of the injustice.

In the Native American struggles for self-determination and acknowledgment of their distinct cultural identity, these contradictions of postmodern identity and the legal subject are writ large, since the postmodern insistence on heterogeneity as opposed to identity and on the passé nature of a discourse of rights and nationalism as belonging to the discredited "narrative" mode comes into focus in these struggles. Here, too, one would wish that postmodernism's optic would cast a revivified look at the law, in particular at the decrepit legal formulations that make up the ongoing history of the Native American presence in American courts of law. The ebullient heterogeneity celebrated by Lyotard does not accord well, as it happens, with the need to deploy a language of the legal subject, in other words, a language of rights and a language of cultural identity, in securing cultural justice. James Clifford has provided a reading of the case of the Mashpee Indians which highlights this gap in postmodern identity.[15]

The trial of Mashpee versus the New Seabury Corporation took place in 1976 as the Mashpee Indians of Cape Cod sought to establish their claims to land bought up by the corporation; in order to do so it was incumbent on them to prove they were a tribe, in other words, to get recognition for themselves in court as a tribe while their request to the Federal government for such legal recognition was still in limbo.[16] "Tribe" as an identity had to be proven in relation to the legal definition proffered by the 1901 Supreme Court decision, containing an antiquated (by any anthropological or disciplinary measure) and actively hostile and ignorant (by any Indian measure whatever) definition of what constituted a "tribe." Thus the legal identity of a tribe was by no means an innocent or innate one, but nonetheless the legal standard was what needed to be demonstrated by the Mashpee, and this they were unable to do. An all-white jury from the Boston area found, in a rather spectacular decision, that the Mashpee had indeed constituted a tribe in 1834 and 1842, but not in the all-important year of 1790, the date when the Indian Non-Intercourse Act was passed, on which many land claims are based, nor in the subsequent years of 1869, 1870, and, most relevantly, 1976. The phantom status of tribal identity, waxing and waning over the years, efflorescing at one juncture and then ebbing forever, itself has a liminal quality— but one that served to deny the Mashpee any grounds as legal subjects. Their identity in this case was entirely predicated on their establishing the legal subject-category of "member of the Mashpee tribe." To be an Indian is a pre-existent cultural identity, of course, but in this instance and many others what was needed to bring about the desired result—the return of their land and thus their land-based cultural identity—revolved around a legal definition of their identity as tribal Indians and required their officially becoming Mashpee Indian legal subjects. To achieve this result an acceptance of the discourse of rights and national identity is not just strategic, but necessary.

This postmodern political dilemma connects with problems in Critical Legal Studies, where that discourse also seeks to "deconstruct" or dissolve the language of rights, scrutinizing rights as innately unstable and indeterminant, and replacing the rights vocabulary with one of "needs." Among the many resulting difficulties is the status of "needs," as identity-groups come under a protectionist shield of

---

[15] J. Clifford, "Identity in Mashpee" in *The Predicament of Culture; Twentieth Century Ethnography, Literature and Art* (1988). See also Torres and Milun "Translating Yonodio by Precedent and Evidence. The Mashpee Indian Case" (1990) Duke L. J. 625.

[16] *Mashpee Tribe v. Town of Mashpee* (D. Mass. 1978) 447 F. Supp. 940, *aff'd, Mashpee Tribe v. New Seabury Corp.* (1st Cir. 1979) 592 F2d 575, *cert. denied* (1979) 444 U.S. 866.

"need" where they remain victims in need of help.[17] Critical Legal Studies has also implied that a rights discourse like that of Native American demands for the upholding of treaties succumbs to a self-defeating legitimation of government power in the first place. Along these lines we can think of the current upheavals in Wisconsin surrounding the spear-fishing rights of the Lac du Flambeau-area Indians, who are fighting for an enhanced and protected fishing domain on the terms of the government's initial dealings with their tribe, on promises made in original treaties, and on the definition of their cultural identity as land-based.[18] The symbolic gestures of the Mexican-American movement of the 1960s and 70s, coalescing in New Mexico in the Tierra Amarilla area and dedicated to the return of property traced back to land-grants honored by the Treaty of the Mexican-American war, had a similar thrust; the battle in the courts revolved around the honoring of these claims as the treaty promised to uphold them, despite the dubious historical circumstances under which the treaty was signed.[19] To seek to dissolve these "rights" away under the acid bath of postmodern multiplicity simply erases the grounds for self-determination, which can only be coded as an identity (collective or individual) possessing rights. Self-determination would seem to entail the embrace of legal subject-hood, as the vocabulary of rights may still be the only viable means to secure that selfhood. A postmodernism that ignores or deplores this necessity reveals its supposition that "rights" are already adequately secured and that the legal arena cannot be bent to a variety of discursive purposes. A related struggle is ensuing in those localities where gay rights activists are applying pressure for the right to marry. Marriage can be subjected to a withering critique as a transparently ideological institution, but in this case too the importance of reserving a vocabulary of "rights" as a legal subject transcends those objections since the political objectives of securing gay marriage rights outweigh any hesitance about the identities pre-supposed by marriage.

A paradox of the postmodern, which any teacher of the humanities can detail, is the coincident and vociferous rise of an identity-based politics hard on the heels of a postmodernist or at least poststructuralist consensus which would seem to question identity at large as an essentialist category. Even where there is some circumspection about making the "mistake" of essentialism (and here I will admit I concur with the assessment that it is a mistake), a separatist identity politics is coming to the fore. With it a kind of "serial identity" politics, along the lines of serial monogamy, is especially often antagonistic and rampant. In this mode identities are seen as additive or cumulative, with smaller and smaller subdivisions to mark more and more specialized identity formations. Part of the impetus for this discursive and political phenomenon arises out of cultural and historical roots in the United States, where an individualizing rhetoric permeates all our major social forms. The community identity models itself on individual identity and coheres around shared attributes which are seen as defining, while the extent to which these community identities arise in relation to a social dominant becomes obscured. Onto this atomizing and even sentimentalizing identity politics a postmodernism of local determination gets grafted, with powerful but often mixed results. Even the brilliantly helpful theorists Ernesto Laclau and Chantal Mouffe seem to articulate this impasse in their certifiably postmodern reconstruction of the social sphere, *Hegemony and Socialist Strategy*.[20] Grafting a dizzying postmodern vocabulary to an incisive political armature, the two arrive

[17] R. Unger, *The Critical Legal Studies Movement* (1986). See also N. Fraser, "Struggle over Needs" in *Unruly Practices* (1989); Williams, "Taking Rights Aggressively: The Perils and Promise of Critical Legal Studies for People of Color" (1987) 5 *Law and Inequality* 103.

[18] See, *e.g. Lac Courte Oreilles Band of Lake Superior Chippewa Indians v. Voight* (7th Cir. 1983) 700 F.2d 341 *cert denied* (1983) 464 U.S. 805.

[19] See *Valdez v. Black* (10th Cir. 1971) 446 F.2d 1071.

[20] E. Laclau & C. Mouffe, *Hegemony and Socialist Strategy* (1985), pp. 191, 193.

at a formulation for radical democracy which would mandate that: "the epistemological niche from which 'universal' classes and subjects spoke has been eradicated, and it has been replaced by a polyphony of voices, each of which constructs its own irreducible discursive identity." They go on shortly thereafter to conclude that this politics is founded on the "affirmation of the contingency and ambiguity of every 'essence,' and on the constitutive character of social division and antagonism." Irreducible, perhaps essential, identities in an polyphonic harmony of voices, the sound can also be heard as the raucous, antagonistic atonality of the social. The one-note song of an irreducible identity is hard to fuse with the dissolving logic of identity, the insistence on internal differences. The laudable goal of opening up social space to a multiplicity of approaches, a postmodern postMarxism, ends up depending on the mobilization of *singular* identities. As long as the postmodern in practice involves such contradictions, the relation between postmodern identity and the legal subject will be in question, too—these confusions in practice will infect the transferring over of postmodern elements to the legal sphere.

Another legally-informed narrative may help to highlight this shortcoming by way of an excursion into another postmodern flavor or type crystallized in the work of Jean Baudrillard, who intersects with both Jameson and Lyotard, despite coming to some remarkably different conclusions. Baudrillard is the coiner of the all-important postmodernist work "simulacrum," his term for the substitution of the screen for the "real" or even the "spectacle" which comprises modern culture. For Baudrillard, we are now, as a result of the technology of the image, so thoroughly imbricated in the image that even the human body is a kind of prosthetic screen.[21] For Baudrillard, there is the autistic ecstasy of communication, where judgment, meaning, and action are impossible. We now live our lives not as actors in pyschic dramas on a stage or in a scene, but as sites of the arbitrary coupling of bits of information, images, termini, and so on that float past us in the hyperreal space of the image-filled simulacrum, an "ob-scene" which has no back side you can get to. For example, Baudrillard analyzes current political events as entirely contained within the simulacral—there is no authentic space anywhere where something else can happen, and even something as fearful as nuclear war is a simulation, a construction in images by a culture that will never have to start the final war because the image of such destruction serves all the purposes. There are echoes of Jameson here: both theorists depend on an idea of the proliferation and takeover of the technologies of postmodern life and on the schizophrenia that induces; Baudrillard, however, has no nostalgia for the realm of history or of concerted political action as does Jameson; his thought is entirely eschatological and apocalyptic, pushed up to the very edge. There is no arena for action, no public discourse. We are seduced by the image and in fact live within it, like the boy in the bubble, tethered to the simulacral bubbles which surround us. The importance of Baudrillard's thought lies first in it powerful evocation of the way images have indeed filled up all the interstices of the world; he is a prophet of that process, which he calls the precession of the simulacral. But Baudrillard's apocalypticism also has affinities to Lyotard's apolitical postmodernism, because it questions any role for agency, any collectivity, any escape from the clutches of the image. Both are happy to put Marxism or cultural critique on ice, for different reasons, but Baudrillard differs too from Lyotard in the nihilism of his postmodernism. For Lyotard still has faith in the effects of art—high modernist art—which he holds to be capable of producing the sublime. Baudrillard's sublime is the monstrous enclosure of the image, the vast screen on which daily life unfurls. There is no antidote to this, least of all art, which itself is thoroughly implicated in the screenings, as it must be.

To segue into the legal subject by way of the world of high art and the

---

[21] See J. Baudrillard, *Simulations* (1983).

simulacral—the recent Mapplethorpe obscenity trial in Cincinnati invoked yet another varient in the postmodern identity/legal subject distinction.[22] The post-humous exhibition of Mapplethorpe's work there called down a trial of the museum director for having shown the photographs, on the grounds that they constituted pornography. Postmodern identity would seem to have it all over the legal subject here, in that Mapplethorpe's work in any number of ways has been identified with a differential logic of identity, an insistence on imagery and the fantasmatic nature of social relations of power and sexuality. This obtains although the artistic form of Mapplethorpe's work might better be conceived as modernist, relying as it does on strict formal symmetries, becoming "post-modern" in its recontextualizing of those aesthetic values onto altogether different arenas of signification. Transcripts of the trial showed high art critical standards of form brought to bear on photographs of, say, penises emerging from unzipped pants; these are amusing enough in their way, but also have something important to say about how a somewhat mystifying postmodernist art must wend its way through legal discourse to be validated *as* art. So problematic have the contours of art become under postmodernism that delineating the boundaries of the mass cultural, the photographic, the popular, the pornographic, the jour-nalistic, and the aesthetic becomes a matter of legal adjudication. The jurors in this trial, to everyone's great relief, were to a man and a woman convinced by the argument that what has been displayed by the museum was art—though art as such, consecrated by high culture, might be very foreign to their own social milieu, they could recognize that even what they *didn't* like could come under that heading. In the churning froth of mobile and multiple sexual identities, of transgressive reformulations of object and subject, in the postmodern wash of identity, the legal subject who came to the fore was the aesthetic individual with the right of freedom of expression—not Mapplethorpe's expression, which could only be vindicated after death in any event, but the rights of Cincinnati museum-goers to see something categorized as art. The strongly simulacral overtones of the trial, the interposition of images of pornography onto unrelated artifacts in the show (like the photographs of children), and the relegation of the objec-tionable works to a viewing ghetto where they were seen from above in a case like a library exhibit, instead of being wall-mounted full size in gallery style, all combined to make this a theater of the "ob-scene," not because of any obscenity in the pictures, but through an all-encompassing "screening," so that one had to have a position on the photographs whether or not one had, like a tiny fraction of the public, seen the pictures under siege. This spasmodic event was inevitably grafted onto a legal discourse of rights with adjudication over the definition of "art" itself. The trial could not begin to encompass all the peculiar, opportunistic, and virulent social meanings of the indictment, but the language of the legal subject prevailed over the overdetermined and commodified scene of the prose-cution. The "legal subject" in this rare instance implied something beyond the consensus of the unlikeability of the images and the desire to get them out of Cincinnati, period—it involved a space for the consideration of the cultural value of art and its duty to venture into the ob-scene.

It is possible then to see a major division in the discussion of postmodernism, one between a utopian postmodernism and the kind of apocalyptic, commer-cialized postmodernism described by Baudrillard and others. In the first instance, postmodernism itself becomes a way of overturning the hierarchies on which modernism is purportedly predicated—looked at in a certain light: the center over the periphery, the West over the third world, men over women, and so on. In providing the critique of these structures, one brand of postmodernism could be called a utopian theory seeking to undermine all such binaries and divisions, installing the play of differences in their stead. Thinkers like Craig Owens and

[22] *Contemporary Arts Center v. Ney* (S.D. Ohio 1990) 735 F. Supp. 743.

others have suggested that postmodernity itself is the "discourse of others," of those who have been disenfranchised from the cultural system. In particular he cites the prominence of sexual difference in postmodern art of the last 15 years and of the female artists who have participated in making postmodernism what it is—for him, a questioning of all difference and a dissolving of natural or essentialized hierarchies.[23]

A postmodernism of this variety has been given the name "resistance" postmodernism, and to this I would register a serious caveat—not to the possibility of resistance, but to its linkage with the postmodern. View in this light, postmodernism becomes a critical took kit, a set of techniques to deploy at will, generally in the realm of textual culture. That vision renders postmodernism with overly broad brush strokes, as providing internal options of a reactionary or progressive kind. What that will mean is an overinvestment in discursive gestures, the often fatuous assumption that an alteration of textual style or nomenclature or the decentering of a discourse in some purely symbolic way sends shock waves to the heart of social domination. That very locution is of course disavowed by postmodernism anyway, since no "heart" or core of hegemony can be posited. This insight could quite profitably be tailored to an understanding of the law, of the legal subject, not as a monolithic construct, but as a permeable membrane within which innumerable sites of conflict and innumerable forms of struggle can be seen to exist.

A primary failure of postmodernism has been the failure to articulate the *location* of postmodernism, where it exists, who has it, and who does not. The conditions of postmodernity only exist in our culture because of the very specific economic and social procedures that go on in the rest of the world, and the "apocalypse now" mentality of much postmodernism has covered over that distinction. The world of the micro-chip, the VCR, and the society of information is predicated on the displacement of labor around the globe, on mass islands of, usually, women, who put together these formations of postmodernity completely outside the circle, charmed or not, of postmodern ruminations. Donna Haraway has called these legions of (mostly) third world women the cyborgs of the postmodern world, who have been turned partly into technological machines by the nature of their work, and partly into celebrated postmodern bodies by Western theory, eager to worship a fragmented, prosthetic Otherness as a privileged place of the postmodern.[24] This is, I think, far too romanticizing and also typical of a postmodern outlook that insists on the glamour of postmodern technological bodies wherever they may appear. By presenting postmodernity as universal, our theory has shown its Eurocentric cast; by presenting postmodernity as total, as either heaven or hell, the specificities of how it is put together as a social reality are lost. This lacuna in postmodernism has been deeply damaging, and its dangers should be readily apparent to legal discourse as well, which needs to remember its own boundedness even in the global reach of the postmodern.     [455–472]

---

[23] See Owens, "The Discourse of Others, Feminists and Postmodernism" in *The Anti-Aesthetic* (H. Foster ed., 1983), p. 57.

[24] D. Haraway, *Simians, Cyborgs and Women, The Reinvention of Nature* (1991), pp. 149–181.

**PIERRE SCHLAG**
**Normativity and the Politics of Form**
(1991)[25]

*L.A. Law's Empire*

On Thursday, March 29, 1990, at approximately 10:00 p.m., Stuart Markowitz was arrested for DWI. Stuart Markowitz is a 50 year old mid-level partner in a small L.A. law firm—a bit of a buffoon, something of a schlemiel, soft around the edges, but not entirely spineless.[26] He is one of the less ego-centred, one of the more principled characters on *L.A. Law*. He is even (at times) surprisingly politically correct on gender issues.

As you might expect, it was an incredible shock to witness Stuart, this soft, kind, harmless man being rudely arrested. You can picture the scene. The cop is a predictable six-foot something, a Nordic blond Visigoth sporting the ubiquitous, standard cop-issue aviator glasses. Clear proto-fascist material. The shock of Stuart's arrest is compounded by our having learned just moments before that Stuart and his wife Ann had planned to go off to a motel to do (as Stuart announced in his best muffled baritone voice) "some unbelievably sinful things."

In a few short T.V. frames, the promise of innocent sex is violently and definitively crushed by the powerful long arm of the law. If you are a member of the legal community, this scene has particular resonance for you: it evokes the iconic intrusion into the marital bedroom condemned in *Griswold* v. *Connecticut*;[27] Orwell comes to mind.[28] Note the image of law here: it is on the wrong side, unaccountably random and awesomely powerful.

Stuart's breathalyzer tests reads .09.[29] This comes to us as somewhat of a surprise. True, Stuart had been seen sipping wine with Ann moments before the arrest, but he certainly did not look drunk, and besides, it's not in Stuart's character to drink and drive. Fortunately, we find out that Stuart will be represented by Michael Kuzak, Stuart's brash, young, sexy, terribly competent, and ruthless partner. In fine form, before taking Stuart's testimony, Michael sits down with Ann and Stuart to explain the law:

> Michael: Peter Himeson is the best toxicologist in the state. If he testifies for us, our stock goes way up. O.K. to the facts ... Now, you had a glass of wine minutes before leaving the restaurant right?
> Stuart: Well, I had wine with lunch so I guess, it was ...
> Michael: Yes, but timing is very important. Let me explain something. It takes thirty minutes for a drink to get into your bloodstream. That means that if you had a glass of wine, just before you got into your car, our expert witness could testify that it wasn't in your system when you were arrested ... This is very important testimony ... So ... When do you think you had that last glass of wine?

Stuart and Ann understand implicitly:

> Ann: He drank it right before we left.
> Michael: Are you willing to testify to this?
> Ann: Yes.
> Michael: Good ... Very good.

---

[25] [From (1991) 139 Univ. of Pennsylvania L. Rev. 801.]
[26] See *L.A. Law* (NBC television broadcast, March 29, 1990).
[27] (1965) 381 U.S. 479 (asking "Would we allow the police to search the sacred precincts of marital bedrooms...?").
[28] See G. Orwell, *Nineteen Eighty-Four* (1949).
[29] He is "above the limit".

Note that Michael has just elicited precisely the testimony he would like the witness to give without once inviting any reference to the truth of the matter. Michael understands, of course, that his role is circumscribed. He cannot overtly suborn perjury, or, more precisely, he cannot knowingly allow Ann or Stuart to lie about the chronology of Stuart's drinking. On the other hand, there is no rule of law, no provision of the ethical code, nothing at all that compels Michael affirmatively to find out the truth about when the drinking occurred.

We thus come to understand that whether or not Stuart will be convicted for DWI has virtually nothing to do with whether or not he was legally drunk at the time of the arrest. It has everything to do with the quality of the performances by various actors (most notably, Michael, Stuart, Ann, the cop, the D.A., and the experts) within the stylized, sometimes highly circumscribed roles that the law has scripted and structured for them.[30]

The image of law presented here is the performance of rhetorical moves within scripted, stylized roles than can be used by the various actors to invoke or suppress institutional power. There are ratios of power among the various actors, and depending how all the actors deploy their power possibilities, it will be *this* outcome rather than *that* one which will be produced. So far Michael Kuzak is performing his role well—so well in fact that he would like to make the case go away before trial. To this end, he has prepared the entire case before going to see the D.A. The provable facts are as follows:

1. Stuart had a .09 blood alcohol level, which is barely over the .08 DWI limit in California.
2. Two witnesses (Stuart and Ann) will testify that Stuart drank the wine just moments before he got into his car.
3. The state's top toxicologist—a highly respected person in the field—will testify that based on this time line, it would have been impossible for Stuart to be drunk at the time of the arrest.

Armed with these rhetorical obstacles to conviction, Michael Kuzak goes to see the D.A., a woman he happens to know by name. He tells her the provable facts. He adds that the case has been scheduled before Judge Matthews—a judge whom both Michael and the D.A. know to be a friend of the senior partner in Michael's firm. She looks skeptical. Michael pleads with her. He asks for a favor: "I need this one." Michael's tone implies: "come on, please, just this one time..."

Michael and the D.A. apparently have a "professional friendship," an informal relation that arises from the repeated contacts of the routine. Very likely they have had cases against each other. It is this kind of professional friendship that sustains the vast informal network through which the long arm of the law does much of its work: plea bargains, settlements, consent decrees, etc. This is the network of the law within the law—*the shadow law.*[31]

The shadow law works smoothly and efficiently in the shadow of the unwieldy bilateral monopolies created by the state's statutory criminal law. The shadow law reduces transaction costs through an institution known as *"the favor bank,"*[32] a huge, constantly rearranging assembly of ties, loyalties, debts, and obligations. To outsiders, it is the secret economy of the law operating in the interstitial spaces

---

[30] This description resonates in autopoietic social theory:
> Legal communications are the cognitive instruments by which the law as social discourse is able to see the world. Legal communications cannot reach out into the real outside world, neither into nature nor into society. They can only communicate about nature and society. Any metaphor about their access to the real world is misplaced.

Teubner, "How the Law Thinks: Toward a Constructivist Epistemology of Law" (1989) 23 Law & Soc'y Rev. 727, 740.

[31] See Mnookin and Kornhauser (1987) 88 Yale L. J. 950.

[32] The "favor bank" is a jurisprudential concept developed by Tom Wolfe. See T. Wolfe, *The Bonfire of the Vanities* (1987), pp. 400–402.

left by the rational structure of explicit doctrinal law. The favor bank is in significant part a feudal institution—hierarchical in structure and operated on principle of loyalty and honor, and on ties of professional friendships, like the one between Michael and the D.A.

In the end, the favor bank, the shadow law, and Michael's performance have done their work: the charges will be reduced to "reckless driving—dry." And that's what matters to us: Stuart is just too nice a guy to be convicted. How does Michael come out? From the perspective of law in the books or law in the law school, Michael has engaged in some very questionable practices. Yet from a purely instrumental perspective, he has done a good job of it. Besides, this is what real law is like—playing the power ratios and manipulating the performances to get the right result. And in our role as TV viewers, we know the right result: it is to get soft, kind, harmless Stuart out of the sex-hating, life-denying, fun-killing, Orwellian grasp of the law.

At the end of this episode, Stuart and Ann are back at their law offices and Stuart drops the inevitable bombshell. "I was guilty: three glasses of wine," he says. This is a brilliant piece of script writing. It is brilliant because it confirms the central point that law is a game of power and manipulation. The lawyers manipulate and control. The law manipulates and controls as it tells its story through the mouths of the various legal actors—the lawyer, the D.A., the suspect, and the witness—all acting in their legal roles. And it is only when the long arm of the law is retracted and the choreographed legal roles have been dropped, that Stuart can tell us that he was in fact drunk.

Did we see this coming? Probably. Could we have missed it? Sure: if we had insisted on believing that the statements made by Michael Kuzak, the lawyer, Stuart Markowitz, the suspect, and Ann Kelsey, the witness, were part of a field of undistorted rational discourse whose ultimate criterion is truth. We could have been taken in. But only if we indulged in one hell of a category mistake. We would have had to misconstrue a field of performances, of performative utterances, of power moves—that is, the field of law—for a field of undistorted rational discourse.

In our role as T.V. viewers of *L.A. Law*, we usually don't make that mistake. We understand that the law represented to us is not simply or even primarily a system of undistorted rational discourse. We understand implicitly that it is an institutionalized arrangement of performative roles and possibilities that both enable as well as delimit the possibilities for truth-telling and deception. We understand that there is a great deal more going on than could possibly be captured by a medium that reduces law to stabilized "propositions," to rational arrangements of "ideas," to overarching "theories."

This is a world in which deceit plays an important part. Ann, Stuart and Michael succeeded in deceiving some of the other characters on the show (including each other). By the end of the show, Stuart even ends up deceiving himself: reflecting upon the fact that by being able to pay $3000 for a top toxicologist, he was able to beat the rap, Stuart says to himself, "I'm just lucky, I guess." This is an extraordinary moment of self-deception. Indeed, it hardly classifies as luck for an upper-middle class, well-connected, white male lawyer to be able to beat an isolated DWI rap. On the contrary, it's part and parcel of what it means to be part of that class. But Stuart abstracts himself away from this unwelcome bit of social self-knowledge, denies to himself that he is part of this web of social power, and avoids any reckoning with the social sources of his power: it's just plain, dumb, ineffable luck. Here we get a wonderful insight into how the average lawyer manages to deal with the web of social power in which he is enmeshed. Like Stuart, the typical lawyer denies that he is of the web. He claims that he is outside or above the web.

One of the striking aspects of *L.A. Law* is that, for all its obvious and not so negligible shortfalls, it is often a better approximation of the world of law practice than the routine academic productions of normative legal thought.[33] This perception is likely to be shared by anyone who has had any actual practice experience, anyone who understands that professional power is the juice that makes the wheels of the law-bureaucracies run. Lawyers tend to see their professional power as resting, "not on rules, but on local knowledge, insider access, connections, and reputation."[34] For instance, "lawyer regulars" within the criminal justice system maintain intimate relations with all levels of personnel in the court setting as a means of obtaining, maintaining, and building their practice: "These informal relations are the *sine qua non* not only of retaining a practice, but also in the negotiation of pleas and sentences."[35]

The favor bank and the shadow law, more than the reason of the better argument, is the stuff of law. The favor bank cannot be seen in *Law's Empire*, but only on *L.A. Law*. *Law's Empire* is predicated on the separation of "law" from the social and on the confinement of law to the space of the rational, the conscious, and the originary. Normative legal thought implicitly assumes that "we are a government of laws, not men."[36] *L.A. Law* reminds us that it is also the other way around. Practicing lawyers know very well that "[i]t makes all the difference which judge is deciding a case."[37]

When a lawyer presents a case to a jury, the opening argument, the direct examinations, the cross, the objections, and the summation all typically aim toward the paramount objective of making the jury believe the lawyer's story line and disbelieve the other side.[38] To this end, the lawyer will establish her authority, credibility, and rapport with the jury. Moreover, she will not presume on them too much but will construct a relatively clear and simple story line. This will be a prototypical story that resonates within the culture and evokes stereotypical responses such as pity, admiration, contempt, fear, and so forth. Each of the trial lawyer's actions in the courtroom will be designed to bolster, repeat, and reinforce that story line.

For the trial lawyer, the substantive doctrine and the law of evidence and of civil procedure, will serve two main functions. In one sense, they will be the filters, the screens through which the stock story-line must pass. In this screening capacity, the positive law is obstructive. But the positive law is enabling as well: it organizes, echoes, and dignifies the lawyer's story-line. In this second sense, the law signals to the jury that this is not any sort of story being told but one that fits a prototypical pattern (i.e., defendant intentionally harmed plaintiff) and that

---

[33] Gillers notes: "I watched many hours of *L.A. Law*. The shows were uneven internally and from week to week. Some were heavy with adolescent humor and crude stereotypes. Others were admirable, occasionally masterful, in their depiction of legal and ethical issues. Lean and subtle, they could inspire class discussion." Gillers, "Taking *L.A. Law* More Seriously" (1989) 98 Yale L. J. 1607, 1620.

[34] Sarat & Felstiner (1989) 98 Yale L. J. 1663 at 1685. As Sarat and Felstiner observe: "Lawyers often suggest that their most important contribution is knowledge of the ropes, not knowledge of the rules; they describe a system that is not bureaucratically rational but is, nonetheless, accessible to its "priests.'

[35] Blumberg, *op. cit.*, (1967) Law and Society Rev. 15, 21; see also J. Carlin, *Lawyers On Their Own* (1962), pp. 105–109 (discussing the mechanics of a small-scale, solo criminal practice).

[36] *Marbury v. Madison* (1803) 5 U.S. (1 Cranch) 137, 163.

[37] A. Dershowitz, *Taking Liberties: A Decade of Hard Cases, Bad Laws, and Bum Raps* (1988), p. 2.

[38] The discourse of lawyers is "a paradigmatic case of strategic, success-oriented communication." Dan-Cohen, "Law, Community and Communications" (1989) Duke L.J. 1654, 1668.

therefore the story warrants a prototypical response (i.e., jurors should make defendant compensate plaintiff).[39]

In crafting this story, the lawyer will consider the self-image of the jurors, their values, and their beliefs about themselves. The lawyer will frame the story with a simple rhetorical structure in mind: believe my story because it will confirm your sense of yourself as decent, courageous, sensible, etc.; believe my opponent's story because in order to believe it, you will have to give up part of your favorable self-image.

Thus, for the effective trial lawyer, truth, rationality, and moral values play a role but only in an instrumental sense—only insofar as they aid the lawyer in effectively manipulating the jury to reach the pre-determined desired outcomes. Control and manipulation are the objective. What matters is not the rationality of a story but whether the story will rhetorically and cognitively produce the desired result; what matters is not moral value, but the moralistic self-image of the jurors.

For the trial lawyer, the field is already in part constituted. As the litigation proceeds, countless factors increasingly limit the trial lawyer's possible strategies. The positive law sets the bounds of possible litigation. Discovery sets the bounds of the possible factual positions in the case. The identity of the judges sets the bounds of permissible evidence. Still, many of the power relations are the creation of the trial lawyer herself. She will establish a relation with the jurors and judge, and in doing so, will influence the jurors' relation with the judge, their task, and opposing counsel.

Neither the truth, nor the rational content, nor the moral effect of this relation matters. What matters is the relation itself: who commands, who silences, who is believed, etc. The trial lawyer knows all this. And the last thing she wants to do is re-present to herself all these relations in terms of a conventional separation and stabilization of truth, rationality, or moral value. On the contrary, to be effective, all of this must be implicitly understood—indeed internalized—as a system of differentiated relations among power, truth, rationality, rhetoric, and deceit. As Dauer and Leff put it:

> A lawyer is a person who on behalf of some people treats other people the way bureaucracies treat all people—as nonpeople. Most lawyers are free-lance bureaucrats, not tied to any major established bureaucracy, who can be hired to use, typically in a bureaucratic setting, bureaucratic skills—delay, threat, wheedling, needling, aggression, manipulation, paper passing, complexity, negotiation, selective surrender, almost-genuine passion—on behalf of someone unable or unwilling to do all that for himself.[40]

All of this, of course, *appears* to be very far from the reigning image of law on the contemporary normative legal thought channel. Listen to Dworkin and experience the dissonance:

> What is law? . . . Law's empire is defined by attitude, not territory or power or process . . .
> It is an interpretive, self-reflective attitude addressed to politics in the broadest sense . . .
> Law's attitude is constructive: it aims, in the interpretive spirit, to lay principle over practice to show the best route to a better future, keeping the right faith with the past.[41]

Listen to Owen Fiss:

---

[39] See S. Winter, "Cognitive Dimensions" (1989) 87 Michigan L. Rev. 2225, 2272–2274 (describing the ways in which the advocate's story-line can persuade by tapping into an existing story-line shared by his or her audience).

[40] Dauer & Leff, "The Lawyer as Friend" (1977) 86 Yale L.J. 573, 581.

[41] R. Dworkin, *Law's Empire*, p. 413.

I continue to believe that law is a distinct form of human activity, one which, as Ronald Dworkin and others have insisted for some years now, differs from politics, even a highly idealized politics, in important ways. Political actors can and often do make claims of justice, but they need not ... Judges on the other hand, have no authority other than to decide what is just, and they obtain the right to do so from the procedural norms that surround their office and limit the exercise of their power.[42]

These visions of law offered by Fiss and Dworkin are a far cry from *L.A. Law*. Against that backdrop, the Dworkin-Fiss visions advertise an extraordinarily idealized, romanticized account of law—impossibly clean and orderly. They certainly seem quite distant from the vision of lawyering offered by Dauer and Leff.

And yet, is there really any contradiction here between the two visions? Does the validation of the Dauer-Leff view of the lawyer-as-bureaucrat somehow falsify the Dworkin-Fiss visions? Or, correspondingly, does the Dworkin-Fiss vision somehow falsify the Dauer-Leff account? The answer, surprisingly, is no. What Fiss and Dworkin describe as the practice of law *is* what Dauer and Leff describe as the practice of law. We have to understand that when Dworkin and Fiss give their idealized or romanticized accounts of law, they are not talking about a separate reality: the Dworkin and Fiss visions are real—and they are realized every day in precisely the ways described by Dauer and Leff. "Laying principle over practice" and "making the law the best it can be" *is* the harassment, *is* the aggression, *is* the manipulation. All this stuff about "deciding what is just" and showing "the best route to a better future, keeping the right faith with the past" *is* exactly what Dauer and Leff's bureaucratic-lawyers say and do as they delay, threaten, wheedle, needle, manipulate, and otherwise kick people around.

Normative legal thought never quite manages to understand this point. Indeed the continued viability, the continued respectability of normative legal thought as an enterprise in the academy *depends upon* its failing to understand this point. Normative legal thought routinely fails to understand this point by relentlessly repeating two errors.

First, normative legal thought believes that in the abstraction of the normative terms from their bureaucratic setting on *L.A. Law*, their meaning, their significance, has nonetheless been preserved.[43] Normative legal thought tends to disavow its own performative dimension; it tends to hide from itself the kinds of social and rhetorical uses to which it is put. Rather uncritically and solipsistically, normative legal thought tends to concern itself only with its own "substantive" propositional normative content and its own normatively sanctioned uses. In this sense, we can say that normative legal thought is not a "serious" enterprise—but rather one that presumes uncritically that its main, or critical, significance is self-determined.

This fixation of normative legal thought on its own "substantive" propositional normative content is sustained by a second kind of prototypical mistake. Having abstracted its own discourse from the bureaucratic setting of *L.A. Law*, normative legal thought tends to assume that its own "substantive" propositional normative content somehow controls the way in which normative legal thought is used—that somehow its propositional normative content regulates the ways in which people get kicked around. Normative legal thought is thus prone to a naïve form of identity thinking where the normative significance of a legal term in the

---

[42] O. Fiss, "The Law Regained" (1989) 74 Cornell L. Rev. 245, 249.

[43] This is a variant of Cover's criticism of the tendency among legal commentators to reduce law to the interpretation of de-contextualized texts. See R. Cover, "Violence and the Word" (1986) Yale L.J. 1601, 1601 (arguing that law cannot be understood apart from its own relation to the violence it occasions): see also R. Coombe, "Same as it Ever Was: Rethinking the Politics of Legal Interpretation" (1989) 34 McGill L.J. 601, 649.

legal academy is blithely assumed to correspond roughly to the same normative significance in law practice. But it's not so.

And rhetorically, it is relatively easy to see that it is not so. We need only ask what kind of role normative legal thought, or Dworkin, could play on *L.A. Law*. The point here is not the usual one of trying to assess whether Dworkin's vision of Law is right or not. Rather, the question is, what *role* can Dworkin *perform*— what role can normative legal thought credibly *perform* on *L.A. Law*? What is the performative significance of normative legal thought?[44]

It is not easy to see what role Dworkin could play. For one thing, it is extremely difficult to imagine a normative thinker like Dworkin on *L.A. Law*. To the extent that we understand Dworkin as the author of *Law's Empire* or *Taking Rights Seriously* (as opposed to Ronald Dworkin, the man), it is implausible that he should become a regular character on *L.A. Law*: there is no leading role on the show for a regular character whose primary (if not sole) mode of communicative interaction is "authentic" normative legal thought.

Perhaps, then, we should think along more modest lines. Perhaps we could introduce Ronald Dworkin in a flashback. Michael Kuzak, faced with a very difficult appeal on constitutional grounds, could remember his old professor from law school. At a critical point in the case preparation, Michael would remember his old professor's words and these would, of course, provide the crucial missing link to win the case. "Yes—I've got it," exclaims Michael Kuzak. The judge "constructs his overall theory of the present law so that it reflects, so far as possible, coherent principles of fairness, substantive justice, and procedural due process, and reflects these combined in the right relation."[45]

No. Dramatically, this does not work. It is not credible. Normative legal thought cannot contribute to the practice of law *in this way*. Its prescriptions and its subtle intellectual moves are simply not important to the practice of law in this way.

Perhaps, then, Ronald Dworkin could be allowed to make a speech at some bar convention about the rule of law and law's empire? Now, this dramatic option does work; this is credible theater. It can be scripted. Ronald Dworkin could even play the part himself. But there is something disturbing about this. The only role we have found for Ronald Dworkin or normative legal thought on *L.A. Law's Empire* is the ritualistic ceremonial one of providing the lawyering profession with a pleasing and admirable self-image. In other words, the one role dramatically possible for the normative legal thought of the legal academy is that of self-image maintenance for legal academics and lawyers.[46] This, of course, raises a disquieting question about the social significance of normative legal thought, suggesting that its primary significance is the performative one of providing and disseminating an appealing rhetoric and self-image for the lawyering profession.

In part, these observations bring us back to the early days of the cls legitimation thesis, when legitimation was a description applied to legal thought, as distinguished from judge-made law. In the early days of cls, Duncan Kennedy suggested that various kinds of legal thought were a kind of legitimation of existing legal institutions and practices.[47] As applied to academic legal thought,

---

[44] American (legal) culture is experiencing a shift from meaning based on constative value to meaning organized in terms of performative value. As this transition accelerates and becomes widely recognized, we experience an erosion of meaning. See Schlag, "Normative and Nowhere to Go," *op. cit.*, pp. 185–186.

[45] R. Dworkin, *op. cit.*, p. 405.

[46] This point is suggested in R. Abel, "Why Does the ABA Promulgate Ethical Rules?" (1981) 59 Tex. L. Rev. 639, 667–68.

[47] In the early days, Kennedy's articulation of the apologetic or legitimating character of academic legal thought was targeted at legal thought—in fact, legal theory. See D. Kennedy, "Cost-Benefit Analysis of Entitlement Problems: A Critique" (1981) 33 Stan. L. Rev. 387, 387–89 Kennedy "The Structure of Blackstone's Commentaries" (1979) 28 Buffalo L. Rev. 205, 209–11.

there is not much doubt that this legitimation thesis was and is right: virtually regardless of what is going on in the courts or the legislatures, most legal thinkers spend their intellectual energies rationalizing (i.e., making rational, coherent, appealing, etc.) whatever it is the courts are doing. Very often this legitimation effort takes the form of criticizing certain opinions or tendencies—but it is always in the attempt, in the effort to redeem, to celebrate, to validate the vast bulk of positive law, the legal institutions, and the thinking and practices of the contemporary American legal community.

While there can be little doubt that normative legal thought is always launched in the enterprise of legitimation, its role may go well beyond apologetics to the actual creation, production, and maintenance of the discourse and rhetoric that enables bureaucratic institutions and practices to organize themselves.[48] The normative legal thought of the academy may thus serve to keep the techniques and strategies of bureaucratic harassment, needling, wheedling, aggression, etc. in working order. There is a great deal to be said for this view. For one thing it helps to explain how the Fiss-Dworkin visions are completely consistent with the Kafkaesque Dauer-Leff vision of bureaucratic lawyering: when lawyers harass, coerce, intimidate, etc. they do it with the nice words, the nice arguments, the nice jurisprudence crafted by normative legal thinkers.

In accordance with this last view, the primary role played by normative legal thought is to constitute students (and to a lesser extent, lawyers and judges) as polite, well-mannered vehicles for the polite transaction of bureaucratic business. *Law's Empire* spells out the proper etiquette for the actors on *L.A. Law's Empire*.[49] This is not as surprising as it might first seem: remember that *Law's Empire* begins with and draws its inspiration from a discussion of courtesy.[50] Courtesy, of course, is nothing if not the studied observance of the idealized self-image of an existing social regime.

So it is certainly plausible to think that normative legal thought's crucial role goes beyond apologetics to the maintenance and refurbishing of the rhetoric deployed on *L.A. Law's Empire*. But such a conclusion is hardly inexorable. After all, there is something quite unorthodox in trying to put Dworkin or any other normative legal thinker on the set of *L.A. Law*—they clearly do not belong there. And if I persist in trying to put them on the stage of *L.A. Law*, they will try vigorously to get off. This is quite predictable; we can expect normative legal thinkers to try to marginalize and deny *L.A. Law's Empire*.

From the perspective of normative legal thinkers, *L.A. Law's Empire* is tosh; it is a fallen and degraded world not worth thinking about or even recognizing. If the world of law practice has become *L.A. Law's Empire*, then so much the worse for law practice—or so normative legal thinkers might argue. But this dismissive posture is not really available to them. Normative legal thought after all does not present itself as a mere intellectual exercise bereft of social or political ambitions. On the contrary, normative legal thought wears its worldly ambitions on its literary sleeves, as the names of its major productions—*Law's Empire* and *The Rule of Law*—indicate.

Owen Fiss reminds us eloquently of these worldly ambitions:

---

[48] On legitimation and apologetics, see Kennedy, "Cost-Benefit Analysis", *op. cit.*, n. 47 at 444–445 (arguing that efficiency analysis is a kind of legitimation for the system of private law).

[49] This is a slightly more gracious and slightly different way of saying that Stanley Fish has already said of Dworkin's theory: it's a nice piece of rhetorical work. As jurisprudence goes, it is in the genre of cheerleading. See S. Fish, *Doing What Comes Naturally*, pp. 390–392; see also Smith, "Pursuit of Pragmatism" (1990) 100 Yale L.J. 409, 444–47 (suggesting that legal pragmatism is a kind of preaching, a kind of jurisprudence-as-exhortation).

[50] See R. Dworkin, pp. 46–70. If one's basic motif for law is "courtesy," it's a pretty good (though not a sure) bet that the analysis is not going to take a searching self-critical turn.

The judge might be seen as forever straddling two worlds, the world of the ideal and the world of the practical, the world of the public value and the world of subjective preference, the world of the Constitution and the world of politics. He derives his legitimacy from only one, but necessarily finds himself in the other. He among all the agencies of government is in the best position to discover the true meaning of our constitutional values, but, at the same time, he is deeply constrained, indeed sometimes even compromised, by his desire—his wholly admirable desire—to give them meaning a reality.[51]

Owen Fiss is entirely right: normative legal thought demands and desires not merely to be performed, but to be enacted in some realm beyond itself—to be realized in the social realm. This sociality of law is true even of the most austere, ascetic formalist approaches that claim that law has an immanent moral rationality.[52] Even for such self-announced formalist accounts, there is a demand that law be not simply thought, but enacted, realized.

To recognize the significance of these worldly ambitions is to recognize that normative legal thought cannot be indifferent to *L.A. Law's Empire*. On the contrary, normative legal thought's ambitions are precisely to rule over the domain currently occupied by *L.A. Law*, to submit the conduct of the various legal actors to some normatively appealing overarching rational pattern. Normative legal thought cannot so quickly dismiss *L.A. Law's Empire*—for that empire is the realm where law is enacted. *L.A. Law's Empire* may be a degraded, fallen world, but it is most assuredly not tosh.

There is another reason why normative legal thought cannot simply dismiss or deny *L.A. Law's Empire*: it is in some senses a more resonant and richer source of intellectual inquiry about law than many of the genteel productions of normative legal thought. Obviously, there are things that *L.A. Law* gets wrong; it is, after all, prime time TV. But despite its romanticization of law practice, the program, in comparison with normative legal thought, is much more consonant with what we are told by psychology, sociology, rhetoric, or even personal experience about the actual practice of law itself. In fact, one would have a very difficult time finding intellectually respectable sources of authority to credit the sort of psychology, sociology, and rhetoric that is (and must be) implicitly or explicitly assumed into methodological—and often—ontological existence by normative legal thought.[53]

Indeed, where is the intellectually respectable documentation to validate the main social and pyschological categories of normative legal thought? Where is the psychological or sociological documentation to authorize normative legal thought's routine invocations of:

the integrity of the sovereign individualist self?
the phenomena of choice, consent, free will?
the concept of unitary intent?
the notion of individual agency?
and so on?

---

[51] Fiss, "The Supreme Court, 1978 Term-Foreword: The Forms of Justice" (1979) 93 Harv. L. Rev. 1, 58.

[52] See Weinrib, "Legal Formalism: On the Immanent Rationality of Law" (1988) 97 Yale L.J. 949, 982, 1012–1013; *ibid.* at 1003 ("[T]he forms of justice cannot be understood detached from the particularity of the external interactions that they govern and from the specific regimes of positive law that actualize them.").

[53] Some normative thinkers attempt to escape this problem by specifying that they are operating within the normative realm—hence, adopting normative conceptions of the person distinct "from an account of human nature given by natural science or social theory." Rawls, "Justice as Fairness: Political Not Metaphysical" (1985) 14 Phil. and Pub. Aff. 223, 232, n. 15.

There isn't much. By and large, normative legal thought has assumed its own psychology, sociology, rhetoric. The sociology, psychology, and rhetoric assumed into existence by normative legal thought is largely the unconscious concretization of its own *posited* aesthetic of social life—an aesthetic inherited from worlds now long since gone. There is little to support the social aesthetic of normative legal thought other than flat and the power of academic inertia. Unfortunately for normative legal thought, its *posited* understandings of the psychological, the social, and the rhetorical are now stunningly anachronistic and strikingly discordant with much of what leading work in the humanities and social sciences have to tell us about human beings and what they do.[54]

To the extent, then, that normative legal thought remains concerned about the adequacy of its representations of the social sphere, it cannot afford to dismiss *L.A. Law's Empire*. To the extent that normative legal thought is or wants to consider itself an "authentic" enterprise, it must recognize the advanced bureaucratization of the practice of law, and strive to understand how its own psychological, sociological, and rhetorical maps are so discordant with those on *L.A. Law's Empire*. [852–870]

## J. M. BALKIN
### Understanding Legal Understanding: The Legal Subject and the Problem of Legal Coherence
### (1993)[55]

*Legal coherence from the standpoint of the socially constructed subject: coherence as rational reconstrubility*

The tests of hypothetical and actual justification envision legal coherence as a feature of an object. The law is coherent if it has certain properties; it has these if it passes a certain test. This approach results in an undecidable dialectic between the requirements of hypothetical and actual justification.

Now we must consider the problem from a different angle. Instead of asking what properties the legal object must have in order to be coherent, we must consider what has to be true of a legal subject in order for the law to be coherent to her. What do legal subjects do when they form judgments of legal coherence and incoherence? What do they bring to the task of legal understanding? What characteristics of subjectivity produce their judgments of legal coherence? Of what features of their thought are judgments of legal coherence the result?

Judgments of legal coherence arise when we understand the law in a particular way. I call this special type of legal understanding rational reconstruction. As explained more fully below, rational reconstruction is the attempt to see reason in legal materials—to view legal materials as a plausible and sensible scheme of human regulation. The experience of legal coherence is the result of our attempt to understand law through the process of rational reconstruction.

---

[54] The point is made most globally by Alasdair MacIntyre, who demonstrates how the history of moral philosophy has evolved along tracks that have little relation to the aesthetics of our own social and psychological practices. See A. Macintyre, *After Virtue* (1984).

[55] [From (1993) 103 Yale L. J. 105.]

Some authors use the term "rational reconstruction" as a test of legal coherence; the law is coherent if it is amenable to rational reconstruction.[56] I do not use the term in this way because this conceals the subject's contribution to legal judgment. Rational reconstruction is not simply a test for properties of or relations between legal norms. It is a way of looking at law.[57] To say that law is amenable to rational reconstruction is to make a claim about both an object and a subject who constructs the object in a particular way so that she may understand it. The law is rationally reconstructible when a legal subject views the law for a certain purpose with a certain result. Implicit in this view is the possibility that she might view the law for a different purpose, or under different circumstances, with a correspondingly different result.

The question of legal coherence is ultimately the question of the conditions of rational reconstructibility. This is a study not only of features of the law, but of how subjects construct the law they understand. Thus, to understand legal coherence we need to ask the following questions?

(1) What is involved in the specific form of understanding called rational reconstruction?

(2) How does this form of understanding differ from other forms of legal understanding?

(3) What features of our experience affect the process of rational reconstruction and hence our judgments about legal coherence?

(4) What effect does the process of rational reconstruction have upon us?

*Rational Reconstruction as an Interpretive Attitude*

Rational reconstruction is the attempt to see parts of the law as a defensible scheme of principles and policies. We rationally reconstruct a part of the law when we seek to apply it to a concrete case. To apply legal rules we must attempt to understand their point, and this requires us to imagine reasonable principles and policies underlying legal doctrines. We need not agree with these principles and policies in all respects; our concern is that they seem consistent and reasonable to us. In considering what is reasonable, we use something more than the principle of non-contradiction; we employ a substantive conception of reason. To rationally reconstruct the law is to attempt to understand the substantive rationality emanating from it.

Consider the common-law doctrines of owner-occupier liability. These doctrines distinguish among the duties that an owner-occupier owes to trespassers, social-guest licensees, and business invitees. We can have many different interpretive attitudes towards these doctrinal distinctions. For example, we can criticize their justice or view them as historical artifacts. We rationally reconstruct these doctrines when we try to understand their point so that we can apply them. We try to imagine the policies and principles that might explain these doctrines and how a reasonable and morally sensitive individual might believe that the doctrines employ sound distinctions. Thus, rational reconstruction is not merely a

---

[56] *e.g.* Andrew Altman, *Critical Legal Studies: A Liberal Critique* (1990), pp. 117–118, 121–23, 127 (viewing C.L.S. arguments as claims that law is not rationally reconstructible; doctrine is rationally reconstructible if it may be seen as conceptually derivable from a single coherent ethical view); Neil MacCormick, "Reconstruction after Deconstruction: A Response to CLS" (1990) 10 O.J.L.S. 539 (offering rational reconstruction as alternative to C.L.S. accounts of law).

[57] MacCormick speaks helpfully of rational reconstruction as an activity, and this approaches my use of the term. MacCormick, *op. cit.*, n. 56, p. 556 (describing rational reconstruction as "the production of clear and systematic statements of legal doctrine, accounting for statute law and case law in terms of organizing principles"). The difficulty is that MacCormick is still concerned with the activity of organising a legal object, and not with the subject who engages in the activity.

criterion or test; it is also a purpose for interpreting and an attitude expressed towards the object of interpretation. The attempt to see the point of doctrines, the attempt to envision ourselves as sympathetic advocates for these doctrines so that we can apply them, is the hallmark of the interpretive attitude I call rational reconstruction.

We might rationally reconstruct these doctrines as follows: When people use their land for business purposes, or for the hope of some economic benefit, they should be held to an ordinary standard of due care. However, when they allow others to come onto their property without expectation of economic benefit, or when they invite people onto property that is not generally held open to the public (for example, when they are merely having their friends over for dinner), they should have less stringent obligations. Finally, when a person invades their land without their permission, they should have the lowest duty of all.

We might believe that these distinctions are unjust and that the law should not make them. Yet the goal of rational reconstruction is not to offer our own account of how doctrine should be constructed. It is to bring a charitable attitude towards the legal object and to envision how it could be a reasonable accommodation of principles and policies that are themselves reasonable. It is to see how the application of these doctrines to concrete situations makes sense. If we find ourselves able to provide such an account, we can say that the law is rationally reconstructible even though it does not fully comport with our ideas of justice. When we can successfully take this attitude towards the law of owner-occupier liability, we will say that this body of doctrine is coherent.

I do not mean to make too much of the simple account of owner-occupier liability just proposed. I do not mean to suggest that this is the only account or even the best account that could be given of these doctrines, much less that everyone would agree that I have provided a substantively reasonable account. Indeed, my argument about the nature of legal coherence assumes that some people will disagree and assert that I have not offered a successful rational reconstruction. I am merely suggesting that when we understand law in order to apply it, we bring an attitude of charity towards the law and that in this task we can and do offer principles and policies, grounds of distinction and grounds of similarity, that seem intelligible, workable, and reasonable, even if we are not wholly convinced that they are morally best. The rational reconstruction of law rests on the possibility of taking this attitude and being able to offer such accounts.

*The Dialectic of Rational Reconstruction and Rational Deconstruction*

Nevertheless, rational reconstruction is only one interpretive attitude we take towards the law. There is another, equally important way of understanding the legal system—an attitude I call *rational deconstruction*. We rationally deconstruct the law when we critically examine legal doctrine to discover its shortcomings. We do not bring the charitable attitude of rational reconstruction to the object of our interpretation. Our goal is not to see the law's substantive rationality, but its failures in that regard.[58]

Consider our rational reconstruction of owner-occupier liability. We might

---

[58] Hence I call this interpretive attitude "*rational* deconstruction" and not simply "deconstruction" because it is grounded in a judgment of substantive rationality. One could engage in deconstruction of a legal text without the desire to offer a normative alternative, or without a belief that the difficulties one found in the text were due to failures of substantive rationality. See, *e.g.* Pierre Schlag, "Le Hors' de Text, C'est Moi: The Politics of Form and the Domestication of Deconstruction" (1990) 11 Cardozo L. Rev. 1631 (criticising normative uses of deconstruction). However, the deconstruction practiced by legal critics is almost always rational deconstruction, because it seeks to criticise law on the basis of some proposed normative alternative.

criticize this account in the following way: It makes no sense for the defendant's duty to exercise due care to depend on the plaintiff's status as trespasser, licensee, or invitee. Absence of an expectation of economic benefit to defendants does not justify limiting the duty to licensees and trespassers. After all, we hold defendants liable for failure to exercise due care in automobile accidents even if they have no economic relationship to their victims or are complete strangers. Similarly, the fact that the plaintiff is a wrongdoer does not eliminate the defendant's duty to exercise due care in automobile accidents unless the plaintiff's wrongdoing is the proximate cause of her injury, so that it was foreseeable from the nature of the plaintiff's conduct that she would be injured. This cannot be said of all cases of trespassing. Hence, we might argue, the doctrines of owner-occupier liability are unprincipled because they draw arbitrary distinctions between individuals and situations. They are not rationally reconstructible and therefore are not normatively coherent.

Just as rational reconstruction involves an attempt to see the substantive rationality emanating from the law, rational deconstruction attempts to recognize how law has failed to live up to the standards of substantive rationality. Rational deconstruction attacks what rational reconstruction defends. To critique a set of doctrines as unprincipled is to critique a proposed rational reconstruction of them; hence, rational deconstruction seeks to show that candidates for rational reconstruction of an area of law are unsatisfactory.

Rational deconstruction of doctrine operates through an appeal to other principles or policies, either implicit or explicit. When we say that a proposed reconstruction of doctrine fails, we are not making a claim about logical contradiction. We are claiming that legal distinctions and similarities have not been adequately justified. When we say that the explanations are not reasonable, we really appeal to standards of justice and sound policy. We appeal to distinctions that would be just, similarities that would be sound. Once again, although coherence and actual justification are not identical, the only way that we can demonstrate incoherence is by an appeal to standards of actual justification. Rational deconstruction makes an argument about a failure of substantive rationality that must employ its own conception of substantive rationality; it offers an argument about justice that invokes its own conceptions of what could be just.

In this way the interpretive stances of rational reconstruction and rational deconstruction employ the dialectic between hypothetical and actual justification. Rational reconstruction constructs a scheme of hypothetical justification by bona fide principles and policies, which is more than logical consistency but less than actual justification; rational deconstruction denies hypothetical justification but proceeds through an attack based on actual justification.

It is important not to confuse these two dialectics. Actual and hypothetical justification are criteria for judging whether legal doctrines are coherent or incoherent. They are tests that an object of interpretation has to meet in order to say that a certain property (coherence) is true of it. In contrast, rational reconstruction and rational deconstruction are interpretive attitudes we have about the legal system; they are the ways in which we look at legal doctrines, which in turn give rise to judgments of coherence and incoherence. The dialectic of actual and hypothetical justification means that we alternate between criteria for legal judgment. The dialectic of rational reconstruction and rational deconstruction means that we alternate between ways of looking at the legal system—sometimes as the repository of a coherent substantive rationality and sometimes as a jumble of conflicting principles and policies.

Although I have described these two interpretive stances as separate, they actually depend upon each other. Rational reconstruction of legal doctrine requires the tools of rational deconstruction in two senses. First, many different accounts of legal doctrine are logically consistent, but not all of them involve morally satisfying principles and policies. Therefore, in constructing a rational reconstruction of doctrine, we must have some way of choosing among the different accounts of the principles and policies that could be said to emanate from existing legal doctrines. Our tool for sorting and judging is rational deconstruction. We reject explanations of legal materials if they seem unprincipled or morally unsatisfying. Rational deconstruction resembles the sculptor's tools that allow her to uncover the statue buried in a block of marble. The sculptor constructs a work of art, but she must do so by eliminating what is inconsistent with her artistic vision. To create she must eliminate; to construct, she must deconstruct. So too the rational reconstructor only achieves her goal by the use of rational deconstruction.

Second, when we rationally reconstruct the law, we often find that we must classify certain legal materials (for example, certain judicial decisions) as anomalies. Even when we judge the law as rationally reconstructible according to a certain story, we will discover that certain parts of it do not fit that story. So we may acknowledge that part of the existing corpus of legal materials are exceptions, mistakes, or wrongly decided cases. Hence, we have two decisions to make: first, whether there are anomalies, and second, which part of the existing legal materials will be considered the anomaly and which part the "real" or "correct" portion of the law that conforms to our story. Different stories will assign these roles to different parts of the legal corpus. Our belief in the rational reconstruction of the law requires us to show that anomalies are exceptional elements of an otherwise coherent whole, elements that could be excised without doing irreparable damage to the fabric of the law. If anomalies are like warts that detract from the beauty of a face, different stories about law may make the same decision a wart or a beauty mark. Indeed, what seemed to be a wart in one story might under another be a central feature of the face. Our belief in the rational reconstruction of the law requires us to show that anomalies are indeed anomalous—that they are like a wart as opposed to a nose. Thus our rational reconstruction—our story of the principles and policies behind the law—must purport to tell us what is central and what is peripheral in legal doctrine.

In order to tell what is anomalous and what is central to our story, we need the tools of rational deconstruction. Through rational deconstruction we decide that two parts of the existing corpus cannot live together in a coherent scheme of principles and policies and that we must choose between them. Rational reconstruction thus makes use of rational deconstruction not only in determining which consistent sets of principles and policies could serve as a rational reconstruction, but also in deciding which parts of the legal corpus must be explained by the rational reconstruction and which parts can be jettisoned as mistaken. There is no rational reconstruction, in other words, without rational deconstruction, just as there is no cup without the void it encloses, and no statue without the space that surrounds it.

If the task of rational reconstruction depends on the prior use of rational deconstruction, the reverse is also true: all rational deconstruction depends on some alternative successful rational reconstruction of existing doctrinal distinctions and similarities, or upon a set of distinctions and similarities that do not presently exist in law but that could exist in a law that is yet to be. To accuse legal doctrine of incoherence is to imagine a set of legal doctrines that might be coherent; to assert that explanations of existing doctrine are not reasonable is to appeal to distinctions and similarities that could be reasonable. If rational reconstruction achieves its aims by rational deconstruction, rational deconstruction lives off the hope of a future rational reconstruction to which the sorry present might aspire.

*Rational Reconstruction and the "Internal Perspective" of Jurisprudence*

Perhaps the most important thing one can say about rational reconstruction is that it is not the only form of legal understanding. It is not even the most central or most important form of legal understanding. We have already seen its mutual dependence upon another form of legal understanding, rational deconstruction. Nor do these two forms of legal understanding exhaust the possibilities. Understanding is a purposive activity. Because there are many different purposes in understanding the law, there can also be many different forms of legal understanding. In order to study the subject's contribution to legal understanding, we must recognize the many different purposes behind legal understanding, as well as the social roles, activities, and contexts that give rise to these purposes. To understand law, we must ask who seeks to understand the legal system and why they seek to understand it.

These distinctions are not always clearly made in current jurisprudential writing. In his discussion of legal coherence, for example, Joseph Raz assumes that coherence is a property of law revealed through the preferred perspective of orthodox jurisprudence, the "internal point of view." It is irrelevant that the law lacks coherence from any other perspective. "Given the admitted priority of the participant's point of view," Raz argues, "even the [outside] observer, *in order to acquire a sound understanding of the law*, must understand it as it would be seen by a participant. *If it must be coherent to a participant then coherent it is.*"[59]

The difficulties here are twofold. First, there are many different types of "participants": laypeople and professional elites, for example. Within the category of professional elites there are litigators, judges, bureaucrats, academics, and so on. Thus, there can be more than one "internal perspective" because there are many different social groups who regard legal rules as norms for conduct. If these different groups disagree about their perceptions of legal coherence, their disagreements must be resolved in some fashion.[60]

Second, within each group of participants there are many different purposes for understanding the legal system, such as predicting what other legal officials will do, arguing for legal reform, or understanding the practical effects of legal norms. These forms of understanding raise the issue of coherence in different ways, and for some of them coherence may even be irrelevant. Thus, there can be more than one "internal perspective," because people who regard legal rules as norms for conduct can have more than one purpose in understanding law.

Consider five different purposes for understanding the law. First, we may wish merely to make sense of the law as a coherent scheme of regulation in order to learn it or apply it. Second, we may want to predict what other legal actors will do. Third, we may wish to describe the law in order to persuade others to interpret the law in our favor. Fourth, we may offer a critical portrait of existing law in the hope of persuading others to change the law. Fifth, we may wish to understand law in terms of its practical effects rather than in terms of the content of its doctrines. Professional elites adopt all of these purposes in understanding law; laypeople adopt some or all of them. Moreover, this list is not intended to be

---

[59] Raz, *The Relevance of Coherence*, 72 B.U.LawRev. 273 at 293 (emphasis added).

[60] Although Raz does not specifically address the point, I assume that he, like most other jurisprudence scholars, would generally resolve such disputes in favor of the perspective of elites. For example, Hart argued that for a legal system to exist it is only necessary that authoritative legal officials hold the internal perspective. See Hart, *The Concept of Law*, pp. 116–117. How conflicts between judgments by different elites (for example, litigators and judges, or judges and academics) should be resolved is quite another matter. I suggest that jurisprudence has rarely emphasised the possibility of such conflicts within elites, assuming instead that the standard of the judge is paradigmatic and that of the litigator, executive official, legislator, or academic is parasitic on this perspective. For a similar criticism, see Roger Cotterrell, *The Politics of Jurisprudence* (1989), p. 230.

exhaustive; there are doubtless other purposes in legal understanding as well. The point is that "understanding law" encompasses many activities. In each of these activities we approach the law in different ways.

When we seek to make sense of the law in order to learn or apply it, we employ rational reconstruction. Yet rational reconstruction cannot serve all of the other purposes of legal understanding. For example, it does not always accurately predict the behavior of legal officials, and it cannot tell us the practical effects of legal norms.

Furthermore, although rational reconstruction asks us to attempt to see the law as a coherent scheme of regulation, other forms of understanding do not impose such a requirement. Thus, in predicting what legal officials will do, we do not always expect that their actions will comport with our own judgments about the most coherent or the most just continuation of the law. We may think that a certain line of cases should be continued in a particular way, but we may doubt that authoritative decisionmakers will agree. On the contrary, we may believe that they will introduce an undesirable incoherence into the law. When we attempt to persuade judges or other legal decisionmakers to interpret law in our favor, the most persuasive account of law for that audience may leave the law far less coherent than we would like, but our goal is to appeal to the decisionmaker's view of coherence, not our own.[61]

When our goal is to persuade others to change the law, our account of law may be specifically designed to show it as partly incoherent, because one of the ways we may seek to convince others to change existing doctrine is to demonstrate its incoherence or the superior coherence of our proposed solution. Here we employ the tools of rational deconstruction. Similarly, when we criticize the decisions of legal authorities, we do not always endeavor to portray the law in its most coherent light. Rather, our goal is to point out its inadequacies.

Finally, if our concern is the practical effects of legal norms, questions of coherence or incoherence may be wholly irrelevant. Because one cannot know the practical effects or practices of application of a legal doctrine in advance, there is no guarantee that the result will be normatively coherent. Moreover, one purpose of studying the effects of legal norms in practice may be to offer critiques based on the arbitrary results we discover.

To be sure, each of the above varieties of legal understanding may intersect with and make use of rational reconstruction. Our predictions about the behavior of legal decisionmakers and our attempts to persuade them may require us to imagine how they would rationally reconstruct the law; if their beliefs are similar to our own, then our own rational reconstruction of legal norms will be helpful in this task. Conversely, if our goal is to persuade others to change the law, we may appeal to an alternative that is rationally reconstructible, at least in the eyes of our audience. Finally, we may find rational reconstruction useful even in our study of the practical effects of doctrines in action. One way to understand the law's effects is to look at the content of authoritative legal norms. Rational reconstruction may be helpful in this enterprise, although a prediction of how others will rationally reconstruct the law may be even more helpful.

Nevertheless, these forms of legal understanding are distinct from rational reconstruction. In predicting what legal decisionmakers will do or in attempting to persuade them to decide in our favor, we must bow to the values and pre-dilections of the legal decisionmakers we attend to. Implicit in our attempts to critique the law and persuade others to change it is a claim that the law is not as coherent as it could be. Our search for the effects of law necessarily contemplates the possibility, which the realists made famous, of a divergence between "law in the books" and law in action. We may not be able to deduce the effects of the

---

[61] See Sanford Levinson, "What Do Lawyers Know (And What Do They Do With Their Knowledge)? Comments on Schauer and Moore" (1985) 58 S. Cal. L. Rev. 441, 455–56.

legal system from the content of the legal norms that form the subject of rational reconstruction. Even our ability to predict what a particular legal decisionmaker will do (i.e., that Justice S will vote to strike down a particular affirmative action program) does not necessarily result in knowledge of the effects of the decisionmaker's act (i.e., the social consequences of holding such affirmative action programs unconstitutional). What people do is not the same as the effects of what they do. One can know the first without knowing the second.

Although we can see connections between the activity and attitude of rational reconstruction and other purposes in legal understanding, we should not assume that rational reconstruction is the master form of legal understanding to which all other forms are subsidiary. One could also see rational reconstruction depending in part on other forms of legal understanding. I have already noted rational reconstruction's debt to the tools of rational deconstruction. Similarly, in order to decide whether legal norms are rationally reconstructible, we may need to understand how they would be applied by others, and we must gauge their practical effects in the real world.

Instead of viewing rational reconstruction as the central case of legal understanding, accompanied by a set of auxiliary or special forms of legal understanding parasitic on it, I propose a different picture: a set of differentiated yet mutually dependent forms of legal understanding that we employ as the need arises to make sense of the world around us. We must not forget that our understanding of law is always in the larger service of making the social world coherent of ourselves. From this perspective, it makes sense to think of legal understanding as a set of related hermeneutic instruments or devices. Thus, legal understanding is less a single entity than a set of complementary tools we employ in the larger task of social understanding.[62] Rational reconstruction then becomes simply one of many devices in our hermeneutical toolbox, a form of understanding that nevertheless may rely upon and interact with others even as they rely upon and interact with it. Legal understanding, then, is a complicated encounter with the social world in which we employ whatever tools of understanding seem appropriate to the task at hand.

The plurality of forms of legal understanding may explain the persistence of the predictive theory of law—that law is what the courts will do—despite the repeated criticisms that have been levelled at it.[63] Jurisprudence professors wrongly seek to judge the predictive theory as a unitary jurisprudential theory. But the predictive "theory" of law is not a jurisprudential theory at all. Prediction is simply one purposive activity among many others that individuals use to understand law. One might think that this approach to law articulates a theory of "what law is" only if one forgot the purposive and situated component of all legal understanding; that is to say, only if one forgot the subject's essential contributions to the cultural object it perceives. Of course, this is precisely the occupational hazard of traditional jurisprudence. In this way the person who understands law for the purpose of rational reconstruction and the person who understands law for the purpose of prediction might each believe that they are engaged in the same enterprise—describing law's nature—and that the other party is mistaken in her assertions. In fact, each is merely projecting her situated, purpose-driven subjectivity onto the object of their study and giving it the name of "the theory of law."[64] Similarly, explaining law wholly in terms of rational reconstruction offers no more of a unitary theory of law than the predictive theory; rational reconstruction is merely one among many purposes in understanding law and can claim neither primacy nor the title of "the internal perspective."

---

[62] See Cotterrell, *op. cit.*, n. 60 at 229.
[63] See Hart, *The Concept of Law*, pp. 40–41.
[64] The most famous statement of the predictive theory is Oliver W. Holmes, "The Path of the Law" (1897) 10 Harv. L. Rev. 457. [See also *ante*, 1007.]

This analysis might also explain why the debate between positivism and some forms of natural law theory also seems never-ending. I am not concerned here with natural law theories that claim that law is simply that which is just, but rather those theories that claim that moral reasoning is inextricably linked to law and legal understanding.[65] These theories are projections of the experience of rational reconstruction, in which we must view the law as the embodiment of substantive reason. The law appears to have a moral component because the very form of understanding through which we apprehend law in order to apply it to concrete cases requires us to imbue law with substantive rationality. Yet once again, this experience of a moral component does not reveal the nature of law so much as the nature of the projection of our subjectivity onto the legal object of our understanding. Other purposes in understanding law need not imbue law with substantive rationality and therefore need not produce the same hermeneutic effect. The natural law advocate is correct that law is inescapably linked to morality only to the extent that a certain activity of legal understanding requires us to see it in that light, but the advocate is incorrect in deeming that form of understanding central or exclusively revelatory of the nature of law.

We must resist the dual temptation of believing in a single internal perspective that reveals the nature of law and then identifying that perspective with rational reconstruction. The temptation arises because rational reconstruction seems to match the type of legal understanding judges employ when the apply the law. The judge's purpose in understanding law is to make sense of a jumbled mass of precedents, statutes, and administrative regulations and to infer from these a coherent scheme of legal regulation that she can apply to the case before her. However, because there are many different purposes in understanding law, and many different social roles in which legal understanding occurs, we cannot pick out one form of understanding practiced by particular legal elites and bestow upon it the title of "*the* internal perspective"—the perspective that, as Raz contends,[66] reveals the nature of law and determines its coherence or incoherence.[67]

Belief in a single internal perspective and its identification with rational reconstruction has several unfortunate ideological effects.[68] First, it makes the other purposes of legal understanding and the other social roles in which understanding occurs irrelevant, conflates them with rational reconstruction, or else relegates them to a peripheral and dependent status. To the extent that alternative forms of legal understanding are recognized, they are depicted as deviations from or modifications of legal understanding that must be understood in terms of their variance from the norm and that may not contradict its conclusions.

Second, this identification makes invisible the subject's contribution to the particular form of legal understanding dubbed "the internal perspective." It divorces this form of understanding from both the purpose giving rise to it and the social group employing that purpose. It presents rational reconstruction employed by judges and other legal elites as legal understanding simpliciter, unconnected to a particular purpose or position. It portrays rational reconstruction as an understanding that does not impose "special" purposes like prediction, political activism, or social scientific study on the legal object, but simply observes the legal object as it is. The social role and purpose of the judge engaged in rational reconstruction become the hidden norm of legal understanding against

---

[65] An example would be Lon L. Fuller, *The Morality of Law* (1964).

[66] Raz, "The Relevance of Coherence" *supra*, n. 59, at 293.

[67] For a similar argument, see Cotterrell, *supra*, n. 60, at 228–31. In Raz's defense, I should note that he has also been critical of the lawyer's perspective in other contexts. See, *e.g.* Joseph Raz, "The Problem About the Nature of Law" (1983) 21 U. W. Ont. L. Rev. 203.

[68] Cotterrell, *supra*, n. 60 at 229 (noting that traditional jurisprudence becomes "mystificatory" and a "professional ieology" when it assumes that what is being discussed is the nature of law rather than a particular mode of thought that lawyers engage in).

which all other forms of legal understanding are seen as special pleading, deviant, irrelevant, or mistaken. Simultaneously, the contributions of the judge's social role and purpose are projected onto the law and given the name "the nature of law."

Ronald Dworkin's theory of law as integrity exemplifies these confusions. Dworkin identifies legal understanding with judicial methods of rational reconstruction; indeed, his goal is to explain the internal experience of judging and to reveal the ideals that lie behind judicial practice.[69] There is nothing wrong with offering a normative or descriptive theory of judicial understanding if it is understood and labelled as such. The problem is that Dworkin believes that explicating this form of legal understanding also explicates the nature of law, or, in Dworkin's language, when "propositions of law are true."[70]

To speak in this way makes the subject, her purposes, and her preconceptions disappear from view. Interpretation has become purposeless and subjectless. For all of his concern with the interpretive character of law, Dworkin's theory depends on making the contributions of subjectivity invisible to the discourse of jurisprudence. The fact that judges are socially situated individuals who interpret the law for a particular purpose and bring a particular set of sociological and ideological predispositions to their acts of understanding becomes irrelevant to Dworkin's discussion of legal understanding. By assigning the contributions of subjectivity to the nature of law, Dworkin makes these contributions invisible and all-powerful. Hence, Dworkin is able to exclude all sociological or ideological analysis—the very analysis of what the subject does bring to the object of understanding—as "external critiques" that can tell us nothing about the nature of law. So hermetically (and hermeneutically) sealed is Dworkin's universe that it becomes impossible to object that the concerns of judges occupy only one rather limited position in the constellation of legal reality and the forms of legal understanding.

This error is compounded by Dworkin's general approach to interpreting social practices, of which legal understanding is only a special case. According to Dworkin, interpretation of social practices is always "constructive interpretation"—an attempt to identify the point of a social practice and to see it in its best light.[71] In this way Dworkin obscures not only the many different forms of legal understanding, but also the many different forms of nonlegal understanding. After all, not all forms of social understanding portray the object of interpretation in its best light. When we describe the injustices of our society in order to convince others of the need for change, we do not attempt to view the object of interpretation in the best possible light; similarly, when we criticize a work of art as badly conceived and executed, we do not describe it in its best light. In both cases, we seek to expose its flaws, blindness, and incoherences. This is not rational reconstruction but rational deconstruction. Dworkin's constructive interpretation is not the only form of cultural understanding. It is cultural understanding for a particular purpose; it is one of the many different activities that are collectively called understanding.

In fact, the plurality of forms of cultural understanding is revealed by Dworkin's own practices of argument in *Law's Empire*; his theory of interpretation is undermined by attending to what he actually does, rather than what he says he is doing. Although Dworkin insists upon the primacy of constructive interpretation,

---

[69] See, *e.g.* Dworkin, *Law's Empire*, p. 94 (arguing that theory of law as integrity is "the best interpretation of what lawyers, law teachers, and judges actually do and much of what they say").

[70] *ibid.*, p. 225 ("According to law as integrity, propositions of law are true if they figure in or follow from the principles of justice, fairness, and procedural due process that provide the best constructive interpretation of the community's legal practice.").

[71] *ibid.*, p. 52.

he does not practice what he preaches, nor could he, given the multiple purposes of understanding. When he describes and criticizes the work of the Critical Legal Studies movement, for example, constructive interpretation and interpretive charity are thrown out the window.[72] Rather, his quite understandable purpose is to point out the inaccuracies and flaws in theories whose conclusions cast doubt on his own. Dworkin may justly be criticized for failing to offer the strongest account of CLS positions before attacking them, which is merely to say that he employs the principles of constructive interpretation and charity inconsistently and opportunistically.[73] But there is a more important objection: he has failed to acknowledge that having offered the strongest account of a position, an important and distinct purpose in understanding is to recognize the flaws and mistakes in the object of interpretation. In legal understanding, this is the moment of rational deconstruction.

That jurisprudential scholarship might identify the nature of law with elite legal understandings of rational reconstruction makes perfect sense from a critical perspective. It is yet another example of the legal subject projecting the contributions of her subjectivity—her social situation and purposes for understanding—onto the object she seeks to understand. Rational reconstruction is how students of law are taught to understand law, how litigators are taught to argue law, and how judges are expected to write law. Rational reconstruction is the most conspicuous form of legal understanding employed by professional elites, and, more particularly, by the most powerful and central of professional

---

[72] Dworkin's interpretations of Critical Legal Studies do not evidence any serious attempt to offer the strongest, most coherent, or best possible interpretation of Critical Legal Studies arguments. Rather, Dworkin dismisses this entire body of scholarship in five pages and two lengthy footnotes. *See ibid.*, p. 271–275. His depiction of C.L.S. "acolytes" as people who "assemble in conferences" to "decid[e] what the movement is," *ibid.*, p. 271, does not seem promising, at least if his goal really is interpretive charity.

According to Dworkin's own theory of constructive interpretation, he should have spent considerable time carefully going over C.L.S. scholarship, trying to make sense of its conflicting assertions, and developing a coherent set of arguments to support its positions. If, as Dworkin argues, "the literature of critical legal studies announces rather than defends [its] claims" about the coherence of the legal system, *ibid.*, pp. 272–273, the constructive interpreter should, like the interpreter of legal doctrine, try to fill in the theoretical underpinnings for herself, so as to make the theory the best it can be. Finally, the constructive interpreter, rather than imposing her own purposes on the enterprise, must attempt to understand what the purposes of the enterprise are to the persons who participate in it, and decide what the best explanation and continuation of those purposes are. She must not assume, as Dworkin appears to, that the theoretical importance of Critical Legal Studies rests solely on whether "its aims are those of law as integrity," *ibid.*, p. 275; that is to say, whether it can be usefully employed to further the development and acceptance of Dworkin's theories about law. This is an exclusively instrumental stance which does not seek true understanding because it does not open itself up to the possible truth of what it seeks to understand. See Hans-Georg Gadamer, *Truth and Method* (Garrett Barden & John Comming trans., 1975), p. 270 (criticizing such instrumental interpretations as attempts to preserve one's own beliefs from question). In short, there is nothing that seems further from the charity-driven account of interpretation offered by Dworkin in chapter two of *Law's Empire* than Dworkin's own interpretation of Critical Legal Studies in Chap. 7 of the same book.

[73] This tendency is not limited to his accounts of radical scholarship. See, *e.g.* Charles Silver, "*Elmer's Case, A Legal Positivist Replies to Dworkin*" (1987) 6 Law & Phil. 381, 382 (noting that "Dworkin rarely asks whether an argument he calls positivistic is the best argument a Legal Positivist could make.").

elites, the judiciary. It therefore becomes what legal understanding is.[74]

Although there is nothing wrong with elites employing distinctive forms of understanding, a difficulty arises when these elites assume that a particular form of legal understanding discloses the real nature of the legal system. By forgetting the different purposes of understanding and the socially situated nature of understanding, they may elevate a particular form of understanding, useful as it may be in a particular context and for a particular purpose, to a universal status.[75] When jurisprudential discussions assume that the activity of rational reconstruction discloses the true properties of the legal system, they engage in this error. That is why attention to the subject of legal understanding is helpful: it asks us to think about who is understanding the law and for what purposes. It reminds us that there is no understanding of the social world without a subject who understands and a purpose for understanding, and hence no understanding of the social world without the contributions of subjectivity.

## D. The Production of Rational Reconstruction

Our argument so far has considered the question of legal coherence sociologically as well as philosophically. Judgments of legal coherence arise from a specific form of understanding—rational reconstruction—that is employed predominantly although not exclusively by legal professionals. We have also noted the ideological tendency to privilege this form of understanding in jurisprudential discussions. This section discusses how judgments of rational reconstruction are produced; it considers how these judgments are affected by the experiences and beliefs of the legal professionals who make them. I discuss three features of subjectivity that shape our judgments of rational reconstruction. The first is the state of our moral and political beliefs, the second is the state of our knowledge about the legal system, and the third is the state of our efforts at rational reconstruction through considering possible conflicts of value between legal doctrines. Finally, I argue that the contributions of subjectivity do not merely lead to disagreements among and mistakes by legal professionals. They also facilitate, regulate, and limit professional judgments of rational reconstruction. They are the source of both disagreement and agreement, of both mistakes and correct judgments as viewed from the perspective of dominant conventions of understanding.

**The Effects of Moral and Political Beliefs on Rational Reconstruction.** The dialectic of hypothetical and actual justification presupposes that our judgments of legal coherence are shaped by our judgments of political morality. Judgments of coherence and incoherence cannot be fully separated from political and moral beliefs because these beliefs help us construct our judgments. Individuals with different political and moral beliefs will tend to define the boundaries of bona fide principles and policies differently; they will also tend to differ on whether balances among them have been struck in a principled and consistent manner. Hence they

---

[74] Note in particular that viewing legal coherence in terms of rational reconstructibility of the content of legal rules projects away considerations of legal application and enforcement by judges, juries, administrative agencies, police officers, social welfare caseworkers, and the like. It focuses our attention on that aspect of law that can be understood through a comparison of the content of legal norms described on paper. Hence we do not focus on exercises of power and injustice that work beneath the economy of rules, the performative aspect of legal doctrine and legal writing, and the irrelevance of much normative legal scholarship to law as it is practiced. See Schlag. "Normativity and the Politics of Form" *ante*, 1283. Schlag's analysis, in turn, recalls Jerome Frank's realist critique. Jerome Frank, *Courts on Trial: Myth and Reality in American Justice* (1949), [on which see *ante*, 989].

[75] See Cotterrell, *supra* n. 60, p. 229; Schlag, *ante*, 1440.

may reach different conclusions about the rational reconstructibility of a particular area of law.

The contributions of political and moral belief to our judgments of coherence and incoherence are most obvious when they produce disagreement. Yet our political and moral beliefs help construct our judgments of legal coherence even when there is considerable consensus. The social construction of subjectivity produces consensus by creating individuals who think, act, and believe in roughly similar ways. Our judgments of political morality are part of the hermeneutical baggage we bring with us in our attempt to understand the legal system; we should not confuse the fact that each of us brings similar baggage with the claim that we bring no baggage at all.

In like fashion, we must resist the temptation to see political ideology as merely an obstacle or hindrance to our understanding of law. Our political and moral beliefs are necessary tools of legal understanding—they make judgments of normative coherence and incoherence possible. Hence, political ideology does not simply distort or detract from legal understanding; it actively assists in the construction of the legal object of interpretation, both in the case in which we disagree with others and the case in which we agree, both in the case in which the coherence of legal doctrines is disputable and the case in which their coherence seems so obvious that it goes without saying.

**The Effects of Legal Knowledge on Rational Reconstruction.** Discussions of legal coherence that treat coherence as a property of a legal object normally bracket away questions about the state of our knowledge of the legal system. In the alternative, they assume a subject with complete knowledge of the legal system, one who sees the law as it really is.[76] The assumption of complete knowledge makes the legal subject irrelevant to questions of coherence; she becomes a mere vessel into which the real content of a law existing independent of understanding is poured. Nevertheless, our actual judgments about the coherence and incoherence of the law must depend heavily on our knowledge of the content of existing legal norms and their effects in application. Our knowledge of "what the law is"—in the sense of what the actual decisions of courts and promulgations of legislatures and administrative agencies are—is remarkably limited, even for individuals who regularly practice law. There is simply a huge amount of law that even so-called experts are not aware of, and their knowledge of the practical effects of existing legal norms may be even sketchier.

If we are not aware of the content of legal norms in many different parts of the law, they cannot figure into our awareness of possible sources of moral conflict and normative incoherence. Moreover, if our knowledge is focused in a few areas of law, our opinions about the coherence of other parts of the law and of the legal system as a whole are likely to be informed by our opinions and our experience of the limited areas we do know. Our judgments about the coherence of the legal system therefore must derive largely from our image of the legal system, an image shaped as much by our ignorance as by our knowledge. We judge based on what we know and do not know, and, equally importantly, on what we do not know we do not know.

Our judgments of legal coherence and incoherence are affected not only by our knowledge of legal doctrines, but also by the amount of cognitive effort we have put into considering the normative consistency among the doctrines we do know.

---

[76] For example, in Ronald Dworkin's theory, the law is coherent to the extent that it is coherent to and ideal judge with perfect knowledge of the legal system. See Dworkin, *supra*, n. 69, p. 265.

After all, justifications that make sense to us at first glance often become problematic on further reflection, and vice versa.[77] However, most people (law professors included) have not thought very hard about the various justifications for the content of most legal doctrines; indeed, they may have neither the time nor the ability to consider all of the possible justifications or conflicts among justifications that might be offered within the many areas of legal doctrine.

The problem is magnified when we move from considerations of coherence in a specific area of law to questions of coherence across doctrinal areas or the legal system as a whole. Few people have considered all the possible conflicts among rules across different areas of law. Compartmentalization of law into different subject areas probably exacerbates this phenomenon; we simply do not think to ask whether the way we argue in tort law is consistent with the principles we use in the law of trusts and estates, the law of mineral rights, or the law of mass communication. In any case, it may well be impossible for any one person or group of persons to develop a global justification and reconciliation of legal materials or a comprehensive understanding of the law's effects. Because we cannot conceive of the legal system as a totality, and because we cannot hope to subject all of the different aspects of the legal system to the most searching analysis, we must fall back on assumptions about the coherence of the legal system based on our limited experiences and our existing ideological commitments. Hence, our judgments about the coherence of the legal system or parts thereof may be as much matters of faith and ideological presupposition as the consequence of reasoned analysis. We construct an imagined legal system from equal parts of ignorance and experience, and it is against this image that we test our visions of justice. Our judgments of coherence are not simply judgments about properties of the legal system, but rather judgments of imaginative reconstructions of the legal system as it is believed to exist. The constructed object of interpretation is also the constructed object of our imagination.

**Rational Reconstruction's Debt to Subjectivity.** My focus on our lack of knowledge and circumspection in our judgments of coherence may seem both obvious and irrelevant. Of course people make mistakes in judgment, one might object, but what has that to do with the question of legal coherence? Legal coherence is a question of what the law really is, not a question of what people mistakenly assume it to be. Yet this objection exemplifies the basic difficulty in accounts of legal understanding that dismiss the contributions of subjectivity. It considers legal coherence purely from the standpoint of an object that is constituted independent of human consciousness. This misunderstands the nature of legal understanding. Legal coherence is a hermeneutic feature of law. It is the result of an interaction between a legal subject and a legal object already constructed by the legal subject. One might wish to abstract away the question of legal coherence from the vagaries and insufficiencies of legal subjects. But this is a fool's errand. *There is no judgment of legal coherence that is not made by a legal subject.* The experience of legal coherence is always by somebody or someone. There is no one else to do the job.

This conclusion may seem unsatisfying because we naturally assume that there is a fact of the matter about the coherence of the law quite apart from the intrusions of subjectivity. But subjectivity is not an intrusion into law—it is a constitution of law. Thus, there is a fact of the matter about legal coherence, but it is of a quite different sort. The fact of the matter is that legal coherence is the product of a hermeneutic interaction. It is the result rather than the object of a process of understanding.

---

[77] See Duncan Kennedy, "Freedom and Constraint in Adjudication: A Critical Phenomenology" (1986) 36 J. Legal Educ. 518, 531–533 (discussing changing appearances of "field" of judicial precedents as we work to understand and employ them).

The inseparability of legal coherence from subjectivity has two important consequences. First, our experience of legal coherence is necessarily grounded in our social situation and in the manner in which we encounter the law. We occupy different positions in society and experience the legal system in different ways. Understandings of the legal system differ for a trial judge in a court of general jurisdiction, a practicing tax attorney, a recidivist criminal, a twenty-three-year-old secretary who has never received any more serious legal sanction than a parking ticket, a businessperson in the midst of a child custody battle, a social scientist, a first-year law student, and a professor of jurisprudence. Merely to list these different social situations is to note the many possible forms of legal understanding and the many different sorts of experiences that individuals can have. Rather than viewing this plurality of experiences as distractions from legal understanding, we should recognize that this is what legal understanding consists in. There are no subjectless encounters with the law.

Second, our experience of legal coherence or incoherence is dynamic. Our experience of the content of the legal system changes over time as we have new experiences, engage in deeper analyses of possible conflicts of value between doctrines, and become aware of the effects of doctrines in action. Our judgments about and understandings of the legal system are always in a process of change. Our continuing experience as individuals in a legal system changes our understandings as to what is in the system, whether particular distinctions and similarities are tenable or untenable, and so on. Legal understanding, and hence legal judgment, is always in a process of flux. It is dynamic, not static, because our knowledge and experience of the object of understanding is dynamic.

One might hope to avoid these conclusions by employing an "ideal observer" theory of legal coherence. Under this theory, we would say that the law is coherent if it would appear coherent to an ideal observer.[78] Thus, although some individuals might incorrectly perceive certain elements of the law as coherent or incoherent, they are mistaken to the extent that their conclusions diverge from those of an ideal observer of law. An ideal observer theory would preserve the subject's centrality to legal understanding while simultaneously offering a standard of objectivity that abstracts away from subjectivity.

The ideal observer view is attractive because it points, however obliquely, to a number of sound intuitions about our experience of the law. First, our views of the law are revisable. Upon further reflection, and given further information, we may sometimes change our minds as to whether a distinction is tenable or untenable, whether a doctrine is just or unjust, and so on. Second, we know that some judgments about the law are better than others, although it does not necessarily follow that all judgments for all purposes in understanding law can be ranked in order from best to worst. Third, we generally believe that legal judgments are better when the individual who makes them has access to more information, and has thought a lot about the issues involved.

The postulation of an ideal observer is an extrapolation from these three eminently sensible views about legal judgment. The extrapolation itself, however, is misguided. Just because our views about law are revisable does not mean that there is a final unrevisable view. Just because some legal judgments are better than others does not mean that there must always be a single judgment that is better than all others. Finally, just because more thought and more information

---

[78] *Cf.* Roderick Firth, "Ethical Absolutism and the Ideal Observer" (1952) 12 Phil & Phenomenological Res. 317 (proposing naturalistic theory of ethics that defines "good" as that which an ideal observer would approve). Ronald Dworkin's Hercules plays a role similar to an ideal observer of law. See Dworkin, *supra*, n. 69, at 265 ("Hercules is useful to us just because he is more reflective and self-conscious than any real judge need be or, given the press of work, could be ... He does what [judges] would do if they had a career to devote to a single decision ...").

generally lead to better judgments does not mean that taking infinite time and possessing all information leads to a univocal, correct judgment.

More importantly, the ideal observer theory fails to grasp the nature of legal knowledge. Knowledge of a cultural artifact like law must always result from our situatedness in a particular social and historical tradition.[79] This situatedness is not a hindrance to cultural understanding but rather the ground of its possibility.[80] The problem of legal understanding is a special case of the problem of human understanding of culture generally. Cultural traditions constitute us as human and make possible our understanding of culture. Hence human beings are always part of culture and not merely disinterested spectators. Even when we attempt to understand a culture that is not our own, we bring our own "cultural software" as necessary tools of understanding. We always understand from a historical and cultural position, just as we always measure velocity or acceleration from a particular point in space. Without a place to start from, we cannot understand anything at all.

It follows that if the understanding of the ideal observer is truly a human understanding, she too must be the product of a particular history and a particular cultural situation. However, this is precisely when an ideal observer theory resists, because it assumes that historical and cultural situatedness is a bias that must be neutralized or abstracted away. The ideal observer approach views as an obstacle to understanding what is in fact a condition of understanding.

If the ideal observer's understanding is truly a human one, we must ask several questions about this observer: Of what culture is she a part? What is her history? What are the wellsprings of her understanding? Merely attempting to answer these questions with respect to an ideal observer shows the limitations of the theory. Shall we say that the ideal observer lives in no culture at all? Then how is she able to understand any culture? Shall we say that the ideal observer comes from a perfect culture? Which culture is that? Shall we say instead that she comes from our culture? If so, what is it about our culture that makes it ideal? Our culture is not homogenous; from what part of our culture does the ideal observer come? If this part is the ideal, does this mean that the other parts of our culture are less than ideal? Similarly, we might wonder, what experiences has the ideal observer had? Shall we say that the ideal observer has had every experience? If she has, what experience does she currently have, since one cannot have all experiences simultaneously?

We are faced with a dilemma. To imagine an ideal observer is either to imagine a person with no culture, no history, and no experiences, who therefore lacks the conditions of human cultural understanding, or else it is to elevate a particular culture, status, position, and history to the level of an ideal standpoint for observation and thus to forget its partiality.

Ultimately, the turn to an ideal observer is an attempt to avoid thinking about the legal subject and to focus sole attention on the object. It is an attempt to avoid worrying about the legal subject's contribution to understanding by imagining a neutral "plain vanilla" subject who is not doing anything in her encounter with the constructed object of her interpretation. This conception throws the baby out with the bath water. It removes the possibility of understanding along with the biases it seeks to excise. Worse still is the danger that an ideal observer theory may confuse the baby with the bath water: it may unthinkingly equate the ideal observer with the theorist's own cultural and historical situation, and thus may make the theorist's own situatedness invisible by defining it as objective. Even plain vanilla is still, after all, a flavor.

---

[79] See John B. Thompson, *Ideology and Modern Culture* (1990), pp. 276–277. This idea is central to Hans Georg Gadamer's ontological hermeneutics.

[80] See Jerome Bruner, *Acts of Meaning* (1990), pp. 11–15, 20–21; Clifford Geertz, *The Interpretation of Cultures* (1973), pp. 50–51, 82–83.

Our discussion of the purposive nature of understanding points to a further difficulty. Ideal observers do not have purposes because they are not human beings. They do not have particular desires, motivations, goals, and urges. They just are. Cultural understanding, on the other hand, is grounded in our individual purposes, desires, and aspirations; these in turn are shaped by our social construction. To understand as a human being is to grapple with the world in a particular way because of who we are and what we seek to accomplish. If we wish to apply the concept of an ideal observer to the concept of human understanding we must ask what purposes the ideal observer has in understanding law. Yet to answer this question requires that we place the ideal observer in a particular context—as a human being with limited physical and mental capabilities, with a particular set of goals and aspirations, and with a history that structures and determines them. To capture the human experience of purposive understanding we must also capture the human finitude and situatedness that from the basis of our motivations and purposes in understanding. At the point at which the ideal observer becomes sufficiently particularized so that we can call her understanding a human one, she has largely lost her status as an abstracted, ideal observer.

My point in making these observations is not to deny that in making judgments individuals share a great deal with others. Much of our subjectivity is intersubjective, and this intersubjectivity is a source of objectivity. Yet what we share with others may be cognitive limitations as much as abilities, ignorance as much as information, faith as much as knowledge, and partiality as much as neutrality. The average observer is by no means an "ideal" observer with unlimited time, knowledge, and capabilities. That is what makes her a human, as opposed to an ideal, observer. Ironically, her imperfections and limitations may be what she has most in common with her fellow citizens.

We can preserve the sound intuitions that motivate the ideal observer theory only if we strip the theory of its pretensions to subjectless objectivity. We can employ the notion of an ideal observer as a shorthand when we are speaking about a particular purpose in understanding and a particular cultural standpoint. There is nothing wrong with saying that for a particular purpose (for example, rational reconstruction), or from a particular standpoint (for example, that of a legal professional), one judgment is better than another, because we understand the context in which we are making our judgments. Our goal should not be to deny that we can and do make appropriate judgments about the law and legal coherence. We should merely recognize the relationship of our subjectivity to the standard of appropriateness. [pp. 121–143]

## B. de SOUSA SANTOS
### The Postmodern Transition: Law and Politics
### (1991)[81]

*Politics and Law in the Postmodern Transition*

*A new theory of subjectivity is needed to account for the fact that we are an increasingly complex network of subjectivities.* Out of the ruins of social collectivism, the collectivism of the self is emerging. The struggle against the monopolies of interpretation must be conducted in a way that leads to the proliferation of political and legal interpretive communities. The controlled dispersal of the legal realm will contribute to decanonize and to trivialize law. The end of legal fetishism will mark the emergence of a new legal minimalism and of micro-evolutionary practices.

I will now try to justify this thesis by bringing my scripts to bear on a

---

[81] [From Austin Sarat and Thomas R. Kearns (eds.), *The Fate of Law.*]

postmodern and critical understanding of law and politics. The last script (interest and capacity) shows that a discrepancy has been growing between the scale of interests in social transformation and the organization of capacities to struggle for them. As some interests become global, the enemy to fight against seems to vanish, which, contrary to what might have been expected, has not facilitated the organization of those wanting to get actively involved in the struggles. This has aggravated the impasse of modern critical theory and, in particular, of orthodox Marxist theory, an impasse that has crystallized in a double reification: the reification of the historical subject and the reification of the political mediation for the deployment of social capacities. The emergence of postmodern critical theory is premised upon the supersession of this double reification.

The reification of the historical subject consists of the a priori historical privilege granted to class and to class politics, that is, and to use Laclau's and Mouffe's words, "the idea that the working class represents the privileged agent in which the fundamental impulse of social change resides."[82] The critique of this reification has been brilliantly made by Laclau and Mouffe. But, contrary to their view, it is neither necessary nor correct to go to the other extreme and conclude that "society has no essence," that is, that it is impossible to account in sociotheoretical terms for the problem of historical determination.[83] In my view, the most important task for social theory today is combining global contingency with local determinisms, structure with agency. If essence is to be conceived in monolithic terms, be it the society, in all versions of holism (starting with Durkheim), or the individual, in the recent theories of methodological individualism, it is only correct to be antiessentialist. But between the essence conceived as a monolithic ontological entity and the nonessentialism of infinite contingencies, there is the middle ground of a pluralist view of essences, of a controlled dispersal of social structures.[84]

As far as the question of the historical subject goes, I think that instead of fixing the a priori priority of a historical subject, as orthodox Marxism did, or instead of sweeping the question of the subject under the carpet of social knowledge, as both structuralists and poststructuralists have done, the task ahead consists of analyzing, in concrete terms, our historical trajectories as subjects both at the biographical and the macrolevel. Modern men and women are configurations or networks of different subjectivities, and, even though the internal differentiation of the self is a historical variable, as Agnes Heller has rightly pointed out, I submit that the differentiation is neither infinite nor chaotic.[85] As I have proposed elsewhere, contemporary capitalist societies consist of four structural places to which four structural subjectivities correspond: the subjectivity of the family corresponds to the *householdplace*; the subjectivity of the class corresponds to the *workplace*; the subjectivity of the individual corresponds to the *citizenplace*; the subjectivity of the nation corresponds to the *worldplace*.[86]

This is not the occasion to provide a full explanation of this analytical framework. It should merely be mentioned that modern men and women are configurations of these four basic subjectivities. Of course, they are also many other subjectivities (for instance, male/female, black/white) but all of them are grounded in four basic ones. On the other hand, the specific configuration of subjectivities varies according to different historical conditions, according to different

[82] Ernesto Laclau and C. Mouffe, *Hegemony and Socialist Strategy: Towards a Radical Democratic Politics* (1985), p. 177.

[83] Nico Mouzelis, "Marxism or Post-Marxism" (1988) New Left Review 167 at 107.

[84] My paper on modes of production of law and social power is an attempt to present such a pluralistic view of structures [(1985) 13 Int. J. of Soc. of Law 302.]

[85] According to Agnes Heller, "the internal differentiation of the Self is itself a variable ... it is not only a historical, but also a 'personal' variable" (*The Human Condition* (1987) *Thesis Eleven* 16 at 4).

[86] Santos, *op. cit.*, n. 84.

periods of our lives, or even according to daily routines or circumstances. We attend the meetings of our children's schools as members of a family, go shopping or read the newspaper as individuals, attend the match of our national team as nationals. In all these occasions or situations we are all four, and perhaps even other subjectivities, at the same time, but as the occasions or situations very, one different basic subjectivity get the privilege of organizing the specific configuration of subjectivities that accounts for our behavior and attitudes. In this respect, the social and scientific construct of a postmodern critical theory is based on the idea that out of the ruins of social collectivism the collectivism of the self is emerging.

The second reification of critical modern theory, the reification of the political mediation for the deployment of social capacities, consists of the reification of the state. This reification is indeed central to liberal political theory, from which critical theory borrows, and consists of reducing the political to a segregated sector of social action, and in conceiving the latter as action of and/or through the state. This reification gained great prominence in the period of organized capitalism and found its most accomplished expression in the political form of the welfare state.

The crisis of this conception is now apparent. Postmodern critical theory is based on two ideas. First, the hyperpoliticization of the state is the other side of the depoliticization of civil society. Confined to a specific sector of social action, the public sphere, the democratic ideal of modern politics has been neutralized or strongly limited in its emancipatory potential.[87] Second, freedom is not a natural human good that has to be preserved against politics as liberal political theory claims.[88] On the contrary, the broader the political realm the greater the freedom. The end of politics will always mean, in one way or another, the end of freedom.

Based on these two ideas and following Foucault, I suggest that there is politics wherever there are power relations. But again I think, and now contrary to Foucault, that we cannot go to the extreme of giving up the task of structuring and grading power forms and power relations. If power is everywhere, it is nowhere. In my view, the four structural places I mentioned before are the loci of four major power forms circulating in our society.[89] These power forms are: patriarchy, corresponding to the householdplace; exploitation, corresponding to the workplace; domination, corresponding to the citizenplace; and unequal exchange, corresponding to the worldplace. There are other forms of power, but these are the basic ones. None of these forms of power is political in itself. It is the combinations among them that make them political, each one, then, political in its own way. Of all four forms of power, only one, domination, is democratic, and even so in a limited degree and in a small group of countries in which the advanced capitalist societies are included. The political aim of postmodern critical theory is to extend the democratic ideal to all other forms of power. Socialism is but the tireless continuing expansion and intensification of democratic practices. This aim, because it has no limit itself, will inevitably show the limit of capitalism, the point at which capitalist social relations will have to block the further expansion of democratic emancipation.

The global but not indiscriminate politicization of social relations will mark the end of the monopolies of political interpretation at the same time that it will ensure than renunciation of interpretation, typical of mass consumption societies, will not follow. While for modern critical theory, the radical democratization of social and personal life had only one enemy, the monopolies of interpretation (be they religion, the state, the family, or the party), for postmodern critical theory

---

[87] *ibid.*, 306.

[88] A critique of the liberal conception of freedom as a prepolitical essence can be read in Hannah Arendt, *Between Past and Future* (1963), p. 149.

[89] Santos, *op. cit.*, n. 84.

there are two enemies, both equally fierce: the monopolies of interpretation and the renunciation of interpretation. To fight against both of them there is only one alternative: the proliferation of political interpretive communities. Softly structured by the specific combinations of subjectivities and of forms of social power, such communities are the social basis of a new political common sense, a new political commitment based on old and new civic virtues in Dewey's sense, that is, virtues that are not poured on us as the metaphysical overflows of any deus ex machina but that, rather, emerge from the familiar and the near. In this sense, Charles Jencks is right when he includes among postmodernist values the idea that "the human presence is back even if it's on the edge."[90] The human presence is back but not as an unreflexive identity dissolved in deep-rooted traditions. Our roots are on permanent display; they are the rhizome that proliferates on the deep surface and on the momentary eternity of our meaningful encounters. Traditional communities in advanced capitalist societies would be of as little use for us as the medieval guilds were for Durkheim when he proposed the reconstruction of the *corps intermédiaires* (between the state and the individual), the lack of which accounted (in his view) for the rampant anomie in French society at the turn of the century.[91]

The proliferation of political interpretive communities represents the postmodern way and, indeed, the only reasonable way of defending the accomplishments of modernity. I mentioned earlier, among such accomplishments, a fairer distribution of economic resources and a significant democratization of the political system in the conventional sense. As with all processes of transition, the postmodern transition also has a dark side and a bright side. The dark side is that, as the reification of class and of state are further exposed, the modern tools used until now to fulfil and consolidate those promises, that is, class politics and the welfare state, become less reliable and less efficient. The proliferation of political interpretive communities will broaden the political agenda in two convergent directions. On the one hand, it will emphasize the social value of extraeconomic or postmaterialist goods such as ecology and peace; on the other hand, it will expand the concept and the practice of democracy in order to incorporate direct participatory (or base) democracy. The success of the struggle for extraeconomic goods will be conditioned by the success of the struggle for economic goods and for a fairer distribution of economic resources. The struggle for participatory democracy will prevent the emasculation of representative democracy. It is in this sense that the promises of modernity can only be defended, from now on, in postmodern terms.

The postmodern understanding of law starts from here. I will concentrate on the topics that, from my point of view, will be most crucial in constructing a new legal common sense.

### The End of the Monopolies of Legality

The movement toward a postmodern understanding of law began in the 1960s with the studies of legal pluralism in complex societies, followed by the focus on the informalization of justice. The theoretical and normative claims behind these studies could be traced back to some of the debates in the continental legal philosophy of the nineteenth century, but they were new to the extent that they were sociologically grounded and informed by a progressive political stance. These studies were also very much part of the dominant sociolegal paradigm, that is, the critical analysis of the discrepancy between law in books and law in action with the purpose of contributing positively to the greater efficiency of the official legal system.

[90] C. Jencks, *Post-Modernism* (1987), p. 11.
[91] Emile Durkheim, *The Division of Labour in Society* (1964).

The problem with these studies was that these two dimensions, the critical and the positive, did not quite match. Explicitly or implicitly, such studies contained a devastating critique of the official legal system, but they were content to contribute to some minor improvements in the operations of the system. With the privilege of hindsight we can say today that, to the extent that these studies addressed themselves to legislators or state bureaucracies, they were bound to fail.[92] The current disenchantment with this scientific agenda, with the co-optation of its critical potential and with the perverse consequences of some of its proposals, expresses that sense of failure. To my mind, such failure could have been avoided if, instead of addressing itself to the state bureaucrats, this scientific agenda had spoken to the people in general or to specific social groups (i.e., different addresses of legal discourse) and tried to generate a new legal common sense in them. The genuine shred of utopian content of these studies lies in the verification that, in the same geopolitical space, there are not one but many different legal orders and that, accordingly, the claim of the state to a monopoly on the production and distribution of law is absurd. As much as we are networks of subjectivities and enter social relations in which different combinations of forms of power are present, we also live in different and overlapping legal orders and legal communities. Each one of them operates in a privileged social space and has a specific temporal dynamic. Since the social spaces interpenetrate and the different legal orders are nonsynchronic, the particular stocks of legal meanings that we activate in specific practical contexts are often complex mixtures, not only of different conceptions of legality but also of different generations of laws, some old some new, some declining some emerging, some native some imported, and some testimonial some imposed.

Corresponding to the four basic subjectivities and forms of power, I identify four basic forms of law that circulate in society: domestic law, that is, the native law of the family; production law, which includes the factory codes and internal regulations of corporations; territorial law, which is the law in the conventional and official sense; and finally, systemic law that regulates the relations among the nation-states and that extends far beyond the domain of international law.[93] There are many other legal orders in society, but these are the basic ones in that they structure the ways in which all the others operate. This controlled dispersal of legal orders has two important implications for the postmodern understanding of law: first, of the four forms of law only one, territorial law, is democratic, even if not completely so. The democratic content of this form of law can only be expanded or merely secured if the democratization of the other forms of law becomes central to the participatory political agenda. Second, relativized in this way, law in general and most particularly state law is trivialized and decanonized (and, accordingly, the distinction between "high law" and "low law" tends to disappear). The emancipatory social value of a given legal order lies in its capacity to secure and expand individual and collective rights (in the last instance, rights are forms of social competence). The modern understanding of law made law sacred and trivialized rights. The postmodern understanding of law trivializes law and makes rights sacred.

*From Modeling to Repetition: Toward a New Legal Minimalism*

Modern state law has undergone many changes in the three periods of the development of capitalism. In the first period, the major legal developments aimed at expanding and consolidating the principle of the market. In the period of organized capitalism, state law was specifically characterized by the consolidation

---

[92] Austin Sarat and Susan Silbey, "The Pull of the Policy Audience" (1988) 10 *Law and Policy* 97.
[93] Santos, *op. cit.*, n. 84.

and expansion of the principle of the state and the principle of the community. In the current period of disorganized capitalism, the trends carried over from the previous period seem, on the surface, to go on undisturbed. At a deeper level, however, some important changes are taking place. I summarize them as the relative cancellation of the symbolic value of law occurring in the transition from maximal law to minimal law.

In the first and, even more so, in the second period, modern state law was typically a maximal law. The political construction of legal reformism as the hegemonic mode of social transformation endowed state law with imperialistic powers that were used to declare the death of a double enemy: social revolution on the one hand and all kinds of popular, nonstate, nonofficial law on the other. The death rituals were performed in different ways in different periods. Out of them emerged state law as a unique, autonomous, and auratic law. The aura, which as in modern art was inscribed from the start in its uniqueness, was further amplified by the prestige of legal science, particularly in continental Europe, and by the social power of law schools both in Europe and in North America. Fixed in the solid sculptures of legal codes, high court decisions, and leading articles in leading scientific journals, modern state law was allowed to make Comte's slogan of "order and progress" come true, and to plan the future sometimes as a repetition of the present, sometimes as modeling of controlled social innovation. Grounded on the persistence of its building materials, modern state law, as much as modern art, adopted an aesthetic of appearance and permanence in which the dynamics of an eternal present contrasted both with the ephemeral past and the trivial future.

In recent years two complementary changes have occurred that undermine the pedestal upon which this legal posture stands. First, the growth of the regulatory state and the high speed of legal repetition and legal modeling have led to the increasing obsolescence of state law. Its solid fixity seems to be melting away as if possessed, like the televised images, by an aesthetic of disappearance rather than by an aesthetic of appearance. Second, both at the infrastate level and at the suprastate level, there have been emerging forms of law that are explicitly liquid, ephemeral, ever negotiable, and renegotiable, in sum, disposable, Among many examples I cite two, one at the level of the infrastate, the other at the level of the suprastate. They are respectively the regulations of subcontracting, that is, the particularistic laws and contracts that regulate the relations of production among corporations and the legislation of the European Community.[94] In their very different ways, both examples bear witness to the emergence of a contextual legality, finely tuned to the momentary interests of the parties involved and to the power relations among them.

For these emerging forms of law, the *hic et nunc* becomes a categorical imperative. The hyperproductivity of the social context is not only tolerated but celebrated. Like some U.S. postmodern art, the "new objectistics" I mentioned before, this postmodern legality "deliberately lowers the level of its own traditional atmosphere in order to reestablish for it a function suited to the times."[95] It is an antiauratic law, an interstitial, almost colloquial law, which repeats social relations instead of modeling them, and in such a way that the distinction between professional and nonprofessional legal knowledge (as much as the discrepancy between law in books and law in action) ceases to make sense. Confronted with this new legal minimalism, the sociologist of law is at pains to even identify and isolate the legal dimension of social relations, a situation that echoes that of legal anthropologists in the so-called primitive societies. The real books of the law are more and more the changing images of social relations. But this explains why the

---

[94] Maria M. Marques (1987) 22 *Revista Crítica de ciências Sociais 69*, Francis Snyder, "New Directions in European Community Law" *(1987) 14 J. of Law and Society* 167.
[95] A. B. Olivia, "New America" 138 Flash Art. 57 at 66.

situation of the legal sociologist is very different from that of the legal anthropologist. The new minimalism is only possible on the basis of a preexistent tradition of auratic, autonomous, highly professionalized law; indeed minimal law is oftentimes developed by professionals trained in the tradition of maximal law. The hyperproductivity of the social context is a complex phenomenon because the latter is to a great extent saturated by modern legality and has been moulded by it. In other words, the contextualization of postmodern legality is a two-way process: as law approximates social reality, social reality approximates law.

This emergent and still very marginal postmodern legality coexists peacefully with modern legality, but as it gains ground it corrodes the symbolic stance of modern legality by forcing it to descend into the materiality of the *hic et nunc*. Slowly but steadily, modern law transits from modeling to repetition, from duration to copresence, and concomitantly from generality to particularism, from abstraction to rematerialization.

## *Law, Microrevolutions, and Neo-Luddism*

The transition from modeling to repetition, from planning to ratification, does not mean that law will disappear completely in the social relations it regulates. Law will go on performing an intensification function through which social relations are rerouted from an ordinary chain of being toward a higher chain of being. The difference will lie in the ways in which such a function will be performed. As law, through its many operators, reaches the understanding that its false utopia is coming to an end, the world as it is becomes more recognizable in the process of its legal intensification. As this occurs, two related phenomena will take place: on the one hand, the limits of social transformation through law will become more apparent; on the other hand, other forms of emancipatory practice will gain or regain social credibility.

Among the limits of law and legal reformism the following will become most prominent. First, state law is one among many forms of law circulating in society, even if it is the most important one. Indeed, it became more and more important in the period of organized capitalism, since the objectives and strategies of reformism and democratization concentrated on state law. In this process, all the other forms of law existing in society were left out of the legal picture and were thus allowed to go on reproducing *status quo* and undemocratic social relations. As this historical process of reduction and occultation is further exposed, the undemocractic nature of law as a whole is unveiled and even the democratic content of state law is put into question. Since the law of the state, while regulating social relations, is forced to interact and negotiate with other forms of law, its reformist and democratic claims must be contextualized and relativized, particularly in view of the hyperproductivity of the social context diagnosed above. A very recent illustration of this can be found in Kristin Bumiller's brilliant analysis of the ways in which antidiscrimination laws may have, in fact, contributed to perpetuating the victimization of the people they were intended to benefit.[96]

The second limit of law and legal reformism is that authentic legal reformism is hard to achieve and that, whenever achieved, it does not sustain its social meaning for very long. Assuming that the undemocratic content of a given network of legal orders is socially exposed, this exposure will, by itself, contribute to the empowerment of those social groups more victimized by the former occultation. The fairer the distribution of power among groups interested in legal reforms, the harder the negotiations to produce reformist laws and the narrower the scope of the reforms. The laws will accordingly become more particularistic and complex. The idea of the simplication of social reality through law that Weber and most

---

[96] Kristin Bumiller, *The Civil Rights Society* (1988).

prominently Niklas Luhmann celebrated as the genius of modern law[97] will come to an end, and this is not in itself a bad thing. But it will definitely decanonize and trivialize law in general and the state law in particular. In an age of audiovisua speed and social acceleration, these effects are likely to be intensified by the constant and ever-stronger pressure to renegotiate regulatory agreements or impositions. Under these circumstances, law will be easily trapped in the dilemma: either to remain static and be ignored, or to keep up with social dynamics and *be* devalued as a normative reference.

The third limit of modern state law has to do with the scale (in cartographic terms) used by law to represent and distort social reality. I have dealt with this topic elsewhere.[98] Here it will suffice to mention that the specific scale used in the representation of reality accounts for the type of phenomena that can or cannot be adequately regulated by law. There are phenomena that, no matter how important in social terms, cannot be adequately dealt with by law because they fall outside the regulation threshold defined by the scale at which that particular law operates. To give examples, we live in a world of Chernobyl and AIDS. In spite of their seriousness, it seems that neither of these problems can be dealt with adequately by state law, one because it is too public or too collective (Chernobyl), the other because it is too private or too individual (AIDS). As these types of limits become more readily identified, the following question will inevitably emerge: if law cannot adequately deal with some of our most serious problems, why should we treat it so seriously?

The principle of the recognizability of the world that presides over the post-modern understanding of law is not confined to the negative function of identifying the limits of law. It opens up to new positivities. On the one hand, the identification of limits maps, by contrast, social spaces in which nonlegal (illegal or alegal) emancipatory practices may take place. On the other hand, since the identification of the limits goes hand in hand with the expansion of the concept of law and its internal fragmentation in a plurality of legal orders, the ideological claim of legal fetishism becomes more untenable and the alternatives to its correspondingly more credible. Such alternatives can be summarized by the concepts of *microevolutions* and *neo-Luddism*.

If we closely analyze the reform/revolution debate at the turn of the century, we will conclude that the debate was about different strategies to achieve basically the same goal, that is, socialism. As reformism got the upper hand, the social transformation to be brought about under its name was gradually scaled down and state law was the instrument used to achieve that objective. It can even be argued, in favor of the relative autonomy of the law, that law reconstructed the scale of social transformation to a level that would maximize the efficacy of legal regulation. From then on, a discrepancy was created between the scale of legal reformism and the much larger scale of revolution, a discrepancy that further discredited the revolution.[99] This created no serious problem in advanced capitalist societies as long as legal reformism kept its ideological hegemony intact. In recent years, however, the situation has been changing. The gradual cancellation of the symbolic aura of law will open a gap in our social imagination. After a century of small-scale legal reformism it is, however, impossible to fill such a gap with the old concept of a large-scale social revolution. A postreformist social revolution can only be a network of microrevolutions to be carried out locally, inside political communities whenever and wherever they are created. To

---

[97]   Niklas Luhmann, *Legitimation durch Verfahren* (1969).
[98]   Santos, "Law: A Map of Misreading" (1987) 14 J. of Law and Society 279.
[99]   I speak of social revolution on the large scale for the sake of intelligibility. In cartographic, technical terms, one should speak of the small scale: larger the real space to be represented in the confined space of the maps, the smaller the scale. See Santos, *op. cit.*, n. 98, 283.

conceptualize such microrevolutions is not an easy task. It may help to proceed by quotation—indeed, a very postmodern way—and try to recuperate, recycle, and reinvent degraded forms of social resistance against oppression. Hence the concept of neo-Luddism. It evokes the destruction of mechanical looms in the first decades of the nineteenth century by English weavers confronted with the introduction of new technologies that would eliminate their autonomy in the work process and further degrade their already wretched life conditions. For many decades, such outbreaks of protest were dismissed as foolish, romantic, and reactionary resistance against the inevitability of progress. In recent times, however, and not altogether by coincidence, the Luddite movement has been reevaluated. The pioneering work of Eric Hobsbawm, followed by others,[1] has contributed to changing the Luddite symbol and converting it into the only rational collective action available to workers before the age of unionization. What is coming into the new political agenda is not the specific means of resistance used by the Luddites but, rather, the invention of forms of social innovation that, like those of the Luddites, confirm and intensify the capacity of autonomous subjectivities to free themselves from the prejudices of legal fetishism.

In the technological age, neo-Luddism will certainly be less violent and naive, but it shall equally bear witness to the intensity of civil engagement and political mobilization only obtainable when the objectives of the struggle are transparent, and the results to be expected are as close as possible to the world of everyday life. Only under these conditions will the struggles be lived as rational, as a mini-rationality that is only total insofar as it is local. Interpretive and transformative communities will generate these struggles through process of rhetorical persuasion that get their argumentative ammunition from the topoi that can be squeezed out of the scripts of partial stories about knowledge, desire, and capacity that referred to previously. It does not matter if such minirationalities are light-weight, portable, or even pocket rationalities, provided that they explode in our pockets. [pp. 105–118]

### C. DOUZINAS and R. WARRINGTON
**"A Well-Founded Fear of Justice": Law and Ethics in Postmodernity**
**(1991)[2]**

"Does he know his sentence?" "No" said the officer. "He doesn't know his own sentence?" "No" the officer said again; he was still for a moment as if expecting the traveller to volunteer some reason for his question, then he said. "There would be no sense in telling him. He experiences it on his own body."

Kafka, *In the Penal Colony.*

### 1. Interpretation and action

Legal judgments are both statements and deeds. They both interpret the law and act on the world. A conviction and sentence at the end of a criminal trial is the outcome of the judicial act of legal interpretation. But it is also the authorisation and beginning of a variety of violent acts. The defendant is taken away to a place of imprisonment or of execution, acts immediately related to, indeed flowing from the judicial pronouncement. Again as a result of civil judgments people lose their homes, their children, their property or they may be sent to a place of persecution and torture.

The recent turn of jurisprudence to hermeneutics, semiotics and literary theory

---

[1] Eric Hobsbawm, *Labouring Men* (1964); Jeffrey Wasserstrom, "Civilization and Its Discontents" (1987) 16 *Theory and Society* 675.
[2] [From *Law and Critique* (1991), vol. II, p. 115.]

has focused on the word of the judge and forgotten its force.[3] The meaning seeking and meaning imposing component of judging is analysed as reasoned or capricious, principled or discretionary, predictable or contingent, shared, shareable or open-ended, according to the political standpoint of the analyst. But as Cover has reminded us, in our obsession with hermeneutics we forget that "legal interpretation takes place in a field of pain and death."[4] The main if not exclusive function of many judgments is to legitimise and trigger off past or future acts of violence. The word and the deed, the proposition and the sentence, the constative and the performative are intimately linked.

Legal interpretations and judgments cannot be understood independently of this inescapable imbrication with—often violent—action. In this sense legal interpretation is a practical activity, other-orientated and designed to lead to effective threats and—often violent—deeds. This violence is evident at each level of the judicial act. The architecture of the courtroom and the choreography of the trial process converge to restrain and physically subdue the body of the defendant. From the latter's perspective, the common but fragile facade of civility of the legal process expresses a recognition "of the overwhelming array of violence ranged against him and of the helplessness of resistance or outcry".[5] But for the judge too, legal interpretation is never free of the need to maintain links with the effective official behaviour that will *en-force* the statement of the law. Indeed the expression "the law is enforced" recognises that force and its application lies at the heart of the judicial act. Legal sentences are both propositions of law and acts of sentencing.[6] Judges whatever else they do, they deal in fear and pain and death. If this is the case any aspiration to coherent and shared legal meaning will flounder on the inescapable and tragic line that distinguishes those who mete out violence from those who receive it.

This necessary distinction and linkage between the constative and performative aspects of legal judgments has passed without much comment in jurisprudence. Hermeneutically orientated legal theory assumes that the rightness, fairness or justice of the interpretative enterprise will bestow its blessing on the active component of the judgment and justify its violence. Theory and practice, word and deed are seen as belonging to the same field, as successive points on an unproblematic continuum. A just interpretation and statement of the law is accepted without more as just action. But is this assumption justified? Does the correct interpretation of the law—if it exists—and the "right answer" to a legal problem—if we can find it—lead to moral and just praxis? Is the law law because it is just or is the law just because it is the law?

To do justice to such questions we turn to some paradigmatic texts which explicitly or impliedly address ethics and the problem of justice. Our reference will be three recent cases from the canon of postmodern philosophy and another three

---

[3] The linguistic and interpretative aspects of the law were always a part of legal theory. They were neglected during the heyday of legal positivism but they have now returned to the forefront of jurisprudence. Law is seen as an exclusively linguistic and meaningful construct and various types of hermeneutics and literary theory are being adopted to explain and justify the operations of the "prison house of legal language." In orthodox jurisprudence R. Dworkin, *Law's Empire* (1986); S. Levinson and S. Mailloux (eds.) *Interpreting Law and Literature: A Hermeneutic Reader* (1988), and S. Fish, *Doing What Comes Naturally* (1990), are clear examples of the linguistic turn. For a more critical approach see P. Goodrich, *Legal Discourse* (1987); P. Goodrich, *Languages of Law* (1990), and C. Douzinas and R. Warrington (with S. McVeigh), *Postmodern Jurisprudence: The Law of Text in the Texts of Law* (1991).

[4] R. Cover, "Violence and the World" (1986) 95 Yale L.J. *1601*.

[5] *ibid.*, p. 1607.

[6] For a more detailed look into the linguistics and pragmatics of sentences as applied to legal texts see C. Douzinas and R. Warrington, "Suspended Sentences", in *Postmodern Jurisprudence, op. cit.*, n. 3, pp. 197–271.

judgments from the House of Lords and the Court of Appeal. The stakes behind the confrontation are high. Can there be a postmodern ethics that while accepting the pragmatic, epistemological and ontological critiques of modern moral philosophy, is not condemned to cycnicism or passivity?

## 2. The ethics of postmodernity

### (a) The Face of the Other

"Driven out of Abraham's house. Hagar and Ishmael wandered in the desert. When their water supply was spent, God opened Hagar's eyes and she saw a well and gave drink to her dying son. But the angels who know the future and the law protested: 'Wilt thou bring up a well for one will one day make Israel suffer?' 'What does the end of the history matter' replied God. 'I judge each for what he is now and not for what he will become.'"

"I judge each for what he is now." If postmodernity recognises the exhaustion of all attempts to ground action upon cognition and reason or some a priori stipulated conception of the Good, it also marks the beginnings of an ethical awareness stepped in the "now" and the event. Emanuel Levinas, the Jewish philosopher of alterity, stands as the figure of the other of Greek archaeology—the ethics of the *arche*, of principles and origins, and of *logos*, reason and logic.[7] The ethics of alterity on the contrary, are based on the shifting relationships between self and Other. It is the unique encounter with the living Other, in his present and unrepresentable corporeality, that opens up the field of ethics.

The Other is not the self's *alter ego*, nor its extension. Nor is the Other the negation of self in a dialectical relation that can be totalized in a future synthesis. Heidegger correctly emphasizes the historical and social nature of self since "the word is always one I share with the Other."[8] But the Other is not similar to self; self and Other are not equal partners in a Heideggerian "we" in which we share our world; nor is it the threatening externality and radical absence of Sartrean existentialism that turns self into an object.

The Other comes first. (S)he is the condition of existence of language, of self and of the law. The Other always surprises me, opens a breach in my wall, befalls the ego. The Other precedes me and calls upon me: where do you stand? Where are you now and not who you are. All "who" questions have ended up in the foundational moves of (de)ontology. Being or the I of the Cartesian *cogito* and the Kantian transcendental subject start with self and create Other as *imitatio ego*. In the philosophy of alterity the Other can never be reduced to the self or the different to the same. Nor is the Other an instance of Otherness or of some general category, an object to a subject that can become a move of dialectics. The sign of another is the face.

The face is unique. It is neither the sum total of facial characteristics, an empirical entity, nor the representation of something hidden, like soul, self or subjectivity. The face eludes every category. It brings together speech and glance, saying and seeing in a unity that escapes the conflict of senses and the arrangement of the organs. Nor is the face the epiphany of a visage, or the image of a substance. Thought lives in speech, speech is (in) the face, saying is always

---

[7] Levinas is the major twentieth-century philosopher who introduces a post-rational ethics as a first philosophy that is not dependent upon cognitive claims and does not lead to totalising systematisations. His most influential books in English are *Otherwise than Being* (A. Lingis trans.) (1981), and *Ethics and Infinity*, (R. A. Cohen trans.) (1985). A good introduction to Levinas' occasionally inscrutable work that owes both to European phenomenology and to the Jewish theological tradition is *The Levinas Reader* (S. Hand, ed., 1981).

[8] M. Heidegger, *Being and Time* (1962), p. 145.

addressed to a face. The Other is her face. "Absolutely present, in his face, the Other—without any metaphor—faces me."[9]

Defying all categorising, the face is more unique than the leaf of a tree in the spring, more concrete than the species of a genus, more particular than the instance of an essence, more singular than the application of a law. In its uniqueness, the face gets hold of me with a ethical grip "myself beholden to, obligated to, in debt to, the other person, prior to any contracts or agreements about who owes what to whom."[10] In the face-to-face, I am fully, immediately and irrevocably responsible for the Other who faces me. A face in suffering issues a command, a decree of specific performance: "Welcome me", "Give me Sanctuary", "Feed me". The only possible answer to the ethical imperative is "an immediate respect for the other himself ... because it does not pass through the central element of the universal, and through respect, in the Kantian sense for the law".[11]

The demand of the Other that obliges me is the "essence" of the ethics of alterity. But this "essence" is based on the non-essence of the Other who cannot be turned into a concept or the instance of a law. "The other arises in my field of perception with the trappings of absolute poverty, without attributes, the other has no place, no time, no essence, the other is nothing but his or her request and my obligation."[12] As the face of the Other turns on me (s)he becomes my neighbour. But (s)he is not the neighbour of the principle. As absolute difference and otherness, my neighbour is at the same time most strange and foreign. Closer than the air I breathe and further away that the starry sky, the Other calls on me but the encounter can be never fully consummated. Our relationship is necessarily non-symmetrical and non-reciprocal. Equity is not equality but absolute dissymmetry.

The ontology of alterity too is based on the absolute proximity of the most alien. When self comes to constitute itself, it faces before the *I*, *I*'s relationship with the Other. The Other has always and already been within self, (s)he disposes and decentres self. The face is a trace of otherness inscribed on the "ground" of self. And if such is the case, all return to self from otherness is exposed to this exteriority which leaves its trace but can never be full internalised. Self is always followed by the Other's demand, never able to return home fully, always in internal exile. I am always persecuted by the refugee and seek asylum from the exile, but (s)he always comes back, always before me, a step behind or a step in front, the not yet which is the always has been.

*Asylos* is (s)he who is not subjected to *syle*, the act and the right of seizure, of plundering and of reprisals, (s)he who is not stripped of her arms, deprived of her possessions, robbed of her due. Asylum is the place that offers sanctuary to the *asylos* from the *syle*. Do we enjoy asylum from the Other? Not in the postmodern ethics of alterity. Πανταχύ συλωμένων, ημων, despaired the Greeks. "Wherever we go we are being plundered. Such is the position of self. The Other persecutes me, puts me in passivity, asks me for sanctuary as (s)he persistently refuses it to me. And if this is the law of ethics, does the law heed its call?

### (b) The Justice of Sentences

The recent writings of Lyotard and Derrida have been answering the call of the Other. In Lyotard's *The Differend*, the singularity of the ethical relationship with the Other becomes the example of a postmodern philosophy of events and

---

[9] Levinas quoted by Derrida in "Violence and Metaphysics", his famous discussion of Levinas' theory in *Writing and Difference* (1978), p. 100.

[10] R.A. Cohen, "Absolute Positivity and Ultrapositivity: Husserl and Levinas" in *The Question of the Other*, (A. Dallery and C. Scott ed., 1989), p. 43.

[11] *Op. cit.*, p. 96.

[12] J.F. Lyotard, *The Difference: Phrases in Dispute* (1988), p. 111.

sentences—and of justice. Derrida in the *Force of Law* declares that justice concerns singularity, individuals, irreplaceable groups, events and lives, "the other or myself as other".[13] Both Derrida and Lyotard seem to share a number of positions on the nature of ethics and the action of justice. As Lyotard's narrative is the more analytical of the two we will start from his story and we will try to weave into it the tales of law and Derrida's aphorisms.

The linguistic mode of ethics is the imperative or, in Lyotard's terminology, the prescriptive sentence.[14] An ethical command cannot be derived from a theory, a concept or a descriptive sentence nor from a general prescription or law, like the Kantian categorical imperative. The demand "Welcome me" of a stranger asks me to act but offers no criteria of choice. The specificy of the ethical moment is that self feels obligated, and acts in response to an inescapable order: "You must". I must act, I am not free not to act, I cannot do otherwise.[15] Criteria of judgment on the other hand follow theoretical and deductive models and attempt to ground ethical action either on the description of a state of affairs to be achieved or on the calculation of consequences.

The specificity and urgency of the ethical command, however, befalls and obligates me before any possibility and without any need for reasons or justifications. Indeed for Lyotard, every sentence is a unique event that happens now. When it occurs, the sentence-event presents a "universe" upon which its four poles or instances and their unique relationship, their "situation", are placed: a sentence first presents its referent, that of which it is about; secondly, the meaning of the case which the sentence presents; the sentence then presents that to which or to whom this meaning is addressed (the receiver), and finally that in whose name the meaning signifies (the sender or addressor). Thus sentences position both subjects and realities and open up worlds of possibilities.

Sentences belong to various incommensurable "regimes": they are descriptive, prescriptive, normative, interrogative. Sentences from the various regimes link together and create "genres" of discourse—science, philosophy, poetry, law etc. Every sentence is a radically unique occurrence but it is always followed by another sentence. Linking between sentences is necessary but what type of linking actually occurs is contingent. Genres act like a gravitational force: they try to attract sentences towards those linkages that promote the function of the genre *e.g.* to know, persuade, seduce, amuse, be just etc. "One will not link unto *To Arms!* with *You have just formulated a prescription*, if the stakes are to make someone act with urgency. One will do it if the stakes are to make someone laugh."[16]

The characteristic of descriptive sentences is that their sender and addressee are potentially interchangeable. They find themselves in a position of equivalence because the referent of the sentences is "reality". Prescriptives on the other hand place addressor and addressee in a situation of radical dissymmetry. Lyotard here follows closely Levinas's ethics of alterity. An ethical command turns the *I* of the addressee into its *you* as the sender of the command becomes master and takes the other's *I* hostage. Self experiences this displacement into the receiver's pole, the "*You*", that the command imposes, as a loss of freedom, knowledge and pleasure. The *I* is tempted to explain or justify his dispossession. New sentences are produced that will transport the *I* back to the sender position; their stake will be to

---

[13] "Force of Law: The 'Mystical Foundation of Authority'" in (1990) 11 Cardozo L. Rev. 949.

[14] The sentence is for Lyotard the basic unit of all discourse and action, the minimum constituent of our world. As such it is a unique event that just happens. We feel that the ambiguously singular nature of a legal "sentence" best encapsulates Lyotard's ambition to theorise the irreducibly unique.

[15] For an ordinary language analysis of the "ideal of obligation" see H.L.A. Hart, *The Concept of Law* (1994), pp. 82–91.

[16] Lyotard, *op. cit.*, n. 12 at 84.

give persuasive reasons for the command and the obedience. For the ethics of alterity, this urge to explain is due to the blindness of the *I*, ego's infatuation with knowledge which, as we saw, presents the Other as symmetrical to self. "The blindness of transcendental illusion resides in the pretension to found the good or the just upon the true, or what ought to be upon what is."[17] But this epistemological narcissism has no object. The *I* cannot put itself in the position of the Other and discover her intentions or deduce them from the sense of the command. To be obligated by an order because self can fully understand its sense would be a crime against ethics. It would both reduce the Other into self and would violate the autonomous underived sense of obligation that ethical prescriptives create. More generally no theory of the good society nor account of justice can furnish criteria for ethical action. Theories are descriptions of determinate states of affairs while the ethical response is indeterminate, something to be done rather than something said.

Kantian philosophy accepts this dissymmetry between prescriptive and constative sentences. According to Kant the data of experience and the metalanguage of scientific principles are homologous, making the passage from observation to theory unproblematic. But in ethics, the object language (*You must ...*) and the metalanguage is not isomorphic. The Good is not given and cannot be apprehended in experience nor are moral judgements the affective reactions of moral agents to empirical properties The knowledge of a state of affairs cannot be the basis of moral knowledge and action. In a move that resembles the operations of the aesthetic in the Third Critique, Kant tries to deduce the ethical command by analogy, *as if* it were a fact of nature amenable to reason. "The 'you must' of obligation is assimilated, via what Kant calls the 'type' (i.e. the form of conformity to the law in general) to the 'I know' of knowledge and the 'I can' of freedom."[18]

The categorical imperative asks us to act as if the maxim of our will may become a principle of universal legislation. The recognition of will's involvement in action is a typically modern move which distinguishes practical from pure reason. But, the injunction to universalize the maxim of the will presents the world as a totality. To act on principles that would be acceptable and willed by all rational people is to assume that self's desire and actions are compatible and coherent with those of all others. The radical first step of the Kantian moral philosophy comes to an end in the assertion that we live in a totalisable community of reason. Furthermore, the categorical imperative installs self as both legislator and subject, sender of the law and its addressee. This is of course the typically modern conception of autonomy or self-determination, the other side of will's enthronement. Within the legal system, laws from now on will be considered just if they are prescribed by those who will have to obey them.

The philosophy of sentences and the ethics of alterity refutes these assumptions. "There is no point in formally distinguishing will from understanding, will from reason, when you decide at once to consider as good will only the will which adheres to clear ideas, or which makes decisions only out of respect for the universal."[19] Similarly the split *we* of the legislator/subject cannot become the horizon of the ethical relationship of the *Thou/I*. The Other cannot be turned into an integral element of a totality or into a monad of an empirical consensus. If the obligation of the ethical command cannot be derived or explained cognitively, neither is it the outcome of autonomy willing the universal law. Without the safe anchorage of a concept and without law, postmodern ethics is left only with responsibility. Indeed with a responsibility for the responsibility created by the suffering face of my neighbour.

---

[17] *ibid.* at 108.
[18] [On Kant, see *ante*, 113.]
[19] Levinas quoted by Lyotard in (A. Benjamin ed.), *The Lyotard Reader* (1989).

*3. The refugees cases*

Our first two cases are very similar.[20] They involved a number of Tamils seeking asylum in Britain. The refugees were fleeing Sri Lanka in 1987 as a result of an offensive by the majority Sinhalese government and the Indian army against the guerilla Tamil forces in the north of the islands. According to the court, parts of the country "have been in a serious state of civil disorder, amounting at times to civil war. The authorities have taken steps [which] have naturally resulted in painful and distressing experiences for many persons innocently caught up in the troubles ... [The] Tamils are the people who have suffered most." (1:198)

In both cases the applicants were refused asylum by the immigration authorities and challenged the refusal in proceedings for judicial review. In the first case the material question was under what circumstances is someone a refugee entitled to asylum; in the second, what can one do to challenge the decision that refused him/her refugee status.

Under Art. 1 of the U.N. Convention on the Status of Refugees, a refugee is someone who "owing to well-founded fear of being persecuted for reasons of race, religion, nationality, membership of a particular social group or political opinions, is outside the country of his nationality and is unable to, owing to such fear, is unwilling to avail himself of the protection of that country". In the first case, the sole point for consideration before the House of Lords was the proper basis for the determination of a "well-founded fear of persecution". The Court of Appeal had held that the test for a "well-founded fear" was qualifiedly subjective. It would be satisfied by showing (a) actual fear and (b) good reason for this fear, looking at the situation from the point of view of one of reasonable courage. Unless an applicant's fear could be dismissed as "paranoid", "fear is clearly an entirely subjective state and should be judged accordingly" (1:195).

The House of Lords reversed, reinstated the immigration decisions and as a result the refugees were sent back to Sir Lanka. The Court held that a genuine fear of persecution could not suffice. The fears should have an "objective basis" which could be "objectively determined" (1:196). Such fears to be justified should be based on "true", "objective facts" that could be ascertained by an objective observer like the Home Secretary or the immigration officers and not solely "on the basis of the facts known to the applicant, or believed by him to be true" (1:200). Once that was accepted, the Secretary of State was entitled to have regard to facts "unknown to the applicant" in order to assess whether "subjective fear was objectively justified." The Secretary indeed had taken into account such "unknown facts", reports of the refugee unit of his department compiled from press articles, "journals and Amnesty International publications, and also information supplied to him by the Foreign Office and as a result of recent visits to Sri Lanka by ministers" (1:198). He had concluded that the army activities, "that amounted to civil war" and "occurred principally in areas inhabited by Tamils" "do not constitute evidence of persecution of Tamils as such" (1:199), "nor of any group of Tamils." As no "real risk" of persecution of the group in general existed, nor a risk "on the balance of probabilities", the Secretary was justified to conclude that none of the applications had been or was likely to be subjected to persecution.

Lord Goff rounded off by assuring the U.N. High Commissioner for Refugees who had intervened in favour of the applicants that he need have "no well founded fear that, in this country, the authorities will feel in any way inhibited from carrying out the U.K.'s obligations under the convention by reason of their

---

[20] *R. v. Secretary of State for the Home Department, ex p. Sivakumaran* and conjoined appeals [1988] 1 All E.R. 193, H.L. (hereinafter cited in text as 1:); *Bugdaycay v. Secretary of State for the Home Department* and related appeals [1987] 1 All E.R. 940, H.L. (hereinafter cited in text as 2:).

having to make objective assessments of conditions prevailing in other countries overseas" (1:203). The U.K. would continue to apply the law and give sanctuary to refugees. The objective test was necessary to ensure that this country—regarded as a suitable haven by many applicants for refugee status—would not be "flooded" with persons who objectively experienced no fear of persecution (1:201).

The second case involved four applicants who were refused asylum by the immigration authorities and wanted to challenge that decision. They claimed that they met the criteria for asylum and that they should not be removed to a country where they feared persecution unless they had exercised a right of appeal against the initial refusal. Now, under the Immigration Act 1971, illegal entrants and those refused leave at a port of entry have a right of appeal against refusal to the immigration adjudicator and further to the Immigration Appeals Tribunal but only after they have left the country. With the beginning of troubles in Sri Lanka, a visa requirement was imposed upon all those arriving from that country. Both those without visa and those refused refugee status at a port of entry should leave the country and appeal against the refusal from abroad. One suspects that people fleeing persecution will experience some difficulty in acquiring genuine travel documents and visas.

The appellants had been designated illegal entrants because they had obtained temporary leave to enter on various grounds and later applied for refugee status. They claimed that under the U.N. Handbook on Refugee Determination Procedures, they had a right to appeal against refusal and that their removal—a precondition for appealing under the Act—would frustrate that right. The House of Lords ruled first that the Handbook had "no binding force in either municipal or international law" (2:946). It went on to endorse the applicants' designation as illegal entrants. At the time of arrival they had misrepresented to the immigration authorities the "true nature and purpose of their visit ... by making statements—which they knew to be false or did not believe to be true" (2:947). Such being the case, to allow the applicants to stay, while all visitors denied leave to enter could appeal after leaving "would be plainly untenable" (*ibid.*). It was prohibited by law and it would discriminate in favour of illegal entrants.

### Criteria of (in)justice (I): Fear and truth

> "Before the Law stands a doorkeeper. To this doorkeeper there comes a man from the country who begs admittance to the Law. But the doorkeeper says that he cannot admit the man at the moment. The man, on reflection, asks if he will be allowed, then, to enter later. 'It is possible', answers the doorkeeper, 'but not at this moment.'"
>
> Kafka, *Before the Law*

The Tamils' cases are (legal) judgments on (administrative) judgments. Are the judgments just? Can we judge their justice? Can we ever be just when facing the refugee? Justice requires that we must read the judgments carefully and justly, to do justice to their word.

A foreigner comes along to the house of the law. He says "I am in fear". He asks to be admitted and to be given sanctuary. The immigration officer/judge demands: "Justify your fear, give reasons for it." He answers: "My father has been killed by the police of my country. My two sisters have been harassed. One of my cousins was arrested, taken to a barracks where he died of injuries. Before dying he gave particulars of friends and relatives including myself. My other cousin has since been arrested and killed."[21] "Ah," says the judge "you must accept that fear is valid when it is based on the facts. And facts being what they are I can find them out as well as you can. Indeed better. I know the true facts

---

[21] This is taken almost verbatim from the second refugees case.

from my newspapers and from reports by my agents and informers on 'the current political, social and law and order position at present pertaining' (2:949) in your country. Let us have a look at the facts. People are being killed in your part of the world, some Tamils in particular. But then people are always killed in your part of the world. On the basis of the true facts as I know them I can find no systematic persecution of Tamils or of any group amongst you. There is no objective basis for your fear as you are under no 'real and substantial risk'. I cannot admit you at the moment."

In this encounter with the refugee the role of the judge has gradually changed. He started as the recipient of the refugee's request but in asking for grounds and reasons and in stating the facts he now claims to be on the same plane as the refugee able to understand his predicament. In other words the past pain of the refugee and his fear of future torture have been translated into an interpretable, understandable reality that like all reality is potentially shareable by judge and victim. But if interpretation is the possibility of constructing interpersonal realities in language, pain, death and their fear bring interpretations to an end.

The claim that fear and pain can be rationalised through the shared understanding of their cause puts the victim in a double bind. Either he is in fear or he is not. If he is, he should be able to give facts and reasons for it which, as they belong to the genre of truth, should match up to the assessment of the judge. If they do not, the refugee is lying. If, on the other hand, he cannot give "objective" justifications for his fear the refugee is again lying. Similarly, when the refugee is inarticulate and cannot explain the "objective basis" of his fear, he is not in fear. But when he can do so, the immigration officer "formed the view that the Applicant, who appeared in good health, was alert and confident at interview, was moving away from Uganda because a better life awaited him somewhere else and that this was not a genuine application for asylum." (2:949)

In the idiom of cognition, fear is either reasonable and can be understood by the judge or is unreasonable and therefore non-existent. In the first instance it is the excess of knowledge and reason on the part of the judge that disqualifies itself. But this translation of fear into knowledge and of the *syle* into reasons and causes assumes that the judge can occupy the place of the refugee and share his pain. Fear, pain and death however are radically singular; they resist and at the limit destroy language and its ability to construct shared worlds.

Lyotard has called this violent double bind an *ethical tort* (*differend*); it is an extreme form of justice in which the injury suffered by the victim is accompanied by deprivation of the means to prove it.

"This is the case if the victim is deprived of life, or of all liberties, or of the freedom to make his or her ideas or opinions public, or simply of the right to testify to the damage, or even more simply if the testifying phrase is itself deprived of authority ... Should the victim seek to bypass this impossibility and testify anyway to the wrong done to her, she comes up against the following argumentation, either the damage you complain about never took place, and your testimony is false; or else they took place, and since you are able to testify to them, it is not an ethical tort that has been done to you."[22]

When an ethical tort has been committed the conflict between the parties cannot be decided equitably because no rule of judgment exists that could be applied to both arguments. The genre and the rules used to judge such cases will not be those of the genre judged and the outcome will be necessarily unjust. The violence of injustice begins when the judge and the judged do not share a language or idiom. It continues when all traces of particularity and otherness are reduced to a register of sameness and cognition mastered by the judge. Indeed all legal interpretation and judgment presuppose that the Other, the victim of the

[22] Lyotard, *op. cit.*, at 5.

language's injustice, is capable of language in general, is man as a speaking animal, in the sense that we, men, give to the word language. And as Derrida reminds us "there was a time, not long ago and not yet over, in which 'we, men' meant 'we adult white male Europeans, carnivorous and capable of sacrifice'."[23] But our communities have long lost any aspirations to a common idiom. We should not forget, therefore, that justice may turn out to be impossible, just a shibboleth.                                    [pp. 115–131.]

## PETER FITZPATRICK AND RICHARD JOYCE
### The Normality of the Exception in Democracy's Empire

*The motif is one of inversion. In its received mode, the exception—the exceptional decision suspending the normal legal order—generates both the sovereign and the law. Here, on the contrary, the exception is found to be of the "normal" law and, thus endowed, law goes to constitute the sovereign. This normality of the exception is then matched with the sovereign claim of democracy's empire. That empire is thence shown to have an oxymoronic quality, democracy and its constituent law being conducive to empire yet ultimately opposed to it. The empire of the United States of America provides a "case".*

### Introduction

Guantánamo is influentially taken to be the paradigm for our time of the state of exception and its attendant sovereign rule.[24] In this rendition, so to speak, Guantánamo is a place of pervasive sovereign control where people are comprehensively contained beyond the law. Yet it has been cogently shown that law flourishes in this very scene supposedly devoid of it.[25] This revisionist account of Guantánamo indicates at least that there is a question about the adequacy of the received version of the exception and its attendant sovereign rule. The abrupt answer offered here is that the exception to the law is itself of the law and that the exception's attendant sovereign rule is constituted by law. Such an answer is then related to the sovereign claim of democracy's empire. In the result, democracy and its law are found to be conducive to empire yet also and ultimately opposed to it. The empire of the United States of America provides a telling "case".

### The Received Exception

The inevitable starting point is Schmitt's pronunciamento: "Sovereign is he who decides on the exception."[26] There is a dual constitution involved here. The immediate one is the constitution of the sovereign. The consequential constitution is that of a distinct legal order. It is the sovereign who, in deciding when a state of exception exists and the normal legal order has to be suspended, also decides what is the normal legal order.[27] The normal order is one of a "boring", repetitive application of pre-existent rules.[28] "In the exception the power of real life breaks through the crust of a mechanism that has become torpid by repetition."[29] The

---

[23] Derrida, *op. cit.*, at 951.
[24] J. Butler, *Precarious Life: The Powers of Mourning and Violence* (2004) 51, 57; G. Agamben, *State of Exception* (2005) tr. K. Attell, 4.
[25] F. Johns, "Guantánamo Bay and the Annihilation of the Exception" (2005) 16 *European J. of International Law* 613; N. Hussain, "Beyond Norm and Exception: Guantánamo" (2007) *Critical Inquiry*.
[26] C. Schmitt, *Political Theology: Four Chapters on the Concept of Sovereignty* (2005) tr. G. Schwab, 5.
[27] id., p. 13.
[28] id., p. 15.
[29] id.

exception is, then and of necessity, illimitable. It "cannot be circumscribed factually or made to conform to a preformed law".[30] Rather, it "frees itself from all normative ties"; it "departs ... from the legal norm".[31]

That is one side of the story. The other has to do with the primacy of law and the sovereign's dependence on it. That side will be recounted shortly. Its intimations are, however, already present in Schmitt's account. The sovereign decision on the exception needs the norm to which it is exceptional. Hence for Schmitt the exception only suspends the legal order. This legal order remains in the wings ever awaiting its return. And return it must if there is to be a sustaining of the norm to which the exceptional can continue to be exceptional. But that is not all. Law invades the realm of the exception, and does so despite the surpassing determinative force which Schmitt would accord the decision on the exception. Law constitutes the terms in which the exception can be decided on: it "suspend[s] itself", and although the sovereign "stands outside the normally valid legal system, he nevertheless belongs to it", and sovereignty remains "a juristic concept" or remains "within the framework of the juristic".[32] Nor is it simply the case that the sealed completeness of the decision on the exception is contaminated by legal matter—rather, the contamination is mutual. The exceptional inhabits the norm. With the operation of the norm, and for Schmitt, the "autonomous moment of the decision recedes to a minimum",[33] but it exists. There is always "space" for the norm in itself to be other than what it may be at any one time, "space" for the entry from within the domain of the legal order itself of what is exceptional to the norm. In like vein, Schmitt recognizes that "every juristic decision" involves a generative creativity, that it cannot simply be read off from what is already there but that it entails "an independently determining moment".[34] The mutual contamination of the exception and the legal order will soon prove crucial for an argument placing the exception in and as law, but what must be considered first is another hugely influential elevation of the surpassing exception and of its attendant sovereignty, an elevation that now becomes pointedly challenging for it incorporates within itself a contamination that for Schmitt seemed merely to derogate from the purity of the separation between the sovereign exception and the legal order.

Agamben's exception has the same components as Schmitt's but the composition of each is different. For Schmitt the decision on the exception "frees itself from all normative ties".[35] Agamben's exception likewise frees itself but not as an occasional suspending of an otherwise distinctly enduring legal order. Rather, the exception now continuously enters into and comprehensively subordinates the legal order:

> Indeed, the state of exception has today reached its maximum worldwide deployment. The normative aspect of law can thus be obliterated and contradicted with impunity by a governmental violence that—while ignoring international law externally and producing a permanent state of exception internally—nevertheless still claims to be applying the law.[36]

The exception "everywhere becomes the rule" says Agamben,[37] and whereas for Schmitt, the exception brings with it "the power of real life [which] breaks

---

[30] id., p. 6.

[31] id., pp. 12, 13.

[32] id., pp. 6–7, 12, 13–14, 16.

[33] id., p. 12.

[34] id., p. 30.

[35] id., p. 12.

[36] Agamben, op. cit., n. 24, p. 87.

[37] G. Agamben, *Homo Sacer: Sovereign Power and Bare Life* (1998) tr. D. Heller-Roazen, 9.

through the crust" of the legal order, for Agamben, the exception itself becomes a power ruling pervasively over life.[38]

The disparity between these lines of thought carries over into the relation between sovereignty and the exception. For Schmitt, as we saw, the sovereign is constituted as "he who decides on the exception", and that power of decision somehow "becomes in the true sense absolute"—something it would have to become if it is to match the illimitable exception.[39] With Agamben it is "life that constitutes the first content of sovereign power", and the "production" of that life is "the originary activity of sovereignty", an originating sovereignty within which "law refers to life and includes it in itself by suspending it".[40] In so doing, sovereignty assumes complete control over that life—a life that is thence decidedly "bare".[41] It is not only that this bare life is produced by sovereignty; it is the very power over bare life that constitutes sovereignty.

That aside, in its encompassing of life, of life that remains infinitely protean if now bare before sovereignty and its law, sovereign power would have to be at least co-extensive with life. How that could be or how it could be known to be is left aptly mysterious. Indeed, where the sovereign of Schmitt and of Agamben comes from is a mystery. Most immediately, it floats on tautology. The decision of Schmitt's sovereign creates the exception which creates the sovereign. Agamben's sovereign is constituted by the bare life it produces. More intriguingly, in both cases there is the evocation of a sacred foundation to sovereignty. Schmitt's sovereign is announced into existence in the opening sentence of a work on "political theology", the gist of which Schmitt explains in this way:

> All significant concepts of the modern theory of the state are secularized theological concepts not only because of their historical development—in which they were trans- ferred from theology to the theory of the state, whereby, for example, the omnipotent God became the omnipotent lawgiver—but also because of their systematic structure, the recognition of which is necessary for a sociological consideration of these concepts.[42]

Part of this systematic structure not exactly recognized by Schmitt is that his sovereign would have to be deiform in order to fuse its determinate presence with the illimitability of the exception. That same fusion endows Agamben's sovereign, only in his case it derives from an ersatz sacred tradition.[43]

Even if a quixotic credence were allowed these grounds of sovereignty, an intriguing irresolution would remain. Schmitt's overweening sovereign, as we saw, remained "a juristic concept" and "belongs to ... the normally valid legal sys- tem", a system able to decide autonomously even if Schmitt would arbitrarily confine this ability "to a minimum".[44] The inability of Agamben's sovereign to contain the law can be discerned more obliquely. The pervasion of this sovereign, its commensuration with life, is qualified by Agamben's finding that this is a catastrophe which is coming rather than already realized, and a catastrophe that could somehow in life be reversed.[45] So, this sovereign is less than comprehensive

---

[38] Schmitt, op. cit., n. 26, p. 15; Agamben, id., generally.

[39] Schmitt, id., pp. 5, 12.

[40] Agamben, op. cit., n. 37, p. 28.

[41] id., pp. 11, 83.

[42] Schmitt, op. cit., n. 26, p. 36. Even more strongly: "The juridic formulas of the omni- potence of the state are ... only superficial secularizations of the theological formulas of the omnipotence of God": C. Schmitt, *The Concept of the Political* (1996) tr. G. Schwab, 42.

[43] For an account and criticism of which, see P. Fitzpatrick, "Bare Sovereignty: *Homo Sacer* and the Insistence of Law" in *Politics, Metaphysics and Death: Essays on Giorgio Agamben's* Homo Sacer, ed. A. Norris (2005) 49–73.

[44] Schmitt, op. cit., n. 26, pp. 12, 16.

[45] Agamben, op. cit., n. 37, pp. 12, 153, 188.

in its effective coverage of life, but the law it supposedly encompasses and sub-ordinates is not so restricted but remains co-extensive with suspended life. This law becomes attenuated or is eventually eliminated only in Agamben's expecta-tion of a new form of life alternative to the coming catastrophe.[46]

## The Law of the Exception

Not without a touch of the tendentious, then, we find Schmitt and Agamben instancing persistent irresolutions in jurisprudence and in the field of law and society. Law is autonomous, or has some significant degree of autonomy. Yet law is receptively subordinated to some other power, usually conceived in terms of society or sovereign. There are various mediations of this divide. In jurisprudence, for example, law has been notably endowed with a "core" of stilled meaning and with a "penumbra" of receptive adaptability.[47] Nothing remotely resembling a general line of division between these categories has been identified. Taking another example, now from the domain of law and society, a "constitutive the-ory" would have it that whilst indeed society constitutes or "shapes" law, law also constitutes or "shapes" society.[48] Again, no dividing line has been identified, and no barrier to stop either pervading the other. The corresponding alternation with Schmitt would have the sovereign generating the legal order *and* law not only retaining an autonomy but also constituently inhabiting the sovereign realm. With Agamben, the contrast, as we saw, was one in which a sovereign power encompassing life subordinated a law of equal extent, yet this same sovereign power also found itself to be less extensive than life leaving the extent of law's own relation to life undiminished.

That these contraries are not simply stark oppositions can be discerned in a more practical perspective on law. The notion of autonomous law usually imports law's providing some determinate reference, some available concentration of enforceable relations between us, some present normative hold on the futurity of our being together. To do all this, however, law has to be continually receptive to the ever-changing quality of those relations and of that futurity. Once, so the moderns say, these two dimensions of law, the determinate and the receptive, could be joined in a transcendent determination. Resort could be had to a deific or sacral resolution much like those evoked by Schmitt and by Agamben. Modernity is bereft of such resort. As the iterative tomes of jurisprudence attest, no resolution is to be found in one side of the division or the other. Law cannot subsist as fixedly determinate. For law to accommodate the ever-pending infinity of possible relation in our being together, it must be utterly receptive. Yet if it were only receptive, it would be purely evanescent and, in the result, a vacuity.

More constructively, and more to our overall point, law is continuously con-stituted in a connecting receptivity to what is ever beyond its determinate self. The call for law always comes from beyond its determinate realization for the time being. If law could not actively and receptively respond to that call, it would wither in cumulating irrelevance. But for law to bring what is beyond into its determinant existence, it must be in a position apart from that existence, a position that opens to, and that can be held open to, what is beyond its deter-minate existence. Yet that same position apart must also be one that resists what is beyond, selecting and gathering it in terms which maintain a connection

---

[46] id., p. 29; Agamben, op. cit., n. 24, p. 64. Compare the law seemingly amenable to the new form of life which Agamben evokes in G. Agamben, *Potentialities: Collected Essays in Philosophy* (1999) tr. D. Heller-Roazen, 165; and G. Agamben, *The Time that Remains: A Commentary on the Letter to the Romans* (2005) tr. P. Dailey, 122.

[47] H.L.A. Hart, *The Concept of Law* (1961) 125, 149.

[48] A. Hunt, *Explorations in Law and Society: Toward a Constitutive Theory of Law* (1993) 174–5.

generatively affirming law's continuing and determinate existence. This position is that of the exception, the exception now as normal.[49] This position is, then, like Schmitt's exception in that it combines being beyond and yet of the existing "legal order".

That self-transcendent position of law also positions the exaltation of the sovereign in both Schmitt's and Agamben's accounts of the exception. "Law itself", says Nancy, "does not have a form for what would need to be its own sovereignty".[50] In its responsiveness to the infinity of possible relation in our being together, law has to be ever changeful and, in some ultimate sense, a vacuity. As such, it cannot in itself, in any formed self, enduringly unite its determinate and receptive dimensions. That same vacuity, however, renders law intimately receptive to power. And it is in the formation of the "modern" national polity that we find a power endowing law, a power concentrated in the persistence of a pre-modern conception of sovereignty.[51] Taking matters that far would help explain the subjection of law to the sovereign within Schmitt's and Agamben's exception. What would still need explaining would be the saturation of Schmitt's sovereign exception with legal matter and Agamben's unwitting extension of law beyond the sovereign power that somehow also encompassed it.

For sovereignty to endow law with determining force, for it to bring together effectively the determinate and receptive dimensions of law, it must share those dimensions with law. In modernity, and like law, sovereignty cannot seek resolution of disparate dimensions in some transcendent reference apart from itself. Hence its starkly dual characteristics delimited by Derrida. Sovereignty, says Derrida, "is undivided, unshared, or it is not"; yet he would ask: "What happens when ... [sovereignty] divides? When it must, when it cannot not divide?"[52] There is some merging of these seeming opposites when Derrida talks about ipseity in terms of "the sovereign and reappropriating gathering of self in the simultaneity of an assemblage or assembly, being together or 'living together,' as we say".[53] Transposing this in terms borrowed from law's dimensions, the determinate dimension could be seen as calling for an experientially undivided cohering; the receptive dimension could be seen as matching the necessity for sovereignty, like any vital organization, to incorporate responsively and assemble the multitude of disparate forces that continually come to (re)constitute it. For this projected assembling, sovereignty must be intrinsically receptive to plurality. To be so receptive, sovereignty must always be incipiently vacuous, always capable of emptying any existent content. So, appropriating another arcanum, Nancy would find that "sovereignty is nothing", "bare", an "empty place".[54] So a "modern" sovereignty, like its exhausted sacral predecessors, must marvellously fuse being determinate with a receptiveness prehensively subjected to that sovereignty's unconstrained efficacy. Such a sovereign power can enclose itself yet extend

---

[49]  This is not to deny that the position apart may provide an opening typically more wide in some legal situations than in others. The situation most frequently instancing the exception, a declaration of emergency, is but an example at the wider end. Congeries of "exceptional" laws can now serve the same function as that performed by the supposed exception to the law (see Hussain, op. cit., n. 25). Standard lamentations, such as Schmitt's, about the spread of discretion and our being moved "further and further from the ground or juridical certainty" (as quoted in Agamben, op. cit., n. 37, p. 172), manage to ignore the intrinsic ability of law to become other to itself. Even the most seemingly stable law carries with it a power of being radically revised or reversed.

[50]  J.-L. Nancy, *Being Singular Plural* (2000) tr. R. Richardson and A. O'Byrne, 131.

[51]  This mode of sovereign appropriation is, of course, not the only way in which law's dimensions have been or are combined.

[52]  J. Derrida, *Without Alibi* (2002) tr. P. Kamuf, xix-xx.

[53]  J. Derrida, *Rogues: Two Essays on Reason* (2005) tr. P.-A. Brault and M. Naas, 11.

[54]  Nancy, op. cit., n. 50, pp. 36, 147.

indefinitely, subsist finitely yet potentially encompass what is beyond its existent content.

To do all this, however, sovereign power cannot simply and purely in itself match the dimensions of law. It has also to be dependent on law. For the sovereign to sustain its being in an importunate futurity, no amount of the present assertion or exercise of power ("exceptional" or otherwise) would suffice. That being is of necessity oriented in a claim of right, a claim that projects sovereign power beyond its determinate dimension and attaches it receptively to what is beyond. Law, then, as the carrier of that right, provides this continuously projected, amenable, and generally enforceable means of combining the determinate and receptive dimensions of sovereignty. In all, as the mutual contamination of Schmitt's law and sovereign intimated, law and sovereignty subsist in a constituent mutuality. It is also possible now to reconcile Agamben's contradiction. In its vacuity law is indeed needful of sovereign assertion, yet law extends beyond such assertion in the cause not just to its own but also the sovereign's continuance "in being".

### Democracy's Exception

Democracy, like law, finds its being in this position of exception—in an opening to what is beyond itself and in bringing what is beyond to itself. There is more here than a simple correspondence between democracy and law. Rather, there is an integral tie in which law creates, and continuously generates, democracy. The necessity for law specifically to do this can be derived from a seeming contradiction in democracy itself.

Democracy is rule by the people, but the people in itself cannot rule. This is the gist of Plato's complaint about democracy in *Republic*.[55] He, or his *dramatis personae*, concentrate on the quality of the democratic individual, but they do so in order to derive the quality of a "corresponding ... democratic political system".[56] Such an individual "indulges in every passing desire that each day brings", submits to "every passing pleasure as its turn comes to hold office, as it were"; and, in all, "his lifestyle has no rhyme or reason".[57] The corresponding political system is promiscuously "open" and potentially "adorned with every species of human trait".[58] It is, in short, this illimitable openness that is the prime and impelling constituent of democracy. Putting this in terms relevant to modern democracy, for Lefort, democracy "inaugurates the experience of an ungraspable, uncontrollable society in which the people will be said to be sovereign, of course, but whose identity will constantly be open to question, whose identity will remain latent".[59] Hence Lefort's thesis that the place of power in democracy is an "empty place"; and the empty throne becomes the "normal" condition.[60] It is not, however, a condition that simply and somehow results from naturalistic traits that Plato, for example, would attribute to it a crucial point that will now be taken up.

The immediate problem is how the people, the demos of democracy, can assume any determinate existence at all, let alone a position of sovereignty. Democracy's pre-modern forms could resort to a defining force of the natural or of the supernatural to selectively constitute the people. With modernity, and as

---

[55] Plato, *Republic* (1998) tr. R. Waterfield, 293–302 (555a–560b).

[56] id., p. 296 (557b).

[57] id., p. 301 (561c-d).

[58] id., p. 296 (557c-d).

[59] C. Lefort, *The Political Forms of Modern Society: Bureaucracy, Democracy, Totalitarianism* (1984) tr. J. B. Thompson, 303–4.

[60] id., p. 303; C. Lefort, *Democracy and Political Theory* (1988) tr. D. Macey, 86, 225–6; S. Žižek, *For they know not what they do: Enjoyment as a Political Factor* (1991) 267–8.

Lindahl incisively notes, "the people" is incapable of coming together to constitute itself as a political unity and from there institute a political and legal order; rather, they come to be a people through the creation of that order.[61] So, this very people, in a feat of what Derrida would call "fabulous retroactivity",[62] is a creation of what it is taken in standard perspectives as creating, a creature of the constitution and of laws made pursuant to it—electoral laws, laws to do with citizenship and immigration, laws to do with mental capacity, and so on. What is more, law produces the definitive processes of democratic, and of sovereign democratic, assertion. Such production extends to the vacuity, the empty place of democracy. In constituting democracy and its definitive processes, this production does so in a way that gives force and effect to this empty place. Law, that is, integrates into democracy's form and processes the ability to be other than what it may determinately be at any one time. With modern democracy, in short, power is purposively constituted or constructed as empty.[63] More specifically, this is achieved through law's sharing in and making operative:

> ...a discourse which reveals that power belongs to no one; that those who exercise power do not possess it; that they do not, indeed, embody it; that the exercise of power requires a periodic and repeated contest; that the authority of those vested with power is created and re-created as a result of the manifestation of the will of the people.[64]

This generative emptiness, then, is embedded in democracy's determinate composition—embedded as a template, no matter how varied its realization. The commensurate ability of democracy to be other than its determinate existence cannot extend to being other to this template securing its emptiness. Democracy then, and like law, imports an "exceptional" position. It is oriented beyond and as other to its determinate existence but still relates and returns to that existence.

### Democracy's Empire

Finally, then, to the question of whether this "normal" exception accords with democracy's empire, relating this to the promised case of the empire of the United States. The issue can be condensed in Jefferson's conceiving of the United States as "the imperial republic". This republic was imperial in that the ability and even the duty of the United States was to expand hugely, but it was republican in that the "territories" so acquired had eventually to be admitted to the union as new states.[65] Imperial expansion beyond the existent range of the republic was justified because of the eventual return to a republican and democratic fold. All of which may seem to accord with the exceptional quality of democracy. Indeed, democracy and its law could be seen in ways as attuned to the imperial. Their vacuity makes them receptive to imperial power, specifically to the assertions of the sovereign of the imperial nation. And their orientation beyond the determinate can serve the expansionary grasp of empire, law having long been part of the "civilizing mission", even if democracy has joined that mission only recently. So, updating the Jeffersonian model to the current formation of American empire so-called, we find its expansionary "influence" is justified by the mantric insistence

---

[61] H. Lindahl, "Constituent Power and Reflexive Identity: Towards an Ontology of Collective Selfhood" in *The Paradox of Constitutionalism*, eds. M. Loughlin and N. Walker (forthcoming).

[62] J. Derrida, "Declarations of Independence" (tr. T. Keenan and T. Pepper) (1986) 15 *New Political Science* 7, 10.

[63] Žižek, op. cit., n. 60, p. 276, fn. 52.

[64] Lefort, op. cit., n. 60, p. 225.

[65] J. Wilson, *The Imperial Republic: A Structural History of American Constitutionalism from the Colonial Era to the Beginning of the Twentieth Century* (2002) 63, 73.

that, in the result, others will be brought within the fold of democracy and the rule of law.[66]

The grand solipsism of empire radically qualifies this easy correspondence with democracy and law. Modern imperialism has been and remains based on national sovereignty, a sovereignty bound in terms that are elevated exemplarily. So, Jefferson's model, which was to be "an empire of liberty", became racially qualified in its application leaving some indefinitely outside the range of achievable civilization.[67] Leaping over to the current scene, we find an imperium officially asserted in terms that are naturalist and divisive, yet transcendent. These are terms laying down "a single sustainable model for national success"; a model in which the market and an economic orthodoxy are enshrined as natural; a model in which certain attendant values are affirmed as "right and true for every person, in every society"; a model in which there has to be limited government and the "unleashing [of] the power of the private sector"; and, more generally, a model in which, conveniently, markets and "societies" have to be "open", especially to foreign investment.[68] This imperative openness turns out to be not quite universal. It excludes the United States which must always, so it is officially ordained, be "strong enough" to counter any "surpassing, or equalling, [of its] power": it must, then, "maintain a military without peer"; and it can use the "global commons" ("space, international waters and airspace, and cyberspace") so as to "project power anywhere in the world from secure bases of operation."[69] If this nationally enclosed predomination were incompatible with the "open" quality of democracy and its law, then we would expect it to find an antithesis when it encountered the rough democracy of the international and its law.

Such proves to be the case. To take a stark example, in his "address to the nation" prior to the invasion of Iraq, a putative President Bush declared: "The United Nations Security Council has not lived up to its responsibilities, so we will rise to ours".[70] This self-elevation of the United States and of its conveniently constituted "responsibilities" did not simply involve the embroiled question of whether the invasion of Iraq was "legal". The breach of international law does not necessarily or usually entail the assertion that, as here, one is superior to it, and superior to the institutions of the international community that create it. The quality of a breach could, however, be quite telling in this respect. Violation of standards, of human rights for example, that are taken to be definitive of the international community, or violation that would seek to undermine the hold of law and its processes, could evidence a hostility or disregard that affirmed superiority at least implicitly. That much could also be extracted from not only the refusal to enter into treaties of a like quality but also from the assiduous undermining of them. And activities of these kinds have been plentiful in the

---

[66] For example, G.W. Bush, *The National Security Strategy of the United States of America* (2002); G.W. Bush, *The National Security Strategy of the United States of America* (2006) introduction, 10–11.

[67] Wilson, op. cit., n. 65, p. 107. For "empire of liberty" see, for example, A. Stephanson, *Manifest Destiny: American Expansion and the Empire of Right* (1995) 22. The phrase was not quite so original in that the British had used it to describe their early empire by way of a contrast with the Spanish. The heavy historical irony is that the "empire of liberty" of the United States was set against British imperialism, among others.

[68] Bush, op. cit. (2002), n. 66, introduction; Bush, op. cit. (2006), n. 43, pp. 4, 27, 31–2.

[69] id. (2002), Part IX; id. (2006), introduction; D. Rumsfeld, *The National Defence Strategy of the United States of America* (2005) 13.

[70] G.W. Bush, "Address to the Nation on Iraq" (17 March 2003) 39 *Weekly Comp. Pres. Doc.* 338, at 339.

recent history of American empire.[71] Any doubt that these activities are super-ordinate may diminish on a reading of the *National Defence Strategy of the United States of America* for 2005 where "our strength as a nation state" is pitted against "those who employ a strategy of the weak using international fora, judicial processes, and terrorism".[72]

## Conclusion

Agamben begins his *State of Exception* with this epigraph, as translated: "Why are you jurists silent about that which concerns you?"[73] Perhaps the point of the question, and accusation, is that jurists should conspicuously condemn the disregard and desecration of the law and legal values in the "exceptional" use of sovereign power he would instance with Guantánamo. In finding that the exception is not *to* but within law, this paper would question a silence that is more "normal", a silence walled in the determinative elevation of naturalist and imperial categories that would deny the responsibility freighted with law's illimitable responsiveness. A like silence diminishes democracy, as we saw. If being modern is to be in a "world of movement, of transformation, of displacement, and of restlessness, this world that is in principle and structurally outside itself, this world where nature does not subsist but steps out of itself into work and into history",[74] then one can only conclude, borrowing that most resonant of titles, "we have never been modern".[75]

---

[71] See, for example, P. Fitzpatrick, " 'Gods would be needed . . .': American Empire and the Rule of (International) Law" (2003) 16 *Leiden J. of International Law* 429, 457–66. Another indicative instance could be that the United States has not notified any derogation from the provisions of the International Covenant on Civil and Political Rights, as provided in Article 4, despite being in breach of several of its provisions. Or perhaps it could not justify a derogation because Article 4 relates to a "time of public emergency which threatens the life of the nation and the existence of which is officially proclaimed". Compare, however, Human Rights Committee, *Consideration of Reports Submitted by States Parties under Article 40 of the Covenant—Third periodic reports of States parties due in 2003: United States of America,* UN Doc. CCPR/C/USA/3, 28 November 2005, Annex I, "Territorial Scope of Application of the Covenant".

[72] Rumsfeld, op. cit., n. 69, p. 5. The terminology could be a tribute to R. Kagan, *Paradise & Power: America and Europe in the New World Order* (2003), widely hailed for its eternal verities about this "new world order", an order in which it is "the weak" who place ultimate reliance on law, the United States having to be strong and act in ways untrammelled by law: at 38–39, 102.

[73] Agamben, op. cit., n. 24, epigraph.

[74] J.-L. Nancy, *Hegel; The Restlessness of the Negative* (2002) tr. J. Smith and S. Miller, 6.

[75] B. Latour, *We Have Never Been Modern* (1993) tr. C. Porter.

17

# CRITICAL RACE THEORY

## Introduction

Critical Race Theory ("CRT") can be seen as a response to (and disillusionment with) the Civil Rights Movement in the United States, and as an off-shoot of Critical Legal Studies.[1] It emerged at the end of the 1980s, has developed strongly since, and has stimulated other minorities so that there is now a "LatCrit" movement[2] (and other movements representing other minorities[3]). Critical race theorists claimed that it was time for "different and blacker voices [to] speak new words and remake old legal doctrines".[4] CRT grew as minority scholars developed a race consciousness form of legal criticism. As Minda explains, " 'Race consciousness' characterizes the jurisprudential perspective of minority scholars who emphasize the need for fundamental changes in the way the law constructs knowledge about race".[5] A product of this consciousness is the racially distinctive body of civil rights scholarship. Central to CRT is the view that racism is "not aberrant but rather the natural order of American life".[6] In an early contribution, Richard Delgado accused civil rights scholarship of being held captive by a group of elite white "imperial scholars" who created a "scholarly tradition" that systematically excluded or minimalised the participation of minority scholars.[7] More recently, he has written of racism as "an ingrained feature of [the] landscape" and of how white elites will "tolerate or encourage racial advances for blacks only when they also promote white self-interest".[8]

---

[1] For the former see R. Delgado and J. Stefancic (1993) 79 Virginia L. Rev. 461; for the latter see A. Harris (1994) 82 California L. Rev. 741. And *post*, 1500. But see Crenshaw, *post*, 1509. For some fascinating insights from jazz see J. Beyer (2000) 88 Georgetown L.J. 537.

[2] *Post*, 1494.

[3] Including Asian-American legal scholarship: see Robert Chang (1993) 81 California L. Rev. 1241, Jim Chen (1994) 80 Iowa L. Rev. 145 and the Colloquy in (1996) 81 Iowa L. Rev. 1467. See also the development of "queer theory": F. Valdes (1995) 83 California L.R. 3, and W. Eskridge, *Gaylaw* (1999).

[4] *Per* J. Culp (1991) Duke L.J. 39, 40.

[5] *Postmodern Legal Movements* (1995), p. 167. And see R. Barnes, *post*, 1496.

[6] *Per* A. Asch (2001) 62 Ohio State L.J. 391, 393.

[7] (1984) 132 Univ. of Penn. L. Rev. 561, 566.

[8] *Critical Race Theory: The Cutting Edge* (1995), p. xiv. See also D. Bell, commenting on *Brown* v. *Board of Education* in (1980) 93 Harvard L. Rev. 518, 524–525.

The main themes of CRT are stated succinctly by Delgado and Stefancic in one of the extracts.[9] In this introduction, accordingly, I take up a few of the more salient themes and issues.

CRT is critical of liberalism. The traditional liberal scholar believed that the legal system would eliminate race discrimination by ensuring that all citizens received the same treatment under law. CRT questions whether formal equality is enough and argues for affirmative action and equality in outcomes. To Bell, "the modern civil rights movement and its ringing imperative, 'We Shall Overcome', must be seen as part of the American racial fantasy".[10]

CRT offers revisionist, racial critiques of civil rights scholarship. In opposition to the colour-blindness of liberal scholars, CRT argues the importance of "race consciousness". To be "race conscious" is to be aware that race is linked to identifiable communities in American society that are "*different* from the community of Anglos in America".[11] And to recognise that "belief in color-blindness and equal process "makes no sense ... in a society in which identifiable groups had actually been treated differently historically and in which the effects of this difference in treatment continued into the present".[12]

CRT believes it can offer "distinct normative insights".[13] Thus, Matsuda claims that those who are "oppressed in the present world can speak most eloquently of a better one".[14] It commonly employs narrative, "story- telling" to tell it as it really is,[15] to bring out the social reality of the victim's story.[16]

Much as it is critical of liberalism, CRT has also developed a critique of the critique of Critical Legal Studies. Crenshaw's article, extracted in this chapter, is paradigmatic of this. She argued that "While Critical scholars claim that their project is concerned with domination, few have made more than a token effort to address racial domination specifically, and their work does not seem grounded in the reality of the racially oppressed".[17] She pointed to the value of rights discourse (routinely rejected by Crits). It offers, she claims, aspirations central to Black demands and performs an "important function in combating the

---

[9] *Post*, 1499.

[10] (1985) 99 Harvard L. Rev. 4, 10.

[11] *Per* G. Peller (1992) Univ. of Illinois L. Rev. 1095. *Cf.* I. Lee (2001) 33 Connecticut L. Rev. 535.

[12] *Per* K. Crenshaw, *op. cit.*, n. 1.

[13] *Per* M. Matsuda (1987) 22 Harvard C.R.—C.L. Rev. 323, 326.

[14] *ibid.*, p. 346.

[15] Patricia Williams's story of being denied the opportunity to shop at a department store (*The Alchemy of Race and Rights* (1991), pp. 44–45) is a classic example. On narrative more generally see K. Abrams (1991) 79 California L. Rev. 971 and L. Pruitt (1997) 50 Arkansas L. Rev. 77.

[16] See M. Matsuda (1989) 87 Michigan L. Rev. 2320 (on racist speech). The best known examples are Delgado's many "Rodrigo's Chronicles", now produced as a book (*The Rodrigo Chronicles: Conversations About America* (1995)). On silence and silencing see Dorothy Roberts (2000) 33 University of Michigan J. of Law Reform 343.

[17] *Op. cit.*, n. 1, p. 1356 and *post*, 1512.

experience of being excluded and oppressed".[18] She also rejects the Crits' view of legal ideology as "induced consent": racism, not liberal ideology, is, she argues, the real source of racial domination.

Some of what CRT says is relatively uncontroversial. Other aspects more so: many, for example, will find it contentious that only minority scholars can understand certain truths. Not surprisingly, there has been a backlash against CRT from, amongst others,[19] black scholars, notably Randall Kennedy.[20] He has argued that race-consciousness critiques of CRT scholars like Bell, Delgado and Matsuda are "bad" for minority scholars, indeed for all scholars because "race-based criteria for intellectual standing are anti-intellectual in that they subordinate ideas and craft to racial status".[21] Kennedy is concerned that race-conscious critiques may have silenced white race scholars:

"If the tables were turned, if a commentator were to read articles by twenty-eight scholars of color, describe deficiencies found in some of them, acknowledge that some black scholars produced work that avoided these pitfalls, but nonetheless conclude that manifestations of these flaws were attributable to the *race* of the twenty-eight authors—there would erupt, I suspect (or at least hope), a flood of criticism."[22]

Kennedy's article led to a symposium in the *Harvard Law Review*.[23] A number of well-respected academics rejected Kennedy's argument. This chapter contains extracts from two of them. Barnes argues for situating CRT scholarship in the need for cultural diversity. In a postmodern world "we have come to realize that *truth* is somewhere, if anywhere, in the symphony of experience" so that the development of social legal principles that vindicates the rights of all "requires a platform for marginalized voices".[24] And Ball that the debate involves conflicting ideologies so that what is required is "translation",[25] "the art of making it possible for people inhabiting different worlds to have a genuine, and reciprocal, impact upon one another".[26]

### The Other "Movements"

Other "movements" have now emerged, out of and/or in response to CRT.

---

[18] *ibid.*, p. 1357.
[19] Not all critics are black: see D. Farber and S. Sherry, *Beyond All Reason* (1997), pp. 52–71, who castigate CRT for anti-Semitism and anti-Asianism. Finkin (1999) 83 Minnesota L.R. 1681 savages it as "rubbish and fascist".
[20] (1989) 102 Harvard L. Rev. 1745.
[21] *ibid.*, p. 1796.
[22] *ibid.*, pp. 1794–1795.
[23] (1990) 103 Harvard L. Rev. 1844–1886. Respondents include Ball and Barnes, extracted *post*, 1506 and 1496.
[24] *Per* R. Barnes (1990) 103 Harvard L. Rev. 1864, 1869–1870.
[25] *Cf.* J. B. White, *Justice As Translation* (1990).
[26] (1990) 103 Harvard L. Rev. 1855, 1857, citing C. Geertz, *Local Knowledge* (1983), p. 155, and *post*, 1506.

Most prominent are Latino-Critical Studies ("Lat-Crit").[27] Latinos/as will soon be more numerous in the United States than African-Americans. The Lat-Crit movement emerged in the 1990s and has analysed such issues as language discrimination, English-only laws, and restrictionist immigration policies and laws.[28] As explained by Berta Esperanza Hernández-Truyol:

> "Latinas'/os' race, ethnicity, and nationhood are conflated, confused and manipulated in and by the dominant society to create, interpret, and enforce a paradigm that renders them others, outsiders, foreign—often in *our* own, *our* parents', and *our* grandparents' country of birth ... Latinas'/os' worlds are subordinated by the dominant normative narrative thereby depriving Latinas/os of *our* normativities, *our* identity."[29]

This is, of course, though it took Lat-Crits to say it, inconsistent with notions of equality and equal participation purportedly inherent in the dominant model. Hence the "exigent need for a LatCrit paradigm that will incorporate *las voces latinas* into the discourse".[30]

Lat-Crits have forged alliances—not always successfully—with blacks and Asians over common issues such as affirmative action. They have debated in-group issues such as discrimination by "lighter" against "darker" skinned latinos/as, and the effect of *machismo* on latinas.[31] They have uncovered the ways in which the black/white binary paradigm of race presupposed in anti-discrimination laws has denied justice to non-black minority groups.[32]

There have also emerged "Whiteness Studies".[33] One of the most interesting—by Ian Haney López, a Latino law professor—shows how American society and courts constructed the category of "whiteness" in naturalisation decisions in cases brought by Japanese, Arabs, Indians and other "near-white" groups.[34]

There are Asian studies too,[35] an increased interest in Native Americans[36] and Gypsies.[37] There is also an interest now in those of Middle-

---

[27] On which see R. Delgado and J. Stefancic (eds.), *The Latino Condition: A Critical Reader* (1998); K. Johnson (2000) 33 U.C. Davis L. Rev. 753 and F. Valdes (1999) 53 Miami L. Rev. 1265.

[28] See R. Delgado and J. Stefancic (1998) 51 C.L.P. 467, 486.

[29] (1997) 72 New York Uni. L. Rev. 882, 911.

[30] *ibid.*

[31] On which see R. M. Gil and C. I. Vázquez, *The Maria Paradox* (1996). See also *op. cit.*, n. 29, pp. 915–918. On "outsider" interest convergence see S. Cashin (2005) 79 St John's L.R. 253 and C. Smith (2008) 40 Connecticut L.R. 1079.

[32] See J. F. Perea (1998) 85 California L. Rev. 1213; and 10 La Raza L. J. 127. See also F. Wu (1995) 15 B.C. Third World L.J. 225, 248 (bipolarity as "an organizational scheme both imposed by and reflected in the law").

[33] See Delgado and Stefancic, *op. cit.*, n. 28, pp. 481–486. See also R. Delgado and J. Stefancic (eds.), *Critical White Studies: Looking Behind The Mirror* (1997).

[34] *White By Law* (1996).

[35] See R. S. Chang, *op. cit.*, n. 3 and Pat Chew (1994) 36 William and Mary L. Rev. 1.

[36] See R. A. Williams, *The American Indian In Western Legal Thought* (1990) and G. Torres and K. Milun (1990) Duke L.J. 625.

[37] See W. Weyrauch (1997) 45 Amer. J. Comparative Law 225; see also W. Weyrauch and Bell (1993) 103 Yale L.J. 323.

Eastern origins.[38] Critical Race Feminism has emerged to address issues such as relations between men and women of colour, sterilisation of black women, and the impact of changes in welfare laws on African-American families.[39] A growing movement too is Critical International Rights. As Hernández-Truyol and Rush explain, "CRT generally, and LatCrit specifically as part of that philosophy, is a movement that at its core is committed to humanitarian conceptions of personhood—conceptions that transcend the limitations of current equality doctrine".[40] Amongst issues addressed are female genital mutilation,[41] sex tourism, the exploitation of third world workers, immigration and welfare.[42] The globalisation of critical theory reconfigures the human rights idea (both domestically and internationally) so that it becomes a truly inclusive paradigm of human dignity and personhood.[43] Some traditional human rights advocates are similarly committed but critical scholars observe they repose too much faith in rights, treaties and other traditional remedies and too little in solidarity.[44]

### But What Does Race Mean?

The word "race" is pervasive in social, political and legal discourse, in the U.S. in particular but elsewhere as well.[45] It is central to debates about affirmative action,[46] racial profiling,[47] hate crimes,[48] health inequities[49] etc. The aftermath of "Hurricane Katrina" in 2005 was seen by many through the prism of race.[50] But what does "race" mean? It has been defined as a biological feature, a local geographic population, a group linked by common descent or origin, a population connected by a shared history, nationality or geographic distribution, a "sub-species", and a social and political construct.[51] There are more and more people of mixed "race". Is "race" thus a meaningful or a useful concept?[52] Sharona Hoffman has argued that "the law should discontinue its use of the term 'race' because it is an unnecessary and potentially pernicious concept".[53] She points to

[38] See J. Tehranian (2008) 40 Connecticut L.R. 1201.
[39] See Adrien K. Wing, *Critical Race Feminism: A Reader* (1997).
[40] (2000) 33 Univ. of Michigan J. of Law Reform 233, 239; and (2000) 5 Michigan J. of Race and Law 817, 823.
[41] L. Amede Obiora (1997) 47 Case W. Res. L. Rev. 275.
[42] B. E. Hernández-Truyol and K. A. Johns (1998) 76 S. Calif. L. Rev. 547.
[43] B. E. Hernández-Truyol, *Human Rights, Globalization and Culture* (2001); Eric Yamamoto, *Interracial Justice: Conflict and Reconciliation in Post-Civil Rights America* (1999).
[44] On distrust of legal systems more generally see M. Olivas (1998) 52 Univ. of Pittsburgh L. Rev. 815, 854–857.
[45] See S. Hoffman (2004) 36 Arizona State L.J. 1093.
[46] See *Grutter v. Bollinger* 539 U.S. 306 (2003).
[47] See K. Johnson (2003) 55 Florida L.R. 341.
[48] C. Chorba (2001) 87 Virginia L.R. 319.
[49] E. Burchard *et al* (2003) 348 NEJM 1170.
[50] See J.V. White in (ed.) D.D. Troutt, *After The Storm* (2006), p. 41.
[51] *Op. cit.*, note 45, p. 1096.
[52] And see M. Rothstein and S. Hoffman (1999) 34 Wake Forest L.R. 849 (on relevance of Human Genome Project).
[53] *Op. cit.*, note 45, p. 1098.

two arguments to justify abandoning the concept: the expressive power of law[54] (discussed briefly previously[55]), and the harms the concept has perpetrated.

The law is an important symbol: it can shape public ideology. It suggests that people can be divided into sub-species and that some of these are inferior to others.[56] There are also significant tangible harms. It ignores those who do not fit into any single "race" category.[57] It "obfuscates political discussion concerning affirmative action, scientific research and social inequities".[58] So when we speak of racial inequality, for example, we could be referring to colour, but equally well to socio-economic status,[59] continent of origin or some other factor (or a combination). Is there thus a case, as Hoffman argues, for replacing "race" in statutes and elsewhere by something more precise? There are a range of alternatives, and which is chosen may depend upon the purpose of the statute and the intended beneficiary class. These issues are beginning to be addressed by critical race scholars.[60]

------

### R. D. BARNES
### Race Consciousness: The Thematic Content of Racial Distinctiveness in Critical Race Scholarship
### (1990)[61]

*I. Distinguishing Themes of Critical Race Scholarship*

As an overview of Critical Race Scholarship, this discussion is by no means complete, but it serves to illustrate the core features of those works that present concepts of racial distinctiveness. Their central elements includes a theory of dual consciousness, a keen awareness of the value of theory for the enhancement of practice, and an explanation of how differentiating characteristics usually compound rather than explain or mitigate racial oppression.

The theory of dual consciousness was captured by W.E.B. DuBois:

> After the Egyptian and Indian, the Greek and Roman, the Teuton and Mongolian, the Negro is a sort of seventh son, born with a veil, and gifted with second-sight in this American world,—a world which yields him no true self-consciousness, but only lets him see himself through the revelation of the other world. It is a peculiar sensation, this double-consciousness, this sense of always looking at one's self through the eyes of others, of measuring one's soul by the tape of a world that looks on in amused contempt and pity. One ever feels his twoness,—an American, a Negro; two souls, two thoughts,

------

[54] See C. Sunstein (1996) 144 University of Pennsylvania L.R. 2021.
[55] Above, p. 1049, n. 88.
[56] *Op. cit.*, note 45.
[57] Note the increase in intermarriage.
[58] *Op. cit.*, note 1, p. 1099.
[59] See R. Fallon (1996) 43 UCLA L.R. 1913.
[60] See T.I. Romero (2007) 37 New Mexico L.R. 245 (referring to the emergence of tri-ethnic jurisprudence).
[61] [From (1990) 103 *Harvard L. Rev.* 1864.]

two unreconciled strivings; two warring ideals in one dark body, whose dogged strength alone keeps it from being torn asunder.[62]

This powerful depiction of dual consciousness delineates the conscious perception of people of color as they are perpetually reminded that their lives,[63] their existence, and their concerns are valued differently,[64] when at all, by the white majority. Their statements and actions are judged by different standards of right and wrong, of morality and immorality. Within their critiques of liberalism and neoconservative justifications for the status of racial minorities, Critical Race scholars pose the debilitating effects of institutional racism as the longstanding, almost impregnable barrier to minority self-determination, thus distinguishing the effects of such discrimination from the difficulties experienced because of the more easily assimilable traits of ethnicity or from status as newly landed in the United States.

Even as people of color are urged to adopt mainstream cultural values, embrace the perspectives of the dominant society, and tailor our aspirations to accommodate the demands of the existing social, economic, and political order, we are invariably relegated to a position of fighting for that to which whites feel entitled.[65] Throughout our lives we receive a pervasive message communicating that we do not truly belong. Implicit in the struggle for equal dignity in our lives and that of our children is the sense that the late nineteenth century doctrine of "white people only" has been replaced with that of "white people first."

One writer describes how as "a black, I have been given by this society a strong sense of myself as already too familiar, too personal, too subordinate to white people. I have only recently evolved from being treated as three-fifths of a human, a subpart of the white estate."[66] Very early on, children of color become aware of the assumptions and expectations that attempt to mark them categorically as second-class citizens unworthy of praise.[67] This "other" consciousness is reinforced across the generations in our familial and community interactions.[68] "We learned from life as well as from books. We learned about injustice, social cruelty, political hypocrisy and sanctioned terrorism from the mouths of our mothers and fathers and from our very own experiences."[69] Many of us remember when we

---

[62] W. DuBois, *The Souls of Black Folk* (1993), p. 3

[63] *See, e.g.* Williams, "Spirit-Murdering the Messenger: The Discourse of Fingerpointing as the Law's Response to Racism" in (1987) 42 U. MIAMI L. REV. 127, 130–32, 156 (providing a moving account of the killing of a black woman by New York City police officers).

[64] *See ibid.* at 140 (arguing that, in society, "soicial costs to blacks are simply not seen as costs to whites").

[65] Mari Matsuda suggests that one of the reasons we do fight is because, although we recognize legal indeterminacy, we have a "core belief in a liberating law that transcends" that uncertainty. Matsuda (1987) 22 Harv. C.R.—C.L. L. Rev. 323, 341.

[66] Williams, "Alchemical Notes: Reconstructing Ideals From Deconstructed Rights" in (1987) 22 HARV. C.R.—C.L. L. REV. 401, 407–08; see also Davis, Law as Micro-aggression in (1989) 98 YALE L.J. 1559 (discussing the degrading treatment of African-Americans in the criminal justice system).

[67] *See* J. KUNJUFU, *Developing Positive Self-Images and Discipline in Black Children* (1984) pp. 1–30; see also Williams, *supra*, n. 63, p. 140 (recounting an incident at age three during which playmates stated that "God had mixed mud with the pure clay of life in order to make me").

[68] Patricia Williams describes an incident in which her family was driving to Georgia to see relatives. On a deserted stretch of highway in South Carolina, police officers pulled over their car. "Throughout the entire fifteen or twenty minutes of our detention, one officer questioned my mother and father in honeyed tones; the other held a double-barreled shotgun through the rear window, pointed at my sister and me." Williams, *supra* n. 63, p. 156, n. 89.

[69] Dalton, "The Clouded Prism" 22 HARV. C.R.—C.L. L. REV 435, 439 (1987).

first *realized* that we were black, and that discovery had a more profound impact than every other thereafter.[70] We do not escape the reality of our experience as members of a racially oppressed group when we enter the legal academy.

In contrast to some white Critical scholars who may seek to transform the existing legal and social order, minorities have insisted on the need to incorporate the concrete, practical realities of oppressed people into agendas for reform. As Harlon Dalton has stated: "whether out of social concern or self-preservation, we learned from the start to harness our brains to the problems of the day. We felt the freedom to play with mind puzzles only after the practical intellectual work of the day was done."[71]

The past and present make us sensitive to the fact that any transformation, whether initiated by those seeking to preserve or to dismantle the *status quo*, might exact the high price of further suffering and marginalization. Thus, for example, although conceding that the use of rights discourse may prove "contradictory, indeterminate, reified and marginally decisive,"[72] Critical Race Theorists contend that for people of color, particularly African-Americans, the symbolic function of rights has served as a formal sanction against invidious treatment and as a tool for empowerment that holds a greater significance than it does for whites.[73]

Finally, the personal and political experiences of Critical Race scholars force them to contend with the complex intersection of race and other characteristics that form the basis for oppression.[74] The discriminatory natures of sexism, classism, and homophobia are often intensified by the added element of race. In addressing issues of false consciousness,[75] for example, as charged by those favoring class struggle as well as those who advocate struggle within the existing order,[76] Critical Race scholars have refused to ignore the difference between race and class as a basis of oppression. Their focus provides a necessary response to the overriding view in much of Critical Legal Studies (CLS) that the poor are disempowered, helpless, and nonculpable co-conspirators in their own oppression and to the tendency of CLS scholars to imply that the focus upon race is misplaced because it hampers efforts to foster class-based resistance to what they view as economic oppression.[77] Critical Race scholars know that class analysis alone cannot account for racial oppression,[78] and they are more likely to focus on such issues as the "invisible ceiling"—the discovery that high socio-economic status will not provide minorities the same freedom and mobility to which whites feel automatically entitled. Virtually all people of color in high-salaried and high-status positions have discovered that money cannot buy everything, not even in

---

[70] As I remember conversations with older black Americans about how racism has touched their lives, there is always a pervasive sense of violation.

[71] Dalton, *supra* n. 69, p. 440.

[72] Williams, *supra* n. 66, p. 404.

[73] See Delgado, "The Ethereal Scholar: Does Critical Legal Studies Have What Minorities Want?" in (1987) 22 HARV. C.R.—C.L. L. REV 301, 305–07, 315, 318.

[74] See, *e.g.* Delgado & Stefancic, "Why Do We Tell the Same Stories?: Law Reform, Critical Librarianship, and the Triple Helix Dilemma" in (1989) 42 STAN. L. REV. 207, 219–20 (critiquing the lack of combined references for racial and gender discrimination in case and statutory law indices).

[75] See Delgado, *supra* n. 73, p. 309.

[76] See, *e.g.* West, "Race and Social Theory: Towards a Genealogical Materialist Analysis" in (1987) *American Left Year Book II* 74

[77] See, *e.g.* A. Freeman, "Antidiscrimination Law: A Critical Review" in (D. Kairys ed. 1982) in *The Politics of Law: a Progressive Critique* 96, 106–10

[78] See, *e.g.* Delgado, *supra* n. 73, p. 321.

the United States. The identity of the purchaser represents as significant a part of the transaction as does the price.[79] In discussing an impending arrangement to lease property, one writer recalls that she was "acutely conscious of the likelihood that, no matter what degree of professional or professor I became, people would greet and dismiss my black femaleness as unreliable, untrustworthy, hostile, angry, powerless, irrational and probably destitute."[80] The acute consciousness of minority scholars often serves as an added impetus to seek concrete changes in the social and political landscape. [pp. 1865–1869]

## R. DELGADO AND J. STEFANCIC
### Critical Race Theory: An Annotated Bibliography
### (1993)[81]

*Introduction*

Critical Race Theory (CRT) took start in the mid-1970s with the realization that the Civil Rights Movement of the 1960s had stalled and that many of its gains, in fact, were being rolled back. Many of us believed that new tactics and theories were needed to understand and come to grips with the complex interplay among race, racism, and American law. Beginning with the ground-breaking works of Derrick Bell and Alan Freeman, the body of CRT scholarship now contains several books and more than two hundred articles. [p. 461]

To be included in the Bibliography,[82] a work needed to address one or more themes we deemed to fall within Critical Race thought. These themes, along with the numbering scheme we have employed, follow:

1. *Critique of liberalism.* Most, if not all, CRT writers are discontent with liberalism as a means of addressing the American race problem. Sometimes this discontent is only implicit in an article's structure or focus. At other times, the author takes as his or her target a mainstay of liberal jurisprudence such as affirmative action, neutrality, color blindness, role modeling, or the merit principle. [. . .]

2. *Storytelling/counterstorytelling and "naming one's own reality."* Many Critical Race theorists consider that a principal obstacle to racial reform is majoritarian mindset—the bundle of presuppositions, received wisdoms, and shared cultural understanding persons in the dominant group bring to discussions of race. To analyze and challenge these power-laden beliefs, some writers employ counterstories, parables, chronicles, and anecdotes aimed at revealing their contingency, cruelty, and self-serving nature.

3. *Revisionist interpretations of American civil rights law and progress.* One recurring source of concern for Critical scholars is why American anti-discrimination law has proven so ineffective in redressing racial inequality—or why progress has been cyclical, consisting of alternating periods of advance followed by ones of retrenchment. Some Critical scholars address this question, seeking answers in the psychology of race, white self-interest, the politics of colonialism and anticolonialism, or other sources.

4. *A greater understanding of the underpinnings of race and racism.* A number of Critical writers seek to apply insights from social science writing on race and

---

[79] For example, after purchasing a building in an elite neighborhood of Cambridge, Massachusetts, in 1987, a predominantly black private day school met with hostile opposition from wealthy neighbors, even though the white school that had operated on the same site for 49 years had never encountered problems.

[80] Williams, *supra*, n. 66, p. 407.

[81] [From (1993) 79 *Virginia L. Rev.* 461.]

[82] [This is not included.]

racism to legal problems. For example: understanding how majoritarian society sees black sexuality helps explain law's treatment of interracial sex, marriage, and adoption; knowing how different settings encourage or discourage discrimination helps us decide whether the movement toward Alternative Dispute Resolution is likely to help or hurt disempowered disputants.

5. *Structural determinism.* A number of CRT writers focus on ways in which the structure of legal thought or culture influences its content, frequently in a *status* quo-maintaining direction. Once these constraints are understood, we may free ourselves to work more effectively for racial and other types of reform.

6. *Race, sex, class, and their intersections.* Other scholars explore the intersections of race, sex, and class, pursuing such questions as whether race and class are separate disadvantaging factors, or the extent to which black women's interest is or is not adequately represented in the contemporary women's movement.

7. *Essentialism and anti-essentialism.* Scholars who write about these issues are concerned with the appropriate unit for analysis: Is the black community one, or many, communities? Do middle-and working-class African-Americans have different interests and needs? Do all oppressed people have something in common?

8. *Cultural nationalism/separatism.* An emerging strain within CRT holds that people of color can best promote their interest through separation from the American mainstream. Some believe that preserving diversity and separateness will benefit all, not just groups of color. We include here, as well, articles encouraging black nationalism, power, or insurrection.

9. *Legal institutions, Critical pedagogy, and minorities in the bar.* Women and scholars of color have long been concerned about representation in law school and the bar. Recently, a number of authors have begun to search for new approaches to these questions and to develop an alternative, Critical pedagogy.

10. *Criticism and self-criticism; responses.* Under this heading we include works of significant criticism addressed at CRT, either by outsiders or persons within the movement, together with responses to such criticism.          [pp. 462–463]

## A. HARRIS
### The Jurisprudence of Reconstruction
### (1994)[83]

*Critical Race Theory and the Politics of Difference*

I have thus far argued that CRT takes as its goal the liberation of people of color while adopting a method of critique that questions the confident certainties embedded in the very concepts "people of color" and "liberation." As the debates over racial essentialism within CRT and the value of legal "storytelling" illustrate, when these postmodernist and modernist narratives clash, postmodernist skepticism threatens to undermine modernist narratives completely.

I do not mean to argue, however, that CRT's reliance on both modernist and postmodernist narratives makes it incoherent. This tension between perspectives is not unique to CRT; it also plagues feminist legal theory[84] and, in a sense, legal

---

[83] [From (1994) 82 *California L. Rev.* 741.]
[84] For a useful summary of the debate between feminism and postmodernism in the legal context, see Dennis Patterson, "Postmodernism/Feminism/Law" in (1992) 77 *Cornell L. Rev.* 254.

scholarship itself.[85] The recent bitter debates throughout academia about the value of deconstruction and postmodernism's "nihilism" and "relativism" suggest the pervasiveness of the problem.

Reacting to the nihilist threat, some writers have argued that postmodernism is antithetical to feminism and should be rejected by feminist theorists.[86] Race-crits could take a similar position, rejecting postmodernist philosophizing in favor of the certainties of universal truth and justice. In my view, however, this response would be a mistake for two reasons. First, postmodernism does not represent an independent alternative to modernism that can be accepted or rejected; it is the voice of modernism's discontents, and as such is not easily stilled. Second, part of the reason why race-crits have tried to distance themselves from traditional civil rights scholarship is precisely that the old verities, the old optimistic faith in reason, truth, blind justice, and neutrality, have not brought us to racial justice, but have rather left us "stirring the ashes."[87] History has shown that racism can coexist happily with formal commitments to objectivity, neutrality, and color-blindness. Perhaps what CRT needs is simply a redoubled effort to reach true objectivity and neutrality. But, then again, perhaps those concepts themselves need reexamination.

If race-crits can neither reject postmodernism nor accept it wholeheartedly without undermining the CRT project itself, what (to ask the legal scholar's perennial normative question) should we do? To talk as if one has the choice to "accept" or "reject" these world views is certainly misleading. We live in a political and legal world shaped by modernism; we cannot step out of it. Nor can we, as good modernist intellectuals, ignore modernism's discontents. As Anthony Cook and others have written, the task should not be to try to somehow resolve the philosophical tension between modernism and postmodernism, but rather consciously to inhabit that very tension.[88] This work requires both a commitment to modernism and a willingness to acknowledge its limits. At its best, it inspires a jurisprudence of reconstruction—the attempt to reconstruct political modernism itself in light of the difference "race" makes.

Race-crits, along with other outsider scholars, have a distinctive contribution to make to this endeavor. The source of this contribution, I argue in this Section, is an engagement with "the politics of difference." Through their commitment both to anti-racism and to affirming the cultural "differences" that the concept of "race" has produced, race-crits bring a distinctive perspective to the jurisprudential "problem of the subject."[89] More broadly, this dual commitment to eliminating oppression and celebrating difference impels race-crits to live in the tension between modernism and postmodernism, transforming political modernism in the process. In this latter project, race-crits are part of a global

---

[85] Thus the emergence of articles written from a "mainstream" perspective that attempt to make sense of outsider jurisprudence by putting it back into a conventional framework. Farber & Sherry's *Telling Stories Out of School* is one example of this genre. For an attempt to construct standards for evaluating legal scholarship that can be applied to outsider jurisprudence and mainstream scholarship alike, see Edward L. Rubin, "On Beyond Truth: A Theory for Evaluating Legal Scholarship" in (1992) 80 Calif. L. Rev. 889.

[86] Robin West, for example, has argued that feminists should reject the antiessentialism of "critical social theory" because it denies women their knowledge of an "antisymbolic, uncultured, natural, loving, female self." Robin West, "Feminism, Critical Social Theory and Law" in (1989) U. Chi. Legal F. 59, 95.

[87] Frances L. Ansley, "Stirring the Ashes: Race, Class and the Future of Civil Rights Scholarship" in (1989) 74 Cornell L. Rev. 993, 1040–1050.

[88] See, *e.g.* Cook (arguing for a reconstructed philosophical framework that "challenges, though never completely overcomes, the dichotomies of self and other, individualism and altruism, and private and public").

[89] See *infra*.

movement by intellectuals in previously colonized nations, not to abandon the Enlightenment ideals of freedom and liberal democracy, but to make good on their promises.

## A. CRT and the Problem of the Subject

Unlike crits, whose primary intellectual-political commitment is to criticism itself, race-crits hold a dual commitment to anti-racist critique and to maintaining the distinctive cultures formed in part by concepts of "race." This dual commitment engages CRT in what I call the "politics of difference."

One notable characteristic about contemporary American left political movements is their obsession with issues of identity.[90] The second wave of the women's movement and the Civil Rights Movement, for example, built their strength on reconceiving their constituents' collective identities; subsequent movements such as Gay Liberation and its contemporary descendants have similarly engaged in "identity politics."[91] In these movements, the construction of one's identity has been both a personal and a political act, linking the individual with a distinct social and political community.[92]

Rather than supporting assimilation to the dominant culture, the new social movements have demanded a recognition of their members' "difference." This claim to equality based not on sameness but rather on difference is at the heart of the politics of difference. Intellectuals' engagement in the politics of difference has resulted in a rejection of the binary distinction between "same" and "different" itself. Instead, these scholars see "identity" as a complex and changing interaction between internal and external forces, between individual agency and structures of

---

[90] For example, from a sociological point of view, Joel Handler describes "new social movements" as follows:

"These movements advocate a new form of citizen politics based on direct action, participatory decisionmaking, decentralized structures, and opposition to bureaucracy. They advocate greater attention to the cultural and quality-of-life issues rather than material well-being. They advocate greater opportunities to participate in the decisions affecting one's life, whether through direct democracy or increased reliance on self-help groups and cooperative styles of social organization. They appeal to value- and issue-based cleavages instead of group-based or interest group issues."

Handler, *op. cit.*, p. 719. Other writers have identified the politics of difference by its distinctive practices or demands. See, *e.g.* CORNEL WEST. *"The New Cultural Politics of Difference" in (1993) 3 Keeping Faith: Philosophy and Race in America* ("Distinctive features of the new cultural politics of difference are to trash the monolithic and homogeneous in the name of diversity, multiplicity and heterogeneity; to reject the abstract, general and universal in light of the concrete, specific and particular; and to historicize, contextualize and pluralize by highlighting the contingent, provisional, variable, tentative, shifting and changing."); Iris M. Young, *Justice and the Politics of Difference*, (1990), pp. 156, 158 ("A politics of difference argues ... that equality as the participation and inclusion of all groups sometimes requires different treatment for oppressed or disadvantaged groups"); see also Kobena Mercer, "1968: Periodizing Politics and Identity" in L. Grassberg *et al.* eds., 1992), pp. *Cultural Studies* 424, 424–425 ("Over the past decade, developments in black politics, in lesbian and gay communties, among women and numerous feminist movements, and across a range of struggles around social justice, nuclear power, and ecology have pluralized the domain of political antagonism.").

[91] For a clear and cogent discussion of identity politics, see Frances Lee Ansley, "A Civil Rights Agenda for the Year 2000: Confessions of an Identity Politician" in (1992) 59 *Tenn. L. Rev.* 593, 599.

[92] For a useful capsule history of racial identity movements, see Manning Marable, *Race, Reform, and Rebellion: The Second Reconstruction in Black America, 1945–1990*, (2d ed., 1991), pp. 137–145.

power.[93] For example, by complicating the notion of "female identity," feminist theorists have tried to move beyond the proposition that gender equality requires either "the same" treatment or "different" (usually meaning "special," and hence disfavored) treatment.[94] Instead, feminist theorists have explored how both "sameness" and "difference" are based on a non-neutral, male standard.[95] Equality in this formulation demands transformation of the existing structure, not just tolerance of or remediation for those who are "different."

Second-wave crits have argued that the reconstruction of political modernism in light of postmodernist critique requires addressing the problem of the subject.[96] Just whom is being spoken of when law review authors recommend that "we" do this or that? What issues are being avoided when legal writers seek to understand the legal system without asking how understanding changes the self?[97] Race-crits, like other intellectuals engaged in the politics of difference, are well situated to speak to "the problem of the subject." The language of race creates, maintains, and destroys subjects, both inside and outside the law. The study of race is in part the study of how individual personalities are melted down into collective subjects. It is also the study of how racialized subjects can be subjected to, yet not represented in, the law. In coming to terms with the long exclusion of people of color from full legal "belonging," race-crits seek not just to expand the subject "we the people," but to turn a critical eye on the legal subject itself. Just as feminist demands for equality require a transformation of traditional understandings of families and markets,[98] race-crit demands for equality under law require a transformation of traditional understandings of the legal subject.

This task forces intellectuals to live in the conflict between modernism and postmodernism. The new social movements based on "difference" have renounced assimilation as the path toward equality and are suspicious of the old

---

[93] For an argument that "practice theory" can reconcile the tension between structure and agency in CLS, see Rosemary J. Coombe, "Room for Manoeuver: Toward a Theory of Practice in Critical Legal Studies" in (1989) 14 *Law & Social Inquiry* 69. For a concise and useful examination of various theories that attempt to explain the interaction of social forces and individual or collective will in the negotiation of "race," ethnicity, and nation, see Edward J. McCaughan, "Race, Ethnicity, Nation, and Class within Theories of Structure and Agency" in (1993) 20 *Social Justice* 82.

[94] See, *e.g.* Christine A. Littleton, *"Reconstructing Sexual Equality" in (1987)* 75 *Calif. L. Rev.* 1279 (arguing that male and female "differences," perceived or real, biological or social, should be costless) [and *ante*, 1184].

[95] See, *e.g.*, Catharine A. MacKinnon, *Feminism Unmodified: Discourses on Life and Law* 32, 34(1987) [and *ante*, 1337].
    Martha Minow has elegantly explored the ways in which "difference" is always a question of context. *Making All the Difference: Inclusion, Exclusion, and American Law* (1990).

[96] Schlag, at 1628; see also J.M. Balkin, *Understanding Legal Understanding: The Legal Scholar and the Problem of Legal Coherence*, 103 *Yale L.J.* 105 (1993) [and *ante*, 1449] James Boyle, *Is Subjectivity Possible? The Postmodern Subject in Legal Theory*, 62 *U. Colo. L. Rev.* 489 (1991).

[97] *See* Balkin, *supra* n. 96, at 107 ("Instead of seeing legal coherence as a preexisting feature of an object apprehended by a subject, we should view legal understanding as something that the legal subject brings to the legal object she comprehends."). As Balkin points out, the question of the "subject" is not simply a psychological inquiry into individuals" "subjective" conceptions of law. Rather, the investigation assumes that "subjects" are members of a common culture, possessing the same or similar "cultural software." *ibid.* at 108.

[98] *See* Frances E. Olsen, *The Family and the Market: A Study of Ideology and Legal Reform*, 96 *Harv. L. Rev.* 1497 (1983).

faith in integration.[99] At the same time, most of these movements are committed to seeking equality, justice, and pluralism within the nation rather than as separate political sovereigns.[1] This political task of giving a new meaning to the phrase "e pluribus unum" thus demands both a commitment to political modernism and a deep skepticism of it.

## B. CRT and Resistance Culture

For people of color, the politics of difference within the United States can be understood within the broader context of global post-colonialism. Edward Said has made a study of how the West justified colonialism, how colonized peoples resisted it, and how the cultural dialogue between colonizer and colonized is evident in the art and literature of each.[2] Since the end of formal colonialism,[3] Said argues, a distinctive "resistance culture" has emerged from formerly colonized peoples.

Resistance culture, as Said describes it, consists of three projects. First is the reconstitution of the formerly colonized nation through consolidating a national language and national culture (a project that is always the product of invention rather than simple "recovery").[4] Second is what Said calls "the voyage in": the "conscious effort to enter into the discourse of Europe and the West, to mix with it, transform it, to make it acknowledge marginalized or suppressed or forgotten histories."[5] Third, according to Said, resistance culture involves "a noticeable pull away from separatist nationalism toward a more integrative view of human community and human liberation."[6]

Reading the history of "racial minorities" in the United States as part of the larger history of western colonialism, race-crits are involved in the project of "resistance culture" as well. Situated within the United States, where separatist nationalism has never been a viable alternative,[7] the domestic politics of difference has focused on Said's first and second projects: the constitution or reconstitution of the subordinated community and the transformation of the dominant community.

Storytelling has contributed to much of the first project. Storytelling serves to

---

[99] See, *Young, ante,* 90, at 159.

[1] The great exception is the movement of indigenous peoples for greater sovereignty. For a legal argument in favor of greater sovereignty for Indian nations, see Comment, *Toward Consent and Co-operation: Reconsidering the Political Status of Indian Nations,* 22 Harv. C.R.-C.L. L. Rev. 507 (1987). For an account of the rise and fall of black nationalism in favor of an integrationist paradigm, see Gary Peller, *Race Consciousness,* 1990 *Duke L.J.* 758. For a defense of the reemergence of nationalism for communities of color, see Williamson B.C. Chang. The "Wasteland" in the Western Exploitation of "Race" and the Environment, 63 *U. Colo. L. Rev.* 849 (1992).

[2] Edward W. Said, *Culture and Imperialism* 209–20 (1993).

[3] Some critics have argued, however, that colonialism never ended, but merely has assumed a new form. See, *e.g.,* Masao Miyoshi, "A Borderless World? From Colonialism to Transnationalism and the Decline of the Nation-State, 19 *Critical Inquiry* 726, 749 (1993) (arguing that transnational corporations continue colonialism).

[4] Said, *supra* n. 82, at 215.

[5] Said, *supra* n. 82, at 216 (emphasis-omitted).

[6] *ibid.* at 216. This last component of resistance culture is arguably more prescription thandescription.

[7] Again, the history of the Indian pations represents at least a partial exception. See Toward Consent and Co-operation, supra n. 18. For criticism of the colonialist structure of Indian law, see Robert N. Clinton, "Redressing the Legacy of Conquest: A Vision Quest for a Decolonized Federal Indian Law", 46 *Ark. L. Rev.* 77 (1993).

create and confirm identity, both individual and collective.[8] As William Eskridge has argued, storytelling helps build new communities: stories of what it means to be gay and lesbian, for example, help individual gay and lesbian people locate themselves within a community and give the gay and lesbian community a collective sense of itself as an agent.[9] At the personal level, this community-building function is similar to what 1970s feminists termed "consciousness raising."[10] Storytelling in this sense is myth-making: the creation of a new collective subject with a history from which individuals can draw to shape their own identities.

Literary and cultural critics have participated in the second aspect of resistance culture, the project of "writing back." For example, in the context of American literary studies, Toni Morrison argues that "Africanism"—the reference in literary works to an imaginary "Africa"—

has become, in the Eurocentric tradition that American education favors, both a way of talking about and a way of policing matters of class, sexual license, and repression, formations and exercises of power, and meditations on ethics and accountability. Through the simple expedient of demonizing and reifying the range of color on a palette, American Africanism makes it possible to say and not say, to inscribe and erase, to escape and engage, to act out and act on, to historicize and render timeless. It provides a way of contemplating chaos and civilization, desire and fear, and a mechanism for testing the problems and blessings of freedom.[11]

Morrison's project is to transform the reader's understanding of the American literary canon by calling her attention to how complexities within American social and political culture have been made into questions of "race."[12] Her effort, however, is not to throw certain works out of the canon and replace them with others, but rather to deepen the reader's understanding both of the works within and without the canon and of how and why canon formation itself takes place.

Robert Williams is engaged in a similar task in his article in this Symposium. Williams points out that the history of the Encounter era in North America is not only one of conflict but also one of mutual accommodation.[13] In telling the story of the English-Iroquois Covenant Chain alliance, Williams does the historical work of adding back to the American legal and political tradition a story of Iroquois creativity and power that has been forgotten or suppressed. Williams engages in the transformational work of "explor[ing] the commensurability of this North American indigenous vision of law and peace between different peoples with contemporary understandings of the problem of achieving human solidarity and accommodation in a multicultural world."[14] By recovering this and other neglected dialogues, race-crits can begin to reconstruct modern political theory.

---

[8] See Richard Delgado, "Storytelling for Oppositionists and Others: A Plea for Narrative", 87 *Mich. L. Rev.* 2411, 2414 (1989) ("[S]tories build consensus, a common culture of shared understandings, and deeper, more vital ethics.").

[9] Eskridge, *supra*, at 624–25.

[10] *See* Elizabeth M. Schneider, *The Dialectic of Rights and Politics: Perspectives from the Women's Movement,* 61 *N.Y.U.L. Rev.* 589, 601–04 (1986) (describing consciousness-raising); see also Catharine A. MacKinnon, *Toward a Feminist Theory of the State* (describing consciousness-raising as a way for individual women to create their own identity and develop a collective identity); Christine A. Littleton, *Feminist Jurisprudence: The Difference Method Makes, 41 Stan. L. Rev.* 751, 764–65 (1989) (reviewing MacKINNON, FEMINISM Unmodified).

[11] Toni Morrison, *Playing in the Dark: Whiteness and the Literary Imagination* LITERARY IMAGINATION 7 (1992).

[12] Said's project is similarly to re-read classics of Western "high" culture in the context of the West's history of imperialism, colonialism, and anti-colonial struggle. See Said, supra. 2, at 57–61.

[13] Williams, at 985–86.

[14] *ibid.* at 995.

## C. CRT as Reconstruction Jurisprudence

Within legal studies, the attempt to use the dissonance between modernism and postmodernism creatively on behalf of people of color is what I call "reconstruction jurisprudence." Mari Matsuda, who coined this term, describes it as having a double meaning. First, reconstruction jurisprudence is meant to distinguish CRT from CLS's project of deconstruction. Race-crits have rejected the project of "total critique" and are committed to transforming modernist paradigms as well as criticizing them. Second, the word "reconstruction" refers to the legacy of slavery in the New World and the unfinished revolutions of the First and Second Reconstructions.

My third connotation for "reconstruction jurisprudence" is the project of "writing back" to white-dominated legal rules, reasoning, and institutions. The first step is the self-conscious formation of identity groups that have been subject to racial oppression and now demand equality—a formation accomplished by collective myth-making. The second step involves the recovery and reworking of what has been lost or suppressed concerning "race" in legal doctrine and policy. The third step is the work of transforming existing jurisprudence and political theory.

These steps do not follow one another in order, but rather are continuous and simultaneous processes. For example, while African America is currently a relatively stable community with a shared sense of history and tradition, Asian American scholars are engaged in the process of community creation. Moreover, the development of Asian American political consciousness will have an effect on African American political consciousness, and both will transform the meaning of "race" itself.

The work of this reconstruction jurisprudence has just begun, and it is too soon to say whether CRT and other forms of outsider jurisprudence will succeed in the ambitious goal of reformulating political modernism. In the next Section, however, I suggest aspirations for CRT toward this end, identify some of the tentative steps race-crits have taken toward this goal, and finally suggest ways in which CRT might further this project.                          [pp. 759–766].

### MILNER S. BALL
#### The Legal Academy and Minority Scholars
#### (1990)[15]

Absent transformation, Priestley will not see oxygen, the colorblind will not see the color purple, and members of the academic establishment will not see colored people. Kennedy says that Bell, Delgado, and Matsuda have not observed the proprieties of the conventional academy. He is correct. They have not. They have set about changing it. He faults them for what he views as their failures of proof. But how does one prove—or translate, or make visible—what is not seen to those without eyes for it?[16] There has to be sight-giving transformation.    [p. 1857]

---

[15] [From (1990) 103 Harvard L. Rev. 1855.]

[16] The science of color perception has explored the role performed by information in or supplied to the eye. Since Newton it has been known that various mixtures of a basic number of colors (three or four) can produce or cause the eye to see all the others. Edwin Land, of camera fame, added a fascinating twist: two beams of the *same* color (he used yellow), projected through a pair of black and white transparencies and combined on a screen, are seen as multiple colors. "[W]e are forced to the astonishing conclusion that the rays are not in themselves colormaking. Rather they are bearers of information that the eye uses to assign appropriate colors to various objects in an image." Land, "Experiments in Color Vision" in (May 1959) *Sci. Am.* 84. The eye does not need much external information but does need some. "It can build colored worlds of its own out of informative materials that have always been supposed to be inherently drab and colorless."

Evocation of guilt is no part of this labor of translation and transformation.[17] If something remains unnoticed, the appropriate response is not to inflict an evil conscience but to try something else. The "something else" chosen by Bell, Delgado, Matsuda, and others—the centrality and significance of the choice elude Kennedy—is storytelling. Although there may be limits to storytelling in contemporary law and legal scholarship,[18] the stories, chronicles, tales, parables, and autobiographical narratives of minority scholars may perform powerfully and affectively, may "get at the curve of someone else's experience and convey at least something of it to those whose own bends quite differently."[19]

My own sense of the situation is that storytelling by Bell, Delgado, Matsuda, and others works both as narrative and as legal scholarship. There is nothing novel or mysterious about stories in law. Lawyers are storytellers, and, more fundamentally, law depends upon story for its meaning and legitimacy.[20] "The affective power—the proof—of the stories at issue here lies in their performance. For the present Response, given its limits, the best argument I can make for the success of these stories as stories is to suggest that they be read.

The more nettlesome question, given that they are good stories, is whether they work as legal scholarship. I think they do, and on several levels. On a basic level, they are executed with erudition and critical ability. Indeed, they are internally self-critical; they speak with appreciation for the limits of mind and of language. It is a talking two ways at once, hard to achieve in forms other than story. On another level they teach us about the felt effects of law and therefore something about its nature: on being an object of property, on being hurt by constitutionally

---

[17] As Mannheim noted, the failure of perception associated with a difference in worlds belongs to "a sphere of errors ... which, unlike deliberate deception, are not intentional, but follow inevitably and unwittingly from certain causal determinants." K. MANNHEIM, *op. cit.*, p. 54. Sloth and immorality do not cause me to misperceive the range of colors to which I am colorblind, and no Jeremiad can stimulate me to perceive them correctly.

[18] See Massaro, "Empathy, Legal Storytelling, and the Rule of Law: New Words, Old Wounds?" in (1989) 87 *Mich. L. Rev.* 2099, 2126 ("The call to context, at its best, simply counsels against complacency."); Winter, "The Cognitive Dimension of the Agon Between Legal Power and Narrative Meaning" in (1989) 87 *Mich. L. Rev.* 2225, 2228, 2255–2267; see also P. Novick, *That Noble Dream* (1988), pp. 622–623 (stating that "the prospect of a revival of narrative seemed to drive historians further apart, not to bring them together").

[19] C. Geertz, *op. cit.*, 156; see also Winter, *op. cit.*, n. 18, p. 2279 (arguing that "empathetic understanding" of others requires an understanding of their expression).

[20] See Ball, "Stories of Origin and Constitutional Possibilities" in (1989) 87 MICH. L. REV. 2280; Their choice of storytelling may align scholars of color with others who have been exploring the moment of narrative in law, recently feminist scholars but also, and earlier, law and literature scholars. Heilbrun and Resnik, "Convergences: Law, Literature, and Feminism" in (1990) 99 YALE L.J. 1915, is a particularly rewarding example of feminist narrative scholarship—in this case, stories about teaching stories in law school—that explores the experience of institutional exclusion of women's voices and the slow, hard work of transformation.

Narrative has been critical to jurisprudence at least since Deuteronomy provided that questions about the meaning of Israel's law were to be answered with a recitation of the exodus story. See *Deuteronomy* 6:20–25.

In one press report of the Kennedy-sparked controversy, an anonymous professor is quoted as saying "Justice O'Connor is going to want more than a story." Rothfeld, "Minority Critic Stirs Debate on Minority Writing" in *N.Y. Times*, January 5, 1990, at B6, col. 3. Justice O'Connor may want something other than a story, but that would be to want something less, not something more. I think it likely that what she will want is more than one story. Even so, there is no reason not to couple practice-based theory with story.

protected speech, on being a minority member of a white law faculty.[21] On yet another level, they teach us how racism and sexism may be hidden but are nonetheless built into the law of the dominant world and dehumanize it. On still another level, they teach us about translation by enacting it and drawing us into the performance. If, as James Boyd White maintains, translation is the center of what lawyers do, they offer in good reading of their stories an essential legal education.[22] [pp. 1858–1860]

If the work of an African-American or a Chicano or a Japanese-American legal scholar successfully performs the duality of affirming and disaffirming the Constitution,[23] the tension of adopting an alien legal system while maintaining one's own and transforming them both,[24] the person—race, gender, and all—of the author is presented and the person of the reader is engaged in response. Race is not to be taken into account in order to compromise some strict, impersonal standard applied to colorless, academic piecegoods; this is not a market in which the concern is to make competition more fair. Race counts because an ethnography of thought is needed when we are trying to find out "how others, across the sea or down the corridor, organize their significative world."[25]

In this difficult, if collegial and promising, work of translation, there is every reason to suppose that we should turn first to the experts, who, in this case, are those at the bottom, largely but not exclusively people of color.[26] Often, and often from necessity, they must live in two worlds, the dominant, dominantly white one, and their own.[27] They are the more likely bilingual, with experience in translation. I seek them out to learn more about my world and theirs, and about the art of translation. This is neither to patronize nor to encourage nostalgia about living at the bottom. It is to challenge conventional references for locating who is at the top and who on the bottom and who therefore may enjoy a view with broad horizons.[28] [p. 1861]

---

[21] I do not mean that they are tools for accessing information. Stories are not language-instruments that convey to a reader certain objects from a real world that exists outside language. Stories create worlds, characters, and experiences and invite us to recreate them in good readings.

[22] See J. White, *Justice A. Translation* (1990) "What Can a Lawyer Learn from Literature?" (Book Review) in (1989) 102 *Harv. L. Rev.* 2014, 2021. Perhaps recognition of the centrality of storytelling and of the success of minority storytelling as legal scholarship accounts for the facts that the "Michigan Law Review" devoted a recent issue to storytelling, see Symposium, "Legal Storytelling" in (1989) 87 *Mich. L. Rev.* 2073, and that the 1990 annual meeting of the Association of American Law Schools includedminority scholars and their stories among its prominent features.

[23] The story of Frederick Douglass comes to mind, as do the stories of Japanese-Americans persecuted during World War II. *See* Ball, *op. cit.*, pp. 2282–2285; Matsuda, "Looking to the Bottom: Critical Legal Studies and Reparations" in (1987) 22 *Harv. C.R.-C.L. L. Rev.* 323, 339–341 and nn.71, 73.

[24] See Matsuda, *op. cit.*, n. 23, 337–342.

[25] C. Geertz, *op. cit.*, n. 19, p. 151.

[26] According to orthodox Christian theological accounts, in the biblical stories, "almost to the point of prejudice—[God] ignored all those who are high and mighty and wealthy in the world in favour of the weak and meek and lowly." 4 *K. Barth, Church Dogmatics* Pt 2, § 64, at 168 (G. Bromiley & T. Torrance eds. 1958). On a theologically-based preference for the poor, see M. BALL, cited above in n. 20, at 186–88.

[27] There may be more than two worlds. Amy Tan, THE JOY LUCK Club (1989) creates asense of having to live in many worlds: Chinese, American, Chinese-American, male, female, past, and present.

[28] Martha Minow observes that feminist analysis "challenges the very reference points that in the past have defined what is central and what is marginal." Minow, "Beyond Universality" in (1989) *U. Chi. Legal F.* 115, 126; see also *ibid.* at 122, 132 (describingmarginality as a social construct).

## KIMBERLÉ CRENSHAW
**Race, Reform and Retrenchment: Transformation and Legitimation in Anti-Discrimination Law**
(1988)[29]

*The new left attack: the hegemonic function of legal rights discourse*

Various scholars connected with the Critical Legal Studies movement have offered critical analyses of law and legal reform which provide a broad framework for explaining how legal reforms help mask and legitimate continuing racial inequality. The Critics present law as a series of ideological constructs that operate to support existing social arrangements by convincing people that things are both inevitable and basically fair. Legal reform, therefore, cannot serve as a means for fundamentally restructuring society. This theory, however, is a general one, the utility of which is limited in the context of civil rights by its insufficient attention to racial domination. Removed from the reality of oppression and its overwhelming constraints, the Critics cannot fairly understand the choices the civil rights movement confronted or, still less, recommend solutions to its current problems.

*The Critical Vision*

In broadest terms, Critical scholars have attempted to analyze legal ideology and discourse as a social artifact which operates to recreate and legitimate American society. In order to discover the contingent character of the law, CLS scholars unpack legal doctrine to reveal both its internal inconsistencies (generally by exposing the incoherence of legal arguments) and its external inconsistencies (often by laying bare the inherently paradoxical and political world views imbedded within legal doctrine). Having thus exposed the inadequacies of legal doctrine, CLS scholars go on to examine the political character of the choices that were made in the doctrine's name. This inquiry exposes the ways in which legal ideology has helped create, support, and legitimate America's present class structure.

**1. The Role of Legal Ideology.** Critical scholars derive their vision of legal ideology in part from the work of Antonio Gramsci, who developed the concept of hegemony, the means by which a system of attitudes and beliefs, permeating both popular consciousness and the ideology of elites, reinforces existing social arrangements and convinces the dominated classes that the existing order is inevitable.[30] After observing the ability of the Italian system to withstand aggressive challenges in the years preceding the ascent of fascism, Gramsci concluded that "when the State trembled a sturdy structure of civil society was at once revealed. The State was only an outer ditch, behind which there stood a powerful system of fortresses and earthworks . . ."[31]

Some Critical scholars place great emphasis on understanding the "fortifying earthworks" of American society. The concept of hegemony allows Critical scholars to explain the continued legitimacy of American society by revealing how legal consciousness induces people to accept or consent to their own oppression.

Although society's structures of thought have been constructed by elites out of a universe of possibilities, people reify these structures and clothe them with the

---

[29] [From (1988) 101 Harvard L. Rev. 1331.]
[30] See generally, A. Gramsci, *Selections from the Prison Notebooks* (Q. Hoare and G. Smith trans., 1971).
[31] A. Gramsci, *op. cit.*, n. 30, p. 238.

illusion of necessity. Law is an essential feature in the illusion of necessity because it embodies and reinforces ideological assumptions about human relations that people accept as natural or even immutable. People act out their lives, mediate conflicts, and even perceive themselves with reference to the law. By accepting the bounds of law and ordering their lives according to its categories and relations, people think that they are confirming reality—the way things must be. Yet by accepting the view of the world implicit in the law, people are also bound by its conceptual limitations. Thus conflict and antagonism are contained: the legitimacy of the entire order is never seriously questioned.

Relating this idea to the limitations of antidiscrimination law, Alan Freeman argues that the legal reforms that grew out of the civil rights movement were severely limited by the ideological constraints embedded within the law[32] and dictated by "needs basic to the preservation of the class structure."[33] These ideological pillars supporting the class structure were simultaneously repositories of racial domination and obstacles to the fundamental reordering of society. For example, Freeman argues that formal equality, combined with the fact that American law does not formally recognize any difference based on wealth, precluded most remedies which would have required the redistribution of wealth.[34] Yet economic exploitation and poverty have been central features of racial domination—poverty is its long-term result. A legal strategy that does not include redistribution of wealth cannot remedy one of the most significant aspects of racial domination. Similarly, the myths of "vested rights" and "equality of opportunity" were necessary to protect the legitimacy of the dominant order and thus constituted insuperable barriers to the quest for significant redistributive reform. Freeman's central argument is that the severe limitations of legal reform were dictated by the legitimating role of legal discourse. If law functions to reinforce a world view that things should be the way they are, then law cannot provide an effective means to challenge the present order.

Some Critics see the destructive role of rights rhetoric as another symptom of the law's legitimating function. Mark Tushnet has offered a four-tiered critique of rights:

> "(1) Once one identifies what counts as a right in a specific setting, it invariably turns out that the right is unstable; significant but relatively small changes in the social setting can make it difficult to sustain the claim that a right remains implicated. (2) The claim that a right is implicated in some settings produces no determinate consequences. (3) The concept of rights falsely converts into an empty abstraction (reifies) real experiences that we ought to value for their own sake. (4) The use of rights in contemporary discourse impedes advances by progressive social forces ...."[35]

Tushnet's first and second arguments crystallize the doctrinal dilemmas faced by the civil rights community. Antidiscrimination doctrine does not itself provide

---

[32]  See Freeman, "Antidiscrimination Law: A Critical Review" in *The Politics of Law*, p. 96.
[33]  *ibid.*, p. 111.
[34]  "[F]ormal equality ... leads easily to evasion of remedial burdens by the rich, since American law sees no formal differences based on wealth ... [A] regime of formal equality will ensure that the dislocative impact [of remedying the economic costs of historical discrimination] is disproportionately borne by lower-class whites (not to mention blacks, who are burdened either way)." *ibid.* See *San Antonio Indep. School Dist.* v. *Rodriguez* (1973) 411 U.S. 1; *Lindsey* v. *Normet* (1972) 405 U.S. 56, 74 ("[T]he Constitution does not provide judicial remedies for every social and economic ill."); *Dandridge* v. *Williams* (1970) 397 U.S. 471.
[35]  Tushnet, at 1363–1364. For a different rendition of the critique of rights which is centred in psychoanalytic theory, see Gabel, "The Phenomenology of Rights-Consciousness and the Pact of the Withdrawn Selves" (1984) 62 Tex. L. Rev. 1563.

determinate results. To give rights meaning, people must specify the world; they must create a picture of "what is" that grounds their normative interpretation.

Tushnet's third and fourth arguments spell out pragmatic reasons to approach rights with caution. According to Tushnet, the language of rights undermines efforts to change things by absorbing real demands, experiences, and concerns into a vacuous and indeterminate discourse. The discourse abstracts real experiences and clouds the ability of those who invoke rights rhetoric to think concretely about real confrontations and real circumstances.

According to Tushnet, the danger that arises from being swept into legal rights discourse is that people lose sight of their real objectives. Their visions and thoughts of the possible become trapped within the ideological limitations of the law. Tushnet suggests that, "[i]f we treated experiences of solidarity and individuality as directly relevant to our political discussions, instead of passing them through the filter of the language of rights, we would be in a better position to address the political issues on the appropriate level."

Peter Gabel suggests that the belief in rights and in the state serves a hegemonic function through willed delusion.

> "[B]elief in the state is a flight from the immediate alienation of concrete existence into a split-off sphere of people's minds in which they imagine themselves to be a part of an imaginary political community—'citizens of the United States of America.' *And it's this collective projection and internalization of an imaginary political authority that is the basis of the legitimation of hierarchy.* It's the mass-psychological foundation of democratic consent."[36]

Hegemony is reinforced through this "state abstraction" because people believe in and react passively to a mere illusion of political consensus.

Gordon, Freeman, Tushnet, and Gabel all assert that these abstractions blind people to the contingent nature of human existence. When people act as if these illusions are real, they actually recreate their own oppressive world moment by moment.

**2. Transformation in the Critical Vision.** The vision of change that Critical scholars express flows directly from their focus on ideology as the major obstacle that separates the actual from the possible. Because it is ideology that prevents people from conceiving of—and hence from implementing—a freer social condition, the Critics propose the exposure of ideology as the logical first step toward social transformation. Emphasizing how ideology obscures the contingency of human relations, Gordon proposes unearthing conventional thought in order to excavate the potential for change. "[T]he point is to unfreeze the world as it appears to common sense as a bunch of more or less objectively determined social relations and to make it appear as ... it really is: people acting, imagining, rationalizing, justifying."[37] Gabel, too, argues that it is necessary to reveal the ways in which "law is actually constitutive of our social existence."[38] He believes that this can best be achieved by experiencing the character of living through legal

---

[36] Gabel & Kennedy, "Roll Over Beethoven" (1984) 36 Stan. L. Rev. 1, 29 (emphasis added). In this piece, the authors acknowledge that the critique of rights is itself in danger of becoming reified. *See ibid.* at 36–37. Elsewhere, Professor Kennedy has advocated "working at the slow transformation of rights rhetoric, at dereifying it, rather than simply junking it." Kennedy, "Critical Labor Law Theory: A comment" (1981) 4 Indus. Rel. L.J. 503, 506. "Embedded in the rights notion," Kennedy observes, "is a liberating accomplishment of our culture: the affirmation of free human subjectivity against the constraints of group life, along with the paradoxical countervision of a group life that creates and nurtures individuals capable of freedom." *ibid.*

[37] Gordon *op. cit.*, p. 289.

[38] Gabel, *op. cit.*, n. 35, p. 1564.

ideas, while at the same time critiquing the ways in which these phenomena "appear in our unreflective consciousness."[39] Reflecting his concern that rights discourse misdirects and abstracts our struggle for a better society, Tushnet also advocates ongoing critique, proposing that popular aspirations for change be recast in the language of "solidarity and individuality," rather than in the language of "rights."

Although Alan Freeman does not offer a transformative strategy in his work on antidiscrimination law, he has advocated delegitimation, or "trashing," elsewhere. Explaining the Critical commitment to trashing, Freeman states that:

> "The point of delegitimation is to expose possibilities more truly expressing reality, possibilities of fashioning a future that might at least partially realize a substantive notion of justice instead of the abstract, rightsy, traditional, bourgeois notions of justice that generate so much of the contradictory scholarship. One must start by knowing what is going on, by freeing oneself from the mystified delusions embedded in our consciousness by the liberal legal worldview. I am not defending a form of scholarship that simply offers another affirmative presentation; rather, I *am advocating negative, critical activity as the only path* that might lead to a liberated future."[40]

Although the focus of their critiques may differ, the Critics all premise their views of transformative possibility on the necessity of critically engaging dominant ideology. Viewing the structures of legal thought as central to the perception of the world as necessary and the *status quo* as legitimate, they believe it is crucial to demonstrate the contingency of legal ideology. Once false necessity or contingency is revealed, the Critics suggest, people will be able to remake their world in a different way.

### A Critique of the Critique: The Problem of Context

The Critics offer an analysis that is useful in understanding the limited transformative potential of antidiscrimination rhetoric. There are difficulties, however, in attempting to use Critical themes and ideas to understand the civil rights movement and to describe what alternatives the civil rights constituency could have pursued, or might now pursue. While Critical scholars claim that their project is concerned with domination, few have made more than a token effort to address racial domination specifically, and their work does not seem grounded in the reality of the racially oppressed.

This deficiency is especially apparent in critiques that relate to racial issues. Critical scholars have criticized mainstream legal ideology for its tendency to portray American society as basically fair, and thereby to legitimate the oppressive policies that have been directed toward racial minorities. Yet Critical scholars do not sufficiently account for the effects or the causes of the oppression that they routinely acknowledge. The result is that Critical literature exhibits the same proclivities of mainstream scholarship—it seldom speaks to or about Black people.

The failure of the Critics to incorporate racism into their analysis also renders their critique of rights and their overall analysis of law in America incomplete. Specifically, this failure leads to an inability to appreciate fully the transformative significance of the civil rights movement in mobilizing Black Americans and generating new demands. Further, the failure to consider the reality of those most oppressed by American institutions means that the Critical account of the hegemonic nature of legal thought overlooks a crucial dimension of American life— the ideological role of racism itself. Gordon, Freeman, Tushnet, and Gabel

---

[39] See ibid.
[40] Freeman, "Truth and Mystification in Legal Scholarship" (1981) 90 Yale L.J. 1229, 1230–1231.

fail to analyze racism as an ideological pillar upholding American society, or as the principal basis for Black oppression.

The Critics' failure to analyze the hegemonic role of racism also renders their prescriptive analysis unrealistic. In the spirit of Alan Freeman's declaration, Critics often appear to view the trashing of legal ideology "as the only path that might lead to a liberated future." Yet if trashing is the only path that might lead to a liberated future, Black people are unlikely to make it to the Critics' promised land.[41]

The Critics' commitment to trashing is premised on a notion that people are mystified by liberal legal ideology and consequently cannot remake their world until they see how contingent such ideology is. The Critics' principal error is that their version of domination by consent does not present a realistic picture of racial domination. Coercion explains much more about racial domination than does ideologically induced consent. Black people do not create their oppressive worlds moment to moment but rather are coerced into living in worlds created and maintained by others. Moreover, the ideological source of this coercion is not liberal legal consciousness, but racism. If racism is just as important as, if not more important than, liberal legal ideology in explaining the persistence of white supremacy, then the Critics' single-minded effort to deconstruct liberal legal ideology will be futile.

Finally, in addition to exaggerating the role of liberal legal consciousness and underestimating that of coercion, Critics also disregard the transformative potential that liberalism offers. Although liberal legal ideology may indeed function to mystify, it remains receptive to some aspirations that are central to Black demands, and may also perform an important function in combating the experience of being excluded and oppressed. This receptivity to Black aspirations is crucial given the hostile social world that racism creates. The most troubling aspect of the Critical program, therefore, is that "trashing" rights consciousness may have the unintended consequence of disempowering the racially oppressed while leaving white supremacy basically untouched. These difficulties are discussed below as they relate to the critiques of Gordon, Freeman, and Tushnet.

**1. Gordon: The Underemphasis on Coercion**. Robert Gordon's explanation of ideological domination illustrates how an exclusive focus on consent leaves gaping holes in his reader's understanding of hegemony. Gordon writes that beliefs are "the main constraints upon making social life more bearable."[42] Yet how can others understand the fact that Black people, although unable to bring about a world in which they fully participate, *can* imagine such a world? Clearly, something other than their own structure of thought prevents Blacks from changing their world. This fact suggests that a more complete explanation of domination requires that coercion and consent be considered together.

The coercive power of the state operates to suppress some groups, particularly when there is consensus among others that such coercion is warranted. Racism serves to single out Blacks as one of these groups "worthy" of suppression. Gordon, however, does not offer any way to understand this. If his exclusive focus on ideological domination is to be taken literally, one is left believing that Black Americans are unable to change their world because they accept the dominant ideology and thus cannot imagine an alternative existence. Yet to say that the beliefs of Black Americans have boxed them into a subordinate existence

---

[41] As Richard Delgado notes, "CLS scholars' idealism has a familiar ring to minority ears. We cannot help but be reminded of those fundamentalist preachers who have assured us that our lot will only improve once we 'see the light' and are 'saved.'" Delgado, "The Ethereal Scholar: Does Critical Legal Studies Have What Minorities Want?" (1987) 22 Harv. C.R.—C.L. L. Rev. 301, 309.

[42] Gordon, *op. cit.*, p. 291.

because of what they believe is to ignore the history of coercive racial sub-ordination. Indeed, it would be difficult for Blacks, given the contradiction between American fiction and Black American reality, to believe as much of the American mythology as whites do.

The most significant aspect of Black oppression seems to be what is believed *about* Black Americans, not what Black Americans believe. Black people are boxed in largely because there is a consensus among many whites that the oppression of Blacks is legitimate. This is where consensus and coercion can be understood together: ideology convinces one group that the coercive domination of another is legitimate. It matters little whether the coerced group rejects the dominant ideology and can offer a competing conception of the world; if they have been labeled "other" by the dominant ideology, they are not heard.

Blacks seem to carry the stigma of "otherness," which effectively precludes their potentially radicalizing influence from penetrating the dominant con-sciousness. If this is the case, then Blacks will gain little through simply trans-cending their own belief structures. The challenge for Blacks may be to pursue strategies that confront the beliefs held *about* them by whites. For Blacks, such strategies may take the form of reinforcing some aspects of the dominant ideology in attempts to become participants in the dominant discourse rather than out-siders defined, objectified, and reified by that discourse. In this sense, the civil rights movement might be considered as an attempt to deconstruct the image of "the Negro" in the white mind. By forcing the political system to respond to Black demands, Black rejected images of complacency and docility that had been invoked by some whites to dismiss Black demands.

**2. Freeman: Failure to Analyze Racism as Hegemonic**. Alan Freeman's dis-cussion of antidiscrimination law suffers from a failure to ground the critique in the historical and ideological conditions that brought about antidiscrimination law. This is puzzling, both because Freeman has written more than any other Critical scholar on antidiscrimination law and because he clearly recognizes the uniqueness of racism as a system of domination. Freeman's work pays too little attention to racism's role in legitimating American society and isolating Blacks. He also overlooks one of the consequences of this history of racism: Blacks have succeeded in diminishing this isolation by relying on and deploying the very ideological "presuppositions" that Freeman attempts to delegitimize.

As I have discussed above, Freeman argues that "needs basic to the pre-servation of the class structure ... compel[led] rejection" of a developing per-spective that would have required an America in which Blacks were substantively better off, not simply the recipients of formally equal treatment. Oddly, in his account none of the needs that forced this retrenchment is connected to racism, that is, white supremacy and racial stratification. In Freeman's account of the sociopolitical and ideological necessities that underlay the Supreme Court's *Brown* decision,[43] the need to respond to racism and race issues, not the need to deal with class issues, gave birth to antidiscrimination law. Freeman's discussion of the forces that led to retrenchment, however, is couched only in terms of preserving class structure. This failure to discuss the retrenchment in racial terms undermines the force of his analysis, especially in light of the racial character of the subsequent political retrenchment.

Freeman argues that affirmative action and other remedial programs conflicted with beliefs in formal equality, vested rights, and equal opportunity. Thus the preservation of these myths compelled the rejection of these remedies, lest whites and people of color discover that these myths were contingent ideas and thus undermine their beliefs in the legitimacy of American class structure.

Freeman implies that the concern that forced the curtailment of affirmative

---

[43]  (1954) 347 U.S. 483.

action was the fear that white would question the legitimacy of the class structure once it was revealed that equal opportunity and vestedness were contingent. Yet a different interpretation suggests that white were unlikely to question the legitimacy of these conceptions, but rather would question the legitimacy of racial remedies that relied upon a suspension of these myths. Indeed, the fact that these promises had been suspended seemed to make whites believe in and cling to them all the more. Freeman fails to analyze the ways in which whites were on the defensive, not because the promise of vestedness had proven unstable, but because Blacks had been grated some privileges at their expense. The most prevalent threat was not that the ideology would be exposed as fraudulent and that whites would attack the ideology, but that there would be a white backlash against Blacks and against institutions perceived as sympathetic to Black interests. This problem could be rectified—as it has been—by narrowing the focus of antidiscrimination law, thereby sacrificing the interests of Blacks in order to appease the majority.

There was something more significant about affirmative action and other civil rights policies that gave rise to a crisis in a way that other more devastating or more common ideological disruptions have not. This suggests that the relatively subordinate status of Blacks serves a stabilizing function in this society. At least one consequence of this "stabilizing" function is that special attention is directed toward the status of Blacks so that ideological deviations arising out of racial issues do not evade popular detection.

**3. Tushnet: The Problem of Pragmatism Without Context.** The problem with Tushnet's critique of rights is perhaps most evident when he rhetorically queries; "Can anyone really think that it helps either in changing society or in understanding how society changes to discuss whether [protestors] were exercising rights protected by the first amendment?"[44] The answer to Tushnet's rhetorical question, given the thrust of his critique, is, of course, no. What really matters, says Tushnet, is not whether people are exercising rights, but whether their action is politically effective. If, however, the inquiry is squarely placed within a historical context, the implied disparity between thinking about change in terms of rights and thinking about politically effective action might be diminished. Perhaps the action of the civil rights community was effective, for example, because it raised the novel idea of Blacks exercising rights. Indeed, thinking in terms of rights may have been a radical and liberating activity for Blacks. Tushnet suggests that thinking in terms of rights is incompatible with feelings of solidarity and is not helpful in determining how to be politically effective. The expression of rights, however, was a central organizing feature of the civil rights movement. Because rights that other Americans took for granted were routinely denied to Black Americans, Blacks' assertion of their "rights" constituted a serious ideological challenge to white supremacy. Their demand was not just for a place in the front of a bus, but for inclusion in the American political imagination. In asserting rights, Blacks defied a system which had long determined that Blacks were not and should not have been included. Whether or not the extension of these rights has ultimately legitimated the subordinate status of Blacks, the use of rights rhetoric was a radical, movement-building act.

Because Tushnet's critique of rights is not sufficiently related to racism, his prescriptive comments are unpersuasive. Tushnet argues that the only circumstance in which rights should be used is when, on pragmatic consideration, they appear useful; he then argues that rights may not be pragmatically useful but instead may actually impede the progress of the "party of humanity".[45]

One wonders, however, whether a demand for shelter that does not employ

---

[44] Tushnet, *op. cit.*, pp. 1370–1371.
[45] See Tushnet, *op. cit.*, pp. 1386–1394.

rights rhetoric is likely to succeed in America today. The underlying problem, especially for African-Americans, is the question of how to extract from others that which others are not predisposed to give. As Tushnet has said himself, rights are a way of saying that a society is what it is, or that it ought to live up to its deepest commitments. This is essentially what all groups of dispossessed people say when they use rights rhetoric. As demonstrated in the civil rights movement, engaging in rights rhetoric can be an attempt to turn society's "institutional logic" against itself—to redeem some of the rhetorical promises and the self-congratulations that seem to thrive in American political discourse.

*Questioning the Transformative View: Some Doubts About Trashing*

The Critics' product is of limited utility to Blacks in its present form. The implications for Blacks of trashing liberal legal ideology are troubling, even though it may be proper to assail belief structures that obscure liberating possibilities. Trashing legal ideology seems to tell us repeatedly what has already been established—that legal discourse is unstable and relatively indeterminate. Furthermore, trashing offers no idea of how to avoid the negative consequences of engaging in reformist discourse or how to work around such consequences. Even if we imagine the wrong world when we think of terms of legal discourse, we must nevertheless exist in a present world where legal protection has at times been a blessing—albeit a mixed one. The fundamental problem is that, although Critics criticize law because it functions to legitimate existing institutional arrangements, it is precisely this legitimating function that has made law receptive to certain demands in this area.

The Critical emphasis on deconstruction as *the* vehicle for liberation leads to the conclusion that engaging in legal discourse should be avoided because it reinforces not only the discourse itself but also the society and the world that it embodies. Yet Critics offer little beyond this observation. Their focus on delegitimating rights rhetoric seems to suggest that, once rights rhetoric has been discarded, there exists a more productive strategy for change, one which does not reinforce existing patterns of domination.

Unfortunately, no such strategy has yet been articulated, and it is difficult to imagine that racial minorities will ever be able to discover one. As Frances Fox Piven and Richard Cloward point out in their excellent account of the civil rights movement, popular struggles are a reflection of institutionally determined logic and a challenge to that logic.[46] People can only demand change in ways that reflect the logic of the institutions that they are challenging.[47] Demands for change that do not reflect the institutional logic—that is, demands that do not engage and subsequently reinforce the dominant ideology—will probably be ineffective.[48]

The possibility for ideological change is created through the very process of legitimation, which is triggered by crisis. Powerless people can sometimes trigger such a crisis by challenging an institution internally, that is, by using its own logic against it. Such crisis occurs when powerless people force open and politicize a contradiction between the dominant ideology and their reality. The political consequences of maintaining the contradictions may sometimes force an adjustment—an attempt to close the gap or to make thinks appear fair. Yet, because the adjustment is triggered by the political consequences of the contradiction,

---

[46] See *Poor People's Movements* (1977), pp. 22–25.
[47] Strikes, for example, are a reflection of the logic of the work institution. It only makes sense for employed workers to use strikes as a tactic. Unemployed workers, of course cannot use the strike to press their grievances.
[48] Reforms necessarily come from an existing repertoire of options. As Piven and Cloward note, "if impoverished southern blacks had demanded land reform, they would probably have still gotten the vote." *Op. cit.*, n. 46, p. 33.

circumstances will be adjusted only to the extent necessary to close the apparent contradiction.

This approach to understanding legitimation and change is applicable to the civil rights movement. Because Blacks were challenging their exclusion from political society, the only claims that were likely to achieve recognition were those that reflected American society's institutional logic: legal rights ideology. Articulating their formal demands through legal rights ideology, civil rights protestors exposed a series of contradictions—the most important being the promised privileges of American citizenship and the practice of absolute racial subordination. Rather than using the contradictions to suggest that American citizenship was itself illegitimate or false, civil rights protestors proceeded as if American citizenship were real, and demanded to exercise the "rights" that citizenship entailed. By seeking to restructure reality to reflect American mythology, Blacks relied upon and ultimately benefited from politically inspired efforts to resolve the contradictions by granting formal rights. Although it is the need to maintain legitimacy that presents powerless groups with the opportunity to wrest concessions from the dominant order, it is the very accomplishment of legitimacy that forecloses greater possibilities. In sum, the potential for change is both created and limited by legitimation.

The central issue that the Critics fail to address, then, is how to avoid the "legitimating" effects of reform if engaging in reformist discourse is the only effective way to challenge the legitimacy of the social order. Perhaps the only situation in which powerless people may receive any favorable response is where there is a political or ideological need to restore an image of fairness that has somehow been tarnished. Most efforts to change an oppressive situation are bound to adopt the dominant discourse to some degree. On the other hand, Peter Gabel may well be right in observing that the reforms which come from such demands are likely to transform a given situation only to the extent necessary to legitimate those elements of the situation that "must" remain unchanged.[49] Thus, it might just be the case that oppression means "being between a rock and a hard place"—that there are risks and dangers involved both in engaging in the dominant discourse *and* in failing to do so. What subordinated people need is an analysis which can inform them how the risks can be minimized, and how the rocks and the very hard places can be negotiated.

### The context defined: Racist ideology and hegemony

The failure of the Critics to consider race in their account of law and legitimacy is not a minor oversight: race consciousness is central not only to the domination of Blacks, but also to whites' acceptance of the legitimacy of hierarchy and to their identity with elite interest. Exposing the centrality of race consciousness is crucial to identifying and delegitimating beliefs that present hierarchy as inevitable and fair. Moreover, exposing the centrality of race consciousness shows how the options of Blacks in American society have been limited, and how the use of rights rhetoric has emancipated Blacks from some manifestations of racial domination.

A realignment of the Critical project to incorporate race consciousness must begin with beliefs about Blacks in American society, and how these beliefs legitimize racial coercion. Thus, this Part examines the deep-rooted problem of racist ideology—or white race consciousness—and suggests how this form of consciousness legitimates prevailing injustices and constrains the development of new solutions that benefit Black Americans.

---

[49] See Gabel, *op. cit.*, n. 35, pp. 1591–1597 (discussing the means by which state officials contain the radicalizing possibilities of social movements via eventual "recognition" of some of the movement's claims).

Racist ideology provides a series of rationalizations that suppress the contradiction between American political ideals and Black existence under white supremacy. Not only does racism legitimate the oppression of Blacks, it also helps to define and privilege membership in the white community, creating a basis for identification with dominant interests. Racism serves a consensus-building hegemonic role by designating Black people as separate, visible "others" to be contrasted in every way with all other social groups. Although not consenting to domination, Black people are seen as legitimate objects of antipathy and coercion by whites.

The Critics are correct in observing that, despite these gains, engaging in rights discourse has helped to deradicalize and co-opt the challenge in the current period, in which racial oppression continues to flourish behind the screen of racial equality. Yet only after race ideology itself and the real differences that formal equality made in transforming race ideology are understood can the paradoxical relationship of transformation and legitimation be fully appreciated. Blacks are ultimately presented with a dilemma: liberal reform both transforms and legitimates. Even though legal ideology absorbs, redefines, and limits the language of protest, African-Americans cannot ignore the power of legal ideology to counter some of the most repressive aspects of racial domination.

### A. The Hegemonic Role of Racism: Establishing the "Other" in American Ideology

Throughout American history, the subordination of Blacks was rationalized by a series of stereotypes and beliefs that made their conditions appear logical and natural. Historically, white supremacy has been premised upon various political, scientific, and religious theories, each of which relies on racial characterizations and stereotypes about Blacks that have coalesced into an extensive legitimating ideology. Today, it is probably not controversial to say that these stereotypes were developed primarily to rationalize the oppression of Blacks. What *is* overlooked, however, is the extent to which these stereotypes serve a hegemonic function by perpetuating a mythology about both Blacks *and* whites even today, reinforcing an illusion of a white community that cuts across ethnic, gender, and class lines.

As presented by Critical scholars, hegemonic rule succeeds to the extent that the ruling class world view establishes the appearance of a unity of interests between the dominant class and the dominated. Throughout American history, racism has identified the interests of subordinates whites with those of society's white elite. Racism does not support the dominant order simply because all whites want to maintain their privilege at the expense of Blacks, or because Blacks sometimes serve as convenient political scapegoats. Instead, the very existence of a clearly subordinated "other" group is contrasted with the norm in a way that reinforces identification with the dominant group. Racism helps create an illusion of unity through the oppositional force of a symbolic "other."[50] The establishment of an "other" creates a bond, a burgeoning common identity of all non-stigmatized parties—whose identity and interests are defined in opposition to the other.

According to the philosophy of Jacques Derrida, a structure of polarized categories is characteristic of Western thought:

---

[50] The notion of Blacks as a subordinated "other" in Eastern culture has been a major theme in scholarship exploring the cultural and sociological structure of racism. *See* Trost, "Western Metaphysical Dualism as an Element in Racism" in *Cultural Bases of Racism and Group Oppression* (J. Hodge, D. Sturckmann & L. Trost eds., 1975), p. 49 (arguing that Black and white are seen as paired antinomies, and that there is a hierarchy within the antinomies, with Caucasians and Western culture constituting the preferred or higher antinomy).

"Western thought ... has always been structured in terms of dichotomies or polarities: good vs. evil, being vs. nothingness, presence vs. absence, truth vs. error, identity vs. difference, mind vs. matter, man vs. woman, soul vs. body, life vs. death, nature vs. culture, speech vs. writing. These polar opposites do not, however, stand as independent and equal entities. The second term in each pair is considered the negative, corrupt, undesirable version of the first, a fall away from it ... In other words, the two terms are not simply opposed in their meanings, but are arranged in a hierarchical order which gives the first term *priority*..."[51]

Racist ideology replicates this pattern of arranging oppositional categories in a hierarchical order; historically, whites represented the dominant antinomy while Blacks came to be seen as separate and subordinate. This hierarchy is reflected in the chart below. Note how each traditional negative image of Blacks correlates with a counter-image of whites:

Historical Oppositional Dualities

| WHITE IMAGES | BLACK IMAGES |
| --- | --- |
| Industrious | Lazy |
| Intelligent | Unintelligent |
| Moral | Immoral |
| Knowledgeable | Ignorant |
| Enabling Culture | Disabling Culture |
| Law-Abiding | Criminal |
| Responsible | Shiftless |
| Virtuous/Pious | Lascivious |

The oppositional dynamic symbolized by this chart was created and maintained through an elaborate and systematic process. Laws and customs helped create "races" out of a broad range of human traits. In the process of creating races, the categories came to be filled with meaning—Blacks were characterized one way, whites another. Whites became associated with normatively positive characteristics; Blacks became associated with the subordinate, even aberrational characteristics.

## B. *The Role of Race Consciousness in a System of Formal Equality*

The previous section emphasizes the continuity of white race consciousness over the course of American history. This section, by contrast, focuses on the partial transformation of the functioning of race consciousness that occurred with the transition from Jim Crow to formal equality in race law.

Prior to the civil rights reforms, Blacks were formally subordinated by the state. Blacks experienced being the "other" in two aspects of oppression, which I shall designate as symbolic and material. Symbolic subordination, refers to the formal denial of social and political equality to all Blacks, regardless of their accomplishments. Segregation and other forms of social exclusion—separate restrooms, drinking fountains, entrances, parks, cemeteries, and dining facilities—reinforced a racist ideology that Blacks were simply inferior to whites and were therefore not included in the vision of America as a community of equals.

Material subordination, on the other hand, refers to the ways that

---

[51] J. Derrida, *Dissemination* (B. Johnson trans., 1981) (emphasis in original), p. viii Otherness is a corollary to the bipolar conceptualizations that characterize structuralist analysis of Western thought. Some Critical legal scholars have seized these bipolar conceptualizations and used them to explain how doctrine attempts to mediate opposing tendencies in the law. See, *e.g.* Kennedy, "Form and Substance in Private Law Adjudication" (1976) 89 Harv. L. Rev. 1685.

discrimination and exclusion economically subordinated Blacks to whites and subordinated the life chances of Blacks to those of whites on almost every level. This subordination occurs when Blacks are paid less for the same work, when segregation limits access to decent housing, and where poverty, anxiety, poor health care, and crime create a life expectancy for Blacks that is five to six years shorter than for whites.

Symbolic subordination often created material disadvantage by reinforcing race consciousness in everything from employment to education. In fact, the two are generally not thought of separately: separate facilities were usually inferior facilities, and limited job categorization virtually always brought lower pay and harder work. Despite the pervasiveness of racism, however, there existed even before the civil rights movement a class of Blacks who were educationally, economically, and professionally equal—if not superior—to many whites, and yet these Blacks suffered social and political exclusion as well.

It is also significant that not all separation resulted in inferior institutions. School segregation—although often presented as the epitome of symbolic and material subordination—did not always result in inferior education. It is not separation *per se* that made segregation subordinating, but the fact that it was enforced and supported by state power, and accompanied by the explicit belief in African-American inferiority.

The response to the civil rights movement was the removal of most formal barriers and symbolic manifestations of subordination. Thus, "White Only" notices and other obvious indicators of the societal policy of racial subordination disappeared—at least in the public sphere. The disappearance of the rhetoric of formal equality and signaled the demise of the rhetoric of white supremacy as expressing America's normative vision. In other words, it could no longer be said that Blacks were not included as equals in the American political vision.

Removal of these public manifestations of subordination was a significant gain for all Blacks, although some benefited more than others. The eradication of formal barriers meant more to those whose oppression was primarily symbolic than to those who suffered lasting material disadvantage. Yet despite these disparate results, it would be absurd to suggest that no benefits came from these formal reforms, especially in regard to racial policies, such as segregation, that were partly material but largely symbolic. Thus, to say that the reforms were "merely symbolic" is to say a great deal. These legal reforms and the formal extension of "citizenship" were large achievements precisely because much of what characterized Black oppression was symbolic and formal.

Yet the attainment of formal equality is not the end of the story. Racial hierarchy cannot be cured by the move to facial race-neutrality in the laws that structure the economic, political, and social lives of Black people. White race consciousness, in a new form but still virulent, plays an important, perhaps crucial, role in the new regime that has legitimated the deteriorating day-to-day material conditions of the majority of Blacks.

The end of Jim Crow has been accompanied by the demise of an explicit ideology of white supremacy. The white norm, however, has not disappeared; it has only been submerged in popular consciousness. It continues in an unspoken form as a statement of the positive social norm, legitimating the continuing domination of those who do not meet it. Nor have the negative stereotypes associated with Blacks been eradicated. The rationalizations once used to legitimate Black subordination based on a belief in racial inferiority have now been reemployed to legitimate the domination of Blacks through reference to an assumed cultural inferiority.

To bring a fundamental challenge to the way things are, whites would have to question not just their own subordinate status, but also both the economic and the racial myths that justify the *status quo*. Racism, combined with equal opportunity mythology, provides a rationalization for racial oppression, making it difficult for whites to see the Black situation as illegitimate or unnecessary. If whites believe that Blacks, because they are unambitious or inferior, get what they deserve, it becomes that much harder to convince whites that something is wrong with the entire system. Similarly, a challenge to the legitimacy of continued racial inequality would force whites to confront myths about equality of opportunity that justify for them whatever measure of economic success they may have attained.

Thus, although Critics have suggested that legal consciousness plays a central role in legitimating hierarchy in America, the otherness dynamic enthroned within the maintenance and perpetuation of white race consciousness seems to be at least as important as legal consciousness in supporting the dominant order. Like legal consciousness, race consciousness makes it difficult—at least for whites—to imagine the world differently. It also creates the desire for identification with privileged elites. By focusing on a distinct, subordinate "other," white include themselves in the dominant circle—an arena in which most hold no real power, but only their privileged racial identity.

## C. Rights Discourse as a Challenge to the Oppositional Dynamic

The oppositional dynamic, premised upon maintaining Blacks as an excluded and subordinated "other," initially created an ideological and political structure of formal inequality against which rights rhetoric proved to be the most effective weapon. Although rights rhetoric may ultimately have absorbed the civil rights challenge and legitimated continued subordination, the otherness dynamic provides a fuller understanding of how the very transformation afforded by legal reform itself has contributed to the ideological and political legitimation of continuing Black subordination.

Rights discourse provided the ideological mechanisms through which the conflicts of federalism, the power of the Presidency, and the legitimacy of the courts could be orchestrated against Jim Crow. Movement leaders used these tactics to force open a conflict between whites that eventually benefited Black people. Casting racial issues in the moral and legal rights rhetoric of the prevailing ideology helped create the political controversy without which the state's coercive function would not have enlisted to aid Blacks.

Simply critiquing the ideology from without or making demands in language outside the rights discourse would have accomplished little. Rather, Blacks gained by using a powerful combination of direct action, mass protest, and individual acts of resistance, along with appeals to public opinion and the courts couched in the language of the prevailing legal consciousness. The result was a series of ideological and political crises. In these crises, civil rights activists and lawyers induced the federal government to aid Blacks and triggered efforts to legitimate and reinforce the authority of the law in ways that benefited Blacks. Simply insisting that Blacks be integrated or speaking in the language of "needs" would have endangered the lives of those who were already taking risks—and with no reasonable chance of success. President Eisenhower, for example, would not have sent federal troops to Little Rock simply at the behest of protesters demanding that Black schoolchildren receive an equal education. Instead, the successful manipulation of legal rhetoric led to a crisis of federal power that ultimately benefited Blacks.

Some critics of legal reform movements seem to overlook the fact that state power has made a significant difference—sometimes between life and death—in the efforts of Black people to transform their world. Attempts to harness the power of the state through the appropriate rhetorical/legal incantations should be appreciated as intensely powerful and calculated political acts. In the context of white supremacy, engaging in rights discourse should be seen as an act of self-defense. This was particularly true because the state could not assume a position of neutrality regarding Black people once the movement had mobilized people to challenge the system of oppression: either the coercive mechanism of the state had to be used to support white supremacy, or it had to be used to dismantle it. We know now, with hindsight, that it did both.

Blacks did use rights rhetoric to mobilize state power to their benefit against symbolic oppression through formal inequality and, to some extent, against material deprivation in the form of private, informal exclusion of the middle class from jobs and housing. Yet today the same legal reforms play a role in providing an ideological framework that makes the present conditions facing underclass Blacks appear fair and reasonable. The eradication of barriers has created a new dilemma for those victims of racial oppression who are not in a position to benefit from the move to formal equality. The race neutrality of the legal system creates the illusion that racism is no longer the primary factor responsible for the condition of the Black underclass; instead, as we have seen, class disparities appear to be the consequence of individual and group merit within a supposed system of equal opportunity. Moreover, the fact that there are Blacks who are economically successful gives credence both to the assertion that opportunities exist, and to the backlash attitude that Blacks have "gotten too far." Psychologically, for Blacks who have not made it, the lack of an explanation for their underclass status may result in self-blame and other self-destructive attitudes.

Another consequence of the formal reforms may be the loss of collectivity among Blacks. The removal of formal barriers created new opportunities for some Blacks that were not shared by various other classes of African-Americans. As Blacks moved into different spheres, the experience of being Black in American became fragmented and multifaceted, and the different contexts presented opportunities to experience racism in different ways. The social, economic, and even residential distance between the various classes may complicate efforts to unite behind issues as a racial group. Although "White Only" signs may have been crude and debilitating, they at least presented a readily discernible target around which to organize. Now, the targets are obscure and diffuse, and this difference may create doubt among some Blacks whether there is enough similarity between their life experiences and those of other Blacks to warrant collective political action.

## D. *Self-Conscious Ideological Struggle*

Rights have been important. They may have legitimated racial inequality, but they have also been the means by which oppressed groups have secured both entry as formal equals into the dominant order and the survival of their movement in the face of private and state repression. The dual role of legal change creates a dilemma for Black reformers. As long as race consciousness thrives, Blacks will often have to rely on rights rhetoric when it is necessary to protect Black interests. The very reforms brought about by appeals to legal ideology, however, seem to undermine the ability to move forward toward a broader vision of racial equality. In the quest for racial justice, winning and losing have been part of the same experience.

The Critics are correct in observing that engaging in rights discourse has helped to deradicalize and co-opt the challenge. Yet they fail to acknowledge the limited range of options presented to Blacks in a context where they were deemed "other," and the unlikelihood that specific demands for inclusion and equality would be heard if articulated in other terms. This abbreviated list of options is itself contingent upon the ideological power of white race consciousness and the continuing role of Black Americans as "other." Future efforts to address racial domination, as well as class hierarchy, must consider the continuing ideology of white race consciousness by uncovering the oppositional dynamic and by chipping away at its premises. Central to this task is revealing the contingency of race and exploring the connection between white race consciousness and the other myths that legitimate both class and race hierarchies. Critics and others whose agendas include challenging hierarchy and legitimation must not overlook the importance of revealing the contingency of race.

Optimally, the deconstruction of white race consciousness might lead to a liberated future for both Blacks and whites. Yet, until whites recognize the hegemonic function of racism and turn their efforts towards neutralizing it, African-American people must develop pragmatic political strategies—self-conscious ideological struggle—to minimize the costs of liberal reform while maximizing its utility. A primary step in engaging in self-conscious ideological struggle must be to transcend the oppositional dynamic in which Blacks are cast simply and solely as whites' subordinate "other."

The dual role that rights have played makes strategizing a difficult task. Black people can afford neither to resign themselves to, nor to attack frontally, the legitimacy and incoherence of the dominant ideology. The subordinate position of Blacks in this society makes it unlikely that African-Americans will realize gains through the kind of direct challenge to the legitimacy of American liberal ideology that is now being waged by Critical scholars. On the other hand, delegiti-mating race consciousness would be directly relevant to Black needs, and this strategy will sometimes require the pragmatic use of liberal ideology.     [pp. 1349–1386]

## KEVIN R. JOHNSON
### Celebrating LatCrit Theory: What Do We Do When the Music Stops?
(2000)[52]

The uninitiated might ask: just what is LatCrit? "LatCrit is a group of progressive law professors engaged in theorizing about the ways in which the Law and its structures, processes and discourses affect people of color, especially the Latina/o communities."[53] In many ways, LatCrit is helping us delve deeper into the impact of the law on Latina/o lives, dispelling popular stereotypes without essentializing or bracketing the Latina/o experience.[54] But the LatCrit project has broader ambitions; it seeks to further (1) "The Production of Knowledge"; (2) "The Advancement of Transformation"; (3) "The Expansion and Connection of Struggle(s)"; and (4) "The Cultivation of Community and Coalition."[55]
[pp. 754–755.]

A cornerstone premise of LatCrit theory is that the various forms of subordination in U.S. society, if not the world, are deeply interrelated and intertwined.[56] Woven together into the American social fabric, racial, gender, sexual

---

[52] [From (2000) 33 *Univ. of California Davis L. Rev.* 753.]

[53] Fact Sheet: LatCrit, in *LatCrit Primer*, unpublished materials distributed to participants at LatCrit IV (1999).

[54] See Gerald P. López, "Learning About Latinos" in (1998) 19 Chicano-Latino L. Rev. 363, 368.

[55] Francisco Valdes, "Foreword: Under Construction—LatCrit Consciousness, Community, and Theory" in (1997) 85 Cal. L. Rev. 1087, 1093–94 and see (1998) 10 La Raza L.J. 1, 7–8.

[56] See Iglesias, (1999) 53 U. Miami L. Rev. 575, 595, 622–29; Kevin R. Johnson, "Racial Hierarchy, Asian Americans, and Latinos as 'Foreigners,' and Social Change: Is Law the Way to Go?" in (1997) 76 Or. L. Rev. 347, 358–362; George A. Martínez, "African-Americans, Latinos, and the Construction of Race: Toward an Epistemic Coalition" in (1992) 19 Chicano-Latino L. Rev. 213, 221–22; Athena D. Mutua, "Shifting Bottoms and Rotating Centers: Reflections on LatCrit III and the Black/White Paradigm" in (1999) 53 U. Miami L. Rev. 1177, 1202–1215. Professor Frank Valdes has referred to this phenomenon as "webs of power." Francisco Valdes, "Piercing Webs of Power: Identity, Resistance, and Hope in LatCrit Theory and Praxis" in (2000) 33 U.C. Davis L. Rev.897.

orientation, class, and other subordinations all warrant careful inquiry.
[pp. 757–758]
Latinas/os must squarely and critically address the problematic aspects of religion on the community.[57]                                                      [p. 766].
The study of the subordination of Latinas is of central importance to the LatCrit project. LatCrit, as an intellectual community, is committed to not replicating the dynamics of subordination.[58] We must continue to analyze how that subordination originates and perpetuates itself through religious and other social institutions.
obp. 769]
LatCrit theory has an enduring commitment to putting theory into practice.[59]
[p. 774]
Although radically different from art, clinical teaching holds the promise of linking theory and practice.[60]                                                    [p. 775]
For many reasons, including globalization, immigration, and technological advancement, to name a few, the local and the global are increasingly intertwined.[61] LatCrit has been central in considering the international.       [p. 777]
We are at a critical juncture in the evolution of LatCrit theory. In the next few pages, I identify future challenges and potential pitfalls. Importantly, although we should celebrate LatCrit theory's early success, we must brace ourselves for growing pains, internal tensions, and external critique.

### A. LatCrit Must Remain Inclusive

Critics might claim that the LatCrit movement has strayed from its Latina/o roots. The "rotating centers" concept captured in the title to LatCrit IV, however, allows us to be inclusive and to consider the subordination of other peoples of color and the relationship to Latina/os' status in the United States. As LatCrit theorists have observed, Latina/o subordination is related to and connected with other subordinations. To fully understand one, we must comprehend them all.

Moreover, the inclusiveness of LatCrit theory is an important source of strength that holds great promise for the future. Inclusiveness has fostered coalitions and mutual self-help. It has built good will and promoted serious scholarship in new and important ways. Inclusiveness allows the LatCrit community to engage in ongoing intellectual ferment and allows it to remain dynamic rather than static.

### B. External Challenges and Internal Tensions

As LatCrit matures, we must anticipate external challenges and continuing, perhaps mounting, internal tensions. The maturation process may well subject

---

[57] See Iglesias & Valdes, (1998) 19 Chicano-Latino L. Rev. 503 511–546.
[58] See Rachel F. Moran, "Foreword—Demography and Distrust: The Latino Challenge to Civil Rights and Immigration Policy in the 1990s and Beyond" in (1995) 8 La Raza L.J. 1, 10 (noting that Latinas/os "often have been attuned to questions of class, rather than race or ethnicity, in formulating a reform agenda"); see also Mary Romero. "Immigration, the Servant Problem, and the Legacy of the Domestic Labor Debate: 'Where Can You Find Good Help These Days!'" in (1999) 53 U. Miami L. Rev. 1045 (analyzing issues of race and class implicated for Latinas in domestic service industry).
[59] See Francisco Valdes, "Foreword—Poised at the Cusp: LatCrit Theory, Outsider Jurisprudence and Latina/o Self-Empowerment" in (1997) 2 Harv. Latino L. Rev. 1, 55.
[60] See Kevin R. Johnson & Amagda Pérez, "Clinical Legal Education and the U.C. Davis Immigration Law Clinic: Putting Theory into Practice and Practice into Theory" in (1998) 51 SMU L. Rev. 1423.
[61] See, e.g. Chang & Aoki, (1997) 85 Calif. L. Rev. 1395 (analyzing how international developments shaped the evolution of Asian American community in Monterey Park, California).

LatCrit to attack, such as that leveled at Critical Race Theory, feminist jurisprudence, and other critical genres.[62] As we prepare for external critiques, we should keep in mind that Critical Race Theory ("CRT") has been vulnerable to attack because critics have ascribed certain intellectual positions as part of CRT orthodoxy. Yet, CRT remains difficult to reduce to fundamental tenets because its fluid and eclectic approach encompasses diverse methodologies from many disciplines.[63] LatCrit should retain the prerogative to define and redefine itself rather than be defined by critics. Constant self-criticism and self-definition is essential to a movement as dynamic as LatCrit.

To fend off external attacks effectively, LatCrit theorists must address internal tensions within the movement. We must support each other and be ready to respond to the future intellectual challenges. Striving to maintain unity, LatCrit theorists must resist the centrifugal pressures toward disintegration.

To this end, LatCrit must keep internal tensions in perspective and learn the lessons of the past. Importantly, LatCrit theorists cannot let the personal dominate the intellectual and allow interpersonal antagonisms to undermine the project. Specifically, we must avoid at LatCrit conferences, the spontaneous "slash-and-burn, hold-no-prisoners, hypercritical attack upon some unfortunate and often unsuspecting target."[64] In that vein, we hopefully will never see the day when so-called "attack scholarship" focuses on each other's work.[65]

We must nip in the bud the development of schisms along gender, class, national origin, racial, and other lines. One way to ease tensions is to recognize and encourage separate investigations of specific group histories, both inside and outside LatCrit. All of these competing strands and thoughts must continue to be included within the umbrella LatCrit intellectual community.

At the same time, we must allow dissent within our ranks. Criticism of ideas and diversity of approaches, of course, remains essential to intellectual growth. LatCrit must continue to emphasize the critical. As scholars, we should be critical of each other's work. Nonetheless, the tone and method by which we criticize is all-important. In voicing dissent and promoting sophisticated intellectual discourse, we must be sensitive to the feelings of others and attempt to offer constructive, not destructive, criticism. An ongoing intellectual scholarly community requires sensitivity to each other, our differences, and our humanity, not a scorched earth approach to scholarship and the views of our colleagues.

In my mind, a wonderful example of constructive criticism was Professor Frank Valdes's presentation at the June 1999 LatCrit conference in Spain.[66] He presented a provocative and devastating thesis—that Spain should seriously consider the payment of reparations for the plunder of the grand indigenous societies of the New World—to a group of Spanish legal scholars. The challenge to Spain from an American ran the risk of causing tension, discord, and hard feelings. Professor Valdes offered a balanced account of the need for an investigation of reparations by Spain for its exploitation of New World natural resources and people. We need this type of constructive and positive engagement both at the live events and in the symposium contributions.      [pp. 781–783]

---

[62] See, *e.g.* DANIEL FARBER & SUZANNA SHERRY, *Beyond, All Reason* (1997); Matthew W. Finkin, "Quatsch!" in (1999) 83 MINN. L. REV. 1681; Anne M. Coughlin, "Regulating the Self: Autobiographical Performances in Outsider Scholarship" in (1995) 81 VA. L. REV. 1229.

[63] See Angela P. Harris, "Foreword: The Jurisprudence of Reconstruction" in (1994) 82 CAL. L. REV. 741, 744–745 [and *ante*, 1500].

[64] Iglesias, *op. cit.*, n. 56, p. 578.

[65] See Keith Aoki, "The Scholarship of Reconstruction and the Politics of Backlash" in (1996) 81 IOWA L. REV. 1467, 1471.

[66] [Johnson's article on "Hurricane Katrina" repays reading: see (2008) 45 Houston L.R. 11. See also R. Aldana (2008) 45 Houston L.R. 73.]

*The Need for Infrastructure*

A LatCrit infrastructure, currently under construction is necessary to ensure the continuity and future of the project.[67] The legal incorporation of LatCrit and the overlapping membership of the planning committee have helped provide necessary continuity and institutional memory. This infrastructure, missing from Critical Legal Studies and Critical Race Theory, hopefully will keep LatCrit moving forward and should help LatCrits avoid getting bogged down in the same old disputes.[68]                                                           p. 785]

## BERTA ESPERANZA HERNÁNDEZ-TRUYOL
### LatCrit as Liberation Theory
### (1997)[69]

To achieve the full possibilities of LatCrit theory as a law reform project, the final part of this Essay proposes a model for LatCrit scholarship and activism that focuses on the interdependence and indivisibility of identities.

### A. Latinas and LatCrit: From Margin to Center

Latinas provide a tremendous challenge to the development of a constructive, nonessentialist model. As multiple-layered outsiders, Latinas have been completely *olvidadas* by the normative structure, in the context of which they constitute far too many deviations from the norm to be manageable in a legal theory universe that looks at one layer of self at a time.[70] Latinas, even the most "*normativas*" among them, differ from the neutral, legal, founding-father-look-alike

---

[67] See Francisco Valdes, "Afterword—Theqriting 'OutCrit' Theories: Coalitional Method and Comparative Jurisprudential Experience—RaceCrits, QueerCrits and LatCrits" in (1999) 53 U. MIAMI L. REV. 1265, 1299–1306.

[68] This criticism has been leveled at Critical Race Theory. See Richard Delgado & Jean Stefancic, "Critical Race Theory: Past, Present, and Future" in (1998) 51 CURRENT LEG. PROBS. 468, 490 ("CRT ... has not changed with the times. It continues focusing on feelings, language, social construction, and the unique multiple consciousness of people of color, while programs vital to the well being and, indeed, survival of minority communities are being terminated right and left.").

[69] [From B. E. Hernández—Truyol, "Borders (En)Gendered: Normativities, Latinas and a LatCrit Paradigm" in (1997) 72 New York Univ. L. Rev. 882.]

[70] These terms are borrowed from the international human rights construct. See, *e.g.* World Conference on Human Rights: The Vienna Declaration and Programme of Action, Pt 1, para. 5, U.N. Doc. A/CONF.157/23 (1993) ("All human rights are universal, indivisible, and interdependent and interrelated."); Report of the International Conference on Population and Development, principle 4, U.N. Doc. A/CONF.171/13 (1994) ("The human rights of women and the girl-child are an inalienable, integral and indivisible part of universal human rights.").

For a discussion of how substantive international human rights can assist in the practice of LatCrit theorizing, see Berta Esperanza Hernández-Truyol. "Building Bridges: Bringing International Human Rights Home" in (1996) 9 La Raza L.J. 69 (discussing how incorporation of substantive human rights into our domestic law can help condition and position of Latinas/os in United States, including with regard to welfare and immigration "reform" legislation); see also "Symposium: International Law, Human Rights and LatCrit Theory" in (1996–1997) 28 U. Miami Inter-Am. L. Rev. 223; Berta Esperanza Hernández-Truyol, "International Law, Human Rights and LatCrit Theory: Civil and Political Rights—An Introduction" in (1996–1997) 28 U. Miami Inter-Am. L. Rev. 223, 224 (discussing human rights laws' positive view of acceptable treatment for all people and how that view allows all people to participate in "global society").

ideal of the (allegorical) reasonable man in sex (meaning gender), race/ethnicity, and culture—not to mention that, statistically speaking, most Latinas will also deviate in terms of language, religion, socioeconomic class, and education. The concept of "the straight white Christian man of property [as] the ethical universal"[71] *is* otherworldly to the Latina.

Latinas' multiple exclusions, to date not considered in discourse, have resulted in barriers to Latinas from actively participating in any of their communities— both the "external" so-called "American" community as well as the *comunidad Latina*—and thus they have been denied visibility, the power to speak, and the potential to be heard. To include Latinas, a LatCrit paradigm must incorporate an internationalist, globalized, feminist, multi/cross-cultural perspective. Such a nonessentialist model brings to the center of discourse the amalgam of Latinas' identities, including race, ethnicity, nationhood, gender, and culture, and will prevent Latinas' exclusion.

In addition, because of the subordinating effect to Latinas of our internal relationship to *la cultura Latina*, a LatCrit paradigm must be sensitive to and develop a roadmap regarding the consideration of culture. In this regard, however, the model also must be careful not to replicate, inadvertently, any of the subjugating effects of the external relationship of the dominant culture to the *cultura Latina*.

Thus, there are two applications and interpretations of cultural conservation that the LatCrit model must avoid. One is the use of culture as a shield by the elite *within* the *cultura Latina* with the desire, purpose, and consequence of keeping Latinas invisible, nonexistent, and disempowered. The other is the use of culture as a sword by a dominant group to eviscerate and subordinate the *cultura Latina*, or a variant of it, as foreign to, and outside of, the normative mold. In other words, LatCrit must avert the mis/use of the protection of culture so as to perpetuate women's subordination in the name of tradition, or to subordinate nondominant subcultures in the name of law—both perfidious results.

In the context of cultural considerations, LatCrit theorizing must support and promote the concept of a benevolent (meaning nondiscriminatory and non-subordinating) respect for culture.[72] A LatCrit paradigm, while embracing and being sensitive to cultural differences, must simultaneously reject oppressive aspects of culture, particularly sex-subordinating or sex-marginalizing practices or beliefs. To attain such cultural pluralism, the subject's position as part of a cultural whole must be considered. Thus, integral to the LatCrit model is the asking of the "culture question"[73] and the evaluation of the obtained information from both

---

[71] As a group, Latinas are the poorest, least educated, lowest skilled, and least likely to hold jobs or obtain training that will facilitate the means of emerging from poverty, of any ethnic or racial group in the United States.

[72] Gayarati Chakravorty Spivak, "The Making of Americans, the Teaching of English, and the Future of Cultural Studies" in (1990) 21 New Literary Hist. 81–89.

[73] International human rights documents provide a model for and support such an approach. While treaties consistently address culture as a basis upon which protections must be afforded, not one cites to culture as the grounds upon which other protected rights may be abridged. See, *e.g.* Convention on the Elimination of All Forms of Discrimination Against Women, G.A. Res. 180, U.N. GAO, 34th Sess., Supp. No. 46, at 195. Annex at art. 2(f), U.N. Doc. A/34/46 (1979) (mandating that States Parties "take all appropriate measures, including legislation, to modify or abolish existing laws, regulations, *customs and practices* which constitute discrimination against women" (emphasis added). The Women's Convention goes so far so as to require that States Parties

"take all appropriate measures ... [t]o modify the *social and cultural patterns of conduct* of men and women, with a view to achieving the elimination of prejudices and *customary and all other practices* which are based on the idea of the inferiority or the superiority of either of the sexes or on stereotyped roles for men and women." (*ibid.,* art. 5(a) (emphasis added).

the object and subject positions with the goal of articulating *teorías* that promote equality, understanding, and full participation rather than imposing subjugating, culture-essentialist perspectives.

A LatCrit project that fails to confront both the internal and external components of Latina oppression will imagine an "equality" that will involve a job market open only to Latinos; a concept of privacy that hides *cosas de familia*, including a few bruises and the occasional black eye; a free market that exploits and undervalues Latinas' services (paying what the market will bear means less when you are female *or* colored so imagine being female *and* colored); a culture hat requires them to be saints; a concept of citizenship that relegates Latinas to second-class membership in all their communities; and a construction of racial, ethnic, and national identities that marginalizes them as foreigners in all their worlds. Thus, it is imperative for LatCrit to emphasize the necessity and demand or Latina participation in the social, political, communitarian, and legal discourse. Absent such pathways for communication and absent such inclusion, Latinas, even those with passports, will remain handicapped traveling their *mundos*.

## B. LatCrit Possibilities

LatCrit as an articulable theoretical construct both presents a great challenge and offers great promise. First, the challenge lies in the great diversity—the panethnicity—of Latinas/os. Latinas/os come from different ethnic, cultural, and racial heritages, as well as from varied national origins. Some are citizens, some are not; some noncitizens are present with, and some without, proper documentation. Many have been in the United States for generations, others are ecent arrivals. Some are monolingual in Spanish, some in English, others are bi/multilingual. Some are homocultural and others can (and some do daily) culturally crossdress. Such apparently cacophonous, heterogeneous demographics would appear to interfere with any attempt at a coherent, cohesive paradigm. This notion of panethnicity, upon an initial consideration, could appear to be an impediment to the articulation of any congruent *teoría*. Ironically, however, such heterogeneity is what holds the promise of LatCrit: the development of a paradigm that accepts, embraces, and accommodates persons as multidimensional entities rather than as conveniently divisible parts of that whole being.

A LatCrit model must deconstruct and reject the existing legal philosophy that fragments worlds by looking only at one aspect of identity at a time.[74] Of course,

---

In fact, the Women's Convention is noteworthy because it even proscribes stereotyping. See, *e.g. ibid.*, art. 10(c) (requiring that States Parties ensure "the elimination of any stereotyped concept of the roles of men and women at all levels and in all forms of education"); see also Charter on the Rights and Welfare of the African Child, July 11, 1990, art. 21, OAU Doc. CAB/LEG/24.9/49. The African Charter on the Rights and Welfare of the African Child expressly balances cultural rights and cultural pretexts to disempower or harm persons simply because of their sex. The Charter requires member states of the Organization of African Unity to "abolish customs and practices harmful to the welfare, normal growth and development of the child, and in particular ... those customs and practices discriminatory to the child on the grounds *of sex* or other status." *ibid.* (emphasis added).

[74] See Berta Esperanza Hernández-Truyol, "Women's Rights as Human Rights—Rules, Realities and the Role of Culture" in (1996) 21 Brook. J. Int'l L. 605, 668 (proposing that, in order to ensure women's full membership and participation in their communities, critical inquiries into lawmaking must include analysis of cultural implications).

this dominant atomistic model is a convenient, superficial, artificially created, normative driven, comparativist construct that facilitates "othering."[75] The analysts, having fabricated their image of the pertinent universe, can handily exclude those who do not fit the mold.[76] The existing "rule of law" driven construct possesses inherent national, racial, gender, religious, sexuality, and cultural hierarchies. The normative Non-Latino/a while ("NLW") legal paradigm essentializes[77] and disadvantages Latinas/os, as we are the multiplicity of our identities, not the atomization of them.

As far as traditional classifications go, LatCrit theory must reject defining identity as anything other than multidimensional because doing so would result in an essentializing of self. Latinas/os are the combination, not the stratification, of our multiple selves. Therefore, under the LatCrit model, rather than independent glyphs carved in stone, notions of personhood, race/ethnicity, nationhood, and cultural citizenship must be viewed as fluid, interdependent, and indivisible.

The central epistemological question to ask in the construction of a LatCrit paradigm is what conditions need to exist in order to have a pluralistic, non-essentialist LatCrit theory. Because all "reality" is socially constructed, the model must incorporate broadbased sources of knowledge and information on race, sex, culture, language, and ethnicity. This re/construction will avoid the flawed structure of the NLW rule of law which evolved as racialized, ethnicized, gendered, and nativistic.

A LatCrit theory, at its core, would insist on the indivisibility, inviolability, and interdependence of identities that are constitutive of personhood. As such, a LatCrit paradigm could eschew the "rule of law" as we know it. Rather than the existing normative comparativist model with the NLoW at the center as the aspirational aim, rather than placing the "elite," the most privileged, at the nucleus, LatCrit would place at the center the notion of full citizenship, the inviolable right of *every* member of society to respect, dignity, and selfhood, with acceptance of identities as indivisible, interrelated, and interdependent rather than splintered.

Adoption of such a model will place LatCrit uniquely in the position of displacing the schisms of the past (namely, "othering" of selves by the majority, "othering" of selves within *nuestra comunidad*, silencing of Latinas' voices, and the eclipsing of Latinas' visibility), developing, expanding, and transforming the content, meaning, and application of legal theoretical constructs. LatCrit can change the landscape of legal discourse.

### Conclusion

LatCrit, using Latinas'/os' cultural, ethnic, and national origin diversity, and Latinas' gendered history and experience, can develop a nonessentialist, pluralistic, egalitarian, and equitable notion of legal discourse and community. Indeed, the central epistemology of norms is social, cultural, and political. Dominance by one group defines, and is constitutive of, social, cultural, and legal realities and identity. The existing, essentialist notion of the "American" has excluded "others" who look or sound foreign to the self-selected norm setters, creating a class of aliens within the borders. This "American" ideal excludes many, particularly Latinas/os, who cannot blend into the "melting pot" because

---

[75] See, *e.g.* Crenshaw (1989) U. Chicago Legal F. 139 160–167 (urging integration of feminist theory with black liberation and antiracist political theory).

[76] See Davis & Wildman (1992) 68 S. Calif 2. Rev. 1367, 1381–1382 (discussing "de-rac[ing]" of Anita Hill during the hearings, making her only a woman within a "white racist conspiracy").

[77] See generally Wildman, *Privilege Revealed* (1996) (discussing how language, social patterns, and laws privilege whiteness).

of the colorizing, feminizing, spanishinzing, and latinizing consequences of their membership. This "American" definition of normativity has created an exclusive/ elite community with *fronteras* denying access to "others."

Consider a postessentialist model in which an individual can freely and comfortably journey in her/his various worlds, engaging in cross-participation, rendering the communities interdependent and indivisible without barriers to knowledge and identity-flows that not only allow traversing the worlds, but help to re/constitute the communities themselves with due regard to the needs and concerns of the varied citizenry. Such unobstructed traveling facilitates information flow from the many perspectives and enhances norm articulation in a pluralistic and inclusive fashion.

The hope of LatCrit lies in the articulation of a system of analysis that, by deconstructing the political normative and rebuilding a participatory and inclusive policy model, can result in praxis. To that end, and in developing such a LatCrit construct, this Essay urges the incorporation of a globalized, feminist, multi/cross-cultural vision of international human rights norms—a perspective that promotes a conception of identity and rights centered on indivisibility, inviolability, and interdependence. Such an expanded, developed, and transformed philosophy can serve to eradicate essentialism, *fronteras*, and margins, providing the pathway for the silenced voices of these borderlands to travel to the center of the narrative.                                    [pp. 920–927]

# 18

# THEORIES OF ADJUDICATION

Modern legal theory has been much concerned to explore the inner workings of the judicial system. The earlier attitude was to regard the judiciary as the priests of the law, the repositories of its ancient rules and traditions; decisions are thus distilled in a mysterious way by the judge *in scrinio pectoris sui*; moreover, he never creates new law but only declares fresh applications of the ancient rule.[1] Despite the traditional doctrine the legal system has been gradually remoulded, albeit often haltingly and inadequately, to meet new social needs. In the meantime judicial orthodoxy still clings to the assumption that it is for the judge to apply the law as it is and not to make new law, and the hieratic tradition may be seen to survive, both in the treatment of the American Supreme Court Judges as High-Priests and Guardians of the Constitution, and in the common law reverence for judicial as against mere juristic utterance.

## THE NATURE OF LEGAL SOURCES

Legal sources are the raw material of the judicial process and, though Salmond argued that they were "merely contingent and not necessary",[2] it is difficult to believe that anything other than a very rudimentary legal system could operate without authoritative sources of law.[3] At many points in this book questions about validity have been discussed. A question that now needs to be posed concerns the validity of the legal sources used by lawyers and judges concerned with the judicial process.

Two prominent views may be distinguished. Salmond's approach is very close in spirit to Kelsen's jurisprudence.[4] "The rule", he wrote, "that judicial decisions have the force of law is legally ultimate and underived. These ultimate principles are the *grundnorms* or basic rules of recognition of the legal system".[5] He believed that these ultimate principles were

[1] But on the medieval attitude towards the power of the court to create new "customs", Plucknett, *Legislation of Edward I* (1952).
[2] *Jurisprudence* (12th ed.), 91 p. 112.
[3] *Cf.* Hart, *The Concept of Law*, pp. 91 *et seq.*
[4] As Stone noted. See 26 M.L.R. 34. See also Ebenstein, *The Pure Theory of Law* (1945), p. 91. On Kelsen see *ante*, Chap. 5.
[5] *Op. cit.*, p. 111. Salmond himself did not use the term "*grundnorm*". His latest editor, Fitzgerald, does. The plural *of grundnorm* is *grundnormen*.

indeed "rules of law" though they differed in some unspecified respects from "ordinary less basic legal rules".[6] This theory has a number of difficulties, not the least of which are concerned with creation and change in the ultimate rule.[7]

Hart's view is different, though he relates it to the rule of recognition. He asserts that Acts of Parliament, and presumably also judicial decisions, have the force of law because judges, officials and private citizens recognise that primary rules are to be identified by reference to certain criteria, one of which is that enactment by the legislature makes law, and another of which would state that certain parts of certain judicial pronouncements bind other courts in the court hierarchy.[8] Thus, to say of a particular statute or precedent that it is a valid source of law is to make "use of a rule of recognition which [the speaker] accepts as appropriate for identifying the law".[9] The rule of recognition exists only as a "complex, but normally concordant, practice of the courts, officials, and private persons in identifying the law by reference to certain criteria. Its existence is a matter of fact".[10] The use of unstated rules of recognition by courts and others in identifying particular rules of the system is characteristic of the internal point of view.[11] The view expressed later in this chapter that rules of precedent are not rules of law but rather rules of practice and that an understanding of them requires detailed study of the actual behaviour of the judiciary follows from Hart's analysis.[12]

### The Common Law

A slightly different question has been raised and partially answered by Simpson.[13] He has tried to explicate the nature of the common law. This is not the same thing as trying to explain *stare decisis* for, as he rightly maintains, the common law existed for many centuries before *stare decisis* evolved. How is one, therefore, to explain how a statement like "it is the law in England that contracts require consideration" can be meaningfully made?

The positivist answer tends to reduce the common law to a system[14] of rules laid down by the will of the law maker. This is clearly unsatisfactory, rather as Austinian attempts to explain judge-made law in terms of tacit command are unhelpful. Simpson prefers instead the view that the common law system is a customary system of law, consisting of a body of

[6] *ibid.*, p. 112.
[7] *Ante*, 267. See also MacCormick, *ante*, 556.
[8] *The Concept of Law*, p. 100.
[9] *ibid.*, p. 108.
[10] *ibid.*, p. 110.
[11] *ibid.*, pp. 55–59, 88–91, 102–103. See *ante*, 379. And see S. Shapiro (2006) 75 Fordham L.R. 1157.
[12] *Post*, 1538.
[13] "The Common Law and Legal Theory" in *Oxford Essays in Jurisprudence* (2nd series, Simpson ed.), p. 79.
[14] But see C. Sampford, *The Disorder of Law* (1989) arguing that it is misleading to think of law as "systematic" (pp. 18–19).

practices observed and ideas received by a caste of lawyers.[15] These ideas, he argues, are used to provide guidance in the rational determination of disputes and in advising clients. This explanation is only partial because it begs further questions about the nature of custom.[16]

## THE INSTITUTION OF ADJUDICATION

Berger and Luckmann have said that, "to engage in judging is to represent the role of the judge. The judging individual is not acting 'on his own', but *qua* judge . . . The role represents an entire institutional nexus of conduct. The role of judge stands in relationship to other roles, the totality of which comprises the institutions of law."[17] An understanding of the judicial process thus requires cognition of this "institutional nexus of conduct".

Every institution embodies some degree of consensus about how it is to operate. There are a number of shared expectations which define the role of the judge.[18] Judges are part of the legal order, that is part of a society in which human conduct is governed by rules. Ideally, rules enable society to function smoothly and efficiently. There are, however, conflicts. Judges are instituted as one of the ways in which society resolves such conflicts. One could posit a society where there were no judges or even prototypes of them, as Hart indeed has done.[19] As he points out, such a society would labour under distinct disadvantages. A society with judges expects them to iron out those trouble cases it takes to them.

It expects them to solve disputes in a rational way. It would not meet these expectations if a judge were to toss a coin. Fuller is right to insist that this does not necessarily rule out "intuitive" or "inarticulate" decisions "provided that there is faith that what is 'intuited' is something that would appear as rational if it could be brought to adequate expression."[20] But this usually will not be so. The paradigm of a rational decision is one reached according to rules, principles or standards. Adjudication according to rules, etc., means that an ad hoc decision-making process is deprecated. It posits that judges must conform to established rules. But this does not mean that the judge has the largely mechanical job of mere application of an existing rule to a new state of facts. At least the function of appellate judges cannot be so characterised.[21] There may not be a rule or the rule itself may be expressed in an open-ended way, directing a

---

[15] *Cf.* Llewellyn's ideas, *ante*, 992.
[16] On which see *ante*, 1088.
[17] *The Social Construction of Reality* (1966), p. 92.
[18] *Cf.* V. Aubert, *Elements of Sociology* (1970), pp. 40–41.
[19] *The Concept of Law* (1994), pp. 91–99.
[20] "The Forms and Limits of Adjudication" in Hart and Sacks, *The Legal Process* (1978) 92 Harv. L. Rev. 353. See also *The Principles of Social Order* (1981), pp. 86–124 and Summers, *Lon L. Fuller* (1984), pp. 90–93.
[21] *Cf.* Cardozo, *The Growth of the Law* (1924) arguing that nine-tenths of a trial judge's rule-enunciation is predetermined.

judge to do what is "fair" or "reasonable".[22] Behind the demand that adjudication according to rules is a rational process of decision-making lies a belief in formal justice that is satisfied by giving like cases like treatment. Such a demand presupposes a standard against which "like" can be measured and this, it must be admitted, is not easy to construct.[23]

The insistence that adjudication must take place according to established rules must not be taken too literally. The rules must not be seen as ends in themselves. Conceptualism (or legalism[24]) is a vice to which lawyers all too readily succumb. Rules are means to an end, purposive instruments. They embody social objectives and policy choices. Thus, when a judge confronts a rule he is not met by a bloodless category but by a living organism which contains *within itself* value choices.[25] The judge must choose and in doing so he makes law,[26] but his choice is limited.

To understand why adjudication according to rules is posited as an *ideal* to which judges should conform one must understand the role that litigants and their advisers perform in the judicial process. The ad-judicative process is one of constant interaction between judges, the legal profession, litigants and the wider public. It would collapse if the volume of business were not kept within manageable proportions. Judges can only cope with a certain amount of work. The knowledge that judges adjudicate according to established rules enables the volume of litigation to be contained.

First, it facilitates the channelling of behaviour[27] so as to keep it within the perimeter of authoritative norm. It helps a planning of social activities within legal limits. Contracts can be entered into and settlements made, property disposed of, fiscal arrangements negotiated on the understanding that a favourable determination would follow if conflicts were to arise. Secondly, it confers on the litigants' advisers the ability to settle a case out of court. As a result less than 10 per cent of claim forms issued in England and Wales result in a trial.

Thirdly, it enables litigants and their advisers to participate meaningfully in the adjudicative process. They can do this because they know what types of evidence to adduce and the boundaries of legal argumentation. Fuller has argued that adjudication is "a social process of decision which assures for the affected party a particular form of participation, that of presenting proofs and arguments for a decision in his favour". He is afforded, "institutionally guaranteed participation". It is,

---

[22] Examples are the Matrimonial Causes Act 1973, s. 25 and the Supply of Goods (Implied Terms) Act 1973, s. 4.

[23] See Hart, *The Concept of Law* (1994), pp. 157–167, following Perelman, *The Idea of Justice and the Problem of Argument* (1963). See also the discussion of this in relation to sex discrimination at 1290–1292.

[24] *Cf.* Shklar, *ante*, 20, and see also *ante*, 985 and 1209.

[25] For a good example cf. the approach of Lord Pearce in *Myers v. DPP* with that of Lords Morris, Hodson and Reid [1965] A.C. 1001. See further Freeman (1973) 26 *Current Legal Problems* 166, 189.

[26] *Cf.* Dworkin's views discussed *ante*, 719.

[27] *Cf.* Llewellyn, *ante*, 1016–1017.

Fuller maintains, the essence of the rule of law that "men affected by the decisions which emerge from social processes should have some formally guaranteed opportunity to affect those decisions".[28] But one cannot direct an effective argument into a vacuum. Lawyers must be able to experience vicariously the judge's process of reasoning. Adjudication, as described here, enables them to do this. Adjudication "in the air" would rob them of any sense of participation.[29]

### *Justiciability*

One consequence that flows from this model of adjudication is that certain disputes become inherently non-justiciable.[30] This does not mean that particular areas of social activity cannot be made amenable to the judicial process: rather, that as at present constituted there are no standards provided and the judge can do nothing other than legislate. Even so a dispute may be justiciable when, although there are not established rules of law, there are at least principles acceptable to lawyers or a high degree of consensus among society as to the proper goals to be pursued or standards against which a judge can reason. When Viscount Simonds in *National Bank of Greece* v. *Metliss* said: "in the end and in the absence of authority binding this House, the question is simply: What does justice demand in such a case as this? ... If I have to base my opinion on any principle, I would venture to say it was the principle of natural justice",[31] he was applying an established standard developed by lawyers and acceptable to the community at large.[32]

Justiciability depends not only on the existence of amenable rules and standards. A dispute is not appropriate for adjudication when it involves a "multiplicity of variable and interlocking factors, decisions on each of which presupposes decisions on all the others."[33] Stone gave as examples of such "polycentric"[34] disputes "the monstrously complex multipartite hearings to determine the normal working week under a labour arbitration such as the Australian or ... the hearing of a case under the United Kingdom Restrictive Practices Act involving the determination of whether a practice admitted for consideration through one of the

---

[28] (1963) Wisc. L. Rev. 3, 19.

[29] But, as Eisenberg points out (1978) 92 Harv. L. Rev. 410, a judge may sometimes have to go beyond the arguments presented by the parties, where they present their case on the basis of an existing rule that the judge thinks should no longer be followed.

[30] On justiciability generally see Marshall in *Oxford Essays in Jurisprudence* (ed. Guest, 1961), p. 265; Summers, 26 M.L. R. 530; Stone, 35 Br. Y. B. Int. L. 124.

[31] [1958] A.C. 509, 525.

[32] *Cf.* Scrutton L.J. in *Holt v. Markham* [1923] 1 K.B. 504, 513 ("well-meaning sloppiness of thought").

[33] *Per* Stone, *Social Dimensions of Law and Justice* (1966), pp. 653–654.

[34] The term is Michael Polanyi's. See his *The Logic of Liberty* (1951), pp. 170 *et seq.* See also Fuller (1960) *Proc. of American Society of International Law* 1–8. On polycentricity see also *ante*, Freeman, *op. cit.*, n. 25.

gateways of 'public interest' is also on all the facts in the interest of the community as a whole".[35]

The difficulties of making polycentric disputes amenable to adjudication are numerous. The problem of representation is particularly acute. In polycentric disputes all interests cannot be represented: the *amicus curiae* brief is but a formal concession to this value. This is one of the biggest obstacles faced by the advocate of prospective overruling.[36] However, the objection to adjudication of polycentric issues must not be insisted upon too strictly. There are polycentric elements inherent in *stare decisis*, as is seen in appellate court development of the law. It is a complex problem and lines cannot easily be drawn.

## STARE DECISIS

To follow past decisions is a natural and indeed a necessary procedure in our everyday affairs. To take the same course as has been taken previously, or as has usually been adopted in the past, not only confers the advantage of accumulated experience of the past but also saves the effort of having to think out a problem anew each time it arises. Accordingly, in almost any form of organisation, precedents have to be established as guides to future conduct, and this applies not merely to legal systems but to all rule or norm-creating bodies, whether clubs, government departments, schools, business firms or churches. There is, however, an inevitable danger that this tendency to follow past precedents may lead to stereotyped procedures and to stultify progress, and much of the working success of any organisation may depend on its ability to apply precedents creatively.[37] The infinite variability of the facts in human situations comes to the assistance of mankind not only by rendering it impossible to apply past rulings purely mechanically, but by providing scope for the gradual moulding of the rules to meet fresh situations as they arise. There is a constant interaction between rules and the factual situations which they govern, for a too rigid observance of the rules may stereotype the very structure and activities of society itself, whereas a freer approach will allow a richer interplay of social forces.

Whilst restraint in exercising the judicial power to overrule precedents makes for stability, abstention can defeat this very stability, for a practice of rigid adherence to precedent will eventually produce an accumulation

---

[35] *Op. cit.*, p. 654. Good examples of such a dispute are *Texaco v. Mulberry Filling Station* [1972] 1 All E.R. 513 and *Lim Poh Choo v. Camden and Islington A.H.A.* [1979] 2 All E.R. 910.

[36] And see Freeman, *op. cit.*, n. 25.

[37] It has been suggested that "vagueness is not incompatible with precision ... A painter with a limited palette can achieve more precise representations by thinning and combining his colours than a mosaic worker can achieve with his limited variety of tiles, and the skilful superimposing of vagueness has similar advantages over the fitting together of precise technical terms". (Quine, *Word and Object* (1960), p. 127). See also Christie 48 Minn. L. Rev. 885.

of outmoded rules which are likely to be blurred by artificial distinctions.[38]

Precedent has thus always been the life-blood of legal systems. It is, of course, particularly prominent in the common law, but barely less so in the modern civil law. The special features of the present-day common law system of precedent may, perhaps, be summarised as (i) a particular emphasis on judicial decisions as the core of the legal system; (ii) a very subordinate role conceded to juristic writings, as against decisions of the courts, in the exposition of the law; (iii) the treatment of certain judicial decisions as binding on other judges; and (iv) the form of judicial judgments and the mode of reporting these.

### The Common Law Approach

What is regarded today as the characteristic attitude of the common law in treating judicial decisions as binding themselves on future courts is quite modern, emerging in the nineteenth century. The earlier view was far closer to the modern civilian attitude, for it regarded decisions as expressions of opinion as to the state of the law whose weight depended on the judge or judges who pronounced them, but which were not actually authoritative in the sense of compelling the judges to follow those opinions, even if they were thought to be wrong.[39] Indeed, the modern common law doctrine could hardly have arisen until there was in existence an established hierarchy of courts and an efficient system of law reporting.

When an overall view is taken of the existing rules of *stare decisis* in English law, it is evident that there is room for a good deal more flexibility than might be supposed.[40] Thus courts of co-ordinate jurisdiction[41] are not bound by each other's decisions (though for this purpose the Divisional Court enjoys a somewhat ill-defined pre-eminence[42]), and a decision of a lower court can only persuade but not bind its superior. And the ruling by the House of Lords in 1898 that it is bound by its own decisions was replaced in 1966 by the recognition that that tribunal, while

---

[38] See Keeton, *Venturing to do Justice* (1969), p. 15 who points out that: "Courts refusing to overrule precedents outright are virtually forced to accomplish reform by devising a labyrinth of rules with dubious and unpredictable implications. Thus, overpowering demands of justice encourage such courts to make casuistic distinctions that produce doubt rather than certainty, irregularity rather than even-handedness and vacillation rather than constancy". *Cf.* Llewellyn's contention that a formal style does not make for predictability.

[39] See *per* Vaughan C.J. in *Bole v. Horton* (1673) Vaughan's Rep., p. 382; Hale, *Hist. Com. Law* (ed. 1739), Chap. IV, p. 63. It is worth contrasting this with Hobbes's view in *Leviathan* II. 26. 24: "All the sentences of precedent judges that have ever been cannot altogether make a law contrary to natural equity".

[40] An excellent illustration of flexibility is the reasoning of the House of Lords in *Conway v. Rimmer* [1968] A.C. 910.

[41] A judge should not reject a decision of a court of co-ordinate jurisdiction unless convinced that the earlier decision is wrong: see *Island Tug Ltd v. S.S. Makedonia* [1958] 1 Q.B. 365.

[42] See, *e.g. Police Authority for Huddersfield v. Watson* [1947] K.B. 842, 848.

treating its former decisions as normally binding, may depart from a previous decision when it appears right to do so.[43] But this direction has made little difference to House of Lords practice. It is clear that it had found little difficulty in circumventing undesirable precedents in the years before 1966.[44] It is equally apparent that the decisive step of overruling *in as many words* a previous decision of the House is too traumatic for many of the law lords to contemplate. Not until 1974[45] did the House of Lords refuse to follow an earlier decision of its own, and only rarely since[46] has the new power been invoked. Dogma has changed: little else. When the opportunity presented itself in *Conway* v. *Rimmer*[47] to overrule *Duncan* v. *Cammell Laird*,[48] at least eight reasons were adduced why *Duncan* should not govern.

As for the civil Court of Appeal, which still adheres to the doctrine that it is bound by its own decisions, both the development of the so-called *per incuriam* rule, as well as an increasing readiness to distinguish earlier decisions viewed with disfavour, has effected a considerable mitigation. Lord Denning favoured the adoption by the Court of Appeal, as regards its own decisions, of the ruling made by the House of Lords. He failed to persuade his brethren and the impetus for change has now gone. It is probable that any change will require legislation.[49] Nevertheless, the basic flexibility of the system is preserved, not so much by the formal limitations on the rule of *stare decisis*, but by the relative freedom with which courts may and often do determine the scope and limits of past precedents and whether to apply them to the fresh circumstances which have arisen, or to distinguish these from the facts and circumstances held to be material in previous cases. In this way, within certain limits, there remains a certain room for manoeuvre, without which no legal system would be workable. Only a totally static society could tolerate a completely rigid system of law.

## Rules of Law or Rules of Practice?

From the point of view of legal theory there has been much speculation as to the authority of the *Practice Direction*.[50] The statement was not part of a judicial judgment. Not being issued in a curial capacity the statement

---

[43] See *Practice Direction* [1966] 3 All E.R. 77. An excellent discussion of this is N. Duxbury, *The Nature and Authority of Precedent* (2008), pp. 125–149.

[44] See Cross, 82 L.Q.R. 203 for an illuminating discussion of the methods used.

[45] *Johanna Oldendorff* [1974] A.C. 479 overruling *The Aello* [1961] A. C. 135 on the test for determining when a ship becomes an "arrived ship".

[46] But see *Kleinwort Benson v. Lincoln City Council* [1998] 4 All E.R. 513. See also *Miliangos v. Frank* [1976] A.C. 443, *R v. G* [2004] 1 A.C. 1034, *Horton v. Sadler* [2006] UKHL 27. Note the House of Lords now operates in a new environment with the Human Rights Act 1998 s. 3 requiring courts to render statutes compatible with human rights jurisprudence. And, of course, a Supreme Court will replace the House of Lords in October 2009.

[47] [1968] A.C. 910.

[48] [1942] A.C. 624.

[49] A view expressed by Lord Simon in *Miliangos v. Frank* [1976] A.C. 443, 471.

[50] See F. A. Mann (1983) 2 C.J.Q. 320, 330–333. And see N. Duxbury, *op. cit.*, n. 43.

can arguably have no legal force. It follows that if rules of precedent have legal force, then a rule modifying them would itself have to have legal force. The whole juridical status of precedent is thus called in question, and not for the first time.[51]

One means of escape from this logical conundrum is to say that rules of precedent are not rules of law but rules of practice. The question as to how a Direction with no legal force could modify rules of precedent would thus be avoided. Glanville Williams[52] has adopted such an approach. He has argued that the binding force of *Tramways*[53] ruling cannot be derived from the binding force of that case as a precedent until we know that the House of Lords was bound by its own decisions. So, he argued, in 1957, the House of Lords was free to overrule its own decisions, including *Tramways*. In view of this the operation of rules of precedent cannot derive from the fact that rules of precedent are legal rules. Consequently, he argued, that such binding force as rules of precedent have, must be based rather on their standing as "rules of practice". It may be readily conceded that Williams' case is logically unanswerable. But, as Stone,[54] has pointed out, this does not dispose of the matter. "Whether this is really a solution still depends on the assumption that 'rules of law' and 'rules of practice' are mutually exclusive categories",[55] or denying that a "rule of practice" may not itself also be a "rule of law". "What, therefore, characterises a 'rule of practice', and are all rules of practice functionally similar? Can a statement, even assuming it was issued in a curial capacity, have binding effect as a 'rule of practice,' any more than as a 'rule of law'?

It is difficult to see, employing Williams' own logic, how the binding force of a rule of practice can be based on some earlier practice, any more than the binding force of a rule of precedent can be based on an earlier precedent laying down such a rule. As Stone suggests the vicious circle can only be broken by positing the characteristics of "practice" that make the rule so observed binding, rather as we can indicate what features of "customary" behaviour make the rules observed binding in the general law. "We might ... say that the hierarchical rules of precedent are binding rules of law, not because some court on some occasion announced them, but rather because of "observed regularities of behaviour conforming to 'the practice' ... a steady manifestation of an *opinio*

---

[51] Duxbury, *ibid*, pp. 131–132 does not agree. There is, he says, no requirement that statements by courts regarding their own practice be made in the course of judgments. Further, the statement was made by the Judicial Committee of the House of Lords whose "proposal" should be no less authoritative than other proposals this chamber makes. More persuasive is Duxbury's third criterion that the argument depends on a "crude" conception of binding force.

[52] See *Salmond on Jurisprudence* (11th ed., 1957), pp. 187–188. This passage is omitted from the 12th edition, edited by Professor Fitzgerald.

[53] [1898] A.C. 375.

[54] See (1969) 69 Colum L. Rev, 1162, 1162–68, 1189–1202.

[55] *ibid.*, p. 1165. Stone compares this logical status with *legal* status.

*necessitatis* by the legislature in all of this".[56] But if we do we must recognise that the "rule of practice *here involved is* also a 'rule of law'."

A distinction can be drawn between *descriptive* rules of practice and *prescriptive* rules of practice. There are, for example, "rules of practice" whereby judges prevent the introduction of evidence which, though legally admissible, might excessively prejudice a party. Failure to do this will not, however, be a basis for reversal on appeal. Such a "rule of practice" is descriptive of past and expected future behaviour, but is not prescriptive for the future. Thus, in *Connelly* v. *D.P.P.*,[57] The House of Lords could disapprove of the rule of practice[58] that a count for murder could not be joined with one for robbery, both having arisen from the same facts. Lord Devlin explicitly stated that the "rule of practice" was not a "rule of law." The Lords' disapproval of the practice did not, therefore, require the appeal to be allowed, as it would have done had the rule been a "rule of law."[59]

In referring, however, to rules of precedent as "rules of practice", one has in mind something less vague and imprecise. For with precedent it is the practice, the behaviour of conforming, reversing, submitting, etc., what Hart[60] has referred to as a "critical reflective attitude", which takes the nature of precedent beyond the merely descriptive, so that the rules become prescriptive for judicial behaviour. If this is so (and ignoring the fact that *Tramways* was the culmination of a long process and not one innovatory step)[61] then the rule in *Tramways* became such with the conduct of other judges and lawyers between 1898 and 1966. "The rule which, immediately on its enunciation in 1898, faced the difficulties described by Glanville Williams, might by 1966, by reason of that practice, have become a rule both *descriptive* of past practice, and also *prescriptive* of a rule of law binding in the future."[62] Similarly, the 1966 Direction *in itself* has no binding effect, but would acquire such when a "degree of conformity to it, and the *opinio necessitatis* grounding this, became manifest in the behaviour of courts".[63] The significance of the Direction must, therefore, be sought in observing and interpreting the differences, if any, in court behaviour before and after it. As has been suggested,[64] and as a glance at *Conway* v. *Rimmer*[65] will readily confirm, the leeways of precedent were sufficiently flexible before 1966 (and still are) for the Lords to develop the law in a creative manner, without recourse to their new weapon.

---

[56]  *ibid.*
[57]  [1964] A.C. 1254.
[58]  In accordance with *R. v. Jones* [1918] 1 K.B. 416.
[59]  But the Lords announced that the challenged "rule" should not have effect "as a rigid rule" in the future.
[60]  See *ante*, 380.
[61]  Earlier cases are *Att-Gen. v. Windsor* (1860) 8 HL 369; *Beamish v. Beamish* (1861) 9 H.L.C. 274.
[62]  *Per* Stone, *op. cit.*, p. 1168.
[63]  *ibid.*
[64]  *Ante*, 1539.
[65]  [1968] A.C. 910.

## The Civil Law

In the modern civil law there is not complete unity of theory and practice, though civilian systems concur in denying absolute authority to judicial precedent and in attaching more weight to juristic writings. In some ways the civil law of France is highly individual and rooted in French historical traditions, but it may usefully serve as an example of the civilian approach.[66] One important feature of civil law systems since the nineteenth century is that they are usually based on a series of codes, so that the fabric of the law is regarded as primarily statutory, the judiciary's task being limited to applying the provisions of the code. But the original theory that the French Napoleonic code was the sole source of law, exemplified by the provision prohibiting the judge from pronouncing by way of general disposition,[67] was soon seen to be impracticable, and for long now the decisions of the courts (*la jurisprudence*) have been acknowledged to play a major role in the development of the law. Moreover, since Gény propounded the judicial role in terms of a *"libre recherche scientifique"*,[68] the creative function of the judiciary has been widely accepted. And yet "debate still continues ... on the issue whether *jurisprudence* is a source of law".[69] Gény's opinion, for long the authoritative one, held that "the rules originating in court decisions had none of the attributes of legal rules," they could merely "propel the formation of custom, whose force derived from the comment of those whose 'interests'

---

[66] For German attitude see Cohn, *Manual of German Law*, vol. 1, pp. 4–6 and, more fully, Dawson, *The Oracles of the Law* (1968), Chaps III (historical) and VI (on the modern caselaw revolution); for the Italian see Cappelletti *et al.*, *The Italian Legal System: An Introduction* (1967), pp. 270–273; for the Spanish see Brown, 5 I.C.L.Q. 364, 367–372. General surveys are found in David and Brierley, *Major Legal Systems of the World* (1985); Merryman, *The Civil Law Tradition* (1985), Chaps. IV–VI. See also K. Zweigert and H. Kötz, *Introduction to Comparative Law* (1998), in particular Chaps B. I and B. II.

[67] But this provision (in Art. 5) must be read together with Art. 4, which provides that a judge who refuses to decide a matter under the pretext of the silence, obscurity or insuffiency of the law is guilty of a denial of justice. The status and role of the French judge was fixed during the Revolution when the judiciary was the enemy. The germ of Article 5 was developed by the Constituent Assembly in 1790 as one of two measures aimed at subjugating the judiciary (Art. 5 is backed by provisions in the Penal Code (Art. 127) which prescribe civic degradation for judges "who intermeddle in the exercise of legislative power". See Dawson, *The Oracles of the Law* (1968), pp. 375–382.) The other curbing measure was the insistence that judges give reasons for their decisions (decisions had, and still have, to be *motivé*).

[68] See F. Gény, *Méthodes d'Interprétation en Droit Privé Positif* (2nd ed., 1932). And see now an American translation published by West Publishing Company for the Louisiana Law Institute (1963).

[69] *Per* Dawson, *op. cit.*, p. 422. He quotes Esmein's opinion expressed in 1952 that this debate is "never closed". Carbonnier states: "jurisprudence is not a source of law; it is no more than an opinion which may, with time, tend to become the law" in *The Role of Judicial Decisions and Doctrine* (Dainow ed., 1974), p. 93. He explains that judgments are encased within a constitutional framework which is intended to prevent them from ever becoming rules of law and he quotes Art. 5 of the Civil Code, and stresses the importance of separation of powers.

the rules affected."[70] But who were the "users of custom" and how was their consent to be obtained? An attempt to answer this has been made by Maury,[71] who has suggested that the "interested" parties will be men of law whose professional judgment "will impose itself" on those affected by the rule. This novel twist to the old concept of *Juristenrecht*[72] has not proved uncontroversial.[73] It shows the wide gap between common and civil law approaches. Certain other differences call for emphasis.

Thus, first, precedents even of superior courts are not recognised as automatically binding subsequently either on themselves or on inferior tribunals, though a leading French lawyer has described them as having "privileged authority".[74] This distinction has tended to diminish, and it is now generally agreed that a decision of the *Cour de Cassation* is to all intents and purposes regarded as authoritative for the future. Yet deviation is not in itself a ground for quashing a decision of a lower court and there have been famous occasions when lower courts, often encouraged by writers of *doctrine*, have resisted innovations of the *Cour de Cassation*.[75] The judicial system under the civil law is far less centralised than that of the common law and judges are far more numerous; in particular there are normally several regional appellate courts of co-ordinate jurisdiction. And although decisions are reported in official series on a scale comparable to that of common law jurisdictions, the judgments of the courts consist usually of a very pithy enunciation (in France embodied in a series of staccato sentences each prefaced by the words "*attendu que* . . .") of the reasons for the decision, without any citation or discussion of authorities.[76] It is here that the importance of juristic opinion comes to the fore, for this (*la doctrine*) is to be found not only in treatises, but in learned annotations appended to reported cases, which compare with the sort of discussion found in the judgments of common law judges, as well as those in contributions to learned periodicals. It has been said that *doctrine* is certainly not a source of civil law, but it is an authority. It has the greatest influence in those areas where there is no established *jurisprudence*, and persistent doctrinal criticism has

---

[70] *ibid.*, p. 417.
[71] Discussed in Dawson, *op. cit.*, pp. 422–424. See also Kahn-Freund *et al.*, *op. cit.*, pp. 139–146. See also Carbonnier, *op. cit.*, at pp. 102–104.
[72] *Ante*, 1081.
[73] See Dawson at pp. 425–426 discussing the criticisms of Dupeyroux.
[74] Carbonnier, *op. cit.*, p. 97.
[75] Examples may be found in Dawson, *op. cit.*, p. 404 and see Kahn-Freund, Lévy and Rudden, *A Source-Book on French Law* (1979), Pt 1, section 2.
[76] In French judgments, individual precedents are not cited as they are in this country. Indeed, the *Cour de Cassation* will quash the decision of a lower court if the only reason given for it is an earlier judgement even of the *Cour de Cassation* itself: such a decision will not be *motivé*. But "decisions of the Cour of Cassation operate as precedents controlling lower courts to a far greater degree than formal opinions acknowledged" (Dawson, p. 405).

sometimes prompted the abandonment of established jurisprudential positions.[77]

## WHY PRECEDENT?

What is the justification for precedent?[78] Why should a court be required to follow earlier judicial decisions? No two cases are completely alike, so if precedents are to constrain they must do so where there are factual dissimilarities.[79]

According to Alexander,[80] three models justifying precedential constraint can be found in the literature.

The "natural model" argues that past decisions naturally generate reasons for deciding cases in the same way as previous ones. Equality and reliance are commonly-cited reasons. Thus, Llewellyn argued that "the force of precedent in the law is heightened by ... that curious, almost universal sense of justice which argues that all men are properly to be treated alike in like circumstances".[81] But what is meant by this? Is Llewellyn suggesting that once a rule is enunciated it is never desirable to depart from it? That cannot be his view.[82] Cahn argued that "if decisions differ, some discernible distinction must be found bearing an intelligible relation to the difference in result".[83] But what is a "discernible distinction"? What is to count as a sufficient reason for ignoring a precedent? Reliance is appealed to as a justification because "not upsetting expectations is a value that courts should take into account".[84] But, as Wasserstrom has pointed out, this is only a substantial argument if it is assumed that there is a legal system which is already committed to adherence to precedent. "A person's reliance would be justifiable if and only if that person was justified in assuming that legal rules would be

---

[77] Carbonnier, *op. cit.*, pp. 106–107. On *doctrine* see Kahn-Freund *et al., op. cit.*, pp. 168–176. Other traditions, like the Islamic, Talmudic and Hindu, lack any notion of precedent: see H.P. Glenn, *Legal Traditions of the World* (2000), pp. 93, 164, 258. And in China "precedents are nowhere to be found" (p. 310).

[78] See L. Goldstein, *Precedent in Law* (1987); S. Perry (1987) 7 Ox.J.of Legal Studies 215; F. Schauer (1987) 39 Stanford L.Rev.571; B.B. Levenbook (2000) 6 *Legal Theory* 185. N. Duxbury, *op. cit.*, n. 43, Chap. 7.

[79] The American Realists doubted whether precedents could ever constrain because there were always factual distinctions: see J. Stone, *Precedent and Law* (1985), pp. 124–129.

[80] "Precedent" in (ed.) D. Patterson, *A Companion to Philosophy of Law and Legal Theory* (1996), pp. 503, 505. See also L. Alexander (1989) 63 S.California L.Rev.I, 5.

[81] "Case Law" in *Encyclopaedia of the Social Sciences* (1930), vol.3, p. 249. See also M. Moore in L. Goldstein, *op. cit.*, n. 78, p. 183.

[82] *Cf.* K. Llewellyn in the *The Bramble Bush* (1960), p. 68, where he points to precedent as "Janus-faced": "there is one doctrine for getting rid of precedents deemed troublesome and one doctrine for making use of precedents that seem helpful".

[83] *The Sense of Injustice* (1949), p. 14.

[84] *Per* L. Alexander in (ed.) Patterson, *op. cit.*, n. 80, p. 505. See also Perry, *op. cit.*, n. 78, pp. 248–250.

unswervingly applied".[85] The argument is, in other words, circular.[86] The reliance argument further calls for a system of precedent which offers little leeway for creativity for this would frustrate predictability and reliance.

The second model is the rule model. Under this model, the precedent court has authority "not only to decide the case before it but also to promulgate a general rule binding on courts of subordinate and equal rank".[87] It is these rules upon which actors justifiably rely. There are different versions of this model and these vary along two dimensions. First, according to the strength by which the precedent court's rule binds the constrained court. However, on no version is the constrained court free to disregard a precedent as it is on the natural model. "The constrained court cannot decide to overrule[88] merely because, having weighed equality and reliance against the advantages of a different rule or decision, it has found the balance slightly tilted in favour of the latter".[89] The second dimension relates to methodologies for identifying the precedent rule. In some versions (in Salmond[90] and Wasserstrom,[91] for example), an attempt is made to locate a statement of a canonical rule in the opinion of the precedent court. In others,[92] the search is for rules that the precedent court "implicitly as well as explicitly used as necessary steps in reaching its decision or facts that it deemed material to its decision".[93] On all versions of the rule model, the identification of the rule must satisfy three conditions (i) it must have a "canonical formulation; (ii) "the rule must be treated separate from the reasoning that led to its adoption by the precedent court; it is only the rule and not the reasoning, that binds the constrained court"[94]; (iii) the formulation of the rule must be fixed at the time of the precedent decision.

The rule model may be criticised. First, it may be difficult to identify the rule and this will undermine the reliance values it is supposed to promote. Secondly, it gives the precedent court "tremendous power"[95] in relation to the constrained court. It would seem to endorse judicial legislation,[96] thus giving precedent courts powers which go beyond the practices of deciding particular precedents. Alexander points out "*Any practice of precedential constraint that distinguishes between overruling a*

[85] *The Judicial Decision* (1961), pp. 68–69.
[86] Reliance could be achieved within a looser system of precedent if prospective overruling were to be adopted. See A. Nicol (1976) 39 M.L.R. 542.
[87] *Per* L. Alexander (1989) 63 S.California L.Rev. 1, 17–18. And see also J. Hardisty (1979) 55 Indiana L.J.41, 53–55.
[88] Or distinguish.
[89] *Per* L. Alexander, *op. cit.*, n. 87, p. 18.
[90] *Op. cit.*, n. 2, p. 177.
[91] *Op. cit.*, n. 85, pp. 35–36.
[92] See, *e.g* J. Stone, *Legal System and Lawyers' Reasonings* (1964), pp. 267–280; A. Goodhart (1954) 22 M.L.R. 117.
[93] *Op. cit.*, n. 87, p. 18.
[94] *ibid.*, p. 19.
[95] *ibid.*, p. 27.
[96] See M. Moore in *op. cit.*, n. 81, pp. 186–187.

*precedent and narrowing/modifying a precedent is not a practice of the rule model of precedent".*[97] Of course, distinguishing is the very life-blood of precedent: a model which cannot account for such a central feature of the practice fails.

The third model is the result model. According to this model, the result reached in the precedent case, rather than any rule explicitly or simply endorsed by the precedent court is what binds. As compared with the natural model, the result model gives the result in the precedential case more constraining scope than it "naturally" carries. The result model can be formulated in two ways. In the first formulation, a constrained court "must decide its case for the party analogous to the winner in the precedent case if the constrained case is as strong or stronger a case for that result than the precedent case was for its result".[98] This is a way of "giving meaning to the injunction 'treat like cases alike' ".[99] In the second formulation, the constrained court is required to decide "analogously to the precedent court if in a world in which the precedent court's decision were correct, the analogous decision by the constrained court would be correct".[1] But whether these two formulations are all that different may be doubted.

Of the three models the second (the rule model), though it has problems, explains most. The natural model does "not represent any sort of legal doctrine of precedent. Although it instructs courts to take account of changes in the world effected by prior judicial decisions, that fully exhausts its force".[2] The result model requires the court constrained by precedent to answer an unanswerable question *viz.,* "What would be a correct decision in a world in which the precedent court's incorrect decision were correct?"[3] The rule model can only work if we can find some way of settling what is to count as the rule. It also asks of us that we accept that precedent courts have a legislative role, and this will not be acceptable to all. Which of the models if any fits the practice of the courts? There can be little doubt that in England it is the rule model.

Alexander has suggested that the three models mirror three different approaches to the nature of law. Using Dworkin's terminology,[4] he argues that the natural model of precedent is "pragmatism", the result model reflects "law as integrity" and the rule model "conventionalism". If this leads us to a conclusion that our courts follow positivistic thinking about law, it may bear out our sense of judicial practice.

---

[97] *Op. cit.,* n. 87, p. 19 (italics in the original).
[98] *ibid.,* pp. 29–30. Alexander describes this *(op. cit.,* n. 87, p. 507) as the "*a fortiori* case" formulation of the model.
[99] *ibid.,* p. 30.
[1] *Op. cit.,* n. 87, p. 507.
[2] *ibid.,* p. 510.
[3] *ibid.*
[4] *Law's Empire* (1986), Chaps 4, 5, 6.

### JUDGES AND DISCRETION[5]

It has long been received opinion that judges filled in the gaps left by rules by using their discretion. Positivistic jurisprudence from Austin to Hart placed emphasis on the part played by judicial discretion. "In these cases it is clear", Hart has written, "that the rule-making authority must exercise a discretion, and there is no possibility of treating the question raised by the various cases as if there were one uniquely correct answer to be found, as distinct from an answer which is a reasonable compromise between many conflicting interests."[6] A competing twentieth-century view was espoused by the Realists who emphasised the paramountcy of the judge's discretion.[7]

So long as discretion was taken as a "given", little attention was devoted to an analysis of it. However, a determined effort has been made by Ronald Dworkin,[8] Rolf Sartorius[9] and others[10] to cast doubt on orthodox opinion. It is the thesis of Dworkin that judicial discretion in what Dworkin calls its strong sense[11] does not exist.

Received orthodoxy held that judges filled in the gaps left by rules of law by using their discretion. By whatever name it is called, in effect they "legislated". Austin saw no problem or danger in this: judges were merely making up for the "negligence or the incapacity of the avowed legislator".[12] Hart saw rules as "open-textured": however smoothly they worked over the great mass of run-of-the-mill cases, at some point their application became indeterminate. "In every legal system a large and important field is left open for the exercise of discretion by the courts and the other officials in rendering initially vague standards determinate".[13]

For Hart there are three reasons for indeterminacy. First, language itself is indeterminate: words contain a central core of certainty of meaning but invariably also a "penumbra of doubt". A statute prohibiting the use of vehicles in a park clearly applies to lorries and buses, but its application to the use of skate boards or to the mounting of a World War II tank on a memorial pedestal is less clear. The judge, according to Hart has a discretion, "a choice", but there are constraints: he may add a new case "because of resemblances which can reasonably be defended as

---

[5]  For the view that this is understood by different writers in different ways, and the attempt to elucidate the issues involved, see Hoffmaster (1982) 1 Law & Phil, 21.

[6]  *The Concept of Law*, p. 132. See also the "Postscript" at p. 272 and 71 Harv. L. Rev. 593.

[7]  Holmes for example referred to "the sovereign prerogative of choice" (*Collected Legal Papers* (1920), p. 239).

[8]  See (1963) 60 J. of Phil. 624, *Taking Rights Seriously* (revised ed., 1978) (hereafter *TRS*), particularly Chaps 2, 3, 4, 13.

[9]  (1968) 78 *Ethics* 173; (1971) 8. Amer. Phil. Q.151. The ideas contained in these articles are substantially repeated in Chap. 10 of *Individual Conduct and Social Norms*.

[10]  For example see Christie (1968) 78 Yale L.J. 1311; Hughes (1967) 77 Yale L.J. 411.

[11]  *TRS*, pp. 31–39, 68–71.

[12]  *Lectures in Jurisprudence* (ed. Campbell), p. 219. See also Hart, *The Concept of Law*, p. 132.

[13]  *ibid.*, p. 136.

both legally relevant and sufficiently close".[14] Secondly, rules use very general standards: reasonableness, just and equitable, a "safe" system of work. And, thirdly, there is indeterminacy inherent in the common law system of precedent.[15]

It would be fair to say that so long as this view was treated relatively unproblematically, there was little attention given to discretion, to its meaning, its role if any and its problems. Nor was it realised how central adjudication was to legal theory.[16] But the positivist account has been subjected to a sustained challenge by Ronald Dworkin. It is the thesis of Dworkin that judicial discretion in, what he calls, its "strong" sense[17] does not exist. Dworkin's understanding of this and his own inter-pretivism were considered in Chap. 7.

## JUDGE-MADE LAW

There remains a consensus of opinion that, within certain narrow and clearly defined limits, new law is created by the judiciary.[18] Attention centres primarily not so much on the *fact* of judicial legislation but rather on the ways in which this occurs, and the motives, attitudes and reasoning which underlie the development of the law by this means, the constitutional and technical hazards of judicial law-making.[19] Thus it is realised that in a sense whenever a court applies an established rule or principle to a new situation or set of facts (or withholds it from these new facts) new law is being created. But this process is inevitably a very gradual and piecemeal one, a step-by-step progression, graphically described in Holmes's phrase of legislating "interstitially",[20] that is, within the interstices of the existing fabric of the law. Sometimes indeed, a

---

[14] *ibid.*, p. 127.
[15] On indeterminacy see J. Coleman and B. Leiter in (ed.) A. Marmor, *Law and Interpretation* (1995), p. 203, and T. Endicott, *Vagueness in Law* (2000).
[16] Realism may have sensed this but legal theory remained peripheral to much Realist writing. The early Realists went even further than positivism in emphasising discretion: Gray's view was that "all law is judge-made law" (*The Nature and Sources of Law*, p. 125).
[17] *TRS*, pp. 31–39, 68–71. An official has discretion in a strong sense when he is "not bound by standards set by the authority in question." Discretion exits in a "weak" sense where standards cannot be applied mechanically but demand the use of judgement. It is also sometimes used in this sense to make the point that the official's decision is non-reviewable.
[18] The most trenchant demolition of the long-prevailing myth is Frank, *Law and the Modern Mind* (1930), pp. 44–45. Lord Devlin has expressed the view that judicial creativity is permissible in the common law but not in relation to statute law. He further opines that activism, as he calls it, must operate "within the consensus" so that where there is not a consensus judges should not act creatively. *The Judge* (1979), Chap. 1. Lord Scarman agrees that the decisions of judges can play only a peripheral part in keeping the law in touch with modern developments (HL, vol. 437, col. 634).
[19] Jaffe, *English and American Judges as Law Makers* (1969), pp. 34–35 raises a number of questions: by what warrant, and in what senses, is the judiciary authorised to make law? What, if any, are the effective limits upon the exercise of judicial power? What problems flow from its being an ad hoc decisional process? Can the judiciary be trusted to move in the right direction?
[20] *Southern Pacific Co. v. Jensen* (1917) 244 U.S. 205, 221.

court may take a bolder step, by laying down a new rule or principle which itself contains the potentiality of creative expansion and development. Even here new law is virtually never created completely *in vacuo*, for the court will strive to follow such analogies as are to be derived from established legal principle and to root its decision so far as may be in the past rulings. Thus was the decision come to in such a leading case as *Rylands* v. *Fletcher*; similarly a court may, as in *Donoghue* v. *Stevenson*, find itself obliged to choose between conflicting lines of past cases, and may settle for a comparatively bold generalisation in favour of one of those choices, while striking out for it a wider field than may have seemed implicit in the earlier decisions.

Nor is it only in the common law field that new law is created judicially, for the same process is at work in the sphere of statutory construction. Modern English legislative theory and practice seeks to fetter the judge by very detailed drafting, which attempts however unsuccessfully to envisage all the situations which the legislator intends to be covered, and by the doctrine that the courts must apply only the words of the statute, and cannot apply them by analogy to new cases not explicitly covered by these words. Yet this approach is of little avail to restrain a court which is mindful to apply what it regards as the real sense or meaning of the statue. Moreover, there are even modern English statutes which resemble the Continental type of legislation, by laying down no more than broad general principles or conceptual ideas, and leaving the courts to expound their meaning and scope.[21]

It is the traditional framework within which a judge operates, and the fact that his whole professional training and background tend to induce caution, that nearly everywhere cause courts to "soft-pedal" the creative side of their activities.[22] This is particularly apparent when a court is being pressed too hard or too far in favour of what it regards as a novel proposition; in such a case it will be very apt to say that however unsatisfactory the law may be, the court merely applies and cannot change the law, which remains the exclusive province of the legislature. Nor indeed, even if one acknowledges the creative side of the judicial process, can one ignore the element of fundamental truth which resides in such an asseveration, for the constricted framework within which judicial legislation functions renders it different in kind from ordinary legislation. The legislature—apart from any constitutional limitations—is legally, if not *de facto*, free to make innovations as it sees fit and deal in an abstract way with all future cases; a court, on the other hand, is limited to the actual issues and the parties before it, and is to an extent restricted by the scope

---

[21] See B. Markesinis (2000) 59 C.L.J. 294 for a comparison with Germany, P. Bobbitt, *Constitutional Interpretation* (1991) on the courts' role in interpreting constitutions of the American type. In relation to the U.K. Human Rights Act 1998 see S. Fredman (2000) 53 C.L.P. 99.

[22] "Men who become judges are all of one type: they do not seriously question the *status quo*; their ambition is to serve the law and not be its master." See Devlin (1976) 39 M.L.R. 1, 8.

of legal aid, and operates within a traditional framework and subject to the force of professional opinion[23] of what is good law, and the possibility of being reversed on appeal. It is, therefore, hardly surprising that courts are fairly reluctant to avow their own creative function, so limited does it appear to any particular court in any individual case. Even in a legal system where the legislative power of the judiciary is explicity conceded, as with the provision of the Swiss Civil Code to the effect that the judge may, in the last resort, fill gaps in the law by applying the rule he would have laid down if acting as legislator,[24] it is significant that this provision has been hardly ever acted upon, the courts preferring to develop new law by interpretation of well-tried and established legal principles.

However, this has not been the German experience. "The German Pandectists, like lawmakers in other countries, had failed to see the problems raised by large concentrations of economic power and new forms of industrial organisation."[25] Further, there was legislative impotence in the face of post-war economic catastrophe. The result was that the courts, spurred on by jurists like Oertmann, filled the gaps. They did this by, what Hedemann has called, "the flight into general clauses". Of these the most notable were Articles 242[26] and 826,[27] which gave enormous scope for judicial participation, the opportunity being grasped with open hands. There was, of course, continuing and increasing resort to general clauses under the Nazis, though Dawson believes that this was "in large part a working out of ideas that had germinated before 1933".[28]

Yet within the severely constricted field of judicial law-making there is scope for the broader or narrower approach according to whether the courts are endeavouring consciously to develop the law relatively freely to meet new social and economic conditions, or whether, in a spirit of conservatism, the aim is to tie legal development pretty literally to the precise enunciations of previous judges. The contrast here is sometimes expressed as between judicial valour and judicial timidity,[29] and certainly we may contrast the bold vision of Lord Mansfield with the outlook of some of his contemporaries, or the black-letter law of Baron Parke with the wide judicial sweep of Blackburn J.; nor are similar contrasts lacking at the present day. Yet even the highest measure of judicial valour must nevertheless heed the restraints to which we have previously referred, though it may find room even within those narrow limits for much useful

---

[23] In France juristic thought, notably that of Maury, has stressed that it is acceptance of newly-made *jurisprudence* by professional opinion that makes the law, so created, law.

[24] Art. 1.

[25] Dawson, *op. cit.*, p. 464.

[26] "The obligor is bound to carry out his performance in the manner required by good faith with regard to prevailing usage."

[27] "Whoever causes injury to another intentionally in a manner offending good morals is bound to repair the injury."

[28] *Op. cit.*, p. 478, Examples of the use of general clauses both before 1933 and after are found in Dawson, *op. cit.*, pp. 461–479, and Schlesinger, *Comparative Law* (3rd ed., 1970), pp. 498 *et seq.*

[29] *Cf.* the respective judgments of Denning and Asquith L.JJ. in *Candler v. Crane, Christmas and Co.* [1951] 2 K.B. 164.

creative work, as witness for instance the effect of the great case of *Do-noghue* v. *Stevenson*. It is sometimes said that today there is little or no scope for the judicial creation of fresh common law principles.[30] But, whilst the scope is much diminished, there is always judicial creativity.

## JUDICIAL REASONING

If, within limits, courts have a choice to decide which way decisions are to go, what is it, if anything, that governs or controls that choice? Certainly not mere logical deduction or inference[31] in the sense of syllogistic reasoning, for legal rules, ideas, and concepts are expressed in words, whose uncertain sphere of operating precludes the statement of legal reasoning in the rigidly defined terms by which conclusions may be logically deduced from stated premises.[32] Nor is this surprising, for not only do legal rules and concepts depend for their usefulness on their very indefiniteness and flexibility, but as Holmes remarked in one of his most striking phrases, "the life of the law has been not logic but experience."[33]

Ordinary language, in which law is necessarily expressed (for how otherwise could its contact with real life be maintained?) is not an instrument of mathematical precision but possesses what has been described as an "open texture."[34] Some part of the meaning of words is

---

[30] See *per* Devlin J. in (1956) *Current Legal Problems*, pp. 11–15. But note the willingness to sweep away the outmoded: *e.g.* the marital rape immunity (see *R. v. R.* [1991] 3 W.L.R. 767 and the *doli incapax* presumption (*C. v. DPP* [1994] 3 All E.R. 190).

[31] For the various types of inferences drawn by courts, see W.A. Wilson (1963) 26 M.L.R. 609. See also Ryle, *The Concept of Mind* (1949), pp. 121–122: "a law is used as, so to speak, an inference-ticket", and Gottlieb, *The Logic of Choice* (1968), for an examination of the concept of rule and rationality with regard to legal reasoning.

[32] MacCormick, in *Legal Reasoning and Legal Theory* (1978), presents an argument in favour of the view that legal reasoning can and should possess a formal deductive structure, though he admits this is not always so, in view of the open-textured character of many legal rules (see particularly p. 52, and pp. 65–66). A. Wilson provides an effective refutation in (1982) *Legal Studies* 269; see also MacCormick's "Brief reply" (*ibid.*, at 286). The contention is whether a so-called logical conclusion can be reached in a legal argument in cases which are not legitimately to be described as "trivial".

[33] *Common Law*, p. 1. It has been suggested that this "striking phrase" is but the progeny of Jhering's more tortuous passage: "Life is not here to be a servant of concepts, but concepts are here to serve life. What will come to pass in the future is not postulated by logic but by life, by trade and commerce, and by human instinct for justice." This is quoted by Zweigert and Siehr in (1971) 19 Am. J. Comp. L. 215, 226. Holmes *had* read this passage. See de Howe, *Holmes, The Proving Years*, vol. II, p. 152.

[34] See F. Waismann, on "Verifiability" in *Logic and Language* (ed. A.G.N. Flew), pp. 1, 119. *Cf.* the discussion between Hart and Fuller, on the "core" and "penumbra" of meaning, in (1958) 71 Harv. L. Rev. 593 *et seq.* See also H.L.A. Hart, *Concept of Law*, Chap. 7. Gottlieb, *op. cit.*, Chap. 8 supports Fuller's advocacy of the role of purpose in the application of rules. He believes that purpose can be used to *preclude* the application of a rule in situations which seem to fall squarely within its language when such application would lead to results entirely alien to it purpose (p. 109). An example would be a statute which prohibited "vehicles" from parks: would the mounting on a pedestal of a truck used in the war fall within the ban? One might object that it would be an eyesore, but aesthetic appearance is not the object of the statute. Unfortunately, the difficulty with "purpose" as a test is its elusiveness and indeterminacy. See Hart, *ibid.*, p. 128. See also Summers, in *More Essays in Legal Philosophy* (Summers ed., 1971), pp. 101, 117–119. And see *ante*, 1546.

given by ordinary usage, but this does not carry one far in those peripheral problems which law courts have to solve in applying words, and legal rules expressed in words. We all know what a highway is, but does it for the purpose of a particular rule, include a pavement or a forecourt? Is a flying-boat a "ship"?[35] Does the rule of negligence impose a duty regarding oral utterances?[36] Such questions do not call so much for logical answers as for *decisions*. Rules of law are not linguistic or logical rules but to a great extent *rules for deciding*[37]

Does this mean that questions for legal decision are really questions of words, whose decision is essentially arbitrary, in the sense that the decision in any particular case might just as well have gone one way as another? The reply to this may be left to Wisdom.[38] As he points out, such a view is to "distort and denigrate legal discussion,"[39] for it ignores the way that rational persuasion proceeds, by setting a problem in a certain context of like and different cases, and showing how certain factors or reasons may be brought to bear in order to satisfy us that one course rather than any other or others is desirable or "right". The mistake here is to expect a chain of deduction or demonstrative reasoning, for this is not how ordinary rational argument works. It is rather a question of presenting a succession of cumulative reasons which severally co-operate in favour of saying what the reasoner desires to urge: "the legs of a chair, not the links of a chain."[40] But this is really the very opposite of the "arbitrary", which suggests a purely haphazard, irrational and fortuitous conclusion though, as Hughes points out, this is not to suggest that the real explanation of the decision, its *motivation*, may not be contained in its reasoning.[41] The essence of legal reasoning is in all essentials, save that the lawyer engages in a more searching inquiry for *precise* reasons for his decisions, comparable to the process of reasoning in ordinary life, whether concerned with ethical or practical problems.[42] Thus when we decide that something is good or desirable, beautiful or ugly, we mean to express a judgement. This may be intended as a expression of a subjective emotion, but more often it involves implicitly or explicitly the idea that we can give reasons in support of that judgement. So too, if a practical

---

[35] *Cf. Polpen v. Commercial Union* [1943] K.B. 161. Or see the similar reasoning of Anscombe, *Intention* (1954), pp. 58–64.

[36] See *Hedley Byrne Ltd v. Heller* [1964] A.C. 465.

[37] *Cf.* A.G.N. Flew, *op. cit.*, pp. 3–4. And *cf.* A.J. Ayer: "The acceptance of a rule does not put us into a strait jacket. We are left free to decide at any given point what the rule enjoins or forbids" *Philosophy in the Twentieth Century* (1982), pp. 147–148.

[38] *Post*, 1577.

[39] See Wisdom, in *Polemic No. 4* (1946) and in *Philosophy and Psychoanalysis* (1953), p. 249.

[40] *Cf.* Hart in Arist. Proc. Suppl. vol. 29, pp. 257–264, who cites *Re Makein* [1955] Ch. 194 as an interesting illustration.

[41] See G. Hughes, in *Law, Reason and Justice* (Hughes ed.) (1969), p. 101. Levi has commented that "the function of articulated judicial reasoning is to help protect the court's power by giving some assurance that private views are not masquerading behind public view" (in *Law and Philosophy* (Hook ed., (1964), p. 281). On this see C. Perelman in 3 Israel L. Rev. 1, 3–4.

[42] The lawyer's reasoning is also fortified by highly developed procedures and techniques, covering such matters as fact-finding and recording and analysing previous decisions.

decision is called for, such as the choice of a profession or of a candidate by a selection committee, the choice *may* be purely arbitrary, but more likely will be based on a weighing of reasons why one rather than another choice is to be made. Such a choice is not *logical* in the sense of being deductively inferred from given premises, but it has a kind of logic of its own, being based on rational considerations which differentiate it sharply from arbitrary assertion.[43]

Legal rulings, not being statements of fact or logical inferences, cannot be treated as in themselves true or false, for such a criterion is inapplicable to decisions involving choice between alternatives. They can however be properly regarded as right or wrong, or good or bad, in the sense that they either are or are not based upon cumulative reasons which are found to be acceptable.[44] Of course the notion of "acceptability" necessarily involves the need for some agreement as to what are ultimately the valid criteria for resolving a dispute, for if there were no such common or widely approved grounds it would be impracticable to settle any dispute whatever.[45] In practice, however, broad agreement of this kind does generally exist in law as in everyday problems, and this is a factor of human social life based on experience, and without which no community could survive or indeed come into existence at all. This does not mean that these so-called ultimate criteria are absolutes in a natural law sense, but simply that it is senseless to ask for justification of criteria which are *ex hypothesi* to be treated as ultimate for a particular purpose and within a particular community. And though their origin may be in some instances ethical, they may equally derive from practical experience, custom, or tradition.

Moreover courts, like ordinary people, may and generally do employ differing criteria, reflecting varying attitudes toward the solution of the problems with which they are called upon to deal. Cardozo's celebrated discussion of the four methods of the judicial process[46] is really concerned to draw attention to such varying criteria as commonly underlie judicial reasoning. Thus custom, tradition, historical development, sociological utilitarianism, and ethics all play their part. As for what Cardozo describes as the method of philosophy, or following along the line of logical progression, what is here involved is not logical deduction in the strict sense but the rational use of *analogy*, whereby a case is compared with like and unlike, so as to determine the "proper" scope of a legal rule. No analogy is compelling in a purely logical sense as leading to a

---

[43]  For an attempt to elaborate a new kind of logic relevant both to legal problems and to everyday reasoning, see Toulmin, *Uses of Argument* (1958).

[44]  *Cf.* Weldon, *Vocabulary of Politics*, p. 44. As Popper has remarked, arguments cannot determine decisions, but this does not mean that we cannot be helped by such arguments; on the contrary, it is most helpful to analyse the consequences likely to result from different alternatives between which we have to choose (*The Open Society and its Enemies*, vol. II, p. 232). *Cf.* Ladd, in *Rational Decision* (Friedrich ed., 1964), pp. 126, 128, where the emphasis is on "rational decisions" rather than correct ones.

[45]  *Cf.* Toulmin, *Reason in Ethics*, Chap. 14.

[46]  *Post*, 1571.

*necessary* conclusion; but as a practical matter human beings do reason by analogy, and find this a useful way of arriving at normative or practical decisions. Here again, even in what Cardozo characterises as the logical method, the basis of this approach is primarily human experience of the efficiency and utility of analogical reasoning.

A standard account of reasoning, like Levi's,[47] which emphasises analogical reasoning, has its limitations. Whilst there is value in similarity judgements, there is also incompleteness. What are the properties to which the similarity claim refers? Just as any two objects may be alike in any number of respects, so two cases may be. Defendants in two cases may both have the surname Brown and may both live in Leeds. They may both be bakers and season ticket holders at Leeds United. It is almost certain that none of these similarities will have any relevance. But what is a relevant property? As White explains: "while relevance and importance of similarities must be restricted *in some way*, there is no *single correct way* to make the necessary restriction".[48] And there will be different views. One answer, though it seems over-mechanical, is to count similarities : this case has more similarities to x than to y so it is to x that the judge should look. But counting similarities is anyway no solution because we must know what to count and what to exclude. "There is no normatively independent way of counting similarities and thus no value-neutral way of deciding which of two conflicting lines of precedent is the correct line to employ in justifying a decision in a case".[49] An additional problem is that most "hard cases" raise a number of different issues. A precedent that is similar to the new case may only be similar in relation to one issue and another case may have greater similarities as regards another. And an inference drawn from analogy may assist a claimant on one issue and a defendant on another. Thus, analogies require evaluation and "in the process they inevitably become embedded in a wider web of legal reasoning which must include non-analogical normative elements".[50]

This has led some to deny the importance of reasoning by analogy for legal reasoning. For Eisenberg[51]: "Reason cannot be used to justify a normative conclusion on the basis of an example without first drawing a maxim or rule". For others, Dworkin for example, reasoning from precedent is, as we have seen, a preliminary phase of legal interpretation. The dimension of "fit" is an appeal to precedent.[52] But meeting the goal of fit is only part of the process. The judge must also "try to show legal

---

[47] *An Introduction to Legal Reasoning* (1949) and *post*, 1582.
[48] "Analogical Reasoning" in (ed.) D. Patterson, *A Companion To Philosophy of Law and Legal Theory* (1996), pp. 283, 585. On the valuable use of analogical reasoning see L. Weinreb, *Legal Reason: The Use of Analogy in Legal Argument* (2005).
[49] *ibid.*
[50] *ibid.*, p. 586.
[51] *The Nature of The Common Law* (1988), p. 86.
[52] *See ante.*, 725.

practice as a whole in its best light".[53] So, according to Dworkin, "jurisprudence is the general part of adjudication, silent prologue to any decision at law".[54] This admission that a judge employs his own convictions[55] because they are believed to be the best morality would require is criticised by Eisenberg. "Almost everyone thinks his own moral convictions are the convictions that the best morality would require, and thinks the method by which he arrives at this conviction is the best method of arriving at moral convictions".[56]

Would it be easier—and perhaps of greater practical value—to seek the normative not in "philosophy" but rather, as Fuller did,[57] in the purposes of law? Or is this an equally difficult goal? Is there likely to be agreement, particularly in hard cases, as to the purposes of a legal rule? Take the oft cited fictional law which prohibits vehicles in parks.[58] Even with precedents providing conclusions the difficult cases will still require the purposes of the law to be teased out and there will not necessarily be consensus amongst interpreters as to what the law is for. There are difficulties both with Dworkin's approach and that of Fuller, but a recognition in both of the limitations of analogical reasoning in law, namely "whether or not a factual similarity between an undecided case and a precedent case is legally significant depends on generalized, or not at least generalizable, normative interpretation".[59]

## STATUTORY CONSTRUCTION[60]

One of the most important of judicial functions is the construction of statutes. It is here that one may discern the widest divergence between common law and continental practice. The former proceeds on the basis that the common law itself represents the basic fabric of the law, into which statutes are interwoven.[61] Hence the practice of drafting statutes in the fullest detail, and the broad assumption that a statute deals only with

---

[53] *Law's Empire*, p. 90.
[54] *ibid.*
[55] And see *ante*, 727.
[56] *Op. cit.*, n. 51, p. 194.
[57] (1946) 59 Harvard L.Rev. 376.
[58] See Hart, *The Concept of Law* (1994), pp. 128–129 and *ante*, 1546.
[59] *Op. cit.*, n. 2, p. 588.
[60] The word "construction," although treated as equivalent to "interpretation" in English legal practice, seems preferable at least in those cases where a court has to do more than extract a meaning from the use of particular words. See Devlin in (1958) 4 J.S.P.T.L. 208; and Ekelöf in *Scandinavian Studies in Law* (1958), p. 88. An excellent comparative study is MacCormick and Summers, *Interpreting Statutes* (1991).
[61] *Cf.* Kahn-Freund's remark that our matrimonial property law "rests on a number of *statutes*, but here is a case in which statutory law has become part of the legal mores to such an extent that the courts do not even bother to mention the legislative basis upon which their decisions rest. The principle of separation of property . . . is a living refutation of that outdated antithesis of principles of the common law as against mere provisions of statutes which you still sometimes find in the more old-fashioned books" (*Matrimonial Property*, The Josef Unger memorial lecture (1971). p. 10).

those cases which fall within its actual wording, and that there is no judicial power to "fill gaps" in a statute by arguments based on analogy,[62] although, as we have seen, this is the acknowledged way in which the common law itself may be developed by the courts. Continental theory, on the other hand, treats statutes (usually, but not necessarily, in codified form) as the basis of the law, but these tend to be drafted in a very general and abstract way, the task being left to the courts to fill in the details of the statutory provisions by reference to a presumed legislative intention. Moreover, it is generally accepted that gaps in the statute may be filled by analogical reasoning, on the footing that the legislature might be presumed to have desired to cover such cases if it had had these in contemplation.[63]

It would seem, therefore, that the English approach[64] is primarily based on ascertaining the plain meaning of the words used, whereas that of the civil law is directed to ascertaining the intention of the legislature.[65] This distinction may appear to explain why continental courts have recourse freely to *travaux préparatoires* or legislative material, whereas English courts were long reluctant to pay much attention to such materials, at least where they are trying to elicit Parliamentary intent.[66]

It is traditional to refer to three basic rules of statutory interpretation. That there are thought to be three rules or canons or conventions[67] can only be explained historically. The earliest "rule" was formulated in *Heydon's Case* in 1584. The mischief rule, as it came to be known, was repeated by Coke and was dominant in the case law until the nineteenth

[62] *Cf. Hancock v. Lablache* (1878) 3 C.P.D. 197, and *Baylis v. Blackwell* [1952] K.B. 154. But Lord Reid has suggested (*Federal Steam Navigation Co. v. Dept. of Trade* [1974] 2 All E.R. 97, 99–100) that words can be struck out of a statute "where without substitution the provision is unintelligible or absurd or totally unreasonable; where it is unworkable; and where it is totally irreconcilable with the plain intention showed by the rest of the statute." See also *Re Beaumont* [1980] 1 All E.R. 266, 270–271.

[63] Where the question of interpreting European instruments is concerned the courts, Lord Denning has assured us, will fill in gaps in "the European way" (*Bulmer v. Bollinger* [1974] 2 All E.R. 1226, 1237). But in *Felixstowe Dock v. British Transport Docks Board* (1976) C.M.L.R. 655, 664–665 he said that "once the bill is passed by Parliament and becomes a statute, that will dispose of all this dicussion about the Treaty. These courts will then have to abide by the statute, without regard to the Treaty at all." The courts have also said that, when interpreting an international convention, they should construe it so as to give effect to its presumed purpose. See *Buchanan v. Babco* [1977] 1 All E.R. 518, 522–523 and *cf.* the approach of the House of Lords [1977] 3 All E.R. 1048; *Ulster-Swift v. Taunton Meat* [1977] 3 All E.R. 641, 646. For the use of *travaux préparatoires* as an aid to the interpretation of international conventions forming part of English law see *Fothergill v. Monarch Airlines* [1981] A.C. 251 and *Quazi v. Quazi* [1979] 3 W.L.R. 833, 840. See, generally, Herman (1981) 1 *Legal Studies* 165.

[64] A good statement of this is in Lord Simon's judgment in *Maunsell v. Olins* [1975] A.C. 373, 391.

[65] On which see Merryman, *The Civil Law Tradition* (1985), Chaps IV–VIII, where this is explained in terms of the growth of state positivism leading to a state monopoly on law-making.

[66] See the view expressed in *Assam Railways v. C.I.R.* [1935] A.C. 455, though the House of Lord, in *Pepper v. Hart* [1993] A.C. 593 has evinced a great willingness to be receptive to such material. *See post*, 1561.

[67] See MacCallum in *Essays in Legal Philosophy* (1968 Summers, ed.), pp. 242–243. Holmes J. described them as "axioms of experience" in *Boston Sand v. U.S.* 108 U.S. 37.

century. The growth of parliamentary supremacy and the articulation of
the separation of powers doctrine led simultaneously with the emergence
of the will theories of law to the development in the early part of the
nineteenth century of what became known as the literal rule. Thus, in
1827[68] Lord Chief Justice Tenderden could refer to the dangers in giving
effect to the equity of a statute: it was better and safer, he opined, to rely
on and abide by the plain words of the statute. The move to literalism
was tempered by the development of the golden rule.[69] At times since then
the literal rule has seemed to be very much in the ascendant. Yet there is
considerable truth in the remark of Lord Diplock that "if one looks back
to the actual decisions of this House [*i.e.*, the House of Lords] on questions of statutory construction over the last thirty years one cannot fail to
be struck by the evidence of a trend away from the purely literal towards
the purposive construction of statutory provisions."[70] This trend has
continued in the 30 years since Lord Diplock made these remarks.

It is wrong to give the impression that there are now three distinct rules
of statutory interpretation.[71] For, whatever status is accorded them (and,
using Dworkin's terminology,[72] "principles" is arguably more accurate
that "rules") it has become clear, as Cross has written,[73] that the three
"rules" have been fused. Driedger[74] has put it this way: "First it was the
spirit and not the letter, then the letter and not the spirit, and now the
spirit and the letter." There seems now to be just one "rule" of interpretation, a revamped version of the literal rule which requires the general context[75] and purpose[76] to be taken into consideration before any
decision is reached concerning the ordinary (or, where appropriate, the
technical) meaning[77] of statutory words. The golden rule is a qualification

---

[68] In *Brandling v. Barrington*, 6 B. and C. 467, 475.
[69] Often attributed to Baron Parke in *Becke v. Smith* (1836) 2M. & W. 191, 195. Its origins
can be traced back earlier, *e.g.* to Parker C.B. in *Mitchell v. Torrup* (1766) Park. 227. See
now *Stock v. Frank Jones* [1978] 1 All E.R. 948, 954, 955.
[70] In *Carter v. Bradbeer* [1975] 3 All E.R. 158, 161. And see *Pepper v. Hart*, n. 66, at 617, *per*
Lord Griffiths.
[71] As Lord Simon does in *Cheng v. Governor of Pentonville* [1973] A.C. 931, where he says
that "English law has not yet authoritatively established any complete hierarchy among
the canons".
[72] *Ante*, 387, and Cross, *Statutory Interpretation* (1987), pp. 35–40.
[73] *Statutory Interpretation* (1987), pp. 18, 194.
[74] *The Construction of Statutes*, p. 2.
[75] Good illustrations of this process are *Davis v. Johnson* [1979] A.C. 264, *Stock v. Frank
Jones* [1978] 1 All E.R. 948, *Nothmann v. L.B. of Barnet* [1978] 1 All E.R. 1243 and
*Johnson v. Moreton* [1978] 3 All E.R. 37 and *Hanlon v. Law Society* [1980] 2 W.L.R. 765,
804.
[76] See *per* Lord Diplock in *Fothergill v. Monarch Airlines* [1981] A.C. 251, 280, and *per* Lord
Scarman in *Shah v. Barnet B.C.* [1983] 1 All E.R. 226, 238, with the added warning that
judges may not interpret statutes in the light of their own views of policy. See also
*Ashworth v. Ballard* [1999] 2 All E.R. 791, *R. v. Secretary of State for Environment, ex p.
Spath Holme* [2000] 1 All E.R. 884 and *A.-G. v. Associated Newspapers* [1994] 1 All E.R.
556.
[77] "What the court is concerned to ascertain is, not what the promulgators of the instrument mean to say, but the meaning of what they have said." *Per* Lord Simon in *Farrell v.
Alexander* [1977] A.C. 59 and see also his speech in *Stock v. Frank Jones* [1978] 1 All E.R.
948, 953.

of this, so that if the judge considers the application to the words in their ordinary sense would produce an absurd result which cannot reasonably be supposed to be the intention of the legislature, he may apply them in any secondary meaning which they are capable of bearing.[78] Reference has been made to the intention of the legislature. But what is meant by this? Much ink has been split in trying to answer that question. Radin[79] suggested it was a fiction. "The least reflection makes clear that the lawmaker ... does not exist ... A legislator certainly has no intention whatever in connection with words which some two or three drafted, which a considerable number rejected, and in regard to which the majority might have had, and often demonstrably did have, different ideas and beliefs."[80] Nor was it relevant for, "when the legislature has uttered the words of statute, it is *functus officio*."[81] Interpretation was a distinct job. It followed that preliminary materials had no relevance.

Landis's[82] reply attempted to distinguish two ideas in the concept "intent." It was "a confusing word, carrying within it both the teleological concept of purpose and the more immediate concept of meaning."[83] Meaning was discoverable: purpose was not. He deprecated the exclusionary rules for, it intent as meaning was to be found anywhere, it was in legislative records.

To Payne,[84] writing in 1956, statutory construction was an act of partnership. There being no *référé législatif*[85] the interpreter was called upon to use his discretion. The legislator delegated to the interpreter the task of determining the particular application of a general rule, rather as it delegated power to make subordinate legislation to a local authority. Just as the latter was circumscribed by the *ultra vires* doctrine, so the former must exercise *discretio*, but not *arbitrium*. In Glanville Williams's words: "a judge has a discretion to include a flying-boat within a rule as to ships or vessels; he has no discretion to include a motor car within such a rule."[86] Parliament often uses general words intentionally in the belief that judges are the most adept in filling in the details.

A most important contribution to this debate has come from Mac-Cullum.[87] He maintains that three distinct, yet rarely distinguished,

---

[78] See Cross, *op. cit.*, p. 15–17; *Maunsell v. Olins* [1975] A.C. 373, 391, *per* Lord Simon; *Pinner v. Everett* [1969] 3 All E.R. 257, 258, *per* Lord Reid; *Lord Advocate v. De Rosa* (1974) 2 All E.R. 849, 863, *per* Lord Simon.

[79] (1930) 43 Harvard L. Rev. 863

[80] *ibid.* at 870.

[81] *ibid.* at 871.

[82] (1931) 44 Harv. L. Rev. 886.

[83] *ibid.* at 888.

[84] (1956) *Current Legal Problems* 96.

[85] On which see Strömholm, 10 *Scandinavian Studies in Law* 178.

[86] (1945) 61 L.Q.R. 303. *Cf.* the oft-quoted U.S. Supreme Court ruling that an aeroplane was not a "motor vehicle" within the meaning of a Federal Statute (*McBoyle v. U.S.* (1931) 283 U.S. 25 (1931).

[87] In *Essays In Legal Philosophy* (Summers ed., 1968), p. 237 (originally in (1966) 75 Yale L.J. 754). See also J. Raz in (ed.) R. George, *The Autonomy of Law* (1996), p. 249, and essays by J. Waldron, L. Alexander and H. Hurd in (ed.) A. Marmor, *Law and Interpretation* (1995), pp. 329, 357 and 405.

questions may be asked of legislative intent: does it exist? Is it discernible? Is it relevant? The complexity of the first two questions leads him to conclude: does enough hang on such appeals [to legislative intent] to make their continuance worthwhile even in the face of the difficulties exposed? "Is it worth our while in terms of the ideological and practical importance of such appeals, to seek institutional changes strengthening the analogies between these appeals and appeals to intentions elsewhere in law and in life generally? ... Legislatures and institutional environments in which they operate are, in a sense, our creatures and can be altered."[88] Perhaps the most constructive part of his article is where he essays a number of models of legislative intent for "one may seek to bring the appeals [to legislative intent] closer to the conditions under which we attribute intentions to corporations, to principals *via* the intentions of their agents, or, above all, to individual men."[89]

But the search for legislative intent goes on.[90] This has led the courts to develop a number of conventions as a means of searching out intent. These may be classified as grammatical rules, such as the *ejusdem generis* rule,[91] and the rule *expressio unius exclusio alterius*,[92] and various presumptions, such as those restricting the construction of statutes which interfere with existing rights affecting the liberty of the subject, or which are penal in effect. But although the books are full of instances where such rules have been ostensibly applied, they are very apt to dissolve

---

[88] *Op. cit.*, p. 272.

[89] *ibid.*, pp. 273–273. The models are set out at pp. 262–271.

[90] *Cf.* Salmond, *Jurisprudence* (12th ed.), pp. 131–140. Nevertheless English Law has usually insisted on relating this intention if any to the date when the legislation was passed; see *Att.-Gen. v. Prince Augustus* [1957] A.C. 436; *Kingston Wharves v. Reynolds* [1959] A.C. 187. But this will not prevent a statute being applied to future circumstances, different though these may be from the situation at the date of the Act, where the language of the statute is apt to cover new situations not foreseeable at the date of the statute. Succeeding generations, therefore, to whom a statute may apply, can only reasonably be held bound by the meaning of its words *to them* (see J. Stone, *Law and the Social Sciences* (1966), p. 60). This advice was Court of Appeal followed by the in *Dyson Holdings v. Fox* [1975] 3 All E.R. 1030 where it was held (contrary to an earlier decision) that a tenant's childless cohabitant was a member of his "family" for the purpose of rent act legislation. James L.J. said: "the popular meaning given to the word 'family' is not fixed once and for all time. I have no doubt that with the passage of years it has changed" (p. 1035). Also in *R. v. Ireland* [1998] A.C. 147 and *Fitzpatrick v. Sterling Housing Association* [1999] 4 All E.R. 705.

[91] A modern authoritative definition of the rule is in Lord Diplock's speech in *Quazi v. Quazi* [1979] 3 W.L.R. 833, 839. It should not be thought that this rule involves a purely rational process. The legislature intends other *like* instances to be covered by their general categorising clause, but what is a "like" case may involve considerations of policy. In *Cleveland v. U.S.* (1946) 329 U.S. 14, a Mormon polygamist was indicted under the Mann Act of 1910 for transporting plural wives across state lines. The Act used the clause "prostitution, debauchery or any other immoral purpose." The Court convicted, holding polygamy to be an immoral purpose, as contrary to Christianity. It is thought that this interpretation went far beyond Congressional intention in passing, what was known as, the "White Slave Traffic Act".

[92] *R. v. Palfrey and Sadler* [1970] 2 All E.R. 12, where Winn L.J. pointed out that *alterius* meant "other of two" and that, in such a case, choice of one excluded the other. But "except in that special case, the maxim had no effect in logic or law" (p. 16). It is not a canon of construction that is applicable to judgments. See *D. v. NSPCC* [1977] 1 All E.R. 589, *per* Lords Simon and Diplock (at 596–597, 615).

away like chaff before the wind whenever the court feels at all strongly that another interpretation is to be preferred. In such cases the court may invoke the so-called rule in *Heydon's Case*, the "mischief" rule, which affords a platform for a broader approach. As for the notion that the court has no power to fill "gaps" in legislation, modern authority[93] supports this, yet if one looks at the way courts actually construe statutes it becomes apparent that courts are frequently engaged in doing just this very thing,[94] and indeed few statutes would prove workable if there were not some judicial freedom in this respect. This much was accepted by Lord Reid.[95] Yet all the reasons for judicial caution to which reference has already been made, operate here with redoubled force, and tend both to limit the degree to which courts will allow such constructions to be pushed, and also the extent to which they are willing openly to avow that they are really exercising a kind of supplementary legislative function.

The refusal of English courts for so long to make use of legislative material[96] did not turn so much on a fundamental difference of principle, but rather on the distinction between actual legislative practice under common law and civilian systems. For whether one accepts the "plain meaning" approach or that of a presumed and largely fictitious legislative intention, there is no reason in principle why courts should not avail themselves of whatever relevant material can be found in explanation or exposition of the meaning of statutes. Even the most literal approach must have regard to the context in which the words appear, and it is purely arbitrary whether that context is confined to the four corners of the statute itself, or may be derived from all the surrounding circumstances out of which that statute arose. English discussion of this question often hinged upon the desirability of the courts having to read the debates in Hansard, in order to find out the meaning of a statute.[97] Yet though continental practice does not forbid courts to peruse parliamentary debates for this purpose, they are generally regarded as having little bearing on the meaning of the language used. "Very few judges will take

---

[93] See Lord Roskill, *Current Legal Problems* (1984), p. 247, 253.

[94] See, *e.g.* such cases as *Rees v. Hughes* [1946] K.B. 517; *Cunliffe v. Goodman* [1949] 2 All E.R. 946; *Chandris v. Moller* [1951] 1 K.B. 240; *Wagg v. Law Society* [1957] Ch. 405; *Baker v. Sims* [1959] 1 Q.B. 114; *Lucy v. Henleys* [1970] 1 Q.B. 393; *Eddis v. Chichester Constable* [1969] 2 Ch. 345 (noted by Jackson (1969) 32 M.L.R. 691); *DPP v. Hester* [1973] A.C. 296.

[95] *Federal Steam Navigation v. DTI* [1974] 2 All E.R. 97, 100. Cross, *Statutory Interpretation*, p. 47 accepts what Lord Reid said as one of the basic rules of statutory interpretation in England.

[96] The earliest clear instance of this refusal appears to be *Millar v. Taylor* (1769) 4 Burr. 2303.

[97] Thus the laxer U.S. practice (which allows such material to be used) has been criticised for the abuses it engenders. So Frankfurter J. (47 Colum.L.Rev. 527, 543) quipped "only when legislative history is doubtful do you go to the statute" and Curtis, another critic, referred to "fumbling about in oceans of legal process for the shoddiest unenacted expressions of intention" (quoted in Law Commission Law Com. 21, p. 33)

the trouble to look these debates up in the official reports."[98] What the courts are really concerned to study are the various reports and comments of expert committees[99] and of the Minister charged with the progress of the bill, which take place at various stages prior to and in the course of the legislative process.[1] The bill itself will probably be drafted in a very general form, so that recourse will have to be had to the various expositions of its provisions and the discussion of disputed points, in order to obtain guidance as to how the bill, when enacted, should be applied. This legislative material is often, as in Sweden, published in a semi-official publication, and its contents are regarded as directives to the courts (though not all are of equal weight), which are less authoritive than the statute itself, but still an instrument for influencing judicial opinion, though a court is free to reject it. The draftsman himself is also expected to draft the bill with an eye on these directives, and Supreme Court judges are often themselves expert draftsmen, having at various times in their careers been engaged in advising upon the preparation and drafting of parliamentary bills. In Sweden, indeed, "they have been appointed to their office because of their capacity for that kind of work rather than because of their experience as judges."[2] Moreover, at least in the smaller continental countries, one or more of the judges dealing with a case may have been concerned in the drafting of a relevant statute, and will be expected to advise the court expertly on this matter, or it may be known which judges or lawyers were so concerned, and these may quite properly be consulted.[3] Continental lawyers see nothing odd in the attitude of those medieval English judges who reproved counsel by telling him: "Do not gloss the statute for we made it and understand better than you what it means."[4]

It is now accepted that the total exclusion of *travaux préparatoires* was

---

[98]  F. Schmidt (1957) 1 *Scandinavian Studies in Law* 170. In France the practice of consulting legislative materials is resorted to less than it was in pre-Gény positivist days. Today, the practice is to consult *travaux préparatoires* only where there is obscurity or ambiguity in the text. See Law Com. No. 21, para. 58.

[99]  In the uniform Commercial Code of the United States, each section is followed by a comment which is not part of the official Code but is used as a valuable aid to construction in litigation, and these comments have frequently been cited by the courts in their judgments on the construction of the Code.

[1]  For an illuminating discussion, see Ekelöf in (1958) 2 *Scandinavian Studies in Law* 77 and Strömholm in (1966) 10 *Scandinavian Studies in Law 175.*

[2]  F. Schmidt, *op. cit.,* pp. 178–179.

[3]  Ekelöf, *op. cit.,* pp. 92–93.

[4]  *Cf.* Plucknett, *Statutes and their Interpretation,* p. 49. But note the approach of Edmund Davies L.J. in *Lucy v. Henleys* (1970) 1 Q.B. 393 in referring to the report of which he was the chairman which led to the Limitation Acts 1963, the interpretation of which was in doubt. He noted that the problem under review had not been contemplated by the committee and added: "I take leave to doubt that such an unhappy outcome was envisaged by the sponsors of the Bill." But he commented: "Unfortunately that is an irrelevant consideration ... the law is found in statutes, not reports" (pp. 405–407).

not justified. There was no doubt that judges in England did consult Hansard.[5] Perhaps the strongest argument for excluding Hansard as an aid to interpretation is that the courts are concerned with the meaning to them, at that time, of words in a statute and less with what the legislature intended the words to mean at some time in the near or distant past.[6]

As far as pre-parliamentary materials are concerned, reports of the Law Commissions, Royal Commissions, etc., the "rule" about non-admissibility when it existed was less straightforward, more in doubt and less easy to justify. But as recently as 1975, the House of Lords was split on the extent to which such material could be used.[7] Both Viscount Dilhorne and Lord Simon were disposed to admit a report of a committee chaired by Lord Justice Greer which formed the basis of the statute under consideration as evidence of intention. Lord Simon, quoting Aneurin Bevan, asked: "why gaze in the crystal ball when you read the book?"[8] But against this, Lord Reid used logic. "If we are to refrain from considering expressions of intention in Parliament it appears to me that *a fortiori* we should disregard expressions of intention by committees or other commissions which reported before the bill was introduced."[9] And Lord Wilberforce cited "constitutional principle" to support excluding reports as evidence of intention. He was concerned lest the courts became "merely a reflecting mirror of what some other interpretation agency might say."[10]

The House of Lords has now decided[11] that, having regard to the purposive approach to construction of legislation the courts had adopted to give effect to the true intention of the legislature, the rule prohibiting courts from referring to parliamentary material as an aid to construction should be relaxed, so as to permit reference when legislation was ambiguous or obscure or the literal meaning led to an absurdity,[12] where the material relied on consisted of statements by a Minister or other promoter of the Bill together if necessary with other such parliamentary material as was necessary to understand such statements and their effect and the statements relied on were clear. It would appear that the

---

[5] Examples are *Letang v. Cooper* [1965] 1 Q.B. 232; *Lucy v. Henleys* [1969] 3 All E.R. 456; *Sagnata v. Norwich Corporation* [1971] 2 Q.B. 614; *Wachtel v. Wachtel* [1973] 1 All E.R. 829; *R. v. G.L.C., ex p. Blackburn* [1976] 3 All E.R. 184, 189; and *Davis v. Johnson* [1978] 1 All E.R. 841, 850–852 and *Hadmor Productions v. Hamilton* [1982] 1 All E.R. 1042.

[6] *Cf. Dyson Holdings v. Fox, ante,* 1558, and see J. Stone, *Law and the Social Sciences,* pp. 58 *et seq.*

[7] *Black-Clawson International v. Papierwerke* [1975] 1 All E.R. 810.

[8] *ibid.* at 847.

[9] *Black-Clawson, op. cit.,* p. 815.

[10] *ibid.*

[11] *Pepper v. Hart* [1993] A.C. 593. See further the discussion by Lord Steyn (2001) 21 Oxford J. Legal Studies 59 and S. Vogenauer (2005) 25 Oxford J. Legal Studies 629.

[12] A useful discussion of absurdity is J. Manning (2003) 116 Harvard L. Rev. 2387.

relaxation of the rule is intended to be narrow, but already the House of Lords has referred to Hansard where there was no ambiguity about the statutory language.[13] It seems to be assumed that recourse to Hansard will reveal legislative intent but there is justifiable concern that this may be misplaced optimism.[14]

A good deal of criticism has been levelled against the way English courts seem to swing from one type of statutory construction to another, one day interpreting a statute very narrowly, and another day favouring a broad approach. Is there room for a more systematic and rational approach? One suggestion put forward by Friedmann[15] and by Lord Evershed, is that statutes might be classified into categories, such as social purpose statutes, and technical statutes, and that different principles of construction might prevail in relation to each category. But it appears doubtful whether such categorisation is really practicable. Lord Evershed, after referring to the old doctrine of the "equity" of a statute,[16] whereby the courts had a certain latitude in stretching it to cover cases not expressly dealt with, makes the interesting suggestion that it might be as well to revive this doctrine and confer on the judiciary the function of rendering an Act just and workable and of giving effect to sensible solutions, unless the terms of the Act itself precluded this.[17] Such a change would doubtless entail a fundamental reversal of the present form of legislative drafting. Draftsmen and courts are at present engaged in a battle of wits, the draftsman seeking to anticipate the restrictive interpretations of the courts by inserting the most elaborately detailed provisions to ensure that particular situations are covered, which often has the unfortunate result of excluding from the effect of the statute equally relevant situations which were not actually thought of at the time.

Another approach, urged by a Swedish jurist, is that statutes should be drafted solely by reference to obvious cases. The courts should then determine the sphere of application of a statute by reference to the underlying purpose of those obvious cases, and should extend the statute to analogous cases, where this would further the purpose of the statute

---

[13] *Warwickshire C.C. v. Johnson* [1993] 1 All E.R. 299. See also *Stubbings v. Webb* [1993] 2 W.L.R. 120, *Chief Adjudications Officer v. Foster* [1993] 2 W.L.R. 292 (use of Hansard to confirm interpretations reached without it), *Miller v. Stapleton* [1996] 2 All E.R. 449 and *Michaels v. Harley House (Marylebone) Ltd* [1997] 3 E.R. 446. See also *R. v. Sec. of State for Environment, ex p. Spath Holme* [2000] 1 All E.R. 884.

[14] See V. Sacks (1982) Statute L. Rev. 143. See, generally, D. Miers (1993) 56 M.L.R. 695 and F. Bennion (1993) 14 Statute L. Rev. 149.

[15] *Law and Social Change in Contemporary Britain* (1951), pp. 239 *et seq.*

[16] See J. Manning (2001) 101 Columbia L. Rev. 1.

[17] "Impact of Statute on Law of England" in Proc. of Brit. Academy, vol. 42, pp. 261–262. See also Lord Evershed, "The Changing Role of the Judiciary in the Development of Law" (1961) 61 Col. L. Rev., p. 761. Lord Evershed puts in a plea that the rules of statutory interpretation should be reconsidered and formulated afresh, and that there should be a recession from the extreme elaboration of statutory form, and a return to a statement of the parliamentary intention so as to give some scope to a principle of interpretation designed to give rational and coherent effect to the statute (p. 789).

ascertained in this way.[18] In fact such a procedure is often in practice adopted by continental courts, even where the court itself, with traditional conservatism, purports to "subsume" a case under the actual principle or wording of a statutory provision. But such a method, at least in this explicit form, cuts right across the traditional English form of drafting and of statutory construction.[19]

An attempt to broaden the approach to statutory interpretation was made in New Zealand by the Acts Interpretation Act 1924, which lays down that "every Act shall be deemed remedial, and shall accordingly receive such fair, large and liberal construction and interpretation as will best ensure the attainment of the object of the Act according to its true intent, meaning and spirit." It is not altogether clear how frequently this provision is expressly cited to or relied upon by the courts, but it does appear to have exerted a silent influence upon professional and judicial attitudes in regard to this matter.[20]

## STATUTORY CONSTRUCTION AND DEMOCRACY

Implicit in every construction of a statute by a court is a theory of democracy. Often this is little more than a rhetorical concern for legislative supremacy. The similarity between the relationship of a principal and agent has been noted[21]: agents do what principals want, not what they themselves may think preferable. But what does this mean? What is the interpreter to do if the statutory language permits of more than one answer? How much discretion, and what kind of discretion does the

[18] Ekelöf, *op. cit.*, pp. 79 *et seq.*, who calls this the "teleological" method. But see the criticisms of a fellow-Scandinavian, in Schmidt, *op. cit.*, pp. 157 *et seq.*

[19] See, however, the most interesting discussion of the scope and method of judicial construction of statutes, *per* Lord Denning in *Escoigne Properties v. I.R.C.* [1958] A.C. 546, 565–566.

[20] For a discussion of this cardinal rule of statutory interpretation see Burrows (1969) 3 N.Z.U.L.R. 253, where it is suggested that this section "merely abolishes the distinction between penal and remedial statutes which existed at common law" (p. 277). "But . . . there can be no suggestion that the New Zealand courts are entitled to go any further, or be any more liberal, than are the English Courts in interpreting 'remedial' legislation" (p. 255). The section is currently in vogue as it enables a court to interpret a provision "as to conform to its ideas of what is socially necessary" (p. 278). However, judicial opinion is agreed that "its comforting philosophy offers no panacea" until legislative intent has been ascertained (*per* Haslam J. in *Nunn's v. Licensing Control Commission* [1967] N.Z.L.R. 76, 78) and that it is really "of limited assistance in the interpretation of statutes in which the true intent cannot be clearly ascertained from the text and historical and circumstantial context" (*per* Turner J. in *Gifford v. Police* [1965] N.Z.L.R. 484, 500). And see *Att. Gen. of New Zealand v. Ortiz* [1982] 3 All E.R. 432, 464, where Ackner L.J. accepted the argument that the Act did no more than abolish the old distinction between penal and remedial Acts and did not mean that the courts are required to adopt a purposive construction in every case. Australia has introduced similar legislation (Statute Law Revision Act 1981 discussed in (1981) Statute L. Rev. 181). D. Farber's empirical study is interesting. It found that it did not matter which theory of statutory construction a judge held since it made no difference to the conclusion reached (see (2000) 94 Northwestern University L. Rev. 1409).

[21] See C. Sunstein (1989) 101 Harv. L. Rev. 407.

interpreter have? Important questions are being raised and a corpus of
literature is developing, particularly in the United States, where assigning
a meaning to the Constitution has always been a fruitful source of controversy.[22] A result is a challenging of orthodoxy.

Thus, for example, orthodox (positivist) opinion holds that the
meaning of a statement is fixed at the end of the process of legislative
enactment. But writers such as Sunstein[23] and Eskridge[24] argue instead
for a dynamic theory of statutory meaning. Both reject the view that
statutory meaning is fixed at the moment of statutory creation. Into this
dynamic process these writers feed "background norms"[25] and larger
public values. Democracy, they argue, is about deliberation and dialogue.
This links to the stand taken by feminism,[26] postmodernism[27] and critical
race theory[28] which call to interpreters to hear voices historically silenced
and to inject at the level of interpretation the interests of the disadvantaged. To Sunstein the courts should self-consciously correct
"malfunctions in the legislative process".[29] He offers an extensive and
rank-ordered catalogue of principles which he claims will enhance such
values as "the promotion of public deliberation, the protection of his-
torically-disadvantaged groups, and the minimisation of naked interest
group transfers". The view held out here is of interpretation as compensation. It has affinities with the "law is politics" position found in
contemporary critical thought.[30]

Issues of the relationship between statutory construction and democracy are also explored by Dworkin's conception of legislatures and courts
as partnership.[31] The view that courts "complement" legislatures can be
traced to Henry Hart and Albert Sacks who conceived of statutory
construction as the "creative elaboration" of meaning by judges.[32] It was
their view that courts had to decide "what meaning *ought* to be given to
the directives of the statute".[33] They acknowledged the primacy of the
legislative role but urged courts to use "good faith and good sense" in
construing ambiguous language so as to ensure that statutory purpose
was effectuated.

To Dworkin the ideal in judging is to find the best justification for each
statute and, in so doing, to enable the polity to become a community of
principle, not just a "rulebook community".[34] Interpretation is thus

---

[22] Not least in the controversy fuelled by the Bork nomination.
[23] *Op. cit.*, n. 16. See also his *Rights Revolution* and *The Partial Constitution* (1993).
[24] (1987) 135 Univ. of Penn. L. Rev. 1479 and *Dynamic Statutory Interpretation* (1994).
[25] *Op. cit.*, n. 16, p. 460.
[26] See K. Bartlett, *ante*, 1359.
[27] See G. Peller and W. Eskridge (1991) 89 Mich. L. Rev. 707.
[28] See G. Torres (1991) 75 Minn. L. Rev. 993; G. Torres and K. Milun (1990) Duke L. J.
    625.
[29] *Per* C. Sunstein (1988) 97 Yale L. J. 1539, 1582.
[30] *Ante*, 1209.
[31] *Ante*, 721.
[32] In *The Legal Process* (1958), p. 1415. See also, *ante*, 1006.
[33] *ibid.*
[34] *Law's Empire*, p. 388.

central to the project to realise the ideals of "political integrity and fairness and procedural due process as they apply specifically to legislation in a bureaucracy".[35] The "chain novel"[36] metaphor is employed once again: judges are to collaborate, to be co-authors in the "chain novel" that is the law-making process.

Similar ideas are to be found in the new breed of American pragmatists.[37] Eskridge and Frickey,[38] for example, argue against "foundationalism"[39] seeing the democratic legitimacy claimed for such theories as a "chimera" because they replicate the problem of indeterminacy.[40] Eskridge and Frickey argue that pragmatism (and hermeneutics) can bring "all the relevant factors and all of our problem-solving skills to bear on difficult questions of statutory meaning in concrete situations" and in so doing achieve "legitimate statutory interpretation through deliberation and candour".[41] And they argue that "even without apparent consensus in society or in the legal community, the interpretation can often create some kind of agreement in the context of a narrow case, and through the case enlighten attitudes in the larger community".[42] The similarity with Dworkin's ideal of judges forging a community of principle cannot be overlooked. More unashamedly pragmatist still is Richard Posner who is critical of traditional approaches to statutory construction because they place "too much emphasis on authority, certitude, rhetoric and tradition, too little on consequences and on social-scientific techniques for measuring consequences".[43] He argues that "the best thing to do when a statute is invoked is to examine the consequences of giving the invoker what he wants and then estimate whether those consequences will on the whole be good ones".[44]

With citizenship now such a key concept, with questions of parliamentary democracy under scrutiny, with a new European dimension to British politics, with the passing of the Human Rights Act 1998 and with statutory construction itself in flux in the aftermath of *Pepper* v. *Hart*, the issues raised by these writers must challenge thinkers in this country to question the legitimacy of different models of statutory construction.[45]

---

[35] *ibid.*
[36] See *ante*, 725 and *ibid.*, pp. 228–250.
[37] See Symposium, (1990) 63 S. Calif. L. Rev. 1; S. Smith argues that Dworkin is a pragmatist (1990) 100 Yale L. J. 409, 412–24 (he rejects this in *Law's Empire, inter alia* at 167, 244, 378 and 410).
[38] (1990) 42 Stanford L. Rev. 321.
[39] Defined by Eskridge and Frickey (*ibid.*, p. 325) as theory that "seeks an objective ground ('foundation') that will reliably guide the interpretation of all statutes in all situations".
[40] *ibid.*, p. 383.
[41] *ibid.*
[42] *ibid.*, p. 384.
[43] *Problems of Jurisprudence* (1990), p. 465. See also, *ante*, 1004.
[44] *ibid.*, p. 300.
[45] A good critical account is B.B. Levenbook (2006) 12 *Legal Theory* 71.

**H.L.A. HART**
**Problems of the Philosophy of Law**
(1967)[46]

*Problems of Legal Reasoning*

There are ... two preliminary issues of peculiar concern to philosophers and logicians which demand attention in any serious attempt to characterize the forms of legal reasonings.

*Deductive Reasoning*

It has been contended that the application of legal rules to particular cases cannot be regarded as a syllogism or any other kind of deductive inference, on the grounds that neither general legal rules nor particular statements of law (such as those ascribing rights or duties to individuals) can be characterized as either true or false and thus cannot be logically related either among themselves or to statements of fact; hence, they cannot figure as premises or conclusions of a deductive argument. This view depends on a restrictive definition, in terms of truth and falsehood, of the notion of a valid deductive inference and of logical relations such as consistency and contradiction. This would exclude from the scope of deductive inference not only legal rules or statements of law but also commands and many other sentential forms which are commonly regarded as susceptible of logical relations and as constituents of valid deductive arguments. Although considerable technical complexities are involved, several more general definitions of the idea of valid deductive inference that render the notion applicable to inferences the constituents of which are not characterized as either true or false have now been worked out by logicians. In what follows, as in most of contemporary jurisprudential literature, the general acceptability of this more generalized definition of valid inference is assumed.

*Inductive Reasoning*

Considerable obscurity surrounds the claim made by more conventional jurisprudential writers that inductive reasoning is involved in the judicial use of precedents. Reference to induction is usually made in this connection to point a contrast with the allegedly deductive reasoning involved in the application of legislative rules to particular cases. "Instead of starting with a general rule the judge must turn to the relevant cases, discover the general rule implicit in them ... The outstanding difference between the two methods is the source of the major premise—the deductive method assumes it whereas the inductive sets out to discover it from particular instances" (G.W. Paton, *A Textbook of Jurisprudence* (2d ed., Oxford, 1951), pp. 171–172).

It is of course true that courts constantly refer to past cases both to discover rules and to justify their acceptance of them as valid. The past cases are said to be "authority" for the rules "extracted" from them. Plainly, one necessary condition must be satisfied if past cases are in this way to justify logically the acceptance of a rule: the past case must be an instance of the rule in the sense that the decision in the case could be deduced from a statement of the rule together with a statement of the facts of the case. The reasoning insofar as the satisfaction of this necessary condition is concerned is in fact an inverse application of deductive reasoning. But this condition is, of course, only one necessary condition and not a sufficient

---

[46] [From *Encyclopedia of Philosophy* (Edwards ed.), vol. 6, p. 264, now in *Essays in Jurisprudence and Philosophy*, Chap. 3, to which page references are made.]

condition of the court's acceptance of a rule on the basis of past cases, since for any given precedent there are logically an indefinite number of alternative general rules which can satisfy the condition. The selection, therefore, of one rule from among these alternatives as the rule for which the precedent is taken to by authority must depend on the use of other criteria limiting the choice, and these other criteria are not matters of logic but substantive matters which may vary from system to system or from time to time in the same system. Thus, some theories of the judicial use of precedent insist that the rule for which a precedent is authority must be indicated either explicitly or implicitly by the court through its choice of facts to be treated as "material" to a case. Other theories insist that the rule for which a precedent is authority is the rule which a later court considering the precedent would select from the logically possible alternatives after weighing the usual moral and social factors.

Although many legal writers still speak of the extraction of general rules from precedents, some would claim that the reasoning involved in their use of precedents is essentially reasoning from case to case "by example": A court decides the present case in the same way as a past case if the latter "sufficiently" resembles the former in "relevant" respects, and thus makes use of the past case as a precedent without first extracting from it and formulating any general rule. Nevertheless, the more conventional accounts, according to which courts use past cases to discover and justify their acceptance of general rules, are sufficiently widespread and plausible to make the use of the term "induction" in this connection worth discussing.

The use of "induction" to refer to the inverse application of deduction involved in finding that a past case is the instance of a general rule may be misleading: it suggests stronger analogies than exist with the modes of probabilistic inference used in the sciences when general propositions of fact or statements about unobserved particulars are inferred from or regarded as confirmed by observed particulars. "Induction" may also invite confusion with the form of deductive inference known as perfect induction, or with real or alleged methods of discovering generalizations sometimes referred to as intuitive induction.

It is, however, true that the inverse application of deduction involved in the use of precedents is also an important part of scientific procedure, where it is known as hypothetic inference or hypothetico deductive reasoning. Hence, there are certain interesting analogies between the interplay of observation and theory involved in the progressive refining of a scientific hypothesis to avoid its falsification by contrary instances and the way in which a court may refine a general rule both to make it consistent with a wide range of different cases and to avoid a formulation which would have unjust or undesirable consequences.

Notwithstanding these analogies, the crucial difference remains between the search for general propositions of fact rendered probably by confirming instances but still falsifiable by future experience, and rules to be used in the decision of cases. An empirical science of the judicial process is of course possible: it would consist of factual generalization about the decisions of courts and might be an important predictive tool. However, it is important to distinguish the general propositions of such an empirical science from the rules formulated and used by courts.

### Descriptive and Prescriptive Theories

The claim that logic plays only a subordinate part in the decision of cases is sometimes intended as a corrective to misleading descriptions of the judicial process, but sometimes it is intended as a criticism of the methods used by courts, which are stigmatized as "excessively logical," "formal," "mechanical," or "automatic." Descriptions of the methods actually used by courts must be distinguished from prescriptions of alternative methods and must be separately assessed. It is, however, notable that in many discussions of legal reasoning these two are often confused, perhaps because the effort to correct conventional mis-descriptions of the judicial process and the effort to correct the process itself have been inspired by the realization of the same important but often neglected fact: the relative indeterminacy of legal rules and precedents. This indeterminacy springs from the fact that it is impossible in framing general rules to anticipate and provide for every possible combination of circumstances which the future may bring. For any rule, however precisely formulated, there will always be some factual situations in which the question whether the situations fall within the scope of the general classificatory terms of the rule cannot be settled by appeal to linguistic rules or conventions or to canons of statutory interpretation, or even by reference to the manifest or assumed purposes of the legislature. In such cases the rules may be found either vague or ambiguous. A similar indeterminacy may arise when two rules apply to a given factual situation and also where rules are expressly framed in such unspecific terms as "reasonable" or "material". Such cases can be resolved only by methods whose rationality cannot lie in the logical relations of conclusions to premises. Similarly, because precedents can logically be subsumed under an indefinite number of general rules, the identification of *the* rule for which a precedent is an authority cannot be settled by an appeal to logic.

These criticisms of traditional descriptions of the judicial process are in general well taken. It is true that both jurists and judges, particularly in jurisdictions in which the separation of powers is respected, have frequently suppressed or minimized the indeterminacy of legal rules or precedents when giving an account of the use of them in the process of decision. On the other hand, another com-plaint often made by the same writers, that there is an excess of logic or formalism in the judicial process, is less easy to understand and to substantiate. What the critics intend to stigmatize by these terms is the failure of courts, when applying legal rules or precedents, to take advantage of the relative indeterminacy of the rules or precedents to give effect to social aims, policies, and values. Courts, according to these critics, instead of exploiting the fact that the meaning of a statutory rule is indeterminate at certain points, have taken the meaning to be determinate simply because in some different legal context similar wording has been interpreted in a certain way or because a given interpretation is the "ordinary" meaning of the words used.

This failure to recognize the indeterminacy[47] of legal rule (often wrongly ascribed to analytical jurisprudence and stigmatized as conceptualism) has sometimes been defended on the ground that it maximizes certainty and the predictability of decisions. It has also sometimes been welcomed as furthering an ideal of a legal system in which there are a minimum number of independent rules and categories of classification.

The vice of such methods of applying rules is that their adoption prejudges what is to be done in ranges of different cases whose composition cannot be exhaustively known beforehand: rigid classification and divisions are set up which ignore differences and similarities of social and moral importance. This is the burden of the complaint that there is an excessive use of logic in the judicial process. But the expression "an excessive use of logic" is unhappy, for when social values and distinctions of importance are ignored in the interpretation of legal rules and the classification of particulars, the decision reached is not more logical than decisions which give due recognition to these factors: logic does not deter-mine the interpretation of words or the scope of classifications. What is true is that in a system in which such rigid modes of interpretation are common, there

---

[47] [Indeterminacy is explored by L. Solum in (ed.) D. Patterson, *A Companion to Philosophy of Law and Legal Theory* (1996), p. 489.]

will be more occasions when a judge can treat himself as confronted with a rule whose meaning has been predetermined.

### Methods of discovery and standards of appraisal

In considering both descriptive and prescriptive theories of judicial reasoning, it is important to distinguish (1) assertions made concerning the usual process or habits of thought by which judges actually reach their decisions, (2) recommendations concerning the processes to be followed, and (3) the standards by which judicial decisions are to be appraised. The first of these concerns matters of descriptive psychology, and to the extent that assertions in this field go beyond the descriptions of examined instances, they are empirical generalizations or laws of psychology; the second concerns the art or craft of legal judgment, and generalizations in this field are principles of judicial technology; the third relates to the assessment or justification of decisions.

These distinctions are important because it has sometimes been argued that since judges frequently arrive at decisions without going through any process of calculation of inference in which legal rules or precedents figure, the claim that deduction from legal rules plays any part in decision is mistaken. This argument is confused, for in general the issue is not one regarding the manner in which judges do, or should, come to their decisions; rather it concerns the standards they respect in justifying decisions, however reached. The presence or absence of logic in the appraisal of decisions may be a reality whether the decisions are reached by calculation or by an intuitive leap.

### Clear cases and indeterminate rules

When the various issues identified above are distinguished, two sets of questions emerge. The first of these concerns the decisions of courts in "clear" cases where no doubts are felt about the meaning and applicability of a single legal rule, and the second concerns decisions where the indeterminacy of the relevant legal rules and precedents is acknowledged.

### Clear Cases

Even where courts acknowledge that an antecedent legal rule uniquely determines a particular result, some theorists have claimed that this cannot be the case, that courts always "have a choice," and that assertions to the contrary can only be ex post facto rationalizations. Often this scepticism springs from the confusion of the questions of methods of discovery with standards of appraisal noted above. Sometimes, however, it is supported by references to the facts that even if courts fail to apply a clearly applicable rule using a determinate result, this is not a punishable offence, and that the decision given is still authoritative and, if made by a supreme tribunal, final.[48] Hence, it is argued that although courts may show a certain degree of regularity in decision, they are never bound to do so: they always are free to decide otherwise than they do. These last arguments rest on a confusion of finality with infallibility in decisions and on a disputable interpretation of the notion of "being bound" to respect legal rules.

Yet scepticism of this character, however unacceptable, does serve to emphasize that it is a matter of some difficulty to give any exhaustive account of what makes a "clear case" clear or makes a general rule obviously and uniquely applicable to a particular case. Rules cannot claim their own instances, and fact situations do not await the judge neatly labelled with the rule applicable to them.

---

[48] [On the authority of law see V. Wellman in *op. cit.*, n. 47, p. 573.]

Rules cannot provide for their own application, and even in the clearest case a human being must apply them. The clear cases are those in which there is general agreement that they fall within the scope of a rule, and it is tempting to ascribe such agreements simply to the fact that there are necessarily such agreements in the use of the shared conventions of language. But this would be an over-simplification because it does not allow for the special conventions of the legal use of words, which may diverge from their common use, or for the way in which the meanings of words may be clearly controlled by reference to the purpose of a statutory enactment which itself may be either explicitly stated or generally agreed. A full exploration of these questions is the subject matter of the study of the interpretation of statute.

## Indeterminate Rules

The decisions of cases which cannot be exhibited as deductions from determinate legal rules have often been described as arbitrary. Although much empirical study of the judicial process remains to be done, it is obvious that this description and the dichotomy of logical deduction and arbitrary decision, if taken as exhaustive, is misleading. Judges do not generally, when legal rules fail to determine a unique result, intrude their personal preferences or blindly choose among alternatives; and when words like "choice" and "discretion," or phrases such as "creative activity" and "interstitial legislation" are used to describe decisions, these do not mean that courts do decide arbitrarily without elaborating reasons for their decisions—and still less that any legal system authorizes decisions of this kind.

It is of crucial importance that cases for decision do not arise in a vacuum but in the course of the operation of a working body of rules, an operation in which a multiplicity of diverse considerations are continuously recognized as good reasons for a decision. These include a wide variety of individual and social interests, social and political aims, and standards of morality and justice; and they may be formulated in general terms as principles, policies, and standards.[49] In some cases only one such consideration may be relevant, and it may determine a decision as unambiguously as a determinate legal rule. But in many cases this is not so, and judges marshal in support of their decisions a plurality of such considerations which they regard as jointly sufficient to support their decision, although each separately would not be. Frequently these considerations conflict, and courts are forced to balance or weigh them and to determine priorities among them. The same considerations (and the same need for weighing them when they conflict) enter into the use of precedents when courts must choose between alternative rules which can be extracted from them, or when courts consider whether a present case sufficiently resembles a past case in relevant respects.

Perhaps most modern writers would agree up to this point with this account of judicial decision where legal rules are indeterminate, but beyond this point there is a divergence. Some theorists claim that notwithstanding the heterogeneous and often conflicting character of the factors which are relevant to decision, it is still meaningful to speak of a decision as *the* uniquely correct decision in any case and of the duty of the judge to discover it. They would claim that a judicial choice or preference does not become rational because it is deferred until after the judge has considered the factors that weigh for and against it.

Other theorists would repudiate the idea that in such cases there is always a decision which is uniquely correct, although they of course agree that many

---

[49] [Goodrich argues that once it is admitted that such "extrinsic" factors operate in the indeterminate area of rule application it is difficult to exclude them from that of the so-called "clear cases." Accordingly, the certainty of the law even in its paradigm instances is "more rhetorical than actual." In this way an attack on the whole structure of legal positivism based on legal sources is directed ((1983) 3 *Legal Studies* 248, 264–266).]

decisions can be clearly ruled out as incorrect. They would claim that all that courts do and can do at the end of the process of coolly and impartially considering the relevant considerations is to choose one alternative which they find the most strongly supported, and that it is perfectly proper for them to concede that another equally skilled and impartial judge might choose the other alternative. The theoretical issues are not different from those which arise at many points in the philosophical discussions of moral argument. It may well be that terms like "choice," "discretion," and "judicial legislation" fail to do justice to the phenomenology of considered decision: its felt involuntary or even inevitable character which often marks the termination of deliberation on conflicting considerations. Very often the decision to include a new case in the scope of a rule or to exclude it is guided by the sense that this is the "natural" continuation of a line of decisions or carries out the "spirit" of a rule. It is also true that if there were not also considerable agreement in judgment among lawyers who approach decisions in these ways, we should not attach significance and value to them or think of such decisions as reached through a rational process. Yet however it may be in moral argument, in the law it seems difficult to substantiate the claim that a judge confronted with a set of conflicting considerations must always assume that there is a single uniquely correct resolution of the conflict and attempt to demonstrate that he has discovered it . . .                                [pp. 100–108]

## B. CARDOZO
### Nature of the Judicial Process
### (1921)

### *The Method of Philosophy*

The work of deciding cases goes on every day in hundreds of courts throughout the land. Any judge, one might suppose, would find it easy to describe the process which he had followed a thousand times and more. Nothing could be farther from the truth. Let some intelligent layman ask him to explain: he will not go very far before taking refuge in the excuse that the language of craftsmen is unintelligible to those untutored in the craft. Such an excuse may cover with a semblance of respectability an otherwise ignominious retreat. It will hardly serve to still the pricks of curiosity and conscience. In moments of introspection, when there is no longer a necessity of putting off with a show of wisdom the uninitiated interlocutor, the troublesome problem will recur, and press for a solution. What is it that I do when I decide a case? To what sources of information do I appeal for guidance? In what proportions do I permit them to contribute to the result? In what proportions ought they to contribute? If a precedent is applicable, when do I refuse to follow it? If no precedent is applicable, how do I reach the rule that will make a precedent for the future? If I am seeking logical consistency,[50] the symmetry of the legal structure, how far shall I seek it? At what point shall the quest be halted by some discrepant custom, by some consideration of the social welfare, by my own or the common standards of justice and morals? Into that strange compound which is brewed daily in the cauldron of the courts, all these ingredients enter in varying proportions. I am not concerned to inquire whether judges ought to be allowed to brew such a compound at all. I take judge-made law as one of the existing realities of life. There before us, is the brew. Not a judge on the bench but has had a hand in the making. The elements have not come together by chance. *Some* principle, however unavowed and inarticulate and subconscious, has regulated the infusion. It may not have been the same principle for all judges at any time, nor the same principle for any judge at all times. But a choice there

---

[50] [Logic is here used as equivalent to argument by analogy; *cf. ante*, 1552, *post*, 1579.]

has been, not a submission to the decree of Fate; and the considerations and motives determining the choice, even if often obscure, do not utterly resist analysis. In such attempt at analysis as I shall make, there will be need to distinguish between the conscious and the subconscious. I do not mean that even those considerations and motives which I shall class under the first head are always in consciousness distinctly, so that they will be recognized and named at sight. Not infrequently they hover near the surface. They may, however, with comparative readiness be isolated and tagged and when thus labeled, are quickly acknowledged as guiding principles of conduct. More subtle are the forces so far beneath the surface that they cannot reasonably be classified as other than subconscious. It is often through these subconscious forces that judges are kept consistent with themselves, and inconsistent with one another. We are reminded by William James in a telling page of his lectures on Pragmatism that every one of us has in truth an underlying philosophy of life, even those of us to whom the names and the notions of philosophy are unknown or anathema. There is in each of us a stream of tendency, whether you choose to call it philosophy or not, which gives coherence and direction to thought and action. Judges cannot escape that current any more than other mortals... [pp. 9–12]

...I have put first among the principles of selection to guide our choice of paths, the rule of analogy or the method of philosophy. In putting it first, I do not mean to rate it as most important. On the contrary, it is often sacrificed to others. I have put it first because it has, I think, a certain presumption in its favour. Give a mass of particulars, a congeries of judgments on related topics, the principle that unifies and rationalizes them has a tendency, and a legitimate one, to project and extend itself to new cases within the limits of its capacity to unify and rationalize. It has the primacy that comes from natural and orderly and logical succession. Homage is due to it over every competing principle that is unable by appeal to history or tradition or policy or justice to make out a better right. All sorts of deflecting forces may appear to contest its sway and absorb its power. At least, it is the heir presumptive. A pretender to the title will have to fight his way. [pp. 31–32]

...Example, if not better than precept, may at least prove to be easier. We may get some sense of the class of questions to which a method is adapted when we have studied the class of questions to which it has been applied. Let me give some haphazard illustrations of conclusions adopted by our law through the development of legal conceptions to logical conclusions.[51] A agrees to sell a chattel to B. Before title passes, the chattel is destroyed. The loss falls on the seller who has sued at law for the price. A agrees to sell a house and lot. Before title passes, the house is destroyed. The seller sues in equity for specific performance. The loss falls upon the buyer. That is probably the prevailing view, though its wisdom has been sharply criticized. These variant conclusions are not dictated by variant considerations of policy or justice. They are projections of a principle to its logical outcome, or the outcome supposed to be logical. Equity treats that as done which ought to be done. Contracts for the sale of land, unlike most contracts for the sale of chattels, are within the jurisdiction of equity. The vendee is in equity the owner from the beginning. Therefore, the burdens as well as the benefits of ownership shall be his. Let me take as another illustration of my meaning the cases which define the rights of assignees of choses in action. In the discussion of these cases, you will find much conflict of opinion about fundamental conceptions. Some tell us that the assignee has a legal ownership. Others say that his right is purely equitable. Given, however, the fundamental conception, all agree in deducing its consequences by methods in which the preponderating element is the method of philosophy. We may find kindred illustrations in the law of trusts and contracts

---

[51] [This approach is sometimes called "the jurisprudence of concepts".]

and in many other fields. It would be wearisome to accumulate them...

[pp. 38–40]

## The Methods of History, Tradition and Sociology

The method of philosophy comes in competition, however, with other tendencies which find their outlet in other methods. One of these is the historical method, or the method of evolution. The tendency of a principle to expand itself to the limit of its logic may be counteracted by the tendency to confine itself within the limits of its history. I do not mean that even then the two methods are always in opposition. A classification which treats them as distinct is, doubtless, subject to the reproach that it involves a certain overlapping of the lines and principles of division. Very often, the effect of history is to make the path of logic clear. Growth may be logical whether it is shaped by the principle of consistency with the past or by that of consistency with some pre-established norm, some general conception, "some in-dwelling, and creative principle."[52] The directive force of the precedent may be found either in the events that made it what it is, or in some principle which enables us to say of it that it is what it ought to be. Development may involve either an investigation of origins or an effort of pure reason. Both methods have their logic. For the moment, however, it will be convenient to identify the method of history with the one, and to confine the method of logic or philosophy to the other. Some conceptions of the law owe their existing form almost exclusively to history. They are not to be understood except as historical growths. In the development of such principles, history is likely to predominate over logic or pure reason. Other conceptions, though they have, of course history, have taken form and shape to a larger extent under the influer reason or of comparative jurisprudence. They are part of the *jus gentiv* development of such principles logic is likely to predominate over illustration is the conception of juristic or corporate personalit' train of consequences which that conception has engendered.

...If history and philosophy do not serve to fix the dir custom may step in.

...It is, however, not so much in the making of ne' of old ones that the creative energy of custom me General standards of right and duty are esta' whether there has been adherence or depart' are usual in the trade. They may be so we' judicially. Such for illustrations is th' make or indorse negotiable paper ; be such that the court will requ' discharge of his duty to prote of care that is commonl prudence. The triers o' attained, must cons man and women dealing to be i the usages of a p. runs throughout th the limits of right a. customary morality, th time. This is the point of c of sociology. They have the interaction between conduct

...The opinion is stea to the study of philo

53
54 Dillon, Law and Jurisprud
55 Printing, etc., Registering C
[From (1945) 61 L.Q.R.]

---

[52] Bryce, *Studies in History and Jurispruc.*

moulds of conduct, which will some day become fixed as law. Law preserves the
moulds, which have taken form and shape from life...                [pp. 62–64]
   ...From history and philosophy and custom, we pass, therefore, to the force
which in our day and generation is becoming the greatest of them all, the power of
social justice which finds its outlet and expression in the method of sociology.
   The final cause of law is the welfare of society. The rule that misses its aim
cannot permanently justify its existence. "Ethical considerations can no more be
excluded from the administration of justice which is the end and purpose of all
civil laws than one can exclude the vital air from his room and live."[53] Logic and
history and custom have their place. We will shape the law to conform to them
when we may; but only within bounds. The end which the law serves will dominate them all. There is an old legend that on one occasion God prayed, and his
prayer was "Be it my will that my justice be ruled by my mercy." That is a prayer
which we all need to utter at times when the demon of formalism tempts the
intellect with the lure of scientific order. I do not mean, of course, that judges are
commissioned to set aside existing rules at pleasure in favor of any other set of
rules which they may hold to be expedient or wise. I mean that when they are
called upon to say how far existing rules are to be extended or restricted, they
must let the welfare of society fix the path, its direction and its distance. We are
not to forget, said Sir George Jessel, in an often quoted judgment, that there is
this paramount public policy, that we are not lightly to interfere with freedom of
contract.[54] So in this field, there may be a paramount public policy, one that will
prevail over temporary inconvenience of occasional hardship, not lightly to
sacrifice certainty and uniformity and order and coherence. All these elements
must be considered. They are to be given such weight as sound judgment dictates.
They are constituents of that social welfare which it is our business to discover. In
a given instance we may find that they are constituents of preponderating value.
In others, we may find that their value is subordinate. We must appraise them as
best we can...                                                      [pp. 65–67]
   ...Social welfare is a broad term. I use it to cover many concepts more or less
allied. It may mean what is commonly spoken of as public policy, the good of the
collective body. In such cases, its demands are often those of mere expediency or
prudence. It may mean on the other hand the social gain that is wrought by
adherence to the standards of right conduct, which find expression in the *mores* of
the community. In such cases, its demands are those of religion or of ethics or of
social sense of justice, whether formulated in creed or system, or immanent in
common mind. One does not readily find a single term to cover these and
d aims which shade off into one another by imperceptible gradations.
s we might fall back with Kohler and Brutt and Berolzheimer on the
ble, but comprehensive something known as Kultur if recent history had
dited it and threatened odium for those that use it. I have chosen in its
m which, if not precise enough for the philosopher, will at least be
iently definite and inclusive to suit the purposes of the judge...
                                                                   [pp. 71–73]


### GLANVILLE WILLIAMS
### Language and the Law
### (1945)[55]


dily growing that semantics is an important prolegomenon
ophy and of the so-called "inexact" sciences, such as


*ence of England and America*, p. 18.
o. v. Sampson (1895) L.R. 19 Eq. 462, 465.

psychology and the social sciences. In the past philosophers have tended to mistake the structure of discourse for the structure of the universe, and a training in semantics helps to prevent this error. In psychology and the social sciences it is coming to be recognized that one of the greatest difficulties is the difficulty of statement, and that many disputes are due to the imperfections of language. Lawyers, perhaps, are not in such need of having the imperfection of language impressed upon them; for every case on construction is an object-lesson in it. Still, even they are not immune from error, as I shall seek to show. Jurisprudence, too, is in my opinion badly in need of semantic analysis. It is ridden with disputes, and many of them turn out on examination to be disputes not as to matters of fact or value-judgment but purely as to the use of words. A student of jurisprudence who comes to the subject armed with an understanding of what is a verbal dispute, will find that his knowledge enables him to pare off the unprofitable matter from his subject. It helps him, in Locke's words, to clear the ground a little, and to remove some of the rubbish that lies in the way of knowledge.                [pp. 72–73]

...Some words, though not equivocal in the sense of having two or more distinct definitions, are yet obviously vague in their meaning, as for example "about", "near", "more or less". Such words, which ought generally to find no place in legal documents, give considerable trouble when they do occur. What I am concerned to demonstrate in this section is that not merely some but all words are capable of occasioning difficulty in their application...                [p. 181]

...The difficulty of using such words as these does not press upon the ordinary man because it usually does not matter to him whether, for instance, he calls a number of stones a "heap" or not. All that matters is that he should make his meaning clear enough for the purpose on hand. Suppose that a housewife is following a cookery book which tells her to add a pinch of mustard to a particular dish. She cannot tell how many grains make a pinch, but she can guess what is meant by a pinch and if she puts too much, or too little, her palate will in due course discover her error.

With law it is different, for in law we make sharp consequences hang upon these words of gradation. The question whether a man is left in freedom or detained in a mental institution depends on whether he is judicially classified as sane or instance,[56] as also does the question whether his dispositions of property are upheld or not.[57] Whether a man is punished or acquitted may turn simply and solely upon whether an attempt to commit a crime was sufficiently "proximate," or upon whether a statement that he falsely swore was "material" to a judicial proceeding; and in a murder case it may be literally a question of life or death whether the accused intended to hurt by means of an act "intrinsically likely to kill."[58] Well may a convict echo the words of the poet—

"Oh, the little more, and how much it is!
And the little less, and what worlds away!"

---

[56] [See the Mental Health Act 1983.]
[57] "The difficulty to be grappled with arises from the circumstance that the question is almost always one of degree. There is no difficulty in the case of a raving madman or a drivelling idiot in saying that he is not a person capable of disposing of property. But between such an extreme case and that of a man of perfectly sound and vigorous understanding, there is every shade of intellect, every degree of mental capacity. There is no possibility of mistaking midnight for noon; but at what precise moment twilight becomes darkness is hard to determine"; *per* Lord Cranworth L.C. in *Boyse v. Rossborough* (1857) 6 H.L.C. 2 at 45, quoted by Hannen J. in *Boughton v. Knight* (1873) L.R. 3 P. & D. 64 at 67.
[58] The terminology is that of Kenny (*Outlines of Criminal Law* (15th ed.), p. 155); but the word "intrinsically" seems to be meaningless in this context. [This is no longer the test but Glanville Williams is likely to be no less troubled by the latest formulation in *R. v. Woollin* [1999] 1AC 82.]

In tort we have one rule for reservoirs, another for duck-ponds; and the Court somehow has to draw the line between the two. A libel is in "permanent" form and a slander in "transient" form; but permanency is a matter of degree. In the law of negligence and nuisance the defendant pays full damages or nothing according as the Court puts his conduct at the "reasonable" or "unreasonable" end of what is in fact a continuous gradation. So also with remoteness of damage. The law of vicarious liability abounds in such puzzles; thus (*a*) the employer of an independent contractor is not liable for him merely because he is employed to do an ordinarily hazardous act, but is liable for him if he is employed to do an extrahazardous act[59]; (*b*) the distinction between a servant and an independent contractor rests on the infinitely variable matter of control; (*c*) the master of a servant who exceeds his authority is responsible for some excess, but not for excessive excess[60] and (*d*) the master of a vanman who deviates from his route and negligently injures a pedestrian is liable if the deviation is a slight one but not if the deviation is such that every yard he goes is a yard away from his employment and not to it[61]—no precise angle being laid down. A contract to be valid must be "certain in its terms," and certainty of meaning is, as it is the object of these pages to show, a question of degree. The "lodger" shades off into the "lessee of a flat"; yet somehow the Courts must draw a line between them, because the relative law is different. In some parts of the law, such as copyright and charities, we must distinguish between a thing that concerns "the public or a portion of the public" and a thing that concerns "private individuals," this resulting in innumerable perplexities.

Judges refuse to be frightened by these difficulties. They are not intimidated from saying that the case is on one side or the other of the line merely because they discover that the line is difficult to draw. Thus in one of the cases working out the limits of the rule against remoteness, where a limitation was upheld as not infringing the rule, Lord Nottingham said: "It hath been urged at the bar, where will you stop if you do not stop at *Child and Bayly's Case?* I answer, I will stop everywhere when any inconvenience appears, no where before."[62] Blackburn J. observed of the rule in *Hadley v. Baxendale*: "It is a vague rule, and as Bramwell B. said, it is something like having to draw a line between night and day; there is a great duration of twilight when it is neither night nor day; but on the question now before the Court, though you cannot draw the precise line, you can say on which side of the line the case is."[63] "Courts of Justice," said Chitty J., "ought not to be puzzled by such old scholastic questions as to where a horse's tail begins and where it ceases. You are obliged to say, 'This is a horse's tail', at some time."[64] Similarly Lord Coleridge C.J.: "The Attorney-General has asked where we are to draw the line. The answer is that it is not necessary to draw it at any precise point. It is enough for us to say that the present case is one the right side of any reasonable line that could be drawn."[65] And Lindley M.R.: "It is urged that it is difficult to draw the line. I admit that it is extremely difficult ... It is always a question of degree. It may be asked. What is the difference between one cart and two, and so on? You cannot draw the line in that way. Nothing is more common in life than to be unable to draw the line between two things. Who can draw the

---

[59]  *Honeywill & Stein v. Larkin Bros.* [1934] 1 K.B. 191.
[60]  *Poland v. Parr* [1927] 1 K.B. 236 at 243.
[61]  Pollock, *Torts* (14th ed.), pp. 70–71.
[62]  *Duke of Norfolk's Case* (1681) 2 Swans. 454 at 468; 3 Chan. Cas. 14 at 36.
[63]  *Hobbs v. L. & S.W. Ry.* (1875) L.R. 10 Q.B. 111 at 121. *Cf.* Scutton L.J. in *The San Onofre* [1922] P. 243 at 253.
[64]  *Lavery v. Pursell* (1888) 39 Ch. D. 508 at 517. See also Pollock C.B. in *White v. Bluett* (1853) 23 L.J. Ex. 36 at 37: "By the argument a principle is pressed to an absurdity, as a bubble is blown until it bursts."
[65]  *Mayor of Southport v. Morriss* [1893] 1 Q.B. 359 at 361.

line between plants and animals? And yet, who has any difficulty in saying that an oak tree is a plant and not an animal?"[66]

So also, judges are not always deterred in framing new legal rules by the consideration that they may be hard to apply. In the words of Bowen L.J.: "It is not a valid objection to a legal doctrine that it will not be always easy to know whether the doctrine is to be applied in a particular case. The law has to face such embarrassments."[67] In the *Pollock-Holmes Letters* Holmes writes: "People in the law as elsewhere hate to recognize that most questions—I think I might say all legal questions—are questions of degree.[68] I have just sent back an opinion of one of our J.J. with a criticism of an argument in it of the 'where are you going to draw the line' type—as if all decisions were not a series of points tending to fix a point in a line."[69]                                    [pp. 183–185]

I have already pointed a number of legal morals in the course of this section, but some general conclusions of legal interest remain to be drawn.

(1) In the first place, the theory here advanced destroys completely and for ever the illusion that the law can be completely certain. Since the law has to be expressed in words, and words have a penumbra of uncertainty, marginal cases are bound to occur. Certainty in law is thus seen to be a matter of degree. (2) Correlatively, the theory destroys the illusion that the function of a judge is simply to administer the law.[70] If marginal cases must occur, the function of the judge in adjudicating upon them must be legislative. The distinction between the mechanical administration of fixed rules and free judicial discretion is thus a matter of degree, not the sharp distinction that it is sometimes assumed to be. This is not to say that judges have an unlimited legislative power. A judge has a discretion to include a flying-boat within a rule as to ships or vessels; he has no discretion to include a motor car within such a rule...                [pp. 302–303]

## J. WISDOM
### Gods
### (1944)[71]

*In courts of law* it sometimes happens that opposing counsel are agreed as to the facts and are not trying to settle a question of further fact, are not trying to settle whether the man who admittedly had quarrelled with the deceased did or did not murder him, but are concerned with whether Mr A. who admittedly handed his long-trusted clerk signed blank cheques did or did not exercise reasonable care, whether a ledger is or is not a document, whether a certain body was or was not a public authority.

In such cases we notice that the process of argument is not a *chain* of demonstrative reasoning. It is a presenting and representing of those features of

---

[66] *Att.-Gen. v. Brighton & Hove Co-operative Supply Assn.* [1900] 1. Ch. 276 at 282. *Cf.*, *per* FitzGibbon L.J. in *Gregg v. Fraser* [1906] 1 Ir. R. 545 at 578–579; "This is in each case a pure question on the construction of a written document, whether the case lies on the one side or on the other of a definite *line* in the mathematical sense—a line without breadth— every case must lie on one side of that line or on the other ... and 'line balls' are barred."

[67] *Dashwood v. Magniac* [1891] 3 Ch. 306 at 364.

[68] [*Cf.* Wilson in (1969) 32 M.L.R. 361.]

[69] *Pollock-Holmes Letters* (1942), vol. ii, p. 28.

[70] The illusion has, of course, been destroyed many times, notably by Dickinson, "The Law behind Law" (1929) 29 Col. L. Rev. 113, 285. But it has extraordinary vitality. One still sees discussions among international lawyers upon the respective merits of legal tribunals and tribunals deciding *ex aequo et bono*, without any express statement by either side that the distinction is one of degree.

[71] [From (1944) Proc. Arist. Soc., reprinted in J. Wisdom, *Philosophy and Psycho-Analysis* (1953). See also Stone, *Legal System and Lawyers' Reasonings* (1964), pp. 325–337.]

the case which *severally co-operate* in favour of the conclusion, in favour of saying what the reasoner wishes said, in favour of calling the situation by the name by which he wishes to call it. The reasons are like the legs of a chair, not the links of a chain. Consequently although the discussion is *a priori* and the steps are not a matter of experience, the procedure resembles scientific argument in that the reasoning is not *vertically* extensive but *horizontally* extensive—it is a matter of the cumulative effect of several independent premises, not of the repeated transformation of one or two. And because the premises are severally inconclusive the process of deciding the issue becomes a matter of weighing the cumulative effect of one group of severally inconclusive items against the cumulative effect of another group of severally inconclusive items, and thus lends itself to description in terms of conflicting "probabilities." This encourages the feeling that the issue is one of fact—that it is a matter of guessing from the premises at a further fact, at what is to come. But this is a muddle. *The dispute does not cease to be a priori because it is a matter of the cumulative effect of severally inconclusive premises.* The logic of the dispute is not that of a chain of deductive reasoning as in a mathematic calculation. But nor is it a matter of collecting from several inconclusive items of information an expectation as to something further, as when a doctor from a patient's symptoms guesses at what is wrong, or a detective from many clues guesses the criminal. It has its own sort of logic and its own sort of end—the solution of the question at issue is a decision, a ruling by the judge. But it is not an arbitrary decision though the rational connections are neither quite like those in vertical deductions nor like those in inductions in which from many signs we guess at what is to come; and though the decision manifests itself in the application of a name it is no more merely the application of a name than is the pinning on of a medal merely the pinning on of a bit of metal. Whether a lion with stripes is a tiger or a lion is, if you like, merely a matter of the application of a name. Whether Mr So-and-So of whose conduct we have so complete a record did or did not exercise reasonable care is not merely a matter of the application of a name or, if we choose to say it is, then we must remember that with this name a game is lost and won and a game with very heavy stakes. With the judges' choice of a name for the facts goes an attitude, and the declaration, the ruling, is an examination evincing that attitude. But *it is an exclamation which not only has a purpose but also has a logic*, a logic surprisingly like that of "futile," "deplorable," "grateful," "grand," "divine."...[72]                                    [pp. 157–158]

---

[72] [For a suggestion that a new model of reasoning can be constructed, based to some extent on the ancient tradition of rhetorical argument, whereby conclusions may be arrived at which are worthy of reliance, even though not susceptible of stringent proof in the strict logical sense, see C. Perelman, *The Idea of Justice and the Problem of Argument* (1963). After a full exploration of this approach, Stone has argued forcibly that too much should not be expected from this new type of rhetorical logic. He points out how much of legal reasonings depends not just on inferences from established legal propositions, but on the use of ideals and established techniques, such as the common law approach to *stare decisis*. Moreover, in a society with conflicting standards and values it is not easy to predicate, as Perelman appears to do, that fundamental propositions from which the law may proceed to its conclusions, can generally be found to command a general consensus. At the most therefore, it would seem that the new rhetoric does not differ very much from the traditional common law approach whereby "good grounds" are sought for justifying particular decisions, such grounds being deployed as cumulatively persuasive rather than logically conclusive. The new terminology seems unlikely to provide more than a new conceptual framework for constructing legal arguments, rather than a novel technique differing in substance from the traditional methods of generations of lawyers both in common law and civil law countries. (See Julius Stone, "Reasons and Reasoning in Judicial and Juristic Arguments" in *Legal Essays to Castberg* (1963), p. 170.]

### D.N. MacCORMICK
### Formal Justice and the Form of Legal Arguments
### (1976)[73]

Justice requires that essentially similar cases be treated in the same way, and that essentially different cases be treated differently. But since that is a purely formal principle, it requires supplementation with some conception of substantive justice to establish criteria of essential similarity and essential difference. Accordingly, it may appear that formal justice considered in itself is an entirely empty value. But that would be a misleading conclusion to reach, as may be seen by considering the bearing of formal justice on the practice of legal argument in its most characteristic function: the justification of claims, defences, counter-claims; above all of decisions, in the context of contested litigation.

Litigation in all its forms is inevitably concerned with particulars; with a particular set of past events upon which one party founds some claim or complaint against another. The parties and the factual issues which concern them are particular and unique. No case for trial can ever be exactly the same in every particular as any other. Disputed questions of fact are particular and resolution of disputes of fact depends upon the gathering and weighing of particular items of testimonial and other evidence with a view to constructing a credible and coherent (credible because coherent) version of past events. Having settled the questions of fact one can proceed to decide about claims or complaints founded on the averments of fact, and can (if one is a judge) issue specific and binding orders to the parties in accordance with one's decision about the claim or complaint. Both in inception and in conclusion, litigation is essentially particular in focus.

Yet, as seems obvious, the justification of the claim or complaint founded on the particular averred facts, or of the decision made about the claim or complaint, can hardly be in terms of the unique and particular. Justification is a matter of universals, not of particulars; certainly, legal argument so far as it is concerned with the justification of claims or complaints or decisions or whatever involves the construction and testing of universal propositions of law (albeit universal only with reference to the jurisdictional areas of the court's competence). It happens not infrequently, of course, that the matters in dispute concern some relatively cut and dried area of law and therefore that the universal proposition advanced in justification of the particular decision is an established rule of positive law (whether derived from statute or from case law) which is uncontroversially capable of being applied once any disputes of fact have been resolved and authoritatively settled.

Of greater present interest, however, are the cases, by no means few in number, in which the law as well as the facts are in dispute. Even if x, y and z can be proved to have happened, as the pursuer avers, does it follow that he is entitled to the remedy r which he claims? For some reason or other the legal answer to that question is in doubt. At any rate sufficiently in doubt to have enabled pursuer and defender to advance opposed contentions as to its correct answer. To settle what is the correct answer is the judge's job. My interest is in showing that and showing why the judge must frame and test generalised propositions (indeed, logically speaking, universal propositions) in framing a satisfactory justification of his answer to the question.

As a first step in that, let me give a concrete illustration, taking for my example a very famous legal decision, the decision of the House of Lords given in the Scottish case of *Donoghue v. Stevenson* in 1932.[74]    [pp. 103–4]

...Lord Atkin found it necessary in justifying his decision in favour of the

---

[73] [From *Etudes de Logique Juridique* (C. Perelman, ed., 1976), vol. 6.]
[74] *Donoghue v. Stevenson* [1932] A.C. 562; 1932 S.C. (HL) 31.

particular pursuer in this case to consider what sort of situation would arise, not just if Mr Stevenson were not liable to Mrs Donoghue, but if manufacturers in general were not liable to consumers in general in relation to latent defects in their products. Essential to the justification of the specific decision given is Lord Atkin's dismissal as wholly unacceptable of the proposition that a manufacturer, any manufacturer, should be held to owe no legal duty of care to consumers of his products. Either manufacturers owe such a duty or they do not. If they do not, many accidents may occur for which the innocent victims will be remedyless although it was known and intended by manufacturers that their products should be used by consumers. If they do, and if it should be possible to show that defects in products are attributable to a failure on the manufacturer's part to take reasonable care, then injured consumers will have a remedy. The former is unacceptable, therefore the latter must be accepted. To decide the case in favour of the pursuer is to affirm the latter as a general proposition...

To summarise: the specific set of events, the specific relations between pursuer and defender, are considered as instances of generic relationships. The question becomes: "What ought to be the legal position of anybody in the pursuer's situation standing in this type of relationship with somebody in the defender's situation?" The various possible answers to that generalised question propounded before the court by one party or another are then tested in terms of the desirability of their consequences. A preferred generalisation is achieved by elimination. The preferred general principle, and the reasons for its being preferred, are advanced as essential elements in the justification of the specific decision...

...It is worth remarking that the whole idea of treating "like cases alike" can in fact be rendered intelligible only if we envisage decisions in individual cases as decisions of principle—indeed, as decisions the principles of which have to be articulated and expounded. What can count as a case relevantly similar to the case in dispute between Mrs Donoghue and Mr Stevenson is a matter which depends entirely on the way in which the relationship between the two of them is to be categorised. Once one has determined that the matter should be treated as being a matter between consumer of consumer goods and manufacturer thereof one has established a basis of comparison with other possible past and future situations. The idea of treating like cases alike presupposes a preparedness to treat cases in terms of general categories of some sort or another. The justification of decisions must be in terms of an assertion of the proposition that whenever a case in a given specified category occurs the decision of the case ought to be so and so and for that reason is now in the present case so and so.

...It might perhaps be objected that such a view as this leaves out of account the possibility of decisions in accordance with equity rather than strict justice. It is sometimes said that equity is a matter of deciding each case on its own special merits without regard to general rules or principles.[75] It seems to me that that view is pure nonsense. I cannot for the life of me understand how there can be such a thing as a good reason for deciding any single case which is not a good generic reason for deciding cases of the particular type in view, that is to say, the "merits" of any individual case are the merits of the type of case to which the individual case belongs...

The question may well be asked how the judge can arrive at possible universal principles of decision and how having arrived at opposed rival principles he can in any rational sense test the one as against the other and choose which to apply.

The doubt about how judges can arrive at relevant principles to test arises from an obvious source. The "facts" of any case being unique and particular there is no end to the possible labels at possible levels of generality which can be stuck on

---

[75] See, *e.g.* sources cited in R. Wasserstrom, *The Judicial Decision* (1961), Chap. 5, esp. at pp. 87–88 and 93. I am in almost complete agreement with Wasserstrom's critique of those arguments.

them. What principles you assert as justifying, or entertain as possible justifications of, your decision, is then determined by how you choose to classify the facts and so there must be an enormously large if not indeed an infinite range of possible principles to be considered. How can you at all, and how can you with any semblance of justice to the parties, narrow down to a reasonable range of principles for consideration?

Let me start by saying how it can be and is in fact done. The point to remember is that legal decision making does not proceed *in vacuo*, but always against a background of a relatively well established set of rules, principles, standards and values. That being so it follows that even in cases of first impression, cases not directly and unequivocally "covered" by some established rule, the court must nevertheless give its decision with an eye upon the surrounding framework of rules and principles within which the new decision is to be located. All the more so in that, for the reasons mentioned, the decision to be given must be justifiable as a decision of principle, in a context in which the principle of the decision is to become, in effect, a new rule of the system.

It follows that not just any principle, but only a principle which is consistent with the existing system, can be accepted as a valid justifying principle of a decision within the system. Of course this means as a minimum that no principle may be asserted which is contradictory to any established and accepted norm of the system, but in practice it means a good deal more as well, as I can best convey in terms of a notion of the overall "coherence" of the system. Not merely should the legal system, or any particular "branch" of it, contain no flat contradictions, but its norms ought to form a coherent whole in the broader and admittedly looser sense of embodying the rational pursuit of a consistent set of values. One of the ways in which this "coherence" is or tends to be secured is evidenced by the way in which judges in their decision making do regularly make appeal to "general principles" of the law, or by the way in which arguments from analogy are regularly used to justify extensions of the law into new ground.[76] So much is this so, indeed, that even the most significant acts of judicial law making in cases of first impression are normally represented as involving no more than extrapolations from, or rationalisations of, or removal of anomalies from the existing law. Lord Atkin's speech in *Donoghue v. Stevenson* gives rather a good illustration of just that practice.

Nor is this mere pretence; in terms of the crucial notion of the overall "coherence" of the legal system it does make sense to envisage the most adventurous of judicial decision making as involving no more than extrapolation, and to accept that there is a genuine if vague limit to the judicial power of law making implicit in the notion that innovation which goes beyond extrapolation is outwith the judicial function, being a matter reserved to the legislature.[77]...

Be that as it may, we are entitled to conclude that novel cases of first impression cannot just be decided according to any old principle of decision which commands itself to the judge out of an infinite range of possibilities, but must be decided in accordance with some principle which is not merely acceptable in itself and for its consequences but which is also coherent with and extrapolated from the existing norms of the system. "Rationality, as it presents itself in law, is always a form of continuity."[78] That implies a very considerable limitation on the range of possibilities available for serious consideration. What is more, it is not only the case that judges deciding such questions do so against the context established by the system, one in which every one of the parties to an issue is entitled to advance before the court all the arguments which he can find in favour

---

[76] N. MacCormick, "Law As Institutional Fact" (1974) 90 L.Q.R. 102, esp. pp. 121–129.
[77] *Cf.* C. Perelman (ed.), *Le Problème des Lacunes en Droit* (1968), esp. pp. 537–522 and 539.
[78] Perelman, *Justice*, p. 164.

of his case. The judge is not left to his own unaided reflection is selecting possible principles of decision for consideration. He has pressed upon him from each side the best arguments of relevant principle which skilled counsel can find in favour of their client's case. [pp. 107–116]

In pursuing the coherence of the system, the judiciary is in fact pursuing and in effect sustaining the consistency of the value system to which the law gives expression. In any system in which the judiciary is expected to play the role of servants rather than masters of the law, it is right that the values of the system should play a larger part in the testing of principles of decision than the judge's own personal values. What is more, especially in a democratic political system, there is good reason to assert that the judiciary ought to play the role of servants rather than masters of the law.

Disputes over the substantive values which ought to be embodied in the legal system, disputes, that is, over questions of substantive justice are in effect clashes of ideology. As such, they could be resolved only if we could find some Archimedean point of argumentation beyond any one of them. Rawls indeed and others before him have claimed to have established such an Archimedean point, but the claim is in its nature perennially open to challenge.

If for no other reason, it seems to be to be of value to pursue the question whether formal and procedural justice has a value independent of particular substantive values embodied in the legal system at any point in time. I think that the answer is "Yes," and I think that the study of legal argument is relevant to that conclusion in spite of, or perhaps because of, the fact that it is a relatively poor source for explicit discussions of substantive justice. [p. 118]


### E. H. LEVI
### An Introduction to Legal Reasoning
(1949)


The basic pattern of legal reasoning is reasoning by example. It is reasoning from case to case. It is a three-step process described by the doctrine of precedent in which a proposition descriptive of the first case is made into a rule of law and then applied to a next similar situation. The steps are these: similarity is seen between cases; next the rule of law inherent in the first case is announced; then the rule of law is made applicable to the second case. This is a method of reasoning necessary for the law, but it has characteristics which under other circumstances might be considered imperfections.

These characteristics become evident if the legal process is approached as though it were a method of applying general rules of law to diverse facts—in short, as though the doctrine of precedent meant that general rules, once properly determined, remained unchanged, and then were applied, albeit imperfectly, in later cases. If this were the doctrine, it would be disturbing to find that the rules change from case to case and are remade with each case. Yet this change in the rules is the indispensable dynamic quality of law. It occurs because the scope of a rule of law, and therefore its meaning, depends upon a determination of what facts will be considered similar to those present when the rule was first announced. The finding of similarity or difference is the key step in the legal process.

The determination of similarity or difference is the function of each judge. Where case law is considered, and there is no statute, he is not bound by the statement of the rule of law made by the prior judge even in the controlling case. The statement is mere dictum, and this means that the judge in the present case may find irrelevant the existence or absence of facts which prior judges thought important. It is not what the prior judge intended that is of any importance; rather it is what the present judge, attempting to see the law as a fairly consistent whole, thinks should be the determining classification. In arriving at his result he will ignore what the past thought important; he will emphasize facts which prior judges would have thought made no difference. It is not alone that he could not see the law through the eyes of another, for he could at least try to do so. It is rather that the doctrine of dictum forces him to make his own decision.

Thus it cannot be said that the legal process is the application of known rules to diverse facts. Yet it is a system of rules; the rules are discovered in the process of determining similarity or difference. But if attention is directed toward the finding of similarity or difference, other peculiarities appear. The problem for the law is: When will it be just to treat difference cases as though they were the same? A working legal system must therefore be willing to pick out key similarities and to reason from them to the justice of applying a common classification. The existence of some facts in common brings into play the general rule. If this is really reasoning, then by common standards, though of in terms of closed systems, it is imperfect unless some overall rule has announced that this common and ascertainable similarity is to be decisive. But no such fixed prior rule exists. It could be suggested that reasoning is not involved at all; that is, that no new insight is arrived at through a comparison of cases. But reasoning appears to be involved; the conclusion is arrived at through a process and was not immediately apparent. It seems better to say there is reasoning, but it is imperfect.

Therefore it appears that the kind of reasoning involved in the legal process is one in which the classification changes as the classification is made. The rules change as the rules are applied. More important, the rules arise out of a process which, while comparing fact situations, creates the rules and then applies them. But this kind of reasoning is open to the charge that it is classifying things as equal when they are somewhat different, justifying the classification by rules made up as the reasoning or classification proceeds. In a sense all reasoning is of this type, but there is an additional requirement which compels the legal process to be this way. Not only do new situations arise, but in addition people's wants change. The categories used in the legal process must be left ambiguous in order to permit the infusion of new ideas. And this is true even where legislation or a constitution is involved. The words used by the legislature or the constitutional convention must come to have new meanings. Furthermore, agreement on any other basis would be impossible. In this manner the laws come to express the ideas of the community and even when written in general terms, in statute or constitution, are moulded for the specific case.

But attention must be paid to the process. A controversy as to whether the law is certain, unchanging, and expressed in rules, or uncertain, changing, and only a technique for deciding specific cases misses the point. It is both. Nor is it helpful to dispose of the process as a wonderful mystery possibly reflecting a higher law, by which the law can remain the same and yet change. The law forum is the most explicit demonstration of the mechanism required for a moving classification system. The folklore of law may choose to ignore the imperfections in legal reasoning, but the law forum itself has taken care of them.

What does the law forum require? It requires presentation of competing examples. The forum protects the parties and the community by making sure that the competing analogies are before the court. The rule which will be created arises out of a process in which if different things are to be treated as similar, at least the differences have been urged.[79] In this sense the parties as well as the court

---

[79] The reasoning may take this form: A falls more appropriately in B than in C. It does so because A is more like D which is of B than it is like E which is of C. Since A is in B and B is in G (legal concept), then A is in G. But perhaps C is in G also. If so, then B is in a decisively different segment of G, because B is like H which is in G and has a different result than C.

participate in the law making. In this sense, also, lawyers represent more than the litigants.

Reasoning by example in the law is a key to many things.[80] It indicates in part the hold which the law process has over the litigants. They have participated in the law making. They are bound by something they helped to make. Moreover, the examples of analogies urged by the parties bring into the law the common ideas of the society. The ideas have their day in court, and they will have their day again. This is what makes the hearing fair, rather than any idea that the judge is completely impartial, for of course he cannot be completely so. Moreover, the hearing in a sense compels at least vicarious participation by all the citizens, for the rule which is made, even though ambiguous, will be law as to them.

Reasoning by example shows the decisive role which the common ideas of the society and the distinctions made by experts can have in shaping the law. The movement of common or expert concepts into the law may be followed. The concept is suggested in arguing difference or similarity in a brief, but it wins no approval from the court. The idea achieves standing in the society. It is suggested again to a court. The court this time reinterprets the prior case and in doing so adopts the rejected idea. In subsequent cases, the idea is given further definition and is tied to other ideas which have been accepted by courts. It is now no longer the idea which was commonly held in the society. It becomes modified in subsequent cases. Ideas first rejected by which gradually have won acceptance now push what has become a legal category out of the system or convert it into something which may be its opposite. The process is one in which the ideas of the community and of the social sciences, whether correct or not, as they win acceptance in the community, control legal decisions. Erroneous ideas, of course, have played an enormous part in shaping the law. An idea, adopted by a court, is in a superior position to influence conduct and opinion in the community: judges, after all, are rulers. And the adoption of an idea by a court reflects the power structure in the community. But reasoning by example will operate to change the idea after it has been adopted.

Moreover, reasoning by example brings into focus important similarity and difference in the interpretation of case law, statutes, and the constitution of a nation. There is a striking similarity. It is only folklore which holds that a statute if clearly written can be completely unambiguous and applied as intended to a specific case. Fortunately or otherwise, ambiguity is inevitable in both statute and constitution as well as with case law. Hence reasoning by example operates with all three. But there are important differences. What a court says is dictum, but what a legislature says is a statute. The reference of the reasoning changes. Interpretation of intention when dealing with a statute is the way of describing the attempt to compare cases on the basis of the standard thought to be common at the time the legislation was passed. While this is the attempt, it may not initially accomplish any different result than if the standard of the judge had been explicitly used. Nevertheless, the remarks of the judge are directed toward describing a category set up by the legislature. These remarks are different from ordinary dicta. They set the course of the statute, and later reasoning in subsequent cases is tied to them. As a consequence, courts are less free in applying a statute than in dealing with case law. The current rationale for this is the notion that the legislature has acquiesced by legislative silence in the prior, even though erroneous, interpretation of the court. But the change in reasoning where legislation is concerned seems an inevitable consequence of the division of function between court and legislature, and, paradoxically, a recognition also of the impossibility of determining legislative intent. The impairment of a court's

---

[80] [For an excellent illustration of analogous reasoning which was accepted by only one of the three members of the Court of Appeal, see *John Carter v. Hanson Haulage Ltd* [1965] 2 W.L.R. 553.]

freedom in interpreting legislation is reflected in frequent appeals to the constitution as a necessary justification for overruling cases even though these cases
are thought to have interpreted the legislation erroneously.

Under the United States experience, contrary to what has sometimes been
believed when a written constitution of a nation is involved, the court has greater
freedom than it has with the application of a statute or case law. In case law, when
a judge determines what the controlling similarity between the present and prior
case is, the case is decided. The judge does not feel free to ignore the results of a
great number of cases which he cannot explain under a remade rule. And in
interpreting legislation, when the prior interpretation, even though erroneous, is
determined after a comparison of facts to cover the case, the case is decided. But
this is not true with a constitution. The constitution sets up the conflicting ideals
of the community in certain ambiguous categories. These categories bring along
with them satellite concepts covering the areas of ambiguity. It is with a set of
these satellite concepts that reasoning by example must work. But no satellite
concept, no matter how well developed, can prevent the court from shifting its
course, not only by realigning cases which impose certain restrictions, but by
going beyond realignment back to the overall ambiguous category written into
the document. The constitution, in other words, permits the court to be inconsistent. The freedom is concealed either as a search for the intention of the framers
or as a proper understanding of a living instrument, and sometimes as both. But
this does not mean that reasoning by example has any less validity in this field.[pp.
1–6]


# R. SARTORIUS
## Social Policy and Judicial Legislation
## (1971)[81]


The strongest and, I believe, the most widely held ground for the view that in at
least some cases judges are not bound to reach a particular decision by authoritative standards, and that they must thus exercise discretion, rests neither on the
claim that there are no authoritative standards other than rules, nor on a denial of
the possibility of in principle identifying, and restricting the judge to a consideration of, legal standards. Rather, the claim is that the necessity for judicial
discretion arises because of the possibilities of conflict among principles and
policies which, because of their authoritative status, may all be relevant to the
decision of a given case. Although the claim is sometimes made that such general
standards do not have predetermined weights, but rather have weight assigned to
them by the legislative fiat of the judge, the argument is even subtler than this.[82]
For what is argued is that if good sense can be made out of the notion that extant
principles and policies have well established weights of varying degrees, then it is
only reasonable to expect that principles of equal weight may come into conflict in
a case where the law contains no further grounds upon which to choose between
them. Since such a case could with equal justification be decided in more ways
than one, and since it can and must be decided in only one way, any decision

---

[81] [From (1971) 8 *American Philosophical Quarterly* 151. See also *Individual Conduct and
Social Norms* (1975).]

[82] My reply to the claim that judges exercise discretion in assigning weights to various legal
standards is implicitly contained in my discussion of the problem of recognition in the
preceding section. I there argued that a principle is relevant if and only if, *and to the
degree to which*, it has what Dworkin aptly calls "institutional support". How this notion
is to be explained is by no means as easy problem, but I ignore it here because I don't
believe that there is a very convincing argument for the existence of judicial discretion *on
this score alone*.

among equally justified alternatives must be recognized as an exercise of the judge's personal discretion . . .

The problem of assigning priorities among competing principles and policies is typically viewed by the proponent of the view that judges are legislators as one of weighing the importance of the purposes which are served by such standards. The position seems to be that when there are no authoritative commitments to which the judge can defer which establish an order of priorities among such purposes, he must then impose his own values, and decide that some substantive goals of the law are more important than others. Now there is a certain sort of model being accepted here of the kind of guidance which could be provided by authoritative legal standards, when, in terms of that model, it is seen that "guidance dries up," it is concluded that judges must exercise discretion.

What is this model of justification? It is one in which a rule or principle at any given level is validated by deriving it from some standard at a still higher level, the process terminating at the point where an ultimate substantive principle is reached which cannot be validated in the manner of subordinate standards, but at best simply be said to be accepted by the members of some relevant group. But the legal system within a pluralistic society such as our own does not contain any such ultimate principle; there simply is no one overriding goal or aim, but rather a plurality of policies and principles which in at least some cases come into quite direct conflict. The reason why on this view there can be no such thing as "the best resolution" of such a conflict on authoritative grounds is because this notion is seen as requiring the existence of an authoritative supreme principle or priority rule which just does not exist. Where the law runs out in this way, and the view is that it inevitably will even where it is construed so broadly as to contain extralegal principles having no authoritative legal basis, the judge "necessarily resorts to his own scheme of values." Indeed, it is this argument, rather than his acceptance of "the model of rules," which I believe is at the root of Hart's conclusion that in at least some hard cases "all that succeeds is success." . . .

Legal rules, principles, and policies do, of course, have purposes, and a corresponding aspect of importance which is to be assessed in terms of the desirability of the aims that they promote and the efficiency with which they promote them. Neither is there any denying that the understanding of such standards typically involves an appreciation of their purposes. But this does not entail, as some have supposed, that the weight which they are to have in the justification of judicial decisions requires that the judge make his own judgment of their importance in this sense. Rather, it may be argued that the only relevant sense in which the judge is entitled to weigh a legal standard is to determine what Dworkin has called its "institutional support" in terms of other established standards. Any judicial decision takes place against the background of an entire legal system containing a wide variety of interrelated and interdependent decisions, rules, principles, policies, etc. In any case, it may be argued, the obligation of the judge is to reach that decision which coheres best with the total body of authoritative legal standards which he is bound to apply. The correct decision in a given case is that which achieves "the best resolution" of existing standards in terms of systematic coherence as formally determined, not in terms of optimal desirability as determined either by some supreme substantive principle or by the judge's own personal scheme of values. Although the degree of weight or importance in this formal or systematic sense which will attach to a given rule or principle will typically reflect the importance in the sense of desirability which it is perceived to have extrasystematically, it is the distinctive feature of the institutionalized role of the judiciary, in contrast to the legislative, that it may not directly base decisions on substantive considerations of the value of competing social policies.

In and of themselves, these considerations do not refute the claim that there are some cases in which the relevant principles, policies, etc., are so finely balanced that there is no one uniquely correct decision, and that the judge in deciding among alternatives having equal weight is, therefore, exercising discretion, it seems that at best they merely force a recasting of the view in terms of the possibility of equal coherence rather than equal importance. This recasting is significant, though, in that it demands an appropriate reformulation of the position in which the judge must be said to find himself before he will be forced to resort to his own scheme of values. For it is one thing to say that either of two possible decisions in a given case would have equally desirable consequences if evaluated in terms of relevant substantive purposes having authoritative status; it is quite a different thing to claim that they both cohere equally well with the entire background body of relevant law. The model of justification in terms of institutions coherence explicitly makes relevant the systematic import of a judicial decision as seen against an enormous and complex body of interrelated authoritative standards; before turning to his own scheme of values, the judge would have to be able to justify the claim that, *all* things considered, there was nothing in this vast body of the law which provided a basis for distinguishing one decision as the correct one. Could such a claim really ever be justified? . . .

I would prefer to conclude that the view that judges are legislators, which is also unappealing, is incorrect. Although it contains a grain of truth, it rests upon a fatal confusion. For there is an important but typically unacknowledged distinction between (a) what can correctly be said from outside the system about the nature and limitations of the judicial process, and (b) how judges are entitled to view the system from within in their role of active participants. Even if a correct philosophical account of the judicial decision process implied that a case might arise in which the issues were so finely balanced that there would be no one uniquely correct decision, it would not follow that in any particular case a judge would be entitled to act as if there was no uniquely correct decision. For unless there was some criterion which would permit a judge to identify a case as one in which there was no uniquely correct result, his institutional role would obligate him to treat each case as one in which there was *the* correct decision to which the litigants were entitled. To the best of my knowledge, though, no such criterion exists. Although one can describe what such a case would be like, in terms, say, of the concept of equal coherence, this does not provide a means for identifying any particular case as one in which there is no uniquely correct result. Indeed, I have suggested above that such a description argues for the practical impossibility of ever being able to identify something as correctly falling under it. Since there is a uniquely correct decision in the vast majority of cases, the lack of a judicial criterion for identifying those in which there is not implies that a judge would never be entitled to treat a case before him as one in which there was no uniquely correct result, for *in all probability* it will not be. The theoretical possibility of the law being indeterminate with regard to what it requires, in other words, does not imply any corresponding indeterminacy with regard to what is required of the judge. [pp. 156–159]

# INDEX OF AUTHORS

References in **bold** type are to selected extracts.

# INDEX OF SUBJECTS

# LLOYD'S
# INTRODUCTION TO JURISPRUDENCE